COUNTRY WISDOM & KNOW-HOW

COUNTRY WISDOM & KNOW-HOW

A Practical Guide to Living Off the Land

From the editors of Storey Publishing's Country Wisdom Bulletins

BLACK DOG
& LEVENTHAL
PUBLISHERS
NEW YORK

Black Dog & Leventhal Publishers
Hachette Book Group
1290 Avenue of the Americas
New York, NY 10104

www.hachettebookgroup.com
www.blackdogandleventhal.com

First Edition: September 2004

Black Dog & Leventhal Publishers is an imprint of Hachette Books, a division of Hachette Book Group. The Black Dog & Leventhal Publishers name and logo are trademarks of Hachette Book Group, Inc.

The publisher is not responsible for websites (or their content) that are not owned by the publisher.

The Hachette Speakers Bureau provides a wide range of authors for speaking events. To find out more, go to www.HachetteSpeakersBureau.com or call (866) 376-6591.

Print book interior design by Ohioboy Design

Library of Congress Cataloging-in-Publication Data has been applied for.

ISBNs: 978-0-316-27696-2 (paperback), 978-1-603-76235-9 (e-book)

Printed in the United States of America

LSC-W

Printing 5, 2022

Introduction

The joy of doing more for oneself, mastering a skill, being more independent, connecting in a very physical way with our land, our property, our earth—that's why we are drawn to this book.

Back in the 1970s, during the "back to the land era" when hippies were homesteading and gas and energy prices were sky high, Storey began to publish a series of small booklets called *Country Wisdom Bulletins,* each one addressing a bite-sized piece of country know-how, a simple skill, some knitty-gritty information. The collection of bulletins grew into the hundreds and eventually over 15 million copies were sold to people eager to discover the fun and satisfaction of doing more for themselves.

And now, collected between the covers of this volume, is a compendium of treasured knowledge from hundreds of *Country Wisdom Bulletins*. If you're like most people, you'll get stuck in it like a fly to old-fashioned flypaper. Whether you want to build a stone fence, make strawberry-rhubarb jam, or plant an herb garden, you'll find this book to be like your grandfather or grandmother at your elbow, showing you how.

Everything old is new again. Enjoy!

Pam Art

Pam Art
President
Storey Publishing LLC

Contents

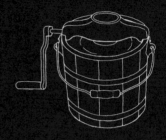

Animals

BIRDS AND BATS

Attracting Birds

Olwen Woodier

Birds can be attracted to your home if you offer food, water, and shelter. Trees and shrubs that yield fruit, berries, seeds, nuts, and cones will provide food. Tangles of wild plants and dense undergrowth left to thrive in chosen areas of your property, log piles, dead trees, and stacked branches will provide shelter, protection, and natural nesting and roosting sites. Nesting boxes can be secured to trees and posts to attract bluebirds, purple martins, wrens, downy woodpeckers, flickers, robins, and other species. Birdbaths or pools can be built to supply water, and feeders, strategically placed around the yard, will furnish supplementary food for the birds when natural sources diminish. Such pockets of refuge can be created on as little as a quarter-acre plot, and costs for a bird haven can be kept to a minimum.

Feeding the Birds

First think about feeding the birds from food supplied by trees and shrubs. Check the listings here to find the plant preferences of a variety of birds. For example, cardinals, whose flash of red brightens many a backyard, prefer to feast on seeds and berries and will nest in grape, holly, honeysuckle, juniper, multiflora rose, and willow.

Your vegetable garden will be a source of animal life to a variety of insect-devouring birds, including the voracious purple martins. Compost heaps are also a good source of free food. Daily deposits of vegetable and fruit peelings, chicken skin, meat fat scraps, and bread crusts will attract birds, particularly jays, crows, and starlings (also squirrels and raccoons), thus eliminating these aggressive species from your feeding stations. When forked over daily in early spring, the compost will be a constant source of insects and worms for fledglings.

To keep the birds in your area all year, it is advisable to provide supplementary feedings. Although the countryside has an abundance of food in the summer, most urban and some suburban landscapes are too manicured to supply sufficient grubs, insects, and weed seeds. If this is your problem, stock your feeders year-round, until you have established generous plant life.

Wintertime, everywhere, is another story. Even if there is no snow, the land will yield precious little food. Once you have decided to put up a feeder, it is essential that it is never left empty since your birds will become dependent on your winter feeding. Small birds must start eating at sunrise in order to replace body weight lost each night in their efforts to keep warm. Those that cannot find enough food to refuel sufficiently for the night ahead will die. If you leave on vacation and your feeders do not hold an adequate supply, ask a neighbor to keep them filled.

While the birds are feasting free in your yard during the summer, you can grow and gather food for the winter. Dried grains, seeds, nuts, berries, and ears of corn harvested in the autumn can be saved for a midwinter treat. Sunflower seeds are a particular favorite of birds and are very easy to grow. To harvest the seeds for later use and prevent the birds from quickly devouring your entire crop, tie a piece of plastic mesh (an orange bag saved for this purpose works well) around the stem of the growing sunflower and wrap it around the seed head.

Continued ➔

Nesting

If your land does not offer suitable nesting cover, homemade birdhouses and nesting boxes are acceptable to many birds, as long as they are built to the right dimensions (See "Building Nestboxes for Backyard Birds). Put the nesting boxes up in the autumn or in early spring.

All types of nesting paraphernalia are to be found at hardware stores, specialist suppliers, and seed merchants. However, it is more rewarding and definitely much cheaper to make your own. Although birdhouses come in varying sizes, the following requirements apply to all.

· Make the entrance hole the recommended diameter.

· Protect the nest from wind and rain.

· Do not set the house in a thickly wooded or shaded area.

· Mount them at the right height. (See table at the end of this section.)

· For mounting, poles and posts are better than trees, which are easily climbed by nest raiders, such as raccoons and squirrels.

· Rough up the inside front of the box to enable young nestlings to climb out.

· Screw together one side of the box to facilitate cleaning. At the end of the summer, discard the old nest to get rid of parasites.

· Bore a couple of small vent holes at the top of one side to give air to the nestlings.

Wood is the best material to use because it breathes and is durable. Try cedar, pine, poplar, and cypress of 3/4-inch to 1-inch thickness. Metal should not be used; on sunny days it will become too hot.

Unless the adult birds are away looking for food, resist disturbing the nest. If done too frequently, there is a strong chance that the nest will be deserted.

You might consider suspending nesting materials from tree branches, clotheslines, or fences. Short pieces of string, yarn, and ribbon; dried grasses and flowers; small dried twigs; small pieces of cloth; cotton; feathers; and animal hair will all be used by nest-building birds.

List of Birds

Here is an alphabetical list of birds common to various parts of the United States that consume a significant quantity of garden bugs and weed seeds. The bird description covers the conspicuous summer plumage of the male. The trees and shrubs listed under **Plant Preferences** provide food in the form of buds, berries, nuts, and seeds. Where more than one bird is mentioned under each species, due to limited space, their plant food and nest choices have been combined. For example, the Western Kingbird might not consume all the plant and animal foods listed, but the Eastern Kingbird will. Under Sparrows and Wood Warblers, only the names of the commonest have been given and the listings for nest choice, plant, feeder, and insect preferences have been generalized.

There are books that can help you learn more about bird identification, birdhouses, and feeders. In particular, I recommend *Audubon Bird Guide* by R. H. Pough; *Birds of North America* by Robbins, Bruun, and Zim; *A Field Guide to the Birds* updated version by Roger Tory Peterson; *Homes for Birds*, Conservation Bulletin 14, Superintendent of Documents (US Government Printing Office, Washington, DC 20402).

BLUEBIRDS

Eastern: blue with rust breast; 5 1/2". **Western:** similar, with blue throat and rust on upper back; 5 1/2". **Mountain:** deep blue above; pale chest, white belly; 6". **Plant preferences:** mountain ash, bittersweet, blackberry, blueberry, wild cherry, dogwood, elder, firethorn, holly, juniper, poison ivy, pokeberry, sassafras, sumac, viburnum, Virginia creeper. **Nest choice:** holes in trees and fence posts, birdhouses. **Insect preferences:** armyworms, cankerworms, centipedes, cicadas, crickets, cutworms, grasshoppers, gypsy moth and tent larvae, leafhoppers and treehoppers, May and woodboring beetles, spiders, wasps. **Feeder food:** dried fruit, peanut butter, suet.

BOBOLINK

Black below, with cream nape; white shoulder patches on lower back; 6". **Plant preferences:** barley, barnyard grass, bristle grass, millet, oat, ragweed, rice, sunflower, wheat. **Insect preferences:** ants, beetles, caterpillars, centipedes, chinch bugs, cotton worms, cutworms, grasshoppers, locusts, weevils. **Nest choice:** in leaves and grasses in meadowlands. **Feeder food:** none.

COMMON BOBWHITE

Red brown with gray tail; white throat and eyebrow stripe; 8". **Plant preferences:** blackberry, blueberry, black cherry, dogwood, firethorn, lespedeza, mulberry, wax myrtle, oak, pecan, pine, plum, pokeberry, privet, raspberry, and a huge variety of weed seeds. **Nest choice:** corn shocks, log and brush piles, grass clumps. **Insect preferences:** cucumber and potato beetles, caterpillars, centipedes, crickets, grasshoppers, katydids, leafhoppers, snails. **Feeder food:** cracked corn, mixed grains, sunflower.

BUNTINGS

Indigo: brilliant blue with darker crown; 4 1/2". **Lazuli:** blue with red chest; white belly and wing bars; 4 1/2". **Plant preferences:** blackberry, bluestem, corn, crabgrass, dandelion, elder, hemp, millet, mulberry, oat, ragweed, rye, wheat. **Nest choice:** blackberry, coralberry, maple, raspberry, rose. **Insect preferences:** beetles, cankerworms, caterpillars, crickets, grasshoppers, wasps, weevils, measuring worms. **Feeder food:** cracked corn, crumbs, mixed grains, nutmeats.

CARDINAL

Red bird with crest; black encircles red conical beak; 7 3/4". **Plant preferences:** a large variety of weed seeds; fruit and berry-bearing trees, shrubs, and vines. **Nest choice:** abelia, camellia, grape, holly, honeysuckle, juniper, multiflora rose, willow. **Insect preferences:** ants, beetles, caterpillars, cutworms, codling moths, leafhoppers, plant lice, scale insects, weevils. **Feeder food:** cracked corn, dried fruit, nutmeats, safflower, squash and sunflower seeds.

CUCKOOS

Yellow-billed: brown above, white below with black splotches under tail; chestnut pinion feathers; 11". **Black-billed:** similar with less distinct tail spots and chestnut wing markings; 11". **Plant preferences:** elder, grape, mulberry. **Nest choice:** near water in alder, apple, cottonwood, crabapple, elm, hawthorn, oak, pine, red cedar. **Insect preferences:** beetles, gypsy moth and tent larvae and pupae, other hairy caterpillars, grasshoppers, locusts, moths, sawflies, spiders. **Feeder food:** none.

DICKCISSEL

Sparrowlike with yellow eyestripe and chest; black V-shaped bib in summer; 5 3/4". **Plant preferences:** alfalfa, clover, millet, oat, panicum, wheat. **Nest choice:** elm, hackberry, mulberry, osage, orange, clumps of tufted grass. **Insect preferences:** ants, beetles, crickets, flies, grasshoppers, katydids, locusts, weevils. **Feeder food:** peanuts, wild birdseed mix.

FINCHES

House: slighter than the purple with more brown on wings and chest; tail less notched and thinner bill; 5 1/4". **Pine Siskin:** streaked olive brown above, lighter below; yellow at base of tail and on wings; 4 1/4". **Purple:** sparrowlike with raspberry head, back, and chest; small heavy beak; notched tail; 5 1/2". **Plant preferences:** alder, ash, birch, box-elder, butternut, canary grass, chickweed, corn, elm, fir, goldenrod, hawthorn, honeysuckle, juniper, larch, maple, mulberry, oat, pine, privet, ragweed, safflower, smartweed, sudan grass, sweet gum. **Nest choice:** alder, box-elder, fir, pine, spruce, willow. **Insect preferences:** aphids, caterpillars, plant lice, weevils. **Feeder food:** bread crumbs, corn, hemp, millet, chopped nuts, rape, sunflower.

Goldfinches and purple finches collect on our store-bought hanging feeder.

FLYCATCHERS

Great-crested: olive brown head and back with white wing bars; gray throat and chest; yellow belly; long rusty tail; 7". **Acadian:** olive drab with white throat and yellowish flanks; white eye ring and white wing bars; 4 3/4". **Traill's:** similar to Acadian, back and sides darker and throat whiter; 4 3/4". **Plant preferences:** blackberry, blueberry, cherry, mulberry, pokeberry, raspberry, sassafras, Virginia creeper. **Nest choice:** great-crested in gourds, woodpecker holes, rustic birdhouses; Acadian in beech, dogwood, hemlock, hickory, sugar maple, oak, sweet gum, witch-hazel; Traill's near water in alder, dogwood, box-elder, honeysuckle, privet, rose, spirea, and willow. **Insect preferences:** ants, bees, beetles, caterpillars, crickets, flies, grasshoppers, locusts, moths, spiders, wasps, weevils. **Feeder food:** none.

GOLDFINCHES

American: yellow body; black cap; black wings with white bars; white rump; 4 1/4". **Lesser:** similar to American, except for green back and rump; 3 3/4". **Plant preferences:** seeds of thistle, burdock, cornflower, hollyhock, lettuce, milkweed, mullein, evening primrose, sunflower, zinnia, and many other weed seeds; birch and alder catkins, evergreen cones. **Nest choice:** in apple, birch, bittersweet, blackberry, dogwood, and hawthorn. **Insect preferences:** aphids, caterpillars. **Feeder food:** bread crumbs, hemp, millet, chopped nutmeats, squash seeds, sunflower, thistle.

GROSBEAKS

Evening: large conical bill; yellow body; black cap and tail; black and white wings; 7 1/4". **Rose-breasted:** large conical bill; black above with white wing bars; white below with splash of deep rose on chest and under wings; 7 1/4". **Plant preferences:** ash, barberry, beech, box-elder, buckwheat, conifers, elm, maple, many wild fruits and berries, sunflower. **Nest choice:** ash, box-elder, conifers, elm, maple, rhododendron, willow. **Insect preferences:** ants, beetles, scale insects, spiders, a large variety of smooth and hairy caterpillars. **Feeder food:** hemp, peanuts, safflower, suet, sunflower.

HUMMINGBIRDS

Eastern ruby-throated: long, thin bills; iridescent bronze green above; dull white below with red throat; 3". **Black-chinned:** long bill; iridescent bronze green above with purple black wings and tail; black throat separated from white underparts by purple band. **Plant preferences:** nectar of amaryllis, azalea, bee balm, cardinal-flower, chinaberry, pink cleome, columbine, coralberry, century plant, citrus tree flowers, dahlia, evening primrose, four o'clock, fuschia, gladiolus, hibiscus, honeysuckle, horse chestnut, red larkspur, tiger lily, torch lily, milkweed, mimosa, morning glory, nasturtium, painted cup, purple penstemon, phlox, petunia, scarlet sage, snapdragon, trumpet creeper, zinnia. **Nest choice:** birch, cotton, hornbeam, oak, oleander, sycamore, willow. **Insect preferences:** ants, beetles, small flying insects, spiders. **Feeder food:** sugar water.

BLUE JAY

Crested; blue above with white wing bars and tail tip; white below with black necklace; 11". **Plant preferences:** beech, elder, oak, pine, and many nut and fruit-bearing trees and shrubs. **Nest choice:** conifers, elm, hackberry, oak. **Insect preferences:** ants, beetles, caterpillars, grasshoppers, gypsy moth (larvae, pupae, and adults), fish, frogs, mice, salamanders, snails, termites. **Feeder food:** bread, corn, fat, nutmeats, peanut butter, suet, sunflower and squash seeds.

JUNCOS

Slate-colored: dark gray with white belly and white-bordered tail; 5 1/4". **Oregon:** black head and breast, chestnut back and flanks; white belly and white-bordered tail; 5 1/4". **Plant preferences:** huge variety of weed seeds including amaranth, barnyard grass, broomsedge, canary grass, crabgrass, ragweed, sudan grass, switch grass, Russian thistle. **Nest choice:** grass tufts, rock piles and crevices, tree roots. **Insect preferences:** ants, beetles, caterpillars, grasshoppers, lacewing flies, leafhoppers, moths, spiders, wasps, weevils. **Feeder food:** pumpkin and squash seeds, sunflower, wild birdseed mix.

Continued ➡

Our covered platform feeder is very popular with blue jays.

KINGBIRDS

Eastern: dark gray above, white below with broad white band across tail tip; 6 3/4". **Western:** light gray head and back with black trail outlined in white; yellow chest and belly with white throat; 7". **Plant preferences:** mountain ash, blackberry, black gum, blueberry, cherry, dogwood, elder, grape, honeysuckle, magnolia, mulberry, pokeberry, sassafras, shadblow, spicebush, sweet bay, Virginia Creeper. **Nest choice:** the Eastern kingbird nests in apple, box-elder, elm, oak, pear, pine, and sassafras; the Western in elm, oak, sycamore, willow, and in bird boxes on stumps and fenceposts. **Insect preferences:** ants, bees, beetles, crickets, flies, gypsy moths, grasshoppers, June bugs, wasps. **Feeder food:** none.

KINGLETS

Golden-crowned: olive above with black, yellow, and orange striped head; dull white below with white wing bars and white eyebrow; 3 1/2". **Ruby-crowned:** distinguished from golden by white eye ring and red crown; 3 3/4". **Plant preferences:** none. **Nest choice:** fir, hemlock, juniper, spruce. Insect preferences: beetles, egg masses of tent, gypsy, and codling moths, plant lice and eggs, wasps. **Feeder food:** nutmeats, suet, sugar water.

HORNED LARK

Brown back; white below with black collar, cheeks, tail feathers, and "horns;" yellow chin; 6 1/2". **Plant preferences:** amaranth, brome grass, buckwheat, corn, goosefoot, oat, panicum, quack grass, ragweed, smartweed, grain sorghum, wheat. **Nest choice:** on the ground in grass clumps. **Insect preferences:** beetles, caterpillars, grasshoppers. **Feeder food:** cracked corn, sunflower seeds.

MEADOWLARKS

Eastern: brown-streaked back; yellow below with black V-shaped collar; short tail with white edging; 8 1/2". **Western:** paler brown and yellower cheeks than Eastern; 8 1/2". **Plant preferences:** barnyard grass, oat, panicum, pine, ragweed, rice, soybean, wild fruits and berries. **Nest choice:** covered grass clumps on the ground. **Insect preferences:** armyworm, caterpillars, cutworm, grasshoppers, weevils. **Feeder food:** corn, millet, peanuts, sorghum, sunflower, wheat.

MOCKINGBIRD

Gray above, with white wing patches; dull white underparts; long tail; 9". **Plant preferences:** wide variety of wild and cultivated fruit and berry trees and shrubs. **Insect preferences:** ants, bees, beetles, caterpillars, chinch bugs, cotton bollworms and weevils, crickets, grasshoppers, lizards, locusts, millipedes, snails, snakes, spiders, wasps. **Nest choice:** in thick low bushes bearing berries, apple, holly, magnolia, orange, sagebrush. **Feeder food:** cheese, dried and fresh fruit, kitchen fat mixes, peanuts and peanut butter, suet.

NUTHATCHES

White-breasted: blue gray back; black cap extending to and around nape; white cheeks and under parts; 5". **Red-breasted:** black stripe through eye; rusty breast; 4 1/2". **Plant preferences:** mountain ash, beech, birch, dock, fir, hickory, maple, oak, pine, ragweed, spruce. **Nest choice:** holes in trees, stumps, hollow logs, (bark-covered) wooden birdhouses near woodland areas. **Insect preferences:** ants, beetles, cankerworm, caterpillars, grasshoppers, moths, moth egg masses, pear-tree psylla eggs, plant lice, scale insects, wood borers. **Feeder food:** bread and doughnut crumbs, kitchen fat mixes, cracked nuts, peanut butter, squash seeds, suet, sunflower.

A nuthatch, downy woodpecker, and chickadee eat from suet cups in this feeder made from a three-inch-diameter tree limb.

ORIOLES

Baltimore (or Northern): orange with black head, neck, wings, and central tail feathers; 6 1/2". **Orchard:** rust red with solid black tail;

otherwise similar to Baltimore; 6". **Plant preferences**: mountain ash, blackberry, blueberry, cherry, box-elder, figs, grapes, hollyhock, huckleberry, peas, sunflowers, and a variety of fruit-bearing trees and shrubs. **Nest choice**: apple, birch, conifers, cottonwood, elm, maple, pecan, poplar, sycamore. **Insect preferences**: ants, beetles, caterpillars, grasshoppers, gypsy moths (larvae, pupae, and adults), Mayflies, plant lice, wasps, weevils, wireworms, wood borers. **Feeder food**: bread, fresh fruit, jelly, nutmeats, suet, sugar syrup.

RING-NECKED PHEASANT

A coppery red and green chickenlike body; green head with red eye patches; a white neck ring; black-barred tail measures about half of its length; 33–36". **Plant preferences**: a great quantity of fruits and berries, grains, weed seeds. **Nest choice**: on the ground in tufts of grass. **Insect preferences**: ants, beetles, caterpillars, crickets, earthworms, fly larvae, frogs, grasshoppers, snails, spiders, toads. **Feeder food**: crabapple, corn, hemp, millet, safflower, sunflower, wheat.

PHOEBES

Eastern: gray brown bird with dark gray head; black bill; white throat; distinct tail wagging; 5 3/4". **Say's phoebe**: light brown back, darker head and tail; rust belly; 6 1/4". **Eastern wood pewee**: similar to Eastern phoebe, but browner; with two distinct wing bars; 5 1/4". **Plant preferences**: some fruit-bearing shrubs and trees (90 percent insectivorous). **Nest choice**: Eastern phoebe on shelves and platforms, with sloping roof under eaves and bridges; likes to nest near water. Say's phoebe under eaves of farm buildings, overhanging cliffs, and banks in sun. Eastern wood pewee in apple, ash, elm, hickory, locust, sugar maple, oak, pine, poplar, red cedar. **Insect preferences**: ants, bees, beetles, caterpillars, crickets, flies, grasshoppers, moths (codling, brown-tail, and gypsy), spiders, wasps. **Feeder food**: none.

ROBIN

Gray brown above with darker head and tail; rusty red breast; 8 1/2". **Plant preferences**: most cultivated and wild fruit and berry trees and shrubs, particularly black gum, mulberry, pokeberry. **Nest choice**: platform boxes on ledges and shelves in barns, porches, sheds, under eaves; and in trees, including apple, ash, box-elder, elm, juniper, oak, poplar, spruce, willow. **Insect preferences**: ants, armyworms, beetles, cankerworms, caterpillars, centipedes, cicadas, cutworms, crickets, earthworms, flies, grasshoppers, leafhoppers, locusts, millipedes, gypsy moth (larvae, pupae, and adults), slugs, snails, sowbugs, spiders, termites, wireworms, weevils. **Feeder food**: bread, corn, dried and fresh fruits, nutmeats, peanut butter, suet.

SPARROWS

Small to medium birds with brown-streaked backs and lighter underparts; stout, conical beaks. Sparrows are distinguished by their distinctive white and black head strips; black or white throats; black, white, or red caps; streaked or unstreaked buff breasts; and variations in song. Those with the widest range in the United States include: chipping, fox, field, grasshopper, Le Conte's, lark, Lincoln's, Savannah, sharp-tailed, song, swamp, tree, white-crowned, white-throated, and vesper. **Plant preferences**: primarily a great variety of weed seeds. In the fall, they eat quantities of wild berries. **Nest choice**: concealed on the ground or low in thick shrubs and hedges. **Insect preferences**: ants, armyworms, beetles, cankerworms, caterpillars,

cutworms, crickets, Japanese beetles and grubs, flies, grasshoppers, leafhoppers, locusts, millipedes, moths, snails, spiders, wasps, weevils. Chipping sparrows, in particular, eat gypsy moths (larvae and adults). **Feeder food**: bread, cracked corn, dried fruit, nutmeats, wild birdseed mix.

SWALLOWS

Barn swallow: deeply forked black tail with dabs of white; black pinion feathers; dark blue head, back, and shoulders; rusty orange underparts; 6". **Purple Martin**: iridescent purple black above and below; black wings and black, forked tail; 7". **Tree swallow**: green head, back, and shoulders; black wings and forked tail; white underparts, 5". **Plant preferences**: some wild fruits and berries, red cedar, Russian olive, Virginia creeper. **Nest choice**: mud and straw attached to beams, rafters in barns, and under eaves; also on a platform box with sloping roof secured to side of the building. The tree swallow nests near water in holes of trees; under eaves; in drainpipes, wooden birdhouses, or gourds with 1 1/2-inch entrance holes, 3–5 feet off the ground. The purple martin nests singly or collectively in wooden birdhouses, large gourds, or in holes in trees and cliffs. **Insect preferences**: variety of flying insects including ants, bees, beetles, flies, gnats, mosquitoes, moths, spiders, wasps, weevils. **Feeder food**: none.

TANAGERS

Scarlet: red body with black wings and tails, 6 1/4". **Summer**: red; 6 1/2". **Western**: yellow body with black tail and wings; red head; 6 1/4". **Plant preferences**: blackberry, blueberry, cherry, elm, fig, grape, mulberry, pokeberry, shadblow. **Nest choice**: apple, aspen, beech, dogwood, fir, hemlock, oak, pine, sweet gum, sycamore, willow. **Insect preferences**: ants, bees, beetles, tent caterpillars, cicadas, dragonflies, flies, gypsy moths (larvae, pupae, and adults), wasps and wasp larvae, weevils, wood borers. **Feeder food**: bread, peanut butter, raisins, suet.

TUFTED TITMOUSE

Crested; gray above, buff below with rust on flanks; 5 1/2". Plant preferences: beech, butternut, hickory, honeysuckle, locust, mulberry, wax myrtle, oak, pecan, pine, safflower, walnut. **Nest choice**: holes in trees, fences, and stumps, or in birdhouses on a tree trunk. **Insect preferences**: ants, beetles, caterpillars, insect eggs, sawfly larvae, scale insects, spiders, treehoppers. **Feeder food**: bread, cake, and cookie crumbs; cracked nuts; peanuts and peanut butter; sunflower.

RUFOUS-SIDED TOWHEE

Black with white breast; large white patches underneath tail; red-dish flanks; 7 1/8". **Plant preferences**: large variety of fruit-bearing and nut-bearing shrubs and trees. **Nest choice**: on the ground, protected by overhanging grasses and brush; or in berry-bearing, sometimes thorny, shrubs and vines. **Insect preferences**: ants, bees, beetles, caterpillars, crickets, flies, grasshoppers, locusts, millipedes, gypsy moths (larvae, pupae, and adults), sowbugs, spiders, treehoppers, wasps. Feeder food: bread, cake, and cookie crumbs; melon seeds; nutmeats; sunflower.

BROWN THRASHER

Red brown above with heavily streaked white below; long tail; long, curved bill; 10". **Plant preferences**: large variety of fruit-bearing trees

Continued →

and shrubs. **Nest choice:** hedges, vines, berry-bearing shrubs, spruce, willows. **Insect preferences:** ants, armyworms, beetles, cankerworms, crickets, cutworms, dragonflies, earthworms, frogs, grasshoppers, lizards, Mayflies, tent and gypsy moths (larvae and adults), spiders. **Feeder food:** bread, cheese, cracked corn, dried fruit, nutmeats, peanut butter, suet, wheat.

THRUSHES

Hermit: brown back; rusty tail; heavily spotted brown-on-white breast; 6". **Veery:** tawny above with lightly spotted breast; 6". **Wood:** brown above with reddish brown head; heavily spotted brown-on-white breast; 7". **Plant preferences:** wide variety of fruit-bearing trees and shrubs. **Nest choice:** in or under apple, beech, birch, blackberry, dogwood, fir, hawthorn, hemlock, honeysuckle, huckleberry, mountain laurel, maple, oak, rhododendron, spruce, yew. **Insect preferences:** ants, beetles, caterpillars, crickets, snails, sowbugs, spiders, weevils, worms. **Feeder food:** bread crumbs, nutmeats, peanut butter, raisins, suet.

VIREOS

Red-eyed: olive brown back; gray cap; white stripe above eye; dull white underparts; 5". **Solitary:** blue gray head; olive brown back; white throat, breast, eye rings, and wing bars; yellow flanks; 4 1/4". **White eyed:** olive brown above, white below with yellow flanks; white wing bars; 6". Warbling: olive brown above, narrow white strip above eye; buff-colored underparts, 4 3/4". **Plant preferences:** alder, bayberry, blackberry, box-elder, cherry, dogwood, grape, holly, magnolia, mulberry, wax myrtle, sassafras, shadblow, snowberry, spicebush, sweet bay, Virginia creeper. **Nest choice:** in alder, apple, ash, aspen, beech, birch, blackberry, camellia, cherry, cottonwood, grape, hawthorn, maple, wax myrtle, oak, pokeberry, spicebush, sweet gum, sycamore. **Insect preferences:** ants, beetles, caterpillars, flies, grasshoppers, moths, spiders, wasps. **Feeder food:** none.

WOOD WARBLERS

These small, slender-billed birds are easiest to recognize during the breeding season (spring and early summer) when the males are decked in their brightest plumage. Many warblers are splashed with yellow; others have characteristic blue, black, or white wing and head markings. In the fall, warblers are duller hued and have indistinct markings, making it difficult to tell them apart. Those spotted most frequently are American redstart, Audubon's, black-throated blue, cerulean, chestnut-sided, hooded, Kentucky, orange-crowned, Parula, pine, prairie, prothonotary, yellow, yellow-breasted chat, yellow-throat, yellow-rumped. **Plant preferences:** almost 100 percent insectivorous. **Nest choice:** beech, conifers, maple, Spanish moss, and a variety of fruit-bearing trees and shrubs. **Insect preferences:** wide variety of insects. **Feeder food:** nutmeats, peanut butter, suet.

CEDAR WAXWING

Crested bird with black mask and chin; brown back; dull yellow belly and yellow-tipped tail; 5 3/4". **Plant preferences:** large variety of cultivated and wild fruit and berry trees and shrubs. **Insect preferences:** ants, beetles, cankerworms, caterpillars, crickets, grasshoppers, Mayflies, and many insects on the wing. **Nest choice:** apple, red cedar, fir, larch, maple, pine, spruce. **Feeder food:** none.

WOODPECKERS

Downy: black and white bars on wings; large white stripe down back; white underparts; red patch on back of head; 5 3/4". **Hairy:** larger than downy, 7 1/2". **Common yellow-shafted flicker:** brown back; white rump with yellow under wings and tail; black moustache; black crescent on chest; red nape; 10 1/2". Common red-shafted flicker: red wings, tail linings, and moustache; 11". **Red-bellied:** black and white "ladder" back; red head; buff cheeks, throat, and breast; 8 1/2". **Red-headed:** completely red head and throat; black back with large white wing patches; white breast; 8 1/2". **Yellow-bellied sapsucker:** black and white striped back, with one long white stripe on wing; red forehead and throat; 7 3/4". **Plant preferences:** variety of fruit-bearing and nut trees. **Nest choice:** holes in dead trees (downy and hairy also nest in live trees) or wooden birdhouses (secured to pole or tree) containing 2 inches of wood shavings or cork chips. **Insect preferences:** ants, beetles, caterpillars, cockroaches, crickets, grasshoppers, insect and moth egg masses. **Feeder food:** rendered fat, nutmeats, peanut butter, suet, sunflower.

WRENS

House: brown; lighter below with finely barred short tail, often cocked; 4 1/4". **Bewick's:** brown above; longer, noticeably rounded, white-fringed tail; white underparts; white stripe above eye; 4 1/2". **Carolina:** rusty brown above and warm buff below; white eye strip; short, cocked tail; 4 3/4". **Plant preferences:** none; almost 100 percent insectivorous. **Nest choice:** holes in trees and walls, hollow logs, in birdhouses, under eaves, flowerpots, discarded hats, boots, and furniture. **Insect preferences:** beetles, caterpillars, crickets, cutworms, flies, grasshoppers, moths, plant lice, scale insects, spiders, ticks weevils. **Feeder food:** bread, nutmeats, peanut butter, suet.

Appendix

Birds are very fussy about their nesting sites. If you want to build a nesting box for birds in your yard, be sure to build them to the exact specifications listed in the table below. Too large an entrance makes small birds vulnerable to attack by larger birds.

Here are some building suggestions from Storey Publishing's *Homemade* by Ken Braren and Roger Griffith.

- Build for the bird's pleasure, not your own. Don't paint the birdhouse with brilliant colors, and paint it at least a few weeks before the birds will occupy it, so the smell of paint will be gone.

- Pick the site carefully. It should be safe from cats, the house should face away from the prevailing wind, and the house should not tilt upward, so that rain enters it. Don't place several houses for the same birds close together. Birds have strong territorial instincts, and several houses close together will promote ill feelings among neighbors.

NESTING BOXES

Species	Floor	Height	Entrance above floor	Diameter of entrance	Height above ground
Bluebird	4 x 4	8–12"	6–10"	1 1/2"	3–6'
Chickadee	4 x 4	9	7	1 1/8	4–15
Great Crested Flycatcher	6 x 6	8–10	6–8	1 3/4	8–20
Nuthatch	4 x 4	9	7	1 3/8	5–15
Phoebe	6 x 6	6	—	—	8–12
Robin	6 x 8	8	—	—	6–15
Barn Swallow	6 x 6	6	—	—	8–12
Purple Martin	6 x 6	6	1	2 1/4	10–20
Tree Swallow	5 x 5	6–8	4–6	1 1/2	4–15
Titmouse	4 x 4	9	7	1 1/4	5–15
Downy Woodpecker	4 x 4	9	7	1 1/4	5–15
Flicker	7 x 7	16–18	14–16	2 1/2	6–30
Hairy Woodpecker	6 x 6	12–15	9–12	1 5/8	12–20
Red-headed Woodpecker	6 x 6	12	9	2	10–20
Bewick's Wren	4 x 4	6–8	4–6	1 1/4	5–10
Carolina Wren	4 x 4	6–8	4–6	1 1/2	5–10
House Wren	4 x 4	6–8	4–6	1–1 1/4	4–10

Easy-to-Build Bird Feeders

Mary Twitchell

Illustrations by Alison Kolesar

Different Foods for Different Folks

Birds that use feeders are either insect eaters (such as the woodpecker, brown creeper, white-throated sparrow, tree sparrow, blue jay, and nuthatch), which prefer animal foods; or seed eaters (such as the house sparrow and junco), which prefer vegetable foods. The insect eaters choose suet (beef fat), while the seed eaters flock to feeders with commercial seed mixtures. Some birds (such as the bluebird, chickadee, and titmouse) eat both kinds of foods.

SERVICING THE SEED EATERS

Seeds are available either as a single variety or in commercial mixes called wild bird seed mixtures. Such mixtures may contain 8 to 10 different seed varieties (usually white and red millet, cracked corn, niger seeds, peanut hearts, wheat, oat groats, sunflower seeds, canary seeds, and milo). These mixes are convenient and half the cost of sunflower seeds (which explains their popularity). However, you may discover that if you don't know the species you are feeding, seeds go uneaten. Birds rifle through your offering, picking out the sunflower seeds and moving on. If this happens, much of your effort and money is wasted, and the filler seeds (oats, rape, wheat, rice, milo) may either rot or attract rodents.

To discover which bird species live in your area, set out test trays with different seeds in each. The trays can be as simple as multiple pie plates or a home-built test tray. If sunflower seeds are the heavy favorite, your population is high in chickadees, titmice, nuthatches, and cardinals; if the millet and cracked corn supplies are depleted, you have a preponderance of tree sparrows, white-throats, and juncos. Then make your own mix or buy only the seeds that are most popular (usually black oil sunflower, millet, and cracked corn).

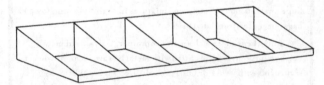

Fill the chambers of a test tray with different types of seeds and set it out in the yard; noting which seeds are eaten most rapidly will let you know which birds are most populous in your backyard.

ALL-PURPOSE MIX

The best all-purpose home seed mixture is 45 percent white proso millet, 35 percent black oil sunflower seeds, and 20 percent safflower seeds.

Sunflower seeds are the most popular; grosbeaks will devour them. The seeds come in three types. The largest are gray-striped seeds. There are also medium-sized black-striped sunflower seeds, and a third type, the smallest, an all-black oil type (these seeds are made into sunflower oil).

Seed eaters prefer the black oil seeds, which have a high percentage of oil and a thin hull; for small birds, the thinner shell makes these seeds easier to open. The seeds are more nutritious, provide more calories for their weight, and of all the sunflower seeds are the least expensive.

Continued ➜

Hull-less sunflower seeds are also available. These are much more expensive but easy for the birds, and for you—there are no scattered hulls to clean up.

Cracked corn, popular with cardinals, sparrows, juncos, bluebirds, and game birds, is water resistant. It is ideal fed daily to birds from an open platform or scattered on the ground. It's inexpensive, but it will attract crows.

Niger seeds, once thought of as for canaries only, are now sold as food for wild birds (redpolls, goldfinches, purple finches, siskins). They're tiny black seeds, imported from India and Africa (Nigeria). Although expensive (twice the cost of sunflower seeds), there is no waste. Special feeders with tiny holes are necessary because the seeds are so small.

White or red proso millet is a major component of commercial bird mixes; it is inexpensive, easy to store, and a favorite of ground-feeding birds, especially goldfinches, juncos, and sparrows.

Peanut hearts, a by-product of peanut butter manufacture, appeal to starlings. Blue jays, titmice, chickadees, goldfinches, woodpeckers, and sparrows will eat whole-shelled peanuts, but so will squirrels. Blue jays and woodpeckers will even crack open the shells.

Safflower seeds attract cardinals but are disliked by crows, grackles, and squirrels. As they are more expensive than sunflower seeds, try mixing the two together to help stretch your supply.

In addition, certain birds have a soft spot for particular treats:

- **Corn on the cob**: Blue jays
- **Coconut**: Chickadees
- **Peanut butter**: Chickadees, tree sparrows, juncos, brown creepers, nuthatches

SETTING OUT SUET

Suet, which contains protein and fat, is a high-energy food. All insect eaters (especially woodpeckers) like suet. They will eat it both summer and winter.

Suet (the hard white fat from beef) is available at the meat counter in the supermarket, or you can use your own fat trimmings from steak or roast beef. In winter use as is; in the heat of summer, suet melts and must be rendered (see the box below) to increase its hardness and to prevent it from turning rancid. Use hardened suet in feeders or pour it into molds of citrus rinds or coconut shells. Freeze unused suet for later use.

To make a simple suet feeder, mix suet and seeds and place the hardened ball in a loosely knitted twine or yarn sack.

BUYING AND STORING SEEDS

When shopping for seeds, visit your local garden center or feed store—they sell seeds in quantity (50-pound, or 23 k, bags). You can also purchase seeds through a mail-order catalog. Buy enough for 4 to 6 weeks, remembering that birds eat more in winter. Supermarkets carry commercial mixtures in 5- to 10-pound (2–5 k) bags but at greatly inflated prices.

Store the seeds in a clean, dry container. Galvanized metal, raccoon-proof trash cans fitted with metal lids are ideal, or you can secure lids with a rock or bungee cords. Don't trust plastic containers; squirrels eat through plastic.

Leave a scoop in the seed can for feeder refilling. A 2-pound coffee can, a 2-quart (liter) plastic soda bottle, or a widemouthed funnel can substitute. For easy pouring, squeeze the sides of the coffee can to create a V in its top edge. To adapt the soda bottle, cut off the top just below the shoulder if you are creating a scoop; to create a funnel, cut off only the bottom and remove the cap.

RECYCLING TABLE SCRAPS

Birds will eat the following table scraps:

- **Snacks:** Popcorn, cheese, potato chips, raisins, currants, nuts
- **Pasta:** Spaghetti, noodles, orzo
- **Fruits:** Apples, pears, berries, bananas, grapefruit, orange halves
- **Stale breads:** Sandwich bread, cake, cookies, breakfast cereal, doughnuts
- **Seeds:** Melon, pumpkin

STEP-BY-STEP RENDERING

Rendering suet for use in hot weather is quite simple. Just follow these easy steps.

1. Cut the suet into small pieces and put them through a meat grinder, or ask your butcher to grind up the suet to make it easier to use.

2. Place the ground suet in a heavy pan or double boiler and cook over medium heat until it begins to melt. Then lower the heat until the fat has congealed. Cool.

3. Reheat again until the suet has melted (the second melting will help it become harder when cooled), then remove from the heat. Pour the melted fat into muffin tins or tuna-fish or cat-food cans and refrigerate until solid.

SWEETENING THE SUET

Other ingredients that may be added to the suet include millet, oatmeal, peanut butter, cornmeal, seeds, nuts, raisins, and cooked rice. Birds love the added tidbits but aren't fussy about what they are.

Some particularly good combinations are:

Combination 1

1 cup (235 ml) melted suet or fat
1/2 cup (140 ml) rolled oats
1/2 cup (140 ml) raisins or peanuts
1/2 cup (140 ml) cornmeal
1/2 cup (140 ml) seeds (sunflower or other)

Combination 2

1 cup (235 ml) melted suet or fat
1/2 cup (120 ml) chunky peanut butter
1 cup (275 ml) sunflower seeds or mixed grains

GRAVEL AND GRIT

Since birds lack teeth, they ingest bits of sand and gravel to grind or pulverize their food. In summer they get the necessary grit by pecking on the ground, but in winter this is impossible. Therefore, add 1 teaspoon (5 ml) of sand to each quart (liter) of feed.

Eggshells, ground and crushed, are useful for the nesting female. They provide her with extra calcium. During nesting season, then, rinse, dry, and pulverize eggshells to add to your feed.

Finding the Best Location

First and foremost, if you're installing bird feeders so that you can bird-watch, be sure that the feeder is visible. Once you've marked out the spots in the yard where bird-watching is best, take notes of which of those sites are safe from predators, available in all weather, and protected from the elements. Birds will also appreciate the following:

- **Fresh food.** Keep food in feeders dry; rain and snow cause the seed to rot quickly.

- **Sturdy fixtures.** Feeders should also be firmly attached or hung, lest a raccoon run off with the entire feeding station.

- **Protection from the wind.** Avoid sites that are exposed to prevailing winds; a sheltered southeastern exposure is best.

- **Adequate vegetation or hiding places.** Birds should find your feeder within 24 hours. If the feeder goes unused for 3 to 4 days, reexamine its location. It may be too exposed—or not exposed enough. Birds need nearby vegetation. Trees and shrubs allow the birds to escape predators, to rest, to assess activity at the feeder before committing themselves, and to retreat to while they open hulled seeds.

- **A gradual introduction to humans.** If the proximity of your house is a problem, let the birds become accustomed to your feeder, then gradually move it closer to the house. Bird feeders hung on a clothesline or pulley system can be slowly reeled in for better viewing.

- **Winter warmth.** Winter feeders need a sunny, sheltered location that will allow the birds to keep warm and the seeds to stay dry. Remember in winter to remove snow from feeder platforms.

- **A hang for hanging feeders.** Locate hanging feeders 5 feet (1.5 m) off the ground and within easy reach from a ladder for restocking. Hanging feeders should be surrounded by open space with a radius of 10 feet (3 m) in all directions.

- **Close quarters for suet feeders.** Hang or attach suet feeders on or close to tree trunks. Insect eaters do not like to fly through open spaces. If the feeder is mounted on a tree, birds can hold on to the trunk while eating. Never nail suet feeders to the house—when the suet begins to melt, it will create unsightly stains.

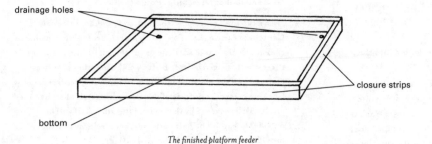

drainage holes

bottom

closure strips

The finished platform feeder

> ## FEEDERS FOR ALL
>
> Having a variety of foods and feeders reduces friction among various birds. To address the feeding needs of all the birds that frequent your backyard, you will need to supply water and four types of feeders:
>
> - A ground or platform feeding tray
> - A suet feeder
> - A hanging feeder stocked with sunflower and other seeds
> - A hummingbird feeder

10 Tips for Building the Best Bird Feeders

1. To make birds feel at home, feeders should look as natural as possible. Adapt stumps or hollow logs; substitute shingle or shake material for milled lumber. If you don't have the perfect natural material, stock lumber (#2 pine, spruce, or fir) is the most versatile. Exterior plywood (CDX) and medium-density fiberboard (MDF) can also be used. Redwood, cedar, and cypress are more expensive but will last longer.

2. Stainless-steel or brass screws are better than steel; they resist corrosion and don't stain the wood. (Stainless plasterboard screws are very easy to use if you have a power drill and a Phillips-head screwdriver.) Brass hinges are preferable to steel ones.

3. Galvanized spiral or ring-shank nails will hold better than smooth ones.

4. The construction directions call for gluing all joints before nailing or screwing. Use an exterior (waterproof) glue.

5. For hanging feeders, choose wire or metal chain, not string (which may rot) and not monofilament fishing line. Squirrels will chew through either.

6. To prevent seeds from getting soaked, drill 1/8-inch (0.3 cm) holes in each corner of any platform bottom, or use wire mesh as the bottom.

7. A deep rim around the feeder bottom decreases seed loss on windy days.

8. Unless it is a hanging feeder (which is meant to sway), firmly mount the feeder to provide a steady perch. Swinging feeders encourage chickadees, titmice, nuthatches, and cardinals, which all like to cling while eating, and discourage blue jays and house sparrows.

9. Directions for hopper feeders (see below) call for 1/8-inch (0.3 cm) acrylic. Glass may be substituted; it is cheaper, but breakable.

10. Feeders can be treated with a waterproof stain. If you prefer to paint, never paint the surface where birds will feed.

Continued →

Platform Feeder

A feeding platform or tray placed above the ground (for example, on a picnic table or windowsill) will attract not only the ground feeders but also chickadees, cardinals, titmice, wrens, blue jays, blackbirds, and grosbeaks. These platform feeders (also called table feeders) are flat, uncovered surfaces that can be as simple as a board or piece of plywood or wooden bowl set directly on the ground or screwed into the top of a low post. Trays, wooden boxes, coconut halves, hubcaps, and/or terra-cotta plant dishes can hold the seeds; drill a few drainage holes in the platform bottom to allow the seeds to dry quickly. A wicker basket or a feeder tray made with a stiff wire or mesh bottom will drain automatically.

Clean feeders regularly. Remove bird droppings, hulls, crushed feed, and other debris. Scrub the feeding surface with a 10:1 solution of water and household bleach. Rinse thoroughly.

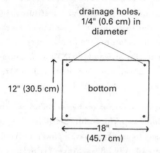

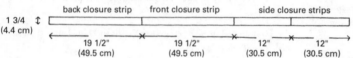

Materials

3/4" x 12" x 18" (1.9 x 30.5 x 45.7 cm) stock
   lumber or CDX plywood 3/4" x 1 3/4" x 63"
   (1.9 x 4.4 x 160 cm) stock lumber or CDX
   plywood

Ten 1 1/2" (3.8 cm) screws or 4 d nails

Glue

Tools

Drill and 1/4" (0.635 cm)
   drill bit

Screwdriver

1. From 3/4" (1.9 cm) stock or 3/4" CDX plywood, cut pieces as illustrated.

2. In the *bottom*, drill four drainage holes, one in each corner, approximately 1/4" (0.6 cm) in diameter.

3. Glue and nail or screw the *side closure strips* to the *bottom*.

4. Glue and nail or screw the *front* and the *back closure strips* to the *side strips* and to the *bottom*.

MOUNTING THE PLATFORM FEEDER

On a window ledge. If desired, screw through the bottom into the window ledge.

On a post. The platform can also be mounted on a 4 x 4 inch (10.2 x 10.2 cm) pressure-treated post by screwing through the *bottom* into the post. To mount the platform feeder on a metal pole, buy 3/4-inch (1.9 cm) galvanized pipe threaded on one end and a 3/4-inch pipe flange. Center and screw the flange to the underside of the platform. Cut the

pipe to the desired length (6 to 12 feet; 1.8 to 3.7 m). Drive into the ground by hitting a board placed over the top of the pipe; if you hit the pipe directly, it will damage the threads. Once the pipe is firmly anchored, thread the flange and platform onto the pipe.

TIN CAN FEEDER

Directions are given for using a 1-pound coffee can (4 inches, or 10.2 cm, in diameter; 5 1/2 inches, or 14 cm, high). Adjust these dimensions if you use a can of a different size.

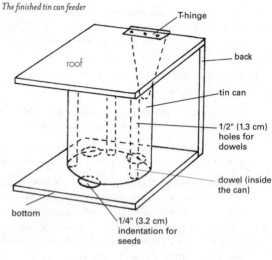

The finished tin can feeder

Materials

3/4" x 6" x 19" (1.9 x 15.2 x 48.3 cm) stock

1 tin can, 4" (10.2 cm) in diameter and 5 1/2" (14 cm) in height (coffee cans are
   usually this size)

One 1/2" x 15" (1.3 x 38.1 cm) dowel

One 4" (10.2 cm) T-strap hinge and screws

Three 1 1/2" (3.8 cm) screws or 6d nails

Tools

Circular saw or handsaw

Drill with 1/2" (1.27 cm) drill bit and 1 1/4" (3.175 cm) paddle bit

Screwdriver

1. From 3/4" (1.9 cm) stock, cut pieces as illustrated.

2. Glue and nail or screw the *back* onto the *bottom*.

3. With a can opener, remove the bottom from the coffee can. Center the can on the *bottom*. Draw a circle around the outside of the can. Remove and, with the paddle bit, drill into the *bottom* three evenly spaced holes 3/8" (0.9 cm) deep (they should *not* penetrate all the way through the bottom) evenly centered on the line that marks the outside of the can, so that half of each drilled circle will be covered by the can and the other half will be outside the can. (The half of the shallow circle outside the can provides a tray from which the birds will get the seeds.)

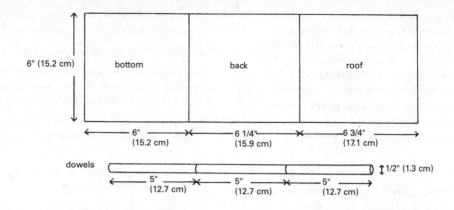

4. Between the holes for seeds, drill three 1/2" (1.3 cm) holes through the *bottom* for the dowels, just inside the line that marks the outside of the can.

5. Cut the dowels to length and insert. Place the can over the dowels; it should fit snugly.

6. Place the *roof* on top of the *back* and mount the hinge, screwing the rectangular leaf into the *roof* and the strap into the *back*. To fill the feeder, simply open the roof and fill the tin can with seeds.

MOUNTING THE TIN CAN FEEDER

On a wooden post. Simply screw through the bottom of the can onto the wooden post.

On a metal post. Screw a 3/4-inch (1.9 cm) flange into the underside of the *bottom*. Drive a 6-foot (1.8 m) length of 3/4-inch galvanized threaded pipe into the ground and screw on the flange (and feeder).

MAKING DO

Any number of household items can be recycled as bird feeders. They won't last as long as the wooden kind, but the birds will enjoy them while they're out!

A coconut feeder will be used by titmice, chickadees, nuthatches, and woodpeckers. Cut a coconut in half. Remove the milk. Drill drainage holes in the bottom to ensure that rainwater doesn't collect; then drill three evenly spaced holes near the outside top edge. Thread a length of wire through each hole, fill the feeder with suet, and hang.

Dried, hollowed-out gourds are very adaptable for feeder use.

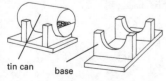

tin can   base

Tin cans can become feeders. Construct a wooden base to keep the feeding can stationary.

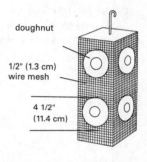

If you tend to accumulate stale doughnuts, make a doughnut feeder for squirrels — it may help lure them away from your bird feeders. These feeders are constructed much like the suet feeder (see below), but with a hole diameter of 4 1/2 inches (11.4 cm). Push a doughnut into the hole and then push sunflower seeds into the doughnut. Hang within reach of squirrels.

doughnut

1/2" (1.3 cm) wire mesh

4 1/2" (11.4 cm)

Single-Sided Hopper Feeder

Hopper feeders such as the singled-sided hopper described here and the two-sided hopper below are favorites of chickadees, titmice, nuthatches, and finches. They can be mounted on poles, but mounting them on trees provides birds with better cover. Hopper feeders can also be suspended from a wire, creating an unsteady perch that some of the birds commonly considered pesky (such as house sparrows and blue jays) don't like.

Materials

3/4" x 5" x 23" (1.9 x 12.7 x 58.4 cm) lumber

3/4" x 1 1/2" x 20" (1.9 x 3.8 x 50.8 cm) lumber

3/4" x 7 1/2" x 6" (1.9 x 19.1 x 15.2 cm) lumber

Two 5/8" (3.8 cm) staples

Thirteen 1 1/2" (3.8 cm) screws or 4d nails

One piece 1/8" x 6" x 3 3/4" (0.3 x 9.5 x 15.2 cm) acrylic

One 2" x 2" (5.1 x 5.1 cm) brass hinge with screws

Glue

Tools

Circular saw

Drill and 1/4" (0.635 cm) drill bit

Staple gun

Screwdriver

Continued ➧

Hopper feeders protect the food from wind and rain; they hold plenty of seeds so they don't have to be refilled as often; and they are easy to clean. Hopper feeders also regulate seed flow (which you can further regulate by increasing or decreasing the size of the hopper opening); however, if the opening is larger than 1/2 inch (1.3 cm), birds may push their heads through and get stuck.

These feeders are more efficient and economical if filled with only one kind of seed; a mixture may result in blue jays eating all the sunflowers, leaving little of interest for others.

1. From 3/4" (1.9 cm) lumber, cut pieces as illustrated.

2. If the feeder will be hung, drill a 1/4" (0.6 cm) hole centered in the top of the *back*, 1/2" (1.3 cm) from the top edge of the *back*. Then glue, screw, or nail the *back* to the *bottom*.

3. Cut the *sides* as illustrated. On each of the *sides*, measure in 1/2" (1.3 cm) from the 90-degree angle, and mark. Draw an angled line from the 1/2" mark to its diagonal corner at the base. Cut a 3/16"

(0.5 cm) deep groove the width of the saw kerf (1/8"; 0.3 cm) along each of these lines. This groove will hold the acrylic door.

4. Glue and then screw or nail the sides onto the *back* and *bottom*.

5. From the *bottom*, measure up 3/4" (1.9 cm) along the groove and insert a staple. Staples will leave a small gap between the acrylic and the *bottom* to allow the seeds to flow continuously.

6. Glue and screw or nail the *side closure strips* to the *back* and *bottom*; then glue, screw, or nail the *front closure strip* to the bottom and *side closure strips*.

7. Hinge the *roof* to the *back*. It will sit on top of the angled *sides* and overhang each by 1/4" (0.6 cm).

8. With the *roof* open, remove the protective coating and slip the acrylic door into the *side* slots. It should rest on the staples.

MOUNTING THE SINGLE-SIDED HOPPER

Fill the hopper and use the hole in its *back* for hanging the feeder.

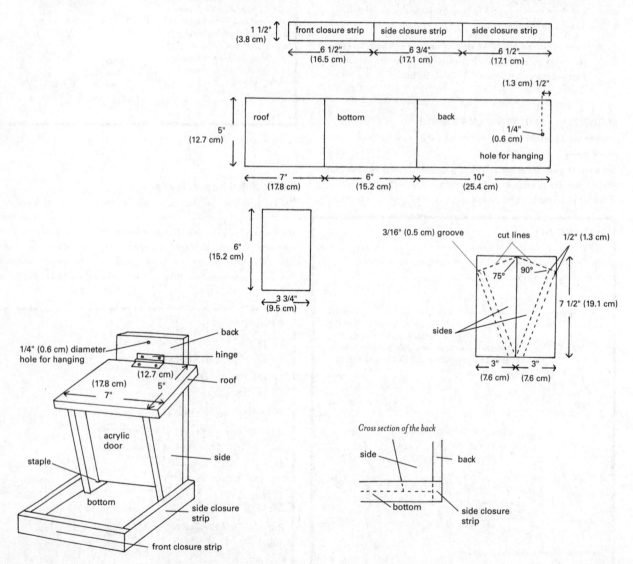

The finished single-sided hopper feeder

Two-Sided Hopper Feeder

Compared with the one-sided hopper, the carpentry involved in building the two-sided hopper is a bit more complicated. However, it allows the mob to feed from both sides—certainly an advantage from the birds' point of view.

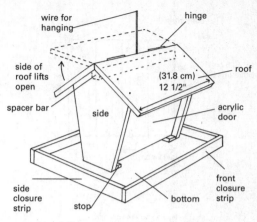

The completed two-sided hopper feeder

Materials

3/4" x 10" x 11" (1.9 x 25.4 x 27.9 cm) lumber

3/4" x 1 1/2" x 45" (1.9 x 3.8 x 114.3 cm) lumber

3/4" x 7" x 25" (1.9 x 17.8 x 63.5 cm) lumber

3/4" x 1" x 5 3/4" (1.9 x 2.5 x 14.6 cm) lumber

3/4" x 3/4" x 6" (1.9 x 1.9 x 15.2 cm) lumber

3/4" x 8" x 9" (1.9 x 20.3 x 22.9 cm) lumber

2 pieces 1/8" x 6" x 6" (0.3 x 15.2 x 15.2 cm) acrylic

Eight 4d nails

Twenty 1 1/2" (3.8 cm) screws or 6d nails

Glue

One 3' (0.9 m) length 15-gauge galvanized wire (optional)

Tools

Circular saw

Hammer

Screwdriver

Hacksaw

Drill and 3/8" (0.953 cm) drill bit

Pliers

1. From 3/4" (1.9 cm) lumber, cut pieces as illustrated.

2. Cut the sides as illustrated. Draw a vertical centerline on the *sides*. At one end, draw lines to either side of the centerline for a 70-degree roof slope. At the bottom of the *side*, mark 1 1/2" (3.8 cm) to either side of the midpoint. Connect these points with the beginning of the roof eaves to create the sloping sides. Cut along these lines.

   Along the sloping edges, cut two grooves 3/16" (0.5 cm) deep for the acrylic. The grooves should follow the angle and be cut 3/8" (1 cm) in from the edge. To cut to the proper depth, adjust the base plate on the circular saw. Check that the acrylic fits in the grooves.

   Cut an identical second *side* with two grooves for the acrylic.

3. For placement of the *stops* and *sides*, draw lines as shown on both the top and underside of the *bottom*. Glue and nail a *stop* into bottom of the *side* using 4d nails. Position the *side* plus the *stop* on the *bottom* as illustrated. Align the centerline of the *side* with centerline drawn on the *bottom*. With 4d nails, glue and nail into the *bottom* through the *stop*.

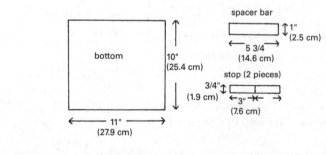

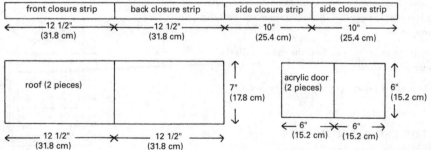

Continued →

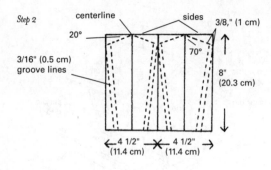

Step 2

centerline   sides

20°   3/8," (1 cm)

3/16" (0.5 cm)
groove lines   70°

8"
(20.3 cm)

← 4 1/2" →✕← 4 1/2" →
(11.4 cm)   (11.4 cm)

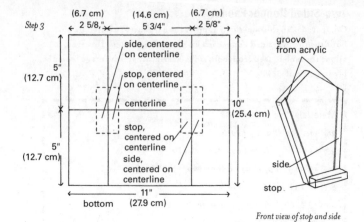

Step 3

(6.7 cm)   (14.6 cm)   (6.7 cm)
← 2 5/8" →   5 3/4"   ← 2 5/8" →

5"
(12.7 cm)

side, centered
on centerline

stop, centered
on centerline

centerline

10"
(25.4 cm)

stop,
centered on
centerline

5"
(12.7 cm)

side,
centered on
centerline

bottom   11"   (27.9 cm)

groove
from acrylic

side

stop

Front view of stop and side

4. Glue and nail a *stop* to the second *side*.

5. At the roof peak, glue and screw or nail through the second (unattached) *side* into the *spacer bar* with one screw or one 6d nail.

6. Align the centerline of the second *side* with the centerline drawn on the *bottom*. Glue and nail (4d) through the *stop* into the *bottom*.

7. Turn over the feeder and glue and screw or nail through the *bottom* into each *side*. Turn right-side up and screw through the first *side* into the *spacer bar*.

8. Insert a piece of acrylic into each set of grooves to be sure the *sides* are plumb and that each piece of acrylic fits. Remove the acrylic.

9. To enclose the *bottom*, glue and screw or nail (6d) the *side closure strips* to the *bottom*; then glue and screw or nail the *front* and *back closure strips* to the *bottom*.

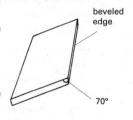

beveled
edge

70°

10. Bevel each side of the *roof* along one of the 12 1/2" (31.8 cm) edges at a 70-degree angle.

11. Place the two sections of the *roof* over the sides. With a hacksaw, cut a continuous hinge into two 5 1/2" (14 cm) lengths. The hinges will fit between the two beveled edges of the *roof*. Screw into place, leaving a 1/2" (1.3 cm) centered gap between the hinges.

12. Remove the protective coating and slide one piece of acrylic into place.

13. Center the hinged *roof* over the *sides* and screw the *roof* section to the *side* that has the acrylic in place. The other section of *roof* will not be screwed; it will allow access to the feeder for cleaning and seed refilling.

14. With the 3/8" (0.953 cm) bit, drill a hole between the two roof hinges and through the *spacer bar*. Drill carefully to avoid hitting the acrylic window.

15. Insert the wire through the hole. Bend the end with pliers so that the wire cannot retract.

16. Remove the protective coating and insert the second piece of acrylic.

MOUNTING THE TWO-SIDED HOPPER

Fill the hopper and hang in an appropriate location.

Suet Feeder

Suet feeders are for insect eaters and are filled with homemade or commercially available suet cakes. These feeders are constructed of a wire weave; plastic or cord mesh will be destroyed by squirrels. The weave gives birds a perch so that they can hang by their feet as they poke their bills into the suet. The feeder can easily be attached to the sides of a hopper feeder (see pages 011–014).

Materials

3/4" x 9" x 5" (1.9 x 22.9 x 12.7 cm) Lumber

One 7" x 9" (17.8 x 22.9 cm) piece 1/4" or 1/2" (0.6 cm or 1.3 cm) hardware cloth

Six 3/4" (1.9 cm) staples

Tools

Circular saw or handsaw

Metal cutting shears

Hammer

Drill and 1/4" (0.635 cm) drill bit

Staple gun

The finished suet feeder

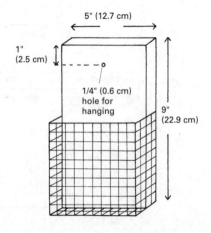

5" (12.7 cm)

1"
(2.5 cm)

1/4" (0.6 cm)
hole for
hanging

9"
(22.9 cm)

1. From 3/4" (1.9 cm) lumber, cut piece as illustrated.

Step 1

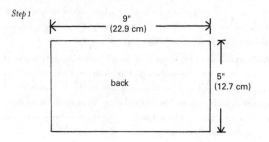

2. With metal cutting shears, cut the hardware cloth to the dimensions shown, and bend. To make the bends, place the hardware cloth on the edge of a sawhorse or 2 x 4 and hammer until 90-degree angles are achieved.

Step 2

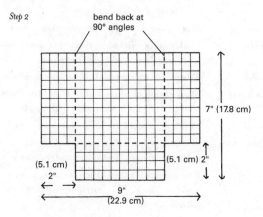

3. Drill a 1/4" (0.6 cm) hole in the *back*, 1" (2.5 cm) below the top edge. Staple hardware cloth to the bottom and sides of the *back*.

MOUNTING

Insert suet cake and attach to or hang from a tree.

Hummingbird Feeder

Put out the hummingbird feeder after the last frost in your area and keep it out all summer. Once the birds have become accustomed to the feeder, you can move it close to the house.

Materials

1 salad dressing bottle

1 rubber stopper (#6 1/2) 1 1/4" (3.2 cm) in diameter with a 1/4" (0.6 cm) center hole (available from homebrew supply shops)

One 1/4" (0.6 cm) diameter plastic tubing with a 120-degree angle at one end

1 S-hook

1 imitation red flower or red decor

1 onion bag or other nylon mesh bag

1 rubber band

---

1. Thoroughly clean and rinse a salad dressing bottle.

2. Fit the bottle with the rubber stopper (also called a bung stopper). Insert the angled tube.

3. Fill the bottle with nectar. (See below for nectar recipe.)

4. Around the tubing, slip a red bow, red plastic flower, or any other piece of red designed to look like a flower.

5. Place the bottle in the mesh bag, securing the bag around the neck of the bottle with the rubber band.

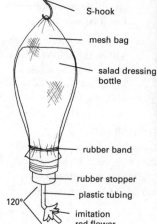

The finished hummingbird feeder

MOUNTING

Slip the S-hook through the mesh and hang the feeder over a flower bed; hummingbirds especially like impatiens and trumpet vines. Adjust the angle of the salad dressing bottle so that the hummers will be able to extract the sugar solution.

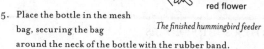

NECTAR FOR HUMMINGBIRDS
1 part white sugar
4 parts water

Combine the sugar and water. Boil the mixture for 1 to 2 minutes to retard fermentation. Let cool, then fill the dressing jar. If there is extra mixture left over, store it in the refrigerator for later use.

Do not substitute honey for sugar; it may quickly ferment and grow mold, which is harmful to birds.

It is not necessary to add red food coloring as long as there is something red to lure your visitors. To prevent unwanted fungi or bacteria buildup, empty the feeder every 3 to 4 days, washing the jar and feeding tube thoroughly with a bottle brush, Q-tip, or pipe cleaner. Rinse, then refill.

Suet Log Feeder

Materials

1 log, 2" to 3" (5.1–7.6 cm) in diameter and at least 24" (61 cm) long

1 screw eye

Tools

Drill and 1" (2.54 cm) paddle bit

Hammer (optional)

Continued ➜

1. Cut the log to 24" (61 cm) in length, if necessary. Bevel the top, if desired.

2. Drill several 1" (2.5 cm) holes halfway through the log and press or hammer suet or a peanut butter mixture into the holes.

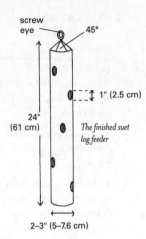

screw eye

45°

1" (2.5 cm)

24" (61 cm)

The finished suet log feeder

2–3" (5–7.6 cm)

MOUNTING

Insert the screw eye in the top and hang from a tree. It's best to use a long section of wire (2 to 3 feet; 0.6–0.9 m) to discourage squirrels.

OTHER SUET FEEDERS

- Fill an onion bag or a nylon mesh container with suet and hang from a tree.
- Fill the crevices of a pinecone with suet or a peanut butter mixture. Secure a wire to the pointed end of the pinecone and hang from a tree branch. The pinecone can also be dipped in melted suet, rolled in birdseed, and chilled to harden.

Bird Food Recipes

Rhonda Massingham Hart
Illustrations by Alison Kolesar

The types of birds that come to your feeder will depend on your geographic location, the time of year, and the types of feeders and food you provide. Different birds have different feeding habits, and a variety of food and feeders will attract the most diverse variety of takers.

Natural Menus

Seed Eaters Most songbirds belong to this broad category. Many eat a combination of seeds and bugs, depending on the time of year. Finches, cardinals, grosbeaks, and sparrows are but a few of the primarily seed-eating birds that are attracted to feeders.

Some Prefer Fruit Birds that might otherwise ignore your feeders, such as Bohemian and cedar waxwings, orioles, or mockingbirds, can often be bribed with orange halves, apple pieces, or other fruit. Sometimes these offerings take a while to be noticed. Don't give up if the first few offerings are not instantly devoured.

Bugs for Supper Bug eaters, such as woodpeckers, nuthatches, and robins, may show little interest in your feeders. But come winter they will flock to suet and suet substitutes. Tempt them in the spring with a squirmy tray of mealworms. Most seed eaters will also indulge in insects in the spring when they are raising young.

Some Sip Nectar Hummingbirds are a delightful addition to any yard. They are primarily attracted to natural food sources, such as flowers and blooming vines and shrubs. They also feed on tiny soft insects found among these blossoms. Hummingbirds will visit nectar feeders on a regular basis if they are kept filled, clean, and free from pests, such as yellow jackets. Also, fruit-loving warblers, orioles, tanagers, and grosbeaks have a taste for the sweet nectar solutions.

NATURAL FOOD SOURCES TO ATTRACT BIRDS

Plant	Birds Attracted
Black cherry	Blue jay, cardinal, downy woodpecker, goldfinch, mockingbird, robin, others
Black walnut	Blue jay, cardinal, downy woodpecker, others
Blueberry	Black-capped chickadee, blue jay, cardinal, robin, mourning dove, starling, scores more
Brambles	Blue jay, cardinal, mockingbird, robin, others
Chokecherry	Black-capped chickadee, blue jay, cardinal, downy woodpecker, goldfinch, mockingbird, robin, others
Dogwood	Cardinal, mockingbird, robin, others
E. White Pine	Black-capped chicadee, blue jay, cardinal, goldfinch, mourning dove, nuthatch, others
Elderberry	Blue jay, cardinal, goldfinch, mockingbird, mourning dove, robin, titmouse, white-breasted nuthatch, others
Gooseberry	Mourning dove, mockingbird, robin, others
Grape	Blue jay, cardinal, goldfinch, mockingbird, robin, mourning dove, others
Hackberry	Cardinal, mockingbird, robin, others
Hawthorn	Blue jay, cardinal, mockingbird, robin, more
Holly	Cardinal, mockingbird, robin, many more
Honeysuckle	Goldfinch, mockingbird, robin, others
Huckleberry	Blue jay, mourning dove, robin, others
Juniper	Downy woodpecker, mockingbird, robin, others
Mountain ash	Robin, white-breasted nuthatch
Maple	Cardinal, goldfinch, robin, others
Mulberry	Blue jay; cardinal; catbird; downy, red-bellied and redheaded woodpeckers; cedar waxwing; eastern kingbird; goldfinch; mockingbird; purple finch; red-eyed vireo; robin; scarlet tanager; wood thrush; yellowbilled cuckoo; many, many others
Multifora rose	Cardinal, mockingbird, others
Oak	Blue jay, cardinal, downy woodpecker, mourning dove, white-breasted nuthatch, others
Olive	Black-capped chickadee, cardinal, mockingbird, mourning dove, robin, others
Red cedar	Cardinal, cedar waxwing, mockingbird, mourning dove, robin, others

Plant	Birds Attracted
Sassafras	Bobwhite, catbird, eastern kingbird, redeyed vireo, robin
Serviceberry	Blue jay, cardinal, downy woodpecker, goldfinch, mockingbird, mourning dove, robin, others
Sumac	Bobwhite, cardinal, Carolina chickadee, eastern towhee, flicker, goldfinch, mockingbird, phoebe, robin, thrushes, warblers, white-eyed vireo, others
Sunflower	At least 42 species
Sweet gum	Black-capped chickadee, cardinal, goldfinch, others
Virginia creeper	Black-capped chickadee, mockingbird, robin, tufted titmouse, white-breasted nuthatch

Garden flowers, such as bachelor buttons, calendula, California poppy, campanula, chrysanthemum, cone flower, coreopsis, cosmos, dusty miller, marigold, phlox, verbena, and zinnia, among others, also attract an array of birds.

FAVORITE HUMMINGBIRD PLANTS

Trees	Hawthorn, flowering crabapple, black locust
Bushes	Azalea, butterfly bush, coralberry, flowering currant, flowering quince, hibiscus, red elderberry, weigela
Vines	Clematis, morning glory, scarlet runner bean, trumpet vine, trumpet honeysuckle
Flowers: Perennials	Bee balm, bleeding heart, columbine, coral bells, dahlia, day lily, delphinium, fox glove, hollyhock, lupine
Annuals	Dianthus (pinks), flowering tobacco, fuchsia, geranium, Impatiens, nasturtium, petunia, salvia

Bird Feeders

Bird feeders come in several types, each designed to serve a specific purpose. **Selective feeders** discourage nuisance-type birds, such as starlings, crows, and house sparrows. These feeders have very short or no perches, which makes feeding difficult to impossible for chunky visitors, while inviting small, agile birds, such as chickadees, finches, and nuthatches to enjoy a free meal. **Non-selective feeders** welcome one and all. Any large, accessible feeder with plenty of parking space may be considered a non-selective feeder. While selective feeders are hung from a branch or line to prevent certain birds from feeding, non-selective feeders can cater to ground birds as well as those that prefer to dine higher up.

Other distinctions in feeders include the type of feed they dispense and the manner in which they release it. Hopper feeders funnel seed down into a feeding tray until the hopper bin is empty. They can accommodate different sized seed and usually have clear sides so that you can monitor the contents. They may be set on a stump, tabletop, or windowsill, attached to a post or hung from branches, eaves, or a pulley string. The latter allows you to reel the feeder in for refills or to gradually move it closer to the window for viewing, as the birds become accustomed to its position. These feeders require very little upkeep as they are virtually self-cleaning. If for some reason the level of food does not go down within a few days, check to be sure the seed is not moldy.

Tube feeders are clear plastic cylinders often designed to release seed at several outlets. They are selective feeders that hang freely and sway with the breeze or the weight of perching birds; conditions which discourage larger birds but beckon to small chickadees, house finches, and others. Shortening the perches to 1/2 inch will limit accessibility to only the smallest customers. Specialized tube feeders dispense tiny thistle (niger) seed, highly prized by goldfinches and siskins, one seed at a time. This is perfectly suited to their habit of flying to a safe place with each seed they find before eating it.

A tray or platform-type feeder can be set near or at ground level to entice a nearly limitless variety of birds. It can hold anything from seeds and nuts to fruit and suet. It is a non-selective type feeder, allowing for the greatest possible variety of birds.

Suet feeders are specially made to hold solid suet or suet mixtures or substitutes. They can be as simple as a hanging mesh bag (such as an onions or oranges bag), a piece of hardware cloth bent to shape and nailed in place, or a large pine cone smeared with fat. Fancier versions can be store bought or created from small logs with holes bored to hold the suet.

Nectar feeders are almost exclusively for hummingbirds. They are clear plastic and usually have red parts to attract the hummer's attention. These feed a sweet liquid mixture through a narrow tube or several small openings. (See Easy-to-Build Bird Feeders)

FEEDING HEIGHT PREFERENCES

Ground Feeders	Tabletop	Hanging or Post	Tree Trunk
Chickadees	Chickadees	Chickadees	Flickers
Jays	Jays	Titmice	Woodpeckers
Game birds	Waxwings	Nuthatches	Sapsuckers
Robins	Grosbeaks	Grosbeaks	Chickadees
Starlings	Starlings	Finches	Nuthatches
Towhees	Finches	Redpolls	Creepers
Sparrows	Redpolls	Siskins	Kinglets
Juncos	Hummingbirds	Hummingbirds	
Cardinals	Cardinals		
Mourning doves			
Pigeons			
Crows			
Cowbirds			
Grackles			
Red-winged blackbirds			

FEEDER TIPS

Here are some tips to help make your bird feeders successful:

- Place feeders so they are easily visible, both by you and the birds. Birds won't eat what they can't see.

- Birds prefer to eat in the sun, but out of direct wind and weather.

- Place near cover.

- Avoid placing directly in front of windows; to the side is better. Birds can be warned away from otherwise invisible glass by closing curtains or putting stickers in windows.

- Use a variety of feeders and food.

- Keep feeders clean and full. Fill at the same time each day.

Continued →

ATTRACTIVENESS AND NUTRITIONAL VALUE

Food	Attractiveness	Nutrition
White bread	High to most birds	Low to moderate
Cornbread	Moderate	Moderate to good
Doughnuts	Moderate to good	Low
White proso millet	High, especially sparrows and juncos	High
Black-oil sunflower	High; many prefer to white millet	Most nutritious of the sunflower seeds
Red proso millet	High	Similar to white millet
Shelled peanuts	High	Rich in protein and calories
Black-striped sunflower	Moderate	Good
Canary seed	Moderate, eaten by birds that like white proso millet	Moderate in protein and minerals
Hulled sunflower	Moderate	High
Milo	Low; a common "filler" in commercial mixes, often scratched aside	Moderate
Gray-striped sunflower	Low	Less oil than others
Buckwheat	Low; except to doves	Moderate
Thistle (niger)	Low; except to goldfinches, siskins, and other finches	High
Rice	Low	Poor
Peanut hearts	Low; except to starlings	High, spoils easily
Oat groats	Low	Good
Flax	Nearly worthless	Moderate
Rape	Very few takers	High fat, protein, and minerals
Corn	High	High, vitamin A, protein
Nutmeats	High	Rich in heat and calories
American cheese	Very appealing to some	High
Cottage cheese	High for young birds	High
Apples	High to many types	Moderate
Berries	High	Good
Orange halves	High to some	Good
Suet	High	High
Peanut butter	High	High

TROUBLESHOOTING

Trilling songbirds and brightly feathered visitors are not the only ones to frequent bird feeders. There are a number of other creatures that can make pests of themselves and in some cases even scare away the birds you are trying to encourage.

Squirrels: Public enemy number one to many bird feeders. They steal or waste food and can damage or destroy feeders in their zeal to empty them. Hang pie pans, metal lids, even old phonograph records up and down support wires of hanging feeders. Use short sections of garden hose or tubing as spacers. Use chew-proof wire. Place feeders at least 8 feet from any take-off point hungry squirrels may try to use. Try suspending feeders from a horizontal line that has been strung with tubing, old plastic pop bottles, or other obstacles. Baffles, spinners, cones, and other barriers are commercially available.

Cats: Provide nearby cover, but keep the immediate area clear so that cats can't sneak up on the feeder undetected. Bell your cat or keep it inside, especially during nesting season. Fence around the feeder area with a 2-to 3-foot tall fence of hardware cloth or chicken wire.

Starlings or House Sparrows: Offer selective feeders with short or no perches, and hang them so they swing freely. Try a counterbalance feeder, which is designed so that the weight of a heavy bird causes the food door to close. Arrange suet feeders so that the only access to the suet is for the bird to hang upside down. Avoid foods that attract these birds, such as baked goods, table scraps, and peanut hearts, and opt for sunflower and millet, if these birds become a nuisance. If the problem becomes severe stop ground or platform feeding for a while.

Rodents: Don't overstock ground feeders, offer only as much as the birds will finish each day. Clean up leftovers and cut down on spilled waste by eliminating commercial seed mixes.

Hawks: Once birds begin to congregate regularly around your feeders, they may attract the attention of such birds of prey as Coopers or sharp-skinned hawks. Help protect your invited guests by providing nearby cover.

Dietary Demands

The nutritional demands of wild birds vary with the season. Even in sub-freezing weather small birds must maintain a body temperature of 105°F. In any season a bird's dietary requirements are substantial. To "eat like a bird" literally means to fill much of every waking hour in the pursuit of food.

To ensure the overall success and effectiveness of your feeding program it is important to have an understanding of the comparative attractiveness and nutritional value of bird foods. Some foods, suet and nuts in particular, are especially high in fat and calories, and are considered "heating foods." Others, like torn white bread or doughnut pieces, seem to be universally favored by many birds, but fall short nutritionally. Even so, they are valuable in establishing a feeder and enticing visiting birds to sample other, healthier offerings.

Personal Preferences

All wild birds have common requirements that you can offer to attract their attention: water, salt, and grit. These are in short supply during cold weather as water freezes up and sandy patches get snowed over.

A clean bird bath (with an inclined floor) is a welcome stop to both drinkers and bathers. Many birds like to eat their food with water. Salt should be offered mixed with other food as it is often ignored if set out alone. Grit is necessary for birds to grind the food they eat and for some mineral value. Offer ground oyster shell, sand, or ground eggshell either alone in trays or mixed with seed or recipes.

The list of other possible offerings is nearly limitless. Some items have a wide appeal, while others are relished by some and rejected by others. Many birds have definite preferences which you can use to tailor your feeding program to include your favorite species. Some foods attract a wide variety of birds and are helpful in establishing business at a new feeder.

FAVORITE FOODS OF FAVORITE BIRDS

Bird	Fruit	Seed	Fat/Protein	Other
Black-capped chickadee and titmice		canary, corn, hemp, melon, thistle, oats, pumpkin, squash, sunflower	bacon drippings, meat scraps, almonds, butternuts, coconut**, hickory, peanuts, pecans, walnuts, peanut butter*	white bread, cornmeal, dog biscuit, doughnuts, pie crust
Bluebird	baked apples, currants, figs, grapes, raisins, strawberries		cottage cheese	biscuits, doughnuts, pie crust
Blue Jay	apples, raisins	hemp, melon, safflower, sunflower, whole or cracked corn	bacon drippings, cooked eggs, meat scraps, suet, peanuts, peanut butter*, peanut hearts, pecans, walnuts	cooked potatoes, potato peelings, white bread, cornbread, cracker crumbs, dog biscuits, doughnuts, chicken feed, eggshells
Cardinal		sunflower, cracked corn, buckwheat	suet	
Cedar Waxwing	apples, cherries, currants, grapes, raisins	sunflower		
Dark-eyed Junco		canary, pumpkin, hemp, white millet, cracked corn, squash, sunflower, thistle	peanut butter*, peanut hearts, suet, pecans, black walnut, rolled oats	white bread, cornbread, dog biscuit, doughnut, pie crust, chicken feed
Evening and other Grosbeaks		apple seeds, cracked corn, melon, millet, safflower, soybean, sunflower	suet, peanuts, peanut hearts, pecans	sugar water
Grouse, Quail, Pheasant		whole or cracked corn, whole oats, soybean		chicken feed, white bread
Goldfinch		cracked corn, canary, white proso millet, black sunflower, thistle	suet, hickory nut, peanut butter*, peanut hearts, English walnuts	chicken feed
Mockingbird	apples, bananas, currants, figs, dates, grapes, oranges, raisins, pears, strawberries, watermelon		suet, cooked eggs, peanut butter*, peanut hearts	white bread, cornbread, doughnuts
Mourning Dove	peanut hearts, pecans		buckwheat, canary, whole or cracked corn, hemp, melon, white proso millet, thistle, milo, oat, sunflower	chicken feed
Northern Oriole	apples, bananas, oranges, grapes, raisins, watermelon	cracked corn, millet, rice	suet, peanut butter*, pecans	honey, jelly, sugar water, syrup, white bread, doughnut, pie crust
Nuthatch		cantaloupe, melon, sunflower	bacon drippings, suet, almonds, butternut, peanut, peanut butter*, peanut heart, black walnut	white bread, doughnut
Pine siskin		sunflower, thistle		salt, ashes
Red-winged Blackbird		buckwheat, canary, millet, niger, oats, whole or cracked corn, sunflower	suet, peanut hearts, chopped pecans	chicken feed, white bread, cornbread
Robin	blueberries, cherries, currants, apples, grapes, pears, raisins, strawberries		suet, American cheese, peanut butter*, peanut hearts, pecans	biscuits, white bread, cornbread, doughnuts, cooked spaghetti
Rufus-sided towhee	grapes	barley, canary, cracked corn, hemp, millet, thistle, oats, sunflower	suet, peanut hearts	chicken feed, white bread, dog biscuit
Scarlet tanager	apples, bananas, cherries, oranges, raisins		suet	sugar water, white bread
Starling	apples, currants, grapefruit raisins	cracked or canned corn, melon, milo, oat groats, whole oats, cooked rice	bacon drippings, cooked eggs, meat scraps, suet, American cheese, peanut butter*, peanut hearts, canned dog food	alfalfa meal, white bread, cornbread, dog biscuit, doughnuts, potato chips, boiled potatoes, cooked sweet potatoes, sauerkraut
Stellars Jay		corn	meat scraps, peanut butter*, suet, English walnuts	white bread
Woodpecker		cracked corn, shelled sunflower	meat scraps, suet, almonds, coconut**, hickory nuts, peanuts, black walnuts	cornbread, doughnuts

*Peanut butter should never be served straight as it can stick to a bird's beak

**Never offer dried, shredded coconut as it swells once inside the bird.

Seasonal Feeding

SPRING

The need for supplemental feeding is at its peak in the early spring. By now the natural foods available from the previous season are long gone, and the current season's growth has not yet started. Birds are about to nest and lay eggs, putting further strain on their winter-weakened bodies. Egg laying requires a high level of calcium which can be supplied with crushed eggshells or ground oyster shell.

SUMMER

Even though natural foods are plentiful in the summer, there is still much you can do to entice birds to come to your feeder. During this season birds must feed not only themselves but their rapidly growing young. This rapid growth demands lots of protein, which turns even the most placid seed eaters into determined bug hunters.

There are several ways you can meet the nutritional demands of summer. Cut down on high energy, heat-producing foods such as suet and nutmeats. Or go a little buggy! Mealworms, the larvae of the *Tenebrio molitor* beetle, are commercially available, easily homegrown, and irresistible to many kinds of birds.

Fledgling Foods. If you feed birds year round, those that raise their young in your vicinity may bring their babies to your feeders. This requires an extreme amount of trust on the part of the birds, for if they have even one frightening experience at your feeder they may never return, let alone bring their fledglings. So sell or bell the cat, keep the field of vision clear, have some cover nearby, and put out some special goodies for the kids.

Nestlings are raised on a partially pre-digested "bug stew." New foods should be soft textured and mild tasting. Offer some of the following dishes to introduce fledglings to new foods while establishing their trust in you and your feeders. Since suet may turn rancid, use the summer suet substitute in very warm weather.

* Cottage Cheese Salad *

Currants, raisins, blueberries, grapes, or mulberries
Cottage cheese

Stir fruit into cottage cheese and set out in shallow containers. Don't set out more than the birds will eat in a day. Better to refill several times a day than to let the salad spoil.

* Baby Bread *

Sugar   *White bread*
Milk

Stir a little sugar into milk until dissolved. Cut bread into pieces and soak in the sweetened milk for a few seconds. Set pieces on feeding tray.

* Cornmeal Mush *

1 part water   *Choice of fruit: Mashed bananas,*
1 part cornmeal   *strawberries, cherries, blueberries, or*
                                       preserves

4 parts water
Salt
For leftovers:

Flour
Shortening or bacon drippings

Mix 1 part water with cornmeal. Bring 4 parts water to a boil and stir in cornmeal mixture and salt. Boil one minute. Remove from heat and pour into serving container, such as an old foil pie plate. Stir in fruit. Chill leftovers, form into patties, dust with flour and fry in shortening or bacon drippings as a treat for older birds.

* Cooked Cereal *

Hot cereal of your choice
    (oatmeal, wheathearts, Farina, etc.)
Pieces of fruit, berries, preserves, or peanut butter

Prepare according to cereal directions and stir in additives. Serve as for Cornmeal Mush.

* Soft Suet *

The softer texture and extra sweetness is much easier for young birds to swallow.

2 parts suet   *1/2 part apple or grape jelly*
1 part peanut butter

Melt suet and allow to cool until it begins to thicken. Stir in peanut butter and jelly. Pour into containers and set out on feeder tray. Consider nailing them down to avoid grand theft.

* Summer Suet Substitute *

1 part flour   *1 part peanut butter*
3 to 4 parts yellow cornmeal   *1 part vegetable shortening*
Dash salt

Mix dry ingredients and stir into gooey. Spoon into containers. Favored by tanagers, thrushes, warblers and many others.

* Hummingbird Nectar *

Sugar   *Red food coloring or grenadine*
Water

Mix equal portions of sugar and water and bring to boil. This helps the sugar dissolve completely and retards fermentation. Dilute to a ratio of four to one by adding 3 parts cold water per part of sugar mix. Add a few drops of red food coloring, or a tablespoon of grenadine to help attract the hummingbirds' attention and to make the feeder contents easily visible. Store unused portions in the refrigerator.

Bees or wasps can become troublesome at hummingbird feeders. They can be discouraged by smearing a little petroleum jelly or salad oil around the dispenser holes.

FALL

During autumn young birds are learning to fend for themselves, and migratory birds are preparing for their long flights by putting on as much fat as possible and by molting into a new set of feathers. These transitions are taxing on the birds and demand optimum nutrition if they are to survive the winter. Starting a winter feeding program early in the fall has the added advantage of luring birds to your feeder that might move on further south if you wait until later in the season to start feeding.

WINTER

Freezing temperatures, chill winds, snow cover, and lack of natural food make winter the most obvious time to keep bird feeders full. Nights are long and temperatures plummet. A study of chickadees found that they could put on as much as 7.5 percent of their body weight during the day, only to have burned it off by the following morning. Birds will be most active in their search for food first thing in the morning and again just before nightfall. Make sure feeders, water, and grit are accessible at these high-demand times.

Freezing weather places a tremendous energy demand on a wild bird's system. Because of this, high fat/high protein/ high energy foods are more important in the winter than any other time of year. They are referred to as "heating foods." Nuts are one example, and suet, the hard, white beef fat found behind the kidneys is a favorite winter offering. It is gratefully accepted by at least eighty different species of North American birds.

Recipes and Food Preparation

PREPARING SUET

The simplest way to offer suet is in large raw chunks, suspended in mesh bags or held in wire holders. Suet can also be prepared by melting and cooling. While there is no difference in nutritional value, prepared suet lasts longer, is less likely to spoil during warm temperature lulls, is less appealing to starlings and other pest type birds, and is easy to work with.

- Cut chunks of suet into smaller pieces or run through meat grinder.
- Melt over low heat until liquid. Allow to cool in pan until solidified.
- Slowly reheat until liquid a second time. At this stage the suet is ready to be poured into molds. It can be poured over or mixed with a variety of other ingredients, or allowed to cool somewhat and spread into drilled log feeders, pine cones, onto tree branches, etc.

Whether served straight or mixed in a recipe, prepared suet lends itself well to a variety of serving forms. Finding suet containers needn't strain your budget, just your imagination. Here are some suggestions:

- Muffin tins
- Tuna fish or cat food cans
- Yogurt cups
- Cottage cheese containers
- Coconut halves
- Log drilled with 1-inch holes
- Cake molds formed by folding foil around bars of soap or other forms.
- Foil lined cookie pan. Use cookie cutter on hardened suet to make shapes.

Pine cones can be spread with suet or suet mixtures and hung from tree branches.

Create suet balls by pouring suet into a rounded mold and removing while still warm and soft enough to manipulate. Set on wax paper and press into shape using the wax paper. When cooled, hang in a mesh bag.

SUET MIXTURES

All by itself suet is a valuable source of energy and very attractive to many birds. Suet cakes, cones, molds, and mixtures simply liven up the menu and keep the birds interested.

* YUMMY CRUMB CAKES *

This recipe combines the high energy of suet, the mass appeal of popular seeds and the extra treat of fruit.

1 1/2 parts wheat or multi-grain bread crumbs

1 part hulled sunflower seeds

1 part white or red proso millet

1/2 part chopped dried fruit (apples, blueberries, raisins, cherries)

6 to 9 parts suet

Dash of salt

Sprinkle of sand

Melt suet, allow to cool, then re-melt. As it cools the second time stir in all other ingredients. Spoon into molds. Once the cakes solidify, place in suet feeders or attach to trays.

* HANGING HEAVEN *

A rich, nutritious mix, appreciated by a variety of birds, especially in winter. Even the feeder is edible!

3 parts suet	1 part brown sugar
1 part cornmeal	1 or more coconuts, split in half
1 part peanut butter	1 part raisins, dried cherries, etc.
Sprinkling of sand	1 part mixed seed or broken nuts

Melt suet, allow to cool, then re-melt. Stir in other ingredients. Cook until the mixture is the consistency of porridge. If too thick, add small amounts of water or milk; if too thin, add flour. Pour into coconut halves. Hang coconut halves from tree limbs or eaves.

* NO SUET SUET *

So tasty you might be tempted to try it yourself!

2 cups water	1/2 cup raisins
1 tablespoon butter	4 cups crunchy peanut butter
1 tablespoon sugar	1/2 cup cornmeal
2 tablespoons cinnamon	1/2 cup whole wheat flour
1 cup oatmeal	1/2 cup millet

Continued →

Boil water with butter, sugar, and cinnamon. Add oatmeal and raisins. Cook one minute and stir in remaining ingredients. Press into containers or mold directly onto tree branches.

Bakery Goods

Just like us, many birds have a craving for the sweetness and texture of baked goods. Gratify their "sweet beaks" with some down home baking, just for them.

* Cornbread *

3 cups yellow cornmeal	1 1/2 teaspoons baking powder
1/2 cup seeds, raisins, nuts, dried berries,	1/3 cup shortening or bacon fat
peanut butter, fruit, or ground meat,	3 cups water
optional	Sprinkling of fine sand

Combine all ingredients, adding the seeds, raisins, nuts, dried berries, peanut butter, fruit, or ground meat to add extra zing. Bake at 425°F for 25 minutes, in a well-greased pan. Allow to cool, turn out of pan. Crumble to serve.

* Fruit Bread *

Birds that love fruit, sweets, and bread, such as tanagers and orioles, find this sweet, fruity bread just to their taste.

2 packages yeast (2 tablespoons)	1/2 cup sugar
1/4 cup warm water	2 tablespoons shortening
2 1/2 cups fruit juice (orange, apple,	1 tablespoon salt
raspberry, etc.)	7+ cups flour

Dissolve yeast in warm water. Let sit while combining other ingredients, except flour. Stir yeast into juice mixture. Add flour, mixing first by spoon, then by hand. Turn out on floured surface and let rest about 10 minutes. Knead about 8 minutes, until surface is smooth and elastic. Divide into loaves and place in greased bread pans. Let rise until doubled in bulk. Bake at 425°F for 25 to 30 minutes. Cool on rack and serve in torn pieces.

Custom Seed Mixes

Most commercial mixes contain a large amount of "filler" seed, such as milo or wheat. While not totally lacking in nutrition, these seeds are not of much value because many birds scratch them aside. Good commercial mixes contain sunflower, safflower, white or red proso millet, cracked corn and even peanuts. If you can't find a mix to suit your particular clientele, whip up a batch of your own.

* 50/50 *

A simple combination sure to draw a crowd.

Black oil-type sunflower seed

Cracked corn

Combine equal parts of each and set out at ground level or in elevated feeders.

* Game Bird Fame *

You will be famous with a variety of game birds and other ground feeders in your areas if you serve this irresistible mixture of their favorites.

2 parts chicken scratch	2 parts whole corn
1 part whole oats	1 part buckwheat
1 part soybean seeds	1 teaspoon grit per quart of seed

Combine ingredients and offer at ground level. Be sure there is nearby cover to allow shy birds a chance to retreat if they feel threatened.

* Come One, Come All *

A healthy mix with vast appeal.

3 parts sunflower seed	3 parts hempseed
3 parts millet	1 part canary seed
1 part finely cracked corn	Grit

Mix and offer at any level.

* Granola Crunch *

The variety in this recipe makes it appealing to many kinds of birds. Use the main ingredients, but don't hesitate to substitute or toss in leftovers, such as bread or cake crumbs, pie crust pieces, dried fruit, cracked corn, or what-have-you. Combine the finished granola with suet for a woodpecker treat.

1 part honey	1 part wheat germ
1 part corn or peanut oil	2 parts raisins or dried berries
2 parts chopped peanuts	2 parts hulled sunflower seed
2 parts white proso millet	2 parts crumbled dog biscuits

Mix and heat honey and oil. In large bowl combine all other ingredients and pour heated liquid over them. Mix and press into shallow pan. Bake at 375°F for 10 minutes. Crumble to serve.

A SPECIAL CRAVING

Many birds regularly risk their lives to glean salt and minerals from roadways. Here is a safer alternative that rewards you for your thoughtfulness with flocks of lingering birds.

* CRYSTALLINE *

Salt

Wood ashes*

Mix salt and ashes with enough water to dissolve and pour over a large rock, stump or wood block. As the water evaporates, crystals form that attract mineral-hungry birds.

   *These can be fireplace ashes as long as they do not contain residues from burning colored (especially red) or slick finished paper.

SERVES UP!

Sometimes the simplest fare can be made intriguing by the way in which it is served. Try these fun favorites.

Corn on the Cob on a Spike. First prepare the dining table. Drive several large nails through an old plank or mill end. Old, weathered wood blends into the surroundings better, both in scent and sight, and is less startling to shy ground-feeding birds. Grease each spike with shortening or salad oil and push an ear of corn (fresh or dried) over each. Set out at ground level near cover.

String 'em Along. Especially appropriate at Christmastime are decorative strands of whole peanuts, popcorn, caramel corn, dried or fresh berries, pieces of fruit, etc. Wrap around trees, hang from window to feeder, weave into holiday wreaths and watch the birds cheerfully dismantle them.

Gourmet Bouquet. Of the many trees, shrubs, and plants that appeal to birds, chances are that you have only a few in your yard. Don't despair. Ask friends and neighbors for cuttings or trimmings of the birds' beloved branches. Collect them when in fruit or seed and arrange them in a bowl or vase on or near the feeding tray. Push the stems into florist styrofoam or a melon to secure.

SPECIAL REQUESTS

Here are some recipes to cater to unique individual cravings.

ROBIN ROUNDS

Perhaps cooked spaghetti reminds the robin of early worms.

Cooked spaghetti	Sprinkling of sand
American cheese, cut in strips	Suet
Chopped apple	

Arrange loops of spaghetti in papered muffin tins. Add cheese and apple and sprinkle with sand. Pour melted suet over mixture and allow to cool. Set out at ground level.

BLUE JAY EGGS

Blue jays love eggs, but they may have to share this specialty of the house with mockingbirds, catbirds, or others.

Bacon drippings	Peanut kernels
Eggs	Dash of salt
Apple pieces	Raisins, pecans (optional)

Melt bacon drippings and break in eggs, crumbling in shells. Scramble with apple, peanuts, and salt. Add raisins, pecans, or other favorite jay tidbits. Offer at ground feeder.

BLUEBIRD HAPPINESS

Bluebirds prefer their apples baked.

1 1/2 cups flour	Sprinkling of fine sand
1/2 teaspoon salt	1/2 cup sugar
1/2 cup shortening	1/2 cup raisins
1 apple, sliced and chopped	1/4 cup water

Combine flour, salt, and sand. Set aside. Bring sugar, shortening, apple, and raisins to boil in water and cook 5 minutes. Combine with flour mixture. Bake at 350°F for 20 minutes. Cook, crumble, and serve at elevated feeder.

CARDINAL CANDY

1/2 part green grapes	1 part sunflower seeds
1/2 part blueberries or black cherries	1 part cracked corn
	Suet
1 part breadcrumbs	Sprinkle of sand

Arrange all ingredients except suet and sand at bottom of foil pan. Melt, cool, and re-melt suet. Pour over other ingredients. As mixture cools, sprinkle with sand and mix well. Place on ground feeder when cool.

DOVE LOVE

Unlike most ground feeders, doves delight in thistle seed. This seed mix will also attract attention from many other birds.

Pecan pieces	Thistle seed
White proso millet	Buckwheat
Cracked corn	

Mix in any proportions and scatter on ground.

CHICKADEELIGHT

Also readily taken by titmice and a number of other birds.

1 part suet	1 part nut pieces (almonds, peanuts, pecans, walnuts)
Bacon drippings	
Chopped meat	1 part sunflower seeds

Melt suet and stir in bacon drippings and meat scraps. Stir in nuts and seeds as mixture cools and thickens. Pour into molds.

Variation: Reserve nuts and seeds. As mixture thickens and cools, fill pine cones. When cones are cooled, spread a second layer of warm suet over them and roll the cones in a mixture of nuts and seeds. Wrap with wax paper and push seeds into suet. Hang from tree branch, feeder, or eaves.

GOLDFINCH GLORY

Suet	Millet
Thistle seed	Hempseed

Pour twice-melted suet over a mixture of these favorite seeds and cool. Place at feeder.

Continued →

GROSBEAK GOODY

1/2 cup sunflower seeds	1/4 cup cracked corn
1/4 cup pecan bits	1 cup suet
1/4 cup soybeans	

Stir seeds and nuts into twice-melted suet. Pour into molds or foil-covered cookie sheet. Cut out pieces from hardened mixture on cookie sheet. Place or hang at feeders.

JUNCO JOY

Cracked corn	White bread
Cornmeal	Sprinkling of sand
Canary seed	Peanut butter

Mix dry ingredients and add enough peanut butter to make a spreadable consistency. Spread on white bread. Cut into pieces and serve at feeding tray.

MOCKINGBIRD MUFFINS

2 cups cornmeal	1 cup buttermilk
1/2 teaspoon soda	1 cup diced meat and fat scraps
1/4 teaspoon salt	Sprinkling of sand

Mix all ingredients and pour into greased muffin cups. Bake at 425°F for 20 minutes. Serve at ground or platform feeder.

SISKIN SATISFACTION

2 parts hulled sunflower	1 part salt or wood ashes
2 parts thistle seed	

Combine ingredients and offer in hanging feeder or elevated tray.

TANAGER TEMPTATION

Apple or banana pieces	White bread
Raisins or cherries	Sugar

Toss fruit and torn bread with white sugar and offer at ground feeder.

WOODPECKER WONDER

Woodpeckers and flickers will flock to this concoction.

4 parts suet	1 part sunflower seeds
Corn oil	1 part nut pieces (almonds, hickory, black
1/2 part raisins	walnut, or peanut)
	Sprinkling of sand

Twice melt suet and stir in 1 tablespoon corn oil per cup of suet. Add raisins, seeds, and nuts. When mixture cools to a spreadable consistency spread on tree bark 6 to 10 feet high.

Building Nestboxes for Backyard Birds

René and Christyna M. Laubauch

Illustrations by Brigita Fuhrmann

Getting to Know Your Birds

The more you know about the birds you are trying to attract, the better. To get started with your nestbox project, you must first appraise the habitat in your area and find out what birds are present. Learn as much as you can about those that make their home in your area, including nest size, nest construction, incubation period, age at fledging, food choices, competitors, predators, and type of habitat required.

The location you select for your nestbox must match the needs of the bird. All locations should have an abundance of food, protective cover, and water; however, different birds find these requirements in different and varied habitats. Some birds live in fields, others in open woodlands, still others along waterways and forest edges. If your nestbox is to be functional, it and its location must meet the basic needs of the bird you are trying to attract. If you put your nestbox in a field, for example, you might be providing an opportunity for Tree Swallows and bluebirds to nest. If you put it in a wooded area, on the other hand, nuthatches might take up residence. And some species, such as the Tree Swallow, require a clear flight path to and from the nestbox. The location and box design that best match the bird's natural nesting choices will be most likely to attract tenants.

Remember also that if the proper food is not available, birds will travel to places where it can be found; consequently, they won't nest in your box.

Designing (Is) for the Birds

At one time or another, we've all seen decorative birdhouses that rival dollhouses in their level of detail. Though they may be nice to look at, these designer birdhouses do little for birds. In fact, the human urge to make birdhouses more aesthetically pleasing is generally misguided and counterproductive. Novelty birdhouses are often undersized; have entrance holes that are too large or too small; are sealed shut, allowing no access to the interior for monitoring or cleaning; lack vent and drain holes; are constructed of wood that is much too thin; or lack other features crucial for success.

A well-designed and -constructed nestbox, on the other hand, is beautiful in a utilitarian sense. Underlying the box's simple exterior are a host of special design features that have taken many years of trial-and-error experimentation to discover. All cater to the needs of the particular species and include a correctly sized entrance hole, a sufficient interior floor size to accommodate eggs and nestlings, and sufficient depth below the entrance hole to help thwart potential predators. Drainage holes, a drip edge, a roof overhang to shed water, and ventilation holes are among the other, more subtle features that will contribute to a successful nesting season in your box.

Good nestboxes should be of sturdy construction and made from at least 3/4-inch-thick (1.9 cm) untreated lumber. The natural cavities that birds use for nest sites have a rough interior surface that provides plenty of footholds for young birds. The nestbox should mirror these cavities. If the box is deep and smooth, a series of horizontal grooves cut into the wood below the entrance can make it easier for the young birds to fledge.

Access to the box should be easy, to facilitate nest inspection and maintenance. The best-designed boxes have a roof that detaches for inspection and a side panel that pivots out for cleaning. Box sides should have ventilation holes or spaces, and floors should have drainage holes. Young birds will suffocate if the box is too hot, and drown or die of hypothermia if they are wet. Native cavity-nesting birds do not need perches to enter nestboxes.

The nestboxes described here are relatively easy to build. Most will attract a variety of birds, although some are specific to one species. Whether you are an experienced woodworker or a novice, read the directions for assembling the box you have chosen to build and study the accompanying illustrations. If you follow the step-by-step instructions, you *will* build a nestbox. Of course there is always room for experimentation, but once you find a design that works for your target species, stick with it—and enjoy. Few things are more satisfying than watching a pair of our native songbirds going about the business of rearing the next generation in a nestbox that you built!

THE BEST (AND WORST) LUMBER

The best choices in wood, in terms of how sturdy, long lasting, rot resistant, attractive, and easy to work with are cedar, pine, and fir. Most important, when selecting wood for your nestbox, make sure that it is untreated lumber. Treated woods and wood preservatives, though beneficial in maintaining the wood, are almost always harmful to birds.

BLUEBIRD OR SWALLOW NESTBOX

No other species (with the possible exception of the Purple Martin) has been studied so extensively with regard to nestbox design as the Eastern Bluebird. Several basic wooden box designs, as well as many variations on the basic plans, have been developed. Indeed, new variations appear in the literature on a regular basis. The design shown here, suitable for both bluebirds and swallows, combines top-opening and side-opening features. An opening top permits less obtrusive monitoring, while the side-opening capability allows for easy cleaning.

Materials

7/8" x 10" x 50" (2.2 x 25.4 x 127 cm) rough-cut (unplaned) cedar. Or use 1" (2.5 cm) rough-cut pine lumber. Roofs should be cut from cedar rather than other woods to prevent cracking.

1/2" x 6" (1.3 x 15.2 cm) maple dowel (optional)

Sixteen 6d (2"; 5.1 cm) galvanized ring-shank siding nails

Three 2d (1"; 2.5 cm) galvanized finishing nails, or wood screws to attach dowel (optional)

Two galvanized #6 x 1 1/2" (3.8 cm) panhead screws and washers

Eyelet screw (optional)

If using planed lumber, 2" x 4" (5.1 x 10.2 cm) piece of 1/4" (0.6 cm) galvanized wire mesh hardware cloth. Attach inside of the front and turn down sharp edges, to aid fledging. Or rout or score inside the front to provide a grip.

Heavy-duty staples or 3/4" (1.9 cm) 18-gauge wire brads to attach hardware cloth

Tools

Table saw, saber saw, jigsaw (bevel cuts are required), or carpenter's handsaw and miter box

Power or hand drill

1 1/2" (3.8 cm) diameter keyhole saw or expansion bit

3/16" (0.476 cm) and 1/4" (0.635 cm) drill bits

Standard or Phillips-head screwdriver, or power drill fitted with screwdriver bits

Claw hammer

Tape measure or yard (meter) stick

Carpenter's square

Pencil

Staple gun (optional)

Sandpaper (optional)

Light-colored exterior latex house paint (optional)

Paintbrush

Cutting and Preparation Notes

Be sure to allow for the width of the saw blade when measuring. The grain of the wood should run longitudinally to minimize warping and cracking. You may want to sand the exterior surfaces of rough-cut lumber to touch.

Drill an entrance hole, with its upper edge situated 1 inch (2.5 cm) below the top of the front. For Eastern Bluebirds and swallows, the diameter of the entrance hole must not exceed 1 1/2 inches (3.8 cm); the bottom of the entrance hole must be located at least 6 inches (15.2 cm) above the floor. For Western and Mountain species, the entrance hole should be 1 9/16 inches (3.9 cm) in diameter.

The Eastern Bluebird

Cutting diagram for Eastern Bluebirds

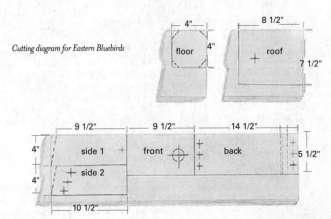

Continued →

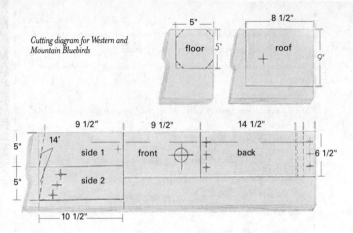

Cutting diagram for Western and Mountain Bluebirds

4. Attach *side 2* (clean-out door) only at the top, using two 4d galvanized finishing nails to create a pivot. **Important:** Use predrilled holes to help ensure that the pivot nails are exactly opposite each other for proper opening. Be sure to leave the necessary ventilation gap on this side as well. Add a centered galvanized #6 x 1 1/2" (3.8 cm) panhead screw and washer near the bottom of this side to line up with the recessed floor in order to secure the side in place.

5. Fit the *roof* into the angled slot cut in the *back* and hold it there by placing a single centered #6 panhead screw or eyelet screw and a washer through the top into the top edge of the front.

Painting/Staining

Boxes need not be painted, but if you decide to do so, be sure to paint only the outside surfaces. Also, do not use paints or stains that contain lead or toxic wood preservatives. Exterior latex house paint is fine. Use only light colors so that the boxes do not heat up unnecessarily when exposed to bright sunlight.

Location

For both bluebirds and swallows, avoid areas where House Sparrows, an aggressive competitor, are common. For bluebirds, place boxes in semi-open country with scattered trees. Keep them away from forest edges and shrubby growth (at least 120 feet, or 37 m, if possible) where House Wrens may be a competitor. A minimum of 2 acres (0.8 ha) of suitable habitat is usually required per nesting pair. Because swallows are territorial and will not nest close to other swallows (but will nest close to bluebirds), mounting paired boxes 15 to 25 feet (4.6–7.6 m) apart can provide housing for both species and alleviate some of the competition. Bluebirds generally require short-grass areas for finding insect prey. Pairs of boxes (or single boxes where swallow competition is not an issue) should be spaced no closer together than 300 feet (91.5 m).

Tree and Violet-Green Swallows, the members of the species most likely to use nestboxes, prefer to nest and forage in open areas near water.

Mounting

Boxes can be mounted in a number of ways, depending on the type of support you have available. Boxes can be nailed, bolted, screwed, or wired to fence posts, iron pipes, wooden posts, or dead trees with sound wood. A pipe flange attached to the bottom of the box allows attachment of 3/4-inch (1.9 cm) or 1-inch (2.5 cm) galvanized pipe. Plumber's hanger iron (perforated galvanized steel), pipe clamps, or wire can also be used to attach boxes to posts or pipes. Using screws or bolts rather than nails allows for easier removal of the box for repairs or relocation.

Boxes should be placed between 4 1/2 and 5 1/2 feet (1.4–1.7 m) above the ground to

Eastern Bluebirds will readily use wooden nestboxes with either a 4-inch-square (10.2 cm) or a 5-inch-square (12.7 cm) floor. For Western Bluebirds, Mountain Bluebirds, and swallows a 5-inch-square (12.7 cm) floor is recommended, as they have larger clutches than Eastern Bluebirds. For this type of nesting box, use 7/8" x 12" x 51" (2.2 cm x 30.5 cm x 1.3 m) or 7/8" x 10" x 60" (2.2 cm x 25.4 cm x 1.5 m) lumber. See the cutting diagrams.

Assembly

1. Cut 5/8" (1.6 cm) off each corner of the floor to create drainage holes. Nail the *floor* to the *back*, recessing it 1/4" (0.6 cm) from the bottom to create a drip edge.

2. Screw or nail *side* 1 to the joined back and floor, leaving a 1/4"-wide (0.6 cm) gap at the top for ventilation.

3. Screw or nail the *front* to the joined *floor* and *side*, again being sure to leave a 1/4" (0.6 cm) recess at the bottom.

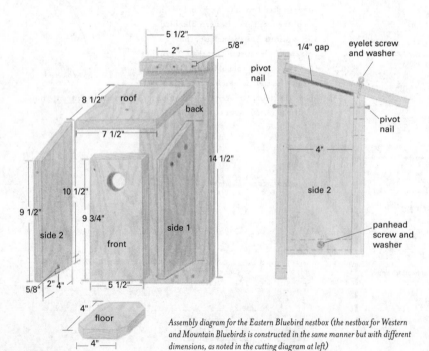

Assembly diagram for the Eastern Bluebird nestbox (the nestbox for Western and Mountain Bluebirds is constructed in the same manner but with different dimensions, as noted in the cutting diagram at left)

facilitate monitoring. Boxes placed less than 4 feet (1.2 m) above the ground may be more vulnerable to predation. On fence posts along active pastures, mount the box on the outside of the post, away from livestock: Cattle and horses have been known to use nestboxes as scratching posts. In general, face boxes toward open country and away from roads.

Western Bluebirds have successfully used hanging boxes in California and Oregon. A specially designed pole has been developed to lift the boxes onto their support hooks.

WREN OR CHICKADEE NESTBOX

The box plan for wrens and chickadees is almost identical to that for the Eastern Bluebird, with the exception of the size of the entrance hole. To make this box suitable for only the most common species of wrens and chickadees, drill the following entrance hole sizes:

- **Carolina Wren.** The largest of our cavity-nesting wrens requires at least a 1 1/8-inch-diameter (2.9 cm) entrance hole.
- **Beckick's Wren.** This intermediate-size wren can enter an entrance hole of 1 inch (2.5 cm) or larger.
- **House Wren.** The smallest and most common of the three nestbox-using wrens, this species finds a 1-inch-diameter (2.5 cm) hole large enough.
- **Black-Capped Chickadee.** One of the most familiar birds in wooded portions of North America, this chickadee requires a 1 1/8-inch-diameter (2.9 cm) entrance hole.
- **Carolina Chickadee.** This southeastern counterpart of the Black-Capped is slightly smaller but also uses a 1 1/8-inch-diameter (2.9 cm) entrance hole.

Of course, all three wrens and both chickadees are accommodated by a 1 1/8-inch-diameter (2.9 cm) or larger entrance. In general, however, size the entrance hole as small as possible in order to exclude birds other than your target species. If the House Sparrow is not a problem, you may want to consider a larger entrance hole, because male House Wrens especially seem to have an easier time bringing sticks into a box with a larger opening.

The Carolina Wren (left), House Wren (middle), and Bewick's Wren (right) are three of the most common wrens that can be attracted to nestboxes.

Location

Wrens are birds of thickets and woodland edges; thus you should locate wren boxes in semi-open habitats near cover such as shrubbery and trees. Their habitat requirements are somewhat intermediate between bluebirds, which prefer more open sites, and chickadees, which will nest in both woodland and edge situations. Place boxes meant for chickadees adjacent to woodland edges, as well as in woodland clearings, where they will receive sunlight 40 to 60 percent of the day.

Mounting

Mount these boxes as you would a bluebird nestbox and from 4 1/2 to 10 feet (1.4–3.1 m) above the ground. Be sure to attach a predator guard to the support pipe, post, or tree.

House Wrens will readily nest in hanging boxes as well. Place 1 inch (2.5 cm) of wood chips or shavings into any chickadee box.

TITMOUSE OR NUTHATCH NESTBOX

The titmouse/nuthatch box plan is identical to that for the Eastern Bluebird, with one exception: The diameter of the entrance hole is 1 1/4 inches (3.2 cm).

Location

Siting the nestbox in an appropriate habitat is, of course, as important as the correct sizing of the entrance hole.

- **Tufted Titmouse.** These birds inhabit mostly deciduous and mixed deciduous-evergreen woodlands with a large variety of tree species that create a dense canopy. In eastern and southern Texas, they also occupy riparian and mesquite habitats. Situate the box in an area with a variety of trees as well as open space, 5 to 15 feet (1.5–4.6 m) above the ground in semishade.
- **Bridled Titmouse.** Essentially mountain dwellers, these birds prefer oak and oak-pine woodlands but will also nest in streamside groves. Mount the box 6 to 15 feet (1.8–4.6 m) above the ground.
- **Oak Titmouse.** Favors live oaks but also uses various types of deciduous woodland. Locate the box in an area with a variety of tree species and adjacent open areas. Mount the box on a tree or post 5 to 10 feet (1.5–3.1 m) above the ground.
- **Juniper Titmouse.** Prefers mixed piñon-juniper-oak woodlands. Mount the box in an area with a variety of trees and open spaces nearby, 5 to 10 feet (1.5–3.1 m) above the ground.
- **White-Breasted Nuthatch.** Mixed deciduous-evergreen and mature deciduous forests are this bird's haunts, although it prefers to nest along forest edges in areas that also contain fields, water, and orchards. Locate the box in a mature forest near a cleared area, 12 to 20 feet (3.7–6.1 m) above the ground.

Mounting

Place boxes on trees for the White-Breasted Nuthatch and Bridled Titmouse and on trees or posts for the other titmouse species. Be sure to use predator guards such as baffles to prevent climbing predators from raiding the nest.

RED-BELLIED WOODPECKER OR NORTHERN FLICKER NESTBOX

Suitable for the Northern Flicker or the smaller Red-Bellied Woodpecker, this design is essentially a larger and deeper version of the standard, slant-top, side-opening bluebird nestbox. It can be attached directly to a tree or post but must be packed with wood shavings and/or sawdust to entice woodpeckers to use it.

Continued ➜

Materials

7/8" x 9" x 10' (2.2 cm x 22.9 cm x 3.1 m) rough-cut (unplaned) cedar. Rough-cut or planed pine may be substituted, but it has a shorter life span.

1/2" x 9" (1.3 x 22.9 cm) maple dowel (optional)

Twenty 1 5/8" (4.1 cm) drywall screws or 2" (5.1 cm) galvanized ring-shank wood siding nails. If using thicker rough-cut lumber, use 2" ring-shank siding nails.

Two 6d (2"; 5.1 cm) galvanized finishing nails

Four 2d (1"; 2.5 cm) galvanized finishing nails (optional)

One right-angle screw

Heavy-duty staples, or 3/4" (1.9 cm) 18-gauge wire brads (optional)

Tools

Table saw, saber saw, jigsaw (two bevel cuts are required), or carpenter's handsaw and miter box

2 1/2" (6.4 cm) diameter keyhole saw (for Red-Bellied Woodpecker, use a diameter of 2"; 5.1 cm), router, or expansion bit to cut entrance hole

Power or hand drill

1/8" (0.318 cm), 1/4" (0.635 cm), and 3/8" (0.953 cm) drill bits

Claw hammer

Phillips-head screwdriver or power drill fitted with screwdriver bits

Tape measure or yard (meter) stick

Carpenter's square

Pencil

Awl or rasp (optional)

CONSTRUCTION TIP

If finished (planed) lumber is used, staple or nail a 3" x 16" (7.6 x 40.6 cm) piece of 1/4" (0.6 cm) galvanized wire mesh (hardware cloth) to the inside of the front, below the entrance hole; be sure to bend the sharp edges under. Alternatively, the inside front can be routed or scored with a sharp tool such as an awl or rasp to provide nestlings with a grip.

Cutting and Preparation Notes

Be sure to allow for the width of the saw blade when measuring. The grain of the lumber should run longitudinally to prevent warping and cracking. Cedar resists warping, and you may want to use it for the roof if you are

building your box of pine. Do not sand either the exterior or the interior of the box, nor paint it.

This wooden box has a 7 1/4-inch-square (18.4 cm) floor. The bottom of the entrance hole should be located at least 16 inches (40.6 cm) above the floor. Drill a 2 1/2-inch-diameter (6.4 cm) hole for flickers or a 2-inch (5.1 cm) hole for Red-Bellieds, being sure to take into account the width of the floor and the fact that it is recessed 1/4 inch (0.6 cm) to create a drip edge. Cut 5/8 inch (1.6 cm) off each corner of the floor to create drainage holes.

Assembly

Cutting diagram

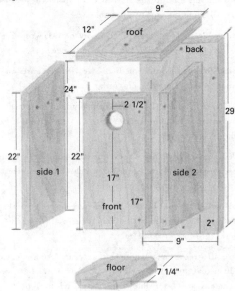

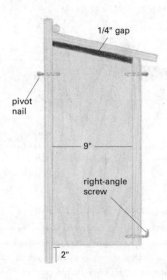

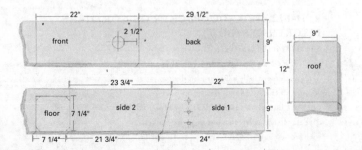

1. Drill three 3/8-inch-diameter (1 cm) holes in a line 1 1/2 inches (3.8 cm) apart near the top of the nonpivoting side for ventilation. The back edge of the roof and the top edge of the front will fit better if cut at a 5-degree angle. Alternatively, you may nail a 1/2-inch-diameter (1.3 cm) maple dowel where the roof and the back meet to prevent rain seepage.

2. Screw or nail the box's longer side (*side 1*) to the back of the box. Note that the shorter side (*side 2*) will be hinged at the top with two galvanized finishing nails.

3. Screw or nail the *front* to *side 1*. A finished (smooth) lumber front must be fitted with a galvanized ladder on the inside, or be roughened up with a rasp, for the nestlings.

4. Attach the *floor*, being careful to recess it 1/4" (0.6 cm).

5. Now attach the shorter *side 2*, using two pivot nails lined up exactly opposite each other (measure first with a carpenter's square). Note that this side is 1/4" (0.6 cm) shorter, to enable it to pivot properly. When it is not open, this side is secured with a right-angle screw; drill a 1/8" (0.3 cm) guide hole for this in the bottom of the *front*.

6. Finally, attach the *roof*, and add the *dowel* if necessary.

Painting/Staining

Woodpecker nestboxes should not be painted or stained. In fact, adding wood slabs with bark to the outside of the box may make it more attractive to woodpeckers. Be careful that the nails you use to attach the slabs do not penetrate the box's interior.

Location

Place the nestbox in semi-open country and in a generally sunny, easily seen (by the woodpeckers) location. For the Northern Flicker, mount 6 to 20 feet (1.8–6.1 m) high; for the Red-Bellied Woodpecker, between 8 and 20 feet (2.4–6.1 m) up.

Mounting

The box may be attached to a dead tree (make sure the wood is sound), a 4 x 4-inch (10.2 x 10.2 cm) cedar post, a 1 1/2-inch-diameter (3.8 cm) galvanized pipe, or another suitable support. Face the box away from prevailing storms, usually southeasterly. Use two 3-inch-long (7.6 cm) lag screws, or bolts with washers centered at the top and bottom ends of the backboard. Predrill holes. Galvanized nails are an alternative, but moving the box will be much more difficult if you decide to use them.

When using a post, bury its end 2 to 3 feet (0.6–0.9 m) into the ground for stability. Be sure to consider this added length when you purchase materials.

It is important to fabricate a predator guard from a 30-inch-wide (76 cm) piece of aluminum sheeting and attach it to the support at least 6 feet (1.8 m) above the ground with galvanized or brass screws.

Red-Bellied Woodpeckers will also use nestboxes that are hung from a flexible wire or chain.

To improve your chances of luring a pair of flickers or Red-Bellieds to your box, be sure to pack the box tightly from top to bottom with wood chips, shavings, or sawdust (other than cedar).

Wood Duck or Hooded Merganser Nestbox

This is the largest box to use the traditional slant-top design. One variation that distinguishes it from boxes for songbirds is its oval entrance hole. This wooden box may be mounted directly over water on a cedar post or attached to a tree near the shore of a permanent water body. A predator guard is essential. Three inches (7.6 cm) of wood shavings must be placed in the bottom prior to each nesting season.

The box has a 10 x 10-inch (25.4 x 25.4 cm) interior floor dimension. It is 17 inches (43.8 cm) deep from the bottom edge of the entrance hole to the floor.

Materials

1" x 12" x 11' (2.5 cm x 30.5 cm x 3.3 m) rough-cut (unplaned) grade 3 cedar. Rough-cut pine can also be used, but it has a shorter life span.

1" x 2" (2.5 x 5.1 cm) piece of lumber, for the doorstop

Thirty 1 5/8" (4.1 cm) drywall screws or 2" (5.1 cm) galvanized ring-shank wood shingle nails. These anchor or grip wood; smooth nails loosen over time. For thicker, rough-cut lumber, use 2" ring-shank nails.

Galvanized hardware cloth, 1/4" (0.6 cm) mesh, 4" x 16" (10.2 x 40.6 cm). Be sure to bend any sharp edges away from the inside of the box before attaching.

#5 staples, or 3/4" (1.9 cm) 18-gauge wire brads

3" (7.6 cm) brass cabinet hinge

Six brass or galvanized flat-head wood screws for the hinge

One piece rigid plastic 1/8" x 1" x 2 1/2" (0.3 x 2.5 x 6.4 cm), for the latch

One brass #8 x 3/4" (1.9 cm) round-head wood screw, to secure the latch

Tools

Table saw, saber saw, jigsaw (two bevel cuts are required), or carpenter's handsaw and miter box

3" (7.6 cm) expansion bit or keyhole saw, to cut entrance hole (you can also use a band saw or router)

Power or hand drill

1" (2.5 cm) diameter keyhole saw or expansion bit

1/8" (0.318 cm), 1/4" (0.635 cm), and 3/8" (.938 cm) drill bits

Claw hammer

Phillips-head screwdriver, or power drill fitted with screwdriver bit

Tape measure or yard (meter) stick

Carpenter's square

Pencil

Staple gun

Rasp or awl

Continued ➜

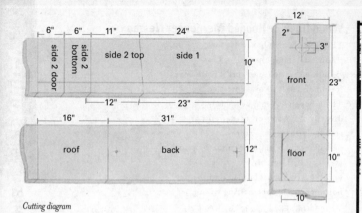

Cutting diagram

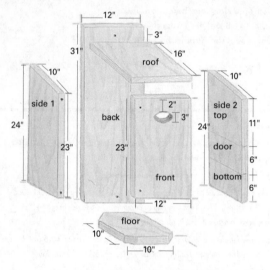

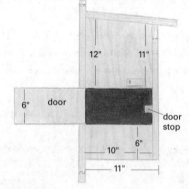

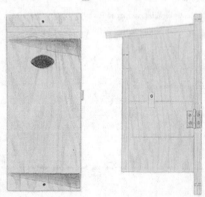

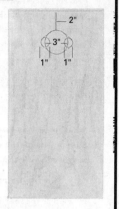

CUTTING THE ENTRANCE HOLE

The horizontal elliptical entrance hole is 4" x 3" (10.2 x 7.6 cm) in size. This is designed to exclude all but the smallest adult raccoons.

To locate the hole, draw a 3"-diameter (7.6 cm) circle, centered 3 1/2" (8.9 cm) down from the top of the *front*. Be sure to do this after the top of the *front* has been beveled down 1/8" (0.3 cm). Now draw 1"-diameter (2.5 cm) circles centered on opposite edges of the 3" (7.6 cm) circle. Cut out these two holes with the keyhole saw or expansion bit. Then cut out the center 3" (7.6 cm) hole with the expansion bit, keyhole saw, or band saw. Use a rasp to smooth off the four edges you have created, until you have a symmetrical ellipse.

Cutting and Preparation Notes

Be sure to allow for the width of the saw blade when measuring. The grain of the lumber should run longitudinally to prevent warping and cracking. Exterior plywood resists warping, and you may want to use it for the roof if your box is built of pine.

Cut 5/8 inch (1.6 cm) off each corner of the floor to create drainage holes. Alternatively, drill four or five 1/4-inch (0.6 cm) drainage holes in the floor. The back edge of the roof will fit better if beveled at a 5-degree angle.

Assembly

1. Screw or nail *side 1* (the one without the access door) to the *floor*.

2. Screw or nail the *back* to the joined *side* and *floor*. Allow for 3" (7.6 cm) of the backboard to extend beyond the top and bottom of the box (for use in mounting).

3. Make sure that the hardware cloth has already been centered on the inside of the *front* and stapled below the entrance hole (use wire brads if you lack a staple gun). Then attach the *front*, making sure that its top is flush with the top of *side 1*. Also, attach the *doorstop* 8" (20.3 cm) up from the bottom of the front (see diagram). Allow for the thickness of the door.

4. Now nail or screw the *top of side 2* (largest portion) to the *back* and *front*.

5. Fit the access door for size; do not attach it now, because it will be hinged at one end. Mark the bottom edge on the front and back with a pencil.

6. Screw or nail the bottom of *side 2* to the *front, back*, and *floor* of the box, making sure that there is a snug fit but that the hinged section above it will open and close freely.

7. Attach the *roof*, making sure that the top of the front and the roof are flush. The back edge of the roof and the backboard should also be flush.

8. Finally, attach the *door* by means of the hinge and 3/4" (1.9 cm) brass or galvanized screws. Use the latch, held in place by a brass round-head screw, to secure it.

Painting/Staining

Painting is not necessary, but if you do wish to paint your box, do so only on the outside with a light-colored exterior latex house paint.

Location

Mount boxes in shallow, freshwater wetland areas no more than half a mile (0.8 km) from water, preferably closer than 1/4 mile (0.4 km). Optimum habitat includes nut- and berry-producing hardwood trees and shrubs bordering permanent streams, ponds, swamps, and lakes. Site the box over water, if possible, or 30 to 100 feet (9.2–30.5 m) from shore, rather than immediately along the shore, where the box may be more prone to raccoon predation. The front of the box should be free of foliage or other obstructions. Heights of 12 to 30 feet (3.7–9.2 m) are recommended by some authors, but these can make maintenance very difficult.

The box must be at least 4 feet (1.2 m) above the normal waterline, and at least 2 feet (0.6 m) above the high-water (annual flood) line. When mounting on land, it should be at least 5 1/2 feet (1.7 m) above the ground.

Boxes can be spaced as close together as 50 feet (15.3 m).

Mounting

The box may be attached to a dead tree (make sure the wood is sound), or mounted on a 4 x 4-inch (10.2 x 10.2 cm) cedar post, or atop a 1 1/2-inch-diameter (3.8 cm) galvanized pipe; 4-inch-diameter (10.2 cm) PVC plastic pipe may also be used for in-water mounting. Be careful not to mount the box with a backward slant, as this admits rainwater. Mount it level or with a slight downward tilt.

Another mounting option over water is to use 4 x 4-inch (10.2 x 10.2 cm) cedar posts fitted with a horizontal board, upon which the nestbox is carriage-bolted. Both posts must be fitted with cone-type predator guards.

Wooden mounting posts should be 16 feet (4.8 m) long. Use two 4 1/2-inch (11.4 cm) lag screws (top and bottom) with 5/16-inch (0.8 cm) washers; predrill guide holes. Loosen the lag screws slightly each spring if you are mounting on a live tree.

If you are mounting atop a 1 1/2-inch (3.8 cm) galvanized metal post, use a threaded pipe flange to attach the pipe to the box. Screw the flange to the bottom of the box first. Do not use pipe strapping as added support where climbing snakes are a problem.

When mounting on a tree, attach a 30-inch-wide (76 cm) metal sheet (or flexible fiberglass wrap) to the trunk to keep predators from reaching the box. The sheet must be loosened annually as the tree grows. You may also attach a wooden tunnel over the entrance.

It is important to put 3 to 4 inches (7.6–10.2 cm) of wood shavings in the box when you clean and refurbish it prior to the nesting season. This should be done in mid-to late winter.

AMERICAN KESTREL, SCREECH OWL, OR NORTHERN SAW-WHET OWL NESTBOX

Nearly all kestrel boxes follow the same basic design: that of an enlarged standard bluebird box. Dimensions vary, however, from plan to plan. In additional to different dimensions, some kestrel boxes, as with bluebirds, are side opening, while others are top opening. The design presented here is side opening. This should make the box easier to monitor and clean, given the heights at which it will be mounted.

Materials

7/8" x 9 3/4" x 8' (2.2 cm x 24.8 cm x 2.4 m) rough-cut cedar board. Rough-cut or planed pine may also be used, but has a shorter life span.

1/2" (1.3 cm) maple dowel (optional)

Twenty-six 1 5/8" (4 cm) drywall screws or 2" (5.1 cm) galvanized ring-shank wood siding nails (use the latter with thicker rough-cut lumber)

Two galvanized 6d, 2" (5.1 cm) finishing nails, for pivot

One brass or galvanized #6 x 1 1/2" (3.8 cm) flat-head wood screw, to hold inside perch

One brass or galvanized #6 x 2" (5.1 cm) panhead wood screw

One washer to fit panhead screw

Heavy-duty staples, or ten 3/4" (1.9 cm) 18-gauge wire brads

Tools

Table saw (two angle cuts are required), or carpenter's handsaw and miter box

3" (7.6 cm) keyhole saw or expansion bit, for cutting entrance hole; 2 1/2" (6.4 cm) keyhole saw or expansion bit for Northern Saw-Whet Owl

Power or hand drill

1/8" (0.318 cm), 3/16" (0.476 cm), 1/4" (.625 cm), and 3/8" (0.953 cm) drill bits

Claw hammer

Phillips-head screwdriver, or power drill fitted with screwdriver bits

Carpenter's square

Tape measure or yard (meter) stick

Pencil

Rasp or awl (optional)

Staple gun (optional)

Sandpaper (optional)

Light-colored exterior latex house paint, for pine boxes (optional)

Paintbrush (optional)

Construction Tip

If finished (planed) lumber is used, staple or nail a 3" x 6" (7.6 x 15.2 cm) piece of 1/4" (0.6 cm) galvanized wire mesh (hardware cloth) to the inside of the front, below the entrance hole; be sure to bend the sharp edges under. Alternatively, the inside front can be routed or scored with a sharp tool such as an awl or rasp to provide nestlings with a grip.

Cutting and Preparation Notes

Be sure to allow for the width of the saw blade when measuring. The grain of the wood should run longitudinally, to minimize warping and cracking. If you use pine lumber, consider using cedar for the roof. You may wish to sand the exterior surfaces, but be sure to leave the inside surfaces rough, to enable the young birds to get a grip when fledging.

Continued ➜

This wooden box has a 7 3/4-inch-square (19.7 cm) floor, although some boxes have floors as large as 8 x 9 inches (20.3 x 24.2 cm). All designs have a 3-inch-diameter (7.6 cm) entrance hole (the Northern Saw-Whet Owl requires only a 2 1/2-inch-diameter, or 6.4 cm, hole; the Screech Owl a 2 3/4-inch, or 7 cm, hole). The bottom of the entrance hole should be located 9 to 10 inches (22.9–25.4 cm) above the floor. An inside perch, which could be made from half of the entrance hole wood, should be screwed 3 inches (7.6 cm) below the bottom of the entrance hole. (*Leave this perch off when building for owls, however.*) When you cut the entrance hole, be sure to take into account that the floor must be recessed 1/4 inch (0.6 cm) to create a drip edge. Cut 5/8 inch (1.6 cm) off each of the four corners of the floor to create drainage holes. Alternatively, drill four or five 1/4-inch (0.6 cm) drainage holes in the floor. Drill three 3/8-inch (1 cm) holes near the top of the nonpivoting side for ventilation.

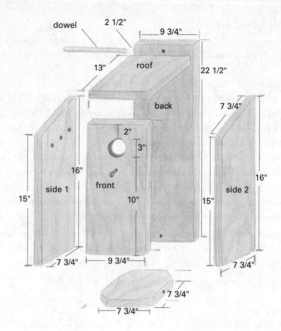

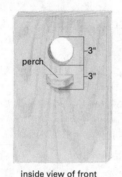

Cutting diagram

inside view of front

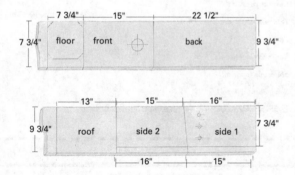

The back edge of the roof and the top edge of the front will fit better if you bevel-cut them at 5 degrees. Or you can nail or screw a 1/2-inch (1.3 cm) maple dowel where the roof and back meet to keep rain from seeping in.

Assembly

1. Screw or nail *side* 1 to the *back* of the box. (*Side* 2 will be hinged at the top with two finishing nails later.)

2. Make sure that the hardware cloth strip and inside perch (the latter only for kestrels) have been fastened below the entrance hole. Then screw or nail the *front* to the *side*.

3. Attach the *floor*, being careful to recess it 1/4" (0.6 cm) from the bottom.

4. Now attach *side* 2, using two pivot nails near the top. Note that the pivot nails must be lined up exactly opposite each other, and that this side is 1/4" (0.6 cm) shorter than the other, to allow it to swing open properly. Predrill a centered 1/8" (0.3 cm) guide hole, then use the panhead screw and a washer to fasten the bottom of this *side* to the *floor*.

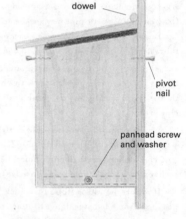

5. Screw or nail on the *roof*.

6. If you have not bevel-cut the back edge of the top, nail or screw the 1/2" (1.3 cm) *dowel* where the top meets the back.

Painting/Staining

You do not need to paint cedar boxes. Pine boxes will last longer if you do, but untreated pine boxes may last approximately 10 years. Be sure to use light-colored exterior latex house paint, and treat only the outside. For owls, boxes can be painted or stained dark brown on the outside only. Do not use paints or stains that contain lead or toxic wood preservatives.

Location

For kestrels, mount the box at least 10 feet (3.1 m) high, and preferably 12 to 20 feet (3.7–6.1 m) up, in open country—farmland, meadows, and abandoned fields. Locate the box 15 to 30 feet (4.6–9.2 m) from a snag, or a tree with dead limbs. Males use such sites as prey "plucking posts." Face the box away from prevailing storms, usually south or east. Space boxes about 1 mile (1.6 km) apart and no closer than 1/2 mile (0.8 km). Kestrels require a minimum of 1 acre (0.4 ha) per pair.

Screech Owls generally prefer open woodland. Locate boxes in shaded areas of open city and rural parks, small woodlots, and apple orchards from 15 to 50 feet (4.6–15.4 m) up in a tree in the woods. Place boxes on straight trunks that have diameters larger than those of the nestboxes. Boxes should be 100 feet (30.5 m) apart. Make sure that there is an unobstructed flying area near the box.

Northern Saw-Whet Owls also tend to nest rather high, so mount the box 14 feet (4.3 m) off the ground, or higher in deciduous, evergreen, or mixed forest, woodlots, and swamps. Place the box in a mature, live tree, preferably near water.

Mounting

Boxes may be attached to metal or wooden poles or large dead trees (of sound wood) with bolts or lag screws. Be sure to wrap a 30-inch-wide (76 cm) sleeve of aluminum around wooden poles or dead trees, to prevent predators from reaching the nestbox. Boxes can also be placed on silos, barns, windmills, or even on the backs of highway signs (be sure to obtain permission from the proper agency first). Where the use of lag screws or bolts is not possible, wrap stainless-steel or galvanized metal banding material around the top and bottom portions of the backboard (but do not try this where climbing snakes are a threat).

It may be wise to make your mounting pole of two telescoping sections, bolted together. This way you can lower it for cleaning and repair without a ladder.

Place only 1 inch (2.5 cm) of wood shavings (not cedar) in the bottom of the box as nesting materials for kestrels; 2 to 3 inches (5.1–7.6 cm) for the owls. Do not use sawdust, as it may irritate the nostrils and eyes of the nestlings.

GREAT CRESTED OR ASH-THROATED FLYCATCHER NESTBOX

This box is basically a larger version of the standard slant-roof, side-opening bluebird nestbox, but with a 2-inch-diameter (5.1 cm) entrance hole. A 1 3/4-inch-diameter (4.4 cm) entrance hole may be sufficient to permit entry by these flycatchers, but most authors recommend the larger size, especially for the Great Crested Flycatcher.

The box has a 6 x 6-inch (15.2 x 15.2 cm) interior floor size. It is 11 7/8 inches (30.1 cm) deep at the back and 8 inches (20.3 cm) from the bottom rim of the entrance hole to the floor. It may be advantageous to add 3/4 inch to 2 inches (1.9–5.1 cm) of wood chips (not cedar, which can irritate nestlings) to the bottom of this box prior to the nesting season.

Cutting and Preparation Notes

Be sure to allow for the width of the saw blade when measuring. The grain of the lumber should run lengthwise, to prevent warping and cracking. Cedar resists warping, so if you are building your box of pine, you may want to use cedar for the roof.

Cut 5/8 inch (1.6 cm) off each of the four corners of the floor to create drainage holes. Alternatively, drill four or five 1/4-inch (0.6 cm) drainage holes in the floor. The back of the roof and the top of the front must be beveled at 5 degrees for a better fit. This amounts to cutting 1/8 inch (0.3 cm) off the edges of both.

Materials

7/8" x 9 3/4" x 6' (2.2 cm x 24.8 cm x 1.8 m) rough-cut (unplaned) grade 3 cedar. Rough-cut or planed pine may be substituted, but it has a shorter life span.

1/2" x 9 1/4" (1.3 x 23.5 cm) maple dowel (optional)

Twenty 1 5/8" (4 cm) drywall screws or 6d (2"; 5.1 cm) galvanized ring-shank wood siding nails

Two 4d (1 1/2"; 3.8 cm) galvanized finishing nails

One right-angle screw

Tools

Table saw, saber saw, jigsaw (two bevel cuts are required), or carpenter's handsaw and miter box

2"-diameter (5.1 cm) keyhole saw or expansion bit, to cut entrance hole

1/8" (0.318 cm), 1/4" (0.635 cm), and 3/8" (0.953 cm) drill bits

Power or hand drill

Claw hammer

Tape measure or yard (meter) stick

Carpenter's square

Pencil

Phillips-head screwdriver or power drill fitted with screwdriver bits (optional)

Sandpaper (optional)

Rasp or awl (if smooth lumber is used, the inside of the front will have to be roughened up)

Assembly

1. Nail or screw *side 1* to the *floor,* being sure to leave a 1/4" (0.6 cm) drip edge below the bottom of the floor (which already has 5/8", or 1.6 cm, cut off the corners, or four 1/4", or 0.6 cm, drainage holes drilled through it). The side should have three 3/8" (1 cm) vent holes drilled horizontally near the top.

2. Nail or screw the *back* to the joined *side* and *floor,* maintaining the 1/4" (0.6 cm) drip edge. You may want to drill a 1/8" (0.3 cm) hole in the center of both the projecting portions of the backboard (above and below) prior to assembly; this can also be done just prior to mounting.

3. Attach the front, making sure that it is flush with *side 1* (the center of the 2", or 5.1 cm, diameter entrance hole should be located 2" down from the top of the front). If you are using planed lumber, you must roughen up the inside of the front, below the hole, with a rasp, awl, or other sharp implement.

4. Now fit *side 2* (the one that will swing out) in place, creating the 1/4" (0.6 cm) drip edge at the bottom and a 1/4" gap at the top. While holding *side 2* flush with the *front,* drill two small-diameter guide holes opposite each other near the top. Insert two 4d

Continued →

(1 1/2"; 3.8 cm) galvanized finishing nails into the guide holes as pivots, but do not drive them in fully. Use the right-angle screw to hold *side* 2, first drilling a small guide hole at the proper point, near the lower edge of the front.

5. Finally, make sure that the pivoting side will open properly with the roof in place and that the roof is centered. Now drive in the two pivot nails fully, then nail or screw the *roof* to the assembled box.

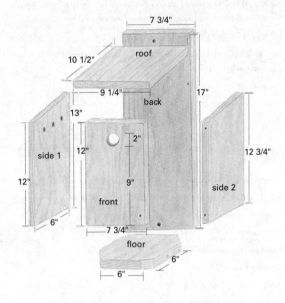

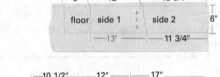

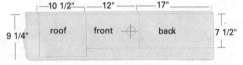

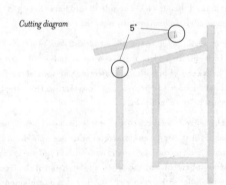

Cutting diagram

Painting/Staining

As with other designs, wood treatment is not necessary. Indeed, flycatchers may be more likely to use unpainted nestboxes.

Location

Site boxes for Great Cresteds in open deciduous, deciduous-coniferous, or coniferous woods, or along the edges of wooded areas. Ash-Throated Flycatchers prefer open woodlands of piñon-juniper, as well as chaparral and riverside groves. They also nest in oak canyons and desert washes. For both species, place boxes about 8 feet (2.4 m) above the ground, although 4 1/2 to 20 feet (1.4–6.1 m) is acceptable. The entrance hole should be clear of obstructing vegetation.

Mounting

Attach boxes directly to tree trunks for these flycatchers. (In central Florida, boxes were successfully mounted on recently cut 6 3/4-inch-diameter, or 17.1 cm, slash pines that had limb stubs left on them.) Drive two 2 1/2-inch (6.4 cm) lag screws through the predrilled holes in the backboard. Be sure to protect the birds from predators by affixing predator guards such as a 30-inch-wide (76 cm) sheet of aluminum wrapped and secured around the trunk.

Where starlings are a problem, you may want to suspend your boxes from a 16-inch (40.6 cm) length of chain or flexible wire. In areas where squirrels gnaw nestbox entrance holes, you may need to screw a metal plate with a 2-inch-diameter (5.1 cm) hole over the outside of the box.

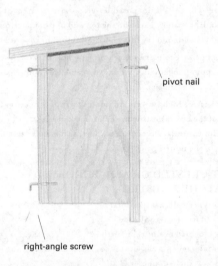

pivot nail

right-angle screw

Easy-to-Build Birdhouses

Mary Twitchell

Illustrations by Alison Kolesar, Jeffrey Domm, and Brigita Fuhrmann

Why Build Birdhouses?

In cities and in the suburbs where we have converted woodlots, forests, marshy land, and open spaces to housing and asphalt, we have depleted natural bird shelter. Yearly cleanup of brush and dead limbs have reduced the number of sites for nest building. Rows of wooden fence posts, once home to bluebirds and wrens, have now been replaced with metal stakes; and wolf trees formerly left as boundary markers are now mercilessly pruned or removed, especially if they are near power lines. Natural shelter is increasingly difficult for birds to find. Yet attracting birds is beneficial; they love to eat the insects we love to swat. Birds eat many times their weight in insects, keep weeds in check (by eating the seeds), and propagate trees and shrubs by inadvertently dropping seeds in flight.

Of the 650 different species of North American birds, approximately 50 will accept a nesting box in which to raise a family. These species look for a protected, secure home. In their natural habitat, cavity nesters drill out holes in dead branches or tree trunks (chickadees, titmice, woodpeckers); use holes vacated by other birds (wrens, bluebirds, swallows, flycatchers); take up residence in hollows caused by lightning, fungal infection, or insects; or use hidden tree crotches for nest supports (warblers, robins, finches).

Above all, the fledglings of cavity nesters need protection from predators. This means a small, enclosed nesting area and a small entrance hole. However, one size of nesting box does not fit all. Before choosing which nesting box to build, decide which birds you want to attract. Your local Audubon Society can provide information on the bird species in your area.

Choosing the Right Materials

The materials from which a birdhouse is made play a large part in attracting and safely hosting birds. If you are making your own, starting out with the best of time-tested materials will increase your chances of success; then again, if you are buying a premade birdhouse, you will still want to make sure that it is made of the appropriate materials.

THE BEST TYPES OF WOOD

Wood is the best material for constructing a birdhouse. It is readily available and easy to work with. Cedar, cypress, and redwood last the longest but are expensive and may need to be predrilled before nailing. Fir weathers well, but pine is probably the most available. Lumberyards carry 3/4-inch (1.9 cm) stock, which is an ideal thickness; it provides adequate insulation from both heat and cold, is durable enough to resist warping, and is easy to use with hand tools. CDX plywood (exterior grade) of 3/4-inch thickness can be substituted. Plywoods made for interior use will quickly delaminate, whereas the layers (plies) of CDX are bonded together with a marine glue that can withstand exposure to different weather conditions.

Rough-cut lumber (before it is planed) and slab ends from a milling operation (sawmill waste with the bark still on) are inexpensive, appropriate, and rustic looking. They may, however, demand more ingenuity and craftsmanship if you're to make the pieces fit.

Gourds are a natural substitute. You can grow them in your garden for next year's supply of nesting boxes.

GLUE

To increase the life of the nesting box, glue all joints before nailing or screwing. The glue will give a weathertight fit and hold the boards together over time. Use an exterior grade of wood glue; it will be yellow in color and is waterproof. The glue will not bond, however, if any of the surfaces have been painted or varnished.

FASTENERS

Galvanized nails will last longer than steel ones; ring-shank nails will hold better than smooth nails. Brass or stainless-steel plasterboard screws are long lived, resist corrosion, and do not stain the wood; brass hinges are preferable to steel ones. Use screws, not nails, when attaching boxes to trees or posts to make seasonal removal easier.

PAINT AND STAINS

There is no need to paint your birdhouse, but if you wish to, use an exterior, water-based (latex) paint. Never paint the entrance—it makes it difficult for birds to get a good foothold. And never paint or stain the inside of the box, as the chemical fumes are hazardous.

If you decide to paint, use dull, drab colors such as green, gray, tan, and light brown and do the painting in fall so that all vapors will have dissipated by spring. The wood may also be treated with a nontoxic linseed oil.

Choosing the Right Design

Although each species has its own specific requirements, all birdhouses should provide the following:

- Shelter
- Protection from the elements (wind, rain, intense sun)
- Ventilation without drafts
- Insulation
- Drainage
- Durability
- Freedom from chemical fumes (such as pressure-treated lumber, preservatives, stains, and paint, especially when they are applied to the entrance or the interior walls of the birdhouse)

The nesting box should also be accessible for easy cleaning between broods, monitoring of the nest-building process and the fledglings, and inspection (so that you can remove unwelcome tenants like mice, snakes, and House Sparrows).

The overall design dimensions (height, length, width), the size of the entrance hole, and the height from the entrance to the floor will vary depending on the species you are trying to attract. Above all, birds like a snug fit. Nesting boxes that are too small cause overcrowding; boxes that are too big make it impossible for the mother to keep the eggs, then chicks, warm. Although the dimensions given with each plan must be followed, you can let your sense of aesthetic embellishment be your guide. Birds don't care whether they are nesting in a French château, a Victorian gingerbread, or an Italian villa.

Continued →

THE RIGHT-SIZED ENTRANCE HOLE

The entrance hole is drilled near the top of the front panel. Its size and shape will vary according to the bird species; for chickadees it is 1 1/8 inches (2.9 cm) in diameter, while for barn owls it is 6 inches (15.2 cm) in diameter. The dimension is based on what is just large enough for the desired species but small enough to exclude predators.

The entrance hole should be at least 6 inches (15.2 cm) above the floor so that the nestlings won't fall out. If the front panel is smooth, it will be difficult for the young to climb up to the entrance hole when the time comes for them to leave. Rough-cut lumber will replicate the rough interior surface of a natural cavity. If you use finished lumber, you'll want to rough up the inside surface from the bottom of the nesting box to the entrance hole to make egress easier for the fledglings—cut multiple grooves 1/8 inch (0.3 cm) deep or tack wooden cleats or wire mesh onto the wall.

ADEQUATE VENTILATION

To keep from becoming hotboxes, birdhouses need good ventilation. Air vents provide even temperatures and fresh air; they also prevent the boxes from being too dark. Vents are easy to include by leaving a 1/4-inch (0.6 cm) gap between the sidewalls and the roof, or by drilling vent holes along the top of each side panel.

EXTENDED ROOF

Regardless of design, the birdhouse roof should slope and overhang on the sides. On the front, the roof should extend 2 to 3 inches (5.1–7.6 cm) beyond the box. This extended eave protects the entrance hole from adverse weather (driving rains, wind, sun) and hinders predators from reaching into the nest.

To encourage water to shed on finished lumber—especially if the roof is level or almost level—cut a groove 1 inch (2.5 cm) in from the outer edge and 1/8 inch (0.3 cm) deep on the underside of the roof. This groove will prevent rainwater from draining back into the interior of the box.

WET-WEATHER DRAINAGE

For the duration of their protected custody, young birds (fledglings) are trapped; not only can they suffocate from excessive heat, but if they become wet, they can die of hypothermia. Any water collecting in the bottom of a birdhouse, which will quickly waterlog the nesting material, is potentially dangerous to the young birds.

A sloping and overhanging roof offers some protection, but to ensure that the nesting box floor will drain properly, cut off the small triangular tip of each corner or drill 1/4-inch (0.6 cm) holes in the floor.

Additional measures to increase water protection include:

- Drilling entrance holes on an upward slant
- Recessing box floors 1/4 inch (0.6 cm) from the vertical sides, front, and back to let the water drip off
- Nailing a small strip of metal or a piece of roofing paper over the ridgeline to prevent the roof from leaking

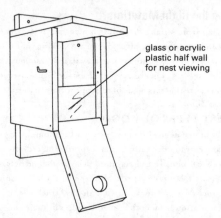
MOUNTING

Boxes can be hung from wire; nailed, screwed, or bolted to trees or wooden posts; or mounted on iron pipes and attached with a metal pipe flange. Whichever method you use, know that your box is well constructed and that its inhabitants are safe from predators.

If hanging your nesting box, use flexible 9-gauge wire or vinyl-coated clothesline. Be sure to use an eyebolt, nut, and washer attached to a sturdy roof; a screw eye can loosen and allow the box to fall.

Boxes can be mounted on top of wooden posts with four L-bracket mounts. If mounting your box to a wooden post or tree, be sure to use a predator guard, as these fixtures are easy for raccoons, cats, and other predators to climb.

Metal pipe and flange mounts are relatively expensive, but also long lived and very sturdy. If mounting your box with a pipe and flange, do not use any pipe less than 3/4" (1.9 cm) in diameter.

PLATFORM VARIATIONS

There are many possible variations of the nesting platform design, as can be seen by the examples shown here. In areas protected from the elements, you can even install nesting platforms that are completely open.

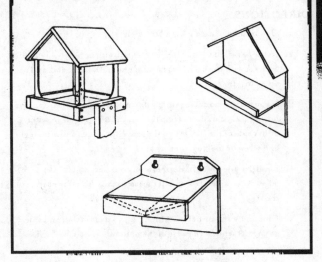

Nesting Platform for Robins, Eastern Phoebes, and Barn Swallows

Robins, phoebes, and Barn Swallows will not use an enclosed birdhouse; they prefer a shelter with one or more open sides. The bottom of the shelf platform (bottom) for Eastern Phoebes and Barn Swallows is 6 x 6 inches (15.2 x 15.2 cm); for robins it is 6 x 8 inches (15.2 x 20.3 cm).

Hang the platform in partial shade, either from the main branch of a tree or under a shed or porch overhang. To help the birds with their nest building, place some clay in a nearby puddle. The birds will use this to cement together the twigs that form their cup-shaped nests.

Robins have adapted well to suburban life and will be easy to lure to backyard nesting platforms.

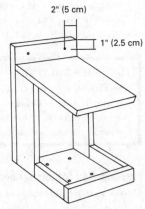

2" (5 cm)

1" (2.5 cm)

The nesting platform for robins, Eastern Phoebes, and Barn Swallows

Materials

3/4" x 7 1/2" x 25" (1.9 x 19.1 x 63.5 cm) wood

3/4" x 8" x 6" (1.9 x 20.3 x 15.2 cm) wood

3/4" x 6" x 11 1/2" (1.9 x 15.2 x 29.2 cm) wood

3/4" x 1 1/2" x 17 1/2" (1.9 x 3.8 x 44.5 cm) wood

Eighteen 1 5/8" (4.1 cm) stainless-steel drywall screws or 6d galvanized ring-shank nails

Two brass or galvanized #6 x 2" (5.1 cm) wood screws and washers to fit

Glue

Tools

Tape measure

Carpenter's square

Pencil

Circular saw or handsaw and miter box

Hand or power drill and drill bits: 1/4" (0.635 cm), 3/8" (0.953 cm)

Phillips-head screwdriver or power drill fitted with screwdriver bit

Cutting diagram

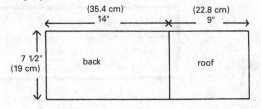

(35.4 cm)
14"

(22.8 cm)
9"

7 1/2" (19 cm)

back

roof

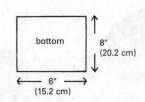

bottom

8" (20.2 cm)

6" (15.2 cm)

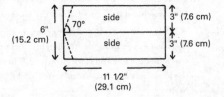

6" (15.2 cm)

70°

side

side

3" (7.6 cm)

3" (7.6 cm)

11 1/2" (29.1 cm)

closure strips

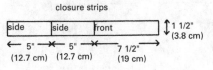

side side front

1 1/2" (3.8 cm)

5" (12.7 cm) 5" (12.7 cm) 7 1/2" (19 cm)

Continued →

DIRECTIONS

1. Cut one end of each *side* at a 70° angle.

2. In the *bottom*, drill four 1/4" (0.6 cm) drainage holes. Then align each *side* with the back of the *bottom*, glue both faces, and nail or screw together.

3. If you will be mounting the platform, predrill two 3/8" (1.0 cm) holes 1" (2.5 cm) down from the top and 2" (5.1 cm) in from either side of the *back*. Align the *back* with the *sides* and *bottom*; glue and screw or nail together.

4. Bevel-cut the *roof* at 70 degrees along one of the 7 1/2" (19.1 cm) edges. Glue and screw or nail the *roof* to the *sides* and the *back* into the roof.

5. Glue and screw or nail 1 x 2 inch (2.5 x 5.1 cm) front and side *closure strips* around the edge of the bottom.

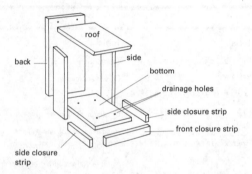

MOUNTING

If you're going to attach the platform to a tree, building, or post, secure it through the back with 2" (5.1 cm) screws and washers.

For robins: Mount a robin platform 6' to 15' (1.8–4.6 m) above the ground.

For phoebes and Barn Swallows: Mount platforms for phoebes and Barn Swallows 8' to 12' (2.4–3.7 m) above the ground.

Appropriately enough, Barn Swallows often find the multitude of open platforms in barns quite inviting.

Gourd Nesting Boxes

Many species will take readily to nesting in gourds. Gourds can be grown like pumpkins—simply plant them in your garden in hills of four or five seeds with the hills 4 to 6 feet (1.2–1.8 m) apart. When fully ripe, harvest the gourds, wash them thoroughly with a disinfectant, and spread them on newspapers to dry. While drying (three to four weeks), turn the gourds regularly and spread them out so that they don't touch one another.

After the gourds have dried, cut a hole to the dimensions required by the desired species. Gourds can be tough—you may need to use a keyhole saw or expansion bit to do this. Then use a serrated knife to break up and remove the hard pith and seeds from the inside.

To shield the entrance hole from the sun and rain, you may wish to add a small canopy made from flexible metal or plastic above it. If so, attach the canopy with silicone caulking and let it dry thoroughly before setting outside.

Attach a fastener to the top of the gourd and hang it from a porch roof overhang, tree limb, or pole.

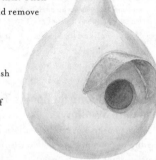

A gourd nesting box with metal canopy

Nesting-Box Maintenance: Predators and Pests

Once you put out bird feeders or nesting boxes, predators become a perpetual concern. Even Fluffy, the once adorable house cat, is turned into terrible Tom and sits crouched and motionless in the grass, soundlessly switching her tail and waiting for the perfect moment to pounce. And clever folks (raccoons and opossums) stake out your yard by night waiting to hector the parents and capture the kids.

Squirrels, mice, or snakes may even have taken up residence before the birds of your choice arrive. Insects and parasites may attempt to cohabit, and there is always the annoyance of sparrows and starlings flitting around trying to distract the mother.

To give your birds their best chance, carefully build to each box's specified dimensions (depth, height, distance to entrance hole, and entrance hole size and configuration). These dimensions not only meet the birds' needs but also minimize the ability of predators to wreak havoc.

For starters, try smearing the mounting pole with Vaseline or a mixture of grease and hot red cayenne pepper. If predators continue to harass the nesting birds, however, you may need to implement some more rigorous measures to safeguard your birds.

SQUIRREL-PROOFING

Teeth and gnawing marks around a nesting-box entrance are signs of squirrels attempting to enlarge its hole. Predator guards made of metal will discourage their activities. Cut the metal 1" (2.5 cm) larger than the opening. Remove a center hole equal in size and shape to the entrance hole and tack the guard in place. Be sure there are no burrs or sharp edges along the metal.

NOEL WIRE RACCOON GUARD

The angled roof and overhang of each nesting box make it difficult for predators to reach into the entrance hole from the roof. However, house cats, squirrels, and—especially if your nest is located near swampy water—raccoons and opossums still may be a problem. They will insert a paw and pull out the young or the eggs. Wood shavings on the ground or around the entrance hole are signs of their activity. To discourage these menaces, use a sharp-edged wire guard that makes for a long, uncomfortable reach.

Noel Wire Raccoon Guard

CONE BAFFLE

If smearing the pole with Vaseline or a mixture of grease and hot red cayenne pepper doesn't work, build a 3-foot (0.9 m) metal cone guard out of 26-gauge sheet metal. The cone should stay in place, but wobble enough to prevent the predator from reaching the nesting box.

To mount a cone on a wooden post: Cut four blocks to 3 x 3" (7.6 x 7.6 cm) and nail to the post just below the nesting box; the blocks will hold the cone guard in place.

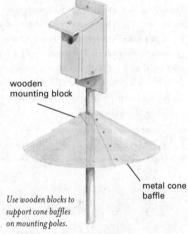

wooden mounting block

Use wooden blocks to support cone baffles on mounting poles.

metal cone baffle

To mount a cone on a metal pole: Fit the pole with a hose clamp, a piece of twisted wire, or a wooden block to support the cone.

METAL SLEEVES AND POLES

If you know you have a flying Wallenda for a house cat, mount the nesting box on a metal pole. Such poles are the most difficult for predators to climb. Other pests (snakes, for example) and particularly persistent cats and squirrels may be more successfully thwarted if the metal support pole is layered with grease and sprinkled with red cayenne pepper.

Sheet-metal guards on a wooden post or tree where the nesting box is mounted offer additional protection and are best installed before the birds begin nesting. Bend an 18-inch-wide (45.7 cm) sheet tightly around the wooden post or tree and tack or nail it in place. Narrower strips of sheet metal may not be sufficient to defeat a springing cat.

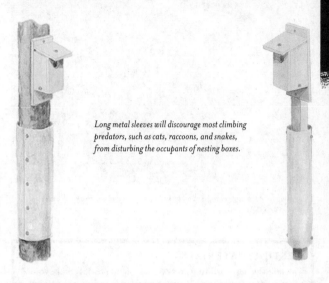

Long metal sleeves will discourage most climbing predators, such as cats, raccoons, and snakes, from disturbing the occupants of nesting boxes.

LEASHING YOUR PETS

Dogs and cats should be leashed or kept inside during nesting time, especially when there are young birds. Bells on collars don't stop cats from being successful hunters.

Attracting Birds to Their New Home

Birds need protective shelter, food, and access to ample water. Make your best attempt to locate nesting boxes in habitat most resembling the bird's natural environment. It may take a year before the birds discover your nesting box, but if it takes longer, reexamine the box and the site. The location you've chosen may not be right for the birds, or perhaps you need to provide some more tempting attractions.

- **Food and water.** Many times birds can be encouraged to nest when the box is close to fruit-bearing shrubs or a birdbath. However, avoid placing boxes right next to a bird feeder.

- **Sheltering foliage.** Check the vegetation around the box. If there is none, there will be nowhere for the mother to shelter the fledglings; if there is too much vegetation, it provides plenty of protection for predators. Or parents-to-be may have already discovered a predator nearby and opted for a safer location.

- **Protected exposure.** Check also that the entrance hole faces south, southwest, or west, and is situated with a clear flight path to its entrance. Do not point the entrance hole in the direction of prevailing winds or storms, or in the path of direct exposure from the afternoon sun. Houses must not overheat. If your summers are extremely hot, point the entrance to the north or east.

- **The right-sized entrance hole.** Ensure that the entrance is the proper size for the species you are trying to entice.

Continued →

Many small cavity-nesting birds, such as chickadees, titmice, and sparrows, will appreciate good cover near their nesting box.

NESTING MATERIALS

To make the nest-building process easier (and possibly make your birdhouse more attractive to potential nest builders), you can offer birds nesting materials. Robins and Barn Swallows need mud. Songbirds use twigs, feathers, straw, grasses, and leaves to build their nests but will be thankful for short threads, string, yarn, tissues, hair (human or horse), lint from the clothes dryer, and bits of cloth. Long threads or wads of cotton may be more dangerous than useful; they can become tangled in a bird's claws. Add wood shavings to the boxes of chickadees and woodpeckers; they'll use the shavings to shape their own nesting cavities.

Look for other nesting facilities in your immediate locale. Your birds may have found safer sites. There also may be too many nesting boxes in the area. Four small boxes (or one large box) per species per acre is the maximum, and more than one box per tree is too much unless the boxes are for different bird species. Birds are territorial, and competition is worst among those of the same species.

Check also that an unwanted occupant (such as a snake, mouse, or squirrel) isn't already nesting in your box.

The Right Time for Installation

Nesting boxes frequently go unused because they are put out too late in the season. You must install nesting boxes before the migratory birds arrive and breeding begins; dates will vary by region, but generally this means January in the South and mid-March in the North.

Setting out new boxes in late fall is ideal. By spring they will have weathered and become more attractive to birds, which might find a brand-new shelter suspicious. This schedule also gives birds that winter over (woodpeckers, swallows, and nuthatches) time to get used to the boxes; they may even roost in them.

Installing boxes in fall has a further advantage: If you will be mounting the box on a pole or post, the ground may still be frozen in early spring. Driving in posts in late fall will be much easier.

Mary Twitchell

Illustrations by Kimberlee Knauf, Frank Riccio, Brigita Fuhrmann, Rick Daskam, and Alison Kolesar

Introduction

Oddly enough, many people who want to attract birds neglect to provide water for them. They may have multiple feeders, which they conscientiously stock year in and year out; yet they fail to furnish water, which is as important to the birds and sometimes harder to find than food. There are, in fact, birds that will ignore all your efforts to entice them to food delicacies, but they'll readily visit a birdbath to drink and disport themselves with abandon.

Providing water is the least expensive method of attracting birds. Oh, you can go to a lot of trouble and expense, but it isn't really necessary. The amounts needed are small and, most of the time, serving it is quite simple. Whether you provide a simple ground basin or a stunning stone birdbath complete with fountain, birds will flock to the newest addition to your garden.

The Basics of Birdbaths

Among the birds likely to visit birdbaths are some of the particularly colorful ones and some that seldom visit feeders. Included are bobwhites, bulbuls (exotic immigrants to southern Florida), indigo buntings, brown thrashers, and cedar waxwings. Meadowlarks are attracted to lawn sprinklers, and white-winged doves will come to surface water.

SHALLOW WATER

Most of the birds that come to feeding stations prefer to drink—and bathe—in very shallow water. If you've ever observed songbirds drinking at a brook or some other natural water source, you will have noticed they generally use the edges. The majority of garden birds prefer the water to be no more than 2 1/2 inches (6.25 cm) deep. Even large birds like jays and grackles are highly suspicious of water more than 4 or 5 inches (10–12.5 cm) deep. All of them prefer a vessel that slopes to the deepest point. Moreover, its surface should be rough so that they can easily keep their footing.

These modest requirements are very easy to fulfill with a run-of-the-mill clay birdbath—a shallow bowl and separate pedestal base. The bowls are also sold separately for two reasons: The tops can be used

Birds prefer shallow water and good footing for drinking and bathing. Avoid slippery surfaces and deep water—they could be deadly.

alone, on the ground; they are also breakable and somewhat more prone to damage than are the bases. Decorated birdbaths of clay are slightly more expensive. Concrete birdbaths are competitive in price with clay ones.

Simple birdbaths made from a clay bowl and separate pedestal are economical, easy to set up, and, best of all, well loved by birds.

That's the bare beginning. Anyone interested in buying one can find baths ranging from the tasteful to the bizarre, made from a wide selection of materials and priced accordingly.

FRESH WATER

Keeping water fresh and abundant isn't much of a chore during warm weather, but those of us who endure cold winters have a problem supplying water when the temperature drops below freezing. If there's snow cover, the birds will get along fine. Some of them—downy woodpeckers, crows, juncos, white-throated sparrows, and black-capped chickadees—will even bathe in snow. But when the ground is bare and natural water sources are frozen, the birds may be in desperate straits.

There are various solutions to the problem. One answer is to put out hot water during freezing weather. However, the container will be a problem. Clay and concrete baths will break if we try to keep them operating in winter by such means. The shallow black pans made by Fortex are splendid for bird watering during freezing weather. They're made of virtually indestructible, heavy, rather soft, neoprene-type plastic. A solid blow to the container will remove ice without damaging Fortex in the slightest, and you may pour boiling water into it with aplomb.

The highly respected John K. Terres, in *Songbirds in Your Garden* (New York: Thomas Y. Crowell, 1968), speaks of the birds standing in hot water in extremely cold weather, apparently warming their feet and enjoying the rising steam. I feel diffident about questioning such an

authority, but that situation would make me extremely nervous. With no evidence to support my conviction, I'm persuaded that such a footbath might actually damage the birds' feet, perhaps inviting frostbite. John V. Dennis in *Beyond the Bird Feeder* (New York: Alfred A. Knopf, 1981), for example, reports that starlings that bathed in a heated birdbath when the air temperature was 10°F below zero promptly froze to death. In the same book he states the startling observation that, in general, birds are very active bathers when the temperature registers 23–26°F. Dennis asserts that birds bathe regularly in winter to keep warm: Proper care of their feathers helps to insulate them from the cold.

Place birdbaths in open areas away from the hiding places of predators.

SAFETY

The use of the pedestal-type birdbath is recommended wherever there are cats because birds with wet feathers fly poorly; besides, they frequently become so engrossed in their bathing activities that they aren't as alert as they might be. The bath itself should be in an open area—on a lawn, for example—so that the birds are less likely to be caught by surprise. When placing a birdbath, be sure that there are some sturdy bushes or trees somewhere nearby where the birds can perch and preen after bathing.

WHEN WATER IS SCARCE

What happens if you don't provide water? If the birds stick around your place despite this oversight, they're more likely to eat any available small fruits and berries—including those prize raspberries, blackberries, or blueberries you may be eager to eat yourself—to get moisture. They'll "bathe" in wet foliage after a rain.

Thirst is probably regulated by the birds' diet. Goldfinches, primarily seed eaters, need a lot of water, while birds such as bluebirds, which eat primarily fruit and insects, will not need as much.

In naturally dry areas, water may be all you need to attract birds. In other areas, however, the birdbath will get more of a workout at some times than at others. During times of sparse rainfall, for example, expect record attendance. During the fall months, water may attract more migrants than your feeding station does (because of the abundance of natural foods).

Birds will use the water about three times as often for drinking as for bathing. In the summertime, they will bathe most often on cool days. Evidently they're not fond of warm water for the purpose and, of course, water warms up quickly in a shallow container. Birds seem to feel a need for bathing most at molting time, in August and September. Presumably it has a soothing effect on skin made sensitive by the molt.

Continued ➜

Other Ways to Provide Water

You can use containers other than birdbaths to provide water for birds. The larger sizes (say, 6 to 12 inches, or 15 to 30 cm, in diameter) of earthenware saucers made for potted plants work fine. Even with only half an inch of water in them, birds will find them quite satisfactory. Robins, catbirds, orioles, and grosbeaks are among those that find such saucers adequate for bathing as well as drinking.

Garden pools can be constructed simply and attractively, beautifying the garden and satisfying the birds at the same time. Keep them shallow and sloping. If there is dry space around the edges, so much the better. Birds are very cautious when entering water to bathe, even if they are regular visitors to the site.

Besides ordinary birdbaths, basins, and saucers, some birders report that natural stone basins that hold only a small amount of water also attract the birds. Such natural basins are easy to clean with a stiff broom. Incidentally, a warning about wading pools: Friends of ours came home from a weekend at their beach cottage to find a catbird drowned in their children's plastic wading pool. Apparently it had misjudged the water's depth and was unable to get out.

Using Water Heaters

If you will be away from the house and unable to provide fresh water in freezing weather when there's no snow cover, you might want to consider using an immersion heater in your watering facility. They're available both at stores that sell poultry supplies and from those that sell wild bird supplies. Relatively inexpensive to operate, they maintain a fixed water temperature of 50–55°F. They can be used in containers that don't normally make good birdbaths—say, a metal or plastic dishpan, 6 to 8 inches (15–20 cm) deep. Put the heater in the bottom with a layer of bricks or stones covering it to provide the correct water depth—about 2 1/2 inches (6.25 cm)—for songbirds. Friends of ours use a large pail instead and float a block of wood on the water. Most of their winter visitors perch on the rim of the pail to drink, but a few of the smaller birds use the wood block itself as a perch. We use floating thermostatically controlled heaters in our livestock tanks in winter, but the tanks themselves have now been placed in the barn. If they were outdoors, I'd float lengths of plank in them to give the birds a perch and an island of safety.

If you decide to heat water for the birds electrically, make sure you use a UL-approved heater designed to be immersed in water, on a circuit protected with a ground fault interrupter (GFI). Make sure your extension cord is of the outdoor, weatherproof variety. Don't try to cut corners and concoct a Rube Goldberg heater that may be dangerous to you as well as to birds and other animals.

HANGING A CERAMIC BIRDBATH

Small and shallow, this is a very easy bath to clean and maintain.

1. Set the saucer in the center of the plywood. Trace a line around the bottom edge of the saucer. Following your line, cut out the center of the circle to create a place to nestle the saucer.

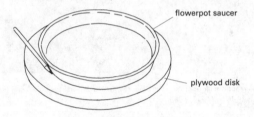

flowerpot saucer

plywood disk

2. Paint the plywood with several coats of acrylic paint. Consider using a layer of marine-grade varnish as the top coat: Bathing birds will keep soaking the wood, and this will help prevent decay.

3. Space the screw eyes equally around the plywood, about 1" (2.5 cm) from the outer edge. Dab a small amount of glue on the threads before you attach the screw eyes. This will keep them secured to the wood.

4. Cut the cord or wire into two equal lengths. Tie one end of a piece of cord to a screw eye. Tie one end of the second piece of cord to an adjacent screw eye. Push the untied ends of the cords through the metal ring and tie them to the screw eyes on the opposite edge of the circle.

5. Put the saucer into the hole in the painted plywood.

6. Secure a sturdy metal screw hook into a tree limb, and hang the birdbath from it, slipping the metal ring onto the hook. (Position the birdbath where it's easy to reach for cleaning and refilling.) Fill it with water and place a few pebbles in the saucer to give the birds a place to stand.

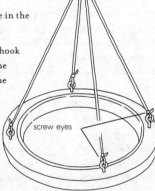

screw eyes

HYPERTUFA BIRDBATH

Hypertufa is a mixture of sand, cement, peat moss, and water that can be poured into a mold and allowed to harden until it forms a lightweight faux stone. There is something about this project that brings out the child in everyone who tries it. Once you get going, who knows what you'll make?

Materials

1 to 2 gallons (3.8–7.6 liters) of clean masonry sand

Water

Portland cement

Milled peat moss

Equipment

Bucket

Round, flat-bottomed plastic container 1 to 2' (30.4–60.7 cm) in diameter, 6" to 8" (15.2–20.2 cm) deep

1. Mix half of the sand (or more, if necessary) with enough water to almost saturate it. This will make a mixture that packs tightly and is hard to disturb. Form the sand into a mound in the middle of the plastic container. Smooth and firm it. You can create a unique and "wild" bath by embedding leaves, twigs, feathers, or small pebbles in the surface of the sand.

You can cut a template from plywood and use it to gently scrape the surface of the sand mold until it has a uniform and smooth shape.

2. Make the hypertufa in the bucket, using equal parts cement, sand, and peat moss. Add water until the mixture is the consistency of cookie dough. Pour into the plastic container. Gently knock against the sides of the container to get good contact between the hypertufa and the sand. Allow the hypertufa to dry for 24 to 48 hours.

3. Remove the birdbath from the plastic container and allow it to cure in a dry place for 4 to 6 weeks.

4. After this first curing period, place the birdbath outside and rinse it frequently to remove chemicals and neutralize cement. It will be safe to use in about three more weeks.

5. You can distress the birdbath to add texture and the illusion of age by hacking, whacking, and chiseling with various tools, such as chisels and hatchets.

Carefully pour the hypertufa mix over the mounded sand and decorative elements.

6. This birdbath is too heavy to hang. Instead, place it on a tree stump, a flat-topped rock, or a stone wall.

MOSAIC BIRDBATH

Use a concrete mix to make a sturdy birdbath that can then be covered with a mosaic. Mosaics are an elegant way to enliven outdoor projects. It is an easy, inexpensive technique to learn. It also very durable. Mosaics found in the ruins of Pompeii and other ancient Roman ruins are evidence of how long they can last.

What you use to make a mosaic is limited only by your imagination. Tile, stone slabs, pebbles, glass nuggets, broken pottery, and tessera are some of the more common materials. For a unique outdoor look, combine river pebbles with lapidary-cut stones, available at craft stores.

MAKING YOUR OWN MIXES

To Make Your Own Ready-Mix Concrete

Concrete is made by mixing cement, sand, gravel, and water. You can add aggregate (often gravel) to concrete to make birdbaths that you can leave plain, brush to reveal the aggregate, or decorate with mosaic.

For small jobs, such as the birdbath, you can purchase ready-mixed concrete. However, if you want to mix your own, simply combine the following ingredients:

-   1 part cement

-   2 parts sand

-   3 parts gravel

To Make Your Own Ready-Mix Grout Mortar

Grout is a fine-grained cement mortar used to fill the cracks between mosaic pieces. You'll find it at ceramic tile supply and hardware stores. To provide a more interesting design, color it using grout dyes available at ceramic tile supply stores. You'll need a pound of grout for every 2 or 3 square feet (60.7 to 91 cm) of mosaic surface. You can buy dry, ready-mixed mortar or make your own by mixing together the following ingredients:

-   1 part Portland cement

-   3 parts sand

-   2 to 3 tablespoons (30–45 ml) cement bonding adhesive per gallon (liter) of water

Continued ➜

Materials

1 to 2 gallons (3.8–7.6 liters) of clean masonry sand

Ready-mixed concrete

Water

Plastic sheeting (like the kind that comes from dry cleaners)

Mastic

Ready-mixed grout

Mosaic pieces

Equipment

Bucket

Round, flat-bottomed plastic container 1 to 2' (30.4–60.7 cm) in diameter, 6 to 8" (15.2–20.2 cm) deep

Trowel

Wire brush

Craft stick

1. To create a sturdy and firm casting medium, wet the sand with enough water to almost saturate it. Form the sand into a mound in the middle of the plastic container. Smooth and firm it. (You can use a plywood template to help make the shape even all the way around.)

2. In a wheelbarrow or shallow plastic pan—wide, shallow containers make it easier for you to get at the clumps of dry concrete—add enough water to the concrete mix to create a "mud" of the right consistency to mold easily. It shouldn't be too runny or too crumbly.

3. Beginning at the bottom and working your way up, use a trowel to drop the concrete mix into the sand mold in a layer about 1 inch (2.5 cm) thick. By superficially chopping into and spreading it, distribute the concrete evenly around the mold. Smooth it with the trowel to press out the air and pack it tightly.

   If you feel that you haven't mixed enough concrete, use what you have in a complete thin coat so that the color will be consistent over the entire inside surface. Then add a second batch to build up the thickness. Aim for 1 to 1 1/2 inches (2.5–3.8 cm) in thickness overall. Keep smoothing the concrete with the trowel to squeeze out air, which makes it stronger. When finished, cover the concrete with a damp towel to allow slow drying and set aside for 24 hours.

4. After 24 hours, lift the concrete gently from the sand. Hose it down and scrub it with a wire brush to remove excess sand and enhance the surface texture. Remember that concrete is soft and weak when first cast, so you can most easily scrape off any unwanted globs at this point. Then replace the damp towel and wrap the concrete casting with plastic. It needs 3 days to fully cure.

5. After 3 days, remove the plastic and damp towel and let the concrete birdbath sit, exposed to the air, for a week.

6. With a craft stick, dab a bit of mastic on the back of each mosaic piece and set it onto the surface of the birdbath. Press to attach firmly. Be sure not to use too much mastic; if it oozes from behind the piece when you press it onto the mosaic, you have too much and it will be difficult to place the pieces side by side.

7. Once all the pieces are securely glued to the birdbath, allow it to dry for 8 hours.

8. You're now ready to finish the mosaic. Place the dry grout in a container and add water, stirring thoroughly with a craft stick, until you have a creamy, workable paste. Be sure to mix in all the dry particles on the bottom of the bowl. Let the grout sit for 10 minutes before beginning to apply.

Until you've had some experience working with mosaics, mix the grout in small batches using a bottle of water kept at the table.

Push the grout between all the pieces that compose your mosaic surface.

9. Wear rubber gloves to protect your skin from the grout. With your hands, apply the grout right over the mosaic pieces, pushing the grout between the mosaic pieces to fill all the gaps and make a level surface. Every crevice needs to be filled to prevent moisture from seeping in and degrading the mosaic.

10. Using a craft stick or paring knife, scrape off the excess portions of grout from the surface, being careful not to scrape out the grout from between the pieces. This part of the process takes a lot of time and attention to detail.

11. Wipe the surface clean with a dry terry cloth towel. If the grout is fully dry, use a damp sponge, but do not use a damp sponge on damp grout—it will pull the grout from the cracks.

12. Allow the grout to dry for 2 to 3 hours, or until hard to the touch, before handling.

13. Place the birdbath on a sturdy, steady support piece, such as a tree stump, a flat-topped rock, a stone wall, or a matching mosaic birdbath stand.

48 inches (1.2 m) high, with the basin formed in the top. The base houses a recirculating pump and water storage tank, with a wooden door providing access. The height of the water plume is up to you.

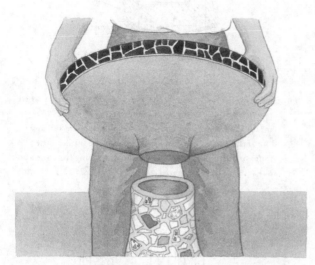

If you feel daring, construct a sturdy matching stand for any shallow birdbath form, such as the concrete mosaic bath described by this project.

The finished stone birdbath contains a gently bubbling spout of water. The sound of the bubbling will attract birds from miles around.

STONE BIRDBATH

A birdbath can be a dramatic landscaping focal point. Add a fountain and it becomes an exercise in elegance. Moreover, when the birdbath is of stone instead of precast concrete or metal, it attains that level of permanence and dignity that characterizes all good stonework. If built of stone natural to the area, it will blend well and be a fitting addition to any lawn. And it will attract birds.

This birdbath, from *Stonework: Techniques and Projects*, by Charles McRaven, would make a magnificent addition to nearly any yard. Now, building anything with running water is more complicated than simple stonework, but a birdbath isn't really a difficult project. Like all stonework, it should be approached a step at a time, which makes the process easier.

A very small fountain pump will suffice for this birdbath. Water is being moved in such a small volume for so short a distance that a large pump is a waste. You may want a small geyser or just a bubbling effect. Either way, not much force is necessary. A larger flow or more pressure will send the water up high where wind will scatter it, and the birdbath will soon go dry.

Do keep an eye on the water level, as the pump will burn out if it runs dry. Evaporation will, of course, lessen the reserve, and birds splash out a lot. As with any recirculating water feature, check the birdbath daily and maintain an appropriate water level.

A stone birdbath is a departure from the usual pedestal birdbath. Because stone looks better as a mass, this project is a round structure,

Materials and Supplies

These materials will create a circular birdbath 48 inches (1.2 m) high and 36 inches (0.9 m) in diameter. For larger or smaller projects, you'll have to adjust the amounts of stone and cement.

Equipment

Hammer

Hand or circular saw

Hoe

Level

Pick

2 pipe wrenches

Pointing tool

Saber saw

Shovel

Square marking pencil

Tape measure

Trowel

Wheelbarrow

Stone

2 tons (1.8 t) stone, mostly 6" (15 cm) thick, relatively short lengths. Corbeling for the top courses will require stones 8 to 10" (20–25 cm) thick.

Concrete

2 sacks Portland cement

250 pounds (0.1 t) sand

500 pounds (0.2 t) gravel, 1" (2.5 cm) or less in size (what quarries call six-to-eights)

Water

Continued ➡

Mortar

4 sacks Portland cement

750 pounds (0.3 t) sand

1 1/2 sacks lime

Water

Wood and Hardware for Door

One 15" x 16" x 1" (38 x 40.5 x 2.5 cm) pine or oak board

Two door hinges, screen door latch or turn block latch, stainless-steel screws

Several 3/4" (1.9 cm) wooden dowels, 9" (22.8 cm) long, tapered at one end

One 10-gallon (38 l) plastic water tank, no larger than 14" x 15" (35.4 x 38 cm)

Small pump, fittings, adjustable hose nozzle, electric cord

1/2" (13 mm) polybutylene pipe, 10' (3 m) long

Other Supplies

One 36" (92 cm) square metal lath

One 36 x 36 x 5/=" (92 x 92 x 1.6 cm) sheet of plywood

Four 2 x 4s (5 x 10 cm), each about 36 inches (0.9 m) long, for form and braces

6' (1.8 m) of pressure-treated 2 x 4s (5 x 10 cm) for door frame

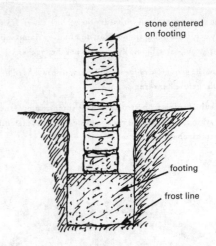

stone centered on footing

footing

frost line

1. Dig a circular footing ditch 12 inches (30.4 cm) wide and 42 inches (1.1 m) in diameter (measured from the outer edge of the footing), to below the frost line.

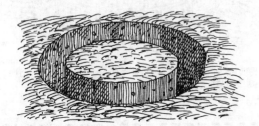

2. Mix the concrete. Start with two shovels of cement, four of sand, and six of gravel. Mix in small quantities in a wheelbarrow or in a portable mixer. Start with the sand, then add the Portland cement. Dry mix, then add water until the mix is wet and loose. How much water you need varies a lot, a key factor being how dry or wet the sand is when you start. Add the gravel last, working it into the wet mix a little at a time.

Concrete should be dry enough to hold shaped peaks when you shovel it into place, but wet enough to level out when it is shaken with a hoe. If water puddles up on it, it is too wet. Excess water will leave air pockets when the concrete dries, which will weaken it.

Mix additional batches of concrete as needed to fill the footing ditch to a depth of at least 6 inches (15.2 cm). (A deeper footing will require more cement, sand, and gravel than the quantities listed under "Stone.") Keep it damp for at least 2 days.

3. Mix mortar, starting with nine shovels of sand, two of cement, and one of lime, plus water.

4. Begin laying stone for the wall, which should be 6 inches (15.2 cm) thick and centered on the footing.

5. Just above ground level, set the door frame—pieces of pressure-treated 2 x 4 (5 x 10 cm) cut to support a 15 x 16-inch (38 x 41 cm) door. (The curve of the wall will accommodate a straight door if the door is recessed a bit.) Anchor the frame to the stonework with stainless-steel screws protruding from the wood so that they can be mortared in.

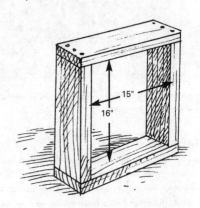

15"

16"

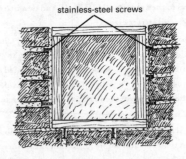

stainless-steel screws

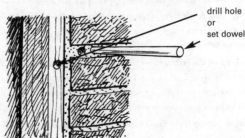

drill hole or set dowel

MIXING MORTAR

A heavy contractor's wheelbarrow is ideal for mixing mortar. The basic mix for stonework is:

- 1 part lime
- 2 parts Portland cement
- 9 parts sand

Lime typically comes in sacks of 50 pounds (22.7 kg). Start with the sand and add the Portland cement and lime, so that the wheelbarrow is no more than half full. A medium-size shovel used for the measuring produces a good batch of mortar.

Mix dry first, using the shovel, a hoe, or both. Then move the dry mix away from one end of the wheelbarrow pan and pour in about half a gallon (1.9 l) of water.

With the hoe, begin "chopping off" thin slices of the dry mix into the water. Work each bit until it's wet throughout, then chop some more. When this water is used up, open a hole beyond the mixed mortar for more water and repeat the process. Be sure you don't leave dry pockets of mix down in the corners as you go. When you get to the end of the wheelbarrow with this process, you should be finished. Take care not to add too much water at a time or the mix can get overly wet. It should stand in peaks.

If the sand is wet from rain, you'll need very little water for the mix. As you get near the end of the batch, use only a small amount of water at a time. It's easy to go from too dry to too wet with just a cupful of water.

The consistency should be as wet as possible without running or dripping. Most masons use very dry mortar because it is neat and easy to clean up later, but it does not bond well to the stone and water leaks through this dry mortar.

If the mix is too wet, add sand, Portland cement, and lime in proportionate amounts and mix until the batch stiffens up. Or you can leave it for 20 minutes or so, until water floats to the surface. Pour this off and repeat. The mortar at the bottom will thicken enough for use, and you can scrape the soft stuff aside to get to it.

As you use the mortar, it will dry out more. This will get rid of too-wet mortar and will mean you have to add water to an ideal mix. Use all mortar within 2 hours of mixing.

6. Drill a 1/2-inch (13 mm) hole in the wood for an electric wire, or leave a hole in the mortar by mortaring in a 1/2-inch (13 mm) dowel that you've tapered so that you can remove it easily after the mortar dries. Set the dowel between stones or between stone and frame.

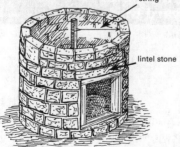

string

lintel stone

7. Continue building the circular wall, measuring often to keep it round and plumb. At the top of the door frame, lay a lintel stone, curved if possible.

8. Lay stone to a height of 36 inches (91.1 cm); then, leaving an inside "lip" of about 2 inches (5 cm), corbel (step) out two or more courses, 2 inches (5 cm) at a time, until the circular wall is 48 inches. (1.2 m) high. Corbeling requires that you use stones that are the full thickness of the wall.

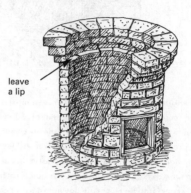

leave a lip

9. Cut a circle of plywood, with a diameter of about 24 inches (60.7 cm), to fit inside the wall, 12 inches (30.3 cm) below the final height. Cut the circumference of the plywood circle to accommodate unevenness in the stone wall. Drill a 3/4-inch (1.9 cm) hole in the center of the disk and another 3 inches (7.6 cm) from the edge.

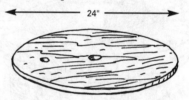

24"

10. Fit a tapered 9-inch-long (22.8 cm) wooden dowel into each hole, then prop the form up with 2 x 4s (5 x 10 cm) that extend to the ground. Position the circular form so that the hole near the outer edge is as far from the door as possible.

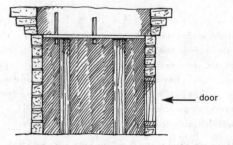

door

11. Mix additional mortar and trowel it onto the plywood form, shaping it into a curved bowl. The mortar should be fairly stiff to keep it from sliding down the sides. When the mortar is 1 1/2 inches (3.8 cm) thick at the bottom of the bowl, cut pie-shaped pieces of metal lath, each about 18 inches (45.5 cm) from point to arc, and lay them overlapping each other by about 2 inches (5 cm) to fit the curve of the bowl.

Continued ➔

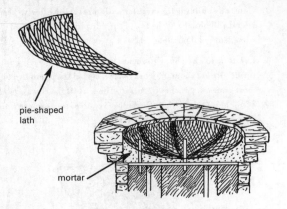

pie-shaped
lath

mortar

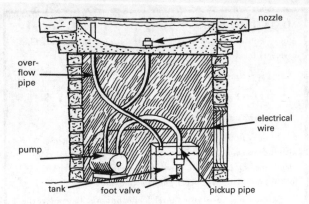

nozzle

over-
flow
pipe

electrical
wire

pump

tank   foot valve   pickup pipe

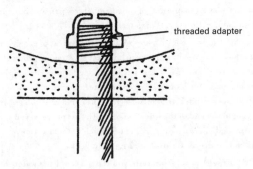

threaded adapter

12. Trowel another 1 1/2 inches (3.8 cm) or so of mortar over the
lath and smooth it out. At what will be water level—say, 2 inches
(5 cm) down from the lip of the bowl—the outermost dowel
should protrude. (When removed later, this will leave an
overflow hole.) Cover the mortar with plastic sheeting and keep
it damp for 4 days. Then remove the plywood form by screwing
drywall screws into it and prying downward with a claw hammer
or crowbar. It should come off the dowels, which can be driven
upward and out with a long punch or another, smaller piece of
doweling. Cut the plywood form into pieces with the saber saw to
get it out the door space.

16. Install the door hinges, the latch, and the door itself. Fill the
tank, then fill the basin, which will prime the pump. Replenish
as needed.

install selected hinge style

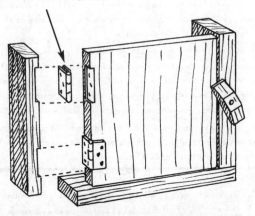

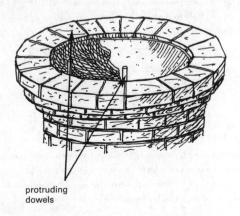

protruding
dowels

13. Now you're ready to put in the pipes. Set the overflow pipe in the
side dowel hole and the nozzle pipe in the center hole. Then apply
mortar around both. Let the mortar cure for 4 days, covered in
plastic, and then caulk. Run the overflow pipe down to the tank,
which can be set on the ground. Run the nozzle pipe down to the
pump. The pickup pipe from the pump should extend to within
1 inch (2.5 cm) of the tank bottom. (Adding a small foot valve
will eliminate the need for repriming the pump.)

14. If you can't find a suitable nozzle, use a threaded adapter, with a
pipe cap, drilled for the size hole that will produce the fountain
volume and height you want. Try several caps with different size
holes, but keep them all smaller than the overflow pipe.

15. Extend the electric wire from the pump through the hole you
left in the door frame or the mortar. Connect it to a breaker in
an electric panel or use a plug-in to an outlet.

Creating a Habitat for Backyard Birds

Dale Evva Gelfand

Illustrations by Kimberlee Knauf, Jeffrey Domm, Elayne Sears, and
Beverly Duncan

Introduction

Most people are familiar with the man-made structures we use to
encourage wild birds to visit our yards, such as bird feeders, birdbaths,
and nesting boxes. Of course, all of these will do the job—but you can

enhance the bird-friendly atmosphere of your backyard to an even greater degree. By planning and developing your backyard as an inviting natural habitat, including diverse native food plants, sheltering shrubs and trees, a water source, and nesting sites, you will encourage birds to stick around, not just eat and run.

Making Your Yard a Habitat

What is *habitat* exactly? The term refers to a combination of food, water, shelter, and space arranged to meet the needs of wildlife. Even a small yard can be landscaped to attract birds, butterflies, beneficial insects, and small animals if you provide the trees, shrubs, and other plants that supply wildlife with shelter and food.

The plants you supply for food and shelter will help determine the wildlife that's attracted to your backyard. And of course any bird feeders, nesting boxes, and water that you provide will make your habitat even more immediately desirable to any bird that happens to be flying over.

The primary rule in what I will call habitat gardening is this: *Practice conservation in your own backyard.* The three most important actions you can take to arrive at this goal are:

1. Plant as many native plants as possible—which by virtue of their indigenous nature are best suited to your region—and do *not* plant any invasive exotic (nonnative) plants.

2. Control pests by natural means—that is, let nature take its course by encouraging beneficial insects (which are often killed off when pesticides are used), bats, and, of course, insect-eating birds to take up residence in your neighborhood.

3. Reduce the size of your lawn, which will cut down on mowing (thereby reducing air and noise pollution) and fertilizing. Although prized in landscaping, these large expanses of clipped green grass are otherwise unproductive spaces that could be filled with plants beneficial to wildlife.

THE PESTICIDE PROBLEM

Insects are a vital food source, especially for songbirds, woodpeckers, and ground birds such as quail and pheasants. As birds do such an excellent job of ridding our yards of insect pests, I can't think of a better reason not to use pesticides—except one: They kill birds! Birds are poisoned when they ingest insects, worms, or seeds from plants or turf that have been treated with chemicals. Especially toxic are:

- **Furadan (Carbofuran),** which comes in both liquid and granular forms. One granule mistaken for a seed will kill a bird instantly.

- **Spectracide (Diazinon),** also available in liquid and granules—and lethal in either form.

- **Dursban (Chlorpyrifos),** which is widely used to kill both house and garden pests but also kills young birds.

- **Kelthane (Dicofol),** a miticide responsible for the deaths of peregrine falcons.

BRINGING BACK BALANCE

Botanists will tell you that many of our native-plant species are on the brink of extinction, and home gardeners play a large role in this botanical annihilation. It's bad enough that we exchange (that is, yank out) native plants for nonnative ones, but these imports don't have any natural checks and balances. So when their seeds or runners escape our gardens—which is inevitable—they can and do overrun our native vegetation, thereby upsetting the entire ecological balance and, especially, eliminating valuable food resources for birds and other wildlife. That makes it imperative that we protect both the birds and our indigenous plants by planting as many native species as possible. (However, you should *not* go dig them out of the woods; buy nursery-propagated material from reputable suppliers only.)

Many of these native species are what have come to be thought of as weeds. But really, the only difference between a weed and a wildflower is a shift in perception—and appreciation. Don't think of that lovely stand of goldenrod as the cause of hay fever (which is erroneous, anyway—the real culprit is ragweed, which often grows with goldenrod and is beloved by birds as a major seed producer); instead, admire the beautiful deep yellow color and the arrangement of flowers on the variously shaped stalks. And while it's true that common plantains don't have much to recommend them to our eyes, birds love them, so consider allowing some to stand in the yard, accompanied by a few more eye-catching grasses like dwarf bamboo, bottlebrush grass, and tussock sedge.

FOUR STEPS TO A GREAT BIRD HABITAT

Birds are no different from the rest of us when it comes to needing the basics for survival of the species. If you can break down your desire to create a bird habitat into just four simple elements, you'll be hosting happy birds for years to come:

1. Food
2. Water
3. Shelter
4. A place to raise young

Of course you want your garden to be appealing to both you and the birds, and the vegetation police aren't going to come after you if you plant several nonnative exotics, be they perennials, annuals, shrubs, or trees—just make sure they aren't of the invasive variety. The point is to plant as many native species as possible, because the greater the variety of plants, the greater the variety of bird (and butterfly) species you'll see in your yard.

Feeding the Birds

Providing a variety of foods is probably the most important part of your wildlife habitat. You can select a diversity of food types from plants that mature at different times, including those that retain their fruits well into and even through winter. Every species has its own dietary needs, which often change with maturity. Food includes the nutritional part of the diet as well as supplements like grit and gravel that many birds need for their gizzards to grind up food.

Continued →

Some birds are omnivorous and eat a variety of foods, while others eat only a few different kinds. But except for the few strict insectivores and carnivores, almost all bird species' diets include some combination of fruits and berries, grains and seeds, nectar, and pine buds and acorns—all of which your garden can supply.

FRUITS AND BERRIES

Fruits and berries are important because they're rich in vitamins and carbohydrates. Sweet fruits like blackberries and mulberries give nesting birds the energy they need to rear chicks; fatty fruits like those of dogwood and maple-leaved virburnum fuel fall migrants and provide nonmigratory species with the resources they need to enter the harsh winter season in peak condition; and winter residents (as well as early-spring arrivals like robins and bluebirds) can avail themselves of supplies of the persistent fruits of hawthorns, crab apples, and sumacs. Some berries, such as those of mountain ash and holly, remain on bushes or trees through the winter—long after they've ripened. In fact, many types of berries aren't even palatable to birds until they've undergone a series of freezes and thaws. And berry-producing shrubs and trees can be quite beautiful; red-osier dogwood, for example, will make everyone happy, providing abundant white berries for food, nesting sites (especially for goldfinches), lovely clusters of white flowers in late spring, and brilliant red stems in winter, brightening up any landscape. Equally beautiful in winter is the aptly named winterberry, whose profusion of eye-catching red berries will attract both birds and their human hosts.

WHO'S COMING TO DINNER?

Some of the birds that will happily eat fruits and berries are:

Bluebirds	Mockingbirds	Thrushes
Cardinals	Nuthatche	Towhees
Catbirds	Orioles	Tufted Titmice
Cedar Waxwings	Quail	Vireos
Chickadees	Robins	Warblers
Cuckoos	Sparrows	Woodpeckers
Doves	Tanagers	
Flickers	Thrashers	
Grackles		
Grosbeaks		
Grouse		
House Finches		
Jays		
Kingbirds		
Kinglets		

- **Summer-fruiting plants** are those that produce fruits or berries from May through August. These include bramble berries such as blackberry, raspberry, and boysenberry (eaten by some 150 species of birds); elderberry (a particular favorite, eaten by 120 different bird species); serviceberry, blueberry, grape, plum, black cherry, and honeysuckle.

- **Fall-fruiting plants** include dogwoods (eaten by some 90 species), buffalo berry, mountain ash, cotoneaster, Virginia creeper, common spicebush, arrowwood, and black tupelo.

- **Winter-fruiting plants** include sumacs (preferred by more than 95 species); crab apple (a favorite of Wild Turkeys), nannyberry, hollies, mountain ash, wild grape, Christmas berry, bittersweet, and winterberry.

NUTS

Nuts, which contain fats and proteins, are actually fruits with a dry, hard shell. The acorns of live oaks—the dominant oak species of the American Southeast—are eaten by at least 15 bird species, including Wood Ducks, Scrub and Blue Jays, and Eastern Meadowlarks. Hazelnuts, found in the plains and prairies, attract several woodpecker species and Blue Jays. The western live oak provides acorns for, among others, the Yellow-billed Magpie, Northern Flicker, Wild Turkey, and Scrub Jay—which, owing to the vast numbers of acorns it stores and hides, is considered the Johnny Appleseed of western oak trees. Some other nuts that attract birds are walnuts, butternuts, hickories, and buckeyes, all of which also provide good nesting habitat. The meats of broken nuts and acorns are consumed by a number of birds, including nuthatches, woodpeckers, flickers, titmice, and towhees.

GRAINS AND SEEDS

Grains and seeds constitute a major food source for many birds. Sunflowers, of course, are a particular favorite of many species, and it's a treat to watch birds eat the seeds "on the fly." Other excellent and well-visited seed plants are asters, coneflowers, and prairie blazing-stars. Grasses and legumes provide both seeds for food and cover for ground nesters. Weeds probably contribute the most to food supplies because of their abundance, and they're frequently favored by birds—if not their human hosts—over what we consider more attractive plants. Pigweed, ragweed, smartweed, dock, and crabgrass, for example, contain tens of thousands of seeds per plant. (Why else do you think they're so darn hard to get rid of?) Assuming you're not willing to go that far in the name of avian hospitality, consider planting other types of grasses and sedges, such as the strikingly beautiful little bluestem grass and a section of buffalo grass, whose low height makes it a desirable "lawn" alternative. Seed-eating birds include sparrows, finches, juncos, blackbirds, chickadees, nuthatches, buntings, jays, meadowlarks, doves, pheasants, towhees, bluebirds, and siskins. If you have a wet spot in your yard, you also shouldn't forget aquatic plants such as wild rice, widgeon grass, pond weeds, and wild celery, as they are favorites of ducks and geese.

A FEAST OF SEEDS

To promote seed production, never deadhead your flowers. If you live in colder regions, leave any flower stalks standing after fall frost for birds to feast on the seeds all winter, and wait until spring to cut back the plants.

CONIFERS

Conifers (evergreens) are also a good source of food—sap, seeds in the cones, as well as berries, buds, and insects in the bark—plus, of course, the trees can't be beat for bird shelter in severe weather. Try to always plant a clump of them in a corner of your yard. Conifer trees and shrubs include pines, hemlocks, spruces, arborvitae, cedars, firs, junipers, and yews. Bird species that are attracted to conifers include jays, siskins, finches, chickadees, grosbeaks, Brown Creepers, nuthatches, warblers, woodpeckers, Wild Turkeys, doves, crossbills, tanagers, and sparrows. Pines also provide roosting and nesting sites for owls and crows, while the sheltering boughs of hemlocks are called home by more than 20 species that roost and nest there, including doves, warblers, robins, cardinals, and thrushes.

NECTAR PLANTS

Nectar plants are a necessity for hummingbirds and orioles (as well as butterflies, bees, and moths). Native perennials and annuals that attract nectar feeders include trumpet honeysuckles, butterfly bushes, cardinal flowers, paintbrushes, bee balms, daylilies, blazing-stars, foxgloves, columbines, hibiscus, wild petunias, trumpet vines, and phlox.

The healthiest and most natural food for a hummingbird is flower nectar.

WHY USE BIRD FEEDERS?

Weather, of course, impacts mightily on natural food sources. Heavy early-spring rains—and, conversely, droughts—and early frosts can drastically curtail food production as well as the natural cycles of nut-producing trees, whose crops can vary from overabundance to practically nonexistent. An early snowfall can cover all the fruit, seeds, and nuts that have dropped to the ground, and sleet and ice storms can make it impossible for wildlife to access food. These are extreme times when natural food sources need to be supplemented with birdfeed.

Bird feeders also allow you to get a good close-up look at many birds of different species. You'll note that it takes a lot of acreage to support any significant number of birds. To get variety and numbers requires careful planning and careful planting. The ideal is a blend of natural foods supplied by the garden and supplemented by feeding stations. By attending to garden and feeders, you can appeal to a tremendous variety of birds.

Installing a Water Source

Water is as essential for bird survival as food—though often a water supply is overlooked as a necessity. Fruit and insect eaters like bluebirds need less water, as much of what they need comes from the foods they consume, which have a high water content. Seed eaters like finches need a lot of water. A ready water source becomes a necessity for all birds during the summer for cooling baths, and in winter when streams and ponds freeze over—especially if there's no snow to "drink" and, yes, occasionally even bathe in. And, from a bird-watching standpoint,

having an immediate supply of water will significantly increase the number of avian visitors to your yard—especially during seasonal migrations.

Providing Shelter

Shelter—or cover—is another, equally important necessity of good bird habitat. It offers birds (and many other forms of backyard wildlife) protection during both waking and sleeping hours. And of course shelter is critically important during birds' nesting and fledging times.

Good cover provides concealment from and impenetrability by predators, as well as refuge from the elements: rain, snow, sleet, wind, heat, and cold. When choosing your bird-habitat plants, make sure to include at least one good clump of evergreen trees and shrubs to provide year-round protective cover from both weather and predators. Excellent choices are pines, junipers, hollies, and live oaks, which all provide food as well as cover. You should also plant deciduous shrubs that offer effective summer nesting sites and shelter from predators.

An important rule: *Good cover should be close to food and water.* The more exposed birds are, the higher their mortality rate from predators. The favor you're doing birds by providing them with feeders is in turn providing opportunists with a free lunch. Hawks learn very quickly where to set up shop for easy pickings, as do any neighborhood cats (or your own).

HEDGES AND HEDGEROWS

Hedgerows—living fences—are invaluable as shelter because they also provide food in a protected environment. Common hedgerow plants that establish themselves naturally are dogwood, redbud, wild cherry, wild grape, and—unfortunately for most of us—poison ivy. Towhees, wrens, and sparrows find such living fences ideal homes. Use rows of conifers and large shrubs to block off a less-than-ideal view and at the same time provide a sound barrier against noise. Windbreaks made up of junipers, spruces, pines—with a crab apple, serviceberry, or chokecherry tucked in the sheltered side—give birds a warm, safe place to rest in northern winters. Come spring, windbreaks provide ideal nesting sites.

Cover can take many forms: trees, shrubs, grasses, flowers, brush piles, field crops (such as corn, grain sorghum, and soybeans), cut banks, hollow trees, nesting boxes, underpasses, abandoned buildings, and fencerows.

STARTING A NEW HEDGE

It is particularly important to get your hedge plants off to a good start. Each one should grow in a bushy form at about the same speed as all its companions. Start with healthy, compact, small plants, if possible.

Begin shearing while the plants are still young, just as soon as they start to grow noticeably—sometimes in the first year, and certainly by the second. Even if you want your hedge to grow to 4 feet, don't wait until it gets to that height before you begin to shape it. In order to have a tall, tight hedge, you should first develop a *small*, tight hedge, then let it grow larger gradually.

Continued →

1. You can dig a hole for each individual plant, but it is easier to get the plants in a straight line and evenly spaced if you plant your hedge in one long trench.

2. If you are planting a straight hedge, use a string stretched taut to mark the line, just as if you were getting ready to plant peas in a garden row. Unless you're installing a mass planting, never plant a hedge more than one plant wide. For easier shearing, set the plants in a single rather than a staggered line, unless you plan to use your hedge only as a high windbreak or snow trap.

3. Set out the plants 2 feet (0.6 m) apart, measuring from the center of each plant. Plant tall-growing hedges, such as a lilac hedge, several feet apart—the exact distance depends on how quickly you want a tight hedge. The farther apart you place them, the longer it will take for the plants to intermingle. Prune the new plants to equal heights.

—Lewis Hill, *Pruning Made Easy* (Storey Books, 1997)

NESTING SITES

Hold that chain saw! As far as birds are concerned, their Park Avenue penthouse is an upper cavity in that dead tree hovering on the far reaches of your property. Snags (the term for standing dead trees) are used for nest sites, roosting, perching (no leaves to get in the way of insect spotting), and even courtship (woodpeckers do their best territorial drumming on the wonderfully resonant wood of a dead tree). The heretofore standard practice of cutting down and removing dead trees—because they were thought to harbor insect pests—has sorely contributed to the massive decline of natural nesting sites, making the competition for those that remain even fiercer. Now it's widely recognized that the many bird species that nest in snags feed heavily on insects and actually prevent serious insect outbreaks. So unless the snags in your yard actually pose a safety hazard to your family or your property, leave them standing—for everyone's benefit!

Many birds like to nest in vines like Virginia creeper, wild grape (not only does it provide food and shelter for more than 50 species, but many birds use its stringy bark as nest material), catbriers, and, yes, poison ivy. Conifers are also preferred nesting sites. Everything from Mourning Doves to cardinals nests in spruce and pine boughs, taking advantage of the dense branches that offer protection from both predators and the weather plus a ready source of food.

Of course, you can substitute or augment natural nesting sites with artificial ones: nesting boxes. Make sure any boxes you erect are placed so that they offer protection from predation, heat, and cold; are close enough to a tree to make that first flight by fledglings a safe one; and are accessible enough to be opened and cleaned at the end of the breeding season.

Planning Your Backyard Bird Habitat

When planning your backyard bird habitat, remember that you have both horizontal and vertical areas to work with. The horizontal aspect of your land is your property itself. The vertical aspects are the canopy of the tallest trees, the shorter understory trees, vines, and shrubs, followed by low-growing plants and ground covers. Because different bird species (and other wildlife) inhabit each section of vertical space, even a small piece of land can include a number of habitats.

THE BASICS OF BIRD HABITAT

Aside from the four habitat essentials—food, water, shelter, and nesting sites—landscaping for birds involves several other basic principles:

- **Diversity.** To attract the greatest number of bird species, include a wide variety of plants in your landscaping plans. Some plants provide food but very little cover; others provide cover but little food.

- **Arrangement.** Habitat components need to be properly arranged. Consider the effects of prevailing winds and drifting snow so your yard will be protected from harsh winter weather. Avoid straight lines and perfect symmetry: Natural habitat has curves and clumps of vegetation. (And remember, birds aren't particularly attracted to a well-manicured lawn, which offers absolutely no protection from predators.)

- **Consistency.** Plant trees, shrubs, and flowers that will provide year-round food and shelter. If you're going to install a birdbath, consider getting an electric immersion heater to keep the water flowing during colder months.

- **Protection.** Birds should be protected from unnecessary dangers. When placing bird feeders and nesting boxes, consider their accessibility to predators. And picture windows can be a death trap for birds. (To prevent this problem, hang closely spaced strings or ribbons on the outside of your windows.) Also, avoid or limit use of herbicides and pesticides—use them only when absolutely necessary and strictly according to label instructions.

- **Hardiness.** One of the best reasons to use native plantings is you never have to worry about their hardiness in your zone. But if you're incorporating some nonnative species into your habitat, make sure the plants are rated for the winter hardiness zone classification of your locale.

- **Soil and topography.** Have your soil tested by your local garden center or county Extension Service office. Plants are often adapted to certain types of soil; knowing what type you have can help you identify the best species to grow in your yard. Also, some plants prefer well-drained slopes to level ground, for example, and it's important to know these preferences, too.

14 SURE-FIRE TIPS FOR ATTRACTING FEATHERED FRIENDS

1. **Limit the size of your lawn.** Wildlife is not particularly attracted to a well-manicured lawn. From a bird's standpoint, your lawn is a wasteland that offers little or no nutritional value and shelter. Instead, use the space for vegetation that will benefit the birds and other wildlife. (And the hours you save on mowing your lawn can be spent

doing *fun* things!) Or let a patch of lawn revert to its natural state as a meadow of wildflowers and native grasses.

2. The farther from the house, the more natural the habitat. Plant traditional garden flowers and vegetable and herb gardens close to your house and increase the amount of native plants and wild areas beyond.

3. Offer a source of water. Be it a birdbath or a garden pool, having water in your habitat is an instant bird magnet.

4. Use native plants. They support themselves and bird populations far better than nonnative plants do.

5. Avoid invasive nonnative plants. Though many of these are advantageous to birds in that they supply food and shelter, their threat to native plants—and therefore the wildlife that depends on them—far outweighs any benefits.

6. Choose plants that will provide food year-round. From early-spring blossoms to fall-fruiting trees with persistent berries, select flowers, shrubs, trees, and vines that will help birds survive everything from the rigors of parenthood to fall migration to overwintering.

7. Plant in vertical levels. Copy nature's design plan and plant canopy trees first. Then fill in with smaller shade-tolerant understory trees and shrubs, followed by flowers and ground covers. Adding these to an existing landscape will enhance the vertical layout that's common in natural landscapes; also, many smaller trees and shrubs are colorful in spring when they flower, and provide berries for fall and winter feed. Birds often use all of these levels—singing from a high branch, nesting in tall shrubs, and finding food on the ground below. Assuming your yard already has at least a tall tree or two, surround them with "islands" of vegetation of varying heights.

8. Plant clumps of same-species shrubs and trees. Doing so allows for pollination, which will boost fertility and produce larger yields of fruits. But avoid straight lines and perfect symmetry. Natural habitat has curves along with its clumps of vegetation.

A clump of shrubs surrounded by native grasses and wildflowers will offer shelter for birds. Many shrubs are also food sources, such as these buddleia, which supply nectar.

9. Plant vines—or leave those that you already have. As far as birds are concerned, vines have it all: food, building supplies, and housing sites. And vines like Virginia creeper provide us with brilliant scarlet early-fall foliage—always a feast for the eyes.

10. Save dead trees. Snags are vital to birds as sites for nesting, roosting, and perching.

11. Don't rake up all the leaf litter. Leave the leaves around the bases of shrubs and trees; the decomposing leaves will attract insects and earthworms that in turn supply ground-feeding birds like towhees and robins with food. Also, the larvae of a number of species of butterflies and moths overwinter in leaf litter, so the wholesale raking up of leaves in fall may be one reason that the butterfly population is in decline.

12. Use natural pesticides, not chemical ones. That is, let the birds do their job. They'll happily devour garden pests in multitudes.

Many woodpeckers make their homes in dead trees, or snags. In future years, other species of birds may nest in the cavities drilled by woodpeckers.

13. Install nesting boxes. With suitable natural cavities in short supply—many of them seized by starlings and House Sparrows—cavity nesters like bluebirds and certain warblers are hard put to find nesting sites. You can help these species by erecting nesting boxes on your property. Before setting out nestboxes, find out which species are common in your area. Make or buy a birdhouse specifically designed for the birds you wish to attract. The size of the entrance hole is critical to prevent the eggs and young from being destroyed by larger birds—always use the appropriate hole size. Other considerations include box size, height above the ground, direction the entrance hole faces, and amount of sunlight. Boxes may need baffles or other protective devices to limit access by cats and other predators.

14. Confer with resource experts. Review your plant list with landscaping resource experts who can match your ideas with your soil types, soil drainage, and the plants available through state or private nurseries. Botanists at a nearby arboretum may be able to help with your selections—and you can also see what many plants look like.

TIME AND MONEY

You can be as economical or extravagant as you choose when planning your backyard bird-habitat-improvement project. Modest changes can be achieved on even a limited budget by purchasing plants through your state or regional foresters or at commercial nurseries late in the season when they're likely to be on sale. If you're limited by funds or space, remember that shrubs provide habitat more quickly and at comparatively less cost than larger shade trees. Or consider joining forces with your neighbors to create a habitat area larger than any one of you could provide alone, thereby multiplying the efforts of all for everyone's mutual benefit. And of course not all the planting needs to be done at once. Consider it a work in progress.

Don't expect too much from your plantings for the first few years. They'll need some time to become established before they can offer adequate food and cover for wildlife. However, you can provide a mixture of habitats with plants, trees, and shrubs in various stages of development. Berry-producing shrubs and other dense cover plants will be the first to provide useful bird habitat. And remember that the less pruning, thinning, and general manicuring you do, the better it will be for the birds. Allow branches to grow down to the ground, and allow some corners to go wild to native plants. If you think it might be difficult to adapt to a "messier" landscape than you've been used to, perhaps start with a habitat that will be a *compromise* between a well-groomed yard and the needs of wildlife.

Continued ➔

Remember, whether you have a small urban or suburban backyard or a many-acre rural lot, the same principles for enhancing bird habitat apply. The greater your efforts to encourage them, the greater your rewards in bird numbers and diversity.

The Right Landscape with the Right Plants

Bird species are extremely variable in their preferences. Some like thick woods, others prefer open meadows, and still others—including sparrows, Blue Jays, cardinals, robins, juncos, and chickadees—are highly adaptable and can be found in many environments. Some are year-round residents while others, like the Cedar Waxwing, will appear for only a few days a year during migration.

No matter what their habits and territory, birds all require the proper habitat. Following are a number of plant species to consider for your backyard bird habitat, each annotated with what hardiness zones, or region, in which it can be best grown. Use this list as a starting point for your landscaping plan. Check with your local Natural Heritage Program, a Cooperative Extension office, or the botany department of a nearby college for lists of plants native to your area. Remember: Naturally adapted plants are a good long-term investment. (And please, don't dig native plants out of the woods—buy nursery-propagated material from reputable sources.)

TREES AND SHRUBS

Trees and shrubs form the backbone of any backyard bird habitat because they provide most of the essentials: food, shelter, nesting sites. Depending on where you live, consider planting some of the following species.

American beautyberry (*Callicarpa americana*), Zones 7–10

American beech (*Fagus grandifolia*), Zones 3–9

Balsam fir (*Abies balsamea*), Zones 3–5

Black cherry (*Prunus serotina*), Zones 3–9

Black gum (*Nyssa sylvatica*), Zones 3–9

Black spruce (*Picea mariana*), Zones 2–5

Buckeyes (*Aesculus* spp.), Zones 3–9, depending on the species

Bur oak (*Quercus macrocarpa*), Zones 2–8

Buttonbush (*Cephalanthus occidentalis*), Zones 5–10

Carolina silverbell (*Halesia carolina*), Zones 4–8

Chokecherry (*Prunus virginiana*), Zones 2–6

Common juniper (*Juniperus communis*), Zones 2–6

Crab apples (*Malus* spp.), Zones 4–8, depending on the species

Eastern hemlock (*Tsuga canadensis*), Zones 3–7

You may find larger birds, such as Ring-Necked Pheasants, foraging under fruit trees.

Eastern red cedar (*Juniperus virginiana*), Zones 2–9

Eastern redbud (*Cercis canadensis*), Zones 4–9

Elderberries (*Sambucus* spp.), Zones: the West Coast's blue elderberry (*S. caerulea*), 5–9; American elderberry (*S. canadensis*), 3–9

Firebush (*Hamelia patens*), Zones 9–11

Flowering dogwood (*Cornus florida*), Zones 5–9

Hackberry (*Celtis occidentalis*), Zones 2–9

Hawthorns (*Crataegus* spp.), Zones 3–8, depending on the species

Hazelnuts (*Corylus americana*), Zones 4–9; (*C. cornuta*), Zones 4–8

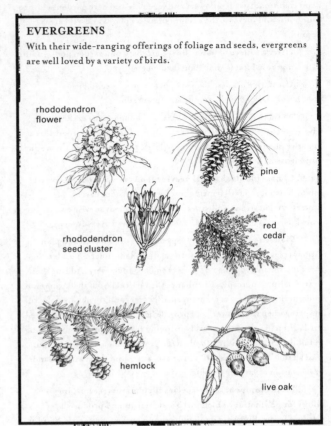

EVERGREENS

With their wide-ranging offerings of foliage and seeds, evergreens are well loved by a variety of birds.

rhododendron flower

pine

rhododendron seed cluster

red cedar

hemlock

live oak

Hickories and pecans (*Carya* spp.), Zones 4–9, depending on the species

Highbush blueberry (*Vaccinium corymbosum*), Zones 3–7

Live oak (*Quercus virginiana*), Zones 8–11

Mountain laurel (*Kalmia latifolia*), Zones 4–9

Northern arrowwood (*Virburnum recognitum*), Zones 2–7

Northern bayberry (*Myrica pensylvanica*), Zones 3–6

Northern white cedar (*Thuja occidentalis*), Zones 2–8

Oregon grape

Oaks (*Quercus* spp.), Zones 3–11, depending on the species

Oregon grape (*Mahonia aquifolium*), Zones 4–8

Persimmon (*Diospyros virginiana*), Zones 4–9

Rhododendrons (*R. maximum*), Zones 3–7; (*R. catawbiense*), Zones 4–8

Serviceberries (aka shadbushes, shadblows) (*Amelanchier* spp.), Zones 4–9

Sheep laurel (*Kalmia angustifolia*), Zones 2–6

Spicebush

Sourwood (*Oxydendrum arboreum*), Zones
4–9

Spicebush (*Lindera benzoin*),
Zones 4–9

Sugar maple (*Acer saccharum*),
Zones 4–8

Sumacs (*Rhus* spp.), Zones: staghorn
sumac (*R. typhina*), 3–8; smooth
sumac (*R. copallina*), 4–9; fragrant sumac (*R. aromatica*), 3–9

Swamp azalea (*Rhododendron viscosum*), Zones 3–9

Sweet pepperbush (*Clethra alnifolia*), Zones 3–9

Wax myrtle (*Myrica cerifera*), Zones 7–10

Western soapberry (*Sapindus drummondii*), Zones 5–9

Wild lilac (*Ceanothus thyrsiflorus*), Zones 8–9

Winterberry (*Ilex verticillata*), Zones 3–9

Witch hazel (*Hamamelis virginiana*), Zones 3–8

Witch hazel

VINES, BRAMBLES, AND GROUND COVERS

Vines, brambles, and ground covers are all essential plants to birds, supplying as they do food, shelter, and even some nesting sites.

American bittersweet (*Celastrus scandens*),
Zones 3–8

Brambles (*Rubus* spp.), including
blackberries, raspberries, and
boysenberries, Zones 3–10

Creeping juniper (*Juniperus horizontalis*), Zones
3–9

Partridgeberry (*Mitchella repens*), Zones 3–9

Trumpet honeysuckle (*Lonicera sempervirens*),
Zones 7–10

American bittersweet

CAUTION

American bittersweet is fast being replaced in the Northeast by the aggressive invader Asiatic (aka, Chinese or Oriental) bittersweet (*Celastrus orbiculatus*), which escaped from cultivatation and is highly invasive. *Do not plant this species!*

Trumpet vine (*Campsis radicans*), Zones 4–9

Twinberry (*Lonicera involucrata*), Zones 5–10

Virginia creeper (*Parthenocissus quinquefolia*), Zones
3–9

Western clematis (*Clematis ligusticifolia*),
Zones 4–10

Wild strawberry (*Fragaria virginiana*),
Zones 4–7

Wild sweet William (*Phlox divaricata*), Zones 3–9

Yellow or Carolina jasmine (*Gelsemium sempervirens*), Zones 6–9

Yellow jasmine

HERBACEOUS PLANTS

While the trees, shrubs, and vines that provide food and shelter are of primary importance when you're planting for the birds, herbaceous plants—perennials, annuals, and grasses—that produce quantities of seeds are also important, especially to seed eaters such as finches, juncos, cardinals, sparrows, and towhees. Seeds from these plants will provide food through the winter. To promote seed production, leave spent blossoms in place (don't deadhead them). Also, don't cut back plants after a killing frost. By leaving plants standing, birds will be able to feast on the seeds through the winter, and many butterfly larvae will overwinter on plant stems as well. It's okay to cut back the plants in spring.

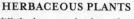

Bee balm

Asters (*Aster* spp.), Zones 3–8, depending on the species

Bee balms (*Monarda* spp.), Zones 3–8

Black-eyed Susan (*Rudbeckia* spp.), Zones 3–9, depending on the species

Blazing-stars (*Liatris* spp.), Zones 3–8

Bleeding-heart (*Dicentra eximia*), Zones 3–8

Columbines (*Aquilegia* spp.), Zones 3–8

Common beard-tongue (*Penstemon barbatus*), Zones 3–9

Common sunflower (*Helianthus annuus*), can be grown as an annual in any zone

Coneflowers (*Echinacea* spp.), Zones 3–9

Coreopsis (*Coreopsis* spp.), Zones 3–9, depending on the species

Desert zinnia (*Zinnia grandiflora*), Zones 5–10

Eastern rose mallow (*Hibiscus moscheutos*), Zones 5–10

Globe thistle (*Echinops ritro*), Zones 3–9

Joe-pye weeds (*Eupatorium* spp.), Zones 4–9

Lupines (*Lupinus* spp.), Zones 4–9, depending on the species

Milkweeds (*Asclepias* spp.), Zones 3–9

Obedient plant (*Physostegia virginiana*), Zones 2–9

Perennial sunflowers (*Helianthus* spp.), Zones 3–9

Prickly pear cacti (*Opuntia* spp.), Zones 9–11 except *O. compressa*, which is hardy in Zones 5–9

Seaside goldenrod (*Solidago sempervirens*), Zones 3–11

Summer phlox (*Phlox paniculata*), Zones 3–8

Yarrows (*Achillea* spp.), Zones 3–9

NECTAR PLANTS FOR HUMMINGBIRDS (AND BUTTERFLIES AND BEES)

Asters (*Aster* spp.), Zones 2–9, depending on the species

Azaleas (*Rhododendron* spp.), Zones 3–9, depending on the species

Bee balms (*Monarda* spp.), Zones 3–8

Butterfly bushes (*Buddleia* spp.), Zones 5–9, depending on the species

Columbine

Continued ➜

Butterfly weed (*Asclepias tuberosa*),
  Zones 3–9

California fuchsia (*Zauschneria californica*), Zones 9–10

Columbines (*Aquilegia* spp.), Zones 3–8

Coneflowers (*Echinacea* spp.), Zones 3–9, depending
  on the species

Coralbells (*Heuchera* spp.), Zones 3–9

Delphiniums (*Delphinium* spp.), Zones 4–8

Jewelweed (*Impatiens capensis or I. pallida*),
  Zones 3–9

Lobelias (*Lobelia* spp.), Zones 2–9, depending on
  the species

Penstemon

Penstemon (*Penstemon* spp.), Zones 3–9, depending on the species

Phlox (*Phlox* spp.), Zones 2–9, depending on the species

Salvias (*Salvia* spp.), Zones 4–9, depending on the species

GRASSES

Many grasses produce abundant seeds for birds to eat. Listed below are just a few species. Many nonnative ornamental grasses also produce abundant seeds, and many birds will also appreciate cultivated grains such as millet, oats, and wheat.

Bluestems (*Andropogon* spp.), Zones 2–7

Buffalo grass (*Buchloe dactyloides*), Zones 3–9

Gama grass (*Tripsacum dactyloides*), Zones 5–11

Indian grass (*Sorghastrum nutans*), Zones 4–9

June grass (*Koeleria macrantha*), Zones 4–9

Little bluestem (*Schizachyrium scoparium*), Zones 3–11

Northern sea oats (*Chasmanthium latifolium*, also known as river oats or
  inland sea oats), Zones 5–9

Purpletop (*Tridens flavus*), Zones 5–10

Switch-grass (*Panicum virgatum*), Zones 5–9

Creating a Bird-Watcher's Journal

Clare Walker Leslie and Charles E. Roth

Illustrations by Clare Walker Leslie

Introduction

You won't find the word *journaling* in your dictionary. It is a word we created as an action form of the noun *journal*. Simply put, nature journaling is the regular recording of observations, perceptions, and feelings about the natural world around you. That is the essence of the process.

mockingbird lands to display striking tail shadow on tombstone

GETTING STARTED WITH BIRD-WATCHING

You don't have any trouble recognizing the robin flitting around the birdbath, or the blue jay busily—or greedily, depending on your point

of view—carrying away sunflower seeds. But what about that little brownish bird? Sparrow, you think. But aren't there roughly 93 different kinds of sparrows? Or maybe it isn't a sparrow at all. Maybe it's one of those other little brownish birds.

That's the state of the art with many of us. So what's the first step? A friend who is an experienced birder is surely the best of all possible aids in learning to identify birds. But even if experienced guidance is available to you, there will certainly be times when you must have recourse to other methods. You'll want to know how to go about the process all by yourself.

In our household, books accumulate as readily as dust. What we consider the indispensable volumes for identifying birds are Roger Tory Peterson's *A Field Guide to the Birds* and *A Field Guide to Western Birds* (Boston: Houghton Mifflin Company).

The first thing to do is to familiarize yourself with the books. Browse awhile. You'll notice that the individual pictures of birds have black lines pointing to those conspicuous characteristics differentiating one bird from another. Now, obviously, you don't intend to memorize every plate in the book. And if you go rushing for your field guide when you see an unfamiliar bird, chances are it'll be long gone by the time you find either the guide or the page in it that you want. So look at the bird while you have the chance.

BRING 'EM IN CLOSE

What you need, of course, are field glasses or, better still, binoculars. Actually, binoculars are easier to find, unless you happen to stumble across field glasses at a garage sale or flea market. Binoculars differ from field glasses (or opera

rusty crown

gray face

notched tail

rusty gray

pink bill

buffy/gray

5 ³/₄"
field sparrow.

glasses or a telescope) in that prisms have been added to the magnifying lens or series of lenses. You'll be able to use them to advantage both earlier and later in the day, and what you're hunting will be easier to find because their field of vision is wider than that of a magnifying lens.

What does that mean? Focus your binoculars on the top of a telephone pole, say, a hundred yards away. Should you try the same thing with field glasses or a telescope, you'll notice that you can see farther to each side of the pole with the binoculars than you can with field glasses or the scope. That's important when what you're trying to locate has a tendency to move around a lot and is not apt to oblige you by perching right next to something you can sight in on easily.

Binoculars come in several degrees of magnification, the usual being 6, 7, or 8. You can get 10 or 20 power, but they're more expensive and somewhat harder to use. You'll find a bewildering variety of binoculars available, in a wide price range. Birding and nature magazines often run articles comparing different kinds of binoculars.

One word of caution about binoculars. Sometimes you'll find advertised what sounds like a great price. The ad may say TEN TO FIFTY POWER MAGNIFICATION. Read the fine print. If it says they're "non-prismatic," they're not really binoculars, no matter what they look like. Non-prismatic binoculars are a contradiction in terms. Binoculars aren't straight tubes. Those bumps contain the prisms. You'd be better off with good, optical-quality field glasses or a telescope than with "non-prismatic" binoculars with molded or poured plastic lenses and phony bumps.

Although binoculars are easiest to use, field glasses and telescopes you might happen to have around the house can also be handy gadgets. The other day we were trying to identify an uncooperative bird on a branch, and our 8x40 binoculars simply didn't pick up the necessary detail at the range. A spotting scope, at 30 power, did the trick.

One of the problems with the scope, however, is that the higher the magnification, the harder it is to hold it steady on the object observed. That's where a tripod comes in handy. If you have a place to keep a scope mounted near a window, it'll be even more useful.

One other possibility is a monocular, which is essentially half of a binocular. Still prismatic, it's used by one eye only. Its drawback is that you can't achieve the three-dimensional quality you get with binoculars.

Beginning Your Journal

The type of journal you use and how you choose to use it are matters for personal decision. Your supplies can be as simple or fancy as you like or as your budget allows.

Common birder's stance. field guide braced between legs

If you are doing a lot of sketching, you may want to buy a small hardbound sketchbook that has smooth, unlined paper. These are available in a range of sizes at art and stationery shops. If you are inclined toward writing as your primary means of observation, and don't mind lines going through your additional sketches, you may want lined paper, in either a hardbound or a spiral notebook.

If you're not ready yet to commit to a hardbound book, or if you're working with a group, individual loose sheets of paper attached to a clipboard or held onto a piece of stiff cardboard with paper clips is fine. Just be careful to keep the completed journal entries in a folder or loose-leaf notebook, organized sequentially by date, so you can refer back to them easily and trace the evolution of your knowledge and style of recording, as well as the ongoing changes of the seasons outdoors.

for COLOR— try Venus Spectracolor or Berol Prismacolor colored pencils. Also try the Derwent water colour pencils. With a brush and some water, they create a nice water color wash.

Knife for clipping branches + sharpening pencils — or metal sharpener

black ball point pen

try varieties of black felt-tipped or rolling ball, inexpensive pens

technical pencil and retractable leads

eraser or eraser stick

* keep at home expensive equipment. It could get lost; technical pens especially

April 10 Wednesday Mt. Auburn, Camb. 8:20 a.m. drizzly, raw 46°F drastic change over last few days

3 duck fly over quacking

In bloom— forsythia Star magnolia apples cherries dogwood— beginning sugar maples pathy sandra * so good to smell again!

magnolias

a shoulder bag or back pack where you can keep everything, ready to go outdoors.

Hardbound journals available in most art or stationary stores— I like the 8"×11" but many students use larger or smaller. Be sure the paper is unlined and smooth.

Identifying Birds

Take note of all the physical characteristics you notice while closely observing a bird, and then look for a matching picture in your guidebook. Ask yourself these questions:

· Does it show any splotches of color?

· What kind of beak does it have? What kind of a tail?

· Does it have a crest or crown patch?

· Any discernible pattern such as stripes or rings?

· Any markings around the eye or head or back or breast?

Continued →

- In flight do you notice any particular characteristic, like gliding or dipping or undulation?

- Do any flashes of white or some other color appear on wings or tail when it moves? Where did you see it?

- What about its shape—is it chunky or slender?

- Does it walk, hop, perch quietly, or flit about?

- Does it say anything?

- What about size? Give yourself some mental image to compare the bird to. Was it about the size of a sparrow (5 to 7 1/2 inches)? A robin (8 1/2 to 10 1/2 inches)? A crow (17 to 21 inches)?

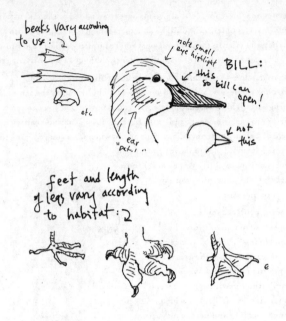

FORM AND FUNCTION

Once you acquire the habit of looking closely at birds so that you can identify them by referring to your field guide, you'll discover that some of their physical characteristics provide clues to their behavior. Some of these physical attributes are related to the feeding behavior of birds.

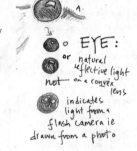

Take note of the size and shape of the bill. Seed eaters like sparrows and finches have short, stubby ones. Cardinals and grosbeaks, with their thicker, heavier bills, can handle larger seeds than, say, a goldfinch. The scissorlike bills of crossbills enable them to extract seeds from pinecones. Woodpeckers have strong bills, like chisels. Warblers and wrens, with their thin, sharplpointed bills, are primarily insect eaters. Birds of prey have hooked bills, ideally suited for tearing meat.

Birds have superb vision, perhaps the sharpest of any animal. Obviously that helps them locate food and contributes to their safety. The position of the eyes on the head is a hint to whether the bird is the hunter (hawks and owls look ahead) or the hunted (woodcocks and grouse have their eyes positioned more to the side and can see farther to the rear than can birds of prey).

Hearing is acute in birds too. Woodpeckers are thought to listen for insects, and owls rely on sound when hunting their prey. Studies have determined the range of hearing in many species. Though many of us may have believed that robins locate earthworms by sound, ornithologists tend to think that the characteristic cocking of the head is related to visual hunting instead.

Look at the legs and feet of the birds you see for further clues to their habits: webbed feet for swimmers, long legs for waders, talons for birds of prey. Birds such as swallows and hummingbirds that take their meals on the wing have small, weak feet. They can perch, but their feet aren't much good for anything else. What a contrast to the thrushes, which forage on the ground!

Color is another hint about behavior. Ground dwellers tend to be duller in appearance than are arboreal (tree-inhabiting) birds. Sparrows, which usually prefer to nest and forage on the ground, are brownish. Grosbeaks and finches, mostly brightly colored, are more active in trees. (There is evidence to suggest that the brightly colored birds aren't as tasty to hunters, either.) Females and juveniles generally tend to be less colorful than males even among arboreal species, doubtless another natural safety device to provide protection for incubating and other relatively helpless creatures.

Increasing Your Birding Knowledge

Be sure to combine indoor study with outdoor observation. Reading books, asking questions, and learning why and how birds do what they do will improve both your knowledge and your ability to accurately depict the birds' activities in your journal.

Journaling Year-Round

Don't let the changing of the seasons slow or stop your journaling activities. As the seasons change, migratory birds will come and go, while the year-rounders will provide a sense of continuity.

some 60 brant in raw umber field

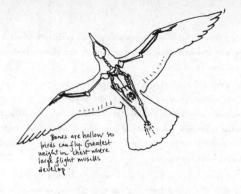

AUTUMN

Observe change in activity and preparations for winter or migrations south among starlings, hawks, geese, and shorebirds.

What fruits are robins, mockingbirds, and sparrows eating?

WINTER

What birds stay through winter and where can you find them? Where do they find shelter? What do they eat? Do they travel in single-species flocks or in mixed-species flocks? How do they communicate in winter? Notice that on bright, sunny days more birds are out singing and flying about.

By February, birds such as pigeons, house finches, and sparrows are actively courting. (And in the wild, great horned owls and mourning doves are, as well.) Winter is pair-forming time for many ducks. Watch them in patches of open water and record their courtship behavior.

Observe the habits of feeder birds: cardinals, house sparrows, mourning doves, and blue jays.

Look for wilder birds: owls, hawks, turkeys, ducks, vultures, and crows.

SPRING

What birds have been with you all winter? Watch for the first birds returning from the South: bay and sea ducks, warblers, and sparrows. What other new birds appear first as part of the spring migration?

What are the arrival dates of the first bird of each species that you see returning in spring? Look for the brightly colored males in breeding plumage; they may look very different from when they passed southward in fall.

Locate a local bird-watcher who can go afield with you, and have him or her help you learn to recognize new kinds of birds.

Observe activities of nearby nesting birds: starlings, house sparrows, crows, robins, and cardinals.

SUMMER

What are five birds that are in your habitat? Are they year-round residents or do they arrive in spring and leave in fall? Are these shorebirds, waterbirds, pelagic or seabirds, hawks, owls, woodpeckers, or songbirds?

Take the time to learn to use a field guide and binoculars for observation. Perhaps you can find a nesting bird and, without disturbing the parents, observe and record the growth of the youngsters. Find a friend, join a group, and go birding with companions.

Learn to identify birds by their calls and habitats.

Practice drawing bird shapes: blue jay, chickadee, magpie, red-tailed hawk, song sparrow, mallard duck, pigeon, herring gull, and common loon.

Drawing Birds

Birds are easier to draw if you learn their basic anatomy and something about the kind of bird you are working with. Incidentally, most bird guides identify groups of bird species from the least evolved (most ancient) to the most evolved (most recent). First listed are loons, then grebes, fulmars, pelicans, ducks and geese, hawks, grouse, herons, cranes, shorebirds and gulls, doves, owls, parrots, woodpeckers, and, last, all the little songbirds. In drawing birds, start with the basic egg shape, then add other geometric forms to build the fundamental structure of the species. Feathers are arranged in groupings, whether on the tail, wing, back, or head. Carefully note the shape of the eyes, bill, feet, and other specific features characteristic to the particular bird you are drawing.

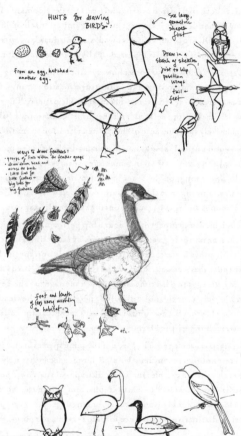

DRAWING FOR OBSERVATION CLUES

Sometimes it helps you get acquainted with local birds if you first draw them from good photos or the drawings in bird identification guidebooks. By drawing particular birds, you fix their most prominent field marks in your memory, and you'll find that you're better able to accurately identify them when you see them in the field. The journal then becomes a great tool for sharpening your observation of birds' movements and activities.

Journal What You Hear, Too

You may find your field guide's written descriptions of song helpful in identifying birds, and perhaps you will want to create journal entries describing what you hear. The guidebook's descriptions mean little to me until after the fact, when I have heard and identified the song.

Continued →

Listening to a recording of birdsongs may prove invaluable. Your local library may have one or be able to get you one. A number of excellent recordings are now available.

Though prenuptial singing is the richest, songs accompany nest building, incubation, tending the young, the departure of the young, roosting, autumn migration, and winter. Through their vocalizations, birds proclaim territory, issue mating invitations and invitations to the nest, request relief from the nest, maintain and strengthen a sexual bond, and abet flock formation.

Birdsong is an essential part of the courtship display. As with courtship displays such as drumming and the whirring of wings, vocal song requires both specialized organs and a certain development of the brain. Song demands more learning (including imitation) than do the calls of birds. Calls are often a single sound, such as squawking, peeping, or screaming. Even if the call is repeated, it's likely to lack variation.

Calls serve a variety of purposes, however, including scolding, warning, begging, summoning, and indicating a location. Songs consist of a series of notes in a somewhat discernible pattern. They tend to be more leisurely, more relaxed, and they first occur as youthful play. They are relatively short because of the limited attention spans of birds.

Females don't usually sing as much as males do, but they're more likely to sing in the tropics than in temperate zones. A female chickadee has only the *fee-bee* song; on the other hand, female cardinals sing as well as their mates. Singing in males is closely correlated with the presence of male hormones and is at its loudest during the breeding season.

Although birdsong is part of the courtship performance, it's used for more than announcing a claim to territory or attracting a mate. Through their songs birds can identify not only their own species but particular individuals as well. That can be very important. Birds may produce, say, 20 eggs in a lifetime and only just manage to replace themselves, which is surely indicative of the perilous lives they lead. They must be able to tell who's who, as well as to recognize the calls that signal distress, hunger, and alarm.

Visual signals aren't enough. Birds of the same species aren't just similar to one another; many females of different species strongly resemble each other. Examples include multitudes of sparrows, purple and house finches, dickcissels, siskins, pipits, and longspurs. No one has yet decided whether birdsong is music or language, poetry or prose, but it must be distinctive at a distance for it to serve its purposes.

Some experts believe birdsong is sometimes used as an emotional release, described as either an excess of energy or an outpouring of sheer joy and called ecstasy song. Such song is produced randomly and is sometimes accompanied by the so-called ecstasy flight. Believing that this activity is motivated by a hope of harmony and escape from discord and boredom will not be easy for everyone to do, but it is interesting to entertain the idea.

Classification of Birds

Taxonomists classify all living things in ever-narrowing categories. Birds are no exception. Beginning at the top, all life on earth is categorized as belonging to either the plant or the animal kingdoms. Birds belong to the animal kingdom; the vertebrate phylum; the class Aves, or birds; followed by order, species, and then subspecies. There are more birds—over 8,500 living species—than any other vertebrate except fishes. The mountain bluebird, for example, is of the animal kingdom, the vertebrate phylum, the class Aves, the order Passeriformes, the family Muscicapidae, the genus *Sialia*, and the species *currucoides*.

Altogether there are 28 orders of birds. Orders are usually worldwide in distribution, but families and groups of genera may be limited to a continent or a zoogeographic region (a large area that has characteristics suitable for them), and genera and species may occur only in certain parts of a continent. An astonishing 85 percent of known species and subspecies of birds are found only in tropical areas, and two-thirds of them are found only in the humid parts of the tropics. Considering this, it's not surprising that 32 of the 44 families of birds that exist only in the New World are found exclusively in the tropics. A dozen of the New World families can be found in the United States. They are migratory and winter in the tropics. Moreover, they prefer the humid, eastern part of the United States.

As you develop your journaling skills, make sure your journal travels with you. A whole new world of birds may await, depending on your destination.

A BIRD-WATCHING FORM

Date _____ Time _____

Location _____

Species _____ Number _____

Sex/Age _____

Body (size, shape, color, wings, tail) _____

_____

Legs and feet (size, length, color) _____

_____

In flight (profile, color, wing/tail, wing beats) _____

_____

Voice _____

_____

Behavior _____

_____

Habitat _____

Sketch _____

Helping Orphaned Wild Birds

Diane Scarazzini

Illustrations by Sarah Brill and Alison Kolesar

Introduction

When faced with a bird in need, most people want to help but don't know how—and also fear doing more harm than good. This bulletin offers some helpful guidelines plus some basic bird knowledge so that you can learn not only how to assist birds in trouble but also which ones really *need* assistance. As individuals, our best strategy is to ascertain if a bird does indeed need help, and then to do what we can to keep him alive until we can transfer him to a qualified wildlife rehabilitator or veterinarian.

The information presented here is not intended to replace doctoring by a professional. Whenever possible, emergency care and handling of wild birds should be limited to individuals who are experienced in treatment protocols for each particular species. Almost every region of North America has at least one licensed and certified wildlife rehabilitator, whose job (as the name implies) is to nurse wild creatures back to health for the purpose of returning them to the wild, and most veterinarians have at least basic emergency skills for helping wild birds. You're merely a way station, a first line of defense—and sometimes a bird's best hope. But always remember: It's a jungle out there, and Mother Nature isn't always kind . . . or pretty.

The ABCs of Baby Birds

The first thing you should know about birds is that they fall into two broad categories based on their development at birth. Knowing whether an orphaned bird is altricial or precocial will help you identify his age and species, which in turn will help you ascertain the best method for helping him.

CHARACTERISTICS OF AN ALTRICIAL BIRD

A bird that is altricial is hatched into a nest naked, eyes closed, unable to do much besides keep his mouth agape for food. Altricial birds must wait for their primary wing feathers to grow—which on average takes about three weeks—before they can leave the nest. Perching birds such as sparrows and chickadees, doves, hummingbirds, crows, and woodpeckers are all examples of altricial birds. Altricial birds pass through predictable development stages as they mature. If you're involved in rescuing an altricial bird, it's important that you be able to determine his development stage.

- **Days 1 through 4:** Mostly naked, feathers develop, mouth gapes for food, has no control of body temperature.

- **Days 5 and 6:** Weight increases rapidly, feathers develop along tracts, eyes open, starts to preen feathers, has some control of body temperature.

- **Days 7 through 9:** Has better motor coordination, fans his wings, flutters feathers, shakes and scratches head, begs for food.

- **Days 9 and 10:** Has control of body temperature, preens, starts to become independent of the nest, responds to parents.

- **Days 10 through 15:** Sleeps in adult position, pecks at food, catches insects, fully feathered, stays apart from siblings.

- **Days 15 through 28:** Preens, may fight with siblings; fledges at any time around this period.

CHARACTERISTICS OF A PRECOCIAL BIRD

Precocial birds develop much differently from altricial birds. The word *precocial* comes from a Latin root meaning "already knowing." While precocial hatchlings aren't yet able to fly, they are born with down, their legs are fully functional shortly after hatching, and they're even able to forage for some if not all of their own food. Many precocial birds are ground nesters, including quail, pheasants, and most types of ducks.

Even though precocial birds have downy feathers, control of their body temperature isn't fully developed until they're at least one month old, so chilling can be a problem if they are away from a parent for too long. Young precocial birds, known as chicks, leave the nest within a day or two after hatching and follow the parents. From the ninth week on, they gain their physical independence and flight ability, though they may be socially dependent on the family throughout the first full year of life.

TO HELP OR NOT TO HELP?

Many wild birds you come across that appear to be in trouble may in fact not need any assistance at all. They are probably doing exactly what they are supposed to be doing for that species in their natural environment at that stage in their development. For instance, many fledglings begin the process of learning to fly after they leap—or, often, are pushed—from their nest. Depending on the species, birds often don't return to their nest once they're out of it, so they may spend several days on the ground literally testing their wings. A well-meaning, concerned individual who tries to "rescue" these birds will in fact *create* a problem instead of solving one.

KNOW YOUR BIRD WORDS

Altricial: Birds that are born naked and helpless (for instance, songbirds).

Precocial: Birds that are born with down feathers and the ability to walk (for instance, ducks).

Hatchling: A newly hatched bird.

Nestling: A baby bird that is completely dependent on its parents for warmth and food; nestlings are too young to leave the nest. This term is usually used to describe altricial birds.

Chick: A young precocial bird.

Fledgling: To *fledge* means to "grow feathers"; fledglings have matured enough to leave the nest but may not yet be able to fly, or may be able to do so only for short distances: They are still cared for by their parents, gradually becoming self-sufficient. This term is usually used to describe altricial birds.

Raptor: Bird of prey.

Pin feathers: The first feathers to emerge on altricial birds.

Talons: The powerful claws of a bird of prey.

Hyperthermia: A dangerously elevated body temperature.

Hypothermia: A dangerously low body temperature.

Of course, there are instances when birds truly are injured or orphaned. Baby birds die from predators, from abandonment, and from exposure after being dislocated from their nest by a high wind or storm. Even when they're successfully off on their own, they can sustain any number of injuries, ranging from gunshots to collisions with cars or windows. Having some information about the normal growth,

Continued →

development, and social interactions of different species may help you determine if a wild bird needs your help.

A bird needs rescuing when:

- The parents are known to be dead, or a nest has been left alone for an hour without the parents returning—a clear indication of abandonment.

- The bird feels cold to the touch or looks sick, lethargic, or weak.

- The bird is a tiny hatchling or nestling that has fallen from its nest. He may be on the ground by himself or with the fallen nest.

- The bird sustained an apparent injury.

- The bird has an infestation of flies, maggots, or other insects.

- The bird is in imminent danger from a life-threatening situation such as predators or tree cutting.

USING COMMON SENSE

A good rule of thumb is: If you have to chase a bird to "rescue" him, more than likely he doesn't need your assistance.

Before you intervene and help a baby bird, observe him from a distance for a few minutes (unless there are factors present that warrant immediate rescue—like an approaching cat). Note his behavior and whether the parents aren't in fact watching over the bird and feeding him. Or the parents may simply be gone for a few minutes, foraging for food. *Don't interfere prematurely!*

Unless the bird is in imminent danger or is very young, it's best to first call your nearest wildlife rehabilitators. They may tell you to transport the bird to them, or they may inform you about special care, handling, or needs until they can get there. They may just as likely tell you to leave the bird alone and watch to see if the parents return. This is especially true in the case of fledglings, which may be out of the nest deliberately. Fledglings can fly successfully from the ground, so your best assistance is merely to keep kids, dogs, and cats away.

If you've ascertained that a bird does, in fact, need assistance to survive, the next step is determining exactly how to help. Often this involves nothing more than replacing the bird in its nest. But sometimes considerably more help is needed. Following are suggestions for some of the more common rescue situations you're likely to run into.

HELPING A GROUNDED BABY BIRD

Sometimes you'll find a baby altricial bird that has fallen from its nest, pushed by a strong wind or by a sibling. Your immediate priority should be warmth, because young nestlings have no control over their body temperature. If the nestling still feels warm to the touch and the nest he fell from is within fairly easy reach, simply climb up and replace the baby bird in the nest. (Be very careful that you don't fall yourself while doing this!) If, however, the baby bird is cool to the touch, you'll need to help him get warm before you can consider how to replace him in his nest.

IF THE BABY BIRD IS COLD

If the baby bird feels cool when you pick him up, he is in danger of becoming hypothermic, a potentially life-threatening situation. Therefore, before replacing the hatchling in his nest, gently warm him in your cupped hands. When the bird feels warm to the touch, so long as

he doesn't appear extremely lethargic or weak, it's safe to replace him in the nest. Always observe the nest for a while to be certain there is parental activity.

IF THE NEST HAS BEEN KNOCKED DOWN

What do you do with a grounded baby bird if its nest has fallen down as well? Simply pick up the nest, replace it in the tree in the spot from which it fell (or reasonably near to it—the parents usually have no problem finding their baby). Then pick up the nestling, warm him in your hands if necessary (see above), and replace him in the nest.

Baby birds can easily become hypothermic, so if a downed nestling feels cool, warm him in your hands before replacing him in the nest.

If you can't reach the nest, or can't warm the baby bird in your hands as you climb to replace the nest, four hands are always better than two. Find a helper who can keep the nestling warm while you replace the nest.

DEBUNKING THE MYTH

You may be thinking "But won't the parent birds reject a baby that's been handled by a human?" Well, don't worry. Birds barely have a sense of smell. The idea that the parents will reject a baby bird touched by humans is a myth—with one exception. Vultures have a very highly developed sense of smell (no surprise here!), but the likelihood of your finding a vulture nestling is minuscule at best.

If the nest was just tipped askew, simply right it and tie both the nest and the branch it was constructed on to other branches with heavy twine or even a length of wire—don't use thin string, because birds can get tangled in it. When the nest has been safely secured, replace the baby bird(s) in the nest and monitor the scene from a safe distance.

IF YOU CAN'T REACH OR USE THE NEST

What do you do if you can't reach the nest to replace the nestling? Or what if the nest has fallen and is too severely damaged to be reused? In this case you'll need to make a substitute nest.

If a nest has been blown or knocked down, a substitute nest can be easily devised from a berry basket and dry leaves or grass.

According to the experts, the best surrogate nest is a plastic berry basket—the kind that holds a pint of strawberries. In fact, it's a good idea to routinely save a few of them so that you'll always have several on hand for emergencies. What makes them ideal, in addition to their size (similar to that of a nest), is that they allow air to circulate and moisture to drain, they won't get soggy and fall apart like a small cardboard box, and they're easy to attach to a tree because of their mesh sides.

Gather dry leaves and grass and fashion them into a cuplike shape within the berry basket. This cupped shape is essential for supporting nestlings. Poke the leaves and grass through the basket's mesh so that it looks more natural to the parent birds. If you don't have a berry basket, you can form a small piece (1 foot, or 30 cm, square) of wire mesh—either chicken wire or hardware cloth—into a cup shape. *Make sure that all sharp wires and edges are bent under so as not to injure the fragile nestling(s) inside.* Again, use dry leaves and grass to form a cup, poking them through the mesh. A small plastic margarine tub can also be used, but be sure to poke drainage holes in the bottom.

WHAT *NOT* TO USE
Never use fresh grass or hay for nesting material; both contain molds and mildew and are damp enough to cause respiratory problems, including pneumonia. Also, never use old nests. They'll likely have parasites and insect infestations of one sort or another.

If possible as you're erecting this makeshift nest, keep the baby out in the open and visible to his parents so that they don't get discouraged and leave. To keep the baby warm, cover a hot-water bottle (a plastic shampoo or dish detergent bottle filled with warm water will do in a pinch) with dry leaves and place the baby on top. Of course, do this only if there's no danger of a cat or dog lurking in the area.

Place the new nest in the same tree as the original, or close by.

MONITORING THE RESCUED BIRD
After replacing the baby bird (and possibly the nest), leave the immediate area and observe from a distance. In cases where you weren't able to reach the original nest and were forced to make a new nest and place it (with the baby bird in it) as close as possible to the original, most times you'll see the parent birds start flying between the two nests. If there are still young in the original nest, they'll start feeding their nestlings in both locations. However, never leave a nest unattended any longer than an hour. If the parents haven't reappeared by then, or if they aren't returning for feedings every 15 minutes or so, you can assume that either the nestlings have been abandoned or the parent birds have rejected your reuniting efforts, and you'll need to bring the babies in and feed them until you locate a wildlife rehabilitator for their long-term care.

Emergency Care of Orphaned Nestlings
If unavoidable circumstances create a delay in getting an abandoned baby bird to your local wildlife rehabilitator, you'll need to know some baby-bird fundamentals to keep the nestling alive. Of utmost importance are feeding the orphan and keeping him warm.

Lacking feathers, nestlings are highly vulnerable and can easily die if chilled. Furthermore, they won't eat if they're cold, which is an equally high priority. (Their normal body temperature ranges from 104 to 108°F, or 40 to 42°C, but since you won't be taking their temperature, you have to make an educated guess.)

Never put a wild bird in a cage, because he can do much damage to his beak and wings. Again, the best temporary housing is a plastic berry basket. For nesting material, don't use cloth or cotton (which can snag on the bird's toenails) or shredded paper (which can entangle them) as the top layer. Instead, use these materials as the bottom layer, shaped into a supportive cup, and cover them with facial tissues or paper towels. Keep the nest in a very warm (80 to 85°F, or 27 to 29°C), quiet, darkened spot away from any drafts. Never place the baby bird in direct sunlight,

where he can quickly become overheated and, unable to move from the nest, die.

Because very young nestlings can't regulate their body temperature yet, a supplemental heat source should be provided. Room temperature is not sufficient unless the bird is almost fully feathered. A covered hot-water bottle or a small plastic shampoo-type bottle filled with warm water and placed beside the berry box will do, but these will soon cool off and need refilling with warm water. A heating pad on its lowest setting and placed underneath half of the box (so that the nestling can move off it and won't become overheated) may be best, because the temperature will remain constant.

The "nest" should be kept clean and dry at all times. Birds usually defecate after eating, so remove the soiled tissues and replace them with clean ones after each feeding.

Emergency Feeding of Orphaned Nestlings
A baby bird's diet must be balanced, easily digestible, and high in protein; it must also provide nutrients for growth, such as calcium for bone development—especially important because birds grow so fast.

Never give a baby bird water. He can easily inhale it into his lungs, which will be fatal. He will receive the water he needs through his food.

IDENTIFY YOUR BIRD
It's important to try to identify the species of baby nestling so that you can provide the proper nourishment. Lacking specific nutrients for any length of time can interfere with proper growth and development and cause other physical problems—even death. A bird identification book can be most helpful with older birds (if you don't already own one, check your local library). Or maybe you know someone who is familiar with birds. Note the bird's characteristics, including size, shape, and color of the beak, feathers, legs, feet, or any markings. It's difficult to distinguish among species when nestlings are very young, but the temporary emergency diet provided here—Emergency Baby-Bird Rations, below—is usually sufficient until you can transfer the bird to a wildlife rehabilitator and make a positive identification.

EMERGENCY BABY-BIRD RATIONS
This *temporary* emergency diet will provide sufficient nutrition until you can get the baby bird to a wildlife rehabilitator. You can also purchase commercial nestling diets from feed stores or garden centers. Always read the directions that come with these feeds carefully, and prepare them accordingly.

1/2 cup (120 ml) canned ground dog food, beef baby food, very lean raw ground beef, or softened dog kibble

1 crumbled hard-boiled egg yolk

2 tablespoons (30 ml) high-protein baby cereal

1. Combine the canned ground dog food, crumbled hard-boiled egg yolk, and baby cereal.

2. Mix in a small amount of water until the gruel is the consistency of oatmeal. For older birds (fledglings), the consistency can be firmer, like that of canned dog food.

Continued →

Keep the mixture refrigerated and discard after 1 day. You can also add to the mixture 1 teaspoon (5 ml) of applesauce (for its nutritive value) or 1 teaspoon (5 ml) of bonemeal (a good source of calcium).

THE FEEDING REGIMEN

Taking care of a baby bird is an enormous commitment of both time and responsibility. Nestlings must be fed from around seven o'clock in the morning until seven in the evening (basically dawn till dusk), roughly every 15 minutes. This feeding schedule must be strictly adhered to in order to provide nestlings with adequate nutrition. They can become severely weak after just one skipped feeding; indeed, an erratic feeding schedule can be fatal. So until you find a wildlife rehabilitator, you must feed your nestling on schedule.

Use the following chart as a guide for the frequency of feedings:

Age	How Often
Hatchling to approx. 4 days	Every 15 to 20 minutes
4–10 days old	Every 30 minutes
10–14 days old	Every 45 minutes to 1 hour
14 days–fledging	Every 2 hours

HOW TO FEED A NESTLING

A young bird will usually raise his head and open his gape (beak) as soon as you tap the side of the nesting box, or even as soon as he hears you coming. Eating is the one thing that nestlings usually have no trouble doing. Your job is to make sure they can do so easily and regularly.

Never use tweezers or anything metal or sharp as a feeding tool. Some items that make handy feeding utensils are:

- The tip of an eyedropper
- A medicine dropper (like the ones veterinarians give out)—squeeze out just a tiny portion of food at a time
- A cotton swab with the cotton removed
- A clean eyeliner brush
- The eraser end of a pencil
- A straw cut on a slant
- The tip of your pinkie

If the bird doesn't open his mouth when presented with food, pick him up, very gently open the back corner of his beak, and insert the food.

When the bird gapes (opens his beak), insert a tiny portion of food down into his throat. (You can use one of the utensils suggested above.) Don't push the food in too far, and give only a small amount at a time or the nestling may choke. If the bird doesn't gape, gently pick him up, open the *back corner* of his beak, and insert the food. Use only light pressure or the beak can be damaged. *Never* open a bird's beak at the tip.

Make sure that the nestling is swallowing the food. If he's not swallowing, he may be cold—try to warm him up. As much as possible, feed the baby bird without touching him so that he won't begin to imprint upon you. Continue each feeding until the bird is no longer interested or refuses any more food.

Helping a Grounded Fledgling

When people see a baby bird on the ground, they often automatically assume that he fell out of a nest or is injured—but this usually isn't the case. Fledglings actually jump from their nests for a sort of flight training and will stay on the ground for a few days, hopping around and making trial flights, taking cover in bushes and high grass. The parent bird will continue to feed the fledgling on the ground until he's able to fly, although at this stage he's also learning to forage for food on his own. Fledglings are better off just left alone unless they are in danger from predators—or kids. Even in this case, you'll be doing more for the bird's welfare by keeping away any cats, dogs, and children in the area until he can get to cover than you would by rushing to his defense. Bring the animals inside or keep them restrained, and instruct the kids not to disturb or chase the bird.

WHAT'S A FLEDGLING?
Fledglings are partially feathered juvenile birds that have matured enough to leave the nest but aren't quite ready to fly and be totally independent.

If you see a fledged bird that is in danger and feel you must rescue it, arrange to bring it to a wildlife rehabilitator as soon as possible. Caring for fledglings causes them far more stress than it would when they're still in the nestling stage, because by now they've developed a fear of humans. This stress can actually kill them. Rehabilitators know how to deal with such things and are far better able to take care of fledglings until they can be released.

Note: Even if you know where the nest is located, don't attempt to replace the bird into the nest. He will probably just jump out again, and you may also scare out any of his siblings still in the nest, thereby compounding the problem.

Emergency Care of Orphaned Precocial Birds

Many birds in this group (which includes ducks, geese, and quail) make their nests on the ground, so nestlings are very vulnerable to predation and injury. Still, if you see a very young duckling or quail chick wandering around by himself, don't immediately panic and scoop the baby up, thinking he's orphaned—unless, of course, the baby is in immediate danger from a predator or a vehicle. First observe him from a distance. These types of birds have very doting and protective parents that will usually respond to the call of an offspring if they have been separated.

If you're sure that the baby is an orphan, place him in a deep container or box lined with newspapers and keep in a warm, quiet place away from household pets and curious children (the box can be covered with a towel for added quiet and privacy). Then call your local wildlife rehabber. If there's a delay in getting the baby to the rehabber, don't panic. Chick care isn't as complicated as nestling care—but needless to say, it's still very important.

KEEPING CHICKS WARM

Because precocial chicks don't have full temperature control until about four weeks of age, they must be kept at a temperature of 85 to 90°F (29 to 32°C), usually by means of a supplemental heat source. (Their box must be big enough that they can get away from the heat source if they want.) Avoid heat lamps that claim to be shatterproof; these emit toxic fumes from their Teflon coating, which can be fatal to birds. To simulate the mother, put a clean dry mop head or even a stuffed animal—anything soft the chicks can nestle against—in one corner of the box.

Contrary to popular belief, baby ducklings should *not* be put into water. Their down feathers are not waterproof, so the babies will become waterlogged and serious chilling will occur—even drowning. In the wild a mother duck will protect her ducklings' downy covering with oil from her own oil gland until their feathers are fully developed and they can generate this oil on their own.

FEEDING THE CHICKS

Feeding these babies is fairly easy. Just set out a starting mash or high-protein poultry or chick starter for them (available from a feed store), and they'll feed themselves. After they are two to three weeks old, they can be switched to a commercial turkey grower mixture. Make sure you read the ingredients list on the package and avoid *medicated* starter mixtures, which contain an antibiotic that can be fatal to chicks. Some other food items that can be added to the mixture are rolled oats, cream of wheat or rice, and mashed hard-boiled egg. The mash mixture should be fed moist; gradually decrease the added water until you're feeding it dry at about four weeks.

Although we've probably all fed ducks at a pond with our leftover sandwich bread, it's best not to give bread to a young duckling because he doesn't have grit in his digestive tract (crop) the way an adult does. The grit helps break down the bread. (Otherwise the bread can cause an obstruction in the digestive tract.)

At about six weeks old, precocial birds should be on an adult diet of cracked corn, mixed grains, trout pellets or fish food, and chopped greens. Add a handful of coarse grit to their feed a couple of times a week. If you prefer, you can obtain a commercial waterfowl mixture from a feed store.

THE PROBLEM OF IMPRINTING

Imprinting is a natural process that occurs with wild birds—to survive in the natural environment, each must learn the social skills of his own species. A nestling learns what species he is soon after hatching, when he's exposed to his parents and siblings. The term *imprinting* refers to this process of socialization.

Precocial species imprint at a much younger age than altricial species, usually within 36 hours of hatching. Altricial species, on the other hand, don't usually imprint until after their sight develops but before they develop fear. The tamer and less frightened of people a wild bird is, the less likely he is to survive and function properly in his own environment.

When you hand-raise a baby bird, imprinting is sometimes unavoidable. He believes that you're his parent. While this may sound cute and harmless, it's potentially very dangerous for the bird. He may:

- Seek out human contact rather than his own species.
- Think that he can reproduce with a human—and while this sounds amusing, birds are killed because of what's perceived as an "attack" on humans.
- Be unable to reproduce with his own species, because he prefers species that look more like what he imprinted on.
- Be unable to survive in his natural habitat.

To avoid imprinting or unnecessary taming:

- Transfer the baby's care to wildlife rehabilitators—they are experienced in such matters—as quickly as possible.
- Minimize exposure to people. Only the caregiver should care for the bird.
- Minimize handling of the bird. Since most precocial birds are self-feeders, handle them only when absolutely necessary.
- If possible, place the bird with a sibling or another of the same species.

The Six Most Important Rules of First Aid for Birds

Injuries and other emergency situations are best treated by wildlife rehabilitators and veterinarians. But some basic first-aid measures should help you out until you can transport the bird:

1. **Give the bird time to recover.** If a bird appears to be stunned but not apparently injured, simply keep the area safe from predators (such as your cats) for 15 to 20 minutes. If the bird does not fly away, then pick it up, place it in a box in a quiet place, and call a wildlife rehabilitator

2. **Handle the bird gently.** Never hold a bird too tightly around his body. Doing so will restrict his chest, and since he doesn't have a diaphragm muscle to assist in breathing, he depends on his chest wall for respiration. If this is restricted with a tight hold, the bird can suffocate.

3. **Keep the bird calm.** For most species, when you want to make an assessment of any injuries, cover the bird's head loosely with a paper towel or lightweight cloth. This will make the encounter much less stressful for him. If you determine that the bird needs to be taken to a veterinarian or a wildlife rehabilitator, keep the bird in a warm, quiet, dark location until you can do so.

4. **Keep the bird warm.** When a bird has a puffed-up look and his feathers seem ruffled, he's cold. Warm him either in your hands or with a hot-water bottle or heating pad.

5. **If you're going to give the bird water, make sure it's in a shallow container.** Never place a deep dish of water in a box with a bird, especially one suffering from poor balance due to injury—he could fall into the water and drown.

Continued →

6. Never keep or transport a wild bird in a metal cage. This could cause additional injury. Instead, use a small cardboard box just big enough to hold the bird. Pad the inside with soft paper towels or tissues.

Helping Injured Raptors

Raptors—hawks, eagles, falcons, owls—are birds of prey that catch and eat live food. Raptors share several distinguishing features: hooked beaks, strong talons (claws), and binocular vision (a characteristic they share with humans).

An injured raptor usually needs immediate specialized care, so always call a wildlife rehabilitator immediately. Raptors are best handled by a person experienced in doing so because they can be extremely dangerous if handled improperly. Raptor beaks are very powerful, and though it's unusual for them to bite, they may open their beaks in a threatening manner. Still, their talons are their major weapons, and they will try to defend themselves. When they grab on to something with a viselike grip, they can inflict serious, cut-to-the-bone injuries!

RAPTOR RESCUE

If a raptor has to be taken out of his immediate situation and you feel you're able to do so, certain safety guidelines *must* be followed. Protective gear must be worn: safety glasses, a pair of heavy gloves, and thick clothing. It's recommended that two people perform the rescue. Have a large cardboard box, with plenty of ventilation holes punched in it, open and ready for transport. Never put a bird in a wire cage.

> ### RAPTOR NOTIFICATION
> Different countries may have different rules concerning raptors, but in the United States, one is universal: If you find an injured Bald Eagle, you must notify the Department of Environmental Conservation in your area (usually within 48 hours).

You'll need a large blanket, coat, or thick towel. Hold it in front of you and approach the raptor from behind. When you're close enough, place the blanket over the bird. He will probably struggle for a while, then quiet down. When handling any raptor, you'll need to control his talons, so grab the bird's ankles immediately. As he eases his struggle, pick him up, making sure his wings are tight against his body and keeping him securely within the blanket. Put the bird in the cardboard box just a little bit bigger than the bird, and remove the blanket. Note where you found the bird when you transport him to the rehabilitator.

Keep the bird in a quiet, warm, dark environment until you can transfer it to a professional.

FEEDING CAUTIONS

Do not feed an injured raptor! Raptors are carnivores, which means they're meat eaters. Out in the wild they eat whole animals—in fact, bones, feathers, and fur clean their crops and are an essential part of their diet. A few species, such as Bald Eagles, Sea Eagles, and ospreys, also eat fish. But the dietary needs of raptors are delicately balanced, and nutritionally incomplete foods such as steak and raw beef can be harmful to them. In addition, injured birds are usually suffering from dehydration, and feeding a bird could cause further damage, as it may not yet be able to digest solid food.

A raptor can go without food for a day or two if absolutely necessary. If you've found an injured raptor, transport it to a wildlife rehabilitator as soon as possible.

RAPTOR CHICKS

If you come across a baby raptor on the ground, it's of utmost importance to notify a wildlife rehabilitator as soon as possible. If you can see the nest and are able to reach it, you can try to replace the baby, but this must be done with extreme caution. First of all, even chicks have sharp talons, so you must wear thick gloves. Their beaks are also very sharp, and they may peck you in self-defense. Also, the parent birds may find your presence very threatening, which can be dangerous for you.

> ### RABIES CAUTION
> Birds don't get rabies, but it's possible for a bird of prey that has eaten a rabid animal to be a rabies carrier. He may carry the live rabies virus in his mouth for a time after ingesting a diseased animal. To prevent the spread of infection and disease:
>
> - Wash your hands before and after handling the bird or his living quarters.
> - Use thin rubber latex gloves under the heavy protective gloves whenever possible when caring for a bird.
> - Provide a clean, dry living area for the bird. Discard the droppings frequently.

If you need to briefly play host to a raptor chick, be sure to seek advice from a wildlife rehabilitator on what to feed it. When birds of prey are very young, they usually eat about every three hours throughout the day and night; this increases to four hours when fully feathered. It's important to give the chick you've rescued the food he was meant to have in nature; feeding improper food for any length of time can eventually sicken or even kill the chick. Yet it may be hard to determine the exact species of raptor you have, because chicks don't have their adult coloration yet.

A simple substitute that will suffice for a short time is lean raw beef cut into small pieces and rolled in bonemeal—feed by hand wearing sturdy gloves. Since the chick needs hair or fur to cleanse his crop, add a little dog or cat fur as a temporary substitution. When feeding, always beware the razor-sharp beaks of even baby raptors and, of course, their sharp talons.

Releasing a Wild Bird

Condemning a wild bird to life in a cage is a terrible thing. Of course, there are times when a bird has injuries or other circumstances that make him unable to resume life in his natural habitat. In such cases the bird belongs with a rehabilitation organization, zoo, or museum, which have special permits to retain animals for display purposes.

But assuming a bird seems healthy enough to return to the wild, use the following criteria to evaluate his potential for release:

- The health of the bird must be optimal.
- He has to be of the proper age for release—that is, able to forage for food on his own, including hunting for and killing live food if he's a bird of prey.

- He must be able to fly or swim without difficulty and must be capable of performing the normal functions of his species.

- The bird has to be able to exhibit social behavior normal for his species, and not be imprinted on humans or any other species except his own.

- He must be in the correct habitat, at the right time of year.

If you've been caring for an orphaned fledgling for just a day or two and he meets all of the above criteria and seems ready to fly, he probably is. If you can find one, check in with a wildlife rehabilitator, and then release the bird.

If you've been caring for an injured bird, the appropriate time for release depends on the extent of his injuries. If the injury was severe—a broken bone, a gash, or a serious mauling by a cat or dog, for example—you should bring the bird to a veterinarian who deals with birds or to a wildlife rehabilitator. He or she can properly care for the bird and determine the right time for release.

How to Locate a Wildlife Rehabilitator

The goal when finding an orphaned or injured bird is to immediately locate a wildlife rehabilitator in your area. Since few rehabilitators list themselves as such in the phone book, you'll probably have to make a few phone calls to secure their names. To start, call:

- Veterinarians, who usually keep a list of referrals for rehabilitators
- A local chapter of the Audubon Society
- In the United States, the nearest office of the Department of Environmental Conservation (DEC), which should have a list of licensed rehabilitators in its region
- The state or provincial fish and wildlife division
- A local zoo, museum, park, or nature center
- Local humane societies, animal shelters, or the Society for the Prevention of Cruelty to Animals (SPCA)
- Other animal welfare organizations

There may be times when you contact wildlife rehabilitators but, due to a heavy caseload of animals or other circumstances, they can't accept any additional birds. In such cases, request that they try to contact another rehabilitator to assist you, or that they give you another referral to call.

The Care of Birds and the Law

Laws and regulations governing the care of wild birds differ from country to country—your local city government should be able to fill you in on what laws apply in your area. In the United States, however, there are some very specific laws that detail the proper care and handling of wild birds. For example, wildlife rehabilitators must have proper permits and licenses to handle and care for wildlife. These include a federal special-purpose permit to temporarily house migratory birds, as well as special permits to handle and temporarily retain Bald Eagles and other federally protected threatened and endangered birds. This rule applies even to veterinarians, who must also be licensed rehabilitators. Any violation of this law can involve a hefty fine and in some cases imprisonment, which is why it's so important to always immediately locate a wildlife rehabilitator, especially when you're dealing with a migratory or endangered bird.

FEDERAL LAWS IN THE UNITED STATES

- *The Migratory Bird Treaty Act* makes it illegal to possess any migratory bird, nest, eggs, or feathers.

- *The Lacey Act* makes it a federal violation to import or export birds or other wildlife across state or national boundaries from the state of origin.

- *The Endangered Species Act* provides special federal protections for species that are threatened with extinction. Wild-life rehabilitators can handle them on an emergency basis, but they must notify the DEC within 48 hours, and they must obtain a special permit to handle this wildlife.

- *The Bald Eagle Protection Act* provides specific protection for Bald and Golden Eagles. A specific permit is required for rehabilitators.

Building Bat Houses

Dale Gelfand

Illustrations by Sarah Brill

Introduction

Why, you may be asking yourself, would anyone want to build a bat house?

Mention the word *bat*, and the image that springs to mind for most people is of a bizarre flying beast, a vicious creature—fangs bared, ready to turn into Dracula, spread rabies, or, at the very least, get tangled in your hair.

While it's true that a number of species of bats have some odd characteristics, the unsavory reputation saddled upon these peaceful mammals is the result of age-old myths, fables, and misconceptions. To this day, bats are frequently associated with witchcraft, vampires, and haunted houses, and their fearsome reputation remains unshakable. It's also unjustified. Not only are bats *not* bloodthirsty, they are, in fact, beneficial to human civilization.

Bats rid the world of billions of insect pests every night, and they act as pollinators and seed dispersers for many different plants. But because bats have been so badly and wrongly maligned, whole colonies are still routinely eliminated. In the United States alone, more than 50 percent of our resident bat species are either declining rapidly or listed as endangered. Much of this decrease in bat numbers can be directly attributed to adverse human intervention, be it through direct killing of the animals as a result of ignorance or cruelty, the use of pesticides on their food supply, or the destruction of their habitat. Even unintentional or well-meant disturbances—from spelunkers inadvertently exploring bats' caves or biologists deliberately entering bats' domains to study their habits and habitats—can have severely detrimental effects on hibernating or maternity colonies.

For this reason, there is a growing movement to preserve natural bat habitats or to provide them with artificial roosting sites. Thanks to efforts by conservationists, both governmental and private organizations (foremost among the latter being Bat Conservation International—BCI—a Texas-based nonprofit organization dedicated to bat conservation, research, and public education), more and more people are now willing, even eager, for bats to make nightly forays into their backyards. An excellent way to make neighborhoods attractive to bats is to

Continued →

provide artificial habitats to augment the decreasing natural ones. Besides, it's only right that since bats do so much for us, we do something for them in return.

Bats and Human Health

If you like the idea of attracting such helpful creatures to your yard, yet fear the health risks of doing so, you can relax. Probably the biggest health risk that people face from bats is their own fearful reaction to them. More people injure themselves in their frenzied escapes from bats swooping for insects—some have even fallen off docks and boats and almost drowned!—than are ever harmed by bats. Incidentally, the myth of bats flying into people's hair is the result of bats being attracted to the insects that often swarm around our heads.

What about rabies? In fact, bats are the least likely of mammals to transmit the disease; fewer than .05 percent of bats contract rabies, and rabies is very rarely spread within individual colonies. Rabies is much more likely to strike dogs, foxes, skunks, and raccoons, which makes any of these animals a much greater rabies threat than a bat. In the rare instance in which a bat does have rabies, even in its rabid state it will seldom be aggressive—unlike any of the aforementioned species—and will only attack in self-defense, when provoked or threatened. According to BCI, in the last 50 years, fewer than 25 Americans have contracted rabies from bats. Most human exposure to infected bats results from careless handling of grounded bats, so simply following the "never handle a wild animal with your bare hands" rule of thumb will usually keep you out of harm's way. (Of course, not all grounded bats are rabid; young pups often become grounded when they're learning to fly.)

Also, contrary to what you may have heard, bats are not filthy (in fact, they groom themselves much like cats) and won't infest the area with dangerous parasites (most bat parasites are so specialized that they can't survive away from the bats, so they pose little threat to people and other animals). As for histoplasmosis, an airborne disease caused by a microscopic fungus found in bat guano—and that also occurs naturally in soils throughout temperate climates—mounting a bat house away from your dwelling should eliminate any problems resulting from droppings. (Hibernating bats don't produce guano, should you have

BAT SPECIES DISTRIBUTION

Nine species of bats that are known to use bat houses are:

Species	Territory	Roosts
Little Brown Bat (*Myotis lucifugus*)	Wooded areas throughout most of Canada and northern half of U.S., except desert and arid areas	Rears young in tree hollows, buildings, rock crevices, and bat houses; most common species to occupy bat houses
Big Brown Bat (*Eptesicus fuscus*)	Most of U.S. and Canada, except extreme southern Florida	Rears young in tree hollows and buildings; hibernates in caves, abandoned mines, and buildings; frequent bat house user; may overwinter in bat houses from Texas to New York
Southeastern Bat (*Myotis austroriparius*)	Gulf States, primarily	Rears young in caves, tree hollows, and buildings; hibernates in caves in northern range and tree hollows or buildings farther south; uses bat houses in Gulf States
Yuma Bat (*Myotis yumanensis*)	Western Canada, Washington, Idaho, Oregon, California, Arizona, extreme western Nevada, eastern Utah, and southern Colorado to western New Mexico	Rears young in caves, in buildings, and under bridges; occupies bat houses from Arizona to southwestern Canada
Northern Long-Eared Bat, Eastern Long-Eared Bat (*Myotis septentrionalis*)	Upper Midwest and east into Canada; south into northern Arkansas, Tennessee, western Alabama, and eastern Georgia	Rears young beneath tree bark, in buildings, and in bat houses; summers beneath tree bark, in buildings, and in caves; hibernates in rock crevices, caves, and mines
Evening Bat (*Nycticeius humeralis*)	East of Appalachian Mountains: from southern Pennsylvania to Florida; west of Appalachian Mountains: north to southern Michigan and Wisconsin, west to south-eastern Nebraska, and south to southeastern Texas	Rears young in buildings, tree cavities, and bat houses; shares nursery colonies with Mexican Free-Tailed Bats
Pallid Bat (*Antrozous pallidus*)	Western and southwestern U.S., mostly in arid areas	Summers in rock crevices, buildings, bat houses, and under bridges; hibernates in deep rock crevices
Cave Bat (*Myotis velifer*)	Southern Arizona and New Mexico into western Texas and Oklahoma, and extreme south-central Kansas	Rears young in caves and building crevices; shares bat houses with Mexican Free-Tailed Bats in Texas
Brazilian Free-Tailed Bat, Mexican Free-Tailed Bat (*Tadarida brasiliensis*)	Southern and southwestern U.S., and north to Nebraska, Colorado, Utah, Nevada, and Oregon	Rears young in caves, buildings, bat houses, and under bridges; migrates to Mexican and Central American caves for winter, except in Florida

bats that winter over, either in a bat house or your house.) And far from being aggressive, bats are quite timid and don't attack people or pets.

Attracting Bats

Bat houses are generally constructed for two basic purposes. Smaller boxes with a capacity for up to 100 bats are used to attract males or nonreproductive females. Larger boxes with a capacity for up to 300 or so bats are good for maternity colonies. Inspections of occupied bat houses have determined that about one-third of bat houses are used by nursery colonies, slightly less than two-thirds by bachelor colonies, and the remainder for hibernation in warmer climates. BCI surveyed bat house owners, who reported an overall occupancy rate of approximately 52 percent, with success rates lower for smaller boxes (32 percent) and higher for larger boxes (71 percent).

There are almost 1,000 species of bats worldwide, each with its particular roosting preferences. The social species, which cluster in caves, buildings, and other shelters, are far more likely to roost in bat houses than their forest-dwelling cousins.

Successfully attracting bats requires both patience and experimentation. If more desirable roosts already exist, your thoughtfully provided bat house may remain vacant. A year to year-and-a-half waiting period is common, and some highly successful bat houses take until the third year to acquire tenants. Trying to attract a maternity colony is the more difficult endeavor, because these colonies return year after year to their traditional roosts and usually won't seek out new quarters unless they've been displaced from their customary home. So while it's possible that your intended maternity bat house will be unoccupied for a number of seasons, by erecting a box, you're providing an alternative shelter in the event that a traditional roost is destroyed or sealed off. You should hang the bat box in the fall or winter—before bats come out of hibernation in April and go seeking a roost.

Bat-Proofing Your Home

Attics are the ideal environment for maternity colonies: They're hot and dry and usually predator-free. Two species—the Little Brown Bat and the Big Brown Bat—are particularly fond of attics. Unfortunately, most homeowners don't like sharing their living quarters with these beneficial creatures and often, in their determination to be rid of what they consider a nuisance or a health threat, either vandalize the roosts or exterminate the animals using poisons. But vandalizing a roost doesn't just threaten the resident bat population; it also allows the resident insect population to flourish, because nature's wonderful system of checks and balances has been destroyed. And using poisons not only kills beneficial bats but also scatters dead and dying bats throughout the house and neighborhood.

The safest and most humane way to evict a maternity colony of bats from your attic or other structure is to seal off the entrances once the colony has left for the winter or before it returns the following spring to hopefully take up residence in its new bat box. If you miss this window of opportunity, wait until August, when the pups are old enough to fly, and install one-way doors. *Bat-proofing must never be done during May, June, or July, when the flightless pups are confined in the roost and would be trapped inside.* Doing so would result in dead and decaying pups or pups entering living spaces in search of a way out—as well as frantic mothers attempting to enter your house, even during the day, to rejoin their young.

For fall, winter, or early-spring sealing, the first step in bat-proofing is to locate the points of entry. The most common are joints that have warped or shrunk, leaving gaps; attic vents that have either broken louvers or torn screening; flashing that has pulled away from siding or the roof; broken clapboards; and chimneys. Start by inspecting the ground around the foundation for bat droppings, which accumulate below their entrances. Next, on a sunny day, climb into the attic and see where light is entering from; conversely, put a bright light in the attic and, after dark, stand outside and see where light is shining through. Bats can enter a hole as small as 3/8-inch (10 mm) in diameter, so be diligent.

Once you've identified the entry ports, seal them. Bats can't gnaw new holes or reopen old ones, so once sealed, they'll stay sealed. Caulk cracks near the roofline and gaps where pipes or wires enter the building. Use metal flashing to seal joints in the house, mortar to seal foundation cracks, and weather-stripping to seal cracks around doors and windowsills. Attic vents and louvers should be sealed with 1/4-inch (6 mm) hardware cloth to allow for proper ventilation, and bird screens should be installed over chimneys. *Only seal up entrances if you are certain the bats have left your building.*

If you must evict a colony after the pups have begun flying, you can do so by installing one-way "doors"—1/4-inch (6 mm) diameter screening or heavy-duty plastic mesh that allows bats to leave on their nightly insect forays but prevents their reentering at dawn. This simple but effective solution works because when bats return to their roosts, they find their entryways by smell, not sight, which means they'll alight on the screening at the point of the opening, not below it. Screening or mesh is inexpensive and available at most garden shops or hardware stores.

Dr. Stephen Frantz, a research scientist for the New York State Department of Health, has studied bats and bat houses extensively. He has developed a plan for one-way doors that is safe and effective.

ONE-WAY DOOR INSTALLATION

1. Using 1/4-inch (6 mm) wire screening or heavy-duty plastic mesh, cut enough material so that it bows out 3 to 5 inches (8 to 13 cm) and completely covers the opening. The screening should extend about 3 feet (90 cm) beneath the hole.

2. Tape the screening in place with duct tape or exterior staples, leaving the bottom open.

3. Leave the door in place for at least four days, or until you're sure that all the bats have left; then remove the one-way door and seal the opening.

Never use a one-way door during May, June, or July to ensure that no pups will be trapped inside and die.

Bat House Construction

Like birds, bats are fussy about their living quarters. It's hard to predict whether the bats in your area will want to move into a bat house that you provide for them. For one thing, shelter is but a third of the essential bat-needs equation, the other two elements being water and an ample food supply.

LOCATION, LOCATION, LOCATION

A nearby permanent water source (a lake, stream, marsh, or river within 1/4 mile, or about 400 m) is ideal for bat habitation. Almost guaranteeing colonization would be adding a combination of nearby fruit orchards, other agricultural endeavors, and natural vegetation. But even if your house isn't within sight of a lake, 100 yards away from an apple orchard, and across the street from a potato farm, you can attract bats if roosts are needed and your bat house meets bat requirements.

Foremost is orienting the box so that it receives enough sunlight in attracting bats to your bat house each day to provide the necessary solar radiation. A recent Pennsylvania State University study found that, at their latitude, all the bat boxes that faced southeast or southwest—so that they received at least seven hours of direct sunlight during the spring and summer—were successful in housing maternity colonies. More northerly areas will likely need to receive more than the seven hours recommended by Pennsylvania State University; more southerly ones can make do with less.

Bat nurseries require a stable temperature of 85 to 100°F (29 to 38°C) for the pregnant females and growing pups, and some species tolerate temperatures as high as 120°F (49°C). In most areas of the North American continent other than the Deep South and the desert Southwest, you don't have to worry about your bat house getting too hot; more likely you'll have to be concerned that it isn't warm enough. (Depending on your location, the air temperature even on hot summer days may well be affected by wind, clouds, and elevation. If you live in a area whose average July temperature is 95°F, or 35°C, but your specific site is on a hillside that gets buffeted by prevailing winds, you should paint your bat house a darker color to compensate for the heat loss.) However, a bat house also needs cooler chambers for the bats to move into in case temperatures do get too high. Attaching black roofing paper to the upper portions of the box, using a tin roof, and cutting a sufficient number of ventilation slits will all greatly reduce overheating.

Also crucial in determining the box site is factoring in whether it's intended to house a displaced maternity colony. If this is the case, the box should be placed as close as possible to the old roost—within 10 to 20 feet (3 to 6 m)—either on the side of a building, a chimney, or a pole. Once the bats have accepted the bat house as their new roost, it can be moved gradually away from the old site *but only during the fall or winter when the bats aren't present.* Don't move the box more than 20 yards (18 m) per year.

When a box is meant to attract a new colony into the area, the ideal site is 12 to 20 feet up on a pole or building, preferably at least 20 feet (4 to 6 m) away from trees, facing south, with an approach unobstructed by vegetation or utility wires, and sheltered from prevailing winds. (Consider mounting four houses in a group, each facing in a different direction to provide a range of temperatures for bats to select from.)

If the box is hung on a building, don't place it in a heavily trafficked area or where droppings will pose a problem, and make sure there's at least 3 feet (90 cm) of open space beneath it so that bats can easily exit; unlike birds, which can take flight from a standstill, most bats need to drop from a perch and catch air beneath their wings before they can fly. To prevent people from walking underneath the bat house, you might consider putting decorative fencing around it or planting some ornamental ground cover such as pachysandra or periwinkle (myrtle) that will discourage foot traffic.

TIMING IS EVERYTHING

Whether you're installing a bat box to attract a new colony or as a new home for a colony in an existing but undesirable roost—say, your attic—the best times for box placement are between January and April or in the fall when they leave for their winter hibernation. Bats come out of hibernation in March and usually arrive at their summer roosts in April. But since in many areas trees are leafless at this time, a location that receives plenty of sunshine in February might be in full shade come June, so house placement might require some preplanning. It might be better to hang a box after a colony disbands at the end of the summer or early fall, when trees are still in full leaf.

When you're looking to move a colony out of a traditional roost, allow the bats to familiarize themselves with their new home, if possible, before expelling them from their old one. Which is to say, let them investigate the new quarters over the course of the summer while they stay in your attic, and in the fall, when they leave for their winter hibernation, you can bat-proof your house so that when they return the following spring, they may well take up residence in the bat box.

If allowing them to remain for another summer isn't an option, install the bat house and bat-proof your own house before the bats arrive in April. Since colonies in part use smell to identify their roosts, consider scenting the new box with their droppings before putting the box in place. To do so, gather a cup of guano from your attic—bat droppings are dry, black, about the size of grains of rice, and accumulated in piles, unlike mouse droppings, which are scattered—and mix with water to a watery-paste consistency; then pour the mixture into the box, allowing it to soak in before hanging the box. **Note:** Wear rubber gloves and a paper filter mask.

As a less odious alternative, some people have had success "aging" their bat boxes by filling them with slightly damp soil for a few days, then dumping out the soil. If scenting the box isn't possible, and new materials are used for construction, allow the box to weather outside for a while before installation to eliminate that new-box smell. You'll be surprised what a difference scenting a box can make in your success rate.

PROPER DESIGN

Building a bat house begins with a suitable design.

Size: Maternity colonies require boxes that are at least 24 inches (60 cm) high and 12 inches (30 cm) wide. Smaller houses will be accepted by male bats or nonreproductive females.

Landing board: Whether large or small, all bat houses need landing boards that extend 3 to 6 inches (8 to 15 cm) below the entrance, preferably covered with 1/8 or 1/4-inch (3 or 6 mm) plastic mesh or hardware cloth.

Opening: Open bottoms are recommended—contrary to European houses, which generally have a bottom—because they won't need to be regularly cleaned of accumulated droppings and parasites, and birds and rodents won't be tempted to take up residence. (Wasps are the only uninvited guests you'll have to worry about; clean out their nests prior to bat occupancy.)

Crevices: Of primary importance is the interior construction, which utilizes carefully spaced baffles, or partitions, to create multiple roosting chambers, or crevices. These crevices allow for larger populations (sardines in a can have nothing on bats in a box) and also regulate and maintain the proper temperature. The designs provided by Pennsylvania State University contain six crevices, which is the maximum recommended by BCI.

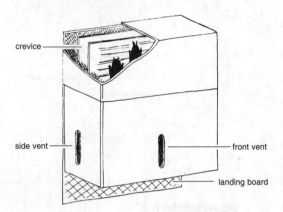

Vents: Vents are critical in bat houses installed in areas where the average high temperature in July is 85°F (29°C) or greater because they modify interior heating, contributing to bat house success in moderate or hot climates. Keeping these vents to 1/2-inch-wide (13 mm) spaces will thwart both unwanted light and avian intruders. A front vent, 3 inches (8 cm) long, should be cut vertically about 3 inches (8 cm) up from the bottom, and two other 3 inch (8 cm) long vents should be cut at either end of the rear chamber of multiple-chambered houses. When maternity houses are paired back to back, an additional 3/4-inch-wide (19 mm) horizontal vent should be cut in the rear, allowing bats to go back and forth between the two houses without having to exit and reenter.

PROPER MATERIALS

Bats seem to show a slight preference for houses that have been constructed of old wood, which, of course, is also environmentally sound. Pennsylvania State University recommends using 3/4-inch exterior plywood for the front and back pieces and 1-inch board lumber of western red cedar, pine, or cypress for the sides and spacers. The interior baffles—made from 1/4-inch plywood—are thinner than the front and back pieces, and they should be roughened to give the bats a good foothold. As an alternative to filing these surfaces, you can attach 1/8- or 1/4-inch (3 or 6 mm) heavy-duty plastic mesh or hardware to the baffles and landing board with 5/16-inch (8 mm) durable galvanized exterior-grade staples. Pennsylvania State University suggests using 1/2 to 3/4-inch exterior plywood for the roof.

To join the pieces, use 1 5/8-inch (41 mm) multipurpose (drywall) screws or galvanized finishing nails and seal them with latex siliconized caulk. Black roofing paper should be applied to the top portion of the box exterior to create a variance in temperature within the crevices. Bat houses mounted in areas where average daily temperatures in July are 80 to 85°F (27 to 29°C) or less should be painted with black exterior latex paint. They should be painted brown, gray, or green where temperatures are 85 to 95°F (29 to 35°C); light brown where they are 95 to 100°F (35 to 37°C); and white where they exceed 100°F (39°C).

BASIC ASSEMBLY INSTRUCTIONS

These instructions apply to each of the three bat house designs featured in this bulletin. Assembly techniques are the same for each of the designs, only the dimensions of the pieces differ.

1. Cut pieces according to plans. Using a jigsaw, cut 3" x 1/2" (8cm x 13mm) vents in the front and side pieces (see designs).

2. Use a knife, saw, or router to roughen all interior surfaces with horizontal scratches or grooves 1/4 to 1/2 inch (6 to 13 mm) apart. It's especially important that the landing board, which is the bottom portion of the back piece, is textured. Attaching a piece of plastic netting to the back and baffles using galvanized staples also gives bats a strong foothold. Make sure that the netting lies flat and does not pucker.

3. Attach the sides to the front using wood screws, caulking first. (*Do not use wood glue* on any part of the bat box, as it can be toxic to bats.)

4. Attach the roof to the sides and front using wood screws. Caulk the seams to seal the roosting chamber.

5. Position the box so that the front rests on a tabletop and the sides and roof extend upward.

6. Attach two interior spacer strips to the inside of the front piece using finishing nails or wood screws. Make sure the strips fit tightly against the roof and side pieces.

7. Place one of the shorter baffles on top of the spacer strips, butting it against the roof piece. Attach the baffle to the spacers using finishing nails.

8. Attach two interior spacer strips to the first baffle using finishing nails or wood screws. Make sure the strips fit tightly against the sides of the box.

9. Place one of the longer baffles on top of the spacer strips, butting it against the roof piece. Attach the baffle to the spacers using finishing nails.

Tools

Table saw	Caulking gun
Jigsaw	Scissors
Variable speed reversing drill	Heavy-duty stapler
Paintbrush	Sander (optional)
Phillips-head drill bit	Router (optional)
Tape measure	

10. Repeat steps 7, 8, and 9 (alternating baffle lengths) until all baffles and spacer strips have been installed.

11. Attach the back of the box to the roof and sides using wood screws, caulking the seams. The back piece should extend below the body of the box to serve as the landing board.

12. Paint or stain the exterior using a latex-based paint or stain. (*Do not stain the interior.*) Apply a second coat of paint or stain.

13. Attach roofing paper to the roof. Caulk the seam at the back where the roof attaches to the back panel.

Continued ➜

071
Country Wisdom & Know-How

Animals

Birds and Bats

14. Tack roofing paper onto the front and sides, extending it approximately 6 inches (15 cm) down from the top. This will help create differences in temperature from the top of the box to the bottom.

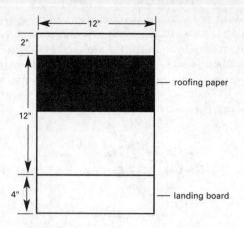

Front View

ROUTER OPTION

If you have a router: After attaching the sides, cut 1/4-inch (6 mm) vertical grooves in the side pieces with a router at 1-inch (25 mm) intervals. Skip the instructions for installing spacer strips and baffles. Instead, simply fit the baffles into the side-piece grooves. Then attach the front, back, and roof as described.

Bat House Plans

Plans for the bat boxes that follow were developed by Pennsylvania State University. BCI features similar bat house designs in its publication, *The Bat House Builder's Handbook*.

SMALL BAT HOUSE

Capacity: 50 Bats

This bat box should be useful when trying to attract bats to an area. It may be accepted by male bats or nonreproductive females, although it's not large enough for most bat colonies.

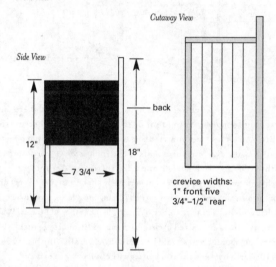

Cutaway View

Side View

back

crevice widths:
1" front five
3/4"–1/2" rear

PIECES FOR BAT HOUSE

Part	Quantity	Dimension	Material
front	1	12" x 12" (30cm x 30cm)	3/4" exterior plywood
sides	2	12" x 7 3/4 " (30cm x 19cm)	1" board lumber
roof	1	12" x 8 1/2" (30cm x 22cm)	1/2"–3/4" exterior plywood
spacer strips	10	1" x 10" (25mm x 25cm)	1" board lumber
baffles (with spacers)	3	10" x 10" (25cm x 25cm)	1/4" plywood
	2	11" x 10 1/2" (28cm x 27cm)	1/4" plywood
baffles (if routered)	3	10" x 11" (25cm x 28cm)	1/4" plywood
	2	11" x 11" (28cm x 28cm)	1/4" plywood
back/landing board	1	18" x 12" (46cm x 30cm)	3/4" exterior plywood

SMALL MATERNITY COLONY BAT HOUSE

Capacity: 150 Bats

This bat box is suitable for small to medium-sized summer maternity colonies (up to 150 bats). If the box is intended to house an evicted colony, it should be installed in the spring *before* the colony is evicted from its current roost.

PIECES FOR BAT HOUSE

Part	Quantity	Dimension	Material
front	1	12" x 24" (30cm x 61cm)	3/4" exterior plywood
sides	2	12" x 7 3/4" (30cm x 19cm)	1" board lumber
roof	1	24" x 8 1/2" (61cm x 22cm)	1/2"–3/4" exterior plywood
spacer strips	10	1" x 10" (25mm x 25cm)	1" board lumber

Part	Quantity	Dimension	Material
baffles (with spacers)	3	10" x 22 1/2" (25cm x 57cm)	1/4" plywood
	2	11" x 22 1/2" (28cm x 57cm)	1/4" plywood
baffles (if routered)	3	10" x 23" (25cm x 58cm)	1/4" plywood
	2	11" x 23" (28cm x 58cm)	1/4" plywood
back/landing board	1	18" x 24" (46cm x 61cm)	3/4" exterior plywood

LARGE MATERNITY COLONY BAT BOX
Capacity: 150–300 Bats

This bat box is suitable for large summer maternity colonies of up to 300 bats. If the box is intended to house an evicted colony, it should be installed in the spring *before* the colony is evicted from its current roost. If a colony larger than 300 bats is to be evicted, two boxes can be installed side by side, or a larger bat box can be used.

PIECES FOR BAT HOUSE

Part	Quantity	Dimension	Material
front	1	24" x 24" (61cm x 61cm)	3/4" exterior plywood
sides	2	24" x 7 3/4" (61cm x 19cm)	1" board lumber
roof	1	24" x 8 1/2" (61cm x 22cm)	1/2"–3/4" exterior plywood
spacer strips	10	1" x 22" (25mm x 56cm)	1" board lumber
baffles (with spacers)	3	22" x 22 1/2" (56cm x 57cm)	1/4" plywood
	2	23" x 22 1/2" (58cm x 57cm)	1/4" plywood
baffles (if routered)	3	22" x 23" (56cm x 58cm)	1/4" plywood
	2	23" x 23" (58cm x 58cm)	1/4" plywood
back/landing board	1	30" x 24" (76cm x 61cm)	3/4" exterior plywood

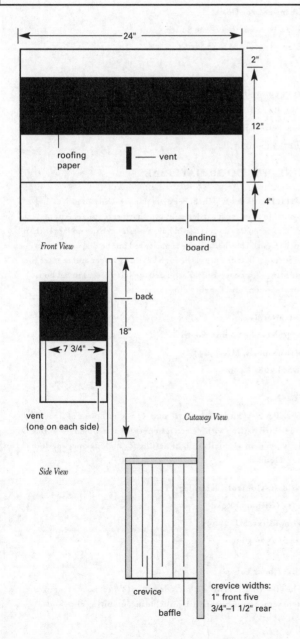

Front View

Side View

Cutaway View

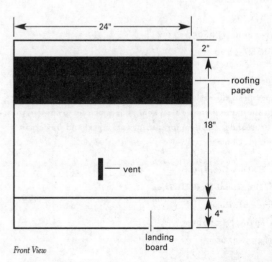

Front View

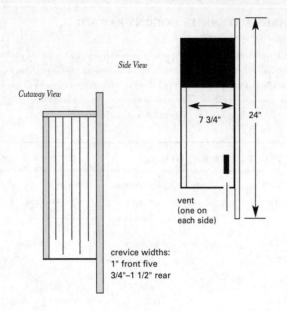

Side View

Cutaway View

7 3/4"   24"

vent
(one on
each side)

crevice widths:
1" front five
3/4"–1 1/2" rear

Bat-Proofing Materials and Suppliers

SEALING MATERIALS

Expanding Foam Insulation/Caulking Compound
Found in most building supply stores, expanding foam insulation is available as an aerosol and can be sprayed into cracks and crevices. The foam expands to fill the opening and then hardens, after which it can be trimmed or painted.

"Flashband"
"Flashband" is a self-adhesive, aluminum-faced sealant that permanently adheres to almost any surface. It can be useful for sealing roof junctions, loose flashing, eaves, and gaps between chimneys and walls. It's easily applied, requires no special tools, and resists water, rust, mold, and mildew. Contact:

The 3E Group
850 Glen Avenue
P.O. Box 392
Moorestown, NJ 08057–0392
(609) 866–7600

Copper Mesh
Copper cleaning mesh is a rolled, flattened strip of knitted copper mesh, similar to flattened steel wool, that can be cut to any length. It won't rust and is excellent for stuffing into cracks and crevices in buildings. Contact:

Otto H. York Co., Inc.
Attn: Industrial Mesh Division
42 Intervale Road
Parsippany, NJ 07006
(201) 299–9200

"Stuff-It"
"Stuff-it" is a copper gauze product useful for plugging holes that are too big to caulk and too small to warrant carpentry repair (such as openings around eaves). It won't rust, stain, or break down. Contact:

Allen Special Products, Inc.
P.O. Box 605
Montgomeryville, PA 18936
(800) 848–6805

Chimney Caps
Designed to prevent damage to chimneys and fireplaces from rain and snow, chimney caps also can be effective at keeping bats out of your home. Contact:

Chim-a-lator Co.
8824 Wentworth Avenue South
Bloomington, MN 55420
(612) 884–7274

Vestal Manufacturing
P.O. Box 420
Sweetwater, TN 37874
(615) 337–6125

ONE-WAY DOOR MATERIALS

Metal Hardware Cloth/Screening/Heavy-Duty Bird Netting
Available from most garden supply or hardware stores. Any material used for one-way doors should have a mesh opening no larger than 1/4 inch (6 cm). (Mesh diameter is measured on the diagonal, from corner to corner.) Bats can crawl through anything larger and reenter the building. For heavy-duty plastic netting (also useful in bat house construction) and fastener clips, contact:

InterNet, Inc.
2730 Nevada Avenue North
Minneapolis, MN 55247
(800) 328–8456

"Bat Net"
The "Bat Net" kit contains a 14' x 20' (4m x 6m) piece of structural-grade bird netting with Velcro fasteners for attachment to buildings. This company also sells rolls of netting for making one-way doors of any size. Contact:

Wildlife Control Technology, Inc.
2513 Girdwood Road
Timonium, MD 21093
(410) 252–4635

"Bat Check Valve"
The "Bat Check Valve" kit includes a 7' x 14' (2m x 4m) length of structural-grade bird netting, including mounting clips and

installation instructions. The company also sells rolls of netting for making one-way doors of any size. Contact:

Wildlife Management Supplies
40 Starkweather
Plymouth, MI 48170
(800) 451–6544

DIATOMACEOUS EARTH

Diatomaceous earth, which scratches the cuticle of insects as they crawl through it, is useful in eliminating bat parasites from an attic after the bats have been evicted.

"Shell Shock"

"Shell Shock" is one of several diatomaceous earth products on the market. It comes from fossilized deposits of microscopic shells produced by one-celled plants called diatoms. Contact:

D & R, Inc.
136 Elm Street
South Williamsport, PA 17701
(717) 322–4885

Perma-Guard

"Perma-Guard" kills insects physically, by puncturing their exoskeleton, disrupting their soft, waxy structure, causing death in a short time by dehydration. Contact:

Fossil Shell Company
P.O. Box 50225
Amarillo, TX 79159

CATS

Cat Toys

How to Make Your Home a Feline Paradise
Lura Rogers
Illustrations by Rick Daskam

Indoors versus Outdoors

Many people feel very strongly about whether or not a cat should be allowed to roam free outside the house. Whatever your opinion, the decision does not greatly affect the nature of in-house furniture and toys. Appropriate furnishings and toys for your cat are important for a cat confined to the house, but good indoor pastimes are also beneficial for the cat that is allowed to go outdoors. Cats need to have a personal space in the house in which they feel secure. They also need exercise as well as stimulating activities that imitate the natural activities of their wild cousins. Toys and structures that promote climbing and chasing are good for both the psyche and the physical health of the domesticated cat.

COZY CAT BEDS

Different cats prefer various types of bedding. Some prefer a flat, firm surface, while others relax more comfortably in a cushioned, bowl-shaped bed. I recommend taking a week or so to observe your cat's favorite places to sleep before choosing a bed for her.

Keeping track of your cat's preferences for napping spots will allow you to customize the perfect bed for her.

KEEPING KITTY'S SLEEPING JOURNAL

To find the perfect bed for your cat to sleep on—one that she will choose over your best sweater, for example—study your cat's sleeping habits and keep notes. Identify the characteristics of each of her favorite sleeping spots, including:

- Firmness
- Surface texture
- Color
- Location (hidden, enclosed, corner, open)
- Light (dark, partial, light, sunny)
- Height (floor, chair, shelf, ceiling)

FINDING THE RIGHT LOCATION FOR A CAT BED

The placement of the bed is just as important as the type of bed you choose. Look back into your kitty journal and see if a pattern of location preference emerges. Does she prefer the corner of the room? Is she often in the sunny window or next to the heater? Does she find comfort on the top shelf of your closet, or does she like to look out from the top of the dining room hutch? Height, warmth, and level of seclusion are just as important to the cat as what she is sitting on, if not more important.

Some pet owners try the multiple-bed approach, especially if their cat is a restless type. Sometimes two or three beds placed in varying degrees of height and seclusion can give your pet more freedom, depending on her mood.

Here are a few suggestions for favorite kitty resting places where you might consider putting a cat bed:

- **The top of the refrigerator.** This perch offers height plus warmth. It lets her observe the action in the kitchen without being underfoot. Many cats find the low hum of the refrigerator comforting, too.

- **In front of a window.** Cats love to watch the business of the outside world, so go with a special windowsill-fitting bed. Or purchase a sturdy folding snack tray and place it and the bed in front of the window.

Continued →

- **The back of the closet.** At first I thought it was just revenge wrought on my favorite black sweater, but cats really love the safety and privacy of the closet. Save your clothes by sacrificing shelf space, and put her bed where she usually sits.

- **The back of the couch.** If matted fur never seems to stay off that spot, try covering it with a nice square of matching or accenting washable cloth. A good place to look for bolt ends and remnants is the local fabric store.

- **The top of the clothes dryer.** Attracted by the warmth and the hum, your cat may think of this as his own personal vibrating bed. The neatly folded towels you just removed from the previous load make this bed all the more attractive. Just make sure you always keep the dryer door closed!

- **Next to a radiator or over a floor heating vent.** Cats love warm spots, and for most the feeling is the warmer, the better! So try setting a cat bed near a heating vent. Your cat may not settle into a bed on the floor, however, so you may need to set it on a small stool or folding table near the heating vent.

OUTWITTING THE CAT

As we all know, cats love to sit on our favorite sweater or other clothing, and it's always something that contrasts with their fur color. To help your cat feel closer to you without ruining your clothing, sleep in an old sweater or soft shirt that you don't mind giving up to your furry pal, then use it to line the cat bed. This quick alternative is comforting to your cat when you're not at home, and it may just save that new cashmere sweater!

ULTRA-SIMPLE HOMEMADE CAT BED

When topped off with fleece and set in a warm, sunny location, this bed will quickly become a cat magnet. Best of all, it's easy to launder—just remove the fleece blanket and throw it in the washing machine. If you suffer the misfortune of a flea infestation, you can wash the bed as well.

An old pillowcase

Old towels, rags, or T-shirts

Needle and thread

A small fleece blanket (a baby blanket works well)

1. Stuff an old pillowcase with layers of rags, worn-out towels, or old T-shirts. Use enough filling to make the bed at least an inch thick and just wide enough to fit inside the condo.

2. Sew up the open end of the pillowcase, again adjusting for size, and add a few stitches around the edge to secure the stuffing, so that it won't bunch up when it's washed.

3. Arrange the cat bed in the area you've selected. Drape the fleece blanket over the bed and tuck in the corners to secure it.

The Best Scratching Posts

As we all know, just about anything that stands upright in the house is apt to become a scratching post for an untrained kitten or cat. Most cats, however, will learn to use a scratching post instead of the couch or table legs if you provide them with one.

There are three important factors to consider when picking out the right scratching post for your cat: height, stability, and surfacing.

GOOD HEIGHT MEANS GOOD STRETCHING

Choose a post that is high enough for your cat. It should at least allow her to fully stretch and extend her upper body and front legs from a sitting position; it can be even taller if you want to combine the benefits of a climbing post. Scratching posts of a good height allow your cat to stretch and strengthen her arm, shoulder, and back muscles. If she can't reach full extension on a permitted scratching area, your cat may take her scratching elsewhere—namely, your living room furniture.

STABILITY AND DURABILITY

A freestanding upright scratching post should have a wide, solid base and should be made of a durable, heavy material, like wood. A popular variation is a simple board-and-carpet piece that attaches to walls and doors, giving cats the sense of a freestanding, treelike structure.

THE BEST SCRATCHING MATERIALS

Carpeting is the most popular surface for cat furniture, including scratching posts, because the cat's claws catch in the nap and carpeting provides a good degree of resistance. The higher the quality of the carpeting and assembly, the longer the post will last before the surface is torn off and shredded.

Some posts offer an unfinished wooden surface to give the cat the sense that she is using a tree, but I find that they splinter quickly and become unattractive.

Another great surface for cat posts is hemp or sisal rope. A thick rope tightly wound around a post provides great resistance for claws and does not deteriorate too quickly. Many pet stores sell a variety of rope-surfaced furniture. In my house, I have covered all of the basement support beams with coarse sisal rope. At first I wound the rope just high enough to serve as a scratching post, but soon I realized that the girls were climbing, and so I extended the rope all the way to the ceiling. Now they consider the basement their own personal jungle gym!

MAKING A SCRATCHING POST

Scratching posts are relatively easy to make. Most carpet supply stores have remnants free for the asking.

A thick piece of plywood at least 24 inches (609.6 mm) square

An 18-inch (457.2 mm) length of 4 x 4 lumber

2 sturdy angle irons with screws to fit them

Small piece of carpet remnant

Sandpaper

Soft marking pencil

Small power drill

Screwdriver

Contact glue

Contact cement

Heavy hemp rope

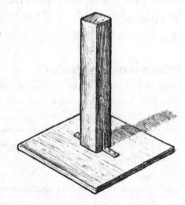

Step 4: Use angle irons to secure the post to the base.

1. Sand the edges of the plywood to remove all splinters.

2. Mark the center of the plywood with the pencil and place the 18-inch length of 4 x 4 lumber upright on it.

3. Mark the placement of screw holes on both the dowel and the board, using the angle irons at opposite sides of the dowel.

4. Drill small holes to start the screws and screw the angle irons tightly in place.

5. Cover the board with a small piece of carpet, gluing it firmly in place.

6. Apply contact cement to the dowel, beginning at the bottom and working a small area at a time.

7. Begin wrapping the dowel tightly with heavy hemp rope, pushing each spiral close to the previous one and adding more glue to the post as you work upward.

8. Finish the top with a tight single knot and nail it in place, so the knot is on the top of the post. Cut the rope a few inches above the knot and ravel the end to make a stiff, brushlike tassel for the cat to swat at.

Cat Condos and Trees

Cat condos can be found in almost any shape and size, ranging from small drum-shaped coves to tall structures with multiple levels and varying types of perches for the lounging feline. Prices for these can range from less than $30 to several hundred dollars, depending on size, quality, design, and complexity.

Simple cat condos are no more than an enlosed "cave" where a cat can seek privacy and repose. Most cats find it more comfortable when the cove is just slightly larger than they are—too much extra room leaves them feeling exposed and defeats the purpose of a protective place to rest. These enclosures are often lined with carpet, and those with a removable bottom are convenient to clean.

More elaborate cat condos and cat trees offer enclosed sleeping spaces as well as a variety of surfaces for lounging, hiding, perching, and jumping, not to mention the all-time favorite of scratching.

MAKING A SIMPLE CAT CONDO

Although building an elaborate cat tree is probably beyond the average person's carpentry skills, a simple condo is not hard to make. I recommend using a wooden crate that is a bit larger than your cat (even larger if the cat is not fully grown). Ask the produce manager of your grocery store for a discarded crate. Do not use a box made of heavy cardboard, because it will not stand up to cat scratching. Carpet remnants are available for the asking at most carpet stores and flooring centers.

Wooden crate

Carpet scraps with short, close pile

Sharp knife

Small saw

Contact glue

Crayon or soft pencil

1. Turn the wooden crate upside down. In one side, use a saw to cut a door big enough for your cat to get through.

2. Lay the carpet upside down and set the box upside down on top of it. Trace around the edges of the box with a crayon or soft pencil so that the dimensions of the top are clearly marked on the back of the carpet. Then cut out that piece of carpet with a sharp knife.

3. Repeat step 2 for all sides of the box except the open bottom.

4. Working one surface at a time and following the bonding instructions on the glue container, glue the carpet pieces onto the wooden box. Be sure the glue goes all the way to the edges, so there will be no loose places for your cat to tear.

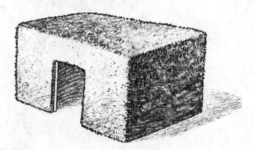

Step 5: Cover all surfaces of the box with carpet.

6. Allow the glue to dry completely. Air the condo outdoors until all traces of glue scent have dissipated.

7. Cut a piece of carpet just barely smaller than the open side of the box. This will be the floor, so it must fit snugly inside the walls when the box is turned upside down over it.

8. Turn the box over on top of the floor carpet and invite your eager cat inside to explore.

THE HOUSEWARMING

Your cat may hesitate to go inside the new condo you've just bought or made, cats being the wary and cautious creatures they are. You can make the condo more inviting by placing a small dish of your cat's favorite food in the back corner, or by lining it with a favorite sleeping surface (that sweater of yours that your cat loves to curl up on will do nicely). Sprinkling a little bit of catnip inside may help, too.

TIPS AND TRICKS FOR BUILDING A CAT TREE

If you have decent carpentry skills and a good imagination, consider designing and building a cat tree, or what we might call a jungle gym, for your cat. A good cat tree will include the following:

- Simple cat condos, or enclosed cat beds

- Plenty of scratchable posts in a variety of textures

- Perches and lounging areas at multiple levels

- Doors and openings that are wide enough for your cat to easily fit through

- Ramps covered in carpet or some nonskid surface that allow your cat to climb from one level to the next

- A wide, solid, heavy base—perhaps screwed to the floor—that will keep the tree from tipping over

Continued ➜

The design of a homemade cat tree is limited only by your imagination. Your cats will appreciate scratching areas, multiple perching platforms, hiding places, and plenty of toys to bat around.

introduced these to the house, my cats didn't leave them alone until the mice were reduced to unrecognizable lumps. I still find bits of fake fur hiding under the couch! The biggest draw of this toy is the frantic motion that the spring creates when the mouse is hit, imitating the movement of a real jittery mouse.

CAT AND MOUSE

You can find faux mice on the front counter of nearly every pet store. I have found, however, that some older cats prefer ones with pizzazz. A small bell attached to the tail spices up a plain mouse for feline senior citizens. And mice filled with catnip, of course, are sure to please even the most finicky of felines.

FEATHERED FUN

Feathers are enticing playthings that almost no cat can resist. A cat's obsession with birds will be greatly satisfied when he has the opportunity to pounce on a bunch of feathers and pretend that he has just hunted down a flock of pesky swallows. Pet stores offer a variety of feathered toys. Some come attached to strings and dowels that you can shake and drag across the floor to captivate your cat. Others are self-supporting and attach to walls for hours of home-alone feline fun. I have even seen motorized versions that spin the fuzz around, but I recommend these only for kittens, since a larger, more aggressive cat is likely to find a way to permanently stop the "flying" and ruin the toy.

Your design is limited only by your imagination and your cat's inclination to explore. You can make everything from scratch, or you can purchase the individual pieces—condos, cat beds, scratching posts, et cetera—and incorporate them into a larger framework.

Of course, not everyone has the time or skills to build a durable and safe cat tree. Thankfully, many commercial cat-tree manufacturers sell expandable cat-tree kits. You can buy a starter kit and any other elements you desire and then fit them together at home in whatever design best suits your cat's temperament.

Classic Commerical Cat Toys

Cats and kittens alike can find hours of entertainment in the right toy. The best approach to finding the best toys for your cat is to start out with cheap versions of each type of toy to see what catches (and keeps) his attention. A plethora of toys is available, from the standard catnip mouse to motorized gerbils to fishing poles with bright ribbons attached. Some toys require a playmate—namely, you. Most he can play with on his own. Which toys your cat will like will vary with age, diet, weather, personality, or just plain mood. Generally speaking, a kitten will find pretty much anything—even a giant rolled-up ball of sticky tape—worth at least half an hour of play. It's finding just the right toys for grown cats that takes a bit of investigation.

THE BIG CHASE

Many cats are motivated by movement. Round toys that roll across the room when batted are great temptations, especially for active cats that like to give chase. My cats love the classic bell in a webbed plastic ball. This toy combines the advantages of the rolling ball with a sound that gets the cats' attention. The cagelike casing also provides a good place to hook claws, so when the cats bat it around, the toy gets caught on a claw and flies in an unexpected direction.

Another cat favorite is a small mouse on the end of a spring, which is attached to the floor by a suction cup. Variations include the same theme attached in different ways to the wall or a table. When I first

---

IS FELIX FANCY-FREE?

Body language is an important clue to determining your cat's mood. If you are unsure about how your cat feels around you or other people, look for these signs:

- A cat sprawled out on her back, showing her belly, is relaxed and feels content and safe in her surroundings.

- A cat with his ears flattened against his head is frightened and angry.

- A cat scurrying madly with her head and body held low has been frightened.

- If your cat lets you play with his paws, he is relaxed, and he trusts you.

- A cat kneading your lap is expressing affection for you, and sometimes also requesting an extended fur rub.

- A cat holding his tail upright with its tip leaning toward his head is curious and playful. If he's walking to you in this tail-high posture, he's coming to say hello.

A cat with tail held high is curious, confident, and ready for action.

WANDS AND FISHING POLES

One of the best interactive toys I have found is the "fishing pole," a long string attached to the end of a plastic wand or wooden dowel. There are several varieties for sale, and a homemade version isn't hard to make. Strings with bells and bright colors help spark interest, but the main fun is in the movement. As you play with your cat, spin and flick the string to imitate the darting freeze-and-flee movements of mice or birds. Even the crankiest old cat can't resist this lure! And your cats will love you for the time you spend with them racing about the house twirling the toy behind you—cats appreciate grown-up silliness just as much as kids do!

FEATHERED FISHING POLE

Bags of feathers in different colors are sold at most craft stores. Although they are eye-catching, be careful of feathers in very bright colors, which may contain dyes that are not safe for your cat to ingest.

Sturdy string, yarn, or twine

A bag of feathers of various colors

A dowel (optional)

1. Cut a piece of string about 3 feet long.
2. Tie a few feathers together and secure to the end of the string with a small amount of nontoxic glue.
3. Tie the free end of the string to the end of a dowel.

Now you have a great flying bird! You can attach this dowel to anything to elevate the bird for free-batting. Another option is to tie the free end of the string to a doorknob or the arm of a chair.

One warning: Do be prepared to sweep up the feather remains, as some cats get very excited about the "kill."

TOYS FOR THE FRUGAL FELINE

Many cat toys are already sitting around the house and can provide hours of fun. Right under our noses, these common articles can become favorite toys. Here are a few ideas for the frugal feline fancier.

PLASTIC EASTER EGGS

Although they are quickly forgotten by humans once the candy is gone, plastic Easter eggs make terrific cat toys. They roll in awkward directions and can be filled with catnip or noisemaking dry cat food. Or try snapping a string into the egg and tying it to a doorknob for an instant batting toy.

CRACKLES AND CRINKLES

When you're done reading the newspaper, tear off a page and crumple it into a loose ball. A newspaper ball is great fun for cats to bat around, and it makes a wonderful crackling noise when pounced upon. My cats now come running whenever they hear the sound of paper being crumpled. Try tossing the balled-up paper in the air for your cat to catch. Many felines are just as good as dogs at catching flying objects, and they're often just as enthusiastic about it.

You can make another great paper toy from a sturdy paper towel. Crumple up a piece of white paper and place it in the center of a paper towel. Bring the towel up around the sides to create a "ghost" shape, and tie it with one end of a 3-foot (.9 m) string. Cats will do back flips for it.

BOXES, BOXES, AND MORE BOXES

As most cat owners know, cats go nuts for packing boxes. They jump in and out, defending their new "castle" against moat monsters on the outside. When they're all played out, they like nothing better than to cozy up inside a box. So whenever you receive a good-size box, leave it on the floor for your cats. When you wake up in the morning, don't be surprised to see your cat snoozing inside with some of her favorite toys.

Smaller boxes also hold great appeal for cats. Kittens, for example, love empty oats boxes. They're small enough to fit inside the boxes and usually love the way the cylindrical boxes roll about the floor. Expect to get hours of amusement yourself watching your kitten in and on this new toy.

Tissue boxes are also great feline sport. Think of this homemade toy as the Rubik's Cube for cats. Take an empty tissue box and insert a Ping-Pong ball inside. Your cat will spend hours trying to fish out this rolling sphere through the narrow opening.

Catnip Creations

There is no end to the varieties of catnip toys available for cats. For several reasons, I don't advise purchasing the inexpensive, poorly constructed toys found at many grocery and discount stores. Most important, the vigor with which these toys are attacked usually reduces the weaker ones to a few threads and scattered leaves within a matter of minutes. If you are fond of sweeping up catnip dust, that may not matter, but practically speaking, the cat won't have much fun with it once it's spilled. Before purchasing a catnip toy, be sure that it is constructed of thick, durable fabric and that its seams are tight and of sturdy thread. Never buy catnip toys made of felt or of loosely woven fabrics such as cotton flannel.

> ### TOYS TO AVOID
> These toys are unsafe for your cats:
> - Plastic bags.
> - Any bag with handles.
> - Soft foam balls, which shred easily.
> - Toys with itty-bitty parts or glued-on pieces.
> - Anything small enough to be swallowed.
> - Empty cellophane cigarette wrappers, which attract cats with their crinkling but can cause choking.
> - Twist-ties; cats love to play with them, but if accidentally swallowed, twist-ties can cause serious damage to a cat's throat and stomach.

Another problem with inexpensive catnip toys is the quality of the herb found in them. Potency and life of the herb depend on freshness and quality. I recommend choosing organic catnip products whenever possible. If you're making your own toys, you can buy organic catnip in bulk at most health food stores and herb shops. It's cheaper than prepackaged catnip and tends to be much fresher.

Continued →

At craft fairs and gift shops, you may find very cute and clever handcrafted catnip toys. These eye pleasers may seem like special treats for your feline friend, but beware of varying quality levels. Some toys are made by dedicated cat owners who make sure that the toys are durable and long lasting. Others may be sloppily made in flimsy bags that tear easily.

Examine these toys carefully before making a purchase. Avoid anything made from felt or other fabrics that are not tightly woven and are quite thick. Check decorations for weakness, and don't trust anything with too much glue. Also, test the freshness of the catnip by squeezing the toy roughly a few times and warming it between your hands. A fresh, herby aroma should radiate from it.

MAKING A CATNIP MOUSE

Making a catnip toy is a fun and simple project, provided you do not invite your cat to join this sewing circle. My favorite fabric to use is denim from a discarded pair of jeans. It is sturdy and thick, but breathable enough to let out the scent.

Piece of denim fabric

Fresh organic catnip, dried and crumbled

Needle and thread

Sewing machine

Table knife or dowel

1. Cut a circle at least 6 inches (152.4 mm) in diameter on the piece of denim, or use the mouse pattern provided.
2. Fold the fabric in half and stitch 1/4 inch (6.3 mm) in from the edge with a tight zigzag. If you're hand-stitching, be sure to use tight and close stitches. Leave an unsewn section along the edge (see diagram) to allow you to turn the pouch.

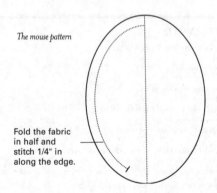

The mouse pattern

Fold the fabric in half and stitch 1/4" in along the edge.

3. Turn the pouch inside out, using a table knife or dowel to push the edge out all the way.
4. Fill the pouch with loose catnip so that it is bulging but not packed too tight.
5. Hand-sew the remaining opening (sew in the mouse's "tail" if you are following the pattern), using either an "invisible stitch" or a series of very tight stitches. Double-stitch or use closely packed overcast stitches. The key to preventing breakage is to leave as little thread as possible exposed to the teeth and claws of the predator kitty.

Caution: When you're making your own catnip toys, be prepared for the cat to show an inordinate interest in anything the catnip has touched, such as newspapers covering your work surface or the manuscript on which you've been practicing making a catnip mouse.

Beyond Catnip: Other Greens Your Cat Will Enjoy

Most cats enjoy munching on plants, and they don't draw any distinction between outdoor and indoor plants. To accommodate your foliage-seeking feline and save your houseplants, consider growing a couple of plants especially for your cat.

CAT GRASS

Cat grass is a sturdy tray of grass especially suited for feline digestion. You can purchase preseeded cat grass beds at most pet and garden supply stores; just follow the sprouting instructions and in a few days you'll have a healthy bed of grass for your cats to chew on. You can also make your own cat grass bed: Fill an aluminum brownie pan with organic seed-starting mix and scatter wheat grass berries over the surface. Cover the berries with about 1/4 inch of soil and set the tray in a warm location that gets a good amount of sunlight. The grass will be ready for feline fun in about a week.

HERBS FOR CATS

Dill and catnip are excellent herbs to offer fresh to your cat. Dill is Mother Nature's tummy soother, a terrific remedy for digestive difficulties of all sorts. Catnip, as we've discussed, is absolutely irresistible to most cats. Purchase a few seedlings of each; once they've matured to a sturdy height, set them out in a high-cat-traffic area.

HOUSEPLANTS VERSUS CAT PLANTS: TEACHING YOUR CAT THE DIFFERENCE

How do you teach your cat which plants are off limits and which plants are available for chewing? First, make your houseplants unavailable. Hang them from ceiling hooks or situate them on high shelves that cats can't access.

Then, offer a green alternative, such as cat grass, dill, or catnip. Place the new grass or herb in the same location as the houseplant that the cat is accustomed to chewing on.

If in spite of green alternatives a houseplant still attracts undue attention from your cat, apply a cayenne pepper— or citrus-based repellent (available at pet stores) to its leaves and stems. When your mighty plant hunter next takes a mouthful or two of greenery, she'll have an experience she won't want to repeat.

Teaching Your Cat Simple Tricks

Arden Moore

Illustrations by Rick Daskam

Feline Psychology

Great teachers know the best ways to motivate their students. To be a successful cat trainer, you need to know what makes your cat tick. If you pay close attention to his actions, you'll discover some or all of the following traits.

Cats prefer set routines. They like to wake up at a certain time, eat at a certain time, and they expect you home at a certain time. They quickly learn your daily schedule and adapt accordingly. Cats' regularity may partially explain why some wake us up a few minutes before our alarm clocks chime. When their inner body clock sounds the signal, it's time to get out of bed and start a new day.

Cats abhor confusion and change. That's why some scoot under the bed when your aunt Dottie pays a surprise overnight visit or when they see packing boxes stacked in your living room.

Cats are place oriented. They feel most comfortable inside familiar surroundings. This is how they differ from dogs. Dogs are people oriented; they want to join their favorite people pals and go to strange new places. Cats prefer to stay at home. Your house is their castle.

Cats love to sleep. Some Rip van Felines will snooze up to 17 hours a day. I've yet to meet a cat with insomnia. They have favorite nap spots that they will risk life and limb to reach, especially if they are sunny, perched up high, or tucked inside closet corners.

Cats are refreshingly honest. They never pretend. They never lie. If they don't want to sit on your lap, they will make like Houdini to figure out a way to wiggle free. It's nothing personal, mind you. They would just rather be elsewhere. But if your cat wants to snuggle next to you, she will unabashedly march over and sit on top of the Sunday newspaper you're trying to read. It's your cat's way of saying, "Hey, look at me. Pay attention to *me*."

How Cat Training Works

My animal behaviorist friends tell me cats can be trained by a pattern of behavior reinforced by rewards. The psychological term for this is *conditioned response*, the very same principle Ivan Pavlov used to elicit responses from hungry dogs using a bell.

Long before you picked up this bulletin, you've been training your cat using the conditioned response approach—probably not even realizing it. Does your cat come zooming into the kitchen each time he hears the whirl of the electric can opener or the *cush* sound a tab top makes when you peel it off a new can of cat food? These sounds signal to your cat that if she goes to the kitchen, there is a good chance she will be rewarded with food.

It is important for you to reinforce a desired behavior with a special signal and reward. Always be consistent. In most cases, cats are motivated by food. Other popular motivators are verbal praise, friendly petting strokes, behind-the-ears scratches, and toys (especially cat wands or toy mice).

IT'S ALL IN THE TIMING

Timing is critical in successful training. Pick a time to teach a new lesson or trick when your cat appears to be a willing student. I've found the best times are just before mealtime or when your cat is in a spirited, frisky, playful mood. Each cat will react differently when a training session commences. Some may ignore you at first, while others may be very curious and eager to learn from the very start.

You should also recognize that your cat trains you. After all, the conditioned response technique can work both ways. Your cat knows that if he rubs against your leg, there is a high probability he will be rewarded with friendly petting. Or if he sits politely by the food bowl and meows sweetly, you will respond by feeding him.

Cat Chat 101

Training success depends on how well you and your cat communicate. Of course you don't speak the same language, and, unfortunately, a handy cat-to-people translation dictionary doesn't exist. No need to fret. The cornerstone of successful training is addressing your cat by her name. This alerts her that you are talking to her, not the dog or your spouse.

When your cat glides into the room and comes into view, offer a friendly greeting and call her by name. Say "Hey, Callie, it's good to see you." Use your cat's name often so that she learns to associate hearing you speak it with happy actions such as getting praise or a tasty treat. Speak in calm, soothing tones so your cat will feel special and part of the household family. She will quickly learn how to interpret your voice tones and body cues if you are consistent in how you deliver them.

Engage in two-way chatting instead of one-way directives like "Time to take your pill, Clipper" or "Murphy, get down from the kitchen counter—*now*." Try making cat sounds. Even if your feeble meow attempts are pure nonsense, your cat will appreciate your efforts.

BODY LANGUAGE BASICS

Cats do most of their communicating through body language. These are some key cat moves you need to recognize:

Note the tail position. Cats rely on their tails for balance, but they are also mood barometers. A cat who holds his tail loosely upright when walking is confident and content. If your cat flicks his tail upright in your direction, he is giving you a warm greeting. If he whips it from side to side or thumps it on the floor, your cat is clearly telling you he is angry or agitated. If he puffs his tail out like a pipe cleaner, your cat is spooked or startled by something or someone.

Read the eyes. The eyes are truly the mirrors to your cat's soul. When a cat looks at you with half-opened, winking eyes, he is making a peaceful greeting: "Hey, I love you." If your cat's eyes are dilated, give him some space. He is nervous or agitated about something.

Check the ears. A receptive cat points his ears forward and slightly outward. A ready-to-fight cat flattens his ears tightly against his head.

Look for leg rubbing. When a cat rubs against your leg or brushes his cheekbone against your hand, he is marking you. It's a form of feline flattery that alerts other scent-savvy animals within range, "Hey, this is *mine*."

CAT CHAT TRANSLATED

If you listen closely, you will notice that your cat's vocabulary goes beyond "meow." Cats rely on various vocal sounds to convey different meanings. What you hear is what they mean. Cats don't clutter their vocabularies with sarcasm, slang, or double meanings. Here are the five most popular "cat-speak" sounds:

Meow. Your cat makes this trademark sound when she demands your attention. She may be saying, "Hey, where have you been all day?" or "Come look out the window with me and check out that sparrow on the bird feeder."

Purr. Cats make this engine-revving sound when they are blissfully happy—like when they're on the receiving end of a massage—or, strangely, when they face a stressful situation, such as a visit to the veterinary clinic. Only cats can purr with their mouths closed while breathing in and out. Try it. It's impossible for humans. Saying "toy boat" 10 times fast without tangling your tongue is easier than trying to mimic a cat's purr.

Chirp. Many cats make strange chirping noises when they see bugs—especially flies buzzing around light fixtures—inside your home. They may also make this noise while pressed up against your back

Continued ➜

window watching birds, squirrels, and other small creatures scurry around outside.

Trill. I truly love this musical trill sound that always seems to end with a question mark. Cats deliver this special chirp only to people they like, not other cats. A chirp can mean "I'm glad you're home" or "Why, yes, I would like that tasty treat you're holding in your hand."

Moan. This elongated "O" or "U" panic or protest call comes from a cat about to regurgitate a hairball or one resisting restraint during a veterinary exam.

Hiss. Plain and simple, this heavy-on-the-S sound comes from a cat warning you to "back off." It is an early warning signal before your cat starts to nip or swat.

Cat-Training Basics

Now that you know how and why your cat acts and chats the way she does, it's time to teach her some tricks. We'll start with the basics.

COME WHEN CALLED

There is a popular saying among cat owners: "Dogs come when they're called; cats take a message and get back to you later." It doesn't have to be that way. As I mentioned earlier, there is a magical bond between cats and can openers. Use it to your advantage. After a few times of opening a can of cat food your cat learns to associate the sound with getting a tasty treat.

Use this food signal to teach your cat the "come" command. Try to teach your cat to come when you call at mealtime. She will pay attention because she wants to eat.

1. Tap your cat's empty food bowl with a metal spoon or make clicking sounds with a child's inexpensive clicker toy in another room.

2. Call the cat by her name: "Bonnie, come here." Tap the bowl or click a few more times until your cat reaches you. Your cat, sensing food is on its way, should race to your side.

3. When the cat comes, praise her and fill the food bowl.

4. Repeat these steps during mealtime and your cat will quickly associate these sounds with getting a full belly.

COME TO A WHISTLE

If your cat ignores your "come" command, try to teach her to scurry your way with a whistle. At mealtime, call your cat by name and whistle. Tap the food bowl if necessary. Praise and give your cat a tasty meal each time she comes. Your cat will associate food with your beckoning whistle in no time.

> **TEACHING COMMANDS FOR SAFETY'S SAKE**
> Teaching your cat to come on command can be a valuable safety tool in cases of emergency, such as a fire or flood, when you need to get your cat out of the house fast.

SIT

This is an important command for your cat to learn. Once a cat can sit on command, he is more receptive to learning other tricks and behaviors. You may want to use a clicker (an inexpensive training tool that makes a clicking noise; it's sold at most pet shops) to help you give the "sit" command. Your cat will learn best—that is, most quickly—if you attempt this command just before mealtime.

> **QUICK TIP**
> If your cat does not sit when you ask him to, gently press down on his hindquarters. Be gentle and patient so you do not frustrate or frighten your cat.

1. Select a quiet place where your cat feels comfortable and safe. Place him up on a table and give him some friendly petting so he feels at ease.

2. Take a single food treat in your hand and hold it in front of your cat. Slowly bring the treat up over your cat's head, giving the "sit" command accompanied by the cat's name, such as "Homer, sit."

3. When your cat tips back his head to follow the treat, he will need to sit down to keep his balance. It's the law of physics. When your cat sits, say "Sit, good sit" and click your clicker if you have one. Immediately hand over the treat.

4. Repeat steps 1 to 3 until your cat obeys the "sit" command without you holding a treat over his head.

5. Once your cat has perfected the "sit" command from a tabletop, practice it when he is walking on the floor.

STAY

No one likes to have to chase a cat around the house to put a collar on or give her a pill. Cats are too quick and agile. Instead, teach your cat the "stay" command. Here's how:

1. Start in an enclosed area such as a screened porch or den—any place the cat cannot escape or hide. If your cat starts to move away from you, say her name followed by "Stay."

2. Extend one arm straight out and, with the palm facing down, move it down steadily toward the floor. Do not chase after your cat. Maintain your standing position. Only after she sits or lies down should you slowly approach her, kneel down, and reward her with "Good girl, Raspberry."

3. Pick your cat up and give her a friendly hug. Then put her back down on the ground.

4. Repeat steps 1 to 3 until she stays in position readily after hearing the "stay" command.

5. Once she heeds the "stay" command inside an enclosed room, practice it in an open area. Soon you'll say goodbye to your cat-chasing days.

SILENT HELLO

Cats have a natural instinct for this trick, and you may find that it becomes your cat's preferred method of greeting. It's also a great trick to teach cats that are slightly skittish—making the initial contact on their terms helps them feel more at ease when they are then petted or picked up. For the first few training sessions, be sure that your cat is in a calm, contented mood before approaching him.

1. Kneel down within arm's length of your cat. Curl the fingers of one of your hands into a soft fist. Slowly raise your arm until it is extended in front of you and your fist is at your cat's eye level.

2. Be patient while waiting for the cat to approach you. If and when he gives your fist a rub or a head butt, give him a scratch behind the ears and then get up.

3. Repeat steps 1 and 2 several times a day as a form of greeting your cat. He will soon learn to come quickly to your hand.

TALK BACK

After a few of these training sessions, your cat will be more apt to respond to your call. Even if she's hiding in the closet, she'll let out an "I'm here" meow when she recognizes your voice. This trick comes in handy when you need to find your cat in a hurry.

1. Position one of your cat's favorite food treats a couple inches from her face. Let her get a good whiff of this must-have morsel.

2. Speak the cat's name a few times. When she answers back, give her the treat.

3. Repeat steps 1 and 2 a few times a day until your cat responds readily. After she has the hang of it, you may want to still offer a treat occasionally so that she continues to associate talking back with a reward.

TOP 12 RULES FOR TRAINING CATS

Here are some pointers that will make training easy and fun for you and your cat:

1. Always say your cat's name to get her attention before giving any command.

2. Be consistent with your verbal and hand signal commands.

3. Pay attention to your cat's moods. Train when your cat is receptive to learning, not when the lessons fit your schedule.

4. Select a quiet time and room where you can be one-on-one with your cat to teach him a new trick.

5. Be positive, patient, and encouraging.

6. Provide food rewards and enthusiastic praise and petting immediately after for each success, no matter how small.

7. Start with the basic commands: come, sit, and stay.

8. Gradually introduce advanced commands, such as "Go fetch your mouse" or "Go to the kitchen door if you want to go for a walk outside."

9. Take advantage of your cat's natural curiosity and love for attention. Let him sniff out new toys and training tools, and always approach training sessions as if they were the ultimate opportunity for pampering your pet.

10. Be flexible; recognize that sometimes your cat just isn't in the mood to perform a trick. Don't try to force training on your feline; she's likely to decide she doesn't want to be trained ever again.

11. Be sure your cat understands each training step before going to the next. If the cat isn't performing the desired behavior, chances are you are moving too quickly.

12. Teach your cat only one new trick or behavior at a time. Cats are not multitasking masters. Keep it simple and short—no more than 10 or 15 minutes at a time.

Teaching Your Cat Classic Dog Tricks

Beyond the basic commands, you are limited only by your imagination and patience when it comes to the more difficult types of tricks to introduce to your cat. Some of my favorites are the classic "dog" tricks of shaking hands, touching an object as directed, sitting up, fetching, rolling over, and jumping up.

SHAKE HANDS

Some cats are natural paw-shakers. Others need much training and patience before they'll get the hang of it.

1. With your cat positioned in front of you, touch his front paw with a small treat and say "Shake."

2. The moment he lifts his paw, gently take it in your hand and shake it. Heap on the praise and give him a small food treat.

3. Repeat these steps in sequence four or five times. Discontinue once your cat delivers a couple of paw shakes or becomes bored and departs for a much-preferred cat nap.

PAW TOUCH

Once your cat has aced the basic tricks, especially the "sit" command, she may be the perfect candidate to touch an object or prop when instructed. You may want to have a clicker tool to help you teach your cat this trick.

1. Place your cat on a sturdy table and give her the "sit" command. Position her about 12 to 15 inches from the edge of the table.

2. Place a small toy, a thick book, or an object that won't tip over when touched at the edge of the table between you and your cat.

3. Hold a small food treat in front of your cat, making sure the object is between the food treat and your cat.

4. Give your cat the "paw" command in conjunction with her name (i.e., "Murphy, paw") as you touch the object with the hand not holding the treat. As soon as your cat reaches for the food with one of her front paws and touches or steps on the object, hit the clicker, if you have one, and say, "Paw, good paw." Immediately give your cat the food treat and praise her.

5. If your cat isn't touching the object, try moving it side to side to entice her into trying to swat at it. As soon as your cat touches the object, press the clicker, say "Paw, good paw," and hand over the treat so your cat begins to associate the object and a food reward.

6. Repeat steps 2 through 5 several times, or until your cat loses interest. Repeat these training sessions daily until your cat seems to understand the "paw" command. Once your cat performs successfully several times over a span of a week, repeat the steps without the clicker. Continue with the food treats.

7. Final challenge: Say the command "Paw, good paw" while pointing to an object on the ground. It doesn't matter whether your cat touches it with her left or right paw or alternates.

FETCH

Cats are born predators. They love to chase, stalk, and capture. Tap into these instinctive drives to teach your cat how to fetch. Select a large, uncluttered room or a long hallway for this trick.

Continued →

1. Take a piece of paper and ball it into a wad about the diameter of a nickel, a tempting size for most cats. Make sure your cat sees you create this paper wad and hears it crinkle between your fingertips.

2. Show your cat the paper wad, toss it over her head, and say "Fetch."

3. Praise your cat as she chases after the paper ball, bats it around, and grabs it in her paws or mouth. Use your hand to motion your cat to come to you as you say "Come here."

4. If the cat brings the paper wad to within a foot or so of your feet, reward her with a treat and lavish praise. You may need to retrieve the paper wad a few times until your cat understands how to play this game.

SIT UP

This is the feline version of the classic begging-dog trick. Cats are too dignified for this behavior, of course; they are simply sitting up, not begging. My cat Murphy does this trick like a pro when it's treat time in my house.

1. When your cat is in a calm, peaceful state and is sitting down, approach him quietly. Hold a treat an inch or so over your cat's head and say "Sit up." If your cat tries to swat at it or stands up, don't give him the treat. Instead, repeat the "sit up" command, and he will soon get the idea that he needs to stand up and balance his weight on his hind feet.

2. The second your cat sits up, give him the treat and deliver praise.

3. Repeat steps 1 and 2 until your cat sits up as soon as you give the command.

Use a treat to teach your cat the "sit up" command.

ROLL OVER

Move over, Fido—any food-motivated cat can learn the art of rolling over. It's a fun trick for showing off your cat's many talents to your friends.

1. Kneel down in front of your cat as he sits on the floor.

2. Hold a treat in your right hand and slowly pass it over your cat's left shoulder to the point that he turns his head to look at it.

3. Say "Roll over" as you keep moving your hand up and over. When your cat tries to grab the treat with his paws, his belly goes up, then he rolls over on his side.

4. Reward your cat with the treat.

5. Repeat steps 1 through 4 several times per session, and repeat training sessions daily until your cat readily obeys the "roll over" command.

Teaching Your Cat to Come Out from Hiding

This trick comes in handy when you need your cat to be within your reach. Always reward her compliance with praise or food.

The instructions here address a cat that is hiding under the bed—a classic feline hideaway spot. If your cat prefers to hide in the back of the closet, under the dresser, or anywhere else impassable to humans, simply adapt these instructions to suit your own circumstances. What's important is to practice over and over again until your cat learns to jump up (or come out or crawl out) of her own volition upon command.

1. Close the bedroom door to prevent your cat's escape and shut out any distractions. Shut any closet doors.

2. Look under the bed and achieve eye contact with your cat.

3. Tap the top of your bed with an open palm and calmly but firmly give the "jump up" command along with your cat's name, such as "Callie, jump up."

4. If necessary, coax your cat out from under the bed using a broom handle. Do not poke or prod, but use a gentle sweeping motion.

5. Be patient but persistent. It could take several minutes for your cat to jump on the bed.

6. Once your cat jumps on the bed, give her a food treat and lots of praise immediately. Let her know you are proud.

7. Leave your cat on the bed and walk out of the bedroom, leaving the door open. This lets your cat know she is free to stay or leave on her own terms.

Teaching Your Cat to Use a Kitty Door

Reward your well-behaved cat with some freedom by installing a cat-sized door (sometimes called a cat-flap door) that permits her to come and go in rooms of your home that are off-limits to dogs. Or install a kitty door from the living room into an enclosed patio so your cat enjoys the feel of the great outdoors in a safe setting.

Now, let the training begin.

1. Introduce the newly installed door to your curious cat by luring her close with some tasty treats. You'll gain her trust if you give her a couple of days to sniff it out.

2. Detach the flap or door. Go to the outside and have a friend stay with your cat on the inside.

3. Call your cat by name and say "Come." Heap on the praise and treats when she ventures through the opening.

4. After a few successes, repeat the "Come" command with the plastic flap or door in place.

5. Repeat the training sessions as often as necessary until your cat uses the cat door with no hesitation. Limit each training session to 10 to 15 minutes. Cats aren't big on lengthy lessons.

CHOOSING THE BEST CAT-FLAP DOOR

To free yourself from doorman duty, follow these tips:

- Select a kitty door best suited for your type of home. Door models are available for installation in existing doors or walls or set up as separate panel extensions to sliding glass doors.

- Size the door to match your cat's size. It should be slightly taller and wider than your cat.

- Factor in the climate in your area. A plastic flip door (made of nontoxic material) performs well in mild climates but not in extremely cold or hot weather.

Fun Feline-Human Interactive Games

There are two types of cat owners: those who spend lots of money on expensive cat toys and those who spend lots of time interacting with their cats using homemade or inexpensive toys. Personally, I prefer to be in the latter group.

Fight boredom for your indoor cat by scheduling a time each day for interactive play. Ten minutes once or twice a day should be enough time to help your cat swat away boredom.

Try these terrific indoor games to strengthen the bond between you and your cat and reinforce some of the basic training commands.

WHY YOU SHOULD PLAY WITH YOUR CAT

Making owner—cat interactive games a regular part of your schedule will:

- Help your cat develop a friendly, fun-loving personality
- Reduce your cat's fear of meeting new people or other pets
- Enhance your cat's self-confidence
- Develop your cat's muscle tone and coordination

PREDATOR PRETENDER

Sharpen your cat's hunting skills by attaching a toy mouse to the end of a sturdy string and flexible pole. Toss the mouse within sight of your cat. When he slinks belly down on the ground and arches his backside in the air, slowly reel in the mouse. This movement proves irresistible to most cats. In no time, your cat will make airborne leaps and on-target pounces on the mouse. Move the mouse up and down and side to side to give your cat a good aerobic workout. This game also keeps his eye-to-paw coordination in top shape.

SHOELACE CHASE

Take a long shoelace, tie a toy mouse to one end, and hold the other end in your hand. Call your cat by name and once you catch his attention, race up and down the hallway with the toy mouse dragging across the floor. Zoom right past your cat. Before long, she won't be able to fight the temptation and will join the chase. Once you've mastered the long hallway route, spice things up by extending the chase in and out of rooms and stairways. Be sure to continually call your cat's name and shower him with accolades for every successful mouse pounce. Both of you will get a great aerobic workout.

CAT IN THE MIDDLE

Cats aren't shy about showing off their leaping and grabbing skills. Ask a friend to play this game with you.

1. Position your cat in the middle of the floor of a large room. Stand or sit about 6 feet from your cat and have your friend positioned at about the same distance on the other side. Hold a toy mouse or paper wad in your hand, call your cat by name, and say "Look."

2. Toss the mouse or paper wad over your cat's head and to your friend. This is a signal for your cat to begin leaping and snagging the airborne object in midflight.

3. Each time your cat "scores," congratulate her. Keep tossing the object back and forth until your cat leaves the room or starts grooming herself. That's her way of telling you, "Hey, thanks for the game, but it's time for me to look glamorous."

HIDE AND SEEK

My cats love this game. The rules are simple. When your cat is next to you in a room, toss a treat across the room. When your cat scurries after it, quietly slip around the corner out of sight. Peek around the corner, call your cat by name, and draw back out of sight quickly. Each time she races to you, reward her with a treat and lots of praise. Repeat this four or five times. This game reinforces your cat's willingness to come on command.

CAT IN THE BAG

Cats can't resist an open bag on the ground. Within seconds, they've plunged inside, and from the outside it looks like the bag is alive. Hone in on your cat's bag attraction with this fun game.

1. Cut the handles off a paper supermarket shopping bag. Cut a circle in the bottom of the bag.

2. Attach a toy mouse to the end of a long shoelace.

3. With the bag placed on the floor with the bottom facing you, fish the toy mouse through the circular opening until it reaches about midway inside the bag.

4. Call your cat so he is facing the open front end of the bag.

5. Gently wiggle the toy mouse and watch your cat raise his haunches, do the rear-end wiggle, and dive inside the bag to capture the mouse. Reel the mouse out of the circular hole.

6. Praise your cat for his hunting prowess.

FLASHLIGHT TAG

After dinner and before bedtime, most cats seem to get their second, or third, wind and need to unleash some pent-up energy. If you have a cat like this, skip the sitcom, bring out your flashlight, and play with your pet. Select a room that has been cat-proofed so your feline doesn't knock over or bump into anything during her determined chase of the light beam. Dim the lights in a room with at least one open wall and plenty of floor room. Cast your flashlight beam on the walls and quickly move it to the floor. Watch your cat take off in hot purr-suit!

085

Lura Rogers

Illustrations by Rick Daskam, Beverly Duncan, Charles Joslin, and Alison Kolesar

Introduction

Centuries before veterinarians existed, cats in the wild instinctively relied on the medicinal powers of plants for healing. They were drawn to specific plants and their leaves, flowers, stems, and roots to cure a wide range of ills and aches, cuts and scrapes.

Today, our domesticated felines are living longer, healthier lives than their ancient ancestors, thanks in part to advances in traditional veterinary medicine. But as veterinarians and cat owners learn more about the benefits of holistic medicine, feline health care is increasingly returning to its plant-based roots.

Mother Nature's green pharmacy offers hundreds of herbs that can be helpful for felines. The "top 10" herbs profiled here earn this acclaim because they are safe to use, are easy to obtain and administer, and address a wide range of common health conditions affecting our feline friends. When used properly, these herbs deliver a bounty of healing goodness, often free of the unpleasant side effects commonly associated with conventional medical prescriptions. They not only treat symptoms but also, and more importantly, often enhance your cat's immune system and address the causes underlying health conditions.

You can buy these herbs in bulk or as tinctures, capsules, and salves from herb shops and natural foods stores. If you're a gardening enthusiast, however, you may want to grow your own, and you'll find the information you need here.

USING HERBS SAFELY

The herbal remedies suggested here are safe and effective; if any precautions are advisable, I've noted them with each herb profile. However, there are a few general safety rules you should abide by:

- If your cat is taking any prescription medicine, I encourage you to seek the advice of a holistic-oriented veterinarian before supplementing with herbal remedies, because herbs and drugs can have harmful interactions.

- If you decide to branch out from the relatively safe and gentle herbs discussed here, you should seek the advice of a qualified professional before giving these new herbs to your cat.

- If you are using a commercial pet preparation, always follow label directions.

- More is not better. Some herbs offer potent benefits in small doses but in larger doses can be harmful. Always follow dosage instructions.

- Consult with your veterinarian before giving herbs to kittens or to pregnant or nursing cats. Their ever-changing physiology may not be able to safely handle doses of nature's medicine.

- Remember that some herbs work best when given regularly, while others are most effective when given on an as-needed basis. Read the herb profiles or consult with a holistic veterinarian or an herbalist for advice on how herbs can best be used for your cat.

Herbal Remedies—and Convincing Your Cat to Take Them

Most cat owners would gladly clean not one but a dozen litter boxes a day rather than attempt to give their cats medicine. I swear cats are psychic. They know what you have in mind before you even reach for the medicine bottle and dash under the bed or some other hiding spot. And even when you do catch them, they contour their bodies and make giving a pill, applying a salve, or administering eardrops a truly unpleasant event for all.

Let me share a little secret on how to outfox your cat. Never attempt to give your cat its medicine in an open area, like the kitchen or living room. The cat has too many escape routes. Instead, corner your cat in a small room, like the bathroom. Shut the door. Speak calmly but confidently. If you have a wiggly cat, wrap it gently in a big bath towel, leaving only its head exposed. Once a cat realizes that there is no escape, it will wave the white flag of surrender. Always finish medicine-giving ordeals with lots of praise and a tasty treat. Then, open the door and let your cat scoot or saunter out, depending on its mood.

HERBAL SHOPPING TIPS

There was a time when "shopping" for herbs was as simple as a walk in the woods. You simply grabbed a handful of whatever you needed. But those handfuls have become teas, tinctures, capsules, and other commercial preparations in a mind-boggling array of choices. If you want to make a smart buy, use these pointers as a checklist for your next herb purchase:

- Purchase products that list both the common name (such as valerian) and the scientific name (*Valeriana officinalis*) of each herb used. Proper identification is important because different plants often go by the same common name.

- Check for an expiration date.

- Choose products that give dosage instructions. Keep in mind that dosages are typically based on an average adult person weighing 150 pounds. Check with your vet to select the proper dosage for your cat.

- Whenever possible, buy only products with certified organic ingredients.

- Limit your purchases to one or two herbs or herbal products. Working with your holistic vet or an herbalist, take the time to see how effective these herbs are for your cat before trying other herbs.

There are many herbal remedies available in the marketplace; most are high-quality products that you can feel comfortable buying and giving to your beloved pet. But if you're willing to commit the time, you can make your own herbal remedies at home—saving yourself some money, allowing you to customize blends for your cat's needs, and guaranteeing the quality of the preparation.

FRESH AND DRIED HERBS

Depending on the herb, you can use its flowers, leaves, stems, or roots in fresh or dried form. If you're growing your own herbs, you can snip fresh cuttings whenever you need them or harvest and dry the herbs for later use. You can also purchase dried herbs in bulk from herb shops and most natural foods stores.

To use fresh or dried herbs, chop them finely and mix them into your cat's food.

HERBAL TEAS

Herbal teas are prepared by two main methods: infusion and decoction. To make an infusion, the herb is steeped. To make a decoction, the herb is simmered over time. Which technique you use depends on the type of herb you've selected.

Infusions. To extract medicinal properties from leaves, flowers, berries, or ground seeds, you infuse them. These ingredients easily release their essential oils when they're steeped in hot water—and they easily lose their value when they're simmered. To infuse a cup of tea, pour 1 cup boiling water over 1 to 2 teaspoons dried herbs or 2 to 4 tablespoons fresh herbs. Cover, let steep 10 to 15 minutes, and strain.

Decoctions. When the recipe calls for tougher herb parts—barks, roots, dried berries, seeds, or rhizomes—you need to use a brewing process known as a decoction. The simmering is necessary to extract the herb's valuable properties. To decoct a cup of tea, add 2 teaspoons dried root to 1 cup water. Cover, bring to a boil, simmer 15 to 20 minutes, and then strain.

Combinations. When you're making a tea with roots *and* leaves, you both infuse and decoct: Simmer the roots 20 minutes, remove the pot from the heat, add the leaves and stir, then cover and steep 10 to 20 minutes.

Note: Let the tea cool completely before giving it to your cat. Store any leftover tea in the refrigerator, where it will keep for up to 3 days.

Some cats will sweetly sip a cup of herbal tea if it contains the healing compounds they need. If your cat refuses to drink the tea, you can pour it over the cat's food. If the cat won't eat "contaminated" food, pour the dosage into a plastic syringe (available from your veterinarian or a veterinary supply house). Hold the cat's head with one hand, applying light upward pressure on the upper jaw with your thumb and fingers. Place the dropper in the side of your cat's mouth where the cheek pouch is, and deliver the herbal liquid in small but steady amounts. This pace makes your cat swallow each time.

TINCTURES

Tinctures for humans are usually alcohol based. However, cats can have trouble metabolizing alcohol. The preferred solvent for tinctures intended for cats is not alcohol but glycerin, a sweet-tasting liquid available in most natural foods stores. Glycerin-based tinctures (also known as glycerites) aren't as potent as alcohol-based tinctures and have a shorter shelf life (1 to 2 years). However, they are nonalcoholic. Glycerites are taken in small amounts—dropperfuls or teaspoonfuls.

There are many good glycerites available commercially. However, if you want to make your own, just follow these steps:

1. **Process the herbs.** When you're using fresh herbs, coarsely chop or mince them. When using dried herbs, powder them in a coffee grinder or mortar and pestle.

2. **Put the processed herbs in a widemouthed jar.** The herbs should make up about one-quarter of the total volume in the jar. Cover them with liquid. For fresh herbs, use twice as much glycerin as herb; for dried herbs, use three times as much glycerin as herb. Blend well.

> ### TINCTURING TIP
> If using glycerin and dried herbs, dilute the glycerin with 1/2 part water per part of glycerin. Use the glycerin at full strength when using fresh herbs.

3. **Seal the jar.** Seal the jar tightly. Put the jar in a dark place, and let it sit for 3 to 6 weeks, shaking occasionally.

4. **Strain and bottle the liquid.** Strain the liquid and decant into smaller bottles, preferably made of dark glass. Store away from direct heat and light.

A tincture can be given like an herbal tea, either by mixing it into the cat's food or by administering with a plastic syringe.

CAPSULES

These supplements are a handy way for your cat to benefit from herbs without too much effort on a daily basis. Capsules are handy if your cat snubs food with any foreign additives but tolerates taking pills. Most herb shops and natural foods stores sell herbal capsules.

You can also custom-blend capsules to fit your cat's needs. Buy some small, empty pull-apart capsules at your local health food store. Use a clean coffee grinder or mortar and pestle to reduce the herbs to a fine powder. Fill each capsule halfway, and close. Since you will not want to do this on a daily basis, be sure to store extras in a well-sealed, dark-colored glass jar, preferably in the refrigerator or freezer.

The quickest method of administering a capsule is to insert the pill into a ball of moist cat food and serve it as a treat. Be sure to follow this up with another soft treat to make sure that your cat swallowed the pill.

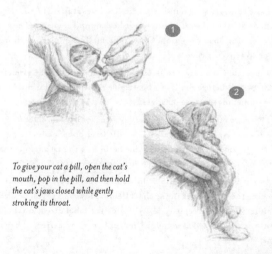

To give your cat a pill, open the cat's mouth, pop in the pill, and then hold the cat's jaws closed while gently stroking its throat.

To give your cat liquid medicine, such as a tincture or tea, hold the cat's head securely and squirt the liquid from a plastic syringe into the cat's mouth.

Continued ➜

If your cat keeps spitting out the pill, here's another option: Hold the cat's head with one hand, applying light upward pressure on the upper jaw with your thumb and fingers. Use your other hand to open the cat's mouth and pop the pill on its tongue as far back as possible. Then hold the cat's jaws closed and massage its throat to induce swallowing. Try blowing a quick puff of air into its face. When the cat blinks, he swallows—it's an automatic reflex (similar to the way we close our eyes when we sneeze).

POULTICES

A poultice is a warm, moist mass of powdered or macerated fresh herb that is applied directly to your cat's skin to relieve insect bites and stings, inflammation, and blood poisoning. It works by drawing out infection, toxins, and foreign bodies embedded in the skin.

Poultices should be made only from herbs that are nontoxic. Your cat will most likely lick off the poultice preparation within an hour of its application. If you've used nontoxic herbs, this is not a problem. In fact, your cat licking off the poultice can contribute to the healing process by getting the herbs into the cat, where they can work internally to promote healing.

A poultice works best if it's prepared from fresh plant parts, but you can use dried herbs if that is what's available. Mash or grind the herb, then mix with just enough boiling water to make a thick paste. Allow to cool to room temperature, then apply directly to the spot that needs attention.

Change the poultice frequently if the wound is bad; less frequently if it is minor. Generally, poultices should be kept in place for an hour, but the time varies with the herb and the severity of the condition.

If your cat keeps licking off the poultice as soon as it's applied, consider getting an Elizabethan collar (a plastic funnel-shaped collar that fits around the cat's neck) from your veterinarian or a pet supply store. Have your cat wear this collar for an hour or so after you apply the poultice. An Elizabethan collar will prevent a cat from licking off a poultice, but it won't prevent the cat from scratching off the poultice. If your cat is particularly determined not to have that poultice and manages to keep scratching it off even while wearing the Elizabethan collar, you may have to bow to its wishes.

Finding the Right Dosage for Your Cat

The easiest and safest way to give herbal dosages is to give them to effect. The basic rule is to start out slowly, with low doses at first. Then, after a month or so, when the cat adjusts to her herbal intake, taper off or add on, depending on her reaction. Often very small amounts of herb are enough to activate a cure.

Expect slow and easy results. Herbs most often need to be given for at least 30 days before you'll see appreciable results. Look for mild and subtle—and long-lasting—changes.

There are many different delivery systems for herbal remedies, some of which are outlined below. Use whichever one is easiest to give to your cat. It is more important to get the herbs into the cat's system than it is to worry about the "proper" way to dose them.

As a general rule, you can administer herbal medicine to your cat following the guidelines in the chart below. However, if you're using a commercial herbal remedy, always follow the label directions, because dosages can vary among different herbs and different herbal forms.

10 Herbs to Know

Without a doubt, catnip rules as felines' favorite herb. It adds zip and zest to our cats, providing us with lots of amusing antics to watch. Beyond catnip, it's easy to be confused about which botanicals to buy. With the dozens of herbs available, you could go broke trying to keep a supply of every one of them.

I'm here to save you time and money. My 10 favorite herbs for cats are easy to administer, offer varied and versatile healing benefits for common cat ailments, are safe to use, and are widely available. Here's the lineup:

- Burdock (*Arctium lappa*)
- Calendula (*Calendula officinalis*)
- Caraway (*Carum carvi*)
- Catnip (*Nepeta cataria*)
- Dill (*Anethum graveolens*)
- Echinacea (*Echinacea angustifolia, E. purpurea*)
- Eyebright (*Euphrasia officinalis*)
- Parsley (*Petroselinum crispum*)
- Rosemary (*Rosmarinus officinalis*)
- Valerian (*Valeriana officinalis*)

BURDOCK (*ARCTIUM LAPPA*)

Parts used: Roots

Of historical note: Burdock root, also known as gobo, is considered a vegetable in Asian cultures. Burdock arrived on the North American continent with early European colonists. Burdock's infamous burrs inspired the creation of Velcro.

Medicinal uses: Burdock has incredible blood-cleansing capabilities and offers excellent support to the liver, urinary tract, and skin. By enhancing kidney function and cleansing the liver, it helps felines clear their systems of waste and toxins. It is especially helpful in easing the symptoms of arthritis and improving skin conditions.

The easiest method of giving burdock to your cat is to grind the root into a powder and sprinkle it on your cat's food. You can also give your cat burdock tea or tincture.

Growing your own: Because of its sticky burrs, not many gardeners enjoy having burdock around. But burdock root is harvested after its first year of growth, and in that first year, burdock produces only a rosette of leaves—no big plant, no flowers, no seeds, and no sticky burrs.

Burdock (Arctium lappa)

To grow this biennial herb, sow seeds in early spring. Burdock grows in just about any location; the plant prefers loam but tolerates most soil conditions. Burdock seeds germinate quickly, and seedlings should be thinned to about 18 inches apart.

Harvesting and storing: Harvest burdock's deep taproot in the fall of the first year or the spring of the second year.

Cautions: In rare cases, burdock leaves cause contact dermatitis. Some felines experience diarrhea with extended use of burdock; if this happens, simply stop giving the herb to your cat.

GENERAL RULES FOR ADMINISTERING HERBS TO CATS

Adapted from *Dr. Kidd's Guide to Herbal Cat Care*, by Randy Kidd, D.V.M. (Storey Books, 2000)

Cat's Weight	Sprinkles (put on the cat's food once daily)	Teas (poured over food or into the cat's water)	Capsules/Tablets (administered orally)	Tinctures (in the cat's water or food or given directly by mouth)
1–5 lbs.	A very small pinch	1/8 cup once daily	Small chip of a tablet or 1/8 to 1/4 capsule 1 to 2 times daily	1 to 3 drops one to three times daily
5–10 lbs.	A small pinch	1/8 to 1/4 cup one or two times daily	1/4 to 1/2 capsule or tablet one or two times daily	3 to 5 drops one to three times daily
10–20 lbs.	A bigger pinch	1/4 cup one or two times daily	1/2 to 1 capsule or tablet one to three times daily	3 to 5 drops one to three times daily
Over 20 lbs.	2 pinches to 1 teaspoon	1/4 to 1/3 cup one or two times daily	1/2 to 1 capsule or tablet two to four times daily	5 to 10 drops one to three times daily

BURDOCK DAILY DETOX SUPPLEMENT

Adapted from 10 *Herbs for Happy, Healthy Dogs*, by Kathleen Brown (Storey Books, 2000)

This daily supplement will help clear your cat's system of toxins. Burdock, nettle, and red clover are great tonic herbs, supporting and strengthening the body's systems. Calendula aids in liver function and gives the immune system a boost.

1 teaspoon dried burdock root

2 cups water

1 teaspoon dried calendula blossoms

1 teaspoon dried nettle leaves

1 teaspoon dried red clover blossoms

To make a tea:

Add the burdock root to the water and bring to a boil. Reduce heat, cover, and let simmer 10 to 15 minutes. Remove from the heat, add the remaining herbs, and steep, covered, 10 minutes. Strain and allow the tea to cool.

To make capsules:

You can also make capsules with this formula, following the instructions given earlier.

To use:

Administer orally, following the dosage guidelines below.

CALENDULA *(CALENDULA OFFICINALIS)*

Parts used: Flowers

Of historical note: Calendula has been prized throughout history not only for its medicinal uses but also as a symbol of victory. Civil War soldiers and cowboys in the Wild West used calendula as a poultice to help heal bullet wounds.

Medicinal uses: Calendula's primary medicinal use is as a topical treatment for cuts and burns. It also works to soothe the itching and irritation of insect bites, poison ivy and poison oak rashes, flea bites,

> **GROWING AT A GLANCE**
>
> Plant Cycle: Biennial
>
> Soil Requirements: Prefers loam but will tolerate most soil conditions
>
> Light Requirements: Full sun, partial shade, or shade

and surgical incisions. Calendula poultices and salves are wonderful for helping to accelerate the healing of minor wounds, bruises, scratches, rashes, and sores. You can also use them on healing incisions to speed recovery.

Taken internally as a tea or tincture or in capsule form, calendula is antimicrobial and antiviral. It stimulates the immune system, calms the nervous system, and aids in liver function.

Growing your own: Also known as pot marigold, calendula is a sturdy annual that grows 12 to 15 inches high. The bright orange and yellow flowers bloom from early summer through autumn, closing up each evening and reopening in the morning. Deadhead throughout the season to encourage further blooming.

Calendula prefers full sun; it does well in just about any soil as long as it is well drained. The herb is easily started from seed. Sow directly in the ground in early spring, when the soil temperature has reached 60°F, or start indoors and transplant later. Space the plants 9 inches apart.

Harvesting and storing: Pluck the flowers in the afternoon, when they are just fully open. Place the flowers on paper towels in an area with good air circulation and out of direct sunlight.

Cautions: Calendula should not be used for pregnant cats. Do not use calendula on wounds that need to drain, such as abscesses; calendula is such a potent healer that it may cause the wound to heal too quickly, trapping the infection inside. Use only the flowers, as calendula leaves and stems contain minute amounts of salicylic acid, which is potentially toxic to cats.

> **GROWING AT A GLANCE**
>
> Plant Cycle: Annual
>
> Propagation: Seed
>
> Soil Requirements: Fertile, well-drained, pH 6.0–7.0
>
> Light Requirements: Full sun to partial shade

FRESH CALENDULA OINTMENT

If you have calendula growing in your garden, you can make a fresh ointment to speed the healing of minor cuts and scrapes.

Fresh calendula petals

Olive oil

Continued →

To make:

Crush the fresh flowers with a mortar and pestle until they are bruised and broken. Add just enough olive oil to create a paste, mixing together well. You can refrigerate any unused portion (it will keep for up to 3 days), but the ointment is most potent when fresh.

To use:

Spread the ointment over your cat's scrape. Reapply as necessary.

CALENDULA PASTE

If you don't have fresh calendula for making an ointment, try making this paste, which is also excellent for helping feline cuts and scrapes heal quickly.

1 part ground dried calendula petals

1 part cornstarch or arrowroot powder

Spring water

To make:

Mix together the calendula powder and the cornstarch. Add just enough water to create a thick paste. Store in a tightly sealed container in the refrigerator, where the paste will keep for up to 2 weeks.

Calendula (Calendula officinalis)

To use:

Spread the paste over your cat's cut or scrape. Reapply as necessary.

CARAWAY (*CARUM CARVI*)

Parts used: Seeds

Of historical note: In colonial times, parishioners often carried caraway seeds in small pouches to prayer meetings; they ate the seeds to curb their appetites and keep their stomachs from rumbling during silent prayers.

Medicinal benefits: Caraway seeds are well-known as kitchen seasonings, but they also help stimulate the appetite and ease occasional bouts of diarrhea and upset stomach. To use, grind or crush the seeds and sprinkle them on your cat's food.

Caraway (Carum carvi)

Growing your own: Caraway is a biennial herb that grows to about 2 feet in height. During its first season the plant produces a rich display of foliage. The following spring new foliage appears, followed by a tall stem topped by an umbel of small white flowers, which give off a dill-like aroma.

Caraway is easily grown from seed. It prefers full sun and a dry, light, well-drained soil. Sow seeds about 2 weeks before the last frost. Thin seedlings so that they are between 6 and 12 inches apart. Once established, the plants are drought tolerant and don't need much watering.

> **GROWING AT A GLANCE**
>
> Plant Cycle: Biennial, Zones 3–8
>
> Propagation: Seed
>
> Soil Requirements: Well-drained, fertile, pH 6.0–7.0
>
> Light Requirements: Full sun

Harvesting and storing: A few weeks after the flowers fade, the small seeds ripen and can be harvested. Harvest the aerial parts as the seeds turn brown. Be sure to get them before they fall on their own. Clip the stalks down far enough so that you can tie them together in bunches. Hang bunches upside down in a warm, dry area, placing a tray covered in paper underneath. After the seeds drop, allow them to dry completely for two weeks before storing them in tightly sealed containers.

Cautions: None.

CARAWAY MILK FOR UPSET STOMACHS

Got a kitty with an upset tummy? Try this stomach-calming recipe. In fact, make a cup for yourself and set out the extra in a dish for your cat. Serve up this recipe only for periodic bouts of indigestion, because the lactose in milk is not good for cats in large quantities. If your cat is lactose intolerant, substitute water for milk and pour the tea over her food.

1–2 tablespoons caraway seeds

1 cup whole milk

To make:

Crush the seeds with a mortar and pestle. In a medium-sized saucepan, bring the milk to a boil, stirring frequently so that it doesn't scald. Turn off the heat and add the crushed seeds. Cover and let steep for 20 minutes, then strain out the seeds.

To use:

Give your cat a small dish of the milk, and add the softened seeds to her food.

CATNIP (*NEPETA CATARIA*)

Parts used: Aerial parts

Of historical note: Catnip has been a favorite of felines for centuries. Its genus name, *Nepeta*, derives from the ancient Roman town of Nepeti, where the herb grew wild in abundance. In those times, the herb was thought to symbolize happiness, love, and beauty.

Medicinal uses: Catnip's leaves, stems, and flowers are filled with compounds that work in harmony to relieve muscle spasms, colds, fevers, diarrhea, and gas in cats as well as people. In cats, catnip acts initially as a stimulant, then becomes sedative. Drawn by its scent, cats chew on the plant to release its active chemical, nepetalactone. Catnip is also an excellent herb for high-strung cats with nervous stomachs.

Give your cat fresh or dried crushed leaves or a glycerin-based catnip tincture. Some people have had success dropping a few leaves in their cats' water bowls.

Growing your own: A perennial member of the Mint family, catnip grows easily in the wild and is hardy in Zones 4 to 9. You'll have to fence off the catnip plants in your garden to prevent them from being conquered by neighborhood cats, or you'll simply have to plant enough catnip so there is plenty to go around. Whatever you do, don't put the catnip in the midst of fragile plants in your garden, or they will surely be flattened.

Plant catnip in full sun; the more sun the plants get, the more nepetalactone they produce. Sow seeds directly in the ground in early to midspring, or start indoors and transplant in late spring. You can also propagate catnip from stem cuttings, which should be taken in spring or early summer and planted about 4 inches deep in soil. If you keep the soil around them moist, the cuttings should root within a week.

Harvesting and storing: Catnip should be harvested in late summer while it is in full bloom. The flowering tips of the plants are the most potent. Cut off the tops and leaves, or pull up the entire plant and hang it upside down to dry; either way, select a shady, dry area. Store the herb in an airtight container out of the sunlight—and out of your cat's reach.

Cautions: Wait until your cat is at least 6 months old before introducing it to catnip. Do not give catnip to pregnant cats.

> **GROWING AT A GLANCE**
> Plant Cycle: Perennial, Zones 4–9
> Propagation: Seed, stem cuttings
> Soil Requirements: Sandy, well-drained, pH 7.0–8.0
> Light Requirements: Full sun to partial shade

DILL (*ANETHUM GRAVEOLENS*)

Parts used: Aerial parts

Of historical note: The name for this tall, elegant plant comes from the Norse *dilla*, which means "to lull."

Medicinal uses: Dill is generally used as a stomach-soothing agent for cats. It can help relieve nausea and flatulence, especially when triggered by a sudden change in diet. The seeds are most potent, but there is plenty of healthy goodness in the foliage and flowers. Feed your cat fresh or dried dill, or give it in tea or tincture form.

Dill
(Anethum graveolens)

Growing your own: Dill is an annual herb that features large umbels of small yellow flowers that bloom from mid- to late summer. The plant's long, thin stalks reach 3 feet in height and should be staked for support.

Dill prefers full sun and well-drained soil. Sow seeds directly in the ground in early spring, after the frosts have gone. Space the plants at least 8 inches apart.

Harvesting and storing: Seeds are best harvested about two to three weeks after the flowers blossom. Cut the stalks and hang them upside down over paper towels in a warm, dark location. The seeds will fall as they dry. Give the seeds another few days to dry completely before storing them in airtight containers.

Cautions: Do not give dill to pregnant or nursing cats, except under the supervision of your veterinarian.

> **GROWING AT A GLANCE**
> Plant Cycle: Annual
> Propagation: Seed
> Soil Requirements: Fertile, well-drained, pH 5.5–6.5
> Light Requirements: Full sun

CARAWAY-DILL TUMMY-SOOTHING CAT SNACK

Try this herbal blend the next time your cat is suffering from stomach upset due to a change in diet.

2 tablespoons caraway seed

2 tablespoons dill seed

1 tablespoon valerian root

1 tablespoon dried rosemary

1 tablespoon dried parsley

1 6-ounce can tuna or chicken in water

3/4 cup cooked rice

3 tablespoons soy sauce

To make: Combine the caraway seed, dill seed, valerian, rosemary, and parsley and grind in a mortar and pestle. Place the canned meat (including the water), rice, soy sauce, and herb mixture in a blender or food processor. Mix well, adding rice or water to adjust the consistency to your cat's liking. Store the unused portion in a tightly sealed container in the refrigerator, where it will keep for up to a week. You can also freeze individual servings to thaw as needed.

To use: Feed your cat 1/4 cup of the mixture per day.

ECHINACEA (*ECHINACEA ANGUSTIFOLIA; E. PURPUREA*)

Parts used: Entire plant

Of historical note: Echinacea was a favorite herb in the medicinal arsenal of Native Americans, who were well aware of its potency. They used echinacea to treat everything from snakebites to burns.

Medicinal uses: Echinacea has tremendous benefits for the immune system, and it also works wonders for respiratory and skin conditions. Give your cat echinacea tea, echinacea tincture, or the fresh leaves, stems, and flowers. You can also apply echinacea as a poultice to relieve pain and swelling associated with insect bites and stings.

Echinacea
(Echinacea angustifolia)

Growing your own: This easy-to-grow perennial produces lovely pink-purple flowers from mid- to late summer. *E. angustifolia* prefers poorer soil that is not overly moist, while *E. purpurea* prefers richer soil and regular watering; both species grow best in full sun.

Echinacea is easily started from seed or by division. Echinacea seeds need to be stratified, so sow them in late fall. Space plants at least 1 1/2 feet apart. Echinacea will reach a height of 1 to 2 feet, and the flowers should be deadheaded to prolong blooming.

Harvesting and storing: Aerial parts—leaves, flowers, and seeds—can be harvested after the plant's second year. Roots can be harvested in spring or autumn of the plant's third year. Allow echinacea to dry in a warm location away from direct sunlight and with plenty of air circulation. Once dried, store the herb in an airtight container. Do not pregrind the roots; leave them whole until you need them, to preserve their potency.

Continued ➜

Cautions: Do not give echinacea to cats with abnormally functioning immune systems, such as cats diagnosed with diabetes or feline immunodeficiency virus (FIV), except under the advice of a qualified physician. In addition, note that many cats have a bad reaction to echinacea, including frothing at the mouth, crying, and hiding. Such reactions usually lessen in severity after the first-time dose.

ECHINACEA-CALENDULA HEALING POULTICE

This quick remedy is excellent for soothing the pain and inflammation of bee stings and minor burns.

1/4 cup fresh echinacea root
1/4 cup fresh calendula leaves
Spring water

To make:

Grind the echinacea and calendula. Add just enough warm water to create a paste.

To use:

Place a dollop of the paste on the wound. Change the dressing as needed.

EYEBRIGHT *(EUPHRASIA OFFICINALIS)*

Parts used: Aerial parts

Of historical note: Eyebright derives its name from its long-time use as a remedy for eye ailments.

Medicinal uses: If your cat has an eye that is weepy, red, and irritated, eyebright—either taken internally as a tea or tincture or used externally as an eyewash—can help clear up the problem. When used internally and externally, eyebright can help treat herpes virus infections, one of the most common eye infections in cats. As an anticatarrhal (mucus-clearing agent), anti-inflammatory, and astringent, eyebright is also helpful in treating upper respiratory disease. For best results, use eyebright in combination with immune-stimulating herbs such as echinacea and blood-cleansing herbs such as burdock.

Growing your own: Eyebright could be considered a robber baron of the plant world. This semiparasitic plant penetrates the roots of a host plant—commonly clover, plantain, or one of the many species of grasses—and absorbs from it the nutrients it needs to grow.

This small annual is delicate in nature, with weedy overtones. The tiny red or white flowers sprout in abundance on thin stems that are scraggily appointed with small leaves.

Eyebright requires a wild area removed from your cultivated garden. Eyebright does

Eyebright
(Euphrasia officinalis)

not transplant well and should be sown directly. To propagate, simply oversow a thin, grassy, moist area with eyebright seed in early spring.

Harvesting and storing: Gather the plant in late summer or early autumn while it is in bloom. Allow it to dry in a warm location away from direct sunlight and with plenty of air circulation. Once dried, store the herb in an opaque airtight container.

Cautions: None.

EYEBRIGHT EYEWASH

This easy-to-make remedy helps ease irritation and clears up any discharge coming from the eye. Be sure to wash your hands before and after treatment. To compound the healing effects, also give your cat an infusion of eyebright internally.

2 cups water
1 teaspoon dried eyebright

To make:

Bring the water to a boil. Remove from heat and stir in the eyebright. Cover and let steep 10 minutes, then strain. Allow to cool to room temperature.

To use:

Using an eyedropper, drip 2 drops of the solution in each of your cat's eyes.

CAUTION

Eye irritations may signal that your cat has a foreign object trapped in the eye, a tear in the cornea, or a more serious infection. Before treating your cat at home, bring it to a veterinarian for a proper diagnosis.

PARSLEY *(PETROSELINUM CRISPUM)*

Parts used: Roots, leaves, and seeds

Of historical note: Ancient Romans wore parsley garlands around their necks at banquets in the hope that the herb would soak up wine fumes and keep them from getting drunk. Europeans during the Middle Ages wore parsley on Good Friday to ward off evil spirits.

Medicinal uses: One of parsley's greatest attributes is its high vitamin content. It is full of vitamins A, B-complex, and C, as well as iron, calcium, and potassium. The root, which is high in potassium, can be used as a diuretic, laxative, and eyewash. Eaten raw or taken as a tea or tincture, the leaves can help alleviate bladder problems and freshen breath.

Growing your own: Parsley does well in most soil conditions in full sun to partial shade. Parsley takes a long time to germinate (typically 6 weeks). To speed up the process, soak the seeds in water for 24 hours before sowing. Sow seeds directly into the ground in early spring, when the soil has reached 50°F. Water the seeds frequently to help speed germination. Thin plants to about 8 inches apart.

Harvesting and storing: Fresh parsley is much more potent than dried, and you can snip fresh parsley as needed throughout the summer. To dry it, hang the plant, or lay the aerial parts on a screen in the shade. Crumble the dry leaves by hand and store in a well-sealed glass container.

Cautions: Do not give parsley to pregnant cats; use sparingly for nursing felines. Do not give parsley to cats diagnosed with kidney disease.

> ### GROWING AT A GLANCE
> Plant Cycle: Biennial
>
> Propagation: Seed
>
> Soil Requirements: Rich, moist, well-drained, pH 5.5–6.5
>
> Light Requirements: Full sun to partial shade

> ### THE INCREDIBLE EDIBLE HERB
> Because parsley is packed with nutrition, and because fresh parsley is so much more potent than dried, you may simply want to serve up your cat's meal with a parsley garnish. Parsley has a "green" taste that most cats enjoy, and your cat may eat it with no encouragement from you.

ROSEMARY *(ROSMARINUS OFFICINALIS)*

Parts used: Leaves, flowers, and stems

Of historical note: Rosemary has long been prized for its stimulating scent and pretty blue flowers. It is said that the flowers took on this beautiful hue when the Virgin Mary hung her legendary blue cloak on the branches of a rosemary bush. The ancient Greeks believed that wreaths of rosemary worn on the head would improve the function of the mind. Considered a symbol of friendship and remembrance, rosemary garlands are often worn at weddings and funerals.

Medicinal uses: This versatile antioxidant herb repels insects, relieves flatulence, and eases muscular and nerve pain. It helps ease the itch and dryness associated with eczema and soothes the soreness of arthritis. You can apply a rosemary poultice or a cloth soaked in a strong rosemary tea on your cat's arthritic joints to draw blood from the area and ease the pain. You can also give rosemary tincture internally to help your cat relax, especially after a scary or traumatic experience.

Growing your own: Rosemary prefers full sun and well-drained soil. This herb is tough to start from seed. I recommend propagating rosemary from stem cuttings, which should be treated with liquid rooting hormone. Keep the cuttings moist but not soggy until a strong root structure has formed.

Because rosemary is a tender plant, it must be brought indoors for the winter in climates cooler than Zone 8. I recommend growing rosemary in pots in these cool-climate areas. You can bury the pots in your garden during the summer and then dig them out and bring them indoors for the winter. Of course, you can also grow rosemary indoors year-round.

Rosemary benefits from a soil "fluffing" each year, which keeps the soil from becoming too tightly packed and preventing air from getting to the roots. Hold the plant gently by the stem at soil level and carefully

Rosemary
(Rosmarinus officinalis)

tip it out of the pot. Fill a bowl with lukewarm water, and dip the rootball in, gently rinsing off most of the old soil. Fill a new pot (or the old one, if the plant has not outgrown it) with fresh soil that has been dampened. Replant the rosemary, being careful to layer the roots with the fresh soil and spread them out evenly.

Harvesting and storing: Rosemary can be harvested at any time. To keep the plant healthy, don't take more than 3 to 4 inches off the end of a branch, and never more than 15 percent of the total plant at any one time. Let the trimmed branch dry; then, rub the needles off the rosemary sprig as you would take needles off a Christmas tree. Store the dried needles in a tightly sealed glass container.

Cautions: Do not give rosemary to pregnant cats.

> ### GROWING AT A GLANCE
> Plant Cycle: Tender perennial, Zones 8–10
>
> Propagation: Stem cutting
>
> Soil Requirements: Well drained, pH 6.0–6.5
>
> Light Requirements: Full sun

ROSEMARY WASH FOR BALD PATCHES

Adapted from 10 *Herbs for Happy, Healthy Dogs*, by Kathleen Brown (Storey Books, 2000)

This recipe is a quick and easy way to treat abrasions, bites, or any injury that tears the hair away. Rosemary soothes the pain, reduces inflammation, and promotes speedy healing.

2 teaspoons rosemary herb

1 cup water

4 teaspoons witch hazel

To make:

Infuse the rosemary in the water, following the instructions on page 6. Strain, then stir in the witch hazel. Store in the refrigerator, where it will keep for several weeks.

To use:

Saturate a sterile cotton pad with the liquid, and apply to the affected area. Repeat twice a day until new hair growth is well under way.

VALERIAN *(VALERIANA OFFICINALIS)*

Parts used: Roots

Of historical note: Valerian has had various roles in history. During the Middle Ages, for example, valerian was valued as a spice and as a perfume; during World War I, soldiers relied on the herb to cope with shell shock and battle stress. And interestingly, valerian attracts not only cats but also rats and earthworms.

Medicinal uses: Valerian root, a potent natural sedative, smells distinctly like a dirty sock. As unpleasant as this smell is to humans, cats are attracted to it. Valerian functions much like catnip: It is at first stimulating, then sedative. Valerian is extremely helpful in soothing jittery feline nerves, as might occur during a move or when a new pet is introduced to the household. Give ground valerian root in capsule form to your cat, or sprinkle it over your cat's food. You can also offer it in tea or tincture form.

Continued ➤

Growing your own: Valerian does best in humus-rich soil; it prefers partial shade but tolerates full sun or full shade. The plant typically reaches 3 to 4 feet in height.

Start seeds indoors in rich soil about eight weeks before the last predicted frost date. The seeds need light to germinate, so cover them with just a dusting of soil at the time of sowing. Keep the soil moist, and make sure the young seedlings receive plenty of sun. Transplant to the garden after the final frost has come and gone. Space plants about 2 feet apart. Valerian can also be propagated by division.

Harvesting and storing: Harvest valerian roots in the spring or fall of their second year. Wash off the dirt, then place them in a single layer on a tray or cookie sheet. Turn the oven to its lowest setting and put the tray inside, leaving the oven door open an inch or two. The roots are ready when they feel dry and hard (this will take several hours, depending on the size of the roots). Once thoroughly dried, store the roots in a tightly sealed glass container to preserve freshness. Grind the roots only when you're ready to use them.

Cautions: Do not give valerian to pregnant or nursing cats.

GROWING AT A GLANCE

Plant Cycle: Perennial, Zones 4–7

Propagation: Seed, division

Soil Requirements: Humus-rich, well drained

Light Requirements: Partial shade

VALERIAN FLEA-FREE CAT BED

Your cat will appreciate the calming effects of this valerian-based pillow, as well as enjoy the absence of fleas in bed.

1/4 cup ground valerian root

Pinch ground rosemary

2 tablespoons dill seed

Thin cushion with a zippered slipcover

Combine the herbs. Distribute the herb mixture in the cushion's slipcover evenly, making sure that there is a uniform layer beneath the cover, then zip shut. You will need to fluff the pillow every week or so to make sure the herbs are evenly distributed. The herbs should be changed once a month, or when they stop releasing a scent.

Note: To make a more comfortable cat bed, remove some of the cushion's stuffing, making a soft hollow for your cat to lounge in.

Breaking Your Cat's Bad Habits

Lura Rogers

Illustrations by Rick Daskam

Introduction

For many of us, cats are our friends and playmates, our most trusted confidants, and our best mood elevators. They keep us amused with their antics and help us cope with the daily stresses of life.

But cats aren't always models of perfect behavior. They aren't born with instant manners. In fact, some cats create more mayhem, mischief, and madness than we can tolerate.

Cats are quite different from dogs. They have no desire to please the "leader of the pack." They don't strive for approval and praise. They are both independent and intelligent, which leaves the frustrated cat owner with a challenging task. But must you put up with a cat's bad habits? Absolutely not! With patience and care, a cat can be trained as well as a dog. It's simply the approach that's different.

The History of Your Cat: Understanding Feline Fancies

Somewhere around 40 million years ago, the first animal to resemble the modern house cat roamed Earth. Similar to today's cat in size and general appearance, with slight differences due to environmental adaptations, this ancient animal proved to be an adept hunter. Research indicates that our household tabby (known by scientists as *Felis domesticus*) is a descendant of the African wildcat (*Felis libyca*).

The first domestic cats appeared around 3500 B.C. in Egypt. By 1500 B.C., cats had earned elevated roles in Egyptian religion. The Egyptians even worshiped a cat deity named Mu. Cats became valued and sacred members of Egyptian society; they not only received special treatment in life but also were included in afterlife mummification rituals.

The Truth about Cats and Dogs

The biggest mistake cat owners make when trying to teach good behavior is assuming that cats learn in the same manner that dogs do. Wrong. Although they are both our furry friends, cats and dogs are two distinctly different species.

Dogs are pack animals that seek a well-defined pecking order. In a dog's mind, there must always be a "top dog"—an alpha dog (usually you, the owner)—who rules the household. Everyone else (people and other pets) then fall into a specific chain of command as perceived by a dog.

Cats, on the other hand, are colony dwellers. Each member has its own role, but no particular cat is in control. There are no alpha cats in the feline way of thinking. That explains why sometimes your cat ignores you.

Feline Behavior Modification: Psychology 101

To correct misbehavior, you need to think a bit like a cat. One of a cat's greatest priorities is the hunt. It's instinctive. Your cat's ancestors survived by hunting small game. Given the opportunity, today's housecats are great hunters of mice, small rabbits, birds, and bugs. They have an innate hunting drive. Watch closely as a mother encourages her young kittens to hone these stalking skills. She may let them chase her waving tail; she may demonstrate for them the proper pouncing technique. Cats of old hunted for survival; cats of today hunt for fun. Watching your kitten play with toys, you can see it practice and improve its stalking and hunting techniques.

Also note that cats have a tendency to use their paws while capturing their prey and that they deftly attack the neck of their victims to immobilize them and prevent injury to themselves. Just by watching your cat play at hunting, you can see that its clever ability to plan and strategize gives it an edge over creatures that depend wholly on physical endurance.

A second important aspect of turning a bad cat into a good cat is your approach to correcting a misdeed. One of the cardinal rules of cat training is: *Never physically punish your cat.* This includes hitting, whacking, throwing, or unnecessarily restraining it. This will result in fear and mistrust of you and fuel a cat's defiant nature.

The Fine Art of Deterring and Distracting

When your cat starts clawing the arm of your cherished upholstered chair or chews a gaping hole in your favorite sweater, you need to react quickly—and appropriately. As emphasized earlier, cats will not respond to punishment. You need to deter and distract them so they cease the misdeed and adopt a more acceptable type of behavior. There are several effective ways to stop a cat caught in the act of misbehaving:

· **Surprises.** Cats hate to be surprised. Shouting "No!" or "Hey!" or clapping your hands loudly will often surprise cats, causing them to stop what they're doing. Most will decide that their antics are not worth the bother of dealing with an obnoxiously loud human.

· **Loud noises.** Rinse and dry an empty aluminum soda can and insert a few pennies. Give it a shake when your cat starts to misbehave. Cats hate loud noises.

· **Finger snapping.** Most cats will be curious enough to stop what they're doing and pay attention to you.

· **Hissing.** If you want to tell your cat that you are displeased, what better way than with cat language? Mimicking a cat's angry hissing may help it understand that this behavior is not acceptable.

· **Water.** Squirt your cats with water from a spray bottle or toy squirt gun. Keep this water "weapon" handy so you can spritz them in the act. A little water won't hurt them or your surroundings.

· **Blow at the cat.** When your cat gets jealous of a good book or another person and won't stop pestering you, simply blow in its face—not too hard, but not too gently, either. Most cats *hate* this, and they'll readily retreat after two or three tries.

Litter Boxes: Hitting the Mark

It's unfortunate but true: According to research done by the American Animal Hospital Association, behavior problems, not medical conditions, top the list as the number-one reason cats are euthanized. And house soiling—urinating and defecating outside the litter box—reigns as one of the most prevalent behavior problems.

A cat's decision to start doing her business outside the litter box may be due to a medical condition, deliberate misbehavior, a change in the household that causes her stress, a dirty litter box, or the introduction of a new type of litter. It pays to be a cat detective and find out what's triggering this litter box avoidance.

FIVE TRAINING COMMANDMENTS

1. **Start early.** Begin teaching proper behavior to your cats when they are kittens. If you have adopted an adult cat, begin the training as soon as you bring the cat into your home. Old habits are hard to break in stubborn-minded felines.

2. **Be consistent.** Always use the same voice commands and hand gestures so you do not confuse your cat.

3. **Never use physical punishment.** Never hit your cat. This only breeds fear and distrust of your outstretched hand.

4. **Don't treat your cat like a dog.** Remember that cats are not dogs, so don't apply the same training principles to them.

You will never be the alpha cat, the leader of the pack. Your cats will not do everything in their power to please you because they consider you simply another member of their colony. You will, however, be able to lay down some general rules for the house.

5. **Work with your cat's unique characteristics.** Recognize that within the feline population, cats possess different personalities. Customize your behavior training to each cat in your household.

CATPROOFING YOUR HOUSE

Remember the Scouting motto to "be prepared"? It's a handy motto to follow as a cat owner. You can reduce a lot of kitty misdeeds if you spend some time removing feline temptations from your house.

It's a win-win situation. You're happy, the cat's happy, and you both can spend more time enjoying each other's company. Here's my handy checklist for catproofing your home:

· Keep breakable items on unreachable surfaces.

· Make sure the furniture cats can jump on is stable.

· Keep dangerous objects out of reach.

· Install childproof latches on cabinets.

· Keep food in sealed containers.

· Keep washing machine and dryer doors closed.

· Do not defrost meat or dairy products unattended on countertops.

· Keep toilet lids down to keep cats from drinking the water.

RULING OUT A MEDICAL PROBLEM

If your cat is relieving himself outside the litter box, your first step must be to rule out a medical problem, such as a digestive or urinary infection. These medical conditions are not always serious, but they may make it uncomfortable for your cat to climb into the litter box or may cause your cat to suffer from incontinence. Symptoms of common urinary and digestive problems include:

· Diarrhea

· Mucus or blood in the stool

· Blood in the urine

· Straining to urinate

· Excessive thirst

If you notice any of these symptoms, or even suspect them, take your cat to the veterinarian immediately. It is wise to confine your cat in a small area or enclosed room while she recovers from a urinary or intestinal disease. This gives her privacy and reminds her that her litter box is nearby. Just make sure she has enough room to sleep. And keep fresh bowls of food and water available, in the corner of the room opposite her litter box.

Continued ➔

DE-SCENT REMEDIES

If your cat has had an "accident," it's important to neutralize any trace of odors that may tempt it—or another cat member of the household—to relieve itself in that location again. Many deodorant sprays simply cover up the odor to human noses, but a cat will smell right through the spray and think that the spot is still acceptable as a bathroom area.

Vinegar is a good neutralizer to use on urine-soiled areas. There is also a good variety of scent neutralizers available at pet stores, but make sure to get one that acts on the actual chemicals of the smell, not one that just covers it up. If the soiled area is a carpet, you should steam-clean it as the last step before bringing the rehabilitated cat back into the environment.

KEEPING A TIDY LITTER BOX

Being the fastidious and picky animals that they are, cats do not appreciate a dirty litter box. Some cats tolerate more than others, but they all have their limits. Cleanliness is especially important in a multi-cat household, even if each cat has his own litter box.

MESS CAUSED BY STRESS

Psychological stress is often the cause of litter box problems. Cats are, by nature, place oriented. They feel most comfortable surrounded by familiar smells and sights. They need a safe haven. Any change in your cat's environment can trigger a stressful reaction. Loud noises, the addition of a new pet or new person to the household, or a move to another place can make your cat feel uneasy and threatened. Even remodeling or redecorating can upset a cat.

If stress is the cause of your cat's poor litter box behavior, you should try to eliminate the stressor. If that's not possible, as may be the case when you've adopted a new pet or moved to a new house, you'll need to help your cat adjust to the new environment. Do your best to help the cat feel that she is in a safe place. Talk to her in a soothing voice as often as possible (even if she's hiding under the couch and refuses to come out). Make sure that her favorite toys and scratching posts are readily available.

Don't punish your cat for not using the litter box; punishment will simply cause her even more stress. Instead, make her feel at home; play with her and talk to her. Keep the litter box area clean. Thoroughly clean the areas in which she has relieved herself. Especially in multi-cat homes, it is important to make sure that all animal "accidents" are fully cleaned and neutralized to prevent other animals from joining in. Set a new object, such as an upside-down washbasin, over that location, or block it off with a baby gate, to discourage your cat from using it again. Do not place an object you value, such as a piece of furniture, over that location—should there be future accidents, you may have to throw it out. And if your cat is relieving herself near the litter box, be careful not to obstruct passage to it.

If your cat is sometimes unable to get to her litter box because the door is closed or dogs or other animals prevent passage, she may give up and begin using another place. Try to accommodate her needs by putting an extra litter box where she can use it without the other animals around, or provide her with a new location that offers constant access, privacy, and protection.

MOVING ADVICE

Moving is an intense stressor for cats. To prevent litter box problems in a new home, don't move your cat and the litter box until you've moved most of the rest of your things—especially your own bed and your furniture. Have some of the cat's favorite toys or her bed readily in sight in the new place. Then move the cat and her litter box at the same time. Put the litter box in the new place you've chosen for it, and confine the cat to that area for a few hours, Spend some time with her there before giving her free range of the new home.

A CHANGE IN LITTER OR LOCATION

A change—subtle or abrupt—can rattle a cat enough to make her refuse to use the litter box. As mentioned earlier, cats are creatures of habit. The simple act of switching litter brands can cause some cats to go elsewhere. The same holds true for relocating the litter box.

In general, most cats prefer the clay, unscented type of litter. Many tolerate the clumping type. Although more pricey, the clumping type is easier to clean, because you remove only the soiled parts, and I think it controls odor better. If you plan to introduce a new litter to your cat, do so gradually. Mix some in with the current type and allow your cat to get used to it. Over a period of 2 to 3 weeks, add more of the new type of litter every time you change it, until your cat is fully adjusted and you can use the new litter unadulterated.

The more finicky your cat, the choosier she will be with her litter box locale. Moving the litter box can confuse or annoy your cat enough for her to avoid using it. She may not like its new location. Figure out environmental factors causing this no-show. The new location may be near a noisy object such as a dishwasher or in an area that gets a lot of foot traffic.

To avoid problems when changing the location of the litter box, first get another litter box, fill it with litter, and place it in the new location. Leave the old one where it is. Once your cat has grown accustomed to using both litter boxes, remove the old one.

BEHAVIOR-INDUCED SPRAYING

If your cat is deemed in good health and the litter box is kept clean and in the same location, odds are good that the cat is deliberately bypassing his bathroom to hit your walls, floors, and furniture.

Spraying is a territorial marking behavior of cats. It is most prevalent in cats that have not been spayed or neutered, especially males. Spraying involves directing a stream of urine onto a vertical surface, including walls and furniture but especially around windows and doors. It occurs more frequently when there are other cats outside, near the house. Your cat may feel the need to "defend" his turf. He may be jealous of a new kitten in the household, your new live-in partner, or an outdoor cat hanging about the yard. Even the presence of other animals' scent can induce spraying—for example, if your cat picks up their scent on your clothing. (If your cat is prone to this type of behavior, after you've spent time around other animals, change your clothes as soon as you get home, before your cat has a chance to get near them.)

TO SPAY OR NOT TO SPAY

Remember, the best way to keep your cat from spraying is to have your pet spayed or neutered. Spaying and neutering reduce hormonal spraying of urine by as much as 90 percent. In addition, it has been shown that spayed and neutered cats live much longer, healthier lives than their "unfixed" brethren.

If you're still reluctant, let me respond to some common reasons for not spaying or neutering:

My cat will miss out on the opportunity to experience motherhood. Like most animals, cats do not eulogize the miracle of birth. They function instinctively, and they probably are much happier if they don't have needy, fussing kittens to take care of.

But all my friends said they would adopt her kittens! Many of your friends, though filled with good intentions, are volunteering a hypothetical home. Do they live in an apartment? Even if their current landlord does not mind, will they be moving during the cat's lifetime? Consider how many children they have and the ages, their financial ability to provide proper veterinary care, and how much time they will have to spend at home with the new "baby." Kittens need lots of care, more than some people realize. Envision yourself as an adoption service, and ask yourself how seriously they have thought about the commitment.

Gee, we can't afford the spaying surgery right now. How about free? Or sharply discounted? Many community organizations concerned with feline overpopulation offer free or low-cost surgeries. Check with your local humane society, a private shelter, or your veterinarian. In the long run, you will save money because your cat will be healthier.

But Fluffy never goes outside! Aside from the spraying, which knows no bounds and may actually be more of a problem for unaltered indoor-only cats, consider the determination of a cat in heat. Once Fluffy hits puberty, outdoors is going to look a lot more interesting, and she will be looking for a way to get out for a night on the town. It takes only a few minutes outside for the damage to be done, and then you have new problems. If your attitude is that you have a male cat and it's not your problem, remember that hormonal motivation for spraying and many other behavioral problems increase with sexual activity.

TEN STEPS TO TOILET TRAINING YOUR CAT

Say good-bye to litter box cleaning! Yes, it's true: Cats can be trained to use the toilets in your home. For you, that means no more buying litter or scooping out smelly litter boxes. Of course, not every cat will tolerate toilet training. But if you have a young, willing cat and a little patience, it can be done.

The golden rule of toilet training a cat: Go slow. Some cats learn quickly; others never do. Be patient.

1. **Prepare the scene.** Leave reminder notes to members of the household to keep the toilet lid up and the seat down. And always leave the door to the bathroom open when the room is not occupied.

2. **Encourage the cat to relieve itself near the toilet.** Place the litter box next to the toilet. Leave it there for at least 2 days.

3. **Gradually raise up the litter box.** Stack something sturdy under the litter box so it is raised by an inch or two. Continue to raise it every few days until it is at the level of the toilet. If at any time your cat seems unhappy or resistant to the change, take it down a level and leave it there for several days.

4. **Rig the toilet for cat litter.** Find a bowl that fits under the seat and will sit inside the bowl of the toilet. I used a double-boiler pan with a lip that rested on the sides of the toilet bowl. This made for easy removal for cleaning and for when humans needed the toilet. (You can be creative here. Find something that works for you, but just make sure it's easy to remove and sits securely.)

5. **Remove the litter box.** Remove the litter box and fill the bowl in the toilet with your cat's regular litter. Don't feel discouraged if your cat resists it at first. Just go back to step 3 and give it some time. Trying to force your cat to do something she's uncomfortable with will just make her mad and leave you with an unpleasant mess.

   Try to be around as much as possible during the first week of training. She needs your encouragement and praise.

6. **Assist with paw placement.** When your cat goes in to use her new bowl of litter, watch the position of her feet. She will most likely either try to sit entirely in the bowl or place her two front paws up on the seat. The more paws she volunteers to put on the seat in the beginning, the better luck you will have. As she gets ready, gently encourage her to place her paws on the seat. If she starts out with all feet in the bowl, encourage the front paws first. Once she does this on her own, work on placing her back feet on the bowl.

   Always be very gentle and talk to her in a soft, reassuring voice. When she does this properly, reward her with a small treat or petting.

7. **Reduce the amount of litter in the bowl.** Once she has the hang of it, begin to leave less and less litter in the bowl. Remove 1/2 to 1 cup per day or two, stopping if she resists using the bowl. Once she is using it with only 1/2 cup or so of litter, you are ready to move on to the next step, which is close to full training.

8. **Use water instead of litter.** Instead of putting litter into the bowl, add a few tablespoons of water. Each day or two, add a little more water. Progress as slowly as your cat's habits demand.

9. **Remove the bowl.** When the bowl is half full of water, it is time to remove it. Your cat may not be comfortable with this, and you may have to replace the bowl of water for a few days, but keep trying. Once she goes in the unaltered toilet, you have reached success!

10. **Celebrate!** When your cat uses the toilet properly, praise and pet her warmly but calmly. Forget the celebratory flush. Cats hate loud noises, so don't congratulate her for using the toilet by immediately showing her how to flush, or the long training may go down the drain—literally!

The Furniture Scratcher

Your cat loves to scratch. In order to understand how to modify her behavior, you must understand why she does it. Cats scratch for a variety of reasons, one of which is plain enjoyment. Scratching also provides an outlet for your cat to mark her territory. There are glands in her paws that leave her scent behind when she scratches. In cat language, it's

Continued ➜

saying, "Hey, this is my couch." Scratching also keeps her claws in shape. Overgrown, neglected claws can get snagged in carpet and cause pain or injury.

So, instead of trying to make her stop, redirect your cat toward more suitable scratching outlets. You'll save your furniture and keep your cat happy.

Again, punishment is not the solution. A cat's urge to scratch is too strong. If you punish your cat, she will most likely wait to claw your furniture until you're not around. And there's a good chance that she will become afraid of you.

Instead, provide your cat with her own scratching furniture. Congratulate her each time she sharpens her claws on it. She will quickly learn that the couch belongs to you, but that nice block of wood or carpeted scratching post is 100 percent her property to shred.

SCRATCHING SOLUTIONS

Scratching is a wonderful form of exercise for a cat. It works and stretches her front legs and manicures her claws. If your cat goes outside and likes to climb, a good scratching post inside can help her get ready for the big tree hunt. If she is an indoor cat, I highly recommend a cat gym to facilitate appropriate climbing as well. It will very likely save your furniture from being treated like trees!

Indoor cats should have at least one acceptable outlet for their scratching desires. Scratching posts are sold in pet and department stores and can be relatively inexpensive. Be sure to pick one that is secure. It should have a sturdy base or be heavy enough so that it won't tip over. If it topples or sways under her pull, she won't use it again. The post should be tall enough to allow her to fully extend, so that she can stretch. Its surface should not be substantially different in texture from the fabric on your furniture or living room rug. Many cats particularly enjoy posts covered in sisal (a thick, natural fiber rope). Sisal shreds into a fine mess, which means that you'll have to do some sweeping up, but your cat will be very happy.

You can make your own scratching post or surface by wrapping sisal around a block of wood and attaching it to a base or the wall, or by duct-taping or stapling an old piece of carpet to the wall or a door frame. If the cat has already begun to destroy a section of the wall, you can cover the space with a nice rectangle of carpeting and she will most likely love the addition.

Place the post near the area your cat most likes to scratch, perhaps next to the couch or by the basement door—wherever the most damage has been done. To increase your chance of success, offer as many scratching alternatives as possible.

Many cats will recognize a scratching post for what it is without any help from you. Other cats, however, may require a little coaxing. To teach your cat to use the scratching post, you can:

- Spend your playtime by the post, and attach toys to it. Play chase-the-string up and around it, so her claws dig in and she can experience it by accident.

- Rub some catnip onto the new post.

- Place the post near her favorite sleeping area; when she wakes up, she has a suitable spot for her full-body scratching stretches.

- Add your scent to the post by mock-scratching it yourself; this will also show her your interest in the new structure. Do *not* pick up her paws and show her what to do. She'll find that quite insulting.

A scratching post should have a sturdy base and be tall enough to allow your cat to extend fully.

Curtain Climbers

So, what do you do if you discover you have a mountain climber for a cat? You know the type—loves to scale the vertical landscape of curtains and draperies. The thicker (and typically the more expensive) the fabric, the better the chance she'll dig in and start her Mount Everest training regimen. A spray bottle may be the surest deterrent to this determined climber.

Kittens are notorious drape and curtain climbers. If you don't stop the behavior early, you'll soon have a full-grown, full-weight cat shredding the curtains and destroying your curtain rods on a regular basis.

If the threat of a spray bottle isn't effective in keeping your cat off the curtains, you can also booby-trap the curtains so that they're no longer so appealing:

- Use tension rods for your curtains, so that your cat's weight will pull them down as she pulls. A few spills will persuade her to stop.

- Use the thinnest thread that will hold the drapery to attach it to the rods. Again, the weight of the cat will break the threads and make the fabric fall. To reinforce the unpleasantness (and reduce the number of times you'll have to restring the drapes), attach a small aluminum can with a few marbles or pennies inside in an inconspicuous place. It will make a racket as the drapes fall, and your kitty won't like that one bit!

Biting and Scratching: Taming the Tiger

Sometimes even the most affectionate cat can become irritated and take a swipe at you or other members of the household. Understanding the motives behind this occasional—or constant—aggression can help you build a better relationship.

If your normally timid or loving cat suddenly becomes aggressive, it may signal a medical problem or injury. Check with your veterinarian. Your cat may have an injury that she does not want touched and may be in pain when you pet her. Or she may be irritated or aggravated by another health-related issue.

Some cats nip very lightly as a sign of affection. It is up to you whether this is acceptable or not. Take into consideration the fact that you may not be the only person around her. Her nips may not be appreciated by other family members or visiting friends. Teaching your cat not to nip people is especially critical if you have small children or infants in the house.

Other cats take to biting and scratching because they're upset or feel unsafe. Environmental changes can heavily influence your cat's behavior. Moving, new family members, or the addition or loss of other pets can influence a cat's mood just as much as a human's. When they feel unsafe or are disturbed by changes in the normal environment, many cats become defensive of their territory and try to take their security into their own paws by becoming physically aggressive.

Other attacks may be due to your cat's issue with its food, water, grooming time, or sleep. As an instinct, some cats are protective of their food as a result of previous competition over food or lack of feeding in a past home. Grooming and nap times leave cats especially vulnerable. Some cats may feel uncomfortable being disturbed while they bathe, and many do not like to be awakened by strange people.

If a dog or other intimidating animal is a guest in your home, or if your cat is wary of a human visitor, be sure to give your cat her own space and do not let the "intruder" sniff out all of her favorite spots. This could lead to resentment-filled scratch attacks on you or on others and, possibly, an unnecessary fight between your cat and the visiting animal.

BREAKING THE BITING HABIT

Immediately react to any unwanted bite or scratch by letting out an exaggerated yelp or "No!" Do not respond with physical aggression. That will only reinforce the nipping, biting, or scratching behavior of your cat. As soon as she has understood that she hurt you, speak in a calm, soothing voice. If she continues to act aggressively or play rough, yell out another "Ouch!" and stop playing.

Ignoring your cat's attempts to get your attention with scratching or biting is the best way to get her to give up. If you feed into this need for negative attention, she will learn that this is a great way to be the center of attention. Turn your back on her, and do not make eye contact. Pretend she isn't there, unless she is hurting you; then make a loud noise or say "No!" If the situation is not solved by these reactions, quarantine the cat in a carrier or the bathroom for a few minutes after one of these aggressive outbursts (like the time-out meted out to a small child who misbehaves).

Cats that seem motivated by sheer nastiness need to have their actions curbed by more than a yelp. A loud noise such as pennies being rattled in a can or clapping along with a shout can be a powerful deterrent. Be sure to make these noises at the moment the aggressive behavior starts, or your cat will not associate the consequence with the action. This is another situation where a spray bottle comes in handy.

TIPS TO SAVE YOU FROM SCRATCHES

- Never pull your hand away from your cat quickly during an attack. She will interpret this as play and chase it, and you will reinforce her behavior.

- Don't play rough with your kitten. When her claws get sharper and her jaws get stronger, it won't be so cute!

- Don't bother your testy cat while she eats, bathes, or sleeps.

- Pay attention to her tail while you are petting her. If it begins to move from side to side in quick, short movements, this is a sign she's ready for you to stop. If you continue, she may lash out and flee. It's better to quit while you're ahead.

- Don't ever react to an attack by hitting your cat. She will feed into your aggressive attitude and will assume that this is your personality. Remember, there is no such thing as an alpha cat in the feline mind.

WHEN YOUR NEW CAT BITES AND SCRATCHES

If you have just adopted a cat and find that it is aggressive, and especially if it also does not like to be touched, the cat may have experienced trauma in the past. Give her plenty of time to adjust, and start her out with a small room of her own so that she can get used to the new house and neighbors. Often this initial fear and distrust is a result of the stress of being adopted into a new home, especially if there are other pets.

To make your new cat's introduction to the new home easier, and to help you bond with her, spend some time alone with the cat in her special space several times a day. Sit in a far corner of the room and talk softly to her. Ask if she would like to come over. Have a toy or two with you, but nothing that requires quick hand movements or a noise more than a quiet bell. If she has experienced abuse, she may be intimidated by a moving hand and by loud noises.

Don't pick her up or corner her. Let her move toward you on her own. This may take a few days, but it is important to let her make the decision herself. She has already been transplanted to a new environment at least once, so now it is her right to take the time she needs to get used to it.

Offer treats, and when she feels comfortable, pet her lightly. If she scratches or bites out of fear, respond with a catlike screech. She will recognize this as a signal of pain rather than a human threat.

AN ARGUMENT AGAINST DECLAWING

Unfortunately, some people choose to have their cats declawed because they are unwilling to take a few simple steps to teach them when and where it is okay to scratch. Rather than invest the time, they make the decision to remove the claws while their pets are still kittens.

Part of the blame belongs to old practices. A decade ago, declawing was practically an automatic procedure for indoor cats. Now we have much more knowledge about the benefits to cats of retaining their claws. And any cat can be taught to scratch only on acceptable surfaces.

Continued ➜

Declawing is the amputation of the cat's digits at the first joint. It is physically painful and emotionally terrifying. Claws are a cat's main line of defense. Even if she is an indoor cat, there is always the possibility of her accidentally getting out. For a cat inexperienced in the outside world, even a few minutes can be terrifying and downright dangerous if she has no claws. She is unable to fight off predators or other cats and cannot climb trees to escape. Her ability to run is also slowed because she can't use her claws for traction.

I urge all readers to use this measure as an absolute last resort, and preferably not at all.

GIVE YOUR CAT A PET-I-CURE

Trimming your cat's nails is another good way to prevent damage to you and your belongings. Some cats are more resistant than others at manicure time, but the younger they are when you start the process, the more cooperative they will be. If you have an older cat, you may need a tag-team approach to nail clipping—at least the first few times, until she gets used to the experience. One person should hold the cat while the other handles the paw and the clippers.

Get your cat used to having her paws touched by gently rubbing the pads behind the claws. Do this for at least a week before attempting a trimming. Press gently on the center pad of her paw to extend the claws.

You will see a pink section toward the toe joint. This area is called the quick. If you accidentally clip this part, your cat will be in pain and bleed. These unfortunate incidents can lead to infections and a loss of any future clipping cooperation on the part of your cat, so be careful!

When clipping your cat's claws, cut just the sharp tip, avoiding the pinkish quick.

All you need to do is cut the sharp tip off the end of her nail. I recommend that you clip only about halfway between the end and the quick. If you are unsure or if your cat is too hard to handle on your own, leave the manicure to pet professionals. Most veterinarians and grooming services offer nail clipping at reasonable prices.

DEALING WITH FELINE SQUABBLES

One problem that many pet owners encounter is disagreement among cats. It is important not to have too many cats in too little space. After all, each cat needs a private place to call its own.

Cats have a wide range of verbal communication, and it's normal to hear an occasional hiss, growl, or air swat among cats that play together. You shouldn't be alarmed by these small squabbles unless they are particularly violent or chronic.

"Verbal" communication among your cats is natural and necessary for setting up a mutual code of rules. Hissing, growling, and an occasional air swat are normal even between cats that usually play, sleep, and eat together. It is possible for cats' relationships to be changed, either positively or negatively, by external stressors such as a move, the addition or subtraction of pets, and other events.

And remember, cats do not want to be treated equally. Each wants you to tend to her individual needs and personality. Giving each cat his own dose of special treatment (such as offering a "secret" treat when the others aren't around) helps keep resentments from forming. If possible, each cat should have his own litter box and his own food dish, and especially his own bed or special nook.

Toilet Paper: The Great Confetti Machine

Some cats regard toilet paper as a marvelous, irresistible toy. After enjoying the show of water spinning and cascading down the toilet bowl, they turn their devious attentions toward shredding a roll of toilet paper.

Here are my tips to help the Save-the-Toilet-Paper Foundation in any cat household:

- Get a covered tissue dispenser that hangs more than halfway over the paper.

- Place the toilet paper on the spindle so that the paper rolls out on the inside, between the wall and the roll, and doesn't dangle temptingly on the outside.

- Balance a plastic cup of water or a small can with marbles or pebbles on top of the roll. When next the cat comes to pull at the toilet paper, she'll be either doused with water or frightened out of the room by a giant noise.

- Make sure spare rolls are kept in a safe place out of paw's reach. Some cats love to rip through the plastic bags to get to their new toys that leave streamers galore. Once she's done it, she'll do anything to get at that "toy" again.

Table-Walking Tabbies

Scoot! Get down! Hey, what are you doing up there? Are these familiar phrases to you and your cat? You're in good company. Cats are height seekers, which explains why they can be found walking across kitchen counters, prancing across high bookshelves, tiptoeing on stair banisters, and tightrope walking on curtain valances.

Meanwhile, we look at their antics in horror and disgust. And secretly, we harbor a little fear that their nimble movements will fail them and they will fall and injure themselves.

There are several ways to deter your cat from leaping up to places where it doesn't belong. Success comes from a little preplanning on your part.

If you're away from home a lot and don't have the time to spend spying on your cat, dissuade your counter climber by covering off-limit surfaces with aluminum foil. Mold the foil around the areas of the couch, chair, shelf, or other pieces of furniture that seem particularly attractive to your cat. Cats aren't fond of digging their claws into or walking on this shiny surface. When you remove the foil, crumple it into a ball and your cat will find it an absorbing toy! (Supervise this playtime to ensure that your cat doesn't try to eat the aluminum foil.)

Double-sided tape is another good deterrent. You can buy this in craft stores and in carpet shops. It is useful on any surface where it is harder to use aluminum foil and that won't be marred by the adhesive, such as door frames, windowsills, and bookshelves. The tape is also less obvious and looks better, though it will need to be replaced as fur and dust stick to it and it loses its effectiveness.

For the persistent kitchen-table walker, take a few cookie sheets with raised edges and fill them with a little bit of water. When your cat leaps onto the table, its paws land in this minipool. It will quickly learn that there are better places to perch.

Taking the Bite out of Chewing

Inappropriate chewing is often associated with teething puppies, who need to massage their tender gums and give their new teeth a workout. But cats can also be champion chewers. If you're not paying attention, their chewing attacks can destroy appliance wires and cords, as well as plants.

There have been a few times when I've gone to dial my phone, only to get no tone and discover the cord severed. My first cat loved to munch on my speaker wires. Many of my houseplants have sacrificed once lush leaves to a munch-minded feline.

Not only is chewing a bad behavior, but it also can be downright dangerous. Cats can be shocked by live wires from electrical cords or become ill from eating poisonous plants. The solution: Survey your home's interior very carefully. Apply cayenne pepper or a citrus-based repellent (available at pet stores) to cords and plants your cat targets. You can also coat wires and cords with pet-deterrent creams and sprays or rub on the juice from a freshly cut citrus peel. If these options don't work, try securing all wires or running them under and behind things to keep them out of your cat's reach.

POISONOUS PLANTS

You don't need to be a horticulturist to have cats, but knowing safe plants from dangerous ones can save their lives. Here's a list of some of the more popular—but poisonous—houseplants that all cat owners should banish from their homes and yards:

- American mistletoe
- Azalea
- Buttercup
- Ficus
- Foxglove
- Horse chestnut
- Hyacinth
- Hydrangea
- Iris
- Jack-in-the-pulpit
- Lily
- Lily of the valley
- Morning glory
- Nightshade
- Onions and chives
- Ornamental tobacco
- Poinsettia
- Poison hemlock
- Poppy
- Rhubarb
- Rubber plant
- Sweet pea
- Tomato vines
- Tulip

Many cats love to chew, especially on houseplants. Be sure that none of your houseplants are poisonous to cats. To satisfy your cat's chewing obsession, you might consider setting out a cat-friendly plant or two for her to munch on.

If your cat displays any of the following symptoms of poisoning, take her directly to your veterinarian:

- No appetite
- Acute diarrhea
- Repeated vomiting
- Swollen tongue
- Tender or painful abdomen
- Convulsions

You might consider growing a couple of plants especially for your foliage-seeking feline. You can grow a tray of grass (premade cat grass beds can be bought, or you can make a simple one from an aluminum brownie pan with soil and some seed), or pick up a catnip plant for your cat to consume.

Roam Control—Escapees!

For the indoor cat, one taste of the outside world can be enough to inspire her to devote a great deal of her time to figuring out a way to get back out there. The best way to prevent escapes is never to let it happen in the first place.

If it's too late for that, preparation is key. Never open the door if you are unable to restrain the cat. If you are carrying something or need to prop open the door, enter the house first and then confine your cat to a smaller room before bringing in the groceries or shopping bags.

Continued ➔

The San Francisco S.P.C.A. (Society for the Protection of Animals) offers this suggestion to thwart escape attempts: "Enlist the help of a friend to hide outside the door with a hose and spray attachment and have him or her spray the cat when you let it out." You may need to do this several times for it to work, but remember that the more times it gets away with it, the harder it will be to get it to stop trying. Some cats are just plain relentless.

Fear of your cat wandering too far from home is another good reason to spay or neuter: A spayed or neutered cat is less prone to roaming.

DOGS

Housebreaking & Training Your Puppy

Pat Storer

Illustrations by Jeffrey Domm

The Basic Nature of a Dog: Leader or Follower?

Dogs are pack animals and by nature need to live in a group situation. A dog's position in the pack can be at only one of two levels: the leader or a follower. Except for very rare individuals, dogs really don't care if they're the top dog or not, but they do need to know what their position is at all times. It doesn't take a puppy very long to accept its new human family as its pack. The real question is, will he be a leader or a follower?

If a dog isn't sure whether he's the leader or a follower, he will try to be the leader until you show him differently. Being the leader is a hard job for a dog. If you show him that you are in the number one position, your dog will easily accept being a follower. With that he gets the security of belonging to your pack.

A Dog's Senses

In order to do a good job of training your dog, it's important for you to understand how a dog experiences his world and what makes a dog "tick." A dog has the same senses as a human, but they are different in several ways.

YOUR DOG'S INSTINCTS

An *instinct* is a behavior pattern that is inherited and not learned. An example is suckling. All mammals are born with the instinct to nurse. They don't have to be taught to do it. Dogs—including your puppy or dog—have inherited strong instincts from their wild ancestors. You may see your dog exhibiting any of the following common instincts.

- **Guarding**: Your dog may guard your yard, your home, or a favorite toy.
- **Pack instinct**: This is the instinct to group together. If your dog is with several other dogs, he will have the instinct to behave as if he's a member of a pack.
- **Prey drive**: Prey drive is the instinct to chase a moving object. In the wild, dogs displayed this instinct when they hunted. Herding, driving, and chasing are all parts of prey drive.
- **Digging, barking, and marking**: These are all natural behaviors of dogs and are familiar to most dog owners.

SMELL

Your dog lives in a world rich with a multitude of scents that we cannot even imagine. The part of her brain that receives messages about scents is over 1,000 times larger than ours. Not only can a dog tell the difference among hundreds and hundreds of smells, but she can also remember them. In addition, a dog's sense of smell is so finely tuned that she's able to notice a very small amount of a particular odor, even if there are many other odors present. For example, your dog is able to pick out your scent on the one object you've touched from all of the others in a pile of identical objects.

HEARING

The dog can hear all of the frequencies that a human can hear—and well beyond. As you will have noticed if you've ever owned a dog before, dogs are able to move their ears in the direction of the sounds they hear. They tune in to different things in sound than humans do.

SIGHT

The dog's sense of sight is sharp when it comes to viewing familiar shapes and moving objects. His ability to distinguish fine details is not as well developed as that of humans, though. A dog is not good at picking out differences in movement or shape, for example. I've tried walking past dogs that knew me with a limping gait or my hair in a much different style, and they have always acted as if they didn't recognize me until I spoke or they could catch my scent.

Earning Your Puppy's Respect, Trust, and Confidence

Your dog needs a leader, and that's you. A puppy must learn self-control and self-discipline. He will learn this as you help him to be obedient. The puppy needs lots of affection, but you must not let him have his way when what he's doing isn't right. He will learn to follow your guidance because he wants to be obedient. You teach your puppy obedience by repeating the same thing over and over and giving praise when he gets it right.

BE CONSISTENT AND FIRM

Decide what behaviors you will allow and what you won't allow from your puppy. The best way to correct a problem behavior is to prevent it in the first place. Don't put your puppy on your lap while you're on the couch if you don't want him to get on the couch as an adult. Never give the puppy a command that you can't or don't enforce. An example is telling a dog "Down" when he jumps on you. Are you going to squat down and put the dog in a down position? Does your dog know the word *down* yet? Is "down" what you really mean, or do you mean "off"? The main thing to remember is that you're trying to communicate with your dog and teach him that you don't want him jumping on you. A better solution would be to say "Off," take the dog's feet and remove them from you, and praise him when his feet are on the ground.

GETTING THE MESSAGE ACROSS

Your dog is a thinking creature, but she doesn't think with words the way you do. In order for a dog to understand us, we have to get a message to her in a language she will understand. We do that by showing her what we want her to do, praising her when she does it right, and correcting her when she does something we don't want her to do.

There are certain dos and don'ts we must remember when living with a dog:

- Praise your dog when she does something you've asked her to do and does it right. Remember to give praise only when the dog earns it.

- Use treats only for training.

- Don't let your dog be confused about who's top dog. For example, don't let your dog go in or out of a door ahead of you or without your permission.

- Don't lose control and get angry or rough with your dog.

- Don't play dominance games such as tug-of-war with your dog. This puts you and the dog on the same level and encourages aggression.

Leash Training

You will need to train your puppy to walk with a leash attached to his collar as soon as possible, so that you can take him to relieve himself. Start out with a soft buckle collar. Let the puppy get used to the feel of it.

Next, attach a short leash to the collar, and let the puppy get used to dragging it around. You must always be within sight of the puppy when he's dragging a leash, because it might get caught and tangled. You can play with the puppy while he drags the leash by putting a little tension on its end.

Now pick up the leash and follow the puppy. If the puppy is obstinate, show him a treat and put light pressure on the leash as you try to guide the puppy to walk on your left side. If he does a good job, reward him with a treat. Don't drag, choke, or force the puppy into perfect position. All you want at this stage is for the puppy to get used to being restrained with the leash. Once he is, you can use the leash whenever you work with your puppy.

USING THE PROPER LEASH AND COLLAR

A soft nylon buckle collar and leash are all you will need in the way of equipment to start out training your puppy. You will add a chain slip collar later, when you begin obedience training.

slip collar

buckle collar

The slip collar on the left is safe and useful only when it is properly placed on your dog, as shown in this drawing. Use it only when you are present, your dog is on a leash, and you are holding the leash. The buckle collar on the right is a good choice for everyday wear. Your dog's rabies and/or identification tags can be attached to the ring.

Crate Training

Wild dogs want to keep their dens clean, so they pick toilet areas away from where they live and sleep. Domestic dogs have inherited this instinct from their wild ancestors. To housebreak your puppy, all you need to do is to reinforce this natural behavior. House-breaking and crate training go together. The crate becomes your dog's "den." That's why crate-training your dog will help in housebreaking him. When you have unruly visitors, his crate is the one place your dog can go (or you can put him) for privacy. Very small children may unintentionally injure or irritate your dog by pulling his hair, tail, or ears. They can walk over his feet and tail, try to climb on his back, and throw objects at him. Your dog has the right to be treated with respect, so the crate is the perfect place for him while they visit.

Crate training is a method of giving your dog a place of his own to sleep, gnaw on a chewable treat, or just get some privacy. The crate feels very much like a den to your dog. When you're going to take your dog with you in a car or truck, or even if you go on vacation, you can take along his crate and he will feel right at home, anywhere.

THE RIGHT-SIZE CRATE

Choose a crate that's large enough for your puppy to enter, turn around in, and lie down in comfortably. The first crate for your pup should be just a tiny bit larger than he is. If the crate is too large, your puppy can divide it into a sleeping area and a potty area. When your puppy is reliably house trained, he's ready for a larger crate. Eventually you will need a crate big enough to accommodate the full-grown dog.

THE RIGHT LOCATION

Pick a spot that will belong to your dog. That's where you'll place her crate. The spot you choose should be in a relatively quiet place where the dog can go to rest. There should be good circulation of air around the crate, but it shouldn't be in the direct path of a heating or air-conditioning vent. The sun shouldn't shine directly on the crate, or the inside could get very hot.

STEP-BY-STEP CRATE TRAINING

1. The first few times you work on crate training, your pup should be a little bit hungry. Place a light-colored towel in the crate. Pick a word you will always use when you're going to put the puppy in the crate: *crate, kennel, pickles* . . . any word will do. Whatever the word is, your dog will soon understand that it means "Go get in your crate." Eventually, you can use that word to tell the dog, from anywhere in the house, to go to her crate—and she will!

2. Show the puppy a food treat, making sure she's really paying attention. Kneel down on the floor in front of the open crate and hold her buckle collar with one hand. Show the treat again, then toss it into the crate. Give your "get-in-the-crate" word. The dog will run into the crate to get the treat.

3. Close the door, but leave it closed only for a minute or so. Don't overdo the length of time. If the dog is quiet, give her praise. Don't open the door if your puppy starts pawing or whining. Open the door only when she stops whining or pawing. Opening at the wrong time will reinforce the behavior you don't want.

4. Let the puppy out, and with another treat repeat the exercise. Over a period of a week or so, increase the time she stays in the crate.

Continued →

MAXIMUM "CRATE TIME" FOR DIFFERENT AGES	
Puppy's Age	Maximum Time in the Crate
8 weeks	3 hours
12 weeks	4 hours
16 weeks	5 hours
6 months	7 hours
1 year	8 hours

Note: Just because your dog is able to stay in his crate for a longer period of time than what's recommended doesn't mean you should keep him in the crate that long.

CRATE TRAINING DOS AND DON'TS

Never use the crate as punishment. If you're angry at your dog and want to banish her, calmly put her in the crate, without scolding her. If you scold your dog as you're putting her in the crate, she may become confused. She may think the crate is for jail time and learn to dislike it, or she may think you're scolding her for going into the crate.

Don't feed your dog in the crate. You can put water in the crate during the day if you must keep the dog confined there for more than a couple of hours.

Be sure the crate is in an area where there's good ventilation. Some short-faced breeds (Chow, Pug, and Boston Terrier, for example) or those with heavy coats (such as the Malamute) need extra holes drilled in plastic crates so that air will circulate properly.

Housebreaking

The more time you spend with your new puppy or dog, the faster she will learn not to urinate or defecate in the house. A puppy is just a baby and must learn what you expect of her. An older dog may have to learn new habits, depending upon how she was housed and trained before.

WHAT DOESN'T WORK

You have probably heard someone say, "If the puppy makes a mistake, rub his nose in it," or, "Drag him to the site of the disaster, point at the puddle or pile, and scold him." Don't use either of those methods. They don't work. All you'll do is frighten the pup and make a mess for yourself to clean up. A dog is so upset when he is being scolded that he can't even begin to understand exactly what you're angry about.

WHAT DOES WORK: 6 SIMPLE STEPS

1. **Watch for the signs.** Be with your puppy as much as possible so that you can learn his different sounds and behaviors. You will soon notice that the puppy behaves in a certain way immediately before he begins to relieve himself—if you see your pup start to circle and sniff the floor, he's almost certainly looking for a place to potty. Watch for this cue and use it to your benefit. You will have only a few seconds to get the puppy outside to the place you want him to use. Don't scold him if you aren't fast enough.

2. **Pick out a potty area.** Pick a spot (in the yard or wherever you choose) that you want your puppy to use as his potty area. Place a piece or two of his stool in that spot. This will act as a cue to the pup. Take him to that spot immediately after eating. Praise him

gently the instant he starts to relieve himself. The praise must be quiet and calm. You don't want to get the pup so excited that he forgets what he started to do. When he's finished relieving himself, shower him with praise and let him play for a few minutes in another area.

3. **Be patient.** Don't play with your pup until he relieves himself. If he doesn't relieve himself within 10 minutes, put him in his crate and try the whole thing over again in 20 minutes or so.

4. **Keep the potty area clean.** Clean up the area every day, leaving a small piece behind as a reminder for a few days. Once you're sure the pup thoroughly understands what the potty area is for, clean up the area completely each day.

5. **Maintain control.** If your puppy is very small, you may have to carry him to the potty spot. Otherwise, try to take him out wearing a collar and leash. Never let the puppy follow you without any type of restraint. Keep a leash and collar by the door.

6. **Introduce the puppy to the house in small steps.** Confine the pup to a single room at first, preferably one with a tile floor. Put a baby gate across the entrance, if possible. You must be able to observe the puppy when he's out of the crate, so don't lock him in the bathroom. The best time to allow the puppy freedom in this room is after he has properly relieved himself outdoors. When the puppy is reliable about staying in the crate, staying in the single room, and relieving himself when he's taken outside, you can gradually allow him more freedom in the house. Don't give the puppy too much freedom too fast. He may find a nook or cranny at the other end of the house that he considers a perfect spot to relieve himself. Go slowly with your puppy and you'll have a more reliable pet.

TRAINING SCHEDULE FOR A 10-WEEK-OLD PUPPY

Playtime can follow any potty break or be part of free time.

6:30 A.M.	Upon awakening, potty break.
7:00 A.M.	Breakfast, followed by potty break—put out water. Free time in one room.
9:30 A.M.	Potty break. Nap in crate, followed by potty break.
noon	Lunch, followed by potty break. Free time in one room.
2:30 P.M.	Potty break. Nap in crate, followed by potty break.
6:00 P.M.	Supper, followed by potty break. Free time in one room.
7:30 P.M.	Pick up water bowl until morning.
9:00 P.M.	Potty break, followed by bedtime.

HOUSEBREAKING TIPS

Whenever your pup or dog is loose on the floor, spend as much time as you can with him. If he starts to relieve himself, lift him gently and carry him to the potty area. Don't yell at your dog, no matter what happens and no matter how much you have to clean up. Here are a few tips to keep your puppy on a fairly regular schedule:

- Feed only dry food until the puppy is house trained. Canned food has a high moisture content and added chemicals that can affect the frequency of your pup's urination.

- Feed on a regular schedule. Take the puppy out immediately after each meal.

- Watch for the puppy to awaken from a nap. Take him out right after a nap.

- Take the puppy out between meals and naps so that he doesn't go more than 2 hours without a potty break.

- Take the puppy out first thing in the morning and last thing at night.

NIGHTTIME POTTY BREAKS

If you're very lucky, your pup will sleep through the night. But if she doesn't, she will need to be taken outside once during the night. This is a rough time for both of you. Your puppy needs to relieve herself during the night because her bladder isn't large enough for her to wait until morning. In a few weeks, this will pass.

If possible, don't wait until the puppy is whining continuously to be taken out. This could cause a whining problem you will have to correct later. Try to get up when you hear the puppy stirring restlessly and before she whines. Take her outside, on the leash and collar, straight to the potty spot. Don't act impatient or the puppy might think she's doing something wrong. If she relieves herself, praise her calmly. If she doesn't relieve herself within the normal length of time, take her back to her crate, put her inside, and go back to bed without a word.

Paper Training

Some people prefer to use the paper-training method of house training. This is convenient for apartment dwellers and for those with little access to an outside area. The puppy is confined to a small area in which the whole floor is covered with newspaper. This should be a noncarpeted area. Since the whole area is covered, the puppy will have no choice but to relieve himself on the paper.

After several days, begin removing some of the paper. The puppy has become used to the idea that he should relieve himself on the newspaper, and he won't eliminate on the area of the floor that's bare.

Eventually, you might use a large litter pan or plastic blanket box with a paper liner in the bottom. Once the puppy is dependably eliminating in the litter pan, you can gradually give him more access to the house. Some people don't use the litter-pan method, but without a litter pan, the dog may think any paper object on the floor is a fair target. I know one dog whose aim was so accurate that he used a TV Guide that was on the floor.

Paper training is often the only house-training alternative. Remember, though, that any newspaper or magazine lying on the floor could be a "target" for your dog.

Common Housebreaking Problems

Here are some common housebreaking problems, and suggestions for dealing with them.

EXCITED URINATION

Dogs that are on the submissive side may squat or lie on their sides or backs and urinate when they get excited. This usually happens when they first see you or even a stranger. It's hard to believe, but this is a compliment from the dog. She's telling you that you're much higher on the ladder of importance than she is. She's also saying that you have her devotion and she will look to you for direction. Most dogs grow out of this, but occasionally a very submissive adult will continue this through her life. Sometimes it helps to teach the dog games, such as retrieving, that build self-confidence. The act of leaving you and going out after the toy is the key factor here. The dog is making a decision to leave your side and pursue an object she wants to catch.

RELIEVING HIMSELF IN THE CRATE

If your puppy or dog urinates or poops in his crate, here are some possible causes and suggested solutions:

- The crate is too large. Get a crate that's just slightly larger than the dog so that when he's lying down, he covers nearly all of the floor.

- The dog or puppy was previously kept in a crate, possibly with a wire bottom or papers in it, and expected to relieve himself without going for a walk or outside. If this is the case, begin to take the dog out for walks to the potty spot very frequently. Give extra praise when he relieves himself outside.

- You're leaving the dog in the crate too long. Get him on a shorter schedule.

- The puppy is sick. Your veterinarian might wish to check for urinary infections or disorders or an upset in the digestive system. There is a defect in some dogs that causes leakage of urine when the bladder gets partially full.

- The puppy or dog won't relieve himself in the potty area and then does relieve himself in his crate when you bring him in. Have you ever caught your dog in the act of relieving himself where he shouldn't have been doing so? Did you scold him? The puppy may think that you don't want him to relieve himself at all, so he waits until you're out of sight to do so.

> **CRATE-CLEANING TIP**
> When you have to clean up a mess in the crate, wash it thoroughly with soap, then rinse with a mixture of 1 part white vinegar and 1 part water.

MARKING

If your dog urinates on your bed, your dad's shoes, or your sister's umbrella, he's trying to let everyone know he's claiming that territory. This dog is confused about just who is in control in the house. You need to straighten him out. This rarely happens with a dog under 8 months of age, and nearly always happens with a male. Females may mark before, during, and after they come into their heat cycle, however.

Continued →

If marking is caused by *hormones*, neutering or spaying the dog will usually cure the problem. I recommend neutering or spaying before the dog is sexually mature.

If marking is a *dominance* issue—the dog is confused about who is in charge—a few brush-up lessons on the leash will remind him that he is not the dominant member of the family. If he hasn't had basic obedience lessons, it's time to get started, right away. Either way, if you use a firm, fair hand in training, the dog will normally stop the behavior. This also works on males in some toy breeds that are notorious for marking if they are not neutered.

Basic Obedience Training

If at all possible, enroll your puppy or dog in an obedience class. Training should be a happy time for both you and your dog. If your dog is treated harshly, she will be afraid or will resent the training sessions. Your dog must eventually understand that she must mind you. Most dogs are followers looking for someone to lead them. Your dog will learn to respect you by the way you treat her and the way you reward her when she has done something that you like.

Sometimes you can unintentionally reinforce undesirable behavior in a dog by saying something in the wrong tone of voice. If the meter reader comes up to the fence and your dog is barking and barking up a storm, and you say—in a nice tone of voice—"Now, that's okay, he's a friend," what your dog is hearing is, "It's good that you're barking. You should always bark at that person." If you want the dog to stop doing something, you must always get her attention first, by calling her name. Then tell her that you don't like what she's doing. Be as simple as possible, with something like: "Sandy, no bark." What the dog understands is, "I don't like what you are doing. Don't do it." A simple "Good dog" in a voice that's pleasant is sufficient to let the dog know she has done something that has pleased you.

There are countless methods for teaching a dog obedience. The method I'll describe here is the most pleasant for both trainer and dog. You will use treats as rewards at first, but eventually you will get the response you want from your dog for praise alone. Your goal is for your dog to work for praise and loving. She will soon learn when you're getting ready to teach her something new.

For the sake of description, I've named the imaginary dog in the next section Maple.

ATTENTION

Before you can get your dog to learn something new, he must be paying attention to you. To get your dog's attention in early training, you must make it worth his while.

Attention: Use a treat to teach your dog to make eye contact with you. Soon he will automatically look to you for directions. Praise him when he does it right.

Attach a leash to your dog's collar. Hold the leash in your left hand. Face your dog and put a tiny treat between your right thumb and index finger. Say, "Maple, watch me." Stroke the treat along the dog's muzzle, past his nose, and up to the outside corner of your right eye. If the dog makes eye contact with you, quietly tell him, "Good dog," and give him the treat. Repeat this several times. Soon, you'll be able to eliminate the stroke along the muzzle to your eye; your dog will give you eye contact just with the command, "Maple, watch me."

SIT

The sit can be easily taught with a treat and a little physical help. Your puppy should be in a relatively calm mood to teach her the sit. With her standing in front of you and facing to your right, show her the treat, say "Sit," and move the treat to her nose and slightly over her head, at the same time lightly pushing down on her rump. If the dog sits, immediately give her the treat and praise. Keep the praise calm so that you can repeat the exercise several times. Within a few tries, the dog will sit without the push on her rump. Then you can tell her "Sit" and not offer the treat until she does. This usually takes only one lesson to learn. If possible, try to have several practice sessions in one day.

Sit: When you teach your puppy to "sit," hold a treat above her nose and use light pressure on her rump. Don't forget to praise her when she does it right!

DOWN

Ask your puppy to sit, with the leash hanging down from her collar. Give the command "Down," stroking with a treat in your right hand from her nose and down her chest to the ground. At the same time, lightly tug the leash toward the ground. If the dog resists after several tries, you may need to lift her front paws from under her with your left hand while pulling down with your right. Don't forget to praise and give a treat.

STAY

This is a very important obedience command to teach your dog. If you ever see your dog entering a dangerous situation, such as crossing a busy road, you'll be happy you taught this.

With the dog in a sitting position, tell him "Stay," give a slight backward pressure to the leash, and pivot in front of the dog so you are

Stay: When you tell your dog to "stay," your hand should look like a solid barrier in front of his face.

facing him. Praise your dog if he doesn't move, then pivot back to his side. Repeat this several times, eventually lengthening the time and distance you are away. When the dog has mastered this in the sit position, you should teach him to stay in the down position using the same method.

HEEL

Obedience should always be taught with the dog walking on the left side of the handler. Since your dog already knows how to walk on a leash, you can easily teach him that "Heel" means to stay next to you without pulling or lagging on the leash. A good place to teach this to a puppy is along a wall or fence, where he won't have an opportunity to wander. Don't crowd him too much, however, or he may begin to lag behind or forge ahead.

Start out with the dog in a sitting position next to your left side. Tell him "Heel" and start off with your left foot, which will act as a cue. Also, give a light tug on the leash. Praise the dog as he stays next to you. Every time you stop, tell your dog to "sit"—assisting him, if necessary, with a slight pressure on his rump with your left hand and a slight upward movement with the leash with your right hand. Don't forget praise for everything your dog does right. When he has mastered the "heel" this far, add changes in your speed and direction, and circle around objects.

Heel: *Teaching your dog to "heel" along a fence or wall helps keep him moving straight ahead. Be sure there's ample space between your dog and the fence so he doesn't feel squeezed.*

COME

An important thing to remember is that when your dog misbehaves, you should never call her to you and then punish her. No dog in her right mind would come a second time!

Once your dog has learned to walk on the leash, put a longer line on her and let her wander and explore. Give the command "Come" and lightly tug on the leash. If the dog comes toward you, lavish her with great amounts of praise and even a treat. If the dog is confused or resistant, reel her in to you without being forceful, and praise her. Soon you can run with the dog on a long line and let her play. At unexpected times, give the command "Come" and praise the dog if she does. If she comes without the need for a tug, give her a treat also.

Solving Common Behavior Problems

Puppies and dogs can develop some behaviors that we don't like. Before you can find a solution, you must understand why your dog is acting this way.

AFRAID OF THE STAIRS

If your puppy will gallop up the stairs, and then stands at the top and refuses to come down, he's normal! Puppies are rarely afraid to go up stairs, because their balance seems to be fine in that direction. But when their head and front feet are facing down, they feel off balance, as if they're going to tumble down.

Solution: Put the puppy just two stairs from the bottom. Call him to you or show him one of his favorite toys or a tiny piece of his favorite treat. The puppy should easily master this short distance. Praise him with great zest. Gradually, over a period of many days, increase the number of steps until he has mastered them all. Be very careful, however, because stairs can be dangerous to puppies if they tumble.

Pups love climbing up stairs, but they may need training to learn how to come down.

CHEWING

All dogs, especially puppies, love to chew. Dogs naturally pick up and carry things in their mouths. The chewing desire is with a dog all through her life, but is strongest when she's teething, from about 5 to 10 months of age.

Solution: Collect a selection of chewing items that are safe for the puppy and "legal" for use in your home. Things you can buy include rawhide and nylon chew toys, knotted ropes, Cresite hard-rubber balls and tugs, and various other dog toys. Place all of the "legal" chewing items in a tub or box. Make sure the puppy knows that anything that isn't from this box is off limits.

Keep the box handy so that when the pup starts to chew on Mom's favorite chair, you can redirect her chewing urge. Scold only when you catch her actually chewing on something that's off limits. Tell the pup "No chew" in a firm voice as you hand her a "legal" item to chew. Praise the pup when she takes the item.

You can teach your puppy that only items from her own box are okay to use as play toys.

Continued ➜

Keep your eyes on the puppy when she's free in the house, until she's well past the critical teething stage. Don't stop watching her until you're sure that chewing is no longer a threat.

Specially designed nylon and hard-rubber chew toys massage your dog's gums and help curb unwanted chewing behavior.

MOUTHING

Mouthing is a dog's habit of putting her mouth on people and other dogs. It's natural for puppies, but it isn't pleasant to people. Puppies need to do a certain amount of mouthing of each other to learn just how hard they can bite in play. But you're not a puppy, and you shouldn't allow your puppy to bite or mouth you. This would put you on the same level as the puppy, as if you were her littermate. As she gets older, she may think she can be dominant over you.

Solution: If your puppy bites, even in a light way, give a loud, convincing "Ouch!" response. If she stops mouthing or biting, or tries to lick your hand, praise her. If she doesn't, repeat the "Ouch!" at the next bite. If the puppy doesn't seem to get your message that the biting is painful, grab her muzzle and say "No!" the next time she bites. If she stops, praise her and give her a chew toy. You must be consistent and never give up. The puppy will eventually learn the lesson.

BEGGING

This is one problem behavior that is created by people. Never give your dog treats when you're eating. No matter how much you would like to share your lunch with your dog, don't let his big brown eyes sway you to give in. Once you've started to give the dog food when you're eating, he will be relentless in begging from you and even other people. Your dog should receive all of his meals in one place or the same dish. Treats should be reserved for play and training times only.

Solution: If your dog has already developed this habit, you will have to resort to scolding him for something he now thinks is fine with you. If your dog is already obedience trained, you could use the "Stay" command when you try to retrain to stop the begging. When the dog begs, say "No!" and take him a reasonable distance away where you can still watch him. Put him at a "Stay," even facing away from you. If the dog breaks the "stay" and still tries to beg, repeat the same procedure. You must be consistent and do this no matter where he starts to beg. Putting the dog in the crate won't give him the correct message. Your dog won't learn that begging is no longer "legal" in your house. The crate shouldn't be used for punishment.

GETTING INTO GARBAGE

This is a problem created by putting tempting tidbits in the garbage and expecting your dog to ignore them. Remember, a dog's nose rules his head.

Solution: Empty the garbage often or keep it out of reach.

JUMPING UP ON PEOPLE

Dogs jump up on people to get attention. Puppies should be taught from a very young age not to jump. The main key in preventing and stopping jumping is not to give the puppy or dog any type of positive attention when she does jump. Don't pet her or talk to her in a way that she might misunderstand as approval.

Allowing a dog to jump up on people will eventually backfire and cause you trouble. The dog might be muddy and get someone's clothes dirty. The person may have his arms full of groceries, including eggs and breakable bottles. The person may be elderly or handicapped. In any case, it's not a good behavior to allow.

Solution: If your puppy is young enough, use a stern voice to say "Off!" as you take her paws off you and place them on the ground. Then praise the dog. If you see that the puppy is coming over and has that "I'm going to jump on you" look, give her a firm "Off" before she jumps and you'll be one step ahead. As she sits down, praise her. For a large dog, you can take a small step forward as she approaches and lift one knee to block her from full-body contact, at the same time giving her a stern verbal "Off." The minute she sits down, praise her.

For a dog that is resistant to the mild solutions above, I suggest that she be taught the "Sit" command. As the dog approaches, give the "sit" command and praise as she sits.

WHINING

Whining can become an irritating habit if it isn't corrected immediately. Spending too much time with your puppy can cause him to be overly dependent on you. He needs to learn to accept being alone, or without your attention, even if you're home or in the same room. Your dog may also whine when he needs to go out or when he's hungry.

Solution: If it's near the time the puppy needs to relieve himself, take him right out to the potty area. Return him to the same spot when he's finished.

If the dog is in his crate, be sure he has some toys to keep his interest. You don't want the puppy to think he's banished or being punished when he's in the crate.

If the puppy isn't in the crate, watch his body language when he whines. Is he trying to get your attention because he needs your help? Maybe his chew toy was taken by another dog or is behind a closed door.

WHINING FOR NO REASON

If you can't find any reason for the whining, ignore it completely. When it stops, you can take the puppy out of the crate and play with her. Never remove the puppy when she's whining, or you will reinforce the whining and it will continue—only stronger next time.

BARKING

Dogs bark for several reasons:

- They sense danger.
- They want something they can't get by themselves: food, water, a toy, a cat in the neighbor's yard, another dog.
- They're annoyed or bored.
- They're joining other dogs in song.

Solution: The first two reasons for barking can be corrected by changing the situation. In the case of the last two reasons, don't allow the dog to bark for so long that it becomes a habit. These are usually problems of an outside dog that has little interaction with his family. Such barking is irritating to almost anyone who hears it, and can cause problems between your family and your neighbors. A barking dog wants attention. Give him plenty of attention. Play fetch, or take him for a healthy jogging expedition before you go to bed. Both of you will sleep more soundly.

DIGGING

This is most often a problem with outside dogs that are bored. When you spend a lot of quality time with your dog, she won't be interested in digging. Dogs dig for several reasons. Terrier breeds were developed to dig out their prey. Other dogs have this instinct also, but to a lesser degree. All dogs have a keen sense of smell and can identify animals, insects, and even certain objects that are under the ground. They'll dig to get to the item.

Solution: If a dog digs to make a den, provide a doghouse or other "den."

If a dog digs to find cool earth to lie on and cool her body in hot weather, find a way to provide cool spots in the dog's pen.

If a dog digs for fun and out of boredom, spend more time with her. If you give your dog plenty of attention, she's less apt to be a digger.

EATING POOP (COPROPHAGIA)

Although it's disgusting for us to realize our dog has done it, this is a natural behavior for dogs, and common among many other animal species. In today's world, it isn't a healthy practice for the dog and it's not healthy for us to be around a dog that does this. Parasites and diseases can be easily transmitted by this behavior. Puppies are prone to this problem a little more than adult dogs are.

Solution: If you have more than one dog, put each one in the potty area separately. Clean up every little speck before you let the dog with the problem enter the area. Stay with him every minute, and scold him with a firm "No!" if he makes any attempt to eat his own feces. There are also products you can add to the dog's food or put on the feces that are said to stop the practice.

ESCAPING

A dog that's loose and out of control can cause huge problems for you, for other people and their property, and for domestic and wild animals. Escaping is also dangerous for the dog.

Solution: Before you ever leave your dog alone in the yard, check every inch of the fence and gates to make sure that there's no way the dog can find an escape route. Once a dog discovers that she can get out of the yard, she will continue trying, even if you repair every place she finds. Check for loose, rusted, or broken wire; cracked or rotted wood; easily opened gate latches; and gaps between the fence and the ground. Make sure that the fence is tall enough to prevent your dog from jumping over, and that it's constructed of a material that will keep your dog from climbing out. If the fence wire isn't buried in the ground, the dog may dig under it. The best way to cure escaping is to prevent it in the first place.

If the dog is continually left alone and isolated, she will become restless and bored. Dogs are intelligent; they know that the grass is greener on the other side if they aren't getting much attention at home. Also, if they aren't neutered or spayed, both males and females will go to all lengths to escape and find a mate. Neutering or spaying is a must for dogs that aren't going to be used for breeding.

Lots of play and exercise will satisfy and tire the dog and reduce the chances that she will search for a way out.

CHASING

Chasing is another natural behavior for dogs. Dogs also use the chase behavior in play. They love to chase and be chased.

Solution: Don't play chase games with your dog unless you both have been through at least basic obedience training and you have pretty good control of your dog. A dog that chases cars feels that the car is "running away" from him, and if he barks at the car and "chases it off," he feels like the winner. Your dog should never be loose and able to do this.

Building a Doghouse

Mary Twitchell

Illustrations by Alison Kolesar

Why Does My Dog Need a Doghouse?

Dogs are social animals; to thrive both emotionally and physically, they need human interaction. Doghouses, therefore, are not meant to serve as permanent living spaces. Dogs belong with their owner and their owner's family. Dogs are best housed indoors or in spaces with access to areas of family activity. Doghouses serve merely as shelters—within a fenced-in area—for canines that have been put outside temporarily.

Sometimes providing a private shelter for your dog is as simple as adapting your house or garage. If you live in a temperate climate, dogs can find shelter from adverse weather in the garage or other outbuilding or beneath a deck. Such adaptations are usually the easiest and cheapest solution, but they're not always ideal. Because dogs depend on their body heat to keep warm, garages and sheds are sometimes too cold, large, wet, and drafty in winter and too poorly ventilated in summer.

For owners who do not have an easy garage-and-yard or other setup, or for owners who want to provide housing that better matches their dog's needs, there are a number of doghouse options to choose from. These include crates, barrels, high-impact plastic houses, and wooden doghouses.

What a Doghouse Is Not

Although doghouses are designed to conserve the animal's body heat, they are not meant to shelter an animal from extreme cold or hot temperatures. Therefore, think of building a doghouse to protect your animal from wind, rain, and snow, but *not* from severe cold or intense heat. If you must put your dog outside during periods when extreme weather is possible, be sure that the animal has access to the moderated temperatures of your home, be it the basement, laundry room, bathroom, kitchen, or utility room.

Continued ➔

Most important, remember that a doghouse is a vacation retreat, a "room of one's own," a space for personal time; it is not a full-time, year-round shelter.

Buying or Building a Wooden Doghouse

Wooden doghouses are available commercially in a variety of styles (Cape Cod, Georgian, ranch) and sizes. There are, however, a few principles that should guide your choices:

- Size
- Entrance placement
- Roof design and materials
- Accessibility for cleaning
- Elevation
- Long-lasting, weatherproof floor supports
- Insulation

SIZING

The most common mistake in sizing a doghouse is to make the quarters too large. As far as dogs are concerned, bigger isn't better. A dog needs only enough room to enter the kennel, turn around, lie down comfortably, and stretch out without feeling the confines of his surroundings. If the kennel is roomier than this, the animal's precious body heat won't be sufficient to warm the space in winter. The goal is to make the house as comfortable and as small as possible for the size of your animal.

Also remember that young dogs grow. If you build a kennel before your dog is fully grown, it may be improperly sized. Postpone construction or build the shelter to the fully grown measurements of your breed.

The *inside* dimensions of a doghouse should be:

Length: 1.3 x length of dog from head to rear (not including the tail)

Width: 1.6 x dog width at the shoulders

Height: 1.5 x dog height at the shoulders

ENTRANCE SIZE AND PLACEMENT

The entrance to the doghouse should be 2 to 3 inches taller and wider than the dog measures at her shoulders. You may want to increase the width to 4 inches if you expect pregnancies. Openings any larger than necessary increase heat loss. Ideally, the dog should be able to look out from the front entrance while sitting or standing; she should not have to lower her shoulders to enter or exit.

The placement of the door opening is crucial. Do not center the door; instead, locate it off center. This allows the dog to curl up to the side of the entrance, keeping her out of the direct path of wind, snow, or rain, yet close enough to easily exit.

ROOFING OPTIONS

There are two types of roofs common in doghouses: a shed roof, or a simple sloping roof, and a gabled roof, which comes to a peak in the center of the house. Your dog's habits may dictate your choice.

The advantage of a shed design is that from her perch on the roof, the dog can see everything that is going on. She can also lie down out of the mud, stretch out in a dry place, or take a break from her nursing pups. The disadvantage of the shed roof is that it gives your dog a raised platform from which to get into trouble. If there are nearby fences to jump, for example, your dog may be tempted.

Do not use roll roofing or asphalt shingles as a roofing material if your dog is likely to relish time on top of the kennel. Asphalt roofing gets extremely hot in summer. Exterior plywood, painted or treated with a nontoxic preservative, is more appropriate.

Whether you choose a gabled or a shed design, the roof should overhang on all sides to ensure easy water runoff. You may even choose to substantially increase the overhang on one side to provide a shaded zone for your animal. Shed roofs should slope to the rear or side so that water runoff doesn't land in front of the door opening. Never build a perfectly flat roof; even the slightest slope discourages rain and snow from collecting.

ACCESSIBILITY

When designing your doghouse, consider how you will clean the inside. Bedding will need to be replaced periodically.

With a larger dog (hence larger doorways), it will be easy for you to crawl in; for a smaller dog, the opening may not be large enough. In this case a roof or a side wall should be hinged for ease of kennel cleaning, for spraying against ticks and fleas, and for removing the pups when necessary.

ELEVATION

The doghouse should not sit directly on the ground. The soil or grass under the kennel can easily become a breeding ground for fleas and ticks. And if your dog uses the adjacent soil for digging and burying, his excavations may cause rainwater to puddle. Soon your animal is living in a wet, unhealthy, soggy mess.

To decrease the collection of water and mud around the doghouse, I have included a floor support system in my designs. The supports raise the kennel a couple of inches off the ground. Cover the area around and under the kennel with a layer of pea gravel. As a further precaution, place the kennel on patio blocks, concrete blocks, bricks, cap blocks, or stones. The additional height will increase summertime ventilation beneath the shelter; the air space will also insulate the shelter from the cold ground in winter if protection, such as straw bales, is provided around the outside perimeter. However, do not raise the kennel so high that your dog has difficulty getting through the door opening.

If you do add blocks beneath the doghouse, space them at the four corners, then check with a 4-foot level to be sure they are level with one another. A tippy doghouse is hazardous, and if it is tipped away from the dog door, rainwater may collect inside.

WEATHERPROOF FLOOR SUPPORTS

The supports beneath the floor will be exposed to water and will rot if they aren't made of pressure-treated lumber. Pressure-treated wood (wood that has been impregnated with pentachlorophenol) will last 30 to 40 years when exposed to weather; untreated wood will last 10 years at best (although somewhat longer in dry, warm climates). Pressure-treated wood is toxic; use it only under the kennel where it is impossible for the dog to chew. Do not use it anywhere else in the construction.

INSULATION

Dog owners who know that people houses have insulation assume that doghouses should as well. They should not. The function of a doghouse is not to provide your dog with a warm place but to provide a dry resting place with a windbreak.

If you insist on insulating the shelter, remember that dogs may inadvertently rip fiberglass batting insulation, and pups may chew it. Besides, fiberglass is a major irritant. Rigid, extruded polyurethane board is a better choice and may be used to insulate beneath the floor and above the roof. It resists moisture and has a high R-value. Cut it to fit between the floor supports (joists), or add it between the joists and floor, nailing through the floor, into the insulation, and then into the joists below. For roof application, place the rigid insulation above the rafters and nail through the plywood roof and insulation into the rafters.

Building a Shed-Roof Doghouse

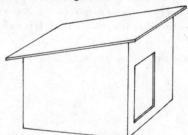

Dogs love to stretch out on the roof of a shed-style doghouse.

Tools

Circular saw	Electric drill with Phillips driver or Phillips
Hammer	head screwdriver
Jigsaw	1" drill bit
Safety glasses	Level
Tape measure	Paintbrush
Pencil	Sandpaper
Combination square	

Materials

A 4' x 8' sheet 5/8" CDX plywood

2 x 4 pressure-treated lumber

2 x 2 lumber

Exterior latex paint or nontoxic wood preservative (linseed oil)

Hardware

16d galvanized nails

2" sheetrock screws or 6d galvanized nails

3" sheetrock screws or 10d galvanized nails

Two 2 1/2" hinges or 1 piano hinge (optional)

A hook and eye (optional)

CONSTRUCTING THE FLOOR

1. Figure the interior and entrance dimensions of your doghouse on a piece of paper. With the circular saw, cut the floor from the sheet of plywood. Set aside.

2. To construct the floor support assembly, cut pressure-treated 2 x 4s to length so that they form a box to fit flush with the outside edges of the floor.

If the length of your doghouse exceeds 16 inches, cut an additional joist for a center support.

Lay the 2 x 4s on edge and nail them together with 16d galvanized nails.

USING THE ILLUSTRATIONS

The illustrations in this and the following plan are for a medium-size (30- to 50-pound) dog. You will have to scale the dimensions up or down to accommodate your animal by adding or subtracting rafters, studs, and floor joists.

---

3. Place the floor on top of the platform box, aligning the outside edges of the plywood with the outside edges of the 2 x 4 box. Nail or screw the parts together using 6d nails or 2-inch sheetrock screws. Be sure to countersink the nail or screw heads.

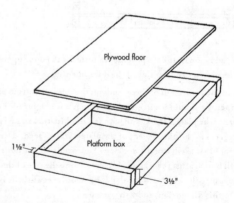

FRAMING UP THE FRONT AND BACK WALLS

4. For the back wall supports, cut a top and bottom plate from the 2 x 2s to the width of the floor.

Cut two vertical corner studs to the height of the wall minus 3 inches (to allow for the thickness of the plates).

If you are building a large structure, you may need intervening studs evenly spaced (or 16 inches on center if your doghouse is over

Continued ➜

32 inches wide). Screw or nail through the top and bottom plates into the studs with 3-inch sheetrock screws or 10d galvanized nails.

Stand up the back wall frame and place it on top of the floor so that its outside edge is flush with the edge of the floor. Nail or screw through the bottom plate and floor into the 2 x 4s of the platform box.

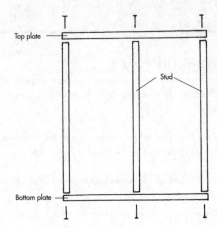

5. For the front wall frame, cut two corner studs that are 6 inches longer than the studs you have just cut for the back wall. Cut top and bottom plates to the same length as those of the back wall.

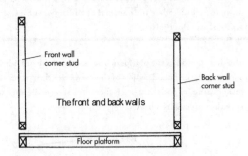

Cut two additional studs to provide framing for the door opening. These will be placed to either side of the door opening.

Mark out the placement of these studs on the top and bottom plates. The door opening should begin 4 inches to the left (or right) of the outside edge of the plates. Mark, and with the combination square, draw a line 90 degrees to the outside face of the plates. Draw a second line to mark the other inside edge of the doorway. Your studs for the door opening will butt against these lines. (To determine the size of the door opening, measure the width of your dog at his shoulders while he is standing. To this dimension, add 2 to 3 inches.)

On a level surface place the two plates so they face each other and nail or screw through the top and bottom plates into the corner and door studs.

The door opening will require a header. From a 2 x 2 cut a piece that will fit between the door studs. For proper placement of the header, measure the height of your dog at his shoulders while the dog is standing and add 2 to 3 inches. This determines the bottom edge of the header. Now nail or screw through the studs into the header. Check that the header is level.

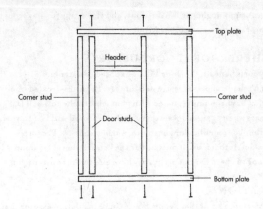

6. Stand the front wall up and place it on top of the floor with its outer face aligned with the edge of the floor. Screw through the bottom plate and the floor into the 2 x 4s of the platform box.

FRAMING UP THE SIDE WALLS

7. For each sidewall, measure the distance between the inside face of the front and back bottom plates. Cut the side bottom plate to length. Align the side bottom plate with the outside edge of the plywood floor and screw through the 2 x 2s and floor into the 2 x 4 platform box.

8. The top plates will need angled cuts at either end. Hold a length of 2 x 2 in place to span the distance between the front and back top plates. Along the inside edges, mark for the angled cuts.

Cut along these lines with the circular saw. Check that the top sidewall plate will fit before using it as a pattern for the second top sidewall plate.

Screw through the back and front top plates into the top sidewall plates.

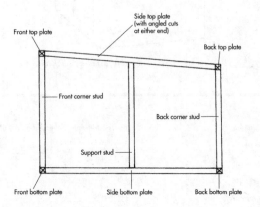

9. The number of vertical studs for the sidewalls will depend on the size of your doghouse. Support should be provided at 16-inch intervals. At the center of either sidewall, measure the vertical distance between the plates and cut two studs (one for either side). One end will be cut at an angle to match the slope of the top plate. Leave a square cut on the other end. Nail or screw the studs into place. Each stud will have to be toenailed into the bottom plate. With the level, check that the studs are plumb.

10. Again, depending on the size of your dog, you may need to add at least one intervening rafter between the front and back top plates. The rafter(s) will be the same length as the side top plates with angled cuts at both ends. Center and nail or screw the rafters into place. If the distance between the top plates exceeds 32 inches (as it may in house designs for multiple dogs), space the rafters at 16-inch intervals.

11. Cut the two plywood sides wide enough to cover the vertical framing and long enough to span the distance between the top of the top plate and the bottom of the raised platform. (Since the floor supports are made of pressure-treated lumber, they should be enclosed to prevent your dog from chewing them. Pentachlorophenol is carcinogenic to humans; it may also be to animals.)

PAINTING THE INTERIOR (OPTIONAL)

12. Before proceeding further, decide whether you will be painting the inside of your doghouse. If so, begin now while you have easy access to the interior. Use an exterior latex paint.

SECURING THE PLYWOOD WALLS

13. Screw or nail the plywood sides to the framing, being sure your hardware goes into the studs. If you miss a stud, retract the screw or nail and adjust the location.

14. The front piece should cover the edges of the plywood sides. Measure the height from the top edge of the front top plate to the bottom of the 2 x 4 platform box.

Once the front has been cut, mark for the door opening. Hold the plywood front in place, and on the inside surface, draw a pencil line along the inside of the door studs, bottom plate, and header. A more accurate method is to mark off the precise dimensions on the face of the plywood. Remember that there will be a 5 5/8-inch lip below the doorway to enclose the bottom plate, floor, and floor support system.

With an electric drill and 1-inch bit, drill holes in each of the four corners. Connect the holes with the jigsaw. Smooth the edges with sandpaper if necessary.

Paint the inside surface of the plywood (if desired) before nailing or screwing it into the studs. Remember to secure it to the door studs and header.

15. The width of the back wall should be measured from outside face to outside face of the sidewalls, and from the top edge of the top plate to the bottom of the raised platform.

Cut out the shape with a circular saw and screw the wall into the corner studs, top plate, and platform box.

ATTACHING THE ROOF

16. To determine the dimensions of the roof, measure the outside width and length of your doghouse, then add 6 inches to each for the roof overhangs. (The roof will overhang 3 inches on all four sides. If you wish to provide shade for your dog on one or more sides, increase these dimensions accordingly.) Cut the piece of plywood. Position the roof on the doghouse, check that it is in the proper location, then draw a line where the back wall and roof meet.

Remove the roof, and on the underside, where you've drawn the pencil line, mount the two 2 1/2-inch hinges or a piano hinge. (The hinge will allow you to inspect and clean the doghouse just by lifting the roof.) Before you set all the screws, set the roof back in place and test the hinging action to be sure you have mounted the hinges correctly. Remove the roof, finish setting the screws, replace the roof, and screw the second hinge leaf into the plywood of the back wall.

17. At the front of the doghouse, mount the eye on the undersurface of the roof and the hook on the front wall. This will ensure that the roof doesn't blow open.

18. If your summers are temperate and the doghouse will be placed in a shady spot, the roof can be covered with roll roofing. However, the asphalt roofing gets very hot if it bakes in the sun; you may prefer painting the roof or coating it with linseed oil.

19. For dog owners wishing to go the extra mile, trim can be added at the four vertical corners, where the plywood pieces meet, and around the door opening. Lattice, gingerbread, wood shingles, or clapboard sliding can also be added.

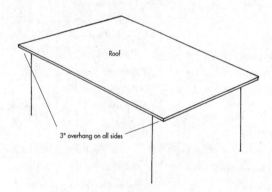

Roof

3" overhang on all sides

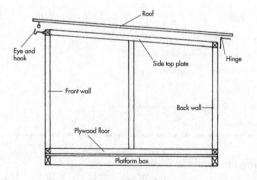

Roof

Eye and hook

Side top plate

Hinge

Front wall

Back wall

Plywood floor

Platform box

FINISHING

20. Once the carpentry is complete, sand any rough edges. Also, check for protruding nails and screws. Cut these off or bend them over.

21. Paint the doghouse with exterior latex paint (to match your house if you wish). Linseed oil is also a good wood preservative.

22. When the paint is thoroughly dry, mount a dog door at the entrance to decrease drafts.

Continued ➜

Building a Gable-Roof Doghouse

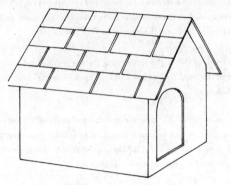

The classic design for a doghouse features a gabled, shingled roof. For a truly aesthetic canine abode, match the shingle on the doghouse to the shingle on your home.

Tools

Circular saw	*Combination square*
Hammer	*Electric drill with Phillips driver or Phillips head screwdriver*
Jigsaw	*1" drill bit*
Safety glasses	*Sandpaper*
Tape measure	*Paintbrush*
Pencil	*Utility knife*

Materials

A 4' x 8' sheet 5/8" CDX plywood	*A bundle of asphalt shingles*
2 x 4 pressure-treated lumber	*Roofing tar*
2 x 2 lumber	*Exterior latex paint or nontoxic wood preservative (linseed oil)*

Hardware

16d galvanized nails

2" sheetrock screws or 6d galvanized nails

3" sheetrock screws or 10d galvanized nails

3/4" roofing nails

Two 2 1/2" butt hinges or 1 piano hinge (optional)

Two hooks and eyes (optional)

Cutting the Walls to Size

1. After you have worked out the dimensions of your doghouse, draw the pieces on the sheet of plywood. Be sure to give matching peaks to the front and back walls. With a circular saw, cut out the pieces and label them.

2. For the precise dimensions of the door opening, measure the height and width of your dog at his shoulders while the dog is standing. To each of these dimensions, add 2 to 3 inches.

On the piece of plywood for the front, mark out these door dimensions, beginning 4 inches from one edge and leaving a 5L-inch lip at the bottom. The door opening will be off center. The top of the opening may be straight, peaked, or curved. At each corner of the opening, drill a 1-inch hole with the electric drill, then connect the holes with the jigsaw. Smooth the edges with sandpaper.

If the inside of the doghouse is to be painted, do so now. Use an exterior latex paint. Set the pieces aside.

CONSTRUCTING THE FLOOR

3. To construct the floor support assembly, cut the pressure-treated 2 x 4s to length so that they will form a box to fit flush with the outside edges of the floor.

If the length of your doghouse exceeds 16 inches, cut an additional joist for a center support.

Lay the 2 x 4s on edge and nail them together with 16d galvanized nails.

4. Place the floor on top of the platform box, aligning the outside edges of the plywood with the outside edges of the 2 x 4 box. Nail or screw the parts together using 6d nails or 2-inch sheetrock screws. Be sure to countersink the nail or screw heads.

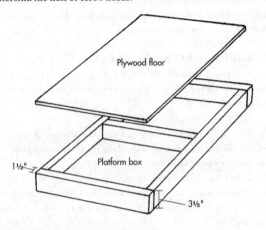

FRAMING UP THE SIDEWALLS

5. Using 2 x 2 stock, cut two top plates and two bottom plates for the sidewalls, each the same length as the floor. Cut 10 (two for each wall and two to frame the door opening) vertical studs, each 3 inches shorter than the height of the sides. Set aside six. If you are building a larger house, place additional studs at 16-inch intervals.

Nail through the top and bottom plates into the studs with 10d galvanized nails or 3-inch sheetrock screws. Stand up the two sidewall frames and place them on top of the floor so that their outside edges are flush with the edges of the floor. Nail or screw through the bottom plates and floor into the 2 x 4s of the platform box.

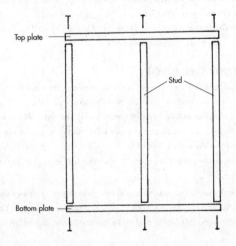

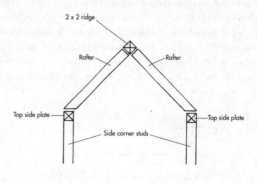

FRAMING UP THE FRONT AND BACK WALLS

6. The front and back walls will sit between the sidewalls. Measure accordingly and cut top and bottom plates for the front and back walls.

For framing the front wall, studs should be added at either side of the door opening. Draw lines on the bottom and top plates to mark the inside edges of the doorway.

To assemble front and back wall frames, nail through the top and bottom plates into the studs with 10d galvanized nails or 3-inch sheetrock screws. Stand up the two frames between the sidewalls with their edges flush with the edges of the floor. Nail or screw through the bottom plates and floor into the 2 x 4s of the platform box. Screw all the corner studs together with 3-inch sheetrock screws.

7. If one of the sides will hinge, check that the plywood piece fits properly. Then set it aside until it is time to install its corresponding roof section.

Hinges should not be necessary on large doghouses; the door opening is usually large enough to let you crawl in for inspections, bedding removal, and cleaning.

SECURING THE PLYWOOD WALLS

8. Align the plywood sides with the outside edges of the corner studs and screw or nail through the plywood into the studs with 2-inch sheetrock screws or 6d nails. Place the painted plywood surface to the inside.

9. The back and front plywood walls should be 1 1/4 inches longer than the floor width so that they overlap the side pieces of plywood. They will also hang 4 1/8 inches below the top of the floor to enclose the floor and floor support system.

Screw these into the vertical corner studs, the top plates, and the floor support box.

FRAMING UP THE ROOF

10. For the roof ridge, cut a 2 x 2 to the length of the floor. Position it between the roof peaks of the front and back pieces. Its outer two faces should follow the line of the peak (gable). Screw through the front and back walls into the ridge.

11. Measure the distance between the 2 x 2 ridge and the outer edge of one top plate. Cut this length from a 2 x 2, cutting one end at a 45-degree angle with the circular saw. The other end should butt tightly against the ridge. Use this rafter as a template for cutting three other rafters. Fasten them all to the ridge ends and top plates.

If your doghouse is large enough to require further rafters, evenly space them at 16-inch intervals.

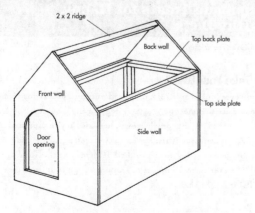

SECURING THE ROOF ASSEMBLY

12. The two pieces of the plywood roof should meet at the ridge and project beyond the top plates and at both gable ends at least 1 to 2 inches. This overhang prevents water from dripping directly at the base of the house.

Place one plywood roof piece at the ridge and center it between the front and back walls. Check that it extends beyond the secured plywood sides. Then screw the roof piece into the rafters, ridge, and top plate.

13. Temporarily tack the removable side in place. Correctly position the second roof piece. Where the two pieces meet at the eave, draw a pencil line. Remove the pieces for mounting hinges or a piano hinge.

Since the slant of the roof makes it impossible to mount the hinge in place, this will have to be done on a work surface and the two pieces installed as one assembly.

Mount the hinge on the side piece, then attach the other hinge leaf to the undersurface of the roof overhang. Before you sink all the screws, experiment to be sure the side will pivot properly.

14. With the roof/side assembly in place, screw through the roof plywood into the rafters and ridge.

15. To secure the side, use a hook and eye at each corner.

PAINTING OR SHINGLING

16. Pitched roofs can be painted or shingled. If you opt to paint the roof, you'll need silicone caulk and possibly aluminum or metal ridging to make the ridgeline watertight. Caulk along the ridge where the two plywood pieces join, or run a piece of aluminum or metal ridge along the seam. Run beads of silicone caulk or roofing tar along both edges where the cap will meet the roof. Nail in place. Do not use roofing nails any longer than necessary.

You may prefer to shingle your doghouse roof, especially if you are trying to match the roof of your home. To apply asphalt shingles, run the first row upside down along the bottom roof edge (slits are toward the peak). Nail to the roof sheathing with 3/4" roofing nails. Cut off excess shingle material with a straightedge and utility knife.

Start the second row directly on top of the first row, but with the slits down (away from peak). Secure with roofing nails placed just above tab slits.

Begin every other row with a half tab so that the slits do not line up. As you reach the peak, cut shingles lengthwise so that they will reach the ridge but not extend over to the other side.

Continued →

Once both slopes are shingled, cap the ridge by cutting the shingles into thirds along the slits. The ridge shingles will run perpendicular to the shingles of the roof slopes. Center each tab at the ridge, bend its sides over both slopes, and nail with two roofing nails. The next tab should cover these nail heads. When you are finished working along the ridge, only two nail heads should show. You can cover these with roofing tar to ensure a tight seal.

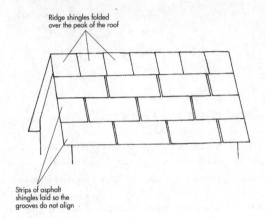

Ridge shingles folded over the peak of the roof

Strips of asphalt shingles laid so the grooves do not align

ENSURING AIR CIRCULATION

Air exchange is important in a doghouse. Warm, stale air encourages bacterial growth, and prolonged dampness may lead to lung problems in your animal.

To promote air movement, cut a small opening in the gable end opposite the door. Cover the opening with wire mesh or screening, and hinge a door to the plywood in the gable end. The door can be latched open with a hook and eye, or latched closed in inclement weather.

FINISHING

17. You can add trim pieces at the four vertical corners and around the door opening to increase the aesthetics of your project.

18. Once the construction is completed, check for rough edges; these should be sanded if necessary. Also eliminate nail and screw tips by bending them over or cutting them off.

19. Paint the doghouse with exterior latex paint (to match your house if you wish); linseed oil is also a good wood preservative.

20. After the paint has thoroughly dried, install a dog door if you wish to decrease the effects of adverse weather on your dog inside.

Choosing the Right Site

Locate your doghouse to take advantage of any natural conditions that will increase the comfort of your animal. The site should be cool, shady, and well ventilated in summer. In winter it should be sheltered from cold arctic blasts. In all seasons it should be draft free, safe, and dry. The doorway should face south and be protected from the worst of rainy, snowy, or windy weather.

Shelters located close to street activity may cause your dog to bark at every passerby. Although you may not be home during the day, this could be very annoying to the neighbors. Locating his shelter near a street also makes it easier for your dog to be stolen or harassed. A doghouse located near your front door will provide invaluable security, though your dog will have to get acquainted with delivery personnel and postal workers.

Pay attention to nearby buildings, barrier fencing, and trees. Once on the roof of a doghouse, your animal may become still more adventuresome and, if nearby structures offer escape avenues, may wander from your yard.

Check street and security house lighting to ensure that it doesn't shine directly at the doghouse at night.

Never place a doghouse on swales, poorly draining soils, or low-lying areas where rain accumulates. Avoid locations near streams or at the base of steep inclines that could experience periodic flooding.

Making a House a Home

Although the carpentry phase is over, there are further steps you can take to ensure that your dog will think of his house as home. Installing dog doors and providing the proper bedding will greatly add to your animal's comfort.

BEDDING

Line the interior floor space of the doghouse with bedding. This will decrease heat loss through the floor. It will also give the dog something to burrow into, further conserving his precious body heat.

For the outdoor doghouse, choose a replaceable bedding material. Straw (the stems or stalks of farm crops), cedar chips, or cedar shavings are ideal and are available from any local feed store.

Hay (the dried top growth of grasses used for feeding livestock) is cheap but should be avoided. Hay gets moldy and can lead to parasite infestations, cause eye and nasal irritations, or give your dog an allergic reaction. Shredded newsprint is also inadvisable for dogs. The ink may rub off and discolor his fur; some dogs are even allergic to newsprint.

Old blankets, oval "cuddlers," or stuffed cushions may be appropriate for your dog when he's napping indoors, but they shouldn't be used in an outdoor shelter. Also avoid carpeting; it is impossible to clean and can quickly become a breeding ground for fleas and other parasites.

With time, the bedding will become soiled with the dirt your dog tracks in; matted with fur, especially when your dog is shedding; and susceptible to flea infestations. You should replace the bedding every couple of months to keep the dog comfortable and the doghouse clean.

Homemade Treats for Happy, Healthy Dogs

Cheryl Gianfrancesco

Why Bake Your Own?

Have you ever looked at the list of ingredients on a box of dog treats? What color are the ones you give your dog—orange, because they're "cheese-flavored"? Or reddish brown, because they're supposed to taste like liver? Now consider this: Have you ever seen a "use by" date or an expiration date on a dog-food product? It seems like this food can last virtually forever! There's no way to know how long your dog's treats have been sitting on the shelf.

And as far as I'm concerned, you should avoid any pet-food ingredients with the words *by-products* and *meal* on the label. Generally speaking, these are food-processing by-products that humans will not consume. Other undesirable—even potentially harmful—ingredients include chemicals, preservatives, artificial flavorings, and artificial colorings. I've come up with the following simple rule for myself: If I cannot pronounce it or I don't know what it is, your dog should not be eating it.

Proper nutrition and regular veterinary care are the two key ingredients for a healthy, happy dog. And I believe that if everyone was aware of the quality of ingredients in store-bought dog food and treats, more people would cook for their pets. The recipes in this bulletin include high-quality ingredients, no fillers, no added colors, and no preservatives or artificial flavorings—and best of all, they're easy to prepare. Making homemade dog treats is one way to take control of your dog's health—and to do something special for your best friend.

ALTERNATIVES TO BAKED TREATS

When you don't have time to bake for your dog, there are many other healthful foods you can offer as treats. Choose dried dates and dried apricots (both without sugar), baby carrots, seedless grapes, and apple slices. Be sure to remove any seeds, and wash fruits and vegetables well to remove pesticides and preservatives before feeding these foods to your dog. Keep portions small. And remember, any time you give your dog new foods, watch for allergic reactions.

WHEN YOU MUST BUY COMMERCIAL PRODUCTS

While I'm a strong advocate of making your own all-natural dog treats, I realize you may not always have the time, or the desire, to do so. If you must purchase dog treats or dog food, be sure to choose products whose primary ingredients (the first few listed on the label) are whole foods, such as chicken, beef, lamb, brown rice, whole wheat, barley, and oats. By-products, meal, corn, and any unpronounceable ingredients, if present, should be near the end of the list of contents. The best treats have a short, simple list of ingredients.

Many pet owners today are concerned about their pet's diet, prompting the development of more healthful, all-natural products. There are plenty of pet specialty stores and Internet resources that offer a wide selection of dog treats and dog foods. Don't be fooled by the packaging or the price—read the ingredient lists and make educated choices.

Tips and Tricks for the Best Treats

Whether you're a seasoned cook or a novice, baking for your dog can be both rewarding and challenging. As I've experimented and created new recipes, I've learned the following tips:

- Be as creative as you like with these recipes! Add different ingredients that you think your dog may like (but remember to try only one new ingredient at a time so that you can identify what your dog is and isn't allergic to).

- Most of these recipes call for whole-wheat flour, but if your dog is allergic to it or you have none in the house, you can use unbleached white flour.

- Many peanut butters contain lots of sugar and salt. In recipes that call for peanut butter, use the all-natural, no-salt- and no-sugar-added type, available at most large grocery stores.

- Do *not* use ingredients that contain any traces of chocolate, onions, seeds from fruits, or caffeine. These ingredients are harmful and, depending on the amount consumed, can be fatal to your dog. (Carob, found in health-food stores, is a nutritious chocolate substitute.)

- Use organic ingredients, if they're available to you. You can find organic products at farmer's markets and natural-food stores.

- If your dough does not seem firm enough, add some flour, 1 tablespoon at a time, mixing or kneading it in until the dough is firm. If the dough is too stiff and crumbly, add water, 1 tablespoon at a time.

- If the dough sticks to your rolling pin as you're rolling it out, pat flour onto the surface of the rolling pin.

- Make it fun! Use a variety of shaped cookie cutters for the treats. (I have not included yields for these recipes, because the quantity depends on the size of the cookie cutter used.)

- Baking times can vary. Check the treats periodically during baking to make sure they're not cooking more quickly than expected.

- Be sure the treats are cooled completely before you serve any to your dog.

Testing for Food Allergies

Just like humans, dogs can have food allergies. If your dog has never been exposed to an ingredient in a recipe you want to try, introduce the treat very slowly. I suggest starting with a simple recipe that has few ingredients. (If you introduce many new ingredients at one time and your dog has a bad reaction, it will be hard to pinpoint which of them caused it.)

1. Give your dog a small piece of the treat—less than half—and wait a few hours, watching the dog for any sign of allergic reaction. This can be as simple as scratching more than usual or as dramatic as vomiting, swelling of face and/or throat, and diarrhea. If any of these more dramatic symptoms develop, contact your veterinarian immediately.

2. If no reaction occurs, give your dog the rest of the treat and wait a few hours, watching for a reaction. If one does occur, do not give your dog any more of that particular treat. Make note of which ingredients were used in the treat, and try making and testing different versions, keeping track of which ingredients are used in each case and which recipes cause your dog to have a negative response. With time and patience, you should be able to isolate the ingredients to which your dog is allergic.

My Favorite Recipes

For most of these recipes, it will take less than 15 minutes to mix the ingredients, cut the cookies, and place them on a baking sheet. Most of the ingredients are inexpensive, and you'll find them at your local grocery or health-food store. Almost all of them are simple, one-bowl recipes—both to save time and because I hate washing dishes!

Note: While these treats are healthful for your dog, they are still treats. They are not intended to be a complete diet.

Continued →

NUT-AND-SEED NIBBLES

Nuts and seeds contain contain a variety of nutrients, including essential fatty acids, that help keep your dog energized and ensure a shiny, healthy coat.

PEANUT BUTTER BISCUITS

4 cups whole-wheat flour

2 cups quick-cooking oats

2 1/2 cups warm water

1/2 cup all-natural peanut butter (no sugar or salt added)

1/4 cup carob chips (available at health food stores)

1. Preheat the oven to 350°F. In a large bowl, combine all ingredients; mix well.

2. On a lightly floured surface, knead the dough until it is firm. If the dough is too sticky, add warm water, 1 tablespoon at a time, while continuing to knead.

3. Roll the dough to a 1/4-inch thickness. Cut with the cookie cutter of your choice. Transfer biscuits to a baking sheet.

4. Bake the biscuits for 40 minutes. Turn off the heat and let the biscuits stand in the oven until hard, 1 to 2 hours.

SESAME COOKIES

1 1/2 cups whole-wheat flour

1 teaspoon baking powder

1/3 cup vegetable oil

1/4 cup pure honey

1 egg

1 teaspoon pure vanilla extract

3 tablespoons sesame seeds

1. Preheat the oven to 375°F. In a large bowl, combine the flour, baking powder, oil, honey, egg, and vanilla; mix well.

2. On a floured surface, knead the dough until it is firm. Shape the dough into quarter-size balls.

3. Place the sesame seeds in a shallow bowl. Roll each dough ball in the sesame seeds, then flatten slightly. Place cookies on a baking sheet.

4. Bake for 10 to 15 minutes, or until the cookies are dry and firm to touch. Turn off the heat; let the cookies stand in the oven until hard, 1 to 2 hours.

MOLASSES PEANUT TREATS

2 cups whole-wheat flour

1 cup quick-cooking oats

1/2 cup wheat germ

1/3 cup water

1/2 cup chopped unsalted peanuts

1 tablespoon all-natural molasses

1. Preheat the oven to 350°F. In a large bowl, combine all ingredients until a firm dough forms.

2. On a floured surface, knead the dough until it is firm.

3. Roll the dough to a 1/4-inch thickness. Cut with the cookie cutter of your choice. Transfer cookies to a baking sheet.

4. Bake for 20 minutes. Turn off the heat; let the cookies stand in the oven until hard, 1 to 2 hours.

SUNFLOWER SEED THINS

1/2 cup chopped unsalted sunflower seeds

1 cup whole-wheat flour

1/4 cup vegetable oil

1 tablespoon water

1. Preheat the oven to 350°F. Place the sunflower seeds on a baking sheet and toast until golden brown, 20 to 25 minutes.

2. In a medium-size bowl, combine the flour, oil, water, and toasted sunflower seeds.

3. Reduce heat to 300°F. On a lightly floured surface, knead the dough until it is firm. If the dough is too soft, chill it for a few minutes.

4. Roll the dough to a 1/8-inch thickness. Cut into rounds using a shot glass or round cookie cutter. Transfer the crackers to a baking sheet.

5. Bake for 30 minutes. Turn off the heat; let the crackers stand in the oven until hard, 1 to 2 hours.

WALNUT WAFERS

2 cups rice flour

1 tablespoon wheat germ

1/4 cup pure honey

1/4 cup vegetable oil

1/2 teaspoon pure vanilla extract

1/2 cup chopped unsalted walnuts

1/4 cup sesame seeds

1. Preheat the oven to 375°F. In a large bowl, combine all ingredients.

2. On a floured surface, knead the dough until it is firm. Divide the dough into 6 equal parts.

3. Using your hands, roll each section of dough into a log shape. Wrap each log in wax paper and chill for 1 hour.

4. Cut the logs into 1/2-inch-thick slices. Transfer the cookies to a baking sheet.

5. Bake for 15 minutes. Turn off the heat; let the cookies stand in the oven until hard, 1 to 2 hours.

MEAT-LOVERS MENU

Unlike commercial treats, which are often made with overprocessed bits and pieces of meat left over from other cuts, these biscuits and cookies are made with top-quality meat. They not only are healthier for your dog, but they taste better, too!

LIVER AND CHEESE BISCUITS

3 1/4 cups whole-wheat flour

1 1/2 cups wheat germ

1/2 cup freeze-dried liver (available at health food stores)

1 cup low-fat cottage cheese

2 eggs

1. Preheat the oven to 300°F. In a large bowl, combine all ingredients.

2. On a floured surface, knead the dough until it is firm.

3. Roll the dough to a 1/2-inch thickness. Cut with the cookie cutter of your choice. Transfer biscuits to a baking sheet.

4. Bake for 1 hour, or until the biscuits are dry and firm to touch. Turn off the heat; let the biscuits stand in the oven until hard, 1 to 2 hours.

BEEF TREATS

1 cup chopped lean beef	1/2 cup vegetable oil
2 cups unbleached white flour	1/2 cup water
1/2 cup wheat germ	1 egg
1/4 cup low-fat powdered milk	

1. Preheat the oven to 350°F. In a skillet, sauté the beef until cooked through. Drain thoroughly.

2. In a large bowl, combine all ingredients; mix well.

3. On a floured surface, knead the dough until it is firm.

4. Roll the dough to a 1/2-inch thickness. Cut with the cookie cutter of your choice. Transfer cookies to a baking sheet.

5. Bake for 30 minutes. Turn off the heat; let the cookies stand in the oven until hard, 1 to 2 hours.

CHICKEN AND CHEESE BISCUITS

2 cups water	1/2 cup shredded low-fat Cheddar cheese
1 chicken leg, skin and bones removed	1/3 cup vegetable oil
3 cups whole-wheat flour	1 egg

1. Pour the water into a small pan and set the chicken in it. Bring to a boil and simmer until the chicken is fully cooked, 10 to 15 minutes. Set the cooked chicken aside; reserve 3/4 cup of the cooking liquid.

2. Preheat the oven to 350°F. In a large bowl, combine the flour, cheese, oil, and egg; mix well.

3. Shred the chicken meat; stir into the dough. Add the reserved cooking liquid; mix until completely combined.

4. On a floured surface, knead the dough until it is firm.

5. Roll the dough to a 1/2-inch thickness. Cut with the cookie cutter of your choice. Transfer the biscuits to a baking sheet.

6. Bake for 50 minutes. Turn off the heat; let the biscuits stand in the oven until hard, 1 to 2 hours.

CATCH OF THE DAY

3 cups unbleached white flour

1/2 cup cornmeal

1/2 cup wheat germ

1 cup water

1/2 cup vegetable oil

1 can (6 ounces) tuna in water, drained, rinsed, and drained again

1 clove garlic, chopped

1. Preheat the oven to 350°F. In a large bowl, combine all ingredients.

2. On a lightly floured surface, knead the dough until it is firm.

3. Roll the dough to a 1/2-inch thickness. Use a fish-shaped cookie cutter (or whatever shape you prefer) to form cookies. Transfer the cookies to a baking sheet.

4. Bake for 30 minutes. Turn off the heat; let the cookies stand in the oven until hard, 1 to 2 hours.

GARLICKY TREATS

Garlic is one of the wonder herbs of the kitchen. It not only adds flavor and zest to recipes, but it also aids the body in fighting off infection, reducing blood cholesterol and blood pressure, and killing parasites. Garlic retains some of its cardiovascular benefits when cooked, but heat destroys its antiviral and antibacterial properties. So these treats will help your dog maintain good heart health, but in addition, if you can stand the odor—or can convince your dog to eat parsley afterward—give your dog half a clove of raw garlic daily as a preventive.

GARLIC TREATS

4 cups whole-wheat flour	1/3 cup vegetable oil
1 1/2 cups water	4 cloves garlic, chopped
1 cup quick-cooking oats	1 egg

1. Preheat the oven to 325°F. In a large bowl, combine all ingredients; mix well.

2. On a floured surface, knead the dough until it is firm.

Continued ➜

3. Roll the dough to a 1/2-inch thickness. Cut with the cookie cutter of your choice. Transfer cookies to a baking sheet.

4. Bake for 50 minutes to 1 hour, or until the cookies are dry and firm to touch. Turn off oven; let the cookies stand in the oven until hard, 1 to 2 hours.

POTATO-GARLIC PANCAKES

2 medium carrots, grated

1 large potato, grated

1/4 cup low-fat shredded Cheddar cheese

1/2 cup unbleached white flour

1/2 cup wheat germ

1/4 cup quick-cooking oats

1 teaspoon vegetable oil

1 egg

1 egg white

1 clove garlic, crushed

1. Preheat the oven to 450°F. Grease a baking sheet with vegetable oil. In a large bowl, combine all ingredients; mix well.

2. Using a tablespoon, form the mixture into small pancakes. Drop the pancakes about 2 inches apart on the prepared baking sheet. Spread each pancake into a circle about 2 inches in diameter.

3. Bake until the pancakes are golden brown, about 15 minutes. Store in an airtight container in the refrigerator.

DOGGIE DESSERTS

Dog treats are, after all, treats. These faux desserts will have your dog begging for more opportunities to sit up, lie down, and fetch—anything for the reward!

BEST-FRIEND BIRTHDAY CAKE

2 cups unbleached white flour

2 teaspoons baking powder

1 teaspoon baking soda

1/4 cup wheat germ

3/4 cup water

1/4 cup vegetable oil

1/4 cup unsweetened applesauce

1 egg

2/3 cup mashed bananas

1/2 cup carob chips (available at health food stores)

1. Preheat the oven to 350°F. Grease and flour an 8-inch square pan. In a large bowl, combine all ingredients; mix well.

2. Pour the batter into the prepared pan.

3. Bake until a toothpick inserted in the center comes out clean, about 25 minutes. Allow the cake to cool completely before frosting.

BIRTHDAY CAKE FROSTING AND GARNISH

1 package (8 ounces) low-fat cream cheese, softened

1/4 cup mashed bananas

2 tablespoons pure honey

1 tablespoon unbleached flour

1/2 cup carob chips (available at health food stores), chopped

1. In a medium-size bowl, combine the cream cheese, bananas, honey, and flour; mix until smooth. If the frosting is not firm, add more flour and continue mixing until firm.

2. Spread a thin layer of frosting on a cooled cake. Sprinkle carob chips over the frosting to decorate.

TEMPTING CHEESE CIRCLES

3 cups whole-wheat flour

1 1/2 cups wheat germ

1 cup quick-cooking oats

1 1/2 cups hot water

1/4 cup vegetable oil

1 egg

3/4 cup shredded low-fat Cheddar cheese

1. Preheat the oven to 300°F. In a large bowl, combine all ingredients; mix well.

2. On a floured surface, knead the dough until it is firm.

3. Using your hands, roll the dough into the shape of a log. Cut into even, 1/8-inch-thick slices. Transfer the slices to a baking sheet.

4. Bake for 1 hour. Turn off the heat; let the cookies stand in the oven until hard, 1 to 2 hours.

CAROB MINT DROPS

2 cups brown rice flour

2/3 cup water

3 tablespoons vegetable oil

1 large egg

1/2 cup carob chips (available at health food stores)

1/2 cup chopped parsley

1/3 cup chopped fresh mint

1. Preheat the oven to 350°F. In a large bowl, combine all ingredients; mix well. The mixture should be the consistency of dough for drop cookies; if it is too thick, add water.

2. Drop the dough by the teaspoonful, 1/2 inch apart, onto a baking sheet.

3. Bake for 15 minutes. Turn off the heat; let the cookies stand in the oven until hard, 1 to 2 hours.

WHOLESOME HONEY TREATS

2 cups rice flour

2 cups unbleached white flour

2 cups whole-wheat flour

2 cups quick-cooking oats

1/2 cup wheat germ

1 3/4 cups water

3/4 cup low-fat milk

1/2 cup pure honey

1. Preheat the oven to 350°F. In a large bowl, combine all ingredients; mix well.

2. On a floured surface, knead the dough until it is firm.

3. Roll the dough to a 1/4-inch thickness. Cut with the cookie cutter of your choice. Transfer the cookies to a baking sheet.

4. Bake for 30 to 45 minutes, or until the cookies are dry and firm to touch. Turn off the heat; let the cookies stand in the oven until hard, 1 to 2 hours.

GINGER COOKIES

5 cups whole-wheat flour	3/4 cup all-natural molasses
1 1/2 tablespoons baking soda	1/2 cup pure honey
1 tablespoon ground ginger	1/4 cup vegetable oil
2 teaspoons ground cinnamon	1 egg
3/4 cup all-natural, unsweetened applesauce	

1. Preheat the oven to 375°F. In a large bowl, combine all ingredients.

2. On a floured surface, knead the dough until it is firm.

3. Chill the dough for 1 hour.

4. On a floured surface, roll the dough to a 1/4-inch thickness. Cut with the cookie cutter of your choice. Transfer the cookies to a baking sheet.

5. Bake for 7 minutes. Turn off the heat; let the cookies stand in the oven until hard, 1 to 2 hours.

CARROT-YOGURT MUFFINS

1 container (8 ounces) plain low-fat yogurt	2 cups whole-wheat flour
1/3 cup pure honey	1/2 cup wheat germ
3 tablespoons all-natural, unsweetened applesauce	1 teaspoon baking powder
	1 teaspoon baking soda
3 carrots, grated	1/2 cup chopped unsalted walnuts
2 eggs	

1. Preheat the oven to 350°F. Line a muffin pan with 12 paper liners.

2. In a medium-size bowl, combine the yogurt, honey, applesauce, carrots, and eggs; mix well.

3. In a large bowl, combine the flour, wheat germ, baking powder, baking soda, and walnuts; mix well.

4. Add the wet ingredients to the dry mixture, a little at a time, mixing well after each addition.

5. Spoon batter into the muffin cups, filling each three-quarters full.

6. Bake until a toothpick inserted in the center of one comes out clean, about 18 minutes.

10 Herbs for Happy, Healthy Dogs

Kathleen Brown

Illustrations by Rick Daskam,

Beverly Duncan, and Charles Joslin

Introduction

Herbs are Mother Nature's green pharmacy. When used properly, they provide a bounty of gentle, safe healing goodness. And they usually are free of the side effects commonly associated with commercial products and medications. Although there are hundreds of herbs, I've selected what I believe are the top 10 herbs for dogs. These herbs earned this ranking because they are safe, easy to obtain, and easy to administer and they address a wide range of common health conditions affecting our canine companions.

The herbal remedies suggested here are safe and effective; if any precautions are advisable, I've noted them with each recipe. However, if your dog is taking any prescription medicine, I encourage you to seek the advice of a holistic-oriented veterinarian before supplementing with herbal remedies, because herbs and drugs can have harmful interactions. If you decide to branch out from the relatively safe and gentle herbs discussed here, you should seek the advice of a qualified professional before giving these new herbs to your dog. And always, *always* follow label directions.

HEALTH IS NOT HERBS ALONE

Certainly, herbs serve a vital role in maintaining your dog's health, but you should also ensure that your dog gets plenty of exercise, is fed a diet that meets its nutritional needs, and receives lots of TLC (tender loving care) from you. All these components work in harmony toward improving the physical and mental health of your dog and extending its life.

Giving Herbal Remedies to Dogs

I remember the first time I had to give my horse a shot. It took quite a while to work up the courage to plunge in the needle, but over time I became comfortable administering medicines of all types to my animals, large and small. Giving herbal medicines to dogs is a snap compared to giving them to horses, but it's still a little intimidating at first. It's a good skill to have, though, because in an emergency you may be the quickest source of help for your dog. In addition, at-home herbal remedies are cost-effective because you don't have to run to the vet every time there's a minor problem. There are several techniques that work well, and with a little practice, you'll become comfortable with them.

HERB SPRINKLES

Fresh or dried herbs can be finely chopped and sprinkled on top of your dog's commercial food or mixed into one of your homemade recipes. Fresh herbs are generally more potent than dried herbs, but dried herbs have a longer storage time, and they're available to everyone, even those who haven't the time or space for gardening.

Fresh or dried herbs can be finely chopped and sprinkled on top of your dog's food.

Continued →

HERBAL TEAS

Sip, savor, smile. Ahhh, there's something relaxing and inviting about brewing and drinking a cup of herbal tea. Well, surprise: Your dog can drink tea to its health, too! Make the tea just as you would for yourself. Cool it completely before pouring it over your dog's chow.

If your finicky dog won't touch food that's been "contaminated" with medicine, simply use a large plastic syringe (available at most veterinarians' offices) to squirt the tea along the dog's lower back teeth. It isn't necessary to open the mouth completely; just insert the tip of the syringe into the side of the mouth toward the back and push the plunger. Then hold the mouth closed and massage the throat gently until the dog swallows.

HERBAL TINCTURES

Tinctures, also known as extracts, are potent liquid botanicals packed into tiny glass bottles with eyedroppers. Tinctures are even easier than teas to give to your dog. Just drip the recommended number of drops into your dog's food or water or pour the dosage into a plastic syringe and squirt it onto your dog's tongue.

If you're using tinctures with an alcohol base, dilute the dose by half in water or mix the drops with a bit of hot water a few minutes before administering to allow the alcohol to evaporate. (For more information, see Appendix G.)

You can administer teas and tinctures by squirting them along the dog's lower back teeth from a plastic syringe.

EARDROPS

Eardrops are used to treat a variety of ear ailments, including mites and various ear infections. In addition, the ear is filled with tiny capillaries, and medicine applied to the ear is absorbed quickly into the bloodstream. To administer, drip a small amount into the ear; tilt the head back; and, holding the ear closed, massage gently. Then do the other ear.

Drip a few drops in the dog's ear, tilt his head back, and hold the ear closed, massaging gently.

HERBAL CAPSULES

Capsules are made from ground herbs packed in a vegetable-gelatin casing. To administer capsules without your dog noticing, hide them in a favorite food, such as meat, peanut butter, or soft bread. To administer the capsule directly, tilt the dog's head back, open the mouth wide, place the capsule over the tongue toward the back, and close the mouth. Hold the mouth closed and stroke the dog's throat gently.

To administer capsules directly, first pry open the mouth and place the capsule on the tongue in the back of the mouth. Then hold the dog's mouth shut while gently massaging the throat until the dog swallows.

Some commercial varieties of capsules come with special coatings that help the herb slide down your dog's throat and pass into its stomach without a fuss. You can also make your own capsules at home. The supplies are available at most health food stores. I recommend purchasing a plastic tray that enables you to fill about 50 capsules at once. The gelatin capsules come in several sizes, most commonly "OO." Making capsules at home is time-consuming, but I think it's worth the trouble, because you can customize the blends your dog needs and ensure freshness and viability too.

Using the Right Dosage

As a general rule, you can administer herbal medicine to your dog three times a day. However, if you're using a commercial herbal remedy, always follow the label directions, because dosages can vary among different herbs and different herbal forms. Most herbs work very gently and slowly, so be patient with your patient.

Below is a general dosage guideline for the different types of herbal remedies you may make at home.

Expect slow and easy results. Herbs most often need to be given for at least 30 days before you'll see appreciable results. Look for mild and subtle—and long-lasting—changes.

There are many different delivery systems for herbal remedies, some of which are outlined below. Use whichever one is easiest to give to your dog. It is more important to get the herbs into the dog's system than it is to worry about the "proper" way to dose.

Watching for Reactions

Most reactions to herbs are caused by allergies. The symptoms of an allergic reaction are generally mild, and they almost always stop when the herb is discontinued. Signs of an adverse reaction are what you'd expect with any human allergy:

- Runny eyes or nose
- Sneezing
- Itching (anywhere on the body)
- Swelling
- Diarrhea or vomiting

When you begin giving your dog an herbal supplement, watch him carefully over the next few days. If you see any of the symptoms noted above, stop giving your dog that particular remedy. Keep track of the ingredients in the remedies your dog is sensitive to; over time, you'll be able to pinpoint the offending ingredient.

GENERAL RULES FOR ADMINISTERING HERBS TO DOGS

Adapted from *Dr. Kidd's Guide to Herbal Dog Care*, by Randy Kidd, D.V.M. (Storey Books, 2000)

The easiest and safest way to give herbal dosages is to "give them to effect." The basic rule is to start out slowly, with low doses at first. Then, after a month or so, when the dog adjusts to her herbal intake, taper off or add on, depending on her reaction. Often very small amounts of herb are enough to effect a cure.

Dog's Weight	Sprinkles (put on the dog's food once daily)	Teas (poured over food or into the dog's water)	Capsules/Tablets (administered orally)	Tinctures (in the dog's water or food or given directly by mouth)
1–10 lbs.	A small pinch	Small amounts (less than 1/4 cup one to three times daily)	1/2 capsule or tablet one to three times daily	1 to 3 drops two or times daily
10–20 lbs.	A bigger pinch	1/4 cup one to three times daily	1/2 to 1 capsule or tablet one to three times daily	3 to 5 drops two or three times daily
20–50 lbs.	2 pinches to 1 teaspoon	1/4 to 1/2 cup one to three times daily	1 to 2 capsules or tablets two or three times daily	5 to 10 drops two or three times daily
50–100 lbs.	2-plus pinches to 2 teaspoons	1/2 to 1 cup one to three times daily	1 to 2 capsules or tablets three or three or four times daily	10 to 20 drops two times daily
Over 100 lbs.	Up to 1 tablespoon	Up to 1 cup three times daily	Adult human dose	Adult human dose

10 Herbs to Know

With dozens of herbs running from A to Z, you could go broke trying to keep supplies of each and every one of them. I'm here to help save you time, money, and frustration. I've selected 10 herbs that are easy to administer even for novices. These herbs are also incredibly versatile and can aid in treating many common canine health conditions. Here's the lineup:

- Calendula
- Chamomile
- Comfrey
- Echinacea
- Garlic
- Marsh mallow
- Peppermint
- Rosemary
- Sage
- Slippery elm

CALENDULA (*Calendula officinalis*)
Parts used: Flowers

Medicinal benefits: Calendula flowers are antimicrobial, antifungal, antibacterial, antiviral, and vulnerary. Externally, calendula flowers are ideal for the treatment of all skin irritations and wounds. Internally, calendula helps reduce inflammation of the digestive system and addresses the toxicity underlying many fevers, infections, and systemic skin disorders. It aids in liver function and can help stimulate the immune system.

Cautions: Although considered one of the safest herbs for both dogs and humans, calendula is potentially toxic to cats, so don't share this herb with your dog's feline friends.

CHAMOMILE (*Matricaria recutita, Chamaemelum nobile*)
Parts used: Flowers

Medicinal benefits: A gentle sedative that is safe for even young animals, chamomile can be used to alleviate anxiety, insomnia, and indigestion. Tests indicate that chamomile reduces aggressive behavior in animals. In addition to being effective against some bacteria and fungi, chamomile's anti-inflammatory activity makes it ideal for inflamed eyes, sore throats, and other irritations. It is an excellent choice for gas, flatulence, and sore tummies, as well.

Cautions: Chamomile should not be used on dogs that are pregnant. In addition, there are occasional reports of dogs being allergic to chamomile, so follow the precautions given above before beginning a daily chamomile regimen. Otherwise, chamomile is safe when used appropriately.

COMFREY (*Symphytum officinale*)
Parts used: Leaves

Medicinal benefits: Historically known as knit-bone, comfrey aids the body in speedy recovery from fractures and breaks. It is anti-inflammatory in nature and boosts circulation, which makes it useful for easing the discomfort and pain of arthritis. It's also helpful in treating cuts, bites, stings, and infections, and it helps repair nerve damage and reduces bruising. Comfrey is very high in protein, which high-energy dogs need plenty of. It also works as a demulcent, making an excellent choice for treating digestive problems.

Cautions: Comfrey should not be given to dogs that are pregnant or nursing or that suffer from liver disease. Comfrey should not be used for extended periods of time.

ECHINACEA (*Echinacea angustifolia, E. purpurea*)
Parts used: Leaves, root

Medicinal benefits: Just as it does for humans, echinacea stimulates and strengthens a dog's immune system. It has antibacterial, antiviral, and antibiotic actions and can fight viral and bacterial infections, particularly upper respiratory infections.

Cautions: Echinacea is safe when used appropriately.

Continued →

GARLIC (*Allium sativum*)

Part used: Bulb

Medicinal benefits: Garlic is one of the wonders of the herb world. It offers potent antibiotic, antiseptic, and expectorant properties. It is excellent for treating coughs, respiratory problems, mucus buildup, and infections of the blood, lungs, intestines, nose, and throat. Externally, it is useful in the treatment of skin parasites and as a poultice for treating abscesses and skin irritations. Garlic is best combined with antioxidant herbs such as basil, parsley, oregano, and thyme, which may counter its oxidative effects.

Cautions: Garlic can cause digestive problems in young animals, so don't give garlic to dogs younger than a year old. It can also cause short-lived diarrhea in animals with sensitive stomachs; if such is the case with your dog, simply discontinue use.

MARSH MALLOW (*Althaea officinalis*)

Part used: Root

Medicinal benefits: As an emollient with high mucilaginous content, marsh mallow is useful in treating gastrointestinal problems, particularly inflammatory and ulcerative conditions, spasm, colitis, diarrhea, and constipation. Marsh mallow also has expectorant properties, which make it ideal for treating dry coughs, congestion, and respiratory disorders. It can be used externally as a poultice to reduce inflammation and relieve skin rashes, abrasions, cuts, and bruises.

Marsh mallow
(Althaea officinalis)

Cautions: Marsh mallow has the potential to exacerbate hypoglycemia, so check with your veterinarian before giving marsh mallow to a dog with low blood sugar. Otherwise, it is safe when used appropriately.

PEPPERMINT (*Mentha piperita*)

Parts used: Leaves

Medicinal benefits: All members of the mint family, including peppermint, are excellent for soothing digestive disturbances, including gas, indigestion, and colic, and for other internal aches and pains.

Cautions: Peppermint is safe when used appropriately.

Peppermint
(Mentha piperita)

ROSEMARY (*Rosmarinus officinalis*)

Parts used: Leaves, stems, flowers

Medicinal benefits: Rosemary is a particularly versatile herb that has antifungal, anti-inflammatory, antispasmodic, carminative, and stimulant properties. Externally, it can be used as a wash in treating abrasions, bites, cuts, and other injuries. Internally, it strengthens the heart and liver and stimulates circulation. Either given as a tea or fed chopped finely with raw parsley and comfrey leaves, it relieves the symptoms of

Rosemary
(Rosmarinus officinalis)

arthritis. Rosemary can also aid in reducing bad breath and is an excellent wash for mouth and teeth.

Cautions: Do not give rosemary to dogs that are pregnant. Otherwise, it is safe when used appropriately.

SAGE (*Salvia officinalis*)

Parts used: Leaves, flowers

Medicinal benefits: Sage has cleansing and astringent actions and antiseptic properties that are useful in healing infections.

Cautions: *Salvia officinalis* is a very safe herb. Artemisia sages (*Artemisia* spp.), however, should not be used internally. Be sure to confirm the botanical name of your sage supply before giving it to your dog.

SLIPPERY ELM (*Ulmus fulva*)

Part used: Inner bark

Medicinal benefits: Slippery elm soothes irritated mucous membranes and eases diarrhea. It's also used internally for stomach ulcers, colitis, sore throats, and coughs and topically for wounds and abscesses.

Cautions: There are rare reports of dogs with allergic reactions to slippery elm. Follow the cautionary guidelines given above when beginning an herbal regimen that includes slippery elm. Otherwise, slippery elm is safe when used appropriately.

Recipes for a Healthy Coat

In this section, you'll find recipes to cleanse and condition your dog's hair and skin, resulting in a healthy, glossy coat. Use these recipes as supplements to a regular brushing and grooming routine, which stimulates the hair's natural oils and encourages healthy growth.

THE "HERB" INGREDIENT

A plant part defined as "herb" means all the aboveground parts of the plant: stem, leaf, and flower.

DAILY SUPPLEMENT FOR A SHINY COAT

This recipe will help keep your dog's coat and skin in the best possible condition.

1 part burdock root

1 part calendula blossoms

1 part crushed garlic clove

1 part nettle leaves

To make a tea:

Decoct the burdock root for 10 to 15 minutes, using 2 to 3 teaspoons of this herbal blend per 2 cups of water, following the instructions in Appendix G. Remove from the heat; add 1 teaspoon each of the remaining herbs; and steep, covered, another 10 minutes. Strain, then allow the tea to cool. Administer orally, following the dosage guidelines given above.

To make a tincture:

Follow the instructions in Appendix G and the dosage guidelines given above.

To make capsules:

To make capsules with this recipe, substitute garlic powder for the crushed garlic clove. Finely powder all ingredients and pour into size 00 capsules. Follow the dosage guidelines given above.

COAT-CONDITIONING MASSAGE

This is a simple but excellent way to condition your dog's coat. Both of you will enjoy the massage.

2 cups water

2 tablespoons nettle leaves

2 tablespoons rosemary leaves

Bring the water to a boil. Pour it over the herbs and steep until cool, then strain. Massage the liquid into your dog's coat. Do not rinse out.

Simple Remedies for Cuts and Scrapes

Dogs are normally quite agile and coordinated, but they are also playful and curious. The latter two traits can get them into trouble. Here are some herbal remedies for minor cuts and scrapes.

HEALING SKIN OIL

This formula is wonderful for skin problems of all kinds, including burns, cuts, and foot pad irritations. The herbs can be used fresh or dried.

1 part calendula blossoms   Tea tree essential oil

1 part comfrey leaves   Lavender essential oil

1 part St.-John's-wort blossoms

To make an infused oil:

If using fresh plant matter, spread it out on clean paper towels and allow the blossoms and leaves to wilt for several hours. Then combine the herbs and infuse in oil following the instructions in Appendix G. Add 1/4 teaspoon of tea tree essential oil and 1 to 3 drops of lavender essential oil per cup of infused oil.

To use, saturate a sterile cotton pad with the infused oil and apply to the affected area.

To make a salve:

These ingredients also make a wonderful salve, which is more easily transportable. Use the infused oil to make a salve following the directions in Appendix G

COMFREY COMFORT

For quick relief from the pain of all types of wounds, bites, stings, and infections, just grab a handful of comfrey—fresh or dried—and make a poultice. If using fresh, rinse the leaves in cold water, then finely chop or mince. If using dried, soak it in water to rehydrate it. Place the wet mass on gauze, a paper towel, or a clean cloth and apply it to the affected area. Secure this poultice in place with a bandage for several hours or overnight.

PAIN-RELIEF POULTICE

This blend, made into a paste, can be applied as a poultice to relieve pain and encourage healing of wounds, bites, stings, and infections.

1 part chamomile flowers

1 part rosemary herb

1/2 part linseed meal

Combine the ingredients with enough water to make a paste. Apply the paste on a square of sterile gauze. Bind in place with bandages or gauze and leave on for several hours or overnight.

CAUTION

If your dog is bitten by another dog, bring your dog to a veterinarian, who can offer treatment to prevent infection.

ANTI-INFECTION WARM COMPRESS

This compress is helpful when applied to a cut or wound, particularly one that is infected or inflamed.

1 cup water

1 tablespoon ground dried echinacea root

1 tablespoon ground dried plantain leaves

Bring the water to a boil. Pour it over the herbs, cover, and steep 20 minutes. Strain. Allow to cool for 10 to 15 minutes; it should be warm, not hot. Saturate a cloth with the tea and apply it to the wound. Bind the compress in place with gauze or a towel and leave on until it cools. Repeat every 2 hours until the inflammation is gone.

ROSEMARY WOUND WONDER

For all but the deepest wounds, many holistic practitioners recommend not bandaging, as a dog's constant licking of the wound keeps it moist and breaks up pus formation. Instead of bandaging, clean the wound with a strong infusion of rosemary and give rosemary infusion internally (follow the dosage guidelines given above) to stimulate healing and strengthen tissue-building action.

BALD PATCHES

This recipe is a quick, easy way to treat abrasions, bites, or any injury that tears the hair away.

2 teaspoons rosemary herb   4 teaspoons witch hazel

1 cup water

Infuse the rosemary in the water following the instructions in Appendix G. Strain, then stir in the witch hazel. Store in the refrigerator, where it will keep for several weeks. To use, saturate a sterile cotton pad with the liquid and apply to the affected area. Repeat twice a day until healed.

Continued ➔

ABSCESS POULTICE

Garlic draws infection from an abscess and helps it heal quickly.

2 or 3 cloves garlic, crushed

2 ounces castor oil

Combine the garlic and oil in a small jar. Place this jar in a pan filled with a few inches of cold water. Bring the water to a boil, reduce heat, and simmer until the garlic in the jar becomes soft, about 15 minutes.

Using oven mitts or tongs, remove the hot jar from the water and allow it to cool for 15 to 20 minutes; it should be warm but not hot. Saturate a clean, damp cloth with the warm oil and bind it over the abscess, using a towel or clean bandage to hold it in place. Allow it to remain on the affected area for several hours. Repeat several times per day.

The garlic-infused oil should be kept in the refrigerator, where it will keep for up to 3 days. Rewarm before using.

ARTHRITIS RELIEF

For an effective massage oil that relieves stiffness and soreness due to arthritis, combine 4 drops rosemary essential oil, 2 drops lavender essential oil, and 2 drops clove essential oil with 2 teaspoons olive oil. Massage gently into the dog's most painful areas.

Recipes for Ear Health

Your dog's ears are vulnerable to a host of diseases and dirt. You should examine them every day, if possible, but at least once a week for mites, dirt, burrs, and other potential irritants. Through early detection and use of some of these herbal recipes, you may be able to stop a small ear problem from becoming a serious ear infection.

ROSEMARY EAR INFECTION WASH

Rosemary is both antiseptic and anti-inflammatory, and it contains salicin, a natural painkiller.

3 parts rosemary herb

1 part witch hazel

Crush the rosemary with a mortar and pestle. Combine the rosemary and witch hazel and let steep in a warm, dry location for 1 to 2 weeks, shaking every day. Strain, then rebottle in a container with an airtight lid. Store in a cool, dark location, where the infusion will keep for up to 6 months.

To use, in the morning grab a cotton ball with long tweezers, dip the cotton into the rosemary infusion, and use it to gently swab the ear. Then drop 1 teaspoon of the infusion into the ear. In the evening, gently swab the ear with a clean cotton ball until it is dry.

TREATING OTITIS

To treat otitis, otherwise known as ear cankers, simply combine 1/2 teaspoon lemon juice and 1 1/2 teaspoons warm water. Drop into the affected ear.

SOOTHING EAR OIL

This herbal oil helps remove foreign matter from the ear and soothe irritations.

1/4 cup olive oil

1 teaspoon cloves

1 teaspoon rosemary herb

1 teaspoon rue leaves

Warm the oil over low heat, then remove from heat and stir in the herbs. Cover and let steep for several hours. Store the oil in the refrigerator, where it will keep for up to 2 weeks. Rewarm the oil before using.

Twice a day, use a cotton swab dipped in the infused oil to clean the ears, then place a few drops of oil in the ears.

Sick Like a Dog

Yes, there are times when your canine companion truly is as sick as a dog. Maybe he got into the garbage and ate some spoiled food and is now paying the consequences with a bad stomachache or a bout of diarrhea. Maybe he's suffering from a cold. Whatever the cause, when your dog's health is under attack, these healing herbal recipes will help restore it.

DIARRHEA RELIEF

Adapted from *Dr. Kidd's Guide to Herbal Dog Care*, by Randy Kidd, D.V.M. (Storey Books, 2000)

Diarrhea is not typically an ailment all on its own; it's usually a symptom of a more serious disorder such as incorrect diet, overeating, eating spoiled food, a bacterial infection, or even allergies to chemical preservatives in processed food. Worms and distemper may also be factors. So if you dog is suffering from chronic diarrhea, bring him to your veterinarian for an accurate diagnosis.

Slippery elm is an excellent remedy for diarrhea. As a demulcent, it coats and soothes the sensitive mucous membranes of the gastrointestinal tract.

1 teaspoonful of powdered slippery elm bark per 20 pounds of your dog's weight

Spring water

Dissolve the powder in a dropperful or two of water. Administer orally. Repeat 4 or 5 times a day until the diarrhea stops.

Caution: Don't use this herb for more than 3 to 4 weeks at a time. Slippery elm is so effective as a coating agent that, over time, it can obstruct the absorption of nutrients.

CAUTION

An occasional case of diarrhea can be curbed with herbs. However, if your dog is suffering repeated bouts of diarrhea, he or she is at risk for dehydration and a host of other maladies. For acute or chronic cases of diarrhea, therefore, bring your dog to a veterinarian for a complete exam.

Chronic or acute diarrhea can be a symptom of or can contribute to a serious health condition and should be treated by a veterinarian.

Flea and Parasite Repellents

Fleas, ticks, and other skin parasites are the bane of all pet owners. You should brush your dog regularly, keeping an eye out for these pesky pests. Regular grooming also helps keep you in tune with your dog's health.

Sadly, if your dog has a serious flea problem, herbs won't help. There are many good herbal flea repellents, but they don't kill fleas, and they don't have much of an effect on flea larvae or eggs. To banish the fleas, you'll have to resort to using one of the chemical-dependent commercial flea powders available in pet shops and most larger supermarkets. *After* you've gotten rid of the fleas, you may be able to depend on herbs to keep the little pests away.

UPSET TUMMY TEA

This tea can ease the discomfort that accompanies occasional vomiting caused by a mild upset stomach. Of course, if the vomiting is prolonged or excessive, you should bring your dog to a veterinarian for a checkup.

1 cup water

1 teaspoon peppermint leaves

1 pinch powdered ginger

1 pinch powdered cloves

Bring the water to a boil. Pour it over the herbs, cover, and let steep 10 to 15 minutes. Give 1 to 2 teaspoons of the tea three times per day. Store any leftover tea in the refrigerator, where it will keep for up to 2 days.

COUGH-RELIEF TEA

Coughing can be a symptom of more serious conditions such as distemper, worms, and lung disorders. It can also be caused by irritation of the mucous membranes. This recipe can help relieve coughing, but if symptoms persist or worsen, consult your veterinarian.

1 tablespoon licorice root	1 tablespoon elder blossoms
1 tablespoon slippery elm bark	1 tablespoon thyme leaves
2 cups water	2 teaspoons honey
1 tablespoon borage leaves and flowers	

Stir the licorice root and slippery elm bark into the water. Bring to a boil; reduce heat and simmer, covered, for 15 to 20 minutes. Remove from the heat; stir in the borage, elder, and thyme; and let steep, covered, 10 to 15 minutes. Strain, add the honey, and let cool. Give 2 tablespoons of this herbal mix before meals.

MINTY HEAT-RELIEF COMPRESS

This compress is useful for relieving mild cases of heat stress in your dog.

1 cup water

3 tablespoons peppermint leaf

Bring the water to a boil. Pour it over the peppermint, cover, and let steep 10 to 15 minutes, then pour over ice cubes. Soak a clean cloth in the cool tea, then place the compress on your dog's chest or belly. Hold in place 5 minutes. Repeat this treatment as necessary to cool the dog.

FLEAS-FLEE LOTION

This herbal rub repels fleas from climbing on your pet and, if they're already there, encourages them to leave.

12 lemons

1 gallon water

Slice each of the lemons in half and put them in a 1-gallon jar filled with water. Place this jar in the hot sun for a week, until the lemons begin to turn moldy; then strain and rebottle. Stored in the refrigerator, this infusion will last for several weeks. Rub this mixture into all parts of the dog's body daily.

FLEAS-FLEE POWDER

If you prefer a powder over a liquid rub, here's one that's helpful in ridding your pet of fleas.

1 part powdered rosemary herb

1 part powdered pennyroyal leaves

1 part powdered rue leaves

1 part powdered southernwood leaves

1 part powdered wormwood leaves

Combine all the herbs. Apply liberally on your dog, remembering under the tail, the inner thighs, the "armpits," and the genital area. You may want to undertake this task outdoors or the powder will end up all over your house.

> **QUICK TIP**
>
> An easy way to protect your dog from fleas is to apply a drop or two of eucalyptus essential oil on top of its head and ears, down the spine, and on the tail.

AROMATIC HOMEMADE FLEA COLLAR

This flea collar discourages fleas from taking up residence on your dog.

1 part chamomile flowers	1 part southernwood leaves
1 part pennyroyal leaves	1 part wormwood leaves
1 part rosemary herb	3 to 5 drops eucalyptus essential oil
1 part rue leaves	

Continued →

Combine all the ingredients and spread across the length of a scarf or bandana. Roll up the scarf around the herbs and tie it around your dog's neck.

Regular application of a flea rinse or powder will rid your dog of these pests and discourage them from returning.

BUGS-BE-GONE TONIC

When mixed with dandelion, garlic helps repel parasites and acts as a general tonic.

1 part crushed garlic cloves
1 part fresh dandelion roots, leaves, and flowers
Apple cider vinegar

Loosely fill a pint jar with the crushed garlic cloves and dandelion. Fill the jar with apple cider vinegar. Seal and leave in a warm place for a month or longer, shaking often. Use it right from this bottle or strain and rebottle. Give I teaspoon per 20 pounds of body weight per day, in food or water.

Resources

American Holistic Veterinary Medicine Association
2218 Old Emmorton Road
Bel Air, MD 21015
(410) 569–0795
Web site: www.altvetmed.com
The association's Web site lists holistic veterinarians by state and specifies the types of alternative medicines that each vet uses.

National Center for Homeopathy
801 North Fairfax Street
Suite 306
Alexandria, VA 22314
(703) 548–7790

Natural Pet Care Catalog
8050 Lake City Way
Seattle, WA 98115
(800) 962–8266
Web site: www.all-the-best.com

PetSage
4313 Wheeler Avenue
Alexandria, VA 22304

(800) 738–4584
Web site: www.petsage.com
Free catalog of products for animals.

Whole Animal Catalog
3131 Hennepin Avenue South
Minneapolis, MN 55408
Web site: www.visi.com/~holistic

The Whole Dog Journal
1175 Regent Street
Alameda, CA 94501
(510) 749–1080
An excellent newsletter focusing on the holistic care of dogs.

RABBITS

Raising a Healthy Rabbit

Nancy Searle

Illustrations by Carol J. Jessop

Why Rabbits?

Raising rabbits is gaining in popularity for many reasons. For example, rabbits can be raised in any type of environment, whether it be country, suburb, or city, and they fit easily into most family settings. A rabbit makes a friendly, low-maintenance family pet and is a good size animal for children as well as adults to care for. In addition, it doesn't take a lot of money to get started with rabbits—this project will fit into most family budgets. Although proper equipment contributes to the success of raising rabbits, it is more important for equipment to be functional than fancy.

Choosing the Right Rabbit

There is an unusually broad range of choices for rabbits. Much depends on whether you want a pet or a wool business. Also influencing your choice may be:

- **Availability.** Is your chosen breed raised in your area? If you select a breed that is popular locally, you will have a greater choice of quality animals.

- **Cost of animal.** You will find that some breeds command higher prices than others.

- **Cost of care.** Other factors, such as breed size, also affect overall costs, since larger breeds need larger housing and consume more feed.

- **Amount of care.** Angoras, which must be groomed daily, take more time than do other breeds.

- **Ease of raising.** Some breeds, such as Netherland Dwarfs and Holland Lops, can be difficult to raise.

After you have evaluated your own needs and preferences, you'll want to select a breed, locate breeders with stock for sale, and then visit a rabbitry to choose your rabbit.

GOOD BREEDS FOR PETS

An increasing number of people keep rabbits as pets. As pets, rabbits can be kept indoors or out, they make no noise, they have few veterinary needs (including no vaccination), their initial cost is low, and daily care is not demanding. These features make rabbits ideal pets for busy, modern families. Any breed may be kept as a pet, but if you want to raise rabbits primarily to sell as pets, you are wise to consider some of the smaller breeds. These include: Netherland Dwarf, Dutch, Mini Lop, and Holland Lop.

GOOD BREEDS FOR FIBER

In recent years, natural fibers and handcrafted items have become very popular. This has brought about a new appreciation for the Angora rabbit breeds. Soft and warm, Angora wool is obtained by pulling the loose hair from the mature coat. Because you are really just helping the natural shedding process, this hand plucking does not hurt the animal. The plucked wool can then be spun into yarn. Although Angora rabbits require some special management (they need to be groomed often), raising them and selling their wool is an excellent business venture.

HOW MANY RABBITS DO YOU WANT?

Whether you are looking for a pet or want to start a small rabbit business, you may want to begin with one rabbit. This allows you to experience both the fun and the work that goes with rabbit ownership. If you enjoy caring for one rabbit, you can get more rabbits as time goes on.

Some new rabbit owners who intend to start a breeding program choose to start with more than one. A reasonable number to begin with is three rabbits, consisting of one *buck* (male) and two *does* (female), known as a *trio*. Ask the breeder to help you select three rabbits that are not too closely related. Look at the animals' pedigrees. The rabbits in your trio may have some relatives in common, but their pedigrees should show some differences in their family trees as well. Your trio should not be brother and sisters. Three rabbits from the same litter are too closely related to be used for breeding purposes.

Whatever number of rabbits you begin with, remember that each rabbit will need its own cage. Don't purchase more animals than you are able to care for properly.

RECOGNIZING A HEALTHY RABBIT

Good health is the most important quality to consider when you select your stock. Look for the following features to determine a healthy rabbit.

- **Eyes.** The eyes are bright, with no discharge and no spots or cloudiness.
- **Ears.** The ears look clean inside. A brown, crusty appearance could indicate ear mites.
- **Nose.** The nose is clean and dry, with no discharge that might indicate a cold.
- **Front feet.** These are clean. A crusty matting on the inside of the front paws indicates that the rabbit has been wiping a runny nose, and thus may have a cold.
- **Hind feet.** The bottoms of the hind feet are well furred. Bare or sore-looking spots can indicate the beginning of sore hocks.

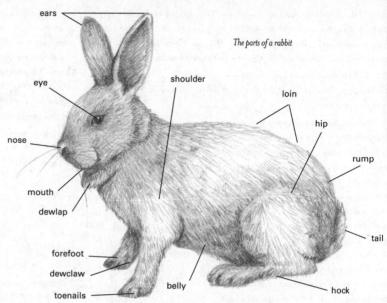

The parts of a rabbit

- **Teeth.** The front teeth line up correctly, with the front top two teeth slightly overlapping the bottom ones.
- **General condition.** The rabbit's fur is clean. Its body feels smooth and firm, not bony.
- **Rear end.** The area at the base of the rabbit's tail should be clean, with no manure sticking to the fur.

Getting Acquainted

A new rabbit has many adjustments to make. Give your rabbit a few days to get used to you and its new surroundings before you handle it a lot.

Get to know your rabbit in a setting where both of you can be comfortable. A good place to get acquainted is at a picnic table covered with a rug, towel, or some other covering that will give the rabbit secure, not slippery, footing. Your rabbit will be able to move around safely on the table, and you can safely visit and pet your rabbit without having to lift it. Rabbits will usually not jump off a table. In spite of this, *never leave a rabbit unattended when it is out of its cage.*

Once your rabbit seems comfortable on the table, practice picking it up. Because the table offers a handy surface to set the rabbit safely back onto, this setting is much better than risking a possible fall to the ground.

PICKING UP YOUR RABBIT

The best way to pick up a rabbit is to place one hand under it, just behind its front legs. Place your other hand under the animal's rump. Lift with the hand that is by the front legs and support the animal's weight with your other hand. Place the animal next to your body, with its head directed

A "football hold" is a secure way to carry your rabbit.

Continued ➜

toward the corner formed by your elbow. Your lifting arm and your body now support the rabbit—just like tucking a football against you. Your other hand is free and can rest on the rabbit's back for extra security. Place the animal gently back on the table and repeat this lift.

To help your rabbit become comfortable with being carried, practice handling skills often, but for short periods of time—10 to 15 minutes at a stretch.

Sometimes an overactive or frightened bunny will struggle and get out of control. When this happens, drop to one knee as you work to quiet your animal. Lowering yourself to one knee lessens the distance the rabbit has to fall and provides a more secure base for a frightened rabbit. You can also easily set the animal on the ground from this position, if necessary. After it's had a short rest on the ground, carefully and securely lift the rabbit again. Even the most mild-mannered rabbit can have a bad day, so be prepared to handle any situation in a calm, controlled manner.

TURNING YOUR RABBIT OVER

After you master lifting and carrying your rabbit, you will want to learn how to turn it over; you'll need to get it in this position in order to better observe its teeth, its toenails, and its sex. You can't see everything about a rabbit just by looking at the top!

If your rabbit starts to struggle while you are holding it, drop to one knee.

Turning a rabbit over puts the animal into a very unnatural position. First, its feet are off the ground so it cannot run away, and second, to make matters worse from its point of view, its underside is now exposed. A wild rabbit in this position is probably one that is about to be eaten by a predator! Your rabbit has good reason to resist this type of handling, so be especially careful and patient.

Practice turning your rabbit over back at the table where you first learned how to lift and carry it. Again, you will want a rug on the table, and wear a long-sleeved shirt.

To turn the rabbit, use one hand to control the head and the other hand to control and support the hindquarters. Place the hand that holds the rabbit's head so that you are folding its ears down against its back, while you reach around the base of the head. If you prefer, you can place your index finger between the base of the rabbit's ears and then wrap your other fingers around toward its jaw. With your other hand, cradle the rump. Now that your hands are in place, lift with the hand that is on the head and at the same time roll the animal's hindquarters toward you. Try to do this movement in a smooth, unhurried manner.

If your rabbit cooperated, you will now be able to let the table support its hindquarters. This will free the hand that was holding the rump to check other things, such as the teeth and toenails. If your rabbit fights against this procedure, it is showing you that this is not its first choice of positions. Keep trying, but be sure to do so in a place where the rabbit hasn't far to fall, and try to support it securely. Your rabbit can injure itself if it struggles and falls.

If you need to turn your rabbit over for a closer look and no table is handy, let the animal rest on your forearm instead of on the table. When you have the rabbit in this position, you get better control over the hindquarters, because they are tucked between your elbow and your body. This is even easier if you sit in a chair; you can then use your legs instead of the table to support your rabbit. In fact, you may find that when you are seated, you can hold your rabbit more securely for grooming and toenail trimming.

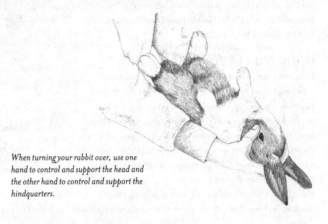

When turning your rabbit over, use one hand to control and support the head and the other hand to control and support the hindquarters.

The Best Housing

Rabbit housing—called a hutch—can be the largest single expense in your rabbit project. Whether you buy or build, you must be sure that your housing—and the environment in which you place it—meets the rabbit's needs. Proper housing contributes greatly to the health and happiness of your animals.

RABBIT HOUSING CHECKLIST

Good rabbit housing must:

- Provide adequate space
- Protect your rabbits from the weather
- Protect your rabbits from other animals
- Be easy to clean

PROVIDING ADEQUATE SPACE

Your rabbit will spend most of its time in its hutch; the hutch should be large enough for the rabbit to move around in, as well as for feeding equipment. When planning how much space you need, the general rule is to allow 1 square foot (0.1 m2) of space for each pound your rabbit weighs. A cage that is 2 feet (60 cm) wide and 3 feet (90 cm) long is 6 square feet (0.6 m2) and would be perfect for a 6-pound (2.7 kg) Mini Lop. Find out how much a mature animal of your rabbit's breed weighs, and use this as a guide to plan the size of its hutch. Young rabbits and bucks may do fine with slightly less space, but does that will be having litters (baby bunnies) will need the whole amount.

After you have figured the width and length of the cage, you must decide how high it should be. Most cages are 18 inches (45 cm) high, although small breeds, like the Netherland Dwarf, need a height of only 12 to 14 inches (30–35 cm).

PROTECTION FROM INCLEMENT WEATHER

Many people who own multiple rabbits keep their rabbitries outdoors. With proper care, rabbits have fewer health problems when raised outdoors and can survive temperatures well below zero. However, you do need to provide protection from winds, rain, and snow. If your cages are inside, you are already providing this protection. If your cages are outside, you will want to add protection as the temperature drops. Most outdoor cages can be enclosed quite easily by stapling plastic sheeting around three sides. If you live where the weather is extremely cold, cover the front with a flap of plastic as well. Do not enclose the whole cage so tightly that the ventilation is poor or that it is difficult to get in to feed and care for your animal.

Take advantage of the winter sun. If your outside cages are movable, place them in a location that receives a lot of direct sun.

Although healthy adult rabbits don't suffer when it is cold, newborn rabbits can easily die from the cold. If you are expecting a litter during cold weather, be sure the doe has a well-bedded nest box. You may want to move the doe into a warmer location, such as a cellar or garage. After the litter is about 10 days old, the cage, with Mom and her nest box of babies, can be moved back outside.

Rabbits are most comfortable when the temperatures are between 50° and 69°F (10° and 20°C). In hot climates, it is important to locate the cage in the shade, and ensure that the cage has lots of air circulation around it. Also provide plenty of cool, fresh water.

In extreme heat, use empty plastic soda bottles to make rabbit coolers. Fill the bottles two-thirds to three-quarters full with water and keep them in your freezer. In periods of extreme heat, lay a frozen bottle in each cage. The rabbits will beat the heat when they stretch out alongside their rabbit cooler.

Wrap plastic sheeting around three sides of your hutch, and nail a separate flap of plastic over the front.

PROTECTION FROM OTHER ANIMALS

A sturdy, well-built hutch will contribute to the safety of your rabbits. Most cages are built on legs or hung above the ground—which also makes the cages safer from dogs, cats, rodents, raccoons, and opossums. Keeping your cages in a fenced area or indoors offers even better protection, but this may be impossible when you are just getting started.

EASY-TO-CLEAN CAGES

Clean cages are important to the health of your rabbits. If your cages are easy to clean, you will be able to do a better job of caring for your rabbits. Cages should have a wire floor that allows droppings to fall

through to a tray or to the ground. Choose all-wire cages or wood-framed cages that do not have areas where manure can pile up. Plan your cages so you can easily reach into them and get around them to clean all parts

---

POOR CAGE MATERIALS

- Do not choose a hutch that is made with poultry wire or with hardware cloth. These products are not sturdy enough for a safe, long-lasting hutch.

- Do not buy a cage made of mesh larger than 1" x 2" (2.5 cm x 5 cm). A larger mesh may be cheaper, but it is not a good idea because baby bunnies can squeeze through.

- Never use a cage that has 1" x 1" (2.5 cm x 2.5 cm) or 1" x 2" (2.5 cm x 5 cm) wire for its floor. Rabbits can get their feet caught in these openings and break or dislocate their rear legs. Instead, look for cages with 1/2" x 1" (1.3 cm x 2.5 cm) floor wire. This smaller mesh gives more support to the rabbit's feet, but the spaces are still large enough to allow manure to pass through.

Proper Nutrition for Healthy Rabbits

Providing proper feed for your rabbits is a very important part of successful rabbit raising. A healthy, balanced diet is based on providing commercial rabbit pellets and fresh water. In the past, rabbit owners had to mix different feeds in order to get the proper nutritional balance for their animals. Nowadays, stores carry feed that is already balanced. Commercial pellets are the best and easiest way to provide proper nutrition for your rabbits. However, commercial feeds do vary, and different feeds are available in different locations. Talk with other breeders and with your feed store clerk to learn about the brands available in your area.

You'll also learn that even under the same brand name there are often several different types of feed. These types of feed are designed to meet the needs of different rabbits at different stages in their lives. The feed ingredient that varies is the protein content. Mature animals usually need a feed that provides 15 to 16 percent protein. Young growing animals and active breeding does are often fed a ration with a higher level of protein, 17 to 18 percent.

UNDERSTANDING FEED LABELS

The U.S. government requires that all rabbit feed contain at least a certain amount of protein and fat. A feed may contain more than these amounts, but not less. The amount of protein and fat is listed on the feed package. The package also lists the fiber content. A package label may say that the feed has no more than 18 or 20 percent fiber, but this tells you only the *maximum* amount of fiber. You also need to know the *minimum* amount it contains. It is very important that rabbits eat feed containing at least 16 percent fiber. If they get less than that, they may have diarrhea.

WATER

No matter which type of feed you provide, your rabbits will not eat well unless you provide the most important nutrient of all—*water*! We often do not think of water as food, but it is essential to your rabbits' health. Rabbits simply do not thrive without a constant supply of clean water.

Continued ➜

SALT

Salt is another ingredient that is important to a balanced feed. It is not necessary to provide a salt spool for your rabbit (and they cause your cage to rust, as well). You may see advertisements for inexpensive salt spools that can be hung in each cage, but the commercial pellets you use as feed already include enough salt to meet your rabbit's needs.

HAY

Many owners also feed hay to their rabbits. Feeding hay will add more time to your feeding and cleaning chores, but rabbits enjoy good-quality hay, and it adds extra fiber to their diet. If you feed hay, be sure it smells good, is not dusty, and is not moldy.

If you choose to feed hay on a regular basis, you will want hay mangers in each cage. Hay mangers are easy to construct from scraps of 1" x 2" (2.5 cm x 5 cm) wire. If you make your own cage, you can use the leftover wire. If your cages are indoors and are of all-wire construction, you can just place a handful of hay on the top and the rabbits will reach up and pull it through the wire. Avoid setting hay inside on the floor of the cage, because it will soon become soiled and droppings will collect on it. This can cause disease and parasite problems.

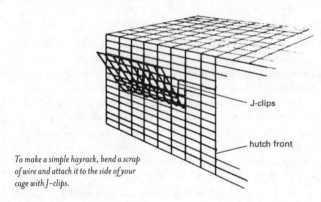

J-clips

hutch front

To make a simple hayrack, bend a scrap of wire and attach it to the side of your cage with J-clips.

WHEN TO FEED

If we study the feeding habits of wild rabbits, we can apply what we learn to feeding our domestic rabbits. In nature, rabbits have learned to stay in a safe place during the day. In late afternoon, hungry wild rabbits come out of hiding. By this time, they are ready for their big meal of the day. Wild rabbits are *nocturnal* animals, active throughout the night and into the early-morning hours.

If our tame rabbits could pick a mealtime, they would probably agree with their wild relatives and choose late afternoon. Using this information, most rabbit breeders feed the largest portion of their rabbits' daily ration in the late afternoon or early evening.

How often should your rabbits be fed? Although different breeders develop a schedule that works for them, two feedings a day—one in the morning and one in the late afternoon—seem to be most common. If you choose to feed twice a day, serve a lesser portion in the morning than in the afternoon.

FEEDING TIME IS CHECKUP TIME

If you have self-feeders and water bottles, you may feel comfortable feeding only once a day. Feeding time, however, is for more than just feeding. Time spent with your rabbits is an opportunity for discovering situations such as:

- Has a youngster fallen out of the nest box?

- Is an animal sick or not eating well?

- Does a cage need a simple repair before it becomes a major repair?

- Does your rabbit need extra water due to extreme heat or freezing conditions? Remember that the overall health of your rabbit will be better if clean, fresh water is available at all times.

Because a lot can happen to your rabbits in a 24-hour period, you should feed, water, and observe your animals at least twice a day. The serious rabbit breeder will see this as a worthwhile investment in time.

Whatever feeding schedule you choose, remember that it is very important to follow the same schedule every day. Your rabbits depend upon you, and they will settle into the schedule that you set. Avoid variation in feeding times. If you regularly feed at 7 A.M, you should do so even if it's Saturday and you want to stay in bed a little longer. Plan ahead for times when you cannot be there to feed your rabbits. Be sure other family members are familiar with your feeding program so that they can help out from time to time. If your family includes more than one rabbit raiser, you can take turns with feeding responsibilities.

HOW MUCH TO FEED

There is no set amount of feed that is right for all rabbits, but the following chart gives you some average amounts.

AMOUNT OF PELLETS NEEDED EACH DAY*			
	Small Breeds	Medium Breeds	Large Breeds
Bucks	2 oz.	3–6 oz.	4–9 oz.
Does	3 oz.	6 oz.	9 oz.
Doe, bred 1–15 days	3 oz.	6 oz.	9 oz.
Doe, bred 16–30 days	3 1/2–4 oz.	7–8 oz.	10–11 oz.
Doe, plus litter (6–8 young), 1 week old	8 oz.	10 oz.	12 oz.
Doe, plus litter (6–8 young), 1 month old	14 oz.	18 oz.	24 oz.
Doe, plus litter (6–8 young), 6–8 weeks old	22 oz.	28 oz.	36 oz.
Young rabbit (weaned), 2 months old	2–3 oz.	3–6 oz.	6–9 oz.
*1 ounce = 28 grams			

In order to use this chart, you need a simple way to measure how much to feed each animal. You can make your own measuring container from empty cans. For example, a 6-ounce tuna fish can filled level to the top holds 4 ounces of pellets. The same can filled so that the pellets form a small mound above the lid gives a 5-ounce serving. You may use a larger can and mark several different levels to indicate the amounts you most commonly feed.

Feed guidelines are exactly what their name says, *guidelines only*. As you get to know your rabbits better, you will find that some need more feed and some need less. A simple way to judge who need more or less is to feel your rabbits regularly. Just a few pats can give you an idea of their condition. If you stroke each rabbit from the base of its head and follow along the backbone, you will soon learn to tell who is too fat and who is too thin. When you run your hand over the rabbit, you will feel the backbone below the fur and muscles. As you feel the bumps of the individual bones that make up the backbone, they should feel rounded. If the bumps feel sharp or pointed, your rabbit can use an increase in feed. (*Note*: Extreme thinness may also indicate health problems.) If you don't feel the individual bumps, it probably means there is too much fat covering them, so that rabbit will do better on less feed.

Stroke your rabbit along its backbone regularly to judge whether it is getting the proper amount of food. The bumps of the individual bones that make up the backbone should feel rounded.

If you need to adjust the feed amount, make the change gradually, not all at once. Unless the rabbit is extremely thin or extremely fat, increase or decrease by about 1 ounce each day. A small plastic scoop that is used to measure ground coffee holds about 1 ounce of pellets. Use this scoop to add or subtract feed, 1 ounce at a time. It will take awhile for the change to show on your rabbit, but you should see and feel a difference in 1 to 2 weeks. It's good to get in the habit of giving each rabbit a weekly check. It takes only a few seconds to feel down the back of an animal. If you check regularly, you will be able to adjust feed before your rabbit becomes extremely fat or thin.

In general, overfeeding is a more common problem than underfeeding. For one thing, overfeeding means it costs you more to care for your rabbits. In addition, if you are breeding your rabbits, you'll find that overweight rabbits are generally less productive than animals of the proper weight. In fact, fat rabbits often do not breed, and an overweight doe that does become pregnant can often develop problems.

SPECIAL CASES

In some special cases, a rabbit's feed may need to be adjusted.

- A young, growing rabbit needs more feed than a mature rabbit of the same size.

- Rabbits need more feed in cold weather than in hot.

- A doe that is producing milk for her litter needs more food than a doe without a litter.

RESPONSIBLE RABBITRY MANAGEMENT

A good schedule will allow you to use your time effectively to accomplish the many tasks that are part of raising healthy rabbits. The chores that are required can be broken down into daily, weekly, and monthly tasks.

THINGS TO DO DAILY

- **Feed and water regularly.** Establish a daily schedule and stick with it 7 days a week.

- **Observe your rabbits and their environment.** Daily observation helps you catch small problems before they become large problems.

- **Keep things clean.** Attend to small cleaning needs so they don't grow into large cleaning chores.

- **Handle your rabbits.** Regular handling will make your animals more gentle, and you will become more aware of their individual condition. This may be impractical in a large rabbitry, but you should strive to handle some of your animals each day.

THINGS TO DO WEEKLY

- **Clean cages.** Solid-bottom cages and cages with pullout trays must be cleaned and re-bedded weekly. On wire-bottom cages, use a wire brush to remove any buildup of manure or fur.

- **Clean feeders.** Rinse crocks with water-and-chlorine-bleach solution (1 part household bleach to 5 parts water). Check self-feeders for clogs of spoiled feed.

- **Check rabbits' health.** If there are animals that you did not have time to handle and check earlier in the week, do so now.

- **Check supplies.** Do you have enough feed and bedding for the coming week?

- **Make necessary repairs.** Have you noticed a loose door latch or a small hole in the wire flooring? Take time to do these small repairs before they lead to larger problems.

THINGS TO DO MONTHLY

- **Check toenails.** You will not have to trim the toenails of every rabbit every month, but you should check each animal and trim those that need it. This is an important management skill to learn, because properly trimmed toenails decrease the chances of your rabbit being injured. Long toenails can get caught in the cage wire and cause broken toes and missing toenails. The time spent trimming toenails will also benefit you; you will be less likely to be scratched when you handle your rabbit.

Trimming toenails is usually a two-person job. With someone holding the rabbit on its back, use one hand to push back the fur so that you can see the nail and the other hand to do the trimming. Trim just the tip of the nail, not the more dense portion, which contains blood vessels.

Build Rabbit Housing

Bob Bennett

The equipment you need to build and outfit a rabbitry is quite limited: hutches, feeders, waterers, and nest boxes. Essential hand tools to build the rabbitry are also few; most households have all but one or two. No power tools are required; nor do you need a large outlay of cash or time. You can construct and outfit your rabbitry as both allow. Interruptions to the construction process will present no problem—you can drop the work and resume it at any point. You can build indoors or out; the materials make no dust or dirt and require no loud banging or sawing. Everything is quite clean and quiet. And simple. If you follow the instructions, your very first efforts will produce a product that functions as well and looks as good as any built by experienced professionals.

The All-Wire Hutch

Successful rabbit raisers consider no other materials for a rabbit hutch than wire and metal. Among other activities, rabbits gnaw and urinate, so you can dismiss wood immediately. If you use wood, they will eat some of it and foul the rest of it. Wire and metal cost less than lumber; no expensive hinges or other hardware are required.

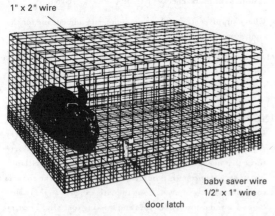

1" x 2" wire

baby saver wire
1/2" x 1" wire

door latch

The basic all-wire hutch. Front, top, back, and sides are 1" x 2" wire. Floor is 1/2" x 1" wire. Door is positioned off center to allow a feeder and waterer at right.

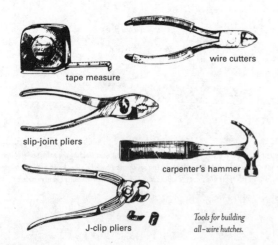

tape measure

wire cutters

slip-joint pliers

carpenter's hammer

J-clip pliers

Tools for building all-wire hutches.

If you need only one or two hutches, perhaps for pet rabbits, buy them from your local farm supply store or send away to a supplier. That's because the welded wire fabric you need is expensive in small quantities (if it is available at all), and it will be cheaper for you to buy one or two than to build them.

To build your own, here are the tools and materials you will need.

Tools

One pair of heavy-duty, 7" or 8" wire-cutting pliers, preferably with flush-cutting jaws.

One pair of ordinary slip-joint pliers.

One tape measure, preferably retractable steel. A 12' tape is best but a shorter one will do.

An ordinary carpenter's hammer.

One pair of special J-clip pliers, available from your farm supply store.

A short length of 2 x 4 lumber; about 3' long is fine.

Materials

A supply of 1" x 2" welded wire fencing, 14 gauge, sometimes called turkey wire. Dimensions will vary as described below.

A supply of 1/2" x 1" welded wire, 14 or 16 gauge, with variable dimensions as described below.

A supply of J-clips, available where you obtain the J-clip pliers.

A door latch for each hutch.

A door hanger for each hutch.

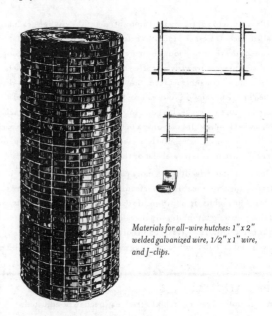

Materials for all-wire hutches: 1" x 2" welded galvanized wire, 1/2" x 1" wire, and J-clips.

Before we actually start hutch construction, let's discuss the tools and materials for a good understanding of what is involved.

ABOUT THE TOOLS

The wire-cutting pliers need to be large enough to give substantial leverage for cutting through 14-gauge wire. A good cutting tool, made of high-quality steel, isn't cheap. If you plan to make more than a few hutches, spend enough to get a good pair. Ideally, the jaws will be fairly narrow so they can get a good bite on the 1/2" x 1" wire. Some rabbit raisers buy a second, smaller pair for working with the smaller mesh wire if they can't find a larger pair with narrow jaws. Unbeveled cutting jaws will make a flush cut; the result will be a smoother hutch with few sharp edges. Less leverage is required with the smaller mesh wire. Plastic handle grips will make your pliers more comfortable, and wearing a leather glove will help prevent blisters.

J-clip pliers are made for use with J-clips. When squeezed tightly around two parallel wires, they produce a clamp unsurpassed for hutch making. It is true that you can use hog rings or C-rings and hog ring pliers; you can even get away with twisting wire stubs or other short pieces of wire around cage sections. These items and techniques will work, but they are time-consuming and usually will not produce as attractive and durable a hutch.

A metal bending brake is probably more efficient than a hammer and 2 x 4 for bending wire, but it is hardly worth the investment unless you build an extremely large rabbitry. If you have access to one, you will save a little time. Power wire-cutting shears are also on the market, but their cost is justified only if you plan to build a great many hutches.

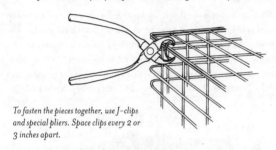

To fasten the pieces together, use J-clips and special pliers. Space clips every 2 or 3 inches apart.

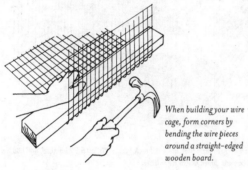

When building your wire cage, form corners by bending the wire pieces around a straight-edged wooden board.

ABOUT THE WIRE

You will need welded wire fencing in both 14-gauge 1" x 2" and 1/2" x 1", or 16-gauge 1/2" x 1". The 14-gauge wire is heavier, better, and more expensive, but is more difficult to obtain in many areas. Instead of 1" x 2" wire you may substitute 1" x 1" or 1" x 1/2". Both of these will make a sturdier cage, but the cage will be overbuilt and not worth the extra expense and extra work (more cutting), unless you plan to raise the giant, extra-heavy breeds of rabbits, or you already have some of this wire available, or are offered some at a bargain price.

Welded wire comes in basically two types—galvanized *before* welding and galvanized *after* welding. Buy the latter. It costs more, but is more rigid and will last longer. Welded wire wears out by oxidation, and wire that is galvanized after welding has more material to oxidize. It will appear thicker, especially at the joints, than wire galvanized before welding, which is smoother to the touch. You can build with wire galvanized before welding but the results will not be as satisfactory.

Sometimes it is possible to find "aluminized" welded wire instead of galvanized. This is very good wire. If you can find some, it makes an excellent hutch.

Some rabbit breeders have experimented with vinyl-covered welded wire. Rabbits love to gnaw, however, and easily can strip the vinyl covering from the wire, which is ungalvanized and soon will rust.

Another point: there is both 1" x 2" wire and 2" x 1" wire. The former has wires every inch of the width of the roll. The latter has wires every 2 inches of the width of the roll. The 1" x 2" is better, but 2" x 1" will work. When calculating dimensions keep in mind that you lose an inch or two each time you cut this wire.

DOOR LATCHES

As you can see from the picture, the recommended door latches are easy to fabricate from heavy galvanized metal that can be riveted or bolted together. These latches are so inexpensive, however, that buying them seems a better use of time, unless you happen to be adept at metal working and already have a supply of bolts or rivets and a riveter. The same can be said for the door hangers.

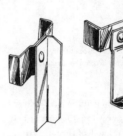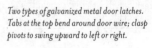

Two types of galvanized metal door latches. Tabs at the top bend around door wire; clasp pivots to swing upward to left or right.

HOW BIG TO MAKE THE HUTCHES

All-wire rabbit hutches consist of little more than boxes with 1" x 2" wire on front, back, top, and sides, and 1/2" x 1" wire on the bottom. How big to make the boxes and how many to make is up to you. Here are a few points for consideration.

Single vs. Multiple Hutches. Making single hutches at a time will give you total flexibility in hutch layout or rabbitry configuration. Rabbits tend to multiply, so your rabbitry is likely to grow and to change shape or design. Single hutches give you the flexibility you might want to get in and out of rabbit raising, to move, or to build totally new facilities. You can move single hutches easily. They appeal more to others who may purchase them from you later and use them in a different arrangement.

Multiple hutch units will save you time overall because you divide them with shared partitions and assemble them faster, with less cutting and fastening. They won't necessarily save you money on materials, however, because single shared partitions demand more costly 1/2" x 1" wire instead of 1" x 2". This additional expense can be debated, however, if you have purchased the 1/2" x 1" in 50' or 100' rolls, and have extra left over anyway. A good compromise is building hutches in 2-unit or 3-unit modules for openers, unless you are determined to start big and have firm plans for a great many hutches. You can also use leftover floor wire for nest boxes, as described later.

Size Considerations. While overall dimensions of hutches are up to you, as they can be made in just about any size up to maximum widths of available wire, there are three other considerations regarding size.

- How much room the rabbit needs. Provide nearly a square foot of floor space per pound of adult doe. A 2 1/2' x 3' hutch will accommodate a medium-size (meat breed) doe and her litter to

Continued ➜

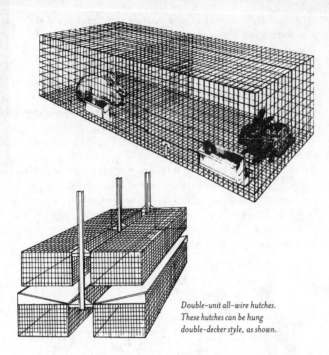

Double-unit all-wire hutches. These hutches can be hung double-decker style, as shown.

weaning time. It will, of course, be sufficient for smaller breeds as well. Hutches for bucks and young growing stock can be half that size or a 2-compartment, 2-door hutch of the same size.

- How big a hutch is convenient for the rabbit keeper. For example, maximum depth front to back should not exceed 2 1/2'. If the hutch is deeper you won't be able to catch rabbits in the back unless you have the reach of a professional basketball player.

- Their location. If you are going to build hutches to fit inside a specific existing building, such as a garage or shed, you may have to adjust the hutch size accordingly (within the above guidelines).

BUYING WIRE

For ease and speed of construction, the ideal situation is to purchase 3 sizes of welded wire. These include a roll of *floor wire* (1/2" x 1") of the desired width, a roll of *top wire* (1" x 2") of the same width as the floor wire, and a roll (or rolls) of side (and *front* and *rear*) wire of the desired height (usually 16" or 18" for the medium breeds, but 24" for the giants and as little as 12" or 15" for the dwarf and small breeds). One can even make a case for buying a fourth size of wire for doors. Available widths for welded wire are 12", 15", 18", 24", 30", 36", 48", 60", and 72".

Two Approaches in Hutch Building

I'm going to describe 2 building schemes—the first if you wish to purchase materials for up to 10 hutches for breeding does of the medium breeds, and the second if you plan to build more than that of the same size. You will be able to decide from these two approaches which will be better for you. Because rolls of less than 100' will cost you more per foot, the first approach will save you money if you plan to build only 10 hutches.

FOR UP TO 10 HUTCHES 2 1/2' X 3' X 16"

Purchase 100' of 1" x 2" wire, 36" wide. Purchase either 26' of 1/2" x 1" wire that is 36" wide or 31' of 1/2" x 1" wire that is 30" wide. If you plan to build all-wire nest boxes, as described later, you will need more of the

1/2" x 1" wire, so plan and buy accordingly. Buy 2 pounds of J-clips. There are about 450 to the pound. Each hutch takes about 90 clips, and you will bend a few out of shape as you get used to working with them.

Here's how to build these hutches one at a time.

Step 1. Cut the Front, Back, and Top. From the roll of 1" x 2" wire, cut a piece 62" long. Cut it flush and, while you're at it, cut the stubs off flush from the rest of the roll. Lay the piece on the floor so it curls down (humps up). Place your feet on one end and gently bend the other toward you, moving your feet forward as necessary to flatten the wire. Take care not to kink it; simply reverse the curve with enough pressure to take the bend out of the roll. Now turn it over before forming 90° corners. This is important so you don't bend against the welded joints, but *with* them. Most rolls of wire come with the 1" wires on top of the 2" wires as you view the roll before unrolling. If your wire is rolled the opposite way, then note it, and do not bend against the welds.

With the wire on the floor , measure 16" and lay your 2 x 4 board across it at that point. Stand on the 2 x 4 and pull the 16" section toward you gently. Hold the 16" end, reach down with your hammer, and gently strike each strand of wire against the 2 x 4 to make a 90° angle. Now turn around, measure 16" from the other end and repeat the bending process. You have just formed the front, the back, and the top. Set it aside.

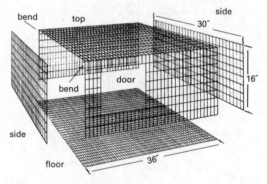

Cutting plan for the individual all-wire hutch, 30" x 36" x 16". This hutch will house a medium-size meat-breed doe and her litter.

Step 2. Cut the Sides. next, cut 30" more off the roll and flatten the resulting 30" x 36" piece as above. Cut it flush and cut the stubs flush off the roll. (As you cut, notice that a slight flick of the wrist down and away from the welds will snap the wire off cleanly with little effort.) Measure 16" up (you are splitting the piece) and cut off flush. The remaining piece will be 30" x 18" (plus stubs). Measure 16" down and cut off 2" (plus stubs). The 2" "waste" strip will be from the center. You will use it later, so set it aside. You now have the sides (ends) of your hutch.

Step 3. Cut the floor. If you bought 36" wide, 1/2" x 1" wire, cut off 30" flush and cut the stubs off the roll. If you bought 30" wire, cut off 36". Do not flatten this piece of floor wire, which curves or humps with the 1/2" wires up, unless it has an extreme curl (perhaps if it is cut from the inside of the roll, where it is curled tighter, in a smaller diameter). The idea is to have the floor of the hutch with the 1/2" wires up to provide a smoother surface for the rabbits, and to keep an upward spring that will eliminate sagging from the weight of the rabbits.

Now you are ready to assemble the hutch. You have cut out all the pieces except for the door and some more 2" strips that you will clip later to the 4 sides near the floor as a "baby saver" feature. More about that later.

Step 4. Fasten the Sides in Place. Place a J-clip in the jaws of the J-clip pliers and fasten the side sections (the 16" x 30" sections) to the front, top, and back sections. After a little practice you will find that squeezing the J-clips on requires a little flip of the wrist or a second squeeze to assure that the clip is tight. Use a J-clip every 4", starting with the corners. Make sure the vertical 1" wires are on the outside of the hutch. That way you will have horizontal wires on the inside where they will make neat, tight corners when fastened to the front-top-back section.

Step 5. Fasten the Floor. After fastening the ends to the front, back, and top, turn the hutch on its top and lay the floor wire on it with the curve and the 1/2" wires down (toward the top of the hutch). Remember that the 1/2" wires provide the smoother floor and that an upward spring will prevent floor sag.

Clip the floor wire on, starting in one corner, again using clips every 4". If the fit is too tight in a corner (this can happen if the 1" x 2" wire is made by a different manufacturer than the one who made the 1/2" x 1" wire), notch out the 1/2" corners of the floor wire.

From what looked like a flimsy beginning, you will find that you now have quite a sturdy hutch. Clipped together, the resulting wire box is extremely rigid.

Now you are ready to cut out the door opening and attach the door.

Step 6. Cutting a Door Opening. Door size and position are very important, so stop and ponder the situation. The door should be located to one side of the front (a 3' side) because you want to leave space on the front for attachment of a feeder and space to fill a waterer, be it a crock, bottle with tube or valve, or automatic watering fount or valve. The door opening must also be large enough to admit a nest box, which you will be putting in and taking out regularly.

If you use an all-wire nest box (which I recommend and explain how to build), a door opening that is 12" wide and 11" high is large enough yet not too large. Remember that, while the door must be conveniently large, you are cutting into the front of the hutch and weakening it somewhat, so a door that is unnecessarily large doesn't do the hutch a lot of good. In any event, be sure to consider the dimensions of the nest box and door together.

For this hutch, I recommend a door opening of 12" x 11" with a door that is 14" x 12" and swings up and in.

Stand the hutch on its back, with the front up and the floor closest to you as you approach it with your wire cutters. Measure 4" over from the left and 4" up from the bottom. Cut the bottom strands to the right to make a 12" opening. Cut up 11" on each side and 12" across the top. *Very important:* Do not cut these strands flush but leave stubs about 1/2" long all the way around the opening. Once you have the opening cut out, use your slip-joint pliers to bend these stubs inward or outward around the outermost wire to form an opening with no sharp projections. This is important because if you cut the stubs off, even with flush-cutting wire cutters, the opening would be sharp. The result would be scratched hands, arms, and rabbits. There are other ways to do it: You could cut them off flush and file them smooth or cover them with flanges of sheet metal. I find leaving stubs and bending them over to be less time-consuming and more satisfactory.

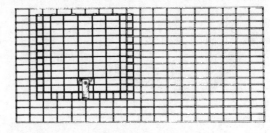

Door overlaps opening by 1" on sides and bottom and swings inward.

Step 7. Attaching the Door. For the door, cut 12" of 1" x 2" wire from the 36"-wide roll. Measure down 14" and cut with all the cuts flush. While you are at it, measure down another 14", cut another door for the next hutch, and set it aside. You will have a piece 6" x 12". Cut the stubs off that and off the end of the roll. Set the small piece aside.

Before you attach the door, attach the latch. Position it up 2" from the bottom of the center of the door. It fits over the strands 2" apart. If you lay it on a bench or the floor you can flatten it easily over the wire with your hammer. If you wait until it's on the door to do this, you will have a difficult time. With the latch on, fit the door *inside* the door opening and clip it with J-clips to the top of the opening.

Use a J-clip on each end and 3 across the middle. Do not give them such a tight squeeze and the door will swing freely. Your door will overlap the sides and bottom by an inch, and the latch should work easily. Give it a drop of oil if it doesn't.

Now swing the door to the top of the cage (the ceiling) and, 5" over from the left edge of the top, squeeze the door hanger onto the top of the cage with your slip-joint pliers. When the cage is upright, the hanger will hold the door up while you reach into the cage. Give the door a push and it will swing loose and shut. The beauty of this door is that it is always inside the cage, not out in the aisle to snag your sleeve. Even if you forget to latch it, your rabbits cannot escape; it will stay shut no matter how hard they push it.

Step 8. Add a "Baby Saver." The hutch now looks finished, and in fact it is usable, but it needs some finishing touches. To prevent baby rabbits from falling out of the hutch if they fall out of the nest box, a "baby saver" is needed.

Take the 2"-wide strip you set aside when you split the 36" wire for front and back sections. "Stagger" it over one end at the bottom and fasten it with J-clips every 6". This will close the openings at the bottom to 1/2" x 1", up 2 1/2" and will prevent the babies from falling through. Cut a 2" strip for the front and another for the back and fasten them on. When you split another front and back section for the next hutch, clip that one on the other end. When you get to the end of the roll, you will find that you will be able to build 10 hutches in this manner and have enough material for the baby saver feature. In the meantime, save the pieces from the door openings and doors for later use as hay racks. We'll discuss them later.

BUILDING MORE THAN 10 HUTCHES

If you plan to build more hutches—even if you don't plan to build them all now—the following is a better plan. It will build up to 36 hutches.

Buy a roll of 1" x 2" "side" wire, 100' long, either 18" or 15" wide (depending upon whether you raise medium or small rabbits), for every 9 hutches you plan to build (4 rolls for 36 hutches). Also buy a 100' roll

Continued ➔

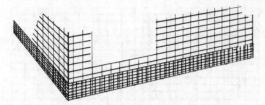

Adding the "baby saver" feature—1/2" x 1" wire fastened around the bottom of the sides of the hutch.

of 30"-wide 1" x 2" "top" wire, a 100' roll of 36"-wide 1/2" x 1" floor wire, and a 50' roll of 12"-wide 1" x 2" "door" wire.

Building Plan. Measure and cut off 11' of the side wire. Form three 90° corners at 30" and 36" intervals around your 2 x 4 and fasten the remaining corner with J-clips. Cut off 3' of the 30" top wire and fasten it on. Cut off 42" of the 36" floor wire. With your 2 x 4 and hammer, bend up 3" at 90° on all 4 sides, cutting out the corners, to form a box. You have now built the baby saver feature right into the floor. Because it is all one piece, the hutch will be considerably stronger this way. Fasten the floor as described earlier, but also fasten the baby saver sides to the front, back, and ends of the hutch. Make the doors as described earlier.

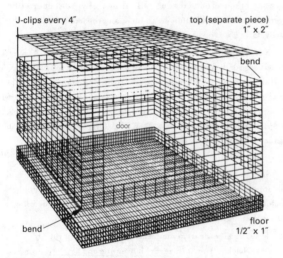

J-clips every 4"

top (separate piece)
1" x 2"

bend

door

bend

floor
1/2" x 1"

Cutting plan for an all-wire hutch when you build 10 or more.

If you decide to build multiple-hutch units with shared partitions, use the 1/2" x 1" wire to divide them. Otherwise, the rabbits may fight through the partitions. Order your wire supply accordingly.

Self-Feeders

To equip this hutch completely, you will want to attach a self-feeding hopper. Farm stores and rabbitry supply houses have them in various sizes. The trough should be positioned about 4" above the floor for small and medium breeds. The hopper portion remains outside the hutch for easy filling by the rabbit keeper. The trough is inside. It takes up no floor space, and it is high enough and narrow enough to keep the rabbits from fouling it.

Successful rabbit raisers have abandoned crockery feeders (which cost as much or more anyway, and often break) for these self-feeders,

which attach with 2 spring wire hooks on each side and, of course, detach easily for periodic cleaning. Tin cans have also gone the way of the crock—they are out. Self-feeders have a lip that prevents the rabbits from scratching pellets out, leaving them hungry and the keeper poor from buying more feed to be wasted. Hopper self-feeders are worth the money and in the long run would save you cash over tin cans even if they were made of sterling silver.

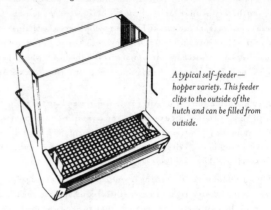

A typical self-feeder— hopper variety. This feeder clips to the outside of the hutch and can be filled from outside.

Hay Racks

You can make 2 kinds of hay racks easily with the small scraps of 1 x 2 wire that remain from door openings. Both are simple to make, so you have no need to purchase manufactured hay racks.

For the first type, simply take a 6–8" square scrap and bend 2" of it to an acute angle of about 30°. With a couple of J-clips, fasten the 2" side to the front of the hutch wherever it is convenient, even on the door. Fill the rack with a handful of hay and the rabbits will pull it through.

Another type of hay rack is especially useful for feeding alfalfa hay, which has leaves that tend to fall from the stems when pulled by the rabbits. Build it about 6–8" over the trough of the feeder on the inside of the hutch. You simply form a box of 1" x 2" wire and J-clips that projects 2" into the hutch up to the roof and as wide as the feeder trough. Cut a slot in the front of the cage the width of the rack minus a couple of inches, and about 3" high. Any hay leaves that the rabbits don't eat on the first attempt will fall into the feed trough for a second chance.

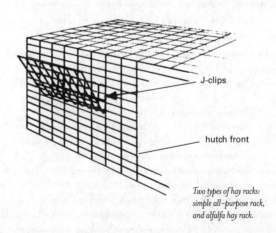

J-clips

hutch front

Two types of hay racks: simple all-purpose rack, and alfalfa hay rack.

138

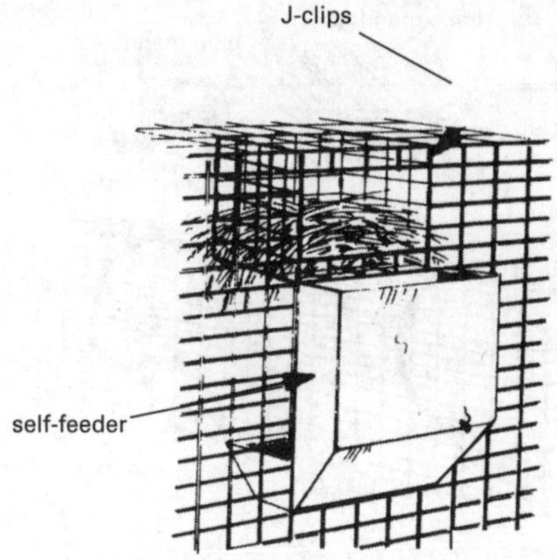
J-clips
self-feeder

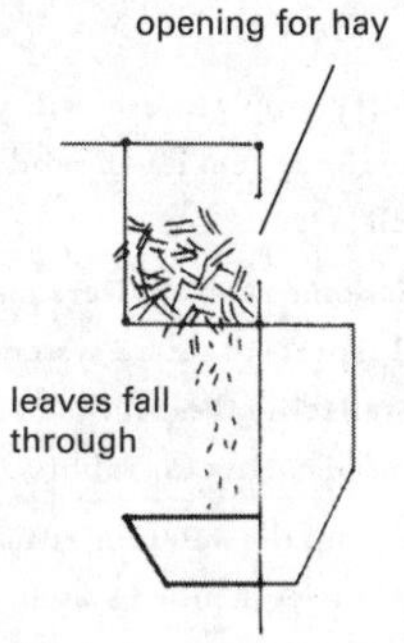
opening for hay
leaves fall through

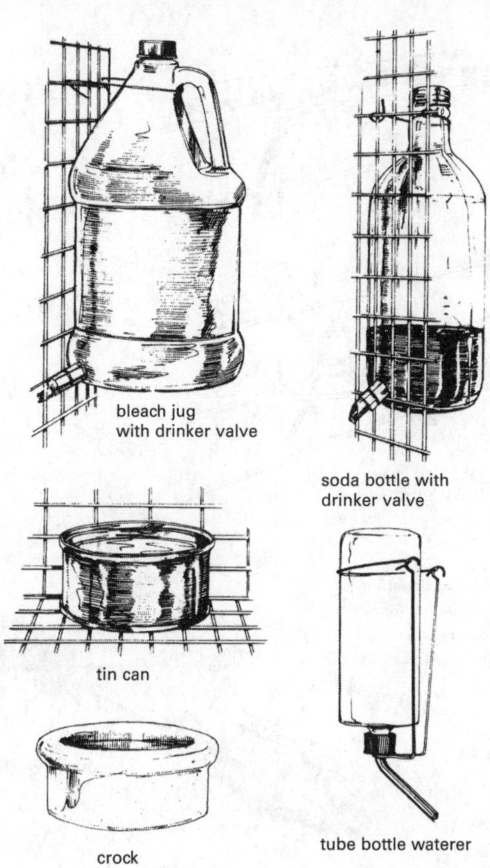
bleach jug with drinker valve
soda bottle with drinker valve
tin can
crock
tube bottle waterer

Manual rabbit-watering devices.

Watering Devices

Rabbits require a constant supply of fresh water to grow and maintain health. Rabbit raisers say water is the best food, because without it a rabbit will not eat properly.

Supplying that water can be the most laborious task in rabbit raising—or you can make it so simple that it practically takes care of itself. Let's review the ways you can supply water to rabbits.

A Tin Can or Other Open Dish. Very poor, as the rabbit will tip it over and go thirsty until you refill it. Difficult to clean, it invites disease. And there is a lot of work involved in refilling if you have many rabbits.

A Crock. Better, because it can't be tipped. If you use crocks, get the kind with a smaller inside diameter at the bottom than at the top. During freezing weather, the water will expand into ice and slide up. Otherwise it will expand out and break the crock. The problem with crocks is that they are, like the tin can, open and susceptible to fouling by the rabbits. They are also labor-intensive, with lots of refilling and washing.

A Tube Bottle Waterer. The plastic bottle with the drinker tube is a big improvement over the can or crock. The enclosed water supply stays clean. No space is taken from the cage floor. They require less washing than crocks. They will not work in freezing weather, but ice doesn't break them.

A Plastic Bottle With Drinker Valve. You make this one yourself because, amazingly, nobody manufacturers one. All it takes is a large heavy plastic bottle, such as one for bleach or soda pop, and a drinker valve designed for automatic watering systems. The bottles are free (unless they are returnable for a deposit); the valves cost a dollar or so and are available at farm supply or rabbitry supply houses.

With a knife or drill bit, make a hole in the bottle near the bottom, as shown in the drawing. Coat the threads of the valve with epoxy cement and screw or push it in. Use wire as shown to hold the bottle onto the cage. A quart or half gallon bottle works well and supplies plenty of water, although you can use more than one per hutch if necessary. The plastic bottle has all the advantages and disadvantages of the tube bottle except that it is cheaper and more durable, can supply more water, and, if large enough, can cut filling time considerably.

A Semiautomatic Watering System. This is a fine way to water a small rabbitry. You need a tank, which need be no more than a 5-gallon jerry can or pail, leading via flexible or rigid plastic pipe to drinker valves at each hutch. You can buy almost everything locally, with the possible exception of the valves, which were developed for use by poultry.

A very simple setup utilizes flexible black plastic pipe that can be fitted out with various adapters, couplings, elbows, and tees. The pipe runs along the outside of the cage, where it cannot be gnawed, about a foot or so above the hutch floor. Using a simple handtapping tool, you make the holes for the valves, which screw in and protrude into the wire case. The rabbits quickly learn to drink from these valves: their licking dislodges a brass tip, letting the water spill into the rabbits' mouths. Another type of valve has a spring-activated stem that opens when bitten and closes when released. The latter are better because they rarely leak.

At least one manufacturer, Borak Manufacturing Ltd., produces semiautomatic watering systems as kits, but you can put your own together from various components in farm supply, hardware, or plumbing supply stores.

Continued →

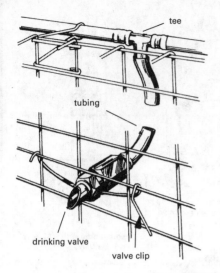

tee

tubing

drinking valve

valve clip

Semiautomatic watering system with detail of drinking valve.

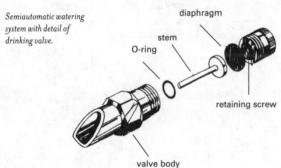

diaphragm

stem

O-ring

retaining screw

valve body

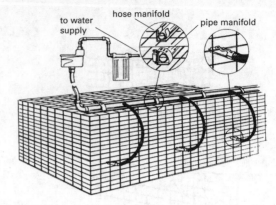

to water supply

hose manifold

pipe manifold

Automatic watering system with detail of pressure-reducing and filtering equipment.

The beauty of the semiautomatic watering system is that you merely fill the holding tank (ideally with a garden hose) and the rabbits drink a constant supply of fresh water that remains clean and takes up no floor space in the hutch. In addition, you can keep this water flowing in the coldest weather by inserting electric heating cables inside the pipes. You can buy these cables in various lengths, depending on how many cages you have, and they can be operated manually or with a simple air-temperature-activated thermostat. Most of them deliver 2 1/2 watts per foot but some produce more heat. Because they are inside the pipe, they need to produce very little heat to keep the water flowing. In severe climates you should use two such cables inside the pipe, activating one with a thermostat and the other manually when the temperature really drops. Without heating cables, you can keep the pipes from freezing by draining them at night. The Borak system is engineered so that you can conveniently disconnect the whole system, if you have a small rabbitry, and take it indoors during freezing nights. All rabbit raisers should consider the semiautomatic system.

An Automatic Watering System. This ultimate system is simply the semiautomatic system with a piped water supply from a well or city water system. It requires the equipment of a semiautomatic system as well as a means of reducing the pressure before water enters the plastic supply pipe to the valves. One way to reduce pressure is a float valve in the tank (like a toilet tank). As the rabbits drink, the float valve allows more water to enter the tank, keeping it constantly full. Pressure-reducing valves are also available. You can keep your float valve and tank system functioning in cold weather by coiling a length of heating cable inside the tank.

Rabbitry supply houses will provide all the materials you require for your watering system if you send them a simple dimensional diagram of your hutch layout.

While some rabbit raisers may be put off by the plumbing and electrical aspects of such a system, you can put one together quite easily. Once installed it takes all the hard work—the hauling and pouring of water—out of caring for rabbits.

To sum up the watering situation, while it is common to begin with crocks or bottles, a piped system can actually cost you less per hutch if you have a large number of hutches and under any circumstances costs very little more. It is important, however, to have all your hutches in place before installing the system, particularly if you will need heating cables, which cannot be shortened or lengthened.

Nest Boxes

Place a nest box in an all-wire hutch on the 27th day after you mate the doe. The littler will be born in it on the 31st day, ordinarily. You must use one because of the open nature of the all-wire hutch. There are basically 3 kinds of nest boxes to choose from.

TYPES OF NEST BOXES

You can make your own nest box from wood. Be sure to cover all the edges with metal; if you do not, they will be gnawed to nothing. For the medium breeds, make the dimensions 10" x 11" of floor space and 8" high. Cut the front down to about 4" for easy use by very young rabbits. Be sure to drill 6 or 7 drainage holes in the floor. Don't put a cover on it as it will become damp. After each use a wooden nest box must be washed, disinfected, and left to dry in the sun.

You can buy ready-made galvanized metal nest boxes. They have removable hardboard floors, but because the tops are partially enclosed, these boxes often become damp. Dampness endangers rabbit health. It's also difficult to see into these boxes for daily inspection of the litter.

You can buy or build all-wire nest boxes with removable corrugated cardboard liners. This is the type of nest box I have used exclusively for many years and strongly recommend. The box is made with 1/2" x 1" floor wire and J-clips, and it has metal flanges covering the top edges to protect the rabbits from injury as they hop in and out.

In very cold weather, use it with the corrugated cardboard liner, perhaps with an extra layer of corrugated cardboard or foam plastic to insulate the floor. Use a new liner, free of any possible germs, for each litter and destroy the liner later. You can cut these corrugated liners from boxes, usually obtainable free.

In warm weather, cut cardboard for only the floor and use a shallower bedding of shavings and straw. Leaving the wire mesh sides open gives plenty of ventilation, which is very important to guard against dampness and extreme heat, two rabbit killers. The open mesh provides you a fine view of the litter's daily progress.

HORSES

Buying and Selling a Horse

Cherry Hill

Illustrations by Kathy Dorn Blackwell

Buying a Horse

If you are in the market for a horse, there are many things for you to consider before you make the final decision on which horse you take home. Above all, invest the necessary time to become familiar with all aspects of choosing and buying a horse. Begin by reading this carefully several times. Being in a hurry is one of the most common pitfalls of horse buying. It can give way to enthusiastic and impulsive but often unwise buying.

Another common error made during horse purchases is pairing a green horse with a green rider. Parents sometimes buy a young horse for a young rider thinking they can "grow up and learn together." Nothing could be further from the truth.

A novice needs a well-seasoned, dependable mount. Often, a beautiful, spirited, but untrained horse may catch your fancy, and it may be difficult to look at other less flashy prospects with objectivity. It is best, however, to follow your head rather than your heart when choosing your first horse. Although you may end up with an older and plainer (but perhaps wiser) horse than you originally dreamed of, the pleasant and safe riding will result in a positive experience. Later, when you are more familiar with training principles, you may be ready to progress to a less trained, more spirited horse.

When buying, it is wise to ask for, and pay for, professional advice—and then listen to it! When your instructor or veterinarian cautions you about a horse, it is for a reason. Conversely, if you are given the "go-ahead" to buy and then you get cold feet, you may not find as good a horse again. When procuring advice, it is best to use the view of an objective professional rather than the enthusiastic recommendation of an equally inexperienced friend. Hire a professional who has no vested interest in the horse sale.

Stay focused. Keep in mind that you are selecting a horse for a particular reason or performance event. There are many decisions and compromises lying ahead, so it helps if you set your priorities clearly at the outset.

If the overall purpose of the horse is to teach you how to ride, rather than how to win in the show ring, the selection process will emphasize different traits. If the horse is intended to be a long-term project rather than a stepping stone, you will have to invest more time, effort, and money in your purchase.

CRITERIA FOR SELECTION

First you must realistically determine how much you can afford to spend on a horse. Remember, the purchase price is just a drop in the bucket when considering the numerous regular costs required for proper horse care. When setting your initial purchase price limit, ask yourself, "Is this the most money I can afford?" Long after the purchase price is but a dim memory, you will continue to pay for feed, tack and equipment, routine vaccinations, deworming, farrier care, dental work, bedding, and so on. Because both (backyard) Clyde and (the World Champion) King of Kings require the same dollar investment for proper care, set your purchase price ceiling as high as you can comfortably afford.

Then begin narrowing the field by considering the factors that, combined, determine a horse's price. Rearrange the following list in accordance with your specific situation.

Temperament. The single most important requirement for a novice's horse (and for that matter, anyone's horse) is a willing and cooperative temperament. The horse should be calm and sensible yet keen. A keen horse is alert and ready to work but under control at all times.

Soundness. For a riding horse, working soundness is essential. An unsoundness is a condition that makes a horse unusable for a particular purpose. An example of a working unsoundness is a lameness that prevents a horse from moving correctly. A breeding unsoundness may prevent a mare from having a foal, but may have nothing to do with her suitability as a good riding horse.

Look for a horse with a kind, intelligent temperament.

Blemishes. Scars and irregularities that do not affect the serviceability of an animal are called blemishes. Although they are not considered unsoundnesses, they often lower the price of a horse. Old wire cuts, small muscle atrophies, and white spots from old injuries may detract from the horse's appearance and may save the buyer money.

A horse with a bad habit such as kicking should be avoided.

Movement and Way of Going. Ideally, a horse should move smoothly and in balance, without stiffness and crookedness. Part of this is inherent and part of it comes from training and conditioning. Be sure you assess the horse at all three gaits. How comfortable is the ride? If you are just starting out, comfort is very important so you might be better off looking for an older model Cadillac.

Conformation. The overall structure of the horse will determine how smoothly and correctly it moves. The conformation should be suitable for the horse activity in which you are most interested. Many horses, however, are quite versatile and can perform in a variety of ways fairly well.

Continued ➜

Breed or Type. A high-level dressage horse will command a greater price than a weekend trail horse. An imported registered horse will likely cost many times the farm-raised, grade horse. If you do not need a registered horse for showing, you should consider purchasing a grade horse. What is most important is to select the type of horse that is best suited for your proposed event.

Manners. A horse's behavior when he is being handled, ridden, and even his behavior in a stall or pen, should be noted. Long-standing behavior is often difficult or impossible to change. Bad habits may lower a horse's price but may provide you with more exasperation and aggravation than the discount is worth. Horses that are difficult to bathe or are slightly grouchy to cinch but perform beautifully under saddle may be an acceptable bargain. However, a horse that turns into a keg of dynamite and refuses to load when shown a trailer may be unusable. A horse that is difficult to shoe can become your farrier's nightmare and a liability for you.

Also remember that a horse's bad behaviors may be at their lowest intensity because of a professional's guidance—the habit may worsen with handling by a novice. Stall vices or bad habits can be dangerous for anyone and should be carefully considered before purchase. Stall vices include, but are not limited to, cribbing, wood chewing, stall kicking, weaving, pacing, pawing, rearing, and tail rubbing. Bad habits include balking, nibbling, biting, striking, kicking, bolting, halter pulling, rearing, and shying. If you are not certain how to recognize these undesirable behaviors, you should take an experienced horseman with you when you go horse shopping.

Sex. Geldings usually make the most suitable horse for a novice because castrated males are reputably more steady in their daily moods. Stallions should never be considered for a first horse unless they are purchased young and with the intention of being castrated and then sent to a professional for thorough training. Mares often make brilliant performers but are often more expensive because of their breeding potential. Also with mares, there can be a period of silliness, irritation, or fussing each month due to the hormonal influences of the estrous cycle.

A horse with a sour attitude that tends to nip is not safe or pleasant to work with.

Health. Many health problems are temporary, so sick horses can sometimes be purchased at a discount. The buyer who plans to nurse a horse back to health must realize, however, that what is saved in purchase price may be expended in time, labor, and supplies. There is also a chance that veterinary bills will be high, as well as a further risk of complications or the development of a chronic condition. Some health problems are permanent and may require a lifetime of care.

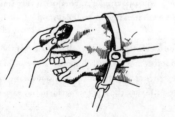

A horse's age can be determined by his teeth by your veterinarian or instructor

Age. Horses in the prime range of five to eight years old usually command the highest prices. They have matured, mentally and physically, enough to be useful; have hopefully already been trained properly; and have many years of service left. Very young horses usually cost less because of their lack of training and experience and because of the risk of developing an unsoundness when put to work. A horse that has been in work and is still sound past five years old will likely remain sound. The assurance is not so great with a two-year-old. An older horse (over fifteen) may have only a few performance years left but may be the perfect choice for a novice.

Level of Performance Training and Accomplishments. Here is where the price tag can shoot skyward in a hurry. Training is time and time is money. The biggest test of the suitability and thoroughness of a horse's training is if the horse does what you want him to do when you are taking a test ride. A good horse does not necessarily have to have a sterling show record. There are many horses with fine training that have never been taken in a show ring. They have been trained by people not particularly interested in competition but who use horses for trail riding, ranch work, lessons, or just pleasure riding. Some horses that have been used exclusively in the show ring may be insecure and unsuitable for work in the real world of rocks and trees.

However, if you are interested in showing, you should look at horses who already have show ring experience. A horse capable of performing consistently in the show ring, and especially one who has a record to prove it, commands a high price. Although awards and points earned in competitions do not tell the whole story, they do highlight a horse as one that has a proven record, not just one that is said to have potential.

Size. Big horses generally cost more, as they can accommodate a wider variety of rider sizes. When considering a small horse, be sure to note whether your legs can be positioned properly for effective use of the aids. When you are mounted and have proper leg position, your heel should not be below the horse's underline. Ask your instructor to evaluate this during your test ride.

Quality. Refinement, class, and presence all increase the price of a horse. The quality horse attracts many buyers. Finely chiseled features, smooth hair coat, clean bone, and charisma all contribute to the horse saying "Look at me!" and, since many people do, the price goes up! Since pride of ownership is a large part of the reason behind buying a horse in the first place, it's nice to own an attractive animal.

Pedigree. The bloodlines of a horse's ancestors dictate, in large part, his quality and suitability to perform in a particular event. However, using a pedigree as the sole selection criterion is not recommended. Using bloodlines along with other observations can be helpful. Certain family lines become fashionable from time to time and command higher prices. Examples of family lines would be Secretariat in the Thoroughbred breed; Bask in the Arabian breed; and Poco Bueno in the Quarter Horse breed. While all of these stallions sired many performance champions, they sired some poor horses too. First be sure you have a good horse in front of you, then look at the papers. If the horse has famous ancestors, that is a bonus.

Color and Markings. Although often the first thing one notices about a horse is his body color and points, it is really the least important criterion for selection unless you are considering the horse for use in halter classes in one of the color breeds. Some registries have formed to promote certain color patterns. For example, the Paint horse is a stock type with tobiano or overo color patterns. The Palomino may be of many breeds, but must conform to certain standards of body and mane and tail color. The Pinto and Buckskin registries are also based on colors.

FINDING A HORSE

Where do you begin looking? If you want to narrow the field to some horses that are in your price range, regularly check bulletin boards of feed and tack stores, local newspapers, shopper's guides, and the classified sections of regional and national horse publications. This may help you get a clearer idea of how much you can spend and what kind of horse you want. Then, unless you are very experienced yourself, I suggest you enlist the aid of a professional to help you evaluate the horses that sound interesting to you.

Enlisting the Aid of a Professional. When you use a professional to help in the selection and purchase of a horse, an unwritten code of ethics is in operation. If you understand the basis of buying and selling etiquette beforehand, you are more likely to emerge a winner from the transaction.

If you have a regular instructor or trainer, he or she will have more long-term incentive than immediate sale profit in mind when helping you to find a suitable horse. Choosing a mount that will work successfully

for your lessons is far more important than a one-time commission. Your instructor should never be expected to perform his or her valuable services without appropriate compensation, however. Looking at horses, testing them, and eventually buying one is time-consuming and often requires traveling many miles. And, the professional's reputation is put on the line every time he or she helps to choose a horse.

If you get a professional trainer or instructor involved in the buying process, you will have to pay for this person's experience and expertise as well as their time and expenses. The buying fee may also include the cost for having the professional be your official representative and negotiator during the actual business transaction. Some professionals add a commission of 10 percent to the price of a horse that they have found for a student. This works fairly well for horses in the price range of $3,000 to $15,000, but it may be inappropriate for horses on either side of that range. A flat fee of $300 might be charged for horses under $3,000 and a negotiable percentage may be used for horses above $15,000.

A finder's fee, on the other hand, is a seller's way of saying thank you to another professional who has referred a customer to him or her. For instance, if you contact Trainer A for a particular type of horse, and he or she sends you to Trainer B from whom you end up buying a horse, Trainer B will likely send Trainer A a check for about 1 to 5 percent of the resulting sale price. So the more professionals who are involved in

SELECTING A HORSE FOR AN EVENT

Type and Performance Event for Which a Type is Suited	Temperament and Other Characteristics	Conformation	Performance Requirements	Examples of Breeds that Excel in this Category
Pleasure (Western Pleasure, Hunt Seat Pleasure, Trail)	Calm, dependable	Well-balanced, smooth, attractive, prominent withers so saddle stays put, good angles and tendons for gait elasticity	Efficient, comfortable mover at all three gaits	Certain individuals in all breeds
Hunter (Hunter Under Saddle, Working Hunter, Hunter Hack)	Coordinated, cooperative.	Neck must be long and supple and tie relatively high at withers and chest to assure greatest length of stride, no exaggerated knee and hock action, knees must be correct, not set back or over, not tied-in	Ability to negotiate obstacles four feet high with balance and efficiency	Thoroughbred, Connemara
Stock (Reining, Cutting, Working Cow horse, Gymkhana)	Energetic but level-headed, cow sense	Well-muscled hindquarters, good lateral muscling overall, inverted V at chest, equal gaskin muscling inside and out, strong hocks and back with rounded croup. No massive shoulders or chest, no sickle hocks, no small hooves	Explosive bursts, lateral maneuverability, and in some cases, cow-sense	Quarter Horse, Appaloosa, Paint
Sport (Dressage, Stadium Jumping, Eventing, Combined Driving, Endurance)	Keen to aggressive, competitive but tractable.	Long, well-set neck with clean throatlatch for flexion, elevated forehand, strong hind legs, good substance of bone throughout. Short back and long underline for increased stride from behind, no long backs or weak stifles. Tough hooves with concave soles, no long, weak pasterns. For jumping, steep croup; for endurance, level croup	Ability to shift weight rearward. High levels of stamina	Thoroughbreds, Warmbloods, Arabians
Animated (Park Horse, Three Gaited and Five Gaited)	Flashy, charismatic	High-set, stylish neck, long well-laid-back shoulder, clean, free-moving joints. Straight legs with long cannons (crooked legs will result in injury at speed). Tennessee Walkers can have shorter, steeper croup and more set to the hock; Saddlebreds, Arabs, and Morgans level croup	Exaggerated flexion of joints with precision and speed	American Saddlebred, Morgan, Arabian

Continued ➔

the sale, the higher the various commissions will be that are tacked on to the sale price, which ultimately comes out of the buyer's pocket.

If you only want to employ a professional's assistance for specific portions of your search, you should expect to pay customary expenses including mileage, meals, and lodging, and a looker's fee of perhaps $25 to $50 per horse evaluated. If, after six horses, at $25 per look plus expenses, the instructor finds you a $6,000 horse he or she might subtract the $150 previously paid from the $600 commission for finding.

If you are a prospective buyer and a regular client of a particular instructor who is helping you with the purchase, here are some guidelines for dealing with a seller. (In some cases, your instructor may be the seller.)

Knowing What You Want. Before you begin narrowing the field, you need to make an accurate statement of your goals and financial capabilities. This provides the professional with essential information and helps to assure a successful purchase and an efficient transaction. Listen to an instructor's advice. A certain horse may have great visual appeal but may not be a practical mount. The instructor should be objective enough to see such distinctions. But if the instructor and the seller are the same person, do not count on his or her objectivity. Employ another professional for a second opinion.

You must be realistic about price and honest about your budget. If you want a top-class show horse but have a small budget, you must be willing to compromise, usually by investing more and expecting less. Many instructors report that a very time-consuming aspect of horse buying is learning what a buyer really likes. A solution may be for you to do the initial looking. You can take the time to narrow the choices down to what you can afford and would be proud to own. This substantially minimizes the instructor's time involvement. If you use this approach, however, you run the risk of missing a prospect that a more experienced eye might have recognized. Like other professional services, you get what you pay for.

STEPS IN BUYING A HORSE

Many barns have records that list the horses currently for sale and those recently sold. In addition to photos and pedigrees, each entry might include performance history, health and farrier records, and important information on conformation defects, unusual conditions, and vices. Prospective buyers are encouraged to browse through the records and take notes to help them decide which horses might fit into their framework.

If you phone ahead to schedule an appointment, most competent sellers will have the requested horses clean and clipped. It is discourteous to arrive for the first visit unannounced and then ask to see everything in the barn. Later on in your relationship with a seller, if you are showing continued interest in a horse, it is OK and actually advisable to arrive unannounced so that you can see your prospect in his natural routine.

Some sellers will allow you to assist in the grooming and saddling of the horses for temperament evaluation. Again, perhaps the first time you should stand back and observe. If you come back a second time, it would be appropriate for you to request to be able to tack the horse, providing you are capable.

Before you take the first trial ride on a horse, the seller may ask you to sign a release or disclaimer of liability in case of accident. Although such a waiver may not hold up in court as a legal document, it does outline your risk in specific terms and proves that said risk was pointed out to you by the seller.

Testing the Horse. The seller is usually equipped to provide you with the appropriate tack to test-ride the horse, but often you can use your own saddle, if you have one. I recommend that you always wear a protective helmet when riding an unfamiliar horse.

Customarily, a horse will be either longed or ridden for you so that you can see the horse's movement. A trainer can best exhibit a horse's talents and level of training. If, after watching the horse move, you or your instructor don't feel he is suitable, it is more polite to say so than to waste time riding a horse that is out of contention.

If the horse seems to be a possible candidate, however, you and/or your instructor should try him out. Depending on the situation, the trial ride may be a casual familiarization or a more formal lesson with coaching.

Advanced maneuvers are best performed by the horse's trainer, not by a prospective buyer. If you are having difficulties resolving a problem with the horse, the seller has the right to step in and initiate a polite closure of the session. Ending with a positive experience for both you and the horse preserves the horse's training and your safety.

Observing the Horse in His Normal Surroundings. In one way or another a seller gives valuable information about each horse in his barn. If you observe carefully and listen attentively, you can gather interesting facts and draw important conclusions about the manners and personality of the horse you are considering.

Bring your own tack to test-drive a prospect. Always wear proper riding clothing and a safety helmet.

However, some of the most honorable and respectful people turn into disbelieving skeptics as they squint and peer at a horse in cross-ties. This seems especially true of inexperienced horsemen who may have read about all the things that can be wrong with horses. It seems as if they feel they need to cleverly uncover a secret unsoundness to prove they are not totally green. It is disconcerting for a seller to be treated with suspicion and can serve to drive a wedge in future negotiations if things go that far.

It is inappropriate for anyone to give an analysis of a horse or his training after seeing him once or riding him for ten or fifteen minutes. You or your instructor would likely alienate a seller by degrading one of his or her horses. Unnecessary detrimental comments have no place when viewing a horse for sale. Save your comments for when you and your instructor have time to discuss the horse privately, perhaps on the way to look at the next horse.

Further Checking a Prospect. After a buyer and seller have been in contact several times, a relationship begins to develop, and it behooves both parties to keep interactions courteous, positive, and businesslike.

You may wish to try the horse out more extensively. Unfortunately, few sellers feel comfortable letting a horse go away on trial. The first week for a new horse and rider, especially in a new setting for the horse, can be rough. It can be dangerous for the rider and damaging to the horse's training, and you may reach an inappropriate conclusion about the horse's suitability. Also, if a horse is out on trial, it is difficult for the seller to show the horse to a backup buyer. If you are a student of a respected instructor, however, and your instructor has safe facilities, a seller may let the horse go out on trial to you under your instructor's supervision.

If you cannot arrange a trial period but you are fairly certain that you have found the horse, it might be best to put a deposit on the horse while you are making up your mind and taking care of the final details, which may require several days to a week or more. During that time, visit the horse and handle him so that you are very sure that if you buy him he is the horse you want.

The Pre-purchase Agreement. If you want the seller to put the horse on "hold" for you, you may be required to sign a pre-purchase agreement. Such a contract will indicate your serious intent. It may also contain a limit to the number of times you may try the horse and may list a deadline for your decision. A pre-purchase contract may also clarify items in writing that you have discussed.

Usually a deposit is required in addition to the contract. When a seller requires a deposit it is to reduce risks for both parties. The deposit will compensate the seller if he loses a sale to another customer because the horse was off the market while you were further

considering him. It will also provide a guarantee to you that the horse will not be sold to anyone else while the contingencies of the contract are being met. The contract will also fix the price at the one originally quoted. A well-designed contract is really a protection for both the buyer and the seller.

The Veterinary Pre-purchase Examination. A pre-purchase veterinary examination is often a contingency in a sales contract and is usually scheduled and paid for by the buyer. Ahead of time, the seller may point out a condition of the horse that may cause it to fail a veterinary exam but still allow it to be suitable for the buyer's purpose. If you and the seller have discussed such a condition, like cribbing, and list it on the pre-purchase agreement, then you have accepted the horse as a cribber if everything else checks out. So, even if your veterinarian suggests that you do not buy the horse because it is a cribber, you had previously acknowledged and accepted the condition. Be sure that you fully understand any habit or condition the horse has before agreeing to accept it.

PRE-PURCHASE AGREEMENT AND SALES CONTRACT

This agreement is made between _____, hereinafter referred to as BUYER and _____
_____, hereinafter referred to as SELLER.

This agreement is entered into between BUYER and SELLER for purchase and sale of the horse described below on the following terms and conditions of sale:

DESCRIPTION OF HORSE. Registered Name_____

Registration Number and Association _____
_____

Tattoo, brand, or other identification (state which)
_____ Date of Birth _____ Sex_____

Color and Markings_____

PRICE. For the total sum of $_____, SELLER agrees to sell BUYER the horse described here and BUYER agrees to buy said horse on the terms set forth here.

PAYMENT TERMS. A deposit of $_____(10% of purchase price) is to be paid at time of offer. This deposit will hold the horse for the BUYER for _____days or until the results of a veterinary pre-purchase exam are available whichever is sooner. This deposit is not refundable if the horse is described as sound for BUYER'S purpose and BUYER does not complete the purchase. This deposit is refundable if the veterinarian fails to pass the animal for BUYER'S intended use. BUYER'S intended use is _____.

The balance of the purchase price $_____shall be paid by the BUYER at time of possession, no later than _____days from the date of veterinary results. Daily board from the time of offer to the time of possession at the rate of $_____per day is also due at time of possession.

CONTINGENCIES. This contract is contingent on the described horse passing a veterinary pre-purchase and soundness examination at the BUYER'S cost with the intended use for the horse being stated as _____.

BUYER understands that the offer is based on the fact that BUYER has knowledge that the horse has the following blemishes, unsoundnesses, conformation defects, vices, or unusual behaviors_____

BUYER states that he knows what the above conditions represent and although discussion of them with a veterinarian is encouraged, since the conditions have been previously noted and accepted by the BUYER, the conditions stated above can not be basis for veterinary exam failure for the purpose of this contract.

WARRANTIES. SELLER warrants that he has clear title to the horse and will provide a bill of sale, appropriate registration transfer papers, and necessary health and transport papers at time of possession.

Signed this _____day of _____, 20_____

_____   _____
    (Seller)   (Buyer)

Important Note: Every state has its own laws regarding the necessary content of contracts. This sample contract is designed to provide you with general guidelines. Check with your attorney or modify a standard sale contract purchased from a business or stationery store to fit your specific needs.

Continued →

The pre-purchase exam should be performed by an equine specialist. You also may wish to retain the opinion and services of an American Farrier's Association Certified Journeyman Farrier as well. Understandably, the greatest emphasis in the examination of a riding horse is centered around the legs and hooves. In examining the hooves, the veterinarian may request that the shoes be removed, so it may be necessary to schedule a farrier to be present to pull the shoes and to reshoe the horse.

Tests and Examination. There is no standard pre-purchase examination. The veterinarian should be informed of the proposed use for the horse, and then you and the veterinarian should confer about what tests will be required to make such a determination. Costs for the exam can run from $30 to well over $300, depending on the number of radiographs required, what lab tests are ordered, how many miles the veterinarian must travel, and how much time is involved in the exam.

A general overall health check is the minimum that should be performed. After palpation and observation, the veterinarian will provide a report—either written or oral, as requested.

If the veterinarian thinks it is warranted, the pre-purchase exam may include X-rays of the lower legs.

After the Veterinary Exam. When a horse has cleared the vet check, you will have a certain number of days (three, for example) to complete payment and pick up the horse. During this time it is the seller's responsibility to have the horse cleared by a brand inspector in states where it is required. The seller must also have the necessary transfer papers available so that at the time of sale, the registration papers can be signed over to the new owner.

If the horse passes the vet exam and you do not follow through with the purchase, the deposit is normally forfeited to the seller for the inconvenience and the time the horse was off the market. If the horse does not pass the veterinary examination, your deposit is refunded or the horse's price can be negotiated in light of the veterinarian's findings.

Other Paperwork. When the final sales transaction is being made, be sure that all the necessary paperwork is taken care of before you give the seller your check. If you are not experienced in paperwork matters, bring someone who is. Registration papers should bear clear title from the seller to you, the new buyer. Be sure the description of the horse on the papers matches the horse you are buying exactly. Brand clearance and ID certification papers should be unmistakably for the horse you are buying. If there is a shadow of a doubt, clear it up before the final sale. Some sellers have been known to use certificates from deceased horses to sell other less valuable horses.

Insurance. Sellers who offer installment sales (those in which you give a downpayment and make periodic payments on the horse) usually require that the horse be insured during the term of the sales contract. The cost of the policy is usually paid for by the buyer.

Mortality insurance pays the value of the horse if the horse dies or if the insurance company agrees that the sick or injured horse should be put down (humanely destroyed). Limited or restricted policies cover specific situations only, such as death by fire or lightning. Full mortality insurance covers all causes of death, including illness and injury. A thorough physical examination is required before a full mortality policy is issued and, even if the horse passes the examination, the insurance company may have standard exclusions for certain causes of death, such as colic.

A Permanent Loss of Use "rider" (amendment) can be added to a policy. At the time of issuance, the intended use of the horse is stated on the policy in specific terms. If the horse is injured and can no longer be used as intended (for jumping or breeding, for example) the owner of the horse can collect about 50 percent of the value of the horse, but the insurance company may have the option to take possession of the horse.

The value of the horse is almost always based on the purchase price, but it can be increased by listing those performance records that affect the horse's value. Insurance rates are based on the value of the horse and vary according to the breed, age, and use of the animal. In general, rates range from 1 percent to 6 percent of the policy value of the animal. So, if you are insuring a $10,000 horse and the rate is 3%, you will pay $300 for the policy.

Due to past horse insurance frauds and unscrupulous activities regarding horse deaths, insurance companies have found it a great risk to insure horses. Some companies no longer offer mortality insurance, and others have been forced to increase rates to protect themselves. Do a good deal of shopping when you select your agent.

Warranties, Express and Implied. In the past, the selling of horses was ruled by the saying *caveat emptor:* "let the buyer beware." The seller was not obligated to inform the buyer about any defects or lack of quality in his animals. That placed the burden on the buyer to keep an eye out for his own protection.

Today, the seller must make good his representation of the horse, where used as inducement to the sale. In this respect, the selling of horses today is ruled by *caveat vendor:* "let the seller beware."

If a seller makes an express or implied warranty about a horse at the time of sale, it is considered a guarantee. According to the Uniform Commercial Code (UCC), all statements of the seller become part of the basis of the sale—in effect, a warranty. The burden then is on the seller to exclude statements and promises to the potential buyer if he or she does not intend to be bound by them as warranties.

But this does not mean the buyer does not have to look carefully at the horse he or she is hoping to buy. If there are defects that can be easily noted by inspection, the buyer is responsible for detecting them. It is up to him or her (or an advisor) to note such defects. A buyer cannot later claim one of these defects as a reason to rescind the sale.

If there is a latent defect or one that is not easily discoverable by ordinary inspection, whether or not it can be basis for rescinding a sale depends on whether the seller knew of its presence. The sale is not fraudulent if the seller did not know of the latent defect.

Suitability for a particular purpose is considered an implied warranty. If a buyer makes known to the seller, in clear terms, the purpose for the horse, the seller's selection and presentation of a horse to the buyer amounts to a warranty that the horse is suitable for the required purpose. This applies mainly to cases where the buyer is relying on the seller's skill and judgement to furnish a suitable horse.

A seller can call various factors about a horse to the attention of a buyer and exclude those items from a warranty. Those items, then, would not be basis for rescinding a sale. A seller can also sell a horse "as is" if it is clearly stated and understood between parties that the horse is being sold without a warranty.

If you feel you have purchased a horse that has been misrepresented, the best thing to do is first discuss the situation with a knowledgeable and experienced professional. Then, if advised, approach the seller and discuss the matter with him. Any reputable seller will try to work out a problem regarding a horse sale.

If you must settle the matter in court, the burden of proof is on you, the buyer. If it is found that there was a breach of warranty, you will probably be awarded the difference between the value of the horse as warranted and its actual value. So if you paid $10,000 for a horse that was only worth $6,000, you would recover $4,000. You may also be able to recover costs for other losses, expenses, or damages.

Selling a Horse

If you have a horse that you have been trying to sell, you know that horse marketing is a very competitive business. Usually there are a good number of horses for sale for every prospective buyer. There are especially a large number of partially trained, out-of-shape, "backyard" horses for sale. It is much more difficult to sell a horse that has not been worked for some time, is overweight, either very lazy or a little bit wild, and not professionally cared for or presented. It is easier to sell a horse at the beginning of the riding season, in the spring or early summer, than it would be at the beginning of the feeding season of fall or winter.

Not many potential buyers will take a seller's word, "He's a wonderful pleasure horse (but he hasn't been ridden for five years)" and buy a horse without being able to test-drive him thoroughly.

If you hope to sell your horse, you must get him in shape, highlight his positive attributes, and direct your sales efforts to the specific market for which he is suitable. Don't hope to sell a horse by saying he is a hunt seat prospect if he has never been in the show ring, let alone never had hunt seat training.

Remember, unless you are selling a very specific age, type, color, or blood-line, there are many other contenders in the marketplace. What makes a horse sell? It can be boiled down to the five P's: Product, Presentation, Performance, Paperwork, and Price.

PRODUCT

We'd all like to own, train, or sell the perfect horse. However, the perfect horse is an ideal we use for comparison and evaluation and will probably never see. Sometimes owners enthusiastically overrate their horses in terms of conformation and ability and inadvertently misrepresent them. Not every horse has the potential to go to The World or The Olympics.

An honest assessment of your horse's quality may best be done by an objective professional. Some charge a small fee for such an appraisal. You may learn that your horse has the conformation to compete in breed halter classes, or place in area reining competitions, or be appropriate for second-level dressage movements. Conversely, you may be informed of detracting points that limit your horse's marketability. Receiving a knowledgeable opinion will help you represent your product realistically.

PRESENTATION

How well you are able to let a buyer know what it is that you have for sale will determine if an appropriate buyer comes knocking on your door.

Advertising. The presentation of your horse to prospective buyers begins with advertising. Advertise your horse in the most appropriate place for his breed, quality, and level of training and accomplishments. It would be a waste of money to advertise twenty-year-old Nell, with her big hay belly and shaggy mane in a monthly color glossy horse magazine. In order to determine where to advertise your horse, you must identify the buyer group he is most appropriate for. Is your horse suitable for a first-time horse owner? For a person who is ready to upgrade? For someone interested in doing a little showing? For a person who wants to raise a foal? For someone who wants to be able to ride right into the winner's circle? For a casual trail rider? For a competitive trail rider? Identify your market and you will have a much easier time attracting the right buyer.

Once you have a good idea of the type of buyer who would be looking for a horse like yours, try to list in detail that buyer's characteristics. Then see if your horse fits the bill. Is the potential buyer an eight-year-old inexperienced girl who lives in the city and wants a horse that she can take lessons on? Or is the buyer a fourteen-year-old boy who lives on a ranch and is looking for a horse that he can take to weekend gymkhanas? Or is the buyer a thirty-something female with some experience fifteen years ago who wants a horse she can ride along the road on weekends? The same horse would probably not be suitable for all of these people, yet quite possibly, your horse might be just the perfect horse for one of them. The more finely you can focus on the type of buyer your horse would be suitable for, the more appropriate your advertising will be.

The simplest, and least expensive form of advertising is the use of bulletin boards. You can pin your ads on boards at your feed store, tack store, and farm supply store. You may even wish to include bulletin boards at supermarkets, Laundromats, and gas stations. One of the best kind of ads is a flattering color photo of the horse, with a simple message, take-home phone number, and other information for interested parties. The description of your horse should include the age, sex, size, color, breed, and price. Be sure the height is accurate by using a measuring stick. Your ad can also describe the personality and training level of the horse. For example:

FOR SALE: Bright sorrel Quarter Horse gelding. Shown in 4-H western classes. Quiet and kind. 15 hands 15 years $1,500. Call George Green at 221–1500.

Newspaper and periodical ads will add costs to selling your horse, and a single ad will rarely do the trick. Sales strategy indicates that keeping a well-written ad running continuously is necessary if you hope to sell your horse. Running a single ad is like throwing away money. Compare costs and readership profile of appropriate advertising mediums: your local newspaper, the nearest city paper, a shopper's guide, a horse shopper's guide, various riding club newsletters, and the classified sections of various regional and national horse publications.

Continued →

Then pare your ad down to bare bones while still retaining its clarity and accuracy.

When people respond to your ad by telephone, be sure you provide them with accurate and honest information. Have a detailed description of the horse and other important information near the phone. Keep a photocopy of important papers with the information. Be sure that everyone at the phone number you listed knows that you have a horse for sale and is willing to be helpful to callers.

If it seems like your horse would be appropriate for a caller, encourage him to come and check your horse. After all, it doesn't cost to look. You might mention to them that when horse shopping, it is best to look at as many horses as possible.

If your ad covers a large geographical area, it would be best if you had good photos or a videotape ready to send to interested parties. A videotape, like photos, must show your horse to his very best advantage. He must be impeccably groomed and on model behavior. The background for photos and videos should be uncluttered so the prospective buyer has a very clear view of your horse. The person operating either the photo or video camera should be experienced and the results should be sharp. Remember, with videos, if a horse makes a mistake, the viewer may play that part of the tape over and over. A poor photo or video is worse than none at all.

Physical Appearance. The physical appearance and manner of you and your horse make a distinct and lasting impression on a prospective buyer.

Health Care. Proper nutrition, deworming, and exercise play the largest part in a horse's overall picture of health. No amount of bathing and coat conditioner will be a substitute for long-term good management.

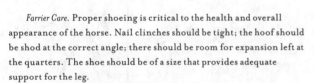

To ensure that the horse you have for sale always has hooves in top shape, schedule competent regular farrier care for all of your horses.

Farrier Care. Proper shoeing is critical to the health and overall appearance of the horse. Nail clinches should be tight; the hoof should be shod at the correct angle; there should be room for expansion left at the quarters. The shoe should be of a size that provides adequate support for the leg.

Keeping your horse on a regular shoeing schedule ensures it will look good whenever someone comes to see it. Before you show your horse, the hooves should be picked clean and the hoof wall should be wiped with a damp cloth. Caution: If you choose to put hoof dressing on just before demonstrating the horse's ability in a dusty arena, you may end up with an undesirable hoof appearance.

Grooming. Although a horse's bloom comes from within, there are certain "last minute" things that will enhance a horse's outward appearance. Clipping a horse according to breed standards and intended use is advisable. Be sure you know what is acceptable. Shaving

When presenting a horse for sale, do not show him to a buyer with a ragged mane and tail, dirty coat, broken hooves, and ill-fitting halter.

Instead, show the horse at his best!

the legs, fetlocks, and coronet may look fine if you are a halter showman but may make the horse appear weak and vulnerable to a prospective endurance rider. Clipping ears, whiskers and eyelashes may turn a customer right on or off depending on their intended use for the horse.

The bridle path should be freshly clipped and not too far down the horse's neck. If you are uncertain what is appropriate for your horse's breed or type, clip the bridle path about 2 to 3 inches from the poll backward.

Tail length and style varies among breeds and performance events. However, to be on the safe side, leave your horse's tail as long as possible. This way the new owner can trim and shape the tail to his or her preference. Be sure the tail is clean and well brushed. Wipe your horse's eyes and nostrils for that finished look. Put your clean horse, either bathed or well brushed, in a freshly bedded stall until the prospective buyers arrive.

Handler's Appearance. The handler's appearance and manner may be more important than you think. The handler or rider should be neat, clean, and dressed conservatively so as not to draw attention away from the horse.

PERFORMANCE

Manners. Manners in the stall, in-hand, and in preparation for riding are important considerations to a prospective buyer. Who wants to buy a horse that is sullen in the cross-ties or wrestles you for a hind foot or has a vise-like jaw when being bridled? You should allow a buyer to observe your horse in a variety of settings and to be involved in the handling, grooming, and tacking of your horse if requested. If a horse has a dangerous bad habit, bring it to the attention of a prospective buyer and price the horse accordingly.

Level of Training. A horse should be safe and cooperative when he is handled. The time for training is not when a customer is present, however. On one occasion, I saw a green two-year-old being shown for sale. I considered the young horse's behavior acceptable—a few steps sideways while being tacked up and a bit feisty on the longe line at first. The handler's actions were not acceptable, however. He jerked roughly, slapped, and yelled loudly at the young horse, who reacted in fear toward the bit and the rider. The prospective buyers were ill at ease watching such a scene. When there was a convenient moment, they slipped away.

Demonstrating a Horse's Ability to a Buyer. As you show your horse to a buyer, be honest, courteous, and informative. First show the horse to the buyer in a halter and lead line. Stand the horse in a level, well-lighted place where the buyers can get around on all sides of the horse and can stand back and get a good view.

It's customary to demonstrate the horse's capabilities thoroughly for the buyer, oftentimes on a longe line. This allows the buyer to see the horse's frame and carriage, its style of movement, and the methods of your training. It's also a convenient warm-up for the horse, tuning it to aids and desired maneuvers.

Whether you are demonstrating ground work or mounted work, be sure your horse is reliable and sound. Indicate to a buyer any habits that a horse has that may cause trouble. It is essential that a horse is in regular work when shown to a prospective buyer. When a horse is fit and ridden daily, his responses tend to be more dependable than if he were just pulled out of a pasture.

You should ride the horse for the buyer first to demonstrate the horse's capabilities. Then if the buyer wishes to try the horse, assist him or her in whatever way you can. Perhaps the buyer brought a personal saddle for the test ride. If it will properly fit the horse, help with the adjustments and offer to hold the horse for mounting. While the buyer is becoming accustomed to the horse, you might want to chat to relax them both or leave them to their work in silence. Be aware of the urge to help verbally. This can be greatly appreciated or resented. Try to get a feel for what the potential buyer would prefer.

You can inadvertently insult someone's riding abilities by claiming with surprise that your horse has "never done that before!" If you are overly defensive about your horse, it may appear as though you are blaming the rider for an error. It is best to accept the responsibility yourself for the horse's behavior since you are the trainer/owner. Perhaps you have made an error in judgment as to the horse's suitability. A good intermediate horse may not be a good beginning horse.

After the trial ride, answer all questions honestly and thoroughly. However, beware of providing too many anecdotes. Not only can storytelling be time-consuming, but it can backfire. What may sound cute to you might sound irresponsible to the prospective buyer. As the buyer prepares to leave, give her something to remind her of your horse. It can be a photo with your name and phone number on the back, an information sheet about the horse, a business card, or a paper with some of the pertinent information on it.

PAPERWORK

Provide an information sheet for prospective buyers that furnishes answers to questions they may have when they're home "thinking it over." Include important health information such as

- breeding records
- major illnesses or injuries
- vaccination and deworming records
- farrier's records

It's a good idea to have a photocopy of your horse's registration papers and/or pedigree to send home with a prospective buyer. If you've ever been on a horse-buying trip, you know that after a while, the horses and their bloodlines can all start sounding alike.

Photos are an inexpensive way to remind your customer what you have for sale. Do not use the pasture shot that Uncle Herbie took from the highway, however. Be sure the horse is flattered—that the image is sharp, clear, and large. It is counterproductive to use anything but a high-quality photo.

Installment Sales. Sometimes in order to entice or accommodate a buyer, you may wish to offer the horse for sale on installments. If you are willing to offer terms to a buyer, draft up several contracts for purchase including pertinent information such as downpayment, number, amount and frequency of payments to follow, late payment penalty, default conditions, insurance requirements until payoff, etc. You can follow a standard loan contract from your bank or office supply store or get ideas from *The Law and Your Horse* (Greene) or *The Business of Horses* (Wood).

Have all the paperwork related to your sale horses handy and organized.

When drawing up the specific installment sale agreement, the following items should be thoroughly discussed and determined between the buyer and seller:

- Whether the buyer will pay interest. If a $1,000 horse is sold for a $500 down payment and two $250 payments two and four months after the sale, the seller may very well not charge interest. However, if an $8,000 horse is sold for a $2,000 down payment and monthly payments over two years, there very likely will be interest.

- When a payment is late. Somewhere in the agreement there should be a statement related to when a payment is late and what the recourse is for late payments. An extra charge (the amount or percentage specified) might be added to the payment or the horse might be repossessed after one or more late payments.

- Who is responsible for selecting and paying for the insurance policy. Usually the seller selects the policy and the buyer pays for it.

- Whether any specific care is required by the seller during the time of installment payments and what recourse will ensue if the buyer is not caring for the horse in the prescribed manner.

Payments are made on a predetermined schedule. The seller legally owns the horse until the last payment is made. At the time of the last payment, the registration papers and other identification papers are signed over to the new owner.

Continued →

The Veterinary Exam. A buyer will usually want to have a pre-purchase veterinary examination performed by a veterinarian of his or her choice. The buyer customarily sets up the appointment and pays for the exam. See the preceding section, Buying a Horse, for a discussion of the pre-purchase exam.

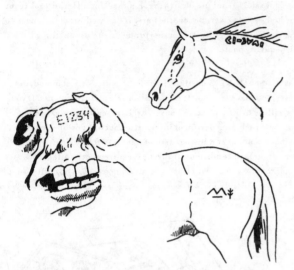

It is the seller's responsibility to be sure all means of identification are correct and registered before the sale takes place.

PRICE

Try to price your horse realistically. Remember, his value is not based on what you paid for him or have invested in him financially or emotionally, but rather on what he is worth to someone else. Be honest about his level of training and potential and find out what people have recently spent for similar animals—those of similar age, sex, breed, level of training, and size. Get several opinions if necessary. Determine your bottom price, then add 10 to 15 percent to it. Horse trading really hasn't changed in the regard that offers and counteroffers still are an expected part of horse sales.

A horse's conformation and training exert the greatest influence on price. Good management and preparation, however, can increase a horse's chances of bringing full market value.

Tack: Care and Cleaning

Cherry Hill

Illustrations by Kathy Dorn Blackwell

Selecting Tack

There is a wide and ever-changing variety of tack and equipment on the market for horsemen. Since every horse activity requires its own specialized equipment, you must know exactly what you need before you buy. There are hundreds of different types and styles of bridles available for your purchase. A bridle for Western pleasure would be unsuitable for eventing. So, if you are not absolutely sure what you should buy, seek the help of a competent professional.

QUALITY

Always buy the very best quality tack and equipment that you can afford. As with other consumer goods, inspect an item and compare it with other similar items for quality of materials, quality of workmanship, and fit. Just because an item is made of leather does not ensure that it is a high-quality article. The various grades and finishing processes of leathers (as will be discussed later) greatly affect an article's serviceability, life, and appearance. And some items, such as halters, made out of synthetic materials, such as nylon, are preferred over their leather counterparts by many experienced horsemen. Quality of materials also refers to hardware as will be discussed later.

Quality of workmanship is evident in the straightness and evenness of stitching, the fitting of seams and parts, the finishing of edges, and the overall appearance of an item. If you are proficient in comparing workmanship of dresses or shirts, use the same sorts of criteria when selecting saddles, horse blankets, and bridles.

The quality of the fit or design of an item of tack can make it easy to use or a nightmare. Tested patterns from well-established companies usually prove satisfactory. Some fledgling companies may produce acceptable items but without the attention to detail. A top-notch horse blanket, for example, would be cut from a pattern with contours to fit a horse's body; a lesser-quality blanket may have very straight seams resulting in a poorer fit.

USED TACK

As you are looking for tack, do not eliminate the possibility of buying used items. Sometimes, by looking on the bulletin board of your tack store or by searching the columns of your local horse news, you can find a used item that will save you a great deal of money. If you are not experienced enough to detect a fatigued saddle tree or a "white elephant" bridle, take a knowledgeable person along with you. No matter if you buy new or used tack or equipment, give it an initial safety check and cleaning before putting it into service. Then inspect it regularly for signs of stress and wear and replace worn portions or have the item repaired as needed.

STORAGE

A tidy, well-organized tack room will assist you in keeping your tack in tip-top shape. A tack room should be dirt and rodent free and be designed so that it consistently has a moderate temperature and humidity. It is best if your tack room is used exclusively for storing and cleaning tack. It is impossible to keep your tack clean if the room also serves as a feed room or tool room.

As you design your tack room, make a list of what you plan to keep there. Your list may include some of the following: everyday saddles, bridles, and blankets; show saddles and bridles; winter blankets, sheets, and coolers; grooming equipment, medical supplies, and records. It will be convenient if you make a space in the room for tack cleaning and small repairs as well.

Take the time to design the room so that it will facilitate proper equipment storage and care. Using a piece of graph paper, draw a proposed floor plan to scale noting the placement of large items such as a desk, saddle racks, and tack trunks. Be sure there are adequate electrical outlets and overhead lights in your tack room.

A tack room should provide enough space for you to keep things in order. Rooms smaller than 8 by 10 feet (the size of a small box stall) get crowded as soon as a few saddle racks and tack trunks are moved in. It is much harder to keep things in good order when they are crowded. If you have from two to ten horses, figure between 100 and 200 square feet for a tack room.

Try to locate your tack room near your grooming and saddling area. Note which way the air flows between the grooming area and your tack room before you decide where to locate the door, or you may find that dirt, hair, and sweepings are blown and tracked into your tack room. The doorway between the grooming area and tack room should be at least 3 1/2 feet wide to easily accommodate you carrying a saddle.

CONSTRUCTION OF THE TACK ROOM

Since leather goods are best kept at moderate temperatures and low humidity, the walls, ceiling, and floor of a tack room should be insulated. Even without a heater or air conditioner, insulation keeps the indoor environment more constant. In some climates, a dehumidifier may be required to keep leather from forming mildew during warm, humid weather. In the winter months, a small space heater may be necessary to prevent medicines from freezing.

Although windows will allow fresh air to flow through a tack room, dirt, one of leather's greatest enemies, usually accompanies the breezes. The rays of the sun shining through window glass can also be a very destructive force to leather. If you want windows, outfit those in direct sunlight with shades, shutters, or awnings. Exterior windows, unless fortified with bars or a heavy screen, decrease the security of a tack room. Plan to fit every door and window with a strong, durable locking device to discourage theft and satisfy insurance requirements. Most tack rooms, however, function quite well without windows.

Hang bridles, halters, and other tack neatly.

Tight doorways and precise wall-to-ceiling and wall-to-floor fit will prevent invasion by dirt, bugs, and rodents, all of which can be damaging to tack and equipment. Dirt floors are a constant source of dust, prevent tight wall-to-floor fit, and defeat the purpose of insulating the rest of the room. Cement floors, although easy to keep clean, are very cold and may crack with settling. An insulated wood floor is warmer and more flexible. The material for the flooring should be durable, water resistant, and easy to sweep. Wood floors should be treated with a sealer. Using a boot scraper or mat to remove mud and snow before entering the tack room will also help to preserve the floor and keep dust to a minimum.

Hanging bridles. A large amount of wall space is required for hanging and storing equipment, especially bridles and halters. Bridle holders with contoured head pieces that approximate the configuration and size of a horse's poll area help to keep bridles in good shape. A half-circle of

wood about 4 inches in diameter and about 2 1/2 inches thick works well. Having a 3/8-inch lip on the forward edge of the curved surface will keep the bridle from slipping off the bridle holder. However, solid wood will not allow a very sweaty bridle to dry out quickly. You may wish to consider using open-framework metal or plastic bridle holders (shaped like horseshoes). Mounting bridle holders 9 inches apart, center to center, provides ample room for convenient use.

Equipment other than bridles, such as halter and lead ropes, longe lines, running martingales, and extra nosebands can be hung on hooks. Figure how many hooks you think you will need, then double the number! If you are short on hooks, you will probably find yourself digging to the bottom of a tangled mass of equipment for the pair of reins you want. Outfit your tack room, grooming area, and barn aisles with plenty of safe hooks.

Saddle racks. Saddle racks can be free-standing or built into the wall. The former style is convenient if you like to rearrange things periodically. Free-standing units can be easily relocated and used as saddle-cleaning stands. If you prefer wall-style racks, be sure to mount them with ample clearance between them for the styles of saddles you use.

No matter what type of saddle rack you choose, be sure it allows the saddle to dry and retain its proper shape. The rack should allow air circulation—the pipes or slats should be well spaced so that the underside of the panels and the stirrup leathers can dry after hard use. The shape of the saddle rack should approximate the contours of a horse's back. Some people use a log or a 55 gallon drum for a saddle rack, but these not only prevent the saddle from drying out but they can spread the saddle out into an unnatural shape. Others use a single rail or rod to rest a saddle on. This may not be as damaging to the tree, but it can mar the gullet (the underside of the front) of the saddle and also cause the saddle to rest in a cockeyed position. It is best if you choose a rack that approximates the size and shape of a horse's back.

Wet saddle blankets and pads are often set to dry by turning them upside down on top of the saddle. This might work well during hot, dry weather or if the blanket does not need to be used again soon. Faster drying can be achieved by locating a blanket rack where it can take advantage of the sun and/or air currents.

Other. Tack trunks are handy for storing items that are not used frequently or for seasonal items such as storm blankets. Trunks take up a lot of floor space, however, so it is best if they are sturdy enough to double as seats or short-term project areas for simple repair work or small cleaning jobs.

Provide a place for everything and keep everything in its place. Having plenty of shelves, cupboards, and cubby holes will help remind you to return an item to its designated spot. That way equipment stays cleaner, lasts longer, and is there when you need it. Bins work especially well for small items such as bandages, protective boots, spurs, and gloves.

Veterinary supplies are best kept in a cupboard. If your tack room is heated to keep things from freezing, your salves, sprays, and dewormers will be ready to use when you need them. An alternative is to insulate and heat a separate cabinet filled with items you want to keep from freezing.

Since it may be most convenient to keep veterinary, farrier, and training records in the tack room, you may wish to use a corner of the room for an office. Outfit a small desk with a good light, your files, pencils and pens, and a calendar.

Continued ➜

If you initially invest the time and effort to set up a tack room to specifically fill your needs, you will find that your tack stays organized and clean and lasts longer, that you will have a base of operations for small horse care and tack care tasks, and that your records will be at your fingertips when you need them. In this way you are protecting your investment in tack and equipment and ensuring that your tack will always be ready, allowing you more time to ride.

Rodents are attracted to the smell and taste of sweat and leather.

Leather

Leather is the preferred material for boots, gloves, and most tack. It is very comfortable because it breathes, allowing evaporation and ventilation, and is self-conforming to the rider and the horse. Leather that is kept dry, clean, and supple is more comfortable for the horse and rider, lasts longer, is safer during stress, and has a first-rate appearance. If you understand some of the aspects of the production of leather, it will help you when selecting leather items as well as providing them with proper care.

CLASSIFICATION OF LEATHER

Lightweight leather from smaller or younger animals such as calves, sheep, or deer is referred to as a *skin* and is used for boots, gloves, and chaps. Heavy leather, predominantly from cattle, is commonly referred to as *(cow)hide*, which comprises the majority of harnesses, bridles, and saddles. Some portions of thick hides can be split into two thinner pieces of leather. Full-grain leather is that which has all of its layers intact. Glove leather, 1/32-inch thick or less, weighs about 3 ounces per square foot, while sole leather, 1/4 - 1/8-inch thick, weighs 12 to 15 ounces per square foot. Most tack is made from 1/8-inch thick leather.

Hides are graded according to quality, taking into account such factors as weight, trim, and blemishes. Hides are said to have a flesh side and a grain (hair) side. The surface of the grain side is often the smooth, exposed surface on tack or clothing, so should be free from defects.

A U.S. Heavy Native Steer, for example, is a grade denoting an unbranded hide weighing at least 60 pounds. It must have been removed from the carcass by a knowledgeable knife resulting in a good pattern, no cuts (holes all the way through the hide from a slip of the knife), and less than five scores (cuts that do not extend all the way through the hide). In addition, the U.S. Heavy Native Steer classification imposes limits on grub holes, injury scars, and rub and drag marks.

Because of the unwieldiness of a full hide, most leather is sold in pieces. A hide is removed from an animal by an incision down the middle of the belly. A second cut made down the backbone results in two sides. Making another parallel cut at about the flank area separates each of the sides into a back strip and a belly strip. The belly strip is thinner, stretchier leather and is about half the width of the back strip.

It usually takes about two sides to make a Western saddle. The skirts and jockeys are generally made from the back, where the hide is thick and tough. Bellies are good for contoured areas such as the stirrups, swells, horn, and cantle because the stretchy leather will conform without bubbling. The ground seat is made from the neck which is thick but not strong and has a lot of fat on it.

LEATHER TANNING

The chemical and mechanical processes that convert hides into leather transform a decomposable commodity into a stable material. A fresh hide is often presoaked before fleshing. Scraping the muscle tissue and fat from the hide exposes the true fibrous skin to the tanning process. After fleshing, the hide is further soaked to remove the balance of dirt, salt, and blood in addition to making the hide flexible.

Hides are soaked in a lime solution to make the hair slip. Once the hair has been removed, the hide must be delimed. Lime is an alkali and if left on the hide, would alter the tanning process by neutralizing the action of tannin, which is an acid. After deliming, the hide can be stretched and dried for use as rawhide or can be tanned and made into leather.

The actual tanning of the leather is accomplished by immersing the hides into a vegetable or chemical solution. Age-old oak bark tanning is still one of the most common and desired vegetable tans today. Tannic acid, the astringent in the tree bark liquor, combines with the proteins in the hide to form a compound that will not rot and that imparts a rich natural color to the leather. The soaking process traditionally takes place in pits in the ground. Depending on the temperature of the ground and the thickness of the hide, tanning is complete in two weeks to two months.

Most saddles and bridles are crafted from oak tanned leather which is thick and firm. Oak-tanned sheepskins, tanned with the wool on, have a hard, heavy skin that makes them ideal for lining saddles.

Chrome tanning is the most popular mineral tan. The soaking process, which takes place in a machine something like a cement mixer, can be completed in a matter of a few days. Such leathers are usually softer, more pliable, lighter in weight, and will stretch more than oak tanned leather. A blue-green or gray-green center to the leather identifies it as having been at least partially tanned by a chrome process. Gloves, boot uppers, and lightweight chaps are made from chrome tanned leather. Chrome tanned sheepskins have a soft, thin skin, which wouldn't wear well on the underside of a saddle but is useful for garments.

Another type of mineral tan uses alum. Alum salts, which naturally occur in the Southwest desert, are used to produce a type of latigo leather with a characteristically bright yellow center. Chrome tanned latigo results in a gray center.

Tanners are not limited to an either/or situation when it comes to tanning methods, however. Often leathers are treated with a combination of soakings. One such example is retan or double-tan latigo. Partially vegetable tanned, the leather is then finished with a soaking in alum salts. Latigo leather has a heavy, waxy feeling and a superior ability to shed water, sweat, and salt. These characteristics are a result of finishing, not tanning.

FINISHING LEATHER

Finishing consists of working the leather, coloring it, texturizing the grain side, and loading the leather with greases and oils. As the leather is drying, the fibers are separated or "broken" by mechanical rollers so that the leather attains the desired pliability. Garment leather is worked longer and more aggressively than skirting leather. Dyeing and texturizing usually takes place before oiling.

While the leather is damp, it is stuffed with the tanner's own recipe of oils and greases. Latigo receives a larger amount and a heavier mixture of oils and greases than skirting leather. This renders latigo more pliable and moisture resistant, while the skirting leather is left firmer and drier. Fish oils, such as cod and sperm, make up the largest percentage of the lubricant, which is forced into the pores of leather, often resulting in a fat content as high as 10 percent of the weight of the hide. Other ingredients include neat's foot oil, paraffin, and tallow.

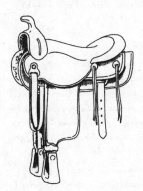

If you take care of your tack, it will have a first-rate appearance and will function safely.

Full-grain leather is that which has all of its layers intact. Shaving or skiving of thick areas may make a full-grain hide an even thickness, but no entire layers have been removed. However, two or more layers of lighter leather can be made from a single hide by running it through a mechanical splitter. The upper split will still have a grain and flesh side. The lower split will have two virtually identical fleshy sides and consequently will have decreased strength because of the absence of the dense grain side.

After shaving and/or splitting, the leather is cleaned with an acid rinse to rid it of bacteria and then it is slicked-out to remove water. While it is still wet, it is set, often by hand, to flatten growth marks. It is now in the russet stage and is hung up to dry. Once dry, it is lightly buffed to remove very superficial scratches. Then it is dyed. Popular colors for tack are London (light brown), Havana (deep brown), and Warwick (near-black). The leather stain can be applied en masse in drums, with a sprayer, or by hand with a cloth.

Decorative patterns on leather can add beauty to a piece of tack and cover up blemishes in the leather. Defects in the leather might have been caused by injury, by the presence of fat molecules in the skin, or by inconsistencies in the tanning process itself. The hide may have been laying crumpled during one of the stages of tanning, or the hide may have been at the bottom of the pit, or perhaps the tanning solution wasn't completely washed out. Many blemishes do not hamper the serviceability of the leather, but they can detract from the appearance of the finished product unless the saddlemaker cuts to avoid the blemishes or conceals the blemishes.

Designs on the leather can be made by a combination of carving and tooling, by hand-stamping, or by embossing. In the first method, the saddlemaker carves the design on the leather with a swivel knife. Then the wet leather is pushed and manipulated with tools of various shapes and patterns in order to give the pattern depth and texture. A newly tooled saddle can feel very rough and bumpy as some of the designs may be raised above the original level of the grain. Although carving has the

potential to weaken the leather somewhat, if properly done, the cut is only made halfway through the density of the grain layer.

Stamping is achieved by pressure from a mallet on various hand-held tools. Embossing is a similar process used by mass-scale saddleries: a mechanically pressurized wheel is rolled over large pieces of leather to leave the desired imprint. Neither stamping nor embossing actually cuts the leather; instead the leather is compressed to form the design.

QUALITIES OF GOOD LEATHER

Good leather will have substance to it. When comparing samples of the same type, the weight in relation to thickness indicates a high fat content, which is the lifeblood of leather. Quality leather is pliable and flexible and will not crease or crack. It has high-tensile strength and is firm, not soft or pappy. When it is bent, it does not bubble and it returns to its original shape.

Quality leather has a fine-grained, smooth flesh side with open pores but no loose or rough fibers. The pores of the grain side should have become sealed during processing, which makes the surface nearly watertight.

CARING FOR LEATHER

Leather's greatest enemies are water, heat, dirt, and the salt from sweat. Fine leather articles should be stored at room temperature and out of direct sun and light. Humidity should be moderate and the room should be well ventilated and as dirt-free as possible.

If a dehumidifier is impractical, discourage mold and mildew by wiping leather articles periodically with a mild acid solution, such as white vinegar and water or a 1:1 ratio of rubbing alcohol and water. If mildew persists, washing with a thick suds of a germicidal or fungicidal soap followed by exposure to air and sunlight will usually take care of the problem.

For routine leather care, follow these three steps to protect your tack: Clean it. Feed it. Seal it.

Warm water and Turkish toweling may be all that is necessary to remove dirt, hair, sweat, and previous applications of saddle soap and oil from tack. Tooled saddles may benefit from the use of a soft-bristled brush, and neglected saddles will require the addition of a cleaning agent to the water. Naturally made oil-based soaps such as Kirkwood's or Murphy's will clean the leather without drying it as detergents and some brands of glycerine saddle soaps will. "Jockeys," or dark spots that can appear under stirrup leathers, for example, may need to be gently rubbed with the end of a wooden match or a dull knife blade to loosen before cleaning with soap and water. Wash, rinse, and wipe.

The basics for good leather care include a sponge, a cloth, saddle soap, and neat's-foot oil.

Continued ➔

Once the leather is thoroughly cleaned and rinsed of soap residue, it should be allowed to dry partially. While it is still damp, the flesh side of the leather should be nourished with oil or grease. Damp leather absorbs oil more readily by drawing it into the pores as the water evaporates.

Leather loses some of its fat every day and needs to be fed. Overfeeding, however, can create a limp, flabby, greasy article with deteriorated threads and weakened leather fibers. Routine light oiling is far superior to a one-time saturation. Beware of compounds that contain petroleum-based products, as they will emulsify the fats in the leather and dry it out. Pure neat's-foot oil is usually a safe choice. One-step leather conditioners and preservers may save some time when used on occasion but may not impart an overall healthy feel to your leather if used on a long-term basis.

Once the leather has had adequate time to dry, the oil must be then sealed into the leather. Two methods can be used for sealing: the soft soap or hard wax methods. This final coat of saddle soap not only locks in the oil, which was added to the tack, but it also makes daily removal of sweat and mud much easier. For articles such as bridles, which don't get very dirty and need to remain supple, apply soft saddle soap directly from the can with a small piece of sheepskin. Let it dry and then buff and polish the piece with a damp chamois. A chamois is a soft undersplit of a sheepskin (no wool) that has been oil-tanned and suede-finished.

For stirrup fenders and leathers, back cinches, and skirts, try the hard wax method. With a clean sheepskin applicator, a small amount of water, a glycerin saddle soap bar, and lots of elbow grease, work up a lather. Apply the foam liberally to areas that especially need protection from sweat and mud and to areas that come in contact with the rider's clothes. Let the foam dry for a half hour or so, then buff and polish the saddle with a chamois.

Leather articles should be covered with fabric when not in use. Fabric offers protection from dust and dirt accumulation while allowing adequate ventilation. Take care of your leather tack items and they will last a long time. And some day, when you least expect it (but most assuredly will appreciate it), they will take care of you.

The most important ingredient to keeping your tack in top shape is elbow grease.

Nylon and Other Fiber Items

Although leather has long been touted as the premier material for tack, some items are more practical, economical, and longer-lasting when made from other materials.

Well-made nylon halters are very sturdy, dependable, and have a long life if well cared for. They are washable and can be sterilized by washing in hot water and disinfectants. They are available in a variety of colors and sizes. Look for halters that are doubled (two layers of nylon) and stitched and are made with high-quality hardware.

Cotton and cotton-blend webbing is often used in the manufacture of longe lines, driving lines, and some English girths. Webbing is very light and washable in cold water.

Western breast collars and cinches are often made of mohair yarn, a fiber made from the hair of the Angora goat. Since mohair will shrink if washed in warm water, only wash mohair items in cold water. You may need to hang the cinch up while drying with a heavy weight on one end so that the cinch does not shrink to an unusable length. Other Western cinches and breast collars are made of cotton, acrylic, and blended yarns and can look very much like mohair yet tend to shrink less. Be sure of the fiber content when you buy and again when you wash.

Hardware

When an item of tack breaks, it is often the hardware that gives way. For everyday working gear, choose hardware that is solid stainless steel or forged brass alloys. Avoid chrome-plated pot metal (sometimes called kangaroo metal), which is cast. Cast metals have a tendency to be weaker and can break when stressed. A cross-section of a broken cast snap reveals a very porous material, unlike the solid structure of forged metal.

The snap on the lead rope that you use to tie your horse must be able to resist a sudden force of 1,200 pounds jerking on it in the event your horse gets frightened and pulls back on the rope. A horse that once learns to break a lead rope can provide a lifetime of headaches. Choose a lead rope with a strong, high-quality bull-snap.

Inspect your tack frequently for rotted stitching, cracked leather, and broken hardware.

This is an example of a poor type of snap to use with horses, as it is far too weak.

When selecting bridles, saddles, and other riding tack, look at the buckles, the rigging rings, the stirrup plates. Are they solid stainless steel (usually stamped) or another forged alloy? Or are they chrome-plated pot metal? Besides being weaker, pot metal hardware will rust once the chrome plating wears off.

When choosing a bit, keep the same principles in mind. A stainless steel or nickel alloy bit will require minimal maintenance and will be accepted well by the horse. A chrome-plated bit will begin to rust where the areas of chrome are thin and will not be as pleasant in the horse's mouth. Aluminum bits are not recommended.

Blankets

Buy the very best blanket you can afford. Be sure it properly fits your horse. Then follow simple rules of good care to minimize costly repairs and maximize the life of your blankets. Top-quality materials alone won't prevent a horse from tearing his blanket if he lives in a stall with protrusions or rough walls. However, blankets made of good materials are easier and more worthwhile to patch. The biggest blanket-buying error is to shop by price rather than by quality.

BLANKET CONSTRUCTION

Purchase well-made domestic blankets. The outer layer of such blankets is usually made of high-quality, tightly woven, durable materials such as Cordura, nylon Pack Cloth, duck canvas, or in the case of coolers, 100 percent wool. Blankets made of acrylic, other fleeces, acetate, or fibers with loose, open, or uneven weaves are easily shredded, shrink unevenly, or may be impossible to thoroughly clean. Many of these import blankets look very attractive when new and have design features of the more expensive, domestic blankets but just do not hold up to normal horse use. What is doubly difficult for the buyer is that many of the import blankets do not have fiber content information on them.

Most nylon products are tough, resist tearing, and provide a smooth, dense surface. Nylon-lined blankets keep the coat slick and don't easily pick up hair and dirt so they don't require frequent washing. Fleece- and blanket-lined blankets accumulate a lot of debris so they are very difficult to keep clean and hard to repair well. In addition, fleece and blanket linings compress over pressure points on the horse's body, such as the shoulders, hips, and withers. Often such blankets are also heavy and result in bare spots or raw spots. Nylon-lined blankets are less likely to cause hair loss. In the case of a horse that is very sensitive, even with a well-fitted blanket, a blanket lined with pure silk can increase comfort.

Polyester or Fiberfill stuffing provides good insulation and is comfortable for the horse. It is light, easy to wash and dry, and allows air to circulate more freely through the blanket. Whether a horse might get wet from external moisture or from his own body heat and sweat, it is important for the moisture to be able to escape from the blanket. Foam-stuffed blankets, unless they are of a very light foam, are not as breathable as polyester, are generally heavier, and are stiffer when dirty.

BLANKET REPAIR

The most frequent blanket repairs are ripped surcingle straps, broken hardware, ripped-out leg-strap holes, and miscellaneous tear holes all over the blankets. Torn stitching of surcingle straps can result from poor workmanship, fatigued thread, or from the horse catching the blanket on something in the stall or trailer. If surcingle straps are left too loose they are an open invitation for damage to the blanket.

Bent or broken buckles, especially the T-shaped hook, often need to be replaced. To do so, your repair person must remove the stitching near the slide, replace the hook and the slide, and restitch. To avoid such a repair, buy blankets with high-quality hardware such as stainless steel or brass. A new type of nylon and polypropylene low-profile, side-release buckle is also being used. This hardware is lighter than metal and won't rust or corrode; however, the side prongs of the buckle have been known to break.

If the rectangular loops where leg straps slide through are not reinforced by a durable material, they may rip out. Often they are

surrounded by vinyl, but some of the vinyls that are commonly used crack. When these slots need to be strengthened, it is best to use leather or a tent material that is a nylon-reinforced vinyl.

Holes in blankets come in all shapes and sizes and are either caused by the horse catching the blanket on something in the stall, the horse chewing the blanket, the horse's neighbor grabbing the blanket, or the horse rubbing or rolling excessively in the blanket. Hoods are also damaged by the horse rubbing, especially around the eyes and ears. Much of the rubbing can be prevented by keeping the horse scrupulously clean. If a hood is damaging the mane, the hood can be lined with silk. If you are putting an expensive blanket on a horse that hasn't been blanketed before, put a sheet over the blanket to protect it until you can assess his tolerance and habits.

Big rips often require replacing a section of outside covering, the polyester insulation, and the inside covering. Sometimes it is easier to start from scratch like this than to try to patch the shreds. When more than one third of a blanket is gone, it is not worth the time to fix it.

BLANKET FIT AND CUSTOMIZING

It is best and usually possible to find a blanket that fits your horse properly. However, if you have a hard-to-fit horse or are trying to utilize a blanket that you already have, customizing can be done such as cutting back at the withers or shoulder, adding fleece at the withers, adding a tail piece, cutting up higher at the tail, moving the front buckles, or making an open front a solid front. Hoods can be customized to make the earholes more comfortable or to adjust the eyeholes. If a blanket shifts around a lot on the horse even with the surcingle straps snug, use a cotton web surcingle (roller) over the blanket to help to keep the blanket in place and prevent potential damage.

BLANKET CARE

Dirt, manure, urine, and sun can be very fatiguing to the integrity of the blanket's material. A dirty blanket is unhealthy and uncomfortable for a horse and makes a mess of a sewing machine during repair. Ideally a blanket should be removed from the horse daily. The underside of the blanket should be checked for debris and lightly brushed or wiped. The horse should be exercised, groomed and then reblanketed.

Washing. If a horse is blanketed daily, the blanket should be washed about once a week; therefore you will need two blankets for each horse. Before blankets are repaired, they should be washed. Most winter blankets will not fit in a home machine and many Laundromats frown on horse laundry. You may have a custom blanket-laundering and repair service in your area.

If you do the washing yourself, use a moderate amount of mild laundry detergent and no bleach, as some horses are very sensitive to chlorine. You may also wish to add an odor eliminator to the wash cycle. Industrial cleaning supply companies carry commercial brands; washing soda is available at the grocery store. Most blankets can be washed in warm water. Exceptions are 100 percent wool coolers (which often must be dry-cleaned), blanket-lined blankets, and those with specifically stated cold-water instructions such as waterproofed blankets or those with leather straps.

Be sure all of the soap gets rinsed out. If you use the proper amount of detergent, most commercial machines (front load heavy-duty) do a

Continued ➡

HORSE BLANKETS

Type	Use	Care
Cotton or cotton/polyester sheet	to keep off dust or flies, used for warmth during cool weather	hand wash, machine wash (cool or warm), or dry clean, hang to dry
Wood Cooler (usually 85–100% wool)	to cool out hot or sweaty horse	hand wash cold or machine wash cold gentle cycle, hang to dry
Acrylic "Baker" blanket	for moderate warmth in a stall	hand wash, machine wash (cool or warm), or dry clean, hang to dry
Cotton duck with blanket lining	for moderate warmth in a stall	hand wash or dry clean, hang to dry
Nylon with fiberfill insulation and nylon lining	for high degree of warmth in a stall	hand wash, machine wash (cool or warm), or dry clean, hang to dry
Nylon with foam insulation and fleece lining	for high degree of warmth in a stall	hand wash, machine wash (cool or warm), or dry clean, hang to dry
Nylon Gore-Tex waterproof laminate	for wind and water protection as well as warmth outside	hand wash, machine wash (cool or warm), or dry clean, dryer OK or hang to dry
Canvas turn-out rug often with blanket lining	for wind and water protection as well as warmth outside	hand wash only and hang to dry

good job of rinsing. It is unlikely that you have a machine at home large enough to wash a winter horse blanket, but if you do, refer to the section under Saddle Blankets that discusses water softener.

You can do a fairly good job of washing a heavy winter blanket at a car wash with a high-pressure sprayer. Clean the bay really well, lay the blanket out on the concrete floor, and spray. However, don't use the car wash detergent; bring your own.

If you are washing a horse blanket at a car wash, once you feel you have the soap out, put in a few more quarters and make sure. Other than the spin cycle of a machine, the best way to get the water out of a blanket is to roll the blanket tightly and squeeze several times each way.

Line-dry all horse blankets. Most don't require reshaping. However, the lining of blanket-lined blankets often stretch way out of proportion while the covering, frequently of cotton duck, will shrink just a little bit. These blankets may have to be stretched back into shape. As the blanket is drying, oil the leather portions with pure neat's foot oil or rub Murphy's oil soap paste into the leather to soften and preserve it.

Blankets can be re-waterproofed with a compound such as Rain Check, a solvent-based wax coating, that can be sprayed on. It is available from canvas or tent shops. Because of its volatile nature, it must be applied with caution and in the open air.

BLANKET FIRST AID

Frequently check the stress points on your blanket: around the surcingles, leg straps, and front buckles. Take care of minor damage before it becomes a big problem. Use your braiding thread and needle to whip a few stitches across the tear until you can have it repaired. Or use duct tape or adhesive tape for a quick and handy first aid for rips. Some tapes, and most tapes that are left on too long, will leave a sticky residue which might have to be wiped off with a solvent-based cleaner before repair can be done. Nylon patch kits for tents also work well as first aid for tears. In some cases such a patch may be good enough to be stitched down and serve as the permanent repair.

Blankets should be cleaned and repaired before they are retired for the season. They should be stored in a trunk, cabinet, or on a shelf in a dirt-free and rodent-proof area. If the blankets are absolutely dry, they can be stored in a sealed garbage bag. However, if there is the slightest bit of moisture, you may open the bag months later to the odor and destructive forces of mildew. Blankets, and especially their insulation, provide irresistible nesting materials for mice. Additionally, blankets that are stored covered with dirt, sweat, or manure attract insects and mice. If you have a particular problem with moths, you may wish to put a few mothballs between the layers of each stored blanket.

Saddle Blankets

Materials for saddle blankets include a wide range of natural and synthetic materials. Ideally a saddle blanket should conform to a horse's back and also allow it to breathe. It is best if the material is absorbent and washable. Wool is a good choice, either as a woven Navajo-type Western blanket or an English felt pad. However, wool requires more care and attention during washing. It can only be washed in cold water and should not be dried in a dryer or it will shrink.

Cotton blankets or pads are absorbent but slow to dry and not particularly resilient or fluffy. Cotton is easy to wash, however. Synthetic fleeces are soft and usually provide thick cushion but are notoriously slippery on the horse's body. They also seem to attract hair and burrs like magnets. Some closed-cell rubber pads provide good cushion and grip but are not absorbent. There are many good synthetic pads available today; each one must be evaluated individually for its intended use.

WASHING SADDLE BLANKETS

In general, when washing saddle blankets and pads, follow these rules. Use a large-capacity washer and an ample amount of water. You may wish to consider placing a wringer washer in your barn exclusively for horse laundry. Do not overload the tub of your washer and try to balance the load, especially with an automatic spinning washer. Use a moderate amount of mild soap. Be sure the blankets are rinsed well. Some detergents, if left as a residue, will cause irritation to your horse's back. If you used too much soap in error or if there is a lot of horse hair on the blankets, you may need to send the blankets through a second rinse cycle.

Using a Water Softener. If you have hard water or want to enhance the cleaning power of your soap or the flushing action of the rinse water, you may wish to use a water conditioner. Sodium hexametaphosphate, a water softener sold under the trade name of Calgon, removes minerals such as calcium and magnesium from water to make it purer and subsequently a better solvent.

Calgon is odorless, nontoxic and has a neutral pH. Washing sodas, on the other hand, are very alkaline, which is undesirable for use on hair and skin. In addition, the sodas remove minerals from the water by precipitation, which results in a sludge in the wash or rinse water. Calgon, on the other hand, holds the minerals in suspension so they can not form scum. It is useful in two ways: to increase the effectiveness of soap and to act as a thorough rinse. With cold, warm, or hot water, Calgon used with soap or shampoo does a better job of cleaning as it prevents the dingy, insoluble scum from forming. As a rinse for a horse's hair or a blanket, a Calgon solution removes the graying dullness caused by previously deposited soap residues. It has a superior ability to combine with and sequester oily and greasy substances, which prevents them from reacting with the horse's skin or becoming trapped in the fibers of a blanket.

How much Calgon to use depends on the hardness of the water. One teaspoon per gallon of water would be adequate for naturally soft water with a hardness of five grains or less per gallon. Two tablespoons per gallon would be more appropriate for very hard water with a hardness score of fifteen grains or more per gallon. At those rates, the 4-pound box available in most grocery stores goes a long way. Do not confuse Calgon with Calgonite. The latter is a cleaner made specifically for automatic dishwashers and contains several harsh detergents. Store the box of sodium hexametaphosphate granules in a cool, dry place and mix as needed.

Drying. Most fleece pads and blankets dry the best in a dryer. Some cotton blankets will shrink a small amount in a dryer so would be best dried on a line. Wool must be line dried and it would be best in a place out of the sun. Some blankets and pads may need a bit of stretching and reshaping before hanging them on the line.

Ropes

Rope is a term used to describe a braided or twisted fiber line 3/16 inch in diameter or larger. Any line smaller than 3/16 of an inch in diameter is referred to as a *cord.* Lead ropes are commonly 5/8 inch or 3/4 inch in diameter. Some of the most common types of ropes associated with horses are two natural fiber ropes, Manila and cotton, and two synthetic ropes, polypropylene and nylon.

TYPES OF ROPES

Manila Rope. Manila rope is made from a brown fiber of a plant related to the banana tree, which grows mainly in the Philippines and is shipped from Manila. Manila rope is one of the least expensive ropes and is the strongest of all ropes made from natural fibers. Ropes made of plant fibers are subject to rot, mold, and mildew if not properly cared for. Manila rope stretches very little, which makes it very popular with

outfitters to secure the loads on their pack animals. Once a knot is properly tied using manila rope, it does not work loose.

One thing to be aware of about ropes in general, and Manila rope in particular, is that when a line is pulled with force across your skin or the skin of your horse, a very painful and potentially serious abrasion results. This is called rope burn. That is why you should always wear well-fitted gloves when handling horses with ropes. And that is also why Manila rope is not recommended for lead ropes or training ropes.

Cotton Rope. Cotton rope is manufactured from the fibers of the cotton plant. It is stretchier than manila rope and is only half as strong. Cotton rope, when new, is bright white and soft when compared to other ropes. This makes it the traditional favorite among horsemen for lead ropes and training ropes. Although a soft rope such as cotton makes rope burns less likely, they are still possible with any type of rope.

Cotton rope has a tendency to fray—the outermost fibers break with use and become ragged, making the rope weaker. If stored wet or dirty, the fibers of a cotton rope will deteriorate and the rope may break when in use. The best care for any rope, and especially cotton, is to keep it clean and dry.

Polypropylene. Polypropylene is a product of the petroleum industry. It has twice the stretch of a cotton rope of equal size and is three times as strong. However, it is a hard, slick rope that is stiff to work with. If used improperly, it can cause extremely deep and serious rope burns. It is not suitable for lead ropes but may have some applications around the barn and wash rack.

Polypropylene is available in a wide variety of colors, yellow being the most common. It is unaffected by gasoline, oil, or other chemicals and is one of the only ropes that will float indefinitely in water. It is, however, one of the ropes least resistant to sunlight and it will melt under a direct flame. Baling twine and high-visibility electric fence wire are examples of polypropylene.

If the end of a twisted rope is left unattended, it will unravel. To keep it from unraveling, you can whip the end with a cord or back-splice it.

Nylon. Nylon, another synthetic fiber, is very popular for lead ropes because it is nearly as soft as cotton and is over four times as strong. In fact, nylon rope is one of the strongest you can buy. It is also the stretchiest rope, which allows it to absorb the energy of a sudden load without breaking. Nylon rope is resistant to abrasion and not noticeably affected by water, gasoline, or sunlight, but will melt under a direct flame. Nylon comes in a variety of colors.

FINISHING ROPES

You must keep the ends of your ropes from unraveling. The way you do this will depend on the type of rope you are working with. Nylon rope and some polypropylene ropes are braided; Manila and cotton ropes are twisted. A twisted rope consists of three strands that spiral alongside each other. Such ropes can have their ends finished or a snap added to an end by a type of weaving called back-splicing. After back-splicing, the rope can be further finished by covering the ends of the strands with cord (called whipping) or tape.

Continued ➜

Tool	Description	Use
Hoof Pick	all-metal hoof-cleaning tool with dull point, may have wooden handle	to remove mud and manure from the sole and clefts of the frog of the hoof
Rubber Curry	oval or round, soft or hard rubber massager with pointed or rounded nubbins	to loosen mud, sweat, and shedding hair and to stimulate the skin; use in a circular motion
Rubber Grooming Mit	shaped like an oven mit but made out of rubber and covered with nubbins	for similar purposes as rubber curry but on sensitive and contoured areas such as head and legs
Mud Brush	very stiff brush	for long or very dirty coats to remove large particles of mud
Dandy Brush	medium-stiff brush	used with a short, flicking motion of the wrist to send dirt flying the head and legs
Body Brush	soft brush	for finishing the coat and brushing off coat and legs
Mane and Tail Brush	long-bristled, human type hairbrush often lubricated with baby oil or silicone	to remove tangles from the mane and tail
Metal Curry	sharp-toothed instrument with concentric metal blades and a wooden handle	to clean mud, dandy, and body brushes; is not used on horse's body itself
Terrycloth	rough, thick cloth of sizes various	use wet or dry to clean eyes, nostrils, anus, udder and sheath, and groom's hands
Stable Rubber	tightly woven, linen-like cloth	to remove the final dust from the hair and to set the coat
Sweat Scraper	contoured aluminum blade	to remove sweat or wash water from the horse's body

Keep grooming tools clean.

The ends of braided ropes are usually finished by heating the fibers to melt them into a seal or by using an iron clamp, called a *ferrule*, to bind a folded end tight.

Inspect your ropes regularly for signs of fraying, rotting, and weakness and replace any ropes that you feel no longer are trustworthy.

Grooming Tools

As a horse owner, you will eventually accumulate a variety of grooming tools and equipment to help you properly care for your horse. Take care to keep your tools clean and in good repair so they last a long time and function properly when you need them.

BRUSH CARE

Brushes are composed of blocks and fibers. The block is the base that contains the bristles. Blocks can be made of wood, plastic, or leather. Wood is the traditional favorite because it feels good in the hand of the groom. Wood can swell and crack if not cared for properly. Plastic blocks are usually lighter than wood and impervious to water. Leather is the most expensive alternative for a brush block and requires the most care.

The bristles should be washed regularly. If the bristles are dirty only halfway up, set the brushes bristle-side down in a shallow pan of warm, soapy water. The water should not reach the base of the bristles in wood or leather blocks. Let the bristles soak for a half hour. Then use the brushes to gently scrub each other. Rinse the brushes thoroughly and shake out the excess water. Place them bristle-side down to dry.

Fine hardwood blocks should last a long time. To increase their lifespan, you may wish to re-lacquer them from time to time. Leather blocks and leather handles on all brushes need oiling from time to time.

BRISTLE FIBERS

Rice Root: A type of body brush with stiff bristles made from the root of rice plants. These brushes are often wire-drawn: the bristles are drawn through one-half of the wooden base, fastened with wire, and the top is screwed in place. The places where the wires are drawn through are large holes to let water drain through.

Palmyra: From Palmyra palm of India. The texture of the fibers medium stiff to stiff. It has a mottled light or dark brown color. Useful for brushing with water.

Bassine: A superior quality of Palmyra. The fibers are coarse and stiff and range in color from dark brown to black. A very durable fiber used primarily for stiff, scrubbing applications.

Tampico: From the Mexican agave plant. Originally an off-white color, it can be dyed to any color. The texture is soft to medium with good durability and acid resistance. It works well with water applications.

Union: A mixture of two or more fibers, usually Tampico and Palmyra. A medium-stiff texture and mottled light brown color with a variety of applications.

Boar: Also known as Chinese bristle. Stiff to very stiff so can be used as a mud brush or for mane and tail but too stiff for body brush.

Horse Hair: Good resilience and texture. Soft to slightly stiff; available in white, gray, and black. Durable and used in fine facial brushes.

Nylon: Synthetic material available in a wide range of diameters, textures, shapes, and length of fibers. Therefore can be soft to stiff. Resilient and durable and resistant to many common chemicals as well as temperature and abrasion.

Polypropylene: Synthetic material either crimped or straight in a variety of colors. Acid, fungus, and rot resistant with long life.

Polystyrene: Synthetic that can be crimped (to add to its water-carrying capacity) or flagged (tips split) to provide a soft brushing surface. Unusually durable and resists moisture and petroleum products.

CLOTHS

Keep a good supply of rags and cloths around the stable, as they are required for a variety of tasks including the cleaning of the horse, the tack, and the groom! Keep a cloth near your tacking area so that you can wipe the bit and bridle when you remove it from your horse. Use a cloth to apply a body-bracing liquid to your horse after a hard workout. Use an old rag to wipe the mud off the hoof wall of your horse before your farrier arrives.

Cloths that are heavily soiled or contain chemicals or are covered with bacteria from a sick or wounded horse must be disposed of or washed separately with special wash additives. For cloths with hoof dressing or fly spray on them, you may need to add a degreaser to your wash water. Contaminated cloths should be discarded, burned, or if desired, can be washed with a disinfectant. Confer with your veterinarian as to the type of disinfectant that you should use depending on your specific situation. If your horse is shedding contagious bacteria from a nasal discharge, for example, you will need to disinfect all items that come in contact with the horse to keep from spreading it to your other horses.

For routine washing, grooming cloths can be laundered with saddle pads and horse sheets and blankets.

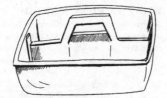

An inexpensive tote is helpful for organizing grooming tools.

ELECTRIC CLIPPERS

Removing hair from certain portions of your horse's body during various seasons may make him easier to care for, cool out, and keep healthy. It is customary to remove several inches of mane just behind the poll to provide an area for the headstall of the halter or bridle to lay

without becoming tangled in mane hair. It is also a common practice to keep the hair on the horse's lower legs relatively short so snow and mud do not build up on the long hair.

These things are accomplished with the help of electric clippers. Electric clippers are a must if you plan to show, as you will want to freshen your horse's tidy appearance frequently with a clip. If you are an ardent winter rider, you may also wish to clip all or part of your horse's winter coat. This will allow you to work your horse in the winter without him sweating profusely. When he does sweat, he will dry out much more quickly and safely with his clipped coat than he would with a heavy winter coat. Of course, if you do clip your horse's body, you will have to provide him with blankets when he is inactive, standing outside in a pen, or inside in a stall.

What type of clippers you will buy depends on what you plan to use them for. In very general terms, there are two types of clippers: heavy duty and light duty. The heavy-duty clippers are suitable for body clipping and leg clipping. They should be designed to be used for extended periods of time—an hour or more, as it takes that long, at least, to body-clip a horse. Such clippers must be able to cool while you are using them. Light-duty clippers are suitable for trimming the muzzle and throat, the ears, bridle path, and perhaps a touch-up on the legs. If you use light-duty clippers for removing the heavy winter leg hair, not only will the blades become dull, but the motor may overheat and burn out as well. Be sure you choose the appropriate clipper for the job.

Clean and oil your clippers after each use and before you store them.

Care of Electric Clippers. Store clippers unplugged in a clean, dry place with the cord bundled up so as not to create a safety hazard. The cord should be inspected periodically, for wear. If there is a thin or exposed spot, cover it with electrician's tape or have the cord repaired or replaced; otherwise you or your horse could be shocked during clipping.

The clippers can be stored in a box or a holster but should never be rattling around unprotected in a trunk with other items. They could damage leather or cloth items with their sharp blades or oily surfaces. Other items in the trunk, such as metal tools or bits, could dull or damage the blades of the clippers.

Every time you use your clippers, you should thoroughly clean them before putting them away. Leaving hair, sweat, and scurf on the blades can result in rusted blades, which will not clip well. After each use and periodically during use, you can dip the tips of the clipper blades (while running) in a shallow container of a commercial blade wash or kerosene. This will cut any gummy residue that has built up on the clipper teeth. While still holding the clippers with blades down, shake the excess cleaner off the blades before resuming use.

If you notice the sound of the motor begins to change while you are using your clippers, it may be that the blades need to be lubricated. Refer to your owner's manual. Some models require oiling. Others recommend a spray lubricant be used directly on the blades. The lubricant cools the blades and removes small particles, thereby reducing

Continued ➔

friction. Be sure the air intake vent on the side of your clippers is unobstructed. Some models have a screen across the air intake opening. Keep this screen free of hair. If clogged, the clippers will overheat.

The cleaner you keep your clipper blades, the longer they will last. The cleaner the horse is that you are clipping, the longer the blades will last. When the blades no longer clip well, refer to your owner's manual to see if there are adjustments you can make to the tension of the blades that may allow the blades to clip a while longer. If you have exhausted your options, it is time to have the blades sharpened. A set of blades can be sharpened many times. It is a good idea to have several sets of various kinds of blades on hand so while one set is away being sharpened, you have another on hand.

Your dollar investment in tack and equipment can easily equal or exceed the value of your horse. Tack that is kept dry, clean, and in good working order is ready when you need it, more comfortable for the horse and rider, lasts longer, is safer during regular work and especially during stress, and has a first-rate appearance. From the standpoint of economics and safety, taking care of your tack just makes sense.

Building or Renovating a Small Barn for Your Horse

Jackie Clay

Illustrations by Alison Kolesar, Elayne Sears, and Jim Dykeman

Introduction

When it comes to providing adequate shelter for domestic animals, horses are among the easiest you'll deal with. Contrary to what you might think, horses are sturdy, adaptable creatures, and their housing requirements are very basic: shade, ventilation, protection from the elements, and comfortable, dry footing. Now, this may sound simple, and it can be, but remember that horses are also large, strong, active, and playful.

Building a horse barn is quite a project—and there is a vast and varied array of plans and books available to help you. But renovating a shelter to make it fit for just one or two horses, or building a sturdy three-sided shelter, can be quite simple, even if you have only basic carpentry skills. And that's what I'll talk about here.

The Fundamentals of Building for Horses

The fundamentals of proper construction for horse housing are:

- **Stay on high ground.** Make sure that the shelter is located on a slight rise or hill, which will ensure adequate drainage away from the structure. Horses need dry footing; otherwise, such foot diseases as thrush and grease heel will result. You wouldn't want to stand in constant mud during a rainy spell, right? Well, neither does your horse.

- **Overbuild rather than underbuild.** A lot of horses are injured kicking through light plywood or sheet-metal walls while playing, knocking 2 x 4s loose, tearing their hides on exposed nails, and—believe it or not—pushing apart walls while scratching their tails. Unlike the case of a garden shed or even a garage, 2 x 4s aren't adequate for horse housing. You'll need to use 4 x 4s or 2 x 6s or greater. I've found that using rough-cut sawmill lumber adds a greater dimension of strength and safety—and costs a lot less.

- **Build a sturdy understructure.** The timber-frame and pole-barn types of construction are the sturdiest, and thus the best choices for horse barns. If the structure you're renovating uses conventional framing with 2 x 4 posts, you'll need to add extra structural support to make the building strong enough to survive years of use by playful, rambunctious horses.

- **Use heavy-duty hardware—hinges, latches, and so on.** Even if you're working with a tight budget, this is no place to scrimp. It's better to employ a set of used, auction-bought hinges than a cheap new store-bought set! Always think heavy, strong, and safe when you're planning, buying material, and building. It's much cheaper to build a safe, long-lasting building or stall than it is to construct a low-priced structure that requires constant repair and remodeling due to horse damage. And it won't take 10 minutes longer to build!

Tips and Techniques for Remodeling

Often the best and most obvious choice for horse housing is simply to modify an existing structure. Unused older cow barns, chicken coops, wooden sheds, and garages can often easily and economically be remodeled to suit a horse. And you don't have to be a professional contractor to build good, solid housing for your horse. Remember, horses can live well in structures as simple as lean-tos and three-sided run-in sheds.

Old one-car garage

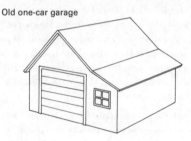

New one-horse barn

Almost any small structure that's still in good condition can be transformed into a shelter for your horse.

WHAT'S A RUN-IN SHED?

A run-in shed is a three-sided shelter that allows horses to come and go as they please, taking advantage of the shed's shade in the heat of the day and the sun's warmth during cold winters. The three sides offer shelter from the wind, no matter which direction it's blowing from; the sloping roof protects against rain, sleet, and snow.

A three-sided run-in shelter

CONSIDERATIONS FOR REUSE

If you're considering modifying an existing structure, here are a few things to keep in mind:

- **Is the structure in the right place?** Is the building set on an elevation so that water will drain away from it? Is it near or in the pasture you intend to use? Does it open to the south? I like a barn to run east–west, facing north, with paddock or pasture access on its southern side. This gives the horses additional protection from sharp, cruel north winds as well as a sunny spot to relax in the afternoon.

- **Is there enough headroom for the horse?** A building with less than 7 feet (2.1 m) of headroom is not a good choice for horse housing. (When calculating headroom, measure the distance from floor to the rafters or support beams that tie the walls together.) Most horses will at some time or another get playful and throw up their heads. You wouldn't want an animal to get injured by hitting rafters or beams.

- **Is the structure strong enough?** Usually an old cow barn is well built, with strong, durable timbers and heavy construction. But the smaller buildings you might be considering, such as chicken coops and small sheds, are often built with 2 x 4s, which aren't strong enough to house a horse without extra beefing up.

- **Is the structure big enough?** You should provide an ample stall—about 10' x 12' (3 m x 3.7 m)—for your horse. Anything larger allows for more exercise inside but takes longer to clean and bed—besides being more costly to keep in bedding. If two horses share the same paddock or pasture, remember that horses "buddy." Often both will occupy a single stall, even when you provide two separate ones, so the stall should be large enough to accommodate a pair (about 10' x 14', or 3 x 4.3 m). Housing for ponies can, of course, be proportionately smaller.

- **Is the structure safe?** Don't, for example, use a corner of a tractor shed or garage for horse housing. Many more fires occur in structures used for equipment and vehicles than occur in livestock shelters. Gasoline and other combustible materials are never a safe mix with horses. I've seen garages burn from a ruptured fuel line dripping gas onto a hot manifold, a backfiring carburetor, and a welder sending sparks into flammable material. For the safety of your animals and your own peace of mind, you don't want to house your horses where you'll have that sort of activity occurring.

- **Is the framework for the roof in good condition?** If your structure's roofing needs replacing, it's simple enough to secure new sheets of corrugated metal. However, if the boards forming the frame that holds up the roof of your structure aren't strong and secure, you'll need to replace them—a potentially expensive proposition.

- **Does the existing structure have a cement floor?** Cement is very hard on a horse's feet and joints, not to mention uncomfortable to lie on. If you choose to use a cement-floored structure, you need to bed your animal with at least 6 inches (15 cm) of sand or sawdust, topped with removable bedding like straw or shavings.

FOUR RULES FOR RENOVATING HORSE SHELTERS

Remodeling considerations depend on the type of care you want to give your horse. The easiest and often the happiest solution is to transform the structure into a stall that's available to your animal at all times. Such a run-in shed allows the horse to be either at pasture, in a paddock, or safely in his stall when a sudden storm comes up or flies become bad. He isn't dependent on you to bring him inside or let him out for exercise or pasturing.

Whether you're renovating an existing structure into a run-in or an enclosed shed, however, follow these basic rules:

1. **Reinforce the frame.** Unless you're working with sturdy pole-building or timber-frame construction that's still in good shape, you'll need to reinforce the corner posts that frame the structure. Use a posthole digger to dig a hole 3 1/2 feet (1 m) deep on the inside corners. If the floor is concrete, you'll first have to knock out a chunk where each inside corner will be, using a sledgehammer (and, of course, wearing eye protection). Into this hole, secure a 6 x 6 post that runs from the ground to a cross beam or rafter. Bolt the post to the existing corner post and use a fresh batch of cement to set it in place. This post will be very strong, firmly anchoring the inside wall of the structure. In a similar manner, set an anchor pole in each corner of the structure and on each side of the door, if there is one. For additional strength, set more reinforcement poles as necessary so that no pole is more than 12 feet (3.7 m) from another.

In addition, if the existing structure was built with 2 x 4 studs and sill plates, you'll need to double up, or add reinforcing members to each stud and section of sill plate. I've even done this using rough-sawed (hewn with a chain saw) logs from our woods, flattened on two or more sides. Nail or screw (using a power screwdriver) each reinforcement member into its matching 2 x 4 stud.

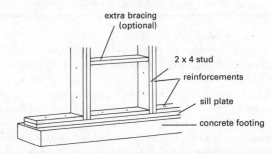

Most outbuildings are constructed with 2 x 4 bracing set on a sill plate, which is set on concrete footing. To make this framework strong enough to shelter a horse, nail reinforcing studs to each 2 x 4 and to the sill plate. You can even add bracing between the 2 x 4s in high-traffic areas.

2. **Reinforce the walls.** If a run-in shed or any of the areas in an enclosed shed with which a horse might come in contact doesn't already have sturdy, 2-inch-thick (5 cm) walls with sturdy planking on the inside of the stall, you'll need to redo the planking (see below). If you want to use plywood or steel sheeting as your siding material, do so on the outside where it won't be exposed to the horse, his activity, and his playfulness.

3. **Examine the roof.** If the roof is not secure and watertight, you'll need to repair or replace it. In addition, examine the framework that supports the roof. If you're working on an older building, this support

Continued ➔

structure may have fallen into disrepair and be in need of reinforcement or replacement.

4. Provide for adequate light and ventilation. If you're working on an enclosed shed, be sure there's at least a small window in the stall for light and ventilation, as well as extra sky panels and windows to allow light to enter the building. This is especially important if you don't have electricity to power artificial lighting in the barn. In the stall, it's best to have a high window about 12 to 18 inches (30–45 cm) tall and 2 feet (24 inches) wide that you can slide open as desired.

PLANKING A RUN-IN SHED

Once you've framed a run-in shed with reinforcing posts, you can start the planking. The minimum thickness of the walls should be 2 inches (5 cm). Again, using rough sawmill lumber gives extra thickness, because it isn't planed. These planks should be spiked using at least 20-penny spikes. (I like to predrill the holes in the planks with a drill bit that's smaller in diameter than the spike to avoid splitting and the resulting weakness.) And as with any livestock building, the planks should be nailed on the *inside* of the structure. Yes, planks on the outside look nicer—but they aren't nearly as strong. A horse can actually kick them off the posts, nails and all! But when he kicks a plank that's nailed in-side, it just goes "bang" and remains in place.

QUICK TIP

Use pressure-treated planks for the bottom two rows of planking, which will save you a considerable amount of money and energy on later replacement of rotted planks. However, I don't recommend using treated planks for the rest of the stall walls. They contain toxic chemicals, and I don't feel they're safe to use where horses may be in constant contact with them, or possibly lick them.

Where economy is of prime importance, consider using 6-inch-diameter (15 cm) logs harvested from your woods or purchased inexpensively from the U.S. Forest Service or a local supplier of firewood. Flatten these logs on both the top and bottom to use as wall partitions in the stall. Another alternative is using thick slabs from a sawmill. (Slabs are the rounded, log-siding-like pieces that are cut off a log before it is sawed into lumber. Depending on the mill and the use the lumber will be put to, these slabs can be quite thick and even, making for a great inexpensive building material.) Both of these choices can result in a very attractive horse stall.

You need to plank the walls of your stall or run-in shelter up at least 4 feet (1.2 m) high inside a building or stall—I like to plank the walls even higher if I'm housing a stallion, a young horse, or a very active animal, because the kicking may well be higher. (See also below for information on building and planking a stall in an enclosed shelter.)

Step 1. Begin planking at the bottom, very close to the floor. If you begin at the top, there's often a large crack left at the floor level, and a horse can get a hoof through a surprisingly narrow opening when rolling and become severely injured. Use a level before nailing or screwing each plank, and adjust each plank slightly to compensate for any irregularities.

In very hot climates, you may want to leave an opening between planks for additional ventilation. Don't let the gap exceed 1 inch (2.5 cm), though, or your horse may begin to chew on the planks. And again, a horse (especially a foal or small pony) can kick his hoof through a very small opening.

Step 2. Plank up at least 4 feet (1.2 m). If you're planking one stall that adjoins another, it's wise to plank all the way up to the ceiling to prevent even friendly horses from biting and kicking at each other in play. This avoids many injuries, and it makes the stall partition last years longer.

Step 3. Build up the sides and back from the top of the planking to the roofline using more 2 x 6 planks, 1-inch (2.5 cm) board-and-batten construction, siding, or sturdy plywood.

Building a Simple Run-In Shelter

Where only one or two friendly horses need to be housed and you don't have an existing structure that lends itself to proper renovation, often the best way to go is to build a simple run-in shed from scratch.

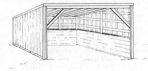

This three-sided shelter is set on a site that drains well. It's planked to 4 feet (1.2 m) on the interior and finished with metal sheeting on the exterior, supported by interior 2 x 6 braces.

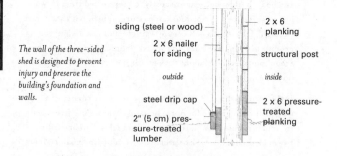

The wall of the three-sided shed is designed to prevent injury and preserve the building's foundation and walls.

siding (steel or wood)

2 x 6 nailer for siding

outside

steel drip cap

2" (5 cm) pressure-treated lumber

2 x 6 planking

structural post

inside

2 x 6 pressure-treated planking

This three-sided shelter typifies pole-building construction. It uses planking on all sides, with pressure-treated planking at the base and a corrugated metal roof.

This type of shelter has an added advantage of not requiring daily bedding and cleaning the way a stall does. This is not to say that the run-in shed should be dirty or wet; still, its very airiness—especially if it's located on a slight hill for good natural drainage—precludes wetness. If you can muck out the shed fairly well once a week and thoroughly clean it twice a year, it will usually remain quite clean.

FIGURING DIMENSIONS

A shed for one or two horses can be quite small—about 12' x 15' to 20' (3.7 x 4.6 to 6.1 m) is adequate. This size allows an animal to move about to escape blowing rain or snow, but it's still small enough to be economical for you and easy to clean. It's best if the shed can be freestanding in the pasture; this allows the horse to take full advantage of its protection no matter where the sun or wind is coming from.

The back wall—often the lowest wall—should be at least 7 feet (2.1 m) high to avoid head injuries to the horse. Depending on the climate and expected snow load, the roof can slope somewhat or be steep enough to allow heavy rain to run off instantly and heavy snow to slide off before damage is done. The front of the shed is generally about 10 feet (3 m) high, which also allows you to clean it (at least in part) with a tractor and a manure bucket or a smaller skid loader.

CHOOSING THE RIGHT MATERIALS

While many run-in sheds are constructed solely out of sheet metal, this is not the best or safest choice for horses. I've seen many, many injuries result from horses kicking through the lightweight metal, kicking a foot under the sheet metal, or ripping open a body part on a torn, projecting piece of metal. Back the sheet metal with rough-sawed 1-inch (2.5 cm) lumber, which is thicker—that is, stronger—than planed lumberyard lumber or 3/4-inch (1.9 cm) plywood. Even so, it's a good idea to line the inside of the shed to 4 feet (1.2 m) up with 2-inch (5 cm) planks for additional safety against kicks.

Give careful consideration to the shed's walls. Besides the common sheet metal, other materials can be used for both economy and horse safety. One of my barns was sided with 4' x 8' (1.2 x 2.4 m) sheets of grooved cedar siding screwed onto 2 x 6 sawmill lumber placed every 2 feet (60 cm) up the barn wall's posts. At 1/2 inch (13 mm) thick, backed by the 2 x 6 planks, I had to repair only one "kick hole" in 12 years—and no damage to the horse!

If you simply must use unbacked sheet metal to side your run-in shed, keep these walls outside the horse paddock or pasture. Locating such a shelter in a corner eliminates two sides that need backing to be strong enough to resist the kicks and bumps a horse is sure to provide. But putting the shelter in the corner of the pasture also eliminates two sheltering sides for the horse should the wind blow from an unusual direction or snow be severe. At any rate, the inside of the shelter must be planked; otherwise, your horse will be at great risk for a serious injury.

FRAMING UP

The frame for the run-in shed is simple. Set used telephone or electric poles 3 feet (90 cm) into the ground, and preferably also into a concrete base, no more than 12 feet (3.7 m) apart. Onto this base, spike or bolt 2 x 6 or greater framework for the walls and roof support. Set 2 x 6 roofing rafters no farther apart than 24 inches (60 cm). You can economize by using 6-inch (15 cm) logs, flattened on two sides, for rafters. Even when using sheet-metal roofing, it's best to use at least 1-inch (2.5 cm) rough-sawed lumber—spaced 2 inches (5 cm) apart if you have to economize—for the rafters. This strengthens the building against strong winds and also keeps the roof on a lot longer.

> **QUICK TIP**
> When using sheet-metal roofing, use screws with gaskets made for this purpose, because they hold much better than nails and prevent leaks.

THE ROOF

You can use asphalt shingles or even rolled roofing, but I really recommend sheet-metal roofing. It lasts longer and, more important, it's fire resistant. (Forest and grass fires can occur almost anywhere; their flying firebrands destroy many buildings after setting fire to a shingled roof.) The roof should extend at least 2 feet (60 cm) beyond the back of the building and 3 feet (90 cm) in front, for added protection from the elements and moisture for both the horse and the building itself.

MAKING PROVISIONS FOR FOOD AND WATER

While some folks feed and water inside their run-in shelters, I prefer to do so outside at some distance from the shed. First of all, nearly every water tank or self-waterer will at some time overflow, causing wet ground. Some horses even like to play in the water, splashing it about or letting it overflow by holding the valve open with their nose . . . just for fun. You don't want this wet inside the shelter. (Also, it's hard to keep the horse from depositing manure in an indoor waterer or tank.)

Feed presents different problems, especially if two horse "buddies" share the same shelter. Even between buddies, fighting at feeding time is common, and you don't want this happening inside the shed. It causes damage to a building and possible injury to a horse. Roughhousing outside, though, is usually of no consequence.

Another reason to locate the feed trough or box outside is for your own safety. All horses are impatient at feeding time, prone to shoving, biting, or kicking in annoyance at not getting their feed *right now*. If you're carrying a bucket of feed and hay bales through the pasture and into the limited, enclosed space of a run-in shed, you have the risk of injury. This is greatly multiplied by every other horse in the pasture sharing the shed at feeding time, no matter how gentle or kind he may be. It is much better to be able to feed the horse(s) from outside the shed and pasture. Locating feed boxes just over the fence provides ideal safety and time efficiency.

Designing the Layout for a Small Barn Renovation

There are many types and styles of economical small horse barns, but all of the good ones have a few things in common:

- They are safe for a horse to live in.

- They are built to last many, many years.

- They are safe and easy to work in.

Sounds simple, doesn't it? And it can be, even if you're planning on renovating an existing structure to make it fit to be called a horse barn. However, it's important to take a good, critical look at the structure and its location before becoming too deeply involved in the project. If it's an older building, you may even want to have a professional contractor examine the integrity of its frame and foundation.

STALL DIMENSIONS

Although horses can certainly be housed in tie stalls (a narrow stall in which the horse is kept tied)—and have been since biblical times—the modern horse often gets less-than-optimum daily exercise. Thus, it's best to house him in a roomy box stall where he can lie down comfortably, walk around at will, and even play a bit when the mood strikes him. Plan for a 10' x 12' (3 x 3.7 m) stall, which is commonly accepted by a single horse and can accommodate a mare and foal as well. A minimum of 7 feet (2.1 m) is required for headroom; 8 feet (2.4 m) is even better. Any less is asking for head and neck injuries.

Continued →

SAMPLE DESIGNS FOR A SMALL BARN RENOVATION

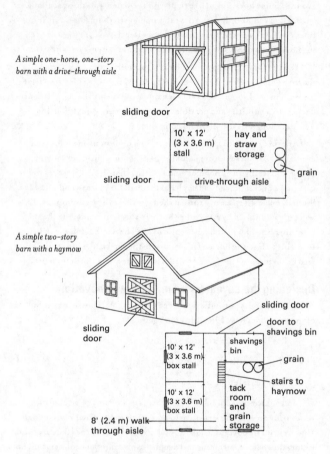

A simple one-horse, one-story barn with a drive-through aisle

sliding door

10' x 12' (3 x 3.6 m) stall	hay and straw storage
drive-through aisle	

sliding door

grain

A simple two-story barn with a haymow

sliding door

sliding door

door to shavings bin

10' x 12' (3 x 3.6 m) box stall	shavings bin
10' x 12' (3 x 3.6 m) box stall	tack room and grain storage

grain

stairs to haymow

8' (2.4 m) walk through aisle

THE FRAME AND WALLS

Like a renovated run-in shelter, the frame of an existing structure being remodeled for use as a small horse barn needs to be reinforced with posts set in concrete and joined to the existing members. Interior walls that will become part of the horse's stall or that the horse might come in contact with need to be renovated accordingly. Exterior walls that the horse will *not* come in contact with simply need to be sturdy and in good shape.

Insulation in a small horse barn is nice but not necessary. Horses do fine in an uninsulated barn, no matter how cold the interior gets, provided they are well bedded, dry, and not in drafts. In fact, more horses are made sick by barns that are too warm than too cold. For this reason, a horse barn should not be heated.

Benefits and Drawbacks of Insulation

Benefits

· The barn will be warmer in the winter and cooler during the summer.

· The barn will be less drafty.

· Water won't drip as frost melts or as cooling and warming temperatures cause heavy condensation.

Drawbacks

· The cost is greater, as is the labor involved in construction.

· Insulation must always be protected from horses, because they will sometimes eat it, then become sick, even to the point of death.

· The barn sometimes becomes too "close," requiring extra ventilation to prevent respiratory problems.

· Insulation provides nesting for rodents.

AISLES AND WALKWAYS

If you're working on a relatively large structure, consider adding a wide inside aisle to your plans. Such an aisle is very handy, especially during winter and wet months. Eight feet (2.4 m) in width is adequate, but 10 feet (3 m) is better and will allow a small tractor and manure spreader to be driven through the barn for quick, easy daily cleaning—a sliding door at each end of the aisle makes for simple drive-through access. An aisle also allows for easy delivery of heavy materials, such as fill dirt for stalls, feed, and bedding. The indoor aisle is also a good place to locate a cross tie where a horse can be groomed and sprayed for flies, have his feet cleaned and trimmed, and have minor veterinary procedures performed.

DOORS

Doors should be a minimum of 3 feet (90 cm) wide and should either slide fully open or be able to be swung easily open on very strong hinges. All stall doors should swing into the aisle, because any bedding shoved up to the door will restrict the opening if the door opens into the stall. Then, if the horse is impatiently waiting to go outside, he may rush into the half-open door and become trapped in the narrow space. The more he fights to free himself, the more severely he can be injured.

FLOORING

As for flooring, my opinion is that the less cement in a horse barn, the better. Concrete is especially slippery to shod horses and causes many falls. It is also, of course, very hard and unyielding, causing injuries to feet and joints. And it's cold, especially when used in the stalls where a horse would like to lie down comfortably to rest. Yes, cement is easy to keep clean, hose down, and so on, but I strongly feel that its minuses far outweigh its pluses. The nicest barn I've ever worked in had used-brick aisles and stall floors made of dry, hard-packed clay. The brick made a less slippery hard surface that was still easy to sweep and hose down—besides looking great. Sometimes used brick is available by the truckload for free or very cheaply at demolition sites. It pays to ask around! Can't afford or can't find used brick? Plain hard-packed dirt, especially if it contains some clay, is fine. You won't be able to hose it down, but you can rake and sweep it clean.

WINDOWS

Every stall should have a decent-sized window—placed high up. This lets the horse look out but doesn't allow him to lean into the protected screen or kick it in play. A window at least 18" x 24" (45 x 60 cm) is good. It should be able to be slid open for ventilation, be screened against biting insects, and be covered with hardware cloth to protect the screen from the horse's inquisitive nose. I prefer using acrylic plastic instead of glass for horse windows, just in case there's breakage. Plastic doesn't shatter, so it's much safer.

WATER

Before you begin any renovations, consider running a water line. Having water in a barn is a great labor saver and will result in the horses having more access to fresh water: Obviously, it's easier and quicker to water the animals where water is readily accessible. Where freezing is a problem, an underground (below the frost line) water line, using economical flexible black poly, can be run from the well or the nearest water source. If you attach this to a frost-free hydrant, which drains completely after use, even a barn that doesn't remain above freezing during the winter can have plenty of water handy. (Take special care to locate the hydrant in a very protected spot so that it can't be damaged by equipment or horses. One of the worst horse accidents I've ever seen happened when a playful horse caught his halter on a frost-free hydrant and tore his head and throat terribly, exposing 6 inches of the jugular vein. Luckily, with immediate veterinary treatment he recovered fully.)

Having water in the barn provides a bonus: fire-fighting ability that just may save your horses and barn in the event of a fire. Always keep at least a 60-foot (18 m) length of hose coiled on the wall, dry and unfrozen. The hose that I designate the "fire hose" isn't used during the winter, just to be sure it doesn't become clogged with ice. My "horse-watering hose" is separate.

HAY, BEDDING, AND FEED STORAGE

While planning the layout of your barn, you need to consider just where your hay/straw, bedding, and grain will be stored. While in some drier climates it's possible to store hay bales outdoors, this practice is wasteful. Not only will some moisture find its way into and between the bales, causing probable mold and spoilage, but even minute condensation can create dusty, moldy hay as well. This mold and dust can cause many health problems in horses, frequently colic and heaves, an asthmalike condition. And no, covering the hay with plastic tarps won't protect it from condensation, even though rain and snow may not penetrate. Fresh hay gives off some heat and moisture, and when it's tightly covered and standing out in the sun, plastic tarps cause it to sweat. This moisture appears all through the hay and will soon produce that dusty, moldy, musty smell.

Having a two-story barn is the ideal situation, but if the structure you're working with doesn't lend itself to this, simply add another box stall specifically for hay and straw, shavings, and grain is as easy solution. If you need more space than this, you can add a "back porch" or shed room off its side, which can double your storage capability quite inexpensively. A simple addition can be made by extending the sloping roof down to a convenient height—6 feet (1.8 m) or so—and walling in from there.

Benefits and Drawbacks of Using a Hayloft

Benefits	Drawbacks
• Lofts make it easy to store and retrieve hay bales.	• Two-story construction is more costly, in both money and labor.
• No horse can get loose and have access to the hay, which causes much destruction.	• To support the weight of the hay bales, strong bracing must be provided underneath, with at least 2 x 8 floor joists or log joists required.
• The barn will be warmer during the winter and cooler in summer due to the insulating properties of the bales.	• The loft must be floored. This can be done with rough-sawed 1-inch (2.5 cm) lumber, but it does cost more and takes a few days longer to construct.
• You'll need less ground area than if you included storage on a single floor.	

The feed room is one place I heartily *approve* of concrete in the horse barn. Not only does the cement keep the bottom tier of hay or straw dry, dirt-free, and mold-free, but it also prevents our little rodent friends from gaining easy access to a free lunch. However, for an added measure of protection, do make sure that the floor has a gentle slope to it, and that it slopes toward a drain.

Do yourself a great favor: Close in the front of the feed storage room and add a sturdy 4-foot (1.2 m) access door. This will almost positively ensure that a loose horse can't get into the feed and gorge himself. A tight-fitting lid on each feed drum will help, but a door is nearly foolproof. A horse can usually get away with eating all the hay he wants, but grain is another story. Pigging out on grain will often cause colic, severe digestive upsets, and founder.

Some feed areas are *too* tight. This causes the hay to sweat, much as if it were under a plastic tarp. Add extra ventilation like a roof ventilator or a small outside window and a window opening into the barn aisle (well screened, of course).

STORING FEED AND BEDDING

Stack straw separately from hay, while providing convenient access to both. If you use wood shavings as bedding, make sure you keep them separate from the hay, which, if ingested, would result in coughing horses. It's best to build a simple plywood bin to store the shavings; a light tarp cover for the bin is an additional help. Locating this bin with an outside access door is a help. That way you can back your truck or trailer up to the open door and simply shovel in the shavings. Any labor saver is great, in my book!

Grain can be stored either in a separate enclosed wooden bin, built on the cement, or in clean, nontoxic 55-gallon (208 l) covered plastic or steel drums. Be sure you know what was in them before you got them. Drums that contained detergents, cooking oil, or other such benign substances are fine. But beware of fuel, chemical, or fertilizer drums. No matter how well you clean them out, your horse can still be exposed to toxic fumes or material. You don't want a "glow-in-the-dark" mount!

A TACK AND TOOL AREA

A single-horse barn can get along quite well without a separate tack and tool area if you use an out-of-the-way corner or even a separate shed to house such items as saddles, bridles, blankets, pitchforks, shovels, and

Continued →

wheelbarrows. But when there are two or three horses in the family, it's best, if at all possible, to include a small tack room in your barn plans.

This room can be small, depending on the amount of tack and tools that will need housing. I've seen a tack room of only 6' x 10' (1.8 x 3 m) function very well, with stacked saddle racks; bridles neatly hung on the wall; a box for winter blankets, summer sheets, leg wraps, and the like; a small cabinet for veterinary and grooming supplies; and tools hung well out of stumbling reach.

Like the feed room, the best tack room is an enclosed, solid-floored room with a sturdy door to keep out rodents, dogs that might chew leather, and dust—not to mention the infamous loose horse. And I've had them in my tack rooms even with a door!

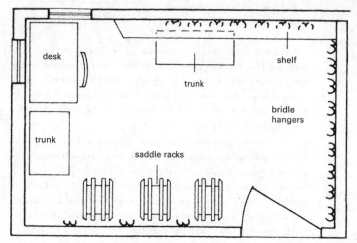

A simple, functional tack room makes good use of shelves, racks, and hangers to keep gear off the floor and out of the way,.

I like to insulate the tack room then, finish it with inexpensive paneling, since it is a place of frequent work and the insulation keeps it cooler in the summer, warmer in the winter. A properly installed small heater, used only when work is in progress, provides safe comfort for the worker.

Any horse supply catalog or tack shop can be the source of ideas for saddle racks, bridle hooks, tool hangers, and other handy items for the tack room. Now, I don't necessarily say "buy." I'm a real do-it-yourselfer; I've gathered many ideas in catalogs or shops that I then rework at home from readily available materials. Not only does this save a lot of money, but it provides an outlet for artistic talents as well, making the tack room truly one of a kind.

FENCING AROUND THE BARN

Finally, always build extra-strong, extra-safe fences near the barn, because there is concentrated activity in that area. Plank, rail, pipe, or some other material that will safely withstand shoving, lunging, and kicking is necessary. During the design stage, plan how your fences will relate to the barn. Some folks prefer to have a wide lane running from the barn door out to a pasture, or separate paddocks. The less contact horses have with the outside walls of their barn, the better. Sooner or later they will do some damage to the siding, whether it be dings and scrapes, chewing, or kick holes.

FIRE EXTINGUISHERS: AN ABSOLUTE NECESSITY

A *must* for the horse barn is a fire extinguisher, kept right beside the door. In fact, one placed next to *every* door is even better. You never know when a fire might start—from electrical failure, wiring damage, lightning, careless smokers, and much more—and it seems as if they always start at night. Having extinguishers handy at the door provides instant help and prevents the panic of having to fight through flames to reach them.

Likewise, at least two fire/smoke alarms are necessary in every barn. Locate them some distance from each other, one near the tack/feed room area, the other at the opposite end of the building. If one fails, the other may save your horses.

Roofing Your Horse Barn

Several roofing materials are available, but the best system I've seen used is plywood covered with corrugated sheet metal. The sheet metal is long lasting, resists hail and wind damage when properly screwed down, seldom leaks, and—its greatest advantage—protects against grass and forest fires. Many barns and other structures are lost to fires started by burning firebrands carried in the wind, and this alone is reason enough to use sheet metal on your barn roof.

But used alone, and on an enclosed barn, sheet metal can cause condensation problems such as frosting up on cold nights. This frost forms on the underside of the roof, to later thaw and drip down on the horses. In most cases you can prevent this by using 3/4-inch (1.9 cm) plywood underneath the sheet metal. This generally prevents heavy condensation problems, plus it will greatly strengthen the roof against wind and heavy snow loads.

In northern areas, where heavy snows are common, be sure your roof slopes steeply enough to quickly shed falling snow. A snow-covered roof may be picturesque, but that pretty white stuff weighs tons—literally—and can weaken or even cave in a barn roof if it stays up there long enough.

Building a Stall

Individual stalls themselves are constructed after the barn is "dried in"—when the shell is built.

Step 1: Reinforce the frame. Set sturdy, 6- to 8-inch-diameter (15–20 cm) poles or squared timbers 3 feet (90 cm) into the ground in a concrete base at each of the inside stall corners. Make sure that these poles are strong and secure, because they form the framework for the stall. (And if you're building a large stall, add additional poles as necessary so that no pole is more than 12 feet, or 3.7 m, from another.)

Step 2: Plank up the walls. Once the corner poles have been set, you're ready to plank the stall. Nail or screw 2 x 6 (or greater) planking to the corner posts to form the walls and front of each stall, up to a height of at least 4 feet (1.2 m). Remember to secure the planks on the inside, or "horse side," of the stall. This provides greater strength and safety than if the planking is fastened to the outside of the poles.

Step 3: Cover the back. Cover the top portion of the back wall with 3/4-inch (1.9 cm) plywood, well supported by underlaying 2 x 6s every 2 feet (60 cm) for strength.

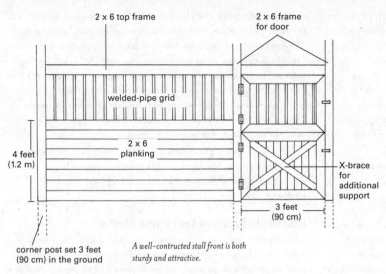

4 feet (1.2 m)

2 x 6 top frame

2 x 6 frame for door

welded-pipe grid

2 x 6 planking

X-brace for additional support

3 feet (90 cm)

corner post set 3 feet (90 cm) in the ground

A well-contructed stall front is both sturdy and attractive.

Step 4: Cover the side walls. What you use to cover the upper portion of the side walls of the stall depends on where they fall in the layout of the barn and your own preferences. The top portion of the side walls can be covered with plywood, like the back wall, or you can use a wire mesh or a welded-pipe grate, like the front wall.

Step 5: Cover the front wall. The top portions of the front wall, including the door, can be covered by a heavy-gauge wire mesh or, better yet, a welded-pipe grate. Construct the pipe grate out of used 3/4- or 1-inch (1.9 to 2.5 cm) galvanized steel pipe, welded onto a 2-inch (5 cm) channel iron the full length of the area to be covered. The pipes should be no farther apart than 4 inches (10 cm)—closer if the horse to be housed has small feet. I've found it very helpful to have one of the pipes set in a hole at the place you plan to feed, rather than welded. This lets you feed without going into the stall by simply sliding the pipe up through the top hole and dumping the feed into the box or pail. Aside from being a great labor saver, it's also safer for you, since accidents sometimes happen at feeding time when an impatient horse rushes to eat.

MAKING DO WITH STOCK PANELS

Many people use livestock panels for the top of their stall fronts. These are inexpensive, very strong, and easily purchased through any farm supply store. They come in 16-foot (4.9 m) lengths and are usually just under 48 inches (1.2 m) high. Shorter "hog panels" are also available should your ceiling height be less or if you decide to plank up higher. The mesh in these panels is about 6" x 8" (15 x 20 cm) and is spaced closer near the bottom quarter of the panel. These livestock panels can easily be stapled to the uprights with long livestock fence staples, and they can be cut down to size using bolt cutters.

One caution about using stock panels in this way: A frisky horse can get his foot through the opening in the mesh. A staid old-timer is probably fine in a stall with a stock panel front, but it's best to line this front with 2" x 4" (5 x 10 cm) welded wire for extra safety. The cost is minimal and may prevent unhappy accidents in the future. Chain link is another alternative, as is the 2" x 4" wire used alone. Either can work, but both will have to be replaced at some point, because with time they'll both sag from being rubbed on, lunged against, and kicked.

Step 6: Frame the stall door. The stall door can be framed with 2 x 6 lumber reinforced with a 2" x 4" (5 x 10 cm) X-shaped brace. Tongue-and-groove 2 x 6s or 3/4-inch (1.9 cm) plywood can be used to build the door, again nailed or screwed on the "horse side," where the pressure will be. Again, this door should be a minimum of 3 feet (90 cm) wide.

A Dutch door (which has a top that opens separately from the bottom) is very nice for a gentle horse, allowing him to hang his head over the lower door to watch goings-on down the aisle. But an aggressive or very frisky horse should be housed in a stall with a floor-to-ceiling door with a small grate at the top for ventilation and also to look out. No horse should be locked up like a prisoner in a stall with no view outdoors and into the aisle. (*Note:* If you're using a Dutch door, arrange a way to fasten its top half open flat against the stall grate. Otherwise it can blow shut in the horse's face. Even worse, he will also quickly learn to play with his new "toy," shoving the door top open again and again just to hear it bang!)

Step 7: Bolt the door to the stall. Whichever style of door you choose, use very strong hinges, bolted to the door for extra holding power. Likewise, the latch should very heavy duty—and horseproof! A simple hook and eye is not good enough. Nearly every horse quickly learns to unhook his stall door and go exploring. A multiple-function hook—which requires a latch to be lifted before the hook can be lifted—or a heavy barrel bolt latch works much more satisfactorily.

Providing Food and Water in the Barn

All horse stalls need to be equipped with the means to provide food and water to the animal occupant. Because horses are such large and playful creatures, you can't just plop down a water bowl and a food dish like you can for Rover and Kitty and say, "There you go." Horses take a bit more planning.

WATER BUCKETS AND HOLDERS

Each stall should have provision for water. This is most easily and economically furnished by hanging a wide, indestructible 5-gallon (19 l) water pail—either rubber or heavy poly—in the stall. While you can just suspend the water bucket from a heavyweight snap around an eyebolt through the stall wall, I like using a welded bracket as well. The bracket is simply two rings welded onto two flat 1/4-inch (6 mm) steel uprights, with a bar or two across the bottom to support the bucket. The flat, upright bracket is bolted to the wall at a convenient height by means of two holes in the wall side of

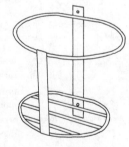

A water-bucket holder

the stall. This bracket can be purchased through most horse supply catalogs or made by a handy do-it-yourselfer with welding skills.

The reason I like the bracket is that it discourages a horse from playing with and dumping a partially full bucket—and they *will* play with the water bucket! The bracket will also help the water pail last longer, because the weight of the water will pull on the bucket constantly, reducing its life.

Continued →

Treated right, rubber pails will last almost indefinitely. I have some that are 20 years old. They look a bit worse for the wear, but they still hold water!

SALT BLOCKS

Each stall should have a salt-block holder so that salt is available to the horse whenever he needs it. A stall block is smaller than a field block—usually about 2 to 4 pounds (0.9–1.8 kg)—and if it's just placed in a tub, the "helpful" horse will soon dump it out onto the floor, where it will quickly disappear.

Instead, fasten a salt-block holder to the wall so you can simply slip in the block of salt from the top. Result: No waste, no mess.

HAY FEEDER

There is quite a debate among horse owners regarding the "right" way to feed horses hay. I feel that the best way is simply to place it on the floor in a clean, dry corner of the stall. This allows the horse to eat in a natural position, and there is absolutely nothing else in the stall for him to get injured on.

But many folks feel that a separate hay feeder on the wall is better. This welded steel bracket with slanted bars on the front allows you to drop in "sandwiches" of hay from the top. Usually a tray sits below to catch the fines, or leaves, preventing waste.

> ### QUICK TIP
> *Never* feed a horse on the floor of a dirty stall. If he is exposed to filth, you may well have a recurring internal parasite problem. If you don't want to use an elevated hay feeder, be sure that the floor of the stall is clean before leaving hay there for your horse to feed on.

A wall-mounted hay feeder is a pretty good setup for most horses. But if a horse is very playful, he can find ways to injure himself on most steel feeders at one time or another. To prevent those sorts of accidents,

A wall-mounted hay feeder

if you choose a steel feeder, be sure to pick one that has rounded, smooth edges, is very solid, and has closely spaced bars. Then locate it by itself on a wall away from the water bucket.

An inexpensive alternative to the hay feeder is a hay net—a poly or nylon net bag that you fill with hay and hang on an eyebolt, just above your horse's head level. This works quite well and is pretty safe (although some creative horses manage to get a foot hung in them). It is awkward to use, however, taking more time to fill than a feeder. In addition, it allows waste of the fines, because they trickle to the ground while the horse eats.

GRAIN FEEDER

It's necessary to supply a separate feeder for grain. This is most handily mounted on the front wall of the stall, where the grain can be poured into it through either a "door" in the pipe stall grate or a "window" cut into a stock panel or wire-mesh grate, framed by welded steel.

A wooden feed box

A grain feeder can be a bucket—held by the same type of bracket as the water pail—or a very sturdy wooden box made out of 2 x 6 lumber. The dimensions of such a box can vary, but it needs to be at least a foot (30 cm) deep or the horse will toss out and waste feed as he eats. For extra strength, instead of nails use screws long enough to get a good bite into the wood. Bolt this box securely on the stall front at or a bit below 4 feet (1.2 m)—depending on the size of the horse. An extra bracing bracket of 2 x 4 lumber or a 4-inch (10 cm) pole cut at an angle will help keep the feeder in place for years.

It's a good idea to put the grain feeder in the opposite front corner from the water pail. Having them side by side, as some folks do, often means having bits of grain in the drinking pail—which quickly ferment.

Finishes to Preserve Your Horse Shelter

After the barn has been constructed, some work still needs to be done. For the barn to last—not to mention remain attractive—it requires an exterior wood finish such as stain, wood preserver, or paint, as well as a nontoxic interior finish both inside and outside the stalls. Of course, if you used sheet-metal siding for the exterior walls, the outdoor finishing will be minimal. But any type of wood construction—whether siding, log, or board and batten—must be effectively protected to withstand the elements and provide you with many years worth of service as a strong, stable shelter for your horse.

THE PROS AND CONS OF PAINT

Paint comes to mind first off, but it's not always a good choice. Paint forms a shell over the wood, and no matter how good the primer and paint are, sooner or later some of the finish will begin to peel and flake. (And if you made the mistake of using a cheap paint or primer—or worse yet, no primer—this peeling will begin all the sooner!)

Never use paint left over from a long-ago job, which you may have discovered in a shed somewhere. Old paint is often lead based, and this is toxic not only to humans but to horses as well—and they are much more likely to ingest some of it.

TIPS FOR USING WOOD STAINS

I feel that stains are a better choice for the finish of horse barns. If you've used very nice wood, such as log construction, you won't want to cover it up with a solid stain that looks like paint. Instead, use a clear stain, which allows grain and texture to show and makes your barn a work of art. If you've used wood siding or 4' x 8' (1.2 x 2.4 m) panels, choose either solid or opaque stain. Solid stain comes in a wide variety of colors and looks like paint on the wall, but the stain *penetrates* the wood, locking into it, so it won't peel or flake off over time. It may fade a bit, requiring another coat in a few years, but it is easily reapplied without scraping and sanding.

Stains are either oil or latex based. Latex stains have the advantage of easy cleanup, but oil-based stains offer better protection to the wood. Stain can be applied to the barn wall with a paint sprayer run by an air compressor, a paintbrush, or a roller. The choice will depend on the type of wood you've used as well as your personal preference.

FINISHES FOR THE INTERIOR

The inside of the barn can receive the same treatment—perhaps in a lighter shade or color than the exterior, since a lighter color reflects more light, making the barn seem less dingy. Be absolutely sure that you use only a nontoxic stain or finish on the interior of the stall; there's always the possibility that a horse may chew or lick it. I've been quite pleased with boiled linseed oil, painted on while still quite hot, as an interior finish for stalls.

If your barn has ceilings, a coat of white solid stain works well and seems to discourage flies a bit. Better yet, give that ceiling two or more coats and you'll be able to scrub off any dirt or fly specks with ease.

Always do any interior painting/staining while the horses are outside, because the fumes can cause respiratory problems. (And of course provide adequate ventilation—open windows and doors and use a fan—for your *own* safety and comfort as you work.)

TIPS FOR ELECTRIFYING THE SMALL HORSE BARN

Electricity is a great help in a barn. But unless you're an accomplished do-it-yourselfer with experience in electrical hookups, leave this job to an electrician. Many fires have been caused in barns because of faulty wiring or improperly installed boxes or light fixtures.

Generally, one light fixture in the aisle placed every 12 feet (3.7 m) along with one in the center of each stall works quite nicely. Add a light in your mow, feed room, and tack area for convenience. And unlike houses, a plug-in outlet every 6 to 8 feet (1.8– 2.4 m) isn't a necessity—but it is very handy to have one outlet on the outside of each stall, in the tack area, and where you have your cross ties and do your grooming.

Of utmost importance, be sure to protect all electric wiring, outlets, and fixtures from inquisitive or rambunctious horses:

- Purchase heavy metal cages to protect lightbulbs from tossing horse heads.

- Protect any exposed wiring with an aluminum conduit. Better still, run the wiring inside a wall or the ceiling.

- Locate any switches or outlets way out of horse reach. If you don't, they will be nibbled and crunched—and the horse may get a bad shock in the process.

- Be absolutely sure that your wiring has been sufficiently grounded to prevent shock and accidents.

- If you ever have to use an extension cord, use a heavy-duty one placed well out of reach of equines, and do away with it as soon as you can. This may prevent an accident or fire.

LIVESTOCK AND MORE

Eggs and Chickens in Least Space on Home-Grown Food

John Vivian

When was the last time you tasted a really fresh egg? One with a high yolk that was a deep, dark yellow, bordering on pink, and a white that stayed together in a plump circle instead of running all over the frying pan? If your answer is, "I guess I never have," you aren't alone. When my wife, Louise, and I first made our move from city to country, I really believed that the lighter colored the yolk, the fresher the egg. It wasn't until our first pullets began laying that I learned the facts, that the yolk color is dependent on the pigments in the feed.

You see, an egg is in many respects a living thing, even if it is not fertile—which is the case with store-bought eggs; a hen will lay her quota of infertile eggs without ever setting eyes on a rooster. And in the time most commercially produced eggs spend in storage or transit, they slowly lose water. You can tell a fresh egg from a stale one easily. Hard-boil it. If the dent in one end where the air pocket was is good-sized, your egg is stale.

We think there's a big difference, too, between poultry raised commercially and raised at home. Here the difference isn't the age of store birds, but the methods and feeds used to raise them.

Commercial eating birds live out their brief spans in totally artificial surroundings. The heat, light, and humidity are all manipulated to generate quick growth. Birds are packed into the broiler factories nearly feather-to-feather.

We believe the difference is quickly apparent, that there's a better flavor and firmer texture to our home-grown chickens.

NUTRITIONAL VALUE AND ECONOMIC SENSE

Now, does it make nutritional and economic sense to raise your own birds for eggs and meat?

Yes, emphatically.

An egg contains everything that goes into a chick that will hatch, ready to walk, peep, feed itself, and do most every chicken thing but fly. It is protein in large part, all usable by the human body. Just a couple of eggs a day will provide an adult with one-quarter to a third of his daily protein needs, with relatively few calories accompanying them.

CHOLESTEROL

Cholesterol is a fat-like substance manufactured by the body, and we can't live without it. Thick deposits of it are found clogging the arteries of some people, so it has been implicated as a factor in arteriosclerosis. And it is found in eggs. This has led many doctors to advise their patients not to eat too many eggs.

The answer should be between you and your doctor. If you are 35 or more, you should have periodic blood tests anyway. If these show you are high in cholesterol, your physician may advise you to cut down on a lot of things, eggs included. Most people who eat normally and exercise regularly will have no problem and presumably can eat as many eggs as they want to. On the other hand, other physicians recommend that any adult should hold his egg consumption to three a week. Growing

Continued ➜

children use the cholesterol in body-building. Louise and I pretty much keep to the three-egg rule, but our two preschoolers gobble down at least one a day. You do as you and your doctor see fit.

There is probably less of a potential health problem from chicken than from any red meat. It is low in calories per unit of protein provided, particularly if you don't eat the skin, and is lowest when broiled.

The fat content can be reduced if you prick the skin to let melted hard fat out while you fry or roast the bird. This puts you lower in calories and saturated type fats than well-marbled beef or any other red meat.

So far as economics go, both eggs and chickens rank high among the animal foods for feed-efficiency. It takes more than twenty pounds of protein to produce one pound of protein in a beef steer, but a chicken can do much better. The protein content of poultry is 25–30 percent. A four-pound live weight broiler will yield about one pound of protein. It takes about eight pounds of a 17 percent protein feed to produce it. That's 1.36 pounds of protein.

It takes about four pounds of an 18 percent diet to produce a dozen large eggs. The eggs are about 13 percent protein, and the dozen consists of about .23 pounds of protein. Thus .72 pounds of food protein produces .23 pounds of egg protein.

Such efficiencies by the chicken in conversion of the protein feed, plus the relative efficiencies of modern poultry management, are why chicken is usually the best meat bargain in the store, and eggs are still cheap.

No home poultry operation can match a commercial factory in capital and labor efficiency and in cheap feed production. Most people, too, agree that a home operation will be a money-loser if it is based on buying all of the chicken feed, though it may be justified purely on grounds of improved quality and food safety. However, if you can produce as much as a quarter of the birds' food needs yourself, you'll probably break even, money-wise. The cooking and table scraps from an average household will provide this for a small laying flock, and from that point on, the more of your birds' diet you raise yourself, the more cash you are ahead. I'll go into the details of this later.

THE LEGALITIES

Before buying any birds or obtaining equipment, be sure you aren't going to be breaking the law. In the old days, nearly every house, in town or country, had a flock of layers out back. But as America grew in population and became urbanized, housing density increased to the point where there were four or five homes where one stood earlier. Too many people too close for the normal smells, crowing, bugs and hen-clucking of a traditional poultry yard to be anything but a nuisance.

Towns grew into cities, expanding out to encompass nearby farms, and soon the farmer's pig lot and barnyard became offensive to the surrounding townsmen. And into law came zoning ordinances, one of the first items in many places being prohibitions against keeping farm livestock within the town or city limits, poultry in particular being singled out as major malefactors.

So, check your municipality's zoning ordinances.

HOUSING AND FURNITURE

The more space you can give your flock, both under cover and out in the open, the better. Nature takes care of any odor problem in a large run, and a deep layer of litter in the house, changed several times a year, does the same for the inside quarters.

EXPENSIVE

Problem is, unless you are a natural carpenter and have a barn full of old lumber you will pay many hundreds of dollars just buying the raw materials, to say nothing of labor costs. Though a well spread out arrangement is highly recommended for both health and attractiveness to the flock, you can make do with considerably less space if you must. At minimum you should provide two square feet of inside floor space and one square foot of above-ground roost per bird. (The roosts can be two or more feet above the floor and the area under them will count as floor space. Make the run as large as you can.)

We've kept as many as twenty-five birds happy with a little five-by-nine house partitioned off one end of the barn and a nine-by-twelve outside run—but not for long. Once they reached broiling weight, all but the half dozen best potential laying hens and a rooster or two went into the freezer. By that time they had figured out the facts of chicken life, and that small space produced more than love spats. It was all-out war as the young roosters battled over the hens, and the hens scrabbled around working up their pecking order.

This is more than a trite phrase, by the way. The birds do have a status system. No. 1 hen can peck everyone but never gets pecked, and so on down the line to the bottom one, which gets pecked by all, but can't peck back.

Toss a strange hen into an established flock and she has to rough it for a bit, as the order must be redefined, with the newcomer usually ending up on the bottom.

One way for the space-short chicken fancier to keep birds is to use cages. Look for the addresses of game and pet bird by-mail sellers in the back of most gardening and outdoor sports magazines. Some of them sell cages and other equipment. Investigate, too, the commercial-type cages with roll-out floors. They are available from agricultural supply houses and feed stores. Many small flock owners use these quite successfully.

Chicken Breeds

The breed you select will depend to some extent on the section of the country you live in. For a reason that is a mystery to me, people in most of the country prefer eggs with white shells, while we New Englanders know full well that the only egg worthy of the name comes in a brown shell. Of course there is not one whit of nutritional difference between the two, and chickens are categorized by far more important criteria than the color of their eggs.

In essence there are three major divisions.

First are the hybrids, developed over the years for maximum egg production. These are most commonly bred from the White Leghorn (pronounced "leegern") breed—a small-bodied temperamental little bird, but a super egg producer. Fed a high protein ration for about six months, then switched to a lower protein, high calcium feed, these little egg machines will produce an egg every day or two for the next year and longer. Still, the commercial factories are lucky if they earn two or three dollars egg money over feed costs per hen—one reason that an egg producer has to have a huge operation to stay in business. The profit on a dozen eggs is computed in pennies—sometimes there is no profit or even a loss, but hopefully he can make five or ten cents per dozen eggs.

The laying breeds don't have much flesh, and male birds (or cockerels) are usually destroyed at hatching. Being hybrids, by and large, the breeding stocks are different for male and female parents, hybrid eggs don't produce good birds, so the hybrid males are of little commercial value. Once their first full year of laying is over the females—pullets as youngsters, graduating to hen status when their first small pullet eggs become full-sized hen fruit—end up being eaten. Many of them are sent to places such as Camden, N.J., where they turn up in chicken and noodle soup and such canned goods.

MEAT-ONLY BREEDS

If you want to raise birds for meat only, you can obtain special broiler crosses, the best known being the produce of a White Cornish male and a White Rock female. Properly called a Rock-Cornish cross hybrid or Rock-X Cornish, these fast-growing birds are stuffed with high-protein feed, slaughtered at about five weeks and sold as one-pound single-serving "Rock-Cornish Game Hens" in fancy restaurants. They're also frozen, inside plastic bags and sold in supermarkets.

Few home-fed producers will be able to come up with a ration that can produce eating birds in that short a time; but they can plan on growing those or any other broiler cross to three-pound fryers in three or four months, and into four-plus pound roasters in another month or so. Fully mature at seven or eight pounds, these birds can replace a turkey on the small family's Thanksgiving table.

BEST FOR SMALL FLOCK

In my view, the best for the small family flock would be any of the multi purpose breeds, hybrid or standard. These are heavy-bodied, large breeds such as the Rhode Island or New Hampshire Reds, Barred or White Rocks and numerous hybrids such as the several kinds of sex-links. Here parents of different breeds and colorations are mated and the offspring come in sex-coordinated colors, males buff and females black, for example. All of these multi purpose breeds produce more eggs than the broiler crosses and more and better meat than the egg layers. However, they don't match up to the special purpose breeds in either category.

We've tried both hybrid and pure-blood, brown-egg laying multi purpose breeds with varying degrees of luck. One white and black-faced hybrid served us well for breakfast eggs and the main course of Sunday dinner for several years. When we decided to try raising chicks from our own eggs we found out that hybrids came out all colors and were not worth much of anything.

Then we kept a series of pure bloods. Rhode Island Reds, with lovely mahogany-red plumage, did well, producing fertile, healthy eggs for a few years until inbreeding produced a club foot deformity in the chicks. Most recently we've run Barred Rocks, with a speckled black and white plumage, to good advantage. The next change will likely be back to a cross that we keep only for one season, then replace. Hatching chicks is fun, but time-consuming.

HOW TO START

Now, my advice to anyone who asks me is to buy day-old chicks—for about $1.30 apiece—from a reputable hatchery, brood them for a month under a warmth-producing infrared light bulb, and raise them in the henhouse from then on. You can buy started pullets, about twenty weeks old, for $8.00 to $13.00 per. However, with the young hens you may be buying all the parasites and diseases the grower has on his farm. One new homesteader we know got a ready-to-lay flock, but before the first egg appeared, all their feathers fell out and they died. There are excellent growers who sell started pullets which will perform and live much better than those raised by the inexperienced grower with inadequate facilities who provides poor management.

My advice again—get young chicks, and not from a friendly neighbor or local farmer. Avoid potential problems and buy them from a hatchery that is U.S. and state-certified to have pullorum-typhoid-clean stock. This automatically avoids the worst poultry diseases.

VACCINATION

You can buy chicks vaccinated against Marek's disease, and the added cost seems worth it even for the small home flock. It is essential for the huge commercial flocks.

With good chicks and a screen over the run to keep out wild birds and their diseases, we've never had any serious problems, and I doubt that you will either.

Chicks are sold in lots of twenty-five at minimum and come as-hatched, or all-male or all-female. Plan to spend $32.00 to $35.00 for twenty-five of most breeds as-hatched, half again as much if you want all pullets in egg-laying breeds or all cockerels in meat-producers.

If you go together with several other neighbors and buy a lot of 100, you can save about $25 over the small-lot size. Find the name of the nearest hatchery from your County Agent, the Extension Service, a

Continued →

Day old chicks in brooder

local feed store or, if you are lucky, in the yellow pages. Several firms sell them by mail, and our first chicks were ordered from the Sears farm catalog. The shipping carton identified the hatchery, one of New England's finest, and we've been dealing directly with them ever since. No reflection on Sears, though.

Brooding and Early Care

Before the chicks arrive, be sure you have all needed equipment ready. For feed, I recommend buying a 100-pound bag of medicated chick starter. This will cost $12 or more, and you will have to get a steel trash can with a tight lid to store it safe from mice or rats. This starter contains all the young birds need to live on, plus a medication against the most serious disease of young chickens, an infection of the gut called coccidiosis. Since the little birds eat very little, a 100-pound bag will last a long time if you keep it free of varmints and in a cool, dry place to avoid mold. We've had one bag last through four batches of chicks.

You can house small lots of birds in a big cardboard box, make miniature feeders and waterers and keep them warm with a 100-watt light bulb around which you fashion a foot-wide cone of aluminum foil. We kept our first chicks in the kitchen in just such an arrangement (and I bet you will, too) until we noticed the dust that even tiny chicks kick up was beginning to settle on everything within range.

The hatchery normally will send the birds by mail. You will receive a note telling when they are to arrive, and the post office will telephone you when they come. Be sure the box, feed, and water are heated up to about 100°F before you bring the chicks home. A fever thermometer placed under the light will help you find the right height for the lamp. If you purchase a commercial brooder such as we use, with a foot-wide bell-shaped infrared lamp holder with a ceramic socket, the directions will tell you how far to have the bulb base from the floor.

Once the chicks are in, they will quickly tell you how well you are regulating their heat. If they cluster together just under the bulb, it's too cold; if they run to the corners

of the box, it's too hot. Ideal is to have them scratching and running all over the box, but napping and feather-ruffling, stretching and such leisure time activities just under the rim of the reflector.

At the end of the first full week, raise the bulb the six or so inches needed to reduce temperature at floor level by five degrees, and do the same for the next three weeks. At the end of a month or up to six weeks in very cold weather, they will be fully fledged, and will be safe from normal spring chill.

If you've used a small carton as a nursery for the first few days, you'll find it is quickly outgrown. We now have a stout wooden box, four feet long, two feet wide and eighteen inches high, with a top of dog-, rat-, and other varmint-proof poultry netting that fits securely over it, especially at the ends. By four to six weeks, the little birds can jump and even flap up a foot or more and are understandably curious about what is happening in the world outside. A loose chick is surprisingly quick and can hide in the most unexpected places. Often your dog or cat will find a chick before you do. Cats will ignore tiny chicks and grown birds, but will chase one- to two-month-old birds out of an instinct that must place the youngsters right in the cat food range.

Henhouse Furniture

Once the chicks are fully feathered—in six weeks to two months—you can put them in the henhouse. First I like to cover the house floor with several inches of leaves. Shavings are also good, being dry, absorbent, and clean. So are pine needles, and other free organic material. The small birds will scrabble around in the covering for a while, and in time the covering will pack down, making a good base for the more permanent litter. The run outside will be sod until the birds get large enough to pick it clean. Then, any time the soil appears muddy, or there is a trace of odor, on goes a six-inch layer of leaves. With a small flock, this treatment is needed on our place only during spring thaw and rains, and the November pre-snow precipitation.

The furniture itself consists of roosts plus feed, water, and supplement containers. Roosts are recommended for laying flocks, not for meat birds. The roosts should be rough boards an inch or two in width, placed about a foot apart. Have at least six inches of roost space for each bird if yours are small, eight inches to a foot for the larger breeds.

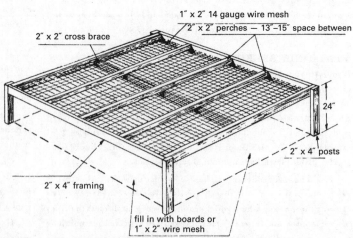

A common roost with perches designed to collect droppings beneath it for several months

The brooder-sized food and water dispensers will serve for a time, but soon you will want to obtain larger scale equipment. Any feed store or the mail order houses referred to earlier sell a wide range of devices. We prefer the domed-type waterer for winter; it can be placed on a heater and the water won't freeze. A five-gallon waterer will keep twenty-five birds happy. Water should be changed daily. The waterer and the heater stand should be placed on a box so the water trough itself is just at the bird's jaw level. That way the birds will kick the least amount of litter into the water.

Feeders

A 30-pound capacity hanging dry feeder will serve for commercial ration or your own home-ground dry feed. For wet table scraps, the type with a pair of chicken head-sized holes running its length is best. Easier to clean, it also prevents the birds from scattering the feed into the litter. And for such home-provided foods as protein-rich meat scraps, I collect those mesh onion bags. They used to be made of string, but now are usually of plastic. A bag filled with meat and fat is suspended by a wire in the middle of the outside run. The birds peck the food out from between the small mesh without getting enough at any one peck that will get lost in the litter. Such meat and fat will decay, smell, and attract all manner of vermin. Of course, any fly eggs that hatch end up as chicken food, but it's best to avoid the problem altogether. It's also best to feed no more than the birds can clean up in one day. We freeze meat scraps, suet, and the like in fist-sized lumps and feed one every couple of days. The onion bags get pretty well pecked apart in time, and greasy to boot, so are discarded after serving well in this recycled capacity.

Summer Feeding

For summer feeding, we find that feed and water containers that can be pen-mounted (on the mesh of the run) are easiest to service. Filling is done from outside the pen, and the only time you need enter the henhouse is to gather eggs. We, and most everyone else we've talked with, agree that the so-called dark nest works best. This is nothing but a box about eighteen inches wide, a yard long, a foot high in the front, and with a hinged roof sloping sharply up and back so the hens won't roost and deposit droppings on it. A perch in front and a hen-sized opening in the middle of the front panel complete this nest. Put it on two-foot legs so the hens can scratch under it, keep it filled with clean straw or wood shavings and the hens will enter happily—one to four at a time—lay and leave, and all you have to do is lift the box roof every morning and evening and gather the eggs.

If you like, you can keep the hens at maximum production all winter by installing a 60-watt light bulb in the house and, either manually or

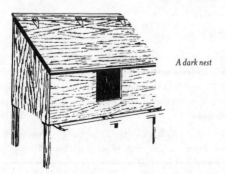

A dark nest

with a timer, be sure they have a full fourteen hours of light each day. A small electric heater in the northern states, to keep nighttime temperatures above freezing, will help too, as the hens will be able to put their energy into egg production rather than keeping warm.

Be sure the birds have fresh, clean water available at all times. Just a few hours without a drink, particularly in warm weather, can knock egg production off by 30 to 50 percent.

Producing Your Own Feed

As stated above, you are better off providing young chicks with a finely ground, medicated commercial feed for their first two months of life. You surely can toss in grass clippings, pieces of lettuce, perhaps finely chopped left-over eggs and shells. It's a good idea to give them a small bowl of rough sand at about two months. They will ingest it, store it in their crops, and begin to prepare for an adult ration.

As you know, "scarce as hen's teeth" is another old bromide with a foundation in barnyard truth. Chickens "chew" with a collection of rocks they store in the gizzard. This organ is not used with finely ground chick starter or the mash fed to commercial birds. Your home flock will need it, though, so keep a pen-located feeder full of rough sand or very small gravel, or with bought grit of a size appropriate to the birds' ages.

You'll also want to supply adequate calcium to the growing birds to strengthen their own bones and for egg shells—although this can be overdone, with too much calcium damaging the birds' kidneys. We routinely crush egg shells and include them with the table scrap feeding. After a meal of steamed clams, I crush the shells in an old gunny sack. (Soft-shelled clam shells crush under the foot, hard shells need a trip through the garden shredder-grinder.) You may want to purchase ground oyster shell, a fine source of soluble calcium that spends some weeks "chewing" in the bird's gizzard, doing double duty. It is very inexpensive.

This is a crucial period for the birds, and some family flock owners prefer to purchase a commercial diet for the birds, not trusting their knowledge of the nutrition needs of the birds at this time.

For the first month or so, each chick will consume only about two pounds of starter mash. After the fourth week, you should switch to a grow mash. There are several formulas, different for broilers and for layers. This should be finely ground, and kept before the birds for another full month. Supplement it with as much home-provided feed as the birds will clean up in a quarter-hour or so, one to three times a day. Feeding after each of your own meals is fine. Chop it all fine, never feed potato peelings unless you cook them first, and it is a good idea to get into the habit of putting trimmings and leavings of all fruit, onions, leeks, garlic, or chives on the compost pile. They won't bother the chicks, but can taint the flavor of the eggs when they start coming along.

After the eighth week, switch to pelletized commercial feed. Notice how the birds eat. They pick out bites with a sideways twist of the head. Much finely ground feed is wasted this way, particularly since at six weeks to two months, you have begun building up a permanent litter in the henhouse. Wasted feed will be scratched in quickly. For litter, add coarse sawdust, wood shavings, ground corncobs, cotton or tobacco waste, chopped cornstalks, wood chips from the road crew—just about anything that will hold together for a reasonable time and that the birds can scratch around in. Build it up to perhaps a twelve-inch depth. Droppings and spilled feed will be worked under in the birds' continual scratching, and the sub-surface composting action of the waste will generate heat by the time fall rolls around. With just a few birds this litter can be

Continued ➜

semi-permanent. You'll have to replace the west spots, under roosts in particular, and once or twice each a year you should rake aside the loose top material and dig out the ammonia-charged hard-packed base layer.

Be prepared for a strong ammonia smell, and either put the stuff right into compost or till it into the garden. We do the latter, so we reserve the cleanout for early spring or late fall. And once again remember that any feed that gets scattered into the litter is lost forever. Best to keep that wastage to a minimum.

THE FEED ITSELF

Now, precisely what is in chicken feed? The original wild chickens lived on what they could come by, seeds, bugs, some greens and grasses. I know of several chicken flocks that range widely, helping control bugs and weed seedlings in established gardens on some larger country places. They get a daily feeding of "scratch"—ground corn just tossed on the ground behind the house. On the odd occasions they may lay in the nest boxes—rather than off in a field, back in the wood pile, or snuggled up cozily on the warm engine of the farm truck. The farmer, when he or she can find the eggs, is getting them for a minimum of bother. Most folks will want to keep the flock confined, and feed it for optimum growth and production.

Basically, you should provide growing birds with a balanced diet (in chicken terms) containing some 20 percent protein. Layers' ration can go down to 15 or 16 percent protein, and egg production will remain high.

Here, just to show you what the commercial feeds consist of, are Leonard S. Mercia's recommendations for a home-mixed complete feed, along with the nutritional components taken into consideration. The wheat middlings referred to, by the way, are little chunks of wheat sifted out in the production of flour.

You'll notice that well over half the feed consists of yellow corn. Figure that an average heavy-bodied layer needs about one pound of corn a week or fifty pounds a year, plus an equal amount of other feeds. Cracked corn is much cheaper than mixed feeds, and you may be able to buy your corn and provide the balance from your kitchen. If you have the land—either your own, a neighbor's vacant lot, or a rented or borrowed plot within easy driving range out in the country—you can do as we do and raise your own. Up to 60 percent of the ration consists of corn, the balance from various scraps from cooking, the gardens, vegetables that go bad in the root cellar, and waste you can obtain from any grocer; stale bread, fat and gristle, lettuce leaves, carrot tops and such, all from various store departments.

At eight weeks the males will be a scrawny broiler size, having consumed about eight pounds of feed. For the remainder of their lives they will eat about a quarter-pound of feed per day—half corn and the balance whatever we can get. Say we keep them until the frost does away with the bugs in early fall, and each will have eaten about twenty pounds of feed—half or ten pounds being corn.

So for the ten or so birds we raise as capons, we need about 100 pounds of feed corn, or a bit less than two standard bushels (each weighing some 55 pounds) shelled from the cob, of course.

For the dozen or so birds we overwinter, the same quarter-pound of feed per day figure holds true. Keeping them at peak egg production after the initial eight-week mash diet period takes about 100 pounds of feed in total, and half of it corn. Feeding them for four pullet months (after two months of chick growth plus the 12-month or so laying periods—16 months in all) requires 1,600 pounds of feed, with 800 pounds of it being corn.

Commercial growers can produce 80 to 100 bushels of corn (on the cob) per acre. This is large-eared "horse corn," not the sweet corn you and I grow in the garden. The commercial yield might be as much as two and one-half tons per acre.

A "NATURAL" LAYING HEN DIET*

To be fed as all-mash to medium size layers kept in floor pens

| | Amount (lbs.) | |
Ingredient	Per 100 lbs.	Per Ton
Yellow corn meal	60.00	1200
Wheat middlings	15.00	300
Soybean meal (dehulled)	8.00	160
Maine herring meal (65%)	3.75	75
Meat & bone meal (47%)	1.00	20
Skim milk, dried	3.00	60
Alfalfa leaf meal (20%)	2.50	50
Iodized salt	0.40	8
Limestone, grd. (38% Ca)	6.35	127
Totals	100.00	2000

| | | Recommended |
| | | (N.E.C.C.) |
Calculated Analysis		(Per Pound)
Metabolizable energy Cal./lb.	1252	1292
Protein	16.07	16
Lysine	0.79	0.74
Methionine	0.31	0.29
Methionine & cystine	0.55	0.54
Fat	3.67	3.33
Fiber	3.15	2.51
Calcium	2.77	2.75
Total phosphorus	0.53	0.50
Available phosphorus	0.44	0.42

Vitamins (units or mgs./lb.)

Vitamin A activity		
(U.S.P. units/lb.)	5112	5290
Vitamin D (I.C.U.)		1000
Riboflavin (mg.)	1.36	1.38
Pantothenic acid (mg.)	3.89	4.05
Choline Chloride (mg.)	411	500
Niacin (mg.)	17.46	16.95

The birds *must* receive *direct* sunlight to enable them to synthesize vitamin D. Unfortified cod liver oil can be fed in place of sunlight to supply vitamin D. The amount of cod liver oil would depend upon the potency of the oil—the need is for 1000 (I.C.U.) per pound of feed.

*(Prepared by Dr. Richard Gerry, Department of Animal & Veterinary Sciences, University of Maine, Orono, Maine)

GROW YOUR OWN

We grow corn on a plot of about an acre and a half, planting sparsely a third of it to the nutrient-gobbling corn, along with beans and squash (Indian style), and rotating the plot so corn occupies the same space only once every three or four years. This way we get the 1,000 pounds or 20 or so bushels of corn we need without depleting the land.

See your County Agent or a good feed store to find the proper strain of corn for your climate and soil conditions. Here in New England we get the shortest season corn we can, so it will mature and dry on the cob before the hard-freeze harvest in early November. Some varieties are bred to resist lodging—getting blown down in Nebraska-type winds. Others resist particular disease, the southern corn blight in particular. Seeding rates and width of rows will vary with corn types, too.

At harvest we pick only the ears, then till stalks and most husks back into the land. During the years we lived on a working homestead, the corn was stored unshelled in a ratproof corncrib and we shelled it as needed. Now, with a place in a country town, we pretty much have to shell it and run it through the shredder-grinder and into 100-pound feed sacks.

Cobs are shredded and bagged separately, to be saved for use as litter for the henhouse.

Then, come the annual cleanout of the henhouse (and the leaves and all that have built up in the outside run), we truck several loads of this rich material up to the corn field and pitch it along the former corn rows. In effect, even on a relatively small place, the poultry operation can be largely a cash-free recycling operation: Chickens eat the feed you grow on their manure, you eat the eggs and poultry, and feed the birds whatever leftovers you may have, eggshells included.

WHAT TO FEED

Notice in the chart showing Mercia's "natural" laying hen diet, many important ingredients will be provided automatically if you feed the birds as we recommend, table scraps included. The suggested animal protein from herring meal and bone meal will come from your meat scraps. If you are a vegetarian, it will come from your protein-balanced diet of beans, corn, soybeans, and other legumes. Calcium from the dried milk will likely come from the milk you or your kids leave. Salt, iodine included, will be in your leftovers, and the protein and calcium from alfalfa (plus calcium from limestone) will be provided from eggshells or clam or oyster shells. And, as the chart says, if the birds are exposed to direct sunlight, the vitamin problem will be even less of a worry.

Of course, all during the garden year, the wastes such as pea vines and carrot tops, should go into the chicken pen. The birds will love it all and do well on it. We just toss the waste and trimmings into the run, and what isn't eaten gets added to the litter. Just be sure you don't put in any woody vines, tree or shrub limbs, though. They will not decay quickly, and can make digging out the run a much harder chore.

YOUR OWN EGGS AND MEAT

Five or six months after you took the carton of peeping chicks home from the post office, the first pullet eggs will appear—seldom in the nest at first. Some may come out with only vestigial shells, in odd shapes and colors, as the hen's equipment gets broken in. All will be about half-sized, but perfectly delicious. Don't worry about a blood speck in an egg, particularly in the first offerings. It's normal, just a bit of strain on the egg-making machinery, and it will disappear in the cooking. In time the eggs will become full-sized and may come on in a considerable quantity the first few months.

Usually there will be some chicken manure on an egg. A gentle rinse under warm water will remove it if you wish, but don't scrub the egg, even if it is covered with those hard bumps that are just extra calcium deposits. The hen coats the eggs with a cuticle or bloom, a natural coating that helps seal in moisture.

An untreated egg will keep for weeks in a properly chilled refrigerator. In the old days they stored washed fresh eggs in a crock of waterglass—a thick, gooey mixture of sodium silicate or potassium silicate and water. Kept in a cool place and protected from air or bacterial action by the waterglass, the eggs would keep for up to six months—or so I've heard.

You can freeze eggs for future cooking use, but I wouldn't plan to use them as-is for breakfast. The texture changes, yolks become thick and gummy, the whites become almost cooking hard. You can improve the texture of frozen eggs by separating the whites from the yolks, adding a good sprinkling of salt per yolk and a pinch of cornstarch or arrowroot per white, then stir each in gently. Don't whip any air into either.

If you like, you can freeze several eggs unseparated. Just add the salt and starch and whip all in together. At 0°F they will keep for nine months or a year, and you'll never tell them from fresh-laid in your cakes. The natural additives will reduce texture change considerably. But don't try them scrambled.

THE MOLT

After a good twelve or fourteen—or occasionally as many as eighteen—months of solid production, your hens will quit laying for the most part and put their energy into molting, which is changing their suits of feathers. Then, after several months' rest, they will start laying again, but never producing as many eggs or for as long as in the first pullet year.

Best economy, really, we find, is to buy a whole new set of chicks, say in March, and keep them segregated for three months, until June. By then our original flock will be down to perhaps a half-dozen birds—some having died, most having gone out of the egg business and into the stewing pot. We shut the older birds in the yard, introduce the youngsters to the house, and after a day (if it doesn't rain) let the generations get acquainted. There will be a lot of chasing around, and the young birds will tend to crowd into a corner where the bottom layer will contentedly let itself get smothered. So, we visit the chickens often during the week or so they need to settle down.

If you have the facilities to do it, it's best to keep the age groups separate. This competition as well as the possibility of spreading disease are factors to be considered.

INTO MEAT

When the young birds are beginning to start laying, the old ones go into the freezer. Same is true of the culls, birds that lose the bright eyes and combs and the cantankerous disposition of good layers. Also out go any birds whose eye rings and legs don't bleach from yellow to white—the color going into the egg yolk—or whose vents lose the plump, moist look of layers and become dry and puckered. A productive bird, by the way, should have rumpled, soiled feathers. Any hen whose plumage remains shiny and clean gets a once-over, a vent inspection in particular, and usually gets the axe.

Continued →

You may not have the stomach to slaughter your birds, and they will sell for $2.00–$4.00 at any country livestock auction. We slaughter our own, both the old hens and extra roosters. Our own preference is to order twenty-five as-hatched chicks for June delivery. Once the young roosters develop enough of the upright stance and larger comb of a male bird, I caponize all but the two largest and feistiest. The desexing operation involves major surgery, as the gonads are located well inside, up along the spine. Look for caponizing sets in the farm supply catalogs. They will come complete with instructions. By November, the June-hatched hens of the year before and the capons of the current year are slaughtered, leaving only the small over-wintering flock of a dozen or so birds. The old hens will be fit for stew and soup only, but the capons will be plump, tender, and wonderful roasters.

The easiest way to kill a chicken is to hang it up, each foot in a rope with a noose or slipknot at the end, and cut the throat just behind the lower beak. Then get away quickly. The bird will flap, scattering blood all over. Once it is bled, swish the carcass for 30–60 seconds in 160° to 180°F water. This is called the hard scald method. Pull out the tail and wing feathers first, and the rest should come all almost in sheets. If they come out hard, you've scalded for too short a time. If the breast skin tears, you scalded too long.

You can clean the birds whole, but it's easiest to split them up the back. Get a strong pair of poultry shears. Cut off the feet, head and end of the neck, and the pointed oil gland at the base of the tail. Be sure to get out all the yellow glandular material. Then, with a sharp knife, cut around the vent in a funnel shape to avoid cutting into the gut. Then cut up the spine and the bird will open like a book. You'll recognize the giblets. Cut the green bile sack from the liver and the tubes from the top of the heart. Split the gizzard, peel off the tough yellow inner lining, dispose of the rest of the innards, including the tubes in the neck and the crop, a sack that may be empty or full of food, located under the skin just at the base of the neck. Oh yes, keep the egg-making machinery of any old hen, including the ropes of developing yolks. Delicious and proof that the bird that went into the stew was homegrown.

MISCELLANEOUS POINTS

Don't worry much about chicken disease; clean out the litter and the run and disinfect the house and furniture twice a year with Clorox, and you should be largely problem-free, if you have bought good stock. Dispose of any bird that looks ill. If it is plump, you may as well eat it. If scrawny and wasted, the bird should be killed and buried. Bloody droppings, especially in young birds, means coccidiosis and a trip to the vet for medication to put in the water. (Several types of coccidiosis don't show symptoms of bloody droppings.)

A hen may go broody on you, acting fussy and wanting to sit on her eggs. Most brooding instinct has been bred out of modern strains, and she won't do a very good job of it. Suspend her in a private cage with wire or flat floor and with small feed and water receptacles for a few days and what the breeders have let remain of the hen's maternal instinct will pass.

Want to raise chicks from eggs? Keep a rooster or two, tolerate the crowing and the jumping on the hens. Then look through the catalogs for an incubator—some will double as brooders—and follow the directions supplied. Eggs need constant heat of about 100°F, water to supply humidity, and a twice-daily turning.

But any way you do it, whether you buy started pullets or incubate your own eggs, you can look forward to eggs and poultry with a flavor—and at a cost—to be found in no supermarket.

Building Chicken Coops

Gail Damerow

Illustrations by Bethany Caskey and Elayne Sears

Twelve Tips for a Successful Coop Design

Some people provide their flocks with perfectly adequate housing by converting unused toolsheds, doghouses, or camper shells. Others go all out, such as the fellow I knew in California who built a two-story structure, complete with a cupola, for his fancy bantams.

No matter how it's designed, though, a successful coop:

- is easy to clean
- has good drainage
- protects the flock from wind and sun
- keeps out rodents, wild birds, and predatory animals
- provides adequate space for the flock size
- is well ventilated
- is free of drafts
- maintains a uniform temperature
- has a place where birds can roost
- has nests that entice hens to lay indoors
- offers plenty of light—natural and artificial
- includes sanitary feed and water stations

ENSURING GOOD DRAINAGE

If your soil is neither sandy nor gravelly, locate your coop at the top of a slight hill or on a slope, where puddles won't collect when it rains. A south-facing slope, open to full sunlight, dries fastest after a rain. Capture that light and warmth from the sun inside the coop with windows on the south side.

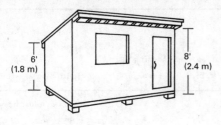

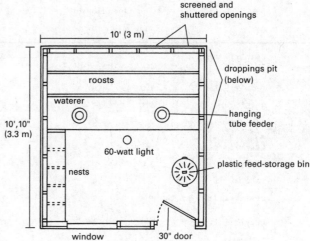

This basic coop plan features roosts over a droppings pit for good sanitation, a window for light, and screened and shuttered openings on the north side to control ventilation. To expand the interior floor space, build the nests on the outside of the coop.

Planning for Easy Access

Simple, open housing is easier to clean than a coop with numerous nooks and crannies. If your coop is tall enough for you to stand in, you'll be inclined to clean it as often as necessary. If you prefer a low coop (for economic reasons or to retain your flock's body heat in a cold climate), design the coop like a chest freezer, with a hinged roof you can open for cleaning.

The coop should have both a chicken-sized door and a people-sized door. The chicken door can be a 10-inch-wide by 13-inch-high (25 x 32.5 cm) flap cut into a side wall, opening downward to form a ramp for birds to use when they enter and exit. To keep predators out, the door should have a secure latch that you can fasten shut in the evening, after your chickens have gone to roost.

SPACE REQUIREMENTS

The more room your chickens have, the healthier and more content they'll be. Except in extremely cold climates, home flocks are rarely housed entirely indoors but have room to roam outside whenever they please. Yet even in the best of climates, chickens may sometimes prefer to remain indoors due to rain, extreme cold, or extreme heat.

Minimum space requirements, including those shown in the chart on the next page, indicate the least amount of indoor space birds need when they can't or won't go outside for an extended period of time. Birds that never have access to an outside run will do better if you give them more space than the absolute minimum. On the other hand, birds that spend most of their time outdoors, coming in only at night to roost, will do nicely with less space.

To encourage chickens to spend most of their daytime hours outdoors, even in poor weather, give them a covered area adjoining the coop where they can loll out of rain, wind, and sun. Encouraging your chickens to stay out in the fresh air has two advantages: They will be healthier, and their coop will stay cleaner.

Providing Adequate Ventilation

The more time chickens spend indoors, the more important ventilation becomes. Ventilation serves six essential functions:

· supplies oxygen-laden fresh air

· removes heat released during breathing

· removes moisture from the air (released during breathing or evaporated from droppings)

· removes harmful gases (carbon dioxide released during breathing or ammonia evaporated from droppings)

· removes dust particles suspended in the air

· dilutes disease-causing organisms in the air

Compared to other animals, chickens have a high respiration rate, which causes them to use up available oxygen quickly while at the same time releasing large amounts of carbon dioxide, heat, and moisture. As a result, chickens are highly susceptible to respiratory problems. Stale air inside the henhouse makes a bad situation worse—airborne disease-carrying microorganisms become concentrated more quickly in stale air than in fresh air.

> ### VENTILATION QUICK CHECK
> Use your nose and eyes to check for proper ventilation. If you smell ammonia fumes and see thick cobwebs, your coop is not adequately ventilated.

Ventilation holes near the ceiling along the south and north walls give warm, moist air a way to escape. Screens over the holes will keep out wild birds, which may carry parasites or disease. Drop-down covers, hinged at the bottom and latched at the top, let you close off ventilation holes as needed.

COLD-WEATHER CONCERNS

During cold weather, you not only have to provide good ventilation, but you also have to worry about drafts. Close the ventilation holes on the north side, keeping the holes on the south side open except when the weather turns bitter cold.

Continued →

MINIMUM SPACE REQUIREMENTS

Birds	Age	Open Housing sq ft/Bird	Open Housing Birds/sq m	Confined Housing sq ft/Bird	Confined Housing Birds/sq m	Cages sq in/Bird	Cages sq cm/Bird
Heavy	1 day to 1 week	—	—	0.5	20	(Do not house heavy breeds on wire.)	
	1–8 weeks	1.0	10	2.5	4		
	9–15* weeks	2.0	5	5.0	2		
	21 weeks and up	4.0	3	10.0	1		
Light	1 day to 1 week	—	—	0.5	20	25	160
	1–11 weeks	1.0	10	2.5	4	45	290
	12–20 weeks	2.0	5	5.0	2	60	390
	21 weeks and up	3.0	3	7.5	1.5	75	480
Bantam	1 day to 1 week	—	—	0.3	30	20	130
	1–11 weeks	0.6	15	1.5	7	40	260
	12–20 weeks	1.5	7	3.5	3	55	360
	21 weeks and up	2.0	5	5.0	2	70	450

*or age of slaughter

From *The Chicken Health Handbook*, by Gail Damerow

WARM-WEATHER CONCERNS

Cross ventilation is needed in warm weather to keep birds cool and to remove moisture. The warmer the air becomes, the more moisture it can hold. In the summer, leave all the ventilation holes open and open windows on the north and south walls. Windows should be covered with 3/4-inch (1.9 cm) screen to keep out wild birds and should slide or tilt so they can be opened easily. Provide at least 1 square foot of window for each 10 square feet of floor space (or 1 sq m of window per 10 sq m of floor space).

Where temperatures soar during summer, you may need a fan to further improve ventilation. Henhouse fans come in two styles: ceiling mounted and wall mounted. The former needs be no more than an inexpensive variable-speed Casablanca (paddle) fan to keep the air moving. A paddle fan benefits birds only if ventilation holes are open and will keep hot air from getting trapped against the ceiling.

A wall-mounted fan sucks stale air out, causing fresh air to be drawn in. The fan, rated in cubic feet per minute, or cfm, should move 5 cubic feet (0.15 cu m) of air per minute *per bird*. If your flock is housed on litter, place the fan outlet near the floor, where it will readily suck out dust as well as stale air. Since some dust will stick to the fan itself, a wall-mounted fan needs frequent cleaning with a vacuum and/or pressure air hose.

Temperature Control

A chicken's body operates most efficiently at temperatures between 70° and 75°F (21–24°C). For each degree of increase, broilers eat 1 percent less, which causes a drop in average weight gain. Egg production may rise slightly, but eggs become smaller and have thinner shells. When the temperature exceeds 95°F (35°C), birds may die.

To keep the coop from getting too hot, treat the roof and walls with insulation, such as 1 1/2-inch (3.8 cm) styrofoam sheets, particularly on the south and west sides. Cover the insulation with plywood or other material your chickens can't pick to pieces. To reflect heat, use aluminum roofing or light-colored composite roofing and paint the outside of the coop white. Plant trees or install awnings to shade the building. An awning can also provide a shady place for birds to rest.

To enhance heat retention in winter, build the north side of your coop into a hill or stack bales of straw against the north wall. Where cold weather is neither intense nor prolonged, double-walled construction that provides dead-air spaces may be adequate to retain the heat generated by your flock. In colder weather, you'll need insulation and, to keep moisture from collecting and dripping, a continuous vapor barrier along the walls. Windows on the south wall will supply solar heat on sunny days (but should be shaded in hot weather).

COLD-WEATHER WARNINGS

In winter, rapidly disappearing feed may signal that your chickens are too cold. Eliminate indoor drafts and increase the carbohydrates in the scratch mix. However, it may also mean that the chickens are infested with worms—take a sample of droppings to your veterinarian for testing. Of course, disappearing feed may not be your chickens' fault at all—make sure that rodents, opossums, wild birds, and other creatures are not dipping their snouts into the trough.

Choosing the Right Flooring

Henhouse flooring can be one of four basic kinds: dirt, wood, droppings boards, or concrete. Which you choose will depend on your budget, the siting of your coop, and how much time you're willing to invest in keeping the floor clean.

DIRT

A dirt floor is the cheapest and easiest to "install," but consider it only if you have sandy soil to ensure adequate drainage. Dirt draws heat away, which can be a benefit in warm weather but a potentially dangerous drawback in cold weather. A coop with a dirt floor is not easy to clean and cannot be made rodent proof.

WOOD

A floor built from wood planking offers an economical way to protect birds from rodents as long as the floor is at least 1 foot (30 cm) off the ground to discourage mice and rats from taking up residence in the space beneath it. However, wood floors are hard to clean, especially because the cracks between the boards invariably become packed with filth.

DROPPINGS BOARDS

Droppings boards of sturdy welded wire or closely spaced wooden battens allow droppings to fall through to the bottom of the coop, where chickens can't pick in them. If you opt for droppings boards, not only will the chickens remain healthier, but droppings will be easier to remove because they won't get trampled and packed down. Start with a wooden framework and to it fasten either welded wire or 1 x 2 lumber, placed on edge for rigidity with 1-inch (2.5 cm) gaps between boards. Build manageable sections you can easily remove so that you can take them outdoors and clean them with a high-pressure air or water spray and dry them in direct sunlight. Like wood flooring, droppings boards must be high enough off the ground to discourage rodents.

CONCRETE

Finished concrete is the most expensive option for a floor, but it's also the most impervious to rodents and the easiest to clean. As a low-cost alternative, mix one part cement with three parts rock-free (or sifted) dirt and spread 4 to 6 inches (10–15 cm) over plain dirt. Level the mixed soil and use a dirt tamper to pound it smooth. Mist the floor lightly with water and let it set for several days. You'll end up with a firm floor that's easy to maintain.

PUTTING DOWN BEDDING

Bedding, scattered over the floor or under droppings boards, offers numerous advantages: It absorbs moisture and droppings, it cushions the birds' feet, and it controls temperature by insulating the birds from the ground.

Good bedding, or litter, has these properties:

- is inexpensive
- is durable
- is lightweight
- is absorbent
- dries quickly
- is easy to handle
- doesn't pack readily
- has medium-sized particles
- is low in thermal conductivity
- is free of mustiness and mold
- has not been treated with toxic chemicals
- makes good compost and fertilizer

Of all the different kinds of litter I've tried over the years, wood shavings (especially pine) remain my favorite because they're inexpensive and easy to manage. Straw must be chopped; otherwise, it mats easily and, when it combines with manure, creates an impenetrable mass. Of the kinds of straw, wheat is the best, followed by rye, oat, and buckwheat, in that order. Any of these, chopped and mixed with shredded corncobs and stalks, makes nice loose, fluffy bedding.

Rice hulls and peanut hulls are cheap in some areas, but neither material is absorbent enough to make good litter. Dried leaves are sometimes plentiful, but they pack too readily to make good bedding. If you have access to lots of newsprint and a shredder, you've got the makings of inexpensive bedding that's at least as good as rice or peanut hulls, although it tends to mat and to retain moisture; in some areas, shredded paper is sold by the bale.

If you don't use droppings boards, start young birds on bedding a minimum of 4 inches (10 cm) deep and work up to 8 inches (20 cm) by the time the birds are mature. Deep litter insulates chickens in the winter and lets them burrow in to keep cool in the summer.

When litter around the doorway, under the roosts, or around feeders becomes packed, break it up with a hoe or rake. Around waterers or doorways, remove wet patches of litter and add fresh, dry litter (and fix the leak, if any, that caused the litter to become saturated).

If you use droppings boards, after each cleaning spread at least 2 inches (5 cm) of litter beneath the boards to absorb moisture from droppings. An easy-to-manage combination is to place droppings boards beneath perches where the majority of droppings accumulate and to have open litter everywhere else. Your chickens won't be able to get to the manure piles beneath the droppings boards, but they can dust and scratch in the open-litter area, stirring up the bedding and keeping it light and loose.

EARNING THEIR KEEP

Scratch—a feed mixture containing at least two kinds of grain, one of them usually cracked corn—can be used to trick chickens into stirring up their coop's bedding to keep it loose and dry. Toss a handful over the litter once a day (traditionally, late in the afternoon when the birds are thinking of going to roost), and your chickens will scramble for it.

Installing Roosts

Wild chickens roost in trees. Many of our domestic breeds are too heavy to fly up into a tree, but they like to perch off the ground nevertheless. You can make a perch from an old ladder or anything else strong enough to hold chickens and rough enough for them to grip without being so splintery as to injure their feet. If you use new lumber, round

Continued ➔

off the corners so your chickens can wrap their toes around it. Plastic pipe and metal pipe do not make good roosts; they're too smooth for chickens to grasp firmly. Besides, given a choice, chickens prefer to roost on something flat, like a 2 x 4.

The perch should be about 2 inches (5 cm) across for regular-sized chickens, or no less than 1 inch (2.5 cm) across for bantams. Allow 8 inches (20 cm) of perching space for each chicken, 10 inches (25 cm) if you raise one of the larger breeds. If one perch doesn't offer enough roosting space, install additional roosts. Place them 2 feet (60 cm) above the floor and at least 18 inches (45 cm) from the nearest parallel wall, spacing them 18 inches (45 cm) apart. If floor space is limited, step-stair roosts 12 inches (30 cm) apart vertically and horizontally, so chickens can easily hop from lower to higher rungs. Either way, make perches removable for easy cleanup and place droppings boards beneath them.

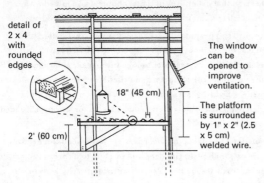

This roost is made from 2 x 4 lumber with rounded edges, mounted for easy cleaning and spaced 18" (45 cm) apart, over a raised platform surrounded by wire mesh to keep chickens from picking in their droppings.

If roosting space is at a premium, step-stair perches and space them 12" (30 cm) apart vertically and horizontally.

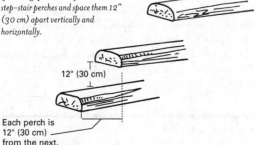

Nests and Nest Boxes

Hens, by nature, like to lay their eggs in dark, out-of-the-way places. Nest boxes encourage hens to lay eggs where you can find them and where the eggs will stay clean and unbroken. Furnish one nest for every four hens in your flock. A good size for Leghorn-type layers is 12 inches wide by 14 inches high by 12 inches deep (30 x 35 x 30 cm). For heavier breeds, make nests 14 inches wide by 14 inches high by 12 inches deep (35 x 35 x 30 cm); for bantams, 10 inches wide by 12 inches high by 10 inches deep (25 x 30 x 25 cm).

A perch just below the entrance to the nest gives hens a place to land before entering, helping keep the nests clean. A 4-inch (10 cm) sill along the bottom edge of each nest prevents eggs from rolling out and holds in nesting material. Pad each nest with soft, clean litter and change it often.

Place nests on the ground until your pullets get accustomed to using them, then firmly attach the nests 18 to 20 inches (45–50 cm) off the ground. Raising nests discourages chickens from scratching in them and possibly dirtying or breaking eggs. Further discourage non-laying activity by placing nests on the darkest wall of your coop. Construct a 45-degree sloped roof above nests to keep birds from roosting on top. Better yet, build nests to jut outside the coop and provide access from the back—chickens won't be able to roost over nests, they'll have more floor space, and you'll be able to collect eggs without disturbing your flock.

An alternative plan for creating darkened nests that are easy to clean is to place a long, bottomless nest box on a shelf. Partition the inside of

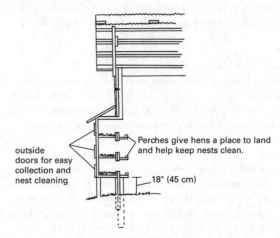

Exterior nests increase floor space and are easy to maintain from outside the coop.

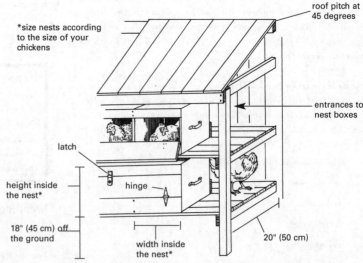

Nest boxes on shelves provide darkened entrances at the back and can easily be cleaned by sliding each box off its shelf.

180

the box into a series of nesting cubicles, with their entrances facing the wall. Allow an 8-inch (20 cm) gap between the wall and the entrances so hens can walk along the shelf at the back. Build a sloped roof above the shelf to prevent roosting. Add a drop panel at the front of the box for egg collection. To clean the nests, make sure no eggs or hens are inside, then pull the box off the shelf and the nesting material will fall out.

Choosing and Siting a Feeder

Feeders come in many different styles—the two most common are a long trough and a hanging tube. Regardless of its design, a good feeder has these important features:

- discourages billing out
- prevents contamination with droppings
- is easy to clean
- doesn't allow feed to get wet

Chickens are notorious feed wasters. Feeders that encourage wastage are narrow or shallow and/or lack a lip that prevents chickens from billing out—using their beaks to scoop feed onto the ground. A feeder with a rolled or bent-in edge reduces billing out. To further discourage billing out, raise the feeder to the height of the chickens' backs. The best way to keep a feeder at the right height as a flock grows is to hang it from the ceiling by chains.

One hanging feeder is enough for up to 30 chickens.

A good feeder discourages chickens from roosting on top and contaminating feed with droppings. A trough mounted on a wall allows little room for roosting. A free-standing trough may be fitted with an anti-roosting device that turns and dumps a chicken trying to perch on it. A tube feeder should be fitted with a sloped cover to prevent roosting; unfortunately, most tube feeders don't come with covers anymore, but you can fashion one from the lid of a 5-gallon plastic bucket. It may not keep chickens from roosting, but it will keep their droppings out of the feed.

This trough has adjustable-height legs and an anti-roosting reel that rotates and dumps any bird that tries to hop on. Allow 4" (10 cm) of trough space for each bird, counting both sides if birds can eat from either side.

REPLENISHING TROUGH FEEDERS

If you use a trough feeder, never fill it more than two-thirds full. Chickens waste approximately 30 percent of the feed in a full trough, 10 percent in a two-thirds-full trough, 3 percent in a half-full trough, and approximately 1 percent in a trough that's only one-third full. Obviously, you'll save a lot of money by using more troughs so you can put less feed in each one.

Since you fill a trough from the top and chickens eat from the top, trough feeders tend to collect stale or wet feed at the bottom. Never add fresh feed on top of feed already in the trough. Instead, rake or push the old feed to one side, and empty and scrub the trough at least once a week.

After having used trough feeders for years, I much prefer tube feeders. Since you pour feed into the top and chickens eat from the bottom, feed doesn't sit around getting stale. A tube feeder is fine for pellets or crumbles, but works well for mash only if you fill it no more than two-thirds full. Otherwise the mash may pack and bridge, or remain suspended in the tube, instead of dropping down.

WHERE SHOULD THE FEEDER BE PLACED?

Placing feeders inside the coop keeps feed from getting wet but encourages chickens to spend too much time indoors. Hanging feeders under a covered outdoor area is ideal for keeping feed out of the rain and for encouraging the flock to spend more time in fresh air. If you have to keep feeders indoors, for good litter management move them every two or three days to prevent concentrated activity in one area.

HOW MANY FEEDERS IS ENOUGH?

If you feed free choice, put out enough feeders so at least one-third of the flock can eat at the same time. If you feed on a restricted basis, you'll need enough feeders so the whole flock can eat at once.

Choosing and Siting a Water Source

A chicken drinks often throughout the day, sipping a little each time. A chicken's body contains more than 50 percent water, and an egg is 65 percent water. A bird, therefore, needs access to fresh drinking water at all times in order for its body to function properly. A hen that is deprived of water for 24 hours may take another 24 hours to recover. A hen deprived of water for 36 hours may go into a molt followed by a long period of poor laying from which she may never recover.

Depending on the weather and on the bird's size, each chicken drinks between 1 and 2 cups (237–474 ml) of water each day—layers drink twice as much as nonlayers. In warm weather, a chicken may drink two to four times more than usual. When a flock's water needs go up during warm weather and the water supply remains the same, water deprivation can result. Water deprivation can also occur in winter if the water supply freezes.

Even when there's plenty of water, chickens can be deprived if they simply don't like the taste. Medications, for example, can cause chickens not to drink. Do not medicate water when chickens are under high stress, such as during hot weather or during a snow.

Large amounts of dissolved minerals can also make water taste unpleasant to chickens. If you suspect your water supply contains a high concentration of minerals, have the water tested. If total dissolved solids exceed 1,000 parts per million (ppm), look for an alternative source of water for your flock.

TEMPERATURE CONTROLS

Chickens prefer water at temperatures between 50° and 55°F (10–13°C). The warmer the water, the less they'll drink. In summer, put out extra waterers and keep them in the shade, and/or bring your flock fresh, cool water often. In cold weather, make sure water does not freeze: Bring your flock warm water at least twice a day (but avoid increasing humidity in the coop by filling indoor fountains with steaming water), use an immersion heater in water troughs, place metal fountains on pan heaters, and wrap heating coils around automatic watering pipes. Water-warming devices are available through farm stores and livestock-supply catalogs.

Continued ➜

To keep water from freezing indoors, set a metal fount on a thermostatically controlled heating pan like this one.

Outdoors, drop a sinking heater, like this one, into the water bucket.

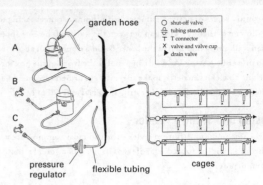

Water enters automatic waterers in one of three ways: through (A) manually filled tank, (B) float valve–regulated tank, or (C) pressure-regulated direct water supply.

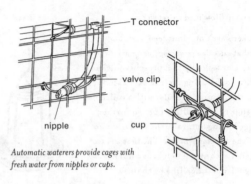

Automatic waterers provide cages with fresh water from nipples or cups.

CHOOSING THE RIGHT WATERER

Chickens should not have to get their drinking water from puddles or other stagnant, unhealthful sources but should be given fresh, clean water in suitable containers. Provide enough of these waterers so at least one-third of your birds can drink at the same time. No less than once a week, clean and disinfect waterers with a solution of chlorine bleach.

Waterers, like feeders, come in many different styles. The best drinkers have these features in common:

· They hold enough to water a flock for an entire day.

· They keep water clean and free of droppings.

· They don't leak or drip.

Automatic, or piped-in, water is the best kind because it never runs out. But piped-in water isn't without disadvantages. Aside from the expense of running plumbing to the chicken coop, water pipes can leak if not properly installed and freeze in winter unless buried below the frost line or wrapped in electrical heating tape. Automatic drinkers can also become clogged, and so must be checked at least daily.

Properly managed piped-in water is handy for birds kept in cages, since it saves the trouble of having to distribute water to each cage by hand. Automatic devices come in two basic designs: nipples and cups.

Nipples dispense water when manipulated by an individual bird. Since birds have to learn how to drink from a nipple, you'll need to spend time watching to make sure all your birds know how to drink and helping those having trouble. One nipple serves up to five birds.

Cups hold a small amount of water, the level of which is controlled by a valve that releases water each time a bird drinks. Cups come in small and large sizes. The smaller size is for birds in cages. The larger size can be used by a flock. Provide one large cup for up to 100 birds.

Inexpensive plastic 1-gallon (3.7 l) drinkers are fine for young birds, but they don't hold enough for many older birds (and usually get knocked over by rambunctious adults). In addition, plastic cracks after a time, and the cost of constantly replacing those inexpensive waterers adds up fast.

Metal waterers are sturdier than plastic and come in larger sizes holding 3 gallons (11 l), 5 gallons (19 l), or more. As in all things, you get what you pay for—a cheap metal waterer will rust through faster than a quality drinker. Whether you use plastic or metal, set the container on a level surface so the water won't drip out. To help birds drink and to reduce litter contamination, set the top edge of the waterer at approximately the height of the birds' backs.

WHERE SHOULD THE WATERER BE PLACED?

Placing the container over a droppings pit confines spills so chickens can't walk or peck in moist, unhealthful soil. Build a wooden frame of 1/2" x 12" x 42" (12.5 x 304 x 1066 mm) boards. Staple strong wire mesh to one side and set the box, wire side up, on a bed of sand or gravel. Place the waterer on top so chickens have to hop up onto the mesh to get a drink.

Offering Access to a Yard

A yard offers chickens a safe place to get sunshine and fresh air. Ideally, it should have trees or shrubs for shade, along with some grass or other ground cover. Since chickens invariably decimate the ground cover immediately around their housing, a large yard is better than a small one, but a small one is better than none at all.

Some chicken keepers contend that confining a flock to a coop with properly managed litter and good ventilation is more healthful than letting them into a yard of packed dirt coated with chicken manure. That's certainly true if the hardpan turns to slush in rainy weather. Sad but true, two sure signs of an unsanitary yard are bare spots and mudholes.

Where space for a run is limited, one way to avoid the barren-yard problem is to level the area and cover it with several inches of sand. Go over the sand every day with a grass rake to smooth out dusting holes and remove droppings and other debris. If available yard space is truly minuscule, you might build your chickens a sunporch with a slat or wire floor and periodically clean away the droppings that accumulate beneath the porch.

On the other hand, if you have plenty of room, keep your flock healthy and take advantage of the cost savings in feed by letting your chickens graze.

RANGE ROTATION

It amazes me that folks who wouldn't dream of planting cabbages or potatoes in the same plot two years in a row never think twice about keeping chickens in the same spot year after year. Even if the coop itself is in constant use—cleaned and disinfected regularly—pathogens and parasites become concentrated in the soil of a constantly used yard.

One way to rotate range is to have two yards that can be accessed from the same doorway, with a gate that can be repositioned so when one yard is opened, the other is blocked off. The disadvantage to this system is that the constant comings and goings of chickens through the single entryway soon kills the grass around the door. When it rains, you have an unsightly and unsanitary situation.

To avoid this mess, you might provide different entries into different yards. By having chicken-sized doors on different sides of the coop, you can periodically close one door and open another. As soon as you switch the chickens to a new yard, rake over their previous entryway, toss on some fresh seed, and let the grass grow while the chickens are away. Rest, sunshine, and plant growth will conspire to sanitize the yard.

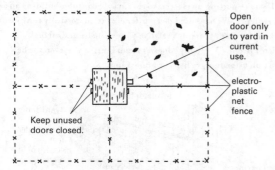

To rotate range without moving the housing, put chicken-sized doors on different sides of the coop and separate "ranges" with electroplastic net fencing.

If chickens must constantly use the same entry, a covered dooryard (of the sort used to provide a shady resting place) helps prevent muddy conditions. Alternatively, put a concrete apron in front of the door and periodically scrape off the muck with a flat shovel. As a third alternative, avoid permanent housing altogether and turn your flock out to pasture.

Raising Chickens Free on the Range

Pasturing chickens on range saves you money by letting your chickens forage for much of their sustenance, and it keeps them healthy by preventing a build-up of parasites and pathogens. But ranging requires a fair amount of ground. It's also labor intensive, since range housing must be moved frequently to new forage areas. Because range housing is moved often, it needs to be light and portable and thus offers little protection against cold weather.

A rudimentary range shelter protects birds from sun and wind. It might be as simple as a roof on posts that can be lifted and moved by two people. For a one-person operation, wheels at one end let you lift the other end and push or pull the shelter to its new location. To protect birds from the elements, enclose those sides of the shelter most subject to prevailing wind and rain.

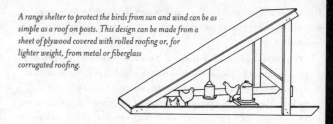

A range shelter to protect the birds from sun and wind can be as simple as a roof on posts. This design can be made from a sheet of plywood covered with rolled roofing or, for lighter weight, from metal or fiberglass corrugated roofing.

For our range shelter, we built a plywood corral topped with a lightweight surplus camper shell. Our camper-top shelter is an improvement over open shelters, since it can be closed up at night for predator protection and insulated against cold weather. Although we bolted it together so it could be taken apart for storage or moving, we've found it more convenient to move the whole thing in one piece. For this purpose, we added two sturdy hooks on each side. By using straps or chains to connect opposite pairs of hooks, we can lift and move the shelter with our front-end loader. If you don't have a loader handy, a pair of wheels at one end or skids at the bottom of the shelter would help you move it without too much trouble.

MOVING A RANGE SHELTER

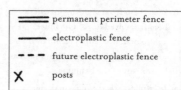

permanent perimeter fence
electroplastic fence
future electroplastic fence
× posts

For total range confinement, move the shelter daily to a new location. For a free-ranged flock, move the shelter when pasture has been grazed down to an inch (2.5 cm) or when bare spots appear.

Total range confinement

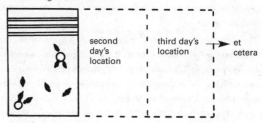

second day's location | third day's location → et cetera

Free range

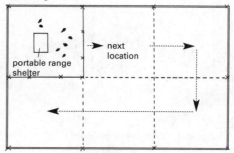

portable range shelter | → next location

HELPING YOUR CHICKENS FIND THEIR SHELTER

Chickens can be decidedly stupid about finding their home after it has been moved. You can help them along by watching for stragglers that insist on bedding down in the old place and by never moving the house

Continued ➜

far outside the previous range—chickens are conservative by nature, and don't like to venture more than about 200 yards (180 m) from their home place.

To avoid the problem of having chickens forget where they live, you might construct the range shelter so that the flock is entirely confined by it. An advantage to range confinement is its superior ability to exclude predators. Its disadvantage is the need to move the shelter more often. Since the unit gives chickens less space to roam, you don't have to move it as far—only to the nearest patch of fresh pasture.

INTRODUCING CHICKENS TO THE RANGE

You can put young birds on range as soon as they feather out, raising them away from older birds while they develop immunities through gradual exposure to the disease in their environment. In a warm climate, a flock can be kept on range year-round. Where winter weather turns nasty, the flock may need to be moved to permanent housing during the colder months.

Despite its many advantages, a distinct disadvantage to putting chickens out to pasture is their greater susceptibility to predators. A good fence goes a long way toward solving the predator problem.

Fencing

Whether your chickens have only a small yard or are free to roam the range, you'll need a stout fence to keep them from showing up where they aren't wanted and to protect them from predators. The fence should be at least 4 feet (120 cm) high so predators won't climb over and chickens won't fly out. It may need to be higher if you raise flyers such as Leghorns, Hamburgs, Old English, or many of the bantams.

The ideal chicken fence is made from tightly strung, small-mesh woven wire. The best fence I ever had was a 5-foot-high (150 cm) chain-link fence that once came with a house I moved into. A chain-link fence isn't one I can recommend, though, because of the exorbitant cost of building a new one.

The most common coop fencing material is "chicken wire," or "poultry netting," which consists of 1-inch (2.5 cm) mesh woven in a honeycomb pattern. Take care to specify galvanized wire designed for *outdoor use.* Chicken wire designed for indoor use rusts away all too soon when used for outdoor fencing. Many people use so-called "turkey wire," which has 2-inch (50 mm) mesh, because it's cheaper than chicken wire, but it doesn't hold its shape as well.

A better though more expensive option is yard-and-garden fencing, which has 1-inch (2.5 cm) spaces at the bottom that graduate to wider spaces toward the top (thus using less wire to keep the cost down). The smaller openings at the bottom keep small chickens from slipping out and small predators from slipping in. Birds and predators can't sneak under if you pull the fence tight and attach it to firm posts that don't wobble. As further insurance, place pressure-treated boards along the ground and staple them to the bottom of the fence.

Downy chicks can pop right through most fences, but they won't stray far if they have a mother hen inside the yard to call them back. Chicks outside the fence are, however, vulnerable to passing dogs and cats. To keep them in, get a roll of 12-inch-wide (30 cm) aviary netting, which looks just like chicken wire but has openings half the size. Attach the aviary netting securely along the bottom of your regular woven-wire fence.

ELECTRIC FENCING

If you need additional protection from dogs and other predators, string electrified scare wires along the top and outside bottom, 8 inches (20 cm) away from your fence. The top wire keeps critters from climbing over, and the bottom wire discourages them from snooping along the fence, pushing against it, or attempting to dig under it.

If you're putting up electric wires anyway, consider building an all-electric fence. We have used electric fencing to successfully confine our chickens for many years. It's relatively inexpensive and virtually predator proof. "Virtually" doesn't mean "entirely"—even the best fence won't stop hungry hawks or opossums.

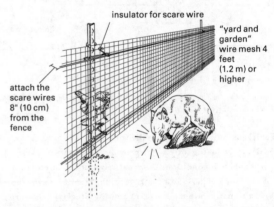

insulator for scare wire

"yard and garden" wire mesh 4 feet (1.2 m) or higher

attach the scare wires 8" (10 cm) from the fence

*Attach wire-mesh fencing to the side of the posts **away** from the chicken yard. Electrified scare wires toward the top and bottom will discourage four-legged predators.*

One good electrified chicken fence is made from electroplastic netting. Chickens can see the netting more easily than they can see individual horizontal electric wires, and the fence comes completely preassembled so it's easy to move when the flock needs fresh ground. Electroplastic net for poultry comes in two basic heights: the shorter version for sedate breeds is a little over 20 inches (50 cm) high; the taller version is 42 inches (105 cm) high.

A controller (the device transmitting electrical energy to the fence) that plugs in will give the fence more zap, especially when fast-growing weeds drain its power, but out in a field you can use a battery-operated energizer of the sort sold to control grazing livestock or to protect gardens. A lightweight net fence with a battery-powered controller lets you easily move the fence each time you move the shelter.

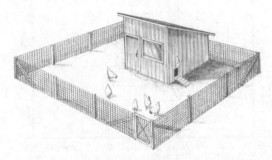

The ideal chicken fence is made from tightly strung, small-mesh woven wire. Yard-and-garden fencing, with 1-inch (2.5 cm) spaces at the bottom that graduate to wider spaces toward the top (thus using less wire to keep the cost down), makes a good secure fence for the coop. The smaller openings at the bottom keep small chickens from slipping out and small predators from slipping in.

For full construction details on electric fencing in general, consult a comprehensive book such as *Fences for Pasture & Garden*.

Although chickens aren't as susceptible to getting zapped as other livestock because of their small feet and protective feathers, they do learn to respect an electric fence. But first they have to know their home territory. Whenever you move chickens to a new coop, confine them inside for at least a day. When you let them into the yard, they won't stray far from home.

Raising Ducks

John M. Vivian

crown
ear
nostril
nail
flight feathers
sex feathers (in drakes)
wing speculum
abdomen
thigh coverts
shank
keel
breast

Raising Ducks

THE KINDS OF DUCKS

There are dozens of species of wild duck, divided mainly into two groups: freshwater or pond ducks and the saltwater varieties. No saltwater duck I know of has been domesticated.

Practically all tame ducks have been bred from the wild Mallard. The male has green head feathers, a white ring around his throat, and variegated plumage in general. The female shares the patterns but not the bright coloration.

Mallards nest from the Arctic Circle to the middle latitudes all around the world. Winters are spent as far south as Borneo and just about anywhere else that the birds can find open water and plenty of food, which in the wild consists of pond weeds and such small aquatic creatures as snails and mosquito larvae.

The other wild ancestor of domestic duck stock is the Central American *Pato*, the Spanish word for duck. From this breed have been developed several color variants of Muscovy ducks—accent on the "Mus." (The name has nothing to do with Moscow, but is a slightly mauled pronunciation of Musk duck.) Muscovies look to be something of a cross between a duck and a goose, and they can get pretty large—the male (or *drake*) often topping ten pounds, the lady (or *duck*) weighing some eight pounds.

Muscovies don't quack, but have a goose-like hiss. (Duck raisers tend to fall into two categories: those who like Muscovies, and those who

don't.) The birds' faces are bare of feathers and covered with red bumps called caruncles, the same sort of protuberances as a chicken's or turkey's comb or wattles, but all over.

Muscovies are relatively slow growers, and unless they are kept tame they can be mean as all blazes. The flesh is perhaps the tastiest of all domestic ducks, if you enjoy the slightly wild, gamy flavor. However, unless you are into breeding your own and hatching the eggs, young ducklings of the species are too expensive to consider raising to eat. The last time I looked, a trio (drake and two ducks) of premium quality cost up to $50 or more, placing them (in our opinion) as fancy fowl, kept mainly for fun and show.

Among the Mallard-based breeds, by far the most common in commercial North American production is the White Pekin—originally developed in Asia, as the name would lead you to believe. Both sexes are all white unless you feed them a lot of corn, in which case the plumage can yellow a bit but does no harm. A British-developed variation is the White Aylesbury.

Perhaps the fastest-growing duck, particularly if its water intake is restricted, the Pekin supplies those five-pound "Long Island ducklings," which weigh about eight pounds live but come equipped with about three pounds of feet, feathers, and other discards. They reach "green duck" slaughter weight in less than two months from hatching.

Our favorite species is the Rouen (or domestic Mallard). Its mature weight is the same as the Pekin—perhaps nine pounds for the drake, eight for the duck. The major advantage from our perspective is that the Rouens, developed in France, share more or less the same sex-differentiating coloration with their wild ancestors, though they are almost three times the size. The color lets you avoid the sex-identification process, necessary when it's time to select young birds for slaughter or breeding.

The breeding flock usually consists of one male to each half dozen or so females. If you are new at bird sexing, you may end up as we did our first year (using the recommended Pekins) with an all-male "breeding" flock. No eggs.

So, for ducks we'll stick with Rouens, for the color difference and also—though they grow a bit more slowly than Pekins—because the flesh is a bit more highly flavored. Their colored feathers make good trout flies and streamers, too.

Now, there are plenty of other breeds of ducks to choose from. The Indian Runners (developed in India from Mallards by all reports) are scrawny little things, but the hens are prodigious egg layers. Khaki

Continued →

Campbells are another laying breed. Indeed, the two are called "The Leghorns of Duckdom" after the small but highly productive chicken breed, Leghorn.

SHELTERS

For chilly nights, and particularly if you intend to winter over a breeding flock, you'll need a house or other shelter providing at least four square feet of floor space per bird. With the large, well-feathered breeds it's not the cold that is a problem, but drafts. Also, since ducks really don't sleep much at night, it's best to be able to shut up the shelter completely. Instinct makes them nervous to begin with—even more so during the night hours when a potential enemy can't be easily seen—so it's best to shut them in. During warm seasons we use shutters on screened windows so air can move out for proper ventilation, yet such duck irritants as moonlight or passing bat shadows won't upset the flock.

There are a few breeds that need special winter quarters in the North, but these are largely the fancy fowl that will require more care than is needed for meat birds. In the South, be especially sure that plenty of water is available at all times, and provide shade for midday and a well-ventilated shelter at night.

Anywhere, make the duck house as rodent- and predator-proof as you can. Rats in particular will clean out an entire season's hatch of ducklings in a night. Raccoons and skunks will take ducks of all ages, as will weasels and ferrets—a danger if you live well out in the country.

So make sure the foundation, bottom boards, door, and windows of the shelter are sound. If you have a fenced yard, bury a good foot of the poultry netting or wire fencing about six inches deep and angling out from the pen. It will stop critters that try to dig in. If you are keeping ducks in a small space, it's also best to put netting over the top of the outside run. This will keep the occasionally venturesome bird from flying out, and also will keep potentially disease-bearing wild birds from flying in to share the ducks' feed.

SANITATION

Now ducks are watery creatures from stem to stern. They need to splash those heads around for one thing. For another, their droppings aren't droppings at all, but great watery splotches that are produced all too frequently for them to be kept in most housing suitable for chickens. Some few wild ducks tuck their flat feet up under their wings at night, but not our meat birds. On a cold night they can become frozen in their own messes, since unlike chickens and pheasants most ducks spend nights on the ground, if they don't have open water. The relatively few tree ducks, such as our native Wood duck, the Mandarins, and some others, are too small to be suitable for meat raising.

The illustrations here will give you a few good ways to keep ducks with minimum bother in a restricted space. Remember, for a large flock you'll almost certainly need a pond or plenty of grazing land. For warm climates and summer in the North, the best foundation for both shelter and fenced run is a six-inch to foot-deep layer of well-drained pea gravel, used with a high-pressure hose. A daily hosing will force the mess down into the gravel, and a weekly raking will get up the loose feathers and blown-in leaves or sticks.

WATERERS

We found that for watering the flock a length of old metal storm gutter was sufficient. The birds couldn't submerge their entire heads, but they learned quickly to dip in one side and then the other, and it was deep and wide enough so they could get their whole bills in to drink. Someday I plan to install a permanent, in-place water supply. But now we just run a length of hose to the trough and let it trickle slowly on warm days. The outflow goes to the compost heap.

In the winter, the daily bucket of warm water still works best for the trio of breeders overwintered with the chickens. The loose, foot-deep layer of litter inside the hen house absorbs the duck mess, as the chickens "till it in" along with their own droppings during their daily scratching.

FEED

The natural diet of ducks consists of about 90% vegetable matter and 10% animal matter (such as insects, slugs, worms, and fish). On the farm, dry food for our overwintered ducks was the same layer mash the chickens got. We ground it ourselves, primarily of field corn mixed in with buckwheat or other small grains. Using short-season corn, a spare third of an acre planting provided us about a dozen 100-pound sacks of corn (shelled). We ground it—cob, much husk, and all—figuring the roughage wouldn't hurt either kind of bird. Supplements were a daily feeding of table scraps—meat, bone meal, fish meal, and fat in particular—to increase protein intake as well as fruits, vegetables, nuts, and seeds. The chickens could peck the supplement out of a mesh onion sack hung in the pen. Duck bills aren't designed for pecking, so their share was offered, chopped, in a heavy ceramic bowl.

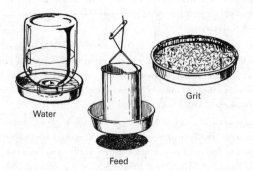

Water

Feed

Grit

Now that we've moved to town for the kids' school years, the animal population is reduced to a few rabbits, a small laying flock of hens, and the ducks that we raise from eggs, then slaughter at two to three months of age. (After six months they get a bit tough.)

Here we feed our birds cracked corn (cheaper to buy than any prepared poultry mash or pellets), plus the household scraps. Many people will need to purchase all their feeds, and some feed companies mix special waterfowl formulas. Some experts recommend more complicated feeding programs, particularly when egg production is a consideration. Perhaps your birds will do better on them. All I can say is that our corn and table scraps, supplemented with much garden residue such as carrot tops, have produced some fine duck dinners.

Ducks need grit, too. Lacking teeth, they grind the feed in their gizzards. So a container of hen-sized crushed rock and another of crushed oyster shells—mainly to supply calcium to the hens—is kept in the run. The water, feed, and grit containers are illustrated.

STARTING YOUR DUCKS

The easiest way to begin with ducks is to buy a batch of day-old ducklings. Perhaps you can get some from a local duck fancier, but more likely you will purchase them from a specialty catalog or a feed store. Our local feed store sells Rouens and Pekins for around $2.00 to $3.00 per duckling. We think that's a little high, so we buy fertile eggs from a near by farm. Some wildfowl order houses sell these too, but they can be hard to find in some areas and usually cost at least $1.00 each.

INCUBATING DUCK EGGS

You'll need an incubator—and the Sears catalog, your feed store, or the specialty houses all sell good ones—but make sure yours has holders for duck eggs, which are larger than chicken eggs.

Before the eggs arrive, set up the incubator. There will be a water pan; fill it and put a small piece of sponge in so that it protrudes a couple of inches (waterfowl eggs need more humidity than chicken eggs.) Set the temperature control at 95°F, and check it carefully with a fever thermometer. The exact temperatures recommended are 99°F. to 100°F. for a forced-air machine, and 101°F. to 102°F. for a still-air machine.

The eggs will likely be pretty dirty, but do not wash them. The mother puts on a coating that helps keep internal conditions right and keeps bacteria out. Any soil that is dry, just flick off with a thumbnail. Put the eggs in the incubator, keep the water and sponge well supplied, turn the eggs twice a day, and at each turning spray them lightly with warm water. On the 25th day, discontinue turnings but continue sprinkling water when the eggs commence to pip.

You can make a candler per the illustration. In just a few days you should be able to see the developing embryo. In a couple of weeks the good (fertile) eggs will be dark nearly throughout. Any that stay clear, letting light through, should be discarded.

The ducklings will begin pipping four weeks to the day from commencement of incubation. You may want to dip each egg in warm water once the first little egg tooth appears, for this will facilitate hatching. There is some disagreement about helping the young ducks from the eggs. If you pull them out too soon, they may die from hemorrhaging, since the umbilical that was attached to the egg's internal membranes won't have sealed itself. Also, we've found that with any species of bird, the youngsters that lack strength to hatch out unaided prove to be unthrifty, and often are deformed and unviable. Let nature take her course.

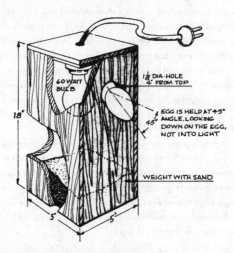

BROODING THE DUCKLINGS

We leave the young ducklings in the incubator until each is fully dry and walking around actively. Then, as each is ready, it goes into the brooder. This is a good-sized box, providing a square foot of floor space for each duckling. Hanging over the middle is an infrared brooder bulb encased in a metal hood.

A layer of absorbent litter several inches thick goes on the bottom. Crushed corncobs are good. Sand is OK but needs frequent stirring. We've used shredded leaves, which work well with a good daily stirring. Ducklings won't scratch and forage as much as chickens do, and you might find the absorbent stuff used in cat boxes will work, so long as the ducks don't eat too much of it. Don't get any with dye, deodorizer, or other potentially harmful additives in it.

Even the smallest ducks will spatter their food and water all around, so plan to change the litter frequently. It is most important that the young ducks be kept dry—thus unchilled—until they are well fledged and have their waterproof suits of feathers on and well buttoned up.

So we provide them with water in a shallow pan with a rock in the center. We move its location at each refilling—as many as a dozen times a day—and make sure the litter under the water pan is well stirred to keep dry. Feed is provided the same way, and at first includes a coarse, crumbled feed or moistened meal. We feed all that they seem to want three times a day.

The third day you can raise the brooder light so the floor temperature is 90°F. The birds will let you know if they are getting the heat they need; if it is too warm for them, they'll run off to the corners of the box. If it is too cold, they will cluster under the lamp. Keep it at

Continued ➜

90°F. until the eleventh or twelfth day, then lower it to 80°F. By now the ducklings will have lost much of their fuzzy cuteness and will be sprouting feathers. At three weeks each bird will weigh almost three pounds—if you've provided it the almost five pounds of feed it should have had—and now it will need more space. Put the birds into a pen with the brooder at 75°F. Then, at four weeks, you can turn it off and let them out into the grass, so long as temperatures are moderate.

FEED FOR YOUNG DUCKS

To encourage maximum growth, ducklings need a diet that provides 20 to 22 percent protein for the first two weeks and 16 to 18 percent from two to twelve weeks. Commercial feed mixtures are available specifically for ducks and geese. If specialized food is not available, they can be fed chick starter (formulated for chickens). However, this is not always advisable because it contains medications for coccidiosis, which is common in chickens but rare in ducks.

For the first several weeks, small pelleted 3/32" or coarse crumbled feed is preferred. From then on, larger pellets 3/16" will give good results. Ducklings choke on fine, powdery mash when fed dry, and up to 25 percent of the feed may be wasted. If used, finely ground feed should be moistened with water or milk to a consistency that will form a crumbly ball when compressed in your hand. A new batch should be mixed at each feeding to avoid spoilage and food poisoning.

During the first two weeks, ducklings should be allowed to eat all the feed they want. From then on, you can limit them to two or three feedings daily. After a month, ducklings can be given one meal in the evening and encouraged to forage in a succulent pasture throughout the day. They should always have access to grit, which aids their digestion.

CONTROLLING THE DUCKS

Many duck keepers render their Mallards, Calls, and Muscovies flightless so they can't get away and also are easier to catch. One way is to snip off the final little joint of one wing when the birds are little. Or you can cut or pull the flight feathers. But we've found no need for this.

Ducks aren't your smartest barnyard creatures, but they can be trained to come when called. Start them young. Use a whistle or duck call, scattering grain or a good supply of succulent greens when they come quacking down. Do this to lure them into the pen in the evening, too.

THE BREEDING DUCK FLOCK

For breeding you should select your largest ducks, but keep the smallest, most active drakes, particularly if you lack a pond. Ducks normally mate on the water, though the smaller breeds can get it done on land. However, a big, 10-pound Rouen is often too heavy to do his job on land. There are all sorts of rules of body and plumage conformation for show breeds, but for meat always pick the biggest ducks (and without a pond small drakes).

Beginning in the spring, each duck will lay 100 to perhaps twice that number of eggs, one a day or so, usually in the early to mid-morning. Shallow, four-foot square nest boxes, filled with straw and placed in the corners of the house, seem to attract most of the ducks. Then let them out to forage for the day and collect the eggs. The females keep producing all spring.

The big meat breeds, the Pekins in particular, are notoriously poor mothers, and if left on their own devices will lay nests full of eggs all over the place and eventually abandon them.

We collect a dozen eggs as they are produced, keeping them at 50°F.-60°F. and turning and spraying, but we do not put them at the high incubating temperature until we have the incubator full. (The eggs will stay alive and ready for incubating for a week at least—probably longer.)

Extra eggs are sold or used in cooking. When the excess becomes too great, we divide each, add a good shake of salt to each yolk, a pinch of cornstarch to each white, stir briefly, and freeze for future cakes and such The salt and starch keep the eggs' consistency more or less unaffected by freezing.

I've heard that ducks will continue to produce eggs from their second spring and on for ages, though the males run out of steam in two or three years. We generally replace the whole flock every year, keeping the best of the newest hatch to breed. As with any strain of livestock, it's best to keep inbreeding to a minimum. We just trade a batch of eggs with another duck fancier every so often.

CULLING THE FLOCK

Culling out the poor producers is less of a problem with ducks than with chickens. Occasionally one may develop a heavy, drooping wing, and it just gets slaughtered early. Ducks penned in sanitary quarters or allowed to forage over sufficient land seldom develop problems.

Slaughtering and Dressing Ducks

Commercial duckling producers hang the birds up on assembly lines, remove most feathers with revolving drums covered with rubber fingers, then coat the whole birds with wax that's removed along with pinfeathers. We don't get quite so elaborate and have found that doing six birds in two three-bird batches is an easy early evening chore.

First, a big old canner is two-thirds filled with water and brought to a boil on the wood stove. (We always wait until after a bug-killing frost to slaughter livestock, so that the weather's gotten chilly enough that the stoves have been put to work again.)

Then I catch three ducks by their necks, hang each to a convenient tree limb by both its feet, and cut the throat just behind the bill. Once the birds are bled, they are dunked one at a time in the now not quite boiling water and are swished around hard. The heat cooks the muscles, causing the feather follicles to release the feathers.

The pinions (flight feathers on wings and tail) are the first to come out, and then the rest. If the hot water bath has been long enough, they come off practically in sheets. If you have the time and patience, remove the outer layer of feathers first. Then remove, wash, and save the soft underlayer of down. Use it in pillows or sell it. Well-washed down brings a few dollars a pound, though it takes a lot of ducks to make a pound of down.

To dress a duck you can go through the bother of opening it up and cleaning it whole. We split ours. First, head and neck end are chopped off. The legs are bent so you can see the joint, and the feet are removed. It takes practice, but there are two ligaments alongside the joint that can be cut, and the feet twist right off.

Then the oil gland—the little pointed thing at the base of the tail—is removed. Be sure to get all the yellow, oil-producing tissue.

Next I cut the skin around the vent in a funnel shape, to avoid the gut. With a good pair of poultry shears, I cut up the duck's back, and it will open up like a book. You'll recognize the heart, liver, and gizzard. Remove the green bile sack from the liver, the tubes from the heart, and split the gizzard. Discard the contents and the tough muscular liner, which peels off easily once you've a good start on it.

Everything else, including tubes and attachments up along the neck, go out. I remove the neck, wing tips, and tail and add them to the giblets to boil up for gravy. Then, with giblets etc. inside, the bird is closed up, using fat flaps . . . close up the ends. All is frozen in a double thickness of freezer paper and kept at 0°F. until we want roast duck. Incidentally, duck freezes and keeps its quality better than chicken.

DUCK DINNER

The secret to roasting a duck is to thaw it slowly in the refrigerator the day before you want to serve it. Remove the bird from the refrigerator the next morning and let it warm to room temperature as you simmer the giblets. Dry it well inside and out several times, so that by roasting time the skin is as dry as it can get. Then go over the fatty parts with a fork (or one of those old multi-spiked ice crushers is good) to pierce the skin so most of the fat will render out.

Cook the bird at 425°F. for 15 minutes, then at 325°F. for 20 to 35 minutes, depending on its size and age. Baste frequently with fresh-squeezed orange juice and rendered fat—but don't begin this until the skin is turning a golden brown.

The affinity of duck and oranges has been known for centuries. For the classic of French cooking, *Canard a l'Orange*, baste with a cup of the best white wine you can afford. When the bird is done, remove it to stay warm, pour off the fat (save it), and add the giblet stock, reduced to one cup. Then add the juice of four fresh oranges (and—optional—one small lemon and a shot of brandy if you like). Make a sweet/sour caramel by melting one tablespoon of sugar in an equal amount of vinegar, then combine all the ingredients and scrape all the good stuff up off the pan bottom.

We like to get out the poultry shears and simply quarter or halve the duck, pour sauce over, and serve with wild or brown rice, a light salad, and a white or rosé wine. If you've the time, you can slice the breast meat, divide drumsticks and thighs, getting as much skin on each piece as possible, and thus serve it a bit more elegantly. But so long as you get the bird dry and render out most of the fat in cooking, that crispy skin and dark, flavorful meat will be a culinary delight, no matter how you cut it.

White Muscovies

Raising Game Birds

Mavis and Monty Harper

Illustrations by Cindy McFarland

There are nearly as many reasons for raising game birds as there are birds. For our family it is their unique beauty, and the fun of raising them; they also provide our table with delicious, inexpensive meals. To many, raising game birds is educational and challenging, to some therapeutic, to others profitable.

No matter which birds you choose, there are some basic rules to follow. Start small enough to enjoy your project, allowing time to study good management ideas and to think about future plans. Remember that the birds are completely dependent on you, and success or failure depends on your management. There is no such thing as luck in game bird rearing: You make it happen.

PURCHASE CHICKS

If you are just beginning, you'll want to purchase chicks rather than breeding stock. The number depends somewhat on the species, but we think 25 chicks is a good workable number. By the time they're at the breeding age you will know whether you want to expand in that area. That, of course, will make greater demands on your time.

Whether you start with day-old chicks or breeders, and no matter how small your flock, purchase only from reputable suppliers. Check for birds that look healthy and vigorous.

Breeders should be young and fully feathered with good body weight. Chicks should appear alert. Bargain hunting is rarely worthwhile—sick chicks die or grow into poor breeders.

To get a list of reputable suppliers of game bird chicks and breeders, write to the U.S. Department of Agriculture, Science and Education Administration, Beltsville, Maryland 20705, requesting the *National Poultry Improvement Plan Directory of Participants Handling Waterfowl, Exhibition Poultry, and Game Birds*.

If you join the North American Game Bird Association, PO Box 218, Elgin, South Carolina 29045, you will receive a subscription to *Wildlife Harvest Magazine*. This magazine has a listing of places that buy and sell birds and equipment. Your state Cooperative Extension Service can also supply names and addresses of other sources of information and supplies.

Varieties of Birds

If you've decided to try raising game birds, and have a small area for this, your next step is to decide which birds to raise. Let's look at some of them.

BOBWHITE QUAIL (NORTH AMERICAN)

A 9- to 10-inch bird, it has beautifully mottled brown or chestnut plumage. Males have a white eye-stripe and brown throat underscored with black; females have a buff line through the eye and a buff throat.

Bobwhite quail

Bobwhites are monogamous, mature at 16–20 weeks, and start laying at 24 weeks. One hen will lay 50–100 eggs during the mating season, or up to 200 eggs per year if light is provided 17 hours a day.

Continued ➜

Mature birds weigh live at 7.5–8.2 ounces; dressed at 6.2–6.4 ounces. Birds are plump-breasted with lighter meat than the coturnix. A serving is 1 1/2–2 birds.

CHUKAR PARTRIDGE

This native of India is a stout, grey bird with light, silky, smooth feathers on its head and a distinctive black band passing across its eyes, circling the face, and ending at a V at the throat. It has orange feet and a beak that grows so fast that the bird must be debeaked regularly. Birds are 12–14 inches long, with broad chestnut bars on the flank. While markings are the same for males and females, the males are slightly larger.

Chukar partridge

These birds are polygamous. They reach maturity at 26–28 weeks. Birds begin laying following the first mating season after hatch unless forced by means of artificial light. Young birds are very susceptible to stress and must be handled carefully. Until they are nearly mature, the birds must be provided warmth on cool nights. Stress may be caused by changing pens or feed, or even a change in the feeding pattern. Chukar are best left in one pen until maturity, at which time they are more hardy.

Mature birds weigh about 1/4 pounds. A serving is 3/4 to one bird.

COTURNIX (PHARAOH) QUAIL

Originally from Japan, this 7- to 8-inch bird has a brown and black coloring, with contrasting white and buff. Males have a reddish tint on the breast, while hens have a grey-mottled breast. They start laying at 6–7 weeks, and reach maturity at 10 weeks. These birds will give you a good return on your time, money, and effort invested; they are excellent breeders and layers, are hardy, and are good meat producers. Dressed weight at maturity is 4–4.4 ounces. A serving is two birds.

Coturnix quail

GUINEA FOWL

Although not considered game birds, guinea fowl are often used as a substitute, and are becoming increasingly popular. While the head is small and rather homely, the body of one breed has pleasing polka-dot plumage. Originally from Africa, the guinea is a shy, flighty, nervous bird, and should be provided with brush, limbs, or hay, and with as much privacy and security for the nests as can be managed. This bird thrives in a woodsy, natural setting as close to its natural state as possible. It loves to perch high in trees, and shrieks loudly when frightened.

Guinea fowl

The mature market weight is 2 1/2–3 1/2 pounds, and the rich, dark meat may be prepared like any game bird's. Serving is 1/4 to 1/3 bird.

Chinese ring-necked pheasant

PHEASANT (CHINESE RINGNECK)

This bird will add beauty to your home. The adult males are brightly colored with golden red, purple, and yellow hues standing out in a varied color scheme distinguished by the iridescent greenish-blue heads, the white rings around their necks, and the striped, 15-inch tails. The hens are light brown, chunky, and drab by comparison. A scarlet area of bare skin surrounds the eye of the cock, and a set of erect blue-black feathers on the side of the head gives him a horned appearance during the mating season.

Pheasants are polygamous; avoid having more than one cock per pen. The birds mature in 26–28 weeks. They begin laying at 7–8 months or following the mating season, unless brought into production earlier by artificial lighting. The adolescent birds are stressed easily and are very cannibalistic. They have sharp, strong beaks and use them on each other. Debeaking and antipick lotion help to prevent this. Giving young birds additional picking food, such as apples, green vegetables, and grain, also helps to draw their attention away from each other. Mature birds dress out at 2 1/2–3 1/4 pounds. A serving is 1/2 bird.

Pigeons and Doves

PIGEONS AND DOVES

Pigeons and doves are very closely related, both being members of the pigeon family *(Columbidae)*. Doves are smaller than pigeons and more delicate in flavor. Pigeons vary widely in size, weight, and color. Both are monogamous and enjoy worldwide distribution.

The nestlings are called squabs, and are fed pigeon milk, a substance rich in protein and fat which is secreted by the lining of the parents' crop and pumped into the mouth of the young by the parents.

Pigeons may be raised in cages in pairs by hanging a nest on the wire inside the pen, or in ground pens. We find that our pigeons do remarkably well by themselves. We let them handle their own marital and family affairs. We simply lend them the use of the barn loft. They raise about five hatchlings a year, with two or three eggs at each clutch. We scatter some grain on the ground; they pick up the spilled feed from other pens and forage the rest. Serving: one pigeon or 1–2 doves.

Housing and Equipment

The two types of housing suitable for game birds are pens built off the ground with a hardware cloth floor (sturdy 1/2-inch mesh) and pens built on the ground with a dirt floor. As you'll see, you must consider sanitation, ease of handling, species of bird, whether they are breeders, whether they are paired off or colony bred, whether they are raised for meat or for breeders, or whether the birds are going to be flight-conditioned for hunting preserves—all of these influence your selection of pens.

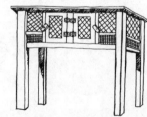

The 2 x 2 x 8-foot pen can be divided into two colony pens, each 2 x 2 x 4 feet, or eight breeder cages, each 2 x 2 x 1 foot.

OFF-GROUND PENS

Our most workable pens are 2 x 2 x 8 feet, and have wire floors. Some are relatively portable, with 40-inch legs; some are permanently attached to posts driven into the ground. They're high enough to protect the birds from predators, especially dogs. The cage door is in the 2 x 8 front wall; the pen slopes back to the 1 1/2-foot wall.

If the pens are out in the open, a 3 x 9-foot wood or metal roof which slopes from front to back is all that is needed.

This size pen provides comfortable housing for about 50 quail, or 30–35 chukar, or 20–30 guinea fowl or pheasants. When the birds reach maturity, we cull and slaughter them, and remove the remaining birds to the ground breeding pens.

PARTITIONING

These pens also work well with a partition dividing them into two 2 x 2 x 4-foot colony breeding pens that can house 20–25 quail or 16 chukar each. Or they can be partitioned into eight 2 x 2 x 1-foot cages for individual pairs or three quail (one male, two female) or chukars.

We find that housing a smaller number of birds in the colony breeding pens reduces cock fights. The birds are also easier to observe, which enables us to pick out the nonproductive or disruptive birds. This, in turn, increases the number of hatchable eggs.

Use 2 x 4's of the frame and legs, strong hardware cloth for the floor, and either hardware cloth or small chicken wire for the sides and top. If the pen is outside, you should plan on a 3 x 9-foot wood or metal roof.

Wire-floored pens are far more sanitary, since the droppings fall through the wire, away from the birds, and can be raked up. The ground can be sprayed with a fly and odor control, thus limiting exposure to bacteria that cause diseases.

GROUND PENS

We use ground pens for mature, larger species, such as guinea fowl and pheasants. Ground pens can provide a natural setting, with shrubs, trees, or brush, if you want to entice the birds to nest. You can also provide more than a day's supply of food and water in such pens. You will need to cover the top with chicken wire. Dimensions of this type can vary according to your needs, but it should be at least six feet high and have a sturdy entrance, so that you can enter it and work there.

We have 6 x 12-foot ground pens built under the loft of our barn where they get the morning sun. Chicken wire covers the sturdy wooden frame of each and extends down into the ground to keep out rodents and other wild creatures. The chicken wire is attached to the beams above, and forms a ceiling, so there are no gaps through which the birds can escape or wild birds can get in, bringing disease. The wire is nailed to thick, wide boards around the pens to discourage dogs.

A ground pen, covered only by chicken wire, should have a south-facing shelter to protect the birds from rain and the summer sun. A portion of this shelter should have solid walls to provide extra protection from winter cold and wind; in cold climates a house with a small entrance should be provided.

Invest in locks for your pens: They will attract friends and children who will want to step inside, not realizing how many diseases they may bring to your flock, or not remembering to close the door after entering or leaving.

The ground in the pen should be raked daily; droppings can spread disease.

WATERERS

When starting, buy an inexpensive waterer that the small birds can't drown themselves in. While automatic waterers can't be beat for convenience, they are neither feasible nor necessary for just a few pens. We use automatic waterers for the larger pens, and screw-on plastic waterers with plastic gallon jugs for the smaller pens with fewer birds. In the brooders and for young quail we use game bird waterers. Automatic waterers cost from $10 to $30; the others cost considerably less.

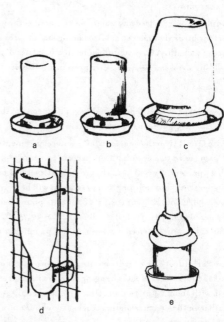

Types of waterers. From left: (a) plastic chick waterer, (b) combination chick/adult jug waterer, (c) screw-on gallon jug waterer for adults, (d) pop-bottle waterer attached to side of pen, (e) automatic waterer.

FEEDERS

Feeders do one job—they dispense feed. For adult birds, any feeder is fine if it minimizes waste feed and keeps droppings out of the feed. We prefer the regular game bird feeders with the enclosed hopper and narrow feed gate for birds of all ages. They cost about $7, and they'll pay for themselves by cutting down the amount of feed wasted. We also use the cheaper (about $5) 36-inch reel feeder troughs. These do waste more feed. Hanging feeders can be suspended off the ground, under a shelter in a ground pen. If these are used, the birds won't scratch feed onto the ground or dirt into the feed.

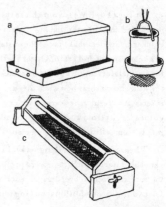

Types of feeders. From left: (a) game chick feeder 12 1/4 inches long and 6 inches wide. This type may also be used for adult birds. (b) hanging 12-quart tube-type feeder, c) 36-inch reel feeder.

Continued →

GETTING READY

In the location and construction of your pens, and the purchase of equipment, you should be concerned with sanitation, good nutrition, and the prevention of stress. Before your chicks or breeders arrive, the pens and equipment should be cleaned. The new birds should be isolated from noises and disturbances, and given time to adjust to their new surroundings. The birds shouldn't be handled until they've adapted to the pens, and they shouldn't be overcrowded. Do not mix species or age groups.

Provide plenty of fresh feed and water. No matter what the weather is, if you feel the birds are under stress from being moved, provide them with a source of warmth. A 60-watt bulb hung in one corner of the pen will do. Avoiding stress is a big step toward preventing diseases.

Feeding

The amount and type of food depend on the age and species of the birds. Here are some of the figures on the various game birds:

Bobwhite Quail (North American). Protein requirements are: 0–3 weeks, game-bird starter with 28–32 percent protein; 4–5 weeks, starter with 24 percent; 6 weeks to adult, grower mash with 18 percent; breeders, 19 percent. Feed consumption to 14 weeks will be approximately 3 1/2 pounds. Our cost, at $8 for a 50-pound bag of food, is 54¢ per bird. Birds of this size sell for $2.50–$2.75. Breeders will eat about 8 3/4 ounces of feed per week, or 7–8 pounds per day for 100 birds.

Chukar Partridge. These birds require a high-protein game bird starter until about 12 weeks of age, changing then to a high-protein grower mash with about 24 percent protein. Breeders should get a breeder mash with 18 percent protein. They eat about 8 1/2 ounces of feed per bird per week.

The estimated consumption of feed from hatch to 14 weeks is 4 1/2– 5 pounds, or 80¢ worth of feed. At that age the bird will consume about 6.5 ounces of feed per week, gradually increasing to about 8–9 ounces per week. Thus you will spend another $1 per bird to raise them to maturity. The price for mature chukar in our area of Georgia ranges from $15 to $17 a pair. Feed grain, apples, and green vegetables to birds over six weeks of age. It prevents picking and cannibalism.

Coturnix (Pharaoh) Quail. Protein requirements are: 0–3 weeks, game bird starter with 28–32 percent protein; 6 weeks–adult, grower mash with 17 percent protein; breeders, breeding mash with 16– 20 percent protein. A breeder will eat about nine ounces of feed per week. Cost to raise to maturity 10 weeks) is 40¢. Retail price of birds is $1.50–$2.

Guinea Fowl. We fed our chicks (keets) game bird starter, *never* medicated chick starter. Laying birds are fed the same rations as laying chickens. Guineas make use of the waste produce from the garden as well as kitchen scraps and grain. Oyster shells and limestone grit are needed for eggshell formation and digestion. Guinea fowl are natural foragers in the wild and do their best when they are allowed to range freely, eating insects. As a result, these are very inexpensive birds to raise. A mature guinea weighs from 2 1/2 to 3 1/2 pounds and sells for $4 to $6. We have no problem selling the keets and mature guineas we raise.

Pheasant (Chinese Ringneck). Protein requirements: 0–6 weeks, game bird starter with 32 percent protein; 7–12 weeks, grower with 20– 24 percent protein; breeders, breeder mash with 16–22 percent protein. Give young birds additional picking food, such as apples, green

vegetables, and grain, to draw their attention away from each other. One bird will eat about 5 1/2 pounds of fed from hatch to 14 weeks, at a cost of about 88¢. The bird will have another 12–14 weeks to go before reaching maturity, and feed to that time will cost an additional 95¢. After maturity the average feed consumption will be 12–14 ounces per week. Mature birds in this area sell for $18 to $22 a pair.

Pigeons and Doves. Since these birds forage for themselves at our farm, eating insects plus spilled feed from under the pens, and are given only an occasional scattering of grain or a tray of grower mash, their feed costs are very low. Pigeons sell for $1.50 to $6, depending on the supplier, breed of pigeon, and its color.

Managing the Breeder Flock

All recommended requirements are meant as suggestions only, based on experience and methods that have worked for us. Every grower of game birds has ideas about managing breeds. However, there are a few basic steps that should be taken, steps that indicate a strong commitment to sound management that will save time, money, and even loss of birds.

FLOOR, FEEDER, AND WATERER SPACE FOR BREEDERS

Species	Floor Sq. Ft./Bird	Feeder Inches/Bird	Waterer Inches/Bird
Coturnix Quail			
ground	2–3	1	0.5
colony	0.25	1	0.5
Bobwhite			
ground	3	1	0.5
breeder pen	0.75–1	1	0.5
breeder cage	0.75	1	0.5
Chukar			
ground	2–3	1.5	1
cage	1	1.5	1
Pheasant			
ground	15–20	2	1
Guinea Fowl			
ground	5–10	2	2

Guard against the impulse to keep, from your own stock, or to buy, more breeders than you have time or space to care for properly. We've found that it is important to assess the time we have to give before expanding our flock or extending our work load. Before we turn on our 17-hours-per-day lights and start our breeders working overtime, we sit down with pencil and paper and determine how many birds of a species we will need for our own use at a given time, based on how many birds we already have in the freezer and whether the chicks will be breaking out of their shells on the day the pole beans in the garden have to be canned. It is more rewarding to manage a small group of healthy birds that you have the time to care for properly than to watch a large group of inferior birds barely existing. Time and money spent on sick birds, weak chicks, breeders of low productivity, and eggs that don't hatch are time and money wasted.

FEED CAREFULLY

In general, we feed our potential breeders a 28–32 percent game bird starter through eight weeks, a 20 percent protein grower through 18 weeks, and then breeder mash with 18–20 percent protein one month before we start collecting eggs for incubation.

Keep a careful record of success and failure, and feed costs per bird. Accurate records will help you to plan future flocks.

Game birds, especially breeders, need plenty of space, food, and water. Properly designed pens and good equipment that minimizes waste are essential for good management. The wrong waterers get the birds wet, keep the pen damp, and leave the birds without water. Feed costs money, and wasted feed shows up on your management record. We put a piece of clean cardboard or large lid under the feeder to catch the spills, then replace the cardboard or wash the lid at each feeding. Our records show waste runs about 30 percent when our feeders are full, 7 percent with two-thirds full, 2 percent when half full, and 1 percent when one-third full.

Disease

Disease prevention and good management are synonymous. Game birds require a clean, dry, and disease-free environment. Good hygiene and sanitation will not assure your success, but without them you can expect failure. A dirty pen can't be disinfected. You must clean the pen first. Frequent attention to detailed cleaning will save you work and problems later on.

Here are a few tips for disease prevention that have been helpful to us:

- Clean and disinfect pens and equipment between broods. Maintain a rigid clean-up schedule, washing waterers with each refill and feed bins weekly.

- Check on the birds often to see that they have feed and water.

- Use wire flooring for breeders if possible, to keep droppings away from the birds and thus prevent problems with internal parasites and infectious disease.

- Don't introduce a new bird into an existing flock until you are sure it has no disease. After taking a bird to a fair, isolate it before returning it to the flock.

- Keep birds penned by age groups, and attend to the younger birds first each day. Older birds are a potential source of infection to younger birds.

- Make periodic checks for disruptions within the flock. Remove any sick birds and provide them with warmth.

- Don't make the birds the center of attention. Put the pens in a quiet place, away from noise, children, visitors, and animals.

- Keep down the mosquito population, the primary source of fowl pox infection.

- Check birds for external parasites such as mites and lice. A dusting pan of sand containing 10 percent insecticide usually takes care of this problem. Read directions carefully before using insecticides or drugs. Better yet, consult your local county extension agent about treatment, proper insecticides, and dosages.

If you have diseased birds, consult a reliable diagnostician, rather than guessing and treating. Your county farm agent can assist you with almost any problems caused by insects, rodents, and disease, or can direct you to a source of help.

DEBEAKING AND CANNIBALISM

Game birds have very sharp beaks that must be trimmed from time to time. Chukar, especially, grow long beaks that interfere with their ability to pick up feed. Pheasants have very strong and damaging beaks. Males should have a quarter of the top mandible clipped to prevent cannibalism and to keep them from harming the females during the mating season. Once started in a flock, cannibalism is hard to control.

If it becomes a problem, put a bushy limb or the top of a pine tree in the pen. This will distract the birds and give the victim a place to hide. Another basic step is to provide high-protein feed. Using antipick lotion and providing various fruits and vegetables, grain, and mineral blocks are also very helpful.

Excessive beak trimming can cut the productivity of the bird. For example, successful mating may be hindered if the male has a sore beak. Do the debeaking before the mating season. You may find, too, that egg production drops after debeaking, because the birds will not pick up as much feed with sore beaks.

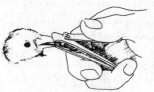

To debeak, clip off a quarter of the upper beak with debeaking clippers.

THE STRESS FACTOR

Stress plays an important role in a bird's susceptibility to disease, because it lowers the bird's body defenses.

The most common unnecessary stresses are overcrowding, inadequate feed, improper nutrients in the feed, random changing of feed, and excessive handling. Handling, debeaking, vaccinations, and moving birds from their accustomed pens are unavoidable stresses. They must be done carefully.

Culling, Sexing, and Turnover

We have a complete turnover of birds each year, choosing from among the younger birds for our new breeders. As we select our breeder stock, we save a few extra birds as a breeding reserve. This allows us to cull undesirables as they show up, while maintaining flock size. By butchering the older birds, culling, sexing, and saving the healthiest birds that are most uniform in color, size, and vigor, we continually improve our stock.

Wintering over a large flock of birds can be expensive. We usually save half as many breeders as we will need, then purchase unrelated eggs when we start up our incubators in early spring. By doing this we introduce unrelated stock, a practice we recommend at least every third year, to prevent inbreeding. If you use the same breeders for more than one season, the results usually are lower egg production and hatchability, weaker chicks, and less disease-resistant birds.

Breeders

MALE-FEMALE RATIOS FOR BREEDERS

Male-female ratios refer to how many hens one rooster can inseminate. In a colony pen of 30 coturnix partridges, 10 males require 20 females.

Continued ➔

Species	Male	Female
Bobwhite (pair or colony pen)	1	1
Coturnix (colony pen)	1	2
Pheasant (ground)	1	4–5
Chukar Partridge (colony pen)	1	3–4
Guinea Fowl (ground)	1	1–3

Pair off breeders or place them in colony pens about four to five weeks before you start collecting eggs. Feed them 18–22 percent breeder mash plus a free choice of egg shell, calcite grit, leafy greens, and some grain to supplement the mash. To stimulate egg and semen production, increase artificial light to 17 hours a day, and maintain temperatures of at least 60 degrees. More than 17 hours of light per day is unnecessary and may prove harmful.

We advise pair mating for bobwhite quail, and colony pens of 30 birds or less for most other species, as long as the correct male-female ratio is maintained (see table). By having a smaller number of birds in the pen, it's easy to spot those with poor performance and poor egg production.

The best method of checking mating ratio and performance is to determine whether the birds are congenial and the eggs are fertile. The fertility of eggs may be determined after the first seven days of incubation by candling them. This process is described below. If you find clear (infertile) eggs, you may want to change the male-female ratio or replace some birds. Too many males can be a problem, since some will interfere with those trying to mate. If you find disruptive or inactive males, replace them from among your reserve of breeders.

Check often on the health of your breeders. Be sure the pens are free of sharp wire, droppings, or a buildup of moldy feed. Make sure the birds have enough feed and water.

If you will be selling your birds, have pulloroum—typhoid tests administered to the breeders. The state Cooperative Extension Service will tell you a laboratory that does these tests. This is a free service to the poultry and game bird industry. The laboratories are staffed by veterinarians who will also treat your sick birds at no charge.

INCUBATION

Begin storing eggs for incubation after the hens have been laying for 3–4 weeks. This wait insures larger, more uniform, and better developed eggs with higher fertility rates. Store eggs for seven days, then mark the date on them and place them in the incubator. If your incubator allows continual incubation, a new batch of eggs may be added every seven days thereafter.

STORING EGGS BEFORE INCUBATION

Egg care is essential. Follow these directions:

- Gather eggs twice daily. Don't incubate eggs that have been exposed to high or low temperatures, are cracked, oversized, weak-shelled, odd-shaped, or extremely dirty. Washing an egg removes the natural protective covering, so try pickling eggs unsuitable for incubation.

- Store eggs, with the small end pointing down, in egg cartons from which you have snipped the bottoms. This lets air circulate around the eggs. You can purchase papier mâché hatching trays for quail, chukar, or regular chicken eggs for a few cents each. These trays save time you would spend turning the eggs, since all you have to do is tilt the eggs morning and evening at a 45 degree angle. This prevents the yolks from sticking to the shell membrane while they are stored.

- Eggs should be stored no longer than seven days at a moist (75 percent relative humidity) 35 degrees F—never in an air-conditioned room. An egg is mostly water and will be useless if the moisture is removed.

INCUBATORS

The two main types of incubators are still air and circulated air. There are several makes and models of each.

Still-air incubators are usually round, metal, or thermal plastic, with a moisture circle or moisture pan in the bottom under the wire mesh floor that holds the eggs. Still-air incubators come in sizes that hatch 50–150 quail eggs, or fewer if the eggs are from a larger bird. Prices range from $40 to $150. We find these little incubators do a marvelous job.

Circulated-air incubators are equipped with electric turners that turn the eggs automatically every two hours. Some have manual or mechanical turners with the crank on the outside to turn the egg trays. The trays hold the papier mâché egg cartons and tilt the eggs at a 45-degree angle at each turn. With the automatic turner you don't have to be home at a certain time to turn the eggs. We think that is worth the extra money. Some models come with a separate hatching tray.

We have both types of incubators and get excellent results. We find that all work well if you follow the manufacturer's instructions to the letter. A mechanical turning incubator costs about $185; an incubator with the automatic electric turner costs about $230; a hatching incubator costs about $175. Humidaire incubators are the Cadillacs of incubators, expensive but very good.

For continual hatching, good sanitation, and best results, a separate hatching incubator is needed, since hatching releases down and microorganisms into the air, and this increases the chances of contaminating other incubating eggs.

A still-air incubator holds 200 quail eggs or 90 pheasant or chukar eggs.

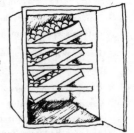

A circulating-air incubator tilts the eggs manually or automatically. It holds 800 quail eggs or 300 pheasant or chukar eggs. For automatic humidity, set a five- or ten-gallon plastic container of water on top of the incubator and connect it to the humidifier with plastic pipe.

GETTING THE INCUBATOR READY

Clean and disinfect the incubator. Make sure you understand how it works before you turn it on. Set up and level the incubator in an enclosed area with a room temperature of 65° to 70°F. An incubator will not work properly in a cold building; the unit will run too long and may burn out.

Supply fresh air without drafts or direct sunlight striking the incubator. Run the incubator for 48 hours to make sure it is working properly and that it cuts off and on at the temperature you are striving for. Fill the moisture pan with water.

INCUBATING THE EGGS
Incubation Period, Incubator Temperature, and Hygrometer Reading

The incubation period for several phases is listed below. The hatch period can be computed by subtracting the "do not turn eggs" figure from the incubation period figure: it averages 3 days. During that time, eggs are placed in a hatcher and left undisturbed until hatch is completed.

Bring the eggs to room temperature (65° to 70°F.) Mark the eggs on one side if you plan to turn them manually. We use colored markers for marking the eggs, with a different color for each setting date. It makes the eggs easier to locate if you have the eggs of one date in more than one tray or incubator. Keep a record of the date set, the date due to hatch, how many eggs are set, and of what species. Check your records often to keep abreast of when the eggs are due to hatch, so that you can have the brooder warm and ready for them.

If you are turning eggs mechanically or by hand, turn them three times a day, until about three days before they hatch. When turning quail eggs in a still-air incubator, we moisten our clean hands, place the palms lightly over the eggs, then make rotating circles as we turn the eggs, making sure all eggs have been turned. Be sure the small ends are pointed downward before you put the incubator lid back on.

The eggs need to cool down once a day after the first week. It takes only five minutes to cool small eggs. Circulated-air incubators are equipped with cooling systems.

Ventilation and humidity are important during incubation, to prevent drying out the normal moisture content of the egg. We use a fine-mist sprayer if the weather is dry or if the incubator is opened frequently, spraying lightly from time to time, throughout the incubation period (but not during a hatch).

The Hatch

About three days before the eggs are due to hatch, open the incubator for the last time before removal of the chicks. Fill the moisture pan with water, turn the eggs one last time, and put the lid back on. Leave it on until the chicks hatch out. Removing the lid or opening the incubator during a hatch lets out the moisture the chicks need to pip and break through the shell.

When the chicks have hatched and are dry (this takes 6 to 24 hours), remove them to a warm brooder. Experts consider a normal hatch to be 60 percent of incubated eggs, but we find a normal average hatch can be 75–80 percent with good management.

CANDLING

Candling is usually done on days 7 and 14 of incubation. Candling an egg is a way of inspecting it to determine if it is fertile or infertile, or has gone stale (the embryo has died). Removing such eggs from the incubator will prevent gases from harming the living embryos of the other eggs.

While commercial egg candlers are available, you can make one from a small corrugated box. Into it you insert a 60-watt light bulb attached to a drop cord, and cut a 3/4-inch hole in the side of the box. To use the candler, place the large end of the egg against the hole. The light turns the egg translucent, enabling you to see into it.

If the egg is fertile, there will be a dark spot with a network of small blood veins radiating outward. If the embryo has died, the blood will have settled away from the embryo toward the edges of the yolk. All clear (infertile) eggs can be removed, boiled, and fed to the guinea fowl. Notice the size of the air space in the egg. It will get larger during incubation. If the air space becomes excessively large, add moisture.

Because of the dark brown spots on coturnix eggs, they can be tested only for infertility. The darker the egg, the harder it is to see inside.

Brooding

Now that you've hatched the birds, you must provide protection, food, and warmth. What you do now determines whether your chicks become healthy birds.

Forty-eight hours before the chicks are to be moved in, clean and disinfect the brooder, and set the temperature at 100°F. This gives you ample time to make adjustments or repair the equipment.

BROODERS

There are automatic, battery-type brooders with thermostats, and hover-type brooders for a large quantity of birds. Poultry and game bird equipment suppliers will provide information on the brooder suited to your needs, plus other aids for raising game birds.

	Bobwhite Quail	Pigeon, Coturnix	Chukar	Pheasant	Guinea Fowl
Incubation Period (days)	23–24	17	23–24	23–26	28
Forced Air Temp. (degrees F., dry bulb)	99.75	99.75	99.75	99.75	99.75
Temp. last 3 days of Incubation (degrees F., dry bulb)	99	99	99	99	99
Still-Air Temp. (degrees F., dry bulb)	101–102	101–101 1/2	101–102	101 1/2–102 1/2	101–103
Humidity	84–86	84–86	80–82	86–88	83–85
Do not turn eggs after (days)	21	15	21	21	25
Humidity during last 3 days (degrees F., wet bulb)	90–94	90–94	90–94	92–95	90–94

Continued →

We use a battery-type brooder that has a thermostat and a green light to show when the heat is on.

You can make a simple, temporary brooder for a few chicks using a large, heavy corrugated box, a wide-mouth jar, and a drop cord with a 60-watt bulb. Don't use a 100-watt bulb—it is too hot and may burn the chicks or set the box afire.

To construct the brooder, cut a hole in the metal jar lid large enough to insert a socket, turn the lid over, insert the socket, screw in the bulb, then screw the lid and bulb onto the jar. Place the jar in the box, which is lined with fine hay, and plug the cord into an outlet. A tinted jar works best; it dims the light. Bright light in a brooder encourages picking and cannibalism. Tape a thermometer to the inside of the box, and check the temperature often. (See Brooding Schedule that follows for proper temperatures.) A piece of plywood placed on the top of the box can be used to regulate the temperature. Sliding it open will let heat escape. Be sure there is ample ventilation. This brooder works only in a room heated to at least 55°F.

Hover-type brooders are ideal in a large room or building. As long as the chicks remain comfortable and warm, many types of brooders are good. Too low a temperature causes the chicks to crowd together and possibly smother one another; too hot and they will die from exhaustion. With either too low or too high a temperature, the chicks are under stress and thus are more susceptible to disease. Good ventilation will remove ammonia buildup, dust, and carbon dioxide, thus reducing the number of disease organisms.

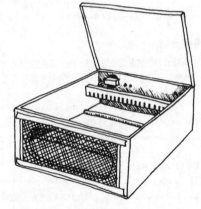

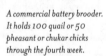
A commercial battery brooder. It holds 100 quail or 50 pheasant or chukar chicks through the fourth week.

BROODING SCHEDULE
Floor, Feeder, and Waterer Space for Brooding and Grow-Off Birds

These ratios are recommendations only because they work for us.

	Battery Brooder 1 to 10 days	Brooder 10 days to 6 weeks	Grow-Off 6 to 14 weeks
Floor Space			
Quail	9 birds/sq. ft.	6 birds/sq. ft.	3–4 birds/sq. ft.
Pheasant	5 birds/sq. ft.	2 birds/sq. ft.	1 bird/sq. ft.
Chukar	6 birds/sq. ft.	3 birds/sq. ft.	2 birds/sq. ft.
Guinea	5 birds/sq. ft.	2 birds/sq. ft.	1 bird/sq. ft.

	Battery Brooder 1 to 10 days	Brooder 10 days to 6 weeks	Grow-Off 6 to 14 weeks
Feeder Space			
Quail	1/2 in./bird	1 1/2 in./bird	1 1/2 in./bird
Pheasant	1 in./bird	1 1/2 in./bird	3 in./bird
Chukar	3/4 in./bird	2 in./bird	2 in./bird
Guinea	1 in./bird	2 in./bird	3 in./bird
Waterer Space			
Quail	2 chick waterers /100 birds	2–1 gallon fountains /100 birds	2 ft./100 birds or 3 to 4 1-gal. fountains
Pheasant	1-gal. fountain /35 birds	1 in./bird	1 in./bird
Chukar	1-gal. fountain /70 birds	3/4 in./bird	3/4 in./bird
Guinea	1-gal. fountain /30 birds	2–1 gal. fountains /30 birds	1 1/2–2 in./bird

Here is a brooding schedule that has given us excellent results:

24–28 Hours before Removing Chicks from Hatcher: Turn on brooder and set at 100°F. Place fresh water in game bird waterers. Game bird chicks are very small, so, to make sure they don't drown in their waterers, we set out a few shallow jar lids with water and marbles. The chicks walk on the marbles and drink the water below. Set out feeders with high-protein game bird starter. We use a mix with 32 percent protein. Set feeders on rough cardboard and scatter feed on the cardboard around the feeder to introduce the chicks to the feed. We provide the chicks with a rough surface to stand on to keep them from becoming spraddle-legged, when the legs spread wide apart as a result of slipped tendons. As you transfer the chick from the hatcher to the brooder, cull out any weak or crippled birds.

1–7 Days: Observe the chicks to see if they are eating and drinking. Refill waterers daily with fresh water, replace cardboard under the feeder, and scatter fresh feed on it. Remove paper-lined droppings tray and wash or clean the flooring of the brooder. Keep temperature at a constant 100°F.

7–14 Days: Reduce the brooder temperature to 95°F. Clean and refill waterers daily. By now the birds know where the feed is, but you can save feed if you continue to place a clean piece of cardboard under the feeder. Keep the brooder clean.

14–21 Days: Reduce the temperature to 90°F. Keep fresh feed and water before the birds at all times. Wash the feeder weekly. Watch for a powdery mildew that can build up on the inside of the feeder. If detected, scrub it off. Powdery feed sticks to the beaks and may cause picking, so replace it with fresh feed. Because ammonia builds up fast, provide plenty of ventilation.

21 Days and After: Reduce the temperature to 85°F., and continue reducing the temperature by 5 degrees each week.

After 5–6 Weeks: Transfer birds to grow-off pens. At this time cull any sick or crippled birds, and lightly debeak others, if you feel it is necessary.

MANAGING GROW-OFFS

Mash-Grain Ratio for Meat-Producing Birds

This is the ratio we use for feeding grain-grower to our meat-producing birds. A pan of grit should also be made available to the birds to aid digestion of grain.

Weeks of Age	Mash-Grain Ratio
0–6 weeks	starter mash only
7–8 weeks	4 parts 20% protein grower/1 part grain
9–12 weeks	3 parts protein grower/2 parts grain
13–16 weeks	2 parts protein grower/3 parts grain
17 weeks—market or slaughter	1 part protein grower/3 parts grain

After the brooding period of five to six weeks, we move our birds to the wire-floored grow-off pens. These are called grow-off (or grow-out) pens because it is here that the birds "grow off" into meat birds or breeders.

These pens are placed in quiet places, the birds aren't crowded, and space is provided for feeders and waterers. Birds that are crowded tend to tread over each other, often rubbing one another bare-backed, and they may pile on top of each other, smothering those underneath.

When you transfer your brood to grow-off pens, feed them a high-protein grower ration with 20–24 percent protein. You may add grain to the feed. If you offer cracked grain, free-choice grit is essential; fine gravel can be substituted.

Grain gives the birds something solid in the crop, and helps keep them from picking on each other. At this stage the birds are inclined to be cannibalistic, so provide enough space, plenty of picking food, such as vegetables or fruit, and grain, and something for distraction, such as boxes or limbs. You may want to supplement the grower mash with grain as a ration for birds grown-off for meat production.

You want these birds to grow off as quickly as possible, so never let them run out of feed or water. We use a grower mash with a digestible protein content of 20 percent, which is high in nutrients birds need for development. About a month before we slaughter our meat-producing birds, we begin feeding the grower-grain ration. It makes them plumb and adds a nice edging of fat.

Slaughtering

A timetable should be prepared so that you will slaughter your game birds when they reach the peak of development.

We butcher most of our quail and pigeons when they are 6–14 weeks old, depending on how we plan to use them. For sauteing, grilling, or broiling, the birds should be very young and tender. The mature birds are best for braising or baking. We slaughter most of the chukar and pheasants at the mature stage, at which point we think they have a better flavor. Guinea fowl may be slaughtered any time and cooked the way you would either game birds or poultry. We love the rich, dark meat and delicious flavor of the mature guinea. Young dove and squab are delicious simply split and sauteed or grilled. The dove has a more delicate flavor than the pigeon.

PREPARATION

About a month before we plan to slaughter, we change our feed formula for all birds except the coturnix. For birds that are 12 to 18 weeks old, we begin feeding a ration made up of three parts grower mash and three parts cracked grain. To mature birds we feed a mixture of one part grower mash to three parts cracked grain.

We butcher our coturnix young, and they remain on a high protein starter ration from hatch to slaughter.

We remove the feed from all birds 24 hours before slaughter so that the birds' crops will be empty when we butcher.

On the day of slaughter we take our largest pots and pans, sharp knives, large bowls, and clean towels to our outside sink under the barn shed. After sterilizing the sink (remember the pigeons), we turn on our gas burner and put on a large pot of water to boil. We have a bucket for feathers and entrails, and fill other buckets with clean, cold water.

HOW TO SLAUGHTER

The quickest and easiest way we've found to slaughter small birds is to hold the bird with one hand firmly around the body, grasp the head and neck between the thumb and forefinger on the other hand, and give a sharp pull, while slightly twisting. The neck will snap immediately. Cut off the head so the bird can be hung by the feet and bled. Another method is to place the live bird on the butcher block and cut off the head with a sharp knife.

We slaughter about 10 quail at one time, or three or four of the larger birds, then pull up our stools to either skin, or scald and pluck.

To skin, break the skin on the breast and with the fingers of both hands, pull the skin and feathers upward and outward, over the wings, legs, and back. The procedure is very simple.

To scald, plunge the bird in 160-degree water for just a few seconds, then pluck the feathers as you would a chicken. Ideally, quail should only be wiped clean with a damp cloth, not put into water or washed after dressing.

SLAUGHTERING LARGER BIRDS

To slaughter the larger birds, we lay the live bird on the chopping block and, with a small axe, chop off the head. After the birds are bled, we skin them or scald and pluck them. (Game birds can be plucked without scalding, but it takes much longer and requires a great deal of patience.)

After removing the feathers, we drop the bird into a bucket of cool water, then finish dressing it by splitting it down the back to the vent, opening the bird, and emptying the contents into a bucket. The final step is to cut around the vent, carefully circling the large entrail so that it isn't cut. We save the liver, gizzard, and hearts of all the birds, for additions to gravy or stuffing.

Starting Right with Bees

Do You Want to Keep Bees?

Your needs to get started are so few.

- The money for equipment. (You'll get it back in a season or two, from your honey crop.)

- A location for your hives. It should be selected so you won't bother your neighbors. Good locations can be found even in cities.

Continued ➜

- Time. The demand is small. Beekeeping fits well with other weekend chores.

- Knowledge. A little will get you started—and you'll never have it all. A beginner's book such as Garden Way Publishing's *Practical Beekeeping* will guide you through most of the problems you may face.

YOUR QUESTIONS ANSWERED

Experienced beekeepers hear the same questions, again and again, from those considering beekeeping. Let's answer some of those questions, and see if we can help you.

I. What will I need to get started?

Your basic start-up needs are listed below. The cost of this start-up equipment may vary, depending upon your regional supplier.

1. One standard ten-frame hive with bottom board, entrance block, outer cover, inner cover, frames, and foundation.

2. A bee veil to protect your face

3. A bee smoker

4. Gloves

5. A hive tool for prying the hive and frames apart

6. A feeder for feeding the bees sugar syrup until they can support themselves with nectar

7. A beginner's book on beekeeping

8. A bee brush

9. A three-pound package of bees, with queens

Basic equipment needed by the beginner includes standard ten-frame hive with frames, at left; bee veil, gloves, and bee smoker, and in front, a basic book, foundation for the frames, hive tool and entrance feeder.

The bees are sold in two- to five-pound screened packages. The three-pound package is recommended over the smaller one since the greater number of bees is needed to keep up the temperature of the bee cluster for raising young bees. This temperature has to be maintained at between 93 and 94°F in the brood area.

Remember, except for the bees, this is basic equipment. Most bee equipment firms have beginner's kits. If you buy one, make certain you buy all of the above items.

As your hive prospers and grows, the bees will need more room, and you'll need more equipment. For the first season, plan to buy the following:

- One deep super, exactly the same as the box of your hive, with frames and foundation. (You of course won't need extra covers or bottom board for this.)

- Two shallow supers with frames and foundations. The bees store honey for you in these.

- Queen excluder, to keep the queen from moving up into the shallow supers and laying eggs.

- Bee escape. This one-way bee escape is used to get bees out of the shallow supers when they are full of honey and ready to be taken off the hive.

This will get you through your first season, and by then you will know what extra equipment you need to fit your plans.

Modern beehive cut away to show interior and placement of moveable frames. Bottom, full-depth hive body; middle and top, shallow hive bodies. (USDA photograph)

2. Can I keep bees at my home?

Almost always, the answer is yes, unless zoning laws prohibit it. A sunny, secluded spot out of traffic is best. Bees take off and land much the same as airplanes at an airport. They follow a definite landing and take-off pattern in front of the hive. Remember this when you set up your hive. Don't have that flight pattern across a sidewalk or road, or a neighbor's path.

Bees dislike irritating noises, such as the roar of lawn mowers, so keep these distractions at least 10 feet from the hive.

And the early morning sun should reach the hive, to wake up the inhabitants and start them out on their rounds.

If there isn't a natural source of water for your hive, provide one. That way your bees won't become a nuisance around your neighbor's home or swimming pool.

3. When should I start with bees?

You've started right now, by reading this. Continue to read about bees as much as you can. If you know an experienced beekeeper, talk with him.

You should make arrangements in January or February to buy bees. Placing your order then is not too early. If you are buying package bees, you should get your order in early because the orders are filled on the basis of first-come, first-served. It is important to get your bees early in the season, in northern states. They must have time to build their combs and raise new bees so the hive population will be large at the time of the main honeyflow.

The earlier you get the bees, the more time they have for building up and making honey. Also, the better the chance they have of producing enough honey to carry them through the next winter and perhaps of making some surplus honey for you the first year. Most beginners don't think about getting bees until the spring flowers start to bloom. By that time it may be too late to get the bees and to give them a chance to do their best. If you get them too late, they may not have time to store enough honey for their winter needs and may die of starvation.

There are several different ways to obtain bees. They may be bought from southern or California beekeepers. You may be able to purchase an established hive of bees from a nearby beekeeper. Or, you might have a nearby beekeeper place a swarm of bees in a hive for you.

When buying an established hive of bees, make certain it has been inspected for disease by a state apiary inspector. Ask for a certificate of inspection signed by the inspector stating that it is free of disease. Don't take anyone else's word for it. Don't take a chance on losing your bees from disease right at the start. You will have enough problems without that one.

Arrange to have your bees delivered at about the time fruit trees bloom your area.

4. What kind of bees should I buy?
You have a choice, and all of them originally were imports to this country.

You probably don't want the *German* or black bees, such as the colonists first brought to this country. They had dispositions that made them hard to handle; when the hive was opened they flew up wildly, much to the dismay of the beekeeper.

You'll find the *Italian* bees the most popular in this country. Their bodies are various shades of yellow, with the abdomen having three or five bands of yellow, bordered with black.

These bees are industrious, and a good queen will quickly build up a strong hive. If you open the hive on a rainy day, when they're unhappy about being unable to fly out to collect, they'll let you know by buzzing angrily around your head. Don't argue with them; close the hive and wait for a sunnier day.

The gentlest of all bees are the *Caucasians*. Some of them are black with soft grey hair, while others look much like the Italians. If they have a fault it is that they will glue together everything in the hive with propolis, a resinous material of plants collected by all bees. This means that you will have to use your hive tool constantly, to break away this glue, when you open a hive of Caucasians.

Carniolans are rarely found in this country. They are originally from the Carniolan Mountains, and are black with grey rings. They' e very gentle, but tend to swarm (divide the colony to start a new one).

Many commercial beekeepers are now offering specially bred hybrid bees. The good strains are productive. To maintain the hybrid strain, the USDA recommends replacing the queen each year.

5. Is it difficult to install the package of bees in the hive?
It sure is, the first time you do it, and the difficulty is largely in your head. There's a bright side to it, too. You'll rarely get more satisfaction out of beekeeping than you will the first time you successfully install a package of bees

---

TWO IS BETTER THAN ONE

"If you can finance it, it is better to start with two colonies of bees rather than one. If you have two, you can compare their progress and have a better idea if something is wrong with one of them. Also, if something happens to one of the queens you can take a frame of brood with eggs from the other hive and give it to the queenless hive. Then the bees can rear a new queen to replace the lost one. Combs of sealed brood may be taken from the stronger colony and given to the weaker to increase the number of bees in the weaker colony. Combs of honey may be taken from one colony and given to the other when food stores become short. If one colony becomes hopelessly weak in number of bees, it may be united with the strong hive, then divided later, when the number of bees warrants such action."

Enoch Tompkins, Garden Way Publishing's Practical Beekeeping

6. Just how do I go about it?
It's a 12-step process, and not as difficult as it may seem as you read about it. A few general hints: Don't feel you have to rush this. Work calmly (it's so easy to tell someone else that) and avoid crushing the bees. Install the bees in the evening. And remember, especially, that they aren't inclined to sting you, after being fed. And now for those steps.

1. **Get the package of bees (three pounds, about 10,000 bees), from the post office,** if they came by mail. The folks there will be happy to get rid of them, may even call you the minute they arrive.

2. **Feed them.** Bring two quarts of water to a boil, remove it from the heat, and add five pounds of granulated sugar. Stir until it has dissolved. Let cool. Place the package of bees on its side and brush on this syrup. The bees may take as much as a pint of this syrup. You'll need the rest later.

3. **Store them,** only if you can't install them right away, by placing them in a dark, well-ventilated place where the temperature is 50°–60°F. Feed them twice daily while stored, and keep them there as briefly as possible, not more than two or three days.

4. **Prepare the hive.** It should be assembled and painted before the bees arrive. Put it in its permanent location. Installing bees is best done in the early evening of a warm, sunny day, but it can be done on a rainy day.

5. **Get yourself ready.** Light your smoker. Don your bee attire and net. Have your hive tool and bee brush handy. You'll also need one small nail. Have the entrance feeder full and ready to put in place. Remove the hive covers and take out five of the brood frames. All of the frames of course should have wax foundation mounted in them, ready for the bees to draw out into the cells in which the honey is stored. Feed the bees as much syrup as they will take, just as you did when they arrived, by smearing the syrup on the wire sides of the package.

6. **Prepare to open the shipping cage.** You'll notice it has a small can of syrup. That's for feeding the bees until they reach you. It also has a queen cage hanging near the syrup can. This holds the queen

Continued ➔

bee and several workers. Working near the hive, tap the package on the ground, hard enough so the bees tumble to the bottom of the package. Pry off the cover of the cage with your hive tool. Remove the queen cage. This also could permit the bees to escape, so block that route with a wad of paper or the original cover.

7. **Look at the queen cage.** She's longer than the workers, and her back lacks the hair they have. Remove the cork (sometimes cardboard) blocking one end of the cage. There'll be a layer of candy underneath. Poke a hole through it with that nail you have, taking care not to injure the queen. Put the cage, candy side up, between the top bars of two frames, letting the pressure of the bars hold it. The bees will find this cage, eat away the candy, and free the queen.

Queen and several workers are packed into tiny wooden shipping cage.

8. **Jolt the bees to the bottom of the package.** Pry out the syrup can, and brush any bees from it onto the open hive. Dump several handsful of bees onto the queen cage. Pour the rest of them into the space left when you removed the five frames. All of them won't spill out. Don't worry. Put the package in front of the hive so the remaining bees will crawl out of it and into the hive.

9. **Replace the five frames.** Replace one at a time, working gently so that you don't pinch the bees. Equalize the space between the frames. Put the inner cover back on. The bees at this point may be trying to escape by climbing up over the hive top. Brush them back with the bee brush, and put the inner cover on gently, so that you don't crush the bees. A small amount of smoke will also drive them back from the top. Replace the outer cover.

10. **Confine the bees to the hive.** Insert the entrance of the entrance feeder into the hive, letting it rest on the hive bottom board. Plug the remainder of the hive entrance with a handful of grass, and that's it. You've installed the bees. Remove your veil and mop your brow. You'll notice you're sweaty, even on a cool day.

11. **Several days later.** For the next five to seven days, do very little. Remove the grass the following day, and replace it with the entrance block. Replenish the syrup if necessary.

12. **After about a week.** Use a little smoke. Remove both covers. Remove the queen cage. Is she free? If so, fine. If not, enlarge the hole in the candy and replace the cage. If she is out, check frames near the cage location to see whether she is laying eggs.

If you find none, you must conclude something has happened to her. Order a new queen, as quickly as possible, and introduce her to the hive as explained earlier.

7. How often should I open the hive?

At first, once a week, and try to do it on warm, sunny days. Check the foundation. Has the cell-like print on it been drawn out into true cells? If this has been done on all frames but those at the ends of the hive,

move those frames into the center, moving one frame each week. Continue feeding the sugar syrup—as much as they will take—until all the foundation has been drawn out.

As the colony gains in numbers, turn the entrance block to provide a bigger entrance. When the foundation has all been drawn, or when the bees can be seen spread across all of the frames, add the super. These two deep supers will comprise the homes for your bees, a place to raise their offspring, store their honey for winter use, and to huddle in a big, warm cluster of bees and endure the winter.

8. And finally, the question asked by everyone: will I get stung?

Yes.

The first time it will really sting; the second time you won't mind it quite as much. And while you'll never get so that you can ignore it, you do reach the point where you tolerate it.

You can avoid many stings. Remember the bees are defending the colony when they sting you, and a worker bee gives up her life when she uses this defense.

Work with the bees in good weather, when they are out of the hive and gathering nectar.

Wear a veil to protect your face, gloves for your hands (although you will soon discard them, as you gain experience) and light-colored clothing. Bees tend to crawl into dark places, so have tight wristbands on your sleeves, and tuck the bottom of your trousers into your socks, or otherwise seal off that entrance.

Use a smoker when working with bees. Watch the reaction of the bees to the smoke. You will soon learn the minimum amount that can be used to achieve results.

And when you are stung, remove the stinger quickly by scraping it with the hive tool or your fingernail. Don't try to pull it out with your fingers. This will only force more venom into your body.

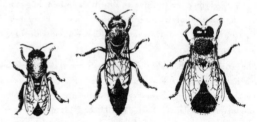

Worker, queen, and drone bees. (USDA photograph)

And finally, make certain you are not one of those who is allergic to bee stings. Most beekeepers eventually develop an immunity to stings. If you become allergic to bee stings, with the effects of the sting growing worse each time, consult an allergy specialist. Such an allergy can become deadly.

And Now...Honey

If you have followed the instructions in the preceding questions and answers, you're well on your way to being a beekeeper. You've felt the surprising jab of the stinger; you know the satisfaction of seeing bees move busily in and out of the hive as they seek out the nectar for the honey you and they will share.

Now you're ready to learn a little more about such things as making yours a productive hive, how to deal with your queen, how to make your bees comfortable for the winter, and get them going again early in the spring. Let's talk over a few of these subjects.

USING THE SMOKER

You have on your veil and your gloves. Your garments are beetight top and bottom, and not even a draft is stirring through them. And you try to fire up your smoker. And it simply won't catch. It's like a charter member of the American Lung Association in its refusal to smoke. What's to do?

First, undress a bit. Get the smoker going before you encase yourself in protective gear.

The trick of getting a smoker smoking nicely is to use the right fuel. Try clean burlap, dry wood shavings, pine needles, or dry rotted wood. Start the fire by lighting a small wad of paper and dropping it into the bottom of the smoker canister. Then gradually add fuel, while slowly working the bellows. And remember, when working with the bees, to give the bellows a pinch on occasion, even if you don't need the smoke, just to keep the fire going. It can be disquieting to find yourself smokeless just when the hive is wide open, and the bees turn restless and need the quieting effects of a puff or two.

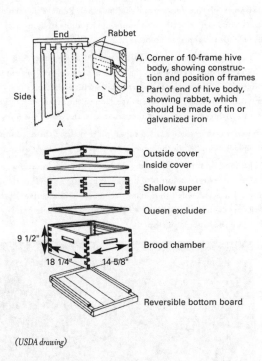

A. Corner of 10-frame hive body, showing construction and position of frames
B. Part of end of hive body, showing rabbet, which should be made of tin or galvanized iron

Outside cover
Inside cover

Shallow super

Queen excluder

Brood chamber

Reversible bottom board

9 1/2"
18 1/4"   14 5/8"

(USDA drawing)

OPENING THE HIVE

When opening the hive, stand to one side of it. Blow two or three puffs of smoke into the entrance. This disorganizes the guards and causes the other bees to fill up with honey.

Wait a minute or two. Now remove the outer cover of the hive. Place it on the ground, top side down. Blow a few puffs of smoke through the center hole in the inner cover.

Pry up one corner of the inner cover with your hive tool. Blow some smoke through that crack as you lift off the cover. Place this upside down in front of the hive, with the end resting on the entrance, so the bees on it can saunter back into the hive.

Remove any supers on the hive, and place them in the outer cover. Check out the brood (bottom) chamber first, wafting smoke over its top before removing the frames for inspection.

REMOVE A FRAME

Try removing the frame nearest you first. Loosen it by inserting the bent end of the hive tool between the top bar of the frame, near one end, and the side of the hive. Repeat this at the other end of the frame. It should be freed from being glued to the inner wall of the hive.

Do the same thing to loosen the first frame from the second. Now you can use the bent end of the hive tool to pry up the frame a bit so you can grasp and lift it with your fingers. Lift slowly and carefully, so that you do not crush any bees, and make the rest irritated.

After inspecting it (the first one should have honey in it), place this first frame against the back or one side of the hive, and pry up and remove the second frame.

What are you looking for? You're trying to check on life in the hive. Is there enough food? There should be at least fifteen pounds of honey in the hive at all times.

Is the queen there? You can recognize her from her size, and from the bees attending her, busily moving near her. Make certain you don't lose her in the grass as you check those frames.

Is she laying? Hold the frame so the sun shines over your shoulder and down into the cells. Look into the cells to see if you can find any eggs or very young larvae. The eggs will look like small white commas attached to the bottom of the cells. These hatch into small, white, grublike larvae and will be curled up in a milky mass of royal jelly or bee milk. If you find eggs or larvae, you know that the queen is present and laying.

NEED ROOM?

Does the queen have enough room for laying? If you find that most of the combs in the brood nest are filled with brood, pollen, and honey, you should provide more room. This can be done by adding a super or by replacing combs of honey with empty combs or with frames containing foundation. The combs of honey may be placed in the food chamber super, if you are using a deep super for the food chamber.

Are the bees building queen cells during the late spring or early summer? This is a sign the bees are preparing to swarm. Queen cells are usually built along the bottom edge of brood combs. They are shaped like peanut shells and hang down from the frame. A quick check for these cells can be made by tipping back the entire super and looking along the bottom edge of the exposed frames.

When you have finished examining a frame (except that first one held out to give yourself working room), place it back in the same order as it was before. Combs in the brood nest may have the lower front corners chewed away by the bees. Make certain that the combs are replaced with that corner toward the front.

After you have finished examining the combs, crowd together those that have been replaced so you will have room for the first frame removed. Replace that one, then crowd all of them together, and equalize the space between them.

During all of this the bees may tire of the game, and fly up in our face or otherwise display hostility. Blow a little more smoke on them when this starts.

Continued ➜

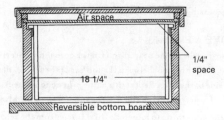

Plans and dimensions of Langstroth ten-frame beehive.

Air space

18 1/4"

1/4" space

Reversible bottom board

Cross section of hive body and frame

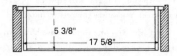

5 3/8"

17 5/8"

Cross section of shallow super

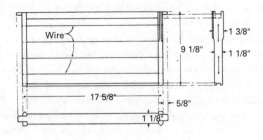

Wire

1 3/8"

9 1/8"

1 1/8"

17-5/8"

5/8"

1 1/8"

Side, end, and top elevation of frame

Inspect each super as you replace it, each time blowing a little smoke over the top of it to keep the bees down from the top of the frames. Complete the task by replacing the inner and outer covers.

Weekly Inspections

Check the hive once a week during the spring and summer. This way you will spot feeding problems or preparations for swarming. If you don't inspect them regularly you can easily lose them.

Summer Management

You now have two full supers comprising your hive. They are there as a home for the bees. Soon you will be adding shallow supers that hold about thirty pounds of honey as compared with the fifty pounds held in the deep super.

Before you add those shallow supers you must make a decision: what type of honey do you want to produce? You have three choices:

1. **Section comb honey.** This requires special frames and experience in dealing with the bees. Wait a few seasons before trying this.

2. **Extracted honey.** This requires a somewhat expensive piece of equipment, a honey extractor that spins the frames, two or more at a time, to force the honey from the cells, after the top layer of wax has been removed from the faces of each frame. Here's a big expense that can be delayed by opting for the third choice, which is:

3. **Chunk or cut-comb honey.** You've seen this in stores, aluminum or plastic square boxes containing a four-inch square of comb filled with honey.

For the moment, all you need to know about this method is that you should buy the frames that have a thin top bar and a divided bottom bar, and use foundation that is *not* reinforced with wire. The reinforced foundation is for producing extracted honey, and makes the foundation better able to withstand the centrifugal force of the extractor. The sheets of foundation for chunk honey are slightly thicker than the very thin sheets made to fit into the comb honey section boxes. The sheets are 5 1/4 x 16 3/4 inches.

WHEN TO ADD SUPERS

Supers should be added soon enough so that the bees are never without room to expand their activities. Watch them as they spread into the second deep super. When they are working on at least eight of the frames, it is time to add a shallow super. With an overwintered hive this can be as early as when fruit trees are blossoming; it will be later with a first-year hive.

Remove the inner and outer covers, and place the first shallow super on top of the second deep super. After a week, check to see the activity there. Look at the frames. Has the queen moved up there to lay eggs? If so, brush her back onto the frames of the top deep super. Place a queen excluder on top of that deep super, whether or not the queen was found up there, then put the shallow super back in place.

Watch that first surplus honey super. When bees are working on eight of the frames, it's time for a second shallow super. Remove the first one and add the second right *above* the deep super, then put the first one back on top of the second, and replace the covers.

The reason for not simply adding super #2 above super #1 is that the "bottom supering" method gets the bees working on drawing out the foundation—building the cells on the blueprint etched on the foundation. It also helps relieve congestion in the brood nest by getting the comb builders up into the super and out of the way of the nurse bees.

When it's time to add a third super, place it above the deep super, then replace #1 and #2 in the same order they were, with #1 on top.

This method is used all during the honeyflow, when the bees are bringing home great amounts of nectar. When the honeyflow slows, any additional supers needed should be placed on top of the hive. In that way, the bees will tend to complete filling the lower supers before working on the super at the top.

The size of frames in shallow and full-size supers are compared. Top photo is frame from a shallow super. Both have new foundation, which has not yet been drawn into cells by the bees.

202

You'll quickly notice that bees tend to work on the frames in the middle of the super, drawing out that foundation into combs. They can be stimulated to draw out the outer foundation by moving it into the center of the super, and pushing those in the center toward the outside.

EXTRACTED HONEY PRODUCTION

If you decide to aim for extracted honey the first year, you'll do a few things differently. You'll load your frames with reinforced foundation, having wires running through it. You can buy this type of foundation, or you can buy plain foundation and do your own wiring and embedding. Frame wiring kits and wire embedders are available from beekeeping equipment suppliers.

You will place supers one on top of the other, so that the first is on top of the deep super, the next one you place is on top of #1, and the third will be on top of #2. Note this is the reverse of the method used for cut-comb honey production.

And for frames filled to overflowing with honey, you will reduce the number of frames in the super from ten to nine or even eight, and space the frames an equal distance apart. The result is that the bees build the combs thicker, putting more honey into each frame. This makes uncapping—cutting off the top layer of wax from each face of the frame—much easier. Don't use this system when starting with only foundation in the frames; wait until the foundation has been used once and the cells are formed, otherwise the bees may build combs in that vast space between the frames.

HARVESTING THE HONEY

You've placed super on super on super, and all are filled with honey. What next?

It's time to enjoy the fruits of your bees' labors. But first you must get it out of those supers. It isn't difficult.

The honey in the frames is ready to be taken when the bees have capped it with a layer of wax. It has a finished, packaged look, and none of the honey will leak out, no matter how you hold the frame.

The super from which you will take honey should be at the top of the hive. Fit a bee escape into the center hole in the inner cover, and place this cover *under* the super. Place the outer cover back over the super. Wait twenty-four hours. In that time most of the bees will find their way down through the bee escape, and its pair of flat spring gates will prevent them from returning to the super.

Now you can take the super off the hive. While still outdoors, remove each frame and check for any remaining bees. If you find them, brush them off the combs near the hive entrance. Take the super inside where you will work on it.

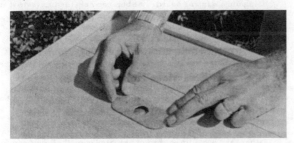

A bee escape is placed in position in hole in inner cover. This cover will be placed under the super containing the honey that is to be removed from the hive. Thus bees in this super can go down into the hive below the inner cover, but cannot return. Most of the bees will find their way out in 24 hours.

CUT-COMB HONEY PACKAGING

You're now ready to package your honey in one of its most delicious states.

You'll need a wire cake rack 12 x 18 inches (or you can make a wooden-framed rack using galvanized hardware cloth), a cookie pan of those dimensions or larger, to catch the drippings, containers for the honey, a guide for cutting honey to fit into those containers, and a spatula to move the chunks from your cutting board (the wire cake rack) to the containers.

Using the knife and guide, trace lines on the comb to show yourself where to cut to divide the comb. If you're using a 4-inch square guide, you should get four chunks from the frame.

Next cut with a sawing motion all around the frame, and place this large chunk on the rack. Cut out the four chunks. There will be some pieces at each end. Place them in a big jar for your own use. Separate the chunks and let the honey drain from the sides. Then place them in the container and seal.

Another method of packing cut-comb honey is to cut the chunks and place them in wide-mouthed glass jars. Heat some honey to 150°F, let it cool, then fill the jar with it. This type of pack is commonly called chunk honey. One chunk is placed in the one-pound jar, and two chunks are placed in the two and one-half pound jar. The honey in these jars tends to crystallize quickly, even though you have heated it to prevent this.

Swarming

There's a roar in the air, like a strong wind. But it isn't that. It's your bees—more than half of them—moving out of the hive you've provided, moving to a location they've selected. Maybe you could have prevented this.

Seeing such a swarm from his own hive is a deflating experience for the beekeeper who realizes "my" bees are "mine" only as long as they elect to remain in the hive.

The beekeeper's first question: "What did I do wrong?"

We should remember, first of all, that swarming is the natural method by which bees increase the number of colonies. Swarming generally takes place in late spring or early summer. Bees are more apt to swarm during the light honeyflow that precedes the major honeyflow. Overcrowding or a failing queen contribute to the desire to swarm. Bees may also swarm when a heavy honeyflow is broken by alternate periods of rainy and fair weather.

The bees will give you fair warning of their plans. They'll build a number of queen cells, to provide the hive with a queen when the reigning queen leaves with the swarm.

Queen cell cups may be present at any time of the year. But when the bees are preparing to swarm they begin to enlarge the cups, and this can be detected because the enlargement will be a lighter colored wax than the original cups.

Bees also begin clustering on the landing board of the hive when they are preparing to swarm. Sometimes such clustering can be misleading, since bees also do it during hot weather, or simply when there is little nectar to collect.

About the time the first queen cell is capped over is when the bees are most likely to swarm. The departure time is generally between 10 A.M. and 2 P.M.

Their journey is a two-part one, which works to the advantage of the beekeeper. They will hover busily near the front of the hive in a large

Continued ➡

mass, then fly off, usually to the branch of a nearby tree. There they await the return of their scouts, sent out to find a new home for the colony.

That waiting period may be a matter of a few minutes or a few days. It is the one and only opportunity the beekeeper has to hive the swarm. And he can rest assured he is dealing with docile bees at this time.

There are only a few steps to hiving the swarm. First, place a sheet or a large piece of plastic under the swarm. Place an empty hive (with frames and empty combs or foundation) on the sheet. If the swarm is close to the ground, shake the branch so the bees fall onto the sheet near the hive. Usually they will scamper into the hive. If the branch is higher up, it may have to be cut carefully, and then can be placed on the sheet.

If the swarm gathers on the side of a tree, a fence post or the wall of a building, the bees may be scooped off with a shoe box and dumped in front of, or into, the hive.

When most of the bees are in the hive, it should be moved to its permanent location.

E. HARRI

SWARM PREVENTION

If you're lucky, you will thus retrieve each swarm from your hives. But your honey production will fall, since the divided colonies will not be as strong that season as the original one.

There are several things that the beekeeper may do to cut down on the possibility of swarming. Here are some of them:

1. Provide plenty of storage room for incoming nectar and surplus honey when nectar becomes available. Keep ahead of the needs of your bees in this respect. Add supers a little before they are needed rather than afterward. Nectar may contain 80 percent water when first brought into the hive. Honey, the end product, contains only about 17 percent water. The bees need room to store and to process the nectar. Make certain that your bees have enough room to do the job properly. When you see that the bees are working on eight frames of your top super, give them another one. If they don't need it, they won't use it.

2. Bees are less likely to swarm when headed by a queen that is less than two years old. Such a queen secretes a larger quantity of glandular substances than an older queen. These substances (pheromones or queen substance) are passed around among the worker bees and inhibit the production of supersedure queen cells. Requeening every year or two helps to control the swarming impulse.

3. Provide the queen with sufficient space for laying eggs. The queen should have empty cells available for egg laying at all times. You may have to remove some combs of honey from the sides of the brood chamber and replace these with empty combs or frames of foundation. Empty combs are best. The

combs of honey may be replaced in the food chamber or given to a colony that needs more honey. Most, if not all, of the combs of the brood chamber should be reserved for brood rearing.

During the winter and early spring, the bees tend to move upward in the hive and bring their brood nest with them. In a two-story hive, additional space for brood rearing may be provided by periodically reversing these two parts of the hive during the spring buildup preceding the main honeyflow. This practice will relieve congestion of the brood nest and help prevent swarming.

4. When a hive becomes congested with bees, and the weather becomes hot, bees may have a problem in keeping the hive cool enough. When you see bees clustering outside the hive entrance on hot days, you should do something to assist them in cooling their hive. This may be done in several ways.

    One method is to give the hive a larger entrance. If the entrance block is still being used, change it to the larger-sized entrance. Or you may wish to remove the entrance block and substitute one that closes only half the entrance. If the entire entrance is open, you may provide more air circulation by propping the front of the hive body up with small blocks of wood at the two front corners.

    Another method of providing additional ventilation is to lift the outer cover of the hive and move it forward so the bottom rear edge rests upon the edge of the inner cover. With the hole in the inner cover open, top ventilation is provide around the edges of the outer cover.

    Ventilation may also be provided by moving the inner cover toward the front of the hive about half of an inch with the outer cover in the position just described. Or the top supers may be staggered to provide half-inch spaces at front and rear.

    In southern states, place your hives where they will be shaded during the hottest part of the day. Or you may want to make a slatted rack of lath to place on top of the hive to provide shade.

5. Provide an adequate supply of water for the bees if there is not a source of fresh running water nearby. Water is used, at times, to dilute the honey for feeding brood. It is also brought into the hive and placed on top of frames and in burr comb to help cool the hive through evaporation. Fresh running water is preferable. This may be provided by letting an outside faucet drip onto a slanting board. The bees can help themselves to it as it runs down the board. If you would rather have the bees farther from the house, a hose may be attached to the faucet and the water allowed to drip onto a board at the other end of the hose. Stagnant water, as a source for bees, is thought to assist in the spread of the bee disease, nosema.

6. Combs of sealed brood may be removed from the brood chamber and empty combs, or frames with foundation, may be put in their place. Place these beside other combs containing brood rather than break up the brood nest by placing them between brood combs. The combs of sealed brood may be placed in a super above other supers on the same hive, or may be given to

weaker hives to strengthen them. Removing sealed brood relieves congestion in the brood nest and gives the queen more room for laying eggs.

SWARM CONTROL

If the bees start building queen cells in spite of your efforts at prevention, then other measures are called for. One of these is to cut out or destroy the queen cells every eight to ten days. They may be destroyed by sticking the point of your hive tool into them in such a manner that the larvae are killed. You must be very thorough in destroying queen cells since if only one is missed the colony is likely to swarm. Before destroying any queen cells, you should check them closely to make certain they are not supersedure cells. If you were to destroy all such cells, your colony might be left queenless (see the paragraphs on supersedure for information on distinguishing one type of queen cell from the other). If the cells are supersedure cells, leave one for the new queen to emerge, and destroy the remainder. Also destroy the old queen, if you can find her.

If destroying queen cells doesn't stop the desire to swarm, you may want to divide the colony and increases our number. If would be better to do that than to risk losing the swarm if it should come out on a day when no one is at home.

DIVIDING A COLONY

There are several methods of dividing a colony of bees. Probably the simplest is to remove four to six combs of brood, with adhering bees and old queen, to an empty hive. Fill the remaining space of both hives with empty combs or frames with brood foundation. Move the new division, with the queen, to a new location. This may be near the old location, but preferably with the entrance turned at right angle

to the parent hive. The parent hive should be given a ripe (capped) queen cell or a new, young queen within two hours, or no later than twenty-four hours, after making the division. Dividing should be done during the middle part of the day when many of the bees are away from the hive.

QUEEN SUPERSEDURE AND REQUEENING

The queen, center of attraction in the hive, is wanted there, by both bees and beekeeper, only as long as she is productive. When her egg-laying ability diminishes, she should be replaced. If the bees do this, it is called supersedure; if the beekeeper acts, it is requeening.

When the bees decide the queen must go, they build several queen cells on the face of the comb, preparing to hatch a new queen. These differ from the cells built in preparation for swarming in that the latter are built along the bottom edge of the comb, and are more numerous. The old queen is killed before the new one emerges.

The best time for *requeening* is during the fall honeyflow. The new queen will have time to produce plenty of young bees before winter.

LONG LIVE THE QUEEN

The beginning beekeeper will marvel at the decisions made in the complex, efficient operation of the hive. One of these is in making certain the hive has a queen—and a productive one.

When the queen is missing or is judged inadequate or defective by the colony, she is replaced.

First step is for the bees to build one or more queen cells, usually along the edge of a comb. These are far larger than the usual cells, and are readily recognized by their peanut-shell shapes. The cell is either built around an egg or larva, or a worker egg is deposited in the cell after it is built.

The queen, in her fifteen days of maturing from egg to insect, is fed royal jelly by the worker bees during her entire period of growth, and it is this rich, abundant diet that produces a queen rather than a worker bee.

First step is to find and kill the old queen, so that the old and the new will not fight to the death of one of them. Look on the combs in the brood chamber for her.

This of course should not be done until the new queen arrives. A queen may be purchased from southern bee breeders, and will arrive in a wooden cage accompanied by a few workers.

The workers must be removed from the cage, since the bees in the hive will accept the queen but look on the alien workers as foes.

Introducing the queen is very similar to the step taken when adding the queen to the hive with the bees you purchased. Poke a hole through the candy blocking the cage entrance. Suspend the cage between two frames of brood with the candy end up. Close the hive, leaves it closed for one week, then check to make certain the queen is out of the cage—and is laying.

Preparing for Winter

A common belief among non-beekeepers is that somehow bees lie dormant in the hive all winter. Not so. That white box with its cap of snow may look dormant, but within it is activity. Bees are massed together over the honeycombs, eating, giving off moisture, maintaining heat within the cluster, changing position in the cluster, and moving the cluster itself from comb to comb to stay in contact with the food supply.

The beekeeper's duty is to simplify all of these steps for the bees. They need food—90 pounds of honey isn't too much—they need protection from such enemies as mice, they need air circulation, since the moisture, not the cold, is their major problem. And, finally, there is strength in numbers. They need a strong colony.

Here are some of the steps you should take in preparation for winter.

1. Requeen if the queen is old. Some beekeepers do this every fall.

2. Provide a windbreak from the prevailing winds. A building, trees, shrubs or walls are fine. The winter sun should reach the hive.

3. Unite weak colonies. A colony should cover at least 20 deep combs in the fall. Weak colonies can be united with stronger

Continued ➔

ones by placing a sheet of newspaper (poke a few small holes in it) on top of the brood chamber of the strong colony, then place the weaker colony on top. They will unite without trouble.

4. Check winter stores. The upper hive body should be full of honey and pollen. The lower hive body should be at least half full of honey and pollen. If there isn't enough, feed them sugar syrup (heat water to the boiling point, remove from heat, add sugar, with two parts sugar to one part water). This is a good time for preventive medicine. Add USDA-approved drugs to the syrup for the prevention of American Foulbrood and the control of nosema. Dissolve the drugs in water before adding them to the syrup. Stir the syrup well to distribute the drugs.

5. Remove queen excluders. You might bar the queen from following the cluster from one super to another, and cause her death.

6. Provide an upper entrance to the hive. It's needed for air circulation, and for an emergency exit in case snow, ice, or dead bees block the lower entrance.

   If the inner cover of your hive has a notch cut in the rim, place this notch toward the front of the hive, and leave open the hole in the center of the inner cover. Push the outer cover as far forward as possible, so there's an open route into the hive.

   Another way to provide an entrance is to drill a three-quarter inch hole in the front and upper part of the top super. Don't drill it into the handhold, or you may get stung when lifting the super.

7. Adjust the entrance block to provide a minimum opening. This provides enough space for the bees, but will keep out mice.

8. Once cold weather hits, leave the bees alone. Opening the hive in cold weather can only cause trouble for the bees.

Instead, think of your bees in the hive. The drones have been forced, protesting vehemently, from the hive, As the temperature reached down into the 50s, the cluster formed, with the bees as well as the eggs, larvae and pupae, kept warm within it. The egg-laying of the queen bee tapers off, and probably stops during October and November.

As temperatures drop, the bees squeeze together; whenever temperatures rise, the cluster expands and the bees shift their position to cover new areas of comb.

The queen stays within the cluster. In late January or early February the colony will remind her it's time for egg-laying; brood will be needed to replace the many bees who die during the winter.

Outside, winter rages, with storms and periods of intense cold. Inside there's a fight for survival going on, with lack of food, moisture build-ups and sometimes even the cold threatening the lives of the many parts of this colony. If they make it, it may be due to that extra effort you made last fall.

Brood combs showing (top) healthy brood necessary for high honey production and (bottom) diseased brood which results in weakened colonies and low honey production. (USDA photograph)

Spring...It's Wonderful

The first hint of spring is a time of worry for the beekeeper.

Did the bees make it through the winter?

Then comes a day when the sun is out, rotting the snow. The beekeeper watches the hive. A bee steps delicately out onto the landing platform, and you almost imagine that she yawns and stretches and welcomes the sun. Soon she is joined by others in what are delicately called cleansings flights, and the snow is soon peppered with yellow dots.

The bees made it through the winter.

Every beekeeper knows what the natural impulse is: to open the hive and check it to see if there is enough food, if the queen is laying, how many bees are left.

Fight that impulse.

Wait for a day when the temperature gets to about 60°F. And make this a quick inspection. Remove the covers. See if there are combs of sealed honey next to the cluster of bees. You can tell by looking between the frames just below the top bars. Perhaps if there isn't honey there you can move a comb of honey from the side of the hive to where it is needed.

Remember, the bees will consume more food at this time. Brood is being reared, and the number of bees in the hive is growing. If you're sure there's food, and its available to the cluster, close the hive and move on.

If the hive is short of honey, you may feed it dry sugar. Place the dry granulated sugar on top of the inner cover in the space provided by the rim. The bees will move up through the center hole and find it. Don't feed sugar syrup at this time. This might cause them to rush out of the hive where they might be chilled and never get back into the hives.

Four-inch eaves trough filled with coarse gravel and equipped with float water-level control makes excellent water supply for bees. (USDA photograph)

If weak colonies are found, they can be united with other weak colonies or strong colonies.

And if a hive of dead bees is found, close up all entrances to it to keep out robber bees. As quickly as possible take it into a bee-tight building where it can be cleaned and inspected for disease.

SECOND VISIT

The second visit to the hive should be made when temperatures reach 70°F, when dandelions or fruit trees are blooming.

Look for the queen. It may be necessary to replace her if she is dead or simply not laying many eggs.

Again, check the strength of colonies. Now is the time to unite two weak colonies for best production of honey this season.

Check the food supply again. Each hive should have three brood combs full of honey. If you have more than one hive, it's often possible to move food from one hive to another to meet your needs at this time. Or give them sugar syrup made of one part sugar, one part water.

Now is a good time to reverse the position of the food chamber and the brood chamber, and to clean dead bees and other debris from the bottom board.

Your bees are now ready for the honeyflow, and already you've seen them returning to the hive, carrying loads of bright yellow pollen.

A good season for bees, and for beekeeping, is ahead.

Work with your bees and they will work for you.

Additional Sources of Information

BEE JOURNALS

There are several magazines devoted to the subject of beekeeping. Some of these are listed below. The publishers are generally glad to send you a free sample copy upon request.

American Bee Journal, Hamilton, IL 62341

Gleanings in Bee Culture, The A.I. Root Co., P.O. Box 706, Medina, OH 44256

The Speedy Bee, P.O. Box 998, Jesup, GA 31545–0998

BEEKEEPERS' ORGANIZATIONS

Most states have a state beekeepers' association. Some also have county or regional organizations. Ask your County Agricultural Extension Agent for information regarding these. Their meetings give you a chance to hear speakers on various aspects of beekeeping. Also, you have a chance to associate with other beekeepers and to ask question and compare notes. You will find it very worthwhile to join your local organization.

OTHER STOREY PUBLISHING BOOKS

These two titles by Richard E. Bonney are available at your local bookstore or directly form Storey Books by calling 1–800–441–5700.

Hive Management: A Seasonal Guide for Beekeepers, ISBN 0–88266–637–1.

Beekeeping: A Practical Guide, ISBN 0–88266–861–7.

Butchering Livestock at Home

Phyllis Hobson

Illustrations by Elayne Sears

Getting Ready

Let's start with the animal. Select the best you have or can get. It is disappointing to spend the time and energy required to butcher an animal, then find the quality of the meat is less than you expected. If you want good meat you have to start with a healthy, well-fed, good-looking animal. It should be bright-eyed, glossy-coated (or feathered), and in top shape for its type.

Pamper your animal for a week or two before butchering. Everything you have heard about contented cows goes for hogs and sheep, too. If possible, keep the animal in a special pen. Keep the stall clean and comfortable. Provide the best feed and hay. Keep the water fresh; you might even put a little molasses in it.

All this pampering is not nonsense. It really makes for better-tasting, more nutritious meat. An animal that is relaxed and contented before butchering has all its chemicals in balance. An animal that is agitated or uncomfortable will have its life-protecting chemicals flowing. The result will be tougher, off-flavor meat that will not keep as well.

The day before you plan to butcher, take out all the grain and hay to give the animal's stomach time to empty. It is easier by far, especially for a beginner, to butcher an animal that is as cleaned out as possible. Keep the water bucket full, though, and put in an extra dollop of molasses so the animal will drink more.

Next, select the right environment. There are only two absolutes. The butchering area must be clean and cold. Within those limitations, you can adapt almost any location. A refrigerated, antiseptically clean room is ideal, but a shed with a freshly scrubbed table is fine. If the weather is right, you can make do with a sturdy tree limb for hoisting the larger animals and a clean tree stump for cutting.

A cold temperature is important. The carcass must be chilled quickly and kept cold. All meat, except pork and veal, must be aged up to a week or two at 32 to 35°F.

If you live in a cold climate, you can provide the proper temperature by butchering large animals in late fall when the temperature has dropped to just above freezing and is likely to stay there for at least a week. Small animals and poultry can be butchered at any time because they can be chilled and aged in a refrigerator. In warmer climates, or in an emergency, large animals can be cut into quarters and chilled in a barrel of ice or a spare refrigerator.

In addition to cold temperatures, you will need some equipment and materials. You will not need all of these tools for every butchering job. If

Continued ➜

you are butchering a chicken, you obviously will not need a gun or hoist. But if you are going to butcher a variety of animals, this is the minimum equipment you will need.

- .22 rifle or a .38 caliber pistol and ammunition
- Hooks (or a chain or rope) for hanging the animal
- Block and tackle or a hoist for large animals
- Good, sharp butcher knives (as many as you can assemble)
- Knife sharpener
- Hardwood (or hard plastic) cutting board or surface
- Meat grinder for making ground meat or sausage
- Meat saw
- Meat cleaver
- Large kettle, tub, or barrel for collecting wastes
- Empty gallon-size plastic bottle for chickens or a killing cone
- Hot water for scalding chickens or hogs
- Lots of clean, cold water
- Plastic apron
- Thin plastic gloves
- Plastic or newspapers to protect floor, if necessary

You can make substitutions in order to make do with what you have or can borrow. You do not need a fancy cutting board, for instance; an old kitchen table will do. If you cannot rent or borrow a meat saw or meat cleaver, you can substitute a clean, well-sharpened hacksaw from your workshop.

The meat grinder can be a hand-cranked food chopper with a meat blade, an attachment to your kitchen mixer, or a food processor.

Start with clean, soap-and-water-scrubbed tools and keep a bucket of hot water nearby to clean the knives as you go along. Keep the knife sharpener handy, too. Knives get dull quickly when they keep bumping into bones. There is nothing more frustrating than a knife that will not cut when you need it.

Speaking of frustration, be sure you have everything ready before you start. You do not want to kill or stun your animal, then discover you have no way to hang it. Make a list of the tools you will need for your job, then assemble them, and check your list before you start.

Now comes the hardest part of the whole project for most of us. If you like animals, you found it is fun to raise them. The end result—a freezer full of meat—is rewarding. The skinning and cutting operations are not difficult. But even experienced hunters sometimes have difficulty killing an animal they know.

The idea is to make it as quick and as painless as possible, for your sake, for the sake of the animal, and for the sake of the meat. Besides, if the kill is painless, you will not dread it so much next time.

The experts tell you to stun, not shoot, the animal; but those of us who are amateurs find it is far easier and more humane to shoot. Stunning an animal by hitting it over the head is a method best left to the more experienced. It is amazingly difficult to knock out an animal that way—even a small rabbit.

Which is where you should start—with a rabbit. It is a good idea to think small and work your way up with butchering. First butcher a rabbit, then a chicken, then a lamb, a calf, a hog, and finally a beef.

Which is exactly what we are going to do.

Rabbits

Rabbits provide high-quality protein at low cost and in a short time. A well-fed rabbit will reach frying size while it is still young and tender. It should be butchered between three months and six months of age. The weight at this age will depend on breed and sex, but the meat should be about half the live weight of the rabbit.

Domestic rabbit meat tastes much like chicken, which the cut-up pieces resemble. Rabbit meat is a little drier, practically fat free, and low in sodium.

Usually rabbits are kept in separate cages, so there is no need to pen the animal before butchering. About twenty-four hours before butchering, take away all grain and hay, but supply plenty of water.

Rabbits can be butchered in any weather, and the meat chilled in the refrigerator. One of the simplest ways to provide a clean environment is to kill and skin the animal outside, then complete the cleaning and cutting operations at the kitchen counter.

Start by breaking the animal's neck. Hold the hind legs about waist high with the left hand (or the right hand, if you are left-handed) and hold the rabbit's head firmly with the right hand. Bend the head up and back as far as possible while pulling the body down. Pull with a firm, steady motion until you feel the neck break, then quickly cut off the head with a sharp knife or an ax.

Hang the carcass by the hind feet to allow it to bleed thoroughly. Meat that is not bled quickly and thoroughly after filling will not keep well. Actually, a rabbit bleeds out quickly and can be held upside down for a few minutes, then nailed to a table or board for the skinning operation. However, it is a good idea to get used to hanging since it is a procedure used with larger animals.

To kill a rabbit, hold the hind legs with one hand while bending the rabbit's head up and back as far as possible as you pull the body down.

To hang the rabbit, insert small hanging hooks or a rope or chain through incisions made between the bone and tendon just above the hocks. It helps to cut off the hind feet and pull back the skin from this area before making the incision with a knife.

When the rabbit has bled out, cut off the tail and front feet. Slit the skin from each hind leg to the crotch and from each front leg to the neck. Do not cut down the middle of the belly.

Beginning at the top of the hind legs, fold the skin over and downward. Gently pull it down, using a knife to cut around the vent and to trim off any fat or tissue. Peel the skin off in one piece as you would a tight sock. The skin will come off inside out.

Take the carcass down, rinse it in running water to remove any blood or hair, and place it on a cutting board or table. With a sharp knife, slit the belly from the anus to the breastbone, being careful not to puncture the bladder or intestines. Cut out the anus to free the intestines, then reach in and pull out the entrails. In them you will find the liver. Attached to it is the gall bladder, a sac of dark green liquid that will give a bitter taste to anything it touches. Cut or pull it free from the liver without breaking the sac. Discard the gall bladder and the entrails, saving only the liver. Reach up into the chest cavity and pull out the heart and lungs. Discard the lungs. Wash and refrigerate the heart and liver.

Wash the carcass quickly in cold, running water. Do not soak. Drain well on paper towels. Cover to keep the meat from drying out, and refrigerate three to five days to age the meat. This not only improves the flavor, it makes the meat more tender.

When it is aged, rabbit meat can be roasted or barbecued whole or cut up and fried or braised. The meat can be stored by freezing, canning, or curing.

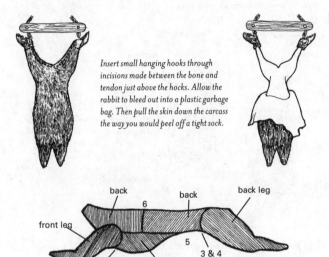

Insert small hanging hooks through incisions made between the bone and tendon just above the hocks. Allow the rabbit to bleed out into a plastic garbage bag. Then pull the skin down the carcass the way you would peel off a tight sock.

Cuts 1 & 2: Cut off both front legs at the shoulder joints.
Cuts 3 & 4: Cut away the hind legs at the hip joints.
Cut 5: Cut through the ribs to separate the breast section.
Cut 6: Cut the back piece in half.

Poultry

Chickens, turkeys, ducks, and geese add nutrition and variety to the diet. Chicken can be fried or broiled, stewed or roasted, and served in cream sauce, casseroles, or with noodles or dumplings. Turkeys, ducks, and geese have long been holiday favorites.

Both chickens and turkeys have a combination of light and dark meat. Ducks and geese have a richer dark meat with a higher percentage of fat.

Young chickens are more tender for frying, but mature birds, which are used for stewing and roasting, have more flavor. Broiler-fryer chickens are best at eight weeks to twelve weeks of age. Stewing or roasting hens and turkeys are butchered at six to twelve months. Ducks and geese are best when butchered at ten to twenty weeks of age.

About 50 percent of the live weight of poultry is edible meat. With younger birds, the percentage is lower because they have a higher ratio of bone to meat than do mature birds.

Poultry should be penned up and denied grain for twenty-four hours before butchering in order to empty the crop and make cleaning easier. Give the bird plenty of water. Geese and ducks often are penned

up four to six weeks before killing in order to fatten them and improve the flavor of the meat.

Here is a simple way to kill chickens, small turkeys, and ducks. Take a one-gallon plastic bottle. Cut off the bottom of the bottle and trim about two inches (more if the bird is large) from the top and handle. Hang the bottle upside down by a rope or small hook to a tree or the side of a building. You can buy a *killing cone* from your farm supply store for the same purpose.

Pick up the bird by the feet and hold it a minute. This head-down position will put the bird to sleep. Insert the unconscious bird upside down into the large end of the hanging plastic bottle or cone and pull the head through the pouring end. Mature geese and turkeys too large to fit one-gallon jugs can be hung by the feet or in a large killing cone.

Open the bird's beak and pierce the back of the roof of the mouth, into the brain, with a sharp knife or ice pick. Immediately pull the head down and cut it off at the neck. Let the carcass bleed out.

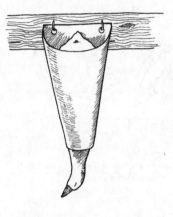

A goose suspended in a killing cone. The head-down position puts the bird to sleep.

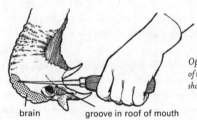

Open the beak and pierce the back of the roof of the mouth with a sharp knife or ice pick.

brain   groove in roof of mouth

As soon as the bleeding stops, scald the bird by dipping it up and down for one minute in hot water (140°F for chickens and turkeys, 160°F for ducks and geese).

Lay the bird on a table and pluck out the wing and tail feathers, then the rest of the feathers. On older birds, singe off any hairs over an open flame. Cut off the feet and wash the carcass thoroughly in running water.

Lay the bird on its back and cut off the tail, including the oil sac just above it. Carefully cut around the vent and cut a slit just through the skin from the vent to the breastbone. Reach in and remove the entrails.

Carefully remove the bile sac from the liver, and clean and peel the gizzard. Cut off the neck and pull out the crop and windpipe from the neck opening. Reach in and remove the heart and lungs from the breast cavity. Wash and refrigerate the neck, liver, heart, and gizzard. Discard the rest.

Continued ➡

Wash the carcass, inside and out, in cold water. Cover and refrigerate forty-eight hours and tenderize the meat. Poultry can then be prepared for the table or stored by freezing, canning, or curing—whole or cut up.

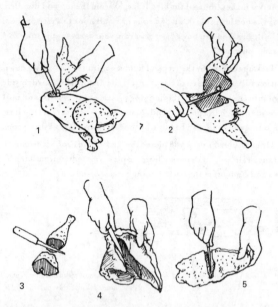

Cut 1: Cut off the wings at the shoulder joints.
Cut 2: Cut off the thighs at the hip joints.
Cut 3: Cut through the joint to separate the leg and thigh.
Cut 4: Cut through the skin at the cavity to the center of the back. Then cut along the ribs to separate the white meat of the breast from bony back pieces.
Cut 5: Cut the breast into two pieces.

Sheep and Goats

Sheep and goats, especially young ones, are small enough for anyone to handle easily; yet the butchering methods are the same as those used on larger livestock.

Sheep and goats can be raised where there is little, or poor, grazing area. The meat of young lambs and kids, three to four months old, has a delicious, subtle flavor when broiled, fried, or roasted. The meat from older sheep, called mutton, or goats, called chevon, tends to be tougher and sometimes needs longer cooking, but it is delicious when used in stews and casseroles, ground into patties, and broiled or braised and pressure-cooked. The hind legs can be cured as hams.

The animals can be butchered at almost any age, but many people consider the meat of very small lambs and kids a special treat. Rams and bucks can be butchered up to one year of age; but for best flavor they should be castrated when they are two or three months old.

A well-fed, three- to four-month-old lamb will weigh 35 pounds to 50 pounds and will dress out at 20 pounds to 30 pounds of meat. Kids do not fatten as well and will weigh less. Mature sheep and large goats will weigh up to 100 pounds. About 60 percent of this is edible meat.

Animals of any size should be confined for a week to ten days before butchering. During this time, keep them calm and well-fed. Mature animals should be starved, but given plenty of water, for twenty-four hours before butchering. Animals less than three months old should have feed withheld for no more than six to eight hours.

Sheep and goats are excitable animals and should be slaughtered when they are preoccupied. Also, since their skulls are fortified for butting, it is difficult to stun or shoot a sheep or goat on top of the head. It is best to shoot it in the brain through the back of the head.

To distract the animal and get it in position for shooting, place a small pan of grain on the ground before it. When the animal's head is lowered to the pan, aim for the spot just under the ear.

Immediately after it drops, slit the throat and hang the carcass by the hind legs. Traditionally this is done by cutting a slit between the tendon and bone just above the hocks and inserting a hanging hook or rope in each slit. However, Paula Simmons, in Garden Way's *Raising Sheep the Modern Way*, recommends a new method of hanging the carcass by the aitchbone (pelvic bone) to produce a more tender meat. This method may be used with any of the larger animals.

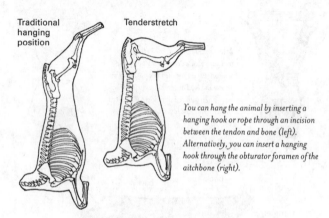

Traditional hanging position   Tenderstretch

You can hang the animal by inserting a hanging hook or rope through an incision between the tendon and bone (left). Alternatively, you can insert a hanging hook through the obturator foramen of the aitchbone (right).

With the animal hanging, cut off the head, tail, and all four feet to the hocks. Cut around the anus and vagina or penis area; then make a slit, just through the hide, between the two front legs and between the two hind legs. From the center of these two cuts, slit down the middle of the belly.

Starting at the hind legs, skin the animal by pulling back the skin with one hand while using the knife to cut it loose with the other.

As soon as the skin is removed, wash off the carcass with a hose or damp cloth. Using a clean knife, make a slit down the abdomen from the pelvis to the breastbone, taking care not to puncture the stomach or intestines. Cut around the anus and tie it off with a piece of twine to keep the contents from contaminating the meat. Reach inside and pull the

Lambs and Kids

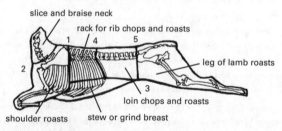

slice and braise neck
rack for rib chops and roasts
leg of lamb roasts
loin chops and roasts
shoulder roasts
stew or grind breast

Cut 1: Saw off both shoulders between the fifth and sixth ribs.
Cut 2: Cut off the neck flush with shoulder.
Cut 3: Remove the breast with a saw.
Cut 4: Cut between the last two ribs. Saw through the backbone.
Cut 5: Separate the loin from the leg at the small of the back. Saw through the backbone.

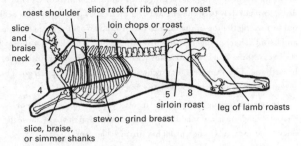

Mutton and Chevon

roast shoulder — slice rack for rib chops or roast

slice and braise neck

loin chops or roast

1 6 7

2

4 5 8

sirloin roast

leg of lamb roasts

stew or grind breast

slice, braise, or simmer shanks

Cut 1: Saw across the carcass between the fifth and sixth ribs.
Cut 2: Cut off the neck even with shoulder.
Cut 3: Separate the right and left shoulders by sawing through the backbone.
Cut 4: Saw off the shanks.
Cut 5: Saw off breast piece.
Cut 6: Cut between the last two ribs. Separate the two pieces by cutting through the backbone.
Cut 7: Cut and saw through at the small of the back. Split the loin by sawing through the backbone.
Cut 8: Cut away the sirloin, leaving it in one piece.

anus inside. Gently pull out the entrails into a container, cutting them loose as you go.

Wash out the cavity with a hose and let it hang in a cold place (32 to 35°F) for five to seven days.

Lambs and kids often are barbecued or baked whole. Larger animals can be cut into roasts and chops, and the scraps ground for patties.

Baby Beef or Veal Calves

Beef calves can be kept in small pastures or barn lots and fed hay and grain, then butchered at six months to eight months of age as baby beef. A six-month-old beef calf that has been well fed will weigh from 300 to 400 pounds, depending on the breed and sex. Approximately 55 to 60 percent of this is edible meat.

Newborn calves also can be set aside as veal calves, kept confined to a stall, and fed nothing but milk for eight to ten weeks. A well-fed veal calf will weigh up to 180 pounds at this age and will yield about 100 pounds of meat.

Baby beef is a lighter-colored, milder-flavored more tender form of beef. The steaks and roasts are smaller. Baby beef may be broiled, pan-fried, or roasted.

Veal is a light, delicate meat that is expensive and difficult to find in the supermarket. Chops and steaks usually are broiled. The meat is very tender and can be used in casseroles and dishes that call for chicken.

Beef calves six months old or older should be confined at least three days before butchering. All feed except water should be withheld the last twenty-four hours. Veal calves should be fed their usual ration of milk up to six to eight hours before butchering.

Kill the calf with a well-aimed shot in the center of the forehead just above the eyes. As soon as it falls, lay the animal on its back and slit the throat lengthwise and push the knife up under the breastbone between the first two ribs. Cut to the backbone on either side of the gullet. This will sever the carotid arteries and allow the animal to bleed well.

Hang the carcass by inserting hooks or a sturdy rope through incisions made just above the hocks or in the pelvic bone on each side. Using a hoist or rope, pull the animal up to a comfortable working height. (This procedure is the same as for sheep.)

When it has finished bleeding, skin the head by cutting across the top and down each side of the face to the corners of the mouth. Skin the face, then the back of the head. Cut off the head. (To use the head, see page 215 on using the by-products.)

Slit the throat lengthwise and push the knife up under the breastbone between the first two ribs.

Cut off the front feet at the joints. Then, working on the underside, slit just through the skin from the end of each front leg to the neck opening and from the end of each hind leg to the anus. Cut around the anus and vagina or penis area and slit just through the skin down the middle of the belly. Be careful not to puncture the stomach or intestines.

Remove the hide by pulling and holding it taut with one hand while cutting it loose with a knife in the other. As soon as the hide is removed, cut a slit just through the abdominal wall, from the anus to the breastbone. Hold the knife inside and cut from the inside out to keep from puncturing the entrails.

Prepare for the removal of the entrails by working out the gullet and windpipe as far as possible through the slit you made in the throat. Tie off the gullet with a piece of twine. If you are butchering a heifer calf, reach into the abdominal cavity and tie off the vagina and anus together. On a male calf, tie off the anus, then reach in and tie off the urethra (the tube to the bladder) and remove the exterior genitals.

Work the intestines free of the backbone carefully cutting it loose with a knife. Ease the anus inside through the opening you made. Let the entrails drop down into a container, cutting away any tissue holding them.

Split the chilled carcass down the center of the backbone with a meat cleaver.

Continued ➡

Hose off the carcass inside and out. Chill the whole carcass for twenty-four hours. Baby beef should hang another four or five days for aging, but veal calves should be cut, without aging, as soon as they are chilled to the bone.

To cut the meat, first split the carcass down the center of the backbone with a meat cleaver or saw. Cut each side into two quarters by cutting between the last two ribs. This will leave twelve ribs on the front quarter and one rib on the hind quarter. Use a saw to cut through the backbone. Lay each quarter on a cutting table and cut as the illustrations show.

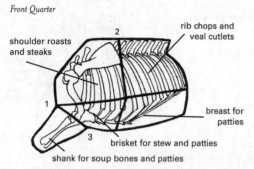

Front Quarter

Cut 1: Saw through the quarter lengthwise, beginning just above the shank and cutting to the center.
Cut 2: Cut all the way across between the fifth and sixth ribs. Saw through the backbone.
Cut 3: Saw off the shank at the joint.

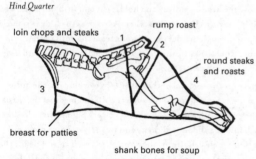

Hind Quarter

Cut 1: Cut across at the socket of the hip joint. Start with a knife, then finish with a saw.
Cut 2: Separate the rump from the round with a knife and saw.
Cut 3: Cut away the breast.
Cut 4: Saw off the shank. Cut through the meat, down along the bone, then saw through the joint.

Hogs

Pork is one of the most versatile meats. It can be served fresh or cured, fried or roasted, barbecued whole, or ground into sausage. Because it is butchered when the animal is quite young, all the cuts are tender, mild-tasting meat. Also, it is the easiest and cheapest meat to raise. A novice with a small pen and no pasture can raise 150 pounds of pork in four to six months.

A hog should be butchered when it is six months to eight months old and weighs about 200 pounds to 220 pounds. Since a hog has a high dressing percentage—about 75 to 80 percent—a 200-pound hog will provide about 150 pounds of dressed meat plus about 20 pounds of lard.

If the hog is on pasture, it should be penned up two or three days before butchering. Take away all feed the last twenty-four hours, but offer plenty of water.

With the animal still penned up, stun it by shooting it in the center of the forehead at point-blank range. It should drop instantly. When it does, immediately turn the animal over on its back and stretch the neck out by forcing the top of the nose to the ground. Working from the head and using a sharp, long-bladed knife, slit through the skin just above the breastbone. Work the knife downward until it slips back under the breastbone. Then cut straight downward as far as the knife will go. This severs the main artery and allows the hog to bleed out well.

Immediately hang the carcass by inserting meat hooks or a rope or chain through incisions made between the tendon and the bone above the hock. Let the carcass hang until it has finished bleeding.

SKINNING

Traditionally the hog is not skinned. Instead the hide is scalded and scraped to remove the hair and dirt. The butchering is then completed with the skin on. When cured, this skin becomes the rind on hams and bacon.

Scalding can be done in any clean container large enough to hold at least half of the carcass at a time. A metal livestock watering tank is ideal because it will hold the entire carcass; but a fifty-gallon barrel can be used.

Place the container under the hanging carcass and fill it half full with hot water (145°F. in warm weather, 160° in cold weather). Add one-half cup of lye to the water and stir with a wooden paddle.

Using a hoist, lower the carcass into the hot water. First dip the front end, then the hind end. Completely immerse each end, then raise and lower it with the hoist, or move it back and forth with your hands. Keep it under the water and in motion for about five minutes in the 145°F. water, or for three minutes if the water is 160°F.

Lay the carcass on a flat surface and scrape off the hair, using a scraper or the dull edge of a knife. Some farmers shave the hair off. When the hair is removed, scrape with a knife or wire brush to scrub out the dirt and remove the outer layer of skin. Rinse off well with cold water and hang again.

If you think all that scalding and scraping sounds like a lot of work, you are right. It is. It also is unnecessary, according to some home butchers. Since no one eats the skin anyway, they see no need to go to all the trouble of scalding and scraping it. Instead, a hog can be skinned just as you would skin a calf, but unless you plan to tan the pig skin, there is an easier way.

First wash off the hanging carcass with a hose. Then cut the skin off in strips about three inches wide. Start the strips with a sharp knife at the top of the carcass and pull them down as far as you can with your hands. Skin the entire animal this way, then remove the head by cutting across the back of the neck just above the ears. Cut through the gullet and windpipe. Let the head drop and wait a minute for the bleeding to finish. Pull down on the ears and cut from the ears to the eyes and then to the point of the jawbone. This cuts off the head but leaves the jowls on the carcass.

Make a deep cut up the center of the hind legs from the foot to the hock. In each incision you will find three tendons. Work them out with the fingers.

EVISCERATING

Place a container under the hanging carcass to catch the entrails and open the abdomen by cutting from the sticking point in the throat upward to the breastbone, being careful not to puncture the stomach. Using the knife as a pry, split the breastbone.

Continue the cut down the belly, being very careful not to cut into the stomach or intestines. Hold the knife down, with the blade pointing out or hold the hand inside to protect the entrails. Cut around the reproductive organs to the anus. To release the intestine, cut around the anus, cutting it free, but not cutting into it. Tie off the end with a piece of twine and work the tied-off end through the hole you cut into the abdominal cavity. Pull the entrails out into the container below, cutting away any tissue holding them. Cut the gullet loose from the chest cavity and pull it out with the stomach.

Hose out the inside of the empty carcass and remove any large pieces of fat, including the long strips of flaky-looking leaf fat that run the length of the carcass. Save them for lard.

CUTTING THE MEAT

While the carcass is still warm, split it down the middle of the backbone with a knife or saw. Leave about twelve inches of skin intact at the shoulders to hold the two sides together.

Pork is not aged like beef but should be thoroughly chilled before cutting or curing. Let it hang for twenty-four hours where the temperature is between 32° and 35°F.

When the carcass is chilled to the bone, cut the skin holding the two sides together and lay each half on the cutting table to cut as the illustrations show.

Pork Cuts

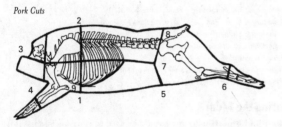

Cut 1: Cut between the fourth and fifth ribs. Use a saw to cut through the backbone.
Cut 2: Cut off the jowl. Trim to a square.
Cut 3: Separate the butt from the shoulder. Trim the shoulder to look like a small ham.
Cut 4: Saw off the front foot.
Cut 5: Cut off the ham at the joint. Trim to round off the corners.
Cut 6: Cut off the hind foot.
Cut 7: Using a saw, cut the center piece in half lengthwise.
Cut 8: Trim the fat back from the loin.
Cut 9: Cut the spareribs from the top of the back.

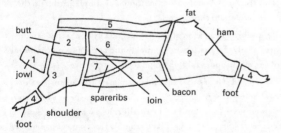

1. *Cure the jowl as a bacon square.*
2. *The Boston butt is cured or ground for sausage.*
3. *The shoulder can be cured as a picnic ham or roasted fresh.*
4. *Simmer or pickle the feet.*
5. *The fatback can be cured or used in lard or sausage.*
6. *Cut between the ribs for loin chops or roast. Pull out the meaty strip of tenderloin and cut the remainder into short ribs.*
7. *Spareribs can be baked or simmered.*
8. *Bacon is cured.*
9. *Ham is cured.*

Beef

Beef is the most universally liked meat. Ask any adult their favorite meal and chances are it starts with a steak; ask a child and it is a hamburger.

The steps for butchering beef are essentially the same as the steps for butchering a rabbit—killing, hanging and skinning the animal, removing the entrails, aging the carcass, and cutting the meat. A 1,000-pound beef calf is not more complicated to butcher than a 3-pound rabbit. Just bigger.

It is a good idea to start with a yearling calf. A grain-fed yearling will weigh from 800 pounds to 1,000 pounds and about 400 to 500 pounds of that will be edible meat. The carcass is not as hard to handle as a 1,200-pound to 1,500-pound older calf, and you will have less invested in it than in an animal you have had to feed for two years.

Pen the calf up a week or two before butchering and give it plenty of feed, quiet, and attention. Keep it in familiar surroundings, if possible, with quiet, reassuring sounds. A softly playing radio nearby is a help. The day before butchering take away all hay and grain, but provide plenty of water.

When you are ready to butcher, halter the animal or tie a rope around the neck and quietly lead it to the tree or shed where you have the hoist in place. Remember, this animal weighs 1,000 pounds or so. After killing it, you will not be able to move it from place to place easily.

When you have it directly under the hoist, tie the animal securely with the head held up and shoot it. Aim for a spot just above the eyes in the middle of the forehead.

Move quickly now. As soon as the calf falls, roll it over on its back and slit the neck from the jawbone to the breastbone. At the breastbone, push the knife under the bone and between the first ribs. Cut to the backbone on either side of the gullet. Turn the knife over and cut downward to sever the carotid arteries.

Immediately insert hanging hooks or a chain in incisions between the tendons and bones at the hocks just above the first joint in the hind legs. Hoist the animal off the ground, upside down, to a comfortable working height. You will need to adjust the height from time to time as you work. As the animal bleeds out, you can help by pumping the front legs up and down a few times.

With this large an animal, the next few steps are easier if the animal is lowered back to the ground and laid on its back. However, if you do not have a hoist that allows you to raise and lower the weight easily, these procedures can be done with the carcass hanging.

SKINNING

Skin the head by cutting through the hide across the top of the skull, then down to the eye and the corner of the mouth on each side. Start peeling off the skin at the point where the throat was cut, loosening the hide free with a knife where necessary.

Cut off the head and remove the cheek meat. Sever the tendons on the front legs by cutting across the legs between the foot and the dewclaws. Cut the skin loose around the feet and make a slit on each to above the knee at the back of the legs. Pull the skin back and cut the foot off at the joint.

Cutting carefully to avoid puncturing the abdominal wall, make a slit just through the skin from the cut you made in the breastbone down the middle of the belly to the rump. Cut around the scrotum or udder and continue to slit the skin on each side up the hind legs to the point

Continued →

they were slit to the hocks. Make similar slits down the front legs from the breastbone.

Pull back the skin on the insides of the thighs on all four legs. Then, using a fresh, well-sharpened knife, start at the belly and remove the hide by grasping the skin and pulling it up and out with one hand while you cut it loose with the other. If you have a skinning knife, this is a good time to use it.

Hold the knife blade slightly outward to avoid cutting into the meat or hide while you remove as much fat as possible from the hide. Skin the front and sides. Then, if you lowered the carcass to the ground, hoist it up again, and finish skinning the back. Skin the tail down a few inches, then cut it off. Keep the skin in one piece. It can be sold or used for leather.

Now take a minute to wash off the skinned carcass. Some experts say not to use water on the meat; certainly you do not want to soak it. But you will find at this point the carcass has more blood and hairs on it than you would like. Use a hose and wipe it down with a dry towel or wash it with a clean cloth dipped in water. Clean off the knives in hot water and place a large container under the carcass.

EVISCERATING

Reach into the throat opening you made and work out the gullet and windpipe as far as possible. Tie the gullet off with a piece of sturdy twine so any stomach contents will not contaminate the meat.

Now cut open the carcass from breastbone to anus, being careful to cut only through the abdominal wall and not to puncture the intestines. Saw through the breastbone and the pelvic arch to lay the carcass open.

Cut the anus loose, tie off the end with a piece of twine, and carefully cut away any tissue holding it. Gently ease the entrails out and into the container below, cutting them loose as necessary. Now split the carcass down the middle of the backbone with a saw or cleaver, and hose the insides of the carcass with cold water.

Let the sides hang in a temperature of 32° to 35°F for six to seven days for yearling calves, up to ten to fifteen days for older beef.

CUTTING THE MEAT

When you are ready to cut the meat, separate each side into two quarters by cutting across the carcass between the twelfth and thirteenth ribs. Since the carcass has thirteen ribs, this leaves twelve ribs on the front quarter and one rib on the hind quarter. Slant the cut at the belly and cut to the backbone, then saw through the spine.

Lay the front quarter on the cutting table, bone-side down, and cut it into five large pieces. Cut up the front quarters first, as shown. Then lower one of the hind quarters from the joist and place it on the cutting table, bone-side down and cut that piece as the illustration shows. Repeat with the other hind quarter. All scraps, as well as any cut you wish to use, can be used for ground beef.

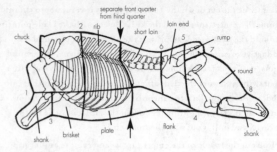

First separate the front quarter from the hind quarter.
Cut 1: Cut from the rib to just above the elbow joint, starting 10 inches from the backbone.
Cut 2: Cut between the fifth and sixth ribs to separate the rib from the chuck, and continue sawing downward to separate the plate and brisket.
Cut 3: Saw off the front shank at the elbow.
Cut 4: Trim away the boneless triangular flank from the belly.
Cut 5: Separate the loin from the round at the hip joint.
Cut 6: Starting at the hip joint, divide the loin into two pieces, the short loin and the loin end.
Cut 7: Remove the rump from the round by sawing across the aitchbone.
Cut 8: Cut off the hind shank by cutting through to the bone on the back side, then cutting along the bone to the joint. Work the knife between the joints.

Preparing the Cuts
Cut the chuck into pot roasts and boned rolled roasts.
Cut between the ribs for rib steaks or use for standing rib roasts.
The front shank should be cut into soup bones.
The brisket is used for corned and ground beef.
The plate is cut into short ribs or ground for beef patties.
Pull out the flank steak and use the rest of the flank for ground beef.
Slice the loin end into sirloin steaks.
The short loin is sliced into porterhouse, T-bone, and club steaks.
The rump is roasted.
Slice the top of the round for steaks, the bottom for pot roasts.
The shank is ground or simmered in soups.

Storing the Meat

Meat is highly perishable and should be used or stored as soon as it is cut. Always keep meat well chilled. Before butchering, decide how the meat is to be stored, which cuts will be frozen or canned, and which will be cured. Be sure you have the space in the freezer or pantry shelves and the materials you will need for the storage method you choose.

FREEZING

No other method of storing meat preserves the fresh texture and flavor as well as freezing. And no other method is as simple. Just trim the meat, wrap it, and freeze it.

Before wrapping, trim off excess fat and any bones that can be removed easily. Fat turns rancid quickly and cuts down on the storage life of the meat. Bones take up too much freezer space.

Do not add salt or other seasonings to meat (including fresh sausage) before freezing. Freeze meats in packages for one meal in the right amount for your family. The smaller the packages, the easier they are to freeze, store, and thaw. Place a double thickness of paper between chops and steaks so they can be separated easily.

The storage life of unsliced, cured meats is two months to three months at 0°F. Ground meats and pork will keep well for four months at that temperature. Veal will keep up to six months. Beef and lamb cuts can be stored up to nine months.

Poultry keeps better when packaged whole, but it is sometimes convenient to cut up chickens and sort the pieces, separating the meaty ones from the bony pieces. If you are freezing several chickens, you may want to package together all thighs, or all drumsticks, or all white meat for special dishes. Package livers separately and use them within three months. Other giblets and poultry meat can be stored up to nine months.

CANNING

Meat and poultry can be canned with excellent results. Canned meats are a delicious convenience. Some meats, notably cured meats, keep longer when canned than when frozen.

Trim off all fat and cut the meat into pieces convenient for use. Remove large bones and cube less tender cuts for use in stews. Form ground meat into one-inch balls or patties, or cook in tomato sauce. Poultry can be cooked and boned or packed raw, with the bone in.

Pack raw meat loosely into clean pint-size or quart-size canning jars or metal cans. Do not add liquid. Cooked meats should be covered with water or cooking liquid. Process pints for seventy-five minutes, quarts for ninety minutes, in a pressure canner at ten pounds of pressure. Follow the manufacturer's directions for sealing cans or jars.

CURING

The curing process not only lengthens the storage life of meats, it also adds its own distinctive flavor. Although hams and bacon are the traditional cuts reserved for curing, any meat can be cured with delicious results. Pork chops and spareribs are good when cured, and the hind leg of mutton or chevon tastes much like ham when cured. Almost any beef cut can be cured for dried beef or corned beef. Cured chickens or turkeys are tasty.

To obtain a good cure, you must provide cool temperatures, the right amount of salt, and the process must be timed carefully.

Cool temperatures. The meat must be kept cold throughout the curing process. If you cannot trust the weather to stay below 40°F, it is possible to cure small batches in the refrigerator in a covered bowl or plastic bag. Sometimes cold storage space can be rented at the local butchering plant.

Salt. Weigh the salt and the meat. The sugar gives the cured meat its flavor, but it is the salt that keeps it from spoiling. Use fine, granulated table salt, not iodized.

Time. Timing is important in curing. If you allow too much time, the meat will be hard and salty; too little, and it will spoil. Meat should remain in the brine or dry-cure one day to three days per pound, depending on the size of the cut and the amount of cure desired. Bacon and Canadian bacon should be cured one day per pound for a mild cure, up to one and a half days per pound for maximum keeping quality. Hams and shoulders should be cured two days to three days per pound. After curing, the meat should hang in a cool place one week to three weeks to age and to let the salt spread evenly through the meat.

There are excellent sugar-cure mixtures on the market, but if you would like to make your own, here is a brine recipe recommended by the United States Department of Agriculture.

BRINE RECIPE

6 gallons water

12 pounds salt

3 pounds white or brown sugar

100 pounds of chilled meat

Dissolve the salt and sugar in the water and bring to a boil. Stir well and chill thoroughly before using. When the meat and brine both are well chilled, pack the meat in a clean stone crock or wooden barrel. Place hams on the bottom, skin-side down, then the shoulders, and finally the bacon slabs, skin-side up. Pack the meat tightly and weight it down so it will not float in the brine. Pour the cold brine over the meat, being certain all the meat is immersed. Keep the container in a cool (under 40°F.) place for seven days.

At the end of seven days, pour the brine into a pan. Remove the meat and repack it, repositioning the pieces for an even cure. Pour the brine back over the meat, and keep it in a cool place until the curing is complete.

After curing, the meat should hang in a cold place one week to three weeks to age. It can then be smoked or used as is.

Using the By-Products

If a 600-pound animal is 50 percent to 60 percent edible meat, you will be left with 300 to 400 pounds of both edible and nonedible by-products when you have finished butchering. Whatever the size of the animal you butchered, you will have a container of entrails and several pounds of hide and bones left over.

Do not throw them away. With a little ingenuity and some work, every bit of the animal can be used.

ORGAN MEATS

The organ meats of large animals—the brains, tongue, heart, kidneys, liver, sweetbreads, and tripe—are even more nutritious than the muscle meats. Liver and kidneys are high in vitamins and minerals and are very flavorful meats. Brains, sweetbreads, and tripe are delicate both in texture and flavor. The tongue and heart are fine textured and mild flavored.

Do not age the organ meats with the carcass. Brains, sweetbreads, kidneys, and tripe are extremely perishable and should be cooked within twenty-four hours after butchering. Liver, heart, and tongue can be stored in the freezer.

Brains and tongue. Immediately after cutting off the head, whether or not it is skinned, soak it in cold water. Rinse well in running water. When the butchering is completed, remove the tongue by making an incision on each side of the head just inside the jaw. Cut through the cartilage at the base of the tongue, pull the tongue out, and cut it off. Remove the cheek meat on each side of the jawbone and add it to the muscle meats. Split or saw the skull open and remove the brains.

Heart. The heart, lungs, and gullet of the animal are attached to the backbone in the chest cavity. Remove them together. Trim the heart and wash well. Discard the lungs and gullet.

Kidneys. Two kidneys will be found in the abdominal cavity on each side of the backbone. Cut through the knob of fat to the kidneys, removing the white membrane covering them.

Liver. Remove the liver with the intestines. Attached to it is the gall bladder, a sac of dark green liquid that will give a bitter taste to anything it touches. Carefully cut or pull the sac from the liver without breaking the sac. Wash and refrigerate the liver. Discard the sac.

Sweetbreads. Sweetbreads are the thymus glands of the calf and lamb. Pork sweetbreads are not used. The gland resembles the heart and is located near it at the base of the neck.

Continued →

Tripe. The lining of the first and second stomachs of calves is used as tripe. Plain tripe is the lining of the first stomach. Honeycomb tripe, the most popular, is the lining of the second stomach. Cut the stomachs from the gullet, slit them open, and turn them inside out. Wash and rinse several times in clean, cold water. Tripe must be simmered in water to cover four hours or more, until tender. Refrigerate it until you are ready to cook it for a meal.

PELTS AND HIDES

Whether you plan to sell it or tan it yourself, the skin of the animal is a valuable by-product. When you have finished skinning the animal, take a minute to put the hide out of harm's way in a dry place in the shade while you continue with the butchering.

As soon as the carcass has been cleaned and gutted and set aside to chill, spread the skin out on a clean surface, fur-side down, and carefully scrape off any fat or meat. At this point, you can salt the green hide to preserve it for a week or so until you have time to tan it.

If possible, weigh the hide and measure one pound of salt for every pound of hide. If this is not possible, allow about twenty-five pounds of salt for a mature beef, fifteen pounds for a small calf, and ten pounds for a sheep or goat. Use about three pounds of salt for a lamb or kid skin and one pound or less for a rabbit skin. When in doubt it is better to use too much salt rather than too little.

Spread out the cleaned and scraped hide to eliminate wrinkles. Dampen the inside of the skin if it has dried out. Sprinkle a layer of salt over every inch of the hide, then rub it in well, using a brush or your hands.

When all the salt is rubbed in, fold in the four edges, loosely roll up the hide, and store it in a cool, dry place. If you must keep it longer than a week, shake out the hide, drain it, resalt it, and roll it up for another week.

The hide can be stored in the freezer for later tanning. After the skin is cleaned and scraped, roll it up and put it in a plastic freezer bag. Do not salt it. Use a vacuum cleaner hose to remove the air in the bag and seal well. Store at 0°F. for no more than a month. (For detailed tanning instructions, see Phyllis Hobson's *Tan Your Hide*.)

FEATHERS

As you pluck poultry, separate the down from the feathers. Spread both separately in thin layers over a flat surface. A window screen works well. Cover with a layer of cheesecloth, fasten the cloth down, and dry it in a well-ventilated place. Use the down for quilted jackets and the feathers to stuff pillows.

BONES AND HORNS

For a delicious, nutritious meat broth and soup base, fill a sixteen-quart pressure canner with the trimmed bones left over from butchering. Half fill the canner with water. Cook at fifteen pounds of pressure for one hour, then turn off the heat, and let the pressure drop. Strain the broth into a clean kettle. Remove whatever meat is left on the bones and add it to the kettle. A kettle full of closely-trimmed bones will yield at least a quart of meat. Chill the broth and lift off the fat. The meat and defatted broth can be canned or frozen. A beef will yield five or six canners full of bones.

This broth is very rich in calcium from the bones, but there are still a lot of minerals left in the bones after cooking. Give some bones to the dogs and bury the rest around fruit trees or among permanent plantings in the garden, where they will slowly leach out and enrich the soil.

Horns can be fashioned into beautiful knife handles, decorative inlays, buttons, toggle fasteners, and zipper pulls.

FAT

A pure, white lard can be made from the back and side fat of pork. It should be rendered over very low heat in a large, heavy kettle. Cut up or grind the fat to speed the process and stir it frequently to keep the pieces from sticking. As the lard cooks out, the cracklings will float to the top. As they do, skim them off and drain them. They are delicious in corn bread. When all the pieces have floated to the top, turn off the heat and let the liquid cool for thirty minutes. Ladle the lard into small coffee cans or plastic containers without disturbing the settlings on the bottom. Strain what is left through a piece of muslin and package separately. Store lard in the refrigerator. For long-term storage, keep it in the freezer.

Use the intestinal fat from hogs and all the fat from sheep and calves to make soap and candles.

SAUSAGE AND BOLOGNA CASINGS

The small intestine of the hog is used for sausage casings. Small intestines from beef are stuffed to make wieners. Large beef intestines are used for bologna. To prepare them for stuffing, first tie off the intestine at both ends with twine, then cut them loose. Remove any fat, untie one end, and carefully strip out the contents by squeezing with the fingers from the top to the bottom. Thoroughly wash the casing, inside and out, first in clear water, then in hot, soapy water, then again in clear water. This is easier to do if two people work together, or if the intestine is cut into several pieces.

Once the casing is cleaned, turn it inside out. With the dull edge of a knife, scrape off the mucous coating on the inside (now the outside). Wash again and soak for several hours in a solution of three tablespoons bleach to one gallon cold water. Rinse, turn right-side-out and rinse again before using.

IN THE GARDEN

Now that you have used up everything else, you are left with the entrails from the animal and some other things, including the blood. Do not waste them; they can add valuable nutrients to your garden.

You can make a rich, humusy compost by adding them—and any other by-products you did not use, except fat—to leaves, grass clippings, garbage, and manure and anything else organic you can find. Add any feathers, hide, or bones you have leftover, too. They will take a few years to decay, but they will keep feeding the soil, wherever they are. Mix it up, cover with a layer of soil, and wait a few weeks, then mix it up again. After a month or two you will have a soft, black soil that will do wonders for your plants.

And think how good you will feel, knowing that none of the animal you butchered went to waste.

Cooking

GENERAL

Cooking with Winter Squash & Pumpkins

Mary Anna DuSablon

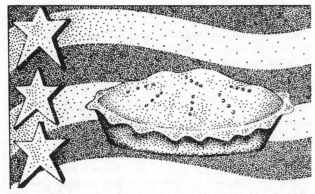

"The American pie is perhaps the most ridiculed of all dishes. It has, however, great popularity and undoubted merits."

Mary Ronalds, *The Century Cook Book, 1896.*

Winter squash and pumpkins are a good source of vitamin A. Squash and pumpkin flesh can be used as a poultice for burns and inflammations. One large glass of juice taken before breakfast is a reliable laxative.

The seeds, high in leucine, tyrosine, and the B complex vitamins, are reputed to be a cure for both roundworms and tapeworms. The seeds are slightly sedative in nature, and it is said that they also calm sexual excitement, which may or may not be an asset. Oddly, these same seeds can cause inebriation of ducks, who are very fond of them.

The leaves and blossoms are also edible. The *young* leaves can be cooked and eaten like any other green if you are looking for novelty. The blossoms should be eaten fresh. When choosing blossoms for any recipe, be sure to take the male flowers, that is, the flower with the longer stem. Leave the female to bear fruit. Squash and pumpkin flowers are delicately flavored.

Types of Squash

Here is a condensed guide to the many strains and hybrids of winter squash. All may be baked, boiled, steamed, frozen, canned, or dried, but special note has been made of some individual differences in these varieties.

Acorn. An acorn-shaped squash with a dark green rind and golden-yellow, sweet-flavored flesh. These squash are especially good for baking and stuffing. One squash will usually serve two people. Can be frozen in halves. For best flavor, use within a few months of harvest, before the flesh turns bright orange.

Banana. A very large squash with a long, cylindrical body and small seed cavity. Usually weighs around 10–35 pounds. Good keeper; thick flesh, fine-grained.

Buttercup. Averaging 3–4 pounds, this drum-shaped squash has a tough, green rind. It cooks extra dry, but its sweet potato flavor is good steamed or baked. Medium to medium-long storage life.

Continued ➜

Butternut. Bottle-shaped or straight, this squash has a pinkish-tan hide and averages 2–4 pounds in weight. Its sweet, nutty flavor and fine texture make it good for pies. Good keeper but will get stringy eventually.

Butterbush. The bush-type butternut squash with reddish-orange flesh and average weight of 1 1/2 pounds. Good keeper; nice for baking and stuffing.

Cushaw. Crookneck or pear-shaped with a light buff or green-striped rind. Cooks and tastes like squash, good for baking and boiling for mashing. Good for pies and canning.

Delicious. Round, yellow or dark green, heart-shaped squash with orange flesh. Good for canning and freezing. Higher in vitamin content than most winter squash; used for baby food.

Hubbard. Comes in green, gold, or blue varieties. With its hard shell, it keeps until spring. Large, nice for large families. Freezes, cans, and dries well. Excellent boiled for mashed squash dishes.

Spaghetti. Not really a winter squash, but it will keep well nonetheless. You can cook this novelty squash in boiling water and then substitute it in any recipe calling for spaghetti. This squash can be cooked and chilled for use in salads, too. Spaghetti squash is oval, with a cream-colored or tan rind and yellow spaghettilike texture inside.

Sweet Dumpling. Very small, sweet, delicious winter squash, weighing only about 1/2 pound apiece. Great baked, plain, or stuffed. Freeze halves.

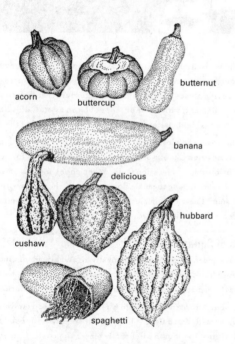

acorn
buttercup
butternut
banana
delicious
hubbard
cushaw
spaghetti

Storage

A ripe squash is easily detected; if your thumbnail cannot penetrate the skin, it is mature. But check the color first. If you test an immature squash and you do penetrate the skin, that squash will not store as long. There is no hurry to harvest winter squash and pumpkins; they cannot over-ripen on the vine. Just pick the mature fruit sometime before the first frost.

When you harvest the fruit, leave a few inches of stem attached, and handle with care. Just because they are large and tough looking does not mean they are invulnerable to rough handling.

Winter squash and pumpkins must be cured before they can be put into storage. This will dry and harden their skins. Ideally, they should be left to cure in a warm, well-ventilated place for about ten days. Look for a spot, perhaps on a sunny porch, or by a woodstove where the temperature ranges between 75 and 85°F.

Ideal storage conditions for these vegetables is in a cool, dry place, approximately 50°F., 50–70 percent humidity, with moderate air circulation. A basement or an attic with a fan might be just the thing. They should be set securely on shelves, not touching each other.

Outside storage might run the risk of freezing your vegetables, and inside the home where temperatures run above 55°F. will cause them to get

stringy. Even under the best conditions pumpkins and winter squash will not stay perfect forever. Eventually the starch content will turn to sugar and the water content will increase. For this reason some people freeze, dry, can, or pickle some pumpkin or squash to use during the late winter months.

BAKING

To get a crusty top on your squash, cut in halves or pieces, remove seeds and fibers. Place the squash flesh side up on an oven rack or baking sheet and bake for 20–60 minutes at 350°F. until fork tender. The time will vary depending on the size of the squash. Brush with butter and seasonings before or during baking, if desired.

To get a soft top, cut in halves, remove seeds and fibers. Brush with butter seasonings and place face down on baking sheet. Or wrap each piece in aluminum foil. Bake 20–60 minutes at 350°F. until fork tender. Baking a whole squash might result in the squash exploding in the oven.

BOILING

Place halved or cut-up and seeded squash in boiling water. Boil for 15–30 minutes or until fork tender, depending on the size of the squash. Do not overcook.

STEAMING

This method is best for retaining nutrients. Place halved or cut-up and seeded squash in the top of a boiler or blancher. Cover and cook for 20–40 minutes, or until fork tender.

PUREE

After you have baked, boiled, or steamed your squash or pumpkin, you can puree it to use in many recipes. Simply remove flesh from rind and put through strainer or food mill. Some food mills, such as the Squeezo, have special large-hole screens that make the job of straining the flesh go quickly.

Preserving

Winter squash and pumpkins must be fully cooked before they can be frozen or canned. You can preserve squash and pumpkin in cubes.

218

FREEZING

Remove seeds and fibers, peel if desired. Cut up and bake, pressure-cook, steam, or boil until tender. Remove the flesh from the shell, then mash hot or dice. Cool quickly. Pack in appropriate containers, leaving 1/2-inch head space. Thaw before using, except in slow-cooking soups and stews.

CANNING

Pumpkins and squash should have a hard rind and stringless, mature pulp of ideal quality for cooking fresh from the garden. Smaller sized pumpkins will give you better results.

Remove seeds and fibers and peel. Cut in 1-inch cubes, cover with water, and bring to boil. Remove cubes from water, reserving cooking water, and pack hot. Fill hot sterile jars with hot cubes, leaving a 1/2 inch of head space, adding 1/2 teaspoon of salt to pints, 1 teaspoon of salt to quarts. Add cooking water that has once again been brought to a boil, leaving 1/2 inch of head space. Adjust lids. Pressure-process at 10 pounds (240°F.), pints for 55 minutes, quarts for 90 minutes.

Substitute home-canned or frozen squash in any recipe calling for squash pulp.

Caution: the USDA considers it **unsafe** to can mashed or pureed winter squash or pumpkins.

DRYING

Take the vegetable directly from the garden, wash, and peel. Remove seeds and fibers, then slice or shred it. Steam for about 5 minutes, then dry at 140°F. until the pieces are tough or brittle. In a dehydrator this should take from 10 to 15 hours; in an oven at 140°F., it should take about 5 hours. When dry, allow the vegetables to cool to room temperature on the trays or oven sheets. Store in tightly sealed plastic bags or glass jars.

When you want to use these dried vegetables in a recipe, simply drop the pieces into boiling water to rehydrate. Then use in your recipe as you would fresh. For best results, use dried vegetables in soups and stews and just toss the dry pieces in the stock or gravy.

Pickled Pumpkin Pieces

No harvest kitchen is complete without a colorful shelf of pickles and relishes. Instead of canning or freezing all your extra pumpkin, why not try pumpkin pickles for a change?

1 large pumpkin

2 cups vinegar

2 cups sugar

4 pieces stick cinnamon

8 whole cloves

4 whole allspice berries

Wash, cut, and peel pumpkin, discard seeds and fibers. Cut flesh into chunks no larger than 1-inch. Place in a colander and set over a pan of boiling water; cover and steam until tender. Do not let pumpkin chunks touch the water or they will become mushy.

While the pumpkin is steaming, combine vinegar, sugar, and spices in a pot, bring to a boil; then simmer for 15 minutes. Drain pumpkin

chunks when ready, place them in the simmering syrup, and simmer for about 5 minutes. Turn off heat and let stand in a cool place 24 hours. Bring back to heat, then simmer for another 5 minutes, removing spices as you find them.

Pack boiling hot in sterilized jars; process 5 minutes in a boiling water bath.

Yield: 3 pints.

Cooking Tips

The tough skin of the winter squash and pumpkin is always removed before, or discarded after, cooking. And although the seeds are edible, they and the stringy pith in the center are also removed when preserving or preparing this vegetable for the table.

There does not seem to be a specific utensil for scraping the seeds and fibers from squash and pumpkin, but the best tool I have found is a serrated grapefruit spoon. It can also be used to scrape the cooked flesh from the shell of squash when you are preparing them for stuffing. Peeling is difficult but it is possible using a parer or sharp knife or both. For some recipes it is worth the trouble, saving time and energy in the long run.

As with all vegetables, winter squash and pumpkins should not be overcooked or drowned in boiling water since this will result in the loss of both nutrients and flavor. Most people bake, broil, pressure cook, or steam them before using in a recipe, but squash can be peeled and cut up for cooking in a small amount of water or broth.

One way to efficiently cook winter squash is to think ahead and stick a few in the oven with a casserole, or in a pot of soup or pan of boiling potatoes for use later in the week. These halved or cut-up pieces can then be cooled and stored in a plastic bag in the refrigerator until you are ready for them. If squash are cooked with other vegetables or on a pan underneath a dripping fruit pie, they will pick up some of the flavors, and this can definitely be a step toward a tastier meal.

After you acquire some experience cooking with squash and pumpkins, the knack of estimating how many cups of mashed pulp per vegetable will get easier. For the time being it is safe to estimate that you will get approximately 1 cup of pulp to each 1 pound of vegetable.

Seeds should be dried or roasted for storage. There is a variety of squash with hull-less seeds, but the majority should be hulled before eating.

The type of pumpkin or squash you use and the age of the fruit will alter the taste of the dish you are preparing. As you season, you will want to taste often and let your palate be your guide.

All "pumpkin pie spices" go well with pumpkin and squash, together or individual: cinnamon, ginger, nutmeg, allspice, mace, and clove. "Poultry seasonings" will blend as well: thyme, parsley, sage, rosemary, marjoram, black pepper, and nutmeg. Other suggestions for seasoning squash and pumpkin are orange peel, nuts, raisins, cranberries, apples, dried fruit, wine, and all sweeteners, including honey and maple syrup.

PREPARING SEEDS

Remove seeds from fibers by hand or with a fine spray of water. This can sometimes be a tedious job but well worth the effort in taste and nutrition. Spread the seeds on paper towels until dry. Pumpkin seeds

Continued ➔

will dry in a few days, if the weather is not too humid. Hull-less seeds may be eaten as is; seeds with tough hulls can be shelled, just like nuts, for the kernel inside.

To roast seeds, put about 1 tablespoon of oil in a bowl and add seeds, toss until lightly coated. Lay on a baking sheet and place in oven at 350°F. for a few minutes. Salt lightly if desired and cool on paper towels.

To fry seeds, put about 1 tablespoon of oil in a skillet, add seeds. Turn heat to medium-high and as seeds begin to "pop," keep a lid handy and shake skillet just as you would if you were making popcorn. When the seeds swell, remove from heat. Salt lightly if desired and cool on paper towels.

Hull-less seeds or kernels, whole or ground, may be added to poultry dressing, salads, muffins—almost any recipe calling for nuts.

If you are growing your own pumpkins, you will find the Triple Treat variety has hull-less seeds. It also has delicious flesh and is a long keeper. Lady Godiva has hull-less seeds also, but the flesh is not recommended for table use.

MAIN DISH RECIPES

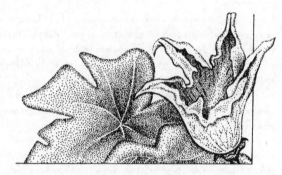

Squash with Sausage Stuffing

Choose the traditional pork sausage, or try something new, such as German sausage, mild Italian sausage, or the Greek sausage flavored with wine and orange peel.

2 large or 4 small squash

1–2 pounds sausage

4 tablespoons oil or butter

1/4 cup chopped onions

1 cup dried bread or cracker crumbs

2 eggs, well beaten

1/2 cup grated cheese

Cut squash in half, remove seeds and fibers. If necessary, cut a slice off the bottom so that the shell will sit flat. Bake upside down in buttered baking dish for 1/2 hour at 350°F. or until barely fork tender.

While squash is baking, precook sausage. Remove from casing if necessary and break up in skillet. Cook over low heat about 15 minutes. Drain. Add butter or oil and onions, and sauté another minute or two. Turn off heat and wait for squash to bake.

When the squash is tender, carefully remove cooked pulp from shell. Add to skillet, then add crumbs and egg. Stir well. Stuff shells,

top with cheese. (We prefer Swiss with pork sausage, Parmesan with Italian, cheddar with German, and feta with Greek.) Bake another 15 minutes at 400°F.

Serve on a plate surrounded by some cooked, seasoned greens such as Swiss chard, spinach, or kale.

Yield: 4 servings.

Time: approximately 1 hour.

Squash with Shrimp Stuffing

Fresh, frozen, or canned shrimp may be used, as long as it is cleaned and cooked. Of course, you may substitute crab or lobster; the better your seafood, the better your dish. Serve with cooked broccoli and hush puppies for a special meal.

2 large or 4 small squash

6 tablespoons oil or butter

1/2 cup diced celery

1/2 cup chopped onion

3–4 cups cooked shrimp or other shellfish

1 cup dry bread or cracker crumbs

1 cup milk

1 egg, well beaten

1/4 cup sherry

1/4 teaspoon thyme

1/4 teaspoon garlic salt

salt and pepper

Cut squash in half, remove seeds and fibers. Cut a slice off the bottom of each piece so that it sits flat, and place upside down in buttered baking dish. Bake until barely fork tender, about 1/2 hour at 350°F.

Sauté celery and onions in oil, then add all other ingredients in order given, stirring after each addition and reserving some crumbs.

Pile into baked squash. Top with the reserved crumbs which have been tossed with a little more oil or melted butter, and bake at 400°F. for about 15 minutes more.

Yield: 4 servings.

Time: approximately 1 hour.

Spaghetti Squash Pot Meal

1 spaghetti squash

water to cover

1 pound lean ground beef

4 tomatoes, quartered

2 large onions, peeled and sliced thickly

1 teaspoon basil

1 teaspoon oregano

3 garlic cloves, peeled and minced

1 can pitted black olives, drained

salt

Wash and halve squash, remove seeds and fibers. Place squash in a large pot, almost cover with water. Bring to a boil, then simmer until flesh is fork tender at largest part, about 15 minutes. Remove squash, boil squash water down until only about 1 quart remains. Turn off. Add ground beef, breaking it up as you put it in.

Using a potholder to hold squash, pull flesh from inside and add to pot, stirring with each addition. Discard skins. Stir in all other ingredients. Bring to a boil, then cover and simmer about 30 minutes or until flavors are blended and meat is cooked.

Yield: 4 servings.

Time: 45 minutes.

Squash Soufflé

We have used both the acorn and butternut squash in this recipe with great results. This is a good recipe to use with home-canned or frozen squash.

3 (packed) cups cooked squash pulp, drained

1 tablespoon flour

4 eggs, separated

1/2 cup yogurt

1/4 cup Swiss cheese, grated

1 teaspoon dried parsley

1/4 teaspoon thyme

salt

Mash pulp, and if necessary, put through food mill processor until smooth. Place in a saucepan; beat in egg yolks and flour. Heat gently, stirring constantly, until mixture begins to set. Do not boil. Take off heat and stir in the yogurt, Swiss cheese, and seasonings.

Preheat oven to 325°F. Beat egg whites until stiff, but not dry, and fold into squash mixture. Pour into a well-buttered 2-quart soufflé or baking dish and bake about 1 hour.

Yield: 4 servings.

Time: 1 hour, after squash is cooked.

Chicken and Pumpkin with Pumpkin Seed Sauce

Making this exotic sauce is reason enough to save your pumpkin and squash seeds. This is an old American Indian recipe.

1 medium pumpkin

2 fryers, cut up

2 cups pumpkin seeds

2 cups fresh popcorn, popped

1 teaspoon chili powder

1 teaspoon cumin

2 garlic cloves

2 cups water

Wash pumpkin, cut in half, seed, take out fibers, and peel. Prepare seeds for sauce by removing most fibers. If you have enough to make 2 cups, roasted or raw, it is nice; more seeds are really not necessary. Cut pumpkin into small chunks, about 1 1/2 inches square.

Put seeds, popcorn, garlic, and water into blender and blend well for about 2 minutes. Add chili powder, cumin, and salt if desired, and blend again.

Spread all the chicken parts in a large roasting pan, including chopped up livers and gizzards. Cover with the sauce. Bake at 350°F. for 1 hour, using the sauce as a baste. About 1/2 hour before serving, add the pumpkin chunks, sticking them between the chicken pieces wherever you can, and basting them, too. (If you are tired of squash, cut the pieces very small and after they have cooked in this fabulous sauce you will not remember what they were.) Serve with cooked spinach or a green salad.

Yield: 6 servings.

Time: approximately 1 1/2 hours.

SOUPS

Pumpkin Soup Tureen

To make a real pumpkin tureen for your pumpkin or squash soup, choose a large pumpkin that sits flat or can be cut to sit flat without major surgery (which might cause it to leak). A bit of stem on the top is necessary. The size depends on how many servings you will be bringing to the table at one time; but do not get too carried away, you can always refill the tureen.

While your soup is simmering, wash the pumpkin well, and on top of the pumpkin draw a lid with the point of a sharp knife. Make the lid slightly larger than your ladle. Carefully cut the lid by inserting the knife in and out, tapering toward the center, so that the lid lifts out in one piece and is larger at its top. This way it will not fall in the soup.

Scrape the seeds and fibers out of the pumpkin, being careful not to pierce the flesh. Find a suitable round plate or tray to form the base of your tureen. You may warm the bowl of your tureen in the oven if you want to, just for a few minutes, but do not heat the lid or else it might shrink. When ready to serve, ladle your soup into the tureen, pop on the lid, and serve with a smile.

Pumpkin Soup

You can use corn chips to decorate this soup. Or serve it in the pumpkin tureen.

Continued →

1 small pumpkin, about 3 pounds, or 3 cups cooked pumpkin pulp

2 tablespoons butter

1/2 cup finely chopped onion

4 cups chicken or vegetable stock

1/4 teaspoon ginger

1/4 teaspoon nutmeg

corn chips

black olives (optional)

To make pumpkin puree, preheat oven to 375°F. Wash pumpkin, cut in half, remove seeds and fibers. Place halves, cut side down on oven rack. Bake about 40 minutes or until flesh is fork tender. Cool slightly; scrape flesh from shell and puree in blender. You can use home-canned or frozen pumpkin.

In soup pot, melt butter and sauté onion until transparent. Add stock, spices, and pumpkin. Bring to a boil, reduce heat, and simmer for about 10 minutes more. Serve with crushed corn chips on top. Or make a ring with the corn chips and use olive slices to make a jack-o'-lantern face on this rich, heavy soup.

Yield: approximately 6 cups.

Time: about 1 hour.

SIDE DISHES

Baked Squash

Cut the small squash into quarters, the larger squash or pumpkins into more pieces. Slice the bottom rind free of any bumps so that the pieces sit flat. Remove seeds and fibers.

Each little "boat" will have a slight cavity for a dab of butter. As the butter melts it can be brushed over the whole piece (or you can just use melted butter to begin with). Each piece can also be brushed with 1 tablespoon of sweetener—brown sugar, honey, fruit juice, maple syrup, sorghum, or molasses.

Bake in an oiled baking dish at 350°F. for about 30 minutes, until fork tender. The squash may be baked at the same temperature you are cooking the rest of your meal, even right in the pan with your roast. Cooking time should be lengthened for temperatures under 350°F., shortened for temperatures higher.

Fried Pumpkin Flowers

15—20 blossoms, try different ones, some wilted, some open,
    some about to open

1/2 cup whole wheat flour

1 tablespoon safflower oil

salt

1/4 teaspoon baking powder

1/4 teaspoon nutmeg

1 cup beer

1/2 cup milk

Wash and dry flowers with paper towel. Blend the remaining ingredients to make batter, and beat until completely smooth. Place a few tablespoons of oil in skillet, enough to coat. Heat oil but do not allow it to smoke. Dip flowers into batter a couple of times to cover, shaking off excess batter. Fry in hot oil turning only once, until crisp. Do not crowd skillet. Add more cooking oil if necessary.

Yield: 4 servings as appetizer or side dish.

Time: about 20 minutes.

Fancy Stuffed Butternut Squash

This stuffing is company fare when used as a surprise dressing in the cavity of a Cornish hen. Add about 1/2 cup of dry bread crumbs to the ingredients in the bowl, then stuff hens lightly. Follow poultry directions for cooking dressed hens; this recipe will stuff 5 or 6 hens.

2 medium butternut squash

1 cup dry wheat bread crumbs

2 large cooking apples, peeled and diced

1/2 cup walnuts, chopped

3 tablespoons chives, chopped

1 teaspoon sage

Split the squash lengthwise, remove seeds and fibers. Rub with butter and bake, flesh side down, on a baking sheets for about 30 minutes.

While the squash are baking, mix all other ingredients in a bowl. When squash have baked, carefully scoop out flesh along with butter and juices, adding to the other ingredients in the bowl. Chop pulp up somewhat and add some salt and freshly ground pepper. Pile mixture into shells, dot with butter, and bake 30 minutes at 350°F. If tops become too browned, cover loosely with aluminum foil.

Yield: 4 servings.

Time: approximately 1 hour.

Fancy Mashed Hubbard Squash

1 medium hubbard squash, or 4 cups home-canned or frozen hubbard squash

1 very ripe banana

1 egg, separated

1/4 cup honey

salt

1 teaspoon honey, warmed

Bake or boil the squash until fork tender. Remove from shell and mash well. Add bananas, 1/4 cup honey, the egg yolk, and a little salt. Beat until smooth. Pile squash in a greased ovenproof bowl (not a long casserole dish) almost all the way to the top of the bowl.

Beat the egg white with a pinch of salt until foamy. Gradually add the teaspoon of *warmed* honey to the egg white, beating until peaks form. With a spatula dipped in cold water, spread the meringue in peaks on top of the squash, bringing it all the way to the edges of the bowl. Bake at 350°F. for about 25 minutes or until meringue browns.

Yield: approximately 8 servings.

Time: approximately 35 minutes after squash is cooked.

Fried Squash

Surprisingly light, this recipe will appeal to people who never knew they liked squash.

1/2 cup whole wheat flour

1 tablespoon safflower oil

pinch of salt

1/4 teaspoon baking powder

1/4 teaspoon nutmeg

1 cup beer

1/2 cup milk

1 small buttercup squash, peeled, seeded, and sliced 1/8-inch thick

oil for frying

1/4 cup catsup

3 tablespoons Worcestershire sauce

In a large bowl, combine flour, oil, salt, baking powder, nutmeg, beer, and milk. Beat until smooth.

Heat frying oil in a large skillet. Dip slices in the batter and place in hot skillet. The batter will not readily cling to the squash, but will give an irregular coating which is both unusual and tasty. Fry a little more than a minute on each side. Coating will get brown and crispy; squash will be cooked. Drain on paper towels.

In a cup or bowl, mix catsup and Worcestershire sauce. When squash slices have cooled somewhat, dip into sauce and eat.

Yield: approximately 4 servings as an appetizer or side dish.

Time: about 20 minutes.

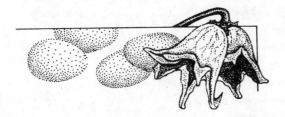

Scalloped Squash

2 tablespoons oil

1/4 cup onion, chopped

1/2 cup green tomatoes, chopped

1 teaspoon parsley

1/4 teaspoon thyme

2 tablespoons flour

1 cup milk

3 cups raw squash, peeled, seeded, and chopped

1 egg well beaten

1/2 cup ricotta cheese (or whipped cottage cheese)

buttered crumbs

Sauté the onion and green tomato in a large skillet for about 3 minutes, stirring frequently. Add parsley, thyme, and flour, and stir well. Cook for another minute or so. Add milk, and heat until somewhat thickened. Turn off heat and add all other ingredients in order given, stirring well after each addition. Pour into a greased casserole dish and bake, covered, for 30 minutes at 350°F. Uncover, top with buttered crumbs, and bake for another 15 minutes.

Yield: 6 servings.

Time: approximately 1 hour.

BREADS AND DESSERTS

Pumpkin Rolls

1/2 cup warm water

2 packages active dry yeast

1/4 cup lukewarm milk

1/2 cup butter

1 cup mashed, cooked pumpkin

2 eggs

1/2 cup honey

1 teaspoon cinnamon

1 1/2 teaspoon salt

5 cups freshly ground whole wheat pastry flour

1/2 cup safflower oil

1/2 cup honey

1/2 pound pecan halves

Warm the milk in a saucepan; remove from heat and add butter to soften. Measure warm water into mixing bowl; add yeast and stir until dissolved. Add milk, butter, pumpkin, eggs, honey, cinnamon, and salt, and beat lightly until smooth. Add flour, a little at a time, mixing well. When dough can be managed, turn out on lightly floured board. Knead until smooth. Let rise until double, about 1 1/2 hours.

While dough is rising, prepare muffin tins by pouring 1 teaspoon oil into each hole, spreading it on sides and bottom. Add 1 teaspoon honey per hole (a plastic honey bear can be a good helper) and 2 pecan halves, broken up somewhat.

When dough has risen, punch down, and shape into balls the size of a walnut. Put three balls into each muffin hole, creating the old-fashioned cloverleaf roll. Cover and let rise for about another hour. Bake at 375°F. for 20–25 minutes.

Yield: 24 rolls.

Time: about 3 1/2 hours.

Pumpkin Bread

Delectable warm with melted butter or topped with cream cheese or apple butter when your sweet tooth needs a nibble.

1 medium pumpkin (3 cups pulp)

1 cup safflower oil

Continued →

1 cup honey

1 cup yogurt

2 eggs

1 teaspoon salt

1 teaspoon cinnamon

1 teaspoon cloves

4 teaspoons baking soda

4 cups whole wheat pastry flour

If starting from scratch, cut pumpkin into halves, remove seeds and fibers and bake flesh side down on a buttered baking sheet for 30–45 minutes at 350°F., or until fork tender. Let cool for a few minutes. Put oil into blender. Using a towel to handle, scrape out hot pulp and put it into blender too, a cup at a time, and blend until smooth. You can substitute 3 cups of canned or frozen pumpkin if desired.

Spoon into a large mixing bowl, then add all other ingredients except flour, mixing very well. Add flour. Stir well, then taste batter. If it isn't sweet enough for you, add more honey. Spoon into 2 oiled 8 1/2-inch by 4 1/2-inch bread pans and bake at 325°F. for 1 hour. Cool in the pan for 15 minutes before removing to rack.

Yield: 2 loaves.

Time: approximately 1 1/2 hours after pumpkin is cooked.

Honey Chiffon Pumpkin Pie

Nancy Zahour of Nancy's Honeybees (6016 Woodward Ave., Downers Grove, IL 60515) gave us permission to use this recipe. She says that it is best served the same day it is made. "Deliciously different for your holiday meals. A Blue Ribbon prizewinning recipe I know you will enjoy!"

Crust:

20 graham crackers (1–2/3 cups)

1/4 cup soft butter

3 tablespoons honey

Crush crackers very fine. Blend honey with soft butter, then mix with cracker crumbs. Press into a heat-resistant, deep 10-inch pie dish. Bake 10 minutes at 375°F.

Filling:

1 tablespoon plain gelatin

1/4 cup cold water

3 eggs, separated

3/4 cup honey

2 cups cooked pumpkin (not pumpkin pie filling)

1/2 cup whole milk

1 teaspoon salt

1 teaspoon cinnamon

1/2 teaspoon ginger

1/2 teaspoon cloves

2 tablespoons honey

Soak gelatin in cold water for 5 minutes. Beat egg yolks, combine with honey, pumpkin, milk, salt, and spaces. Cook in double boiler until thick, stirring constantly. Remove from heat, add softened gelatin, and stir until dissolved.

Beat egg whites until frothy, add 2 tablespoons of honey gradually, and continue beating until whites stand in stiff peaks. Fold stiffened whites into pumpkin mixture gently but thoroughly. Turn into graham crust and chill several hours.

Yield: 6 to 8 generous servings.

Traditional Pumpkin Pie

Pumpkins have always been an American staple food as illustrated in this anonymous early New England verse:

For pottage, and puddings, and custards, and pies.
Our pumpkins and parsnips are common supplies.
We have pumpkins at morning and pumpkins at noon;
If it were not for pumpkins, we should be undoon.

2 8-inch pastry shells, unbaked

2 1/2 cups mashed cooked pumpkin (May be home-canned, frozen, or commercially prepared)

2 15-ounce cans condensed milk

4 eggs

1/2 teaspoon salt

2 teaspoons cinnamon

1 teaspoon nutmeg

1 teaspoon ginger

1/4 teaspoon cloves

1 cup brown sugar (more if desired)

Combine all ingredients in a large bowl and beat until smooth. Pour into pastry-lined pie tins. Bake at 375°F. for 50–55 minutes, or just until a silver knife inserted 1 inch from the side of the filling comes out clean. The center may still look soft but will set as it cools. Serve at room temperature or cold—always with whipped cream.

Yield: 2 8-inch pies.

Time: approximately 1 hour after pumpkin is cooked.

Squash Cornbread

The best cornbread you will ever eat!

1 cup cooked squash puree

3/4 cup corn meal

1 egg, beaten

2 teaspoons baking powder

1 teaspoon salt

1/2 cup frozen or fresh kernel corn

1/4 cup oil

To make fresh squash puree, peel squash, and boil in water to cover until soft. (Add a tablespoon of poultry seasonings and a few grinds of pepper to the cooking water if desired.) Puree cooked (home-canned or frozen) squash in blender or food processor.

Beat egg lightly, then beat into the puree. Add the other ingredients and mix lightly. Pour thick batter into well-buttered cast iron skillet (8 inches across). Dot with butter, bake at 350°F. for 40 minutes.

Yield: lots of cornbread for 4.

Time: approximately 1 hour.

Squash-Oatmeal Cookies

3/4 cup butter

3/4 cup honey

1 cup grated raw winter squash

1 egg

2 cups whole wheat pastry flour

2 teaspoons baking powder

1 1/2 cups rolled oats

1 cup raisins

Allow butter to come to room temperature and mix well with honey. Beat in squash and egg. Add flour and baking powder, and mix well. Then add oats and raisins, and stir well again. Drop by teaspoonfuls onto greased cookie sheet and bake at 400°F. for about 12 minutes.

Yield: about 50 cookies.

Squash or Pumpkin Cake

You will receive many compliments when you serve this cake. Frost with your favorite recipe for coconut icing or spread on a mixture of 1/2 cup cream cheese, 1/4 cup butter, and 1/2 cup honey.

4 eggs

1 1/2 cups oil

1 cup honey

1/2 cup sugar

2 cups grated raw squash or pumpkin

2 cups whole wheat pastry flour or white flour

2 teaspoons baking powder

1 1/2 teaspoons baking soda

1 teaspoon salt

2 teaspoons cinnamon

1 8-ounce can pineapple, well drained

1/2 cup nuts

Place eggs, oil, honey, and sugar in blender, in that order, and blend until smooth. Add the squash, a little at a time. Pour into a large mixing bowl, add all dry ingredients and stir well. Fold in nuts and pineapple. Pour into greased 9- by 13-inch pan. Bake at 350°F. for 35–40 minutes until done.

Yield: 1 large cake.

Time: approximately 1 hour.

Cooking with Dried Beans

Sara Pitzer

Illustrations by Janet Rabideau

Kinds of Beans

As you browse through the recipes, you may discover some calling for a bean you can't find where you live, because a few beans still seem to be popular only in certain parts of the country. In these cases, just substitute another similar bean. The following list and descriptions should help you.

WHITE BEANS

Baby Limas. These are the same baby limas you grow in your garden. You can dry your own if you grow extra. And you can buy them anywhere. They are one of the faster cooking beans.

Butter Beans. These are the large limas you grow in your garden. These, too, are a good variety to dry yourself. You can buy them everywhere in the country in grocery stores.

Great Northern Beans. Great northerns are a meaty, plump bean, somewhat larger than navy beans, commercially grown mostly in Idaho. They are good to use when you want the cooked bean to be quite soft or when you want to make a puree. You can buy them all across the country.

Continued →

Marrow Beans. Marrows look something like a fat baby lima. They're similar in size and texture to great northerns and are interchangeable with them. Although you may not find them in all grocery stores, they're generally sold everywhere in the country.

Navy Beans, Pea Beans, Small White Beans. Although we have 3 names, they seem to represent only 2 bean varieties. Commercial labeling on them is confusing. Navy beans, which are grown mainly in Michigan, are smaller than great northerns, but larger than the small whites grown in California. "Pea beans" sometimes refers to navy beans and sometimes means a small white bean (though not necessarily grown in California). To confuse matters more, some packages are marked, "Navy Pea Beans." Don't worry too much about the names. These beans are pretty much interchangeable, although the small white (or pea) bean is smaller and firmer than the standard navy beans. These beans are available, under one name or another, everywhere. Usually they are the cheapest of the white beans.

PINK AND RED BEANS

Red Kidney Beans. Of all the kidney beans, these are the darkest, being deep red when dried and turning almost purple-black when cooked. They are often used in chili and are grown from coast to coast. They do well in the home garden and are a good choice for drying yourself.

Light Red Kidney Beans. Another popular choice for chili, these look just like dark red kidney beans except for being lighter in color. When cooked they look like pintos and pinks, a rosy brown. They're available from coast to coast, although some grocery stores carry only red or light red, not both. They can substitute for dark red kidney beans.

Cranberry Beans. Sometimes called "shellouts," cranberry beans are a mottled pink and beige bean, a little smaller than kidney beans, typically found in the East and practically impossible to find on the West Coast.

Pinto Beans. These are common in the West and Southwest and look like cranberry beans except they are pale pink spotted with brown.

Pink Beans. Pinks look like pintos without the spots. Pinks, pintos, and cranberry beans are interchangeable. You never know where you will find pink beans. They seem to be available all over the country, but not in all grocery stores.

Small Red Beans. These beans are a bright red, sometimes called a red pea bean and sometimes called "Mexican chili bean." They are smaller, firmer, and less mealy than kidney beans. Common in the West and Southwest, they are hard to find in some parts of the East, but when you can find them, they make a nice change from kidney beans and give a completely different character to chili. When you can't get them, any of the other pink or red beans may be substituted, although the results will be somewhat different.

PEAS

Black-Eyed Peas, Yellow-Eyed Peas. Both of these are oval, with a black or yellow spot in the curve. They are actually beans, but are always called "peas" in the south where they are traditional. They cook faster than most dried beans and have a smooth, rather than mealy, texture when cooked. Although you can use black-eyed and yellow-eyed peas interchangeably, which is good because the yellow variety is hard to find in some places, nothing else substitutes properly for them. But you can find one variety or the other almost everywhere.

Chick-peas, Garbanzos, Ceci Peas, Spanish Peas. Four names apply to one bean. Chick-peas are round but irregular, pale yellow, with

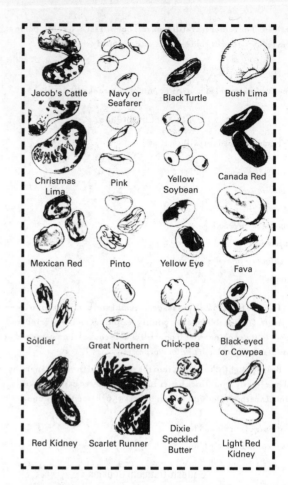

Jacob's Cattle — Navy or Seafarer — Black Turtle — Bush Lima

Christmas Lima — Pink — Yellow Soybean — Canada Red

Mexican Red — Pinto — Yellow Eye — Fava

Soldier — Great Northern — Chick-pea — Black-eyed or Cowpea

Red Kidney — Scarlet Runner — Dixie Speckled Butter — Light Red Kidney

wrinkled skins and very firm texture. Small stores often do not carry them (except sometimes canned), but you can find them in virtually all larger supermarkets and natural food stores. No other bean substitutes.

Split Peas. Split peas really are peas and they really are split. You can buy green or yellow, with the yellow ones somewhat less common than the green. The two are similar in taste and can be used interchangeably in any recipe where color is not a factor.

Whole Dried Green Peas. Although not as popular as split peas, whole green peas show up in most grocery stores. They are another good grow-and-dry-it-yourself project. You can begin with garden peas you didn't get to pick when they were young and sweet. Just let them mature until the pods dry, then shell them out.

BEANS WITH EXOTIC FLAVOR

Lentils. People have been eating lentils since biblical times. Today they're available almost everywhere. They're a brownish olive-drab color, although some natural food stores carry red lentils which, actually, are orange in color. Both kinds look something like miscolored split peas, except that each whole lentil is about the size of one half of the divided "split" pea. Older recipes recommend long soaking and cooking for lentils. Newer lentil varieties, the kind you find in stores today, cook much more quickly than their predecessors and don't have to be soaked at all any more. Red and brown lentils taste somewhat the same, but absolutely nothing else tastes like a lentil—there's no substitute.

Black Beans, Turtle Beans. Black beans have been popular in South America for many years, but because of their musky-spicy taste which blends better with Latin seasonings than those typically North American, black beans have been slow to catch on in the United States. Gourmet cooks consider them the "Cadillac" of beans, but that still limits them to a small corner of the eating populace. There are many varieties of black bean, ranging in size between navy beans and kidney beans. When you nick the skin of a cooked black bean, it is white underneath.

Soybeans. This is the only bean that supplies complete protein without being supplemented by grains or dairy products. It used to be difficult to find soybeans anywhere except in natural foods stores, but these days they're increasingly visible on grocery store shelves. Soybeans are easy to grow in your garden if your season is long enough for them to mature before the frost—they need about 20–30 days more than most snap and wax beans, depending on the variety. No soybean recipes are included in this collection because whole books are devoted to that single versatile bean.

GROW YOUR OWN BEANS

The above list by no means covers all the kinds of dried beans you might encounter. Not only will you find lesser-known varieties limited to small regional pockets, but also you will discover that the home gardener who lets green and yellow snap beans grow to maturity and then dries them will produce beans of every shape and color. One popular oddity, the decorative scarlet runner, planted mainly for its flowers, produces a large, spectacular dried bean splashed with red. It's delicious, but probably available nowhere commercially.

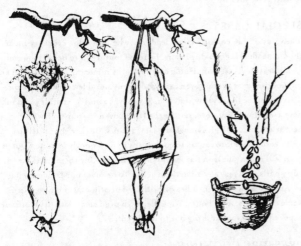

Beans are threshed when the plants and the pods are thoroughly dry. Here's an easy system. Hang a burlap cylinder from a branch. Tie off the bottom opening. Fill the bag with beans and beat with a blunt stick. The beans will fall to the bottom of the bag and can be poured out into a container.

If you want to dry your own beans, the simplest way is to leave some of the beans on the vine until the hulls have dried and begun to open, and then to shell out the beans. However, this method invites insect problems, and you may lose as many beans as you can save. A better method is to pull up the plants and allow them to dry in an airy place. Once the hulls are brittle, you can shell out the beans easily. Then put the shelled beans in the oven on warm for about an hour to kill any insects or larvae.

You'll find that beans you grow and dry yourself often cook faster and are less firm than commercial beans; this is because of differing varieties and because your own beans may be stored a shorter time.

Store beans in a tight container in a cool, dry, dark place. I keep mine in Mason jars in the pantry, rotating older jars to the front when I add newer ones.

Although cookbooks tend to be conservative in their estimates of how long you can keep dry beans (*The Woman's Day Encyclopedia of Cookery* says 1 year on your kitchen shelf), properly dried and stored beans will keep indefinitely without significant deterioration.

Cooking Information

Here are a few tips for those of you who have never cooked dried beans before.

WASHING AND SOAKING

Always wash beans thoroughly and remove foreign objects and bad beans. You *can* cook beans without soaking them first, but it takes forever and they end up unevenly cooked, with poor texture. For generations the method for soaking beans was to cover them with cold water and let them stand overnight in a cool place. It's still a good method.

The home economists of the California Dry Bean test kitchen prefer a variation on the old method, worked out by the USDA: the overnight salt soak. For each cup of dried beans, add 3 cups of cold water and 1 teaspoon salt. Allow to stand overnight, as with the old method. Testers say the salt in the water helps the beans absorb moisture more evenly, which results in better shape and more even cooking. However, if you are trying to reduce the amount of salt in your diet, you would want to avoid this method.

The Quick-Soak Method. The quick-soak is good when you haven't planned ahead to soak beans overnight. Put the beans in a large pot, cover them with water, bring to a boil, and cook for 2 minutes with a lid on the pan. Then remove the pan from the heat and let the beans stand, covered, for 1 or 2 hours. This is equivalent to as much as 15 hours of plain soaking.

SIMMERING

No matter how you soak the beans and no matter what recipe you plan to use, the next step is to simmer the beans until they are tender. In past years, nutritionists urged cooks to simmer the beans in their soaking water. Today no one's quite sure. Nutritionists have determined that the loss of nutrients in discarded soaking water is minimal, and some cooks feel that cooking in fresh water makes the beans taste better and also helps cut down on what Julia Child calls the "root-ti-toot-toot" problem. However, any digestive problems you have with beans settle down as you eat them more regularly and your body becomes accustomed to the B vitamins and extra fiber provided by beans. And most people wouldn't be able to tell by taste whether beans had been

Continued →

TIMETABLE FOR COOKING BEANS

	Soaked beans cooked tender *regular method*	Soaked Beans cooked tender *pressure cooker*	Unsoaked beans cooked tender *pressure cooker*
Baby limas and butter beans	30 to 60 minutes	not recommended	not recommended
Great northern and marrow beans	2 1/2 to 3 hours	8 minutes	20 minutes
Navy, pea, and small white beans	3 to 3 1/2 hours	10 minutes	30 to 35 minutes
Kidney, pink, cranberry, and pinto beans	2 to 2 1/2 hours	5 to 7 minutes	20 to 25 minutes
Small red beans	3 to 3 1/2 hours	10 minutes	30 to 35 minutes
Black-eyed peas	30 to 50 minutes	not recommended	not recommended
Chick-peas	4 hours	15 to 20 minutes	45 minutes
Split peas*	40 to 60 minutes	not recommended	not recommended
Whole dried green peas	60 to 70 minutes	not recommended	not recommended
Lentils*	30 to 40 minutes	not recommended	not recommended
Black beans	2 1/2 hours	8 to 10 minutes	25 to 30 minutes

Soaking may be eliminated; cooking time then approximately doubles.

All cooking times here are the minimum; longer cooking times may be necessary depending on the dryness of the bean. Hard water also lengthens cooking times.

cooked in fresh water or soaking water. So, ultimately, it doesn't seem to matter much one way or the other. I still follow the old cooks' advice of cooking in the soaking water when it tastes sweet and replacing it with fresh when the soaking water tastes bitter. It is important to remember that if you use the salt soak, you should cook in fresh water or you will end up with oversalted beans.

One old-time simmering trick you should avoid is putting baking soda in the cooking water to speed up cooking. Don't do it; it destroys vitamins in the beans.

If you have trouble with beans foaming as you cook them, you can add a tablespoon of oil or butter to the cooking water, or you can tilt the pan lid and lower the heat until the foaming subsides.

The simmering time to make beans tender varies considerably depending on the variety of bean, how long it's been stored and how dry it is. If time matters at all, add tomatoes, vinegar, or wine toward the end of the simmering, otherwise the acid will slow the cooking.

When you're planning, it's best to allow a little extra time for beans, just in case they take longer than the recipe suggests. You'll know they're done when the skins begin to break open and a bean is tender all the way through when you bite into it.

KEEPING IT SIMPLE

All this discussion of how to cook beans, combined with the comparatively long cooking times of most of the recipes, could make you feel that cooking beans is a complicated, time-consuming process. It is not. Indeed, there's not much you can do to spoil a bean—it tolerates overcooking, fluctuating temperatures, and even interrupted cooking. As for time, beans do take a lot of it, but it's not *your* time. You don't have to watch or stir them through most of the cooking, and if you use low heat and proper utensils, you don't even have to be in the house for most of it.

The only thing that seems crucial in cooking beans well is long, slow cooking at low, low temperatures, rather than shorter cooking at high

temperatures. The beans develop their own flavor; their skins are less inclined to fall off; and when the skins to come off, they gradually disintegrate into the bean broth.

SPECIAL CASES

The value of slow cooking might lead you to believe a slow crockery cooker should be ideal for cooking beans. I haven't found this to be so. However, a well-seasoned cast-iron Dutch oven, barely simmering on the back of an old woodstove or in your oven can produce memorable beans. Cast iron distributes the heat evenly and holds it steady; beans like that. If you don't have a woodburning stove, setting the Dutch oven in your oven with the heat at about 200°F gives much the same results. Be sure your kettle is well-seasoned before you try to cook beans in it. A poorly seasoned Dutch oven will release an iron flavor into the beans, making them taste like rusty nails, and may also turn them gray. (To be sure your Dutch oven is adequately seasoned, rub it heavily with lard or other fat and heat it in a warm oven for several hours. Wipe the dutch oven clean with dry cloths or paper towels. Avoid washing it with detergents.)

PRESSURE COOKING

However desirable it may be to cook beans slowly, sometimes you need them in a hurry. You can cook them quickly in a pressure cooker, if you're *careful*. An entire generation of us grew up with mothers who were forever telling tales about vegetable soup on the ceiling. Because beans tend to foam and can clog the vent in a pressure cooker, you need to take special precautions to keep your beans off the ceiling.

You need not soak beans for pressure cooking, just wash them and put them into the cooker with about 3 or 4 cups of water for each cup of beans. Bring the beans to a boil, put on the lid of the pressure cooker according to the manufacturer's instructions, and set the gauge at 15 pounds. Use the cooking times listed above to figure out the proper cooking time. Keep the heat adjusted so that the jiggle of the pressure gauge is steady but not frantically fast. At the end of the cooking time, hold the pressure cooker under cold running water to reduce the pressure. Vent any remaining steam and open the pressure cooker according to the directions for your particular pressure cooker.

For safety, you should never fill your pressure cooker much more than one-third full when cooking beans. A little fat added to the cooking water will help keep foam down, but lima beans foam too much to be successful in the pressure cooker; split peas and black-eyed peas can be risky, too. For chick-peas, however, the pressure cooker is a great gift because they take so long to soften with ordinary cooking methods.

Recipes

SOUPS AND STEWS

MANY BEAN SOUP

1/3 cup great northern beans

1/3 cup dried baby limas

1/3 cup lentils

1/3 cup pinto beans

1/3 cup red beans

6 cups water

1/2 teaspoon salt

1 medium onion, coarsely chopped

1 celery rib with leaves, coarsely chopped

2 garlic cloves, minced

1 bay leaf

2 ham hocks

1/4 cup salt pork cubes

Soak the beans together overnight or use the quick-soak method. Put the beans in a kettle with 6 cups of the soaking water or use fresh water. Add the salt, onion, celery, garlic, bay leaf, ham hocks and salt pork. Reduce the heat, cover the pan, and simmer until all the beans are tender and some are beginning to fall apart, probably about 3 hours.

Cool the ham hocks so you can remove any meat on them and return the meat to the beans.

Time: 3 hours (after the beans are soaked)

Yield: 6 servings

PUREED BEAN SOUP

1 cup marrow beans

4 cups water

1/2 teaspoon salt

1 medium onion, chopped

1 medium carrot, chopped

1 celery rib with leaves, chopped

1 clove garlic, minced

1 bay leaf

2 tablespoons butter

1 cup chicken broth or vegetable stock or milk

2 tablespoons chopped parsley

2 tablespoons chopped chives

Soak the beans overnight or use the quick-soak method. Put the beans into a kettle with 4 cups of the soaking water or use fresh water. Add salt. Bring to a boil, lower the heat, cover the pan, and simmer until the beans are very tender, at least 2 hours.

Add the chopped onion, carrot, celery, garlic, and bay leaf. Cook about 30 minutes longer, until the vegetables are soft. Remove the bay leaf, and puree the bean mixture in the blender, food processor, or food mill. Stir in the butter and as much stock or milk as you need to thin the soup to a consistency you like. Return the soup to the heat until it is very hot, but if you thinned it with milk, be careful not to let it boil.

Chilled bean puree soup is a summer gourmet specialty in some French restaurants. To serve the soup chilled, proceed exactly as you would for serving it hot, but instead of returning it to the pan to reheat, cool it further, and refrigerate it at least 6 hours. It tends to thicken as it cools, so you may need to add more milk or stock. Also, test the seasoning, you may want to zip it up a bit more for serving chilled. Garnish with the parsley and chives.

Time: 2 1/2 hours (after the beans are soaked) for hot soup, plus 6 hours chilling time (or overnight) for cold soup

Yield: 6 to 8 servings

Continued ➜

SPLIT PEA SOUP

1 pound (about 2 1/4 cups) green or yellow split peas

6 cups chicken or vegetable stock

2 tablespoons butter

1 teaspoon salt

1 whole clove

1 medium onion, chopped

1 celery rib with leaves, chopped

1 small clove garlic, minced

1 carrot, chopped

1 small potato, unpeeled and diced

1 cup diced cooked chicken or turkey (optional)

Wash and sort the split peas. Put them in a 6-quart kettle with all the other ingredients except the chicken or turkey. Bring to a boil. Lower the heat, cover the pot, and simmer, stirring occasionally to keep the peas from sticking to the bottom of the pan, for 2 to 3 hours. The peas and vegetables should be very soft and begin to fall apart. The thicker part of the soup will tend to sink to the bottom of the pan and should be stirred up before serving, or you can puree the soup before serving. Stir in the chicken or turkey, just about 5 minutes before serving. Parmesan cheese makes a good garnish.

Time: 2 to 3 hours (if peas are soaked first; preparation time after soaking is 30 to 40 minutes)
Yield: 6 to 8 servings

BLACK BEAN SOUP

1 cup dried black beans

4 cups water

1/2 teaspoon salt

1 celery rib with leaves, chopped

1 medium onion, chopped

1 leek, white part only, chopped

2 ham hocks

1 bay leaf

1/2 teaspoon dried thyme

2 tablespoons dry sherry

2 hard-cooked eggs

Soak the beans overnight or use the quick-soak method. Drain the beans and put them into a kettle with 4 cups of fresh water. Add all the remaining ingredients, except the eggs and sherry. Bring to a boil, lower the heat, cover the pan, and simmer until the beans are tender and the meat is falling off the ham hocks, about 3 hours.

Remove the ham hocks and set aside to cool. Scoop out about 1/2 cup of the cooked beans and puree the rest in a blender, food processor, or food mill. Return the puree to the pan, add the reserved beans and all the bits of meat you can pick off the ham bones. If the soup seems too thick, thin it with a little hot water or stock. Bring almost to a boil, then stir in the sherry. Serve garnished with thin slices of hard-cooked egg.

Time: 3 hours (after the beans are soaked)
Yield: 6 servings

WEIGHTS AND MEASURES OF BEANS

1 cup dried beans = 2 to 3 cups cooked beans

1 pound dried beans = 2 1/4 to 2 1/3 cups dried beans

1 pound dried beans = 6 to 7 cups cooked beans

IT'S EASY TO SPROUT BEANS

Wash 1 cup of dried beans and pick out any which are broken. Soak them overnight in warm water. Drain. Place the beans in a glass jar and cover the mouth with a screen or cheesecloth and keep the jar in a warm, dark place for 3 to 5 days. Rinse the beans gently with warm water, draining thoroughly each time, at least 3 times a day, more often if the weather is very warm. Sprouts are ready when they are 1 or 2 inches long. Rinse them thoroughly in cold water, drain well, and store in a covered container in the refrigerator. The sprouts will keep about 4 days. One cup of dried beans yields 4 cups of sprouts.

CASSOULET

2 cups great northern or marrow beans

1 cup water

6 cups stock

3 garlic cloves, minced

1 large onion, chopped

2 celery ribs with leaves, chopped

2 tablespoons chopped parsley

1 bay leaf

1/2 teaspoon dry thyme leaves

1/2 teaspoon salt

1/4 teaspoon pepper

a bone from a cooked pork roast or 3 pork chops, browned

1/2 cup dry white wine

10 chicken thighs or drumsticks or wings (or a combination)

1/2 pound smoked sausage

Soak the beans overnight or use the quick-soak method. Drain the beans and put them into a kettle with 1 cup fresh water, the stock, garlic, onion, celery, parsley, and seasonings. Bring to a boil, cover the pan, reduce the heat, and simmer for 1 hour. Then add the pork bone or chops. Continue simmering another 1 1/2 hours or until the beans are tender.

Turn the beans into a large baking dish. Cut the pork into small pieces and add it to the beans. Pour on the wine. Arrange the chicken pieces on top of the beans, cover the casserole, and bake in a 200°F oven for about 6 hours. Check the beans occasionally to be sure they have lots of liquid. If they appear to be drying out, add stock. Cassoulet should be almost soupy, not as thick as ordinary baked beans.

While the beans are baking, cut the sausage into small pieces and brown it in the skillet. Drain off as much fat as possible. About 30 minutes before you want to serve the cassoulet, stir in the sausage, raise the oven heat to 350°F and bake about 30 minutes with the cover removed to brown the top of the beans and chicken. Be sure to keep adding stock, if necessary, to keep the beans juicy. (You can omit the browning step if you're busy. It's mainly for appearance's sake. If you do, just stir in the sausage and finish baking at the lower temperature in a covered casserole.)

Baking time for cassoulet is flexible. Shorten it to as little as 2 hours or extend it to 8 hours or more. Raise or lower the oven heat accordingly. Long, slow cooking gives superior flavor.

Time: 4 1/2 to 10 1/2 hours (after beans are soaked); may be started a day ahead

Yield: 10 servings

LOUISIANA RED BEANS AND RICE

2 1/3 cups (1 pound) red kidney beans

3 cups water

1/2 teaspoon salt

2 or 3 ham hocks

1 medium onion, chopped

1 garlic clove, minced

1 celery rib with leaves, chopped

1 bay leaf

1 pound sausage

2 cups cooked brown rice

chopped green onion

grated cheddar cheese

Soak the beans overnight or use the quick-soak method. Drain and put them in a kettle with 3 cups fresh water. Bring to a boil, reduce the heat, cover the pan, and simmer for about 30 minutes. Add the salt, ham hocks, onion, garlic, celery, and bay leaf. Simmer 2 hours or longer. Add water if the mixture gets too thick. The beans will be tender in 2 hours, but longer simmering makes the flavor richer.

About 30 minutes before serving, remove the ham hocks, and cool them until you can remove the meat from the bones. Cut the meat into

small pieces and return it to the kettle. Meanwhile, cut the sausage into small pieces and fry until brown. Drain away the fat and stir the sausage into the beans. Simmer over very low heat to blend the flavors.

To serve, spoon the beans over the rice on a large platter and garnish with generous amounts of chopped green onion and grated cheddar cheese.

Time: 2 1/2 hours minimum (after beans are soaked)

Yield: 8 to 10 servings

LENTIL-RICE STEW

1/4 cup olive oil

1 large onion, sliced

1/2 cup raw long-grain brown rice

2 cups lentils

1/2 teaspoon salt

6 cups water

1 cup canned tomatoes

6 cups coarsely chopped raw chard

coarsely ground black pepper

vinegar

yogurt or sour cream

Heat the olive oil in the bottom of a heavy saucepan or Dutch oven. Sauté the onion and rice in the oil over medium high heat until the onions are golden and the rice grains are coated with oil and look translucent. Add the lentils, salt, and water. Bring to a boil, reduce the heat, cover the pan, and simmer until the rice is done, about 45 minutes. By then the lentils should be tender too; if not, simmer about 20 minutes longer. Add water if the mixture becomes too thick.

When everything is tender, add the tomatoes and cook 10 minutes longer. About 5 minutes before serving, stir in the chopped chard and steam with the lid on just until the greens are wilted. Season with the pepper and vinegar, top with yogurt or sour cream.

Time: 1 1/4 hours

Yield: 8 servings

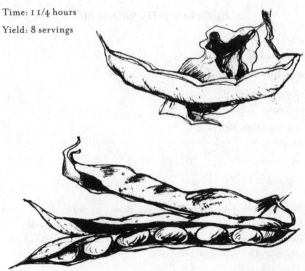

Continued ➡

While the zucchini is steaming and cooling, sauté the onion in the butter until tender. Combine this mixture with the cottage cheese, rice, beans, eggs, salt, and chopped zucchini centers. Spoon the mixture into the hollowed out zucchini shells. Arrange the shells in a long, shallow pan or on a cookie sheet.

Cover loosely with aluminum foil. Bake in a 350°F oven for 25 minutes. Remove the soil, sprinkle the grated cheese on the zucchini, and bake uncovered about 5 minutes more, just until the cheese has melted.

Time: 50 minutes (after beans and rice are cooked)
Yield: 8 servings

OTHER MAIN DISHES

BEAN-RICE SQUARES

1 cup dried beans (or 2 cups cooked beans)

3 cups water (for cooking dried beans)

1 egg, beaten

1 cup milk

1/2 teaspoon salt

1 teaspoon Worcestershire sauce

1/2 teaspoon dry mustard

1/4 cup chopped green onion

1 cup cooked brown rice

1 1/2 cups grated cheese: Swiss, cheddar, or a combination

Soak the beans overnight or use the quick-soak method. Put the beans in a kettle with 3 cups of the soaking water or fresh water. Bring to a boil, lower the heat, cover the pan, and simmer until the beans are tender, about 2 hours. Cool slightly and drain.

Mix the cooked beans with all the other ingredients and pour into a well-greased 8 inch square baking pan. Bake 40 to 45 minutes at 325°F. The mixture should be just set, like a custard, but not dried out.

Time: 40 minutes (after beans are cooked); 2 hours and 45 minutes for uncooked beans (after the beans are soaked)
Yield: 4 servings

ZUCCHINI STUFFED WITH BEANS

4 medium zucchini

1/2 cup finely chopped onion

2 tablespoons butter

1 cup cottage cheese

1 cup cooked brown rice

1 cup cooked pink or red beans

2 beaten eggs

1/2 teaspoon salt

1 cup grated cheese

Trim the ends of the zucchini and steam the squash in a small amount of boiling water for 8 minutes or until barely tender. Cool. Cut each zucchini in half lengthwise, scoop out the centers, discarding any large seeds and dice the rest of the centers.

SIDE DISHES

BOSTON BAKED BEANS

Here's standard baked bean recipe in the New England tradition. You'll note the absence of tomato or catsup. That's because the colonists did not eat tomatoes and, in fact, thought they were poisonous until after 1800.

2 cups small white beans

6 cups water

1/2 teaspoon salt

3/4 cup salt pork cubes

1/4 cup brown sugar

1/4 cup molasses

1/2 teaspoon dry mustard

Soak the beans overnight or use the quick-soak method. Put the beans in a kettle with 6 cups of the soaking water or fresh water. Add the salt. Bring to a boil, lower the heat, cover the pan, and simmer the beans until tender, about 2 hours.

Mix the beans and all the cooking water in a baking dish with the salt pork, sugar, molasses, and dry mustard. Cover the casserole and bake the beans at 225°F for 6 to 8 hours or longer. Check occasionally to see if you need to add more water. You may raise the heat and shorten the baking time, but the long, slow cooking produces tastier beans.

Time: 8 to 10 hours (after beans are soaked)
Yield: 8 to 10 servings

FRIED CHICK-PEAS WITH GARLIC

Chick-peas are indestructible; it's almost impossible to cook them too long. When you prepare chick-peas for cooking, wash them extra carefully because the dust and sand sometimes imbedded in the wrinkles of their skin cling tenaciously.

1 cup dried chick-peas

3 cups water

1/2 teaspoon salt

3 tablespoons olive oil

1 clove garlic

lemon juice

black pepper

After a thorough washing, soak the beans overnight or use the quick-soak method. Drain the soaking water. Put the beans into a kettle with 3 cups fresh water. Add the salt. Bring to a boil, reduce the heat, cover the pan, and simmer until the chick-peas are tender, about 4 hours. Check occasionally to be sure the beans are still covered with water and add more water as needed. When the beans are tender all the way through (bite into one to test), drain and cool them.

Heat the oil in a heavy skillet and swirl the garlic around in it a few seconds before adding the beans. Keep the heat medium high and stir the chick-peas around in the skillet gently for about 10 minutes, or until they form a crispy, brown crust on the outside. Put the chick-peas into a serving dish, remove the garlic, and season with lemon juice and pepper.

Time: 15 minutes (after chick-peas are cooked)

Yield: 2 servings

HUMMUS

This is pureed chick-peas. It's Middle Eastern and is usually served with Arab or pita bread, but it's good as a spread on whole wheat bread or as a dip for raw vegetables, too.

2 cup cooked chick-peas

1 clove garlic

1/4 cup lemon juice

1/4 cup olive oil

cold water

2 tablespoons chopped fresh parsley

Puree the chick-peas and garlic in a food processor, blender, or food mill. Mix in the lemon juice and olive oil. Add a little water, if needed, to make a soft mixture. Sprinkle the chopped parsley on top and chill at least 1 hour before serving.

Time: 1 hour and 10 minutes (after the chick-peas are cooked)

Yield: 6 to 8 servings

Cooking with Tofu

Mary Anna DuSablon
Illustrations by Sue Storey

Tips for Cooking and Storing Tofu

The water content in all tofu differs occasionally, whether store-bought or homemade. You may have to adjust the liquids in your recipes accordingly. Remember, it is easier to add more liquids to a recipe than more dry ingredients.

- To make a firmer or drier tofu, place the tofu on your drainboard, wrapping it with cheesecloth or paper towels. Place a saucer or small dish on top of the tofu and a 1-pound can on top of the dish to press the water out of the tofu. Drain for at least 15 minutes. Parboiling the tofu will also result in a drier product.

- If you wrap tofu in a clean towel and twist and wring the water out, you will have a crumbly, dry tofu—good in stir-fry dishes.

- To use tofu as a thickener for sauces and gravies, make your sauce or gravy thinner than usual. Then whip the tofu in, using a wire whisk. The texture will not be smooth, but it is an interesting consistency, and your sauce will be richer in protein.

- Plan to use fresh, sweet tofu in desserts, salads, and drinks. Cook with tofu that is older or slightly bitter.

- Tofu will last in the refrigerator about 1 week. It will stay fresher if you change the water every other day.

- Refrigerated tofu will begin to turn pink around the edges when it is about to go bad. It can be revitalized by parboiling, but should be used soon. To parboil, place the tofu, whole or in slices, in a saucepan; then cover with water. Bring to a boil, then reduce the heat and simmer for about 3 minutes. Remove the tofu with a slotted spoon.

- When your tofu smells yeasty or sour, it should be thrown out.

Soybeans are easy to grow. They prefer a sandy loam, well fertilized with lime, potash, and phosphoric acid; but the plant is not too fussy. Sow seeds in early spring, and harvest for dried beans when the plant is brown and bare of leaves, and only the dried pods remain.

Continued →

COMPOSITION OF FOODS*

100 Gram Portions	Protein (GRAM)	Fat (GRAM)	Carbohydrates (GRAM)	Calcium (MG)	Iron (MG)
Tofu	7.8	4.2	2.4	128	1.9
Ground beef (cooked)	24	20	—	11	3.2
Eggs	13	11.5	0.9	54	2.3
Cream cheese	8.2	37.6	2.4	62	0.2
Sour cream	3	20.4	4.3	102	.04
Cow's milk	3.5	3.7	4.9	117	—
Yogurt	3	3.4	4.9	111	—

100 Gram Portions	Sodium (MG)	Potassium (MG)	Vit. A (I.U.)	Vit. B1 (MG)	Vit. B2 (MG)	Vit. B3 (MG)
Tofu	7	42	—	0.06	0.03	0.1
Ground beef (cooked)	47	450	40	0.09	0.21	5.4
Eggs	122	129	1,180	0.11	0.30	0.1
Cream cheese	250	74	1,541	0.02	0.20	0.1
Sour cream	41	118	839	0.03	0.15	0.04
Cow's milk	50	140	150	0.03	0.17	0.1
Yogurt	47	132	140	0.03	0.16	—

Nutritive Value of Foods, Home and Garden Bulletin #72, USDA: Washington D.C. (1970).

Nutritive Value of American Foods: In Common Units, prepared by Catherine F. Adams, USDA: Washington D.C. (1975).

The No-Nonsense Guide to Food and Nutrition, Marion McGill and Orrea Pye, Butterick Publishing Company: New York (1978).

FROZEN TOFU

Tofu can be stored in the freezer for up to 3 months. During the freezing process the tofu will undergo a radical change: all of the water in the tofu, about 86 percent of the total weight, will melt away when thawed, leaving a soft, fine-textured, fine-grained, spongy product especially suited for mixing with meats or using as a meat substitute.

It will take approximately 12 hours to freeze the tofu. Drain it first; then place it in a plastic bag. Frozen tofu may turn a pale yellow or brown color.

A wonderful way to prepare frozen and thawed tofu is batter-dipped. Sliced into 1/2-inch slices, dipped into batter and fried, it can be served alone or on a sandwich with melted cheese on top. Cut into smaller pieces, perhaps 1/2-inch cubes, and batter-fried, it becomes an appetizer—superb when dipped in a seafood cocktail sauce with plenty of horseradish.

BATTER-DIPPED TOFU

1 pound tofu, frozen, thawed, and drained

1 cup unbleached flour

1/2 teaspoon salt

1/8 teaspoon pepper

1 teaspoon dried dill weed

1 egg

1/4 cup milk

3 dashes hot sauce

oil for frying

Cut the tofu into 1/2-inch cubes or slices. Combine the flour with the seasonings. In a separate bowl, beat the egg, and add the milk and hot sauce. Heat the oil in a heavy skillet. Dip the tofu in the flour, then in the egg mixture, and again in the flour. Fry until browned, about 3 minutes on each side.

YIELD: 8 TO 10 SLICES

TIME: 20 MINUTES

TOFU ON THE SIDE

SWEET POTATO PANCAKE

1 cup cooked sweet potato, mashed

4 ounces tofu

2/3 cup fresh bread crumbs

1 tablespoon onion, minced

a few dashes of curry powder

1/4 teaspoon salt

2 tablespoons unbleached flour, spread on a saucer

2 tablespoons oil

Using a fork, mix all the ingredients, except the flour and oil, in a small bowl. Mash the tofu as you mix and blend. Form the mix into 4 thin patties, and dip each side in the flour.

Heat the oil in a heavy skillet, and fry the pancakes over medium-low heat for about 10 minutes on each side. The pancakes should be golden brown and crusty on the outside, soft and rich inside.

YIELD: 4 PANCAKES

TIME: 25 MINUTES

EGG-FREE MAYONNAISE

3/4 cup oil

2 tablespoons lemon juice

1/4 teaspoon prepared mustard

1/4 to 1/2 teaspoon salt

8 ounces tofu

Put all of the ingredients into the blender in the order given. Process until smooth, using a rubber spatula to scrape the sides of the glass. The oil separates again during storage, so stir before using.

YIELD: 1 1/4 CUPS
TIME: 5 MINUTES

OLIVE NUT SPREAD

This spread is good on crackers and even better broiled on a slice of bread. For the best flavor, make this spread in advance and refrigerate it overnight.

1/2 pound tofu, crumbled

10 pitted olives, green or black

1/3 cup pecan or walnut halves

1 1/2 ounces cream cheese

dash Worcestershire sauce

1 small garlic clove, minced

a few tablespoons of olive juice, dill pickle juice, or beer

Place all the ingredients in a blender and process until smooth. Use a spatula to scrape down the sides of the blender to assist the process. Add more juice or beer, a little at a time, to achieve a moist, easily spread consistency. Refrigerator for at least an hour to combine flavors.

YIELD: APPROXIMATELY 1 1/4 CUPS
TIME: 10 MINUTES PLUS CHILLING TIME

POPPY SEED DRESSING

This dressing is great on a spinach-mushroom salad, topped with fresh orange slices or mandarin orange segments from a can. Use less honey if you do not like sweet dressings.

1/4 cup oil

1/4 cup cider vinegar

2 tablespoons lemon juice

1/4 cup honey

6 ounces tofu

1 tablespoon poppy seeds

Place all the ingredients in your blender in the order given. Blend until smooth.

YIELD: 1 1/4 CUPS
TIME: ABOUT 5 MINUTES

MARINATED SALAD

1/4 cup vegetable oil

2 tablespoons cider vinegar

1 teaspoon honey

1 teaspoon soy sauce

1 teaspoon dry oregano

1/4 teaspoon garlic salt

a few grinds of black pepper

1 small onion, sliced thinly

1 pound carrots, sliced into 1/4-inch rounds

1 pound green beans, sliced in 1-inch lengths

12 ounces tofu

Pour the oil, vinegar, honey, soy sauce, and seasonings into a large mixing bowl. Add the vegetables and tofu, and toss lightly but thoroughly. Place in a refrigerator container with a tightly fitting lid, and chill several hours, shaking gently or turning upside down occasionally.

YIELD: 6 SERVINGS
TIME: 30 TO 35 MINUTES, PLUS CHILLING TIME

TOMATO TOFU SALAD

This is a very light, protein-packed summer salad.

1/4 cup vegetable oil (olive oil is best)

1/4 cup lemon juice

1/8 teaspoon salt

1/8 teaspoon pepper

1/2 teaspoon dried basil

4 scallions, chopped

1 cup sliced mushrooms

2 medium tomatoes, chopped

8 ounces tofu, cut in 1/2-inch cubes

Combine the oil, lemon juice, and seasonings. Add the vegetables and tofu. Toss gently. Chill for a half hour before serving.

YIELD: 4 TO 6 SERVINGS
TIME: 45 MINUTES

GREEN ONION DIP

8 ounces sour cream

8 ounces tofu

1 garlic clove

3 green onions, chopped

1 teaspoon Worcestershire sauce or soy sauce

salt to taste

In the order given, put all of the ingredients into your blender or food processor, and process until smooth. Serve with chips or fresh vegetables—or pile into hot baked potatoes.

Other dips can be made using various herbs, vegetables, or cheeses to season the tofu and sour cream—just combine your own experience and creativity.

YIELD: APPROXIMATELY 2 CUPS
TIME: 3 TO 5 MINUTES

Continued ➜

SOUPS

CREAM OF MUSHROOM SOUP

2 cups chicken or vegetable stock

1 cup chopped mushrooms

1 small onion, quartered

1/3 cup brown rice

dash garlic salt

4 ounces tofu

1/2 cup milk

salt to taste

Place the stock, mushrooms, onion, rice, and garlic salt in a saucepan. Bring to a boil; then simmer, covered, until the rice is thoroughly cooked. This will take 30 to 50 minutes. Pour this soup into your blender, and add the tofu and milk. Blend 1 minute, until smooth but still hearty. Salt to taste. Serve immediately, or rewarm slightly if necessary.

YIELD: ABOUT 3 CUPS
TIME: 50 TO 55 MINUTES

HEARTY VEGETABLE SOUP

1 quart water

3 tablespoons soy sauce

2 teaspoons parsley

1 carrot, chopped

1 potato, diced

2 tomatoes, chopped

1 cup cabbage, chopped

1 cup corn

1 cup summer squash or cucumber, diced

1 cup peas or pea pods

8 ounces tofu, cut in bite-size pieces

2 cups spinach or Swiss chard leaves

salt to taste

Place all the ingredients, except the spinach and salt, in a soup pot and stir well. Bring the soup to a boil, then simmer for 30 minutes. Add the spinach for the last 5 minutes of cooking. This makes a good meal served with corn bread or rye bread fresh out of the oven.

YIELD: 4 SERVINGS
TIME: APPROXIMATELY 1 HOUR

Thoroughly dry beans can be stored in burlap bags, or loosely covered plastic containers, and kept in a well-ventilated area.

MAIN DISHES

TOFU BURGERS

These burgers are good hot or cold—they are great on sesame buns.

1 pound tofu

2 cups rolled oats

1 tablespoon catsup

1 tablespoon Worcestershire sauce

1 small onion, minced

1 teaspoon prepared mustard

1 teaspoon salt

1/4 teaspoon pepper

2 tablespoons butter or safflower oil

garnishes: lettuce, sliced onions and tomatoes, sprouts, pickles (optional)

Crumble the tofu in a large mixing bowl. Place the oats in your blender and whirl until you have a coarse flour. Add the oats to the tofu, and blend well with a wooden spoon. Add all of the other ingredients, except the garnishes, blending well. Wet your hands and form thin burgers with the mix, making the burgers the size of your bread or bun.

Heat the oil in a heavy skillet. Fry the burgers at a low temperature, about 8 minutes on each side.

Serve on buns or rolls, trimmed with sprouts, lettuce, sliced onions and tomatoes, pickles, or whatever else tickles your fancy.

These burgers freeze well once fried and can be reheated by frying gently in a small amount of oil.

YIELD: 6 LARGE BURGERS
TIME: 15 TO 20 MINUTES

QUICHE

Combining cheese, milk, whole wheat, and tofu will give you a perfect combination of proteins—nutritious as well as delicious!

Crust:

1 cup whole wheat pastry flour

dash of salt

2 tablespoons butter

2 tablespoons oil

2 tablespoons ice water

Filling:

1/2 pound spinach

2 green onions

3/4 cup milk

2 eggs

6 ounces tofu

1/4 teaspoon salt

few grinds of pepper

dash of nutmeg

1/2 cup Swiss or Herkimer cheese, shredded

Mix the flour and salt together in a bowl; then add the butter, using a fork to cut it in. Add the oil a little at a time, continuing to cut with the fork until the mixture looks crumbly. Add the ice water and stir until the mixture starts to cling together and can be formed into a ball. Add more ice water if necessary. Flatten the pastry and roll it out between sheets of waxed paper. Spread the crust in an 8-inch pie pan. Poke holes in the crust with a fork. Place in a preheated oven for 5 minutes at 400°F.

Chop the spinach, and wash it by placing it in a dishpan filled with cold water. Swish the chopped spinach around; then let it sit in the water another minute or so to allow the dirt to settle on the bottom. Remove the spinach, and set it aside to drain. Chop the green onions.

Put the drained spinach and chopped onions in a saucepan, covered, over a high heat. The spinach and onions will be soft in about 2 minutes, cooking in the water left on the spinach leaves. Leave the lid off for another minute or so to evaporate all of the remaining water.

Then place the vegetables in the waiting pie shell. Put all of the remaining ingredients except the cheese into your blender and process until smooth. Pour this into the pie shell on top of the spinach. Top with cheese and bake at 375°F for about 50 minutes, or until a clean knife inserted 1 inch from the side of the pan comes out clean. Cool for at least 10 minutes before serving.

Variation: Instead of spinach you can add lean bacon pieces, fried crisp and drained well. Six strips of bacon, broken or cut into bite-size pieces, will suffice. Or you can make a combination quiche of 1/4 pound of wilted spinach and 3 strips of crisp bacon.

YIELD: 5 SERVINGS

TIME: APPROXIMATELY 1 1/2 HOURS

TOFU-NUT LOAF WITH MUSHROOM SAUCE

This dish may remind you of meatloaf. It makes a very hearty, informal supper dish. Served cold with horseradish, it tastes amazingly like cold meat.

Tofu Loaf:

1 cup rolled oats

1 cup walnuts

1 pound tofu

1 medium onion, grated

1 carrot, grated

1/2 green pepper, minced

1 teaspoon salt

2 teaspoons sage

2 teaspoons thyme

1 tablespoon oregano

Mushroom Sauce:

3 tablespoons butter

1 shallot or 2 scallions, minced

1/2 pound mushrooms, chopped

3 tablespoons unbleached flour

1 1/2 cups milk

dash of garlic salt

a few drops of hot sauce

salt to taste

Preheat your oven to 375°F. Put the oats into your blender and blend until you obtain a coarse flour, stirring with rubber spatula between blendings if necessary. Transfer the oat flour to a large mixing bowl. Put the walnuts into the blender and blend coarsely; then add the nuts to the oats in the bowl.

Crumble the tofu into the bowl and add all of the other ingredients (the vegetables should total 1 cup). Mix well, even beat some, until all ingredients are blended, and the contents of the bowl has a fluffy, but firm, texture. Butter a large shallow casserole dish then add the contents of the bowl, shaping into an oval or a rectangle in the center of the dish. The loaf should be no more than 2 inches high. Bake at 375°F for 45 minutes, adding half the mushroom sauce during the last 10 minutes of cooking.

To make the mushroom sauce, melt the butter in a skillet, then add the shallot and the mushrooms. Sauté until slightly cooked. Add the flour and blend well. Add all of the other ingredients and bring to a boil, stirring frequently. Turn off the heat. Pour half the sauce over the Tofu-Nut Loaf during the last minutes of cooking time, and serve the rest as gravy.

YIELD: ABOUT 6 SERVINGS

TIME: ABOUT 1 HOUR

GRILLED CHEESE-TOFU SANDWICH

Slice tofu thinly and place enough on one slice of bread to cover it all the way to the edges. Top with thinly sliced cheddar cheese. For a little excitement, add sliced pickles, sliced onions, or a few dashes of hot sauce. Put another slice of bread on top and butter both slices (outsides) for grilling; or dip the sandwich into a mixture of beaten egg and milk and fry as you would French toast.

CURRIED VEGETABLES

Creamy cubes of tofu contrast nicely with the texture of the bite-size vegetables. This is a vegetable toss taken out of the ordinary.

Continued ➜

4 tablespoons oil

1 clove of garlic, minced

a few dashes of curry powder (more to taste)

6 ounces tofu, cubed

1 bunch broccoli, chopped

2 large carrots, sliced thinly on the diagonal

1 onion, sliced thinly

2 tomatoes, chopped

salt to taste

Heat the oil in a large skillet or wok. When the oil is hot, but not smoky, add the minced garlic. Sauté for a minute. Remove the garlic, and add a few dashes of curry powder and the tofu cubes. Sauté the cubes stirring frequently, for about 3 minutes.

Add the vegetables one at a time. First add the broccoli and sauté for about 2 minutes; then add the carrots and onion. Continue stirring and tossing over low heat. When the carrots are tender and the onions appear translucent—after 3 minutes or so—add the tomatoes to heat through, about 2 more minutes. Salt to taste.

This makes a great meal served with rice. Try a little yogurt on the side.

YIELD: 5 TO 6 SERVINGS
TIME: 20 TO 30 MINUTES

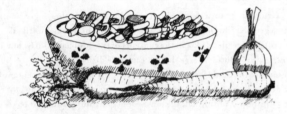

CHINESE DISHES

EGGPLANT SZECHUAN STYLE

This recipe calls for sesame oil, which adds a smoky taste, and hot sesame oil, which is very hot, and vegetable oil. Vary the proportions of oils to achieve different tastes. The recipe offered here is quite mild.

1 small eggplant (1/2 to 3/4 pound)

1 teaspoon salt

1 tablespoon hot sesame oil

1 tablespoon sesame oil

1 tablespoon vegetable oil

1/2 teaspoon salt

1/4 cup soy sauce

1 pound fresh or frozen string beans

8 ounces tofu, cut in 1/4-inch cubes

2 tablespoons sesame seeds (optional)

Peel the eggplant, and cut it into 1/4-inch cubes. Sprinkle the eggplant with 1 teaspoon of salt, and allow it to sit for 5 minutes or

more. The salt will draw out the bitterness in the eggplant. Rinse the salt off before cooking the eggplant.

Heat the oils in a wok or large skillet. Add 1/2 teaspoon salt, then the eggplant. Fry the eggplant over high heat for 5 minutes or until the eggplant becomes quite soft. (If the oil starts to smoke, reduce the heat.) Add the soy sauce and continue stirring for another minute. Add the string beans and tofu, and continue cooking until the string beans are tender but not soft. Toss in the sesame seeds and serve immediately with plenty of hot rice.

YIELD: 4 SERVINGS
TIME: 25 MINUTES

BEAN CURD SOUP

1 quart homemade chicken stock, clarified if desired

1/4 cup finely minced green onions (reserve some tops)

2 tablespoons dried green seaweed or finely chopped spinach

8 ounces tofu, cut in 1/2-inch cubes

4 tablespoons celery leaves, chopped fine

soy sauce

The appearance of this soup is greatly enhanced if you use clarified soup stock. To clarify stock, start with only fresh meat, bones, and vegetables. After simmering the stock at least 1 hour, let the stock boil down, uncovered, until you have a good strong flavor. Strain the stock through a cheesecloth. Briefly place a piece of paper towel on top of the soup to remove any surface grease. Place the stock in a clean soup pot with one egg white and one broken egg shell. Bring to a boil and let simmer until the soup is beautiful and clear. Strain through a cheesecloth. You now have clarified your soup stock.

Bring the stock to a boil, then add the green onions and dried seaweed or spinach. Cover the pot, and boil the stock for about 5 minutes; then turn off the heat. Add the tofu cubes and wait a minute or two, until they are heated through. Just before serving, garnish with the green onion tops and celery leaves. Serve in rice bowls with wide spoons, accompanied by a good soy sauce.

YIELD: 4 SERVINGS
TIME: 2 HOURS

BRAISED TOFU

1 pound tofu, sliced 1/4-inch thick

2 tablespoons vegetable oil

1 clove garlic, sliced thinly

1/2 teaspoon ginger or 3 thin slices of fresh ginger root

3 scallions, chopped

3 tablespoons soy sauce

1/4 cup sauterne

Slice the tofu and spread it out on a flat surface covered with a towel. Weight the tofu with a heavy plate to squeeze out any excess water. Allow the tofu to stand for at least a half hour. Or, use frozen tofu that has been thawed and drained.

Heat the oil in a wok or heavy, 10-inch skillet. Add the garlic and ginger. Gently place the tofu slices in the oil. Fry over medium heat for 2 minutes on each side. Sprinkle the scallions and pour the sauterne and soy sauce on top of the tofu.

Cover. Reduce the heat to low and braise the tofu for 15 minutes. Serve immediately.

YIELD: 4 SERVINGS AS A SIDE DISH

TIME: 40 MINUTES

STIR-FRY VEGETABLES

1 tablespoon oil

2 tablespoons soy sauce

2 teaspoons honey

2 garlic cloves, minced

1 tablespoon ginger root, grated

2 cups snow pea pods

2 cups bean sprouts

2 cups bok choy (Chinese cabbage), chopped on a diagonal

1/2 cup green onions, chopped lengthwise

8 ounces tofu, cut in small cubes

Place the oil, soy sauce, honey, and seasonings in a heavy skillet or wok, and heat until sizzling. Spread the mixture around. Add the vegetables and stir fry, gently mixing and tossing over the high heat. Add the tofu. Stir fry until the vegetables begin to look cooked, the tofu is well seasoned, and the bean sprouts have lost their "raw" taste. Serve immediately.

YIELD: SERVES 4 AS A SIDE DISH, OR 2 AS A MAIN COURSE, OVER RICE

TIME: APPROXIMATELY 15 MINUTES

HOT AND SOUR SOUP

1 tablespoon salt

1/2 teaspoon honey

2 tablespoons soy sauce

2 tablespoons cider vinegar

1 teaspoon black pepper

1 tablespoon sesame oil

1 fresh scallion, chopped

1 teaspoon ginger, freshly minced

1/4 pound fresh lean pork, cut in matchstick–size pieces (optional)

1 teaspoon soy sauce

1 teaspoon corn starch

5 cups water

1 cup fresh mushrooms, chopped fine

1 pound tofu, chopped fine

1 cup celery or cucumber, chopped fine

2 1/2 tablespoons corn starch

2 tablespoons cold water

1 egg beaten

In a large bowl combine the first eight ingredients. Set aside. Mix the pork strips with the soy sauce and corn starch.

Bring water to a boil in a large saucepan. Add the pork strips, stirring well. Keep the contents of the pan boiling as you add the mushrooms, tofu, and celery. Boil 3–5 more minutes and thicken with the corn starch combined with water. Stir to a boil, then add the beaten egg.

Remove from heat immediately and pour over the ingredients in the large bowl. Mix gently and serve hot.

YIELD: 8 SERVINGS

TIME: 1 HOUR

DESSERTS

BANANA-APPLE SHAKE

For best results, chill all the ingredients and the glasses before you begin.

Bananas can be frozen (and used in this shake) by removing their skins and cutting them, if desired; then placing them in a plastic bag. They will keep for at least a month.

1/2 cup apple juice or cider

1/4 cup ripe banana

1/4 cup tofu

In a measuring cup, put 1/2 cup of apple juice. Add enough ripe banana to make 3/4 cup of liquid. Last, add enough tofu to bring the level to the 1-cup line. Dump all ingredients into the blender and blend until very smooth, about 40 seconds. Serve in a chilled glass with a straw.

YIELD: 1 SHAKE

TIME: 3 MINUTES

HEAVENLY PIE

Crust:

2 cups crushed graham crackers

1/4 cup melted butter

2 tablespoons honey

Filling:

8 ounces cream cheese, softened

8 ounces tofu

1 egg

6 ounces carob or milk chocolate morsels, melted

1 teaspoon vanilla

whipped cream (optional, for serving)

To make the crust combine the cracker crumbs, butter, and honey. Press into an 8-inch pie pan.

Continued ➡

In a food processor, or with a mixer at medium speed, blend together the cream cheese, tofu, egg, chocolate, and vanilla. You will find that scraping down the sides of the bowl periodically with a rubber spatula will be necessary to allow you to blend all the ingredients. Be sure that all the cream cheese lumps are incorporated.

Spoon the chocolate filling into the pie pan. Bake at 350°F for 30 to 45 minutes. Chill well before serving. Decorate with whipped cream if desired.

YIELD: SERVES 6 TO 8

TIME: 1 HOUR PLUS CHILLING TIME

MILK SHAKE

1 scoop carob or chocolate ice cream

1 scoop tofu

1 ounce carob chips, melted or 1 tablespoon chocolate syrup

1/2 cup milk

Blend the ingredients together until frothy and smooth.

YIELD: 1 SHAKE

TIME: 2 MINUTES

Cooking with Honey

Joanne Barrett

Illustrations by Nancy Anisfield

What Is Honey?

Flowers secrete a sweet liquid called nectar. Bees collect this nectar and carry it back to the hive, where it is thickened into honey. During the hot summer months, bees store much more honey than they can use, and the beekeeper harvests this surplus. Honey can be obtained in several forms.

- **Comb honey.** Honey can be left in the wax combs, just as the bees store it. Comb honey is delightful to eat, wax and all, spread on a warm slice of fresh bread or a muffin. Since the bees have sealed it in wax, it keeps all the original flavor months later.

- **Liquid honey.** This honey is spun from the combs and bottled. Most commercial honey is warmed before bottling so it will remain liquid. Liquid honey is the easiest and most commonly used form for cooking.

- **Crystallized honey.** This is extracted honey which has been bottled unheated. It will undergo a natural process of granulation and will retain its original flavors better than heated honey. It has a nice, easily spread consistency, and many people prefer their honey this way when they become familiar with it. Slow warming in a pan of water will reliquify crystallized honey if this is desired.

THE FLAVORS OF HONEY

There are as many flavors of honey as there are flowers. In early summer we get honey from wild berries and locust trees. The main honey flow occurs up here in the North during July, and we harvest a delicious light honey made from the blossoms of clover, alfalfa, and wild flowers. As the season progresses, the later flowers, goldenrod and aster, darken the color and make the flavor more pronounced. Honey can be as dark as molasses, as those who know buckwheat honey can attest. Its dark color and distinctive flavor cannot be mistaken. If one type of flower predominates in an area, the honey will have its flavor. Most of you have probably seen orange blossom, tupelo, or sourwood honey for sale.

Generally, the lighter the honey, the milder is its flavor and the better it is for general cooking.

Cooking Tips

Honey is a liquid sweet, and unlike sugar, it adds a special flavor to foods. It tends to absorb moisture, which enables baked goods to stay fresher for a longer time.

There are a few basic cooking techniques which are helpful to know when preparing food with honey.

- Substitute the honey cup for cup of sugar, but decrease the amount of liquid in the recipe by 1/4 cup.

- If you find that honey is too sweet cup for cup of sugar, substitute 3/4 cup of honey for each cup of sugar and reduce the amount of liquid by 2 to 3 tablespoons.

- Measure the honey in a cup after the oil or fat in a recipe, or coat the cup or spoon with oil. This keeps the honey from sticking to the cup so you get all the honey out.

- Honey is acidic. In baked goods where as much as 1 cup of honey is being substituted for sugar, if no baking soda is called for, add 1/2 teaspoon of baking soda.

- Honey works best in most recipes as a liquid. It can then be added slowly to the other liquid ingredients in the recipe.

- Crystallized honey can be measured cup for cup of liquid honey; the two can be used interchangeably in cooking. But crystallized honey tends to make baked goods denser. What I do is measure the crystallized honey in a metal measuring cup, put the metal cup in a pan of warm water, double-boiler style, until the honey liquifies. Then I add the liquid honey to my ingredients—after it is cooled.

- When substituting honey for sugar in a recipe, bake the food longer and at an oven temperature 25°F. lower than the original recipe called for.

- Most honey breads and cakes improve in flavor and texture if they are baked and wrapped a day before eating.

BEVERAGES

HONEY ROOT BEER

For this recipe, you will need a 1-gallon jug with a tight-fitting, screw-on lid to prevent leaking and loss of carbonation.

2 quarts warm water

1 3/4 cups honey

1 1/2 ounces root beer extract

1/4 teaspoon dry bakers yeast

warm water to fill jug

Fill a 1-gallon jug half full with warm water. Add honey, root beer extract, and dry yeast. Swirl the jug until the honey, extract, and yeast are completely blended. Add enough warm water to fill the jug to 1/2 inch from the top. Carefully rotate the jug to mix the ingredients. Then cap it tightly. Lay the jug on its side in about 70°F. for 24 hours. (I wrap the jug in a towel in case the jug leaks or should break.) Refrigerate until it is cold.

MAKES 16 8-OUNCE SERVINGS.

COCOA

2 full tablespoons unsweetened cocoa (carob powder can be substituted)

2 full tablespoons honey

2 cups warm milk

1/4 teaspoon vanilla

2 tablespoons powdered milk (optional)

Blend the cocoa and honey in a cup. Slowly add a small amount of warm milk to make a syrup. Pour the syrup into the remaining milk and add the vanilla. (If you want richer cocoa put it into a blender and add the powdered milk.) Heat the cocoa until hot, but not boiling, and serve.

MAKES 2 SERVINGS.

HONEY LEMONADE

1/2 cup honey

1/2 cup hot water

Juice of 4 medium-size lemons

4 cups cold water

Blend honey with hot water to make a syrup, and pour it into a pitcher. Add lemon juice. Pour in cold water and stir. Serve icy cold.

SERVES 6.

MILK SHAKE

3 tablespoons honey

1 cup fresh fruit (strawberries, sliced peaches, blueberries)

2 cups milk

1/2 pint vanilla ice cream

Stir honey and fresh fruit together. In a blender, combine fruit-honey mixture and milk. Whirl to blend, then add the ice cream and blend again. Serve in cold glasses.

MAKES 2 SERVINGS.

FRUIT PUNCH

1/2 cup honey

1 cup hot water

2 6-ounce cans frozen cranberry juice cocktail concentrate

3 cups cold water

4 cups unsweetened pineapple juice

juice of 4 medium-size lemons

1 quart ginger ale

12 ounces (1 1/2 cups) frozen strawberries

Blend honey with hot water to make a syrup and pour into a punch bowl. Add the cranberry concentrate and cold water. Add pineapple juice, lemon juice, and ginger ale. Float the strawberries on top and add ice.

MAKES 20 PUNCH-GLASS SERVINGS.

HONEY VERSUS SUGAR

Honey is generally considered to be more nutritious than white sugar. This is because the refining process removes all the trace minerals and vitamins from the sugar cane. Honey does contain minerals, but both honey and sugar have insignificant vitamin content. Brown sugar, which can be made in your kitchen just by combining white sugar and molasses, compares more favorably to honey in terms of food value.

Continued ➡

BREAKFAST FOODS

GRANOLA

5 cups rolled oats

1 cup wheat germ

1 cup chopped almonds or cashews

1 cup sunflower seeds

1/2 cup sesame seeds

1/2 cup coconut

1/2 cup powdered milk

1/2 cup vegetable oil

1 cup honey

2 teaspoons vanilla

1 cup dried fruit (optional)

Mix the dry ingredients in a large bowl. Warm the oil and honey together. Pour the oil, honey, and the vanilla into the dry ingredients and mix thoroughly. Put the mixture in a large, shallow roasting pan (the larger the pan, the crisper the granola). Bake at 250°F. for 1 hour, stirring every 10 to 15 minutes. Dried fruit can be added after baking.

MAKES 20 4-OUNCE SERVINGS.

BAKED APPLES

4 large cooking apples (Cortland or Rome)

4 tablespoons honey

4 teaspoons chopped walnuts

cinnamon

1 cup heavy cream

Wash and core the apples. Place them in a shallow baking dish. Put 1 tablespoon of honey into each apple. Add 1 teaspoon chopped walnuts to each apple and sprinkle with cinnamon. Cover the bottom of the pan with cold water. Cover the dish with foil and bake at 350°F. in the oven for 40 to 60 minutes, or until the fruit is tender. Serve warm with heavy cream.

MAKES 4 SERVINGS.

GERMAN PANCAKE

3 eggs

1/2 cup milk

1/2 teaspoon salt

2 tablespoons oil or melted butter

1/4 cup powdered milk

1/2 cup whole wheat pastry flour

butter to grease pan

3 large cooking apples

1–2 tablespoons cold water

1/4 cup warmed honey

cinnamon

Combine the eggs, milk, salt, oil, powdered milk, and flour; blend until smooth. Pour the batter into a well-buttered, 10-inch, cast iron frying pan. Bake for 10 minutes at 450°F.; then decrease the oven temperature to 350°F. and bake until the pancake puffs up at the sides (about 10 to 15 minutes) and is brown.

While the pancake is baking, slice the apples, combine with 1 to 2 tablespoons of water, and cook slowly over low heat until soft. Spread the cooked apples over the baked pancake, drizzle on the honey, and sprinkle it all over with cinnamon. Serve immediately—or your pancake will fall!

MAKES 4 SERVINGS.

Yeasted and Quick Breads

Honey breads are rich and golden and they stay fresh much longer than those baked with sugar.

BAGELS

2 cups whole wheat flour

2–3 cups unbleached white flour

1 tablespoon salt

3 tablespoons honey

1 tablespoon yeast

1 1/2 cups very warm water

1 egg white, beaten

1 tablespoon cold water

In a large bowl, thoroughly mix 1 cup whole wheat flour, 1/2 cup unbleached flour, salt, honey, and undissolved yeast. Gradually add warm tap water and beat for 2 minutes with an electric beater at medium speed. Add 1/2 cup unbleached flour. Beat at high speed for 2 minutes. By hand, stir in enough additional flour to make a soft dough. Turn onto a lightly floured board; knead until smooth and elastic.

Place the dough in an ungreased bowl. Cover and let rise in a warm place for about 20 minutes. (The dough will *not* double in bulk.) Punch down. Turn onto a lightly floured board.

Cut the dough into 12 equal parts. Roll each piece into a long strip. Pinch the ends of the strip together to form a circle. Place on an ungreased baking sheet. Cover and let rise for 20 minutes.

Boil 2 inches of water in a shallow pan. Lower the heat and add a few bagels at a time. Simmer for 7 minutes. Remove from the water and place the bagels on a towel to cool. Cool for 5 minutes.

Place the bagels on ungreased baking sheets. Bake at 375°F. for 10 minutes. Remove from the oven and brush the tops with the combined egg white and cold water. Return to the oven and bake about 20 minutes, until golden brown.

MAKES 12 BAGELS.

WHOLE WHEAT BREAD

This is a basic hearty bread and the secret of its success is in kneading it until the dough is satiny.

3 cups warm water

2 cakes or tablespoons yeast

1/2 cup honey

6–7 cups whole wheat flour

1/4 cup oil or melted butter

2 teaspoons salt

Place the warm water in a large mixing bowl and sprinkle in the yeast. Allow 5 minutes for the yeast to start bubbling. Stir in the honey, 3 cups of the flour, the oil, and the salt. Beat this mixture by hand until smooth. Slowly add the remaining flour cup by cup, until the dough becomes easy to handle. Turn the dough onto a lightly floured board and knead until it is smooth and satiny in texture. Use more flour if the dough is still sticky.

Place the dough in a lightly oiled bowl. Cover and let it rise in a warm place (85°F.) until it is double in bulk (about 1 hour). When doubled in bulk, punch it down, divide it into two parts and shape into loaves. Place into 2 greased loaf pans. Cover and let it rise again until it doubles in volume.

Bake in a preheated oven at 350°F. for 50 minutes or until the top is well browned. Remove from pans to cool.

MAKES 2 LOAVES.

BRAN MUFFINS

You can make a lot of these and freeze some. The honey and molasses make them so good.

3 cups whole wheat pastry flour or unbleached white flour

2 cups bran

1 cup powdered milk

3 teaspoons baking powder

1 teaspoon baking soda

1 teaspoon salt

2 cups water

4 eggs, beaten

1/2 cup vegetable oil

1/2 cup molasses

3/4 cup honey

1 cup chopped dates or raisins

Combine the flour, bran, powdered milk, baking powder, baking soda, and salt in a large bowl. Add the water, eggs, and oil and stir; then add the molasses, honey, and fruit. Stir until the batter is smooth. The batter will be quite moist. Spoon the batter into buttered muffin tins and bake in a 350°F. oven for 15 to 20 minutes. Be careful not to overcook these muffins.

MAKES ABOUT 36 MUFFINS.

BLUEBERRY MUFFINS

4 tablespoons honey

2 tablespoons melted butter

1/2 cup milk

2 eggs, beaten

1 1/2 cups unbleached flour

2 1/2 teaspoons baking powder

1/2 teaspoon salt

3/4 cup blueberries

Combine the honey and melted butter. Add the milk and eggs. Mix together the flour, baking powder, and salt; add to the honey mixture to make a smooth batter. Stir in the blueberries. Fill a greased muffin tin 2/3 full and bake in a 400°F. oven for 20 minutes. Serve warm.

MAKES 12 MUFFINS.

RAISIN BREAD

Whole Wheat Bread Recipe—substitute half or all of the whole wheat flour with unbleached white flour

6 tablespoons melted butter

1/2 cup warmed honey

1 cup raisins

4 teaspoons cinnamon

2 tablespoons melted butter

Prepare the dough as for the bread recipe. After the dough as risen once, punch down and divide it in two. Roll each piece of dough on a floured board into an oblong shape, 1/4 inch thick. Spread each piece with the melted butter, honey, raisins, and cinnamon. Separately roll each piece of dough up as for a jelly roll and pinch the seams to seal. Tuck the ends under and put each loaf in a well-greased bread tin.

Continued ➜

Brush the top of each loaf with a tablespoon melted butter. Bake in a 350°F. oven for 45 to 50 minutes until golden brown. Remove from the pans to cool.

MAKES 2 LOAVES.

BANANA BREAD

2/3 cup honey

1/2 cup oil

3 eggs, beaten

3 ripe bananas, mashed

1/4 teaspoon salt

1 teaspoon vanilla

2 cups unbleached flour or whole wheat pastry flour

1 teaspoon baking soda

Beat together the honey and oil, then add the eggs. Add the mashed bananas, salt, and vanilla; mix well.

Sift together the flour and baking soda. Gradually blend the flour mixture in with the banana mixture until the batter is smooth. Grease 1 large or 2 small loaf pans, pour in the batter, and bake in a 350°F. oven for 45 to 60 minutes depending on the size of the pan. Lower the oven temperature if the bread is browning too quickly.

MAKES 1 LARGE LOAF, OR 2 SMALL ONES.

APPLE CRESCENT LOAF

Yeast Dough:

1 cake or tablespoon yeast

1 cup milk scalded, cooled to lukewarm

1/4 cup honey

3 tablespoons oil or melted butter

1/2 teaspoon salt

2 eggs, beaten

2 cups unbleached white flour

1 1/2 cups whole wheat flour (do not use whole wheat pastry flour)

3 tablespoons melted butter

Apple Filling:

4 apples

2 tablespoons water

1/2 cup raisins

1/2 cup walnuts (optional)

1/4 cup honey, warmed slightly

1 1/2 teaspoons cinnamon

Soften the yeast in milk with 1 teaspoon of the honey in a small bowl. Blend the rest of the honey, butter or oil, salt, and eggs in a large bowl. Add the yeast and milk and stir in the white and whole wheat flours. Turn the dough onto a lightly floured board and knead lightly, adding a small amount of flour if necessary. Turn into a lightly oiled bowl, cover, and let rise until double in bulk—about 1 hour.

Peel, slice, and stew the apples in 2 tablespoons of water until soft. Allow to cool slightly.

Roll out the dough into an oblong shape, 1/4 inch thick. Brush with 2 tablespoons of melted butter. Spread the apples, raisins, and nuts over the dough. Drizzle the honey over the apples and sprinkle on the cinnamon. Roll the dough up as for a jelly roll. Put it on a greased cookie sheet and shape into a crescent, turn the ends under and slit the top in a few places to expose the filling. Cover and set in a warm place to rise slightly.

Brush the top with the remaining tablespoon of butter and bake in a 375°F. oven for about 30 minutes.

MAKES 1 LOAF.

CASHEW NUT COFFEE CAKE

Batter:

1 egg, beaten

3/4 cup milk

1/4 cup vegetable oil

1 teaspoon vanilla

1/2 cup honey

1 1/4 cups whole wheat pastry flour

1/2 cup wheat germ

1/4 cup powdered milk

2 teaspoons baking powder

Topping:

1/2 cup chopped cashews

1/4 cup warmed honey

1 tablespoon melted butter

1 1/2 teaspoons cinnamon

Blend the egg, milk, oil, and vanilla in a bowl. Slowly add the honey, beating the mixture the whole time. In a separate bowl, combine the dry ingredients and gradually stir into the liquid mixture. Pour the batter into a well-greased 8-inch by 8-inch pan. To prepare the topping, mix the cashews, honey, butter, and cinnamon together. Slowly drizzle the topping over the batter. It will sink down into the batter as the cake bakes. Bake at 350°F. for 30 to 35 minutes.

SERVES 9.

DRESSINGS, MARINADES, AND SAUCES

HONEY FRENCH DRESSING

1/2 cup olive oil or vegetable oil

2 tablespoons cider vinegar

1 tablespoon honey

2 teaspoons catsup

1 small clove garlic, minced

1 teaspoon soy sauce

1/4 teaspoon salt

1/4 teaspoon paprika

dash cayenne pepper

Combine all of the ingredients in a jar and shake well until blended. Store in the refrigerator.

MAKES ABOUT 2/3 CUP OF DRESSING.

LEMON MARINADE FOR CHICKEN

1 tablespoon melted butter

1 tablespoon olive oil

1/2 cup honey

1/2 cup lemon juice (flavor to taste)

1 medium chicken, cut in pieces

1 lemon sliced into rounds

Combine the butter, olive oil, honey, and lemon juice in a small bowl. Put the chicken pieces in a large bowl and pour the marinade over all, carefully coating each piece. Let the chicken sit for a few minutes. Place the chicken in a baking pan and arrange the lemon rounds on top. Cover the pan with foil and bake for approximately 45 minutes in a 350°F. oven. Uncover the pan for the last 10 to 15 minutes.

This recipe makes 1 1/4 cups of marinade, enough for 1 medium chicken.

- If you like, spoon off some of the fat and make a gravy from the pan drippings. It is good served with rice or bulgur.

- Substitute orange juice and oranges for the lemons in the recipe if you wish.

BARBECUE SAUCE

1 cup tomato sauce

1/3 cup catsup

1/4 cup honey

1 teaspoon soy sauce

2 teaspoons prepared mustard

1 teaspoon molasses

2 tablespoons minced onion (optional)

Combine all of the ingredients together in a jar and blend. Keep refrigerated. Makes about 1 3/4 cups.

For a sweeter sparerib, brush the ribs with warmed honey first, and then baste with the barbecue sauce during the last 30 minutes.

PICKLE MARINADE FOR CUCUMBERS OR BEANS

Keep a crock of this marinade in the refrigerator and just keep replenishing the vegetables.

1 1/4 cups cider vinegar

1 1/2 cups water

1/3 cup olive oil

1 1/2 teaspoons dry mustard

1 teaspoon salt

2 tablespoons dry dill weed or 1/2 cup fresh dill

1/2 teaspoon oregano

3 cloves garlic, minced

1/4 teaspoon fresh-ground black pepper

1 tablespoon honey

1/2 teaspoon red pepper

Mix all the ingredients in a saucepan. Bring the marinade to a boil and simmer for 4 minutes. Pour the marinade over sliced pickling cucumbers or steamed green beans in a crock or glass jar. Refrigerate for at least 12 hours before serving.

MAKES 3 1/4 CUPS.

HONEY CRANBERRY SAUCE

4 cups cranberries

1—1 1/2 cups water

1 1/2 cups honey

Wash the cranberries. In a saucepan, mix together the cranberries, 1 cup of water, and honey. Bring the mixture to a boil and cook until the cranberries pop open and are translucent. Add more water if necessary. Chill before using and keep in the refrigerator.

MAKES ABOUT 3 CUPS.

- A half cup of this sauce mixed with an additional cup of honey can be used as a glaze for ham. Cover a scored ham with this glaze during the last 45 minutes of baking.

- Try this sauce on vanilla ice cream.

Continued ➜

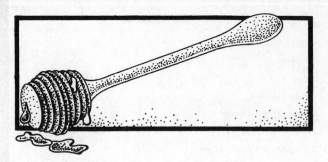

HONEY FRUIT SALAD DRESSING

4 ounces cream cheese

2 tablespoons honey

1/4 cup yogurt

2 tablespoons heavy cream

2 tablespoons lemon juice

Mash the cream cheese until soft. Add the honey, yogurt, and cream. Cream until smooth. Add the lemon juice.

MAKES 1 CUP OF DRESSING.

SIDE DISHES

COLESLAW

1 cup mayonnaise

4 tablespoons half-and-half

1 teaspoon cider vinegar

2 teaspoons prepared mustard

4 teaspoons honey

1/2 teaspoon salt

1 teaspoon celery seed

1 medium head cabbage, shredded

2 carrots, grated

Mix all of the dressing ingredients in a small bowl. Pour over the shredded cabbage and carrots. Gently toss until the vegetables are well coated.

MAKES 8 SERVINGS.

GLAZED CARROTS OR ONIONS

1 tablespoon butter

1 tablespoon honey

1 pound carrots, cut in strips and steamed until tender or 1 cup tiny onions cooked and drained

Heat the butter and honey slowly in a pan. When melted, add the carrots or onions and carefully stir to coat thoroughly. For carrots sauté only until glazed, 5 to 7 minutes. Then serve plain or with chopped fresh mint or cinnamon or nutmeg. For the onions, cook slowly until browned—about 20 minutes.

SERVES 4.

HARVARD BEETS

2 1/2 teaspoons cornstarch

1/4 cup water

1/4 cup vinegar

1/2 cup honey

3–4 whole allspice berries

1/2 stick cinnamon

12 small beets, cooked, peeled, and sliced or cubed

twist of lemon peel

1 tablespoon butter

Combine the cornstarch and water in a saucepan and blend until smooth. Add the vinegar, honey, and spices. Boil for 5 minutes.

Let the sauce cool for at least 30 minutes. Before serving add the beets, the twist of lemon, and the butter. Heat until it starts to boil.

SERVES 6.

CUCUMBER SOUR CREAM SALAD

2 envelopes unflavored gelatin

2 cups boiling water

1/4 cup honey

1/4 cup lemon juice

1/2 cup plain yogurt

1/2 cup sour cream

2 teaspoons dried dill weed

2 cucumbers, peeled and sliced

Thoroughly dissolve the gelatin in the boiling water. Add the honey and lemon juice; stir well. Chill this mixture until it has the consistency of an egg white. Mix the yogurt, sour cream, dill weed, and cucumbers together. Blend this into the chilled gelatin. Pour into a mold and refrigerate until firm.

MAKES 8 SERVINGS.

DESSERTS AND SWEETS

PEANUT BUTTER CANDIES

1/2 cup peanut butter

1 cup dry powdered milk

1/2 cup honey

3/4 cup coconut or crushed nuts (optional)

Combine all of the ingredients in a bowl and stir until well blended. Pat it into a buttered 8-inch by 8-inch pan, chill, and cut into squares. Or, make the dough into small balls and roll into coconut or crushed nuts, then chill.

HONEY CHOCOLATE LAYER CAKE

2 cups sifted unbleached white flour

1 1/4 teaspoons baking soda

1/2 teaspoon salt

1/2 cup butter

1 cup honey

2 eggs, well beaten

2 ounces unsweetened chocolate, melted and cooled

3/4 cup milk

Sift the flour and then measure it. Combine the sifted flour with the baking soda and salt and sift 3 times. Cream the butter in a large bowl; gradually add the honey in a slow stream, creaming it thoroughly. Slowly add the eggs, beating after each addition. Then add the chocolate and blend again. Add the sifted, dry ingredients alternately with the milk. Blend thoroughly.

Turn the batter into 2 greased 9-inch pans. Bake in a 350°F. oven for 25 to 30 minutes. When a carefully inserted toothpick emerges clean, the cake is done. Do not overcook.

MAKES 10 SERVINGS.

HONEY CHOCOLATE BROWNIES

1 cup butter, softened

1 1/2 cups honey

3 eggs, beaten

1 teaspoon vanilla

1/2 teaspoon salt

4 ounces unsweetened chocolate, melted and cooled

1 cup unbleached white flour

1 cup chopped walnut

Beat the butter with an electric mixer until creamy. Slowly add the honey in a steady stream, mixing constantly. Add the eggs, vanilla, and salt. Add the melted chocolate alternately with the flour. Stir in the nuts carefully. Turn the batter into a well-greased 9-inch by 13-inch by 2-inch pan and bake at 350°F. for 20 to 25 minutes. Watch for burning, turn down the oven if it browns too quickly.

MAKES 24 BROWNIES.

HONEY CREAM CHEESE ICING

2 tablespoons honey

8 ounces softened cream cheese

Beat the honey into the softened cream cheese until smooth and well blended. Spread on a cooled cake. Refrigerate the cake if this icing is used.

MAKES ENOUGH FROSTING FOR ONE 8-INCH BY 8-INCH CAKE.

APPLE CRISP

Filling:

4—5 tart cooking apples, peeled and sliced

1 teaspoon lemon juice

1/4 cup honey

1/2 teaspoon cinnamon

1/4 cup water

Topping:

1 cup oatmeal

1/4 cup wheat germ

1/4 cup flour

1/2 cup honey

1/4 cup soft butter

Combine the apples, lemon juice, honey, and cinnamon. Place the apple mixture at the bottom of a greased 2-quart casserole dish or an 8-inch by 8-inch baking pan and add the water.

Mix the topping ingredients together and sprinkle on top of the apples. Bake in a 350°F. oven for 30 minutes. Serve warm with heavy cream.

MAKES 4 SERVINGS.

POPCORN BALLS

You will need a candy thermometer for this recipe.

8 cups popped popcorn (1/3 cup before popping)

1/2 cup light molasses

1/2 cup honey

1 1/2 sticks butter

pinch of salt (optional)

Make 8 cups of popcorn and put it in a large bowl. Cook 1/2 cup of molasses with the 1/2 cup of honey until the thermometer reads 270°F or "hard crack." Stir in the butter and salt.

Slowly add the mixture to the popcorn, stirring with a wooden spoon until all the popcorn is coated. Butter your hands lightly and shape the popcorn into balls. Set the balls on wax paper and let them harden. To store them, wrap each one in wax paper.

MAKES 16 BALLS.

Continued ➡

HONEY DATE BARS

Filling:

1/2 pound pitted dates, cut in pieces

1/2 cup honey

1/4 cup water

Dough:

1 cup rolled oats

1 cup unbleached flour

1/4 teaspoon salt

1/2 cup honey

1/2 cup butter, melted

1/2 teaspoon cinnamon

Put the dates, honey, and water in a pan and cook slowly until thickened. Allow to cool.

Combine the oats, flour, salt, honey, butter, and cinnamon in a bowl. Mix well.

Pat half of the oat mixture on the bottom of a greased 8-inch by 8-inch pan. Spoon all of the filling on the oat mixture. Top with the other half of the dough. Spread the dough with a knife to cover all of the date mixture. Bake in a 325°F. oven for 30 minutes. Cut into squares while warm.

MAKES 16 SQUARES.

GINGERBREAD MEN

1/2 cup softened butter

6 tablespoons honey

1/4 cup blackstrap molasses

2 cups unbleached flour

1 1/2 teaspoons baking soda

1 1/2 teaspoons cinnamon

1 1/2 teaspoons ginger

Combine the butter, honey, and molasses. Add the dry ingredients and stir until a dough is formed. Divide the dough in half and knead each ball gently. This dough is soft and buttery. Roll each ball to a thickness of 1/4 inch on a lightly floured board and cut out the dough with a cookie cutter. Place on a greased cookie sheet. Bake in a 375°F. oven for 5 to 7 minutes. Watch carefully since they burn easily. Decorate with your favorite icing.

MAKES 12 MEN.

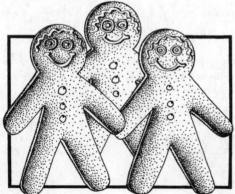

CHOCOLATE ICING

2 tablespoons cornstarch

1/4 cup water

2 squares of unsweetened chocolate

2/3 cup honey

1/2 cup brewed coffee

1 teaspoon vanilla

1 tablespoon butter

1/4 teaspoon salt

Blend the cornstarch with the water. Then combine this mixture with all the other ingredients in the top of a double boiler. Cook, stirring often, until the ingredients have blended and the icing becomes thick. Cool.

MAKES ENOUGH FOR ONE DOUBLE-LAYER CAKE.

CARROT CAKE

This cake can be iced with the honey cream cheese icing and decorated with a few walnuts.

1/4 cup butter, softened

1/2 cup oil, mild in flavor

3/4 cup honey

2 eggs, beaten

1 1/4 cups unbleached flour

1 teaspoon baking soda

1 teaspoon cinnamon

1 1/2 cups grated carrots

1/2 cup coconut

1/2 cup walnuts

With an electric mixer, blend the butter and oil. Slowly pour in the honey and eggs (one at a time) while mixing. Combine the flour and baking soda and sift into the liquid. Add the cinnamon. Stir in the grated carrots, then the coconut, and finally the chopped nuts. Pour the batter into a well-greased 8-inch by 8-inch pan and bake in a 350°F. oven for 35 minutes.

SERVES 9.

HONEY ICE CREAM

You will need a 2-quart (or larger) ice cream maker to make this recipe.

3 eggs, separated

2 cups milk

I cups honey

2 tablespoons vanilla

1/4 teaspoon salt

2 cups heavy cream, whipped

6 ounces grated semi-sweet chocolate or 1 1/2 cups of mashed fresh fruit

Separate the eggs, and in a double boiler make a soft custard (just thick enough to coat a spoon) of the egg yolks, milk, and honey. Add vanilla and salt and chill. Beat the egg whites and carefully fold in chilled custard. Whip the cream and fold into the chilled custard and egg-white mixture. Add chocolate or fruit. Follow the usual procedures for making ice cream with an ice cream maker.

LEMON CREAM CHEESE PIE

Crust:

2 cups crushed graham crackers

1/4 cup melted butter

2 tablespoons honey

Filling:

1 cup heavy cream

8 ounces cream cheese, softened

1/4 cup honey

3 tablespoons lemon juice

rind of half a lemon, grated

Combine the graham cracker crumbs, butter, and honey. Set aside 2 tablespoons of this mixture as a topping. Press the rest of the crust firmly on the sides and bottom of a 9-inch pie pan.

Whip the heavy cream and set aside. Whip the cream cheese until soft. Drizzle in the honey while mixing. Add the lemon juice and grated rind and blend. Fold the whipped cream into the cream cheese. Spoon the filling into the crust and top with the reserved crust mixture. Refrigerate at least 3 to 4 hours.

SERVES 8.

MORE USES FOR HONEY

Canning? Honey can replace all of the sugar generally used in canning, preserving, and jelly making. A syrup made from honey may be somewhat darker in color than a sugar syrup, and will tend to darken fruits such as peaches and pears. No matter. The honey intensifies the fruit flavor. Remember that honey has a tendency to foam considerably when it is heated. Use a large cooking kettle and watch the pot carefully to avoid having it boil over. Also, since honey contains some liquid, it will be necessary to cook the product slightly longer than usual to evaporate this liquid.

For syrups, use these proportions: 2 cups of honey to 3 3/4 cups of water for tart cherries, plums, apples, and strawberries; 1 cup of honey to 2 cups of water for pineapples, raspberries, peaches, black cherries, and blueberries

Beatrice Trum Hunter, Sugar & Sweeteners, Garden Way Publishing

---

Cooking with Yogurt

Olwen Woodier
Illustrations by Nancy Anisfield

Ingredients for Making Your Own Yogurt

It may be possible to buy good commercial yogurt; but once you have made your own, never again will you be satisfied with store-bought. Yours will be deliciously fresh and free from additives—preservatives, dyes, or stabilizers (such as gelatin, pectin, cornstarch, vegetable gums, or carrageenan). Homemade yogurt is also 65 to 70 percent cheaper. If this hasn't convinced you that it is more rewarding to make your own, let me mention that yogurt takes no more than 15 minutes to prepare, and the 3-hour to 4-hour fermenting time needs little or no supervision.

To make yogurt, certain beneficial active bacteria must be mixed with *warm milk* and kept at a constant temperature for several hours until coagulation takes place. These active bacteria are called the *starter* or culture. *Non-fat milk solids* are often added to create a thicker consistency and to increase the protein content. *Sweeteners may* be added before or after fermentation time.

MILK

You can vary the taste of your yogurt by using whole, evaporated, skim, low-fat, pasteurized, or raw milk. You can also use the milk of sheep or goats. Whichever type of milk you choose, make sure it is absolutely fresh. "Ripe" milk will produce a sour yogurt.

If calories are not important, instant non-fat dried milk, half-and-half, or heavy cream can be added to give a thicker, creamier texture. Or you can make yogurt from reconstituted (fat-free) milk powder. All of the yogurt recipes in this bulletin have 1/3 cup of instant, non-fat dried milk per quart added. This adds an extra 20 calories per cup of yogurt and can be eliminated if the caloric content is more important than texture.

THE STARTER

The starter can make quite a significant difference in the quality and flavor of your yogurt. For your first homemade try, purchase a special culture powder such as Yógourmet, a Canadian import found in the dairy section of some supermarkets or at health-food stores. Or use unpasteurized "plain" commercial yogurt (which was made from pasteurized milk). Once you have made your own yogurt, you can then save some to start the next batch. You will use 1 rounded tablespoon per quart of milk.

After using your homemade starter for 4 to 6 batches, you may notice a deterioration in both the flavor and texture. This is the time to reintroduce a fresh starter. However, if you make yogurt every day or so, the starter can be kept going because the bacteria will feed on the fresh milk sugar, which it needs if it is to survive indefinitely.

SWEETENERS

Homemade yogurt can be made as sweet or as tart as you like, simply by adjusting the fermentation time. When the natural sweet flavor fails to satisfy, experiment with sweeteners—honey, malt, molasses, maple

Continued ➤

sugar, maple syrup, preserves, corn syrup, brown sugar, fructose, dextrose, and artificial and dietetic sweeteners.

Equipment for Making Yogurt

Not much is required for making yogurt. You can buy yogurt-making machines that will keep your yogurt at the steady warm temperature that is best for incubating. But you can easily improvise. Here is what you will need.

- candy thermometer (or yogurt spoon thermometer supplied with yogurt makers)
- 1 1/2-quart to 2-quart saucepan
- measuring spoons
- large jug or bowl for mixing
- wire whisk
- various containers with lids: glass or porcelain jars; stainless steel, enamel, or porcelain bowls

Unless your equipment is sterilized, there may be some undesirable bacteria present, which can destroy your yogurt culture. I usually run my utensils through a dishwasher cycle (if they are clean, the rinse cycle is adequate) just before I begin to heat the milk. That way, the utensils are prewarmed, and I know that my equipment is absolutely clean. An alternative is to immerse the utensils for 1 minute in a pot of boiling water.

THE BASIC RECIPE

1 quart whole milk

1/3 cup instant non-fat dried milk (Optional. It produces a thicker texture and increases the protein content by 2 grams/cup.)

1 rounded tablespoon plain yogurt or recommended quantity of powdered culture

1. Scald the milk. Attach your candy thermometer to the side of the saucepan, pour in the milk, and place over low heat. Scald the milk until bubbles form around the edge of the pan, and the thermometer registers 180°F. (This scalding process kills undesirable bacteria.)

2. Cool the milk. Remove the pan from the heat, stir in the dried milk, and cool to somewhere between 90 and 120°F. before adding the starter. If the temperature is too high the culture will be destroyed; yet if it is too low, the culture will not be activated.

The cooling process can be hastened by pouring the mixture into a chilled bowl and refrigerating for several minutes. If I'm in a hurry, I just warm the milk to 110°F. but I find that the yogurt is not quite as sweet or as thick.

3. Add the starter. When the milk is cooled, add the yogurt culture. Do not use more than the recommended amount of starter. Too much interferes with the growth of the culture, making the yogurt sour and watery. Stir or whisk the mixture until smooth.

4. Incubate the yogurt. Pour the yogurt mixture into a large or several small, warm containers and cover. You are now ready to start the incubation process. This will take 2 to 5 hours at a more-or-less constant temperature—110°F. is ideal. If the temperature remains around 110°F the yogurt will be sweeter than if incubated around 120°F.

If you are using a yogurt-maker you will have no problem maintaining a constant temperature. However, if you don't mind coping with a little guesswork in the beginning, there are plenty of uncomplicated and reliable alternatives for incubators.

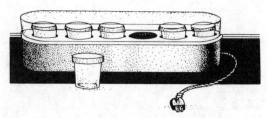

There are several brands of commercial yogurt makers on the market. Each contains an electric unit which keeps the special yogurt containers at an even temperature. Some come with automatic timers.

In the Oven. If you have a gas oven with a constant pilot, simply place the covered containers directly on the oven shelf. (My gas oven maintains a constant 105°F. and ferments the yogurt in 2 to 3 hours.) If you have an electric oven, preheat the oven to 150°F., turn off the heat, and leave the oven light on if possible to maintain the warmth.

In Warm Water. Put the covered containers in a pan of 110°F. water and cover. Then, place the pan over a pilot light on top of a gas stove; or place the pan by the side of a wood-burning stove (not too close); or cover the pan with a folded blanket (or 2 or 3 towels) and place it on a heating tray or heating pad set on low.

In a Thermos Flask. Pour the warm milk mixture into a prewarmed thermos flask.

In a Crockpot. Preheat a crockpot on low for about 15 minutes until it feels very warm to the fingertips. Put in the covered containers of yogurt mixture, cover the crockpot, and turn off the heat. At approximately 35-minute to 45-minute intervals, heat the crockpot on low for 10 to 15 minutes.

5. Test after 3 hours. Do not move or shake the containers during the incubation period or the yogurt will not coagulate properly. After 3 hours, test for thickness by tilting the containers gently. If firm, remove and refrigerate for several hours to thicken further. If a tarter flavor is desired, leave the yogurt to incubate for another hour or so.

WHAT WENT WRONG?

Problem	Cause
Yogurt won't thicken	Starter was inactive
	Not enough starter was used
	Incubating temperature was too hot or too cold
	Milk was too hot or too cold when starter was added
	Culture was stirred or moved while incubating
	Utensils were not clean
Yogurt is too thin	Starter is old
Whey separates from yogurt	Yogurt incubated too long
	Culture was stirred or moved while incubating
Yogurt is too tart	Yogurt incubated too long

MORE YOGURT RECIPES

You can make different flavored yogurts, with different textures, if you vary the basic recipe. Try these recipes, too.

THICK CREAMY YOGURT

This yogurt does not have to be drained when used in cooking, unless you are making yogurt cheese.

1 13-ounce can evaporated milk (1–2/3 cups)

2 1/3 cups whole milk

1/3 cup non-fat dried milk

1 rounded tablespoon yogurt

Follow the procedures outlined for the Basic Recipe.

RICH YOGURT

1 13-ounce can evaporated milk (1–2/3 cups)

2 1/3 cups water

1/3 cup non-fat dried milk

1 rounded tablespoon yogurt

Follow the procedures outlined for the Basic Recipe.

SKINNY YOGURT VARIATIONS

Here are 3 yogurt recipes for weight-watchers.

Variation #1 (104 calories per cup)

4 cups skim milk

1/3 cup non-fat dried milk

1 rounded tablespoon yogurt

Variation #2 (124 calories per cup)

4 cups low-fat milk

• cup non-fat dried milk

1 rounded tablespoon yogurt

Variation #3 (104 calories per cup)

1–2/3 cups non-fat dried milk

4 cups water

1 rounded tablespoon yogurt

FLAVORED YOGURT

Scald 1 quart of milk and stir in 1/4 to 1/3 cup of sugar, honey, maple syrup, chocolate syrup, malt, molasses, or artificial sweetener. If other flavors are desired, after dissolving the sugar or honey, stir in 1 tablespoon of extract such as vanilla, lemon, almond, peppermint, or instant coffee. Another time, try adding 1 teaspoon of ground spices, such as cinnamon, nutmeg, mace, ginger, or your own special combination. Add the instant non-fat dried milk, cool the mixture to 110°F., then stir in the culture. Pour into warm containers, cover, and incubate.

For jam, preserve, and peanut-butter flavors, put 1 tablespoon of the flavoring into the bottom of 1-cup containers and pour the warm milk-yogurt mixture over. Cover and incubate as usual.

If fresh, canned, or dried fruit is desired, it is best to make such additions to the yogurt *after* it has incubated. The acid content of some fruits can curdle the milk-yogurt mixture and prevent proper fermentation.

Whenever you are flavoring yogurt, always remember to leave 1 cup plain so that you will have fresh starter for the next batch.

Tips for Cooking with Yogurt

There are many ways to use yogurt. In Middle Eastern and Indian cooking, yogurt is more likely to be incorporated into meat and vegetable dishes than consumed as a snack or for dessert. Once you have a quart or 2 of homemade yogurt in the refrigerator, you'll find many ways to use it up. In fact, you will be surprised at how quickly it disappears. Here are a few ways I use yogurt.

In Baked Desserts, Breads, and Pancakes. Yogurt makes these foods light and moist. If your yogurt is thick or solid, and you want to substitute yogurt for the liquid, use 1 1/4 cups of yogurt for each cup of liquid called for in the recipe. But if there is whey (a watery liquid) separated out on top of the yogurt, your yogurt is liquid enough. Just stir the yogurt well, and measure it cup for cup for the liquid in the original recipe. When using yogurt in baking, add 1/2 teaspoon of baking soda per cup of yogurt to counteract the acid content.

In Marinades. Yogurt is a great tenderizer, and it particularly enhances chicken, lamb, and pork.

As a Low-Calorie Substitute in Sauces and Dressings. Yogurt can be substituted for mayonnaise, sour cream, and cream cheese when some of the whey is drained off.

Substitute For	Drain	Yields
Mayonaise	10–15 minutes	2 cups yield 1 1/2 cups
Sour Cream	30 minutes	2 cups yield 1 cup
Cream Cheese	6–8 hours	3 cups yield 1 cup

Continued →

STABILIZING YOGURT

Yogurt curdles when heated by itself or when added directly to hot foods and hot liquids that have not been thickened with flour or cornstarch. To avoid this separation of the curds and whey, stabilize the yogurt by mixing it with egg yolks, egg whites, cornstarch, or flour. Yogurt that is drained to a thick "sour cream" consistency can be spooned on top of hot foods without stabilizing.

To drain yogurt, line a strainer or colander with 2 to 3 layers of cheesecloth, or a linen tea towel rinsed in cold water and wrung out. (I find that it is easier to scrape drained yogurt off linen tea towels than cheesecloth.) Place the lined strainer over a pan or bowl. Pour the yogurt into the strainer. Refrigerate while the yogurt is draining.

To stabilize yogurt, pour 1 to 2 cups of yogurt into a cold saucepan, and beat until a smooth liquid forms. In a separate bowl, mix 1 egg yolk, or 1 egg white, or 1 tablespoon of cornstarch, or 1 tablespoon of flour with 1 tablespoon of cold water or cold milk. Beat until smooth. Add to the yogurt. Slowly bring the mixture to a boil, stirring constantly. Reduce the heat to its lowest point, and simmer uncovered for 5 minutes, until it has thickened. Add to the hot cooked food and reheat briefly.

Some people allow their yogurt to drain off at room temperature. During the 8-hour period it takes to drain yogurt to a cream cheese consistency, the yogurt will usually develop a tarter flavor. If this is acceptable, the cheesecloth or linen towel can be gathered around the yogurt, tied with a string, and suspended from a hook above a bowl to catch the whey. You can use the whey in place of stock or water in soups, stews, rice, or baked dishes.

Another way to stabilize yogurt is to make a sauce. Melt 2 tablespoons of butter or margarine in a saucepan. Add 2 tablespoons of flour. Stir and cook for 1 minute. Add 1 to 2 cups of yogurt, and stir constantly until smooth. Remove the sauce from the heat when it starts to bubble around the edges. Season with salt, pepper, herbs, Parmesan cheese, or curry, as desired.

BREAKFAST WITH YOGURT

FRUIT SHAKE

2 cups plain or vanilla yogurt

1 1/2 cups (12 ounces) peaches, apricots, or strawberries

1/4 cup wheat germ

1/4 cup honey

Place all the ingredients in a blender, cover the container, and process for 20 seconds, until smooth.

YIELD: 4 SERVINGS

TIME: 2 MINUTES

BANANA EGGNOG

1 cup plain or vanilla yogurt

1 banana, cut up

2 tablespoons honey

2 teaspoons vanilla extract

1 egg

Place all the ingredients in a blender and process for 20 seconds, or until smooth.

YIELD: 2 SERVINGS

TIME: 2 MINUTES

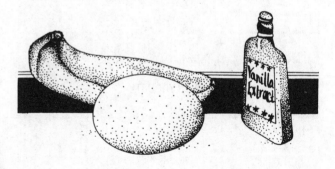

PANCAKES

2 cups plain yogurt

3 large eggs

1/4 cup vegetable oil or melted shortening

2 tablespoons vanilla extract

1/4 cup honey or sugar

1 1/2 tablespoons baking powder

3/4 teaspoon baking soda

2 cups unbleached flour

1 cup chopped fruit or corn kernels (optional)

Place all the ingredients in a large bowl or blender, and beat or blend until smooth. (For a lighter pancake, allow the mixture to rest for 30 to 60 minutes at this point.)

Grease a skillet or griddle and place over medium-high heat. Using a serving spoon or pouring directly from the blender, drop the mixture onto the hot griddle a few tablespoons at a time. Turn the pancakes when bubbles appear on top, cooking approximately 1 minute per side. This recipe can be used for waffles.

YIELD: 4 GENEROUS SERVINGS
TIME: 30 MINUTES

MUFFINS

This batter will keep several days under refrigeration.

2 eggs

1/3 cup vegetable oil

1/2 cup honey or maple syrup

1 1/2 cups plain yogurt

1 cup whole wheat flour

1 1/2 cups unbleached flour

2 teaspoons baking powder

1 teaspoon baking soda

1/2 cup chopped nuts or 1 cup blueberries

Preheat the oven to 400°F. Grease the muffin trays.

In a small bowl, beat together the eggs, vegetable oil, and honey. Stir in the yogurt.

In a large bowl, stir together the flours, baking powder, and baking soda. Make a well in the center of the flour, and add the liquids. Stir together until the dry ingredients are moist (a lumpy mixture makes tender muffins). Gently stir in the chopped nuts or berries. (If you plan to refrigerate the mixture overnight, add the berries just before baking.) Fill each muffin cup approximately O full.

Bake 20 to 25 minutes or until a skewer, inserted in the center, comes out clean. Remove from the muffin tray immediately and cool on a wire rack, or serve hot.

YIELD: 18 MUFFINS
TIME: 30 TO 35 MINUTES

FRUIT SCONES

1 1/2 cups unbleached flour

3/4 teaspoon baking soda

1/2 teaspoon baking powder

3/4 cup whole wheat flour

1/4 cup sugar

6 tablespoons butter or margarine

1 large egg

3/4 cup plain yogurt

1/2 cup raisins or chopped dates

Preheat the oven to 425°F.

Sift the unbleached flour, baking soda, and baking powder into a large bowl. Add the whole wheat flour and sugar. Mix together. Cut the butter into several pieces and rub into the flours with your fingertips until the texture resembles peas.

In a small bowl, beat the egg, stir in the yogurt and raisins. Pour into the flour mixture and, using a fork, stir until a soft dough is formed.

Lightly flour a baking tray. Scoop the dough onto the tray and pat into a round approximately 3/4 inch thick. Bake for 20 minutes or until a skewer, inserted in the center, comes out clean.

Serve warm with butter and jam. This also makes a delicious dinner bread—substitute 1 tablespoon of dried herbs for the raisins.

YIELD: 6 TO 8 SERVINGS
TIME: 30 TO 35 MINUTES

SALADS AND APPETIZERS

Drained yogurt can be substituted in any of your favorite recipes that call for sour cream.

SALMON SPREAD

3 ounces cream cheese

2 cups plain yogurt, drained 30 minutes to yield 1 cup

1 teaspoon cider vinegar

14 ounces salmon (or tuna)

4 scallions including the green part, sliced thinly

1/2 teaspoon ground black pepper

1 teaspoon dried dill, crumbled

2 cloves garlic, crushed

Place the cream cheese in a bowl and mash until soft. Add 1/4 cup of the yogurt and the vinegar. Beat until the consistency is smooth. Stir in the rest of the yogurt.

Drain the salmon, turn into another bowl, and flake with a fork. Add the scallions, pepper, dill, and garlic, and mash together. Blend thoroughly into the yogurt mixture. Chill. Serve on toast, in scooped out tomatoes, or over lettuce.

YIELD: 4 SERVINGS
TIME: 45 MINUTES

YOGURT HERB CHEESE

Drain 3 cups of very fresh yogurt for 6 to 8 hours, or overnight, in the refrigerator. Scrape into a bowl, and add 2 cloves of crushed garlic, 1/2 teaspoon of crushed pepper (about 20 turns on the pepper mill), 1 teaspoon each of crushed dried herbs—thyme, basil, and oregano—and a 1/4 cup of chopped chives or parsley. If this seems a little too tart for your taste, whip 1/2 cup of heavy cream to a thick, but not fluffy, consistency, and beat into the yogurt cheese. Refrigerate so that flavors can blend.

Continued →

DEVILED EGGS

12 hard-boiled eggs, peeled

2 teaspoons mild curry

2 cloves garlic, crushed

1/4 cup chopped watercress or parsley

1 cup plain yogurt, drained 30 minutes to yield 1/2 cup

Cut the boiled eggs in half, scoop out the yolks into a bowl. Mash the yolks with the curry and garlic. Add the chopped watercress and drained yogurt. Blend together. Spoon into the egg white halves and chill. Serve on lettuce.

YIELD: 6 SERVINGS

TIME: 10 MINUTES, PLUS CHILLING TIME

CUCUMBER SALAD

1 cup plain yogurt

1 clove garlic, crushed

1/2 cup sliced scallions

1/4 teaspoon ground black pepper

1 teaspoon finely minced ginger root or 1/2 teaspoon ground ginger

2 cucumbers, peeled and sliced thinly

Mix the yogurt, garlic, scallions, and seasonings together. Toss with the sliced cucumbers. Refrigerate for 1 hour before serving.

YIELD: 4 SERVINGS

TIME: 10 MINUTES, PLUS 1 HOUR CHILLING TIME

SALAD DRESSINGS AND SAUCES

For all of these recipes, drain the yogurt first if you want a thicker dip consistency.

BLUE CHEESE DRESSING

This sauce is great as a dip for raw vegetables or as a topping for baked potatoes.

1/4 cup mayonnaise

1/4 cup blue cheese, mashed

2 cloves garlic, crushed

1 cup plain yogurt

2 tablespoons chopped parsley

1/2 teaspoon ground black pepper

Mash the mayonnaise, blue cheese, and garlic together in a bowl. Stir in the yogurt. Blend in the parsley and pepper.

YIELD: 1 2/3 CUPS

TIME: 10 MINUTES

HOT GRAVY FOR ROASTS

1 cup yogurt

1/2 cup vegetable or meat broth

2 tablespoons unbleached flour

salt, pepper, herbs to taste

Combine the yogurt, broth, and flour. Refrigerate until needed.

Remove excess fat from the roasting pan. Stir the yogurt mixture into the remaining pan juices. Cook over medium heat, stirring constantly, until the gravy is thick and smooth. Thin with more broth or water, if desired. Season with salt, pepper, and herbs to taste.

YIELD: APPROXIMATELY 2 CUPS

TIME: 10 TO 15 MINUTES

FRESH HERB SAUCE

Excellent with chicken and with raw vegetables.

1 cup plain yogurt

1/2 cup fresh herbs (basil, tarragon, or lemon thyme)

1/4 cup chopped shallots or the white part of leeks, chopped

1 small clove of garlic, crushed

1/2 teaspoon ground pepper

Place all the ingredients in a bowl and blend together well.

YIELD: 1 3/4 CUPS

TIME: 10 MINUTES

SWEET AND SOUR SAUCE

This is delicious on cold meats or deep-fried fish.

1 cup plain yogurt

1/4 cup chopped sweet pickles

2 teaspoons sweet pickle juice

1 clove garlic, crushed

Place all the ingredients in a small bowl and mix together.

YIELD: 1 1/4 CUPS

TIME: 5 MINUTES

HOT SAUCE

Try this on clams on the half-shell.

1 cup plain yogurt

1/4 cup chili ketchup

2 dashes of Tabasco or Worcestershire sauce

2 tablespoons grated horseradish

Place all the ingredients in a small bowl. Mix together thoroughly.

YIELD: 1 1/3 CUPS

TIME: 5 MINUTES

MAIN DISHES

GOULASH

2 pounds boned beef round or veal shoulder

1/4 cup unbleached flour4 tablespoons vegetable oil

1 large onion, chopped

2 carrots, sliced thinly

2 cloves garlic, crushed

8 ounces mushrooms, sliced

1 cup whole tomatoes, cut up

1/2 cup wine (red for beef, white for veal) or dry vermouth

1 1/2 cups stock or water

1/2 teaspoon pepper

1 bay leaf

1 tablespoon paprika

2 cups plain yogurt, drained approximately 30 minutes to a sour cream consistency to yield 1 cup

1/4 cup chopped parsley

Roll the cubed meat in the flour. Heat 2 tablespoons of the oil in a 4-quart Dutch oven and brown the meat on all sides for about 5 minutes. Remove to a plate.

Heat the remaining oil; add the onion, carrots, garlic, and mushrooms to the pan. Cook over low heat for 5 to 10 minutes, stirring frequently. Return the browned meat to the pan. Add the tomatoes, wine, stock, pepper, bay leaf, and paprika. Stir to mix. Cover the pot and cook over medium heat until the liquid starts to bubble. Reduce the heat to low, and simmer for 1 1/2 hours or until the meat is tender.

Put the yogurt in a bowl, sprinkle with chopped parsley, and serve separately. Goulash is delicious served over rice or noodles.

YIELD: 4 TO 6 SERVINGS

TIME: 2 HOURS

MOUSSAKA

Meat Layers:

2 eggplants (about 1 pound each), peeled and sliced lengthwise, 1/4-inch thick

2 tablespoons vegetable oil

2 tablespoons olive oil

1 large onion, chopped

4 cloves garlic, crushed

1 1/2 pounds ground lamb or ground beef

2 teaspoons oregano

1/2 teaspoon cinnamon

1/2 teaspoon mace

1/2 teaspoon nutmeg

Custard Topping:

1 1/2 cups plain yogurt

3 eggs, beaten

2 tablespoons flour

1/4 cup grated Parmesan cheese

1/2 teaspoon nutmeg

1/4 teaspoon cinnamon

1/4 teaspoon ground pepper

Lightly salt each side of the eggplant slices and allow to drain in a colander for 1 hour.

Combine the oils and heat 2 tablespoons in a skillet. Add the onion and garlic. Cook for 5 minutes. Add the ground meat, oregano, 1/2 teaspoon each of cinnamon, mace, and nutmeg. Brown the mixture for 5 to 10 minutes. Drain off the excess fat.

Wipe the eggplant slices with paper towels. Arrange the eggplant on an ovenproof tray, and sprinkle with the remaining 2 tablespoons of oil. Broil on the highest position for approximately 2 minutes each side.

Preheat the oven to 350°F.

Place a layer of broiled eggplant slices in an 8-inch by 8-inch baking dish. Cover with a layer of ground meat. Continue to alternate the eggplant with the ground meat mixture, ending with an eggplant layer. Bake for 20 minutes.

To make the custard topping, combine the yogurt, eggs, flour, Parmesan, 1/2 teaspoon nutmeg, and 1/4 teaspoon each of cinnamon and ground pepper.

Remove the eggplant and meat dish from the oven when the 20 minutes are up. Cover with the yogurt mixture. Continue baking for 25 to 30 minutes, until the custard is set and golden.

YIELD: 4 TO 6 SERVINGS

TIME: 2 1/4 HOURS, PLUS 1 HOUR TO DRAIN EGGPLANT

Continued ➔

CHICKEN TANDOORI

This is also good as a barbecue.

1 1/2 cups plain yogurt

4 cloves garlic, crushed

1 small onion, chopped finely

2 tablespoons lemon juice

2 tablespoons vegetable oil

1 teaspoon ginger

1 teaspoon turmeric

1 teaspoon cumin

2 teaspoons ground coriander

1/4 teaspoon ground pepper

4-lb. frying chicken, cut up and skinned

Combine the yogurt, garlic, chopped onion, lemon juice, oil, ginger, turmeric, cumin, ground coriander, and pepper in a large baking dish. Cut several deep slits in the chicken pieces and place in the dish with the yogurt mixture. Turn to coat each piece thoroughly, cover, and refrigerate for 24 hours, or as time permits. Turn the pieces of chicken occasionally.

Preheat the oven to 350°F. Bake the chicken pieces for 1 1/4 hours, or until tender, basting several times.

YIELD: 4 SERVINGS

TIME: 2 HOURS, PLUS 2 TO 24 HOURS MARINATING TIME

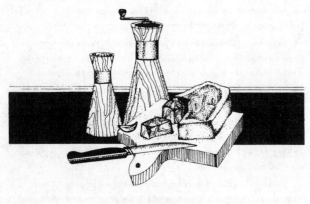

SESAME KABABS

2 pounds boneless lamb or pork, cut in 1-inch cubes

1/2 pound button mushrooms

1 pound cherry tomatoes

2 medium zucchini, sliced in 1/4-inch rounds

1 cup plain yogurt

2–4 tablespoons soy sauce

1/4 cup tahini (sesame seed paste)

2 cloves garlic, crushed

2 teaspoons fresh grated ginger root or 1 teaspoon ground ginger

Thread the meat and vegetables on 8 skewers. Place the skewers in a long roasting dish.

In a bowl, combine the yogurt, soy sauce, tahini, garlic, and ginger, and blend until the mixture is creamy. Pour over the skewers. Cover and refrigerate 4 to 6 hours, turning the skewers occasionally so that all sides sit in the marinade.

To barbeque, allow the coals to burn 30 to 40 minutes before bringing the meat out. The coals should be grey, not red. Arrange the grill so that it is approximately 4 inches from the coals. Place the skewers on the grill. Give a quarter turn every 3 to 4 minutes, brushing with the yogurt mixture each time.

YIELD: 4 TO 6 SERVINGS

TIME: 50 MINUTES, PLUS MARINATING TIME

SOUPS

You can use yogurt as a low-calorie substitute for heavy cream in any chilled soup. Or use it as a thickener in a hot soup.

ZUCCHINI-SCALLION SOUP

2 tablespoons butter or margarine

12 large scallions including the green part, sliced finely

2 cloves garlic, crushed

2 medium zucchini, peeled and grated

1/2 teaspoon ground pepper

1 1/2 teaspoons dried basil, crumbled

1/4 cup flour

1 cup stock or water

1/2 cup milk

1 cup plain yogurt

Heat the butter in a skillet, and cook the sliced scallions and garlic over low heat for 3 minutes. Add the zucchini, and cook for 10 minutes more. Stir in the pepper, basil, and flour. Cook for 2 minutes. Add the stock, raise the heat to medium, and cook, stirring constantly, until the mixture thickens—about 3 minutes. Lower the heat, add the milk, and cook for 5 minutes more. When the soup is hot, blend in the yogurt and pour into warm soup bowls.

YIELD: 4 SERVINGS

TIME: 30 MINUTES

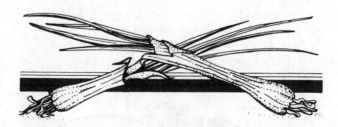

TOMATO-CUCUMBER SOUP

1 pound fresh ripe tomatoes

1 cucumber, peeled, seeded, and cut in 1-inch pieces

2 sticks of tender celery heart, cut in 1-inch pieces

1 large carrot, pared and cut in 1/2-inch pieces

2 cloves garlic

1 cup tomato juice or broth

1/2 teaspoon ground pepper

1 cup plain yogurt

1/4 cup chopped parsley

Place all the ingredients, except the yogurt and parsley, in a blender or food processor. Process until smooth. Stir in the yogurt. Refrigerate until chilled. Garnish with the chopped parsley.

YIELD: 4 TO 6 SERVINGS

TIME: 20 MINUTES, PLUS CHILLING TIME

DESSERTS

YOGURT BERRY PIE

Crust:

1 cup unbleached flour

8 tablespoons butter or margarine (1 stick)

2–3 tablespoons cold water

Filling:

2 cups of berries (strawberries, raspberries, or blueberries)

1/2 cup sugar or 1/3 cup honey

2 1/2 tablespoons cornstarch

2 cups plain yogurt, drained 30 minutes or more to yield 1 cup

---

SUBSTITUTING YOGURT FOR CREAM CHEESE IN CHEESECAKE

If a cheesecake recipe calls for 3 8-ounce packages of cream cheese, drain 9 to 10 cups of yogurt for 6 to 8 hours to get 3 packed cups. Since most cheesecake recipes include flour and/or eggs, there will be no need to stabilize the yogurt—it will act just like cream cheese—for fewer calories.

To make the pie shell, pour the flour into a large bowl or food processor. Cut the butter into thin slices, and drop into the bowl. Using a pastry blender, 2 knives, or the processor, work the mixture until it has the texture of large crumbs. Pour in the cold water, and mix until the pastry forms a ball. Remove from the bowl, place on a piece of wax paper, and flatten the dough into a 6-inch circle. Cover and refrigerate for 15 to 30 minutes.

Meanwhile, make the filling by placing the berries in a saucepan over low heat. Mix the sugar and cornstarch together, and stir into the berries. Cook over medium heat, stirring frequently, until the mixture thickens—about 10 minutes. Remove from the heat and cool.

Now, preheat the oven to 425°F. Roll out the pastry on a floured board until it is approximately 1/8 inch thick. Fit the crust into a greased 9-inch pie tin, and trim the edge to about 1/2 inch above the rim. Roll the overlapping pastry toward the outside. Flute the edges. Line the pastry with waxed paper and cover with a handful of dried beans. Prick the sides to let air escape. Bake 20 minutes and cool.

Stir the drained yogurt into the cooled berry mixture, and return to the refrigerator.

When both the berry filling and pie shell are cool, pour the chilled mixture into the chilled pie shell and refrigerate no more than 2 hours (otherwise the crust will become soggy).

Top with sweetened yogurt, whipped cream, or ice cream, if desired.

YIELD: 6 TO 8 SERVINGS

TIME: 1 HOUR

FROZEN YOGURT

2 cups yogurt, plain or flavored

1/4 cup honey

1/2 cup evaporated milk or heavy cream

1 egg, beaten (optional)

flavoring: 1/2 cup drained fruit, chopped or pureed; or 1 tablespoon vanilla extract; or 2 tablespoons lemon or lime juice; or 4 tablespoons orange concentrate; or 1/2 cup chopped nuts (replace the honey with maple syrup); or 3 tablespoons chocolate sauce and 1 tablespoon instant coffee, dissolved in 1 teaspoon hot water, for mocha

For the thickest consistency, drain the yogurt for 30 minutes before blending it with the other ingredients, and be sure to include an egg in the mixture.

Combine all the ingredients (except nuts) in a blender or food processor, or use rotary beaters, and beat only until the mixture is smooth. Stir in the nuts. Pour the mixture into an ice cream machine, and freeze according to the manufacturer's instructions.

If you do not have an ice cream maker, pour the yogurt mixture into a dish, cover, and freeze for 30 minutes. Remove the mixture from the freezer and beat until smooth. Return to the freezer for 1 hour, or until the yogurt is the desired firmness.

YIELD: 3 SERVINGS

TIME: ABOUT 2 HOURS

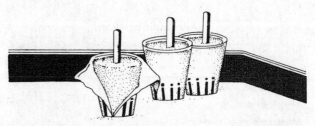

To make yogurt popsicles, spoon soft-frozen yogurt, as soon as it comes out of the machine, into small paper cups. Then, insert a popsicle stick into each cup. Freeze the yogurt for 3 to 4 hours. Peel off the paper cups before serving.

Continued →

257

CHOCOLATE/CAROB CAKE

1/2 cup (1 stick) sweet butter

1 cup brown sugar or 3/4 cup honey

1/4 cup (unsweetened) cocoa or carob powder

2 large eggs, beaten

1 tablespoon vanilla extract

1/2 cup plain yogurt

1 cup unbleached flour

1 teaspoon baking powder

1/2 teaspoon baking soda

Preheat the oven to 350°F. Grease a loaf pan and dust with flour, or line with wax paper and grease again.

Melt the butter in a large saucepan. Remove from heat, and stir in the sugar and cocoa or carob. Beat in the eggs, vanilla, and yogurt. Sift in the flour, baking powder, and baking soda. Beat for approximately 1 minute, until thoroughly blended. Turn into the prepared pan and bake for 45 minutes, or until a skewer inserted into the center comes out clean.

Allow the cake to rest in the pan for 5 to 10 minutes before turning out onto a wire rack. Peel off the waxed paper gently. This is delicious to eat warm.

This recipe also makes great cupcakes. Grease 12 2 1/2-inch muffin cups and bake 15 to 20 minutes. Turn the muffins out onto a wire rack immediately.

YIELD: 6–8 SERVINGS

TIME: 1 HOUR FOR LARGE CAKE, 30–35 MINUTES FOR CUP CAKES

YOGURT FROSTINGS

Any yogurt, plain or flavored, when drained for 30 to 60 minutes, will make delicious frostings and fillings for cakes.

First drain 2 cups of yogurt to yield 1 cup. Then flavor with

- 2 tablespoons honey or brown sugar and 2 tablespoons carob powder or
- 2–3 tablespoons lemon, strawberry, raspberry, or apricot preserves or
- 2 ounces of melted semi-sweet chocolate.

APPLE COBBLER

Filling:

1/2 cup brown sugar or 1/3 cup honey

2 tablespoons flour

1 teaspoon cinnamon

1 teaspoon grated orange or lemon peel

6 apples, sliced and peeled

2 tablespoons butter or margarine

Topping:

1 1/2 cups unbleached flour

2 teaspoons baking powder

1/2 teaspoon baking soda

1/4 cup brown sugar or 3 tablespoons honey

1/4 cup butter or margarine

1 cup plain, vanilla, or lemon yogurt

Preheat the oven to 400°F.

Mix the sugar, flour, cinnamon, and grated peel together. Grease a 2-quart dish and layer half of the apples. Sprinkle with half of the sugar mixture, add the rest of the apples and cover with the remaining sugar mixture. Dot with the butter, cover, and bake for 20 minutes.

While the apples bake, combine the flour, baking powder, baking soda, and sugar. Rub in the shortening until the mixture resembles coarse crumbs. Stir in the yogurt. Drop by the tablespoon on top of the hot fruit. Bake at 400°F for 30 minutes.

YIELD: 6 SERVINGS

TIME: 1 HOUR

Cooking with Cranberries

Lura Rogers

Illustrations by Alison Kolesar

Selecting and Storing Cranberries

Cranberries are among the simplest fruits to judge and keep. A bright red berry is a fresh berry, packed with flavor. Beware of any berries with wrinkly skins or squishy bodies. The fresher the berry, the more time you'll have to think up new ways to eat it! Size is not a prerequisite for a good berry. I have found many a little berry that has packed a mighty punch while its big brother lumbered lazily along.

In most areas, shoppers can choose to buy organic produce. Organic cranberry crops are grown without pesticides or fertilizers. They yield fewer berries per year at a higher price. The cost to consumers is slightly greater, but so is the fruit's wholesomeness, an important consideration for many.

Whole cranberries usually keep for several weeks in the refrigerator; in the freezer, they last at least 9 months. Whole frozen cranberries can be substituted for fresh in many recipes, and older frozen berries may be used in recipes that require you to cook the berries. Do be aware, however, of the differences among store-bought varieties of frozen cranberries—some are presweetened and cut, and this variety will not work well in many recipes.

Sweetened dehydrated cranberries and canned jellies and sauces are readily available in supermarkets. Cranberry juices are found in a plethora of forms, including unsweetened concentrates, ready-to-mix concentrates, juice blends, organic juices, and more. Cranberries can even be found in pill form in the supplement section of health food stores.

Cranberries and Health

The cranberry is the focus of quite a bit of medical research. You may have heard about the cranberry's ability to improve urinary tract health, but did you know that cranberries have been used to relieve symptoms of urinary tract infection since at least colonial times? More recently, several studies at leading universities have concluded that the proanthocyanidin compounds present in the cranberry prevent offending bacteria from adhering to the walls of the bladder and urinary tract.

The cranberry has other bacteria- and fungi-fighting properties that are still being researched, including those that inhibit growth of *Candida*, *E. coli*, and *Staphylococcus* bacteria. Researchers have discovered that cranberry consumption may prevent and possibly reverse gum disease and stomach ulcers. (Although we think of the acidic cranberry as an ulcer's worst nightmare, it is actually bacteria that perpetuates most ulcers.)

And there's more! Along with other popular antioxidant fruits, such as blueberries, apples, and grapes, our little red friends have recently been found to contain large quantities of phenols, which prevent cellular oxidation. This makes the cranberry a cancer-fighting agent, thanks to a high percentage of flavonoids (these include anthocyanins, which give the cranberry its festive red). Also, the cranberry's antioxidant properties make it a hero for heart health, reducing atherosclerosis by preventing oxidation of cholesterol in the bloodstream.

Cranberries Make the Meal

COUNTRY INN GRANOLA

The currants in this recipe are made from dried Zante grapes, native to Greece. They are quite different from the tiny berry called a currant.

10 cups rolled oats (not instant oatmeal)
1/4 cup pure Vermont maple syrup
3/4 cup dried blueberries
3/4 cup dried cranberries
1/2 cup dried apples, chopped
1/2 cup slivered almonds
1/2 cup Zante currants
1/2 cup chopped pecans
1 tablespoon kosher salt
1 cup granulated sugar
1 cup light brown sugar, firmly packed
1 cup apple cider or apple juice
1/4 cup (1/2 stick) butter

1. In a large mixing bowl, combine the oats, syrup, blueberries, cranberries, apples, almonds, currants, pecans, and salt.

2. In a saucepan over low heat, dissolve the granulated and brown sugars in the cider and bring to a simmer. Continue simmering until the amount is reduced by one third, then add the butter in small pieces, stirring with a wire whisk.

3. Drizzle the cider syrup over the oat mixture, stirring well to prevent clumping.

4. Spread the mixture on a baking sheet and cool at room temperature for 30 minutes. Store in an airtight container, or freeze.

YIELD: 14–16 SERVINGS

CRANBERRY ANADAMA BREAD

Anadama keeps well in the fridge or freezer, and it also makes incredible toast.

2 1/2 cups water
2/3 cup stone-ground cornmeal
1/2 cup dark molasses
4 tablespoons (1/2 stick) butter
2 1/2 teaspoons salt
2 envelopes active dry yeast
1/2 cup warm water (105–115°F)
1/4 cup plus 1/2 teaspoon sugar
1 1/2 cups fresh or frozen cranberries
Zest of 1 orange
7–8 cups all-purpose flour

1. Place the water in a large saucepan and bring to a boil.

2. Lower heat to medium-high and slowly add the cornmeal, stirring with a wire whisk. Cook until thickened, about 5 minutes, then add the molasses, butter, and salt. Set aside to cool.

3. While the cornmeal mush is cooling, dissolve the yeast in the warm water in a bowl and add 1/2 teaspoon of the sugar. Stir, then set aside. In a food processor, process the cranberries, the remaining 1/4 cup sugar, and the orange zest for 30 seconds, just long enough to chop the berries and incorporate the sugar.

4. Once the cornmeal has cooled to room temperature (too much heat will kill the yeast and prevent the bread from rising), add the yeast and cranberry mixtures. Add flour gradually, until the dough becomes difficult to stir, then transfer to a well-floured counter.

5. Continue to knead in the remaining flour until the dough is smooth and elastic and bounces back when you poke it. Place in a lightly oiled glass bowl and cover with a dish towel. Move the bowl to a warm (not hot), draft-free place to rise for about 45 minutes, or until it doubles in bulk (on top of the refrigerator works well).

6. Grease two 9- x 5-inch loaf pans. Flour the counter again and turn out the dough, kneading it to press out the large air bubbles. Once the dough is elastic, cut it in half with a sharp knife and place each half in a loaf pan. Cover with towels and allow to rise in the same draft-free space until the dough has reached the top of the pans, about 1 hour.

7. Preheat oven to 350°F. Bake for 45 minutes, or until the surfaces of the loaves are nicely browned. When you tap a loaf, it should sound hollow. Remove from pans to cool on a rack.

YIELD: 2 LOAVES

Continued →

CRANBERRY–APPLE PANCAKES

2 cups all-purpose flour

2 tablespoons plus 2 teaspoons sugar

2 tablespoons baking powder

1 teaspoon salt

4 eggs

1—1 1/2 cups milk

1/2 cup fresh cranberries, halved

1/4 teaspoon ground allspice

1/2 cup chopped Cortland apple

1. Mix the flour, 2 tablespoons of the sugar, the baking powder, and the salt. Whisk the eggs, then add to the flour mixture. Gradually add the milk until the batter has the consistency of a thick pudding.

2. In a separate bowl, toss the cranberries with the remaining 2 teaspoons of sugar. Add the allspice, toss, then add the apples and toss again.

3. Ladle the egg batter onto a hot greased skillet to make a pancake 4—5 inches in diameter. As soon as the batter has set, sprinkle a handful of the fruit mixture evenly into the pancake and cook until the surface of the pancake bubbles. Flip pancake and cook until firm and lightly browned.

YIELD: 12 PANCAKES

CREAM OF SWEET POTATO AND CRANBERRY SOUP

Cranberry Purée

1 1/2 cups fresh cranberries

1/2 cup port

1/4 cup sugar

Sweet Potato Soup

2 shallots, chopped

1 carrot, thinly sliced

1/4 cup (1/2 stick) butter

3 cups chicken or turkey broth

1 1/2 pounds sweet potatoes, peeled and cut into 1-inch cubes

1/2 pound red potatoes, peeled and cut into 1-inch cubes

1/2 pound parsnips, peeled and cut into 1-inch cubes

1/4 teaspoon ground ginger

1/4 teaspoon ground mace

1/4 teaspoon ground nutmeg

1/4 teaspoon white pepper

Kosher salt to taste

1. To prepare the cranberry purée, simmer the cranberries, port, and sugar over medium heat for 5—10 minutes, until the skins of the cranberries split and the liquid begins to thicken. Transfer to a blender or food processor and purée. Using a fine sieve and a spatula, remove the solids from the purée and discard them. Cover and refrigerate.

2. To make the soup, in a large pan, sauté the shallots and carrot in the butter until the vegetables are softened. Add 2 cups of the broth, the sweet and red potatoes, parsnips, ginger, mace, nutmeg, and white pepper. Cook, covered, over medium-low heat for 30 minutes. Test a few pieces of each vegetable to make sure all pieces are soft all the way through, then transfer to a blender or food processor to purée. Once all of the soup has been puréed, add the remaining 1 cup of broth gradually to desired consistency, then add the salt to taste and adjust the seasonings.

3. To serve, pour soup into bowls and pipe cranberry purée decoratively onto the soup's surface.

YIELD: 4—6 SERVINGS

FRUITED CHICKEN SALAD

Cranberries and chicken make a fine marriage. This dish is perfect for a summer picnic or a cool supper.

2 large chicken breasts, boned, cooked, and cubed (about 4 cups)

2 celery stalks, chopped (about 1 cup)

1 can (11 ounces) mandarin oranges, drained

1 cup halved cranberries

1/4 cup mayonnaise

3 tablespoons low-fat milk

Juice of half a lemon

2 tablespoons finely chopped fresh parsley

2 teaspoons celery seed

2 teaspoons finely chopped fresh savory or 1 teaspoon dried savory

Salt

Bibb lettuce

1. In a large bowl, combine the chicken, celery, oranges, and cranberries. Set aside.

2. Thin the mayonnaise with the milk and lemon juice. Add the parsley, celery seed, savory, and salt to taste. Mix well.

3. Combine the dressing with the chicken mixture and refrigerate. Serve cupped in leaves of Bibb lettuce.

YIELD: 6 SERVINGS

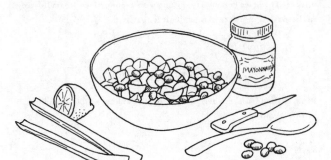

THE VERY BEST STUFFING

1 1/2 cups dried cranberries

1 cup white rum

5 cups coarsely crumbled fresh corn bread (about 1 1/2 loaves)

2 cups chopped pecans

4 stalks celery, chopped

2 Cortland apples, chopped

1 Vidalia onion, chopped

2 teaspoons dried marjoram

2 teaspoons freshly ground nutmeg

2 teaspoons dried sage

2 teaspoons dried thyme

1/2–1 cup chicken or turkey broth

1. Soak the dried cranberries in the rum for at least 3 hours.

2. In a very large mixing bowl, combine the corn bread, pecans, celery, apples, onion, marjoram, nutmeg, sage, and thyme. Add the cranberries and rum. About an hour and a half before the turkey is done, add 1/2 cup of the broth to the stuffing and mix well. If the stuffing is too dry, add more broth until it is slightly moist but not mushy. Spread the stuffing in a baking pan (a lasagne-type pan works well), cover tightly with aluminum foil, and place in the oven.

3. When the turkey has about 15 minutes left to cook, remove both it and the stuffing from the oven and scoop some stuffing into the turkey. (Be very careful when you take off the aluminum foil cover; there will be a good amount of steam built up!) Put the turkey back in the oven to finish off, and spread the rest of the stuffing evenly over the bottom of the baking pan. Return the pan to the oven, uncovered, until the turkey is done. If members of your family prefer a crispy stuffing, leave this in the oven while you carve, taking care to check it for signs of burning.

4. Serve the cooked-inside stuffing and the crispy pan-baked stuffing separately to offer different textures to suit individual tastes.

YIELD: 8 CUPS

THANKSGIVING LEFTOVER MASH

Typically made with leftover turkey, this recipe is also delicious with leftover chicken or game hen. If you can't wait for a day with leftovers, grab an already-roasted bird from your grocery's deli counter. The potatoes, as well, should be precooked—keep this in mind a few nights in advance, and this will be a speedy meal to prepare. You'll find dried cranberries in the bulk foods section or the snack aisle of your supermarket.

1–2 tablespoons extra virgin olive oil

1 pound cooked, unpeeled mini-potatoes, quartered

1 pound cooked, diced turkey

1 cup dried cranberries

3 shallots, finely chopped

2 tablespoons fresh marjoram, chopped (may substitute 2 teaspoons dried, crumbled)

1/3 cup sour cream

1/4 cup half-and-half

1/2 teaspoon salt

Freshly ground black pepper

1. Heat a large cast-iron skillet on medium-high, then heat enough olive oil to amply coat the bottom of the pan. Add the potatoes and the turkey and toss with a sturdy pair of tongs. Add the cranberries, shallots, and marjoram and toss once more. Reduce heat to medium, and cover the pan.

2. Mix the sour cream and half-and-half in a small bowl until smooth. Add the salt and several coarse grinds of pepper and stir. Add the sour cream mixture to the potatoes and turkey and mix well.

3. Cover skillet and let sit for 5 minutes, then stir well. Cook, covered, for another 10 minutes or so on medium heat, stirring occasionally, then uncover and raise heat to medium-high. Watch that the mash does not stick to the pan too much or get too dry. If it does, drop a tablespoon or two of olive oil onto a clear spot in the pan, let it heat up, and toss the mixture into the hot oil.

4. Cook, uncovered, at medium-high until crisp and browned, and stir frequently to prevent burning. Add salt and pepper to taste and serve hot.

YIELD: 4 SERVINGS

CRANBERRY PORK CHOPS

The ease of preparing these chops makes this scrumptious dish even more appealing!

6 pork chops

4 cups cranberries, chopped

1 medium onion, chopped

1 cup honey

Salt and freshly ground pepper

Continued ➔

1. Preheat oven to 350°F.

2. In a large skillet, brown the pork chops on both sides over medium heat. Add salt and pepper to taste.

3. Combine the cranberries, onion, and honey in a bowl.

4. Place the pork chops in an ovenproof casserole dish. Spread the cranberry mixture over the pork chops, and cover. Bake for 1 hour.

YIELD: 6 SERVINGS

DRINKS, SAUCES, AND SIDES

RED SNAPPER

3 ounces cranberry juice cocktail

1 jigger Amaretto di Saronno

1 jigger Crown Royal

1 slice orange, to garnish

In a shaker, mix the cranberry juice, amaretto, and Crown Royal with crushed ice and pour into an old-fashioned glass. Garnish with the orange.

YIELD: 1 SERVING

CRANBERRY–PINEAPPLE SMOOTHIE

1 1/2 cups plain yogurt

1 cup crushed ice

1 cup fresh ripe pineapple

3/4 cup fresh diced or frozen cranberries

Juice of half a lemon

Superfine sugar, to taste

1. Place the yogurt, ice, pineapple, cranberries, and lemon juice in a blender and mix until the ice has been adequately blended. Add sugar to taste.

2. Divide into two glasses and insert straws.

Variations: You can replace the yogurt with the same amount of coconut milk or vanilla ice cream. Try serving with a scoop of ice cream floating in the glasses, or a slice of fresh fruit for garnish.

YIELD: 2 SERVINGS

MY FAVORITE FRUIT SMOOTHIE

Ripe, chilled fruits are best, except for the banana, which should never be refrigerated.

3 peaches

3/4 cup fresh cranberries

1 banana

3/4 cup freshly squeezed orange juice

1/2 cup rice milk or milk

3 scoops vanilla ice cream or substitute

Maple syrup or superfine sugar

1. Place the peaches, cranberries, banana, orange juice, and rice milk in a blender and mix until smooth. Add the ice cream and blend.

2. Adjust consistency with more ice cream if the mixture is too thin; add milk if it's too thick.

3. Add maple syrup to taste.

YIELD: 2–3 SERVINGS

NON-DAIRY CRANBERRY SPRITZER

3/4 cup fresh ripe or frozen cranberries

3 hulled strawberries

1 tablespoon mint, finely diced

1 liter ginger ale

Candied ginger, to garnish

1. Purée the cranberries, strawberries, mint, and 1/2 cup of the ginger ale in a blender until completely liquefied.

2. Distribute the mixture evenly into four glasses, and insert a long spoon in each.

3. Pour the ginger ale to 1 inch below the tops of the glasses and stir gently, then remove the spoons and insert straws in each glass. Garnish the edges of the glasses with scored pieces of candied ginger.

YIELD: 4 SERVINGS

ASIAN FUSION TEA

6 tablespoons Gen-Mai Cha tea or other loose green tea

3 cups boiling water

1 1/2 cups cranberry juice

1/2 cup pure maple syrup

6 tablespoons amaretto

1. Brew the tea in the boiling water, covered, for 5–7 minutes. Add the cranberry juice and maple syrup and return to low heat to warm.

2. Pour 1 tablespoon of amaretto into each of six teacups, then pour in the cranberry tea. Serve with a smile.

YIELD: 6 SERVINGS

CRANBERRY COULIS

Serve this dish with grilled pork chops for a mouthwatering meal. And wear kitchen gloves when handling the chiles to keep the caustic juices away from your skin.

2 jalapeño chiles

2 tablespoons kosher salt

1 sweet red pepper

1 can (10 ounces) cranberry sauce

3 drops liquid smoke

1. Preheat the broiler. Place the jalapeños on a baking sheet. Broil evenly by turning frequently with tongs until the skins are black. Remove the jalapeños from the baking sheet and place them in a brown paper bag with the salt, shake a few times, then leave in the bag to steam.

2. Repeat this process with the red pepper, steaming it in the bag with the jalapeños.

3. Allow the red pepper and jalapeños to steam together for at least 10 minutes, then remove all peppers from the bag and run them under cold water, rubbing the skins off with your fingers. Seed the peppers and chop coarsely.

4. Place the cranberry sauce and liquid smoke in a blender, and begin to process. Add the pieces of pepper a few at a time, until all have been incorporated and liquefied. Store the coulis in the refrigerator for up to 1 week.

YIELD: 2 CUPS

CRANBERRY BUTTER

1 cup (2 sticks) butter or margarine, softened

2 tablespoons confectioners' sugar

1/3 cup cranberries, mashed

Mix all ingredients in a blender or food processor and blend until smooth. May be kept, refrigerated, for up to 2 weeks.

YIELD: 1 1/4 CUPS

CRANBERRY SALSA

Serve this salsa with blue corn chips, broiled salmon, pork chops, or game or mix a half cup with three mashed ripe avocados for a fun twist on guacamole. Wear kitchen gloves when handling the chiles.

2 cups fresh cranberries

1 medium Spanish onion, medium diced

3 tablespoons extra virgin olive oil

1 medium orange bell pepper

1 medium yellow bell pepper

1 tablespoon kosher salt

1 habanero chile, seeded and diced fine

1 jalapeño chile, seeded and diced fine

1 ripe peach, diced medium

2 fresh scallions, thinly sliced

4 tablespoons chopped fresh cilantro

2 tablespoons chopped fresh mint

3 tablespoons granulated sugar

Juice of 1 fresh lime

1. Preheat oven to 425°F.

2. Combine the cranberries and onion in a bowl with 2 tablespoons of the olive oil. Spread this mixture on a baking sheet and roast for 10 minutes or so, until the onions are slightly brown and the skins of the cranberries begin to split. Set aside to cool in a large mixing bowl.

3. Turn oven to broil.

4. Place the orange and yellow bell peppers on a baking sheet. Broil, turning with tongs regularly, until the skin of each pepper is black and blistered. Remove from the oven, place in a paper bag with the salt, and roll the top of the bag. Give it a good shake to distribute the salt and set aside to steam for 10 minutes.

5. While the bell peppers are steaming, add the habanero, jalapeño, peach, scallions, cilantro, mint, sugar, and lime juice to the bowl with the onions and cranberries. Mix well.

6. Remove the bell peppers from the paper bag and run under very cold water, rubbing with both hands. The blackened peels should come off easily. Halve the peppers, scoop out the seeds, and dice the peppers. Add diced peppers to the bowl and mix.

7. Scoop 1 1/2 cups of the mixture into a food processor and purée until smooth. Stir the purée into the remaining mixture. Refrigerate the salsa for a minimum of 2 hours before serving.

YIELD: ABOUT 4 CUPS

Continued ➜

CRANBERRY PRESERVES

Preserves, unlike jams or jellies, feature whole berries.

4 cups sugar

4 cups water

2 pounds fresh cranberries

Zest of 2 oranges

Juice of 2 limes

1. Dissolve the sugar in the water and simmer over medium heat for 10 minutes. Add the cranberries, zest, and lime juice, and increase heat to high. Stir constantly to prevent burning as you allow the syrup to thicken and reduce, about 20 minutes.

2. Distribute into sterilized jars and refrigerate for up to 2 weeks, or process in boiling water according to the manufacturer's instructions for 10 minutes (up to 1,000 feet altitude; adjust processing times for elevations over 1,000 feet).

YIELD: 10 JARS

CRANBERRY CHUTNEY

This is great with any white meat, hot or cold, and with ham or cold roast beef.

4 cups fresh cranberries

1 cup chopped Vidalia onion

3/4 cup fresh squeezed grapefruit juice

3/4 cup apple cider vinegar

1/2 cup apple cider

2 teaspoons grated grapefruit zest

1 tablespoon minced fresh ginger

1 teaspoon allspice

1 teaspoon cinnamon

1 cup maple syrup

1/2 cup brown sugar

1 1/4 cups pecans, chopped

1. Bring the cranberries, onion, juice, vinegar, cider, zest, ginger, allspice, and cinnamon to a boil.

2. Once the mixture has reached the boiling point, lower the heat and simmer for 10 minutes.

3. After 10 minutes, add the maple syrup and brown sugar, stirring. Continue to stir every few minutes for an additional 15 minutes, or until the chutney has thickened sufficiently. Stir in the pecans.

4. Remove from heat and spoon into sterilized jars. Refrigerate for up to 2 weeks, or process in boiling water according to

the manufacturer's instructions for 10 minutes (up to 1,000 feet altitude; adjust processing times for elevations over 1,000 feet).

YIELD: 5 JARS

CHUTNEY HINT

If you forget to stir a sugary batch, the bottom of the pan may scorch and create a layer of burned chutney. Refrain from scraping the burned bits up into the rest of the batch, or you'll spoil it. When you jar the chutney, take great care that you don't dislodge the burned parts. Tilt the pan and scoop from the chutney that slides to the sides of the pan. Sacrifice the layer of "good" chutney that doesn't slide.

CRANBERRY JELLY

For a tangy twist to the old peanut butter and jelly sandwich, try this jazzy delight.

8 cups fresh cranberries

5 cups water

5 cups sugar

3 ounces liquid pectin

1. Simmer the cranberries in the water, covered, over medium heat for 15 minutes. Strain the cranberry mixture through a sieve, and measure 6 cups of the pulp/juice that results.

2. Place the juice in a heavy-bottomed cooking pot over medium-high heat. Add the sugar, stirring well, and bring to a boil. Add the pectin and boil for 1 minute.

3. Remove from the heat and, with a slotted or mesh spoon, skim off the foam. Pour into hot sterilized jars and refrigerate for up to 2 weeks, or process in boiling water according to the manufacturer's directions for 10 minutes (up to 1,000 feet altitude; adjust processing times for elevations over 1,000 feet).

YIELD: 10 JARS

THE BEST CHOCOLATE CHIP COOKIE

The contrast of the tangy cranberries with the sweet chunks of chocolate in these cookies is delightful. When made with dried cranberries, the cookies are a bit sweeter.

8 tablespoons butter, softened

1/4 cup granulated sugar

1/3 cup light brown sugar, firmly packed

1 large egg

1/2 teaspoon pure vanilla extract

1 cup plus 2 tablespoons all-purpose flour

1/2 teaspoon baking soda

1 1/2 cups fresh chopped cranberries or 1 cup dried cranberries

1 cup semisweet chocolate chips

1/2 cup walnuts, chopped

1. Preheat oven to 375°F. Beat the butter and the granulated and brown sugars in an electric mixer until light and fluffy. Add the egg and vanilla and mix well, scraping the sides of the bowl with a rubber spatula.

2. In a separate bowl, mix the flour and baking soda with a whisk or fork until well blended. Add to the butter mixture slowly, scraping sides of the bowl. Mix well. When all of the flour mixture has been added, remove and scrape beaters.

3. Add the cranberries, chocolate chips, and walnuts to the dough and stir in carefully. Spoon onto ungreased baking sheets, in tablespoon-sized dollops about 2 inches apart. Bake for 20 minutes, rotating the baking sheets in the oven every 5 minutes to ensure even baking. Let cool on the sheets for a few minutes before transferring to wire racks for complete cooling.

YIELD: 2 1/2 DOZEN

CRANBERRY–GINGER PINWHEELS

These are festive, impressive, and easy to transport—a great gift cookie.

3/4 cup whole-berry cranberry sauce (canned is fine)

1/4 cup ginger preserves

1 tablespoon cornstarch

3/4 cup brown sugar, firmly packed

1/2 cup (1 stick) butter, softened

1 egg

1 3/4 cups all-purpose flour

1 teaspoon baking powder

1/4 teaspoon ground allspice

1/4 teaspoon ground nutmeg

1/4 teaspoon salt

1. To make the filling, over medium-high heat, bring the cranberry sauce, ginger preserves, and cornstarch to a boil, stirring constantly, then refrigerate.

2. To make the dough, use an electric mixer to cream the brown sugar and butter. Add the egg and beat until light.

3. In a separate bowl, mix the flour, baking powder, allspice, nutmeg, and salt. Add these slowly to the brown sugar mixture, 1/2 cup at a time, scraping the sides of the bowl with a rubber spatula. Refrigerate the entire bowl, covered, for 1 hour.

4. On a floured work surface, press or roll the chilled dough into a rectangle, about 16 inches by 8 inches. Spread the chilled cranberry filling uniformly over the dough, leaving clear a 1/2-inch strip on each long side.

5. Roll from the long side of the rectangle, slowly and carefully so you do not press out the filling. Cut the roll in half and wrap the two rolls in plastic wrap. Refrigerate for at least 2 hours or up to 1 day; the rolls may also be frozen for up to 3 months.

6. Preheat oven to 375°F and grease several baking sheets. Slice the rolls into 1/2-inch-thick pinwheels and place about 2 inches apart on the prepared sheets. Bake for 9–12 minutes, or until golden brown, then transfer to a rack to cool completely.

YIELD: 3 DOZEN

POLENTA–CRANBERRY CAKE

Try serving this with a warmed cranberry conserve and a sprig of mint.

4 packages active dry yeast (1 ounce total)

2 tablespoons warm water

1 3/4 cups all-purpose flour

1 1/3 cups dried cranberries

2 tablespoons brandy

2 cups yellow cornmeal

3/4 cup sugar

1/4 teaspoon salt

1 1/3 cups chopped dried Calimyrna figs

2 apples, peeled, cored, and chopped

2/3 cup freshly squeezed lime juice

1 cup water, 98°F

4 tablespoons unsalted butter, melted

2 tablespoons extra-virgin olive oil

1 egg, beaten

1. Butter a 10-inch round pan and dust with cornmeal.

2. In a small bowl, dissolve the yeast in the 2 tablespoons of water. Measure 2 tablespoons of the flour into the yeast mixture. Using a wire whisk, blend well to make a paste. Cover with plastic wrap and set in a warm place for 30 minutes.

3. In another small bowl, let the cranberries soak in the brandy and set aside, stirring occasionally.

Continued ➞

4. Stir to combine the remaining flour and the cornmeal, sugar, and salt in the large bowl of an electric mixer. Add the cranberries and brandy, figs, apples, and lime juice. Using the dough hook, mix the batter, scraping the sides diligently with a rubber spatula. Add the water, butter, olive oil, and yeast mixture, which should have a spongy consistency. Mix thoroughly.

5. Turn the batter onto a lightly floured work surface and knead for a few minutes until the dough is smooth and elastic. Transfer the dough to the prepared pan and cover with a clean dish towel. Let rise in a warm, draft-free spot for 1–2 hours, or until the dough has reached the top of the pan.

6. Heat the oven to 375°F. With a pastry brush, coat the top of the cake lightly with the egg. Bake for 50 minutes, or until a tester inserted in the center comes out clean. Cool in the pan for 15 minutes, then invert and gently lift the pan off the cake. Turn right-side up on a wire rack. Cool completely.

YIELD: 12 SERVINGS

CRANBERRY–PEAR CRISP

Serve with vanilla ice cream for a mouthwatering combination.

Filling:

5 cups sliced, peeled pears (canned are fine if they are well drained)

1 1/2 cups fresh or frozen whole cranberries

3/4 cup firmly packed brown sugar

2 tablespoons all-purpose flour

2 teaspoons orange zest

1 teaspoon ground nutmeg

Topping:

1 cup rolled oats (not instant oatmeal)

3/4 cup firmly packed brown sugar

1/2 cup all-purpose flour

1 teaspoon ground cinnamon

1/2 cup butter (1 stick), melted

1. Preheat oven to 375°F. To make the filling, place the pears and cranberries in an 8- x 8-inch baking pan, distributing evenly.

2. In a separate bowl, mix the sugar, flour, zest, and nutmeg, and sprinkle over the fruit. Shake the pan a few times to let the mixture settle in.

3. To make the topping, mix the oats, sugar, flour, and cinnamon. Continue stirring as you drizzle in the butter. Sprinkle the topping evenly over the fruit.

4. Bake, covered, for 15 minutes. Uncover and bake 10–20 minutes longer, until the topping is crisp and the fruit is bubbling. Serve warm.

YIELD: 6 GENEROUS SERVINGS

MINI CRANBERRY CHEESCAKES

Make these impressive little snacks for a potluck or a dinner party, and they will go fast!

Cheesecakes:

1 cup graham cracker crumbs (about 15 crackers)

4 tablespoons butter, melted

1/4 teaspoon ground allspice

1/4 teaspoon ground nutmeg

8 ounces cream cheese, softened

1/3 cup sugar

1 large egg

2 tablespoons sour cream

1 tablespoon freshly squeezed lemon juice

1/2 teaspoon pure vanilla extract

Topping:

1/4 cup water

1/3 cup sugar

1 cup fresh or frozen cranberries

2 1/2 teaspoons cornstarch

1. Preheat oven to 375°F. To make the cheesecakes, combine the graham cracker crumbs, butter, allspice, and nutmeg in a bowl and stir well. Distribute evenly between two 1-dozen capacity mini-muffin pans, and press into the bottom and sides of depressions to create shells. Refrigerate.

2. In the large bowl of an electric mixer, beat the softened cream cheese with the sugar until smooth, then add the egg, sour cream, lemon juice, and vanilla, and beat well, scraping the sides of the bowl with a rubber spatula as it turns.

3. Spoon the cream cheese filling into the graham cracker shells or pipe in with a pastry bag. Bake the cheesecakes for 10 minutes, switching the positions of the pans after 5 minutes. Turn off the oven and open the door, but do not remove the pans. This allows the cakes to cool slowly so that the tops do not split. After 30 minutes, remove from oven and let cool completely in pans.

4. To prepare the topping, whisk the water, sugar, cranberries, and cornstarch in a heavy-bottomed saucepan over medium-high heat. Bring to a boil, stirring constantly. Reduce heat to low and simmer for 1 minute, whisking intermittently. Set aside to cool.

5. Once the cheesecakes and topping have cooled, carefully remove the cakes from the pans and spoon the topping onto the center of each, distributing cranberries evenly. Cover and store in the refrigerator, taking care that the wrap does not cling to the topping and pull it off.

YIELD: 24 CHEESECAKES

CRANBERRY–LEMON POUND CAKE

This cake is splendid with a cup of tea on a winter afternoon.

2 3/4 cups sugar

1 1/2 cups (3 sticks) butter, softened

1 teaspoon lemon zest

1 teaspoon pure vanilla extract

1/2 teaspoon lemon extract

6 eggs

3 cups all-purpose flour

1 teaspoon baking soda

1/2 teaspoon salt

8 ounces sour cream

1 1/2 cups fresh cranberries, chopped

1. Preheat oven to 350°F. Grease and lightly flour a 10-inch Bundt pan or a 9-inch tube pan.

2. Using an electric mixer, beat the sugar and butter in a large bowl until light and fluffy. Add the lemon zest and the vanilla and lemon extracts, then add the eggs one at a time, continuing to beat thoroughly between additions and scraping the sides of the bowl with a rubber spatula.

3. In a separate bowl, mix the flour, baking soda, and salt. With the electric mixer running, add to the egg mixture 1/2 cup of the flour mixture alternately with 1 ounce of the sour cream. Scrape the sides of the bowl frequently. Mix well to combine, then remove the beaters.

4. Fold in the cranberries and pour the batter into the prepared baking pan.

5. Bake for 1–1 1/4 hours, or until a toothpick inserted in the center comes out clean. Allow to cool for 15 minutes, then remove from the pan to cool completely.

YIELD: 12–14 SERVINGS

Great Blueberry Recipes

Karen Matthews

Illustrations by Mary Rich

Cooking with Blueberries

FRESH VERSUS FROZEN

Fresh blueberries can be frozen for winter use: Just rinse the fresh blueberries, pat them dry, and put them in freezer containers. They will keep all winter in your freezer.

There is little difference between cooking with fresh and cooking with frozen blueberries. Nutritionally, while the calories remain the same—90 calories and .7 grams of fat per cup—other nutritional values per cup are somewhat different:

Nutrient	Fresh	Frozen
Calcium	22 mg	17 mg
Vitamin A	150 units	120 units
Ascorbic acid	20 mg	12 mg
Iron	1.5 mg	1.3 mg
Potassium	117 mg	134 mg

WILD VERSUS CULTIVATED

For cooking purposes, there is a slight difference between the small, intensely flavored wild blueberries and the larger, milder-flavored cultivated ones. If you are fortunate enough to have a choice, use the smaller wild berries for bread recipes that make batters and the larger, cultivated ones for recipes in which the blueberries blend into a sauce or thick filling.

BREAKFAST SPECIALS

BLUEBERRY PANCAKES

This batter keeps well for several days in a sealed container in the refrigerator. Make extra to have on hand for a quick midweek breakfast, or add a tablespoon of chocolate chips to the batter for a late-night snack.

1 1/2 cups flour

2 tablespoons sugar

2 teaspoons baking powder

1 cup milk

1 egg, beaten

2 tablespoons vegetable oil

1 tablespoon butter

1/2 cup blueberries

1. In a medium bowl, mix together the flour, sugar, baking powder, milk, egg, and vegetable oil.

2. In a large skillet, melt the butter over low heat. Pour 1/4–1/2 cup of batter into the pan and sprinkle blueberries over the top. Fry until the bubbles that form in the batter leave small holes when they burst. Then flip and cook on the other side until golden brown.

3. Serve with maple or blueberry syrup.

MAKES 6–8 PANCAKES

Continued ➔

BLUEBERRY STICKY ROLLS

This is great for a fancy breakfast, and not much more complicated than making muffins. If you have any leftovers, top them with whipped cream and you have a fantastic blueberry shortcake for dessert!

3/4 cup plus 2 tablespoons sugar

1 cup water

6 tablespoons butter or margarine

1 1/2 cups plus 2 teaspoons flour

1/2 teaspoon vanilla

1/2 teaspoon ginger

1/2 teaspoon cinnamon

3/4 teaspoon salt

1 1/2 teaspoons baking powder

1/2 cup milk

3/4 cup blueberries

1. Preheat the oven to 350°F.

2. In a medium-size saucepan, combine 3/4 cup of the sugar, the water, 2 tablespoons of the butter, 2 teaspoons of the flour, the vanilla, ginger, cinnamon, and 1/2 teaspoon of the salt. Cook over medium heat to a full boil, stirring constantly. Remove from heat and set aside.

3. In a large bowl, mix together the rest of the flour, sugar, and salt with the baking powder. Then cut in 2 tablespoons of the butter until you have a crumbly mixture. Add the milk and mix gently until a dough forms.

4. Turn the dough onto a floured surface. Sprinkle lightly with flour and pat into a loaf. Roll out the loaf to form a 9 x 12-inch rectangle. Spread the remaining butter on the dough and arrange the blueberries evenly over its surface.

5. Roll up the dough like a jelly roll. Cut the roll into 9 slices and arrange them, evenly spaced, in a greased 9 x 9-inch pan. Pour the sauce from step 2 over the rolls.

6. Bake for 25–30 minutes, until golden brown on top. Cool before serving.

MAKES 9 SERVINGS

BLUEBERRY CRÊPES

These elegant little goodies will impress the most sophisticated brunch bunch. They're even fancier with blueberry syrup poured over them. The batter can be made the night before—it's actually easier to handle if has set for a while before you make the crêpes.

1 egg, beaten

1/2 cup flour

3/4 cup milk

1/2 cup sugar

1/2 cup blueberries

1/2 teaspoon vanilla

Butter

1/2 cup cottage cheese

1. In a medium bowl, mix together the egg, flour, milk, and 1/4 cup of the sugar until batter is smooth.

2. Pour the blueberries into a small saucepan, fill it with water so that the berries are just covered, and heat. When they begin to simmer, add the vanilla and the remaining 1/4 cup of sugar. Simmer for 2–3 minutes, then remove from heat.

3. Coat a frying pan with butter. Pour 2–3 tablespoons of batter into the pan and tip the pan in all directions to make the batter spread out. Fry over low heat until the batter looks slightly darker and dry. Flip, then fry the other side until golden brown. Rebutter the pan again before making the next crêpe.

4. When all of the crêpes have been made, put 2–3 tablespoons of the cottage cheese across the middle of each one. Then put 2–3 tablespoons of the blueberry mixture on the cottage cheese and fold each side of the crêpe over the mixture to form a roll. Serve with blueberry syrup, whipped cream, or both!

WHITE CHOCOLATE CHIP–BLUEBERRY BRUNCH CAKE

If you want to make this with dark chocolate chips, add a teaspoon of cinnamon to the batter.

3 eggs

1/2 cup milk

1 cup butter, softened

1 tablespoon baking powder

1 cup sugar

1 teaspoon vanilla

2 cups flour

1 tablespoon lemon juice

1 cup blueberries

1 cup white chocolate chips

1. Preheat the oven to 350°F.

2. In a large bowl, beat together the eggs, milk, butter, baking powder, sugar, and vanilla until well blended. Add the flour and lemon juice and mix until thoroughly blended.

3. Gently fold in the blueberries and the white chocolate chips.

4. Pour the batter into a greased 9 x 9-inch pan. Bake for 45–50 minutes, or until a knife inserted into the center comes out clean.

BLUEBERRY–SOUR CREAM SCONES

Scones should be served warm right out of the oven. These are very good with a little honey or butter. Brush the tops with melted butter or a beaten egg before baking to give them a more golden, glossy crust.

1 cup flour

1/2 cup instant oats

2 tablespoons baking powder

3 tablespoons sugar

1/4 teaspoon salt

3 tablespoons butter

1/2 cup blueberries

2 eggs, beaten

1/4 cup sour cream

1/4 cup milk

1. Preheat the oven to 375°F.

2. In a large bowl, mix the flour, oats, baking powder, sugar, and salt.

3. Cut in the butter and add the blueberries, beaten eggs, sour cream, and milk. Stir until the batter is just moistened.

4. Turn onto a lightly floured surface and roll out to 1/2 inch thickness.

5. Cut into desired shape and bake for 12–15 minutes. Serve warm with butter.

MUFFINS

PEACHY BLUEBERRY MUFFINS

This recipe works best with fresh, firm peaches, but you may also use canned.

2 cups flour

1 cup brown sugar

1 tablespoon baking powder

1 teaspoon salt

1 1/2 teaspoons cinnamon

1/2 teaspoon ginger

2 eggs, beaten

1/2 cup milk

1/4 cup vegetable oil

1/2 cup blueberries

1/2 cup diced, peeled peaches

1. Preheat the oven to 375°F.

2. In a large bowl, mix together the flour, sugar, baking powder, salt, cinnamon, and ginger.

3. In another bowl, mix the eggs, milk, and oil.

4. Add the wet ingredients to the dry ingredients. Stir until just moistened.

5. Fold in the blueberries and the peaches.

6. Fill greased muffin tins about 3/4 full of the batter.

7. Bake for 15–20 minutes, or until a knife inserted into the center comes out clean.

8. Cool and serve.

MAKES 1 DOZEN MUFFINS

CLASSIC BLUEBERRY MUFFINS

1 3/4 cups flour

1/2 cup sugar

1 tablespoon baking powder

1/2 teaspoon salt

1 teaspoon cinnamon

4 tablespoons butter

1 egg, beaten

2/3 cup milk

1 teaspoon vanilla

1 cup blueberries

1. Preheat the oven to 375°F.

2. In a large bowl, mix the flour, sugar, baking powder, salt, and cinnamon. Cut in the butter.

3. In another bowl mix the egg, milk, and vanilla.

4. Pour the wet ingredients into the flour mixture. Stir until just moistened, then carefully fold in the blueberries.

5. Fill greased muffin tins about 3/4 full of the batter. Bake 20 minutes, or until a knife inserted in the center comes out clean.

MAKES 1 DOZEN MUFFINS

Continued ➜

BLUEBERRY CORNMEAL MUFFINS

1 cup flour

3/4 cup cornmeal

4 tablespoons sugar

1 tablespoon baking powder

1 teaspoon salt

1 teaspoon cinnamon

1 egg, beaten

3/4 cup milk

1/4 cup vegetable oil

1 cup blueberries

1. Preheat the oven to 400°F.

2. In a large bowl, mix the flour, cornmeal, sugar, baking powder, salt, and cinnamon.

3. In another bowl, mix the egg, milk, and oil.

4. Pour the wet ingredients into the dry ingredients. Mix until just moistened, then carefully fold in the blueberries

5. Fill greased muffin tins about 3/4 full of the batter. Bake 18–20 minutes, or until a knife inserted into the center comes out clean. Cool for 5–10 minutes before serving.

MAKES I DOZEN MUFFINS

SALADS AND SALAD DRESSINGS

BLUEBERRY VINAIGRETTE

This is a wonderful dressing for any green salad. On a hot summer day it makes a delicious cool salad even more refreshing.

1/2 cup salad oil

1/2 cup Blueberry Vinegar (see recipe that follows)

1 tablespoon sugar

1 teaspoon nutmeg

1/2 teaspoon ginger

1/4 teaspoon salt

1. In a container with a cover, mix the oil, vinegar, sugar, nutmeg, ginger, and salt. Shake to blend before using.

2. Use to dress a salad or serve on the side.

MAKES ABOUT I CUP

BLUEBERRY SPINACH SALAD

To make this into a dinner salad, add 2–3 sliced boiled eggs and 2–3 grilled boned chicken breasts cut into strips.

1 cup clean spinach torn into bite-size pieces

1 cup clean iceberg lettuce torn into bite-size pieces

1 small cucumber, peeled and diced

1 tomato, diced

1 small can of mandarin orange slices, drained

3/4 cup fresh blueberries

1/2 cup Blueberry Vinaigrette

1. In a large bowl, toss together the spinach, lettuce, cucumber, tomato, and mandarin oranges.

2. Add the blueberries and vinaigrette. Toss lightly.

3. Refrigerate until ready to serve.

SERVES 4–6

BLUEBERRY PASTA SALAD

2 cups cooked pasta

1 tomato, diced

1 small cucumber, diced

1 stalk of celery, sliced thin

1/2 green pepper, seeded and diced

1/2 cup fresh blueberries

1/4 cup Blueberry Vinaigrette

Salt and pepper to taste

1. In a medium-size bowl, mix the pasta, tomato, cucumber, celery, and pepper.

2. Add the blueberries, vinaigrette, and seasonings. Toss lightly.

3. Refrigerate until ready to serve.

SERVES 4

SOUPS

BLUEBERRY POTATO SOUP

This is a light but filling soup. It's best when chilled for several hours before serving. You can make it the day before and let it chill in the refrigerator overnight.

4 medium potatoes, peeled and quartered

4 scallions

3 cups chicken bouillon

1 cup blueberries

1/4 cup mint leaves, shredded

1 cup half and half

1. Simmer the potatoes and scallions in the bouillon for 25–30 minutes, until the potatoes are soft.

2. Remove from heat and add the blueberries and mint leaves.

3. Put aside 2 cups of the mixture.

4. Puree the remaining mixture in a food processor.

5. Put the pureed mixture and the 2 cups set aside in a large bowl.

6. Chill in the refrigerator for at least 2 hours before serving.

SERVES 4–6

COLD BLUEBERRY SOUP

2 cups blueberries, washed and patted dry

2 cups water

1/2 cup maple syrup

1/2 teaspoon cinnamon

1/2 teaspoon ginger

1 cup sour cream

2 tablespoons fresh mint, shredded

1. Simmer the blueberries, water, maple syrup, cinnamon, and ginger for 8–10 minutes. Then remove from heat and cool.

2. Stir in sour cream and mint. Chill for 2–3 hours before serving.

SERVES 4

JAMS, SPREADS, SYRUPS, AND SAUCES

BLUEBERRY GINGER JAM

This is a spicy blueberry jam that will add zing to your morning toast. It goes very well on scones or spread on pancakes.

5 cups blueberries

1 tablespoon lemon juice

5 cups sugar

2 tablespoons cinnamon

1 tablespoon ginger

1/2 cup mint leaves, shredded

1 package fruit pectin

3/4 cup water

1. Select containers that can tolerate heat as well as freezing. Submerge them in boiling water for 15 minutes.

2. Wash the blueberries. Remove all stems and debris. Put the blueberries into a large bowl.

3. Add lemon juice, sugar, cinnamon, ginger, and mint leaves. Mix well and set aside for 15 minutes.

4. Put the pectin and water into a small pan and boil, stirring constantly, for 1 minute.

5. Add the pectin to the blueberry mixture, stir constantly for 5 minutes.

6. Fill the containers to 1/2 inch of the top and seal immediately.

7. Cool and transfer to the freezer.

8. Thaw when ready to serve. Keep refrigerated after opening.

BLUEBERRY MARINADE

This delightful and different marinade is delicious with chicken, fish, and beef. Pour it over four servings of the chosen meat and leave it in the refrigerator overnight. The next day it will be ready for the grill!

2 cups blueberries

1 cup Blueberry Vinegar (recipe follows)

3/4 cup extra virgin olive oil

1 teaspoon tarragon

1 teaspoon thyme

1 teaspoon shredded mint leaves

1/2 teaspoon salt

1/2 teaspoon pepper

1. In a small saucepan, combine the blueberries and vinegar and boil for 1 minute.

2. Remove from the heat and add the olive oil, tarragon, thyme, mint, salt, and pepper.

3. Refrigerate until ready to use.

BLUEBERRY SYRUP

2 cups blueberries, washed and patted dry

1 cup water

1/2 cup sugar

1 tablespoon cornstarch

1 teaspoon lemon juice

1 teaspoon cinnamon

1/2 teaspoon ginger

1. In a small saucepan, combine all of the ingredients. Turn heat on low and bring to a simmer. Simmer for 5 minutes.

2. Use a potato masher to mash the berries, then simmer for another 5 minutes.

3. Remove from heat. Cool before serving.

MAKES ABOUT 1 PINT

Continued →

BLUEBERRY VINEGAR

Blueberry vinegar can be used in any recipe that calls for vinegar. It will give most dishes an interesting tang and color. You can keep it in a sealed container in the cupboard—but it's so pretty, you may want to put it in a decorative glass container and keep it out on display.

1 cup ripe blueberries

2 cups white vinegar

1. In a medium saucepan, bring the vinegar to a boil. Turn off the heat and add the blueberries.

2. Allow to cool, then transfer to a container. Drape a towel over the container so that it is completely covered.

3. Let sit for one week in a cool, dry place.

4. Strain to remove the blueberries. Pour the vinegar into a sealed container until ready to use.

MAKES ABOUT ONE PINT

DESSERTS

BLUEBERRY ORANGE CAKE

2 eggs

4 tablespoons butter

1 cup sugar

2 cups flour

2 teaspoons baking powder

1/2 teaspoon salt

3/4 cup orange juice

1 cup blueberries

1. Preheat the oven to 375°F.

2. With a mixer, beat the eggs, butter, and sugar on high for 2 minutes. Add flour, baking powder, salt, and orange juice. Stir until smooth, and then fold in blueberries.

3. Pour the batter into a greased 8 x 11 pan. Bake for 30–40 minutes, or until a knife inserted into the center comes out clean. Serve cooled.

SERVES 8

BLUEBERRY SOUR CREAM CAKE

4 tablespoons butter

1 cup sugar

3 eggs

2 teaspoons vanilla

1 1/2 cups flour

2 teaspoons baking powder

3 cups blueberries

2 cups sour cream

1. Preheat the oven to 350°F.

2. In a large bowl, cream the butter and 1/2 cup sugar.

3. Add 1 egg and 1 teaspoon of the vanilla. Beat thoroughly.

4. Add the flour and baking powder.

5. Spread the batter, which will look slightly dry, evenly in a greased 9-inch springform pan. Spread the blueberries over this.

6. Beat together 2 eggs with 1/2 cup sugar, 1 teaspoon vanilla, and sour cream.

7. Pour the sour cream mixture over the blueberries.

8. Bake 55 minutes, until golden brown. Cool before serving.

SERVES 8

EASY PIECRUST

Even if you have had bad experiences trying to make piecrust, give this a try. It's easy and reliable—you can't miss with this one.

3 1/2 cups flour

2 teaspoons salt

1 cup vegetable oil

8 tablespoons cold water

1. Put the flour and salt into a large bowl.

2. Add the oil and mix with a fork until a crumbly mixture forms and there is no loose flour left.

3. Add the water and stir just until it is absorbed into the dough. Do *not* knead this dough.

4. Divide the dough in half. On a floured surface, roll out half for the bottom crust and half for the top crust. As you roll out the dough, sprinkle it with flour whenever it starts to become sticky.

5. Add the desired filling and follow directions for baking in the specific recipe.

MAKES CRUST FOR A 10-INCH, TWO-CRUST PIE

BLUEBERRY-LIME PIE

1/2 prepared piecrust recipe

1 envelope lime gelatin

1/4 cup cold water

3 egg yolks

3/4 cup sugar

3/4 cup lime juice

1 1/2 cups whipping cream

2 cups blueberries

1. Preheat the oven to 400°F.

2. Prepare the piecrust for the bottom of a 10-inch pie pan and bake for 15 minutes.

3. Put the gelatin in a pan and add the water.

4. On low heat, dissolve the gelatin. Remove from heat and cool.

5. In a small bowl, beat the egg yolks, sugar, and lime juice.

6. Add the egg mixture to the cooled gelatin.

7. Heat again on low, stirring constantly, until the mixture thickens to the consistency of mousse. Remove from heat and cool.

8. Beat the whipping cream until stiff peaks form. Fold into the lime mousse.

9. Fold in the blueberries.

10. Pour mousse into the piecrust.

11. Refrigerate for 4 hours before serving.

SERVES 8

BLUEBERRY YOGURT PIE

1/2 prepared piecrust recipe

3 cups blueberries

1 cup sugar

1 cup flour

1/2 teaspoon salt

3 eggs, beaten

1/2 cup plain yogurt

1/2 cup brown sugar

4 tablespoons butter

1 cup crushed walnuts

1. Preheat the oven to 350°F.

2. Clean the blueberries and spread them on top of the piecrust.

3. In a large bowl, mix together 1 cup sugar, 1/2 cup flour, and salt. Beat in the eggs and yogurt.

4. Pour the yogurt mixture over the blueberries in the piecrust.

5. Mix 1/2 cup brown sugar and 1/2 cup flour. Cut in the butter until you have a crumbly mix.

6. Sprinkle the mix over the pie, then sprinkle the walnuts on top of it all.

7. Bake for 45–55 minutes, until delicately browned.

SERVES 8

FRESH BLUEBERRY PIE

This is a great pie to make with the kids. It requires no baking and no sharp knives. You will need to use the range for a few minutes, so an adult should do that step, but most of the preparation is mixing and measuring!

1 3/4 sticks softened butter

1 cup sugar

1 cup graham cracker crumbs

1/2 cup flour

1 1/4 cups water

1 tablespoon vanilla

3 cups blueberries

1. Mix 1 stick soft butter with 1/4 cup sugar and the graham cracker crumbs. Press the graham cracker mixture into the bottom of a 9-inch pie plate.

2. Melt 3/4 stick of butter in the microwave on medium for 50 seconds. Add the flour and 3/4 cup sugar to the butter. Mix well.

3. Put the mixture into a saucepan and add the water. Heat on medium low, stirring constantly, until the mixture thickens. Then stir in vanilla.

4. Remove from heat; allow to cool. Then fold in the blueberries.

5. Pour the mixture into the pie plate on top of the graham cracker crust. Refrigerate until ready to serve.

SERVES 8

BLUEBERRY–BANANA CREAM PIE

This is a spectacular summer dessert pie—cool and light as well as tasty and unusual. Serve it with a warm summer breeze and the fragrance of your favorite flowers.

1/2 prepared piecrust recipe

2/3 cup sugar

1/4 cup cornstarch

1/2 teaspoon salt

3 cups milk

4 egg yolks, beaten

2 tablespoons soft butter

1 tablespoon vanilla

2 cups blueberries

2 sliced bananas

1. Preheat the oven to 350°F.

2. Prepare the bottom crust for a 10-inch pie pan.

Continued →

3. Bake the piecrust for 15 minutes until golden brown.

4. Remove the piecrust from the oven and set aside to cool.

5. Mix sugar, cornstarch, salt, milk, and egg yolks in a medium saucepan.

6. Turn heat on medium and stir constantly until the mixture thickens. Remove from heat.

7. Mix in the butter and vanilla.

8. Cool in the refrigerator for 10 minutes.

9. Fold in blueberries and banana slices, and pour mixture into the piecrust.

10. Chill for 4 hours before serving.

SERVES 8

BLUEBERRY BUCKLE

1/2 cup melted butter

3/4 cup brown sugar

1 beaten egg

1/2 cup half and half

2 cups flour

1 teaspoon cinnamon

2 teaspoons baking powder

1 teaspoon salt

2 cups blueberries

2 tablespoons sugar

1. Preheat the oven to 350°F.

2. In a large bowl, beat the butter, brown sugar, and egg.

3. Add half and half, flour, 1/2 teaspoon cinnamon, baking powder, and salt. Fold in 1 cup of the blueberries.

4. Pour into a greased 8-inch square pan. Sprinkle 1 cup blueberries, 1/2 teaspoon cinnamon, and sugar over the top.

5. Bake for 50–60 minutes, or until a knife inserted in the center comes out clean. Serve warm.

SERVES 8

BLUEBERRY BETTY

Here's a great way to use up bread that's just starting to turn stale.

2 cups blueberries

2 tablespoons lemon juice

3/4 cup brown sugar

4 cups bread cubes without crusts

1/4 cup sugar

1 teaspoon cinnamon

1. Preheat the oven to 350°F.

2. Mix together the berries, lemon juice, and brown sugar. Put half the blueberry mix into a greased 9-inch square baking dish.

3. Mix together bread crumbs, sugar, and cinnamon. Put half the bread mixture over the berries in the baking dish.

4. Spoon the remaining blueberry mixture over the bread mixture. Top with the remaining bread crumb mixture.

5. Bake for 25 minutes. Serve with ice cream or whipped cream.

SERVES 6

BLUEBERRY–WHITE CHOCOLATE OATIES

1 1/2 cups flour

1/2 teaspoon baking soda

1 teaspoon cinnamon

1/2 teaspoon salt

1 egg, beaten

1 cup sugar

1 cup melted butter

1/4 cup molasses

1/4 cup milk

2 1/4 cups instant oatmeal

1 cup white chocolate chips

1 cup blueberries

1. Preheat the oven to 350°F.

2. In a large bowl, mix the flour, baking soda, cinnamon, and salt. Add the beaten egg, sugar, melted butter, molasses, and milk. Stir until smooth.

3. Stir in the oatmeal and white chocolate chips, and fold in the blueberries.

4. Drop by large tablespoonfuls on a cookie sheet. Bake 10–12 minutes, until lightly browned. Cool before serving.

MAKES 2 DOZEN

BLUEBERRY KUCHEN

This dish is actually better after it has been frozen and thawed. It's the ideal dish to make ahead of time and keep in the freezer until you need it.

1 stick melted butter

3/4 cup brown sugar

2 eggs, beaten

2 teaspoons vanilla

1 1/2 cups flour

1/2 teaspoon baking powder

1/2 teaspoon salt

2 cups blueberries

1 cup crushed walnuts

1 tablespoon sugar

1 teaspoon cinnamon

1. Preheat the oven to 350°F.

2. In a large bowl, beat the butter, sugar, eggs, and vanilla.

3. Mix in the flour, baking powder, and salt.

4. Pat the dough into the bottom of a greased 10-inch pie pan.

5. Sprinkle the blueberries, walnuts, sugar, and cinnamon over the dough.

6. Bake for 45 minutes, or until golden brown. Cool before serving.

SERVES 6–8

BLUEBERRY KUGEL

1 package (8 ounces) cream cheese

1 cup sour cream

1 cup sugar

2 teaspoons vanilla

4 eggs, beaten

1/2 pound flat noodles, cooked

2 cups blueberries

1. Preheat the oven to 350°F.

2. In a large bowl, beat together the cream cheese, sour cream, and sugar.

3. Add the vanilla, eggs, and noodles.

4. Fold in the blueberries.

5. Pour into a greased 9 x 11-inch baking pan.

6. Bake for 55 minutes, or until knife inserted in the center comes out clean. Serve cooled.

SERVES 8–10

BLUEBERRY INDIAN PUDDING

This hearty dessert is especially good topped with whipped cream or maple syrup. If you dislike a heavy texture, use 1/2 cup white flour instead of the 1/2 cup cornmeal.

2 cups blueberries

4 cups water

1/2 cup cornmeal

1 cup honey

2 eggs, beaten

1 teaspoon cinnamon

1/4 cup white flour

1. Preheat the oven to 350°F.

2. Boil the berries in the water for 5 minutes.

3. Mash the berries with a potato masher.

4. Add the cornmeal, honey, eggs, cinnamon, and flour. Mix together thoroughly.

5. Refrigerate for 2 hours.

6. Pour into a greased 9 x 11-inch baking pan. Bake for 1 hour.

SERVES 8–10

Green Tomato Recipes

Phyllis Hobson

Preserving Green Tomatoes

CANNED SLICES

Wash, core and slice green tomatoes. Pack loosely in quart canning jars. Cover with boiling water to 1/2 inch of top of jars. Add 1/4 teaspoon of salt to each jar if you wish. Process 20 minutes in boiling water bath.

To use, drain slices and prepare according to the recipes for green tomatoes as a vegetable, main dish or dessert.

FREEZING GREEN TOMATOES

Wash and core green tomatoes without peeling. Cut in slices or cubes and spread in a single layer on a cookie sheet covered with waxed paper. Freeze, then remove from sheet and package frozen pieces in containers or plastic bags. Use in almost any of the following recipes for vegetables, main dishes, salads or desserts. Frozen slices may be dipped in flour and fried in hot oil without thawing. Salt and pepper to taste.

DRIED GREEN TOMATOES

Peel and core green tomatoes and chop in cubes 1/2 inch or less in size. Drain. Line cookie sheets with waxed paper or aluminum foil and spread cubes one layer deep. Dry in commercial food drier or place outdoors in a well-ventilated, sunny location. Bring indoors at night to protect from dew. When perfectly dry, store in glass jars. Soak one hour in an equal amount of water before using in any recipe calling for chopped green tomatoes.

GREEN TOMATO BUTTER

6 pounds (12 to 18 medium) green tomatoes

2 tablespoons powdered ginger

2 teaspoons powdered cinnamon

1 teaspoon powdered allspice

5 pounds brown sugar

Juice of two lemons

2 cups water

Coarsely chop green tomatoes without peeling or coring. Add remaining ingredients. Simmer over low heat two to three hours, until mixture is thick, stirring frequently. Run through colander or strainer to remove seeds and any hard bits of pulp. Reheat to boiling and pour into hot, sterilized pint canning jars. Seal immediately.

MAKES 4 PINTS.

Continued ➔

GREEN TOMATO MARMALADE

24 medium green tomatoes

4 oranges

3 1/2 pounds granulated sugar

Core and peel green tomatoes and cut in thin slices. Wash and peel oranges and cut peeling into thin strips. Cut oranges into thin slices. Combine tomato slices, peeling and orange slices with sugar in a kettle and let stand overnight. In the morning, place kettle over low heat and gradually bring mixture to a boil, stirring occasionally. Simmer gently about two hours, until thick. Pour immediately into hot, sterilized jelly jars and seal.

MAKES 6 PINTS.

GREEN TOMATO PRESERVES

5 pounds green tomatoes

4 pounds granulated sugar

2 lemons, thinly sliced, with peeling

Core and peel tomatoes and chop fine. Add sugar and let set overnight. Drain liquid into a large kettle and boil rapidly until thickened. Add chopped green tomatoes and lemon slices. Cook until thick and clear. Pour, boiling hot, into hot, sterilized pint canning jars. Seal immediately.

MAKES 6 PINTS.

GREEN TOMATO PICKLES

EASY GREEN TOMATO DILLS

Wash small green cherry tomatoes but do not peel or core. Pack loosely in quart canning jars. To each jar add:

1 peeled garlic clove

1/2 teaspoon mixed pickling spices

1 sprig fresh dill

1 small piece hot red pepper (optional)

In a saucepan combine:

2 cups water

2 cups vinegar

1 tablespoon flaked pickling salt

Bring to a boil and stir to dissolve salt. Pour over tomatoes in jars to within 1/4 inch of tops. Seal jars at once. Let set six weeks to cure before eating. Keep refrigerated after opening.

INDIAN PICKLES

8 medium green tomatoes, cored

8 medium ripe tomatoes, cored and peeled

3 medium onions, peeled

3 sweet red peppers, cored and seeded

1 large cucumber

7 cups celery, chopped

2/3 cup flaked pickling salt

6 cups vinegar

6 cups brown sugar

1 teaspoon dry mustard

1 teaspoon white pepper

Coarsely chop all vegetables. Sprinkle with salt and let stand overnight. In the morning, drain, discarding liquid. Combine with remaining ingredients in an open kettle. Place over low heat and bring to the simmering point slowly. Cook 30 minutes, stirring occasionally. Pack into hot, sterilized jars and seal at once. Process 10 minutes in boiling water bath.

MAKES 5 OR 6 PINTS.

SWEET PICKLE SLICES

2 quarts sliced green tomatoes

3 tablespoons flaked pickling salt

2 cups vinegar

2/3 cup brown sugar

1 cup granulated sugar

3 tablespoons mustard seeds

1/2 teaspoon celery seeds

1 teaspoon powdered turmeric

3 cups thinly sliced onions

2 large sweet red peppers, chopped

1 hot green or red pepper, chopped (optional)

Combine tomato slices and salt. Let stand overnight, then drain, discarding liquid. In an open kettle, heat vinegar to boiling and add sugars and spices. Simmer 5 minutes, then add onions and simmer another 5 minutes. Add drained tomato slices and peppers and return slowly to a boil. Simmer 5 minutes more, stirring occasionally with a wooden spoon. Pack, boiling hot, into hot, sterilized jars to 1/4 inch of tops, making sure syrup covers vegetables in each jar. Seal at once. Process 10 minutes in boiling water bath.

MAKES 4 TO 6 PINTS.

SWEET PICKLE RELISH

1 gallon (about 32) green tomatoes

2 medium onions

4 green peppers

2 sweet red peppers

1/2 cup flaked pickling salt

1 teaspoon mixed pickling spices

1 tablespoon celery seed

3 (3-inch) cinnamon sticks

3 cups vinegar

1 cup water

2 cups sugar

Wash and core tomatoes. Peel onions. Core and seed peppers. Run all through coarse blade of food chopper. Mix in salt and let stand overnight. In the morning, drain well, discarding liquid. Tie mixed pickling spices in a cheesecloth bag and add to vegetables and remaining ingredients in an open kettle. Slowly bring to a simmer over low heat, stirring occasionally. Cook 30 minutes. Remove cinnamon sticks and cheesecloth bag and discard. Ladle relish into hot, sterilized jars and seal at once. Process 10 minutes in boiling water bath.

MAKES 12 PINTS.

PICCALILLI

32 medium green tomatoes

1 large head cabbage

4 medium sweet red peppers

1 large onion

1/2 cup flaked pickling salt

1 1/2 cups brown sugar

2 tablespoons mustard seed

1 tablespoon celery seed

1 tablespoon prepared horseradish

4 1/2 cups vinegar

Wash and core tomatoes and cabbage. Core peppers and remove seeds. Peel onion. Run all through coarse blade of food chopper. Sprinkle with salt and mix well. Let set overnight and drain thoroughly in the morning, pressing to remove as much liquid as possible. Discard liquid. Meanwhile, add sugar, spices and horseradish to vinegar and bring to a boil. Simmer 15 minutes, then strain vinegar over vegetables and discard spices. Heat vegetables to boiling and pack into sterilized pint jars to within 1/2 inch of tops. Process 10 minutes in boiling water bath.

MAKES ABOUT 6 PINTS.

Using Green Tomatoes as a Vegetable

STEWED GREEN TOMATOES

3 medium onions

2 tablespoons cooking oil

6 large green tomatoes

1/2 cup water

2 tablespoons butter or margarine

1 tablespoon sugar

1/2 teaspoon salt

Peel and thinly slice onions. Sauté in cooking oil until transparent, but not browned. Meanwhile, peel and core green tomatoes and cut into 1/4-inch slices. Add to skillet and sauté, stirring gently two to three minutes. Add water, cover and simmer 10 minutes, until tomatoes are soft. Season to taste with butter or margarine, sugar and salt.

SERVES 6 TO 8.

FRIED GREEN TOMATOES

1 medium green tomato per person

Flour

Salt and pepper

Cooking oil

Wash, core and slice tomatoes in 1/3-inch slices. Do not peel. Dip each slice in flour, season to taste with salt and pepper and fry until golden in hot oil. Drain on paper toweling, then serve hot with butter or margarine.

BROILED GREEN TOMATOES

Select one large green tomatoes for each two servings. Wash and core tomatoes and cut in halves. For each half, dice 1/2 slice bacon. Arrange uncooked bacon bits on tomato halves and sprinkle with Parmesan cheese. Broil 10 minutes, or until bacon is crisp and tomato top is lightly browned.

Using Green Tomatoes in Main Dishes

GREEN TOMATO CROQUETTES

2 cups canned or fresh tomatoes, chopped and drained

Cracker crumbs, finely rolled

Salt and pepper to taste

Hot oil for frying

To the chopped tomatoes add enough cracker crumbs to make a mixture easy to handle. Shape into 1 1/2-inch balls or cylinders four inches long. Roll in cracker crumbs or flour and fry in hot cooking oil at least two inches deep. Serve as a meat substitute or accompaniment.

SERVES 6.

SPINACH LOAF

2 eggs, well beaten

1 cup cooked spinach, chopped

2 1/2 cups green tomatoes, chopped and drained

1 cup cheddar cheese, shredded

1 cup soft bread crumbs

Salt and pepper

3 slices bacon, diced

1 tablespoon minced onion

1 tablespoon green pepper, chopped

2 tablespoons flour

Combine eggs, spinach, 1 cup green tomatoes, cheese and bread crumbs. Season to taste with salt and pepper and put in a greased loaf pan. Bake in 350°F oven 30 minutes. Serve hot with sauce made by frying diced bacon until crisp. Sauté onion and green pepper in bacon fat. Add remaining 1 1/2 cups chopped green tomatoes and stir fry 3 to 5 minutes, until tomato is cooked. Stir in flour and cook until thickened. Season to taste and pour over loaf.

SERVES 6.

Continued →

CHEESE LOAF

2 cups canned or fresh green tomatoes, chopped and drained

1 egg

Day-old bread crumbs

1 cup cheddar cheese, grated

Salt and pepper to taste

1 tablespoon onion, finely chopped

1/2 cup catsup

Combine green tomatoes and egg. Add as much bread crumbs as the mixture will absorb. Add cheese, seasoning and onion and shape into a loaf. Bake in 350°F oven 30 to 40 minutes, until the loaf is firm and beginning to brown. Decorate top with catsup and return to oven 5 minutes more. Serve as a main course.

SERVES 4 TO 6.

GREEN TOMATO OMELET

1 tablespoon onion, minced

1/4 cup green tomato, chopped fine

2 tablespoons butter or margarine, melted

2 eggs, well beaten

Salt and pepper

Sauté onion and green tomato in melted butter or margarine in a small skillet over low heat until onion is transparent and green tomato pieces are lightly browned. Spread evenly over bottom of pan and pour beaten eggs over all. Season to taste with salt and pepper. Cook over low heat. As egg begins to firm, lift edges and tilt pan to allow liquid to run underneath. Cook until bottom is golden brown and top is set but still moist. Fold over and serve hot. Increase ingredients in proportion for larger omelets or make one or more omelets per person.

MAKES ONE OMELET.

SCALLOPED EGG — GREEN TOMATO CASSEROLE

6 hard-cooked eggs, peeled and sliced

1 1/2 cups cubed green tomatoes, drained

5 tablespoons butter or margarine

3/4 cup soft bread crumbs

3 tablespoons flour

1 1/2 cups milk

1/2 teaspoon salt

Cover bottom of a casserole dish with half of egg slices. Top with half of green tomato cubes. Repeat. In a saucepan, melt 2 tablespoons butter or margarine and add bread crumbs. Stir well, then empty onto piece of waxed paper and set aside. Melt remaining butter or margarine in saucepan and stir in flour. Gradually add milk and salt and cook over low heat, stirring constantly, until thick. Pour sauce over eggs and green tomatoes in casserole and top with buttered bread crumbs. Bake in 350°F oven 30 to 45 minutes.

SERVES 4 TO 6.

SPANISH CASSEROLE

1 pound ground beef

1 small onion, minced

1 tablespoon green pepper, chopped

1 tablespoon sweet red pepper, chopped

1 1/2 pounds firm green tomatoes, thickly sliced (about 5 cups)

1/2 teaspoon salt

1/4 teaspoon garlic salt

1/4 teaspoon ground cumin seed

Dash of cayenne

1 cup tomato sauce

1 1/2 cups canned or frozen whole kernel corn, cooked

Sauté beef, onion and green and red peppers in medium skillet. Add remaining ingredients and mix well. Pour into oiled casserole. Bake 30 to 45 minutes in 350° oven.

SERVES 6.

BUSY DAY CASSEROLE

1 pound ground beef

1 small onion, chopped

1/2 green pepper, chopped

1 clove garlic, minced

1 teaspoon salt

2 cups tomato sauce

4 medium green tomatoes, sliced

1 cup cheddar cheese, shredded

Sauté ground beef, onion, green pepper and garlic until meat loses its red color. Add salt and tomato sauce and cook over low heat 15 to 20 minutes, until thickened. Spread one-half of the green tomato slices in the bottom of a greased casserole dish, top with one-half the cheese, then with one-half the ground beef mixture. Repeat layers. Bake 30 minutes in 350°F oven.

SERVES 6.

Using Green Tomatoes in Desserts

GREEN TOMATO PIE

Pastry for two-crust pie

2 cups green tomatoes, cut in 1/2-inch cubes

Pinch of salt

1 tablespoon flour

1 tablespoon lemon juice

1 tablespoon butter or margarine

1 teaspoon powdered cinnamon

1/4 teaspoon ground nutmeg

1 cup sugar

Line a 9-inch pie pan with one-half the pastry. Roll out remainder for top and cut four 1-inch slits in the center. Combine remaining ingredients and fill pie shell. Top with rolled-out pastry and crimp edges to seal. Bake 45 minutes in 350°F oven.

SERVES 6.

OATMEAL CRUMBLE

3 cups canned or fresh green tomatoes, chopped and drained (reserve 1/4 cup juice)

1/2 cup brown sugar

1/4 teaspoon powdered cinnamon

1/4 cup reserved juice

2/3 cup flour

1/8 teaspoon salt

1/4 teaspoon baking soda

2/3 cup uncooked rolled oats

1/3 cup sugar

1 tablespoon butter or margarine

1/4 cup butter, margarine or vegetable shortening, melted

Spread chopped green tomatoes in the bottom of a greased shallow baking pan. Sprinkle with brown sugar and cinnamon which have been mixed. Dot with 1 tablespoon butter or margarine cut into pieces. Pour juice over top. In a mixing bowl, combine flour, salt, soda, oats and sugar. Stir in melted shortening to make a crumbly mixture. Spread evenly over the green tomato mixture. Bake in a 350°F oven until lightly browned. Serve warm plain or with cream.

SERVES 6.

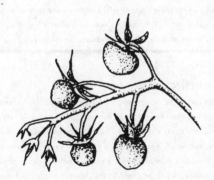

GREEN TOMATO SPICE CAKE

2 cups green tomatoes, chopped

1 1/2 cups sugar

1/2 cup vegetable shortening

2 eggs, beaten

2 teaspoons baking soda

1 teaspoon salt

1 teaspoon powdered cinnamon

1/2 teaspoon ground nutmeg

1/2 teaspoon powdered cloves

2 cups flour

1/2 cup seedless raisins

1/2 cup walnuts, chopped

Simmer chopped green tomatoes and 1/2 cup sugar until tomatoes are well cooked and transparent. Strain through a colander or sieve to remove seeds, cores and skins. There should be 1 1/4 cups pulp. Cool. Cream remaining 1 cup sugar and shortening until fluffy. Add the eggs. Blend soda into cooled tomato pulp and add gradually to creamed mixture, beating well after each addition. In a separate bowl, combine salt, spices and flour. Gradually add all but one cup of the flour mixture to the batter, beating well. Finally, add raisins and nuts to remaining 1 cup flour and mix to coat well. Add, all at once, to batter and beat well. Pour into a well-greased and floured square cake pan and bake in 350°F oven 35 to 40 minutes, until lightly browned and the touch of a finger does not leave an impression. Serve plain or frosted.

GREEN TOMATO BREAD

8 to 10 medium green tomatoes

2/3 cup seedless raisins

2/3 cup boiling water

2/3 cup vegetable shortening

2 2/3 cups sugar

4 eggs

3 1/3 cups flour

2 teaspoons baking soda

1 1/2 teaspoons salt

1/2 teaspoon baking powder

1 teaspoon powdered cinnamon

1 teaspoon powdered cloves

2/3 cup pecans, or walnuts, coarsely chopped

Peel and core green tomatoes. Discard seeds. Run cut-up pieces through blender until smooth and creamy. You should have 2 cups pulp. Set raisins to soak in 2/3 cup boiling water and set aside to cool. In a large mixing bowl, cream shortening and sugar until fluffy. Add eggs, 2 cups tomato pulp and the plumped raisins and water in which they were soaked. Beat well. In another bowl, combine flour, soda, salt, baking powder, cinnamon, cloves and nuts. Add, one cup at a time, to mixture in large bowl, stirring well after each addition. Divide batter into two 9 x 5-inch greased loaf pans and bake in 350°F oven 1 hour, 10 minutes, or until toothpick inserted in center comes out clean.

Fast and Easy Ways to Cook Vegetables

Penny Noepel

Variety is more than the spice of life . . . it is a key element in good nutrition. Vegetables add variety to our meals with their colors, flavors and textures. We can add to this variety in a number of ways:

Continued ➡

- Change the shape/form of the vegetable as in slicing, dicing, grating etc.

- Use different methods of preparation/cooking

- Serve a vegetable with or in a sauce

- Combine two or more vegetables for a new taste treat

Vegetables are most flavorful and nutritious, however, with a minimum of preparation. For this reason they are the ultimate convenience food. Most can be eaten with just a rinsing off or a little scrubbing under running water. When cooking, use only a minimum of water (if any) and don't overcook!

A WORD ABOUT SODIUM

Although sodium is a necessary nutrient, it occurs naturally in adequate amounts in foods (including vegetables); we don't really need to use salt in our cooking. Babies who don't get salt in their food don't miss it, but those of us who have acquired a taste for salt seem to think that it makes foods, especially vegetables and eggs, taste better. Because some people, primarily older persons, find that salt and salty foods cause fluid retention, and because sodium is associated with high blood pressure, many cooks are choosing to leave it out of cooking.

A sensible approach is to moderate our use of salt, in the same way we moderate our intake of fats and sugars. Salt in modest amounts is found in some of the recipes in this bulletin. Feel free to cut down or leave it out if you wish, or if your doctor recommends that you do so.

NUTRITION NOTES

All vegetables contain complex carbohydrates, and most Americans don't get enough complex carbohydrates in their diet. Vegetables also contain some protein—about 2 grams per 100-gram (1/2 – cup) serving. Three servings of vegetables contain about as much protein as one ounce of lean meat. The quality of vegetable protein is enhanced when meat, dairy products, grains, or beans are eaten at the same meal (or within an hour or two of each other).

Vegetables and fruits are also high in food fiber (roughage), particularly when eaten raw and with their skins on. Peas, green and dried beans, apples, and celery are all excellent sources of roughage.

To conserve the food value of cooked vegetables, use only a small amount of water (or none) and cook until just tender. Stir-fried vegetables should be tender yet crisp. Save the cooking liquid, if any, to use in soups, stews, and sauces. Or drink it!

All vegetables are not created equal. The color of a vegetable can indicate vitamin content. Generally, the darker green or the deeper orange, the more vitamin A. Broccoli, dark leafy green vegetables, carrots, yams, sweet potatoes, and hard-skinned winter squash are especially good sources of vitamin A. Vitamin C is destroyed by contact with air and by prolonged cooking. To minimize its loss, prepare your vegetables shortly before cooking, or eat them raw.

Nutritionists recommend three to five servings of vegetables daily, including dark green or orange vegetables three or four times a week.

Which Will It Be—Fresh, Frozen or Canned?

Vegetables are best fresh, and the fresher the better. Nothing beats vegetables harvested right from your own garden moments before a meal.

Next best to fresh is *frozen*. Frozen vegetables are harvested at the peak of maturity (ripeness), quality, and nutrition, and quickly processed to retain as much of their wholesomeness as possible. Because frozen vegetables have been partially cooked by blanching, they require less cooking time than fresh vegetables.

Canned vegetables need only reheating. Since some of the vitamins, minerals, and flavor are in the vegetable liquid, plan to save the liquid for use in soups, stews, sauces, or vegetable juice cocktails. Although canned vegetables are inferior in taste and texture to fresh or frozen, they are convenient to keep on hand for instant or emergency uses.

If you are preparing a recipe that calls for a small amount of vegetables and you want to avoid waste, it is easy to get just the amount you need from a supermarket salad bar. Suppose you want 1/2 cup of sliced mushrooms, a few strips of green pepper, or 1/4 cup of black olives for garnish. Buy just what you need and none will go to waste.

Storing Vegetables

Correct storage is vital to vegetables' taste and freshness, and necessary to preserve their vitamin content. Some vegetables need to be wrapped or covered in the refrigerator to prevent moisture loss.

STORAGE GUIDE FOR FRESH VEGETABLES

Store in a Cool Room, Away from Bright Light: Mature onions, potatoes, sweet potatoes, waxed turnips, winter squash.
Refrigerate Covered, or keep in vegetable crisper: Asparagus, beans (snap or wax), beets, broccoli, cabbage, carrots, cauliflower, celery, corn (if husked), cucumbers, leafy greens, leeks and scallions, parsnips, peas (if shelled), green peppers, radishes, summer squash, turnips (unless waxed). **Refrigerate Uncovered**: Lima beans and peas in pods, corn in husks. Vegetables kept in a refrigerator's vegetable crisper will keep well for several days or longer. If you don't have a crisper, a closed plastic bag is a good substitute. **Store at Room Temperature**: Tomatoes.

STORAGE POINTERS

For optimum nutritive value, color, and eating quality, harvest or hold vegetables the least possible time before preparing and cooking. As vegetables mature their sugar turns to starch, which is why older peas and corn are less sweet. You can add a pinch of sugar when cooking older vegetables, but *never* add baking soda. This was done in past generations to keep a bright green color, but properly cooked vegetables retain their lively green color anyway. Baking soda in cooking water destroys many nutrients—especially the B vitamins.

Cooking Methods

STEAMING

This is an easy, practical, and economical way to cook vegetables. No other method preserves the flavor, color, and texture of fresh or frozen vegetables quite so well.

If you don't own a steamer, you can suspend a colander over boiling water in a saucepan, or buy an inexpensive collapsible steamer-basket. Put a small amount of water (no more than one inch) in a saucepan with a tight-fitting lid, bring the water to a boil, and cover. Adjust the heat so the water will keep boiling but not boil away. Steam until the vegetables are just tender. Allow three to five minutes longer than you would to cook the same vegetable in boiling water.

BOILING

Place vegetables in a saucepan or pot with 1/2–1 inch of water. Cover and bring to a boil, then reduce the heat and boil gently until vegetables are just tender. Drain the liquid to keep the vegetables from getting soggy. Season lightly with salt, pepper, and butter, if you wish. (If you have used salt in the water, probably no more is needed.)

Save the flavorful cooking water and keep it in a jar in the freezer. When it's full, time to make soup!

Pots and pans are available that can cook food with very little water. Such utensils are sometimes called waterless cookware.

STIR FRYING

This is a quick-cooking method, ideal for mixed, tender vegetables. The vegetables are thinly sliced (sometimes on an angle) and cooked quickly in a tiny amount of very hot oil in a wok, frying pan, or electric skillet. I prefer electric woks or skillets for their large, uniformly hot cooking surfaces. Allow two teaspoons of oil for one pound of vegetables. Peanut oil is a good choice because of its high smoking point. Vegetables which need longer cooking are put in first, and the more tender ones added later so that they'll all be done at the same time. The Chinese use peanut oil, but you can use any vegetable oil except olive oil.

MICROWAVING

Just a sprinkling of water (or none at all) is needed to retain the bright colors, flavors, and textures of the vegetables. You can cook them in the same dish from which they will be served. Vegetables reheat well in the microwave, and they usually—but not always—cook faster than in conventional ovens. The cooking time is determined by several factors: the size, shape, maturity, and density of the vegetables or vegetable pieces, and the quantity and placement of the vegetables in the unit. The timetables in your instruction book are only a guide, and approximate at best. Microwave ovens vary in wattage: the larger ones usually have the highest wattage and require the least cooking time; compact models may have as few as 400 watts and therefore require almost half again as much cooking time. Get to know your oven and keep a record—your experience will be your guide.

Microwave ovens almost always have cold spots. Because of this and the fact that food cooks more slowly in the center of the oven, you should stir the vegetables halfway through the cooking process. Sometimes it's possible to arrange the vegetables (or other food) in a ring, thus avoiding the center of the oven, for more even cooking.

VEGETABLES ON THE GRILL

When you're cooking outside on a grill or hibachi, it's easy to cook your vegetables along with the meat. Simply place sliced vegetables such as carrots, onions, squash, cauliflower, peas, etc., on a square of heavy-duty foil. Add a few teaspoons of water (but not to summer squash), a little butter or margarine, and lightly salt if you wish. Fold the packet, overlapping the foil to make a sealed envelope. Place it on the grill and cook until the vegetables are tender. To shorten cooking time, cut less tender vegetables, such as carrots, into thinner pieces.

Vegetables placed directly on the grill take on a barbecued flavor, and cook in less time than in foil. Some vegetables, such as onions and carrots, need to be partially cooked beforehand, especially if they are to join other vegetables on skewers, as in vegetable kabobs. Mushrooms, green peppers, cherry tomatoes, onions, and chunks of zucchini are especially good this way, and can be enhanced by brushing them with Italian dressing or a marinade, or by marinating ahead of time. Young zucchini can be split lengthwise and brushed with oil to which seasoned salt, or a combination of onion powder, garlic powder, salt, pepper, and paprika have been added. Grill, turning occasionally until just tender and slightly brown—10 to 20 minutes or more, depending on size and the heat of the grill. Delicious!

Asparagus

- Break off the lower part of the stalk at the point where it snaps easily. Clean stalks well. Now gather them into a bundle and secure it with string or a rubber band. Stand the bundle upright in a tall pan in about one inch of water. Cover, or invert a bowl over the pan to form a tall steam chamber (or use a tall coffee pot). Bring the water to a boil and steam for 3–4 minutes, or until the stalks are tender. Now remove the string or rubber band, and serve the asparagus with a little salt, pepper, and butter.

- Cut asparagus stalks into one-inch lengths. Cook in a pot or a covered skillet in a very small amount of water, or place in a steamer. Cook until just tender, about 3 minutes.

- Place asparagus spears in microwave-safe covered dish with the tips toward the center. Or cut the spears into short lengths and place the tip pieces in the center of the dish. Microwave on high until tender. The time depends on the power (wattage) of your oven, but it will be about 2–3 minutes.

ASPARAGUS SALAD

Simply place cold, cooked asparagus on a lettuce leaf and pour on a small amount of your favorite salad dressing. Or marinate cold, cooked asparagus in Italian dressing and serve it on lettuce with deviled eggs on the side.

Beets

Boil or steam beets until they're tender. After being plunged into cold water, the skins will slip off quite easily, or you can peel them before cooking. If you don't peel them first they'll keep their color when steamed, pressure-cooked, or microwaved. Cutting them into different shapes such as julienne, slices, or wedges, or grinding them into "jewels," will save cooking time as well.

The next time you're preparing beets, try a piece raw—surprisingly good!

Continued →

281

BEETS IN ORANGE SAUCE

1 cup cooked beet "jewels" (beets ground, or finely chopped in a food processor)

1 tablespoon corn starch

1 teaspoon butter

1/2 cup orange juice

Combine the above ingredients and boil 1 minute. The beets may be shredded (before or after cooking) rather than ground.

MAKES 2 SERVINGS.

Broccoli

Cut off the thick stems (these can be peeled and sliced lengthwise for crunchy, low-calorie nibblers). Wash the dark green leaves (nutrition-packed) and broccoli branches. Slit the stem once or twice lengthwise to allow for even cooking. Stand the branches in a pot with flowerets up, or place them in a steam basket. Put a small amount of water in the pan, cover it tightly, and cook until just tender. Serve with butter, margarine, lemon juice, or sprinkled with Parmesan cheese.

Stir-fry or steam the lower stems (thinly sliced across the grain). They are tender and delicious, and add a nice texture, similar to water chestnuts.

Raw broccoli is good added to salads, and makes good dippers.

GREEN DUMPLINGS

1 cup ricotta or cottage cheese

1 cup chopped cooked broccoli or spinach (or 1/2 package frozen, chopped spinach)

salt, pepper, parsley to taste

1 small egg, beaten

1/2 cup flour

Make sure the vegetable is chopped fine. Mix all the ingredients together, then roll the dough into little balls and roll them in flour on a flat surface. Cook gently in boiling water or chicken broth for about 8–10 minutes. Serve with butter and grated cheese.

MAKES 2–3 MAIN DISH SERVINGS.

Cabbage

Quick Steamed Cabbage

- Finely shredded cabbage cooks in a steamer or a small amount of salted water in 3–5 minutes. Drain and serve hot with a bit of butter.

- Cook shredded cabbage for 2–3 minutes in a covered microwave-dish. No water is necessary.

QUICK CORNED BEEF AND CABBAGE

A filling and economical main dish.

1/2 cup chopped onion

1–2 tablespoons hot fat or oil

3 cups finely shredded cabbage

1/2 of 12-ounce can corned beef

1/2 teaspoon salt

1/4 teaspoon pepper

1/2 cup water

Sauté the onion in the hot fat, then stir in the remaining ingredients. Cover and cook for 6–8 minutes.

MAKES 4 SERVINGS.

FRESH CABBAGE MAKES A NICE DINNER VEGETABLE

Shredded, it takes only a few minutes to cook. For the best flavor and to retain nutrients, use only a small amount of water, or steam the cabbage. Cook until just tender. Leftover cabbage can be added to soup, either canned or homemade.

CABBAGE SOUP...A GENERAL RECIPE

Make this soup using the stock from your New England Boiled Dinner. Mash any leftover vegetables (potatoes, carrots, turnips) and add cabbage, shredded if necessary. Add 1–2 teaspoons of caraway seeds and simmer for 20–30 minutes.

Carrots

CARROT RAISIN SALAD

Shred raw carrots. Moisten them with mayonnaise, or mayonnaise thinned with orange or pineapple juice. Add raisins if desired.

Crushed pineapple makes a nice addition to this salad, or add a little shredded coconut.

CARROT CUCUMBER SOUP

3 medium carrots

1 1/2 cups milk

1 pint (2 cups) sour cream, yogurt, or buttermilk

1 medium cucumber, cut up

3 green onion bulbs

1 1/2 teaspoons garlic salt

1/2 teaspoon allspice

dash pepper

Chop the carrots in a blender with 1/2 cup water, then cook until tender. In a blender, place the milk, sour cream, cucumber, onion, garlic salt, allspice and pepper. Chop. Pour into a bowl. Stir in the cooked carrots. Chill. Garnish with cucumber slices, carrot curls, or fresh dill.

MAKES ABOUT 4 1/2 CUPS.

Celery

You don't have to entertain guests to enjoy an appetizer of stuffed celery. It goes nicely with fruit juice or tomato juice cocktail.

STUFFED CELERY

Wash celery stalks and dry them. There's no need for peeling unless the strings are tough, which may be the case if you're using the outer stalks (I save these for soup, or to chop and use in salads or sandwich fillings and casseroles). Fill the crisp, tender celery stalks with any of the fillings listed below. Chill well. Before serving, cut into bite-size pieces, about 1 inch long.

Fillings

- Mix softened cream cheese with seasoned salt to taste, adding a little onion powder or garlic powder (optional).

- Into a 3-ounce package of cream cheese, stir 4 chopped stuffed olives and 10 minced, blanched almonds, or a few walnuts and 1 tablespoon mayonnaise.

- Mash 2 tablespoons of blue cheese with a 3-ounce package of softened cream cheese, a small can of deviled ham, and some minced green pepper.

CELERY LEAVES

The outer, darker green leaves are stronger tasting and are good for flavoring, or for adding to green salads. The inner, lighter leaves are delicate and are nice chopped and added to sandwich fillings, salads, and soups. You can easily make cream-of-celery soup by cooking the chopped leaves and outer stalks in chicken broth until tender. Add to an equal amount of medium cream sauce, and season to taste. Blend until somewhat smooth.

Corn

CORN PUFF

1 cup sweet corn (cooked and cut from cobs, or frozen, or canned)

1 egg, slightly beaten

1/2 cup milk

1 tablespoon butter, softened

1 1/2 tablespoons flour

1/2 teaspoon salt

dash pepper

Preheat the oven to 350°F. Mix all the ingredients together, combining well. Bake in greased individual souffle or other baking dishes, or in a small casserole dish. To serve 4, double the ingredients and bake in a quart casserole.

MAKES 2 SERVINGS.
BAKING TIME: APPROX. 1/2 HOUR

CHILI CORN

To cook on the grill.

3–4 ears corn

1/4 cup (1/2 stick) butter

2 tablespoons chopped green pepper

1 tablespoon pimento

1/2 teaspoon salt

1/4 teaspoon chili powder

Husk the corn just before preparing this. Whip the butter until light. Stir in the green pepper, pimento, salt, and chili powder. Place each ear of corn on a square of double thickness heavy-duty aluminum foil. Spread them with about 2 tablespoons of the butter mixture. Wrap securely in foil, twisting the ends. Roast directly on medium coals 10–15 minutes, turning once.

MAKES 3–4 SERVINGS (1 EAR PER SERVING).

Foil-wrapped corn may also be baked in a preheated 425°F oven for about 25 minutes.

Cucumbers

EASY CUCUMBER SALAD

This recipe provides some guidelines—the amounts are up to you and your taste.

Peel cucumbers and slice them as thinly as possible. Put them in a bowl and add chopped or thinly sliced onions, salt and pepper, a dash or more of vinegar, a few teaspoons or tablespoons of cottage cheese, some fresh basil, and just enough salad dressing to suit you. For a good dressing, combine equal amounts of mayonnaise, catsup, and water with a dash each of onion and garlic powder, or fresh, minced garlic.

SHORT-CUT PICKLES

A "non-recipe" just for fun!

Buy a jar of your favorite pickles. When they're all gone, or even as you're still using them, put fresh cucumber or zucchini slices, quarters, or spears into the jar with the pickle juice. Refrigerate. After a few days or a week, your pickles will have absorbed the flavor and be similar to the pickles you purchased.

Dark Leafy Greens

NUTRITION NOTE

You can't beat the dark leafy greens for good nutrition. All are excellent sources of vitamins A and C. They contain appreciable amounts of iron, calcium, and potassium, and are the lowest in calories of any foods—fewer than 25 calories per 1/2 cup serving.

This class of vegetables includes such familiar favorites as spinach, beet greens, and Swiss chard, and the less common but equally tasty and nutritious collards, kale, and turnip greens.

All of the dark green leafy vegetables can be cooked in the same way. Use only a tiny amount of water and cook until just tender. You can easily remove the heavy ribs from larger leaves by pulling the leafy parts away from the center section. The stems and ribs of spinach, beet greens, and Swiss chard are tender, but should be placed in the bottom of the pot where they will get a little more moist cooking. Greens can also be steamed or cooked in the microwave. They require

Continued ➔

little cooking time. Small pieces of fresh, leafy greens make nice additions to tossed salads for color contrast, texture, and enhanced nutrition.

Kale is crinkly and a pretty blue-green color. Pieces of kale are often used as an attractive garnish in restaurants, and in seafood and deli displays.

If you are restricted in the use of salt, a simple sprinkling of lemon juice or vinegar will perk up the flavor of vegetables. Some people prefer lemon juice or vinegar on their cooked greens instead of the customary butter, salt, and pepper.

Eggplant

EASY LOW-CALORIE EGGPLANT PARMESAN

The amounts in this recipe do not need to be specific. Use your judgment to suit your own taste. Allow 2–4 slices per person if served as an entrée; 1–2 slices if served as a vegetable side dish.

eggplant (either peeled or unpeeled) cut into 1/2 inch-thick slices
salt (optional)
Italian seasoning—or a generous shake of basil and oregano
spaghetti sauce, or a meaty tomato-based sauce
Monterey Jack cheese, grated or sliced
Parmesan cheese, grated

Preheat the oven to 350°F. Place the eggplant slices in a casserole or baking dish (or in a lightly oiled or non-stick skillet if you want to cook this quickly on the top burner). Sprinkle with salt and seasonings or herbs. Top with the sauce or saucy meat. Now place the cheese on top of each slice and sprinkle with Parmesan cheese. Bake, covered, for about 10 minutes. Uncover and cook until the eggplant is tender and the cheese is bubbly (about 20 minutes).

MAKES 2 SERVINGS.

Green Snap Beans

Formerly called string beans, green beans and yellow wax beans are essentially stringless these days. It isn't even necessary to remove the tail, which is quite tender. Only the tougher head needs removing. Beans can be cut in several ways to add variety and eye appeal. Slit them lengthwise in several thin strips for French beans, cut them on the diagonal, or cut them crosswise in tiny round slices.

As with other vegetables, cooking beans until just tender preserves color, texture, and taste. Steaming is ideal and takes only 5–10 minutes, depending on the size and maturity of the beans. Green beans also perform well stir-fried with other vegetables.

- For an elegant touch, sauté slivered almonds in a little butter a few minutes over moderate heat, until the almonds turn golden. Toss with fresh-cooked beans and serve hot.

- Chopped onions cooked the same way do wonders for tender green beans.

- Sautéed mushrooms added to hot green beans create a simple but delicious side dish.

GREEN BEAN SALAD

A good way to use leftover green beans.

Simply add chopped onion to leftover green beans and marinate for an hour or so in your choice of dressing. Serve on a bed of lettuce or sprouts.

Mushrooms

FRESH MUSHROOM SAUTÉ

8 ounces mushrooms, more or less
2 tablespoons butter or margarine
2 teaspoons flour
salt and pepper

Wash the mushrooms and cut them through the caps and stems into thick slices or halves. Melt the butter in a skillet and add the mushrooms. Sprinkle them with flour, and toss to coat. Now cover the skillet and cook over low heat until tender, about 5–6 minutes, stirring occasionally. Season to taste with salt and pepper.

SERVES 2 AS A VEGETABLE OR 4 SERVINGS AS A MEAT ACCOMPANIMENT.

CREAMED MUSHROOMS

Prepare and cook mushrooms as above, but increase the flour to 1 tablespoon. Slowly stir in 3/4 cup light cream, half-and-half, or evaporated milk. Cook and stir until the mixture thickens. Serve over toast points.

Peppers

STUFFED PEPPERS

6 green peppers
1 1/4 cups minced, cooked meat
1 1/4 cups bread crumbs, moistened with water or stock
1 cup water or stock
1/2 teaspoon salt
1/8 teaspoon pepper
1/2 onion, grated

Preheat the oven to 350°F. Cut a slice from the stem end of each pepper. Remove the seeds and parboil peppers for 5 minutes. Mix the meat, crumbs, salt, pepper, and onion. Stuff the peppers with this mixture and place them in a baking pan. Add water or stock, and bake for about 1/2 hour, basting frequently.

MAKES 6 SERVINGS.

RAW PEPPERS

Peppers are delicious raw. Cut into strips, they make tasty nibblers for the relish tray. Cut in chunks, they make good dippers.

> **FREEZING**
>
> Chopped peppers, celery, onions, parsley, and chives are easy to freeze. Simply chop, spread out on cookie sheets, and when frozen, put into a plastic bag or rigid container and freeze.

Potatoes

Potatoes are an excellent complex carbohydrate food. They're virtually fat- and sodium-free, and contain only 85 calories per potato (2 1/2-inch diameter). They're also a good source of potassium and vitamin C, and contain iron, thiamine (B1), and niacin (B2).

CAMP-STYLE MASHED POTATOES

Scrub fresh, relatively new potatoes and (without peeling) cut them into quarters or eighths, depending on the size of the potato. Cook, tightly covered, in a 1/2 inch of slightly salted water until tender, or cook, covered, in a microwave. Mash, draining off water only if necessary (save it and add it back if possible). Add sour cream to taste and some butter or margarine if you can afford the extra calories. Quick, easy and delicious.

OVEN FRESH FRIES

A low-fat treat.

2 medium potatoes

2 teaspoons oil

salt

Preheat the oven to 450°F.

Peel the potatoes and cut them into long strips about 1/2 inch wide. Dry the strips thoroughly on paper towel, then toss them in a bowl with oil as if you're making a salad. When the strips are thoroughly coated with the oil, spread them in a single layer on a cookie sheet and cook in the oven for about 35 minutes. Turn the strips as needed to brown on all sides. Sprinkle with salt before serving.

MAKES 3 SERVINGS (ABOUT 85 CALORIES EACH).

POTATO PANCAKES

2 eggs

2 tablespoons flour

2 tablespoons milk

2 tablespoons butter, melted

1/2 teaspoon salt

dash pepper

1/2 small onion, peeled

3 medium potatoes, peeled

Mix the eggs, flour, milk, butter, salt, and pepper. Now grate the potatoes and onions and add them to the batter. Stir only until the potato shreds are coated. Drop the batter by 1/4-cup measures onto a hot, greased griddle or skillet to form 4-inch pancakes. Brown both sides and serve immediately with apple sauce.

MAKES 8 PANCAKES (3–4 SERVINGS).

Note: A food processor makes shredded potatoes in a flash.

Spinach

SPINACH SQUARES

4 cups uncooked fresh spinach, chopped (about 10 ounces)

2–3 tablespoons butter or margarine

3 eggs

1 cup flour

1 cup milk

1/2 teaspoon salt

1 teaspoon baking powder

3/4–1 pound Monterey Jack or cheddar cheese, grated

Preheat the oven to 350°F.

Wash the spinach well and pat or spin it dry. Melt the butter in a 9-inch by 13-inch pan in oven. Meanwhile, beat the eggs in a large bowl. Add the flour, milk, salt, and baking powder. Stir in the cheese and spinach. Mix well and pour into the buttered pan. Smooth the surface and bake for about 35 minutes. Cool for 20 minutes before cutting into 1-inch squares.

If you want to freeze these, arrange them on a cookie sheet and place it in the freezer. Once they're frozen, put them into a plastic bag. Reheat on a cookie sheet for about 20 minutes at 350°F, or if at room temperature, 20–35 seconds in a microwave oven.

MAKES 50 1-INCH SQUARES AS AN APPETIZER, OR 8 SERVINGS AS AN ENTRÉE.

SPINACH SALAD

1/4 pound bacon

1 hard-cooked egg

1 red onion, sliced and separated into rings

1 10-ounce package of spinach (fresh)

French salad dressing

Fry the bacon until it's crisp, then drain and crumble it. Dice the egg. Slice the onion and separate it into rings. Wash the spinach well and pat or spin it dry. Combine the other ingredient and pour on just enough French dressing to please. Toss lightly and serve.

MAKES 5–6 SERVINGS.

Continued ➜

Sweet Potato

SWEET POTATO PUDDING

1 cup mashed sweet potatoes

1–2 tablespoons brown sugar

1 egg, well-beaten

1 tablespoon melted butter

1/2 teaspoon salt

1/2 cup milk

1/2 teaspoon cinnamon (optional)

Preheat the oven to 350°F.

Combine all the ingredients and blend well. Pour into a buttered casserole dish, individual custard cups, or souffle dishes. Bake for about 30 minutes or until done.

Although this is usually served as a vegetable, I think it makes a tasty dessert. If you desire, put a tablespoon of marshmallow fluff or miniature marshmallows on each dish halfway through baking. Or top cooked and cooled pudding(s) with spiced whipped cream. As a dessert, serve warm or at room temperature.

MAKES 2–3 SERVINGS.

Tomatoes

STUFFED TOMATOES

This is a nice lunch or supper entrée.

Stand a fresh, firm-but-ripe tomato upright and slice it down into fourths, cutting only 2/3 of the way through. Spread the sections slightly apart. Put a mound of cottage cheese (flavored, if desired) or tuna salad in the center of each tomato. Serve them on a bed of shredded lettuce, or in a lettuce cup.

SCALLOPED TOMATOES

2 cups bread crumbs, dry or fresh

2 1/2 cups stewed or canned tomatoes

salt, pepper, sugar, onion powder, other seasonings to taste

2 tablespoons butter or margarine

Preheat the oven to 350°F.

Cover the bottom of a greased 1 1/2-quart baking dish with 1 cup bread crumbs. Add the tomatoes and season to taste.

Stir the remaining crumbs in melted butter and cover the tomatoes with them. Bake until well-browned, about 15 minutes.

MAKES 6 SERVINGS.

Turnips

The large, yellow variety of turnip is also known as rutabaga. Turnips in the grocery store are often coated with wax to keep the natural moisture in and to protect the firm texture so important to good quality. When peeled and cut into strips for eating raw, turnips are similar in taste and texture to carrot sticks. For a milder turnip flavor, or to help your family learn to eat turnips, mix hot, mashed turnips with mashed potatoes. Turnips require more time to cook than most any other vegetables. They also seem to require ample water. Cutting them into small pieces will save cooking time, or you can dice them in a food processor to make turnip jewels. This form can be boiled in a little water or cooked in a microwave.

Zucchini

Zucchini squash is very low in calories (less than 20 calories per half-cup serving) unless you use a cooking method which adds fat (100 calories per tablespoon). Yet you can use merely one tablespoon of oil to cook enough zucchini for 4 people, and the 25 extra calories per person are well worth the enhanced flavor.

Zucchini Favorites

- Brush an electric skillet or heavy frying pan with vegetable oil (not olive oil). Heat to 350°F or medium-high heat until the pan is piping hot. While it's heating up, cut the zucchini into 1/2-inch slices and quickly place in skillet in single layer. Cook slices, turning once until they're crisp and golden-brown. Sprinkle them lightly with salt. Serve hot.

- Stir-fry thinly sliced zucchini and onions in a minimum of hot oil (start with a teaspoon and add more if you need it), using very high heat and stirring frequently until the vegetables are tender-crisp. Sprinkle with a little salt or soy sauce.

- Stir-fry chunks of green pepper, onions, and zucchini until just tender. Add some tomato sauce or spaghetti sauce and stir. Cook some ramen noodles, drain, and cover with a slice of Swiss, Monterey Jack, or other cheese and top with the tomato-vegetable sauce.

ZUCCHINI QUICHE

1 cup biscuit mix

1/2 cup evaporated milk

4 eggs (unbeaten)

3–4 cups chopped or grated zucchini (about 1 pound)

1 cup sharp cheddar cheese, grated

1 teaspoon fresh chives, onion, or parsley

Preheat the oven to 350°F.

Mix well with a fork in a large bowl. Bake in a quiche pan or a large pie plate for 30 minutes or until brown. Let stand a few minutes before serving. It tastes just as good if reheated the next day.

MAKES 4–6 SERVINGS.

Cooking with Edible Flowers

Miriam Jacobs

Text illustrations by Mary Rich and Laura Tedeschi

COMMONSENSE CAUTIONS

Because edible flowers are new to many people, it's important to point out some safety issues. The most obvious one is that not all flowers are edible; in fact, quite a few are poisonous. *Eat only those flowers you are positive you can identify.* Do not experiment on your own; if you're unsure whether a flower is edible, don't add it to the menu until you've confirmed with an expert—a horticulturalist, a reference guide, or a nursery owner, for example—that it's safe to eat. In addition, if you have asthma or allergies, you will want to be just as cautious with edible flowers as you would be with other foods.

There's another "rule" when it comes to eating flowers: Eat them only if you are positive that they have been grown organically. Never eat flowers picked at the side of the road; they are polluted by automobile emissions. You should avoid flowers from a nursery as well; they most likely will have been sprayed with pesticides. Don't forget: Because flowers are not usually considered a food, they are likely to be sprayed with stuff you absolutely should not ingest. Pick them in your own garden (if you garden organically), find a nursery or herb shop that offers organically grown flowers, or get them from trusted friends with organic gardens.

The Best Blossoms for Eating

If your only criterion is that they be nonpoisonous, then many flowers are edible—but not all of them are yummy. Following are the best-known, most delicious edible flowers:

- Basil
- Chamomile
- Chives
- Dill
- Hibiscus
- Lavender
- Marigolds
- Nasturtiums
- Roses
- Sweet pea*
- Violas (pansies, Johnny-jump-ups, and violets)

*Note: Other parts of the sweet pea plant are poisonous—only the flower is edible!

Once you've prepared some of the recipes in this booklet, you'll be ready to experiment with other flowers. Again, be sure you can identify them! Try cooking with the blossoms of some of the following plants:

- Bee balm
- Borage
- Dandelion
- Daylily
- Fennel
- Honeysuckle
- Marjoram
- Mint
- Oregano
- Rosemary
- Thyme
- Yucca

Preparing Flowers for the Dinner Table

Flowers are among the most delicate of foods, and they need special care. Before you can eat or process flowers, you first need to wash them. Because of their fragile nature, the best method of washing is simply to rinse them quickly in cold water and gently shake off the remaining drops of water.

Fresh flowers don't keep particularly well, so it is best to use them freshly picked. If this isn't practical for you, you can also harvest them with their stems and place them in a vase with some water, just as you might do with any bouquet.

You can also dry flowers to save them for later use. Use a commercial dehydrator, if you have one, or simply place the blossoms on paper towels, where they will be dry in a day or two. Long-stemmed flowers can be hung to dry from racks, much like herbs. Store the dried flowers in airtight containers in a cool, dark location. As with all dried produce, be sure that the flowers are thoroughly dry before you pack them away, as excess moisture can cause mold to form.

The Best Dressings

The simplest way to use edible flowers is in salads. When doing so, be sure to use a mild dressing to avoid drowning out the flowers' delicate flavors. Serve the dressing on the side; pouring dressing over the flowers will quickly discolor them.

MUMU'S SWEET DRESSING

My mom made the following sweet dressing for fruit salads. Try it on salads that include roses, violets, pansies, or lavender.

3/4 cup (177 ml) mild-flavored vegetable oil, such as safflower

1/3 cup (79 ml) honey

1/4 cup (59 ml) freshly squeezed lemon juice

Place all ingredients in a blender and blend for 10 seconds. Any leftovers should be refrigerated and will keep for 1 week.

MAKES 1 1/3 CUPS (316 ML)

SAVORY SALAD DRESSING

For more savory salads, which might include basil flowers, nasturtium, and dill flowers, try this basic dressing.

3/4 cup (177 ml) extra-virgin olive oil

1/4 cup (59 ml) balsamic vinegar

1 tablespoon (15 ml) Dijon-style mustard

1/4 teaspoon (1.3 ml) salt

1/4 teaspoon (1.3 ml) freshly ground black pepper

Continued ➜

Place all ingredients in a blender and blend for 10 seconds. Any leftovers should be refrigerated and will keep for 2 weeks.

MAKES 1 CUP (237 ML)

Basil Flowers

I used to feel guilty when my basil bolted. But then I learned that you can eat the flowers! Basil flowers taste a little like the leaves and therefore make a great addition to any dish in which you use basil, such as pasta or pizza.

BASIL FLOWER SALAD

This unusual salad is easy to make and adds a touch of class to any dining table.

1 small head romaine lettuce

1 avocado

1/4 cup (59 ml) freshly grated Parmesan cheese

A handful of basil flowers

Oil-and-vinegar dressing

1. Wash the lettuce and tear the leaves into bite-size pieces. Place the lettuce in a serving bowl.

2. Peel and pit the avocado and cut it into bite-size pieces. Sprinkle the avocado pieces over the lettuce, then sprinkle Parmesan cheese over all.

3. Sprinkle basil flowers over the salad. Serve immediately, with dressing on the side.

MAKES 4 SERVINGS

BASIL FLOWER FRITTERS

2/3 cup (158 ml) flour

1/2 teaspoon (2.5 ml) salt, plus a pinch more if desired

1/4 teaspoon (1.3 ml) freshly ground black pepper

A pinch of ground cayenne pepper (optional)

1 egg yolk

1/3–1/2 cup (79–118 ml) beer (or nonalcoholic beer)

Vegetable oil, for frying

12 basil flower stalks

1. Line a plate with a double thickness of paper towels. In a small bowl, combine the flour, salt, black pepper, and cayenne. Add the egg yolk; mix until well blended.

2. The amount of beer to add depends on the humidity in the room. Add a little beer, whisking constantly; continue adding beer until the mixture is the consistency of thick pancake batter.

3. Fill a deep frying pan (or any thick-bottomed pan) with about 2 inches (5 cm) of oil. Set over high heat. Drop a little bit of batter into the oil and watch it carefully; when the batter starts to

brown, reduce the heat to medium. Pick up a basil flower stalk by the stem and swish it in the batter, making sure to coat the whole stalk except the part you are holding.

4. Place the batter-covered stalks into the hot oil, a few at a time. Fry until brown on both sides, turning once. (Take extreme care to keep your hands and forearms well away from the spattering of hot oil!)

5. Transfer the fritters to the paper towel–lined plate. Sprinkle with salt if you like; serve immediately.

MAKES 12 FRITTERS

TOMATO PESTO SOUP

This cold, fragrant, garlicky soup is perfect on a hot day. Make the tomato base early in the morning, when you won't mind having the stove on for a few minutes. Let the base cool in the refrigerator all day, and in the evening you can have delicious soup in 5 minutes.

2 tablespoons (30 ml) extra-virgin olive oil

1 medium onion, chopped

2 cloves garlic, chopped, plus 1 whole clove

2 pounds (908 g) very ripe tomatoes (about 6 medium tomatoes), chopped

1 cup (237 ml) loosely packed basil leaves

1 tablespoon (15 ml) lemon juice

1/4 cup (59 ml) freshly grated Parmesan cheese

A handful of basil flowers

1. Heat the oil in a large frying pan over medium-high. Add the onion; sauté until soft. Add the chopped garlic; sauté for 1 minute longer. Add the tomatoes; cook the mixture, uncovered, until the tomatoes are soft, about 15 minutes. Remove from heat and let stand until cool; then chill until serving time.

2. Place the basil leaves, lemon juice, and whole garlic clove in a blender. Add the chilled tomato mixture; blend well.

3. Pour the soup into individual soup bowls. Sprinkle each serving with Parmesan cheese and basil flowers. Serve cold.

MAKES 4 SERVINGS

FRESH TOMATO SAUCE

This homemade fresh pasta sauce hands-down wins out over the processed and preserved canned sauces of the grocery store.

2 pounds (908 g) ripe tomatoes (about 6 medium tomatoes)

2 tablespoons (30 ml) extra-virgin olive oil

1 onion, chopped

2 cloves garlic, minced

1/4 cup (59 ml) loosely packed basil leaves

1 cup (237 ml) basil flowers

Salt and freshly ground black pepper

1. With a sharp knife, make a shallow cross-shaped cut in the bottom of each tomato.

2. Bring a large pot of water to a boil. Turn off the heat and drop the tomatoes into the water. Let stand for a few minutes, until the skin looks loose. Remove the tomatoes from the water; let stand until slightly cooled. Peel off the skins and discard; coarsely chop the tomatoes, reserving any juice.

3. Heat the oil in a medium saucepan over medium-high. Add the onion; sauté until translucent. Add the garlic; cook for 1 minute more. Add the tomatoes and any juice; cook for 5 minutes. Remove from heat; let stand until slightly cooled.

4. Pour the tomato mixture into a food processor fitted with a metal blade; add the basil leaves. (You might have to do this in several batches.) Process the sauce to the desired thickness; you can make it completely smooth or leave it slightly chunky if you prefer. Return the sauce to the saucepan and season to taste with salt and pepper; heat to serving temperature.

5. To serve, pour the sauce over cooked pasta; sprinkle with basil flowers.

MAKES ENOUGH SAUCE FOR 4–6 SERVINGS OF PASTA

Chamomile

To dry chamomile flowers, pick them and lay them on a clean cloth or screen to dry in the sun. If they are not dry by the end of the day, finish drying them in the oven on very low heat. When the blossoms are thoroughly dry, store them in an airtight container.

CHAMOMILE TEA

This is a very soothing tea, great after a stressful day.

1 cup (237 ml) boiling water

1 teaspoon (5 ml) dried chamomile flowers

1 teaspoon (5 ml) honey or 1 lemon slice

1. Pour the boiling water into a teapot. Add the chamomile flowers; let steep for about 5 minutes

2. Pour the tea through a sieve into a cup. Serve immediately with honey or a slice of lemon.

MAKES 1 SERVING

Chive Blossoms

Chive blossoms are usually the first edible flowers to bloom in my garden, and they do so without any help from me. The strength of their flavor varies widely, so taste them before using them in a recipe. To use chive blossoms, cut the purple florets off the stem or simply pull them off in bunches.

COLD YOGURT, CUCUMBER, AND CHIVE BLOSSOM SOUP

For a more filling soup, add cold cooked and peeled shrimp.

2 cups (473 ml) plain yogurt

1/2 cup (118 ml) walnut halves

2 cloves garlic, minced

1/2 teaspoon (2. 5 ml) salt

1 large cucumber, peeled

6 chive blossoms, divided

1. In a food processor fitted with a steel blade, combine the yogurt, walnuts, garlic, and salt. Process until the walnuts are completely ground.

2. Pour the yogurt mixture into a bowl; set aside. Replace the food processor bowl (you do not have to wash it first). Fit the food processor with a coarse grating blade. Grate the cucumber.

3. Add the grated cucumber to the yogurt mixture; stir well. Chill until serving time.

4. Pour the soup into serving bowls. Remove the flowers from two of the chive blossoms and sprinkle them over the soup. Float the remaining whole chive blossoms on the soup as a garnish.

MAKES 4 SERVINGS

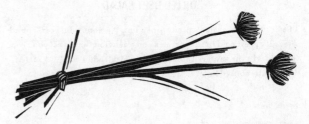

Continued →

HOME FRIES WITH CHIVE BLOSSOMS

1/4 cup (59 ml) extra-virgin olive oil

4 cups (946 ml) boiled or steamed potatoes, sliced

Salt and freshly ground black pepper

8 chive blossoms, florets snipped off and separated

1. Heat the oil in a heavy-bottomed frying pan over high.

2. Add the potato slices; cook until the bottoms begin to brown. Using a large spatula, turn the potatoes; sprinkle with salt and pepper to taste. Sprinkle with chive florets.

3. Continue cooking until the bottom is brown. Serve immediately.

MAKES 4 SERVINGS

CHIVE VINAIGRETTE

This recipe comes from my friend Joel Goodman, who also gave me some of his abundant chive blossoms to make it with. Be a little patient while adding the oil, and you will have a rosy dressing that is creamy, sweet, sour, and oniony all at the same time.

1/4 cup (59 ml) lemon juice

1/4 cup (59 ml) rice vinegar

1 tablespoon (15 ml) honey

8 chive blossoms, florets snipped off and separated

1 small clove garlic

1 cup (237 ml) extra-virgin olive oil

Salt and freshly ground black pepper

1. In a blender, combine the lemon juice, vinegar, honey, chive blossoms, and garlic. Blend until the blossoms are thoroughly liquefied.

2. With the blender running, add the oil a little at a time, blending completely after each addition, until all the oil is in and emulsified. Season with salt and pepper to taste. If you're not going to use the dressing right away, cover and refrigerate; it will keep for 1 day.

MAKES 1 CUP (237 ML)

Dill Flowers

Dill flowers taste like a combination of dill and anise. They're a great way to decorate dishes flavored with dill: Floating dill flowers in vichyssoise, for instance, is a pretty and delicious presentation.

DILLED BEET SALAD

The beets tint this salad a pretty pink. This is a wonderful year-round salad: It's great cold in the summer and a delicious way to eat your root vegetables in the winter. To turn it into a meal, add 1 cup (237 ml) of diced, fully cooked ham.

2 beets, peeled

3 medium potatoes, boiled and diced

3 hard-cooked eggs, chopped

2 medium Granny Smith apples, diced

1/4 cup (59 ml) minced onion

1/2 cup (118 ml) mayonnaise

1 teaspoon (5 ml) apple cider vinegar

1/4 teaspoon (1.3 ml) salt

1/4 teaspoon (1.3 ml) freshly ground black pepper

2 tablespoons (30 ml) dill flowers

1. Grate the beets in a food processor or by hand. In a large bowl, combine the grated beets, potatoes, eggs, apples, and onion.

2. In a small bowl, combine the mayonnaise, vinegar, salt, and pepper.

3. Pour the dressing over the beet-potato mixture and toss well. Sprinkle with dill flowers. Serve immediately or chill first.

MAKES 4 SERVINGS

DILLED SWEET POTATO

This recipe is for one very hungry person, and that is how it developed: I was famished and wanted something filling and satisfying. Of course you can double or quadruple the recipe if you're feeding others!

1 large sweet potato, peeled and cut in chunks

2 cloves garlic

1/4 cup (59 ml) chopped pecans

1 tablespoon (15 ml) extra-virgin olive oil

1 teaspoon (5 ml) butter

1 teaspoon (5 ml) sweet miso

3 dill flowers

1. Fill a large pot with about 1 inch of water. Bring to a boil. Place the sweet potato and garlic in a steamer basket and place in the pot, over the boiling water. Cover and let steam until the potato is tender.

2. Mash the sweet potato and garlic. Add the pecans, oil, butter, and miso; mix well.

3. Sprinkle the dill flowers over the potato mixture; serve immediately.

MAKES 1 SERVING

CUCUMBER–DILL FLOWER SALAD

1 medium cucumber

2 teaspoons (10 ml) salt

2 tablespoons (30 ml) apple cider vinegar

1 tablespoon (15 ml) sesame seeds

1 tablespoon (15 ml) dill flowers

1. Peel and thinly slice the cucumber. Sprinkle the salt over the cucumber slices and rub it into the surfaces. Place the cucumber slices in a colander and let drain for about an hour.

2. Using your hands or the back of a spoon, press any remaining moisture out of the cucumber. Transfer the slices to a serving bowl.

3. Sprinkle the cucumber slices with vinegar; toss to coat. Sprinkle with sesame seeds and dill flowers. Serve cold.

MAKES 3 OR 4 SERVINGS

DILL POTATO SALAD

Potato salad is a summertime must. Here the dill flowers add visual appeal and a subtly different layer of dill flavor.

6–8 new potatoes, diced

1 chive (white part only), minced

1/3 cup (79 ml) mayonnaise

1/3 cup (79 ml) chopped pimento-stuffed olives

1 tablespoon (15 ml) minced fresh dill

1 teaspoon (5 ml) Dijon-style mustard

1/2 teaspoon (2.5 ml) salt

4 dill flowers, flowers only

3 dill flowers stalks, for decoration

1. Fill a large pot with about 1 inch (2.5 cm) of water. Bring to a boil. Place the potatoes in a steamer basket and place in the pot, over the boiling water. Cover and let steam until the potatoes are tender.

2. In a medium bowl, combine the chive, mayonnaise, olives, dill, mustard, salt, and the four dill flowers. Add the warm potatoes to the dressing and toss to coat. Let stand until cool.

3. Spoon the potato salad into a serving bowl and decorate with the flower stalks. Serve immediately.

MAKES 4 SERVINGS

Hibiscus

I do not have hibiscus in my garden, but I can buy the dried flowers at my local herb shop. If you do grow this pretty flower, by all means dry the red petals yourself.

HIBISCUS TEA

This dramatic-looking red tea is very fresh and tart. It is also delicious iced.

1 teaspoon (5 ml) dried hibiscus flowers

1 cup (237 ml) boiling water

Honey

1. Place the dried hibiscus flowers in a warm teapot. Pour the boiling water over the flowers; let steep for 1 minute.

2. Pour the tea through a sieve into a cup. Sweeten with honey to taste; serve immediately.

MAKES 1 SERVING

PINK HIBISCUS RICE

This rice dish has a most unusual pink-purple color. The hibiscus gives the rice a slight tartness, while the currants make it sweet.

1 cup (237 ml) uncooked basmati rice

2 cups (473 ml) water

2 teaspoons (10 ml) dried hibiscus flowers

1/3 cup (79 ml) dried currants

1/4 teaspoon (1.3 ml) salt

Fresh hibiscus flowers (optional)

1. Place the basmati rice in a colander and rinse under running water until the water runs clear.

2. Place the water in a saucepan; add the dried hibiscus flowers. Bring the water to a rolling boil over high heat; add the rice, currants, and salt. Stir once; when the water returns to a boil, cover the pan and reduce the heat to very low. Simmer the rice mixture for 20 minutes.

Continued →

3. Fluff the rice; serve immediately. Top with hibiscus flowers, if desired.

MAKES 3 OR 4 SERVINGS

HIBISCUS STRAWBERRIES

The tart flavor and deep red color of hibiscus tea go perfectly with strawberries. Make this beautiful fruit salad in a clear glass bowl so you can really appreciate the vivid color.

1 tablespoon (15 ml) dried hibiscus flowers

1/2 cup (118 ml) boiling water

1 tablespoon (15 ml) honey

1 pint (473 ml) fresh strawberries, hulled, divided

1. Place the hibiscus flowers in a bowl; pour the boiling water over them. Let steep for 3 minutes.

2. Pour the tea through a sieve into a bowl or glass measuring cup. Add the honey; stir well. Let stand until cool.

3. Transfer the tea to a blender; add 2/3 cup (158 ml) of the strawberries. Blend until smooth.

4. Slice the remaining strawberries. Pour the hibiscus-strawberry sauce over the sliced berries, then chill for 1 hour. Serve cold.

MAKES 3 OR 4 SERVINGS

Lavender

The somewhat floppy, gray-green lavender leaves and long spikes of purple flowers create a soft corner in the garden. You can use the entire spike for decorating or for flavoring (try cooking it in milk for an unusual and delicious beverage!). However, for flavoring sugars and more delicate decorative concoctions, use only the small purple flowers.

LAVENDER CUSTARD

This easy-to-make custard is redolent with the delicate fragrance of lavender blossoms.

4 cups (946 ml) milk, divided

5 lavender spikes, divided

5 eggs, beaten

1 cup (237 ml) sugar

1 tablespoon (15 ml) vanilla extract

A pinch of salt

1. Preheat the oven to 350°F (177°C). In a double boiler set over simmering water, combine 1 cup (237 ml) of the milk and three lavender spikes; cook, without boiling, for 10 minutes.

2. Pour the lavender-scented milk through a sieve into a large bowl. Whisk in the remaining milk. Add the eggs, sugar,

vanilla, and salt; whisk well. Pour the mixture into a large, ovenproof, ceramic mold.

3. Stand the mold in a roasting pan. Carefully pour water into the roasting pan until it reaches a depth of about 2 inches (5 cm).

4. Bake the custard until a wooden skewer inserted in the center comes out clean, about 1 hour. Let stand until cooled to room temperature; if you're not going to eat it right away, keep it refrigerated.

5. To serve, loosen the edges with a knife and invert the custard onto a serving platter. Decorate with the flowers from the remaining lavender sprigs.

MAKES 4 SERVINGS

HERBES DE PROVENCE

This is a great holiday gift to make for friends and family, so be sure to dry extra lavender when your crop comes in. Add a tag with a recipe for the herb mixture.

1/4 cup (59 ml) dried thyme

3 tablespoons (45 ml) dried marjoram

2 tablespoons (30 ml) dried summer savory

1 teaspoon (5 ml) dried rosemary

1/2 teaspoon (2.5 ml) dried sage

1/2 teaspoon (2.5 ml) dried lavender flowers

Combine all the ingredients and store in an airtight jar. Crush the herbs between your fingers before adding them to food.

MAKES ABOUT 2/3 CUP (158 ML)

LAVENDER SUGAR

Keep in mind that most flavored sugars have a very mellow taste that won't stand up to strongly flavored dishes. Use your lavender sugar to add a subtle new flavor to mild foods such as vanilla icing and chamomile tea.

1/4 cup (59 ml) lavender flowers

1 cup (237 ml) granulated sugar

1. Dry the lavender flowers completely.

2. Alternate the sugar and flowers in several layers in an airtight container. Let stand for at least 2 weeks.

3. Sift the sugar to remove the flowers; store the sugar in an airtight container.

Variation: You can also make this with beautiful bits of lavender in the sugar. Combine the dried flowers and sugar in a food processor and process until the lavender is finely ground. (You can also pulverize the lavender in a coffee or spice grinder and then add it to the sugar, but be sure the grinder is very clean first. Otherwise, the lavender will pick up whatever flavors might linger.)

MAKES ABOUT 1 CUP (237 ML)

FROSTED LAVENDER STICKS

Excerpted from *Herbal Sweets*, by Ruth Bass (Storey Books, 1996)

Sugared, lavender flowers are a crisp, pretty nibble. For variety, substitute violets or rose petals for the lavender.

12 stalks fresh lavender flowers

1 egg white, beaten until frothy

1/2 cup (118 ml) granulated sugar

1. Dip the flowers of the lavender stalks in egg white, then roll in or dust with sugar. If you are worried about eating uncooked egg whites, substitute the proper amount of pasteurized, dried egg whites.

2. Air-dry on waxed paper

MAKES 1 DOZEN STICKS

SWORDFISH STEAK EN PROVENCE

Flour for dredging

Salt and freshly ground black pepper

1 2-inch-thick (5 cm) swordfish steak (about 1 pound; 454 g)

1 teaspoon (5 ml) Herbes de Provence

5 tablespoons (75 ml) butter

1/4 cup (59 ml) white wine

1. In a shallow bowl, combine the flour, salt, and pepper. Dredge the fish steak in the flour.

2. Press the herb mixture into the surface of the fish.

3. Melt the butter in a large skillet over medium heat; add the fish. Cook the fish for about 8 minutes, then turn it over.

4. Continue to cook for another 7 or 8 minutes, until the fish flakes easily when tested with a fork.

5. Transfer the fish to a warmed platter. Add the wine to the pan and turn the heat to high; cook until the liquid is boiling, scraping the pan to incorporate any remaining bits of fish. Pour the sauce over the fish and serve immediately.

MAKES ABOUT 4 SERVINGS

Marigolds

I've raised easy-to-grow potted marigolds for years, but I had no idea until recently that their flowers are edible! You eat only the petals, which are slightly bitter, but they are a great addition to salads and the following recipes.

MARIGOLD PILAF

2 tablespoons (30 ml) butter

1/4 cup (59 ml) diced onion

1 cup (237 ml) uncooked white rice

1 clove garlic, minced

1/2 teaspoon (2.5 ml) salt

2 cups (473 ml) water

1/4 cup (59 ml) raisins

3 tablespoons (45 ml) minced marigold petals

1 whole marigold

1. Melt the butter in a heavy saucepan over medium-high heat. Add the onion and sauté until transparent. Add the rice, garlic, and salt; mix well until all the rice is covered with butter.

2. Add the water, raisins, and minced marigolds; bring to a boil. Cover the pan, reduce the heat to low, and simmer for 20 minutes.

3. Fluff the rice and transfer it to a serving bowl. Carefully tear the petals from the remaining flower and sprinkle them over the rice. Serve immediately.

MAKES 3 OR 4 SERVINGS

Nasturtiums

Nasturtiums provide multiple pleasures: They are easy to grow, they have lovely bright flowers, and both the flowers and leaves are edible!

SAUSAGE AND PEPPERS WITH NASTURTIUM BLOSSOMS

This classic mix is equally tasty spooned over steaming hot pasta and scooped onto crusty French bread. Since this dish reheats very well, make it while the day is still cool and then simply warm it up for a hearty and flavorful supper.

2 tablespoons (30 ml) extra-virgin olive oil

1 onion, sliced, rings separated

2 cloves garlic, minced

1 red bell pepper, cored and cut into strips

1 green bell pepper, cored and cut into strips

Salt and freshly ground black pepper

1 pound (454 g) link-style chicken sausage, fully cooked, cut into 1-inch (2.5 cm) pieces

1/4 cup (59 ml) white wine

1/4 cup (59 ml) freshly grated Parmesan cheese

1 cup (237 ml) nasturtium blossom petals

1. Heat the oil in a large frying pan over medium-high. Add the onions; sauté until they start to turn brown. Add the garlic; cook for 1 minute longer. Add the peppers; cook, stirring often, until the peppers wilt. Add salt and pepper to taste.

Continued ➤

2. Add the sausage and wine to the pan. Cover and cook until the sausage is heated through, about 8 minutes.

3. Spoon the sausage and peppers into a serving bowl or over cooked pasta. Sprinkle with Parmesan cheese and nasturtium petals. Serve immediately.

MAKES 4 SERVINGS

NASTURTIUM SALAD WITH MARIGOLD-PETAL DRESSING

This lovely salad uses both the leaves and the flowers of this versatile plant.

For the dressing:
1 cup (237 ml) extra-virgin olive oil
1/4 cup (59 ml) apple cider vinegar
1 tablespoon (15 ml) Dijon mustard
1/4 cup (59 ml) marigold blossom petals, minced

For the salad:
4 cups (946 ml) mesclun salad mix
1 cup (237 ml) nasturtium leaves
A handful of nasturtium blossom petals
Marigold petals

Making the Dressing:
Whisk together the oil, vinegar, and mustard, then stir in the marigold petals.

Making the Salad:

1. Wash and thoroughly dry the salad mix. Line the salad bowl with the nasturtium leaves and place the salad mix in the center.

2. Sprinkle the nasturtium and marigold petals over the salad. Serve the salad with the Marigold-petal Dressing on the side.

MAKES 4 SERVINGS

Roses

Experiment with the roses in your garden to discover which are the most flavorful. Since fragrance and flavor are so closely linked, traditional nonhybridized roses probably provide the most flavor.

Don't be tempted to make a rose-flavored dish from that gift of a perfect dozen roses: All commercially grown roses are heavily sprayed with non–food grade pesticides and fungicides and are definitely *not* for human consumption.

ROSE STRAWBERRY JAM

This uncooked jam won't keep for very long, but it retains all the bouquet of fresh roses. To be sure you have a sweet jam, cut off all the white at the bottom of each rose petal. Rose water can be purchased in many specialty shops and Middle Eastern groceries.

3 1/2 cups (828 ml) sugar
2 cups (473 ml) rose petals
1 cup (237 ml) fresh strawberries, washed and hulled
2 tablespoons (30 ml) rose water
1/4 teaspoon (1.3 ml) orange extract
1/2 cup (118 ml) water
1 tablespoon (15 ml) lemon juice
1 package (3 ounces) liquid fruit pectin

1. Combine the sugar, rose petals, strawberries, rose water, and orange extract in a food processor fitted with a steel blade. Process, scraping down the sides several times, for 30 seconds.

2. In a small saucepan, combine the water, lemon juice, and pectin over high heat; bring to a boil. Boil the mixture for 3 minutes and then add it to the rose mixture in the food processor. Process until well mixed, about 30 seconds.

3. Pour as much jam as you will eat in the next month into clean jars. Pour the rest into freezer bags. Let jars and bags stand at room temperature overnight to set. Refrigerate the jam you will eat now and freeze the rest. (The frozen jam will keep for 2 to 3 months. Thaw as necessary.)

MAKES ABOUT 4 HALF-PINT JARS

RAS AL HANOUT

This spice mix can be used the way curry is used in Indian cooking; just like curry, its fragrance and flavor are nearly indescribable. It is the ground dried rose petals that make it so distinctly North African. Make this as a gift for special friends and add a recipe card so they'll know how to use it. Grind the cardamom, nutmeg, pepper, and coriander yourself if you can, but good-quality, store-bought spices will also give you amazing results.

1 tablespoon (15 ml) cinnamon
1 teaspoon (5 ml) ground cardamom
1 teaspoon (5 ml) ground nutmeg
1 teaspoon (5 ml) ground cumin
1/2 teaspoon (2.5 ml) freshly ground black pepper
1/4 teaspoon (1.3 ml) turmeric
1/4 teaspoon (1.3 ml) mace
1/4 teaspoon (1.3 ml) ground coriander
1 cup (237 ml) dried rose petals

Sift together all of the spices to remove any little stems and pieces. Toss with the rose petals and store in an airtight jar.

MAKES ABOUT 1 CUP (237 ML)

PERSIAN LAMB AND SPINACH STEW

This dish is my fantasy; it is possible that no person of Persian descent has ever cooked or eaten it! But the flavors and aromas sent me right to Scheherazade's tales. Serve this stew with Marigold Pilaf and pita bread.

2 tablespoons (30 ml) flour

2 tablespoons (30 ml) Ras al Hanout

1/2 teaspoon (2.5 ml) salt

2 pounds (908 g) shoulder blade lamb chops

1 tablespoon (15 ml) extra-virgin olive oil

4 cloves garlic, minced

4 scallions, chopped

2 cups (473 ml) water

1 10-ounce (292 g) package frozen spinach

Juice of 1/2 lemon

4 cups (946 ml) hot cooked white rice

1 cup (237 ml) plain yogurt (optional)

1. In a shallow bowl, combine the flour, Ras al Hanout, and salt. Dredge the lamb chops in the flour mixture; reserve the leftover flour mixture.

2. Heat the oil in a deep frying pan over medium-high. Add the lamb; brown on all sides (you may have to do this in two batches).

3. Add the garlic and scallions; sauté for 1 minute. Sprinkle the reserved seasoned flour over the mixture in the pan; stir well. Carefully add the water (it might splatter a bit), spinach, and lemon juice; stirring and scraping the pan constantly, bring the stew to a boil. Reduce heat, cover, and simmer for 45 minutes, stirring occasionally.

4. Scoop the hot stew over rice. Top each serving with a dollop of yogurt if desired; serve immediately.

MAKES 4 SERVINGS

CHERRY CLAFOUTI WITH ROSE-FLAVORED ICE CREAM AND ROSE-SCENTED WHIPPED CREAM

Cherries and roses go together very well, and in this dessert they pair up in three different ways. Although this dish involves many steps, it is very easy to make. If you like it a lot, you'll want to get a cherry pitter: It makes pitting the cherries a breeze.

For the clafouti:

1 1/2 pounds (681 g) fresh cherries, halved
    and pitted

3 eggs

1 cup (237 ml) milk

2/3 cup (158 ml) sugar

1/2 cup (118 ml) flour

1/4 cup (59 ml) butter

2 teaspoons (30 ml) vanilla extract

1 teaspoon (5 ml) rose water

For the ice cream:

1 pint (473 ml) good-quality vanilla ice cream

2 tablespoons (30 ml) rose water

For the whipped cream:

1/2 cup (118 ml) whipping cream

1 tablespoon (15 ml) sugar

2 teaspoons (30 ml) rose water

Making the Clafouti

1. Preheat the oven to 400°F (204°C) and butter a casserole dish. Place the cherries in the casserole.

2. Combine the eggs, milk, sugar, flour, butter, vanilla, and rose water in a blender. Blend the batter until smooth; pour the batter over the cherries.

3. Bake the clafouti for 45 minutes. (Note: Because this cake has a custardlike center, a toothpick inserted in the center will not come out clean.)

Preparing the Ice Cream

1. Let the ice cream stand at room temperature until slightly softened.

2. Transfer the ice cream to a large bowl; add the rose water and beat with a stiff spatula until combined. Return the ice cream to the freezer.

Making the Whipped Cream

1. Pour the cream into a chilled bowl. Beat the cream with an electric mixer until it starts to thicken.

2. While beating constantly, add the sugar and then the rose water. Beat until stiff.

Serving the Clafouti

Scoop ice cream and whipped cream onto warm servings of clafouti; serve immediately.

MAKES 6 SERVINGS

Continued →

NECTARINE–ROSE PETAL SALAD WITH RASPBERRIES AND PINE NUTS

This salad is built on soft but deep flavors and scents. It's a special dish for a summer meal, served perhaps with a glass of sauterne, Kir, or simply raspberry iced tea.

2 cups (473 ml) Boston lettuce leaves, washed and dried

1 cup (237 ml) rose petals, divided

4 ripe apricots, halved and pitted

1 cup (237 ml) raspberries, divided

1/2 cup (118 ml) pine nuts

Mumu's Sweet Dressing (see above)

1. In a large bowl, toss together the lettuce and half of the rose petals.

2. Cut the apricot halves into slices. Place the apricot slices in the bowl. Sprinkle with 3/4 cup (177 ml) raspberries and the pine nuts.

3. In a food processor or blender, combine the remaining raspberries with the salad dressing. Process until berries are pureed.

4. Sprinkle the remaining rose petals over the salad. Serve immediately, with the dressing on the side.

MAKES 4 SERVINGS

Sweet Pea Flowers

These delicate flowers are a beautiful decoration for any salad or cake. They have little flavor but offer a pleasant crunch. I have both white and purple sweet pea flowers in my garden; they look especially lovely when used together.

PEACH CAKE WITH SWEET PEA FLOWERS

Peaches are in season just when your sweet peas bloom, so it makes sense to combine them!

3 medium fresh peaches

3/4 cup sugar

1/4 cup (59 ml) butter, softened

1 egg

1/2 cup (118 ml) milk

1/4 teaspoon (1.3 ml) orange extract

1 1/2 cups (355 ml) flour

2 teaspoons (30 ml) baking powder

1 tablespoon (15 ml) sugar

Sweetened whipped cream

9 sweet pea flowers

1. Butter and flour a 9-inch-square (23 cm) pan. Preheat the oven to 375°F (191°C).

2. Cut the peaches in half around the pit and twist the halves apart. Remove the pit; slice each peach half into four sections.

3. Combine the sugar, butter, and egg in a food processor fitted with a steel blade. Process, scraping the sides occasionally, until well blended. Add the milk and orange extract; process until combined. Add the flour and baking powder; process until combined.

4. Scrape the batter into the prepared pan. Place the peach slices on the batter in three rows, moving the batter into the corners as necessary. Sprinkle with sugar.

5. Bake the cake until a toothpick inserted into the center comes out clean, about 30 minutes.

6. Cut the cake into nine pieces. Top each serving with whipped cream and a sweet pea flower.

MAKES 9 SERVINGS

SNOW PEA SALAD WITH SWEET PEA FLOWERS

8 ounces (225 g) fresh snow peas in their pods

1 teaspoon (5 ml) sesame oil

1 teaspoon (5 ml) tamari

1 teaspoon (5 ml) balsamic vinegar

8 sweet pea flowers

1. Pull the strings from the snow pea pods. Steam the peas in a steamer basket until they turn bright green, about 1 minute. Immediately plunge the peas into a bowl of ice water or rinse them under very cold water until they are cool. (If you do not stop the cooking in this way, they will continue to cook and turn olive drab.) Dry the snow peas.

2. Combine the oil, tamari, and vinegar in a small bowl; whisk until well combined. Pour the dressing over the snow peas.

3. Just before serving, decorate the salad with the sweet pea flowers.

MAKES 4 SERVINGS

Violas

Pansies, Johnny-jump-ups, and violets (all members of the Viola family) tend not to have a pronounced taste, but they are so beautiful that they are a joy to cook with. Of the three, violets have the most flavor and fragrance.

HONEYED STARFRUIT, PEACH, AND PANSY SALAD

This is a gorgeous and delicious salad: sweet, tart, crisp, soft, green, orange, and purple—an absolute delight to the eye and palate.

For the salad:

3 cups (711 ml) baby lettuce mix, washed and dried

2 fresh peaches

1 starfruit

A handful of pansies

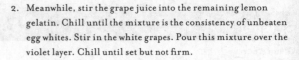

For the dressing:

I cup (177 ml) extra-virgin olive oil

1/2 teaspoon (2.5 ml) salt

1/2 teaspoon (2.5 ml) paprika

1/3 cup (79 ml) honey

1/4 teaspoon (1.3 ml) mustard

1/4 teaspoon (1.3 ml) freshly ground black pepper

1/4 cup (59 ml) lemon juice

Making the Salad

1. Divide the lettuce among four serving plates. Cut the peaches in half around the pit and twist the halves apart. Remove the pit; slice each peach half into four sections. Cut the starfruit into slices.

2. Divide the peaches and starfruit among the four salads.

Making the Dressing

1. Mix all the ingredients in a jar. Cover and shake until blended.

2. Drizzle the dressing over the salads. Just before serving, sprinkle the pansies over the salads.

MAKES 4 SERVINGS

CHILDREN'S VIOLET GRAPE PARTY MOLD

1 package (3 ounces) lemon-flavored gelatin

2 cups (473 ml) boiling water, divided

5 violets

3/4 cup (177 ml) white grape juice

1 cup (237 ml) seedless white grapes, halved

1 package (3 ounces) grape-flavored gelatin

3/4 cup (177 ml) cold water

1 cup (237 ml) seedless purple grapes, halved

Grape leaves and additional violets for decoration (optional)

1. Place the lemon-flavored gelatin in a bowl. Pour I cup (237 ml) of boiling water over the gelatin; mix well. Pour a little of the gelatin into a 4-cup (946 ml) mold, so it just covers the bottom. Place the violets upside down in the gelatin, making sure the flowers are partially covered with gelatin. Chill the mold until the gelatin is set but not yet firm.

2. Meanwhile, stir the grape juice into the remaining lemon gelatin. Chill until the mixture is the consistency of unbeaten egg whites. Stir in the white grapes. Pour this mixture over the violet layer. Chill until set but not firm.

3. Place the grape-flavored gelatin in a bowl. Pour I cup (237 ml) of boiling water over the gelatin; mix well. Add 3/4 cup (177 ml) of cold water and mix. Chill until the mixture is the consistency of unbeaten egg whites. Stir in the purple grapes. Pour this mixture over the white grape layer. Chill until firm.

4. Unmold the dessert onto a serving platter. Decorate the edges with grape leaves and violets if desired.

MAKES 8 SERVINGS

PANSY PEAR PANCAKES

This is a pretty pancake for a special breakfast. The flowers will fade a little during cooking, and you won't want the pancakes to brown too much, so don't make these in a cast-iron skillet and don't let the pan get too hot.

1 cup (237 ml) flour

1 tablespoon (15 ml) light brown sugar

2 teaspoons (30 ml) baking powder

1/4 teaspoon (1.3 ml) salt

1 cup (237 ml) vanilla yogurt

1 tablespoon (15 ml) safflower oil

1 egg

1 tablespoon (15 ml) water

1/4 cup (59 ml) finely diced pears

2 tablespoons (30 ml) butter

9 pansies

Wildflower honey, brown sugar, or maple syrup

1. Sift together the flour, brown sugar, baking powder, and salt into a bowl. In another bowl, combine the yogurt, oil, egg, and water; whisk until well blended. Add the pears; mix well.

2. Pour the wet ingredients into the flour mixture and stir until just combined.

3. Heat a frying pan or griddle over medium. Add a little butter; heat until melted. Pour a scant 1/4 cup (59 ml) of batter into the pan for each pancake. Gently press a pansy, face up, into the center of each pancake. Cook until the edges of the pancake are dry; turn and cook briefly on the other side.

4. Serve the pancakes flower side up with honey, brown sugar, or syrup.

MAKES 4 SERVINGS

297

Salsas!

Glenn Andrews

Illustrations by Mary Rich and Laura Tedeschi

A Few Words about Chiles

Many, if not most, homemade salsa recipes center on fresh chile peppers. Before we begin, then, here's a brief look at the sorts of fresh chile peppers you're most apt to run across, arranged roughly from mild to scorching. Canned peeled green chiles are also an excellent product, as are canned jalapeños and sliced, pickled jalapeños. All three can be found in most supermarkets. Canned chipotle peppers (smoked jalapeños) are harder to find, but well worth a search. They're usually spelled *chilpotles* on the can labels. These are packed in *adobo*, a smoky, spicy sauce that's worth the price of the cans all by itself.

Anaheim (*Capsicum annuum* var. *annuum* 'Anaheim'). Sometimes known as the New Mexico chile or the Californian chile, this is the one of the mildest in the chile family—it's not terribly hot—and has a somewhat sweet flavor, similar to that of a bell pepper. The Anaheim matures from bright green to red, and usually grows to about 7 inches long and 2 inches wide.

Poblano (*Capsicum annuum* 'Poblano'). This dark green or red chile is also relatively mild, although a bit hotter than the Anaheim. It has a triangular shape and ranges from 2 1/2 to 6 inches long. When the poblano is dried, it becomes known as the *ancho*.

Jalapeño (*Capsicum annuum* var. *annuum* 'Jalapeño'). The jalapeño is probably the best known of all hot peppers, and it's available almost everywhere. Some are a lot hotter than others—you can't tell by looking. Jalapeños are thick fleshed, and grow to about 2 inches long and 1 inch wide. Green jalapeños will ripen to shades of yellow or red. When a jalapeño is smoked, it becomes a **chipotle**, which many people think the tastiest of all chiles. (To substitute for a chipotle in a recipe, use a jalapeño and a few drops of "liquid smoke.")

Serrano (*Capsicum annuum* var. *annuum* 'Serrano'). Serranos are short (about 2 inches long), fairly thin, smooth skinned, and quite hot. They're usually used green, although they're sometimes available in red.

Tabasco (*Capsicum frutescens*). Tabascos are shorter, thinner, and hotter than serranos. They ripen from yellow to red (they're especially tasty when yellow) and grow to about 1 inch in length.

Bird or **Thai pepper** (*Capsicum annuum* var. *glabriusculum*). These peppers are tiny (about 1 1/2 inches in length) and very hot. They ripen from green to red and have an elongated, pointed shape. They're often used in Caribbean, West Indian, and Asian cuisine.

Habañero (*Capsicum chinense*). Searingly hot! These small peppers (about 2 inches in length) are shaped like Chinese lanterns. They're available in light green, orange, red, or deep purple. True, experienced chile fanciers talk about the fruity flavor—others just scream. Be sure to wear protective gloves when handling.

Preserving Your Salsas

Fortunately, salsas are very easy to make. Most of them don't require any cooking, and even the raw salsas will keep nicely for three or four days under refrigeration. Salsas made from dry chiles will usually keep longer (up to about three months) in your refrigerator.

The best method of preserving is to freeze your salsas. They might lose some texture, but they will still taste great. Just put the salsas into zip-seal freezer bags or plastic containers and pop them into your freezer. In the freezer, salsas have a shelf-life of eight to ten months (except for cirus salsas, which have a shelf-life of only four to six months). To use, let them defrost in the refrigerator.

The salsas recipes in this book should not be canned without first consulting with a specialist in home canning safety. Because of the serious repercussions possible with canning homemade salsa recipes, the United States Department of Agriculture (USDA) recommends that you use only scientifically tested salsa recipes specifically formulated for home canning.

USDA-tested recipes for home canning salsa can be found in USDA canning publications available from your local state coperative extension service as well as the *Complete Guide to Home Canning*, a free USDA publication available at many local grocery stores and cooperative extensions.

It's important to preserve your salsas properly in order to prevent the growth of *Clostridium botulinum*, the bacterium that causes botulism. To ensure complete safety in preserving, if you are unsure whether or not a salsa recipie can be safely canned, don't can it. It will taste just as good if you freeze it instead.

Salsa Recipes

> **WARNING**
>
> Be sure to wear rubber or latex gloves when handling hot peppers! Take care not to touch your face—especially not your eyes—and wash your hands very thoroughly with soap and water afterward.

RED SALSAS

CLASSIC RED RESTAURANT SALSA

1 pound Roma or plum tomatoes, minced

1/2 teaspoon minced garlic

3 tablespoons tomato paste

1 serrano or jalapeño chile, seeded and minced

1/4 cup minced onion

1/4 cup minced cilantro

Combine all of the ingredients in a small bowl and let sit, covered, at room temperature for half an hour before using. (Or you can chop all of the ingredients roughly and then run them in a food processor, leaving quite a bit of texture. Again, let the salsa sit before serving.)

MAKES ABOUT 1 1/4 CUPS

SALSA RANCHERO

Here we have a country salsa, more informal than most. It's primarily a tomato salsa, with just a touch of spice.

3/4 cup minced onion

1/2 teaspoon minced garlic

1 jalapeño, minced

1 pound tomatoes, peeled, seeded, and chopped

1/4 cup water

1/2 teaspoon oregano

1/2 teaspoon sugar

1/4 teaspoon salt

Put all of the ingredients in a medium-size nonreactive saucepan. Bring to a boil, then turn the heat down and simmer for 15 minutes, or until the onions and tomatoes are soft. If you want a smooth sauce, run it in a blender or food processor. This salsa will keep for weeks if refrigerated.

MAKES ABOUT 2 CUPS

FRESH TOMATO SALSA

Excerpted from *The Herbal Palate Cookbook*, by Maggie Oster and Sal Gilbertie (Storey Publishing, 1996)

2/3 pound tomatoes, peeled, seeded, and finely chopped

1/2 cup finely chopped sweet green pepper

1/4 cup finely chopped onion

1 jalapeño, cored, seeded, and finely chopped

1 garlic clove, finely chopped

2 teaspoons minced fresh cilantro

1 teaspoon olive oil

1/2 teaspoon salt

Prepare the salsa by combining all of the ingredients in a medium-size bowl. Use immediately, or cover and refrigerate for up to 3 days.

MAKES ABOUT 1 1/2 CUPS

TOMATILLO SALSA

Excerpted from *The 10% Low-Fat Cookbook*, by Miriam Jacobs (Storey Publishing, 1996)

This is a very mild red-and-green salsa. Roasted poblano peppers are not very hot, and the tomatillos are pleasantly tart. If you like your salsa with more zip, add some hot sauce, cayenne, or diced jalapeño.

8 medium tomatillos, husked, rinsed, and quartered

1 poblano, roasted (see the box below) and chopped

1/4 cup chopped red onion

1/4 teaspoon vegetable-broth mix

1/4 cup water

1/8 teaspoon lemon juice

3 tablespoons minced fresh cilantro

In a medium-size saucepan, combine the tomatillos, poblano, onion, broth mix, water, and lemon juice. Bring the mixture to a boil, then reduce the heat. Let simmer for 15 minutes; remove from heat. When the mixture has cooled, blend in the cilantro. Serve at room temperature or chilled.

MAKES 8 SERVINGS

HOW TO ROAST PEPPERS

Roasting peppers is a fairly simple process. You can use a dry griddle, a gas or electric broiler, or a charcoal or gas grill—or simply use tongs to hold the pepper over a gas flame. Turn the pepper as it cooks until it's charred (really blackened) all over. Then place it in a paper or plastic bag, close tightly, and let it "sweat" for 10 to 15 minutes. Open the bag, remove the pepper, and slip off its skin. Rinse under lukewarm water. Cut off the stem, slice, and remove the seeds and ribs.

PICO DE GALLO

3 ripe tomatoes, chopped

2–3 jalapeños, seeded and minced

1/4 cup minced fresh cilantro

1/4 cup minced onion

Combine all of the ingredients. Refrigerate for at least an hour before serving. This salsa keeps 3 or 4 days if refrigerated.

MAKES ABOUT 1 1/2 CUPS

CHERRY TOMATO SALSA

Excerpted from *Mustards, Ketchups & Vinegars*, by Carol Costenbader (Storey Publishing, 1996)

Serve this spicy dip with tortilla chips or as a topping for warm crabmeat, shredded fresh spinach, and cheese.

1 pound cherry tomatoes

1 large shallot, minced

1 clove garlic, minced

2 tablespoons chopped fresh cilantro

1 tablespoon white wine vinegar

Salt and freshly ground black pepper to taste

2 teaspoons fresh lime juice

2 jalapeños, seeded and chopped

In a food processor or blender, process the tomatoes until they have a rough consistency. Transfer to a large bowl and add the remaining

Continued ➜

ingredients. Cover and refrigerate for at least 2 hours to allow the flavors to blend.

This salsa will keep in the refrigerator for 2 to 3 days.

MAKES ABOUT 2 CUPS

SALSA CON QUESO

Excerpted from *Tomatoes!*, by the Editors of Garden Way Publishing (Garden Way Publishing, 1991)

2 tablespoons vegetable oil

1 medium onion, diced

2 medium red tomatoes, finely diced

8 ounces low-fat cream cheese

1/2 pound Monterey Jack cheese, grated

1 jalapeño, seeded and finely diced

2 teaspoons chile powder

In a medium-size skillet, heat the oil and sauté the onion for 5 minutes. Add the tomatoes and simmer for 5 minutes more. Reduce the heat and add the remaining ingredients. Cook, stirring constantly, until the cheeses are melted. Serve warm.

SWEET TOMATO SALSA

Just a year or two ago, this luscious cooked salsa would have been called a chutney. Try some instead of barbecue sauce on spareribs.

1/4 cup chopped onion

2 tablespoons chopped fresh ginger

2 cloves garlic

3/4 cup cider vinegar

1/2 cup sugar (or 3/4 cup for a sweeter salsa)

2 tablespoons minced chiles (Anaheim or New Mexico)

1 dash each cinnamon, cloves, and nutmeg

1 1-pound can chopped tomatoes, undrained

Run all of the ingredients except the tomatoes in a food processor or blender. Combine with the tomatoes in a medium-size saucepan. Simmer gently, stirring occasionally, until the mixture is almost as thick as marmalade.

Keep under refrigeration or put in jars while still very hot. Serve cold or at room temperature.

MAKES ABOUT 3 1/2 CUPS

GREEN SALSAS

SALSA VERDE

Excerpted from *Peppers, Hot & Sweet*, by Beth Dooley (Garden Way Publishing, 1990)

This fresh, delicate sauce is wonderful with grilled vegetables, hard-cooked eggs, fresh crusty bread, or mild cheese.

2 cloves garlic, minced

1/2 cup chopped fresh parsley

1/2 cup chopped fresh cilantro

1 Anaheim chile, seeded and chopped

1 medium green bell pepper, seeded and chopped

Zest and juice of 1 lime

1/2 cup extra-virgin olive oil

Salt and freshly ground black
    pepper to taste

In a small bowl, combine all of the ingredients thoroughly. This salsa will keep for 2 to 3 days in the refrigerator.

TOMATILLO SALSA VERDE

This is a mild salsa. To make it hotter, add more chiles or use a hotter variety.

8 tomatillos, husked, rinsed, and chopped

3 tablespoons chopped fresh cilantro

1/2 cup chopped green Anaheim or New Mexico chiles (or use a 4-ounce can of peeled green chiles)

1 teaspoon minced garlic

2 tablespoons chopped onion

Run all of the ingredients together in a food processor or blender — or mince everything very finely by hand. Refrigerate, covered, for at least an hour.

MAKES ABOUT 1 1/2 CUPS

FIRE-ROASTED SALSA VERDE

This salsa is best if used within a few hours of making it.

3 poblanos

3 jalapeños

1 teaspoon minced garlic

1 tablespoon minced onion

1 tablespoon lime juice

1/2 teaspoon salt

Roast both kinds of chiles until their skins are nicely blackened. Remove the skin and seeds, and put the remaining pulp in a food processor or blender along with the rest of the ingredients. Run the machine until the salsa is the consistency you wish. (It can be totally smooth or slightly chunky.)

MAKES A LITTLE MORE THAN 1 CUP

GUACAMOLE

1 large ripe avocado

1/4 cup minced white onion

Juice of 1 lime

1 medium tomato, finely chopped

1 jalapeño or Anaheim or New Mexico chile, seeded and minced

Salt to taste

1 tablespoon chopped fresh cilantro

1 small clove garlic, minced

Cut around the avocado lengthwise. Twist the two halves to separate. Remove the stone. Now just hold each half upside down and squeeze the avocado meat out into a bowl. (Or simply peel the avocado, if you prefer.)

Chop the avocado meat coarsely (or mash it with a fork, if you prefer a smoother guacamole), then add all of the other ingredients.

Serve immediately, or keep in the refrigerator for a few hours by sprinkling on some extra lime juice, then pressing plastic wrap onto the surface.

MAKES ABOUT 1 CUP

HOT AND SWEET TOMATILLO SALSA

8 tomatillos, husked, rinsed, and quartered

1–2 jalapeños (fresh or pickled), cut up coarsely

2 green onions, cut in 1-inch pieces

2 tablespoons fresh cilantro or parsley, stems removed

1 1/2 tablespoons honey

Juice of 1 lime

Run all of the ingredients together in a food processor or blender, turning off the machine and scraping down the bowl several times with a spatula. Stop processing when the salsa is just slightly chunky. This salsa keeps 3 or 4 days under refrigeration.

MAKES ABOUT 1 CUP

LIME CILANTRO PASTE WITH SALSA

Excerpted from *Mustards, Ketchups & Vinegars*, by Carol Costenbader (Storey Publishing, 1996)

Here's a green-and-red salsa that can be served "fresh" from the freezer. Prepare when fresh cilantro is plentiful, and then combine with fresh tomatoes for a quick piquant salsa, or spread on toasted pita bread as a -low-calorie appetizer.

6 cloves garlic

2 jalapeños

1 cup cilantro leaves, washed and dried

2 tablespoons fresh lime juice

2–3 medium tomatoes, seeded, drained, and chopped

Pinch of salt

2 tablespoons olive oil

Process the garlic, jalapeños, cilantro, and lime juice in a blender or food processor until they form a paste. Place the paste in ice cube trays and freeze until needed. The paste cubes will keep for several months. (Once frozen, you can transfer them to a separate freezer container and label, if desired, then return to the freezer.)

To use, remove the paste cubes from the freezer and let them defrost. Once they're thawed, place them in a mixing bowl and add the tomatoes, salt, and olive oil. Mix well and serve immediately.

MAKES 1 1/4 CUPS

HOTTER-THAN-HADES SALSAS

XNIPEC, OR DOG'S NOSE SALSA

In the Mayan language, xnipec means either "dog's nose" or "dog's breath."

1 red onion, diced

1/3 cup freshly squeezed lime juice

5 habañeros, stems and seeds removed, diced (for greater hotness, don't remove the seeds)

2 Roma or plum tomatoes, diced

Salt to taste

Soak the diced onion in the lime juice for at least 30 minutes. Add the other ingredients and run in a food processor or blender, adding a little water if desired. This salsa is best when used within an hour or two of being made.

MAKES ABOUT 1 1/2 CUPS

Continued ➜

CHIPOTLE SALSA

This one is dark, smoky, hot, and generally wonderful.

Broiling the tomatoes is a Mexican trick, and a good one to know. When tomatoes are at their ripest in late summer, broil them in quantity, run them in a food processor or blender, and store them in batches in your freezer to use in salsa or other recipes.

4 ripe tomatoes

1/2 large white onion, chopped

Juice of 1 lime

2 teaspoons olive oil

1 teaspoon minced garlic

2 minced chipotles from canned chipotles in adobo, plus 1/2 teaspoon or more of the adobo sauce in the can

Cut out and discard just the core from the tomatoes, and place them in a shallow pan. Broil, turning as the sides char, until they're fairly evenly dark brown or even black.

Put the tomatoes, skins, seeds, and all, into a food processor or blender and run until they're thoroughly chopped. Add all of the other ingredients and give them a quick whirl together. This recipe will keep for 7 to 10 days in the refrigerator.

MAKES ABOUT 1 1/2 CUPS

YUCATÁN KNOCK-YOUR-SOCKS-OFF SALSA

They love this incredibly fiery salsa in the Yucatán (where it's known as Salsa Picante à la Yucateca). Just remember that the habañero chile is about 300 times hotter than the hottest of jalapeños. Be sure to use rubber gloves when handling these scorpions! (And remember that eating peanut butter on a cracker is supposed to be a good way to calm down a chile-burned mouth.)

6 habañeros

1/4 cup lime juice

1/4 teaspoon salt

Wearing rubber gloves, toast the chiles on a hot, dry griddle, turning them constantly with tongs until they're soft. Now remove the stems and put the chiles in a food processor or blender with the lime juice and salt. Process very briefly, pulsing just until the chiles are chopped. (You don't want a puree.)

MAKES ABOUT 1/2 CUP—WHICH SHOULD BE PLENTY!

FRUIT SALSAS

WATERMELON SALSA

This is one of the most refreshing of all salsas. It also can be used as a highly unusual fruit salad.

2 cups watermelon in 1/3" cubes

1/4 cup minced green onion

1/4 cup minced jicama or water chestnuts

2 tablespoons minced fresh cilantro

3 tablespoons minced mild (or not-so-mild) chiles

1 tablespoon balsamic vinegar

Combine all of the ingredients and chill for an hour or more, to give the flavors a chance to mingle.

MAKES ABOUT 2 1/2 CUPS

PINEAPPLE SALSA

Pineapple salsa is perfect with any plain- or charcoal-broiled chicken or fish.

1 cup finely chopped pineapple (if you're using canned pineapple, don't use the "crushed" variety)

2 tablespoons finely minced onion

3 tablespoons chopped fresh cilantro or mint

1 serrano, seeded and finely minced

Combine all of the ingredients in a small bowl and refrigerate for at least half an hour.

MAKES ABOUT 1 1/4 CUPS

RED ONION, MANGO, AND CHILE SALSA

Excerpted from *The Herbal Palate Cookbook*, by Maggie Oster and Sal Gilbertie (Storey Publishing, 1996)

This salsa makes a wonderful complement to grilled swordfish, grilled steak, stews, steamed vegetables, rice, or beans.

1 1/2 cups chopped mango

1 1/2 cups chopped papaya

1 cup finely chopped red bell pepper

1 cup chopped fresh cilantro

1 1/2 cups finely chopped red onion

1/2 cup finely chopped fresh chile peppers

6 tablespoons lime juice

2 1/2 tablespoons red wine vinegar

2 tablespoons lemon juice

2 tablespoons olive oil

2 teaspoons cumin

1 teaspoon salt

1 teaspoon freshly ground black pepper

In a large bowl, combine all of the ingredients and mix well. Cover and let stand for 2 hours, allowing the flavors to blend, before using.

MAKES 4 SERVINGS

KIWI SALSA

Who knows if this cooling salsa is used in New Zealand—but that's where kiwis come from! You'll like this with lamb or chicken.

1 pound kiwis, peeled and minced

1 Anaheim or New Mexico chile, minced

Juice of 1 lime

1 tablespoon minced fresh mint

1/2 teaspoon sugar

Combine all of the ingredients. Keep refrigerated until needed.

MAKES ABOUT 1 1/2 CUPS

NECTARINE AND APPLE SALSA

Try this with grilled pork chops or chicken, or as a morning treat with toast or bagels and cottage cheese.

3 large nectarines or peaches

1 tart (Granny Smith, for example) cooking apple, peeled, cored, and chopped

1/2 cup chopped fresh cilantro

1/4 cup honey

2 tablespoons freshly squeezed lime juice

1/4 teaspoon allspice

1/4 teaspoon cinnamon

Skin the nectarines or peaches by dunking them for 30 seconds in a saucepan of boiling water, then plunging them into a bowl of ice water. The skins will come right off. Chop the fruit and put it in a bowl. Add the rest of the ingredients, cover the bowl, and chill for at least an hour.

MAKES ABOUT 1 1/2 CUPS

THREE-CITRUS SALSA

Excerpted from *The 10% Low-Fat Cookbook*, by Miriam Jacobs (Storey Publishing, 1996)

This citrus salsa will perk up any number of dishes that need a fresh, bright accompaniment. It complements fish entrées particularly well.

1 orange

1/4 lemon

1/2 grapefruit

1/3 cup minced cucumber

1 tablespoon minced shallot

1 teaspoon minced fresh mint

1 teaspoon balsamic vinegar

Peel the orange, lemon, and grapefruit. Remove the white pith and loosen the sections, discarding the membranes. Cut each section into thirds. Combine the citrus chunks with the cucumber, shallot, mint, and vinegar. Refrigerate until ready to serve.

MAKES 4 SERVINGS AS A SIDE DISH

VEGETABLE SALSAS

SWEET ONION SALSA

There are at least three varieties of sweet onions available in this country: Vidalias (from Georgia), Walla Wallas (from Washington), and Mauis (from Hawaii). Sweet Onion Salsa is especially nice on steak or grilled fish.

1 large sweet onion, minced

Cold water

1 tablespoon balsamic vinegar

1/2 teaspoon sugar

3 tablespoons thinly sliced green onions

3 tablespoons minced fresh parsley (preferably flat-leafed Italian)

2 teaspoons minced jalapeños

Cover the minced onion with cold water. Let sit for 30 minutes, then drain in a strainer and pat dry with paper towels.

Combine the onion with all of the other ingredients in a fairly small bowl and refrigerate, covered, for at least an hour, stirring from time to time.

MAKES ABOUT 1 1/2 CUPS

CUCUMBER-MINT SALSA

1 cup peeled, seeded, and minced cucumber

1/2 cup chopped onion

1/4 cup chopped fresh mint (or dill) leaves

4 teaspoons seasoned rice wine vinegar

2 teaspoons olive oil (optional)

Combine all of the ingredients in a small bowl. Let sit for 30 minutes at room temperature.

MAKES ABOUT 1 1/2 CUPS

Continued →

NOPALITOS SALSA

The taste of nopalitos is hard to describe, but they're fresh, clean, and just faintly tangy. Combined with garlic and chiles, they're sublime. The jicama in this salsa gives a nice little crunch, too.

1 11-ounce jar or can nopalitos, chopped by hand (do not process)

1/4 cup peeled and diced jicama

3 Roma or plum tomatoes, diced small

1/2 cup minced green onion

3 tablespoons minced fresh cilantro

3 tablespoons red wine vinegar

1 tablespoon olive oil

1 jalapeño, minced

1 teaspoon minced garlic

Combine all of ingredients in a bowl. Chill, covered, for at least 2 hours, stirring occasionally.

MAKES ABOUT 2 CUPS

BLACK BEAN SALSA

1/2 cup minced onion

2 tablespoons olive oil

1 teaspoon cumin

Juice of 1/2 lime

1/4 cup orange juice

Sections from 1 navel orange, cut in half

1/2 cup black beans, soaked, cooked, and drained (or use a 1-pound can of black beans, well rinsed)

1/4 cup chopped fresh cilantro or parsley

Cook the onion in the olive oil until limp, then add the cumin and cook for 2 or 3 minutes more. Add all of the other ingredients. Keep covered and chilled until needed.

MAKES ABOUT 2 1/2 CUPS

Some Great Ways to Use Salsas

- As a condiment with any poultry, meat, or fish
- As a glaze when cooking chicken
- In sandwiches, as a low-fat alternative to mayonnaise
- In scrambled or deviled eggs, or in egg salad
- To dress up the taste and appearance of any vegetable
- As a topping for any cream soup
- As a sauce for pasta
- With cream cheese, served on crackers as an appetizer

CHILE CON QUESO

Chile con queso, which translates as "chile with cheese," is served hot, as a dipping sauce for corn chips. In other words, it's the hot and spicy equivalent of Swiss fondue. But unlike fondue, it's brimful of exciting

flavor and easy to make, not fussy. It keeps well over a warming candle or low flame, too. And it's much better than nachos!

1 tablespoon butter

1/4 cup minced onion

1 medium tomato, peeled, seeded, and chopped

1/2 pound cheddar cheese, shredded

4 ounces cream cheese, cut up

1/2 cup salsa (use one of the classic red salsas)

1. In a medium-size saucepan, melt the butter and sauté the onion for a few minutes, until it's limp. Then add the tomato, cheddar, cream cheese, and salsa, and cook over moderately low heat, stirring often, until hot and well blended.

2. Keep the mixture in its saucepan, or transfer it to a decorative flameproof pot. Serve surrounded by corn chips—perhaps a mixture of the yellow and blue corn kinds.

MAKES ABOUT 3 CUPS

POTATOES MONTEREY

These are scalloped potatoes, but unlike any you've ever had! They go well with any plainly cooked meat or poultry.

2 pounds russet potatoes, peeled and thinly sliced

3/4 cup red or green salsa of your choice

1 cup shredded Monterey Jack cheese

1 1/3 cups chicken broth

2 tablespoons butter

1. Preheat the oven to 350°F.

2. Place half of the potato slices in a buttered 9 x 13-inch baking pan. Spread the salsa over the potatoes, followed by the cheese. Top with the rest of the potatoes. Pour the chicken broth over all, then dot the top with small pieces of the butter.

3. Bake until the potatoes are tender, the broth has been absorbed, and the top is slightly brown (about an hour and a half), tipping the pan every 20 minutes and spooning the liquid over the potatoes.

MAKES 6 SERVINGS

HADDOCK WITH CITRUS SALSA

Excerpted from *The 10% Low-Fat Cookbook*, by Miriam Jacobs (Storey Publishing, 1996)

16 ounces haddock

Juice of 1 lime

Juice of 1 orange

1 teaspoon tamari soy sauce

1 recipe citrus salsa of your choice

1. Place the haddock in a shallow bowl. Combine the lime and orange juices with the soy sauce and pour over the haddock. Cover the bowl and let marinate in the refrigerator for at least 1 hour.

2. Just before you're ready to eat, preheat the broiler and remove the haddock from the marinade. Broil the haddock until cooked through. (The length of time will depend on the thickness. Allow 7 to 8 minutes for 1 inch of thickness.) Serve with citrus salsa on the side.

MAKES 4 SERVINGS

BAKED EGGS WITH SALSA AND CHEESE

2 tablespoons red or green salsa of your choice

2 tablespoons cream or sour cream (nonfat is all right)

2 eggs

3 tablespoons shredded cheddar or Swiss cheese

1. Preheat the oven to 350°F.

2. In a small buttered individual baking dish, combine the salsa with the cream or sour cream. Break the eggs on top of this, then sprinkle on the shredded cheese.

3. Bake for 10 minutes, or until the eggs are as set as you want them. (I like mine with the whites firm, but the yolks still soft.)

MAKES 1 SERVING

SALSA-GLAZED SPARERIBS

3 pounds spareribs (preferably baby back ribs)

Salt and freshly ground black pepper

1/2 cup salsa

1. Preheat the oven to 425°F.

2. Cut the ribs into serving sections of 3 or 4 ribs each. Sprinkle both sides with salt and pepper.

3. Place the ribs on a rack in a roasting pan, bone-side up. Bake for 30 minutes, turn them over in the pan, and bake for 15 minutes more. Then spread the salsa on the ribs and bake for a final 15 minutes.

MAKES 4 SERVINGS

MOCTEZUMA CHILAQUILES

1/3 cup vegetable oil

12 corn tortillas, each cut into 6 wedges

1 1/2 cups shredded cooked chicken

2 cups salsa of your choice (spicier recommended)

1 cup sour cream

1 1/4 cups shredded Monterey Jack or cheddar cheese

1. Preheat the oven to 350°F.

2. In a medium-size skillet, heat the vegetable oil over moderately high heat, and in it cook the tortilla wedges, a few pieces at a time. Drain on paper towels.

3. Now assemble the dish: Put one-third of the tortilla wedges in the bottom of a deep baking dish. Top with one-third of the chicken, then one-third of the salsa, followed by one-third of the cheese. Repeat twice, ending with the last of the cheese.

4. Bake for 20 minutes.

MAKES 4–6 SERVINGS

BREADS

Basic Bread Baking

Glenn Andrews

Illustrations by Mary Rich

Introduction

There's something so elemental about a good bread. It's satisfying! It makes you feel well fed. And if it's a bread you've made yourself, you also feel a lovely sense of gratification. In addition, you can make breads you'll never find in any store or bakery—and, of course, you can brag to your friends.

Basic Techniques of Breadmaking

The same techniques are used to make most yeast breads: proofing, combining the ingredients, kneading, rising, shaping, baking, and cooling.

Proofing has two functions—it gets the yeast off and running, and it's the best way to be sure that the yeast is still active. To proof, stir the yeast into lukewarm (95° to 110°F; 35°–43°C) water, usually along with a little sugar or other sweetener, and let it sit for 5 minutes, or until foamy. If you don't see any signs of life after 5 minutes, your yeast is dead. Toss it out and start over with a new supply.

Combining the ingredients is done differently for different breads; check each recipe. But if you're using a food processor to combine and knead, put all the dry ingredients into the bowl first and give them a buzz before adding and processing the other things.

Kneading finishes up the combining process and gives your bread texture. Many do this in a food processor, pulsing on and off until a nice dough is formed, then giving the dough a final turn or two on a

Continued ➜

floured board. If you have a heavy-duty mixer with a dough hook, you can knead using the mixer.

Traditional kneading is done on a floured board, with floured hands. Form the dough into a pancake shape. Using the heels of your hands, push the dough away from you. Then fold it over and rotate it a quarter turn. Keep doing this, adding more flour to the board and your hands as necessary, until the dough is elastic and has lost its stickiness. A "perfect" dough has been accurately described as feeling like a baby's bottom! Others have said that it feels like an earlobe. Doughs containing rye flours will always seem a little sticky, though.

GLUTEN

Gluten is a substance created when the protein in wheat flour is combined with a liquid. The amount of protein in the flour governs the amount of gluten. You can purchase boxes of wheat gluten to add to recipes—especially whole-grain recipes—to help them rise better. The way gluten works is that it forms an elastic network (think kitchen sponge here) that traps the carbon dioxide being released by the yeast. This is what makes your bread rise.

You will see the phrase "a floured surface" in many of the recipes. Many of you will use a bread board. Others, a lucky few, will use a slab of polished marble. Still others will use a countertop. All of these surfaces work well. I'm happy to have a marble slab, which I leave out on a counter at all times, but I think it's mostly for aesthetics!

Rising. After the dough has been kneaded, place it in a greased bowl and turn it around until it's greased on all sides. Cover. (Some will tell you to cover with a damp cloth, but I've found that any sort of cover works just fine—and in most cases is preferable to the damp cloth, because you don't always want to add any extra moisture. Plastic wrap or foil works well. I even cover bowls with dinner plates on occasion!) Let it sit in a warm place (ideally between 80° and 85°F; 27°–29°C) until doubled in size. This will usually take about an hour. A gas oven with a pilot light works well. In a cold electric oven, place a pan of boiling water on the bottom rack. See the specific recipe instructions for the number of rising times.

You will know that a dough has doubled in size when it doesn't bounce back, even a little, after you poke a hole in it with two fingers.

Punching down. Just bang your fist into the center of the risen dough—this is fun! Turn the dough over and punch again, then fold it a bit; keep folding and punching until the dough is thoroughly deflated. (You can also turn out the dough onto a floured surface and knead just a little to accomplish this if you find it necessary.)

Shaping. Flatten the dough into a rectangle whose shorter end is the length of the bread you want or of the pan you're using. (Flattening it with a rolling pin is a good idea, because it will get rid of any air pockets in the dough.) Roll up the dough tightly from the short end, then pinch the ends and tuck them under. For a round loaf, flatten the dough into a square, then tuck the edges under.

Baking. Breads can just bake on baking tins or, if they're in pans, right on the oven's racks. But for breads that aren't baked in pans, it really is nice to use a baking stone, which approximates a professional baker's brick oven. These are rather expensive, though. So you might

want to try an easy substitute: Go to a store that sells ceramic tiles and purchase some unglazed terra-cotta or quarry tiles. They're always inexpensive. They usually come in 6-inch (15 cm) squares, so if you buy nine of them, you'll have an area 18 inches by 18 inches (45 cm) at about one-sixth the price of a baking stone. Use these to line a regular oven rack.

Failing this, put your loaves on baking sheets that you've sprinkled with a little cornmeal.

Testing for doneness. The classic way to find out if a loaf has baked enough is to remove it from the pan and rap it with your knuckles. If the bread sounds hollow, it's done. If you don't hear a hollow sound when you rap on the loaf, put it back in the oven for a few minutes more. (You don't need to return it to its baking pan.)

MAKING ROLLS

Any of the basic white or whole-wheat doughs can be formed into rolls. If you haven't made rolls before, a good one to start with is the cloverleaf. Just make small balls of dough and stick three of them in each greased standard-size muffin tin hole. (Balls of dough the size of large marbles are what to aim for.) Cover loosely and allow to rise until double, then bake in a preheated 350°F (177°C) oven for about 20 minutes, or until light brown.

Don't try this with any of the batter bread doughs or with rye dough, which is usually too soft and sticky. However, those doughs, as well as all the basic ones, can be made into miniature loaves if you have the right little bread pans.

Finishing the bread. Sometimes it's nice to rub the top of a baked, warm loaf with a little soft butter or some milk, since it will give the loaf an appealing shine. Another technique is to brush the top of an unbaked loaf with an egg wash consisting of an egg (or just the yolk) beaten with 2 tablespoons of water. With or without these touches, let the finished, baked loaf sit on a rack until it's completely cool. (The late James Beard used to call cutting into an uncooled loaf of bread "infanticide"!) To avoid major problems removing the bread from the pan, first make sure to thoroughly grease the pan. If the bread then sticks after baking, let the pan sit first on one side for a few minutes, then on the other.

Keeping bread on hand. When the bread is thoroughly cool, put it into a bag and keep it at room temperature. Or freeze it. Bread can be frozen and thawed any number of times. But if you want the bread sliced, it's best to do this before you freeze it: Bread that has been frozen is difficult to slice.

Basic Bread Recipes

As you may have gathered by now, I feel that it's too bad that so many people are scared off by dogmatic rules about breadmaking. Bread is very forgiving. No matter what you do, the chances are very, very good that you will turn out a creditable loaf of bread. If you don't, it's not such a big deal. The ingredients you've used aren't expensive. Just toss out the loaf, if you must, and try again!

WHITE BREADS

Recently, white breads have fallen out of favor with the health-food crowd. But white flour, with its high gluten levels and forgiving nature, is a natural—and healthy—basis for beginning to bake bread.

BASIC WHITE BREAD

There are many recipes in the world for a good, basic, home-style white bread. I just happen to feel that this is the best. The recipe can be cut in half, but as long as you're going to go to this much trouble, it seems to me you might as well make two loaves!

2 cups (475 ml) milk

3 tablespoons butter, divided

2 tablespoons sugar (can be omitted or the amount cut down)

1 tablespoon salt

2 packages dry yeast

1/2 cup (120 ml) lukewarm (95° to 110°F; 35°–40°C) water

6–6 1/4 cups (1,650–1,720 ml) white flour

1. Heat the milk in a medium-size saucepan. Add 1 tablespoon of the butter plus the sugar and salt. Stir until dissolved.

2. Stir the yeast into the lukewarm water in a large bowl. Make sure it's dissolved, then set aside to proof for 5 minutes.

3. Add the cooled milk mixture to the proofed yeast. Beat in the flour, 1 cup (275 ml) at a time, then turn out the dough onto a floured surface and knead.

4. Place in a greased bowl and turn the ball of dough around so it's greased on all sides. Cover. Let rise in a warm place until doubled.

5. Punch down the dough, turn it out onto the floured surface again, and knead once more, briefly.

6. Shape the dough into two loaves. Place them in two well-greased, large (9-inch; 22.5 cm) loaf pans. Cover. Let rise once more.

7. Preheat your oven to 400°F (205°C).

8. When the loaves have doubled in size, slash their tops in two or three places. Melt the remaining butter and brush half of it onto the loaves.

9. Bake for 40 minutes, then brush the loaves with the remaining tablespoon of butter. Bake for 5 minutes more, then remove from the pans and allow to cool on a rack.

MAKES 2 LARGE LOAVES

CINNAMON RAISIN BREAD

When you've made the dough for Basic White Bread, you're well on the way to making Cinnamon Raisin Bread, which is a favorite with so many people.

1 recipe Basic White Bread dough

1 1/2 cups (415 ml) raisins

1/2 cup (120 ml) warm water

1 1/2 teaspoons cinnamon

3 tablespoons sugar

2 tablespoons white flour

1. While the white bread dough is rising, combine the raisins with the water in a small bowl and let sit, stirring from time to time.

2. When the dough has risen, punch it down and put it on a lightly floured surface. Divide into two sections. Roll each into a rectangle that's about 3/4 inch (19 mm) thick.

3. Combine the cinnamon and sugar and sprinkle over the dough.

4. Drain the raisins and sprinkle them with the 2 tablespoons of flour. Toss well to combine, then spread them evenly over the two dough rectangles. Press the raisins in lightly.

5. Now roll the loaves one at a time. Starting at a short end of a rectangle, roll up the dough into a log, tucking in any raisins that escape. Roll tightly, but not so much so that the skin of the dough tears.

6. Seal the seam of the log by lightly pinching its edges together with your fingers. Place the loaf, seam-side down, in a greased 9-inch (22.5 cm) bread pan. Repeat with the other rectangle of dough.

7. Cover and allow to rise in a warm place until the dough has risen well above the edges of the pans. This may take close to 2 hours.

8. Preheat your oven to 400°F (205°C).

9. Bake for 45 minutes, checking often to make sure that the raisins on top of the loaves aren't burning. If they are, cover the tops of the loaves lightly with foil.

10. Remove from the pans and allow to cool very thoroughly on a rack before slicing.

MAKES 2 LOAVES

FRENCH BREAD

A true French bread will go stale in about half a day, because it contains no fat. So that's not the sort of recipe I'm giving you. This bread might as well be called Italian (and it does make a wonderful garlic bread). So call it whatever you want! The ice cube trick will give you somewhat of an approximation of a French baker's oven, and I think you'll find that it's fun to do.

Continued ➜

I make this in a food processor, putting the flour and salt into the bowl, then adding first the yeast mixture, then the combination of the rest of the water and butter.

1 1/2 packages (or a scant 3 1/2 teaspoons) dry yeast

4 teaspoons lukewarm (95° to 110°F; 35°–40°C) water

1/4 teaspoon sugar

1 cup (235 ml) cold or room-temperature water

2 tablespoons butter

3 1/2 cups (965 ml) white flour

1 teaspoon salt

2 tablespoons cornmeal

1. Proof the yeast in the warm water along with the sugar.

2. Put the cold or room-temperature water and butter into a small saucepan and slowly heat just until the butter has melted. Cool briefly. Combine all the ingredients except the cornmeal, then knead well, form into a ball, and allow to rise, covered, in a greased bowl until doubled.

3. Punch down, knead briefly, and let rise again in the greased bowl.

4. Punch down again and form the dough into a loaf that's about 13 inches (32.5 cm) long. Sprinkle the cornmeal on a baking sheet. Place the loaf on this and let it rise once more.

5. Preheat your oven to 450°F (232°C).

6. Using a very sharp knife or single-edge razor blade, cut three long diagonal slashes in the top of the loaf. Put the baking sheet in the oven.

7. Immediately throw four ice cubes onto the oven floor. (This will create the steam that would be present in a French baker's oven.) After 5 minutes, throw in four more ice cubes. Ten minutes after that, turn the oven down to 400°F (205°C) and bake for about 20 minutes more.

8. Cool on a rack.

MAKES 1 LOAF

PORTUGUESE SWEET BREAD

If you live in New England, you can probably buy Portuguese Sweet Bread in a supermarket, since so many Portuguese sailors and their families ended up living in that region. (Your own will be better, though.) It's not the sort of "sweet bread" you might expect—just a light and delicious egg bread.

1 package dry yeast

1/2 cup (140 ml) plus 1 teaspoon sugar

1/4 cup lukewarm (95° to 110°F; 35°–40°C) water

1/4 cup (1/2 stick) soft butter

1/4 cup (60 ml) warm milk

2 eggs, lightly beaten

1 1/2 teaspoons salt

2 1/4 cups (620 ml) or more white flour

1. Proof the yeast with 1 teaspoon of sugar and the warm water in a large bowl.

2. Meanwhile, combine the butter with the warm milk in a small bowl, then add the rest of the sugar and mix well. Add this to the yeast mixture and stir well. Remove and reserve about one fourth of the beaten eggs; add the rest to the mixture in the large bowl, along with the salt.

3. Add 2 cups (550 ml) of the flour, 1 cup (275 ml) at a time, mixing it in with your hands right in the bowl. Move it to a floured surface and keep on kneading, adding more flour as needed, until the dough is smooth and elastic.

4. Put in a buttered bowl, covered, to rise until doubled.

5. Punch down and shape into a ball. Put into a 9-inch (22.5 cm) buttered ovenproof skillet or a large bread pan. Cover (but not tightly) and allow to double again.

6. Preheat your oven to 350°F (177°C).

7. Brush the top of the loaf with the remaining beaten egg and bake for about half an hour.

MAKES 1 LARGE LOAF

CHALLAH

There are many ways to describe Challah. It's an egg bread. It's a braided bread. It's a ceremonial bread for Jews—and just an excellent bread for all others.

If you're not worried for religious reasons about combining meat and dairy products at the same meal, you can make your Challah with milk instead of water, and butter instead of margarine.

3 packages yeast

1 1/3 cups (315 ml) lukewarm (95° to 110°F; 35°–40°C) water

1 tablespoon sugar

3 tablespoons softened margarine

1 tablespoon salt

4 eggs

5 cups (1,375 ml) or a bit more white flour

1 tablespoon water

Poppy seeds

1. Proof the yeast in the warm water in a large bowl along with the sugar.

2. Stir in the margarine, salt, and three of the eggs, one at a time. Now add the flour, 1 cup (275 ml) at a time. You will have a very stiff dough.

3. Turn out the dough onto a floured surface and knead for about 10 minutes, until it is smooth and elastic.

4. Place the dough in a large greased bowl, turning it so it is greased on all sides. Cover and let rise until doubled in size.

5. Punch down the dough and divide it into six sections of equal size.

6. Working with one section of dough at a time, roll it out on your floured surface between your hands to make a rope that's about 1 inch (2.5 cm) in diameter.

7. Take three of these ropes and braid them into a loaf, pinching it to seal at the top and bottom and tucking the ends under. Place the loaf on a greased baking sheet.

8. Repeat with the remaining three ropes of dough. Place this loaf on the same baking sheet if there's enough room—there should be about 6 inches (15 cm) between the loaves.

9. Cover lightly and allow to rise again until almost doubled. Preheat your oven to 400°F (205°C).

10. Combine the remaining egg with the 1 tablespoon of water and brush the loaves with this egg wash. Sprinkle with poppy seeds.

11. Bake for 35 to 40 minutes.

MAKES 2 LOAVES

WHEAT AND OTHER GRAINS

If you limit yourself to making white breads, you miss out on a whole bunch of healthy, hearty breads that are just as easy and forgiving as white breads are.

HEARTY WHEAT BREAD

This is an old German-influenced recipe, but it fits right in with today's ideas of how to eat—there's no fat and no sugar!

1 package dry yeast

1 1/2 cups lukewarm (95° to 110°F; 35°–40°C) water

1 teaspoon salt

3 cups (825 ml) whole-wheat flour

1 cup (275 ml) white flour

1. Proof the yeast in the warm water in a large bowl.

2. Add the remaining ingredients and knead on a floured surface. Grease a bowl, or spray it with nonfat cooking spray; let the dough rise there, covered, until doubled.

3. Form into a loaf and place in a roughly 8 x 4-inch (20 x 10 cm) bread pan. Cover. Allow to rise again.

4. Preheat your oven to 375°F (190°C). Bake the loaf 25 to 30 minutes.

MAKES 1 FAIRLY SMALL LOAF

KATIE'S BULGUR BREAD

Here's a robust and tasty Middle European type of bread, with a few additions by a clever cook, my daughter Katie Doherty.

Bulgur is the same thing as cracked wheat, so you could call this bread that, if you like. Bulgur just sounds a bit more exotic.

1 cup (275 ml) bulgur wheat

3 tablespoons butter

1 1/2 cups (355 ml) boiling broth (chicken, beef, or vegetable)

1 1/4 cups (295 ml) cold water

2 teaspoons salt

1/4 cup (60 ml) honey

1/4 cup (60 ml) molasses

1 teaspoon caraway seeds

1 package dry yeast

3/4 cup (180 ml) lukewarm (95° to 110°F; 35°–40°C) water

3 cups (825 ml) whole-wheat flour

3 cups (825 ml) white flour

1. Put the bulgur wheat and butter in a large bowl. Stir in the boiling broth and let sit for half an hour. Add the cold water, salt, honey, molasses, and caraway.

2. Proof the yeast in the warm water and add to the bulgur mixture.

3. Now stir in the whole-wheat and white flours and knead well. Let the dough rise until fully doubled, then shape into two loaves. Put in greased 8 x 4-inch (20 x 10 cm) bread pans. Let rise again until the dough reaches the tops of the pans.

4. Preheat your oven to 375°F (190°C). Bake the loaves for 40 to 45 minutes.

MAKES 2 LOAVES

BASIC MIXED-GRAIN BREAD

Here you can add whatever pleases you. Make a three-grain bread, a five-grain one, or whatever you like. One suggestion: Keep a written record of what you use and how you feel it works out, so you'll be able to repeat your favorite combinations (although there's a lot to be said for constantly trying new flavors, too).

1 package dry yeast

2 cups (475 ml) lukewarm (95° to 110°F; 35°–40°C) water (or use milk for half of this)

2 tablespoons honey or sugar

1 1/2 cups (415 ml) (total) any combination of: cornmeal, barley flour (or pearl barley, soaked or parboiled), raw oats, millet, triticale, quinoa, rice flour, soaked or sprouted wheat berries—whatever you want! (Or use a mixed-grain cereal from a health-food store or co-op.)

1 tablespoon salt

2 cups (550 ml) whole-wheat flour

3 cups (825 ml) white flour

Continued →

1. Proof the yeast in the warm water with the honey in a large bowl.

2. Stir in the combination of grains and the salt, then the whole-wheat flour and 2 cups (550 ml) of the white flour.

3. Turn out onto a floured surface and knead in the rest of the white flour.

4. Let rise in a greased bowl, covered, until doubled.

5. Punch down. Shape into two loaves and place in greased 8 1/2 x 4 1/2-inch (21 x 11 cm) pans. Let rise until doubled again.

6. Preheat your oven to 350°F (177°C).

7. Bake for about 1 hour.

MAKES 2 FAIRLY SMALL LOAVES

CARAWAY RYE BATTER BREAD

This recipe is primarily for those who don't find that kneading is necessary to their mental health, but it's also a nice bread that you'll be proud to make.

If you don't want a caraway rye bread, just (guess what?) omit the caraway seeds.

2 packages yeast

4 tablespoons sugar, divided

1 cup (235 ml) lukewarm (95° to 110°F; 35°–40°C) water

1 cup (235 ml) milk

1 egg

1/4 cup (60 ml) salad oil

1 tablespoon salt

2 tablespoons caraway seeds

2 cups (550 ml) rye flour

1 1/2–2 cups (415–550 ml) white flour

1. Proof the yeast along with 1 tablespoon of the sugar in the warm water in a large bowl.

2. Add the milk, egg, salad oil, and salt. Combine well.

3. Combine the rye and white flours, then stir the caraway seeds and the remaining sugar into the flour. Beat into the liquid mixture, 1 cup at a time, the rye flour, then enough of the white flour to make a stiff batter.

4. Cover the bowl and allow the batter to rise for 30 minutes (it should not double in size).

5. Stir down the batter, then spoon it into two 8 x 4-inch (20 x 10 cm) bread pans.

6. Preheat your oven to 375°F (190°C). When the batter in the pans has risen just slightly (about 15 minutes), put them in the oven. Bake for 35 to 40 minutes, then remove from the pans at once and allow to cool on a rack.

RAISIN PUMPERNICKEL BREAD

Raisin Pumpernickel is a New York tradition. It's quite black in color and quite delicious to taste. You can make it into great sandwiches (for instance, try one with ripe Brie and prosciutto) or just eat it by the slice.

1 package dry yeast

3/4 cup (180 ml) lukewarm (95° to 110°F; 35°–40°C) water

1/4 cup (60 ml) molasses

1 1/2 teaspoons salt

1 tablespoon dry cocoa

1 teaspoon instant coffee granules

1 cup (275 ml) rye flour

1 cup (275 ml) white flour

1 cup (275 ml) whole-wheat flour

1/2 cup (140 ml) raisins

2 tablespoons cornmeal

Egg wash (1 egg beaten with 2 tablespoons water)

1. Proof the yeast in the water with the molasses.

2. Stir the salt, cocoa, and coffee granules into the rye flour, then stir this into the yeast mixture. Mix well.

3. Combine the white and whole-wheat flours, and add about 1 1/2 cups (415 ml) of this to the yeast and rye flour mixture.

4. Turn out onto a floured board and knead in the rest of the flour. Let the dough rise in a greased bowl, covered, until doubled; this may take an hour or even two.

5. Punch the dough down. Put the raisins onto your floured board, plop out the dough onto this, and knead well, until the raisins are well incorporated. Let the rough rise again, then shape into a round loaf.

6. Sprinkle the cornmeal on a baking sheet and place the loaf on it. Let it rise, covered, until doubled once again.

7. Preheat your oven to 375°F (190°C).

8. Cut across the top of the loaf in two or three places with a single-edge razor or a sharp knife. Brush with the egg wash; wait 5 minutes and repeat.

9. Bake for 40 to 45 minutes.

MAKES 1 LOAF

SPECIALTY BREADS

Unique flavors, special ingredients, and new techniques give these breads their special flavors.

ONION BREAD

When I lived in Manhattan, a bakery near me made an onion bread I had a hard time resisting. Now I no longer live there, but I've learned to make my own!

1 package dry yeast

1 cup (235 ml) lukewarm (95° to 110°F; 35°–40°C) water

2 teaspoons sugar

2 teaspoons salt, divided

3 cups (825 ml) white flour

2 tablespoons melted butter

2/3 cup (185 ml) minced onion

1. Using a large bowl, proof the yeast in the lukewarm water along with the sugar. Add 1 teaspoon of the salt.

2. Beat in 2 cups (550 ml) of the flour. When well mixed, beat in 1/2 cup (140 ml) more.

3. Turn out onto a board or other surface on which you have spread 1/2 cup (140 ml) more flour. Knead well, until all the flour has been incorporated and the dough is shiny and elastic.

4. Put in a greased bowl. Turn the dough around in it. Cover. Let rise until doubled in size, about 1 hour.

5. Punch down the dough and divide it into halves. Put each in a greased 9-inch (22.5 cm) round cake pan.

6. Brush the top of each loaf with butter and sprinkle on the onion, then, using your fingers, poke down the onion pieces into the dough. (The tops of the loaves will look dented.)

7. Let rise until doubled again (the loaves do not need to be covered).

8. Preheat your oven to 450°F (232°C) (very hot).

9. Sprinkle remaining salt on the loaves. Bake for about 20 minutes.

MAKES 2 ROUND LOAVES

CHEESE BREAD

You probably won't be able to buy cheese bread anywhere, but making your own is a snap—and a highly worthwhile way to spend your time! You'll love it plain or toasted, or as the base for an appetizer, or made into croutons, or...

1 package dry yeast

1 tablespoon sugar

1/2 cup (120 ml) lukewarm (95° to 110°F; 35°–40°C) water

1 1/4 cups (295 ml) milk

2 1/2 cups (690 ml) grated or shredded Cheddar cheese

3 tablespoons salad oil

1 1/2 teaspoons salt

5–6 cups (1,375–1,650 ml) white flour

1. Proof the yeast in a large bowl along with the sugar in the lukewarm water.

2. Beat in the milk, cheese, and oil, then add the salt and 2 1/2 cups (690 ml) of the flour and mix well.

3. Add another 2 1/2 cups (690 ml) of flour and turn out onto a well-floured surface. Knead until smooth and shiny, adding more flour if necessary.

4. Put the dough in a greased bowl, turning it around, then cover and let it rise until doubled in size.

5. Punch down the dough and divide it in two. Shape into two loaves and place them in greased 9-inch (22.5 cm) bread pans. Cover lightly and let rise again until once more doubled. Preheat your oven to 350°F (177°C).

6. Bake for about 40 minutes.

MAKES 2 LARGE LOAVES

MONKEY BREAD

I've read that Nancy Reagan insisted Monkey Bread be served at most White House dinners when she was the first lady. An odd choice, many thought, but there's no getting around the fact that it is quite delicious!

2 packages dry yeast

1 cup (275 ml) white (granulated) sugar

1/2 cup (120 ml) lukewarm (95° to 110°F; 35°–40°C) water

1 cup (2 sticks) room-temperature butter, divided

1 1/2 tablespoons salt

1 cup (235 ml) lukewarm (95° to 110°F; 35°–40°C) milk

4 eggs (or 3 eggs and 2 egg yolks)

6 cups (1,650 ml) or more white flour

1/2 cup (140 ml) light brown sugar

1. Proof the yeast along with the white sugar in the lukewarm water in a large bowl.

2. Stir half the butter (that's 1 stick) and the salt into the warm milk. Don't worry if it doesn't completely dissolve. Add this to the proofed yeast mixture. Add the eggs. Mix very thoroughly.

3. Now start adding the flour, 1 cup (275 ml) at a time, mixing it in well each time. After about 5 cups (1,375 ml), the dough will become rather difficult to handle, so turn it out on a

Continued ➜

well-floured surface and add more flour until you have a dough that is no longer sticky and can be kneaded. This may take another 2 cups (550 ml) of flour (making a total of 7 cups; 1,925 ml).

4. Knead very thoroughly, until the dough is absolutely manageable. Put it into a greased bowl, turning to coat it all over. Cover and let rise until doubled in size. Punch down the dough. Let it rest for 5 minutes, then turn it out onto a lightly floured surface.

5. Let the dough rest where it is while you melt the remaining stick of butter and combine it with the brown sugar.

6. Now comes the fun: Make the dough into balls the size of Ping-Pong balls. Working with one a time, dip the balls into the brown sugar mixture and place in a well-buttered tube pan (like an angel food cake pan). There should be some of the brown sugar mixture left; just pour it over the top of the pan.

7. Cover the pan loosely and allow the dough to rise once more, this time to the top of the pan. Preheat your oven to 375°F (190°C).

8. Bake for an hour or a few minutes more. Test for doneness by tapping the top of the bread—if it's done, it will sound hollow. Turn out of the pan onto a plate.

9. If you serve the bread warm, you and your guests can pull off little globes of dough. Otherwise, the bread can be cooled and sliced. I have no idea which way it was served in the White House, but suspect that, at least for formal dinners, it was sliced.

MAKES 1 VERY LARGE LOAF

Making Quick Breads

Barbara Karoff

Introduction

Quick breads are an old favorite of mine. Because I've found that most general cookbooks, and even most baking books, include few recipes for quick, non-yeast loaves, I long ago began collecting recipes. I use and change them frequently, and, in these busy times, I believe you will share my enthusiasm for these simple and delicious baked goods.

And because few of these batters require kneading or time to rise, most loaves are ready for the oven in 10 to 15 minutes. Mixing time is brief, in part, because the cardinal rule about quick breads is: *Do not overmix.* Overmixing results in tough breads. Mix batters with a wooden spoon or rubber spatula just enough to combine the wet and dry ingredients. A few lumps are all right. Electric mixers, food processors, or blenders do not produce good quick breads.

Equipment requirements are as simple as the mixing rule. A wooden spoon, a couple of bowls, measuring cups and spoons and baking containers are all that are necessary. A wire whisk is a handy time-saver.

Most recipes were originally designed to fill one or two approximately 9 x 5-inch loaf pans. The one I use is closer to 8 1/2 x

4 1/2 inches but it doesn't make any difference. Don't be put off by pan sizes.

As I've baked quick breads over the years, I've come up with a variety of baking containers to meet my needs and suit my whims and I hope you will too.

Any oven-proof casserole, bowl, or pan will work. Of course baking times will vary, but they do in different ovens anyway, so keep a tester handy. As soon as it comes out clean when inserted in the center of the loaf, and the bread begins to pull away slightly from the sides of the pan, the bread is done.

I urge you to experiment with casseroles, small ramekins, and au gratin dishes. I've baked successfully in one-cup porcelain ramekins. The little round loaves these containers produce are an interesting change and just right for one hungry person.

Please watch carefully the first time and make a note of the actual time required when bread is baked in a particular pan size. Not only pan size, but the material of which the pan is made, affects the baking time. The times below are approximate and are intended to serve only as a guide.

Pan Size/Type	Approximate Baking Time
1-cup porcelain ramekin	15 to 20 minutes
3-cup au gratin dish or pie pan	15 to 20 minutes
9-inch x 5-inch loaf pan	about 1 hour
5 1/2-inch x 3-inch loaf pan	30 to 40 minutes
1-quart casserole	40 to 50 minutes

Listed below are a few tips to make your quick breads even quicker—and more fail-proof.

1. Never beat the batter. I repeat this because it is so important.

2. Allow thick bread batters which do *not* contain baking powder to rest in the pan for 10 minutes before baking. A lighter loaf will result.

3. Fill pans or other containers no more than two-thirds full.

4. Place filled pans in the center of the oven.

5. No need to preheat the oven. Save energy instead.

6. Test about 10 minutes before you think the loaf will be done.

7. Use whole wheat *pastry* flour instead of regular milled whole wheat flour for a lighter loaf. It's processed from soft wheat which contains less gluten. (Gluten is something else that makes quick breads tough.)

8. Seek out and experiment with special flours. A store that sells in bulk allows you to purchase just the amount you need. Special flours include amaranth, buckwheat, cornmeal, graham, millet, oat, quiona, rice, rye, soy, triticale, and whole wheat. Don't forget wheat germ, oats, and bran as well.

9. Add nuts and dried fruits to the dry ingredients to coat them with flour so they don't sink to the bottom of the loaf.

10. Mix dry ingredients together in a large bowl. I like to combine them with a wire whisk to distribute the leavening agents evenly and to add air to the mixture.

11. Mix wet ingredients together in another bowl (use the same wire whisk) and, with a spoon, stir them quickly into the dry ingredients.

12. Do not combine wet and dry ingredients until you are ready to bake, or some of the leavening action will be lost.

13. When loaves are done, cool them in the pans for 10 minutes; then remove to a wire rack. If they cool completely in the pans, condensation will make them soggy.

BASIC QUICK BREAD RECIPE

This is a basic recipe to which you can add different flours, spices, nuts, seeds, and fruits. It is not very interesting as it stands, so use it as a basic guide to create your own special breads. Keep the addition and substitution rules in mind and go for it.

1 1/2 cups unbleached flour

1/2 tablespoon baking powder

1/2 teaspoon salt

1/4 cup softened butter or margarine

1/2 cup sugar

1 egg

3/4 cup milk

In a large bowl combine the flour, baking powder, and salt. In another bowl cream the butter and sugar. Stir in the egg and mix well. Stir in the milk and add the liquid mixture quickly to the dry ingredients. Stir just enough to moisten completely. Spoon the mixture into greased pans and bake at 350°F until a tester comes out clean. Cool in the pans for 10 minutes and then remove to a wire rack to cool completely.

Sweet Quick Breads

DRIED FRUIT BREAD

Full of unexpected fruit flavors, this loaf is a winner every time.

l cup dried pears	l cup unbleached flour
l cup dried peaches	l cup whole wheat flour
l cup golden raisins	2 teaspoons baking powder
1 1/2 cups water	l teaspoon baking soda
l cup pitted dates	1/4 teaspoon salt
1/2 cup dried cherries (optional)	1/2 teaspoon nutmeg
3 tablespoons butter or margarine	1/2 teaspoon cardamom
3/4 cup sugar l egg	2/3 cup liquid from cooking the fruit
Grated peel of 1 orange, orange part only	2/3 cup unsalted sunflower seeds

Place pears, peaches, and raisins in a sauce pan with water to cover and simmer gently for five minutes. Drain and reserve liquid. Chop the pears and peaches coarsely. Cut the dates in thirds and add them, along with the cherries, to the other fruit. In a large bowl cream the butter and sugar together. Add the egg and grated peel, and mix well. In another bowl combine the flours, baking powder, soda, salt, and spices. Add them to the creamed mixture alternately with the fruit cooking liquid. Fold in the fruits and seeds, and mix just enough to combine thoroughly. Spoon the batter into greased pans and let stand 15 minutes. Bake at 350°F until a tester comes out clean. Cool in pans for 10 minutes and then remove to a rack to cool completely.

BUCKWHEAT-CURRANT BREAD

This loaf is dense and moist and bursting with wonderful Old World flavor. Add nuts if you like. It's even better the next day.

1/2 cup currants	1/2 cup brown sugar, packed
1 3/4 cups buttermilk	1 teaspoon salt
2 1/3 cups buckwheat flour	1 teaspoon baking powder

Combine the currants and buttermilk in a small bowl and allow to stand while assembling the other ingredients. Combine the flour, sugar, salt, and baking powder in a large bowl. Add the currants and buttermilk and mix until just combined completely. Spoon the batter into greased pans and bake at 325°F until a tester comes out clean. Cool in the pans for 10 minutes and then remove to a rack to cool completely.

WHOLE WHEAT WALNUT BREAD

This unsweet loaf successfully breaks the rule about the ratio of whole wheat to unbleached flour. It's chock full of walnuts and is wonderful for breakfast.

3/4 cup unbleached flour	1 cup walnuts, coarsely broken
1 1/2 cups whole wheat flour	3 tablespoons vegetable oil
2 1/2 teaspoons baking powder	1 1/2 cups buttermilk 1 teaspoon baking soda
1/2 cup brown sugar, lightly packed	

In a large bowl combine the flours, baking powder, soda, sugar, and nuts. In another bowl combine the oil and buttermilk and stir them quickly into the dry ingredients. Spoon the batter into greased pans and bake at 350°F until a tester comes out clean. Let cool in the pans for 10 minutes and then remove to a rack to cool completely.

HONEY-PECAN BREAD

A solid loaf filled with crunchy oats and nuts. It's just slightly sweet.

l cup unbleached flour	l teaspoon baking soda
1/2 cup rye flour	1/2 teaspoon salt
1/2 cup whole wheat flour	l cup chopped pecans
1/2 cup rolled oats	1 1/3 cups yogurt
1/2 cup bran	4 tablespoons honey
l teaspoon baking powder	

In a large bowl combine the flours, oats, bran, baking powder, soda, salt, and pecans. In another bowl mix the yogurt and honey, and then combine this with the dry ingredients, mixing just enough to blend completely. The batter will be stiff. Spoon the batter into greased pans and bake at 350°F until a tester comes out clean. Cool in the pans for 10 minutes and then remove to a rack to cool completely.

Continued ➔

RHUBARB BREAD

This loaf is quite moist with a delicious sweet-tart flavor. It's difficult to slice until cooled completely. It's definitely more mellow the next day.

1 1/2 cups brown sugar, lightly packed

2/3 cup vegetable oil

l egg

l teaspoon salt

l cup buttermilk

1 1/2 cups rhubarb, finely diced

1/2 cup walnuts, chopped

1 1/4 cups unbleached flour

1 1/4 cups whole wheat flour

1/4 cup wheat germ

l teaspoon baking powder

In a large bowl combine the oil and sugar. Add the egg, salt, and buttermilk, and mix thoroughly. Stir in the rhubarb. In another bowl combine the nuts, flours, wheat germ, and baking powder, and add the dry ingredients to the rhubarb mixture all at once. Stir just enough to combine. Spoon the batter into greased pans and bake at 350°F until a tester comes out clean. Cool in the pans for 20 minutes and then remove to a rack to cool completely.

APRICOT-ALMOND BREAD

Almonds and apricots are a time- and taste-tested combination. Cardamom and nutmeg complete the flavor magic.

1/2 cup sugar

2 tablespoons butter or margarine

l egg

l cup buttermilk

1/2 cup bran

1/2 cup wheat germ

l cup almonds, coarsely chopped

l cup dried apricots, coarsely chopped

l cup unbleached flour

l cup whole wheat flour

1/2 teaspoon nutmeg

1/2 teaspoon cardamom

1 tablespoon baking powder

1/2 teaspoon baking soda

1/2 teaspoon salt

In a large bowl cream the butter and sugar until fluffy. Add the eggs and buttermilk and mix well. In another bowl mix the bran, wheat germ, nuts, apricots, flours, spices, baking powder, soda, and salt. Add them to the creamed mixture and mix just enough to combine thoroughly. Spoon the batter into greased pans and bake at 350°F until a tester comes out clean. Cool in the pans for 10 minutes and then remove to a rack to cool completely.

NANCY'S CHRISTMAS BREAD

This bread is filled with fruits and nuts and spices—a "fruitcake" for those who don't like fruitcake. Enjoy it for the holidays and throughout the year

4 cups unbleached flour

l cup sugar

1 teaspoon baking soda

3 teaspoons baking powder

1/2 cup almonds, chopped

1 cup assorted dried fruit, chopped

1/2 cup walnuts, chopped

l teaspoon cinnamon

1/2 teaspoon ground cloves

1/2 teaspoon ground ginger

1/2 teaspoon grated nutmeg

2 eggs, beaten

2 cups buttermilk

2 tablespoons butter or margarine, melted

2 tablespoons cognac

In a large bowl combine the flour, sugar, baking soda, baking powder, fruits, nuts, and spices. In another bowl combine the eggs, buttermilk, butter, and cognac. Add the wet to the dry ingredients and, in this case, mix thoroughly. Spoon the batter into greased pans and bake at 350°F until a tester comes out clean. Cool in the pans for 10 minutes and then remove to a rack to cool completely.

APPLE-SPICE BREAD

Applesauce and currants and lots of other good things go into this bread. Try substituting 1/2 cup of bran for half the oats, or leave out the apple and increase the applesauce to one cup. However you make it, it's better the next day.

3/4 cup unbleached flour

3/4 cup whole wheat flour

l teaspoon baking powder

l teaspoon baking soda

1/2 teaspoon salt

l teaspoon cinnamon

1/2 teaspoon nutmeg1/2 teaspoon mace

l teaspoon allspice1/3 cup butter or margarine

1/4 cup brown sugar, lightly packed

2 eggs

3/4 cup unsweetened applesauce

l large apple, peeled, cored, and chopped

l cup rolled oats

3/4 cup walnuts, coarsely chopped

l cup currants

In a large bowl combine the flours, baking powder, soda, salt, and spices. In another bowl cream the butter and sugar. Add the eggs, applesauce, and apple, and mix well. Stir the oats, nuts and currants into the dry ingredients, and then add the wet mixture and mix just enough to combine thoroughly. Spoon the batter into greased pans and bake at 350°F until a tester comes out clean. Cool in the pans for 10 minutes and then remove to a rack to cool completely.

BANANA-BRAN BREAD

This is a healthy and flavorful update of my favorite old Banana Nut Bread.

1/4 cup butter or margarine

1/4 cup sugar

l egg

1 1/2 cups coarsely mashed banana

3/4 cup unbleached flour

3/4 cup whole wheat flour

1 cup bran

2 teaspoons baking powder

1/4 teaspoon salt

1/2 teaspoon baking soda

2/3 cup almonds or peanuts, coarsely chopped

1/2 cup crystallized ginger, chopped (optional)

2 tablespoons water

l teaspoon vanilla

In a large bowl cream the butter and sugar until fluffy. Add the egg and mix thoroughly. Add the banana. In another bowl combine the flours, bran, baking powder, salt, soda, nuts, and ginger. Add the dry ingredients to the creamed mixture. Stir in the water and vanilla, and spoon the batter into greased pans and bake at 350°F until a tester comes out clean. Cool in the pans for 10 minutes and then remove to a rack to cool completely.

CRANBERRY-NUT BREAD

This is an old New England favorite. The tart-sweet flavor improves the next day.

1 cup whole cranberries, coarsely chopped	1/2 teaspoon baking soda
1 cup walnuts, coarsely chopped	2 eggs, lightly beaten
1 tablespoon unbleached flour	2 tablespoons vegetable oil
2 cups unbleached flour	Grated rind of 1 orange, orange part only
1 cup sugar	Juice of 1 orange
1/2 teaspoon salt	Boiling water
1 1/2 teaspoons baking powder	

Combine the cranberries and nuts with one tablespoon of flour and set aside. In a large bowl combine the 2 cups of flour, sugar, salt, baking powder, and soda. In a one-cup measure combine the eggs, oil, orange rind, and juice. Add enough boiling water to measure 1 cup and add this mixture to the dry ingredients and combine well. Fold in the cranberries and nuts. Spoon the batter into greased pans and bake at 350°F until a tester comes out clean. Cool in the pans for 10 minutes and then remove to a rack to cool completely.

SAVORY QUICK BREADS

BLUE CHEESE BREAD

Many years ago I was introduced to the intriguing combination of sweet wheat meal crackers spread with sharp blue cheese and I loved it from the start. This bread recreates the flavor combination.

1/3 cup butter or margarine	2 teaspoons baking powder
1/2 cup sugar	1/4 teaspoon baking soda
2 eggs	2/3 cup milk
1 1/2 cups unbleached flour	1 cup crumbled blue cheese
1/2 cup whole wheat flour	1 tablespoon poppy seeds

In a large bowl cream the sugar and butter until fluffy. Add the eggs and blend well. In another bowl combine the flour, baking powder, and soda. Add the dry ingredients alternately with the milk to the butter mixture. Stir in the cheese and seeds, and spoon the batter into greased pans. Bake at 350°F until a tester comes out clean. Cool in the pans for 10 minutes and then remove to a rack to cool completely.

DOUBLE CUMIN BREAD

This bread is a natural with chili or other Mexican-style food. It's better the second day.

3 cups unbleached flour	1 1/2 teaspoons salt
1/4 cup sugar	3 eggs
2 tablespoons baking powder	1 1/2 cups milk
4 teaspoons ground cumin	1/3 cup vegetable oil
1 teaspoon cumin seeds, toasted	
1/2 teaspoon dry mustard	

In a large bowl combine the flour, sugar, baking powder, ground cumin, cumin seeds, mustard, and salt. In another bowl whisk together the eggs, milk, and oil, and add the liquid ingredients to the dry. Mix until just moistened. Spoon the batter into greased pans and bake at 350°F until a tester comes out clean. Cool in the pans for 10 minutes and then remove to a rack to cool completely.

BEER BREAD

Someone once said of this recipe that it is so simple they were embarrassed to tell anyone. It really is that simple and it's equally delicious. Beer gives the loaf a robust, yeasty flavor. It's wonderful eaten soon after it emerges fragrant from the oven and it makes toast like no other.

BASIC LOAF

3 cups self-rising flour	One 12-ounce can beer
3 tablespoons sugar	4 tablespoons butter or margarine, melted

Combine the flour, sugar and beer in a bowl. Scrape it into a well-greased loaf pan or 1-quart soufflé dish. Bake at 375°F for about 50 minutes. Pour the melted butter over the top and bake 10 minutes longer. Cool on a rack.

Variation I Add 1/2 cup minced herbs and parsley.

Variation II Use brown instead of white sugar, add 1 tablespoon cinnamon, 1/2 teaspoon nutmeg, and 1/2 cup walnuts, chopped.

Variation III Increase flour to 4 cups. Add 2 eggs, 2 cups sharp Cheddar, grated, 1/4 cup vegetable oil, 1 teaspoon each thyme and oregano, and 12 ounces beer. Mix all ingredients and bake as above.

IRISH SODA BREAD WITH SEEDS

Slightly sweet, rich and utterly delicious, this is my favorite of the many Irish soda breads I've made and eaten.

3 1/2 cups unbleached flour	2 teaspoons caraway seeds
1/2 cup sugar	1 cup golden raisins
1 teaspoon salt	2 eggs
1/2 teaspoon baking soda	2 cups sour cream
2 teaspoons baking powder	

In a large bowl combine the flour, sugar, salt, soda, baking powder, seeds, and raisins. In another bowl whisk together the eggs and sour cream, and add them to the dry ingredients. Mix just to moisten thoroughly. Spoon the batter onto a greased and floured 8-inch round cake pan or other flat baking dish. Form the dough into a round and cut a cross on the top with a sharp knife. The dough is sticky. Bake at 350°F for about an hour, or until the loaf sounds hollow when tapped and a tester comes out clean. Remove to a rack to cool completely.

Continued →

SAVORY OLIVE BREAD

For a different flavor replace the pimiento-stuffed olives with Calamata, Niçoise, or other flavorful black olives. It takes time to remove the pits but it's worth it.

2 cups unbleached flour	1/4 cup butter or margarine, softened
1/2 cup cornmeal	1 cup sharp Cheddar cheese, grated
2 1/2 tablespoons sugar	1 egg
2 teaspoons baking powder	1 cup buttermilk
1/2 teaspoon baking soda	5 slices bacon, cooked crisp, chopped
1/2 teaspoon salt	1 cup pimiento-stuffed olives, chopped
1 teaspoon dry mustard	
Pinch dried red pepper flakes, or to taste	

In a large bowl combine the flour, cornmeal, sugar, baking powder, soda, salt, dry mustard, and red pepper flakes. Cut in the butter with a pastry blender or combine with fingers until it is well blended. Stir in the cheese. In another bowl whisk together the egg and buttermilk and add it to the dry ingredients. Stir until just blended and then fold in the bacon and olives. Spoon the batter into greased pans and bake at 375°F until a tester comes out clean. Cool in the pans for 10 minutes and then remove to a rack to cool completely.

SAVORY TOMATO BREAD

This loaf bursts with tomato flavor and is a fine accompaniment for soup or salad or a simple meat dish. Other ingredients you might add include chopped sun-dried tomatoes, tomato paste, ketchup, pesto, or pine nuts.

1 1/4 cups whole wheat flour	1/2 cup grated Parmesan cheese
1 1/4 cups unbleached flour	2/3 cup tomato puree
1 teaspoon salt	2 or 3 cloves garlic, pressed
1 tablespoon baking powder	2 eggs
Pinch of baking soda	1/4 cup olive oil
1 teaspoon oregano	1 tablespoon honey

In a large bowl combine the flours, salt, baking powder, soda, oregano, and cheese. Drain the juice from a 14-ounce can of whole tomatoes and puree the tomatoes. There should be about 2/3 cup. If the measure is short, make it up with milk. Add the pressed garlic, eggs, olive oil, and honey to the tomato puree, and mix well. Add this mixture to the dry ingredients and mix just enough to combine completely. Spoon the batter into greased pans and bake at 350°F until a tester comes out clean. Cool in the pans for 10 minutes and then remove to a rack to cool completely.

CHEDDAR-DILL BREAD

This cheesy loaf is especially good warm. Substitute other herbs for the dill if you like.

4 cups unbleached flour (3 cups white, 1 cup whole wheat is best)	2 teaspoons salt
	2 teaspoons dried dill weed
2 tablespoon baking powder	Ground black pepper, to taste

3 cups sharp cheddar cheese, coarsely grated	2 eggs
1/2 cup green onions, chopped	2 cups milk

In a large bowl combine the flours, baking powder, salt, dill weed, and pepper. Add the cheese and onions and toss to coat. Beat the eggs and milk together and stir into the dry ingredients. Spoon the batter, which will be stiff, into greased pans and let rise 10 minutes. Bake at 375°F for about 45 minutes or until a tester comes out clean. Cool in the pans for 10 minutes and then remove to a rack to cool completely.

SAVORY PUMPKIN BREAD

The flavors of India take the spotlight in this unusual loaf.

3/4 cup unbleached flour	1 tablespoon curry powder
3/4 cup cornmeal	1/4 teaspoon ground cumin
1 teaspoon baking powder	1/8 teaspoon cayenne
1/2 teaspoon baking soda	1/2 teaspoon salt
1 tablespoon sugar	1 cup cooked pumpkin puree (canned is fine)
3 tablespoons butter or margarine	2 eggs
1/2 cup onion, minced	6 tablespoons buttermilk

In a small bowl combine the flour, cornmeal, soda, baking powder, and sugar. Melt the butter in a skillet and cook the onion, curry powder, cumin, cayenne, and salt over medium heat until the onion is soft. In a large bowl beat together the pumpkin, eggs and buttermilk. Stir in the onion mixture and then the flour mixture until just moistened. Spoon the batter into greased pans and bake at 350°F until a tester comes out clean. Cool in the pans for 10 minutes and then remove to a rack to cool completely.

TUSCAN COUNTRY BREAD

If fresh sage is available, the mild flavor is distinctive and delicious. If you use dried leaves, 2 tablespoons are enough.

1 cup unbleached flour	1/4 teaspoon ground black pepper to taste
1/2 cup whole wheat flour	1/4 cup olive oil
1/2 cup cornmeal	1 egg
1/4 cup chopped fresh sage leaves	1/2 cup milk
1/2 tablespoon baking powder	1/4 cup dry white wine
1/2 teaspoon salt	

In a large bowl combine the flours, cornmeal, sage, baking powder, salt, and pepper. In another bowl combine the olive oil, egg, milk, and wine. Stir the wet ingredients into the dry ingredients and mix until just blended. Spoon the batter into greased pans and bake at 350°F until a tester comes out clean. Cool in the pans for 10 minutes and then remove to a rack to cool completely.

ONION-ZUCCHINI BREAD

This is a perfect loaf for picnics or for snacking. Try adding a tablespoon or two of pesto and/or 1/2 cup of toasted sunflower seeds or pine nuts. Bake in a shallow pan, au gratin dish, or pie tin.

3 cups unbleached flour	3/4 cup onion, chopped
2 tablespoons sugar	1/3 cup butter or margarine, melted
1/2 cup grated Parmesan cheese	
4 teaspoons baking powder	1 cup buttermilk
1/2 teaspoon baking soda	2 eggs
1 teaspoon salt	3/4 cup grated zucchini

In a large bowl combine the flour, sugar, cheese, baking powder, soda, and salt. In another bowl combine the onions, butter, buttermilk, eggs, and zucchini. Stir the wet ingredients into the dry ingredients just enough to moisten. Spoon the batter into greased pans and bake at 350°F until a tester comes out clean. Cool in the pans for 10 minutes and then remove to a rack to cool completely.

CORN QUICK BREADS

CUSTARD CORN BREAD

A slightly sweet custard layer forms on the top of this unusual cornbread as it bakes. It can be made in an 8-inch square or round pan or in individual ramekins.

2 eggs	1/2 cup unbleached flour
1 cup milk	1/2 teaspoon baking soda
1/2 cup buttermilk	1/2 teaspoon salt
3 tablespoons sugar	1/4 teaspoon nutmeg
3/4 cup cornmeal	2 tablespoons butter or margarine, melted

In a large bowl beat together the eggs with 1/2 cup milk and all of the buttermilk. Stir in the sugar, cornmeal, flour, soda, salt, nutmeg, and butter, and mix until well blended. Pour the batter into well-greased pans or ramekins and top with the remaining milk. Do not stir the milk into the batter. Bake at 325°F until the center appears set when shaken lightly. The top should be lightly browned. Let stand 15 minutes before serving warm.

MEXICAN CORN BREAD

Bake this wonderfully flavorful corn bread in a 6-cup casserole dish or in a 9-inch skillet.

One 8 1/2-ounce can cream style corn	3/4 cup milk
1 cup cornmeal	1/3 cup butter or margarine, melted
2 eggs	1/2 cup sharp Cheddar cheese, grated
2 tablespoons butter or margarine	One 4-ounce can diced chilies, drained1 teaspoon salt
1/2 teaspoon baking soda	

Preheat the oven to 400°F. In a bowl combine the corn, cornmeal, eggs, salt, soda, milk, butter, half the cheese, and the chilies. Mix well. Put 2 tablespoons butter in the baking casserole or skillet and place it in the oven until the butter is hot and melted but not brown. Immediately pour the batter into the baking container. Sprinkle the top with the reserved cheese and bake at 400°F until the tester comes out clean. Let rest a few minutes and serve hot.

FROM THE DAIRY

Making Cheese, Butter, & Yogurt

Phyllis Hobson
Illustrations by Sue Storey

This material was taken from *Making Homemade Cheeses & Butter* by Phyllis Hobson, Garden Way Publishing.

If you have a couple of goats or a cow on your homestead (and if you do not you are missing one of the most satisfying aspects of country life), you are sure to find yourself with several gallons of surplus milk on hand. Few families, even those with several milk drinkers, can keep up with the output of a good cow on green pasture, and most goats will average a gallon of milk a day during the summer months.

You can make butter and buttermilk, of course, or you can make yogurt; you can freeze packages of butter or cartons of whole milk for the less bountiful winter months; you may even want to can the milk.

But the best solution to a surplus of milk is cheese—the most delicious, nutritious method of preserving milk yet devised.

Even if you do not have a cow or goats of your own, chances are good that you can find a source of fresh milk from a farmer or at a dairy where you can buy raw milk that is free from chemicals. During the summer months, when the animals are eating lush pasture and the milk is plentiful, you often can buy milk at a lower price.

The instructions for making cheese sound complicated, but the process is really much simpler than baking a cake. For each recipe read the Basic Directions through first, then read the specific recipe. Read each step carefully as you go. With only a little practice you can become an expert at making cheese.

As you gain confidence, you will learn the variables of cheese making—the degree of ripening of the milk and its effect on the flavor, the length of time the curd is heated and how that affects the texture, the amount of salt, the number of bricks used in pressing and the effect on moisture content, and how long the cheese is cured for sharpness of taste. All of these variables affect the finished product and produce the many varieties of flavor and texture. The more you learn about it, the more fascinating cheese making will become.

Kinds of Cheese

There are basically three kinds of cheese: hard, soft, and cottage.

Hard cheese is the curd of milk (the white, solid portion) separated from the whey (the watery, clear liquid). Once separated, the curd is pressed into a solid cake and aged for flavor. Well-pressed, well-aged cheese, will keep for months. Most hard cheeses can be eaten immediately but are better flavored if they are aged. The longer the aging

Continued ➔

period, the sharper the flavor. The heavier the pressing weight, the harder the texture. Hard cheese is best when made of whole milk.

Soft cheese is made the same way as hard cheese, but it is pressed just briefly. It is not paraffined and is aged a short time or not at all. Most soft cheeses can be eaten immediately and are best eaten within a few weeks. Cheeses such as Camembert, Gorgonzola, and Roquefort are soft cheese which have been put aside to cure. They do not keep as long as hard cheese because of their higher moisture content. Soft cheese may be made of whole or skim milk.

Cottage cheese is a soft cheese prepared from a high-moisture curd that is not allowed to cure. Commercially it usually is made of skim milk, but it can be made of whole milk. Cottage cheese is the simplest of all cheese to make.

Equipment

The list of equipment needed to make cheese is long; but do not let that scare you off. Improvise with your equipment. Most of the necessary utensils are already in your kitchen. A strainer can be made by punching holes in a restaurant-size can, but a colander or large sieve works best. A floating dairy thermometer works fine for cheese making, but almost any thermometer that can be immersed will do. A coffee can, a few boards, and a broomstick can be transformed into a cheese press.

Equipment

cheese form	long-handled spoon
follower	large knife
cheese press	2 pieces of cheesecloth, 1 square yard each
2 large pots	6 to 8 bricks
strainer	1 pound paraffin
thermometer	

CHEESE FORM

You can make your own cheese form from a 2-pound coffee can by punching nail holes in the bottom of the can. Be sure to punch the holes from the inside out so the rough edges are on the outside of the can and will not tear the cheese. The cheese form is lined with cheesecloth and filled with the wet curd, which then is covered with another piece of cheesecloth before the follower is inserted for pressing. The excess whey drains from the curd through the nail holes in the can. You can also buy cheese forms.

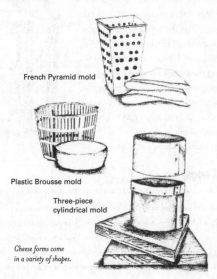

French Pyramid mold

Plastic Brousse mold

Three-piece cylindrical mold

Cheese forms come in a variety of shapes.

FOLLOWER

A follower is a circle of 1/2-inch plywood or a 1-inch board cut just enough smaller in diameter than the coffee can so that it can be inserted inside the can and moved up and down easily. The follower forces the wet curd down, forming a solid cake in the bottom of the can and squeezing out the whey.

CHEESE PRESS

Cheese presses can be bought, substituted for by an old-fashioned lard press, or you can make your own in an afternoon with some scrap wood and a broomstick. (See illustration.)

To make your own cheese press, take a piece of 1-inch plywood or a 1-inch by 12-inch board and cut the wood to make 2 pieces about 11 1/2 inches by 18 inches each. Drill a hole about 1 inch in diameter in the center of one of the boards; whey will drain through this hole. In the other board, drill 2 holes, 1 inch in diameter each, 2 inches from each end. These holes should be just big enough so that the broomstick can move through them easily.

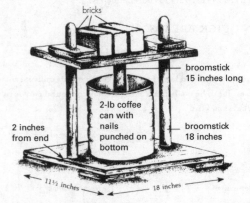

bricks

broomstick 15 inches long

2-lb coffee can with nails punched on bottom

2 inches from end

broomstick 18 inches

11½ inches

18 inches

A cheese press can be made from scrap wood, a broomstick, bricks, and a 2-pound coffee can.

You can buy a cheese press for about $170.

Cut the broomstick into 3 lengths: 2 pieces 18 inches long and 1 piece 15 inches long. Nail each 18-inch length of broomstick 2 inches from the ends of the bottom board, matching the holes in the top board. Nail the other length to the center of the top board, and nail the round follower to the broomstick at the other end. Nail 2 blocks of wood to the bottom or set the press on 2 bricks or blocks so that you can slide a container under the drainage hole to catch the whey (an ice cube tray works great).

The curd is poured into the cheesecloth-lined cheese form (coffee can) which is set on the press. The ends of the cheesecloth are folded over the curd. The follower is set in place, and the top board is weighed down with 1 or 2 bricks. The weighted follower exerts slow pressure on the cheese, forcing the whey out. Up to 4 bricks may be added later to make a firmer cheese.

CONTAINERS

For a container, I set a 24-quart hot-water canner inside a 36-quart canner, double-boiler style. I recommend them because they are lightweight (4 gallons of milk can get heavy), and they are porcelain enamel covered (aluminum is affected by the acid in the curd). The 24-quart canner holds 4 or more gallons of milk, is not too deep to cut the curd with a long-bladed knife (such as a bread knife), and is easily handled. These pots can be sued at canning time to process tomatoes, peaches, and other acid fruits and vegetables.

Ingredients

To make cheese you need raw goats' or cows' milk, a starter, rennet, and salt. You can add color if you like your cheese bright orange color, but I prefer cheese in its natural, creamy white color.

MILK

Raw whole milk from goats or cows makes the richest cheese, but partially skimmed milk can be used. Preservatives are often added to milk that is labeled "pasteurized," so only raw milk can be used; otherwise, your milk may not form curds. Neither can you use powdered milk. For one thing, it has been over-processed; for another, skim milk makes a poor quality cheese.

Use fresh, high-quality milk from animals free from disease or udder infections. It is very important not to use milk from any animal that has been treated with an antibiotic for at least 3 days after the last treatment. A very small quantity of antibiotic in the milk will keep the acid from developing during the cheese making process.

The milk may be raw or pasteurized, held in the refrigerator for several days or used fresh from the animal. It must be warmed to room temperature, then held until it has developed some lactic acid (ripened) before you start to make the cheese. It should be only slightly acid tasting; more acid develops as the cheese is made.

It is best to use a mixture of evening and morning milk. Cool the evening milk to a temperature of 60°F and hold it at that temperature overnight. Otherwise it may develop too much acid. Cool the morning milk to 60°F before mixing with the evening milk.

If you use only morning milk, cool it to 60 or 70°F and ripen it 3 or 4 hours. Otherwise it may not develop enough acid to produce the desired flavor and may have a weak body.

If you are milking 1 cow or only a few goats, you will have to save a mixture of morning and evening milk in the refrigerator until you have a surplus of 3 or 4 gallons.

When you are ready to make the cheese, select 10 or 12 quarts of your very best milk. Remember that poor quality milk makes poor quality cheese. Plan that 4 quarts of milk will make about 1 pound of hard cheese, slightly more soft cheese, or about 1 quart of cottage cheese.

STARTER

Some type of starter is necessary to develop the proper amount of acid for good cheese flavor. Different starters will produce different tastes. You can buy buttermilk, yogurt, or a commercial powdered cheese starter, or you can make a tart homemade starter by holding 2 cups of fresh milk at room temperature for 12 to 24 hours, until it curdles, or clabbers.

RENNET

Rennet is a commercial product made from the stomach lining of young animals. The enzyme action of rennet causes the milk to coagulate (curdle) in less than an hour, making the curd formation more predictable for cheese making. Rennet is available in extract or tablet form from drug, grocery, or dairy supply stores. You can buy it in health food stores or in the special cheese making sections of gourmet food shops. Or you can order it by mail.

Because natural rennet is of animal origin, many vegetarians prefer not to use it in making cheese. For that reason, a new, all-vegetable rennet is available in health food stores.

SALT

After you have made cheese a few times, you will learn the exact amount of salt that suits your taste, but some salt is needed for flavor. Our recipes call for a minimum amount. You can use ordinary table salt, but flake salt is absorbed faster. Morton flake salt is available in some stores.

Basic Steps for Hard Cheese

1. Ripen the Milk. Warm the milk to 86°F and add 2 cups starter; stir thoroughly for 2 minutes to be sure it is well incorporated into the milk. Cover and let it set in a warm place, perhaps overnight. In the morning, taste the milk. If it has a slightly acid taste it is ready for the next step.

2. Add the Rennet. With the milk at room temperature, add 1/2 teaspoon rennet liquid or 1 rennet tablet dissolved in 1/2 cup cool water. Stir for 2 minutes to mix the rennet in thoroughly. Cover the container and let it remain undisturbed until the milk has coagulated—about 30 to 45 minutes.

3. Cut the Curd. When the curd is firm and a small amount of whey appears on the surface, the curd is ready to be cut. With a clean knife, slice the curd into half-inch cubes. First slice through every half-inch lengthwise. Then slant the knife as much as possible and cut crosswise in the opposite direction. Rotate the pan a quarter turn and repeat. Stir the curd carefully with a wooden spoon or paddle and cut any cubes that do not conform to size. Stir carefully to prevent breaking the pieces of curd.

To cut the curd, use a clean, long knife and slice the curd at half-inch intervals. Then slant the knife as much as possible and cut through the curd at a slant. Rotate the pan a quarter turn and repeat the pattern at right angles to the first cut.

Continued →

4. Heat the Curd. Place a small container into a larger one filled with warm water, double-boiler style, and heat the curds and whey slowly at the rate of 2 degrees every 5 minutes. Heat to a temperature of 100°F in 30 to 40 minutes, then hold at this temperature until the curd has developed the desired firmness. Keep stirring gently to prevent the cubes of curd from sticking together and forming lumps. As it becomes firmer, the curd will need less stirring to keep it from lumping.

Test the curd for firmness by squeezing a small handful gently, then releasing it quickly. If it breaks apart easily and shows very little tendency to stick together, it is ready. The curd should reach this stage 1 1/2 to 2 1/2 hours after you added the rennet to the milk.

It is very important that the curd be firm enough when you remove the whey. If it is not, the cheese may have a weak, pasty body and may develop a sour or undesirable flavor. If it is too firm, the cheese will be dry and weak-flavored.

When the curd is firm, remove the container from the warm water.

5. Remove the Whey. Pour the curd and whey into a large container which you have lined with cheesecloth. Then lift the cheesecloth with the curd inside and let it drain in a colander or large strainer. A 1-gallon can with drain holes is convenient for this step.

When most of the whey has drained off, remove the curd from the cheesecloth, put it in a container, and tilt it several times to remove any whey that drains from the curd. Stir occasionally to keep the curd as free from lumps as possible.

Stir the curd or work it with your hands to keep the curds separated. When it has cooled to 90°F, and has a rubbery texture that squeaks when you chew a small piece, it is ready to be salted.

Be sure to save the whey. It is very nutritious and is relished by livestock and household pets. We save the whey for our chickens and pigs, but many people enjoy drinking it or cooking with it.

6. Salt the Curd. Sprinkle 1 to 2 tablespoons of flake salt evenly throughout the curd and mix it in well. As soon as the salt has dissolved and you are sure the curd has cooled to 85°F, spoon the curd into the cheese form which has been lined, sides and bottom, with cheesecloth. Be sure the curd has cooled to 85°F.

7. Press the Curd. After you have filled the cheese form with curd, place a circle of cheesecloth on top. Then insert the wooden follower and put the cheese form in the cheese press.

Start with a weight of 3 or 4 bricks or 10 minutes, remove the follower, and drain off any whey that has collected inside the can. Then replace the follower and add a brick at a time until you have 6 to 8 bricks pressing the cheese. When it has been under this much pressure for an hour, the cheese should be ready to dress.

Pressing is extremely important. If you want a hard, dry cheese, you will need 30 or more pounds of pressure for a 2 1/2 to 3 pound cheese.

8. Dress the Cheese. Remove the weights and follower and turn the cheese form upside down so the cheese will drop. You may have to tug at the cheesecloth to get it started. Remove the cheesecloth from the cheese and dip cheese in warm water to remove any fat from the surface. With your fingers, smooth over any small holes or tears to make a smooth surface. Wipe dry.

Now cut a piece of cheesecloth 2 inches wider than the cheese is thick and long enough to wrap around it with a slight overlap. Roll the cheese tightly using 2 round circles of cheesecloth to cover the ends.

Replace the cheese in the cheese form, insert the follower, and press with the 6 to 8 bricks another 18 to 24 hours.

9. Dry the Cheese. At the end of the pressing time, remove the cheese, take off the bandage, wipe the cheese with a clean, dry cloth, and check for any openings or cracks. Wash the cheese in hot water or whey for a firm rind. Seal the holes by dipping the cheese in warm water and smoothing with your fingers or a table knife.

Then put the cheese on a shelf in a cool, dry place. Turn and wipe it daily until the surface feels dry and the rind has started to form. This takes from 3 to 5 days.

10. Paraffin the Cheese. Heat 1/2 pound of paraffin to 210°F in a pie pan or disposable aluminum pan deep enough to immerse half the cheese at one time. Be sure to heat the paraffin over hot water—never over direct heat.

Hold the cheese in the hot paraffin for about 10 seconds. Remove and let harden a minute or so, then immerse the other half. Check to be sure the surface is covered completely.

11. Cure the Cheese. Now put the cheese back on the shelf to cure. Turn it daily. Wash and sun the shelf once a week. After about 6 weeks of curing at a temperature of 40 to 60°F, the cheese will have a firm body and a mild flavor. Cheese with a sharp flavor requires 3 to 5 months or longer curing. The lower the temperature the longer the time required. It's a good idea to test your first cheese for flavor from time to time during the curing period. One way is to cut the cheese into 4 equal parts before paraffining and use 1 of the pieces for tasting.

How long to cure depends on individual taste. As a rule Colby is aged 30 to 90 days and Cheddar 6 months or more. Romano is cured at least 5 months. Other cheeses are cured sometimes no more than 2 or 3 weeks. The cooler the temperature in the curing room, the longer it takes to ripen. Once you have the temperature and time to suit your taste, you will know exactly when your cheese will be ready.

Remember, these are *general* instructions to be used for hard cheese. When you follow the specific recipes, you will find many variations, particularly for processing temperatures and pressing times.

Recipes for Hard Cheese

CHEDDAR

There are several ways to make cheddar. To make my version, follow the Basic Directions through Step 5, removing the whey. Then place the dubs of heated curd in a colander and heat to 100°F. This may be done in the oven or in a double-boiler arrangement on top of the stove. It is important to keep the temperature between 95 and 100°F for 1 1/2 hours.

After the first 20 to 30 minutes, the curd will form a solid mass. Then it should be sliced into 1-inch strips which must be turned with a wooden spoon every 15 minutes for even drying. Hold these strips at 100°F for 1 hour. Then remove from the heat and continue with the Basic Directions, beginning at Step 6, salting the curd. Cure for 6 months.

COLBY

To make a small colby cheese, add 3 tablespoons of starter to 1 gallon of lukewarm milk. Let it stand overnight to clabber, then proceed with the Basic Directions through Step 4, heating the curd.

When the curd is heated to the point where it no longer shows a tendency to stick together, remove the container from the heat and let it stand 1 hour, stirring every 5 minutes.

Now continue with Step 6, removing the whey. After pressing the curd for 18 hours, the cheese can be dried a day or so and used as a soft cheese spread or ripened for 30 days.

MOZZARELLA

Mozzarella is a delicate, semi-hard Italian cheese which is not cured but is used fresh. It often is used in Italian dishes.

Follow the Basic Directions to Step 3, cutting the curd. Instead of cutting the curd with a knife, break it up with your hands. Heat the curd to as hot as your hands can stand. Then stir and crumble it until the curds are firm enough to squeak.

Proceed with the Basic Directions at Step 5, removing the whey, and continue to Step 8, dressing the cheese. At this point, remove the pressed cheese from the cheese form and discard cheesecloth wrapping. Set the cheese in the whey which has been heated to 180°F. Cover the container and let stand until cool.

When cool, remove the cheese from the whey and let drain for 24 hours. The cheese is now ready to eat or use in recipes.

FETA

Feta is a white, pickled cheese made from goats' or ewes' milk. To make this salt-cured cheese, follow the Basic Directions through Step 3, cutting the curd. In the next step the curd is heated to no more than 95°F and drained when less firm than most hard cheeses.

To remove the whey, the curds and whey are poured into a cloth bag which is hung for 48 hours until the cheese is firm. Feta is not pressed in a cheese form. When firm, the curd is sliced and sprinkled with dry salt, which is worked in with the hands. The cheese is then returned to the cloth bag which is twisted and worked to expel most of the whey and firm the cheese. After 24 hours, the cheese is wiped off and placed on a shelf to form a rind. It is ready to eat in 3 to 4 days.

Recipes for Soft Cheeses

Soft cheeses usually are mild and aged little, if at all. They do not keep as long as hard cheese. Soft cheeses are not paraffined, but are wrapped in wax paper and stored in the refrigerator until used. Except for a few soft cheeses that are aged, they should be eaten within a week or so for best flavor.

The simplest soft cheese is fresh curds, which Grandmother made by setting fresh warm milk in the sun until the curds separated from the whey. The most familiar soft cheese is cream cheese which is made by draining curds for a few minutes in a cloth bag.

If you gather from this that the making of soft cheese is not nearly as complicated as hard cheese, you are right. Here are some of the simplest recipes.

SWEET CHEESE

Bring 1 gallon of whole milk to a boil. Cool to lukewarm and add 1 pint of buttermilk and 3 well-beaten eggs. Stir gently for 1 minute, then let set until a firm clabber forms. Drain in a cloth bag until firm. The cheese will be ready to eat in 12 hours.

CREAM CHEESE

Add 1 cup of starter to 2 cups of warm milk, and let it set 24 hours. Add to 2 quarts of warm milk and let it clabber another 24 hours. Warm over hot water for 30 minutes, then pour into a cloth bag to drain Let it set one hour. Salt to taste and warp in waxed paper. It may be used immediately for sandwiches, on crackers, or in recipes calling for cream cheese. Refrigerate until used.

Another method of making cream cheese is to add 1 tablespoon of salt to 1 quart of thick sour cream. Place in a drain bag and hang in a cool place to drain for 3 days.

CHEESE SPREAD

Let 2 1/2 gallons of skimmed milk sour until thick. Heat very slowly until it is hot to the touch; do not allow to boil. Hold the milk at this temperature until the curds and whey separate. Strain through cheesecloth and allow the curds to cool a little, then crumble with your hands. Makes 4 cups crumbled cheese. Let it set at room temperature 2 to 3 days to age.

To the 4 cups crumbled curds, add 2 teaspoons of soda and mix in with your hands Let it set 30 minutes. Add 1 1/2 cups of warm milk, 2 teaspoons of salt, and 1/3 cup of butter Set over boiling water and heat to the boiling point, stirring vigorously. Add 1 cup of cream or milk, a little at a time, stirring after each addition. Cook until smooth. Stir occasionally until cold. Makes 1 1/2 quarts of cheese spread.

To make a flavored cheese spread, add 3 tablespoons of crumbled bits of crisply fried bacon, or 1 tablespoon of chopped chives, or 4 tablespoons of chopped, drained pineapple.

DUTCH CHEESE

Set a pan of curded milk on the back of a wood-burning stove and heat very slowly until the curd is separated from the whey. Drain off the whey and pour the curd into a drain bag. Hang and let it drain for 24 hours. Chop the ball of curd and pound until smooth with a potato masher or round-end glass. Add cream, butter, salt, and pepper to taste. Make into small balls, or press in a dish and slice to serve.

GERMAN CHEESE

Put 2 gallons of clabbered milk in an iron pot over low heat and bring it to 180°F in 45 minutes. Drain off the whey and put the curds in a colander. When the curds are cool enough to handle, press it with your hands to extract any remaining whey. The warmer you work it the better. Put the drained curd in a dish and add 2 teaspoons of soda and

Continued →

I teaspoon of salt, working in well with your hands. Press the curd with your hands to form a loaf. Let it set for I hour, when it will have risen and be ready to slice. It will keep several days in a cool place.

If the cheese is dry and crumbly it may have been heated too much or pressed too long. If it is soft and sticky it was not heated enough or not pressed enough.

CHEESE BALLS

To each pint of drained curd, add 2 ounces of melted butter, I teaspoon salt, a dash of pepper, and 2 tablespoons thick cream. Work together until smooth and soft. Make into small balls to serve with salad.

Cottage Cheese

Cottage cheese may be eaten as a spoon cheese or strained (or put through a blender) and used as a low calorie dip or in recipes calling for sour cream. It is best eaten as soon as it is chilled, but it will keep up to a week in the refrigerator.

Homemade cottage cheese does not contain preservatives, so it does not keep as long as the commercial variety usually does.

Method 1

Bring I gallon of whole or skimmed milk to 75 to 80°F and add I cup of starter. Cover and set in a warm place 12 to 24 hours or until a firm clabber forms and a little whey appears on the surface.

When a clabber is formed, cut into half-inch cubes by passing a long knife through it lengthwise and crosswise. Then set the container in a larger pot containing warm water Warm the curd to 110°F, stirring often to keep it from sticking together. Be careful that you do not overheat.

When the curd reaches the proper temperature, taste it from time to time to test for firmness. When it feels firm enough to your liking (some people like their cottage cheese rather soft; others like it quite firm and granular), immediately pour it into a colander lined with cheesecloth, and drain for 2 minutes. Lift the cheesecloth from the colander and hold under tepid water, gradually running it colder, to rinse off the whey. Place the chilled curd in a dish, add salt and cream to taste, and chill thoroughly before serving.

Method 2

Add I cup of starter to I gallon of freshly drawn milk. Cover and set in a warm place overnight. In the morning, add half a rennet tablet dissolved in 1/2 cup of water. Stir I minute. Cover again and let it stand undisturbed for 45 minutes. Cut the curd into half-inch cubes, set the container in a larger pot of warm water, and warm the curd to 102°F. Proceed as in Method I, once the curd has reached the desired temperature and firmness.

Method 3

Add I cup of starter to 2 gallons of warm skimmed milk. Stir well and pour into a large roaster pan with a lid. Place in a warm (90°F) oven (heat off) overnight or for about 12 hours. In the morning take out I pint of the clabbered milk and refrigerate it to use as a starter for the next batch. Turn on the oven and set at 100°F. Heat the clabber in the oven for I hour, then cut into half-inch cubes. Do not stir or move pan

unnecessarily. Leave the milk in the oven until the curds and whey are well separated. When the curd rises to the top of the whey, turn the heat off and let it set until cool. Dip off excess whey; then dip out curds and put them into a cheesecloth-lined colander to drain. Pour curds into a dish and add salt and cream to taste.

Method 4

Heat I quart of sour milk in the upper part of a double boiler over hot water. Heat until lukewarm, then line a large strainer with cheesecloth dipped in hot water and pour in the milk. Over the milk pour I quart warm water. When the water has drained off, pour another quart of warm water over the milk. Repeat. When the water has drained off for the third time, gather the ends of the cheesecloth to form a bag and hang to drain overnight. Add salt to taste.

Method 5

Pour 2 quarts of clabbered milk into a large pan. Into it slowly pour boiling water, continuing until the curds start to form in the milk. Let set until the curds may be skimmed from the top. Mix curds with cream. Salt lightly.

Making Butter

Butter can be made from sweet or sour cream in a variety of equipment ranging from an electric mixer or blender to a plain glass jar with a tight-fitting lid.

If you make butter often, you may want to buy a churn. They vary from the large, old-fashioned, wooden-barrel churns which will accommodate up to 5 gallons of cream to the small, glass-jar, wooden-paddle churns that are still sold by Sears, Roebuck in hand-operated or electric models.

Sweet cream butter takes longer to churn than sour cream butter. If the cream is very fresh it may take several hours to turn to butter. Sour cream churns into butter in 30 to 35 minutes. Both sweet and sour cream churns quicker if they have been aged 2 to 3 days in the refrigerator. Sweet cream butter is sometimes preferred for its mellow, bland flavor. Sour cream butter has a richer taste.

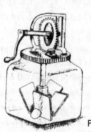

Forerunner to the electric butte churn.

Barrel churn.

SWEET CREAM BUTTER

If you make butter once a week from the cream accumulated during the week, it will give the cream time to ripen a little, which improves the taste and makes it easier to whip. Or leave the cream a day or so at room temperature until it begins to clabber.

Pour the cold, heavy cream into a chilled mixing bowl. Turn the mixer slowly to high speed and let the cream go through the stages of whipped cream, stiff whipped cream, and finally two separate products—butter and buttermilk. In a churn, turn slowly for 15 to 20 minutes. It is only during the last stage as the butter separates from the buttermilk, that the process needs attention. Then you must turn the speed to low or it will spatter wildly. When the separation has taken place, pour off the buttermilk. (Save the buttermilk. It's great for making biscuits or pancakes or to drink.)

Now knead the soft butter with a wet wooden spoon or a rubber scraper to force out all the milk, pouring the milk off as you knead. When you have all the milk out, refill the bowl with ice water and continue kneading to wash the remaining milk from the butter. (Any milk left in will cause the butter to spoil.) Pour off the water and repeat until the water is clear.

You now have sweet butter. If you want it salted, add a teaspoon of flake salt. Uncolored butter may be an appetizing cream white color, but if you want it bright yellow, you can add butter color.

One quart of well-separated, heavy cream makes about one pound of butter, and about a half quart of buttermilk.

SOUR CREAM BUTTER

Ripen cream by adding 1/4 cup of starter to each quart of heavy cream. Let it set at room temperature for 24 hours, stirring occasionally. Chill the ripened cream 2 to 3 hours before churning.

When it is chilled, pour the cream into a wooden barrel or glass-jar churn. If desired, add butter coloring at this point. Keep the cream and the churn cool and turn the mechanism with a moderately fast, uniform motion. About 30 to 35 minutes of churning usually will bring butter, but the age of the cream, the temperature, and whether the cream is from a morning or a night milking will affect the length of time required.

When the butter is in grains the size of wheat, draw off the buttermilk and add very cold water. Churn slowly for 1 minute, then draw off the water.

Remove the butter to a wooden bowl and sprinkle it with 2 tablespoons of flake salt for each pound of butter. Let stand a few minutes, then work with a wooden paddle to work out any remaining buttermilk or water, and mix in the salt. Taste. If the butter is too salty, wash with cold water. If it needs it, add more salt.

While working, keep the butter cold. If it should become too soft during hot weather, chill the butter until it hardens before finishing.

Yogurt

Making yogurt essentially is the same as making cheese starter. The milk is warmed to 100 to 110°F, the culture is added, and the mixture is kept at the desired temperature for several hours. At about 100°F you can make yogurt in 5 to 6 hours, but you can leave it 10 to 12 hours if like a tarter flavor.

It is important to keep the mixture at the proper temperature for the necessary length of time in order to allow the culture to develop. If you have a yogurt maker, simply follow the manufacturer's directions. If you don't use your ingenuity.

WITH A THERMOS
Almost fill a thermos (preferably wide mouth) bottle with warm (100°F) milk. Add 2 tablespoons of plain yogurt and mix thoroughly. Put the lid on and warp the thermos in 2 or 3 terry towels. Then set in a warm, draft-free place overnight. (On winter nights, over the furnace register is a good place.)

IN AN OVEN
Pour 1 quart of warm milk in a casserole dish and add 3 tablespoons of plain yogurt. Stir well and cover casserole. Place in warm (100°F) oven with the heat off. Let it set overnight.

ON A HEATING PAD
Set an electric heating pad at medium temperature and place in the bottom of a cardboard box with a lid. (A large shoe box works well.) Fill small plastic containers with warm milk, add yogurt starter to each, and mix well. Put on lids. Wrap heating pad around containers, then cover with towels to fill box. Put lid on box and let set undisturbed for 5 to 6 hours.

IN THE SUN
Pour warmed milk into a glass-lidded bowl or casserole. Add yogurt starter and cover with the glass lid or a clear glass pie plate. Place in the sun on a warm (not too hot) summer day and let set 4 to 5 hours. Watch it to make sure it is not shaded as the sun moves.

ON THE BACK OF THE STOVE
Grandmother made her clabber by setting a bowl of freshly drawn milk on the back of the stove after supper. She added 1 cup of starter to each 2 quarts of milk and let it set, loosely covered with a dish towel, on the back of the cooling wood range overnight. If you are fortunate enough to have a wood range in your kitchen this method works beautifully.

Cheese Making Supplies
You can buy cheese making supplies from the following companies. Write for their catalogs.

Chr. Hansen's Laboratories, Inc.
9015 Maple St.
Milwaukee, WI 53214

Lehman's Hardware
P.O. Box 41
Kidron, OH 44636
(330) 857-5757
info@lehmans.com

New England Cheesemaking Supply Company
P.O. Box 85
Ashfield, MA 01330

Maggie Oster
Illustrations by Alison Kolesar

Simply put, making ice cream and other frozen desserts yourself makes good sense and is a lot of fun. The flavors you can make are literally limitless, and the ingredients are readily available. Your ice cream will cost less than the premium brands and be vastly superior to the cheaper brands. Most importantly, you can control what goes into your ice cream, making it as sinfully rich or as austerely slimming as you want, with no unnecessary ingredients. If you decide to use an ice cream freezer, new ones are available in a wide range of sizes, are relatively inexpensive, and are easier than ever to use.

Homemade ice cream need no longer be a "once-in-the-summer" treat. Why not enjoy it year round?

The Ingredients

The basic ingredients of ice cream include a dairy product such as cream or milk, a sweetener, and a flavoring. By making your own ice cream you can interchange ingredients to suit your tastes and resources.

MILK PRODUCTS

Having your own cow or goat means an abundant supply of fresh milk and is ideal in terms of wholesomeness, availability, and cost. But purchased milk products will also yield a better product than store-bought ice cream, and you'll still save money. For strict vegetarians, ice cream, sherbet, and frozen yogurt can be made from soy milk.

Whipping Cream. With 36 percent butterfat, this naturally makes the creamiest dessert with that superb cream flavor, but you will pay a price at both the checkout and calorie counters. Most kinds available in grocery stores are ultra-pasteurized and contain emulsifiers and stabilizers.

Light cream. Also called coffee cream, light cream has 20 percent butterfat. It produces a relatively rich ice cream with fewer calories.

Half-and-half. A mixture of milk and cream with 12 percent butterfat, half-and-half makes a satisfactory ice cream with a hint of richness.

Whole Milk. Fresh, whole milk contains 3 1/2 percent butterfat. It is the basic ingredient in most ice creams and sherbets.

Low-fat milks. Low-fat (2 percent butterfat), 99 percent fat-free, and skim (less than 1/2 percent butterfat) milks are useful when you want to limit calories, but you will get a coarser texture in the ice cream.

Nonfat dry milk. An economical choice, nonfat dry milk is handy because it needs no refrigeration prior to reconstituting with water. Mix instant dry milk granules in the proportions recommended on the package. To reconstitute non-instant dry milk powder, combine 1 part powder with 4 parts water, or for a richer ice cream, use 2 parts powder. A blender works well for this, or first mix the powder with a small amount of water to form a paste before adding the remaining water.

Buttermilk. Originally the liquid leftover in the churn after butter was made, today buttermilk is made by adding a bacterial culture to pasteurized skim milk. Its thick, creamy texture, low calories, and tart flavor make it a useful ingredient in many frozen desserts.

Evaporated milk. Evaporated milk is made by removing some of the water from fresh milk, adding various chemical stabilizers; it is then sealed in cans and heat-sterilized. Used undiluted, evaporated milk gives a richer taste and smoother texture to ice cream than plain whole milk.

Yogurt. You can make yogurt with fresh whole, low-fat, skim, or nonfat dry milks and even soy milk. Frozen yogurt made with any of these products will have the characteristic tart, tangy flavor. It is very economical to make your own yogurt. If using purchased yogurt, be sure to buy brands with live bacterial cultures, preferably with no flavoring, or only those with preserves at the bottom and no additives.

Sour cream. Made from light cream and inoculated with a bacterial culture, commercially available sour creams may have texture-enhancing additives. Sour cream helps make ice cream rich and tangy.

Soy milk. As high in protein as cow's milk, soy milk has only one-third as much fat—and it is unsaturated fat to boot. When making ice cream, add 1/4 cup vegetable oil for every 3 cups soy milk to make a richer product. Soy milk powder is available, or soy milk can be made by soaking soybeans overnight, grinding, cooking with water, and straining off the milk.

SWEETENERS

Much controversy rages over the relative merits of various sweeteners. For simplicity, the recipes here call for the two most readily-used sweeteners, honey and white sugar. Other sweeteners can be easily substituted. A proportion of 3/4 cup granulated white sugar or 1/3 cup honey to each 4 cups of dairy product is usual when making ice cream. Syrups and honey tend to give a smoother texture because they control crystal formation.

However, sugar also adds to the overall solids of the mixture in a way that is different from honey and syrups. A high solid content lowers the freezing point for the mixture, causing the ice cream to freeze more solid and be easier to scoop. Honey and syrups often have a higher moisture content than sugar which also affects the product. A little experimenting should give you an idea of the different results to be obtained by using various sweeteners.

Granulated white sugar. Granulated white sugar is the most common sweetener, however, it is totally devoid of nutrients.

Brown sugar. Brown sugar is white sugar with molasses added, which gives it traces of vitamins and minerals. Brown sugar adds a distinctive taste, and should be used in the same proportion as white sugar, though lightly packed.

Honey. Depending on its own taste, honey may add a slight or a strong flavor to your ice cream. Darker honeys are usually stronger and sweeter. Honey that is labeled unfiltered, raw, or uncooked will have traces of vitamins and minerals. Half as much honey is needed to sweeten ice cream as white sugar.

> ### SUGAR SUBSTITUTES
> To make ice cream, 1 cup white sugar is equal to each of the following:
>
> - 1/2 cup honey
> - 1/2 cup molasses
> - 2/3 cup maple syrup
> - 1/3 cup crystalline fructose
> - 1 1/2 cups maltose
> - 1/2 cup sorghum
> - 1 cup brown sugar lightly packed

Unsulphured molasses. A by-product of the sugar refining process, molasses contains some iron, calcium, and phosphorus. It has a distinctive flavor that is appropriate only with certain flavors of ice cream. Use 1/2 cup of molasses for 1 cup of white sugar in recipes.

Maple syrup. This ingredient adds not only sugar, but also its own unique flavor to foods. Be sure to use only pure maple syrup, free of additives, not flavored pancake syrup. Substitute 2/3 cup maple syrup for 1 cup of white sugar.

Light corn syrup. Sometimes used in making fruit ices and sherbets, light corn syrup produces a light, smooth texture with no flavor effect. It is a mixture of refined sugars, partially digested starches, water, salt, and vanilla. A less expensive, homemade sugar syrup or honey may be preferred.

Dark corn syrup. A distinctive flavor, dark corn syrup has the same drawbacks as light corn syrup. Use dark honey or molasses instead.

Fructose. A sugar found naturally in fruit and honey, fructose does not have an adverse affect on a person's blood sugar level. As it is two-thirds sweeter than white sugar, it can be used in smaller quantities. Substitute 1/3 cup crystalline fructose for 1 cup sugar; liquid fructose varies in concentration, so follow label directions. Although called fruit sugar, the commercially available forms are usually made by extensive refining of corn, sugar beets, or sugar cane.

Maltose. Maltose is most frequently found as barley malt or rice syrup, both the cooked liquid of fermented grain and with a subtle flavor. It does not create blood sugar fluctuations, but maltose is less sweet than other sugars so more must be used. Substitute 1 1/2 cups maltose for 1 cup of white sugar.

Sorghum. A molasses-like product, sorghum is made from a plant related to corn. When using sorghum substitute 1/2 cup sorghum for 1 cup of white sugar.

Flavorings

This is where your creativity really has a chance to flower in ice cream making. Always use pure extracts and the finest ingredients, whether it be vanilla, chocolate, carob, fruits, nuts, coffee, or liqueurs. Using home-grown fruits and nuts is not only a source of pride, but the way to be sure of the best ingredients at a reasonable cost.

FILLERS, STABILIZERS, AND EMULSIFIERS

These make a smoother frozen product with smaller ice crystals. They also add body and richness, and increase the amount of air that can be incorporated. Since one of the reasons to make your own frozen desserts is to avoid additives, you may choose not to use these. But if you do, it's best to select ones that add to the nutritional content. Remember, though, these also add extra cost.

Eggs. An excellent inexpensive source of complete protein, eggs also contain certain minerals and vitamins. The egg yolks in custard ice cream help to thicken and add richness. Beaten egg whites also add body and richness as well as making a smoother, fluffier product. Ice creams with eggs also store longer in the freezer.

BE CAREFUL WITH EGGS

The U.S. Department of Agriculture strongly recommends that you *do not use* raw eggs, raw egg yolks or raw egg whites in making ice cream, in order to avoid salmonella poisoning. Use eggs only where they can be cooked. Cook all custard mixtures to a temperature of 160°F, to kill any possible bacteria.

Cream of tartar. A natural fruit acid made from grapes, cream of tartar can be used to increase volume, to stabilize, and to firm egg whites. Add at the beginning of beating, using 1/4 teaspoon to 2–4 whites.

Arrowroot. The powdered starch of several tropical plant roots, arrowroot is an excellent thickener, or filler. Easy to digest, it is clear when diluted and has no chalky taste like cornstarch. As arrowroot is more acid-stable than flour, it works well with fruit. It is effective at lower temperatures and when cooked for a shorter period of time than other thickeners. Use 1 1/2 teaspoons arrowroot in place of 1 tablespoon flour or cornstarch.

Cornstarch. A finely milled corn with the germ removed, cornstarch may be used as a thickening agent in cooked custard mixtures to make a smoother ice cream. It has little food value. Use 1 tablespoon in 2 cups cooked liquid when making custard ice cream.

Whole wheat flour. Whole wheat flour can be used as a thickening agent in cooked custard mixtures to make a smoother ice cream. It will contribute a slight amount of food value. Use 1 tablespoon in 2 cups cooked liquid when making custard ice cream.

Unflavored gelatin. Unflavored gelatin is a protein extracted from animal parts, then dried and powdered. It helps to make a smoother ice cream. Dissolve it in water and cook before adding to other ingredients. Use 1 1/2 teaspoons in a 1 1/2 quart batch of ice cream.

Agar. A sea vegetable high in minerals, agar can be used in place of unflavored gelatin. Agar is available as a concentrated powder, flakes or sticks, and unlike gelatin, it gels without requiring chilling. It is flavorless and highly absorptive. Use 1 1/2 tablespoons to 1 quart of liquid.

SALT

Salt is frequently used in foods as it heightens and enhances flavors. While an essential element in the body's health, too much salt can cause problems. It can be omitted from ice cream with little notice.

Equipment

Ice cream freezers for home use come in sizes ranging from 1 quart to 2 gallons. Some are elaborate and expensive, but most are relatively inexpensive and still very functional. In deciding which ice cream freezer to buy, consider such factors as cost, when and how you want to use it, durability, portability, and storage space needed. A large freezer can be used to make small amounts as well as party-size quantities.

Old-fashioned ice cream churns. These churns are available as either hand-cranked models or as electricity powered units. A large plastic, fiberglass, or wood tub holds a smaller, metal can. The ice cream mixture is placed inside the can along with a dasher or paddle and the assembly is covered. To freeze the ice cream, a brine solution of ice and salt is placed in the tub around the metal can. Turning the crank-and-gear assembly on top of the can rotates the dasher or paddle and mixes the ice cream. The dasher extends the height of the can and scrapes the ice crystals at the edge of the can to the inside. Churning is usually finished in 20 minutes.

Continued →

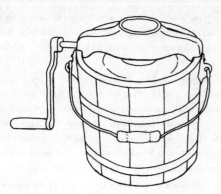

Old-fashioned hand-crank model

In-freezer ice cream churn. Such churns include a 1-quart unit with a dasher, metal can, plastic tub, and electrical assembly that uses the frigid air of a deep freezer or refrigerator freezer rather than ice and salt to freeze the mixture inside. Churning is usually completed in 1 1/2 hours.

Self-contained ice cream churns. These models come in sizes slightly more and slightly less than 1 quart. Using their own freon freezing unit and powdered electrically, they can make ice cream in 20 minutes. Although expensive, their ease of operation, speed, and lack of mess make them appealing.

With any of these machines, be sure to follow manufacturer's directions and care instructions. With all machines, it is important to wash, rinse, and thoroughly dry after each use. Wipe around electric motors and gear housings with a dampened, well-squeezed sponge followed by a dry towel.

Ice. Ice is cheapest when made at home. Plan ahead and make plenty, figuring on 8 ice cube trays or 6 pounds of ice to make 1 1/2 quarts of ice cream. Ice can be crushed to provide the most surface area for heat exchange, but cubes work reasonably well. Ice can be crushed by putting in a burlap or other heavy sack and hitting with a hammer.

Salt. Salt lowers the freezing temperature of water. Use table salt with ice cubes, and coarser, more slowly dissolving rock salt with crushed ice. For a 1 1/2-quart batch of ice cream, you will need 1 1/2 cups table salt or 1 cup rock salt. Additional salt will be needed if the ice cream is hardened in the churn.

Other Equipment

Measuring spoons	Whisk
Measuring cups	Wooden spoon
Glass measuring cup	Electric mixer or rotary beater
Saucepan	Shallow pans such as 8-inch round or
Blender, food processor, or food mill	square cake pan or ice-cube tray
Fine strainer	Rubber bowl scraper
Glass, ceramic, or stainless steel bowls	Freezer storage containers

Basic Procedure for Churned Ice Cream

1. Prepare ice cream or other frozen dessert mixture, pour in bowl, cover, and chill for several hours in the refrigerator. This will give a smoother product with less freezing time.

2. Wash the dasher, lid, and can; rinse and dry. Place in the refrigerator to chill. Keeping the equipment cold will make the process of freezing your mixture go faster.

3. Pour chilled mixture into the can, making sure it is not more than two-thirds full to allow for expansion. Put on the lid.

4. Put the can into the freezer tub and attach the crank-and-gear assembly.

5. Fill the tub one-third full of ice. Sprinkle an even layer of salt on top about 1/8-inch thick. Continue adding ice and salt in the same proportions layer by layer until the tub is filled up to, but not over, the top of the can. The salt-to-ice ratio affects freezing temperature and, therefore, freezing time. Too much salt and the ice cream will freeze too quickly and be coarse; too little salt will keep the mixture from freezing. Many factors influence the ratio, but the best proportion seems to be 8 parts ice to 1 part salt, by weight.

6. If using ice cubes, add 1 cup of cold water to the ice-and-salt mixture to help the ice melt and settle. If using crushed ice, let the ice-packed tub set for 5 minutes before beginning to churn. While churning, add more ice and salt, in the same proportions as before, so that it remains up to the top of the can.

7. Start cranking slowly at first—slightly less than 1 revolution per second—until the mixture begins to pull. Then churn as quickly and as steadily as possible for 5 minutes. Finally, churn at a slightly slower rate for a few more minutes, or until the mixture turns reasonably hard.

8. For electrically powdered ice cream churns, fill can with mix and plug in the unit. Allow to churn until it stops in about 15 to 20 minutes. Most kinds have an automatic reset switch that will prevent motor damage by stopping when the ice cream is ready. If the freezer becomes clogged with chunks of ice, the motor may shut off or stall. Restart by turning the can with your hands.

9. When the ice cream is ready, remove the crank-and-gear assembly. Wipe all ice and salt from the top. Remove the lid and lift out the beater. The ice cream should be the texture of mush. Scrape the cream from the beater. Add chopped nuts and fruit or sauce for ripple, if desired. Pack down the cream with a spoon. Cover with several layers of wax paper and replace the lid, putting a cork in the cover hole.

10. Ripen and harden the ice cream by placing in a deep-freezer or refrigerator freezer, or repack in the tub with layers of ice and salt until the can and lid are completely covered. Use more salt than for making the ice cream. Cover the freezer with a blanket or heavy towel and set in a cool place until ready to serve, about an hour.

TIPS FOR CHURN-FROZEN ICE CREAM

· Make sure batter is well-chilled before freezing.

· Never fill can more than 3/4 full; 2/3 is preferred.

· If hand-cranking, be sure to start slowly until you feel a pull.

· Proportions of salt to ice will vary according to content with those mixtures high in sugar or alcohol needing more salt and those low in sugar or high in butterfat needing less.

Basic Procedure for Still-Frozen Ice Cream

1. Prepare the ice cream mixture as directed and pour into a shallow tray such as a cake pan or ice-cube tray without the dividers.

2. Place the tray in the freezer compartment of the refrigerator at the coldest setting or a deep freezer for 30 minutes to 1 hour, or until the mixture is mushy but not solid.

3. Scrape the mixture into a chilled bowl and beat it with a rotary beater or electric mixer as rapidly as possible until the mixture is smooth.

4. Return the mixture to the tray and the freezer. When almost frozen solid, repeat the beating process. Add chopped nuts and fruits, liqueur, or ripple sauce, if desired.

5. Return to the tray and cover the cream with plastic wrap to prevent ice crystals from forming on top. Place in the freezer until solid.

TIPS FOR STILL-FROZEN ICE CREAM

- Use as little sweetener as possible.
- If using whipped cream, beat only to soft peaks for maximum volume and better flavor.
- If using whipped cream, add to mixture when well-chilled or partially frozen.
- Use lowest freezer temperature possible.
- Do not freeze ice cubes and ice cream at the same time in a refrigerator freezer.
- Have refrigerator freezer unit defrosted.
- Do not open the freezer door during freezing of the ice cream unless absolutely necessary.
- Add nuts and chunk fruits when the mixture is partially frozen.

Recipes

Each of these recipes makes 1 1/2 quarts or about 6 servings. The recipes can be decreased or increased to accommodate smaller or larger ice cream freezers. If making still-frozen ice cream, these recipes will fill 2 shallow pans.

BASIC VANILLA ICE CREAM

Whether cooked or uncooked, this simple, fast version can be made as rich or as low-calorie as you desire. Variations are infinite.

1 quart heavy or light cream or half-and-half or 2 cups each heavy and light cream

1 cup sugar or 1/3 cup honey

1 tablespoon pure vanilla extract

The above ingredients can be mixed and used as is or the cream can be scalded. Scalding concentrates the milk solids and improves the flavor.

To scald, slowly heat cream in a saucepan until just below the boiling point. Small bubbles will begin to appear around the edges. Stir

for several minutes, then remove from heat. Stir in the sweetener. Pour into a bowl, cover, and chill. When completely cooled, add the vanilla. When thoroughly chilled, follow directions for either churned or still-frozen ice cream.

Variations on the Basic Recipe

Super Creamy Vanilla Ice Cream

To the Basic Vanilla Ice Cream recipe: soften 1 1/2 teaspoons unflavored gelatin in 1/4 cup water and add with sugar to scalded milk. Continue cooking over low heat until gelatin is dissolved. Or, substitute 1 1/2 tablespoons agar.

Ice Milk

To the Basic Vanilla Ice Cream recipe, substitute whole, low-fat, skim, or reconstituted dry milk for the cream.

Ice Buttermilk

To the Basic Vanilla Ice Cream recipe, substitute buttermilk for the cream and do not scald.

Ice Sour Cream

To the Basic Vanilla Ice Cream recipe, substitute sour cream for the cream and do not scald.

Ice Soy Milk

To the Basic Vanilla Ice Cream recipe, substitute soy milk for the cream, without scalding. Combine soy milk, sweetener, flavoring, and 1/4 cup vegetable oil and whirl in a blender.

BEYOND VANILLA

Once you're mastered vanilla, you will want to try these quick and easy flavor variations.

BRANDIED CHERRY ICE CREAM

To the Basic Vanilla Ice Cream recipe: add 1 1/2 cups pureed fresh dark sweet cherries to the cream mixture just before freezing. Omit the vanilla and add 1/2 teaspoon almond extract and 1/2 cup kirschwasser, or cherry, or chocolate cherry liqueur.

BURNT ALMOND ICE CREAM

To the Basic Vanilla Ice Cream recipe: substitute light brown sugar, lightly packed, for white sugar. Toast 1 cup blanched, chopped almonds in a 350°F oven until golden and add when ice cream is mushy.

BUTTER PECAN ICE CREAM

To the Basic Vanilla Ice Cream recipe: add to the mushy ice cream 2/3 cup chopped pecans that have been sautéed in 3 tablespoons butter until golden.

CARAMEL ICE CREAM

To the Basic Vanilla Ice Cream recipe: melt the sugar called for in the recipes in a heavy skillet until golden. Carefully pour in 1/2 cup boiling water. Stir until dissolved and boil for 10 minutes, or until thick. Add to hot cream mixture.

Continued →

CAROB CHIP ICE CREAM

To the Basic Vanilla Ice Cream recipe: add 1 cup finely chopped carob nuggets to cream mixture just before freezing.

CHOCOLATE ICE CREAM

To the Basic Vanilla Ice Cream recipe: melt two to six 1-ounce squares of bitter or semi-sweet chocolate (depending on personal preference) in a small pan over low heat and add to scalded milk. Increase sugar to taste, usually doubling the standard quantity.

CHOCOLATE CHIP ICE CREAM

To the Basic Vanilla or Vanilla Custard Ice Cream recipe: add 1 cup finely chopped chocolate chips to cream mixture just before freezing.

COFFEE ICE CREAM

To the Basic Vanilla Ice Cream recipe: add 3 tablespoons instant coffee, espresso, or grain beverage dissolved in 4 tablespoons hot water, or 3/4 cup brewed coffee to cream mixture just before freezing.

COFFEE-WALNUT ICE CREAM

To Coffee Ice Cream, add 3/4 cup chopped walnuts when the ice cream is mushy.

FRUIT ICE CREAM

To the Basic Vanilla Ice Cream recipe: add just before freezing 1 1/2 cups fruit puree stirred with 2 teaspoons fresh lemon juice to heighten flavor and 2 tablespoons sugar or 1 tablespoon honey.

Use fresh or unsweetened frozen fruit such as strawberries, peaches, apricots, cherries, blueberries, raspberries, blackberries, mangoes, or plums. If you use pineapple, be sure to use canned, not fresh, pineapple. Fresh pineapple contains an acid that breaks down proteins, including milk protein, and will keep your ice cream from hardening properly. Fruits with seeds such as raspberries or blackberries should be drained after pureeing.

GRASSHOPPER ICE CREAM

To the Basic Vanilla Ice Cream recipe: add 1/4 cup each green crème de menthe and crème de cacao to chilled cream mixture just before freezing.

MAPLE-WALNUT ICE CREAM

To the Basic Vanilla Ice Cream recipe: use 1/2 cup pure maple syrup for the sweetener and add 3/4 cup chopped walnuts when ice cream is mushy.

PECAN PRALINE ICE CREAM

To the Basic Vanilla Ice Cream recipe: lightly coat an 8-inch cake pan with vegetable oil and put in 1 cup chopped pecans. In a heavy skillet, slowly melt 1/2 cup sugar with 1 tablespoon water, stirring occasionally, until the mixture turns a light brown. Pour over the pecans. When the caramel has hardened, break it into very small pieces. Add to the ice cream when mushy.

PEPPERMINT CANDY ICE CREAM

To the Basic Vanilla Ice Cream recipe: add 1/4 cup crushed peppermint stick candy to the milk while it heats, stir until dissolved. Add 1 teaspoon peppermint extract to chilled cream mixture. Stir in 1/4 cup crushed peppermint stick candy to ice cream mixture when mushy.

PISTACHIO ICE CREAM

To the Basic Vanilla Ice Cream recipe: add 1 teaspoon almond extract with the vanilla extract. Add 1 cup finely chopped pistachio nuts when the ice cream is mushy. If you want green ice cream, add several drops of green food coloring with the extracts.

ROCKY ROAD ICE CREAM

To any Chocolate or Carob ice cream: add 1/2 cup chopped nuts and 1/2 cup marshmallow bits to ice cream when mushy.

RUM-RAISIN ICE CREAM

To the Basic Vanilla Ice Cream recipe: soak 2/3 cup raisins in rum to cover until plump. Drain and dice raisins. Add rum and diced raisins to ice cream when mushy.

SWIRL ICE CREAM

To the Basic Vanilla Ice Cream recipe or another appropriate recipe: remove dasher after freezer stops. With a knife or narrow spatula, stir in 1 cup thick dessert sauce or jam just enough to create a swirl effect. Use dessert sauces such as caramel, butterscotch, blueberry, carob, chocolate, or marshmallow, and jams such as strawberry, blackberry, raspberry, peach, apricot, or apple butter.

MEATS

Easy Game Cookery

Phyllis Hobson
Illustrations by Elayne Sears

A successful hunt should mean good eating at the table, not hard work in the kitchen. The best ways to cook game are the easiest.

Basic Techniques

For best flavor, game animals should be skinned, game birds plucked, and fish scaled or skinned as soon as possible. The entrails should be removed and the meat washed and chilled. You may want to take large game animals to a butcher or a locker plant for processing. With smaller game, chances are you will do it yourself.

All fat should be trimmed from the meat. Although most game animals do not develop the heavy layer of fat characteristic of domestic livestock, their fat is strong tasting and even a small amount will affect the flavor of the meat. The trimmed meat can be basted with cooking oil, butter, or margarine. Ground meat can be mixed with pork or beef fat.

Large and small animals and game birds (but not fish) should be aged to improve the flavor and tenderize the meat. Small game animals and game birds should be wrapped in a damp towel or put in a plastic bag and kept in the refrigerator for a few days to age. One to two days will age young animals and up to four days is good for older, tougher meat. In cold weather, large game may be hung in a cold garage or unheated basement where the temperature does not go above 40°F. Or, the carcass can be cut into large chunks and stored in a refrigerator.

After aging, large game should be cut into roasts, steaks, stew meat, and so on. Small animals and game birds may be cut up or left whole.

The more tender cuts from young game animals can be fried, broiled, sautéed, or cooked on the open grill—just as you would the steaks and chops of beef, pork, and lamb. To fry the steaks, dredge the pieces in flour, season with salt and pepper, and brown in heated oil over low heat. Turn once to brown on both sides and let the meat slowly cook to tender goodness.

Smaller pieces of boneless meat can be sautéed in hot butter or margarine over medium heat. Stir frequently and do not flour. Either way, be careful not to overcook game. Otherwise, it will become tough and dry.

The meat from older animals should be braised or stewed to break down and tenderize the fiber. To braise, first fry or sauté to brown the meat, then add 1/2 to 1 cup liquid, cover, and cook over very low heat until tender, adding small amounts of liquid if necessary.

Meat from more mature game and the tougher cuts from young animals can be fried if they are first tenderized. There are several ways to tenderize meat.

- **Use a commercial tenderizer.** Commercial tenderizer made from a natural enzyme, will soften the tough muscle tissue in a few minutes. Follow the directions on the package.

- **Marinate.** Place meat slices in a shallow bowl or baking dish and pour over it a coating of French dressing; tomato juice, water, and lemon juice; water and vinegar; or your favorite marinade. Refrigerate 24 hours, turning several times.

- **Pressure-cook.** Stew or braise at 15 pounds of pressure for 15–20 minutes, following the manufacturer's directions.

- **Break down the fiber.** Tenderize by pounding with a meat mallet, chopping, or grinding the meat.

- **Parboil.** Simmer for 15 minutes over low heat in just enough water to cover. Then discard the water and bake, fry, or braise. Parboiling also removes some of the gamey taste from strongly flavored meat.

About that gamey taste. Most people like it—once they have acquired the taste. It is like ripe olives or Limburger cheese; few people like it the first time. But for many people, the different flavor of game is the reason they look forward to the opening of the hunting season. They welcome the change from the monotony of beef, pork, and chicken on the dinner table. If you have not yet acquired the taste, there are ways you can minimize the strong flavor of wild game. Here are a few.

- **Soak it.** Cover the meat with water in which 3 tablespoons of salt or 3 tablespoons of vinegar have been mixed. Soak the meat for 30 minutes. Be careful, though; soaking too long can make the meat soft and watery.

- **Disguise it.** Baste a roast with marinade or gravies rich with garlic or spices. Serve steaks and roasts with flavorful sauces and gravies.

- **Stuff it.** Fill the cavity of whole animals with sliced onions or orange halves. Discard the stuffing after baking.

- **Combine it.** Make stew or ground meat with half game and half beef or pork. Cook a venison stew or pot roast with potatoes and carrots.

- **Parboil it.** Simmer the meat in water before frying or baking. Discard the cooking water.

- **Hunt early in the season.** The meat of large game animals becomes much stronger in taste with the approach of the mating season.

Small Game

Skin the small game as the illustration indicates. When the skin has been removed, cut the abdomen just through the muscle and remove the entrails, being careful not to burst the bile sac. Save the heart and liver and discard the rest. Wash the carcass under running water, wrap in a damp towel, and refrigerate—1 day for young animals and up to 4 days for older animals.

Small game may be fried, braised, or baked whole or cut in severing pieces. Tougher cuts and meat from older animals should be cooked as you would older chickens.

Cut up your small game in the sequence shown.

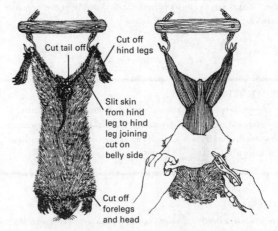

The process of skinning a muskrat can be adapted to any small game. (1.) Cut off the head, tail, and forelegs. (2.) Cut just through the skin around the hock of each leg. (3.) Hang the animal by the hind legs (or fasten it to a table). (4.) Slit the skin from the hind leg to hind leg and foreleg to foreleg through the neck opening. (5.) Working from the top, fold the skin over and peel it off, wrong side out, as you would a tight sweater.

RABBIT

Rabbit meat is fine grained and mild flavored. The meat of young animals can be used as a substitute for chicken fryers. Meat from older animals needs slow, moist cooking to make it tender.

Continued →

RABBIT WITH VEGETABLES

1 wild rabbit, cleaned and cut up

1/4 cup flour

1 teaspoon salt

1 teaspoon curry powder

dash of paprika

1/4 cup cooking oil

4 small potatoes, scrubbed but unpeeled

4 whole carrots, scrubbed and cut into 3-inch lengths

1 small onion, sliced

1 cup water

1 bay leaf

salt and pepper

3 tablespoons flour

1/2 cup cold water

Dredge rabbit pieces in flour mixed with salt, curry powder, and paprika. Brown in hot oil in a heavy skillet. Cover and bake for 30 minutes at 350°F. Add vegetables, water, and bay leaf. Season with salt and pepper. Cover and bake another hour. Remove meat and vegetables to serving dish. Discard bay leaf.

Blend 3 tablespoons flour and 1/2 cup water and gradually add to liquid. Cook, stirring constantly, until thickened. Pour over meat and vegetables.

SERVES 4–6.

SOME TIPS

It's a good idea to wear rubber gloves when skinning or cleaning any game animal. Never, never dress an animal that looks sick or in poor condition. Bury it, as soon and as deeply as possible, without touching it.

SQUIRREL

Squirrel meat is similar to rabbit except it has a stronger flavor. Most rabbit recipes can be used for squirrel. If the animal is old, simmer it in gravy until tender.

SQUIRREL SKILLET PIE

1 squirrel, cleaned and cut up

1/2 teaspoon salt water to barely cover

1/2 cup celery, chopped

1/4 cup sweet red or green pepper, chopped

1/4 cup flour salt and pepper

1/4 cup butter or margarine1/4 cup minced onion

2 packages canned, ready-to-bake biscuits

Cover squirrel pieces with salted water. Add chopped celery, cover, and simmer until the meat is tender. Remove the meat, but save the cooking

liquid. When the meat has cooled, pull it from the bones, leaving it in fairly large pieces. Set aside.

In a large iron skillet, melt butter or margarine over low heat. Add onion and peppers and cook about 5 minutes, until onion is transparent but not browned. Blend in flour and cook until the mixture bubbles, stirring constantly. Pour in 2 cups cooking liquid. Cook until thick and smooth, stirring constantly. Season to taste with salt and pepper. Add meat and reheat to boiling. Top with canned biscuits and bake at 350°F. for 10–12 minutes, until biscuits are browned.

SERVES 4–6.

OPOSSUM

Opossum is a rich food; and it is not for everyone. But to those who like it, there is nothing better than roast 'possum. It was once a staple of the winter months in the South.

BARBECUED OPOSSUM

1 whole opossum, cleaned

2 quarts cold water

1 teaspoon salt

1 small hot pepper

1 cup barbecue sauce

Cover whole opossum with cold water. Add salt and hot pepper and simmer over low heat for 30 minutes, just until tender. Discard cooking water and place opossum in a baking pan. Bake at 350°F until crisp and golden, basting frequently with barbecue sauce.

SERVES 6.

PORCUPINE

Skin a porcupine just as you would a rabbit. Dress it and wipe with a damp cloth. The meat is especially good with this unusual stuffing.

STUFFED PORCUPINE

1 whole porcupine, cleaned and dressed salt and pepper

3 cups sauerkraut

1 apple, cored and coarsely chopped

2 tablespoons melted butter or margarine

Sprinkle porcupine inside and out with salt and pepper. Stuff lightly with sauerkraut mixed with chopped apple. Truss or sew up and place in an uncovered baking pan. Bake at 350°F for 1 to 1 1/2 hours, until tender, brushing frequently with melted butter or margarine.

SERVES 4–6.

RACCOON

Skin and dress a freshly killed raccoon. Carefully remove the brown, bean-shaped kernels under each front leg and on both sides of the spine. Wipe with a cloth dipped in vinegar and water.

ROAST RACCOON

1 raccoon, cleaned and cut up

1/2 cup flour

1 teaspoon salt

1/4 teaspoon pepper

1/4 cup cooking oil

2 medium onions, peeled and sliced

2 bay leaves

Dredge the meaty pieces of raccoon in flour that has been seasoned with salt and pepper. Brown pieces on both sides in cooking oil in a heavy skillet. Pour off excess oil. Add onions and bay leaves and cover. Bake at 350°F. for 2 hours, until tender.

Simmer bony pieces in water to cover until tender. Strain and season the broth, then use it to make gravy.

SERVES 6.

MUSKRAT

A very clean animal, the muskrat feeds only on plants and roots, which gives the meat a sweet flavor. It tends to be soft, though, and should be crisply fried.

CRISPY FRIED MUSKRAT

1 muskrat, cleaned and cut up

2 eggs, well beaten

1 tablespoon milk

2 cups commercial biscuit mix

1/2 cup catsup

3/4 cup cooking oil

Cut muskrat as you would rabbit or squirrel. Use only the meaty pieces. Reserve the bony pieces for soup or gravy. Dry pieces with a paper towel, then dip in eggs mixed with milk. Dip in biscuit mix, then in catsup, and again in biscuit mix. Fry in heated oil until crisp and golden brown.

SERVES 4–6.

WOODCHUCK

When skinning a woodchuck, take care to remove the red scent glands between the forelegs and the body. Because of its strong flavor, woodchuck should be parboiled in salt water for 20 minutes before baking or using in this recipe.

WOODCHUCK CASSEROLE

1 woodchuck, cleaned, parboiled, and cut up

1 teaspoon salt

1/8 teaspoon pepper

1 teaspoon ground thyme

4 large bay leaves

8 slices bacon

1 cup water

1 cup dry bread crumbs

1/2 teaspoon seasoned salt

Arrange a layer of meat in an oiled casserole. Combine salt, pepper, and thyme and sprinkle half the mixture over the meat. Lay 2 bay leaves and 4 bacon slices over the top. Repeat layer. Pour 1 cup water over all. Cover and bake at 350°F. for 1–2 hours, until tender. Remove lid and sprinkle with bread crumbs, then seasoned salt. Bake 30 minutes longer, uncovered.

SERVES 4–6.

Large Game

The method of cleaning and skinning large game is the same as for small animals, although larger animals are more difficult to hang and skin because of their size.

Hang the animal by the hind legs in a cool place as soon as possible after killing. To skin the carcass, cut around each of the ankles, and pull the legs through. Cut off the head and feet and discard. Strip the skin from the hind legs down, carefully cutting it away as you go.

To clean, slit the flesh up the front from the tail to the throat and take out the entrails. Remove the bile sac from the liver without bursting the sac. Refrigerate the heart and liver and discard the other entrails.

Wipe the carcass thoroughly inside and out with a cloth dipped in a solution of 1 cup water and 1 tablespoon vinegar.

FIELD DRESSING YOUR DEER

Dress your deer immediately after tagging. Roll the deer over on its back, rump lower than shoulders, and spread the hind legs. Cut along the centerline of belly from breastbone to base of tail. First, cut through the hide, then through the belly muscle. Avoid cutting into the paunch and intestines by holding them away from the knife with the free hand while guiding the knife with the other.

With a small, sharp knife, cut around the anus. Tie off with cord and draw it into the body cavity so it comes free with the complete intestines. In doing this, avoid cutting or breaking the bladder. Loosen and roll out the stomach and intestines along with the genital organs. Save the liver if desired. Cut around the edge of the diaphragm which separates the chest and stomach cavities, then reach forward to cut the windpipe and gullet ahead of the lungs. This should allow you to pull the lungs and heart from the chest cavity. Save the heart if desired. Drain all blood from the body cavity.

From *Dressing Out Your Deer*, Special Circular 119, The Pennsylvania State University, College of Agriculture Extension Service, University Park, PA.

Continued →

331

To skin a large game animal: (1) With the animal hanging by the hocks, cut off the head, tail, and all four feet. (2) Slit the skin between the hind legs, and between the two forelegs, and down the center of the belly. (3) With a sharp knife, cut around anus to loosen it. (4) Using a skinning knife, work the skin loose from the hind legs and begin to peel it off. Work the skin down, pulling it away from the carcass and cutting away any tissue.

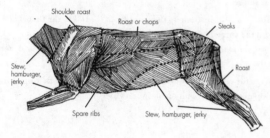

Butcher your large game as shown.

Let the meat hang at a temperature of 35–40°F. for 1–2 weeks. This aging process tenderizes the meat and gives it flavor.

The meat now is ready to be cut according to the illustration.

The following are easy recipes that can be used for any large game.

ROAST GAME

4 tablespoons cooking oil

1 tablespoon vinegar

1/4 cup catsup

2 tablespoons Worcestershire sauce

1 clove of garlic, chopped

Combine all ingredients. Cover and refrigerate overnight. Use as a basting cause for roasting any large game roast. Bake at 250°F. 4–6 hours, basting frequently.

WOODMAN'S STEW

2 pounds lean, boned meat, cut in 1-inch cubes

1 cup flour

1 teaspoon salt

1/8 teaspoon pepper

1/2 cup cooking oil

2 cups water

2 cloves garlic, minced

1 medium onion, chopped

4 tablespoons vinegar

1 teaspoon grated lemon rind

2 tablespoons Worcestershire sauce

Dredge meat cubes in flour mixed with salt and pepper. Brown on all sides in heated cooking oil in a Dutch oven. Remove the meat, and to the fat in the pan add 3 tablespoons flour left from dredging. Stir in well, then add remaining ingredients. Return meat to gravy and cook over low heat (or a campfire) 1 1/2–2 hours, until tender.

SERVES 6 AT HOME OR 4 IN THE WOODS.

VENISON

Although usually thought of as deer meat, venison is the meat from any antlered game animal, including deer, caribou, elk, and moose.

The meat from young animals is tender, with a mild flavor. It is cooked as you would cook beef. The texture is similar to veal or beef; but without the marbled fat of beef, it tends to be dry.

The meat from old animals or mature bucks during the mating season may be tough or strong tasting and should be marinated or basted with barbecue sauce.

The following recipes can be used interchangeably with any antlered game.

VENISON STEW

2–3 pounds venison roast, cut in 1-inch cubes

1/2 cup flour

1 teaspoon salt

1/8 teaspoon pepper

1/4 cup cooking oil

2 cups boiling water

1 bay leaf

2 beef bouillon cubes

12 small whole onions, peeled

6 medium carrots, peeled and cut into 2-inch chunks

1 package frozen green lima beans

3 tablespoons flour

1/2 cup cold water

2 large green peppers, seeded and cut in rings

Dredge venison cubes in flour that has been mixed with salt and pepper. Brown on all sides in cooking oil. Add boiling water and bay leaf. Cover and simmer over low heat for 30 minutes. Discard bay leaf. Add bouillon cubes, onions, and carrots. Simmer 45 minutes longer. Stir in lima beans and cook for an additional 15 minutes.

With a slotted spoon, remove meat and vegetables to a serving dish, leaving cooking liquid in the pan. Blend 3 tablespoons flour and

1/2 cup cold water in a cup and gradually add to hot liquid. Cook, stirring constantly, until smooth and thickened. Pour over meat and vegetables. Top with green pepper rings. Broil 5 minutes, until browned on top.

SERVES 6.

VENISON SAUERBRATEN

1 large venison roast

2 medium onions, chopped

2 bay leaves

12 peppercorns

6 whole cloves

2 teaspoons salt

1 cup apple cider

1/2 cup cider vinegar

1 cup boiling water

1/4 cup cooking oil

12 gingersnap cookies, crushed

2 teaspoons brown sugar

In a large mixing bowl, cover venison with a mixture of onions, bay leaves, peppercorns, cloves, salt, cider, vinegar, and boiling water. Cover tightly and refrigerate 3–7 days, turning meat several times a day. The day before serving, drain meat and strain the liquid, discarding onions and seasonings. Brown meat in oil in a Dutch oven or crock pot. Add strained liquid, cover, and cook over low heat for 3–4 hours in a Dutch oven, or 12–24 hours in a crock pot. Remove meat to platter. Turn heat to high over cooking liquid and add the gingersnaps and sugar. Cover and simmer 5 minutes. Serve as a gravy with the meat.

SERVES 4–6.

BEAR

Bear meat is dark and well flavored. The layer of fat should be trimmed off or it will give the meat a strong gamey taste.

Bear meat, like pork, is a carrier of trichinosis, so it must be cooked to well done (185°F.) or frozen 3–4 weeks before cooking.

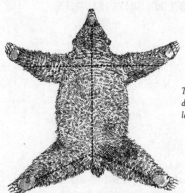

To save a bear pelt, slit the skin down the belly and between the legs as shown.

BEAR STEAKS

1 bear round steak, about 3/4-inch thick

1/2 cup flour

1/2 teaspoon salt

1/8 teaspoon pepper

1/4 cup cooking oil

1 can condensed cream of celery soup

1 cup milk

Trim any fat from steak. Cut in serving-size pieces and sprinkle with flour mixed with salt and pepper. Pound with a meat mallet or the edge of a saucer until all flour is worked into meat. Brown on both sides in hot oil. Combine soup and milk and pour over meat. Cover and bake at 300°F. for 1 hour. Uncover and bake 15 minutes longer.

SERVES 6.

WILD BOAR

The texture and flavor of wild boar meat is much like that of pork, except there is little fat. The meat has a gamey taste because of the animal's diet. Like pork, wild boar must be cooked to well done (185°F.) or frozen 3–4 weeks before cooking.

Boar is cleaned, dressed, and cooked in the same way as pork. Very young animals are barbecued whole.

WILD BOAR ROAST

1 large loin roast of boar, trimmed of fat

1 1/2 teaspoons salt

1/2 teaspoon powdered thyme

1 1/2 teaspoons dry mustard

1/2 teaspoon powdered ginger

1 1/4 cups orange juice

3/4 cup honey

1 unpeeled orange, thinly sliced

Place roast in shallow baking pan. Combine salt, thyme, mustard, and ginger and rub over the meat. Bake 1 hour at 300°F., then baste with 1/4 cup orange juice. Bake 1 hour more, basting 3 more times with 1/4 cup orange juice each time. Combine remaining 1/4 cup orange juice and honey and baste with this mixture. Bake 45 minutes longer or until meat thermometer inserted in center registers 185°F. Baste often with liquid in bottom of the pan. Garnish with orange slices.

SERVES 6.

Game Birds

Game birds, like other game animals, should be cleaned as soon as possible after being killed. The entrails are removed after the birds are plucked.

For easier plucking, work quickly, while the bird is still warm. Dip the beheaded bird into a pot of water in which a cake of paraffin has been melted. The water should be hot enough to melt the paraffin, but not hot enough to cook the skin.

Pluck the feathers off in handfuls, singe off the fuzz over an open flame and remove any pinfeathers with a knife or a pair of tweezers. If the bird is to be stewed, it may be easier to skin it.

Game birds should be aged in the refrigerator for 1 day for young, tender birds, up to 4 days for older birds.

Roast game bird slowly over an open fire or in a slow oven turning frequently and basting with butter or margarine or your favorite basting sauce.

ROAST WILD GOOSE

2 cups bread crumb

1/4 cup butter or margarine, melted

1/4 cup chopped orange, peeled

1/4 teaspoon grated orange rind

3/4 cup celery, diced

1 cup cooked pitted prunes, chopped

1/2 teaspoon salt

1 wild goose, cleaned and aged

salt and pepper

Sauté bread crumbs in melted butter or margarine. Add chopped orange, orange rind, celery, prunes, and salt. Stuff goose cavity lightly and place in roasting pan. Sprinkle with salt and pepper. Bake at 300°F. for 1 1/2 hours, basting frequently with pan drippings.

SERVES 6.

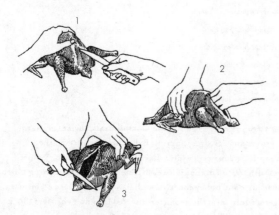

Preparing a game bird is similar to preparing domestic fowl.

1. Slit the skin from vent to breast bone.
2. Reach into the body cavity and remove entrails.
3. Cut off tail.

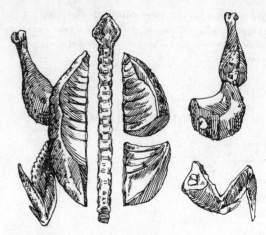

Cut larger game birds into breast pieces, wings, and legs and thighs. The bony back pieces usually are discarded or simmered in water to make soup stock or gravy.

ROAST WILD DUCK

2 wild ducks, cleaned and aged

1 teaspoon salt

1/8 teaspoon pepper

1/4 teaspoon crushed rosemary leaves

1 medium onion, thickly sliced

1 unpeeled apple, cored and sliced

2 stalks (ribs) celery, cut in chunks

1 unpeeled orange, sliced

1/2 cup butter or margarine, melted

1/4 teaspoon pepper

1/4 teaspoon crushed rosemary leaves

Wipe ducks dry. Blend salt, pepper, and rosemary and sprinkle over ducks, inside and out. Combine onion, apple, celery, and orange and stuff each cavity with half the mixture. Put ducks on roasting rack, breast sides down. Roast 30 minutes at 325°F. Combine butter, pepper, and rosemary and baste ducks with this mixture. Roast 1 hour longer, basting occasionally, until tender. Empty cavities and discard contents of ducks before serving.

SERVES 4–6.

QUAIL ROASTED IN GRAPE LEAVES

6 dressed quail

4 tablespoons butter or margarine, melted

salt and pepper

12 grape leaves

1 tablespoon water

juice of 1 lemon

6 slices buttered toast

Wipe quail dry. Brush inside and out with 2 tablespoons melted butter or margarine. Sprinkle with salt and pepper. Wrap each bird in 2 grape leaves and place in a baking dish. Bake at 350°F. for 45 minutes, until tender. Arrange toast on platter. Remove birds to platter, discarding grape leaves. Add remaining butter, water, and lemon juice to the pan drippings and simmer over low heat, stirring constantly. Pour over quail on platter.

SERVES 6.

EASY PARTY PHEASANT

1 pheasant, cleaned, aged, and cut up

1 can condensed cream of mushroom soup

1/2 cup apple cider

1 1/2 tablespoons Worcestershire sauce

1/2 teaspoon salt

2 tablespoons minced onion

1 clove garlic, crushed

1/2 cup fresh mushrooms, sliced paprika

Place pheasant pieces in baking dish. Combine remaining ingredients, except paprika, and pour over pheasant. Sprinkle with paprika. Bake at 300°F. for 1–1 1/2 hours, until tender.

SERVES 4.

RICE-STUFFED GROUSE

2 large grouse, cleaned and aged

1 teaspoon salt

1/8 teaspoon pepper

1 1/2 cups brown or wild rice

1 teaspoon salt

4 cups boiling water

2 tablespoons butter or margarine

1 cup celery, chopped

3 tablespoons minced onion

1/2 cup fresh mushrooms, sliced

pinch of sage

pinch of dried thyme

pinch of dried savory

6 slices bacon

Sprinkle the cavities of the birds with salt and pepper. Refrigerate. Meanwhile, cook the rice in salted water until tender, about 45 minutes. Sauté celery, onion, and mushrooms in melted butter or margarine and add to cooked rice. Stir in herbs. Stuff grouse lightly with the mixture. Place in a baking pan and cover the breasts with bacon slices. Bake at 300°F. for 1 1/2 hours, until tender. Remove bacon during the last 30 minutes of baking.

SERVES 4–6.

Fish

Most fish must be scaled before cleaning. To make this job easier, first soak the fish for a few minutes in cold water. Then, holding it down firmly, scrape with a dull knife from the tail to the head. Be sure you have removed all the scales near the base of the fins and head.

To clean, use a sharp knife to slit the belly from vent to gills and remove the entrails. Discard. Cut around and remove all fins and cut off the head. Rinse quickly in cold water and wipe dry. Do not soak in water after cleaning.

Small fish usually are cooked whole, with the tail on, but larger fish may be cut crosswise into steaks or lengthwise into fillets.

To cut a boneless fillet, use a sharp knife to cut the meat away from the backbone from the tail to the head. Cut the piece loose and lift the entire side of the fish in one piece. Turn the fish over and repeat the process on the other side. You will have two boneless fillets per fish. The remainder of the fish may be discarded or used for soup.

To skin catfish, nail the fish to a solid surface and cut through the skin around the head. Using a pair of pliers, pull the skin down to the tail. Cut off the head and tail and remove entrails as above.

Cook fish quickly but gently. All fish, regardless of age, are tender and may be baked, poached (never stewed), fried, or broiled. Fish should be cooked over low heat just until the flesh flakes easily with a fork.

BAKED TROUT

1 whole fresh trout, cleaned

lemon juice

salt and pepper

Dip trout in lemon juice and arrange in oiled baking pan. Season with salt and pepper. Bake at 350°F for 20–30 minutes, until done.

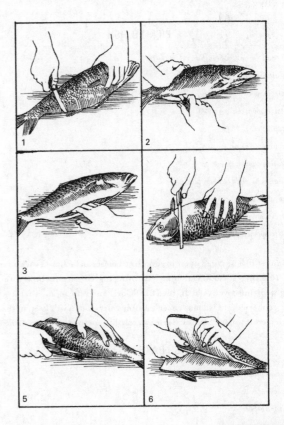

Continued ➜

To clean fish:
1. *Scrape off scales.*
2. *Insert knife at vent and slit up to head.*
3. *Remove entrails.*
4. *Cut off head, fins, and tail.*
5. *Cut the fillet from head to tail.*
6. *Cut along backbone from tail to head to remove fillet.*

ROLLED FISH FILLETS

1 tablespoon butter or margarine

1 small onion, finely chopped

6—8 fish fillets

salt and pepper

2 cups tomatoes, canned or fresh

1/2 cup fresh mushrooms

1 cup cold water

2 tablespoons butter or margarine

2 tablespoons flour

Melt butter or margarine in skillet. Sauté chopped onion for 2 minutes over low heat, stirring constantly. Spread onion over bottom of skillet. Season fish fillets with salt and pepper and roll them up, jelly-roll style. Arrange rolls in skillet over onions. Top with tomatoes, mushrooms, and water. Simmer 10 minutes, until fish is cooked. Remove fish to platter and cook tomato sauce until it thickens. Season with salt and pepper and thicken with butter and flour that have been blended. Pour over fish on platter.

SERVES 6.

PICKLED FISH

16 small fish or 4 medium fish, cut into pieces

1 teaspoon salt

water to cover

4 tablespoons cooking oil

1 cup water

1 cup cider vinegar

4 tablespoons minced onion

2 teaspoons mixed pickling spice

1 sweet red pepper, chopped fine

2 teaspoons salt

1/4 teaspoon pepper

Simmer fish in salted water to cover until meat can be flaked with a fork, 8—10 minutes. Cool. Combine remaining ingredients in a bowl with a tight-fitting cover. Add drained fish. Cover and refrigerate, turning 2 or 3 times a day. Fish may be served after 2 days, but it will keep in the refrigerator up to 2 weeks. Serve as a relish, appetizer, or main dish.

FISH BAKED IN MILK

6 whole fish, cleaned and scaled

3 cups hot milk

salt and pepper

3 tablespoons flour

4 tablespoons butter or margarine

Wash fish and wipe dry. Place in baking pan and cover with hot milk. Bake at 350°F. for 20—30 minutes, depending on thickness of fish. Remove fish to platter, sprinkle with salt and pepper. Thicken milk in pan with flour and season with butter and salt and pepper. Pour sauce over fish.

SERVES 6.

OVEN-FRIED FISH

1/2 cup cooking oil

8 medium fish, cleaned

1 egg, well beaten

1 cup cracker crumbs

Pour oil in baking pan. Heat in a 350°F. oven. Dip fish in beaten egg, then in cracker crumbs, and arrange in preheated baking dish. Bake until browned, about 20 minutes.

SERVES 8.

FISH SOUP

8—10 small fish, cut into 1-inch chunks

4 quarts water

5 sprigs parsley

2 carrots, sliced

2 stalks (ribs) celery, sliced

1 medium onion, chopped

2 lemon slices

2 teaspoons salt

1/8 teaspoon pepper

1 cup cream

2 egg yolks

3 tablespoons chives, minced

In a soup kettle, simmer fish chunks, water, and vegetables 1 hour. Add lemon slices and simmer 5 minutes more. Strain stock and season to taste with salt and pepper. Blend cream, egg yolks, and chives. Pour hot soup over mixture and stir well.

SERVES 6.

Cooking with Fresh Sausage

Charles Reavis

The Basics

Before we investigate the wonderful things that you can do with your homemade sausage, let's take a brief detour and describe the sausage-making process. If you've made sausage before, consider this as a mini-refesher course, or, if you are a consummate *wurstmacher*, skip over this section and go straight to the recipes. If you've never made sausage before, then this section will give you a bare-bones description of the process. For a more detailed account of making sausage you might want to consult a good sausage-making manual, such as *Home Sausage Making*, Revised Edition, Garden Way Publishing, 1987.

There are three basic essentials you need to make your own sausages: meat, something with which to grind the meat, and some herbs and spices with which to flavor it. You needn't stuff the sausage into casings, expecially if you are going to use it in a recipe that calls for sausage as an ingredient and not simply as a stand-alone part of a meal.

If you've never made sausage before, try this simple recipe for Italian-style sweet sausage adapted from *Home Sausage Making*, Revised Edition.

With a food grinder or food processor, grind or chop 2 pounds of lean pork. Add 1 teaspoon of crushed fennel seed, 1/2 teaspoon of freshly ground black pepper, and salt to taste (approximately 1/4 to 1/2 teaspoon per pound is a good starting point). Mix the seasonings into the meat to distribute them evenly. Your hands make the best mixing tool. That's all there is to it. You can leave it bulk, form it into patties, or, if you're a traditionalist, stuff it into natural hog sausage casings. If you choose to stuff it into casing, follow this procedure.

Casing come packed in salt and are available from your local butcher. They must first be rinsed in cold water and allowed to soak for about 30 minutes before you stuff them with the sausage mixture. To stuff the meat into casings, use either the funnel attachment that came with your food grinder or purchase a sausage funnel (for a dollar or less) from a restaurant supply or kitchenware store. After the casings are stuffed, twist or tie off the individual links.

The best part about making homemade sausage is the myriad of wonderful things you can make with it. Here are some examples:

TURKEY SAUSAGE FAJITAS

Although no one seems quite certain where fajitas originated, this Tex-Mex dish has become quite popular. Traditionally made with beef skirt steak, this recipe takes advantage of turkey's naturally low-fat content to create a dish that is both easy to prepare and good for you.

2 tablespoons olive or vegetable oil

2 pounds fresh Spanish-style turkey sausage, removed from the casing and crumbled

1/4 cup lime juice

1/4 cup tequila

3 garlic cloves, finely minced

1 teaspoon oregano

1 teaspoon ground cumin

12 (approximately) large (8 to 10 inch) flour tortillas

Toppings:

Green onions, minced

Fresh cilantro (Chinese parsley), minced

Black and green olives, chopped

Lettuce, shredded

Jalapeño peppers, fresh or pickled, sliced

Salsa fresca (Mexican-style tomato sauce, bottled or homemade)

Sour cream or yogurt-based sour cream substitute

Heat the oil in a large skillet and add the sausage. Sauté the sausage until it loses its pink color. Add the lime juice, tequila, garlic, oregano, and cumin. Sauté until the liquid evaporates and the sausage is browned. Set aside and keep warm.

Soften the tortillas by wrapping in aluminum foil and heating in a 325° F. oven for 10 to 12 minutes or wrapping in a clean dish towel and microwaving on high for 2 to 3 minutes.

Each person assembles his or her own *fajita* by spreading some of the reserved sausage mixture on a tortilla and adding the toppings to suit his or her individual taste. Fold up the bottom of the filled tortilla and then fold in the sides to enclose. Serve.

Serves 4 to 6.

SAUSAGE-STUFFED MUSHROOMS

Although this hors d'oeuvre is elegant and sophistated, it is very easy and quick to prepare. It can be prepared ahead of time, refrigerated, and then reheated just before guests arrive.

18 large mushroom caps

2 tablespoons butter

1/4 pound sweet Italian-style or country-style fresh bulk sausage

2 tablespoons finely minced onions

2 tablespoons olive oil

1/4 cup dry bread crumbs

2 tablespoons dry sherry

1 tablespoon oregano

1 tablespoon chopped fresh parsley

1 garlic clove, very finely minced

Salt to taste

Fresh ground pepper to taste

1/4 pound mozzarella cheese, grated

Wash the mushrooms and remove the stems. Finely chop the stems and set aside.

Melt the butter in a large skillet and sauté the mushroom caps for 2 to 3 minutes, or until they are slightly golden, but remove the caps before they are noticeably shrunken. Remove them with a slotted spoon and drain on a paper towel.

Add the sausage and onions to the skillet and sauté for 5 minutes, or until the sausage loses its pink color and the onions are crisp-tender. Drain off the fat and add the oil to the skillet along with the reserved mushroom stems and sauté for 2 minutes.

Remove from the heat, add the bread crumbs, sherry, oregano, parsley, garlic, salt, and pepper and mix well. Add the cheese and stir through.

Place an equal amount of the sausage mixture in each mushroom cap. Place the caps on a greased baking sheet. At this point either refrigerate or place the baking sheet under a preheated broiler for 1 to 2 minutes, or until the cheese is bubbly. Serve hot.

Serves 6 to 8.

Continued →

RED POTATO SALAD WITH KIELBASA AND YOGURT DRESSING

Tiny new red potatoes in their jackets make this the perfect late summer luncheon salad, but larger red potatoes cut into cubes work just as well.

2 pounds tiny new red potatoes or about 5 to 6 large potatoes

8 ounces plain yogurt

1/4 cup white vinegar

1 teaspoon Dijon-style mustard

1 tablespoon sugar

4 garlic cloves, finely minced

1 teaspoon summer savory

1 teaspoon basil

1 teaspoon thyme

1/4 cup sliced green onions

1/4 cup finely chopped celery

1 tablespoon finely shredded carrot

1 pound fully cooked kielbasa, thinly sliced

2 tablespoons minced fresh parsley for garnish

Wash the potatoes and cook them in a large pot of simmering water for approximately 15 to 25 minutes (depending on the size of the potatoes). Drain and rinse under cold water. If larger potatoes are used, cut them into 1/2-inch-thick cubes. Set aside.

In a large mixing bowl, combine the yogurt, vinegar, mustard, sugar, garlic, savory, basil, and thyme. Add the onions, celery, and carrot and mix thoroughly. Add the kielbasa and the reserved potatoes and stir through. Cover and chill thoroughly before serving.

Serves 6 to 8.

RABBIT SAUSAGE SALAD WITH THREE GREENS

When made with wild rabbit, rabbit sausages have a dark color and a decidedly gamy taste. When made with domestic rabbit, however, they are mild and the color of cooked breast of chicken. Either way, they help make this a very unique and delicious salad, suitable as the main course for a luncheon.

8 ounces fresh rabbit sausage in links

2 tablespoons vegetable oil

4 cups red leaf lettuce, torn into pieces

4 cups green leaf lettuce, torn into pieces

4 cups romaine lettuce, torn into pieces

1 small red onion, thinly sliced and separated into rings

6 large fresh mushroom caps, thinly sliced

2 tablespoons rice wine vinegar

1 teaspoon Dijon-style mustard

1/3 cup vegetable oil

Salt to taste

Freshly ground black pepper to taste

Sauté the sausages in the 2 tablespoons of oil until lightly browned and cooked through, about 10 to 12 minutes. Drain on paper towels and when they are cool enough to handle, cut them into 1/2-inch-thick pieces. Set aside.

In a large mixing bowl, combine the three lettuces and mix thoroughly. Divide the lettuce mixture, then the onion rings and the mushrooms among 4 to 6 salad plates. Place the reserved sausage pieces on the top of each salad.

In a small mixing bowl, combine the vinegar, mustard, and the 1/3 cup of oil. Mix well. Add the salt and pepper to taste. Just before serving, dribble the vinaigrette dressing over each salad.

Serves 4 to 6.

JAMBALAYA

Jambalaya is a Cajun dish that has many variations. This version has shrimp, ham, and smoked sausage.

2 tablespoons olive oil

1 pound smoked sausage in a link, such as kielbasa, smoked chorizo, or any other highly spiced variety

1 cup chopped sweet onions

1 cup chopped sweet green pepper

1 cup chopped celery

4 garlic cloves, minced

1 pound cooked ham (preferably dry-cured), diced

4 cups canned whole tomatoes, crushed, with juice

1 6-ounce can tomato paste

1 cup dry red wine

1 cup water

1 teaspoon thyme

2 bay leaves

1 teaspoon crushed red pepper

Salt to taste

Freshly gound black pepper to taste

1 cup white rice, uncooked

1 pound large, fresh shrimp, peeled and deveined

Heat the oil in a large skillet or saucepan and sauté the sausage until it is evenly browned. Remove the sausage and when it is cool enough to handle, cut it into 1-inch-thick pieces. Set aside.

Sauté the onions, pepper, celery, and garlic in the skillet until they are slightly wilted, about 8 minutes. Add the ham, tomatoes, tomato paste, wine, and water. Stir to mix well. Add the thyme, bay leaves, red pepper, salt, and pepper and bring to a boil. Add the rice, reduce the heat so that the mixture simmers gently, cover, and cook 20 minutes.

Add the shrimp and the reserved sausage pieces, cook an additional 10 minutes, or until the shrimp is pink. Remove the bay leaves and serve.

Serves 6 to 8.

VENISON SAUSAGE STEW

Venison is one of those meats that you either hate or you love. This recipe tends to tame the somewhat characteristic gamy flavor of venison and so even those who don't usually care for game meats might find this stew to their liking.

2 tablespoons vegetable oil

2 pounds fresh bulk venison sausage

4 cups coarsely chopped onions

4 garlic cloves, minced

1 12-ounce bottle dark ale

4 cups hearty beef stock

1 teaspoon thyme

1 teaspoon marjoram

2 cups crushed tomatoes

2 cups carrots, cut into 1/2-inch dice

2 cups potatoes, cut into 3/4-inch cubes

Salt to taste

Freshly ground black pepper to taste

1/4 cup chopped fresh parsley

1 tablespoon cornstarch

2 tablespoons cold water

Heat the oil in a large skillet and sauté the sausage until it is evenly browned. Remove it with a slotted spoon and place it in a large Dutch oven.

Sauté the onions and garlic in the skillet until the onions are crisp-tender. Remove the onion mixture with a slotted spoon and place it in the Dutch oven with the sausage.

Pour the ale into the skillet and cook over high heat, stirring, to deglaze the pan. When the liquid is reduced by half, pour it into the Dutch oven.

Add the beef stock, thyme, marjoram, and tomatoes. Cook over medium heat until the mixture comes to a a boil. Reduce heat, cover, and simmer for 1 hour.

Add the salt and pepper to taste and the parsley.

Mix the cornstarch with the cold water and add it to the stew. Cook, stirring, until the stew thickens. Serve.

Serves 6 to 8.

SAUSAGE CHILI

The argument still rages over whether "real" chili has beans or no beans, ground meat or cubed meat, tomatoes or no tomatoes. We're not going to settle all the arguments here, but we can certainly add our own two cents—or rather our homemade sausage—to the pot and fan the flames of controversy.

2 pounds of at least three different kinds of fresh sausage in links, such as Italian, chorizo, kielbasa, etc.

2 tablespoons olive oil

2 cups coarsely chopped onions

2 cups coarsely chopped sweet green pepper

4 garlic cloves, minced

1 12-ounce bottle beer

2 cups crushed tomatoes

2 cups tomato puree

2 Jalapeño peppers (or to taste), seeded and chopped

4 cups canned red kidney beans with their juice

Salt to taste

Freshly ground black pepper to taste

Remove the sausages from their casings and brown the meat in the oil in a Dutch oven. Remove the sausage with a slotted spoon and set aside.

Drain off all but 2 tablespoons of the drippings. Sauté the onions, green pepper, and garlic in the remaining drippings until they are slightly wilted. Add the beer and cook, stirring, to get the brown bits from the bottom of the pot.

Return the reserved sausage to the pot. Add the remaining ingredients and simmer gently, uncovered, for 1 hour. Serve.

Serves 6 to 8.

HUEVOS CON CHORIZO

Huevos con chorizo, or eggs with sausage, is sort of a Mexican omelet, but much, much spicier. This is definitely not a dish for those who are watching their cholesterol.

2 tablespoons vegetable oil

1 pound fresh chorizo sausage, removed from the casing

1 cup finely chopped onions

1 garlic clove, finely minced

12 eggs

3/4 cup milk

1 teaspoon oregano

Salt to taste

Freshly ground black pepper to taste

Heat the oil in a large skillet and sauté the sausage until it is evenly browned. Remove it with a slotted spoon and set aside.

Drain off all but 2 tablespoons of the drippings and sauté the onions and garlic until they are crisp-tender. Return the reserved sausage to the skillet.

In a large mixing bowl, beat the eggs with the milk, oregano, salt, and pepper. Pour the egg mixture into the skillet. Cook as you would an omelet, tilting the pan from side to side, lifting the cooked edges of the egg mixture, allowing the uncooked egg to flow under the cooked part. Cook just until all the egg is set but remains moist, about 6 to 8 minutes. Serve.

Serves 6 to 8.

Continued →

CHICKEN SAUSAGE VINDALOO

Vindaloo is traditionally an incendiary curry made with chicken. Try this interesting variation with a fresh batch of chicken sausage. Be forewarned, however, this dish is HOT!

2 tablespoons vegetable or peanut oil

1 pound fresh bulk chicken sausage

2 cups coarsely chopped onions

6 garlic cloves, minced

1 tablespoon minced fresh ginger

2 teaspoons ground cumin

1/2 teaspoon ground cinnamon

1 teaspoon ground allspice

2 teaspoons turmeric

2 tablespoons cayeene pepper

1/4 cup chopped and seeded Jalapeño peppers

2 teaspoons crushed red pepper

2 teaspoons tamarind paste*

2 teaspoons brown sugar

1 cup crushed tomatoes

1 cup chicken stock

1/4 cup cider vinegar

Salt to taste

Heat the oil in a large skillet and brown the sausage. Remove it with a slotted spoon and keep it warm.

Add the remaining ingredients to the skillet and heat until the mixture bubbles. Add the reserved sausage, reduce the heat, and simmer, covered, for 30 minutes. Serve with steamed rice.

Servies 4 to 6.

*Available in Indian groceries and in large supermarkets.

TORTELLINI AND SEAFOOD SAUSAGE SALAD

Tortellini are pieces of pasta shaped like little caplets and stuffed with meat or cheese. Cheese tortellini are best used in this recipe.

1 pound frozen cheese tortellini

1 pound fresh seafood sausage in links (any variety)

1 cup broccoli florets

1 cup cauliflower florets

1/2 cup thinly sliced carrots

1/2 cup chopped sweet green pepper

1/2 cup chopped sweet red pepper

1/4 cup red wine vinegar

1 tablespoon Dijon-style mustard

1/2 teaspon sugar

Salt to taste

Freshly ground black pepper to taste

1/2 cup extra virgin olive oil

Cook the tortellini according to the package directions. Drain, rinse under cold water, drain again thoroughly, and place in a large mixing bowl.

Steam the sausage until cooked through and firm, about 8 to 10 minutes. Rinse under cold water, drain, cut into 1/2-inch-thick pieces, and add to the tortellini.

Steam the broccoli, cauliflower, and carrots just until crisp-tender, about 2 minutes. Rinse under cold water, drain, and add to the tortellini. Add the red and green pepper to the tortellini.

Mix the vinegar, mustard, sugar, salt, and pepper together in a small bowl. Add the olive oil in a stream, whisking, until it is combined.

Pour the vinaigrette mixture over the tortellini and mix well. Transfer the mixture to a large serving bowl, cover, and refrigerate for 30 to 40 minutes or until chilled through. Serve cold or at room temperature.

Serves 8 to 10 as a side dish or 4 to 6 as a main dish.

VEAL SAUSAGE WITH MARSALA AND MUSHROOMS

Any mildly flavored fresh veal sausage can be used in this classically Italian recipe.

1/4 cup olive oil

1 pound fresh veal sausages

4 garlic cloves, crushed

1 cup finely diced onions

1 pound fresh mushrooms, sliced

1/2 teaspoon oregano

1/2 teaspoon basil

1/2 teaspoon thyme

Salt to taste

Freshly ground black pepper to taste

1 cup marsala wine

Heat the oil in a large skillet and sauté the sausages until they are browned and cooked through. Remove them with a slotted spoon and keep them warm. Drain off all but 2 tablespoons of the oil.

Add the garlic, onions, mushrooms, oregano, basil, thyme, salt, and pepper to the skillet and cook over medium heat, until the mushrooms are cooked, about 10 minutes.

Add the wine to the skillet and return the reserved sausages to the skillet. Simmer until the liquid is reduced by half, about 10 minutes. Remove the sausages.

Increase the heat to high and cook the sauce until it is syrupy, about 5 minutes. Place the sausages on a serving platter and pour the sauce over them. Serve.

Serves 4.

PORK SAUSAGE WITH ORANGE AND PINEAPPLE SAUCE

Almost any pork sausage will do in this recipe but breakfast-style sausages would make this dish excellent as part of a brunch buffet.

2 tablespoons vegetable oil

1 pound fresh pork sausages

1 cup orange juice

1 cup pineapple juice

1/4 cup brown sugar, packed

1/4 teaspoon allspice

1 teaspoon finely minced fresh ginger

3 tablespoons dry white wine, chilled

1 tablespoon cornstarch

Orange slices for garnish

Heat the oil in a large skillet and brown the sausages. Drain off all but 2 teaspoons of the oil.

Mix the orange juice, pineapple juice, brown sugar, allspice, and ginger and pour it over the sausages in the skillet. Sauté gently, covered, 25 to 30 minutes, or until the sausages are cooked through.

Mix the wine and cornstarch and pour it into the skillet. Increase the heat and cook until the sauce thickens. Place the sausages on a serving platter and pour the sauce over them. Garnish with fresh orange slices and serve.

Serves 4.

BARBECUED SHRIMP SAUSAGE

This is a quick and simple recipe that makes a perfect supper dish on a warm summer evening.

1 pound fresh shrimp sausage in links

1 8-ounce bottle French Catalina-style salad dressing

1 tablespoon finely minced garlic

1/4 cup finely minced fresh parsley

Place the sausages in a large mixing bowl. Combine the remaining ingredients and pour over the sausage. Allow the sausages to marinate at room temperature for 30 minutes, or cover and refrigerate for several hours. If refrigerated, allow the sausages to warm almost to room temperature before proceeding.

Thread the links of sausage on metal skewers. Prepare a hot charcoal fire or ready the gas grill.

Barbecue the sausages until they are cooked through, about 10 to 15 minutes depending on the intensity of the heat. Baste occasionally with the remaining sauce. Serve.

Serves 4.

TURKEY SAUSAGE WITH MUSHROOM WINE SAUCE

The wine sauce perks up the turkey sausage, giving this dish an irresistible aroma.

2 teaspoons vegetable oil

1 pound fresh bulk turkey sausage

1 1/2 cups chicken stock

1/2 cup dry sherry

1/4 cup cold water

1 tablespoon cornstarch

2 cups sliced fresh mushrooms

Salt to taste

Freshly ground black pepper to taste

Heat the oil in a large skillet and add the sausage. Brown the sausage well. Add the chicken stock and sherry and cook over medium heat until the sausage is cooked through, about 10 minutes.

Mix the water and cornstarch and set aside.

Add the mushrooms to the skillet and cook 5 minutes. Add the reserved cornstarch mixture to the skillet and cook, stirring, until the sauce is thickened. Serve hot over rice or noodles.

Serves 4 to 6.

FETTUCCINE WITH SEAFOOD SAUSAGE ALLA PUTANESCA

Alla putanesca is an Italian term which usually means the dish will include olives and anchovies. This recipe is no exception.

2 tablespoons olive oil

1 pound fresh seafood sausages (any variety)

1 cup chopped onions

1 tablespoon chopped garlic

1/2 teaspoon crushed red pepper or to taste

4 anchovy fillets, minced

1/2 cup dry red wine

4 cups whole canned tomatoes with their juice, broken into small pieces

1/4 cup oil-cured black olives, pitted and coarsely chopped

1/4 cup oil-cured green olives, pitted and coarsely chopped

1/2 teaspoon basil

1/2 teaspoon oregano

Freshly ground black pepper to taste

1 pound fettuccine

Continued ➜

Heat the oil in a large skillet and sauté the sausages until they are lightly browned and cooked through. Remove them with a slotted spoon and put them on a platter to keep warm.

Add the onions, garlic, red pepper, and anchovies to the skillet. Sauté until the onions are translucent, about 10 minutes.

Add the remaining ingredients except the fettuccine and simmer 30 minutes until the sauce is reduce slightly and begins to thicken. Cut the sausages into bite-sized pieces and return them to the sauce.

Boil the fettuccine until it is *al dente*. Drain it and put it in a large serving bowl. Pour the sauce over the fettuccine and serve.

Serves 6.

LAMB SAUSAGE CURRY

Cumin, turmeric, cloves, and cinnamon give this dish a traditional curry flavor.

2 tablespoons vegetable oil

1 pound fresh lamb sausages

2 cups diced sweet white onions

2 tablespoons finely minced garlic

1 tablespoon finely minced fresh ginger

2 teaspoons ground cumin

1 teaspoon ground cloves

1 teaspoon tumeric

1 teaspoon cinnamon

2 teaspoons (or to taste) cayenne pepper

2 cups chicken stock

1/2 cup tomato paste

Heat the oil in a large skillet and sauté the sausages until they are evenly browned. Remove them with a slotted spoon and keep them warm.

Discard all but 2 tablespoons of the drippings and add the onions, garlic, and ginger. Sauté until the onions are just slightly wilted, about 5 minutes.

Return the reserved sausages to the skillet along with any juices that have accumulated in the dish. Add the cumin, cloves, turmeric, cinnamon, cayenne pepper, and chicken stock. Cook, uncovered , over medium heat for 20 minutes, or until the sausages are cooked through and the liquid is slightly reduced.

Add the tomato paste, stir through and cook 10 minutes, or until the sauce has thickened. Serve hot with rice or bread.

Serves 4 to 6.

PRESERVING, PICKLING, CANNING, DISTILLING

Food Drying Techniques

Carol Costenbader

Illustrations by Alison Kolesar, Judy Eliason, and Charles Joslin

Drying Food

Drying was one of the earliest methods of preservation humans found to save food from times of bounty to use when food was scarce. As far back as pre-biblical times, fishermen dried and smoked fish, and farmers dried olives and dates in the hot, dry climate of the Middle East.

Drying is by far the simplest and most natural way of preserving food. Little in the way of equipment is needed, but climate is everything. If you are fortunate enough to live in a warm, dry region, all you need is fresh food and a little time. The faster food can dry without actually cooking, the better its flavor will be when it's reconstituted. If you live in a relatively moist climate, you will want to learn to use a more active drying method—a dehydrator, your oven, or in some cases the sun. As always, the finished product will be only as good as the original, so start with the very best fresh food.

The concept of drying food is quite simple. When all the moisture is removed from the food, the growth of organisms that spoil food is stopped. Bacteria, mold, and yeasts can be supported only in an environment that has adequate water for them to grow. Properly dried fruits have about 80 percent of the water removed, and properly dried vegetables have about 90 percent of the water removed. Thus you can count on keeping your home-dried foods for six months to two years, depending on the storage temperature (see chart). Remember that cooler storage temperatures are better. Food kept at 70°F does not keep as long as food stored at 52°F.

Food Preparation for Drying

Use only blemish-free fruits and vegetables. Fruit should be fully ripe but not overly ripe. The smaller the piece of food to dry, the less time it will take to dry properly. Try to keep all the pieces about the same size, so each piece will dry at the same rate.

BLANCHING

Proper blanching, which heats the food without actually cooking it, deactivates the enzymes that cause food spoilage. For use in the drying process, steam-blanching is the only method recommended for vegetables.

The method of dipping produce in boiling water, used in many areas of the world, is not recommended because it adds more water to the produce and therefore increases drying time. Because the food is heated longer and at a hotter temperature, it also robs the food of nutrients and does not fully protect the produce from spoilage organisms. If you must boil fruits and vegetables, use about 3 gallons of water to every 1 quart of food, drain and chill the pieces in ice water to stop the cooking and then pat dry.

To blanch using the steam method, you'll need a steamer, a large Dutch oven, or your canner with lid. Use a wire basket with legs, a basket that fits in the top of the pot, or a colander that will allow 2 or more inches of water to boil without touching the produce. Steam 1 minute longer than the time given if you live 5,000 feet or more above sea level (see chart). After blanching, drain the food, then chill in ice water to stop the cooking. Drain again and dry on towels.

Blanching can be done in a microwave oven, but only in small quantities. Wattages vary, so consult the manufacturer's instructions.

To steam-blanch, place produce in a steamer basket in a pan over at least 2 inches of water.

To cool, pour produce into an ice-water bath. When cool, transfer to a towel to dry.

Four Types of Drying

Drying meat and produce involves the simple process of exposing the food to mild heat and moving air. This can be done by placing food in the sun, in a dehydrator, in the open air, or in an oven.

AIR-DRYING

The process of air-drying is very similar to sun-drying. Puffs of dry air circulate around the food, absorb the moisture, and carry it away. Keep the food out of direct sun to prevent loss of color.

Try air-drying steam-blanched green beans by stringing them on a cotton thread and hanging them under the eaves of the house or porch or in a well-ventilated attic. Depending on the conditions, in two or three days you will have dried, pliable "leather britches," great for adding to soups. Bring the beans inside at night to prevent dew from collecting on them. Keep them out of direct sun: It will make them lose all color.

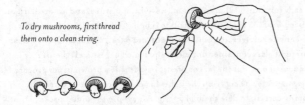

To dry mushrooms, first thread them onto a clean string.

To dry mushrooms, wipe them clean, string using a needle and thread, and hang in an airy location. Or you can place clean mushrooms on several thicknesses of newspaper; turn them several times as the day progresses, and change the newspapers as moisture is absorbed. Place the mushrooms in a dry, airy spot (in direct sun if you wish, but don't forget to bring them in at night.) In one or two days the mushrooms will be almost brittle.

After the drying process, both the green beans and the mushrooms must be heated in a 175°F oven for 30 minutes to destroy insect eggs. Condition the produce (see Post-Drying Methods) and then store in a cool, dry place for up to six months.

SUN-DRYING

Because sun-drying takes more time, pretreating the produce by blanching or another method is much more important. The ideal temperature is about 100°F with low humidity. If you are blessed with a climate like that, do try sun-drying. In other climates, use caution. Low temperature and high humidity is the perfect combination for spoilage to occur before drying can be accomplished.

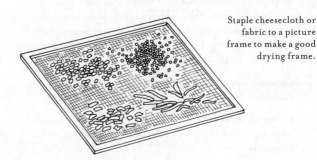

Staple cheesecloth or fabric to a picture frame to make a good drying frame.

Staple cheesecloth or fabric to a picture frame to make a good drying frame.

Sun-Drying Equipment To make sun-drying equipment, I like to use old picture frames purchased from flea markets. First, clean the frames with a cloth dampened with soap and water. Then seal the frames with mineral oil. Stretch a clean, 100 percent cotton sheet or cheesecloth over a frame and secure with a stapler. Some people use screens from their windows. This is fine, but don't use a screen with galvanized wire as it can impart off-flavors to the food. Arrange the prepared produce on the cloth, then place the frames in direct sun, bracing them so that air can circulate on all sides. (Bring them in at night to prevent dew from collecting on them.) You can turn the produce over halfway through the drying process (after about two days). In about two to four days you will have leathery, pliable produce. This is great for sun-dried tomatoes.

To destroy any pest eggs that may still be in your homegrown foods, remove the produce from the frames and freeze it for two to four days below zero or heat it in a tray in your oven 10 to 15 minutes at 175°F (see Post-Drying Methods). Whether you freeze or heat the produce, bring it to room temperature and then store in airtight jars for up to six months.

Continued ➜

You can either purchase a commercial dehydrator or make your own.

become quite long. Allow 4 to 12 hours, depending on the items and quantities being dried. Food should be dry but pliable when cool. (Test one or two pieces.)

While some authorities claim that it's possible to dry food in a microwave oven, I don't recommend it, because the microwave will cook your produce before it dries.

Post-Drying Methods

After the food is dried, condition it by pouring it into a large open container such as a big enameled canner pot. Don't use a container that is aluminum or that is porous, because it might affect the flavor or consistency of the dried food. Put the pot in a warm but dry and airy place. For the next 10 days or two weeks, stir it once or twice a day. Don't add newly dried food to the batch in the pot, as you want it all to finish drying at the same time.

DEHYDRATOR

Using a food dehydrator is simple: You fill the trays with prepared produce, set the timer, turn on the dehydrator, and go about your business. Although a commercial dehydrator can be expensive, it will pay for itself over several seasons. Comparison shopping is difficult, since most commercial dehydrators are sold through mail order. Plan on writing for information before ordering. Many of these companies also have Web sites on the Internet that can be accessed by searching "dehydrator" or "food drying." There are several features to consider before you buy:

- Underwriters Laboratories (UL) should approve the dehydrator for safety.

- Be sure you order a size that you can easily accommodate in your house and that will allow you to dry the right amount of produce or meat at a time.

- Trays should be lightweight and sturdy. Plastic screens are easier to clean and are better than metal. Metal screens can corrode, retain the heat longer, and may scorch food.

- If your model has a door, make sure that it opens easily and can be completely removed.

- The controls should be easy to read. Control settings to adjust vents for airflow and to regulate the heat are important, and an automatic built-in timer is useful.

- The materials used in the outside cabinets vary greatly. Consider how easily you can move the cabinet, clean it, and store it. Look for double-walled insulation, also.

- Look for dehydrators that use less electricity.

OVEN-DRYING

The most labor intensive of all the methods, oven drying is an effective (although possibly more expensive) process. In this method, place the food directly on oven racks or cover the racks with clean, 100 percent cotton sheeting or cheesecloth.

Preheat your oven to 145°F. Check the temperature periodically with an oven thermometer. Ovens vary, so you may need to experiment with a setting between 120°F and 145°F. My gas oven dries produce best at 145°F. Use a wooden spoon to prop open the door to let the moisture escape. Be sure not to have your oven too full, or the drying time will

PASTEURIZING

Pasteurizing is the partial sterilization of food. Because outdoor drying and oven-drying are less exact, pasteurizing dried food is recommended.

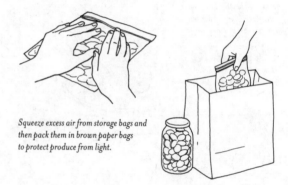

Squeeze excess air from storage bags and then pack them in brown paper bags to protect produce from light.

The longer you wish to keep the dried food, the more the need for pasteurizing increases. Pasteurizing ensures that insect eggs and organisms that cause spoilage are destroyed, allowing food to be stored for a longer period.

There are two ways to pasteurize:

- Heat. Spread the dried produce on trays in a thin layer and leave in your 175°F oven for 10 to 15 minutes. Cool.

- Freeze. Using plastic storage bags, place dried produce in a zero-degree freezer two to four days. This destroys fewer vitamins than does the oven method. The freezer must be at zero. The freezer compartment of a refrigerator will not do.

PACKING AND STORING

Dried food should be packed promptly in a "user-friendly" quantity ready for your meal preparation. As light, moisture, and air are hard on dried foods, a cool, dry, dark place is best. (This does not necessarily mean the refrigerator, which is moist and dark.) Completely fill a clean, airtight glass container or a clean zip-sealed bag with all the air squeezed out. Put the jars or plastic bags inside a brown paper grocery bag to protect them from the light. Label the dried foods carefully, being certain to date them properly. Always use the oldest package first.

If summer's heat becomes a problem, switch to the refrigerator, but make certain the packaging is absolutely airtight to guard against moisture.

REHYDRATING

To rehydrate dried produce, first cover it with boiling water. Let the produce stand for several hours to absorb the water, then cook the produce in the soaking liquid that is left. Vegetables take longer to rehydrate than fruits because they lose more water to dehydration. Cooking time will be much shorter than for produce not rehydrated before cooking. In the case of dried beans, drain the rehydrated beans and cook them in fresh water, because the nitrogen released by the beans in the soaking water is difficult to digest. Cook until tender.

Drying Herbs

HARVESTING AND AIR-DRYING HERBS

Herbs should be harvested when their essential oils are at the highest level, usually right before flowering or bolting time (when they form seeds). The best time of the day to harvest them is before the hot sun wilts them but after the dew has evaporated. Cut them within 6 to 8 inches of the base of the plant. Some herbalists recommend not washing the leaves unless they are filled with grit or beaten down from rain, as washing depletes some of their essence. You might try hosing the plants the night before you plan to pick them. Give them a good shake and make certain they are upright and not weighted down with water. The next day they will be grit-free and won't require washing after harvesting.

To dry the cut herbs, tie together small bunches of them with garden twine and hang them with leaves pointed downward in an airy, warm, dry place that's not in direct sunlight. Gravity will force the essential oils downward into the leaves.

Never hang herbs over the stove, refrigerator, or freezer. Heat from these appliances causes deterioration. Also, don't store your purchased herbs and spices in cabinets above these appliances.

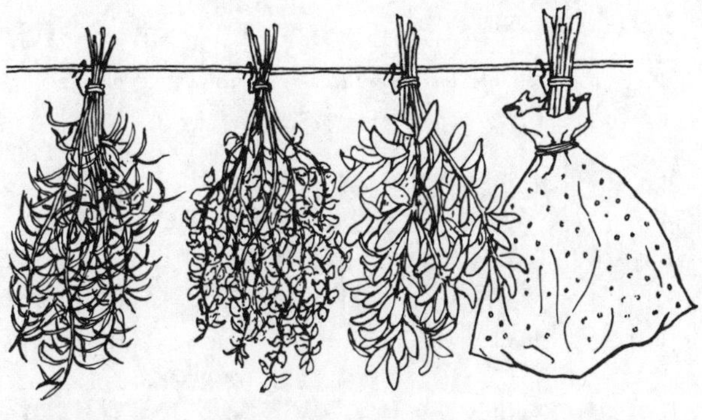

Hang herbs upside down on a wire, string, or drying rack to dry. If dust will be a problem, dry them inside small paper bags with holes or slits for air circulation.

If you plan to use a dehydrator, consult the manufacturer's directions for drying herbs.

Before storing, test for remaining moisture. Put dried herbs, stems and all, in airtight containers in a warm place for a day or two. If there is moisture present on the inside of the container, it is better to take the herbs back to the drying process. When the herb leaves are completely dry, put them on a tray and into a warm oven for 2 to 3 minutes to further dry them. Remove the leaves from the stem by stripping them off. Store the leaves, undisturbed, in a cool place with no direct sun, ideally in a dark glass container and/or inside a kitchen cabinet. Crush the leaves between your hands for cooking as needed: The crushing releases the pungent flavors and aroma. A mortar and pestle can be used to grind the leaves into powder. Either way, deterioration sets in within six months to a year, so plan on starting over with new batches the next season.

Drying Meats

Meats are dried in much the same way as fruits and vegetables, but the drying temperature must be held at 140°F to 150°F to prevent spoilage. Except when you're making meat jerky, all meats must be cooked before drying. To obtain the longest possible storage time, one year, use only the freshest lean beef and store the finished product in zip-seal bags in the freezer. Dried meats will keep for two months in the refrigerator.

Meat jerky, which can be marinated for additional flavor before drying, has a much shorter shelf life than dried meat that is cooked first. It will keep two to six months, but it is easy to prepare and very convenient to use. I store jerky in the freezer in zip-sealed bags.

Pork does not perform well because it contains more fat than lean cuts of beef and the fat can turn rancid. Chicken should not be used either; it also contains too much fat for successful drying, and may present a health hazard. As stated before, lean beef is the most reliable choice for dried meat.

DRYING BEEF

In a heavy saucepan, cover with water 2 pounds of lean beef cut into 1-inch cubes (lean lamb may be used); boil, covered, for about 1 hour. Spread the pieces in a single layer on trays or cookie sheets and dry them in the oven at 140°F to 150°F for 4 to 6 hours. Prop open the oven door with the handle of a wooden spoon to let the moisture escape. To test, cool a cube and cut it open to check for moisture in the center. After 4 to 6 hours, continue drying the meat but lower the temperature to 130°F; dry until there is no moisture in the center of the cubes. An oven thermometer will help you maintain a stable low temperature.

To rehydrate, use 1 cup of boiling water over 1 cup of meat. Let stand 3 to 4 hours. Use in stews, casseroles, or soups. Plan to marinate for flavor if necessary.

You can speed up the rehydration process by simmering the meat and water, in the same 1:1 ratio, in a covered saucepan for 40 to 50 minutes.

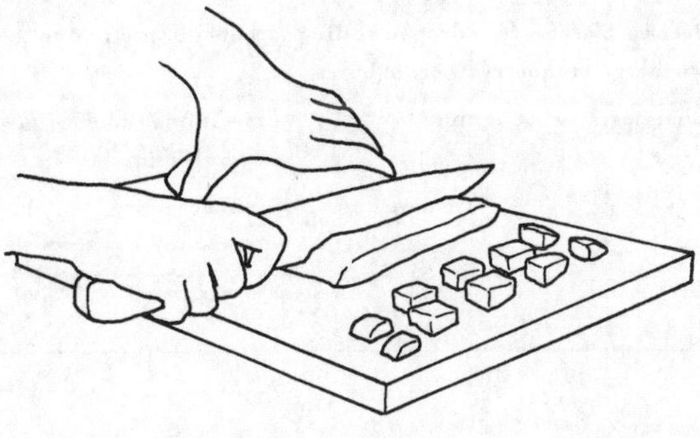

Cutting meat into small pieces aids the drying process.

Continued →

DRYING VEGETABLES AND FRUITS

Best Vegetables/ Fruits for Drying	Preparation	Preferred Pretreat Method	Oven or Electric Dehydrator (hrs)	Sun/Air (days)	Final Consistency	1 cup dry = cups cooked	Cooking time (min.)	Storage time at 52°F (months)
VEGETABLES								
Beans (green, wax, yellow)	trim or shell, string to air-dry	steam-blanch 4–6 minutes	12–14	2–3	leathery	2 1/2	45	8–12
Beans (all others)	shell, pick over mature beans	steam-blanch 5 minutes	48	4–5	hard		120–180	8–12
Corn	shuck, cut kernels off after blanching	steam-blanch whole 10–15 minutes	8–12	1–2	dry, brittle	2	50	8–12
Mushrooms	wipe clean, string to air-dry or air-dry on paper	steam-blanch 3 minutes if not air drying	8–12	1–2	leathery	1 1/4	20–30	4–6
Okra	slice	steam-blanch 5 minutes	8–12	1–2	dry, brittle	1 1/2	30–45	9–12
Peas	shell	steam-blanch 3 minutes	12–18	2–3	shriveled	2	40–45	8–12
Peppers (chile)	string whole, air-dry	not necessary	not recomm.	2–3	shriveled	1 1/2	use directly	16–24
Peppers (bell)	slice or chop	not necessary	12–18	1–2	leathery	1 1/2	30–45	
Tomatoes, Italian	slice in half lengthwise, remove seeds, air-dry	not necessary	6–8	1–2	pliable, leathery	1 1/2	30	6–9
FRUITS								
Apples	peel, core, slice	juice or ascorbic dip, or steam-blanch 5 minutes	6–8	2–3	pliable, leathery	1 1/4	30	18–24
Apricots	slice, pit	juice or ascorbic dip, or steam-blanch 5 minutes	8–12	2–3	pliable, leathery	1 1/2	30–45	24–32
Bananas	peel, slice	honey, juice pectin, or ascorbic dip, or steam-blanch 5 minutes	6–8	2	brittle	.....	not recomm.	12–16
Berries: blackberry, blueberry, cranberry	drop in boiling water to burst	honey or pectin dip	12–24	2–4	hard	.....	not recomm.	18–24
Cherries	pit	pectin, juice, or ascorbic dip	12–24	2–4	hard	1 1/2	30–45	36–48
Figs	remove stem	not necessary	36–48	5–6	shriveled	....	not recomm.	18–24
Grapes	remove from stem	break skin	24–48	3–6	shriveled	....	not recomm.	18–24

DRYING VEGETABLES AND FRUITS

Best Vegetables/ Fruits for Drying	Preparation	Preferred Pretreat Method	Oven or Electric Dehydrator (hrs)	Sun/Air (days)	Final Consistency	I cup dry = cups cooked	Cooking time (min.)	Storage time at 52°F (months)
Peaches	peel, pit, slice, or halve	honey, pectin, or juice or ascorbic dip	10–12	2–6	leathery	1 1/4	20–30	18–24
Pears	peel, slice, or halve	ascorbic dip, or steam- blanch 2 minutes	12–18	2–3	leathery	1 1/2	20–30	18–24
Plums/prunes	pit, halve, or leave whole	break skin	12–18	4–5	shriveled	1 1/2	20–30	24–32
Strawberries	halve	honey dip	8–12	1–2	hard	.....	not recomm.	18–24

Jams, Jellies, & Preserves

Imogene McTague

Jelly A flavorful addition to any meal, a gift for every occasion.

Jelly is made from strained juices. It should be clear, colorful, firm enough to hold its shape, soft enough to spread easily.

To make jelly you'll need the following:

· A large enamel or stainless steel kettle
· Jars and lids
· Jelly bag or cheesecloth
· Potato or other masher
· Wooden stirring spoons
· Damp clean cloth
· Rack for cooling jars
· Measuring cups
· Candy thermometer
· Vegetable brush
· Paring knife
· Timer
· Slotted spoon

Here are the steps you will follow:

1. *Extract the juice.* Slightly unripe fruit is best for jelly. Wash it. Pare only pineapple, core only quince. Cut up into kettle. Mash lower layer of berries. Add small amount of water only if fruit lacks enough juice to prevent scorching. Apples and plums require water. Start over low heat, gradually increasing heat as juice builds up. Cook until fruit is soft, about three minutes for berries, and fifteen to twenty-five for harder fruit.

2. *Strain juice.* Put cooked fruit in damp jelly bag, and let juice drip into bowl. Pressing or squeezing bag will cloud the juice—and the jelly. Juice can be frozen or canned, and used later for making jelly.

A jelly bag can be made from four layers of cheesecloth which are tied at the four corners and suspended over a bowl. An equally effective method is to place the layers of cheesecloth over a colander. In either case, dampen the cheesecloth before ladling the pulp into it.

3. *Test for pectin.* Put 1 tablespoon of juice in a glass. Add 1 tablespoon rubbing alcohol. Shake gently. *Don't taste.* Pectin should form a transparent glob, indicating high pectin content. Use equal amounts of juice and sugar in making jelly. If two or three globs form, pectin content is less, and you should use 2/3 to 3/4 cup sugar to 1 cup juice. If smaller globs form, use 1/2 cup sugar to 1 cup juice. Pectin level can be raised by adding tart apple juice to juice prepared for making jelly.

Some juices such as apple and crab apple, cranberry, quince, gooseberry, and red currant, are high in the pectin so essential for jellies to jell. The low-pectin fruits include raspberries, blueberries,

Continued →

strawberries, blackberries, apricots, peaches, pears, cherries, and grapes.

The high-pectin fruits, particularly underripe apples, are often used in combination with low-pectin fruits to make jellies.

Other recipes call for the addition of commercial pectin. *Liquid* pectin is added *after* the sugar has been added to the juice and the combination has been brought to a boil. *Powdered* pectin is added to the unheated, unsweetened juice. Use the type pectin called for in the recipe; for example, don't use powdered pectin if liquid pectin is called for.

Recipes calling for added pectin require more sugar; those without added pectin have to be cooked longer to reach the jelly stage.

4. *Cook to jelly stage.* Measure juice into kettle. Simmer 5 minutes in open kettle. Skim off froth. Add sugar. Boil rapidly.

Honey and corn syrup may be substituted for sugar in many recipes. The U.S. Department of Agriculture suggests these formulas:

Without Pectin	With Pectin
Light corn syrup may be used in place of one-fourth of the sugar in jelly recipes.	(Powdered) Up to 1/2 sugar (Liquid) Up to 2 cups sugar

Two cups honey may replace 2 cups sugar. However, when a recipe makes less than six 8-ounce glasses, only 3/4 to 1 cup sugar should be replaced by honey.

5. *Test for jelly stage.* Jelling point (use candy thermometer) is 220°F. (or 8 degrees above boiling temperature for water where you live). Or let jelly drip off spoon. Jelly point is reached when jelly comes off spoon in a sheet. Begin testing 10 minutes after boiling starts. When ready, remove from heat, skim off foam with slotted spoon.

6. *Seal the jelly.* Ladle or pour the hot jelly into hot sterilized jars, leaving 1/8 inch headroom. Wipe rim with a clean damp cloth to remove any jelly that could spoil seal. Take Mason lids from hot water and place on jar. Screw the band on tightly.

Place closed jar in rack in simmering water. Add water to bring it 2 inches above the tops of the jars. Put on cover, bring water to a full rolling boil and time for just 10 minutes. Remove jars immediately, and place on rack to cool.

7. *And finally* . . . let cool, label, and store in a cold, dry place.

WARNING: NEW CANNING STANDARDS

Many of the recipes here may indicate that after being sealed, jars filled with jelly should be immersed in a boiling water bath for 5 minutes. This is no longer true. New canning standards from the USDA recommend that the boiling water bath should be extended to a longer period of 10 minutes.

Please disregard instructions in any recipe that call for a 5-minute boiling water bath; instead, be sure to immerse your canned jelly in boiling water for a full 10 minutes.

Pitfalls

Cloudy Jelly
Juice not properly strained
Jelly bag was squeezed
Too much unripe fruit
Delayed pouring into jars
Overcooking

Stiff Jelly
Too much pectin
Overcooking

Weak Jelly
Insufficient pectin
Too much water
Not enough acid
Cooked in too large amounts
Note: Additional cooking or more pectin *sometimes* will remedy this.

Spoiled Jelly
Too little sugar
Improper sealing

Bubbles
Improper pouring
Improper sealing

Floating Fruit (Jams and Preserves)
Too much unripe fruit
Insufficient cooking

Crystal Formation
Improper cooking; too long, too short, too slowly
Too much sugar

APPLE OR CRAB APPLE JELLY (Without Pectin)

4 pounds apples

4 cups water

3 cups sugar

Use hard, tart fruit. Wash apples, discard stems and blossom ends. Cut apples into small chunks. Place in kettle. Add one cup water per pound of apples. Bring to a boil and simmer 25 minutes. Place fruit and juice in suspended cheesecloth jelly bag. Allow juice to drip overnight. In the morning, measure 4 cups of juice into kettle, add sugar, heat, and stir until sugar dissolves. Bring to a boil and cook rapidly until jelly test is met. Skim off foam. Pour into hot glasses and seal.

MAKES FOUR TO FIVE 8-OUNCE GLASSES.

BERRY JELLY

(Blackberry, black raspberry, dewberry, elderberry, loganberry, red raspberry, strawberry, youngberry)

3 quarts berries

7 1/2 cups sugar

6 oz. liquid pectin

Wash and crush berries. Extract juice by using a jelly bag. Measure 4 cups juice into kettle. Add sugar. Bring to full boil, stirring constantly. Reduce heat and add pectin. Reheat to full boil and stir for one minute. Remove from heat, skim, and ladle into hot glasses and seal.

MAKES EIGHT 8-OUNCE GLASSES.

Note: 1/4 cup lemon juice may be added to blackberry, elderberry and black raspberry mixtures.

SOUR CHERRY JELLY

3 pounds red sour cherries

1/2 cup water

7 cups sugar

6 oz. liquid pectin

Wash, stem, and crush fruit. Add water and bring to a boil. Reduce heat and simmer 10–12 minutes. Extract juice with a jelly bag. Combine three cups juice and sugar. Heat until sugar is dissolved. Bring to a boil and remove from heat. Add pectin. Stir and remove scum. Pour into sterilized glasses and seal.

MAKES ABOUT SEVEN 8-OUNCE GLASSES.

GRAPE JELLY (Without Pectin)

Concord grapes (slightly underripe)

Water

Sugar

Wash, stem, and crush grapes. Measure amount of crushed fruit and pour it into kettle. Add one-eighth as much water as fruit. Bring mixture to a boil, reduce heat, and simmer for 15 minutes.

Strain juice through a suspended cheesecloth jelly bag, allowing juice to extract overnight. Never squeeze bag as this makes juice cloudy.

In the morning, measure juice and add 3/4 cup of sugar for each cup of juice. Cook one quart of juice at a time and heat until mixture meets the jelly test. Pour into glasses and seal.

If for some reason mixture does not successfully pass jelly test, add amount of liquid pectin recommended on pectin bottle directions and reheat.

Jams

Jams are made from crushed fruit with or without added pectin. This is one of the most economical fruit concoctions to make, since it calls for but one cooking, and even the pulp of the fruit is used.

Making it is simple. Wash the fruit. Prepare it by cutting hard fruit into small pieces, and crushing soft fruits. Measure the amount. Put it into the kettle. Add the sugar or honey. Bring it to a boil, stirring frequently so it doesn't scorch. When it reaches 221°F (or 9 degrees above the boiling point of water in your area) it's cooked. This may take as much as a half hour. Remove it from the heat, skim off the foam and stir jam for about 5 minutes, letting the jam cool. This prevents fruit from floating to the top of the jam. Then pour the mixture into sterilized jars and seal (see step 6 under Jelly).

BERRY JAM (Without Pectin)

Blackberry, black raspberry, blueberry, dewberry, elderberry, gooseberry, huckleberry, loganberry, red raspberry, strawberry, youngberry

2 pounds crushed fruit

2 pounds sugar

* Lemon juice

Crush fruit. Seedier berries may be put through food mill. Combine fruit with sugar. Heat to boiling point, stirring frequently. Reduce heat and cook until desired consistency is reached.

*Add 1/4 cup lemon juice to blackberry, elderberry, and black raspberry mixtures. Mix thoroughly.

Ladle into sterilized jars and seal.

MAKES SEVEN 8-OUNCE JARS.

Continued ➜

CRANBERRY JAM

2 pounds cranberries

3 cups sugar

Wash and stem. Cook in small amount of water until skins break. Puree by putting berries through food mill.

Return to kettle. Add sugar, cook, and stir to desired consistency.

Pour into hot, sterilized jars and seal.

MAKES ABOUT THREE PINTS.

PEACH OR PLUM JAM

2 quarts prepared fruit, crushed

3 tablespoons lemon juice

6 cups sugar

3 oz. liquid pectin

Peel and seed fruit. Crush and combine with lemon juice. Cook slowly for 10 minutes. Add sugar. Bring mixture to a boil. Stirring constantly, continue cooking for 10 minutes. Remove from heat and add pectin.

Pour into sterilized jars and seal.

MAKES FOUR PINTS.

RHUBARB JAM

2 pounds prepared rhubarb

3 cups sugar

1 lemon, juice and rind

3 oz. liquid pectin

Wash and cut rhubarb into small pieces. Combine with sugar and let stand overnight. Heat mixture. Add lemon juice and grated rind; stir. Add pectin. Bring to boiling point and stir for one minute. Remove from heat, skim, ladle into sterilized jars and seal.

MAKES SIX PINTS.

ROSE-HIP JAM

4 cups rose-hip puree

5 cups sugar

1 tablespoon lemon juice

Collect hips after the first frost. Prepare puree by covering hips with water and simmering until they are soft. Put pulp through food mill. Combine pulp, sugar, and lemon juice. Bring to a boil; reduce heat. Simmer until desired consistency is reached. Ladle into hot sterilized jars and seal.

MAKES TWO TO THREE PINTS.

STRAWBERRY JAM

2 quarts crushed strawberries (about 4 quarts uncrushed)

6 cups sugar

Wash, hull, and crush berries. Combine them with sugar. Heat slowly, bringing to boil, and stirring. Continue to stir as mixture cooks until thick. This may take as much as 45 minutes.

Ladle into hot sterilized jars, seal, and process.

MAKES ABOUT FOUR PINTS.

Butters

Butters are much like jams. They should be thick, but easily spreadable. During cooking, keep heat low and stir frequently to avoid burning.

Butters should be kept in canning jars, to insure a good seal and a long storage life. Ladle butter into sterilized jar, leaving 1/4 inch headroom, quickly take lids from hot water and place on jar, then screw band on tightly. Process in boiling water bath by putting jars in kettle of simmering water, adding enough water to bring level 2 inches over tops of the jars, putting on cover, bringing water to a full rolling boil and timing for just 5 minutes. Remove jars immediately and place on rack to cool.

APPLE BUTTER

6 pounds apples (24–36 medium apples)

2 quarts water

1 quart sweet cider

3 cups sugar

Cinnamon, ground

Clove, ground

Wash the apples and cut into small pieces, leaving the skins and cores. Add water and boil apples until they are soft (about 30 minutes). Put through a food mill or rub through a sieve.

Boil down the cider to half its volume, add hot apple pulp, sugar and ground spices to taste, and cook until thick enough to spread without running. Stir occasionally to prevent sticking or scorching. Ladle into hot, sterilized canning jars, leaving 1/4 inch headroom, and seal. Process in a boiling water bath for 5 minutes.

MAKES FIVE OR SIX PINTS.

Preserves

Fruit retains its shape in preserves, and is clear and shiny. The aim is to have clear syrup, as thick as honey, or thicker—almost to the point of jelling. Syrup may not reach—or may pass—that stage. If syrup is too watery when fruit has reached the clear, shiny stage, remove the fruit with a slotted spoon, place it in hot, sterilized jars, then continue to cook syrup until it reaches the desired consistency. If it is too thick, add small amounts (1/4 cup at a time) of boiling water to delay the syrup reaching the jelling point before the fruit is clear.

All preserves should be processed in boiling water bath for five minutes. (See Butters.)

CHERRY PRESERVES

5 pounds cherries

4 pounds sugar

Wash, stem, and pit cherries. Layer fruit in kettle with sugar, ending with a layer of sugar on top. Allow mixture to stand overnight. In the morning, bring to a boil, stirring frequently. Allow mixture to simmer for 30 minutes until fruit is tender and sugar is dissolved. If a thicker consistency is desired, strain off juice, reheat it, and cook until it thickens, or add 1/2 bottle pectin. Ladle into hot sterilized jars, seal, and process in boiling water bath for 5 minutes.

MAKES FOUR PINTS.

For spiced preserves add 1/2 teaspoon each of ground cinnamon and cloves before boiling.

PEAR PRESERVES (WITH GINGER)

2 pounds pears

3 cups sugar

2 cups water

1 lemon, juice and grated peel

1/4 cup chopped preserved ginger

Peel, core, and slice pears. Combine with sugar and water. Simmer until fruit is soft and sugar is dissolved. Add lemon juice, grated peel, and ginger. Cook until mixture reaches desired consistency.

Ladle into sterilized jars, seal, and process in boiling water bath for 5 minutes.

MAKES FIVE 8-OUNCE JARS.

PLUM PRESERVES (BLUE DAMSON)

12 cups prepared plums

3/4 cup water

8 cups sugar

Wash fruit. Cut in half and discard pits. Combine plums with water and sugar. Simmer, stirring frequently, until sugar is dissolved. Bring mixture to a boil, stirring constantly; continue cooking until mixture reaches desired consistency.

Ladle into sterilized jars, seal, and process in boiling water bath for 5 minutes.

MAKES TWELVE 8-OUNCE JARS.

PUMPKIN PRESERVES

4 pounds prepared pumpkin

5 cups sugar

1/2 teaspoon ground cinnamon

1/2 teaspoon allspice

Peel and cube pumpkin into 1/2-inch cubes. Add sugar; allow to stand overnight. Add spices. Cook mixture slowly, stirring frequently, until pumpkin is tender and clear.

This recipe is for immediate use. Do not can or store in sealed containers. Refrigerate.

MAKES THREE TO FOUR PINTS.

TOMATO-PEAR PRESERVES

1 orange

2 lemons

3 pounds tomatoes (small and firm)

2 pounds pears

5 cups sugar

2 tablespoons crystallized ginger

Squeeze orange and lemons; reserve juice. Cut citrus peel into narrow strips. Cover with water, bring to a boil, reduce heat, and simmer 15 minutes. Drain. Scald tomatoes and remove skins. Peel and core pears and slice. Combine lemon juice, peels, tomatoes, pears, and remaining ingredients. Heat to boiling. Reduce heat and simmer until desired consistency is reached, about 2 hours.

Ladle into hot sterilized jars, seal, and process 5 minutes in boiling water bath.

MAKES FOUR PINTS.

WATERMELON RIND PRESERVES

3 pints watermelon rind, prepared

2 quarts of water in which are dissolved 4 tablespoons salt

2 cups ice water

1 tablespoon ground ginger

4 cups sugar

1/4 cup lemon juice

7 cups water

1 lemon, sliced

Remove fruit and green from rind. Cut rind into one-inch cubes and soak overnight in salt water. Drain and soak again in ice water for two hours. Drain. Spread ginger over rind, cover with water and cook until tender.

Combine sugar, lemon juice, and 7 cups water. Boil until sugar is dissolved, add drained rind and boil for a half-hour, then add sliced lemon and cook until melon rind is clear. Ladle into hot, sterilized jars, seal, and process in boiling water bath for 5 minutes.

MAKES THREE PINTS.

Continued ➡

STRAWBERRY PRESERVES

3 pints strawberries

5 cups sugar

1 1/2 cups lemon juice

Wash and stem berries. Add sugar and let strawberries combine with it for four hours. Bring to boiling, stirring, and add lemon juice. Cook until berries are clear and syrup reaches desired consistency. Pour into a shallow pan and let cool overnight. Ladle into hot, sterilized jars, seal, and process in boiling water bath for 5 minutes.

MAKES ABOUT FOUR HALF-PINT JARS.

Favorite Pickles & Relishes

Andrea Chesman

Wood engravings by Charles Joslin

Whether sweetly piquant, mouth-puckeringly sour, or flaming hot and pungent, pickles and relishes bring zest to the table. They enliven mundane meals, brighten salads, add panache to picnics and potluck suppers, and provide very special gifts. And with modern methods, it takes just a few hours in the kitchen to transform the seasonal bounty of your garden into a year-round source of pickled delicacies.

Most of the recipes that follow are for fresh-pack pickles: produce prepared and packed raw into jars. Often vegetables are short-brined—salted and allowed to stand for a few hours—before packing. This makes them crisp. Then a boiling syrup or brine is poured over them. The jars are sealed and processed briefly in a canner, unless they are to be refrigerated or frozen.

Also included are recipes for traditional brined pickles, the ones you used to find in big crocks at the general store. In this method the vegetables, most often cucumbers, are cured for several weeks in brine before being packed into jars and processed or refrigerated. Brining is a fermentation process. It works best at 70 to 80°F. Bacteria generate lactic acid from sugars in the vegetables, which gives the cured pickles a distinct, sharp flavor.

INGREDIENTS

The difference between a good pickle and a great one is usually the freshness of the ingredients. Select young or even slightly immature, unbruised fruits and vegetables. Ideally they should be harvested early in the day, before the sun wilts them, and processed immediately. Since this isn't always possible, chill your produce quickly and thoroughly to ensure a crisp pickle. This is particularly important with cucumbers. If you don't have a garden, buy from local farmers, roadside stands, or farmers' markets. If you must buy from the supermarket, avoid fruits and vegetables that have been waxed. No matter where it comes from, always wash and drain produce thoroughly before use.

Cucumbers come in two types, pickling and slicing. A good pickling cucumber is thin-skinned and small. It may be warty. Slicing cucumbers, when still small, are acceptable for sliced pickles such as bread and butters, and they are fine in relishes, but they rarely make good dills.

Most pickle recipes call for vinegar, salt, herbs and spices, water, and a sweetener. It is best to use commercially made vinegars. To safely preserve pickles, the vinegar must have 4 to 6 percent acetic acid, and homemade vinegar may not be strong enough. For the same reason, never reduce the amount of vinegar in a recipe. *White vinegar* is most commonly used because it does not color the pickle. *Cider vinegar* has a rich, somewhat mellow flavor and less bite. It is preferred for many sweet pickle and chutney recipes. *Malt vinegar*, with a delicate, almost sweet flavor, is used in a few recipes. While you may substitute one vinegar for another, keep in mind that it will change the flavor. *Salt* both flavors and preserves. It preserves first by drawing water from the food to make it crisper, and second, by creating a hostile environment for microorganisms. Always use pure pickling salt or dairy salt, and do measure exactly.

The traditional *pickling herbs and spices* are dill, mustard seeds, celery seeds, garlic, pepper, cloves, and prepackaged mixed pickling spices. But the seasoning possibilities are endless, and recipes here include summer savory, basil, fennel, coriander, tarragon, hot pepper, and nutmeg, to name just a few. Herbs and spices must be fresh and, if you want a clear brine, they should be whole rather than ground. Many recipes call for tying them into a cloth bag for easy removal. Cheesecloth, muslin, and stainless steel tea balls work well, too.

EQUIPMENT

Always use stainless steel, glass, or ceramic pans, bowls, and utensils. The salts and acids in pickles react with metals to produce an off-flavor. A *food processor* is a great timesaver and gives uniform results, thus improving the texture of the pickle.

Mason jars with two-piece lids are the most readily available. The dome lids cannot be reused, but the screw-bands can. Old-fashioned *bail-wire jars* are also used for canning. The glass lid is sealed to the glass bottom with a non-reusable rubber ring. *(Beware of scratches and chips in the lid or rim, which may prevent a perfect seal.)* For slow-brined pickles, glass, plastic, or ceramic *crocks* are useful. Wash containers thoroughly in soapy water, rinse, then sterilize with boiling water. Whatever type of equipment you use, always follow the manufacturer's directions in preparing for canning.

CANNERS

The United States Department of Agriculture recommends processing pickles in a boiling-water bath canner. A boiling-water bath is basically a large kettle in which jars are immersed, with a wire rack to keep jars from banging around and make them easier to get in and out. Though not approved by the USDA, steam canners are popular among some picklers. A steam canner has a shallow well to hold water, a rack to hold jars above the water, and a dome lid to keep in the steam. In either case, you have to place the filled jars in the canner and wait for it to reach a full boil before you start counting the processing time. Because they heat up more quickly, steam canners cannot guarantee that your food will be sterile, as does a boiling-water bath canner. However, steam canning offers the advantages of faster boiling time and, because they are heated for a shorter time, crunchier pickles. For the convenience of all picklers directions for both methods are included in this book.

Pickling Tips

When packing jars, a wide-mouth funnel and wooden spoon pack vegetables neatly and firmly. Run a chopstick or spatula between food and side of jar to remove trapped bubbles. Add more brine if necessary to correct headspace. Yields are approximate: have an extra jar or two ready.

After processing, place jars on a towel or wooden rack in a draft-free place. Cool undisturbed for 24 hours, then test seals. On screw-band jars, lid center should be depressed and not pop back. On bail-wire jars, tip until the contents push against lid. There should be no bubbles. Refrigerate unsealed jars and use within two weeks.

To store, wash, label, and date jars. Keep in a dark, dry cupboard between 32 and 50°F to avoid vitamin loss and fading. Most pickles should be stored at least six weeks to develop flavor.

WHAT WENT WRONG?

Problem	Cause
Soft or Slippery Pickles	Scum not skimmed from surface daily (slow-brining)
	Pickles not well covered by brine
	Jars stored in a warm place
	Water too hard
	Blossom end not scrubbed
	Jars did not seal properly
Shriveled Pickles	Brine too strong
	Syrup too sweet
	Vinegar too strong
	Cucumbers not fresh
Dark Pickles	Water too hard
	Used copper, brass, galvanized metal, or iron equipment
	Canning lids corroded
	Cucumbers lacking in nitrogen
Hollow Pickles	Cucumbers overmature or sunburned
	Proper headspace not maintained
Lids Didn't Seal	Nonstandard jars or lids used
	Jars not sufficiently processed
	Jar rim not wiped well

A number of the recipes that follow do not require processing in a canner, because the pickles are refrigerated or frozen instead. Most of these can be found under the heading "Refrigerator and Freezer Pickles"; those appearing elsewhere are marked with an asterisk(*).

For slow-brined pickles: Hold cucumbers under brine with a weighted plate. Fermentation should begin within two days. Taste occasionally to see if pickles are sour enough for you. Refrigeration halts curing. Fermentation is complete when gas bubbles stop rising to top of crock, between second and fourth week. Tap crock side when checking for bubbles.

Sweet and Sour Pickles

SWEET GHERKINS

5 quarts cucumbers, 1 1/2–3 inches in length (about 7 pounds)

1/2 cup pickling salt

8 cups sugar

6 cups white vinegar

3/4 teaspoon turmeric

2 teaspoons celery seeds

2 teaspoons mixed pickling spices

8 1-inch cinnamon sticks

1/2 teaspoon fennel (optional)

2 teaspoons vanilla extract (optional)

First day. Morning: Wash cucumbers thoroughly; scrub with vegetable brush; stem ends may be left on. Drain; place in large container and cover with boiling water. *Afternoon (6–8 hours later):* Drain; cover with fresh, boiling water.

Second day. Morning: Drain; cover with fresh, boiling water. *Afternoon:* Drain; add salt; cover with fresh, boiling water.

Third day. Morning: Drain; prick cucumbers in several places with a table fork. Make a syrup of 3 cups sugar and 3 cups vinegar; add turmeric and spices. Heat to boiling and pour over cucumbers. (The cucumbers will be partially covered at this point.) *Afternoon:* Drain syrup into pan; add 2 cups sugar and 2 cups vinegar. Heat to boiling and pour over pickles.

Fourth day. Morning: Drain syrup into pan; add 2 cups sugar and 1 cup vinegar. Heat to boiling and pour over pickles. *Afternoon:* Drain syrup into pan; add remaining 1 cup sugar and vanilla; heat to boiling. Pack pickles into clean, hot pint jars and cover with boiling syrup, leaving 1/2 inch headspace. Seal. Process for 5 minutes in a boiling-water bath or steam container.

YIELD: 7 TO 8 PINTS.

Continued →

BREAD AND BUTTER PICKLES

25 cucumbers, sliced medium thick (about 10 pounds)

1/3 cup pickling salt

5 cups white vinegar

5 cups sugar

2 teaspoons mustard seeds

1 teaspoon powdered cloves

In a large glass, ceramic, or stainless steel bowl combine cucumbers and salt and let stand for 3 hours. Then drain.

In a medium-size saucepan, combine remaining ingredients and bring to a boil. Add cucumbers, but do not reboil.

Pack cucumbers and syrup into hot, sterilized pint jars, leaving 1/4 inch headspace. Seal. Process in a boiling-water bath or steam canner for 5 minutes.

YIELD: 7 TO 8 PINTS.

SUNSHINE PICKLES

4 cups ripe cucumbers, peeled and cut into chunks

1 tablespoon pickling salt

1 medium-size onion, sliced

1 sweet red pepper, sliced

1/2 cup white vinegar

1 teaspoon celery seeds

1 cup sugar

1 teaspoon mustard seeds

Prepare cucumbers and mix well with salt. Cover with tap water. Let stand for 2 hours; drain.

Combine remaining ingredients in a large saucepan. Add cucumbers and cook until just fork tender. Ladle pickles and syrup into clean, hot pint jars, leaving 1/2 inch headspace. Seal. Process in a boiling-water bath or steam canner for 10 minutes.

YIELD: 2 PINTS.

PATTY SPEAR'S SOLAR GLOW HONEY SPEARS

12 large ripe cucumbers, peeled and seeded

6 large onions, sliced

1/2 cup pickling salt

1 gallon water

3 cups cider vinegar

1 cup water

2 cups honey or maple syrup

2 tablespoons mustard seeds

2 teaspoons celery seeds

2 teaspoons turmeric

Slice cucumbers into spears. Combine salt and water in a large glass, ceramic, or stainless steel bowl. Add cucumbers and onions and soak overnight.

The next morning, combine remaining ingredients in a large kettle and cook for 5 minutes. Add drained cucumbers and onions. Heat to boiling. Ladle mixture into clean, hot pint jars, leaving 1/4 inch headspace. Seal. Process in a boiling-water bath or steam canner for 10 minutes.

YIELD: 5 TO 6 PINTS.

Dill Pickles

KOSHER DILL PICKLES

4 pounds cucumbers, 2–4 inches long

3 1/2 tablespoons pickling salt

1 1/2 tablespoons mustard seeds

3 cups water

3 cups white vinegar

6 bay leaves

6 cloves garlic

6 fresh dill heads or 1 1/2 tablespoons dill seeds

Wash cucumbers and remove blossom ends. Combine salt, mustard seeds, water, and vinegar in a saucepan. Heat to boiling.

Into each hot, sterilized quart jar, put 1 bay leaf, a piece of garlic clove, and a piece of fresh dill. Pack with cucumbers. Top each jar with 1 bay leaf, 1 garlic clove, and 1 dill head. Fill with the hot liquid, leaving 1/4 inch headspace. Seal. Submerge in a boiling-water bath for 10 minutes. Turn heat off when all jars are in the canner. Be sure jars are covered with boiling water. Remove at once when 10 minutes are up. Or process in a steam canner for 10 minutes. Ready to eat in 2–3 weeks.

YIELD: 2–3 QUARTS.

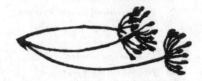

*REFRIGERATOR DILLS

2 dill heads

3 cloves garlic

2 tablespoons mixed pickling spices

2 bay leaves

1 gallon pickling cucumbers

1 cup white vinegar

pickling salt

Place dill, garlic, pickling spices, and bay leaves in bottom of a gallon jar. Fill with cucumbers, cut in halves or quarters if large.

Combine vinegar, water, and pickling salt in a medium-size saucepan. Bring to a boil, then cool. When cooled, pour it over cucumbers and refrigerate.

After 3 days, cucumbers and brine can be put into small jars. Keep refrigerated.

YIELD: 4 QUARTS.

*FRESH-PACK DILL PICKLES

8 cups small pickling cucumbers

4 dill heads

2 cloves garlic

2 slices horseradish root (optional)

4 cups water

1 cup white vinegar

1/4 cup pickling salt

Wash and dry cucumbers. Prick a few holes in each.

Place I dill head in each sterilized quart jar. Add I garlic clove and I slice of horseradish root to each. Pack with cucumbers and top with remaining dills.

Combine water, vinegar, and salt in a medium-size saucepan. Heat to boiling, then cool to room temperature. Pour over cucumbers. Be sure they are covered. Seal. Store in the refrigerator for at least 8 weeks before eating.

YIELD: 2 QUARTS.

Refrigerator and Freezer Pickles

REFRIGERATOR PICKLES

6 medium-size cucumbers, sliced thinly

3 medium-size onions, sliced thinly

1 medium-size green pepper, chopped

1 medium-size red pepper, chopped, or 1 small jar pimentos

2 cups white vinegar

3 cups sugar

1 tablespoon pickling salt

1 teaspoon celery seeds

Prepare vegetables, mix well, and pack into clean jars.

Combine remaining ingredients in a medium-size saucepan. Heat just until sugar dissolves. Pour over vegetables. Chill at least 24 hours before eating. These pickles will keep for a few months in the refrigerator.

YIELD: 4 QUARTS.

SPICED FREEZER PICKLES

8 cups thinly sliced cucumbers

2 tablespoons pickling salt

1 large onion, sliced

1 1/3 cups sugar

1 cup white vinegar

3/4 cup water

1 tablespoon mixed pickling spices

1 tablespoon celery seeds

1 teaspoon dry mustard

Mix cucumbers and salt. Cover with water. Let stand overnight. Rinse well and drain. Add onion.

Combine remaining ingredients in a medium-size saucepan and cook over low heat until the sugar is dissolved. When liquid is cool, strain, then pour over cucumbers. Place in plastic freezer bags and freeze. Defrost in refrigerator 8 hours before serving.

YIELD: 2 QUARTS.

FREEZER MINT PICKLES

8 cups thinly sliced cucumbers

1 green pepper, minced

2 tablespoons pickling salt

1 1/2 cups sugar

1 cup cider vinegar

1/2 cup water

12 fresh mint leaves or 1 teaspoon mint extract

4 allspice berries

Combine vegetables and sprinkle with salt. Mix well and let stand for 2 hours. Rinse in cold water. Combine sugar, vinegar, and water and pour over vegetables. Mix well. Add mint and allspice. Refrigerate overnight.

The next morning, pack pickles in freezer containers and freeze. Defrost in the refrigerator for 8 hours before serving.

YIELD: 4 PINTS.

FROZEN CUCUMBERS

2 cups sugar

1 cup white vinegar

2 teaspoons pickling salt

2 teaspoons celery seeds

7 cups thinly sliced cucumbers

1 cup sliced onions

1 cup chopped green peppers

Combine sugar, vinegar, salt, and celery seeds in a large glass, ceramic, or stainless steel bowl. Add prepared vegetables and mix well. Let stand overnight.

Continued →

Place vegetables and brine in freezer containers or bags and freeze. Defrost in the refrigerator for 8 hours before serving.

YIELD: 6 PINTS.

Pickled Fruits and Vegetables

SPICED PICKLED CABBAGE

4 quarts shredded red or green cabbage

1/2 cup pickling salt

1 quart white vinegar

1 1/2 cups sugar

1 tablespoon mustard seeds

4 teaspoons grated horseradish

1 teaspoon whole cloves

4 cinnamon sticks

Layer cabbage and salt in a large kettle or crock. Let stand overnight. The next day, drain cabbage, pressing out all juice. Rinse thoroughly and drain again. In a saucepan, Combine vinegar, sugar, mustard seeds, and horseradish. Bring to a boil. Tie cloves and cinnamon in a cheesecloth spice bag and add to saucepan. Simmer for 15 minutes.

Pack cabbage into clean, hot pint jars and fill with vinegar mixture, leaving 1/4 inch headspace. Remove air bubbles by running a nonmetallic spatula down sides of jars. Seal, and process in a boiling-water bath or steam canner for 20 minutes.

YIELD: 4 PINTS.

PICKLED GREEN BEANS

This recipe makes a hot bean.

4 pounds green beans (about 4 quarts)

5 cups white vinegar

5 cups water

1/2 cup pickling salt

1/2 teaspoon dill seeds per jar

1 clove garlic per jar

1/2 teaspoon whole mustard seeds per jar

1/2 teaspoon crushed red pepper per jar

Wash beans and cut to fit jars. Combine vinegar, water, and salt and bring to a boil. Into each clean, hot pint jar, place 1/2 teaspoon dill seeds, 1 garlic clove, 1/2 teaspoon mustard seeds, and 1/2 teaspoon red pepper. Fill with beans. Pour hot brine over beans, leaving 1/4 inch headspace. Adjust seals. Process in a boiling-water bath or steam canner for 10 minutes.

Allow jars to sit for a minimum of 4 weeks to develop full flavor.

YIELD: 7 PINTS.

BEANS ORIENTAL

8 cups green beans (2 pounds)

4 cups white vinegar

1 cup water

2 tablespoons soy sauce

2 tablespoons cooking sherry

1 1/2 cups sugar

1 tablespoon ground ginger or shredded ginger root

1/2 teaspoon cayenne pepper

4 bay leaves

4 cloves garlic

Wash beans and cut into 4-inch pieces. Combine vinegar, water, soy sauce, sherry, sugar, ginger, and cayenne in a medium-size saucepan. Bring to a boil. Place 1 bay leaf and 1 garlic clove in each clean, hot pint jar. Pack tightly with beans. Cover with hot syrup, leaving 1/4 inch headspace, and seal. Process in a boiling-water bath or steam canner for 10 minutes.

YIELD: 4 PINTS.

PICKLED BEETS

10—12 pounds beets

1 quart cider vinegar

2/3 cup sugar

1 cup water

2 tablespoons pickling salt

Cut tops and roots off flush with beet. Scrub thoroughly. Place beets on a rack in a large roaster. Cover and bake at 400°F until tender, about 1 hour for medium-size beets. Meanwhile, preheat hot water and jars in canner.

In a saucepan, mix vinegar, sugar, water, and salt. Heat to boiling. When beets are tender, fill roaster with cold water. Slip skins off beets. Pack in clean, hot pint jars, whole or cut. Add brine to cover. Leave 1/2 inch headspace. Process in a boiling-water bath or steam canner for 10 minutes.

YIELD: 7 PINTS.

MIDDLE EASTERN CAULIFLOWER PICKLES

These pickles turn a shocking pink. A perfect gift pickle.

3 heads cauliflower (4 1/2—5 pounds)

3 cups white vinegar

6 cups water

2 tablespoons pickling salt

1 tablespoon cumin seeds

6 slices horseradish root

3 small beets, cooked and sliced

Wash cauliflower and cut into small flowerets. Steam over boiling water for 1 minute. Do not overcook. In a medium-size saucepan combine vinegar, water, salt, and cumin seeds. Bring to a boil and simmer for 5 minutes.

In the meantime, place 1 slice horseradish root and a couple of beet slices in each clean, hot pint jar. Pack tightly with cauliflower. Cover with hot brine, leaving 1/4 inch headspace. Seal. Process in a boiling-water bath or steam canner for 15 minutes. Allow the jars to sit for at least a few days for full color to develop.

YIELD: 6 PINTS.

ZUCCHINI DILL PICKLES

3 quarts zucchini or other summer squash

1/4 cup pickling salt

2 1/2 cups white vinegar

2 1/2 cups water

6 cloves garlic

3 springs fresh dill

18 peppercorns

3 grape leaves

Cut squash lengthwise into sticks to fit jars. Combine salt, vinegar, and water. Bring to a rolling boil.

Place 2 garlic cloves in each clean, hot quart jar. Arrange squash in jars; add dill and peppercorns, and top with grape leaves. Pour in hot pickling juice, leaving 1/4 inch headspace. Seal and process in a boiling-water bath or steam canner for 10 minutes.

YIELD: 3 QUARTS.

QUICK DILLED PEARL ONIONS

4 quarts white pickling onions (about 6 pounds)

1/2 cup pickling salt

2 tablespoons sugar

4 cups white vinegar

4 cups water

8 fresh dill heads

4 teaspoons mixed pickling spices

16 peppercorns

Peel onions. Combine salt, sugar, vinegar, and water in a large saucepan. Bring to a boil. Add onions and simmer for 3 minutes.

Meanwhile, place 2 dill heads, 1 teaspoon mixed pickling spices, and 4 peppercorns into each clean, hot quart jar. Pack with onions. Pour

in hot brine, leaving 1/4 inch headspace. Seal. Process in a boiling-water bath or steam canner for 10 minutes.

YIELD: 4 QUARTS.

*SWEET PICKLED PEARS

To substitute peaches, dip briefly in hot water, then rub off fuzz with a towel. Stick each peach with 4 cloves instead of 3.

1/2 peck pears (6–7 pounds) cloves

2 pounds brown sugar

2 cups cider vinegar

1 ounce stick cinnamon

Wash pears. Pare only if skins are tough. Large pears may be quartered. Stick each pear with 3 cloves. Boil sugar, vinegar, and cinnamon for 20 minutes. Add pears, and cook in syrup only until tender when pricked with a fork. Fill hot, sterilized jars with fruit, add hot syrup, and seal.

To store the fruit in a crock instead of jars, fill with pears, cover with syrup, and place a plate on top to hold pears beneath syrup. Store in a cool, dry place, or refrigerate.

YIELD: 3 TO 4 QUARTS.

Relishes

PEPPER RELISH

12 red peppers

12 green peppers

12 onions

2 quarts boiling water

2 cups white vinegar

2 cups sugar

3 teaspoons pickling salt

Chop peppers and onions. Cover with boiling water. Let stand for 5 minutes and drain. Combine vinegar, sugar, and salt. Add vegetables and boil for 5 minutes. Pour into hot, sterilized jars, leaving 1/4 inch headspace. Seal. Process in boiling-water bath or steam canner for 5 minutes.

YIELD: 6 PINTS.

GREEN TOMATO RELISH WITH HONEY

12 green tomatoes

4 large onions

1 sweet red pepper

1 sweet green pepper

1 tablespoon pickling salt

1 cup dark honey

1 cup white vinegar

1 tablespoon mustard seeds

1 tablespoon celery seeds

Chop tomatoes, onions, and peppers coarsely. Drain. Add remaining ingredients and mix. Cook slowly until tender, about 20 minutes. Put into clean, hot pint jars, leaving 1/2 inch headspace. Seal. Process in a boiling-water bath or steam canner for 10 minutes.

YIELD: 5 PINTS.

CORN RELISH

8 cups raw corn cut from the cob

3 cups chopped onions

1/2 cup chopped green pepper

1/2 cup chopped sweet red pepper

3/4 cup packed brown sugar

1/2 cup white corn syrup

7 teaspoons pickling salt

1 tablespoon dry mustard

3 cups cider vinegar

Mix all ingredients thoroughly. Cover and boil for 15 minutes, stirring often. Pour into clean, hot pint jars, leaving 1/2 inch headspace. Seal. Process in a boiling-water bath or steam canner for 15 minutes.

YIELD: 4 TO 5 PINTS.

SWEET PICKLE RELISH

4 cups chopped cucumbers (4 medium-size cucumbers)

2 cups chopped onions

1 green pepper, chopped

1 sweet red pepper, chopped

1/4 cup pickling salt

3 1/2 cups sugar

2 cups cider vinegar

1 tablespoon celery seeds

1 tablespoon mustard seeds

Combine cucumbers, onions, and peppers in a large bowl. Sprinkle with salt and cover with cold water. Let stand 2 hours. Drain thoroughly. Press out excess liquid.

Combine sugar, vinegar, and spices. Heat to boiling. Add vegetables. Simmer for 10 minutes. Pack hot into clean, hot half-pint jars, leaving 1/4 inch headspace. Seal. Process in a boiling-water bath or steam canner for 10 minutes.

YIELD: 7 TO 8 HALF-PINTS.

TOMATO CHUTNEY

6 pounds ripe medium-size tomatoes (about 24)

6 pounds tart green apples (about 12 medium-size)

2 pounds onions (about 6 medium-size)

1/2 pound red peppers (about 3)

1/2 pound sweet green peppers (about 3)

1 cup minced celery

5 cups cider or malt vinegar

2 1/2 cups sugar

4 tablespoons pickling salt

1 pound sultana-type raisins

Peel and chop tomatoes, apples, and onions. Chop peppers. Combine with the celery, vinegar, sugar, and salt in a large kettle.

Boil rapidly, stirring constantly, until mixture is clear and slightly thick. Add raisins and boil 20–30 minutes more. Keep stirring to avoid scorching. When sauce is reduced to 7 pints, put into clean, hot pint jars and seal. Process in a boiling-water bath or steam canner for 15 minutes.

YIELD: 7 PINTS.

CONNIE'S PEAR CHUTNEY

10 cups (about 5 pounds) sliced, firm, ripe pears

1/2 cup finely chopped green pepper

1 1/2 cups seedless raisins

4 cups sugar

1 cup chopped crystallized ginger

3 cups cider vinegar

1/2 teaspoon pickling salt

1/2 teaspoon allspice berries

1/2 teaspoon whole cloves

3 cinnamon sticks, 2 inches long

Place pears and next 6 ingredients in a saucepan. Tie allspice and cloves in a cheesecloth bag and add along with cinnamon. Cook slowly until pears are tender and mixture thick, about 1 hour.

Remove spices. Ladle into clean, hot half-pint jars, leaving 1/2 inch headspace. Seal. Process for 10 minutes in a boiling-water bath or steam canner.

YIELD: 10 HALF-PINTS.

Making & Using Mustards

Claire Hopley

Mustard is growing in popularity. As Americans cut calories and cholesterol, mustard is taking over the role mayonnaise once held as an all-purpose condiment. Mustard works as a sandwich spread, a sauce base, a salad dressing ingredient, and a coating medium, as well as a spice.

You can buy mustard in several forms. The most basic form is the seed. There are three types of mustard seeds: black (*Brassica nigra*), brown (*Brassica juncea*), and white (*Brassica hirta*). The black and brown seeds are tiny and hard, while the so-called white seeds, actually a golden beige, are larger. Black seeds are hard to find. Confusingly, the brown seeds, which are deep reddish black, are often sold as black mustard seeds. You can buy them, and also the milder white mustard seeds, packed in small bottles in the spice section of supermarkets, or more economically, in bulk in health food stores and oriental groceries.

Another way to buy mustard is to purchase the yellow powder, which is commercially prepared from the seeds. The English brand, Colman's, is widely available, and it now also comes in a coarse-ground form. You may also find powdered mustard in bulk in health and other specialty food shops.

The third way to buy your mustard is ready-made. Until a few years ago that meant buying the bright yellow ballpark mustard popular for slathering on hot dogs, or for gentler tastes, choosing a sweetish German-style mustard or a mild Dijon mustard from France. Today, mustard comes in many varieties. It may be spiked with wine or spirits, fired up with chilies or horseradish, or sophisticated with herbs or spices. It can be smooth or coarse. It may be European, but it's just as likely to be American, made by a small company specializing in interesting food.

To use mustard as a flexible multipurpose ingredient, it helps to understand the way it works. The fiery bite comes from the reaction of liquid with chemicals in the seed. The reaction is most intense about 10 minutes after the mustard is mixed, then declines quickly. From this it follows that the hot Chinese mustard served with egg rolls or the powerful paste mustard the British eat with their roast beef must be made fresh. For milder tastes, mustard can be made ahead of time. Salt and sugar both preserve the flavor. Acid and heat both weaken the fire-reaction, so mustard made with vinegar or wine, and mustard used in a cooked sauce, are milder. Add mustard near the beginning of the cooking time if you want flavor without pungency; towards the end if you want it strong and hot.

John Evelyn, author of *Acetaria: A Discourse of Sallets* published in 1699, told his readers that mustard seeds should be "bruis'd with a polished Cannon-Bullet, in a large wooden Bowl-Dish." Don't let a shortage of cannon-bullets prevent you from grinding your own mustard. An electric coffee or spice grinder does a fast and perfect job. You can also use a pestle and mortar.

The recipes below make small quantities, usually enough to fill a container about the size of a small baby-food jar. But you can multiply the quantities so you have enough to give to friends.

You can keep mustard 3–4 weeks in the fridge, though remember, it loses its potency the longer you keep it.

BALLPARK MUSTARD

2 tablespoons powdered mustard

1 tablespoon turmeric

1/4 teaspoon salt

1 teaspoon sugar

water or mixture of water and white vinegar to mix

Put the mustard, turmeric, salt, and sugar into a small bowl. Gradually add water or water and vinegar, stirring to make a smooth paste of the consistency you want. This is the mustard for hot dogs and other sausages. It can also be used in potato salads.

HONEY MUSTARD

4 tablespoons mustard powder

2 tablespoons water

1 teaspoon vinegar

1 tablespoon vegetable oil

2 tablespoons honey.

Mix the mustard to a stiff paste with the water and vinegar. Stir in the oil until the mixture is smooth, then stir in the honey. Pour into a sterilized jar. This mustard is a good spread for sandwiches made with boiled ham or other cold cuts. Serve it also with baked ham, pork, and barbecued meats.

SPICE MUSTARD

1 tablespoon curry powder

1 teaspoon cinnamon

1/4 teaspoon powdered cloves

1 tablespoon vegetable oil

3 tablespoons mustard powder

1 teaspoon sugar

1/4 cup water

Put the curry powder, cinnamon, and cloves in a small frying pan over medium heat. Let them heat through for about 4 minutes, stirring to prevent them from burning. Stir in the oil. In a small bowl, combine the oil and spice mixture with the mustard and sugar. Add the water and stir to a smooth paste, adding a bit more water if necessary. Good with barbecues and with Indian or Middle Eastern food.

HORSERADISH MUSTARD

1/2 cup powdered mustard

1/8 teaspoon white pepper

1/4 cup water

1 teaspoon salt

1 teaspoon brown sugar

1 clove of peeled garlic

1/2 cup white wine or cider vinegar

1–2 tablespoons grated or prepared horseradish

Continued →

Combine the powdered mustard, pepper, and water in a bowl. Put the salt, sugar, garlic, and I tablespoon of horseradish in a blender, and blend them together, then strain into the mustard mixture. Transfer to a small pan, and simmer over low heat, stirring all the time, until it has slightly thickened. When the mustard has cooled, stir in half the additional horseradish to add texture. Add the remainder if you like. If the mixture is too thick, thin with additional water or vinegar.

This startlingly hot mustard is definitely only for those who like strong condiments. It's good with beef, ham, and hearty sausages.

LEMON MUSTARD

1/2 cup yellow mustard seed

4 teaspoons mustard powder

grated zest and juice of 1 medium lemon

1 tablespoon white sugar

1/4 teaspoon saltpinch cayenne or red pepper (optional)

3/4 cup water

Grind the mustard seeds in a spice grinder or a blender until they look like coarse corn meal. In a small saucepan, mix them with the mustard powder, lemon zest and juice, sugar, salt, and cayenne (if using). Stir in the water and then place over medium heat and bring to simmering point. Cook for 5 minutes, stirring all the time. Let cool. To store, pack into a small sterilized jar and keep in the fridge.

This is a good mustard to serve with chicken, fish, and steak. Note that at first it tastes pungent but cools down and tastes very lemony after a day or so. For a hotter mustard, add more cayenne.

QUICK GREEN PEPPERCORN MUSTARD

One 8-ounce jar Dijon mustard

1 teaspoon mustard powder

1–2 tablespoons green peppercorns

Mix I tablespoon of Dijon mustard with the mustard powder. When it is smooth, stir in the remaining Dijon mustard. If using green peppercorns packed in brine, drain them, discarding the liquid, then add them to the mustard. If using dried green peppercorns, soak them for 1/2 hour in water before adding to the mustard.

Put the peppercorn-mustard mixture into a blender and blend until smooth. For a coarser mixture, simply mash the peppercorns into the mustard. Good with steak and as a sandwich spread.

TARRAGON MUSTARD

1/2 cup coarse-ground mustard

1 teaspoon powdered mustard

1/2 cup dry wine

1/4 cup red wine vinegar

1 tablespoon brown sugar

1/2 teaspoon salt

2 teaspoons dried tarragon

Put the coarse-ground mustard, the mustard powder, the wine, and the vinegar into a small saucepan; stir over low heat until the mustard

powder is blended in, then cover and cook over the lowest possible heat for 20 minutes. Check and stir occasionally to make sure it doesn't stick to the pan. Remove the cover, add the sugar and salt, increase the heat, and let the mustard bubble, stirring often for another 5 minutes. Stir in the tarragon.

You can use this mustard right away as a warm sauce with chicken, broiled pork chops, or fish. Or, let it cool and pack into a small sterilized jar. It thickens as it cools. You can replace the tarragon in this mustard with other dried herbs. Try it with thyme, oregano, or basil.

MAPLE MUSTARD

1/4 cup white mustard seed

1/2 cup mustard powder

2 tablespoons white cider vinegar

1/2 cup pure maple syrup

pinch salt

Grind the mustard seed until it is medium coarse. In a small bowl mix it with the mustard powder, the vinegar, and the maple syrup. Taste and add salt to season. Pour into a sterilized jar. This mustard is good with ham, sausages, and pork.

COLESLAW

1 tablespoon dry mustard

1 teaspoon sugar

1/4 cup white vinegar

1/2 cup mayonnaise

3 cups shredded white cabbage

1/2 cup shredded carrots

1/2 cup shredded red or green pepper

salt to taste

Put the mustard and sugar in a large bowl. Stir to a paste with the vinegar. Stir in the mayonnaise. Toss the cabbage, carrots, and pepper together. Add to the mayonnaise mixture and toss again. Chill and serve with fish or cold cuts.

SERVES 4–6.

EGG SALAD

3 hard-boiled egg

ssalt and pepper to taste

1–2 radishes, washed and sliced

1 tablespoon tarragon mustard

1 tablespoon mayonnaise

tomatoes or endive for stuffing

Shell and chop the eggs. Put them in a small bowl and season with salt and pepper to taste. Add the radish slices and then the mustard and mayonnaise, and mash. Use to stuff tomato halves or endive leaves for an hors d'oeuvres tray. Also good in sandwiches.

SERVES 4.

POTATO SALAD

6–8 large baking potatoes

pepper and salt to taste

1 medium onion, chopped

12 radishes, washed and quartered

2 teaspoons powdered mustard or 1 tablespoon of ballpark mustard

1 cup mayonnaise

4 hard-boiled eggs

3 radishes, washed and sliced

Put the potatoes, unpeeled, in a large pan; cover with water and boil until fork tender. Drain. Peel the potatoes. (Keep an oven mitt on your hand to do this.) Cut each into 5 or 6 pieces and put them in a salad bowl, seasoning them with salt and pepper as you go. Scatter the chopped onion and quartered radishes among the potatoes. Mix the mustard to a paste with a little of the mayonnaise, then stir in the remaining mayonnaise. (If using ready-made ballpark mustard, blend it with the mayonnaise.) Pour the mayonnaise mixture over the potatoes and toss gently. Taste for seasoning and add more if necessary.

Cover the salad with a cloth and cool in the fridge. Shell the eggs and cut into slices or quarters. Arrange the egg and the radish slices on top of the salad and serve.

SERVES 6–8.

ROASTED LEMON-MUSTARD CHICKEN

One 5–6 pound roasting chicken

2 cups dry breadcrumbs

grated zest and juice of 1 lemon

2 tablespoons chopped fresh parsley

2 tablespoons butter

1 cup boiling water

1 tablespoon lemon mustard

For the sauce:

4 teaspoons lemon mustard

3/4 cup white wine

4 teaspoons flour

1/2 cup water

1/4 cup juices from the chicken

salt to taste

Preheat the oven to 400°F.

Remove the giblets from the bird. Rinse the cavity and rub lightly with salt. Set aside.

To make the stuffing, place the breadcrumbs in a bowl with the lemon zest and juice, and the parsley. Put the butter in another bowl and pour the boiling water on it. Stir until the butter has melted, then mix in the mustard. Combine the 2 mixtures and pack into the cavity of the bird. (If the stuffing is too dry, add a little more water.)

Put the chicken into a Dutch oven; cover, and cook for 30 minutes. Baste with the juices; reduce the temperature to 350°F; cover and cook for another 30 minutes. Baste again and cook uncovered at 375°F for another 20 minutes, or until the skin is golden and a thin skewer inserted into the thickest part of the thigh produces a clear (not pink) juice. Do not rely on pop-up timers; they don't emerge until the bird is overcooked and dry.

While the chicken is in the final stages of roasting, make the sauce. Put 3 teaspoons of mustard in a small saucepan with the wine. In a bowl, mix the flour with the water, starting with half the water and gradually adding more until you have a thin paste. Add this mixture to the ingredients in the pan and bring to a boil, stirring all the time. When the mixture has thickened, add the 1/4 cup of juices from the roasting chicken and simmer for 6–7 minutes, stirring as necessary to prevent sticking. Taste for seasoning and add salt and the remaining spoonful of mustard. Serve in a sauce boat with the sliced roasted chicken.

SERVES 6–8.

BEEF ROLLS WITH PEPPERCORNS AND MUSTARD

1 cup finely chopped mushrooms

1 small onion, finely chopped

2 teaspoons green peppercorns

2 tablespoons chopped fresh parsley

1 1/4 cups red wine

2 slices wheat bread, crusts removed

2 teaspoons horseradish or green peppercorn mustard

8 sandwich steaks

1 tablespoon Dijon or an additional tablespoon of the horseradish or green peppercorn mustard

Preheat the oven to 375°F.

If the peppercorns are dry, soak them in water for 1/2 hour; if packed in liquid, use them straight from the bottle. Put the mushrooms, onion, 1 teaspoon of peppercorns, and the parsley into a small saucepan with 3/4 cup of the wine. Cover and simmer for 5 minutes or until the mushrooms and onions are tender. Crumble the bread and add to the mixture. Beat each sandwich steak with a rolling pin or mallet. Spread a little of the hot mustard onto the steak, then spoon on a portion of the mixture and roll up the steak into a sausage shape. Place each one, seamside down, in a greased baking dish.

Pour the remaining 1/2 cup of wine over them, cover with a lid or aluminum foil, and bake for 8 minutes. Pour the accumulated liquid into a small saucepan and keep the beef rolls hot. Stir the remaining peppercorns into the liquid in the pan and boil for 3 minutes. Remove from the heat and add the Dijon or other mustard. Spoon the sauce over the beef rolls. Serve with vegetables.

SERVES 4–8, DEPENDING ON THE SIZE OF THE SANDWICH STEAKS.

Continued →

1 1/2–2 pounds bluefish

1 tablespoon olive oil

2 tablespoons lemon mustard

1 tablespoon melted butter

1/3 cup hot milk

2 teaspoons chopped fresh dill

few drops fresh lemon juice

Preheat the broiler. Place the bluefish in a greased shallow pan and sprinkle the surface with olive oil. Place 2–3 inches from the broiler and cook for 5 minutes for 1/2-inch-thick fish, up to 10 minutes for inch-thick fish. While it is cooking, put the mustard into a warmed sauceboat. Just as the fish is ready, stir in the butter, milk, and dill. Taste and add a few drops of lemon juice to sharpen the sauce to your taste. Serve with the fish. (This sauce also goes well with salmon, mackerel, and shrimp.)

SERVES 4.

Making & Using Flavored Vinegars

Glenn Andrews

Illustrations by Brigita Fuhrmann

Introduction

Seasoned vinegars are lovely, both to keep for your own use and to give away as special gifts. There are many excellent seasoned vinegars on the market, but yours will be better—fresher, more flavorful, and more unusual. (The price differential is nice, too.)

These vinegars are simple to make. You're limited only by the range of your imagination—and imaginations have a wonderful way of opening up when you begin to stretch them. Start by making some of the versions I'll give you, then create your own, adding whatever herbs, spices, and flavorings sound good to you.

Making Flavored Vinegars

Many flavored vinegars can be made right in the bottles in which you will store them or give them away—as long as you have enough time at your disposal to allow for the gradual build-up of flavor by the steeping process. You simply insert the flavoring ingredients into the bottle, add the vinegar—and wait.

If, however, you suddenly decide in mid-December that you want to give your aunt Minnie some marvelous vinegar for the holidays, you're going to have to speed up the process. To do this, first bruise your seasoning ingredients—smash them as best you can with a garlic press, pepper mill, coffee grinder, or even a hammer. (In the case of fresh herbs, just crumple them up a bit.) Then place them in a jar with a cover (a mayonnaise jar works well), heat the vinegar to the boiling point, and pour it into the jar.

Keep the jar at room temperature, covered. Start tasting the vinegar in a day or two (putting a few drops on a small piece of bread is a good way to do this) so you will know when the flavor is just right. In many cases, the vinegar will be ready in just a few hours.

When you decide to go with the vinegar the way it is, strain out the flavoring ingredients. Now carefully examine the vinegar. If you can see small particles floating around, or if it looks at all cloudy, run it through a coffee filter until it's clear.

Put another small supply of the seasoning ingredients (this time left whole) into the bottles, mostly for looks, and pour in the vinegar.

Other vinegars, such as raspberry, are best made by cooking the main ingredients briefly in the vinegar, then steeping. No matter which method you use, there's very little effort involved and the rewards are tremendous.

All the vinegars will keep indefinitely. If you plant to keep them on hand for a long time, though, it's wise to sterilize the vinegar you use as a base to avoid further development of the cloudy-looking "mother." Because of vinegar's excellent preservative properties, any sprigs of herbs, etc., that you add will stay fresh looking.

The instructions below all make about two cups of vinegar. To make more, just multiply the ingredients.

WHAT BASE VINEGARS TO USE

In each of the sets of instructions below, I've suggested that you use a certain vinegar. There's always a reason for my choices. Red wine vinegar adds to the color of raspberry vinegar; white wine vinegar shows off the Thyme, Lemon Peel, and Black Pepper Vinegar, and so forth. However, please feel free to follow your own inclinations and preferences.

Here are the vinegars you can find in most grocery stores. (You don't need to use the most expensive brands. You'll be making them special enough to please the most epicurean taste.)

Red wine vinegar—Attractive to the eye; mildly gusty.

White wine vinegar—Off-white; delicate in taste.

Champagne vinegar—Not too different from white wine vinegar.

Japanese or Chinese rice vinegar (white or red)—Very subtle, delicate flavor (but be aware that the "seasoned" variety contains sugar).

Distilled white vinegar—Colorless; very acidic; best for such unsubtle uses as Hot, Hot, Hot Vinegar.

Apple cider vinegar—Light brown; strong flavor of apples.

Malt vinegar—Dark brown; very strong but pleasant flavor; can be hard to find except in Canada (where it's used on French fries!) or in England (where it's the preferred condiment for fish and chips).

Sherry vinegar—Brown; strong flavor of sherry; usually imported from Spain; rather expensive.

Of all these possibilities, the best for making most flavored vinegars are the first four—red wine, white wine, champagne, and Japanese rice vinegars. For most purposes, the others have too strong a flavor of their own. (Exceptions: such pungent vinegars as the ones made with hot peppers, shallots, garlic, or onion.)

RASPBERRY VINEGAR

Many people consider this the very best of all the flavored vinegars. Because it's made with fresh fruit, the procedure is a little different from the usual. Don't omit the sugar or honey; this vinegar needs a touch of sweetening to bring out its full flavor.

2 to 2 1/2 cups fresh red raspberries, lightly mashed (an equivalent amount of frozen raspberries can be used, but if they're presweetened, don't add the sugar or honey)

2 tablespoons sugar or honey

2 cups red wine vinegar

Combine all the ingredients in the top of a nonaluminum double boiler. Place over boiling water, turn down the heat, and cook over barely simmering water, uncovered, for 10 minutes.

Place in a large screwtop jar and store for 3 weeks, then strain to separate the vinegar from the berries, pressing on the berries to get out all the juice. If your vinegar is cloudier than you wish, run it through a coffee filter. Pour into the bottle(s) you plan to use, adding a few fresh berries.

MAKES ABOUT 2 CUPS.

Shortcut: Paul Corcellet, maker of one of the finest commercial raspberry vinegars, also markets an excellent raspberry syrup that you can find in many fancy-food stores. A little of it added to some red wine vinegar will give you an instant raspberry vinegar, which may not be quite as tasty as what you can make but is still very good.

BLUEBERRY VINEGAR

This ultra-chic and ultra-good fruit vinegar is made in exactly the same way as the raspberry vinegar above.

Use your choice of red or white wine vinegar. The red will give a darker color, but it will have a purplish tinge.

An attractive way to bottle this vinegar, after it has been heated, stored, strained, and possibly filtered, is to put some fresh, large blueberries and a small cinnamon stick in each glass jar. The blueberries will stay fresh indefinitely, the cinnamon stick will swell (and add to the flavor of the vinegar), and the look will be extremely appealing.

PEACH, APRICOT, AND OTHER FRUIT VINEGARS

Follow the same system for vinegars made from any fruit, but use white wine vinegar as the base. Can you imagine peach vinegar sprinkled on a fruit salad—or apricot vinegar mixed with mayonnaise and used in a chicken salad? I strongly recommend them.

Peel apricots, peaches, or nectarines before using by dipping them momentarily in boiling water, then removing the skin with your fingers. If they're big, cut the fruits immediately. Continue as you would for Raspberry Vinegar, above.

Herbal Vinegars

Your individual taste and the matter of what fresh herbs are available to you will determine what you use in your herbal vinegars.

You can use one herb or a combination of as many as you like. In addition, you can combine herbs with other flavorings.

I'll give you one example each of a one-herb vinegar, a mixed-herb vinegar, and one with other flavors added. In each case, you'll find a few other suggestions. After that, you're on your own.

I prefer white wine or champagne vinegar for all of these, simply because the herbs show up so well in them when you gaze admiringly at the bottles. White rice vinegar gives the same effect, and is pleasantly mild. Distilled white vinegar, to me, is a bit strong-tasting and tends to overpower the herbs.

BASIL AND OTHER SINGLE-HERB VINEGARS

A pattern to follow—you can use any fresh herb. Dill, for instance, is always enjoyed, as is chervil. Tarragon is one of the greatest vinegars of all. Chives make a subtle vinegar—be sure to use a lot of them in the bottles. For small-leaved herbs such as thyme, use an extra sprig or two.

4 large sprigs fresh basil

2 cups white wine or champagne vinegar

Put the basil sprigs into a pint bottle and pour in the vinegar (or divide everything between 2 smaller bottles). Seal. Store for 2 to 3 weeks before using. (For quicker, though not easier, herb vinegar, see the instructions on page 362.)

ROSEMARY-TARRAGON VINEGAR
(and Other Herb-Combination Vinegars)

If I had to pick a favorite of the herb vinegars, this would be it. Rosemary and tarragon are a terrific flavor combination, and the sprigs of the two herbs look fascinatingly exotic together.

But there are other good combinations. Any herb goes well with any other herb. You could use several herbs in combination, too. Oregano and dill are interesting together, as are basil and savory.

2 large sprigs rosemary

2 large sprigs tarragon

2 cups white wine or champagne vinegar

Make this just as you would the basil vinegar above. If you're dividing it between two bottles, make sure to put a sprig of rosemary and a sprig of tarragon in each.

THYME, LEMON PEEL, AND BLACK PEPPER VINEGAR
(and Other Combination Vinegars)

Aside from the fact that it's so good-tasting, the appealing look of this vinegar makes it one of the best to give as a present. Other flavoring ingredients to combine with herbs include dill seeds, whole allspice, white peppercorns, cinnamon sticks, orange peel, tiny hot dried red peppers, and celery seed. The mixture known as pickling spice makes

Continued →

an unusual vinegar, too. (Unless you want a hot vinegar, though, be sure to remove the small chili peppers from the pickling spice.)

1 large sprig of fresh thyme

1 long spiral lemon peel

2 heaping teaspoons black peppercorns

2 cups white wine vinegar

Put the thyme, lemon peel, and peppercorns into one 1-pint or two 8-ounce bottles. Add the wine vinegar. Seal the bottle. Store for a month before using, giving the bottle a very gentle shake every day or two. (See the instructions on page 362 if you need to make this vinegar for more immediate use.)

Note: If you're using two 8-ounce bottles, use two smaller sprigs of thyme and two smaller spirals of lemon peel. Put one of each plus 1 heaping teaspoon of peppercorns in each of the two bottles.

THREE-PEPPERCORN VINEGAR

The peppercorns involved are black, white, and green. To make a Four-Peppercorn Vinegar, you could add pink peppercorns, though they are the object of a controversy involving possible toxicity, so I don't recommend them.

This is a desperately chic vinegar. It's also very good.

1 teaspoon black peppercorns

1 teaspoon white peppercorns

1 teaspoon green peppercorns, from a jar or can

2 cups white wine vinegar

Bring the vinegar to a boil. Remove from the heat and add the black and white peppercorns. Let sit until cool, then pour into your bottle(s). (If you're using more than one bottle, divide the peppercorns evenly.) Now add the green peppercorns. Store for 2 or 3 weeks before using. There's no need to strain.

HOT, HOT, HOT VINEGAR

Use with caution—though you can vary the fierceness of this vinegar by the number of hot peppers you use. Distilled white vinegar or apple cider vinegar are the ones to use here, because of their strength of flavor.

You will find this handy to have on hand. Not only will you have an instant source of hotness for certain Mexican and Oriental dishes, but you will also always be in possession of fresh hot peppers, since they keep perfectly in the vinegar. You can pull one out, cut off a little of it to use in your cooking, then put the rest of it back into the bottle.

For the very hottest vinegar: Fill a jar with clean, dry hot peppers. Pour in enough vinegar to cover. Seal. Store for a week or two before using. I use a mixture of jalapeños and the smaller, hotter serrano chilis, but you can use any hot fresh peppers you have or are able to find.

For a milder vinegar: Use milder chilis (of course), and smaller amounts of them—or substitute pieces of red or green sweet peppers for part of the chilis. They will add flavor, but not heat.

SPICED JAPANESE RICE VINEGAR

Dieters will be happy to know that this soft, gentle vinegar can be used as a salad dressing all by itself, with no added oil or salt!

1 small, peeled shallot or garlic clove

10 black peppercorns

1 quarter-sized piece of fresh ginger, peeled

2 cups Japanese white or red rice vinegar

Put the shallot or garlic clove, the peppercorns, and the piece of ginger into a bottle. (You may have to cut the piece of ginger in half if the top of the bottle is small.) Add the rice vinegar.

Seal the bottle and store for about 2 weeks before using.

SEVEN-PEPPER VINEGAR

Anything with a name this outrageous is fun to give as a gift, but this also happens to be a very good vinegar. Here's how you arrive at the large number of peppers:

Black peppercorns

White peppercorns

Szechuan peppercorns

Green peppercorns

Sweet green peppers

Sweet red peppers

Hot chili peppers (to make an Eight-Pepper Vinegar,

you could use red and green hot peppers)

2 cups white wine vinegar

Make this vinegar exactly as you would Three-Peppercorn Vinegar, with these exceptions: Add the Szechuan peppercorns along with the black and white ones, then mince the sweet peppers and chilis very, very finely and add them to the vinegar at the same time as the green peppercorns. This vinegar does not need to be strained; the vinegar will preserve the fresh ingredients. If you're not familiar with Szechuan peppercorns, you'll find them in the Chinese food section of most supermarkets and, of course, in any Asian market. They add much flavor but no heat.

GARLIC, SHALLOT, OR ONION VINEGAR

Garlic, shallot, or onion vinegar is a good bet for giving a quick shot of pungency to almost anything non-sweet that you're cooking. Shallot vinegar is the mildest of the three and is usually well liked by even those who run screaming at the thought of garlic. Onion vinegar isn't subtle at all, but that's fine. Garlic vinegar—well, garlic lovers think it enhances everything short of chocolate ice cream.

As to what vinegar to use: Garlic and onions seem to demand a vinegar with strength of its own, hence good choices would be apple cider vinegar or white distilled. Shallots, being more delicate, get along well with wine vinegars.

1/3 cup chopped garlic, shallot, or onion

2 cups vinegar (see above for the sorts to use)

Simply combine the chopped garlic, shallot, or onion with the vinegar in a screw-top jar. Store for 2 or 3 weeks, then strain and bottle, inserting the appropriate thing in each bottle—a peeled clove of garlic or shallot or either a piece of onion or a tiny white onion, peeled.

PROVENÇAL VINEGAR

The flavors of Provence in the South of France are glorious. Here's an easy way to add a touch of them to your food.

1 small sprig of thyme

1 small sprig of rosemary

1 small bay leaf

1 large clove garlic, peeled

Orange peel—1 strip about 1" by 4"

1 pint white wine vinegar

Put the thyme, rosemary, bay leaf, garlic, and orange peel into a 1-pint bottle (or put smaller amounts in each of two 8-ounce bottles). Add the wine vinegar. Seal. Store for a month before using, giving the bottle a very gentle shake every day or two. (If you need this vinegar for more immediate use, follow the instructions on page 362.)

Recipes Using Flavored Vinegars

These recipes are just to get you started using the vinegars you've made. Try these to get the general effect of what can be done, then start inventing your own ways to use them—either by substituting them for the vinegars in other recipes, or by just splashing them in whenever you sense that they'd add a little magic to a dish you're cooking.

If you haven't yet made the vinegar called for in a recipe you want to try, you can substitute others.

PORK CHOPS DIJON WITH SHALLOT VINEGAR

To me, these are the best pork chops there could ever be.

2 tablespoons butter or margarine

4 3/4-inch-thick pork chops, trimmed of most of their fat

2 tablespoons Shallot Vinegar

1 teaspoon Dijon mustard

1/2 cup heavy or medium cream

Salt and freshly ground pepper to taste

Melt the butter in a large frying pan over low heat. Add the pork chops and cook, still over low heat, turning occasionally, for about 30 to 35 minutes or until brown and tender. Remove from the pan and keep in a warm place. Now turn up the heat just a little and deglaze the pan by adding the vinegar and stirring well, scraping up any brown bits. Next, stir in first the mustard, then the cream. Simmer, stirring for 2 or 3 minutes, then serve over or under the chops.

SERVES 4.

SZECHUAN CHICKEN SALAD

Spicy but not really hot, this is a marvelous dish. (If you want it hotter, you can add a few drops of Hot, Hot, Hot Vinegar to the pan containing the other flavoring ingredients.) The warm sauce should be poured on at the last minute, but everything can be prepared, ready to go, well in advance. The Szechuan peppercorns and hoisin sauce are available in most supermarkets.

4 check breast halves (2 whole breasts)

1 one-inch piece of fresh ginger, peeled

3 large scallions

1/4 cup salad oil

2 tablespoons Spiced Japanese Rice Vinegar

1 teaspoon Szechuan peppercorns, finely ground in a coffee mill, peppermill, or mortar and pestle

1 tablespoon hoisin sauce

1 tablespoon honey

1 tablespoon tamari or other soy sauce

1/2 teaspoon pressed or finely minced garlic

1/4 cup peanuts or cashews (optional)

Drops of Hot, Hot, Hot Vinegar (optional)

Romaine lettuce, shredded

2 medium tomatoes, cut into wedges

Cut a slice the size of a quarter from the ginger and cut one of the scallions into 1-inch pieces. Put these in a fairly large pot with 2 quarts of water. Bring to a boil, then add the chicken breasts, turn down the heat, and simmer for 15 minutes, covered. Remove from the heat and allow to cool for half an hour.

Meanwhile, mince the rest of the ginger and the remaining scallions. Put these in a small pot with the salad oil, the Spiced Japanese Rice Vinegar, the Szechuan peppercorns, *hoisin* sauce, honey, tamari, garlic, and the nuts, if you're using them. Taste the mixture and then, if you want, add just a little Hot, Hot, Hot Vinegar. Set aside for the moment.

When the chicken is cool, remove the skin and bones and tear the meat into shreds. Place in a heat-proof bowl. Make a bed of the shredded romaine on individual plates or one large platter. At serving time, bring the pot with the ginger-oil mixture to a boil, then pour it over the chicken shreds. Mix well, and serve over shredded romaine. Place the wedges of tomato around the outside of the lettuce.

SERVES 4.

Szechuan Chicken Salad can also be made with leftover chicken. It won't be quite as good, but it will still probably be the best leftover chicken dish you've ever tasted.

Continued →

CHICKEN BRAISED WITH BASIL VINEGAR

Fabulous dishes of this sort turn up in the cooking of both France and Italy. The flavor of the herb vinegar permeates the chicken and creates a small amount of simple but succulent sauce.

4 tablespoons olive oil

1 three-pound chicken, cut up or quartered

Salt and freshly ground black pepper to taste

1/4 cup Basil Vinegar

Rub the chicken with a little salt and pepper. Heat the olive oil in a large frying pan over medium heat, then brown the chicken all over in this. Remove the chicken pieces to a shallow baking dish, pour on the vinegar and bake, uncovered, at 350°F for 35 to 40 minutes, basting 3 or 4 times.

SERVES 4.

FRENCH POTATO SALAD

The French have a great approach to potato salad. Quite unlike our usual American picnic version, which is cold and laden with much mayonnaise, theirs is served warm and features vinegar, oil, and subtle seasonings.

For a classic French Potato Salad, the potatoes are peeled immediately after boiling, but many cooks now use small new potatoes, preferably red, and leave the peel on.

2 pounds "boiling" potatoes, new or older (see above)

3/4 cup salad oil (or, to be very French, use olive oil)

2 tablespoons Thyme, Lemon Peel, and Black Peppercorn Vinegar

1/4 cup minced onion or scallion

Salt and pepper to taste

2 tablespoons minced parsley

Boil the potatoes in salted water until just tender. Meanwhile, combine the oil, vinegar, and salt and pepper in a small saucepan. Now either peel the potatoes or don't (see above). Either way, slice them into a bowl while still hot. Bring the dressing in the saucepan just to a simmer, add the onion or scallion and parsley, and pour the mixture over the hot potato slices at once. Toss gently. The salad is ready to eat now, though its flavor will be even better if you allow it to sit for at least 30 minutes, then reheat.

SERVES 4 TO 6.

Making the Best Apple Cider

Annie Proulx

Even if you've never made cider before, with a little care and selectivity in the apple department, with a few essential pieces of equipment, and with a little help from your family and friends, you can make a better and more flavorful cider yourself at home than most commercial mills ever do. If you've got a discerning palate, a supply of good cider apples, and an interest in fresh apple nectar, you may want to start up your own quality sweet cider business after a few seasons of experimentation.

To make good sweet cider, you need a balanced mixture of apple varieties—some bland for the "base" juice, some tart and acidic to liven the cider up, a few bitter apples with astringent tannins to give body and character, and some aromatic apples for bouquet and outstanding flavor. You will need a grinder to reduce these apples to a pulp, and a press to exert pressure on the pulp so that the fruit cells rupture and release their juice. You need containers to hold the fresh-pressed cider, and, if you're not going to drink it all up within a few weeks, a cold storage place—refrigerator or freezer—is essential lest your sweet cider ferment its way to a potent hard cider.

Equipment for Cider-Making

Only a few years ago cider-making equipment was scarcer than hens' teeth, but the back-to-the-land movement has motivated an increasing number of manufacturers to turn out butter churns, spinning wheels, horse-drawn farm machinery—and apple grinders and cider presses.

Much of the new equipment is more efficient, easier to clean and lighter in weight than the machines great-grandpa used which were heavy with cast iron and oak. The new grinders feature stainless steel or cast aluminum rollers or breaker teeth, and can be bought ready-made or in kit form. Don't try to put apples through grape or soft fruit crushers—they can't take it.

Small hand and hydraulic presses are available from a growing number of manufacturers, and plans for building your own cider press are available as Report No. 8 from the New York Agricultural Experiment Station, Geneva, N.Y. 14456. This is also the home of the largest orchard of apple varieties in the United States; over a thousand apple varieties are maintained here, many of them true cider apples.

The Grinder: This is usually a hand-powered oak frame set with stainless steel or aluminum cutters or toothed rollers, with a commodious hopper on top which can accommodate up to a bushel of fruit. They are available from several sources, either ready-made or in kit form. Electrically powered grinders vary from the professional hammermill to a small grinder powered by a 3/8" home electric drill.

The Press: A surprising variety of presses is available to the home cider-maker: small single-tub hand-operated screw presses are ready made and in kits; double-tub screw presses ready made; single- and double-ratchet system tub presses ready made; small hydraulic hand presses with cheese racks which are miniature versions of the large commercial presses; and replicas of nineteenth century presses with some modern modifications.

Pressing Bags and Cloths: If you are using a cheese-rack press, where each rack of apple pomace is enfolded in a nylon press cloth, and the racks are stacked in layers before pressure is exerted, you need press cloths. Usually they come with the press, but replacements can be bought from many sources. If you use a tub press, you'll need a sturdy, porous nylon press bag into which the pomace is poured. They are strong and easy to clean.

Filter Cloth: To filter out stems, seeds, and large chunks of apple pomace from the fresh juice, a layer of cheesecloth or nylon filter cloth is fine. The tastiest and most nutritious cider will be somewhat cloudy with tiny pectin particles in suspension. Filtering sweet cider until it is brilliantly clear is a lot of unnecessary work that takes the desirable pectin out of the cider—purely a cosmetic procedure.

Primary Container: This is the bucket, bowl or vat in which you catch the fresh cider as it pours from the press. It should be stainless steel, odorless polyethylene plastic or nylon, glass, or sound, unchipped enamel. Do NOT use galvanized metal containers such as old milk cans, aluminum, copper, or other metal containers, or chipped enamel. The acid in apple juice will react very quickly with the metal and give your cider unpleasant off-flavors.

Plastic Siphon Tubing: A four-foot section of plastic quarter-inch diameter tubing makes a neat efficient job of filling cider jugs and bottles.

Plastic Funnel: For filling five-gallon carboys and other large vessels.

Storage Containers: Earthenware cider jugs stoppered with corks were the traditional cider containers. These can still be found, both old and new, for a price. Most cider makers are thrifty folk who will be content to use clean plastic or glass jugs with screw tops for sweet cider. If you plan on freezing cider, use plastic containers and leave room for expansion under freezing conditions.

SUPPLIERS OF CIDER PRESS KITS, ACCESSORIES, AND SUPPLIES

All Seasons
Homestead Helpers
P.O. Box 99
Jeffersonville, VT 05464
(802) 644–2658

Cumberland General Store
#1 Highway 68
Crossville, TN 38555

Day Equipment Corp.
1402 E. Monroe St.
Goshen, IN 46526
(219) 534–3491

Happy Valley
Manufacturing
16577 W. 327th Street
Paola, KS 66071–9516
(913) 849–3013

Jaffrey Manufacturing Co.
Box 23527-ME
Shawnee Mission, KS
66223
(913) 849–3139

Lehman's Non-Electric
Catalog
1 Lehman Circle
P.O. Box 41
Kidron, OH 44636
(330) 857–5757

National Filter Media Corp.
1717 Dixwell Avenue
P.O. Box 4217
Hamden, CT 06514
(203) 248–5566
Sells nylon press cloths

Which Apples Make the Best Cider?

Hard cider may take the skill of a cellarmaster to make a marriage of the fruit varieties that will weather the rigors of fermentation and grow more beautiful through the flavor changes of aging, but in sweet cider the ideal is an orchard-fresh apple aroma crowning a rich fruit drink. For the best sweet cider you must choose apples whose blended flavors give a juice as piquant and fresh as a bite of ripe apple just off the tree.

DIFFERENCES IN APPLES

Apples may appear to differ only in color, shape, and flavor, but for the cider maker there are other important differences. All apples contain the same basic properties: they are made up of 75 to 90 percent water, several sugars (glucose, levulose and sacchrose), malic and other acids, tannin, pectin, starch, albuminoids, oils, ash, nitrogenous substances, and trace elements. Most apples contain roughly the same amount of

sugar—between 10 and 14 percent—and though a dessert apple tastes much sweeter to us than a cooking apple or a tart wild apple, it's not because the dessert apple contains more sugar, but because higher levels of malic acid in "sour" apples mask their sweetness. A good rule of thumb is that a sweet-tasting apple is low in malic acid.

The tannin content, acid levels, and aromatic oils determine the value of the different varieties for cider makers. Tannin causes an astringent puckering sensation in the mouth, and malic acid contributes a tingling sourness. They give body and zest to a hard cider, and, in moderate proportions, contribute to the perky freshness of a good sweet cider.

In North America most cider is made from culled or surplus dessert apples. The sugar and acid levels in these apples are good for both hard and sweet cider, but there are few aromatic types, and most dessert apples are sadly deficient in tannin, so are not ideal for cider. The cider maker can overcome this latter deficiency by blending in wild apples or crab apples. Both have good levels of tannin.

"PERFECT" CIDER APPLES

There are "perfect" cider apples, those varieties which have good balance of aromatic oils, sugar, tannin, and acid, but they're rare and becoming rarer. The Roxbury Russet, Golden Russet, Ribston Pippin, and the Nonpareil were long treasured as fine single-variety cider apples. These antique varieties are hard to find today, so most cider makers have to make do with the varieties at hand, and balance their cider through blending. Most of the best ciders and apple juices of the world are blends, and the better for it.

BLENDING

Rather than "shotgun" blending, where as many different varieties are available are fed into the press in one giant cider gamble, a system of judicious blending gives a more predictable, superior product. Popular varieties can be grouped by their cider characteristics, and the trick is to get your hands on the types needed to round out a blend.

There are thousands of different apple varieties, many of them members of the same apple family with strong similar characteristics. The McIntosh group is popular and widespread, and several of them unwittingly blended in a cider could produce a batch of juice overpoweringly scented with McIntosh perfume. Macoun, Cortland, Spartan, Jonamac, and Empire are all McIntosh descendents. In the same family, but further removed and so better candidates for blending with the very aromatic McIntosh are Quinte, Ranger, and Caravel.

"Wild" apples make better hard cider than "tame" apples—the cultivated varieties—but in sweet cider a straight or high percentage of wild apple juice in a blend can make a cider that is too bitter and sharp for tastes acclimated to sweet juice drinks. Hard cider made from wild apples is more palatable than the fresh juice because the second stage malolactic fermentation neutralizes most of the malic acid. However, if wild apples are available, and your cider base is bland and lacking in character, you can blend in wild apple juice or crab apple juice as you would the juice of domestic varieties with higher acid and tannin levels.

"WILD" APPLES

What are "wild" apples? They are not the fruits found on old domesticated cultivars standing beside cellar holes or in neglected long-abandoned orchards. Although disease, vermin, and poor nutrition can make the fruits of these trees look like their wild cousins, they are still of proper family no matter how scruffy, and the apples will have the

Continued ➜

family characteristics. Wild apples are the naturally seeded offspring of known cultivars, or are from trees which have grown up from rootstock suckers bearing fruit of an unknown type and quality. (Not all wild apples are good cider material; some are mushy and characterless. Taste sample before you gather them, and if they are bland and insipid, pass them by.) Since apples do not breed true to seed, but are propagated by grafting, the seeds of the familiar orchard varieties which escape captivity and grow to maturity tend to bear fruit which resemble those of their ancient ancestors, the crab apples.

SOME THINGS TO THINK ABOUT

Apples unacceptable for the market and surplus apples have long provided the bulk of cider fruit in North America. This may be a good way to utilize a perishable commodity, but unfortunately the cider press has also been used to clean up the orchard of battered windfalls, natural drops, and even decaying fruits. The best ingredients make the best products, so to avoid the plague of off-flavored or vinegary cider, use only sound, ripe fruit. Immature apples have low sugar levels and are too acid and starchy for cider, while drops which have been on the ground for a while can taste moldy. Brown-spotted and rotten apples are loaded with vinegar-inducing acetobacter. Windfalls can also contain a toxic substance known as patulin. Both unripe apples and aging drops make very poor cider, sweet or hard.

How to tell when an apple is ripe? Twist it clockwise on the stem. If the apple comes off the tree readily, it is usually ripe. A further test is to cut the apple open and look at the seeds. If they are dark brown, the apple is mature. Light tan or pale white seeds mean the fruit is not ready for harvesting. Sometimes in late summer or September high winds will knock down many maturing fruits which are not quite ripe. Do not be tempted to use these for cider. Instead, use them for apple or herb-flavored jelly.

McIntosh, Winesap, and Delicious apples should never be used to make a single variety cider. Winesap has an unpleasant, bitter flavor by itself, and Delicious, which is very low in acid, makes a bland, insipid cider. It does have good sugar levels and pleasant aromatic oils, and can be used as a suitable base with more lively varieties such as Jonathan or Newtown blended in. McIntosh has a uniquely penetrating aroma which drowns out other desirable cider characteristics. Use it in blends if you like the McIntosh essence, as some people do.

In the final analysis, blending is a process of taste trial and error until you hit on a combination of varieties that fits your palate. This will be your unique, personal cider, unlike any other.

FINDING APPLES

If you do not have apple trees of your own, you may want to plant several varieties of fast-maturing semi-dwarf trees strictly for cider production. If you decide to gather wild apples from the wayside or from an abandoned orchard, be sure to get permission from the owner of the land; he or she may be planning on using them for cider too. Experimental Station orchards often have hard-to-find varieties for sale to the public. Commercial orchards and pick-your-own orchards are other apple suppliers.

If your cider fruit comes from an orchard that has been heavily sprayed, you may want to wash the apples, then cut off the stem and blossom ends before milling them.

Steps to Making Cider

The flavor and quality of your cider will depend not only on the varieties and proportions of apples you use in your cider blend, but also on the summer weather as the apples ripened, on orchard care, on mellowing techniques, and your own personal taste. Make cider outside, preferably on a cool, breezy day. The low temperature will reduce the risk of bacteria growth, and the breeze will keep away the tiny vinegar flies that can infect your new cider with *acetobacter*, the bacteria that make vinegar—and disagreeable sour cider.

An extremely important part of quality control in cider making is cleanliness. All materials and equipment must be clean and sanitary. The press, grinder, and all utensils should be scrubbed and hosed down with plenty of clean water (no soap) after each day's run is over, even if you plan on pressing again the next morning. If your equipment is in a cider house, the walls and floors must be hosed down at the end of the run also, to prevent the growth of acetobacter and to avoid providing pleasant surroundings for the dreaded vinegar flies. Dirty cider equipment leads directly to ruined cider.

1. **Apple harvest and "sweating":** Harvest or buy only mature, ripe, sound apples. Do not use unripe apples or windfalls. Immature apples make inferior cider. Windfalls are loaded with undesirable bacteria which will contribute unpleasant off-flavors to the juice.

A GUIDE TO CIDER CLASSIFICATIONS

High Acid	Medium Acid	Low Acid
Close	Baldwin	(Neutral Base)
Cox's Orange Pippin	Cortland	Ben Davis
Esopus	Empire	Delicious
Spitzenberg	Fameuse	Golden
Gravenstein	Golden Russet	Delicious
Jonathan	Idared	Grimes Golden
Melba	Jerseymac	Lindel
Newtown	Lobo	Rome Beauty
Northern Spy	McIntosh	Westfield Seek-
Quinte	Rambo	No-Further
Rhode Island	Roxbury Russet	
Greening	Sops of Wine	
Ribston Pippin	Spartan	
Vista Belle	Wayne	
Wealthy	Winesap	
	York Imperial	

Aromatic	
Cox's Orange Pippin	Astringent (Tannin)
Delicious	Dolgo Crab
Fameuse	Geneva Crab
Golden Delicious	Lindel
Golden Russet	Mont Royal
Gravenstein	Newton
McIntosh	Red Astrachan
Ribston Pippin	Siberian crab apples
Roxbury Russet	Most wild apples
Wealthy	Young American
Winter Banana	crab apple

Store the harvested apples in a clean, odor-free area for a few days to several weeks, "sweating" them until they yield slightly to the pressure of a firm squeeze. This mellowing procedure improves the flavor of the cider and makes the apples yield up their juices more readily. Never use rotten or decaying apples. Keep the different varieties separate if you want to make a balanced blend after pressing.

Be extra careful washing the apples if they have been sprayed.

2. Selecting apples for blending: You can expect to get about three gallons of cider from every bushel of fruit. A bushel of apples weighs forty-five pounds. Depending on the varieties you are able to gather, you can make a good blend based on the following amounts of fruit in each category.

Neutral or low acid base: 40 to 60 percent of the total cider. This bland, "sweet" juice will merge and blend happily with sharper and more aromatic apples.

Medium to high acid: These tart apples can make up 10 to 20 percent of the cider. Use any of the listed varieties which please your palate.

Aromatic: 10 to 20 percent of these fragrant apples will give your cider bouquet. Most of the aromatic oils are concentrated in the apple skins, but these cells are difficult to rupture. An efficient grinder helps.

Astringent (tannin): 5 to 20 percent of the total juice. Go easy with these tongue-roughening varieties. Too many will give your cider a fierce puckering action on the taste buds. The North American varieties which are high in tannin are also high in acid, so blend them carefully.

3. Washing: Just before grinding, wash the apples in a large tub of clear, cool water. Squirt a garden hose at high pressure directly on them. This helps get rid of unwanted bacteria and orchard detritus. Toss out any rotten or moldy fruit.

4. Milling or grinding: Dump the washed apples into the hopper of the grinder and reduce the fruit to a fine, mushy pomace. In ancient times apples were pulped for cider in stone troughs by men swinging heavy nail-studded clubs called "beetles." North American dessert apples are quite soft and make a pulp that may be even too mushy for efficient pressing. Wild apples give a more manageable pomace. Very small batches of apples can be mushed in a food mill or chopper, but this is impractical if you want to make more than a gallon or two of cider.

If this is your first cider-making experience, keep the apple varieties, the ground pomace, and the juice separate and blend to taste later. When you have worked out a desired mixture with known quantities of varieties, next time you can grind the mixed apples all together. Many cider makers enjoy experimenting with new blend ratios every fall. That's what makes good, individual ciders. Do not let the pomace stand, but press it immediately.

Grind the apples to a pulp.

5. Pressing: If you are using a single-tub screw press or ratchet press, place the nylon press bag in the tub and fill it with apple pomace. Do not use galvanized or metal scoops which react with the acid in the pomace. Tie or fold the bag closed, and slowly apply increasing pressure to the pulp. Don't hurry the process—you may burst the bag of pomace. As the juice flows out you can tighten the screw or pump the ratchet to bring the pressure up again. It will take about twenty-five minutes for the juice to come out, no matter what kind of press you use.

If you have a double-tub press, you can set up a continuous cider-making operation with one or two helpers. As one person grinds the apples which fall in pomace form down into the rear tub beneath the grinder, the other tightens the screw or ratchet which presses the pomace in the front tub. When the juice has all been extracted, the front tub slides forward out of the press, and the pomace is dumped. The back tub, now full of fresh-ground pomace, slides forward to be pressed, while the just-emptied tub is popped under the grinder in the rear of the press for a new load of pomace. This "continuous" method yields about eight to ten gallons of cider an hour, and is good exercise for whomever twirls the grinder handle.

Continued →

Place the pressing disc in position.

Press the juice from the pulp.

The small hydraulic presses are designed to press pomace which has been loaded into a number of slotted racks, each lined with a sturdy but porous nylon press cloth. The pomace is dumped onto a press cloth laid over a rack. Then the cloth is folded over on each side to completely enclose the pomace, and another rack placed on top of it. The process is repeated until six to eight layers or "cheeses" are stacked up. The hydraulic press, usually operated by a foot pedal, then exerts pressure, and the press stands until all the juice has flowed from the pomace, about half an hour. This is the type of press in large size, most often seen at commercial cider mills.

Catch the fresh cider in a clean stainless steel or plastic or sound enamel container. Do not allow your cider to come in contact with other metals. If you are planning to blend the juices from different varieties rather than mixing predetermined ratios of apples before grinding, keep the pressed-out juices separate, but covered and cool until you have a chance to blend. Put the pressed-out pomace to one side.

Catch the juice in a container.

6. Blending the juices: If this is your first cider, it will be helpful in future autumns to know the proportions of different apple varieties you used to make the delicious beverage. A few scribbes on the spot in a small notebook can save you time and headaches next year. Serious cider drinkers will eventually invest in a hydrometer to measure the sugar content of the juice, and an acid tester for determining acid levels. Others prefer to blend strictly by judicious tasting.

Take quart samples of each kind of juice. Use a measuring cup to figure exact amounts, and try for a good balance of juices. Taste-test for tannin content first. Add small amounts of high-tannin cider to the neutral or low-acid cider base until the level of astringency is pleasing to you. Look for a sensation of dryness or puckering in your mouth when you are trying to isolate a tannin taste reaction from an acid reaction. A lot of tannin in a juice will make your tongue feel rough, as though each taste-bud were standing on end. A lot of acid in a juice tastes sour and sharp, but without that dry, puckery sensation. Next, add in aromatic juice, then cautiously blend the high acid juice until the cider is lively, fragrant and well-balanced. Referring to your notes, blend your bulk juice to the same proportions. The cider is now ready for filtering and storage.

Experimental Station-tested balances of juice types for tasty sweet cider can be your primary blending guide. The total cider consists of ten equal parts.

And enjoy.

3 to 6 parts: low acid or neutral juice for the cider "base"
.5 to 2 parts: high tannin juice
1 to 2 parts: aromatic apple juice
1 to 2 parts: medium to high acid juice

Ratios can vary considerably, depending on personal taste.

7. Filtering: Not so many years ago Americans preferred glassy clear cider with the pectin content removed by filters and enzymes. Current preferences lean toward natural, unadulterated, unrefined foods, including the faintly hazy, natural sweet cider which has passed through only a light layer of cheesecloth or nylon mesh to catch impurities and flecks of pomace. The pectin and crude fiber in a natural sweet cider supplies bulk in the diet and regulates the digestive system. Pectin has also been linked in recent experiments with regulating cholesterol levels in humans. Most nutritionists now recommend sweet cider with its natural pectin content as superior to the crystal-clear type.

Storing and Preserving Sweet Cider

Refrigeration: Cider can be stored for short periods in clean glass or plastic jugs, or in waxed cardboard containers in a refrigerator at normal refrigeration temperatures. Depending on the condition of the fruit used to make the cider and the cleanliness of the grinding and pressing machinery, it can stay fresh-tasting from two to four weeks. If the machinery was not properly cleaned and harbored substantial colonies of yeasts and bacteria, you can expect fermentation to begin soon, or undesirable bacteria may grow.

Freezing: After refrigeration, the preferred method of preserving cider is freezing it in plastic or waxed cardboard containers. Most families use the half-gallon size as the contents can be consumed in a couple of days, but if large quantities of cider are at hand, this is a bulky procedure. Allow two inches in the necks of the containers for expansion during freezing. Defrost the cider for a day in the refrigerator when you want to drink it. You can keep frozen cider for a year with little deterioration in quality.

Pasteurizing in Bulk: Cider can be stored almost indefinitely on the pantry shelf by pasteurizing the juice and the preserving it in bottles or canning jars. This is the hot pack method using sterilized bottles with crown caps or regulation canning jars with new lids. If you use bottles and caps, you will need a bottle capper to affix the caps. You also need a metal-stemmed high temperature thermometer, such as the kind used for candy-making or deep frying. You will need a large kettle to sterilize the containers and keep them hot, and a stainless steel or unchipped enamel kettle in which to heat the cider. The acids in the juice will react with other metals and taint the cider. Bring the cider up to a temperature of 160°F and hold it there for fifteen seconds. Fill and cap the containers, place them on their sides on several layers of paper in a draft-free place, allow them to cool, then check to be sure they are properly sealed. Store in a cool, dark place.

Hard Cider

Making fine hard cider can be as complex a process as making fine wine. Only the basic steps to making a simple farm cider are covered here, but a natural hard cider to, which no sugar has been added, can attain a respectable 6 or 7 percent alcohol if fermented to dryness.

WHAT IS HARD CIDER?

Hard cider begins where sweet cider leaves off. The fresh-pressed apple juice (called "must" by hard cider makers) is poured into a fermentation vessel. The fermentation which follows is often in two stages. In the first phase, the natural yeast flora in the apple juice feed on and convert the natural hexose apple sugars into alcohol. When the sugars are exhausted, alcohol production ceases. At this point a secondary fermentation may take place, either in the fermentation vessel or the storage bottles. This is the fermentation of the malic acid in the cider by lactic acid bacteria. The result is lactic acid, a more mellow and subtle-tasting acid than the familiar sharp malic acid of fresh apple juice, and carbon dioxide bubbles.

BARRELS—TRADITIONAL BUT TROUBLESOME

Cider was traditionally fermented in barrels, and many people still believe that good hard cider needs an oak barrel. However, barrels are temperamental, difficult vessels now just about obsolete in commercial hard cider operations; preferred are high density polyethylene tanks and glass-lined steel vats.

If you are making hard cider for the first time, your chances for a good-flavored cider will be vastly improved if you use five-gallon glass carboys or polyethylene containers for fermenting. Glass carboys are sometimes available from bottled water supplies, and the less expensive poly containers are found everywhere at discount and hardware stores. They are cheap, light, unbreakable, easy to clean, and take screw-on, air-tight fermentation locks. Both can be purchased from wine supply stores. Two mail-order wine and cider-making equipment suppliers are:

Vynox Industries, Inc.
400 Avis St.
Rochester, N.Y. 14615

Happy Valley Ranch
Rt 2, Box 83
Paola, KS

MAKING BASIC HARD CIDER

The single cardinal rule to making hard cider is *never let air come in contact with the cider at any stage of fermentation or storage.*

1. **Blend the fresh-pressed sweet cider** immediately after pressing. Do not allow the juice to stand exposed to the air more than necessary. Exposure to air increases the chance of contamination by acetobacter which will convert your cider to vinegar.

2. **Strain the blended must** into your fermentation vessel right to the top in a cool, clean area. A clean, unheated cellar is ideal. Don't make cider in any place where strong-smelling substances such as oil storage tanks, gasoline, rubber, cleaning materials, onions, or root crops are stored. The cider will readily absorb such odors and have peculiar and unpleasant off-flavors. The higher the temperature, the faster the cider will ferment, but a slow fermentation rate makes a better quality cider. A good temperature range is 50°F to 60°F though decent ciders have been made in warmer areas.

Set aside a gallon of fresh sweet cider, covered, in the refrigerator for topping off the working cider. Leave the top of your fermenting vessel open. The liquid will not be contaminated by air at this stage because the cider is giving off gas. Within a few days the cider will be visibly "working" and will boil over a thick foam as it casts off impurities and detritus in the first vigorous stage of fermentation. Keep the foam wiped off the sides of the container. Add a little fresh cider daily to keep the liquid level high, for as long as the cider is working and the level is up to the top of the opening, the chances of air-borne acetobacter contamination are nil.

As the foaming subsides, screw on a water fermentation lock and allow the cider to ferment at its own pace. This process can take from a few weeks to five or six months, depending on the temperature of the cellar, the amount of natural sugar in the juice, the vigor of the natural yeasts and the chemistry of the apples. When the bubbling in the waterlock subsides, the yeasts will have exhausted the sugar in the cider; the cider has now fermented to dryness and is drinkable.

Continued →

3. Siphon the finished cider with plastic tubing into sterilized bottles, and cap them with crown caps, available from wine supply stores, or screw-on caps or corks. Store the bottles on their sides if you use corks so that the liquid will keep the corks swollen and tight-fitting. A cool, dark corner of the cellar is a good place to store the precious golden fluid, now your own natural hard cider. You may drink it right away, or years from now.

If you are making cider for the first time with a new press, the natural yeasts on the apples may not build up in sufficient quantity to give you a good, vigorous fermentation. Many cider makers find it helpful to guarantee a good ferment by adding a commercial champagne or white wine yeast to the must when it is poured into the fermentation vessel.

Cider makers who want a more potent drink, or who suspect that the natural sugars in the fresh apple juice are low because of a cold, rainy summer, may want to add sugar to the must for a higher alcohol content. A hard cider with an alcohol content of less than 5.7 percent does not keep well. By adding about one cup of sugar per gallon of must before fermentation, your finished cider will have roughly 10 to 11 percent alcohol. Adding too much sugar can stop the fermentation process.

Old New Englanders often added raisins instead of sugar; a few handfuls of natural raisins to a five-gallon jug of juice supply the fermentation process not only with additional sugars, but with wine-type yeasts from the raisin skins.

Making hard cider without a few instruments to measure sugar and alcohol levels is a seat-of-the-pants procedure. Some of this b'guess-and-b'gosh cider can be very good, depending on the expertise of the maker, the weather, the apples, and the luck of the game.

THE BEEFSTEAK MYTH

Somewhere along the line word has gotten out that hard cider needs a big juicy beefsteak tossed into it to "ripen it up." What happens most often when this is done, is putrefaction, not fermentation, resulting in a foul liquid that not even the devil could drink. In the old days, a fermenting cider sometimes stopped bubbling in the midst of the process (known as a "stuck fermentation") and the desperate cider maker, not realizing that the problem was a lack of nitrogen in the juice, knew only that adding a piece of meat to the barrel would start the fermentation process up again. The decomposing meat added enough nitrogen to the cider to boost the fermentation. The people who drank this cider, with its rank off-flavor, called it "scrumpy." Today, "nutrient tablets" sold by wine supply houses will restart a stuck fermentation without recourse to the meat counter.

VINEGAR

From the giant acetator towers of commercial vinegar factories to the forgotten gallon cider jug in the pantry, vinegar is made many ways. Though a lot of vinegar has been made by accident, the best is made with care.

Vinegar is the result of a secondary fermentation of hard cider. Acetic bacteria, or acetobacter, in the presence of oxygen will change the alcohol in hard cider to acetic acid. The bacteria is either airborne, transported directly to the cider on the feet of vinegar flies attracted by the yeasts, or deliberately introduced in a culture. Since it is the *alcohol* which converts to acetic acid, leaving a jar of sweet cider open to the air and hoping for good vinegar to develop is a chancey undertaking. The

yeasts in the cider must convert the sugars to alcohol before acetic acid can develop. Since many bacteria and molds in the air feed on the fruit sugars in sweet or partially fermented cider, there is a considerable risk of making a foul moldy liquid instead of a sharp zesty cider vinegar, unless you start out with a hard cider which has been fermented to dryness.

To make good vinegar, first make hard cider, as explained earlier. (Before going on to the next stage, remember never to make vinegar anywhere near sweet, fermenting, or stored cider; the risk of acetobacter contamination is high.) Pour the hard cider into a wide-mouthed container—glass, glazed pottery, stainless steel, or enamel—for the maximum exposure to oxygen and acetic bacteria. Cover the container with several layers of cheesecloth to keep out insects or mice. Don't worry about the acetobacter—they'll pass right through the cloth. The vinegar crock should be left in a fairly warm place in dim light. Sunlight has an inhibiting effect on the development of the vinegar.

The conversion of the alcohol in the cider to vinegar can take several weeks or several months. If you have made a natural hard cider without adding sugar, it should contain about 6 percent alcohol. This will convert into an equal amount of acetic acid. A 6 percent acetic acid vinegar is a good table strength. Anything more, acid will have to be diluted with distilled water, for it will be extremely sharp to taste.

Mother of Vinegar: When the cider has changed to vinegar, you will notice the gelantinous mass of acetobacter floating in the crock. This is the famous "Mother of Vinegar" or "vinegar mother" and it has value. A good vinegar mother can be sold, bought, or traded, for it serves as a catalyst which speeds up the conversation of your hard cider to vinegar. Vinegar makers in a hurry can buy vinegar mother at many health food stores.

Bottling: Full strength vinegar made from completely fermented hard cider can be simply poured into sterile bottles, capped, and stored. If you make vinegar from incompletely fermented cider which still contains sugar, you must pasteurize the vinegar in a hot water bath if you want it to keep for any length of time. When capping vinegar bottles use coated lids, cork-lined crown caps, rubber and glass covers or just corks. Metal lids must be coated, as the acetic acid in vinegar is highly corrosive to metals.

WHAT TO DO WITH LEFT-OVER POMACE

After the pressing is over you will face a mount of damp pomace—the skins, cores, seeds, stems and pulp which has been wrung free of juice. Many people view this mass of browning pomace with dread—a waste product which has to be gotten rid of somehow. But pomace has many uses, and if you can't do something with it yourself, try swapping it with someone who can. Farmers and sheep raisers are delighted to have pomace to feed to their stock. Here are some other uses.

Ciderkin and Mock Cider: Ciderkin was a popular children's drink in the old days, and it's still refreshing and tasty to modern palates. It is made by soaking the still aromatic pomace which contains plenty of sugars, yeasts, and flavor, in water overnight. Then run the reconstituted pulp through the press again. The result is a delicate, sweet cider drink which can be enjoyed straight from the press. If sugar and yeast are added to this juice it can be fermented into a mock cider.

Feed for Livestock: One part of pomace blended in with four parts of cattle or sheep feed makes an excellent animal food. Stock relishes pomace, though feeding it straight in large amounts can cause diarrhea. Many sheep raisers like to finish lambs for the fall market by feeding them apple pomace for several weeks. Pigs also enjoy pomace. If you don't raise animals yourself, try swapping or selling your pomace to someone who does.

Seedling Stock: Did you ever wonder where nurserymen get all those sturdy rootstocks used for grafting cultivars onto? Most of them are the strong seedlings sprouted from the seeds in the pomace of commercial cider mills. If your pomace hasn't been smashed up in a hammermill, you can start your own apple-crab nursery by spreading some of the seediest pomace in a freshly turned field, or by starting individual seeds in an apple seedling bed. When the trees are several years old they can be used as rootstock for your favorite budded or cleft-grafted cultivars. You can let these trees grow to maturity, too. This will take a long time, but who knows, one of them might turn out to be the greatest cider apple of all time. It's a gamble.

Compost: Pomace is so acid it must be composted for two years before it can be applied to the garden. By that time composting temperatures will have sterilized the seeds, or you'll have pulled out any sprouts by hand. To compost pomace thoroughly, build layers; a layer of pomace, a sprinkling of lime, then a layer of soil, and repeat until the pile is built.

Brush Reducer and Weed-Killer: The high acidity of fresh pomace discourages the growth of many plants. Spread it where you want to keep down weeds and brush.

Wildlife: Deer standing knee-deep in the pomace piles or chipmunks scurrying by, cheeks bulging with apple seeds—something for everyone.

Building Homebrew Equipment

Karl F. Lutzen & Mark Stevens
Illustrations by Randy Mosher

Introduction

Take one step into a homebrew store, or flip through the pages of any magazine about homebrewing, and it's easy to see that homebrewing can be an expensive hobby. From the counterflow wort chiller to a refrigerated keg system to a complete brewery, a serious homebrewer can spend thousands of dollars on a homebrewery.

Most of the products offered by the many homebrewing equipment manufacturers and suppliers have been produced with the needs and wants of the consumer in mind. Companies in the brewing industry are constantly coming up with products that they hope will make the brewing process easier, yet also allow the homebrewer to make a better beer. Many of the best-selling homebrewing supplies and "accessories" were created by homebrewers like yourself who developed a product that greatly aided them in their quest for "professional"-quality ales and lagers.

Despite the dizzying number of gadgets on the market, there is one thing to take solace in—brewing is a simple science. No matter if you are a beginner using strictly kits or a professional at a 30,000-gallon-a-year microbrewery, beer is still made using the same five basic steps: making wort, boiling, cooling, fermenting, and packaging (carbonating). You can make award-winning beer using a simple starter

kit. Yet there is equipment that doesn't come with the beginners' kit that will help you produce a higher-quality beer. Wort chillers, mashing and lauter tuns, and kegging systems are not required equipment for beginners, but most experienced homebrewers cannot produce their product without them.

All of the equipment described here can be purchased at your local brewing supply store or at one of the growing number of national homebrewing supply distributors. But building this equipment yourself offers two attractions: 1) You will save money; and 2) you can make changes to the equipment as is necessary to work in conjunction with your work or storage space, or existing equipment.

The projects here are designed for anyone from beginning to advanced brewers, kit brewers to all-grain masters. Most presuppose brewing experience (i.e., you will have a rough idea about how to use homemade equipment), and all require a working knowledge of and access to common tools found in a workshop (drills, saws, hardware, etc.). We hope you enjoy making these products and, with their help, succeed in achieving the ultimate goal—excellent beer.

The Rolling Carboy Carrier

The best way to move carboys is with rolling carboy carriers. They can be made at a minimum cost (we were able to make the rolling carboy carrier with only scrap wood from our work shed), they can be assembled quickly, and they provide a much safer and easier way to handle glass carboys. You basically construct a platform with a lip to keep the carboy in place and then put caster wheels on the bottom so that it can be rolled from the brewery area to the fermenter area. This doesn't solve the problem of moving carboys up and down stairs, but if you brew and ferment on the same level, it's a real back-saver.

The best way to move a carboy is with a rolling carboy carrier like this.

MATERIALS FOR A ROLLING CARBOY CARRIER

1	13"x13" platform of 3/4" plywood
4	1"-wide x 12"-long strips of 3/4" plywood
4	swivel coasters
16	#10 3/4"-long wood screws

Directions

1. Cut out the platform and strips from a 3/4" plywood sheet.

2. Glue and clamp the strips to the platform in the pattern illustrated.

3. Attach the swivel casters with the wood screws 1" in from the edges (be sure to drill pilot holes first).

4. Set the carboy on the platform, fill, attach airlock, and roll into the fermenter closet or corner.

Continued →

The Carboy Stand

Milk crates provide an easy way to build an inverted carboy stand for the BrewCap system. A carboy stand is a necessity if you want to effectively drain your carboys after sanitizing them, or if you are interested in using the BrewCap (made by BrewCo in Boone, North Carolina). The BrewCap was developed to allow brewers a more effective way to remove the expended yeast and trub that settle at the bottom of the carboy. With your carboy in an inverted position, the BrewCap holds two tubes in place: The short one extends into the neck and removes the expended yeast and trub, and the long one extends to the top of the inverted carboy and is a pressure-relief mechanism. Using a BrewCap, you will no longer need to siphon the wort into a secondary fermenter, and it is a completely closed system.

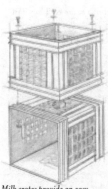

Milk crates provide an easy way to build an inverted carboy stand for the BrewCap system.

Directions

1. Saw a hole in the bottom of one of the milk crates (the "top" crate) large enough that the neck of the inverted carboy extends through the hole.

2. Set the second crate (the "bottom" crate) on its side and face the open side toward you; cut a large square hole in the top of the crate to accommodate the neck of the carboy and the hoses.

3. Fasten the two crates together using bolts, washers, and nuts.

Immersion Wort Chillers

One of the longest steps of the extract brewer's brewing process (other than the wort boil) can be the cooling of the wort. Especially if you still are using the ice bath and diffusion method of cooling your wort, you know how long it takes to get the 200° wort down to a temperature appropriate for pitching the yeast. The immersion chiller can reduce your cooling time to 15 minutes.

Immersion chillers are usually built from a coil of copper tubing with connectors on each end to which hoses are attached (garden hoses are often used). One connector is run to a source of cold water; the other is run to a drain for expelling the hot water. The immersion chiller offers a simple, effective way to quickly cool hot wort. Cooling wort quickly is important for two reasons. One: You can achieve a more effective cold break, which is the point when suspended proteins drop out of suspension as the wort is cooled. And two: You reduce the amount of time the wort is exposed to possible airborne pathogens.

BASIC IMMERSION CHILLER

Chillers are readily available from many homebrewing supply stores for $30 to $35; however, they can also be built at home for a bit less than

that. One advantage to building the chiller yourself is that you can adapt the plans to suit your own needs. We'll describe a few ways that chillers can be adapted to work more effectively.

When you build a wort chiller, the most critical aspect is the tubing you choose. Copper works well because it efficiently transmits heat energy and is readily available at fairly low cost. Stainless-steel tubing would work, but it costs more. Aluminum also works fine, but some brewers feel that it tends to give the beer a metallic taste. There is, however, no real evidence of such flavor problems. Your tubing should be 3/8" in diameter. If you use a thinner tube, you will achieve potentially greater efficiency because the thinner tube will give you more surface area per volume. However, chillers made from 1/4"-diameter tubing tend to take much longer to cool wort and are prone to clogging. Using a 3/8"-diameter tubing gives you good efficiency and acceptable cooling times, and it avoids clogging.

You can buy an immersion chiller like this one for about $30, or you can make one yourself.

Note: *Lengths of copper tubing greater than 20' usually come in a large coil. Most hardware stores will want to sell you a full box containing 50' to 60' of tubing. Shop with a friend and build two wort chillers if your hardware store will not sell you a cut length (or maybe find a new hardware store!). You could also build two chillers and use the double-coil chiller method that we describe on page 375.*

Note: *Before you begin, you should know that you can easily crimp your copper tubing and ruin that section of it. Once it's crimped, cut out the crimped section and attach a coupler by soldering (lead-free, please). If you don't have a spring tubing bender, buy one when you buy your copper tubing. It will help make the 90-degree bends without crimping the tubing.*

One other point: You should plan to leave enough copper tubing on the ends so that they stick out over the sides of the pot. Once in a while you may get leaks from loose hose clamps; if the tubing–hose connection is outside the pot and it does leak, the water will not drip into the wort.

Directions

1. Turn the copper tubing into a coil. If the copper tubing came in a coil, you can wind it into a tighter coil by hand. This is done by holding one end and turning the coils into ever-smaller coils. You can coil the copper tubing for your immersion chiller by wrapping it carefully around a soda keg if you have a soda keg handy. The final diameter must be small enough that there is at least 2" between the interior sides of the brewpot and the coil. Leave about 18" to 24" on one end.

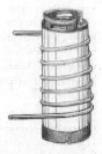

Use a soda keg to bend your tubing.

2. Bend the short end of the tube at the top of the coil 90 degrees out from the coil.

3. Bend the longer end 90 degrees so that the length of the tube goes back up toward the top of the coil.

4. Bend the top part of the long length out from the coil.

5. Cut the garden hose so that each length is at least 5' or 6' long.

6. Slide a clamp over each cut end of the hose.

7. Slip one hose length over one end of the coil. Repeat with the other hose at the other end of the coil.

8. Tighten the clamps to hold the hose lengths firmly to the coil.

That's it! Your immersion chiller is ready to use, and it should have cost you less than $25.

We recommend testing the chiller before brewing a batch of beer, just to convince yourself that everything works and to satisfy yourself that there will be no surprises when the time comes to use the chiller. We tested our chiller by boiling a brewpot full of water, to which we had added 1/2 gallon of white vinegar, and seeing how long it would take to cool it. The vinegar is important because it will clean the outside of the chiller and prepare it for use in the wort.

In addition to the chiller, you will need a hose that's long enough to run from your faucet to the chiller. If you're using the chiller in your kitchen, as most people do, you may need to twist off the end of your faucet to reveal the threads. These threads should accept a standard hose fitting, but many kitchen faucets need a threaded adapter to accept a hose connection. These are available at most hardware stores for $1 to $2. Some homebrew supply shops also sell the adapters. If you can't get the end of your faucet off, or if you just don't want to mess with it, you can buy a rubber adapter that will fit over the end of the faucet, avoiding the need to unscrew the faucet sprayer.

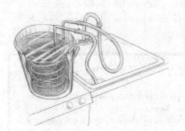

When you are ready to use your immersion chiller, sanitize it by putting it into the boil for 15 to 20 minutes. When the boil is done, attach the hoses—and chill out.

When you're ready to use the chiller, sanitize it by setting it down into your brewpot 15 to 20 minutes before the end of the boil. The heat will destroy any bacteria and other microorganisms on its surfaces. Then when the boil is done, simply attach the hose to your faucet, set the other end of the hose in the sink, and turn on the faucet. Five gallons of wort should cool from boiling to below 80°F in about 15 to 20 minutes. The time will depend on the flow rate and temperature of the water.

DOUBLE-COIL IMMERSION CHILLER

If you had no choice but to buy a 50' or 60' length of copper tubing, or if you are worried about wasting water, want faster cooling times, or have a cold-water supply that just isn't cold enough, you can build a chiller with two coils that are connected by a length of hose (see illustration below). Set one coil in a bath of ice water, the other coil in

the hot wort, and then run water through the chiller. This is more efficient both because you are cooling the water before it gets to the brewpot and because you are using a single coil with a greater difference in temperature between the cooling fluid and the wort. Thus the heat-exchange process works more efficiently.

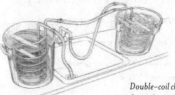

Double-coil chiller. This one calls for two coils: the first to lower the temperature of the cold water, the second to chill the wort.

Counterflow Chillers

If you want to run wort through your chiller, instead of running the chiller through your wort, a counterflow chiller is the best way to go. We'll describe several you can build yourself.

PVC PIPE COUNTERFLOW CHILLER

The PVC pipe counterflow chiller is one of the more popular counterflow chiller designs to emerge over the last several years. It is fairly simple to build and use, and it works faster than most immersion setups. However, as with all counterflow chillers, the inside of the copper tubing needs to be cleaned carefully before and after use because any trace of beer left behind can lead to infection.

The PVC pipe chiller involves taking a 2' length of a large-diameter PVC pipe; inserting a copper coil inside; drilling two holes, one for bringing in cold water and another for expelling hot water; attaching fittings for water hoses; and then sealing the ends. To use: Pump hot wort through the coil while simultaneously pumping cold water through the pipe.

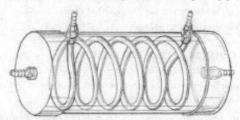

The PVC counterflow chiller (cutaway view) allows cold water to flow through a section of large-diameter plastic pipe, while hot wort circulates through the small-diameter copper coil installed inside the plastic pipe.

MATERIALS FOR A PVC PIPE COUNTERFLOW CHILLER

1 2' length of 6" PVC pipe
2 PVC pipe caps (also called end-caps)
4 3/8" compression x 3/8" MPT adapters
4 1/2" hose barb x 3/8" FPT connectors
10' of 3/8" copper tubing
1/2" heat-resistant hose
1/2" PVC hose
25' inexpensive garden hose, 1/2" diameter
PVC cement
Epoxy cement
Teflon tape

Continued ➡

Directions

1. Drill a 1/2"-diameter hole in each end-cap.

2. Insert the compression end of a 3/8" compression x 3/8" MPT adapter into each end-cap and seal with epoxy.

3. Drill a 1/2"-diameter hole 2" from both ends of the PVC pipe.

4. Coil the copper tubing and insert it into the PVC pipe.

5. Place a compression nut and ferrule on each end of the coil.

6. Insert the compression end of a 3/8" compression x 3/8" MPT adapter into each hole in the PVC pipe.

7. Thread the compression nuts onto the adapters and tighten. Seal the adapters with epoxy cement.

8. Coat the inside rim of an end-cap and the outside of one end of the PVC pipe with PVC cement. Place end-cap on pipe and repeat for other end. Be sure all sealing surfaces are evenly coated with the PVC cement to avoid leaks.

9. Wrap a couple of turns of Teflon tape around each 3/8" MPT, thread on the hose barbs, and lightly tighten. Do not overtighten.

10. Add the hoses and you're done! The key to success, however, is making sure you sanitize the inside of the copper tubing.

You may want to build a small stand for the chiller using strips of wood. Otherwise the pipe has a tendency to move around. You can either cut a rounded curve in two end pieces, or you can build a four-sided rack—whatever works for you.

Another method for "controlling" your chiller is to wrap a length of 16-gauge wire around the pipe just below one end-cap and twist the ends into a double wire. Bend the end lengths 90 degrees up past the end-cap, make a hook, and hang it from the brewpot handle. Remember: the simpler, the better.

HOSE COUNTERFLOW CHILLER

In the hose counterflow chiller, a copper tube is inserted inside a standard garden hose and the wort is pumped, or siphoned, so that it runs in a direction opposite to the water flow.

Before we delve into a description of making a chiller from scratch, we need to mention that the tube fittings can be bought already made. These fittings are produced by Listermann Manufacturing and are sold under the name Phil's Phittings. This fitting kit sells for about $15 and really makes building a chiller easy work.

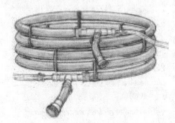

A hose counterflow chiller coiled up and ready for action

> ### MATERIALS FOR A HOSE COUNTERFLOW CHILLER
>
> *50' of 5/8" I.D. (inside diameter) garden hose*
> *50' of 3/8" O.D. (outside diameter) soft copper tubing*
> *6 1 1/2"-long pieces of 1/2" copper pipe*
> *2 1/2" copper tees*
> *2 1/2" copper end-caps*
> *6 hose clamps*
> *Plastic zip ties or wire*

Directions

1. Cut off 8" from each end of the hose and save for Step 9.

2. Insert a 1/2"-long copper pipe into each end of the copper tees and solder them in place.

3. Drill a 3/8"-diameter hole in the end of each copper end-cap. (Hint: Start with a 1/8" drill and work up to a 3/8" drill.)

4. Place an end-cap on one end of the long leg of the tees and solder into place.

5. Uncoil the copper tubing and feed it through the garden hose.

6. Place a hose clamp on both ends of the hose.

7. Feed the end of the copper tubing through the tee assembly and onto the hose, then tighten clamp. Repeat for other end.

8. Solder the 3/8" tubing to the end-caps to seal.

9. Attach the hose ends to the short legs of the tees with hose clamps.

10. Wind the hose and tubing assembly into a coil around a large cylinder, such as your brewpot.

11. Secure the coils together with wire or zip ties.

12. To sanitize the chiller before using it for the first time, run a very hot solution of 75 percent water and 25 percent vinegar through the copper tubing.

> ### PLUMBING SETUP
>
>
> *In a hose counterflow chiller, a copper tube is inserted in a garden hose. Water flows through the hose (and over the tube) in one direction, while hot wort is pumped through the tube in the opposite direction.*

Mash Tuns

Making a mash tun means you are now going to make all-grain beers. Making all-grain beers does take more time, but we think it is well worth the control you gain when you produce your own malt sugars (instead of purchasing them in the form of liquid or powder extract). Three different mash tuns are presented here, and all three can be adapted for lautering and sparging as well.

The most important consideration when designing and building a mash and lauter tun is the ability of the vessel to hold hot (up to 180°F) liquid. A mash tun must be large enough and sturdy enough to hold at least 6 gallons of liquid. It should also be insulated; if it is not insulated, it should be made of an appropriate material that will allow you to apply direct heat to maintain the right mash temperature. The mash tuns described here can also be used as lauter tuns with the addition of a sparge water sprayer and a false bottom.

MASHING IN A PICNIC COOLER

Large, chest-style picnic coolers make ideal mash tuns because they are well insulated and inexpensive. For a 5-gallon setup, look for a 34-quart cooler (about $10 to $15). The next size up is usually the 48-quart cooler, which will handle 10- or 15-gallon batches without a problem. Although 48-quart coolers are larger than you'd really want when doing 5-gallon batches (they may give you a shallow grain bed), quite a few homebrewers use that size without a problem. For very large batches, 60- or 80-quart coolers are reasonable. One consideration when choosing a cooler is its resistance to heat. If you can find a brand that claims to withstand 170°F temperatures, you're ahead of the game. If not, you're still okay. Most of them don't warp too badly, and even if they do, they'll still hold heat well enough to mash—and besides, they're cheap. Building a new one every year or so is no big deal.

manifold

picnic cooler

Once you have the cooler, you may need to drill out a drainage plug if it doesn't already have one. Because we're using 1/2" diameter CPVC pipe for this project, drill a 5/8"-diameter hole (the outer diameter of a 1/2"-diameter CPVC pipe). Although the drainage hole in a cooler is usually on the side, having the hole in the bottom is actually a bit more workable in many situations. Next, you'll have to build a drainage manifold to lay in the bottom of the cooler.

MATERIALS FOR MASH-TUN CONSTRUCTION

6' of 1/2"-diameter CPVC pipe
4 90-degree elbows for 1/2"-diameter CPVC pipe
5 tee connectors for 1/2"-diameter CPVC pipe
Food-grade silicone or epoxy sealant
1/2"-diameter I.D. (inside diameter) poly tube
Picnic cooler
Tools
Hacksaw
5/8"-diameter drill bit and drill (if the cooler does not have a drain)

Directions

1. Measure the length of the cooler bed. Subtract 4" and cut four lengths of CPVC tubing to that length.

2. Measure the width. Subtract 4" and divide by three. Cut six lengths of CPVC tubing to that length. Cut one of these lengths in half. Now use a hacksaw and cut thin slots in all the pipes, about one-third of the way through. Assemble the manifold as shown in the illustration above.

3. You can glue the manifold together, but it will be easier to clean if you make it easy to disassemble. One idea that works well is to permanently glue the two end units together, and then just piece together the four long rods when it's time to brew.

One other idea that seems to work well is to replace the CPVC with copper pipe, which is readily available at most plumbing supply stores and is fairly inexpensive and easy to work with.

You could add a valve to the manifold outlet if you wish, but a simple and less expensive approach is to use a length of vinyl hose, a hose clamp, and a pinch-cock-type (siphon) clamp. Push a length of hose over the outlet tube and secure it with the hose clamp. Feed the hose through the siphon clamp. This will be your valve. By closing and opening this clamp, you can adjust the flow of your runoff. If you wish to use a valve, CPVC ball valves are available for about $3 to $5. Compression fittings with gaskets are also available for CPVC tubes, and if your cooler does not already have a drain plug in the wall, consider using one of these. Before drilling through the wall, remember that you could also go through the bottom rather than the side.

MASHING IN A WATER COOLER

The large, cylindrical water coolers that you often see on the back of construction trucks or on the sidelines of pro football games make ideal mashing vessels. They are available in sizes that are large enough for home mashing, and they are well insulated. The brand most often used by homebrewers is the Gott cooler, which is made by Rubbermaid.

Round water coolers make great mash tuns. You can use a vegetable steamer as a false bottom or, better yet, a colander.

This cooler is known to withstand the heat of a mash without warping, as often happens with cheaper coolers. The 10-gallon size is the one you'll want; it usually runs about $50 at outdoor or construction supply stores, although it can be found at discount warehouses for as little as $30.

An easy way to use the cooler is to put a vegetable steamer in the bottom of the cooler and then set the grains on that. We've found this works acceptably well, but it does tend to let a lot of grains through. Another idea is to get a colander that's smaller than the circumference of the cooler and set it upside down in the bottom of the cooler. You may want to rig some kind of drainage device, such as the JSP EasyMasher (available from Jack Schmidling Productions), to go inside the colander. Phil's Phalse Bottom (available from Listermann Manufacturing) is an excellent choice for use as a drainage system with the Gott coolers, and this is the method that we recommend. The Phil's Phalse Bottom is simply a heavy plastic cone with perforations. It's available at many homebrew supply shops.

You can also build a manifold, much like that described in the picnic cooler mash tun directions.

With the Gott cooler masher, you will need to install a valve of some kind. The push-button spigot is inadequate (unless you want to hold in the button for the hour or so that a sparge might take).

MODIFIED KEG WITH FALSE BOTTOM

Modified kegs, if not the most commonly used mash tun, are probably the most talked about and respected. Kegs are sturdy and inexpensive, and they work well. You can apply heat directly to them, and you can

Continued →

modify them with false bottoms and valves to make sparging simple. They are also easy to clean.

The first thing you will need is a legally obtained keg. Do not think that paying the deposit for a full half-barrel, consuming the contents, and then keeping the keg is a legal means of acquiring one. It is not. Instead, you will need to talk to the distributors in your area. Sometimes they are willing to help, and sometimes they'll barely give you the time of day. Other sources are salvage yards and scrap-metal dealers. Before you begin to modify your own keg, you will need an assortment of gear.

A modified keg with false bottom makes a long-lasting mash tun.

Note: *You are working with stainless steel, which is tough stuff. The basic rule when working with it is, the slower, the better. Take your time!*

MATERIALS FOR MODIFYING A KEG

3/8" copper tubing
8"-diameter perforated stainless steel for false bottom
1 3/8" compression nut and ferrule
2 3/8" male pipe thread (MPT) x 3/8" compression adapters
1 1/2" I.D. (inside diameter) stainless-steel washer
2 1/2" I.D. (inside diameter) nylon washers
1 3/8" ball valve with 3/8" female pipe thread (FPT)
12" square perforated stainless steel
Permanent marking pen
Lightweight oil
Teflon tape

Tools

Hearing and eye protection. *You are about to embark on the noisiest job you've ever started.*
Variable-speed saber saw or reciprocating saw. *A two-speed unit is not good enough; the slowest setting is still too fast.*
Five bimetal saw blades (32 *teeth per inch or better*). *You may need more. A small angle grinder would work fabulously for cutting a keg.*
Center punch (or nail and hammer)
3/8" electric drill, variable speed preferred
Assortment of drill bits
Grinding wheel

Directions

1. Without a blade in the saw, set the saber saw against the inside top of the keg. You are finding out how close you can cut to the handles, as the saw body will be the limiting factor.

2. Mark a point where the blade will be cutting. Draw a circle around the top inside of this mark. In our case, we were able to make an opening 12" in diameter in our keg.

3. With a center punch (or nail and hammer), mark a point 1/8" from the line inside this circle.

4. Drill a 1/4" hole at that point. (It is easier if you drill a smaller hole first and then enlarge it.)

5. Install a blade in the saw, oil it, and at a slow speed carefully cut out the top of the keg. Plan on spending at least 45 minutes on this phase.

6. With the grinding wheel in the drill, grind off all sharp edges.

7. Mark a point 3/8" above the bottom weld line.

8. Drill a 1/2"-diameter hole. (Again, start small, then enlarge the hole.)

Note: *You are done cutting and about to start assembling your mashing vessel. This is a good time to scrub the interior of the keg. It will save time later. Also, clean all parts before final assembly. That, too, will help.*

9. Place the stainless-steel washer and then a nylon washer on the pipe-thread end (the large end) of a 3/8" MPT x 3/8" compression adapter.

10. Insert this into the 1/2"-diameter hole. It will fit tightly, and you will have to use a wrench to finish the job. You may have to enlarge the hole slightly beyond 1/2".

11. Place the other nylon washer over the pipe threads.

12. Wrap Teflon tape around the threads.

13. Thread on a 3/8" ball valve and tighten. Be sure to use a wrench on the inside to hold the adapter in place.

14. Drill a 3/8"-diameter hole in the center of the perforated metal (false bottom).

15. Bend the end of the 3/8"-diameter copper tubing to 90 degrees. This bent end goes through the false bottom.

16. Set the false bottom and tube assembly in the bottom of the keg.

17. Measure and cut the copper tubing so that it fits into the inside 3/8" compression fitting.

18. Attach the tubing to the 3/8" compression fitting with a compression nut and ferrule.

19. Add a 3/8" MPT x 3/8" compression fitting to the ball valve output. By using a 3/8" compression nut, you can either connect this to your counterflow chiller or add a small piece of 3/8" copper tubing for a spigot and attach a vinyl hose.

Note: *Instead of using the adapters, washers, and all, you could just take the keg and have two 3/8" female nipples welded to the hole. A welded nipple will also be easier to clean and sanitize. You would need a 3/8" male nipple to attach the ball valve and a 3/8" MPT to 3/8" compression adapter to attach the copper tube. Wrap the male threads with Teflon tape before installing.*

Before you start brewing for the first time, fill the keg with 12 gallons of water and add 1 gallon of white vinegar. Bring the mixture to a full boil and boil it for about 15 minutes. Drain. Now everything should be ready for your first batch in your new mash tun.

SPARGING TIPS

To introduce sparge water to the grain bed in your picnic cooler, water cooler, or modified keg mash tun, you can construct a simple sparge sprayer out of CPVC pipe. Simply obtain two lengths of thin CPVC supply line (3/8" will be fine) and cut one to the length of your cooler or to the diameter of your modified keg (the other length will be slighter longer than the width of your cooler or the diameter of your keg). Next, cap one end of this pipe and drill very small holes in the pipe (see illustration below).

To do this, we acquired a couple of 1/32" drill bits from a hobby shop (they break easily!) and drilled holes about 1/2" apart on one side only along the entire length of the pipe. Glue the second length of CPVC, which is cut a bit longer than the cooler's width or keg's diameter, to the long tube and at a right angle to it. The second pipe simply supports the sprayer and provides stability when it's positioned over the top of the cooler.

Now push the vinyl tube over the end of the CPVC tube. Depending on the size of your hose, you may have to add a hose barb adapter to hook the CPVC to the vinyl hose. If you use 1/2"-diameter CPVC pipe, a 5/8"-diameter I.D. (inside diameter) poly hose will fit tightly over the end. Then siphon the sparge water into the sprayer.

This is a bottom view of the sprayer: The holes need to point down to spray onto the grain bed.

Kegging

If there's one gadget that marks the transition from the casual homebrewer to the die-hard hobbyist, it's the keg system. Bottles are fine when you're starting out and not sure how dedicated you are to the hobby; but once you're hooked, the advantages of kegs over bottles are just too obvious to be ignored.

When you bottle, you've got 50-some bottles to wash and sanitize for every batch, and it takes a lot of time to fill and cap each one. Whereas beginning homebrewers worry about the cost of kegging setups, experienced homebrewers willingly spend the money. It's a trade-off between time and money.

MAKING A KEG SYSTEM

There are, of course, benefits to bottles too. They're easy to carry and hand out to friends. They're easy to store for long periods of time. They're easy to send to competitions. As we've said, it's a trade-off. You can still fill bottles with a keg system setup, and we've included the counter-pressure bottle filler project just for you.

The kegs used by homebrewers are usually used soda kegs. These are available at many homebrew supply shops. Many homebrewers get their kegs by buying excess kegs from local soda-bottling companies, from restaurants, or from junk dealers.

A complete kegging setup includes: a stainless-steel keg, a CO2 tank, a regulator with pressure gauge, and various taps, hoses, and connectors.

When you buy from these sources, you'll need to refurbish the keg. Homebrewers often refer to these kegs as Cornelius kegs, after one of the companies that makes them. Yours may or may not be a Cornelius keg; it could be a Firestone or John Wood.

If you've ever thought about getting into kegging and want to use refurbished soda kegs, now may be your last chance. Soda companies are increasingly abandoning kegs for plastic bags. Now easy to come by cheaply, the supply of kegs will dry up once the soda companies switch.

There are two important things to know about any keg you're buying: size and lock type. Most homebrewers use 5-gallon kegs, the most commonly available size. You can also find 3-gallon and 10-gallon kegs. Foxx Equipment sells new kegs in both 3-gallon and 5-gallon sizes. The locks can be either the pin type or the ball type. You can tell which is which by looking at the hose connectors (fittings) on your keg. If there are two knobs (pins) sticking out from the base of one fitting and three knobs sticking out from the base of the other, it's a pin lock. You slide steel hose connectors over these pins and then twist to lock the hoses onto the keg. Ball-lock valves, which are smooth all the way around, use a locking ring to attach the hoses. Whichever type of lock you prefer, get several kegs, and make sure they all have the same type of lock (or get two CO2 supply lines).

The CO2 tanks are large steel cylinders containing pressurized carbon dioxide. They are available in different sizes—the smallest used by homebrewers is referred to as a 5-pound tank, the largest, a 20-pound tank. A 10-pound tank is also available. The 20-pound tank is preferred by many of the more serious homebrewers because it means fewer trips to a gas supplier to get it filled. At the top of the CO2 tank is a valve handle for turning the flow on and off. The regulator and gauges attach to a threaded nut on the side of the tank.

The regulator reduces the high pressure of gas coming out of the cylinder to the pressure you want going into your keg. This is accomplished simply by turning a screw on the regulator. Attached to the regulator is a gauge that shows the pressure of gas leaving the regulator. If you've got a second gauge, it shows the pressure of gas coming into the regulator (the pressure of the CO2 tank). Many regulators also come with a check valve, or there is one attached to the gas-out line.

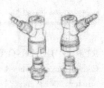

Typical pin and ball locks commonly found on kegs used by homebrewers. A pin lock has knobs or pins that fit into each other. A ball lock has a locking ring.

You'll also need a keg connector on each valve: one for the gas line to the CO2 tank, the other to your tap. The two connectors are different, and you'll need one of each. Further, the connectors are not interchangeable, making it impossible (well, in theory it's supposed to be impossible) to connect a line to the wrong valve (assuming you put

Continued →

the right connector on the right line). You may also need a barbed connector to attach to your regulator.

Most homebrewers use a plastic tap faucet attached to a length of plastic hose as their tap. The plastic taps, which are inexpensive and can be taken apart for easy cleaning, are often listed in supply catalogs as "picnic faucets." If you happen to get your hands on an extra refrigerator, you can modify the fridge and put a tap in the door.

PORTABLE TANKS AND CO2 SOURCES

Very small portable CO_2 tanks, which you can fill from your larger supply tank, are also available to homebrewers who want to take a keg to a party without bringing along a big pressure tank. You can find portable tanks in sizes as small as 3H ounces. West Creek Home Brewing also has some nifty gadgets for handling CO_2, such as a cap for charging a PET (polyethylene terephthalate) bottle to 30 psi as a portable CO_2 source.

Another source of tanks and gas is your local compressed-gas dealer. This could be a welding shop or a business dealing exclusively with compressed gas. Check your phone book for more information. These places sometimes offer what is called a "lifetime lease" on a tank. Effectively you buy a tank and every time you need a refill you bring in the tank, pay the refill charge (for a 20-pound tank, it's usually less than $20), leave the empty tank, and walk out with another filled and certified tank. You never have to worry about a bad tank—a rare event in any case. The vendor takes the empties and recertifies them (if necessary), then fills and "sells" them to someone else. A lifetime lease may cost about $75.

Note: *Tanks are required to have certificates showing that they have been pressure-tested. This is done (if needed) when you fill the tank. If a tank fails a pressure test, the certifier will drill a hole in it, preventing it from being used again.*

REFURBISHING USED KEGS

Okay, you've managed to obtain some old kegs from a soda bottler…what next? Now you've got to clean out those kegs and replace the rubber seals.

Most homebrew supply stores either have these parts or can get them. Foxx Equipment also sells all the gaskets as well as replacement poppets (spring valves inside a fitting) and other parts. Gaskets cost anywhere from about 25 cents to about a dollar each, and $5 will get you a complete set. Poppets are cheap too, usually less than $2 apiece.

MATERIALS FOR REFURBISHING A USED KEG

Rubber gasket for the lid
Rubber O-rings for the two valve fittings
Rubber O-ring for the gas dip tube
Rubber O-ring for the liquid dip tube

Directions

1. Release any pressure left in the keg. Use the pressure relief valve if the keg's got one; otherwise, press down with a screwdriver on the gas-in line.
2. Remove the lid by lifting up on the bail (the release handle).
3. Use a wrench to remove the two valve fittings. There will be tubes attached to the fittings inside the keg. Pull these out, too.
4. Examine the poppets. If they are damaged or worn, replace them.
5. Clean the keg with TSP, B-Brite, iodophor, or similar cleaner, as described below.
6. If the liquid (long) and gas (short) tubes are plastic, consider replacing them.
7. Replace O-ring gaskets on the liquid tube and gas dip tube.
8. Replace O-rings on the outside of the valve fittings.
9. Reassemble the tubes and fittings, screwing them back onto the keg.
10. Replace the gasket on the lid.

CLEANING SODA KEGS

Although homebrewers often praise stainless steel because it is easily sanitized, keep in mind that older beer kegs (and some kegs from Europe) are aluminum, and some of the cleaning agents used for stainless steel can damage aluminum.

The best sanitizing solutions to use with kegs are iodophor and trisodium phosphate (TSP). Use a plastic scrubber to loosen deposits or settled matter on the insides of kegs. TSP can be left to soak in the keg; if you get a used keg, soaking it overnight or for a couple of days will not hurt the surface. You can also store your unused kegs with a TSP solution in them.

Sometimes a layer of beer matter can settle and harden onto the bottom of a keg; this is referred to as "beer stone." If beer stone begins to build up in your keg, you can remove it with an acid solution. Let the keg soak for 2 to 6 hours. Use food-grade phosphoric acid in a solution at a strength of 1.7 to 2.0 pH and a temperature of 120° to 130°F. Then scrub the stone with a plastic abrasive. The acid dairy rinse is perfect for removing beer stone. Beverage line cleaner may also be useful.

When you're cleaning kegs, keep in mind that household bleach should never be used. Bleach is an effective sanitizer for glass and plastic surfaces, but it will corrode stainless steel. Stick to iodophor or TSP.

MODIFYING REFRIGERATORS FOR KEGS

The first order of business for accommodating kegs to fit your refrigerator is to remove the shelves. A soda keg sits about 2 1/2' high, a 5-pound CO_2 tank about 1 1/2' high. You'll probably want these to sit upright, so removing the shelves is a necessity. You may also want to look at the bottom shelf to see how it's supported. Often the bottom shelves are made of glass and are supported on the sides by molded plastic, and sometimes in the middle by a brace. You may want to remove this shelf and replace it with something a bit sturdier, such as a piece of 1/2" plywood braced under the middle and sides by 2" by 4" braces. A keg weighs about 50 pounds when full, so the shelf and supports need to be pretty strong.

Most homebrewers like adding tap handles to the outside of the fridge so they don't have to open the door every time they want a beer.

This is a fairly straightforward modification. The tap handles and shanks that go through the door are available from Foxx Equipment and most likely your local homebrew store. The size you get will depend on the thickness of your refrigerator door (or side wall). If you're drilling through the side wall, be aware that some refrigerators have gas lines running in the walls. If you puncture one of these, the refrigerator will be useless. If the side of the refrigerator is warm to the touch, it probably contains gas lines.

MATERIALS FOR MODIFYING A REFRIGERATOR

Beer shank	*Beer faucet*
Wall flange	*Tap handle*
Flanged jam nut	*Drip tray*
Tail piece and hex nut	

Directions

1. Measure the thickness of the refrigerator wall before ordering your shank. You'll probably want about a 4" or 5" shank, but the length depends on the thickness of the refrigerator wall.

2. Drill a hole through the refrigerator wall to accommodate the shank.

3. Put the wall flange on the shank.

4. Insert the shank through the door.

5. Apply a small amount of caulk around the area where the shank passes through the door, inside and out, and secure with the flanged jam nut on the inside.

6. Attach the tail fitting with the hex nut onto the shank on the inside.

7. Screw the faucet onto the outside of the refrigerator.

8. Screw the knob onto the faucet.

9. Screw the drip tray onto the refrigerator about 1' or so below the faucet (allow enough space to accommodate your largest beer glass).

10. Attach your beer line to the barbed tail fitting, then tighten the hose clamp.

11. Connect to your keg and enjoy.

If you store beer in a keg in a refrigerator, install a tap on the door or side wall. You won't have to open the door each time you want a beer, and it looks professional.

COUNTER-PRESSURE BOTTLE FILLER

With your keg system in full operation, you probably find that you have a lot of extra time on your hands with no more bottles to fill. We suggest you use that free time to build a counter-pressure bottle filler. The counter-pressure bottle filler lets you store and carbonate your beer in a Cornelius keg and then apply CO2 pressure to fill a bottle, purging air and nearly eliminating the chance of oxidized aromas and flavors. It also fills bottles gently and retains the carbonation in the beer.

A counter-pressure filler assembly lets you store beer in a keg, then use CO2 pressure to fill bottles. Note the No. 2 stopper, which you place in the opening of your clean and empty beer bottles.

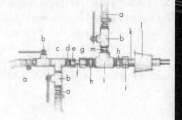

Parts List

a — 1/4" MPT x 1/4" hose barb

b — 1/4" MPT x 1/4" FPT on-off valves

c — 1/4" FPT tee

d — 1/4" MPT x 1/4" comp adapter

e — 1/4" compression nut and ferrule (not shown)

f — 18" long 1/4" copper or stainless tubing

g — 3/8" compression nut with 3/8" O.D. (outside diameter) O-ring (instead of ferrule)

h — 3/8" comp x 3/8" MPT adapter

i — 3/8" FPT tee

j — 3/8" compression nut with ferrule (not shown)

k — 3/8" copper or stainless tubing, 2" long

l — #2 stopper with 3/8" hole

m — 3/8" MPT x 1/4" FPT adapter

MATERIALS FOR A COUNTER-PRESSURE BOTTLE FILLER

3	1/4" MPT x 1/4" hose barbs
1	1/4" FPT tee
1	3/8" FPT tee
1	1/4" MPT x 1/4" compression fitting
2	3/8" MPT x 3/8" compression adapters
3	1/4" MPT x 1/4" FPT on-off valves
1	1/4" compression nut and ferrule
2	3/8" compression nuts and ferrule (only one ferrule needed)
1	3/8" O.D. (outside diameter) O-ring
1	3/8" MPT x 1/4" FPT adapter
1	No. 2 drilled rubber stopper
1	5/16" hose tee for gas line
1	18"-long, 1/4"-diameter tube (stainless steel, brass, or copper)
1	2"-long piece of 3/8"-diameter tube
	Teflon tape

Directions

1. Wrap the male connectors with Teflon tape.

2. Assemble according to the diagram. You'll want the tee for hooking up the CO2 gas line as shown in the illustration.

To use the counter-pressure bottle filler, first sanitize it with iodophor. Do not use chlorine bleach. Connect everything as shown in the illustration. Insert the filler into a clean bottle. Make sure the stopper seals well, then turn on the gas valve (valve A) to pressurize. Turn off the gas valve A. Turn on the beer valve (valve B). Open the

Continued →

bleed valve (valve C). As the gas escapes from the bleed valve, the beer in the keg will be at greater pressure than that of the bottle and will slowly fill it. When it gets full, close the beer valve (valve B). Remove the filler, then close the bleed valve (valve C) and cap the bottle. If you close the bleed valve too soon, there will be pressure in the bottle and there will be a spray of foam when you remove the filler.

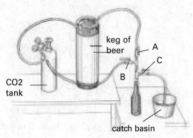

To use a counter-pressure bottle filler, turn on gas valve (A) to pressurize. Then turn off gas valve, and turn on beer valve (B) and open the bleed valve (C). Gas will escape from the bleed valve and the beer in the keg will be at greater pressure than that of the bottle and will slowly fill it.

TRANSFERRING LIQUID UNDER PRESSURE

Once you have a kegging system with a CO2 tank and regulator, you can use pressurized carbon dioxide to move liquids from one vessel to another without having to rely on siphons and gravity. For example, you can force-rack beer from one carboy to another under CO2 pressure, avoiding the worries of starting the siphon and reducing oxidation risk by purging vessels with a blanket of CO2 gas. Transfers can thus take place in a "closed" environment, which means that the vessels are never open to airborne contamination risks.

1. Seal up the container holding the liquid.
2. Attach a tube from the liquid to the empty vessel.
3. Attach a gas-in line to the carboy cap, keg, or whatever.
4. Slowly open the gas line.

If you have a kegging setup, there is no need to siphon beer from your carboy. Use your CO2 cylinder and a racking configuration like this.

Brewery Design

If you have committed to all-grain brewing and use modified kegs as your brewing vessels, you will want to arrange your vessels in such a way as to take advantage of process flow and gravity. A tower design, the most common, is time-tested and has been used for hundreds of years, if not thousands. It starts with grain on the highest level of the brewery, where it's milled and sent down a chute into the mash tun. From there, the mash is lautered (run off and sparged) and the liquid is piped down a level to the brew kettle. After the boil, the hot wort is chilled and sent down another level to the fermenter.

BUILDING A TOWER BREWERY STAND

The stand is best set up in a permanent location. Using modified kegs as brew vessels, the overall dimensions are 7' high by 4 1/2' wide by 1 1/2' deep. Construct it from 1" angle iron, or use uni-struts (steel angles with predrilled holes) if you do not have access to a welder. The top level should be 5' high, the second level 36" high, and the bottom level about 12" off the ground. The width and length of each level of platform will depend on the size of your brewing equipment. Generally, for modified kegs, about 18" square will work for the shelves. Widen the middle level for the longer dimensions of a picnic-cooler mash tun.

Make sure you have a small stepstool for filling the top pot, as you do not want to lift a full pot to that height. This is a good application for a pump. If you wish, a single, large propane tank can be strapped onto the outside of the frame instead of messing about with two or three bottles. Indeed, there may be a substantial savings on propane costs in doing this. Many places charge a flat rate to fill a 20-pound bottle, regardless of how much is left in the tank. If you brew many batches, it may be a better idea to connect to a large outdoor propane tank and really save some money.

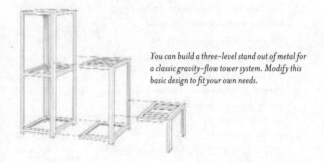

You can build a three-level stand out of metal for a classic gravity-flow tower system. Modify this basic design to fit your own needs.

MATERIALS FOR A TOWER STAND

Legs
- 4 60" x 1" lengths of angle iron
- 2 36" x 1" lengths of angle iron
- 3 12" x 1" lengths of angle iron

Shelf supports
- 24 18" x 1" lengths of angle iron with ends cut to 45 degrees

Cooker shelf cross member
- 6 17 3/4" x 1" lengths of angle iron

Shelves for propane bottles
- 3 18" square sections of expanded aluminum or steel

Heat shields
- 2 18" x 24" long thin aluminum sheets
- 3 low-profile 125,000 BTU cookers with bolting brackets on bottom (Camp Chef—Low Profile)

Directions

1. Cut out all materials as indicated above.
2. Assemble four shelf supports into a square.
3. Select three shelf frames for the top cooker shelves.

4. Measure the distance between the bolt holes on the cookers. Add 1 to this number and subtract from 18. Divide by 2. Measure in this distance from the ends, and set two cross members at this point and weld. Do the same for the other two shelves.

5. Set the cookers in the center of one of the shelves, mark the mounting holes onto the frame, and drill holes into the cross members. Do the same for the other two shelves. (Do not mount the cookers yet.)

6. Clamp the 60" legs onto one of the cooker shelves and weld.

7. Clamp a propane bottle shelf 1" from the bottom of the 60" legs and weld.

8. Clamp and weld a second propane shelf 28" from the top of the bottom shelf.

9. Clamp and weld the two 36" legs onto another cooker shelf.

10. Clamp the last propane shelf 1" from the bottom of the 36" legs and weld.

11. Weld the middle shelf assembly to the first shelf assembly.

12. Clamp the two 12" legs onto the last cooker shelf and weld into place.

13. Weld this short shelf assembly onto the main shelf assembly.

14. Bolt one propane cooker onto each of the cooker shelves (top shelves).

15. Using either screws or pop rivets, attach a heat shield to the legs next to the center cooker; then do the same for the bottom cooker. These prevent the bottles of propane from getting too hot.

16. Put the expanded metal sections on the propane-bottle shelf frames. These sections do not need to be anchored to the frames, but you can do so if you wish.

17. Set the assembly in its permanent home.

18. Add propane bottles, and connect them to the cookers. *Check for gas leaks at all connections!* (A mixture of dish soap and water applied to each connection will bubble if there is a gas leak.) Leaks can be sealed with Teflon tape.

19. Add kettles and you are ready to brew.

The completed stand for a gravity-flow tower system: As you can see, it is best set up in an extremely well-ventilated location.

Note: *If you take this to a professional welder and he makes some recommendations that are different from those stated here, please listen to him. He may suggest improvements that could strengthen the system.*

Many homebrewers use other types of mashing vessels, such as picnic coolers with manifolds. These, too, are easily adapted to the gravity-flow tower model. Simply put a burner and a pot for heating water on the top level. Put the cooler mash tun, complete with sparge apparatus, on the second level; then run a tube from the hot-water pot to the sparge apparatus. Finally, drain the mash tun directly into a brew kettle on the lower level.

To build such a stand, assemble the large- and small-shelf stands as described in the gravity-flow tower system. The center shelf will need to be 28" wide for a 48-quart cooler, or 36" wide for an 80-quart cooler. As you will not be adding the low-profile cooker to this shelf, the stand will also need to be 6 to 8" taller, depending on the style of cooker used. Weld this center stand to the tall and short stands. Be sure to use a heat shield next to the burner to prevent melting the cooler.

Making Homemade Wine

Robert Cluett

Illustrations by Sue Storey

Wine is the easiest alcohol to make. It does not require the fastidious temperature control involved in brewing beer. Unlike distilled spirits, it requires no still and does not invite the curiosity of the revenue agents—unless you undertake to sell the wine you produce, and we do not recommend doing that. You can make fine wines from grapes or other fruits, or you can make it from vegetables, grains, or flowers.

As with any specialty, winemaking has a language all its own. Before we go any further, let me introduce you to some of the terms.

Champagning: The process of trapping carbonation into a still wine with a second, sealed ferment.

Cider: The customarily low-alcohol (6 to 9 percent) wine made from apples. Sometimes made sparkling, usually made still.

Fining: The removal of small-particle cloudiness from a wine.

Maderize: To cook a wine until it is like a Madeira. Wines stored at too high a temperature often will be said to be maderized.

Must: The dense liquid from which a wine begins. The point at which must stops being must and starts being wine is indefinite, but is generally conceded to be about SG (specific gravity) 1.030, or the point at which 60 percent of the sugar is converted into alcohol to give an alcoholic content of at least 7 percent.

Pearl: The carbon dioxide bubbles in a very slightly fermenting wine. Some wines, designed for a texture between champagne and still wine, are bottled when there is still a slight pearl in them.

Perry: Cider made from pears. See *cider*.

Plonk: A corruption of the French *blanc*, commonly used to denote a common white wine of French origin.

Rack: To siphon wine from one vessel to another.

Specific gravity: The density of a liquid as a fraction of the weight of water. A wine must with a lot of sugar in it will weigh between 8 percent and 12 percent more than water, hence will have a specific gravity (SG) of between 1.080 and 1.120. When these musts ferment out to the point where no sugar is left, they will give wines that weigh between 0.7 percent and 1.2 percent less than water (alcohol being lighter than water). The more alcoholic a finished dry wine is, the lower its SG.

Vinify: Literally, "to turn to wine."

Equipment

You do not need much equipment to make wine at home. Many of the items listed here may already be in your home. The rest should be available at any store that sells winemaking equipment. If there are no

Continued ➡

such stores in your area, you can order equipment from the suppliers listed in the back of this bulletin.

ESSENTIAL ITEMS

These are the pieces of equipment you will need to get started in home winemaking. **Air locks:** These let carbon dioxide gas out of the carboy and prevent air from getting in. Buy one for each carboy.

Carboys: Large glass vessels used as secondary fermenters. Carboys hold 5 gallons of liquid. You need an extra empty carboy to rack wine into, so buy one more carboy than you plan to make batches of wine.

Funnel: Buy a large one.

Hose and J-tube: For siphoning and keeping the siphon level above that of the dead yeast in the bottom of the vessel.

Hydrometer set: Includes a hydrometer to measure the sugar content in the must and a tall tube.

Nylon bag: Select a fine-mesh or medium-mesh bag, measuring 2 feet by 2 feet. It is used with a mallet to make a homemade juice extractor.

Plastic sheet: To cover the vat.

Spoon: A long-handled wooden spoon works best; but a plastic one is an acceptable substitute. Used for stirring the must.

Strainer: Any large kitchen sieve will do.

String: Take a string that is 4 inches less than the circumference of your vat, and tie the ends to a 3-inch rubber band. Then you have an elastic tightener to hold the sheet on the vat.

Titration kit: Measures the acidity of the must.

Vat: You will need a large vessel, or vat, for the initial fermenting stage. I am partial to a 17-gallon garbage pail.

HELPFUL BUT NOT ESSENTIAL ITEMS

Corker: For inserting corks in bottles.

Crown capper: Needed if you intend to make sparkling wines or ciders.

Crusher: Necessary for any large-scale operation that works directly from fresh fruit. It is not necessary for 10-gallon or 20-gallon batches. Crushers can be rented, but if you intend to go to press frequently you will probably want to own your own.

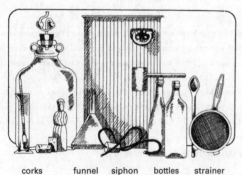

corks   funnel   siphon   bottles   strainer

Basic winemaking equipment.

De-stemmer: For taking stems off fresh grapes. A large wooden spaghetti server makes an adequate substitute.

Filter and pump: These are used as a last-ditch method of clarification. I have used one once in 250 batches of homemade wine.

Gallon jugs: These are useful in the stage between carboy and bottle. Sometimes restaurants give them away.

Vinometer: Measures alcohol in wines that are fermented out and dry; it is not useful for wines with residual sugar in them.

Wine press: Device for pressing fruit either before or at the end of the first fermentation in the vat. It is necessary if you are making over 100 gallons a year of fresh grape or fresh fruit wine.

Ingredients

Listed below are the ingredients you will need, in addition to fruit, to make wine at home.

ESSENTIAL INGREDIENTS—LONG SHELF-LIVES

Acid blend: Raises acidity level of low-acid must and flabby finished wine.

Campden Tablets: Disinfects fresh must and wines during racking.

Grape tannin powder: Enhances the flavor and gutsiness of cider, perry, and wines made from concentrates.

ESSENTIAL—BUT PERISHABLE—INGREDIENTS

Disinfectant: Solution of water and potassium metabisulfite crystals, kept in gallon jug. Absolutely essential for cleanliness.

Pectic enzymes: Removes the pectic haze from fruit wines and is put into the must just before yeast. It has a 3-month shelf life.

Yeast culture, liquid or powdered: Essential to fermentation, the yeast organisms turn sugar to alcohol. It has a one-year shelf life if kept unopened in the original sealed jar or packet.

OPTIONAL INGREDIENTS

Finings: A powder used to remove microscopic particles that cloud wine.

Glycerine: Adds finish to table wines.

Oak chips: For adding barrel taste, especially to red wines.

Pure unflavored grain or grape alcohol: Fortifies port, sherry, and Madeira.

Sorbic acid (potassium sorbate): Stabilizes the wine before bottling.

Vitamin C tablets, 250 mg: Protects white wines from oxidation.

Basic Techniques of Winemaking

There are only 4 requirements for successful winemaking.

- *The weight or sugar content should be enough to read 1.060 to 1.080 on a hydrometer scale.* (All hydrometer readings in this book are given in the form of *specific gravity* (SG), that is, a fraction of the weight of water.)

- *The acidity of your must should measure .55 to .80 percent to prevent early deterioration.* Obtain this reading with your titration kit.

- *Proper temperatures must be maintained.* During the first 10 days of fermentation, the temperature of the must should measure at a maximum of 76°F for red wines and 70°F for fruit wines and white wines. The temperature of the must should never dip below 55°F. Remember that a fermenting must will generate quite a bit of heat.

Winemaking: Step by Step

1. *Wash the fruits, remove all stems and leaves. Then crush the fruit.*
2. *Add crushed Campden Tablets.*
3. *Test the must with a hydrometer and titration kit.*
4. *Add the yeast starter.*
5. *Cover the must tightly with a plastic sheet and secure it with a string.*
6. *When the weight of the must reaches SG 1.025 to 1.030, transfer the must to a carboy and fit the top with an air lock.*
7. *Rack the wine into a secondary fermenter.*
8. *Fine the wine with a special gelatin solution and rack again.*
9. *Bottle the wine.*

- *Absolute cleanliness.* This means keeping air out of contact with fermenting juice and wine, and it means meticulous sterilization of all equipment both before and after use. To sterilize equipment, use a sulfite solution made from crystals that are available from your wine-supply dealer.

Given these things, you need only a live yeast culture, some primitive equipment, and some patience in order to make good wine. We shall deal with all these things in detail—except, that is, the patience, for which I do not have the space or the time. As we go along, you will see that there is nothing complicated or even difficult about making wine.

There are 8 stages of winemaking, and we will take you through the first 7: preparation, primary fermentation, secondary fermentation, aging in the carboy, fining (an optional stage), finishing and bottling, and cellaring. Drinking the wine is the final stage, and you are on your own for that.

The processes we describe take days, weeks, and months. There is time to master each step as you go along. You will make your wine one stage at a time, beginning with the preparation.

PREPARING THE EQUIPMENT

Careful sterilization of all gear with a sulfite solution is essential. Here are a few rules for cleaning equipment.

- Never use detergent; use only a chlorine solution (and only for stains) and a sulfite solution, mixed in your own cellar with a gallon of warm water and a packet of crystals from a winemakers' supply store.

- Glassware should be rinsed inside with warm water first, then drained, then rinsed with sulfite solution. If the glassware is going to be stored, it should be stoppered with a small amount of solution in it (1/8 inch on the bottom). Bottles about to be used immediately *may* be rinsed again with water, but it is not necessary.

- Corks and screwcaps should be sterilized by a 60-second total immersion in sulfite solution; do not boil corks.

- If fruit pulp sticks to your gear, use a *plastic* abrasive pad and hot water to remove it.

- When putting away our primary fermenters for a while, rinse with sulfite solution, cover with a plastic sheet, and secure with a tight string.

PREPARING THE FRUIT

After you have removed all the stems and leaves from your washed fruit, it is ready for crushing. You can use a commercially available crusher for this stage, or you can improvise with a large plastic container and

Continued ➔

wooden mallet. With white grapes, as well as with many tree fruits, press out the vegetable matter in a press, so the must consists of nothing but juice. With red grapes, you will ferment first for 5 to 10 days and then go to the press. If you are making no more than 35 or 40 gallons a year, you can use a medium-mesh or fine-mesh nylon bag to get the effect of a pressing. Just crush your fruit in the bag, then squeeze the juice out.

The Garden Way cider press can be used to crush fruit for wine.

Add hot water and other ingredients (see recipe section) to the crushed fruit, and you will have a must, or a liquid that is nearly ready to ferment. Add to the must some Campden Tablets, which will keep it free from debilitating organisms.

TESTING THE MUST

First, test the must with a hydrometer. If the must weight is between 1.080 and 1.095, you won't want to tinker. If it is below 1.080, you will want to add sugar; if it is above 1.095, you will probably want to cut the must somewhat with water, unless you want a very sweet or alcoholic wine. Temperature has a large effect on specific gravity readings, and hydrometers are calibrated to be accurate when the must is at 60 or 68°F.

Measure specific gravity with a hydrometer. Some hydrometers are calibrated to read accurately at 60°F, others at 68°F. Make sure you are reading your hydrometer at the proper temperature. To read a hydrometer, ignore the way the liquid curves against the stem and tube because of surface tension, and take the reading from the level portion of the liquid.

Next, test the must for acidity with a titration kit. If it is a red must and the acidity is .65 percent, or a white must and the acidity is .75 percent, you will be happy indeed. If your acidity is too low, add an acid blend (citric, malic, or tartaric). With shipped California grapes, the natural acidity will be too low. If it's too high (and with Eastern grapes, it may well be), you may want to cut the must somewhat with a sugar and water solution of weight 1.090, or with a dilute low-acidity must made from a hot-climate concentrate (also available from wine-supply stores). Some of my friends ferment their Eastern grapes at a natural acidity of 1.5 percent, but they are patient people: that kind of acidity level makes for either a disagreeable little wine or a long wait—about 5 years (wine loses acidity over time).

You can get to this stage of the process much more quickly and easily by using a grape concentrate from a winemakers' supply store or by using grape juice shipped to a juicer in your nearest urban area. You should not be put off by previous unhappy experiences with concentrates. In the last few years, Wine-Art Ltd. of Toronto, a marketer of home wine products, has been selling concentrates from Australia that make wines indistinguishable from those made with fresh grapes.

ADDING THE YEAST CULTURE

The last item of preparation is adding a yeast culture, which should have been mixed with a starter solution 2 to 3 days before the must was crushed or put together. Here is a formula for starting yeast for a 5-gallon batch of wine.

3 ounces frozen orange juice concentrate

24 ounces water

6 ounces sugar

2 rounded teaspoons of ordinary yeast nutrient

Put the frozen orange juice, water, and sugar into a 2-quart saucepan, and bring the mix to a boil on the stove. When the mix boils, remove it from the heat, add the nutrient, and cover the pot until the mix cools to room temperature.

Transfer the starter mix to a sterilized 1-gallon jug, add the yeast culture, and stopper the jug with an air lock. After 24 to 36 hours, "islands" of active yeast should appear on the surface of the liquid. Give the jug a swirl every 6 to 8 hours. When the solution gets to an active ferment (much CO_2 is expelled through the air lock when you swirl), it is ready to add to the must.

Always prestart your yeast for any batch of wine 3 gallons or more. The recipe given above will handle any quantity of wine from 3 to 12 gallons; for larger quantities you will want to double, triple or quadruple the recipe. For smaller quantities, add the yeast culture directly to the must from vial or packet, since the smaller quantities of must will dilute the culture less than larger ones.

PRIMARY FERMENTATION

After you have adjusted weight and acidity, and added a yeast culture, the vat in which this first (primary) fermentation goes on should be covered with a tight-fitting plastic sheet, fastened with string. Once a vigorous, rolling ferment is started (24 to 48 hours), stir the must and push down the "cap" (the vegetable crust that will form on the top) twice a day. Use a well-sterilized wooden spoon.

Weigh the must every day after the third day, to see how rapidly the fermentation is going. A weight loss of .007 to .015 per day is good, more than that indicates that the must should be moved to a cooler place.

To secure the plastic sheet over the primary fermenter, I have invented an elasticized fastener I call "Cluett's String." I take a string that is 4 inches shorter than the circumference of my primary fermenter. Then, I tie the string to a 3-inch rubber band. This makes an easy-to-use string that secures a tight cover over the fermenter.

Test the must frequently with your best piece of winemaker's test equipment—your nose. The smell of a fermenting must is pervasive, at least in the space in which it is fermenting, sometimes throughout the house. If there is an aroma in addition to those of fruit and CO2 coming from the wine, do not be disturbed unless that aroma has a strong sulphur or vinegar cast to it. In that case, turn to our troubleshooting section.

When the weight reaches 1.025 to 1.030, transfer the wine to glass carboys with a siphon and J-tube. If you are making a red wine, press out the residual fruit left in the fermenting vat. (Here again, the nylon bag is a useful alternative to a press.) Stopper the carboys with air locks filled with sulfite solution to permit CO2 to escape and prevent air contact with the wine. Leave the wine in the primary fermenter for 5 to 10 days.

SECONDARY FERMENTATION

The next step is to rack the wine into freshly disinfected carboys for the secondary fermentation. To rack wine from a primary to secondary fermenter, place the vessel with the wine in it on a shelf or table at least 30 inches high. Put the sterilized carboy or jug on the floor. Take a 5-foot or 6-foot length of clear tubing with a J-tube on the end, and place the J-tube into the wine, on the bottom of the vessel. Apply suction on the plastic hose to fill it, and put the discharge end quickly into the vessel you are filling. When the wine is completely transferred, rinse and sterilize both the used vessel and the plastic tubing. Change the disinfectant in the air locks.

Until you are very experienced, check the weight of your wine at this point, too. A weight of 1.005 to 1.010 will be average, though a wine that started off very heavy (1.100+) will be fermenting slower at this point because its high alcohol content will inhibit yeast action. A wine with a vigorous yeast in it may well be below 1.000. As long as the wine is sending even the occasional bubble up through the air lock, it is actively fermenting.

AGING

Rack your wine again in another 6 to 12 weeks, adding 1 crushed Campden Tablet per gallon. I prefer a 6-week interval, especially with fruit wines. Three months after the second racking, you should rack again, adding more Campden Tablets. After this, rack every 6 months.

Change the disinfectant in the air locks every 3 months. SO2 in solution is highly volatile, and fruit flies, which tend to carry vinegar bacteria on them, are massively persistent. Fresh disinfectant in the air lock is the best way to keep them out.

To rack the wine to a secondary fermenter, use a plastic J-tube and siphon the wine from the first carboy to the second. Keep the original carboy 30 inches higher than the fresh carboy. Be sure that the end of the tube is completely submerged in the wine. This arrangement prevents the wine from coming in contact with air.

FINING

At the sixth month (perhaps even as soon as the sixth week with Cluett's Plonk, or the third month was some of the lower acidity wines from concentrate), you may want to fine your white wines.

Fining, the removal of small-particle cloudiness from a wine, was originally done with bull's blood or egg white, but both these items are messy. Far better to use a gelatin-based fining sold under several brand names. The most commonly used brand is Sparkalloid.

The special gelatin, in hot solution, is poured into a carboy of wine and coagulates around the small particles that cloud the wine, carrying them to the bottom of the carboy. After it has done its work completely (1 to 28 days), you can rack the clear wine off the fined gunk that has settled to the bottom of the vessel. The wine can then be stabilized (by adding 1 teaspoon of sorbic acid per gallon) and put into jugs or bottles, or simply left in the carboy to age further.

FINISHING

Between the seventh and the twelfth month you will bottle most white wines, some reds, and most other fruit wines. Make sure that there is no threat of renewed fermentation in the wine; if that occurs after the wine is bottled, you will get some nasty explosions in your cellar.

Preventing renewed fermentation can be done in either of 2 ways. One way is to keep the wine under an air lock until it reaches a weight between .993 (for a starting weight of 1.080) and .990 (for a starting weight of 1.100), and not bottle before. This can involve an indefinite wait. Fermentation can stick at weights like .996 or .998, which indicate *some* residual sugar in the wine and probably *some* residual live yeast. Wines can sit for 18 and 24 months at .998 and then suddenly reignite after a change in the weather. It seems to me best to stabilize the wine by adding 3/4 teaspoon of sorbic acid (potassium sorbate) per gallon, whatever the weight of a wine when bottling.

There is an alternative to bottling: aging the wine in a gallon jug between carboy and bottle. With wines for which I have further plans, such as champagning, I use an air lock on the jug; other wines get 3/4 teaspoon of sorbic acid and a screw cap. Using the gallon jug has many

Bottle capper

advantages. With jug wines like Cluett's Plonk, bottling is just a chore. It is far preferable to have a 4 wide-mouth, stoppered, 1-liter carafes that can be kept in the refrigerator. The wine will last nicely for 5 to 6

Continued →

weeks. A further advantage is that the gallon jug leaves you flexibility for blending wines, especially reds. Some of your wines will be too dark, some too light, some too tannic, some too smooth (yes, *too* smooth, a forecast of short life). Such wines, so long as they do not taste outright bad, will often benefit from being blended with wines of opposite character. I keep a few gallon jugs of elderberry-enriched Petite Syrah on hand to give backbone and color to the pale, pale California Carignane of which I make a carboy or so each year.

At this point (seventh month) you will probably want to add a packet of oak chips (available from your wine-supply dealer) to your better reds for about a month. This process adds oak tannin and barrel flavor to the wine and is generally beneficial. To remove the chips, rack the wine again.

After the oaking, which you may want to do a second time on some wines, taste the wine for finish, or ability to hang on the palate. First, swirl an inch of wine around in a large wine glass. If it leaves several glycerine streaks down the side of the glass (so-called legs), you have a good sign. Second, put the wine into your mouth, squeeze it into the corners back of your teeth and under your tongue, and then swallow. If the flavor of the wine and its intensity last after swallowing, then you have a second and wholly convincing good sign. If the wine throws no or few legs, or if it quits quickly after being swallowed, then add 4 ounces of glycerine to the carboy and repeat the 2 tests about 8 weeks later, adding more glycerine if the wine is still unleggy or faint-hearted on the palate. Some time around the eighteenth month, stabilize and bottle your better reds.

BOTTLING

I always bottle and cork my better wines. Although some people swear by plastic screw caps, most serious amateurs prefer cork. Cork breathes slightly and allows the very slow process of oxidation that facilitates the aging of the wine. The better the wine, the more worthy it is of being placed under cork.

Do not use recycled corks. Use new, waxed corks from a reliable supplier. And, the better the wine, the longer the cork you will need; your cork should be at least 1 1/4 inches long, with a diameter slightly larger than that of the mouth of the bottle.

Before bottling, prepare the corks. Place them in water that just has been boiled (never boil the corks), cover the vessel, and leave them for 5 minutes. Then place them in a sulfite solution, pushing them down in the solution to make sure they have been covered fully by the sulfite. Then they are ready to use, and you can siphon your wine into a sterilized bottle. Recycled *glass*—not plastic—bottles are okay, but make sure that they have been completely cleaned and rinsed with sulfite solution.

I always bottle and cork my better wines. You can use recycled glass soda bottles. These are some of the traditional bottle shapes. From left to right: Burgundy, sauterne, Rhine.

Many devices for driving home corks are available—from $2.00 wooden gadgets to $150.00 production-line devices. My own recommendation is the San-Bri handcorker from France, which retails for about $10.00 and is both quick and reliable. This corker has a metal collar for squeezing the cork and a piston for driving it home.

When you cork the wine, do not countersink the cork; keep it level with or slightly above the very top of the bottle opening. One further suggestion: If you use a hand corker of any kind, put the filled bottles into divided wine cases before corking them; this prevents the bottles from spontaneously overturning, spilling wine or breaking glassware.

As for putting a plastic or metal seal over the top and neck of the bottle, I do not recommend it. The capsule is strictly a decorative device, and it impedes the breathing of the cork.

CELLARING

After bottling, you are usually in for a wait of 6 months or more, possibly much more. Periodic checking is the key to timing the consumption of the wine at its peak point. Unless a wine is hideously astringent (in which case an annual check is enough), opening a new bottle every 6 months will be enough to keep you abreast of a wine's progress. You should always remember that patience can be a great healer of the problems of a wine. Several of my friends have produced wines they pronounced "undrinkable" at an early stage, only to see the wines turn highly drinkable some 3 to 5 years later. Don't give up too soon.

Much is made of "correct" storage and some of the myths are downright silly. There are, however, 4 basic rules for cellaring that have the force of sacred writ.

- Store wine away from light, especially direct sunlight or fluorescent fixtures; these kinds of light maderize wine, or make it go off in flavor.

- Store corked wines on their sides. If they are stored upright, the corks dry out, and air gets to the wine, ruining it eventually.

- Wine storage temperature should never go over 75°F, except for brief spans of time. At 75°F, wine begins to oxidize.

- Temperature in a wine storage area should be as steady as possible; changes should be gradual. A 68°- to 73°F storage area is far preferable to one whose range is 45 to 65°F, even though the first one makes a closer approach to the dangerous 75°F figure. Rises in temperature force wine through the cork; drops cause air to be sucked back in. The greater the changes in temperature a wine suffers, the greater the premature aging of the wine from overbreathing.

Follow these guidelines, and your cellar (or closet) will never ruin a well-made bottle of wine.

Day-to-Day Summary

The list below provides a day-by-day summary of all that I have described to this point.

Day 1	Start your yeast culture.
Day 3	Crush and de-stem the fruit. Add Campden Tablets. Weigh, test for acidity, adjust for sugar and acid balance. Press (white and most fruit wines), add yeast to the must in premixed starter.

Day 4 or 5	Break up the cap and stir. Do this daily there-after until wine reaches a specific gravity of 1.030.
Day 10	(Or when the wine reaches a specific gravity of 1.030.) Press out the grapes in red wines. Rack all wines into carboys and stopper with air locks and sulfite.
Day 25	Rack into fresh carboys. Add Campden Tablets.
Month 3	Rack again, and gain 3 months later, and every 6 months thereafter.
Month 7	(Or sooner.) Fine whites. Stabilize and bottle most whites, some reds. Red wines may be oaked.
Month 8	Check reds for finish. Add glycerine if needed.
Month 12	White wine bottled in month 7 is probably drinkable. Beaujolais from France and other light reds may also be ready to serve.
Month 18	Bottle better reds, wait minimum of 6 months to drink them.
Month 24 to year 40	Wines become drinkable and reach their age limits.

The rate of maturation, especially in red wines, will vary enormously with the style of vinification. You can vinify with the stems left on the grapes and get much more tannin and acidity into your wine; this will mean early harshness but longer life. Similarly, the more complete your pressing of the grapes, the more tannin, acid, and coloring matter will go into the wine. To vinify a red wine lighter, press sooner (but leave the wine in vat until its weight reaches 1.030), and press more lightly. Filtration, too, will make a lighter, faster-maturing wine.

Troubleshooting

Because each of us has a distinct style of going about things, we each will evolve a distinctive set of winemaking problems—and solutions for them. There are, however, certain problems that plague about 95 percent of the winemaking population. I have had all of them except mycoderma and vinegar, and these two I have suffered through vicariously with neighbors. What follows is a handy guide to the Universal Ills of Winekind, ordered by their probable place in the life of the wine.

1. *Stuck starter:* the yeast will not ignite. *The cause:* either the starter was too cool or the yeast too old. *The cure:* move the bottle to the top of the refrigerator or get new yeast. Prevent it next time by keeping the starter at a temperature of 68 to 72°F, and deal only with a first-class supplier.

2. *Stuck ferment in the primary fermenter* (first week to 10 days) has 4 probable causes.

- If the must or wine gets too hot (above 76°F), the heat will kill the yeast. *The cure:* move to a cooler place; add freshly started yeast culture. Prevent it next time by watching the temperature carefully.

- If the must is too cool (under 58°F), the yeast will not ignite. *The cure:* move the must to a warmer place. Watch the temperature carefully.

- If the must is too heavy (SG 1.115 or more), the sugar will inhibit fermentation. *The cure:* cut the must with water and acid blend. To prevent it, add the sugar in stages, rather than at the beginning. (I presume in this case you want a wine that is alcoholic or sweet or both.)

- If there is not enough nutrient for the yeast, fermentation is inhibited. This is especially likely with blueberry, pear, and peach must. *The cure:* add nutrient and fresh yeast culture. Next time, use a good recipe and follow it exactly.

3. *Stuck ferment in the secondary fermenter* (carboy) can be caused by all of the above. There is also a chance that the wine sticks (often at SG 1.012) for causes that are utterly mysterious. *The cure:* add "supernutrient," a magnesium and vitamin B mix that gives you a stronger kick than the ordinary ammonia and uric acid nutrient. If that fails, add fresh yeast culture. If that fails, wait for the wine to clear, and add it in a 1 to 5 ratio to other wines that are in a healthy secondary fermentation. Otherwise, resign yourself to having made a sweet wine. Before you bottle this wine, stabilize it.

4. *Hydrogen sulfide* (rotten egg aroma) is a special threat to low-acid wines, notably Cluett's Plonk and any wine made from vinifera grapes that have been shipped a long distance. It is recognizable by the unmistakable aroma of rotten eggs, and it usually occurs in the second to fourth week of the wine's life—although I have had it happen in hot weather during the fifth day. The cause is dead yeast and dead fruit pulp working together in low-acid wine. *The cure:* pour the wine (do not siphon) into a fresh carboy with 1 Campden Tablet per gallon. Use a funnel and make sure the wine is well-aerated. This is the only exception to the general rule to keep air out of wine. The prevention is to rack more often and watch acidity levels.

5. *Mycoderma* appear as grey islands of organisms on the wine; they are caused by poor sanitation. *The cure:* immediately strain the wine through fine cotton mesh and add 2 Campden Tablets per gallon. Once mycoderma have covered the entire surface of the wine, however, the wine is lost and must be thrown out. Prevent this by keeping your equipment sterilized and keeping air out of your wine.

6. *Vinegar smell and taste* is caused by poor sanitation. There is absolutely no cure, the wine is lost. Next time, keep your equipment sterilized and keep air out of your wine.

7. *Browning* occurs in white wines from using overripe fruit or allowing the wine to be in contact with air. There is no real cure, but the browning can be halted by adjusting the acid balance, adding ascorbic acid (250 mg/gallon), and keeping air out. Prevent browning by avoiding overripe fruit and contact between wine and air.

8. *Stuck fining* happens when the wine is too warm or too low in acid. *The cure:* add 1 tablespoon of acid blend to the carboy, decrease the temperature by 5°F. If this fails—and it will occasionally fail—rent a filter and pump from your friendly local supply house and use them. The next time, fine your wine at the proper temperature (65°F and under) and acidity (.06 or more).

9. *Explosion or spontaneous degorgement* is caused by residual sugar and live yeast in the wine when bottled. *The cure:* unbottle all remaining wine of that batch to a carboy, add potassium sorbate, and rebottle. Prevent this by reading the hydrometer carefully and stabilizing the wine before bottling.

10. Bottle odor when wine is opened has 2 causes.

- If there is a sulphur odor, it means there was much sulfite in the bottle when it was filled. *The cure:* decant the wine an hour before drinking; leave the decanter unstoppered. The SO2 will evaporate. Next time, when you bottle your wine, rinse the bottles with water after sterilizing them; or keep them upside down after sterilizing.

Continued →

- A mildew odor probably indicates a rotten cork. Sometimes it is caused by mildewed fruit. There is no cure; but open 2 or 3 bottles from the same batch to see if all are affected. If all the bottles have a mildew taste in the wine, scrap the batch. If only some bottles have mildew in the wine, recork the sound bottles. Prevent this problem with strict attention to sanitation. Also, pick over your fruit and remove suspect berries before you crush.

11. *Undue harshness* is caused by too much acidity, tannin youth, all 3, or any 2 thereof. *The cure:* patience, and blending with wine of opposite character. Give the swine at least a few months before blending. Prevent this by using the best suppliers you can find for your fruits and concentrates.

Recipes

These recipes were selected to cover cider, still wines, and champagne; the major kinds of materials (grape, other fruit, grain, and flower); and the tree and vine fruits most likely to come into the hands of home winemakers. If you are in possession of a material not specifically covered here (rice, for example), you can make a reasonable wine from the recipe in our group that is closest to your material. In the case of rice, for example, use the recipe for wheat.

Once you find that a recipe works reasonably well for you, you might find it interesting to try variations. For example, you can make a wine taste *drier* by adding a rounded teaspoon of acid blend per gallon. This, in fact, does not make the wine any drier (that is, lacking in sugar); it simply makes it more tart. You can make a wine *sweet* by starting with a SG of 1.115 or by stopping fermentation with sorbic acid at SG 1.002 to 1.005. You can give a wine *longer life* by adding extra tannin to the must before the yeast culture is added, or by the addition of stem, pip, or freeze-dried whole grapes. You can give a wine *more alcohol* by adding extra sugar to the must, preferably in stages after the fermentation has begun.

The recipes do not specify the amount of yeast needed. Here is the rule to follow. If you are making 3 gallons or less, simply add 1 packet or 1 vial of wine yeast culture to your must, when the must cools to 70°F or less. If you are making over 3 gallons, it is best to start your yeast in the way described above, then add it to the cooled must.

Where fruit concentrates are called for, I have not specified the exact amounts for some of the other ingredients. You will find instructions for adding the proper amounts of tannin, yeast nutrients, water, pectic enzymes, and so on, on the concentrate labels.

We will not repeat our injunctions about keeping everything absolutely sterile. In addition to this, it is a good protection to add a crushed Campden Tablet for each gallon of must at the beginning of fermentation, and to add an additional crushed Campden Tablet every second racking. When dealing with concentrates of juices, always ask the supplier about the need for Campden Tablets.

CLUETT'S PLONK

This makes an all-purpose dry white wine, ready to drink in 6 to 10 weeks.

1 unit (100 ounces) apricot concentrate

1 unit non-Labrusca white grape concentrate

corn sugar (75 percent of what is called for on concentrate labels)

grape tannin (as per labels)

yeast nutrient (as per labels)

acid blend (1 1/2 ounces less than combined total on labels)

warm water (as per labels)

yeast culture

pectic enzyme (as per labels)

Mix all the ingredients, except the yeast and pectic enzyme in a 17-gallon plastic vat. The water temperature should be 105 to 110°F. Cover the vat with a plastic sheet secured with a string. Put the vat in a place that is room temperature (65 to 75°F). Wait 24 hours, then measure the specific gravity and adjust to 1.080. Add water if the SG is too high; add sugar if it if too low. Measure acidity, and adjust to .55 to .60 percent by adding acid blend or water. If you add water, add sugar also to bring SG to 1.080. When the acid and SG levels are satisfactory, add the yeast culture and pectic enzyme.

Rack into carboys 5 days after fermentation starts; rack again in 10 days. This wine, with its high pulp content and low acidity, is very vulnerable to hydrogen sulfide and must be racked often. That's bad news, but one does not get a ready wine this quickly without paying a price.

THIS RECIPE MAKES 2 5-GALLON CARBOYS OR 50 BOTTLES—ALMOST A MONTH'S DRINKING.

FLOWER WINE

With honeysuckle and clover, some winemakers like to stabilize the wine with sorbic acid, then add sugar to SG 1.005 or 1.010 before bottling.

2 quarts flowers (dandelion heads, clover blossoms, or honeysuckle blossoms)

1/4 pound raisins, chopped

juice and peel of 2 oranges

juice and peel of 2 lemons

3 pounds sugar

1 ounce acid blend

1/4 teaspoon grape tannin

1 gallon boiling water

yeast culture

Gather the flowers on a dry, sunny day and make sure they are fully open. Remove the green parts, and put the flowers in a 2-gallon plastic vessel with the peel *only* of the oranges and lemons. Add boiling water. Cover the vat and secure, stirring the mixture every 12 hours to keep flowers saturated. After 4 days, strain off the liquid and press the pulp. Add to the liquid all the other ingredients, including the juice of the oranges and lemons, stirring well to dissolve the sugar. Adjust the must to SG 1.100. Ferment to SG 1.030, and remove to a gallon jug with air lock. Rack in 3 weeks, then in 3 months. When the wine is clear, stabilize and bottle.

THIS RECIPE MAKES 5 BOTTLES OR 1 GALLON—ALL DRINKABLE IN A YEAR.

APRICOT OR PEACH WINE

5 pounds apricots or peaches

1 gallon boiling water

2 1/4 pounds sugar

1 tablespoon cider blend

1/2 teaspoon yeast nutrient

1/2 teaspoon pectic enzyme

yeast culture

Stone the fruit and cut it up, placing it in a 2-gallon plastic vessel. Add the boiling water and steep for 2 days; strain out and press the fruit. Then add the sugar and acid blend. Adjust the must to SG 1.095. Then add the nutrient, pectic enzyme, and yeast, stirring well. Stir daily. At SG 1.030, remove to gallon jug with an air lock. Rack in 3 weeks, then at 3 months. When clear, stabilize and bottle.

THIS RECIPE MAKES 1 GALLON OR 5 BOTTLES.

CHAMPAGNE, COLD DUCK, AND CANADA GOOSE

The tax collectors, who levy heavier by far on bubbles than on alcohol, have made these wines much prized. Actually, the carbonic gas in such wines disguises true flavors, so champagning is an excellent expedient for wines that are free of mildew and vinegar, but still do not taste quite up to snuff.

For these sparkling wines, you will need 25 26-ounce pop bottles with crown cap tops and a capper.

1 5-gallon carboy of fully fermented wine that was started at SG 1.080 or less and has not been stabilized with sorbic acid

water

acid blend

10 ounces sugar

1 packet dry champagne yeast

If the wine you are using started at SG 1.090, add 1/9 of its volume in water, plus a level tablespoon of acid blend for each half gallon of water. If the wine you are using started at SG 1.095, add 1/6 its volume in water, plus acid blend at half a tablespoon per gallon of water.

Sterilize the bottles; then rinse them with plain water. In each bottle, place a rounded teaspoon of sugar and a few grains of the dry yeast. Fill the bottles to within 3 inches of the top. Cap with sterilized crown caps. Shake vigorously, and do so again on the seventh and thirtieth days. Before and after shaking, keep bottles upright.

After the thirtieth day, leave them for 2 months. At that point, remove a cap and check for fizz. If it's good, you can start drinking. If it's slightly torpid, you can start drinking anyway; but if you recap and wait another 90 days, your patience should be rewarded with more bubbles. This recipe makes 24 bottles or 2 cases, plus a test bottle.

Cluett's Plonk is an excellent champagne base; the bubbly from it has been compared by *cognoscenti* to the champagne made at Chateau Margaux. Another interesting base for bubbly is a mixture of 3 or 4 different carboy ends brought together in a gallon jug when you are

bottling; for this, you need only 5 bottles, 2 ounces of sugar, and 5 crown caps. The end product has been called Cold Duck and Canada Goose in North America and Hegel's Synthesis in Eastern Europe.

CIDER OR PERRY

A festive drink, 7 1/2 percent alcohol, with a distinct pearl. Great for summer parties! To make this recipe you will need 5 26-ounce soda bottles and 5 crown caps.

3 pounds apples or pears

2 Campden Tablets

1 gallon boiling water

25 ounces sugar

3 teaspoons acid blend

1 teaspoon yeast nutrient

1/2 teaspoon grape tannin

1/2 teaspoon pectic enzyme

yeast culture

Remove stems from fruit, cut the fruit into quarters, and crush it in a large plastic vessel. Dissolve Campden Tablets in the boiling water, and pour the water over the fruit, stirring the mix well. Tightly cover the vat. After 72 hours, pour off the liquid and press out the fruit. Add the sugar, acid blend, nutrient, and tannin. Adjust the must to SG 1.060. Then add the pectic enzyme and yeast culture. Cover. Stir twice daily for 5 days or so, measuring the SG daily. At 1.030, transfer the fermenting must to a glass vessel with air lock.

Continue to measure the SG at 2-day to 3-day intervals, until it reaches 1.010. At that point, transfer the wine to sterilized *and* rinsed bottles, capping them with sterilized crown caps. The bottles should be filled to within 3 inches of the cap. Store the bottles upright. When the liquid is clear, the cider or perry is ready to drink. When serving, be careful not to disturb the sediment on the bottom of the bottle.

THIS RECIPE MAKES 1 GALLON OR 5 BOTTLES.

ELDERBERRY WINE

6 ounces dried or 3 1/2 pounds fresh elderberries

8 ounces raisins, chopped

2 1/2 pounds sugar

4 teaspoons acid blend (optional)

1 teaspoon nutrient

2 Campden Tablets

1 gallon hot water

1/2 teaspoon pectic enzyme

yeast culture

vitamin C tablets

Combine the elderberries and raisins in a primary fermenter and add the sugar, acid blend, nutrient, Campden Tablets, and hot water. Cover. When the mix has cooled to 70°F, adjust the must to 1.100. Add the pectic enzyme and yeast culture. Cover with plastic sheet and secure

Continued →

with a string. Stir the must daily for 7 days. Strain out the fruit and siphon the liquid to a glass vessel with an air lock. *Do not press the fruit.* Pressed elderberries put out a hideous green gunk that ruins every piece of equipment with which it comes in contact. Beware.

Rack the wine in 3 weeks, again every 3 months. When the wine is clear and stable, bottle it, adding a 250 mg. vitamin C tablet per gallon.

MAKES 1 GALLON OR 5 BOTTLES.

POTATO OR CARROT OR PARSNIP WINE

4 1/2 pounds potatoes or carrots or parsnips

peel and juice of 2 oranges

peel and juice of 2 lemons

1 gallon boiling water

2 1/2 pounds sugar

1 teaspoon yeast nutrient

1/2 teaspoon pectic enzyme

1/2 teaspoon grape tannin

yeast culture

Scrub and dice the vegetables, removing the skins and all the discolored parts. Add the peel *only* of the fruit. Add the water and boil until the vegetables are tender. Let stand for 1 hour. Strain into a plastic vessel and add sugar. Cover. When the liquid is cool, add the other ingredients, including the juice of the oranges and lemons. (Some people at this point like to add ground ginger, ground cloves, and/or chopped raisins.) Adjust to SG 1.085. Stir daily for 5 days. Move to a glass vessel with an air lock. (If you added raisins, strain the wine first.) Rack in 3 weeks, again at 3 months. When the wine is clear, stabilize and bottle it. It will reach its peak of palatability in 6 to 15 months.

MAKES 1 GALLON OR 5 BOTTLES.

APPLE OR PEAR WINE

8 pounds apples or pears

2 Campden Tablets

1 gallon boiling water

2 pounds sugar

juice of 2 lemons or 4 teaspoons acid blend

1 teaspoon yeast nutrient

1/2 teaspoon pectic enzyme

1/2 teaspoon grape tannin

yeast culture

Remove stems from the fruit, cut the fruit into quarters, and crush it in a large plastic vessel. Dissolve Campden Tablets in the boiling water, and pour the water over the fruit, stirring the mix well. Tightly cover the vat.

After 72 hours, pour off the liquid and press out the fruit. Add sugar, adjusting the SG to 1.090. Then add lemon juice (or acid blend), yeast nutrient, pectic enzyme, tannin, and yeast culture. Cover. Stir

twice daily for 7 days. Remove to a glass vessel with an air lock. Rack in 3 weeks, again at 3 months. When the wine is clear, stabilize and bottle.

THIS RECIPE MAKES 1 GALLON OR 5 BOTTLES.

RASPBERRY OR PLUM WINE

This recipe will yield a dry and modest fruit wine of roughly 11 percent alcohol. Some rustics like both a more robust and a sweeter fruit wine. If you be one of these, increase the sugar to 3 1/2 pounds, adding it 2 pounds at the beginning, 1 pound on the fourth days, 1/2 pound on the sixth day.

3 pounds fruit, de-stemmed and de-stoned

2 teaspoons acid blend

2 Campden Tablets

2 pounds sugar

1 gallon warm water (100°F)

1 teaspoon yeast nutrient

1/2 teaspoon grape tannin

1/2 teaspoon pectic enzyme

yeast culture

Crush the prepared fruit in a plastic vessel. Add all the ingredients, except the pectic enzyme and yeast. Stir thoroughly to dissolve the sugar. Cover with a plastic sheet. When the mix cools, adjust the must to SG 1.085. Add the pectic enzyme and the yeast culture. Cover and secure, stirring twice daily for 6 days. At that time, or whenever the must reaches SG 1.030, remove to a glass vessel and secure with an air lock. Rack in 3 weeks and again at 3-month intervals for 1 year; then stabilize and bottle the wine.

THIS RECIPE MAKES 1 GALLON OR 5 BOTTLES.

WHEAT WINE

Often a delight and a surprise. When made sweet—with 3 1/2 pounds of sugar—it can be a very nice dessert wine.

1 pound whole wheat berries

1 1/2 pounds raisins

1 gallon boiling water

peel and juice of 1 lemon

peel and juice of 2 oranges

2 pounds sugar

1/2 teaspoon acid blend

1/4 teaspoon grape tannin

1/2 teaspoon yeast nutrient

1/4 teaspoon pectic enzyme

yeast culture

Crush the wheat, using a rolling pin and bread board, and add it with the chopped raisins to a 2-gallon vessel. Add boiling water, the peel *only* of the oranges and lemons, the sugar, the acid blend, tannin, and the nutrient. Move to a spot at room temperature.

When the mix cools, add the juice of the fruits. Adjust the SG to 1.100. Add the pectic enzyme, and the yeast culture. Cover and secure; stir daily for 5 days. After 7 days, strain (do not press) into a 1-gallon jug with air lock. Rack in 3 weeks and again in 3 months. Bottle the wine when it is clear and stable.

MAKES 5 BOTTLES OR 1 GALLON.

UNIVERSAL WINE RECIPE*

We offer you here the universal wine recipe chart of Mr. Stanley F. Anderson, of Vancouver, B.C. You will find it handy at times when you have picked a large quantity of ripe fruit that you want to ferment before it spoils—or when a quantity of ripe fruit has been dumped on you by a zealous acquaintance. The steps you should take are as follows:

1. Get a vessel (preferably plastic) that holds about 1 1/2 times the volume of the crushed fruit. This can range from a 2-gallon plastic pail for 5 pounds of fruit to a 45-gallon plastic drum liner for 350 pounds of grapes.

2. Multiply or divide the quantities shown on the chart, and get the appropriate ingredients from a winemaker's supply house, if you do not already have them. Get Andovin yeast if you can, otherwise use some other high-grade winemaker's yeast, and prestart it as explained above.

3. Prepare the fruit as indicated on the chart.

4. Mix all the ingredients, crushing the Campden Tablets before adding them, and stirring the must well to dissolve the added sugar. Put it in a place that is between 65 and 75°F. Add the yeast culture.

5. Cover with a plastic sheet and secure with a string.

6. Stir twice a day and follow the steps outlined above.

*This recipe first appeared in *The Art of Making Wine* by Stanley Anderson and Raymond Hull (Longman). Used with permission.

Winemaking Supplies

Your local shop is the place you should deal with first. Check your local Yellow Pages under "Brewing Supplies" or "Winemaking Supplies."

A second source is the Home Wine and Beer Trade Association. They can supply you with names, addresses, and phone numbers of suppliers in your area. Call (813) 685–4261, fax (813) 681–5625, or send a self-addressed stamped envelope to

Home Wine and Beer Trade Assoc.
P.O. Box 1373
Valrico, FL 33594
E-mail: hwbta@aol.com
Website: www.hwbta.org

Fruit	Weight of Fruit to Yield 1 Gallon	Preparation of Fruit	Water	Acid Blend	Campden Tablets	Yeast Nutrient	Sugar	Raisins	Pectic Enzyme	Grape Tannin	Wine Yeast
Apples	8 lb.	Crush	1 gal.	4 tsp.	2	1 tsp.	2 lb.	None	1/2 tsp.	1/4 tsp.	1 pkt.
Apricots	3 lb.	Destone	1 gal.	2 tsp.	2	1 tsp.	2 1/2 lb.	None	1 1/2 tsp.	1/4 tsp.	1 pkt.
Blackberries	4 lb.	Crush	1 gal.	1 tsp.	2	1 tsp.	2 1/2 lb.	None	1/2 tsp.	None	1 pkt.
Blueberries	2 lb.	Crush	1 gal.	3 tsp.	2	1 tsp. energizer	2 1/2 lb.	1 lb.	1/2 tsp.	None	1 pkt.
Sweet cherries	4 lb.	Crush	1 gal	3 tsp.		2	1 tsp.	2 1/2 lb.	None	1/2 tsp.	1/4 tsp.
Sour cherries	3 lb.	Crush	1 gal.	2 tsp.	2	1 tsp.	2 1/2 lb.	None	1/2 tsp.	1/4 tsp.	1 pkt.
Cranberries	4 lb.	Crush	1 gal.	None	2	1 tsp.	3 lb.	1 1/2 lb.	1/2 tsp.	None	1 pkt.
Concord grapes	6 lb.	Crush	1 gal.	None	2	1 tsp.	2 1/2 lb.	None	1/2 tsp.	None	1 pkt.
California grapes	20 lb.	Crush	None	1 tsp.	2	None	None	None	None	None	1 pkt.
Loganberries	2 lb.	Crush	1 gal.	2 tsp.	2	1 tsp.	3 lb.	None	1/2 tsp.	None	1 pkt.
Peaches	3 lb.	Destone	1 gal.	3 tsp.	2	1 tsp.	2 1/2 lb.	None	1/2 tsp.	1/4 tsp.	1 pkt.
Plums	4 lb.	Destone	1 gal.	2 tsp.	2	1 tsp.	2 1/2 lb..	None	1/2 tsp.	1/8 tsp.	1 pkt.
Raspberries	3 lb.	Crush	1 gal.	2 tsp.	2	1 tsp.	2 1/2 lb..	None	1/2 tsp.	1/4 tsp.	1 pkt.
Strawberries	5 lb.	Crush	1 gal.	2 tsp.	2	1 tsp.	2 1/2 lb.	None	1/2 tsp.	1/4 tsp.	1 pkt.

Note: all teaspoon measures in this table are level teaspoons.

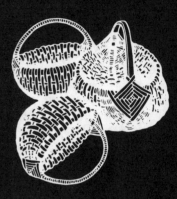

Crafts

FOR THE HOME

Stenciling

Judy Tuttle

Stenciling

Stenciling is suitable for any kind of room, both in new and in older homes. Designs can be applied on rough plaster walls, where larger designs are usually more effective, and on smooth walls or wallboard, wood or plaster. Stenciling can be applied to floors or paneling and also is impressive on brick. Old wallpaper can be painted and then stenciled, and if the wallpaper has a texture, the finished product is all the more interesting.

Almost any paint can be used for the background. It can be flat, satin finish, semi-gloss, latex, or oil-based. Stenciling can also be done over wood stains, varnishes, polyurethanes, or shellacs, but slippery materials such as glass, glossy paints, waxed surfaces, and vinyl will resist paint and for that reason shouldn't be used as a base for stenciling.

The paint you use to stencil is easier to work with if it is oil-based. Latex pain dries too quickly and builds up on the stencil.

TRACING DESIGN

Any design you find can be traced first and then changed to suit your situation. If you want an idea of how it might look on your wall, color your tracing with felt-tipped markers and tape it up where you would be applying it. You can have a design enlarged or made smaller by professional copying firms, or you can do it by hand by copying your design onto a piece of graph paper and then recopying the lines in each square onto graph paper with larger squares.

An average-sized ceiling border runs about seven inches vertically, but the height can be adjusted according to taste and the size of the room.

Materials

Heavy waxed stencil paper (obtainable in art supply stores). You can see through it to trace the stencil.

Pencils—well sharpened to trace the design onto the waxed paper.

A piece of plywood or heavy cardboard or fiber board on which to cut the stencil.

X-Acto knife

Oil-based paint (1/2 pint of one color will probably do a room)

A three-inch trim roller

Paint thinner

Stirring stick

Roller tray or piece of glass about the same size

Newspaper

Yardstick or tape measure

Clean rags

Cotton batting and pieces of sheeting (for blobs)

A level

A plumb line (for creating a straight horizontal or vertical line in a room which is not exactly square, such as an old house).

A chalkline (for laying out long straight lines).

A roll of 3" tape with one half gummed and one half plain used specifically for stenciling stripes. Can be found in hardware stores.

CUTTING THE STENCIL

You must decide before you cut your stencil how many colors to use. If you plan to use one color, place the waxed paper over the design and trace the outline with a pencil, bearing down hard to cut through the wax. Be sure to center the design to provide a border of at least 1 1/2 inches on all sides. Place the waxed paper with the traced design on a piece of smooth plywood, glass, or other smooth material that can be used as a drawing board. Hold the stencil down firmly with one hand while holding the knife as you would a pencil with the other hand. Simply cut on the lines of the design, lifting out the parts of the design you wish the paint to go through. If you have a long line in your design, it is best to break it up in several places to help make the stencil stronger.

If you plan to have a two-colored stencil, you must cut two separate stencils, one for each color. Place your waxed paper over the design you wish to use, centering it and leaving borders of 1 1/2 inches. Trace only the parts of the design that are to be the first color. Place the traced design on the drawing board and cut the stencil for the first color.

Then tape this cut stencil paper onto the original drawing and put another piece of stencil paper on top. On this second piece of stencil paper, trace only the parts of the design that are the alternate color. You will then need to trace some parts of the design that you cut for the first color to use as registration marks. Registration marks let you see through the stencil to the design you have already put on the wall so you will know where to place the stencil to apply the second color.

Remove the first piece of stencil paper from the original design and cut the stencil for the second color and the registration marks. For each new color you add, you will need to cut another stencil.

When you have cut both stencils for a two-color design, you are ready to begin stenciling.

IF YOUR CEILING IS NOT LEVEL

Before measuring for your border design, you must determine whether your ceiling is level. You may be able to tell whether it dips or rises from corner to corner by eye, but if you aren't sure, place a level along the ceiling in various spots. The bubble on the level will tell you whether the ceiling rises or dips and where. If you find that the ceiling is so uneven that a design following its lines will look peculiar, you can draw a straight line using the level as a guide.

Begin in one corner of the room. Place the level against the ceiling. Move it up or down until the bubble indicates that the level is exactly horizontal. Draw a light line using the level as a guide. Then put one end of the level on the line you have just drawn. Move it up or down until the level is exactly horizontal again, and extend the pencil line as far as the level reaches. Repeat this process until you have a level line extending all the way across the room.

MEASURING FOR A BORDER DESIGN

If you have chosen a design that is repeated (not a continuous or running design such as a vine), you will need to figure how many times to repeat your design along the horizontal line you have drawn. Measure your design and add to that measurement the amount of space you will want between designs. If you have a design that spans 4 inches and you would like 4 inches between each design, you will have a total of eight inches. Divide the 8 inches into the entire length of the horizontal line where the border will be placed, and the answer will give you the number of repeats to be stenciled on your wall. If the number doesn't come out even (which will mean you will have a part of a design or a part of a space at the end of your wall), you can adjust the amount of space between designs, making that space longer or shorter until you end with either a whole design or a whole space. If your border design is to go all the way around the room without being interrupted, be sure to measure the whole way around the room and divide that number of inches by the total number of inches in the design and the amount of space you want between designs. If you have chosen a 4" design and you want the designs 4" apart, divide 4" plus 4" or 8" into the total number of inches around your room. A 12Ð by 12Ð room has 576" around it. Divide 576 by 8. You will have 72 designs around the room spaced 4" apart. When you finish, your final design will be spaced perfectly next to the very first design you applied.

MEASURING FOR AN ALL-OVER DESIGN

If you have chosen an all-over design covering your wall, you must divide your wall area into square blocks or sections. Decide how far apart you would like your designs, and then, using a measuring tape, square off the room by measuring down from the ceiling and across the baseboard on perfectly vertical and horizontal lines and placing dots where each intersection will be.

Use only dots rather than drawing in the lines to save yourself the work of removing the pencil lines when you finish stenciling. When the surface is squared off, you can decide whether you'd like your design to be in the center of each square, in the center of every other square, at the intersections of the squares, or at the intersection of every other square.

An interesting effect results from placing one design at every other intersection and printing a different design at the intersections that were skipped. A variation of this idea is to run a continuous pattern to every other intersection and print a different design at the center. Sometimes, because of the way a pattern is shaped, you may want to divide the wall into rectangles that are not square.

MEASURING FOR A FLOOR

When measuring a large area, such as a floor, to be stenciled with an over-all design, a chalkline is very helpful. I find the center of the room to square off the floor so the design will be placed as evenly as possible in the room. To find the center of the floor, measure the length of the room along both walls and divide the number in half. Place a dot at each half-way mark and connect the dots across the room. Then measure the width of the room along both walls, divide the number in half, and place dots at each half-way mark. Connect those dots across the room. Where the lines intersect is the center of the room. Also, you have drawn the first two lines for squaring off the room. Check to see that the angles formed are exactly 90°, because a quarter of an inch mistake at

Continued ➜

the center of the room can be as much as a 2-inch mistake at the outside of the room.

An easy way to draw a long line running across a room is to snap a chalkline. Have one person hold the chalkbox at the center dot along one wall while another person takes the string across the room and places the end on the dot which indicates the center of the line on the other side of the room. Holding the chalk-filled string taut, snap the string on the floor by raising it up six inches or so at one end and letting go. A chalk line running straight across the room will be the result of the string snapping against the floor.

When you have two intersecting lines drawn across the room meeting in the center at right angles, you have a basis for dividing the rest of the room into squares. You measure along those lines, placing dots where the intersection of each square will fall.

If you plan to have a border along the edges of the floor, first measure out from the wall and snap a chalkline where the border will run. Then follow the directions for finding the center of the room and divide the remainder of the room into squares ending at the line marking the placement of the border rather than at the walls.

GETTING READY TO PRINT ON YOUR WALLS

Gather all your materials and set up a work area before you begin to apply paint. I spread newspapers in a small area on the floor, perhaps 3 feet by 3 feet. You will not need newspapers throughout the room, because stencil prints are applied so dry there are never drips. On the newspaper, I place my paints, my roller tray or glass, one for each color in my design, my stirring rods, one for each color I plan to use, paint thinner, a pile of clean newspapers and clean cloths and a large paper bag to use as a waste basket. Make sure you have enough space to work without being crowded, and try to set up your work area where the light is good. When your work area is set up, you are ready to begin printing.

You do not have to move furniture or even take down drapes unless they are in your way. You should however have a clean, waxless surface on which to print. Wax can be removed with paint thinner. Dirt should be scrubbed from any surface that hasn't been newly painted in order to assure that the paint will stick.

STENCIL PRINTING

Printing takes a little practice in order to know how much paint to use on the roller. Beginners would do well to practice one or two designs in a closet or woodshed or somewhere where the first designs won't show. Use very little paint or the paint will seep under the edges of the stencil and spoil the design. I use the stirring stick that I used to stir my oil-based paint after opening it. I lift the stick out of the paint and dribble the paint left on the stick onto the paint tray or pane of glass in a sort of S motion. Doing this only once or twice usually puts enough paint onto the paint tray and afterward the roller, to print several designs. You can test whether there is enough paint on the roller to print evenly by rolling paint onto a piece of clean newspaper. If you need more paint to cover a small space on the newspaper of about three inches by three inches, dribble one more stirring stick full of paint onto the paint tray or glass. Now you are ready to stencil.

To print with a roller, place the stencil on the wall in the spot measured for it. Holding the stencil with one hand, roll over it with the roller several times until all the holes in the stencil are filled with paint.

A stencil print is the most attractive, I think, when the paint shading is varied, heavier in some of the cut outs and lighter in others. You can accomplish this by rolling over the holes more often on some parts of the design and less on the other parts. Another way to accomplish this is to bear down more heavily on some parts of the design as you apply the paint. Roll the paint in different directions so the total effect won't have a one-direction quality.

Another method of printing is rubbing with a cotton blob. A cotton blob is made by wrapping a piece of cotton batting about the size of a walnut in a 3" by 3" square of cotton cloth. I use old sheeting. Pull the corners of the sheeting together, then wrap elastic band around the end near the cotton. What sticks up will be your handle. Hold the handle and dip the blob into the paint on the glass or tray. Blot it on newspaper until the paint no longer squishes out and you have made a relatively dry paint spot. Holding the stencil with one hand, blot and rub the cotton blob over the holes in the stencil until you have applied as much color as you wish. Cotton blob printing is useful for hard-to-reach spots, places where the roller won't fit, and very small touches of color on a design where it seems impractical to print with a roller.

PRINTING THE CONTINUOUS DESIGN

If the design you use is to be a running design (one without an end, such as a vine) make sure the beginning and ending holes on the stencil are identical. For the first design, place the edge of the stencil along the ceiling or along the horizontal line you have drawn with a level and print the design. Then, lift the stencil and place the first holes of the design over the last part of the design you have just printed at the point where they match. Repeat the printing process. Continue until you have gone all around the room. Since it is unlikely that the first printed design and the last one will work out exactly, begin your printing in the least conspicuous part of the room so the mismatch will show up the least.

CORRECTING A MISTAKE

The most common problem of beginning stencilers is applying too much paint and having it squish and blot up under the design, spoiling its effect. If the first design you apply looks like this, don't despair, because mistakes are relatively easy to repair. Put paint thinner on a clean cloth as soon you notice your mistake and rub off the design. Allow the paint thinner to evaporate until it can no longer be seen on the wall—only a minute or two—and look at the spot where the design was. If the background paint shows a shiny spot, blot on some of the background color with a rag and allow it to dry. Then reapply the design. Most of the time the background paint will be satisfactory after you have removed the mistake, and you will be able to try again right away. Any spots or mistakes should be removed before the paint dries to have the paint thinner work on it. If, however, you find a place you wish changed after the paint is thoroughly dry, sand the spot lightly, reapply the background paint, and proceed with your painting.

STENCILING HARD-TO-REACH PLACES

When you reach a corner with the continuous design, bend the stencil as close to the wall as possible, folding it right around to the next wall. Make sure it stays on the horizontal line, for it may tend to slant downward after the corner. Your roller will not fit in the corner, so use a cotton blob to apply paint. If you find it difficult to hold the stencil and go around the corner at the same time, use a little masking tape to hold the stencil.

When you reach spots where your stencil won't fit, it can be bent just as it is in going around a corner, or you can leave an appropriately sized space and continue around the room. When you have finished with the stencil except for those spots, cut the stencil to fit the tight area and print with the cotton blob. If the area is too small for any kind of a stencil, sketch in the part of the design you need with a pencil and fill it in with a small brush. The change in texture won't be noticeable in the over-all effect.

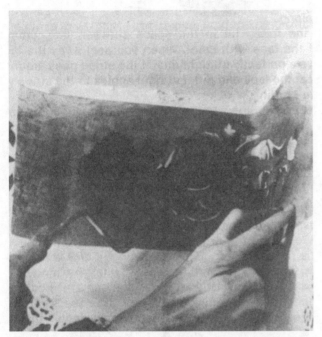

To make a running design go around a corner, bend the stencil into the corner and proceed as on a flat wall. Don't worry about the spots where the roller won't fit. These blank spaces are too close to the corner to be noticeable in a completed room. If you feel you must fill them in, do so with a cotton blob or a small artist's brush.

THE SOLID STRIPE

With some designs, you may want to print a solid stripe. Lay out the size of the stripe with a ruler, placing dots indicating where the stripe will run. Buy the special tape used for making stripes at a hardware store. It is about 3 inches wide and is gummed along one-half of its width. Place the gummed side along the dots you have made on both sides of the stripe, but before you print, carefully measure the distance between the stripes of tape to make sure your stripe is of uniform width all the way along.

Using the roller, fill in the space between the gummed halves of the tape with paint. When you peel away the tape, you'll have a perfectly straight line. If the stripe goes around a corner, tear the tape and put it at right angles to the stripe you have been printing.

If you are stenciling a stripe on the floor or paneling, the paint will not go into the cracks, and the overall appearance will show some breaks in the color. Fill in the cracks with the color of the stripe, using a small paint brush.

PROTECTING YOUR WORK

If you have finished stenciling an area where the design could wear off, such as a floor, apply several coats of a polyurethane to give it the protection it needs. Polyurethane will darken the colors slightly. This darkening is most noticeable over very light colors and increases with the amount of polyurethane applied. If you have stenciled a floor, the polyurethane will flow thickly into any wide cracks and be more noticeable there. I solve this problem by applying a little of my light color over the polyurethane in the cracks with a small artist's brush. The polyurethane can be applied as soon as the paint is thoroughly dry, and any touch-up can be done when the polyurethane is no longer tacky.

CLEANING UP

As you stencil a room, you will find that the stencil becomes sticky with paint. You may have difficulty holding it in place, and if it moves only a fraction of an inch it will make a blurred impression. When you feel the stencil has become too sticky, stop printing. Lay the stencil on newspapers in the work area and pour a little paint thinner all over the stencil. With a clean rag, gently wipe away the paint. With another rag, clean off the paint thinner from both sides of the stencil. When the stencil is wiped dry on both sides, work may be resumed.

You may need to clean the stencil every 8 to 12 feet of work, depending upon the consistency of the oil-based paint. The thicker it is, the more often you will need to clean the stencil. Remember that the stencil will tear, especially on the small parts close to another cut-out area, so don't be too vigorous in your cleaning.

STENCIL DESIGNS

Continued ➜

397

398

Quilting Basics

Debra Rogers-Gillig

Illustrations by Brigita Fuhrmann

Clay's Choice

Nine-Patch

Broken Dishes

Picking Out Your Fabric

Picking out fabric is easily one of the best parts of quilting; maybe the most difficult as well. It is a quilter's market right now with fabric manufacturers catering to the "country look." Quilt shops and fabric stores are filled with calicoes, wonderful larger prints, every imaginable shade in solids—the choices can be overwhelming!

Where do you start? Think about your project. Will it go in a particular room? Is it a gift for a baby? A wedding present? The quilt's purpose and recipient can help determine which colors and patterns to use.

A few other suggestions: First, go to the fabric store with plenty of time, and go alone or with a patient adult friend. Second, look around at *all* the fabric; don't just grab the first three bolts and run. There may be a particular fabric you just *have* to use; this can be a good starting point for adding coordinating fabrics, picking and choosing as you try different combinations. Third, try to use a light, a medium, and a dark

fabric in your quilt, and to vary the size of the prints. By varying the scale of the prints and the values of the colors, you add depth and spark to your quilt. "Viney" all over prints, oversize prints, and stripes will also add variety and interest. Don't try to match every color! Remember, variety adds interest.

One hundred percent cotton fabrics are recommended as they are easier to handle than the thinner polyester blends.

Once you have decided on your fabrics, the next question is how much to buy. I always buy more than I need to make allowances for mistakes, to compensate for shrinkage, and in case I change the pattern.

PREPARING THE FABRIC

Pre-wash all fabric, whether it's brand new from the fabric store or scraps from previous projects. Pre-wash all materials to rid them of dust, dirt, excess dyes and sizing. Darks and lights should be washed separately to prevent bleeding. Prewashing also preshrinks the fabric, hopefully eliminating any distortion caused by one fabric shrinking more than the rest when the finished piece is washed.

Next, cut off all selvedges—the very tightly woven edges. You do not want to use this edge in your quilt. It acts differently and may distort the block.

Press all fabric. Nothing's worse than trying to trace templates on top of wrinkles!

Supplies

I. *Pattern Tools*

  A. *Ruler (18" transparent)*

  B. *Template plastic (11" x 18" sheet available in craft shops)*

  C. *Permanent fine line marker (not ballpoint)*

  D. *Old scissors for cutting template pieces*

  E. *Sharpened pencil*

  F. *Small manila envelopes for template pieces*

II. *Cutting and Sewing Tools*

  A. *Good fabric scissors (for fabric only!)*

  B. *Straight pins*

  C. *Needles*

    1. *hand sewing needles (sharps)*

    2. *long, thin needle for basting*

    3. *quilting needles (betweens)*

  D. *Thread*

    1. *hand or machine (size 50 cotton wrapped polyester recommended)*

    2. *any inexpensive thread for basting*

    3. *quilting thread*

  E. *Thimble*

III. *Fabric and Quilting Needs*

  A. *Quilting fabric (100% cotton recommended)*

  B. *Batting, the filler between the quilt top and the backing*

  C. *Quilt backing (100% broadcloth recommended)*

Continued ➡

QUILT PATTERNS

At the end of this section, you will find actual size pattern pieces for several different blocks (enough for a variety of pillows or a sampler wall-hanging). There are dozens of excellent pattern books available at quilt shops or your local library. Some books contain actual size templates, while others have patterns that you must enlarge.

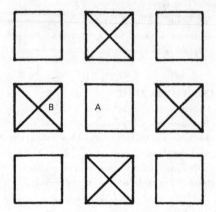

We will use a 12-inch Ohio Star block as our example. You can see that the block is easily divided into nine sections. Piece A is a 4-inch square and piece B is a right triangle with a long side of 4 inches. These are the only two pattern pieces for the entire block! By varying fabrics and placement within the quilt a great variety of different looks can be achieved.

MAKING TEMPLATES

Lay the template plastic on top of the pattern pieces and trace accurately (use a ruler for all straight edges). If you plan to hand-piece your quilt (sew the pieces together with a needle and thread), pattern pieces will be cut on the inside line. If you will use a sewing machine to piece your quilt, pattern pieces will be cut on the outside line. Cut out these pattern pieces using your old scissors. Mark all information onto each pattern piece. Don't forget to include the grain line. Cutting quilt pieces on the straight grain of the fabric is important to keep the quilt from being pulled out of shape, resulting in a distorted and inaccurate block.

CUTTING OUT PATTERN PIECES

For a hand-pieced quilt: Place the template on the wrong side of the fabric, with the marked grain line parallel to the lengthwise edge of the fabric (where the selvedge used to be). Trace around the template carefully with a sharp pencil (on light fabrics) or a permanent fine-line marker (for darker fabrics). The line you are marking is the sewing line; it must be smooth and straight.

Reposition the template so that there is 1/2 inch between the marked lines. Cut out pattern pieces by cutting midway between marked lines, leaving a 1/4-inch seam allowance outside all lines.

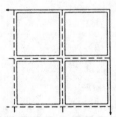 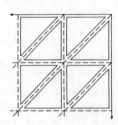

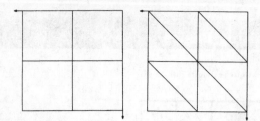

For a machine-pieced quilt: Place the template on the wrong side of the fabric, with the marked grain line parallel to the lengthwise edge of the fabric (where the selvedge used to be). Trace around the template carefully with a sharp pencil (on light fabrics) or a permanent fine-line marker (for darker fabrics). Lines must be smooth and straight.

Reposition the template to trace the next pattern piece. There is no need to leave space between pattern pieces as the lines you are drawing are the cutting lines for each piece.

MAKE A TEST BLOCK

It is a good idea to make a test block to ensure the accuracy of the pieces and to see if you are satisfied with the color choice and placement. It's far better to discover mistakes at this point before you have 20 blocks cut and sewn!

HAND PIECING

Hand sewing is done using a crewel or a sharp needle, strong thread, good light and lots of patience.

Lay out the block pieces in front of you.

Start by sewing the smallest pieces together first. In this case, one B triangle to another B triangle at their short sides. Place the pieces right sides together and pin them point to point on the drawn line.

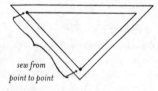

sew from point to point

Join the pieces together by sewing them with a small running stitch, making sure you are on the marked line on both sides of the pieces. Be accurate or the block won't fit together!

Pin and sew another set of triangles together. Then pin the two sets of triangles together to form a square. Refer to the block layout to ensure proper color placement.

In joining the sets of triangles, it is best to use the butted seam technique. Pin the sets together point to point, on the marked line. Pin also at the middle, butting the seam allowances together, leaving them freestanding.

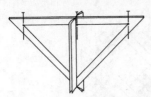

Stitch the pieces together, sewing from point to middle point, stopping, making a backstitch (for reinforcement), and then passing the needle through the seam allowance to continue stitching. Do not stitch down the seam allowance. It is left free to be pressed whichever direction is best.

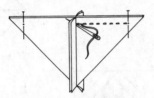

As a general rule, a light fabric would be pressed toward a darker fabric. Otherwise the darker seam allowances would show through the lighter fabric, causing distractions. Another point on pressing—do it lightly! You don't want to distort the seams or the sharp points of your newly sewn angles.

Next, make three rows. For the first row of the Ohio Star block you will pin a square to a square of triangles to another square, again point to point. Stitch.

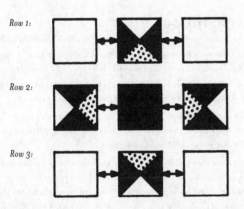

Row 1:

Row 2:

Row 3:

Join the rows together, pinning and sewing on the drawn lines, using the butted seam technique.

Remember, the key to sewing pieced blocks is to visually break the design down to straight lines. Stitch the smallest pieces first, then make rows, and finally join the rows to make a block.

MACHINE PIECING

Piecing patchwork blocks by machine involves a few differences from sewing clothing on the machine.

Template patterns for machine pieced quilts include the 1/4-inch seam allowance. The lines you draw onto your fabric are the cutting lines. There are no sewing lines on machine-pieced pattern pieces.

In quilting you are dealing with 1/4-inch seam allowances as opposed to 5/8-inch seams in commercial dressmaking patterns. Measure the presser foot of your sewing machine. Many are a convenient, accurate 1/4 inch in width. If yours is not, measure and mark the throat plate with masking tape 1/4 inch from the needle hole.

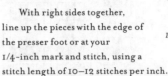

1/4"

With right sides together, line up the pieces with the edge of the presser foot or at your 1/4-inch mark and stitch, using a stitch length of 10—12 stitches per inch.

After a seam is sewn, it must be pressed to one side before it is sewn down to another piece. Press lighter fabrics toward darker ones.

SETTINGS

Once the blocks have been made, the next step is to set them together. There are many ways of doing this, including butting the blocks together, alternating with plain blocks, using lattice work to set off the blocks, and setting the blocks on point.

Whatever setting you decide on, be sure to figure and buy adequate yardage. Most sales clerks in fabric and quilt shops are very knowledgeable and more than willing to help you decide how much of each fabric you will need. When cutting and sewing plain blocks, lattice work and/or borders, remember the 1/4-inch seam allowances.

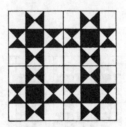

Continuous Blocks

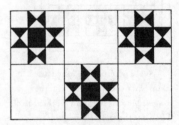

Alternating with Plain Blocks

Alternating Plain Blocks

Setting with alternating plain blocks has the advantage of clean, seam-free areas waiting to be filled with quilting. This setting is made by sewing a patchwork block to a plain block to a patchwork block and so on until the row is completed. The next row would alternate by starting with a plain block sewn to a patchwork block sewn to a plain block, etc. Then the rows would be joined together and borders could be added if desired.

Lattice or Sashing

Lattice or sashing around each block serves two purposes; one, to frame or show off each block (this is especially effective in setting off sampler blocks where each block is different and competing for attention) and two, to increase the quilt size.

Lattice strips should be no wider than 1/4 the width of the block they are framing.

Blocks with Lattice Work

Continued ➡

However, a strip that is too narrow will also take away from the overall design of the quilt.

Sew the strips to the blocks as follows:

1. Cut short strips to set between the blocks. These should be the same length as the block.

2. Sew the strips between the blocks to form rows.

3. Using rows as measurement, cut the necessary strips for the vertical latticework. Sew to each row.

4. Join the rows.

5. Cut and sew the outside strips. These may be wider than the inside lattice strips but should not be any narrower. Sew vertical sides first, then sew horizontal sides. These strips may be the end of the quilt top or you may add more borders to make the top larger.

Avoid seaming the long lattice strips whenever possible. Cut the longest lengths first and set them aside. Then cut the shorter strips. If you don't have enough fabric for long, unseamed strips, consider putting in corner squares.

Triangle A is one half of the 12-inch block. Triangle B is one quarter of the 12-inch block.

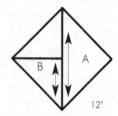

Blocks Set on Point with Latticework

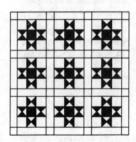

SETTING BLOCKS ON POINT

Setting a quilt "on point" simply means placing the blocks on the diagonal. Again they may be set as continuous blocks, with latticework or with plain blocks.

Blocks Set on Point (Diagonal) with Plain Blocks

The rows of blocks are still sewn using straight seams but the quilt is assembled in diagonal lines, using triangles to complete the top.

MARKING THE QUILT

After the quilt top is completed, the markings for the actual quilting should be done. Stitching 1/4 inch around each piece (outlining) is a traditional look and easily accomplished by eye or by using 1/4-inch masking tape (available at quilt and fabric shops). Lay the tape right next to the seam line. Stitch beside the tape, not through it.

Another option is to stitch next to the seam (stitch in the ditch) which raises the piece slightly and hides the quilting stitch on the front (good for beginners with shaky stitches).

There are many plastic quilting stencils available for borders, blocks and latticework, ranging from floral designs to intricate feather and cable borders to simple hearts. These can be marked onto the quilt top with a chalk pencil, a silver pencil (both of which brush or wear off the fabric) or a wash-out pen. The wash-out pen enables you to mark the fabric with a distinct blue line, making the quilting design easier to see. When the quilting is completed, the blue lines are removed using a damp cloth. (There has been some controversy involving these pens regarding the long-term effect of the chemicals on the fabric and the reported phenomena of the reappearing line. I have not personally experienced any problems with these pens.)

With marking, it is best to experiment to see which method works best for you in regard to your particular project. Always experiment on a leftover scrap of fabric, not the finished top. I do not recommend using regular pencil as it will not wash out.

BACKING, LAYERING AND BASTING

The backing of a quilt is the bottom layer. Broadcloth and muslin, both 100% cotton, are good choices for this as they are easy to quilt through and are the same weight and texture as the fabrics in the top. (Sheets are too tightly woven, making them difficult to quilt through.)

The backing should coordinate with and complement the quilt. It is better to use one of the fabrics used in the quilt top than something totally different. A solid will show the quilting stitches much more than a print. A print will also disguise the use of different colors of quilting thread if you plan to stitch some areas of the quilt top in different colors.

Measure the completed top. Add three inches to all four sides to figure the minimum size piece required for the backing. For example, a quilt top measuring 72 by 90 inches would need a backing of 78 by 96 inches. Broadcloth and muslin are usually available in 43- to 45-inch widths requiring that the back be pieced. This means buying two lengths of 96 inches or 5 and 1/3 yards of fabric (you may want to buy extra in case of shrinkage).

Pre-wash the fabric and remove the selvedges. Cut into two equal lengths and press. With right sides together, stitch long side using a 1/4-inch seam allowance. Press seam to one side.

Stretch the backing, right side down, onto the floor and tape it down. (I pin mine directly to the living room carpet.) It is important to get and keep the backing straight, taut and wrinkle-free. You don't want to quilt in pleats or wrinkles.

Layer the batting on top of the backing, patting it smooth. Then layer the top, right side up. Pin through all three layers, starting in the center and working out to the edges. Using a long, thin needle and basting thread, start in the center and work out to the edges basting through all three layers. Work in a grid 3 to 4 inches apart. Don't skimp in this step—basting adequately is necessary to keep the layers from shifting and bunching during quilting. Remove the pins after basting.

Don't be fancy—take large stitches. They will be removed after the quilting is completed.

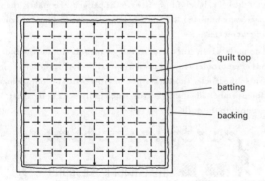

quilt top

batting

backing

QUILTING

Quilting is the actual stitching together of all three layers. Aside from its practical purpose of holding the batting in place, keeping it from lumping and shifting especially after being washed, quilting adds depth and interest to the quilt.

The quilt stitch is nothing more than a simple running stitch, as small and even as possible. Start with an 18-inch length of quilting thread and tie a single knot at one end. Using a "between" needle, go

into the fabric, popping the knot through the top, dragging it through the batting to secure it. No knots are to be seen on the top or the back of the quilt. Now come back up where you wish to begin quilting. Always start at the center of the quilt and work out to the edges. This will ease out any fullness.

Insert the needle at an angle. Using the needle straight up and down can result in crooked stitches on the back. And use a thimble. Besides protecting your finger, it enables you to quilt longer.

You can read about quilting and watch others stitch, but quilting must be done to be learned and perfected. Good, even, tiny stitches come by practice and more practice. Experiment with different size needles and types of thimbles and battings to find out what's best for you. Try using a 14-inch hoop or a large frame or just holding the quilt in your lap. Only by trying several methods will you discover your own.

Hoops and frames were designed to keep the three layers taut and straight during quilting so that no bulges or pleating occurs, especially on the back. However, don't be discouraged if you can't manage the hoop. (I can't, but that hasn't stopped judges from awarding prizes to my quilts!) Lap quilting without the use of a hoop can turn out beautiful results. Just make sure the quilt is thoroughly basted so that the layers don't shift in handling.

Quilting needles, called betweens, come in different sizes ranging from 7 to 13. The higher the number, the smaller the needle and the tinier the stitch.

The length of the stitch should be the same as the distance between stitches. Try to take 2 to 3 stitches on the needle at one time. This will help keep a straighter line as you stitch.

A common problem for beginners is that the stitches on the front may be even but the stitches on the back vary in size; some stitches are barely visible. There are many factors that can contribution to this problem: Inexperience in handling the three thicknesses of fabric and batting, the length of the quilting needle, the weave of the fabrics used (tightly woven materials such as a chintz are wonderful to look at but can be difficult to quilt through), and taking too many stitches at a time.

Don't worry that some inconsistencies in stitch length (from the front to the back) may persist. Practice makes a difference.

A quilting thread is ended the same way it is started, by making a knot and dragging it through the batting. Bring the needle around and through the held thread to make a single knot. Insert the needle through the top and still on the quilting line. Pop the knot through the fabric and drag it through the batting. Do not go through the backing. Come up through the top 2 inches from the quilting line and clip the thread.

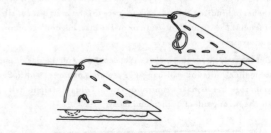

Once the quilting has been completed, remove the basting threads carefully so as not to tear or rip out any quilting stitches. Now the quilt is ready for binding.

Continued →

TIEING A QUILT

Of course, quilting is optional. There is no reason you cannot "tie" a quilt as long as it is done sufficiently to keep the batting from shifting.

Once the quilt top has been completed and the backing prepared, you can proceed to tie the quilt. Spread the backing, right side down, onto a large clean flat surface. Pin or tape the backing straight and taut. Place the batting onto the backing patting it smooth. Layer the top, right side up, onto the batting. Pin through all three layers, starting in the center and working out to the edges. Pin approximately 6 inches apart.

Using crochet cotton thread or a washable yarn and a long thin needle, stitch and tie double knots throughout the quilt, making sure you go through all three layers. The ties should be no more than 5 to 6 inches apart in any direction. Any more than that and the batting may bunch and shift after the quilt has been washed. Tie according to your block design—in the corners of each block, the middle and along each edge—somewhere where the ties do not obstruct the design of the block.

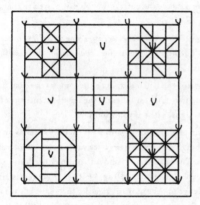

Remove all pins and release the quilt from the floor or table. Now the quilt is ready for binding.

BINDING

There are two ways of finishing off a quilted piece—either a separate binding or bringing the backing up and over to the front.

For a separate binding, first measure the perimeter of the quilt (the sum of the lengths of all four sides) and then add 12 inches (for easing or mitering the corners and overlap at the beginning and end of stitching). For example, a quilt measuring 72 by 90 inches would have a perimeter of 72 + 90 + 72 + 90 = 324. Add 12 inches and you will need 336 inches of binding. You will have to piece this from strips, cut all pieces from the straight of the grain or on the bias, but don't combine bias and straight.

Cut the strips 2 1/2 to 3 inches wide, depending on the size of your quilt. Smaller quilts and wall-hangings can use a narrower width. Sew the strips together to make a continuous strip. Fold the strip in half lengthwise, wrong sides together, and press.

Matching the raw edges, pin binding to the quilt top. Start the binding in the middle of the bottom edge of the quilt and continue to the corner. Leave a small pleat of binding at the corners to form a miter. Using a 1/4-inch seam allowance, stitch up to the pleat and backstitch. Break your stitching, lift up the presser foot and push the pleat to the other side. Insert the needle and continue stitching down the next side.

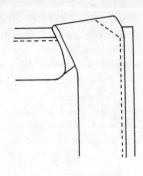

Overlap the binding end where you started and cut off any excess. Using a 1/4-inch seam allowance, stitch through all layers by machine. Either miter or ease the corners as you sew. Fold the binding to the back and slip stitch the entire binding closed.

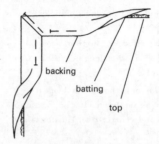

backing

batting

top

The second method of finishing a quilt simply involves bringing the backing up and over to the top. Trim the excess batting within 1/2 inch of the top. Trim the extra backing within 2 inches of the top. Fold under the raw edge of the backing approximately 1/2 inch and then fold it again onto the top, overlapping at least 1/4 inch. Pin through all thicknesses. Miter or ease the corners as you slip-stitch the edge.

A separate binding is recommended when the quilt has a curved or scalloped edge or is a large bed covering that may suffer abrasion from dragging on the floor or being stepped on.

LABELING YOUR QUILT

Last but not least, sign your quilt. In quilting stitches on the front, in cross-stitch, in embroidery or even permanent ink on a piece of muslin sewn on the back, label your quilt as to the pattern, the maker, the year the piece was completed and any other pertinent information. You are making memories.

I do my labels in cross-stitch on 18-count aida cloth using two strands of embroidery floss. I use a simple alphabet for the lettering, and finish the label with a back-stitch or cross-stitch border. Sometimes the label is embellished with a cross-stitch quilt block design that corresponds to the quilt.

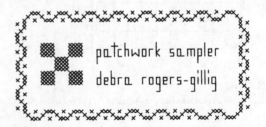

patchwork sampler
debra rogers-gillig

QUILT CARE

Most quilts made today can be washed. Use a mild soap or one especially made for quilts such as Ensure by Mountain Mist, Inc. Wash in warm or cold water on a delicate cycle or hand wash in the bathtub.

Dry in a large dryer, also on a delicate setting. Placing a couple of dry towels in with the quilt may help absorb the tumbling of the quilt. Or lay the quilt flat on a sheet to dry. Hanging a wet quilt on a clothesline causes too much strain on the batting and the stitches and may damage the quilt.

Dry cleaning is not recommended as some fabrics may react to the solvents by running or discoloring.

Pieces that are not soiled but merely "dusty" such as wall-quilts may be freshened by putting them in the dryer with a couple of damp washcloths or hand towels on an air-only cycle. This removes the dust without having to wash and soak the piece.

Never store your quilts in a plastic bag. The fibers need to breathe. Condensation may build up and stain a quilt sealed in plastic. A zippered pillow case is a safer alternative as well as special acid-free boxes and tissue paper usually available by mail order.

Be careful of the amount of light your quilts receive. Give your wall-hangings a rest after 3 to 6 months of display. Any light, not just direct sunlight, can cause fading.

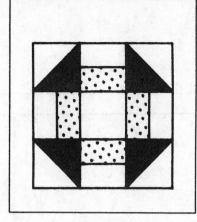

Monkey Wrench

QUILT PATTERNS

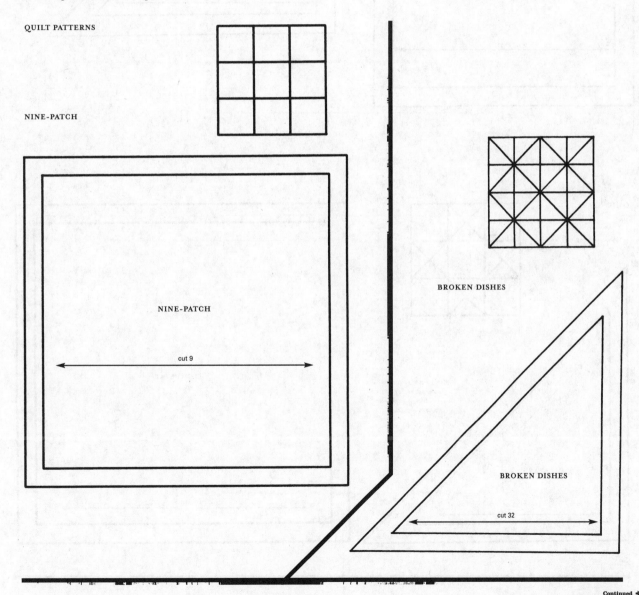

NINE-PATCH

NINE-PATCH

cut 9

BROKEN DISHES

BROKEN DISHES

cut 32

Continued →

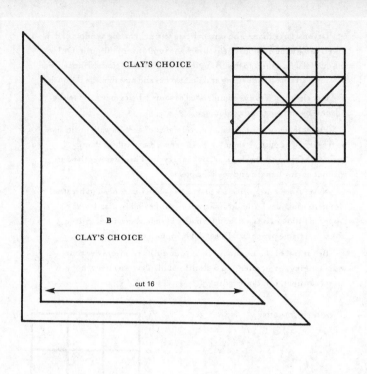

CLAY'S CHOICE

B
CLAY'S CHOICE

cut 16

A
CLAY'S CHOICE

cut 8

OHIO STAR

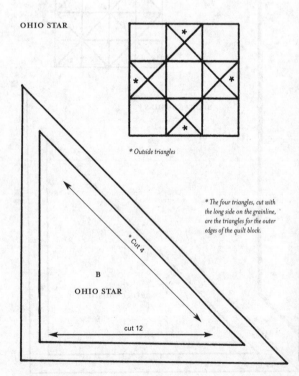

* Outside triangles

* The four triangles, cut with the long side on the grainline, are the triangles for the outer edges of the quilt block.

* Cut 4

B
OHIO STAR

cut 12

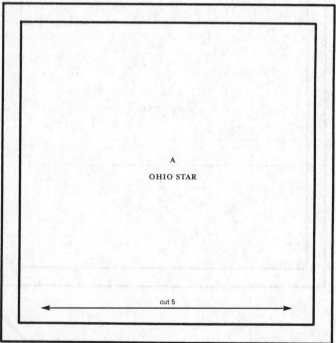

A
OHIO STAR

cut 5

MONKEY WRENCH

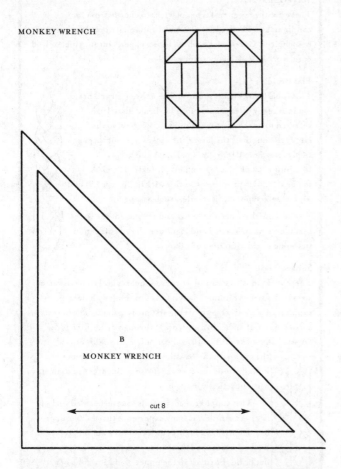

B

MONKEY WRENCH

cut 8

C

MONKEY WRENCH

cut 8

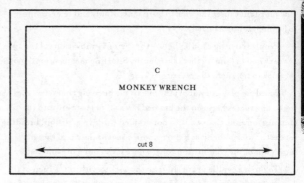

A

MONKEY WRENCH

cut 1

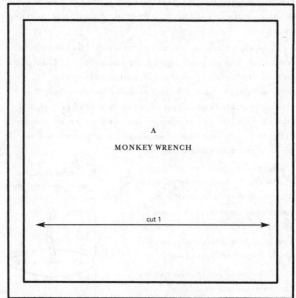

Making Hand-Dipped Candles

Betty Oppenheimer
Illustrations by Laura Tedeschi

Candlemaking Basics

To understand how to dip candles, you must first understand a few key concepts about how candles burn, and what supplies are required to make them burn well. A candle flame burns because of the two main ingredients: fuel and wick. When you light a candle, the wick catches fire and that fire heats to melting a small pool of wax just below the flame. The wick draws up that liquid wax to feed the flame, and the wick burns away at the top. In a good candle, the fuel (wax) burns more quickly than the wick does.

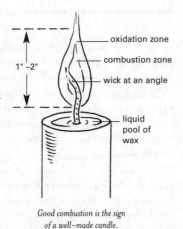

oxidation zone

combustion zone

wick at an angle

1" –2"

liquid pool of wax

Good combustion is the sign of a well-made candle.

When you're burning your candles, watch the wick and flame in order to determine whether you have achieved good combustion. A candle that is burning well will have a 1- to 2-inch, steadily burning flame. The wick should bend over at approximately 90 degrees or stick straight up into the oxidation zone at the top of the flame so that the tip is almost to the edge of the flame and can burn to ash. The wax should form a liquid pool surrounding the wick—not so big as to spill over but not so dry that the wick has no liquid to pull up.

ALL ABOUT THE WICK

The relationship of the wick to the wax, in terms of burn rate, is what determines whether a candle will burn well—or at all.

Before the invention of braided, mordanted wick, a variety of twisted fibers were used to carry the flame of a candle. Since they did not curl predictably—modern wicks bend over an exact 90 degrees—the wick stayed in the hottest part of the combustion zone and smoked as it carbonized.

Now, a wick is a braided (plaited) bundle of cotton threads, or plies, that has been mordanted, or pickled in a chemical solution. The mordant, or pickling, used on a wick is essentially a fire-retardant solution. It sounds strange to say a candle wick is treated to retard burning, but a candle's fuel (wax) should burn before the wick does so the wick can act as a fuel delivery system between the wax and the flame.

Continued ➡

The mordant causes the wick to burn more slowly and to decompose fully when it is exhausted.

People burning candles before the various innovations of the 19th century had to "snuff" them frequently. Snuffing means snipping off the wick to 1/2 inch, to prevent smoking.

Braiding plays an important role in the burning characteristics of a wick. The spaces between the braided plies allow more air into the combustion zone than would a nonbraided cord. In addition, braiding forces the wick to bend as it burns, which means the tip of the wick moves out of the combustion zone, where it can burn off completely.

To burn a candle properly, trim the wick to within 1/4 inch of the wax surface before lighting. This cuts down on the excess carbon that builds up on the wick and prevents the candle's flame from becoming too big.

It is difficult to pinpoint exactly what wick you should use for a candle, but there are general guidelines you can follow. Most commonly available candlemaking supplies will indicate which wick is recommended for the wax and type of candle you are making. For example, a wick package will say, "Use this wick for all 1 1/2-inch-diameter candles." This is a good place to start, but be aware that your choice of wax may have as much impact on the success of a candle as the choice of a wick for a particular-size candle.

Suppliers of wick material usually classify candles by diameter: for example, extra small (0–1 inch), small (1–2 inches), and medium (2–3 inches). Within these size guidelines, certain types of wick work better with certain candle shapes and types of wax.

Wicks for dipped candles are usually flat-braided or square-braided. Most suppliers' labels indicate the wick's best use, but this information will give you some familiarity with the choices.

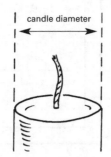

candle diameter

Candle diameter plays an important role in wick selection.

TYPES OF WAX

Wax is the fuel that burns in the flame of a candle. Generally speaking, candle wax can be liquefied between 100°F and 200°F and is solid at room temperature. There are waxes from animal, vegetable, and mineral (petroleum) sources. Commercially refined waxes are used in food and pharmaceutical coatings, cosmetics, industrial casting, lubricating, finishing leather and wood, and a host of other applications. Only a few of the commercially available waxes can be used in candlemaking.

Nowadays, most candles are made of paraffin or beeswax or some combination of the two. But over the centuries, candlemakers have used a wide variety of waxes. Here's a list of the traditional and modern choices for the candlemaker.

Bayberry. This wax is obtained from boiling the berries of the bayberry shrub. The wax naturally floats to the surface and is skimmed off and made into candles. Bayberries were so named because the Pilgrims first found them growing along Cape Cod Bay. But these bushes are found as far north as Nova Scotia, as far south as the Carolinas, and as far west as upstate New York. At present, bayberry wax is very expensive because the berries are not as plentiful as they were in colonial times. They are known for their sage green color and spicy

WHICH WICK?

There are three general types of wicks to choose from for candlemaking. For tapers, flat braid and square braid are the two best choices. Cored wicks, which have a paper, cotton, zinc, or lead core, work best with container candles.

Flat Braid

This is basically what it sounds like—a three-strand braid made of many plies per strand. Flat-braided wick is referred to by the number of plies in the wick, so the larger the number, the larger the wick. Common sizes are 15 ply (extra small), 18 ply (small), 24 and 30 ply (medium), 42 ply (large), and 60 ply (extra large). A major U.S. wick producer says this wick is "for use in rigid dipped self-supporting candles, such as tapers."

Because these braids are flat and tensioned, the wick bends over when burned and may burn slightly off center, in the side oxidation zone of a flame.

Square Braid

These wicks look like round-cornered squares and come in various sizes with various numbering systems. One major wholesale supplier of wick uses a numbering system ranging from 6/0 (extra small) to 1/0, then beginning with #1 through #10, which is the largest. The wicks with /0 after the number are regular braid, and the ones with the # symbol in front of the number are loosely woven, so they are fluffier and larger in diameter without actually being heavier.

This supplier recommends square-braided wicks for beeswax candles. It is my experience that a 1/0 square-braided wick is roughly equivalent to a 30-ply flat braid. Square-braided wicks tend to stand up straighter than a flat braid, burn off in the upper oxidation zone of a flame, and keep a flame centered in its candle.

As a beginning candlemaker, you will have your best success with wicks by following the instructions in the catalogs or on the packages provided by the supplier. If a wick does not burn well, use the troubleshooting guidelines offered in this bulletin (see pages 24–25), or go back to your supplier and describe what has occurred; suppliers are only too happy to answer questions.

aroma. Today, most bayberry candles available at a reasonable price are actually paraffin candles scented with bayberry essential oil. However, some specialty candlemaking-supply houses do offer bayberry wax.

If you wanted to create bayberry candles today, you would need 10 to 15 pounds of berries to make a pound of wax, enough for three to five pairs of dipped tapers. The berries would have to be boiled, the impurities filtered out, and the wax used for either dipping or pouring into molds.

Beeswax. Beeswax is the secretion of honeybees. They use it to build the combs where they store their honey and incubate their larvae. When bees secrete wax, they form it into the hexagonal shapes we associate with honeycombs. Amazingly, all bees, all over the world, have the ability to create hexagons with their wax—and each hexagon has angles

within 3 to 4 degrees of each other! The layers of hexagons are offset from one another and result in the optimal use of space and engineered strength to allow 1 pound of hive wax to hold 22 pounds of honey! When beekeepers remove the honey for processing, they melt down the wax and sell it in blocks for cosmetics and candlemakers.

Beeswax has a wonderful sweet smell, which varies depending on the type of plants and flowers on which the bees feed. Natural beeswax is golden yellow to brownish in color, and contains bee and plant parts. It can be filtered to remove the impurities or bleached to a pure white. It is among the most desirable materials for candlemaking, as it burns slowly with a beautiful golden glow and smells sweet. It can also be mixed with paraffin to create a more affordable but long-lasting candle.

Petroleum Waxes. Paraffins are the most commonly used waxes in candlemaking. They come in a variety of melting-point ranges. Paraffin is a by-product of the process of refining crude oil into motor oil. Crude oil is distilled into fractions, or cuts, in a pipe still. Crude oil is heated at the bottom of this tall pipe and separates according to temperature into petroleum products, from heavy lubricating oil to hydrocarbon gas. Waxes from light lubricating oils are chilled and sweated or distilled off, based on their melting points. These waxes are further refined through hydrogenation and end up with very specific properties.

Generally, candlemaking paraffins are rated by melting point: low, medium, or high. Most candles require using waxes with a melting point of 125° to 150°F. When you are purchasing wax from a craft store or from a candlemaking supplier, the wax will be labeled with its melting point and intended use. Most of the time you will be adding stearic acid to the paraffin to increase its hardness and opacity.

Avoid grocery-store paraffin. The paraffin used for candles is not the same as what is sold in grocery stores for sealing jam jars. This type of paraffin has a much lower melting point than candle wax and makes very soft, drippy candles. As candlemaking is alive and growing as a do-it-yourself craft, waxes are readily available at most craft stores, even in small towns.

Synthetic Waxes. These are a class of waxes used as additives for hardening paraffin or making it pliable. Some of them are highly refined petroleum-based waxes while others are synthetic polymers that act like wax.

Tallow. There were three kinds of rendered animal fat used in candles before the 19th century—mutton fat, from sheep; beef fat; and pig fat. Of the three, mutton was considered the best and pig the worst. Mutton burned longer than the other two, tended not to smoke, and did not smell as bad. Pig, on the other hand, burned rapidly with a thick smoke and a foul smell. You may want to experiment with historical candlemaking, if only to increase your appreciation of how far the craft has come. Be sure to conduct your experiments in a well-ventilated area!

Vegetable Waxes. Candelilla and carnauba waxes are used primarily in wood and leather finishes. Candelilla is a reedlike plant, covered by waxy scales, that is native to northern Mexico and southern Texas. Carnauba is a palm grown in Brazil.

WAX ADDITIVES

There are a number of substances that can be added to wax when you want to achieve special effects in the appearance or characteristics of your candles. Here are a few of the common ones:

Microcrystallines. These are highly refined waxes that serve various purposes for the candlemaker, such as increasing layer adhesion for overdipping and increasing tackiness for wax-to-wax adhesion or modeling wax. There are two major types of micros—the soft, pliable kind, used to increase the elasticity of wax, and the hard, brittle type used to increase the durability of candles. The supplier's information will make clear what each micro is for.

Stearic Acid. While not really an acid in the caustic sense we usually associate with the term, this candlemaking essential is an animal or vegetable fat refined to a flake or powder form. Its name comes from the stear, meaning "solid fat, suet, or tallow." It is, in fact, a natural offshoot of the soapmaking craft. When fat is mixed with wood ashes (alkaline or lye), the chemical reaction produces soap and glycerin through the process of saponification. Mixing the soap with acid produces stearines. Chemical companies today still perform the same chemical reactions to produce soap, glycerin, and stearic acid from animal and vegetable fats.

Stearic acid causes two reactions when mixed with paraffin. It lowers the melting point and, when cooled, makes candles harder, which prevents bending or slumping. The reaction between wax and stearic acid is remarkable because at critical percentages and temperatures, wax and stearic acid change their individual chemical structures to become one composition. Their combination creates a hard candle with an excellent, strong crystalline structure.

Stearic acid also makes otherwise translucent paraffin more opaque. Depending on what you're trying to do, you may want to reduce or eliminate the stearic acid from certain applications, such as overdipping a layer on top of flowers when you want the flowers to show through the translucence of the natural paraffin. Stearic acid is generally sold as Triple-Pressed Stearic Acid. Do not use stearic acid with reactive metal containers or utensils, such as copper, because it is an oxidizer.

Synthetic Polymers. These are synthetic microcrystallines that serve various purposes, such as increasing luster and pliability and raising the melting point of wax. There are also various other additives that help prevent color fading and so forth.

A word of caution: Microcrystallines and polymers should not be used in percentages over 2, since they thicken wax and can cause wick problems. You may need to use a slightly larger wick if you are using high-melting-point micros. They can be used to offset the thinning effect of adding an essential oil for scent, however.

Dipping Candles

The wax formulas and wick types specified in this recipe are meant to be guidelines. The relationship among a wax's melting point, the selected wick type and size, and a finished candle's diameter is critical in determining the successful burning characteristics of a candle. Remember to take notes so that you can repeat your successes or make adjustments for your next batch of candles.

Keeping notes is very valuable and will save you lots of time in the long run. Your candlemaking notebook is an ongoing history of what worked and what didn't, if you jot down what materials and temperatures you used, and add notes later about how well the candles burned. My general rule is to write down everything I would need to know if I wanted to explain what I've done to someone else in a few weeks. What would that person want or need to know?

Continued →

MELTING WAX

The best method for melting wax is to use a double-boiler system. Start with a heavy metal pot for the water, a smaller pot for the wax, and a trivet to hold the smaller pot off the bottom of the double boiler. Your smaller pot should be taller by at least 2 inches than the tallest candle you plan on making.

If you have a deep-fat fryer, slow-cooker, or other concealed-element heater (Crock-Pot), you can use that instead of a double boiler. The important thing is that the wax should not come into direct contact with a heat source.

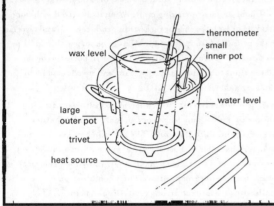

Materials

You will need at least 6 pounds of wax to dip three pairs of 10- by 7/8-inch tapers, more if your dipping can is very widemouthed. Only about half this wax will become candle. The rest is there only to give you the depth you need in your dipping can to completely submerge the candles. Other ingredients are:

- Wick (medium-sized, 1/0 square braid, or 30-, 36-, or 42-ply flat braid)
- One of the following wax formulas:
  - Formula A: 100 percent beeswax
  - Formula B: Paraffin with 5 to 30 percent stearic acid (I like 10 to 15 percent)
  - Formula C: 6 parts paraffin, 3 parts stearic acid, 1 part beeswax
  - Formula D: Paraffin and beeswax mixed in any proportion (keep notes so you know what worked!)
  - Formula E: 60 percent paraffin, 35 percent stearic acid, 5 percent beeswax
- Color, as desired
- Scent, as desired

Equipment

Double boiler or concealed-element heater

Dipping can, at least 2 inches taller than desired length of finished candle

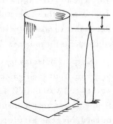

Make sure your dipping can is at least 2 inches taller than the candles you are making.

1 small piece of cardboard

Small weights such as washers, nuts, and curtain weights

Water bucket tall enough to submerge your entire candle

Hook or peg to hang candles on

Step-By-Step

1. Measure a length of wick equal to twice the length of the desired candles plus 4 inches. For example, if you want 10-inch candles, make the wick (2 x 10) + 4 = 24 inches.

2. Tie one small weight on each end of the wick.

3. Cut a 2-inch square of cardboard. This will be your candle frame. Cut a 1/2-inch-deep slash on opposite sides of the cardboard. Fold the wick in half to find its center point. Align this center point with the center of the cardboard (1 inch from the edge). Push the two lengths of wick into the slashes. If you cut a 24-inch piece of wick, you will have two lengths of wick, both approximately 11 inches long, hanging from each side of the cardboard with a 1-inch space between them.

4. Heat the wax in double boiler or heater setup. The wax must be 10 degrees above its melting point—155°F for medium-melting-point paraffin and stearic acid, 165°F if you used the beeswax formula. Add color and scent if desired.

Dip the wicks into your hot wax and pull out smoothly and slowly for a good start to your dipped candles.

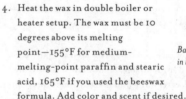

Basic tapers are repeatedly dipped in hot wax to build diameter.

5. Fill dipping can with wax to 1 inch from the top. Add wax as needed throughout the process to keep it at this height.

6. Dip the wicks down into the wax until only about 1 inch of the wicks shows below the cardboard. Hold for 30 seconds. This will allow all the air bubbles to leave the wicks. Pull the wicks up slowly and steadily when you see no more bubbles.

7. Hang the wicks by the cardboard on a peg or suspended dowel until wax feels cool. Do not let the wicks bend. You can speed up this cooling process by dipping the growing candles into water between each wax dip. If you decide to do this, be sure all the water droplets have come off the candles before you redip or you will have wax-covered water bubbles in your candles. These are unsightly and will cause the candles to sputter when you burn them.

8. When the wax feels cool, redip the wicks. Dip in quickly, up to the same point on the wicks as the first time, and pull out slowly and steadily. When the wax is cool, repeat this process once

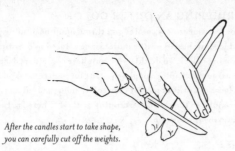

*After the candles start to take shape,
you can carefully cut off the weights.*

more. You should see a small wax buildup. If not, allow your dipping wax to cool by 5 degrees and do these two dips again.

It's a good idea to rotate your cardboard frame each time you dip to avoid bowing the candles. It also helps to be able to see the other side of the candles every other dip to be sure you are getting a smooth layering effect.

9. Continue dipping all the way up to the tip of the growing candles, cooling between dips (the cooling time will increase as the candles thicken), until the tapers are at least 1/4 inch thick at their widest point. The candles will be heavy and stiff enough to weight themselves down at this point, so you can carefully slice off the bottom of each, taking the wick end and weight. The cleaner and straighter you cut the bases, the nicer your finished candle bases will be, but you can also repeat this process later in the dipping to form the finished bases.

To reuse the weights, melt off the wax by dropping into hot wax.

10. Continue dipping until the candles are the desired diameter, 7/8 inch being the most common. Replenish the wax in the dipping can throughout this process as needed to maintain the depth necessary to completely submerge your candles. If the bases are elongated by drips or are uneven as you approach the finished size, trim with a knife and proceed with the last few dips. These dips will round over the bases, giving them a nice shape.

11. Some candlemakers raise the temperature of the wax to 180–200°F for the last two or three dips to improve layer adhesion. Some candlemakers use higher temperature wax, or a higher stearic acid content for the last several dips so that the candle has a harder outer coating and drips less when burned. In my experience, if you have the proper wax-to-stearic-acid ratio for the candle, this is not necessary.

12. If you want a shiny surface on your candles, dip them into cool water immediately after the last dip. Hang the candles on a hook or peg for at least an hour to cool further, then store flat and out of direct sunlight.

Troubleshooting Dipping Problems

It takes time to become a master dipper, and understanding wax temperature is probably the most crucial factor in the process. Shaping the candles and avoiding surface blemishes are also difficult. Following are a few tips for diagnosing trouble.

WHILE DIPPING

- If the candle appears to melt, the wax is too hot, or you are lingering too long in the hot wax.

- If the wax is thick and lumpy, the temperature is too cool.

- If your candle is not growing with each successive dip, the wax is too hot, or you are lingering too long in the hot wax.

- If the candle surface is blistering, the wax is too hot, or you are lingering too long in the hot wax.

- Because the wax shrinks as it cools, successive dips should be of relatively close temperatures and the candle must be cool but not cold when you redip it.

SURFACE BLEMISHES

Surface blemishes can be caused by the wax being too hot or too cold. If the wax is too hot or has too high an oil content, you may get blisters filled with air. If the wax is too cold, it will go on lumpy and thick.

LAYER ADHESION

Good temperature control means good layer adhesion. Layer adhesion is the melding together of successive dips. Poor layer adhesion can result in a candle that breaks apart in concentric circles, like an onion. Good layer adhesion will produce a candle that's a solid rod of wax that will come apart only if intentionally broken.

If you are having problems with layer adhesion, try changing the following during the dipping process:

- Lengthen the submersion time.

- Shorten the time between dips.

- Raise the wax's temperature.

- Increase the ambient (room) temperature or eliminate drafts in your work area.

In fact, the four items listed above—submersion time, time between dips, wax temperature, and room temperature—are all critical. They should be recorded in your notebook and explored whenever you're having trouble dipping quality candles.

Other Dipping Projects

Once you have mastered dipping candles, you can begin to try more advanced methods of finishing your candles. From adding a color or series of colors over a white candle core, to twisting, to creating wax matches, you will learn that dipping is only the beginning.

OVERDIPPING FOR DRIPLESS CANDLES

If you've ever watched a commercially made, dripless candle burn, you're probably noticed that the wax on the outside of the candle melts more slowly than the wax inside. This phenomenon is caused by more than the wax's proximity to the wick. Dripless candles are often overdipped with a layer of wax with a higher melting point than the rest of the candle. This lets the wax close to the wick be consumed by the flame before it can drip.

Overdipping creates a hard outer shell on your candle. You can also use a translucent overdip to adhere decorations to the candle's surface. For this technique, use paraffin without stearic acid. You can overdip any candle you make using the same wax as the candle itself with the addition of 10 percent hardening microcrystalline. No additives are necessary for a beeswax overdip. Beeswax has a higher melting point than most paraffins, so if you want a beeswax look on a paraffin core, submerge the candle two or three times in liquid beeswax. You can overdip beeswax candles with beeswax without any problems.

Continued ➜

Materials

High-melting-point wax

5 to 30 percent stearic acid by weight (depending on technique; see above introduction)

Cool water (optional)

Equipment

Double boiler or concealed-element heater

Pliers

Bucket

Instructions

1. Melt the wax at least 20 degrees above its melting point.

2. In order to ensure good adhesion of an overdip wax, the candle should be warm, not cold. Hold it your hands until it is warm to the touch or keep it in a warm place until you are ready to dip it.

3. Holding the candle's wick with your hands or in a pair of pliers, submerge the whole candle in the overdip, then pull it out slowly and steadily. Work quickly so you don't melt the candle; be aware that it will be soft and pliable for several minutes. A second dip is not necessary but you may decide you want one to thicken the outer layer.

4. If your wax is not deep enough to submerge the whole candle, you can do half, flip it over, and do the other half. If your candle is a spiral with diagonal layers, overdip following the angle of the spiral to conceal the overlap of the overdipping.

5. For a glossy finish, plunge the candle into cool water immediately.

ACCENTING THE TAPER

Dipping creates a natural, slim taper, but you can make this shape more pronounced. Once you've dipped the wick once, follow these instructions for the next three dips.

1. Visually split the length of the candle into quarters. Dip the candle into the wax leaving only the top quarter exposed. Cool.

2. Immerse the candle for a second dip that reaches only to the halfway point of its length. Cool.

3. Make a third dip that covers only the bottom quarter of the candle. Cool. After the above dips are made, some candlemakers make a taper dip one-third up, and then two-thirds up, to smooth over the first lines. Try this if you find your taper lines are too noticeable.

4. Continue dipping the candle (full length) until it has reached the desire diameter.

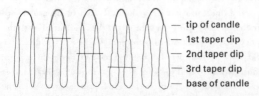

- tip of candle
- 1st taper dip
- 2nd taper dip
- 3rd taper dip
- base of candle

OVERDIPPING AN OUTER COLOR

It is not necessary to use colored wax throughout the dipping process. A dipped (or purchased) white candle can be colored by overdipping it in one or more colors. To do this, you must have containers deep enough to submerge the candles completely—one for each color. You have to melt a large quantity of wax for each color, enough to submerge the whole candle, in the above overdipping method. There are two methods for achieving the overdip.

Method 1

1. Choose any wax formula from page 408. Melt wax either in your wax-melting pot or in individual cans for each color. Add color and scent to each can as you please. Many people use a small percentage of microcrystalline hardener in their overdip formula too.

2. Dip the whole candle, or part of it, in one color. If you want to have two or more colors on the outside of the candle, dip the large end first, then turn the candle over and dip the tip end into a different color. By blending colors at a central band of stripes, you can create some beautiful colors on your candles.

Method 2

This alternative can be used when you have only a small quantity of a particular wax and want to use it to color a candle by overdipping.

1. Assemble deep cans for dipping—one for each color—in a double boiler or heater setup. Fill each can three-quarters full of hot (at least 150°F) water.

2. In smaller cans, combine melted wax with color. Pour the colored wax into one of the deeper cans on top of the water. Keep the water hot so the wax stays melted.

3. Dip the candle through the wax into the water. As you draw it out, the wax will adhere to the candle. You have to work fast, because the hot water will start to melt your candle.

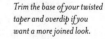

The drawback of this method is that sometimes water adheres to the candle and is coated with wax, forming a bump on the surface of the candle.

TWISTED TAPERS

When you're dipping candles, you'll notice they're very pliable while warm. While they're in this pliable state, you can create some very interesting effects. I find the following twisted tapers particularly beautiful in beeswax. Dip candles as directed until they are about 1/2 inch at the base. Remove the cardboard spacer and twist the two candles around each other. With your fingers, form the base into a 7/8-inch stem to fit in a holder, and you have a double-wicked twisted taper. You can overdip these twisted tapers to make them look more connected.

Trim the base of your twisted taper and overdip if you want a more joined look.

Flattened, then twisted, this taper looks quite elegant.

You can make braided candles the same way, using three or more candles.

FLATTENED TAPERS

After dipping a taper to the desired diameter, flatten it with a rolling pin, leaving the base round so it will fit into a holder. If you grasp both ends of the still-warm candle, you can twist the flattened wax. Or you can shape a taper into leaves or petals..

WAX MATCHES (VESTAS)

If you are someone who lights a lot of candles at one time and has nearly burned your fingers trying to light them before the match burns down, you need wax matches, or vestas. A vesta is a wick coated with only two or three layers of wax that can be lit and used as a long match for lighting many candles. Vestas are easy to make. Follow the basic dipping directions, but make enough wax for only three dips, using medium-sized wicks.

DIPPING MANY CANDLES AT ONCE

There are many ways to do production dipping, limited mostly by the size and shape of your dipping can or tank. In addition to the cardboard-frame technique I explained in the basic dipping instructions, there are other frames a candlemaker can use to make space between candles so they don't stick to one another. Just remember, the more apparatus you use, the more wax-coated "stuff" you will need to snip and melt off.

Any frame you use will become coated with wax that will have to be scraped or melted off. The more surfaces entering the wax, the faster the wax will be consumed, so be prepared to have more wax melted to complete the candles. Some candlemakers stop partway through the process and reclaim, by scraping, as much wax as they can to remelt for continued dipping. Depending on your frame system, this may or may not be possible.

Cleaning Up

I suggest you work on a covered surface so that wax will be caught on a disposable covering. If your candlemaking grows to the point that you have a surface just for candles, it's nice to have a smooth countertop that can be scraped clean of wax so you can save the wax for future projects.

NEVER, NEVER...

NEVER pour wax down the drain! It will solidify and cause you tremendous (and expensive) plumbing problems. Pour extra wax into cups or tins. After it's cooled, store the wax in plastic bags for reuse. You will be able to recycle all the wax you don't use up.

It's not a good idea to pour your double-boiler water down the drain either. Although it's mostly pure water, it probably contains some wax. You can either pour it outside, or allow it to cool thoroughly and remove the solid wax from the surface before pouring the water down the drain.

WAX ON YOUR CLOTHES

If you get wax on your clothes, you have a few options for cleanup. Try one of the following procedures.

- Wait until the wax cools; if it is sitting on the surface of the fibers, scrape it off.

DIPPING-FRAME ALTERNATIVES

As you become more experienced, you might want to try other dipping methods, especially if you plan on dipping a large number of tapers.

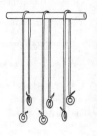

Use hollow rods such as drinking straws and metal tubes as frame spacers and make a continuous looped wick knotted inside the tube with the spacers at the top and bottom of each planned candle.

The simplest way to dip multiple wicks is to hang or knot several wicks over a rod that can be suspended somewhere, for example between two chairs, while the candles cool. If you have a very large dipping tank, you will be able to dip an entire rod's worth of candles at once. If not, you can dip the pairs one at a time, moving the rod in and out of the wax to coat each wick.

You can buy round, metal dipping frames made to fit into some of the available round dipping cans. These have a central post with a hooked top like a coat hanger with four or more protruding rods at the top and bottom on which to thread the wicks. These are modeled after the romaine, a circular dipping system of old, used to lower wicks into cauldrons of hot wax. If you are handy with metal, you can make one of these from old coat hangers or similar-gauge wire.

If you have an oblong dipping tank, you can make a dipping frame from wood or metal, with wick wound around it and spaced properly for the size of candles you plan to make.

- Put the cloth in the freezer and chip off the wax when it's most brittle.

- Place the cloth between layers of kraft paper and iron the wax out of the cloth and into the paper, changing the paper frequently to prevent the wax from redepositing onto the cloth.

- Boil the cloth in water, then wash and dry it. A caution here: When you pull the cloth out of the water, wax can be redeposited in a different place.

- Take the garment to a dry cleaner, letting him know you have a wax stain. Dry-cleaning solvent dissolves wax, but it's best for the cleaner to know about the wax for preliminary spot treatment.

Safety Equipment and Procedures

The importance of safety in candlemaking cannot be overstated. You must be aware of this fact at all times: Making candles requires the use

Continued →

of flammable materials around a heat source. Avoid working around open flames unless it is absolutely necessary.

Always heat wax in a double boiler or in a heating vessel with encased elements. When using a double boiler, never let the water boil away. Replenish the water frequently to maintain the proper level.

Never leave burning candles unattended.

Keep these items handy for extinguishing a fire, and know how to use them:

- Fire extinguisher (ABC type)
- Metal pan lid to starve a fire of oxygen
- Baking soda to smother flames
- A damp cloth or towel

If a fire starts while you are making candles, turn off the source of heat and use an extinguisher, pan lid, baking soda, or damp towel to deplete the oxygen level available to the fire and smother it.

Never use water to extinguish a wax fire! This can cause wax to splatter and increase your chances of being burned.

Decorating Your Candles with Wax

There are a variety of ways you can use special wax techniques for colors to put finishing touches on your candles. You can create candles unlike anyone else's or duplicate beautiful centerpieces you've seen elsewhere.

WARM THE WAX

Before you begin decorating candles, be sure they are warm. They should be at least 85°F, warmer if possible. When I'm decorating my candles, I keep them near the woodstove or heater. In candle factories, they have a "warm room" set up with heaters and temperature controls to keep the wax at a constant 85 to 90°F.

DECORATIVE OVERDIPPING

Overdipping lends itself to several decorative techniques in candlemaking. You can color the outside of a white candle, create a series of colored stripes or ripples, refresh a faded candle, or attach decorations.

Creating Stripes. To make a simple stripe design with overdipping, wrap pieces of masking tape around the places on a candle where you do not want a stripe. For example, if you have a plain white candle that you want to stripe with dark blue, apply the tape everywhere you want to maintain the candle's original white color. Now overdip it in colored wax, let it cool, and carefully remove the tape. To make stripes without masking tape, dip a white candle in one color (red) from its bottom to its halfway point. Turn the candle over and immerse it in a second color (yellow) from its top to a point where it overlaps the first color at least an inch. This overlap will produce a stripe of a third color, in this case orange.

DECORATING WITH SHEET WAX

Decorating Wax is smooth-surfaced sheets designed to be cut into shapes and stuck onto candles. You can buy a pack with 22 different colors to play with. In addition to making one-of-a-kind shapes or figures to decorate your candles, you can also try the millefiori technique.

Millefiori, which means "thousand flowers," is a technique used throughout history by glassmakers. The round, flowerlike motifs are created by making logs, or canes, out of glass, or, in this case, wax. When the log is sliced, each slice is a duplicate of the same design. These slices can be used as a repeat pattern on the surface of a candle. You can press the shapes onto your warmed candle.

FLOWER, LEAF, AND HERB APPLIQUÉ

You can attach relatively flat bits of plants and natural fibers to candles with variations of the overdipping technique. These can be pressed flowers and herbs or freshly dried materials. Do not use stearic acid in the wax, as it will make the overdip opaque and obscure your decorations.

Remember, when decorating your candles, flammable surface treatments can be dangerous! These materials must be used with caution. I've seen dried flower petals on a candle surface catch fire. This form of decoration is best used on larger-diameter candles where the wax pool will be contained and the surface will remain relatively unmelted. Never leave a burning candle of any type unattended.

Begin by attaching the plant or fiber decorations by one of the following methods:

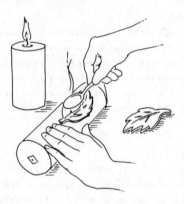

- Pin the flowers to the surface of the candle with straight pins.
- Dip the plant material in melted wax and then attach it to the candle while it is still hot.
- Heat the back of a spoon or use a heat pen to warm the surface of the candle, and then adhere the plant parts to the softened wax.

Once the plant material is adhered to the candle, overdip the entire candle in clear wax. Be sure to pull it out of the overdip slowly, particularly as the decorations emerge, to prevent wax from dripping down the sides.

While the overdip wax is still hot, carefully push on all the tips and corners of the leaves and flowers so they are fully adhered to the candle's surface. Remove the pins. Overdip again to cover any prints and pinholes, then plunge the candle into cool water for a shiny surface.

TROUBLESHOOTING

No matter how careful you are, you will occasionally make candles that don't come out quite right. This chart will help you identify the problem, its possible causes, and solutions.

PROBLEM	POSSIBLE CAUSES	SOLUTIONS
Lumpy	Wax too cold	Increase wax temperature
	Candle too cold when redipped	Keep candle warmer between dips; redip sooner
	Wick not fully saturated during first (priming) dip	Hold wick in wax at least 30 seconds during first dip
Wax not building up	Wax too hot	Decrease wax temperature
Blisters, surface bubbles	Candle too hot	Wait until candle cools more before redipping
Air between layers	Wax too hot	Lower wax temperature
	Wax too cool	Increase wax temperature
Base of candle getting tapered	Candle too cool	Keep candle warmer; redip sooner
	Wax too hot	Lower wax temperature
	Time in wax too long	Decrease time in wax; add more taper lines at base
Flame drowns	Wick too small to absorb and burn off enough	Increase wick size liquid wax

PROBLEM	POSSIBLE CAUSES	SOLUTIONS
Flame drowns	Wax too soft	Use wax with higher melting point or add more stearic acid
Drips	Burning in draft	Shelter candle from drafts
	Wax too soft	Use harder wax; overdip with harder wax
Flame sputters	Wick too small	Use larger wick
	Water in wax or wick	Make sure no water droplets remain on candle cooled by dipping in water
Smokes	Burning in draft Wick too large; consumes wax faster than it can melt	Shelter from drafts Use smaller wick
Won't stay lit	Wick too small to melt enough wax to fuel	Use larger wick
	Wax too hard for wick to melt	Use softer wax
Small flame	Wax too hard	Use softer wax
	Wick too small	Use larger wick
	Wick clogged with pigment	Use oil-soluble dyes
Wick burns hole only down candle center	Wick too small	Use larger wick
	Wax too hard	Use softer wax
Flame too large	Wick too large	Use smaller wick

Continued →

Candle Storage Tips

- Candles must be stored flat. This is particularly true of long tapers, which tend to bend if airspace is left beneath them.

- Store candles in a place that stays cool and dark year-round. Temperatures above 70°F for prolonged periods of time can soften the candles, which can bend or even stick together at these high temperatures. But if they are wrapped and stored properly, your candles should be able to withstand summertime heat.

- Do not refrigerate or freeze candles. This can cause them to crack!

- Candle colors may fade if continuously exposed to light, so be sure to cover the box or close the drawer or cabinet where you store your candles.

- Candle scents can dissipate if the candles are not wrapped in an impermeable covering such as plastic.

Decorative Candle Wrapping

Candles make wonderful gifts, whether or not you make them yourself. They are a great addition to gift baskets because they add color and texture, and because they're useful.

TISSUE PAPER

For a single candle, simply roll tissue paper securely around it and tape or tie with ribbon. To wrap pairs or multiple candles, roll the paper completely around the first candle, then insert the second one so that it does not touch the first and continue rolling. This way, the candles are separated from each other by a layer of paper and serve as stiffeners for each other.

FABRIC AND RIBBON

For gift-giving, I like to wrap the bottom half of a candle in fabric or interesting paper tied with a bow. This allows the top half of the candle to be exposed so people can see, feel, and smell it. If necessary, add a piece of cardboard for extra stiffness before wrapping. This method works best for undecorated candles, since the fabric wrap might cover or clash with the design of the candle.

Making Baskets

Maryanne Gillooly
Illustrations by Brigita Fuhrmann

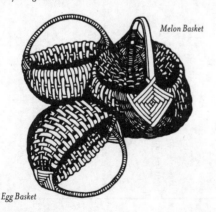

Melon Basket

Egg Basket

TOOLS AND MATERIALS

Tools

Fine sandpaper	Awl
Tape	Pencil sharpener
Pencil	Spring-type clothespins
Tape measure	Towel
Bucket or dishpan (for soaking the reed)	Clippers or snips
Scissors	

Materials

2 basket hoops, 10-inch size (3/4-inch wide)*

1 bundle #7 round reed (for spokes)**

1 bundle 3/16-inch flat reed (for lashing);

1 bundle 1/4-inch flat reed (for weaving)

*The amount of reed you buy, a 1-pound bundle, will make three 10-inch baskets, so you may want to purchase four extra hoops to make two extra baskets. Half-inch wide hoops can also be bought.

**The millimeter size on round reed varies from company to company, so check when ordering. This #7 round reed is 5 MM size. The size is listed in millimeters in the catalogs.

DEFINITION OF TERMS

Handle, the top portion of the vertical hoop.

Handle bottom, the bottom portion of the vertical hoop.

Lashing, the weaving used to bind the two hoops together.

Rim, the horizontal hoop that forms the edge of the basket.

Spokes, the round reeds that form the framework of the basket and provide the warp to weave over and under.

Weaver, the piece or reed or other material used to weave.

Melon Baskets

STEP 1. HOOPS

Start with the two 10-inch hoops. Sand them with fine paper if their edges are rough. Put one pencil mark on the outside of one hoop. Measure half-way around the hoop, about 16 inches, and mark the halfway point. Measure and mark two similar points on the other hoop.

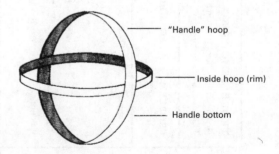

"Handle" hoop

Inside hoop (rim)

Handle bottom

Select a side of one hoop that has no seams or marks and mark it with a piece of tape. This will be the handle. Place this handle hoop on the outside of the other hoop, and have them meet at the pencil marks.

STEP 2. FOUR-FOLD LASHING

The next step is to weave the four-fold lashing that will bind the two hoops together and serve as a place for the ends of the spokes to rest.

The 3/16-inch reed that you use, like other reeds, has a right, or smooth side, and a wrong, or rough side. If you bend one end back and forth you can quickly identify the splintery side and the smoother right side.

Select one of the longest pieces of 3/16-inch reed. Place it in a pan of lukewarm water. When the reed is pliable (this takes about 3 minutes), remove it and shake off any excess water.

Place the crossed hoops in front of you, making certain that the hoops are even on the pencil marks. Start with one crossed section facing you, with the taped handle on top. Follow closely the instructions and the steps below.

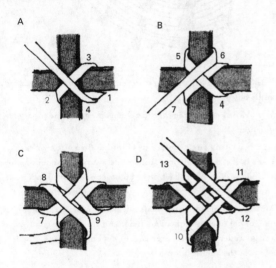

Step A. Place the soaked piece of reed behind the handle bottom at point 1 with the wrong side against the back of the handle bottom. Leave about an inch of the end to be tucked into the weaving as the lashing progresses. From point 2, bring the reed up and across to point 3, with the right side showing, then straight down and behind the rim to point 4.

Step B. Picking up at point 4, bring the reed up and across to point 5, then behind the handle to point 6. You have now formed an X across the hoops. Keeping the reed next to the previous row, bring the reed down and across to point 7.

Step C. Picking up at point 7, bring the reed straight up and behind the rim to point 8, then down and across to point 9. Now bring the reed behind the handle bottom to point 10.

Step D. Picking up at point 10, bring the reed up and across to point 11, then straight down and behind the rim to point 12. Bring the reed up and across to point 13.

At this point you can see the diamond shape of the four-fold lashing. Continue the pattern for eight rows. They can be counted on the back, behind the lashing. Make each row snug to the previous one. There will be a slight overlap on the front of the lashing.

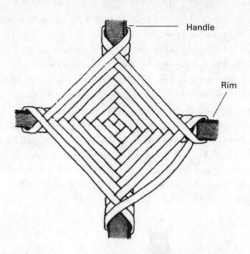

To finish the lashing, cut the end at an angle, with the scissors, then slide the reed under the last row at one of the corners. Use the awl or the pointed end of the scissors to tuck the end in firmly behind the lashing and the hoop.

Repeat this lashing on the other side. Double-check that the hoops are even on the pencil marks.

STEP 3. SPOKES

The spokes form the basic structure and shape of the basket, in this case the round or "melon" shape.

Cut ten pieces of #7 round reed 15 1/2 inches long. Sharpen both ends of each spoke with a pencil sharpener. Soak these only if they are so crooked that they will not form rounded arcs.

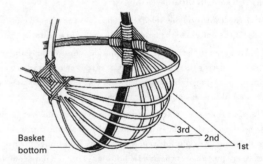

Place five spokes on one side of the basket bottom, tucking the pointed ends inside the pocket formed by the four-fold lashing. First place the two spokes nearest the rim and the bottom of the handle. Then place two more, one next to the top spoke and the other next to the bottom one. Finally, place the fifth spoke in the middle.

Repeat the placement of the spokes on the other side of the basket bottom.

STEP 4. WEAVING

You now have the basic form or framework of the basket. The two hoops are firmly joined by the four-fold lashing and the spokes are evenly spaced and firmly in place.

The weaving begins at the base of the lashing and proceeds from one side of the rim to the other. You might expect that weaving would be continuous, starting at the base of one lashing and continuing under

Continued ➡

the framework until you have reached the lashing on the other side. But that isn't the way it is done. Instead, when the first piece of reed is completely woven in, you begin weaving at the base of the lashing on the other side. The weaving alternates from one side of the basket to the other as each weaver, or piece of reed is used up, until, at the bottom of the basket, the framework is completely filled in with weaving.

The weaving is done in a simple over-one, under-one pattern. However, in the beginning, there isn't enough space between the spokes to weave in and out. So you will notice that the directions call for several steps to follow until eventually, as you continue to weave toward the center of the basket, there is enough space to weave through each spoke. This process is called breaking down. Study the diagrams and follow the instructions exactly, and you will have no trouble with it.

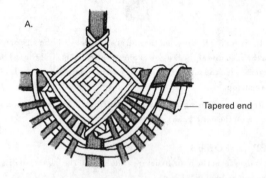

A.

— Tapered end

Before beginning to weave, soak a piece of 1/4-inch reed in lukewarm water until it is pliable. This, too, takes about three minutes. It will fray and crack if soaked too long. Taper one end of the reed by cutting it diagonally with the scissors.

With the lashing on one side facing you, tuck the tapered end into the space at the bottom of the lashing, with the right side down.

Fold the reed to the right, so the right side is up. Weave it under all five spokes, treating them as one unit. Carry the red over and around the rim to the inside of the basket, back out (the wrong side is now out) and over all five spokes, then under the handle bottom.

Continue to the left side by bringing the reed out and over all five spokes on the left, then under and around the rim to the inside, and back out again. The right side is now out. Weave back under the five spokes, then out and over the handle bottom again. You have completed one full row. See Step A.

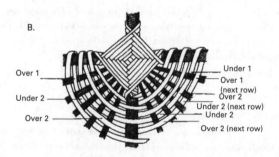

B.

Over 1 —
Under 2 —
Over 2 —

— Under 1
— Over 1 (next row)
— Over 2
— Under 2 (next row)
— Under 2
— Over 2 (next row)

Continue this pattern for one more complete row, again ending at the handle bottom.

Now the pattern changes, as shown in Step B.

Continuing to the right, weave under two spokes, over the next two, under the last one, and then over and around the rim. Weave to the left now, over one spoke, under two, over two, and under the handle bottom. Continue this pattern on the left by weaving over two, under two, over one, under and around the rim. Then weave back, under one, over two, under two, and over the handle bottom. You have completed one row of this new pattern.

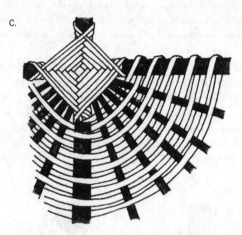

C.

Repeat this step so that you have woven two complete rows ending at the handle bottom.

Your weaving can now change to a simple over and under pattern, as shown in Step C.

You are starting on the outer side of the handle bottom. Weave under one spoke, over one spoke, under one, over one, under one, over and around the rim. Weave back down and over one spoke, under one, over one, under one, over one, and under the handle bottom.

Continue this pattern on the left side, weave over one, under one, over one, under one, over one, and under and around the rim. Weave back and go under one spoke, over one, under one, over one, under one, and over the handle bottom.

This pattern will be continued for the rest of the basket.

When the weaver is used up, secure it with a clothespin and repeat this breaking down process on the other side of the basket. The reason for alternating from side to side is that it's easier to make the basket more uniform in shape.

STEP 5. PIECING

You now have used up a weaver on each side of the basket. You're ready to add a new piece.

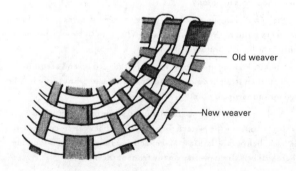

— Old weaver

— New weaver

Soak another reed until it is pliable. Start on the side you finished first, remembering that you are alternating from one side to the other. Place the new weaver right on top of the first one and overlap it by 3 or 4 inches. This should be done away from the rim. If the weaver ends near the rim, cut it back so the piecing stays in the middle. If the first weaver ended with the wrong side showing, lay the new weaver on top of the old one with the wrong side showing. Thus the pattern of rows alternating right and wrong sides will be continued.

The end of the new weaver can be tucked under a spoke or the handle bottom to hide it.

Proceed with the weaving as before by continuing with the new piece.

STEP 6. COMPLETING THE WEAVING

Continue weaving from one side of the basket to the other. Do not, however, weave past the middle with either side of the weaving. If one section of weaving reaches the middle and there is some reed left, stop, clip the reed with a clothespin, then weave the other side until it reaches the middle.

When the weaving nears completion, the reed from each side is joined by overlapping one on top of the other, just as you did in piecing. You may need to cut one or both reeds to have them overlap by 3 or 4 inches, and not near the rim.

If you followed these directions exactly, the weaving pattern will be correct, so that the two reeds don't meet weaving over and under the same spoke.

But if you didn't and they do, you can do one of two things:

1. Gently push the weaving apart on each side (toward the rims) just enough to squeeze in another row of weaving and thus make the pattern correct.

2. If the space is too small for another row of weaving, take out the last uneven row. Then fill in the gap by gently pushing the weaving from each side toward the middle.

Finish by cutting any long ends, stray fibers, or wisps of reed. The basket should sit level. If it doesn't, soak it for a few minutes, then gently press down on the inside bottom, to form it so that it will sit level. Then I usually put a smooth round rock inside to weigh it down, and leave it to dry for a day or two.

STEP 7. THE HANDLE

The handle can be left with the wooden hoop showing, or it can be covered in a variety of ways. Here are several ways:

1. The Simple Wrap.

Select a piece of 3/16-inch reed long enough so the handle can be wrapped without piecing. Soak it, then push one tapered end, right side down, into the space between the hoop and the top of the lashing. Fold the reed over and, with the right side now showing, begin to wrap rows of reed around the handle. Each row should be snug to the last one.

Continue wrapping around the handle to the other side. Cut the reed at an angle and short enough to push down into the space at the top of the lashing. An awl can be a great help in getting the end securely down inside the lashing.

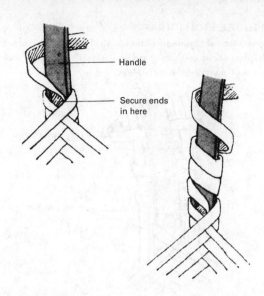

Handle

Secure ends in here

2. THE WOVEN WRAP.

Using the same wrap as in the simple wrap, a variety of patterns can be achieved by weaving over and under another strand of reed.

Secure both the soaked weaver and a length of thin reed, soaked, at the top of the lashing. This reed should be just a bit longer than the handle, it must reach from one lashing to the other.

Wrap the weaver once around the handle, going over the shorter reed. Next, pick up the reed and wrap the weaver under it. Continue this pattern, going over and under the reed, until all of the handle is covered. Secure the ends into the top of the lashing on the opposite side.

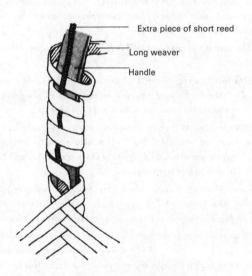

Extra piece of short reed

Long weaver

Handle

This pattern can be changed easily by weaving over or under the reed a different number of times. It could be over two, under two; or over two, under one; or over one, under two. A handle bigger than this one could be woven over and under three or more times.

Try changing the shape or color of the short reed. Or, with a wider handle, try adding two short reeds to weave through.

Continued ➡

3. FIGURE EIGHT WRAP.

Cut two pieces of #7 round reed the length of the handle. Sharpen the ends, place one on each side of and parallel to the handle and tuck them inside the pockets behind the lashings.

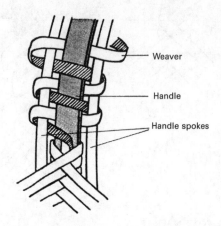

Weaver
Handle
Handle spokes

Select a lengthy weaver, soak it until it is pliable, then secure one end, wrong side down, in the space at the top of the lashing. Fold it over and weave it under and around one side spoke, under the handle, then up and around the other side spoke and over the handle. Continue weaving in this manner until the handle is completed. Secure the end of the weaver in the space at the top of the lashing on the opposite side.

Dyes

Dyeing basket materials offers you a chance to use your imagination. It's a lot of fun. The flat and round reed, the spokes, and even some wild materials can be dyed. Or a whole basket can be dyed one color when it is completed. I prefer to dye my materials separately so that I can use more than one color in a basket.

The easiest and fastest method is to dye with packaged commercial fabric dye.

One small package of dye (1 1/8 pounces) will dye about a pound of reed. I mix the commercial packaged dye in our stainless steel kitchen sink, but a large, old pot or metal container can be used.

Mix according to package directions, using hot water right from the tap. Stir until well dissolved. Wet the reed before placing it in the dye bath. Leave the material in until it is the shade you want. Don't forget that it will look lighter when it dries.

I like to leave some reed in the dye for about 30 minutes, replace it with some that I leave in for 15 minutes, then replace that with some that I dye for just a few minutes. That gives me three shades of the same color.

Remove the reed from the dye bath with a stick or old wooden spoon, rinse it in clear water, and place it on lots of paper towels to drain. Then hang it to dry completely. I use out clothesline in the cellar for this, but any place outside in the shade will do.

When dyed reed is soaked later for weaving, some of the color may come out. Use separate soaking pans for each color.

If you have a large pot, you can dye a finished basket. First, try a test piece of reed to make certain the color is right. Then wet the basket, place it in the dye bath, and move it about with a stick. Take it out when it reaches the right shade, pat it with paper towels, and hang it up to dry. Leave some towels underneath to catch the drippings.

Some of my students have had excellent results using the stains sold for staining wood. Thin these with turpentine or mineral oil.

Acrylic or latex paint can also be thinned and applied directly to the basket with a brush. In each case, test with a small piece of reed to make certain the color is what you want.

You can also apply mineral or linseed oil to a basket. The oak basket hoops look especially beautiful when coated with oil.

If you're planning to use the basket for food, use a finish that is non-toxic, or leave the basket natural.

NATURAL DYES

Using dyes from natural materials requires time and patience, but is rewarding. The only dye I know of that does not call for a mordant (fixative) is black walnut hulls. The colors obtained from natural materials, without using a mordant, are not as longlasting nor as vivid, but paler and more subtle. I prefer them that way and feel better not using the many chemicals required in mordanting.

To use black walnut hulls:

Soak 1/2 pound of walnut hulls overnight in 3–4 gallons of water.

The next day boil the hulls in the water for an hour.

Let cool, then strain the dye through cheesecloth.

Wet the reed, and leave it in the dye until it is the desired shade.

To get a darker brown, try more hulls or less water.

This procedure can be used with coffee, tea, or any other natural materials.

Variations

You now know how to weave a 10-inch basket, color it in different ways, and decorate its handle. It's time for us to experiment, to try new and different methods of weaving and variations on materials. Let's see what they are.

HOOPS

The basic basket can be changed in many ways by using a different size or shape of hoop. Round hoops come in sizes from 4 to 18 inches, and widths of 1/2 to 3/4 inch. Oval hoops are available in several sizes. Try combining oval and round hoops, using one for the handle and the other for the rim. There are also "D" frames available for wall baskets and square frames for market baskets. All of these can be made using the same procedure as the basic basket.

Basket hoops, too, are offered in different woods—poplar, oak, hickory. Hard wood is preferred, but a beginner can start with less expensive plywood.

My favorite basket has wild grapevine for the hoops and spokes. I gather vines about H inch thick, peel off the bark, and twine the vine into a circle. Make two circles of the size desired, insert one inside the other, and follow the steps using in weaving the basic basket.

You can use thick vine for a large basket, thin vine for a small one. Because of the irregularities of the vine, I usually use a three-fold, instead of a four-fold lashing.

Other vines can be used, such as honeysuckle, wisteria, or whatever is native to your area. Even the thicker, purchased round reed can be twined into hoops and used to make especially attractive handles. So...experiment.

Whether you try a large, small, round, or oval basket, be sure to adjust your materials accordingly. By this I mean that for baskets smaller than the basic one, use narrower reed for weaving and a smaller size spoke. Just the opposite for a larger basket.

THREE-FOLD LASHING

A different type of lashing can be made to secure the basket hoops together. The three-fold lashing is a little easier, so if you have difficulty with the four-fold lashing, try this one. While I think the four-fold lashing is more secure and attractive, in some cases, such as with a grapevine basket or any basket without a handle, it is necessary to make a three-fold lashing. The following intructions are for a 10-inch basket.

Mark the loops and set them in place. Soak a 3/16-inch weaver, then begin the lashing on one of the crossed sections of the hoops.

Step A. Place the reed, wrong side out, behind the handle bottom at point 1. Leave about an inch of the end to be tucked into the weaving as it progresses. At point 2, bring the reed up and across to the top of the rim on the right side to point 3. Bring the reed straight down behind the rim to point 4. Bring the reed up and across to the rim on the left side of point 5, then down behind the rim to point 6. This forms an X across the hoops, and only the right side of the reed should be seen.

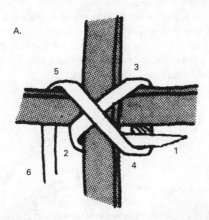

Step B. At point 6, twist the reed so that it lies flat over the handle bottom with the right side showing. At point 7, twist again, and bring the reed under and around the rim to point 8, then back down to point 9. Twist and bring the reed under the handle bottom to point 10.

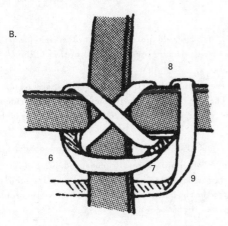

Step C. At point 10, twist the reed and bring it over and around the rim to point 11, then back down to point 12. Twist the reed and bring it over the handle bottom to point 13.

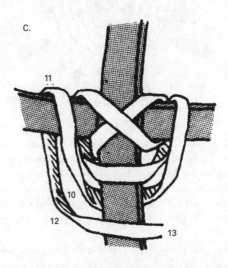

Step D. At point 13, twist and bring the reed under and around the rim to point 14, then down to point 15. Twist and bring the reed under the handle bottom to point 16. Continue in this manner for four or five rows. Note that the twisting in all cases is so that the right side of the reed will show. Stop at the handle bottom and secure the weaver with a clothespin. Repeat this much of the lashing on the other side of the basket.

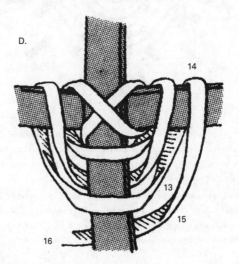

PLACING THE SPOKES

With this method of lashing, the spokes have to be placed as the weaving progresses. At this point, two spokes should be added on each side. Cut four spokes from #7 round red, making them 15 1/2 inches long. Sharpen both ends of each spoke. Place one spoke in each of the spaces in the lashings, as shown.

Pick up the weaver where you secured it, and begin weaving over and under each spoke. Weave from rim to rim as in the weaving of the basic basket. After weaving two rows, secure the weaver with a clothespin at the handle bottom, and repeat this much on the other side of the basket.

Continued →

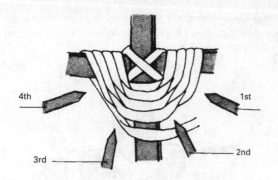

4th
1st
3rd
2nd

Round Reed	MM Size*	Hoop Size
#4 round reed	2 3/4	4-inch or smaller basket
#5 round reed	3 1/4	6-inch or 8-inch basket
#6 round reed	4 1/2	8-inch or 10-inch basket
#7 round reed	5	10-inch or 12-inch basket
#8 round reed	5 3/4	12-inch or 14-inch basket

*The MM (millimeter) size differs among many suppliers. Check when ordering.

You will now add more spokes on each side of the basket. Cut and sharpen six spokes, three for each side. Four of them should be 13 inches long, two should be 15 inches long. Place them as shown below, with two 13-inch spokes under each side of the basket rims, two others on each side of the handle bottom, and the 15-inch spokes in the middle between the two original spokes. Push them into the weaving to secure them.

Starting again on top of the handle bottom, continue to weave over and under, going through all five spokes on each side of the basket, and around each rim.

If you make a basket smaller than the 10-inch basic basket, you will need fewer than ten spokes—and a bigger basket will require more than ten spokes.

On the larger baskets, since the pocket of the lashing won't hold more than five spokes on each side, the extra spokes must be added after the weaving has started. Here's how we do it.

ADDING EXTRA SPOKES

With larger baskets the space between spokes shouldn't be more than 1 1/2 inches. If it is, extra spokes must be added. To add spokes, complete weaving the same number of rows on each side of the basket. Measure the length of the still-exposed areas of the other spokes, add about 2 inches to this length, and cut spokes that length. Sharpen both ends of the spokes, then insert them as shown below.

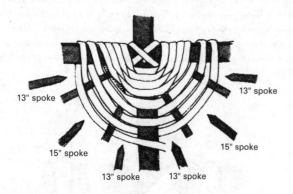

13" spoke
13" spoke
15" spoke
15" spoke
13" spoke
13" spoke

When the reed is used up, repeat the weaving on the other side, until that weaver is used up. If you are delayed in doing all of this and the reed becomes too dry for weaving, soak what remains while holding the basket close to the surface of the water.

Continue the weaving, piecing, and finishing as described for the basic basket. For a variation, however, you can complete an equal number of rows on each side with the 3/16-inch reed, then switch to 1/4-inch reed, doing the piecing for this at the handle bottom.

SPOKES

Spokes form the framework and determine the shape of the basket bottom. By varying their length and placement, spokes can be used to construct round baskets, egg-shaped baskets, or any variation in between. As you become more familiar with the basic principles of basket-weaving, you will be able to make a shape that pleases your eye without using any measurements.

This thickness or size of the spokes must vary according to the size of the basket. Here is a table of the spoke sizes that go best with various sizes of baskets.

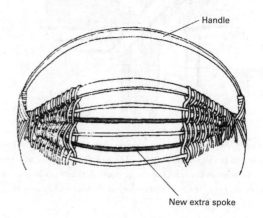

Handle

New extra spoke

You will, of course, add spokes in pairs, two on each side of the basket. The weaving then continues by including the additional spokes.

For a variation on any basket, try placing extra spokes on top of the rim. They can be longer than the rim, to form a wide ridge or lip on the basket, or they can be smaller, to close in the opening of the basket.

Tuck the spokes into the pocket of the lashing, on top of the rim.

Weaving and other procedures are unchanged. Just continue each row of weaving past the rim and over the extra spokes. Treat the last spoke as you do the rim in the basic basket. Bend the weaver around it and continue weaving back down.

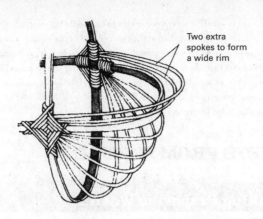

Two extra
spokes to form
a wide rim

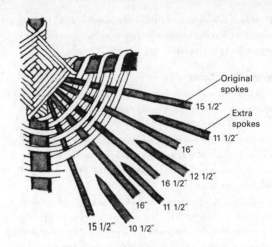

Original
spokes

15 1/2"

Extra
spokes

11 1/2"

16"

12 1/2"

16 1/2"

16"   11 1/2"

15 1/2"   10 1/2"

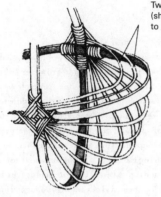

Two extra spokes
(shorter than the rim)
to close in the opening

bend. Weave around that spoke, and back down to within one or two
spokes of the previous bend on the other side.

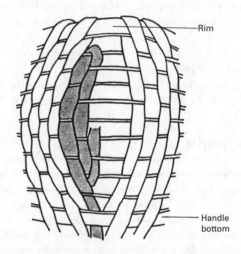

Rim

Handle
bottom

Continue weaving through progressively fewer spokes until you
have reached the widest part of the space. Then reserve the process by
increasing the number of spokes you weave over until the area is
completely filled in.

Egg Baskets

An egg basket can be made by following the earlier instructions for
making the basic basket. The one difference is that the spokes must be
of different lengths.

Here are the lengths of the spokes you will need for a 10-inch egg
basket:

4 spokes 15 1/2 inches long

4 spokes 16 inches long

2 spokes 16 1/2 inches long

Extra spokes, added after the weaving measures 3 inches on each
side:

4 spokes 11 1/2 inches long

2 spokes 10 1/2 inches long

2 spokes 12 1/2 inches long

The diagram shows the pattern of the spokes on one side of the
basket. Repeat the pattern on the other side.

Because of the shape of the egg basket, the weaving will completely
fill the rim, and cover the handle bottom, while the middle sections
remain unwoven.

This space can be filled in by continuing with a weaver you are
already using, or starting a new one, overlapping the earlier weaver at
the handle bottom. Weave over and under in the usual manner, until
you reach the first or second spoke nearest the rim. Bend the weaver
over the spoke, as you would at the rim, and continue weaving to the
other side. Again, bend the reed over the first or second spoke near the
rim and weave all the way back within one or two spokes of the previous

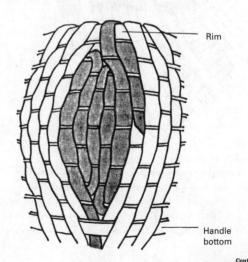

Rim

Handle
bottom

Continued ➡

Treat each unwoven space in the same manner, using this step-like procedure. With an egg basket of this size, you may have to weave only a few rows to fill in the middle.

Weaving Variations

In hoop-constructed basketry, the weaving pattern remains constant, but many variations can be achieved by using different weaving materials. In this way you can add color, texture, and interest.

Flat reed used for weaving comes in widths from 3/16 to 1 inch. Try weaving with different widths. Be sure to keep the width of the reed proportional to the basket size—too wide a reed, for example, will look cumbersome in a small basket.

It is also possible to weave with some of the small, round reed. It is available in sizes from #0 (1 1/4 MM size) to #17 (15 3/4 MM). The thicker round reed, from about #5 up, is primarily used for spokes. I like to weave with round reed at the beginning of the weaving. The lashing can also be done in #2 round reed.

Add interest by weaving in some wild materials. Your choices include thin vines, strips of bark, cattail leaves, and cornhusks. Even twine, seagrass, and wool fabric strips can be used. Experiment with these and others.

As for colored reed, the sky is the limit. Dye your own and make rows of various colors.

Be certain, whenever changing colors or weaving materials, to do the piecing at the handle bottom. Each new row should be started at that central point.

Exterior Weaving

When the basket is completed, extra weaving, usually in a contrasting color, can be done along the outside of the rim and the handle bottom.

Soak a piece of narrow reed until it is pliable. Insert one tapered end into the side of the lashing, then weave over and under each piece of reed along the rim. When the weaving reaches the other side, cut the end and slide it into the side of the other lashing. The next row of weaving should be done just below the first row. Alternate the weaving so that the second reed goes under where the first reed went over.

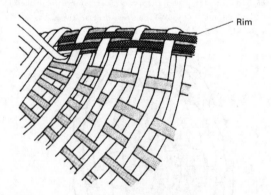

Rim

Repeat this exterior weaving on the other half of the rim. A knife or slender tool, such as a small screwdriver, is very helpful for gently lifting up the reed so the weaver can slide under it. Usually, with a 3/4-inch hoop, only two rows of exterior weaving can be done along the rim. It will, of course, depend on the width of the reed you are using.

There is usually enough room along the handle bottom to fit three rows of exterior weaving. Insert the tapered end of the weaver into the bottom of the lashing, weave around to the other side, cut, and secure the other end into the bottom of the lashing on that side. Repeat for two more rows, making sure that the weaving pattern is the opposite of the first row. I sometimes like to use a different color in the middle row and repeat that color in the handle.

GIFTS FROM NATURE

Making Grapevine Wreaths

Gayle O'Donnell
Illustrations by Alison Kolesar

All About Grapevine

The wild grapevine generally appears as a stringy, woody, tangled web of reddish-brown twigs and branches, which seem to grow every which way. The vines are always visible throughout the seasons. Young leaves sprouting off the bare vines appear pinkish towards the middle to the end of April depending on where you live, becoming large and round, toothed, sometimes heart-shaped and often lobed as they mature. They form heavy, leafy canopies by summertime as they drape themselves over bushes and stone walls and hang from trees. In the autumn the leaves turn a rich yellow color, then drop to reveal their delicious fruits, exposing the abundant reddish-brown vines among the vegetation.

Grapevine comes in all shapes, sizes, and lengths; in shades of reddish-browns, tans, greens, and greys. There is a very old vine that is as thick as a baseball bat, vine so long that kids can swing on it, and vine as thin as yarn. It can have all kinds of natural bends, twists, and angles. Older vine can be rather long, thick, and branched. It usually has a couple of layers of bark, the outer bark being loose and shaggy. The vine underneath is generally of a tan color. Despite their size, the older vines are amazingly flexible.

Young vines are the newer shoots which haven't had many years in the elements. There is usually a single, tough, stringy layer of bark in shades of browns to reds to purples, and some varieties have a waxy feel to the bark. These vines are generally less branched, can be quite long, and have wonderful new curling tendrils. Underneath the bark, the vine is very green. This vine is still flexible but it does tend to break more easily. Vines can take on a silver-grey color from being very old and weathered, the same way cedar and other woods change color with age.

PICKING ATTIRE

Picking attire for collecting grapevine should consist of old clothes including long pants, long sleeves, and gloves to avoid cuts, scratches, splinters, and the like. Don't wear a sweater because the vine's branches and tendrils will get hooked in it and everything else, from clothes to jewelry to glasses to shoelaces. It is not a bad idea to wear eye protection to guard from falling debris or being poked in the eye with a branch.

The vines should be gathered fresh. Some sources suggest soaking vines that are not fresh in water until pliable, but I find it just as easy to pick fresh vines. The vines are flexible, pliable, and can be bent and twisted quite easily. As they dry out, they keep their shape very well. The vines don't have to be used immediately. After it is picked, the vine can remain outside unused for a few weeks, more or less, depending on the size of the vine and the weather. The thicker and heavier the vine is, the longer it can sit outside, especially if the weather is cold and/or wet. The thinner the vine and the drier and hotter the weather is, the more quickly it will dry out. As long as there is some flexibility to a cut vine there is no problem in using it. You'll know soon enough if it is too dry as you use it.

The ideal and the most pleasant time for gathering vines is in the fall. By this time the big yellow leaves have nearly all dropped or they come off easily when the vine is pulled down, and the juicy purple grapes are ripe for picking, if the birds and animals haven't gotten to them first. I continue to pick grapevine throughout the winter, though not nearly as much as in the fall.

The leaves begin to bud about mid-April, and the vines are still easy to find and gather. But, as spring turns to summer, the leaves quickly grow rather large, new shoots sprout, and suddenly there is lush, green growth everywhere. The big leaves, long shoots, and new tendrils make the vines very heavy, and if picked during the summer, you must cut off and discard this new growth—none of it is good for crafting. New green shoots are too fleshy, like plant stems, and they have yet to develop the layer of bark which begins to appear later in the fall. The leaves can be used for rolling or stuffing, however.

LOCATING GRAPEVINE

Locating patches of grapevine is easy. Friends, relatives, or neighbors may have grapevines on their property. Take a walk in the woods; take a ride down an old country road. Scan the roadsides. Look up at the trees and into the bushes. In the summer, the size and appearance of the leaves stand out among the surrounding vegetation. Look for the heavy, leafy canopies formed by all the new growth. In late fall and winter look for the stringy, reddish-brown, web-like growth. Think of it as the plant's skeleton. The color stands out well against stone walls, bare shrubbery, and the greyish trees, and even more so against the white snow.

After finding a good patch of grapevine in the autumn, the first thing you should do is to get permission to pick, if possible. Most of the time, if you ask a landowner if you may trim his vines, he won't object. Then, stand back and study the area for a moment. You must be sure you are picking fresh live vine and not old dead vine. From a distance, you can't really tell after the leaves are gone unless you remember seeing leaves during the summer. You'll have no trouble spotting live areas of grapevine during the growing season, but after the leaves and grapes have dropped, the only way to tell is to feel and bend the vine. Live, fresh vine bends without breaking, and when cut, looks green and moist inside. Old dead vine is brown, dry, and brittle, and is not useful for crafting.

Scatter your picking areas so that the vine has time to grow back, which it seems to do rather quickly. I have found that I can go back to many areas year after year, picking the new growth and older growth that I had missed or bypassed a year or two before. You also may find different varieties of grapevine by picking in other areas. Other varieties may have different colored vines or bark, different textures or appearances, different shaped leaves, and different lengths of vine.

CUTTING GRAPEVINE

Focus on just one branch and trace it to its beginning. It may be growing directly from the ground or it may keep branching off larger and thicker sections of vine. It may grow one hundred feet straight up into a tree or it may be short and full of branches that cover fences, stone walls, and bushes, depending on what it has to climb on.

With a pair of clippers, cut the vine at the thickness you want. Don't pull it up out of the ground—as long as you don't uproot the vine, it will grow back. Then start to yank, jerk, pull, and tug until the vine loosens and can be pulled free. Each time one vine is freed, you'll discover many more vines that were buried or hidden. Beware of pulling grapevine from dead tree limbs. A good strong vine will bring the dead wood along with it, and sometimes an entire dead tree!

If the grapevine you want is climbing high up in a tree, first try to pull it down instead of cutting it. That way, if you can't pull it down, at least it can continue to grow and produce grapes. If you cut it and then can't free it, it is a waste. If you are pulling on a vine that has a few branches, try loosening one branch at a time.

Grapevines, and any other vines that climb by tendrils, are generally very easy to pull down because the tendrils are the part of the vine which attach and curl around other branches and such. Vines without tendrils such as bittersweet, twist and twine their stems around themselves and other branches, and cannot be pulled down easily.

Preparing Your Vines

After picking and transporting the vines to a working area, the process of cleaning, separating, and sorting begins. There sits a mountain of grapevines just waiting to be lovingly crafted and woven into all kinds of beautiful wreaths, baskets, and unique works of art, but first it must be divided up into some kind of manageable amounts. It is much easier to work if you can see what you have to work with.

I start by pulling out and cleaning the thickest, heaviest vines and putting them in one pile. Cleaning is nothing more than cutting off any smaller unwanted branches, broken or dead ends, leaves, and so on. The longest and biggest of the heavy vines, about one-half inch up to about three-quarters of an inch in diameter, are mostly used for weaving giant outdoor wreaths for houses, garages, or barns. These huge vines, which tend to be long, old, shaggy, and without many tendrils, are amazingly flexible despite their size, and it's fun to see what monster creations you can make!

Next, I take all of the leftover branches of vine, examine and clean each one individually, and then see what each branch has to offer. If there are any long, thin, single vines sprouting off a branch, I clip them off and make a second pile. These single vines, similar in thickness to heavy twine, are ideal for basket weft, delicate heart wreaths, tiny wreaths, lashing or sewing, or other small projects.

The vine branches that are left over go into a third pile of medium-sized (about the thickness of a pen or pencil), approximately five feet in length or longer, branched or single. These pieces can be used for almost any wreathmaking. Branched vines make nice, full wreaths. Other vine branches may be good for solid wreaths or smaller wreaths.

As you can see, very little goes to waste!

SUPPLIES AND EQUIPMENT

Now that the vines have been sorted, it is time to design and create. There is no need to go out and buy any special tools for crafting with grapevine. You probably have most of these things around your house or workshop.

Garden Clippers. These are perfect for grapevines, from cutting down the vines to clipping off dead or broken branches to trimming your creation. A good, heavy pair of scissors will work just as well.

Continued →

Pliers. Regular pliers are useful when making forms out of coat hangers. Needlenose pliers may come in handy to insert or pull out a vine you can't grasp with your fingers.

Masking Tape. Masking tape can temporarily hold grapevine pieces together until they are secured by wrapping or weaving. Cut off or pick out once the area is held together.

Awl or Screwdriver. The awl or any long thin instrument can be used to open up a passageway between vines for inserting another vine.

Coathangers. These can be bent into a variety of shapes with a pair of pliers and wrapped in thin vine.

Hot Glue Gun. A good tool for attaching decorations to grapevine, but use with care—hot glue can burn. Use a stick to push the glued pieces together instead of your finger.

Tacky Glue. A good, clear-drying glue for attaching decorations to grapevine, but slow-drying.

Unscented Hairspray. An inexpensive way to apply a layer of lacquer to dried flowers, weeds, and such with fuzzy or fly-away flowers or seed pods.

Designing Wreaths

Traditionally, wreaths have been a part of the holiday season, but the use of wreaths goes back to ancient cultures. The Greeks and Romans used them as headdresses or head garlands made out of leaves, greens, and tree boughs such as olive, laurel, oak, pine, holly, and mistletoe. The ancient Olympians were given wreaths of olive or laurel as their prizes, Jesus wore a wreath or crown of thorns, and both Julius Caesar and Napoleon wore crowns of laurel, which symbolized triumph and eternity.

Crown comes from the Latin word, *corona*, which means wreath, crown, or garland, and the circle symbolizes eternity. Wreaths have been worn by royalty for centuries, and by the addition of jewels, stones, and metals, have become the ornate crowns we associate with royalty today. Unfortunately, it is not clear as to when wreaths as head ornaments became home and wall decorations.

Wreaths are no longer limited to front door decorations. Today wreaths of all shapes, color combinations, and sizes can be found in every room of the house; as well as in churches, offices, banks, restaurants, and other businesses. They appear in all decorating styles and in every season of the year.

A grapevine wreath has a pleasing natural look that is so popular these days. And because it is natural, there is no need to strive for perfection. No wreath or grapevine creation can or should be perfectly even, perfectly round. But it will be perfectly natural and unique. There is no right or wrong way to craft with vines, so it is impossible to make a "bad" wreath!

A grapevine wreath, whether simply decorated with a full paper bow, serving as a frame for pictures, mirrors, little scenes or still lifes, or gracing a table as a unique centerpiece, can go as far as your imagination and creativity allow. The possibilities are endless! Now get the clippers ready.

Round and Full Wreath

TIPS FOR WORKING WITH GRAPEVINES

- Grapevine creations are meant to be uneven, irregular, imperfect, even lopsided. Its natural state and beauty should be stressed.

- Pick fresh, live vine. It is quite flexible and can be bent, shaped, and twisted easily. Dead grapevine is of no use.

- Begin with the thicker end or butt end of the vine and work towards the thinner end or the tip.

- Incorporate natural bends, angles, and forks into your project for shaping and added reinforcement.

- Spend time searching through the piles of vine for a particular piece that will work well for what you are doing—a certain thickness, a certain length, a fork, and so on.

- To remove bark from the vine easily, gently bend the vine back and forth so the bark cracks and separates.

- Young vine is sometimes very long and thin, great for small wreaths and rings, but it snaps more easily than older vine.

- Try to readjust your wrapping to avoid placing the knobs on a curve or a bend. Breakage will occur if you try to make the vine bend on or near the knobby areas from where the tendrils or stems sprout. It will bend nicely between the knobs.

- You can pull and twist the vine just so far before it cracks, splits, or breaks. By working with the vine, and with time, patience, and practice, you will develop a feel for the material and discover just how far it will go, what it can do, and how to maneuver it.

- If your vine does break at any point, simply tuck the broken end into the weaving, and begin in that general area with another piece of vine.

- In wreathmaking, start a bit smaller than the size you wish to end up with. Wreaths tend to increase in size as you wrap and add vines.

- Often, some of the tendrils will get buried as you wrap and twist the vines. Pick and stretch them out as you go along if you want them exposed. When making a wreath, determine which side is the front and bend the tendrils on the backside toward the center or to the sides. Cut off any tendrils that will prevent the wreath from laying flat against a wall.

Materials needed

clippers

some medium-weight branched vines approximately 6 feet or more in length a few long, single vines

1. Select two or three vines, line up the butt ends together, and hold them all in one bundle. Bring the ends around to form a circle and make a simple overhand knot. The circle will stay together and you can check your measurement. Pull the knot tighter if you want a smaller wreath, let it out a little if it is not big enough.

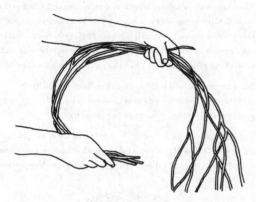

Start with two or three vines, butt ends together. Form a circle and make a simple overhand knot.

2. Coil the remaining vines around the circle you just made, grasping the vine circle in one hand as you coil with the other. (Think of the way you would coil up a length of hose or rope.) Tuck the ends of the vines into the circle. Your wreath may or may not be as thick as you want it, depending on the lengths of the vines you started with. For more fullness, add another few vines. Insert the thicker ends into the circle and coil these vines around in the same manner as before, tucking in the ends. Now you have a loose circle of vines which has to be held together somehow.

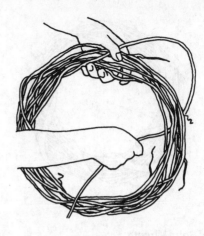

3. Next, select a long single length of vine. This piece will be used to wrap in and out around the circle, holding the vines and any loose ends all together. Tuck the thicker end of this vine into the circle, finding a snug spot. Grasp the other end and begin to thread it in and out, in and out, all around the circle of vines. Go around as many times as you can with that piece. When it runs out, tuck the end into the wreath, again finding a snug spot.

No one can tell you when your wreath is done. It's all up to you. A wreath is finished when you like it, when its appearance is pleasing to you. Then give it a final trim, as much or as little as you like.

A second method to achieve a full wreath is by piling up single rings or circles of vine. This is a method I use when the vines are not long enough to coil or when I accumulate a lot of short, leftover pieces. As long as the vine is long enough to make a knot, you can make a single ring; and a pile of rings will make a wreath.

For a 12-inch diameter wreath, make a variety of circles between 10 and 12 inches across. Pile them all up together until it appears to be the thickness you want, staggering the knot areas. Then continue as in step 3 by selecting a long single vine to wrap in and out around all the rings.

Simply insert the end into the pile of rings you are holding and thread this piece in and out, going completely around a few times until all rings and ends are secured.

VARIATIONS

*   Vary the tension of the wrapping vine in step 3. By wrapping it loosely, your wreath will look lighter and fuller. By pulling it tighter, the wreath will be more compact.

*   Vary the thickness or appearance of the wrapping vine. A much thicker wrapping vine around a circle of many thin vines will emphasize the pattern of the wrap. A stripped green vine, a shaggy brown vine or a silver-grey vine can also be wrapped around the vine circle to emphasize different colors and textures.

*   Vary the direction and placement of the wrapping vine. By adding additional vines and wrapping in opposite directions, you can create a variety of patterns. Also, the number of times the vine is wrapped around the circle adds to the pattern. Let your creativity go wild—experiment with thicknesses and colors of vine in different combinations for a variety of patterns and appearances.

Continued ➔

Using a larger wrapping vine

Round and Solid Wreath

Materials needed

clippers

long, single vines of medium weight or more

1. Beginning with one length of vine, form a circle and make a simple overhand knot. Check your measurement.

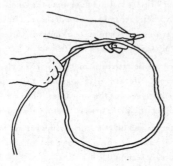

2. Grasp the far end of the vine and immediately begin to thread it in and out, in and out, twisting the vine around itself. Tuck the end into the twisting vines as you come to the end of that length. If you clip the end at an angle it will slide between the vines more easily.

3. Add another single length of vine by cutting that end at an angle and sliding the pointed end into any snug spot created by the twisting vines in the area you ended. This is where those knobby areas of the vine are helpful—they can help to wedge the new piece in. Keep pushing the vine into a space until the knobs get caught inside and it is hard to pull the vine out.

4. Continue threading this vine in and out following in the same direction, and tuck the end in as before. Repeat this step until your wreath is as big as you want it to be. The more pieces you add, the heavier, sturdier, and wider it becomes. Wreaths made this way look tight and solid, with a spiraling and rope-like pattern. It is possible to make a wreath from one exceptionally long piece of vine!

Variations

- For a two-layer look, wrap a wreath all in one direction as above. Then take an additional length of vine or two and wrap in the opposite direction for the second layer. You can wrap as few or as many times around as you like. Again this is where you can let your creativity run wild. You can always unwrap the vine and try something else if you don't like the pattern you have created.

- For an open but still solid appearance, keep alternating directions each time a new vine is added. The multi-layered result gives an interesting, criss-crossing pattern.

- Experiment with peeled vines. Removing all the bark and cutting off any tendrils will give you a very smooth, wooden, clean-looking wreath and will emphasize the pattern better than shaggy vines.

Criss-cross Wrapped Wreath

Oval Wreath

This is a very easy wreath shape to achieve, and it offers more ways to decorate because it can be hung horizontally or vertically. As with any other wreath, design it the way you want to—large or small, tight or loose, shaggy or peeled.

One way to form an oval is simply to push it into shape while you are making the wreath. Because the vines are still fresh and green, they can

be pushed, pulled, and somewhat molded into shapes. Begin with a round wreath and after you've made a few rounds, simply grasp the sides of your wreath with your hands and push toward the middle until your desired oval shape is created. Continue to wrap and push, wrap and push, until your wreath is completed. As it dries, the shape will remain.

Tie a rope around the middle of a newly-made round wreath to create an oval.

Another way to shape an oval is to incorporate a naturally curved piece of grapevine into the wreath. You may have come across one while sorting the vines. This piece can be added to strengthen the curve of the oval.

You can make an oval wreath out of a newly finished round wreath by tying it into shape. Wrap a piece of rope or strong twine around the middle, and tie it up as the wreath becomes the oval shape you desire. Let it dry a few days before removing the rope.

Teardrop Wreath

A teardrop-shaped wreath is another unique design; decorate it point up or point down. This is a perfect example of what a vine with a wide fork or natural angle can be used for. While sorting the grapevines, you should have come across quite a few vines with natural right angles or wide forks.

1. Select a good-size medium weight vine which has either a sharp angle or wide fork. Trim off any unwanted branches.

2. This wreath is also started by the knot method, just as the previous wreaths were, but the beginning vine has the angle. As you wrap and add additional vines, the natural angle will keep the point sharp. An additional angled piece or two may be added to reinforce the point. Once again, you may use single vines, heavy vines, or branched vines, you can wrap it tight or loose, you may criss-cross or follow one direction, just as long as you include natural right angles to make the point sharp.

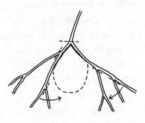

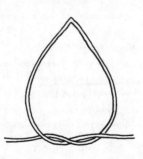

Thin and Dainty Heart

Materials needed

coat hanger

pliers

clippers

a pile of long, thin, single vines approximately 6 to 8 feet in length or longer

1. Make a heart form out of a coat hanger: Hook your index finger on the bottom of the hanger (a) midway from the ends and pull down (fig. 1). This makes the bottom point of the heart. With pliers, round out sides (b and c) to form the curves of the heart (fig. 2).

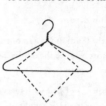

Fig. 1   *Fig. 2*   *Fig. 3*

Flip the top of the hanger to the inside (fig. 3) and finish rounding out the curves evenly. Bend the hook back and forth until it breaks off.

2. Starting at the bottom point of the heart form, simply twist the vine in and out around the frame, leaving the end sticking out about an inch, until you come around to the center point.

3. Using your hand to guide the vine, make a loop around the point. (A loop is nothing more than the bottom half of a "figure 8.") Remember that vines will bend best between the knobby areas. If the vine is not positioned right at this point of the construction to make a loop, slide the vine up or down a bit at the bottom to reposition it.

4. Continue wrapping in and out around the other side of the form until you end up back at the bottom point where you started. Round one complete.

5. Give the vine the slightest bend with your fingers so it is positioned upward and continue wrapping tightly around the wire for the second time around. When the vine ends, tuck it between the twisting vines, insert another length and continue. Try to make good loops around the top point. If possible, reposition or rewrap the vine so you can get a nice bend. If you can't, don't worry about it. If the vine should break while forming a loop, just tuck the end in and start fresh with another piece of vine. The subsequent loops should be placed higher or lower than the first one, but again you may need to reposition or rewrap the vine to avoid a bulky center area.

Continued ➡

6. As the vines build up around the form, determine which will be the front side so you can concentrate on making sure that that side is the best one. It is easy to insert additional vines by sliding them into the loop area, or insert them into the bottom point area. Continue until the wire form is completely covered, then give it a final trimming. Should you discover a spot where the wire is still showing, simply tuck in a small stick or some bark to cover the spot.

Decorating Suggestions

Don't go overboard covering up all your hard work with decorations. All you need is a splash of color here and there. Here are some suggestions:

- Attach a simple paper twist bow. It comes in many colors, is easy to work with and is weather resistant.

- Spray paint your wreath to match your décor.

- Peel off all the bark and clip off all the tendrils for a smooth, clean, wooden look. Or leave the short twigs in the tendrils and the shaggy bark as is for a rough, rustic, primitive look.

- To achieve a wild look, keep adding pieces of vine with lots of nice tendrils, and pick out or stretch out any tendrils caught up between the vines.

- Turn a full, thick wreath into a unique table centerpiece. Lay it flat and use it to hold hors d'oeuvres on toothpicks with a bowl of dip or sauce in the center. Or place a fat candle in the center with hurricane glass over it.

- Collect bird nests, feathers, reindeer moss, lichens, shells, nuts, pine cones, berries, twigs, bark, seed pods, reeds, and grasses for free, natural decorations.

- Small toys, wooden decorations, Christmas ornaments, and dolls make unique additions to wreaths.

- Using a grapevine wreath as a base, overwrap it with another vine of a different texture and color such as bittersweet or Virginia creeper.

- Use a round or oval wreath to frame a mirror.

- Cut out old greeting cards, photographs or calendar pictures. Glue onto stiff cardboard and frame with a grapevine wreath.

- Add dried herbs from your garden or dried autumn field and meadow flowers such as Queen Anne's lace, Joe Pye weed, St. John's wort, yarrow, rabbit's foot clover, sweet everlasting, tansy, black-eyed Susan, or bee balm.

MAKE A FALL BITTERSWEET WREATH

To make a fall bittersweet wreath, use a grapevine wreath as the base. Lay the bittersweet in a circle on top of the grapevine like a crown. Using a long single piece of grapevine, lace it in and out over the bittersweet so it is lashed to the wreath. This way the bittersweet isn't being moved around, disturbing the beautiful berries. Also, when the season is over or the berries have faded, the bittersweet can easily be taken off by undoing the thin grapevine. Now decorate the wreath for Christmas by tucking in a few pine branches and some holly or winterberry. Wire on a few pine cones and add a red bow.

Now that you have learned to make a variety of wreaths, put your creative wheels into motion. Wreaths and rings of all shapes and sizes can be joined, stacked, lashed, and intertwined to make baskets, trees, and sculptures of all kinds. Countless designs are possible; there is nothing you can't try!

Just remember to have fun, don't worry about perfection, and you'll enjoy your original masterpiece for years to come.

Making Potpourri

Madeleine H. Siegler
Illustrations by Karen Rager

Introduction

Fragrance has the power to arouse forgotten emotions and events. It activates the brain in a unique way. It can stimulate and exhilarate, or it can dull the senses. Animals respond to it much as humans do. A sleeping cat is very much awake when a bag of catnip is opened; the dog snoozing on porch steps is suddenly alert when the scent of cat is in the air. The nose remembers even when the body rests.

In my years spent working with fragrance I have seen this memory function at work many times. Weary travelers stopping to visit the herb gardens would suddenly look years younger when a certain aromatic plant took them back to their childhood. Customers in the shop would beg for more of a certain potpourri when some element in the fragrance recalled a long-forgotten happy memory.

One dictionary defines potpourri as a combination of various incongruous elements; and also as a mixture of dried flower petals and spices kept in a jar and used to scent the air. The phrase *pot pourri* comes from the French. The literal translation is "rotten pot." The moist method of making potpourri from fresh rose petals does result in a rotting process of sorts.

The art of blending potpourri incorporates these two definitions. Some of the recipe ingredients may appear incongruous; combine them all and they play their part in creating fragrance. Basically you will be using dried petals and spices, mixing them with necessary fixatives and oils to create a lasting and pleasing aroma with which to enhance your surroundings.

A really fine potpourri has one predominant aroma and many subordinate ones. Expensive perfumes are blends of as many as 150 fragrances; one of my best potpourris contains 20. As with soup making, the more you put in, the richer the result.

Learning to capture the scent of roses and lavender, recognizing such exotics as frankincense and myrrh, vetiver and tonka bean, and knowing how to blend them all together is creatively rewarding and can add a fresh dimension to life.

If you maintain gardens you have a source of fragrant and colorful materials to dry and use; a sentimental bouquet can bloom forever in your jars of potpourri.

Potpourri must have one or more elements from each of the following fine categories to have a lasting fragrance.

A—Fragrant Leaves and Flowers

Roses	Scented geraniums	Thyme
Mint	Marjoram	Bay leaves
Lemon balm	Rosemary	Costmary
Lavender	Lemon verbena	Sweet woodruff

B—Spices and Seeds

Allspice	Cloves	Cardamom
Anise	Star anise	Lemon peel
Nutmeg	Coriander	Orange peel
Mace	Cinnamon	Vanilla bean

C—Oils, Essential or Fragrance

Ambergris	Neroli	Sandalwood
Jasmine	Rose geranium	Clove
Musk	Cinnamon	Lime
Rose	Lemon	Bitter orange
Bergamot	Sweet orange	Ylang-ylang
Lavender		

D—Fixatives

Orris root	Calamus	Myrrh
Benzoin	Tonka bean	Oakmoss
Cellulose fiber	Vetiver	Frankincense

E—Petals and Leaves for Color

Pansies	Amaranth	Nigella
Calendulas	Ferns	Salvias
Carnations	Daffodils	Delphinium
Rose leaves	Geraniums	Uva-ursi (bearberry)
Tulips	Asters	Feverfew
Larkspur		

CATEGORY A—FRAGRANT LEAVES AND FLOWERS

Of all the flowers you may dry to use in potpourri, only roses and lavender will retain their aroma. All the leaves listed have scent glands not easily destroyed by drying; they keep their fragrance indefinitely.

The best roses for fragrance are the antique varieties. (Consult any good nursery catalog.) We enjoy gathering many petals from the sturdy rugosa roses so common here, but they cannot compare in aroma with my antique gallica and damask roses.

Lavender blossoms hold their perfume almost forever. They contain more oil for their weight than any other fragrant flower. All varieties of lavender are fragrant; my preference for potpourri is *Lavandula vera*.

Costmary (*Chrysanthemum balsamita*) is an old herb that holds its shape and minty smell for years. For potpourri use, press or air-dry the leaves.

Lemon verbena (*Aloysia triphylla*) has slender 3-inch leaves smelling more like a lemon than a lemon. Leaves do not crumble when stirred and shaken repeatedly. This plant is a tender perennial, equally at home in a large tub or in the garden.

Lemon balm (*Melissa officinalis*), an easily grown perennial herb, makes a fine cup of tea. It will yield its lemony smell long after it has been picked and dried. Caution: The leaves crumble easily, so handle carefully.

Sweet marjoram (*Origanum marjorana*) is truly a culinary herb. Its sweetness makes it a good addition to light floral potpourris.

Spearmint (*Mentha spicata*) is a perennial usually associated with cold summer drinks and hot herb teas. It is equally at home in the salad bowl, Mediterranean cooking, and potpourri. All the mint varieties have a place in potpourri blends.

Rose geranium (*Pelargonium graveolens*) is just one of more than a hundred geraniums bearing fragrant leaves and small flowers. The leaves may smell spicy, fruity, woodsy, or flowery. Old-Fashioned Rose is my favorite for potpourri use. To keep the leaves green when drying, spread a single layer on a tray and refrigerate for several days. Cover all food items or they may smell like roses!

Rosemary (*Rosmarinus officinalis*) is an herb prized for appearance alone, but nearly indispensable in cooking. It adds its sharp spicy odor to many good potpourri recipes where its green needlelike leaves also add good color.

Sweet woodruff (*Galium odoratum*) is covered with white starry flowers in May, when the 6-inch stems are best cut for making May wine. Odorless when fresh, the leaves develop a strong vanilla fragrance when dry.

Uva-ursi (*Arctostaphylos uva-ursi*) is a trailing vine or low shrub with a long history of medicinal herb use. The leaves are the potpourri-maker's pet because they are small and green, and hold their shape. They are quite inexpensive to buy.

If you have access to any of these plants gather them at their peak in midsummer, dry carefully, and store for later use. Long-stemmed herbs such as mint or lemon balm can be bunched, tied, and hung to dry in a warm, airy spot out of direct sun. Dry single leaves and short sprigs on shallow trays. Store all dry materials in paper (not plastic) bags until needed.

CATEGORY B—SPICES AND SEEDS

You may already have many things from this category in the cupboard. Here you will learn new uses for them.

Allspice (*Pimenta officinalis*) is the dried unripe fruit of an evergreen tree of the myrtle family. In their native West Indies these trees grow to great heights. The hard, small, brown berry is highly aromatic, with a flavor that combines cinnamon, nutmeg, and cloves. Thus its name. Ground allspice adds zing to many cooking recipes, and it also has a place in many potpourris.

Anise seed (*Pimpinella anisum*) is produced from the flowers of an annual plant that can be easily grown in the garden. Native to the West Indies, it is grown there on a commercial scale. The flavor is sweet and slightly licorice, the aroma pleasant and long-lasting.

Star anise (*Illicium verum*) is the large seed pod from a flowering tropical evergreen. The star-shaped pod may be from 1 to 2 inches in diameter and is highly scented of licorice. Used in Oriental cooking, it is very useful in spicy potpourri blends.

Continued ➔

Cinnamon may be either true cinnamon (*Cinnamomum zeylanicum*) or cassia, from another cinnamon tree of the laurel genus. The hard stick cinnamon used to stir mulled cider is the latter. For potpourri we prefer the true Ceylon cinnamon which is soft, can be broken with the fingers, and has a sweeter odor. All cinnamon is produced by stripping thin layers of bark from the tree branches. It is then peeled, soaked in water, and formed into the tight rolls called quills. Cinnamon sticks may be purchased in any length from 1 inch to 16 inches.

Cardamom (*Elettaria cardamomum*) is the seed pod from a flowering shrub native to India and also cultivated in Central America. The pods are usually bleached white and are from 1/4 to 1/2 inch long. Both the outer pod and the black seeds inside have a very special pungency. Crushed seed is favored in Scandinavian cookie recipes. This spice is very expensive.

Coriander (*Coriandum sativum*) is a small tan seed from a lacy flower of the annual herb cilantro. This herb enjoys considerable popularity in cooking despite the unpleasant odor of the leaves. The seed, on the contrary, has a warm, sweet fragrance. Inexpensive, it is used in baking and is a major ingredient in one of my favorite potpourris. Because of its low cost, it can be used freely.

Cloves (*Carophyllus aromaticum*) are one of the best-known spices and surely one of the most interesting. They resemble short, round-headed nails; their name is the French word for nail, *clou*. They are the tightly closed flower bud of a large, shapely evergreen tree native to the East Indies. The entire crop must be hand picked, and the timing is crucial. If the buds open into flowers they are useless to the spice trade. The flavor is strong, the aroma heavy and long-lasting. Another variety, sold under the name Rajah, is twice the size. These are good for potpourri use if you fortify the faint aroma with clove oil.

Nutmeg (*Myristica fragrans*) is the inner kernel of a peach-sized fruit from a tropical tree with laurel-like leaves. The fruit makes a bland, sweet jelly. The seed pod contains three layers, one of them quite unexpected. Just inside the pulp is a thin, brittle shell encased in a bright red, irregular covering resembling red candle wax. This thin layer, the aril, is carefully removed and dried. It then turns orangey brown in color and is sold as the spice we call mace.

The remaining thin shell is cracked to reveal the brown nutmeg. Heaps of discarded nutmeg shells surround the spice-processing plant on the island of Grenada, which grows one-third of the world's supply. The natives use them for mulch and for surfacing parking lots; it makes for fragrant parking. Mace has a much sweeter aroma and flavor than the spicy-bitter nutmeg. Since it takes 400 pounds of nutmegs to yield one pound of mace, the mace is naturally far more expensive. Only two of my better potpourris include it.

The easiest way to crush a few nutmegs for potpourri use is with a pair of blunt-nosed pliers.

Vanilla bean is the seed pod of a tropical orchid common in many hot countries. The fruit resembles a bush bean. A six-month fermenting process is needed to produce the luscious aroma and flavor of vanilla, thus the high price.

Orange and lemon peel are familiar to everyone. Peel may be purchased all dried and diced, but home-dried peel has far more aroma. Orange peel is especially useful. Rinse them and remove pulp and white lining. Chop in a food chopper or cut into thin strips with scissors. Spread on a shallow pan and dry in a warm place. (Try the top of your refrigerator.) When crispy dry, store in a glass jar for future use.

To double the aroma and usefulness of the peel, stud wide strips with whole cloves before you dry them. The resulting fragrance will be perfect for adding to a spicy or floral potpourri.

CATEGORY C—OILS, ESSENTIAL OR FRAGRANCE

One or more of these fragrant oils are used in every recipe to enhance and perpetuate the aroma you want to achieve. There are two types used: essential and fragrance. Here, "essential" does not mean fundamental or necessary. *Essential oil* is the essence extracted from a plant. For example, nearly every lavender oil you buy will be a pure or essential oil. The oil present in the flowers is extracted by steam distillation. If you pack 600 pounds of fresh lavender flowers into a copper tank, cover it securely, and run steam through it, you can obtain about one pint of pure oil. It will drip out of a pipe in the tank into a collecting jar, while the steam condenses to water and runs out of another pipe. The resulting oil is then stabilized and sold as *essential oil*.

In a recipe calling for strawberry oil, you will be using a *fragrance oil*. This is produced chemically in laboratories. The chemist analyzes the smell of strawberries, knows what chemicals contain those components, and blends them to produce a fragrance similar to strawberries.

Basic fragrances important to many traditional potpourris, such as musk and ambergris, were once obtained from animals. They are now reproduced synthetically. You may find great differences in the quality of chemically produced oils; buy very small amounts at first. There is a lot of poor quality oil on the market today, but there are also many sources of very good oils.

The list given is far from complete; these are the oils called for in my recipes. You may recognize many of the scents. Four oils listed are all derived from the orange. Sweet orange smells like orange soda. Neroli, bergamot, and bitter orange are products of another type of orange. Bergamot oil adds a nice note to many rose potpourri blends; it is also the flavoring ingredient in Earl Grey tea. The oil, sprayed on the plain tea leaves, gives this tea its distinctive aroma and flavor.

Ambergris was originally obtained from the excreta of whales. Greatly in demand for fragrance, it was always in short supply and high-priced. Today it is made synthetically. Musk, favored by royal houses 200 years ago, came from the musk deer. The animals were killed to obtain the gland containing the oil. Today all musk oils are made chemically and vary greatly in their scent.

In using oils, remember they are highly concentrated and should be measured exactly as directed. Too much of one can ruin a batch of potpourri. If kept in brown glass bottles, tightly closed, and stored in a dark place, they will remain useful for years. Only poorly made oils lose fragrance quickly. All essential oils are volatile, and will evaporate when exposed to air for long periods.

CATEGORY D—FIXATIVES

A fixative has one main purpose in your finished potpourri. It preserves your scents. It has the ability to reach out and grab the combination of aromas in the jar and hold on to them. Some fixatives will add fragrance of their own, some are scentless.

Orris root has been commonly used for a fixative for over 200 years. It is the tuber or corm of *Iris germanica*, usually called Florentine iris. Italian perfume makers in Florence first discovered its usefulness. This variety of iris grows abundantly in many European countries; most orris root used in this country is imported. When dried and powdered or chipped, it takes on a characteristic violet scent and also its ability to "fix" other scents.

Calamus (*Acorus americanum*) is commonly called sweet flag. An easily grown perennial with a creeping rootstock, it still grows wild in some areas. The slender root has a sweet taste and smell when dried.

Oakmoss (*Evernia pranastri*) is a nearly white moss with a lovely earthy aroma. It is also known as chypre and gives its name to a whole class of fragrances. Its cost is reasonable and the results long-lasting; use this one freely.

Vetiver (*Vetiveria zizanioides*) is called khus-khus in many old recipes. A grassy tropical perennial, its stems reach six feet. The numerous thin, tough roots of this plant provide the fixative with the wet, woodsy scent. It grows profusely on the island of Grenada in the West Indies, where our guide said his grandma dug and dried its roots and put them in her trunk to keep things smelling good and to keep insects out. It is one of my own favorites.

Vetiver is cultivated in Louisiana where, with luck, you may find fans for sale woven from the tough fibers of the root. Such a fan will keep its sweet smell forever. Humidity (or a light spray with water) draws out the aroma. For potpourri use purchase the root uncut if you can; the fragrance will be much stronger if you cut it as you use it.

Tonka bean (*Dipterix odorata*) is also known as tonquin bean. It is the inner kernel of the pit of a peach-sized tropical fruit. The tough pit requires considerable force to crack in order to reach the much-prized tonka bean. The strong vanilla fragrance is immediately present and increases as the beans dry. The most common use for them is in blending aromatic pipe tobaccos. They are toxic for cooking and should be used only in perfumery.

Frankincense and myrrh are both gum resins from India and the Middle East. They are among the oldest aromatics known in the world of fragrance. The light gray, waxy frankincense is from a large tree, *Boswellia thurifera*, while myrrh, looking like orangey-brown gravel, is the product of low shrubs and is difficult to gather. Frankincense is also known as olibanum. It has a sharp yet sweet odor when heated. Myrrh, used also in healing lacerations, has a less balsamic odor. Both these fixatives were in use long before the birth of Christ, as temple incense and for embalming the dead.

Benzoin is a gum resin from a shrub grown in Thailand. Old recipes will call it benjamin. This is a useful fixative for recipes not calling for orris root. It is said to have a quality that fuses all other aromas in a potpourri and brings them together. It looks like granitic gravel.

Cellulose fiber is a surprising fixative. When it became available, few potpourri makers could believe that such a common product could be used in our good recipes. It is actually ground corn cob, sold in pet shops as cage litter. The cost is minimal when compared to other fixatives. Since it is softer than orris root it will absorb considerably more oil, which means that what you save on fixative you may spend on oil.

The ratio of 1 teaspoon (1/8 ounce) of oil to 1 cup cellulose fiber provides enough fixative and fragrance for about 8 cups of potpourri. Mix the oil and cellulose fiber in a jar, shake well, and let it blend for 24 hours before using.

Fiber's biggest advantage is that no one seems to be allergic to it, which many people are to orris root. Although I still depend on orris root for most of my recipes, I have made many successful potpourris using cellulose and oil for the fixed fragrance.

In recipes calling for more than one oil, I recommend that you use separate jars. Measure the amount of cellulose needed into each jar, add the drops of oil, let each mellow overnight, then add to the botanicals.

CATEGORY E—DRIED PETALS AND LEAVES

While it is true that only roses and lavender flowers retain their scent after drying, most blossoms and many leaves are worth drying to add color and dimension to your potpourri.

Some mixtures of dried rosebuds, lavender, leaves, spices, and fixatives can look quite drab. Add a few bright red tulip petals, deep pink larkspur, or true blue delphinium and the mixture glows with light. Lemon-scented potpourris are a good place for yellow shades. Dry calendulas for this purpose.

Most flowers will dry well if spread in a single layer in shallow boxes placed in a warm, airy location. Direct sunlight is acceptable if the temperature is high enough to dry the petals quickly, say in 24 hours. Prolonged exposure to bright light will fade colors.

Pansies and ferns lose all their appeal if dried in shallow boxes. Better results come from pressing them in a thick catalog or paperback book with non-glossy pages. Place the pansies face down as flat as possible on the page, cover with the next pages. Repeat until all flowers or pages are used, weight the book with any heavy object, and leave it for a week or ten days. You will have a good supply of flat, dry flowers to add their pretty faces to potpourri. Ferns and lacy leaves, dried the same way, retain their good green color.

Floral designers have little patience with fallen petals and blooms. They sweep them up and discard them at the end of the day. Should you know anyone who works in either fresh or dried flower design, you may well have an unfailing source of potpourri flowers.

Putting It All Together

The dry method is the usual way we mix potpourri, both on a small scale at the kitchen table and in large amounts commercially. The hobbyist uses a glass jar, the commercial operation uses a cement mixer. For this process all ingredients must be dry. Simply measure out the botanicals, add the properly prepared spices, then stir in the oils and fixatives.

Some recipes suggest that you add the oil to the fixative and let this mellow for a day or two before incorporating it into the other ingredients. I do this only when using cellulose fiber. For all my recipes calling for orris root I have consistent good results when I put the botanicals and spices in the jar, stir well with a wooden spoon, place the orris root on the surface, and then start adding the oils. Most of the oil is immediately absorbed by the orris root; the remainder clings to rosebuds or bits of vetiver or moss. At the last I thoroughly stir and shake, or pour the mixture back and forth several times until I feel sure that every bit of oil-soaked orris root has said "hello" to every other ingredient.

Always remember that the fragrance you achieve when the mixing is finished is not your final one. All dry potpourris need to age at least three weeks to mellow and tone down. Trust your recipe, not your nose, when you smell a freshly made batch. Shake it daily, let it rest in a dark place, and notice the gradual mellowing of the scent. If at the end of three weeks you are still not satisfied with the fragrance, modify it by adding a few drops of whatever you think it needs.

Continued ➜

NECESSARY TOOLS

Most of the material you will need for making potpourris can be found in your own kitchen or purchased inexpensively. Things I consider necessary include:

- An old three-speed blender (for cracking whole spices).
- Several old measuring cups and set of spoons.
- Clean glass jars. One-quart mayonnaise jars are fine for small batches.
- Flat wooden paddles or spoons for stirring.
- Dieter's scales for measuring ounces.
- Inexpensive glass eyedroppers. Ideally, use a clean one for each oil.
- Storage space. Once you start this hobby, all the products can take up lots of space. Love will find a way. Most of my supplies share my clothes closet.

If you proceed beyond small batches, you will need 5-gallon containers. I use the food-grade plastic pails available at bakeries. Lightweight plastic will not do. Glass, stoneware, and stainless steel are the containers preferred by the professionals in this business. Since buying oils at the Fragonard factory in France where they package all oils and perfumes in aluminum, I must add this metal to the suitable container list.

Recipes

Nearly every mixture is a blend of different fragrances just as a fine perfume is a blend. In perfumery top notes, middle notes, and base notes are carefully balanced to create the distinctive aroma sought by the perfumer.

A typical rose potpourri might use a top note of coriander, a middle note of cinnamon, and a base note of musk to create a new and richer scent.

All scents are classified to fit one of these categories; remember the need to have some from each when you experiment on your own.

The first recipe is a basic rose potpourri. This might be the one to try if you have received a bouquet of roses and want their memory to live on. You need to purchase only an ounce of cut orris root and a small vial of rose oil. Coarsely cracked whole spices would be best, but for your first attempt you might use ground spices from the cupboard.

SMALL ROSE JAR

2 cups dried rose petals and leaves	1 1/2 teaspoons orris root
1/2 teaspoon each of cinnamon, cloves, allspice	6 drops rose oil

Combine the first four ingredients in a quart jar. Add orris root and drop the oil onto it. Shake well. Age for three weeks, shaking daily. The result is a light rose fragrance that keeps well.

CLASSIC ROSE POTPOURRI

Combine thoroughly in a gallon jar:

1 quart rose petals	1/2 cup patchouli leaves
1 to 2 cups lavender flowers	1/4 cup sandalwood chips
1 to 2 cups rose geranium leaves	1/4 cup vetiver root
	1 cup rosemary

Mix, then add:

2 teaspoons cracked frankincense	1 teaspoon myrrh
1 teaspoon coarsely ground cloves	1 teaspoon crushed Ceylon cinnamon
2 tonka beans, ground or broken	

Mix together, then add:

1 cup orris root	30 drops rose oil

Stir all together thoroughly and age for three weeks. This is a rich blend with hints of garden and woods mingled with the strong rose scent.

RAY'S FAVORITE POTPOURRI

2 1/2 cups rose petals	2 tablespoons mace blades*
1 cup lavender	1 tablespoon crushed cloves
2/3 cup whole coriander	1 teaspoon each of lavender, rose, cinnamon, and clove oil
1/3 cup orris root	
2 tablespoons crushed Ceylon Cinnamon	2 teaspoons musk oil

* Note: If whole mace is not available, substitute powdered mace or two crushed nutmegs.

Combine the rose petals, lavender, coriander and other spices in a 1-gallon jar. Sprinkle the orris root on the surface. Add each of the oils, stir in well. Stir daily and age for three weeks.

The scent will not please you when you first mix this one. In three weeks it will have mellowed; it will be even better in three months. It is rich enough to hold its scent for months on end even when displayed in an open container. Ray's Favorite is perfuming the air even as I write this.

LAVENDER BOUQUET

In this recipe I have added spices and two fixatives: oakmoss and orris root. This blend is very nice for sachet bags. To heighten the color for display, add light blue petals such as delphinium or bachelor button.

4 cups lavender flowers	1/2 cup crushed Ceylon cinnamon
1 cup oakmoss	1 vanilla bean
4 teaspoons cracked cloves	1/2 cup orris root
2 teaspoons cracked allspice	1 teaspoon each oils of lavender and bergamot

Combine the first five ingredients in a gallon jar. Cut the vanilla bean into small pieces and add. Stir it all well. Scatter the orris root on surface and add the oils. Now stir very well, cover, and let age.

MAINE WOODS AIR

1 cup fir balsam tips	*1/2 cup hemlock cones*
1/2 cup rose hips	*1/4 cup oakmoss*
1/2 cup juniper berries	

Combine everything in a jar with the oakmoss on top. Sprinkle 10 drops fir balsam oil onto it. Stir well, shake and age.

This mixture allows for countless variations. For the holidays I add red sumac berries and red rose petals, and package it with a tiny red and white striped candy cane. Many fragrance oils are available with Christmasy smells: Merry Berry, Christmas Pine, Elfin Christmas.

NEW ENGLAND BAYBERRY POTPOURRI

Most of us know the warm, balsamic aroma of bayberry candles, since every gift shop seems to sell them. My version of bayberry potpourri came into being many years ago when we were vacationing along the coast and noticing the wonderful fragrance of this shrub. With imagination, you can make a potpourri with almost the same aroma.

1 cup uva-ursi leaves	*1/2 cup cellulose fiber and*
1/2 cup oakmoss	*1/2 teaspoon bayberry oil*
1/2 cup juniper berries	

Mix the cellulose and oil and allow to set for 24 hours. Then add the other ingredients. Shake and age. You may want to adjust the scent with more leaves or more oil. Package this one in a large clamshell.

SPICY LEMON VERBENA POTPOURRI

The very name lemon verbena conjures up pleasant memories for many people. To me it has a sweet, warm, comforting scent—not as sharp as lemon, not as sweet as orange. It makes a pretty green and yellow potpourri.

2 cups lemon verbena leaves	*1 tablespoon benzoin granules*
1 cup calendula petals	*1/2 cup cellulose fiber*
1/2 cup crushed ceylon cinnamon	*1/2 teaspoon best lemon verbena oil*
2 tablespoons cracked cloves	

Allow the oil and cellulose to blend for 24 hours. Combine all other ingredients, shake well and age. If at end of three weeks the fragrance is not quite strong enough, add more oil in more cellulose fiber.

SACHETS FOR MOTHPROOFING

Several pleasant-smelling herbs, available from the supply sources listed or easily grown in your garden, will repel moths. I grow wormwood, southernwood, and tansy for "herbal mothballs." Other herbs to grow for insect repellents include santolina, pennyroyal, and mint. In late summer cut the long stems, bunch them with elastics, and hang them in the warm attic to dry. Later, strip and combine them in a five-gallon pail ready for use.

Each herb has its own strong and pungent scent. To temper the somewhat acrid odor I add handfuls of cedar shavings and lavender flowers to each pail (they in themselves are also moth repellents).

Just two or three botanicals are enough to make herbal moth balls. You do not need fixatives or oils for this. To hold the mixture, cut 6-inch squares of any firm fabric. Put about 1/4 cup of blend in center of square. Gather the corners up to make a ball; tie tightly with a long length of yarn. Make a double bow with loops big enough to slip over a coat hanger. Use half a dozen in a closet, or one or two in your sweater drawer. These have been tested for many years. They remain effective as long as the scent is there, at least two years.

Hints to Help Make Potpourri Mixing Easier

- If you lack just one ingredient for a recipe, try substituting. Any green leaf can replace uva-ursi. Most flowers except lavender can be replaced by another. Rose geranium oil can be used for rose geranium leaves. Sandalwood oil can replace sandalwood chips.

- Most recipes call for rose petals. Either petals or the more expensive rosebuds could be used in any recipe given here.

- Few of the recipes call for a wide variety of bright-colored petals. Add any you have to any recipe to provide required bulk.

- Keep careful records when experimenting with new blends. Never trust memory. My best Asian potpourri is lost forever because I did not take my own advice.

- Copy any recipe and tape it to the jar. Date it. Later you know at a glance just what is there.

- Body chemistry is an individual thing. Each person reacts differently to scent. What pleases one may not smell good to another.

- Store all botanicals (home grown and purchased) in a cool, dry place. Check periodically for insect infestation. All commercial products are fumigated before being sold; even so, outbreaks of insects may happen. Any contaminated botanical can be saved by freezing for ten days. Less time would kill any live insects but not their eggs.

Uses for Potpourri

There is a place for your potpourri in every room of the house. Covered containers will prolong fragrance. Candy jars, antique sugar bowls, covered baskets, wooden boxes and modern plexiglas cubes are all fine containers. Covers are needed to prolong the scent you have created.

- Potpourri aromas last indefinitely if the mixture is kept covered the same length of time it is open. In other words, open a jar when you are using the room and cover it when you leave.

- In some areas of our home I keep open containers. These must be refreshed after about four weeks, except for Ray's Favorite, which

Continued ➜

will last about six months. Refresh with a few drops of 100 proof alcohol, which reactivates the fixative and oil. Add more oil and fixative if there is no alcohol handy. Some users routinely stir the blend and add more oils, plus perhaps a few perfect dry flowers on top.

- Sweet bags, as described in *The Toilet of Flora*, are a fine way of keeping fragrance in the living room. Make these from any square of fabric. Put half a cup of potpourri in each square, tie shut, and tuck the finished balls behind chair or couch cushions.

- For a man's den or bachelor apartment, try fir balsam or spice blend. Citrus-spice is especially effective against stale smoke odors. Cloves have long been the remedy for mustiness in trunks, storage areas, and basement rooms.

- Lavender bags are one sure way of freshening clothes closets. I like to combine cedar, a moth repellent, with lavender for a sweeter aroma. Hang these over the closet rod for lasting aromas among the clothes. Replace after one season.

- I keep sachets in my suitcase. It smells good when I get it out to pack, and the fragrance lingers on my clothes. Doing this became a habit after I spent a month in an apartment in Portugal. The large wooden wardrobe had a musty smell—but rosemary grew everywhere. Sprigs of this herb soon made things smell better.

Sources of Potpourri Supplies

The Herb and Spice Collection
P.O. Box 118
Norway, Iowa 52318–0118
This thick catalog is free for the asking.
Not only do they offer oils and botanicals for potpourri, but many other herbs and herbal products.

Create Something Special Catalog
Lorann Oils
4518 Aurelius Road
P.O. Box 22009
Lansing, Michigan 48909
A catalog to serve candy makers more than potpourri makers.
You will not find rose petals or lavender here, but they handle an excellent line of oils including some that are hard to find elsewhere. Free.

Tom Thumb Workshops
Route 13
P.O. Box 357
Mappsville, Virginia 23407
From them you can buy oils and botanicals for potpourri, also their own potpourri blends. They also sell craft accessories and crafted gift items. Send long self-addressed stamped envelope with request.

Home Sew
Bethlehem, Pennsylvania
18018–0140
The best mail-order source I know for lace, ribbon, notions. Free catalog and prompt service.

Making Natural Milk Soap

Casey Makela
Illustrations by Randy Mosher and Laura Tedeschi

Introduction

Soapmaking is a blend of science and art. Once you have mastered the technique of mixing fats and alkalis to make soap, you can unleash your imagination. Learn the basics of soapmaking, then experiment with colors, shapes, scents, and textures to create one-of-a-kind handicrafts.

Soap is created when a fat is mixed with an alkali. When the two ingredients combine, a chemical reaction occurs. This reaction is known as *saponification*.

Soap can be made with either animal or vegetable fats. In this bulletin, vegetable fats are used, since they complement the gentle nature of milk-based soaps. The alkali used most often in home-based soapmaking is sodium hydroxide. It's commonly called caustic soda or lye.

Milk has long been revered as a cosmetic ingredient. It's an excellent moisturizer and has been heralded throughout the ages as a skin softener that even the most delicate skin types can trust. Milk makes soap richer, creamier, and less drying to the skin.

Milk: The Natural Cosmetic

No one knows who first added milk to soap, though milk has been used as an ingredient in cosmetics and therapeutic treatments in different cultures for thousands of years. Centuries ago, Cleopatra indulged in luxurious milk baths to preserve her legendary beauty. The soothing and moisturizing qualities of milk have made it an increasingly popular ingredient in commercial soaps, especially over the last 30 years.

Milk is rich in proteins, vitamins, and minerals. Chemically, milk is a lipoprotein: It's made up of lipids plus protein. (A lipid is an organic substance that's insoluble in water and is usually somewhat greasy to the touch.) Lipids, found in most skin creams in the form of animal or vegetable oil or wax, help seal in moisture.

Milk is unique in its natural ability to moisturize and nourish the skin. It is a fragile miracle of nature that cannot be synthetically reproduced. But its gentle properties are easily destroyed.

Not All Milk Is Created Equal

The composition of milk can vary drastically among animal species. Even within the same species, there are individual differences. Among other components, milk contains proteins, vitamins, and minerals. These individual ingredients can cause variations in soaps.

The amount of protein in both cow's and goat's milk is 3.5%. Milk has even more protein than eggs. Naturally, soap made with milk is also protein rich. This unique property makes milk-based soaps a favorite for delicate complexions.

Milk also has lots of vitamin A, which is converted from carotene by the liver. Carotene levels can fluctuate according to the lactating animal's diet. Animals that graze on lush, springtime green pastures produce milk that is higher in carotene.

Carotene affects the color of milk. Low levels cause milk to be very white, while high levels make it appear more off-white or creamy yellow. Soaps made with milk may have subtle color variations from the different levels of carotene.

436

Milk is an important source of minerals. In addition to calcium, milk contains potassium, sodium, magnesium, and phosphorus, plus small amounts of other minerals such as lithium and strontium.

The percentage of ash in milk reveals the amount of minerals that it contains. Milk ash is white milk that has been dried and then burned until it forms a fine, pale powder. The ash content of goat's and cow's milk is similar: Goat is 0.79% and cow is 0.73%. The ash in milk helps it to remain stable when it is combined with lye during the soapmaking process.

COW'S MILK OR GOAT'S MILK?

Which is the best milk to use for soapmaking? The answer is—it depends. Both goat's and cow's milk make excellent milk soaps. If you live near both a cow and a goat dairy, you have the best of both worlds. If you do not have easy access to goat's milk, your choice has been made for you: Use cow's milk and don't give the question another thought.

WHOLE MILK, 2%, SKIM, OR POWDERED?

In soapmaking, fat is critical to the saponifying process, so the fat content of milk is important. The standard fat content of commercial, processed cow's milk is 3%. Milk that is sold as low in fat has 2% fat content, while skim has almost no fat at all. Powdered milk has nearly all of the fat removed as well. Use milk that has the highest fat content possible for the best soapmaking results. Do not be tempted to use low-fat, skim, or powdered milk: Use whole milk.

RAW OR PASTEURIZED?

Where it is available, raw (unpasteurized) whole milk fresh from the farm has one advantage over milk from the store: Raw milk has a higher fat content than commercial milk. It is not unusual to find that the fat content of raw cow's milk exceeds 4%. Raw whole milk, if available, is the best choice, though pasteurized whole milk purchased from the grocer works fine.

HOMOGENIZED OR NOT?

In cow's milk, the fat globules are large and buoyant. When cow's milk is undisturbed, the fat globules rise to the top and form cream. Cow's milk is homogenized, or blended, until the fat globules are small enough to remain suspended in the milk. The fat globules in goat's milk are much smaller than those in cow's milk. A very thin cream line may occur in goat's milk that has been left undisturbed for eight or more hours, but most of the cream remains suspended in the milk, so homogenization is unnecessary. Whether or not the milk is homogenized does not affect its qualities for soapmaking, as homogenization does not change fat content.

CREAM OR HALF-AND-HALF?

Whipping cream, heavy cream, and half-and-half can be used in place of whole milk in soapmaking. The resulting soap is superfatted, because of the higher fat content found in the cream-based products. When you use cream, the proportion of lye to fat is changed. In addition, not all of the fat is bound chemically during the saponification process. Using cream for milk-based soaps results in a moisturizing cleanser. When experimenting with creams, substitute an equal amount of cream for either part or all of the milk in the recipe.

Note: In goat's milk, the fat globules are much smaller and more difficult to separate from the milk. To obtain goat's cream, you will need to use a cream separator. It's well worth the effort, however. Goat's cream makes soap extra rich.

Making Molds

The following recipes make approximately 8 pounds of soap, which means that if you want 4-ounce soap bars, you will be making 32 bars of soap with each batch. You need to make or buy molds to hold all that soap while it sets up.

Common soap molds include wood and even cardboard boxes lined with plastic or baker's paper. You should avoid any material that will corrode or leach color into the soap, so choose the molds carefully. Boxes should be about 14" x 20" x 2" deep, and the plastic lining should be smooth and wrinkle free.

Many companies sell premade soap molds. Candy and candle molds can be adapted to soapmaking, too, giving you a wide range of shapes and sizes for your homemade soap. But the cost of enough molds for 8 pounds of soap can be prohibitive.

Instead, try using white vinyl window expanders or PVC pipe to make molds for your milk-based soaps. (A window expander is used on the top of vinyl windows as a gap filler during window installation.) You can purchase expanders from most vinyl window manufacturers. The expanders usually come in 16' lengths with interior measurements of 1 1/2" high x 3 1/4" wide. Use white window expanders, as saponifying soap can absorb colors from a mold.

Line the molds with silicone bakery paper to prevent the soap from sticking. The paper can usually be purchased at bakeries in small amounts. Although you can reuse the molds, you will need to use new paper each time you make soap.

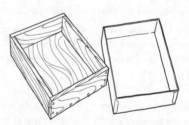

Wooden or even cardboard boxes can be used for soap molds if you line them with plastic.

BASIC MOLDS

1. Cut the expander into lengths of 69 7/8 inches.

2. Seal the ends with a piece of taped PVC or vinyl, or use duct tape.

3. Cover the inside of the ends with plastic packing tape to ensure a good seal on the mold. The mold ends should be sealed inside and out.

Cut white vinyl window expanders and line them with plastic to make soap molds.

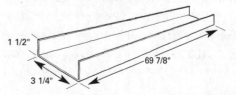

1 1/2"

69 7/8"

3 1/4"

Continued →

4. Measure and mark the upper edge of the frame every 2 1/4 inches with an indelible marker. These are the cutting marks. Each mold will contain 31 bars.

5. Cut the full sheet of bakery paper into thirds.

6. Fold each third of paper so that it will fit into the mold.

7. Fit the bakery paper into the mold, smoothing out any wrinkles so that the surface of the soap will be smooth.

8. Lubricate the lined mold with spray-on corn oil. The mold is now ready for use.

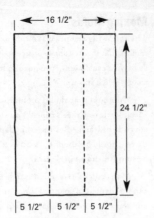

Cut the full sheet of bakery paper into thirds on the dotted lines. One sheet is enough to line one mold with overlap between sheets.

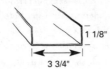

Working with Lye

There are a few safety precautions to follow when working with lye. Lye is a powerful and dangerous chemical that must be handled with great caution. Read this section carefully before you make soap.

You can purchase sodium hydroxide, or lye, in your grocery store in 12-ounce (340-g) containers. This is the amount needed for recipes in this bulletin and it's convenient to have the lye premeasured in a disposable container.

Lye cannot be handled with bare hands, and its fumes must not be inhaled. Lye is harmful or fatal if swallowed. Until the fat/lye mixture fully saponifies into soap (approximately 48 hours after being poured into the mold), it will burn the skin on contact.

Occasionally, the soap mixture separates after the liquid has been poured into the mold. If this happens, you must discard the batch of soap. You might be tempted to pour the batch back into the saucepan and reheat it to encourage saponification. This will not work and is extremely dangerous.

The liquid is highly corrosive and lye is very sensitive to being heated. The goal of soapmaking is to temper lye's hot nature. If you heat it, you can cause the lye to become chemically aggressive and lose control over the process. Never reheat the mixture.

Follow these safe practices when working with lye:

- Read and follow the precautionary statements on the lye container.

- Make sure the product you purchase contains only sodium hydroxide. Read the label carefully; some brands contain additives that will interfere with the saponification process.

- Always wear safety glasses. Don't risk exposing your eyes to the lye.

- Always wear rubber gloves. If you spill any lye on your skin, immediately wash the affected area in cold water.

- Work in a well-ventilated room, near an open window if possible. Do not inhale the fumes. Leave the room immediately for a few minutes when the milk and lye are first mixed if the fumes become too strong.

- Thoroughly clean every utensil, container, counter, and tabletop that was used for soapmaking immediately after the soap is poured into the molds.

TIPS FOR A SAFE WORK ENVIRONMENT

There are important precautions that you should take before soapmaking can safely begin. The process will take your undivided attention from start to finish, so allow yourself plenty of time free from distractions, phone calls, and other interruptions.

- *Work* on a stable surface. The work surface should be a roomy, stable area such as a cleared kitchen countertop. Avoid rickety tables.

- Cover the work surface. Cover all work surfaces with newspaper or plastic to protect them from accidental splashes or spills.

- Lay out the equipment. Lay out and organize the soapmaking equipment so it is easily accessible. Once you start to mix the ingredients, it will be too late to look for equipment.

- Dedicate the equipment to soapmaking. Soapmaking equipment is laboratory equipment. It should be used only for soapmaking. Never use it for cooking once it's been used to make soap.

- Start with new equipment. Foodstuffs can ruin a batch of soap. It's best to invest in new soapmaking equipment. You can find everything you need at a kitchen supply store or a supermarket.

- Do not allow children to help. Young children should be supervised away from the soapmaking work area. Older children may observe from a safe distance, though they should leave the room when the milk and lye are first mixed because of the fumes. Rubber gloves and safety glasses are a must for their protection—even if they are not helping in the process.

BEFORE YOU MAKE THE FIRST BATCH

Soapmaking is a process that cannot be hurried. This is especially true with milk soap. Every batch will be slightly different, even if you follow the recipe exactly every time. Allow for each batch to develop its individual character in its own time. Keep the following points in mind before you make your first batch:

- Soapmaking is a lengthy process. At first, it will take you several hours to make a batch of soap. Because the batch must be continually stirred while portions are blended, it's much easier to work with another person.

- Take careful notes. If you document every detail of each batch, right down to the weather, you'll create a running record that will tell you what works best.

- Choose quality ingredients. Do not lessen the quality of your soap by cutting corners to save a few pennies. Soap that is not as lathery, long lasting, nice smelling, or as even colored as it should be will waste the time and money you have invested.

- Measure accurately. Soapmaking is a science. For best results, measure as precisely as possible. This means measuring by weight, not volume. A good digital scale will give you accurate control and your records will be more detailed and dependable.

- Be patient. Once the soap is poured into molds, it must be allowed to sit for 24 – 48 hours until it is hard enough to be cut. Then, bars must be allowed to cure, undisturbed, for six weeks.

Preparing the Milk

You'll need to prepare the milk at least two days before you make the soap, as it must be frozen and then thawed before use. Freezing milk increases its stability, making it more effective in the soapmaking process.

In addition, milk must be pasteurized before it can be used as an ingredient in soap. Commercially sold milk is already pasteurized. Raw milk purchased fresh from a farm and goat's milk have not been pasteurized.

To pasteurize milk, slowly heat it to 155°F (68°C), measuring with a glass candy thermometer. Hold the milk at this temperature for 1 minute, then cover the pan and allow the milk to cool.

Once the milk has cooled, pour it into a freezer-safe container (don't use glass), leaving room for expansion. Allow the milk to freeze solid. The milk can be stored in the freezer for several months. Remove the milk from the freezer and thaw the day before you're ready to make soap. Once it has thawed, the milk is ready to use.

Basic Equipment

Many of the tools you'll need to make soap are probably already in your kitchen. Remember to use the soapmaking equipment for soapmaking only. You will need:

- Plastic wrap and newspaper to cover work surfaces
- Two 8-quart (7.5-l) stainless-steel saucepans.

  Note: *Never use aluminum containers or your containers and soap will be ruined.*

- Digital scale
- 4-quart (3.7-l) stainless-steel saucepan
- Ice-water bath: Fill the sink with cold water, then add 4–6 trays of ice cubes
- Several 8-ounce plastic cups
- 16-ounce (454-g) glass measuring cup
- 2 heavy-duty plastic or stainless-steel spoons.

  Note: Never use wooden spoons; the lye will destroy the wood fibers.

- Glass candy thermometer
- Plastic ladle
- Blender
- Plastic spatula
- Narrow-blade putty knife
- Trisquare
- Molds
- Curing rack

Note: *Large plastic bread racks work well as curing racks. Don't use wood, aluminum, or steel curing racks, as these materials react with the soap while it is curing, ruining both the rack and the soap.*

Let's Make Soap!

Understand the safety precautions of working with lye. Caustic soda is very dangerous and can cause serious burns. Carefully read and follow the safety instructions each time you make soap.

The first time you make a basic, milk-based soap, you can expect the process to take about 3 hours. After you become more experienced, you'll need about 1 1/2 hours, including cleanup and barring any unforeseen chemical complications. Before you begin, review the list and set aside the ingredients and equipment. Reread the safety precautions for working with lye.

Cover all work surfaces with plastic or newspaper. Lay out your soapmaking equipment so it is within reach, including the molds. Wear gloves and safety glasses at all times.

Well-made milk soap is created with the maximum amount of milk that can be included in proportion to the lye and fat used in each batch. There has to be a substantial amount of milk in every batch to react properly with the lye. Ideally, each 4-ounce bar of soap should have 1 1/2 – 2 ounces of its weight in milk.

Fine cosmetic soaps are often made with a combination of liquid vegetable oils and vegetable shortening. Vegetable shortening usually comes from soybeans. It is economical and readily available at grocery stores and makes an excellent milk-based soap. Olive oil is a good moisturizer. Using extra-light olive oil reduces its slight odor and makes a lighter-colored soap. Safflower and canola oils add foaming action to soap, helping to create the luxurious lathers associated with good soap.

The biggest challenge in making milk-based soap is adding the lye to 6 cups of milk. It can be tricky to combine the caustic chemical with such a large volume of milk. For best results, practice making several batches of soap using the basic recipe before making soap with added ingredients.

You'll need help at several points during the process. Working with a partner makes the soapmaking experience much easier and more enjoyable.

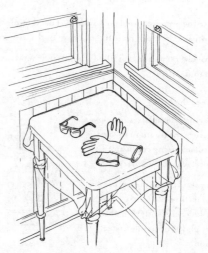

A safe and stable work area and good safety equipment are the most important factors in successful soapmaking.

Continued →

BASIC MILK-BASED SOAP RECIPE

3 pounds (1.36 kg) pure vegetable shortening

17 ounces (482 g) extra-light olive oil

12 ounces (341 g) safflower oil

8 ounces (227 g) canola oil

3 pounds (1.36 kg, or approximately 6 cups) cold milk, prepared for soapmaking

12 ounces (312 g) pure lye (sodium hydroxide)

1 ounce (28.4 g) borax

1/2 ounce (7.1 g) white sugar

1/2 ounce (7.1 g) glycerin

YIELD: 32 (4-OUNCE) BARS

Prepare the Fats and Milk

1. Melt the vegetable shortening in an 8-quart saucepan over low heat.

2. Add the liquid oils to the shortening. Heat the combined ingredients just until the shortening is completely melted, then immediately remove from the heat. Take care not to overheat or scorch the oils, or you will ruin them for soapmaking. Set aside the oil mixture until you are ready to add the lye/milk mixture.

3. Create an ice-water bath by filling the sink with cold water and adding 4–6 trays of ice cubes to the water.

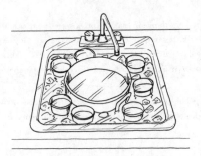

4. Place the prepared, cold milk into a 4-quart stainless-steel saucepan. Carefully place the saucepan in the ice water.

5. Place several plastic cups filled with water around the floating pan to stabilize it.

Add the Lye to the Milk

1. Wearing safety glasses and gloves, measure the lye into a 16-ounce glass measuring cup, using a digital scale for accuracy.

2. Very slowly pour the lye into the cold milk in the ice-water bath, stirring constantly with a heavy-duty plastic or stainless-steel spoon.

Caution: *This pouring process should take no less than 15 minutes. It's very important to introduce the lye slowly into the milk so that the lye does not reach extreme temperatures and react with the milk, causing the milk to burn.*

3. Use a candy thermometer to monitor the temperature of the lye/milk mixture constantly, taking care not to let the temperature fall below 80°F (27°C). You want to keep the mixture cool enough to prevent the milk from scorching, but warm enough to prevent the milk and lye from saponifying. Saponification occurs between the milk and the lye at this temperature because there is enough fat in the milk to cause this action. The two main mistakes you might make at this point are allowing the lye/milk mixture to get too cool and letting it sit too long before combining it with the oils. Both of these scenarios could cause the mixture to congeal into a noxious and useless custard-textured mass that would need to be scooped out of the pan instead of poured. So guard the temperature and keep stirring. Keep the temperature of the mixture right at 80°F, and remove the lye/milk mixture from the ice-water bath as soon as the lye and milk are combined. You will notice that the milk turns a bright yellow once the lye has been successfully combined with the milk.

Combine All Ingredients

1. Over low heat, reheat the oils to a temperature of 125°F (52°C), taking care not to scorch the oils. Remove from the heat.

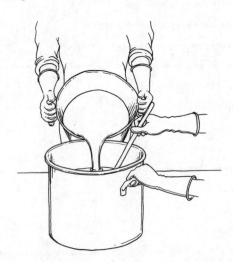

2. Slowly pour the lye/milk mixture into the oils.

3. Add the borax, sugar, and glycerin. Stir the mixture constantly, taking care not to splash any. The mixture will begin to warm as the lye reacts. You might also notice that the mixture doesn't want to combine and that it separates readily if you stop stirring. Just be patient.

Blend the Soap Mixture

1. Using a plastic ladle, scoop evenly mixed amounts of the soap mixture into the blender. Fill the blender halfway.

Caution: *Secure the lid on the blender carefully before turning it on!*

2. Run the blender for 1 minute on medium speed, remembering to keep stirring the remaining soap mixture at the same time. The liquid in the blender will turn a pale cream color.

3. After 1 minute, pour the contents of the blender into the second 8-quart saucepan. This is where having a partner is critical—you now have two saucepans to stir and the blender to operate.

4. Repeat steps 1–3 until all of the original mixture of oils and lye/milk has been blended.

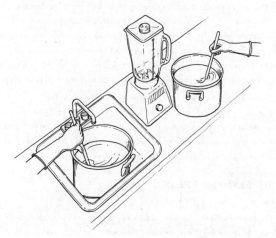

5. Quickly wash out the first saucepan and dry thoroughly.

6. Now do the same thing all over again, transferring from the full saucepan to the blender for 1 minute, and then into the now empty saucepan.

7. After the second blending, the liquid is ready to pour into molds. You should see little or no separation of the oils from the rest of the mixture. After the second blending, the mixture should have thickened up somewhat, but even if it seems a little thin, it will still be ready for the molds. If it really seems too thin, you can blend it a third time.

Pour the Soap into the Molds

1. Pour the mixture into the prepared mold(s). To prevent the soap from seeping through the bakery-paper liner, use a spatula to press down on the liner until the soap flows over the liner and weighs it down.

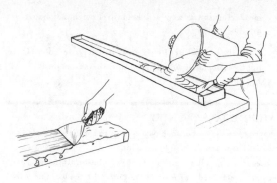

2. Once a mold is full, you can screed the surface with the spatula to smooth out the surface of the soap: Slowly pull the flat edge of the spatula across the entire surface of the mold, from one end to the other.

3. Allow the saponifying liquid to sit uncovered and undisturbed in a draft-free area. After 12 hours, you may notice sweatlike beads of moisture on the surface of the soap. These usually evaporate, but if they don't, you can gently wipe them off with a paper towel before cutting the bars.

4. After 24 hours, use the narrow-blade putty knife to cut the bars. Set the trisquare parallel to each 2G-inch mark to guide a straight cut. Then slice each bar straight down with the putty knife, sliding it from one side of the mold to the other. Do not wait more than 24 hours to cut, or the soap will become too brittle.

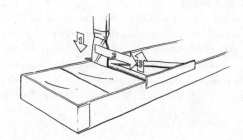

5. Cut the entire strip of bars, then remove one bar to check its hardness. If the bar holds its shape, remove all the bars and place them on the curing rack. If the soap does not hold its shape, allow it to remain in the mold for another 24 hours. Check it every 4 hours until it is ready.

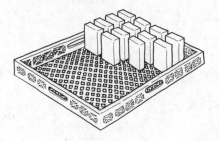

6. As soon as the bars are ready, place them on the curing rack. If you stand the soap bars on the narrow ends, a bread rack

Continued ➜

measuring 26 1/2" x 22" will hold three batches of soap, or 96 bars.

7. Allow the bars to cure for six weeks in a dry, cool room. Cover lightly with plastic wrap to protect the bars from dust.

FAILURE TO SAPONIFY

It happens to the best of soapmakers once in a while—a batch of soap refuses to saponify. When you hit a stubborn batch that refuses to set up, starting over is the best solution. If the mixture becomes overheated, the milk will not mix with the lye. The milk will change from an orange color to a burnt orange and float to the top of the mixture. There is no alternative but to dispose of the batch and start over.

Another problem might occur when the lye/milk mixture cools too long before being combined with the oils. The mixture will become custardlike and will have to be scooped out of the pan. You can still add it to the oils, though. Usually the blender will mix it well enough so that it poses no further problems. The lye/milk mixture will be easier to work with if you maintain the temperature so it can be poured out of the pan.

Occasionally the soap separates after it has been poured into the molds. The mixture will not saponify. Again, the only solution is to discard the batch and start over.

Selecting a Scent

As with natural colors, many natural scents are destroyed during saponification. Synthetic perfumes and colors offer a wide array of choices, but lack the character and goodness of natural products.

Fragrances and colors from natural ingredients often go hand in hand. For example, adding cornmeal makes the soap golden yellow with a sweet corn smell. Cinnamon produces a brownish soap that smells like that spice.

SOAP SCENTS

The following are strong enough to withstand the saponification process.

Almond	Orange
Cinnamon	Patchouli
Citronella	Peach
Cloves	Pennyroyal
Eucalyptus	Peppermint
Jasmine	Rose
Lavender	Rosemary
Lemon	Sage
Musk	Vanilla

ESSENTIAL OILS OR FRAGRANCE OILS?

Essential oils are highly concentrated extracts derived from the leaves, berries, flower, petals, twigs, bark, or stems of plants through distillation or expression. The oils usually bear the scent or fragrance of the original plant. Essential oils are also believed to have therapeutic properties. Prices for essential oils vary and can be quite high, depending on the plant type. But a little goes a long way.

Fragrance oils are synthetically produced imitations of plant essences. They are far less expensive than essential oils and are less vulnerable to spoilage.

Making and Using a Flower Press

Deborah Tukua

Illustrations by Alison Kolesar and Judy Eliason

Making Your Flower Press

A flower press is a simple tool used to flatten and dry flowers and foliage. Presses are very easy and inexpensive to make, and, because they apply even pressure, you will get better results than you will by using a book. All flower presses work the same way: They flatten the botanical materials in them, and they use paper or other absorbent material to help dry the flowers you are trying to preserve. Once the flowers are dried, you will be able to remove them from the press and store them for use in your projects.

You can purchase a flower press from a craft store. But commercially available presses tend to be quite small and lightweight, which limits the types and numbers of botanicals you can press. You might want to use a purchased press as your portable field press, and build one of the models here for your main press.

BASIC FLOWER PRESS

Plans by Lowell Tukua

This is a reasonably large and very sturdy flower press. It is versatile, with lots of space for pressing many flowers.

Materials

2 12" x 12" x 5/8"-thick pieces of plywood (you can use other wood, such as pine shelving, if it is available)

4 6" x 1/4" carriage bolts (rounded head for flush mounting)

4 1" flat washers with 1/4" hole

5 1/4" wing nuts (large wings for easy tightening)

2 1" x 2" x 12" boards

Tools

Pencil	*Nails or screws*
Straightedge or metal ruler	*Small brush*
Drill	*Polyurethane*
Hammer	

Assembly Instructions

1. On one of the 12" x 12" pieces of plywood, measure in along each side of the board 1 3/4" and mark with a pencil. Using a straightedge and your measurements, draw a line along each side of the board at your 1 3/4" markings.

2. Place and align the marked board on top of the other 12" plywood board. Drill a 5/16" hole at the four intersections of your drawn lines. Drill through both boards, then set aside the unmarked one.

3. Insert two of the bolts through the holes in the marked board. When only the head of the bolt is visible, use a hammer to drive the head into the wood until it is flush with the board. Repeat with the other two bolts.

4. Nail or screw (predrill the holes for screws) the 1" x 2" pieces of wood over these bolts to hold them in place. This will serve as the base of the flower press.

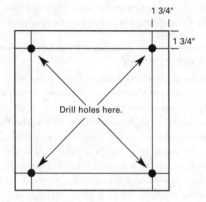

5. Turn over the baseboard with the bolts facing up and place the unmarked 12" x 12" board over the holes. Put on the flat washers and wing nuts, and your flower press is built. Brush on a coat of poly-urethane and let it dry completely before using.

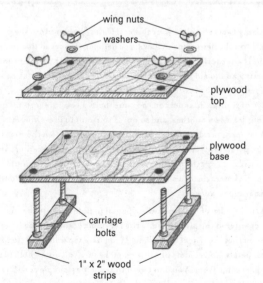

VARIATION: THE C-CLAMP FLOWER PRESS

Plans by Lowell Tukua

Here's an easy variation of the previous flower press. Using C-clamps instead of bolts and screws allows you to use every inch of space in the press.

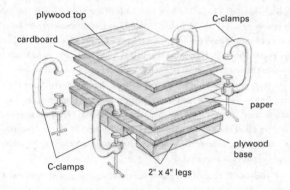

Tools

Wood glue	Pencil
Screwdriver	Polyurethane
Ruler	Brush

Materials

2 12" x 16" x 3/4"-thick pieces of plywood

1 4'-long 2" x 4", cut into four 1'-long pieces

4 3" C-clamps

16 2"-long wood screws (plasterboard screws work best)

Assembly Instructions

1. Cut the plywood and boards according to the specifications on the materials list. The two pieces of 3/4" plywood will serve as the top and bottom of the press.

2. Glue and, after the glue has set, screw the four pieces of the 2 x 4 to the bottom of one of the pieces of plywood (see illustration). These will serve as legs, while also providing gaps where the C-clamps will be positioned. Set the first 2 x 4 strip about 1/4" from the edge. Set the second strip parallel to the first, but about 3/4" away from it. The third strip will fit tight up against the second, with no space between. Then leave another 3/4" space between the third and final strips, which should be about 1/4" from the edge of the board.

3. Apply at least one coat of polyurethane to protect the wood of your flower press. Let this dry completely before using.

4. When you use the press, the C-clamps will fit in the two gaps between the legs of the press.

Using the Flower Press

With a few tips to help you get started and some basic supplies, you can begin using your new flower press immediately.

Continued →

TOOLS AND MATERIALS

Blotting paper or newsprint. The easiest and least expensive paper to use in your press is newsprint. In fact, many people begin pressing using newspapers or pages from an old phone book. While this kind of recycling is always a great idea, you many run into problems with the ink staining your flowers. Instead of using printed paper, call or visit your local newspaper. They often have roll-ends of unprinted newsprint that are too short to use on the press. They sell or give these away (our local paper gives them away for educational use and otherwise sells them for a very reasonable fee). If you do get a roll, you will have to trim or fold the paper to the size of your press. But even a short roll will last you for many seasons of flower pressing. You can also buy newsprint pads in craft, hobby, and office supply stores. If you buy pads, you can get the size you need and save yourself the task of trimming. If you are eager to start, try using the old telephone book until you get unprinted paper. You will need to change the paper in your press frequently, so an ample supply of paper is a very good idea.

Cardboard. You will also need four to six rectangles of cardboard cut to the dimensions of your flower press. They can be cut from cardboard boxes or purchased from craft and hobby stores. Lay one sheet directly on the inside base of the press. Then add four to six sheets of paper, and then another piece of cardboard. Repeat as often as necessary for the amount of materials you will be pressing, but always end the stack with a piece of cardboard and then the top of the press.

A PORTABLE FLOWER PRESS

Although both of the flower presses I've just discussed can easily fit into your car, neither is suitable for carrying into the field. Because you should press your flowers as soon as they are picked, you might consider buying or making a more portable field press to use until you can get your plants home to the big model.

Some ideas for portable presses are:

- A large telephone book or an outdated encyclopedia will suffice as a temporary press. Simply place the botanical materials in the book and secure with string or elastic bands. Add weight by stacking books.

- For smaller pressing projects, you can use a pair of paperback books with their covers removed. Place your flowers between the books and secure with strong elastic bands. If the books are thick, place materials every 20 to 30 pages inside the books as well as between them and secure.

- A handy portable press can be made from four pieces of cardboard cut to 8 1/2" x 11" dimensions (or 5" x 7", if you prefer a smaller temporary press). Place several sheets of blotting paper or some paper from an old telephone book between the cardboard pieces. Wrap twine around the outside length and width of the cardboard and tie firmly in a bow.

Tweezers. Both before they enter the press and after they are dried, your plant materials are fragile and easily damaged. And some of them will be quite small. You should get into the habit of handling them with a good pair of tweezers. The kind I prefer have a long, curved gripping surface; they came from a dentist. Try your local drugstore or medical supply store for a pair you will be comfortable using.

Boxes and paper for storage. Unless you will be using them as soon as they come out of the press, you will need to store your pressed flowers. Some projects require a large quantity of botanicals; you may have to store some while pressing others. The best way to store them is to lay them on construction paper or newsprint in flat boxes or shallow drawers. You can stack dried flowers and foliage, separating each layer with a layer of paper. Flowers should retain their color for two years. They will keep longer, but colors will start to fade.

Pressing Flowers

The basic procedure for pressing flowers is very simple. You will pick what you want to press place it carefully between two sheets of paper in your press, date the sheet the flowers rest on, and seal the press. But there are some guidelines that will improve the quality of your pressed flowers.

MICROWAVE PRESSES

At least one company sells a microwave flower press. Made of plastic, it works the same way traditional presses do, with absorbent paper and pressure, but uses the microwave to speed the process. People who have tried this microwave technique say that the colors stay truer and that the microwave-dried botanicals are not as brittle as traditionally dried flowers. Drying times in the microwave range from 20 seconds to 4 minutes, depending on the materials used. If you want to try microwave-drying, try using two heavy, microwave-safe plates with paper towels between them. Sandwich the flowers between paper towels on one plate, making sure they do not touch or overlap. Place the other plate on top. Start drying in 20-second increments on the high setting. The thinner and more delicate the flowers, the less time they should spend in the microwave.

Using tweezers, place your flowers, leaves, or stems into the press directly on the newsprint. Allow space between flowers so that none touch. If any overlap, they will probably stick together. For convenience in sorting and to aid in organizing, place like flowers on the same sheet of paper. If you're pressing a variety of botanicals, place flowers and foliage of similar thickness on the same sheet. Press flower stems on one section, leaves on another, and so on. If you want to press blooms with thick layers of petals, it is best to separate the petals from the stems and dry the petals separately. Also, flowers with thick, round centers are best separated; dry the petals on one sheet and the flower centers on another. (Later, you can arrange the petals in a design similar to their original appearance.)

On the edge of the paper, use a pencil to note the date that the flowers entered the press. Also, write the name of the herb or flower or leaves on that sheet next to the date. If you have separated the stems, leaves, petals, and centers of a flower, make sure you note which plant each part came from. You don't want to assemble a purple coneflower for a project and accidentally use the leaves from an ivy!

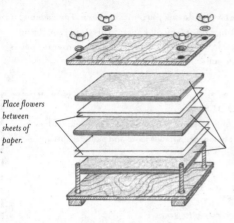

Place flowers between sheets of paper.

Place cardboard at the top and bottom of the press. Also add cardboard on top of each paper/flowers/paper layer.

After one sheet of paper has been filled and labeled, lay two sheets of paper on top. If the flowers are relatively flat and thin, such as pansies, these two sheets are all you'll need; just add more flowers and more paper on top, then a cardboard divider. If the plants are thicker, cover them with a sheet or two of paper and add a piece of cardboard. Then lay a sheet of paper on the cardboard, add more plants, and repeat. Make sure that there is always a piece of cardboard against both the wooden base and the top of the flower press, with ample blotting paper between each cardboard divider. Both of the presses described in this booklet can hold up to five cardboard divider sections with paper and plants sandwiched between.

Finally, make sure that each of the four bolts (or clamps) of the flower press is tightened evenly. Equal pressure is key to getting good results with your press.

THE THICK AND THIN OF PRESSING

If you do not want to separate the thinner parts of your plant from the thicker parts, here are a couple of ideas to help you press the entire plant successfully.

Place pads of blotting paper over the thinner parts of your flower to even up the pressure in the press.

Cut pieces of foam slightly larger than the thin part of your flower. If you have a flower with a thicker center, cut a hole in the foam and lay it over the flower.

Check your flowers the day after you put them into the press. If the paper shows any signs of dampness, you will need to change it; use tweezers to transfer the plants to fresh paper. Check them again the following day. If moisture is again present, change the paper again. If the paper and flowers do not remain absolutely dry, then some or all of the flowers may mold in the press, spoiling others nearby. If this happens, you will need to discard the moldy plants and paper; restock your flower press with clean, dry paper and fresh flowers; and start the procedure again.

Allow botanicals to press for four to six weeks before removing. You may check them periodically while they are drying, but do not move them unless necessary.

STORING PRESSED FLOWERS AND FOLIAGE

Remove your pressed flowers the same way you put them into the press: with tweezers. Pressed flowers, herbs, and foliage can be stored until you have accumulated the desired quantity and variety. Store in a dry place, away from direct sunlight.

Check stored flowers periodically for mold and mildew, especially if you live in a humid area. Promptly discard anything with a trace of mold or mildew to avoid losing the remainder of your stored botanicals. In humid regions, consider placing a packet of silica gel (you can purchase this at a craft store) in the box with your botanicals. Also, try to store the boxes in a well-ventilated area to prevent damage from moisture.

THE SECRET TO PRESSING LOVELY ROSEBUDS

When you're working with a rosebud, detach the bud from the stem and press each separately. You may also choose to remove the leaves and press them separately. If the leaves on your stem are not all perfect, simply pick perfect leaves of similar sizes and press them instead. Discard those with brown spots or holes. Press only the freshest and closest to perfect. When you use the rosebud, you will simply reconstruct it from the best leaves and stems you have pressed.

Using a sharp pair of scissors or a utility knife, cut the rosebud in half vertically. Then lay the two halves in your press, cut-side down. This reduces the thickness and moisture of a bud and, at the same time, doubles the number of rosebuds available for your projects.

GETTING THE BEST RESULTS

Flowers that grow from bulbs generally have a high moisture content and therefore do not press well. Examples include daffodils, crocuses, amaryllis, and tulips. Of course, there may be other flowers that you will not have success in pressing. An experienced flower presser may be able to press the most difficult flowers, like calla lily, while a beginner might fail. But don't be afraid to experiment, even with some of the flowers listed above. If you fail, you have still learned something, and all you have lost is a couple of sheets of paper and some time.

There are ways to help ensure success, however. Follow the basic guidelines below for the best results.

- Until you become experienced, try to use freshly picked flowers, not those taken from a florist's bouquet: Most of the latter are full of water, and this increases the likelihood of mold or mildew. If you do use purchased flowers, check often in the first few days to make sure they are not too wet in the press.

- Pick flowers in dry weather, just after the morning dew has evaporated. Never pick flowers to press right after a rain.

- Pick flowers and foliage without blemish (no brown spots or insect damage). Preferably, pick the newest, youngest, freshest-looking blooms.

- Press all specimens immediately upon picking. This is especially crucial in hot weather. When you're in the field, carry along a temporary press. Otherwise, your flowers may wilt before you

Continued ➔

return to your press. If you're gathering plants from your lawn or garden, lay them in a basket.

- Unless it's a windy day, try placing your specimens in the press while on the porch or patio to keep cleanup to a minimum.

Getting Started

Now that you have pressed your first flowers, it is time to use them in projects. The key to a successful project is to lay out your design first, arranging it exactly as you want it. When you have it just right, then begin gluing it down. Even the most experienced designers work this way.

GLUING BASICS

Once you have laid out your design, you are ready to glue it to the chosen background. Begin by squirting white glue into a bottle cap. You will need very little glue, but it must be applied carefully so that it doesn't leak out around the edges of the flowers. Keep a supply of toothpicks handy.

Start with the layer of flowers you positioned first. For example, if you are reassembling a flower you took apart to press, start by gluing down the petals as you want them. Then glue the center over the petals to hide their inside ends.

GLUING TOOLS

Much like pressing, affixing flowers to a background requires few tools; more important are a steady hand and patience. Still, the following will come in handy:

Bottle caps

Plastic party toothpicks

Tweezers (same as the ones used for pressing)

White glue

PRESSABLE FLOWERS, FOLIAGE, AND HERBS

Flowering Trees, Shrubs, Bushes, and Vines

Common Name	Color(s)	Zones
Azalea	White, pink, purple	3–9
Catalpa	White with yellow stripes, purple	4–9
Crape myrtle	Pink, white, purple, red	7–10
Flowering dogwood*	White, cream, pink	5–8
Elderberry flowers	White	6–8
Hydrangea	Blue, pink, white	4–10
Ligustrum	White	3–9
Pinxter flower	Pink	7–9
Redbud*	Purple-red	5–9
Weigela	White, pink, red	4–9
Wisteria	White, purple, pink with purple tips	6–9

Garden Flowers, Wildflowers, and Flowering Herbs

Common Name	Color(s)	Zones
Aster	Pink, yellow, white	3–10
Begonia centers	Yellow flower center	All
Buttercup	Yellow	4–8
Catnip	White with purple spots	3–7
Chickweed	White	All
Clover	White, magenta	4–9
Curly dock	Red	All
Daisy varieties*	White, yellow	3–8
Dandelion	Yellow-gold	5–7
Dianthus	Red, pink, white	4–10
Fire pink	Red	3–8
Fleabane	White, pink	2–8
Goldenrod	Yellow	5–9
Impatiens	Various	All
Indian blanket	Red with yellow tips	2–10
Johnny-jump-up*	Yellow, white, and purple mix	4–8

Garden Flowers, Wildflowers, and Flowering Herbs Cont.

Lantana	Various	8–10
Lavender	Lavender	5–10
Lobelia	Blue-purple	4–10
Mullein	Yellow	5–9
Pansy*	Various	4–8
Phlox	Red, pink, lavender, white	4–8
Pickerelweed	Purple-blue	3–11
Plumbago	Blue	4–9
Purple coneflower	Purple	3–9
Queen Anne's lace*	White	7–10
Rose varieties	Various	2–9
Salvia	Red	5–10
Skullcap	Blue	5–8
Statice	White	8–9
Sunflower	Yellow	5–9
Viola	Various	6–9
Violet	White, purple	4–9
Wood sorrel	Rose-purple	3–10
Yarrow	White	4–8

Greenery and Foliage

Common Name	Characteristics	Zones
Artemisia	Striking silver leaves	3–7
Bottlebrush	Thick green leaves	10–11
Carrot tops	Lacy	All
Elderberry	Long, slender leaves	6–8
Galax	Turns red in fall	5–8
Gardenia	Dark, shiny green	8–10
Ivy*	Cascades of leaves	5–10
Maidenhair fern*	Green, lacy fronds	3–11
Redbud	Heart-shaped leaves	5–9
Wisteria leaves*	Clusters of slender leaves	6–9
Wood betony	Small, fernlike leaves	5–8
Yarrow	Fernlike, soft-toothed leaves	5–7

* easiest to press

Carefully lift each piece with tweezers. Dip the flat end of a toothpick into the glue and gently dab a small amount onto the back of each flower as you are ready to apply it to the background. Be careful not to apply too much glue, and try not to get it on your tweezers. It's a good idea to keep a damp cloth handy in case of accidents.

Work from the bottom layer up, gluing your botanicals to their base, overlapping where your design dictates. When you are finished, either throw away the bottle cap or wash it to keep for the next project. If you are using plastic toothpicks, you can wash and reuse them. Wooden toothpicks should be thrown away.

Simple Projects for Beginners

FRESH-PRESSED-FLOWER PLATES

The next time you have a dinner party or feel festive, you can create unique dinner or serving plates. You will need two clear glass plates for each place setting or serving plate. They should be of the same size and design. You will also need some ferns and some flowers in full bloom. They can be used fresh for this unique project, because the glass plates will serve as a temporary flower press.

Lay down one glass plate and arrange some greenery on the surface. Select one large flower for the center, or several smaller blooms to rest on top of the greenery. When you've arranged them the way you want, simply press another clear glass plate on top to sandwich them under glass. Trim off any greenery that overhangs the edge of the plates.

The plates can be made up to half a day ahead or the night before and stored in the refrigerator until needed. If you are making multiple place settings, you can stack them in the refrigerator. But remember to remove them about 20 minutes early to give any frost a chance to clear from the glass plates.

Variation. Cover a cardboard circle larger than your dinner plates with autumn leaves, taping them in place at the center and completely covering the cardboard at the edge. Place dinner plates over these bases for a festive autumn table.

DECORATED GIFT SOAPS

Start with a bar of either homemade or purchased soap and some small dried flowers. Simply moisten the surface of the bar and apply the chosen dried flowers or leaves. If your design consists of multiple flowers that overlap, melt a little paraffin or beeswax and brush gently onto the underside of each botanical. Press into place on the soap according to the design. Let the bar dry completely; then cover with plastic wrap.

PLACE MATS

Materials

1 12"x17" piece of burlap

1 piece of muslin or other fabric 2"–4" smaller than the burlap

Spray adhesive

Tweezers

Pressed flowers, greenery, and leaves (for this project, they need be pressed for only a day or so, just until they are flat and dry)

White glue

Plastic toothpicks

Clear contact paper

Scissors or pinking shears

1. Glue the muslin to the burlap using a spray adhesive and let dry. This will give you a stiff background to compose on.

2. With the tweezers, lay out your pressed flowers and foliage on the fabric until you are satisfied with the design.

3. Glue the botanicals to the fabric and let dry.

4. Remove a couple of cross threads on all four sides of the burlap to create a slight fringe effect.

5. Cut two pieces of contact paper to the same dimensions as the burlap. Apply one piece to the bottom of the burlap mat, then cover the top with the second, being careful to apply smoothly without any creases or bubbles in the surface. Trim around the perimeter of the place mat with pinking shears or scissors. Your place mats are ready to delight everyone at mealtime!

Intermediate Projects

MINIATURE FRAMED FLOWERS

Look for small, pretty picture frames in brass, gold, silver, or wood tones and shaped in circles, ovals, or squares. Some square mini-frames also have heart-shaped centers. With small frames, start by trying a single-bloom display. One mini-frame is often used to display a large pansy. Select a simple background fabric such as linen, muslin, or shantung in a solid color and mount the fabric on the cardboard piece that comes in the frame. Tape the fabric to the cardboard on the back. Find the center of your frame and mark it lightly with a pencil as a general reference for applying your bloom. Select your bloom and glue into place. Place in the frame after the glue has dried. These look especially great displayed in a group.

Variations:

Mini-collage. Use tiny flowers that you have collected and dried. After you have covered the board in the back of the frame with a solid, neutral-colored fabric or heavyweight paper, lay the frame on top and lightly mark the inner four corners. There is no need to cover the whole piece of fabric with flowers, only the portion that will be visible when framed. Just make sure that the flowers completely cover the pencil markings that you made on the backing. To plan your design, start close to the center and overlap flowers in an appealing arrangement. Once the area within the markings has been covered, begin gluing flowers into place on the backing. Remember to glue the bottom layer of flowers first.

Topiary shapes are very popular and can be easily re-created in frames. Simply sketch a circle, star, heart, or other shape on the backing and fill it in with flowers. A mini standard rose is a good idea, but any topiary shape will work. Simply use a stem or thin leaf for the trunk and flowers or a paper pot at the base.

Bouquet. The flowers in this project are designed to resemble a bouquet of fresh flowers. For a romantic look, select a cream-colored ceramic frame and background fabric for this lovely bouquet of flowers. A 3 1/2" x 5" ceramic frame sets off a bouquet of small blooms to perfection. Matting is not necessary; indeed, it would detract from the soft, romantic look of the ceramic frame. Start by taping a piece of cream-colored fabric

Continued ➜

to the cardboard insert that came in the frame. Arrange all flowers with stems pointing downward to mimic a bouquet. It's okay, however, if the flowers used in this bouquet design do not all have stems attached; feel free to take artistic license by borrowing thin stems from other botanicals. The base of the bouquet is where the majority of the stems should appear, as they would in a real bouquet. When your design is finished, carefully glue the botanicals to the backing. For a nice finishing touch, tie a bow of thin ribbon and glue it across the flower stems as if the tied bow were actually holding the bouquet together.

Embellishing matting. This is an easy way to add a personal touch to standard matting. Any of the materials that you have successfully pressed and stored can be used to embellish matting. First determine how the matting will be used—to frame a photograph, watercolor, print, charcoal drawing, or the like. Then select pressed botanicals in a range of colors that complement the picture. For balance, decorate around all four corners, in an L shape around the bottom corners, or along opposite sides. As always, lay out your design with the print or photo underneath first, to get a preview of how the finished product will look. After you are satisfied with the design, glue it down. Allow the glue used on the botanicals to dry completely before you place the matting in the frame.

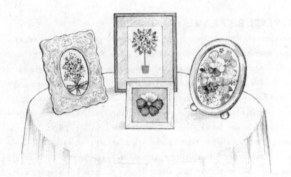

DECORATING CANDLES

It's a simple matter to embellish tapered or pillar-style candles with pressed flowers. Choose the candles you wish to work with, and select from your pressed materials flowers compatible with the candle colors. Arrange the materials until you are happy with the design. When embellishing tapers, try using one simple flower and a couple of leaves. If you're working with chunky pillar candles, create a band of daisies or pansies around the base.

Pour a little glue into a bottle cap or jar lid. Using the toothpick or a very fine artist's paintbrush, apply glue, covering the entire back of each botanical. Press onto the candle. If any glue shows on the candle, wipe it

clean with the tip of a damp sponge or cotton swab, making sure not to wet the flowers. When you're working with tapered candles, you can seal the flowers with paraffin if you wish; this will make the decorations less fragile.

Care should be taken when burning candles, especially narrow tapers, that have dried-flower decorations added. As the candle burns down to the level of the dried materials, make sure the flame does not touch them. For this reason, it is often best to decorate only the base of tapers. When the candle burns down to the level of the decoration, it's time to replace the candle anyway. With pillars and wider tapers, the flame does not come close to the outside of the candle, so the fire danger is minimal.

EMBELLISHING WOODEN BOXES

Any box with a flat lid is suitable for this project. A trio of floral-embellished Shaker-style boxes in graduated sizes would make a lovely accent to any room in the home. Dogwood blossoms, baby's breath, and Johnny-jump-ups are ideal, because they are flat. The box you select will need to hold glue, so avoid highly polished or lacquered boxes. To ensure that the glue will adhere to the wood, lightly rub a piece of fine sandpaper only within the area that will be covered by the decoration. Then select your pressed materials and lay them out, gluing when the design is complete. If any glue seeps out from under the pressed flowers, immediately wipe it off with a damp cloth, being careful not to wet the pressed flowers.

To protect the flowers on the lid of each box, spray two or three even coats of sealer across the arrangement, allowing the sealer to dry between applications. Most craft and art supply stores stock spray sealer.

BOOKMARKS

The flattest of foliage and flowers is necessary for this project. When a protective film covering is applied, bulky materials will cause uneven lumps on the surface. Bookmarks can be made on ribbon or stationery paper or a combination. Choose a width of ribbon to complement the flowers you will be working with, but generally, a bookmark should not exceed 2" in width and 8" in length.

To make a bookmark, select a 1"- to 1 1/2"-wide satin ribbon and cut to a length of 16". Fold in half. At the bottom of the ribbon, opposite the folded end, cut an upside-down V no more than 1" deep. Apply a thin bead of glue across the notched bottom to hold the two ends together. Decorate with delicate dried botanicals like ferns and Queen Anne's lace, gluing these to the ribbon. Seal with clear contact paper or laminate. If you are new to working with laminates, or if you have trouble getting a smooth seal, practice before attempting the final project. One effective method is to peel off the backing slowly, working from the top, rather than peeling off the backing all at once and trying to apply the entire piece of laminate.

For different looks, try using different materials. Ribbons come in an amazing variety of fabrics, from gold to calico. Different colors and different flowers create moods that range from elegant to rustic. Or you can use paper instead of ribbon: Decorate stiff paper or poster board with dried flowers and seal. Tie a complementary yarn string to the top to dangle out of the book. You could even try affixing your dried flowers directly to the laminate or contact paper back, sealing with the top piece of laminate to create a stained-glass bookmark.

Advanced Project

FERN AND PANSY COUNTRY HEART TRAY

Materials

Fabric

Antique tray with glass

Hardboard backing

Tape

Maidenhair fern

Heart template (optional)

Glue and bottlecap

Tweezers

Party toothpicks or a small artist's brush

Pansies

A couple of smaller flowers (optional): one blue and one white, such as Johnny-jump-up or violet, and chickweed or aster

Spray sealer

Duct tape or veneer pins

2 screws, and picture-hanging wire (optional)

1. Select a color and type of fabric that will complement the flowers you are using and cut the fabric in a rectangle that is at least 4" larger than the antique tray.

2. Place this fabric facedown on a table and place the hardboard backing from the tray down on top. Fold the fabric over the hardboard and tape.

3. Arrange the fern of your choice in a heart-shaped design. Trace a heart template lightly onto the fabric if you need to. Then glue down the fern, using tweezers to hold the foliage while you apply glue with a toothpick (or a thin artist's paint brush).

4. Now place one large pansy at the bottom, where the heart would come to a point. Next, place two smaller pansies overlapping at the top on either side, as shown in the illustration. The rest of the pansies should be placed among the fern wherever you choose. Glue the pansy flowers into place. Then use the optional smaller flowers to fill in bald spots as desired within the remainder of the heart until you're satisfied. Glue the botanicals into place.

5. A light spray of sealer can be applied directly onto the pressed foliage and flowers and allowed to dry. Try to keep the sealer off the fabric, as it may cause slight discoloration. **Hint:** *Lay wax paper over the design and carefully trace your design. Cut out and place the wax paper over the project before spray-sealing to protect the fabric.*

6. After the design has completely dried, place the cleaned glass in the frame and insert the hardboard backing—pressed flower design combination. Seal the spot where the hardboard meets the tray back with duct tape or veneer pins.

7. If your tray will sit on a table or shelf, you now are finished. To hang it, insert a small wood screw into each side of the tray and string picture-hanging wire between the two.

Tips for Preserving Your Projects

Most of the pressed floral designs presented in this booklet can be sprayed with a thin coat of sealer. Various sealers can be purchased at art supply or craft stores. However, you should take great care when you apply them. Because the sealer is applied to the design once it has been affixed in its final form to the backing fabric, you could damage or discolor the fabric by overspraying the adhesive. To help avoid ruining your background fabric, lay a piece of tracing paper or wax paper over the entire picture. Trace the outline of the pressed-botanical design onto the paper and cut that part out. This will give you a protective shield for the portion of the project that does not need to receive the spray sealer. It is best to apply the sealer outdoors on a warm sunny day. Natural light helps you see exactly how much sealer is coming out. It is always better to apply two thin coats than one heavy coat; you do not want the sealer to run. Lay the design flat for a few moments after spraying to avoid any running of the sealer in case you oversprayed. Follow the manufacturer's recommendations for use. Under no circumstances should you leave the pressed floral designs out in the sun for more than a few minutes.

If the pressed flowers are wedged firmly between a sheet of glass to the front and

Continued ➜

fabric, padding, and hardboard closed in to the back, this may be all the sealer that is needed for preserving the floral work for years of lasting enjoyment.

How your design is displayed will also affect its longevity. If you sell or give away pressed botanicals, include a card with the following notations: "This artistic creation is made of pressed flowers and foliage. In order to ensure many years of enjoyment, do not place this in a room with high humidity or moisture or near a window that receives a lot of sunlight." These few guidelines should help keep your flowers as lovely as they are now.

Making Prints from Nature

Laura Donnelly Bethmann
Illustrations by Alison Kolesar

Field Collecting

While gathering materials on your home ground may keep you quite busy, roaming in the great outdoors will expand your possibilities. Wear proper clothing and footgear, and be aware of poison ivy, poison oak, and poison sumac. Obtain a field guide of the wildflowers and plants in your region so you will recognize poisonous plants if encountered and be able to identify your newfound specimens. Attempt to contact property owners before removing plants from even seemingly remote locations. If you see lovely wildflowers growing along a roadside or in a meadow, go to the nearest house or business to find the landowner and get permission to collect plants. If in doubt, check town, county, or city records for property ownership. State and national parks don't allow removal of anything, but it doesn't hurt to ask the park superintendent.

Rare and endangered species should never be disturbed. Local gardens, conservation groups, or your state department of natural resources can provide a list of threatened plants.

EQUIPMENT FOR FIELD COLLECTING

The following items are useful to keep close at hand in your car or in your backpack for collecting specimens.

- Notebook, self-stick note pads, self-stick labels for bags, and waterproof marker.
- Scissors and/or hand pruners for cutting stems, twigs, and woody plants. If you have an interest in collecting leaves and flowers from trees, you may also need to purchase long-handled pruners.
- A trowel for digging up plant specimens.
- Zip-seal plastic bags to store specimens.
- Spray bottle of water to keep specimens from wilting.
- Lightweight plant press, or, if you're traveling by car, newspapers and some weights . Delicate plants, especially, should be pressed quickly.
- Container of water for transporting cut flowers or whole plants that you want to print fresh, not pressed.
- A field guide or two describing the wild plants found in your region of the country.

TRANSPORTING SPECIMENS

Place your collected materials in plastic bags. Inflate the bags before closing (zip the seal, leaving one or two inches open, blow air into the opening to inflate, and seal completely) to provide a protective air cushion.

If you can't press specimens immediately upon returning home, store them in the refrigerator. Do not leave them in plastic bags unrefrigerated. Plants that have wilted during transport may revive in the refrigerator. Herbs, tree leaves, and other plants can be stored successfully under refrigeration for one to three weeks. When collecting wildflowers, cut and transport them in a container of water or press them on site.

To collect an entire plant, dig it up with as much root as possible and gently shake off excess soil. Using a spray bottle of water, spray once or twice inside a plastic bag large enough to accommodate the plant, insert the plant, close the bag, and label it.

Pressing Techniques

Good results in nature printing depend on well-pressed specimens. Folded, wrinkled leaves and petals produce poor nature prints. It's very important to take the time to press your specimens carefully. See *Making and Using a Flower Press* for pressing procedures.

REMOISTURIZING DRY PLANTS

Plants needs to be supple to accept ink or they will crumble. If you are using plants that were collected in autumn or winter and have become brittle or plants that have dried in the press, you will need to soften them up before use. For this task, you will need a plastic bag, newspapers, a spray bottle of water, and weights.

Leaves. Using the spray bottle, mist dried leaves on both sides. Lightly spray inside the plastic bag, as well. Put the leaves inside the bag, seal it, and let them rest a few hours or overnight. Once they are pliable, they are ready to press. Dampen several layers of newspaper and sandwich the now pliable plants between the layers. Cover with a sheet of plastic or plastic bag and add weight. Most leaves will press flat within 30 minutes to an hour.

Plants. To remoisturize a dry, pressed plant, begin by placing the plant between layers of dampened newspaper, cover that with plastic, and place a weight on top. A pressing time of 30 minutes to overnight will be required, depending on the plant. Check the plant occasionally and spray the newspaper again if it becomes dry. But beware: Leaving plant material in a damp press for too long encourages mold growth.

Flowers. Dry, pressed flowers should remain in a damp press for only a few minutes and must be handled with care. Many flowers are too delicate to use when not fresh, although some, such as dogwood, Queen Anne's lace, lavender (in bud), and red clover, can be pressed for up to a year and remoisturized for use.

Printing Supplies and Equipment

Nature printers use some of the traditional tools and supplies of printmakers, painters, and craftspeople, but useful supplies can also be found in pharmacies, junkyards, or auto supply stores, or even lying around the house. Nature printing lends itself to most media, so if you already have art or craft supplies, you can probably make use of them in nature printing. It is easy to get carried away with wanting to try all the wonderful art products on the market, but that can be expensive. If you

450

are unsure of where to begin, buy only the minimum printmaking supplies needed to experiment.

PIGMENTS

Most nature printers use block printing inks. These produce excellent results, are readily available, and come in small and large tubes and cans. They are applied to plants with a brayer, bristle brush, or dabber. Begin with just one tube of black ink or, at most, one tube each of black, white, red, yellow, and blue. You can mix these colors to create new colors, shades, and tints.

Inks are either oil-based or water-based. To use oil-based inks for nature printing, you must add linseed oil, poppy seed oil, or other oil preparations made for printmaking, which reduces the tack (stickiness) of the ink and results in a more even application, fewer roller marks, and easier printing. Clean up oil-based inks with solvents such as kerosene or mineral spirits. Keep in mind that solvents are flammable, volatile, potentially toxic, and should be used in a well-ventilated area. Carefully follow label directions. Special hand cleaners are available for removing ink, or you can wear latex gloves.

Many water-based inks are difficult to use for nature printing. They dry too quickly on the palette during printing sessions because they are mixed with water. Graphic Chemical and Ink Company, however, has a line of water-based inks that use a water-soluble vehicle for mixing instead of water. (You can write to them at P.O. Box 27, Villa Park, Illinois 60181 or call them toll-free at 800–465–7382.) These inks perform as well as oil-based inks do, and when dry, will not wash off, making them a good choice for use on fabric and other washable surfaces, in addition to paper. Many water-based colors are nontoxic and have no fumes. All water-based inks clean up with mild soap and water.

The behavior of inks can be altered by adding other products. *Extender* dilutes ink color, making it more transparent. *Cobalt drier* or *Japan drier* speeds up the drying process. *Sureset* compound reduces the tack of ink for better distribution, but also keeps ink from drying, so a drier should accompany the use of Sureset. When using a drier without Sureset, add a drop of oil of cloves (available at a pharmacy) to keep the ink mixture from drying too fast on the palette. All of these products should be added to ink in minute amounts.

THE PALETTE

The best palette to use for preparing oil- or water-based ink, and for inking plant specimens, is a sheet of window glass. I use a 16-inch by 20-inch sheet of glass for every four or five colors and a separate glass sheet for inking the plants. The glass is available in any size you require from a hardware store or glass cutter. The raw edges of cut glass can be a safety hazard, but a professional glass cutter can polish them for you. Windows removed from old car doors (complete with safe, polished edges), a sheet of Plexiglass, a white-glazed dinner plate, a disposable paper palette, or freezer paper from the supermarket also work well. When using a clear palette of glass or plastic, place a white sheet of paper underneath to improve visibility when you're rolling out ink.

PALETTE KNIVES/INK SPREADERS

Palette knives are for mixing and spreading inks on the palette in preparation for rolling out with a brayer. You can also make your own disposable ink spreaders from matboard scraps cut with a utility knife into strips approximately one inch by two inches.

PIGMENT APPLICATORS

The most common methods for applying ink or paint to printable objects require brayers, brushes, or dabbers.

Brayers. Soft rubber brayers (hand-inking rollers) or polyurethane brayers are used for rolling ink onto the plants. Brayers come in a variety of sizes from a 1/4-inch long to eight inches long. Expensive composition or gelatin brayers, available in larger sizes, are suitable only for oil-based inks.

Brushes. You may want to use bristle brushes to apply ink to plants. Flat or round brushes are available in sizes appropriate to every need. Good-quality synthetic or ox-hair blend brushes are moderately priced and do a fine job.

Dabbers. Dabbers are a traditional tool. The easiest way of obtaining suitable dabbers is to make them yourself from a variety of items, some of which you probably have around the house. Soft foam cosmetic sponges or dense foam blocks made for young children (often labeled bath blocks) are ready-to-use dabbers.

Method 1: Nature printer John Doughty makes simple dabbers by fasioning a handle from a bottle cork, 35mm film roll canister, or wooden dowel (about one inch wide) and covering that with dense, adhesive-backed vinyl foam. You simply remove the top layer of clear plastic, cut the foam to fit your handle, and adhere. The adhesive makes the foam easy to use, and its density provides a fine, absorbent surface for applying ink.

Method 2: Dabbers can also be made from one-quarter-inch-thick sheets of continuous (not shredded) polyurethane foam, available in craft and fabric shops or carpet stores. Cut a foam circle about three times wider than the width of the handle you are using, wrap it around one end, and secure it with a rubber band.

Just about any elongated item will serve as a handle. Try recycling empty correction fluid, medicine, or sample-size cosmetic containers. For smaller dabbers, use flat-top clothespins, dried-up markers, or unsharpened pencils. Large dabbers can be made by covering the bottom end of plastic soda bottles of varying sizes. Use whatever items you have on hand to suit your needs.

Make as many dabbers as you will need for a printing session. The foam is disposable, although it can be cleaned and reused. If you're using a children's foam block, the dried, inked end of it can be shaved off with a single-edge razor blade to expose a new surface.

PAPER

To begin, a pad of newsprint paper and a roll of sumi (kozo) paper will provide inexpensive but receptive surfaces for practice. Cut rolled paper to size as needed and tape the corners to keep it flat while working. As your control and skill in nature printing develop, you will want to invest in better quality, long-lasting papers, reserving the newsprint and sumi for test printing.

Continued ➜

OBTAINING DESIRED SIZE

Cutting paper with scissors is the obvious way to trim it to the desired size, but folding and tearing paper preserves the fibrous look of deckled edges. First, wash and dry your hands thoroughly before handling paper. Even if your hands look clean, the natural oils on skin can stain or be absorbed by the paper, thereby resisting or discoloring water-based pigments. Work on a clean, flat surface.

For European or American papers, fold to desired width or length, making a firm crease. Be careful not to wrinkle the paper. Now, open the paper and refold in the opposite direction, pressing firmly along the crease. Repeat once or twice, weakening the paper fibers along the crease each time. Open the sheet, lay it on the table, and hold one side in place with your hand. With your other hand, grip the edge of the other side, and gently pull away, tearing on the crease. Or place a ruler or straightedge on the crease and gently tear the sheet along the edge.

The fibers of most Japanese and Chinese papers are much longer and need to be dampened before tearing. Fold and crease once, open the sheet, quickly drag a wet watercolor brush in a straight line along the crease, and gently pull the paper apart.

PRINT PRESSING TOOLS

Our versatile, tactile hands are the most readily available printing tool. Pressure from the heel of the hand, or thumbs and fingers, applied to an inked plant in contact with a printing surface will transfer ink from the plant to that surface. Other tools for pressing, tamping, rubbing, or rolling by hand are large, flat spoons, printmaker's barens, clean brayers, dowels, and rolling pins. If you have access to a flat-bed printing press, use it for nature printing. Or make a "walking" printing press that uses the weight of your whole body—the second-best thing to a professional printing press.

MAKING MISTAKES

Before you begin nature printing, keep in mind one important aspect of making art: Mistakes are going to occur. Even though errors simply indicate experimentation, many of us are afraid to make them. But the only real risk involved is in acquiring knowledge about how not to do something. More importantly, mistakes are a crucial part of learning and should be recognized as such.

HOW TO MAKE A "WALKING" PRESS

A "walking" printing press does not require any special supplies—just a sheet of plywood, a felt blanket, a sheet of newsprint, and printmaking paper.

1. Find a sheet of plywood larger than the plants you plan to print. For most prints, a 2-foot by 3-foot sheet is adequate.

2. Lay half of the felt blanket on the plywood leaving the rest to double over the top layer. Then place a sheet of newsprint on the blanket to keep it clean.

3. Large or generally unwieldy plants should be laid inked-side up on the newsprint in the press, with the printmaking paper then positioned face down on top. Small or easy-to-handle inked plants can be laid inked-side down on printing paper, which is then set on the press.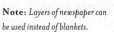

4. Over the plants and printing paper, lay another sheet of newsprint, and cover all with the remaining part of the blanket.

5. The press is ready for walking. With or without your shoes on, baby-step along the blanket to distribute your weight over the inked plants and paper sandwiched inside.

Note: *Layers of newspaper can be used instead of blankets.*

Basic Nature Printing Methods

The basic procedure for nature printing is a simple direct printing process: A pigment-covered natural object is pressed onto paper or another receptive surface, revealing a delicately textured, life-size image of itself. Not quite as easy as it sounds, however, nature printing takes practice to master, especially if you aren't used to working with artists' tools and materials such as inks and paints.

BASIC DIRECT PRINTING

The basic direct printing method requires a clear work space, such as a large table, in a well-lit area where you can keep all materials close at hand.

I recommend that you use Graphic Chemical water-based block printing ink and water-soluble vehicle. The vehicle is a mixing agent that keeps the ink fluid and workable on the palette for hours, even days. The Graphic Chemical water-based inks are made to be used with a water-soluble vehicle. These inks do not mix with water as other water-based inks do; water is only used for cleanup. You can use another brand of water-based ink, but be aware that inks mixed with water instead of vehicle are more difficult to work with.

Oil-based printing inks perform similarly to Graphic Chemical water-based ink, except that they use oil as a mixing agent and require solvents for cleanup. If you choose to use a different brand of ink, you should adapt the following directions as necessary.

For basic direct printing you will need the following materials:

- Water-based block printing inks (such as Graphic Chemical brand)
- Water-soluble vehicle (such as Graphic Chemical brand)
- Soft rubber brayers in assorted sizes and/or bristle brushes and dabbers
- Palette (sheet of glass) and palette knife or ink spreaders
- Tweezers
- Paper for practice printing
- Printmaking papers
- Water and mild liquid soap
- Paper towels
- A variety of pressed leaves and plants

INKING

Prepare for inking by setting up a clear work area and assembling all of your materials within easy reach. Be sure to have a practice sheet of newsprint or sumi paper ready.

1. To ink palette, squeeze a 1/4-inch blob of ink near the top edge. Place the tip of a palette knife or ink spreader in the middle of the ink and draw it straight down the palette, making a thin smear about 3 or 4 inches long.

2. Dip the corner of a clean spreader into the can of vehicle and mix a few drops of it into the ink smear with the same downward-drawing motion for several seconds. Lay the spreader at the top of the palette.

3. Select a sturdy, flat leaf. Choose a brayer to accommodate the size of the leaf. Roll the brayer back and forth along the ink smear on your palette, allowing the ink to just coast the brayer—you do not need to apply heavy pressure. Slightly widen and lengthen the ink by rolling the brayer back and forth, thinning it out, and obtaining even distribution on the brayer. The ink should be very tacky and shiny; if it feels dry and looks dull, add another drop of vehicle. Don't add too much or the ink won't dry and your print may remain sticky for weeks.

   A very thin layer of ink is optimal for successful printing. If your ink layer is still heavy after rolling, scrape some off with the spreader. When the ink is an even, translucent film on the palette, you are ready to ink the leaf.

4. Lay the leaf underside up on a clean area of the glass and roll the inked brayer gently over it from stem to tip. Roll the brayer over the ink on the palette again to get an even layer of ink on it and re-ink the leaf a second time, and perhaps a third. The leaf should now be sufficiently coated.

ALTERNATIVE INKING METHODS

If you are using a bristle brush instead of a brayer, work the brush back and forth through the ink and vehicle to charge the bristles with a moderate amount of ink. Then brush the leaf surface gently from the center to the edges until evenly coated.

If you are using a dabber instead of a brayer, you need to alter the application method accordingly. Begin by spreading the ink and vehicle with an ink spreader over the palette in a slightly thicker coat than needed for a brayer. Using a dabber, dab into the ink layer. Dab off the excess ink on a clean area of the palette. Then, using some pressure, dab ink over the leaf until a thin, even coating of color appears.

PRINTING

The most readily available printing tools are our hands. By feeling the structure of the plant beneath the thin paper covering with your fingertips, you also absorb tactile knowledge about the plants you're printing, almost without realizing it.

5. Carefully, lift the leaf by its stem with tweezers, position it over the paper, and place it inked-side down. To avoid spotting or smearing, the leaf should not be moved once it touches the paper.

6. Cover the leaf with a piece of newsprint or paper toweling. If you prefer to see the leaf while you press it, cover with a piece of sturdy plastic such as clear freezer bag. Cut plenty of cover sheets a little larger than your plant to have on hand during your printing season.

7. Press with your hands. For a small leaf, press with the heel of your hand. For a large leaf, press your left thumb (or right thumb, if you are left-handed) firmly at the center of the leaf to anchor it, then use the thumb, fingers, or heel of your other hand to successfully press all around the leaf, radiating from the center outward to the edges and feeling the leaf's structure under the sheet of paper. Be careful not to shift the leaf. You can also try a gentle rubbing motion. The body of the leaf is more likely to adhere to the paper than the stem is, so press the body of the leaf first, the stem last.

8. Slowly, remove the paper covering. Wipe the ink off the end of the tweezers, then grasp the stem of the leaf and lift it straight up and off the print. Lay the leaf on the glass, ready to ink again.

Continued ➔

9. Lay prints in a row to air dry thoroughly for one to four weeks before storing, mounting, or framing.

CLEANUP

10. Soak brayers in a sink of soapy water for one or two minutes, then wipe ink off with a sponge, rinse, and dry. Soak brushes in a glass of soapy water (do not immerse handle) for one or two minutes, wipe off ink, rinse well under running water, and lay horizontally to dry.

11. Clean foam dabbers by successively pressing them on scrap paper until most of the excessive ink is removed. Save to reuse for future printing sessions with same ink color.

12. Scrape excess ink from glass palette. Spray palette with water, let stand a minute, and wipe clean.

13. Leftover ink can be covered with a loose-fitting lid or plastic wrap and stored for future use.

Advanced Direct Printing Techniques

To start, try printing with just one color ink, according to the directions for direct printing. After you've had some practice, experiment with multiple colors and alternative ink application methods. Here are a few techniques to try.

COLOR VARIATIONS

- Paint the protruding veins of a leaf with a contrasting color from the leaf body. To do this, after inking the underside of the leaf with one color, gently roll a brayer inked with a different color over only the veins of the leaf before printing the entire leaf.

- Apply a thin wash of one or more watercolor paints to add color and depth to a finished print once the ink has dried.

- Experiment with combining colors by smearing and then rolling two or three colors side by side on your palette to fit the width of a 3 1/2-inch (or larger) brayer. Roll the brayer back and forth until an even film appears showing each distinct color.

INK APPLICATION

- Try inking leaves and plants on both sides, then using a folded sheet of paper, create a double print.

- Make an indirect print as a result of your direct print. The negative image left on the brayer after inking a leaf can be rolled onto a printing surface, thus creating an indirect print. Another way to capture this image is to roll a large, clean brayer over an already-inked object and then roll it on a printing surface. This method works best with the very sensitive composition brayers and polyurethane brayers, although soft rubber brayers also work.

PRINTING WHOLE PLANTS AND LARGE SPECIMENS

Large and complex flowering plants present particular challenges and difficulties for the nature printer, and you must use your judgment and imagination in determining how to print each plant as you're presented with it. The following step-by-step description of procedures for printing a hibiscus demonstrate some of the diversity of techniques and adaptability necessary to achieve success in printing these specimens. But, remember that every nature printer has her or his own way of working. You may discover other techniques that work well for you. Nature printing is never an assembly-line process.

The bright magenta hibiscus usually blooms from late summer through early fall. It grows three to five feet tall, and the flowers average seven inches across.

Equipment. Use the following materials to make this hibiscus print:

- Water-based block printing inks (such as Graphic Chemical brand)
- Water-soluble vehicle (such as Graphic Chemical brand)
- 3-inch brayer
- 1-inch brayer
- Watercolor paints
- Watercolor brushes
- Watercolor palette
- Container of water
- One 22-inch by 30-inch sheet of Evanescent paper
- Newsprint
- Tweezers
- Ink spreaders
- Glass palette
- Flowering hibiscus plants

Pressing. The hibiscus plant requires no pressing at all since its leaves are flat. To keep them for winter use, put them in a press. When you remove the leaves from the press, moisten them slightly between sheets of damp newspaper. The flowers can only be printed fresh.

Because the flower petals have a slight curve, pressing usually creates wrinkles. Simply cut several long stems of the hibiscus and other flowering plants you plan to print and put them in cases of water so you can prepare each petal, leaf, and stem as you are about to print it. Also, this will enable you to refer to the natural form of the plant in the vase as you compose the picture of it.

Printing the flower. The flowers are the focus of this print and dictate the placement of the leaves and stems, so the flower should be printed first. Begin your print by removing the six ray petals of the hibiscus one by one, and inking and printing each in turn. Using both light and dark colors adds variation and achieves a sense of dimension.

Trim some of the petals at the point where they join to create the curved appearance they have when the blossom is whole. The wide petals can be inked with several passes from a 1-inch brayer, covering a portion of the petal each time to avoid wrinkling, and then print it by hand pressing. The petals disintegrate after just one pressing and can not be used again.

The pistil must be flattened before being inked and printed. Instead of actually printing it, I usually draw it in with a pencil and paint it later with watercolor. The stem is handled in this way, as well. To appear natural, the entire stem shouldn't be visible.

Printing the leaves. The hibiscus leaves can be printed in the "walking" press (see page 452), laid out in a natural formation overlapping and cascading across the paper. They should look like they're generating from the stem. You could add a very light "stem" pencil line (later erased) to guide leaf placement.

Displaying Finished Prints

For the best protection and enhancement of nature prints on paper, mat and frame them under glass or plastic. Choose mat colors and frame moldings to complement the nature prints. A frame contains the art, separating it from the surroundings. A mat creates a visual space around the art for viewing and air space between the art and the glass, allowing air circulation which greatly reduces the possibility of bacterial growth.

Consult a professional framer, visit a do-it-yourself frame shop, or purchase foam board backing sheets, ready-made frames and hardware, and pre-cut mats available in standard sizes from art and craft suppliers. When matting and framing nature prints that have been produced on archival or acid free papers, be sure to mat and back them with museum quality or, at least, acid free materials to extend the life of the art. These materials are more costly, but provide proper protection for valued artwork.

DISPLAY IDEAS AND TIPS

- Crop nature prints so that the margin is even all around, slip prints into sturdy clear plastic envelopes, and tack them into a wall or wall-mounted cork strips.

- Mount a length of molding to a wall, with lip facing up, and line up firmly backed or matted prints.

- Plate stands or small table easels make appropriate holders for matted prints and for nature-printed herbals or journals.

- Store unprotected prints in mylar or acid free paper envelopes in a cool, dark, airy place.

- Acrylic box frames are inexpensive and come in a large variety of sizes, and it is very easy to insert and remove prints so they can be changed frequently. Make a wall arrangement with several box frames to be changed seasonally or just to accommodate your latest nature prints.

- Nature prints on soft Asian papers, such as sumi, can be fastened on very inexpensive wooden embroidery hoops for interesting wall art or a pleasing gift. Use fabric markers for lettering or a border (regular markers bleed on soft papers).

Mounting prints. Mounting removes wrinkles resulting from pressing papers into crevices of fish, shells, and other objects when printing, and creates a firm base for prints made on soft, lightweight Asian papers. Artists' spray adhesives are an easy solution for small nature prints. Spray the back of the print and attach it to heavy paper or board (follow label directions). Don't use this method for artwork you value, as spray adhesive products are not permanent, and, in time, will discolor the paper. Dry

mounting with inert adhesives applied with heat can be a viable alternative. Consult a reliable, professional frame shop for this service.

Wet mounting with wheat or rice paste is the traditional method. The wet mounting process can be reversed with water, and the artwork removed from the backing.

GIFTS AND DECORATIONS

Making Gingerbread Houses

Rhonda Massingham Hart
Illustrations by Alison Kolesar

Create a Family Tradition

Family traditions set us apart and pull us together. In the remembering, they often become the center of what life was all about. What better way to set the mood for memories than the warm, spicy-sweet scent of gingerbread enveloping a kitchen strewn with candies and other marvelous makings of a gingerbread house? If ever an endeavor deserves to become a family tradition, the making of gingerbread houses does. There is something for everyone to appreciate and enjoy.

Country Chapel

Begin with a Plan

Select a gingerbread project from the blueprints below, and decide on the scale in which you wish to work. Bigger is not always better. Clever design and a flair for details are just as dramatic as enormous proportions. Enlarge the plans on graph paper or by using the zoom feature of a copy machine. A house from 8 to 12 inches square is large enough to incorporate plenty of eye-catching details.

Next, draw each feature (front, side, roof) onto lightweight cardboard (empty cereal boxes are good) in the actual size the pieces are to be. Once the templates are cut out, make sure everything fits together. Tape the template pieces together, then check and adjust the fit. Taking a few minutes now for this step may save you unnecessary frustration later. Mistakes are easily corrected at this stage—before they are even made.

Kitchen Supplies

Mixer or hand-held beater	Large and small mixing bowls
Clean, hard surface for rolling out dough	Cake decorating bags and tips
Rolling pin	Plywood or sturdy cardboard base, cut to size of finished project
Cookie sheets	
Aluminum foil	Canned goods (for holding walls in place while the glue dries)

Continued →

Making the Gingerbread

Like many culinary treasures, there are many recipes for gingerbread. This is my own, born of trial and error, but if you have an old family recipe, by all means dust it off.

GINGERBREAD

1 cup butter, margarine, or shortening

1 cup brown sugar

1 cup molasses

5 cups flour (all purpose, bleached, or unbleached)

1 1/2 teaspoons cinnamon

1/2 teaspoon cloves

2 teaspoons baking soda

1/2 teaspoon salt

1/3 to 1/2 cup water

In a large mixing bowl beat butter until softened. Add sugar and beat until fluffy—at least three minutes. Add molasses and beat well. Combine dry ingredients and add to the batter a little at a time, mixing in each addition. You will have to use your hands to work in the last additions.

Divide dough into thirds and shape into balls. Cover with plastic wrap and chill for several hours, preferably overnight.

Roll out one ball to approximately 3/16-inch thick on a piece of aluminum foil. Dough must be sufficiently chilled before rolling to prevent stickiness. Lightly flour the foil, your hands, and the rolling pin, before rolling to prevent pulling. Or roll between a sheet of foil on the bottom and a sheet of wax paper on top.

Position the pattern templates on top of the dough at least 1 inch apart to allow for a little spreading of dough during baking. Carefully cut out the pieces, using a pastry wheel or paring knife, and *gingerly* lift the scraps away from the cutout shapes, and return them to the refrigerator. If your house calls for texturized woodgrain, panels, brick, etc., score these effects into the gingerbread before baking (see tips below).

Carefully slide the foil (with the cutouts on it) onto a cookie sheet. Bake at 375°F for 9 to 11 minutes. Bake until just firm, never browned. In ovens that do not produce even heat, bake one sheet at a time, centered in the oven. Once all of the dough has been used, form the scraps into another ball and roll out again. Avoid rolling the dough out more than twice if you plan to eat your gingerbread—this extra handling makes it tough.

When the pieces have finished baking, remove from the oven and allow to cool on the cookie sheets. As soon as the pieces come out of the oven, check the edges and, if necessary, trim with a sharp knife so that the pieces will fit together. Lay the corresponding templates over each piece and check to be sure the sides are square with those of the template. The dough will have spread somewhat, but the basic shape should be the same. The dough hardens as it cools, making it more difficult to trim later.

Allow the gingerbread plenty of time to cool on racks before you begin construction. If you can't start right away, slide the fully cooled pieces onto foil-covered cardboard or back onto the baking sheets, wrap with foil or plastic wrap, and store flat. Gingerbread will stay reasonably fresh for several days.

DECORATING INGREDIENTS

Bread sticks – rafters, beams, pillars, logs

Candy canes – pillars, support beams, fenceposts, lightposts

Coated candies (M&M's) – tree decorations, Christmas lights

Cereal – colored loops for Christmas chains, tiles, small wheels, flat types for shingles

Chocolate bars – door, shutters, shingles

Cinnamon candies – red roofing tiles, paving stones, flowers

Crystallized flowers – frosted garden flowers, rare jewels, lady's corsage

Foil wrapped chocolate kiss – church bell, roof decoration

Frosting – mortar, snow, flowers, siding, hair, ribbons & bows

Fruit leather – window shades, fabric (from leather to whatever)

Gumdrops – bushes, flowers, ornaments

Gum candies – sliced into shingles, shaped into flowers

Hard candies – melted for stained glass windows, mirrors, reflecting pools; crushed for colored gravel, beads, gems

Ice cream cones – trees, tower turrets, hats, hoop skirts

Icing – garlands, flowers, snow, bows, siding

Licorice – railings, edgings, exposed beams, fireplace bricks

Licorice ropes – rope, edging, window pane dividers, harness

Lollipops – road signs, people, trees, bushes

Marshmallows – snowballs for snow forts, snowmen

Marzipan or fondant – anything you can shape it into

Nuts – stones; (slivered almonds) shingles

Powdered sugar – light dusting of snow, frost

Pretzels – fancy ironwork fences, bed headboards, scrollwork

Pretzel sticks, dry bread sticks – logs, winter trees, firewood

Rock candy – rocks, stepping stones, stone walls

Round crackers or cookies – wagon wheels, doors, tabletops

Shredded wheat – roof thatching, hay, hair

Silver dragees – doorknobs, ornaments, jewelry (not edible)

Sprinkles – flowers, Christmas lights, ornaments

Wafer cookies, crackers or candies – roof shingles, siding

Windows and doors

Windows and doors can be cut out of the pattern pieces before baking or simply iced onto the walls.

When cutting out doors and windows, don't worry if they don't hold their shape perfectly when lifted out. You can always cut an extra door or window from rerolled scraps. Or substitute a graham cracker or candy bar with sections for an elegant, molded door or window.

Frost and pipe icing over a solid wall to achieve the effect of ornate doorways and fancy windows (frost in with yellow or light orange to look as though they are lit from the inside or grey, blue, or violet for an unlit window).

FORMING AND BAKING TIPS

- Be sure the cookie sheets are cool—no warmer than room temperature—for each batch of gingerbread. Hot cookie sheets cause the dough to soften and spread before it can set up.

- Not all parts of a gingerbread house should be cut from the same thickness of dough. Cut the major structural components (main supporting walls) of the thickest dough, 3/16- to 1/4-inch thick, and chimneys, trim, and other decorative pieces from dough rolled thinner, but not less than 1/8-inch thick. This makes the finished house more stable and it is easier to fit together small pieces, such as dormers and chimneys, if they are made of thinner gingerbread.

- Baking time will vary according to the thickness of the dough. Thicker pieces of gingerbread need to bake slightly longer than thinner pieces. Bake different thicknesses of dough on separate cookie sheets.

Logs and fenceposts

To create gingerbread logs or fenceposts, roll small balls of dough with your palms to form "snakes" about 1/2-inch thick. These are thicker than rolled-out dough and must bake longer. The exact time will vary, so keep an eye on them while baking.

Stone chimneys and towers

Construct a chimney or tower by first building the basic shape from gingerbread. Give it that "made-of-stone" look by applying a base of frosting and either pressing (candy or nut) stones into the mortar or creating stones with icing.

TEXTURIZING TIPS

You can create wood grain, boards, bricks, a woven surface, or shingled roof by texturizing the dough pieces before baking.

Create the planks for a gingerbread barn by scoring the dough with a knife. Gently press into the dough with the knife edge, being careful not to cut all the way through.

Or roll the dough out over a very clean, floured, texturized surface, such as a woven placemat. Cut out the pattern pieces and transfer to foil or a baking sheet by placing the sheet over the rolled-out dough and carefully flipping the placemat, dough, and sheet over in one smooth motion. Slowly peel the placemat from the dough pieces.

You can also use icing to look like paneling or bricks. Smooth a layer of colored icing (or frosting) on the gingerbread, then pipe the same color or a contrasting color of icing over the frosting to make parallel lines.

ICING, FROSTING, AND FONDANT

Royal Icing makes a fine glue for holding the house together, can be spread or piped on for decoration, and can be colored any shade you wish. But this icing is made with raw eggs, and *it should not be eaten.*

Almost Buttercream Frosting is the frosting we all grew up on—spreadable and edible. Use it to assemble and decorate gingerbread works that are to be eaten. It can be used as paint, to pipe on fancy accents and decorations, and as glue, to hold pieces together.

Don't use both frosting and icing on your gingerbread house—the colors may bleed from one to the other.

Fondant makes an edible modeling clay for all kinds of special effects. Use it just as you would sculptor's clay to create accent pieces, such as cups and saucers, candlesticks, decorations, paving stones, flowers, braided rag rugs, etc.

ROYAL ICING

3 egg whites

1 1/2 pounds powdered (confectioners) sugar

Food coloring, if desired

Beat egg whites until frothy. Gradually beat in sugar until icing reaches the desired consistency. The more you whip the icing the fluffier it gets. Icing that is less fluffy is best for piping out details, such as siding, roof or window designs; fluffier icing makes good glue for holding the pieces of the house together. Add food coloring a few drops at a time, or a smudge at a time if using the paste type, and mix in thoroughly. Immediately wrap and refrigerate leftovers.

ALMOST BUTTERCREAM FROSTING

1/2 cup white shortening

3 1/2 cups powdered confectioners sugar

1 teaspoon vanilla (use clear vanilla to avoid discoloring frosting)

1/4 teaspoon almond or coconut extract

3 to 4 tablespoons milk or hot water

Food coloring as desired

Beat shortening and flavoring for about one minute, then slowly add half of the sugar, mixing in well. Add half of the milk or water and mix well. Gradually beat in the rest of the sugar and just enough milk or water to reach the desired consistency, whether for piping or spreading. Stir in food coloring.

FONDANT

1/3 cup light corn syrup

1/4 cup white shortening

1/4 teaspoon flavoring (peppermint, cherry, almond extract, etc.)

1 pound powdered (confectioners) sugar

Food coloring as desired

Beat all ingredients, except about 1 cup of the powdered sugar, in large mixing bowl at medium speed until well mixed. Liberally sprinkle a clean cutting board or countertop with powdered sugar and knead in

Continued ➜

enough to form a smooth ball that holds together, but is not sticky. Wrap in plastic until ready to sculpt.

PUTTING IT ALL TOGETHER

There are many steps to successful gingerbread house construction. The biggest tip to finishing a house you can be proud of, all in good cheer, is to allot yourself enough time for each of those steps. The most time-consuming part of the project is waiting for the icing to dry. Here is a timetable to guide you through the project. You could combine any or all of these steps into one day, but experience has shown this to be the "less stress" method.

Day One—Draw out templates, check for fit

Day Two—Mix dough, allow to chill overnight

Day Three—Roll out, cut, and bake dough; cool

    Install glass windows

    Mix up and apply decorative icing to pieces

Day Four—Piece together walls, roof and other features

    Apply finishing touches

Step 1—A firm foundation

For a steady anchor, to define the limits of your display, and for ease of moving and storing, you will need a sturdy base. Cut plywood or heavy cardboard to the size and shape desired. Cover with wax paper or aluminum foil taped together on the bottom. Frost or ice the entire base, or only where the walls of the house will contact it.

Step 2—Ice first

Except for the roof of the gingerbread house, most decorative icing should be applied before putting the house together. It is easier to ice straight lines (to make clapboards or bricks) and to pipe fancier icing on gingerbread that is lying flat, than on an assembled house where the walls are vertical. So ice first, and allow plenty of time for the icing to dry before piecing your house together.

Tint icing to any color you desire, and use a metal spatula or butter knife to spread the icing as evenly as possible over the surface of each piece. Pipe on contrasting icing for trim and other effects.

Glass in windows (see below for making glass). Along the inside edge of the window pipe or spoon on a generous amount of icing and carefully press the glass in place. Allow to dry until icing is hard.

Step 3—Put up walls

Start with the biggest walls of the house. Pipe a generous line of icing along the meeting edges of two walls and press together. Ice the bottom edges of the walls before setting them in place to help secure them to the foundation. Position side walls between front and back pieces to make the front of the house more attractive. Place canned goods on either side of the walls to hold them in place while the frosting dries.

Run icing along the meeting edges of the next two pieces, press them together, and settle into position, making sure all iced edges fit squarely together. Again, use cans for support.

As you press the iced edges together, icing will ooze from the seams. Before the icing dries, run a metal spatula or butter knife along the seams to tidy up. Later, you can pipe an even line or a decorative edging along the seams to hide any unevenness where the walls meet.

Step 4—Build chimneys, dormers, bay windows, and towers

As the major walls of your gingerbread house dry, the smaller structures can be pieced together. When the icing holding them together is dry enough that they can safely be handled, join these structures to the house. Apply icing to all edges that will touch and gently ease into place, holding for a moment or two. Support with cans as needed. Chimneys and dormers will be added once the roof is in place.

Step 5—Ice again

After the walls are thoroughly dry, from an hour or two to overnight, pipe a line of icing along the seams from the inside. This extra bit of glue helps to make the house more solid. Let dry again.

Step 6—Roof it

Ice along the top edges of the walls and edges where the roof pieces will meet. Set one side of the roof in place, then the second. Carefully adjust the two pieces until they meet at the top. Press firmly so that the icing smushes together. Add dormers and chimneys.

Be sure to allow the icing plenty of time to dry before adding snow, shingles, reindeer, etc. To secure shingles or roof ornaments, first frost the roof with snow, then gently press the objects into place. If laying shingles (slivered almonds, cereal, fondant, etc.), apply a strip of frosting a little wider than a row of shingles to the bottom of the roofline. Press the shingles into place. Then frost the next row up, press the next row of shingles into place so that they overlap the first row a little bit, and continue on until the top of the roof. If shingles don't match up perfectly at the peak of the roof, cut smaller shingles or camouflage the peak under a blanket of snow.

Step 7—Finishing touches

From whimsy to realism, the finishing touches are what make your gingerbread house spring to life. Detailed icing, landscaping, figurines, snow and roof decorations are the last features to add to your edible art.

You will find many ideas under the list of supplies at the beginning of the bulletin. But let your own imagination be your guide. Enjoy, and many happy mistakes!

Victorian House

LANDSCAPING AND SPECIAL EFFECTS

Some dandy, yet deceptively simple tricks will transform even the plainest gingerbread house into a showplace. How about stained glass windows in your church or a shimmering frozen pond, complete with ice skaters? Piece of cake!

Window glass and ponds

Sugar candies do something marvelous when heated—they melt. Keep heating and they caramelize, creating the effect, when cooled, of murky glass. To make glass-like windows or frozen ponds, melt hard candies on foil-covered baking sheets in the oven and let cool.

For or a stained glass effect, crush colored hard candies and make little piles of three or more different colors right next to each other on the foil. As they melt they will merge together. Use enough candy so that the finished puddle will be slightly larger than the opening that needs glass.

When the glass cools, attach by heavily icing the inside of the window cutout and pressing the glass into place. Allow to dry before handling the piece.

Set off a pond with a few ice skaters or a graceful fondant swan. Cut the figures from gingerbread using a cookie cutter or make a template. Decorate with icing and other goodies, ice a bit of aluminum foil to the base of skates to glint in the winter sun. Secure in place with icing.

Fretwork and railings

To create these pieces, tape a pattern for the fretwork or railing to a piece of cardboard, cover the pattern with wax paper, and secure. The wax paper must be taped tightly in place to prevent it from moving around as you trace the pattern with icing onto the wax paper. Make a few extras of individual pieces, just in case, and allow to dry completely. When dry, carefully peel the wax paper away from the fretwork, then glue the fretwork in place on the house with dabs of frosting. For sturdier fretwork pieces, peel back the wax paper and repipe icing along the back side of the pieces. Once this second coat is dry, the fretwork will be twice as strong (and less likely to break).

Trees and bushes

It takes only a few landscape pieces to truly set a lifelike scene. Large green gumdrops become well-trimmed bushes; a row of them becomes a hedge. Cut them into smaller shrubs, or stack them together for a topiary effect. Create larger evergreens by attaching small green gumdrops to ice-cream cones, or pipe green icing around ice-cream-cone trees with a decorative tip (try star or leaf tips) for a similar effect.

The garden path

Pathways are easily created by first laying down a path of frosting mortar, then pressing the stones (mixed nuts, rock candy, broken crackers, etc.) or bricks (cut pieces of red licorice, red cinnamon candies, square crackers or cereal, etc.) into place.

Fences

Build fences with candy cane or pretzel stick posts or rails and pretzel gates. Secure to base with frosting. Populate fenced areas with animal cracker, cookie cutter, or template figures, decorated to suit the scene and held in place with frosting. Or mold figures from marzipan paste or fondant and decorate—this is especially fun for kids.

Snow

Whip up a blizzard. Use lots of frosting around and atop the gingerbread house to create a wintry effect. For icicles hanging from eaves, pipe through a large tip or opening cut from a homemade icing bag. Begin by piping just at the edge and drawing the tip down to allow the icing to dangle over. Let dry and add more icing later if desired.

For a mere dusting of snow, sift powdered sugar over the scene. If a sifter is not handy, shake a little sugar through a strainer.

Blueprints

Use these gingerbread patterns to make your templates. Enlarge them on graph paper or by using the zoom feature of a copy machine. (You may have to enlarge several times to get the size you want.) An 8- to 12-inch square gingerbread house is a good size, but you're the boss. Feel free to experiment!

STARTER HOME

A lovely little house for the first-time home builder. This is the basic gingerbread house from which your imagination can take you to whatever lengths you are willing to go. Attach a candy bar door and a hard candy chimney. Frost the roof thickly and press in decorations. Add a front porch by extending the front roof line and supporting it with candy cane pillars.

If you feel adventuresome, add dormers and/or a chimney using the blueprints below.

COUNTRY CHAPEL

From a simple country church to a grand cathedral, this basic pattern can be embellished as you wish. Stained glass windows will set a magical mood.

Piece the main part of the church together as per general instructions. Place the smaller stair piece on top of the larger one to create a short stairway, and position the entryway at the top of the stairs. Use licorice, icing, or candy canes cut to size to make the cross. Don't forget an ice-cream-cone steeple!

VICTORIAN HOUSE

Finished Victorian House is shown on page 458.

A little more challenging, this Victorian has a bay window and delicate fretwork that give it the feel of old San Francisco.

Choose bold colors of icing for the walls of this Painted Lady. Pipe fretwork onto wax paper then glue in place with a thin line of fresh icing. Cut out windows or paint them in with icing as you wish. How about a fancy yogurt-covered pretzel for a front gate?

Continued →

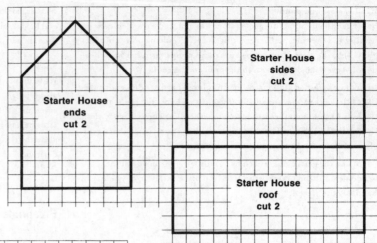

Starter House
ends
cut 2

Starter House
sides
cut 2

Starter House
roof
cut 2

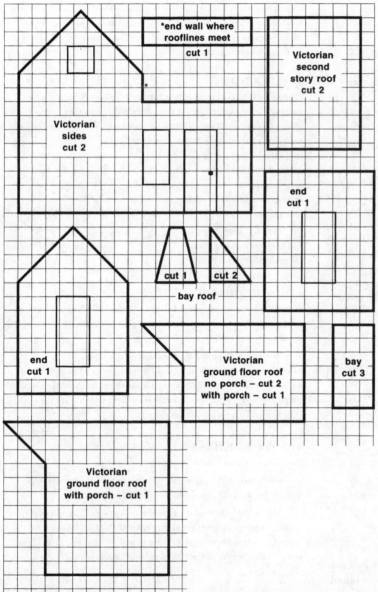

*end wall where
rooflines meet
cut 1

Victorian
second
story roof
cut 2

Victorian
sides
cut 2

end
cut 1

cut 1 cut 2

bay roof

end
cut 1

Victorian
ground floor roof
no porch – cut 2
with porch – cut 1

bay
cut 3

Victorian
ground floor roof
with porch – cut 1

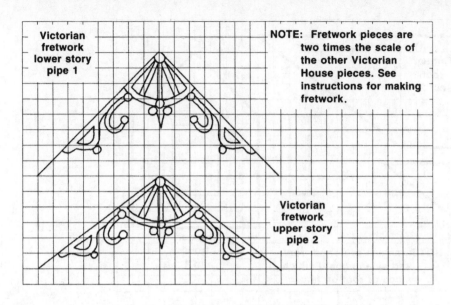

Victorian
fretwork
lower story
pipe 1

NOTE: Fretwork pieces are two times the scale of the other Victorian House pieces. See instructions for making fretwork.

Victorian
fretwork
upper story
pipe 2

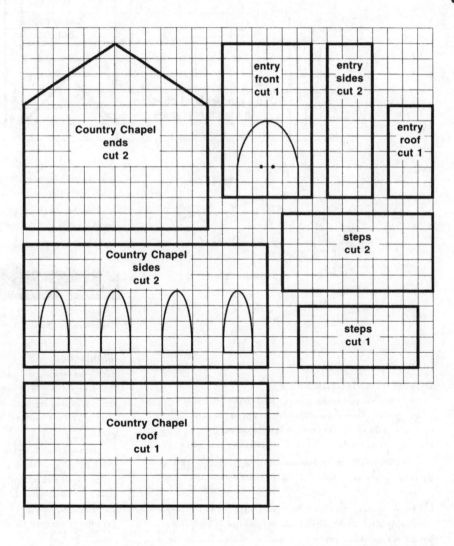

Country Chapel
ends
cut 2

entry
front
cut 1

entry
sides
cut 2

entry
roof
cut 1

steps
cut 2

Country Chapel
sides
cut 2

steps
cut 1

Country Chapel
roof
cut 1

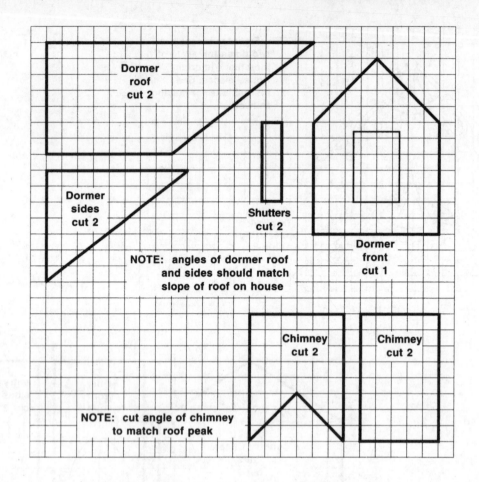

Dormer
roof
cut 2

Dormer
sides
cut 2

Shutters
cut 2

Dormer
front
cut 1

NOTE: angles of dormer roof
and sides should match
slope of roof on house

Chimney
cut 2

Chimney
cut 2

NOTE: cut angle of chimney
to match roof peak

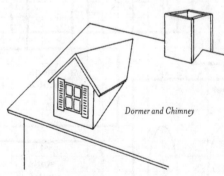

Dormer and Chimney

DORMERS AND CHIMNEYS

Dress up your gingerbread house with dormers or a chimney using the pattern pieces. Match the angles where the dormer or chimney meets the house to the slope of the roof. When you cut out the template pieces, check to see that the dormer or chimney will meet flush with the roof.

Use thinner dough for these decorative, nonsupportive pieces. Roll out the gingerbread to about 1/8 inch thick for dormer and chimney pieces.

Piece decorated dormers and chimneys together and allow to dry thoroughly before attaching to house. Apply a line of icing along the bottom edges of dormers and chimneys where they will meet the roofline of the house. Press gently into place and support until secure. Allow to dry thoroughly.

Decorate house roof and dormer roofs after dormers and chimneys are in place.

Making Homemade Candy

Glenn Andrews
Illustrations by Sally Sussman

Introduction

What's the very best present you can give to the traditional person who "has everything"? My vote goes to homemade candy. It's also the perfect present for almost any occasion that comes along, whether a birthday, Christmas, for a hostess gift or as a "little something" for your child's teacher.

Dress up your homemade candies with attractive packaging. Stores which sell candy-making or cake decorating supplies (look in the Yellow Pages) also sell little fluted paper cups and folding boxes that will make your candies look highly professional. Ask a local bakery if they will sell you boxes and the larger fluted cups suitable for large truffles. Try a florist's or craft shop for unusual shades of tissue or wax-like paper.

If originality is what you want, you can package your candies (or at least the individually-wrapped ones such as caramels or taffies) in sand pails, balloon wine glasses, French jelly glasses, apothecary jars, coffee mugs or anything else that strikes your fancy.

With the exception of truffles, which need special handling, all of these candies travel well and can be shipped. Just make sure they won't rattle around in their boxes and won't be crushed.

Before you start your candy-making, please read the section on ingredients which follows. Following the section on ingredients is one on the taking of your candy's temperature, a procedure which is vital for the success of certain candies. Glance at this even though you're already well-versed in temperature-taking, since there's a brand new shortcut way to do it.

Ingredients

The only ingredient I want to implore you to use is pure, real vanilla. Not artificial vanilla or vanillin or the strange (and toxic, some say) product sold in large bottles in Mexico. The difference in taste is unbelievable.

No, on second thought, I also want to urge you to use only real chocolate. There are artificial "chocolate" chips and morsels out there; avoid them. Filled and molded chocolate candies require a special chocolate; it's discussed in the section on "Designer Chocolates." For other purposes, use the standard chocolate (semisweet, chips or unsweetened) available in all grocery stores.

The choice between butter and margarine is up to you. My own feeling is that it's fine to use margarine in such highly-flavored candies as chocolate fudge, but that butter is essential for the more delicate concoctions—vanilla buttercreams, for instance. (A "vanilla margarinecream" would sound rather silly, and wouldn't taste the same at all.)

Avoid artificial food colors and flavorings as much as you can. There are pure extracts on the market (though sometimes only in health food stores). Buy them and use them. Some of these will also impart a faint tinge of natural color. Some health food stores also carry natural food colors.

Except in Salt Water Taffy, where it is inescapable, there is no added salt in any of these recipes. (The nut brittles, however, do taste better with salted nuts.)

You also won't find sugar substitutes here. If you want to use them, though, follow the substitution instructions on their packages, remembering that Nutrasweet can't stand up to being cooked for any length of time.

Temperatures

I try to avoid this whenever possible, but there are times when you simply have to take your candy's temperature.

Of the three ways to do this, by far the simplest is to cook your candy in an electric fryer-cooker. Mix the ingredients before plugging it in, then set the dial for the temperature you want. When the light goes out, you're there.

A more traditional way is to use a candy thermometer. (Check its accuracy by heating it in water—when the water boils, it should read 212°F.)

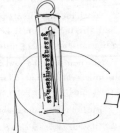

candy thermometer

Or you can put a little of the mixture into some very cold water, form it into a ball with your fingers and check results as below:

Soft-ball stage	234–240°F.
Firm-ball stage	244°–250°F.
Hard-ball stage	265°–270°F.
Soft-crack stage	275°–280°F.
Hard-crack stage	285°–300°F.

BRITTLES

Brittles seem like nice, healthful treats, to the point where I have known a doctor to recommend them to someone trying to lose weight. Unfortunately, this is an illusion, since they are loaded with sugar. But they're very good, and they are low-fat—and they're easy to make.

All brittles should be made only when the weather is dry. They will keep indefinitely if you put them in airtight tins.

PEANUT BRITTLE

Butter to grease a cookie sheet

1 1/3 cups sugar

1 6 1/2 ounce can "cocktail peanuts"

Before you start, butter a cookie sheet very thoroughly.

Cook the sugar in a frying pan over low heat until it has melted and turned a light brown. Stir in the peanuts, then pour onto the baking sheet.

Now immediately start stretching the candy by pressing it out with the backs of two spoons. Don't touch it with your hands, as it will be very hot. Keep this up, working quickly, until the brittle is no more than 1 peanut deep.

When the candy is completely cool, break it into pieces. Keep in an airtight tin.

OTHER NUT BRITTLES

Substitute whatever nuts you want for the peanuts in peanut brittle, above. Salted nuts make the best-tasting brittles, and cashews are particularly good for this purpose.

CARAWAY COMFITS

This is my version of a confection that was very popular in eighteenth century England. It's supposed to be good for the digestion, but more importantly, it's marvelous-tasting and a nice change from nut brittles.

Butter to grease a cookie sheet

1 cup sugar, granulated or raw

6 tablespoons caraway seeds

Before you start, butter a cookie sheet very thoroughly.

Cook the sugar and caraway seeds together in a frying pan until the sugar has melted and is just beginning to turn color.

Continued →

Pour onto the buttered cookie sheet and immediately start stretching it out with the backs of two spoons. Don't touch, since it will be very hot.

When completely cool, break into brittle-sized pieces.

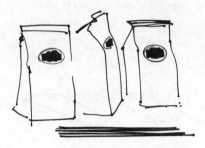

BENNE CANDY

Benne (pronounced benny) is sesame seed. It makes an outstanding candy.

1 1/2 cups sesame seeds

Butter to grease a pan

2 cups sugar

1 teaspoon real vanilla

Spread the sesame seeds in a medium-sized pan and bake at 350°F. until toasted. (This takes just a few minutes; keep an eye on them to prevent burning.)

Butter a cookie sheet very thoroughly.

Cook the sugar in a frying pan, stirring most of the time, until melted. Remove from the stove and very quickly stir in the vanilla and sesame seeds.

Pour onto the cookie sheet. When the candy has cooled a little, but is still warm, mark it into squares with a knife. When completely cool, break into squares.

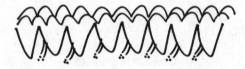

FUDGE

Is there anyone who doesn't like fudge of one sort or another?

If you're giving your fudge as a gift, you'll save yourself a good deal of trouble and mess if you take the gift boxes you plan to use and line them with waxed paper or foil. Spray with a non-stick spray, then let the fudge cool slightly before pouring it directly into the boxes.

ALWAYS-CREAMY CHOCOLATE FUDGE

If you've had problems making a truly creamy chocolate fudge, this is the recipe for you:

1 tablespoon butter or margarine (plus more to grease the pan)

6 ounces evaporated milk

2 1/2 cups sugar

1 12-ounce bag real chocolate semi-sweet chips

1/2 ounce unsweetened baking chocolate

3 1/2 ounces marshmallow cream (half of a 7-ounce jar)

1/2 teaspoon real vanilla

1/2 cup broken walnuts or pecans (optional)

Combine the butter, sugar and evaporated milk in a saucepan. Bring to a rolling boil and cook for exactly 6 minutes.

In the meantime, put the chocolate chips, unsweetened chocolate and marshmallow cream in the large bowl of a mixer. (No mixer? No matter. You can do the bearing by hand.)

At the end of the 6 minutes of furious boiling, pour the hot mixture over the ingredients in the bowl. Beat until smooth, then add the vanilla and the nuts, if you're using them. Pour into a roughly 10 x 10-inch pan and allow to cool before cutting.

Since there's no such thing as too much chocolate fudge, you might want to multiply all of the ingredients by three and use a large jelly-roll pan.

BROWN SUGAR FUDGE

Also known as penuche, panocha, ponoche, etc

2 cups granulated sugar

2 cups brown sugar

1 cup heavy cream

2 tablespoons butter (plus more to grease a pan)

1/4 cup water

1 cup broken walnuts or pecans (optional)

Butter a roughly 10 x 10-inch pan.

Put all the ingredients except the nuts in a large saucepan. Bring to a boil, stirring only until the butter and sugars have melted. Cook at a rolling boil for exactly 5 minutes.

Now pour into the bowl of a mixer. (No mixer? Make something else unless you feel a need for biceps-building.) Beat until the mixture is thick and lighter in color and has lost its gloss.

Stir in the nuts and spoon into the buttered pan.

Allow to cool very thoroughly before cutting into small squares.

VANILLA FUDGE

A very white and creamy variation.

2 tablespoons butter (plus more for greasing a pan)

3 cups sugar

1 1/2 cups half and half

1/4 cup corn syrup

1 tablespoon vanilla

1 cup broken walnuts or pecans (optional)

Grease a roughly 8 x 8-inch pan.

Combine the butter, sugar, half and half and corn syrup in a medium-sized saucepan. Stir until it comes to a boil, then continue cooking, stirring only from time to time, until it reaches 235°F. (the soft-ball stage).

Remove from the heat. When cool enough to touch comfortably, add the vanilla, transfer to the bowl of a mixer and beat until the mixture has thickened and lost its gloss. Stir in the nuts and spoon into the buttered pan. Cut into squares when thoroughly cool.

KATIE'S COCOA FUDGE

The easiest of all fudges, and one of the very best.

1/2 cup cocoa

1 pound confectioners' sugar

6 tablespoons butter or margarine (plus more to grease a pan)

1/4 cup milk

2 teaspoons real vanilla

1/2 cup chopped walnuts or pecans (optional)

Combine all the ingredients except the nuts in a double boiler. Cook, stirring, over barely simmering water until the butter is melted and the mixture is smooth. Add the nuts, if you're using them.

Pour into a small buttered pan and allow to cool before cutting into squares.

CARAMELS

Caramels are among America's favorite candies. However, they are adversely affected by even small amounts of moisture in the air, so you have to wrap each little candy in plastic wrap.

VANILLA CARAMELS

A rather hard caramel, which softens slightly after it's wrapped in plastic or encased in chocolate.

2 cups sugar

1/2 cup corn syrup

1 1/2 cups medium cream

4 tablespoons butter (plus more for greasing a baking pan)

1 1/4 teaspoons vanilla

Cook the sugar, corn syrup, cream and the 4 tablespoons of butter in a medium-sized saucepan, stirring often, to the firm-ball stage (246°F.).

Remove from the stove and stir in the vanilla. Pour onto a well-buttered marble slab or baking tin.

When thoroughly cold, cut into small squares and wrap each in a little piece of plastic wrap.

COFFEE CARAMELS

1 cup sugar

1 cup light corn syrup

1 cup evaporated milk

1/4 cup double-strength coffee (can be decaffeinated)

4 ounces butter (plus more for greasing a baking pan)

1/2 teaspoon vanilla

Cook the sugar and the corn syrup in a medium-size saucepan to the firm-ball stage (246°F.), stirring often. Combine the evaporated milk and coffee and add, along with small pieces of the butter, to the hot mixture. (Add very slowly so the boiling won't stop.) Keep boiling, stirring constantly, until the mixture is back at 246°F. (the firm-ball stage).

Remove from the fire, stir in the vanilla and pour into a well-buttered baking pan. When thoroughly cold, turn out of the pan, cut into squares and wrap.

CHOCOLATE-HONEY CARAMELS

Oil for greasing a marble slab or tin

1/2 cup honey

4 1-ounce squares unsweetened chocolate

8 tablespoons butter

1/2 cup sugar

First, thoroughly oil a marble slab or a baking tin.

Now combine all the other ingredients in a medium-sized saucepan. Bring to a boil, then turn down the heat and simmer, stirring, for 10 minutes. Remove from the heat for 1 minute, then return to the stove and cook, still stirring, for another 5 minutes.

Pour onto the slab or tin. Using a table knife, push the caramel into a rectangle, about 1/3-inch deep. Let it cool a bit, then cut into 1-inch lengthwise strips. Separate these by dextrous wiggling of your knife, then cut across at 1-inch intervals, again wiggling your knife. Remove from the slab or tin when thoroughly cool. Wrap separately.

Continued ➔

mint wafers and coffee

Mint or Fruit Wafers

The perfect finale to a simple meal. You could add a little food coloring to these, but it's truly unnecessary, especially if you only make and serve one flavor at a time.

2 cups sugar

7 tablespoons water, divided

3/4 teaspoon cream of tartar

A few drops of mint or fruit flavor extract

Remove 3 tablespoons of the sugar and put it in a small bowl. Put the rest of the sugar and 6 tablespoons of the water in a large saucepan and bring it to a boil. Boil for 3 minutes, then remove from the fire.

Now combine the cream of tartar, the last tablespoon of water and the flavor extract with the 3 tablespoons of sugar in the bowl. Add this to the boiled mixture and stir gently for about 3 minutes, or until it begins to take shape.

Drop by teaspoonful onto a sheet of foil or waxed paper.

DESIGNER FILLED CHOCOLATES

When you want to give a magnificent present to someone, make these wonderfully sinful candies. Though they're easy to make, they've been

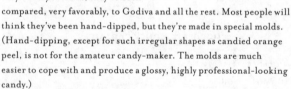

butter creams

compared, very favorably, to Godiva and all the rest. Most people will think they've been hand-dipped, but they're made in special molds. (Hand-dipping, except for such irregular shapes as candied orange peel, is not for the amateur candy-maker. The molds are much easier to cope with and produce a glossy, highly professional-looking candy.)

First, take a trip to a store where they sell candy-making supplies. (Look in your Yellow Pages. No luck? Try cake decorating supply stores.) You'll need coating chocolate, which comes in 1-pound bags of disks, and candy molds (a different design for each sort of candy you plan to make). None of these things will set you back any large amount of money, and the molds can be used over and over. Resist the filling mixes—you're going to make your own.

Disks of coating chocolate come in dark (semisweet) and milk-chocolate (very sweet). If you're aiming at candies which resemble the best on the market, buy the dark chocolate. Don't try to use any other sort of chocolate for molding unless you're already a pro. Other varieties, including the "couverature" chocolate sold in large blocks at a very high price, requires "tempering" by an elaborate, several-step, temperature-controlled process.

If you don't want to take a trip to a candy-making supply store, but still yearn to make mouth-watering filled chocolates, see "Non-Designer Chocolates," below.

BASIC BUTTERCREAM FILLING

(Also known as Uncooked Fondant)

Use this filling, just as it is, to make vanilla buttercreams. Add other ingredients to it to make a wide variety of different buttercreams (see below).

1/3 cup butter, at room temperature

1/3 cup white corn syrup

1 1/2 teaspoons real vanilla

3 cups confectioner's sugar

Combine all the ingredients. The mixture will keep, well wrapped and refrigerated, for weeks and weeks.

GENERAL DIRECTIONS FOR FILLED CHOCOLATES

First, assemble the things you'll need:

Disks of coating chocolate (preferably dark)

A small jar (an 8-ounce screwtop Mason-type jar is ideal)

A small saucepan half-filled with hot (but never, at any point, boiling) water

A small spoon

Plastic candy molds (one for each sort of candy you want to make)

Filling

Waxed paper

Put enough coating chocolate disks into the small jar to fill it about halfway. Place this in the pan of hot, but not boiling, water. Don't have so much water in the pan that the jar floats.) Make sure that you never let any water get into the jar.

When the wafers are melted, stir well. Then, using the small spoon, put a little chocolate in each of the depressions in the candy mold. Move it around with the spoon so each depression is thoroughly, but thinly, coated. Place in your freezer until firm—about 15 minutes or less.

Now place a small ball of filling in each little chocolate-coated hole. Press it in gently so it's level, then top with a thin layer of melted chocolate, making sure that the filling is completely enclosed by chocolate. Put back in the freezer for another few minutes, or until the chocolate on top is firm.

Unmold by holding the candy mold upside down about an inch over a sheet of waxed paper. Tap gently on the mold while flexing it just a bit and the beautiful, shiny little candies will pop right out. (If by chance they don't, just freeze a bit more.)

If you're making quite a bit of candy, keep adding more wafers to the jar of chocolate, then stirring as they melt. When your candy-making session is over, let the chocolate in the jar cool to room temperature, then close it tightly and keep it, still at room temperature, ready for the next time.

NON-DESIGNER FILLED CHOCOLATES

Don't pass by the delights of such things as vanilla buttercreams just because you haven't been to a candy-making supply store. You won't end up with professional-looking high-gloss, nicely-shaped candies, but the flavor will be all there.

Use any of the buttercream filling variations below (except liquid cherries). Form it into small balls, then dip these into melted regular chocolate (unsweetened is spectacular; semi-sweet is also excellent), turning to coat all sides. Put on waxed paper to set.

VANILLA BUTTERCREAMS

Vanilla Buttercreams are the queen of candies, to some of us. If you've made the basic buttercream filling and used that when you followed the instructions for the general method for filled chocolates, you have just made the best Vanilla Buttercreams you've ever tasted. (But if you want a really strong vanilla taste, you can add a few more drops of that heady flavoring.)

OTHER BUTTERCREAMS

In each case, start with 1/2 cup of the basic buttercream filling, which will make approximately 2 to 3 dozen buttercreams, depending on the size of the mold you use. (The fairly large "bonbon" molds use about a teaspoon of filling for each candy.)

Flavor the 1/2 cup of filling as suggested below, then follow the general directions for filled chocolates, above.

COFFEE BUTTERCREAMS

Add 3/4 teaspoon instant coffee powder (decaffeinated, if you wish).

CHOCOLATE BUTTERCREAMS

Add 2 tablespoons melted coating chocolate.

MAPLE-WALNUT BUTTERCREAMS

Add 2 tablespoons finely minced walnuts and 1/4 teaspoon maple flavoring extract. (Real maple syrup would soften the filling too much, but soft maple sugar would be an excellent alternative for the basic buttercream filling.)

LEMON, ORANGE, LIME, ETC. BUTTERCREAMS

Add a few drops of flavor extract to taste, then, if you must, add just a little food coloring. Lemon buttercreams, in particular, are lovely.

MINT OR WINTERGREEN PATTIES

Add a few drops, to taste, of mint or wintergreen flavor extract. While mint or wintergreen patties could be made in a regular mold, they'll look more authentic made in a special mint patty mold.

CHOCOLATE-COVERED LIQUID CHERRIES

I used to think that liquid cherries were created by injecting the liquid into the candy with a hypodermic needle. Perhaps in some candy-making operations this is true. With this system, though, you put a thinned-down buttercream filling inside the chocolate along with the cherry and somehow, miraculously, in a day or two it becomes a liquid. Use a candy mold with extra-large depressions.

Maraschino cherries and their juice
Basic buttercream filling
Coating chocolate

Following the general directions for filled chocolates, line each depression in the mold with chocolate and freeze briefly.

Now put a cherry into each chocolate-lined hole. Some cherries are too big, so cut them in half. Stir enough maraschino cherry juice into some basic buttercream filling to make a very soft consistency—a little softer than mayonnaise. Put a very small amount of this on top of each cherry.

Cover each cherry with a layer of coating chocolate, making extra-sure that you've sealed the fillings so the liquid can't leak out. Freeze for about 15 minutes—then turn out onto waxed paper.

The centers will start to liquify in about 2 hours, but will be at their best after 2 days.

MARZIPAN

Marzipan can bring out the artist in you. No other sort of candy-making is quite as much fun as shaping your marzipan mixture into tiny potatoes, apples, and so forth.

You can buy prepared marzipan in almost any supermarket (sometimes under the name "almond paste"). Technically, almond paste is different from marzipan, but the little rolls of almond paste available in stores work quite well for marzipan-molding and taste good, too. Making your own, though, isn't hard to do and is, of course, better in every way, including cost.

Almonds

For a stunning gift, place assorted marzipan fruits and/or vegetables on an attractive serving plate (which will be part of the present). If you like, nestle the marzipans in a little shredded cellophane of the sort used for Easter baskets, then cover it all with plastic wrap and top with a bow.

Continued ➜

BASIC MARZIPAN MIXTURE

Think of this as the clay with which you will do your sculpting.

1 cup blanched almonds

2 cups confectioners' sugar

1/2 teaspoon almond extract

2 egg whites, lightly beaten

Grind the almonds very fine by putting them through a meat grinder 3 or 4 times or by running them in a blender or food processor, being sure to stop the machine before you've created almond butter. Add the confectioner's sugar and almond extract, then mix in the egg white a teaspoon at a time, using just enough to make a nice clay-like mixture.

General Instructions for Marzipan

The only marzipan shapes which don't need coloring are little potatoes. For the others, you can work food coloring into the marzipan itself or, using an artist's brush, paint the colors of your choice on the sculpted shapes. I recommend the latter procedure. Let the shapes dry for an hour or two, then paint them, using and mixing your food colorings just as though they were paints. To dilute a color, add water.

To be really fancy, you can make stems of leaves from green-tinted decorator's frosting, but this isn't at all necessary. Twigs and tiny leaves from artificial flowers can be used, too—but make sure they're clearly evident, so they won't be eaten.

Make your shapes all about the same size. Thus strawberries will be more or less life-size, but oranges and lemons will be much smaller than the real fruits. Raspberries, on the other hand, should be larger than life.

MARZIPAN POTATOES

Make irregular little potato shapes. Poke small holes in them to be the eyes. Roll in cocoa to which you've added a little confectioner's sugar. To make them look as though they were sprouting, you can stick a sliver of blanched almond or a few shreds of coconut in each "eye."

MARZIPAN STRAWBERRIES, LEMONS OR ORANGES

All these shapes benefit from being rolled against the finest side of a four-sided grater to give a dimpled affect. Paint a nice strawberry-pink, lemon-yellow or orange-orange.

MARZIPAN APPLES

Make small balls of marzipan, then poke them in at the top and bottom. Judicious use of very light yellow plus areas of reddish food coloring will give the effect of the lovely little "lady apples" sometimes available in grocery stores. Or make Macintoshes, if you'd rather! A whole clove stuck in the bottom of each apple looks good, as do 2 or 3 slivers of cinnamon stick in the top.

CHOCOLATE-COATED MARZIPAN

Chocolate and marzipan make one of the world's great combinations. See the general instructions for filled chocolates, substituting marzipan for the buttercream filling.

For larger candies, make little finger-sized logs of marzipan and dip them in chocolate according to the instructions above.

TRUFFLES

Truffles are the "in" candy, in spite (or perhaps because) of their usual high price. They're also the chocoholic's favorite. Luckily, they're easy and comparatively inexpensive to make. No one has ever accused them of being low-calorie, though.

Truffles can be any size, from little marbles to golf balls. A nice way to serve or give them is in small fluted paper cups, obtainable at candy-making or cake-decorating shops. Keep the cream-based truffles refrigerated or frozen. If you wish to ship truffles to a friend, use Kentucky Bourbon Balls or other variations of cookie-based candies.

BASIC MIXTURE FOR TRUFFLES

1/4 cup heavy cream

6 tablespoons cocoa

12 ounces real chocolate chips

6 tablespoons butter, at room temperature (soft)

1 teaspoon real vanilla

Combine the cream, cocoa and chocolate chips in a small saucepan. Stir over very low heat until the chocolate has melted. Remove from the fire and stir in first the vanilla, then the soft butter.

Chill until firm enough to work with, then form into whatever size balls you wish.

COCOA-COATED CHOCOLATE TRUFFLES

This is the way truffles, the candies, started out. The idea was to make them look like freshly-dug French mushroom-like truffles.

Roll balls of the truffle mixture or any of the variations below in cocoa, then put on waxed paper to dry. Keep refrigerated or frozen until ready to serve.

CHOCOLATE-COATED TRUFFLES

The expensive truffle in candy shops is usually coated with chocolate rather than cocoa these days. If you think you, too, would prefer this approach, here's what to do:

Follow the recipe, above, for truffles (or use any of the variations below), but instead of rolling the balls in cocoa, dip them (using two spoons) in melted semi-sweet chocolate, especially the coating chocolate you'll find discussed under Designer Chocolates. Melted white chocolate can be used instead. Place on waxed paper until set.

LIQUEUR TRUFFLES

Follow the basic recipe for truffles, but eliminate the vanilla, adding instead 1 tablespoon of Grand Marnier, Amaretto, Kahlua, or any other liqueur.

MOCHA TRUFFLES

Follow the basic recipe for truffles, but add, along with the chocolate, 1 tablespoon of instant coffee granules, regular or decaffeinated. For a stronger coffee flavor, mix more instant coffee powder with the cocoa for rolling. (Ratio: 3 parts cocoa to 1 part coffee powder.)

MINT-CHOCOLATE TRUFFLES

To the basic recipe for truffles, add, instead of the vanilla, either one tablespoon of Créme de Menthe or a few drops of mint flavor extract.

KENTUCKY BOURBON BALLS

These were around long before the name "truffle" began to be applied to candies. They're terrific—but not to be fed to children.

1 cup confectioner's sugar

3 tablespoons cocoa powder

2 tablespoons light corn syrup

1/4 cup bourbon

3 cups crushed vanilla wafers (use a rolling pin or food processor)

More confectioners' sugar and/or cocoa powder for coating

Stir the confectioner's sugar and the cocoa powder together in a medium-sized bowl. Mix the corn syrup and bourbon together and stir into the dry mixture. Now add the crushed vanilla wafers and combine very thoroughly.

Form into 1-inch or larger balls. Roll in confectioners' sugar, cocoa, or a combination, and put on a rack to dry. Coat again, if you wish, after half an hour.

CHOCOLATE-RUM BALLS

Substitute dark rum for the bourbon in Kentucky Bourbon Balls.

CHOCOLATE-ORANGE-GINGER BALLS

Here's a variation you can serve to children. Children can have fun making these little balls, too.

Follow the Kentucky Bourbon Ball recipe, substituting orange juice for the bourbon and ginger snaps for the vanilla wafers.

TAFFY

This is the candy immortalized in the taffy-pulling parties you may have read about as a child. While it's best known as an amusing group operation (in other words, it's good for quite a few laughs), it's perfectly possible to pull taffy all by yourself. Old-time kitchens often had "taffy hooks" permanently attached to a wall.

Each piece of taffy must be individually wrapped. Use squares of waxed paper, twisted at each end. Keep the wrapped taffies in a tightly closed tin.

How to Pull Taffy

Let your cooked taffy sit just until barely cool enough to work with. (If it gets too cool, you can warm it in a 350°F. oven for 3 or 4 minutes.) Form it into one or more balls. Now start pulling:

Use just your fingertips and thumbs, well-coated with cornstarch or butter.

Working fast, pull a lump of the candy between the fingertips of one hand and the other until it's about 15 inches long. Now double it up and pull again. Repeat until the candy is porous and hard to pull.

Stretch into a rope about 1-inch in diameter. Cut with greased scissors into 1-inch pieces. Wrap.

MOLASSES TAFFY

2 cups unsulphured molasses

1 cup sugar

2 tablespoons cider or white vinegar

2 tablespoons butter (plus more to grease a pan)

Combine all the ingredients in a large saucepan. Stir while bringing to a boil and cooking to 265°F. (the hard-ball stage). Pour onto a buttered platter or baking tin. Using a spatula, turn the edges toward the center to speed cooling. Pull.

SALT WATER TAFFY

They'll tell you in Atlantic City that Salt Water Taffy was discovered by a taffy-maker on the Boardwalk who used water from the Atlantic Ocean in desperation one day. Since the oceans aren't what they used to be, I suggest that you make your own salt water.

2 cups sugar

1 cup water

1/4 cup corn syrup

1 teaspoon salt

Butter to grease a large pan or platter

Flavoring and coloring (see below)

Continued ➜

Combine the sugar, water, corn syrup and salt in a large saucepan. Stir until the sugar has dissolved, then boil to 265°F. (the hard-ball stage). Pour onto the platter or pan. Turn the edges toward the center with a spatula. Pull. (See above.)

Add whatever flavoring and colorings you wish to use as you pull. For this size batch, use 1 teaspoon vanilla or other extract or 1/4 teaspoon flavoring oil (available at pharmacies) and about 3 drops of food color.

Holiday Gifts from Nature

Illustrations by Brigita Fuhrmann, Judy Eliason, and Alison Kolesar

Introduction

For years, I shopped for Christmas and Hanukkah gifts in the conventional way—going to crowded malls, waiting in long lines, spending too much money, and emerging with gifts that were "good enough" but seemed to be missing something.

Then it occurred to me to combine my lifelong interest in crafts such as wreath making with my desire to give more unique and personal holiday gifts. Creating gifts from nature is infinitely more pleasurable than shopping in stores, and it saves money. Equally important, making your own gifts saves time. You can work on gift projects at the time of year that suits your own schedule best, organizing your work in stages or doing it all in larger blocks of time.

After reading this booklet, you will be able to create the projects described here as well as use your imagination to improvise on variations. The step-by-step instructions are simple and basic, suitable for both the novice and the experienced crafter. In some cases, packaging ideas are also suggested, but for many of these projects, the gift in itself is already a beautiful presentation.

WREATHS

As one of the oldest holiday traditions, wreaths have become ubiquitous in December. In certain parts of the country, it has even become customary to keep them up until spring as a way to brighten the long winter months. Wreaths make wonderful holiday gifts, not only as seasonal decorations for doors, mantelpieces, or centerpieces, but also—in herbal versions—for year-round decorating anywhere in the home.

Best of all, wreaths are easy and inexpensive to make. When you're ready to present your handmade wreath, simply add a hand-printed tag that lists the ingredients or contains a holiday wish.

QUICKIE SPICE WREATH

adapted from *Herbs for Weddings & Other Celebrations*

These adorable aromatic wreaths can be created in miniature to use as favors or made large to serve as decorations. For a variation, apply the project steps below to a Styrofoam ball, and present it as a topiary decoration. Once all the ingredients below are assembled, you'll be ready to make many spicy wreaths. Why not organize a workshop?

What You Will Need
Stryofoam rings

Brown florist's tape or textured fabric

Hanger

Glue

Assortment of dried materials from herb garden or spice cupboard

1. Use Styrofoam ring of desired size purchased at any craft shop or cut from cardboard, and wrap with brown florist's tape or textured fabric.

2. Attach a small hanger at the back.

3. Cover the wreath generously with glue. Embed bay leaves; small nuts, pinecones, or acorns; bits of cinnamon bark; vanilla beans; whole aniseed, dill, cumin, caraway, poppyseeds—anything dried from your herb garden or spice cupboard. Whole cloves and star anise are both especially fragrant and attractive. For color, glue on cardamom, dried orange peel, petals, rose hips, candied ginger, pistachios, whatever is available. Look around you, especially on the spice shelf in your favorite store, with an eye toward color, size, shape, and texture as well as fragrance.

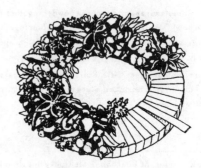

For an aromatic miniature wreath, attach a variety of dried pods and spices to a small wreath form.

4. Allow your wreath to dry thoroughly.

5. Fasten on a bow, if you wish.

HANDMADE HOLIDAY WREATH

adapted from *Christmas Trees*

Single-faced wreaths, made by wiring the greens on only one side of a wreath ring, are designed for hanging on a wall or door, or to use as a centerpiece. Double-faced wreaths, with greens on both sides of the ring, are preferred by most people because they are more bushy and, since the wreath wire is hidden, they can be hung in windows.

What You Will Need
Tips of seasonal greens such as fir, holly, boxwood, pine or spruce

Hand pruners

Crimped wreath ring of desired size

23-guage wire

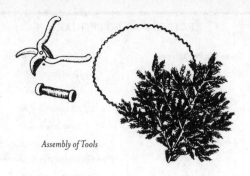

Assembly of Tools

1. Wind a few twists of wire around the wreath ring to fasten it securely.

2. Place a bunch of two to four tips of greens on one side of the ring. Wire the base of the bunch to the ring with two or three tight wraps around. Select some good bushy greens for this first bunch, because it must hide the base of the last bunch you'll insert. If you are making a double-faced wreath, flip the ring over, and use the same method to wrap a similar bunch onto the back side. Place it almost, but not quite, opposite the first one.

3. Lay another bunch of greens over the base of the first bunch, hiding the wire, and wire this one to the ring. Continue in this fashion all the way around the ring. If it is a double-faced wreath, continue wiring on both sides, gently turning the ring over after each bunch is secured.

Securing greens to the ring

4. When you reach the spot where you began, tuck the base of the last bunch underneath the tops of the first that you wired. Wire it in carefully, so neither the stems nor the wire show.

5. Cut or break the wire and fasten it tightly with several twists to one of the wires or to the ring itself.

WREATH-MAKING TIP
Since the upper and lower sides of greens such as fir, holly, and boxwood look quite different, they must be "faced" when placing them on the ring so the pale side won't show. Pines look the same on both sides, so this facing is not necessary.

Herbal Creations
The eloquence of herbs is never more apparent than at holiday time. They speak of many things—of ancient wisdom and future joy. Gifts made from herbs are not only a pleasure to give, they are equally

delightful to make! You can use fresh, dried, or pressed herbs in any quantity available to you. Pick and choose from the projects below gifts that suit each person's lifestyle best, and build upon the suggestions with your own improvisations.

HERB BOUQUET

adapted from Herbs for Weddings & Other Celebrations

Basic flower arranging is a breeze if you follow the principles outlined below. Vertical, horizontal, or triangular designs are traditional and easiest to accomplish, and they usually work well for herbal arrangements, whether large or small. Choose a beautiful vase and plan your arrangement with its size in mind, deciding in advance how tall and how wide the arrangement should be.

What You Will Need
Vase in desired shape, color and size
Herbs, foliage, and flowers of varying lengths, the longest being twice the height of the vase

1. Position the tallest and longest side stems of your herbs, foliage, or flowers first. Use a ruler if you need to. This is the skeleton of your arrangement; never extend outside this framework.

2. Fill in these outermost perimeters with slightly shorter materials, both herbs and foliage, fleshing out your pattern.

3. Tuck more herbs and greens in between. I call this the "poke and shove" method of flower arranging. Don't be timid. Although your bouquet may look sparse and funny at first, poke and shove to your heart's content. Be assured it will work.

4. Fill in from behind as well as in front, angling materials as necessary to conform to your original basic pattern. Stems of varying lengths will give the proper fullness, depth, and dimension. The arrangement should not have the uniform appearance of a clipped hedge.

5. Finally, place your flowers strategically here and there, angling them so that all their faces are visible from all perspectives. If you have enough flowers, tuck a few in the back to complete your arrangement properly.

6. Add decorative elements such as baby's breath or bows last, if desired.

7. Mist thoroughly, swathe in sheets of plastic, and keep shaded and cool until time to present your beautiful fragrant bouquet.

Create oversize bouquets in large vases.

Continued ➜

POTPOURRI PARASOL

adapted from Herbs for Weddings & Other Celebrations

This unique fragrance packet makes a welcome gift for anyone who likes pretty things. It is surprisingly easy and inexpensive to create. Why not make several?

What You Will Need

2 pieces of calico fabric (in holiday colors if desired), 10" x 10"

One 8-inch and one 22-inch length of 1/2-inch lace and coordinating thread

One 12-inch pipe cleaner

1/4 cup fragrant potpourri

One narrow satin ribbon (12 inches long)

1. Enlarge the parasol pattern shown here, and use it to cut two pieces from the calico. The long sides of each piece should measure approximately 9 inches.

2. With the wrong sides of the calico together, stitch the sides together, taking 1/4-inch seams. Turn right side out, and press with a warm iron.

3. Hand sew or machine stitch the 22-inch length of lace around the top edge of the parasol pouch so that the lace ruffles rise upward. Hand stitch the 8-inch length of lace around the bottom edge, lace ruffles downward. Be careful not to stitch across the bottom opening of the pouch.

4. Insert the pipe cleaner down the middle of the parasol. Position it so that approximately 2 to 3 inches show at the bottom. Stitch in place across the bottom.

5. Gather the bottom of the parasol with basting stitches and pull it closed. Secure the pouch with tiny stitches.

6. Stuff the parasol with your favorite potpourri (see below for the recipes).

7. Baste around the top and gather to close. Hand stitch the top closure carefully, securing with tiny stitches. Tie the narrow satin ribbon in place just below the lace edge, and make a bow.

8. Bend the upper portion of the pipe cleaner to form the handle.

Potpourri-filled parasols make thoughtful holiday gifts.

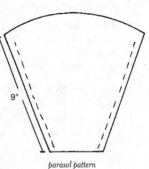

9"

parasol pattern

RECIPES FOR POTPOURRI

Rose Jar Potpourri

Rose petals, dried

1/4 cup Kosher salt

1/4 ounce each ground cloves, mace, and allspice

1/2 ounce ground cinnamon

1/4 pound lavender flowers

1/4 ounce toilet water or cologne (preferably lavender)

A few drops of rose oil

2 ounces of orrisroot

Mixed Bag Potpourri

1 quart dried herbs and flowers

1/2 cup patchouli

1/4 cup sandlewood chips

1/4 cup vetiver roots

1 teaspoon each frankincense, myrrh, ground cloves, and ground cinnamon

1 tonka bean, finely chopped

1/4 cup ground allspice

10 drops rose oil

1 cup ground orrisroot

Carefully and gently mix together the ingredients of your potpourri. Store in a tightly closed container for 3–4 weeks until well blended.

Nature Prints

Simple nature prints make beautiful gifts that can be worn, framed, or displayed. This centuries-old process of recreating images from the natural world requires only a natural object, pigment, and a printable surface such as paper or fabric. It is a low-cost process that yields unlimited possibilities, restricted only by your imagination and the natural objects available to you. Described below are two of my favorite nature printing projects for holiday giving.

LEAF-STAMPED STATIONERY

adapted from Nature Printing with Herbs, Fruits, & Flowers

Leaf stamping is an easy way to create beautiful gift packets of stationery for letters, memos, postcards, and envelopes. The design possibilities are endless for place cards, note cards, holiday cards, labels, and gift wrap as well. Almost anyone will appreciate a gift of hand-printed stationery, whether they use it for handwritten letters or computer-printed and faxed messages.

Leaf stamps can be used to ornament stationery, cards, envelopes, labels, and invitations.

What You Will Need

Stamp pads (colors of your choice)

Tweezers

Variety of small leaves

Typing paper, copier paper, or stationery of your choice

Envelopes to fit selected paper

1. Using a stamp pad and tweezers, ink several small leaves on both sides. Turn over each leaf once or twice while pressing it on the stamp pad to ensure enough ink has adhered. (Note: Stamp pad embossing inks and powders create glossy, raised designs that look very professional. However, some printers and fax machines may not accept paper with glossy, raised designs.)

2. Arrange the inked leaves on a piece of stationery as you would like them to print.

3. Position an envelope face down over the leaves on the stationery as you would like it to be printed, and press with the heel of your hand. Inking the stationery and the envelope at the same time will allow you to design a matched set.

4. Remove envelope and leaf carefully and allow printed paper to dry before packaging as a gift.

Variation: To create two prints at once, simply place a second sheet of stationery facedown over leaves in Step 2.

HAMMERED PRINT T-SHIRT

adapted from *Nature Printing with Herbs, Fruits, & Flowers*

This printing technique requires no paint or ink. Naturally occurring pigments, such as green chlorophyll, are released when a young, juicy leaf is pummeled on natural fiber fabric. The resulting pigmented design is then set in a mineral bath.

Hammered-leaf and fabric-paint nature prints can be combined on a T-shirt.

What You Will Need

Fresh, young leaves

Natural fiber T-shirt or fabric, prewashed and ironed

Hammer with a flat end

Newspapers

Waxed paper

Transparent tape

Salt or washing soda

Wood ashes (optional)

Water

Iron

1. Lay a section of newspaper topped with a sheet of waxed paper on a hard, flat surface.

2. Spread the T-shirt or fabric on the surface so that the area to be printed on is smoothed with no wrinkles and then arrange the leaves you intend to print. Secure all edges of each leaf to the fabric with tape (see Figure 1). Cover leaves with another sheet of waxed paper.

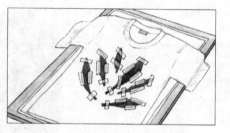

Figure 1

3. Hammer leaves for several minutes until prints appear (see Figure 2). Replace the waxed paper cover as needed, if it rips. Some leaves may print better than others, and coloration will vary. Very fragile leaves disintegrate quickly. You may want to experiment first on a piece of scrap fabric, and then select the leaves that work best.

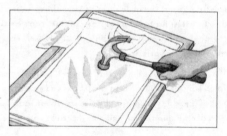

Figure 2

4. To set colorfastness, soak the T-shirt or fabric in a solution of 1/2 cup salt to 2 gallons tepid water for ten minutes, or in a solution of 2 tablespoons washing soda dissolved in 2 gallons tepid water for ten minutes. Rinse thoroughly and dry outdoors or in a dryer. Iron fabric smooth.

5. Then gift wrap your finished project in some of your favorite hand-printed or store-purchased paper. Or simply roll up the T-shirt or fabric neatly and tie it with a beautiful satin ribbon.

Variation: For a reddish-brown color, follow directions in step 4 for a mineral bath and rinse, then immediately soak in 3 gallons of cold water mixed with 1 cup of wood ashes for five minutes. Rinse again, dry, and iron.

Continued →

Holiday Ornaments

Handcrafted ornaments made from natural objects are wonderful and unique gifts. Each ornament lends an enduring festive element to its surroundings and can carry the holiday spirit on through the rest of the year. Best of all, these ornaments are easy and inexpensive to make. Make the natural world an integral part of your holiday celebrations with these fragrant and lovely ornaments.

APPLE CONE TREE

adapted from Herbal Treasures

These are delightful and aromatic gifts. You can change the color of the ribbon or the apples to make a decorated cone for any holiday occasion. If your dried apple slices have not been treated with a sealer, keep the apple cone tree away from areas of high humidity.

What You Will Need

1 large (6 to 8 inches tall) pine cone

Dried apple slices (approximately 1 1/2 cups)

Small sprays of baby's breath

3 or more 6-inch lengths of 1/8-inch ribbon

Glue gun and glue sticks

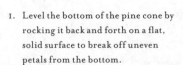

1. Level the bottom of the pine cone by rocking it back and forth on a flat, solid surface to break off uneven petals from the bottom.

2. Cut a large, dried apple slice in half and fold to form a cone shape. Glue the ends together and allow to dry. This will form the base of the apple cone tree. Apply hot glue to the tip of the cone-shaped apple slice and place the pine cone over the tip. Allow to dry.

3. Starting at the top of the pine cone and using the smallest apple slices first, insert the apple slices between the cone petals, skin side out, to test for fit before gluing. To glue, run a small bead of hot glue along the edge of the apple slice and insert the slice between the cone petals.

4. Glue small sprays of baby's breath scattered around the cone. Tie 6-inch lengths of ribbon into small bows and glue them on the edges of the cone petals. You can also tie ribbon onto small pieces of cinnamon sticks, and glue the sticks onto the cone.

Variation: You can scent the cone by adding a few drops of essential oil along the edges of the cone petals.

POTPOURRI POMANDER

adapted from Herbal Treasures

This decoration, with its sweet, old-fashioned look, makes a delightful gift. You can use an apple or orange for your base if you prefer, although the Styrofoam ball tends to last longer.

What You Will Need

Crochet yarn or fine wire (of a length sufficient to hang the pomander)

3-inch Styrofoam ball

Clove or toothpick

Oakmoss

Glue

Velvet ribbon for a bow

An assortment of flowers and spice, such as allspice, balm-of-Gilead buds, 1-inch cinnamon sticks, tiny heather flowers, whole rose hips, sandalwood chips, sunflower petals, or others (see Assortment A and Assortment B below)

1. Thread the crochet yarn through a long darning needle, knot the two ends together, and push the needle through the center of the Styrofoam ball. Push a clove or a 1-inch piece of toothpick through the knot at the end of the yarn, and pull this end tight against the ball to prevent the yarn from pulling through. If you are using wire, double it and force the center folded point through the ball. Fold back 1 inch of wire on each of the two loose ends and tuck these up into the ball securely to keep the wire in place.

2. Place the oakmoss on a sheet of newspaper. Coat the ball in glue and roll it in the oakmoss until it is completely covered. Allow to dry.

3. Arrange the flowers and spices over the oakmoss, using plenty of glue.

4. Make a bow out of the velvet ribbon, using multiple loops and long streamers if desired. Attach the bow to the top or bottom of the pomander.

Variation: Add a few drops of essential oil in several places over the surface. The oakmoss will act as a fixative. Refresh with oil from time to time.

COMBINATIONS FOR YOUR POMANDER

Assortment A	Assortment B
Rosebuds and petals (pink)	Hibiscus flowers (maroon)
Star anise (brown)	Calcitrippae flowers (deep blue)
Cloves (brown)	Statice flowers (pink/purple)
French lavender (purple)	Roman chamomile (cream)
Everlastings (yellow)	White cardamom seeds (cream)
Malva flowers (black)	Uva-ursi leaves (green)

MINIATURE TUSSIE MUSSIES

adapted from Herbal Treasures

Miniature tussie mussies make elegant holiday ornaments and are a perfect way to use pieces of herbs and flowers that have broken off from wreaths.

What You Will Need

Styrofoam

8-inch lengths of fine wire

Very small sprigs and pieces of flowers, herbs, and spices

Glue

Narrow width of lace

Sturdy white paper

Florists tape

Short length of 1/4-inch wide ribbon

1. Cut a piece of Styrofoam about the size of a nickel. Double a length of wire and push the folded center point through the center of the Styrofoam circle to make a handle. Leave about an inch of the loose ends protruding from the bottom (see Figure 1). Thread the cord under the wireloop on top of the styrofoam, and tie it off to make a loop handle.

Figure 1

2. Push the stems of the herbs into the Styrofoam. If you have one, use a single, tiny rosebud in the center. Use glue to affix any herb, spice, or flower that doesn't have a sturdy stem. Use single florets of rosebuds, statice, tansy, or other flower to make a tiny bouquet on the Styrofoam, filling in the spaces with tiny whole cloves, tiny sprigs of baby's breath, leaves of boxwood, or other tiny blossoms. Allow to dry.

3. Wrap the lace around the base of the tussie mussie, cut to fit, and glue around the edge. Cover the bottom with a fitted circle of white paper, first snipping off any stem ends that may protrude.

Figure 2

4. Wrap together the two loose ends of the wire with florist's tape. Then finish off with a tiny bow of ribbon in a matching or complementary color.

PRESSED HERB ORNAMENT

adapted from *Herbal Treasures*

As herbs bloom, save the tiny blossoms and a few leaves. Press and dry these snippets to use in this wonderfully elegant and delicate holiday ornament.

What You Will Need

Pressed and dried small cuttings from herb plants (good choices are thyme, sage, lavender, marjoram, rue, hyssop, the individual florets of chive and bee balm, and the smaller leaves of bay and costmary)

2 microscope slides

Transparent glue

Sewing needle or pin

1/8-inch wide satin or grosgrain ribbon

1. Arrange the cuttings of herbs on a microscope slide. Secure carefully with tiny drops of glue applied with the point of a needle or pin. Allow to dry.

2. Cover the arrangement with the other microscope slide. Secure at the corners with additional glue droplets. Press until dry.

3. Make a 1-inch loop of the ribbon and glue it to the center of the top edge. When the loop is dry, make a border with the rest of the ribbon, covering the raw edges of the glass. Beginning at the top center, glue the ribbon in place all the way around, ending at the center and leaving 4–5 inches of ribbon at each end. Allow to dry.

4. Tie the ends of the ribbon in a bow around the hanging loop. Trim the ends to an attractive length.

Holiday Gifts Kids Can Make

Illustrations by Alison Kolesar and
Edward A. Baldwin Publishing

Children love Christmas, and part of the joy and excitement of the season is in the making of decorations and gifts for family and friends. This bulletin is a collection of projects that will delight parents and children alike.

Whatever the talent level, this bulletin includes something for everyone. There are projects suited for the smallest of crafters, as well as creative challenges for those with more experience. All the instructions are simple and clear to assure success.

Many of the projects are made with items found in nature. The use of readily accessible materials makes the projects affordable, preserves the beauty around us, and gives the gifts a feeling of timelessness. Most

Continued ➡

important of all, parents and children will be creating something more precious than gifts. They will be making memories of holiday times spent together.

Gifts From Nature

Use the Tempera Nature Printing or Bubble Printing methods to create cards, stationery, gift wrap, prints to frame, or decorative mats for photos.

BUBBLE PRINTING

adapted from *Nature Printing with Herbs, Fruits and Flowers*

The bubble pattern is found frequently in nature: in rushing water, honeycombs, seedpods, and the tiny world of cell structure.

What You Will Need
Mild liquid soap
Several colors of water-soluble bottled pen ink
Wide-top containers or jars
Drinking straws
Printing paper or plain-colored gift-wrapping paper

1. Set out a container for each ink color. Put one inch of liquid soap in each container. Add one tablespoon of ink and one straw to each container, and mix.

2. Blow through the straw until bubbles come up over the top of the container.

3. Remove the straw and lay a sheet of paper on top of the bubbles. On contact, the pattern will appear on the paper. Repeat the process with the other ink colors on the same sheet of paper to make a multicolored design.

4. Thin paper will buckle as it dries. To flatten, apply a warm iron to the dried bubble print. These designs make delightful pictures just as they are, or you can add nature prints of leaves and other natural objects.

TEMPERA NATURE PRINTING

adapted from *Nature Printing with Herbs, Fruits and Flowers*

Many of the printing supplies used by adults, such as oil-based inks, can be used by older children under the supervision of an adult. However, young children should use only nontoxic supplies. While most water-based ink is nontoxic, there is a simpler method using tempera paint, which contains materials that are safe for children. It is inexpensive, and washable with soap and water.

Tempera paint alone produces poor prints. A combination of tempera, honey, and glycerin forms a workable mixture that coats objects evenly and doesn't dry while you're working with it.

What You Will Need
Liquid tempera (Crayola brand, or other good-quality paints)
Dabbers (make your own by attaching a piece of foam to an elongated object such as a bottle cork or wooden dowel)
Small containers or cups for mixing tempera recipe
Glycerin (from a pharmacy)
Honey
Freezer wrap
Masking tape
Tweezers
Paper (typing, copier, or newsprint)
Flat leaves (you can flatten curved leaves in a telephone book with weight on top for about thirty minutes)

Tempera prints can be cut out and combined with other media and glued to a three-dimensional, free-standing frieze made of sturdy folded paper.

1. Begin by preparing the tempera paints. For each color, mix eight parts tempera with three parts honey and two parts glycerin.

2. Prepare the work space. If working outside, keep out of the wind and direct sunlight or the paint will dry too fast. Cover tabletop or other flat surface with newspapers or a washable covering. Tear a sheet of freezer wrap to serve as a palette. Attach freezer-wrap corners to the tabletop with masking tape.

3. Place a few drops of tempera mixture on the freezer-wrap palette. Too much paint on leaves results in a poor print. Use the dabber to thinly spread the tempera on the palette. Make an area of paint larger than the leaf you will be printing.

4. Fold a piece of printing paper in half, open it again, and lay it next to the palette.

5. Place a leaf in the middle of the spread tempera and dab the leaf, pressing all around until it's covered with a thin, even coat of paint. Pick up the leaf with the tweezers, turn it over, and repeat paint application on the other side.

6. Pick up the leaf carefully with tweezers and place it on one half of the printing paper. Don't move the leaf once it is on the paper. Fold the other half over the leaf and press on top with the help of your hand. If the leaf is larger than the heel of your hand, hold the paper down with one hand and press all around with the heel or fingers of the other hand, or use a gentle rubbing motion.

7. Open the folded sheet and carefully remove leaf with the tweezers. Notice that double printing doesn't produce a mirror image: Leaf veins are usually more prominent on the underside, showing more detail. If your prints are heavy, too much paint was used. If they appear pale and vague, use a little more paint.

8. Lay prints flat to dry.

APPLE PRINT HOLIDAY GIFT WRAP

adapted from *An Apple A Day!*

Make apple-printed gift wrap by stamping on plain-colored paper. Then wrap your presents in your own printed creations!

What You Will Need

Three large apples

Knife

6 colors of finger or tempera paints in holiday colors

6 paper plates or pie tins

Newspaper

Colored construction or gift-wrap paper

Smock

1. Get your grown-up helper to cut each apple in half crosswise.

2. Get a grown-up to help you cut a holiday design on the flat surface of an apple half. In the examples, the shaded areas are removed; the flat raised areas will print.

3. Pour a different color paint onto each paper plate. Spread out the newspapers over your worktable and place a piece of colored construction paper on top.

4. Carefully dip the flat surface (the design) into the paint, and then press it on the paper (see Printmaking Tips).

5. Remember to clean up your work space thoroughly. Throw out the paper plates, put the apples into the compost or garbage, recycle the newspapers, and wash your hands. By the time you are done, your pictures should be dry!

PRINTMAKING TIPS

- You will get the best results if you use one apple for each color. If you mix your paints, they will turn gray!

- The paint may make the apples slippery and hard to hold onto. Try using corn-cob holders to get a better grip.

For The Birds

Share the holiday spirit with our feathered friends and create festive outdoor displays on which to watch them feed on a winter's day.

CHRISTMAS TREE BIRD FEEDER

adapted from *Let's Grow!*

Transform a living tree in your yard, or, after you finish with your Christmas tree, stake it outside and decorate it for birds to use as a feeding station.

DECORATE YOUR TREE WITH

Pine cones stuffed with peanut butter

Strings of cranberry, popcorn, and dried fruit

Small mesh bags of suet

Nosegays of wheat or other grains

Half rings of oranges filled with birdseed

Small ears of corn

Small dried heads of sunflowers

ABOUT FEEDING THE BIRDS

Once you begin feeding the birds, they will depend on you for food. Don't let them down. Stock a few feeders, so birds can move to another if frightened by a predator. Put feeders near shrubs or trees, so birds can perch there to check out the situation before they feed.

You can rig a simple feeder from a half-gallon milk carton or a gallon plastic jug.

If you are very patient, you may be able to coax a chickadee to take a sunflower seed right from your hand. Stand very, very still and call gently, "Chickadee-dee-dee." It may take a few days of trying before a black-capped friend feels brave enough to visit your hand.

PEANUT BUTTER LOG

adapted from *Birdfeeders, Shelters & Baths*

This quick and easy bird feeder is one that can be successfully made by young children and their parents. You may also want to sprinkle some wild birdseed on the peanut butter for an added treat. Then, hang it up and go sit down on your back porch and wait for the crowd to arrive!

What You Will Need

One 12" length of 2 x 2 rough wood

Small screw eye

Peanut butter

Nylon cord

1. Measure and cut the 12-inch piece of 2 x 2. Do not sand it. The rougher it is, the better.

2. Using a 1-inch bit, drill holes through the center of one side and the top and bottom about 4 inches from each end of the other side.

3. Attach a small screw eye at the top.

4. Fill the holes with peanut butter and go find a branch to hang the project from. Use nylon cord to attach the project.

BAMBOO BIRDCALL

adapted from *Everything You Never Learned About Birds*

Try something new by making your very own birdcall. Then use it to invite the birds over to feast from your bird feeders!

What You Will Need

A piece of bamboo, * 1" in diameter*

A piece of bamboo, * 3/4" in diameter*

A bottle cork

Sandpaper

Continued ➔

Cotton balls

A small piece of soft cloth

Fine string

Note: Bamboo is available from most craft stores

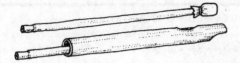

1. Cut the 1-inch-thick bamboo between the nodes to get a single piece, 9 1/2 inches long.

2. Cut the narrower piece of bamboo to get one length 11 inches long, with a node at one end.

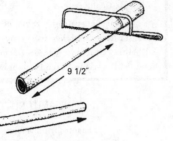

9 1/2"

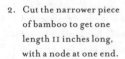

node

11"

3. Carve a little slit 4 inches from one end of the wider piece of bamboo. Carefully enlarge the slit to form a round opening.

4. On the side opposite the carved V, starting 3/4 of an inch from the end of the tube, carve an angled mouthpiece opening as shown.

carve out

4"

5. Slice the cork in half lengthwise. Sand the rounded side of the cork so that a 1" length is beveled.

3/4"

6. Shove the cork into the mouthpiece end of the wide bamboo. The flat side of the cork should be toward the round opening in the front; the beveled side toward the mouthpiece in the back. Poke the cork into the bamboo tube until about 1/4 inch shows through the front V hole. Cut off any extra cork sticking out the top. Sand the mouthpiece and the beveled end of the cork so that the edges are smooth and tight.

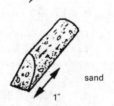

sand

1"

7. Carve a narrow groove all around the thinner bamboo, about 3/4 inch from the end without the node. Put a pair of cotton balls on either side of the bamboo, just above the carved groove. Wrap the cotton balls in a small circle

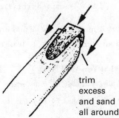

trim excess and sand all around

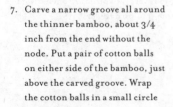

of cloth and tie tightly in place with your fine string or thread. The string should sit in the carved groove. This is the stopper for your birdcall.

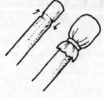

8. Insert the stopper into the wide bamboo tube. As you blow in the mouthpiece, pull the stopper up and down. Try to tweet like a bird.

Festive Cooking

What would the holidays be like without festive food to enjoy? Gifts from the kitchen are guaranteed to please all who receive them. Whether you paint some bread with colorful designs or make some edible ornaments, you are sure to have some cooking fun with these projects!

STAINED-GLASS HOLIDAY COOKIES

adapted from Hearts and Crafts

You will love making and giving this beautiful dessert. You can arrange the cookies on a plate and serve them to your friends, or hang the cookies on the Christmas tree or in the windows and let them catch the light.

What You Will Need

1/2 cup margarine	Red raspberry jam
1/2 cup sugar	Large bowl
1 egg	Wooden spoon
1 3/4 cups flour	Plastic wrap
1/2 teaspoon baking powder	Aluminum foil
1/2 teaspoon salt	Cookie sheet
1 teaspoon vanilla	

1. Mix the margarine in the bowl with your wooden spoon to soften it. Add the sugar and egg and beat until it is creamy. Add the remaining ingredients. Mix until the batter is smooth and stiff. You might need to take turns with a grown-up helper or a brother or sister—mixing dough is tiring work!

2. Cover the dough in the bowl with plastic wrap, and refrigerate for at least two hours.

3. Preheat the oven to 375°F. Place a piece of aluminum foil on the cookie sheet.

4. Take a small piece of the dough and roll it out into a rope that is about 1/4 inch thick. Form your rope of dough into a holiday shape—small or large, whatever you decide to create. Some ideas are stars, trees, hearts, candy canes, stockings, and wreaths.

5. Fill the inside of the ornament with raspberry jam. Spread at least 1/4 inch thick.

6. Bake the cookies for at least 10 minutes. The jam must bubble in order for it to harden as the cookies cool.

7. Let the cookies cool on the cookie sheet. Peel the aluminum foil off the back of each cookie.

PAINTED HOLIDAY BREAD

adapted from *Hearts and Crafts*

Here's an extremely simple and healthy way to let your artistic talent shine through in the kitchen! Grab your paintbrush—a brand-new brush or one that has only been used for food—and let's go!

What You Will Need

1/2 cup milk	Small bowl
4 drops each of red and green food coloring	Brand-new paintbrush
White bread	Toaster

1. In separate small bowls, mix half of the milk and one of the food colorings.

2. Set your slice of bread on the counter or work surface and use the paintbrush and milk "paint" to paint a holiday design on your bread. Make one large design or several small ones. Paint only one side of the bread, and be sure not to let the bread get too soggy!

3. When your picture is done, put the bread in the toaster on a low setting. The heat from the toaster will bake your design into the bread.

4. Use the bread just as you would use any other. You can make a whole batch and store it in the refrigerator or in the freezer, so that you always have some on hand.

SALT-DOUGH JEWELRY

adapted from *Hearts and Crafts*

This is a very simple way to make yourself and those you love look festive. String a red-and-green beaded necklace or create some holiday pins and hair barrettes. You can paint your jewelry or leave it natural.

What You Will Need

2 cups whole-wheat flour	Spatula
1 cup salt	Toothpick
3/4 cup water	Timer
Mixing bowl	Nylon cording
Cookie sheet	Pin backs and/or plain
Nonstick cooking spray	barrette pieces
Rolling pin	Watercolors and paintbrush (optional)
Cookie cutters in various holiday shapes	Dish towel

1. Combine the flour, salt, and water in the bowl, and mix with your hands until it forms an elastic dough that is easy to knead with your hands. This may take some experimenting—if it is too dry, add a little more water; if it is too wet and sticky, add a bit more flour.

2. Coat the cookie sheet with nonstick spray.

3. Roll a small piece of dough into a ball. Put it on the table and use a rolling pin to roll it out until it is about 1/4 inch thick.

4. Using your cookie cutters, cut out as many shapes as you can. Use the spatula to move the cut-outs to the cookie pan.

5. To make beads, take small pieces of dough and rub them into little balls with your hands. Place these on the cookie sheet, and put a hole through the middle of each one. Make sure that the hole is big enough for the nylon cording to be threaded through.

6. Preheat your oven to 170°F. Ask your grown-up helper to put the cookie sheet in the oven. Set a timer for one hour.

7. After the hour is up, carefully check the jewelry pieces. If they are hard when you tap them, they are done. If you can indent them with your finger, put them in for another 15 minutes. Pieces thicker than 1/4 inch usually take longer than one hour to "cook." Don't burn yourself when you test the clay! Let them cool for at least a half hour before using them.

8. Now your jewelry is ready to paint, if you like. Paint with the watercolors and let dry.

9. When your jewelry is cool, it is ready to be made into necklaces, pins, and barrettes. String beads on nylon cording (found at fabric stores). Other pieces can be made into pins or barrettes by gluing pin backs or plain barrette pieces (from an arts-and-crafts store) onto the backs with white glue, or by using a hot-glue gun.

CREPE PAPER ORNAMENTS

adapted from *Easter Eggs by the Dozens!*

Bright bits of broken color splash out and surround crepe-paper ornaments. With bits of colored paper and blown eggshells, you can make great ornaments to decorate your house. This is one of the fastest, easiest, and liveliest ways to make great-looking mosaics. The vivid shades of tissue paper bring sparkling life to plain, white eggshell. Whether overlapping in random abandon or carefully placing in a pattern, these fragments of intense holiday colors are real attention-getters with their stained-glass appearance.

Continued ➔

What You Will Need

Clean, dry, blown white eggs

Tissue paper in three or four holiday colors

White glue

Small paintbrush

Shallow container (for thinned glue)

Finish

1. Decide on the look you want. Choose one or two light colors and a dark and a medium shade for high contrast. It's easy (and quick) to start with a random design and work your way into more complex patterns later.

2. If working a planned pattern, keep the shapes simple, such as triangles or squares, and combine in a pleasing order. Basic quilt block patterns are a fine choice, but any type of geometric repetition works well.

3. Cut tissue paper shapes by folding paper over itself (up to eight thicknesses) and cutting out all the pieces at once. Place the tiny pieces in a dish or bowl.

4. For a random, or crazy-quilt look, cut or tear the pieces into small, irregular shapes.

5. Pour a little glue into shallow dish. Thin with water to the consistency of milk.

6. Brush the thinned glue onto a piece of tissue paper and place it, glue-side down, on the egg. Lightly press into place. Continue gluing, placing, and pressing until the entire egg surface is covered. Overlapping pieces will blend to create new shades. Torn pieces will blend more subtly than the sharp, distinct lines of cut pieces.

7. If you are working a pattern with open spots, cover the whole egg first with torn bits of white (or light-colored) tissue, let dry a few minutes, then apply the pattern pieces.

8. When dry, apply a coat of spray finish to prevent the dye in the paper from bleeding.

Colonial Crafts

Drying flowers and plants was considered an art during colonial times. In the fall, the colonists dried all sorts of natural materials from which they made toys and winter bouquets. Try making these traditional crafts from days gone by.

CORN HUSK DOLLS

adapted from Let's Grow!

Children in colonial times made corn husk dolls after the harvest in the fall.

What You Will Need

Dried corn husks and corn silks

Water

Yarn or string

Scissors

Fine-point colored markers

White glue and brush

1. Prepare the husks by soaking them in warm water until they bend without cracking. Slit some into narrow strips to use for tying, or use yarn or string.

2. To form the head, lay several husks on top of each other. Fold in half. Tie under the fold to make the head. The part below the head will make up the body.

3. Slip some folded husks between the body husks, below the tie. Let them stick out on both sides to form arms. Tie at the place the "wrists" should be, and cut off the extra length of husk at the end of each "hand."

4. Tie the body husks again under the arms, to make a waist. For a girl doll, arrange the lower part of the husks into a skirt. For a boy doll, separate the husks into two parts and tie at the "ankles."

5. Glue corn silk on the head for hair. Add facial features with colored markers.

6. Use extra husks, corn silk, twigs, and buttons to make a broom, a rake, a pocketbook, a hat, or the like, for your doll.

ORANGE POMANDER

adapted from An Apple A Day!

A few wealthy colonists had hothouses in which they were able to grow oranges. Spicy orange pomanders make wonderful holiday gifts and decorations. Hang your pomander in the kitchen, bathroom, or a closet. Its spicy scent will last for years.

What You Will Need

1 perfect orange	*1 teaspoon allspice*
1 ounce whole cloves	*1/8 teaspoon ginger*
1 tablespoon cinnamon	*An 18-inch length of ribbon*
1 teaspoon nutmeg	*Bowl and skewer*

1. Push the stem ends of the cloves into the orange—just close enough to touch. Cover the orange completely with cloves.

2. Mix the cinnamon, nutmeg, allspice, and ginger in the bowl. Roll the orange pomander in the spice mixture. Leave the pomander in the bowl in a warm spot for two or three weeks. Roll it in the spices occasionally to help the orange dry, harden, and shrink.

3. Have a grown-up helper pierce the pomander orange lengthwise with the skewer. Thread a double length of ribbon through the top of the pomander. Tie a knot and a bow at the bottom and make a loop for hanging at the top.

Gardening

GENERAL INFORMATION

Improving Your Soil

Updated and Revised

Stu Campbell

Illustrations by Susan Berry Langsten

A Little Background

The key to understanding your garden soil is to understand what it is and what it is becoming.

WHAT'S IN SOIL

Soil particles. About 95 percent of soil consists of minerals. Most of this mineral material has been weathered into particles smaller than pebbles and gravel; these are classified by decreasing size as sand, silt, or clay. You can visualize the relative size of soil particles by thinking of a grain of coarse sand as a large beach ball, a particle of silt as a marble, and a particle of clay as a pinpoint. Sand includes particles with a diameter smaller than 2 mm but larger than 0.05 mm; it feels gritty between your fingers. Silt ranges from 0.05 mm down to 0.002 mm, too small to see with the naked eye. Pure silt feels smooth and fine like talcum powder or white flour. Clay includes anything smaller than 0.002 mm. That's about one 1/1000 as large as the average grain of coarse sand, so fine it can be seen only with the aid of a powerful microscope. Pure clay feels very smooth, and if wet it feels sticky and clings to your fingers. Soils contain a mix of particle sizes; the relative proportions of each determine texture (whether a soil is silt loam, sandy clay loam, silty clay, etc.).

Organic matter and humus. Only 3 to 5 percent of soil's total weight is organic matter, formerly living creatures (primarily plants) in various stages of decomposition. But you should never underestimate the importance of this once living material. It's something that must be renewed constantly if the soil is to stay in good condition. It's an important source of phosphorus, nitrogen, and sulfur (major nutrients that plants require), plus the main source of food (energy) for microorganisms.

Humus is a term that gardeners use all the time, but that few really understand. It's more than just rotting organic matter. True humus is well aged, fine and dark, and decomposed to the point where the original material can't be recognized any longer. Yet it's much more resistant to breaking down than is organic material in earlier stages of decay; some humus lasts many, many years in the soil. It's a bit like Jell-O in texture; the humus that surrounds soil particles helps hold them together into nice, porous crumbs.

Air and water. When we're standing on the ground it feels pretty solid, but only half of soil is solid particles. The other half is a combination of space (air) and water. When everything is just right, there is plenty of room for air to occupy the spaces between soil particles. These spaces are known as soil pores. They allow gases such as oxygen and carbon dioxide to move in and out of soil, so that plant roots won't asphyxiate.

When too much water saturates soil, it fills all available air spaces and plant roots can't get any oxygen. Ideally, about half of the "empty" space in soil is filled with water. If present in the right amount, water should encase each soil particle in a thin film of moisture. An alphabet

Continued ➜

THE SOIL'S PROFILE

Soil exists in more or less horizontal layers; you can see this layercake effect if you dig down about 3 feet. The thickness and nature of the layers will vary in different soils because of differing interactions among the site's original rocks, climate, slope or shape of the land, animals, plants, and microorganisms, which together shape a particular soil. A typical soil profile, or cross section showing all the layers, is illustrated below.

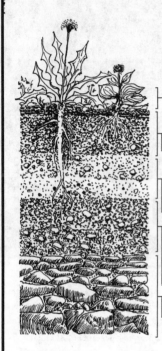

Organic layer. A thin layer of plant material in various stages of decomposition. Absent if the soil has been bulldozed or cultivated.

Topsoil. The top layer of soil, darker and more crumbly than deeper layers, where most nutrients, roots, and soil organisms exist. The deeper this layer, the better.

Subsoil. Usually lighter than topsoil because it contains less humus. Much of the water plants need is stored here, plus some nutrients. Often contains two or more distinct layers.

Parent material. Rubble that hasn't yet weathered enough to look like soil.

Bedrock. The underlying layer of solid rock, usually too far down to find by digging.

soup of chemicals is dissolved in this soil water, including plant nutrients; as a result, it's often called the soil solution. The only way these vital minerals can move through soil and be absorbed by plants is when they're dissolved in water.

WATER AND AIR IN THE SOIL

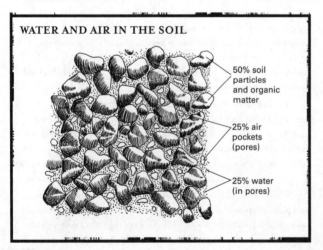

50% soil particles and organic matter

25% air pockets (pores)

25% water (in pores)

Most plants need an astonishing amount of moisture. Water is what keeps many plants upright, by filling cells until they're turgid, or stiff. That's why some plants wilt and flop over when deprived of water. Plant roots will grow remarkably deep in search of water and nutrients. Alfalfa roots have been known to bore as deep as 30 feet, and if the root system of a single wild oat plant were put end to end and measured, the whole thing might total more than 54 miles—not even counting the tiny root hairs.

Some Specifics

Everybody has had some experience with soil, even if it was just wiping sticky clay off boots or pouring sand out of sneakers after a walk on the beach. Chances are you know more about different soils than you think.

There are six things a plant needs to grow successfully:

1. light
2. mechanical support (to keep the plant from falling over)
3. heat
4. air
5. water
6. nutrients

Except for light, the soil has a role in providing all of these things. We've all heard the adage "A chain is only as strong as its weakest link." Plant production is similar. It can be only as successful as the most limiting of these six plant-growth factors. Soil should allow roots to grow easily to form a good anchor, breathe, get moisture, and permit microbial activity—which controls nutrient supply. Here are some specifics to help you understand how to make your soil a hospitable environment.

LOAM, SAND, SILT, OR CLAY?

If you have a choice of soil (and most of us do not), sandy loam is just about ideal. It is "light," as they say, crumbly, and rich in humus. But don't be discouraged if your soil is something less than perfect. Almost any soil of other-than-excellent quality can be improved in fairly short order by working in generous helpings of leaves, manure, grass clippings, compost, or some other form of organic matter.

To evaluate a particular soil, consider both its texture and its structure. A soil's texture simply refers to the size of the particles that make up the soil, which determines whether you have sandy soil, clay, or ideal loam. Structure describes the way these particles are clumped into aggregates, or crumbs. Loose crumbs are good because they increase soil pore space, and therefore its aeration and drainage. They are held together by well-decomposed organic matter (humus). Good structure is far more important than good texture. That's a good thing, because texture is something you learn to live with but structure can be changed. Good structure is something you can create, and it will compensate for any less-than-ideal texture.

Loam. Soil with a nicely balanced mix of soil particles is called loam. An average loam might contain about 40 percent silt particles, 40 percent sand, and 20 percent clay. This mix gives it a nice balance of properties: It retains a good amount of nutrients and doesn't dry out too fast after it rains, yet doesn't stay soggy. Loam has what gardeners call good tilth, meaning that it's easy to work. If it's dry to slightly moist, you can crumble a fistful simply by poking it gently with your finger.

Most soils are some type of loam, but usually they're some variation such as clay loam or silty clay loam and thus share some of the characteristics of those other soils.

The word *loam* is also used more loosely for ideal soil, which means that in addition to having a loamy texture, it's full of rotting organic matter and has been treated well, so it retains its naturally good structure.

Sandy soil. Soils referred to as sandy contain at least 70 percent sand particles by weight. To tell if your soil is sandy, pick up a handful and rub it between your fingers; if it falls apart almost instantly and feels mostly gritty, it contains a lot of sand. While gardeners frustrated by clay soil may wish they had sand, these soils aren't entirely easy either. Sand absorbs and holds heat well, but that's an advantage only in cool climates. Sandy soils absorb rainfall well, but they can drain too quickly and tend to dry out. They don't retain nutrients for very long, so typically they need to have fertilizer added often and in smaller amounts to counteract leaching (the washing away of nutrients by water). The best way to improve sandy soils is to add organic matter, which acts like a blotter to hold moisture and nutrients in the soil. Sandy soils with abundant organic matter can be very fertile and easy to work. More common (and more manageable) than strictly sandy soils are sandy loams, or a variation such as sandy clay loam. An average sandy loam soil contains 50 to 70 percent sand, with the remainder a mix of silt and clay.

Gardeners refer to sandy soil as "light," in spite of the fact that a given quantity of sand probably weighs a good deal more than a similar quantity of clay, which they tend to call "heavy." Actually "lightness" or "heaviness," in gardening lingo, describes not weight but how easily a soil can be worked.

Silty soil. Soil has to contain at least 80 percent silt particles to be classified as silt. Such soils have properties between those of sandy and clay soils, much like loam; as a result, silty soils are classified (by the U.S. Department of Agriculture) as a type of loam. True silt soil is pretty rare; most soils with 40 percent or more silt particles are silt loams, silty clay loams, or silty clay. These soils are most common in river deltas or areas that were once the bottoms of lakes and ponds.

Clay soil. Soils classified as clay contain at least 40 percent clay particles. These tiny specks are very rich in mineral nutrients, but they're shaped like plates or flakes and can stick together like slices of bread buttered on both sides. Clay soils, often called "heavy" soils, tend to hold water too well. If mistreated, they're prone to compaction and can form a water-resistant crust after a heavy rain; when they finally do dry out, they can form rock-hard lumps that make the soil practically unworkable. Clay soils are very slow to warm up in the spring. To check for clay, pick up a handful of moist soil. Can you roll it into a thin sausage that holds together even if you poke it gently? If so, add a few drops of water; if it looks shiny, feels sticky, and clings to your fingers, your soil is full of clay.

The best way to make clay soils more manageable is to add lots of organic matter. This will lighten such soils by increasing the amount of pore space, thereby increasing both drainage and air flow. Adding coarse sand may seem like a good idea, but it's not. Sand is solid particles, so it's not nearly as effective at increasing pore space as is organic matter.

Organic matter has the added benefit of promoting good structure (formation of loose crumbs), which will make clay soils behave more like loam. Another way of promoting good structure in clay soils is keeping bare soil mulched where heavy rains are common; this minimizes crust formation and keeps a summer thunderstorm from pounding flat all the nice soil crumbs. Water dry soil well and wait overnight; let wet soil dry out a couple of days. Squeeze a handful to make sure it's not sticky; moist soil forms a mostly solid lump that easily breaks apart if you poke it.

Calcium can be helpful in maintaining good structure in clay soils, but be careful not to add too much or you'll end up in even more trouble. If a pH test shows your soil is acidic, add calcium in the form of limestone. If your soil is neutral or alkaline, use gypsum (calcium sulfate) if tests show a calcium deficiency; gypsum supplies calcium without changing soil pH.

Peat or muck soils. Occasionally, a soil will contain unusually high amounts of organic matter. If soil contains more than 50 percent organic matter (usually only partially decomposed), it's called a peat soil; if organic matter makes up 20 to 50 percent, it's called a muck soil. (*Muck* is an old term for well-aged and well-rotted organic matter in which the original plant material can no longer be recognized because most has become humus.) These soils are very dark in color and are typically found in areas that were once wetlands.

These are sometimes dug out of swamps and sold by unscrupulous dealers as "soil improvers." More often than not they're a waste of money. When spread dry in the garden, they can blow away to the next county on the first slight breeze. Good commercial compost is a much better investment. Don't, by the way, confuse peat soil with peat moss, which is a good source of organic matter for soils that need its acidity.

SOIL LIFE

The relationships among growing plants, the soil, and the countless billions of microscopic creatures that exist in just a few cubic inches of it are incredibly complex. There are more than enough unanswered questions to keep microbiologists and soil scientists hard at work unraveling the mysteries for the next several centuries at least. Still, there are some simple generalizations that can be made. For one thing, it's safe to say that the more you feed your soil with organic matter, the more microbes increase in both numbers and activity, and the more fertile and productive your soil becomes.

Soil organisms do several essential things: (1) They decompose organic matter, creating humus and releasing nutrients in organic matter by changing them to forms plants can absorb. The availability of nitrogen, phosphorus, sulfur, iron, and manganese is largely controlled by microbial action. (2) Larger organisms such as insects, earthworms, and even small mammals help pulverize and mix soil, and mix organic matter into the soil, as they move around. (3) A few specialized bacteria (*Rhizobium, Azotobacter,* and *cyanobacteria* or blue-green algae) can "fix" nitrogen by absorbing it from the atmosphere and converting it into forms plants can use; in the case of legumes, the bacteria live in root nodules and get food in return in the form of carbohydrates manufactured by the plant. (4) Other specialized fungi (mycorrhizae) form mutually beneficial relationships with plant roots, increasing the roots' absorption of nutrients. (5) Many microorganisms produce enzymes, growth hormones, and vitamins that benefit plants. (6) Soil bacteria and fungi transform many compounds that are toxic to plants and animals into nontoxic substances.

Continued →

Microorganisms in the soil include bacteria, fungi, actinomycetes, and algae. Though they make up only a small portion of the soil by volume or weight (between 1 and 8 percent of the total organic matter in the soil), their populations may be huge. One gram of soil may contain more than a trillion bacteria! These tiny soil organisms constantly compete with each other, and whole groups of them live and die as conditions in the soil change. The waste products and tiny dead bodies of one set of microbes may be food for another.

The soil life—microbes—of most interest to gardeners consists of those that require oxygen (aerobic organisms). Both in the soil and in the compost pile, these are the organisms that do the best job of breaking down raw organic matter and converting it to humus. If there isn't enough oxygen (air), they'll die out and less efficient anaerobic organisms will take over; anaerobic organisms are responsible for the bad smell of a wet, gooey compost heap.

Besides oxygen, aerobic organisms need a steady supply of carbon as their energy source; this is supplied by organic matter. They also need a continuous supply of nitrogen, which they use to synthesize essential compounds including DNA and proteins. Most kinds of organic matter contain enough nitrogen to supply the needs of decomposer organisms. But a few types are low in nitrogen (or, more accurately, excessively rich in carbon): sawdust, wood chips, bagasse (sugar-cane residue), and straw. To break these down, microorganisms have to "borrow" nitrogen from the soil temporarily. In the short term, this can deprive plants of nitrogen—which is one of their most essential nutrients. There are two simple fixes. If you want to add any of these materials directly to the soil (as mulch, or mixing in as a soil amendment), you'll need to add a good source of nitrogen at the same time. (All manures are good nitrogen sources; other options include alfalfa meal and ordinary garden fertilizer.) Or leave the material outdoors for a few months—until the sawdust or wood chips turn gray—before using.

EARTHWORMS

Any discussion of garden soil would be incomplete without mentioning the earthworm, the gardener's best friend. An earthworm eats its way through the soil, ingesting and digesting organic matter. As the organic material passes through the earthworm's body, it is ground with the help of tiny stones in the worm's gizzard. The "castings" excreted by earthworms are very high in humus (and so perfect as a soil conditioner) as well as rich in the forms of nutrients most easily absorbed by plants. This wiggly gardener can produce its weight in castings each day.

Earthworms also do a lot to solve the problem of soil compaction. Plants do best where there are plenty of pore spaces for roots to grow into. Earthworms do a fine job of loosening and aerating the soil as they go about their day-to-day business of consuming organic matter. Their burrows make passageways for roots. Burrows also allow more water to seep in—rather than just running off the surface—when it rains or when you irrigate. Slightly sticky substances in earthworm castings help soil particles hold together loosely into crumbs, promoting good soil structure.

The more earthworms, the better off is your garden. To increase the number of earthworms, increase the amount of organic matter in your soil. If you are continuously adding vegetable matter, you are almost automatically increasing the earthworm population.

DRAINAGE: MANAGING AIR AND WATER IN THE SOIL

Let's face it, it's impossible to garden successfully in soil that's waterlogged. Drainage is an important factor to consider when judging the quality of any soil. Plant roots and soil organisms have to breathe, so they depend on air that penetrates between the soil particles. Earth that is drowned—so saturated that water fills all soil pores and leaves no space for air—gets no oxygen. Sometimes "poor" soil is simply a matter of poor drainage, not missing nutrients.

Compaction of soil particles (right), resulting from heavy machinery or footprints, can cause soil to be drowned. This condition cuts off the air supply to the soil and to the roots beneath the surface.

The water table is the point where water stops percolating downward through the soil. This usually occurs wherever the water reaches bedrock or impervious subsoil. Where the water table is very high (close to the surface), even a moderate amount of water can cause a garden to be swamped. "Puddling" happens when there's so much water that finer particles float to the surface. There the muddy solution will be heavy and gummy, and later may crack as it dries out. Puddling is a symptom of soil that's begging for additional organic matter.

Drowning is the most complete way of cutting off the air supply to the soil. But there's another way that's every bit as dangerous. This is called compaction, and it occurs when people walk or drive machinery over the same plot of ground time after time. Eventually, more and more pore spaces, or tiny air pockets, get pressed out. What was once fairly good topsoil can in pretty short order become too dense to support healthy plant growth. Soils with a lot of clay are especially susceptible. Repeated compaction can create an impervious layer known as hardpan hidden below the surface; in extreme cases, roots won't be able to push through this layer. If you see a well-worn track where grass won't grow in otherwise healthy lawn, suspect compacted soil. Soil that holds puddles long after it rains, especially where there isn't a low spot, is another sign of compaction.

If you have a drainage problem, try to figure out what's causing it. Garden spaces can sometimes be drained by digging ditches to direct the water out of the area, and low spots can often be filled in by changing the grade of the land. Near a house, redirecting a downspout may solve the problem. Installing underground drainage pipes works only if the pipes are sloped correctly; even if installed by an experienced person, the pipes can shift or fill in over time and stop working. Is compacted soil causing the poor drainage? Dig down to see if there's a compacted layer of hardpan below the surface; if so, one of the best remedies is to break up the impervious subsoil so that the water can get through. If you have a serious drainage problem and relocating the garden isn't an option, your best bet is to build raised beds.

There are times when soil lacks enough moisture, and this, of course, forces the growing and decomposing processes to grind to a halt. Water can be lost in several ways: (1) It moves downward—percolates—through the soil, and then moves away laterally when it reaches the water table. Too-rapid percolation, as in unimproved sandy soil, causes nutrients to leach away. (2) It can run off the surface of a soil that doesn't absorb moisture well, often taking some of the soil along with it as erosion. Soils that are compacted or low in organic matter may shed more water than they absorb. (3) It is lost through evaporation or transpiration. Plants transpire just as people perspire; it's basically the same thing—living organisms giving off moisture to the atmosphere.

The best way to manage air and water is to keep soil abundantly stocked with organic matter. Humus and organic matter promote the formation of good soil structure and help stabilize soil crumbs so they can withstand cultivation and pounding by rain. By increasing the amount of pore space, organic matter improves drainage and air flow. At the same time, organic matter acts as a sponge to keep water (and nutrients) from draining away too quickly in sandy or gravelly soils.

CULTIVATION

Cultivation—loosening up and working soil with a garden fork, hoe, or rotary tiller—serves several purposes. It mixes organic matter and applied fertilizer into the soil. It breaks up large soil clods into smaller pieces that, when raked, form a nice smooth seedbed. It temporarily improves aeration, especially in heavy clay soils. When done properly, it can reduce rather than increase compaction.

But there are certain dangers involved in cultivating. For instance, never attempt to till earth too early in the spring before the frost has gone out of it, or before it has dried from soggy wet to nicely moist. Working any wet soil can damage its nice crumb structure. Working clay when it's too wet can cause it to puddle or form lumps that later bake hard as a rock in the sun. Before cultivating, give any soil the "fist test."

The fist test is the simplest way to tell if your garden is dry enough to be dug or tilled. If you pick up a handful of soil and can squeeze water from it, it's obviously too wet. If the soil compresses into a tight or sticky ball and stays that way, it needs more drying time. If it's dry enough to crumble slightly in your hand, it's friable—that is, ready to be worked. (If it's really dry, you're better off watering it and waiting a few hours to dig; you'll breathe in less dust that way!)

It is possible to stir things up too much. Soil organisms need some time to do their work without being disturbed. Cultivating too often only overstimulates them, burns up organic matter more quickly, and cuts down their productivity in the long run. Besides, too much cultivation can break down soil structure, destroying the aggregates you worked so hard to build.

Simple Fixes

A few simple tests can tell you what your soil needs. You can use the following tests to tell you more about your soil's structure and pH. Correcting flaws in these two areas will make a world of difference to your garden and lawn success.

SOIL TESTING

Dig a narrow pit with a regular spade, trying to keep the walls as vertical as possible. When you're down a couple of feet, shear off a slice of soil from one side of the pit and drop it on a hard surface. If it breaks apart into chunks or blocklike clods, the structure is probably poor. To check how stable your soil structure is, place a nice crumbly handful into two glasses. Slowly add water to one glass and compare it with the soil in the other glass. If the wet crumbs dissolve, your soil structure needs work; if the crumbs remain intact when wet, pat yourself on the back.

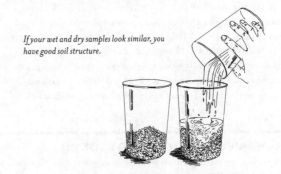

If your wet and dry samples look similar, you have good soil structure.

A pH test is something you can easily do yourself. It will tell you whether your soil is acidic, alkaline, or just right (the ideal pH is slightly acidic, 6.3 to 6.8). Inexpensive test kits are available at any garden center; for a bit more money, you can get a pH meter that gives you instant results. The pH of the water you mix your soil sample with can distort your results; use distilled water for accuracy. To get the most reliable picture of the pH, take two or more tests for each different garden area (lawn, vegetable garden, flower bed) and average the results. Always test soil pH before adding limestone, both to keep you from wasting money and because too much limestone will give you alkaline soil, which is just as difficult in its own way as is acidic soil.

A more detailed chemical analysis of a soil sample is also something you might try yourself, though it's hard to get really accurate results. There are a number of good home test kits available. Sometimes, if you're not experienced, such simple tests can lead to strange or downright erroneous conclusions; if you get an odd result, repeat the test with a new soil sample. (See Appendix C: How to Take a Soil Sample.)

To get a good picture of your soil's chemistry, it's safest to send a soil sample to your local Cooperative Extension Service or a private testing laboratory. You'll get a detailed report that includes recommendations for correcting pH and just how much fertilizer your soil needs. If you suspect your soil might be high in lead, you'll need a professional soil test to confirm it. The Cooperative Extension Service can give you names of private soil labs; their tests often cost a bit more but in return you'll get more-detailed results, explanations, and recommendations. Be sure to specify if you want organic recommendations; most places can provide this but you may have to ask for it. Testing services are normally very busy in the spring; it may speed things up if you submit your sample early. Better still, do it in the fall when things aren't so hectic.

Continued ➜

BALANCING ACIDITY AND ALKALINITY (pH)

It may seem funny to talk about acidity and alkalinity before nutrients, but they really come first. If the pH of your soil is way off, all the fertilizer in the world isn't going to do you much good. By bringing pH into balance, you bring more nutrients within reach of your plants without adding any fertilizer. Very acidic or alkaline conditions upset the soil's chemical balance, locking up existing nutrients so plants can't absorb them. Some nutrients dissolve more readily in slightly acidic soil, others when the soil is more alkaline. The ideal pH (slightly acidic) is a compromise; soil scientists have found that the greatest availability of nutrients occurs when the pH falls between 6.3 and 6.8. If soil contains lots of organic matter, many plants will grow tolerably well when the pH is 5.5 to 8.0 (organic matter helps buffer pH and increases plants' ability to tolerate any less-than-ideal conditions, including acidity and alkalinity). If you apply limestone regularly, it's a good idea to get your soil's calcium and magnesium levels checked periodically; if you use wood ashes to correct acidity, test potassium levels as well.

HOW MUCH LIME TO USE TO RAISE PH

The following recommendations are approximate, because each soil is slightly different. Start with these amounts and retest pH before adding any more. Sandy soils need less calcium to correct acidity; you need to spread lime on them more often, though. Clay soils have large reserves to fill and therefore need more calcium, but you won't need to lime as often. Soils rich in organic matter also need more lime; double the recommended amounts for such soil. If you soil is very low in organic matter, reduce amounts by about 25 percent until you've built up your soil's humus.

Ground calcitic limestone supplies only calcium; it's the best choice for most soils. (You can substitute finely ground oyster or clam shells.) Use dolomite limestone only if your soil tests low in magnesium; too much magnesium will lock up important nutrients. Wood ashes, which are rich in potassium, will also raise soil pH. If you use the amounts of wood ashes listed here, don't add fertilizer containing potassium (such as 5–10–10) or you'll throw off the nutrient balance of your soil. Wood ashes work quickly to change pH but can be too strong for new seedlings; mix them in well at least three weeks before planting.

RAISING PH FROM 5.5 TO 6.5

Approximate amount of lime needed per 100 square feet

Soil Texture	Calcitic Limestone	Dolomite Limestone	Wood Ashes
Sandy (light)	2 1/2 lbs.	2–3 lbs.	3–4 lbs.
Loamy (medium)	6 1/2 lbs.	6 lbs.	8 lbs.
Clay (heavy)	9 lbs.	7–8 lbs.	9–10 1/2 lbs.

Acidic soils are common in areas of heavy rainfall, as rain leaches out chemicals such as calcium and magnesium that counteract acidity. But if you're living on top of a limestone deposit, in those areas your soil could be alkaline, so test the pH to make sure. If you know your soil is acidic, avoid using pine needles or peat moss, which contribute more acidity. Well-aged manure is a good source of organic matter for acidic soils because it's slightly alkaline and rich in calcium and magnesium.

The easiest way to counteract acidity is by spreading limestone. Fall is the best time, because it takes a while for limestone to become available in soil. To avoid shocking soil organisms, don't add more than 5 pounds of limestone per 100 square feet at one time. Wait six months (and ideally retest soil pH) before adding more.

HOW MUCH SULFUR TO USE TO LOWER PH

The following recommendations are approximate. To reduce stress to plants and soil organisms, add no more than 1 1/2 pounds of sulfur per 100 square feet at one time (for heavy clay soils, 2 pounds). If you need to lower the pH by more than one unit, spread 1 pound in spring and another in fall. Retest the soil before spreading any more the following spring.

LOWERING PH FROM 7.5 TO 6.5

Approximate amount of sulfur needed per 100 square feet

Soil Texture	Powdered Sulfur	Aluminum Sulfate	Iron Sulfate
Sandy (light)	1 lb.	2 1/2 lbs.	3 lbs.
Loamy (medium)	1 1/2 lbs.	3 lbs.	5–5 1/2 lbs.
Clay (heavy)	2 lbs.	5–6 lbs.	7 1/2 lbs.

Alkalinity, the opposite condition from acidity, is typical of extremely dry regions. But just as pockets of alkaline soil occur east of the Mississippi River, pockets of acidic soil occur in arid regions west of the Mississippi. Even more so than acidity, alkaline conditions cause soil nutrients to become locked up and unavailable to plants. Fortunately, many alkaline soils have large nutrient reserves; once the alkalinity is corrected, they can be quite fertile.

Annual soil tests are a good idea for such soils for two reasons. First, you may not need all the nutrients in a typical balanced fertilizer (such as 5–10–5 or 5–10–10), so you can save money by buying only the nutrients you need. Second, alkaline soils are sometimes prone to high salt levels, and you'll need a soil test to tell you what kind of salt problem you have.

If your soil is alkaline, seek out acidifying forms of organic matter: chopped oak leaves, leaf mold, ground bark, aged sawdust, peat moss, pine needles, and pine or cypress bark mulch. Some concentrated, synthetic fertilizers such as ammonium sulfate are acidifying and may be helpful if used in small amounts (large amounts can harm soil organisms); divide the recommended dosage into at least three or four parts and apply three or four times throughout the season.

Moderately alkaline soils are managed much like acidic ones, except sulfur is substituted for limestone to lower the pH. Powdered (elemental or agricultural) sulfur is the best form to use because it works in six to eight weeks, lasts six months or more, and is pure sulfur. Aluminum sulfate (alum) is faster-acting but doesn't last as long and large amounts can harm soil organisms. Iron sulfate is similar but supplies iron. These chemicals should be worked into the soil and watered thoroughly afterward.

Chlorosis. While the green-veined, yellowing leaves of chlorosis may look like a plant disease, this problem is usually caused by improper soil pH. Chlorosis occurs because the plant is unable to take up iron from the soil through its roots. This is usually not because the soil lacks iron, but because an imbalance makes existing iron unavailable. Chlorosis often develops when acid-loving plants such as azaleas, rhododendrons, blueberries, and camellias are grown in ordinary or alkaline soils. It can develop on many plants grown in overlimed or extremely alkaline soils. The long-term solution is to lower the soil pH with a combination of sulfur and acidifying mulches such as pine needles. But plants showing chlorosis need immediate help. Any garden center sells iron in chelated form; chelating agents help keep iron in a more usable form for plants. Most forms of chelated iron can be absorbed by plant leaves for immediate use; apply as directed. Liquid seaweed (also available at garden centers) mixed to the appropriate dilution and sprayed on plant leaves will also provide a temporary fix.

Salinity. Overly salty soil can be a problem in arid or semiarid areas and at the seashore. Too much salt burns leaves on mature plants, slows down seed germination, and stunts plants. White salt deposits on the surface of soil are a classic sign of saline soils, which contain a mix of salts. Saline soils can be created by irrigation where dry air causes high evaporation rates; poor drainage is almost always part of the problem. If your pH is over 8.5, there's a good chance you have sodic soil; this contains high sodium levels that make gardening a challenge!

If you suspect a salinity problem, get a professional soil test to find out whether your soil is saline or sodic. Ask the testing laboratory or your local Cooperative Extension Service for advice on how to manage these soils. It will help to add lots of organic matter to your garden beds, preferably an acidifying type such as leaf mold or ground bark. Have your water tested, too; if your tap or irrigation water is high in mineral salts, it will contribute to the problem. Try collecting rainwater in a barrel placed under a downspout to cut back on your use of tap water. Don't use softened water on plants, as it's too high in sodium; install a faucet that bypasses your water softener.

NUTRIENT BALANCE

Just about everyone who gardens recognizes that nitrogen (N), phosphorus (P) and potassium (K) are major nutrients necessary for plant life and growth. They're the ones used in greatest quantities by plants, which is why they're included in standard fertilizers. But don't underestimate the importance of the other major nutrients. They are calcium (Ca), magnesium (Mg), and sulfur (S). After the big three, calcium is most often added, though in some soils it's already abundant and so is not needed. Gardeners who lime their soils regularly to correct acidity won't have to worry about calcium. Magnesium is often already present in soils, too; acidic, sandy soils are sometimes deficient, but that's easily fixed by using dolomite limestone to correct the acidity. Soils kept well stocked with organic matter from compost or manure shouldn't need additional sulfur, especially if they're fertilized with organic fertilizers.

Plants need other nutrients, too, but in smaller amounts. These trace elements or micronutrients include iron, manganese, copper, boron, zinc, molybdenum, chlorine, and cobalt. Micronutrients are just as essential for plant growth as the major elements, but in much smaller quantities. For example, corn needs more than 4,500 times as much nitrogen as boron in its diet.

Micronutrients aren't a problem for many gardeners. Keeping the soil pH within the 6.3–6.8 range and spreading compost or manure every year or two will maintain adequate levels. Where soils are very alkaline, it may be hard to keep the pH acidic enough to keep micronutrients readily available to plants. In such areas, try foliar fertilizers such as liquid seaweed; these are poured over plants so leaves can absorb the nutrients before they get locked up by alkaline soil. Intensely cultivated vegetable gardens may benefit from a balanced general micronutrient boost every few years. Seaweed (kelp), granite dust, rock phosphate, and greensand (all available from garden centers or mail-order sources) are good for this; they release nutrients so slowly, there's no danger of creating an imbalance.

It's important to remember that nutrients don't do plants much good unless they're in balance. An excess of one nutrient may cause others to be locked up out of plants' reach. And too much fertilizer is usually worse than too little. Overfertilizing (especially too much nitrogen) makes plants more susceptible to pests and diseases, reduces winter hardiness, and causes poor quality in flowers, most vegetables, and fruits. If plants are growing poorly, try to find out what's causing the problem. If the problem is compacted soil, overliming, or acidic soil, throwing on fertilizer is just throwing away money.

WHEN TO IMPROVE YOUR SOIL

Many people ask, "When is the best time of year for soil improvement?" The answer is "Whenever you have time." You can improve soil any time simply by covering bare areas with organic mulch; earthworms will mix this into the soil for you. For faster results, you can dig in organic matter any time the soil isn't frozen or soggy. Before you plant a perennial bed, at the beginning or end of the growing season for annuals and vegetables, and between successive crops in the vegetable garden are the easiest times to do this. The more decomposed the organic matter you mulch with or mix in, the sooner it will improve the soil.

If you start in spring, use the most well-decomposed organic matter you can get, such as compost or well-aged manure. Mix it into vegetable beds when you cultivate the soil, along with any fertilizers recommended by a soil test. Once the soil warms up, spread it as mulch around perennial flowers and crops such as berries. Spring is also a great time to start a compost pile with materials from cleaning up the garden; mix in some fresh grass clippings or manure to help the pile heat up.

In summer, you can grow any of the green-manure crops in bare areas of the garden. If you have a big garden, you might develop a system of rotating vegetable crops with green-manure crops. Some, such as fava beans and soybeans, do double duty because they're also edible.

After each annual crop has finished bearing, till it back into the soil while it's still tender and green. Once crop residues have been allowed to decompose in the soil for a few days, plant another succession vegetable crop or a green manure crop.

In the fall, you can use "raw" forms of organic matter because they'll have plenty of time to break down before spring. If you're tilling the garden, dig in a layer of chopped leaves or sawdust or whatever is close at hand. (If your soil's acidic, add ground limestone now so it has time to act before spring.) There's still time to plant a green-manure crop now to grow your own soil amendment right where it's needed; winter rye is hardy enough even for the coldest regions if planted in September. Any bare soil should be "put to bed" properly by mulching with a thick layer of leaves or hay to prevent erosion; these can be turned under in spring.

Continued →

SOIL AMENDMENTS

Any material that helps improve soil structure can qualify as a soil amendment. This might be organic matter, gypsum (calcium sulfate, which can improve the structure of hard, very alkaline soils), or an "artificial" soil conditioner such as perlite or vermiculite (either is expensive compared to organic matter and so is usually used only in soil mixes for containers). Organic matter is by far the best soil amendment. It offers many additional benefits besides improving structure. It reduces fertilizer requirements by supplying small amounts of nutrients in ideal slow-release form, and by helping to hold on to existing nutrients so they don't wash out of soil. It improves the soil's ability to hold moisture at the same time that it improves drainage. It lightens and improves drainage of clay soils, while helping sandy soils retain water and nutrients. It provides food for beneficial soil organisms while it helps suppress harmful soil organisms (including nematodes and some plant diseases). It improves the soil's ability to absorb rainfall while reducing soil erosion.

IMPROVING DIFFICULT SOILS

It may sound like an oversimplification, but it bears repeating over and over again: When in doubt about the quality or workability of a soil, add organic matter such as compost. You can't go wrong.

GOOD SOURCES OF ORGANIC MATTER

Alfalfa meal

Coffee grounds

Compost (commercial or homemade)

Corn cobs (ground or chopped) and husks

Grass clippings

Green manures (cover crops)

Hulls from buckwheat, oats, cocoa, and rice

Leaf mold

Leaves (chop with lawnmower)

Manure (cow, sheep, goat, or rabbit)

Oilseed meals (cottonseed, linseed)

Pea and bean pods and vines

Peanut shells

Peat moss and sphagnum moss

Pomace from apples, grapes, or cranberries

Rotted wood

Sawdust

Sewage sludge (composted)

Shredded brush trimmings

Spent hops (brewery wastes)

Straw

Tea leaves

Vegetable parings

Weeds (preferably without seeds)

Wood chips and shavings

Subsoil. Whenever good topsoil gets stripped away by bulldozers or erosion, all that remains is poor subsoil. If you're in a brand-new subdivision and the lawn is growing very poorly, this may be your situation. Unless you're dealing with solid rock, it's more economical to bring subsoil to a state of fertility than to try to haul in loads of new topsoil from somewhere else. (It's difficult to know what you're getting when you buy "topsoil" anyway.) The best and most efficient way to improve very poor soil is to grow a series of green-manure crops for a whole season. Plant buckwheat, which tolerates poor (and acidic) soil, and follow with rye; when grown in succession, these green manures have the added benefit of suppressing weeds.

Start by testing the soil pH to make sure it's not too far from neutral; add limestone to correct extreme acidity or sulfur to correct extreme alkalinity (see Balancing Acidity and Alkalinity, above). Mix into the soil and water if rains are lacking. Wait a few weeks before proceeding, to give the lime or sulfur time to work. (Also, spreading lime and fertilizer causes some of the nitrogen in the fertilizer to evaporate!)

Spread an inch of compost or other well-decomposed organic matter over the area. Also sprinkle the area with an all-purpose, balanced fertilizer; organic fertilizers are great because they contain important micronutrients and release their nutrients slowly. Read the label and don't exceed listed application rates. Mix these into the top 6 to 8 inches of soil. While you can use a garden fork for small areas, a rotary tiller is a great help for larger areas (you may be able to rent one, or to hire someone to rototill for you).

Buckwheat needs warm temperatures, so plant after all danger of frost has passed. Spread seeds evenly over the area; you'll need 3 to 4 ounces for 100 square feet, or 2 to 3 pounds for 1,000 square feet. Rake to cover seeds with soil; if possible, spread a thin layer of straw or grass clippings. Let the buckwheat grow until it just starts to bloom. Till it into the soil and immediately plant another crop of buckwheat. Till the second crop into the soil when you see the first blossoms.

Follow the buckwheat with winter rye, which is hardy enough to be sown in September in cool climates. (You'll need 4 to 6 ounces for 100 square feet, or 3 to 4 pounds for 1,000 square feet.) Turn it under in spring as soon as the soil can be worked; you'll need to wait three to four weeks after turning under before planting anything else. This gives you some time to get your soil tested. After an intensive season of green manures, even very poor soil or subsoil should be capable of growing some vegetables.

Hardpan and compacted soil. If your soil drains poorly even without low spots, you may have a layer of hard clay or compacted soil below the surface, known as hardpan. Sometimes these layers are so dense that roots can't grow through. For small gardens, the best solution is double-digging. Dig a trench the depth of one shovel along one edge of the bed (place removed soil on a tarp for easy moving). Use a garden fork to loosen the soil in the bottom of the trench (you don't have to turn it over; plunge the fork in as deep as you can and wiggle back and forth to break through compacted soil). Dig a second trench alongside the first, turning removed soil into the first empty trench and again loosening soil in the bottom. Continue across the garden, using the soil from the first trench to fill your last trench. For large gardens, the easiest treatment for hardpan is to grow green-manure plants with deep, very tough roots, such as sweet clover and alfalfa. For lawns, invest in a broadfork (or U-bar), a giant version of a garden fork. When soil is barely moist and not wet, drive the fork deeply into the ground and wiggle back and forth; repeat over the whole compacted area. You can greatly improve your chances of preventing hardpan by keeping heavy tractors out of your garden, minimizing use of large tillers, and not driving on lawn when the soil's wet. Avoid working the soil when it's wet (wet soil compacts easily), and encourage earthworms by adding organic matter every year.

Poorly drained (soggy) soils. If water collects in puddles after every rain, you have a drainage problem. It may be caused by a water table close to the surface, a low spot where water collects from surrounding areas, or hardpan. Poorly drained soil stays much colder and so delays planting in spring. The easiest solution is to raise the soil level in your garden beds by at least 4 inches. Use a mix of good-quality topsoil and compost. If your soil has lots of clay or if you suspect compaction or hardpan, double-dig the beds (see above) before spreading the soil-compost mix.

Soil diseases. Microorganisms are not only in the soil; they're also in and on just about everything! Disease-causing microbes (pathogens) are no exception. Fortunately, they have to compete with nonpathogenic microorganisms for food, vitamins, and moisture; when there's a healthy population of beneficial microbes, the pathogens normally lose. Beneficial bacteria produce chemicals that actually inhibit the growth of disease-causing microbes. These wonder compounds are known as antibiotics (penicillin and streptomycin were first obtained from soil organisms).

When double-digging a bed, use a garden fork to loosen the soil in the bottom of the trench before filling with the soil dug from the next trench.

The best way to keep your soil healthy is to keep it stocked with organic matter, as this will keep the beneficial microbes well fed. Trying to sterilize or fumigate the soil with strong chemicals is counterproductive because that will kill everything in the soil, including the beneficial organisms. Don't be preoccupied with disease organisms in the soil. If plant diseases are a problem, contact your local Cooperative Extension Service for a specific remedy that controls the disease without killing off all the life in the soil. The solution may be as simple as mulching to keep soil from splashing onto plant leaves.

Shallow soils. It's easy enough to determine soil depth by digging with an ordinary spade. If you have a lot less than 8 to 12 inches of topsoil, see the section on subsoil above. If you're on ledge and you can dig only a short distance without hitting bedrock, you'd better look for another spot to grow things for the moment. Many roots need to penetrate to a depth of 18–24 inches in search of moisture

and nutrition, and a garden with such a shallow layer of soil dries out rapidly. If you don't mind spending money, the quickest fix is to buy enough good-quality topsoil—or better yet a mix of 1/4 to 1/2 compost and topsoil—to make raised beds.

In the final analysis, it always comes back to organic matter as the universal medicine for improving soils. You can add organic matter in the form of mulch, dig it in as a soil amendment, grow it as green manure, or spread it alongside plants as a sidedressing. Gardening requires a continuous soil-improvement program. It's just part of the overall picture. Once you get in the habit of practicing good soil management, you'll be amazed at what an interesting, rewarding, and sometimes—though not always—easy job it can be.

Starting Seeds Indoors

Ann Reilly

Why Grow Plants From Seed?

In today's busy world, many of us look for the easiest and quickest way to achieve a goal. Buying plants at the nursery is a fast and simple way to get a garden growing. Why bother starting your own plants from seed? There are several reasons you might want to do so.

Each year, seed companies introduce new annuals with larger or more colorful flowers and vegetables with more luscious fruit. You may want to try new perennials from faraway places—or perhaps you have an "old-time" favorite. It's not always possible to find nursery plants of these varieties, and if you want to have them you must grow them from seed.

Growing your own plants from seed is more economical, a serious consideration if you have a large garden.

Some plants do well *only* when grown from seed. These include some annuals, like California poppy, sunflower, sweet pea and nasturtium, and vegetables such as beets, carrots, radishes and peas.

Children may be introduced to gardening by growing their own seedlings. Watching them witness the wonder of "creation" is a reward in itself.

And, finally, there is a certain satisfaction, come July, to look around a thriving garden and know that you were responsible for starting these plants from the very beginning.

Before You Germinate

WHAT IS A SEED?

Seeds are produced by flowers and are the result of the joining of the male and female flower parts. The male part of the flower is known as the *stamen* and is made up of the *anther* and the *filament*. The anthers contain the pollen which is transferred to the female part of the flower, where fertilization takes place. This female part is called the *pistil* and is made up of the *stigma*, the *style*, and the *ovary*.

Continued →

After fertilization (also called pollination) takes place, the seeds grow in the ovary until they ripen and can be harvested. Pollination is achieved by insects, the wind or by hand.

When differences occur naturally within a species, these are known as *varieties*. Those that are man-made are called *cultivars* (which stands for cultivated varieties). *Hybrids* are crosses between selected parents, and improvements of them. When choosing seed, it is important to study hybrids carefully to select the exact flower color or shape and type of vegetable that best suits your preferences and growing conditions.

Hybrids are valued for their increased flowering, uniformity, flower size, productivity or disease resistance. They are more expensive than open-pollinated seeds because of the cost of research and production; many seeds, such as those of petunias and impatiens, are greenhouse produced, and pollination is done by hand.

Since hybrids are crosses between two different parents, it is important not to save seeds from hybrid plants as they will not grow into the same plant and will usually be inferior. Seeds from non-hybrids, however, can be saved and grown the following season.

The outside of the seed is called the *seed coat*; its purpose is to encase the other parts and offer protection. With some seeds, such as lupines, sweet peas and false indigo, the seed coat is very hard and must be softened or nicked for germination to occur.

Inside the seed is the *embryo*, which is a small dormant plant, and the *endosperm*, which is a food source the plant uses during germination and in early stages of growth. The lower part of the embryo becomes the root, the upper part the growing tip, and in the center is (are) the *cotyledon(s)*. Cotyledons are the first signs of growth, although they are not true leaves.

In order for a seed to germinate, it must be mature and viable, and receive the proper combination of moisture, temperature, light and air. When these requirements are met in the proper amount and order, the embryo grows, the seed coat bursts, the roots anchor, and the top begins to develop.

SPECIAL TREATMENTS

Most annuals, vegetables and herbs germinate easily without a lot of fuss; a few, however, need special help. Perennial seeds, in general, need more attention than others. The reasons for this are varied: the seed coat may be too hard, preventing moisture from getting through; the embryo may be dormant; the seed might contain a chemical substance that inhibits germination; or it may need either complete darkness or constant light to germinate. Fortunately there are ways to deal with these various conditions.

Soaking. The soaking of seeds before sowing may be necessary for two reasons: to soften a hard seed coat, and to leach out chemicals that could inhibit germination. Place seeds in hot, but not boiling, water (190°F). For maximum contact of the seeds with the water, place the seeds in a shallow dish and cover them with 2–3 times their depth in water. Soaking for twenty-four hours will usually be long enough, but if instructions or experience dictate that a longer time is necessary, change the water once a day. After the soaking period, sow the seeds immediately and don't let them dry out.

Soaking is also a trick to speed up the termination of slow-to-germinate seeds. The embryo absorbs moisture, which gives the seed a head start on germination.

Scarification. Hard seed coats prevent or slow down the absorption of water and therefore germination. Scarification is the breaking of the seed coat by nicking it with a file, sandpaper or a small scissor. Be careful not to cut too deeply into the seed coat so you don't damage the embryo.

When seeds are too small to be handled, soften the hard seed coat by soaking the seeds in water as described above.

Stratification. Some seeds, particularly perennials, have an immature or dormant embryo when they are harvested. The seeds must be subjected to a moist-cold treatment before they are sown; this process is known as stratification. Lettuce and delphinium seeds become dormant if they are stored at a temperature over 75°F for more than a few weeks and must be chilled in order to germinate.

To stratify, mix the seeds with two to three times their volume in moistened sowing medium and place them either in the freezer or refrigerator.

You could also sow the seeds directly in their sowing flats and place the entire flats in the freezer or refrigerator, but this would take up more room.

Stratification will not work if the seeds are chilled in the packet or in water; seeds treated this way may never germinate. In general, seeds require six weeks to three months to stratify.

Stratification can also be done outdoors, provided your winter temperature drops to at least 40°F. You can sow the seeds either in the ground or in flats; if you do the latter, place the flats in a cold frame or on the north side of the house, away from drying winds and sun. Sink the flats into the ground up to their top. Seeds will germinate in the spring if placed outdoors in the fall. It takes longer this way, but often works better.

WHAT YOU'LL NEED TO GET STARTED

You need seeds, of course, and you'll also need a few more supplies to be successful at starting plants from seed.

Containers. Basically, anything that can hold media and is the right size can be used as a container to germinate seeds. There are many types of containers commercially available that are easy to use and reuse.

Seed-sowing flats should be about 3 to 3 1/2 inches deep and can be of any size, depending on how many seeds you intend to germinate. Generally the ones you buy are made of plastic or fiber. The fiber ones are not as good as the plastic ones since they cannot be sterilized and therefore should not be reused. They also dry out more quickly. On the other hand, their porosity ensures good aeration, so they do have advantages.

Peat pots are good for seeds that resent transplanting, and for larger seeds. These pots are round or square, usually 2 1/2 to 3 inches across, and are a combined germinating-growing-transplanting unit. Seeds are sown directly into the pot, and then later the pot is planted along with the plant. Peat pots are also useful for transplanting seedlings sown in flats.

Peat pellets, the most popular being the Jiffy products, are made of compressed peat. When placed in water they expand into a germination-growing-transplanting unit, similar in idea to the peat pot. They are best for larger, reliably germinating seeds and seeds that resent transplanting.

To keep peat pots and pellets properly watered and protected, place them in a plastic tray or container.

A new germinating method uses what are known as plugs, which are cone- or cylinder-shaped transplants. You can buy plug trays, which may have up to 200 plug holes. The holes are filled with medium, and one seed is sown into each plug. The unit goes from germination to transplanting without disturbing the roots.

You can make your own containers from things lying about the kitchen, such as coffee cans, paper cups, aluminum baking trays, milk or juice containers or plastic food storage containers. Before you use them, wash them well with soap and water and rinse them in a bleach solution (1 ounce or 1/8 cup bleach per 2 gallons water) to prevent diseases that might kill your seedlings.

Containers have two basic requirements in addition to cleanliness. The container should be 3 to 3 1/2 inches deep for proper root development. Less than that and the roots will not have enough room to grow and will dry out too quickly. Deeper containers waste medium and serve no purpose.

Containers must also have excellent drainage. Purchased containers will already have drainage holes in the bottom. If you make your own containers, be sure to punch out some drainage holes in the bottom.

Germinating Media. The best media for germinating seeds are sterile, soilless mixtures of peat or sphagnum moss with vermiculite and/or perlite. You can make these yourself, using from 1/3 to 1/2 sphagnum or peat moss, with the remainder vermiculite or perlite or a combination of the two. Experiment and choose the combination that works best.

The easiest way to obtain your germinating medium is to buy it ready-made. Many are available that are a combination of peat or sphagnum moss with vermiculite and/or perlite and enough fertilizer to get the seedlings off to a good start. This same mix can be used for transplanting and growing in containers.

The "perfect medium" has 50 percent solid material, 25 percent air spaces (in which roots grow and obtain necessary oxygen), and 25 percent moisture. A good mix is light, sterile, and firm but airy. It drains properly, yet retains the right amount of moisture for plant development. It helps eliminate damping-off, reduces the need for constant watching and expert judgment, promotes ideal growth and lets you grow even the most difficult plants from seeds.

ENVIRONMENTAL CONDITIONS

Germination Temperature. Correct temperature is one of the environmental conditions critical for seed germination. While most seeds require temperatures of 70 to 75°F to germinate, some require cooler temperatures.

Although the temperature in the room of a house may be 70°F, the medium in the germinating flat will be lower because it cools down as the surface moisture evaporates. To keep the medium at 70°F or above, gentle bottom heat is recommended. This heat may be obtained from a warm spot, such as on top of the refrigerator, or from a heating cable or heating tray.

Heating cables and trays may be spread out wherever seeds are germinated, whether it be on a windowsill or countertop or under fluorescent lights, with the germinating containers placed on top of them. They will heat flats to 70–75°F. When the flat gets warm enough

(add a thermometer to your equipment list), simply pull the plug. Some have a built-in thermostat which automatically turns the system on and off. Waterproof soil heating cables may also be used in outdoor beds and cold frames.

If seeds are germinated indoors during the heat of summer, room temperatures will probably go high enough so that heating cables and heating trays will not be necessary (unless the house is air conditioned).

When cool temperatures are required, germinate the seeds indoors in an unheated garage, attic, basement or porch which must, of course, have a source of natural or artificial light. Outdoors, this temperature is achieved in early spring or fall. Sow directly into seed beds, or set the flats outside in a spot protected from sun and wind, or in a cold frame.

Moisture and Humidity. Moisture and humidity are also critical. The germinating medium must be kept evenly moist, but never soaking wet. If there is too little moisture, germination will not occur; too much and the seeds will rot. If a good medium is used, watered thoroughly and allowed to drain for several hours before sowing, the moisture level should be "perfect."

It is best to slip your seed flats into plastic bags or cover them with glass until the seeds germinate. This will keep the level of moisture and humidity just right, so the seed flats will not have to be watered often, if at all, before germination. This will eliminate the problems caused by overwatering, forgetfulness, or accidentally dislodging tiny seeds before they germinate.

Light. The final environmental factor, but one equally as important as the others, is light. Some seeds require light to germinate, while others need a complete absence of it to sprout. If light is needed for germination, the solution is not to cover the seeds. If darkness is necessary, cover the seeds completely with medium, unless they are too fine to be covered. In that instance, place the seed flats in total darkness or cover them with a material like newspaper or black plastic to block out the light until germination occurs.

Once germinated, all seedlings need ample light to develop into strong, healthy plants. In fact, seedlings have the highest light intensity requirements of all plants. Using fluorescent lights or growing seedlings in a greenhouse is best, but if you do not have these available, an unshaded south window will do well.

Light is necessary to enable the plants to convert water and carbon dioxide into sugar (its food) in a process known as photosynthesis. If the light intensity is too low, which often happens during the short days of winter or prolonged cloudy periods, the plants will be unhealthy, tall and spindly.

Other Needs. There are a few other supplies needed to make seed germinating successful. *Labels* are very important, for no matter how good your memory is, you can't possibly remember which seed is in what flat, or when it was sown. Heavy white plastic markers are widely used, for they are durable and reusable. You can write on them in pencil, and your markings will stay there until you erase or wash them off. Keep them with your plants after you've moved them into the garden for your own information or in case a friend asks about a certain plant or variety. If you have good success with a variety, you'll want to know what it is so you can grow it again.

Young seedlings have to be watered carefully so they don't become damaged or dislodged. You can either water the plants from the bottom or with a *mister*.

Continued ➔

A *record book* is a last good "extra." If you keep records this year, you'll appreciate being able to double-check next year on what you planted, when, how long it took to germinate, whether you started it too early or too late, and whether you grew too few or too many of a particular plant.

Now that you have everything together, it's time to sow. Read on!

While You Germinate

The type of seed you are going to germinate and grow determines when the seeds should be sown and how they should be handled. *Annuals* are plants that grow, flower, set seed, and complete their life cycle the same year the seeds are sown. *Biennials* have a two-year life cycle; seeds sown this year will flower next year and then set their seeds and die. Most vegetables are annuals and are sown and harvested in the same year. Herbs may be annuals or *perennials*. Most perennials die to the ground each winter and come back each spring, living for varying numbers of years, depending on the genus and/or species.

Annuals are started indoors or in seed beds outdoors, depending on the type of plant. Most are *frost-tender*, and should not be set in place outside until all danger of frost has passed (this date may be determined from your local County Agent). Some annuals are *hardy*, which means they may be sown in early spring as soon as the soil may be worked, and will not be killed by frost.

Vegetables, like annuals, are started either indoors or outdoors in spring, depending on the type of plant and how much time it requires before harvesting. Annual herbs are started like other annuals and vegetables, while perennial herbs are grown like other perennials.

Biennials and perennials are started in spring or summer up to two months before frost so the plants will be of sufficient maturity to be transplanted into their permanent location before cold fall weather sets in. Perennials requiring stratification are often sown outdoors in late fall or early winter for spring germination.

SOWING SEEDS INDOORS

Why start seeds indoors? There are a number of reasons. Many annuals and vegetables have such a long growing season that they won't flower or fruit if they don't get a head start indoors, especially in the north. Others may not need to be started indoors, but will flower or be productive for a much longer time if started early. Plants with fine seeds should be started indoors to protect them from the ravages of weather. Indoor seed starting eliminates worrying about weeds, insects, diseases and excessive heat. When intercropping, you'll make more productive use of your land if you start with plants instead of seeds.

Annuals that must be started indoors include begonia, coleus, geranium, impatiens, lobelia, African marigold, petunia, salpiglossis, salvia, browallia, ornamental pepper, vinca, gerbera, lobelia, monkey flower, cupflower, poor-man's orchid, wishbone flower, pansy and verbena.

While many vegetables are sown directly into the garden bed, others must be started indoors since the growing season, in all but the warmest parts of the country, is not long enough for them to produce. These include broccoli, brussels spouts, cabbage, cauliflower, celery, eggplant, leeks, okra, peppers and tomatoes. Lettuce, onions, and melons are often started indoors as well.

Containers and Media. Start your sowing process by assembling your containers and making sure they are clean and have drainage holes.

If the container is made of fiber or peat, it must be soaked thoroughly before medium is placed in it or it will act as a wick and pull moisture out of the medium later on. Fill the container with water and allow it to absorb all that it can, draining off the rest, or place the flat or pot in a larger container of water until it has absorbed all it can. When the flat is thoroughly moistened, place a layer of stones or gravel in the bottom.

To judge how many seed flats to prepare, use this rule of thumb: A 5 1/2" x 7 1/2" flat will hold 100 seedlings from large seeds, 200 seedlings from medium seeds and 300 seedlings from fine seeds. Always sow about twice as many seeds as the number of plants you want since all of the seeds won't germinate, and some seedlings will be lost in the thinning and transplanting processes.

The container should be filled with premoistened sowing medium to within 1/4 inch of the top. One of two methods may be used to moisten the medium. You can wet the medium in a plastic bag or a pot before placing it into the container (four cups of medium and one and one-half cups of water should be enough for one 5 1/2" x 7 1/2" flat), or put it in the container dry and let it draw up water from the bottom. Do this slowly so the medium won't separate. Dry medium is very difficult to evenly moisten with top watering. Once the medium is moist, make sure it is leveled out and patted down firmly, especially in the corners.

At this point, drench the sowing medium with a solution of benomyl fungicide (1/2 tablespoon per gallon of water) to prevent "damping-off" disease. The medium should be moist but not wet for sowing; if the medium is allowed to drain for approximately 2 hours after moistening and drenching, it should be perfect.

Fiber and peat containers and sowing medium should never be reused for seed sowing, for they may not be sterile. Any leftover medium from previous sowings can be used for transplanting or in containers.

If compressed peat pellets are to be used, soak them in water until they reach full size, which will take only minutes. These peat pellets or small peat pots should be used to sow and grow seeds that don't like to be transplanted later on (see below for a complete list). Sow two to four seeds per pellet or pot in case they don't all germinate; remove all but the strongest seedling as soon as they germinate.

Sowing. Gather together your seeds and double-check to see if they need any special treatment before sowing, such as soaking, scarification or stratification. Check the time required to germinate and grow to the point where they are transplanted outdoors so that seeding is done at the proper time. If a seed is supposed to be started six to eight weeks before planting outdoors, don't start it four weeks or ten weeks before. Immature seedlings started too late will not be large or strong enough to move outside when it's time, and those started too early will be too tall, lanky or mature to transplant well. Seedlings are best transplanted all-green and not in bud or flower.

You may not want to sow all of the seeds in each packet, just in case something goes awry and you have to start all over again.

If you're sowing two types of seed in the same flat, be sure you pick ones that have the same temperature requirements and germinate in approximately the same length of time.

It is best to sow seeds in rows, as it makes transplanting easier, so make depressions the thickness of the seed in the top of the medium with a label or pencil. Very slight depressions are needed for fine seeds and those that need light to germinate, since they must not be covered by the medium.

Write the name of the plant and the date of sowing on a label.

Cut the seed packet open across the top. Sow the seeds as carefully and evenly as you can. You can hold the seed packet in one hand, squeeze it together slightly, and tap it gently with your finger or a pencil. A few seeds should fall out with each tap; if too many come out at one time, they may be separated with a pencil.

As an alternative, crease a piece of paper and transfer the seeds into it. Let the seeds roll out or tap the paper with a pencil. Plastic seed sowers may also be used; these are clear plastic tubes with a hole at one end. Larger seeds may be individually placed by hand; large, flat ones should be sown vertically in the flat to decrease their chances of rotting.

Some seeds, like those of petunias, impatiens, and begonias, are very fine and dusty, and extreme care must be taken that they are evenly spread over the sowing medium. This is the one case where broadcasting rather than sowing in rows might be necessary and more practical.

Be careful when sowing that seeds aren't planted too close together. Seedlings need room for root growth, light and air circulation. In addition, transplanting later on of properly spaced seedlings will be easier and done with less damage.

Very fine seeds, such as snapdragon, petunia, ageratum and begonia, should not be covered with medium after sowing, but merely pressed into the surface of the sowing medium with a pencil, label or a very fine mist from a rubber bulb sprinkler. To germinate, seeds must be in contact with moistened medium, not air. All other seeds, except those that need light to germinate, should be covered with one or two times their thickness with dry sowing medium, and then watered carefully with a fine mist of room temperature water. Rubber bulb sprinklers are recommended because they deliver a fine spray that will not dislodge the seeds.

Seeds that need light to germinate should not be covered with medium but merely pressed into contact with medium. Those seeds that need darkness, as long as they are not fine, should be completely covered with sowing medium. Fine seeds that need darkness to germinate are treated in one of two ways. Either place the flat in a dark spot until germination occurs, or cover the flat with black plastic or some other material to block the light until the seeds have sprouted.

The seed flat is now ready for germination. Place the entire flat into a plastic bag and tie it tightly, or cover the flat with a piece of glass or plastic. Either of these methods will keep the humidity high enough so that the seed flat should not need to be watered before germination, thereby reducing the chance of drowning or dislodging the seeds. When using a plastic bag or sheet, be sure it does not touch the top of the medium. Extra labels or toothpicks set at the corners of the flat will keep the plastic off the medium.

Pelleted Seed. Some very fine seeds, such as petunia, coleus, pinks and snapdragons, are sometimes *pelleted* (coated), to make them easier to handle and space properly. The coating increases their size and protects the seed; generally these seeds germinate more reliably and quickly. Do not cover the pellets when sowing, but merely press them gently into the surface.

Germinating. Once your seed flat is ready, place it in a location where it will receive the proper light and temperature for seed germination. If you have an area in the house, such as a spare room, attic, or basement, where your seed garden would be out of sight and where a water spill or other accident wouldn't cause a problem, so much

the better. If not, you can use the kitchen, den or bedroom—wherever you have the space. If you will be using a windowsill, it's wise to protect it from moisture.

With very few exceptions, seed flats should be placed in good light but not in direct sun while germination is taking place, or under fluorescent lights.

The use of a soil thermometer will ensure that the medium is the right temperature for germinating.

The germination times given in the tables below are average ones and may vary by 25% in either direction, depending on environmental factors. Don't give up too early if your seeds don't germinate. If, however, too much time has gone by, try to figure out what went wrong and start again.

Even though the glass or plastic covering on the seed flat should minimize the need for watering, check the medium once in a while to make sure it isn't drying out.

Condensation on the plastic or glass does not necessarily mean the flat has been overwatered; a change in temperature may cause moisture to form. Feel the medium to be sure. If it is too wet, leave the glass or plastic off for several hours to dry it a little, and then cover it again. Don't, however, let the medium dry out completely at any time.

Once the seeds have started to germinate, remove the plastic or glass from the seed flats. Gradually move the seedlings into full sun or strong light; sudden changes in light may injure tender seedlings.

Germinating Under Lights. If you have the space, germinating seeds under lights is the more productive method. You won't have to worry about short and cloudy days or limited space on windowsills. Light gardens can be situated anywhere as long as electricity is nearby and the temperature is right.

You can purchase one of the many fluorescent lights available for indoor gardens, but since seedlings need light in the blue and green area of the spectrum to grow properly (yellow, orange and red wavelengths promote flowering), you can also use common household cool white lights.

Except for those seeds requiring darkness to germinate, place seedling flats under lights for twenty-four hours per day until germination occurs. After that, the light duration should be cut down to twelve to fourteen hours per day. Once the plants start to grow, the light source should be 3–6 inches above the top of the seedlings. To accomplish this, you'll need a system to either raise the lights or lower the shelves as the plants grow.

If the leaves turn downward or look burned during growth, the lights are too close. If the seedlings are starting to grow tall and spindly, the lights are too far away.

Seedling Care. In the following weeks, how you care for your seedlings is critical. Water, of course, is most important. The root systems of the new seedlings are not yet well developed, so the medium must always be kept moist, but never completely wet, or the seedlings will suffer from poor aeration. If the medium starts to lighten in color, that is a sign that it is drying out. Check every day to see if water is needed. Watering from the bottom is best until the seedlings reach a fairly good size, since watering from above can dislodge young plants or knock them over. If you do water from above, water the medium between the seedling rows.

Continued ➜

Most plants will grow successfully at normal room temperatures of 60–70°F. Those that require cooler germination temperatures will usually like cooler growing temperatures as well.

If seedlings are grown on the windowsill or at the edge of the light garden, they should be turned regularly so they will grow straight and evenly.

Once the first true leaves have developed (the first growth you will see are the cotyledons, which are food storage cells), it is time to start fertilizing. No food is needed prior to this point, since the seedling is using food that was stored in the seed. Use a soluble plant food such as Hyponex, Miracle-Gro, or Peters at one-quarter the label strength when seedlings are small, increasing to one-half the label strength as the plant matures. It is better to fertilize with this weak solution once a week instead of feeding with full-strength solution once a month; growth will be more even and burning of the seedlings will be avoided. When bottom-watering young seedlings, mix the fertilizer into the water; later on, the seedlings can be fertilized from above.

Transplanting. It is possible to plant seedlings directly from the seed flat into the garden, but this is generally not advised. The seedlings should be transplanted to a larger container first or at least thinned so they will not be crowded, leggy, weak or susceptible to damage. One transplanting is usually enough, and will guarantee good, strong root development and easier adjustment of the plant to the garden. Seedlings started in individual pots do not need to be transplanted.

After the seedlings have developed four true leaves, it is time to transplant or thin. If thinning, leave at least 1 inch between seedlings in the flat. Larger seedlings will need more space. These seedlings may now be left to grow until it is time to transplant them into the garden, although they will benefit from transplanting at this point into their own pots.

There's one interesting fact to be aware of when thinning or transplanting seedlings: the weakest seedlings in annual mixtures such as snapdragons and phlox often produce the most unusual colors and types. For a good balance, transplant all seedlings, large and small.

When transplanting, first water the seedlings thoroughly. Peat pots, pellets or small plastic pots are best for transplanting. If the seedlings are being transplanted into peat pots or flats, wet the containers as well, and don't forget to premoisten the medium to be used for transplanting. Seedlings can also be transplanted into flats; those with dividers or compartments lead to more compact root development and easier transplanting, without shock to the roots.

You may use the same medium you used for germinating for transplanting, or use leftover medium from previous seed sowings. It is not critical that medium for transplants be sterile.

Fill the container with pre-moistened medium to just below the top of the container. With a label or pencil, open a hole in the center of the medium, deep and wide enough to fit the seedling's roots.

Using a label, spoon handle, fork, or similar tool, gently lift the seedlings from the flat. Separate them carefully so as not to break any more roots than necessary. A small amount of medium should cling to the seedling's roots. Always handle a seedling by its leaves and NEVER by its stem; if damage is accidentally done, the seedling will grow a new leaf, but never a new stem.

Lower the seedling into the hole you made in the medium, placing it slightly deeper than it was growing in the seed flat, and gently press the medium around the roots. Don't forget to put a label in the container!

Peat pots and pellets should be set into an empty tray or flat to keep them intact and to catch excess water.

Transplants will often droop or wilt because they have lost some of their roots. They will recover quickly if properly cared for. Keep the transplants in good light but not full sun for several days, increasing the light intensity gradually. If you've transplanted during cloudy weather, the containers can go right onto the windowsill; if you grow under lights, the transplants can go under the fluorescents right away. If the plants become tall and spindly later on, they're not getting enough light.

Water when necessary, never allowing the transplants to wilt, and keeping the medium evenly moist but not soaking wet. Once a week, when watering, add soluble fertilizer at one-half the recommended label strength.

Several plants benefit from pinching while in the transplant stage. Single-stemmed plants such as snapdragons, dahlias, and chrysanthemums will be more bushy and colorful if pinched. Those that are getting too tall before the weather is right for outdoor planting should also be pinched. Simply reach into the center of the plant and nip out the growing tip.

Once roots show through the container walls, the plants are ready to be moved to the garden. If it's too early for outdoor planting, they may be held in the container for up to four weeks until the weather is right.

Hardening Off. One week before indoor-grown seedlings are shifted outdoors to the garden, start to harden them off. This process acclimates the soft and tender plants, which have been protected from wind, cool temperatures and strong sun, and gradually gets them used to their new environment.

Move the trays or flats of potted plants outside into a sheltered, shady area such as a porch, cold frame or under a tree or shrub. If it gets cold at night, move them back inside. After two or three days, give them half a day of sun, increasing the exposure gradually to a full day. Make sure the transplants are well watered during this "hardening off" period. If at all possible, don't place transplants on the ground if slugs are a problem in your area.

After You Germinate

After your seeds have germinated and the seedlings are growing strong and healthy, it's time to plant them into the garden.

PLANTING INTO THE GARDEN

Double-check planting dates before you start moving plants outside. Most annuals and vegetables must wait until danger of frost is past to be placed outside; some can go out earlier. Tomatoes, eggplant and peppers should wait a little longer until the ground has completely warmed up.

Plan the garden in advance. Select plants for sun and shade, and check planting distances.

The soil must be well prepared in advance to get the most from your flowers, vegetables or herbs.

Before moving your plants into the garden, water both the ground outside and the transplants. This will cut down on transplanting shock.

It's preferable to do your transplanting on a cloudy day or late in the afternoon so the heat of the sun won't cause excess wilting. If you've used individual peat pots or peat pellets, transplant shock and wilting will be held to a minimum.

Dig a hole about twice the size of the root ball. Set the transplant into the hole so the root ball will be covered by 1/4 inch of soil, and press soil firmly about its roots so there is good contact between the soil and the roots.

Seedlings in peat pellets can be planted as they are. When planting a peat pot, peel whatever you can off the pot before planting so the walls of the pot will not confine the roots. Be sure the peat pot is completely covered with soil so it will not dry out and act as a wick, allowing moisture to escape from around the roots.

If your transplants have been growing in flats that are not compartmentalized, very carefully cut out a root ball with a knife or a trowel. If the transplants have been growing in individual plastic pots or flat compartments, turn them upside down and tap them on the bottom, and they will come out easily.

The newly-set-out plants may look a little sparse at first, but they will grow and fill in quickly, and you won't want them to be overcrowded. Adequate spacing also cuts down on disease.

Water well immediately after transplanting and again every day for about a week until the plants are well established and growing. Some transplants may wilt at first, but misting them every day or shading them will help them to quickly revive.

From this point on, a few simple maintenance practices will ensure a successful garden and a lot of enjoyment.

FROST PROTECTION

If an unexpected late frost occurs after transplanting, you will need to protect your tender seedlings from frost damage. This can be done by placing Styrofoam cups or Hotkaps over the plant when frost threatens and removing them when the temperature warms up.

Seeds That Require Special Treatment

SEEDS THAT NEED LIGHT TO GERMINATE

Achillea species—YARROW; *Ageratum Houstonianum*—FLOSSFLOWER; *Alyssum montanum*—BASKET OF GOLD; *Anethum graveolens*—DILL; *Antirrhinum majus*—SNAPDRAGON; *Aquilegia* species and hybrids—COLUMBINE; *Arabis* species—ROCK CRESS, WALL CRESS; *Begonia* species—BEGONIA; *Brassica oleracea* Acephala—ORNAMENTAL CABBAGE; *Browallia speciosa*—BROWALLIA; *Campanula* species—BELLFLOWER; *Capsicum annuum*—ORNAMENTAL PEPPER; *Chrysanthemum Parthenium*—MATRICARIA, FEVERFEW; *Chrysanthemum x superbum*—SHASTA DAISY; *Coleus x hybridus*—COLEUS; *Coreopsis grandiflora*—TICKSEED; *Doronicum cordatum*—LEOPARD'S-BANE; *Gaillardia x grandiflora*—BLANKET FLOWER; *Gerbera Jamesonii* hybrids—TRANSVAAL DAISY; *Helichrysum bracteatum*—STRAWFLOWER; *Impatiens Walleriana*—IMPATIENS; *Lactuca sativa*—LETTUCE; *Lobularia maritima*—SWEET ALYSSUM; *Lynchis chalcedonica*—MALTESE-CROSS; *Matthiola* species—STOCK; *Moluccella laevis*—BELLS-OF-IRELAND; *Nicotiana alata*—FLOWERING TOBACCO; *Papaver orientale*—ORIENTAL POPPY; *Petunia x hybrida*—PETUNIA; *Platycodon grandiflorus*—BALLOON FLOWER; *Primula*

species except *P. sinensis*—PRIMROSE; *Reseda odorata*—MIGNONETTE; *Salvia* species—SALVIA (Red flowered varieties); *Sanvitalia procumbens*—CREEPING ZINNIA; *Satureja* species—SAVORY; *Tithonia rotundifolia*—MEXICAN SUNFLOWER.

SEEDS THAT NEED DARKNESS TO GERMINATE

Borago officinalis—BORAGE; *Calendula officinalis*—POT MARIGOLD; *Catharanthus roseus*—PERIWINKLE; *Centaurea Cyanus*—BACHELOR'S-BUTTON; *Consolida ambigua*—LARKSPUR; *Coriandrum sativum*—CORIANDER; *Delphinium* species—DELPHINIUM; *Foeniculum* species—FENNEL; *Gazania rigens*—TREASURE FLOWER; *Lathyrus odoratus*—SWEET PEA; *Myosotis* species—FORGET-ME-NOT; *Nemesia strumosa*—NEMESIA; *Papaver* species except *P. orientale*—POPPY; *Phlox* species—PHLOX; *Primula sinensis*—CHINESE PRIMROSE; *Salpiglossis sinuata*—PAINTED-TONGUE; *Schizanthus x wisetonensis*—BUTTERFLY FLOWER, POOR-MAN'S ORCHID; *Tropaeolum majus*—NASTURTIUM; *Verbena* species—VERBENA; *Viola* species—VIOLA, VIOLET, PANSY.

SEEDS THAT REQUIRE SOAKING BEFORE SOWING

Abelmoschus esculentus—OKRA; *Armeria maritima*—THRIFT, SEA PINK; *Asparagus officinalis*—ASPARAGUS; *Hibiscus* species—MALLOW; *Ipomoea* species—MORNING-GLORY and other closely related plants; *Lathyrus latifolius*—PERENNIAL PEA; *Lathyrus odoratus*—SWEET PEA; *Liriope Muscari*—LILYTURF; *Lupinus* species—LUPINES; *Pastinaca sativa*—PARSNIPS; *Petroselinum crispum*—PARSLEY.

SEEDS THAT NEED STRATIFICATION BEFORE SOWING (COLD TREATMENT)

Angelica Archangelica—ANGELICA; *Aquilegia* species and hybrids—COLUMBINE; *Brassica oleracea Acephala*—ORNAMENTAL CABBAGE; *Dicentra spectabilis*—BLEEDING-HEART; *Dictamnus albus*—GAS PLANT; *Helleborus niger*—CHRISTMAS ROSE; *Hemerocallis* hybrids—DAYLILY; *Lavandula angustifolia*—LAVENDER; *Machaeranthera tanacetifolia*—TAHOKA DAISY; *Phlox paniculata*—PHLOX; *Primula* species—PRIMROSE; *Trillium ovatum*—WAKE-ROBIN; *Trollius europaeus*—GLOBEFLOWER; *Viola* species—VIOLA, VIOLET, PANSY.

SEEDS THAT MUST BE SCARIFIED (NICKED OR FILED) BEFORE SOWING

Baptisia australis—WILD BLUE INDIGO, FALSE INDIGO; *Hibiscus* species—MALLOW; *Ipomoea* species—MORNING GLORY and other closely related plants; *Lathyrus* species—PERENNIAL and SWEET PEA; *Lupinus* species—LUPINES.

SEEDS THAT NEED COOL TEMPERATURE (55°F) TO GERMINATE

Aubrieta deltoidea—FALSE ROCK CRESS, PURPLE ROCK CRESS; *Cheiranthus Cheiri*—WALLFLOWER; *Dictamnus albus*—GAS PLANT; *Erigeron* species—MIDSUMMER ASTER, FLEABANE; *Eschscholzia californica*—CALIFORNIA POPPY; *Heuchera sanguinea*—CORALBELLS; *Iberis sempervirens*—CANDYTUFT; *Lathyrus latifolius*—PERENNIAL PEA; *Lathyrus odoratus*—SWEET PEA; *Matricaria recutita*—CHAMOMILE; *Moluccella laevis*—BELLS-OF-IRELAND; *Nemophila Menziesii*—BABY-BLUE-EYES; *Papaver* species—POPPY; *Penstemon* hybrids—BEARD-TONGUE; *Phlox Drummondii*—ANNUAL PHLOX; *Rosmarinus*

Continued ➜

officinalis—ROSEMARY; *Thymus* species—THYME, MOTHER OF THYME.

SEEDS THAT SHOULD BE SOWN AS SOON AS POSSIBLE (THEY ARE NOT LONG-LIVED AND SHOULD NOT BE STORED)

Angelica Archangelica—ANGELICA; *Chrysanthemum coccineum*—PYRETHRUM, PAINTED DAISY; *Delphinium* species—DELPHINIUM; *Dimorphotheca sinuata*—CAPE MARIGOLD; *Geranium sanguineum*—CRANESBILL; *Gerbera Jamesonii* hybrids—TRANSVAAL DAISY; *Kochia scoparia*—BURNING BUSH; *Salvia splendens*—SCARLET SAGE.

HARDY ANNUALS (SEEDS THAT MAY BE SOWN OUTDOORS IN EARLY SPRING AS SOON AS SOIL CAN BE WORKED AND WILL NOT BE AFFECTED BY LATE SPRING FROSTS)

Allium Ampeloprasum—LEEK; *Allium Cepa*—ONION; *Anethum graveolens*—DILL; *Anthriscus Cerefolium*—CHERVIL; *Arctotis* species and hybrids—AFRICAN DAISY; *Beta vulgaris*—BEET, SWISS CHARD; *Borago officinalis*—BORAGE; *Brassica* species—BROCCOLI, BRUSSELS SPROUTS, CABBAGE, CAULIFLOWER, CHINESE CABBAGE, COLLARDS, KALE, KOHLRABI, MUSTARD, TURNIP; *Centaurea Cyanus*—BACHELOR'S-BUTTON, CORNFLOWER; *Consolida ambigua*—LARKSPUR; *Coriandrum sativum*—CORIANDER; *Daucus Carota* var. *sativus*—CARROT; *Eruca vesicaria*—ROCKET; *Eschscholzia californica*—CALIFORNIA POPPY; *Gypsophila* species—BABY'S-BREATH; *Lactuca sativa*—LETTUCE; *Lepidium sativum*—GARDEN CRESS; *Lobularia maritima*—SWEET ALYSSUM; *Machaeranthera tanacetifolia*—TAHOKA DAISY; *Matricaria recutita*—CHAMOMILE; *Mentzelia Lindleyi*—BLAZING STAR; *Moluccella laevis*—BELLS-OF-IRELAND; *Nemophila Menziesii*—BABY-BLUE-EYES; *Origanum Majorana*—MARJORAM; *Pastinaca sativa*—PARSNIPS; *Petroselinum crispum*—PARSLEY; *Phlox Drummondii*—ANNUAL PHLOX; *Pisum sativum*—PEA; *Raphanus sativus*—RADISH; *Reseda odorata*—MIGNONETTE; *Spinacia oleracea*—SPINACH.

SEEDLINGS THAT RESENT TRANSPLANTING (SOW SEEDS WHERE THEY ARE TO GROW OR IN INDIVIDUAL POTS)

Anethum graveolens—DILL; *Anthriscus Cerefolium*—CHERVIL; *Beta vulgaris*—SWISS CHARD, BEET; *Borago officinalis*—BORAGE; *Brassica* species—MUSTARD, RUTABAGA, TURNIP; *Carum Carvi*—CARAWAY; *Coriandrum sativum*—CORIANDER; *Daucus Carota*—CARROT; *Eruca vesicaria*—ROCKET; *Eschscholzia californica*—CALIFORNIA POPPY; *Foeniculum* species—FENNEL; *Lavatera* hybrids—TREE MALLOW; *Linum* species—FLAX; *Lupinus* species—LUPINE; *Nigella damascena*—LOVE-IN-A-MIST; *Papaver* species—POPPY; *Pastinaca sativa*—PARSNIP; *Petroselinum crispum*—PARSLEY; *Phlox Drummondii*—ANNUAL PHLOX; *Pimpinella Anisum*—ANISE; *Pisum sativum*—PEA; *Raphanus sativas*—RADISH; *Reseda odorata*—MIGNONETTE; *Sanvitalia procumbens*—CREEPING ZINNIA; *Sesamum indicum*—SESAME; *Spinacia oleracea*—SPINACH; *Trachymene coerulea*—BLUE LACE FLOWER; *Tropaeolum majus*—NASTURTIUM; *Zea mays*—CORN.

ANNUALS

Species	Germination time in days	Indoor sowing—number of weeks before transplanting outdoors	Outdoor sowing—number of weeks before last frost	Outdoor transplanting—number of weeks before last frost	Planting distance in inches
Ageratum Houstonianum AGERATUM	5–10	6–8	last frost	last frost	9–12
Amaranthus species JOSEPH'S-COAT, LOVE LIES BLEEDING	10–15	3–4	last frost	last frost	12–24
Antirrhinum majus SNAPDRAGON	10–14	6–8	2	last frost	6–8
Arctotis stoechadifolia AFRICAN DAISY	21–35	6–8	4	4	10–12
Begonia semperflorens WAX BEGONIA	15–20	10–12	—	last frost	6–8
Brassica oleracea ORNAMENTAL KALE AND CABBAGE	10–18	6–8	—	first frost in fall	12–15
Browallia speciosa BROWALLIA	14–21	6–8	—	last frost	8–10
Calendula officinalis POT MARIGOLD	10–14	4–6	6	4	10–12
Callistephus chinensis CHINA ASTER	10–14	6–8	last frost	last frost	6–15
Capsicum annuum ORNAMENTAL PEPPER	21–25	6–8	—	last frost	6–8
Catharanthus roseus VINCA, PERIWINKLE	15–20	10–12	—	last frost	8–10
Celosia cristata CELOSIA, COCKSCOMB	10–15	4–6	last frost	last frost	6–12

ANNUALS CONT.

Species	Germination time in days	Indoor sowing—number of weeks before transplanting outdoors	Outdoor sowing—number of weeks before last frost	Outdoor transplanting—number of weeks before last frost	Planting distance in inches
Centaurea Cyanus BACHELOR'S-BUTTON	7–14	4–6	6	4	6–12
Chrysanthemum species ANNUAL CHRYSANTHEMUM	10–18	8–10	last frost	last frost	12–15
Cleome hassleriana SPIDER FLOWER	10–14	4–6	last frost	last frost	24–30
Coleus X hybridus COLEUS	10–15	6–8	—	last frost	10–12
Consolida ambigua LARKSPUR	8–15	6–8	4–6	4–6	12–24
Coreopsis tinctoria CALLIOPSIS	5–10	6–8	last frost	last frost	8–10
Cosmos bipinnatus COSMOS	5–10	5–7	last frost	last frost	9–18
Dahlia hybrids DAHLIA	5–10	4–6	last frost	last frost	6–30
Dianthus species DIANTHUS, PINKS	5–10	8–10	last frost	last frost	6–12
Dimorphotheca sinuata CAPE MARIGOLD	10–15	4–5	last frost	last frost	6–8
Eschscholzia californica CALIFORNIA POPPY	10–12	—	4–6	—	6–8
Euphorbia species ANNUAL POINSETTIA SNOW-ON-THE-MOUNTAIN	10–15	6–8	last frost	last frost	8–12
Gaillardia pulchella BLANKET FLOWER	15–20	4–6	last frost	last frost	8–12
Gazania ringens TREASURE FLOWER	8–14	4–6	last frost	last frost	8–12
Gerbera Jamesonii TRANSVAAL DAISY	15–25	8–10	—	last frost	10–12
Helianthus species SUNFLOWER	10–14	—	last frost	—	24–36
Helichrysum bracteatum STRAWFLOWER	7–10	4–6	last frost	last frost	9–12
Iberis species CANDYTUFT	10–15	6–8	last frost	last frost	6–8
Impatiens Balsamina BALSAM	8–14	6–8	last frost	last frost	10–12
Impatiens Walleriana IMPATIENS	15–20	10–12	—	last frost	8–12
Ipomoea species MORNING-GLORY	5–7	4–6	last frost	last frost	12–15
Kochia scoparia BURNING BUSH	10–15	4–6	last frost	last frost	15–18
Lathyrus odoratus SWEET PEA	20–30	—	6–8	—	12–15
Lavatera hybrids TREE MALLOW	15–20	—	4–6	—	18–24
Lobelia Erinus LOBELIA	15–20	10–12	—	last frost	4–6
Lobularia maritima SWEET ALYSSUM	8–15	4–6	4	2	5–8
Machaeranthera tanacetifolia TAHOKA DAISY	25–30	6–8	4–6	4–6	6–8
Matthiola incana STOCK	7–10	6–8	last frost	last frost	12–15
Mimulus species MONKEY FLOWER	8–12	10–12	—	2	6–8
Mirabilis Jalapa FOUR-O'CLOCK	7–10	4–6	last frost	last frost	12–18
Moluccella laevis BELLS-OF-IRELAND	25–35	—	6–8	—	12–15
Nemesia strumosa NEMESIA	7–14	4–6	last frost	last frost	6–8
Nemophila Menziesii BABY-BLUE-EYES	7–12	—	6–8	—	6–9
Nicotiana alata FLOWERING TOBACCO	10–20	6–8	last frost	last frost	10–12
Nierembergia species CUPFLOWER	15–20	10–12	—	last frost	4–6
Pelargonium X hortorum GERANIUM	5–15	12–15	—	last frost	10–12
Petunia X hybrida PETUNIA	10–12	10–12	—	last frost	10–12
Phlox Drummondii ANNUAL PHLOX	10–15	—	6–8	—	6–8
Portulaca grandiflora ROSE MOSS	10–15	4–6	last frost	last frost	12–15
Reseda odorata MIGNONETTE	5–10	—	4–6	—	10–12
Salpiglossis sinuata PAINTED-TONGUE	15–20	6–8	—	last frost	8–12

Continued →

ANNUALS CONT.

Species	Germination time in days	Indoor sowing—number of weeks before transplanting outdoors	Outdoor sowing—number of weeks before last frost	Outdoor transplanting—number of weeks before last frost	Planting distance in inches
Sanvitalia procumbens CREEPING ZINNIA	10–15	—	last frost	—	5–7
Schizanthus X wisetonensis POOR-MAN'S ORCHID	20–25	10–12	—	last frost	12–15
Tagetes erecta AFRICAN MARIGOLD	5–7	4–6	—	last frost	12–18
Tagetes patula FRENCH MARIGOLD	5–7	4–6	last frost	last frost	6–8
Thunbergia alata BLACK-EYED SUSAN VINE	10–15	6–8	last frost	last frost	10–12
Tithonia rotundifolia MEXICAN SUNFLOWER	5–10	6–8	last frost	last frost	24–30
Torenia Fournieri WISHBONE FLOWER	15–20	10–12	—	last frost	6–8
Tropaeolum majus NASTURTIUM	7–12	—	last frost	—	8–12
Verbena X hybrida VERBENA	20–25	12–14	—	last frost	6–8
Viola X Wittrockiana PANSY	10–20	6–8	—	4–6	4–6
Zinnia elegans ZINNIA	5–7	4–6	last frost	last frost	6–18

PERENNIALS

Species	Germination time in days	Indoor sowing—number of weeks before transplanting outdoors	Outdoor sowing—number of weeks before last frost	Outdoor transplanting—number of weeks before last frost	Planting distance in inches
Achillea species YARROW	10–12	6–8	A	B	12–18
Alcea rosea HOLLYHOCK	10–14	6–8	A	B	18–36
Alyssum montanum BASKET OF GOLD	7–14	6–8	C	B	6–8
Anchusa azurea SUMMER FORGET-ME-NOT	14–21	6–8	A	B	18–30
Chrysanthemum coccineum PYRETHRUM, PAINTED DAISY	20–25	6–8	A	B	10–12
Chrysanthemum X morifolium GARDEN CHRYSANTHEMUM	7–10	6–8	C	F	8–18
Chrysanthemum Parthenium FEVERFEW	10–15	4–6	C	B	6–12
Chrysanthemum X superbum SHASTA DAISY	10–14	4–6	A	B	12–18
Coreopsis grandiflora TICKSEED	20–25	6–8	G	B	12–15
Delphinium species DELPHINIUM	8–15	6–8	A	B	12–24
Dicentra spectabilis BLEEDING HEART	30+	8–10	I	B	24–30
Dictamnus albus GAS PLANT	30–40	6–8	I	B	30–36
Digitalis species FOXGLOVE	15–20	6–8	A	B	15–24
Doronicum cordatum LEOPARD'S-BANE	15–20	6–8	A	B	12–15
Echinacea purpurea PURPLE CONEFLOWER	10–20	6–8	A	B	18–24
Erigeron species MIDSUMMER ASTER	15–20	6–8	D	B	10–12
Gaillardia X grandiflora BLANKET FLOWER	15–20	4–6	C	B	8–15
Geranium sanguineum CRANESBILL	20–40	8–10	C	B	10–12
Geum species AVENS	21–28	6–8	A	B	12–18
Gypsophila species BABY'S-BREATH	10–15	6–8	A	B	18–24
Helleborus niger CHRISTMAS ROSE	14–20	6–8	H	B	12–15
Hemerocallis hybrids DAYLILY	21–50	9–15	D	B	18–36
Heuchera sanguinea CORALBELLS	10–15	6–8	D	B	9–15
Hibiscus Moscheutos MALLOW	15–30	6–8	A	B	24–36
Hosta species PLANTAIN LILY	15–20	6–8	A	B	10–12
Iberis sempervirens CANDYTUFT	16–20	8–10	C	B	6–9
Kniphofia Uvaria RED-HOT-POKER, TRITOMA	10–20	6–8	C	B	18–24
Lathyrus latifolius PERENNIAL PEA	20–30	4–6	C	B	10–12

PERENNIALS CONT.

Species	Germination time in days	Indoor sowing—number of weeks before transplanting outdoors	Outdoor sowing—number of weeks before last frost	Outdoor transplanting—number of weeks before last frost	Planting distance in inches
Liatris species GAY-FEATHER	20–25	6–8	A	B	12–15
Linum species FLAX	20–25	—	A	—	10–12
Liriope Muscari LILYTURF	25–30	8–10	J	B	6–12
Lunaria annua MONEY PLANT	10–14	6–8	C	F	12–15
Lupinus species LUPINE	20–25	6–8	C	B	18–24
Lychnis chalcedonica MALTESE-CROSS	21–25	6–8	A	B	12–15
Lythrum Salicaria LOOSESTRIFE	15–20	6–8	C	B	18–24
Monarda didyma BEE BALM	15–20	4–6	A	B	12–15
Myosotis scorpioides FORGET-ME-NOT	8–14	6–8	I	B	8–12
Oenothera species EVENING PRIMROSE	15–20	6–8	J	B	6–12
Papaver species POPPY	10–15	—	D	—	12–18
Penstemon hybrids BEARD-TONGUE	20–30	8–10	D	B	12–18
Phlox paniculata PHLOX	25–30	8–10	I	B	24–36
Physostegia virginiana FALSE DRAGONHEAD	20–25	6–8	A	B	15–18
Platycodon grandiflorus BALLOON FLOWER	10–15	6–8	A	B	12–18
Polemonium caeruleum JACOB'S LADDER	20–25	6–8	D	B	15–18
Primula species PRIMROSE	21–40	8–10	D	B	6–8
Rudbeckia hirta GLORIOSA DAISY	5–10	4–6	A	B	12–18
Santolina Chamaecyparissus LAVENDER COTTON	15–20	6–8	A	B	18–20
Scabiosa species PINCUSHION FLOWER	10–15	6–8	A	B	10–15
Sedum species STONECROP	15–30	6–8	—	B	6–8
Sempervivum species LIVE-FOREVER	15–30	6–8	—	B	4–8
Senecio species DUSTY-MILLER	10–15	8–10	A	B	8–10
Stokesia laevis STOKES' ASTER	25–30	8–10	A	B	12–15
Thalictrum aquilegifolium MEADOW RUE	15–30	8–10	I	B	12–18
Tradescantia species SPIDERWORT	25–30	8–10	A	B	12–15
Trillium ovatum WAKE-ROBIN	180+	—	I	—	10–12
Trollius europaeus GLOBEFLOWER	50–60+	—	I	—	8–10
Veronica species VERONICA, SPEEDWELL	15–20	6–8	A	B	12–15
Viola species VIOLA, VIOLET	10–20	8–10	G	B	6–8

KEY:

A Sow outdoors from early spring through summer up until two months before first fall frost.

B Plant outdoors from early spring through summer up until two months before first fall frost.

C Sow outdoors in early spring.

D Sow outdoors in fall or early spring.

E Sow outdoors in late spring or early summer.

F Plant outdoors in early to mid spring.

G Sow outdoors in fall or from early spring through summer up until two months before first fall frost.

H Sow outdoors in spring after danger of frost has passed.

I Sow outdoors in fall.

J Sow outdoors in fall, spring or early summer.

Continued ➜

VEGETABLES

Species	Germination time in days	Indoor sowing—number of weeks before transplanting outdoors	Outdoor sowing—number of weeks before last frost	Outdoor transplanting—number of weeks before last frost	Planting distance in inches
Abelmoschus esculentus OKRA	10–14	4–6	last frost	last frost	15–18
Allium Ampeloprasum LEEK	10–14	10–12	—	4–6	6–8
Allium Cepa ONION	10–14	8–10	6–8	4–6	6–8
Apium graveolens CELERY	21–25	10–12	—	last frost	10–12
Asparagus officinalis ASPARAGUS	14–21	12–14	last frost	last frost	12–15
Beta vulgaris SWISS CHARD	7–10	—	4–6	—	6–8
Beta vulgaris BEET	10–14	—	4–6*	—	4–6
Brassica juncea MUSTARD	9–12	—	4–6*	—	6–8
Brassica Napus RUTABAGA	7–10	—	early summer	—	6–8
Brassica oleracea KALE, COLLARDS	10–14	4–6	4–6	4–6	12–15
Brassica oleracea CAULIFLOWER	8–10	5–7	—	2	18–24
Brassica oleracea CABBAGE	10–14	5–7	—	4–6	15–18
Brassica oleracea BRUSSELS SPROUTS	10–14	8–10	early summer	early summer	18–24
Brassica oleracea KOHLRABI	12–15	3–4	4–6	4–6	6–8
Brassica oleracea BROCCOLI	10–14	5–7	—	2	18–24
Brassica Rapa CHINESE CABBAGE	10–14	4–6	early summer	early summer	12–18
Brassica Rapa TURNIP	7–10	—	4–6*	—	4–6
Capsicum annuum PEPPERS	10–12	6–8	—	last frost	18–24
Cicer arietinum CHICK PEA, GARBANZO BEAN	6–10	—	last frost	—	8–12
Cichorium Endivia ENDIVE	7–14	6–8	early summer	early summer	8–12
Cichorium Intybus CHICORY	7–14	4–6	3–5	3–5	6–8
Citrullus lanatus WATERMELON	5–7	3–4	last frost	last frost	24–30
Cucumis Melo MELON	5–7	3–4	last frost	last frost	15–18
Cucumis sativus CUCUMBER	7–10	4–6	last frost	last frost	12–15
Cucurbita species SQUASH, PUMPKIN	7–10	3–4	last frost	last frost	24–48
Cynara Scolymus ARTICHOKE	12–15	6–8	—	last frost	36–48
Daucus Carota CARROT	14–21	—	4–6*	—	2–4
Glycine Max SOYBEAN	12–15	—	last frost	—	4–6
Lactuca sativa LETTUCE, LEAF LETTUCE,	7–10	4–5	4–6*	4–6*	6–12
HEAD	7–10	8–10	4–6	4–6	10–12
Lycopersicon Lycopersicum TOMATO	5–8	5–7	—	last frost	18–24
Pastinaca sativa PARSNIP	21–25	—	6–8	—	3–4
Phaseolus limensis LIMA BEAN	7–10	3–4	last frost	last frost	4–8
Phaseolus vulgaris GREEN BEAN	6–10	—	last frost*	—	3–8
Pisum sativum PEA	7–10	—	6–8*	—	2–3

VEGETABLES CONT.

Species	Germination time in days	Indoor sowing—number of weeks before transplanting outdoors	Outdoor sowing—number of weeks before last frost	Outdoor transplanting—number of weeks before last frost	Planting distance in inches
Raphanus sativus RADISH	4–6	—	6–8*	—	1–2
Solanum Melongena EGGPLANT	10–15	8–10	—	last frost	24–30
Spinacia oleracea SPINACH	8–10	—	6–8*	—	4–6
Tetragonia tetragonioides NEW ZEALAND SPINACH	8–10	4–5	last frost	last frost	15–18
Vigna unguiculata COWPEA	7–10	—	last frost	—	3–4
Zea Mays CORN	5–7	—	last frost	—	10–14

*Make successive sowings or plantings every 2 weeks.

ANNUAL HERBS

Species	Germination time in days	Indoor sowing	Outdoor sowing	Outdoor transplanting	Planting distance
Anethum graveolens DILL	21–25	—	4–6	—	8–12
Anthriscus Cerefolium CHERVIL	7–14	—	4–6	—	8–10
Borago officinalis BORAGE	7–10	—	6–8	—	10–12
Carthamus tinctorius SAFFLOWER	10–14	6–8	last frost	last frost	10–12
Coriandrum sativum CORIANDER	10–14	—	4–6	—	8–10
Cuminum Cyminum CUMIN	10–14	6–8	last frost	last frost	20–24
Eruca vesicaria ROCKET	5–8	—	4–6	—	12–14
Foeniculum species FENNEL	10–14	—	last frost	—	8–12
Matricaria recutita CHAMOMILE	10–12	4–6	4–6	4–6	6–12
Ocimum basilicum BASIL	7–10	6–8	last frost	last frost	10–12
Origanum Majorana MARJORAM	8–14	6–8	4–6	4–6	6–8
Petroselinum crispum PARSLEY	14–21	—	2–4	—	6–8
Pimpinella Anisum ANISE	18–20	—	last frost	—	6–8
Satureja hortensis SUMMER SAVORY	10–15	6–8	—	last frost	8–12
Sesamum indicum SESAME	5–7	—	last frost	—	8–10

PERENNIAL AND BIENNIAL HERBS

Species	Germination time in days	Indoor sowing	Outdoor sowing	Outdoor transplanting	Planting distance
Allium Schoenoprasum CHIVES	10–14	6–8	4–6	4–6	6–8
Angelica Archangelica ANGELICA	21–25	6–8	late fall	4–6	24–36
Artemisia Dracunculus SIBERIAN TARRAGON	20–25	6–8	4–6	2–4	15–18
Carum Carvi CARAWAY	10–14	—	late fall	—	10–12
Hyssopus officinalis HYSSOP	7–10	6–8	4–6	4–6	15–18
Lavandula angustifolia LAVENDER	15–20	6–8	6–8	4–6	10–12
Levisticum officinale LOVAGE	10–14	6–8	late fall	4–6	30–36
Marrubium vulgare HOREHOUND	10–14	—	6–8	—	12–15
Melissa officinalis LEMON BALM	14–16	6–8	4–6	4–6	10–12
Mentha species MINT	12–16	6–8	4–6	4–6	10–12
Nasturtium officinale WATERCRESS	7–10	6–8	4–6	2–4	3–4
Nepeta species CATMINT	7–10	6–8	4–6	4–6	6–15
Poterium Sanguisorba BURNET	8–10	6–8	2–4	2–4	12–15

Continued →

Species	Germination time in days	Indoor sowing—number of weeks before transplanting outdoors	Outdoor sowing—number of weeks before last frost	Outdoor transplanting—number of weeks before last frost	Planting distance in inches
Rosmarinus officinalis ROSEMARY	18–21	6–8	4–6	4–6	12–18
Ruta graveolens RUE	10–14	6–8	4–6	4–6	6–12
Salvia officinalis SAGE	14–21	6–8	4–6	4–6	12–18
Satureja montana WINTER SAVORY	15–20	6–8	—	last frost	12–15
Thymus species THYME	21–30	6–8	4–6	4–6	6–8

NOTE: For some herbs it is not recommended to start plants indoors, but this may nevertheless be accomplished successfully if you sow into individual pots to eliminate transplant shock. Start the seeds indoors 6–8 weeks before transplanting outside.

Gardening in Clay Soil

Sara Pitzer

Illustrations by Alison Kolesar

NUMBER ONE RULE FOR CLAY GARDENERS!

Never Work It Wet!

To understand why not, watch a potter at the wheel. She'll take a lump of wet clay, throw it onto the wheel, wet it some more, then wet her hands before she starts turning. As the pot takes shape, she repeatedly spreads water on it. The water helps firm the clay tighter and tighter, alters its density so that, when heated, it will become solid as a rock.

Although gardening in clay presents serious challenges, clay has its advantages, too. First, clay tends to be fertile. Amish farmers looking for new areas in which to settle favor clay fields because they so often yield productive crops. Also, clay, unlike sandy soil, holds moisture, retains nutrients, and anchors plant roots securely.

Both the benefits and the problems are the result of clay's basic character: it is composed of extra fine particles which stick together tightly. The gardener's challenge is to loosen the mass.

You can have a good garden in clay if you use elbow grease rather than heavy equipment to loosen the clay; if you enrich it and improve its tilth; and if you use long-term strategies to maintain the health of the soil. Use a tiller or turn the earth in beds with a spade and improve the soil with both commercial products and natural materials from your own locale. But number one, you should never work it wet.

Ways to Improve Clay Soil—Inorganic Additives

Once you have stopped working clay soil wet, the next step is to improve the composition and structure of the soil by adding inorganic and organic materials to make it less dense.

The following inorganic additives act as barriers to keep clay loose by getting between the clumps so they can't stick together. My reading and experience suggest that you need to replenish such materials every few years because they gradually disappear from the soil. I've never quite figured out where everything goes. At least not things like sand and ashes.

LIME

Don't ignore the standard advice to take soil tests before beginning your garden to check the pH and to spot mineral or chemical imbalances. Clay tends to be slightly acid and applying a *light* dusting of lime, in the form of ground limestone or dolomite, is standard practice for many gardeners, except those who plant lime-hating plants such as blueberries. In addition to raising the pH of clay to make it less acid, lime makes the clay particles come together in larger clumps, creating looser, less dense soil.

Also, lime releases phosphorus and potash from the soil making it available for your plants. Lime is not actually a fertilizer, but it will help make acid soils more fertile, as well as more neutral in pH.

Of the products available, do not choose quicklime, which will burn and kill plants. Hydrate of lime is safe enough applied according to directions, but it is so fine that rain carries it away from root-level in the soil too quickly for plants to benefit from it. The best choice, ground dolomitic limestone, is sandy to the touch and dissolves slowly.

Dolomitic limestone should be available in any agriculture or garden store. Unlike faster forms of lime, it contains magnesium, a trace element plants need to grow strong. The recommended application for dolomitic limestone is 70 pounds per 1,000 square feet. Add it in the fall or early spring immediately after you have turned the soil, well before planting time. It's important to spread the limestone evenly because it stays where you put it in the soil.

Because it dissolves slowly, ground limestone should be applied only every two or three years once you have the soil in condition.

You should test the soil every year as you start gardening. It may take a couple of years to get the pH properly adjusted, but once adjusted more lime may be unnecessary.

Neutral soil has a pH of 7; fractions above 7 indicate alkaline soils, fractions below 7 indicate acidic soils. For most plants anything in the range from 6 to 8 will be acceptable. Garden vegetables, annuals, grass, and many shrubs prefer a slightly acid soil dipping toward 6. A few plants, such as rosemary, lavender, and clematis appreciate extra lime.

LIME TIP

If a bag of dolomitic limestone gets wet and turns hard as a rock, don't throw it away. With a hammer and a little patience you can turn it back to sandy powder and spread it as before.

GYPSUM

If you don't want to change the pH of your soil, try using gypsum, also known as sulfate of lime. You can add it with an acid mulch if you want to make a place for acid-loving plants such as gardenias, camellias, blueberries, or roses. Like lime, it will help clay form into larger clumps, thus loosening its density. Gypsum is usually applied at the rate of 5 pounds per 100 to 500 square feet.

SAND, VERMICULITE, PERLITE

The main problem with these additives is their expense. Their advantage is that they don't decompose as quickly as organic matter. Once you've added them they're there for a long time. Each of the three, or all in combination, can be helpful, if you can afford them; they help keep clay loose once you've started working on it. However, don't rely on them alone. You already know that without organic matter, clay and sand make a brick. Clay and perlite or vermiculite without organic matter make slightly lighter bricks.

Sand. The best sand to use is coarse, sharp sand with rough edges you can feel. River sand, which is finer and smoother, will tend to stick to the clay—creating just the opposite effect of what you want. Builder's sand is better.

Vermiculite. You won't need a magnifying glass to look at vermiculite, as it contains mica. It is mined and heated to produce large, fluffy granules full of pockets which hold water and air, and thus water-soluble nutrients plants need. Vermiculite comes in several sizes, from a fine grain size the size of coarse sand, to a coarse grain size nearly as large as small pebbles. While the fine grades work well for starting seeds, use a coarse grade if you're adding it to clay. Horticultural-supply houses sell vermiculite in large bags.

Sometimes swimming pool companies can be a good source for low-cost vermiculite. Don't use insulating vermiculite; it may contain mold and mildew preventatives that would damage plant growth as well. In addition to its cost, the main disadvantage of vermiculite is that it works its way to the surface, rather than staying mixed in as sand does.

Perlite. Perlite also tends to float to the top. Perlite is a volcanic material that is heated to make it expand. It has rough edges and holds water well. It's also dusty. To avoid inhaling the fine powder, apply it wet. A sieve works wonders. Put the perlite into the sieve, or any container with holes in the bottom, and run water from a hose over the perlite as you walk over your garden plot. Perlite, like sand, keeps soil loose. Some gardeners, however, find perlite visually unattractive as it remains a stark white against the soil.

OYSTER SHELL

In some coastal areas ground oyster shell is available economically. It adds calcium (important for getting tomatoes to set blossom), gradually sweetens the soil, and, like sand, helps keep clay loose. Oyster shell, like wood ashes, however, would not be appropriate to add to alkaline soils.

WOOD ASHES

Unless you heat a large house with wood, it's hard to generate enough wood ashes. But it's worth some trouble to get them. Ashes provide potash and phosphorus to the garden and their texture helps keep clay loose. The usual application is about 5 to 10 pounds of ashes per 100 square feet of garden, applied well before planting time. Spreading ashes in the fall works well, but most of us need a winter of burning to acquire any significant volume, which means we have to spread them in early spring.

Wood ashes will also help sweeten the soil, though the effect is much slower than with limestone. It's important to keep wood ashes covered and dry until you use them because rain leaches out the nutrients. Also, don't use wood ashes where new seeds are germinating or young plants are just putting out roots, nor should you spread them in areas where acid-loving plants grow.

Ways to Improve Clay Soil—Organic Additives

Because organic additives decompose readily, you have to replenish the soil annually with these materials.

MANURES

Enriching clay soil with organic matter requires a lot of material. For me, discovering the local duck growers was like finding a new wonder of the modern world. For $20 a dump truck load I could get it fresh and hot (and odiferous!) or aged.

Information about the most readily available manures:

Horse manure. We liked duck best, but the Amish neighbors worked wonders with horse manure. They mixed it with lots of straw and let it age in big heaps until it cooled down. The main problem with horse manure, unless you're near a stable, is finding it.

Chicken manure. Although fine where available, chicken manure notoriously burns plants because of its high nitrogen content.

The problem can be compounded if little litter is mixed in. If you use chicken manure, let it age longer than other manures and mix it with something like oak leaves to spread out the nitrogen.

Turkey manure. Turkey manure is replacing duck manure in my locale; I have no personal experience with it yet, but other gardeners report that it's like working with chicken manure.

COMPOST

What gardener doesn't sing the merits of compost? It seems you never have enough, and composting can become an obsession as one strives for finer and richer compost.

You can make compost by piling up garden and kitchen wastes with grass clippings, shredded leaves, and dead houseplants, and keeping it all moist. Eventually you'll produce compost. If you get more artful, you'll probably get your compost sooner. Either way, finished compost mixed with lime or gypsum will do wonders in the initial loosening of your clay.

LEAVES

Shredded leaves, especially oak leaves, decompose into fluffy humus that greatly helps clay. One effective way to use leaves is to mix them with wood ashes (to compensate for the leaves' acidity) and grass clippings (to add nitrogen) and dig everything in while the mixture is still in a coarse, partially decomposed state.

SAWDUST

It takes a lot of sawdust to make a difference, but it's often available by the truckload (usually you have to do the hauling) from sawmills. It's better not to work it into the clay until after the sawdust has decomposed because it takes so much nitrogen from the soil in the decomposition process. If you're in a hurry, you can add blood meal, grass clippings or fresh manure, dig the sawdust in right away, and let everything mellow together for a few weeks.

PEAT MOSS

Peat is the additive you hear about the most because it is commonly available—though expensive—in manageable baled form. It's hard to imagine a gardener who hasn't worked with peat and who doesn't keep some on hand. In theory, peat should create some acidity on your site; in reality it doesn't seem to, especially if you sprinkle in a few wood ashes. Lots of gardeners never use anything else.

There are two main problems in using peat, however. It is hard to wet down, and therefore must be very moist before you work it in, or the bed will never absorb moisture evenly. Furthermore, peat tends to break down rapidly—you have to keep adding more. Recently there's been some concern that heavy use of peat is depleting peat bogs, which has sent horticulturists scurrying for substitutes. However, other producers of peat, especially in Canada, say there is no problem; we have plenty. For the time being it seems reasonable to rely on peat when less expensive local materials aren't available.

ACID/ALKALINE ADDITIVES

To make soil more acidic (lower the pH), add:

       oak leaves

       bark

       coffee grounds

       pine straw or pine needles

       woodchips

To make soil more alkaline (raise the pH), add:

       oyster shell

       dolomitic lime

       wood ashes

Watering Clay Soil

Overhead watering and even rain can make a disaster area of unprotected clay by compacting and crusting the surface so that it gets hard in the sun. Subsequent water then runs off instead of being absorbed. Mulch is part of the answer. Clay soil holds moisture better than sandy soil, and once you have it well mulched you shouldn't have to water except in periods of drought and excessive heat. For one thing, the rain that does come will do more good because the mulch will keep it from running off. The mulch also slows evaporation.

When you do have to water, avoid overhead sprinkling. In addition to the crusting and compacting problems it causes, it wastes water. If you must water, try to set up some sort of drip irrigation. Setting a drip system under the mulch layer is especially effective as the object is to direct water to the roots and soil around the plants and not encourage fungus problems on their leaves or on top of the mulch.

The gardening magazines advertise some effective, though expensive, drip systems. Less costly approaches involve canvas soaker hoses or even something as simple as punching more holes in an already leaky hose and plugging the open end with a cork. Where your object is to keep a particular plant, such as a shrub or tomato plant, well watered, the easiest way may be to pierce a small hole into a couple of plastic gallon jugs and sink them part way into the ground or simply set them near the base of the plant. Then, to water that plant, simply fill the jugs regularly. The water, to which you could easily add fertilizer, will drip slowly into the root area.

Plants Especially Suited for Clay

Here is a general guide for choosing what to plant in clay soil. The bigger the seed and its germinating shoot, the better it probably will do in clay. The thicker and more aggressive plant roots are, the better they will do in clay. The more blunt a root crop is, the better it probably will do in clay.

PLANTS FOR CLAY SOIL

Baptisia alba (white wild indigo)

Chrysanthemum

Coreopsis

Cosmos

Daylily

Echinacea (coneflower)

English ivy

Flowering quince

Lemon balm

Larkspur

Honeysuckle

Marigold

Mint (except Corsican mint)

Mother-of-thyme

Salvia

Sassafras

Sedum (adding sand and small gravel helps)

Snapdragon

Spreading juniper

Stokesia

Yarrow

For example, pole beans do better than haricots verts; mints and chrysanthemums do better than most varieties of thyme; turnips and rutabagas do better than parsnips. Burpee's stubby carrot 'Short 'n Sweet' or Park Seed's round carrot 'Kundulus' will do better than any of the long slender varieties.

When you grow annual and perennial flowers you'll usually do better with local-market varieties that are sold for their vigor than with more delicate choices that thrive in the Pacific mist or along the banks of the British Isles. If you start annuals or perennials from seed, start them in a light propagating mix to transplant outside later.

Among the herbaceous perennials, those described as "invasive" are a good choice. Almost anything that spreads with stoloniferous roots or by creeping along the ground does well in clay.

If you love plants you don't see here, remember that all the work you've put into making your clay friable opens up new possibilities. Take heart from a North Carolina nurseryman who suggests trying anything that takes your fancy, because you never know what you'll be able to get away with until you try.

Gardening in Sandy Soil

C.L. Fornari

Strategies for Success: Using Amendments

Few of us start out with a garden full of perfect loam, but just because we are given a sandbox to garden in does not mean we are powerless to improve it. There are many simple and inexpensive methods you can employ for successful gardening in sandy soil.

SOIL AMENDMENTS

Amending the soil simply means adding what is lacking. What is lacking in sandy soils is something for both water and nutrients to hold on to. The addition of clay or silt to a sandy garden is a soil amendment, and, indeed, rock powders are available to use in this way. Although rock powders improve the soil structure somewhat and provide slow-release nutrients, they are too expensive to be used extensively by most home gardeners. If you have a local source of clay—and are willing to do the back-breaking work of hauling it to your garden—the amendment of sandy soils with clay particles will help improve your soil structure. However, there are easier ways to improve sandy soils.

You can purchase loam, or topsoil, from a garden center or nearby farm to add to your soil. However, when buying topsoil in sandy areas, "buyer beware." Often what is sold as loam in sandy areas is quite sandy itself. Check the loam before you buy it. When it is delivered, be sure to feel the loam *before* it is dumped from the truck. If it feels sandy, why pay for what you already have? Send it back.

Incorporating organic matter is the most common way to amend sandy soils. Organic material is widely available in many forms, and you can purchase it or make it yourself. No matter how it is produced or where it comes from, organic matter acts like a sponge to hold both water and nutrients in the soil. It is also the perfect medium for the many beneficial fungi and bacteria that make a healthy garden soil.

Peat Moss

Gardeners have been amending their soil with peat moss for many years, and it does, indeed, make a fine organic addition to the soil. It is available at any garden center, and is clean and odorless.

There are, however, some important concerns about using peat moss. First, it comes in a dry, compressed state that is difficult to saturate. But a far more serious concern is that the bogs from which peat is derived take centuries to form. By using peat moss in vast quantities we are fast depleting what is virtually a nonrenewable resource.

I feel that the ecological concerns raised by the use of peat moss far outweigh its value as a soil amendment. There are other ways to improve sandy soil—try some of the following suggestions.

WHICH ORGANIC MATTER IS BEST?

Sand requires lots of material to keep the soil structure intact. Keep in mind that the processes that turn organic materials into finished compost continue after the compost is spread in the garden; compost continues to decompose in the ground. It isn't possible to apply organic matter to your sand and be done with it; amending the soil is an ongoing process.

Whether you amend the sand in your garden with composted manure, leaf mold, homemade compost, or seaweed does not make much difference; organic matter is organic matter. It is important, however, that it be inexpensive and easily obtained because then you're likely to put large amounts of it in your garden.

Homemade Compost

Most gardeners find that a combination of organic matter works best. Homemade compost is the first choice: It's free, it's right in your own backyard, and it's made from materials that would otherwise be thrown away, such as kitchen wastes, grass clippings, and leaves. Composting recycles the plant refuse from your own garden and improves your soil in the process.

Manure

You may be able to find someone who can deliver loads of cow manure to your garden. Manure is an excellent amendment for sandy soils, but it should be aged or composted before you apply it—fresh manure can burn the roots of tender plants.

Composted and dehydrated manure is also available by the bag at any garden center and most hardware stores. Although it is more expensive than having a truckload dumped on your property, you'll be able to purchase manure in manageable amounts. Dehydrated or composted manure in bags is easily transported to your garden, and lifting bags from the car to a wheelbarrow is less messy than shoveling manure from a pile!

Other Sources of Soil Amendments

Many towns are now composting the wood chips and leaves that residents drop off at a dump or transfer station. This compost is often available free or for a minimal charge; check with your local municipal waste department to see if compost is available in your area.

Continued ➜

Many garden centers and landscaping firms sell compost along with the usual topsoil and wood chips. Ask to feel any compost before buying it to be sure it has not been mixed with sand in the composting process. Be sure to find out if the compost has been made from industry by-products or processed municipal sewage; the composted sewage products are fine for shrubs, trees, and ornamental gardens, but may not be suitable for vegetable beds.

GREEN AMENDMENTS

There are times when the composting process can take place right in the garden. You can dig green amendments directly into the soil, saving composting time.

Green manure

Late-growing crops such as alfalfa, buckwheat, and annual ryegrass make excellent green amendments in vegetable gardens or large annual flower beds that are tilled every spring. Sow seeds for cover crops after the garden is cleared in the fall, and plow the young plants under in the spring.

Leaves

Fallen leaves make wonderful organic soil amendments. If you're going to use the leaves in the soil of a perennial bed or shrub border, compost them first. A compost of leaves that are partially or fully broken down is called *leaf mold*. Leaves are high in carbon, so leaf molds often need added nitrogen to aid in decomposition.

When dried leaves are added to the soil, nitrogen from the soil helps break down the leaves. Because sandy soils are not naturally high in nitrogen (the nitrogen leaches out quickly), don't add these leaves to a garden where plants are growing; the decaying leaves take nitrogen away from the plants. Gardens that are empty throughout winter can be amended with dried leaves, however, because there are no plants to compete for nitrogen. Rake leaves that fall on your lawn directly onto the vegetable garden or annual flower beds in the fall. Turn them in before a hard frost or as soon as the ground is workable in spring.

Seaweed

Gardeners living near the ocean have an ample supply of green amendments at hand—seaweed. Seaweed is high in nitrogen, so it may be placed right onto the garden as a mulch or dug into the soil.

Fertilizing

Because sandy soils don't hold nutrients, you'll have to be more vigilant about supplementing minerals in a sandy garden. This does not mean that you should use fertilizers with reckless abandon; the overuse of fertilizers is more harmful than using none at all. It's a good idea to have your soil tested by your local extension service to find out exactly what your soil needs.

Nitrogen tends to leach out of soils quickly, and with the frequent watering that your sandy soil requires, it is probably low in nitrogen. Composted cow manure used as a soil amendment will add a small amount of nitrogen, but in most sandy soils manure alone is not enough.

Organic fertilizers are excellent for sandy soils because they release their nutrients into the soil more slowly than do chemical fertilizers. They also add organic matter, and those who garden in sand need all the organic matter they can get! Organic fertilizers can be spread in late fall and again in early spring. As always, read the label and follow directions.

Plants in sandy soil may need a boost from a liquid feed in the midseason of their growth—usually in June, but in hot climates that may be in late April or May. You can make a liquid feed from any of the instant-mix chemical fertilizers available, or from one of the many organic seaweed or fish emulsion products on the market. Again, follow directions, and fertilize *after* your plants have been well watered. Never fertilize a wilted plant.

Mulch

Covering the surface of soil with a layer of mulch is always a good idea, but for those who garden in sand it is essential. Mulch is commonly applied to keep down the weeds, and it certainly does this well. But of more importance to gardeners in sandy soil is the capacity of mulch to hold moisture in the soil. And in retaining moisture, mulch also slows the leaching of nutrients.

There are several materials that can be used for mulch, both synthetic and organic. In general, sandy soils benefit most from the use of organic mulches—they add desperately needed organic matter to the soil as they decompose.

PROBLEMS WITH MULCH

When mulch is applied properly, there are few problems associated with its use. Because sandy soils are often low in nitrogen, the main concern when using mulch is that the decomposition of materials high in carbon takes nitrogen from the soil, leaving sandy soil severely depleted. Solve this problem by applying an organic source of nitrogen to the surface of the soil before you spread the mulch. Cottonseed meal, blood meal, fish emulsion, and a thin layer of grass clippings are all good sources of nitrogen. If you follow a regular fertilizing program, you can let the mulch do its job of suppressing weeds and retaining moisture without worry.

Choosing Plants

It makes good gardening sense to landscape with plants that do well in your soil conditions and in your climate. Although it is possible to grow moisture-loving plants in sandy soils, choose primarily those that will thrive in your augmented sand.

Plan your garden so that you group plants according to their preferences. If you do decide to grow some things that prefer a moister soil, for example, plant them all in one bed to simplify your garden's demands for both soil amendments and watering.

SANDY SOILS AND pH

Because sandy soils are usually acidic, plants that thrive in earth with a low pH are good choices. Ask your Cooperative Extension Service to test your soil. In general, lawns, vegetables, and perennials grow best in neutral soils—that is, those that measure 7 on the pH scale. Because low pH levels limit the availability of nitrogen from organic material, you may have to add nitrogen-yielding sources (such as lime) more often. Test the soil that is in your flower beds, vegetable gardens, and lawns before adding lime (or any other source of nitrogen) to find out if your soil needs it.

If the soil in your area is acidic, choose plants for your home landscape that grow well in this type of soil. Although it is possible to add lime to flower and vegetable beds to maintain a near-neutral pH, it's another story to adjust *all* of the soil around your property. Because the roots of shrubs and trees reach out great distances, you'll do better to use plants that thrive in what is naturally there.

Plants for Sandy Soils

The following plants are tolerant of—or even prefer—sandy soils. This list is by no means exhaustive; check with your Cooperative Extension Service or a local nursery for suggestions of other plants that thrive in your region.

GROUND COVERS AND GRASSES

Latin Name	Common Name
Arctostaphylos Uva-ursi	mealberry
Calluna vulgaris	heather
Chasmanthium latifolium	wild oats
Cotoneaster horizontalis	rock cotoneaster
Deschampsia cespitosa	tufted hair grass
Epimedium x versicolor	barrenwort
Erianthus ravennae	Ravenna grass
Hedera Helix	English ivy
Juniperus chinensis 'Procumbens'	Japanese juniper
Juniperus horizontalis	creeping juniper
Miscanthus sinensis	eulalia
Molinia caerulea	moor grass
Parthenocissus quinquefolia	Virginia creeper
Rosa Wichuraiana	memorial rose
Spartina pectinata	prairie cordgrass
Thymus spp.	thyme
Viola labradorica	Labrador violet

ANNUALS

Latin Name	Common Name
Brachycome iberidifolia	Swan River daisy
Celosia cristata	cockscomb
Cleome hassleriana	spider flower
Coreopsis tinctoria	calliopsis
Cosmos spp.	cosmos
Eschscholzia californica	California poppy
Gaillardia pulchella	blanket flower
Gazania rigens	treasure flower
Gomphrena globosa	globe amaranth
Helianthus annuus	common sunflower
Ipomoea spp.	morning-glory
Pelargonium spp.	geranium
Perilla frutescens 'Crispa'	beefsteak plant

Latin Name	Common Name
Phlox drummondii	annual phlox
Portulaca grandiflora	portulaca
Portulaca oleracea	purslane
Rudbeckia hirta	black-eyed Susan
Sanvitalia procumbens	creeping zinnia
Schizanthus spp.	butterfly flower

PERENNIALS

Latin Name	Common Name
Achillea spp.	yarrow
Ajuga reptans	carpet bugleweed
Anthemis tinctoria	golden marguerite
Arabis spp.	rock cress
Armeria maritima	thrift/sea pink
Artemisia spp.	wormwood
Asclepias tuberosa	butterfly weed
Aster novae-angliae	New England aster
Aster tataricus	Tartarian aster
Aurinia saxatilis	basket-of-gold
Baptisia australis	blue false indigo
Belamcanda chinensis	blackberry lily
Cassia marilandica	wild senna
Chrysanthemum nipponicum	Nippon daisy
Coreopsis grandiflora	tickseed
Coreopsis verticillata	threadleaf coreopsis
Echinacea purpurea	purple coneflower
Echinops spp.	globe thistle
Erica spp.	heath
Eryngium spp.	sea holly
Euphorbia spp.	spurge
Gaillardia grandiflora	blanket flower
Geranium macrorrhizum	bigroot geranium
Gypsophila paniculata	baby's breath
Helianthus spp.	sunflower
Hemerocallis spp.	daylily
Iberis spp.	candytuft
Kniphofia Uvaria	red-hot-poker/torch lily
Lavandula angustifolia	English lavender
Liatris spp.	gayfeather/blazing star
Lychnis chalcedonica	Maltese cross
Lychnis Coronaria	rose campion
Malva moschata	musk mallow
Nepeta cataria	catnip
Oenothera spp.	evening primrose/sundrop
Perovskia atriplicifolia	Russian sage
Phlomis spp.	Jerusalem sage
Phlox subulata	moss phlox

Continued →

Latin Name	Common Name
Potentilla spp.	cinquefoil
Rudbeckia spp.	coneflower
Salvia officinalis	sage
Santolina spp.	santolina
Saponaria ocymoides	soapwort
Sedum spp.	stonecrop/sedum
Sempervivum spp.	house leek
Solidago spp.	goldenrod
Stachys spp.	betony/woundwort
Tradescantia spp.	spiderwort
Verbascum spp.	mullein
Yucca spp.	yucca

SHRUBS AND TREES

Latin Name	Common Name
Acer Ginnala	Amur maple
Amelanchier stolonifera	serviceberry, shadbush
Aralia spinosa	devil's-walking stick
Berberis thunbergii	Japanese barberry
Buddleia alternifolia	butterfly bush
Caragana arborescens	Siberian pea shrub
Chaenomeles speciosa	flowering quince
Cornus racemosa	panicled dogwood
Cotinus Coggygria	smoke tree
Cupressus glabra	smooth-barked cypress
Cytisus spp.	broom
Kolkwitzia amabilis	beautybush
Lavandula spp.	lavender
Ligustrum spp.	privet
Lonicera Morrowii	gray honeysuckle
Myrica pensylvanica	bayberry
Philadelphus coronarius	mock orange
Pinus Banksiana	jack pine
Pinus nigra	Austrian pine
Pinus parviflora	Japanese white pine
Potentilla atrosanguinea	cinquefoil
Potentilla fruticosa	shrubby cinquefoil
Prunus maritima	beach plum
Quercus rubra	red oak
Rhodotypos scandens	jetbead
Rhus spp.	sumac
Rosa rugosa	rugosa rose
Viburnum Lentago	nannyberry
Vitex Agnus-castus	chaste tree

Wide Row Planting

Dick Raymond

Why Wide-Row Planting?

This is a good question. But maybe a better question would be: Why narrow-row planting? Think about it. Is there any good reason to arrange all your vegetables in single file? No one has ever given me a satisfactory answer to this.

Wide-row planting is simply a matter of broadcasting seeds in bands anywhere from ten inches to three or more feet wide. I started experimenting with it many years ago and have been continually amazed and excited by the results. One of the most surprising things I found is that it can actually be easier and involve less work than conventional gardening methods. But there are many other benefits as well, and I'd like to share them with you now.

1. INCREASES YIELD

Just about anyone can grow two to four times as much produce when they start using wide rows. The reason for this is obvious. In a wide-row garden, more square feet of garden space is actually producing food and less is wasted on cultivated areas between rows.

But won't individual plants produce less when they are more crowded? Yes, there will usually be a slight decrease in production *per seed*—perhaps about 25 percent. But since a wide row contains so many more plants than a regular row, there is a big increase in production *per square foot*.

For example, if you compare a single row to a row that is twelve inches wide, you can expect up to three times as much produce per foot from the wide row. With rows that are more than a foot wide, you can sometimes get four or five times as much produce.

Let's look at it another way. A fifty-foot single row of peas might yield about twenty servings. That same length of wide row might yield sixty or more servings. Think of how much less you would have to buy at the store.

2. SAVES TIME

If you try wide-row planting, you will spend much less time weeding and harvesting. This is partly because you have to move around much less. When you bend down to pull weeds or pick peas in a regular row, you can only reach about three feet in either direction. When you bend over a wide row, you have far more growing area right at your fingertips. You can pick or weed the equivalent of nine to fifteen feet of single row without moving.

You can also save some time early in the season. Seeds planted in wide rows do not have to be exactly spaced. Random distances will work just as well. This means that at planting time, you don't have to be quite as careful about distributing the seeds evenly. You can thin them easily after they come up with an ordinary garden rake. I will explain how to do this in a later section.

Plants in a wide row will have to be watered far less, in many cases not at all. This is another time-saver. Once the plants have grown tall enough to shade the ground, moisture will be held there. Any weeds that germinate after the plants are well established will not have much of a chance to grow. The only place they will appear is on the sides of the row.

3. SAVES SPACE

Say, for example, that you would plant a row of onions thirty feet long to have enough to feed your family. To get the same number of onions, you would only have to plant a row ten feet long if the row were one foot wide. If you planted a row that was two feet wide, it would need to be only five feet long. By planting shorter rows you leave yourself space to plant more varieties of vegetables than you could before. This is a big help if your garden space is limited.

4. SAVES MULCHING

A wide row shades the soil beneath it, keeping the soil cool and moist. Last year, during two very dry spells (when all of my neighbors were complaining about watering every day), my wide rows of beets, lettuce, carrots, peas, and beans did very well with no watering at all.

Wind has a strong drying effect on plants. A staked tomato plant that sticks up in the air may take twice as much moisture out of the soil as one which is allowed to run along the ground. The staked plant transpires, or releases more moisture to the atmosphere, because it is more exposed to the winds. Only those plants on the edge of a wide row feel the drying effects of the wind.

Many people like to mulch their gardens, covering the soil with a layer of material, either organic matter such as hay or straw, or a sheet of plastic material. What they are doing is keeping the sun from reaching the soil so that weed seeds do not germinate and water does not evaporate.

In a wide row, you are doing almost the same thing. I like to think of a band of growing foliage as creating what I call a "shade mulch." It's even better because you cut out all the expense and labor of hauling in enormous amounts of mulching material. You may still want to mulch between the rows, so that you have to do no weeding, but in most cases you should never have to mulch between the plants themselves.

5. MAKES HARVESTING EASIER

Some folks think that it is difficult to harvest peas or beans. But in a wide row all you need to do is to take a stool, sit down next to the row (or even *in* the row) set a basket next to you, and gather in a peck or so of produce. When you are finished, you can move up the row, sit down again, and pick another peck. You may miss a few peas or beans this way because there will be so many, but a few ripe pods will enrich your soil if you till the plants back in when they have finished bearing.

The same thing is true of all other wide row crops. Since they produce so much more per foot of row, you can pick a lot more from a single location.

6. PERMITS COOL-WEATHER CROPS IN HEAT

Shading the ground keeps it cooler. Crops such as spinach will "bolt," or go to seed, quite quickly once the weather gets warmer in early summer. A wide row will continue to produce tender green leaves much longer than will a single row.

Anyone who has ever grown spinach knows that it is difficult to raise enough. A single row of spinach one hundred feet long might fill a twenty-pound bag. In a row fourteen inches wide and one hundred feet long you should be able to pick as many as five or six twenty-pound bagsful.

Most gardeners find it impossible to grow what we call English peas in warmer climates because the weather gets too hot and dry for them to do well. I have received many letters from such places as Texas and Hawaii, where people tell me that they are able to grow peas for the first time using the wide-row method. Even here in Vermont peas will not do well in July or August—sometimes not even in September. I find that if I use a variety of Wando, which will stand some heat, I am able to grow peas from early spring until late fall.

7. IMPROVES QUALITY OF CROPS

Soil experts tell me that a crop that grows in an even environment—without being overly moist after a rain and too dry during a sunny spell—will be far superior to one that has been growing under varied conditions. I won't say that vegetables grown in wide rows will be larger than those grown the conventional way. But I can assure you that the texture and consistency of the produce will be greatly improved. Smaller vegetables grown in wide rows will be crisper, tastier, and more moist. They will also be less prone to diseases because they will have less dirt splashed on them by raindrops.

8. REDUCES INSECT DAMAGE

Many good gardeners realized some time ago that healthy plants are less frequently attacked by insects. It is also true that by keeping the soil temperature constant, there is less likelihood of nematodes invading your plants. Wide rows are a lot closer to growing conditions that you find in nature. Somehow non-isolated plants are less attractive to a

Continued ➡

horde of chewing insects and pesty worms. And even if a small section of a row does get infested, there will be more than enough left over for you and your family.

9. MAKES COMPANION PLANTING EASIER

If you decide to adopt wide-row planting, you will see that precise seeding arrangements for companion planting are not necessary. You can spread more than one type of seed in a wide row. It is not complicated at all to plant radishes with just about anything else, or to sow beet or carrot seeds among onions. Carrots and beets will help each other in a wide row. When you pull a small beet or carrot you are automatically cultivating and aerating the soil, as well as leaving a small cavity for the other bulbs or roots to expand into.

10. FREES GARDENER FOR VACATION

Many people like to take a week or so off in the summer for a short vacation. But they worry about leaving their gardens for such a long time. Some hire youngsters to help, or ask neighbors to come in and do some cultivating so that the garden is not overrun with weeds when they come home. With wide rows there is no need to worry; the only place you should have weeds when you return is between the rows.

If you own any kind of good cultivating equipment, cleaning out the weeds between the rows should be no problem at all. You can forget about watering while you are gone too, although if it was very dry while you were away, you might want to give everything a good soaking when you return.

11. KEEPS PLANTS CLEANER

In wide-row planting, little mud splashes up on lettuce, chard, spinach or anything else during a heavy rain.

Cleaner produce is healthier produce. One of the reasons such crops as peas are often grown on brush or wire fences is to keep the plants off the soil. Peas grown in three- to four-foot-wide rows will support themselves, saving the extra time and expense needed to make any kind of supporting trellises. The whole row may sway to one side or the other, with the wind and rain, but only a small portion of the crop, those plants on the edges, will lean over enough to touch the ground.

Head lettuce can be damaged by splashing soil. In a wide row, the only splashing it will receive will be at the edge of the row.

12. MAKES THE GARDEN MORE BEAUTIFUL

The beauty of wide-row planting is a plus that can't be ignored. Wide rows have a full, lush look that is quite striking. Expect to hear voices of surprise from your neighbors, and expressions of pleasure as well, as they see the blocks, bands, and strips of green vegetables that you're growing.

Soil Preparation

Good soil preparation can help you get more out of any garden, but when you use wide rows, it can be especially rewarding. Planting, thinning, cultivating and every other operation related to wide rows is so much easier when you have a loose, loamy soil that is rich in organic matter. And it will help your crops healthier, more nutritious and more productive as well.

Unfortunately, few people are blessed with soil like this to start with. Some of us have clay, some of us have sand, and some seem to have an abundant crop of stones. But with the right preparation, we can garden successfully on any of these and plant wide rows on all of them.

First, if you can get your hands on any sort of organic matter, you should add it to your soil. This might be in the form of grass clippings, compost, leaves, spoiled hay, weed-free manure or any other kind of dead or decaying vegetable matter. This should be tilled or spaded into the soil to a depth of four to six inches. Be sure to do this early enough so that the materials are well-decayed before planting time. It is often best to do this in the fall.

While you are preparing your soil, you should also be thinking about fertilizer. Wide-row planting does not require any special fertilizing techniques, but if it is at all possible, you should take a soil sample and have it tested. This is the best way to insure that your soil has a balanced supply of nutrients. Your County Extension agent can help you with this.

If a soil test is not possible, there is a rule of thumb you can use to determine the approximate amount of fertilizer to apply. Use 1,000 square feet of garden space as a standard area measurement. Spread a ten- or twelve-quart bucket of commercial fertilizer, such as 10-10-10 or 5-10-10, on the area and mix it into the top three inches of soil. If you choose an organic fertilizer, use an equivalent amount; and work it into the soil early in the spring.

A soil test is also the best way to determine whether your soil requires lime. But again, if you are unable to test and you know that your garden has not been limed for several years, you can use the same rule of thumb: A twelve-quart bucket of lime for every 1,000 square feet of garden space. Broadcast the lime over the area and mix it into the top four to six inches of soil. Liming can be done at any time, although fall is usually best because the lime itself will have time to work into the soil before spring.

Before planting, you should have your soil broken up to the point where it is loose and crumbly. When soil reaches this condition, we say that it has "good tilth." You can work the soil by hand, but renting or borrowing some sort of power equipment will save you lots of sweat and possibly a sore back. I use a roto tiller with tines in the rear for all my soil preparation and find it to be the ideal tool for the job. It leaves a mellow, smooth seedbed that requires little, if any, raking.

NOTE: Once you have worked up the soil, be careful not to walk on any of the areas where you will be planting seeds. This is important if you want the best possible results with your wide rows.

Planning the Garden

Before you begin planting, you should sketch out on paper exactly where you are going to plant each vegetable and herb in the garden. As you do this try to keep in mind which crops are hardy and can stand some cold. Be sure the tender crops are set out in full sunlight. Take note of the high spots and low spots in your garden, the places that may be wet, and those that may dry out early. You should also know which plants can stand a lot of moisture and those that do not do well with "wet feet." You know your garden plot better than anyone else, and can judge best how to take advantage of all its little quirks and oddities.

STAKING OUT THE GARDEN

Once your garden is planned on paper, you can begin laying out the rows. For a ten-inch-wide row, you can stake it out very much the same way that you would lay out a single row. Use a string attached to two stakes. Run the string across the garden area, pulling it tight along the ground. Once you have established this straight line, pick up a regular steel garden rake, hold one side of it next to the string, and run it down the length of the garden. This will give you a marked-off band that you can spread the seeds in.

For wider rows, you can use two strings and stretch them out parallel to each other. Then stand on the outside of the strings and rake the area between them. In both cases it is not necessary to rake the entire garden—just the areas within the rows where the seeds will be broadcast.

As you rake the seedbeds, you will also be smoothing and leveling them by removing all the clumps and organic matter that has not yet decomposed.

You'll remember that we plant seeds somewhat thicker in a wide row than we might in a single row. This means, to use peas as an example, that you should sprinkle the seeds about an inch and a half apart in the entire area you have just prepared with the rake.

The same is true of lettuce seeds. Sprinkle them closer together than you might in a narrow row.

Keep in mind that a seed should be planted to a depth that is four times its own diameter. Obviously if you are planting large seeds such as peas, you will want to have a lot more soil over them than you would over small lettuce seeds.

In order to germinate, a seed should come in contact with warm, moist soil on all of its sides. This is why we firm the soil around a newly planted seed by gently packing the earth.

How do we cover seeds in wide rows? Lettuce seed, because it is so small, will need a maximum of a half-inch of covering. After you have sprinkled seeds into the row, tap them gently with the back of a wide hoe or rake so that you press them into the soil a bit. Then, using a hoe or rake, pull some soil from outside the wide row to cover the seed. Level it off carefully with the back of the rake, and firm it down again, so that the seeds are covered with enough firm soil to equal four times their own diameter.

Larger seeds such as peas can be covered the same way. Of course, you will need more soil to cover them. (They will need an inch to an inch and one-quarter of covering.) If you have organically rich soil that does not pack down too much, you might walk on these larger seeds once they have been spread to be sure they have a good contact with the soil. Later you can pull soil from the side of the row, and firm it down with a hoe. All of this is quite easy to do if your soil has been prepared well.

Continued →

CROPS THAT DO WELL IN WIDE ROWS

Here is a list of vegetables and herbs that can be grown in wide rows:

"Small" Seeds

Anise	Kale	Peppermint
Beets	Kohlrabi	Radishes
Caraway	Leeks	Rutabagas
Carrots	Lettuce	Salsify
Chard	Mustard	Spearmint
Chives	Onions	Spinach
Collards	Oregano	Summer Savory
Cress	Parsley	Sweet Marjoram
Dill	Parsnips	Turnips
Endive		

"Larger" Seeds and Transplants

Beans of all kinds

Cabbage

Garlic

Onion Plants (sets)

Peas (English, crowder, field, Southern)

Shallots

Thinning and Weeding a Wide Row

Many people think that thinning a wide row would be difficult, but it is actually one of the simplest operations. First of all, the crops in the " 'Larger' Seeds and Transplants" category in the list above should be properly spaced when planted and should not need to be thinned. Most of the crops in the "Small Seeds" category, however, *will* need to be thinned as soon as they come up. This can be done quickly and easily with an ordinary garden rake. Just drag it across the row so that the teeth dig into the soil about a quarter to half an inch. Don't press down too much, though, or the teeth will dig in too deeply. One thinning should be all you need to do with the rake.

It is very important to do this thinning while the plants are still very small. It may look like a terrible mess at first, but in a few days it will look just fine again and you will have saved countless hours of tedious hand-thinning. At the same time you will have completed your first weeding and cultivation of the row.

After a week or two, your plants will get too large to drag a rake over them, but they still need cultivation. There also needs to be a way to cultivate large-seeded crops such as peas and beans. To do these jobs, I invented a tool I call an In-Row-Weeder®. It is a special kind of rake with long, flexible tines. It is designed so that you can drag it right over a row of established plants without injuring them, yet at the same time it will cultivate the soil and kill all the tiny, sprouting weeds there.

The first few weeks after your crop comes up is the most critical time for weeds in a wide row. If you can keep them under control during this period, you will have it made for the rest of the season. After several cultivations with a tool such as the In-Row-Weeder, most of the weed seeds that are close enough to the surface to germinate will have been killed. Since the In-Row-Weeder disturbs only a thin layer of soil, it doesn't bring up any additional weed seeds from deep in the soil. Remember also that as the wide-row crop gets larger, it will begin to shade the soil and further discourage the weeds.

Once again, the important thing is to get the weeds while they are still very tiny. Once they get too large, you will be forced to do a lot of hand-weeding. Don't wait until you see the weeds before you cultivate within the wide rows.

Harvesting from a Wide Row

Harvesting from a wide row is a simple matter. Just keep picking the largest vegetables whatever they are. Harvest the biggest carrots, the largest beans and so on, and leave the smaller ones so they can continue to grow. This way few vegetables should get overripe, seedy or woody tasting.

When you are harvesting greens, such as spinach, chard and lettuce, don't be too dainty about it. Cut off all the leaves of a plant to within an inch of the ground. It will grow more leaves.

A plant's main purpose is to grow seed so that it can produce another generation. As long as you prevent it from going to seed, it will continue to try. You will be amazed at the number of times you can cut back a leaf crop in a wide row and have it continue to produce. It's the old story. Keep your garden picked and it will continue to grow more. Let it go to seed and it is finished.

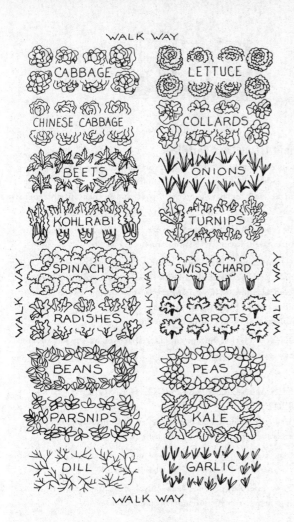

WALK WAY

CABBAGE	LETTUCE
CHINESE CABBAGE	COLLARDS
BEETS	ONIONS
KOHLRABI	TURNIPS
SPINACH	SWISS CHARD
RADISHES	CARROTS
BEANS	PEAS
PARSNIPS	KALE
DILL	GARLIC

WALK WAY

Planning Your Garden Two Seasons Ahead

No good gardener can afford poor planning. Successful and abundant harvests are as much a matter of thinking ahead as they are a question of knowing what you are doing. You should know, for instance, that "legumes"—peas and beans, for example—contribute far more nitrogen to the soil than they take out. Take advantage of their soil-building qualities by planting something like carrots, lettuce or onions in the same space where you had legumes the year before.

You can win the war with weeds, and have a far more lush garden by planning not just for this coming season, but three seasons ahead. One of the greatest joys of gardening happens on those cold winter evenings when you sit down at the kitchen table with a stack of seed catalogs and start choosing your crops, diagramming the garden plot for the next summer, and making plans for succession plantings. Don't be content with short-range goals. If you're really going to get into serious gardening, draw up a long-range "master plan." The key to your plan lies in movable wide-row cover crop strips.

First, divide your garden into lanes that are four to six feet wide. What you should plan to do is rotate cover crops (sometimes called green manure crops) from one of these strips to the next in a three-year cycle. Each time you plant a cover crop in one of the strips you will be accomplishing several things. You will practically eliminate all the weeds; you will add organic matter to the soil; you will add natural fertilizer; and you will break the soil into finer particles so it will be easier to work in the future.

There is nothing wrong with planting an edible cover crop. You may want to buy five or ten pounds of peas and broadcast them into one whole wide-row strip in the early spring. Once the peas have been harvested, till the plants back into the soil where they will add lots of nitrogen. You can do exactly the same thing with beans.

Soy beans are another legume that can be used as a cover crop. They don't need to mature and be harvested for them to do your soil a lot of good. That same year a cover crop of beans, soybeans, or peas can be followed by either a second cover crop or crops that you can store for the winter—carrots, beets, or late broccoli and cauliflower. You could also plant more beans, spinach, lettuce, and best of all, kale. (You should be able to get two wide rows into each six-foot strip.)

If the strip you plant with a cover crop the first year is in a part of the garden that has had a lot of weeds in the past, plant buckwheat a couple of days after you have tilled under the first edible cover crop. This will discourage the weeds and make the soil a whole lot easier to work the following year.

Fine-seed crops such as onions, carrots, spinach, lettuce and dill germinate very slowly. Plant them in a place that is as weedfree as possible. Next year they should grow where the cover crops were planted this year, while the next year's cover crop is moved over to the next strip. The year after next—the third season—large seed plants such as squash, cucumbers, melons, corn, tomatoes and potatoes, should be planted in the first strip (see the diagram). Continue this kind of soil building rotation for as many years as you like.

After the harvest each fall, put a "winter blanket" cover crop over the whole garden (except for your perennials which will need to be covered with mulch). Annual ryegrass is one of the best winter protection cover crops there is. The difference between it and the perennial rye or "winter" variety of rye, is that it will grow lush and green until snow comes, but will be completely dead by spring.

The brown mat of dead grass will protect your soil from any damage caused by continuous freezing and thawing as well as from erosion. It will also allow the microscopic soil life to keep working longer into the cold months. If you plant a perennial grass such as Balboa rye or winter wheat, it will come up again in the spring, and you will have to till it in and let it decompose before you can do any early planting.

Continued →

This is the simplest and best way I know to mulch your garden and at the same time keep using available square feet of space to produce food.

Once you have established some of the patterns for wide row planting that I have suggested, the sky's the limit. There will be no end to the different possibilities and variations that the system offers. There are all kinds of opportunities to be creative. I hope you'll experiment a little. If you do, I'm sure that in a couple of years, there will be a lot you can teach *me* about wide row planting. I hope so. Learning something new about gardening is almost as much fun as growing so many vegetables that I can give some away!

Cover Crop Gardening

Meet the Green Manures

Green manuring—the growing and turning under of crops to fertilize and improve the soil—is an age-old practice that is gaining popularity again.

One reason has been the rising costs of chemical fertilizers.

Even more important is the development of equipment that has made the task of turning under crops an easy one. Once gardeners turned these under with spades. It was hard work, and time-consuming, but many gardeners thought it was worth it, even then. Now the gardener can quickly chop up a crop—and that speeds decomposition—and mix it with the soil, using equipment designed for the job.

But why raise green manures? Why plant cover crops, or catch crops? The answer is simple. All these crops will improve the soil. They add something valuable to it, or prevent something valuable from disappearing.

Green manures add huge amounts of organic material to the soil, cover crops prevent erosion, catch crops prevent the leaching away of nutrients, and all overlap in their contributions.

Let's look more closely at the benefits you can expect from these crops.

Benefit 1. Buy Less Fertilizer

If you are an experienced gardener, you know that you can't have rich, productive soil unless you put something back into it. For many, chemical fertilizers have been the answer, and an increasingly expensive answer.

By growing green manures you can improve the soil and cut your fertilizer needs in half at the same time.

Green manuring is a way to speed up the natural system of creating rich soil. Soil has been built up over the centuries as natural vegetation died and decomposed. By raising crops, then chopping them up and tilling them under, this same process is accelerated, and the benefits to the soil are much more quickly apparent.

The result is that the amount of fertilizer you have to buy and use can be reduced sharply.

GREEN MANURES HELP UNLOCK SOIL NUTRIENTS

Large supplies of nutrients may be locked up in insoluble rocks or minerals. Green manures can help unlock some of this supply.

One way that green manures can make more of these nutrients available is by increasing the activity of microbes in the soil.

These microbes produce weak acids that eat away at soil minerals, causing them to release nutrients for plants to use.

Some green manure crops can extract nutrients from insoluble minerals. Rye, buckwheat, and sweet clover can extract phosphorus from some insoluble minerals. When crops like these are grown in poor soil and turned under, the phosphate they mine from the earth is released to plants grown later in the same area.

514

Benefit 2. Cut Nitrogen Purchases

Nitrogen is one of the most plentiful elements. It's in the air we breathe. Tons of it hang in the air over each acre of our gardens, free for use if we can get it down into the soil.

At the same time, nitrogen bought through commercial channels has shot up in price, because production of it demands use of expensive petroleum products.

There is a way to get this nitrogen free, and in large quantities. You can plant legumes as green manures. Legumes—alfalfa, beans, peas, and vetch are some of them—have the ability to host bacteria that can fix nitrogen in the air. The legume seed is inoculated by coating it with a strain of nitrogen-fixing bacteria suited for the particular legume, then planted. This inoculant is widely available in seed stores. When the seeds sprout and grow, the bacteria enter the developing root hairs, take nitrogen from the air and fix it in nodules on those root hairs.

Alfalfa, the best of the nitrogen-fixing crops, can add as much as 200 pounds of nitrogen per acre. That's the same amount of nitrogen you would get from spreading a ton of 10–10-10 commercial fertilizer on that acre. And think of the extra organic material you are adding to the soil and thus enriching it.

THE FORCE OF A RAINDROP SPLASH

A drop of rain striking bare soil is like an explosion. Small particles of soil splash into the air and scatter in all directions. On bare ground which has poor soil structure, one hard rain can move tons of soil per acre. On a slope, most of this soil will land downhill from its original location, and it can cause even more erosion than flowing water.

Green manures can help this problem in several ways. They shield the soil from the force of a driving rain. The plants absorb the force of the raindrops and the water flows gently into the ground. The roots help hold the soil in place and there is almost no loss to erosion.

Benefit 3. Stop Those Weeds

If weeds are your problem, and you think weeding or poisonous, expensive herbicides are the only answer—read on.

Green manures, particularly buckwheat and ryegrass, are effective against weeds by making the weeds know they're not wanted. You till the soil, preparing it for a planting of a green manure. This exposes thousands of weed seeds that have been waiting for light and warmth to begin growing. And begin to grow they do, but so does that green manure crop, and the green manure

grows so fast that it soon overpowers the weeds and crowds them out. It's that simple.

Peas and beans, broadcast or planted in wide rows, will do this, too, and they have the advantage of providing a crop for your dinner table.

Thus, every time you grow a green manure crop and till it under, you are reducing the number of weed seeds in your soil. A few such crops and the weeds will no longer be a problem.

Benefit 4. Improve Your Soil Structure

Pick up a handful of good soil. It is soft, dark and has a spongy "give." Smell it. Not unpleasant at all. Rich.

Examine it closely. Notice how it separates into small granules. These are called "aggregates" and explain the soil's looseness. Clay particles, microscopic in size, fit together very tightly, leaving little space for air, water or roots. When the soil is well aggregated, these clay particles are molded into rounded granules that have spaces between them. They fit together loosely like a pile of pebbles rather than tightly like bricks. Water and roots can penetrate those spaces between the granules.

Green manures play a big role in the formation of these granules. First the plants protect them from being shattered by raindrops. When the crop is turned under, the micro-organism population is increased many fold. And it is this population that produces polysaccharides, the glue that holds together the material in each aggregate. A good green manure can produce several thousands of pounds per acre of this glue.

HIDDEN BENEFITS

A gardener sees only the leaves and stems of the green manure crop, and this vegetation is only part of the plant's contribution to the soil. Don't forget the root system.

Few realize how large a root system can be. A scientist grew a single rye plant in a box for four months, then measured the roots. His findings were almost unbelievable—nearly 14 million roots with a combined length of 387 miles. This means roots reaching down, loosening soil, and bringing up minerals. It means, too, hundreds of pounds of organic material decaying in the soil.

Benefit 5. Increase the Life In Your Soil

By turning under lush green manure crops, you can create conditions so that the millions of organisms in your soil will flourish.

And the list of jobs they will do for you is tremendous:

- They decompose organic matter in the soil and release nutrients that plants can use.

- They create humus, organic matter that helps the soil to hold water and retain nutrients.

Continued →

- They help dissolve nutrients tied up in the insoluble minerals of the soil.
- Some of them even take nitrogen from the air and make it available to your crops.

HELP THE EARTHWORMS HELP YOU

The green manure gardener provides ideal conditions for earthworms. He offers them food in large amounts as he tills under those green manure crops. He gives them protection, too, a cool, protected soil in the summer, and insulation during the fall, when a sudden frost across bare ground would kill them before they could move deep into the earth.

What does the gardener get from them for this food and protection?

More than he gives. Earthworms will increase in numbers. They will eat and eat, and pass more than 50 tons of materials per acre through their systems.

The product of this is castings, and compared with topsoil, castings are exceedingly rich, containing twice the calcium, 2 1/2 times the magnesium, five times the nitrates, seven times the phosphorus and eleven times the potassium of topsoil.

Benefit 6. Save Time and Energy

Composting and green manuring are alike in that both are excellent ways to improve the soil in your garden. And the greatest difference between them is the amount of work required to achieve this.

Composting is one of the most valuable tools of the gardener, providing him with rich and nutritious food for his garden. But it is hard work. You must select a site and build an enclosure. You must find the proper materials to compost, providing a source of carbon as well as a source of nitrogen, on a ratio of about 15 to 30 parts of carbon to one part of nitrogen. The pile must be built up, and should be turned several times.

Compare this with green manuring. The seed bed is prepared, the seeds are sown and covered, then the gardener waits until the crop has grown. He turns it under, an easy task with tractor-drawn disks and plows, or rear-tined rotary tillers.

The only carrying involved was carrying that seed to the garden. In composting, materials must be carried to the pile, and the compost carried to the garden and spread.

Green manuring provides uncounted pounds of inexpensive organic material, and it grows right where you need it.

Think of green manuring as a way of composting on a large scale. Instead of making piles of compost, you are turning your whole garden into an efficient compost pile.

Benefit 7. Stop Wasting Nutrients

When the growing season is over, a lot of nutrients are left in the soil. What will happen to them?

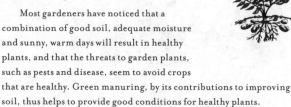

Some, of course, will remain in the soil until next season. But much of that goodness may be leached away and lost.

To avoid this loss, plant green manures, and this time call them catch crops, to underscore their ability to catch and hold nutrients that might otherwise leach out of the soil, or cover crops, if they are left over the winter.

This approach is particularly valuable in the south, where soil life stays active all winter, breaking down organic matter and releasing nutrients. In such areas of mild winters with heavy rainfall, nutrients that would be lost can be caught and held until needed.

Planting these crops is a way to store safely over the winter the soil nutrients, because they can't be lost while they are a part of growing plants or undecayed plant material.

Benefit 8. Growing Healthier Plants

Here's the real reason for any activity in the garden—to grow healthier plants that produce the tastiest crops.

Most gardeners have noticed that a combination of good soil, adequate moisture and sunny, warm days will result in healthy plants, and that the threats to garden plants, such as pests and disease, seem to avoid crops that are healthy. Green manuring, by its contributions to improving soil, thus helps to provide good conditions for healthy plants.

Green manures seem to contribute even more. They seem to suppress plant diseases carried in the soil, doing this by encouraging the beneficial soil life. Diseases develop when the balance of power is upset and the disease organisms outnumber and overpower the good organisms. By growing a green manure crop and turning it under, we can often increase the beneficial organisms so they regain control. Potato scab and snap bean root rot are examples of diseases that can be eliminated with the right green manures.

Benefit 9. Improves Soil's Ability to Hold Water

The gardening books say that most crops should have "moist but well-drained soil." Fine, but what do you do if your soil is sandy, and so dries out quickly, or if it is clay and crusts when drying?

The answer: Green manures...

In the sandy soils the green manures turned under will increase the amount of organic matter in the soil and greatly increase its ability to hold water. With clay, the soil structure will be improved by the green manures, enabling the water to soak in much more readily.

Compacted subsoil called hardpan may prevent water from draining down through or from working back up to the surface by capillary action. Grow a crop with strong, deep taproots, such as alfalfa or clover. These taproots penetrate into the subsoils and loosen them. When the crops are turned under, the roots decay, leaving columns through which water will travel.

GROW YOUR OWN MULCH

Don't overlook the possibility of cutting a green manure crop and using it as mulch in another part of your garden.

By doing so you can transfer benefits of the green manure crop immediately to that part of the garden where you are growing food crops.

The mulch will conserve moisture, smother weeds, encourage soil life, improve soil structure, and prevent erosion.

Benefit 10. Make Your Garden More Attractive

Vegetable gardens can be a pleasure to view in the summer, and an eyesore in the fall.

You can change that by growing green manures.

Most gardens, after the crops have been collected, have a bare and desolate look. Some are a mass of blackened squash vines, posts on which tired tomato plants still cling, and weeds in unlikely patches.

Others are bare, with the gardener having raked and removed the trash, and left the soil exposed to the erosive blasts of winter.

Then there's the garden that is soft with a thick mat of green. It belongs to the green manure gardener. You'll notice some patches which are green are higher than others. That's because he doesn't wait to plant his whole garden with green manures, but fits them in when and where he can. He will harvest a row of vegetables, and quickly spread seed. Or he may even plant between rows while the crops are still growing.

Gardeners in the north can have a green garden right up to the first snow by planting a crop such as annual ryegrass. A heavy, rich growth will appear in only a few weeks.

Southern gardeners have a much bigger variety from which to choose. Crimson clover and blue lupine are two good selections. Vetch, field peas, annual sweet clover and bur clover are others. In both the north and south, a wide band of kale can be grown to provide a contrast, and to offer good eating for many months.

CROPS

SPRING AND SUMMER SEEDING	Seeding Rate (Pounds Per Acre)	Seeding Rate (lbs./1000 sq.ft.)	Depth to Cover Seed (in.)	Adapted to Soils of Low Fertility	Areas of U.S. Where Best Adapted	Comments
Legumes						
Alfalfa	20	1	1/2	—	all	Has deep roots and is excellent for mulch. Needs a pH of 6 or higher. Should grow a full season.
Beans, Snap	—	15	1 1/2	*	all	Broadcast in wide rows. Harvest before turning under.
Beans, Soy	90	5	1 1/2	*	all	Can be turned under early or be allowed to mature and be harvested.
Clover, Alsike	10	1/2	1/2	—	North	Good for areas too wet or acid for red clover.
Clover, Red	10	1/2	1/2	—	North & Central	Needs a pH of 6 or higher. Should grow a full season. Can be cut for mulch.
Clover, White	10	1/2	1/2	—	all	Needs a pH of 6 or higher. The giant variety, Ladino, is best for green manure.
Cowpeas	90	5	1.1/2	*	South & Central	Fast-growing crop for hot, dry, weather. Drought resistant.
Hairy Indigo	10	1/2	1/2	*	Deep South	Needs warm, well-drained soil. Highly resistant to root-knot nematode.

Continued ➜

SPRING AND SUMMER SEEDING	Seeding Rate (Pounds Per Acre)	Seeding Rate (lbs./1000 sq.-ft.)	Depth to Cover Seed (in.)	Adapted to Soils of Low Fertility	Areas of U.S. Where Best Adapted	Comments
Legumes						
Lespedeza	25	1	1/2	*	South	Good for restoring poor, eroded, acid soil.
Sweet clover, white	15	1/2	1/2	*	all	Needs a pH of 6 to 7. Should grow a full season. Has strong, deep taproot.
Sweet clover, yellow	15	1/2	1/2	*	all	Similar to white variety but does better under dry conditions.
Nonlegumes						
Buckwheat	75	2	1/4	*	all	Fast-growing warm-season crop. Grows in most any soil and can smother weeds.
Millet, Pearl	30	1	1/2	*	all	Fast-growing warm-season crop. Good for smothering weeds.
Sudan Grass	35	1	3/4	—	all	Makes rapid, vigorous growth during the hottest part of the summer.

LATE SUMMER AND FALL SEEDING

	Seeding Rate (Pounds Per Acre)	Seeding Rate (lbs./1000 sq.-ft.)	Depth to Cover Seed (in.)	Adapted to Soils of Low Fertility	Areas of U.S. Where Best Adapted	Comments
Legumes						
Bur Clover	30	1	1/2	—	South	Will re-establish itself each fall if allowed to go to seed every five years.
Crimson Clover	30	1	1/2	—	South & Central	One of the best winter annuals from New Jersey southward.
Lupine, Blue	100	2 1/2	1	—	Gulf Coast	Most widely used of the lupines. Needs moderate fertility.
Lupine, White	150	4	1	—	Deep South	The most winter-hardy lupine. Needs neutral, fairly fertile soil.
Lupine, Yellow	80	2	1	*	Florida	Least winter-hardy of lupines. Does well on moderately acid, infertile soil.
Pea, Field	90	5	1 1/2	*	South	Needs well-drained soil with pH above 5.5. Can be spring-planted in the North.
Sweet clover, Yellow Annual (Sourclover)	15	1/2	1/2	*	South	A good winter annual for the Southwest. Needs a pH of at least 6.
Vetch, Common	60	2	3/4	—	South	Less winter-hardy than hairy vetch and less suitable for sandy soil.
Vetch, Hairy	40	1 1/2	3/4	—	all	The most winter-hardy vetch and the best for most situations.
Vetch, Hungarian	60	2	3/4	—	South	Better adapted to heavy, poorly-drained soils than other vetches.
Vetch, Purple	60	2	3/4	—	Gulf Coast	Least winter-hardy but produces more green material than other vetches.

SPRING AND SUMMER SEEDING	Seeding Rate (Pounds Per Acre)	Seeding Rate (lbs./1000 sq. ft.)	Depth to Cover Seed (in.)	Adapted to Soils of Low Fertility	Areas of U.S. Where Best Adapted	Comments
Nonlegumes						
Barley	100	2 1/2	3/4	—	all	Prefers pH 7 to 8. Spring varieties must be used in the North.
Bromegrass, Smooth	30	1	1/2	—	North	A fibrous root system and cold-hardiness make this a good winter cover crop.
Kale	15	1/2	1/2	—	all	Plant in late summer and it will grow on into the winter. Can be eaten anytime.
Oats	100	2 1/2	1	—	all	Tolerates a wide pH range. Not good on heavy clay. Spring varieties must be used in the North.
Rye	100	2 1/2	3/4	*	all	Winter rye is the most hardy of the small grains and a very important winter cover crop.
Ryegrass, Annual	35	1	3/4	*	all	One of the best winter cover crops. Grows rapidly in the fall. Dies before spring in the North and is easy to till under.
Wheat	100	2 1/2	3/4	—	all	Prefers pH 7 to 8.5 and fertile soil. Winter variety is very cold-hardy.

Green Manuring Methods

Use your imagination in planting green manures and cover crops. There's sure to be a crop that will fit into your situation. If you have lots of room and good tilling equipment, you have a greater choice of approaches, but there are possibilities for even the smallest areas. Here are three basic methods for green manuring. Try them, experiment a bit, and find out what works best for you.

A. ROTATION

For a two-year rotation divide your garden into two plots. Plant garden crops in one, and manures for the entire season in the other. Switch uses of the two plots the next year. A three-year rotation works the same way except that only one-third of the garden is planted to green manures each year. Either way, perennials such as asparagus and berries are kept in a separate part of the garden.

B. WINTER COVER CROP

Winter cover crops protect the soil from erosion and temperature extremes, and add organic matter when they are turned under in the spring.

Annual ryegrass is good in the north for space where you will plant early crops the following spring. Hairy vetch, kale and winter rye will resume growth in the spring, so plant where later crops, such as corn, squash and melons, will be planted. Choices in the South include

Continued →

crimson clover, bur clover, yellow sweet clover, vetch, field peas, lupine, rye, oats, barley, and wheat.

C. SPOT PLANTING

When there's a bare spot in your garden, fill it with a green manure, possibly an edible one such as beans or peas. In the fall, after the last cultivation, plant between the rows. Cowpeas, buckwheat, and ryegrass are fast-growing and quickly fill vacant spots.

How to Plant Them

1. PREPARE SOIL

Turn under crop residues and weeds, and let them decompose. Rototill soil to fine texture. Add fertilizer and lime if they are needed.

2. SOW SEED

Broadcast by hand. See chart to determine amount of seed needed.

3. COVER SEED

Rake it in, or go over area with rear-mounted rotary tiller set at a very shallow depth. Roll it or simply walk on seedbed.

4. WATER IF DRY

If weather is hot and dry, water the plot so the seeds are moist until they put down roots.

SOIL TEST RECOMMENDED

Does your soil need fertilizing before you plant green manures? Is it too acid? A soil test will give you the answers. It is available through the Cooperative Extension Service as well as from private laboratories. It's either free or inexpensive, and can result in better crops.

When to Turn Under a Green Manure

Here are some guidelines for determining when green manures should be turned under, to get maximum benefit from them.

One rule is: Don't let them go to seed. A crop of buckwheat is an excellent soil conditioner, but if it is permitted to go to seed, and that buckwheat comes up again in a vegetable crop, suddenly the buckwheat looks and acts suspiciously like a weed, since it is a plant growing where it is not wanted.

Another rule is to plant a vegetable crop soon after turning under the green manure. In that way you avoid loss of the nutrients.

Are you trying to add minerals to your soil? Then turn under the crop while it is still fairly young, green and succulent. The acids produced as the green material rots will free locked-up soil nutrients. The soil will be ready for planting in as little as two weeks.

Do you want to build up the organic material in your soil? Then let the crop mature. The woody material will last in the soil much longer, and assist you to increase the humus in the soil. If you do this, you should wait six or eight weeks before planting another crop.

How to Turn Them Under

You can use any method that will chop up the green manure crop, then get it down into the soil where you want those nutrients to be. Choose the one that best meets your needs.

BY HAND

If you are energetic, or if your garden is fairly small, turning by hand works well. Use a shovel or spading fork. The job is easier if you cut the crop first with a power mower or a scythe.

WITH A TRACTOR

The crop can be disked or plowed into the soil if you have a tractor, or you can hire someone to do it for you. This method can be used for several acres. Tractors tend to compact garden soil.

A FRONT-END TILLER?

Front-end tillers, designed to cultivate the soil between rows, aren't good for this job since they won't dig through a heavy plant cover into the ground. Also, the tines tangle.

The Best Tool for Green Manuring

A rear-mounted rotary tiller is ideally suited for turning under a green manure crop in either a large or small garden.

The forward motion of the tiller is controlled by the wheels so it takes little effort to operate.

Since the tines turn many times faster than the wheels, tangling is not a major problem. Crops that are two or more feet high can be tilled under in just a few passes.

A rotary tiller is better than a plow for turning under green manures. A plow slices off a long strip of earth and turns it upside down or on its side. This leaves the vegetation in a mass, not mixed with the soil.

A rear-mounted tiller chops up the plants and mixes the material with the topsoil, together with plenty of air. Since the organic matter is more uniformly distributed through the soil this way, it will decay and release its nutrients much more quickly.

The tiller can handle small sections of the garden that would be difficult to get at with larger equipment. Also it is light enough so that soil compaction is no problem.

From beginning to end, each step of a good green manuring program is made more easy by the tiller.

It is good for preparing the seedbed, since it leaves a smooth surface, ideal for sowing seed. By setting the tiller to a shallow depth, it will cover those seeds.

Finally, its big job comes when it is time to till under those green manures.

Buckwheat

A FAST-GROWING CROP FOR POOR OR WEEDY SOIL

It's hard to beat buckwheat as a green manure that answers many requirements. It will grow in wet or dry areas. It can be planted in soils from which almost all nutrients have been depleted, and, while the crop won't be outstanding, it will start the soil back to a more healthy state. Buckwheat is especially good for loosening up tough sod and discouraging weeds in a new garden area.

Wait until after the last spring frost before planting it. You'll see it emerge a few days after planting. Within a week it will begin to shade the soil. It comes up so quickly weeds don't get a chance to get started. It will even smother out quackgrass, if the quackgrass is tilled thoroughly before the buckwheat is planted.

Give the buckwheat a full season and it will prepare a new garden site for you. Till the area in the spring, then plant

the buckwheat. Wait until it blossoms, then till it under. Wait about three days, then plant a second crop. When this blossoms, then till it under. Wait about three days, then plant a second crop. When this blossoms, till it under and plant an annual ryegrass. The next season you will have an ideal garden site.

Or you can let that second crop of buckwheat reach maturity, then mow it. The seeds will germinate and grow the following spring. Till the crop under when you wish to use the space.

Ryegrass

ONE OF THE BEST CROPS FOR WINTER PROTECTION

The most versatile of the winter cover crops is annual ryegrass. It grows fast in home gardens when planted after garden crops are harvested and will keep growing until the cold of winter hits it. While it is killed by extreme cold, the

grass forms a heavy mat that will continue to protect and insulate the soil. By spring it can be tilled under in time to plant early crops such as peas.

Get the annual variety of ryegrass rather than the perennial variety which is longer lived but doesn't grow as rapidly. Also, don't confuse ryegrass with rye, which is a grain. Both have their places among the green manures, and winter rye will be discussed later.

Don't delay too long in the fall before planting the ryegrass cover crop, since you want it to have good growth before being killed by the

cold. Garden residues should be turned under soon after the crops are harvested, and while those residues are still green. Plant ryegrass between the rows of late-bearing crops, such as those in the cabbage family, or carrots.

Consider using annual ryegrass among your perennial garden crops. It can help in many ways, such as adding humus to the soil and cutting back on the weeding you must do. One way to try this is to plant it in your asparagus bed after the last harvest. The thick growth will eliminate the need for weeding for the rest of the summer. The ryegrass will die in the winter and will not interfere with the asparagus shoots that come up the following spring.

The Legumes

Remember: Legumes will increase the amount of nitrogen in your soil. A special kind of bacteria, rhizobia, lives in nodules on their roots and can take this plant nutrient out of the air and fix it in a form that plants can use. Peas, beans, alfalfa, clover, and vetch are some of the well-known legumes.

Nitrogen will be fixed only if the right bacteria are in the soil. Make sure they're there by coating them on the seed in the form of an inoculant. These inoculants are available in most seed stores, and are bought as black powders that are mixed with water. Be sure to get the right one for the crop that you are planting. For example, all soy beans are inoculated with one type of rhizobia, while another type is associated with most of the clovers.

Continued →

ALFALFA

Alfalfa is a high-protein forage crop to consider if you use rotation plans for green manures. It is a perennial that can add much to your soil, and it should be allowed to grow for at least a year before being turned under. This pays off, because a year-old growth of alfalfa can supply up to 200 pounds of nitrogen as well as tons of organic material per acre, when it is turned under. Many gardeners cut it while it is growing, and use the cuttings for mulch elsewhere in the garden. This makes excellent mulch, and provides nitrogen to the soil as it decays.

Alfalfa has a high proportion of root growth, with those roots reaching as much as thirty feet down into well-drained soils. The roots mine nutrients from the subsoil, and make alfalfa very drought-resistant because they can draw moisture from great depths. When the crop is turned under, these roots add a wealth of organic matter and improve the soil far below normal tilling depth.

Alfalfa has two requirements: the soil should be well-drained and not too acid. The pH level should be between 6 and 7.5.

In the north, plant alfalfa in the spring and turn it under the following spring. Many plant it in the fall in the south. Do this early enough so that the plants are established before winter, but late enough to avoid the summer's heat and drought.

The Vetches

Several varieties of this viney legume are valuable soil-improvement crops. Since they are annuals and like cool weather, they make good winter cover crops for the Southeast and the Pacific Coast. Hairy vetch is the only variety hardy enough to survive northern winters. Vetches will grow in a wide variety of soil and do not require as much lime as most legumes. They demand a fairly

fertile soil and adequate rainfall because they are shallow-rooted and not very drought resistant. They make a good cover crop because they form a large mass of roots in the surface soil and will yield a lot of nitrogen.

Hairy Vetch is the most widely used because of its winter hardiness. Even in the south it is often the best choice because it doesn't begin growth during temporary warm spells in winter, only to be killed by severe freezing later. Vetch is susceptible to root-knot nematodes and either should not be planted where these are a problem, or should be planted late enough to avoid these parasites.

In the North, hairy vetch can be planted later than any other legume. The best time is from August to the middle of October, depending on your latitude. It is a slow starter, so don't look for much growth in the fall. Plant it with a nurse crop such as winter rye or oats which will control the weeds until the vetch is established. The nurse crop will also protect the vetch against the cold of northern winters. This combination makes an excellent green manure that does well in both sandy and clay soils. Don't sow either crop too thickly, or one may choke out the other.

Common Vetch can't be grown where temperatures drop below 10°F. It grows well on the Pacific Coast, does poorly in light, sandy soils.

Hungarian Vetch is between the two previous vetches in winter hardiness. It does better than both in heavy, poorly drained soils.

Purple Vetch is the least winter-hardy, and its growth is limited to the Pacific and Gulf coasts. It will grow all winter and thus its large mass of green material can be turned under early in the spring.

Clovers

EXCELLENT DEEP-ROOTED SOIL-IMPROVEMENT CROPS

If your ancestors were gardeners or farmers, they knew it for generations back: plant clovers to improve your soil. This was practiced for years before the chief reason for its contribution was understood, that clover, like other legumes, could absorb nitrogen from the air and thus enrich the soil.

Clover is still one of our best green manures, with species for many purposes.

Most of the clovers grown for green manures are planted in the spring and allowed to grow a full year. Crimson clover, an exception, is an annual that can be planted in the fall where winters are mild, then turned under in the spring.

Red Clover. A perennial that grows one or two feet high and once was the most common forage plant in this country. If not cut before it sets seed, it will usually die the year it is planted. It prefers well-drained soil that is not too acid. Because it won't tolerate as much heat and dryness as alfalfa, it is mainly a northern crop. It has a strong taproot, with many branches. Red clover will produce a large mass of green material, plus nitrogen.

Alsike Clover. this clover looks much like red clover except that its flowers are pink or white. It is a forgiving crop, since it will grow in poorly drained areas and in soil too acid or alkaline for red clover. Its root system is less extensive, but it's a strong nitrogen producer.

White Clover. The usual white clover plant is a low, creeping perennial often found on lawns. However, one variety, Ladino, is much larger and has been used increasingly in the North as a forage crop. It is a good green manure, tolerating excessive moisture, demanding heavy feeding and producing rich organic matter.

Crimson Clover. This clover is popular where winters are mild, and where it is planted in the fall. It makes rapid growth in the spring, and decomposes rapidly when it is turned under, so it contributes much organic material to land that is quickly ready for such warm season crops as corn, beans, melons and squash.

Sweet Clovers

EXCELLENT SOIL-IMPROVERS WITH POWERFUL TAPROOTS

Look below the surface of your garden when putting a value on those biennial legumes, the sweet clovers. Their root systems work in many ways to improve your soil.

The sweet clovers have a strong taproot that will dig its way into hardpan and subsoils. This means the plants are bringing up for use minerals not reached by other plants. And when the plants are turned under, those roots decay quickly, leaving deep channels filled with organic material.

The sweet clover roots, too, have a greater ability than most crops to extract nutrients from insoluble forms of phosphorus and potassium, such as rock phosphate and feldspar. Later crops will benefit from the sweet clovers when they use these nutrients. And as with other legumes, the roots of sweet clovers house the bacteria that can extract nitrogen from the air.

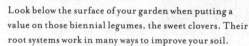

Sweet clover has one requirement: It wants a pH above 6.0, so you may need to add lime. It will tolerate both wet and dry conditions, and extremes of cold and heat.

The two common varieties are white and yellow sweet clover. The white-flowered variety usually produces a greater bulk of green material, while the yellow will grow under drier conditions. Both are usually planted in the spring, and in the first year develop a single branched stem and a strong taproot. The following spring many stems come out of the buds that remain dormant on top of the root through the winter.

The best time to turn it under is in the spring when this second growth reaches six to eight inches tall. By turning it under at this time you get 75–80 percent of its potential soil improvement value and at the same time you clear the way to plant the warm-season crops.

If you turn it under in the fall, till it thoroughly. Otherwise many of the dormant buds will survive the winter and sprout in an unwelcome fashion in the spring.

There are annual varieties of sweet clover such as the Yellow Annual, sometimes called sour clover. This is used as a winter cover crop in the south and is not winter hardy in the North.

Planting Cover Crops of Beans and Peas

Beans and peas are excellent cover crops and equally good eating. For a cover crop, they are planted in wide rows. Both are legumes, so add nitrogen and organic material to your soil.

If you use a rear-mounted tiller, broadcast the seeds, trying to spread them so they are about two inches apart. Set the tiller so that it tills about two and one-half inches deep, then run over the plot in high gear. This will cover the seed.

If you are doing the work by hand, broadcast the seeds in one strip, cover them with soil from the adjacent strip, then plant that strip, and cover, getting the seeds under about an inch and a half of soil.

Next, in both cases, firm the seedbed, either rolling it or walking on it. Water if it is dry. You won't have to thin the plants, and they should be thick enough to crowd out the weeds.

Controlling Garden Weeds

Barbara Pleasant

Illustrations by Regina Hughes

Weed Seeds and Self-Propagation

When planting seeds, we gardeners operate within countable numbers—say, 25 seeds for a planting of squash, or a few hundred for a nice row of zinnias or beans. But most garden weeds produce so many seeds that it's a small exaggeration to call their version of seed production a *seed rain*. In a good year, a healthy crabgrass plant can drop 100,000 seeds, and lambsquarters can beat that number five times over. Along with amazing numbers, weed seeds (and the roots of tenacious perennial weeds) have an almost supernatural gift of longevity. For example, if you were to bury an assortment of weed seeds a foot deep and leave them there for five years, when you finally brought them to the surface you could expect about 25 percent of them

to sprout. Try the same experiment with seeds of cultivated onion or lettuce and germination will be zero.

THE WEED SEED BANK

All gardeners can assume that every square inch of their garden soil contains weeds. Some of them may have been there for years, while others dropped or blew in only yesterday. The seeds that exist naturally in any soil are called the soil's *seed bank*. And just as with the dollars in your checking account, repeated withdrawals will make the balance go down. If no deposits are made (by allowing weeds to drop seeds or importing weed-seed-bearing manure or topsoil, for example), you can make your balance go lower and lower—maybe by as much as 25 percent a year in the first three years. But you will never completely bankrupt your soil's weed seed bank, for some seeds will always blow in or perhaps hitch a ride on the feet of a passing bird.

PROTECTING YOUR GARDEN FROM WEED SEEDS

To drive the balance in your soil's weed seed bank close to bankruptcy, the most important thing to do is to prevent weeds from shedding their seeds. Use mulches, cover crops, smother crops, cutting and mowing, hoeing, and hand weeding to keep weeds from developing and shedding seeds into your garden soil. Where weeds are allowed to grow and reproduce freely, about 95 percent of the weed seeds in the bank come from weeds that shed seeds in previous seasons.

THE MYTH OF WEEDY MANURE

Some gardeners are reluctant to use manure to enrich their soil for fear that it contains many weed seeds. Yet the number of weed seeds in manure depends on what the animals eat and can be very high or close to nothing. As long as the animals that produce the manure you put in your garden do not subsist on weeds, you can use the manure with confidence to improve your soil's structure and fertility. Also keep in mind that it's easier to control weeds than it is to grow healthy flowers and vegetables in weak, infertile soil.

SOLAR-POWERED WEEDS

Many weed seeds are extremely tiny. All seeds contain food energy that the new sprout uses for its initial growth, and the tinier the seeds, the fewer food reserves the plants have to sustain them during and just after germination. So how do plants that are handicapped by minuscule seed size survive? They take the energy they need from the sun.

Here are several ways to deny weed seeds the light they so desperately need:

1. **Resist the temptation to overhoe.** Avoid constantly turning up the soil so that new weed seeds (which were previously buried) are close enough to sunlight to take advantage of its energy. Sunshine cannot help seeds that are buried deep, so hoeing or cultivating only the very top of your soil will result in fewer weed seeds germinating than if you were to go deeper, and thereby drag weed seeds up into the "germination zone."

2. **Mulch your soil.** Mulching exposed soil also limits the life-giving sunshine small-seeded weeds need, as does maintaining a thick canopy of foliage over the soil. Scientists have found that one of the reasons fewer weeds emerge from soil that is partially shaded by plants is that a foliage canopy changes the type of light that filters through. In other words, it's not just weed *plants* that

Continued ➝

are set back by shade; many weed seeds require bright unfiltered light to trigger germination.

3. **Provide shade.** The constant shade of nearby plants may also keep some weed seeds from germinating by limiting changes in soil temperature. The daytime warming and nighttime cooling that take place in open soil encourage the germination of some weed seeds. Shade decreases those temperature changes, which also helps reduce the number of weed seeds that come to life.

UNDERGROUND WEEDS

New annual weeds usually sprout from seeds, but hardy perennial weeds have other ways of making sure they stay alive. True, long-lived perennial weeds like bindweed and johnsongrass produce seeds, but they're usually small or relatively few in number. Instead, many perennial weeds reproduce vegetatively, without flowers or seeds, or by producing seeds as an afterthought. For example, new quackgrass plants can sprout from bits of root; nutsedge and wild garlic grow from corms left behind in the soil when the mother weed is pulled; and bermudagrass and johnsongrass sprout from pieces of rhizome (a sort of stem-root structure) that become brittle and break off when you try to dig out the plants.

These vegetative plant parts often succeed at reproduction where seeds fail because they contain substantial food reserves to help tide the new plant over until it's ready to stand on its own. Most weeds capable of multiplying by spreading vegetatively *and* by making seeds take care of first things first: They develop aboveground runners or underground buds (or rhizomes or corms) *before* they attempt to flower.

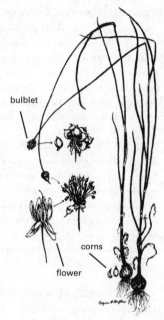

bulblet

corns

flower

Wild garlic (*Allium vineale*)

Keep this in mind when managing weeds that spread into colonies. Although you might wait until flower buds form on annual weeds to chop them down, attack spreading perennials early and often to make sure you don't work any harder than you really need to.

The Secrets of Weed Survival

Weeds find much of their strength in numbers, which is the main strategy they use to take over your garden. In addition to the seed-production bonanza that allows them to self-propagate successfully, many weeds have evolved to grow as ferocious competitors or resource-stealing companions to the "good" plants that we often cultivate.

THE WEEDY ADVANTAGE: CROP MIMICRY

The most successful weeds are closely keyed to the cultural sequence of certain crops, almost as if they are natural partners. For example, the pretty flower called bachelor's button (*Centaurea cyanus*) joined the ranks

of weeds in Europe 300 years ago (and more recently in the Pacific Northwest) since it became an unwanted companion to winter wheat. Bachelor's buttons like everything about winter wheat—the time it is planted, the soil in which it grows, and also the way it is harvested.

Scientists call this near perfect fit between weeds and cultivated plants *crop mimicry*. Perhaps you've seen mimicry at work in your garden when you thought you were growing a wonderful tower of pole beans, only to find morning glory vines overpowering your beans one day. Get to know any and all resident weeds that have this trick up their sleeve and focus your control efforts on them before they bamboozle you.

GETTING RID OF VINE WEEDS

Weeds that grow as vines pose special problems, for their growth habit makes it possible for them to invade the garden virtually unnoticed. Get to know all of the vining weeds that turn up in your garden so you can eliminate them when they're young, before they get a stronghold on your favorite plants.

If you miss a few and discover them after they've tied themselves in knots around your plants (but before they've begun to flower), you don't need to untangle the stems and pull them out unless you really want to do so. Instead, sever the base of the vine with pruning shears and let it die while still bound around other plants. Pulling out an extensive vine may mangle its support plant so badly that it's not worth doing.

MASQUERADING WEEDS

As you become a seasoned gardener, you will gradually become an expert at recognizing the seedlings you want to grow, as well as your weeds. This does not happen overnight. The truth is that some weeds look like cultivated plants, which is part of their self-preservation strategy. Shirley poppies look like dandelions, lambsquarters can look like radishes (at least for a while), and sorrel looks a bit like spinach. If you're new at this who's-who-of-weeds game, delay weeding until you see a pattern in the plants, instead weeding around the row you planted. With time, recognizing the true forms of weeds and cultivated plants will be automatic.

WEED-TO-PLANT WARFARE

Besides great timing, weeds use other strategies to assure themselves of long, prosperous lives. The most successful weeds grow so fast that they have no trouble stealing the space, light, nutrients, and water that we hoped would go to our lettuce. Crabgrass, one of the fastest-growing plants on the planet, is a prime example.

Some weeds are downright detrimental to other plants. They exude chemicals from their roots that act as poison to other plants, or perhaps they "sabotage" the site in other ways. Nutsedge hosts soil-dwelling bacteria that destroys soil-borne nitrogen, the most important nutrient for most growing plants. Bermudagrass roots give off chemicals that slow the growth of other plants, including peach trees. This plant-to-plant chemical warfare is called *allelopathy*.

Several weeds provide textbook cases of allelopathy in action. When lambsquarters starts flowering, the roots release toxic levels of oxalic acid into the soil. Velvetleaf carries toxic substances to its leaves, which rain then washes into the soil. Scientists are now confident in saying that several weeds—quackgrass, Canada thistle, johnsongrass, giant foxtail, black mustard, and yellow nutsedge, among others—hinder other plants while they are alive through competition for resources and allelopathy, and after they are dead by releasing plant-killing chemical residues.

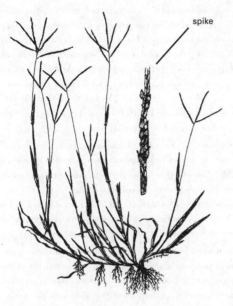

Smooth crabgrass (*Digitaria ischaemum*)

Some weeds go even farther by enlisting the cooperation of soil-dwelling bacteria in an attempt to keep other plants from crowding their space. Ragweed, crabgrass, prostrate spurge, and some prairie grasses may be able to counteract the work of rhizobium bacteria, the soil-dwelling microorganisms that help legumes (like peas and beans) fix nitrogen from the air.

Perhaps you've noticed that when gardening conditions take a turn for the worse—during droughts or plagues of grasshoppers, for instance—weeds tend to fare better than cultivated plants. This edge cannot be attributed to allelopathy. Cultivated plants like beans and corn have been selected over hundreds of years to grow in the pampered sites of gardens and cultivated fields, where they are lavished with good soil, generous spacing, and supplemental water. Weeds, on the other hand, growing wild and untended, have developed very large root systems that may be measured in feet rather than inches. While bean roots may reach down a foot or so, the deepest roots of redroot pigweed grow down three times as far!

This is both good and bad. In light of the primary mission of most garden weeds—to heal over and restore open soil—deep-rooted weeds not only survive but also pull nutrients from deep in the subsoil up to the surface. But it's bad news for gardeners, since weeds constantly interfere with the welfare of our plants. All gardens have weeds, and all good gardeners must find ways to get rid of them.

Fighting the War Against Weeds

Getting to know the weeds that inhabit your garden space is crucial to reducing their numbers. First we'll look at large-scale measures that have a broad impact on all weeds—methods that can shrink the balance in your garden's weed seed bank in a big way. These methods include cover cropping, using smother plants, and mulching.

COVER CROPS

Weeds are naturally discouraged when the soil is well covered with healthy plant life. Plants that can be used to temporarily or permanently cover arable ground are called *cover crops*. Some cover crops are allowed to grow and are then mowed down or turned under, while others can be used as permanent companions for vegetables and fruits. Either way, cover crops discourage weeds and help improve the soil at the same time.

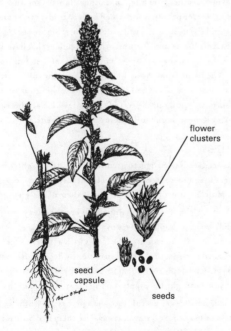

Redroot pigweed (*Amaranthus retroflexus*)

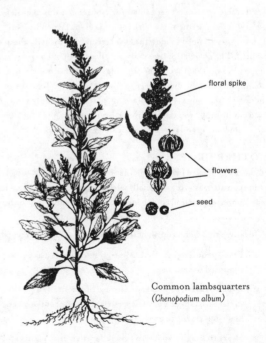

Common lambsquarters
(*Chenopodium album*)

Continued ➡

You need to think through how you intend to use cover crops to make them really work for you. Grain-type covers, such as annual rye, cereal rye, and wheat, produce a huge amount of top growth, and the roots tend to be quite extensive, too. For these reasons, it's impossible to plant a crop into an established stand of uncut grain. However, you can allow the grain to grow from fall to spring and then mow it down and allow the stubble to dry where it falls. To plant in this dry mulch, open up a small space here and there and plant in those open hills. Vine crops such as watermelon, cantaloupe, and sweet potatoes often do very well when grown this way.

Some cover crops grow best during the winter months, flower in spring, and then cease growth through much of the summer, just when you want to use the space to grow vegetables. The best example is the subterranean clover (*Trifolium subterraneum*), a European legume. Subterranean clover does not grow and spread during the summer months as most other clovers do, so it's an ideal cover crop for places where you will grow summer crops like corn. In a study done in New Jersey, a cover crop of subterranean clover controlled morning glory and weedy grasses in corn better than herbicides, and slightly increased the corn yield to boot!

You can even use weeds themselves as cover crops, provided you turn them under *before* they have a chance to develop viable seeds or mow them so often that flowers never have a chance to develop. For example, let's say that you cleaned out the bed where you grew spring lettuce and three weeks later found a strapping stand of pigweed, lambsquarters, and other weeds in its place. If you let these weeds grow for a few weeks and then turn them under, you can consider that space cover-cropped.

COVER CROPS AND WIDE-ROW PLANTING

Many people who grow large gardens plant their crops in wide rows and keep the walkways between the rows in mixed cover crops, such as a mixture of white clover, red clover, and buckwheat. The cover-crop rows serve as a habitat for spiders and other beneficial insects, and the clovers help enrich the soil by fixing nitrogen from the air. As long as these between-row stands remain thick, few weeds are able to grow there.

Of course, you don't get habitat for more than a dozen beneficial insects without putting some work into this plan. Depending on rainfall, you will need to mow the cover-crop rows (usually about once a month). The cover clippings make excellent mulch, however, and if you use a mower that throws the clippings out a chute on the side, you automatically mulch adjoining crop rows as you mow. To make sure your beneficial insects always have a place to go, try to mow only some of the mixed cover-crop rows on a given day, or, better yet, plan your mowing so that alternating rows are mowed in alternating weeks.

SMOTHER CROPS

You can use cultivated plants to smother out unwanted weeds, too. This method consists of sowing a specially selected companion crop that forms a weed-suppressing ground cover beneath your crop plants. The only trick is to provide enough water for both the primary crop and the smother crop.

Ideally, a smother-crop plant should have these four characteristics:

1. **Fast-sprouting**, so it will come up at least as fast as the weed it's supposed to smother.

2. **Broad-leaved**, so that leaves spread horizontally over the soil's surface will shade out weed seeds trying to sprout or weed seedlings trying to grow.

3. **Short in height**, so it won't get taller than crop plants and shade them out, too.

4. **Shallow-rooted**, so it won't seriously compete with the crop plants for space, nutrients, and water.

Agricultural scientists are starting work that may result in a new generation of plants specifically designed to work as smother crops, but for now gardeners can think in terms of lettuce, mustard, and other leafy greens, as well as fast-growing bush beans and field peas. None of these are exactly right for the job. Lettuce often sprouts slowly, most leafy greens grow upward instead of outward, and beans and peas eventually get quite tall. Yet you can help with these shortcomings. For example, you might broadcast turnips a week ahead of summer squash but basically grow the two together. The squash will quickly overtake the turnips, but it will take a while for weeds to do the same—especially under the dark canopy of big squash leaves.

When investigating the use of short-lived smother crops to control weeds in corn, scientists in Minnesota thought yellow mustard might do the trick. However, they found that when the corn and mustard were planted together, the mustard grew so quickly that the corn had to compete with it, and yields suffered. But if the mustard had been planted two weeks after the corn, the corn would have gotten the head start it needed, and the story may have had a happier ending.

The Minnesota scientists did learn that yellow mustard suppressed 66 percent of nasty weeds, which included yellow foxtail, green foxtail, lambsquarters, and redroot pigweed. If you translate this idea into a scaled-down version for a small garden, you might substitute a leafy green that you intend to eat young, such as arugula (also known as rocket), and plant it just after sunflowers or another tall crop. Instant edible smother crop!

In my spring and fall gardens, I routinely use lettuce as a smother crop, interplanting it with broccoli and always alongside peas. If left unsmothered, the open soil in the beds would be overrun with chickweed, henbit, and wild violets. With the help of lettuce (especially fast-growing leafy types), I must weed my spring garden only once or twice, and always get two crops instead of one from a limited amount of space.

In warmer weather, you might use other plants as smother crops. I often sow crowder peas in unoccupied beds in midsummer and thin back the stand (by pulling out individual plants) before sowing late crops of carrots, beets, parsley, and other vegetables that have a hard time sprouting when the days are so hot that the soil heats up and dries out daily. The shade from the legumes helps keep the soil moist enough to facilitate germination. When the carrots or other crops attain the status of sprouts, I pull out the rest of the peas, which all the while have been fixing nitrogen in the soil and suppressing weeds.

MULCHES

Almost all weed seeds need light to germinate and grow. Light functions like a trigger to some weed seeds that wait in the soil for years, deactivated by darkness. Mulches control weeds by depriving them of life-giving light.

The best mulches for suppressing weeds are the ones you already have. In fall, spread chopped leaves over empty beds to keep chickweed and henbit at bay. If you run over the leaves with a lawn mower before you pile them on your soil, they will sufficiently decompose over the winter so you can simply turn them under in spring. Stockpile extra leaves to use around garden plants during the summer months.

Pine tree needles are useful, too, though they are acidic and tend to help naturally acidic soil stay that way. Use them to discourage weeds around plants that like acidic conditions, such as strawberries, azaleas, and rhododendrons.

Environmentally minded lawn-keepers are advised to let grass clippings rot where they fall, but they also make great mulch. I hook the bagger on my mower when I cut my backyard; then the clippings go straight from the bag into flower beds.

You can go for years without buying mulch materials, but in the end weathered wheat straw may be worth its modest price. Unlike hay, which usually contains zillions of weed seeds, wheat and oat straw are normally pretty clean. If you can find some that's been rained on (so its value as animal food is low), buy it. Besides suppressing weeds by depriving the seeds of light, wheat and oat straw are believed to leach out chemicals that act as natural herbicides. But as long as you use them to mulch plants that are beyond the seedling stage (such as established berries or transplanted tomatoes and peppers), wheat and oat straw both have strong track records of increasing yields.

SLUGS IN THE MULCH

The one disadvantage of organic mulches is that slugs and snails just love them. I went for years without serious slug problems and then accidentally imported thousands of baby slugettes in a load of rotted leaves. Two weeks of steady trapping with beer traps got the problem under control, but in some climates beer is not enough. Where slugs rule the night, try topping off a paper or cardboard mulch with sawdust, or stop mulching altogether until you get the slugs under control.

To trap slugs with beer, fill a small shallow container (like a plastic margarine tub) with beer and set it in the soil in the evening so that only the rim sticks up above the soil line. Early in the morning, go out and gather your drunken, drowned slugs. Reload the traps each night. Don't worry if you trap snails along with your slugs, for they are basically slugs with shells.

Leaves, grass clippings, straw, and other materials that rot are called organic mulches, and the material they eventually become—called humus—is nature's most fundamental soil conditioner. Yet these organic mulches do have a flaw when it comes to weed control. Some weeds can grow through them, a feat that becomes easier as the mulches compact, wear thin, and decompose.

You can enhance the weed-controlling ability of any organic mulch by placing sheets of newspaper or cardboard beneath it. Lay down two to six sheets of newspaper directly on the ground, or cut cardboard boxes to make them flat and spread them over the soil in a single layer. Top off these paper mulches with leaves, grass clippings, or straw. Newspapers can also help stretch your mulch supply, since you'll need only about a 1-inch-deep blanket of organic mulch instead of a 3-inch one (the usual depth required to keep weed seeds in the dark).

BOARD IT UP

Tough perennial weeds have a habit of showing up when you're not prepared to deal with them. I keep a few short, broad boards handy and throw them on top of knots of bermudagrass to slow them down until I have a chance to dig them out. Colonies of quackgrass and johnsongrass can be held in check with boards, too, until you have time to give them the careful digging they deserve.

STORE-BOUGHT MULCHES

Mulching materials are usually easy to find in gardening centers. Many stores offer several different types, including the following:

Woven black or green polyester fabric mulch (such as the product called WeedBlock) are the most expensive kinds of roll-out mulches to buy, but they are long-lasting and work just great. Water and air pass through them, but the openings are too small for weeds. A good-quality fabric mulch will last several seasons when used in shade or when protected from sunshine with an organic mulch. Gardeners who like their gardens to look extra neat and manicured love these products, and often cover them with bark nuggets or pine straw for a more natural look.

Spunbound black polyester mulches (such as Weed Barrier Mat and Weed Shield) are as easy to use as the woven types, and about as long-lasting when protected from strong sun. Tearing can occur when used in places that get heavy foot traffic. The cost is slightly less than the woven version.

Perforated black plastic is widely available at discount stores. It's basically heavy black plastic with little holes punched into it for rain to trickle through. Hot sunshine causes the plastic to degrade, so without a topping of organic mulch, the stuff is good for only one season. Relatively inexpensive, this type of mulch heats up the soil below it, so it's better in cool climates than in hot ones. An extra plus is that little soil moisture evaporates through the plastic, so you have to water less often.

Roll-out paper mulch (such as BioBlock) degrades over the course of a season, so you never have to pick it up—just till it under. When topped with an organic mulch, paper mulches perform beautifully, without the disposal problems of plastic. The cost is modest as well.

Hands-On Weeding

Weeds are terribly hardy creatures. Despite all the hard work you may put into preventative measures against them, there will be weeds in your garden. Whether you hoe or weed by hand, you'll be getting to know the weeds in your garden personally, one by one.

Hoeing can be done standing up, but most hand weeding requires you to squat, kneel, or sit while you get the job done. My preference is to sit, and I do it on a dense foam pad that I've had for years. A neighbor uses an old stadium seat, and the garden catalogs sell kneeling pads made especially for this purpose. All weeders need one of these or something equally effective, both to keep their clothes clean and to make weeding easier.

ABOUT HERBICIDES

Herbicides are chemicals that kill plants. Conventional farmers rely on them heavily, but gardeners are better off using them only for emergencies. It's a purity issue, for all chemical herbicides are highly toxic and definitely do not fit into the descriptive category of "earth safe."

You will not find me recommending so-called natural herbicides, either, for I have been disappointed with how well they work. Spray-on organic herbicides are basically soap sprays, and they do manage to kill the top parts of young seedling weeds. However, they are useless against older plants, and even young treated weeds often manage to grow back from their uninjured roots. Considering the time involved in mixing and applying these products, their short-term benefits, and the ever-present risk of injuring nonweeds, I think they're a poor substitute

Continued →

for more traditional methods of weed control such as hands-on weeding.

Old-time methods of chemical control involving salt and vinegar aren't safe, either, for they destroy many soil-dwelling microcritters and may make soil unfit for plants. For weeds, there are no environmentally safe miracle cures that come in bottles.

WEED DISPOSAL

What are you to do with your weeds once you get them out of the garden? Young weeds often can be laid on the surface of the soil, where they will dry into mulch, or you can chop them into your compost heap when they are succulent and green. But watch out if the weeds are already in flower, even if you don't think they are carrying mature seeds. Some weeds, like chickweed and purslane, can continue to develop seeds after you pull the plants from the soil.

Some of the toughest weeds have a miraculous talent for surviving the heat and stress of the hottest compost heap. However, these same weeds may be dried to death and then composted after they are thoroughly dead. Here is a drying method that may work for you.

First, pull out the troublesome weeds. Pile them loosely in a wheelbarrow and park it in the sun for a day or two. If rain is expected, move the wheelbarrow to a dry place (such as a garage) so the weeds won't get wet. Then dump the weeds in a pile that cooks in the sun and never gets watered. In rainy weather, you can stuff the weeds into a black plastic bag.

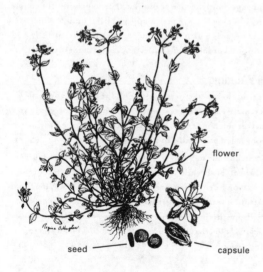

Common chickweed
(*Stellaria media*)

To make sure the plant parts are thoroughly dead, spread them out and wet them down. If you see no signs of life, chop a mix of these nastiest of nasty weeds into your compost heap.

Beware of Cultivating Invasive Plants

If not strictly disciplined, some cultivated plants spread so much that they become pesky weeds. You can restrain their exuberant growth in several ways, but you still have to keep a close watch on them.

Some can be kept in place by growing them in containers partially sunk into the ground, with the rim an inch or two above the soil to keep the roots from spreading. Others, like mint, are best grown between a wall (or paved area) and a space that is regularly mowed. Tall spreaders like Jerusalem artichoke and tansy are best handled by planting them far from closely managed beds in areas where they can dominate other weeds rather than cultivated plants.

Here are 14 notorious spreaders and suggestions for handling them—provided you want them badly enough to put up with their invasiveness.

Crown vetch (*Coronilla varia*)

An excellent ground cover for steep, eroded banks, crown vetch becomes a monster when grown in or near pampered places like gardens. It spreads via seeds and fleshy underground stems, some of which are more than 6 feet long. Avoid planting crown vetch on banks that slope toward your garden. Slopes that end at a street or ditch are more suitable sites.

Honeysuckle (*Lonicera* spp.)

This plant's wonderfully fragrant blossoms come at a cost—runaway growth that requires a commitment to trim and prune at least twice a summer. Even well-behaved named cultivars of bush-type honeysuckles bear close watching. The trailing types demand a place of their own. If allowed to mingle with other plants, they insist on strangling their neighbors.

Jerusalem artichoke (*Helianthus tuberosus*)

Grown for its nutty-tasting edible roots, this perennial sunflower dominates space with its height (up to 9 feet) and by seeds and sprouting roots. Never till over a dormant cache of roots, or you'll spread them everywhere. Dig all roots from the outside of the colony yearly, in early winter, to keep the colony from getting too huge.

Mint (*Mentha* spp.)

The mints spread via ropelike creeping underground roots, called rhizomes, which can sneak several feet—even under thick mulch or concrete. Grow them adjacent to mowed areas so you can enjoy the fragrance of the cut leaves where you mow. Or grow them in large containers and cut back the faded flowers to keep the plants from dropping seeds. Some strains are better behaved than others.

Morning glory (*Ipomoea hederacea*)

In warm climates, the same annual morning glories that are breathtakingly beautiful on a trellis can become very pesky weeds as they twine around any other plant that's upright. Grow them far from vegetable and flower gardens, preferably surrounded by a large area of mowed grass.

Mugwort (*Artemisia vulgaris*)

This herb is valued in fragrance gardens for its camphorlike aromatic foliage, but it's a rampant spreader that will quickly overtake other plants. Monitor new seedlings and young plantlets that pop up on the outside of the clump. Promptly pull up the ones you don't want. Cut back plants as soon as they flower to keep them from dropping seeds.

Oxeye daisy (*Chrysanthemum leucanthemum*)

This lovely wild (but non-native) daisy can become a nuisance, especially in the Northwest and Midwest. But in most places, you can control oxeyes by mowing or hoeing out unwanted plants. If you like the daisies but not where they're growing, dig them early in spring and move them to your chosen spot.

Purple loosestrife (*Lythrum salicaria*)

A dramatically beautiful perennial, purple loosestrife has become such a problem in the wetlands of the upper Midwest that its cultivation there is now illegal. Until reliable sterile strains become commercially available, choose something else for your garden, like a nice monarda.

Snow-on-the-mountain (*Euphorbia marginata*)

One of the largest and showiest members of the spurge family, snow-on-the-mountain spreads via seeds and has become a resented weed in parts of the Midwest. The leaves are poisonous to livestock, and the milky sap causes skin irritation, so handle with care. A much smaller *Euphorbia*, cypress spurge, is often grown as a ground cover and can become invasive if its spread is not controlled by the gardeners who grow it.

Tansy (*Tanacetum vulgare*)

Although tansy is useful for attracting beneficial insects (and possibly repelling destructive ones), it rapidly gains dominance over other plants with its tall, robust stems, and then produces thousands of seeds. Cut it back after the flowers have hosted their mini wasp party, and promptly dig out plants that pop up where you don't want them. Better yet, grow tansy in containers so you can move it around and let different plants enjoy its beneficial aura.

Toadflax (*Linaria vulgaris*)

Also known as butter-and-eggs, this delicate little wildflower sometimes gets carried away with itself, especially in northern areas where cool weather enables it to set seeds very successfully. Plant in impoverished soil where other plants refuse to grow.

Trumpet creeper (*Campsis radicans*)

When properly managed, this perennial woody vine is a fine addition to a low-maintenance landscape. To limit its spread, clip off all the green seedpods you can reach before they are fully mature. Prune as needed to confine the vine to its allotted space in your garden.

Violet (*Viola papilionacea*)

There are good violets and bad ones, and the common blue violet of the eastern United States is too naughty for cultivated space. Pretty flowers in early spring are no excuse for the tenacious roots of this native species or the way it reseeds so heavily that it smothers out nearby plants. Have no fear of the better-behaved violets, like Johnny-jump-ups and yellow violas, or the native birds-foot violet.

Yarrow (*Achillea millefolium; Achillea Filipendulina*)

Both species of yarrow are enthusiastic spreaders, so keep a close eye on them. Cultivated forms of both species are prettier and better behaved than the strains often sold as wildflowers, but they still need to be monitored. Pull up or dig out unwanted plants. When mowed twice a year, *Achillea millefolium* can make a nice ground cover.

Using Beneficial Insects

Rhonda Massingham Hart

Illustrations by Judy Eliason, Mike Belanger, and Alison Kolesar

Bugs You Can Love

These days the healthiest gardens are all abuzz. A garden teeming with insect life is a sure sign of a well-balanced miniature ecosystem. Impossible under the rain of pesticides and insecticides often accepted as "conventional" pest controls, a varied population of insect life will benefit the garden as no spray ever could.

Of course, all gardeners have problems with insects at one point or another. The number of garden insect pests staggers the imagination. Flies, moths, and butterflies fill the air; cutworms, nematodes, and others choke the soil; and caterpillars, beetles, and a bevy of bugs try to invade everything in between. What's a gardener to do?

The answer may be a surprising, *nothing*. Or at least as little as possible. Certainly don't resort to toxic chemicals. For while they *may* kill off a large number of bugs in one fell swoop, you might be surprised at the actual cost of such control measures. Not so much in dollars and cents, but the cost in contamination of food, soil, groundwater, and insect gene pools.

Chemicals are responsible for a great many modern ills, from increased cancer rates to birth defects. These chemicals often are not merely present on the surface of crops. Some are absorbed by the soil and taken up by the plants' roots, which circulate the toxins throughout the plant, infiltrating the entire system of the plant. Chemicals not immediately absorbed by plants eventually make their way to the water table, into wells and other water supplies.

But contamination of food, soil, and water is not the only evil of toxic pesticide use. Wiping out complete bug populations can wreak more havoc on your plot than doing nothing to control them. Pesticides kill indiscriminately: the good die right along with the bad and the ugly.

There are also the inevitable reactions of *resistance* and *resurgence*. There are always a few survivors of a pesticide attack. These few quickly reproduce new generations, at least as well equipped to withstand chemical assault as their parents. Mutations occur through successive generations until invincible "superbugs" evolve.

At the same time, smaller populations of secondary pests find the competition suddenly eliminated. Not only the competition, but all the predators and bug parasites have vanished with them. Uninhibited, these secondary pests can become primary problems.

So what *is* a gardener to do? If you must resort to pesticides, opt for botanical derivatives, which break down quickly into harmless components, or try the many other organic remedies available, from pheromone traps to soap sprays to bacterial bug "bugs." Never overlook the importance of sound cultivation practices, such as soil, weed, and water management. Try a "patchwork" garden, arranging plants into mixed beds or rows. This slows many a pest who prefers to munch his way down neat rows of his favorite fare. Handpicking bugs and eggs is

Continued ➡

a valuable practice—just be sure to familiarize yourself with those you find. You wouldn't want to squish a friend!

One of the best methods is to take your cue from Nature herself, and employ "good" bugs against those "bad" pests. Encourage predators and parasites, as well as vital pollinators, by including a mix of flowers and herbs among your plantings. You may be in for a treat once beneficial insects come to your rescue. Some will help with pest-control problems, stalking and parasitizing your pests; others will help to improve crop production by pollinating plants; and still others will help to build ever healthier soil by adding organic matter and working the soil to improve fertility and drainage.

The Soil Builders

EARTHWORMS

To list earthworms among the natural wonders of the earth would only begin to pay them due tribute. A single slimy, squirming worm in the hand may not *seem* like a living miracle, but the combined forces of trillions perform vital, literally earth-shaping tasks every day, everywhere.

Earthworm bodies are virtual humus mills, manufacturing nutrient-rich castings (manure) from nearly anything found in the soil. As they burrow through the earth in their constant search for food, they leave tunnels that improve soil aeration as well as drainage and water retention. All this underworld activity also gives both subsoil and topsoil a thorough mixing.

Actually, worms are not insects. They belong to a vast classification of animals called annelids, the ringed or segmented worms. The order Oligochaeta is but a fraction of this diverse group, to which the three thousand or so different kinds of earthworms belong.

The earthworm is a marvel of underground engineering, perfectly designed for his soil-dwelling role. Long, slender, and tapered at either end, the body is made up of many segments. Large night crawlers may have over one hundred fifty segments, while manure worms possess fewer than a hundred. These segments are formed of circular muscles, which make the earthworm incredibly strong for his size. In the course of a day he may shove aside many stones and other bits of debris sixty times his own weight.

The average North American garden-variety worms measure about 4 to 8 inches in length. Most are reddish in color, some with alternating yellowish rings, others are a deep maroon, and some even greenish. All are slimy, the result of a highly efficient kidney system that pumps out fluid wastes through pores located all along the body. This mucus helps them to glide through the soil. Worms have no eyes, though they are sensitive to light, and no ears, though most are unbelievably attuned to vibrations. Though earthworms have a tiny "brain," it can be removed without any apparent effect. And earthworms have five hearts!

The worm's existence is primarily one of digestion. All of his essential organs are located in the front one-third of his anatomy, but his digestive tube runs the entire length of his body. An earthworm has the ability to regenerate a lost or injured tail, but contrary to childhood beliefs, the tail cannot regrow a new head.

Earthworms make their way through the soil by a combination of muscle contractions and by swallowing much of what lies in their path. Digestive fluids neutralize acids, raising the pH levels of acidic

soils. The castings also tend to neutralize alkaline soil, which makes earthworms a valuable asset for balancing soils.

The worm's organically rich castings are made up of essential, water-soluble nutrients, easily accessible by plants. Compared to topsoil they contain five times as much nitrogen, seven times as much phosphorus, eleven times as much potash, and three times as much magnesium. Noting that earthworms convert anything available into fertile manure, the Greek philosopher and naturalist Aristotle dubbed these creatures the "intestines of the earth."

Each worm can recycle his own body weight daily. The concentration of earthworms varies from region to region, but estimates from one hundred fifty thousand to two million per acre are common. With each producing up to his own one or two ounces of body weight in castings every day, even if they were active only half the year they would still produce from 5 to 50 *tons* of instant compost per acre, per year!

Besides eating, a worm's other primary function is reproduction. Any two worms can mate and reproduce because each has both male and female reproductive organs. Both sperm and eggs are released into a thick envelope of mucus, where fertilization occurs. Gradually, as the slime dries, it draws closed at either end into a lemon-shaped capsule.

From two to twenty eggs will hatch within two to three weeks. In two to three months they are mature enough to reproduce, doing so every seven to ten days—up to 1,500 worms each year per individual. A worm's needs are simple—moisture, moderate temperatures (from 60° to 70° F. is optimal), oxygen (provided by their tunneling), and food (anything small enough to fit into their mouths). They avoid light; direct sunlight for more than a few minutes is fatal. Many come up to feed at the surface at night or after a rain, as the vibrations from falling raindrops alert them to the moist conditions.

Some species, like the common night crawlers, dig deep tunnels, converting and mixing subsoil as well as topsoil, and carrying bits of leaves or other organic debris down into the lower layers. Others work only the top few inches of soil, many rising to the surface to deposit their castings.

Supply plenty of organic matter, even by scattering or lightly burying biodegradable trash, such as kitchen scraps or newsprint; maintaining soil moisture to a depth of at least 2 inches; and avoiding the use of chemical pesticides. Provide protection from natural enemies such as moles, birds, snakes, ants, and centipedes.

Earthworms can be purchased from commercial growers to supplement or to start a population of your own. Buy capsules or just-hatched worms rather than full-grown breeders, as they are much more apt to adapt to new surroundings. Interestingly, when smaller species of worms are raised with larger varieties, the little guys will assume the identity of their neighbors and grow to a larger size, but only if raised with them from the hatching stage.

Vermiculture, or the raising of earthworms, is a worthwhile endeavor in its own right. Worms can be raised in anything from a shallow box to massive in-ground pits. All that is required is bedding material, food, moisture, darkness, and worms. A wooden box 1 foot deep, 2 feet wide by 3 feet long, with 1/2-inch holes drilled into the bottom for drainage and aeration, should serve the needs of a four- to six-person family. Fill the box with shredded cardboard, newspaper, or computer paper, or animal manure, leaf litter, or peat moss. Throw in a handful of soil or powdered limestone to provide grit, mix well, and wet thoroughly. Add two pounds of worms per pound of food (kitchen scraps, etc.) that you plan to have available per day.

Keep your worm box covered with a piece of black plastic, heavy fabric, or old rug to conserve moisture and block light. Bury your peelings, coffee grounds, bread crumbs, pizza crusts, leftovers, and other material every few days, rotating the feeding site each time. The worms will turn your trash into treasure!

The Pollinators

Plant pollination is the single most important step in plant production. Without this essential function, no amount of watering, weeding, or feeding will produce a harvest. No matter how carefully you choose your seed or stock, no matter how diligently you cultivate, control pests, or pamper your plants, without pollination your efforts will truly be fruitless.

SOME CROPS THAT RELY ON INSECT POLLINATION

Alfalfa	Celery	Flax	Pear
Almond	Cherry	Grape	Pepper
Apple	Citrus crops	Lettuce	Plum & prune
Apricot	Cole crops	Lima bean	Red clover
Artichoke	Cotton	Muskmelon	Soybean
Asparagus	Cranberry	Nectarine	Strawberry
Avocado	Cucumber	Olive	Sweet clover
Bean	Date	Onion	Tomato
Beet	Eggplant	Peach	Watermelon
Carrot	Fig	Peanut	

Excerpt from Agricultural Handbook No. 496, "Insect Pollination of Cultivated Crops"

Pollination is the process by which plants propagate their species. It is the plant's way of uniting male and female cells to produce the seeds which, in turn, become the next generation of that plant. It is one of the most important types of plant reproduction, though by no means the sole method.

Many plants have evolved other kinds of self-perpetuation, such as sending off runners, and man has devised other ways to duplicate plants he favors, such as root cuttings. Even so, many cultivated crops rely on plant pollination.

Pollinated plants produce both male reproductive cells, *pollen*, and female reproductive cells, *ovules*. These develop within an exquisitely specialized apparatus, called a *flower*. Some flowers are both male and female, while others are either all male or all female. Corn bears male pollen-producing tassels and female silks, on different parts of the plant. Some plants mature pollen and ovules at different parts of the plant. Some plants mature pollen and ovules at different times, making cross-pollination necessary. Other plants can pollinate themselves, transferring pollen among different blossoms, while others require entirely different cultivars (species of a related plant) to get the job done.

Pollination is complete once the male pollen has been transferred to the female ovules, resulting in fertile seeds. Only after the fruit sets can we tell whether or not the faded flower has performed its intended duty. Of course, certain garden crops (lettuce and other greens, broccoli and related cole crops, onions and other alliums, turnips, radishes, and carrots, to name a few) do not reach the flowering stage in many home plots. But pollination is vital if you want to have seeds for next year's garden. Many gardeners let a few of their choicest plants flower and go to seed, carefully collecting, curing, and saving the seed for the following year.

Many catalysts are credited with helping plants accomplish their reproductive goal. Corn crops depend on the breeze. Certain types of cacti rely on nectar-feeding bats. Man will manipulate the process to his advantage to produce hybrids that excel in those qualities he prefers. Many factors affect whether pollination occurs. We can influence flower formation by adjusting temperature, water availability, and soil fertility, but none of these can assure the completion of this important process.

By far the most important of the pollinators for plants grown and harvested by man are insects. Honeybees are among the most renowned pollinators, but bumblebees, hover flies, wasps, butterflies, and other insects also contribute to this essential cause.

POLLINATORS AND THEIR WORK

Honeybees (*Apis* spp.)

Busy bees gather nectar and pollen from more than 250 kinds of plants. As they work inside the blossoms, sticky globs of pollen grains cling to their hairy legs and bodies. When the workers move from one flower to the next, the male pollen is transferred to the female ovules, thereby pollinating the receiving plant. This relationship benefits both the bug and the blossom. For while the plants depend on the insects to complete their life cycle, the insects rely on the plants' nectar and pollen to feed their colonies.

There are four species of honeybees, the most productive being the domestic *Apis mellifera* of which there are several races, including the popular German (or European) and Italian, as well as the notorious "killer" African bees. There are no honeybees actually native to the United States, however, only immigrants.

Continued ➤

Honeybees are easily identifiable as amber-colored insects buzzing amidst flower blossoms. These are sterile female workers, who grow to about 1/2 inch in length. The males are larger and stockier, with oversized compound eyes that come together at the top of the head. Longer yet, but more slender than the males, is the queen. She is rarely seen outside the nest. All bees have short antennae, three pairs of legs (the workers bearing pollen baskets on the hind legs), and clear wings.

The population of a colony, or hive, may grow to as many as one hundred thousand bees, each the offspring of a single queen. She begins egg-laying in late winter, depositing her eggs in specially made "brood cells." A virtual egg-laying machine, she will lay up to two thousand eggs *daily* during the warmer months.

The vast majority of eggs develop into the sexually undeveloped female workers who are the lifeblood of the colony, performing specialized tasks, intricately designed for the benefit of the hive. Bee colonies are highly organized, perfectly functioning societies. Besides the nurse bees tending the developing larvae, members of the queen's "court" attend to her every need. Other workers are foragers, collecting pollen and nectar, or carpenters, building the wax combs that house the developing young and store food. Guard bees are posted at the hive entrance to keep away intruders. They are known to fan the entrance with their wings in hot weather.

All workers can sting, but can do so only once as the act results in fatal injury. The queen also stings, but usually only when fighting for her throne, and her life.

The population of the colony rises and falls with the seasons, reaching a peak in late summer and dwindling throughout the winter. Bees do not hibernate, but cold weather finds them clinging together in a ball for warmth.

The farther your garden is from a hive, the fewer bee visitors you may expect. Most foraging occurs within a quarter-mile of the colony, though when pickings are exceptionally poor the workers may venture out several miles. Poor foraging sites will be bypassed for more promising areas, but in general the bees try to keep their commute to a minimum. They have devised an ingenious system of body language, or bee dances, to direct other foraging members of the hive to the best gathering spots.

Some plants provide better bee fare than others, thereby inviting the pollinators to work among and around them. Alfalfa and sweet clover are sought after by bees and also produce good honey. Fireweed, mints, and black and purple sage are also attractive. Orchard blossoms draw thousands of workers as do mixed flower gardens and—possibly most importantly—wild flowers and weeds. Blossoms that hold little appeal to us may well be the mainstay of the colony's diet when other plants are not in bloom.

Bees also need water, and will make use of an accessible water supply, especially in hot weather. Normally, the droplets of dew collected on plants is sufficient.

The most important consideration in maintaining a healthy working bee population is allowing them a poison-free workplace. Practice organic pest controls. Switch from chemical fertilizers and herbicides to animal manures, compost, leaf mold, and the like. Bees are very susceptible to insecticides. They may become lethargic or erratic, depending on the poison. Workers die out in the field as well as back at the hive. House bees have the sad task of moving the bodies of their fallen sisters out of the hive. As they push them out the hive

entrance, piles of the dead will form near the base of the hive. Entire colonies may perish.

Commercial growers often ensure pollination of their crops by renting hives from professional beekeepers. The beekeeper maintains the colony and harvests the honey crop, while the grower benefits from the pollinators' work.

Beekeeping is a rewarding hobby that can be practiced almost anywhere. A wooden hive, placed in a sheltered area and stocked with a queen and a healthy colony, will provide prolific pollination as well as many pounds of honey. See *Starting Right with Bees*, for more information on beekeeping.

Bumblebees (*Bombus* spp.)

Some species of bumblebee is native to almost anywhere on earth, from the cold northern Canadian slopes to tropical rain forests or isles. Dozens of species are found throughout the United States, and most of these are important pollinators of a variety of crops.

Bumblebees are instantly recognized as large, loudly buzzing, flying balls of black and yellow or orange fluff. Their large size (some are over an inch long) and menacing buzz command respect and often a generous berth. Actually, bumblebees are relatively docile creatures, no more testy than most honeybees, but unlike their sisters whose sting results in fatal self-injury, bumblebees can sting repeatedly.

Social insects, as are other bees, bumblebees follow a less stringent regime. There are still distinct classes of drones, workers, and the specialized queen, but a bumble queen never surrenders her life to become an egg-laying machine as does the Royal Honeybee. She continues to forage occasionally and is more intimately involved with her progeny than is her counterpart.

Bumblebees do not maintain year-round colonies; instead they vacate their nests each fall and establish new ones every spring. Young queens, hatched the previous autumn, strike out each spring, feeding on pollen and nectar to build up their strength. They carefully hunt for a suitable nest site, such as overgrown ditchbanks, forgotten garden corners, or untended flower boxes. Abandoned mouse runs are a favorite find. There the queen builds a wax egg cell, provisions it with pollen, and seals from eight to fourteen eggs inside. She continues to forage, storing extra nectar in wax honey pots to hold her over during bad weather. She will actually brood the eggs like a mother hen, resting on top and warming them through body heat generated by moving her wings.

The eggs hatch into tiny wormlike larvae within days. They develop rapidly, and soon spin cocoons within their sealed chambers to undergo their metamorphosis into adult bees.

As these larvae undergo their transformation, the Queen Mother prepares new nursery cells atop the pupating cocoons. When this first batch of workers emerges, they will help to care for the next, and so on, until the colony numbers hundreds of bees.

Cold weather signals that the end is near. The queen stops laying eggs. No more workers emerge from the nursery cells, only drones and new queens. After a time the entire hive dies out, except for the new queens who, having mated, carry the seeds of the next generation of colonies. They fly off in search of a sheltered spot in which to hibernate through the winter. Spring days awaken them to start the cycle again.

Bees have many natural enemies as well as diseases. Insect-eating birds and large robber flies attack them on the wing. Badgers, skunks, and other animals will dig them from their inground nests, eating both stored nectar and bees. Mice, shrews, and other small vermin invade the nest and desecrate the contents.

Though some bumblebees do develop the ungrateful habit of cutting away part of the flower to gather nectar, thereby avoiding contact with pollen or ovules and shirking any responsibility of pollinating the plant, the vast majority are indeed important pollinators. They flock to wildflowers and flowering herbs such as oregano and thyme. They will make use of manmade nests such as a 6-inch cube placed just beneath the soil surface. They even adapt well to live in a greenhouse where they will mate, nest, and carry out their normal life cycles.

Hover Flies (*Family Syrphidae*)

Following bees, the runners-up for Most Important Pollinators are the hover flies, or flower flies as they are also known. The adults feed on nectar and the honeydew secreted by various plant pests. Pollen is transferred among the many blossoms they visit as they make their feeding rounds.

Hover flies are tremendously accomplished fliers. Aptly named, they can hover in place while feeding, appearing to rest in midair, despite any breeze. Suddenly, they dart away, moving forward, backward, or to the side with equal ease and effortless grace.

At a glance many hover flies closely resemble small bees or wasps. Though some are solid dark colors, others sport the same bright, contrasting yellow and black bands as do many bees and wasps. Buzzing while they work, many even sound like bees. But, despite the superficial likenesses, there are many differences. Most common hover flies are smaller and more slender than bees. They have only two wings rather than the bee's four. Unlike bees or wasps, hover flies do not bite or sting.

Much of the credit for their intricate flying abilities goes to their sensitive vision. Though hover flies are no more able to make out images than most other insects, their oversized eyes instantly recognize and interpret even the slightest movements. By quickly adjusting to any changes in their position relative to stationary objects, they can ride the breeze seemingly oblivious to its effects.

Though all hover flies feed on nectar, there is a weird and wonderful variety of larval feeding habits. Some larvae are scavengers, surviving on debris, plant residues, even liquid rotting animal manures. Some combine their beelike camouflage and scavenger tactics to coexist in beehives as resident housekeepers, feeding off the residues of the hive. Still others are significant insect predators, heartily downing aphids, mealybugs, and other soft-bodied bugs.

These useful flies will flock to flower gardens and can be easily enticed to those that include such favorites as cosmos, coreopsis, gloriosa daisies, dwarf morning glory, marigolds, spearmint, baby blue-eyes, and meadowfoam.

Wasps (*Hymenoptera*)

The category of *wasps* includes a diverse array of insects from the buzzing, stinging picnic pests to tiny, barely visible parasitic organisms. One common thread prevalent throughout this varied group, however, is that the adult forms feed on flower nectar. As such, many aid in the cause of flower pollination. Flowering herbs or small single-flowered blossoms are easiest for the smallest wasps to access, and are equally appreciated by even the largest of the bunch.

Like the hover flies, wasps will earn their keep by preying on the pest insect population.

Read more about them in the section on predators.

Butterflies (*Lepidoptera*)

Butterflies of many species regularly visit a variety of cultivated plants, including lettuce and strawberries. Some are pests, like the white cabbage butterfly, menacing cole crops as they deposit their eggs, which hatch into downy, green, destructive caterpillars. But others are aiding the cause of pollination as they add their own colorful animation to the flowers they grace.

One look at a nectar-feeding butterfly's mouth reveals an instrument highly specialized for its task. Though there are hundreds of variations, the basic structure is composed of the *proboscis*, a tubelike adaptation used to literally siphon the sweet nectar from within the flower. Other mouthparts are greatly reduced, except for feelerlike *labial palps*.

As the butterfly approaches a likely-looking prospect, he may venture near, then abandon several possibilities before alighting on his choice. This is probably due to the fact that his large, bulbous, compound eyes are capable of making out clear images only up close: what looks like a tempting blossom from a distance may turn out to be a bit of litter once it comes into focus. Many butterflies have taste receptors in their feet, so they can further distinguish, upon landing, whether or not they have found their sweet reward.

Ultraviolet reflection, as well as flower color, plays a significant part in drawing the drinker to the nectar he seeks. Once alighted, blossom in sight, he gingerly approaches and inserts his proboscis into the neck of the blossom, all the way down into the nectar reserves of the flower. He may spend only a second or two, or savor a long, leisurely slurp. As he feeds, grains of pollen adhere to his hairy legs or underbody and hitch a ride with him to the next flower. Since butterflies often visit a regular circuit of blooms, they can be very effective in pollinating those they patronize.

To attract these lovely insects to your garden, include a variety of blossoms. See "Planning a Butterfly Garden."

PREDATORS

Well-pollinated crops in fertile, humus-rich soil definitely have the edge. They are disease-resistant, productive, and a joy to behold. In general, they are even less susceptible to insect damage than less vigorous plants. Unfortunately, outbreaks of plant-eating pests can occur even in well-tended plots. But don't despair. Help may already be lurking in the shadows.

While greedy garden pests gorge themselves on the fruits and veggies of your labor, just one link up the food chain are carnivorous cousins waiting to come to your rescue. Among the most potent of biological control agents are the natural enemies, the predators, of bugdom. They may be hunters, who consume their victims—eggs, larvae, or adults—on the spot, or they may be parasites, whose hatching larvae do in the various stages of garden villains. In either case, they are upstanding insect citizens and outstanding pest exterminators.

Continued ➔

THE PREDATORS

Ladybugs/Ladybird Beetles (*Hippodamia convergens*)

Most of us recognize the adult form of this gardeners' darling, but true to insect form, the other stages of development bear no resemblance to the familiar adults. Adult ladybugs may well have inspired the endearment "cute as a bug." Bright orange-red, rounded little beetles, they average about 3/8 inch long and are nearly as wide. Like all insects, they gad about on six legs, theirs being short, black, and spindly. Their red wing covers are decorated with a sprinkling of black spots, the number, size, and placement of which vary with the species. White markings embellish the shiny black thorax, or center segment. Their heads are also shiny black.

But don't dare to compare the youngest maidens with the adults. Eggs laid on plants pestered by aphids or other ladybug prey may be mistaken for those of some despicable pest. Learn to spot the clusters of small, oval, bright yellow eggs.

Tiny, yellow, and black, multisegmented larvae hatch from these eggs and go through several stages, or *instars*, the last being the largest and the hungriest. Each larva may devour several hundred aphids, earning them the nickname "aphid wolf." Within about twenty days from hatching, these plump, feasting larvae undergo a brief metamorphosis, from which a tender, pale adult beetle emerges. The bright color and markings develop quickly.

Adult egg-laying beetles can put away two hundred aphids per day. Their life expectancy is only a few weeks, but these mature insects produce several generations per season, ensuring a constant supply of hungry ladybugs.

Both larvae and adults are active daylight hunters. They will prowl the garden, especially plants targeted by soft-bodied pests; the adults will even take wing in their search for food. All this activity is one of the prime reasons that ladybugs have such high nutritional demands. Upon spotting their prey, the ladybugs grasp it with powerful jaws and consume it live. The habits of such prey as aphids, scale, etc., are such that large, nearly immobile groups are often found together. The ladybugs will stay in one place, gorging on their fill of pests, continuing on their endless search only after cleaning up the immediate infestation.

In the western United States, ladybugs migrate in the fall to mass hibernating sites high in the mountains. Eastern varieties may congregate under garden litter for the winter. Warming spring temperatures trigger the beetles to migrate and disperse. During most of the year, nearly every North American habitat can claim some native species of ladybug.

Invite the neighborhood ladies to make themselves at home in your garden by incorporating their favorite flowering plants into your landscape. Angelica, buckthorn, euonymus, and yarrow will entice them. Special favorites include marigolds (especially the dainty, single-flowered Lemon Gem variety), butterfly weed, and tansy. By tucking some of these in among crops susceptible to aphids and other ladybug fare, you can lure the beetles to potential trouble spots, effectively curtailing outbreaks before they start. Lemon Gem makes a pretty border plant and can be used to edge the garden plot or beds of vulnerable crops.

In times of sparse food supplies (for instance once the aphid or other pest populations are under control), help our ladybugs along with an occasional garden party. Commercial beneficial bug food supplements are sold under names like Bug Chow and BugPro, or you can whip up your own. Dissolve one part sugar into four parts water for a temporarily sustaining homebrew. These mixtures simulate the sweet honeydew secretions given off by aphids and many of the ladybug's other prey. Sprinkling a few drops around the lower leaves of target plants may help to keep your gals from going hungry, or from straying. These sugar concoctions may also encourage mold growth on plants, so don't overdo it.

A special consideration for ladybugs and certain other aphid eaters is ant control. Ants and aphids have a *symbiotic* relationship, each benefiting from the other. Ants protect and maintain aphid "herds" in return for the precious drops of sweet, sticky honeydew. They will attack any marauding beetles or larvae in defense of their flocks. Boric acid is an effective organic means of ant control. Sprinkle some along their trails. Sticky bands of tacky material, either homemade or commercial preparations such as Tanglefoot, placed around the base of plants, will protect them from climbing ants. Be sure to keep the barriers free from any debris the ants might use as a bridge, including each other!

Ladybugs are widely available through mail order from numerous seed and garden catalogues or from many garden supply centers. A pint contains about 7,000, enough to cover about 5,000 square feet. By taking some precautions, you can improve the odds that a good percentage of the beetles will remain in your garden.

Remember that the first impulse a ladybug has upon waking from her winter's sleep is to migrate. Instinct tells her she must move on to find food. Spring warmth, rough handling, and hunger will all add to her restlessness.

If you just open the container and scatter them to the breeze, chances are you'll never see them again. Instead, consider things from the ladybug's point of view. Hose down the release area thoroughly prior to setting them free. This will create a cool, moist area. Release them in the cool of the evening to further lull them (remember, ladybugs are active during the day). Don't toss them from the container, but gently place groups of them about the plants most in need of their attention. The less shaken up they are, the less likely they are to make a quick getaway.

Ground Beetles (*Family Carabidae*)

If you happen to see a large, ugly, black beetle scurrying for cover from the light of day, resist that urge to stomp it. Ground beetles are fierce enemies of the likes of slugs, snails, cabbageworms, cutworms, armyworms, corn earworms, codling moths, gypsy moths, Colorado potato beetles, flea beetles, aphids, mites, thrips, and other garden pests.

Of the twenty-five hundred known species, some exist almost everywhere in North America. Ground beetles are found in a variety of colors from shimmering, metallic purples, blues, greens, and bronzes to flat black. Built like a tank, the average ground beetle comes heavily armored by a hard shell, and many are ominously large.

The basic black *Carabus nemoralis* is a relentless hunter who grows to well over an inch in length and will grab on to prey many times its own size, including small children's fingers. They stalk the night for slugs, snails, and other nocturnal pests, hiding out by day under rocks, boards, or in other sheltered spots.

Another common large ground beetle, *Calosoma scrutator*, has been dubbed the fiery searcher, both for his vivid purple, black, and green iridescence and for his merciless hunting technique.

Some other ground beetles are as tiny as 1/16 inch, but still are fearsome predators of the smaller nightlife.

Females of some species lay their eggs in carefully prepared hollows in the ground and actually stand guard over them while they incubate. As many as fifty eggs may be deposited together, or hundreds may be laid singly in prepared mud cells. The voracious larvae emerge within a few days to a few weeks, and immediately begin chowing down on garden pests. Each grub may devour as many as one hundred caterpillars before pupating into an adult. Feeding habits range from the gruesome to the dainty. Some species, such as the fiery searchers, revel in ripping their victims apart to get at the tender insides, while others merely puncture a small hole into the side of their prey and neatly suck out the contents.

Each year a new generation is produced, but various beetles may live from two to five years, hibernating in the soil or crevices through the winters.

Syrphid Flies (*Family Syrphidae*)

We already know about these good-guy flies in disguise, many of whom look like wasps or bees but harmlessly provide the vital service of pollination. But there's more. These useful creatures work double time to make our gardens more abundant and prosperous. For while the adults are busy performing their important task, the larvae provide yet another valuable service.

Syrphid, or hover or flower fly, larvae are a diverse bunch, as previously mentioned. However, a significant group are active predators of small insects such as aphids, mealybugs, thrips, and leafhoppers. During its active juvenile life a single larva can consume up to one thousand aphids or other small prey.

Hatching from small, white, oval eggs throughout the growing season, the larvae are greenish to grey or brown. Like miniature slugs, they are fat little maggots whose bodies taper to the head. However, they have the benefit of short, stumpy legs (called *prolegs*, common among caterpillar-type larvae) to aid their mobility. Their mouthparts feature tiny hooks with which they grab their prey and suck out the body fluids.

The larvae grow up to only 1/2 inch or so, heartily eating their way to full size. At this point, they pupate and undergo the metamorphosis into the adult. As winter approaches, those larvae who have entered the pupal stage remain dormant and hibernate through the winter.

Tachinid Flies (*Family Tachinidae*)

Found the world over, tachinid flies are important parasites of a variety of pests, including Mexican bean, Japanese, and other beetles; many caterpillars and cutworms; an assortment of bugs; and grasshoppers. Though many of the adults are humble nectar sippers, the larvae are ruthless carnivores, devouring their parasitized victims from the inside out.

Of the nearly thirteen hundred species found throughout North America, many resemble large, bristly houseflies. Shades of brown, grey, or black with faint markings are common. Size ranges from about 1/4 inch to 1/2 inch long. They fly about searching for hosts in an identifiable "seeking" flight. Once alighted on plants, they hustle across leaf surfaces in their quest.

Females deposit eggs in a variety of ways, all designed to get them into a host. Some types scatter thousands of miniscule eggs on foliage where the host routinely feeds, with the hope that they will be consumed along with the pest's regular meal. Others deposit their eggs right on the host, while still others make dead sure the job is done by puncturing the body of the host and inserting their eggs within. Once inside the host, the eggs hatch and the larvae develop by sucking the body fluids. Small stages even receive their oxygen through the blood of their hosts, while larger parasites resort to drilling air holes through the victim's body, or similarly accessing its breathing tubes.

Wild buckwheat is a favorite of the adults, and a small planting should draw scores of these pest-control experts to your garden.

Green Lacewings (*Chrysopa carnea, et al.*)

Delicate, demure lacewings flittering through the twilight sky, daintily sipping at flower nectar or nibbling pollen for their daily repast, belie the merciless predation of their youth. Lacewing larvae, whose raging appetites have earned them the alias "aphid lions," relentlessly stalk and devour hundreds of aphids throughout their brief childhood. Other soft-bodied insects, such as small worms, mites, thrips, leafhoppers, scale, immature whiteflies, and insect eggs form part of the larvae's diet.

Adult lacewings portray the essence of delicate frailty. Barely 3/4 inch long, they are slender insects with long, threadlike legs and antennae. Their wings are so fragile and transparent that except for a shimmer of iridescence when seen at certain angles they seem nearly invisible. Only the lacelike pattern of veins is distinguishable, hence their common name. Colored a soft, pale green, with large, coppery colored eyes, they blend well with their surroundings.

Adults are night fliers and can easily be observed apparently struggling towards bright lights. Their flight is labored and oddly clumsy for such a graceful-looking creature.

Female lacewings fly to any suitable plant to lay their eggs. This is generally one infested with prey for her children-to-be. Realizing the voracious appetites her newborns will possess, she ingeniously designs her nursery to prevent cannibalism. Secreting a tiny spot of sticky goo from her abdomen, she quickly draws it up into a fine silken stalk, which dries and hardens instantly. Atop this isolated perch she deposits a single, pale, pearly green egg. Several dozen of these curious one-egg nests may be grouped together or randomly scattered throughout the foliage.

Within days the eggs hatch into miniature larvae resembling tiny dull brown alligators with giant piercing jaws. These little guys immediately set off in search of their first meal. By grasping their prey between powerful jaws, injecting digestive juices into their victims, then slurping up the liquefied innards, each hunting "lion" can put away more than two dozen aphids or similar tidbits daily. After two

Continued ➜

or three weeks of feasting, the larva spins a cocoon and undergoes the transformation into the elegant adult. During the summer an entire lifetime may take no more than one month, but as winter approaches, larvae and some adults take shelter and hibernate until spring.

Though new generations of egg-laying adults can be produced throughout the summer, lacewing populations may not survive a harsh winter. However, they are readily available through mail-order catalogues or garden supply outlets. When sent through the mail, they are most often shipped in a medium containing supplementary food, such as moth eggs, and a dispersing agent, like rice hulls, both for physical separation of the eggs and as an aid in releasing them. Considering that ten thousand lacewing eggs will fit into the well of a thimble, it is obviously helpful to make them physically manageable.

Place the lacewing eggs out in the garden as soon as they begin to hatch. Suppliers recommend one thousand eggs per 200 square feet of garden if infested, or per 900 square feet as prevention against emerging pests. Simply sprinkle the contents in and around susceptible plants, then monitor to see if the hungry larvae are keeping pests in check. Repeat applications are often advised.

Since the larvae will devour any soft-bodied pest in its path, they rarely go hungry. Adults, however, depend on a ready supply of pollen, nectar, or honeydew. You can entice them to stay in your garden by providing an assortment of blossoms, including angelica, red cosmos, coreopsis, tansy, goldenrod, and Queen Anne's lace. When these kinds of food are in short supply, the population will dwindle either through migration, death, or reduced reproductive ability. By keeping an eye on their numbers you should be able to spot when a handout is warranted.

Commercial beneficial bug foods are available, or provide your own by sprinkling small amounts of one part sugar to four parts water here and there.

Praying Mantis (*Family Mantidae*)

Reverently poised upon a beanstalk, forelegs raised as if in prayer, the deadly praying mantis waits for an unsuspecting meal to happen within its reach. Even though aphids, beetles, various bugs, butterflies, caterpillars, leafhoppers, small birds and animals from frogs to shrews—even each other—are all acceptable fare, praying mantises alone will not put much of a dent in their populations. This is because despite their large size and menacing appearance, mantises are actually dainty eaters. They maintain a slow-paced lifestyle that requires less food than you might expect.

Suddenly, a caterpillar lumbers near and the statue-like mantis strikes. Enlarged, spine-covered forearms grasp the struggling insect as it thrashes about. One quick bite from the accomplished killer through the base of the victim's neck area severs crucial nerves, effectively paralyzing the prey.

Slowly, delicately, as if relishing every morsel, the hunter enjoys her meal, eating it alive.

Mantises, by their sheer size and strange appearance, are fascinating to watch. Unhurried, they generally allow the interested observer a fulfilling view. Their long, slender bodies may grow a full 5 inches or more in length. They have huge, bulging eyes and swiveling heads, the better to see approaching prey; powerful, spiny forearms, the better to grasp and hold it; and strong, chewing jaws, the better to consume it. Most come in shades from off-white to pale brown or green, which serve to blend in against the background. Not only an asset to their passive sit-and-wait hunting style, this camouflage helps to make them less obvious to birds and others eager to prey on so large and slow a meal.

When old enough to mate, the male mantis must question at some point whether it is really *worth* it. The female simply regards him as nothing more than a potential meal, and he must proceed with *extreme* caution if he is to accomplish his goal intact.

Upon spying his ladyfair, the suitor freezes in his tracks. Ever so slowly he approaches her from behind, taking over a half hour to move only inches. When finally he is close enough, he hops up and clasps his betrothed in a mating embrace.

If, however, the female sees him or is disturbed in the process, she will turn on him and literally bite his head off! Interestingly, this does nothing to impair the decapitated male's mating ability, and he continues to engage his mate until the act is completed. At this point, the now fertilized female devours the unlucky fellow, requiring him to satisfy her hunger as well.

Of the eighteen hundred species, many occur throughout the United States, most being relatively cold-hardy. Females lay as many as one hundred eggs in foamy, sponge-like egg cases that they create and deposit on branches or suspend from twigs or stems. These egg cases can be collected, refrigerated through the winter, then set out in the garden in the spring. Three egg cases, whether collected locally or purchased through the mail or from your garden center, are usually enough to patrol about 5,000 square feet of garden. You can draw native mantises to your plot by planting cosmos, raspberries, or other brambles, or by allowing a stand of weeds to flourish. Those for sale are usually a large Chinese variety. Though these are said to be more active hunters, they are also less cold-hardy and will not overwinter in many areas.

Predatory Wasps (*Family Vespidae*)

This family includes various hornets and wasps, perhaps the most familiar of which are the yellow jackets and paper wasps. Aggressive predators, wasps search out a range of garden pests, from fat, plodding caterpillars to quick, darting spiders.

Like bees, wasps form highly ordered societies based around a solitary egg-laying queen. Hundreds to thousands of workers perform the myriad daily tasks, both within the colony and in the field as foragers. Drones fulfill but one function in life, then perish. Just like the beehive, the wasp colony functions as a sterling example of cooperative effort and teamwork. However, there are some remarkable differences.

As intricately organized as the wasp colony is, it is all the more amazing that each colony is but a fleeting civilization. Each year, every individual in the nest dies, with the sole exception of newly hatched queens. These new queens mate soon after emerging and leave the colony forever to search for a sheltered spot in which to hibernate through the winter. With the coming spring they will emerge to establish colonies of their own.

Some species nest underground, some in other sheltered spaces such as tree hollows or deserted buildings, and others build their paper nests suspended from tree limbs or overhangs. All are built in essentially the same way, from chewed wood pulp and plant fibers glued together with saliva. The first brood of young is tended by the solitary queen. Unlike bees, who feed royal jelly and pollen to their young, the wasp mother includes a protein-rich mash of partially digested, regurgitated insect stew. After these young pupate and emerge as workers, they take over the duties of the nursery, leaving the queen to concentrate on egg-laying. By the end of the season the population of the colony can number into the thousands.

Though wasps have a nasty reputation for stinging, you can still benefit from their presence if you take a few precautions. Work in the cool of the evening or early morning when they are least active. Never dare a wasp: quick motions or crowding the nest may be perceived as a threat and dealt with accordingly. Avoid using scented products like colognes, hairsprays, and suntan lotions when working in the garden or other areas that wasps frequent. Also, don't invite them to investigate you by wearing bright colors, especially blues and yellows; instead opt for white or beige.

The adults feed on pollen, and will make good use of a flower patch, especially if it is stocked with their favorites, such as various daisies, strawflowers, goldenrod, or yarrow. They will also flock to ripe (especially overripe, even slightly fermenting) fruit, sweets, or meat. Ask anyone who has ever shared a picnic with one!

Parasitic Wasps (*Hymenoptera*)

As pest-control agents go, it's hard to find a more effective clan than the parasitic wasps. There are thousands of varieties, some parasitizing many species, others zeroing in on a single host. The victims have virtually no defense from these tiny invaders. Once attacked, they are doomed to certain death.

Trichogramma wasps are among the best known of these tiny terrors. They are egg parasites, killing the pest before it has a chance to develop and do any damage. They will control more than two hundred kinds of pests, including cabbageworms, hornworms, corn earworms, cutworms, armyworms, loopers, borers, and nearly every type of moth or butterfly. They can be found working in all kinds of habitats and depending on the temperature and humidity may live from only one week to as long as two months.

Depending on the host's egg size, the female Trichogramma may lay from one to several of her own eggs inside. This stops any further development by the egg, for the developing embryo is consumed and replaced by the quick-growing parasite. Since only a fraction of hatching pest eggs ever make it to reproductive maturity, eliminating

them prior to hatching significantly reduces numbers of subsequent stages.

Adult trichogramma wasps depend on small, single-flowered blossoms for nectar. Again, a small wildflower garden, with an assortment of blooms from spring until frost, will help to keep them in your plot.

Trichogrammas are available commercially either by mail or through some garden centers. They are shipped as minute eggs glued to small squares of black paper, resembling sandpaper. The thousands of eggs glued to these squares are actually moth eggs with the developing parasites inside. They should be released into the garden as soon as they begin to hatch, and by that time will be barely visible on the paper as tiny moving brown specks. Until this time, keep them at approximately 80° F. and shield them from direct sunlight. Distributors recommend several releases at two-week intervals for best results and advise either placing them on the ground near plants or stapling small pieces of the cards to leaves.

Braconid and chalcid wasps are small, usually dark though occasionally gaily colored, parasitic wasps. They range in size from a mere 1/32 inch to almost 1/4 inch in length. Belonging to a vast group found almost everywhere, these parasites claim a variety of hosts, including aphids, scale, mealybugs, and the soft bodies of the larvae of many beetles, moths, and butterflies, but they use a slightly different tactic than their Trichogramma cousins. Using exaggerated ovipositors, they carefully insert their eggs into the active, moving body of the host. As the eggs hatch inside the body, they feed on the host's internal tissues and fluids until they are ready to pupate and emerge in the adult form.

Some species dig out a hole through their victim's flesh and move to the outside of the body to spin tiny, silken cocoons. You can spot parasitized victims such as aphids by their bloated, discolored appearance, or later as "aphid mummies," mere shells of the bugs they once were; certain caterpillars are recognized by the load of pupating cocoons they carry.

Also included in the list of parasitic wasps are the *ichneumon wasps*. They range from very tiny to a frightening 2 inches long. Long ovipositors account for a good portion of their overall length and are used to deposit eggs in or on the host insect. They have the distinction of being the largest family of insects, with more than three thousand different kinds found in North America. Many are brightly patterned with yellow and black, while others wear more sedate shades of brown.

Host-specific parasites are constantly being discovered and evaluated. Many occur naturally and/or are already available commercially. *Encarsia formosa* is a parasitic wasp that attacks the greenhouse whitefly. *Edovum puttleri* is another small wasp that parasitizes only the eggs of the Colorado bean beetle in the same way the Trichogramma parasitizes its many hosts.

Pediobius foveolatus is yet one more tiny, dark villain of the pest insect world. It attacks the larvae of bean beetles, leaving nothing but a mummified shell. So tiny are many of these insects that they are often mistaken for gnats or else overlooked entirely. If we begin to think smaller and smaller, there may well be an entire world of untapped biological control agents just waiting to be recognized and put to work!

FLOWERING PLANTS

Growing Scented Geraniums

Mary Peddie, Judy Lewis & John Lewis

Illustrations by Alison Kolesar

General Classifications

The following descriptions are general, but they should help you to identify the plants you grow. Today there are probably more than 200 different scented geraniums available, and over a hundred more that have surreptitiously crept into the category. This includes flowering types, such as the Unique pelargoniums, and those with distinctive leaf shapes, like the grape-leaved pelargonium. Those we list in this book are true scenteds, with distinctive and individual aromas.

THE ROSE-SCENTED PELARGONIUMS

This is the largest and most beloved group of scented geraniums. There are two distinct leaf patterns, both triangular, in this group. One is more or less lobed; botanically it is *Pelargonium capitatum*.

The other pattern is deeply cut and, in fact, may be quite open. This is *P. graveolens*, from which most of the hybrids have been developed. However, the crossovers are so numerous and so ancient it is impossible to distinguish all of them.

THE MINT-SCENTED PELARGONIUMS

Here we have an easily identified group. The mint or peppermint geranium has a large, hirsuit (fuzzy) leaf and is named *P. tomentosum* because of its wooly texture. It has the habit of spreading exuberantly, and is one of the few scenteds which require mottled shade for optimum growth. Although few in number, the mint geraniums are a valuable addition to any collection. Mint has been crossed with others to produce deeply lobed leaves with dark centers.

THE FRUIT-SCENTED PELARGONIUMS

There are several distinct fruit types. Citrus is the largest group and contains many long-recognized citrus varieties. One, a hybrid of ancient origin, *P. x nervosum*, is the lime geranium, which truly does smell like limes. The 'Mabel Grey', introduced to the United States in 1973, is more lemony than lemons. Most of the citrus varieties are distinctly shrubby, with serrated leaves. Some have dark green leaves; others such as the 'Mabel Grey', are a light green. Variegated citrus scenteds, such as 'French Lace', have been grown for more than a hundred years.

Other fruit-scented types may have only one or two varieties or cultivars in each category. The apple, or *P. odoratissimum*, meaning very fragrant, is exactly that. True apple geraniums simply smell like fresh apples. All of the fruit-scented types seem to hybridize readily, and there are a number of charming offspring, including two different strains of Old Spice: one is more like the apple, the other has the grey cast of a nutmeg.

THE PUNGENT-SCENTED GERANIUMS

Most of the plants in this group belong to, or are closely related to, the *P. quercifolium* or oak-leaf-shaped group. Some growers note a eucalyptus scent, others think of them as pine, and indeed, our experience has been that these and other sharp scents may be quite clearly detected in selected plants. Some gardeners may find the pungent group more pungent than pleasant. Many have quite distinct coloration on the leaf and bloom profusely, and thus deserve a place in the garden. The *quercifolium* species hybridizes easily, even with geraniums that are not considered scented. The results are interesting and vigorous, but not necessarily sweet-smelling.

SPICE-SCENTED PELARGONIUMS

This classification has relatively few members but is exemplified by the long recognized *P. fragrans*, or nutmeg geranium. Others, such as 'Cinnamon Rose' with its spicy rose scent, may be placed in this category or left in the rose group, since the leaves more closely resemble that parentage. Ginger, *P. x nervosum* 'Torento', is frequently classified as *P. torento*, but this has no botanical standing. New cultivars, such as 'Apple Cider', are definitely spicy, and regardless of leaf shape, color, or texture, belong in the spice group.

OTHERS

Of course there are others—scented-leaf cultivars or species that defy classification. In the past few years it has been customary for some growers to include the pelargoniums known in England as the Uniques as scenteds. This is a dubious addition, for the foliage may be only slightly pleasant. Like the common zonal geranium, the foliage may well be odoriferous! However, these plants cross with many of the species in the scented group and do have quite distinctive blossoms, a desirable attribute.

Thus it is obvious that much depends on a specific plant and the eye of the beholder. And when it comes to classification of the scenteds by our sense of smell, the matter becomes most subjective.

Scenteds in the Garden

As natives of the temperate regions, pelargoniums require warmth and good drainage, but in many countries they thrive in a variety of soils. Generally they prefer full sun (in the Sun Belt shield them from the afternoon sun), but many tolerate partial shade. Only the mint geraniums, the old *P. tomentosum* and the newer *P. tomentosum* "Chocolate Mint", require shade. They make a wonderful groundcover around an established tree. "Pungent Peppermint" and "Joy Lucille" are much more tolerant of the sun.

For best results in a garden of scenteds we recommend soil amendments, fertilizers, and plant food.

Often these terms are used interchangeably, but the primary use of a soil amendment is to change the basic character of a soil, to make it more porous, more alkaline, or more water-retentive. Fertilizers provide nutrients for a plant, but these are not all readily available and sometimes must be broken down even further before they can be absorbed by the plant. A plant food, usually applied as a water-soluble chemical compound, feeds the plant immediately.

Some products may do all three, but plant food, for example, ordinarily is consumed by the plant and does not alter the soil. Sometimes a water-soluble compound is labeled "fertilizer" when in the strictest sense it is only a plant food.

TRANSPLANTING OUTDOORS

To transplant a 6-inch potted geranium in the garden, dig a hole 12 inches deep and about 9 inches across. Add soil amendments as necessary. In sandy soil place a 1-inch layer of peat moss at the bottom of the hole. In clay soil place a 3-inch layer of sand for drainage. Set plant in place, loosening the roots from the root ball as necessary. Fill hole with good topsoil. Water well, but water the soil, not the foliage of the plant. As a rule, scented geraniums do not like to get their leaves wet.

Large plants in the garden benefit from a top dressing of mulch, but it should be of a porous material, which does not stay damp. Cedar, eucalyptus, and pine bark are good organic mulches available commercially. Rock, gravel, sand, and products such as Turface are attractive inorganic materials.

WATERING

Geraniums are best watered with a soaker hose. Only in very dry areas is an occasional sprayer application of water needed. In their native habitat the pelargoniums are often found in small patches of soil between rocky outcroppings. The large fleshy roots can grow to several feet in a single summer, and will eagerly seek water and nourishment. When watering, it is best to give the scenteds a deep watering, rather than a sprinkle on top. They have few small feeder roots on the surface.

HINTS FOR BIGGER AND BETTER PLANTS

Soil amendments, fertilizers, and plant foods produce large, showy plants in one season. Ideal soil contains plant nutrients and holds some moisture, but drains well, permitting oxygen to permeate the interstices between soil particles. Clay soils, although difficult for the gardener, often contain many nutrients that are released under favorable conditions. They can be amended with gypsum and humus. Sandy soils do not contain enough nutrients and need to be amended with humus, peat, or compost, but provide good drainage. Plants in sandy soils require regular fertilization and an occasional plant food application. In a good rich loam, fertilization may not be required during the entire growing season.

In such a rich soil, an application of iron chelate in mid-August gives plants that are to be brought indoors an extra boost. Cuttings taken about three weeks after an application of iron chelate will root well and produce nice small plants for a windowsill. In those parts of the country where the scenteds grow all year, some fertilization is required to maintain healthy plants, especially if they are being cut regularly or require water frequently. Frequent watering leaches nutrients from the soil.

In a sandy soil fertilize every thirty days with a general-purpose fertilizer. It is wise to alternate the types of fertilizers and plant foods by using (1) fish emulsion, (2) a water-soluble chemical combination, or (3) an organic fertilizer such as dehydrated manure. Read the label carefully. To induce more blooms, decrease the amount of nitrogen in the fertilizer.

Container-grown geraniums thrive on a variety of fertilizers and plant foods; but again, alternate the types used. A 5–10-10 or similar formula is a safe combination. Do not overfertilize, but if you have to water frequently, remember that the water is leaching away plant nutrients, which must be replaced. An application of one of the timed-release fertilizers is good insurance. Several good brands are available at garden centers.

It takes about fifteen weeks for boom buds to form in the tips of the scented geraniums. If you want to enjoy blossoms, do not pinch

severely. To keep plants healthy and sturdy indoors during the winter, they must receive a lot of light. A south window with supplemental light insures growth, and a fan moving air over them makes them branch and stay stocky. The scenteds thrive indoors; part of this may be due to the reduced humidity found in most homes. They do not tolerate misting or high humidity often required for tropical houseplants.

PESTS AND DISEASES

The scenteds are robust plants, occasionally subject to mealybugs, whiteflies, and, infrequently, red spider mites or leaf miners. In the garden these insects rarely cause a great deal of damage. You will find the scenteds are "home base" for praying mantises, who do their part in making off with injurious insects.

Indoors, pests invariably find the sweetest-smelling of any collection. Apparently insects enjoy them as much as we! Use any insecticidal soap or a chemical houseplant insecticide; read and follow directions carefully. Stem damage, overwatering, and cold encourage disease. In midwinter move plants to a sunny window where they will get good and ample light; see that they have good ventilation. Water sparingly.

Fungus and virus infections are uncommon but possible. If stems become soft and dark, or leaves wilt and look dull, isolate the plant. Repot in fresh growing medium and cut back all damaged parts. Sterilize clippers after use. Do not attempt to take cuttings from an infected plant.

If a plant does not put out vigorous new growth, discard plant and soil. Sterilize the pot in a 20 percent chlorine solution before reusing.

Twelve Wonderful Plants to Grow

For a summary of plant characteristics, refer to the chart below.

P. X CAPITATUM
"ATTAR OF ROSE"

This popular rose scented acquires some of its popularity because of the romantic name. Not all "Attar of Rose" strains are heavily scented. This cultivar was once thought to have been introduced commercially for oil extraction to replace the rare true rose extract from Turkey. However, no record of it exists before 1907, when it was introduced to the trade in Britain by Cannel and Sons, a popular nursery operation closely allied to Kew Gardens. It is very similar to the *P. capitatum*, which was probably the source of the oil. *P. capitatum* is a fast-growing plant with weak and trailing stems. This cultivar is a slightly compact plant that is branched and has tri-lobed leaves, gently notched and somewhat light green in color. One strain has pink flowers; another produces a more lavender shade.

Select a vigorous, strong-scented "Attar of Rose". It is an excellent garden plant, likes full sun, and can stand a good deal of aridity. As a houseplant it requires abundant sun but infrequent watering. In midwinter it tends to become "leggy" and does best if pinched back severely in early fall.

Continued →

P. X GRAVEOLENS "GREY LADY PLYMOUTH"

"Grey Lady Plymouth" displays a pencil-thin line of creamy white about the border of its sage green leaves. It is quite fragrant, and its deeply lobed leaves add much interest to the garden. The "Lady Plymouth", its sister plant, is quite similar but boasts a wider margin of creamy white on the leaves, which are more a true green and have a slightly less pronounced scent.

This is a very adaptable houseplant. In confinement it seldom grows to more than 18 inches and maintains its compact size under most light conditions. A look-alike plant is the silver-edged rose, which is quite grey in color but does not evidence the line of white around the leaves. Some cultivars have pink flowers, others tend toward lavender hues.

P. X GRAVEOLENS AND P. X JATROPHOLIUM "ROBER'S LEMON ROSE"

Introduced by Ernest Rober in the 1930s, this old-time favorite has leaves that look like those of a tomato plant. It is bushy, and the irregularly lobed leaves are rather thick. It grows upright, with light lavender flowers. This particular plant is a favorite of many, but in recent years the lemon/rose fragrance so keenly described in the 1930s seems to be lacking from much of the stock available. It is a good garden specimen, and tolerates the dryness of most winter-heated homes with remarkably good grace.

"Rober's Lemon Rose" is a very long-lived cultivar. It does not train well as a standard because of its size and has a tendency to shoot off in odd directions. Grafted specimens are quite striking. It can be shaped as a topiary.

P. X CAPITATUM "SNOWFLAKE ROSE"

This large plant is a good example of the difficulty faced in tracing down the ancestry of many of the scented cultivars. Some catalogs list it as *P. adcifolium*, which is a name of no botanical meaning. Old authorities list 'Scheidt's Ice Crystal Rose' and 'Both's Snowflake Rose'. Later books call the snowflake *P. x capitatum logii*.

It is an irregular form of the round-leafed rose, and may be splotched, streaked, or flecked with white. The variegation is probably due to a virus, since Snowflakes will revert to plain green leaves once they are grown in an optimum environment. By carefully selecting the most colorful cuttings, one can successfully propagate this rose-scented geranium through many generations. In the garden it will meander over a 4-foot circle in one season, although it seldom grows more than 20 inches high. It is a good basket plant, but unruly in a pot on the windowsill.

P. ODORATISSIMUM (APPLE GERANIUM)

At last we come to a scented with a reasonable heritage. Scientists of the 1700s, including Linnaeus, L'Hertiers, and Aiton, knew of it and listed it in their works. A low-growing mound, the oval, almost rounded, pea-green leaves arise from a crownlike growth. Although not a true trailing geranium, the increasing diameter of the crown and the profuse white flowers borne on very long-stemmed growth make it an ideal hanging

basket plant. Hang it in the breezeway and the gentle winds that turn and twist the basket help to release the fresh scent of apples. In the garden it will spread to an 18-inch circle, but because of its height it is at its best in a border.

Apples are easily grown from seed, but they readily cross-pollinate with others, particularly nutmeg. It is recommended that seed-bearing plants be isolated. Cuttings should be made from the crown or from the nodes on the blooming stem. There are several delightful cultivars, and at least two different strains of old spice. One is more like the apple parent, the other favors the nutmeg side of the family. Both are pleasantly spicy.

P. X CRISPUM "FRENCH LACE"

Again, a scented with clear-cut lineage. This is sometimes called the "Variegated Prince Rupert". "Prince Rupert", an old cultivar from the *P. crispum* group, appears on lists in the early 1800s. Like all the *crispums* the leaves of "French Lace" are many, small, and tri-lobed; they are distinguished by narrow variegation. It is best to keep this one pinched to make it grow into a compact upright form. Otherwise it has a tendency to "grow informally," as one grower described it.

This elegant geranium requires more heat than its sire and is subject to disease in cold or dampness. From the leaves come the clear scent of lemon. A very good pot plant, "French Lace" surprises one with small, almost showy lavender flowers in midwinter. Water carefully when needed. It is at home in the garden, and prefers full sun and airy, breezy conditions.

P. CITRONELLUM "MABEL GREY"

This handsome upright plant is more lemony than lemon. It was introduced to the United States from England in the 1970s via South Africa, according to one authority, although another says it came from Kenya. Whatever its origin, all gardeners should be glad it arrived. "Mabel Grey" makes a wonderful standard because of its upright growth pattern. After much deliberation, it was placed on the International Registry of Geraniums in 1983 as a separate species. This was a great relief to many growers who were hard-pressed by their experiences and observations to accept "Mabel Grey" as a mere hybrid of already known varieties.

The most successful cuttings are from the stem shoots. This treatment results in standards with incomparably sturdy stems that support a fragrant yellow-green ball. In midwinter it blooms with sudden beauty, a bright pink flower with carmine blotches and streaks.

Although more difficult to propagate than some other specimens, it has some resistance to cold, and several close relatives, such as "Angel" and "Frensham". It is a collector's item, included here because of its desirability.

P. X RADENS "CINNAMON ROSE"

The deeply dentate, spicy, rose-scented green leaves of "Cinnamon Rose" are easily distinguished from other dentate rose-scented varieties by the crisp, almost harsh, texture of the leaf, protruding veins, and the rows of cells rolled under at the edge of each leaf. There is much confusion about this nomenclature: some plants sold as Cinnamon may be incorrectly classified.

This particular 'Cinnamon Rose' grows upright and rapidly in the garden and is unexcelled to train as a standard. In a year stems may be 24 inches tall, more than 1 inch in diameter, and supporting a ball of foliage 14 inches across. The leaves are excellent for use in jelly or syrup.

P. X FRAGRANS (NUTMEG GERANIUM)

Another old favorite, long known and grown. Because of its similar size and shape, it is often linked with the apple. Although they are alike in many respects, such as their ability to cross-pollinate and their abundant small white flowers, apple and nutmeg are two distinct species. Nutmeg leaves are grey-green, soft, and lobed; the flowers are more distinctly marked with red splotches, and the stems are woody and branched. The sharp spicy fragrance may or may not resemble the smell of nutmeg, apparently depending on the way the plant is grown and the particular strain.

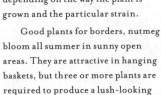

Good plants for borders, nutmeg bloom all summer in sunny open areas. They are attractive in hanging baskets, but three or more plants are required to produce a lush-looking display. They were much favored by the Victorians, who even wrapped sweet butter in nutmeg leaves for an unusual butter for tea sandwiches. This plant requires some care, since the lower leaves tend to become discolored. Variegated cultivars available include "Snowy Nutmeg" (occasionally listed as "Showy Nutmeg" or "Golden Nutmeg"). The white variegation is not always a stable characteristic.

P. TOMENTOSUM (MINT GERANIUM)

Again, a clear-cut species, known and grown in cultivation for over 300 years. The very strong mint scent and huge velvety leaves make this a favorite in any collection. Garden specimens may grow to be 36 inches across, but mint geranium spreads laterally and is seldom more than 18 inches tall. It requires some shade for such a luxuriant display. The plant does well in large containers and does not demand the amount of water its size and texture would seem to require. It should be watered well when necessary, but overwatering results in yellowed leaves and soft growth.

This has been crossed with others to produce such remarkable plants as "Chocolate Mint", "Joy Lucille", and

a decidedly upright "Pungent Peppermint". The leaves of this species are used in crafts such as wreaths, and in the kitchen as a flavoring agent for pound cakes and chocolate sponges.

P. QUERCIFOLIUM "FAIR ELLEN"

The oak-leafed species has many cultivars, from the "Giant Oak", which simply gallops over the ground in a garden, to the "Village Oak", small and self-contained. "Fair Ellen" falls somewhere in between. It has the deeply dentated and serrated leaves that distinguish all of the *quercifolii*, but its deep maroon center and veining add much interest. This is a profuse bloomer for a scented, with lavender blossoms tinged with carmine.

Although not as imposing as some of the family, this particular cultivar remains a favorite. The cool temperatures and long days of winter cause this plant to become leggy. In the house, however, it will produce abundant blossoms in December and January given adequate light. Strangely enough, all the *quercifolii* tolerate—in fact require—a good deal of water.

P. X DOMESTICUM "PINK CHAMPAGNE" ET AL.

This complex hybrid is known to have been crossed with one of the Martha Washington pelargoniums, themselves a complex cross. The "Pink Champagne" is an unusual geranium, included because it is a vigorous plant with a striking pink blossom. No mention of it appears in any catalog until after 1960, so it is presumed to have been introduced in the last part of this century. On the other hand, it is quite possible it was known in the late 1800s under another name and has merely reemerged.

Because of its mixed breeding the plant should only be propagated from tip cuttings, and any seedlings or root growths ruthlessly destroyed—unless, of course, you want to spend several years trying to unravel its geneology.

So do enjoy these wonderful old-new plants. Don't pamper them. Pinch them when they become leggy, water them when they are dry, and groom them by removing yellowing leaves and spent flowers. They will reward you with wonderful odors, fascinating textures, luxuriant growth, and an insatiable desire to find new and different types.

Pelargonium Propagation

Once you have acquired a plant or two, you will want others. But the collector discovers that plants of like appearance may differ in their chief charm—scent. When you have found one you like, propagate it vegetatively—with cuttings—to assure that it will be duplicated. "Mother plants," as they are often called, should be strong and vigorous. Water them well several hours before taking cuttings. Cut "slips" 3 to 6 inches long with a very sharp knife or nurseryman's clippers, sterilized with alcohol. The best cuttings are from a stem that "snaps." Stems that bend may be soft and young, and those that refuse to snap are often woody. Both the very tender and the woody stems take longer to "strike," or produce roots.

Continued →

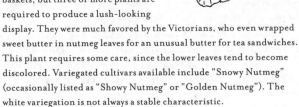

Cut below an internode at an angle and remove lower leaves and stipules. Lay the cuttings out for 24 hours to "callus." This stimulates the growth of new cells—a callus—on the wound. Filtered light, a dry atmosphere, and no more than 70°F assures the best callusing. Placing cuttings in a frost-free refrigerator for 12 to 36 hours assures good callusing. It is not necessary to use a rooting hormone on geraniums. However, if you are going to root them in sand or soil, the fungicide contained in rooting compound may prove helpful.

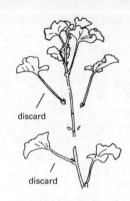

discard

discard

An old-fashioned pot-in-pot rooting bed is a time-honored way of rooting plant material. Use a large, broad, squat clay pot, a small clay pot, a small cork, and rooting medium of 1 part commercial growing mix and 1 part perlite, thoroughly mixed. Soak new pots overnight in water or thoroughly scrub old pots because using.

Put small pieces of nylon hose over the holes on the inside of the large pot. Fill loosely to within 1 inch of the top with damp rooting medium. Put a cork in the hole in the small pot. Scoop out the rooting medium in the center of the large pot and place the small pot firmly in the center of that hole, its rim even with or slightly above the rooting medium.

Stick the callused cuttings upright into the medium. Keep the corked, small pot filled with water. Put this nursery in a warm place in filtered light. In two weeks or so the cuttings will develop roots. Transplant to 3-inch pots using a commercial medium. When plants are growing vigorously, transplant again to a larger container or to the garden. Again, houseplant potting soil is not suitable for geraniums. A professional growing mix provides an optimum growing medium. See chart below for suggested mixes.

Geraniums will root quite well in many other media such as clean sand or well-drained garden soil. Select a sheltered place in mottled shade in the garden. Remove soil or make a trench, and fill with ordinary sand. Make cuttings as described above and insert into the rooting bed, which should be kept damp. Check daily and remove wilted or discolored leaves or cuttings. Although the success rate is not so great, the use of small "cutting beds" is time-tested and can result in many beautiful plants.

GROWING FROM SEEDS

Occasionally, scented pelargonium seeds are offered in a catalog. They may be quite good, or very ordinary, since hybridization occurs frequently. Gathering seeds from a rose-scented geranium you particularly favor is no guarantee that the resulting plants will be equally strong-scented. Wrap hanging baskets of nutmeg or apple in netting to capture the tiny, coiled, bristled seed and its nectar stem. If hanging baskets are isolated, or only one variety is grown, a true apple or nutmeg will result.

Seed should be scattered on top of a very light, porous seed medium. As the spiral nectar tube absorbs water, it straightens out. This straightening movement acts something like a screwdriver, and the seed is screwed or drilled into the medium to the proper depth. The fresh seeds of many species germinate within ten to twelve days, although no exact figures are available for different cultivars.

The cultivars have very diverse flower parts. Many of them flower, but the pistil (female) may develop long after the stamens (male) have produced pollen and dried up. Some stamens produce only infertile pollen. Some stamens are very short, the minute amount of pollen they carry lost in the petals of the flower. Many seeds that develop are themselves infertile. This apparent lack of foresight on the part of Mother Nature may in fact be insurance that the stronger species and the better cultivars tend to survive.

Thus the surest way to propagate pelargoniums you wish to have multiplied is vegetatively with cuttings.

The following chart is based on twenty years of observing, growing, and enjoying scented geraniums in zones 3, 4, 5, and 6. The category "Add Trace Elements" simply means that these particular species or cultivars do best with added minerals. Extra minerals can be added through additional fertilizers or by using blood meal, bone meal, or Epsom salts in small quantities. Use only if the plants do not grow well, have yellow leaves, or otherwise evidence lack of vigor.

The required pH is for the most part neutral; however, a few varieties seem to grow better and bloom more frequently if they are occasionally fertilized with a slightly acid fertilizer. Even an occasional drink of cold tea or tea leaves scattered over the soil benefits these geraniums.

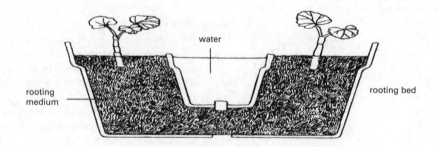

water

rooting medium

rooting bed

GROWING & USAGE CHART
Based on Garden Plants Grown in Zones 3, 4, 5, and 6

	Height	Ordinary Soil	Rich Loam	Add Trace Elements	pH	Border	Bedding Plant	Standard	Bonsai	Hanging Basket	Houseplant	Culinary Use	Potpourri	Topiary Subject
Attar of Rose	2'	X			N		X			X	X	X	X	
Skeleton Leaf Rose	4'	X		X	N		X	X			X		X	
Fern Leaf	3'	X		X	N		X				X		X	X
Nutmeg	18"	X		X	A	X			X	X	X	X	X	
Rose, *Capitatum*	2'	X			N		X			X	X		X	
Rose, *Graveolens*	3'	X			N		X				X	X	X	
Grey Lady Plymouth	3'	X			N		X				X	X	X	
Cinnamon Rose	4'	X			N		X	X			X	X	X	
Rober's Lemon Rose	4'	X		X	N		X				X		X	
Mint, *Tomentosum*	1'		X	X	N	X				X	X		X	
Ginger	2'	X		X	A		X				X		X	X
Southernwood	2'	X		X	N	X			X		X			X
Snowflake	2'	X		X	A		X			X	X		X	
Prince of Orange	2'	X		X	N		X				X		X	X
Fingerbowl	2'	X		X	N	X	X		X		X	X	X	X
French Lace	18"	X		X	A	X	X		X		X		X	X
Pink Champagne	3'	X			N		X	X			X		X	
Coconut	12'	X		X	N	X				X	X		X	
Lime	2'	X		X	N	X	X			X	X	X	X	
Apple	1'		X	X	N	X				X	X	X	X	
Apricot	3'		X	X	A		X	X			X		X	
Strawberry	2'		X	X	N	X	X				X		X	X
Oak Leaf	3'	X			N		X	X			X		X	
Fair Ellen	2'	X			A		X				X	X	X	
Mabel Grey	4'		X	X	N			X			X		X	X

10 Steps to Beautiful Roses

Maggie Oster

Ilustrations by Brigita Fuhrmann

Introduction
More and more, people are discovering that roses can be a valuable addition to the landscape. No other shrub can bloom almost continuously from early summer until frost. And no other shrub comes in such a wide range of growing habits.

No other plant produces the quantity or quality of blooms each year, even the same year of planting. The fresh-cut roses alone will return your purchase price many times over. No doubt, roses are one of the best gardening buys around. To insure a return on that investment, let's go through the 10 easy steps to successfully growing beautiful roses.

Step 1 — Choose Well
Originally there were between 150 and 200 rose species found growing in the wild. From these have evolved the thousands available today that are divided into four major types: bush, climbing, shrubs and ground cover, and tree roses.

Continued ➜

BUSH ROSES

Usually upright-growing, bush roses need no support and grow from less than six inches to over six feet tall, depending on the variety and climate. Bush roses are further subdivided into five categories: hybrid tea, floribunda, grandiflora, miniature, and heritage, or old, roses.

Hybrid tea roses are the most popular, with their classic long-stemmed, narrow buds opening into large blooms. Plants flower throughout the growing season in a wide range of colors, and they are generally three feet or more tall.

Floribunda roses were developed in the mid-1940s. Generally, they are very hardy, compact plants, growing two to three feet tall. They bear large quantities of medium-sized flowers in short-stemmed clusters all summer long. These are considered among the easiest roses to grow and are also among the best for landscaping.

Grandiflora roses usually grow five to six feet tall and bear large flowers in clusters on long stems continuously during the growing season. Because of their height, they are excellent plants for accent or for a background planting.

Miniature roses are a small version of almost every other category, but they usually grow less than two feet tall. Blooms and foliage are proportionately smaller as well. Most are extremely hardy and vigorous. They make excellent additions to the garden as edgings, mass plantings, accents or container plantings.

Heritage, or old, roses are a diverse lot of plants that were developed by plant breeders prior to 1867, a date established by the American Rose Society as a delineation between "old" and "new" roses. Most of these are direct descendants of species roses, with many varying plant and flower forms, hardiness and characteristics. Some of the heritage rose types include the Albas, Bourbons, Centifolias, Damask, Gallicas, Mosses, Noisettes and Rugosas.

CLIMBING ROSES

Roses do not actually climb like beans or peas, but rather some kinds do have such long, flexible canes that they can readily be attached to supports like arbors, trellises, posts or fences. Just about every type of bloom and color is available in climbing roses. There are two main types

of climbers: large-flowered and ramblers. Large-flowered climbers have thick, sturdy canes growing about ten feet along; plants bloom continuously or off and on throughout the summer. Ramblers have longer, thinner canes; they bear clusters of small flowers once in late spring or early summer.

SHRUB AND GROUND COVER ROSES

Growing broadly upright with slightly arching canes, most shrub roses are very hardy, low-maintenance plants. Size, depending on variety, ranges from 4 to 12 feet tall. Plants usually have many canes and lots of leaves. This makes them a good choice for hedges as well as background and mass plantings. Most rose flower types and colors are available, and plants may bloom only in the spring or throughout the season, depending on the variety. Shrub roses often produce red, orange or yellow seed pods, called hips, after blooming. These are high in vitamin C and can be used in teas and cooking or left on the plant for the birds to eat during the winter.

Ground cover roses have limber, arching canes that trail along the ground producing slightly mounded plants. There are both spring-blooming and repeat-blooming varieties.

TREE ROSES

Any rose that is bud-grafted onto a straight, sturdy trunk is a tree rose. The trunk may be one to two feet tall for miniature and floribunda roses, or three to four feet tall for hybrid teas. To create a weeping effect, climbers are budded onto six-foot trunks. Tree roses require special winter protection in all but the mildest areas.

SHOPPING FOR ROSES

As with many garden plants, roses can be purchased either locally at a nursery or garden center or from a mail-order company. Either way, check the package or catalog for the rose grade. Roses are graded according to their growth at the time they are packaged or potted. The top grade is #1. These plants must have three or more healthy canes at least 3/8-inch in diameter. Number 1 plants generally grow faster and produce more blooms in the first season.

The next grade is #1–1/2. These plants have two or more canes thinner than 3/8-inch. They are a little slower to develop in the garden and require a bit more attention. The #2 grade plants have one or two thin canes. They are useful for large mass plantings, or when you can provide plenty of care and attention.

Roses are sold either as dormant, bare-rooted plants or planted and growing in containers. There are pros and cons to either type.

Most mail-order companies offer dormant, bare-root roses with a wide selection of varieties. These roses are kept in cold storage until shipped at the proper planting time. Miniature roses are usually shipped year-round, or whenever the customer desires, fully growing and blooming. Something new are tissue-cultured roses, produced by a special micro-propagation technique. These are shipped at planting time, also fully growing.

Local nurseries, garden centers and other retail outlets also offer dormant roses in the spring. When buying locally, be sure plants have been kept cool and moist. Canes must be smooth, plump, and green or reddish, not dry, shriveled, wrinkled or excessively sprouted.

Bare-root, dormant roses are planted in early spring, when the soil is workable and severely freezing weather is over. In milder climates, bare-root roses may be planted in late fall or winter.

Also available locally are roses planted in containers and actively growing. These have the advantage that you can add them to the garden at any time during the growing season, but they are more expensive and there are fewer varieties from which to choose. Check the canes and foliage for health and vigor.

Once the different types, grades, and dormant versus growing roses are understood, the big question is: "What are the best roses for my garden?"

There are several ways to arrive at an answer. One is to visit local public rose gardens to see which plants are doing well in your climate. Another is to talk with neighbors or others in your area who grow roses, discussing the ones that have done well for them. Joining the local rose society is a good way to meet these people. By joining the American Rose Society you gain access to rose gardeners and information both locally and nationwide. For information on membership, write the American Rose Society, P.O. Box 30,000, Shreveport, LA 71130–0030. For $2.50 plus shipping from the same address, a yearly-updated "Handbook for Selecting Roses" can be purchased; the handbook contains an alphabetical listing of rose varieties, each with a numerical rating from 1 to 10.

Based on these ratings, some of the best roses in each of the categories are:

Hybrid Teas—Mister Lincoln, First Prize, Dainty Bess, Pascali, Pristine, Granada, Peace, Precious Platinum, Duet, Color Magic and First Prize.

Floribundas—Europeana, Cherish, Simplicity, Sea Pearl, Anabell, Gene Boerner, Little Darling and Iceberg.

Grandifloras—Aquarius, Gold Medal, Pink Parfait, Queen Elizabeth and Prima Donna.

Miniatures—Beauty Secret, Starina, Rise 'n' Shine, Mary Marshall, Magic Carrousel, Holy Toledo, Lavender Jewel, Jean Kenneally, Minnie Pearl and Pacesetter.

Climbers—Altissimo, Don Juan, Jeanne Lajoie, Sombreuil, America, Royal Sunset and Handel.

Shrubs—Dortmund, Hansa, Ruskin, Will Scarlet, Wanderin' Wind, Golden Wings, Applejack, Cornelia and Bonica.

Heritage—Souvenir d'Alphonse Lavallee, Apothecary's Rose, Celsiana, Crested Moss, Souvenir de la Malmaison, *Rosa hugonis*, Mme. Hardy, Nastarana and Charles de Mills.

Sometimes roses are wanted for a specific purpose or a special reason. The following selections are somewhat personal and arbitrary, but should provide a springboard in choosing varieties for your yard:

Fragrant Roses—Fragrant Cloud, Granada, Papa Meilland, Mister Lincoln, Duet, Dainty Bess, Angel Face, Gold Medal, Intrigue, Sutter's Gold, Tiffany, Sweet Surrender, Double Delight, Climbing Crimson Glory, Don Juan, Royal Sunset, *Rosa rugosa*, Blanc Double de Coubert, Frau Dagmar Haustrup, Sparrieshoop, Stanwell perpetual, Duchesse de Branbant, General Jacqueminot, Honorine de Branbant, Mme. Hardy and Salet.

Hybrid-tea Roses for Hot, Dry Climates—Double Delight, First Prize, Granada, Mister Lincoln, Peace, Royal Highness and Sutter's Gold.

Hybrid-tea Roses for Hot, Humid Climates—Double Delight, Fragrant Cloud, Honor, Lady X, Mister Lincoln, Paradise, Pascali and Peace.

Especially Hardy Hybrid-tea and Grandiflora Roses—Fragrant Cloud, Lady X, Pink Parfait, Pristine, Swarthmore, First Prize, Granada, Mister Lincoln, Paradise, Pascali and Peace.

Most Disease-resistant Hybrid Tea, Grandiflora, and Floribunda Roses—Precious Platinum, Duet, Aquarius, Queen Elizabeth, Cherish, Simplicity, Pascali, Pristine, Sea Pearl, Anabell, Gold Medal, Europeana, Rose Parade and First Edition.

Step 2—Provide a Great Location

No matter how great the rose variety or the quality of the plant, if put in a less-than-ideal location, you'll be waging an uphill battle. A very simple way to have success with roses is to consider the site before planting.

The first consideration is sunlight. Roses need at least six hours each day for vigorous, healthy growth. If you have a choice between morning and afternoon sun, choose morning. It's important for the dew to dry off quickly as wet foliage is a breeding ground for disease. Actually, afternoon shade is beneficial in hot climates.

If one area of the yard has better soil than another, that area should be your first choice. But, as discussed later in Step 3, the soil can be improved, so don't let that limit where you use roses in the landscape. Roses are very tolerant of different soil types, especially if the soil is improved with organic matter.

Soil drainage is particularly important, but even that can be corrected, either with tiling or raised beds. To check drainage, dig a hole 18 inches deep and fill with water. If not empty in several hours, there is a problem.

Avoid planting roses near large trees with shallow roots, such as silver maples or poplars. Also avoid planting under eaves or gutters where falling water, snow, or ice can be damaging.

An area with good air movement helps to quickly dry foliage from moisture of dew, rain or sprinkler systems. Too much wind, especially in winter, can damage canes.

One aspect that people sometimes forget to consider is access. Having roses close to the house or a part of the yard that you regularly pass will mean that you will enjoy your roses more and take better care of them. Ready access to water is especially critical to summer maintenance.

Step 3—Super Soil

There are a few people who have the wonderful garden loam that is described in books and magazines. One is more likely to have a soil that is predominantly clay or sand. If you live in a subdivision, the probability is good that the soil is a relatively infertile subsoil.

Fortunately, soil can be helped with additives and fertilizer. If you have not gardened previously or are on a new site, have your soil tested by a laboratory. Call your County Extension Service office (usually listed under county offices in the phone directory) for information on how and where to take a soil sample.

Continued →

The results will tell you about the soil, including the fertilizer needs and the pH. Roses grow best in a slightly acid soil with a pH of 6.0 to 6.5. The lab or extension office will be able to provide information on how to raise or lower the pH, if necessary. At this time, check your soil for drainage as described in Step 2.

If you're going to plant roses among other plants that are growing well, then no special preparation is needed. For a newly planted area, first remove any sod. Next, till or dig the soil to a depth of at least 12 inches, removing any stones or large rocks. Spread a 4-inch layer of an organic material, such as peat moss, compost, leaf mold or dehydrated cow manure evenly over the soil surface. Also spread on the recommended fertilizer. Till or dig this into the soil, incorporating well. The site is now ready for planting.

Step 4—Planting Perfectly

Properly planting roses does not require any special know-how. It is, however, helpful to plant bare-root roses at the correct time and to follow certain procedures to ensure success. The following planting times and spacing as well as rose-planting steps were developed by All-America Rose Selections, a national rose-testing organization.

PLANTING TIMES

Region	Planting Time
Pacific Northwest	February – March
Pacific Southwest Seaboard	January – February
Southwest	late December – January
South Central	late January – February
Mid-South	December – January
Subtropical	December – January
North Central	April – early May
Eastern Seaboard	March – early April
Northeast	April – early May

SPACING

Region	Hybrid Tea/Grandiflora	Floribunda
Pacific Northwest	3–4 ft.	2.5–3.5 ft.
Pacific SW Seaboard	3–4 ft.	2.5–3.5 ft.
Southwest	3–4 ft.	2.5–3.5 ft.
South Central	2.5–3 ft.	2–3 ft.
Mid-South	2.5–3 ft.	2–3 ft.
Subtropical	3–4 ft.	2.5–3.5 ft.
North Central	2–2.5 ft.	2–2.5 ft.
Eastern Seaboard	2.5–3 ft.	2–3 ft.
Northeast	1.5–2 ft.	1.5–2 ft.

PLANTING BARE-ROOT ROSES IN 5 EASY STEPS

1. Prepare the site as previously described, if necessary. Dig each hole 15 to 18 inches wide and deep. Mix a quart of peat moss, compost, or other organic material with the soil removed from the hole. Form a blunt pyramid of some of this soil mixture in the planting hole.

2. Remove any broken or injured roots or canes and canes less than pencil-size in thickness. Position rose on soil pyramid so the bud union (the swelling at the stem base) is just above the ground level after the soil settles in mild climates or about one to two inches below the surface in climates where winter temperatures fall below freezing. Spread roots in a natural manner down the slope of the pyramid.

3. Work soil mixture around the roots to eliminate any air pockets. Firm the soil around roots and add more soil until the hole is three-quarters full.

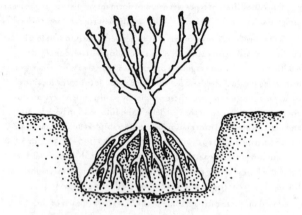

4. Fill hole with water, allowing it to soak in, then refill with water. After water drains the second time, check to see that the bud union remains at the proper level; if not, add soil as necessary. Fill remainder of hole with soil and tamp lightly. Trim canes back to eight inches, making cuts one-quarter inch above an outward-facing bud at a 45-degree angle.

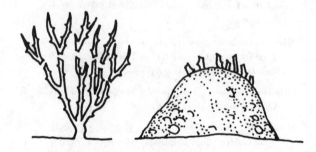

5. Mound soil around and over the plant to six inches deep. This protects canes from drying out. When buds sprout, gradually and gently remove soil mound, probably within two weeks or so, checking every two or three days. Loosen name tag so it does not constrict cane. When vigorous growth starts, apply plant food according to manufacturer's directions.

Step 5—Mulching

Although not everyone agrees with me, I have found that using an organic mulch is a great boon not only to growing roses but also for all gardening. Mulching reduces the need for weeding and watering by inhibiting weed growth and slowing down soil moisture evaporation. Plus, over a period of time, it adds nutrients to the soil.

Before mulching, remove weeds and lightly loosen the soil surface. Spread two to four inches of mulch over the bed, leaving several inches of space unmulched around the base of each rose.

Over a period of time the mulch will deteriorate, the length of time depending on the material. Usually some new mulch must be added at least once each year. There are a variety of materials that make effective mulches. Use whatever is locally available and cost effective. Some of the possibilities are wood chips and shavings, shredded bark, pine needles, cottonseed or cocoabean hulls, chopped oak leaves, partially decomposed compost or ground corncobs.

These mulches will tie up soil nitrogen as they decompose, so use a fertilizer with a higher percentage of nitrogen than normally recommended for roses.

Another type of mulch that is becoming readily available is the porous black plastic or landscape-fabric mulches. These can be laid down first, then holes cut in them for planting, or they can be put down after the roses are planted. These mulches necessitate using a water-soluble fertilizer. To improve appearance, cover with a layer of bark chips or gravel.

Step 6—Watering

An ample supply of soil moisture, coupled with excellent drainage, is essential for vigorous and healthy rose plants. Because of the variations in the type of soil, climatic conditions, and growth stage of the rose, it's difficult to give hard-and-fast rules for watering. A sandy soil will need more frequent watering than a loamy one; hot, dry air causes rapid transpiration of plant moisture; young plants also have a greater need for soil moisture than established plants. These are some of the basic considerations; learn to observe and use common sense.

Assuming you have well-drained soil, a good rule-of-thumb is to never let more than the top inch or so of soil dry out during the growing season. This may necessitate watering as frequently as every couple of days during the height of summer. Mulching plays an important role in conserving water, especially under these conditions.

Water in the early morning, so if foliage gets wet it can dry out before dark, thus inhibiting diseases. Water should be applied slowly to the base of the plant. Soaker hoses, drip irrigation systems, or a bubbler attachment for the end of the hose are various solutions; these also have the advantage of keeping water from splashing onto leaves and spreading diseases. Many gardeners create a basin, or dike, at the perimeter of the foliage spread to concentrate water at the roots.

Most importantly, water slowly and deeply. The soil should be soaked at least 12 to 18 inches deep. To check this, dig down after a specified period of time. Reduce or lengthen watering period accordingly. A light watering is almost worse than none at all. Light watering encourages shallow roots that cannot adequately anchor the plant, are subject to fertilizer and cultivation damage, and need ever more frequent watering.

Step 7—Feeding

There are just about as many opinions on fertilizing roses as there are people growing them. The main agreement is that to produce that lush, healthy foliage and those gorgeous flowers, plenty of any kind of fertilizer is needed.

A basic fertilizer program for roses that repeatedly bloom throughout the summer includes three feedings. The first is in early spring, just as the buds begin to break. Plants should be fertilized again when flower buds have developed and, finally, about six weeks before the first fall frost in your area.

Additional or more frequent feeding will be needed if the soil is sandy or in warm climates with an extended growing season. Many expert rose gardeners also add several feedings of a water-soluble fertilizer during the summer.

Plants don't know if the fertilizer package says rose food or not, so a general-purpose dry granular garden fertilizer like 10–10-10 if plants are mulched, or 5–10-10 if they are not, will be sufficient for the first two feedings. Use a formulation without nitrogen, such as 0–10-10 for the last feeding before frost. Use about 1/2 cup for each rose bush. Scratch into the soil around the plant, without letting the fertilizer touch the canes or bud union, then water well.

If you decide to use commercial rose fertilizer or a water-soluble or foliar fertilizer, always follow manufacturer's directions.

The rose varieties that only bloom once, such as many of the species and heritage roses, only need to be fertilized once a year, in early spring.

Newly planted roses should not be fertilized until about a month after planting.

For those who like to use organic-type fertilizers, a popular recommendation is dehydrated cow manure and bone meal in the spring, and fish emulsion or manure tea for the other feedings.

Step 8—Pruning

Any type of pruning, whether of fruit trees, ornamental trees and shrubs, or roses, seems to be one of the most intimidating aspects of gardening. But without pruning, most of the hybrid tea, grandiflora, and floribunda roses will become a tangled, misshapen mass with a few small blooms. Actually, it's hard to make a mistake in pruning, and the benefits will far outweigh your fears.

The basic tools you'll need are a good-quality, sharp, curved-edge pruning shears; a long-handled lopping shears; a small, fine-toothed curved pruning saw; and a pair of heavy leather gardening gloves.

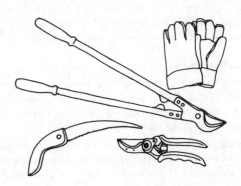

Most pruning cuts are made at a 30- to 45-degree angle at a point 1/4-inch above an outward-facing bud eye. A bud eye is a dormant growing point on the crotch between a leaf stalk and the cane, or stem. Pruning directly above a bud eye stimulates growth, which results in a new shoot. Because roses need good air circulation to prevent the spread of diseases, it's best to have most branches growing outwards from the center. This is why pruning cuts are made just above an outward-facing bud eye.

A trick for minimizing injury to the plant is to have the cutting blade of the pruning shears on the lower side of the cut.

Continued ➔

How much to prune depends on the result you want. Gardeners raising roses for competition usually prune back a great deal, as this produces a few very large flowers. Lighter pruning results in more flowers that are slightly smaller.

Pruning is done in early spring after the winter protection has been removed and just as the buds begin to swell (often about the time of daffodils blooming). Remove all wood that has died over winter. You've reached healthy wood when the center of the cane is white. As you prune, remove any weak or crisscrossing canes as well as any damaged or broken canes.

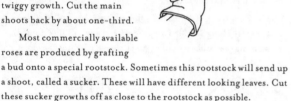

Through the growing season, the only other pruning necessary is to remove any diseased foliage or canes and the faded flowers, cutting the stem just above the first live-leaflet leaf below the flower.

Many of the new shrub-type roses need only minimal pruning of dead, diseased or damaged growth. Most heritage and species roses, as well as climbing roses that bloom once a year, bear flowers on growth from the previous year. Prune these plants as soon as flowering is finished. Remove any small, twiggy growth. Cut the main shoots back by about one-third.

Most commercially available roses are produced by grafting a bud onto a special rootstock. Sometimes this rootstock will send up a shoot, called a sucker. These will have different looking leaves. Cut these sucker growths off as close to the rootstock as possible.

Step 9 — Pest Control

Just as with other garden plants, healthy, vigorous roses that are grown in humus-rich, fertile soil with plenty of water will be much less susceptible to pests than weak, untended plants. Also, try to choose varieties that are more resistant to pests and that are the best grade possible.

Preventative maintenance helps to keep pests in check. Immediately remove and destroy any diseased foliage and flowers during the growing season as well as in the fall before applying winter protection. Use the correct pest control as soon as pests are spotted, not after the infestation or disease has become a major problem. Many pests are prevalent just at certain times of the year, so learn to use control measures only when necessary.

When treating roses with pesticides, always be sure to very carefully follow the manufacturer's directions. Do not mix different pesticides together unless the label specifies compatibility. Also, repeat applications at the specified intervals at least three times in order to kill newly hatched eggs or spores.

Pesticides can be applied as either a dust or a spray. When applying either one, it is advisable to wear one of the small dust masks available at hardware stores. Dusts require no mixing, so are ready for immediate use, but the residue can be unsightly. They are especially handy for spot applications. Dusts usually last slightly longer than sprays, unless it rains. Apply dusts when the air is still.

A broader range of materials are available as spray concentrates, plus there are many different types of spray applicators. Choose one that is easy for you to use, the appropriate size for the number of plants, and within your budget. When spraying, be sure to cover both sides of the leaves, spray in the early morning the day after thoroughly watering the plants, and always clean out the sprayer after each application.

Step 10 — Winter Protection

How well a plant survives winter's low temperatures is a measure of its hardiness. Some plants are naturally more hardy than others. Plant hardiness is also affected by the plant's health going into winter; a vigorous, healthy plant is much more likely to overwinter well than a weakened, sickly one.

Where winter temperatures do not go below 20°F, no winter protection of roses is needed. In areas with colder temperatures, varying degrees of protection are necessary. As mentioned previously, some roses are hardier than others. Try to select varieties that are the hardiest possible. If you must grow ones that are more tender, be prepared to provide extra care or to replace plants.

The objectives in providing roses with winter protection are to prevent the temperature around the plant from going below a certain point, to decrease the damaging effects of freezing and thawing, and to prevent canes from whipping about, which causes roots to loosen.

Preparation for winter should be done just before the first hard freezing weather in the fall or early winter. First, remove all rose leaves that have fallen to the ground around the plants as well as any foliage still attached to the stems. This reduces places where diseases can overwinter. Apply a final spraying of fungicide. Work in a feeding of 0–10–10 around each plant, watering in well. Prune roses to one-half their height and tie canes together with twine.

Many of the newer shrub roses as well as some of the floribundas and miniatures need only minimal winter protection. The following guidelines are for the widely available hybrid tea and grandiflora roses as well as for any other rose varieties of questionable hardiness.

In areas where winter temperatures drop to 0°F, the base of each rose must be protected by an 8-inch mound of soil, coarse compost, shredded bark or other organic material. If using soil, do not pull up soil from the rose bed; instead, bring it in from another part of the garden. This soil will have to be removed the following spring, while organic materials can be spread out as mulch.

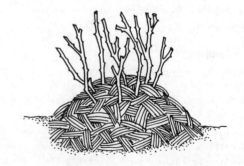

Where winter temperatures fall below 0°F, the mound is made progressively deeper, or up to 12 inches in the northern plains. Some gardeners cover this with another 8 to 10 inches of loose mulch, such as pine needles, oak leaves, pine branches or straw. Where winds are severe, this can be contained in wire or paper cylinders. If temperatures stay below 15°F for extended periods, caps, cones or baskets over the two layers of mulch are recommended.

The large-flowered, repeat-blooming climbers need special care in areas with winter temperatures falling below -5°F. Put a mound of soil or organic material around the base of the plant, detach the canes from supports and lay them on the ground, covering with soil, pine branches or mulch. A very hardy climber that does not need such protection is Dortmund.

Suppliers

Most mail-order nursery companies carry some roses, and there are also companies that specialize in roses, usually either modern-day hybrid, heritage or miniature roses. The following companies are just a sampling of these. If you're looking for specific varieties, especially if they are unusual, an excellent source of information is the annually updated *Combined Rose List*. The 1989 edition is $11.50 (New York residents add sales tax) from Beverly Dobson, 215 Harriman Road, Irvington, NY 10533. This book lists every rose in commerce, matched with practically every source.

Catalogs free unless otherwise indicated.

The Antique Rose Emporium
Route 5, Box 143
Brenham, TX 77833
Catalog $2.00

Carroll Gardens
P.O. Box 310
Westminster, MD 21157

Country Bloomers Nursery
20091 East Chapman Avenue
Orange, CA 92669

Roses by Fred Edmunds
6235 S.W. Kahle Road
Wilsonville, OR 97070

Heritage Rosarium
211 Haviland Mill Road
Brookeville, MD 20833
Catalog $1.00

High Country Rosarium
1717 Downing
Denver, CO 80218

Historical Roses
1657 West Jackson Street
Painesville, OH 44077

Jackson & Perkins Company
Medford, OR 97501–9810

Justice Miniature Roses
5947 S.W. Kahle Road
Wilsonville, OR 97070

V. Kraus Nurseries
Carlisle, Ontario
Canada LOR 1HO

Krider Nurseries
P.O. Box 29
Middlebury, IN 46540

Moore Miniature Roses
2519 East Noble Avenue
Visalia, CA 93277

Nor'East Miniature Roses
58 Hammond Street
Rowley, MA 01969

Pickering Nurseries
670 Kingston Road
Pickering, Ontario,
Canada L1V 1A6
Catalog $2.00

Stocking Rose Nursery
785 North Capitol Avenue
San Jose, CA 95133

Thomasville Nurseries
P.O. Box 7
Thomasville, GA 31799
Website: http://thomasvillenursery.com/

Easy-Care Orchids

Mary Carol Frier

Illustrations by Harriet Olds

Introduction

When you shop at a garden center, the orchids in bloom are unmistakable. The foliage appears tough but looks somehow tropical, and the flowers are immediately arresting, with their strange form, subtlety of color, and compelling perfume. If you want to bring these beauties home with you but worry that you won't be able to keep them alive or make them flower, think again. Many orchids are no more difficult to care for than the average houseplant.

Light and Temperature: The Keys to Growing Orchids Successfully

Like all plants, orchids need light to grow; the trick is to have the right amount of light. Since most orchids grown as houseplants originate from the tropics, the optimal day length is generally a consistent 12 hours of light, followed by 12 hours of darkness. To begin the bloom sequence, most orchids need a slightly greater intensity of light than they normally require. For example, the popular Phalaenopsis, or moth orchid, normally prefers bright, indirect light, but in the fall months it requires brighter light to stimulate the bloom sequence that results in flowers the following winter or spring.

After light, the correct temperature is the next important requisite for growing and flowering orchids successfully. Most orchids grown as houseplants will thrive with temperatures in the low 60s (Fahrenheit) at night and the high 70s to low 80s during the day. Conventional orchid-growing wisdom fine-tunes the concept of temperature even further, splitting orchids into three cultural groups—warm, intermediate, and cool—depending on their temperature requirements. This division is useful for optimizing growth but not really necessary for the windowsill grower. Getting the light level right for your orchid varieties is far more important.

Note: The harm of overly hot conditions in your window can be lessened by running a fan that disperses *moist, moving* air over the plants. The moisture in the air acts as a "heat sink" and dissipates the heat of the sunlight streaming in the window. To generate airborne moisture, run a small humidifier in the plant-growing area or set the orchid pots over (not in) pans of water.

Continued →

OTHER CONCERNS: HUMIDITY AND FERTILIZER

After light and temperature, the relative humidity in your orchid-growing area becomes important. Humidity serves as a buffer to smooth out temperature fluctuations and encourages the even rate of transpiration that orchids prefer. The more humid the orchid's native enviroment, the more humid it will prefer your windowsill to be. Phalaenopsis and Paphiopedilum orchids are both native to the tropics of Indonesia, so they prefer environments with about 60 to 70 percent humidity. Orchids with thick leaves and pseudobulbs, like Cattleyas, prefer a lesser humidity of 40 to 50 percent. Orchids with pseudobulbs but with thin leaves, such as Oncidiums, prefer conditions somewhere in the middle, at about 50 percent relative humidity.

Fertilizer is an important component of successful orchid culture, although it's not nearly as important as light, temperature, and humidity. Any balanced product designed for houseplants will suffice. You may want to switch to a blossom booster fertilizer, with its high phosphorous content, about 3 months before your plants usually bloom; however, if you are using a balanced fertilizer, blossom booster isn't really necessary.

> **DEFINITION**
> Pseudobulb: A fleshy, bulbous growth between the stem and the leaf.

Cattleya

Cattleyas and their hybrids are not demanding in a full southern exposure. In their native South and Central American environment, Cattleyas grow halfway up a tropical forest tree or on a shrub on a grassy hillside or in a forest glade. In these locations, Cattleyas receive very bright light and dappled sun as the day progresses. You should try to create similar conditions for your Cattleya. In general, the cultural requirements of a Cattleya are as follows:

- **Light:** Provide bright light year round, with direct sun during the fall and winter.

- **Temperature:** Prefers 55–60°F nights and 70–85°F days.

- **Humidity:** Keep the relative humidity at 40 to 50 percent.

- **Fertilizer:** Fertilize with half-strength houseplant food every two weeks.

- **Watering:** Allow to dry out a little between waterings.

Outdoors, the air always has a moving quality, even on the stillest days. Of all the orchids, Cattleyas seem to benefit the most from having a small fan running in their growing area. If the fan moves *moist* air around them, it dissipates the effects of afternooon heat or occasional direct sun, when the window tends to heat up.

> ### TAKING YOUR CUE FROM THE PLANT
> When you've acquired experience in growing Cattleyas, you will begin to notice that they vary in physical appearance. Some have thicker pseudobulbs; some thinner leaves; some almost no pseudobulbs. Their appearance offers a clue to their watering and light requirements. In general, the thicker the leaves and pseudobulbs, the more the plant should dry out between waterings and the more light it should have. Cattleyas with naturally thin leaves should be grown with less light and more even moisture in the pot, much like Oncidiums.

Cymbidium

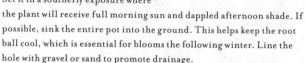

Cymbidiums are native to the low mountains of India and eastward to China and Japan. Their native habitat usually has a 6-month rainy season followed by a 6-month dry season, at the end of which the plant blooms. To grow Cymbidiums successfully, you must reenact this cycle in your "program" of culture, as follows.

In early spring, repot your orchid if needed. When night temperatures reach 45°F, move the plant outdoors. Set it in a southerly exposure where the plant will receive full morning sun and dappled afternoon shade. If possible, sink the entire pot into the ground. This helps keep the root ball cool, which is essential for blooms the following winter. Line the hole with gravel or sand to promote drainage.

During spring and summer, water the plant copiously. Feed with a balanced, half-strength fertilizer every week to promote strong pseudobulbs. Mist with cool water during very hot weather.

In late summer, cut back on the watering, waiting until the plant's soil is nearly dry before you water. Stop fertilizing.

In fall, when the first killing frost is forecast, bring the plant inside. Set the plant in an area where it will receive full sun during the day and where nighttime temperatures will drop to the 50s. Keep the plants on the dry side. Flower spikes looking like asparagus spears—at least until they are an inch or two long—will soon arise from the bases of the pseudobulbs.

> ### PREPARING FOR LIGHT FROSTS
> Cymbidiums should be left outdoors until a killing frost is forecast. These orchids will, however, tolerate light frosts, so long as they are protected. If a light frost is expected, drape an old sheet over the plant to keep the frost's icy crystals off the orchid's leaves. Failure to do this results in leaf die-back severe enough to inhibit blooming.

In winter, when new growths of flowers or leaves appear, begin watering copiously again. Flowers are close at hand.

Cymbidium blooms last 4 to 6 weeks. Given proper care and attention, a Cymbidium will yield three or four—and sometimes more—impressive flower spikes, a tribute to your orchid-growing skill.

Dendrobium

Because the *Dendrobium* genus is so diverse, the guidelines below are very general in scope. Notes about specific varieties follow.

- **Temperature:** Prefers 60–65°F nights and 75–85°F days.
- **Light:** Needs bright light year round with direct sun in fall and winter. Prefers to be outdoors in the summer when night temperatures are 60°F or better; place in a location with full morning sun followed by light afternoon shade. Do not be alarmed if the plants drop some leaves when you bring them indoors in the fall. This is their way of matching plant size with the light available.
- **Humidity:** Prefers 40 to 60 percent relative humidity.
- **Watering:** Likes to almost dry out between waterings; water well when actively growing.
- **Fertilizer:** Feed every 2 weeks with half-strength houseplant fertilizer when it is actively growing. Do not fertilize when the plant appears dormant.

Phalaenopsis-type Dendrobiums

The Phalaenopsis-type Dendrobium is the easiest to grow in this genus; it thrives in the temperatures found in most homes. This type of Dendrobium will do especially well in a full southern exposure; run a small fan in the growing area that moves *moist* air around the plant to mitigate the heat of the abundant sunlight.

Nobile-type Dendrobiums

In their native environment, nobile-type Dendrobiums experience distinctive wet and dry seasons. As you would expect, the plants grow vegetatively in late spring and summer, rest in fall and early winter, and bloom in late winter and spring. Their flowers are so spectacular and tropical looking in the dead of winter that they are worth the extra effort it takes to get the plants to bloom. They prefer to be outdoors in the summer.

In the fall, nobile-type Dendrobiums should be brought indoors when nighttime temperatures reach 50°F. When they are indoors, water them only every two weeks or so; they will not be growing vegetatively and will not require much water. Place them in a location that is very bright but cool (around 70°F during the day). Some people simply hang them up out of the way in a small home greenhouse. However, be sure the plants aren't sitting in a hot, stagnant location. Take a look at them as you water them to be sure that they haven't acquired any insect inhabitants and that they are not burning from overly bright or hot conditions. When you see growths in the notches between leaves and canes, start watering and feeding again because the wonderful blooms have almost arrived!

ENCOURAGING YOUR DENDROBIUM TO BLOOM

A common problem for Dendrobium growers is plants that grow well but produce lots of little "suckers" (*keikis*) instead of flowers. This is caused by conditions that favor vegetative growth, that is, plentiful food and water but low light. To encourage flower production, discontinue feeding and be sparing with water. A good time to begin this austerity program is when you bring the plants indoors in early fall. Resume the heavy feeding and watering in the spring or when plants begin to show new growth.

Tropical foliage and sweet-scented flowers make Phalaenopsis-type Dendrobiums favorite orchids for home windowsills.

Oncidium

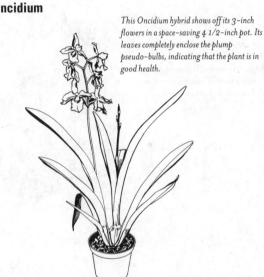

This Oncidium hybrid shows off its 3-inch flowers in a space-saving 4 1/2-inch pot. Its leaves completely enclose the plump pseudo-bulbs, indicating that the plant is in good health.

In their native environment of South and Central America, Oncidiums live in lightly shaded conditions. Therefore, with the exception of the thick-leaf mule-ear type, Oncidiums prefer a shaded environment or morning sun and shade the rest of the day. Most have thin leaves, so they are prone to burning. The plants in this group do vary by the temperature they prefer, based on the altitude at which their jungle ancestors grew.

Oncidiums do best in eastern exposures, which usually have bright light but afternoon shade and cooler temperatures, or in shaded southern exposures. Western exposures can work if afternoon heat can be dissipated; you can use fans to move moist air around the plants

Continued ➧

during the warmer spring and summer months. You can also hang your plants outside in a tree when nighttime temperatures are reliably above 50°F.

Generally speaking, Oncidium cultural requirements are as follows:

- **Light**: Provide bright light year round, with some direct sun during the fall and winter months.
- **Temperature**: Prefers 55–60°F nights and 75–80°F days. Keep daytime temperatures below 82 degrees for Oncidiums with large flowers (more than 2 inches in diameter).
- **Humidity**: Maintain 50 percent relative humidity.
- **Watering**: Plants with thin leaves and pseudobulbs should be kept in evenly moist soil. The thicker the leaves and more prominent the pseudobulbs, the more the plants need to dry out between watering.
- **Fertilizer**: Fertilize with half-strength houseplant fertilizer every 2 weeks

Paphiopedilum

Attractive gray-green leaves enfold the flower spikes of this Paphiopedilum Maudiae *hybrid. This variety boldly combines maroon, green, and white in flowers that last almost 2 months.*

Paphiopedilum's habit is semiterrestrial, and it requires a fine aggregate medium to thrive. But the key to successful Paphiopedilum culture is to take note of the leaf color and then grow as described below.

For the Mottled-Leaf Paphiopedilum:

- **Light**: Provide bright, indirect light; be sure that the light is not so bright that it causes leaves to heat up or bleach out.
- **Temperature**: Prefers 60–65°F nights and 70–85°F days.
- **Humidity**: Maintain relative humidity at about 60 percent.
- **Watering**: Keep the soil evenly moist.
- **Fertilizer**: Fertilize with half-strength, balanced fertilizer every 2 weeks.

For the Plain-Green-Leaf Paphiopedilum:

- **Light**: Provide bright, indirect light; in fall and early winter, be sure the plant receives some direct sun.
- **Temperature**: Prefers 55–60°F nights and 70–85°F days.
- **Humidity**: Maintain relative humidity at about 50 percent.
- **Watering**: Keep the soil evenly moist.
- **Fertilizer**: Fertilize with half-strength, balanced fertilizer every 2 weeks.

To encourage the bloom cycle in your Paphiopedilums, provide plants with cool (50–55°F) night conditions in fall and early winter. Flower buds develop slowly but are worth the wait; each flower may last 2 months or more.

Phalaenopsis

You are caring for your Phalaenopsis properly when each leaf is slightly larger than the previous one, as shown in this juvenile plant.

Here is a quick summary of Phalaenopsis culture:

- **Light**: Provide bright light, but never so much that leaves become hot to the touch.
- **Temperature**: Prefers 60–65°F nights and 70–85°F days.
- **Humidity**: Keep the relative humidity at 60 percent; top-dress the pot with wet-sheet moss if the air is dry.
- **Watering**: Keep evenly moist.
- **Fertilizer**: Fertilize with half-strength balanced fertilizer every 2 weeks.
- **Blooming**: In fall, needs brighter days and cooler nights to initiate bloom sequence.

Potting Orchids

The health of your orchids depends on the condition of their roots. The medium you use and your potting technique will directly affect the health of these roots. There are two rules for optimal roots:

Rule #1: Repot orchids every 2 years.

Rule #2: Place your orchids in a chunky potting medium, which creates plenty of air space around the roots.

WHEN YOU BUY AN ORCHID...

When you buy an orchid, assume that it has been in the pot at least a year, and repot it within the next year.

Label each orchid pot with the orchid's botanical name and the date it was potted. This helps you care for the plants when they are out of bloom and hard to identify, and it will also help you remember when it is time to repot them.

Repotting your orchids every 2 years prevents root dieback caused by stagnating potting mix. Why is stagnant mix such a problem? Orchids have air-loving roots. In their native environment, most orchids perch in trees with their roots wrapped tightly around its trunk, they clink to rocks, or they grow in loose forest litter that has lots of air space in it.

CHOOSING THE RIGHT POT

Because they grow in their native environments with their roots surrounded by air, orchids depend on *constant* humidity in the air to provide most of the moisture they need. On the home windowsill, humidity fluctuates drastically, which can make most orchids seriously ill. Therefore, the cornerstone of serious orchid culture is to provide optimal humidity consistently. Potting plants appropriately is an important part of providing this essential constant for orchids.

Pseudobulbs are fleshy, bulbous growths between the stem and leaf of an orchid. They allow orchids to store moisture and can protect the plants during unstable humidity conditions. Cattleyas, for example, have prominent pseudobulbs, which allow them to withstand uneven external moisture levels. Dendrobiums store moisture in their thick canes as protection against dry conditions, which surely visit them in their native habitat. Orchids without pseudo-bulbs, such as Phalaenopsis and Paphiopedilum, are most at risk in an unevenly humid environment because they have no internal stores of moisture and wither in the dry or hot conditions that often visit the home windowsill.

Orchids with Pseudobulbs	Orchids without Pseudobulbs
Cattleyas and their relatives	Phalaenopsis
Oncidiums (except Equitants)	Paphiopedilums
Dendrobiums (thickened canes, rather than proper pseudobulbs)	Equitant Oncidiums
	Phragmipediums
Cymbidiums	

Not only can orchids with pseudobulbs withstand wet/dry cycles, they also, in fact, need them. Therefore, orchids with pseudobulbs are best potted in clay pots or even slotted orchid pots, which facilitate drying out slightly between waterings. Orchids without pseudobulbs do best in plastic pots. Potting mix dries much more slowly in a plastic pot than in a clay pot, so plastic pots promote the even moisture level these plants need.

In some garden centers you may encounter orchids mounted on bark slabs or tree fern to more closely mimic the way the plants grow in nature. While it's true that orchids grow this way in nature, it's also true that nature provides an even 70+ percent relative humidity and moving air for these plants. Don't attempt to grow these mounted plants on your home windowsill until you have found a way to replicate these natural ambient conditions. For most windowsills, pots are best.

POTTING TECHNIQUES

Orchids grow on tree bark and rocks in nature, so this is what you should pot them in. A simple homemade orchid potting medium comprises bark, bark mulch, and perlite. These materials are inexpensive and commonly available; as a potting mix, they will hold together without rotting or compressing, and thus endangering the roots, for the 2 years between pottings. The proper proportions to use depend on the orchid being potted.

Step-By-Step Potting

1. Use the chart below to determine the proper proportions of potting ingredients for the orchid you are potting. Mix the ingredients together. Add water until the mixture is moist and crumbly, then let it sit for several hours. Working with moist mix will lessen the transplant shock your plants experience.

2. Thoroughly water the plants a few hours before transplanting. This makes the roots more pliant and less likely to break. If you are repotting an orchid with lots of roots growing out in the air, soak the whole plant in a bucket of tepid water to soften the roots.

3. Select a clean pot that will comfortably house the plant's roots; the roots should not be "lost" or "jammed" in the pot. Use a *clean* pot. If you are reusing pots, clean and disinfect them with a 20 percent bleach solution and rinse thoroughly.

4. Put a layer of Styrofoam packing "peanuts," small stones, or gravel in the bottom of the pot. If you are using gravel or stones, first clean them in a 20 percent bleach solution and rinse thoroughly.

5. Gently remove the orchid from its old pot. You may have to scrape roots from the sides of the pot to get the plant out.

PROPORTIONS FOR POTTING INGREDIENTS

Seedling-grade bark chunks are 1/8 to 1/4 inch in diameter, while medium-grade bark chunks are about 1/2 inch in diameter. Bark mulch is pulverized bark, commonly known as bark "fines." Any fine aggregate, such as coarse peat, chopped tree fern, or sphagnum moss, can also be used. Coarse perlite is a porous rock; it provides lasting pore spaces in the mix and holds moisture on its rough surface as well. It is a small but critical ingredient in orchid mixes. The proportions given here make 8 cups of finished mix, enough to fill three or four 4-inch pots.

Orchid	Bark (cups)	Bark Mulch (cups)	Coarse Perlite (cups)
Cattleya	3 (medium grade)	4 1/2	1/2
Cymbidium	1 (medium grade)	6 1/2	1/2
Dendrobium	3 (medium grade)	4 1/4	3/4
Oncidium	2 2/3 (seedling grade)	5	1/3
Paphiopedilum	2 (seedling grade)	5 1/2	1/2
Phalaenopsis	2 1/2 (medium grade)	5	1/2

Continued →

6. Remove dead roots. Dead roots look mushy and pull away from the plant with just a gentle tug. Live roots are plump and firm.

7. Set the orchid in its new pot.

   Orchids with horizontal rhizomes, such as Cattleya, Oncidium, Dendrobium, and Cymbidium, should be potted with the oldest part of the plant set against the side of the pot to allow room for the plant to grow toward the front of the pot. If your plant has withered, leafless pseudobulbs, strip them off.

   Orchids with upright stems, such as Phalaenopsis and Paphiopedilum, should be centered in the pot. If you are repotting a very old plant with a long stem, you may want to snap off the oldest part so that the plant will sit properly in the pot. Remove any old leaves below the roots.

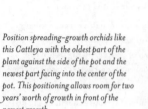

Position spreading-growth orchids like this Cattleya with the oldest part of the plant against the side of the pot and the newest part facing into the center of the pot. This positioning allows room for two years' worth of growth in front of the newest growth.

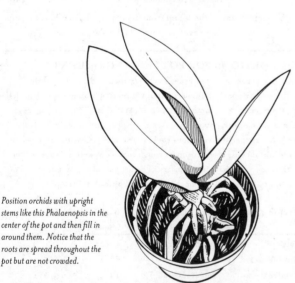

Position orchids with upright stems like this Phalaenopsis in the center of the pot and then fill in around them. Notice that the roots are spread throughout the pot but are not crowded.

DIVIDING ORCHIDS

If you are repotting a plant with more than seven mature pseudobulbs, the plant can be divided so that each division has three or four mature bulbs. The piece with the youngest bulbs is called the "front" division. The oldest part of the plant is the "back" division. Back divisions are slower to establish than front divisions. It may take the back division an extra year to grow to blooming size.

---

8. Holding the plant in the proper position in the pot, fill in around the roots with damp potting mix, tamping the mix firmly as you work. Tapping and shaking the pot from side to side will help get the mix down around the roots without damaging them.

9. Cover all the roots with mix.

   Orchids with horizontal rhizomes *must* be planted with their rhizomes at the surface of the mix. The rhizome is the center of the plant's growth; all roots and new leaves and bulbs rise from it. It must be at the surface of the mix to do an effective job.

   Orchids with upright stems should be potted so the mix just reaches the root line, where roots emerge from the stem.

10. If your plant is floppy or wobbly after you have tamped the mix firmly around it, loosely tie the plant to a stake. The plant will need this support to grow properly.

11. Pick up the plant, pot and all, to gauge its weight. Put it down, water it until the potting mix is thoroughly wet, then let the pot drain. Lift the pot again; it should feel heavier. If the pot doesn't feel appreciably heavier, continue watering until it does.

12. Put the plant in a low-light location until it begins to grow, which can take anywhere from days to weeks. When you see new growth (leaves growing or new roots developing), transfer the plant to its normal growing conditions and begin fertilizing (see the descriptions of the individual orchids for their fertilizer preferences).

Pests, Diseases, and Cultural Problems

Good cultural practices are the best way to prevent and eliminate pests and diseases. The stronger your plants are, the more resistant they are to infection. Even with good care and attention, however, orchids are sometimes subject to pests and diseases. Use this section as a guide to common problems.

GOOD CULTURE REPELS TROUBLE

Make sure the growing environment is as best-suited for your particular orchid as possible. Plants under stress are more susceptible to pests and diseases.

PESTS

Orchids are not often bothered by insects, but as with any other plant, a weak or young orchid can attract pests. And plants spending the summer outdoors, even healthy plants, can be troubled by slugs and insects like millipedes. Your best defense is observation of your collection and quick action if you spot a problem.

If you spot insects that chew on foliage and stems, try removing them with soap and water or just your fingers and a tissue. If more insects show up a day or two later, use a horticultural oil spray or insecticidal soap, following the instructions on the bottle. The best time to spray is either early in the morning or late in the day. Try not to spray in the middle of the day, because some sprays can exacerbate the effects of the sun, causing the plant's leaves to burn, and other sprays dry off quickly—and lose their potency—during the daytime warmth.

Most sprays sold for home use are "contact" sprays, which means that the spray must come in direct contact with the pest to be effective. If you miss an insect, it will still be doing damage the next day. Often the spray's label will suggest multiple applications at set intervals to completely eradicate a pest.

Insects that live or spend part of their lives in the potting medium are much harder to detect and control. Mealybugs and fungus gnats fall into this category. If you suspect that your orchid is infested with a soil-borne pest, the best thing you can do is remove the plant from its pot, discarding both the pot and the potting mix. Carefully wash the roots and spray them with insecticide (following the label instructions), then set the plant in a new pot with fresh potting mix. *Note:* When using any chemical spray, be sure to follow label directions exactly and use the product in a well-ventilated space.

Remember, for a pesticide to be most effective, your orchid must be as healthy as possible and must not be suffering from any physical stress. In other words, if you are going to apply a pesticide, be sure that your orchid is provided with optimal growing conditions—light, temperature, humidity, water, and fertilizer.

DISEASES

Pests such as insects, slugs, and spiders are the most prevalent problem in the home orchid collection, but diseases caused by fungi, bacteria, and viruses are also problematic.

Fungi are generally slow-acting and leave dry, black spots on leaves or dry, black lesions on pseudobulbs and stems. Many pseudobulbs are sheathed in a papery velum that thins and turns brown and black as the pseudobulb matures. This is natural and is *not* due to a fungal infection. When you peel back the velum you should see bright green growth. If this growth has broad, black streaking, you have a fungal problem.

The easiest solution to fungal infections is to cut them out with a clean blade and dust the cut with a fungicidal powder, following the instructions on the label. Disinfect any cutting tools you use between cuts to make sure disease is not spread between plants.

Many insects, such as aphids and thrips, move readily from plant to plant, feeding on a plant infected with a virus and carrying that virus to the next plant they infest. Viral infections cannot be cured, so plants infected with viruses should be discarded. Infected plants often have foliage or flowers streaked with thin, black or brown broken lines or blotched with lighter yellow or green. They may also have streaky,

malformed flowers. In the later stages of a viral infection, the plants themselves become malformed. These are not attractive plants!

Bacterial infections cause watery brown lesions to develop and often progress quickly. A plant with a watery brown spot 1 inch in diameter can be dead just 2 days later. So you have to act quickly! Cut out the spot with a clean blade and dust the cut with a bactericide, following the label directions.

CULTURAL PROBLEMS

A cultural problem is your plant's response to a stressful, or inadequate, environment. Most are easy to detect and correct.

Sunburn. Also called leaf scorch, sunburn is a common orchid cultural problem. Sunburn is caused by excessive light intensity, often combined with low humidity. When the leaf tissue "cooks" in the excessive light, a light tan lesion, usually oval in shape, results. Sometimes fungal spores will invade the damaged tissue, turning it black around the edges. So long as the blackened area doesn't become larger, no action is needed. Sunburn produces only cosmetic damage, but its presence should be a warning that the light and humidity conditions are harmful to the plant.

Root dieback. This more serious cultural problem is caused by decayed, stagnating potting mix. You should suspect dieback if the leaves or pseudobulbs of your orchid go limp and look withered, especially if you know the plant hasn't been repotted recently. Withering is also symptomatic of severe underwatering. Check the condition of the roots and repot if necessary.

Cracking. Occasionally a new leaf grows so quickly and becomes so heavy that it cracks along its midrib. Phalaenopsis orchids growing under warm, humid conditions are most prone to this condition, but other types can develop it, too. The cracking does not damage the plant, but it is unsightly. If the environmental conditions are corrected, new, healthy leaves will grow to cover the cracked leaves the following year.

Pleated leaves. Oncidiums can develop new leaves that look "accordion pleated." This pleating occurs when new, developing leaves receive insufficient moisture, causing the tissue to collapse and "pleat." Subsequent growths will be normal. To avoid this problem, keep the planting medium moist and the ambient humidity constant.

Bud blast. Withered flower buds are the most distressing problem the orchid grower faces. The orchid plant is finally in spike and flowers look imminent, but the buds dry up and fall off overnight. This condition, called bud blast, is caused by overwhelming stress to the flower buds, most often a sharp, rapid change in temperature, humidity levels, or both. Weak plants with poor root systems are most vulnerable, and Phalaenopsis seems to be the most affected. However, even if your Phalaenopsis has dropped some buds, it will usually continue to set buds on the end of the spike as long as the temperature and humidity problems are solved.

A MEDICINE CHEST FOR ORCHIDS

Since most orchid pest infestations and diseases should be addressed immediately, it's helpful to keep a well-stocked medicine kit nearby. Items to stock include:

· Horticultural oil or other pesticide of your choice

· Slug bait (if your plants spend time outdoors)

Continued →

- Fungicidal powder
- Sterile sharp knife or razor blades
- Pest and disease identification book
- Potting supplies and clean pots

The best thing you can do to maintain the health of your plants is observe them. One of the pleasures of having an orchid collection is examining it every day to see what is happening: new growths, flower spikes, open blooms. Sometimes plants seem to hide their flower buds until the last moment when they happily surprise you. Take the time to spot pests and diseases before they ruin your good efforts!

APPENDIX: LIGHT AND TEMPERATURE REQUIREMENTS FOR COMMON ORCHIDS

Orchid Name	Light Requirements	Light in Foot-candles*	Preferred Temperature (°F)	Temperatures Tolerated (°F)
Cattleya	Very bright indirect light in southern exposure; sun in winter	2,500–3,500	Nights: 55–60° Days: 70–85°	Nights: 50–55° Days: Above 85° occasionally; rarely in excess of 90°
Cymbidium	Full sun with light afternoon shade	3,500–4,000	Nights: 50–55° (standard); 55–60° (miniature) Days: 75–80°	Nights: 30° Days: 85°, so long as rootball is cool
Dendrobium	Very bright light in southern exposure; sun in fall/winter	3,000–4,000	Nights: 60–65° Days: 75–85°	Nights: 55° Days: Above 85° occasionally; rarely in excess of 90°
Oncidium	Bright indirect light sun in eastern exposure	1,500–2,500	Nights: 55–60° Days: 75–80°	Nights: 50° nights Days: Up to 85°
Paphiopedilum (mottled leaf)	Indirect light	1,000–1,500	Nights: 60–65° Days: 70–85°	Nights: Down to 55° occasionally Days: Above 85° occasionally
Paphiopedilum (plain green leaf)	Indirect light	1,000–1,500	Nights: 55–60° Days: 70–85°	Nights: 45–50° occasionally Days: Above 85° rarely
Phalaenopsis	Indirect light	800–1,200	Nights: 60–65° Days: 70–85°	Nights: 55° occasionally Days: Above 90° occasionally

*You can use an inexpensive light meter to measure illumination, measured in foot-candles, in your orchid's growing area.

Long-Lasting Hanging Plants

Rhonda Massingham Hart

Illustrations by Alison Kolesar

Become a Basket Case!

Hanging gardens. The mere thought is at once romantic, intriguing, and intimidating. For sheer attention-getting, nothing beats cascades of color bursting from containers. The effect is multiplied when the show defies the law of earthbound expectations and takes to the air. Hanging baskets bring cheery color to eye-level and sensuous scents right under your nose. Some even tempt your taste buds with dangling fruit.

Best of all, these mini-gardens offer their gifts to the neediest of places. They brighten dark corners, sweeten still breezes, soften stark lines, and bring drama to the drab. The impact of a lush, hanging arrangement can lighten a heavy heart, if only for a moment. And anyone can create them! All it takes is a little basic know-how and creativity to design hanging baskets to complement any setting, from a shady retreat to a sun-drenched patio.

Choosing the Best Ready-Made Basket

In the spring, especially around Mother's Day, every store, from garden centers to corner grocery markets, gets into the plant business. Ready-made hanging baskets can be found suspended from anything that will hold them. So even if you're not quite ready to create your own designer plants, you can still enjoy the splendor of your own little hanging paradise. Just follow these tips for bringing home the best baskets.

- **Check the weight.** The basket should feel heavy for its size. Light-weights have been allowed to dry out and may suffer permanent stress.

- **Inspect the foliage and flowers.** Reject any baskets that show obvious pest infestation, disease, or damage. Part foliage with your hands, and look on the underside for bugs, discolored spots, or broken stems. If you find obvious problems, do the management a favor and bring such baskets to their attention.

- **Check the soil level.** The planting medium should come within 2 inches of the top of the container. Too little soil causes roots to become crowded and stresses the plant(s).

- **Consider your site.** Choose plants that tolerate, or better yet, prefer, your growing conditions. Buy shade lovers for shady areas, sun lovers for bright spots, etc.

Create Your Own

The real fun starts when you decide to design and plant your own hanging baskets. You can cater to your own tastes and color schemes, select from a wide range of varieties not available in nursery-grown baskets, and save money, too.

CHOOSE THE RIGHT BASKET

Any container that appeals to your eye, has not been used to contain any sort of toxic substance, is at least 3 inches deep, and has drainage holes in the bottom can be put to use as a hanging container. Just be aware that what the "basket" is made of makes a difference, and each material has its advantages and disadvantages.

COMPARISONS OF BASKETS

Material	Characteristics
Pulp	Inexpensive, lightweight, absorbs water, breathes well
Wooden	More expensive, heavy, attractive, breathes well
Plastic	Moderately priced, lightweight, less attractive
Clay	Moderately priced, heavy, absorbs water
Ceramic	Expensive, very attractive, moderately heavy
Wicker	Inexpensive to costly, rots if kept wet, attractive
Wire	Lightweight, durable, allows for planting at different levels
Metal	Heats up quickly in the sun which may damage roots, heavy

Bear in mind that hanging plants require lots of water (more on this later) and that well-watered soil is heavy. Consider total weight when choosing containers. For instance, earthenware pots are attractive plant containers, but can weigh more all by themselves than the plant and soil combined. On the other hand, lightweight decorative wicker baskets won't hold up over time.

WICKER TRICK
To get the effect of a wicker planter, use a slightly smaller plastic container as the planter and nest it in the wicker basket.

PICK THE PROPER PLANTING MEDIUM

Don't use dirt! When used in containers, even the best garden loam compacts, which squeezes oxygen away from the roots and hinders water absorption. Instead, use a planting mix. You will find that there are two kinds available: soilless and soil-based. Soilless mixes are composed mainly of shredded peat. While lightweight and porous, they contain no nutrients and tend to break down over time, which also causes problems with aeration and water absorption. Soil-based mixes retain nutrients and are easy to wet, both initially and after planting, but they are also heavy. Soilless mixes are fine for temporary baskets, such as annuals that will be tossed at season's end. Soil-based mixes are the best choice for perennial baskets that are to be maintained over time.

Planting mediums can be purchased pre-mixed or you can whip up your own. Mixing your own allows you to work in bloom-boosting amendments, such as bonemeal, dolomitic limestone, or slow-release fertilizer.

HOMEMADE PLANTING MIXES

Soil-Based Planting Mix
- 1 part high-quality soil
- 1 part peat moss
- 1 part perlite, vermiculite or clean, sharp builder's sand
- 1 part compost (optional)

Soilless Planting Mix
- 1 part #2 grade vermiculite
- 1 part peat moss

To either mix add 1 tablespoon superphosphate, 2 tablespoons ground limestone, and 4 tablespoons steamed bonemeal per gallon of medium, or substitute a fertilizer mix of your choice.

WATCH THAT HARDWARE

Be realistic about hangers, hooks, and support structures. Flimsy hangers are disasters in waiting. Macrame hangers, braided or twisted rope, and good quality chain are decorative and strong. Wire hangers that come attached to nursery-grown baskets are plain but suitable. Beware of delicate, screw-in hooks that can give under the stress of a heavy hanging planter. Look for hooks that list the weight-load they will

Continued ➜

bear on the package. Swivel hooks are great for rotating baskets for even sun exposure. Finally, be sure to hang the basket from a sturdy support.

Choose the Best Varieties

Some plants just seem to be destined for the swinging life of a hanging basket! Trailing plants spill over container edges like kaleidoscopic waterfalls. Annuals provide quick color for the season, while perennials perform encores. Listed here are some old favorites and new twists.

INDOOR OPTIONS

No gardeners worth their salt can leave their passion at the patio door. Bring it inside with a few easy-to-grow hanging houseplants. Here are some that will thrive in the low light and humidity of indoor growing conditions.

VARIETIES THAT FLOURISH INDOORS

Common Name	Characteristics
Achimenes	Does well indoors near a sunny window. Red, pink, lavender.
Asparagus Fern	Keep from direct sunlight and maintain even moisture.
Baby's Tears	Likes semi-shade and high humidity. Misting helps.
Begonias (Tuberous)	Keep moist indoors; misting helps. Needs sunlight to keep in bloom; position near an open sunny window when possible, but avoid direct sunlight. (See below for cultivars and description.)
Chenille Plant	Fuzzy red "cat tails" sprout in summer, adding interest to an already attractive plant. Requires plenty of light and humidity indoors (misting helps). Can be moved outside, away from direct sunlight, for the summer.
Christmas Cactus	('Dark Marie', 'Eva', 'Frieda', 'Madisto', 'Saane') Glossy green leaves; pink, rose or mauve blooms. Blooms appear when days get shorter and nights cooler, Bloom is best if plants receive partial sun. Water after the soil has dried slightly and mist regularly.
Cissus	Related to grapes. Ignore neglect and thrive despite poor conditions. Avoid overwatering.
Creeping Charlie	Well-suited to semi-shade and household conditions. Keep evenly moist.

Common Name	Characteristics
Creeping Fig	('Bellus', 'Rikky', 'Sonny') Shiny heart-shaped leaves in pure greens or variegated varieties. Grows quickly. Requires some light, but avoid direct sunlight except in early morning or evening. Allow to dry slightly between waterings.
English Ivy	An attractive vine that tolerates a range of conditions, but prefers cooler house-hold temperatures. Will thrive in low light if exposed occasionally to sunlight. Allow soil to dry slightly between waterings and mist regularly for best results. Can be grown outdoors in mild (zones 5 and up) climates.
Ferns	Low light. Keep evenly moist and mist daily.
Kalanchoe (manginii and other species)	Winter-blooming succulent with sparks of bright yellow, orange, or red. Likes bright, but filtered light. Allow to dry out for a day or two between waterings.
Pothos	A tough plant to kill! Will survive in nothing but water for months at a time or potted-up for years. In good, moist soil and with filtered sun the vines grow at an amazing rate and can be trained over door frames, windows, or along trellises or walls.
Donkey Tail	Long, fleshy, braidlike stems of gray-green resemble a thick rope. Needs protection from drying winds and sun. Allow to dry somewhat between waterings.
Spider plant	A living air filter. Graceful arching blades of green and white erupt from the center of the pot. Occasional stems sprout "baby" plants along their length. Tolerates low light and dry periods.
Wandering Jew	Different varieties produce a range of different colored and variegated vines, from soft green to gleaming, silvery purple and dark green stripes. The more sunlight they receive, the more brilliant the color display. Water before pot begins to feel dry.
Wax plant	Thick stems and leaves are easily held as cuttings in water. Prefers a semi-sunny spot and even moisture. Mist regularly.

PERENNIAL VARIETIES AND HABITS

Common Name	Habits	Cultivars	Color/Size
Achimenes	Prefers semi-shade or shade.		Red, pink, lavender
Begonia (Tuberous)	Semi-shade is best, but they will tolerate some sun. Keep moist.	'Non-Stop' 'Illumination' 'Giant Cascade Double'	White, yellow, salmon, orange, pink and red Pink, scarlet White, yellow, orange, red, pink
Bougainvillea	Need lots of sun. Bring inside when temperatures dip near freezing. Do best in a large (14 inches or more) container filled with coarse soil. Keep soil moderately dry and mist regularly for best results.	'Crimson Jewel'	Magenta; bold-colored bracts provide show of color
Fuchsia	For most, avoid direct sunlight and cold temperatures. Morning sun, sheltered from afternoon sun is best. Keep evenly moist—mist, if necessary, and give two daily waterings in hot weather. Water wilted plants immediately. Brightly colored, pendulous blossoms are irresistible to hummingbirds. Dark-colored, single blossom varieties withstand more sunlight than lighter shades. Woodier, upright specimens are hardier, tolerate extremes better than tender plants.	'Swing Time' 'Dollar Princess' 'Blue Eyes', 'Dark Eyes'	White with rose-colored sepals
Miniature Rose (trailing types)	Sun, good drainage, and plenty of water. Check water daily.	'Acey Duecy' 'Cinderella' 'Gourmet Popcorn' 'Jackpot' 'Loveglo' 'Minnie Pearl' 'My Honey' 'Over the Rainbow' 'Red Delight' 'Sachet'	Red White mini White Yellow Coral pink Pink blend Bright orange Red and cream Red Mauve

ANNUAL VARIETIES AND HABITS

Common Name	Habits	Cultivars	Color/Size
Black-eyed-Susan Vine	Likes full sun.	'Susie'	Orange, yellow, white; many with dark eye
Browallia*	Takes sun, but prefers semi-shade. Keep moderately moist. Mist.	'Bell'	Blue, white
Geranium	Prefers a sunny or semi-sunny location. Allow to dry slightly between waterings. Trailing. Full and upright. Upright but will fill in a basket nicely.	Ivy-leaf 'Martha Washington' Zonal types	Red, pink, salmon, lavender, white, and bi-colors
Impatiens	Semi-shade to shade. Allow to dry out slightly between waterings. Bred to be upright and compact.	Various	White, pinks, lavender, coral, red

Continued →

Common Name	Habits	Cultivars	Color/Size
Impatiens	Prefers semi-shade, but tolerates full sun if kept well-watered. The over-flow of growth and profusion of bloom makes it a natural for hanging baskets.	New Guinea Hybrid	White, pink, lavender, red, orange
Lobelia	Likes a sunny spot, but tolerates semi-shade. Allow to dry slightly.	'Fountain' 'Trailing Sapphire'	Blue, crimson, lilac, white Blue with white eye
Lotus Vine*	Makes a delicate counterbalance to mixed plantings. Tolerates full sun to part-shade. Let dry between waterings.		Lacy, filigree-like, silvery gray-green foliage on 2- to 3-foot-long trailing stems
Nasturtium (trailing)	Likes sun. Tolerates drought and weak soil. Overfeeding retards bloom. Water after soil has dried somewhat.	'Semi-Tall Double Gleam' 'Hermine Grasshof'	Yellow, orange, red Double-flowered, orange
Nierembergia*	Prefers sun or semi-shade. Heat tolerant. Pest-free. Allow soil to dry somewhat between waterings.	'Mount Blanc' 'Purple Robe'	White Violet-blue with yellow eye
Nolana paradoxa	Full sun. Tolerates hot dry weather well. Water when soil is nearly dry.	'Blue Bird'	Sky blue
Pepper Plant	Relative of the red hot chili pepper bears bright, perky, upright, inedible peppers. Full sun required. Keep soil moderately moist, allowing it to dry slightly between waterings and mist regularly.		Yellow, orange and red
Petunia	Likes lots of sun, keep well-watered.	'Supercascade' 'Supertunia'	White, pink, red, rose, purple
Portulaca	Loves sun and heat. Tolerates poor nutrition. Allow to dry somewhat between waterings.	'Sundial'	White, yellow, apricot, orange, scarlet, pink, fuchsia
Swan River Daisy	Prefers sun or light shade. Allow to dry somewhat between waterings.		Delicate, small daisy-like flowers of clear lavender float atop draping mounds of finely divided foliage throughout spring and summer
Sweet Alyssum	Sparkles in sun or partial shade. Sweet fragrance. Let soil dry between waterings.	'Snow Crystals', 'Carpet of Snow' 'Royal Carpet'	White Purple
Verbena*	Full sun. Allow to dry slightly before watering. Trailing types from cuttings.		White, lavender, pink, red, bi-colors
Vinca vine	Cold hardy. Takes full sun. Allow to dry slightly between waterings.		Variegated vine

*Perennials grown as annuals.

UNUSUAL VARIETIES FOR HANGING BASKETS

Common Name	Habits	Cultivars	Color/Size
Cucumbers	Vines will climb hanging ropes and tumble over edges of container. Plant 3 to 4 seeds per basket.	'Salad Bush' Hybrid	A smaller variety developed for container gardening
Peas	Compact vines tumble out of container. Cool-season crop; can be sown indoors in late winter and brought outside during the day. Plant seeds 4 inches apart. Need even moisture.	'Sugar Bon', 'Maestro' 'Petit Provencal'	Tiny gourmet peas

Common Name	Habits	Cultivars	Color/Size
Pumpkin	Need large containers, constant moisture, and regular feedings. Plant 3 to 4 seeds per basket.	'Jack Be Little' 'Baby Bear'	Mini-pumpkins on 2-foot-long vines 6-inch, fine-grained pumpkins produced on 3- to 4-foot-long vines
Strawberries	Need full sun and plenty of water for best production.	'Picnic' 'Hanging Harvest' 'Serenata'	Everbearing; start from seed indoors in winter; produces fruit in 4 months; developed especially for containers; remarkable for generous production of pink ornamental blossoms
Thyme (creeping)	Outstanding display of subtle color, pleasing texture, and heady scent. Allow to dry out between waterings. Keep in full sun.		
Tomatoes	Keep well watered.	'Tumbler'	Cascading habit a natural for hanging baskets; early producer (as little as 50 days); will set fruit near a sunny window

PLANTS FOR SUN

Black-eyed-Susan Vine	Pelargonium
Blue Bird	Petunia
Bougainvillea	Portulaca
Cucumbers	Pothos
Dollar Princess Fuchsia	Pumpkins
Herbs	Strawberries
Miniature Roses	Sweet Alyssum
New Guinea Impatiens	Tomatoes
Nasturtium	Verbena
Lobelia	Vinca Vine
Peas	

PLANTS FOR PARTIAL SHADE

Asparagus Fern	Lobelia
Begonia	New Guinea Impatiens
Browallia	Nierembergia
Cissus	Pothos
Creeping Charlie	Spider Plant
Donkey Tail	Sweet Alyssum
English Ivy	Wandering Jew
Fuchsia	Wax Plant
Impatiens	

Get Your Fingers Dirty

For some of us this is the best part—we get to play in the dirt! Here's where your careful planning and consideration pays off.

START FROM SEED

There is a phenomenal range of choices available as seed, which is great since seed is cheaper than transplants. Given moisture, warmth, and adequate light, the seeds will, in time, develop into those glorious images you have in your mind's eye. There's the catch—time. Be patient, it's worth the wait.

If you have a sunny window, grow lights (fluorescent shop lights do quite nicely), or best of all, a greenhouse, you can start annual baskets early. If you must wait until baskets can be started outside, you will have to wait until mid-season to enjoy the fruits (or flowers) of your labor.

Start seeds in flats or directly in the planters. Generally direct seeding into the planters works best with large-seeded plants, such as nasturtiums. Plant only one type of seed per basket for the most predictable results. Here are five simple steps to sure success:

1. To start seeds fill the flats or baskets with well-moistened planting medium.

2. Sow seeds. The general rule of thumb is to plant at a depth equal to roughly 2 1/2 times the widest part of the seed. Check the seed packet for special instructions.*

3. Keep in a warm, moist place until seedlings sprout. Covering the flat or basket with clear plastic wrap helps retain moisture, like a mini-greenhouse.

4. Once seedlings emerge, provide light. Either move to a sunny window (or greenhouse) or position about 4 inches beneath grow lights.

5. When the plants are about 2 inches tall, thin them to about 4 to 6 inches apart if growing in baskets, or transplant.

* Some seeds germinate best in light. For best results don't cover ageratum, coleus, impatiens, lobelia, petunia, portulaca, snapdragon, or sweet alyssum when sowing.

Continued ➔

HANDLE WITH CARE

Whether you start your own transplants or bring home store bought, transplanting is an exciting time. Tender new plants spring from their ordered world of flats or transplant packs to mingle with a jumble of unfamiliar new friends. Treat them kindly to make the transition an easy one.

Some plants, bougainvillea in particular, languish if you mistreat their tender roots. Be very gentle when handling any rootballs, just to be on the safe side. Here are a few tips for tranquil transplanting:

1. Begin by choosing young, healthy transplants. Try to find some not yet in bloom. Avoid any that have brown or yellowed leaves, or that have overgrown their containers. Check the bottom of the pack for escaping roots.

2. Fill the container with damp planting medium to within about 2 inches of the top edge.

3. Using your fingers or a small garden trowel, hollow out a spot in the center of the basket for the center plant. Remove the transplant from its container, gently separate roots if they are matted together or prune away excess if necessary, and place in planting hole. Firm soil around the base of the transplant so that it rests at the same level it did in the pack. (Tomato plants are an exception to this rule; transplant them deeper than they originally grew. This causes new roots to form along the length of the stems, which makes for stronger plants.)

4. Repeat Step 3, moving around and out from the center. Finish by planting perimeter plants.

Get Tough

Whether you just brought home a nursery-grown basket overflowing with mature growth or have finally decided your direct-seeded basket of nasturtiums looks presentable enough to set out, don't rush out to hang it just yet.

Tender new plants, even those mature-looking nursery grown specimens, need a little toughening up before they are ready to face the rigors of the real world. The process is referred to as *hardening off* and involves a physical toughening of plant tissues. It prepares plants for drying winds and wavering temperatures, the likes of which they never encountered in the greenhouse or nursery pack. Hardening off significantly reduces plant stress. Plants that have just been transplanted have already been subjected to a fair amount of vigor-sapping stress and may really suffer if doled out another dose.

Hardening off is easy to do and takes only a few days and a little patience. Rather than hanging the basket and leaving it to fend for itself, set it out in a protected place for about 1/2 hour the first day. The second day leave it out an hour or so. Double the exposure each day and gradually move it nearer to where it will hang for the season.

Hang 'Em Right

There are a few more things to consider when hanging baskets for display. If the basket is a houseplant, or will be spending much time indoors, light is crucial. While many houseplants prefer the shadowy environment found indoors (that's why we call them "houseplants"), all but the most reclusive need some level of sunlight. Orchestrate your indoor plants around a south or southwest facing window, if possible. Arrange those with the greatest craving for sunlight nearest the windows and those that have it made in the shade further back.

Another consideration for indoor hanging plants is drippage. Few plants will tolerate standing in water, so good drainage is essential. Be sure to either position hanging houseplants so that excess water drainage will not ruin carpets and floors, or rig a drip saucer into the hanging arrangement.

Finally, never overestimate the strength of your ceiling. Don't hang baskets from phalange-type ceiling hooks, even if the manufacturer says they will bear the weight. The manufacturer isn't guaranteeing your ceiling—just the hook! Locate a ceiling joist with a stud finder (or tap along the ceiling every few inches until you locate the joist) and affix a sturdy hook directly into the solid lumber. Another solution is to locate a stud in the wall and install a strong bracket from which to suspend the hanger. Stairwells, rafters, and strong window frames also make good choices from which to hang baskets.

When hanging outdoor baskets consider these guidelines. As for indoor plants, be sure that the light level is appropriate for the plant (or plants) in the basket. The problem outdoors is usually just the opposite of indoors—rather than not getting enough light, try to position the basket so it won't be fried by direct sunlight. Afternoon sun is the strongest, so if possible, arrange planters so that they receive morning sun, with some afternoon protection. Refer to Recommended Varieties to see which plants prefer more light than others. But even sun lovers, when grown in containers, require lots of moisture, so position baskets where it is convenient for you to water regularly. Finally, be sure the support is strong enough to hold the basket.

Where and at what height you hang baskets can be used to striking advantage. By hanging several baskets in a row at varying heights you can divide a room or section off a corner of a covered deck or patio. Create a circle, stairstep effect, or spectacular entryway, by strategically arranging baskets.

Keep Hanging Baskets Healthy

Plants in hanging baskets are living in an extremely artificial environment. This works both for and against them. In their favor, plants that are sensitive to cold can be whisked indoors at a moment's notice. On the other hand, the plants are confined; the roots cannot reach out further into the soil in search of water or nutrients. They are also at great risk from temperature extremes, since the roots are surrounded on all sides by air. Hot, dry air causes rapid drying; cold, damp air can contribute to disease and plant stress. So for healthy, happy plants, be prepared to dole out a little pampering.

WATER WELL

Drying winds combine with exposed foliage and limited root space to create a huge demand for moisture. Fuchsias are a classic example—all that lush growth and showy flowering results in a constant thirst. It seems almost impossible to overwater. But there are a few easy watering rules.

Check for moisture before you water. If you can push your finger into the soil an inch and still feel dampness, the basket can probably wait another day before watering. Wet-feeling soil can definitely wait, but dry soil needs water now. Another test is to lift up the basket from the base. If it feels light, water now. Finally, a glance will tell you if a plant is entering distress from lack of water. Wilting is a sure sign that plants need water—unless, you have already *overwatered* so much that the plant has contracted root rot.

Water every day if necessary. In general, more frequent watering is required for plants in small baskets and plants that are naturally thirstier (and in this unnatural environment all plants need more water than in their natural habitat). Plants also require extra water during hot, dry, or windy weather.

Use safe water. Don't use water treated by a water softener. Some water softeners use chemicals that are harmful to plants. In warm conditions, avoid watering straight from the garden hose. A splash of cold water on a warm plant can damage foliage and roots. Likewise, water that has been lying about in a garden hose in the sun can become superheated, and may scald plants. Check water temperature before use.

Dunk 'em. Plants already stressed from lack of water can be thoroughly saturated by filling a bucket or sink with warm water and immersing the pot until the soil at the top of the basket is moist. This takes longer than applying water at the top, but is more effective. Soil in planters that have dried out forms airspaces that water trickles through quickly when watered from the top. By allowing water to wick up from the bottom, these air spaces are filled by water as it is absorbed into the organic matter in the soil mix.

FEED FOR FABULOUS FLOWERS AND FOLIAGE

Life in a basket has its limitations, and one of them is that the roots can't go out to eat. It's up to you to provide all their nutritional needs. These needs vary with the season. During periods of active growth, they eat like kids. During dormant periods they fast. Knowing when, how, and how much to feed your hanging baskets is important, and there are lots of choices. Don't fret—it's very basic stuff.

Just like us, plants need the most nutrition when they are growing. The best type of fertilizer to use often boils down to a matter of convenience. Powders must be mixed; liquids may be used as is or diluted. Most products are applied to the soil, but some are also recommended for foliar feeding, meaning they are sprayed onto the leaves and absorbed into the plant. Slow-release pellets are applied once, then gradually dissolve each time the plant is watered to release a constant flow of nutrients; pegs may be inserted directly into the soil as another form of slow-release feeding. There are organic and chemically based formulas. Each method and formula has its proponents.

There are two hard and fast rules for feeding plants: First, always read and follow label directions when applying fertilizers (or any chemical for that matter). Second, never apply fertilizer to dry soil. Plant nutrients are only absorbed by roots when dissolved in water, so water in well. Underwatering results in under-diluted fertilizer, which results in root burn.

Fertilizing every two weeks is more effective than a large dose every month or so. Dilute a 20-20-20 fertilizer (the numbers stand for the percentage of nitrogen, phosphorous, and potassium in the product) to half the strength recommended on the label. Plants growing in soilless mixes (that contain no nutrients of their own), should be fed a weak solution of fertilizer every time you water.

Gauge whether or not your plants are receiving adequate nutrition by their reaction over time. Plants with yellow leaves may be suffering from a lack of nitrogen. If leaf edges turn brown for no apparent reason (the plant appears healthy otherwise), suspect fertilizer burn. Too much fertilizer can also cause lower leaves to drop or the entire plant to wilt. A whitish crust on the soil surface may signify a build-up of chemical salts.

To save an overfertilized plant, water the soil until it runs through the bottom of the basket and allow the water to continue running to leach out excess chemicals. A more stringent course is to wash the soil away from the roots and repot the plant in fresh soil mix.

STAY IN SHAPE

The shape of a hanging basket can be an image of free-flowing grace or one of tangled confusion. Flowers may grace the foliage or dry up and cling on like embarrassing relatives. The look of your hanging baskets is in your hands.

The silhouette of a hanging basket is determined by two things: the natural growth habit of the plant in question, and the interference (I mean, well-planned guidance) of the gardener. The trailing plants listed above are fine choices for hanging baskets precisely because they tend to hang over the edge of their container and gracefully cascade down the sides. But if you desire a fuller, bushier form, you can manipulate the plant into the type of growth you wish. Conversely, if a vine is putting out side runners at the expense of the willowy trailing stems you had envisioned, you can change its course with a few snips.

For plants that are running on the long, skinny side take a pair of scissors, a sharp knife, or pruners, and snip the plant off (no more than a third), even if it's in full bloom. Plants respond by focusing energy into buds that lay along the sides of the stem which soon develop into side branches, filling in gaps with growth.

To encourage long, delicate danglers, snip off branches that form at the side of the main stem. This focuses the plant's energy into growing lengthwise. Continue to pinch out new buds along the sides of the stem to force growth into length.

Continued ➜

As the flowers begin to fade, pinch off the old blossoms. This important step, called *deadheading*, will clean up the ragged appearance left by dead and faded flowers and encourage further bloom. Even generously blooming annuals have but one purpose in flowering—to set seed. Once the blossoms fade, those that have been fertilized with pollen begin to swell and form seed. This process robs the rest of the plant of the energy and tendency to produce more flowers. The plant has no reason to continue to flower if its objective of reproducing (through setting seed) has been accomplished. Happily for us, annuals are so programmed to set seed that they will continue to do so until exhausted or killed by frost. So, the more future seed pods you pluck off, the more the plant will work to replace them by producing more flowers.

WATCH FOR PESTS AND PROBLEMS

Dangling there in its self-contained world, your hanging basket is no more protected from pests and problems than any other plant in the vicinity. You still have to watch for bugs that target your plant(s), diseases, and problems particular to living in a container.

One of the advantages of mixed baskets is that the diverse array of plants serves to break up bug radar. Rather than finding one juicy mass of its favorite geranium, an aphid population may detect nothing recognizable amid a mixed planting of geranium, sweet alyssum, nasturtium, vines, and ornamental grass. Organic gardeners have used this technique of companion planting (combining different types of plants in the garden) for years. It is one effortless line of defense in the unending competition between bugs and gardeners.

Indoor plants are often plagued by aphids, mites, mealybugs, scale, and whitefly. Insecticidal soaps or horticultural oils are effective. For persistent problems, pesticides containing malathion are effective.

Outdoors aphids and mites are common problems. A stiff stream of water from the garden hose will usually knock them off the plant. Hanging roses are subject to the same ills as any roses, including aphids. Systemic food and pesticides are a sure way to keep them healthy. Apply as per product label. For many pests that attack hanging baskets, the best cure is simply a shot of water from the garden hose.

Among the diseases that most often beset hanging plants are various fungal maladies. As seedlings emerge in flats or baskets they are susceptible to *damping off*, in which the young plants appear to have been pinched off at the base. They topple over and die. The best remedy is prevention. Practice good hygiene in your planting regimen by using only fresh, sterilized soil mix and fresh water to start seeds. Fungicides containing captan are effective. Once the problem is evident, remove any afflicted plants and the soil immediately surrounding them to prevent the disease from spreading.

Another common disease caused by a fungus is gray mold, or botrytis. It strikes young plants and houseplants with equal glee. Like damping off, it is better to prevent it than to treat it. When starting seeds, don't crowd them too closely together in the flat or in the basket. In order to insure adequate air circulation, give each baby at least an inch of space to call its own. Also, be very careful not to injure seedlings, as wounds are a prime port of entry for opportunistic fungi.

Plants that have been overwatered may suffer from a form of root rot. Plant roots need oxygen, and waterlogged soil has had most of the oxygen squeezed out. Roots begin to die and rot, and the plant suffers.

Other problems that plague hanging baskets are particular to growing in containers or under artificial conditions. They are commonly caused by improper growing conditions. Avoid extremes or fluctuations in temperature, humidity, or soil moisture, and place plants so that they receive the required amount of sunlight.

Perennial Pleasure

Annuals deserve due praise for their uplifting gifts of quick and constant color, but come season's end they're goners. Perennials, though, have more to offer. Given a little preparation, they will joyously stage a comeback performance season after season after season.

WAIT OUT WINTER

As the long, balmy days of summer surrender to the dwindling daylight and crisp air of autumn, plants seem to slip into a state of decline. Actually, they are shedding unnecessary frills, such as flowers, fruit, seed pods, and perhaps spare leaves, in preparation for winter. In other words, they are downsizing for the off season.

Nature signals plants that winter is coming through a complex physical/chemical system. Plants react to shorter day length, longer angles of the sun's rays, cooler nights, and perhaps other stimuli, with changes in their hormonal production and cellular structure. The plant gradually falls into near dormancy. As sad as it is to see the glory of the season wane, there is good news. Dormant hanging baskets are a snap to store for the winter. The constant cravings for food, water, and sunlight vanish. All the plant needs now is a cool place to rest and an occasional drink.

To prepare and carry a hanging basket through the winter follow these easy steps:

- **Keep abreast of evening temperatures.** If even a hint of frost threatens, bring baskets in for the night. Baskets can be kept happily blooming for weeks into the fall if protected from the cold. Most hanging basket plants are not cold hardy, though, and will not survive a freezing night forgotten on the porch.

- **Keep an eye on basket plants as fall advances.** Stop feeding and cut back on watering. This will encourage the physical hardening the plant must undergo to survive the winter. Once they begin to enter dormancy, bring them in. The time of year varies from place to place and with each new winter. Some may have to come in as early as late September, while others may hold out through November.

- **Place the plant in a dimly lit, cool, but not freezing spot (45–50°F), for the winter.** Be sure it's a spot in which the plants won't be totally forgotten. They will still need water every 3 or 4 weeks. The garage is fine if you are in an area that doesn't dip much below 40°F in the winter. A corner of the basement, a root cellar, beneath stairwells—anyplace that stays cool, but does not freeze, will do.

- **Check plants periodically.** Don't be discouraged if they drop leaves; some fuchsias even defoliate completely. As long as they don't freeze or dry out, they'll make it.

NEW PLANTS FROM CUTTINGS

Save the pruned cuttings; they can be used to propagate new plants for next season. For fuchsias, trim cuttings to 2 1/2 inches, long enough so four sets of leaves remain on the stem. For geraniums and bougainvillea, take 4-inch cuttings, with the bottom of each cutting resting just below a node. Pinch out the top set of leaves and the bottom set, leaving two sets of leaves on the stem. It's important to be able to tell the top end of the cutting from the bottom. To keep track, cut the bottom off straight across and slice the top at a 45 degree angle. Using this method several cuttings can be obtained from each stem.

Dip the bottom end of the cutting in a rooting hormone and place in a well-moistened cutting mix of half perlite, half vermiculite. Cover with a clear plastic to hold in humidity. Salvaged deli containers work great for this, just be sure to poke a few drainage holes in the bottom. Cuttings root in 4 to 6 weeks.

Rejuvenate in Spring

Bringing back perennial baskets for a new season's encore is a rewarding experience. Most will pull through better than the ones just described. Around the first of April bring the baskets into bright light. This can be achieved with shop lights or a sunny window. Water liberally and watch the new growth sprout!

This is also a fine time to cut back the roots of potbound plants and to repot if necessary. Fuchsias, in particular, react poorly to being rootbound and will perform better in a larger basket once they have outgrown their old confines. Repot into the next-sized basket from the one the plant outgrew, say from a 10-inch basket to a 12-inch.

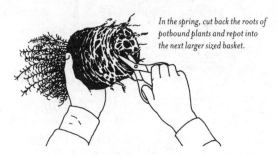

In the spring, cut back the roots of potbound plants and repot into the next larger sized basket.

What if a second-year (or third, or so on) plant doesn't bloom? Be patient. If winter storage temperatures were too warm (above 50°F); if the plant was stressed by insufficient moisture; or if spring time light levels were too low, flowering will be delayed. But even late bloomers catch up by July or August.

Flowering Shrubs

Patricia R. Barrett

Illustrations by Alison Kolesar and Elayne Sears

Introduction

Shrubs are among the most versatile of garden plants. They can fill the landscape with color, shape, and texture all year long—flowers in the spring, lovely foliage in the summer, berries and bright leaves in the autumn, and distinctive shapes and evergreen leaves in the winter.

A shrub is usually defined as a plant that has multiple trunks or stems and does not grow to a height of more than 20 feet. Of course, nature sometimes doesn't choose to go along with such well-planned categories. But we can safely say that shrubs are woody and perennial, or will live more than two years.

Shrubs do include both evergreen and deciduous plants, those that drop their leaves in the fall. But when we speak of flowering shrubs, we usually mean deciduous shrubs. Shrubs can grow in all parts of the United States and Canada, although most shrubs will fail if the temperature drops to −40° to −50°F. Some shrubs are native plants, such as bayberry, sumac, and witch hazel, but many of the familiar shrubs, such as lilac and forsythia, come from China and Japan. Many of our shrubs today are not original species but rather hybrids, results of crossbreeding. Modern plants have been bred for hardiness as well as for a wide variety of bloom color and flower shapes.

LEARNING ABOUT SHRUBS

If you are new to gardening and can barely tell a forsythia from a yew, then before you purchase plants for your garden, learn something about the different shrubs. Walk around a well-planted neighborhood in the early spring. Look at the varieties of shrubs that are in bloom. Chances are you will see numerous azaleas and rhododendrons coloring the borders of many houses. If you see someone in the garden, ask the person what kind of shrub it is. Most gardeners love to talk about their plants and can give you lots of information.

If you have an arboretum nearby, visit it and learn about the different shrubs that are growing there. If they do well at a nearby arboretum, chances are they will also do well for you. Shrubs at most arboretums are well labelled so this will help you in your quest. But, if you can't find the name, bring along a guide that has good photographs of different plants to help with your identification. Other good places to look at mature shrubs are college campuses and cemeteries.

Once you have observed shrubs you will see that they tend to grow in different shapes that can be used singly or in combination to create different effects in the home garden. These shapes are: rounded spreading, prostrate, low spreading, open spreading, globular, columnar, weeping, and pyramidal.

When you see a shrub you like, whether it is for the shape, leaf texture, or color, learn the Latin name rather than the common name. There are two names for plants: the first is the generic name and indicates the plant's genus. A genus is a group of plants that are closely related and have a common ancestor. The second name identifies the species, or a particular member of the genus.

DESIGNING WITH SHRUBS

When you have a list of shrubs you like, remember to consider both the nature of the plant and the function you want it to perform in the landscape. Some flowering shrubs are so lovely they can stand alone as a specimen plant, but many shrubs can serve more than one purpose. They may also provide a protective screen from a neighbor, or act as a windbreak, or provide food for hungry birds with its berries. Think about what you want the plant to do before you plant it.

Continued →

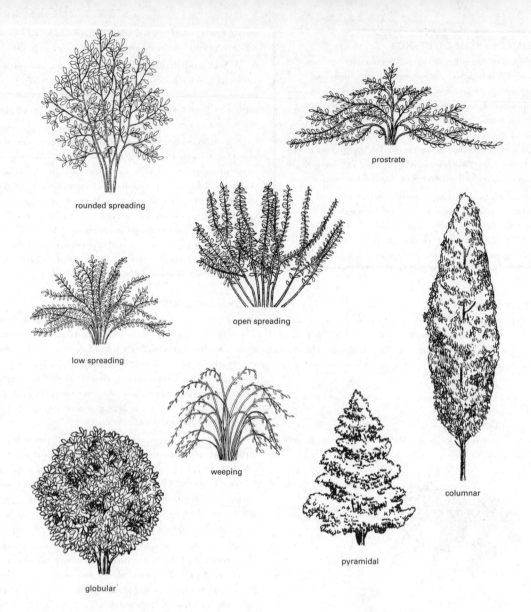

rounded spreading

prostrate

open spreading

low spreading

columnar

weeping

globular

pyramidal

Before you plan or plant any kind of shrub garden, keep in mind:

· Shrub shape and eventual size

· Color of flowers, berries, and foliage

· Texture of foliage

· Bloom time

· Function of shrub

FOUNDATION PLANTINGS

Some common uses of shrubs are to plant them next to the house to hide exposed concrete, to accent the terrace or steps, or to help the house blend into its site. These plantings are called foundation plantings. Foundation plantings need to have interest throughout the year and need to be slow growing. You do not want a shrub that will quickly grow to 30 feet, and you do not want to have to keep pruning plants to keep them in shape.

Shrubs planted near the house should complement the house and not be ungainly. Many flowering shrubs do not exceed 3 feet in height. Think about the viburnums, brooms, cotoneasters, *Potentillas*, spireas, and barberries. In addition to these plants, other shrubs have varieties that stay small, or grow very slowly, making them good choices for foundation plantings.

HEDGES

Shrubs are often used in hedges, which can be a screen for your yard or can be used to define different areas of the yard, keeping children out of some areas or marking spaces for sitting and gardens.

If you want to plant just a single line of shrubs, it is better to plant one kind of shrub rather than mixing a variety of plants. Remember that the shrubs will grow wider as well as taller, so plant accordingly. Fill half the space you want to eventually fill to allow for this eventual growth.

BORDERS

A border is any grouping of plants designed to please the eye. The primary purpose of any border in the garden is to be decorative. Shrub borders have the added advantage of also being able to act as windbreaks, barriers, and screens. For your border to be successful and one you enjoy for many years, consider it an intricate garden made up of many varieties of plants.

Choosing and Planting Shrubs

Remember that most shrubs can grow in both sun and shade to varying degrees. Flowering shrubs tend to need some sun in order to bloom. And some shrubs, such as *Pieris japonica*, grow best in almost constant shade.

Be sure to look at the amount of light available to the shrubs you are planning to plant. Is the sunlight direct or is it filtered through neighboring trees? Is it morning sun or late afternoon sun? If there is no shade, will the plants be in bright sunlight for most of the day? All of these are considerations before choosing your shrub. Keep them in mind when you go to the nursery.

BEFORE YOU SHOP FOR YOUR SHRUB, REVIEW THESE QUESTIONS:

- Will it grow well in the location chosen?
- Will it fit into the alloted space?
- Does it have the right amount of light for its growing conditions?
- Is it hardy for the area?
- Will it bloom or produce fruit at the right time?

BUYING SHRUBS

You can buy shrubs through catalogs, from specialized nurseries, or from local garden centers. Many garden centers today have plants that are grown elsewhere, but some nurseries still do grow their own stock to sell. If you can find a local nursery that grows its own shrubs, you can be assured the plant will be hardy in your area.

When buying at a local nursery, you can see different plants and choose a specific one for the characteristics you desire. The plants are also probably larger than those you would receive from a mail-order catalog. But you do not want to choose a shrub that is too large. They are likely to be more expensive than the smaller ones and may not transplant as well when you get them home.

Nursery owners recommend that you buy young plants at about half the size of what they will be at maturity. That means if you are buying a plant that will grow to be 6 feet tall, purchase one that is about 3 feet tall now. The plant you buy should look healthy—no brown in the leaves, no dead stems. Plants should look as if they are well watered. Do not buy one that is wilted or very dry looking. It may not make it.

The staff at the nursery will help you pick out the best stock. Look for shrubs that have a number of stems that branch out from the central stem. Look for dense, bushy plants that have a number of buds on the branches. Ask if your nursery will guarantee the plant. Many will for a year after purchase.

You may have to order shrubs by mail if you want an unusual variety. It is best to order from a reliable nursery source that specializes in unusual shrubs. Check to see how the plant is sent and specify when you want it delivered to your area. Many reliable nurseries will stand behind what they sell and are quick to reimburse you if the plant is damaged in transit.

HOW SHRUBS ARE SOLD

Shrubs are sold in three ways: bare rooted, balled and burlapped, and container grown.

Bare-rooted plants are usually the least expensive, but if you see them for sale they are probably the ones to avoid. If the roots have been exposed to the air and sun and have not been kept moist, they are worthless. Mail-order houses, however, often ship bare-rooted plants wrapped in sphagnum moss and wrapped well in plastic to keep the moisture in the roots.

Balled-and-burlapped shrubs are dug out of their growing medium so that a ball of soil surrounds the roots. This is then wrapped in burlap and tied. These plants are found in nurseries where they are grown because they are not shipped as easily as plants grown in containers. I have had great luck with balled-and-burlapped plants and recommend them.

Container-grown plants are often not as satisfactory as those that are balled and burlapped. Often plants that have been placed in containers will later die when planted in the garden because of root damage at the time they are dug. What you want with a container plant is one that has been grown in the container and not simply dug from the field and placed in the container.

Nursery owners will usually tell you how the plant was grown, but if not, look at the container; if you see lots of roots tightly packed on the outside of the ball of soil once the plant is lifted from the container, it probably is okay and was grown right where it is now. But if the ball of soil is loose and crumbly, the shrub probably was not grown in the container and may not do well when transplanted.

HOW TO PLANT

Once you have your shrub, the best thing to do is to plant it within a few hours of purchase. If you can't plant immediately, place the shrub in the shade and keep it moist. Wet the ball or water the container.

If the shrub is bare rooted, never let the roots dry out. Fill a bucket with water and add some soil. Dip the roots in this mixture so all are coated. If you can't plant right away, leave the shrub in the bucket until you can. If you cannot plant for a while, make a trench in the garden and lie the roots in the trench, cover with soil, and shade the top of the plant from the sun. Water well.

No matter what kind of shrub you have to plant, one common need of each is a big hole. Preparing the hole and the planting medium for your shrub is very important to its future growth.

Since you will only plant the shrub once, it is worth doing a good job the first time. The hole you dig should be bigger than the width of the roots when they are spread out in their natural position. The extra room in the hole can be used for an additional amount of loose soil and humus to be added around the roots of the shrub. When you dig, take out the topsoil, the first 5 to 7 inches of soil, and place it on a tarp beside the hole. Then take out the rest of the soil, the paler soil that lies beneath the topsoil, and take it to the compost pile. Add some organic matter and fertilizer to the topsoil you saved. Mix well and begin filling the hole.

The organic matter you add to the soil can be leaf mold, compost, decayed leaves, or sawdust. It will help with drainage and aerate the

Continued →

soil somewhat for the health of the roots. If you use peat moss, wet it thoroughly before using.

This proper soil conditioning before you plant your shrub will help the plant's growth for years to come. This is the time to take extra care and be sure the plant is getting what it will need for its growth.

Once you have dug your hole and the soil mix is ready, planting is not difficult. If your shrub is bare rooted, prune the roots and some of the top growth. Remove any weak or broken branches.

When you plant a bare-rooted shrub, place it in the hole and spread out the roots with your hands so they reach out toward the sides of the hole. Then place a small amount of soil in the hole and cover the roots using your hands to tap the soil carefully. When the roots are covered and the hole is nearly filled, firm the soil with your foot. Do not plant the shrub deeper or shallower than it was planted before you purchased it.

Now water the shrub being sure to saturate the soil around the shrub. When the water has drained away, fill in the hole using the remaining topsoil mixture. Make a rim with the soil to hold the water in around the shrub and water thoroughly again.

If the shrub is balled and burlapped, follow the same procedure and leave the burlap in place. Cut any ropes that are tying the ball together and pull the burlap down from the neck of the plant. Do not leave any burlap exposed above the soil as it will tend to act as a wick and take water away from the plant's roots. Make sure the material covering the ball is burlap and not a plastic material that will not break down in the soil.

Container-grown plants need just as much, if not more, attention when being planted. Sometimes they are grown in a soilless mix and need as much organic matter as you can work into the soil to make their transition a painless one. Slide the shrub out of the container or, if necessary, cut the container off. If the roots are tightly bound, make cuts in them with a knife to stimulate new growth. Try to move some of the roots out of the ball and spread them out in the hole as you plant the shrub. This will encourage the plant to send out new roots. If you prune the roots, be sure to prune the top growth of the plant also.

Shrubs you have just planted need extra care. They are very susceptible to water loss and need to be watered often. Once the plants are established they can endure dry periods.

THE SOIL'S PH LEVEL

Many flowering shrubs grow well in soil that is mildly acid, that is, it registers between 6.0 and 7.0 on the pH scale, just slightly on the acid side of the neutral level of 7.0. Many of the more popular flowering shrubs, such as rhododendrons and azaleas, blueberries, and bayberries, require very acidic soil with a pH of 4.5 to 5.5. Leaves of these plants will turn yellow in a neutral or alkaline soil because they cannot get enough iron. If the pH is lowered, the iron is freed in the soil and the plants are able to absorb it.

Many garden centers and extension services will test your soil for its pH level. If you need to make your soil more acidic to grow some of these shrubs, you may add finely ground sulfur or iron sulfate. If you are going to use sulfur, you have to apply it a month or two in advance of planting as it reacts slowly in the soil but it lasts a long time. Iron sulfate acts quickly but needs to be reapplied every two or three years. Read the package instructions and apply according to the pH level of your soil.

If your soil is too acidic for the shrubs you want to grow, you can easily correct it by adding finely ground limestone to the planting soil.

Work it into the soil where the shrubs are planted and spread it on the ground between the shrubs. About five pounds of limestone added to every 100 square feet of garden area will raise the pH level about 1 unit. Again, limestone needs to be added well in advance of planting.

WHEN TO PLANT

Although many gardeners still think that spring is the only time to plant shrubs, others are beginning to realize that fall is an even better time. Some tender shrubs and shrubs of questionable hardiness for your area should be planted in the spring, but others can wait until fall. Container-grown plants, if properly cared for, can be planted any time the soil can be worked. In the North, it is best to give the plants an early start so they are somewhat established before the ground freezes, so plant early in the fall. In the South, where the soil seldom freezes, planting can extend throughout the winter. Fall-planted shrubs will probably bloom the following season while spring-planted ones may not flower the first season.

Caring for Shrubs

Caring for shrubs is not difficult. Even the busiest homeowner can take care of a number of flowering shrubs and be rewarded with bloom and healthy, long-lived plants.

WATERING

Newly planted shrubs do need water if they are to flourish. Any week when there hasn't been a good soaking rain means you need to give the shrubs a good watering. Sprinkling water over the soil's surface does not work; you have to soak the shrubs. Perforated hoses lined around and under the shrubs are good for soaking. Or, you can use a hose and let the water dribble into the soil around the plant for several hours.

When shrubs are planted in the fall, you need to water until the winter snows or rains arrive. Shrubs set out in the spring need weekly watering until late fall. After the plants have been in the garden for a season, they need little watering, except during dry periods, or if you have very sandy soil.

FERTILIZING

If you have taken care when planting your shrubs, they will need little fertilizing. Overfertilizing can create plants with long stems and few flowers. Too much fertilizer with newly planted shrubs can cause root burning, which will weaken or even kill the plants. However, if you have planted your shrub carefully, and if after a few months it fails to grow any new stems or its leaves turn yellow, you may want to apply fertilizer.

The type of fertilizer you use will depend on the shrubs. For those that do not require acid soil conditions, a common garden fertilizer is fine. A typical mix for feeding shrubs is 5–10–5. That is, it contains 5 percent nitrogen, 10 percent phosphorus, and 5 percent potassium. Usually just 1/4 to 1/2 cup of this mix is sufficient for an average-sized shrub. Fertilize in the early spring. Fall fertilizing may encourage new growth which can be damaged by winter frosts.

MULCHING

A mulch will help the soil around your shrubs stay moist and cool throughout the year. A mulch is any covering over the soil of a porous, organic material that will allow water to penetrate the soil. Mulches also cut down on weeding and improve the soil as they disintegrate.

Mulch materials vary. Good choices are leaves (crumbled or shredded), wood chips, hay, grass clippings, pine needles, or coarse peat moss. Apply mulch right after planting in a layer about 2 inches deep. Do not get the mulch too near the stem of the shrub, and do not pile it too thickly as it can cut off air that roots need. Water before applying any mulch.

PRUNING

Pruning is the one word in gardening that causes fear, even in the most experienced grower. When do I prune what? If I prune this at the wrong time, will I kill it? What if I prune too much? Not enough? The list of pruning fears is long and many gardeners feel it is easier to forget the whole thing, sometimes until it is too late.

Pruning doesn't have to be that frightening. It's really done for a purpose and once that is known the rest is easy. Some flowering shrubs need to be pruned annually, some just occasionally, and some hardly ever need pruning. Any shrub that you have to prune more than once a year to keep it in place is probably in the wrong place.

All shrubs need a certain amount of pruning if only to remove the dead or damaged branches. Lower branches in shrubs that do not get much light tend to die and will be the first to get diseased. So once a year it is a good idea to remove these. Early spring is a good time to do this cleaning routine before the leaves appear and hide some of the damage. Cut off the dead wood as close to the stem as possible. Next, cut the branches that are broken and take off any branch that rubs on another or crosses over it in any way.

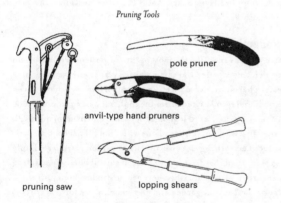

Pruning Tools

pole pruner

anvil-type hand pruners

pruning saw

lopping shears

When you prune, you want to get the best form and show of flowers you can. To do this, it is best to prune regularly. Before you start, try to visualize the look of the plant after you have pruned off a branch.

Rejuvenation is a natural part of annual pruning. Many shrubs that send up new shoots will benefit if you take a few of the older stems off at ground level each year (spirea, mock-orange, and deutzia).

When a shrub gets out of hand, it needs severe pruning. But do not cut every branch back the first year. Cut some back to the first main side shoot, then next year cut the remaining branches. Afterward, shape. Many shrubs that grow in a pendulous form need to have their old wood cut out at ground level (forsythia, weigela).

Plants that do not need to be pruned, other than to remove dead wood:	
azalea	*Laburnum*
Cercis	pieris
Halesia	magnolia
Kalmia	spring-flowering viburnums

Plants that need to be pruned right after they bloom:	
boxwood	*Hydrangea macrophylla*
flowering quince	lilac
forsythia	pieris
winter hazel	some viburnums and spireas

REJUVENATING OLD SHRUBS

If you look at your shrubs closely, you will see that they regenerate themselves by sending up new stems from the ground. To continue this process, it is a good idea each year to remove some of the oldest stems. Cut them down to about 2 to 3 inches off the ground. If you take out a few old stems each year, the shrub will always have stems of different ages coming along.

Sometimes you will find that you will have to do a major job of rejuvenation. If you move into a house and find shrubs that are very overgrown, you can work wonders with pruning. Cut every stem all the way back to the ground in early spring. It will not kill the shrub and will force numerous canes to grow from the stumps. These will not bloom for a few years, but when they do the blossoms will be plentiful. If you feel you need to do a drastic pruning job, do not be timid. Get out the pruning saw and cut stems back until they are 2 to 5 inches high.

Propagating Shrubs

You may wonder why you would ever want to duplicate a shrub, thinking that one would be enough. Perhaps your Aunt Sally has some wonderful shrub from long ago that you'd love to have in your own garden. Or, you may like a shrub that is already growing on your property and would like one just like it for another spot in the yard. If you are not in a rush for a full-sized plant, propagating could work for you. The other advantage to propagation is that the shrub is free.

This savings can readily be seen if you want forty plants for a long hedge and they can be grown from a plant you already own. It is also gratifying to be able to say when someone asks where you got that fabulous buddleia, "I grew it myself."

Propagating most shrubs is not all that difficult. Several methods work depending on the type of shrub you want to propagate. A few of the simplest ways to multiply plants are division, cuttings, and layering. These work well with most of the common shrubs.

DIVISION

Division works well on lilacs, oakleaf hydrangeas, Kerria, deutzias, many spireas, deciduous azaleas, Siberian dogwood, and other shrubs that send out underground branches. The stems grow out of the ground near the plant. These can be dug up in early spring and planted elsewhere.

Look for a sucker that has grown at least 12 inches above the ground. Cut a circle around the sucker so it will be severed from the main plant.

Continued ➔

Dig this small plant carefully and be sure to bring up all its deep roots. Replant at the original depth and water well.

CUTTINGS

Softwood cuttings. Many shrubs can be easily propagated by means of softwood cuttings. These are pieces of the stems taken in late spring from new growth. Cut 4- to 6-inch pieces at an angle from the ends of healthy branches. Dip these pieces in a rooting hormone and place them in a suitable rooting medium.

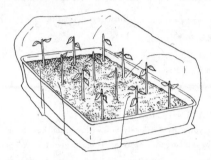

Cuttings placed in a suitable rooting medium and covered with a clear plastic bag.

Coarse sand, peat moss, or a mix of the two are good rooting mixes to use for cuttings. Perlite or vermiculite can also be used. Any container that has good drainage will work as long as it is deep enough to hold about 4 inches of the rooting medium.

Cover the cuttings with a clear plastic bag or a big glass jar. Place in bright light but not direct sunlight. The cuttings will take about a month or two to root. Remember to water them often. You can also place the cuttings outside in the shade, but remember to keep them watered.

When new leaves appear, it is a signal of root growth. The stems can be transplanted to a good potting soil mix but should wait in a cold frame until the following spring to be planted in the garden.

Shrubs that propagate from softwood cuttings include: mock-orange, boxwood, quince, evergreen azalea, clethra, *Potentilla*, deutzia, euonymous, *Tamarix*.

Hardwood cuttings. Hardwood cuttings are a bit more complicated than the softwood. These are 6- to 8-inch cuttings taken from a plant when the wood is mature in late fall or even midwinter. Take cuttings that have at least three or four nodes and cut at a slant. Then slice an inch or so off the bottom bark away from the stem to make it easier for roots to grow. Dust this cut area with rooting hormone. Tie the cuttings in bundles and bury the bundles in a cold frame or in the garden over the winter.

In early spring, dig up the cuttings and place in a narrow trench in the garden. Bury them so that only the top bud is above the ground. You should soon see leaves sprouting above the ground. Leave in the trench for an entire season until planting in the garden.

Shrubs that propagate from hardwood cuttings include: *Buddleia davidii*, *Erica*, hibiscus, rhododendron, *Salix*, spirea, weigela.

LAYERING

Layering is a simple process of bending the supple branches of some shrubs to the ground and anchoring them in the ground until they have rooted. It is an easy but slow process and can take about a year for roots to develop.

Select a young healthy stem from the shrub—one that is long enough to reach the ground—and bend it. Where it touches the soil make a notch with a knife so that a root will grow there. Dust the cut with rooting hormone and remove the leaves from either side of the wound. Bend the branch to the ground again and secure it with a rounded wire, a stone, or a forked stick. Pile a mix of peat and humus to a depth of 5 inches over the branch. Keep this soil moist throughout the season.

Layering

When the wounded area has rooted, remove it from the main shrub and plant it elsewhere.

Shrubs for layering include: rhododendron, *Daphne Genkwa*, *Erica*, fothergilla, *Kalmia*, *Potentilla*, *Pyracantha*, *Rhus*, *Rosa*, stewartia, *Syringa*.

Easy-Care Water Garden Plants

Charles W. G. Smith

Illustrations by Elayne Sears, Kathy Bray, Louise Riotte, and Brigita Fuhrmann

Introduction

Water gardens are often the most beautiful gardens around any home. The blending of water and earth, garden plants with water plants, creates a harmonious balance. The sound of moving water relaxes the body and mind as it inspires the soul. Yet water gardens can be intimidating, too. At first glance they can seem to be complicated places filled with unfamiliar plants with unusual needs. But like just about everything else growing, water garden plants are simpler to care for than they first appear. The beautiful but undemanding water garden plants described here are sure to brighten your spirits as well as your garden and give you pleasure for years to come.

Water lily   Submerged plant   Floating plant

A water garden should have a balance of aquatic plants, including those that root in the pond bottom and spread up to the water's surface, such as lilies; submerged plants, which never rise to above the water's surface; and floating plants, whose roots never reach the pond's bottom.

Submerged Plants

In nature, the water of ponds is purified in part by plants that grow entirely underwater. These plants are usually rooted in the sediment of the pond bottom and grow up through the water toward the surface many feet above. Seen from the surface, the long and slender stems seem like graceful green strands suspended in the water.

Submerged plants, like all green plants, produce food through photosynthesis and release oxygen in the process. The oxygen produced during photosynthesis is released directly into the water and acts as a purifier. Some plants, such as anacharis (*Egeria densa*), produce so much oxygen that a stream of tiny bubbles often can be seen rising from the plants. For this reason submerged plants are frequently called "oxygenating plants" in catalogs and garden centers.

GROWING SUBMERGED PLANTS

Submerged plants are among the easiest of aquatic plants to grow. They do best in water 2 to 3 feet deep but will grow well in as little as 1 foot of water. In cold climates, the plants should be overwintered in areas of the pool that are at least 2 feet deep. For proper oxygenation, you'll need one container of submerged plants for every 2 square feet of pond surface area. The plants are usually sold in bunches of a half dozen long, leafy stems, often without roots and held together with an elastic band or twist tie. Follow these steps for planting your new water-garden residents.

1. While you prepare their new pots, you'll want to keep the submerged plants in water. Place them in a container with enough water to completely cover them and set the container in a cool, shady place.

2. For a bunch of a half dozen plants, select an 8-inch-wide plastic pot and fill it to about 2 inches from the lip with clean, moist sand. Shallow growing containers, called pans, work better than standard-shaped pots for submerged plants.

3. Make a hole in the center of the sand that is twice the diameter of the bunch of plants and about 2 inches deep. Place the plants into the planting hole and gently firm sand around the plants. Be sure that you place the cut ends, not the growing ends, of the plants into the sand. Completely cover the sand with a layer of washed pea stone or coarse gravel.

4. Remove the elastic band or twist tie from the plants, and water the container with pond water until the sand is saturated.

5. Carefully place the container in the pond. Space the plants evenly around the deep areas of the pond. The plants take root very quickly and will begin to grow even before the roots have become established.

PROTECT NEW PLANTS FROM FISH

For many water garden fish, such as koi and goldfish, submerged plants are an all-you-can-eat salad bar. If there are fish in your water garden, you can protect new plants from them with a mesh barrier. Make a dome with 1-inch metal screening or a net of bird netting and place it over the plants. Secure the barrier to the gravel; I like to bend a very large paper clip into a long, U-shaped pin to hold the screen to the bottom of the container.

PROPAGATING SUBMERGED PLANTS

Submerged plants are as easy to propagate as they are to grow. Once the plants have doubled in size, they are large enough to propagate. Simply take cuttings at least 6 inches long from the tops of the plants and plant as directed above.

EASY-CARE SUBMERGED PLANTS

Most submerged plants fall in the category of "easy care." Once you have the plants in the water, they don't require much in the way of maintenance. For information on hardiness zones in North America, see Appendix A.

Anacharis (*Egeria densa*)

Zones 7–11

Dwarf Sagittaria (*Sagittaria subulata*)

Zones 5–11

Elodea (*Elodea canadensis*)

Zones 4–11

Fanwort (*Cabomba caroliniana*)

Zones 6–11

Hornwort (*Ceratophyllum demersum*)

Zones 5–11

Floating Plants

Floating plants have leaves, stems, flowers, and roots like other aquatic plants, but they are not anchored to the pond bottom. Instead, their roots hang down into the water, and the plants are free to move over the surface of the pond on any casual breeze. Many floating plants, like water hyacinth, have hollow, swollen growths called bladders that help the plants float. Others, like water lettuce, are cup shaped, like the hull of a boat, a design that keeps them above the water.

GROWING FLOATING PLANTS

Floating plants are generally tender perennials and grow best in warm water and full sun to partial shade. The roots, which hang beneath the plant, cleanse the water, improving its clarity and quality. Many floating plants are so easy to grow that the challenge is not in growing them but in controlling them. Some floaters, like water hyacinth, are banned from sale in warm regions because they are so vigorous that they have become noxious weeds. In northern areas, floating plants can be easily controlled by simply removing any extra plants. The plants can be overwintered in an aquarium indoors or left to succumb to the first killing frost.

Floating plants come in many different shapes and sizes, from tiny fairy moss with its small needlelike leaves to the bold upright form of water lettuce. Floating plants are sold like fish, enclosed in a plastic bag with some water, which allows the plants to float freely. Larger floating plants are sometimes sold with their roots wrapped in a moist towel and their tops exposed to the air.

Since the plants float on the water, they require nothing but a pool of warm water for growing—no containers, no potting mix. Simply set the floating plants in your garden pool once the water temperature reaches 70°F. They'll soon be growing and spreading abundantly.

Continued →

PROPAGATING FLOATING PLANTS

Most people don't have to try to propagate floating plants—they do it very well with no assistance from us. The original, or mother, plants placed in the water at the beginning of the season will often produce small plants all summer long.

EASY-CARE FLOATING PLANTS

Growing these floating plants is just about as easy as it gets. All you need to do is place them in the pond and stand back.

Fairy Moss (*Azolla filliculoides* or *A. caroliniana*)

Zones 8–11

Velvet Leaf (*Salvinia natans*)

Zones 10–11

Water Fern (*Ceratopteris thalictroides*)

Zones 9–11

Water Lettuce (*Pistia stratiotes*)

Zones 9–11

Water lettuce

Marginal Plants

The term "marginal plants" is a catchall for just about any plant that thrives in the shallow water or sodden soil of wetlands and pond edges. Marginals range from bold perennials such as yellow flag iris to airy, delicate plants like water forget-me-not. Marginal plants often serve to frame the water garden, providing height, texture, ambience, and color to the edges of pools and softening hardscape elements such as stones. Marginal plants also provide shelter and food for many creatures, from birds to butterflies to frogs, that are attracted to the water's edge. In natural ponds the plant's roots serve as biological filters that help cleanse the water.

GROWING MARGINAL PLANTS

Marginal plants require either soil that is consistently moist to wet or sodden soil that stands beneath shallow water. Many gardeners have a difficult time adjusting to the idea of planting a beautiful perennial in sopping soil, but that is just what marginal plants need to thrive.

Marginal plants can be planted directly in the soil along the edges of ponds or tucked into containers that are sunk into the ground. Many marginals are very vigorous, potentially invasive plants that are better behaved when confined to containers. Some marginal plants will still "jump the pot" and spread, their roots sneaking through drainage holes or creeping over the lip of pots. Water garden pools constructed with preformed or flexible liners serve to restrain any such ambitious plants. Natural ponds with earthen bottoms, on the other hand, can act as a nursery for many vigorous plants. In such cases care should be given when deciding which plants to add to the water garden; you and your neighbors may be living with the choice for a long time to come.

After purchasing the plants from the garden center or mail-order catalog, plan on repotting them into new containers with fresh potting mix. Select a container that is either the same size as or slightly larger than the nursery container. A container that is the same size will restrict the growth of many plants and can reduce the overall size of the plant, while a larger container can encourage growth, resulting in a larger plant. However, many marginal plants will grow vigorously even if their roots are restricted in a smallish pot.

1. Fill the new container with fresh potting mix (see the box below), and water the mix until it is wet but not drippy. Dig a hole in the mix large enough to accommodate the root ball of the plant.

2. Remove the plant from the original pot and gently loosen its roots. Allow some of the old potting mix to fall away. Place the plant in the new container so the top of the root ball is an inch or two below the lip of the pot, then firm more potting mix around the root ball.

3. Cover the soil of the container with a layer of washed pea stone or coarse gravel to the lip of the pot.

EASY-CARE MARGINAL PLANTS

There are thousands of different marginal plants that hail from a wide range of climates. While some are finicky plants, many more—including the ones listed here—are very easy to grow, and that makes the water garden even more enjoyable.

Arrowhead (*Sagittaria latifolia*)

Zones 4–11

Cattail (*Typha* spp.)

Zones 3–11

Creeping Jenny (*Lysimachia nummularia*)

Zones 3–8

Cattail
(T. latifolia)

Green Taro (*Colocasia esculenta*)

Zones 9–11

Horsetail (*Equisetum* spp.)

Zones 5–9

Japanese Iris (*Iris ensata*)

Zones 4–9

Lizard's Tail (*Saururus cernuus*)

Zones 4–9

Marsh Marigold (*Caltha palustris*)

Zones 4–8

Parrot's Feather (*Myriophyllum aquaticum*)

Zones 6–11

Pickerel Weed (*Pontederia cordata*)

Zones 5–11

Siberian Iris (*Iris siberica*)

Zones 3–9

Swamp Milkweed (*Asclepias incarnata*)

Zones 3–8

Sweet Flag (*Acorus calamus* 'Variegatus')

Zones 5–11

Thalia (*Thalia dealbata*)

Zones 6–11

Umbrella Plant (*Cyperus alternifolius*)

Zones 10–11

Water Canna (*Canna* cvs.)

Zones 8–11

Water Arum (*Peltandra virginica*)

Zones 5–9

Water Clover (*Marsilea mutica*)

Zones 6–11

Water Forget-Me-Not
(*Myosotis scorpioides* syn. *M. palustris*)

Zones 5–9

Water Mint (*Mentha aquatica*)

Zones 5–9

Water Poppy (*Hydrocleys nymphoides*)

Zones 9–11

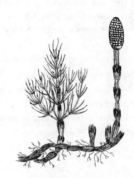

Equisetum arvense

Pickerel weed

Sweet flag

Whorled Loosestrife (*Lysimachia punctata*)

Zones 5–9

Yellow Flag Iris (*Iris pseudacorus*)

Zones 5–8

Water Lilies

Perhaps no other plant is more familiarly identified with water gardens than water lilies. There are many species and varieties of water lilies, but this large group of plants can be divided into smaller categories that have easily recognizable characteristics.

Hardy water lilies thrive in cool and warm climates from Zones 3 to 11. Their leaves have smooth edges and float on the water. They may be solid green or green spattered with maroon blotches. The blossoms, in shades of white, red, pink, or yellow, begin to appear when the water temperature reaches about 70°F. The flowers of hardy water lilies float on the water's surface, open in the early morning, and close by early to midafternoon. On cloudy days the flowers may open only partially; on dark, dreary days they may remain closed.

Tropical water lilies are warm-loving plants that are not hardy in regions cooler than Zone 10. Their leaves are often more oblong than the circular pads of hardy water lilies and usually have a ragged or toothed edge. The color of the foliage ranges from green to green marked with dark red blotches. The blossoms of tropical water lilies have a wider range of colors than do those of hardy water lilies, with flowers in white, pink, apricot, red, lilac, and blue-violet. Tropical water lilies are either day blooming or night blooming, though both types carry their flowers a few inches above the water. The blossoms of day-blooming types usually open in mid-morning and begin to close in late afternoon, while night-blooming types usually open a few hours after dark and close before or near dawn. Some night-blooming tropical water lilies will keep their flowers open on dark, cloudy days.

GROWING HARDY WATER LILIES

The easiest way to pot hardy water lilies is to have someone else do it for you. Most garden centers have a water garden section where potted water lilies are already happily growing in a pool. All you have to do is buy the plant and bring it home to your water garden. If you want to do your own potting, choose a container suited for your needs. A large container will hold multiple plants of a small variety or one vigorous plant. Check with your supplier about the proper size container for the plants you choose. Be sure to use a potting mix specially designed for water lilies and other aquatic plants, which will be heavier than the standard potting mix.

Hardy water lilies can remain in the pond over the winter if the water surrounding the plants does not freeze. In fall, cut back the leaves and stems and place the plants in the deepest part of the pond.

Hardy water lilies require some care in the planting. Follow these steps closely.

1. Fill the container with moist aquatic potting mix to within a few inches of the lip of the pot. Place aquatic plant fertilizer tablets near the bottom of the pot, within the first few inches of soil. Water the medium to settle it.

2. Place the plant atop the medium and spread the fleshy roots evenly over the surface of the soil. The top of the crown should be an inch or two below the lip of the pot. Cover the plant with

Continued ➔

an inch of soil and water gently with a soft spray of water to settle the mix again.

3. Add a layer of pea stone or coarse gravel over the mix and water one more time.

4. Set the pot on a shallow shelf of the pool so that the crown is covered with just a few inches of water. Allow the plant to remain in the shallow water for a few days to get to know its new home. When plant growth resumes, set the container in the water garden at the depth designated for the variety.

Hardy water lilies carry their flowers on the water's surface and have smooth-edged, rounded leaves.

EASY-CARE HARDY WATER LILIES

As a group, hardy water lilies are generally easy to grow. Some cultivars are especially noteworthy, however, because they combine an easy-to-grow disposition with other desirable qualities such as beauty and fragrance.

Nymphaea **'Arc en Ciel'**

Nymphaea **'Charlene Strawn'**

Nymphaea **'Ellisiana'**

Nymphaea **'Fireball'**

Nymphaea **'Helvola'**

Nymphaea **'Lily Pons'**

Nymphaea **'Odorata'**

Nymphaea **'Pink Beauty'**

Nymphaea **'Radiant Red'**

GROWING TROPICAL WATER LILIES

Tropical water lilies differ from hardy water lilies in many ways, not simply in their tolerance to cold. Tropical water lilies are usually more vigorous than hardy water lilies, growing faster and producing larger plants, though often requiring shallower water. The tropical types also usually produce much larger, more abundant, more fragrant flowers.

Tropical water lilies are planted in much the same manner as hardy water lilies, with a few refinements. In general, to accommodate their vigor, tropical water lilies require slightly larger containers than do hardy water lilies. Another difference lies in how the plants are purchased: Hardy water lilies are purchased either as small plants or

as rootstocks with crowns and roots; tropical water lilies are purchased as plants. When potting tropical water lilies, follow the steps outlined for potting hardy water lilies. After potting, place tropical water lilies directly in the water garden at the preferred depth.

OVERWINTERING

Many people grow tropical water lilies in cool regions and lift and store the tubers over the winter. While this is a relatively simple process, it does take some practice to do successfully and falls outside the definition of "easy care."

Remember that tropical water lilies require warmer water temperatures than hardy water lilies and are not hardy in regions cooler than Zone 10. Avoid setting plants into the water garden until the water temperature is above 75°F. The plants will begin to produce flower buds when the water temperature remains above 80°F. In colder water the plants may go dormant.

Tropical water lilies carry their flowers above the water and often have leaves with ragged or toothed edges.

EASY-CARE TROPICAL WATER LILIES

Tropical water lilies are well known for their vibrant, eye-catching flowers. Though having more stringent requirements for growing environments than hardy water lilies, these plants are still relatively easy to grow. The following varieties are especially versatile and charming and are often more forgiving of marginal growing conditions.

Nymphaea **'Emily Grant Hutchings'**

Nymphaea **'Green Smoke'**

Nymphaea **'Margaret Randig'**

Nymphaea **'Pink Capensis'**

Nymphaea **'St. Louis Gold'**

Nymphaea **'Suwannee Mist'**

Nymphaea **'Texas Shell Pink'**

QUICK TIP

If you see a water lily with a lilac to purple flower, it has to be a tropical day-blooming variety.

Lotuses

The intricately beautiful blooms and dramatic foliage of the lotus makes it the royalty of water garden plants. Lotus blossoms are fragrant, multipetaled, and rich in color. They resemble water lily blossoms but are different enough to be easily recognized. As the flowers disappear, the distinctive seed pods emerge and become decorative items all by themselves. The pods are frequently dried and used in arrangements. Lotus flowers open early in the morning and close by late afternoon. This regimen usually occurs for three days, after which the blossoms fade, though in some varieties the blossoms last a little longer.

As distinctive as lotus blossoms are, the foliage is more so, with large, circular leaves with the stem right in the center. The leaves are also waterproof. Raindrops bead up on the leaves' surface and run off into the pond. Both the flowers and the leaves are held well above the water's surface, sometimes reaching up to 6 feet above the water.

Most lotus varieties are so vigorous and produce such large plants that they are suitable only for large ponds. But there are some dwarf varieties that are small enough to grow and bloom in even a half-barrel container.

GROWING LOTUSES

Perhaps no other plant conveys a sense of tropical grandeur like lotuses, but the plants are actually hardy from Zones 5 to 11. Though the plants are hardy, they will not overwinter well if they have not had a period of hot weather during the summer. The heat allows the roots to grow and develop, storing the energy they need to grow strongly the following spring. In cooler climates, smaller pools, such as tubs or half barrels, warm faster in spring and often provide the time needed for lotus roots to grow. In small pools the easiest plants to grow are dwarf varieties.

Lotuses are best grown in containers deeper than those reserved for water lilies. A deep container allows a lotus's roots to grow large enough to produce the thick rhizome needed for the plant to overwinter where it is marginally hardy. A container for a standard size lotus is about 16 inches wide; use smaller containers for dwarf varieties. Check with your supplier about the proper size container for the plants you choose. Be sure to use a potting mix specially designed for aquatic plants, which will be heavier than the standard potting mix. Be sure that the water in your garden pool has warmed to at least 70°F before you plant lotuses.

Here's how to plant your lotus root.

1. Fill the container with about 2 inches of aquatic plant potting mix and firm gently. Press aquatic plant fertilizer tablets into the mix, then fill the container to about 2 inches from the lip of the pot.

2. Water the mix to settle it and place the lotus root horizontally on the growing mix so that the root tip sticks up slightly above the lip of the pot. Cover the root with coarse gravel, and water well to settle the gravel around the root. Lotus roots are brittle and break easily, so be gentle when planting.

3. After planting the root and thoroughly watering the mix, place the container into the pool where the lotus will grow. Be sure to put the plant in the pool at the depth designated for the variety.

Lotuses have impressively large leaves and exotic flowers, lending a sense of grandeur to the water garden.

LOTUS CARE THROUGH THE SEASONS

Many lotuses will survive even the chill of Zone 5 winters if they are set at the bottom of a deep pool well out of reach of the ice above. The trouble with this scheme is that deep pools take a long time to warm again in spring, and the lotus just doesn't get growing soon enough. To remedy this, grow dwarf varieties, and after the first few frosts of fall cut back the stems and set the plants in the deepest section of the pool along with the water lilies. In spring, set up a half barrel or other small growing container in a sunny spot, line it with black plastic, and fill it with water. The plastic will absorb the sun's heat and warm the water faster. When the ice has melted from the water garden, retrieve the lotus container and set it in the water-filled half barrel. Once the plant begins to grow, fertilize it with aquatic plant fertilizer, following the label instructions. Move the lotus, container and all, from the half barrel to the water garden when the water temperature in the water garden reaches 70°F.

EASY-CARE DWARF LOTUS VARIETIES

While all lotuses have similar growing requirements, dwarf varieties are more versatile and fit more easily into most garden plans. The smaller size of dwarf lotuses allows these plants to be equally at home in a half barrel on the patio or in a large backyard water garden. In addition, the smaller leaves of dwarf lotuses are less apt to overpower other plants in the pool, providing the balance that is a basic part of any water garden.

Nelumbo **'Angel Wings'**

Nelumbo **'Baby Doll'**

Nelumbo **'Ben Gibson'**

Nelumbo **'Carolina Queen'**

Nelumbo **'Charles Thomas'**

Continued →

Nelumbo **'Momo Botan'**

Nelumbo **'Momo Botan Minima'**

Bog Plants

In catalogs and garden centers, just about every marginal plant is called a bog plant. But true bog plants live in bogs—habitats dominated by sphagnum peat moss—and are a class unto themselves. The moss grows atop itself, forming thick mats of acidic organic material that decays very slowly. Peat mats are very infertile places, offering few nutrients to any plant willing to grow there. The plants that do colonize bogs are some of the most fascinating plants you will ever see, precisely because the harsh environment has spurred some unique strategies for acquiring the nutrients they need.

Many of the most fascinating bog plants are also carnivorous, catching and digesting insects in wonderfully ingenious ways. These carnivorous plants also make excellent plants for the water garden, provided, of course, you make a little bog for them to live in.

MAKING A BOG GARDEN

A bog garden is a simple thing to make and can add lots of interest to your water garden. A small preformed liner or flexible liner will do just fine.

1. Dig a shallow basin near the water garden but separate from the main pool. Line the basin with the preformed or flexible liner, then drill a few holes in the liner to allow a slow seepage of water through the water barrier.

2. In a clean trash can or other large container, combine equal parts peat moss and sand. Blend the ingredients, then moisten the mix with clear, warm water. Let the water soak in until all the ingredients are thoroughly moist; blend gently until the mix is uniform.

3. Transfer the moist mix to the lined basin and fill it nearly to the top. Plant your bog plants in the mix, then place a layer of fibrous sphagnum moss over the mix and water again.

4. Check the bog every few days to be sure it remains wet but not drippy.

EASY-CARE BOG PLANTS

With their exotic flowers, strangely shaped leaves, and often carnivorous nature, bog plants are perhaps the most fascinating of water garden plants. As a group these plants have evolved to take advantage of specifically boggy environments, and so they are a little more temperamental than most water garden plants. Some bog plants, however, are more easygoing than others.

Round-Leaved Sundew (*Drosera rotundifolia*)

Zones 4–9

Pitcher Plant (*Sarracenia purpurea*)

Zones 3–8

Venus Fly Trap (*Dionaea muscipula*)

Zones 7–10

The traps of the Venus fly trap are designed to lure and capture food. When insects brush against delicate hairs inside the traps, they snap shut, capturing the insect inside. The traps then release digestive enzymes that break down the insect, much like the human stomach digests food.

VEGETABLES AND MORE

Grow the Best Tomatoes

Revised and Updated

John Page

Illustrations by Elayne Sears, Alison Kolesar, Ann Poole, and Susan Berry Langsten

The Nature of Tomatoes

The tomato is actually a perennial; if the weather never got cold and if summer or tropical conditions continued to prevail, it would keep on growing for a long time. But as it is grown in virtually every part of the United States, the tomato acts more like an annual, and is treated by gardeners as if it were annual—which means it has to make it from seed to seed in a single growing season.

We consider the tomato to be a heat-loving crop. It doesn't do well until the soil warms up to 65°F or more, and until nighttime temperatures get up into the 50s. This occurs in late May in our northern areas; but if we planted seed at that time, the season wouldn't be long enough to get ripe tomatoes most years. Therefore, we have to lengthen the season by getting the plants started indoors or under protected conditions so that they are already several weeks into their growing season when soil and air reach optimal temperatures.

As we go south and reach the rough climatic equal of Chesapeake Bay, it becomes possible to start with seed in the garden and get ripe tomatoes each year. But even in these warmer areas, why not get your first tomato plants started inside, before the outdoor weather is ready? They will ripen earlier, and you can also plant seed when the time comes. Then you can have fresh tomatoes over a longer season.

Tomatoes come in two different types, determinate and indeterminate. Determinate tomatoes produce fruit at the ends of their branches. They stop growing while they are fairly short. Indeterminate types, in contrast, produce fruit at intervals along their ever-growing stems. They keep growing throughout the season until frost stops them. Most gardeners will not care whether they are growing determinate or indeterminate tomatoes. Staking and pruning are the only activities that could cause trouble if you don't know which type you are working on. Seed packets, labels, and catalogs should always say which type you are buying.

Determinate tomato plants (left) have flowers on the ends of their branches, and indeterminate varieties (right) flower along their stems.

Growing Conditions

Unless you are fortunate in soil and site, some parts of the garden offer better growing conditions than others. Give tomatoes one of the good sites. The soil must be well drained with full sun. If it isn't well drained, you'd better do some drainage work. If it isn't in full sunlight, you'd better do some forestry work. Once you have selected a good site, don't plant tall peas or corn to the south of the tomatoes; these cast shadows on sun-loving tomatoes. If you have a choice, choose a south-facing slope and avoid north-facing slopes.

SOIL

We say the kind of soil necessary to grow tomatoes well isn't different from the soil conditions necessary for growing any other vegetable well, except that when we say this about tomatoes, we really mean it. They like the best of what your garden has to offer. You can chisel a little on corn and beans, but not on tomatoes. You will need to know what sort of soil you are dealing with, so start with a soil test that measures pH, nutrients, and texture if you don't already have that information.

Then put the pH up there to 6.5 or thereabouts with lime. It won't do any harm to use high-magnesium lime, as long as you don't have a magnesium test to tell you you don't need it. Your starting pH and soil condition will determine how much lime you need, but you can count on needing about 2 1/2 pounds of limestone per 100 square feet of sandy soil, 6 1/2 pounds for loamy soil, and 9 pounds for clay soil to raise your pH from 5.5 to 6.5.

Once it is limed, you can make a garden soil out of some pretty poor earth by tilling in rotted manure at the rate of one pound per square foot. If you have already burned out the organic matter with years of gardening, till in a dose in the fall and another in the spring.

If you don't have and can't get well-rotted manure, get a load of fresh manure, but get it a year early. In a year's time, it will be the "well-rotted manure" people are always writing about. Any kind of manure will do, but cut the amount in half if you opt for poultry manure.

If you are gardening a new piece of soil, your soil test will help you to determine levels of phosphorus and potassium as well as give you the lime requirements. The rotted manure will correct most deficiencies. So get on the manure program, which takes care of both fertility and organic matter problems.

If you really can't get manure, then you'd better go the "green manure" route, along with commercial fertilizer with frequent soil tests to keep the soil on an even keel. Soil that is manipulated to grow good tomatoes will grow good vegetables in general.

Gardeners should stop complaining about their soil being too light, too sandy, or too heavy, like clay. The solution to all of these is to keep the level of organic matter high. Manure, green manure, and compost all keep sand from behaving like sugar and clays from behaving like brick. Few of us, indeed, start with a soil that isn't too heavy or too light, and it's your job to make what you have good enough to grow tomatoes. It really isn't that difficult. If you keep up with adding compost or manure every year—or even every spring and fall—you will end up with great soil, no matter how you started out.

If you have a real clay, carting in sand to lighten the soil is a bit like trying to desalinate the ocean beach with a garden hose. But at least it raises the elevation of the garden.

GREEN MANURES

Green manures are simply a cover crop planted before the desired crop (in this case, tomatoes) and then cut and either dug or tilled into the soil. Beans and other legumes are examples of a good green manure: They add nitrogen to the soil they grow in, as well as adding organic matter when they are dug into the ground.

The best way to use green manures is to begin planning for your tomato garden the year before you want to plant. The first year, plant peas and beans in the garden. Harvest what you want to eat and preserve, then cut down and till the plants under. Wait a couple of weeks, then plant a cover crop like rye or buckwheat. Chop it up with a string trimmer or scythe and till it under in the fall.

If you don't want to start an entire year ahead, you can simply collect dried leaves, grass clippings, garden plants, and other garden refuse in the fall. Chop it up with a hoe or string trimmer and mix it into your garden soil where the tomatoes will go. In the spring, you will have good, rich soil to work with and your tomatoes will thrive.

Starting Indoors

We start the plants, from seed, six or seven weeks before the frost-safe date when we plan to turn them loose in the great outdoors. If you don't have the right place or the inclination to do this, simply buy started plants from your local greenhouse when it is time to set them out in the garden. The potential problem with this is that they get to choose the varieties you will plant, and their selection is usually limited compared to a good seed catalog. So we start our own plants.

Continued ➡

WHEN TO SOW THE SEED

Under the home conditions that most of us have, starting seed in early in February or even March gives us leggy, long, tangled, brittle plants that have had to tolerate poor growing conditions far too long. Little is gained in the long run by extending the six- to seven-week period between planting of seed and setting out in the garden on your "frost-safe" date.

Frost-safe dates are a myth, but along about Memorial Day in the north country you have to have a little faith—and some coats or tarps ready to cover the plants in case of unanswered prayers. If you wait much longer, you'll get only green tomatoes in the fall.

THE POTTING SOIL

Make yourself a good potting mixture. I use 50 percent of my silt loam garden soil, 50 percent peat moss, and 10 percent compost or rotted manure for fertility. You say this doesn't add up? It has added up for me for years.

You should sterilize the soil if you are afraid of the damping-off organism wiping you out. Or go out and buy some sterilized soil already mixed, instead of using garden soil. Just don't be 100 percent sure it's sterile, okay? Otherwise, make up your own mix. If you can stand the odor in the kitchen, you can sterilize it by baking it at 180°F for 30 minutes. Frankly, I think this is a lousy way to treat living soil. I don't sterilize, but instead use vermiculite as described in the next section.

WHAT YE SOW

Now get yourself a dish about the size and shape of a bread pan. The aesthetic qualities of the dish are strictly secondary to the fact that it should have good bottom drainage—good-sized holes and lots of them. Fill it with your good, loose potting soil. Then pack it down well, leaving about 3/4-inch between the soil and the top of the container. At this stage you saturate the soil with water.

Scatter the seed evenly over the surface. If you are buying an expensive hybrid, you may have only 25 seeds in the pack. This is all

Germinate seeds in a pan of soil mix. Layer vermiculite on top to prevent damping-off.

right if you need only a dozen or so tomato plants. If they give you 200 seeds in the packet, and you need only a dozen, then scatter only 25 of the seeds around on the soil surface. It's a poor gardener who can't get a dozen plants from 25 seeds. Now you can cover the seeds with a sprinkling of soil if you wish, or you can let them germinate on the surface of the damp soil. In any case, here is where you can usually take care of the damping-off organism. Scatter 1/4 to 1/2 inch of vermiculite

over the surface. Then put newspaper over your dish and leave it there for five or six days. The seeds don't need light to germinate and the newspaper holds the moisture in. When the seeds start to sprout, remove the paper and let them have light. The plants are growing up through dry vermiculite. As long as it stays dry, you shouldn't have any damping-off disease problems. Keep it dry by bottom watering or watering around the edge of the dish. Plants of this size use precious little water anyhow.

POTTING TIME

About two weeks after germination, three weeks after planting, it is time to give each little plant a pot of its own for the next few weeks. You can use peat pots, foam coffee cups, tin cans, paper cups, clay pots, or anything that suits your fancy as long as it has drain holes and won't fall apart before setting-out time. Some folks use eggshells, but I'd want turkey eggs if I were to go this route.

Before you start to pot the plants, water them well an hour or two before you disturb their roots, which you will. While they are imbibing water, fill your pots with loose potting soil and then pack the soil firmly. Punch a hole in the center with your finger. Then take a seedling—I use a fork to remove it from the soil—and place it into the hole at the same depth it was before. Pack the soil tightly around the roots. I repeat, tightly around the roots. Water the plant well at this time. Then put your 1/2 inch of vermiculite on the surface and go on to the next. Whenever you move a plant, break the roots as little as possible, and never let the roots dry out.

If you are growing several kinds of tomatoes, it is at this stage that you'd better get your labeling system down. You may think you can remember, but in 10 days you won't be able to tell a 'Roma' from a 'Big Boy'. And you won't find out until you have tomatoes. If your idea of fun is a mystery garden, then feel free not to label.

From here on the little plants need light, lots of light. If there isn't enough outside light, supplement it with artificial light. You can use a mix of fluorescent and incandescent light if you don't have the regular plant lights. Or just use fluorescent. One of the best systems is to hang a fluorescent light just a couple of inches above the plants. As the plants grow, raise the light to keep it at the same relative height. I'd keep the plants on 16 hours of light and 8 hours of darkness daily.

Water them only when they show a little wilt. Tomatoes are not a swamp plant. Bottom watering is still preferable. If they get long and leggy, they aren't getting enough light. They do not need hot temperatures at this stage. Old-timers always grew them in the cool windows, and around 60°F would be fine.

If they are in a full-sun window and have been exposed to several dark, cloudy days, they may show sunburn when the sun comes out suddenly. Tape a piece of newspaper up on the window for a day to acclimate them to the sun again. (Greenhouse operators use whitewash instead of newspapers.)

Into the Garden

As the days get warmer, the soil thaws, and spring advances, it is time to think of moving your plants into the garden. Timing will depend on your location, and on the severity and duration of the winter. Tomato lovers walk a thin line. You want the last frost to have passed and the soil to be warming up toward the ideal 65°F, but if you wait too long, you will have green tomatoes at first fall frost. From year to year, your transplanting time may vary by two weeks or more.

HARDENING OFF

Moving the plants from the indoor to the outdoor environment without damaging them is called hardening off. About a week or 10 days before transplanting them into the garden, you must begin acclimating them little by little to the cooler temperatures, to the direct sunlight, and to some wind. Let them see sun for an hour at first and work them up to 5 to 6 hours a day. If it is going to stay over 50°F, leave them out overnight. And make sure they have plenty of water. Air circulates much more outside than it does in your house, and it will dry the plants more quickly. After a week of hardening, they'll be able to take what Mother Nature has to offer when you set them out. Failure to harden off the plants can result in your having to go out and buy plants to replace all of those that didn't take the shock.

SETTING OUT THE PLANTS

Spacing will vary with your method of growing. If you are going to let the plants sprawl on the ground, each needs 4 by 4 feet. For those that are to be staked, caged, or trained, 3 by 3 feet is adequate.

If your soil tends to be on the wet side, set the plant out on a mound 4 to 6 inches higher than the surrounding soil. If the land is particularly dry, set the plant down in a depression, hoping that rainwater may concentrate around its roots a bit. Water plants well an hour or two before transplanting so that they will not dry out during the move.

If you have nice sturdy plants, set them straight into a hole dug with your hands or a trowel. Set them about 2 inches deeper than they are in the pot. Don't disturb the roots any more than necessary. If they are in a peat pot, crush the peat pot well or cut out the bottom so that roots can escape easily. After planting, remove a couple of the lower leaves by picking them off. This brings the top into balance with the roots, which you may have injured a little in your transplanting manipulations.

If your plants are long and leggy—much stem and few leaves—lay the plant down on its side in a trench instead of in a hole. Prune off the lower leaves, leaving just the top leaves of the plant exposed, and bury part of the stem along with the roots. Roots will soon form on the stem, and at this stage the growth of the top will take care of itself in rapid fashion. We call this "layering."

Immediately after planting, water the plant well. Some folks water the plant after it is placed in the hole and again after it has been covered. This is called "mudding-in" and is common when planting woody plants. It forces all the air away from the roots. After the initial watering, go back and water only plants that show wilt. Otherwise, leave them alone. They don't need to be drowned.

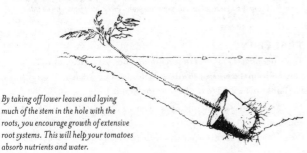

By taking off lower leaves and laying much of the stem in the hole with the roots, you encourage growth of extensive root systems. This will help your tomatoes absorb nutrients and water.

If possible, set out the plants on a cloudy day. If you can't, plant in late afternoon and hope for clouds for the next day. Strong sunlight can burn the leaves of new plants, even after hardening off.

Think about Mulching

Some people can't wait to bury these newly set-out little plants under a couple of feet of mulch. In fact, some folks put the mulch down and then dig a hole in it and do the planting. I'd much prefer, and strongly recommend, that you let the soil get well warmed up before insulating it with mulch. The soil should be warm enough to mulch by the time the tomato plant is as big as a basketball. Then a good hay or straw mulch 5 to 6 inches deep has several benefits. It preserves moisture and evens out the supply between rains. It keeps the tomatoes up off the ground as they develop. The mulch eventually rots to improve the soil's organic matter. And, of course, it discourages weed growth.

Black plastic mulch is okay, but it is real work to put it down and take it up. It is effective in evening out moisture supply, and it does absorb a lot of heat and speed things up to begin with. I prefer hay as a mulch for tomatoes, but I do reluctantly use plastic for melons here in the subarctic of southern Vermont. Another idea is to use biodegradable paper mulch, which will decompose in the soil.

Black plastic mulch can be difficult to put down, but will keep away all weeds and will lengthen the growing season by absorbing heat and holding moisture and warmth in the soil.

Supporting Your Plants

Tomatoes do not really climb. They are rangy, spreading plants that, if left to their own devices, will spread almost as far as a squash vine will. Most people choose to restrain them and try to keep them upright. The secret is to remember that they will not attach themselves to anything, but will simply lean against any support.

I've always had a sneaking suspicion that we tie our tomatoes to stakes to satisfy us more than the tomato. If you lay down a thick layer of mulch, you can leave your tomatoes to sprawl as they choose. They will grow perfectly well and produce a good crop if you never lay your hand on them or direct them after you lay down the mulch.

STAKING

Because staking requires pruning, only indeterminate types of tomatoes should be staked. There are several advantages to staking. You may get a few tomatoes a few days earlier. If you are going to prune suckers, you just about have to stake them, because it is difficult to sucker a plant that is sprawling on the ground. Staking gets the plant up off the ground where it may or may not get less damage from passing insects, birds, or mice. You can grow a plant in about half the space. When you get around to harvesting, your fruit is hanging there, so you don't have to hunt for it. Staked plants look good too, as if somebody actively grew tomatoes, rather than just let them grow. There should be fewer disease problems because plants should dry out quicker due to improved air movement around them.

Conversely, staking is a lot of work: driving the good solid stakes and tying the plant to the stake, an exercise you can engage in

Continued →

during many spare moments. Because you do a little pruning both intentionally and unintentionally while staking, you probably get less yield per plant. Because you plant them close, you can probably get more tomatoes per yard of space. You do expose the fruit to sunburn. I have staked my last tomato patch, though I will continue to stake one or two of the small salad tomatoes to get some for early salads.

STAKING TOMATOES

Set stakes when you set out your transplant, and keep in mind that your tomato plant will get quite tall by fall. Stakes should be 6–8' tall and no thinner than 1" x 2". Drive them deeply (6–8") into the ground; your tomato plant will get heavy as it grows and bears fruit.

As your tomato plant grows, tie it to the stake using coarse twine or fabric. Knot the tie around the stake, then around the plant.

When the plant becomes as tall as its stake, pinch off the growing point at the top. Remove any new flowers that form; this will direct the plant's energy into the fruit it has already set.

FENCE ME IN

If staking is too much work, but you still want your plants growing vertically instead of horizontally, buy some tomato cages. Unlike stakes, cages are suitable for both determinate and indeterminate types of tomatoes. Made of heavy-duty wire, they are usually narrow at the bottom and wider at the top, with strong wires protruding 10 inches or so at the bottom. Drive the wire ends into the earth around your young plant, and it will naturally grow up through the cage. At the end of the season, you can remove the cages and stack them for storage.

If you are thrifty or a confirmed do-it-yourselfer, you can make tomato cages from concrete reinforcing wire or other wire fencing. The key here is to make sure the wire weave is open enough for you to reach your hand in and

A cage made of large-mesh wire will keep your plants off the ground and tidy. Stake the cage to the ground for support.

pick a huge tomato. Chicken wire will keep your plants tidy, but you will only be able to visit your tomatoes, not actually pick them. So choose an open-weave fence, and cut it into 6-foot lengths about 4 feet tall. This will give you a circular cage about 19 inches in diameter and plenty tall enough to support your tomatoes. When you cut the wire, loop the ends into hooks that will link together. Then, in the fall, you can unhook them and flatten the cages for storage.

You will have to support these cages with stakes, since they cannot be driven into the ground like purchased cages. Just drive stakes into the ground on either side of your plants. Make sure the stakes are the same distance apart as the diameter of your cage. Then set the cage down over the stakes and make sure it is a snug fit. Or use one stake (place it to the north of the plant so it will not shade the tomatoes) and tie the cage to the stake. Once your plants grow into the cages, they will not go anywhere in almost any wind.

PLATFORMING

Other ways of keeping tomatoes off the ground include letting them grow up through a snow fence or other material that is held off the ground about a foot. This keeps them off the ground, but I can do that with hay mulch, and I haven't got to worry about the platform collapsing in an early snowstorm. Besides, I think rabbits hide under these horizontal fences and use them for raiding parties elsewhere in the garden.

TOPLESS TABLE

A friend of mine was as confused as I about whether to stake or cage or platform, so he devised a method that did the job well. He made a little table about 16 inches square out of some thin wood strips. The four legs were about 18 inches long. But he didn't put any top on his table. He simply shoved the four legs into the ground around his tomato plant. As it grew up through, it sort of looped itself over the edge of this topless table, and he had the best of both worlds. It sure beats tearing up old bedsheets and tying tomatoes by moonlight. When you price the cage wire, this may not sound too bad.

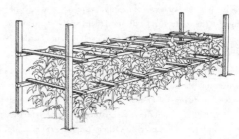

A combination of a topless table and a platform can be used over a large bed. If you use this method, it becomes simple to throw a tarp over the plants in the fall if frost is predicted.

TRELLISING

Tomatoes lend themselves to several methods of traditional and nontraditional trellising for the hopelessly tidy gardener. Several methods can be used to trellis your tomatoes.

Cut open-mesh fencing into sections 2 1/2 feet wide, leaving wire ends on one side. Loop the wire ends of one panel around the edge of the next panel. Set this fence in a zigzag pattern down a row of tomato plants with one plant framed by two panels. The panels will support the plants, and at the end of the season, you can simply fold the fence flat for storage.

If you don't have or want to buy fencing, you can trellis your tomatoes very easily with nothing but stakes and some heavy-duty twine. Simply set tall stakes (6 to 8 feet tall) at each end of a row of tomatoes. Starting low when the plants are small, tie one end of the twine to a stake and weave back and forth between the plants. Tie at the other stake. Now do the same thing a little higher starting from the other end, making sure you are weaving back and forth opposite from the first string; every plant should have support on both sides after you are done. As the plants get bigger, repeat higher up the stakes. If your row is very long, add a center support stake, or your middle plants are at risk of keeling over, bringing down the whole trellis.

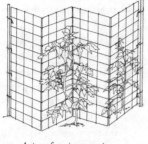

A zigzag fence is one way to trellis your tomato plants.

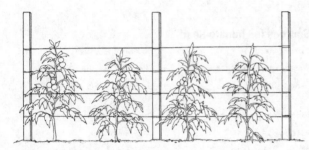

Twine woven between stakes is an effective tomato trellis.

HANGING TOMATOES

Last, there is the hangman's method of supporting tomatoes, used by frustrated derrick operators. Here we run a tight wire above the tomatoes, then we lasso the tomato now and then and pull it up toward the wire and let it hang there until we get a new hold. A variation of sorts on this is the espalier method, where we keep the branches pinned and shaped to a fence or a wall: beautiful and effective if you have a place and the time to really put your heart and talent into it.

Controlling Leafy Growth

In the fall, you often see tomato plants nearly bare of leaves, just a stalk and the ripening fruit. The theory here is that with less green to support, the plant puts its energy into the fruit. Also, fewer leaves offer less shade, an advantage in the dwindling sunlight of autumn. You can start the process while the plant is still growing, if you have the time and energy.

SUCKERING

People ask me if I sucker my tomato plants. I tell them no. It's hard to sucker plants that grow on the ground as they get larger and denser. Many people ask this because they don't know what a sucker is and are trying to find out because somebody they know attached some degree of importance or urgency to getting rid of suckers. Suckers are simply the little vegetative growths that arise at the junctions of the stem and the side branches. They have no useful purpose, as far as I know. Prune them if you are a sucker-pruner. Pinch them if you are a sucker-pincher. Let them go and things will get pretty dense and green, often requiring some topping.

TOPPING

Now and then, in a good growing year with frequent rains, the tomato plant will go on a wild vegetative binge in August. This requires some pretty drastic surgery. If you have a couple of plants, you can nip off some of the fast-growing leaves with pruning shears and let the sun into the stem area. If you have a dozen or more plants, you can make a few slashing motions with a sickle or a corn knife and do the same thing. It wouldn't do any harm to do a little pruning out on the ends of the branches after you get first fruit ripe to size, anyhow. It will let in the sun to keep ripening, and put the vigor toward maturing the fruit rather than growing late-season leaves. Topping is sort of a lazy man's way of suckering.

Care and Maintenance

To hear gardeners talk about it, tomatoes are the most difficult crop in the home garden. Not so. But you will have better results with a few pointers about what conditions they prefer and how to achieve those conditions.

FERTILIZER

Tomatoes like rich, fertile soil. And they are large, vigorous growers, which means they will benefit from occasional applications of fertilizer or compost during the growing season. You can apply a good organic fertilizer like fish emulsion, or well-broken-down compost every two or three weeks beginning after blossoming. Because tomatoes are sensitive to nutrient levels in the soil, they often let you know what they need. For example, a white edge around the leaves may mean they need more potassium. Thin stems and yellowing leaves may indicate a nitrogen deficiency. Too much nitrogen will cause your plants to be all stem and foliage and few fruits. And purple leaf stalks indicate a deficiency of phosphorus.

SIDE-DRESSING

One of the best ways to get nutrients to your plants is to side-dress them. Side-dressing is a method of feeding plants without disturbing their root systems at all. Simply apply compost in a circle around each plant or in two lines on either side of your rows.

Beware of side-dressing with nitrogen until flowering is well under way. It promotes foliage growth in excess and will delay flowering. Once flowers appear, side-dressing a little can result in more vigorous plants and more fruit, providing there isn't already enough nitrogen present. You can side-dress with an ounce or so of 5–10–10 commercial fertilizer in a ring around the base of the plant. Don't get it on the leaves; it may burn. You can use a quart of manure tea, made by mixing 1 part manure and 2 parts water, and stirring daily for a couple of weeks. Great stuff for side-dressing, but don't overdo it.

Continued →

Side-dressing in a circle (above) or double line (below)

WATERING

The secret to good watering is good mulching. If you've mulched to even out the water supply between rains, don't water tomatoes until you see wilt. Then water them well and leave them alone. Frequent light watering makes shallow root growth and weak roots. What we want are roots that are reaching down and out for water. At any stage of the tomato's growth, overwatering is undesirable. Roots need a balance of both soil gases and nutrient solutions in the soil pores.

WEEDS

Get weeds by pulling when they are little. Mulch out weeds at the proper time. Keep herbicides away from tomatoes in the home garden. If the plant has any vigor at all, it will soon shade out any weeds you can't reach with a hoe. If you can't control weeds in tomatoes, better take up golf.

Harvesting

Tomatoes and frost don't get along, so you must either harvest them ahead of a frost or cover them so that the frost won't damage them. Neither the leaves nor the fruit will take much cold.

The "ripe-off-the-vine" superiority theory of the tomato is all right with me. But I wouldn't take much of a chance on frost just to prove the theory. When a green tomato starts to show a whitish color on the blossom end, you can pick it, lay it out on newspapers on the porch or the garage floor, and it will ripen off pretty normally. As far as my taste goes, it is as good when ripe as one from the vine. Some folks say

this is not so, by golly! I have ripened off many tomatoes a month or six weeks after picking them green. Half-grown ones will eventually ripen if they are fairly free of disease.

I'd suggest you use the smaller, firmer green ones for your green tomato pickling and preserves, and give the larger ones a chance to ripen, to extend your fresh tomato season and give you sizable ones for processing.

I do not try to ripen them indoors. They ripen too fast, and I want to extend the season. I use old coats and blankets to protect them from freezing as cold becomes more intense. As early November comes, we fill up the vegetable compartment with the ripe ones, give away or process the rest, and call it quits for the year.

I realize that some people pull the whole plant and hang it upside down on the withering vine. All right, if you have hanging room. Some folks bury them in hay. I guess it works, but mine ripen without the hay. In any case, keep them dry while ripening. Wetness will bring on more spreading of rot organisms and more decay.

Sources for Tomato Seed

Burpee Gardens
Warminster, PA 18974
1–800–888–1447

Park Seed
1 Parkton Avenue
Greenwood, SC 29647

Johnny's Selected Seeds
RR1 Box 2580
Albion, ME 04910
207–437–4301

Shepherd's Garden Seeds
30 Irene Street
Torrington, CT 06790
860–483–3638

SAVING SEEDS

Tomatoes are either hybrid or open pollinated. If they are hybrid, they will not breed true from the seeds. If you have an open-pollinated variety, however, you can save the seeds for planting next year.

1. Look for the healthiest plant that suits your needs, whether it fruited early, bore well, or had the tastiest fruits. Mark the plant or plants you have selected by tying a colored flag to the stake, cage, or trellis near the plant.

2. Leave a tomato or two on the plant until

they are just past perfect eating ripeness, but not rotting. This will guarantee that the seeds are mature. Pick the fruit, cut the tomato in half, and use a spoon to scrape out the seeds.

3. Each seed is encased in a membrane about the consistency of jelly. To improve germination rates next spring, it is a good idea to get rid of this membrane before you dry and store the seeds. To do this, you will ferment the seeds. Place them in a

jar and add about 1/4 cup of water. Put the cap on the jar, but don't screw it on tightly. Keep the jar on the kitchen counter. The contents will turn murky and will begin to smell a bit

ripe. Stir daily. The good seeds will sink to the bottom and the infertile ones will float along with the fermented pulp. After 2 or 3 days, pour off the floaters and the liquid. Then dump the good seeds into a strainer and wash them well.

4. Spread out the rinsed seeds on several layers of newspaper to dry. After a few days, they should be dry and will not stick

to the newspaper. If they seem to dry slowly, change the newspaper underneath every day. When thoroughly dry, place the seeds in an airtight container (like a babyfood jar) and store in a cold, dry place—a refrigerator, freezer, or cold pantry.

—Adapted from *Step-by-Step Gardening Techniques Illustrated*. Written by Nancy Bubel and illustrated by Elayne Sears.

Potatoes, Sweet and Irish

D.J. Young

Potatoes are among the most productive, in terms of food value per unit of space, of the many vegetables in the home garden. And when we say "potatoes" we are referring to two separate species, Irish and sweet, seemingly with little in common except the name, yet with much in common when added to the garden and family food fare.

Both have become as American as the beef steak, which is best with a baked Irish potato; or the highly spiced southern smoked sausage that demands a baked sweet potato as its companion on the breakfast table. The Irish potato's food value is next to rice among the world's food staples. The sweet potato has its roots set deeper in the South, and is grown commercially from New Jersey southward and westward to Southern California. It ranks high in nutritional values.

Add to those food and gastronomic values the small amount of work necessary to grow these two gems, and what gardener could resist adding them to his garden calendar? So, let's discuss Irish potatoes first, then the sweet.

The Irish Potato

BEST SOIL TYPES

A silt or sandy loam, high in organic matter, with good drainage, is the ideal soil for growing Irish potatoes. But if you are not blessed with

the ideal, it is not a sign that you should deprive yourself of some good home-grown spuds. Soils can be built up or reclaimed.

Plenty of organic matter—leaf mold, manures—will do much for a clay soil. A few cubic feet of sand will help lighten an otherwise heavy soil. Soils that are too sandy can be improved with organic matter.

The ideal size potatoes (6–8 oz.) cut in four equal wedges. Each piece is used as a seed. (potatoes shown: Red La Soda)

Continued →

Be sure you have good drainage. Poor drainage will promote rot in the seed before it sprouts, and possibly in the forming of young tubers.

FERTILIZATION AND SOIL pH
Different types of plant life require different diets of nutrients. What the particular plant produces determines the diet. There are many plant food requirements, but the major ones are nitrogen, phosphorus, and potash.

The nutrient requirements of your soil must be established, but it is not enough to pick up a USDA bulletin and read that a 6–12-6 (six percent nitrogen, twelve percent phosphorus and six percent potash) fertilizer at the rate of eight pounds per 100 feet of row is recommended for Irish potatoes. This recommendation is given as an average requirement. It may be too little or too much for your particular soil's existing nutrition level.

That level must be established before determining an effective fertilization program. It can be learned through a soil test which you can have done by your local Extension Service agent, whose office is generally at the county seat. Soil tests are usually free.

The soil test result given to you will be accompanied by a recommended fertilization program. Follow it strictly. If recommendations are for eight pounds of 6–12-6 per 100 feet of row, get out the bathroom scale, figure out your needs and weigh out the proper amount. Don't guess. Too much can be worse than not enough.

The soil test report will also include the pH level, indicating the acidity or alkalinity of your soil. The pH reading is from 0 to 14. A low reading, from 0 to 7, indicates an acid soil, 7.0 is neutral, and any reading above that indicates an alkaline soil. Most common vegetables do best on a soil with a pH reading of 6.5, but authorities recommend a pH no higher than 6.5 for Irish potatoes. My best potato harvest was made from a soil that tested 4.8 after harvest.

The higher soil pH reading may promote potato scab, while a pH lower than 5.0 will halt the speed of this fungus disease. Your potatoes will tolerate a low pH better than a high pH, so avoid any use of lime.

The organic gardener will find nutrients in manure and composts, plus ground rock phosphate as one source of phosphorus, and greensand or granite dust as possible sources of potash. While wood ashes are a source of potash, needed by potatoes, they shouldn't be used for potatoes because of the high lime content in them.

If the soil test shows a marked deficiency in phosphorus and potash, an application of 10 to 15 pounds of the rock phosphate and an equal amount of the greensand or granite dust per 100 feet of row is recommended. The nitrogen needed will come from the manure, or from compost, made without the addition of lime.

Avoid spreading fresh manure on land to be used for potatoes. An ideal way to prepare the land is to grow soybeans or some other legume on the site the previous year, then rototill this crop under in the fall and add compost or rotted manure, spreading as much as 10 wheelbarrow loads per 100-foot row.

The rock fertilizers can be applied in the previous summer or fall, but if applied the year you grow potatoes, they should be spread several weeks before planting time to give the ingredients time to be broken down in a form the plants can use.

CHOOSING A VARIETY
There are many varieties of Irish potatoes. Look for the varieties best adapted to your region and its climate. That choice can best be made after talking with your Extension Service agent, the seedman and growers in your area. The seedman usually stocks varieties that are in greatest demand and most suitable to your region, so you can't go very wrong in following his advice.

Most regions have a choice of two or more varieties. It then becomes a matter of taste or purpose, a choice between a white variety which bakes best, or a red, some of which are good all-purpose varieties, or a variety for winter storage, such as the Katahdin or Russet Burbank.

If diseases are a problem in your area, look for potatoes resistant to them. For example, Irish Cobbler is resistant to mild mosaic, Early Gem is scab resistant, and Sebago is resistant to both blight and scab. Get recommendations from your seedman.

USE CERTIFIED SEED
Regardless of your choice of variety, use of certified seed is advised. You are safe when purchasing your seed from a reputable seed dealer, as he is not likely to put a seed potato on the market that is not certified. But if you want to be certain, ask the dealer to let you see the tag on the container. Each container (usually a sack) of seed potatoes must carry certification by the shipper that his potatoes meet certain standards if they are to be offered as certified. These standards are: True strains of the variety stated, free of diseases.

Don't use Irish potatoes bought at the supermarket as seed. Their use, besides resulting in possible crop failure because of impure strain, may introduce diseases in the garden soil that will carry over to future crops. In addition, these potatoes may have been treated with chemicals to slow their rate of sprouting, and so will be unsatisfactory for planting.

Gardener planting Irish potatoes under straw in early February. Seed pieces have been pressed firmly to ground level; a six-inch layer of rice straw is being placed on top.

A completed lazy bed. Soil is placed on top of the straw to hold it down until the potato sprouts emerge through it. The potatoes will form on or near the surface of the ground. When mature, they can be selectively harvested on an as-needed basis.

584

PREPARING THE SEED

The ideal potato seed is a 1 1/2 to 2 ounce block with two or more eyes, obtained by cutting a six to eight ounce potato into four equal quarters. Any block from this cutting with less than two eyes should be discarded. A large seed piece will withstand injury better than a smaller piece; and the multiple eyes will generate several sprouts, increasing the production per hill.

After the seed potatoes have been cut, the seed pieces should be left at room temperature for about twenty-four hours before planting. Exposing the cut sides of the potato pieces to air causes them to firm up, reducing the chances of rotting in the ground before sprouting.

You will need seven to ten pounds of potatoes per 100 foot row and should harvest at least three bushels of mature potatoes. A good gardener will get five to six bushels.

WHEN TO PLANT

The Irish potato, like other annual vegetables, will be best during certain seasons. Being primarily a cool weather crop, it does best when planted in early spring or in the fall. (Fall sowing will be covered later.)

To determine your sowing date, establish the last killing-frost date in your area, then back up about 20 days. Since the potato takes about 20 days to sprout, danger of frost should have passed by sprouting time. If frost is predicted after the potatoes have sprouted, cover the young sprouts with soil to prevent damage in the event the frost is severe. A light frost may burn the top leaves, but will not damage the entire plant.

SOWING THE SEED (TWO METHODS)

You're ready now to sow your spring potato crop. You have a choice of two methods. One is the conventional row method commonly used on the farm. The other may be new to you. Both have their merits, so experiment with them and make your choice.

Planting Irish potatoes under straw, hay, leaves or mulch of some other material, called the "lazy bed method" in some gardening circles, offers definite advantages to the small gardener. It eliminates practically all cultivation after sowing, permits a significant increase in space utilization, is safer in soils where scab may be a threat, and permits easy harvesting on an as-needed basis.

The lazy bed is set up on a rectangle not more than six feet wide (less if your reach is short) to allow you to reach the middle from the sides without stepping on the bed. The length is determined by the amount of potatoes you wish to plant, or the available space. Some plant an even wider bed, planning not to move across it once the potatoes have been planted, but it is convenient to have it narrow enough to reach into, for harvesting a few early potatoes, or to pull the occasional weed that may find its way up through the mulch.

When preparing the bed, cultivate the soil deeply and, if heavy rains are a problem in your area, give the final bed a slightly rounded contour or a slight slope to permit drainage. Place the potato chunks, cut side down, twelve inches from the sides and ends, spacing them twelve inches apart in each direction. Thus, for example, on a 6 x 12 foot bed, you can place four chunks across and ten on the length, or forty plants.

After the chunks are in place and pressed down firmly in the soil—no need to bury them—spread a layer of straw, hay or shredded leaves on top of them. If you use bailed hay, six-inch pads will do the job. If you use loose hay, spread it 12 to 18 inches thick. That loose hay will pack down and disintegrate gradually, and if it isn't deep enough,

there's a danger of potatoes showing through, greening and thus becoming inedible. And, once the plants have come up and spread, it's difficult to add additional mulch.

If there's a chance the mulch will blow away, weight it down with wire, wooden slates or a sprinkling of soil. The first rain will usually mat down this layer and hold it in place.

After that chore is completed, forget about cultivation and weeding. (That's why some call this the "lazy bed" method.) Calculate how few potatoes you could have planted in rows in that 6 x 12 foot space: Two good rows with 10 plants each, or 20 plants.

The lazy bed method may not have its advantages in large scale growing because of the need for large quantities of mulch, but its advantages in the home garden will become apparent once tried. The mulch requirement is not on a scale that the gardener can't meet. If it is necessary to buy the hay, one or two bales will be sufficient for the average small garden.

Row Planting: One method of row planting is to hoe or dig a trench about a foot wide and six inches deep. If there's a question about the richness of the soil, put a two-inch layer of compost in this trench and work it into the top layer of soil. Plant potato chunks, cut side down, a foot apart and three inches deep. As plants emerge, hoe soil up to them, gradually filling the trench and building a row-long hill about eight inches high. If you desire, you can mulch at this time, to keep soil cool and to discourage the weeds. By hilling the potatoes, you give them an ample area of loose soil in which to spread out and grow. The rows in this method should be about twenty-eight inches apart.

If heavy rains are a problem in your area, make certain that standing rain does not remain between rows after these rains. Hoeing the mounds higher will help with this problem, and protect the potatoes from rotting underground due to the standing water.

GROWING IRISH POTATOES IN THE FALL

Irish potatoes can be planted as a fall crop in any section of the country where there is a 90-day period relatively free from extreme heat just prior to the first killing frost, and thus fall growing is popular in many southern areas. The Irish potato, being a cool weather crop, needs a fairly cool period to mature, but it can withstand short periods of heat rather well. And since a severe frost will kill the plant, it must be given time to mature before the first fall killing frost.

A gardener should determine the first average killing-frost date in his area, then count back about 90 days to establish his sowing date. The gardener may find the first-frost date for his garden different from

A second sowing is being done near the first. Second sowing is taking place about 30 days after the first one; note potato plants from the first sowing coming through the straw.

Continued →

Gardening · Vegetables and More

published average frost dates for his region. The most reliable source for information is the local Extension Service office.

The same planting methods that were used in the spring can be used in the fall. If you are in a long growing season area and thus could grow consecutive crops, avoid using the same bed that was used for the spring crop. Introduction of another potato crop shortly after harvesting one will give the fungi a chance to progress, possibly out of control.

If you choose the row method of planting, but are limited in space, use the following method of setting up rows in a small area. It is ideal for the gardener with limited space.

MORE IN LESS SPACE

Using a 5 x 9 foot space, for example, would limit you to two rows using the farming technique of building rows. But it is possible to construct three rows in this space, if rows or mounds are constructed on top of the potato chunks.

Mark off rows eighteen inches apart, and cut furrows two inches deep and twelve inches broad along these lines. Place the potato chunks in these furrows, spacing them eight inches apart. Hoe up the mound on the top of the seed and top off with mulch.

This row-building scheme will give more than 30 percent increased production over the farm method of row building, and will furnish rows substantial enough to house the developing tubers, if the mounds are maintained during the potato's developing period. Keeping the rows mulched is a good way to avoid erosion during heavy rains.

Row building scheme for the gardener with limited space. The potato seed is placed in a two-inch deep furrow, and row built on top of the seed. This method allows rows to be spaced closer than when the row is built first, then opened and closed for the seeds.

HARVESTING AND STORAGE

Pick a relatively dry period for your final harvest. Wait until the vines are dead and dry. This is a sign that your potatoes are fully matured.

Use a potato hook or fork on plants in a row, and work carefully, trying to avoid puncturing or otherwise damaging the potato skins. If you used the lazy bed method, pull or rake back the layer of mulch and pick up your crop. Dig under the top several inches of soil occasionally, to see whether any have hidden there.

Let the potatoes dry for one or two hours, then move them into storage. If the potatoes are to be used in the next month or six weeks, they can be stored in a dark area with temperatures as high as 70°F. For winter storage, fully mature potatoes should be stored in the dark, at temperatures of 38–40°F, and with a relative humidity of 85–90

percent. They will keep this way for at least five or six months. Darkness is essential for these potatoes. Light will promote greening, making them inedible. Higher temperatures cause early sprouting and shriveling.

The storage area should have some air circulation. I get good results with a home-made storage box with one-inch holes in the sides and ends. My potatoes are placed inside between layers of straw, so air can circulate around them. This box is neat and handy.

Effort spent at providing a good storage facility is effort well spent. You have exerted effort, time and some cash growing and harvesting a crop of your favorite variety. Now you are looking forward to enjoying them for weeks or months. Store them well.

Growing Sweet Potatoes

Introducing that delicious, nutritious product of warm-belt gardens, the sweet potato. Eaten and beloved throughout the United States, it is a major commercial product in Louisiana, North Carolina, Texas, and Virginia. Gradually, the growing area has spread, particularly for home growing, and this spread has been aided by the development of more hardy varieties, and the use of such aids as black plastic to raise the soil temperature, and cloches to protect the emerging plants. Northerners may find it a challenge to grow them in their gardens.

Ideally the crop should have 130 to 150 frost-free days, with most of them up to 80–85°F and with moderate to high humidity. Planting should be well after the last frost, when the soil has warmed to about 70°F.

Sweet and Irish potatoes are alike only in name and the ways they are prepared by the cook.

Growing conditions are widely different. So is the method of propagating. The Irish potatoes are started by using small potatoes or chunks of larger ones as seed. The sweet potatoes are started by using the whole potato to grow plants, and these plants are transplanted to the potato bed.

Seed potatoes should be selected from hills producing from 4 to 5 medium sized tubers, such as shown here.

The initial source of these plants is the potato designated as *foundation seed stock*. Foundation stock is exactly what the term "foundation" means: a base upon which anything is started. It may be compared to the certified Irish potato seed.

The plants are produced by planting the foundation seed stock potato in specially constructed hotbeds. When the plants are six to seven inches long, they are pulled with the roots from the foundation seed

Select from good producing hills medium size potatoes as shown here. Store for next year's seed stock, away from those potatoes stored for consumption.

potato and transplanted to the potato bed. When they are used in that manner, they are called *draws*. The draws are sometimes cut about one inch above ground in the hotbed. When used this way, they are called *cuttings*. They are allowed to grow a little taller to compensate for the part left in the hotbed below the cut. When cuttings are taken, the original sprout will continue growing, creating another plant.

Draws or cuttings supply the initial plants for the *first* potato crop. From this crop a grower selects hills producing the best quality and largest quantity of potatoes, and from these hills selects potatoes to produce draws and cuttings for his next year's crop. These potatoes are called *seed stock*. They are different from the foundation seed stock only in the sense that they are derived from the foundation seed stock.

A grower can produce his own seed stock for four or five years without losing the desirable characteristics of any particular variety. Periodically, new foundation seed stock should be used to renew those characteristics.

The foundation seed stock, or the seed stock, when placed in a hotbed to produce draws or cuttings, is called the *mother potato*.

HOW TO START

A beginning grower of sweet potatoes has a choice of several methods to get started. He can purchase draws or cuttings, if he has a source nearby. He can obtain seed stock from a reliable grower and produce his own draws and cuttings in his home hotbed. If these options are not open to him, he should contact the Extension Service to obtain a supply of foundation seed stock.

To avoid the many diseases infesting sweet potatoes, I recommend a start with foundation seed stock, with the grower producing his own seed stock from year to year. This will assure him that diseases will not be introduced in his soil by infested seeds or plants, and that he has a pure variety for maximum production.

SOIL TYPES

The type of soil affects the yield and quality of the sweet potato in as many ways as there are soil types. An extremely rich, heavy soil will produce a high yield, but the potato will be low quality. A light, sandy soil of poor fertility will produce a high quality potato, but the yield will be low. These are the opposite of what one might expect.

However, reference to quality tends more toward the formation and appearance of the root than its qualities for eating. A short, well-formed potato that will grade U.S. No. 1 looks better than a slightly elongated tuber graded U.S. No. 2. The taste is the same. Only in extreme cases where the root is six to eight inches long and two inches or less in diameter, a condition found where potatoes are grown in extremely heavy clay soils, will the texture tend to become stringy.

The ideal soil is a light, sandy or silt loam, with a firm clay subsoil, with good drainage and moderate fertility. The moderately fertile soil is a compromise to get a good potato and still harvest a fair crop. The clay sub-soil forms a foundation below the sandy or silt loam; it contributes forming a tuber of good appearance.

You can't do much to change such things as that clay sub-soil. But as time goes by soils can be built up to a satisfactory condition. Use of organic matter and winter cover legumes go a long way in a soil improvement program. Due to their remarkable ability to condition the soil, legumes are highly recommended as a soil conditioner, regardless of the primary soil base.

FERTILITY AND SOIL pH

Because soil fertility affects both the yield and the quality, an accurate fertilization program is essential for best results in growing sweet potatoes in the home garden.

Recommended commercial fertilizers include 4–12-8, 5–10-0, or 6–12-6. A gardener reading this information may be confused. The type and amount of fertilizer required can be determined only by testing to learn the existing fertility level of the soil, then working out a fertilizer program based on the results of that test. As recommended in the Irish potato growing section, this can be done with the help of the Extension Service agent. Generally speaking, the sweet potato requires essentially the same type but less nutrients than the Irish potato.

The organic gardener, who will have his own plan of fertilization, should avoid use of fresh stable manures. The sweet potato is an excellent host for many rot bacteria, and some authorities claim stable manures promote their growth.

The sweet potato does best with a pH of 5.0. Agricultural soil sulfur (to lower pH) or lime (to raise it) can be applied from October to December to stabilize the pH at the desired level.

Soil sulfur is also helpful in the control of soil rot, a fungus that infests sweet potatoes, but it should not be applied for that purpose arbitrarily, as too much is harmful to the plants, as well as upsetting the pH balance of the soil.

CHOOSING A VARIETY

Many varieties of sweet potatoes are grown in the United States. Several factors will influence a choice of variety. Some varieties are better for shipping purposes, some are favored by home gardeners. The choice may be limited to the variety that grows best in a particular region, or the availability of foundation seed stock, seed stock or plants. Because of the many factors that may influence your choice, we will limit our discussion to three varieties which we believe fall within specific categories.

The Unit 1 Porto Rico, slowly being replaced by new varieties, is still regarded by many as one of the best for fresh market and storage. Since it cures well, it is a favorite choice of the gardener who can get foundation seed stock or plants. I grow this variety; I recommend it.

Continued →

A relatively new variety is the Heartogold. It has white skin with bright orange flesh. For unexplained reasons, it does not market very well. Some say it is because of the white skin, an unnatural color for a sweet potato skin. But it is high in quality and can be eaten immediately after harvest without a curing period. These qualities make it very desirable for the home gardener.

Some may find the Heartogold's disadvantages outweigh the advantages. It bruises easily when harvesting, therefore does not store well. Also, foundation seed stock or plants may be hard to get, since it is not in great demand by commercial growers.

Centennial is favored by many commercial growers, especially in Louisiana, where it is recommended for all regions. It outyields all other commercial varieties, and stores and ships very well. Foundation seed stock, seed stock or plants are widely available.

Disadvantages are that in cool climates the Centennial plants may emerge later than others, and it requires more heat to sprout. The latter disadvantage is nullified where hothouses are used to grow plants.

THE FOUNDATION SEED STOCK

The sweet potato production cycle begins with the foundation seed potato. It is the base upon which future propagations are derived. It is grown by the Extension Service, or under its direct supervision. It is available only through the county agent; it cannot be purchased through normal seed outlets.

In the South, growers place their orders for foundation seed stock with the county agent in early January. The foundation seed stock is distributed by the county agent, rather than being shipped direct to growers. (Since this procedure may vary in different areas, it is advisable to contact the area county agent during late fall to determine his procedure in obtaining foundation seed stock.)

After receiving the foundation seed stock, the grower will bed it to get plants for sowing the first year's crop.

Besides being the source of plants for the first year's crop, the foundation seed stock is also the source of seed stock for several years. As explained earlier, the seed stock is different from the foundation seed stock only in that it is derived from the foundation seed stock. It serves the same purpose—to produce plants for sowing.

Rows should be built sufficiently high and wide to accommodate the developing tubers, such as shown here. Vine cuttings are shown in place, ready for setting.

Foundation seed stock can't be bought in less than one-bushel quantities. That's more than most gardeners need, since one bushel will produce about 1,000 plants at the first cutting, and more than 2,500 in several cuttings. Friends often combine their orders and purchase the minimum one bushel.

THE COLD FRAME OR HOTBED

We strongly recommend that a gardener grow his own seed stock each year, unless he is in an area where sweet potatoes are grown commercially and disease-free cuttings or draws are available each year.

To do this, he will need a cold frame or hotbed, which is a cold frame equipped with some means of artificial heat. Since soil temperatures between 70° and 80°F are needed to promote sprouting, this is the best means of controlling the temperature at that level. Further, a sterile soil is needed in the bedding area to avoid diseases, and use of this method furnishes an isolated environment that can be sterilized.

A cold frame or hotbed for producing plants need not be elaborate or expensive, and can be built quickly with wooden sides and a glass or plastic removable top. In cool climates, sunlight alone may not maintain the required temperatures, and electrical heating units, with pre-set thermostats, or more expensive hot water pipes may be needed.

Many gardeners will have extra room in existing units for the few potatoes required. A two-foot square area is large enough.

Vine cuttings such as shown here are ideal for use as plants. They can be taken either from the hotbed, cut above ground away from the mother potato, or from the vines of the first sowing. When embedded in the soil, each joint in the vine will develop root. One of the cuttings shown here is already developing root.

A first step in having a disease-free cold frame or hotbed is to change the soil each year, getting new soil from an area that hasn't been under cultivation for several years. A good place to get this soil is on a high point in a wooded area. Although the pH of the soil may be low, this will not adversely affect the production of plants.

Before adding the new soil, remove the first six inches of soil, where the germs and insects that could affect the seed potato will probably be found. Then add twelve inches of new soil. This raises your soil level six inches, affording good drainage.

Soil can be sterilized with chemicals or steam. Since steam is not practical for the small gardener, the chemical Vapam can be used effectively by following the manufacturer's directions on the container. Plan ahead, if Vapam is used, since a waiting period of about 30 days between treatment and planting is recommended.

The organic gardener who avoids use of chemicals might try my method. I use boiling water. I get sterile soil.

Follow this procedure for effective results: Prepare about five gallons of water for an area measuring three feet square. Install a three-inch layer of soil, then pour boiling water over it. Continue this until twelve inches of soil have been added, then pour boiling water over that and cover the surface with plastic for forty-eight hours to keep the heat in the soil as long as possible.

Wait a few days to let the soil dry—but not too dry—before using the area. Bed the mother potatoes by covering them with two inches of the sterile sandy soil in the hotbed. Dampen the soil and cover with a black polyethylene plastic. This will absorb and hold the heat from the sun. If the transparent top of your bed is removed, you do not have to worry about excessive heat. This material is used successfully throughout the deep South, where it is very hot.

After the sprouts begin pushing up the plastic, remove it to let them harden. Continue maintaining the temperature level until the sprouts are about nine to ten inches tall. At that height, they are ready to cut and transplant.

Bedding time will depend on the climate. In my area of the South, we bed in February to have plants for early sowing in April. This is about sixty days from bedding the potatoes to planting. Determine when you will be able to plant by learning the last spring frost date, then count back at least sixty days to determine your bedding date.

PRODUCING SEED STOCK

While many gardeners purchase cuttings or draws each year, the gardener who produces his own seed stock usually has best results, since he has control over the selection of that seed stock, and can achieve better production in this way.

Here's how to grow seed stock: From the mother (seed) potatoes in your hotbed, take cuttings instead of pulling them with the roots as draws. This means that you will cut the draws about one inch above the ground. This reduces the chances of transmitting diseases from the hotbed to the planting bed.

Better stock will result if you plant late, but still early enough to harvest before frost. In the deep South the sowing time for seed potatoes is June. In cooler regions, only one sowing may be possible, so that the single sowing can be all-purpose for seed stock and consumption.

Plant in soil that has not had sweet potatoes planted in it for at least three years. This will help discourage diseases in your seed stock.

When harvesting, select the best roots from the most prolific hills, hills that produce four or five roots of medium size, free of any signs of insects or fungus injury. Store at 85°F, away from any stored for consumption.

When planting, place vine tip about 5 inches deep in the row. If soil is dry, pour water in the hole before firming-up the soil around the cutting. When using vine cuttings from the first bedding, cut about 10 or 12 inches long, and fold the cut tip when bedding. This will permit more vine to be in the ground, developing a better root system.

WHEN TO PLANT

For an early crop, plant in the spring as soon as cuttings are available from the hotbed and soil temperature in the garden is about 70°F. Sweet potato cuttings do not grow very well when the soil is colder than that.

Successive sowings can be made thereafter, if desired, as soon as there are new growths from the hotbed; or, as will be explained, when vine cuttings are available from the initial sowing.

Small row of 10 hills in a small home garden. This small row should produce 40 to 50 potatoes, above-average food value for the unit of space used when compared with the other vegetables.

HOW TO PLANT

Build rows about three feet wide and one foot high to accommodate the potatoes that will develop, and space the rows about three feet apart. The rows should be prepared about ten days ahead of planting, and the recommended fertilizer should be mixed into the top six inches of topsoil.

When taking plants from the hotbed to transplant into the row, cut the sprout (now referred to as a cutting) about one inch above ground. The sprout should be about nine or ten inches tall in the hotbed, so that the cutting is at least eight inches long.

Continued ➤

Cutting the sprout is recommended over the old practice of pulling the sprout—referred to as a *draw* when used in this manner—to transplant, as it reduces the possibility of transmitting diseases from the mother plant to the planting row. It also allows the sprout to continue growing, producing another cutting.

Plant them four inches deep, spaced twelve inches apart. Firm soil around them, and if soil is dry, water them.

If you wish to make a second sowing shortly after the first, but don't have enough sprouts for cutting, you may take ten or twelve-inch tips of vines from the first sowing, after they have started running. This practice is favored by many as an excellent way to propagate a second or third sowing.

Sweet potato sprouts, when pulled out of the hotbed with the roots, as illustrated with the two on the left in this photo, are called draws; when cut above ground as shown on the right, and used as plants in that manner, they become known as cuttings. The latter procedure is recommended over the use of the entire draw as a plant. It reduces considerably the transfer of diseases from the hotbed to the planting row.

Cuttings obtained from a distant source can be stored without worry. If they are kept damp and cool by wrapping the cut tips in damp newspapers, they will remain viable for several days, even if they appear withered. They are very sturdy.

CULTIVATION
A minimum of cultivation is necessary or advisable because of shallow roots. After the vines start running, pulling by hand weeds that come through the vines will suffice.

HARVESTING
Your potatoes should be ready to harvest about 130 to 150 days after planting. This may vary somewhat due to climate and soil. Potatoes planted early in rich soil in a warm climate may mature earlier, so after 130 days dig one hill to see if they are mature. If the root is not fully developed (approximately two and one-half inches in diameter), or the skin is tender, wait another 20 days before harvesting.

Harvest before frost, using a spading fork and digging deeply. The roots are way down, the tip of some as much as one foot. Separate the

bruised potatoes, which you will want to use first as food, from the ones you will want to store for later consumption, or for seed stock.

Store initially in a well ventilated area at 85°F for 15 to 20 days. This is a curing period that will help your potatoes keep better for longer periods. After the curing period, store at a temperature of 60°F, but not below 50°F at any time. For short periods of time (30 to 60 days over the curing period) they will keep well at 80°F.

Storage facilities need not be elaborate. Refer back to storage suggestion for Irish potatoes and duplicate that facility. Both boxes can be stored in the same area, making it doubly handy for the cook.

A small commercial patch of sweet potatoes at harvest time.

Grow the Best Peppers

Weldon Burge

For American gardeners, peppers are second only to tomatoes in popularity. They produce well in limited space, are virtually free of pests and diseases, and are fairly easy to grow. The plants are attractive in the garden; many people grow several varieties just for their decorative touch.

Bell peppers are the most popular and familiar, but in recent years there has been heightened interest in the vast selection of peppers—many of which are only available if you grow them yourself. If your only experience with peppers has been green bell peppers for stuffing, roasting, or slicing, you've barely scratched the surface.

Peppers, particularly the hot varieties, have gained popularity as more and more ethnic foods come into vogue, including Spanish, Italian, Mexican, Indian, Hunan, Szechuan, Thai, Indonesian, Vietnamese, and Arab dishes. The fruits provide a diversity of shapes, sizes, colors, and flavors that add variety to your garden and pizzazz to your cooking.

PEPPER CLASSIFICATIONS
Peppers are members of the Nightshade Family, which includes the tomato, potato, and eggplant. Although they are herbaceous perennials, they are generally grown as annuals.

In parts of Europe, peppers are called *capsicums*, their botanical name. Some historians believe the name came from the Latin *capsa*, or "box," because of their shape. Others believe the name came from the Greek word *capto*—"I bite."

If you thumb through several seed catalogs, you will find that peppers often defy classification—or at least provide some confusion. For example, "Cayenne," "Jalapeño," and "Bell" are all type names, each representing a group of peppers that may contain many cultivars. Yet, a seed catalog may offer a variety called "Cayenne" or "Jalapeño." This list shows common groupings with some representative varieties.

Pepper Group	Representative Varieties
ANAHEIM	Anaheim Chili
ANCHO	Ancho/Poblano
BELL	Big Bertha, California Bell
CAYENNE	Long Red Cayenne, Ring of Fire Cayenne
CHEESE	Yellow Cheese Pimento
CHERRY	Sweet Cherry, Cherrytime
CUBAN	Pepperoncini, Cubanelle
JALAPENO	Early Jalapeño, Jalapeño M
PIMENTO	Pimento Select
SMALL HOT	Serrano Chili
TABASCO	Tabasco
WAX	Sweet Banana, Hungarian Wax

To add to the confusion, the same variety of pepper may have different names in different contexts. For example, an Ancho pepper is the dried version of the fresh Poblano pepper—however, it can be found under both or either name in seed catalogs. This is particularly confusing in ethnic cookbooks. A Mexican cookbook may call for Habaneros; a Jamaican recipe may call for Scotch Bonnets—both are the same pepper.

If you need help with the different groups and names, send for the guide *Capsicum Pepper Varieties and Classification* (Circular #530) available for $1.00 from the Bulletin Office, Box 3AI, New Mexico State University, Las Cruces, NM 88003.

For the sake of simplicity, we'll divide the vast number of varieties into two groups: sweet peppers and hot peppers.

Sweet Peppers

There are probably plenty of green bell peppers in your local supermarket; perhaps some overpriced yellow and red bells, and maybe some Italian frying peppers. Very little else.

If you're looking for green peppers for stuffing, roasting, or slicing for salads or crudités, many bell varieties will suffice. They range in size from the enormous (Big Bertha, King of the North) to the miniature (Jingle Bells, Little Dipper). The green peppers are actually immature fruits. Allowed to ripen, most turn red or yellow with a sweeter, milder flavor and a finer texture. In fact, those expensive "gourmet" red and yellow bells are merely green peppers that have matured.

Sweet peppers range far beyond the bell peppers. You can select from the long frying types (Cubanelle, Biscayne, Italia), the small cherry varieties (Cherrytime, Sweet Cherry), and the pickling types (Sweet Pickle, Sweet Banana, Pepperoncini).

The following is only a sampling of the many sweet peppers available from seed catalogs.

SWEET PEPPER VARIETIES & SOURCES

Variety	Description	Days to Harvest*	Sources
ACE	An extra-early bell pepper variety that has high yields even in cold climates—good for Northern gardens. The fruits are up to 4" long with medium-thick walls; ripens to red early. Resistant to blossom drop, so nearly every flower creates a fruit.	50	9,17
ARIANE	A Dutch bell pepper variety that ripens into a gorgeous deep orange. The large, blocky fruits are heavy; the flesh is thick, crunchy, and juicy.	68	16
BELL BOY	An all-purpose bell variety that is prolific, disease and drought resistant. Sweet and mild, medium size, thick-walled, and uniform—perfect for stuffing. All America Winner.	72	4,5,17
BELL TOWER	A midseason bell pepper recommended for all regions. Heavy, thick-walled fruits ripen from dark green to red. Disease resistant.	70	9,17
BIG BELL	Noted for its huge yields of sweet bells, ideal for stuffing.	72	4
BIG BERTHA	The Mother of the Bells! Produces prolific yields of blocky, thick-walled peppers that grow up to 8" long and 4" across—and often weigh over a pound each!	73	4,5,17, 18,19
BISCAYNE	Cubanelle type, perfect for frying. Elongated fruits are blunt-ended and tapered, usually harvested when light green. Well-branched plants provide canopy o prevent sunscald.	63	11,19
CALIFORNIA WONDER	Probably the most familiar and best stuffing peppers. Can be tough to grow in Northern gardens. Fruits are 4" long and 3 1/2" across; excellent cooked or served on a crudité tray.	75	4,5,6,17
CANAPE	Recommended for short-season areas and Northern gardens; tolerate summer heat and drought. Each plant produces about 15 fruits; the peppers are tapered, 3 1/2" long and 2 1/2" wide, ripening to a bright red.	65	6,18
CHERRYTIME	An early cherry pepper variety with impressive yields. The 2" round, red fruits are excellent for pickling whole. For sweetest flavor, wait until the fruits are red to harvest.	53	9

Continued →

Variety	Description	Days to Harvest*	Sources
CHOCOLATE BELL	A dark brown bell pepper that's larger and matures later than Sweet Chocolate. The blocky, sweet fruits are 3–4" across. Resistant to mosaic.	70	2,17
CORNO DI TORO	The red and yellow "Bull's Horn" peppers from Italy. The 6–8" tapered fruits are twisted like their namesake. Although considered a frying pepper, can be used in salads and (the less twisted fruits) are also great for stuffing.	70	3,12,15,16,19
CORONA	Holland import, turns orange when ripe. Medium size, bell-like fruits on compact plants.	66	9
CRISPY	Early bell hybrid that lives up to its name. The fruits have thick, crunchy walls; turns red early, too. Blocky peppers are 3 1/2" long and 2 3/4" across.	70	2,5
CUBANELLE	The standard frying pepper. Large, smooth tapered fruits up to 6" long; best harvested at yellow-green stage, when the fruits walls are still firm—they'll be sweeter when they ripen to red, but won't hold up as well.	68	12,14,17,19
ESPANA	Another frying pepper that produces large yields of tapered, 6–7" fruits with medium-thin walls; ripens from green to red. Excellent disease resistance.	72	6
GEDEON	Huge, elongated pepper with thick walls; ripens to red.	78	2
GOLD CREST	Earliest golden bell type. Fruits are blocky and small to medium size. Plants produce heavily and have good disease resistance.	62	9,12
GOLDEN BELL	Another golden bell. Larger than Gold Crest with blocky fruits up to 4" across—great for stuffing. Fruits ripen from light green to a deep golden color.	68	6,18
GOLDEN SUMMER	Similar to Golden Bell, with large 4"-wide fruits that have thick walls and sweet flavor. Plants grow 20" tall with a canopy of leaves that protects the peppers from sunscald.	70	3,4,5,11
GYPSY	Wedge-shaped fruits are 4 1/2" long and 2 1/2" wide at the shoulders; crisp, sweet flesh; turns from light green to orange to red. An early variety that can tolerate cool weather and is disease-resistant. Compact plants are great for containers, with as many as 16 peppers maturing at once on each plant. An All America Winner.	65	2,4,5,6,11,17,18,19
HONEY BELLE	Large, elongated fruits ripen from green to gold. The plants are vigorous and prolific.	74	6
ISLANDER	A lavender bell variety with pale yellow flesh; actually ripens in stages from violet to a very dark red. The fruits are medium-sized and have thick, juicy walls.	56	9
ITALIA	Similar to Corno Di Toro frying peppers and other long, sweet Italian peppers. The fruits are 8" long and 2 1/2" across at the shoulders; ripens early from green to red.	55	9
IVORY CHARM	A white bell variety that matures from a cream to a soft yellow color with no green at all. The plants produce early and show good disease-resistance.	67	16
JINGLE BELLS	A miniature bell that is ideal for containers; bears early and prolifically. Fruits are 1 1/2" by 1 1/2" that turn red at maturity.	60	6,12,
JUPITER	Midseason bell. Produces large, nearly square fruits that are thick-walled and crunchy.	74	6,19
KEY LARGO	Cubanelle type, superb for frying. Yellow-green fruits grow up to 7" long and 2 1/2" across at the shoulders, are thin-walled and crisp, and turn bright orange-red at maturity.	66	6
KING OF THE NORTH	An early green bell pepper recommended for the North. Fruits are 6" long and about 4" across with thick walls and a mild flavor, particularly after it ripens red.	65	5
LA BAMBA	Fruits grow up to 5" long and 3" wide with medium-thick walls and a delightful flavor. Great for slicing, stuffing, or roasting.	76	6
LADY BELL	This bell variety produces abundantly even in short seasons; the fruits are larger and more uniform than most other early types.	71	6
LILAC BELLE	Another lavender bell that shows no green at all; holds its purple color for a long time before turning a deep red. Excellent disease resistance.	68	2,5,16
LIPSTICK	Elongated, smooth, cone-shaped fruits are 4–5" long, tapering to a blunt point; they turn from a dark green to a glossy red at maturity. The flesh is thick, crunchy, and juicy with a sweet flavor that's perfect fresh for salads or roasted. Produces early; tolerates cool weather. The plants are often covered with the attractive fruits.	53	9

Variety	Description	Days to Harvest*	Sources
LITTLE DIPPER	A miniature bell pepper. The fruits are only 2" long and 1 3/4" across, ripening from green to red. Wonderful for stuffing or roasting. Produces early and prolifically.	66	2
MARCONI	Similar to Corno Di Toro but larger and more flavorful. Up to 12" long and 3" across at the shoulders, ripens to yellow and red. Great for frying or sliced into salads.	70	3
MONTEGO	A Cubanelle type for the Caribbean. The large, heavy fruits grow up to 9" long and 3" at the shoulders, ripening from white to eyellow to red. The thick flesh is juicy and mild, perfect for salads, crudités, or cooking. The compact plants produce early.	60	9
NORTH STAR	This medium-sized bell pepper is especially recommended for the Northeast; bountiful even in short, cool seasons.	60	2,9,19
OROBELLE	A main season golden bell, slightly larger than other gold varieties. The blocky fruits grow to 4 1/2" long and 4 1/2" across. Grows well in the North.	70	9,19
PARK'S EARLY THICKSET	One of the earliest, high-yielding bells. The fruits are medium-sized, maturing to a scarlet red.	45	11
PARK'S POT HYBRID	This space-saving bell variety is just 10–12" tall, perfect for containers or small gardens. The plants bear heavily and early.	45	11
PARK'S SWEET BANANA WHOPPER	The first hybrid Sweet Banana—a distinct improvement! The fruits are larger and have thicker walls.	65	11
PARK'S WHOPPER IMPROVED	A main season green bell pepper. The fruits are 4" long and 4" across, with thick walls excellent for stuffing or slicing. Matures red.	71	11
PEPPERONCINI	Traditional, mild pickling pepper recommended for antipasto. Dries well. Fruits are thin and tapered, growing up to 8" long. Picked green for pickling, but will ripen to red.	65	7,12,14, 16,17,19
PURPLE BEAUTY	Compact plants have thick foliage to protect the fruits from sunscald. Peppers are up to 5" long with a rich purple color that holds through cooking. Ripens red.	65	3,4,5,6, 11,17,19
PURPLE BELLE	Another bell variety that changes from green to deep purple to red. The fruits are 3 1/2" long, borne on compact plants.	72	17
SECRET	Unique color! The fruits have deep purple skin, but the flesh is a light green; ripens to a dark red. Plants produce early and prolifically.	60	9
SWEET BANANA	Attractive wax-type peppers are great for frying or pickling. Tapered fruits grow up to 6" long with thin walls. Plant may simultaneously bear fruits ranging in color from light green to yellow to orange to red. Can be used ornamentally in the garden.	72	2,4,5,6,
SWEET CHERRY	Like Cherrytime, this variety produces round fruits about 1 1/2" across, starting green and turning red; perfect for pickling.	78	12,15,17
SWEET CHOCOLATE	Similar to Chocolate Bell, only earlier; tolerates cool weather well. The fruits are medium-sized and slightly tapered. The flesh under the chocolate skin is brick red; the peppers won't lose their color when cooked.	58	3,9
SWEET PICKLE	Recommended for pickling. Plants bear fruit in a variety of colors at once. Compact plants grow only to 15"—great as an ornamental or potted plant.	65	11
VALENCIA	An orange bell. The fruits are 4 1/2" long and wide; rich in vitamin A when ripe.	70	11
VIDI	A French hybrid that, like other European bells, is about twice as long as it is wide. The fruits are 7" long, maturing to red. Good disease resistance; grows well in relatively poor conditions.	75	3,16,19
YELLOW CHEESE PIMENTO	Fruits are large and squash-shaped; ripens green to yellow to orange.	73	17
YOLO WONDER	A standard green bell pepper that is thick-walled, blocky, growing to about 4 1/2".	76	17

* Refers to the time after transplanting of seedlings which were started 8–10 weeks earlier. Time to harvest also refers to when the pepper is generally picked; many gardeners may prefer to wait until the pepper fully ripens or matures, which may be weeks later. Check current seed catalogs for availability and pricing.

Continued ➧

Hot Peppers

Like sweet peppers, hot peppers have many shapes, colors, and flavors. They range in "heat" from the slightly pungent Anaheims to the blistering Habañeros.

Many people believe the smaller the pepper, the hotter it is. Or that red peppers are hotter than green ones. Not true! Serranos are picked green and are longer than the chunky Jalapeños, but they are far hotter than Jalapeños. *Variety* determines how hot a pepper will be, not color, shape, or size.

Growing conditions such as soil quality, moisture, and temperature also influence the hotness of a pepper. A Cayenne will always be hotter than an Anaheim. But a Cayenne grown in New Mexico, where the soil is poor and the climate is arid, will be hotter than the same variety grown in New York, where it is cool and damp. That's why some of the hottest chilis come from Mexico and the Southwest.

WHAT MAKES HOT PEPPERS SIZZLE?

Researchers at New Mexico State University have identified at least six compounds in hot peppers that pour on the heat, but the chief chemical ingredient is capsicin, a crystalline alkaloid that acts as an irritant.

The degree of heat in hot peppers can be measured on a scale using Scoville units. Created by William Scoville in 1912, the scale refers to the parts per million of capsicin in a pepper variety. Scoville discovered that the human tongue can detect as little as 1 part per million of the substance. A mild Anaheim may reach 1,400 on the scale, but a Tabasco could reach 50,000 and a fiery Habañero up to 350,000!

HOW HOT IS HOT?

Pepper Variety	Scoville Heat Units
ANAHEIM CHILI	250 – 1,400
JALAPEÑO	4,000 – 6,000
SERRANO CHILI	7,000 – 25,000
CAYENNE	30,000 – 35,000
CHILE PEQUIN	35,000 – 40,000
TABASCO	30,000 – 50,000
HABAÑERO	200,000 – 350,000

Planning for the Best Production

With peppers more than most other vegetables, matching the right variety with the right location is essential. But, before you open a seed catalog, first consider *your* needs.

If you're satisfied with green bell peppers, a good nursery will have some varieties. But if you want a greater variety, you'll have to start from seed. Here is where planning is key.

Peppers vary widely in their regional adaptation. California Wonder may be wondrous in California, but it has lackluster production in Maine. If you live in a short-season area, in the North or in the mountains, select early varieties that mature in 50–70 days. If you live in the South or in a long-season area, choose main season and late-maturing varieties.

For advice on what varieties are best adapted to your local environment and soil conditions, talk with fellow gardeners, your County Extension agent, or your state university Extension Service. Look for varieties that are resistant to common diseases, notably Tobacco Mosaic Virus or Potato Virus Y.

I like to experiment, searching by trial and error for the best varieties for my garden. Grow a few different varieties each year and you'll quickly discover that some produce more or taste better than others. Eventually you'll find some "favorites" that you can count on year after year!

When ordering pepper seeds from catalogs, keep in mind:

- A single seed packet contains more seeds than most home gardeners can use in one season. Pepper seeds can be saved for up to four years, but they become increasingly less viable. Buy one or two fresh packets each year and trade different varieties with friends.

- Unless the seed catalog states otherwise, the "number of days to maturity" refers to the days *after transplanting* until the plant produces a full-sized fruit. You must add 8–10 weeks (50–70 days) for the time between sowing and transplanting, and 3–6 weeks (20–40 days) if you want the fruits to fully ripen.

GETTING A JUMP ON THE SEASON — STARTING PEPPERS INDOORS

In areas that don't have long, warm seasons, peppers must be started indoors to produce a harvest before the fall frosts.

Many people think peppers should be started at the same time and under the same conditions as tomatoes. But peppers take longer and require a higher temperature to germinate and are more finicky concerning climate. You've got to start them earlier and transplant them later than tomatoes.

Establish the last expected frost date in your area (your Extension agent or fellow gardeners can be of assistance), then count backwards 8–10 weeks to determine when to start your pepper plants. For many of us, that means January or February. If you receive your seed catalogs in November or December, you must act quickly.

Seeds will sprout in about a week at a temperature of 70°–80°F. Keep in mind that sprouting is uneven at any temperature, and that germination rates vary from variety to variety. Hot peppers can be *very* slow to germinate.

You can start your seeds in flats, but you'll have to transplant them into pots when their first true leaves appear. I prefer to soak the seeds, pre-sprout them, then plant them in individual containers.

To break the seeds' dormancy, soak them for a few hours in lukewarm water. For the slow-to-germinate hot pepper varieties, soak them in warm, salted water (1 tbsp. per quart) for 2–3 days. (Don't leave the seeds in the solution for more than 3 days or they may not germinate at all!) After soaking, place the seeds between moist sheets of cloth or paper towel, put them in a plastic bag, and put the bag in a warm place. The top of a refrigerator is perfect.

Check the seeds frequently. When they sprout, plant them 1/4-inch deep in peat pots, six-packs, or other small containers filled with a commercial potting soil or an equal mix of friable loam, leaf mold, and sharp sand. As with any seedlings started indoors, you must guard against damping-off disease, a soil-borne fungi that can decimate your crop. The best precaution is to use a sterile potting mix and be careful not to overwater.

Peppers are fussy about temperature in the seedling stage. After you've planted your sprouts, provide bottom heat at about 68°F, if possible. Once the true leaves appear on the seedlings, move them to a location that receives full sunlight—a sunny southern window with no cold drafts will suffice. Daytime temperatures should average 70°–80° and night temperatures about 60°–70°F. Lower temperatures may inhibit growth and higher temperatures may make the plants weak and scrawny at transplanting time; both will reduce yields later in the summer. Water the seedlings from the bottom and fertilize lightly until you can move the plants into the garden.

PREPARING THE PERFECT GARDEN SITE

Choose an area where the peppers will receive a maximum amount of direct sunlight. For best production, peppers need 6–8 hours of full sun each day—much the same as tomatoes.

Although peppers often grow well in poor soil (particularly the small, hot varieties), they produce higher yields when provided the proper soil conditions. Peppers are heavy feeders that produce a long harvest, so don't skimp on soil preparation.

Peppers prefer a deep, fertile (but not too rich), sandy or gravelly loam that drains well. If your soil is heavy, a raised bed is your best solution—fill it with a mixture of loam and sand. If you can't construct a raised bed, be sure to incorporate massive amounts of organic matter into the bed, preferably during the preceding fall, to give it plenty of time to work its magic. If your soil is excessively sandy, the organic-matter treatment will provide needed nutrients and help the soil retain moisture.

Whatever your soil conditions, you have everything to gain by preparing the soil with organic matter. Peppers need plenty of nutrients to reach optimum size and production, and they need it steadily throughout the season. If the soil is too rich with nitrogen early in the season (as can happen with chemical fertilizers) the plants may produce luscious foliage at the expense of flower and fruit production. This isn't as likely to happen with a balanced mix of organic matter.

If you have disease problems in your garden, refrain from using compost in your pepper bed, particularly if you've dumped potato peelings in the compost pile. Even the hottest compost can't maintain high enough temperatures at the edges of the pile to eliminate all bacterial diseases. If you want to add organic matter, instead of compost, use well-rotted manure, well-rotted sawdust, or leaf mold.

I've found a combination of organic and slow-release chemical fertilizers works best. When the temperatures stabilize in the early spring and I can work the soil, I blanket the area with about 2 inches of compost, sprinkle it with 5–10-10 fertilizer, and work it all in. If weather permits, I do this about a week before transplanting, as the peppers are hardening off.

Peppers are moderately tolerant to an acid soil (pH 5.5–6.8), but highly acidic soils should be limed according to soil test recommendations. Dolomite limestone contains the magnesium that peppers need to prevent leaf drop, which results in sunscalded fruits.

In the North, for early peppers in cold soils, cover the prepared bed with a plastic mulch at least a week before transplanting your seedlings. This will heat the soil nicely and will be less of a shock to young pepper roots. A brown polyethylene mulch is preferred to black or clear plastic mulches; it doesn't build up as high a soil temperature and has been shown to increase yields by 20%.

MOVING SEEDLINGS INTO THE GARDEN

Peppers will never fully recover from a cold shock. If they're not killed outright by an unexpected frost, they'll produce poorly all summer. The plants grow best with daytime temperatures of 70°–80°F, so wait until well after the last expected frost in your area before transplanting.

Before transplanting, harden off your pepper plants to get them acclimated to the garden. Place seedlings in a warm, sheltered area that is partially shaded—they should receive sun for a few hours each day. Move the plants back indoors overnight if temperatures are expected to drop below 60°F. After a week or so of this hardening-off process, the pepper plants should be accustomed to outdoor conditions.

When the weather is consistently moderate, you can move the plants into the garden. I usually wait until night temperatures are above 60° and never fall below 55°F. A soil thermometer is helpful. When the soil 4 inches below the surface is 65° or higher in the morning, you can transplant your peppers. If you've prepared raised beds covered with a plastic mulch, you may not have to wait as long!

TRANSPLANTING AND SPACING

The ideal pepper transplant has about 5 true leaves, is as tall as it is wide, and has only a few tiny flower buds or none at all. Plants sold at garden centers are often large and loaded with blossoms. The root systems are too small to support the plants in the garden. You probably can salvage such a plant by trimming back a substantial amount of the foliage before transplanting. This gives the roots time to spread through the soil, and encourages a bushier growth and better production.

HOT PEPPER VARIETIES & SOURCES

Variety	Description	Days to Harvest*	Sources
AJI	*C. baccatum* species; slender, cylindrical, 4" long, ripens to orange-red; medium hot to hot. Cultivated for 4,000 years in the Andes.	80	8,14,15
ANAHEIM CHILI	One of the easiest to grow! Relatively mild; tapered fruits grow to 8" long; matures from green to red. Dry or use fresh. Often used for salsa verde and picante sauces.	80	1,3,6,7,8 12,13,14, 15,16,19
ANAHEIM TMR 23	Mildly hot Anaheim with medium-thick flesh; fruits grow up to 7" long. Popular choice for commercial canneries.	77	2,4,5,11, 19

Continued ➜

Variety	Description	Days to Harvest*	Sources
ANCHO/POBLANO	Best adapted to areas with hot, long summers. Large plants grow up to 4' with 30 or more peppers per plant. Fresh it's called Poblano and is great for chiles rellenos. Dried it is called Ancho and is excellent for moles and sauces. Mildly pungent, heart-shaped fruits are 3–4" long; ripens from blackish green to brownish red.	80	1,2,4, 7,8, 9,12,13, 14,15,16, 19
CALIENTE	Productive, early chili that can be used fresh, but is easy to dry and use as seasoning. Straight fruits grow up to 6" long, have thin flesh, and are medium-hot. Ripen to red early.	65	9
CAYENNE	Pencil-thin, 6" red peppers are smaller than Anaheim and considerably hotter. Excellent for drying and grating for homemade chili powder.	75	3,13,16
CAYENNE LONG SLIM	Another red-hot cayenne variety that is no bigger around than a pencil and matures to a red-orange.	70	4
CHILE PEQUIN	One of the "bird peppers"—so called because of the fondness birds have for the fruits. Plants grow to 12" tall and 18" wide, bearing a prolific crop of 1/2" long lava-hot peppers.	80	10,12,13
COPACABANA	Similar to Hungarian Wax, only earlier. The tapered fruits are smooth, up to 8" long, and mature from a waxy yellow to an orange-red.	65	6
EARLY JALAPEÑO	Recommended for Northern gardens.	60	9,12,16
FIESTA	An ornamental adapted for container gardening. Can be used in the garden if moved indoors before frost. Compact, bushy plants grow only 9" tall, but produce an abundance of long, slender fruits that change from creamy white to orange and finally to red. Fiery hot!	80	17
HOLIDAY TIME	Another ornamental (or Christmas) pepper that matures earlier than Fiesta. Green, purple, and red fruits are hot. An All America Winner.	65	12,17
HABAÑERO	The hottest pepper you can grow! Most famous as the key ingredient in hot Jamaican "jerk" sauces. Belongs to the species *C. chinense*; also called Scotch Bonnets in Jamaica and the West Indies; the major pepper grown throughout Brazil. Needs a long, hot season to fully reach its pungent potential. The small 1–2" fruits are square to bell-shaped, maturing to bright orange, yellow, red, or brown. *Handle with care!*	90	1,2,3,8, 9,11,12, 14,15,16, 17,18,19
HOT PORTUGAL	Early, produces tapered, 6" long fruits that ripen to a glossy scarlet.	64	6,12,17
HUNGARIAN WAX	A standard, all-purpose hot pepper that can be grown in the North; bares early, produces well in cooler weather, and is prolific. The wrinkled yellow peppers turn deep, dark red at maturity, grow 6–8" long, and are mildly hot. Popular for canning, fruits can be stemmed, seeded, and dried, then ground for homemade paprika.	70	2,3,4, 5,6,7, 8,9,12, 15,17,19
JALAPEÑO	Perhaps the most familiar hot pepper, particularly in Southwest cuisine. Produces early, setting fiery fruit throughout the summer. Fruits are 2–3" long with rounded tips. Harvested when dark green, but will turn red. Excellent canned or pickled, whole or as a relish; adds distinctive flavor and flame to a variety of dishes and salsas.	72	3,4,5,13 17
JALAPEÑO M	Improved Jalapeño variety. The medium-hot, thick-walled fruits grow 3" long and 1 1/2" wide at the shoulders.	75	2,6,11,19
LARGE RED CHERRY	Fruits are nearly round, growing up to 1 1/2" wide.	80	2,6,17
LONG RED CAYENNE	Fruits are 5" long but only 1/2" wide, and are often twisted and curled. Recommended for drying.	75	2,17
MANZANO	*C. pubescens* species with unique purple flowers and apple-shaped fruits that ripen to orange, red, or bright yellow. Requires long growing season.	150	1,8,14

Variety	Description	Days to Harvest*	Sources
NUMEX BIG JIM	Large, slender fruits grow to 10" and ripen to a fire-engine red; mildly hot, recommended for Tex-Mex recipes. Plants produce prolifically.	75	4,5,13,12
PASILLA BAJIO CHILE	When used fresh, called Chilaca. Cylindrical fruits grow 6–8" long and 1" wide; mild to medium heat. "Pasilla" means "little raisin"—referring to the brown, wrinkled fruits after drying. Delicious fresh or dried; particularly tasty in moles and sauces.	80	16
PIMENTO SELECT	Mildest pimento you can grow. Fruits are thick-walled, ripening from green to bright scarlet. Recommended for canning.	73	4
RELLENO	Also known as the "green chili." Long, slender fruits grow up to 6 1/2" long and 2 1/2" Wide at the shoulders. Mildly hot; excellent for canning or making chiles rellenos.	75	4
RING OF FIRE CAYENNE	Earliest and most productive Cayenne variety for Northern gardens. Wonderful, fresh or dried.	60	12,15,17
SERRANO	Similar to Cayenne, only smaller and hotter. The plants are heavy producers of finger-shaped fruits, 1–2" long and slender, usually picked when dark green but will ripen red. Excellent canned or pickled, or thread on a waxed string (dental floss) for drying.	75	1,2,3,4, 5,7,14, 15,16, 18,19
SUPER CAYENNE	Plants grow 2' tall—ideal Cayenne for container growing; very attractive when loaded with thin, red peppers. The fruits are 3–4" long and fiery hot. An All America Winner.	70	11,18,19
SUPER CHILI	Hotter than Jalapeños, but not as hot as Cayenne. The cone-shaped, thin-walled fruits are borne upright on the plants, and grow only 2 1/2" long. Harvest when green or red. As a bonus, the plants work well ornamentally, even indoors in containers.	62	4,5,11, 16,19
TABASCO	*C. frutescens* species. Infamous as the main ingredient in the fiery sauce that shares its name. The small, pointed fruits mature from yellow to orange to red. The plants grow up to 3' tall; each plant can produce over 100 peppers. The fruits are easiest to dry right on the plants. Produces best where the season is long and hot.	80	8,12,14, 16,19
TAM MILD JALAPEÑO (JALAPA)	A milder variety for those who like the flavor of Jalapeño but not the heat. Heavy yields of 2 1/2" fruits; can be used when green, but better flavor when red. Excellent when used on pizza or nachos, in sauces or pickles, or simply sliced with Monterey Jack cheese.	70	4,5,11,19
THAI HOT	Almost as hot as Habaneros! The 1" fruits are like firecrackers! The mound-shaped plants reach a height of 18", blanketed with tiny peppers of green and red held erect above the foliage. The plants can be used ornamentally, particularly in patio containers or even in an annual flower bed. Bring in the house before the first fall frost to enjoy as a houseplant. Widely used in Asian dishes; but go easy—a few fruits go a long way.	75	3,11,12,14
YELLOW CAYENNE	Tapered fruits are 8" long and 3/4" wide; ripens from yellow to dark red.	68	2
ZIPPY	Similar to Cayenne, but much milder. Fruits are 6" long but only 5/8" wide. Usually harvested when green, but matures to red. More zesty than hot, the peppers can even be used in salads or crudité trays.	57	2

* This refers to the time after transplanting of seedlings which were started 8–10 weeks earlier. Time to harvest also refers to when the pepper is generally picked; many gardeners may prefer to wait until the pepper fully ripens or matures, which may be weeks later. Check current seed catalogs for availability and pricing.

Continued →

Studies at the University of Texas and the University of Florida show that close spacing results in more and larger fruit. The leaves of each full-grown pepper plant should be touching those of surrounding neighbors. I've found that most bell peppers should be spaced 18 inches apart and hot peppers about 12 inches.

Peppers need a healthy dose of nutrients at transplanting time to put on enough growth to support large yields. For each plant, dig a hole about 6 inches deep. Add a 2-inch layer of organic matter and a handful of 5–10–10 fertilizer; mix it well with the soil at the bottom of the hole. An old gardening trick is to toss in a book of matches—the sulfur in the matches will make the soil more acidic, which will please the pepper. (Make sure there is some soil between the matches and the roots of the transplant.) A sprinkling of colloidal phosphate will help prevent blossom end rot.

Set each seedling lower in the ground than it was in its pot. If your pepper plants are in peat pots, be sure to bury the entire pot below the soil surface. If any of the peat pot material is above the soil surface, it will act as a wick, drawing water from the plant and eventually killing it. Backfill around the plant and carefully tamp it down with the heels of your hands. Mulch lightly around the base of the plant.

AFTER TRANSPLANTING

Immediately after transplanting, water thoroughly to remove any air pockets in the soil and help settle in the roots. The plant will quickly develop a sturdy root system and will soon tap the nutrients you placed at the bottom of the hole.

To protect young plants, you may want to cover the bed with a floating row cover like Reemay to deter flying insects, keep the plants warm, and prevent wind damage. When the peppers begin to blossom, remove the cover to allow bees and other insects to pollinate the plants.

If an unseasonably cool night threatens after you've transplanted the peppers, protect the plants with Wall O' Waters, cloches, plastic milk jugs, or another form of heavy covering. Don't forget to uncover the plants the next morning or the plants may cook in the noonday sun!

What Do Peppers Need?

WATER!

Remember, peppers are natives of the American tropics, where the humidity is high and it rains almost daily from May to October. Peppers need water from the time you transplant your seedlings until the end of the season. How much depends on where you live and what kind of summer you're having. But wherever you garden, the key to watering peppers is *moderation*. If the soil is too dry, the plants will wilt and refuse to produce fruit. On the other hand, peppers won't tolerate waterlogged roots. The plants will start shedding leaves, exposing fruit to sunscald, or will simply shut down altogether. Too frequent waterings also leach water-soluble nutrients from the topsoil.

A deep, weekly watering that is the equivalent of 1 inch of rainfall is preferred. However, if it is unusually hot and dry for long periods, or if your garden soil is sandy and drains too quickly, you may need to water more frequently. Peppers respond splendidly to trickle or drip irrigation.

The critical time for watering is from flowering through harvest. If the plants are stressed from lack of water, many buds and blossoms will drop. Don't heed the common belief that you can ripen fruits sooner by withholding water or otherwise stressing your pepper plants. Pampered plants will bear far more and better quality peppers.

THE IMPORTANCE OF MULCH

Watering may not be enough during the hot, dry, breezy days of summer when plants transpire moisture rapidly from their leaves. In addition to water in the soil, there must also be enough humidity—the primary benefit of mulch.

A thick, finely-shredded, organic mulch not only keeps weeds at bay and helps the soil retain moisture, it also keeps the humidity high around your peppers. The idea is to supply a wide evaporative area under each plant that will continually pour on the humidity. A mulch made of a mixture of grass clippings, straw, and shredded organic matter works best in my garden. Starting an inch or two from the plant's stem, apply the mulch about 6 inches deep, extending just past the dripline of the plant.

Wait until summer heat begins to peak before applying such a mulch, however. A thick organic mulch will keep the soil cool around the roots—great during the summer, but not in the spring when you want the soil warm. Before applying organic mulch, remove any plastic mulch. This allows the organic mulch to add nutrients to the soil beneath as it breaks down.

PROVIDING A BALANCED DIET

Like most vegetables, peppers need *nitrogen* for sturdy stems and foliage, *potassium* for strong roots, and *phosphorus* for fruit production. The trick is to time feedings right.

Give the plants potassium and phosphorus initially and later in the summer when blossoms appear, with small doses of nitrogen. The 5–10–10 you applied at transplanting time will get the peppers off to a good start. In the third month of growth, when blossoming starts, the plants need more nutrients. Pull back the mulch and side-dress the plants with a sprinkling of 5–10–10 and some bonemeal around the dripline—don't fertilize at the base of the plants. Carefully work the mixture into the soil and replace the mulch. When the fruits are about an inch long, repeat the process.

Peppers often produce lots of flowers but few fruits. This is generally caused by a lack of magnesium. To jump-start production, spray your plants with a solution of Epsom salts just as they start to blossom. This topical application will provide all the magnesium required. Mix 2 teaspoons of Epsom salts in a quart of warm water and spray it on the leaves and blossoms; repeat the process two weeks later. The plants will turn a dark green—followed by a flush of fruit!

Harvesting Peppers

Peppers are fruits, like cucumbers, that are traditionally harvested in an immature stage. Many gardeners, however, have learned that allowing peppers to ripen fully on the vine improves their quality. Peppers can be harvested any time, but the flavor doesn't really develop until maturity.

The dilemma is this: Prompt harvesting improves yields. If you allow the fruits to mature on the plants, they will produce fewer peppers. If you pick the fruits throughout the season, the plants will continue to produce—but you may have fewer ripened peppers. The determinant may hinge on where you live.

In mild, long-season areas, you can allow the peppers to ripen fully before harvest and still expect a second crop. In short-season areas, however, yields will be reduced if you leave all the fruit on the vine until full maturity. The plants wouldn't have time to flower and fruit again before a killing frost. You may have to sacrifice high yields for taste—or vice versa. Seek a balance; leave some peppers on each plant to ripen, and harvest the others throughout the season as they become table-sized.

When picking peppers, it's easy to break off a branch or uproot the whole plant if you're not careful. Use a sharp knife or heavy scissors or shears to harvest the fruits, cutting the tough stems rather than tugging on the plants and risking damage. Leave about 1/2-inch of stem on each pepper. When frost threatens, harvest the remaining fruit—the plants won't survive freezing temperatures.

If possible, eat the peppers on the day you pick them. If not, leave them on the kitchen counter where they'll continue to ripen for the next few days. Don't enclose them in plastic wrap or a plastic bag or toss them into the vegetable crisper of your refrigerator! If you have too many peppers to use right away, consider the following storage options.

Storage

FREEZING

Probably the easiest way to store peppers is in your freezer. Although peppers can be frozen whole, they hog freezer space. A little preparation is recommended.

Choose firm, thick-walled fruits that are blemish-free. Wash them, cut out the stems, remove the seeds, and cut them according to intended use. If you want to use them for stuffing, cut them in half lengthwise. If you want to use the peppers for seasoning in winter soups, stews, casseroles, and spicy sauces, dice them. Cut them into rings or strips for frying. You don't need to blanch the peppers; just pack them into freezer containers or bags; seal, label, and freeze.

Frozen peppers will be soft when thawed, but the flavor will still be there.

CANNING

You can also preserve peppers by canning them. Because they're low-acid fruits, they must be canned under pressure, however. I find it easiest to pickle them. You can pickle your peck of peppers in much the same way you would cukes—either in a crock or processed in jars.

Select a large crock with a lid. Wash the container thoroughly with salt water to make sure it is sterile. Wash the peppers as well, and preferably leave them whole as you put them in the crock. If you're using small peppers, cut two slits in each fruit to allow for complete pickling. If the peppers are extremely large, stem and core them, then cut into quarters. I like to add a few small hot peppers to a crock full of sweets, just to spice things up a bit.

For a simple brine, mix 4 cups of water, 4 cups of vinegar, and 1/2 cup of pickling salt. Add a clove or two of crushed garlic and some fresh herbs. Many people use dill as they would with cukes. But for a really different, pleasant flavor, try adding a few sprigs of fresh mint. Pour the brine over the peppers and cover. Place the crock in a cool place out of the sun and the peppers should be ready to eat in about 2 weeks.

You can also store your pickled peppers in jars. Simply fill cleaned jars with your peppers, then add the garlic and herbs. Bring the brine to a boil and pour it over the peppers, covering by 1/2-inch. Screw on the caps and process in boiling water for 15 minutes. Store the jars in a cool place.

DRYING

Peppers, particularly the thin-walled hot varieties, are easily sun-dried or hot air-dried. It's best to use fully-ripe, red or orange fruits. Even sweet peppers can be dried, but I've found that hot peppers work best.

The easiest way is to allow the fruits to dry right on the plant—either in the garden or by harvesting the entire plant and hanging it upside down in a place that's warm and dry with good air circulation. An open garage or garden shed will work nicely in late summer. Many gardeners thread peppers on a string (dental floss is recommended) and hang them in the kitchen to dry while using them as decoration.

When using tough-skinned peppers, like most of the bell varieties and some hot peppers like Jalapeño and Poblano, it's best to peel them before drying. If you roast them first, the skins are easily removed and the peppers retain that wonderful roasted flavor as they are dried.

Most small peppers can be dried whole, but the larger types need some preparation to speed up the process. Select fully ripe, unblemished fruits. Core and cut the peppers into rings or strips. Then spread them evenly in a single layer, with none of them touching, on a rack to dry. This can be done in the oven at a low temperature for 6—12 hours, in a food dehydrator, or even outdoors in a cool, dry, airy spot that receives direct sunlight. Turn the peppers occasionally to make sure they dry evenly.

The key to drying peppers is to do it s-l-o-w-l-y. The slower they dry, the better they'll retain their color and flavor, and the longer they can be stored. When the peppers are crisp and brittle, they're ready for storage. Place them in airtight containers and store them in a cool, dark area.

When you want to use your dried peppers, you have many options. You can use dried strips as seasoning on meats. Soak whole dried peppers for a few hours (or simmer them) until tender to be used for stuffing. An excellent way to use dried peppers is for grinding into your own powdered seasonings. Remove the stems and seeds from the peppers and grind them to the preferred consistency. A small electric coffee grinder will work fine, but be sure to clean it thoroughly after use. If you're grinding hot peppers like Cayenne, be sure to wear rubber gloves during the process. And be careful not to inhale the powder, or you'll be in for a very nasty surprise! Store the ground peppers in airtight containers to preserve their flavors and pungency.

Sources

1. **Alfrey Seeds**
   P.O. Box 415, Knoxville, TN 37901

2. **W. Atlee Burpee & Co.**
   Warminster, PA 18974

3. **The Cook's Garden**
   P.O. Box 535, Londonderry, VT 05148

4. **Henry Field's Seed & Nursery Co.**
   415 North Burnett, Shenandoah, IA 51602

Continued ➜

5. **Gurney's Seed & Nursery Co.**

   110 Capital St., Yankton, SD 57079

6. **Harris Seeds**

   60 Saginaw Dr., P.O. Box 22960,
   Rochester, NY 14692–2960

7. **Horticultural Enterprises**

   Box 810082, Dallas, TX 75381

8. **J. L. Hudson, Seedsman**

   P.O. Box 1058, Redwood City, CA 94064

9. **Johnny's Selected Seeds**

   Foss Hill Road, Albion, ME 04910–9731

10. **Native Seeds/Search**

    2509 N. Campbell Ave., Tucson, AZ 85719

11. **Park Seed Co.**

    Cokesbury Road, Greenwood, SC 29647–0001

12. **The Pepper Gal**

    P.O. Box 23006, Ft. Lauderdale, FL 33307

13. **Plants of the Southwest**

    1812 Second St., Sante Fe, NM 87501

14. **Redwood City Seed Co.**

    P.O. Box 361, Redwood City, CA 94064

15. **Seeds of Change**

    1364 Rufina Circle, Sante Fe, NM 87501

16. **Shepherd's Garden Seeds**

    30 Irene St., Torrington, CT 06790

17. **Stokes Seeds Inc.**

    P.O. Box 548, Buffalo, NY 14240

18. **Thompson & Morgan Inc.**

    P.O. Box 1308, Jackson, NJ 08527–0308

19. **Tomato Growers Supply Co.**

    P.O. Box 2237, Fort Myers, FL 33902

Grow the Best Asparagus

Michael Higgins

In the early spring, when other fresh vegetables are unavailable, how pleasant it is to have one of the tastiest vegetables ready to harvest. And it is reassuring to know that the harvest will continue each spring for years

to come. A well-prepared asparagus bed, in good soil, should produce abundantly for up to twenty-five years. If you can be patient in the beginning, you will be rewarded by a wonderful return for your labor.

A gourmet treat, expensive when purchased (and never as fresh), asparagus can be grown in almost any garden where there is a cold or dry season to provide it with a dormant period. As a vegetable, the versatile asparagus can be cooked in many ways and dried, canned, or frozen for off-season eating. Low in calories, high in flavor, each serving of four spears (sixty grams) contains only ten calories, with two grams of carbohydrates and one gram of protein. Asparagus is a very good source of thiamin and a good source of vitamin A and riboflavin.

The asparagus plant is a beautiful addition to any location. Few garden sights are more attractive than early dew glistening in the feathery, dark green foliage of the summer plants. In the fall, the asparagus fern turns a bright yellow, and when snow is on the ground, the light brown brush bends high over the white.

CHOOSING A SITE

Although asparagus *can* be grown almost anywhere, good production is based on a carefully chosen site. Plant your asparagus where it will be neither crowded (especially by trees) nor in the way. Remember, asparagus is a perennial, so plan for a permanent location. Allow four feet between the asparagus row and any other planting. Some gardeners put all their asparagus in a single row along the edge of the garden or in a row dividing the flower garden from the vegetable garden. The tall summer and fall foliage makes a pleasant background for an area of colorful flowers. Do not put your bed where the plants will shade nearby crops, unless you want to use that shade to advantage when you need a cool spot to put in midsummer lettuce or other plants that require some shade.

Asparagus itself requires full sun; a slight slope facing south will help to give it an early start. It should not be subjected to strong winds. If a windy location is all you have, it may be necessary to stake the plants once the harvesting season is over.

Ideally, the soil should be a well-drained, rich, sandy loam; heavier clay soils should be conditioned with plenty of organic matter. If you have no place to put your asparagus but in a poorly drained spot, raised beds can help a great deal. To make a raised bed, dig the soil deeply. Add additional organic soil to raise the level of the bed one foot. The sides of the bed can be contained by concrete blocks or railroad ties. Or you can let the sides of the bed slope down naturally. The bed will remain in its loose, "fluffed up" condition as long as you do not walk on it.

Finally, since you may need to irrigate occasionally, a handy water supply can be important.

Starting Plants

You can start your asparagus from seeds or from roots. Growing from seeds is cheaper; growing from roots yields quicker results. When you start from seed, you can plant extra and then select the best plants. Then you will not have to worry about root damage from shipping. In addition, the United States Department of Agriculture is now warning gardeners about a prevalent disease, fusarium rot, and claims that the only way to guarantee disease-free plants is to start with treated seeds. You can treat your own seeds and you may be able to obtain free seeds from a gardening friend with an established bed.

The major disadvantage of planting seeds is the wait before the harvest—about three years, or one year more than you will have if you start with roots. In general then, starting your plants from seeds gives you more control over the quality and is quite a bit less expensive, but does take more time and effort.

If you decide to start from roots, you can save money by obtaining some or all of your plants from the wild. Wild asparagus occurs very widely in sunny, open locations such as old fields and in sandy soil along riverbanks. Also, it often is found along roadsides. These plants may have been polluted from automotive exhausts or defoliants and should not be eaten; however, the roots can be transplanted to your garden. Wild asparagus is not easy to spot in the early spring but can be recognized easily in the summer or fall by the tall feathery foliage that is distinctive to asparagus. So locate a patch in the year preceding your planting time.

Some authorities suggest that varieties growing in the wild have developed natural immunities to help the plants fight off disease. Wild spears tend to be thinner than garden asparagus, but many find them more highly flavored.

In the early spring, dig the wild roots, taking a clump of earth at least a foot across and as deep as you can go—at least a foot deep—for each plant. Some root damage is inevitable since the roots spread laterally for several feet, and the roots in a clump will be intertwined. Remove any weeds, then plant the soil ball in a trench in the garden with the soil ball and the roots several inches deeper than where you found them. Firm the soil, water, and treat as you would any one-year root.

If you want to begin your bed by purchasing year-old bare root crowns, select a variety suited to your area and one resistant to asparagus rust. Here are some recommended varieties. Call your local county extension office for more specific recommendations for growing in your climate.

- California U.C. 157   West Coast
- Roberts strain of Mary Washington   East and Midwest
- Rutgers Beacon   East and Midwest
- Waltham Washington   East and Midwest
- Viking   Northern regions

Before starting plants from seeds, you may want to treat the seeds for a protection against fusarium root rot.

- Soak the seeds for two minutes in a solution of one part laundry bleach and four parts water.

- Rinse the seeds for one minute under cool, running water.

- Plant in soil that has not grown asparagus previously.

The seeds can be started indoors or in a garden seedbed. To start indoors, sow the seed twelve to fourteen weeks before transplanting in the spring when the soil warms up (late December in the Southwest and mid-February in the East).

Use potting soil or a mixture of peat moss, vermiculite, and compost. Plant the seeds three-quarters of an inch deep in two-inch diameter pots (two seeds per pot) or sow the seeds two inches apart in flats. Cover the flats with clear plastic to create a miniature greenhouse and keep the moisture and temperature stable. The temperature should be kept between 75 and 80°F during the day and about 65°F at night. Remove the plastic once the seedlings appear.

Full sunlight is important to the young seedlings. Artificial lights should be used if the plants receive less than twelve to fourteen hours of sunlight a day.

When the soil has warmed up, transplant your seedlings into a temporary garden location. These new plants are not mature enough to be planted deeply in their permanent location. The young seedlings will look like miniature asparagus plants—very ferny. Although asparagus is hardy and reasonably frost-tolerant, it is a good idea to harden off the plants before transplanting. Ten days before you are ready to transplant, cut back on the amount of water and fertilizer you supply. Leave the seedlings outdoors for a few hours each day in a sheltered, sunny location. Gradually build up the time the plants are left outside until they are out night and day. Then you are ready to transplant. Select a temporary location and space the seedlings three inches apart in rows two and one-half feet apart. Only the hardiest of these plants will be selected for the permanent bed.

To start outdoors, sow the seed in a nursery plot of good soil about two weeks before the time tomatoes are normally put in the garden in your area. Select a temporary location and place the seeds one inch deep and three inches apart in the row, with rows two and one-half feet apart. Since asparagus seed is slow to germinate, you may want to mix in some radish seeds to sow in the same row. The radishes will come up early to mark the row and help you see where to weed. Plant three to four seeds for each crown you will want in the permanent bed, and thin to leave the best seedlings.

Whether started indoors or out, the plants will be ready to be moved to their permanent location the following spring. When the plants are still dormant and the ground has thawed, carefully dig the roots with the soil ball intact and plant in prepared trenches.

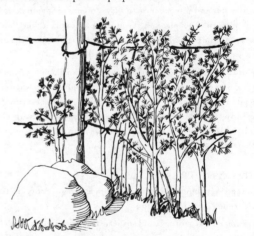

Look for wild asparagus in the summer or fall in sunny open locations, like the edges of old fields. The tall, feathery green foliage is very distinctive.

Making the Permanent Asparagus Bed

Asparagus spears have been known to grow ten inches in one day, and there are records of shoots weighing a third of a pound each! These plants are supported by powerful roots that often extend five or six feet downward and almost that far to each side. This kind of growth requires a well-prepared site as well as continued attention. Your soil should be rich with organic matter. A soil test to check on the acidity and the levels of nitrogen, phosphorus, and potassium will also help in planning. If

Continued →

you do not have access to a home garden soil test kit, get a soil sample container from your county extension agent, take a sample in the summer before planting, and send it in to be analyzed.

SOIL PREPARATION

In the fall prior to planting roots, till in rich organic material such as manure, compost, or animal bedding, or sow a green manure crop. A green manure, or cover, crop is a technique for growing your own fertilizer by growing a crop simply to till into the ground. This will add organic matter and nutrients to the soil. Winter vetch or rye are good green manures. If you are planning to till in leaves, corncobs, animal bedding, or any other relatively coarse material, shredding prior to working them into the soil is sometimes helpful.

If your soil test has indicated a deficiency, add rock phosphate, bone meal, greensand, or wood ashes for phosphorus; wood ashes or greensand for potassium; or an organic fertilizer, such as cottonseed meal, if nitrogen levels are low. If the test shows an acid soil (any pH lower than 6.5 or 6.8) add lime, preferably dolomite for its magnesium content. In clay soils, five and one-half pounds of dolomite will raise the pH of 100 square feet one degree. Light, sandy soils will require only two pounds per 100 square feet. The lime will also improve the soil texture by binding soil particles and allowing air and moisture to be absorbed more readily.

In early spring in the North, or in late fall in the South, till or cultivate deeply to destroy all the weeds and work in the cover crop. Then you will be ready to plant.

CARING FOR THE ROOTS

If the plants have arrived in the mail, open them at once. Sprinkle the roots with water and cover them with a layer of moss or damp newspaper. Keep the stock in a cool place until you are ready to plant, but plan to plant as soon as possible. Take care not to expose the roots to the drying sun or wind.

Before planting the roots, some gardeners soak them overnight in a mixture of water and well-matured compost and plant only when the sky is overcast or in the evening. Strange as it may seem, the best time for putting in any bare root transplant is on a gloomy, cool day with a heavy mist or light drizzle. If you are planting more than one row, cover and water these roots before going to the next row.

DIGGING THE TRENCH

Opinions do vary about the best way to set in asparagus roots. To trench or not to trench is the big question.

Some recent gardening books advocate the simple "no-trench" method. To plant by this method, you mark your row, open a shallow furrow, and plant the roots so that the crowns—the points where the roots converge—are about a half inch below the surface of the ground. Then you cover and firm the soil surface. This method is easy but has one major drawback: the roots are so close to the surface that cultivating and weeding become very difficult. Also, incorporating the necessary amounts of organic materials will be impossible with the roots laced so shallowly. You can grow asparagus with the no-trench method, but your harvest will probably not be those two-inch-thick spears that keep coming year after year!

Most experts, therefore, recommend the tried-and-true trench method. The asparagus trench can be twelve to fifteen inches wide and from twelve to fifteen inches deep. Allow four to five feet between trenches.

If you want to extend your harvest over the longest possible period, vary the depth of your trench. In the spring, the plants that are nearest the surface will send up shoots for an early harvest. Those planted a little deeper will produce later, and the deepest roots will come up later still. You can add about three weeks to the harvest in this way.

Here is how to dig a trench for planting the asparagus at different depths. Dig a trench fifteen inches deep and eighteen inches wide for one-third of the bed. As you remove dirt, put the top five inches of the soil on a ridge on one side of the trench, the bottom ten inches on the other side. You will use some of this ridge of soil (the "top" soil) to fill in the trench once the asparagus is in place; the rest of the ridge of soil will be used to fill in the trench during the growing season, as the shoots emerge.

Dig the second third of the bed twelve inches deep and eighteen inches wide. As you remove the dirt, put the top five inches of dirt on one side of the trench, the bottom seven inches on the other side. For the last third of the bed, dig a trench nine inches deep and eighteen inches wide.

PLANTING THE ROOTS

Fill the bottom eight inches of the deepest part of the trench with compost, well-rotted manure, or rich topsoil. Add seven inches of compost to the second third of the trench, four inches to the shallow end of the trench. Make a slight (one-inch to two-inch) mound every eighteen inches along the trench. Place an asparagus root crown carefully over each mound, spreading the roots out in a circle around the crown, making sure that the small buds on each root are facing up. Two inches of good soil should be placed over the crowns and firmed by hand. Using the "top" soil you dug from the trench, fill in between each mound so that the soil in each third of the trench is level, then water well. Fill in the rest of the trench gradually during the first growing season as the shoots appear. By June, the ridged-up soil should be in the trench, and the entire bed should be level.

During this first season it is especially important not to let the roots dry out. Water once a week, if necessary, enough to wet the soil eight inches deep. Too much water is also harmful—do not let water stand in the trench.

In the spring, the plants that are nearest the surface will send up shoots for an early harvest. Those a little deeper produce later, and the deepest roots come up later still. These later-producing plants, of course, can be harvested a corresponding length of time longer at the end of the season.

You can make the planting simpler by digging the entire trench fifteen inches deep, yet still extend the harvest by using mulch. After you have planted your asparagus as described above, put about five inches of a heavy mulch, such as shredded leaves, over the whole bed. Early in the spring, rake the mulch away from those rows that you want to produce first. The soil will warm up in the bare rows while the mulch will keep the other rows cool and delay the appearance of shoots. It is important to remove all but a fine layer of mulch as soon as the first spears begin to show. This will keep slugs away from the emerging spears. Also, shoots coming up through heavy mulch sometimes have a tendency to curl over.

Digging your entire trench fifteen inches deep has the additional advantage of keeping the asparagus roots deep enough to enable you to use a rototiller for cultivation.

CULTIVATION

A productive asparagus plant has a balance between healthy roots and foliage growth. Both are essential for steady, long-term production. Roots need space; do not plant any other deeply rooted crop within four feet of any asparagus row. After the first season, the deep roots of the asparagus plant will normally draw in enough moisture. However, if dry spells occur, two inches of water applied every two weeks should be sufficient.

It is important to keep the beds weed-free; be especially careful to prevent perennial weeds, such as dock and dandelion, from getting established. In the early spring, weed control and plant feeding can be assisted by tilling or shallowly working in manure or other fertilizers or soil conditioners applied the previous fall. The dried asparagus ferns from the previous season should be tilled in. A light mulch, especially after the first of June, will discourage weed growth and keep the soil loose. Weeds that do appear should be removed as soon as possible. After the cutting season, a heavy mulch of nonacid materials (straw, grass clippings, ground corncobs, well-rotted sawdust) will help keep weeds down and protect soil moisture during the warm months. In the fall, apply manure or other organic fertilizers.

Never cut or remove the foliage until the asparagus has become completely dormant; these ferns produce the energy that the roots store. Only the female plants produce berries (seeds). If you are not trying to save seed for new plants, remove the seeds as soon as they appear.

Harvesting

Although commercial growers usually harvest spears when they are eight to twelve inches high, most gardeners feel that asparagus tastes best when the shoots are about five inches tall. If you are more concerned about quantity, you can wait until the spears are mature, eight or nine inches tall. Experiment with harvest sizes; but do harvest before the heads start to open. This will keep the beds in strong production. It may mean daily harvesting in hot weather. Snap or cut the asparagus at ground level, and be careful not to injure the buds below the surface.

How much should you harvest? It depends on the inherent capacity of the plants themselves. There is no real limit to the number of spears that can be harvested. Plants have been known to produce more than a hundred spears per season and a single asparagus spear may grow as much as ten inches in one day under ideal conditions! This explains the need to be attentive to the plants' requirements for space, moisture, and nutrients.

The first year after planting or transplanting roots, harvest only a few spears or none at all. Those first spears may be hard to resist; so if you do harvest, one or two stalks from each plant should be the limit. The second year you can harvest for two weeks, the third year for four weeks, and in the fourth and following years for eight weeks. These are, of course, only general guidelines. The vigor of the plants, as indicated by the number and size of the shoots, should determine the harvest. Small, slender stalks (the size of a pencil or less) should be left alone. Best production may be expected when the bed is from five to ten years old, and the average length of production for a bed is from fifteen to eighteen years. At that point you will have to decide whether declining production warrants putting in a new bed.

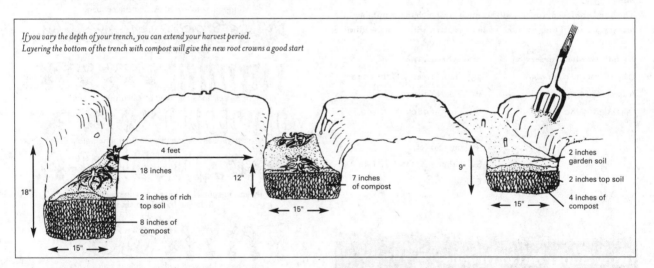

If you vary the depth of your trench, you can extend your harvest period.
Layering the bottom of the trench with compost will give the new root crowns a good start

4 feet
18 inches
12"
18"
2 inches of rich top soil
8 inches of compost
15"
7 inches of compost
15"
9"
2 inches garden soil
2 inches top soil
4 inches of compost
15"

Hot weather may interfere with your harvest when the cutting season is half over, especially if you have used the no-trench method or have staggered planting depths to extend the season. The high temperatures (a week in June with temperatures in the eighties, for example) coupled with the continued harvesting, will cause the plant to overproduce, leading to an eventual decline in plant vigor. You can circumvent this by keeping the soil temperature cool. Ridge five to six inches of soil carefully over the row. This will lower the temperature around the crown and increase spear size. Level the bed with a rake after the last harvest.

Older books on asparagus growing frequently suggest techniques for bleaching or producing a spear with a white base by excluding sunlight from

Continued →

that portion while it is growing. However, modern sources agree that this is extra work for a result that is purely cosmetic. Naturally green asparagus is more tender, better flavored, and richer in vitamins. Bleached spears must be peeled and this further reduces the vitamin content.

Suppliers

There are many reliable sources of asparagus roots and seeds. The best sources may be located in your growing region; it is always best to buy seeds or plants that have been produced in your area, they are more suited to local climate and conditions. If you cannot find asparagus locally, here are a few of the suppliers you might want to order from.

Roots

Buy only year-old roots; two-year and three-year crowns are only more expensive, not better.

Allen Plant Company
P.O. Box 310
Fruitland, MD 21826-0310
(410) 742-7123

Gurney Seed and Nursery Co.
110 Capitol Street
Yankton, SD 57079
(605) 665-1671

Indiana Berry and Plant Co.
5128 West 500 South
Huntingburg, IN 47542
(812) 683-3055

Seed

The number of seeds you buy will be much greater than the number of plants you want. This will allow you to be selective with young seedlings.

Nichols Garden Nursery
1190 N. Pacific Highway
Albany, OR 97321
(541) 928-9280

Stokes Seeds, Inc.
737 Main Street, P.O. Box 548
Buffalo, NY 14240
(716) 695-6980
or
39 James Street
St. Catharines, ON L2R 6R6
Canada

Grow Super Salad Greens

Nancy Bubel

Illustrations by Carol MacDonald

Fitting Greens into Your Garden

There are greens you can grow in every season—even winter. Some garden greens, like spinach, grow quickly and last just a short time. Others, such as chard, remain ready for picking all season long. Heat lovers, such as amaranth and New Zealand spinach, need warm weather to grow in; but they are the exception. Most greens thrive in cool weather. Some, in fact, such as kale and Chinese cabbage, are at their best after frost.

SUCCESSION PLANTS

With some planning, you can pick your own fresh greens from spring through winter. The secret of a continuous harvest is succession planting. You might, for example, plant early spring spinach, followed by green beans bearing in August, with a quick crop of radishes put in after the beans finish. Your summer greens can be grown in the rows where spring peas or scallions have finished. For a fall harvest, you can transplant kale, cabbage, and other good fall greens into spaces left by early radishes or beets. Fall spinach and escarole can follow summer-harvested onions. Most green vegetables do well when seeded right in the row, but you might want to raise some seedlings in flats and have them ready for transplanting to the garden, both to get an early spring start and to save growing time in midseason.

INTERCROPPING

Another way to fit more greens into your garden is to tuck a quick-maturing leafy vegetable, such as spinach or leaf lettuce, in the wide space between your tomato, melon, or squash transplants. By the time the spreading vegetable needs all the room you have allowed for it, the leafy vegetable will have been picked and eaten. Shade from larger vegetables nearby sometimes helps to keep some spring vegetables, such as spinach, producing for an additional week before going to seed in the summer warmth and longer days.

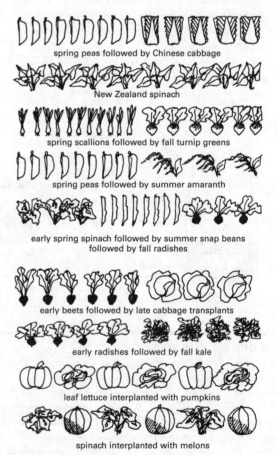

spring peas followed by Chinese cabbage

New Zealand spinach

spring scallions followed by fall turnip greens

spring peas followed by summer amaranth

early spring spinach followed by summer snap beans followed by fall radishes

early beets followed by late cabbage transplants

early radishes followed by fall kale

leaf lettuce interplanted with pumpkins

spinach interplanted with melons

By using succession planting and intercropping, you can grow an extensive variety of greens in a small space.

Making a Raised Bed, 3 feet by 6 feet.
1. Dig a 6-foot trench, 1 foot wide and 1 foot deep. Remove the dirt to a garden cart.
2. Widen the trench by digging up additional soil.
3. Continually throw the loosened soil well ahead of where you are digging.
4. Add 2 or 3 bushels of compost or manure.
5. Pat the raised sides of the bed smooth and rake the top.

What Greens Need

The secret of growing any special crop is to find out what it needs and to meet these needs as closely as you can. Greens do have certain general requirements (and some individual ones as well), but these are not hard to meet.

COOL TEMPERATURES

With some exceptions, most greens grow best and taste best in cool weather—spring, fall, and sometimes winter. Luckily, there are a few that prefer hot weather, so you need never be without garden greens as long as you can keep planting. And some—like parsley, chard, cabbage, and others—will produce all summer and into the fall in spite of heat.

RICH SOIL

Since they grow quickly and leafily, greens need plenty of nitrogen—a pretty rich soil. Chard and parsley, both deep-rooted plants, are exceptions here. They do well in soil that is not especially rich, perhaps because their roots can delve deeply to find nourishment in the subsoil that other more shallow-rooted plants miss.

Compost, animal manure, and turned-under green manure plantings, such as clover or rye, will boost both fertility and humus content of the soil. Humus is especially helpful to shallow-rooted greens because it holds moisture at root level, available when the plant needs it. For a quick boost during the growing season, you might also want to give your leafy greens an extra dose of manure tea, blood meal, or diluted fish emulsion (available at garden stores and hardware stores).

Green Manure Plantings. These soil improvers are dug or plowed under while still tender and green, before they go to seed. Legumes, such as clover, vetch, and

In hot weather, most greens will bolt to seed and become bitter tasting.

soybeans, add nitrogen to the soil. Rye has an extensive root system which is as valuable as the top growth for soil enrichment. Examples of good seasonal green manure crops are clover for spring, buckwheat for summer planting, rye for late summer or early fall planting.

Adjusting Soil Acidity. With the exception of parsley, most greens like soil that is nearly neutral or only slightly acid. If your soil grows especially good blueberries, potatoes, azaleas, and rhododendrons, it may be on the acid side. You can test for soil acid levels with a home soil testing kit, available at most garden supply stores. To sweeten acid soil for greens, add limestone, powdered oyster shell, wood ashes, bone meal, chalk or marble dust. Spread about ten to fifteen pounds of limestone on a ten-foot by twenty-foot garden plot.

Proper spacing is important. Thin most greens so that they just miss touching.

WATER

For tenderness, rapid growth, and mild flavor, greens need a good supply of water. If a week goes by without an inch of rain, you will get better greens and more of them if you water the plants. Shallow-rooted greens, such as lettuce, are more adversely affected by drought than deeply rooted chard or parsley.

Great Greens to Grow

What greens should you add to your next seed order? We suggest, for starters, growing some familiar greens—lettuce and chard, perhaps. Then choose one you have tasted but have not grown—maybe endive, collards, or kale. To assure a continuous supply, you might also want to agree with a friend to grow different greens and trade your surplus. Then next year, try some more new varieties, until you arrive at a succession of greens that is just right for your garden and your family.

The greens listed here can be grown in conventional narrow rows or in wide rows (twelve to twenty-four inches) or in raised beds. In wide

Continued ➡

rows or raised bed plantings, space the plants the same distance apart in all directions, using the recommended row spacings given here.

We recommend wide-row plantings for most greens. The wide rows enable the plants to shade the soil, keeping it cooler. Also, it prevents mud from splashing up onto the foliage. These leaf lettuce seedlings should be thinned so the leaves just miss touching.

CABBAGE

Although it is usually grown for its solid head, cabbage offers a bonus in the green leaves loosely surrounding the head. Save these nutritious, darker green leaves to make stuffed cabbage. Jersey Wakefield and its yellows-resistant form, Jersey Queen, are among the best-tasting cabbages for fresh eating. The heads are not quite as tightly wrapped as the more solid storage cabbages, such as Penn State Ballhead, but the flavor is excellent.

Cabbage

Planting. Cabbage likes rich, moist soil and plenty of sun. Both the young seedlings (if properly hardened) and the mature heads can stand a few degrees of frost, so cabbage can be one of the first vegetables in your garden patch, and the last vegetable out. It is safe to set the seedlings out two to three weeks before your average last frost date. Better not put them out much earlier than that, though. Although the cold may not kill them, it often makes the heads tough and fibrous. Early cabbage can be spaced eighteen inches apart. Fall cabbage, with its larger heads, should be spaced to allow two feet between plants.

To get a head start in spring, raise seedling cabbages indoors (under fluorescent lights or at a sunny window), planting seed about four weeks before your safe planting-outside date. Cabbage seeds tend to germinate very thickly, so try to space them about an inch apart. Thin the seedlings to a two-inch spacing so that they will not be forced to develop long weak stems in a search for light.

Care. Late cabbage appreciates a side-dressing of manure tea when heads begin to form. If the cabbage looper, the larva of the white cabbage moth, is eating holes in your cabbage, try spraying with Dipel or Thuricide, commercial preparations of a bacterial disease, *Bacillus thuringiensis*, that affects only moth and butterfly larvae. Sometimes maturing cabbage heads split after a thorough rain. To prevent this, twist or pull the stalk to break some feeder roots so the head will absorb less water.

Harvest. Pick cabbage as soon as the head is solid enough to be worth using. You might also harvest a second crop of small heads that grow around the stump after the main head is removed. To encourage this bonus crop, cut the heads off carefully, leaving a good three inches of stump. Within a month, you will see new, secondary heads forming.

Mature, solid heads of cabbage store well in root cellars. Pull the plants up, root and all, and wrap each head in newspaper. Then place the heads, roots up, on slatted shelves in a cold, but not freezing, dark place.

SWISS CHARD

Old Faithful to many gardeners, Swiss chard produces all summer and fall from spring-sown seeds. It often lives over the winter with some protection, thanks to its deep, strong root. Chard comes in both the regular form—white stalks and puckered green leaves—and the red-stalked rhubarb chard, a bright note in the summer greens garden. Mature chard grows twenty to twenty-four inches high.

Swiss chard

Planting. Sow about eight seeds to the foot, four or five weeks before your last frost date, and thin the plants to stand eight to ten inches apart. (Eat the thinnings!)

Care. Mulching in dry weather helps to keep tender leaves coming, but chard has such a deep root that it is pretty independent. It is one leafy green that thrives in poor soil. In good soil, no side-dressings are needed. Insects are seldom a problem with chard.

Harvest. Pick the leaves as soon as they grow to a height of six to eight inches, and continue to pick all summer. When the plants grow large, take only the smaller inner leaves, up to ten inches or so. The larger outer leaves have a coarser flavor and are not as tender. If the plant gets ahead of you, you can cut the stalks down to a height of three to four inches in midsummer, and it will produce tender new leaves in a few weeks. Compost your tough cuttings, or feed it to your livestock.

COLLARDS

A nonheading member of the cabbage family, the collard plant has a strong central stem, twenty-four-inch to thirty-six-inch stalk, and many nutritious spoon-shaped leaves. Collards are hardy, robust, and easy to grow.

Planting. Start seedling plants indoors for a summer crop, planting seeds three or four weeks before your safe planting-outside date, which can be two to three weeks before the date of your average last frost. For a fall harvest, sow seeds in the garden row in late spring. Space the plants two feet apart.

Collard greens

Care. A side-dressing of manure tea or diluted fish emulsion when the plants are half grown is a nice extra, but not really necessary unless your soil is poor. Combat flea beetles and cabbage moth larvae as suggested under cabbage.

Harvest. The flavor of collards is best after a frost. Pick the individual leaves and also the central rosette of leaves on the top of the plant.

ENDIVE AND ESCAROLE

Endive has narrow, curly, fringe-cut leaves growing in an open crown like a loose-leaf lettuce. It has a slightly bitter flavor that adds zest to salads and soups when mixed with other greens. Escarole is a broad-leafed form of endive with a somewhat milder, good-bitter tang. When blanched, the leaves have a very mild flavor.

Escarole

Planting. For the spring crop, plant endive and escarole indoors and set out plants a month before the last frost. An early crop is best because escarole will turn bitter and go to seed in hot weather. The best crop is the one you pick in fall, from plants started in July and transplanted into the garden, or from seed sown right in the row. Thin the plants to a twelve-inch spacing. (If you intend to tie them up to blanch the leaves, eight inches apart is enough.)

Care. Endive and escarole require little care, other than normal attentiveness to keeping weeds down and soil moisture up. Insects do not seem to be interested in these good salad plants. Like most leafy greens, endive and escarole are at their best when grown quickly in moist, good soil. If your soil is marginal, give the plants an extra dose of manure tea or fish emulsion fertilizer. If you do tie up the leaves to blanch them, do it on a dry day, or the moisture on the crown will encourage spoilage.

Endive

Harvest. Pick individual leaves in early fall if you are short of garden greens, or let the whole head develop and cut the entire crown off if you have plenty of plants. You can also cut just the central rosette of leaves, leaving the outer leaves. A new smaller center will grow back within a month.

Endive and escarole are more frost hardy than lettuce and often live until late fall. Sometimes they will even live over the winter in a cold frame, if given extra protection like a light blanket of leaves or straw. If you have flourishing endive plants in your garden at the time of hard frost, you might want to try lifting a few of them and bringing them into a cool basement or unheated porch. They will be a cut above anything you can buy at the store in the dark of December. If you replant the heads in buckets, they should last another two weeks at least.

KALE

This super vegetable earns its place in any garden because it is very high in vitamin content, low in calories, winter-hardy, and almost pest-free. Kale is another member of the large and varied cabbage family, the brassicas. It has deeply ruffled, sturdy leaves on a stem that reaches a height of eighteen to twenty-four inches. There is a spring-growing kale—the variety Hanover—but since the flavor is greatly improved by frost, most gardeners raise kale as a fall crop.

Planting. For fall kale, plant seeds in the row or in flats for transplanting, in May or early June. If you do not have space in the garden then to sow seeds, keep the seedlings growing in flats until you have an empty row or can find space for them between other plants. Space the plants about eighteen inches apart.

Care. Since kale spends a good many months in the garden, a good layer of mulch will help to reduce your seeding chores and to maintain soil moisture as well. Kale has fairly shallow roots for such a hardy vegetable. Since it produces over such a long period of time, many gardeners like to give their kale an extra feeding in early fall. Insect pests are rare, except for aphids, which sometimes attack the weaker plants. Try hosing them off with a strong spray of water.

Harvest. For most people, kale harvest begins right after the first frost, and continues all winter when the kale is well mulched and/or protected by a blanket of snow. Pluck individual leaves, counting on one or two per serving. Kale does not mush down and lose volume when cooked as many other greens do. Wintered-over plants often produce a new crop of tender, young leaves in spring before going to seed.

HEAD LETTUCE

Most commercially grown head lettuce is rather heavily sprayed with pesticides. And yet it is so easy to grow your own which, in a healthy garden surrounded by different kinds of plants, needs no spraying at all. The crisp, crackling heads are a real ego-builder for the gardener; they look lovely in the row and on the table.

Head lettuce (Ithaca)

Planting. The important thing with head lettuce is to get it going well while the weather is still cool, because it gets bitter and bolts to seed in hot weather. To do this, you will need to raise your own plants, sowing seeds in flats indoors five to seven weeks before the safe planting-outside time—about one month before your frost-free date. Light frost will not hurt the seedlings, but they should be covered if there is a threat of heavy frost. Space the seedlings a foot apart when you plant them out, and snip off the outer leaves, so there will be less surface area for the disturbed rots to support. For fall head lettuce, sow seed outdoors in late July or early August.

Care. Lettuce has a very shallow root system, so it needs rich soil and a steady supply of moisture. Mulch will help to keep the roots cool. You may need to water the plants if a week goes by without rain. Insects do not bother lettuce, but slugs can be a problem in a wet season. Trap them under halved grapefruit rinds or in jar lids into which you have poured beer or baker's yeast solution.

Bottom rot is a fungus disease that produces rusty spots on leaves and eventual rotting of the plant, starting on the bottom leaves. It affects lettuce varieties that have ground-hugging bottom leaves more than those that grow upright. Preventative measures include adequate spacing between plants, crop rotation, and not planting lettuce in poorly drained ground.

Harvest. This delicate crop must be used and enjoyed while it is in its prime, so start cutting the first heads while they are still small. As you work your way down the row day after day, the heads will grow larger and firmer, until the hot weather comes; then they turn bitter and go to seed.

Continued →

LEAF LETTUCE

One of the earliest garden greens, and all the more appreciated after a cold, leafless winter, leaf lettuce and butterhead lettuce contain more vitamins A and C than head lettuce.

Leaf lettuce (Buttercrunch)

Looseleaf lettuce, which forms a ruff of individual, loosely joined leaves, is earliest of all, ready in forty-two to forty-eight days from seed. Black-Seeded Simpson, one of the earliest at forty-two days, is also one of the best, with crinkly, tender leaves. Oakleaf and Salad Bowl are other good looseleaf lettuces. Salad Bowl is slower to go to seed in hot weather, although all looseleaf lettuces do send up seed stalks and form bitter leaves when weather turns really warm. Ruby looseleaf lettuce is popular with many gardeners and chefs for its red-tinged leaves.

Butterhead lettuces form a loose, soft head of wrapped leaves, blanched in the center, with dark green outer leaves. They tend to be somewhat more crisp than looseleaf lettuces. Bibb and Boston are good butterhead kinds; but they go to seed rapidly in warm weather. Kagran is not as crisp as Buttercrunch, and has lighter green leaves, but stands summer heat even better.

Planting. Sow lettuce seed as soon as the ground can be worked in early spring. Lettuce seed germinates well in cold weather; in fact, very hot weather may severely retard germination. (You can get around this difficulty by prechilling the seed for summer plantings and covering them very lightly, if at all, when you put them in the ground.) The seed is fine and, under good conditions, germinates well, so be sure to avoid sowing it too thickly, which just wastes seed and crowds the plants. You might want to mix the seed with a cup or so of sand and sprinkle the mixture down the row. This also shows how far you have planted, in case you are interrupted—you know, the wind takes your hat, the cat starts to rake the other end of the row, the children arrive home from school. Plant seeds every seven to fourteen days in small patches for a continuous crop.

Care. Keep the lettuce well thinned; there should be just enough space between plants so that the leaves just miss touching. With their shallow root systems, leaf lettuce and butterhead lettuce need a good supply of moisture and plenty of nitrogen in the soil. In summer, try giving the leaf lettuce some shade by growing it in the shadow of pumpkin vines, sticking leafy twigs in the soil beside it, or draping netting over it. If you keep the lettuce cool, it will not go to seed quite as soon.

Harvest. Lettuce planted in early April is ready for the first pickings in late May. You can pick individual leaves at first, but whole plants are crisper.

PARSLEY

More than a garnish, French curly and Italian parsley are easy-to-grow, vitamin-rich plants that can be eaten every day. If you grow a surplus, you can dry some for winter.

Planting. Unlike most other greens, parsley does well in acid soil. It even tolerates light shade and does not mind heavy soil either. A very agreeable plant! The only complaint we gardeners have about parsley is that the seed is slow to germinate. To cut a week or two from the usual three-week to four-week germination period, soak the seed briefly in water to cover, drain, and place it in a plastic bag for a week before planting. Seed can be planted as early in spring as the ground can be worked. It is a good idea to scatter a few radish seeds along the row to mark the place so you don't forget and plant something else there.

Care. Just keep parsley weeded and enjoy picking. Mulch can help to prevent splashing of mud on the leaves, as well as to control weeds and keep the soil moist. Parsley develops a fairly deep tap root so it does not need a lot of extra water or fertilizer; nevertheless, it appreciates a boost if conditions are lean.

Harvest. You can start snipping the perky green leaves as soon as they are big enough to be worth picking, and the stems are long enough to permit cutting. Keep the plant cut back by continuously picking the new growth; new, tender leaves will continue to appear. If you want to pot up a parsley plant to grow indoors over the winter, choose a young one. The deep tap root of mature plants suffers in transplanting.

To dry parsley, chop the leaves or cut with kitchen scissors, spread them on a cookie sheet, and place the sheet in an oven at the lowest possible setting—about 140°F—for several hours, until the leaves crumble readily. Leave the oven door open an inch or so.

ROMAINE

Also called cos lettuce, romaine is a sweet lettuce that has closely folded leaves growing in a rather firm, upright head. The plant grows nine to twelve inches tall, with tender green leaves on top and thicker, crisp stalks at the base. Early varieties, such as Cosmo MC, mature in fifty-eight days from seed; midseason types, such as Winter Density, take around sixty-four days. (Both are available from Johnny's Selected Seeds.) Paris White Cos, one of the older standard romaine varieties, may take as long as eighty-three days from seed to picking.

Romaine

Planting. Start seedlings indoors for an extra-early spring crop, or plant the seeds in the row in early spring. Start fall seedlings outdoors in late July or early August. Space the plants about a foot apart in the row.

Care. Like other lettuces, romaine is about 95 percent water, so it needs a steady supply of moisture. Plenty of nitrogen will encourage good leafy growth. Humus in the soil will hold water within reach of the plant's shallow roots.

Harvest. Pick whole heads as soon as they begin to head up. Hot weather will cause bolting and leaf-tip burn (brown-edged leaves).

SPINACH

Spring spinach appears on the table soon after the first green onion tops and just before the first lettuce. That's the time to enjoy it—before the weather gets hot, and the spinach bolts to seed. In most varieties of spinach, the ground-hugging rosette of thick green leaves is deeply crumple, or "savoyed," as the seed catalogues say.

Spinach

Planting. Plan to sow spinach seeds as soon as the ground has dried out enough to dig. Sow the seeds one inch apart. Thin the plants to three inches apart as they grow. Late July or early August plantings will give you a fall crop of spinach. To improve germination in hot weather, chill the seeds for several days before planting. Tiny seedlings of September-planted spinach will often live over the winter under mulch, ready to resume growing in spring. Winter Bloomsdale is a good variety for wintering-over.

Care. Spinach grows quickly when it has good soil, cool weather, and plentiful moisture. Lime your spinach row if your soil is acid (see What Greens Need, above). Since early spring months are often wet and muddy, it is a good idea to mulch around the spinach to keep those low-growing leaves out of the mud.

Harvest. Pluck individual leaves as soon as they are large enough to be worth taking. Eat all the thinnings, and pull or cut whole plants. Count on about forty-five days from seed to harvest for spinach. You can shear the plants off in midspring, leaving a two-inch stub; they will grow back for one more cutting. Enjoy spinach as the fleeting special spring treat that it is. When days grow longer and warmer, it will grow tough and bitter and go to seed no matter what you do.

Grow the Best Root Crops

Weldon Burge

Soil Preparation

The key to growing the best root crops is in proper soil preparation. Root crops need a loose, friable soil that is deeply worked and drains well. They also require more phosphorus and less nitrogen than leaf and cole crops, and heavy feeders like corn and melons. An overabundance of nitrogen, in fact, causes some root crops to produce bushy tops and hairy, spindly, or forked roots.

Till the seedbed to a depth of 6 to 8 inches. As you do so, work in plenty of organic matter to improve the soil. This is particularly helpful if you have a clay soil. I use a balanced compost containing a variety of organic materials, including leaves, wood ashes, old straw, weeds, pine needles, and garden residues. The compost helps the soil retain moisture without getting waterlogged, allowing air to circulate around the roots, and keeps the soil thriving with beneficial microorganisms and earthworms. I also add clean sand to help drainage, then rake the soil to remove all rocks and clods.

If you use a commercial fertilizer, select 0–20–0 (also known as superphosphate) for your root crop bed. Rock phosphate is an excellent source of phosphorus, and superphosphate is simply rock phosphate treated with acid to make the phosphorus more accessible in the soil. Sprinkle the fertilizer over the bed, about 8 pounds per 100 square feet of garden, and rake it into the top inch of soil where young feeder roots can best use it. Bone meal is also high in phosphorus but releases its nutrients slowly over the season. Use it with long-season root crops like parsnips and salsify.

RAISED BEDS

Experienced gardeners agree: root crops produce best in raised beds, planted in blocks rather than single-file rows. If you have a heavy clay or shallow soil, growing long root crops like carrots, parsnips, and salsify is next to impossible without a raised bed.

Why grow root crops in raised beds?

1. Root crops are cool-weather vegetables. The earlier you can plant them in the spring, the better. A raised bed warms and dries out faster than surrounding ground, permitting earlier sowings. This is particularly beneficial in areas that receive much spring rain. Raised beds drain well and seldom puddle after a downpour.

2. A raised bed has deeper, looser topsoil and more concentrated nutrients than surrounding ground, allowing for better root development. The beds are easier to prepare, and you have better control over the soil's friability and fertility.

3. Because you can walk in the pathways between the beds, rather than on the beds themselves, soil compaction is eliminated.

4. Raised beds are easier to weed and harvest because they are 6 to 12 inches higher than the ground. I usually sit on the frame as I'm working in the bed. Root crops must be sown and thinned, a back-breaking chore without a raised bed!

5. Using the square-foot method in each raised bed, I've found it much easier to plan and sow root crops in succession, sowing a block at a time. I get double the production that I would in a single-file row. Close spacing in blocks saves limited garden space, smothers weeds, keeps the soil cool and moist, and makes thinning and harvesting easier.

My raised beds are contained in 4' x 8' frames, 6 inches high, made of pressure-treated lumber. When starting a new bed, I stake out a 4' x 8' area, then dig it by hand with a spade to a depth of about 12 inches. I construct the frame over the prepared area, then fill the frame with a mixture of topsoil, compost, sand, and peat moss. Nothing could be better for growing the tastiest carrots and parsnips!

I've discovered only one disadvantage for growing root crops in a raised bed. The perimeter dries out faster than the rest of the bed. If not watered regularly, plants near the edge of the bed can bolt and produce tough, bitter roots. A mulch often prevents this problem.

Root Crop Descriptions

When planning your seedbeds, consider the root crops you already enjoy and those you'd like to try, then open some seed catalogs and do some armchair shopping.

Following are capsule descriptions of each of the major root crops—their particular growth habits, sowing and growing tips, recommended varieties, and suggestions for kitchen preparations—to help you along.

Beets
(Beta vulgaris)

THE BEST VARIETIES

My favorite spring varieties are Early Wonder, Red Ace, and Ruby Queen, but don't limit your selection to just those. If you plan to pickle or can beets, plant the long slicing varieties, Cylindra, Forono, and Formanova. These carrotlike beets are smooth and tender, without side

Continued ➔

roots. Slices are bite-size and uniform canning.

If you're tired of red-stained sinks, bowls, and kitchen counters, try Golden beets. They don't "bleed" like their red relatives. They don't become as woody or as poor in flavor when left in the ground too long (but they taste better when small). They have bright orange skin and succulent yellow flesh, a wonderful alternative to regular red beets. If you have trouble getting your kids to eat red beets, try some Golden beets. The only disadvantage with Golden beets is their low germination rate, which means only that you have to sow the seeds thicker than you'd normally plant beet seeds.

Albino White beets don't bleed either. But they remind me too much of turnips. I prefer a beet with color. Try Chioggia instead, an Italian specialty beet with alternating rings of white and bright pink.

The best beets for winter storage are Detroit Dark Red and Long Season, also known as Lutz Green Leaf and Winter Keeper. The latter is particularly recommended, for it produces large roots that can remain in the soil, under a heavy straw mulch, all winter long without forfeiting quality.

SOWING AND GROWING

Beets thrive in cool weather, so plan spring and fall plantings. Although they can't tolerate scorching summer heat, they can stand a light frost. I plant beets about two weeks before the last frost in spring (garden conditions permitting), sowing them in succession every two weeks until June. Then I make one large planting about ninety days before the first frost in the fall.

A beet "seed" is actually a fruit containing several seeds. When they germinate, a small clump of plants results, requiring thinning. I sow the seeds about 2 inches apart in square-foot blocks, about 1/2 inch deep. The seedlings sprout in about two weeks if the soil temperature is below 50° F; one week at 65° F. To avoid pulling up whole clumps of seedlings, carefully pinch out the unwanted plants when thinning. Thin the beets to about 3 to 4 inches apart (closer for Cylindra beets), then mulch with clean straw.

The quality of home-grown beets depends on rapid, uninterrupted growth with a steady moisture supply. If your soil is heavy, soften it by working in plenty of sand and organic matter. Otherwise, the beets will be spindly and as tough as bullets. Beets like a pH of 6.5 to 8.0 and won't produce well in acidic soil. Sweeten the soil with about a pound of lime for each square yard of bed. Hot, dry soil toughens the roots, making them fibrous. Keep the soil moist, not saturated, for the best-tasting beets. A light mulch around the young beets also hinders weeds and helps the soil retain moisture for plumper, juicier beets.

Beets are especially sensitive to boron deficiency. To avoid blackspot, sickly growth, and poor taste, make sure your soil contains this trace element. It's difficult to test for boron, but only minute amounts are needed. Mulching with compost is all that's necessary. Use a variety of organic materials and you shouldn't have boron problems.

HARVESTING AND STORAGE

The best beets are young, only 1 to 2 inches in diameter, about the size of a golf ball. The only exception is Long Season. The large roots may develop woody centers, but these slip out easily after cooking.

Storage beets, harvested in late fall, shouldn't be pulled until a frost threatens, preferably after a dry spell. Where winters are mild, store the roots right in the ground under 8 to 12 inches of straw to keep the soil from freezing. Otherwise, pull the beets and let them "cure" in the sun a few hours before topping and moving them into the root cellar or basement. Top the roots, leaving about 1/2 inch of stems above the crowns, then pack them in moist sand. Stored beets need high humidity and a temperature just above freezing, about 35° F. If properly handled, they'll store for three to four months.

Beets can be stored briefly in the refrigerator vegetable bin if placed in a plastic bag previously punched with holes for ventilation. Beets are also easily canned, pickled, or frozen.

Carrots

(*Daucus carota* var. *sativus*)

THE BEST VARIETIES

Most gardeners grow carrots for the same reasons—high yield in a limited space, showy foliage, and, of course, their great taste. Unfortunately, many novice gardeners make the mistake of sowing long carrots like Goldpak and Imperator in a heavy clay soil, resulting in forked, malformed roots. After that first failed attempt, they refuse to grow carrots again. If you've had trouble growing carrots, consider the following tips.

The trick to growing carrots is selecting varieties that will produce best in your garden's soil conditions. The long, slender carrots sold commercially require a soil so deep, friable, and smooth that they're virtually impossible for most home gardeners to grow. Unless you have a deep, loose soil free of obstructions, best plant shorter varieties like Nantes Half Long, Goldinhart and the Chantenay types. A new variety, A-Plus, is recommended for its higher vitamin A content.

If your soil is extremely heavy, try the beet-shaped carrots, like Gold Nugget, Kundulus, Oxheart and Planet. Beet-shaped carrots offer high yields in a small space. These are the best carrots for the patio garden. Because they can be grown close together and have short roots, they can be planted in window boxes or any container at least 6 inches deep.

Experiment until you find the varieties that grow the best in your garden. Carrots are easy to grow when you use the proper varieties. No matter what type of soil you have, you can find a variety that will produce well in your garden.

SOWING AND GROWING

Soil preparation is important for tasty carrots. During early stages of growth, the carrot's taproot must meet no resistance in the soil. If a root meets a rock or impenetrable clay, it will branch or simply stop growing. Carrots need a stone-free, deeply worked soil that drains well. Too much water and the carrots may develop cavity spot—black spots near the crown of the root which break down, leaving unsightly rotting cavities. Improper soil conditions account for most of the problems experienced with carrots.

Carrots produce best in raised beds. Till the soil to a depth of at least 8 inches, adding plenty of compost. Organic matter lightens the soil, helps retain moisture, and remedies boron and manganese deficiencies. No manure, please, unless well rotted. Excess nitrogen causes branching and hairy, fibrous roots. Potassium, on the other hand, promotes solid, sweet carrots. Wood ashes contain highly soluble potassium, which reaches the plants quickly. As you prepare the bed, work wood ashes into the top 4 inches of the soil, where feeder roots thrive. Then rake the bed smooth of rocks and clods.

Carrots are cool-weather vegetables, so start sowing about two weeks before the last expected frost in your area, garden conditions permitting. Make successful plantings every three weeks until July. Make furrows about 3/4 inch deep, spacing the furrows 4 inches apart. Place a 1/2-inch layer of sifted peat moss in the bottom of each furrow, sow the seeds sparingly on top, then cover the seeds with about 1/4 inch of the peat moss. To help germination, cover the bed with burlap bags, soak them, and keep the bed moist until the carrots sprout. Remove the burlap and water the beds daily until the seedlings are well established, then mulch with clean straw.

When sowing the seeds, try to space them 1/2 inch apart—no easy task but worth the effort when it comes time to thin. Because carrots are slow to germinate, gardeners often mix radish seeds with the carrot seeds to mark the rows.

The first few weeks after sowing determine if you'll have a bumper or a bummer crop. Carrots can't tolerate a deep planting in a dry bed, so the trick is to offer them a shallow sowing with even moisture. The seedlings grow slowly and can't compete with weeds. Hand weeding is recommended until the carrots are 2 inches tall. Thin the carrots to 3-inch spacings, then mulch with chopped leaves, pine needles, and compost to keep the weeds at bay. Mulching also helps the soil retain moisture and prevents "green shoulder," which is caused by exposing the crowns of the carrots to the sun, making the roots bitter.

HARVESTING AND STORAGE

Most varieties are ready for harvest in less than three months. The largest carrots will have the darkest, greenest tops, but don't leave the roots in the ground too long or they'll be tough. Most carrots are at their prime when they're about an inch in diameter at their crowns.

When harvesting, drench the bed with water first, making the carrots easier to pull. When you find a carrot large enough, grasp the greens at the crown and gently tug with a twisting motion. If the greens snap off, carefully lift the roots with a spading fork. Use damaged roots first and store unblemished roots for later use.

There are three ways to store fresh carrots: leave them in the ground under a heavy mulch, store them in a root cellar or underground barrel, or keep them in the crisper bin of the refrigerator. The thick-cored varieties store the best. If you want to preserve them longer, you can freeze or can them with little difficulty.

Celeriac

(Apium graveolens var. rapaceum)

Most gardeners love fresh, crunchy celery, but few grow it. Celery is a difficult crop, requiring a long season of mostly cool, moist weather and plenty of pampering. Celeriac, on the other hand, gives you the flavor of celery, is easy to grow, doesn't need blanching, and is a wonderful winter keeper.

Celeriac is a member of the parsley family, and closely related to celery, carrots, and parsnips. Sometimes called "celery root" or "celery knob," it is prized for its hairy, softball-size root that tastes like celery with a sweet hint of anise, and has a nutlike texture. The "root" is really the swollen stem base of the plant, with rough brown skin and white flesh like a turnip.

Celeriac fetches more than $3 per pound at gourmet shops. Considering that a packet of seeds (costing about $1.25) can produce several hundred plants, gardeners can truly celebrate this close cousin of celery.

THE BEST VARIETIES

Celeriac is an Old World vegetable thought to have originated in Mediterranean regions, although ancient Chinese texts show that Asiatic people also grew it. It didn't become popular in Europe until the 1700s. Now, it's a common winter vegetable in France, Germany, most of Eastern Europe, and the Scandinavian countries.

Americans still haven't discovered celeriac. Almost no hybridizing is done here. Large Smooth Prague is the most familiar variety, but newer hybrids have far better quality. Try Alabaster, Globus and Marble Hall. The best variety I've grown is Jose, which resists pithiness and hollow heart and has sharp white flesh. Because it is compact and tolerates close spacing, Jose is the best celeriac for the small garden.

SOWING AND GROWING

Like celery, celeriac requires a long growing season, 100 to 120 days. In short-season areas, seedlings must be started indoors. I start my seeds indoors in late February, about 10 to 12 weeks before the last frost. Presoak the seeds overnight to hasten germination, then sow the seeds sparingly in 2 1/2-inch pots. Celeriac seeds take up to three weeks to sprout, so keep the soil moist and warm (70° F) until the seedlings appear. Never allow the soil to dry out. When the seedlings are about an inch tall, thin to the strongest plant per pot.

Celeriac needs a little cold weather before summer, but the seedlings shouldn't be transplanted until outside temperatures rise above 45° F or they'll produce stalks at the expense of fat bulbs. Most gardeners wait until the apple blossoms fall before moving their plants into the garden. I usually harden off the seedlings in a cold frame the last week of March, then transplant them into the garden the first two weeks of April. Space the plants about 8 to 12 inches apart in the bed, then cover them with a cloche or spun-bonded material to protect them from an unexpected frost. To give the plants a good start, add some soluble fertilizer to your watering can, fill with water, and soak the soil around each plant immediately after transplanting.

Although celeriac is less susceptible to heat and drought than celery, the plants grow best in a deep, rich soil that supplies plenty of moisture, yet drains well. Till the soil to a depth of at least 8 inches, working in plenty of well-rotted manure, compost, wood ashes, and sand to provide drainage. Celeriac thrives when the soil pH is between 6.0 and 6.5.

When the plants are established in the garden, supply ample water throughout the summer, especially during dry spells. Remember, wild varieties of celery and celeriac grow in marshy

Continued ➜

regions. If the plants don't receive steady moisture throughout the season, the roots become fibrous and tough. When the plants are 5 inches tall, mulch them with chopped leaves and straw to retain soil moisture and hinder weeds. A drip irrigation system is a godsend when growing these thirsty vegetables!

When the bulbs start to form, trim off most of the lateral roots at the soil surface. This keeps the bulbs round and fiberless. Also, remove side shoots and withered leaves. To blanch the celeriac for whiter, milder roots, hill soil around them two weeks before harvest.

To extend the season well into the winter, mulch the plants under a thick layer of clean straw after the first frost. In mild areas, celeriac can winter over. In the North, it will safely store in the ground about 4 to 6 weeks after the first frost.

HARVESTING AND STORAGE

Like most fall root crops, celeriac should remain in the ground until after a few frosts. The cold weather converts starch in the roots into sugar, improving the flavor. The bulbs should be 2 to 4 inches in diameter. To harvest, loosen the soil around the roots and gently tug them free. Trim the hairy roots and remove all the leaves but the small cluster at the crown.

Celeriac stores best between 33° and 40° F. with a high humidity. Unwashed, the bulbs will keep in the refrigerator for about a week. If you can't use them that quickly, they'll store a month or two in moist sand or sawdust in a cool root cellar or basement. If your soil doesn't freeze hard, it's easier to keep the celeriac right in the garden under an 8- to 12-inch mulch of straw, to use as needed. If you do this, be sure to use the bulbs before spring arrives. The plants will resume growth, forfeiting the bulbs' sweet, nutty flavor.

Rooted Parsley

(*Petroselinum hortense* var. *tuberosum*)

Although largely unknown in the United States (except in the gardens of gourmets), rooted parsley has long been popular in Europe, where it's commonly roasted with meats or added to winter stews and soups. Also known as Hamburg or Dutch parsley, its few available varieties are now carried in some American seed catalogs. The parsniplike roots have a flavor somewhere between celeriac and parsley. The foliage can be used like regular parsley, although the flavor is inferior.

THE BEST VARIETIES

Rooted parsley is usually listed in seed catalogs as Hamburg Rooted parsley. Short Sugar and Early Sugar are two improved Hamburg types, recommended for their high sugar content.

SOWING AND GROWING

Like carrots, rooted parsley tolerates a poor soil if steady moisture is supplied. Don't plant them in a soil that has been freshly manured or is high in nitrogen. This causes excessive top growth and forked, hairy roots. Simply till the bed to a depth of at least 8 inches, then rake the soil smooth of rocks and clumps.

Because rooted parsley requires a long growing season, about 100 days, I start seedlings indoors in late February or early March. If you live in an area that has mild winters, try planting a fall crop for harvest next spring. Parsley is extremely hardy, and the rooted varieties are no different.

Like parsnips, rooted parsley is slow to germinate. Use fresh seed every year, and soak the seed overnight in tepid water to promote sprouting. I plant the seeds in peat pellets, then place the pellets in a sunny windowsill until seedlings appear, up to a month later. Germination is best at 55° to 65° F. When temperatures outdoors are above 45° F, I move the seedlings into their bed, spaced 4 inches apart. Mulch the bed with clean straw, and water the bed often to keep the plants healthy.

HARVESTING AND STORAGE

Like parsnips, rooted parsley becomes sweeter after a few frosts. Because it's a biennial, rooted parsley can be stored in the garden under a heavy layer of mulch. The roots can be dug and stored in a root cellar or basement in damp sand, but the roots freshly pulled from the garden as needed have a fuller, sweeter flavor.

Parsnips

(*Pastinaca sativa*)

Parsnips are superb winter keepers, one of the few vegetables that can stay in the garden even under snow. Like other root crops, they take up little garden space yet produce high yields. True, they look like rough, anemic carrots. But they have a superb texture and sweet, nutty flavor beyond description. Gardeners who ignore parsnips have probably never tasted them at their best. Properly prepared, they're absolutely scrumptious!

THE BEST VARIETIES

Parsnips are easy to grow. They have no major disease or pest problems. But there are a few tricks for growing the large, sweet roots. First, buy fresh seed each year. Seeds more than a year old germinate poorly, if at all. I plant All American, which matures in about 105 days, and Cobham Improved Marrow, which has a high sugar content. Gladiator, Harris Model, and Hollow Crown parsnips are also excellent.

SOWING AND GROWING

Parsnips should be planted in early spring, about the same time as peas and radishes. Like carrots, they require a deeply tilled, well-prepared soil. I till the beds as early as I can, raking the soil smooth of rocks and clods. I work in plenty of peat moss, leaf mold, and clean sand to soften the soil and promote drainage. Avoid nitrogenous material like manure, which encourages lush top growth and pencil-thin, hairy roots. Like other root crops, parsnips thrive in a soil rich in potassium and phosphorus, so work in a dusting of wood ashes (potash) for good measure.

The seeds germinate slowly (up to three weeks), even in the best garden conditions. To hasten germination, some gardeners soak the seeds overnight or treat them with boiling water before planting. I simply start the seeds indoors between moist sheets of paper towels. Presprouted seeds have a better chance of survival. When the tiny white roots of the sprouted seeds are about 1/4 inch long, they're ready to plant. Be careful not to break the small roots or allow the seeds to dry out.

A trick for growing monster parsnips is to plant them in conical holes. It's the method most often used by prize winning parsnip growers. Drive a crowbar into the soil to a depth of about 2 feet, rotating the bar in a circular fashion until the hole is about 6 inches across at the top. Then fill the conical hole with a mixture of sand, peat moss, and sifted soil, leaving a slight depression at the top of the hole. Place two or three sprouted seeds in the depression, then cover with 1/2 inch of sifted sphagnum moss and water. Space the holes 8 inches apart each way in the bed.

As the seedlings grow, keep the beds evenly moist, but not saturated, until they have three or four leaves on each. Then thin to one strong plant per hole and mulch the beds. A 2- or 3-inch straw mulch will control weeds, help the soil retain moisture, and maintain a cool soil temperature. Parsnips grow slowly, and mulching is the best way to pamper them.

If the parsnips receive inadequate moisture during the summer, they'll be tough and likely to split and rot with the fall rains. During dry spells, water the beds deeply once a week.

HARVESTING AND STORAGE

Aside from mulching and regular waterings, the plants can be left alone until harvest, which isn't until winter or after a few frosts. The colder temperature changes starches in the roots into sugar. Store the roots right in the ground where they grew, digging them as you need them throughout the winter, knowing they'll be sweet and delicious. Mulch the parsnips with up to 12 inches of straw to keep the soil soft enough to dig. Even if there's snow on the ground, you can have fresh, tasty parsnips.

Harvest the roots before the soil warms in the spring, before new tops start to grow, or the roots will be bitter and tough. Usually that's no problem, for I use all the parsnips before the end of winter.

When harvesting parsnips, don't try to pull them as you would carrots. Use a spading fork to loosen the soil and lift the roots from the ground. Leave the dirt on the roots until you're ready to use them, for the roots tend to shrivel when exposed to air.

KITCHEN PREPARATION

Parsnips taste best straight from the garden. Wash and gently scrub the roots, then briefly steam them to make paring easier. For even cooking, halve or quarter the roots to cook the cores to the perfect degree of tenderness. With larger roots, remove the woody core entirely and use the tender outer flesh.

Many people ruin the taste of parsnips by overcooking them until they're mushy and bland. The sugar in parsnips dissolves in water. To retain their delightful flavor, don't boil the roots. That's a common mistake made when preparing parsnips. Brown them in butter or sauté them in oil, keeping the heat low to avoid scorching the sugar in the flesh. Or simply bake them. You can mash, bake, or fry them like potatoes. Make fritters or parsnip pancakes, even pies, or glaze them like candied sweet potatoes. They're also delicious steamed until tender and served with peas drenched in melted butter.

Radishes

(Raphanus sativus)

According to legend, radishes originated in China. They are still highly appreciated in the Orient, particularly in Japan where the Daikon

radish is a major food. The ancient Greeks prized radishes above all other root crops. Here in America, thousands of years later, almost every gardener grows radishes. However, few gardeners grow good radishes, roots that are mild and crisp rather than hot and as pithy as corks.

THE BEST VARIETIES

There are two basic types of radishes: spring and winter.

Most of us are familiar with the crunchy spring varieties, like Cherry Belle, French Breakfast, White Icicle, Plum Purple and Champion. These should be planted in early spring, to mature quickly in cool weather for the best production. Most spring varieties mature in less than a month, making them some of the first vegetables harvested in the garden.

The winter radishes are superior in many ways. They hold their quality in the garden longer, tend to be larger than spring varieties, store better, and have a sharper flavor. A popular winter radish is China Rose, which grows almost 3 inches in diameter and 6 inches long. Black Spanish radishes have black skins and crisp white flesh, slightly more pungent than China Rose, but excellent cooked or pickled. A novelty winter radish, Sakurajima, is a giant that can weigh more than 15 pounds, but requires more than 95 days to reach that size. There is also a wide range of Japanese Daikon radishes to choose from. Experiment with several varieties to sample their diversity in taste, texture, and color.

SOWING AND GROWING

For the best radishes, give them a friable soil, cool weather, uninterrupted growth, and constant moisture. As soon as your garden soil is workable in the spring, don some warm clothes and get to work. Don't forget to plant some radishes in the fall, when they're likely to give you the best production.

I usually make small weekly plantings during April and May, then again in August and September. (In the South, plant them a little earlier in the spring and a little later in the fall.) Because most radishes are ready for harvest in less than a month, these succession plantings guarantee a steady supply for my dinner table.

Till the radish bed to a depth of 8 inches (especially if you plan to sow the longer varieties like White Icicle), mixing in plenty of organic matter to loosen up the soil and help it retain moisture. Then make furrows with a yardstick, spacing the furrows about 3 inches apart. Sow the seeds at a depth of 1/2 inch, trying to space the seeds about 1 inch apart.

When making succession plantings, keep in mind that the longer the radish, the better it tolerates heat. I plant the round varieties first (Sparkler, Cherry Belle), the blunt radishes next (French Breakfast), and finally the slender, tapered one (White Icicle). In the fall, I simply reverse the process, planting some winter radishes like Black Spanish and China Rose in late August. The fall varieties, if mulched with straw, can remain in the garden through the winter to be harvested as you need them.

When the seedlings are about 2 inches tall, thin them to 3-inch spacings. If you don't thin them, you'll end up with lush greens and

Continued →

shriveled, inedible roots. Mulch the bed with compost to maintain stable soil moisture, which could mean the difference between perfect and pitiful radishes. If the soil is too dry, the radishes will bolt and become pithy and pungent; too wet and the roots will split and rot. Never let the radish bed dry out, but don't keep it mucky either.

HARVESTING AND STORAGE

When the radishes mature, check them frequently. Many gardeners fail with radishes because they leave them in the ground too long. When the radishes are ready, pull them whether you need them or not, cut off the leaves, then put the roots in a plastic storage bag in the vegetable bin of the refrigerator. Our family loves salad, so the radishes don't last long!

Winter radishes are excellent winter keepers. Although they can be stored in moist sand in a root cellar, they're best left in the garden under a heavy straw mulch and harvested as needed.

Salsify and Scorzonera

(*Tragopogon porrifolius* and *Scorzonera hispanica*)

Salsify is greatly appreciated in Europe, where the 8- to 10-inch roots are prized for their unique "oyster" flavor, exquisite in soups or fried in rounds. Early American colonists from England also valued salsify. Thomas Jefferson grew a large plot of the roots at Monticello, and nineteenth-century cookbooks regarded salsify as a standard crop. The plants have even become naturalized in parts of the United States and Canada. Yet, in the past century, the vegetable has fallen out of favor with the American gardeners. Maybe it's time to give this wonderful vegetable some space in our gardens again.

THE BEST VARIETIES

Often called the oyster plant or vegetable oyster, salsify is a biennial member of the daisy family, native to the Mediterranean region. The plants produce large, grassy leaves growing up to 4 feet high, resembling daylilies.

Improved Mammoth Sandwich Island is the standard variety in this country, but most gourmets agree that Black Salsify, or Scorzonera, has superior flavor. These roots have black skins and delightful white flesh. Gigantia is a European strain of Scorzonera recommended for its firm, smooth flesh and rich flavor.

SOWING AND GROWING

Salsify has a culture similar to parsnips, requiring a long growing season and a deep, friable soil worked to a depth of about 10 inches. Avoid using fresh manure or high-nitrogen fertilizers with salsify, or you're likely to harvest hairy, forked roots. Like parsnips, salsify is a low-maintenance crop; once established in the garden, the plants need only occasional weeding and watering.

Sow seeds in the spring, around the same time as you would parsnips. Use fresh seed each year. Salsify germinates slowly, so plant thickly at a depth of 1/2 inch. When the seedlings are 3 inches tall, thin to 4-inch spacings. Be careful when thinning and weeding, for the seedlings resemble blades of grass and are often eliminated by unknowing gardeners. Once thinned, mulch the salsify bed with clean straw. Unlike other root crops, salsify tolerates drought without loss of quality, but grows best in a soil that's watered deeply once a week.

HARVESTING AND STORAGE

Like parsnips, salsify is a biennial, perfectly hardy left in the bed until needed. The roots improve in flavor after a few heavy frosts. Cut off the tops, then mulch with straw to keep the soil from freezing solid. As with parsnips, it's best to dig the roots with a spading fork rather than trying to pull them like carrots. Harvest salsify before new growth begins in the spring, unless you intend to use the young shoots.

Although salsify can be stored in moist sand in a root cellar, it tends to get tough and shriveled, and the oyster flavor deteriorates with long storage. The roots can be stored a few days in plastic bags in the refrigerator, but for the best eating, dig the roots fresh from the garden just before kitchen preparation.

Turnips & Rutabagas

(*Brassica Rapa* and *Brassica Napus*)

The turnip was one of the first vegetables cultivated by man. A member of the mustard family, the turnip was at one time as popular as the potato. In the past century, however, the vegetable has fallen out of favor with American gardeners, despite new varieties that mature quickly and taste superb.

Although a different species, rutabagas are usually grouped with turnips (as I'm doing here!). The rutabaga is really a weedy offshoot of the cabbage, producing a larger root than the turnip. Popular in Russia, Scandinavia, the British Isles, France, and Canada, rutabagas are often called swedes or yellow turnips. In the United States, rutabagas are grown even less than turnips, although they store better than turnips and have sweeter, yellow flesh.

THE BEST VARIETIES

The most attractive and familiar turnip is the Purple Top White Globe. The large white roots have purple shoulders, and the flesh is firm and mild if harvested early. An improved Purple Top, Royal Crown, matures faster and holds its sweetness longer in the garden.

Tokyo Cross, an F-1 hybrid and All-American Winner, is also a popular variety. This turnip can be grown like a radish, maturing in less than 40 days, making it superb for early spring and late fall crops. The sweet, tender white roots grow up to 6 inches wide without getting pithy, but they're milder if pulled younger. Tokyo Cross is also disease resistant. A similar variety, Just Right, is recommended for fall crops.

Other recommended turnip varieties are Market Express, White Lady, Ohno Scarlet, De Milan, and De Nancy. A Vermont heirloom variety, Gilfeather, is a superb fall storage turnip.

There are also some varieties grown primarily for their greens. Shogoin is the best known, but it bolts quickly. All Top and Seven Top are preferred, for they are slower to bolt and produce a large crop of greens. They don't produce edible roots, however. Truth be told, the greens from any turnip variety are perfectly edible, if harvested young.

The best of the rutabaga varieties are Laurentian, Burpee's Purple Top Yellow, and American Purple Top. All three are excellent winter keepers.

SOWING AND GROWING

Turnips are easy to grow in cool weather. Spring and fall crops are usually possible, although a fall crop is preferred. They'll tolerate light frosts, so plant early in the spring, about a month before the last frost if possible. An early heat wave, however, will make the roots bitter. This is particularly a problem in the South. A fall crop, when turnips mature in cold weather, results in more tender, sweeter roots and greens. Sow eight weeks before the first fall frost, even later for fast-maturing varieties like Tokyo Cross and Market Express.

Turnips are excellent for planting in spaces where other crops—beans, spinach, peas—have come and gone. Although the main turnip root goes no deeper than the topsoil, many finer roots reach as far as 4 feet into the ground. Before sowing, loosen the soil in the bed to a depth of at least 10 inches, working in plenty of compost, sand, and wood ashes. Don't use highly nitrogenous material unless you only want greens.

The easiest way to sow turnips is to broadcast the seed over the bed, then thin the seedlings later. Sow thinly, for germination is high, almost 100 percent. After broadcasting the seeds, lightly rake the bed to just barely cover the seed, no deeper than half an inch, and water well to get them started.

When the seedlings are 3 inches tall, thin them to 3-inch spacings for the smaller varieties and 5-inch for the larger Purple Top types. Use the thinnings for greens. (Don't thin the turnips if you're growing them for greens only.)

The key to growing tasty turnips is to grow them fast and give them regular waterings. After thinning, mulch the turnip bed with shredded leaves, well-rotted sawdust, and grass clippings. The roots require constant moisture but won't tolerate waterlogged soil. Water deeply once a week, more often during drought periods. Shallow, erratic watering causes bolting. If you use a drip irrigation system, you'll have no problem.

Rutabagas should be grown only as a fall crop, maturing in cold weather and stored in the root cellar for winter enjoyment. Plant them in mid-June or about 90 days before planned harvest shortly after the first frost. Sow the seeds about 1/4 inch deep at 8-inch spacings. Provide plenty of moisture until the seedlings are growing strong, then mulch well and water deeply once a week.

HARVESTING AND STORAGE

Most turnip varieties mature in two months or less. The plants seem to double in size each week, so watch them carefully. Although most varieties will grow to be 6 inches in diameter, they're tastier and more tender when they're no larger than a golf ball. Harvest the greens before hot weather in the spring, or they'll be too strong and tough to eat.

Unfortunately, turnips don't store as well as rutabagas. Because of their high water content, turnips dehydrate quickly when exposed to air. In some parts of the South, turnips can be left in the ground for most of the winter under a mulch of straw and harvested as needed. In the North, however, turnips should be pulled before a hard freeze and put into storage. Don't clean the roots if you keep them in a root cellar or the refrigerator. They'll store longer and won't bruise as easily. Ideally, turnips should be stored in high humidity with a temperature between 30° and 40° F.

Some gardeners can turnips, although I've never tried it. The best way to keep turnips is to process and freeze them. Pare and dice the roots, blanch them for three minutes, plunge them into ice water, drain and pack in freezer bags. If you prefer, mash and puree the turnips before freezing.

Harvest rutabagas after a few frosts, but before the ground freezes. Cut the tops and store them like carrots in a root cellar or basement. Good roots will keep up to six months if stored just above freezing with 90 percent humidity.

Grow the Best Corn

Nancy Bubel

Illustrations by Sue Storey

Sweet corn is a gardener's vegetable, one of the most eagerly awaited summer crops. By growing your own, you can have it at its best: sweet, tender, juicy kernels, five minutes from the patch. Fresh sweet corn is so good that it needs no sauces or fancy recipes; simply steam and serve. Many gardeners like to eat raw corn while husking it. Corn is a vigorous plant that responds to generous fertilizing, so it is satisfying to grow.

Kinds of Corn You Can Grow

Usually, selecting a vegetable variety to grow is a pretty easy choice—mainly because you do not have that many varieties to choose from. But if you have ever counted the varieties of corn offered in most seed catalogs, you know that selecting a variety of corn to grow involves considering a lot of different factors.

TYPES OF CORN

Let's consider, first, the characteristics of each of the different kinds of corn you might want to grow.

Sweet Corn. This demanding variety is so good that it is worth extra soil feeding and careful timing to pluck its perfection from the corn patch. Some early sweet corn is ready as soon as fifty-five days from planting, making it possible, in some areas, to follow the corn with a fall vegetable crop or a soil-improving cover crop. Sweet corn thrives on hot weather, plenty of soil lime and nitrogen, good drainage, and abundant moisture.

Kernels of sweet corn contain a relatively small amount of starch and a large amount of water containing sugar in solution. When dry, the kernels shrink and wrinkle. The characteristic sweetness and tenderness of sweet corn are actually caused by a genetic defect that keeps the starch grains in the kernel few and small and prevents the conversion of soluble sugars into more starch.

Sweet corn is generally less robust in germination and growth than dent corn, flint corn, or popcorn. Also, it is somewhat more demanding of rich soil, and often less disease-resistant.

Popcorn. Ears of popcorn are shorter than those of most kinds of sweet corn, and the kernels are smaller. Each kernel contains a small

Continued →

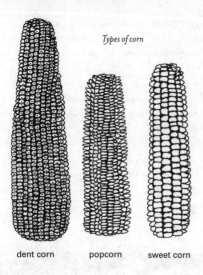

Types of corn

dent corn   popcorn   sweet corn

central core of soft starch around the germ, surrounded by a larger outer layer of hard starch. The kernels pop when heat expands the moisture in the center of the kernel, and the resulting steam bursts the hard, starchy coating.

Like sweet corn, popcorn does well in hot weather and well-drained, limed soil; but it will thrive on somewhat leaner soil and less moisture than sweet corn. Most popcorn varieties need 90 to 100 days to mature. Some, like strawberry popcorn, are also decorative and frequently grown for roadside stands.

Flint Corn. You do not hear much about flint corn, but it is a useful and delicious staple corn, good for year-round storage. The kernels are hard and smooth, not shriveled like sweet corn or indented like dent corn. The hard kernels can be ground to produce a sweet, nutritious meal for use in making muffins and cornmeal crackers, mush, and bread. Flint corn needs a rather long growing season—about 110 to 120 days—but it is more tolerant of cool weather and prolonged dampness than sweet corn. Flint corn can be found in varieties colored red, blue, black, orange, and mahogany.

Dent Corn. Dent corn, also called field corn, has a dimple at the tip of each kernel, caused by the rapid drying of the soft starch at the center of the kernel. Immature field corn can be sweet, and it is perfectly good to eat—although it is neither as tender nor as sweet as sweet corn. Both the plant and the cob are large. You might want to raise small plots of dent corn for feed if you keep animals. The kernels contain more soft starch than flint corn. They can be ground in a hand or powdered mill.

Flour Corn. Varicolored like flint corn, flour corn has much more soft starch in the kernel. It grinds to a fine flour, rather than the coarse meal produced by flint and dent corn.

Super-Sweet Corn. These varieties sound like the answer to a gardener's dream. Most of the new extra-sweet corn varieties are not only sweeter than standard corn to start with, they also hold their sugar content for a longer time after picking, because conversion of their sugar to starch takes place more slowly. It is not true, though, that they increase in sweetness after picking, only that their sugar content twenty-four hours after picking is higher than that of day-old regular sweet corn, a quality that has made these varieties especially useful for sale at roadside stands.

This extra sweetness has been achieved by tinkering with the genes of standard sweet corn. As is usual in nature, though, something's got to give. In this case, some plants tend to have spotty germination, lower vigor, and sometimes ears incompletely filled with kernels. Breeders are working on these problems, and at least one new extra-sweet-corn type shows improvement in germination and seedling vigor.

The other limitation that has discouraged many backyard gardeners from growing the super-sweets is the fact that their quality suffers if the plants receive pollen from any other kind of corn plants, even different varieties of sweet corn.

The latest improvement in super-sweet corn has been the development of the everlasting heritage varieties. These extra-sweet ears are not affected by cross-pollination. Because they do not require isolation to ensure sweetness, these new varieties should be easier to fit into a backyard garden patch.

Good Soil for Corn

Corn is a member of the grass family. If you think of it as a great, big, fast-growing, tasseled grass, you will appreciate what a hearty appetite it has. To support the rapid development of its stout stalk, long stiff leaves, and heavy ears, corn needs a ready supply of plant food, especially nitrogen, which fosters leaf growth. Most gardeners sensibly plant corn in the richest soil on the place.

ENRICHING THE SOIL

Enrich the soil well in advance of planting. If possible, plow under a one-inch layer of manure the preceding fall. You can also grow a green manure crop, such as buckwheat, oats, clover, rye, winter wheat, or vetch. In the spring, before planting corn, turn this cover crop under.

CORN ANATOMY

Brace roots: An arching crownlike group of aboveground roots originating low on the cornstalk and growing down into the ground. Corn grows so fast and is so tall that it needs an extensive root system.

Ear: A cylindrical arrangement of corn kernels growing on a cob. In a good year, most plants produce two ears.

Endosperm: Material stored in the seed for the purpose of nourishing the embryo plant. In corn, the endosperm is the part we want to eat.

Husk: The protective leafy membrane that encloses each ear of corn.

Kernel: An individual grain of corn. It's not exactly a seed, but rather a ripened plant ovary containing a single seed.

Leaves: Serve to produce food for the fast-growing corn plant and also to channel rain and dew toward the thirsty roots.

Silks: The pollen-receptive female part of the corn plant. Each thread of silk leads to an ovary, and each one that is pollinated grows into a kernel of corn.

Tassel: The pollen-bearing male flower of the corn plant.

Tillers: Extra stalks growing from the base of the plant, usually one on each side. They help to nourish the plant and should not be removed.

Humus. Humus-rich soil contains more air spaces, making it easier for roots to grow. Even more important in the case of corn is the fact that humus acts like a sponge, holding from five to ten times its own weight in water, and gradually releasing it as needed. Nutrients must be dissolved in water in order for plant roots to absorb them; so you can see the value of humus as a reservoir for the rich broth that has percolated through the soil after rain.

Green manure crops and compost build humus. Many gardeners bury their summer household garbage in the center of their corn rows. Any organic materials that you can compost and add to the soil will benefit your corn.

Lime. Corn needs a good supply of lime. The average recommended lime application is a half ton per acre every five years, or as needed. For the home garden, one three-gallon bucketful applied to a plot measuring 50 feet by 20 feet (1000 square feet) every three to four years should be sufficient.

CROP ROTATION

Rotate crops to prevent one-sided depletion of soil nutrients. Corn needs a lot of nitrogen. Peas, clover, soybeans, and other legumes have bacteria living in nodules on their roots that add nitrogen to the soil, as much as 100 pounds per acre in the case of alfalfa. To make the best use of this free fertilizer, plant corn right after a legume crop, which can be either a crop of garden vegetables (peas, beans, limas, soybeans) or a hay or green manure crop like alfalfa, clover, or vetch.

Some gardens have special soil problems, such as a hardpan layer of soil, six to twenty-four inches deep. The hardpan is so dense that plant roots cannot penetrate it to get the nutrients they need from the subsoil. If this is your problem, you could substitute a planting of cowhorn turnips (sown at the rate of two pounds per square acre) for one of the other recommended cover crops. The deep roots of the turnips help to break up the subsoil, and leave drainage spaces when they are turned under to decay and add organic material to the soil. Alfalfa, which is slow to get established the first year and needs well-limed soil, is another deep-rooted cover crop sometimes used for this purpose.

Even if you do not find it possible to plant all the recommended cover crops, you should still hopscotch your corn plantings around the garden, alternating corn with root crops, leafy crops, legumes, and fruit-bearers (like tomatoes and strawberries), in order to keep the soil in balance.

PREVENT EROSION

Corn is hard on the soil in two ways: it uses up many nutrients, and it leaves the soil exposed to erosion from wind and rain. A closely followed cover-cropping system helps to prevent erosion by keeping the soil covered with soil-holding plants. There is hardly ever any bare soil exposed to the elements under this system. In a very small corn patch, you can mulch during the summer and leave the mulch and corn stubble over winter to catch snow and blown leaves and protect the soil. If your garden is on a hill, run your corn rows around the hill rather than up and down, so that rain will not run in long paths, which tend to cut into the soil and wash it away.

Planting Corn

Hungry as we are for that first taste of fresh sweet corn, planting it too early will result only in wasted seed and row space. Some like to

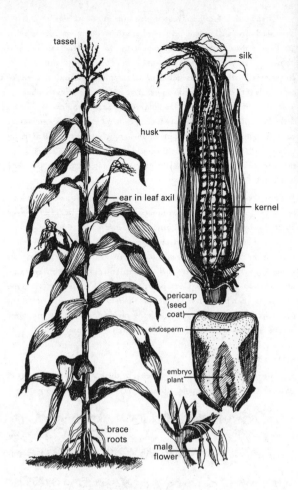

gamble on a small extra-early planting, and there is nothing wrong with that—as long as you know what you are up against.

TIMING

Timing corn plantings late enough to be safe, yet early enough to satisfy the restless green thumb and hungry palate—that is one of the arts of gardening. The native Americans made their first planting when the new oak leaves in their neighborhood were the size of squirrels' ears, and that is still a good guide. It is usually safe to plant early corn about a week before the date of the last expected frost in your area.

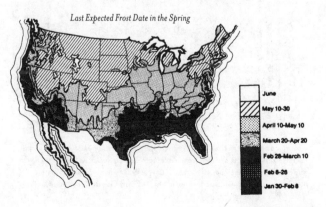

Last Expected Frost Date in the Spring

June
May 10-30
April 10-May 10
March 20-Apr 20
Feb 28-March 10
Feb 8-28
Jan 30-Feb 8

Continued →

Corn seed, even when treated with a fungicide like Captan, as most seeds are, will not germinate where the soil temperature is below 50°F—the absolute minimum temperature for germination. For early plantings, when the soil temperature ranges between 50 and 60°F, treated seed will germinate much more completely than untreated seed, especially if the treated seed you use is one of the varieties that has been bred to withstand cold soil, like Polarvee or Early Sunglow. When the soil is too cold, seed rots before it can germinate. Rotting seed attracts corn maggots, giving you two problems: an uneven stand and an insect infestation. Early-planted seeds should not be in touch with fresh manure, or they will be more likely to rot than to germinate while soil is still cool.

For a continuous harvest, make repeated plantings—either every two weeks, using small blocks of space, or every three weeks with larger blocks for better pollination. Since early, midseason, and late sweet corns have successive maturation times, many gardeners plant them at about the same time. There is no point in putting midseason or late varieties in the ground extra early; later plantings almost always catch up to the too-early ones. Corn plantings made in midsummer to ripen in early fall can be sown in the pea patch right after the removal of the pea crop. Use an early, quick-maturing variety for these late plantings because growth is slower in September when days grow shorter.

SPACING
Spacing is determined, to some extent, by the kind of corn you plant. In general, corn rows are made thirty to forty inches wide. Choose the

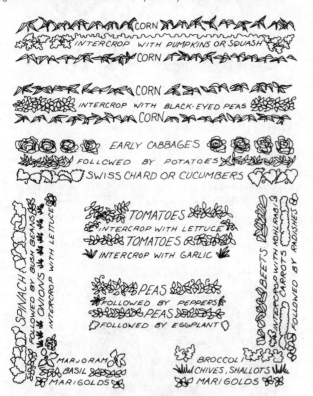

A plan for a small garden based on both intercropping and succession plantings. The corn is interplanted with squash and shell beans. Note that the corn is located on the north end of the garden so that it will not shade other crops. It was planted in a four-row block to ensure pollination. (adapted from Success with Small Food Gardens *by Louise Riotte, Garden Way Publishing.)*

narrower spacing for short plants and hand cultivation, the wider to accommodate machines and extra tall plants, to leave room for broadcasting fall cover crops between rows, and when interplanting squash and beans. Early corn varieties grow fairly short plants: four to six feet tall, with relatively small ears. The midseason corns are taller: six to eight feet. Late corn is even taller and more robust: seven to ten feet, with long ears. Many varieties of popcorn have shorter stalks: three to five feet. These can be spaced somewhat closer than the largest corns—rows two to three feet apart, with dwarf plants four to six inches apart. Larger popcorn varieties should be spaced eight to ten inches apart. Plant popcorn about the time of your last frost.

In the row, the usual practice is to sow seeds of sweet, dent, and flint corn 4 inches apart and thin to 8 to 12 inches apart, using the wider spacing for late corn and sowing more thickly (but thinning the same) when planting early corn in cold soil. Cover seed no more than 1 inch deep for early planting, up to 1 1/2 to 2 inches deep later in the season. Some gardeners prefer the hill system; they plant three seeds close together every 30 inches, and they do not thin the plants.

Corn in Small Gardens
Most gardeners who have the space grow large patches of corn to have enough for freezing as well as eating fresh. Where space is limited, though, it is still possible to grow corn for immediate use, which is when it is at its best, anyway. This can be done in two ways.

- Devote a small square of the garden, say 10 feet by 10 feet, to a single planting of corn. For greater production, this small plot should be generously mulched, irrigated, and given side-dressings of manure tea (see below). Space your plants 8 to 12 inches apart in the row. You can, however, reduce the separation between rows to 2 1/2 feet, if you are able to hand-cultivate this small plot.

or

- Plant a solid block of corn—with plants spaced ten inches apart each way—in a raised bed, which can be worked from all sides. Popular bed sizes are three feet wide and six to ten feet long.

Interplanting. Squash and climbing beans can be interplanted with corn, an old Indian trick that makes good use of garden space. You can plant squash and pumpkins along with corn in the end row, and the vines will ramble into the corn patch and mulch the ground. Or plant a bean seed or two beside each young corn seedling left after thinning the row. The beans return nitrogen to the soil, and the corn stalks support the bean vines. Rows should be more widely spaced to prevent shading of one row by another.

Pollination
Corn is pollinated by the wind, which blows pollen from the tassels of one plant to the silks of another. For well-filled ears with no missing kernels, each silk must receive a grain of pollen. So naturally, you will want to lay out your corn rows so that the wind will carry pollen from corn plant to corn plant, not from corn to other garden plants. The best way to ensure complete pollination is to plant corn in blocks at least four rows wide.

HOW CROSS-POLLINATION AFFECTS CORN

With most vegetables, cross-pollination between varieties does not show up until the resulting seeds are planted and growing. Corn is different, though. Each pollen grain releases two sperm. One sperm fertilizes the plant embryo and the other joins the nuclei in the endosperm to determine the nature of the stored material in the seed. Because of this unique double fertilization, the kernel that forms on an ear of corn this year can be affected by this season's crossing. If the silks on an ear of sweet corn receive pollen from dent corn tassels, for example, the kernels that grow from these dent corn pollen grains will be starchy and tough like dent corn, not sweet and tender, like sweet corn. Popcorn, flint corn, and flour corn may also cross with sweet corn. If only a few grains of odd pollen are involved, the quality of the ear suffers little, if any; but if half the silks of an ear or sweet corn are fertilized by pollen from popcorn tassels, then you will have an ear of corn that is not so sweet, but it will not pop too well either. You might have noticed, in growing white or bicolor corn next to yellow corn, that you get a few maverick white kernels in the yellow ears if the wind shifts during tasseling. Crossing between regular sweet corn varieties does not usually affect flavor.

Buildings, hedges, or several rows of tall plants like sunflowers can effectively bock the transfer of pollen and reduce the necessary isolation distance between corn varieties. Broom corn, which is actually a sorghum, looks like a corn relative but is not related closely enough to cross, and may be planted close to all kinds of regular corn (*Zea mays*) without fear of crossing.

Saving Seed. If you want to plant corn next year from seed you save this year, the plants from which you save seeds should be pollinated only by their own variety, or the next crop will not come true. If you want to maintain a strain of Golden Bantam, then the seed you save must be pollinated only by Golden Bantam corn plants. So you will have to plan your planting schedule so that no other corn crop within 500 to 1300 feet is in tassel at the same time as your seed crop. You can guarantee this by planting early corn next to late corn, for example, because the early corn will have shed its pollen by the time the late corn is in tassel.

There should be at least two weeks' difference between maturity dates of different varieties to eliminate all chance of cross-pollination. Plants raised for seed must be more strictly isolated from other tasseling varieties than those raised for food. The reason for this is that a few odd kernels on a cob may not affect its eating quality, but if you plant them, these kernels (seeds) will not grow into the kind of corn you are aiming for.

If they are to germinate well in the next growing season, seeds must be allowed to ripen fully on the plant. So leave your seed ears on the stalk for about a month past the time when they would have been just right for eating. Frost will not hurt well-dried seed corn. It is a good idea to hang the seed ears, with husks pulled back, in a well-ventilated spot to dry some more after picking. Even if you need only a handful of seed corn, save and mix the seed from several plants so your corn will not become inbred.

You can store your seed corn on the ear in cans, or shelled in jars or cans. Keep it as dry as possible and in a cool, dark place. Heat and moisture use up stored nutrients in the seed and reduce germination rates. If kept completely dry and quite cool, corn seed can remain usable for as long as five years. To be on the safe side, most gardeners count on planting seed corn no older than two to three years.

Care of the Growing Crop

Care during the growing season should help the plants to make the most of their natural advantage of efficient metabolism. Since corn needs all the light it can get, you will want to avoid planting other tall plants nearby that might shade the young corn plants on their way up. And you will want to make sure that each plant has every opportunity to make good use of the rich soil you have provided. Thin the seedlings to their proper spacing—eight to twelve inches apart. Crowded corn plants shade each other and compete for soil nutrients. Leave the tillers (those extra stalks growing from the base of the plant) on the plant. Although their function is not completely understood, it is generally agreed that corn grows better if the tillers are not removed.

CULTIVATION

When the plants are small, weeds should be eliminated—or at least kept under control, because they use up soil nutrients, and the fast-growing weeds can shade out young corn seedlings. When chopped down young and tender, weeds contribute a certain amount of green manure. If weeds are hoed down until the plant is knee-high, it is usually not necessary to do much cultivating after that. Some gardeners hill up the rows—draw soil toward the plants from the middle of the rows—when plants are knee-high. This helps to encourage strong root formation. Once they have reached that height, corn plants have extensive roots, which could be damaged by hoeing too close to the plant.

When growing small blocks of corn, some gardeners like to mulch to discourage weeds and retain soil moisture, and this is a good practice to follow as long as you wait until the soil is thoroughly warm before spreading mulch.

WATER

Irrigation is not always possible—many corn patches are far from a hose outlet—but in a dry season it can boost your corn yield. Plant food taken from the soil can be absorbed only in solution. And, of course, most plant tissues are composed largely of water. Furthermore, a full-grown corn plant can lose as much as a gallon of water a day in hot summer weather by evaporation through its leaves. If weather is dry, and if you are able to water your corn plants, watering is most effective at the time of tasseling and when the kernels are forming. If you do irrigate your plants, soak the soil at least four inches deep. Surface dampness only encourage the development of shallow roots, which quickly die when the soil dries again.

FERTILIZING

For really spectacular corn, try side-dressing the plants twice during the growing season with liquid plant food, such as diluted fish emulsion (available in most lawn and garden stores) or manure tea.

To make manure tea, put several shovelfuls of manure into a burlap or cloth sack and suspend this large "tea bag" in a large bucket of water—at least five gallons. Cover the brew and let it steep for several days. Then pour out one to two quarts of the murky water into a three-gallon bucket or watering can. Dilute the concentrated tea with water until it is the color of weak beverage tea. Pour it around the base of each plant. Refill the large bucket with water and let it steep again.

Soak the soil around each plant with the manure tea or fish emulsion once just after the final thinning, when the seedlings are about eight inches high, and again when the plant is knee-high. Many

Continued →

gardeners think such side-dressing is worth their while, both to give the plants a boost and to maintain soil fertility. In good rich soil, though, you should get a good corn crop without this extra step.

Harvesting

Sweet Corn. Sweet corn is at its tender, sweet, juicy best for only a few days. That moment of perfection occurs about eighteen to twenty days after the silks have been pollinated. This is the milk stage, when the kernels contain as much moisture as they will ever have. The juice in the kernels is milky, and the usual test of readiness is to puncture a kernel with your fingernail to see if milky juice spurts out. If you are too early, the juice will be watery. Too late (about twenty-eight days beyond pollination), and the kernels will turn doughy as the moisture recedes and sugar turns to starch. Here are some other signs of ready-to-pick corn.

- Dark green husks. If the husks are yellow, the corn is probably old and tough.

- Brown, but not brittle, silks.

- Well-filled ears. It is important to know your variety here, though. The varieties Wonderful and Candystick, for example, have very slim ears and can be ready before you realize it, if you are waiting for those ears to fill out.

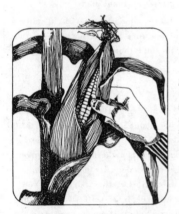

Sweet corn is at its harvesting best at the "milk stage." If you puncture a kernel at this time, the juice in the kernel will be milky. If you are too early, the juice will be watery.

Your harvest dates may vary somewhat from the maturity dates you see listed in the seed catalogues. Eighty-day corn, for example, is not always ready exactly eighty days from planting. Prevailing temperatures and rainfall, soil quality, and even microclimate conditions in your own garden can easily add several days to the growing period.

Sweet corn should be eaten or processed as soon as possible after picking, because in standard varieties the sugar starts to change to starch as soon as the ear is plucked. Cooling the corn helps to slow this process. If you do not cook the corn immediately after picking, leave the husks on the ears, and store the corn in plastic bags in the refrigerator, If you have never tried raw sweet corn, treat yourself to an ear or two while husking.

Popcorn. Leave the ears on the stalk until the kernels are hard and dry. They need to develop a hard skin to contain the small burst of steam that builds up inside each kernel when it is heated, or the pop will be just a sputter, and the interior contents will not puff up. Pull off the ears and peel back the husks. It is a good idea to hang the ears in a dry, airy place to cure for a week or two after picking. You can tie several ears together by the husk and drape them over a nail, or you can string a wire

and hang a series of ears along its length. Or you can husk the ears and store them in open baskets.

Flint Corn. Most people grow flint corn for grinding, so it must be good and dry when picked. Kernels should appear glazed, and cannot be indented by a thumbnail. Damp corn will mold in storage and gum up the grinder. If the weather is dry enough, leave the ears on the stalk well into the fall, until they are thoroughly dry. If you must pick the ears before they are fully dry, complete the drying process in an oven, over a pilot light, or near a wood stove.

Dent Corn. Like flint corn, dent corn should dry completely on the stalk before picking. The whole plant should be brown and dry and each kernel well indented before the corn is picked for storage. For immediate use as animal feed in early fall, ears can be hand-picked and husked as needed. When the corn is good and dry it will be easier to remove from the husk and easier to grind for household use. Dent corn can be left in the field and gathered as needed, but in areas where snow is common, it is best to harvest the ears while you can still get a cart into the field. Heavy snow or roaming deer can do away with a lot of ear corn left on the stalk over winter.

Dry flint, dent, seed corn, and popcorn by suspending the ears from a wire or rope, with their husks pulled back.

Storage

In the frontier settlements of nineteenth-century America, having enough food meant having sufficient corn. Today we enjoy a much wider variety of foods, but corn can be a source of a great many delicious dishes, from steamed sweet corn to cornmeal mush, crackers, muffins, corn pudding, popcorn, tortillas, chapaties, corn chowder, succotash, stewed dried corn, and others. We have more ways to keep corn now, too. Here is how you can store your corn crop.

FREEZING

Freezing is strictly for sweet corn. For whole-kernel corn, scald ears of husked corn in boiling water to cover for four minutes. Chill, then cut the kernels off with a sharp knife. Then package and freeze. To freeze whole ears, scald small ears for seven minutes, medium ones for nine minutes, and large ears for eleven minutes. Then, drain, chill, and package.

CANNING

Again, canning is a method almost exclusively used for sweet corn, although in a pinch one could can use green (immature) dent corn. Corn

620

is a low-acid vegetable and must be canned under pressure. Never use hot water bath or open-kettle methods.

To can whole-kernel corn, cut the kernels from the cob and put into clean jars, leaving a one-inch space at the top. Do not pack the corn tightly. Pour boiling water over the corn to cover it, leaving a one-inch head space. Put caps on jars. Process pints for fifty-five minutes, quarts for one hour and twenty-five minutes, at ten pounds of pressure.

Caning Whole-Kernel Corn
1. *Cut the kernels from the cob.*
2. *Pour into clean jars, leaving a one-inch head space.*
3. *Pour boiling water over the corn to cover it, leaving a one-inch head space. Cap the jars.*
4. *Process at ten pounds of pressure, pints for fifty-five minutes, quarts for one hour and twenty-five minutes.*
5. *Test the seals.*

EAR STORAGE

Popcorn can be stored on the ear in discarded nylon stockings or mesh bags, or in cans; or it can be shelled and kept in jars in a cool, dry place. To shell popcorn, rub two ears together or put an old sock over your hand and rub the kernels off. One-half cup of popcorn kernels should yield about four quarts of popped corn. If you try some and it

does not pop well, it is probably too dry. Add one tablespoon of water to three cups of kernels and shake; then cap and leave for one to two days. Kernels should not be kept wet, though, or they will mold. Some folks say that popcorn pops better when it has been refrigerated.

Flint and dent corn can be stored on the ear in bins or cribs, or in cans; or it can be shelled by hand or hand-cranked machine and kept in cans, as long as it is well dried before being covered.

Corn Varieties to Grow

The following list of corn varieties is just a sampling of the many delicious strains available. Each seed house carries a different assortment, and there are many more good corn varieties out there to try. These are some of the most widely grown selections. Perhaps some of them will become your family favorites.

SWEET CORN

Type	Where Available
Early	
Polarvee: 53 days	Stokes
Spancross: 60 days	Olds, Burgess, Shumway
Earlivee: 60 days	Johnny's, Stokes
Sprite: 68 days bicolor	Harris
Midseason	
Quicksilver: 72 days; 3 weeks earlier than Silver Queen	Harris
Wonderful: 82 days	Harris
Butter and Sugar: 80–84 days	Farmer, Twilley, Harris, Stokes, Park, Herbst
Golden Bantam: 83 days open-pollinated	Vermont Bean Seed Co., Nichols, Farmer, Johnny's
Country Gentleman: 92 days open-pollinated	Nichols, Burpee, Shumway
Stowell's Evergreen: 99 days; an oldie grown since the mid-1800s	Johnny's, Farmer, Shumway
Black Mexican: 86 days Vermont open-pollinated, kernels blue-black at maturity	Nichols, Burpee, Olds, Vermont Bean Seed Co.
Mixture of yellow hybrids	Shumway, Olds
Late	
Jubilee: 87 days	Farmer, Herbst
Honey Cross: 87 days wilt resistant, tight husks	Burpee
Silver Queen: 92 days large, late, and delicious	Twilley, Stokes, Farmer, Shumway, Burpee, Harris, Park, Herbst
Honey and Cream: 92 days bicolor	Nichols, Burpee, Herbst

Continued →

Type	Where Available
Super-Sweet Varieties	
Earliglow: 70 days everlasting heritage	Herbst
Kandy Korn: 89 days everlasting heritage	Herbst, Olds, Nichols, Stokes, Burpee, Twilley, Vermont Bean Seed Co., Burgess
Florida Staysweet: 84 days less trouble with germination and seedling vigor; needs isolation	Harris, Park, Herbst
Iochief: 89 days; needs isolation	Shumway, Burgess, Park, Burpee, Farmer
Illinichief: 85 days needs isolation	Burgess, Farmer, Twilley, Stokes, Shumway
Wilt-Resistant Varieties	
Honey Cross: 87 days	Burpee
Golden Cross Bantam: 75 days; hybrid	Vermont Bean Seed Co.
Comanche: 70 days	Stokes, Seedway
Bellringer: 79 days	Harris
Comet* white	Seedway
Bi-Queen: 92 days bicolor	Burpee

POPCORN

Rhodes Yellow Pop: 118 days 2–3 ears per stalk	Johnny's
White Hull-less Hybrid*	Farmer
Strawberry: 105–110 days open-pollinated	Farmer, Harris, Olds, Shumway
White Cloud: 95 days hybrid	Stokes, Park, Olds, Harris
South American* 2–3 ears, golden kernels	Shumway

FLINT CORN

Longfellow: 117 days	Johnny's
Garland: 110 days	Johnny's
Indian Flint: 105 days multicolored ears, but meal is white	Nichols
Rainbow Flint* multicolored ears, but meal is white	Olds
Nichols Hominy Corn: 78 days	Nichols

HIGH-LYSINE CORN

Crow's Hybrid Corn Co., P.O. Box 306, Milford, IL 60953

Pioneer Hi-Bred Inc., 221 N. Main St., Tipton, IN 46072

FLOUR CORN

Mandan Bride: 98 days multicolored ears	Johnny's

DENT CORN

Type	Where Available
Seneca Hybrid: 103 days	Johnny's
Reid's Yellow Dent: 85 days	Park
Many varieties of dent corn	Crow's, Pioneer Hi-Bred

*No maturation time available

Addresses of Seed Companies Mentioned

Burgess Seed and Plant Co.
905 Four Seasons Road
Bloomington, IL 61701

Burpee Seed Co.
Warminster, PA 18991

Farmer Seed and Nursery Co.
Faribault, MN 55021

Herbst Brothers Seedsmen Inc.
1000 North Main Street
Brewster, NY 10509

Johnny's Selected Seeds
Albion, ME 04910

Nichols Garden Nursery
1190 North Pacific Highway
Albany, OR 97321

L. L. Olds Seed Co.
P.O. Box 7790, 2901 Packers Ave.
Madison, WI 53707

Geo. W. Park Seed Co. Inc.
Greenwood, SC 29647

R. H. Shumway Seedsman, Inc.
628 Cedar St., P.O. Box 777
Rockford, IL 61105

Stokes Seeds Inc.
737 Main Street, Box 548
Buffalo, NY 14240

Otis Twilley Seed Co., Inc.
P.O. Box 65
Trevose, PA 19047

Vermont Bean Seed Co.
Garden Lane
Bomoseen, VT 05732

Growing Garlic

Glenn Andrews

Illustrations by Charles H. Joslin and Brigita Fuhrmann

Growing Garlic

Garlic (*Allium sativum*) is a member of the same Lily family as onions, leeks, and shallots. It is one of the oldest known foods—its use has been traced back as far as 3000 B.C. Through all those years, it has been prescribed for virtually every known human complaint, from infertility to arthritis.

You grow garlic by planting individual garlic cloves. The plants grow to 1 to 2 feet tall, and, as the plants mature, the bulb divides into a cluster (or head) of cloves covered and held together by a thin, papery skin.

It's possible to get yourself a nice little head of garlic by just taking a clove of garlic you have sitting around in the kitchen and sticking it in the ground in fall. Come spring, the chances are good that your little clove will have become a whole head.

But it will be a small head, and there's no absolute certainty that this method will work. (It usually does, though.)

For a good crop of garlic, you'll be amply rewarded if you do it right. This means using good soil, well prepared, plus planting in the right place, at the right depth, watering, weeding, and then harvesting at the right time. Seem like lots of work? Luckily, this isn't hard.

WHERE TO PLANT

Garlic needs full sun to develop properly, so choose a spot where the sunshine will hit it all day long. You can get away with partial sun for many other sun-loving plants, but garlic is not one of these. Well, you'll still get garlic in a location that receives sun only, say, half the day, but it won't be as large as it would have been in total sun.

SOIL

As is true with any root vegetable, success in growing garlic starts with excellent soil.

Superb soil is sometimes hard to come by, though. (I once asked an organic farmer if I could buy some of his soil. He gasped and said, "I'd rather sell you one of my children!") So you'll probably have to settle for improving the soil you have. The addition of compost or humus and well-rotted manure will do the trick in most cases.

You want a soil that is rich in nutrients and of a consistency that will pass the "snowball test." Pick up a handful of your soil. Pack it gently into a snowball shape. Now break it open, again gently. If the ball forms nicely and if it yields and crumbles when you carefully press on it, you have good soil consistency.

If, however, you can't easily form a ball from the soil, it contains too high a proportion of sand. The solution: Add some compost or humus.

If your "snowball" won't crumble easily, then you know that there's too much clay. The solution for this: Add compost or humus and sharp sand.

The pH of the soil is important, too. Most garden centers sell inexpensive pH-testing kits. What you're looking for is a pH of between 6.0 and 6.8. A lower reading than this means your soil is too acid. The application of a little lime will take care of that. If your soil reading is over 7.0, your soil is alkaline. Digging in some garden sulfur, plus some extra compost, will take care of that.

But hey, we're talking about "perfect" soil here. Hardly anyone reaches perfection in their garlic-growing soil. You should do fine if you just come close! And remember that adding compost or humus will help, no matter what.

If you want to use a commercial fertilizer, look for a 10–10–10 mix. This means that the three main components of the fertilizer—nitrogen (N), phosphorus (P), and potassium (K)—each comprise 10 percent of the fertilizer. If you prefer an organic fertilizer, look for a blend with nearly equal numbers (like 3–2–2 or 5–5–5). Whichever you choose, follow the package recommendations for use. Too much is as bad as none.

Let's assume that your soil is now close to the ideal composition. What's left for you to do to it? Digging and loosening! If you've added compost, humus, sand, lime, or commercial fertilizer, you've probably worked the garden bed already. Now make sure the bed is well dug and the soil is loose to a depth of 1 foot. Picture yourself as a garlic clove that has been put into the ground. You want to become an entire head of garlic, but if the soil around you is compacted and stiff, you'll waste energy trying to grow.

If some kindly soul has provided you with nice loose soil, however, you have (literally!) room to grow.

WHEN TO PLANT

The usual advice given to would-be garlic growers is to plant in fall. However, the ideal planting time varies with your preference as well as where you live.

Northern gardeners will be well advised to plant in fall (for instance, in late September) before the first frost, then, after 3 or 4 days of watering, apply a mulch to help protect the garlic through the cold winters. Good mulches include shredded leaves or grasses (but not quack grass), peat moss, cocoa shells, and seaweed.

Gardeners in such semitemperate growing zones as Ohio feel it's best to plant their garlic in early spring—March or, at the latest, April.

Those in the Deep South have more latitude. Floridians will probably do best if they plant, just as in the North, in fall, looking forward to the cooler days of winter.

WHAT TO PLANT AND HOW TO PLANT IT

Professional garlic growers refer to "garlic seed." What they mean is the cloves of garlic themselves. Thus when you plant cloves of garlic from a grocery store, you are planting "seed."

Garlic seed of very high quality can be bought from mail-order sources (see below). If, though, you use store-bought garlic for your seed, use only the large cloves from the outside of good-size heads. If you want to use "seed" from home-grown garlic, store it in whole heads until your next planting season. Separated cloves dry out too fast.

If you are planting in fall in a cold climate, put the cloves 2 to 4 inches deep. Otherwise, plant them about 1 inch deep. In either case, the cloves should be placed pointed end up. They should be set at 3- to 5- inch intervals, with at least 18 inches between rows.

You will find that garlic sprouts very quickly—sometimes in as little as 3 days. However, it has a long way to go before each clove becomes a new head.

WATERING

It's very important to water your newly planted cloves thoroughly for their first 3 days in the ground. After this, you can settle down to a routine similar to that you would use for any other root vegetable—watering only every few days. You don't want to let the soil dry out, but you also don't want to drown your bulbs.

INSECTS

Garlic is not attacked by many insects. It can, in fact, be considered a deterrent to infestations that might affect other crops, which makes it popular as a companion planting with other garden favorites, including tomatoes, fruit trees, and roses.

One exception to the no-pest rule is the onion maggot larva, which turns up only occasionally. It shows itself in the cloves when they are harvested, but can be spotted earlier when you see a premature dying of the leaf tips.

The best thing to do when you see this symptom is to pull up and discard the offending plant. (Don't worry; it's very rare. You will probably never encounter this nasty little maggot.)

Continued →

Harvesting

Garlic has its own way of letting you know when it's ready to harvest.

Start by watching to make sure the garlic plants do not flower. This takes energy away from production below ground. If it looks like your plants will flower, break the stem to frustrate this development.

When the tops of the stalks start to turn brown, it's time to harvest. Dig the cloves up carefully, so you don't damage them with your shovel or spading fork. Avoid pulling the heads out by hand because of possible breakage.

Note: If you're desperate for some nice, fresh garlic before the stalks begin to brown, and if you don't mind small cloves, go right ahead and do a bit of early harvesting. Just try to let most of your crop reach maturity before you dig it up.

Unless you are planning to make garlic braids, brush off any loose dirt, then spread the heads out on the surface of the soil to dry. Leave them there until dry or until you are threatened by rain, then store at room temperature somewhere where they will receive plenty of air.

BRAIDING GARLIC

Braiding your garlic heads is probably the very best way to preserve them and keep them on hand throughout the year, since you hang the braid and air can circulate around it. Also, garlic braids make truly sensational presents—as long as you're sure the recipient is a garlic lover!

The soft-necked garlics work the best for braiding. Start making the braids as soon as you pull the heads from the ground, so the stems will still be pliable.

Some say to rinse the heads off. I think that's asking for trouble, so I suggest that you simply brush away any soil. Be sure to use heads that have their leaves attached.

Make the braids on a flat surface. Start with three fat heads of the garlic. Braid their leaves together, then start adding other heads (like French-braiding hair). For braids you plan to give away, or if you care a lot about the looks of the braid, put the heads so closely together that the leaves don't show. Otherwise, a little space between the heads will make it easier to remove them one at a time as needed.

You may find it reassuring to use some light wire to reinforce the braids.

When you've done as many heads as you want, braid the last of the leaves and tie off with raffia or twine—forming a loop for hanging.

Hang the finished braids where they'll get the benefit of a lot of air circulation.

Varieties of Garlic

There are a number of varieties of garlic. Each has its fans. The garlic you'll most commonly encounter is white or, more accurately, creamy.

But you'll also encounter quite a bit of "red" garlic. Many—but not all, by any means—people feel that it's the tastiest.

There are "hard-necked" garlics and also "soft-necked" ones, which are used for braiding.

Here are the names and details of some of the garlics grown in this country. Many of these are descendants of garlics brought here by immigrants from Italy, Spain, France, and Germany. These first four are available from Weavers Garlic Shedd, whose address you'll find below.

Northern white. These bulbs are very large, easy to peel, and winter hardy. Strong flavor. The skins are white, but the cloves are tinged with red.

German red. Cloves are light brown, with a touch of purple. Easy to peel. Stores well. Hot, spicy flavor.

Italian purple. White skinned, with purple stripes. Easily peeled and a good keeper. Spicy, biting flavor. The favorite of many.

Silver skins. A nice garlic in every way, but grown primarily because it is soft necked, and thus suitable for braiding.

And here are three garlics from Shepherd's Garden Seeds.

Spanish rojo (formerly known as Morado de Pedronera). Red-skinned cloves. Tasty; easy to peel; a good keeper. Shepherd's suggests using some of the early, tender greens in stir-fries.

Gilroy California late garlic. Originally brought to California by immigrants from Italy. Large, easy-to-peel cloves. A soft-necked variety, good for braiding.

Early Asian purple skin. Popular in China—and best grown in warm climates in the Southeast and Southwest.

And then there's "elephant" garlic, named for its very large size. The cloves are at least two or three times bigger than the largest "regular" garlic you'll find. Bulbs (heads) can often weigh a pound, or even more. Elephant garlic is also quite a bit milder than other varieties, thus most people, or at least real garlic lovers, find it disappointing. (The somewhat disillusioning truth is that it isn't a garlic at all—it's a leek!)

Sources for Garlic Seed

Remember that what's known as the "seed" of garlic is the clove of the pungent herb. You can use cloves from heads of garlic you buy at a market, or you can know exactly what sort of garlic you're growing by ordering from one of these places.

Dakota Gardens and Herbs
R.R. 6, Box 363
Minot, ND 58703

Weavers Garlic Shedd
29822 Ashburn Lane
Shedd, OR 97377
(541) 491–3920

Shepherd's Garden Seeds
30 Irene Street
Torrington, CT
06790–6658
(860) 482–3638

All the Onions

Revised and Updated

Betty Jacobs

Illustrations by Elayne Sears, Charles Joslin, Alison Kolesar, and Louise Riotte

Bulb (Common) Onions

Botanical Name: *Allium cepa*, Cepa Group

Other Names: (Fr.) *oignon*; (Ger.) *Zwibel*; (It.) *cipolla*; (Sp.) *cebolla*

Life Span: Half-hardy perennial, usually grown as a long-season annual

HOW TO CHOOSE THE RIGHT VARIETY

The right variety is more important for onions than it is for most other vegetables. If you pick a variety adapted to the wrong part of the country (say, trying to grow the sweet Vidalia-type onions in the Northeast), you could end up with nice scallions but no bulbs. The formation of bulbs in different varieties is controlled by how the plants respond to day length. When daylight reaches the right number of hours for that variety, the onion plant stops putting out leaves and starts producing a bulb. The eventual size of the mature bulb depends on how much leaf growth the plant has produced at the time bulb formation starts. If the onion plant hasn't achieved enough top growth (either because it was planted too late or because the variety needs a different day length), the plants won't be able to make bulbs. A cool start encourages the heavy leaf growth necessary for building up good-sized bulbs. Variety alone doesn't ensure good onions; you also need to provide fertile soil, so plants get the nutrients they need to produce good top growth.

Onions are grouped into short-day, long-day, and intermediate varieties. *Short-day* onions are adapted to growing in southern climates (south of 35° latitude), as they need only 11 or 12 hours of daylight to stimulate bulb formation. They also need mild winters (where temperatures don't go below about 20°F), as they're planted in late fall and grow through the winter. Bulb formation is triggered when days start to get longer in spring. The long winter growing season gives these varieties plenty of time to produce lots of leaves, so they can develop impressively large mature onions by late spring or early summer. The extra-sweet onion grown in Vidalia, Georgia ('Granex 33' or 'Yellow Granex') is a short-day variety.

Gardeners north of 35° latitude need to grow *long-day varieties*. (The 35° runs approximately through Flagstaff, Albuquerque, Memphis, and Charlotte.) These put out leaves during the long days of northern summers; they don't start making bulbs until the days start getting shorter (14 to 15 hours) as summer wanes.

Intermediate-day varieties, as you might expect, fall somewhere between the other two. They don't need the extra-long days of northern areas, but they need a long growing season. They can be planted from seeds sown outdoors in fall anywhere south or west of Zone 7 (below 35°N latitude and up the West Coast through the Pacific Northwest). Intermediate-day varieties can be grown in the North, but only if started from transplants rather than seeds or sets; otherwise, the growing season won't be long enough to form good bulbs.

There's usually a trade-off between sweetness and storage quality in onion varieties. The onions with the sweetest flavor typically don't store as well as the more pungent types. Many of the largest and sweetest onions are short-day varieties. Many of the best keepers are long-day varieties; while these have a pungent flavor when raw, they lose their bite when cooked and also become milder in storage.

When choosing a variety, read the descriptions you'll find in seed catalogs. A catalog should tell you which varieties grow best in what areas, the number of days from planting to maturity, the shape and flavor of the bulb, and whether it is suitable for eating raw, cooking, pickling, and/or storing.

> ### DID YOU KNOW?
> The onion is one of the oldest vegetables known. It belongs to a genus of about 280 species of bulbing plants, all having a very distinctive smell. There are hundreds of cultivated varieties, which vary in appearance, pungency, and keeping qualities. They are widely distributed over the Northern Hemisphere, mostly in regions with a temperate climate.

SEEDS, TRANSPLANTS, OR SETS?

You can start your onions by sowing seeds, by buying started plants, or by planting sets. Starting onions from seeds gives you the widest choice of varieties (so be sure you choose one that's the right day length). It takes 100–120 days for most varieties to develop mature bulbs, so plan on starting seeds indoors where the growing season is shorter. You can, of course, use the immature onions as scallions (green onions) sooner. If stored in a cool, dry spot, onion seeds should remain viable for two years.

Buying plants gives you a small choice of varieties, but it enables you to produce an edible crop more quickly. While relatively expensive, it's a good choice if you live where the growing season is short and want to produce the largest onions. You can often find flats of seedlings at local garden centers, and now you can order pencil-thick transplants from many standard seed companies. Mail-order transplants are shipped at the appropriate planting time for your area; while they may arrive looking tired from their journey, they recover quickly if planted soon after arrival.

Planting sets gives you even less choice of varieties (unless you've grown your own the previous year; see below for how to do so). But you'll

Continued →

get green onions very quickly, and the bulbs will mature three or more weeks before those grown from seeds. Sets are also available by mail order, for less expense than transplants. They're a good choice for short-season areas, or where onion diseases have been a problem (sets and transplants are more disease-resistant than are direct-seeded onions).

How to Grow Good Onions

SOME RECOMMENDED VARIETIES

Here are a few onion varieties for different areas of the United States. There are many more that are equally good. Check catalog descriptions or ask your local Cooperative Extension Service or garden center. Varieties sold as sets usually do well in most regions; they may be described only as "red," "white," or "yellow" sets.

Long-Day Varieties for the North

Plants: 'Yellow Sweet Spanish' (large and mild); 'Walla Walla Sweet' (large, white with yellow skin, one of the sweetest onions for the North); 'Red Burgermaster' (red-and-white flesh). *Note:* Transplants of intermediate-day varieties also grow well in the North.

Sets: 'Stuttgarter' (yellow, good for storage); 'Ebenezer'

Seeds: 'Early Yellow Globe' or 'New York Early' (early maturing, yellow); 'Yellow Sweet Spanish' (large bulbs); 'White Sweet Spanish'; 'Copra' (one of the best keepers); 'Southport Red Globe' (red skin, pink to white flesh); 'Mars' (relatively early, red)

Intermediate-Day Varieties for Middle Latitudes

Plants: 'Stockton Red' (good keeper; transplants do well in all regions)

Sets: 'Stuttgarter'; 'Ebenezer'

Seeds: 'Early Yellow Globe'; 'Candy' (white flesh, one of the sweetest, also grows well in the North); 'Red Torpedo' (mild, nonbolting, disease-resistant)

Short-Day Varieties for the South

Plants: 'Yellow Granex' or 'Granex 33' (very sweet, type grown in Vidalia, Ga.); 'White Bermuda' or 'Crystal Wax' (very sweet)

Sets: 'Ebenezer'

Seeds: 'Yellow Granex' or 'Granex 33' (very sweet, large); 'Texas Grano '1015Y' or 'Texas Supersweet' (very sweet, large, disease-resistant); 'White Bermuda' or 'Crystal Wax' (very sweet); 'Red Burgundy' or 'Red Hamburger' (sweet, red skin, red-and-white flesh); 'Yellow Bermuda' (white flesh, small necks)

Onions prefer a loose, crumbly, well-drained, fertile soil with a pH between 6.0 and 7.0. If you have any doubt about whether your soil is well drained, grow onions in raised beds, that is, 4 inches (10 cm) higher than the surrounding soil. Incorporate lots of organic matter to improve drainage and fertility. You can add organic matter at any time, but it's best to do this well before planting. That means the fall before planting, where onions will be planted or transplanted in spring; or a month or two before where onions will be planted in spring. Spread a couple of inches (about 5 cm) of compost or well-aged manure over the planting area and turn under with a garden fork or till in. If a soil test shows your soil is acidic, it's a good idea to add lime at the same time that you add organic matter; add only enough lime to raise the pH to the ideal range, as too much is worse than too little.

A week or so before planting or transplanting, spread a balanced fertilizer (such as 5–10-10) at the rate recommended on the fertilizer label for vegetables. Rake the soil to create a level planting surface.

STARTING ONIONS FROM SEEDS

To give the onions the longest possible growing season, seeds should be sown outdoors in fall where winters aren't too severe (Zones 7 and warmer). In Zone 7, sow onion seeds (intermediate-day or short-day varieties) from late August to mid September; in the warmer parts of Zone 8 and Zone 9, sow in October (short-day varieties). In colder zones where the growing season is long enough (100 to 120 days; the actual length of time needed depends on the variety), you can sow seeds outside in early spring. Plant seeds a month before the final spring frost, when the soil has warmed to at least 45°F (about 7°C). In areas with shorter seasons, start seeds indoors.

START ONION SEEDS INDOORS

Where the growing season is short, start onion seeds indoors 10 to 12 weeks before the last expected frost. Onion seeds will germinate in 7 to 10 days if kept between 64° and 77°F (16°–25°C). They'll germinate at a temperature as low as 45°F (8°C) but will take longer. Once they sprout, grow seedlings under fluorescent lights or in a greenhouse or cold frame.

1. Fill a seed flat with sterile potting soil, and tap it down gently.

2. Shake seeds thinly over the soil, so that they're well spaced.

3. Cover seeds with no more than 1/4 inch of fine soil. If some seeds show through the next day, sprinkle a little more soil over them, but never bury them deeply.

4. Stand the whole flat in a tray of water, so that the water comes only about three-quarters of the way up the sides of the flat. The water will be drawn up into the soil. Remove the flat from the water as soon as the soil surface looks damp. Let the surplus water drain out of the flat. Keep in a warm spot to speed germination.

5. As soon as the onions start to show, move to a bright spot such as under fluorescent lights. Once they've sprouted, they don't need as much warmth.

6. Keep seedlings moist by bottom watering when they begin to look dry. Once the little plants are well up, you can water them with a fine spray from above. Thin to four seedlings per inch, or three plants to each 1- or 2-inch-diameter cell.

7. When the onions are about as thick as a pencil, they should be hardened off. Put the flat outside for longer and longer periods for a few days, starting with the warmest time of day, and eventually leave them out all night. This hardening off should take about two weeks.

8. To make the seedlings easier to transplant, lift them and wash the soil off the roots, trim any extra-long roots, and trim the green leaves to about 5 inches (12.5 cm) long.

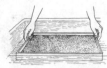
Bottom watering keeps seedlings moist.

Allow 1/2 ounce (14 g) of seeds for every 100 feet (30 m) of row. Plant seeds 1/2 inch apart in rows, spacing rows 12 to 18 inches apart. Cover seeds with 1/4 to 1/2 inch of soil.

Many gardeners thin their rows twice, the first time when the seedlings are very small and the next time when the plants are large enough to be enjoyed as scallions. Thin young seedlings to 2 inches apart, then harvest scallions as needed to leave mature plants 4 inches apart to form bulbs. (Final spacing should be 6 inches for large varieties.)

STARTING ONIONS FROM SETS

Sets are small, dry onion bulbs that were grown the previous year but not allowed to mature. They produce the earliest onions; they're also a good choice if you want to grow large onions where the growing season is short. A pound of sets will plant about 50 feet of row (.5 kg for 15 m). Sets can be planted outdoors four to six weeks before the last expected frost. Press sets into the soil so the stem ends point up and they're not more than 1 inch (2.5 cm) below the surface, and 4 to 6 inches apart. Or plant the sets more closely (2 inches apart) and harvest the thinnings as scallions, eventually leaving 4 to 6 (10–15 cm) inches between plants. In this case you'll need about twice as many sets for the same amount of row (2 pounds for 50 feet; 1 kg for 15 m).

GROW YOUR OWN SETS FROM SEEDS

By planting seeds too late (about mid May), you can ensure that they won't have time to mature and will form only very small bulbs, or sets. When replanted the following spring, these tiny bulbs can finish developing; because they get a head start on the season, they'll form good-sized bulbs in much less time as soon as they get the right day-length signal.

Choose a sunny area of well-worked, weed-free soil. Sow the seeds thickly and don't thin the seedlings; this will help to keep bulbs small. Don't fertilize the seedlings; you don't want to encourage too much top growth or you'll end up with bulbs that are too large. (Overly large sets may bolt to seed the following spring.) Water as required. Lift them in late summer or as soon as the tops are dry. The bulbs, which should be under 3/4 inch (approximately 2 cm) in diameter, will form no flower buds in cool storage. The following year, the bulbs will quickly produce edible "green" onions or, if left in the ground until late summer, will grow into good-sized bulb onions.

TRANSPLANTING ONIONS

Whether you've raised your own seedlings or bought plants, onions can be transplanted out about a month before the last frost date (they can handle temperatures as cold as 20°F, about -7°C). If you've grown your own, be sure to harden them off first. Mail-order transplants will arrive already hardened off.

Transplants should be set out about 1 inch deep (or at about the same level they were growing). Space standard varieties 4 inches apart, larger varieties 6 inches apart. If you plan to eat a lot of scallions, space transplants 2 to 3 inches apart and thin every other one to leave a final spacing of 4 to 6 inches (10–15 cm). If you prefer to plant in standard rows, space rows 12 to 18 inches apart. Onions also grow well in wide rows, which allow you to grow more plants in a smaller garden.

In wide rows, onions are spaced 4 to 6 inches (10–15 cm) apart in all directions in 4-foot-wide (1.2 m) beds. This method works well in raised beds. Two great advantages of this method are that you never have to walk on the beds—as anyone kneeling down can reach halfway across a 4-foot (1.2 m) bed to weed and cultivate—and no space is wasted between rows. Make your wide rows as many feet long as necessary to give you space to grow the quantity of onions you require.

Here's an example of how to calculate how many plants you'll need for wide-row planting. Assume a spacing of 5 inches (12.5 cm) between onions, with 4 inches (10 cm) from the edge of the bed to the first onion and 4 inches (10 cm) to the back edge of the bed, and you'll end up with eight onions per row. Every 5 inches (12.5 cm) along the bed will give you another row of eight onions, so a bed 5 feet (1.5 m) long will give you room for 12 rows. A wide bed 4 feet x 5 feet (1.2 x 1.5 m) therefore provides space for 8 x 12 = 96 onions. If you like to eat a lot of scallions, you can fit in even more onions by spacing plants 2 1/2 inches (6.25 cm) apart in at least a few of the rows and gradually thinning alternate plants as scallions or small onions.

CARE DURING GROWTH

Whichever way your onions are started, they'll all need the same care. Keep them free of weeds. Onions tolerate far less crowding from weeds than can many other vegetables. Because onion roots grow close to the surface, keep cultivation shallow. At no time while they're growing should soil be drawn up around the plants. Onions do better growing on or near the surface. For the largest onions, pull away the soil from the upper two-thirds of the bulb.

After plants have been growing for a month or so, they'll appreciate side-dressing with fertilizer, or a foliar feeding with liquid seaweed or fish emulsion; repeat in another month. Avoid giving onions too much nitrogen; you want to encourage good growth, but too much nitrogen will give you more leaves than bulb. Stop feeding plants about a month before harvest, or as soon as the necks start feeling soft.

If any of your onions send up a flower stalk, pull them up and eat them. Bulb onions that have started to bolt won't store well, so it's best to eat them before the flower stalk gets very big.

Onions need even moisture to grow well. A thin layer of mulch (1 to 2 inches of fine compost or chopped leaves) helps keep the soil moist and reduces weeds, but pull the mulch away from plant bases once bulbs begin forming. Water plants regularly until the tops start to yellow, then withhold water to help skins ripen for better storage. When the leaves have turned yellow and about a quarter have fallen over, bend tops over to direct energy from the leaves into the maturing bulbs. The back of a garden rake is handy for this job.

Continued →

HOW TO HARVEST ONIONS

Once the tops have been bent over, it will take a few days (depending on the weather) for the leaves to dry enough to harvest your onions. When the tops are quite dry, lift the bulbs and leave them in the sun to dry, long enough so that any dirt on their roots is dry. To prepare for storage, you can braid the long dry tops and hang the braids. Or just cut off the tops, leaving 1 inch (2.5 cm) of stem on each bulb, and trim back the roots. Place trimmed onions in slatted crates, net bags, or old nylon stockings (tie a knot between each onion, and cut the stocking when you want to use an onion).

Cure onions for several weeks by keeping them in a shed or under cover where air can circulate freely. While the weather is still dry and before frost is expected, move the onions into a dry, cool, frost-free, and (preferably) dark storage place.

SWEET, VIDALIA-TYPE ONIONS

There are a few tricks to growing the large, sweet onions called 'Vidalia' after the place in Georgia that made them famous. Their sweetness is a combination of the right variety, an exceptionally long growing season, and fertile soils low in sulfur. The largest, sweetest onions can be grown only in the South and in mild areas of the West because they're short-day varieties that are planted in fall and grown through the winter. They need winters that don't get below 20°F (7°C). If planted in early spring, these varieties will still produce good onions, but the bulbs won't be as large or as sweet as those grown through the winter.

The best varieties for sweet onions are 'Yellow Granex' or 'Granex 33' (the type grown in Vidalia, Georgia), 'Texas Grano 1015Y' or 'Texas Supersweet' (any variety with "Grano" in the name), and improved Bermuda types such as 'Excel'. In parts of the Northwest with winters mild enough for fall planting, the intermediate-day variety 'Walla Walla Sweet' produces large, very sweet onions. A new intermediate-day variety, 'Candy', also produces very sweet onions from spring planting in most parts of the country.

If onions are stressed by low fertility or lack of water while they're growing, their flavor will be more pungent, so it's important to keep plants well fed and watered. Sulfur also increases pungency; one secret to the sweetness of onions grown in Vidalia is the low sulfur content of the soils there. While you can't change the sulfur content of your soil, you can avoid increasing it by steering clear of fertilizers that contain sulfur (such as ammonium sulfate). Stop fertilizing about 30 days before you expect to harvest in order to keep onions as sweet as possible.

When the necks are well contracted and the skins are brittle, curing is complete. The ideal storage conditions for onions are quite cool, 36°F (2°C), and fairly dry, 60 to 70 percent relative humidity. Storage temperatures must not get above 45°F (7°C).

Use thick-necked onions first; they're not as good keepers as thin-necked bulbs. In general, sweet varieties don't store as well (because they have a higher water content), so eat them first. Pungent varieties last the longest and often become sweeter in storage.

BRAIDING ONIONS

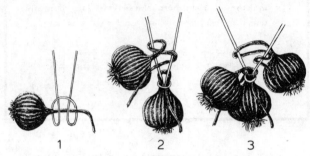

1. Loop string around onion top.

2. Braid in second onion as shown.

3. Repeat with third onion and others.

SCALLIONS (GREEN ONIONS) AND PICKLING ONIONS

As already mentioned, the thinnings of immature bulb onions make good scallions. If you want just scallions, you can also plant varieties developed to form no bulbs, or only small ones. The bestknown variety of bulb onion grown specifically for scallions is 'White Lisbon'. It's easy to grow from seeds and is grown the same way as onions for bulbs. In climates with mild winters, a fall as well as a spring sowing is recommended so scallions can be harvested almost year-round. In hot climates, fall sowing is mandatory.

There are also a number of varieties of bunching onions such as 'Evergreen White' and 'Evergreen Hardy White' that produce long, thin, nonbulbing stems. These make good scallions that will stand over the winter months.

Pickling onions should have small bulbs, so they don't need a rich soil. You can also grow them spaced closely together to help keep bulbs small; thin seedlings to no more than 2 inches apart.

Suggested Suppliers

Most seed catalogs offer either onion sets or transplants as well as seeds; many offer garlic, shallots, and Welsh or bunching onions. Here are a few good sources to get you started.

Filaree Farm
182 Conconully Highway
Okanogan, WA 98840
(509) 422–6940
e-mail: filareenorthcascades.net;
http://www.filareefarm.com
Specializes in garlic

The Gourmet Gardener
8650 College Boulevard
Overland Park, KS 66210

(913) 345–0490

Seeds for onions, leeks, chives, garlic chives; sets and seeds for shallots;
garlic sets

Le Jardin du Gourmet
P.O. Box 75
St. Johnsbury Center, VT 05863
(802) 748–1446

Seeds for onions, chives, garlic chives; garlic sets; shallots (sets or seedlings); Egyptian onions;
leek plants

Nichols Garden Nursery
1190 North Pacific Highway
Albany, OR 97321–4580
(541) 928–9280

Sets for Egyptian onions, shallots, several types of garlic, elephant garlic;
seeds for chives, garlic chives, leeks, onions, Welsh and bunching onions;
onion plants

Shepherd's Garden Seeds
30 Irene Street
Torrington, CT 06790–6658
(800) 482–3638

Seeds for onions, leeks, chives, garlic chives; onion plants;
garlic sets; shallot sets

Thompson and Morgan, Inc.
P.O. Box 1308
Jackson, NJ 08527–0308
(800) 274–7333

Seeds for onions, leeks, chives, garlic chives, Welsh onions;
sets for onions, shallots, elephant garlic

FRUITS AND BERRIES

Grow the Best Blueberries

Vladimir G. Shutak and Robert E. Gough
Illustrations by Nancy Anisfield

Would you like to grow blueberries in your own yard and enjoy fresh fruit for 8 to 10 weeks during the summer? You can, if you collect a few basic guidelines about location, soil, and culture.

You know that there are a lot of different kinds of blueberries besides the highbush blueberry—dryland, evergreen, mountain, rabbiteye, half-high, and low bush. We are going to talk about the highbush blueberry only—the kind most common to commercial growers and the home gardener.

Highbush blueberry plants are easy to grow, relatively pest-free, and need little maintenance; they also fit very easily into most landscape plans. The plant has delicate white bell-shaped flowers in the spring, delicious fruit in the summer, bright crimson leaves in the fall, and red, or yellow-colored branches in the winter.

Where Can You Grow Blueberries?

Highbush blueberries can be grown in most areas of the United States; however, don't plant them in an area where winter temperatures frequently fall below −20°F. Also, because they need winter chilling, don't plant blueberries in areas where there is not at least 800 hours (about 2 months) of temperatures below 40°F. You can extend these limits somewhat by planting new cultivars especially developed for extreme northern and southern areas. In most cases these cultivars are crosses between highbush blueberry and rabbiteye for southern locations and low bush blueberry for northern locations.

BEATING THE CLIMATE LIMITATIONS

You can extend the general temperature area limitations if you select a location within your area which is known to be warmer or cooler than the surrounding area—this is called a microclimate.

For instance, if you have an area protected from the cold northern winds, it will be warmer than an exposed area. It will also reduce drying injury. You can create an area like this by providing a windbreak by planting trees or putting up a fence on the north side of the planting. Frequently, you can also take advantage of existing windbreaks provided by buildings—yours or your neighbor's.

Any structure—even a driveway—near your plants which absorbs and/or reflects heat, may help to maintain higher temperatures. If you are looking for a cooler area, select an exposed area with good air movement. A northern slope or an area which is shaded from the late afternoon sun (after 3:00 P.M.) will provide a cooler environment.

REDUCE FROST DAMAGE

If you live in an area where late spring frosts are likely, locate the plants on a northern slope. This will delay the bloom in the spring and reduce chances of frost damage. A gentle slope is also recommended because it will provide better air drainage, help dry the air, and reduce fungus diseases. Do not plant in areas surrounded by buildings or dense stands of trees because both will cause poor air circulation.

PROVIDE FULL SUNLIGHT

For best production, plant your plants where they can receive 8 hours of sunlight per day. Too much shade results in spindly growth, reduces yield, and decreases the quality of the fruit.

Continued →

GREEN MANURE CROPS

A green manure crop is usually a small grain crop that is tilled under before it matures. The decaying tops and roots provide organic matter and some nutrients to help build up the soil. This process increases soil aeration, water-holding capacity, and stimulates microbial activity in the soil.

Some of these grains grow best in summer and will not tolerate a frost. Others will survive the winter and are useful in preventing soil erosion during this time. Some commonly used green manure crops are listed below, along with their time and rate of seeding.

Crop	Seeding Time	Seeding Rate per 1,000 sq. ft.	Time to Turn Under
Winter rye	Early fall	2 lb.	Very early spring
Buckwheat	Early summer	1 lb.	Early fall
Ryegrass	Early fall	1/2 lb.	Early spring
Millet	Early summer	1 lb.	Early fall
Soybean	Early summer	1 lb.	Early fall

Provide a Good Soil Environment

The best plants are grown on soil that has met 3 major requirements. First, it must be acid (sour) and fertile. Second, it should have a lot of organic matter; and third, it must have good water drainage. If you don't have this kind of soil, don't get discouraged. You can change the soil so that you do have good soil for blueberries and we will tell you how to do it.

MAKING SOIL ACID

The best soil pH (acidity) for growing blueberries is between pH 4.5 and 5.6. This is also good for rhododendrons and azaleas. If your soil is higher than 5.6, you should add powdered sulfur. You may have to experiment a little with amounts for your soil conditions. In general, 24 pounds of sulfur for each 1,000 square feet should lower acidity by 1 full pH point. If your pH is too low, your soil is too sour, and limestone should be added to sweeten it. Again, the exact amount will depend upon your location, but about 150 pounds per 1,000 square feet will raise the pH by 1 pH point.

There are several home soil test kits you can buy. These generally will indicate soil pH and fertility. However, because most of these rely upon color tests, you may have a difficult time interpreting them. You will probably be better off having your soil tested through your local county extension agent's office. There is usually only a modest charge for these services, and they will tell you how to take soil samples.

INCREASING THE ORGANIC MATTER

Blueberry soils should have a lot of organic matter. You can increase the level of organic material by adding compost, peat moss, leaves, straw, and other organic materials (except sewage sludge).

You must have good soil drainage with a water table no closer to the soil surface than 18 inches. A good way to test this yourself is simply to dig a hole about a foot deep and fill it with water. If the water disappears within about an hour and a half, the drainage is okay. If it doesn't you'd better find another spot. But remember, swampy areas can be planted as a last resort, if you either install a costly system of drainage ditches or plant the bushes on small mounds as they grow naturally in swamps.

PREPARING THE SOIL

Preparing the soil for highbush blueberries means building up organic matter and adjusting the soil pH. The best way to start is to plant a green manure crop of buckwheat in the early summer prior to planting the blueberries the following spring. In late summer, measure the soil pH and adjust it to be between 4.5 and 5.0 by spreading either ground limestone (to raise the pH) or ground sulfur (to lower the pH) just before turning the buckwheat under. In early September, till the area again, and plant a crop of winter rye. This will reduce soil loss from erosion during the winter months, as well as add additional organic matter. In early spring, turn under the winter rye and whatever other organic materials you can find—rotted manure, compost, and peat moss—and bring the soil to a fine texture by thorough harrowing or rototilling. Complete this and let the soil settle for at least 2 weeks before planting.

If you are only planting a few bushes, you can prepare individual planting holes. Dig the holes approximately 2 feet in diameter by 2 feet deep in the early spring. Use a mixture of equal parts of loam, sand, and organic matter, such as rotted sawdust, compost, or peat moss to fill the hole when planting. A word of caution! Be sure the sawdust or compost component of the mix is well rotted. Undecomposed organic matter, such as fresh sawdust, can severely stunt the plant.

Selecting Plants

Blueberry plants are available from nurseries as rooted cuttings or as older plants. Generally, we recommend buying dormant, vigorous 2-year-old plants, 12 to 18 inches high. Younger, smaller plants may be less expensive, but they require greater care, while the cost of older plants frequently is not justified. Obtain plants from a reputable nursery to assure trueness to name. To get the cultivars and quality that you want, place your order at least 6 months before planting.

ESTIMATING QUANTITIES

You can figure out how many bushes you need by remembering the following points:

- A plant 6 to 8 years old or older can produce up to 10 quarts of fruit per bush, if you take good care of it.
- Each mature bush may have a total spread of 4 to 5 feet.
- Bushes are usually spaced about 6 feet apart within rows and about 8 to 10 feet apart between rows.
- In hedgerows, space bushes 4 feet apart.

Blueberries are borne on 1-year-old shoots. Each overwintering flower bud can produce 5 to 15 berries, which typically ripen over a 6-week period.

CULTIVARS

Cultivar is just a shortened word for the term "cultivated variety." There are hundreds of different cultivars of highbush blueberries, and some will be best for you.

If you look in most seed catalogs, you will find that most mailorder operations will list only a few cultivars of blueberries. That's too bad, because cultivars have some definite geographic preferences. The list below gives cultivars by region to help you choose the best variety. Even better than choosing from a list is enlisting the aid of your local county extension agent. These agents can tell you what cultivars other growers in your area have grown successfully.

You want to choose more than one cultivar to grow. Why? You will have a longer picking season and a better crop if you plant early, midseason, and late-ripening cultivars. Also, although blueberries are considered self-fruitful, you will get a greater yield and larger fruit that ripens earlier if you interplant several cultivars.

This listing is based on United States Department of Agriculture recommendations. Approximate order of ripening is indicated by the letters "e" for *early*, "m" for *midseason*, and "l" for *late*. There are **many** cultivars that are not included in this list, so **don't forget** to have that chat with your extension agent.

Geographic Area 1: North Florida, Coastal Plain of Georgia, South Carolina (south of Charleston), Louisiana, Mississippi, Alabama, East Texas, lower Southwest, and Southern California (Los Angeles and south)

Cultivars

Flordablue

Sharpblue (for trial only)

Geographic Area 2: Mountain and Upper Piedmont regions of Area 1

Cultivars

Morrow (e)	Patriot (m)
Croatan (e)	Bluecrop (m)
Harrison (e)	Berkeley (m)
Murphy (e)	Lateblue (l)
Bluetta (e)	

Geographic Area 3: Richmond, VA, south to Piedmont and Coastal Plain Carolinas, Tennessee, lower Ohio Valley, east and south Arkansas, lower Southwest, and mid-California

Cultivars

Morrow (e)	Bluecrop (m)
Croatan (e)	Patriot (except in coastal plain
Harrison (e)	areas) (m)
Murphy (e)	

Geographic Area 4: Mid-Atlantic states, Midwest, Ozark highlands, mountain regions of Area 3, northern California, Oregon, and Washington

Cultivars

Bluetta (e)	Lateblue (l)
Collins (e)	Elliott (l)
Patriot (m)	Herbert (l)
Bluecrop (m)	Elizabeth (l)
Blueray (m)	Berkeley (m)
Darrow (l)	

Geographic Area 5: New England and cooler areas of the Great Lakes States

Cultivars

Bluetta (e)	Blueray (m)
Collins (e)	Meader (m)
Patriot (m)	Berkeley (m)
Bluecrop (m)	Northland (m)

Planting

You can obtain blueberry plants from the nursery bare-rooted, canned (potted), or balled-and-burlapped. The latter two are best because they usually can be planted without disturbing the roots too much.

Bare-rooted plants often are shipped in plastic covers. Remove these as soon as the plants arrive. If you can't plant immediately, heel the plants in by placing the roots in a trench and mounding soil around them. If the ground is frozen, put them in a cool, protected place, such as a garage, and cover the entire plant with damp peat moss or sawdust.

Try to plant during the afternoon of a cloudy day.

Although blueberries can be planted in the fall, spring planting is safer and is recommended in most areas. Do this as soon as the ground can be worked in the spring. This means as soon as the ground has dried

Continued ➜

out enough. Prune off any damaged or excessively long roots, any weak or broken wood, and all flower buds, since fruiting the first year may stunt the bush.

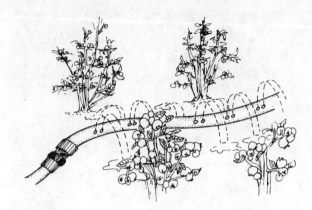

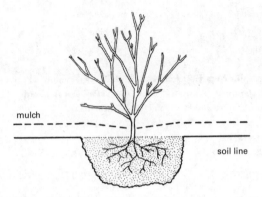

Plant your blueberry bush 1 to 2 inches deeper than it was planted in the nursery. Plant the bush in an oversized hole filled with a loam/peat/sand mixture.

Plant your bushes 1 to 2 inches deeper than they were in the nursery and 4 to 6 feet apart in rows spaced 8 to 10 feet apart. In large plantings, do not separate cultivars by more than 2 rows from others with similar ripening seasons. After you put the plants in the hole, fill it three-fourths full of either soil or a loam-peat-sand (1 to 1 to 1 proportions) mixture, and flood it with water. After the water has seeped out, fill the remainder of the hole and pack firmly with your feet. Water the plant thoroughly with a starter solution to encourage rapid growth.

Caring for Your Blueberries

Highbush blueberries are easy to grow. All you have to do is fertilize them 2 or 3 times a year, prune once a year, and make sure they have enough water. We will discuss their needs in this section. You always should pay attention to the general health—or as we call it, vigor—of your plants. A mature, vigorous bush should have dark green foliage and should produce 2 or 3 new shoots from the base of the plant each year. About half of the new growth on the bush should be longer than 5 or 6 inches and a few new shoots should be 12 to 18 inches long.

IRRIGATION

Blueberry plants require a constant moisture supply for best growth. The highbush blueberry plant has an exceedingly fine, fibrous root system that is mostly located within the dripline of the bush and within the top foot of soil. It is, therefore, relatively shallow and quite susceptible to drought stress under poor soil conditions.

When should you water? First, try the "feel test" to determine whether the soil needs moisture. Squeeze a soil sample in the palm of your hand. If the ball formed is weak and easily broken, soil moisture is adequate. If it is not easily broken, the soil is too wet; if no ball is formed, then it is too dry.

A soaker hose efficiently provides water to the shallow roots without wetting the berries, which could cause them to split.

If irrigation is necessary, water during the early morning, but don't wet the bushes when berries are beginning to ripen. If you wet the berries at this time they may split. You can use ground flooding or a soaker hose. This will conserve water and prevent wetting of the bush. Apply about an inch of water during each watering.

Blueberries flower in early to late May, depending on the cultivar. The flowers are not especially tolerant of cold or frost.

POLLINATION

As we mentioned earlier, blueberry plants are generally self-fruitful, but interplanting cultivars will improve yields because some cultivars, such as Earliblue and Coville, do not produce enough good pollen.

Bees are necessary for good cross-pollination. If the wild population is small, we recommend you provide 1 hive of bees for every 300 blueberry bushes. Bees should be introduced into the field before one-fourth of the earliest cultivar reaches full bloom. Place the hives near the center of each planting. If you are planning to do any insecticide spraying following bloom be sure to remove the bees.

FERTILIZATION

All plants remove nutrients from the soil. If these are not replenished, the plant will soon lose vigor and crop production will be reduced. You can replace major nutrients by periodic application of recommended fertilizers.

We usually recommend fertilizers such as 5–10-10 or 10–10-10. Since these are more concentrated than "organic" fertilizers, they are applied in smaller quantities. We find that commercial fertilizers are more readily available, easier to handle, free from weed seeds, more consistent in nutrient content, and more readily available to the plant than organic materials, and that is why we prefer commercial fertilizers over "organic" ones.

Make the first fertilizer application about a month after planting. Apply about a half-cup of 5–10-10 or 10–10-10 per bush. Just spread the fertilizer around the plant in a broad band at least 6 inches but not more than 12 inches from its base. Repeat the application in early July. If the plants show low vigor, fertilize again in the fall when the leaves drop. Make the last 2 applications at the same rate as the first. If you have mulched around your bushes, double the rate of the first application and omit the second.

You should increase the rate of fertilizer each year until mature plants (after 6 to 8 years in the field) are receiving about 1 pound* per plant, two-thirds applied at the beginning of bloom and the other third applied 5 to 6 weeks later. Since most fertilizer nutrients move vertically in the soil, proper fertilizer placement is important.

If your mature plants are not vigorous, a late autumn application (when the leaves drop) of about 1 pound of fertilizer per bush will increase nutrient reserves in the plant and promote an early spurt of growth in the spring. Don't try this on your vigorous bushes, and do not apply the fertilizer too early in the autumn, since an early application could encourage late autumn shoot growth that will winterkill. When possible, rake in the fertilizer after application.

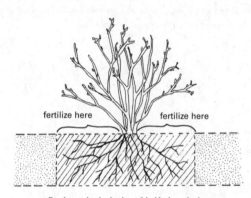

fertilize here   fertilize here

Fertilize under the dripline of the blueberry bush.

* Complete fertilizers (10–10-10, 5–10-10, etc.) and superphosphate weigh about 7.5 oz. per cup; urea, ammonium sulfate, and ammonium nitrate weigh about 5.5 oz. per cup.

In sandy soil, where leaching is rapid, additional fertilizer may be required. This can, however, present a danger of root injury from the higher salt concentrations. You can offset poor growth in sandy soil by burying up to 3 bushels of a peat moss/soil mix (1 to 1 proportions) or compost per plant beneath the dripline—if you only have a few bushes to worry about. Plant roots will grow into these areas, invigorating the plant.

Be sure to fertilize every year regardless of whether a crop is produced.

You can use "organic" fertilizers if you want. Compounds such as blood meal, cottonseed meal, tankage, and well-rotted manure will provide some of the major nutrients. Most of these will also provide valuable organic material that will improve soil texture and aid plant growth. You should use combinations of these materials to provide for a more balanced fertilization. Don't use bone meal or wood ashes, because they tend to sweeten the soil.

Don't apply organic fertilizers after the early summer, because they could stimulate late fall growth of the plants if applied too late. The amount to apply will be determined by the plant vigor.

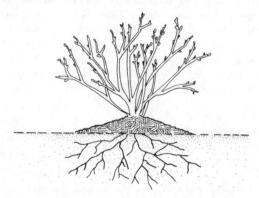

Maintain a 6-inch deep layer of sawdust mulch at all times.

Soil Management

Blueberry plants do not compete well with weeds for water and nutrients. Therefore, they should either be cultivated frequently or thoroughly mulched. In most areas of the country, mulching is perhaps the wisest and best soil management practice. We recommend it highly for the homeowner. Nearly any organic material—grass clippings, pine needles, straw, peat moss, buckwheat hulls, or wood chips—can be used.

SAWDUST MULCH

We have used sawdust as a mulch very successfully for 35 years and strongly recommend it. Sawdust is a relatively inexpensive material. Like all organic mulches, it retains soil moisture, reduces soil temperature fluctuations, and adds valuable organic matter to the soil.

In addition, we have found that sawdust, in particular, substantially increases plant vigor and produces higher crop yields.

The type of sawdust used does not matter. However, softwood sawdust is usually coarser in texture and decomposes more slowly than hardwood sawdust, and this is desirable. Although fresh sawdust can be used as a mulch, it is better to use aged material.

Apply the sawdust immediately after planting to soil that has been thoroughly moistened. Apply the mulch 4 inches deep and sloped toward the plant. Add additional mulch each year to build up and maintain a 6-inch depth at all times. The area beneath the plant or, preferably, the entire plantation can be mulched.

One bushel of moderately dry sawdust is equivalent to about two 5-gallon buckets, and weighs about 45 pounds. Plan to use about 5 bushels for each plant, depending on the size of the plant.

Breakdown of the sawdust will tie up some of the nitrogen in the soil. This may cause a nitrogen deficiency in the plant. To correct this, apply additional nitrogen fertilizer each time you add new mulch. We recommend the application of 2 pounds of ammonium nitrate or 6 pounds of 10–10-10 for each 100 pounds of sawdust mulch. You can

Continued →

correct nitrogen deficiencies with organic fertilizers that contain as little cellulose material as possible. Fish emulsion or blood meal are suitable. Exact quantities are dependent on the extent of the deficiency and the age of the plant. Remember, this is in addition to the regular fertilization.

OTHER MULCHES

Some of the other organic mulches you can use may present particular problems which you should know about in advance. For example, grass clippings from lawns previously treated with herbicides should not be used. Peat moss, buckwheat hulls, and wood chips are relatively expensive, and the former may crust on the surface, restricting moisture penetration. Straw mulch may introduce weed seeds and present a considerable fire hazard. Inorganic materials such as black polyethylene may also be suitable but have not been fully tested.

HAND CULTIVATION

If you choose to cultivate, start in the early spring and continue the practice as weeds grow throughout the growing season. Hand cultivation, with a hoe, should be very shallow (less than 1 inch) to avoid damaging the roots. Be careful not to knock fruit off the bush—ripening fruit drops especially easily. Since cultivated soil loses moisture more rapidly than mulched soil, be sure to water frequently enough to maintain enough soil moisture for good plant growth.

Pruning

There is a mystique to pruning fruit trees and bushes; it always seems to make gardeners nervous. But pruning is one of the important factors in developing and maintaining high production in your blueberry plantation. So let's eliminate some of the mystery by understanding the bearing habit of this plant.

Most flower buds, each containing up to a dozen flowers, are produced at the tips of the current season's growth. They are formed during the summer and early fall for next year's bloom. Since flower buds are only formed on new wood, stimulation of new growth through proper pruning and fertilization is necessary. Pruning should start immediately after planting and be continued each year in the early spring just as the flower buds begin to swell. The only tools needed will be a lopping shears, a hand shears, and maybe a handsaw.

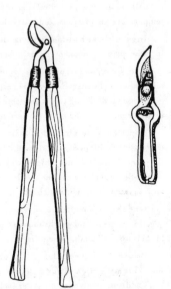

Lopping shears (left) are the best tool for removing large canes; hand shears (right) can be used for making fine cuts.

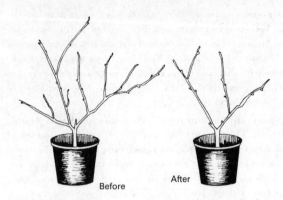

Lopping shears (left) are the best tool for removing large canes; hand shears (right) can be used for making fine cuts. Pruning a blueberry bush at planting.

PRUNING AT PLANTING

At planting time, you should remove all weak, diseased, and broken wood and all flower buds.

AFTER ONE YEAR

Again prune any diseased or broken wood. Vigorous plants may be allowed to bear up to a pint of fruit (2 to 30 flower buds). Remove any additional buds.

AFTER TWO TO FIVE YEARS

Continue similar pruning practices for the next 2 to 5 years. If the plants appear vigorous, do not remove more flower buds than is necessary during pruning. During this time, the emphasis should still be on producing healthy bushes and not on fruit production.

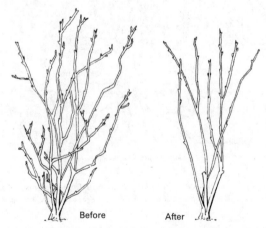

Pruning a blueberry bush after 2—5 years in the field.

If well-grown bushes were started as healthy 2-year-old plants, they may be considered mature bushes after 6 to 8 growing seasons in the field.

PRUNING MATURE BUSHES

After you have removed all dead and diseased wood, thin out the bush by removing one-fourth of the main branches. These can be cut at an angle slightly above the ground level or to a low, vigorous side shoot.

634

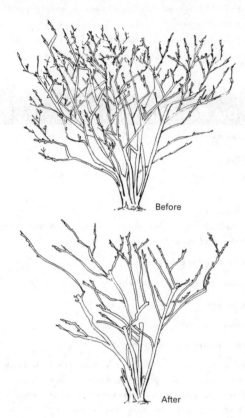

Pruning a mature blueberry bush.

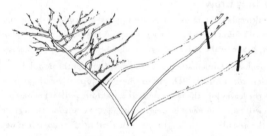

The heavy black marks indicate where cuts should be made to remove weak wood from a mature bush.

This should be done each year, always removing the oldest canes. Branches older than 5 years are less productive. Failure to remove enough old wood, or inadequate fertilization, will result in an insufficient number of new branches arising from the base of the bush.

After cutting out the main branches, thin the remainder of the bush, removing twiggy or bushy growth clusters, weak lateral shoots, and interfering branches. Unpruned bushes degenerate rapidly into a thick, twiggy mass of unfruitful wood.

Blueberry bushes that have been neglected for several years may be rejuvenated and returned to good production by severe pruning. Cut these back to the ground, leaving only short, 2-inch to 3-inch stubs. The whole bush may be done at once (1-year method) or half the bush

may be done 1 year and the other half in the following year (2-year method). By using the 1-year method, the entire crop is lost for one season. The 2-year method does allow the plant to bear a portion of the crop each year of the rejuvenation process.

Protection from Birds

Birds present one of the worst problems of any pest. They are especially frustrating for the small grower in a suburban or other densely populated area. Nearly any kind of bird will destroy the ripening fruit and, at times, will even eat the flower buds on the plant. Nationally, blueberry crop lost to birds is estimated to be between 2 and 4 million dollars per year.

Many people are opposed to destruction of the birds. Since federal and state laws concerning shooting, trapping, and poisoning are quite complicated, and since these measures are not very effective, we will limit our discussion to alternative bird control methods.

NETTING

The most effective type of bird control device is netting.

You can cover entire plantations or individual bushes for nearly 100 percent bird protection. A durable, synthetic netting, often made of nylon and treated to resist deterioration from ultraviolet radiation, will usually last for several seasons. Place the netting over the bushes as the first fruits begin to ripen, and remove it after harvest is completed. When protecting individual bushes, envelop the plant completely with the netting, tying the netting around the base of the plant and using scrap lumber supports to keep it off the bush. Whole plantations can be enclosed with netting, but it does require support posts and wires to keep the netting sufficiently high over the plants to allow easy access to the bushes. An alternative to the complete use of netting is to construct a "cage" for the plants from 1-inch-mesh poultry fencing. A combination of the two materials, with poultry fencing on the sides and flexible netting on the top, is quite frequently used.

The blueberry's worst enemy is not insects or diseases, it is birds! Plastic netting, specifically for bird control, is shown here. Hardware cloth or chicken wire will also work well.

Continued ➜

VISUAL REPELLENTS

Hawklike balloons, rubber snakes, and aluminum pie plates may be partially effective near the beginning of the ripening season. However, birds soon will become accustomed to these objects and will henceforth and forever after ignore them. In fact, it has been reported that some birds nest in the balloons and use them as strategic airbases from which to launch their midseason raids.

AUDITORY REPELLENTS

One type of auditory repellent depends upon simple noisemakers, such as firecrackers, propane cannons, and radios. These are often placed on a timer, so that they are switched on at irregular intervals. Regular timing will frequently acclimate the birds to the timing of the sounds. They may then feed twice as fast between the noise sequences. A second type of auditory repellent depends upon the recordings of bird distress calls to frighten the pests. A third type utilizes the production of high frequency sounds to frighten the birds. This type appears to be the most effective of the auditory repellents.

Controlling Diseases and Insects

In many areas blueberries can be grown without the use of sprays. This is especially true if plants are maintained in vigorous condition, are planted in an optimum location, and are grown under good, sanitary conditions. This includes removing old leaves, berries, and prunings from the site and practicing good weed control. We have tried to maintain optimal conditions and have found that often no sprays, or only 1 to 2 sprays per year, were necessary. However, the pest problems may be more severe in some areas. This will require spray control measures.

Many people prefer not to use synthetic pesticides. We suggest that these people use a botanical insecticide, such as rotenone; a natural pest pathogen, such as *Bacillus thuringiensis*; a natural predator; or handpick the larger insect pests. Some of these control measures may not be very effective or may be too costly to use, in which case the grower will have to consider using a synthetic insecticide. In addition, if diseases are present, you will have to use a synthetic fungicide, if you want to produce any fruit at all.

All pesticides, including "organic" pesticides, have varying degrees of toxicity. Use all recommended precautions when applying these, and be sure they are stored in their original containers under lock and key at all times. Keep them out of the reach of children.

The degree of acute toxicity is indicated on the package by the label warning statement. Those compounds that are considered "highly toxic" have the words *DANGER* and *POISON* and a skull and crossbones on the label; we recommend you never use these. Moderately toxic compounds have the word *WARNING* on the label; slightly toxic compounds are labeled *CAUTION*; and relatively nontoxic compounds have no signal word on the label. Make sure you observe the specified time interval between last application and fruit harvest.

Harvesting

To get the highest quality berries, harvest 4 to 6 days after the berry turns completely blue. If picked earlier, the berries will not be as large and the flavor will not be fully developed. Berries picked when not completely ripe will ripen off the bush, but they will be of poorer quality. Since overripe berries shrivel and may drop, the entire planting should be harvested about once a week, or more frequently during high temperatures.

Since harvesting goes more quickly if both hands are free for picking, tie a container around your neck or attach it to your belt.

Grow the Best Strawberries

Revised and Updated!

Louise Riotte

Illustrations by Ralph Scott

Introduction

If there is one fruit every homesteader and suburbanite should grow, it is strawberries, for strawberries are:

· The first fruit of the season.

· The quickest to bear of any fruit.

· Easy to grow.

· Expensive in stores.

· Better quality when home grown.

And no matter where you live, there is a variety that will thrive and do well in your region. Though they do best in the cooler, moist regions, they can be grown in hot, dry climates, especially where windbreaks can be provided and supplemental watering is possible during the critical months of July, August, and September.

How They Grow

Set healthy plants in moist soil in your prepared bed in early spring. They will produce new roots in a few days. A few days later, each plant usually has several new leaves of normal size.

For those plants that send out runners (most of the popular varieties do), runners will begin to emerge in June. Growing from where the leaves join the main stem, these runners will form new plants, which will take root near the original plant. New runners then grow from the new plants, and in this way a succession of independent new plants soon is growing around the original plant.

Plants produce blossoms the first year, and these will develop into fruit if they are not pinched off. Do pinch them off, which will encourage your plants to develop strong root systems and vigorous growth. Your reward will be next season's abundant crop of large, healthy, delicious berries.

In the fall, the growing points in the crown change into blossom buds. The buds grow rapidly, and by the end of October they can readily be seen by opening the crowns. In vigorous plants, buds also develop in many of the leaf axils. The number of leaves on a plant in the fall is a good indication of the following year's production: The more leaves, the more berries the plant will produce the next spring.

Plants become dormant in the fall, and the older green leaves and connecting runners die.

In the spring of the fruiting year, the buds that developed last fall develop into blossoms. The first one to open on a cluster contains the most pistils (female elements), is the largest, and becomes the largest fruit with the most seeds. The next one to open becomes the next largest fruit, and later ones become successively smaller fruits.

Strawberries in mild weather mature about 30 days after blooming. In warm weather they will mature more rapidly.

Selecting Your Best-Bet Berries

There are three distinct fruiting habits in strawberries. The first, and most common, is the summer-bearer. These produce one large crop of fruit once during the season, usually for about two weeks. Many people prefer these so that freezing and canning will be done once and put away, usually before gardeners are overwhelmed with the chores in the rest of the garden. Depending on your growing season and region, you can get early-, mid-, or late-season bearers.

Everbearers produce a crop in the spring, and then either produce smaller crops every six weeks or so or produce one more crop in the fall. If you want strawberries throughout the growing season, consider everbearers.

Alpine strawberries are the closest descendants of wild strawberries. They are perennial and are often grown as borders or even ground covers. Unlike the other types of strawberries, these plants can be grown from seed, and will bear throughout the growing season. Their fruit are small and often intensely flavored.

Most strawberry plants spread by sending out runners. Smaller plants grow on these runners. Many growers kill or remove the mother plant after a good fruiting season and then the daughter plants become the primary fruit bearers the following year. They in turn send out runners, and so on.

VARIETIES

There are many strawberries to choose from. Decide whether you want summer bearing, everbearing, or alpine (or some combination of them) and then choose your plants according to your growing season, region, and special conditions.

Every variety has a different set of characteristics. Commercial growers look for varieties that are firm and will ship well. Sometimes they sacrifice taste for these qualities. Some berries are known for being large and perfect looking. Some are known for sweetness, and some freeze better than others. Growers for the restaurant market care about the look and color (both outside and inside) of the strawberry. Listed below are some of the most popular varieties and some general notes.

CLIMATE AND CONDITIONS

Climate and local weather conditions affect the table quality of strawberry varieties, and it often varies greatly from season to season. Often it improves toward the end of the season.

Temperature. In New York and New England, 'Midway' develops better quality than in Maryland. 'Sparkle' is a good dessert variety in the North. Temperature also greatly affects the flavor of strawberries. Varieties grown where there are sunny days and cool nights have better flavor than those grown where there are cloudy, humid days and warm nights.

Firmness. Most varieties produce firmer fruit in cool temperatures. In New England, New York, and Michigan, 'Catskill' and 'Sparkle' produce a firmer fruit than they do farther south. In Maryland, they grow too soft for shipment.

Frost injury. Strawberries may escape frost injury if they blossom after most danger from frost has passed or if they have short blossom stems and blossoms that remain under protecting leaves. But varieties that have a long flowering season will develop some fruit despite frost. The flowers of 'Tennessee Beauty' and 'Sparkle' are late-blooming and are protected by leaves.

Varieties that escape frost more often are 'Pocahontas' and 'Catskill'. In the North and West, where frosts are unusually serious, everbearing strawberries are grown. If their first blossoms are killed, they produce a new set of buds.

Home garden varieties. Choose strawberry varieties for the home garden according to where you live, the size of your garden, and the way you intend to use the berries. A local strawberry grower, or the Extension Service, can often give excellent advice for your locality.

Preparing to Plant

Plants are usually obtained from commercial nurseries. Buy disease-free and nematode-free planting stock. Order early and specify a delivery date, close to the date you want to set out your plants, if you are ordering by mail. It is a good idea to buy your stock either from local nurseries or from ones located in a climate similar to yours.

It is easier to get nursery-grown plants in the spring than in other seasons, and spring planting is usually recommended for northern and eastern regions. In southern areas, fall planting is often desirable.

POPULAR STRAWBERRY VARIETIES

Variety	Flavor	Notes
SUMMER BEARING		
EARLY		
'Dunlap'	Excellent	Very hardy. Sweet. Drought tolerant and resistant to most foliar diseases. Zones 4–8.
'Earliglow'	Excellent	Good for freezing, jams. Highly productive, many runners, and very disease resistant. Zones 4–8.
'Surecrop'	Excellent	Good for freezing/canning. Does well in poor soils, drought. Disease resistant. Zones 4–8.
MIDSEASON		
'Catskill'	Good	Very hardy. Good northern variety. Large fruit. Resistant to leaf scorch and verticillium wilt. Susceptible to red stele.
'Midway'	Excellent	Does best in heavier clay and loamy soils. Resistant to verticillium wilt and red stele. Zones 4–8.
'Cavendish'	Excellent	Very hardy northern berry. Very resistant to red stele. Good for freezing/jams.
'Honeoye'	Excellent	Hardy. Excellent for freezing. Resistant to rot. Good northern plant.

Continued ➡

Variety	Flavor	Notes
'Pocahontas'	Good	Does best in areas with little frost. Good for jams/freezing. Large berries.
'Robinson'	Good	Very vigorous. Does well in poorer soils. Tolerates drought. Large fruit. Hardy. Midwest and Northeast.
LATE		
'Sparkle'	Excellent	Most popular variety. Produces many runners. Freezes/cans well. Does well in clay soils. Very hardy.
'Tennessee Beauty'	Good	Resistant to leaf spot and leaf scorch. Does best in warmer climates. Slightly tart flavor. Zones 5–8.
EVERBEARING		
'Ozark Beauty'	Excellent	Disease resistant. Prolific. Good for freezing and canning. Zones 4–8.
'Shortcake'	Good	Burpee only. Larger than most ever-bearers.
'Tribute'	Excellent	Large fruit, disease resistant. Good for freezing/jams. Grows well in South, milder areas of Pacific Northwest.
'Tristar'	Excellent	Disease resistant. Excellent in hanging baskets. Light runner production. Fall crop is heaviest. Zones 5–8.
ALPINE		
'Red Alpine'	Excellent	(*Fragaria vesca*) Small plants. Intense-flavored berries. No runners. Very hardy perennial.
'Mignonette'	Excellent	Large (1-inch) fruit. Very prolific. Good edging or ground cover.

If you have a healthy, established strawberry bed, you can get planting stock from it for your new bed. Very early in the spring, transplant from your garden the most vigorous of the young plants that are growing alongside the bearing rows. Select plants only from plantings that are free of diseases and insect infestations.

CARING FOR YOUR PLANTING STOCK

When plants arrive early from the nursery, they can be held in cold storage for several days.

If they are shipped in a plastic bag, keep them in it. If not, place them in a large freezer bag. A fine place to store them is in the vegetable crisper section of your refrigerator. For longer periods, the dormant plant can be held at between 28° and 34°F.

The new plants should be checked over. There are usually only one or two small leaves on each plant. I always remove all but one of the leaves. Notice the roots. They should be fresh and bright.

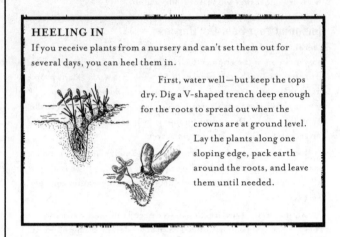

HEELING IN

If you receive plants from a nursery and can't set them out for several days, you can heel them in.

First, water well—but keep the tops dry. Dig a V-shaped trench deep enough for the roots to spread out when the crowns are at ground level. Lay the plants along one sloping edge, pack earth around the roots, and leave them until needed.

LOCATING YOUR PLANTING

In selecting a site for a strawberry planting, consider air and water drainage, slope of land, and direction of land exposure.

If late-spring frosts are frequent in your locality, choose a site on ground slightly higher than the surrounding areas. There will be less danger of frost damage on higher ground, because cold air drains to adjoining low ground.

A site that slopes gradually and is less liable to soil runoff is better than one that slopes steeply.

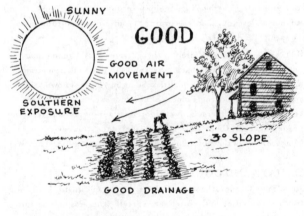

For an early crop, select a site that slopes toward the south. Select one that slopes to the north if you wish to delay ripening.

SOIL REQUIREMENTS

Strawberries are a joy to grow because they're not fussy about soil and can be grown successfully on almost any type that contains a good supply of organic matter. Growers wishing to produce early fruit prefer sandy soil.

Strawberries will thrive in well-drained soil that is moist but not wet. Plants are often killed when wet ground freezes in the winter. Wet soil also inhibits plant growth and may lead to damage by red stele root rot.

If you are uncertain about your soil, get a soil test. The pH preference of strawberries is between 5.0 and 6.5.

Established plants should not be limed.

Avoid planting on newly plowed sod. White grubs and wireworms can be troublesome.

PREPARING THE SOIL

Strawberries will grow best in well-prepared soil that is high in organic matter. Don't plant on land where persistent weeds such as quackgrass, purslane, and chickweed are abundant.

Ideally, soil preparations will begin from one to three years before the soil is used for strawberries. The chief aim will be to enrich the soil with as much organic matter as possible.

If cultivation the previous year included seedbed preparation, cultivation, and either turning under a green manure crop or adding stable manure, only harrowing or tilling is needed to prepare the soil for the strawberry plants.

If these were not included, at least one year of advance preparation is necessary. Plant a green-manure crop or add stable manure. If the soil is very deficient in organic matter, two green manure crops are recommended.

Recommendations for adding manure call for as much as 2 bushels per 100 square feet. In family-sized gardens of one-quarter acre, the gardener can add as much as 1 to 2 tons of the more potent hog and poultry manure, and four times that amount of horse and cow manure. It should be applied in the fall and turned under.

The strawberry is a forgiving plant, and will grow in widely different soils, with varying amounts of organic matter. For the strawberry crop you'll be able to boast about, careful preparation of the soil and the addition of organic matter in large amounts are essential.

INSECT CONTROLS

Two insects often found in poorly prepared strawberry beds are the white grub and the strawberry root aphid.

White grub

The white grub, larva of the June bug, dines on strawberry roots. Avoid having it become a nuisance by not planting on newly cultivated areas. If those grubs are a problem in your area, you can get rid of them by plowing or rototilling the soil in the fall so that the winter cold will kill them.

Aphid

Strawberry root aphids are most common when strawberry plantings follow corn, grass, or weeds, so avoid this.

WHEN TO PLANT

Most strawberries are planted in early spring, when temperature and moisture conditions are best.

Late-set plants, unless they have been kept in cold storage, seldom grow as well as early-set plants. Also the average yield from plants set out in late summer will not be as large from plants set out in early spring. However, as with many other rules, there are exceptions.

Where the land must be fully utilized and rainfall is dependable, plants of those varieties that bud in late fall and early spring—such as 'Pocahontas'—may be set out in late summer to bear the following year. This is common in the South. If you set out plants at this time, plow a large quantity of composted manure into the soil before planting. Later put on a fall mulch of straw, manure, or compost.

If the season is very dry or very wet, or if a winter mulch is not used, the plants set out in the fall may be killed by low winter temperatures. On very heavy soils, if early autumn planting is necessary, be sure to protect the plants with a mulch in winter. On such soils it often is preferable to plant in late spring with dormant cold-storage plants.

Autumn-set plants should be large and have well-developed root systems. Care must be taken to set them out in moist soil, and irrigation usually is necessary for them to get a vigorous start.

How to Plant

In the early spring, wait for a cloudy, cool day with no wind to dry your plant roots. You should have a prepared bed rich in organic matter and with a pH of about 6. Your plant roots should be moist, and you should have decided on a training system. You are ready to plant.

Training Systems

Three systems are commonly used in training strawberries:

- Hill system. No runners are allowed to grow.
- Spaced matted-row system. Some runners are allowed to grow.
- Matted-row system. Most runners are allowed to grow.

The first two are recommended with irrigation and in intensive cultivation. Use the matted-row system where there is danger from white grubs, drought, or severe winters. Hill-system plantings are most often used for home gardens, especially where there is some winter protection. Twenty-five plants will produce enough strawberries for one person.

HILL SYSTEM

Plantings are made either in double or triple rows, with plants 10–12 inches apart in the rows, and with 12 inches between rows. Leave a 14-inch alley between each group of rows.

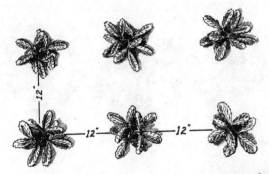

Continued ➜

To thin and space: Cut off runner plants that appear the first summer. A hoe or cutter made for the purpose can be used. The hill system is usually preferred by the home gardener with limited space. It produces larger but fewer berries. However, if a "mother" plant dies, it leaves a vacant space in the row.

SPACED MATTED-ROW SYSTEM

Set the plants 18–24 inches apart in the rows, with a 42-inch space between rows. Planting an acre under this system requires 6,225 plants for the 24-inch spacing, and 8,300 plants for 18-inch spacing.

To thin and space: The runners are trained by hand so that runner plants are 6–8 inches apart. Establish plants by covering the tops of the runners with soil as soon as they begin to enlarge. The plant bed should be 18–24 inches wide, with 24 inches of alley between rows. Retain this space in thinning.

MATTED-ROW SYSTEM

Spacing is the same as for the spaced matted-row system. Because there is no runner placement, and less weeding, growing strawberries in matted rows costs less per acre than growing them in spaced matted rows.

Under this system, individual plants may be crowded, however, and the yields and individual fruit size may be smaller than with the spaced matted-row system.

To thin and space: This, the lazy man's system, is the easiest way to grow strawberries, and for effort expended will give you the largest number of berries. But they will be smaller. Allow mother plants to set runners at will until you have a solid bed of plants as wide as your space permits. There usually will be 2–8 inches between plants. Try to keep the beds 18–24 inches wide, with alleys 24 inches wide between rows. Cut all runners that extend into the alleys after the desired stand of plants is established. During late summer or autumn, thin the plants so that 3–4 inches remain between each plant. Remove surplus runners while hoeing.

Cultivating

To control weeds, cultivating may be necessary as often as once a week during the first season. Hoe as often as necessary to clean out any weeds that may spring up between plants.

As you work, hoe and cultivate toward the plants. This will keep the roots from being killed by exposure to air. But keep the crowns of the plants at ground level at all times. If you are using a cultivator on a large planting, set the teeth on each side so they will not stir the soil more than 1 inch deep near the rows. This will prevent loosening the plants or cutting their roots.

Generally speaking, no cultivating is done in the spring of the fruiting year. If recommendations for cultivation and mulching have been followed, it is not likely that weeds will be a serious problem before the crop is picked. If you are planning to renew your planting, you then should cultivate and hoe just as you would for a newly set area.

REMOVE THOSE BLOSSOMS

Culture of newly set-out strawberry plants should be directed toward vigorous growth rather than flowering or bearing. During the first season, remove blossom stems on the plants as soon as they appear. This is done to strengthen the plant and also to increase the number of runner plants. Look into the future, as I try to do, and know that blossom removal, hard as it may be to do, is a definite advantage. This is because early-formed runner plants will bear the most fruit the following year. You will get your reward—you just have to wait a little longer for it.

MULCHING

I've always considered mulching one of the most important operations in caring for a strawberry bed. It's especially important in northern sections as winter protection. The crowns of any plants that remain unprotected are often severely injured by low winter temperatures. This becomes noticeable the following spring, evidenced by weak growth and reddish foliage. Eventually, when the berries ripen, the plants may wilt and collapse. Mulching will also prevent the plants from being heaved out of the ground as the result of a hard freeze and eventual thawing of the earth.

Mulching keeps down weeds, keeps the berries clean, and conserves moisture during the growing season.

It prevents infecting organisms in soil from splashing up on plants during rains. Also raindrops splashing on bare soil detach particles that are carried away by surface water—and good, organic soil should not be lost.

What you will use for your mulch is not as important as the fact that it is being used. Many materials will serve. Small-grain straws and marsh hay are among the best mulching materials, but there are others that are satisfactory. You may use pine needles, ferns, composted manure, hay, Sudan grass, mixtures of kafir and sorghum fodders, and mixtures of spring oats, straw, and sorghum fodders. If Sudan grass, kafir, or sorghum is used, it is well to run it first through a hay crusher. Crushing allows the material to dry rapidly and therefore reduces the risk of moldy or rotten mulch.

If you want to use black plastic mulch, spread it across the entire row, then anchor it by burying the edges in soil. Cut small slits where the plants bulge up in the plastic, and carefully work the foliage through the slit. Runners will be put out by the mother plant. You can select the healthiest, cut small slits under them, and push them down into the soil.

If you mulch your plants well, you will have less work the second season. You will have eliminated the need for cultivation, and any weeds that appear can be pulled easily by hand.

Fertilizing

If you prepared your soil in advance of planting, and if your strawberry plants are growing vigorously and have dark green leaves throughout the summer, it is probable that they have an adequate supply of fertilizer. Use fertilizers only when a soil test or poor plant growth shows that they are needed.

If soils are poor, cottonseed meal or a complete commercial fertilizer can be applied as a side-dressing from four to six weeks after planting. If a need for fertilizer is seen later, plan to apply it in August and September when the fruit buds that determine the next season's crop are forming.

On a dry day, scatter about I pound of 10–5-5 or 8-8-8 on each 80 square feet of the bed. Brush the fertilizer off the leaves to avoid damage.

Organic gardeners may prefer to use cottonseed meal for this application, spreading it at a rate of about 4 pounds per 25 feet of strawberry row.

Irrigating

Strawberry plants are particularly benefited by irrigation if there is dry weather either in the summer when the plants are getting established or in the spring from blossom time through the fruiting season. Strawberry plants are shallow-rooted, with most of the roots in the upper 3 inches of soil, so they tend to need water during periods of dryness.

Sprinkler or surface irrigating systems may be used. For large plantations, the most common sprinkler irrigation systems consist of 4-inch portable aluminum pipes with 3-inch pipes attached to them laterally. The rotating sprinkler heads are mounted at 40-foot intervals on the lateral pipes. About 1,100 feet of lateral 3-inch pipe is needed per acre.

Use an eyelet hose sprinkler system for home gardens. This is a flat plastic tube with small holes spaced along its upper side. With suitable pressure, an eyelet hose will irrigate three or four rows at a time. This is the system that I use and prefer. The droplets fall in a soft, gentle, misty spray. I take care, however, to water when there are no strong winds blowing, since much of the water is lost through evaporation during windy periods. For me, the best time is usually the early-morning hours.

Furrow irrigation, a form of surface application, is used where the land has sufficient slope to let the water flow slowly down the furrows. For this type of irrigation to be effective, the soil must be of fairly heavy texture so that the irrigation water will flow the full length of the furrow, which should not be more than 250 feet long.

For sandy soils with a gentle slope, a porous canvas hose may be useful, but with this method only one or two rows can be irrigated at one setting of the hose.

One of the most valuable uses of irrigation is to prevent blossom damage during cold spells in the spring. A spray that is applied continuously will protect blossoms when temperatures drop as low as 25°F. This spray must be started before the temperatures dip below freezing, and must be continued until the temperature has risen above 32°F and all ice has melted. The amount of water used need not be large, and can be kept to a minimum by using small nozzles.

Protection Against Winterkill

It is normal for strawberry plants gradually to become hardier in the autumn, so that by winter they can stand colder temperatures. However, if a sudden cold snap with temperatures lower than about 20° occurs before the plants have time to do this, they may be severely damaged. Temperatures of 15°F or lower often kill unhardened plants.

Plants also may be killed if alternate freezing and thawing of soil heaves the plants out of the ground, breaking their roots. Mulching the plants is the best protection against these dangers.

But don't apply the mulch too soon or the plants will not develop hardiness, thus increasing the danger of winter injury.

As soon as a temperature of 20°F or lower has occurred, the plants will have become hardened. This is the time to apply the mulch. Use a loose organic material such as wheat straw. I do not like to use leaves because of their tendency to pack.

In northern states, cover the plants with 3 or 4 inches of the mulch. In the South, a lighter mulch may be applied. It can be thin enough so that an occasional leaf protrudes.

In the spring, rake all but a light covering of mulch into the alleys between the rows. This should be done as soon as new strawberry leaves begin to grow. Later, if necessary, the mulch can also be used to cover the plants temporarily during cold nights to protect the blossoms from frost injury.

SPRING FROST CONTROL

Here are three ways to avoid frost damage if frosts occur during the spring blossoming period:

1. Use mulch.

2. Operate a sprinkler irrigation system.

3. Use heaters.

If the planting was mulched during the winter, and the mulch was raked into the alleys in the spring, simply rake it back over the plants if a frost is feared. This is an easy and relatively safe way to avoid blossom damage.

For sprinkler protection, heads that produce a mist rather than a heavy stream of water are ideal. See explanation under "Irrigation."

Heating is the third possibility but it is generally practical only for large planting. It is less effective than sprinkler irrigation. If heaters are used, 100 per acre will be needed when the temperature drops to 26°F.

Continued ➜

Harvesting

This is the time we have been looking forward to—when we can enjoy the fruits of our labor, have plenty of delicious fresh strawberries to eat, make others into desserts, and freeze or can for future use.

Picking strawberries still is a hand job—even on large plantings. No machine presently available can remove berries from plants at the right degree of ripeness without injuring them.

The most natural way to pick strawberries is not the best way. That way is to grasp the berry and pull. This bruises the strawberry, and usually leaves the cap on the plant, opening the center of the fruit to spores of decay organisms. Fingers gradually get dirty and sticky using this method, and the dirt gets on the berries.

Instead, grasp the stem close to the cap, twist, and pull, leaving as short a stem as possible attached to the cap to avoid puncturing other strawberries and exposing them to rot. Don't pile them high in the picking container; this will crush and damage them.

Strawberries should be harvested at the right stage of ripeness. Overripe berries are soft and easily injured in marketing, lose flavor, and don't keep well. Immature berries lack both a full flavor and a fine appearance. Consider how you will use the berries as you pick them. If you must keep the fruit for a few days, pick it when it is pink rather than ripe red. If berries are to be used or eaten immediately, they should reach full ripeness. Berries remain in this ideal condition for only one to three days, depending on the variety.

Weather conditions usually determine the frequency of picking. Berries ripen fast in warm weather and more slowly in cool weather. You should pick berries at least every four or five days. Ideally the gardener will pick every day, and reap the best flavor and the least loss from spoilage. While picking, the gardener should pick any spoiled berries, taking them from the row so they will not contaminate others.

Pick strawberries early in the day. They are firmer then and easier to handle than when picked in the heat of the day. Rains will not halt the ripening of the fruit, so it may be necessary to pick when the berries are wet. While this is not ideal, it usually will not cause serious difficulties.

If picked berries are dirty, chill them for an hour or two, then wash them through one or two cold waters.

Louise Riotte

Raspberries in the Home Garden

The brambles, raspberries and blackberries, are among the most popular of all bush fruits, ranking second for most families only to the strawberry. I have found them easy to grow and very rewarding, for they produce the most fruit with the least amount of effort. Blackberries will be considered separately, so let's start with the raspberries.

Raspberries bear a light crop the second year after planting but you can expect a full crop a year later, and annual crops thereafter for the life of the planting. And plantings that are well cared for may produce good crops for ten years or more.

Another big advantage I've found with raspberries is the relative ease of controlling insects and diseases as compared with the sometimes difficult, expensive and messy job of applying several sprays each year to fruit trees. The berries often need **no** spraying, but if they do, it may be done with a hand sprayer or duster.

While generally raspberries thrive best in cooler regions, I have had no difficulty growing them in my area of southern Oklahoma, and have been particularly successful with the black ones, such as the **Cumberland** variety. The red variety, **Latham**, has done well for me, too, but may be expected to do much better farther north.

Raspberries come in a brilliant spectrum of colors—red, black, purple and yellow—and many varieties come early, midseason, late or as everbearers. Those bearing one large crop each year generally are referred to as "July-bearers."

The so-called "everbearers" are becoming increasingly popular, since they bear two crops each year and extend the season. If you have the space, plant both types.

Red raspberries include **Fallred** (everbearer), **Latham** (late), **Newburgh** (midseason), **September** (everbearer), **Southland** (everbearer), **Sunrise** (early) and **Taylor** (late). Some excellent varieties for the North, originated at the New York Experiment Station at Geneva, are **New Heritage**, a vigorous grower of medium-sized, very firm berries, which may be picked about September 1st. The sturdy, erect canes require no support. Two other excellent new varieties, **Hilton** and **Milton**, will be available soon as virus-free stocks can be increased.

Some good, proven varieties of black raspberries are **Allen** (early), **Blackhawk** (late), **Bristol** (midseason), **Cumberland** (midseason), **Dundee** (midseason), **New Logan** (early) and **Morrison** (late). Two fine varieties originated at the New York Station are **Huron**, which has large and glossy black berries of good quality, and **Jewel**, a vigorous variety whose large, glossy black fruits are of very high quality. The plant is not susceptible to any serious disease and only slightly susceptible to mildew.

The "purple" raspberry is a cross between reds and blacks. Varieties include **Amethyst** (midseason), **Clyde** (late) and **Purple Autumn** (an everbearer). **Sodus**, also an old favorite among the purples, is hard to beat.

Yellow raspberries include **Amber** (very late), **Fallgold** (an everbearer) and **Forever Amber** (a yellow member of the black raspberry family). This last has medium-sized yellow-to-amber berries, which have a delicate black raspberry flavor and aroma.

Names of raspberry varieties seem almost endless when you look through nursery catalogs and it is difficult not to become confused. Each one, seemingly, has its own good qualities and differs from the others in size, quality, color or bearing season. It may be well for you to do a little detective work before you purchase. Check with your county agent, friends and neighbors, to find out what will grow best in your area and select types best adapted to your section of the country. One-year-old No. 1 grade plants are best for establishing new plantings. Make every effort to secure virus-free plants.

LOCATING YOUR RASPBERRY PATCH

Never try to grow raspberries in soil that is too acid—a pH of 6.0 is preferable—and determine your conditions by sending a soil sample to your State Agricultural College or Experiment Station. If you do not know where to send your sample, call your county agent.

To take a soil sample, dig deeply in four or five places in your plot, mix the earth together in a clean box and then send about a pint of this mixture. There probably will be a small charge for the test.

If the report shows an acidity below pH 5.8 or 6.0 you will need to give your plot a good application of lime. A one-hundred-foot row should have about 40 pounds of agricultural lime scattered on the ground, preferably in the fall before setting out plants in the spring. The lime should be dug or tilled into the ground, and if this is done in the fall, follow up by seeding the ground with rye.

If you're planning a hedge or single row of raspberries, lime, till and seed to rye a strip six or eight feet wide. You will need about six quarts of rye seed, which should be raked or cultivated into the ground.

In selecting your raspberry plot, bear in mind that the planting will remain there for 7 to 10 years, so put it to one side of your garden where it will not interfere with yearly cultivation. Try to choose a piece of ground that has goodly amount of humus in it. If the soil is lacking, work into it a very heavy application of farmyard manure before sowing the rye. Manure with a lot of straw in it is excellent. If manure or

compost if not available, gather grass clippings, weeds, wild grass or old vegetable plants from the garden. Till these into the ground with 50 pounds of purchased dried sheep manure. Do not use dried weeds with mature seed heads (as the seeds may sprout), but young, green weeds will decompose quickly.

Old leaf mold from a nearby woods can be used, but be sure to add lime even if the soil test shows alkaline or neutral, for leaf mold is acid, and the lime will be needed to counteract the condition. Old, weathered hay which is no longer fit for animal consumption, also may be used, or alfalfa and peanut hay, which are particularly high in nitrogen.

SPRING CARE

In the spring, as soon as the soil can be worked, dig or plow in the rye. Do not use any fertilizer at this time. Then let the ground remain in the rough until you are ready to set out your raspberry plants. (This should be done about the time beans are planted in the garden in your section of the country.)

If you buy your plants from a reliable nurseryman you should order them in January or early February at the latest; let him decide when to send them to you. As soon as they arrive will be the right time to set them out in your locality. Unless you live in the far South or Southwest, spring is best to set out plants.

When the plants arrive, remove them from their packing at once (unless they are frozen—in which case let them thaw slowly in a cold room), and soak them in a tub of water to which enough soil has been added to make the water muddy. Muddy water not only freshens up the plants, but the particles of mud stick to the fine, hairlike roots. This helps the plants get a good start when they are set out.

FALL PLANTING

I believe there is much to be said for fall planting if you live in a section of the country, as I do, where winters are **not too severe**. Raspberries set out during the autumn months will start growth early the following spring—just as soon as weather conditions are favorable and usually before it is feasible to do any spring planting. Thus, fruits planted in the fall get off to a quicker start and are apt to make better growth than spring-planted fruits. This advantage is particularly evident during the first season of growth.

Soil frequently is in better condition for planting, also, during the fall than in the spring, when sometimes it is so wet that planting must be delayed to prevent puddling or serious compaction. Raspberries should **never** be planted if the soil is excessively wet. Store the plants in a cool place and wait until things dry out. Then your soil will not pack.

Avoiding compaction is very important, because of the **leader buds**. When your raspberries arrive from the nursery you will note several small, pale-colored, yellow-green growths on the stems just above the roots. Once the plant is set in the ground the buds soon will push their way upward and become little shoots, but packed soil will slow them down or make it impossible for them to come through.

In raspberry language these shoots are called canes. And they must have all the help you can give them, for they need to hurry and grow very fast. Their life lasts for only a little more than a year. You can see what an advantage it is, then, to plant in the fall if possible, so these little shoots can come through and grow quickly.

Another possible advantage of fall planting is the fact that nursery plants are generally fresher at this time than in the spring. Most

Continued →

frequently (but not always) nurseries dig their plants in autumn and store them bare-rooted during the winter. In this way, plants are available for early shipment the next spring. Although winter storage is not particularly detrimental, transplanting operations cause less of a setback when plants are replanted soon after they are dug.

Fall planting is best done in late October or early November, before the soil is frozen. The greatest drawback to it is possible heaving and winter-killing. Heaving of plants during the winter is caused by alternate freezing and thawing of the soil, and usually occurs when there is a lack of protecting snow. You can achieve equal or better protection by mulching your fall-planted bushes to a depth of six or eight inches with straw, hay, grass clippings or some similar material.

In extremely cold climates you can avoid winter-killing by mounding soil about a foot deep around your plant and over the roots. This mound should be removed in the spring.

HILL OR HEDGE SYSTEM?

If you intend to make a hedge row of your berry patch, set the plants about three feet apart in the row. If you want more than one row, be sure that they are not closer than five feet apart. If, on the other hand, you choose to set the plants in the hill system, the plants should not be set nearer than four or five feet apart each way. As the plants attain their full growth, the individual hills should be staked and the plants tied to each stake with heavy binding twine.

The hill system has the advantage of allowing free air circulation around individual plant clusters. When the hedge row system is used, often the rows are allowed to grow too thick and too wide. This causes berry mold and a chance for plant disease due to inadequate air circulation and lack of sun. If enough space is available, I feel the family wanting six to a dozen plants to supply its own needs will find the hill system the best to use.

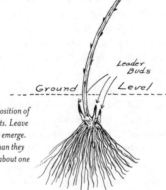

Newly planted raspberry plant showing position of leader buds placed on stem just above roots. Leave soil loose at surface of ground so buds can emerge. Set red raspberries 2 to 3 inches deeper than they were in the nursery, set black and purple about one inch deeper.

HOW TO PLANT

Set your plants in holes large enough to contain the roots without crowding. Set red raspberries two to three inches deeper than they were in the nursery, and set black and purple raspberries about one inch deeper. Yellow raspberries, considered to be members of the black raspberry group, are also set about an inch deeper. You can determine this nursery depth by the dark brown color line on the cane.

Be sure to press dirt firmly about the plant roots. Do this by stepping around the plant, watering well to prevent air pockets. If the weather is dry put on a light mulch.

Red raspberry plants should be cut back to 8 to 12 inches after planting. The canes, or the "handles" of black and purple raspberries should be cut off at ground level, removed from the planting and burned.

If there are any wild brambles growing around or near your new planting, they should be dug up and destroyed to prevent the possibility of their carrying disease.

CULTIVATION

During the first season, cultivate the raspberry plants each week. Take care not to cultivate too deeply (as this may injure the feeder roots) and do not get too close to the plants. Continue cultivation until about August 1st but not after this, since it is important for the new canes to "harden off" in preparation for the winter. Cultivation after August 1st could stimulate new growth which in colder climates will winter-kill.

At this time you may cut off the original plant canes which you set out, as they will not bear again. The fruit will appear next year on this year's new canes.

If you have let weeds grow, cut them down before they go to seed and use them with all the other plant material you can find for mulch. It is good to place a layer of leaves four to six inches deep around the plants. Any kind will do, but if they are maple leaves do not use quite as many, as they have a tendency to pack. Oak leaves are the best, but they should be sprinkled with a little lime since they are very acid. If you use the mulch system—which I find very satisfactory—you will have nothing to do after August 1st other than put the mulch on about mid-October.

If you prefer to cultivate instead of mulching, stop cultivation by August 1st and in mid-September rake into the ground a heavy sowing of rye. Take care not to get the rye too close to the plants or it will be difficult to remove the following spring.

Use leaves close to the plants, let the rye grow over the fall and winter, and in early spring dig or till it into the ground. Again, do not till or cultivate too deeply near the plants. When you work the rye into the ground it is good to add some well-decomposed compost, too.

If you use the mulch system, till the mulch into the soil in the early spring, also adding a light application of compost or well-decayed manure. This should be done early, whether it is rye or another mulch. If you wait too long, you will break off the new raspberry canes which will have started into growth. Again place more mulch on the raspberry patch—weeds, straw, leaves—anything organic that is available.

PRUNING

Understanding how raspberries grow and bear fruit helps us to understand why they should be trained and pruned by certain methods. They bear their fruit on **biennial** canes, but the roots and crowns are **perennial**.

All brambles send up new shoots or canes from the crown of the plant during each growing season. Red and yellow raspberries develop new shoots from **both** the crown and roots.

These new canes, whether from crown or roots, will grow vigorously during the summer, initiate flower buds in the fall, overwinter and then bear the following season. This fruit is borne on the leafy shoots which arise from lateral (side) buds on the one-year-old canes. Once having borne their crop, the canes start a gradual process of drying up and begin to die back shortly after the fruit is harvested. They should be cut and burned. New shoots soon will begin developing to repeat the cycle and provide next year's fruiting canes.

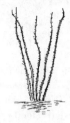

Raspberry plants left unpruned will become a mass of brambles. Prune for larger fruit and easier care. Unpruned plant at left is shown at right after being properly cut back. Cut canes of red raspberries back to about 30 inches.

In late March or early April before bud growth starts, trim back last year's growth of canes. These will be the canes that bear this year. Remember, this second season's bearing canes will be neither numerous nor large, for raspberries take three years before there is sufficient growth for a large crop. This first pruning should see the canes cut back a quarter of their growth.

The second pruning takes place after the canes bear fruit. As soon as the berries have all been picked, cut the canes which bore fruit (and any others that are broken) close to the ground. Remove and burn them. This will permit the new shoots to have sun and air, and will reduce the possibility of disease spreading from the old canes. Be sure to thin out any weak new canes, giving the ones you decide to keep sufficient growing room.

By the third season, if you have either mulched or cultivated according to directions, you should have fine, husky plants, 7 to 10 feet tall. From the third season on you should cut these back in late March or early April about a third of their length. Do this before their bud growth starts.

After old canes have borne fruit they should be cut off close to the ground, moved elsewhere, and burned. This will help to prevent disease.

PRUNING EVERBEARERS

While cutting the canes after they fruit and die back is the approved method for most raspberries, the everbearers have a different lifestyle.

They bear fruit twice on the same cane. The new shoots bear a crop at the tips in the fall and bear again the next season farther down on the canes.

For this reason the fruit canes of the everbearers should not be pruned after bearing the fall crop, since this would remove the fruiting wood for the spring crop.

For those who prefer one large crop to two smaller ones there is still another way. Everbearing varieties will provide abundant fruit on primocanes (canes of the current season's growth), and thus it is possible to grow them only for the fall crop. This is accomplished by mowing all of the canes to within two or three inches of the ground in the spring, before growth starts. In the fall only the abundant crop on the primocanes is harvested. There are several advantages in doing this: it eliminates all the labor of hand pruning, winter-injured canes present no problems, and fungus diseases are held to a minimum as well.

GROWING RED RASPBERRIES

In training the reds, you either may keep all suckers pulled (which will limit your number of plants to just what you started out with), or you can let some of the suckers grow within the row to form a hedge. For a hedge, set your plants three feet apart; for individual bushes set them four feet apart. For either, if you plant in parallel rows, space the rows five feet apart.

Keep the soil well cultivated for the first few months after planting. Start applying mulch about the middle of the summer after the canes for next year's growth are well up. This will conserve moisture and keep down weeds.

The following spring all of last year's dead canes should be cut out and removed. Head back the new ones to about 30 inches. They will then put out lateral branches which will bear fruit in midsummer. Leave five to eight fruiting canes per hill for mature plants, and at this time also remove any weak canes.

Red raspberries properly pruned usually are able to stand well without support, but if they need help here is what to do:

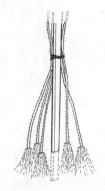

Red raspberries may be trained and pruned to the staked hill system. Do not bunch canes up too tightly or they will not have good air circulation.

Drive a stake beside each plant and tie the canes loosely to it. Do not bunch them up too tightly or they will not have good air circulation. If you are growing your reds hedgestyle, set posts at the end of each row, stretch a wire between them and tie the canes to the wire.

To keep your raspberries within bounds you will have to control their enthusiasm for producing unwanted suckers. With the hill system, these should be pulled up from the very start. If you want your raspberries to establish themselves as a hedge, let the suckers develop in the row about 10 inches apart. Pull up any that appear at the sides. Once the hedge is established keep all new ones pulled. And when I say "pull up" I mean exactly that! Cutting them just makes them grow again even more eagerly.

If red raspberries grow well in your climate you can propagate indefinitely from the first variety you plant. Just dig up healthy suckers and plant them in a new location.

GROWING BLACK RASPBERRIES

Black raspberries are, if anything, even more eager than the reds to continue propagating themselves. They are constantly arching over their canes and burying the tips in the ground, and every time they do this the tips take root and a new plant grows. If unchecked you will soon have a jungle, so restrain them properly.

Pruning should begin with the blacks as soon as the new shoots are 18 to 20 inches tall. At this height the tops are pinched off to make the canes branch. This makes them sturdier and easier to manage, and if it is not done they become long and sprawling. This operation, called **tipping**, will prevent the bush from growing taller and also keep your plants under control so they cannot form tip plants. And it makes them put out laterals which will bear the following year. By late summer or early fall the laterals will be several feet long, and a number of fruit buds will have developed. During the winter both the canes and the laterals will "sleep" in what is called dormant rest.

Black and purple raspberries and erect blackberries are pinched back 3 to 4 inches after the primocane has reached the desired height in the summer. This will result in the development of lateral shots.

While blacks should not be planted quite as deeply as the reds, it is good to give them more space—five feet apart within the rows and the rows also five or six feet apart. Cultivate the soil and follow a mulching program just as for the reds.

In the spring, while the canes are still dormant, the laterals should be cut back to five or six buds. The choice is yours: the more fruit buds you leave the more berries; the fewer the buds the larger the fruit.

Here is something it is well to remember, too. If you want to grow both red and black raspberries you should put a considerable distance between the two types This is because the reds sometimes carry a disease that does them little or no harm but may prove near fatal to the blacks. (Diseases and Insect Pests—Turn to the following section on blackberries for full notes on the few disease and insect problems that are encountered in growing raspberries.)

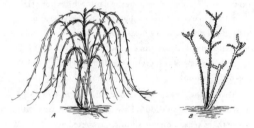

*Left: Black raspberry plant before pruning.
Right: Same plant after pruning.*

GROWING RASPBERRIES IN THE NORTH

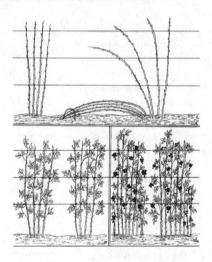

A. In the fall, after the first killing frost, prune long raspberry canes back to 6 feet. Bend canes down and lay them flat on the ground, parallel to the row, securing them so they will not pull back up again. Dig a trench between rows ½ feet wide by 8 or 9 inches deep. Mound soil from the trench over the canes. This is well worth the effort where winter temperatures are severe.

B. Straighten canes after uncovering and tie to the supporting wires. Cut them back if they are longer than 6 feet. Allow about four canes to each root.

C. In early summer new canes will start from base of plant. Again choose four healthy sturdy canes and allow them to develop. Try to choose canes about 6 to 8 inches apart. Remove canes, by cutting off at ground, that have borne fruit.

HARVESTING

Delicious and desirable as it is, the raspberry fruit is also delicate and perishable, so use care in harvesting. Pick the fruit often and when fully ripe. Reds are best when they are a deep garnet and begin to push away from the stem.

I find they are of the best flavor when picked in the late afternoon, and I always pick in small baskets and never press them down. Also I pick only the best, for there is often a surprising difference in the quality of the berries growing on the same plant.

After picking I remove the berries to a cool storage place as soon as possible. If washing is necessary I place them in very cold water (or chill them first in the refrigerator), and wash quickly, draining them on paper towels. I like to serve them well chilled, and in a shallow dish, so they will not be crushed. And they look very attractive in a large saucer or a shallow bowl so they can be seen and admired. This is a fruit that is also fun to "eat with your eyes."

Growing Better Blackberries

There's no doubt about it. While raspberries with care can be easily grown in the South, they will do much better in the North and East. Blackberries, on the other hand, are a pushover for those who live in a more temperate climate. Yet, by careful choice of variety they can also be grown in colder regions.

Check the "Hardiness Chart" at the end of this bulletin to find the variety that will do best in your zone. Note that **Alfred**, given winter protection, will even grow in Zone 4. Also the fine new variety, **Darrow**, originated at the New York Experiment Station is noteworthy among blackberries for its vigor, reliably heavy production, firmness and good quality. The plants appeared hardier than all other selections and varieties in the Station planting. Berries are 1 inch long, 1 inch wide, long, conic, and are glossy black. They begin ripening early (or about the same as **Eldorado**) and continue over a long period. **Darrow** also does well for me in Southern Oklahoma and I prefer it to all other varieties.

Actually there are two types of blackberries—erect and trailing—and they differ primarily in the character of their canes. Erect blackberries have arched, self-supporting canes. The trailing blackberries (also called dewberries, ground blackberries, or running blackberries) have canes that are not self-supporting and must be tied to poles or trellises in cultivation.

The two types also differ in fruit characteristics. Fruit clusters of the trailing blackberry are more open than those of the erect blackberry. Trailing blackberries generally ripen earlier and are often larger and sweeter than the erect type.

CHOOSING A PLANTING SITE

Always consider the availability of soil moisture, for this is the most important factor in choosing a planting site for blackberries. As the fruit grows and ripens, it will need a large supply of moisture. During the winter, however, the plants are harmed if water stands around their roots, so drainage is also important.

Almost any soil type, except very sandy soils, is suitable for blackberries as long as the drainage is good. The exact pH preference is between 5.0 and 6.0, but this can be slanted a little either way.

In areas where winters are severe, the slope of the planting site is important. Blackberries planted on hillsides are in less danger of winter injury and damage from late spring frosts than those planted in valleys. In sections where drying winds occur frequently, the plantation should be sheltered by surrounding hills, trees or shrubs.

PLANTING

Blackberries should be planted as soon as you can prepare the soil—in early spring in the North, in late winter or early spring in the South.

Preparing the Soil

Prepare the soil for blackberries just as thoroughly as you would for a garden. For best results, plow to a depth of about nine inches as soon as the soil is in a workable condition. Just before setting the plants the soil should be disked and harrowed. This, of course, applies to the larger planting. For a home garden go over the area with a rotary tiller.

Just as with raspberries, it is a good idea to seed and plow under one or two green-manure crops before establishing a new blackberry planting. This may be rye, vetch or cowpeas. This thorough working gets the soil in good condition for planting, and the added organic matter and nitrogen help the plantation to produce an early fruit crop.

As with raspberries, you can take a soil sample of the area to be planted and make any corrections needed beforehand. The pH preference of blackberries is between 5.0 and 6.0—much the same as for raspberries. They do well in ordinary soil, thriving best in clay loam that is moist yet well drained.

Spacing the Plants

Plant erect varieties of blackberries five feet apart in rows that are eight feet apart. Space vigorous varieties of trailing or semitrailing blackberries, such as Thornless Evergreen, 8 to 12 feet apart in rows 10 feet apart. Space other trailing varieties four to six feet apart in rows eight feet apart.

In the central states, set erect varieties two feet apart in rows 9 to 10 feet apart, and let the plants grow into hedgerows.

Setting the Plants

When setting out my plants I am always careful not to let the planting stock dry out. If I cannot plant the stock as soon as it arrives, I protect the roots from drying by heeling in the plants.

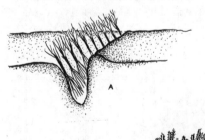

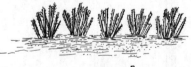

When your stock arrives open and examine it as soon as possible. If you cannot plant at once, store it for a few days by covering the roots with some type of moist material and store in a cool place, away from wind and sun so it will not dry.

If you must hold it more than 2 or 3 days it should be heeled in. Dig a trench (A) and bury the roots in the ground. (B) Pack soil firmly around the roots to prevent air pockets and keep the soil moist until ready to plant.

Be sure to plant in permanent location before buds begin to swell.

Continued ➜

To heel in, I dig a trench deep enough to contain the roots. Then I spread the plants along the trench, roots down, and cover the roots with moist soil.

If the plants are dry when I receive them, I soak the roots in water for several hours before planting or heeling them in.

When I am ready to set the plants in their permanent location I dip the roots in a thin mud made with clay and water (or I keep the plants in polyethylene bags). This coating helps to protect the roots from rapid drying while the plants are being set.

Before setting the plants, I cut the tops back so they are about six inches long. The six-inch top is useful as a handle when setting the plants and will serve to show their location.

Proper planting depth for strong, well-rooted blackberry.

I find the best way to make a planting is to cut a slit in the soil with the blade of a mattock or shovel, pressing the handle of the tool forward to open the slit. Then I put the root of the blackberry plant in the hole, setting it so it is about the same depth as it was in the nursery. Then I withdraw the blade of the mattock or shovel and pack the soil firmly around the root with my heel.

Intercropping

During the first summer after the blackberry plants have been set, I find it possible to grow vegetables between the rows. Such vegetables as cabbage, cauliflower, beans, peas and summer squash are good for intercropping. Do not, however, try to grow grain crops, since they are not cultivated and they take too much moisture and nutrients needed by the blackberry plants.

TRAINING PLANTS THE WAY THEY SHOULD GO

Blackberry plants are best trained to trellises. While erect types can be grown without support, many of the canes may be broken during cultivation and picking. Trellises will pay for themselves by reducing this damage.

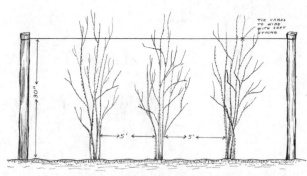

Trellis for Blackberries

Erect blackberry plants can be grown without support, but many of the canes may be broken during cultivation and picking. Trellises will often pay for themselves by reducing this damage.

A simple trellis may be made by stretching wire between posts set 15 to 20 feet apart in the row. Use a single wire attached to the post about 30 inches from the ground.

Tie the canes to the wires with soft string where the canes cross the wire. Avoid tying the canes in bundles.

While many trellis arrangements and methods of training are used by blackberry growers, I believe the simplest method of trellis construction and training is as follows:

Build trellises by stretching wire between posts set 15 to 20 feet apart in the row. For erect blackberries, use a single wire attached to the posts about 30 inches from the ground. For semi-trailing and trailing blackberries it is best to use two wires, one about three feet and the other about five feet from the ground.

I like to tie the canes to the wires with soft string. Erect varieties are best tied where the canes cross the wire. Then tie trailing canes horizontally along the wires or fan them out from the ground and tie them where they cross each wire. Because the canes need air circulation around them they never should be tied in bundles.

TO PRUNE AND THIN

The crowns of blackberry plants are perennial, new canes arising from them each year. These canes are biennial—that is they live for only two years, and during the first year they grow and send out laterals (side branches). Small branches grow from buds on the laterals in the second year, and the fruit is borne on these buds. After the laterals bear fruit, the canes die.

Be sure to prune the laterals back in the spring, so the fruit will be larger and of better quality (than fruit from unpruned laterals). Pruning is best done before growth starts, and the laterals should be cut back to a length of about 12 inches.

Growing blackberries is almost too easy, especially with the erect types which send up root suckers in addition to the new canes (that arise from the crown). Don't let all these root suckers grow, or your blackberry planting will soon turn into a thicket.

Take care during the growing season to remove all suckers that appear between the rows. And you must pull the suckers out of the ground. Those that are pulled will not regrow as quickly as those that are cut down.

Cut off the tips of erect blackberry canes when they reach a height of 30 to 36 inches. This will make the canes branch. Also tipped canes are much sturdier and are better able to support a heavy fruit crop than untipped ones.

In summer, just as soon as the last berries have been harvested, it is wise to cut out all the old canes and burn them. At this time I like to thin out the new canes as well, leaving three or four canes of erect varieties, four to eight canes of semi-trailing varieties, and 8 to 12 canes of trailing varieties.

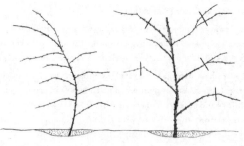

Blackberry

Pruning makes the difference. Note sturdy plant on the right. This plant was pruned during the summer and will be pruned the following spring where the black marks indicate.

648

If you live in an area where anthracnose and rosette are serious diseases problems for blackberries, cut out all the canes—both old and new—after fruiting. Then fertilize and cultivate to promote growth of replacement canes for the next year's crop. These two diseases seldom are troublesome except in some areas of the South.

If suckers are allowed to form within the rows of erect blackberries, thin them to about five or six per lineal foot of row.

FERTILIZING

In a large planting, barley, oats or buckwheat make excellent cover crops for blackberries because they do not live over the winter. They should be worked into the soil in autumn and additional humus added if possible. These crops also help in giving winter protection to berry canes. For the smaller home planting, compost or well-decomposed manure are helpful. It is believed now by most authorities that chemical fertilizers such as the nitrates increase cane growth, but not the formation of more fruit.

Some varieties of blackberry are self-sterile and need a pollenizer. Two varieties in the garden, which blossom at the same time so that the blossoms may be crossed, often give better fruit results.

Blackberries, as I said earlier, need a moist soil during the fruiting season, and poor quality berries often result on dry soil. The moist condition in the soil can best be assured by the use of abundant compost.

CULTIVATING

Blackberry plantings should be cultivated thoroughly and frequently. Don't let grass and weeds get a start and become difficult to control. Begin cultivating in the spring very early, just as soon as the soil is workable. Cultivate throughout the season as often as necessary to keep weeds down. As often as once a week, if you must. Discontinue cultivation at least a month before freezing weather normally begins.

To avoid harming shallow roots of the plants, cultivate only two or three inches deep near the rows. For a large planting, a tractor-mounted grape hoe or a rotary hoe may be used for cultivating in the rows and under trellises. A tiller works best for home plantings.

Winter cover crops help prevent soil erosion, add humus to the soil and also shield the canes during the winter from drying winds. It is a good idea to sow a cover crop at the time of the last cultivation. In addition to those already mentioned, such crops as cowpeas, spring oats or rye may be used, drilled in the middles and leaving 12 to 15 inches next to the plants free of cover crop. Plant a cover crop best suited to your area and winter conditions. Then turn it under the following spring.

TO FOIL THE BIRDS

Birds are sometimes troublesome in and around the blackberry patch. If you find this to be true, try luring them away by planting mulberries, elderberries or chokecherries which they often prefer. With these fruits to attract them they will leave the blackberries alone.

HARVESTING

Pick your blackberries as soon as they become sweet. Be sure they are fully ripe, for the fruit is not ready for picking when it first turns black. You may need to do a little testing and tasting. Berries that are picked at the proper time, handled carefully and stored in a cool place will stay in good condition for several days. Berries that are over-ripe or injured spoil quickly.

The fruit should be fully ripened but firm. Pick often—for most varieties every other day. Pick early in the day and try to finish before the hottest part of the day. Blackberries do not spoil as quickly if picked in the morning as when picked in the afternoon. Do not crush or bruise the fruit—place it carefully in the baskets—and as soon as each basket is full, place it in a basket carrier, which should always be kept in the shade.

Great Grapes

Grow the Best Ever

Annie Proulx

Who Can Grow Grapes?

Grapes have the reputation of being fragile and difficult to grow. Many northern gardeners, convinced that all grapes are too tender for their fierce winters and uneven spring temperatures, do not even consider trying to grow them, yet some vines will flourish in regions of every state and in several Canadian provinces. Since 1843 when Ephraim Bull of Concord, Massachusetts, finally succeeded in breeding the native grape he named for his town, after more than 20,000 tries, grape breeders and hybridizers have developed literally thousands of different grape varieties suited to an amazing range of climates and soils. A good rule of thumb is that if wild grapes grow in your area, you can grow plump and tasty domestic grapes of some kind.

Even in New England, successful commercial and amateur vineyards are proliferating. Several winemakers in the best southern New England sites are actually growing *Vitis vinifera*, the prima donna European wine grapes—a gardening feat once believed impossible in this region. Hardier cultivars (*cultivated varieties*), such as the Beta and Blue Jay, will grow in the northern states and southern Canada, bred to withstand winter temperatures that plunge to 30°F below zero! Really determined vine growers can coax even the most delicate vines to fruition in a hothouse. In an especially sheltered, sunny, well-drained site—an optimum microclimate—you may be able to grow cultivars beyond their normal range. Northern grape growers have worked out wine growing, or viticultural, practices that protect and encourage their vines despite frost and snow. In the South Atlantic and Gulf states, Muscadine grapes will succeed where other cultivars cannot.

You can grow grapes successfully if:

· You choose the most suitable cultivars for your area, grapes that will ripen before killing frosts get them, or that will withstand hot, humid summers.

· You plant them in the most sunny, sheltered, well-drained place possible.

· You learn—and practice—every special growing technique that will give you and your grapes the edge over climatic vagaries.

· Don't give up if one variety fails to flourish. Only trial and error will enable you to match the best cultivar to your vinery.

Continued →

THE BEST CLIMATE

The best grape climates are regions where the growing season is 150 to 180 days, where relative humidity is low, and where summer rains are sparse rather than frequent. A week of cloud and rain in the final week of ripening may result in extensive crop losses.

Grape growing will be difficult or impossible in arid desert regions without irrigation, in places with extremely short growing seasons, or with very severe winter temperatures.

SOMETHING TO THINK ABOUT

You should have a good idea of what you will do with your grape crop before your vineyard gets off paper. A quarter-acre of vines—about 100 plants—can give you a ton of fruit at harvest time. A ton of grapes fills 50 to 60 bushel baskets. Depending on the grape cultivar, this means up to 200 gallons of juice or wine.

If you are thinking of growing grapes commercially, even on a small scale, you should know that the costs of establishing a vineyard (posts, wire, vines, pesticide sprays, and hired labor) are estimated at about $4,500 an acre. The major cost is in the hired labor. Cultivation, vine training, pruning, pest control must all be done when the vines need it, or the crop may fail. The home grower who can attend to his or her vines without hiring paid help is way ahead of the game. Remember, too, that it takes three to four years before the vines will produce a crop.

GRAPE YIELDS

- 10 Concord vines grown 8 to 10 feet apart will yield about 50 quarts of juice a year.

- Each vine of bunch grapes will give between 5 and 15 pounds of fruit every season.

- One to two bushels of grapes yields enough juice to fill a 5-gallon carboy.

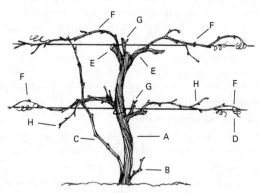

The major parts of a grapevine consist of the trunk (A), suckers (B), young replacement trunk (C), tendril (D), arm (E), cane (F), spur (G), and shoot (H).

Grape Growers' Vocabulary

Arms: The favored canes left on the vine after the rivals are pruned off. These arms produce fruiting shoots and canes for next year. After a season's production they are usually pruned off during the next dormant season and replaced.

Canes: The mature shoots late in the season. The word also means the year-old dormant wood of the preceding season. Most canes are pruned out during the dormant period before the new growth begins in the spring.

Cordon: *See* Trunk.

Cultivar: A cultured variety of plant especially developed for commercial or domestic cultivation. Cultivar is just a short form of cultivated variety.

Renewal canes: *See* Spurs.

Shoots: The young, succulent growth of the present season. Shoots grow from last season's buds and send out leaves, flowers, and fruit. When mature, they become the fruiting canes of the next season.

Spurs: Short, one- or two-bud canes deliberately left on the vine to become the arms and canes of the future.

Stripping: The process of removing all new growth in the event of frost damage.

Trellis: A number of wires strung on posts to support the fruiting arms of the vine.

Trunk: The main stock of the plant, also called the cordon. Some tender varieties may have two, or even three, trunks.

Basic Grape Types

There are basically three types of grapes: native wild grapes, *Vitis vinifera*, and hybrids.

The twenty-four to thirty species of wild grapes native to the United States comprise more than half of the world's species. The most familiar is the Fox Grape (*Vitis labrusca*) from which the Concord with its characteristic "foxy" taste was developed, the Riverbank Grape, the Frost Grape, and the Muscadine Grapes of the South, of which the yellow-green, plum-flavored Scuppernong is best known. Some of the wild grapes are still gathered and used for jelly. The best have been hybridized by grape breeders in their search for hardy, disease-free, delicious fruits.

In the late nineteenth century vines were sent from the United States to Europe that carried *phylloxera*, a burrowing plant louse that feeds on grapevine roots. Although the American vines were resistant to phylloxera, the European wine grapes were not, and great and noble vineyards were devastated, especially in France. Today European vineyards are planted with *Vitis vinifera* grafted on native American rootstocks which are by nature resistant to phylloxera.

Vitis vinifera are the famous grapes of Europe from which the great wines come; and Riesling, Cabernet Sauvignon, Chardonnay, Pinot, and many others are the grapes that have made wine history. From their Mediterranean homelands, *Vitis vinifera* have been transplanted all over the world from South Africa to Russia. In the United States they grow especially well in California, Oregon, and Washington; but they are being successfully harvested and pressed elsewhere, even in New England. Some of the familiar dried raisins come from *Vitis vinifera*, but this crop is almost exclusive to California since it calls for a very long sunny season for the berries to develop the necessary amount of sugar.

There are also complex crosses involving *Vitis vinifera*, native American grapes, and the resulting hybrids themselves. Decades of intensive hybridizing by grape breeders have given commercial and home grape-growers many cultivars suited to nearly every climate from the cold north to the hot, humid Gulf Coast, and to a wide range of soils, from acid to fairly alkaline. These "bunch grapes," as they are often called, are used for table fruit, wine, fresh and canned juice, jellies, and cooking. They are the mainstay of the home grape-grower.

Many of the French hybrids carry the names of their breeders, as Georges Couderc, Seyve-Villard, who specialized in hybrid vines for warm climates; Baco, whose hybrids are important in the New York wine industry; and Seibel, who developed hundreds of specialized vines. Usually a number is attached to the name. For example, Seibel 13053 is a very early, hardy blue grape also known as Cascade. There are also American and Canadian hybrids, usually bearing simple place names, such as Niagara, Buffalo, Seneca, and the Canada Muscat. The Experimental Station in Geneva, New York, is one of the major American centers for grape hybridization. The Geneva-based New York State Fruit Testing Cooperative Association (NYSFTCA) annually offers its members promising new varieties of dessert and wine grapes developed at the Geneva station and elsewhere for home trial and testing.

The bunch grape hybrids are popular and extensively grown. They are easy to work with, bear early and regularly, and, like other grapes, are long lived, with a span of fifty years. Some cultivars are best for eating fresh, such as Seneca; others, like the Concord, are used in juice and jelly; some, like Foch and Seibel 9549 (De Chaunac) make very good wines.

Planning Your Vineyard

CHOOSE THE RIGHT CULTIVARS

The USDA has developed maps outlining four basic grape regions: the early-ripening grape area; the midseason-ripening area; the late-ripening area; and the unique Florida and Gulf Coast area. These regional maps are a good general guide for selecting grape varieties to grow. In addition you should talk to your extension agent and, if possible, other grape-growers in your neighborhood. There is no substitute for experience in the vineyard.

If you intend to grow grapes commercially, even on a small scale, you will want to stick with dependable, safe cultivars that will not fail you at harvest time. If you are more adventurous, growing only for your own use, and if you don't mind an occasional crop failure, experiment with cultivars a bit beyond your range and join the NYSFTCA to try the latest from the fruit breeders' laboratories.

CHOOSING THE BEST SITE

Choosing the right place for a vineyard is always important; for a northern gardener, it is a crucial decision. You may not be aware of it, but your land forms miniclimates of its own. Northern slopes are colder and receive fewer hours of sunlight.

Northern growers usually seek southeastern, southwestern, or southern exposures on long, gentle slopes with good air drainage—where the frost will roll down past the vines and settle in the flat lands and the valleys. Spring frosts probably cause more harvest losses than cold winters because a late frost at flowering time can severely damage the season's crop of grapes. Although planting on a northern slope leads to late flowering, which in turn reduces the risk of frost harm, such slopes lose too many hours of precious sunlight so vital to the fruit's maturation and ripening process.

Most vineyards lie on slopes. Vineyards on northern or southern slopes with rows running east and west, not only hold the soil in place, they take advantage of the prevailing westerly winds that quickly dry and aerate the grape foliage, reducing the chances of disease. Grapes are extremely sensitive to dampness. Hot, humid conditions, as in parts of the South, are conducive to numerous diseases and fungi that attack grapes.

Some of the most favorable sites for vineyards are south or east or southeast of large lakes. Temperature changes in spring and autumn are slow and moderate in these locations, with less chance of untimely frosts. Winds off the lake keep the grape foliage dry and healthy.

Be as deliberate in placing your vineyard as you would an orchard; grapevines live and bear for more than fifty years.

THE SOIL

There is a winegrower's saying in Burgundy: "If our soil weren't the richest in the world, it would be the poorest." The classic European wine grapes are largely grown in chalky, sandy, or shale soils where nothing else will thrive. Such soils encourage the plant to put its energy into the fruit rather than foliage. Although these famous, "noble" soils are poor in some nutrients, they are rich in the mineral elements which contribute markedly to the final flavor and aroma of the great wines.

Fortunately for grape lovers elsewhere, the vine will grow in many different soil types. Well-drained, deep, fertile loams are excellent, yet grapes will thrive on soils containing clay, slate, gravel, shale, and sand. Gravelly, stony soils, generally drain well, and they absorb and reflect the sun's warmth to give the vine bottom heat.

Very dry and very wet soils are bad for grapes. A soil that drains poorly is quite unsuitable, as are shallow soils underlaid by hardpan, gravel, or sand. Very rich soils with high levels of organic material tend to make vines with excessive foliage, or bearing a heavy crop of late-ripening, low-sugar fruit. Leaner soils are more desirable as they give comparatively modest crops of fruit that mature earlier and have considerable sugar in the berry.

Have your soil tested for grape growing. A complete soil test will tell you the pH level, levels of mineral and trace elements, and make the necessary recommendations for soil improvement. If you are thinking of growing grapes commercially, you must have a complete fertilizer analysis. Often soils are not only deficient in nitrogen, phosphorus, and potash (the familiar NPK), but must have small amounts of boron, magnesium, calcium, and zinc added to produce grapes of good quality. It is estimated that in New England it may take as much as between 500 and 750 pounds of NPK per acre per year to produce four to six tons of quality grapes and the next year's new wood.

Preparing the Vineyard for the Vine

Grapes do not tolerate weeds or competitive grass. Therefore, land intended for a vineyard is usually plowed, disced, and planted to some row crop the year before the vines are set out. This reduces the number of weeds substantially.

The vineyard should be plowed deeply and should be very well disced, so that the soil is thoroughly pulverized before the vines are set out. Since grapes are usually grown on a slope in "clean cultivation" (no plant competitors allowed nearby, the vine set in bare soil), the risk of erosion is considerable. If your slope is more steep than gentle, your

Continued ➔

local soil conservation service specialist can help you plan the most advantageous contour rows for your vines. Good topsoil is eroding in this country at a frightening rate, and every care must be taken to prevent erosion.

BUILDING A TRELLIS

Grapes require some system to support their eager vines. While grapes can be grown ornamentally along fences, for best harvest results, the vine should be trained to grow on a trellis system designed for ease of pruning and maximum sunlight. An overgrown, dense vine will not receive enough sunlight to ripen the fruit.

The trellis should be built for sturdiness and longevity. It is particularly important that the posts which support the trellis wires be strong and well-set. The end posts must be the strongest; they should be heavy and well-braced, set three feet deep and angled outward so they will not be pulled over by the weight of the mature vines. In each row the end posts should be positioned four feet from the last plants in the row. Every two or three vines, set in the line posts to carry the trellis. Remember that the posts must support the weight of the heavy foliage and fruit, and during windstorms the stresses can be powerful.

Grapevines should never be set right up against a post, for the plants will outlast any wooden post, and the roots will be disturbed when the post has to be replaced. Moreover, many wooden posts are treated with preservatives that can harm the vine. Long-lasting wooden posts are made of black locust, white oak, red cedar, and osage orange. Posts made of other wood may be treated with creosote to make them last longer.

Better than wooden posts, but quite expensive, are steel or concrete posts. But, steel posts also act as lightning rods in a vineyard on an exposed hill. Lightning has been known to run along the trellis wires and destroy a row of fruiting arms. Grape-growers who live near granite or other stone quarries may be able to get their hands on stone posts that are beautiful and last forever.

Once the posts are set, putting up the trellis wire is not unlike putting up a fence. The standard trellis consists of two or more strands of no. 9 wire stapled to cross arms on each post. The staples are not driven snug, but allow the wires to slide back and forth beneath them, so that the wires may be tightened at the end of the row with a turnbuckle when the weight of the vines causes them to sag.

PLANTING THE VINES

Grapes should be planted as early in the spring as the soil can be worked north of Arkansas, Tennessee, and Virginia. Farther south the vines can be planted in the autumn. It is important that the plants make themselves at home and get established before the long hot days of summer begin.

Order your grape stock from a nursery as nearby as possible; if you can, pick out and pick up the plants yourself. Slow delivery and delays in transit are unfortunately the rule rather than the exception with mail-order stock; vines often arrive late, dried out, and weakened. The best stock is strong, sturdy, one-year-old plants with large fibrous root systems; two-year-old plants are more expensive, and they will not bear any sooner.

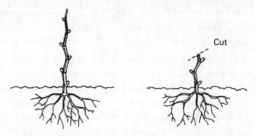

Plant the vine at the same depth it grew in the nursery. Prune it back to a single stem or three buds tall.

Dig a good hole in the worked-up soil, large enough to spread out the vine's roots comfortably. Never stuff a grapevine into a cramped miserly hole. Pack the soil firmly around the roots, leaving no air spaces that can increase the chances of disease. Plant the vines at the same depth they grew in the nursery, then prune them back to a single stem two or three buds tall. If it is early spring and the soil is moist, you need not water at planting. Later in the spring you may want to water well after planting. Watering helps the soil close in around the roots.

Space most hybrid cultivars eight to ten feet apart in the row, with the rows ten to eleven feet from each other. Less vigorous vines, like Delaware, can be closer together—seven or eight feet apart in the row.

Caring for Your Vineyard

CULTIVATION AND SOIL MANAGEMENT

Cultivation seems to stimulate tired vines like a Swedish massage revives an exhausted executive. Grapevines thrive with shallow cultivation, no deeper than three or four inches lest the roots be damaged, at least several times in the spring and early summer. A rototiller is very useful for this chore, but there are vine growers who cherish the hours in their vineyard with a grape hoe, one of mankind's better inventions. A session with the grape hoe will leave very few weeds behind for hand pulling.

If your vines are planted on a steep hillside, practice "trashy cultivation" to control soil erosion. Trashy cultivation means leaving some herbiage growing and some rough pockets and hillocks of soil to hold water in tiny pools rather than allowing it to run off a smooth surface and carry precious topsoil with it. It is better not to be scrupulously clean in cultivating, but to cultivate just enough to keep the weeds down and the vines up. There is always another year for the vines, but when the soil is gone—it is gone forever.

Weak vines usually perk up with cultivation. Sometimes vines that are doing poorly need only a shot of nitrogenous fertilizer, sometimes a complete fertilizer. Work organic material into the soil—rotted manure, old hay and straw, and grape pomace—all build the soil and give the vine considerable amounts of plant nutrients. If you are not sure what fertilizers you need, see your county agent and have the soil tested for grape growing conditions.

Sometimes the soil is so rich that the vines grow too lustily. These excessively vigorous plants may blossom heavily but set fruit sparsely and with reluctance. Grape gardeners have learned that sowing a rapid-growing cover crop such as rye or oats will take some of the nutrients away from the too-vigorous vines, restrict their growth, and force them to set their fruit. Normal cultivation should follow after the fruit sets. The same ploy worked just before the grapes ripen often makes

The Italian grape, or grading, hoe is useful for cultivation.

With smooth cultivation (left), as you might do in your vegetable garden, all weeds are removed and the soil is left smooth. Trashy cultivation (right) leaves rough pockets of soil and a few weeds; it is recommended to prevent soil erosion.

better quality fruit and helps next year's bearing wood mature more thoroughly.

TRAINING

Training is the business of shaping young vines into a particular system of growth by judicious pruning. There are scores of these systems, such as the Four Arm Kniffen, the Umbrella Kniffen, the Geneva Double Curtain, the Munson, the Keuka High Renewal, and many more. The Single Stem Four Cane Kniffen System is the most popular in the eastern United States and suits most bunch grapes well. However, the Geneva Double Curtain System was especially developed for vigorous cultivars like Catawba, Niagara, and that old favorite, Concord. Both the Kniffen and the Geneva Double Curtain are briefly described here. If you wish more information on training systems, consult USDA Farmers' Bulletin Number 2123, "Growing American Bunch Grapes" by grape authority J. R. McGrow. Bulletin Number 811, "The Geneva Double Curtain System for Vigorous Grape Vines," is available from the New York Agricultural Experiment Station, Geneva, New York, 14456.

The Four Arm Kniffen System (for moderately vigorous vines). For this system two wires are strung across the posts, as illustrated. The lower wire is strung about 30 inches from the ground. The top wire is run 24 inches to 30 inches above the lower wire.

Begin training in the autumn of your vine's first season, after it has become dormant. Choose the strongest-looking cane and tie it with binder twine to the top wire. (Do not use wire, plastic twine, or long-lasting cord to tie grapes; these will last so long they may strangle the growing vine.) Nip off the cane just above the top wire, then cut off *all* the other canes. If the vine did not grow any canes long enough to reach the top wire, don't worry, the plant is building up its root system. Simply tie the strongest cane it made to the bottom wire and nip off the other growth. If the vine was laggard and you do not have a cane that will reach even the bottom wire, cut the cane right back to a single stem with two or three buds as you did after the initial planting, and wait until next year. Patience is only one of the grape-grower's virtues.

In the dormant period following the second or third growing season, choose four of the strongest canes for the *arms*. Count off about

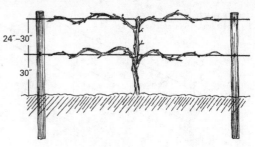

This established vine has been trained to the Four Arm Kniffen System.

ten buds along the length of each arm, and prune off all other growth, except for *renewal spurs*. Tie each arm along its horizontal wire. Near each arm's source, leave an auxiliary arm two or three buds long for renewal spurs. Every year in the dormant season the arms will be replaced by the renewal spur canes, and new sets of renewal spurs will be started. In that way, each vine will have new arms every year.

Northern gardeners with their short growing seasons will find that extending the Kniffen System trellis a foot higher so that there is more space between the wires lets greater amounts of sunlight strike the vines, and this extra sunshine can make the difference between harvest baskets full of ripe grapes or a row of frost-blasted immature bunches.

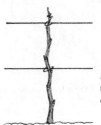

In the autumn of the vine's first season, select the strongest cane to become the trunk, tie it to the top wire, and cut off all other canes.

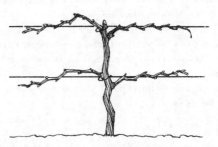

In the dormant period following the second or third growing season, choose four of the strongest canes for arms and prune back the rest, leaving two or three buds for renewal spurs.

The Geneva Double Curtain System (for vigorous vines). This system is designed to get greater amounts of sunlight on the vines, making more and better fruit.

Three wires are used in this system; the center trunk support wire is set 52 inches from the ground, and the two cordon wires support the arms. A vine can be trained so that its arms extend 16 feet along the wires.

With the Geneva Double Curtain each vine is usually allowed to have two trunks of a more efficient use of the trellis space. Five-bud

Continued →

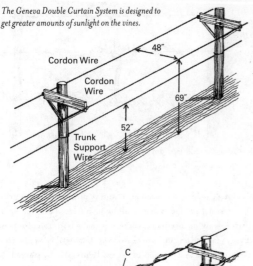

The Geneva Double Curtain System is designed to get greater amounts of sunlight on the vines.

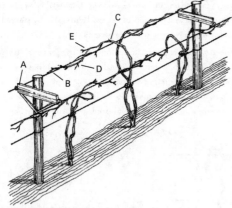

An established vine trained to the Geneva Double Curtain System (A = cordon wire support; B = cordon wire; C = cordon; D = fruiting cane; E = renewal spurs).

fruiting canes are left on the cordons, and the renewal spurs are one-bud stubs. If the canes were allowed to grow at their own will, the system would turn into a mass of random greenery. However, every year the fruiting canes are tied into position by hand so that they will grow downward. The leaves receive the sun; with grapes it is sunlight on the leaves which causes the fruit to ripen rather than on the fruit clusters themselves. The effect of this system in midseason is a double curtain of foliage, hence the name.

PRUNING

Once the young vines are properly shaped on the trellis to the system you want and begin producing, they are mature vines and must be maintained by heavy annual pruning. Many beginning grape gardeners are timid about pruning and hesitate to slash away healthy growth. But grape growers must learn to be ruthless, for the vines cannot give a decent crop without thorough pruning. There is a limit, however; too much pruning will discourage the vines.

Pruning grapevines is a fairly simple operation.There are no ladders to climb, no "wrong" cutting angles to worry about, no special tools are required. Most grape pruning jobs can be done with hand pruners.

Vines should be dormant when they are pruned. Where the winters are mild, pruning can be done at leisure throughout the winter. But

never prune or handle frozen canes; they are brittle and snap off easily. If your winter temperatures are severe, and you expect a certain percentage of canes will be killed by the cold, hold off on pruning until the early spring when you can see which canes have made it through the winter.

It is possible to prune late in the spring. The vines will leak sap rather alarmingly, but the practice does not seem to injure them. But late pruning and handling after the spring growth has begun will almost certainly injure many tender buds.

How much to cut off? This is the burning question for the beginning grape-grower. The answer varies with the cultivar. The different grape varieties are divided into "long cane," "medium cane," and "short cane" vines, and different handling is recommended for each.

- *Long cane:* These vines should keep between thirty and sixty buds on each plant after they are pruned. Serious vine growers weigh the pruned wood on a balance scale. They leave a basic thirty buds on the vine, plus ten more buds for each pound of year-old wood pruned out.

- *Medium cane:* Leave twenty-five basic buds plus an additional ten for each pound of wood pruned out.

- *Short cane:* These cultivars bear large clusters of grapes and should be severely nipped back. For the first pound of cuttings taken off, only four to six buds are allowed to remain. A scant two buds are granted for each additional pound of wood removed.

Just as artists begin a painting by "roughing out" a sketch, experienced pruners begin by roughing out the whole vine to conform to its particular training system. They leave plenty of extra buds as a margin, weigh the cuttings, then "fine prune" the vine to its proper balance. After a few seasons the eye and the hand are all that's necessary to tell how much to take off.

Long Cane	Medium Cane	Short Cane
Beta	Blue Lake	Seibel 9110 (Verdelet)
Caco	Catawba	Seyve-Villard
Campbell Early	Concord Seedless	5–276 (Seyval Blanc)
Concord	Delaware	
Fredonia	Ellen Scott	Seyve-Villard 12–375 (Villard Blanc)
Foch	Golden Muscat	
Niagara	Himrod	Seyve-Villard 18–315 (Villard Noir)
Worden	Interlaken Seedless	
	Landot 244 (Landal)	
	Moore Early	
	Seibel 5279 (Aurore)	
	Seibel 13053 (Cascade)	
	Seneca	
	Steuben	
	Stover	
	Vidal 256	

New Trunks for Old. It is not unusual for vine trunks to grow feeble through disease or damage and falter after some years. It is faster, takes less work, and means less crop loss to develop a new trunk than to take out the whole vine and start over.

To renew a trunk, allow a healthy sucker from the base of the damaged trunk to develop. Train it up the trellis just as though it were a young vine.

At the end of two seasons the basic form of the new trunk and its arms will be established. Start decreasing the canes on the old trunk system so that the new trunk can gather the strength to put out a crop. At the end of the third season, cut out the old trunk altogether during the dormant period.

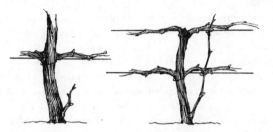

To replace a feeble trunk, allow a healthy sucker to develop (left) and train it up the trellis like a young vine (right).

The Killing Spring Frost. Northern gardeners and grape growers learn to develop a sixth sense for weather changes that mean a late frost and are usually able to protect their plants from the damaging ice crystal formations. But sometimes the worst happens, and the tender new growth on the vines is badly damaged by a killer frost. If the damage is severe, you can still get a partial crop by *stripping* the new growth to force secondary buds to develop. If the frost damage is light and has just hit the tips, do *not* strip. You still may get only a partial crop through incomplete fruit set, but that's all you'd get with stripping, too.

Stripping is something of a last resort, the difference between some grapes and no grapes. With your hands or a pair of hand pruners completely strip the vines of *all* new growth, both the frosted and the unfrosted shoots. (Partial stripping is not good; it leads to malformed vines that will be difficult to prune in following years.) The stripped vine will be forced to develop secondary buds, which will flower and fruit and give you a partial crop.

PROPAGATION

Bunch grapes usually grow on their own roots and do not have to be grafted onto special rootstocks. They are easily propagated from cuttings taken from the previous season's growth, a simple procedure with good and economical results.

Cuttings should be taken fairly early in the dormant season to avoid the possibility of getting winter-damaged wood. Select matured canes at least one-third inch in diameter. Avoid spindly or thick canes.

From vigorous cultivars like Beta or Concord, take canes with the buds three to five inches apart, and be sure there are at least three buds on the section you cut. From less vigorous vines, such as Delaware, choose canes that have the buds closer together, and cut four-bud sections.

Mallet cuttings include a small heel of two-year-old wood, and are more apt to root strongly than the one-year growth.

Bundle the cuttings with the buds pointing in the same direction and store them over the winter to plant in early spring if you live in the north. Southern grape-growers can set out cuttings in the grape nursery any time during the dormant season. The cuttings can be kept over the winter by burying them in well-drained soil covered with heavy mulch, or by packing them in moist sand or sawdust and storing in an unheated cellar. A small amount of cuttings can be kept in the refrigerator in plastic bags if they are packed in moist peat moss or sawdust.

In the early spring set out the cuttings in prepared soil that is weed-free, fertile, and in good tilth. The rows should be two to four feet apart, and the plants set four to six inches apart within the row. Set the cuttings firmly with one bud above the soil. Keep the nursery bed weed-free through the growing season. The following spring the yearling plants are ready to go into the vineyard.

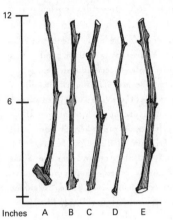

Bunch grapes can be propagated by cuttings. Cutting A is a mallet cutting; B and C are good cane cuttings; D is too thin; and E is too thick.

Grafting. Special rootstocks to improve the vigor of weak cultivars, or that are resistant to phylloxera or nematode infestations of the soil, or that hasten or delay wood maturity, or are adapted to dry and alkaline soils are available. Scions from the desired varieties may be grafted or chip-budded onto these stocks, but since not all stocks and scions are compatible, it is best to check with your nursery, county agent, or state extension service for information on the rootstocks that suit your special problems and the best grafting techniques.

Layering. Layering is a good propagation technique when you need to fill a vacancy left by a deceased vine in the vineyard. A young plant fresh from the nursery may have trouble competing with mature vineyard neighbors, but a layered vine will usually do very well.

Layering is best done in spring. Choose a sturdy cane on a vine neighbor near the vacancy. At the place you want the new vine to grow, dig a shallow trench three or four inches deep and fill it halfway with rich, well-worked soil. Bend down the chosen cane so it lies in the trench with two buds protruding above the surface, and two or three buds lie below the soil. Pack the soil down firmly. You may have to put a brick on it to hold the cane down. Let the cane tip grow freely through the summer. In the autumn dormant period the connection with the parent plant can be severed if the new vine has done well. Otherwise, let it develop a strong root system through another season.

Continued ➜

Diseases and Pests of the Grape

Humans are not alone in loving grapes; the sugar-rich berries and succulent vines and roots are banquet material for hundreds of insect species. Few birds can resist a vine of ripe grapes. Indeed, eighty-four species of birds feast on grapes, as do black bears, coyotes, foxes, possums, raccoons, skunks, and squirrels. White-tailed deer enthusiastically nibble foliage and canes. Nets, fences, alarms, scarecrows, flapping and noise-making objects, deterrent scents, and many other items are sold each year to grape-growers anxious to protect the fruits of their labor.

A few of the grape-damaging insects are: *Japanese beetles; curculio; cutworms* that gnaw the buds at night; *thrips* that suck the plant's vital juices; *rose chafers* that devour buds, blossoms, new fruits, and leaves; the larvae of *grape moths* that devour the pulp of the berries; *flea beetles*, partial to the vine and its leaves; and the infamous *phylloxera*, a sucking louse which destroyed the pure viniferous vineyards of Europe in the nineteenth century.

Organic gardeners find grapes one of the most difficult crops to grow well without sprays. Still, there are those who claim good results by keeping a well-situated vineyard isolated, scrupulously clean, and by encouraging birdlife in the vineyard, at least until the fruit begins to ripen. Knocking the insects off the vine with a jet of water from the garden hose is a deterrent, as are the practices of sprinkling soot, lime, or ashes on the leaves in the morning when the dew is still on the plants. The more visible creatures such as slugs, chafers, and Japanese beetles can be hand-picked off the vines and drowned. Some gardeners find placing a jar of decomposing rose chafers under the vine makes a nasty odor that sends survivor chafers away. Since rose chafer larvae must feed on grass roots, clean cultivation will keep these pests at bay.

In their natural state, grapes grow high in the tops of trees where they are well-ventilated. Wild grapes are hardy, bothered by few insects or diseases. Man has brought the domestic grape down to his level and pays for the convenience of its artificial posture by watching numerous fungus diseases attack the vines in damp, ill-ventilated, shaded, crowded conditions. *Bird's eye rot*, or *anthracnose*, spots the fruit, leaves, and new sprouts; *black rot* shrivels the berries; *dead arm* eventually moves from the arms to the main trunk and kills the vine; *downy mildew*, a fuzzy gray fungus killer is a bad problem with *Vitis vinifera* and hybrids in eastern vineyards.

Sprays. There are many different fungicides and insecticides on the market for combating grape pests. Commercial growers are forced by economic necessity to depend on a heavy spray schedule to make a profitable crop. Home growers can experiment with organic methods and light, but regular, applications of botanical sprays such as hellebore and pyrethrum, if they are willing to take less than full crops and accept blemished fruit.

Consistent quality and quantity grapes may be possible only by following a scheduled chemical spray program. Many home grape-growers will be able to get away with only three sprays a season, but in vineyards where disease or insects have a stranglehold on the vines, and if there is a long run of wet weather, as many as ten or twelve spray applications may be necessary.

Because spray programs must be tailored to suit the particular vineyard with its own special problems, no cut-and-dried schedule can be applied equally to all. Growers have to recognize the particular pests or diseases that menace their grapes and select and apply the proper spray at the right time. Your county agent is the first one to consult. A helpful guide is Farmers' Bulletin Number 1893, "Control of Grape Diseases and Insects in the Eastern United States," free from the Office of Communication, U.S. Department of Agriculture, Washington, D.C. 20250.

Since new pesticides (and new restrictions on old pesticides) are constantly appearing, always check with the county agent or nearest Cooperative Extension Service for the latest recommendations on effective, safe pesticides.

Harvest

Granted healthy, pruned, well-nourished plants; good cultivation; plenty of sunshine—and a bit of luck—you will find yourself the possessor of heavy clusters of gloriously fragrant blue, purple, red, or golden grapes at harvest time. But are they really ripe? Color is a poor indicator of grape ripeness. Some people judge by taste. Others look at the seeds: green seeds mean unripe grapes, brown seeds show maturity. A change in stem color from green to brown is another index to ripeness. Winemakers, who need completely ripe grapes with high sugar levels, will test a little of the fresh juice with a hydrometer.

Although the difference in quality between ripe and unripe grapes is considerable, northern gardeners may be forced to pick early by the threat of impending frost. Unfortunately, grapes do not continue to ripen after they are picked.

Bird damage just before complete ripeness is a problem everywhere; netting, available from nurseries and garden suppliers, is a good investment. If you are a bird fancier you can always leave one or two vines uncovered, as a reward to the birds who picked insects off your vines earlier in the season.

If you have only a few vines, or if you cannot locate any netting, you might want to bag your clusters of grapes with small, white paper bags well on in the season. Brown paper bags give the fruit a disagreeable baggy flavor like a damp grocery sack. Do not use plastic bags. Bagging keeps grapes safe from birds and early frosts. Cut the bottom corner off the bags to let rain water drain out rapidly.

Protect your grapes from birds by bagging your clusters. Be sure to cut off a bottom corner to allow rain to drain.

Cut

When you harvest, always snip off the clusters of fruit with a pair of grape or pruning shears; "picking" grapes is not easy, for the wood is tough and you usually end up with mangled and torn stems, squashed grapes, and a bad temper.

ENJOYING THE HARVEST

Wine is the outstanding product of the grape; but grapes also have a place of honor in the kitchen and on the table. Although grape lovers claim the best way to enjoy a ripe, fragrant cluster of delicious grapes is to eat them out of hand in the sunny vineyard, grapes make excellent pies, jams, jellies, juices, compotes, and conserves.

Grape Cultivars

Plant your vineyard with grape cultivars selected for their suitability to your climate. (R = red; B = blue; R–B = red to blue; W = white or green)

EARLY CULTIVARS

Beta (B): An extremely hardy, vigorous, and productive grape. The small berries have a wild flavor, high sugar and high acid content. Makes excellent juice and jelly.

Blue Jay (B): A cold, hardy, early grape used for juice, jelly, and the table when thoroughly ripe. Unlike most grapes listed here, it needs cross-pollination.

Edelweiss (W): This vine, like the Swenson Red, comes from Minnesota. It is very hardy, and makes a decent white wine that is below average in sugar. It grows where few other grapes can.

Foch (Kuhlmann 188–2) (B): A very early grape, but only moderately productive. It has small berries in tight little bunches. It is a very popular grape with winemakers, making a Burgundy-type wine. Birds love it, so nets are needed.

Himrod (W): Hardier than Interlaken Seedless but ripens a few days later. Large, loose clusters of sweet yellow grapes that are almost seedless make it a superior table grape and a popular roadside-market fruit.

Interlaken Seedless (W): Only moderately vigorous and productive, somewhat tender to cold, and often needs a careful spray program. A delicious and popular eating grape, almost seedless. A good roadside-market seller.

Red Amber (R): Another of the very hardy vines which produce sweet, medium-sized table fruit.

Seibel 5297 (Aurore) (W): Very early, vigorous, extremely hardy, and very productive, this fine vine gives pinkish grapes in medium-long loose clusters. The fruit is delicious to eat and makes an excellent, delicate white wine.

Seibel 13053 (Cascade) (B): Very early, vigorous, moderately hardy, and productive, this vine makes a superior rosé wine and a good blending wine for Foch.

Seneca (W): Productive, moderately vigorous, and hardy. Gives medium-sized clusters of superb, crisp berries of outstanding table quality with a sweet, winy flavor. Often named the outstanding white dessert grape. Powdery mildew is often a problem.

Swenson Red (R): A very hardy, early, vigorous vine, the juice has a good acid-to-sugar ratio and is used to make white and rosé wines. This cultivar, along with Beta and Edelweiss, can take temperatures of 30°F below zero and colder without root, trunk, or arm damage or complete winterkill. All three are prizes for the northern grape-grower.

Van Buren (B): A vigorous, productive, very early Concord-type grape. Its succulent flesh makes it a favorite with northern growers who cannot grow Concord.

MIDSEASON CULTIVARS

Caco (R): A vigorous, moderately productive, and hardy vine whose large fruits are attractive if not particularly outstanding. A table fruit and roadside-market grape.

Catawba (R–B): Vigorous, productive, and hardy with large clusters of big grapes. A commercial grower's favorite for wine, juice, and table.

Concord (B): The leading commercial grape in North America with the familiar foxy flavor. It is vigorous, productive, hardy, but needs at least 170 frost-free days to ripen properly. It is used for juice, jelly, and specialty wines. This seedless cultivar is a favorite with pie fanciers.

Fredonia (B): This vigorous, productive, and hardy vine gives large berries with a mild Concord-like flavor. A sort of Fredonia, McCampbell, is an excellent roadside-stand seller with its large clusters of big, bursting berries.

Golden Muscat (W): This fine, golden-yellow grape is vigorous, moderately productive, and hardy. It likes a somewhat cool summer with plenty of sun to ripen properly. A table grape with a mild, foxy taste.

Landot 244 (Landal) (B): Moderate vigor and production. Fully ripened fruit makes good wine.

Moore Early (B): This is hardy, but only moderately vigorous and with poor productivity. Its charm lies in its being a Concord type that ripens about two weeks earlier than Concord, though the fruit often cracks.

Niagara (W): A foxy-flavored, large-berried fruit. The vine is hardy, vigorous, and productive. Good table fruits.

Seibel 9110 (Verdelet) (W): Vigorous, but not a steady producer. Apt to be sensitive to cold. The grapes are a beautiful yellow-gold, an excellent dessert grape which also makes good wine.

Seyve-Villard 5–276 (Seyval Blanc) (W): A medium vigorous vine with good disease resistance, largely grown for the superior quality white wine it makes.

Steuben (B): Vigorous, productive, somewhat hardy and disease resistant, Steuben is an increasingly popular commercial grape. The sweet grapes in their long, tapering clusters have an unusual spicy flavor.

Worden (B): Hardy, productive, and vigorous, the vine gives large Concord-type grapes of equal quality with Concord. Fruit sometimes cracks. Good juice and jelly grape, ripening about ten days earlier than Concord.

LATE-SEASON CULTIVARS

Delaware (R): Hardy, but medium to low vigor and production. The small grapes ripen from pink to deep mahogany with a high sugar content. These are table grapes of considerable popularity.

Ellen Scott (R): A vigorous and productive vine that is not very hardy. Susceptible to disease. It is usually grown as a table and juice grape in the South. The fruit is large and juicy.

SeyveVillard 12–375 (Villard Blanc) (W): Vigorous, very productive, highly disease resistant. A regular producer of large, loose clusters of grapes widely planted for wine and used also for dessert grapes.

Continued →

Seyve-Villard 18–315 (Villard Noir) (B): This is a standard grape in southern France, a late red of low vigor but quite hardy. It makes a sound but ordinary good red wine—*un vin ordinaire*.

Vidal 256 (W): A very vigorous, hardy, heavy producer. It is grown for wine, which has a good aroma and is neutral, clean, rated good to very good. If hit by spring frost damage, it can still produce a moderate secondary crop.

GULF COAST AND FLORIDA CULTIVARS

Blue Lake (B–R): The vine produces in early midseason and gives the grower clusters of small grapes with a unique aromatic spiciness. The fruit is poor for shipping or storing; it is usually made into juice and jelly.

Stover (W): This special vine must be grafted and is then moderately vigorous, productive, hardy, and resistant to Pierce's Disease. It must be sprayed for foliage diseases. Produces white table fruit of quality superior to Blue Lake.

WINE GRAPES FOR EAST COAST GROWERS

The New York State Fruit Testing Cooperative Association (NYSFTCA) lists the following *Vitis vinifera* cultivars. (West Coast growers will have little trouble locating a source of *Vitis vinifera* stock through county agents and extension service recommendations.)

Cabernet Sauvignon (R): A variety that gained its fame through the red wines of Bordeaux. An outstanding grape for the finest Médoc clarets, it rarely ripens well enough at Geneva to make a notable wine.

Chardonnay (W): One of the more hardy *vinifera* cultivars, this is the grape that makes white burgundies.

Gamay (R): This grape makes red wine and is temperamental. Grown in Burgundy its wine is ordinary; in Beaujolais, it is superb. In California plantings, the wine from the mountain vineyards in Santa Cruz are markedly superior to the Gamay wine of the Napa Valley. It is a late ripener. The NYSFTCA notes that it is more productive than the other *V. vinifera* they list.

Gewürztraminer (W): The spiciest flavored wine grapes and the basis of many delicious Alsatian and German fruity wines. Less hardy with the Geneva, NY, climate than White Riesling and Chardonnay, it has produced excellent wines there.

Pinot Noir (R): One of the greatest and most famous fine wine grapes, this is the source of the great red Burgundies and Champagne. The vine is infamous for being "difficult." At Geneva it has made the best red wines of their collection, but not of a quality to compare with the wine it makes in France. The Geneva-made wine was notably lacking in color and body.

White Riesling (W): The source of the noble wines of Alsace, the Moselle, and the Rhine, White Riesling is one of the great grapes of the wine world. It is grown not only in Europe, but in Chile and California, and it makes a flowery, aromatic wine. At Geneva this variety has made outstanding white wines and appears to be, with Chardonnay, the most promising *Vitis vinifera* for growing in the north.

Information for Grape-Growers

SOURCES FOR GRAPE VINES

Gurney's Seed & Nursery Co., 110 Capital Street, Yankton, SD 57079 (605–665–1930)

Henry Leuthardt Nurseries, Inc., P.O. Box 666, Montauk Highway, East Moriches, NY 11940–0666 (516–878–1387)

Indiana Berry and Plant Co., 5218 West 500 South, Huntingburg, IN 47542 (812–683–3055)

Inter-State Nurseries, 1800 Hamilton Road, Bloomington, IL 61704 (309–663–9551)

J.E. Miller Nurseries, Inc., 5060 West Lake Road, Canandaigua, NY 14424 (800–836–9630)

Kelly Nurseries, 1706 Morrissey Drive, Bloomington, IL 61704 (309–663–9551)

Mellinger's Inc., 2310 West South Range Road, North Lima, OH 44452 (800–321–7444)

Northwoods Retail Nursery, 27635 South Oglesby Road, Canby, OR 97013–9528 (503–266–5432)

Spring Hill Nurseries, 110 West Elm Street, Tipp City, OH 45317 (513–667-4079)

Stark Brothers Nurseries and Orchards, P.O. Box 10, Louisiana, MO 63353–0010 (800-325-4180)

KITCHEN HERBS

Grow 15 Herbs for the Kitchen

Sheryl L. Felty

Illustrations by Charles Joslin

Essentials for Growing Herbs Outdoors

Herbs will prosper in most types of good garden soil, especially a fertile, well-drained, sandy loam. Since most herbs are native to the poorer, rocky soils of the Mediterranean, they are able to make a fine showing under less than optimum conditions. However, if you are considering a long-term perennial bed, it is advisable to make your soil the best possible.

Most soils benefit from the addition of organic matter such as compost, chopped leaves, or peat moss. Organic matter improves the texture of soil, making light or sandy soil more fertile and able to hold a greater amount of water and loosening heavy or clay soil.

Most herbs require well-drained soil (the exception being some types of mint). Well-drained means that water seeps down into the soil at a fairly constant rate, so there is never a pool of standing water on the soil surface resulting in soggy roots for the herbs. Do not plant in poorly drained areas unless you plan to build raised beds.

All soils should be tested before you start growing. The information you get from your soil test will give you a clear understanding of your soil and its needs. You can buy a soil test kit and do your own; or for a minimal cost, you can send your soil off to a soil testing lab for analysis. Your local county extension service agent will help you with this.

A soil test will determine the soil pH (degree of acidity or alkalinity). A pH of 7.0 is neutral; below 7.0 is acidic; above is alkaline. Most herbs prefer a pH in the range of 6.0 to 7.5. If your soil is below 6.0, then it is too acid and you need to "sweeten" it with lime or wood ash. Apply five pounds of lime to each ten-foot by ten-foot area to raise the pH one point. Add the lime the fall before planting to give it sufficient time to work into the soil.

A soil test will also tell you what nutrients are available in your soil and what, if any, are lacking. The major nutrients a plant needs for growth are nitrogen, phosphorus, and potassium. These are the main ingredients in most chemical fertilizers. However, all plants need other essential elements for good growth. Some of these are calcium, magnesium, sulfur, and the many trace minerals. Most herbs require only small amounts of fertilizers and are sensitive to overfeeding.

The best time to fertilize herbs is in the early spring, just as they are planted or when they start to put on new growth. I prefer to use organic fertilizers like compost, alfalfa meal, bone meal, blood meal, or cottonseed meal. Well-rotted or dehydrated manures can also be used. Fresh manure contains too much ammonia and may burn plants. If the plants look as if they could use a lift later in the season—indicated by yellowing foliage and sparse growth—give them a shot of liquid fertilizer mixed with water. My preference is fish emulsion or seaweed.

You can use a complete chemical fertilizer such as 5–10-10, if you desire. Add a couple of tablespoons around each perennial shrub in the early spring. Mix it into the soil and water well to send the nutrients down to the roots.

Most perennial herb gardens benefit from a layer of mulch. Mulch is material spread on the soil surface to maintain even soil temperatures and moisture content. It also discourages weed growth, primarily because it blocks out light, which prevents weed seeds from germinating. Mulching the herb garden cuts out a large percentage of the time you would ordinarily spend watering or weeding.

Organic mulches decompose and add fiber and nutrients to the soil. There are several good mulches to use in your herb garden.

- chopped straw, leaves, or hay (Do not use hay that has gone to seed.)
- chopped bark
- grass clippings
- peat moss

Container Growing Indoors

So you want to grow herbs but you do not have the garden space? Or you simply cannot go through another winter without fresh herbs to liven up your meals? Do not despair. Herbs are some of the easiest plants to grow in containers. All they need is adequate light, warm temperatures, fertilizer, and humidity to thrive.

Choose herbs that you often use in cooking, or those that are hard to find in stores. It is preferable to select compact, low-growing herbs like thyme, marjoram, savory, parsley, sage, basil, or chives. You certainly would not want a six-foot angelica plant on your windowsill! Help your herbs stay bushy by pinching off the terminal ends of the shoots.

Pots made out of porous materials are desirable because they allow excess water to seep through. Most herbs cannot tolerate "wet feet." That's why I prefer clay pots to the plastic ones. Whatever type of container you choose, *a drainage hole is a must.*

Use a suitable growing mixture. A sterilized potting soil mix is the best bet. Bags of soil mixtures are available in most gardening stores.

Help your plants stay bushy by pinching off the terminal ends.

Continued ➔

Place a small piece of broken pottery or a few pebbles in the bottom of the container to keep the soil from spilling out of the drainage hole. Fill the container about halfway with the soil mix. Place the herb cutting or transplant in the pot and pack soil around it, leaving a one-inch headspace. Water well.

Herbs are sun lovers. They should receive at least five to six hours of direct sunlight a day. Grow-lights can be used if you lack sufficient natural light. A combination of warm and cool white fluorescent tubes is recommended. The lights should be laced about six inches from the tops of the plants and should shine eight to ten hours a day, if they are the only light source.

Herbs prefer day temperatures of 65 to 70°F; night temperatures about 10° cooler. Most houses tend to be dry in the winter. The more humidity you can put in the air, the better.

Let your plants dry out between waterings. Too much water has probably killed more container-grown herbs than too little. Feel the soil and be sure it is dry about an inch down. Water thoroughly so that it flows out of the drainage hole. Plants are like people—they prefer a warm bath to a cold shower!

Potted herbs thrive on small, regular doses of water-soluble fertilizer. Treat them with a *dilute* solution of liquid seaweed or fish emulsion once a week. (Halve the recommended dosage.)

Although insects and diseases are rarely a problem with garden-grown herbs, you may occasionally encounter a pest on indoor herbs. There are several common culprits.

Red spider mites. Cause a yellowish, mottled discoloration of the foliage. May be seen with a hand lens. Wash the plant with a soapy water solution.

White flies. Tiny, mothlike, white pests that suck the sap out of the leaves. They rise like a little cloud when the plant is disturbed. Wash with a soapy water solution. Pyrethrum insecticides successfully combat white flies.

Damping off. This disease is often a problem on overwatered herbs or newly started transplants. Be sure your potting mix is sterilized. Do not overwater. Thin plants to allow good air circulation.

Getting Plants Started

Many annual and biennial herbs are easily started from seed sown directly in the garden. Or you can get a jump on the growing season by starting your plants from seed indoors, then transplanting when the soil warms up. With the exception of tarragon, all the herbs mentioned in this bulletin can be propagated by seed.

Prepare the soil in the early spring, as soon as the ground warms up and is easily worked. Rake over the seed bed and break up any clumps of soil or organic matter. After you have a fine granular surface, scatter the seeds lightly on the top of the soil. Most herb seeds are very small and need only a fine covering of soil. Mist the seedbed with water and do not let it dry out until germination.

You can also expand your garden by propagating by division, layering, or cuttings. A neighbor with an established herb garden may be able to provide you with plants this way. To propagate by division, dig up a section of the roots of an established plant in the fall or early spring, separating them into smaller clumps with a shovel or small knife, and replant. Chives, mints, oregano, rosemary, sage, tarragon, and thyme lend themselves to root divisions.

Some herbs benefit by being divided into smaller clumps every few years; this is a good way to expand your garden. Dig up a section of the roots of an established plant, shake off the excess soil, separate into clumps. Replant in new holes to which a two-to four-inch layer of compost has been added.

Some herbs form roots along stems that touch the ground. These herbs can be propagated by layering. Simply mound the soil over the stem to encourage rooting. Layering is effective with mint, oregano, rosemary, sage, and thyme.

You can also propagate herbs with cuttings. Take a three-inch to four-inch shoot cut from the tip of the current season's growth. Strip all but the top two leaves from the shoot, dip the cut surface into a hormone rooting powder, and plant in a loose growing medium. Once the plant is established, transplant it into the garden, if desired. This method works for marjoram, mint, oregano, rosemary, sage, tarragon, and thyme.

TRANSPLANTS

Many kitchen herbs are set out from transplants or young seedlings that have been growing for eight to twelve weeks. These plants get off to a faster start and may be larger at the end of the season than the directly seeded herbs.

Space the transplants at the distance recommended on the seed package for each herb. Small herbs are usually planted eight to twelve inches apart; larger types may be separated by as much as three feet. Although the spacings may look too roomy at first, in no time the plants will fill out the area.

To successfully grow transplants you will need the following materials:

- seedlings trays, flats, or peat pots
- sterilized soil mix
- fresh seeds
- water mister
- clear plastic bags

Pour the sterilized soil mix into the flats. Gently sprinkle the seeds on the surface of the soil. Cover lightly with soil. With the mister, dampen the top of the soil. Put the flats into plastic bags to create a miniature greenhouse. (This promotes speedier germination.) Place the covered flats in a warm location (about 70°F) and check on them every few days until you notice small sprouts appearing. Remove the flats from the bags and place them in a sunny window or under grow-lights. Thin out the herb seedlings to stand two or three inches apart. Dense populations are plagued by a lack of aeration and potential disease problems. Once the herbs are larger, you may wish to transplant them into separate or roomier containers to encourage strong root and leaf development.

Before you set your transplants out in the garden, harden them off so they are accustomed to outdoor living.

- Cut back on the ration of water and fertilizer about ten days before you plan to transplant.

- Set the plants outside for a few hours on a warm, sunny day. Place them in a sheltered location so they will not be windblown.

- Gradually build up the time they are left outside each successive day, until you finally leave them out day and night.

GOOD SCENTS

The fragrance of many aromatic herbs can spice up and perfume your daily existence. Aromatic herbs can scent bathing waters, soaps, powders, oils, sachets, and potpourris. Here are a few ideas.

- **Breath fresheners.** Chew on a sprig of mint.

- **Herbal bathing waters.** Angelica, mint, rosemary, thyme. Add the herbs directly to the water or place them in a small piece of cheesecloth. Use very hot water and let the herbs steep for ten minutes. Hop in and enjoy.

- **Sachets and potpourris.** Mints, thyme, rosemary, sage, dill, savory. Combine the herbs and let them sit in a closed container for the scents to marry.

  For sachets: Grind the herbs into powder and place in a small fabric bag or pillow. Place in drawers for fragrance.

  For potpourris: Place the herbal mixture in an open-topped container to scent the room.

- **Catnip mice.** Crush freshly dried catnip and sew into little pillows or merry mice. A feline favorite!

Varieties of Herbs

There are hundreds of varieties of herbs to grow and enjoy, but only about fifteen varieties are regularly used in most kitchens. Do experiment with as many different varieties as you can (and Betty Jacob's *Growing and Using Herbs Successfully*, Garden Way Publishing, is a good book to consult for more information about additional varieties). But if you want to start small, consider planting the herbs described here.

ANGELICA

Angelica archangelica

Angelica blooms in its native Lapland on the eighth of May, the feast day of Michael the Archangel. Legend has it that the angel proclaimed angelica a cure for the plague.

Angelica is considered a biennial because it usually flowers, goes to seed, and dies in its second year. However, it sometimes takes three or four years to flower, making it the exception to the biennial rule.

Angelica
(Angelica archangelica)

Angelica prefers rich, moist soil in a partially shady location. Be sure to plant it in the back of the garden as it often reaches five or six feet in height.

The plant is majestic, with large, light green, serrated-edged leaves and thick, hollow stalks. Early in the summer, angelica blossoms with huge clusters of white flowers.

Propagate by fresh, viable seed. Once a planting is established, it will reseed itself. Harvest the leaves and stems early in the season while they are still tender and colorful.

Angelica is an aromatic used to flavor liqueurs and wines. The candied stems decorate many fancy pastries. The tips and stalks may be cooked with tart fruit to impart a natural sweetness.

BASIL

Ocimum basilicum

In its native India, basil is a sacred plant, and its culture supposedly bring happiness to the household. In Italy, a gift bouquet of basil is a sign of romance.

Basil is a tender annual, very sensitive to frost. It is easily propagated by seed sown directly in the garden after the soil has warmed up. Basil likes a soil rich in organic matter and thrives on an extra dose of compost. Plant it in full sun and be sure to water it weekly in dry weather.

Basil, Sweet
(Ocimum basilicum)

This fast-growing plant reaches about two feet in height and has large, egg-shaped leaves that curl inward. In midsummer, small spikes of white flowers shoot up from each stalk. Pinching out the blooms, or the tips of each stem before they flower, will make the plant bushy. The leaves can be harvested throughout the summer from the growing plant.

There is a "Dark Opal," or purple, variety of basil that beautifully offsets the greens and the grays of the kitchen herb garden. It also imparts a rich magenta color to white vinegar.

Basil has a pungent flavor that superbly complements all types of tomato dishes. Pesto, a green sauce served on pasta, is made from ground basil leaves, garlic, olive oil, nuts, and cheese.

To dry basil, harvest just before it blooms. Hang, screen dry, or freeze.

CATNIP

Nepeta cataria

A member of the mint family, this herb is a feline favorite. Cats love to roll in it, rub on it, chew it, play with it, and otherwise hamper the growth of your patch. But to watch them frolic is sheer delight!

The plant is a hardy perennial growing about two to three feet tall. Fragrant, velvety, gray green, heart-shaped leaves on squarish stems are characteristic of the plant. Pink flowers bloom off the terminal

Catnip
(Nepeta cataria)

Continued ➤

ends of the shoots from midsummer on. If you keep the flowers pinched off, the plants will be bushier.

Propagate by seed or root divisions.

Cut catnip just before the flowers open and hang to dry. Store in airtight containers to preserve the volatile oils. Sew little cloth pillows or fancy mice and stuff with the crushed herb. These make wonderful gifts.

CHIVES

Allium schoenoprasum

Chives are native to the East, and for centuries they were used to ward off evil and promote psychic powers.

The plant is a hardy perennial, reaching twelve to eighteen inches in height. The leaves—dark green, hollow spears—poke up through the soil in the early spring, almost before anything else. Mauve blue flower balls bloom on hard, green tendrils from midsummer on. These should be cut to keep the plant growing but can be left later in the season to keep foraging bees happy.

Chives
(Allium schoenoprasum)

Chives prefer full sun, rich soil, and plentiful water. Mulching around the plants is helpful to keep competitive weeds and grasses at bay.

Propagate by seeds or root divisions. A small plant will quickly enlarge and should be divided every three or four years to keep the plant healthy. Simply cut through the plant with a shovel or sharp knife in the early spring, allowing at least ten small, white bulbous roots per new clump. Set the divisions ten inches apart.

Harvest chives as soon as the spears are a few inches long. Snipping out entire spears encourages tender new growth. Chives do not dry well. Freeze for winter use.

The delicate onion flavor of chives is used extensively in cooking. Chives can be added to omelettes, soups, cheeses, salads, or fish. Sour cream and chives fattens up many a baked potato.

DILL

Anethum graveolens

Dill has been used in the culinary arts for centuries, with the famed dill pickle being the most notable product.

Dill is a hardy annual that closely resembles fennel. However, it usually develops only one round, hollow main stem per root, and the feathery branches are a bluish green. Yellow flowers bloom in clusters of showy umbels. The dill seeds are dark brown, ridged, and strongly flavored. Dill grows two to three feet tall and can be planted in groupings to keep the plants supported in windy weather.

Dill
(Anethum graveolens)

Propagate by seed sown directly in the garden. It does best in full sun in sandy or loamy, well-drained soil that

has a slightly acid pH (5.8 to 6.5). Enrich your soil with compost or well-rotted manure for best dill growth. Once you have grown dill, it will reseed in the following years.

Dill weed and dill seed are both used in cooking; the weed is mild and the seeds are pungent. Dill weed can be harvested at any time, but the volatile oils are highest just before flowering. It adds a delicate flavor to salads, vegetable casseroles, and soups. The seed heads should be cut when the majority of seeds have formed, even though some flowers may still be blooming. Whole dill heads look striking in jars of homemade pickles and flavored vinegar. Dill seeds add zest to breads, cheeses, and salad dressing. The seeds may be threshed from the heads after drying.

FENNEL

Foeniculum vulgare

There are two types of fennel grown: the herb fennel, grown for its leaves and seeds, and Florence fennel, grown primarily for its bulbous leaf stalks.

Herb fennel is a hardy biennial that often becomes a perennial in favorable climates. The plant reaches three to four feet tall and has thick, shiny green, hollow stalks; feathery branches; yellow flowers that bloom on showy umbels; and sweetly flavored, ridged seeds.

Fennel
(Foeniculum vulgare)

Fennel prefers a rich, well-drained soil in full sun. Add lime if the pH is below 6.0. Propagate by seed in the early spring to give it sufficient time to flower and go to seed. The leaves should be harvested just before the plant flowers.

Fennel is closely related to dill and the two should not be interplanted because they may cross-pollinate, resulting in dilly fennel or fennelly dill!

Fennel is favored in all types of fish cookery and is often used to flavor sauerkraut.

MARJORAM

Majorana hortensis or *Origanum majorana*

Throughout history, marjoram has symbolized sweetness, happiness, and well-being. Shakespeare called it the "herb of grace."

Marjoram is a tender perennial native to the warm Mediterranean. In colder climates, it is grown as an annual. The plant reaches eight to twelve inches in height and has short, branched, squarish stems. The small, oval leaves are grayish green and covered with a fuzzy down. Little balls or knots grow out of the leaf clusters and the end of the branches in the midsummer. From these, white or pink flowers emerge.

Marjoram
(Marjorana hortensis)

Marjoram thrives in a light, rich soil in full sun. It prefers a neutral pH. Since it has a shallow root system, mulching around the plant helps to retain soil moisture and keep the weeds down.

Marjoram seeds can be sown directly in the garden after the soil has warmed up. Germination is slow—usually about two weeks. Keep the seedbed moist until the plants have sprouted. Marjoram can also be started from cuttings, layering, or division. Set transplants about a foot apart.

Marjoram is highly aromatic and its flavor improves with drying. Harvest just before the flowers open.

Marjoram is traditionally used in sausages and stuffings.

MINT

Mentha species

Peppermint, spearmint, apple mint, and curly mint are but a few varieties of the fragrant mints used in gum, jelly, and liqueur.

Mints are hardy perennials often attaining three feet in height. They are notorious spreaders and will invade the surrounding garden territory if they are not confined. They prefer a moist, rich soil and will do well in full sun to partial shade.

Mint is known by its squarish stems and its tooth-edged leaves. Clusters of white or purple flowers bloom off the terminal ends of the shoots.

Mint
(Mentha *species*)

Propagate by seed or divisions. Older mint plantings can be divided up every four or five years. Separate the roots into foot-sized clumps with a sharp shovel. These divisions are a nice present for a gardening friend.

The leaves may be harvested and enjoyed fresh throughout the summer. To dry mint, cut the stalks just above the first set of leaves, as soon as the flower buds appear. Hang to dry for ten to fourteen days.

Mint jelly is a favorite accompaniment to lamb roasts and chops. Minted peas are a summertime treat.

OREGANO

Origanum vulgare

Oregano's fame bubbles from the flavor it imparts to pizza and other Italian specialties.

Some confusion has arisen about the relationship between oregano and marjoram. They are close relatives and oregano is often called wild marjoram.

Oregano is a hardy perennial growing eighteen to thirty inches tall. The oval, grayish green, hairy leaves grow out from the nodes. White or pink flowers make their showing in the fall.

The plant does best in a well-drained, sandy loam soil. If the pH is

Oregano
(Origanum vulgare)

below 6.0, add lime before you set out the plants; oregano likes a sweet soil and a plentiful supply of calcium. Oregano thrives in full sun in a location sheltered from high winds. Mulch over the plant if winters are severe.

Oregano may be propagated by seed, divisions, or cuttings. Because the seeds are slow to germinate, you will get best garden results by setting out young plants spaced fifteen inches apart.

To dry oregano, cut the stems an inch from the ground in the fall, just before the flowers open. Hang to dry.

PARSLEY

Petroselinum crispum

The Greeks believed that Hercules adorned himself with parsley, so it became the symbol of strength and vigor. Parsley was also associated with witchcraft and the underworld; it was never transplanted because this supposedly brought misfortune to the household.

Parsley is a hardy biennial, often grown as an annual. There are two main types of parsley: the Italian flat-leaved and the French curly.

Parsley
(Petroselinum crispum)

During the first growing season, the plant develops many dark green leaves that are grouped in bunches at the end of long stems. Italian parsley leaves are flat and fernlike; French parsley leaves are tightly curled. Umbels of yellow flowers are borne on long stalks. The plant reaches twelve to eighteen inches in height.

Parsley thrives in rich soil, endowed with plentiful organic matter. It prefers full sun for optimum growth, but it will survive in partial shade.

Parsley can be planted from seed sown directly in the garden. However, since it takes three to four weeks to germinate, it is often more reliable to set out young plants. Space parsley transplants about eight to ten inches apart.

Parsley can be picked fresh throughout the season. To preserve for winter use, cut the leaves in the fall and dry or freeze them.

Parsley is a popular kitchen herb, found with the fanciest steak or the most common stew. It is a rich source of many vitamins and minerals, including vitamins A, B, and C; calcium; iron; and phosphorus.

ROSEMARY

Rosmarinus officinalis

Rosemary has been called the "herb of remembrance." This title may date back to the Greeks who used it to strengthen the memory. It has appeared in religious ceremonies, particularly weddings and funerals, to symbolize remembrance and fidelity.

Rosemary
(Rosemarinus officinalis)

Continued ➡

The perennial evergreen shrub grows two to six feet high, depending on the climate. It has woody stems, bearing thin, needlelike leaves that are shiny green on the upper surface and a powdery, muted green on the under surface. Blue flowers bloom on the tips of the branches in the spring.

Rosemary is a tender plant and must be sheltered or taken indoors for the winter in northern latitudes. It thrives best in a warm climate and prefers a well-drained, alkaline soil. Apply lime or wood ashes to acid soils testing below pH 6.5.

Rosemary is usually started from cuttings or root divisions because seed germination is slow and poor. This herb is a good candidate for container growing, allowing you to move it into protected quarters for the winter.

Harvest any time for fresh use. Hang to dry for winter supply.

Rosemary is a highly aromatic herb often used to flavor meat dishes. Use only a few needles per pot as the taste is overpowering.

SAGE

Salvia officinalis

Although it is a prized culinary herb today, during past centuries sage was mainly cultivated as a medicinal herb. The name Salvia comes from the Latin, salvere, meaning "to save," and it was believed that drinking a strong sage tea improved health and prolonged life. Needless to say, it was found in every herb garden.

Sage is a hardy perennial, native to the Mediterranean. It grows two feet or so in height and has velvety, textured, patterned, grayish green leaves. The stems become woody as the plant matures and should be pruned out to keep the plant producing. Lavender flower spikes bloom in the fall.

Narrow-Leaf Sage
(Salvia officinalis)

Sage can be started from seed, cuttings, or divisions. Since the plant takes a long time to mature, transplants are usually set out. Space the plants two feet apart.

Sage prefers a well-drained soil in full sunlight. Enrich the soil with compost before planting, and add lime if the pH is below 5.8. Water well while the plants are young.

Harvest sparingly the first season and increase your quota yearly. The leaves can be picked any time; but it is recommended that two crops a year, one in June and another in the fall, be harvested to keep the plants less woody. Hang to dry in small bunches.

The flavor of sage is recognizable in stuffings. It especially complements heavy meats and game. Its flavor may overpower lighter herbs.

SAVORY

Satureia hortensis (summer); *Satureia montana* (winter)

Of the two savories grown for kitchen use, the summer variety is the mild annual and the winter is the sharper-flavored perennial.

Both savories have narrow, pointed, dark green leaves that grow out of the nodes. Small branches often arise just above the leaves. Lavender or pink flowers bloom in the late summer. Winter savory grows eight to ten inches tall; summer savory is slightly taller. Since they are small plants, the savories are good for container growing.

The savories prefer a somewhat dry soil and will survive even where the land is not too fertile. For the best flavor, plant them in full sun.

Summer Savory
(Satureia hortensis)

Summer savory is planted from seed sown directly in the garden in the early spring. Winter savory is propagated by cuttings or divisions. Space both varieties twelve inches apart.

To harvest for winter use, cut the stems in the fall, just before the flowers bloom. Cut winter savory sparingly. Summer savory can be pulled out of the ground, since it will die anyway after one season. Hang to dry.

These herbs are notably associated with bean dishes, ranging from soups to casseroles. Savory is also an ingredient of bouquet garni.

TARRAGON

Artemisia dracunculus

Tarragon has a high standing, especially in French cuisine where it lends itself to béarnaise sauce and *les fines herbes* (a French herb blend).

Tarragon is a perennial plant, the best varieties coming from the European countries. The Russian variety is weedy and lacks the essential oils. One way to distinguish between varieties is this: the Russian tarragon produces viable seed, the European rarely does.

Tarragon grows two to three feet tall and tends to sprawl out late in the season. The long, narrow leaves, borne on upright stalks, are a shiny, dark green. Greenish or gray flowers may bloom in the fall. Since it rarely sets seed, tarragon should be propagated by cuttings or divisions.

French Tarragon
(Artemisia dracunculus)

Tarragon prospers in fertile soil with plentiful water and sunlight. It is advisable to mulch over the roots in the late fall to protect the plant from winter injury. Since tarragon becomes a rather large plant, it is often divided up every three or four years to make it easier to manage.

This herb may be harvested throughout the summer. To dry for winter use, cut the stalks a few inches from the ground in the early fall. Hang or screen dry.

664

THYME

Thymus vulgaris

Native to the Mediterranean, this aromatic, perennial herb has many well-known varieties including: lemon thyme, creeping thyme, and garden or common thyme. It is a favorite plant of bees.

Thyme is a short plant, only about eight to ten inches tall. The leaves are small and narrowly oval, usually a dull grayish green. The stems become woody after a few years. Pink or violet flowers arise from the leaf axils in the early fall.

Thyme flourishes in sandy, dry soils in full sun. It is an excellent candidate for rock gardens.

Propagate thyme by seeds, divisions, or cuttings. The seeds are slow to germinate, so it is best to set out transplants. Space thyme fifteen inches apart. Older, woody plants can be rejuvenated by digging up the plant and dividing it in the early spring. Fertilize with compost or seaweed.

The leaves can be harvested for fresh use throughout the summer. To dry thyme, cut the stems just as the flowers start to open. Hang to dry in small bunches. Harvest sparingly the first year.

Thyme is one of the three essential herbs used in poultry stuffings; the other two are parsley and sage.

*Thyme
(Thymus vulgaris)*

Harvesting Herbs

The crisp days of autumn and the first frosts do not have to mean an end to cooking with herbs. Centuries ago it was discovered that herbs dry well, retaining their essential oils to enhance winter meals.

To preserve the maximum flavor and color of your homegrown herbs, harvest the herbs on a sunny day after the dew has dried from the leaves. If the herbs are dirty or have been sprayed with chemicals, it is a good idea to hose them off with a fine mist the day before you harvest. By not washing them after they are cut, the herbs will dry faster and you reduce the risk of losing some of the precious oils.

Pick leafy herbs just before the flowers open, when the flavor is at its peak. If the seed is to be used, allow the plants to bloom and complete their cycle. Harvest the seed heads before the seeds are scattered to the wind to produce next year's crop.

To harvest perennial herbs, cut the stems a few inches above the ground with scissors or a sharp knife. If you cut them back halfway in June, you may be able to reap a second crop in the fall. Cut sparingly the first season so the plant will have adequate reserves to make it through the winter.

When harvesting annuals, I often pull up the entire plant, since it has completed its life span and will die shortly. Then I wash or gently rub the soil off the roots.

Biennials can be harvested either like perennials, cut from the stalk, or pulled from the ground like annuals.

DRYING

Hang drying is the most popular method of preserving homegrown herbs. Tie the freshly picked herbs in small bunches and hang them upside down in a warm, dark, airy place. Some people place the herb bundles in paper bags with air holes punched in them to reduce their exposure to light and dust. If you have a dark, airy attic or similar room you may be successful without the bags. Try both methods and see which you prefer.

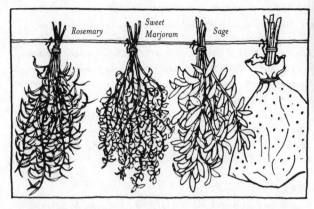

Tie freshly picked herbs in small bunches and hang them upside down to dry in a dark, airy place. Some people place the bundles in paper bags with air holes punched in them to reduce exposure to light and dust.

The herbs should be thoroughly dry in about two weeks or when they crumble to the touch. Do not allow them to hang indefinitely as this reduces their quality.

Strip the leaves off the stalks and crush finely if they are to be used in cooking. Tea leaves should be kept whole. Seed heads can be stored whole or threshed to separate the seeds from the chaff.

HINTS FOR DRYING HERBS

Don't try to pick herbs as you might daisies. Cut them. Pruning shears are fine for this. Leave four inches of stem on leafy annuals. Cut only one-third the growth of leafy perennials. In both cases this permits further growth—and further harvesting.

The delicate flavors of herbs can be spoiled by heat and faded by sun. The flowers and green leaves or herbs should be dried at very low temperatures and away from direct sunlight. Good air circulation is important in order to dry herbs quickly and thus preserve their flavor.

Dry the leaves on the stems. It's easier to strip them off when dry than when green, and it's easier to dry them on the stem.

If a commercial dehydrator, oven, or homemade dryer is used, most herbs should be dried separately in order to keep their distinct flavors from blending. This precaution is not necessary, of course, with outdoor drying.

Store large batches of herbs in several small glass jars. Small containers will retain the flavors better than large ones, which lose aroma each time the jar is opened. To keep dried herbs at their best, always keep jars tightly covered in a dry, cool, dark place. If there is no dark storage area, jars may be kept in paper bags or in a covered can or box.

Do not store herbs in a cabinet near a stove, radiator, or refrigerator. The heat from them can cause loss of flavor.

Phyllis Hobson, *Food Drying*, Garden Way Publishing.

Continued ➜

Screen drying works best with small quantities or with leaves or seed heads that have been stripped off the stem. Spread a single layer of herbs evenly over the fine mesh and place it where air can circulate freely around the entire form. The herbs should be dry in a week or two. Once they are dry, store them immediately to reduce the loss of the precious oils.

Oven drying is a highly debated topic: some people appreciate its speedy results; others denounce it because they say it vaporizes the volatile oils. If you want to give it a try, here is how it is done. Heat the oven to 150°F. Scatter the herbs on a baking sheet and put it in the oven, leaving the door ajar. Stir every few minutes. Remove the tray as soon as the herbs are crisp.

Store dried herbs in dark, airtight containers. Herbs lose their color when exposed to light. The flavor of herbs is not retained indefinitely. The volatile oils and flavor of powdered herbs perish a little quicker than that of the whole leaves.

FREEZING

Some of the thick, leafy herbs, like parsley and basil, and those that do not dry successfully, like chives, can be frozen. Frozen herbs have the same pungency as fresh, although they lack the crispness.

To freeze herbs, gently wash freshly picked herbs, if necessary. Blot dry. Strip the leaves off the stalks, chop or leave whole. Pack into bags or containers, label, and freeze.

Herbs can also be frozen in ice cubes. Simply chop the herbs, pour into an ice cube tray, pour water over them, and freeze. Pop them out of the tray and into the pot as needed.

Cooking with Herbs

If you want to cut back on your dietary salt, try using herbs as flavorings. Here are time-tested guidelines to cooking with herbs.

- Add most herbs about thirty minutes before the end of cooking time. Simmer them slowly with the food to release the flavor and retain the volatile oils.

- Dried herbs are more potent than fresh—one teaspoon dried equals one tablespoon fresh.

- Experiment with herbs! Try them in old recipes, taste new ones, combine herbs.

- Use moderation. Some herbs may be overpowering if too much is used. Familiarize yourself with the strongly flavored ones—sage, rosemary, thyme, and oregano.

HERB VINEGARS

Vibrant yellow and magenta vinegars add zing to a salad. A variety of herbs is used to flavor vinegars: basil (both the green and red types), fennel, tarragon, dill (both the weed and the seed heads), mints, and thyme. Most types of vinegars can be used; however, white and wine are preferable because their flavor is milder and marries better with the herbs.

To make herb vinegar, place one cup of bruised or finely chopped herbs into an old-fashioned canning jar with a glass lid. Add one or two cloves of garlic, if desired. Pour one quart of vinegar over the herbs. Cover and place in a warm spot for two to three weeks. Taste it at that time and see if the flavor suits your fancy. If it is too weak, add more chopped herbs or allow it to set for another week or so. Strain and pour into festive bottles, adding a fresh sprig of herb to each one. Seal. Store the bottles in a cool, dark place.

It is not advisable to use metal lids, strainers, or spoons when making the vinegar because this sometimes adds an off-flavor, and vinegar will rust metal.

HERBS AND THEIR USAGE

Herb	Interplant Ideas	Culinary Suggestions	Medicinal Uses	Gifts/Niceties
Angelica		Natural sweetener for tart fruits. Candied stems.	Digestive aid, spring tonic, bronchial problems and colds.	Fancy pastries decorated with candied stems.
Basil	Companion to tomatoes. Dislikes rue.	Tomato dishes, minestrone soup, pesto sauce for pasta, fish, zucchini casseroles.	Colds, colic, headaches, laxative.	Pesto sauce in decorative jars, purple basil vinegar, potted basil, dried herb.
Catnip	Deters flea beetles.		Upset stomachs, menstrual troubles, calms nerves.	Handmade catnip toys, fresh cuttings, tea leaves.
Chives	Companion to carrots.	Omelettes, soups, green salads, cheese, fish, vegetable dishes.	Digestive aid.	Fresh cream cheese and chive spread, container chives.
Dill	Companion to cabbage and its family members. Dislikes carrots.	Weed: salads, fish, vegetables. Seed: pickles, salad dressings, heavy meats, breads.	Insomnia, flatulence (gas).	Jars of homemade dill pickles, dill vinegar, fresh vinegar, fresh dill
Fennel	Plant alone.	Salmon and oily fish, salad dressings, breads and rolls, apple pie.	Depresses the appetite, kidney and urinary problems, colic.	Freshly baked seeded rolls and breads, fennel oil.

Herb	Interplant Ideas	Culinary Suggestions	Medicinal Uses	Gifts/Niceties
Marjoram	Throughout the garden.	Poultry seasoning, meats and game, sauces and marinades, soups, egg dishes.	Colds and congestion, colic, headaches.	Bouquet garni, sachets, tea, herb butter.
Mint	Companion to cabbage and tomatoes.	Summertime beverages, fruits, minted peas, salads, candies.	Digestive aid, colds, flu, stimulant.	Mint jelly, mint tea, candies, sachets, root divisions.
Oregano	Throughout the garden.	Pizza, spaghetti, Italian dishes, tomatoes, soups, vegetable casseroles.	Nervous headaches. Oregano oil relieves toothaches.	Dried Italian seasoning mix, container grown herbs, oil.
Parsley	Tomatoes.	Soups, stews, salads, all vegetables, steaks, fish, garnish.	Kidney stones, diuretic (promotes urine flow).	Bouquet garni, tea, fresh sprigs, potted parsley.
Rosemary	Sage, beans, broccoli, cabbage, carrots.	Meats and game, marinades and sauces, lamb, breads.	Eases nervous afflictions, strengthens the memory.	Meat marinade mix, sachet, tea, hair rinse, potted rosemary.
Sage	Rosemary, carrots, cabbage. Dislikes cucumbers.	Poultry stuffing, pork, cheeses, breads.	Headaches, tonic, digestive aid, whitens teeth.	Sage cheese, stuffing mix, tea, hair rinse.
Savory	Beans, onions.	All bean dishes, stuffings, fish, soups, vegetable dishes and juices.	Colds, colic, asthma. Tonic.	Bouquet garni, tea, container herb, sachets.
Tarragon	Throughout the garden.	Sauce béarnaise, fish, eggs, cold summer salads, soups, vegetable juices.	Tonic and elixir.	Flavored vinegar, tarragon jelly, les fines herbes mix.
Thyme	Cabbage.	Meat, chicken, fish, soups, stews, sauces, salads.	Headaches, antiseptic.	Bouquet garni, tea, sachets cuttings.

Growing & Using Basil

Ellen Ogden

Illustrations by Alison Kolesar

Growing and Culture

STARTING SEED

Start basil seed indoors four to five weeks before the last danger of frost. Fill pots or seed-starting trays with a moistened medium of potting soil, lightened with sand or vermiculite. Plant seeds a scant 1/8 inch deep. (A good rule of thumb is to plant any seed at three times the depth of its size.) Press the soil gently over the seeds, water lightly, then cover the containers with a clear plastic to prevent loss of moisture. Label the containers with the variety names and the date of sowing.

Place the containers in a warm spot, on top of the refrigerator, or in any place you might place bread to rise. Basil seed germinates best at temperatures around 75°F. Germination will take up to one week.

Once the seedlings emerge, remove the plastic wrap. Move the plants to the brightest place you have or they will stretch for the light and become spindly and weak. Water the seedlings only as needed. The key is not to overwater, but to keep the soil moist. Basil prefers to dry out a little between waterings, but not to the point of wilting. Provide plenty of light and warmth until the seedlings are ready to be planted in the garden.

Plant basil outdoors after all danger of frost is past. A protected area is best if your garden is prone to low temperatures. Cutworms can be deterred by sprinkling a circle of wood ashes around each new transplant. After the first two weeks, the plants should be established, and cutworms won't be able to hurt them.

COMPANION PLANTING

According to gardening lore and tradition, companion planting (planting certain plants next to each other in the garden) is one of the best ways to increase vigor and control insect damage. Basil is an especially valuable companion plant, partially due to its strong fragrance. Plant basil near tomatoes and peppers to repel insects; basil will increase the vigor of your asparagus, so plant some there, too. One source recommends that you liberally sprinkle seed around your manure pile or near your front door to repel flies and mosquitoes.

Plant basil in herb gardens, vegetable gardens, flower gardens, or containers. The plants provide an excellent edible landscape because of their striking foliage and beautiful blossoms. Attractive flowers to combine with sweet basil in containers include nasturtiums, zinnias, marigolds, or even other basils like the green and purple ruffles. Shorter, compact bush-type varieties like spicy globe or green bouquet make excellent formal edging plants. And scented basils can provide a range of sweet fragrances around a deck or sitting area.

Basil is very useful, so make sure you have enough for your needs: Six plants for pesto and tomato seasoning, plus at least two each of the purple and scented varieties for making vinegars and oils. And one

Continued ➜

plant each of the lettuce-leaf basils for summer salads and barbecue. Plan on a minimum of two of the bush basils for container growing throughout the year. Stagger your plantings for a continuous supply of fresh basil.

When grouping several basils together in one garden plot, keep in mind the height and space requirements of each to insure good growth and an attractive arrangement. For example, green and purple ruffles are bushy plants, 18 to 24 inches tall; fine green bush basil will grow 12 to 18 inches tall. In the bush-type family, however, there is a tiny, compact mounded basil called spicy globe that grows only 4 inches tall and would be best grown in front of the ruffles kinds in the garden border. The same is true for lemon-scented basil, which is a delicate plant and not a vigorous grower as compared to the cinnamon-scented variety. Allow a front row spot for lemon basil, next to some showy flowers to mask its narrow leaves.

SOIL, WATER, LIGHT, AND TEMPERATURE

Since basil is a leaf crop, it needs good, fertile soil. Don't overdo it, though. The flavor of herbs comes from their essential oils, and too much nitrogen will yield lush growth but a low oil content. Soil pH necessary for good growth falls in the 6.4 to 7.0 range, the same as for corn or tomatoes. Well-rotted manure mixed into the soil before planting, or a feeding of fish emulsion and liquid kelp used as an organic fertilizer, helps to keep nutrient levels balanced and abundant.

Basil is a sun worshiper, and it grows best in the heat of the summer. Cold soil or air will cause basil to grow slowly. Basil requires at least six hours of full sun every day.

Drip irrigation is a better way to water basil than sprinklers, because cold water on the leaves of plants can cause black spots.

To keep a pot of basil for the winter, either take a cutting from a garden plant in late summer and root it in a slightly moist sterile potting medium, or sow a few seeds in pots during mid-summer to mature in the late fall. Don't expect the plants to put out much new growth during the dark days of winter without supplemental light. Some basils do better than others as indoor plants. The bush types with their tiny compact leaves and growth habit tend to endure the stress of indoor living better than other varieties.

Sweet Basil

Basils for Every Use

Basils contain essential oils that give them their individual characters. Each variety is composed of different proportions of alcohols, terpenes, aldehydes, ketones, and phenols. The proportions of each help determine the fragrance and flavor, whether sweet or pungent, of each variety.

Plant form is another distinguishing factor among the basils. Growth habit, size, shape, and color can all be determined by the variety name. Each variety has its own benefits, and thus there are basils for every use. There are over sixty basil cultivars available to gardeners around the world. Most are primarily culinary, though many are also ornamental and some of the rare forms have been preserved for their historic past.

SWEET BASIL
(Ocimum basilicum)

Sweet basil is the most familiar and widely grown type. The leaves are medium green in color, smooth and shiny, yet slightly ridged. The flavor is strong, with sometimes a touch of licorice. Genovese sweet basil is best used fresh or dried. The leaves are easy to harvest—pick the leaf clusters from the top. Most American companies simply list it as "sweet basil," but there are a few elite European strains such as sweet Genovese that are slower bolting and less likely to become bitter after long cooking in sauces.

1. **Common Basil:** A distinctive clovelike scent to the oval-shaped leaves is characteristic of common basil. The leaf edges cup slightly inward and upward along the inner spine of the leaf, forming a point at the end. White flowers will develop from the center stalk, but the flower buds should be pinched off to retain the best flavor in the leaves. Leaves measure 2 to 3 inches long and 2/3 inch wide.

2. **Sweet Genovese Basil:** Glossy, long, almond-shaped leaves are favored for their true, sweet flavor. A favorite for fresh use on sliced tomatoes and in salad dressings. May be dried successfully. Plants are productive and vigorous, growing 12 to 18 inches tall and 8 to 12 inches across. Widely grown under glass greenhouses in Italy.

BUSH BASIL
(Ocimum basilicum 'Minimum')

Bush basils are a group of upright, bushy plants covered with tiny aromatic leaves. The plants are very ornamental, as the tiny leaves are in just the right proportion to the overall form, resembling a bonsai tree. These basils are especially good for pot or container growing. When harvesting bush basil, take the whole branch and then strip off the leaves. This type of basil is preferred by many chefs because of the exceptional flavor the leaves release when crushed. Some cooks believe that bush basils make the very best pesto.

1. **Fine Green Basil:** Fine green basil is the largest of the bush types. Neat round plants grow to a height of 12 to 18 inches and a width of about 12 inches. True sweet basil aroma and taste, with closely placed leaves measuring 1/2 inch in length. Fine green basil retains its flavor even after flowering. An excellent border plant in the vegetable garden mixed with flowering annuals.

2. **Green Bouquet Basil:** The same familiar sweet scent of basil, but the leaves and plant are shorter with a more compact habit of growth. Green bouquet forms a very pretty, compact, ball-shaped bush 8 to 12 inches in height. The leaves measure 1/4 inch to 1/2 inch in length.

Bush Basil

3. **Spicy Globe Basil:** In the bush basil category, spicy globe is the smallest and most compact plant. It grows into a tidy, umbrella-shaped form, growing 4 to 5 inches in height and width. The bright green leaves are about 1/4 inch long and grow in clusters. This tiny basil makes a nice kitchen herb grown on a sunny windowsill because it is so ornamental.

PURPLE BASIL

(*Ocimum basilicum* 'Purpurascens')

Some purple leaf basils are so striking that they are often grown solely for their ornamental qualities. The first of these was opal. It has the same leaf shape as traditional green basil, but the color of the leaves is very deep purple. The flowers of purple basil are a soft lavender color. Both the leaves and the flowers make a nice accent in salads and create a colorful basil vinegar. These dark leaves contrast well with gray-leaved plants such as artemisia in a garden border.

1. **Opal Basil:** The showy purple leaves on this basil won it the All-America award for excellence. It was hybridized in 1962, combining a colorful Turkish species with the aromatic sweet basil. It needs encouragement to grow, but once established, opal basil will grow 10 to 12 inches tall and measure 8 to 10 inches in width.

Dark Opal Basil

2. **Purple Ruffles Basil:**
Similar to opal in color and form, purple ruffles is a more vigorous grower and its leaves are larger. Dark purple leaves are sharply notched and crinkled in texture. Also a winner of the All-America award. Plants are 18 to 24 inches tall, with lavender to rose flowers. A great combination plant to use with green ruffles.

LETTUCE-LEAF BASIL

(*Ocimum basilicum* 'Crispum')

Lettuce-leaf basil has large, wide leaves. The flavor is less pronounced than the other green basils, but the mildness has benefits—it's excellent for long cooking in tomato sauce. Try this big-leaved type torn into bite-sized pieces in salads with butterhead lettuce and ripe tomatoes. The huge leaves of mammoth basil are ideal for drying, wrapping fish or chicken for the grill, or stuffing with other vegetables.

Lettuce-leaf basil needs a lot of space to grow—as much as 18 inches between plants. Because lettuce-leaf basil does not take to potting up at the end of the summer, it is better to start plants in pots and keep them there.

1. **Mammoth Basil:** Mammoth basil has the largest leaves of any lettuce-leaf basil, 4 to 8 inches in length and almost as wide. Plants grow to 18 inches tall, so it is best used as a mid-border plant. Mammoth basil will not produce a seed head as quickly as the sweet or the bush varieties. It has similar scent to that of sweet basil but the flavor is milder.

2. **Napoletano Basil:** Napoletano is an Italian variety with large crinkled leaves draping from the main stem, giving the plant a tropical appearance. Plants and leaves are slightly smaller than those of mammoth basil. The flowers are white and come later than the other types of basil.

3. **Green Ruffles Basil:** Large crinkly leaves with serrated edges. Flavor is mild, and the plants are vigorous. A recent introduction to American seed catalogs. A close cousin to the purple ruffles, these two plants make a nice combination when grown together in the ornamental or herb bed.

Lettuce-Leaf Basil

SCENTED BASIL

(*Ocimum basilicum odoratum*)

There are a number of basils that have flavors reminiscent of other plants. Cinnamon basil, lemon basil, and licorice or anise basil all fit in this category. Both cinnamon and licorice basil are beautiful plants with dark foliage and prominent, deeply colored stems. The flowers are soft lavender and the characteristic aroma of each is quite strong. Lemon basil is a less vigorous grower, yet once established it provides a wonderful harvest.

Lemon Basil

Scented basil can be used in place of regular sweet basil in any recipe where you might want a hint of something different. Chutney and fruit preserves are enhanced by the scented basils, which impart a delicate flavor and aroma. Custards and sorbets benefit from their light perfume. Place scented basil at the garden gate as a fragrant welcome to all who enter.

1. **Lemon Basil:** Lemon basil has light green, narrow leaves and a distinct lemony aroma. The flavor is mild, but a nice addition to stir-fry vegetable dishes. Lemon basil was introduced to the United States in 1940 from Thailand, although it has been known in England since the 16th century. Lemon basil is a bit harder to grow than other basils, since it does not transplant well and it has a tendency to go to seed. Handle transplants gently or direct seed for best results. This plant will grow to a height of 12 inches and to a width not much more than 8 inches. Keep the seed heads pruned for more vigorous growth.

2. **Cinnamon Basil:** The spicy scent of cinnamon basil fills the air each time a leaf is picked or a plant is brushed when passing it in the garden. Dark bronze leaves and rosy pink flowers are attractive. These are vigorous plants and will grow 12 to 18 inches tall and 8 to 10 inches wide. Cinnamon basil has aromatic qualities that are good in jellies, custards, fruit salads, or marinades for meats. The flavor of dried cinnamon basil is minimal—not nearly as satisfactory as fresh. Pick the branches whole and add them to herbal wreaths; spray with a mister occasionally to refresh the fragrance.

Continued ➜

3. **Licorice or Anise Basil:** The leaves of anise basil are dark green with a hint of mulberry. Flower stalks are rosy lavender, making this a beautiful garden plant. Anise basil is frequently used in Asian cooking, imparting a sweet fennel-like flavor. It's not limited to this cuisine, though, and it is especially good with poached pears and melon. Tomato-based dishes are also enhanced by the clean, tart flavor. Anise basil grows to 16 inches tall.

HARVEST

To get the largest yield and best quality of leaves from your plants, pick leaves from the main stem or branches just above the suckers growing in the leaf nodes. By removing the top leaves, the remaining suckers will begin to produce more branches. The more the basil is pruned and harvested in this method, the bushier the plants will become.

For the best flavor, harvest basil just before the flowers develop. Flavor changes begin to take place in the leaves when the flowers open, robbing the leaves of their essential oils. Keep the plants pruned by pinching flower buds off with your fingers or by snipping off the tops with scissors.

Fertilize the plants with manure tea or fish emulsion after harvest to stimulate new growth from the suckers, and in a few weeks you'll be able to pick again.

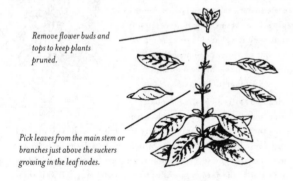

Remove flower buds and tops to keep plants pruned.

Pick leaves from the main stem or branches just above the suckers growing in the leaf nodes.

Preserving Basil

Fresh basil should not be placed in the refrigerator; it is too cold in there for the tender leaves. Place the cut stems in water and basil will sit happily on the windowsill for a week.

To dry basil, harvest clean leaves after the morning dew is off. Do not wash the leaves prior to drying—brush off any dirt if necessary. Tie the leaves in small bunches of three to five stems, securing them with wire or a rubber band. Hang the bunches upside down in a warm, dark place for two to four weeks. A warm oven will work as a dehydrating unit, drying basil in a few days. Spread the leaves out in a single layer on a cookie sheet. Set the oven to the lowest possible temperature until the basil has completely dried. Using either method of drying the basil will not maintain its green color, but its flavor will remain. Spread out newspaper on a table and crumble the dried leaves. Store in a tightly sealed container away from direct sunlight.

The scented basils, especially the lemon and cinnamon varieties, make a nice addition to sachets or dried wreath arrangements when the leaves have been dried. Harvest the stems at midday or in the afternoon when moisture is no longer on the leaves. Group in small bunches and hang upside down in a warm, dry place. Keep the leaves whole and attached to the stems if wreaths are to be made. For sweet-smelling potpourris, crumble and mix the leaves with fruit peels and fragrant oils.

When using dried basil for cooking, measure out the amount called for in the recipe and crush the herb between your fingers or into the palm of your hand as you add the herb to the cooking pot. If dried basil loses its flavor, it may be restored by spreading it out on a cookie sheet and baking it in an oven set at a low temperature.

Whole basil leaves can be frozen, although they will turn black. Harvest the basil, strip off the leaves, and immerse them in water to wash off any soil. Dry the leaves in a salad spinner or colander and then place them between paper or cloth towels to absorb excess moisture. Pack the leaves in plastic bags, seal, and store them in the freezer.

Or, in a blender or food processor, chop 2 cups basil with 1/4 cup olive oil. Place the mixture into ice cube trays or small jars with lids and freeze. After they have frozen, cubes of basil may be transferred to plastic freezer bags. Use the cubes in stews, soups, or sauces. Or mix up a quick pesto just by adding cheese and garlic.

Recipes

SWEET BASIL RECIPES

MARINATED FRESH TOMATO SLICES WITH SWEET BASIL

3 large ripe tomatoes

2 tablespoons chopped fresh basil

3 tablespoons extra virgin olive oil

2 tablespoons lemon juice

1/2 teaspoon sugar

Salt and freshly ground pepper to taste

Slice the tomatoes into 1/4-inch slices. Place into a deep pie dish. Sprinkle the fresh chopped basil evenly over the tomatoes. In a small bowl or jar, mix together the olive oil, lemon juice, sugar, and salt and pepper. Pour this dressing over the tomatoes and basil. Marinate at room temperature for 1 hour. Spoon the dressing over the tomatoes occasionally while they marinate. Serve at room temperature.

SERVES 4.

BASIL PESTO

2 cups fresh basil leaves, removed from the stem

1/2 cup fresh parsley leaves

1/2 cup olive oil

2 garlic cloves, peeled

Salt and freshly ground pepper to taste

1/4 cup roasted pine nuts (pignoli)

1/4 cup fresh Parmesan or Asiago cheese

In a blender or food processor, purée the basil, parsley, oil, garlic, and salt and pepper. Add the nuts and the cheese and process briefly until the pesto reaches the desired consistency.

MAKES 2 CUPS.

SPAGHETTI WITH PESTO

2 quarts water

1 tablespoon oil

1 pound dry spaghetti

2 tablespoons butter

1/2 cup pesto (see recipe above)

In a large pot, bring 2 quarts of water to a boil. Add the oil and the spaghetti, then cover the pot and return to a boil. Stir gently and turn off the heat. Allow the spaghetti to sit in the pot and cook for 5 to 8 minutes. Test the spaghetti for doneness, then drain in a colander. Toss with the butter. Place in a warm bowl or return to the pot. Spoon the pesto over the spaghetti, tossing to coat. Serve hot.

SERVES 4.

PURPLE PESTO

2 cups opal or purple ruffles basil

1 tablespoon sun-dried tomatoes

2 cloves garlic, peeled

6 tablespoons Asiago cheese

1/3 cup pine nuts (pignoli) or walnuts

1/2 cup olive oil

Combine all of the ingredients except the oil in a blender or food processor. Slowly add the oil. Blend to the desired consistency and toss with freshly cooked pasta

MAKES 2 CUPS.

PESTO ON PIZZA

1 1/2 cups warm water

1 tablespoon baker's yeast

1 teaspoon sugar

1 1/2 cups unbleached white flour

1 cup whole wheat flour

1/2 cup wheat germ

1 teaspoon salt

1/2 cup pesto (see recipe above)

Toppings such as peppers, tomatoes, cheese, and onions

In a large mixing bowl, combine the water, yeast, and sugar. Stir and set aside for 5 minutes to allow the yeast to grow. Meanwhile, sift together the two flours, the wheat germ, and the salt. Add to the yeast mixture, stirring until well blended. Turn out onto a floured surface and knead for 5 minutes until the dough becomes smooth and elastic. Place the dough in a lightly oiled bowl, and cover with a damp dishtowel. Place in a warm place to rise for 1 hour, or until double in bulk.

Preheat the oven to 450°F.

Remove the dough from the oiled bowl and divide it into two equal parts. Roll out one half on a lightly floured surface until it's 1/4 to 1/2 inch thick and 9 inches round (or the size of your pizza pan or pizza stone). Fold the dough in half, put it in the pan or on the pizza stone, then open it up and roll the edges to form a raised crust. Bake the crust in a preheated oven for 5 minutes. Remove from the oven and spread 2 to 3 tablespoons of the pesto evenly over the crust. Return to the oven and bake 5 minutes more. Add the desired toppings and continue to bake until the pizza is lightly brown on top, approximately 10 minutes.

MAKES TWO 9-INCH PIZZAS.

POTATO AND BASIL GRATIN

1 cup cold water

1 cup milk

1 pound red potatoes, thinly sliced

1 bay leaf

1 clove garlic, peeled

4 tablespoons butter

1 cup chopped fresh basil

1/2 cup grated Cheddar cheese

1 cup cream

Preheat oven to 375°F.

Pour the water and milk into a saucepan, then add in the sliced potatoes, bay leaf, and garlic. Boil for 10 minutes, just until tender. Drain.

Grease a 10-inch baking dish with 1 tablespoon of the butter. Layer the potatoes and basil in the baking dish. Sprinkle on the grated cheese, then pour on the cream. Dot with the remaining butter. Bake for 45 minutes, or until the top is golden brown.

SERVES 4 TO 6.

BASIL CHEESE TOASTS

1 thin baguette or French bread loaf, cut into 1/2-inch slices

Olive oil

1/2 cup packed fresh basil leaves

8 sun-dried tomatoes (softened in oil), quartered

1/4 cup freshly grated Parmesan cheese

Continued ➜

Preheat the oven to 400°F.

Brush both sides of each slice of bread with the olive oil. Bake on a baking sheet about 6 minutes until lightly toasted.

In a small bowl combine the basil, tomatoes, and cheese, and blend. Spread the mixture on each piece of bread, place on a cookie sheet, and return to the oven to bake about 5 minutes.

MAKES 18 TO 24 TOASTS.

GRILLED BLUEFISH WRAPPED IN MAMMOTH BASIL LEAVES

8 to 10 mature fresh mammoth basil leaves

1 1/2 pounds bluefish

4 tablespoons pesto (see recipe above)

Heat outdoor grill as you would normally do. Soak the mammoth basil leaves in water. Slice the bluefish into strips 2 inches wide, making 8 slices. Spread pesto on each strip of fish. Wrap each fillet in a mammoth basil leaf, securing with a toothpick or wooden skewer. This may be done ahead of time, while the fire is cooking on the grill. Place the wrapped fish pieces on the hot grill over glowing coals, 6 inches from the heat. Cover the grill and steam the fish for 5 minutes on each side.

SERVES 4.

BOURSIN

1 clove garlic, peeled

1/2 cup fresh basil leaves

1/4 cup chives

One 8-ounce package cream cheese

1/4 cup black olives, pitted

In a food processor, chop the garlic and herbs. Add the cream cheese and blend until smooth. Add the olives and chop briefly. Transfer the mixture to a small bowl and serve with crackers or spread on pieces of French bread, topped with thin slices of roast beef.

MAKES 1 CUP.

CINNAMON BASIL GLAZE FOR HAM

1/2 cup brown sugar

1/2 cup cinnamon basil leaves, coarsely chopped

1/4 cup honey

2 tablespoons Dijon-style mustard

Mix all of the ingredients in a small bowl until blended into a paste. Rub one-half of the mixture all over a ham before baking and baste with the remaining mixture during the last 45 minutes of baking the ham.

MAKES ENOUGH TO GLAZE ONE MEDIUM-SIZED HAM.

CINNAMON BASIL JELLY

1 1/2 cups cinnamon basil leaves

2 1/4 cups cold water

3 tablespoons lemon juice

3 1/2 cups sugar

One 3-ounce pouch liquid pectin

Finely chop the basil and place in a saucepan with 2 1/4 cups cold water. Bring to a full boil, cover, remove from the heat, and allow the mixture to steep for 15 minutes. Pour the mixture into a jelly bag or a fine strainer and let it drip. There should be about 1 3/4 cups of basil "tea."

Put the basil "tea" into a large saucepan along with the lemon juice and sugar. Cook the mixture over high heat, stirring constantly until the mixture comes to a full rolling boil (a boil that can't be stirred down). Boil for 1 minute, then remove from the heat. Stir in the pectin and ladle the liquid jelly into sterilized half-pint jars. Wipe the rims of the jars clean and seal with proper lids. Turn the jars upside down for 30 minutes to seal the lids, then turn them right side up and allow the jelly to set and cool.

MAKES 4 HALF PINTS.

LEMON BASIL RICE

2 tablespoons butter

1/2 onion, finely chopped

1/2 sweet red pepper, finely chopped

1 cup uncooked brown rice

1/2 cup lemon basil leaf

1 bay leaves

1 tablespoon parsley, chopped

2 1/2 cups chicken broth or water

Melt the butter in a saucepan over medium heat. Sauté the onion until golden. Add the red pepper and sauté for about 5 minutes. Add the rice and cook, stirring, for 3 to 5 minutes. Add the lemon basil, bay leaf, and parsley. Stir in the broth or water. Cover and bring to a boil. Reduce the heat and simmer for 25 minutes until the liquid has been absorbed and the rice is tender.

SERVES 4.

LEMON BASIL DRESSING

1/8 cup lemon basil leaves

Juice of 1/2 lemon

1 clove garlic, minced

2 tablespoons honey

1/4 cup olive oil

2 to 4 tablespoons plain yogurt

In a small bowl combine the basil, lemon juice, minced garlic, and honey. Add the olive oil in a stream while stirring with a whisk. Blend well. Stir in the yogurt.

Spoon this dressing over plates of fresh fruit such as grapefruit, oranges, and kiwis. Or try it with soft bibb lettuce, avocado, and thin slices of red onion.

MAKES 1/2 CUP.

BAKED FISH IN ANISE BASIL TOMATO SAUCE

1/4 cup anise basil

1 1/2 pounds scrod or flounder fillets

4 tablespoons olive oil

1/2 yellow onion, thinly sliced

1 garlic clove, peeled and chopped

1 teaspoon oregano or sweet marjoram

1 cup chopped tomatoes, with their juice

Preheat oven to 450°F.

Grease a baking dish with butter. Sprinkle 1/8 cup of the anise basil leaves into the dish as a bottom layer, then place the fillets into the dish, overlapping if necessary.

Heat the olive oil in a skillet and sauté the onions until golden. Add the garlic, the remaining 1/8 cup anise basil, and the oregano or marjoram, stirring for 2 to 3 minutes. Stir in the chopped tomatoes and their juice. Simmer for 15 minutes.

Spoon the tomato mixture over the fillets. Cover the baking dish with aluminum foil and bake for 5 to 8 minutes. Serve hot.

SERVES 4 TO 6.

BASIL VARIETY SOURCE CHART*

Variety	Comments and Sources
Camphor	Gray-green leaves and a strong camphor scent *Richters; Well-sweep*
Cinnamon	Dark foliage; ornamental; makes good jelly *Widely available*
Fine Green (*Piccolo verde fino*)	Best for salad as small leaves don't need chopping *Cook's Garden; Shepherd's Garden; J.L. Hudson*
Green Bouquet	Super-compact small-leaf type; good for containers *Richters*
Green Ruffles	Green form of purple ruffles *Cook's Garden; Richters; W. Atlee Burpee; Well-sweep*
Holy (Sacred)	Hairy leaves; primarily ornamental or for potpourri *J.L. Hudson; Johnny's Selected; Park Seed; Richters; Well-sweep*
Lemon	Resents transplanting; good for chicken and seafood *Widely available*
Licorice (Anise)	Quite ornamental and hardier than most basils *Widely available*
Mammoth	Best variety for drying and long cooking *Cook's Garden; Richters*
Napoletano	Lettuce-leaf type, like mammoth, but leaves a bit smaller *J.L. Hudson; Redwood City; Shepherd's Garden; Well-sweep*
Opal	Deep purple foliage is ornamental; makes good vinegar *J.L. Hudson; Richters*
Purple Ruffles	Improved "opal" type; larger leaves; more consistent color *Widely available*
Spicy Globe	Super-compact small-leaf type with strong aroma *Cook's Garden; Richters; Stoke's Seeds*
Sweet Genovese	Best pesto type; productive *Widely available*

*Adapted from *The Cook's Garden* by Shepherd and Ellen Ogden (Emmaus, PA: Rodale Press, 1989). Used by permission.

Growing and Using Thyme

Michelle Gillett

Illustrations by Charles H. Joslin, Mary Rich, Brigita Furhrmann

Varieties of Thyme

Thyme will grow happily in a sunny window box or container. I like to keep a pot of thyme on my windowsill all winter so I can snip the leaves whenever I need to flavor a sauce or a stew. But thyme, which is a sun lover, will not do so well without lots of sun. It would be interesting to experiment with different flavorings by planting a window box with different varieties of culinary *thyme*.

Here's a list of some of the best-known varieties: **Garden thyme** (*Thymus vulgaris*), also known as common or English thyme, is a shrubby plant that grows about 12 inches tall and is essential for cooking. It has pale pink blooms and gray leaves that give off a very strong scent. Thymol, the oil distilled from its leaves and flowers, is a powerful antiseptic. I like to dry the leaves of this variety to have on hand to add to dishes.

Garden thyme

Lemon thyme (*Thymus x citriodorus*) is a spreading plant, smaller than garden thyme, with dark green leaves and deep pink flowers that bloom in June. The smooth leaves have a nice spicy-lemon smell. Like garden thyme, it is an invaluable ingredient for cooking. There are more than 50 forms of this thyme, but actually only 3 are grown for cooking uses. One has gold-and-green leaves; the other has a thin white edging on green leaves. Lemon thyme has a milder flavor than garden thyme but, because of its strong citrus aroma, it is better in teas than in savory dishes. It's delicious with chicken, in fruit salads, and in breads. Use it in place of grated lemon peel. Both garden and lemon thyme should be cut back at the end of flowering and divided every 2 years.

Lemon thyme

Mother-of-thyme (*T. serpyllum*), also known as **wild thyme** (*T. praecox* subsp. *arcticus*), is a carpeting plant. One cultivar, 'Coccineus', has magenta-purple flowers. Another cultivar, 'Splen-dens', has pinkish lavender flowers and tastes spicy. 'Albus' has white flowers and tastes a little like anise. These low-growing thymes are not great for cooking but make wonderful, fragrant ground covers.

Mother-of-thyme

Caraway thyme (*T. herba-barona*) tastes like caraway seeds and should be used to flavor vegetable dishes such as turnips, carrots, and cabbage, or

Continued →

used in breads. It is also nice as flavoring for game and meat and combines well with wine and garlic in cooking.

Azores thyme (*T. caespititius*) has a strong citrusy-pine smell. It is used as a flavoring. As a substitute for or in combination with lemon thyme, it creates an even stronger citrus flavor. It is grown from seed and has 1/4-inch-long slightly sticky, slender leaves, long woolly stems, and pink, lilac, or white flowers that bloom in late spring to summer. It grows in mounds and is perfect for rock gardens.

Caraway thyme

Gardening with Thyme

As long as you don't live in a swamp, thyme is one of the easiest herbs to grow, something that might account for its popularity as a garden and culinary herb. The best place to plant thyme is in a sunny, dry spot that mimics its Mediterranean origins. Any site with poor stony soil on a slope is ideal for thyme, which makes it one of the few plants that will thrive in an otherwise bare spot in your yard. In ordinary gardens, thyme may need a raised bed to keep it happy.

Thyme is a spreading, evergreen perennial that can grow up to 18 inches tall. It can be cut into a hedge or used as a border planting. Creeping varieties make nice scented ground covers, and can even be used as a lawn substitute in low-traffic areas of your yard. Thyme can weather a drought but might not survive in extreme cold unless it is sheltered and dry. Almost all thymes are hardy to Zone 4, but poor drainage during the winter may kill them. If you live in a very cold climate, you might want to bring your thyme plants indoors for the winter.

Most thymes are grown easily from seed. Sow the seed in spring, and keep the ground moist until the first signs of growth appear. Thin plants to 12 inches apart when small. Variegated plants need to be raised from cuttings, divisions, or from pieces of stems that have roots attached. The rarest varieties should be started indoors and then transplanted outside. Thymes tend to become woody, so divide plants every 2 to 3 years. If, after a few years, the plant gradually begins producing fewer leaves, you might want to consider replacing it. Creeping varieties can take over a rock or herb garden and need to be cut way back so that they don't crowd out other plants. Thyme roots are woody with hairlike brown threads and grow underground for some distance. The stems are woody at the base and then become shiny and wiry at the top. Leaves are tiny—no more than 1/4 inch long—and are wide at the base and narrow at their tips. They are slightly furry, which is what gives them their grayish tinge.

Thymes bloom in late May for about a month. The flowers are two-lipped and tiny and grow in clusters at the ends of the stems. Their color, depending on the variety, ranges from pale purple to lilac, white, or shades of pink.

Harvesting and Preserving Thyme

Most herb gardeners choose to harvest in the morning, when the essential oils in the plant are strongest. But it really depends on what you want the thyme for. If you are making a sauce for supper, go out and snip away. Don't deprive yourself of fresh herbs simply because it's the wrong time of day.

But to harvest for storage, let the dew dry in the morning sun, and then pick. It's best to harvest thyme when it's in full flower, and dry it in the shade to preserve the color. You can take up to one-third of the plant at each harvest. Just make sure that you water and feed plants after you harvest them so that you'll get a second growth. For best flavor, feed with liquid seaweed or half-strength liquid fertilizer. Too much fertilizer will reduce essential oils in the plant, so don't overdo it.

When I am drying herbs for cooking, I like to wash them first. I bring the harvested thyme into the kitchen and give it a quick rinse under tepid water. Then I line the counter with dish towels and place the thyme on top of them to dry. Or you can use a salad spinner to get most of the water off.

There are so many ways to dry herbs. One of the quickest drying methods is microwaving. Place the leaves on a double layer of paper towels. Because thyme has small leaves, microwave for only 1 or 2 minutes on high. Check after each minute to make sure you are still drying it, not cooking it.

If you don't have a microwave, you can dry thyme in a conventional oven by placing it in a single layer on cookie sheets. Set the oven on warm (100° to 125°F) and cook for 10 to 15 minutes. Don't forget to leave the oven door slightly ajar so that moisture can escape. If you need to chop the leaves for tea, or you prefer chopped thyme for cooking, you can crush them with a rolling pin or grind them in a coffee grinder.

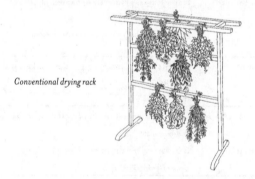

Conventional drying rack

Freezing is another quick and effective way to preserve thyme. Put small, loose bundles of thyme sprigs in plastic bags as soon as they are cut. Seal each bag and put it in the freezer right away. Don't forget to label and date it! If you need thyme for a recipe, don't worry about defrosting it first; you can chop thyme while it's still frozen.

The old-fashioned way to dry herbs also works well with thyme. After picking a bunch, tie the stems together and hang upside down in a dry place. As long as the air is not extremely humid, thyme should dry very quickly. When it is dry, strip the leaves from the stems and store the leaves in airtight containers.

STORING DRIED THYME

Try to keep leaves whole to keep the oils intact. Dark, airtight bottles are the best containers for storing thyme. Or you can store it in zipper-locked bags in a tin or other container. Make sure you label every container and bag with the name of the herb and the date you packaged it. And don't keep dried thyme any longer than 6 or 7 months; after that, it loses its strong flavor and aroma.

Cooking with Thyme

Thyme is a mainstay of the kitchen. It is used in stuffings, stews, soups, stocks, and as a flavoring with strong-tasting vegetables. It blends wonderfully with garlic and wine and mushrooms. And here are some ideas for using thyme varieties:

- Lemon thyme is delicious with fish and poultry.
- Caraway thyme can be rubbed on roasts.
- Orange thyme adds zest to chicken.
- Nutmeg thyme can be added to custards, breads, and puddings.

Thyme is generally cooked as an ingredient in a dish rather than added to a recipe at the end for last-minute flavoring. Thyme flowers can be used to garnish certain dishes. Seafood, pasta, and ragouts are enhanced by the sweetness of flowering thyme sprigs.

SOUP

True comfort food, soup is perfect winter or summer, lunch or dinner. In the winter try using dried thyme, or buy fresh thyme from your local supermarket or greengrocer.

CARROT AND THYME SOUP

With vitamin C from the carrots and thyme's medicinal gifts, this soup is a delicious way to ward off winter colds.

8 ounces carrots, grated

4 shallots, chopped fine

8 sprigs garden thyme, or 2 teaspoons dried thyme

1 garlic clove, chopped fine

1 tablespoon lemon juice

3 pints chicken or vegetable stock

Salt and pepper to taste

1. Simmer all the ingredients in a covered saucepan for 30 minutes.
2. Remove the thyme sprigs (leave the leaves that have come off) and discard. Serve with salad and crusty bread.

SERVES 6

MAIN DISHES

Thyme is traditionally paired with the lighter meats (chicken, turkey, and pork), but don't be afraid to try it with all your proteins.

PORK CHOPS SAUTÉED WITH THYME

This is a mouthwatering, hunger-satisfying recipe—and an easy one.

1/2 cup all-purpose flour

Salt and pepper to taste

8 thin (1/2 inch thick) pork loin chops

4 tablespoons unsalted butter

4 tablespoons olive oil

16 sprigs fresh thyme, or 2 teaspoons dried thyme

1. Season the flour with the salt and pepper. Lightly coat the pork chops with the flour.
2. Heat half the butter and oil in a large skillet and sauté half the chops for 5 minutes on each side.

3. Put some thyme under each pork chop so that it sticks to the meat. Remove the chops and keep warm.
4. Add the rest of the butter and oil to the skillet, and cook the remaining chops in the same way. Arrange on a platter and serve.

SERVES 4 TO 6

LEMON THYME CHICKEN

This is a great recipe for the first thyme of the summer. It's delicious with rice and salad. Serve it on the terrace or deck.

2 tablespoons lemon juice

2 tablespoons olive oil

2 tablespoons butter

1 teaspoon dried lemon thyme, or 1 tablespoon chopped fresh lemon thyme

1 clove garlic, minced

Salt and pepper to taste

2 whole chicken breasts, cut in half to make 4 pieces

4 chicken thighs

1. In a small pan, combine the lemon juice, olive oil, butter, chopped thyme, garlic, and salt and pepper. Stir over low heat until the butter melts.
2. Put the chicken pieces in a broiler pan with a rack and brush with the lemon-butter mixture to coat on all sides.
3. Broil with the skin-side up until done. (The time will depend on the thickness of the meat.)
4. Garnish with fresh thyme sprigs.

SERVES 4

BROILED THYME LAMB CHOPS

This is another quick and easy recipe. It's delicious with rice and stewed tomatoes or ratatouille.

1 tablespoon olive oil

1 tablespoon vegetable oil

2 cloves garlic, minced

1/2 teaspoon dried thyme, or 1/2 tablespoon chopped fresh thyme

Salt and pepper to taste

4 rib lamb chops

1. Preheat the broiler and broiler rack.
2. In a bowl, combine all the marinade ingredients. Add the lamb chops and make sure they are coated well on all sides.

Continued →

3. Cover the bowl and let the lamb chops marinate for 20 minutes.

4. Broil the chops 4 to 6 inches from the heat for 5 minutes on each side.

SERVES 4

THYME AND ONION PIE

This onion pie is both inexpensive and fragrant with thyme. It can be made with a prepared pie shell, a flaky pastry of your own, or this baking-powder biscuit crust. This recipe comes from *Onions Love Herbs, a Fresh-from-the-Garden Cookbook*, by Ruth Bass.

Crust

1 cup flour

1 1/2 teaspoons baking powder

1/2 teaspoon salt

2 tablespoons butter

1/2 cup low-fat milk

Filling

3 tablespoons butter

4 large yellow onions, chopped (2 cups)

1 tablespoon minced fresh thyme

3 eggs

1/2 teaspoon ground cloves

1/2 teaspoon salt

Freshly ground black pepper

1 cup low-fat yogurt

3 slices Canadian bacon or thinly sliced ham

1. Preheat oven to 350°F. Sift the flour and combine with baking powder, salt, butter, and milk for the crust.

2. Roll out the dough to a 1/4-inch thickness and line the bottom of a 9-inch pie pan, leaving extra around the edge.

3. Double over the extra dough and crimp into a fluted rim around the pan.

4. Bake the crust for 5 minutes, remove from the oven, and increase the oven temperature to 400°F.

5. While the crust is baking, make the filling. Melt the butter in a large skillet, and sauté the onions with the minced thyme until the onions are soft but not browned. Remove from heat.

6. In a small bowl, whisk the eggs. Add the eggs, cloves, and salt and pepper to taste to the onions and toss gently. Then add the yogurt. Pour the mixture into the pie pan.

7. Cut the Canadian bacon or ham into small squares and arrange decoratively over the top of the onion mixture.

8. Bake about 15 minutes, or until the meat is crisp and the crust is light brown.

9. Cut into wedges and serve immediately

SERVES 4 TO 6

THYME SCRAMBLED EGGS

Thyme lends a delicate flavor to this morning fare. Serve it with fresh fruit or steamed asparagus to guests for Sunday brunch. Or eat it for breakfast on a tray with a cup of coffee and a glass of juice. In bed!

1 loaf rich bread, cut into
    8 1/2-inch-thick slices

1 stick unsalted butter

8 slices Canadian bacon

12 eggs

1/2 cup chopped fresh thyme

1/4 cup sour cream

6 thyme sprigs for garnish

1. Preheat the oven to 250°F.

2. Cut the bread slices into 8 rounds with a cookie cutter. Melt 3 tablespoons of the butter in a large nonstick skillet over medium heat and brown the bread rounds evenly on both sides. Place them on a baking sheet in a warm oven.

3. Melt 2 tablespoons of the butter in the skillet and sauté the bacon for 1 minute on each side. Remove the bacon and arrange it in a shallow baking dish. Cover and keep warm in the oven. Clean the skillet and wipe it dry.

4. Whisk the eggs in a large bowl with the chopped herbs and sour cream until well blended. Melt the remaining 3 tablespoons of butter in the skillet. Add the egg mixture and cook slowly, stirring with a wooden spoon until the eggs are scrambled but slightly moist.

5. Arrange 2 toast rounds on each plate, cover with bacon, and spoon the eggs on top. Garnish with thyme sprigs.

SERVES 4

SIDE DISHES

Potatoes and other root vegetables are especially compatible with thyme. One of my favorite recipes is to cut up any root vegetables I have on hand (potatoes, squash, sweet potatoes, onions), sprinkle with olive oil and dried thyme, and roast until the vegetables are soft. Delicious.

ROAST POTATOES WITH THYME

These flavors blend to make a warming, rustic dish. Eat it by the fire on a snowy winter night. Remember to use only potatoes that are firm and have no discolored spots. And don't store potatoes in the refrigerator; the starch will change to sugar there and give them an odd-tasting, sweet flavor.

1 1/2 pounds small, firm potatoes (Yellow Finns are good)

2 tablespoons olive oil

2 heads garlic, separated into cloves, peeled

8 sprigs thyme

1 tablespoon water

Salt and pepper to taste

1. Preheat the oven to 400°F. Scrub the potatoes well and arrange them in a shallow baking dish in a single layer.

2. Toss them with the oil, the garlic cloves, sprigs of thyme, and water. Add salt and pepper to taste.

3. Cover the baking pan tightly with aluminum foil and bake for 40 minutes. Test for doneness by pricking with a knife. The potatoes should pierce easily. When they are done, remove them from the oven and loosen the foil to let some heat escape.

SERVES 4

CORN BREAD STUFFING

Everyone has a favorite stuffing recipe. I always like to test new ones, or to experiment with the tried-and-true ones. This is a fairly basic recipe that can be changed according to your tastes. Add raisins or chestnuts, pecans, sausage, or bacon. Whatever you add or take away, though, keep the thyme. There is no stuffing recipe that can exist without thyme's flavor!

2 cups chopped onions	1 cup chopped celery
2 garlic cloves, minced	Corn bread, cut into cubes
1 stick butter	1 teaspoon dried thyme
1/2 cup chopped shallots	2 eggs, beaten
1 1/2 cups peeled and chopped apples	Salt and pepper to taste

1. In a large skillet, sauté the onions and garlic in the butter over medium heat until they are soft.

2. Add the shallots. Cook until soft.

3. Stir in the apples and celery; cook about 10 minutes or until soft. Drain.

4. Combine the corn bread cubes, the onion and celery mixture, and the seasonings. Toss; stir in the eggs. Stuff the turkey!

YIELD: ABOUT 5 CUPS

Mail-Order Sources for Seeds

Caprilands Herb Farm
Silver Street
Coventry, CT 06405

Companion Plants
7247 North Coolville Ridge
Road
Athens, OH 45701

The Cook's Garden
P.O. Box 535
Londonderry, VT 05148

Dabney Herbs
P.O. Box 22061
Louisville, KY 40252

Fredricksburg Herb Farm
402 Whitney
P.O. Drawer 927
Fredricksburg, TX 78624

Harris Seeds
60 Saginaw Drive
Rochester, NY 14692

Johnny's Selected Seeds
Foss Hill Road
Albion, ME 04910

Meadowbrook Herb Garden
Route 138
Wyoming, RI 02898

Pinetree Garden Seeds
Box 300
New Gloucester, ME 04260

Shepherd's Garden Seeds
30 Irene Street
Torrington, CT 06790–6658
(860) 482–3638

Taylor's Herb Garden, Inc.
1535 Lone Oak Road
Vista, CA 92084

Related Titles of Interest from Storey Communications, Inc.

The Big Book of Gardening Secrets by Charles W.G. Smith A thorough guide to every aspect of backyard gardening. Readers will find step-by-step, illustrated instructions and scores of professional secrets for growing better vegetables, herbs, fruits, and flowers, plus tips for extending the growing season and natural pest control. 352 pages ISBN 1–58017–000–5

Contained Gardens: Creative Designs and Projects by Susan Berry and Steve Bradley

Container gardening offers endless possibilities for limited space, supplementing color in a garden, and moving the garden indoors. Step-by-step techniques for creating dozens of designs, color themes, groupings, and using unique planters. Also plant-care advice, watering tips, and container suggestions. 160 pages ISBN 0–88266–899–4

Fresh-from-the-Garden Cookbooks by Ruth Bass

Interest in cooking with herbs continues to grow now that fresh herbs are available year-round. Take advantage of this trend with this unique series. These beautifully designed books, each with more than 30 imaginative recipes, are highlighted by two-color scratchboard drawings throughout and printed on recycled, flecked paper. Series titles are: Herbal Breads (ISBN 0–88266–923–0), Herbal Soups (ISBN 0–88266–924–9), Herbal Sweets (ISBN 0–88266–922–2), Herbal Salads (ISBN 0–88266–925–7), Tomatoes Love Herbs (ISBN 0–88266–931–1), Onions Love Herbs (ISBN 0–88266–934–6), Peppers Love Herbs (ISBN 0–88266–932-X), and Mushrooms Love Herbs (ISBN 0–88266–933–8).

Gifts for Herb Lovers: Over 50 Projects to Make and Give by Betty Oppenheimer

Herb lovers can create herbal body cream, herb-printed notecards, herbal vinegar, an herb drying rack, and much more. 128 pages ISBN 0–88266–983–4

Growing & Using Herbs Successfully by Betty E.M. Jacobs

This helpful guide, beautifully illustrated with delicate botanical drawings, teaches readers how to plant, propagate, harvest, dry, freeze, and store 64 of the most popular herbs. 240 pages ISBN 0–88266–249-X

The Herb Gardener: A Guide for All Seasons by Susan McClure

This very popular book provides complete instructions on every conceivable aspect of herbs in the home and garden. 240 pages ISBN 0–88266–910–9 (hardcover), 0–88266–873–0 (paperback)

The Herbal Body Book: A Natural Approach to Healthier Hair, Skin, and Nails by Stephanie Tourles

How to transform common herbs, fruits, and grains into safe, economical, and natural personal care items. Contains over 100 recipes to make facial scrubs, hair rinses, shampoos, soaps, cleansing lotions, and moisturizers, lib balms, toothpaste, powders, insect repellents, and more! Each recipe include preparation time, yield, and storage and usage tips. 128 pages ISBN 0–88266–880–3

Continued →

The Herbal Palate Cookbook by Maggie Oster and Sal Gilbertie

This beautiful, full-color collection features 150 simple yet elegant recipes for appetizers, salads, soups, main and side dishes, breads and muffins, desserts, and drinks. An herb identification section contains color photographs and instructions for growing herbs in containers. 176 pages ISBN 0-88266-915-X

Herbal Treasures: Inspiring Month-by-Month Projects for Gardening, Cooking, and Crafts by Phyllis V. Shaudys

A compendium of the best herb crafts, recipes, and gardening ideas. 320 pages ISBN 0-88266-618-5

The Pleasure of Herbs: A Month-by-Month Guide to Growing, Using, and Enjoying Herbs by Phyllis Shaudys

This lively book is brimming with information about herbs and herb growing and features both indoor and outdoor cultivation, recipes, and craft projects. 288 pages ISBN 0-88266-423-9

Growing & Using Cilantro

Glenn Andrews

Growing Cilantro

Cilantro, like all herbs, is best at its very freshest. And the best source for fresh cilantro is your own backyard.

SEED VERSUS TRANSPLANTS

What's the best way to approach growing cilantro—starting from seed or buying and using plants?

Well, plants *are* available, from mail-order sources and in garden stores (and even supermarkets from time to time), but I can't really see any purpose in buying them. By the time a plant reaches you, its life is just about over! So start with some seed (yes, even the dried coriander seed in your spice cabinet might sprout and grow fine cilantro).

But if you're really in a rush to use some cilantro in your cooking, you can always buy some cut sprigs tied in bundles or in plastic bags. You can find these in most supermarkets these days. Quite often, you'll find that the cilantro in the supermarket still has its roots attached. This is the best sort to buy. To begin with, the roots will help the herb last longer. But there's more to it than that. The roots are not only edible, but also highly prized—at least by the citizens of Thailand!

So start your plants from seed. Germination is fast and the rewards are well worth the effort.

BASIC GROWING TIPS FOR CILANTRO

Plant the seed from 1/8 to 1/4 inch deep in light, well-drained soil. Keep uniformly moist until germination, which will take place in 14 to 16 days.

Conventional wisdom (and the instructions on most seed packets) will tell you the plants should be spaced 18 inches apart. I feel that this goes back to the days when cilantro was fairly unknown in this country and the plant was almost always grown as coriander, for its seed.

My advice to you is to plant the seeds much closer together than that. I wouldn't put them any farther apart than 2 inches. Think of it as a loose-leaf lettuce—say, a 'Black-seeded Simpson'. You want to be able to use the young plants as you thin them. In other words, start by picking every fourth little plant, then every third, then every second. If you want, you can let the remaining plants grow to their full height of 2 to 3 feet and harvest the coriander seed. (If you become fond of the roots, though, they are best harvested before the plant goes to seed.)

DECISIONS, DECISIONS

You'll have to figure out if you want to grow your cilantro for seed (in which case call it coriander) or for its green leaf. Or—better yet—for both.

Because cilantro is so very quick to bolt (produce seed stalks and seed), raising it for seed is easy. Just plant it in summer in full sun, keep it on the dry side, don't feed it (or not much, at any rate), and you'll soon have seed.

On the other hand, to achieve the largest possible amount of greenery from your cilantro, go in the other direction: Plant in spring or fall in a partly shady location, and keep it nicely watered and fed. A water-soluble fertilizer such as sea kelp (an organic 4-4-4 seaweed fertilizer) or Miracle-Gro is a good idea for cilantro. Nitrogen (the first number in fertilizer formulas) produces lush foliage, so make sure your fertilizer has at least as much nitrogen as phosphorus and potassium (the second and third numbers, respectively). It helps, too, if you choose a strain of cilantro that the grower claims is slow to bolt.

Of course, as with any annual herb, pinching out flower stems (in this case, the thick stems with fennel-like foliage) as they appear will help slow down bolting. Any annual's one aim in life is to reproduce itself. If you let it produce seed, it will consider its work done, turn up its toes, and die. But if you thwart it—don't let it create seed—it will keep on growing.

If you're aiming for both greenery and seed, I suggest you start out using the conditions suitable for greens production, then just let some of the plants go to seed, which they certainly will!

When harvesting the seeds, which will be about 45 days after planting, make sure they're fully ripe by smelling them. When they're ready, they will be brown and will smell deliciously spicy.

To keep up a steady supply of green cilantro, try planting a new batch of seed every 2 or 3 weeks. This way you will always have a new batch of tender greens coming, and if you lapse on care, not everything will go to seed.

GROWING IN CONTAINERS, INDOORS OR OUT

Because cilantro is a tender annual, you won't be able to have its delicious (once you're used to the taste!) leaves year-round in most parts of the country unless you grow it indoors in the winter.

Luckily, this isn't at all hard to do.

Use flowerpots, if you wish, but give some thought to using things that may be a bit more decorative. Casseroles, for instance, or soup tureens, or smallish salad bowls. A Bundt pan! A group of coffee cups or mugs!

Use any standard potting soil, plus a layer at the bottom of gravel or broken pots to provide drainage. As with planting in the ground, cover the seed with 1/8 to 1/4 inch of soil. Keep evenly moist for the 14 to 16 days until germination.

With container planting, you can try a little trick that cilantro appreciates—keep it dark until germination occurs. Just cover the container loosely with newspaper or foil.

After germination, don't worry too much about how much light the seedlings receive. After all, you want to retard their maturation, don't you? I personally think that the middle of my dining room table, as a centerpiece, is the perfect place for a pretty pot of cilantro.

Remember cilantro for outdoor containers, too, especially in spring and fall. (It does like coolish weather.) Aside from the containers you might want to use indoors, don't forget window boxes and tubs of various sizes for your outdoor plantings.

And always remember that cilantro's life span is so short (at least as far as the greenery goes) that you should replant every 2 or 3 weeks.

Selecting Cilantro and Keeping It Fresh

Suppose you don't have any fresh cilantro on hand. What can you do? That's easy for almost everyone—just go to your local supermarket and look in the produce section for little bundles or bags of it. (If you're lucky enough to have a local green market, so much the better!)

However, unless you're very experienced, you may become confused. Cilantro bears a very strong resemblance to flat-leaf, or Italian, parsley. That's a resemblance only in looks—they taste entirely different. So if it isn't labeled, tear off a leaf and taste it. (Or ask permission to do so, if you feel you should.) Even if you've never tasted cilantro before, you'll know, from the moment you bite into it, that it's not parsley!

Choose cilantro that is bright green, crisp, and fresh looking, without any yellow or brown leaves, and certainly without any slimy-looking spots.

When you get the cilantro home (or after you've picked some of your own), there are several ways to prolong its freshness:

- You can put it in an airtight container in your refrigerator—a zipper-locking plastic bag will do just fine. (This system seems to work the best.)

- You can treat it as though it were a little bouquet of flowers and either keep it loosely covered in your fridge or just put it on a windowsill in water.

- You can wrap it in damp paper towels and place it inside a plastic bag. Keep refrigerated.

Preserving Fresh Cilantro

Most herbs dry beautifully. You can simply hang them upside down or microwave them and get fine results. The flavor will be strong and true.

But not so cilantro—the flavor disappears when the herb is dried. (Reputable spice companies do sell dried cilantro, but I wonder if anyone ever buys it a second time!)

Freezing cilantro doesn't work well, either. So what are you left with? Not much!

One thing you *can* do is make a cilantro butter. Soften unsalted butter and combine it with chopped cilantro and lemon juice. Proportions: 4 parts butter, 2 parts cilantro, 1/2 part lemon juice. This freezes quite nicely and will give you a touch of cilantro flavor whenever you need it.

Or you can make cilantro oil. Place cilantro leaves in a glass screw-top jar. Top with twice the quantity of salad oil. Put on a windowsill and leave undisturbed for 3 weeks. Now strain out the cilantro and season the oil with a little salt. Keep refrigerated.

Another possibility is cilantro in vinegar. White wine vinegar is probably the best to use because of its delicate nature. Champagne vinegar would do well, too—and isn't as expensive as it sounds. Just put some fresh cilantro in a screw-top jar. Cover with vinegar, screw on the top, and let the jar sit in a dark place. The cilantro will wilt and its color will fade, but there will be some taste left. The vinegar will have a very strong taste of cilantro after even just a day.

As Coriander—Whole Seed or Ground

Coriander seed (as opposed to the green leaf, which takes getting used to) is a spice everyone seems to love. It's gentle and somewhat sweet and has just a hint of citrus.

After you harvest the seed (which should be brown and smell great), keep seeds in a well-sealed container until you want to use them or until it's time to grind. The best way to do the grinding is in an electric coffee mill, if you happen to have one, but the old mortar-and-pestle routine works well, too. By the way, I have read over and over that if you ever use your coffee grinder to grind spices, you should never use it for coffee beans again. Nonsense! The blades of the grinder are stainless steel and clean very easily. And even if they don't, what's wrong with a little touch of spice in your coffee?

This bulletin is about cilantro, so I won't be giving you a bunch of recipes using coriander. I'm sorry, too, because it's such a very nice spice. I'll just give you a hint or two on its use:

- Combine ground coriander with minced fresh ginger and butter, and stuff the mixture under the skin of a chicken before broiling.

- Mix ground coriander with equal parts of black pepper and dry ginger and a little salt; rub into a pork tenderloin; let sit 15 minutes; brown quickly in just a little oil; roast at 400°F for 20 minutes, turning a time or two.

- Mix with chopped green onions and use to season cooked peas.

- Add with a little orange zest to carrots.

- Or add it to stuffings; mix it into eggs before scrambling; add it to the spices in gingerbread or spice cookies; and so on, and on, and on!

Cooking with Cilantro

Just one little cautionary word as you begin your adventures with cilantro: Start slowly. Use only a little cilantro in any given dish until you get used to it. Then use as much as you want—and you'll want a lot!

However, I have to tell you that there's another school of thought about this, which applies when the cilantro is cooked (as in the Thai Beef Salad on the next page). In this case, use a fairly large amount of the lovely herb—cooking tames the flavor and makes it more acceptable to those who haven't yet acquired a taste for it.

CONDIMENTS, APPETIZERS, AND SNACKS

Most Americans have tried salsa—which might be their only experience with cilantro. The herb's unique flavor adds spice to all kinds of other condiments, too.

CILANTRO AND COCONUT CHUTNEY

This chutney is an unusual and downright brilliant accompaniment to any curried dish. (It also makes a good accent to any plainer meal.) Make it within a day of serving so its freshness will be maintained.

A purist would tell you to use only unsweetened dried coconut, which it's possible to buy in Asian groceries or most health food stores. To me, though, sweetened coconut tastes just fine.

25–30 stalks (with leaves) cilantro

1 jalapeño chile, seeded and chopped

3 tablespoons water

1 tablespoon lemon juice

1 cup dry coconut

1. Run the cilantro, chile, water, and lemon juice together in a food processor or blender until pureed. Stir in the coconut and form the mixture into a cake.

2. Chill, covered, until ready to serve.

CILANTRO CHEESE SPREAD

This is on the order of Boursin or the wide range of garlic and herb cheeses that are so good to spread on crudités or crackers. Cilantro makes it extra special.

8 ounces cream cheese or Neufchâtel (a lower-fat version)

2 tablespoons white wine

3 tablespoons minced cilantro

1/2 teaspoon freshly ground black pepper

1/2 teaspoon (or to taste) minced or crushed garlic

1. Mash everything together in a small bowl. Cover and keep chilled until almost ready to use.

2. Serve with crackers or raw vegetables—sliced jicama is especially pleasant with this spread.

SERVES 8 OR MORE

SALSA VERDE

It's only recently that a shopper can go into the average supermarket in this country and find not only cilantro but also tomatillos. Since these are the two main ingredients in Salsa Verde, you have to wonder how any "green sauce" was made in North American kitchens in the past. I suppose a lot of green sweet bell pepper was used.

Now, however, every major supermarket chain (and some of the minor and independent ones, as well) will be happy to sell you all the cilantro and tomatillos you could possibly want—and on every day of the year, too. So you have no excuse for not making this classic sauce.

Ah, but are you asking, "What in the world are tomatillos?" They are often referred to as Mexican green tomatoes, but they're not in the tomato family at all. They're ground cherries! They're green and round and do look a lot like unripe tomatoes, except that each has a paperlike husk. This must be removed before you use the tomatillos, and then you have to rinse off the somewhat sticky substance underneath. (If they're not available, substitute unripe regular tomatoes—or use canned tomatillos, which you can find in stores with a Latino customer base.)

This is a mild salsa, though in restaurants, green salsas are usually hotter than the red kind. To make it as hot as you like, add more chilies or use hotter varieties.

8 tomatillos, husked, rinsed, and chopped

1/3 cup chopped cilantro

1/2 cup green Anaheim or New Mexico chilies, chopped (or use a 4-ounce can of peeled green chilies)

2 serrano chilies, seeded and minced

1 teaspoon minced garlic

1/4 cup chopped green onion

1. Run all the ingredients together in a food processor or blender—or mince everything very finely by hand. If you use a machine, it's nice (but not absolutely necessary) to stop before the mixture becomes totally smooth.

2. Refrigerate, covered, for at least an hour, to give the flavors a chance to blend.

YIELD: ABOUT 1 1/2 CUPS

CILANTRO GUACAMOLE

Those who love cilantro and also think that guacamole is one of the greatest inventions of this or any other age are going to go berserk over this combination. For that matter, Cilantro Guacamole might be a good way to introduce someone to cilantro. (But cut the amount you use here in half, remembering that it often takes time and experience for someone to learn to appreciate this herb.)

1 large ripe avocado

1/4 cup minced white onion

Juice of 1 lime

1 medium tomato, finely chopped

1/4 cup (or more) chopped cilantro leaves

1 jalapeño, Anaheim, or New Mexico chile, seeded and minced

Salt to taste

1. Cut around the avocado, lengthwise. Twist the two halves to separate. Remove the stone. Now just hold each half upside down and squeeze the avocado meat out into a bowl. (Or peel the avocado, if you prefer.)

2. Chop the avocado meat coarsely (or mash it with a fork, if you like a smoother guacamole), then add all the other ingredients.

3. Serve right away—or hold in the refrigerator for a few hours by sprinkling on some extra lime juice, then pressing plastic wrap onto the surface. (You may have heard that the best way to keep

guacamole in good shape for a while is to bury the avocado seed in the mixture. All I can say is: maybe! But the method given above really does work.)

SOUPS AND SALADS

Cooking mellows the taste of this pungent herb, while its bright color and flavor spice up salads.

GREEN GAZPACHO

An old saying has it that there are as many versions of gazpacho, the brilliant soup-salad of Spain, as there are Spaniards. As far as I know, though, Green Gazpacho isn't one of these, since it's my own invention. It's refreshing, and I actually prefer it to the usual red gazpachos. See what you think!

2 pounds green tomatoes or tomatillos

4 scallions

2 medium-size cucumbers

1/2 cup chopped green pepper

Juice of 1 lemon

1/2 cup chopped cilantro leaves

1 teaspoon or more jalapeño sauce (or use 1 small green chile, seeded)

2 cups chicken broth

Salt and freshly ground black or white pepper to taste

1. Coarsely chop the tomatoes. (If you're using tomatillos, remove the papery husks and rinse the tomatillos well.) Chop the scallions. Chop the cucumbers, peeling them first if the skins have been waxed.

2. Put all the ingredients in a blender or food processor. Run the machine just until everything has been chopped finely—stop before it becomes a puree.

3. Refrigerate, covered, until very thoroughly chilled—overnight is not too long.

SERVES 4–6

CILANTRO-CURRY CHICKEN SALAD

This is the dish, as made by my old friend Margaret Heath, that showed me how delicious cilantro can be. It uses a fairly small amount of cilantro—add more if you and your guests already love this pungent herb.

1 cup mayonnaise

2 teaspoons curry powder (or more, if you want a strong curry flavor)

2 tablespoons minced green onion

1/4 cup minced celery

1/4 cup (or more) chopped cilantro

4 cups cooked, chopped chicken

A little salt and freshly ground pepper, if desired

Lettuce leaves

1. Combine all the ingredients except the lettuce in a medium-size bowl, mixing them in the order given.

2. Serve on lettuce leaves.

SERVES 4

THAI BEEF AND CILANTRO SALAD

They use a lot of cilantro in Thailand, usually in combination with some of their other traditional flavors. This salad is a good example of this—and a fine one-dish meal, as well. The combination of large amounts of lightly cooked cilantro and fresh ginger yields an amazingly warm and buttery sensation.

You can find Asian fish sauce in all Asian markets—and also in many supermarkets. If you don't have it, though, you can substitute a few dashes of Worcestershire sauce, which contains a high proportion of anchovy and thus gives somewhat the same effect.

For the dressing:

1/4 cup rice wine vinegar

2 tablespoons peanut oil

2 teaspoons Asian fish sauce (see above)

1 teaspoon sugar

1 serrano chile, seeded and minced

For the salad:

1 pound fairly lean ground beef (chuck, for instance)

1 teaspoon minced or pressed garlic

1/4 cup minced or grated fresh ginger

1/2 cup chopped cilantro

1 head Boston or Bibb lettuce

1/4 cup radishes, cut into small matchsticks

1 sweet green pepper, seeded and cut into thin strips

1. Make the dressing by combining all its ingredients in a fairly large bowl. Put aside for the moment.

2. Brown the chopped beef with the garlic in a skillet over medium-high heat. When brown, add the ginger and cilantro and cook and stir for 3 or 4 minutes. Add to the dressing.

3. When you're ready to serve, line a salad bowl or four large plates with the lettuce leaves. Top with first the beef and dressing mixture, then the radishes and strips of green pepper.

SERVES 4–6

SIDE DISHES

Surprising new flavors result when you mix cilantro with vegetables. After you've acquired the cilantro bug, you will find yourself sprinkling it on many dishes.

Continued →

FRAGRANT RICE

This rice has so much personality of its own that it's best served with plainly cooked chicken, chops, steaks, or burgers.

It can be made with any rice. Long grain, for instance. Or brown rice (adjust the amount of liquid and the cooking time). Or one of the rices that are fragrant in themselves—basmati, for example, or jasmine rice. Or experiment with such "new" rices as Texmati or Wild Pecan (which is not wild rice and doesn't contain pecans!).

2 tablespoons butter	1/4 cup chopped cilantro
2 tablespoons olive oil	1/4 cup raisins or dried currants
1/2 cup onion	2 tablespoons lemon juice
1 teaspoon minced garlic	2 1/2 cups chicken broth or water
1 1/2 cups raw rice (see above)	Salt and freshly ground black pepper to taste
1 tablespoon minced fresh ginger	

1. Heat the butter and oil in a medium-size saucepan over medium heat. Add the onion and garlic and cook until somewhat soft.

2. Now add the rice, ginger, cilantro, and raisins or currants. Cook and stir for 3 minutes, then stir in the lemon juice and the broth or water. Bring to a boil, turn down the heat, cover the pot, and simmer for about 18 minutes, or until the rice is tender. Season to taste with salt and pepper.

3. This dish can be served now or reheated later over very low heat, stirring often.

SERVES 4–6

GEORGIAN RED BEANS

No, I'm not talking about Georgia, the state just north of Florida. This is the country of Georgia, to be found just south of Russia. A lot of cilantro (often paired with mint, basil, or dill) gets used in the vibrant cooking of Georgia, and this is one of the many areas of the world where it seems to be common knowledge that cilantro and dried beans make a remarkably good team. (It baffles me why the United States has been so slow to discover cilantro. Well, at least we're catching up now.)

1/2 pound dried kidney beans	2 tablespoons chopped cilantro
1 cup minced onion	1/2 tablespoon chopped mint
2 teaspoons minced garlic	1/2 tablespoon chopped basil
1 serrano chile, seeded and minced	1/2 tablespoon chopped celery leaves
1 tablespoon wine vinegar	Salt and freshly ground black pepper to taste

1. Wash the beans and pick through them. Put in a medium-size saucepan. Cover with water. Bring to a boil. Cover the pot and let it boil for 1 minute. Let sit for 1 hour, then drain, cover with fresh water, and simmer for about 2 hours, or until the beans are tender. If you find you need more moisture during the boiling, add only boiling water.

2. Add all the other ingredients and mix well.

3. Serve either hot or as a room-temperature salad.

SERVES 4

CORNCAKES WITH CILANTRO

These are not breakfast pancakes. Brunch or a light lunch or supper? Yes, definitely. They're savory and unusual. In fact, they're the very sort of thing I always hope to be served (but seldom am) when I'm invited to a brunch.

You can prepare the batter several days ahead—this will make it all the better. Just keep it refrigerated until you're ready to cook.

2 eggs	1/2 teaspoon salt
2 cups buttermilk	1/2 cup chopped cilantro
6 tablespoons melted butter	1/2 cup minced scallions
1 cup flour	Salad oil for the griddle
1/2 cup yellow cornmeal	Sour cream or yogurt and salsa for serving
2 teaspoons baking soda	

1. Stir the eggs, buttermilk, and melted butter together in a medium or large bowl or pitcher. Mix thoroughly.

2. Stir the flour, cornmeal, baking soda, and salt together in a smaller bowl, then stir in the cilantro and scallions.

3. Now mix the dry ingredients into the wet ones, stirring just enough to moisten the dry ingredients. Don't worry if there are some lumps.

4. When you're ready to cook, heat a griddle until a little water sprinkled on it dances around. Oil the griddle lightly and pour or spoon on some of the batter. (Most people like to use about 3 tablespoons of batter per pancake.) Cook until bubbles form on the top of the pancakes and begin to dry out. Now turn the pancakes and cook for about a minute on the second side. Keep going until the batter is gone or you're worn out.

5. Pass bowls of sour cream or plain yogurt and salsa.

YIELD: ABOUT 30 PANCAKES

MAIN DISHES

For new cilantro users, moderation is the key. You might not want to add cilantro to every course. But give these centerpieces a try for a wonderful taste adventure.

CHICKEN CALYPSO

This Caribbean invention is as succulent a chicken dish as you will ever encounter. But don't bother to make it if you don't have any cilantro—it just won't be the same.

However, if you don't have a plantain, you can substitute two fairly firm bananas.

1 3 1/2-pound chicken, cut into quarters	3 cups diced tomatoes (may be canned)
2 tablespoons olive oil	3/4 cup chicken broth
1 cup chopped onion	1/3 cup chopped cilantro
1 teaspoon minced garlic	3/4 teaspoon ground cumin
1 ripe (black-skinned) plantain, in 3/4" slices (or use 2 firm bananas)	1/4 teaspoon hot sauce (or more, to taste)

1. Brown the chicken on all sides in the olive oil in a large skillet. Remove. Add the onion, garlic, and sliced plantains to the pan and cook, stirring often, until lightly browned.

2. Add the rest of the ingredients and cook for 5 minutes. Then add the chicken pieces, turn down the heat, cover, and simmer gently for 30 minutes.

SERVES 4—AND IS NICE SERVED ON RICE

THAI FRIED CHICKEN

As far as I know, the people of Thailand are the only ones who use the root of the cilantro plant in their cooking. Try it! You'll discover one more facet of this remarkable plant—and a very good dish, as well.

It would take you a long time to grind this much black pepper, but don't cheat and use the ready-ground kind. The easy way is to use an electric coffee grinder. Then, continuing your life of ease if you can, grind the coriander roots, fresh ginger, and garlic in a small food processor, adding your ground black pepper at the end.

20 coriander roots	3 tablespoons freshly ground black pepper
10 large cloves garlic	8 small chicken thighs
1 quarter-size piece fresh ginger	3 cups oil for deep-frying

1. Make a paste by grinding the coriander roots, garlic, and fresh ginger, and adding the ground black pepper. (See above for the easiest way to do this.) Rub the paste all over the chicken thighs and allow them to sit for at least an hour in the refrigerator, so the flavor permeates the meat.

2. Heat the oil in a deep-fat fryer or wok to 375°F and deep-fry the thighs until golden. (Stick a small knife into one to make sure it's done all the way through to the bone.)

SERVES 4

CILANTRO-LIME BROILED SALMON STEAK

Here's a fish dish that's fast, simple, low in fat—and a true dazzler. In 20 minutes, you can have salmon fit to serve to your fanciest friends (or yourself!).

4 salmon steaks, cut 3/4" thick	1 1/2 tablespoons olive oil
3 tablespoons chopped fresh cilantro	1/4 teaspoon salt
3 tablespoons freshly squeezed lime juice	3 grinds of a pepper mill
1/2 teaspoon minced garlic	Baking spray

1. Preheat your broiler. Put the salmon steaks in a pan. Make a marinade with the other ingredients and pour it over the fish. Marinate for about 10 minutes.

2. Spray your broiling rack with the nonstick baking spray. Put the salmon steaks on the rack and dab each one with a spoonful of the marinade.

3. Broil, 6 inches below the heat source, for 3 minutes. Turn, dab on a bit more marinade, and broil for another 3 or 4 minutes.

SERVES 4

QUESADILLAS

I used to be a snob about quesadillas. I didn't feel they were worthy of the name unless they were made as little turnovers of *masa* (corn tortilla dough) filled with cheese and perhaps a few other odds and ends. At the very least, I felt they should be made of a folded-over corn tortilla filled in a similar fashion. In either case, I felt they should be then lightly fried. I certainly and especially scorned the typical restaurant "quesadilla," which all too often resembles a taco salad!

But then my friend Paula Murphy made me one of her version of quesadillas—and I forgot all about my preconceived ideas. I love them.

Here's what to do. Paula does all this right in front of her guests, grating the cheese directly onto the bottom tortillas. This is fun to watch, but not totally necessary. It's perfectly possible to get the quesadillas ready to cook before your guests arrive.

If you want to serve your quesadillas as finger-food appetizers, cut each one into eighths, pie-fashion.

1 pound "pepper jack" cheese

1 bunch scallions or 1 medium-size onion

Canola or other salad oil

8 large flour tortillas

1/2 cup chopped cilantro leaves

1. Grate or shred the cheese. Mince the scallions or onion. Heat a tablespoon of salad oil in a large skillet over medium heat.

2. Place one quarter of the cheese on a tortilla. Top with first the minced scallions or onion, then the cilantro. Put another tortilla on top of all this.

3. Place your assembled quesadilla in the heated skillet. Cook until the bottom tortilla is stiff and has begun to brown. Now flip it over and brown the other side.

4. Place the cooked quesadilla on a serving plate and keep it warm while you cook the other three, one at a time, adding more oil as needed.

SERVES 4

LULE KABOB WITH CILANTRO

In the Middle East, this would be made on flat metal skewers, which are heated before the meat mixture is wrapped around them. I'm giving you an easier way, but if you have flat skewers and a little courage . . . go for it!

There's one ingredient you might have trouble finding—sumac, a pleasantly sour dried-spice powder. It turns up in many fancy food stores, and in just about all Middle or Near Eastern stores. If you can't find it, don't worry. Just leave it out. (Do *not* use berries from poison sumac bushes!)

2 pounds very lean ground lamb (ground beef can be substituted)	1/2 cup soft bread crumbs
	Salt and freshly ground black pepper to taste
1/2 cup coarsely chopped onion	1 tablespoon sumac (optional—see above)
1/2 cup chopped cilantro, divided	Wedges of lemon
1/2 cup chopped parsley, divided	

1. Combine the ground lamb, onion, half the cilantro, half the parsley, and all the bread crumbs, salt, and pepper in the bowl of a food processor. Run the machine briefly, until everything is well combined. Preheat your oven broiler.

2. With wet hands, form the meat mixture into eight ovals. Place these on an oiled broiler pan. Broil until golden brown all over, turning the patties frequently.

3. Serve sprinkled with the remaining cilantro and parsley, along with the sumac, and with lemon wedges on the side.

SERVES 4 WITH 2 PATTIES APIECE

Growing & Using Oregano

Sara Pitzer

Illustrations by Charles Joslin

Growing Oregano

First, ignore the popular belief that herbs do best in poor soil. That's like saying people do best in bad climates! They can get along, but they get along better where the weather is nice. Although oregano will grow in everything from clay to wet sand, and appears in relatively infertile places in the wild, cultivated oregano does best in light loam with a neutral to slightly alkaline pH. In soil that tends to be acidic, working in a sprinkling of wood ashes or dolomitic limestone is a good idea. (Remember those "chalklands.") If the soil is heavy, add sand or perlite,

because oregano needs good drainage. Grow oregano in full sun, except in the South where it will tolerate some shade. For container growing, use any standard, packaged potting mix, preferably one that does not include fertilizer, adding a sprinkling of dolomitic limestone or a handful of wood ashes to counter the acidity of the peat moss that is the basis of virtually all potting mixes. If the potting mix seems heavy, add also a handful of sand or perlite per 6-inch pot to insure good drainage. In cold, too-wet potting mix, oreganos refuse to spread their roots—they pout and rot.

You can grow oregano from seed, order plants from catalogs, or buy plants at nurseries. While growing from seed produces the least reliable results, because oreganos don't always come true from seed, you may enjoy the experiment—and you will get lots of plants, at least some of which will be what you want, or will turn out to be so interesting they will become what you want.

STARTING FROM SEED

You can sow oregano seed outside directly where it is to grow, or start it inside to transplant in late spring. The seed is very fine so prepare an outside seed bed with extra sand and rake smooth. Growers differ in their opinions of best times to sow outside. Ideal germination temperature is about 70°F., which means you'll see fastest germination if you wait until the ground has thoroughly warmed up before sowing. Other growers have had success sowing the seed anytime after the temperature stabilizes at about 50°F. Scatter the seed thinly and gently tamp in with the back of a hoe but do not cover—oregano seed germinates better with light.

Indoors, you have several options for starting oregano seed. The old-time way is to fill flats with damp sphagnum moss, sprinkle the seeds on top, cover the flat with glass, and place in a warm place. Several seed-starting systems now on the market can help indoor sowers achieve greater success. Any of these seed-starting systems except the APS can be set on a propagation mat for gentle bottom heat which speeds germination.

You can also achieve pretty good results by using the plastic and Styrofoam trays in which some grocery store produce items are sold. Simply punch holes in the bottom to allow for drainage, fill with moistened, light potting mix, sprinkle the seed on top, and cover loosely with clear plastic wrap. The warmth on the top of a refrigerator or television set makes a good substitute for a propagation mat. However you start the seed, gradually remove the plastic cover as the sprouts push up to avoid rotting.

Once they have at least two true leaves, preferably more, seedlings should be "hardened off" for about a week before planting outside when the ground is thoroughly warm. To harden off, choose a spot that is cooler than where they've been sown, but not as cold as it may still be outside. The location should have bright light but not direct sun. A porch or cold frame or even a sheltered spot up against the house will do fine. Be sure to protect seedlings if the nights are very cold. Gradually move them out into a less-protected place by exposing them a few hours longer each day.

STARTING WITH PLANTS

If you buy your oregano plants at a nursery, rely more on appearance, aroma, and taste of the plant than on the label to know what you're getting. Some plants sold in nurseries as oregano are nearly tasteless, so if you're planting them for culinary use be brazen about pinching off a leaf and tasting it before you buy. The best way to know exactly what you are getting is to buy your oregano plants from a reliable herb farm or nursery where labeling is taken seriously and the people who work there are familiar enough with the growth habits of the individual varieties to advise you.

SEED-STARTING SYSTEMS

- The Accelerated Propagation System (APS) marketed by Gardener's Supply Company, is an insulated Styrofoam growing tray with capillary matting that wicks water from a reservoir underneath the seed tray. A clear plastic "greenhouse" cover holds in humidity and admits light. Germination with this system is remarkable—both germination rate and speed are higher than by any other method for many gardeners, including me. The units work best with professional germinating mix, a fine-textured blend of sphagnum peat and vermiculite, which you can also buy from Gardener's Supply, but you'll want to dust on a little extra dolomite to suit oregano's preference for limey conditions. The units come in several sizes. The ones with twenty-four cells per tray are best for oregano. Sprinkle a few seeds in each cell and thin later, if necessary, for strong transplants.

- Burpee sells Seed 'n Start trays. These are ten-cell plastic growing containers already filled with Burpee Seed Starting Formula, a tray for bottom watering, and a clear plastic cover to maintain humidity and let in light. These packs can be ordered as kits complete with oregano seed. Burpee also has self-watering seed starter trays with individual pots that allow you to lift out a single pot to pour in water into a channel-system tray, watering the pots from the bottom.

- Park Seed Company's Park-Starts Seed Starters are polystyrene 2 1/2 x 3 x 6-inch blocks with eighteen perforated planting cells. The perforations are filled with cylinders of pasteurized peat moss held together with a flexible water-absorbing binder. The cylinders are premoistened so all you do is sprinkle seeds on top. The blocks come with trays for bottom watering. Plants started this way come out as flexible little plugs that are easy to transplant.

- Shepherd's Garden Seeds sells Kord Fiber flats made from recycled pressed pulp in two sizes, 6 x 10- and 12 x 10-inch, as well as a commercial quality seed starting mix they recommend for use with the fiber flats. The flats are easy to move around and can be reused many times.

You may be surprised at how many different varieties of oregano are available to grow indoors and out—at least a dozen hardy and several tender ones, including the dittanies, which need winter protection. Aside from the difference in hardiness, oreganos all need about the same growing conditions—sun and friable, well-drained soil with a neutral to slightly limey pH.

Origanum vulgare. The hardy oregano most often grown is *Origanum vulgare*, of which there are several varieties, including dark oregano, compact oregano, and golden creeping oregano. Dark oregano (*Origanum*

vulgare var.) grows upright to a height of 2 feet, with 1/2-inch deep-green leaves and full, almost sharp, flavor. Compact oregano (*Origanum vulgare* 'Compactum Nanum') has good strong flavor, too, but grows only 2 to 3 inches high, spreading rapidly. It's good as a ground cover and in rock gardens. Because of its low growth habit it's also good for growing in a pot in a cool window indoors for winter seasoning. Golden creeping oregano (*Origanum vulgare* 'Aureum') grows to about 6 inches high. Especially suited to rock gardens, its golden-yellow leaves and spreading growth habit can make an entire bed look sunny. The plant is not only highly decorative, but its flavor is more mellow than the darker oreganos.

Origanum laevigatum. For ornamental use outside, *Origanum laevigatum* 'Herrenhausen' makes a wonderful show with deep purple flowers on strong 2-foot stems. The leaves are dark green. *Origanum laevigatum* 'Hopleys', which grows to about 18 inches, has showy flowers of dark lavender that bloom all summer. This is a good one for cooler climates; it's grown in England for hardiness. The flowers dry well. Another very hardy plant is *Origanum tytthanthum* 'Khirgizstan', which grows to about 18 inches and has full, bushy growth with glossy green leaves and rich pink flowers. This one also has fine flavor. A trailer grown for its flowers, though its leaves have the characteristic resinous odor, *Origanum* x 'Barbara Tingley' has soft textured leaves and lavender flowers that emerge from bracts drooping appealingly from the stem tips. *Origanum pulchellum* is also grown for its trailing foliage, which is silver gray, and for its cascading pink flowers. *Origanum* 'Kent Beauty' is a trailing herb with silver veins on oval leaves. The lavender flowers, which resemble hops, are good for drying to use in everlasting bouquets.

Origanum dictamnus. The tender dittany oreganos (*Origanum dictamnus*) are somewhat more difficult to grow than their hardy relatives but they're so pretty, especially in baskets, that it's worth the effort. These grow 6 to 10 inches high, need warmth in winter, and are finicky about water. The soil in which they grow should *almost* dry out between watering but not completely. If you find a block of potting mix dried out enough to shrink from the sides of the pot, you can be sure the dittany in it won't make it. On the other hand, the mix should never be so wet that you can squeeze it into a ball. The most vigorous of this group, dittany of Crete, can grow up to a foot in height. Its oval leaves are a fuzzy silver-white, the flowers are pink, and when grown successfully, this plant can be spectacular. But this is not an easy plant. At one time Thompson and Morgan offered cuttings of dittany of Crete as a houseplant but had trouble propagating enough to meet their orders. When we did receive rooted cuttings, many of us had trouble keeping them going. More difficult still is *Origanum dictamnus x microphyllum*, a miniature version with tiny leaves, that grows like a small shrub. In Greece dittanies grow wild in cracks in limestone walls. But in cold climates dittanies only survive as houseplants that enjoy an outdoor vacation in summer.

CARE

All oreganos look better if you cut them back hard once or twice a summer. When you grow oregano for culinary use and drying, cut the plants back to the base just before they flower. When you grow the showy oreganos for use in dried arrangements, cut the stems when they are in full flower. When you are growing oregano primarily for its ornamental value as a plant, indoors or out, you'll want to enjoy the plants' flowers and hold off pruning until the flowers begin to fade.

Continued ➜

Preserving Oregano

When you need to keep oregano for a few days, cut the stems close to the ground and then place the oregano, unwashed, in a resealable bag. Squeeze out as much air as possible before you seal the bag. The herb will stay in good condition in the refrigerator for about as long as lettuce would.

Air drying. For longer storage, the time-honored way of preserving most herbs is air drying. This is easy. Simply cut the stems, tie them together in bunches, and hang them upside down in a dry, dark place or in a paper bag for about two weeks or until the leaves fall from the stems when you rub them. A faster method is to lay the cut stems on a cookie sheet and keep them in a barely warm oven for about half a day. You can use the same approach with a dehydrator, following the manufacturer's directions for time and temperature. Any of these techniques will produce pretty good results—certainly providing better seasoning than you often get from commercially produced dried oregano, which tends to taste like pencil shavings.

Salt preserving. For fullest flavor, try preserving oregano in salt. This method, described by Mary Ann Esposito in her cookbook *Ciao Italia* results in a dried herb of such full flavor and aroma it almost seems fresh. Esposito says the method was used by the ancient Egyptians, Greeks, and Romans to preserve various herbs. Esposito uses coarse sea salt and sterilized pint jars; I have had success with less expensive kosher salt and cookie tins, sanitized but not sterilized, in the dishwasher.

Harvest the oregano early in the day. Wash it to remove all grit and dry it gently with tea towels. Spread the herbs out on a table or countertop for about half an hour to make sure all remaining moisture evaporates. Cover the bottom of your containers with about an inch of salt. Pluck sprigs of oregano from the main stem and lay them, not touching, on the bed of salt. Cover with about half an inch more salt and lay in more oregano sprigs. Continue layering in this way until the salt is about an inch from the top of the container. The final layer should be salt. Close the container and place it in the refrigerator or a cool place. The oregano will be dried in about a week and will keep almost indefinitely. To use, lift the oregano sprigs out of the salt. Almost no salt will cling to the leaves. You can rinse the leaves or use them as they are.

Freezing. Freezing oregano in tomato juice works well for adding to spaghetti and pizza sauces. Put about a tablespoonful of fresh oregano leaves in each cell of an ice cube tray. Fill the cells with tomato juice and freeze. After the cubes are frozen, remove them from the tray and seal in plastic freezer bags. You may use water instead of tomato juice, but using the juice avoids watering down your sauce as you season it.

Cooking with Oregano

A funny thing about those American soldiers who discovered oregano when they discovered pizza and Italian red sauces in Italy during World War II—they may not have realized it, but these same soldiers had enjoyed similar flavors at home when they ate poultry stuffings seasoned with marjoram. But in stuffings, the marjoram was teamed with thyme and sage. Since sage overpowers every other flavor, the marjoram didn't come through as a separate flavor. It took the combination of tomato sauce and oregano to bring the flavor of the *Origanums* to American attention.

Like marjoram, the oreganos team nicely with other herbs, and it would be a shame to limit them to tomato-based, Italian dishes.

Especially when used fresh, oregano leaves go well with cream sauces, eggs, and cheese.

When you use dried oregano instead of fresh, use about half as much. If you keep a pot of oregano growing in the house you'll have fresh oregano for those recipes where it really matters, and you can use dried oregano in soups and sauces where the fresh taste is less critical. The differences in flavor between dried and fresh oregano are interesting—both are good and each has its place. Because the essence of oregano is in its volatile oils, always add it to cooked dishes at the last minute. In butter and spreads it doesn't have to be cooked at all. And vinegar and oil infused with oregano provide another flavor that, while obviously oregano, is distinctly different from its taste in fresh or dried forms.

GREEK-STYLE FETA

This is served with bread and olives for breakfast in some restaurants in Athens.

1 block feta cheese (about 8 ounces)
3 tablespoons extra virgin cold-pressed olive oil
1 tablespoon coarsely ground black pepper
1/4 cup fresh oregano, chopped, or 1 to 2 tablespoons dried oregano

Rinse the feta, dry it with a paper towel, and place it in a shallow serving dish. Pour the olive oil over, sprinkle on the black pepper and oregano. Cover the cheese lightly with plastic wrap and allow to stand at room temperature for about an hour before serving with ripe olives and French bread.

CREAMY MUSHROOMS WITH HERBS

This recipe is an adaptation of a dish served at Grandview Lodge in Waynesville, N.C.

2 tablespoons butter
1 pound small white mushrooms
1/4 cup dry white wine
A dash of hot pepper sauce
1 tablespoon flour
1 cup sour cream
1/4 cup Parmesan cheese, freshly grated
2 tablespoons fresh oregano, chopped

Melt the butter in a heavy skillet and sauté the mushrooms until they just begin to brown. Add the wine and hot sauce. Remove pan from the heat just as the liquid evaporates. Mix flour and sour cream thoroughly, then stir into the mushrooms. Combine grated cheese and oregano and sprinkle over the mushrooms.

Serve with thin slices of toasted whole wheat bread as an hors d'oeuvre or with a salad and sliced tomatoes for a light supper.

MAKES 4 TO 6 SERVINGS

MARINATED TOMATOES

Save this recipe for summer when you have good fresh tomatoes and herbs.

4 medium-sized ripe tomatoes

2 tablespoons chives, chopped

1/4 cup fresh oregano, chopped

1/4 cup extra virgin cold-pressed olive oil

1 tablespoon balsamic vinegar

Coarse sea salt and coarsely ground pepper

Oregano sprigs for garnish

Choose firm, meaty tomatoes. Cut them in slices about 1/2-inch thick, and lay the slices in a shallow dish. You may need to make more than one layer. Combine the chopped chives, oregano, olive oil, and vinegar. Pour over the tomatoes and cover with plastic wrap. Allow to stand at room temperature about 30 minutes before serving. Sprinkle on salt and pepper to taste.

MAKES 6 SERVINGS

BOILED HERB DRESSING FOR POTATO OR CHICKEN SALAD

This dressing is especially tasty in chicken salad prepared from chicken cooked according to the recipe for Greek Chicken below.

1 1/2 tablespoons sugar

1/4 teaspoon salt

1 tablespoon flour

3/4 cup water

1/4 cup vinegar

2 eggs

1 teaspoon dry mustard

2 teaspoons butter

2 tablespoons fresh chopped oregano leaves

Mix together the sugar, salt, and flour in a small saucepan. Stir the cold water gradually into the dry ingredients. Stir in the vinegar. Beat the eggs and set aside. Turn on the heat and gradually cook and stir as the mixture simmers until it is thick enough to coat a spoon. Remove from the heat and allow to cool slightly while you mix the dry mustard with a small amount of the cooked ingredients and stir it into the pan. Pour about 1/4 of the boiled mixture into the beaten eggs, stirring rapidly with a fork or wire whisk as you do so. Then beat the egg mixture back into the pan. Return the pan to the heat and cook and stir on medium heat for about two more minutes. Remove from the heat and drop in the butter and oregano but do not stir. Set the pan in a bowl of ice to cool completely. After the dressing has cooled, beat the herbs and butter into it until it is smooth. Cover tightly and chill until ready to use.

MAKES ABOUT 1 1/4 CUPS DRESSING

ITALIAN BEAN SALAD

Here's a flavorful change from most bean salads—it's not as sweet as many of the old recipes. An old-world version is made with kidney beans, but pintos have more tender skins.

2 cups cooked or canned pinto beans, drained and rinsed

1 small clove garlic, pressed

1 teaspoon fresh gingerroot, finely minced

1/2 teaspoon dried oregano

1 green onion, minced

A dash of hot pepper sauce, such as Tabasco

1 tablespoon lemon juice

1/4 cup seedless raspberry jelly

1 tablespoon red wine vinegar

1/4 cup olive oil

Sprigs of fresh oregano for garnish

Combine all the ingredients and mix well. Cover tightly and chill at least overnight, longer if possible. The salad will keep for up to 7 days and tastes better after the first day or so.

MAKES ABOUT 2 CUPS

ITALIAN STYLE SALAD OF FRESH TUNA AND HERBS

You can substitute solid white canned tuna for the fresh tuna steaks, but the results are not as spectacular.

1/2 pound fresh tuna steaks

2 tablespoons olive oil

1 tablespoon dried oregano

1/2 cup chopped celery

2 green onions, chopped

1/4 cup chopped dill pickle

1 hard-cooked egg, chopped

2 tablespoons fresh oregano leaves, chopped

1 tablespoon capers

1/2 cup mayonnaise

Oregano sprigs and sliced tomatoes for garnish

Rub the tuna with the olive oil and dried oregano and allow to stand for 20 minutes while you start the charcoal. Grill the steaks until they are white all the way through. Any translucent spots indicate that the fish needs to cook a little longer. Remove from the grill and cool. Break the tuna into small pieces and refrigerate. When the tuna is thoroughly chilled, assemble the salad by mixing together the remaining ingredients and stirring them gently into the tuna. Refrigerate at least 30 minutes before serving. Garnish with oregano sprigs and sliced tomatoes.

SERVES 2

TOMATO SOUP WITH OREGANO

This light, low-fat tomato soup is full of flavor. The fresh oregano contrasts delicately.

2 tablespoons olive oil

1 medium onion, chopped

2 carrots, peeled and chopped

1 cup canned tomatoes (or cooked fresh)

Zest of one lemon

2 cups chicken or vegetable stock

2 tablespoons lemon juice

1/2 cup cooked rice

1/4 cup fresh oregano leaves (not chopped)

Heat the oil in a saucepan and sauté onions and carrots until the onion is soft. Add tomatoes, lemon zest, and stock. Simmer 30 minutes or

Continued ➤

until carrots are completely tender. Cool and purée in the food processor until smooth. Stir in lemon juice and reheat. To serve, place a spoonful of cooked rice in each bowl, pour soup on top, and garnish with a generous sprinkling of oregano leaves.

This soup is also good cold. Instead of reheating, chill several hours after puréeing. Omit the rice and add a spoonful of chopped raw cucumber to each bowl instead. Garnish with a dollop of yogurt as well as the oregano.

MAKES ABOUT 4 CUPS

GREEK CHICKEN

You need lots of fresh oregano to make this, but it's delicious and embarrassingly easy.

1 roasting chicken	1/2 lemon, cut in quarters
1 large handful oregano	Olive oil
1 whole bulb fresh garlic	

Rinse the chicken and pat dry with paper towels. Wash the oregano but don't worry about drying it. Separate the garlic into cloves and peel the cloves. Stuff the oregano, stems and all, into the cavity of the chicken. Put in the cloves of garlic and the lemon quarters. Tie the legs of the chicken together with a piece of string. Rub the chicken all over with olive oil and place in a shallow baking pan. Roast, uncovered, at 350°F about 20 to 30 minutes a pound, or until a meat thermometer inserted in the fleshy part of the thigh registers 190°F. It is not necessary to baste the bird as it roasts.

To serve, allow the chicken to cool until you can handle it, then remove all the meat from the bones and arrange it on a serving platter. Garnish with fresh oregano and lemon slices. Serve warm.

SERVES 6

LEAN HERB SAUSAGE

This Italian-style sausage is seasoned with oregano. The sausage marries well with tomato sauce and makes a nice pizza topping. Mixed with ground beef, it makes good meatballs.

1 teaspoon salt

1 tablespoon paprika

1/2 teaspoon fennel

1 tablespoon dried oregano

1 teaspoon black pepper

1 pound lean ground pork or use boneless pork chops, chopped in a food processor

Combine all the spices in a small dish and mix well. Stir into the ground pork and mix thoroughly, but do not pack. Refrigerate for several hours. If you want to taste the sausage to correct the seasoning when you're making it, fry a bit in a pan; do not taste uncooked sausage. To serve, shape lightly into small patties and brown in a heavy skillet. To use on pizza, dot the surface with small raw sausage pieces before baking.

THE ULTIMATE PIZZA

Using both fresh and dried oregano gives this pizza an extra dimension—a layering of flavors similar to the Paul Prudhomme practice of combining several different kinds of pepper. An automatic breadmaker makes this one of the easiest meals imaginable; even if you make the dough by hand it's very simple. The uncooked sauce is quick and tastes refreshingly light and fresh.

The crust

1 package active dry yeast	1 teaspoon salt
1 cup unbleached white bread flour	1 teaspoon dried oregano
1 cup whole wheat bread flour	1 teaspoon sugar
1 tablespoon corn meal	1 teaspoon olive oil
1 tablespoon wheat germ	1 cup warm water

Bread machine. Put all ingredients into the pan in the order listed, select the manual setting, and press start. Allow dough to rise until doubled.

By hand. Dissolve the yeast in the warm water and then beat in the remaining ingredients. When the dough forms a ball, turn it out onto a floured board and knead until smooth and shiny. This should take only a few minutes. Put the kneaded dough into a buttered bowl, cover with plastic wrap, and let rise until doubled.

To finish the crust, deflate the dough, let it rest for a few minutes and roll out into a circle about 16 inches in diameter or roll into a rectangle to fit a cookie sheet. Place the dough on a pan sprayed with no-stick vegetable cooking spray, and place the pan on the lower rack in a preheated 425°F oven for about 5 minutes. The dough should be baked through, but not browned. Remove from oven and cool. You can either freeze the crust or proceed with the recipe.

The sauce

1 10 3/4-ounce can tomato purée	1 tablespoon fresh oregano, minced
2 cloves fresh garlic, pressed	1 tablespoon Parmesan cheese

Combine all the ingredients. Brush the partially cooked pizza dough with olive oil and spread the sauce evenly over it. Add cheese and toppings. Place the pan on the bottom rack in a 450°F oven. Bake about 15 minutes, depending on your oven.

MAKES ONE 11 X 16" PIZZA

OREGANO BREAD

Perfect with creamy pasta dishes and soups. It takes a little time to bake yeast breads but, after cooling the loaves thoroughly, you can freeze some for instant bread-and-soup suppers later.

2 envelopes active dry yeast	1 tablespoon dried oregano leaves
2 cups warm water	1 tablespoon dried parsley leaves
1 teaspoon sugar	4 teaspoons salt
1/4 cup vegetable oil	6 1/2 cups (approximately) unbleached white flour
2 tablespoons honey	
1/2 cup wheat germ	

Sprinkle yeast over warm water in a large bowl. Stir to dissolve. Add sugar, and let stand until the mixture bubbles. Add oil, honey, wheat germ, seasonings, and 2 cups of the flour. Beat until smooth and shiny; then beat in enough more flour to make a dough you can handle. Turn dough out onto a floured board and knead until smooth and elastic. Place in a greased bowl and let stand in a warm place until dough doubles in bulk—about an hour. Punch down and shape into four long, skinny loaves on greased cookie sheets. Brush the tops lightly with oil. Cover and let rise in a warm place until almost double in bulk—about 45 minutes. Cut three diagonal slashes on top of each loaf. Bake at 400°F for about 30 minutes. Do not wrap the loaves until they are completely cool.

MAKES FOUR LOAVES

EASY VEGETARIAN LASAGNA

The sauce

1 tablespoon olive oil

1 green onion, chopped

3 fresh mushrooms, sliced

2 cloves fresh garlic, pressed or minced

1 teaspoon dried minced onion

1 28-ounce can crushed tomatoes

1 teaspoon dried oregano

6 to 8 dried lasagna noodles

Sauté the green onion and mushrooms in olive oil until barely soft. Pour in the crushed tomatoes and bring to a light simmer. Add the fresh garlic, dried onion, and dried oregano. Simmer about 20 minutes, until the mixture is saucelike. Spread about 1/2 cup of the sauce in the bottom of a 6 1/2 x 10 baking dish. Lay in three or four of the uncooked lasagna noodles so that the edges of each noodle just barely overlap.

The filling

1 15- or 16-ounce container of light ricotta cheese

2 eggs

1 tablespoon fresh chopped oregano (or 1 teaspoon dried)

A pinch of nutmeg

1 to 2 cups chopped broccoli, cauliflower, carrots

2 to 4 tablespoons water

3 to 4 slices provolone cheese

Oregano for garnish

Use a fork to beat together the ricotta, eggs, oregano, and nutmeg until the eggs are thoroughly incorporated. Spread the filling evenly over the noodles.

Steam the chopped vegetables 2 minutes and immediately drain thoroughly. Spread vegetables over the ricotta filling.

Arrange the remaining noodles over the vegetables. Pour sauce over all, pushing the noodles away from the sides of the baking dish to allow the sauce to run down into the lasagna. You may not need all the sauce to cover the lasagna. Save any extra sauce to heat and serve on the side. Add 2 tablespoons of water to the lasagna pan. Cover with aluminum foil and crimp tightly against the sides of the pan.

Place the lasagna in a cold oven. Set the heat for 350°F, and bake for 15 minutes, then reduce heat to 325°F and bake for an hour more. Test to see if the noodles are tender. If not, add another tablespoon of water, re-crimp the aluminum foil and return the lasagna to the oven for an additional 20 minutes or so. When the noodles are tender, remove the foil, arrange the cheese slices over the top of the lasagna, and return to the oven just long enough to melt the cheese. Remove from oven and allow to stand at least 30 minutes before serving. Garnish with a generous bouquet of fresh oregano sprigs.

MAKES 6 TO 8 SERVINGS

Growing and Cooking with Mint

Glenn Andrews

Illustrations by Alison Kolesar

The Many Varieties of Mint

The Mint Family includes basil, summer savory, and marjoram, but the ones we're concerned with here are the actual *Mentha* varieties, including pennyroyal.

Mint is a hardy perennial, dying back in the winter in cold climates and emerging in the spring. It is best propagated by cuttings or plants, not seeds. (It will root readily in water, though not if your water is heavily treated with chemicals.) Some seed catalogs offer mint seed, but often with the warning that mints grown from seed are not uniform and that their flavor will range from spearmint to peppermint.

The two most popular mints are spearmint and peppermint, but there are many other varieties. Perhaps you can find a friend who will be happy to give you plants or cuttings, or you may find just what you want at a local nursery. In either case, you might want to break off a leaf, scrunch it up in your fingers and smell it, then take a taste. You'll know right away whether you're going to like it. (I've been doing this for years and have never been reprimanded. But then, I've never been caught!) Here are some of the varieties that exist:

Spearmint (*Mentha spicata*). The old favorite of cooks around the world. If you can only have one mint, I strongly recommend that you choose either spearmint or applemint, which has a similar taste. This is not just a matter of personal taste; spearmint is milder than peppermint and seems to lend itself better to many sorts of dishes. Its leaves are larger, too, which comes in handy in cooking, and the plants thrive almost anywhere. The plant has bright green leaves, which are shaped like spearheads. It grows to 2 feet, sometimes higher.

Spearmint

An interesting variety is *Mentha spicata* 'Chewing Gum', which has a strong spearmint flavor and mahogany foliage, and the scent of chewing gum.

Peppermint (*Mentha x piperita*). This mint features purple stems with dark green leaves, and is great for tea and for medicinal uses. It does have one problem: it should be moved every 2 to 3 years. Some cooks find it a bit harsh for culinary use. This plant typically grows to 2 feet.

Applemint (*Mentha rotundifolia*). This is every grandma's favorite mint. It has excellent flavor, but wilts quickly after picking. The

Continued →

light green leaves are somewhat woolly in appearance and the plant typically grows to 3 feet.

English applemint (*Mentha suaveolens*). This variety is easily grown (even more so than most mints), and doesn't need as much moisture as others. It is very good for all sorts of cooking and its light green foliage is good for making candied leaves. It grows to 2 feet in height.

Pineapplemint (*Mentha suaveolens* 'Variegata'). This variety has a pleasant aroma similar to a ripe pineapple, and is nice in iced tea. The plant's green leaves are edged with white, and it typically grows to 2 feet in height.

Peppermint

Orangemint (*Mentha x piperita* 'Citrata'). Also known as bergamot mint and Eau de Cologne mint, or Lavendar mint, this mint seems to vary in scent from plant to plant, hence the multiplicity of names. It is especially enjoyable in teas (hot or iced), punches, potpourris, and salads, and is the choice mint for Mint Juleps (see next page). The plant has dark green leaves, and grows to 2 feet tall.

Chocolate mint (*Mentha x piperita* 'Chocolate'). The aroma is as evocative of chocolate-covered mint patties as the name. Usually used in conjunction with sugar—in desserts and ices, the plant has dark green leaves and grows to 18 inches in height.

Orangemint

Variegated Scotch mint (*Mentha x gentilis* 'Variegata'). This plant has a mild spearmint taste. Its appeal is in its coloring: striking gold and green variegated leaves. It grows to 1 foot tall.

Corsican mint (*Mentha requiennii*). This mint makes a superb and extremely aromatic ground cover, especially in moist shade, where many plants fail. It has tiny leaves, and the plant itself is extremely small—it grows to about 1 inch in height. This mint is not reliably hardy in cold climates.

Horsemint (*Mentha longifolia*). This is one of the wild mints. Its flavor and aroma are between spearmint and peppermint. The plant is covered with fine white hairs, and grows to 2 feet tall.

Native mint (*Mentha arvensis*). This plant is the original wild mint native to the northern reaches of North America. It is suitable for any mint use. This mint is easy to spot because its tiny lavender flowers don't form on stalks, rather they grow in little circles around the stem just above the spot where each pair of leaves emerges. The plant grows to 2 feet.

English pennyroyal (*Mentha pulegium*). Another good ground cover, this mint spreads rapidly. It is famous as an insect repellent, because it smells somewhat like citronella. English pennyroyal is very low-growing and mat-like, but flower stalks grow to 18 inches in height. It cannot withstand frost, so for those who live in cold climates, this is one mint perhaps better grown from seed.

Growing Mint

Whatever mint you choose, you now have to decide where to plant it. The old wisdom says to plant your mint directly under or next to an outside water faucet. This system really works beautifully, and tells you

something about the nature of mint—it needs lots of water. But soggy, boggy soil won't do; mint needs good drainage.

Mint also thrives best with a little shade in the course of the day. Three hours of sun is perfect, but it's an amenable plant and will try to get along with somewhat more or less. In fact, commercial growers get good results planting mint in full sun.

Like most herbs, mint doesn't need a lot of fertilizer, although it does appreciate a little well-rotted compost twice a summer. Don't apply fresh manure as it could spread rust disease.

The main thing mint needs is a home of its own. It's a wanderer. Don't try to include it in a lovely little well-mannered herb garden, as it will take over. One preventative for this is to sink a 6-inch piece of metal edging to define where you want the mint to grow. (Some say to make the edging go down 18 inches.) Others will tell you to plant it in a bottomless bucket or flower pot. But it is simpler just to give mint its own spot of land, which you can then refer to as the "mint patch."

I've read that one way to make mint stay where you want it to be is to cut down through the roots with an edger, but in my experience, new sprouts will appear wherever you do this, as though you're offering the mint a challenge. One way or another, it's hard to imagine ever having a shortage of mint once your patch is established!

Keep mint from wandering by edging around your mint patch.

As the mint grows, snip off all buds before they have a chance to flower. And as you pick mint, make your cuts right above the spot where leaves come out of the stem. You'll usually find that two new sprigs will emerge from the spot where you removed one.

As fall approaches, if you live where there will be frost, don't cut mint back more than halfway.

Trim mint just above the spot where leaves come out of the stem.

Keeping Mint on Hand

Even with the portable window box trick, there's still a small period of each year when you have to do without fresh mint.

For cooking purposes, this shouldn't bother you too much, as long as you have preserved a good quantity of mint by drying or freezing it.

Before you can dry or freeze mint you need to harvest, which means large-scale mint-picking. This can be done two or three times throughout the summer, as long as you remember to remove the buds before they flower. It's best to harvest your mint crop in mid-morning on a sunny day. The early-morning dew will be gone, and the mint will be at the height of its vigor. As I mentioned before, don't cut the plants back more than halfway as fall approaches.

Next, most authorities will tell you to wash the mint, then carefully and quickly dry it—a tricky process. To me, this is totally unnecessary if you've grown your own mint and know it is uncontaminated by pesticides or weed killers. Do, however, brush it off to remove any dirt that may be clinging to the leaves.

DRYING MINT

Drying is the age-old way of preserving all herbs, including mint. The old ways involve either setting the mint sprigs on trays to dry or gathering the stems into bundles, tying them together, and hanging them, heads down, to dry. This latter way is picturesque and pretty; herbs hanging from a rafter in an old kitchen add a great air of colonial thrift!

But neither of these ways of drying yields a superior product. Mint dried in these ways may mildew, it may lose much of its flavor, and its color may fade.

It's only recently been discovered that the perfect way to home-dry herbs is in the microwave oven. (I was glad to learn of something to do with mine aside from thawing frozen foods!) The system couldn't be simpler. Barring a microwave oven, a food dehydrator is also a great way to dry mint. There are many on the market now. They are easy to use and dry foods quickly without losing their flavor.

MICROWAVE MINT

To dry mint in the microwave oven: Put a double layer of white paper towels on the floor of a microwave oven. On this spread out a handful or two of fresh mint, in one layer. Make sure you have removed any hard, woody stems; soft, new stems can be dried right along with the leaves. Do not cover.

Microwave on high for 4 minutes, and that's it!

You now have absolutely perfect dried mint! Store in an airtight bag or container in a dark place and it will give you many months of cooking pleasure.

FREEZING MINT

Mint freezes fairly well, though it becomes limp and can't be used for a garnish the way fresh mint can. But it has all the flavor and color you could want and is great in many dishes. Freezing mint is even easier than the almost-instant drying method described above.

To freeze mint, simply pack clean mint sprigs or leaves in airtight bags or freezer containers and put them in your freezer! (If you do feel you have to wash the mint first, be sure it's thoroughly dry before it goes into the freezer.)

SUBSTITUTING DRIED MINT FOR FRESH

As with any herb, fresh is better than dry. But dry mint is excellent and is called for in many Middle Eastern recipes. There's a simple rule of thumb: Use I part of dry mint for every 3 parts of fresh mint called for in a recipe.

In some situations you need the look and texture of fresh greenery. So go ahead and substitute the dry mint for fresh—but add as much minced leaf lettuce, parsley, or spinach as the amount of mint called for.

Cooking with Mint

In these recipes, I have not specified which mint to use. Any mint is a great mint! Personally, I tend to be partial to spearmint, applemint, and orangemint. But use what you prefer.

MINTED CHEESE SPREAD

You've had commercial herb-and-garlic cheese, I'm sure, and perhaps black pepper cheese. They're popular and good, but this one's better.

8 ounces cream cheese

1 tablespoon milk

1 tablespoon white wine

1/2 teaspoon freshly ground black pepper

1 medium garlic clove, finely minced

1 tablespoon minced fresh mint (or 1 teaspoon dry mint and 1 tablespoon minced parsley, lettuce, or spinach)

1/2 tablespoon minced chives (optional)

Combine all the ingredients (a food processor works well for this, but it can also be done with a fork). Chill, covered, for several hours. Serve with toast squares or crackers. It will keep refrigerated and covered for up to a couple of weeks.

MAKES ABOUT I CUP

ZUCCHINI-MINT SOUP

This is a terrific, fresh-tasting soup. Needless to say, it can be made with any other summer squash—it just won't be as green.

2 tablespoons butter or margarine

2 large onions, minced

6 zucchini, about 4 inches long, thinly sliced

4 cups chicken broth

1/4 cup minced mint

Salt and freshly ground black pepper to taste

Melt the butter in a medium-sized saucepan and sauté the onions over medium heat until they're nicely limp. Add the squash, stir well, then add the chicken broth. Cover and simmer until the squash is tender—say 15 minutes. Season to taste.

Now purée the soup by running it in a food processor or blender or through a food mill. Then stir in the mint. Serve now or chill first, if you prefer a cold soup. (But if you do serve it cold, check the seasoning before serving.)

SERVES 4

COLD CUCUMBER-MINT SOUP

The old phrase "cool as a cucumber" should perhaps be changed to "Cool as Cucumber-Mint Soup." What a treat to have some of this in your refrigerator when the hottest days of summer threaten to wilt you!

Continued →

2 tablespoons butter or margarine

3 medium-sized cucumbers, peeled and thinly sliced

1 medium onion, thinly sliced

3 cups chicken broth, divided

1/3 cup minced mint

1 cup cream, milk, sour cream, or yogurt

Salt and white pepper (freshly ground if possible) to taste

Melt the butter in a medium-sized saucepan, and cook the cucumber and onion slices until they are limp and somewhat translucent. Add 1 cup of the chicken broth and run in a food processor or blender or through a food mill.

Add the remaining 2 cups of broth, then chill. When cold, add the mint and 1 cup of whichever dairy product you choose. Season to taste.

SERVES 4

POTATOES WITH GARLIC AND MINT

This is one of the most tempting of all potato dishes, and well illustrates garlic's affinity for mint. I'm giving you two versions—one to be made in a microwave oven, one in a conventional oven—since the microwave way does seem to imbue every fiber of the potatoes with the other flavors. (And yet not everyone owns one of these space-age marvels.)

1 1/2 pounds small potatoes (if you can find Yukon Gold or other yellow potatoes, they're especially pretty here)

2 teaspoons minced garlic

1/4 cup olive oil

1/4 cup minced mint

Salt and freshly ground black pepper to taste

Conventional oven: Poke holes in the potatoes with a fork, then bake at 400°F for 1 hour. Now cut them up into convenient-size pieces and toss with the other ingredients.

Microwave oven: Cut the potatoes into small pieces. Put them into a microwave-safe dish with all the other ingredients except the mint. Cook, covered for 10 minutes on high (or for 15 minutes in a low-power oven). Stir in the mint.

SERVES 4 TO 6

MARINATED LAMB CHOPS WITH MINT BUTTER

When I want a real treat, I often turn to these chops.

4 lamb chops (thick loin chops if you're feeling flush, otherwise shoulder chops)

Salt and freshly ground black pepper to taste

3 tablespoons olive oil

1 tablespoon minced mint leaves

Sprinkle the lamb chops on both sides with salt and quite a bit of freshly ground black pepper, then sprinkle on the olive oil and the mint leaves. Marinate the chops for at least an hour at room temperature, turning them over several times. Marinating them for 2–6 or more hours will impart more flavor to the meat.

Meanwhile, make the mint butter (see below).

Broil the chops over fairly hot coals or on a rack in a hot broiler until brown on both sides. Serve with a little of the mint butter on top of each chop.

SERVES 4

MINT BUTTER

This herb butter is especially good on lamb chops, but it's also great added to any vegetable just before serving. It can be made in larger quantities and kept refrigerated or frozen until you need it.

3 tablespoons unsalted butter, at room temperature

2 tablespoons minced mint

2 teaspoons minced chives (optional)

1 teaspoon fresh lemon juice

Salt and freshly ground black pepper (optional)

Combine all the ingredients in the order given. Chill until needed.

MAKES ABOUT 4 TABLESPOONS

HONEY-GLAZED CARROTS WITH MINT

Try these with your Thanksgiving turkey—or to add a touch of bright color and a lot of fantastic taste to any meal.

1 pound carrots, peeled only if they're old

3 tablespoons butter or margarine

3 tablespoons honey

2 tablespoons minced mint

Slice the carrots fairly thinly on the diagonal, so you have long oval pieces. Put into a medium-sized saucepan with enough water to cover and boil gently, covered, for 10 to 15 minutes or until barely tender. Drain.

Add the butter or margarine and the honey to the saucepan, and cook and stir over medium heat, uncovered, until the carrots are glazed—just a few minutes. Add the mint and cook and stir for 2 minutes more.

SERVES 4

NEW POTATO SALAD WITH MINT

Any potato salad would benefit from the addition of a little mint, but salad made of new potatoes becomes quite spectacular when given this treatment.

This is one case where dried mint cannot be substituted for fresh.

1 1/2 pounds new potatoes (particularly red ones), scrubbed but not peeled

1/2 teaspoon salt

1/2 cup mayonnaise

6 grinds of a pepper mill

1/4 cup minced scallions

2 tablespoons minced red or green sweet peppers

1/4 cup minced mint leaves

Boil the potatoes in water to cover for about 10 minutes, or until tender, but not falling apart. Drain, then cut them into halves if they're very small, quarters if they're a bit bigger.

Mix all the other ingredients in a medium-sized bowl, then stir in the potato pieces. Chill.

SERVES 4 TO 6

TABOULEH

Tabouleh (sometimes spelled Tabouli) is a Middle Eastern salad which has become very popular in this country.

Why? Well—it's unusual, and that's a plus to many people. It's also good for you, and it can be—should be—made ahead. But most important of all, it's an excellent dish!

Don't let only 1 cup of wheat make you think this is a small portion—the wheat expands considerably as it soaks.

1 cup cracked wheat (also known as bulghur or bulghur wheat)

3 cups water

3 tablespoons minced fresh mint

3 tablespoons minced parsley

3 tablespoons minced scallions

3 tablespoons olive oil

3 tablespoons freshly squeezed lemon juice

Salt and freshly ground black pepper to taste

Romaine or other crisp lettuce

Soak the wheat in the water for 1 hour, then squeeze out all the water you can and spread the wheat out onto paper towels or a cloth to dry for 20 minutes.

Now put the wheat in a dry bowl and mix in all the other ingredients. Serve on romaine or other lettuce leaves.

Garnish, if you wish, with bits of cucumber and tomato, but don't mix them in, since their juices will dilute the salad's flavor.

SERVES 4

MINT MARINADE AND BASTE FOR KEBABS

This recipe is particularly good on lamb kebabs, but it will also add spice to other meats, poultry, and vegetables.

1/2 cup wine vinegar

1/2 cup chopped mint leaves

1/4 cup minced onion

1 small clove garlic, minced or pressed

2 tablespoons salad oil

Salt and freshly ground black pepper to taste

Combine all the ingredients, then use to marinate meat for about 2 hours. Put meat onto skewers, then baste with the same mixture every time you turn the meat as it cooks.

For vegetables, skip the marinating. Just baste as they cook. Try chunks of eggplant, tomatoes, or summer squash, such as zucchini.

MAKES ABOUT 1 CUP

A PROPER KENTUCKY DERBY MINT JULEP

Kentuckians—and the honorary ones who go there for the Derby or who celebrate this great horse race elsewhere—care deeply about their Mint Juleps. Most recipes require the use of silver julep cups, but don't worry if you don't happen to have them—these will still taste great.

These directions will make 1 mint julep. To make more, just multiply all the ingredients by the number of people you plan to serve.

1/2 tablespoon sugar

1 tablespoon minced mint leaves (fresh only)

1 tablespoon water

Crushed ice—lots of it

1 1/2 ounces Kentucky bourbon

A large sprig of fresh mint

1 straw, cut in half

Put the sugar and minced mint leaves into a small bowl. Using the back of a wooden spoon or a special wooden muddler made from lignum vitae which can be bought in good hardware stores, mash the sugar and mint until a paste is formed. Add the water and stir for a minute or two more.

Fill your julep cup or glass half full of crushed ice. Pour in the bourbon and the sugar-mint mixture, then fill the rest of the glass with more crushed ice. Stick the large sprig of mint into the glass along with the straws.

Put on a tray, then place in your refrigerator or freezer for 1 hour to frost the glasses or cups.

SERVES 1

CRYSTALLIZED MINT LEAVES

These little beauties can be eaten as candy, but their best-known use is as a garnish for desserts. They'll keep for months in airtight tins. (But be sure to store them in layers separated by sheets of parchment paper or plain white paper.)

You can use the same system for home-grown, unsprayed violets, pansies, borage, crabapple blossoms, or rose petals. The mint's the best, though!

1 cup water

2 cups sugar

1/4 teaspoon cream of tartar

4 drops lemon juice

About 1 quart (not packed) large fresh mint leaves (spearmint is most often used)

Put the water in a large, deep pan. Add the sugar and cook over medium-high heat, stirring, until the sugar is dissolved. Now stir in the cream of tartar and continue to cook until the syrup reaches the soft-crack stage—about 280°F. Remove from the heat and set the pan in a bowl of ice water. Stir in the lemon juice.

When the syrup has cooled enough so it won't burn your fingers, start coating the mint leaves (or blossoms) with it. Drop in a small handful at a time, stir gently, then remove them to parchment or white (typewriter) paper with a slotted spoon, separating them with your fingers.

When thoroughly dry, your crystallized gems can be stored on paper in airtight tins.

There are simpler ways of making crystallized mint leaves and other flowers, but since they involve raw egg white, I can't recommend them. Raw egg whites are not recommended for human consumption due to the concern about possible salmonella poisoning. Too bad, too. But the method given above isn't nearly as tricky or difficult as it may sound.

Patti Barrett

Illustrations by Judy Eliason, Alison Kolesar, and Brigita Fuhrmann

Types of Lavender

Lavender has many varieties of varying degrees of hardiness. In places like California it is possible to grow many tender species of lavender, whereas in the Northeastern United States these tender plants will not make it through the winter and must be treated as annuals (replanted each spring). Some of the hardier varieties will make it through the colder weather with protection, up to and including zone 4, but if it's a hard winter with little snow cover even these hardy plants may not last. It is a good idea to experiment with a few varieties, seeing which work best where you garden. In this way you may find some species that you cannot live without and will plant every spring and others that are hardier and will live for many years without replanting.

HARDY LAVENDERS

Native to the Mediterranean area, hardy lavenders are sometimes known as English lavenders. They are well-suited to English climate conditions and like the long hours of summer daylight without excessive heat. All of the hardy lavenders have gray foliage and flowers arranged in a spike. The flowers are generally lavender in color.

Hardy lavenders are considered perennials though they can be grown as annuals in areas where they will not winter-over well. They don't grow quite as tall as the tender lavenders and they flower only once a year. Some of the world's finest oil of lavender comes from the flowers of these plants. This oil is very intense in fragrance—it is from these plants that we get the lavender oil that is distilled into perfume.

These garden lavenders can live through the winter in zones 5 through 8. They are mostly shrubby plants and have narrow gray leaves. The old plants can look good throughout the winter as they sit in the garden with their woody stems. New growth is more green than gray.

The narrow leaves of different varieties vary in size on different parts of the plants, and some flower spikes are tapered while others are blunt. The stems that carry the flowers are square, rise above the foliage, and harden after the plant goes to seed.

Some of the varieties in this group include:

Dwarf Munstead, *Lavandula angustifolia* 'Dwarf Munstead'

This cultivar, named after gardener and garden writer Gertrude Jekyll's home in England, is the earliest to bloom, showing flowers in the second year from seed. Its flower spikes are a true lavender color, and the two-lipped flowers are closely packed together at the ends of the stems. It is a low-growing, compact bush with many heads of lavender-blue flowers growing on stems that are about 4 inches in length. A popular variety, Munstead does well in garden beds or can be planted in containers.

Folgate Blue, *Lavandula angustifolia* 'Folgate Blue'

'Folgate Blue' has a growing habit similar to 'Dwarf Munstead', but has "bluer" flowers and grows into a slightly larger bush.

Grey Hedge, *Lavandula angustifolia* 'Grey Hedge'

'Grey Hedge' is a taller variety than 'Dwarf Munstead' or 'Folgate Blue', with silver-gray foliage. The flower spikes are thin and pointed, and the flowers are mauve.

Hidcote Purple, *Lavandula angustifolia* 'Hidcote Purple'

Known for its dark purple spikes, which can be striking in a garden setting, 'Hidcote Purple' grows nearly 24 to 30 inches high and has lovely long blossoms.

Old English, *Lavandula angustifolia* 'Old English'

Leaves on 'Old English' are broader and greener than those of 'Grey Hedge'. It has narrow, mauve-colored flower spikes.

Seal, *Lavandula angustifolia* 'Seal'

A tall plant that can reach 3 feet in height under the right growing conditions, 'Seal' is a free-flowering plant with very long stems. The leaves are gray-green and flowers a blue-mauve. It can bloom for extended periods of time, up to four months, in gardens where it thrives.

Twickel Purple, *Lavandula angustifolia* 'Twickel Purple'

'Twickel Purple' is unusual in that its spikes grow in a fan formation. It is smaller than 'Hidcote Purple' with long, deep mauve flower spikes.

Broad-leafed Lavender, *Lavandula latifolia*

This is a much broader-leafed plant that is less free-flowering than those above. It has received the most attention commercially because of its fragrant oil. The foliage of *Lavandula latifolia* is a clear gray color and slender. Branched stalks carry flower spikes similar to those of many lavenders, although they aren't as showy as most. In France, *Lavandula latifolia* is also known as aspic lavender, said to be a name that refers to a belief that small poisonous snakes lived in the plant. But it may be more likely that the name comes from the word "espic," meaning "spike."

Dutch Lavender, *Lavandula x intermedia*

Dutch lavender is a cross between *Lavandula angustifolia* and *Lavandula latifolia*. It has narrower leaves than the latter and is broader than the former. The flowers are in long, branched spikes. These plants bloom later than the low-growing lavenders and tend to have a good strong scent.

Pink Lavender, *Lavandula angustifolia* 'Rosea'

Pink lavender has about the same growth characteristics as 'Folgate Blue', upright with narrow leaves. Its flowers, as its name describes, are a light pink that stand out well against the silver-gray foliage.

White Lavender, *Lavandula angustifolia* 'Alba'

White lavender has spikes of white flowers. Its leaves are long compared to other varieties, growing broad and quite silver. It is not abundantly free-flowering but has a pure lavender fragrance. Some white lavenders are dwarf, growing to just 6 inches high with short, narrow, gray leaves and tiny heads of white flowers.

Woolly Lavender, *Lavandula lanata*

Lavandula lanata is a sweet-scented lavender. It is a short shrub, 2 to 3 feet tall, and can grow as wide. The leaves are a light gray, about two inches long, and look thin because the margins are rolled under. The plant has a woolly appearance that comes from many tiny hairs on the leaf and stem surfaces. The flower spike can be up to a foot long, and is unusual in that several small flower heads can grow along the spike. Dark blue flowers cover the heads.

TENDER LAVENDERS

Native to Spain and southern France, tender lavenders are sometimes known as French lavenders. They are distinguished from other lavenders by the colored bracts at the tops of the flower heads. These bracts are so showy that they are often mistaken for the flowers, but are really only colored leaves.

These are known as the "tender" lavenders because they need to grow in full sun and in a richer soil than the hardy varieties. The tender lavenders may grow up to three feet in height in frost-free areas. Flower stems of tender lavenders tend to be weaker and more arching than the hardier types, and leaves tend to be more green than gray.

LAVANDULA STOECHAS

Lavandula stoechas is the lavender of history that was used as a disinfectant from the time of ancient Rome until the Middle Ages. The gray-green pointed foliage of this variety has a distinct pungent, soft camphorous fragrance.

The flower spike of *Lavandula stoechas* is compressed into an irregular globe shape on which small lavender flowers hide between flat purple bracts. Two long purple bracts point upward from the top of the flower head, reaching as high as 1 1/2 inches in length.

In France, where this variety is common, the plants grow along the southern coast in acid soils. The plant's name, *stoechas*, comes from Stoechades, an ancient name for the islands on the Mediterranean harbor off today's Hyères, France.

LAVANDULA DENTATA

This plant has dainty green leaves, toothed along the margins. Also called Spanish or French lavender, the fragrance of its foliage is a bit camphorous with a hint of balsam. The small, lavender flowers on long stems open successively on the thin cone-shaped head, which is topped with lavender bracts. They flower prolifically much of the year. The scent is not as lasting as that of the English lavender. In warm conditions, *Lavandula dentata* can grow as much as three feet in height and width if not pruned.

LAVANDULA DENTATA CANDICANS

This is similar to *Lavandula dentata* but the foliage is heavier and grayer. It is hardier than *Lavandula dentata* and a more vigorous grower.

LAVANDULA STOECHAS SSP. PEDUNCULATA

Also known as Spanish lavender, this is an upright perennial with long, narrow, green-gray leaves and long, magenta-purple bracts.

LAVANDULA VIRIDIS

Lavandula viridis, also known as the green lavender, is a perennial with long, narrow, sticky green leaves and a pine-lavender scent. It has medium-length stalks. The bracts and the tiny flowers, set in a greenish cone, are creamy white.

LAVANDULA HETEROPHYLLA

Lavandula heterophylla, also known as sweet lavender, has silver-gray leaves which are sometimes toothed along the edges. The plants can grow up to three feet in height and have deep lavender flowers.

OTHER LAVENDERS

Lavandula multifida

These lavenders, while not that common, are interesting plants. They have green, fern-like leaves from which the name *multifida* (meaning "much divided") comes. The plants are upright in growth with strong, square stems. Flowers occur in winged spikes and are deep lavender. The flowers bloom for up to six months at a time, with most of them coming on in late summer. Native to North Africa and Portugal, these very tender plants need protection in winter.

Lavandula pinnata

This is a delicate lavender with lilac-blue flowers that will appear almost year-round if the plant is sheltered. It has soft, gray-green leaves. The entire plant is covered with short white hairs giving it a slightly fuzzy appearance. *Lavandula pinnata* can grow up to three feet in height.

Growing and Culture

PROPAGATION

Tender lavender is fairly easy to propagate by seed, cuttings, or layering. Hardy lavendar is best propagated by cuttings or layering.

By seed. To start seed indoors, choose a seed flat with good drainage and fill it to within 1 inch of the top with sterile potting mixture.

Water liberally but gently with a fine spray that will not disturb the seeds. Place the seed flat in a plastic bag. You should not have to do any more watering until the seedlings come up, in about 14 days. Put them

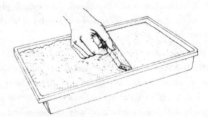

Sift a 1/2-inch layer of clean sand over the top. Level the surface with a flat board.

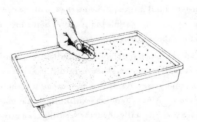

Spread the seed over the soil, evenly and not too thickly, then press the seeds in with the flat side of the board.

Continued →

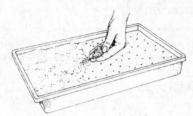

Sprinkle soil over seeds until they are just covered.

Use a flat board to firm the soil a second time.

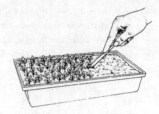

Using a ladle, spoon handle, fork, or similar tool, gently lift the seedlings from the flat.

in a place where the temperature remains at about 70–75°F. As soon as the seeds germinate, remove the plastic covering and place the seed flat in an unshaded south window or under fluorescent lights.

Keep the soil mixture moist, but never completely wet, or the seedlings will rot. If the medium starts to lighten in color, that is a sign that it is drying out. Check every day to see if water is needed. Watering from the bottom is best until the seedlings reach a fairly good size, since watering from above can dislodge young plants or knock them over. If you do water from above, water between the seedling rows.

If seedlings are grown on the windowsill or at the edge of the lighted area, they should be turned regularly so they will grow straight and evenly.

Once the first true leaves have developed, use a soluble plant food at one-quarter the label strength; increase to one-half the label strength as the plants mature.

It is possible to plant seedlings directly from the seed flat to the garden, but this is generally not advised. Seedlings should be transplanted to a larger container first, so they will not be crowded, leggy, weak, or susceptible to damage. A flat with dividers or compartments leads to more compact root development and easier transplanting, without shock to the roots.

After the seedlings have developed four true leaves, it is time to transplant. First water the seedlings thoroughly. Fill the new container with pre-moistened soil mix to just below the top of the container. With a label stick or pencil, open a hole in the center of the mix, deep and wide enough to fit the seedling's roots.

Using a ladle, spoon handle, fork, or similar tool, gently lift the seedlings from the flat. Separate them carefully so as not to break any more roots than necessary. A small amount of soil mix should cling to the seedling's roots. Always handle a seedling by its leaves and *never* by its stem; if damage is accidentally done, the seedlings can grow a new leaf, but never a new stem.

Lower the seedling into the hole you made, placing it slightly deeper than it was growing in the seed flat, and gently press the soil mix around the roots.

Keep the transplants in good light but not full sun for several days, increasing the light intensity gradually. If you've transplanted during cloudy weather, the containers can go right onto the windowsill; if you grow under lights, the transplants can go under the fluorescents right away. If the plants become tall and spindly later on, they're not getting enough light.

Water when necessary, never allowing the transplants to wilt, and keeping the medium evenly moist but not soaking wet. Once a week, when watering, add soluble fertilizer at one-half the recommended label strength.

One week before the indoor-grown seedlings are shifted outdoors to the garden, start to harden them off. This process acclimates the soft and tender plants, which have been protected from wind, cool temperatures, and strong sun, and gradually gets them used to their new environment.

Move the flats of plants outside into a sheltered, shady area such as a porch, cold frame, or under a tree or shrub. If it gets cold at night, move them back inside. After two or three days, give them half a day of sun, increasing the exposure gradually to a full day. Make sure the transplants are well watered during this hardening off period. Don't place transplants on the ground if slugs are a problem in your area.

By stem cuttings. Hardy lavender is difficult to start from seed. Often its seeds do not produce plants identical to the original, and it may take up to a month to germinate. A better way to propagate these plants is with cuttings from established plants at least three years old in the spring or fall. Instead of simply clipping a 2- to 3-inch-long sideshoot, some gardeners prefer to pull a healthy sideshoot downward so that a piece of older wood comes along with it. Dust the cuttings with root-promoting hormone powder to help prevent rotting and speed up rooting. The health of the stem you choose for a cutting is most important to the success of the project. Avoid thin, crooked stems or those that show any yellowing or brown leaves. Place the cuttings 3 to 4 inches apart in moist, sandy soil. Keep the plants pruned during the first year to encourage branching.

By layering. You can also propagate lavenders vegetatively by layering—covering low-lying stems with soil until they root. Both layering and cuttings will ensure that the new plants will keep the qualities of the parent plant. Choose a healthy stem and remove the leaves from the part you are going to bury. Hold down with a curved twig or wire, and check regularly to see when roots develop. Allow the new plant to grow in place until the following year, then carefully cut the stem and re-plant the new plant.

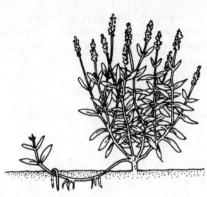

To propagate lavender by layering: Choose a healthy stem and remove the leaves from the part you are going to bury. Hold the bare section of stem down with a curved twig or wire, and cover it with soil.

PLANTING LOCATION AND SOIL CONDITIONS

When growing lavenders in the garden be sure to pick a site that is very well drained and receives at least six hours of direct sun. The amount of humus in the soil is most important to lavender growth, so be sure the garden area you choose is rich in compost. If the soil is sandy or full of clay, mix large amounts of compost into the soil before planting. Lavenders like a moderately alkaline soil with a pH between 6.5 and 7.

Any aid to growth the first summer is helpful as lavender plants are small the first year and subject to winterkill. Once established, plant 12 inches apart—or more, depending on the mature size of the variety.

Lavenders take well to a light mulch around the roots. A light straw mulch or a mulch of an inch or two of sand around the base of the plants can increase winter survival.

Most plants need protection in the winter. Pine boughs, light straw, or even covering a larger plant with a bushel basket can help in winter climes. When choosing a planting site, try to avoid areas that get sharp winds in the winter. When planting lavender in colder climes, the nearer the protection of a house or a stone wall, the better.

CONTAINER GARDENING

Tender lavenders can also be grown in pots. Choose a container that is about 2 to 5 inches larger in diameter than the root ball of the plant. Make sure the pot has good drainage holes, and choose a growing medium that drains well. If roots are soggy for any length of time, a root rot quickly develops and will kill the plant. A soilless mix of peat, vermiculite, and perlite can work well. Many pre-mixed soilless planting mediums can be found at local garden centers.

Container-grown lavenders can be outdoors all summer long. During the summer the plants will need plenty of water and fertilizer. Apply a liquid fertilizer of 20–10–20 about once a month. After bringing them inside in the fall, give the lavenders a lot of sunlight. Stems will weaken if they don't receive enough sun. Artificial light indoors can work well and you may be rewarded with bloom in mid-winter!

PRUNING

Pruning lavenders, whether in pots or in the ground, will keep them attractive. As much as one-half the stem length can be taken off without any damage. Frequent pruning may delay bloom, so it should be done in very early spring or in the fall after most blooming has occurred. In the spring, pruning old bushes back to new shoots toward the base of the bush, can stimulate new growth and help the plants from becoming too woody. (It also gives a good supply of cuttings for new plants!) Pruning again right after flowering—cutting back and shaping the plants—is another good idea. A small hedge of well-clipped lavenders make an excellent border for a small herb or flower garden.

HARVEST

One of the most pleasant aspects of growing herbs is when it comes time to harvest them. The lovely, fragrant blossoms of lavender are especially easy and rewarding to harvest as they hold up well with little care. Pick the mature herb early in the morning, just after the dew has had a chance to dry. This is so the essential oils—what gives the plant its fragrance—won't lose their quality when exposed to the heat of the sun. It is best not to pick lavender when wet as it will take longer to dry. A cool, sunny, dry morning is best for picking.

Spikes of lavender should be cut as soon as most of the flowers in the head are open but before any begin to fade. The stems should be cut where they meet the leaves, and the stalks tied in bundles in large brown paper bags—so that the flowers do not touch the paper—and hung in a dry, airy, warm place out of any direct sunlight.

The stems can also be spread on a cloth-covered screen in a shady room that is well ventilated. Keep moist heat away from the lavender stems while they are drying.

Too hot and sunny a drying place will evaporate the essential oil and fade the colors. When dry, the flowers should be stripped from the stalks (if you want to use just the flowers) and kept in dark glass, airtight containers, for use later.

You can also dry lavender by simply bunching it together and hanging it upside down. It will not keep the attractive scent for long, but it will keep its color and shape and can be used later in dried arrangements. This also works to dry lavender that has been previously used in a mixed flower arrangement.

MAINTENANCE

After harvesting is a good time to side dress the plants with a bit of lime or compost. If you are lucky enough to have early bloom and live in a warm climate, you will be rewarded with a second bloom before too long. Those of us in colder regions are usually happy with one harvest. In the north, prune lavenders back after harvesting, when the plants will soon need to be protected from the harsh winter conditions.

Uses of Lavender

Lavender seems to be gaining in popularity lately. Everywhere you look there seem to be lavender-scented items for the bed and bath as well as a wide variety of lavender oils and essences to create your own scented delights. And its scent is just that—a real delight. It evokes fields of summer sun and grandmother's houses of long ago that seemed to be naturally filled with its thick fragrance, creating a healing atmosphere one longs to imitate in today's harried world.

MEDICINAL USES

Lavender has been used medicinally for years. Dioscorides in the first century B.C.E. said lavender was good for "griefs in ye thorax," and today many caregivers like to place lavender in sick rooms and hospices to ease a patient's distress.

Continued ➜

Just smelling the fresh herb is said to relieve headaches, and herbalists of yore were certain it cured everything from cramps to migraines, tremblings, and passions of the heart. The oil was believed to be anti-aphrodisiac, which might explain its popularity in Victorian times.

While lavender has been used for washing since ancient times, in European folk tradition it is also regarded as a useful wound herb and a worm remedy for children.

TOILET WATER FOR EASING HEADACHES

1 1/2 cups dried lavender flowers

1 pint cider vinegar

1 cup rosewater

Place lavender in glass jar, pour on vinegar and leave for a week in a cool, dry place, shaking each day.

After a week, strain through muslin and stir in rosewater. Use on temples to give relief from headaches caused by fatigue.

Many parts of the lavender are used for medicinal purposes. Flowers are less potent than the essential oil of the herb, and are useful for nervous exhaustion, headaches, and indigestion.

Flowers

- **Infusion.** For nervous exhaustion, tension headaches, or during labor. Also can be used for colic and indigestion.
- **Tincture.** Take up to 5 ml. twice a day for headaches and depression.
- **Mouthwash.** Use as a mouthwash to help with bad breath.

Essential Oil

- Add a few drops of the oil to a calendula cream for skin trouble.
- Add a few drops of the oil to water for sunburn soother.
- Dilute 8 drops of oil in water to use as a hair rinse.
- Add lavender to your favorite unscented oil and use as a massage to ease tension headaches. Or use the essential oil itself. At the first sign of a headache gently massage the oil into the temples and around the head and neck.
- Apply undiluted oil to insect bites and stings.

LAVENDER AND OATMEAL BAG FOR THE BATH

Every mother knows oatmeal baths are good for the skin, as oatmeal softens water. Add lavender and you have a bath that not only smells good but also softens and soothes. Add whatever other herbs you like to the bag as well.

1 cup oatmeal

1/2 cup or so fresh or dried lavender flowers and tops

Another bunch of fresh herbs such as rosemary, lemon balm, and thyme

Combine all ingredients and place in the center of a square of cotton or muslin. Gather up the corners and tie tightly to make a bag. Hold this under the running tap water—but not too hot. While bathing, rub the bag over skin to get extra benefits.

DREAM PILLOW

Place this bag under your pillow at night to relax those jagged nerves.

1/2 cup dried lavender

1/2 cup dried hops

1/2 cup dried lemon balm

Mix all ingredients and fill small cotton or muslin bag. Place under pillow.

TAKE TIME TO SMELL THE FLOWERS

Lavender flowers are always good to have on hand. Keep a bowl of flowers in your bedroom or bring to the hospital when visiting a sick friend. Lavender flowers have always been thought to calm the nerves. Sniff lavender each day and get rid of tension!

Cooking with Lavender

Lavender, surprisingly, can be used in cooking and gives a fresh delightful scent, as you might expect.

LAVENDER SUGAR

To use with cookie recipes that follow.

Mix a cup of dried lavender blossoms with a cup of sugar. Keep mixing as you use, because it tends to separate while it sits.

LAVENDER COOKIES I

1 cup butter	*2 cups flour*
1/2 cup sugar	*Lavender sugar (recipe above)*
A dash of salt	

Cream the butter and sugar together. Add the salt and flour. Mix with mixer or wooden spoon thoroughly. Chill the dough in refrigerator.

Preheat the oven to 350°F.

Form dough into small balls and roll in the sugar mix. Place on ungreased cookie sheets and bake 10 to 12 minutes. Cool on racks.

LAVENDER COOKIES II

1 cup plus 2 tablespoons all-purpose flour	*4 tablespoons butter*
1/3 cup lavender sugar	*2–3 tablespoons sweet white wine*
A pinch of salt	*16 leaves fresh lavender, well minced*

Sift the flour, all but 1 tablespoon of the sugar, and the salt into a bowl. Rub in the butter until the mixture resembles bread crumbs. Make a well in the center and add the wine and lavender leaves and stir in gently. Let sit for 15 minutes, stirring every few minutes, until bonded. Then gather into a dough.

Roll out dough on a floured board until 1/8-inch thick, and use a serrated knife to cut strips about 1 inch by 3 inches. Place on a greased baking sheet, twisting cookies if you like, to make them look like bows.

Bake for 8–10 minutes in 375°F oven.

LAVENDER LEMONADE

Steep 1/2 cup dried lavender flowers in a quart of boiling water for about 5 minutes. Strain and use the liquid to make up part of the water in a frozen lemondade (or limeade) mix. Delightful flavor and fragrance!

LAVENDER CRAFTS

FRAGRANT DRAWER LINERS

An old-fashioned, sweet-smelling trick.

Cut two pieces of cheesecloth 1/2-inch larger than the size of the bureau drawer. Cut two pieces of thin cotton padding a bit smaller than the drawer. Lay one piece of cotton flat on a table, sprinkle it with a layer of lavender, cover with the second piece of cotton. Baste the cheesecloth around the edges, then make tackings of threads through the cloths.

This will scent the whole drawer, and is easy enough to make that you can make more of them each season.

LAVENDER HOT PAD

Whole *Lavandula dentata* flower heads or English lavender flowers can be quilted into a padding for a fragrant tea cozy or a hot pad for the table. The warmth will bring out the fragrance of the herb. Cut two 10-inch squares of quilted fabric. With right sides together, stitch around three sides. Turn right side out. Fill with another pillow made of lightweight cotton fabric and stuffed with lavender. Sew the opening closed with a hem stitch.

LAVENDER-SCENTED CANDLE

Scented candles are expensive to buy but not that difficult to make. Lavender makes a delightful scented candle and is just one more way to enjoy this fragrance in your home.

2 pounds paraffin wax

2 colored crayons or a colorant for wax (optional)

2 cups lavender blossoms, or 4 cups fresh flowers

Candle molds (old cans work well)

Petroleum jelly

Candle wicking

Break up the wax into small pieces and melt in a bowl over a saucepan of hot water. Keep heat very low and watch carefully; paraffin is extremely flammable. Stir in coloring, if using.

Remove from heat and then add the lavender. Coat the molds with petroleum jelly, and drop a length of wick into each mold, so that it touches the bottom. Hold the other end around a pencil resting across the mold's rim to keep the wick centered as you pour in the hot wax.

When the wax cools to a gel, pour it into the molds. Allow the candles to set overnight.

Growing & Using Dill

Glenn Andrews

Illustrations by Mary Rich, Lavonne Francis, and Charles Joslin

Growing Your Own Dill

If you've never grown annual herbs before, dill might be a good one to start with. It will thrive, in spite of almost everything you might do to it!

I strongly suggest that you grow your dill from seeds, sown right where you want the plants to be, rather than either buying plants and transplanting them or starting the seeds indoors early in the spring, then moving them outdoors. Despite the fact that dill really is a cinch to grow, it does have fragile stems that could easily be crunched in the course of being transplanted. I have even seen it listed as being impossible to transplant. I doubt this, but it certainly wouldn't be an easy task.

At any rate, I can't see any point in trying to transplant dill. The seeds can go in the ground in early spring, and they germinate very well and quite quickly.

OBTAINING SEEDS

The first thing you have to do is decide whether you want your dill plants to give you mostly greens to use as herbs or seeds to use primarily in pickles. There's a third choice, too—you can use the green part for a while, then let the plants go to seed.

If that third choice is what you want, you'll find packets of seeds for planting in nearly every supermarket and most hardware and garden stores.

WHERE, WHEN, AND HOW TO PLANT

Dill, like other herbs and vegetables, is a true sun lover. The ideal spot for it is in full sun, but it's an agreeable plant and will also do well with a half day's sun.

Because it grows to be up to 3 feet (0.9 m) tall, your dill is best positioned in the back of your herb garden, so it won't overshadow (literally) your other plants.

For that matter, dill will thrive in a spot where it's mixed in with flowers and/or vegetables. Its frondlike leaves can create the same effect in the garden that ferns do in a flower shop bouquet. Just, as mentioned above, make sure it won't rob anything else of sun—or be robbed of sun itself by other vigorously growing plants.

As to when to put the seed into the ground, dill is a plant that loves coolness. If you live in a region where there are heavy frosts, plant the seeds in early spring. The backs of seed packets will tell you to wait until the date of the average last frost, but you can cheat a bit on that! Since germination takes from 10 to 21 days, you can at least plant that far ahead of the average last hard frost.

If, however, you live where there are no hard frosts, you can sow the seeds from midfall to early spring.

Continued →

Either way, it's a good idea to lay in a good supply of seeds and sow every 10 days or so. In the case of the cold-region garden, you'll find that your best dill crops will come from seeds sown in spring or early fall.

I've read many times that herbs actually prefer to grow in poor soil. I used to believe this and acted accordingly, but now I'm convinced that any herb will do better if it grows in good, fertile soil. Treat the soil where you'll be growing dill as you would any other where you want a good crop: Prepare it deeply; add compost; work in some well-rotted manure; rake it well.

Plant the seeds 1/8 to 1/4 inch (3 to 6 mm) deep, and press down gently. Keep well watered until the little plants poke their heads up through the soil.

Again, I have a quarrel with conventional wisdom in regard to the spacing of your plants. You'll be told, over and over, to thin your dill plants until they are 2 feet (60 cm) apart. I, on the other hand, suggest that you leave them in little clusters in which they are no more than 1 foot (30 cm) from each other. Even 6-inch (15-cm) spacing will work out well. But either way, you are just about guaranteed a great crop.

Can you plant dill seeds in containers? Of course. But do remember that you're going to have very tall plants, so plan accordingly, using rather deep containers.

HARVESTING AND PRESERVING YOUR DILL

There are, of course, two approaches to harvesting your lovely crop of dill—one for the dillweed, the other for the dill seeds. Naturally, they have to be done at different times.

During the growing season, it's great to just go out in your garden and pick the amount of dill you need for your next meal. That's the ideal way.

But if you have a big crop and wish to preserve it, try drying it in a microwave oven. Simply spread the dill in a single layer on paper towels and microwave on high for 3 minutes. The result will delight you—you'll have bright green, perfectly dry, totally delicious dill. After microwaving, remove and discard the hard stems and crumble the leaves with your fingers. Store in an airtight container away from bright light to best preserve the flavor.

Like any other annual, dill will rapidly bolt to seed if you give it a chance—in other words, if you let it flower by not keeping it cut. (Remember, too, that after the plant flowers, you won't get any more of the lovely greenery from it.) So keep cutting the dill until the time comes when you want to swing into seed production. At that time, leave the plant alone until it flowers and seeds form. Make sure the seeds are thoroughly dry. Then cut off the umbels (the more or less umbrella-shaped seed heads), place them in a bag (a paper grocery bag, for instance), and, using your fingers, remove the seeds. Store in an airtight jar.

Appetizers

The original meaning of the word *appetizer* had to do with having a tidbit at the beginning of a meal to act as a stimulus to the appetite.

Some people, however, have been known to make a whole meal (although not necessarily one that meets the food-pyramid criteria) from appetizers. Here are a couple of good ones to get you started.

DILL DIP FOR CRUDITÉS OR CRACKERS

When you're in need of a quick dip, preferably made from things you're apt to have on hand at all times, here is a perfect one. You can serve it immediately after putting it together, but it does benefit from and will be slightly improved by a sojourn in the refrigerator.

Yes, you can use low-fat sour cream and mayonnaise.

2/3 cup (155 ml) sour cream

2/3 cup (155 ml) mayonnaise

2 tablespoons minced onion or chives

1 tablespoon minced celery or 1/2 teaspoon celery seeds

1 tablespoon minced fresh dill or 1 teaspoon dillweed

1. Combine all the ingredients in a small bowl.

2. Cover and refrigerate overnight if you have time. Otherwise, serve at once. In either case, use as a dip for any raw or lightly blanched vegetables.

MAKES ABOUT 1 1/2 CUPS (355 ML)

DILL ROLL-UPS

These are handy little numbers to bring out when an appetizer seems appropriate. They taste good, too! You can keep them, ready to go, for several days in your refrigerator or for several months in the freezer.

3 ounces (90 g) cream cheese or Neufchâtel

2 tablespoons sour cream

1 tablespoon horseradish

1 tablespoon minced fresh dill or 1 teaspoon dillweed

20 slices prosciutto, chipped beef, or very thin cold cuts of any sort

1. Mash the cream cheese or Neufchâtel (which is just a reduced-fat version of cream cheese) with the sour cream, horseradish, and dill.

2. Spread this mixture on the prosciutto, chipped beef, or whatever you're using. Roll up into little cigarlike bundles.

3. Cover with plastic wrap and refrigerate until just before you want to serve the roll-ups. Then cut into slices and serve. (Or freeze, well wrapped. In this case, bring them out to room temperature about 15 minutes before serving time, so you'll be able to slice them without any problems.)

SERVES 12–14

Soups

Some of the nicest soups you'll ever encounter are the ones that have been livened by the judicious use of a smidgen or two of dill.

Here are recipes for some of these soups, but remember that dill can work miracles on canned soups as well. For starters, sprinkle some dry dill ("dillweed") on a canned cream of chicken or green pea soup. You'll be surprised! Better yet, try some of these homemade soups.

6 cups (1.4 l) chicken broth

1/3 cup (90 ml) raw rice

1 tablespoon minced fresh dill or 1 teaspoon dillweed

1/2 cup (140 ml) chopped scallions (optional but nice)

4 eggs

Juice of 2 lemons

Salt and freshly ground black pepper

HOT CABBAGE BORSCHT

Borscht, a great Russian soup, comes in two distinct forms—a hot cabbage-based version and a cold one based on beets. As far as I can see, they only have two things in common: their name and the fact that each absolutely has to contain or at least be garnished with dill.

Here's the hot version, the perfect soup for a wintry day. You'll also find Cold Beet Borscht, a beautiful summer soup, on this page.

To make hot borscht into a truly full meal, add some sliced Polish sausage that you've sautéed for about 5 minutes.

1 head cabbage

1 cup (275 ml) sliced carrots

1 cup (275 ml) sliced celery

1 purple-topped turnip, peeled and diced

1 large beet, peeled and diced

6 cups (1.4 l) beef broth

1 6-ounce (180-g) can tomato paste

Salt and freshly ground black pepper

2 large onions, thinly sliced

1 teaspoon minced garlic

3 tablespoons bacon fat or olive oil (or a combination)

3 medium potatoes, peeled and diced

1/4 cup (70 ml) minced fresh parsley

6 tablespoons minced fresh dill or 2 tablespoons dillweed

1/2 cup (120 ml) or more sour cream

1. Simmer the cabbage, carrots, celery, turnip, and beet in the beef broth in a large stockpot over medium heat for about 5 minutes.

2. Stir in the tomato paste and season with a little salt and pepper (you can add more later). Cover and simmer over low heat for 2 hours.

3. Sauté the sliced onions and minced garlic in the bacon fat and/or olive oil in a small saucepan over fairly low heat for 5 minutes, then add, along with the diced potatoes, to the stockpot. Simmer gently, covered, for another half hour.

4. Taste, adding more salt and pepper if needed. Combine the parsley and dill and stir 3 tablespoons of the mixture into the soup.

5. Serve in large soup plates or bowls, passing the sour cream and the rest of the mixture of parsley and dill for diners to add as they will.

SERVES 6–8

AVGOLEMONO SOUP

Avgolemono, or Greek egg and lemon soup, has been one of my favorite foods since I first tasted it years ago at the Paradise Inn of the Green Olive Tree in New York. Now I've learned that it's sometimes made with dill—and that it's even better that way!

1. Place the chicken broth in a fairly large saucepan over high heat. Bring to a boil. Add the rice; turn down the heat; cover the pot and simmer for 30 minutes, at which point the rice should be tender.

2. Stir in the dill and the scallions (if you're using them).

3. Put the eggs in the bowl of a blender or food processor. Beat until frothy, then add the lemon juice and beat just a bit more.

4. Now, with the machine still running, dribble in about 2 cups (475 ml) of the boiling broth.

5. Stirring constantly, pour the egg mixture into the pot with the remaining broth.

6. Now you have a choice. You can serve right away, and it will be delicious. Or you can make it even better by heating and stirring for 5 minutes.

SERVES 4–6

MUSHROOM SOUP WITH DILL

This particular recipe is based on a highly acclaimed dish from the Sugar Mill Inn in Franconia, New Hampshire.

1/4 cup (1/2 stick) butter, divided

2 cups (550 ml) chopped onions

3/4 pound (340 g) mushrooms, chopped

1 tablespoon minced fresh dill or 1 teaspoon dillweed

2 cups (475 ml) chicken broth, divided

2 teaspoons soy sauce

1/2 teaspoon paprika

2 tablespoons flour

1 cup (235 ml) milk

Salt and freshly ground pepper

1/2 cup (120 ml) sour cream (low fat if you wish)

Freshly squeezed juice of 1/2 lemon

1. Melt 2 tablespoons of the butter in a medium-size saucepan over medium heat. Add the onions and cook a few minutes until they are limp, stirring occasionally.

2. Add the mushrooms, dill, and 1/2 cup (120 ml) of the chicken broth, along with the soy sauce and paprika. Stir well; then reduce the heat, cover the pot, and simmer for 15 minutes.

3. Now (or meanwhile!) melt the remaining 2 tablespoons of butter in another medium-size saucepan over medium heat. Make this into a white sauce by whisking in the flour, stirring for 3 or 4 minutes, then adding the milk. Stir until thick and smooth.

4. Add the remaining broth and the mushroom mixture to the white sauce. Simmer covered, over low heat for 15 minutes.

Continued →

5. You can stop here, if that pleases you, and reheat just before serving. At any rate, when you're ready to serve, stir in the sour cream and the lemon juice.

SERVES 4

CHILLED CUCUMBER-DILL SOUP

Remember this soup (in time to make some for yourself!) the next time a hot day threatens to undo you. It's a refreshing little survival trick. (But it's good heated, too, in case the weather changes.)

3 cucumbers (see below)

4 cups (950 ml) milk or light cream

1 cup (235 ml) sour cream (low fat is all right to use here)

2 tablespoons minced fresh dill or 2 teaspoons dillweed

Salt

1 dash cinnamon

1 teaspoon freshly ground white pepper

1. If you are using unwaxed English seedless cucumbers, simply chop them into smallish chunks. If, on the other hand, you're forced to use waxed regular cucumbers, peel and seed them, then cut into pieces.

2. Put the cucumber pieces and all the other ingredients in a food processor or blender and run the machine until the soup is completely smooth.

3. Chill for at least 2 hours. Taste just before serving—you may need to add more salt and pepper at this point.

SERVES 4–6

COLD BEET BORSCHT

As promised, here's the other borscht, the cold one made with no vegetable other than beets. It's every bit as good as the kind made with cabbage and many other vegetables and served hot.

This soup is not at all hard to make, but for an occasional emergency, there is an excellent cold borscht available in jars in the kosher foods section of most supermarkets. I've found that a jar of this lurking in my refrigerator can be a big help on the hottest of summer days. I just pour it into a bowl, plop on some sour cream, sprinkle on some dill, and there I am with a lovely cold soup, all set to go.

1 1/2 pounds (680 g) raw beets

6 cups (1.4 l) water

2 tablespoons light brown sugar

1/3 cup (75 ml) freshly squeezed lemon juice or vinegar

Salt and freshly ground black pepper

Sour cream and dill for serving

1. Scrub the beets well; then either grate them and add them to the water, brown sugar, lemon juice, and salt and pepper in a medium-size saucepan or simply run all these ingredients together in a food processor before putting into the saucepan.

2. Cook over medium heat, uncovered, until the beets are tender—about half an hour. (Or microwave them in a microwave-safe container for 10 to 12 minutes.)

3. Chill thoroughly.

4. Serve with a dollop of sour cream and a good sprinkling of minced fresh dill (or a combination of minced fresh parsley and dillweed) on each bowl of soup.

SERVES 4–6

Meat, Poultry, and Fish

Lamb stew with dill! Beef stroganoff with dill! Dill-braised chicken! Fish fillets with dill! I'd have a hard time choosing my favorite of these—and so, I dare say, will you.

BEEF STROGANOFF WITH DILL

The first time I ever tasted Beef Stroganoff with Dill was at the home of a friend who had recently returned from a trip to Russia. As the other guests and I exclaimed over the goodness of the dish and the unusual taste brought by the dill, she offhandedly said, "Oh, that's the way they do it in Russia"! It's originally a Russian dish (or so it seems), so they should know, I guess. In any case, dill is a wonderful addition.

Use the most tender beef you can afford. Tenderloin is perfect. (This is a dish that doesn't spare your wallet or your waistline, but it's worth it!)

1 1/2 pounds (680 g) tenderloin of beef

3 tablespoons olive oil

3 tablespoons butter

2 tablespoons minced onion or shallot

1 tablespoon minced fresh dill or 1 teaspoon dillweed

Salt and freshly ground black pepper

8–12 ounces (235–355 ml) sour cream

1. Cut the beef into the thinnest possible strips. (It helps to freeze the meat partially before slicing.) Set aside.

2. Melt the olive oil and butter in a large skillet over medium-high heat. Add the strips of beef and brown quickly.

3. Add the onion and cook, stirring, for just a minute or two.

4. Remove from the heat. Add salt and pepper to taste, then stir in the dill and sour cream. Reheat very gently, not allowing the sauce to boil.

5. Serve with noodles.

SERVES 4–6

LAMB STEW WITH DILL

This is one of the most mouthwatering dishes in the world, in my opinion. But if this recipe sounds a bit long to you, and you find the list of ingredients a bit daunting, you can create a pretty good facsimile by making your own favorite Irish lamb stew and adding to it 1 tablespoon vinegar, 1 tablespoon sugar, and 1 tablespoon minced fresh dill or 1 1/2 teaspoons dillweed.

2 pounds (900 g) stewing lamb, cut up

2 medium onions, peeled and quartered

2 large potatoes or turnips (or use one of each), peeled and diced

Salt and freshly ground black pepper

1 bay leaf

3 tablespoons minced fresh dill or 1 tablespoon dillweed, divided

2 tablespoons butter

2 tablespoons flour

1 tablespoon vinegar

1 tablespoon sugar

1 egg yolk, slightly beaten

1. Put the lamb, onions, and potatoes in a large saucepan. Pour on enough boiling water to cover. Add some salt and pepper, the bay leaf, and 1 tablespoon of the minced fresh dill or 1 teaspoon of the dillweed. Cover. Cook over medium heat for 1 hour, or until the meat and vegetables are tender.

2. Drain, measure, and reserve the broth that has formed in the stew. If you don't have 2 cups (475 ml) of it, add a little water. Return the lamb and vegetables to the saucepan.

3. In a medium-size saucepan over medium heat, melt the butter and stir in the flour. Cook and stir for 3 or 4 minutes, then add the 2 cups of broth reserved from the lamb. Stir until the sauce bubbles and is smooth and thick. Add the remaining dill and the vinegar and sugar. Season with salt and pepper.

4. Simmer the sauce mixture for 2 or 3 minutes; then remove from the heat and stir in the egg yolk.

5. Stir the sauce mixture into the meat and vegetables.

SERVES 4

CHICKEN BAKED WITH WHITE WINE AND DILL

Aside from the fact that this is a wonderful dish, it has other virtues—there's almost no work, and none of the work has to be done at the last minute. You will want to serve this recipe along with something to use the scrumptious juices you'll have. Rice would be good, as would noodles or any other pasta, or mashed potatoes—or even toast.

1/4 cup (1/2 stick) butter

2 tablespoons olive oil

2 tablespoons minced fresh dill or 2 teaspoons dillweed

8 chicken pieces (for instance, 8 thighs)

1 cup (275 ml) chopped onion

1/2 cup (120 ml) white wine or dry vermouth

1. Preheat your oven to 400°F (205°C).

2. Put the butter and oil in a baking pan and place it in the oven briefly until the butter is melted.

3. Add the dill to the butter and oil and roll the chicken pieces in this combination. Leave the chicken in the pan, skin-side up. Top with the onion.

4. Bake for 15 minutes, then add the wine. Turn down the oven to 300°F (150°C) and bake, undisturbed, for another 50 minutes, or until the chicken is done.

SERVES 4–8

DILL-POACHED FILLETS OF FLOUNDER

Here is the secret to moist fish fillets: slow-poaching in an aromatic broth. And what could be more aromatic than a leek broth heavily seasoned with dill? You can, naturally, substitute any other flat fillets of fish.

2 cups (475 ml) chicken broth

3 medium-size leeks

Salt and freshly ground black pepper

1 1/2 pounds (680 g) flounder fillets

2 tablespoons heavy cream

1 tablespoon minced fresh dill or 1 teaspoon dillweed

1. Bring the broth to a boil over high heat in a large, flat pan (such as a skillet) that has a lid.

2. Meanwhile, back at the chopping board, trim the leeks, cutting off the roots and almost all of the green leaves. Cut in half lengthwise and rinse carefully under running water. Now cut into 1/8-inch (3-mm) slices.

3. When the broth has reduced by half, turn down the heat and add the slices of leek. Simmer for 5 minutes. Add the salt and pepper to taste (and do taste it—the broth may contain quite a bit of salt).

4. Add the fish fillets to the pan. Cover and turn off the heat! (I did mention slow-poaching, didn't I? This system will work beautifully if you are using an electric stove, since the burner will hold a certain amount of heat. If not, you may have to keep the burner lit, but the least amount possible.) Check for doneness after 4 minutes. The fish is done when the tip of a sharp knife goes in with no resistance at all. If it isn't quite ready, keep checking at 1-minute intervals.

5. Stir in the cream and the dill.

6. Serve topped with the leeks and some of the broth.

SERVES 4

Eggs and Cheese

Toss a little dill in the mix when you make scrambled eggs. Or perhaps brighten a cheese casserole with a touch of this glorious herb. Or, of course, try this recipe!

DILL AND ONION QUICHE

This is one case where it's important to use fresh dill, since it's to be sprinkled on the quiche as it is served. If that's impossible, though, you could combine minced parsley (especially the flat-leafed Italian sort) and dried dillweed in a ratio of 1 tablespoon parsley to 1 teaspoon dillweed.

Continued →

Also, when I make this dish myself, I mix the eggs, cheese (which can just be in cubes), cream, and 1 1/2 teaspoons of dill, along with the nutmeg, salt, and pepper, together in a food processor or blender.

1 9-inch (22.5-cm) deep-dish piecrust (a frozen crust is fine)

3 large sweet onions (such as Vidalia, Maui, Walla Walla, or Texas Sweet), thinly sliced

3 tablespoons butter

1 tablespoon olive oil

5 eggs

3/4 pound (340 g) Swiss cheese

1/2 cup (120 ml) heavy cream or half-and-half

3 tablespoons minced fresh dill or 1 tablespoon dillweed (see note above), divided

Pinch of nutmeg

Salt and freshly ground black pepper

1. Preheat your oven to 350°F (177°C).

2. Bake the piecrust for 15 minutes.

3. Cook the onions in the butter and olive oil over medium heat until they're limp. Place in the bottom of the partly cooked piecrust.

4. Beat or whisk the eggs in a large bowl. Shred and add the cheese. Now add the cream, half of the dill, and the nutmeg, salt, and pepper. Pour onto the onions in the crust.

5. Bake for 40 minutes. Remove from the oven and allow to rest for at least 10 minutes. Sprinkle on the remaining dill when serving.

SERVES 4–6

Vegetables and Salads

I can't think of a single vegetable that isn't improved by the simple addition of a little dill. While I can't lead you through every possible vegetable in the course of these pages, here are some wonderful examples of what you can do.

In salads, too, dill can be a star. Just mince or chop some of the herb and sprinkle it on any salad, or try it in your best piquant salad dressings.

GLAZED CARROTS WITH DILL

I think everyone can use one more recipe for carrots, especially if it's a really good (not to mention unusual) one such as this!

2 cups (550 ml) thinly sliced fresh carrots

2 tablespoons butter

1 teaspoon Dijon mustard

1 tablespoon sugar

1 tablespoon minced fresh dill or 1 teaspoon dillweed

Salt and freshly ground black pepper

1. Cook the carrots in water to cover until tender. Drain.

2. Combine the cooked carrots with all the other ingredients in a medium-size saucepan and cook over medium-low heat, stirring often, until glazed and lovely.

3. Taste to make sure the seasoning is the way you want it.

4. Either serve at once or set aside for an hour or two, then reheat.

SERVES 4

BAKED BRUSSELS SPROUTS WITH DILL AND VINEGAR

Liven up your Thanksgiving dinner (or any other meal) with a surprise dish such as this one.

Although this recipe serves only four, you can multiply it by three or four, cooking it in a larger baking dish, of course. Also, you can stop for an hour or two between the boiling and the baking stages of this dish, if you wish.

1 pound (454 g) small fresh brussels sprouts

1 tablespoon red wine vinegar

2 tablespoons minced fresh dill or 2 teaspoons dillweed

Salt and freshly ground black pepper

1. Preheat your oven to 350°F (177°C).

2. Trim the sprouts and cut a little cross into the base of each one.

3. Cook the sprouts in a medium saucepan in boiling water to cover for 10 minutes.

4. Drain into a colander, then quickly drench with cold water to prevent any further cooking at the moment.

5. Put the sprouts into a small, buttered baking dish. Stir in the vinegar, dill, and salt and pepper, and cover (using foil if necessary). Bake for 10 minutes, then remove the cover and bake for 5 minutes more.

SERVES 4

DILLED NEW POTATOES

My whole family is very fond of tiny little potatoes, preferably straight from a farm. But little potatoes are usually available in supermarkets, too. Recently, I've seen them in exorbitantly priced little plastic containers, labeled "gourmet potatoes"! They're a favorite food just boiled or baked and served with butter, but they're even better when given the dill treatment.

1 pound (454 g) small potatoes (all pretty much the same size)

1 tablespoon minced fresh dill or 1 teaspoon dillweed

1/4 cup (70 ml) minced scallions

1 tablespoon butter

Salt and freshly ground black pepper

1. Peel a small strip around the middle of each potato. (This will enable the flavors to get all the way through the vegetable. It looks cute, too! However, it's not essential, so skip this step if you wish.)

2. Put the potatoes in a medium-size saucepan. Cover with water and boil, uncovered, until tender.

3. Drain off the water (perhaps saving it to make soup or bread at another time). Add the dill, scallions, butter, and salt and pepper to the potatoes and cook together for just a minute or two.

SERVES 4

RED POTATO SALAD WITH DILL

Once upon a time, "proper" cooks would never have dreamed of leaving the skin on when they made a potato salad. All that has changed now, and "red potato salad" is considered the way to go . . . especially when the salad is seasoned as nicely as this one.

2 pounds (900 g) red potatoes

3 tablespoons balsamic vinegar or lemon juice

3 tablespoons canola or olive oil

1 cup (275 ml) minced mild onion

1 celery stalk, minced

1 sweet pepper (red, green, or whatever color you choose), minced

3 tablespoons chopped fresh dill or 1 tablespoon dillweed

Salt and freshly ground black pepper

1/2 cup (120 ml) mayonnaise (optional, but many people feel that potato salad must include mayonnaise—and it certainly does no harm!)

1. Boil the potatoes in salted water until just tender. Drain, then quickly cut into bite-size pieces. (Don't peel the potatoes—you're supposed to see those red skins!) Put potatoes into a bowl.

2. While the potatoes are cooking, make a vinaigrette with the balsamic vinegar and the canola oil. Pour over the pieces of potato while they are still hot.

3. Add the rest of the ingredients and toss well.

4. Chill, covered.

SERVES 4–6

WINTER SQUASH WITH DILL

I love this recipe. Winter squash is a fine thing and very good for you, but it does need some jazzing up, in my opinion. Just the simple touches of dill and sour cream here turn it into a culinary star.

In many markets these days, you will find winter squash (usually butternut) that has been peeled, cleaned of its seeds, and sometimes even cubed for you. This is a huge boon and I urge you to have no compunction about taking advantage of it. Another shortcut is to buy frozen mashed squash. Again, don't be ashamed of making life easier for yourself. Frozen mashed winter squash is a fine product—and a tremendous help to the cook.

2 pounds (900 g) winter squash, peeled, seeded, and cubed (or two 10-ounce (285 g) packages frozen mashed winter squash—see above)

1 tablespoon minced fresh dill or 1 teaspoon dillweed

1/2 cup (120 ml) sour cream (low fat if you wish)

2 teaspoons sugar

Salt and freshly ground black pepper to taste

1. If you are using uncooked cubed winter squash, put it in a medium-size saucepan, cover with an inch (2.5 cm) or so of water, bring to a boil, and cook until very tender. If you're using frozen squash, just thaw it.

2. Drain the boiled squash cubes well, then mash. Put into a medium-size saucepan or the top of a double boiler. If you're using frozen mashed squash, thawed, just put it in the pan.

3. Add the dill, sour cream, sugar, and salt and heat the mixture gently, stirring over low heat or gently boiling water.

4. Grind on some pepper (quite a bit of it, in fact) just before serving.

SERVES 4–6

JARED'S BAKED ACORN SQUASH

Here's another approach to winter squash. Serve it with something simple—sausages, say, or plainly cooked chicken breasts. If you're a vegetarian, it makes a fine Thanksgiving dinner!

As you will see, this recipe contains cider. You can buy cider in its own season and freeze it until needed. It keeps beautifully.

2 large acorn (or Des Moines—same thing) squash

1 1/2 cups (415 ml) chopped onion

2 celery stalks, diced

1 apple, diced (peeled if it's a tough-skinned variety)

2 tablespoons butter

1 tablespoon olive oil

3 cups (825 ml) soft homemade bread crumbs

1/2 cup (140 ml) grated sharp Cheddar cheese

1/2 tablespoon minced fresh dill or 1/2 teaspoon dillweed

1/3–1/2 cup (75–120 ml) cider

1. Preheat your oven to 350°F (177°C).

2. Split the squash in two and remove and discard all the seeds and stringy material from inside. (A spoon is a handy tool for this procedure.) Place, cut-side down, on an oiled baking sheet. Bake until tender; about 30 minutes should do it.

3. Meanwhile, sauté the onion, celery, and apple gently in the butter and olive oil in a medium-size saucepan over moderately low heat. When they've become somewhat soft and translucent, stir in the bread crumbs, cheese, and dill. Now add the cider bit by bit until you have a nice cohesive (but not wet) mixture.

4. Pack the stuffing mixture into the squash halves, letting it mound up. Bake for about 20 minutes, or until brown.

Pickles

When you say "dill," most people think immediately of pickles. Dill pickles are everywhere, gracing every deli sandwich, right there with the potato chips. But what most people don't know is that you can easily make your own dill pickles, and they'll be better than any you can buy. So please, give these a try. They're dazzlingly good!

Continued ➜

I can't give you elaborate, detailed instructions for making pickles, sterilizing jars, using hot-water baths, and so forth. So I suggest that you consult any good book on preserving and/or pickling; for instance, there's Storey Books' *Big Book of Preserving the Harvest*.

For all cucumber pickles, use only small, unwaxed 'Kirby' cucumbers, which you can find in most markets. For dill seeds on the stem, use an herb that has matured and gone to seed, but has not become so ripe that the seeds have fallen off and disintegrated.

COUNTRY DILL PICKLES

These resemble the country store pickles our grandparents enjoyed, the ones they fished out of big barrels or crocks.

Those were (and are) "cold-pack pickles," the theory being that the vinegar and salt in the brine would prevent the development of any toxins. But now that most of us are so afraid of food poisoning, I'm giving you another version, one where boiling vinegar and water are involved and the jars are sealed.

1 tablespoon mixed pickling spices	*2 quarts (2 l) vinegar*
4 heads and stems of dill	*1 quart (1 l) water*
4 garlic cloves	*1 cup (275 ml) kosher or other coarse salt*
4 quarts (4 l) 'Kirby' pickling cucumbers	

1. Sterilize four 1-quart jars (try to find and use the widemouthed jars).

2. Divide the pickling spices among the jars. Put one head of dill, complete with its stem, into each jar. Peel the garlic cloves and put one into each jar.

3. Scrub the cucumbers well, then place in the jars, cramming them in as best you can.

4. Put the vinegar, water, and salt in a medium-size nonreactive saucepan and bring to a boil. Pour over the cucumbers, filling the jars to within 1/2 inch (13 mm) of the top. Seal.

5. Restrain yourself. Try not to eat the pickles for at least a week!

MAKES 4 QUARTS (4L)

SENFGURKEN

These wonderful morsels came into my life as a rescue mission. I had absentmindedly let some cucumbers in my garden go past what is usually considered the proper point of ripeness. They had become yellow and downright huge.

After making and tasting these, I always have let some cucumbers reach this point so I could make Senfgurken. If you don't have a garden of your own, perhaps you can talk a friend or even a roadside stand

operator into providing you with some nice ripe cucumbers (especially if you give them some of the Senfgurken in return).

4 large yellow cucumbers (the kind you would normally consider overripe)
1/2 cup (140 ml) kosher or other coarse salt
4 cups (950 ml) water
4 small sprigs dill, with seeds
2 teaspoons mustard seeds
6 cups (1,650 ml) sugar
4 cups (950 ml) white vinegar

1. Peel the cucumbers and split them in two lengthwise. Using a spoon, scoop out and discard the seeds. Cut the cucumbers into bite-size chunks.

2. Make a brine from the salt and water. Soak the cucumber chunks in this for at least 8 hours.

3. Sterilize four 1-quart (1-l) jars, preferably the widemouthed kind.

4. Divide the dill and mustard seeds among the jars.

5. Place the sugar and vinegar in a fairly large saucepan and boil over high heat until a light syrup is formed. Add the chunks of cucumber, drained from their brine, and cook for a few minutes, just until they begin to look somewhat translucent.

6. Divide the chunks among the jars and pour on the syrup in which they've been boiled. Seal the jars. Don't eat them for at least a week.

MAKES 4 QUARTS (4 L)

DILLY BEAN PICKLES

Not all dill-flavored pickles are based on cucumbers. In the South, for instance, you'll find okra dill pickles, which are pretty darn good, as are those made from Jerusalem artichokes. Carrots have been made into dill pickles, and so have small green tomatoes.

And then there are "dilly beans." These used to be available in fancy food stores in jars. Perhaps they still are, though I haven't seen them for quite some time.

So make your own! They make a remarkable little appetizer, and I've even seen people use them instead of an olive, twist of lemon peel, or pickled onion in a martini.

2 quarts (2 l) green beans, all the same size	*4 large sprigs dill*
2 teaspoons salt	*7 cups (1,645 ml) more water*
2 quarts (2 l) water	*1 cup (235 ml) cider vinegar*

1. Trim the tops and tails off the green beans. Remove any strings, if necessary. (It hardly ever is these days; the strings seem to have been bred out of most strains of green beans.)

2. Combine the salt and 2 quarts of water in a fairly large saucepan. Bring to a boil and stir until the salt is dissolved. Add the beans and cook for 5 to 7 minutes, or until crisp-tender. Drain well, discarding the water.

3. Meanwhile, sterilize two widemouthed quart jars or eight 1-cup (235 ml) ones. Pack the green beans into the jars, dividing the dill among them.

4. Combine the 7 cups (1,645 ml) of fresh water with the vinegar in a medium-size saucepan and bring to a full boil. Pour into the jars. Seal. Let sit for at least 2 weeks before using.

MAKES 2 QUARTS (2 L)

Growing & Using Rosemary

Bertha Reppert

Growing Rosemary

Rosmarinus officinalis grows best outdoors where winters are mild. Its name is from the Latin *ros marinus*, translated as "dew of the sea," which tells us something of its cultivation demands. It adores the sandy, well-drained shores of the mighty Mediterranean, where it basks in full sun while enjoying misting by the "dew of the sea."

For those of us who harbor pet rosemaries indoors every winter, certain requirements are the secret of growing rosemary houseplants successfully: coolness, sun, good drainage, and frequent misting.

I cannot emphasize enough the importance of these conditions. For those whose rosemary plants have perished from indoor container cultivation, give these essentials a try, especially the misting, and success will be yours. In fact, misting and humidity are so vital to rosemary's health and vigor, I recommend keeping a spray bottle handy at all times. It only takes a few seconds to mist a dozen plants (and people will benefit from the moisturized air as well).

Careful attention to watering is also vital to the well-being of a potted rosemary, indoors or out. Underwatering can be bad, but overwatering is a disaster. Your rosemary roots will rot, leaving you so quickly it will take your breath away. Rosemary can be unforgiving.

Proper drainage—never permitting water to accumulate in its saucer and allowing the plant to dry out between waterings—will prove to be a good precaution. Placing pots on a bed of pebbles in a large pan also works well. After the water drains off onto the stones, the evaporation of the water will give the rosemaries the moist humidity they require.

Warning: If you double-pot your rosemary using a decorative container, add drainage to the outer pot so the plant never sits in excess water. Monitor double-potted plants frequently.

When a sunny south, east, or west window is not available, try growing rosemary under horticultural grow-lights (actually any cool fluorescent fixture will work). This works surprisingly well and will brighten a dark corner to boot. Remember, rosemary requires at least six hours of sunlight every day to flourish. An unheated sunroom is ideal.

Any potted plant will eventually exhaust available soil nutrients. Monthly feeding with a good houseplant fertilizer is usually suggested. I like to alternate several different brands in small amounts applied frequently.

Occasionally we treat our rosemaries to a dose of Epsom salts. It kills bugs while also providing a nutritional element—magnesium.

Used in the ratio of 1 teaspoon per quart of tepid water, it is the "secret ingredient" that encourages sturdier stems and stronger fragrance.

Outdoors, rosemary will thrive in the garden, wallowing in the freedom to spread out and grow vigorously. In climates with moderate or warm winters, rosemary layers itself, especially on sun-drenched, well-drained banks, and has been called a "weed." We feed our garden rosemary bonemeal, superphosphate, and a bit of lime every fall. These fertilizers can be made available to the plants as needed. Compost and mulch are excellent additions, useful to keep down weeds while gently feeding the plants. In very hot areas, mulch is crucial to help stabilize soil temperatures that can otherwise mount to 130°F.

Rosemary is not reliably hardy north of Zone 7. In colder areas, light frosts signal the time when the plants should be put into pots to winter indoors. Rosemary withstands cold down to 28°F, so I pot my plants up in September, allowing them time to adjust their roots to confinement before being brought indoors in mid-November.

On a sunny fall day, potting the plants is a pleasant task. I assemble fresh potting soil mixed with sand and compost; drainage materials (recycled packing peanuts are lightweight and available); pots, matched or assorted, of all sizes; and a pair of good, sharp pruning shears. Instead of crowding the roots, I clip them to fill the pot comfortably. A little judicious top pruning may also be necessary. I talk to them, water them well, then set them aside in light shade to settle comfortably into new homes.

Outside in their pots, rosemary plants cheerfully withstand quite cold nights, especially if wrapped in plastic. In turn, the misty cool mornings are just what they need to settle into their pots and fortify themselves against impending life indoors—an environment frequently hot and dry with poor light.

On mild days in winter, I put my collection outside for a breath of fresh air. If weather reports are favorable, they can stay outside for several days, much to their liking. Moving the plants is a bit of a nuisance but well worth the effort. I can hear the grateful rosemaries whisper, "Thank you."

Propagating Rosemary

Starting rosemary is not difficult. Seeds are sometimes undependable, but there are other ways. If you would like to try that method, here is how: Start seeds in a pot of dampened perlite. Why perlite? Because it provides better drainage. Vermiculite and peat moss hold too much water. Even the seeds of rosemary will resent excessive water. Label and date your seeds, place the pot in a clear plastic bag, close the top, and set it aside. Germination, sometimes a mere 10 percent, usually takes two to three weeks, although it may be a bit faster with bottom heat. Watch through the plastic to witness the miracle of birth.

When this happens, open the bag to sun and air and start watering carefully. To prevent damping off—a condition caused by soil-borne organisms that destroy seedlings—water and mist your babies with chamomile tea (boil one tea bag in 2 cups water until golden yellow; strain, cool, and keep it handy in a mister). Chamomile is a natural fungicide that effectively takes care of seeds vulnerable to damping off.

Because seeds take time to sprout, after which it can take up to two years to obtain a nice-sized plant, I find it practical to buy a few plants to use for propagation. Once you have a rosemary or two, you can easily cultivate new plants by rooting cuttings. For this method of propagation, sever a 6-inch stem of rosemary from a major branch, if possible pulling it off with a heel (a bit of the old wood) by gently tugging downward.

Continued →

Remove all leaves from the lower 2 inches of stem to prevent rotting, dip the heel into rooting powder, thrust it into good, friable soil in a shaded location, and cover it with a quart jar to prevent the loss of moisture until your cutting develops roots and can live on its own.

Easier still, a long stem of rosemary can be propagated by layering. Simply pin the long stem, while it is still attached to the mother plant, to nearby soil. Use a U-shaped fern pin or heavy wire to anchor it firmly. Scrape the stem slightly at the bend where it touches the soil and apply a tiny bit of rooting powder to encourage roots.

When your stem shows signs of growth and a gentle tug resists your pull, you can sever the new plant from the old and plant it elsewhere. Water, then shade it slightly until it stops wilting and has nestled in.

Another interesting—and carefree—way to expand your inventory of rosemaries is in "willow water." This is only possible in the spring, when 12-inch cuttings of pussy willow root readily in tap water. New roots of pussy willow suspended in water will fill the jar with rooting hormones, forcing any companion sprig of rosemary to also form roots. This homemade rooting liquid was used by monks in ancient monasteries who observed that willow's propensity for rooting in water could be transferred to other plants in the same water. Try it! It may be medieval, but it is exciting to see roots appear where there were none. I recommend colored glass containers to moderate the burning effect of strong sun on new roots.

On the other hand, if you are eager to get growing with rosemary, I strongly suggest you buy a plant or two. Instant gratification will be yours, as you can start harvesting small bits immediately.

Harvesting and Preserving

In summer and in warmer climates, rosemary grows abundantly. This is a good time to snip bunches that may be hung and air-dried. Use rubber bands to hold the clusters of branches together. Then hang them out of the light in a dry, reasonably darkened spot away from windows. When thoroughly dry, remove the leaves and store them in tightly lidded, dark containers away from sun, heat, and humidity.

For immediate use, wash your harvest and roll it tightly in a clean terry towel to dry. In a towel, rosemary will stay fresh in the refrigerator for as long as two weeks. You can freeze the unused stems.

Taper off your harvesting come fall, when no more than a third of your bush should be taken. It will need all its strength to get through the long winter, especially if it will be brought indoors.

Using Your Rosemary

Now that you have conquered growing rosemaries, the real fun lies in using them. Of course, in most instances, dried rosemary can also be utilized. Crush it or heat it to release the fragrant oils.

POTPOURRI CRAFTS

Assorted dried flowers, herbs, spices combined with a fixative such as orris root (1 ounce per gallon of dried material), and fragrant essential oil will blend into a scented and useful potpourri. Add a cup of dried rosemary leaves "for remembrance" to a quart of your mixture. It will create a memorable souvenir of a wedding, funeral, anniversary, birthday celebration, or any special occasion. Rosemary potpourri can be:

- simmered to freshen the air;
- glued to Styrofoam forms of all sizes;
- placed in open bowls as fragrant decorations;
- wrapped in 6-inch squares of fabric as sachets to put in small drawers; or
- used for party favors.

SIMPLE, EFFECTIVE MOTH CHASER SACHETS

1 cup rosemary leaves, dried

1 cup lavender blossoms, dried

1 cup cinnamon bark, crushed

Mix well to make half a dozen lovely drawer sachets to use as favors or small gifts.

SCENTS FOR HOME AND PERSONAL CARE

Rosemary is indispensable for cosmetic or household chores.

Soap. Melt down small slivers of soap. Then add a few drops of rosemary essential oil (a concentrated, volatile, natural substance extracted directly from the plant) for a therapeutic bar said to deter acne and wrinkles and to promote cleansing.

ROSEMARY SOAP BALLS

12 small, personal-sized bars of soap, broken into small pieces

1 1/2 cups boiling water

1/2 cup rosemary, fresh or dried

Steep rosemary in water for 20 minutes. Strain and pour over soap. Heat together until mushy. When the rosemary tea has been absorbed and the entire mixture is lukewarm, form small soap balls. Allow to dry thoroughly (may take three to four days) before packaging in jars or individually in fabric. If color is desired, use bits of wax crayon in the melt-down.

Shampoo. Dark hair benefits enormously from the oils in rosemary. Boil 1/2 cup fresh rosemary in 1 cup water. Then strain and add the decoction to a pint bottle of your favorite shampoo. According to directions on a bottle of rosemary shampoo I purchased years ago in London, you should "allow the lather to remain on the hair for five minutes or longer and it will intensify the color, cause the hair to grow, and quicken the wit."

Pets. If your pets are shedding excessively, it's rosemary to the rescue. A few drops of the essential oil of rosemary on a pet's brush will help ease shedding.

Bath. A few drops of the essential oil of rosemary mixed well into your bath will perfume the air as well as relax a weary body and alert all the senses.

SOME DECORATIVE USES

Used decoratively since the earliest times, rosemary has found its niche in gardens, homes, and hearts. Its charm and heady perfume cannot be denied.

Garlands, chaplets, and wreaths are but a few of the ways to enjoy rosemary decoratively. I gather every dead branch to weave, while still supple, into a large wreath. On state occasions, I adorn my wreath with a nosegay of fresh rosemary and ribbons.

Wreaths. Wreaths are easily crafted by pinning fresh rosemary cuttings to a straw wreath. Other herbs may be included. Use fern pins and overlap the little bunches, always going in the same direction, covering the stems with each succeeding bunch.

Chaplets. Rosemary chaplets are just as easy. Form grapevine or honeysuckle into a circle that fits the head. Bind short rosemary sprigs to it with sturdy thread or wool, always overlapping and continuing in the same direction. Suitable for crowning a bride (with the addition of flowers) or a young communicant, such circlets were worn by Roman and Greek scholars of old to promote thinking, emphasizing the importance of simply smelling rosemary. Today we call this aromatherapy.

Decorations. You might like to try some of these quick and easy decorative hints for enjoying your rosemary:

- Bouquets and centerpieces smell sweeter when enhanced with stems of rosemary.

- Tiny tussie-mussies are adorable; several bunched sprigs caught with narrow ribbons can be tucked into a white doily to wear, carry, or lay next to a photo "for remembrance."

- Garnish a large roast lavishly with rosemary tips.

- Stick a sturdy stem of rosemary into a fresh orange for an old-world traditional New Year's greeting.

- If a rosemary standard has perished, poke the frame full of colorful dried flowers for an attractive, maintenance-free decoration.

- Wire a few rosemary sprigs into a tiny circlet to wreath a gift bottle of wine or rosemary vinegar.

- Use tiny circlets of rosemary as napkin rings.

- Make clever notepapers by photocopying rosemary pieces on a white paper doily background.

- Train a 3-foot rosemary standard to dominate a small garden of low-growing herbs such as thyme.

- Using porous cheesecloth or old nylons, wrap small snippets of rosemary tightly against eggs you intend to hard-boil for Easter. Placed in a hot dye bath for 20 or 30 minutes, they come out colored, decorated, and ready to serve. The white tracery of rosemary is a lovely touch.

- Homemade rosemary baskets are special. Choose a loosely woven basket and weave 6-inch pieces of fresh rosemary into the existing frame. They become part of the basket as they dry.

- Tie a generous sprig of rosemary into the bow of an important gift—"for remembrance."

Cooking with Rosemary

Cooking—or eating—food with rosemary appeals to everyone. When I was married 50 years ago, I was given Betty Crocker's wartime cookbook. Determined to learn to cook and surpass my mother's

Germanic cuisine, I proceeded to take Ms. Crocker's advice on filling my spice cupboard properly. Rosemary came as a surprise to me.

I surmised it grew on a pine tree. It looked like pine needles, smelled like pine, tasted piney. What a revelation when I found my first rosemary plant some years later at an Italian greengrocer who sold herb plants! Now rosemary has become my favorite.

Start with small amounts until you develop a taste for this adventurous flavor. Remember the rule—1 teaspoon dried equals 1 tablespoon fresh. The dried herb with captured concentrated oils can be very strong when heated or crushed. Therefore a smidgen may be all you need in the beginning—a teaspoon or a tablespoon can be overpowering. In any recipe, add rosemary to your taste.

SOME EASY TIPS

1. Use rosemary to transform cauliflower into company fare.

2. Cream chopped fresh rosemary into softened butter or cream cheese for a hot bread treat.

3. Garnish orange slices with rosemary.

4. Try rosemary on spinach, eggplant, peas, or squash.

5. Serve the flowers as an attractive edible garnish.

6. Skewer shish kebabs on 12-inch lengths of rosemary.

7. Enhance a variety of Mediterranean dishes with just a pinch of rosemary.

8. Use several sprigs of rosemary, tied together, as a flavor-enhancing basting brush for sauces.

9. Add a few leaves to any marinade.

10. Try using rosemary in your fruit salad—you'll be amazed!

SCARBOROUGH FAIRE SEASONED SALT

Using a well-herbed seasoned salt can automatically reduce your salt intake. The herbs that replace the salt will tease the palate into accepting less salt. For those on reduced salt—or salt-free—diets, these welcome flavor enhancers are helpful and nutritious. They are the most popular items sold in any culinary shop.

4 tablespoons parsley, dried and finely crushed

3 tablespoons sage, dried and finely crushed

2 tablespoons rosemary, dried and finely crushed

1 tablespoon thyme, dried and finely crushed

1 cup salt

Mix thoroughly and package in a large-holed shaker. Useful on meats, fowl, fish, and vegetables. Note: For salt-free diets, remove the salt for an all-herb seasoning.

Continued →

HERBED OLIVES

This recipe is typical of southern Spain (Andalusia) and is a popular form of tapas.

1 7-ounce jar green Spanish olives, drained and lightly crushed	*1/2 teaspoon thyme*
	1/2 teaspoon fennel seed
1/2 teaspoon ground cumin	*2 bay leaves*
1/2 teaspoon oregano	*4 garlic cloves, peeled and crushed*
1/4 teaspoon rosemary	*4 tablespoons cider vinegar*

In a jar (you can use the original olive jar), combine the olives, garlic, and bay leaves so they are evenly distributed. Add all herbs and vinegar. Fill jar to the top with water and shake to thoroughly mix ingredients. Marinate for several days at room temperature. Store in refrigerator but serve at room temperature.

SERVES 12 AS A NIBBLE

OLIVE CHEESE NUGGETS

A welcome appetizer at any party. Make these well in advance and you will find them easy to bake at the last minute as a hot treat. They are also good cold.

1/4 cup butter	*1/2 teaspoon paprika*
1/4 pound Cheddar cheese, grated	*1/2 teaspoon ground rosemary*
3/4 cup all-purpose flour (or slightly less)	*36–40 medium stuffed olives*

Preheat oven to 400°F. Blend butter and cheese. Add flour, paprika, and rosemary. Blend well and form a dough. Using about 1 teaspoon dough, flatten dough in the palm of your hand and wrap it around an olive. Bake on ungreased cookie sheet for 12 to 15 minutes, until light golden brown. Serve immediately.

ROSEMARY FISH

Izaak Walton, a 17th-century English writer, recommended this seasoning: "Cook fish with a handful of horseradish, a handsome faggot of rosemary, some thyme and a sprig of savory."

ROSEMARY JELLY

Herbal jellies always come as a delightful taste surprise. They are a delicious way to enjoy herbal flavors on toast or hot biscuits, suitable for any meal or teatime. On first bite you encounter the citrus flavor but then, suddenly, the tang of rosemary activates the taste buds.

2 heaping tablespoons fresh rosemary, chopped (or 1 tablespoon dried, whole)	*3/4 cup water*
	3 1/4 cups sugar
1/4 cup lemon juice	*3 ounces liquid pectin (one Certo pouch)*
1/2 cup orange juice	*Several sprigs rosemary, for garnish*

Boil rosemary, lemon juice, orange juice, water, and sugar for seven minutes, stirring constantly. Strain. Return to boil. Add 3 ounces liquid pectin (one Certo pouch) and boil vigorously for one minute, stirring constantly. Skim off any foam that may rise. Immediately fill sterilized jars, adding a small sprig of rosemary for decoration. Seal with paraffin and label. Hint: Collect attractive juice or wine glasses for a pretty presentation.

FILLS 6 TO 8 SMALL GLASSES

SMOKED ROSEMARY APPLES

This unusual garnish or condiment requires a pot with a rack and a tight lid. The apples are pretty decorated with curls of orange zest taken from the orange before juicing.

Juice of 1 orange	*1 tablespoon liquid smoke*
Several dried rosemary stems	*2 apples, sliced*

Place the juice, rosemary, and liquid smoke in the bottom of the pot with apple slices piled on the rack. Smoke for 30 minutes or until soft.

MAKES 4 TO 6 SERVINGS

EUREKA POTATOES ROSEMARY

A straggly rosemary that needs trimming is the signal to plan on potatoes seasoned with fresh rosemary. You will need quite a bit of the fresh herb. Don't even think about serving potatoes (except french fried) without the kiss of rosemary—they are made for each other. A strong seasoning, rosemary can be added successfully to dehydrated mashed potatoes reconstituted according to package directions.

6 medium-sized potatoes, pared	*1/2 teaspoon black pepper*
3/4 cup hot milk	*1 teaspoon baking powder*
2 tablespoons butter	*1/2 cup fresh rosemary, minced*
1 teaspoon salt (optional)	

Cook potatoes 30 minutes, drain, and mash. Add everything except rosemary and beat vigorously until fluffy. Add rosemary and serve.

MAKES 6 TO 8 SERVINGS

PATRIOTS' PUNCH

We devised this superb recipe for herbal tea during the U.S. Bicentennial celebration. Depending upon the occasion, we divide it into two punch bowls, half according to this recipe and the other with dry white wine added.

5 tablespoons dried peppermint, whole	*1 small can frozen lemonade concentrate*
3 tablespoons dried sage, whole	*4 tablespoons instant tea*
2 tablespoons dried rosemary, whole	*2–3 gallons cold water*
1 quart water, boiled briskly	*Lemon slices, whole cloves, and rosemary for garnish*
1 cup sugar (or to taste)	

Steep herbs in boiled water for 5 to 10 minutes until well flavored. Strain and add remaining ingredients. Serve iced with lemon slices stuck with whole cloves and garnished with rosemary.

MAKES 50 SERVINGS

EASY ROSEMARY ROAST CHICKEN

The combination of rosemary and garlic is unbeatable. We enjoy it on almost everything, even crusts of toasted bread. You might try these bold seasonings on lamb, beef, or pork chops.

3 garlic cloves, peeled and crushed	1/2 teaspoon freshly ground pepper
1 teaspoon dried rosemary, crushed	1/4 cup vegetable oil
1 teaspoon salt (optional)	1 whole chicken (about 2 1/2 pounds)

Mix together the garlic, rosemary, salt, and pepper. Rub half of the seasoning inside washed chicken. Rub half of the oil over outside of chicken and sprinkle with remaining seasoning. Place chicken in roasting pan and drizzle with remaining oil. Roast at 275°F until brown and crisp, basting with pan drippings every 15 minutes, for one hour.

MAKES 4 SERVINGS

ROSEMARY–LEMON VERBENA TEA CAKE

Perhaps you wouldn't dream of making a cake with a mix. This recipe transforms a convenient mix into a moist cake you can serve with pride—and rosemary.

1 package yellow cake mix	1/2 cup oil
4 eggs	2 tablespoons lemon juice
1 cup water	1 tablespoon fresh rosemary, finely chopped
1 package instant vanilla pudding mix	2 tablespoons lemon verbena, finely chopped

Mix all ingredients for 2 1/2 minutes. Put in lightly greased Bundt pan. Bake at 350°F for 40 minutes. Cool 15 minutes in pan. Remove and glaze with:

Glaze

1 cup powdered sugar

2 tablespoons lemon juice

Combine and drizzle over warm cake.

MAKES 12 TO 20 SERVINGS

GOLDEN RAISIN ROSEMARY MUFFINS

A favorite in our household, this is always a treat—sometimes hot for dinner, sometimes cold for tea. We use the recipe to make muffins or loaves of bread.

3/4 cup milk	1/2 cup granulated sugar
1/2 cup golden raisins	2 teaspoons baking powder
1 teaspoon dried rosemary leaves	1/4 teaspoon salt
1/4 cup butter	1 large egg
1 1/2 cups all-purpose flour	

Simmer milk, raisins, and rosemary for two minutes in a small saucepan. Remove from heat, add butter, and stir until melted. Let cool. Heat oven to 350°F. Grease muffin cups or line muffin tin with foil baking cups. Mix flour, sugar, baking powder, and salt in a large bowl. Whisk egg into milk mixture. Pour over dry ingredients and fold in with a rubber spatula until dry ingredients are moistened. Scoop batter into muffin cups. Bake about 20 minutes or until done. (Can also be made in one regular loaf pan or two small ones, 3" x 9 1/2"—bake 35 minutes or until done.)

MAKES 12 LARGE, OR 24 MEDIUM, MUFFINS

THE ROSEMARY HOUSE OPEN HOUSE COOKIES

Attended by hundreds, our semiannual Open House parties are known for delicious refreshments that are beautifully presented. The recipes must be economical, generous, and yummy. These cookies qualify.

1 cup butter or margarine	1 teaspoon baking powder
2 cups sugar	1 teaspoon baking soda
2 eggs, beaten	1/2 teaspoon salt
1 cup sour cream	3 teaspoons dried lemon balm, crushed
1 orange, juice and grated rind	3 teaspoons dried rosemary, crushed
3 1/2 cups all-purpose flour, sifted	

Mix butter and sugar. Add eggs and sour cream, orange juice, and rind. Blend in the sifted dry ingredients and herbs. Drop by teaspoons onto greased cookie sheets. Bake at 350°F for 10–12 minutes.

Glaze

1 cup powdered sugar

1 lemon, juice and grated rind

Mix glaze and frost cookies while still hot.

MAKES A BUNCH!

ROSEMARY BISCUITS

Although this is a foolproof made-from-scratch recipe, rosemary transforms packaged biscuit mix and can be used in shortcut baking. It is equally robust in dumplings, breads, pasta, and the crusts of quiche.

2 cups all-purpose flour

4 teaspoons baking powder

1/2 teaspoon rosemary, dried (or 1 1/2 teaspoons fresh)

4 tablespoons shortening

1/4 cup milk

Combine dry ingredients; add shortening. Blend in milk. Knead about six times. Pat out to 1/2" thick and cut with biscuit cutter. Bake in 450°F oven for 12–15 minutes.

MAKES 12 BISCUITS

Bibliography

Bown, Deni. *The Herb Society of America Encyclopedia of Herbs and Their Uses.* London and New York: Dorling Kindersley, 1995.

Continued ➜

French, Jackie. *Book of Rosemary*. London and Australia: HarperCollins, 1993.

Friend, Hilderic. *Flower Lore*. Rockport, MA: Para Research, 1981. (Reprint of 1884 volume.)

Gordon, Lesley. *A Country Herbal*. New York: Mayflower Books, 1980.

Hill, Madalene and Gwen Barclay. *Southern Herb Growing*. Fredericksburg, TX: Shearer Publishing Co., 1987.

Hollis, Sarah. *The Country Diary Herbal*. Avenel, NJ: Winga Books, 1995.

Schafer, Violet. *Herbcraft*. San Francisco: Yerba Buena Press, 1971.

Smith, Keith Vincent. *The Illustrated Earth Garden Herbal*. Thomas Nelson Australia Pty. Ltd., 1978.

Growing & Using Tarragon

Glenn Andrews

Illustrations by Charles Joslin and Mary Rich

Growing Tarragon

Tarragon is unusual in that it does not seed. Ever. To grow tarragon you must have a cutting or division from an existing plant. If you see seeds for tarragon, they are probably for Russian tarragon, which does seed (this is one way to tell them apart), and grows easily from those seeds. Mexican tarragon also grows from seeds or cuttings.

WHICH TARRAGON TO USE

For cooking, you want to find French tarragon (which, for simplicity, we will call tarragon from now on). It isn't always easy to find the right plants. Some companies actually market Russian tarragon seed labeled simply TARRAGON, but all you have to know to protect yourself is that true French tarragon cannot reproduce from seed.

You'll find both French and Russian tarragon at various nurseries and plant shops and even at many supermarkets. With luck, they will be labeled. My advice to you is to distrust the labels, though. There are few things as disappointing as learning the hard way (when you use it) that you have a tarragon that has no taste. So ask permission to break off a leaf, scrunch it between your fingers, smell it, then taste it. Better yet, find a trustworthy friend who grows tarragon and get a cutting you know is the right stuff.

PROPAGATING FROM CUTTINGS

Because of tarragon's tenderness, cuttings are best taken from stems. For the same reason, it's best to use hardwood cuttings, from the previous year's growth, or perhaps sturdy semisoft-wood cuttings, from the current year's growth. Be sure to take branch tips, preferably with a terminal bud. The best time to take cuttings is in summer when the plant is strong. If you are planting the cuttings outdoors, put them in the ground early enough in the season to give them time to develop before cold weather sets in.

Tarragon

ROOT DIVISION

There are two ways to root-divide your tarragon.

The first method is to start in early spring by loosening dirt around the roots. Then use a spade to cut through the roots to make a division, lifting it out of the ground with the spade. If your tarragon is healthy, replace dirt around the remaining roots. Rinse the dirt off the roots of the division and set in a pot of light soil, preferably with added perlite, covering only the roots. Water with care, but avoiding saturating. Most tarragons die not from cold but from too much moisture rotting the roots.

The second method of root division will yield several smaller plants rather than two larger ones. When new shoots start to show through the soil, dig up the entire plant and wash away the soil from the roots. Any root that has a shoot attached can be separated and replanted. If there are rotted roots, cut them away, but do not root-trim the plant otherwise. Replant the separated plants and in approximately two weeks you should have a few new plants to share with friends.

Even if you don't want to give away divisions, it's a good idea to divide the plant every few years anyway, as the tangled roots and woody stems make the plants seem tired and less vigorous. In that case, choose the healthiest-looking pieces of root to replant.

CARE AND HARDINESS

Tarragon will go dormant over the winter, but should be up again and thriving by springtime. Don't be downhearted if your plant shows no signs of life early. Once the weather and the soil warm up, it should bound right back.

Some say to mulch your plant heavily when winter comes, but there are others who say not to bother. In fact, I gave a plant years ago to some friends who live in Maine, where 40-below weather is not at all uncommon, and it has thrived without any winter overcoat at all. It does help, though, to have the plant in a spot where it will be protected from harsh, cold winds. The farther north you are, and the more exposed your garden, the more you should consider mulching. Dried leaves, pine needles, evergreen boughs, straw, even matted-down newspapers will make a good mulch. The most important thing, again, is to make sure the plant is not overwatered. Too much water will rot the roots and kill the plant.

The same is true if you are in a very warm climate—Florida, for instance. Your main concern will be to avoid overwatering. So if you have a lawn sprinkler system, as most Floridians and Californians do, position your tarragon where it will be protected from any deluges. Cut it back from time to time to about half (and see below for how to preserve what you take off).

The ideal spot in your garden for French tarragon is sunny but sheltered. Full sun is best, but your plant will tolerate partial light shade. The soil should be fairly rich, deeply dug, and definitely well drained. Position the plants so the level of soil is 1 to 1 1/2 inches above the top of the roots. Tarragon prefers a pH of 5.5–6.5, so if your soil tends to be acidic, mix in some wood ash in to help it thrive.

HARVESTING AND PRESERVING

You can harvest leaves or sprigs throughout the growing season. But stop in early fall to give the plant a chance to recover before winter sets in. Most herbalists say you should pick in early morning after the dew has dried. The essential oils in herbs are strongest then. Once you have picked the leaves, wash to remove any dirt and set on a clean towel or paper towel to dry. Use immediately or preserve.

There are several ways to preserve the leaves you remove from the plants.

First, you can immerse them in wine or vinegar. The color will fade a bit, but the flavor will be fine. You can then use the wine or vinegar in cooking and also use the leaves as you would fresh tarragon.

Next, you can dry them. Traditional drying (hanging for a week or more) is not the best method for tarragon, as a significant amount of flavor is lost this way. A better method of drying is to use the microwave. Try putting leaves or sprigs on a paper towel and microwaving them on high power for about 3 minutes. Check them every 60 seconds or so. They are done when they are dry to the touch but have not lost any color. Store in airtight containers away from direct light. If you see moisture beads in the containers, dry again in the microwave.

Or you can dry them in the refrigerator. Modern frost-free refrigerators are not only cool, but dry as well. To dry herbs in the fridge, place a layer on paper towels on cookie sheets, place a bunch in a mesh bag and hang from a magnetic hook in the fridge, or place a bunch in a bowl. The time it takes them to dry will depend on your refrigerator, its contents, and the method of drying. If you are drying in a bowl, stir the herbs a couple of times a day so they are all exposed to the air. Do not cover herbs drying in the fridge. And be careful that your fridge contains nothing with a strong odor, as this might affect the flavor of the drying tarragon.

The last method of preserving tarragon is to incorporate it into recipes like Tarragon Mustard, Frozen Tarragon Cubes, and Béarnaise Butter, or one of the other goodies in this bulletin.

Recipes

Tarragon is best known as a flavoring for eggs, poultry, and fish. But that is not the entire tarragon story. It is a very versatile cooking herb.

CONDIMENTS, SAUCES, AND SEASONINGS

Here you'll find tarragon in many guises. Any of them will add a fabulous burst of flavor to your cooking, and they're all well worth making to have on hand.

TARRAGON VINEGAR

Making this vinegar is an excellent way to keep a touch of tarragon available at all times. The vinegar itself is a wonderful addition to your larder, and when you need fresh tarragon, simply remove the required amount from the vinegar. It will look just a little washed out, but that's all right!

Sorry, but this is one case where you simply can't substitute dry tarragon. The fresh herb is the only way to go. But it keeps for months, so make a store in the summer when you have fresh tarragon, and enjoy until the new harvest is ready. And don't be afraid to experiment with other herbs and spices. Rosemary and tarragon are a good pair.

4 large sprigs tarragon

2 cups white wine vinegar (or rice vinegar, if you can't find the white wine variety)

1. Put the tarragon sprigs in a bottle. Add the vinegar. (A small-mouthed funnel comes in handy here.)

2. Let sit for at least two weeks to allow the flavor to develop.

3. Can be made in any quantity. Just remember the ratio of a large sprig of tarragon to every half-cup of vinegar. This treat will keep—at room temperature—as long as you want it to.

Tarragon and Garlic Vinegar. Nothing could be simpler. Just follow the instructions for Tarragon Vinegar, above, and add a large, whole peeled garlic clove for each cup of vinegar.

Tarragon Wine. Broiled chicken is remarkably good when you baste it with this wine as it cooks. In fact, use this for any dish in which you want the taste of tarragon along with a touch of white wine.

This is made exactly like Tarragon Vinegar, but with a dry white wine instead of vinegar for your base. It, too, will keep indefinitely.

FROZEN TARRAGON CUBES

When you have a supply of these little cubes in your freezer, you will never suffer from a lack of minced "fresh" tarragon. If the tarragon sprigs you use are supple and tender, the stems can be used right along with the leaves. If the stems are woody, it's best to strip off and use only the leaves.

4 cups, packed, tarragon sprigs (see above)

1/2 cup olive oil

Garlic, optional (see below)

1. Put the tarragon in a food processor. Start the machine and add the olive oil gradually until the mixture reaches a pastelike consistency. (You may not have to add all the oil.) If you want to add the garlic, do so now.

2. Put the tarragon paste into ice cube trays and place in your freezer.

3. When the paste is frozen, put the cubes into one or more plastic bags, label, and continue to keep frozen.

4. Use whenever fresh tarragon is called for and wherever it sounds like a good idea. (A few "good ideas" for you: Add a cube or two to scrambled eggs, any rice dish, or on top of any vegetable.)

Variation: If you don't want to add garlic, you can add other herbs. Make sure you label your cubes as plain, garlic, or mixed herb.

TARRAGON MUSTARD

3 tablespoons dry mustard

2 tablespoons mustard seed

1/2 teaspoon salt

1 dash turmeric (optional—it's mostly for color)

2/3 cup less 1 tablespoon boiling water

1/4 cup Tarragon Vinegar (above)

1/4 cup white wine

Continued →

1. Put the dry mustard, mustard seed, salt, and turmeric (if you're using it) into a fairly small saucepan. Stir in the boiling water. Let sit for 45 minutes.

2. Now add the Tarragon Vinegar and white wine. Pour the contents of the pan into a food processor and run the machine until the mixture is smooth. (It's all right for it to be a little lumpy, though, because of the mustard seeds.)

3. Return to the saucepan. Cook over very low heat, stirring and scraping, until the mustard has thickened slightly.

4. Remove to a jar. Cover when cool, then keep under refrigeration. ("Keep it cool and it'll stay hot," as an old ad for some sort of mustard used to say.)

MAKES A LITTLE LESS THAN 1 CUP

BÉARNAISE SAUCE

Béarnaise, one of the loveliest of all sauces, would not be béarnaise without tarragon. There are many complicated recipes for it, but this is one of the simplest and best. It is especially good with steak (or hamburgers) or broiled chicken.

1 egg

1 egg yolk

1 tablespoon Tarragon Vinegar

1 tablespoon minced shallots

2 tablespoons heavy or sour cream

Pinch of cayenne or 3 drops Tabasco or other hot sauce

Pinch of salt

4 tablespoons butter

1 1/2 teaspoons minced fresh tarragon or 1/2 teaspoon dry (but try to use the fresh)

1. Place all the ingredients except the butter in the top part of a double boiler or in a small bowl that will fit over a saucepan. Whisk well.

2. Put the double boiler top or bowl over—not in—hot, but not boiling, water. Whisk while the mixture heats.

3. When the sauce begins to thicken, stir in the butter, just a teaspoon or two at a time. Now add the tarragon.

4. If you want the sauce to be thicker, cook and stir a bit more.

5. Serve at room temperature.

MAKES ABOUT 1/2 CUP

APPETIZERS

The appetizers given here are for "nibbles" to either start a meal or serve along with drinks (alcoholic or non). Because of tarragon's distinctive flavor, I suggest you serve only one of these at any gathering in order to avoid culinary redundancy. For me, though, it would be hard to choose just one!

CREAMY TARRAGON DIP

This dip is aptly titled "Creamy" because of its consistency and the way it looks, but it's possible to make it comparatively free of butterfat (if that's what you want) by using Neufchâtel instead of cream cheese and low-fat mayonnaise. Either way, it's a lovely creation.

1 8-ounce package cream cheese or Neufchâtel

1/2 cup mayonnaise

1/4 cup milk (more if needed)

1 tablespoon Tarragon Vinegar

1/2 teaspoon sugar

1 tablespoon minced fresh tarragon or 1 teaspoon dry

1 tablespoon minced scallion

1. Combine all the ingredients by mashing or running them together in a food processor. Refrigerate, covered, until needed.

2. Serve with an assortment of fresh vegetables, cut into appropriate sizes. (Cocktail tomatoes, broccoli or cauliflower florets, snow peas, and carrot sticks work well here.)

3. If the dip becomes too stiff after being refrigerated, thin it down by adding just a little milk.

MAKES ABOUT 2 CUPS

TARRAGON PUFFS

These can be made with the sort of crescent rolls that come in a little cylinder in the dairy section of most supermarkets, or you could use puff pastry (your own or store-bought). You can freeze the puffs before or after baking.

3 ounces cream cheese or Neufchâtel

1 tablespoon milk

1 tablespoon minced fresh tarragon or 1 teaspoon dry

Freshly ground black pepper

1 roll refrigerated crescent rolls

1 egg, lightly beaten (optional)

1. Preheat your oven to 375°F. Lightly grease a flat baking tin (a cookie sheet, for instance, or a jelly-roll pan).

2. Mash the cheese with the milk, tarragon, and a little black pepper (just two or three grinds from a pepper mill).

3. Open the package of crescent rolls and divide into four rectangles on a lightly floured surface. Press the seams of each rectangle, then spread with the cream cheese mixture.

4. Roll up each rectangle from the long side. Then cut each roll into six sections. Place them, nicely separated and seam-side down, on the prepared baking tin. Brush each with a bit of the beaten egg. (This is optional, but gives the puffs a nice glaze and a highly professional look.)

5. Bake for about 12 minutes, or until lightly browned.

MAKES 24

SOUPS

Soup is probably the greatest comfort food of all, and soups with a touch of tarragon are the best!

TARRAGON-TOMATO SOUP

If you, like most of us, grew up on canned tomato soup, and still enjoy it, you'll find this version is quite a bit better. (Of course, you could always just add a little tarragon to your canned soup, but . . .)

2 cups minced onion

2 tablespoons butter

6 large, very ripe tomatoes, peeled, seeded, and chopped

2 1/4 cups milk

Salt and freshly ground black pepper

1 tablespoon minced fresh tarragon or 1 teaspoon dry

1. Cook the onion in the butter in a medium-size saucepan over fairly low heat until it is soft but not brown.

2. Add the chopped tomatoes and simmer all together, covered, for 15 minutes.

3. Add the milk and the salt and pepper to taste and simmer for another 10 minutes. If you want a creamier soup, add a little cream with the milk.

4. Add the tarragon and simmer for another 2 minutes. Serve hot.

SERVES 4

WHITE BEAN AND TARRAGON SOUP

If you'd rather have a more pronounced smoky flavor, you can cook a ham hock along with the beans rather than adding the ham at the end. Or if you don't want any ham at all, do add 2 or 3 drops of liquid smoke (available in most supermarkets) along with the chicken broth.

1/2 pound navy or great Northern white beans

3/4 cup minced onion

1 teaspoon (or more) minced garlic

2 tablespoons olive oil

6 cups chicken stock or vegetable broth

1 tablespoon minced fresh tarragon or 1 teaspoon dry

1/4 cup finely chopped ham

1 tablespoon freshly squeezed lemon juice

Salt and freshly ground black pepper

1. Wash the beans. Cover with 4 inches of water and let sit overnight. Drain well. (An alternate method, preferred by quite a few: Put the dry beans in a saucepan. Cover with 3 cups of water. Bring the water to a boil and cook for 2 minutes. Remove the pan from the heat, cover, and let sit for 1 hour. Drain and continue with the recipe.)

2. Sauté the onion and garlic in the olive oil in a large saucepan or stockpot over medium-low heat until soft but not browned.

3. Add the beans and the stock. Cover the pan and simmer over low heat for about 1 hour, or until the beans are soft.

4. Add the tarragon, ham, and lemon juice. Season to taste with salt and pepper. Serve now or reheat and serve later.

SERVES 4 TO 6

COLD TARRAGON SOUP

I love this soup as a first course, but I can easily see it being lunch all by itself or perhaps with some plain rolls on the side.

If you want a somewhat more substantial soup, sprinkle on about a third of a cup of chopped cooked shrimp just before serving. Also, you can line each soup bowl with soft, buttery lettuce such as Boston or Bibb.

1 package plain, unflavored gelatin

1/4 cup cold water

5 cups chicken broth

2 tablespoons chopped fresh tarragon or 2 teaspoons dry

2 teaspoons lemon juice

3 teaspoons minced parsley

1. Stir the gelatin into the cold water, mixing well. Set aside.

2. Bring the chicken broth to a boil over medium-high heat, then turn the heat down to medium-low and simmer for 7 minutes. Stir in the gelatin mixture.

3. Remove from the heat and let sit for 10 minutes, then stir in the tarragon.

4. When the soup has cooled, cover it and refrigerate for 4 hours or more.

5. To serve, stir the soup gently, then divide it among four bowls. Sprinkle each with 1/2 teaspoon of lemon juice and some of the parsley.

SERVES 4

MEAT, POULTRY, AND SEAFOOD

Some of the very best uses for tarragon fall into this category. Nothing (in my opinion, anyway) can equal what this fragrant herb does to any meat, poultry, or fish.

When you are barbecuing, try throwing sprigs of tarragon on the coals just before you do the cooking. Older, woody sprigs work best for this purpose, simply because they will dissipate more slowly on the fire, but younger ones will add flavor as well.

Continued ➜

BEEF STEW WITH TARRAGON

The red wine helps give this stew a beautiful brown color, but you can substitute water and a tablespoon of lemon juice.

3 tablespoons oil

1 pound stewing beef, in 1 1/2-inch cubes

3 tablespoons flour

1/2 cup red wine (or see above)

Water

3 medium potatoes, peeled (if you wish) and cut into 1-inch cubes

1/2 pound carrots, peeled and cut into 1-inch cubes

1 teaspoon minced garlic

1 tablespoon minced fresh tarragon or 1 teaspoon dry

2 tablespoons Worcestershire sauce (optional, but nice)

Salt and freshly ground black pepper

1. Heat the oil in a medium-size saucepan over moderately high heat. Brown the meat in this, then stir in the flour and cook for 2 or 3 minutes more. Remove from the heat.

2. Add the red wine and enough water to barely cover the meat. Cover the pot and simmer over low heat for 1 hour.

2. Add the vegetables and enough more water to cover them. Cook, covered, until they are tender.

3. Add the tarragon, Worcestershire sauce, and salt and pepper to taste. Simmer for another 10 minutes.

4. Either serve at once or cool, then refrigerate for several hours or overnight. (If you do wait, remove any fat from the top of the stew.)

SERVES 6

PORK TENDERLOIN WITH ORANGE AND TARRAGON

Pork tenderloin is very tender and tasty—especially in this orange- and tarragon-flavored dish. The butter and oil and sour cream keep this recipe out of the low-fat class, but you could always use lower-fat sour cream.

1 1/2 pounds pork tenderloin

Salt and freshly ground black pepper

1/4 cup flour

1 tablespoon butter

1 tablespoon olive oil

1 1/2 teaspoons minced fresh tarragon or 1/2 teaspoon dry

1/4 cup frozen orange concentrate, thawed but undiluted

1/4 cup sherry

1 cup sour cream

1. Cut the pork into 1/2-inch medallions. Pound them between two sheets of heavy plastic or butcher's paper with a meat mallet or heavy skillet until they are 1/8 inch thick. Sprinkle them with salt and pepper to taste and coat lightly with flour.

2. Heat the butter and olive oil in a large skillet over medium-high heat. Add the pork medallions and cook for 2 or 3 minutes on each side, until brown. Remove from the pan and keep warm.

3. Stir the tarragon, orange juice concentrate, and sherry into the skillet. Cook over medium-low heat until reduced by half, scraping up the brown bits on the bottom of the pan as you go.

4. Lower the heat and stir in the sour cream. Cook (but don't let the mixture boil) for 2 minutes, then return the medallions to the pan and cook, turning several times, for 2 or 3 minutes more, until the meat is hot.

SERVES 4 TO 6

CHICKEN BREASTS WITH TARRAGON

You'll find that this recipe bears a strong resemblance to Veal Piccata, one of the classic dishes of Italy.

2 whole chicken breasts (4 halves), boneless and skinless

2 tablespoons flour

Salt and freshly ground black pepper

2 tablespoons butter

1 tablespoon olive oil

Juice of 1 lemon

3 tablespoons capers, rinsed

1 1/2 teaspoons minced fresh tarragon or 1/2 teaspoon dry

1. Put the chicken breast halves, one by one, between two sheets of plastic wrap. Flatten them to about 1/4 inch or less, using a meat mallet if you have one or a soda bottle or rolling pin or heavy frying pan if you don't. Cut the flattened breasts in two on the diagonal.

2. Mix the flour with the salt and pepper on a plate. Dip the breast pieces in this, coating both sides. You may need a little more flour.

3. Heat the butter and oil in a large frying pan, then brown the breast pieces in this on both sides. If the pieces don't all fit, brown just a few at a time, removing them to a plate as they're done.

4. With all the chicken out of the pan, add the lemon juice, capers, and tarragon. Bring just to a simmer, then add the chicken and cook gently, turning, until everything is hot. Serve at once.

SERVES 4

GROUND TURKEY PATTIES WITH TARRAGON

Most supermarkets carry ground turkey, but few people know what to do with it! There are two problems: dryness and lack of taste. This recipe solves both of those problems in fine style and gives you an interesting and tasty main dish.

1 pound ground turkey

1 egg

1 cup minced onion

1/2 cup minced celery

1/2 cup minced green pepper or peeled green chile

2 teaspoons lemon juice

2 teaspoons water

1 1/2 teaspoons minced fresh tarragon or 1/2 teaspoon dry

Salt and freshly ground pepper

1 1/2 tablespoons olive oil

1. Combine the ground turkey in a medium-size bowl with the egg, onion, celery, green pepper, lemon juice, water, tarragon, and salt and pepper. Form into four patties.

2. Heat the oil in a frying pan over medium heat and cook the ground turkey patties in this for about 4 minutes on each side, or until the meat in the center looks cooked. Don't cook beyond this point or the patties will be dry.

SERVES 4

MUSHROOM AND TARRAGON BAKED FISH

2 pounds fillets of white fish

1/4 cup dry white wine

1 tablespoon minced fresh tarragon or 1 teaspoon dry

1 1/2 cups sliced mushrooms

1/2 cup sliced scallions

Salt and freshly ground black pepper

1/2 cup freshly made bread crumbs

1 1/2 tablespoons butter, melted

1/2 tablespoon olive oil

1. Preheat your oven to 400°F.

2. Put the fish fillets in a lightly greased 9 x 9-inch baking pan, being careful to overlap the thin ends of the fillets so they won't overcook.

3. Drizzle on the wine, then sprinkle on the tarragon, strew on the mushrooms and scallions, and season with the salt and pepper. Top with first the bread crumbs, then a mixture of the melted butter and olive oil. (Or use all butter if you'd rather.)

4. Bake for 7 minutes. Serve at once

SERVES 4 TO 6

CHEESE AND EGGS

Tarragon has a natural affinity for and seems to bring out the best in both cheese and eggs. Try adding a little to your favorite recipes—for instance, tarragon does wonders for scrambled eggs—or sample some of these gems.

SHIRRED EGGS WITH TARRAGON

Do you know Shirred Eggs? If not, you certainly should. Perhaps you know them by the name Baked Eggs instead. Whatever the name, they make a marvelous dish for breakfast or a light lunch, or even a Sunday-night supper.

2 tablespoons soft butter (or use a cooking spray)

2 tablespoons minced fresh tarragon or 2 teaspoons dry

8 eggs

Salt and freshly ground black pepper

1. Preheat your oven to 325°F.

2. Use the butter (or spray) to coat four very small baking dishes or ramekins. Sprinkle on the tarragon, then add two eggs (out of their shells) to each dish. Cover each dish tightly with foil.

3. Bake for 12 minutes.

4. Remove the foil. Sprinkle with a little salt and freshly ground black pepper.

Variation: Another way to shir eggs is by adding the tarragon to some heavy cream (about 2 tablespoons for every two eggs). Pour a little of this in the dishes before adding the eggs, then pour the rest on top. I'm crazy about eggs shirred in this fashion, but in these fat-conscious days, the method seems too politically incorrect to deserve its own recipe!

SERVES 4

TERRY'S TARRAGON OMELETTE

My friend Terry makes a super-omelette, and he does it with a minimum of fuss. Sometimes he puts a slice of Cheddar or other cheese in the omelette before it's ready to serve. Other times it's a blob of jelly or jam. Sometimes, at my request, it's both!

1 tablespoon butter

2 eggs

2 tablespoons milk

1 1/2 teaspoons minced fresh tarragon or 1/2 teaspoon dry

1. Melt the butter in a 6-inch nonstick frying pan over medium-low heat.

2. Break the eggs into a small bowl. Add the milk and tarragon and stir briskly with a fork.

3. Pour the egg mixture into the frying pan. Cook, undisturbed, until firm.

4. Tip the pan over a serving plate, folding it over with a wrist motion. Voilà!

SERVES 1

CHEESE, SHALLOT, AND TARRAGON TART

This lovely tart can be frozen and reheated—if, by any chance, you can resist eating it right away. If you wish, you can substitute onion for the shallots.

12 ounces Gruyère or Swiss cheese, or a combination, grated

1 9-inch piecrust in a pie pan but not baked

2 cups thinly sliced shallots

2 cloves garlic, thinly sliced (optional)

3 tablespoons butter (or make half of this olive oil), divided

1 large tomato, thinly sliced

1 tablespoon chopped fresh tarragon or 1 teaspoon dry

1. Preheat your oven to 375°F.

2. Put the grated cheese into the pie shell.

3. Sauté the sliced shallots and garlic over medium heat in 1 tablespoon of the butter until they're a bit soft. Place in the pie shell on top of the cheese.

4. Using the same pan, unwashed, cook the sliced tomatoes gently in the remaining 2 tablespoons of butter over moderately low heat for just a few minutes. Sprinkle on the tarragon. Place the tomatoes on top of the shallots and garlic in the pie shell. Pour on the juices remaining in the pan.

5. Bake for 25 minutes, or until the edges of the crust are a light brown.

6. Let sit at room temperature for 10 minutes before slicing and serving.

SERVES 4 TO 6

VEGETABLES

To me, tarragon does wonders for any vegetable! But there are certain recipes where it really shines. Here are a few of my favorites of these.

You'll also find recipes featuring vegetables in the salads section.

CARROTS À L'ORANGE WITH TARRAGON

To put it simply, these are the very best carrots you've ever tasted. If you don't want any alcohol content, cook the carrots for a few minutes after you add the rum. (But don't omit the rum—it's the secret of the dish.)

1 pound carrots

3/4 cup water

1 teaspoon salt

4 tablespoons butter

3/4 cup orange juice

Grated zest (just the yellow part) of 1 lemon

1/2 cup sugar

4 whole cloves

1 1/2 teaspoons minced fresh tarragon or 1/2 teaspoon dry

1 tablespoon rum

1. Peel the carrots and slice them about 1/4 inch thick. Put into a medium-size saucepan with the water and salt and cook over fairly high heat until the water disappears.

2. Add all the rest of the ingredients except the rum. Lower the heat to medium-low and cook, stirring often, until the carrots are tender and a thick sauce is formed.

3. Add the secret ingredient—the rum.

4. Serve now or reheat when needed.

SERVES 3 OR 4

FRIED LEEKS WITH TARRAGON

When you're out to impress, cook these leeks with tarragon. True, they're a bit time-consuming to make, but very well worth it. Anyway, the biggest part of the work is getting the leeks ready to fry, and that can be done well ahead of time.

4 leeks, each about 1 inch thick

Vegetable oil for frying (see below for amount)

1 egg

Salt and freshly ground black pepper

1 1/2 teaspoons minced fresh tarragon or 1/2 teaspoon dry, divided

1/2 cup (approximately) flour for dredging

2 teaspoons Tarragon Vinegar (page 324)

1. Cut off and discard the green part of the leeks. Now trim the base of each leek, and slice them in half lengthwise, stopping short of the base, so they'll hold together. Rinse very well under running cold water to get rid of the dirt that's inevitably lurking in every leek ever grown.

2. Steam the leeks for about 10 minutes, or until tender, over boiling water. Remove to paper towels and let rest for at least 20 minutes.

3. Heat the oil to about 360°F in a heavy frying pan. Use just enough to cover the bottom of the pan amply. (No frying thermometer or electric wok? Heat until a drop of water sizzles in the oil.)

4. Beat the egg in a soup plate and add salt and pepper and half the tarragon. Put the flour in another soup plate. Now dip each leek first in the egg, making sure it's thoroughly coated, then in the flour.

5. Fry until brown and beautiful, turning often. Drain quickly on paper towels, then sprinkle with the vinegar and the rest of the tarragon and serve at once.

TOMATOES PROVENÇAL

You may find that this is the handiest item in your vegetable and side dish repertoire. It goes with just about everything, is simple and quick to make, and always tastes good. Other herbs can be used instead of or with the tarragon, if you want to experiment.

2 medium-size tomatoes

2 teaspoons Dijon mustard

Salt and freshly ground black pepper

1 tablespoon minced fresh tarragon or 1 teaspoon dry

1/2 cup soft, freshly made bread crumbs

2 tablespoons olive oil

1. Preheat your oven to 350°F.

2. Cut the tomatoes in half through their middles. Turn upside down on paper towels for about 15 minutes to drain off any excess moisture.

3. Put the tomatoes in a shallow pan. Spread the cut side of each half with a quarter of the mustard, then sprinkle on the salt and pepper and tarragon. Top with the bread crumbs. Drizzle on the olive oil.

4. Bake for 20 minutes, or until the bread crumbs are a light brown.

SERVES 2 TO 4

(RECIPE CAN BE MADE IN ANY SIZE YOU WISH)

SALAD DRESSINGS

You could just strew some fresh tarragon on a green salad and have a very good thing. But for very special dressings, try some of these.

TARRAGON-HONEY-MUSTARD SALAD DRESSING

A teenager of my acquaintance said, "Wow—this stuff even makes lettuce taste good!" Who could ask for a higher recommendation?

3 tablespoons honey

3 tablespoons cider vinegar

1/3 cup mayonnaise

1 tablespoon Dijon mustard

2 teaspoons finely chopped onion or scallion

1 tablespoon minced parsley

1 tablespoon fresh tarragon, minced, or 1 teaspoon dry

1/4 teaspoon salt

3/4 cup salad oil (or use part olive oil)

1. Dissolve the honey in the cider vinegar by heating them gently together—for instance, in a small bowl in a microwave oven.

2. Allow to cool, then mix with all the other ingredients. (A food processor will do a good job on this.)

3. Keep refrigerated.

MAKES ABOUT 1 CUP

CYBELE SALAD DRESSING

This is my version of the dressing that used to be served in a now gone (and badly missed) Boston restaurant. At Cybele, they used it on Boston or other soft, buttery lettuce, arranged fanned out on a salad plate. As I recall, the only other thing on the plate was a few cherry tomatoes. Lovely!

2 tablespoons wine vinegar

3 tablespoons heavy cream (or you could get by with half-and-half)

1 teaspoon lemon juice

1/2 teaspoon minced garlic

1 teaspoon minced fresh tarragon or about 1/3 teaspoon dry

1 teaspoon Dijon mustard

2 tablespoons olive oil

1/2 cup salad oil (canola is a good choice)

1. Combine all the ingredients in a screw-top jar and shake well.

2. Keep under refrigeration.

MAKES A LITTLE LESS THAN 1 CUP

Growing & Using Sage

Patti Barrett

Illustrations by Elayne Sears, Charles Joslin, and Mallory Lake

Introduction

Sages (*Salvia* spp.) are some of the most popular and widely grown herbs in the world, valued for their culinary, ornamental, and medicinal qualities. Sage species are rich in essential oils and have a wide range of aromas and uses. The leaves dry well, making them usable year-round. Easy to grow, with many cultivars to choose from, sage is sure to please both the beginning and the more experienced gardener with its versatility, beauty, aroma, and flavor. Today sage can be found in the herb garden, the flower bed, and the container garden. The herb continues to grow in favor as gardeners and cooks rediscover its many uses. These include culinary seasoning and restorative teas as well as simple cosmetic preparations, including a popular hair rinse.

Starting Sage from Seed

Whether you are sowing indoors or directly outdoors, starting from seed is one of the simplest methods of propagating sages. Plan your container sites or garden beds carefully: Young seedlings need good drainage and plenty of sun.

STARTING INDOORS

You can grow sage indoors from seed to mature plant. However, if you intend to transplant young seedlings outdoors you should start your seeds three to four weeks before you anticipate the last frost in your region.

Sowing Seed

You can start your seeds in pots or trays filled with either a packaged seed-starting mix or a potting soil mixed with some vermiculite or sand. These materials are available at garden centers or garden-supply shops. Cover the bottom of each container with a layer of pebbles or gravel to ensure good drainage. Moisten your pasteurized planting medium and then fill

Continued →

the containers with it. Press the soil firmly until it has a level surface about 1/2 inch below the rim of the container. Scatter the sage seeds over the surface of the soil. Sage is particularly susceptible to damping off (a fungus disease that frequently kills young seedlings) and needs some light in order to germinate. Cover the seeds with a very shallow layer (a dusting) of vermiculite (grade #4), a sterile medium that will allow plenty of light to reach the germinating seeds.

To ensure sufficient moisture as the seeds germinate, cover your trays or pots with a piece of glass or clear plastic wrap. You'll want to keep the soil temperature within the range of 65° to 75°F.—use a warming tray, or place the containers in any warm spot in your house, such as near a radiator or on top of the refrigerator. Indoors, germination should occur in two to three weeks.

Caring for Seedlings
Once the seedlings emerge, you can remove the glass or clear plastic covering. Then move the small plants to a sunny window, or place them under grow-lights. If they're in a window, rotate them frequently so that they grow upright rather than bending in the direction of the light source. If they seem to be growing too thin and tall, it may be because the light isn't bright enough. Water, but don't overwater: Let your soil dry out between waterings.

When the seedlings have developed two to four leaves, they're ready for more room. Transplant them into individual containers. If you intend to eventually plant the sage outside, consider using peat pots, which can be placed directly in the soil and will decompose over time as your plants grow. Fill the containers with a moist soil-based potting mix. Using a butter knife or tongue depressor, gently prick out (remove from the pot) the seedlings. Caution: Handle the seedlings by their leaves, as the stems can be damaged easily. Set them into the new pots, cover the root systems carefully with soil, and water sparingly. Again, keep the plants in a sunny window or under grow-lights.

Pricking young plants from their container.

Hardening Off
Before you set your sage plants out in the garden, you'll want to harden them off. Put the seedlings out in the sun for a few hours each day, but bring them inside for cold nights. Gradually extend the length of the stay outdoors until the plants are ready to survive outside. Young sage plants should not be set into the garden until after all danger of frost is past.

> **SAGE HARDINESS**
> Sage species vary widely in hardiness. Many sages are annuals in the North but do well as perennials in southern gardens. Some species are hardy in most parts of the United States, but others must be treated as annuals throughout the country. For example, pineapple sage, *Salvia elegans*, is hardy only up to zone 8 but can be grown as a lovely annual in the North. Refer to the individual species reference or consult a gardening reference book to determine the hardiness of your sage species.

Transplanting
Transplanting young plants to the garden should be done on a gray, overcast day, or, ideally, during a gentle rain. Weather like this will give the plants time to adjust to their new surroundings without a hot sun shining down on them. Choose your site carefully: Most full-grown sages will prefer a sunny locale (full sun in the North and partial shade in the South) in well-drained soil that ranges in pH from 6.0 to 7.0. Sage needs room to grow, so place the young plants 18 to 24 inches apart. A mature, three-year-old common sage (*Salvia officinalis*), with good growing conditions, can be three feet tall and just as broad.

STARTING OUTDOORS
Sage can be sown directly into the garden, as well. Wait until any threat of frost has passed and the soil has warmed to about 50°F. To see whether your soil is ready, take a handful and squeeze it. Watch how it reacts as you open your hand. If it remains compacted in a tight ball, you're better off waiting—the moisture content may be too high. If the soil falls away slowly from the compacted ball, though, it's ready for planting. Spade the ground, clear out any weeds, and rake the soil smooth. Make a shallow trench in the ground about 1/4 inch deep and sow the seeds along it 1 inch apart. Spread a light cover of vermiculite over them and water carefully, making sure not to wash away the topsoil or seeds. Keep a careful record of where you put your seeds, using clear labels.

Sage doesn't like to be crowded, so thin the young seedlings when the second pair of true leaves have formed on your plants. Weed out congested areas of young plants until the remaining plants are evenly spaced about 18 to 24 inches apart. If you have lots of young sage plants, you may want to consider giving some away to friends. A single plant can supply more than enough leaves for the culinary use of one family.

Care and Maintenance in Your Garden
Some sages, such as clary sage, will tolerate dry soils, but most prefer regular watering in rich, well-drained soil (although established sage plants are also usually drought-tolerant). Your sage plants will thrive in soil with a pH of between 6.0 and 7.0. Remember to water new transplants well until they are fully established in your garden. For perennial sages, mulch the roots well for winter.

In the spring, prune your sages well and fertilize them with a fertilizer high in phosphorus and potassium but low in nitrogen (such as a 5–10-5 or 5–10-10 fertilizer mix). Sages can be pruned up to three times a year—in the North, however, refrain from pruning after September, as it may stimulate new growth which is subject then to winter-kill. Mature sage plants tend to become woody and less productive with age. After about three years you may want to replace any garden sages with new plants.

Indoor and Container Gardening

Sage grows well in containers both indoors and outside. Use a planting medium that's lighter than garden soil: Mix about 2 parts loam with 1 part peat moss and 1 part vermiculite (grade #2) to keep the soil friable. The most important requirement for growing sage in pots, planters, or tubs, however, is good drainage. All growing containers need to have drainage holes in their bottoms. If you want to use decorative jardinieres, don't plant directly in them—keep the plants in pots that fit inside. This way each pot can be frequently checked for signs of stagnant water.

> ### TRANSPLANTING ESTABLISHED PLANTS
> If you're planning to pot up your garden sage plants and bring them indoors in the fall, you may want to attempt this with younger plants that were started in the middle of the summer. Older plants do not transplant as well as younger plants, which adjust more easily to indoor conditions. Remember, sage is just as good dried as fresh. Rather than nursing an unhealthy transplant of a mature sage plant, you may just want to keep a supply of its leaves and dry them.

Outdoors. Sage is a good candidate for a rooftop container garden, as it withstands winds well. Its woody stems also make it tough enough for high-altitude gardens—you will often find it growing wild in the windswept hills of the West—so it's a natural for a city garden, planted on a roof terrace or even a fire escape. If the container is large enough to allow for adequate root growth, sage can be cut back in the fall to sprout again in the spring.

Indoors. With good drainage and sufficient access to light, sage will thrive indoors. A window with a southern exposure and at least half a day of sunlight is best for common sage (*Salvia officinalis*) and most other sage species. Sage can also be grown under artificial lights—a hanging fluorescent grow-light installed about 6 inches directly over the plants will work well.

If the sage you're raising indoors becomes tall and spindly, it's not getting enough light. If you've been using artificial light, make sure the source is close enough to the tops of the plant. If your plant has been in the window, you may want to try another spot in the house or invest in a lighting system.

Harvesting Sage

When to harvest? A general rule for herbs, if you intend to use them for oil distillation or drying, is to harvest just before they flower. However, you can harvest sage leaves for immediate use throughout their growing season. Pick the leaves early in the day, but after the dew has dried from them. If you wait until later in the day the sun will have drawn out some of the essential oils, and some of the herb's essence will be lost. If possible, wash the sage plants in the garden the night before picking—use a watering can or hose to gently water the plants, including under the leaves. This allows you to skip washing the leaves after harvest.

Sage is easily dried in bunches and is aromatically pleasant to have in the kitchen while drying. Gather the clean, cut branches into small bunches and tie tightly. Hang them out of bright light and in a place with good air circulation. You can also place each bunch in a brown paper bag to dry, especially if you have a large quantity of herbs to preserve. The paper absorbs the leaves' moisture without removing their essential oils, and the bag keeps light away from them, preserving the color. Pull the mouth of the bag around the ends of the bunched stems to cover them completely, and tie it together with some string, leaving an extra length so you can tie it up to hang. Don't let the herbs touch the sides of the bag. Open the bag after a week or two to check on the drying. If the leaves are crisp and can be easily crumbled, roll the bag gently between your hands—the leaves of the plant will fall to the bottom of the bag, making the stems easy to remove.

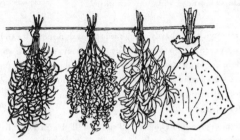

rosemary   sweet marjoram   sage   drying in a paper bag

Collect the herbs in bunches and hang them to dry.

If your sage leaves do not dry completely, they may mold, and they also have a tendency to turn into a fluffy mass in a mortar and pestle. If this is the case, the leaves may need to be helped along in the drying process, especially if you intend to grind them into a powder. To dry them completely, spread the leaves on a cookie sheet. Place the sheet in a 150°F oven. Leave the oven door ajar and keep a close eye on the sage leaves—if you can smell the sage as soon as you put the leaves in the oven, then lower the oven temperature. Stir every few minutes. Remove the tray as soon as the herbs are crisp.

When the leaves are ready to crumble when touched, they should be stored. Grind them and bottle the powder. Or, if the leaves will be used for tea, place the whole leaves carefully into containers so that they won't disintegrate. Store dried sage in dark, airtight containers in cool, dark places.

Choosing the Best Sage for Your Garden

Sage belongs to the Labiatae family, which includes many of the culinary herbs. The sage genus (*Salvia* spp.) includes more than 750 species widely distributed throughout the world. Most *Salvias* prefer to grow in dry, gravelly sites; their stems are usually square in cross section; and their leaves tend to grow in pairs and are usually oval or lance shaped. Sage flowers are arranged in whorls on a slender spike with a two-part corolla: three lobes below, two lobes above. They come in shades of red, blue, white, purple, and pale yellow.

Each species of sage has its own particular features and reasons to grow—or not to grow—in the garden. More and more varieties of sage, with different growth, sizes, habits, shapes, and colors, are now being offered to the home gardener, and many will be desirable tenants in your garden.

Continued →

COMMON SAGE (*Salvia officinalis*)

Common sage is one of the seasonings most often used in a traditional stuffing recipe, and we often associate its strong scent and flavor with our Thanksgiving turkey dinner. This is the sage species most often available in plant stores and seed catalogs. The pointed, gray-green, wrinkled leaves of this shrubby plant are about 2 inches long and 3/4 inch (or less) wide; they have finely toothed margins and a velvety feel, produced by small hairs on the veined surface. Leaves can linger on the woody stems all winter long. *Salvia officinalis* can grow to about 2 feet in height with a spread of up to 3 feet and has showy bluish lavender, pink, or even white flowers.

common sage

Common sage is a hardy plant outdoors and indoors. It can be grown as a perennial up through zone 5 and as an annual elsewhere. Soil pH for common sage and other herbs should fall in the 6.0 to 6.7 range. Mix a good compost or well-rotted manure into garden soil before planting and fertilize with fish emulsion or organic liquid fertilizer.

Common sage grows best in full sun in well-drained soil. It likes cooler weather and can be difficult to grow in the hot South, where the heat and humidity predisposes the plants to infestation with powdery mildew. Common sage should not be situated near plants that need frequent watering, such as basil. It's a good idea to mulch sage plants during severe winters with a light salt hay or a covering of pine boughs. Prune them back severely in the spring, cutting off any deadwood.

Varieties of *Salvia officinalis* may have blue, white, or pink flowers in the late spring. Of its many cultivars, these are of particular interest:

Salvia officinalis 'Albiflora'. Zones 5–8; an elegant sage cultivar; green and gold variegated leaves and white blossoms; useful for cooking; can be tender in the North—treat as an annual; will grow up to 24 to 32 inches high and spread up to 3 feet.

Salvia officinalis 'Icterina'. Golden sage; zones 7–9; a striking addition to the garden with green leaves trimmed in yellow; does not winter well in the North, but does so very well in the South; will grow up to 24 to 32 inches high and spread up to 3 feet.

Salvia officinalis 'Purpurascens'. Purple sage; zones 7–9; has soft, purple/gray leaves, which are strongly flavored and make an excellent tea; grows much like common sage, up to 24 to 32 inches high and spreading up to 3 feet.

Salvia officinalis 'Tricolor'. Zones 7–9; gray-green leaves are streaked with white, purple, and pink; is not reliably hardy in the North but makes a beautiful display in the garden; will grow and spread 18 to 24 inches.

PINEAPPLE SAGE (*Salvia elegans*)

Native to Mexico, this tender perennial, hardy only in zones 9 and 10 and treated as an annual in colder areas, has a pineapple-like scent. The pointed, light green leaves are about 3 1/2 inches long and covered with soft downy hairs. Pineapple sage is a favorite among gardeners for both outdoor and indoor growing, as it grows quickly and becomes full and lush within one growing season. The stems are fuzzy when young, but harden to woody in late summer. Pineapple sage will grow up to 3 feet in both height and spread.

In the late fall and winter, the plants produce striking narrow, tubular, red-to-pink flowers—in the North, we seldom see pineapple sage bloom before frost arrives. The flowers can grow to 1 inch in length and are very attractive to hummingbirds and butterflies.

If you bring pineapple sage in from the garden, check it carefully for disease before placing it with other plants. It will also need periodic checking for red spider mites and whitefly while indoors. Pineapple sage is a very tender plant, so if you keep it indoors, be sure to give it plenty of light and keep it away from cold drafts.

If you live in zone 9 or 10, where pineapple sage is hardy, cut the stems down to about 8 to 12 inches tall after the plant has flowered. Mulch the roots well for winter. Watch for spring growth and apply a fertilizer at that time.

Pineapple sage can be found in garden centers that specialize in herbs, and is worth growing in the herb border. Its fragrant leaves can be included in teas, potpourris, or floral bouquets. Its scent and light green leaves make it a delightful garnish. Pineapple sage is best used fresh, as the dried leaves lose much of their flavor. The dried flowers, however, are excellent in potpourris; their red color can last for years.

SCARLET SAGE (*Salvia splendens*)

Scarlet sage is a very tender perennial, hardy only in zones 9 through 10 and treated as an annual almost everywhere in the United States. As an annual, it will grow up to 3 feet in height; in warmer zones, as a perennial, it can attain heights of up to 8 feet. The stalked leaves are bright green, and the flowers are usually a brilliant scarlet (although they can sometimes be pink, lavender, or purple).

Scarlet sage is the most common of ornamental sages. It prefers full sun, and will flower continuously from early summer until frost. The red Salvia commonly sold in garden centers is most often scarlet sage. It's a welcome addition to a hummingbird garden—hummingbirds love the brilliant blossoms.

Plant *Salvia splendens* in full or partial sun, leaving about 12 to 18 inches of space between the plants. Scarlet sage needs regular watering and will wilt in dry soil.

CLARY SAGE (*Salvia sclarea*)

This long-leafed biennial sage, hardy through zone 4, is an unusual garden plant. Its wrinkled, strong-smelling leaves have toothed margins and are covered with grayish hairs, and its flowers (which appear in the second year) are bicolored lilac or pink and creamy white. Hummingbirds are attracted to the wide-lipped flowers in midsummer; the green seeds form later in the season, attracting goldfinches to the garden.

clary sage

Clary sage grows well in dry soils. Seeds germinate quickly, and seedlings may be set out when danger of frost is past. The plant may self-sow. Clary sage can reach a height of 3 feet, and will spread up to 2 feet.

Salvia sclarea has a very strong odor. In Great Britain it's used as a substitute for hops, and in Germany to flavor wine. The leaves of clary sage can be battered and fried. It's also valuable in dried-flower arrangements, as well as in medicinal preparations: It's considered an aid to digestion and can be used in compresses for swellings or to draw out splinters.

OTHER VARIETIES OF SAGE

Salvia argentea. Silver sage; an erect, branched variety with white flowers tinged with pink or yellow; the large leaves are covered with silvery hairs; will grow 2 to 4 feet in height.

Salvia azurea. Blue sage; native to the Great Plains from Minnesota south to Texas; lovely blue flowers; as a perennial, it can grow as tall as 5 feet.

Salvia coccinea. Texas sage or scarlet sage; a perennial in zones 8 through 10 and grown as an annual elsewhere; a shrubby plant that can be found from South Carolina to Florida, and west to Texas, Mexico, and tropical America; profuse red or sometimes white blossoms about 3/4 inch long; will grow up to 3 feet in height and spread to 18 inches.

Salvia farinacea. Mealycup sage or mealy blue sage; violet-blue flowers on long branches that are good for propagation by cutting; blooms from late spring to first frost; can grow as high as 3 feet; native to Texas and New Mexico.

Salvia lavandulifolia. Narrow-leaved or Spanish sage; long, grayish, woolly leaves with a balsam-lavender scent; hairy stem has covering of fine hairs; blue-violet flowers; can grow up to 20 inches in height and will spread up to 2 feet.

Salvia leucantha. Mexican bush sage; gray-green leaves with abundant spikes of lavender flowers; thrives in hot, dry conditions and will tolerate dry, sandy soil; not winter-hardy; can grow to 4 feet in height.

Salvia viridis. Tricolor sage or red-topped sage; upright annual with medium-green leaves and pink, rose, white, or purple flowers; may rebloom if deadheaded; can grow up to 18 inches but will spread only about 8 inches.

Culinary Uses of Sage

Although sage was used as a medicinal tea and a food preservative for many centuries, it was not used as a food flavoring until the 17th century. The English found many uses for the herb, including the one most common today—as a stuffing for meats. One of the most popular uses of sage in England today is in Derby cheese, in which fresh sage leaves are layered with a Cheddarlike cheese to create a green-marbled effect.

Sage works well alone or with other pungent herbs such as rosemary, summer and winter savory, bay, thyme, and oregano. Combinations of these herbs add a rich taste to soups or stews.

The following recipes are just a sampling to get you started on experimenting with sage in your own cooking.

CONDIMENTS, APPETIZERS, AND SNACKS

These recipes for snacks and spreads will give you a great head start on any meal. Experiment with the amount of sage and other herbs until you find the flavor that suits you best.

PEPPER SAGE CHEESE

Serve with crackers at a high tea.

1 pound plain lowfat yogurt

1/4 teaspoon freshly ground black pepper

1/4 teaspoon chili powder

2 teaspoons olive oil

12 fresh common sage leaves

1. Suspend a damp cheesecloth over a container (or spread the cheesecloth inside a colander). Set the yogurt on the cheesecloth, place in the refrigerator, and let drain overnight.

2. Add pepper and chili powder, and work the cheese mix until smooth. Form into a ball.

3. Spread oil over the surface of the cheese, and then press the sage leaves around the ball. You may garnish with blossoms.

SAGE VINEGAR

All the equipment used in making herbal vinegars must be sterile. Wash all containers and utensils in warm soapy water and rinse with hot water.

Fill a clean glass bottle or jar with common sage and white wine vinegar or cider vinegar. Use 1 cup of loosely packed fresh leaves (or 1/2 cup dried) to 2 cups of vinegar. Cover the container tightly and let macerate for 3 weeks at room temperature in a dark place, shaking the container gently every day or two. Strain and taste. For a stronger flavor, repeat with fresh herbs. Pour into clean, sterilized bottles. Insert a sprig of sage for decoration, cap tightly, and label.

HERB BUTTER

Wash the herbs in the garden the day before you pick them.

1–2 garlic cloves, crushed

Salt and freshly ground pepper

1/2 pound butter, at room temperature

1 teaspoon each fresh rosemary, lemon thyme, oregano, and common sage

1. Blend the garlic, salt, and pepper into the butter. Then add the herb leaves. You can do this by hand or in a food processor.

2. Refrigerate the mixture for 3 hours or more to allow blending of flavors. It can also be frozen for up to 3 months.

USES FOR HERB BUTTER

· Freeze in small plastic molds to use later.

· Roll into a cylinder, wrap in plastic, and chill. Slice off rounds as needed.

· Use a butter curler to create rounds.

Continued ➔

- Roll out and use cookie cutters for various decorative shapes.

- Whip the butter and then pack into earthenware crocks or small dishes.

CLARY-SAGE FRITTERS

Clary-sage fritters can be dipped into confectioners' sugar if you're serving them as a sweet; they also can be served plain with meat as garnish.

1 egg

A pinch of salt

1/2 cup white wine or beer

1 cup flour

Leaves of dried clary sage

Oil for frying

1. Separate the egg. Beat the white until frothy; beat the yolk lightly.

2. Stir the pinch of salt and the wine or beer into the flour and add the yolk. Blend well. Then fold in the beaten egg white.

3. Prepare a saucepan for frying by coating with oil and heating.

4. Dip small leaves of dried clary sage into the batter. Fry in the oil. Remove when brown and puffy.

FRENCH COUNTRY PÂTÉ

Pâté makes a delicious appetizer for a crowd when served with crackers or dark bread.

1 pound pork liver, finely ground in food processor

1 pound ground veal

1 1/2 pounds ground pork

Slightly less than 1/2 pound pork fat

1 egg

2 cloves garlic, pressed

Salt and freshly ground pepper

1/4 cup port or Madeira

1/2 teaspoon dried marjoram

1/2 teaspoon dried basil

1/2 teaspoon dried common sage, or 1 teaspoon fresh

1/4 teaspoon dried thyme

1/4 teaspoon dried tarragon

2–3 bay leaves, for top of pâté

1. Heat your oven to 350°F. Mix together all of the ingredients except the bay leaves. Scoop the filling into a loaf pan or pâté pan. Press the filling down and put the bay leaves on top.

2. Cover the pâté with a double layer of foil; punch a few holes in the foil so steam can escape. Set in a water bath and bake for 1 1/2 to 1 3/4 hours. Serve when cold.

6 TO 8 SERVINGS AS A FIRST COURSE

SAGE STUFFINGS

Pungent sage has long been used to flavor stuffing. Try these traditional (and not-so-traditional) recipes for dressings—use them to stuff a turkey or chicken or as a substitute for the usual potato, rice, or noodle side dish.

FRESH SAGE CHICKEN STUFFING

Since you may have fresh sage leaves even in late November, this is a good recipe to have come Thanksgiving: In larger quantities it can stuff a turkey.

1 loaf of slightly stale bread, old-fashioned white or a darker type

1/2 cup chopped onion

1/3 cup chopped celery

4 tablespoons fresh common sage, chopped, or 2 tablespoons dried

3 tablespoons chopped fresh parsley

Salt and freshly ground pepper

Cube the bread (or break it into small pieces with your hands). Add the onion, celery, and herbs. Season with salt and pepper to taste.

MAKES 4 TO 6 CUPS

"YOUR OWN" PACKAGED DRESSING

1 stick margarine or butter

2 1/2 cups chicken stock or canned chicken broth

1 onion, chopped

6 stalks celery, diced

Freshly ground pepper

1/2 bunch fresh parsley, chopped

4 tablespoons fresh common sage leaves, cut into strips

Salt to taste

1 16-ounce package plain bread dressing

1. Heat the oven to 425°F. Butter a 3-quart casserole dish.

2. In large saucepan, bring the butter, chicken stock or broth, onion, celery, parsley, sage, and salt to taste to a boil. Cook for about 10 minutes.

3. Put the dressing into a bowl and pour the warm mixture over it. With a spatula or spoon, mix until well combined. Let cool.

4. Blend again, adding pepper to taste. Pack into the casserole and bake for 30 minutes.

MAKES 3 CUPS

CORN-BREAD SAGE STUFFING

10 tablespoons butter

1 1/2 cups finely chopped onion

1 pound well-seasoned sausage meat

1 turkey or chicken liver (if available)

6 cups coarsely crumbled corn bread

1/4 cup heavy cream

Salt and freshly ground pepper

1–2 teaspoons dried common sage

1/4 cup finely chopped fresh parsley

1/4 cup sherry

1. Melt 8 tablespoons of the butter in a large skillet and add the onion; cook over medium heat for 6 to 8 minutes or until lightly colored. Scrape the onion into a mixing bowl.

2. Add the sausage meat to the skillet and cook over medium heat. Break up the meat with a fork as it cooks. When it's browned, transfer to a sieve set over small bowl to catch the drippings.

3. In the same pan, melt the remaining butter. When the foam subsides, add the liver. Brown for 2 to 3 minutes, then chop coarsely and combine with the onions in the mixing bowl. Add the drained sausage meat, corn bread, salt and pepper to taste, sage, and parsley.

4. With a large spoon, stir the mixture together. Then moisten with the sherry and cream. Taste for seasoning.

MAKES 8 TO 10 CUPS

MAIN DISHES

Here are some great recipes for wonderfully flavorful meals. Again, experiment with the amount of sage and other herbs until you find the flavor that suits you best.

ROAST QUAIL WITH FRESH SAGE

1 bunch of fresh common sage

10 quail

1/2 pound thick-cut bacon, cut in half

Salt and freshly ground pepper

1 cup red wine or stock

1. Heat the oven to 450°F.

2. Tuck a few leaves of sage into each quail. Tie the legs. Place a large sage leaf on top of each breast. Cover with a piece of bacon.

3. Place each quail on top of another piece of bacon in a roasting pan. Sprinkle with salt and pepper to taste.

4. Roast for 10 minutes. Turn over and roast for 15 more minutes. Remove the birds to a serving platter and surround with bacon.

5. Remove the grease and any remaining bits from the roasting pan and place in a saucepan on top of the stove. Add the wine or stock and bring to a boil. Cook until reduced by about half and serve on the side.

10 SERVINGS

SUMMER VEGETABLE SOUP

The soup:

1 leek, chopped

1 onion, diced

2 cups carrots, diced

8 small new potatoes

1 medium tomato

1 pound fresh cranberry beans or broad beans, shelled

6 sprigs fresh common sage

10 cups water

1/2 pound string beans

1 zucchini, cut into cubes

1/4 pound linguine, broken into short pieces

The pistou sauce:

4 garlic cloves, smashed

1/3 cup basil, chopped

1/2 cup freshly grated Parmesan

1/4 cup olive oil

1 medium tomato

1. Over medium-low heat, sauté the leek and onion until they're just turning brown. Add the carrots, potatoes, chopped tomato, and cranberry or broad beans. Add the sage and the 10 cups of water. Bring to a boil, then lower the heat and simmer, covered, for 45 minutes, or until the vegetables are soft.

2. About 25 minutes before serving, add the string beans, zucchini, and linguine. Add more water if needed. Mix well and continue cooking.

3. While the soup finishes, make the pistou sauce: Place the garlic, basil, and Parmesan in a food processor and blend until grainy. Continue processing while adding the oil slowly until the mixture is smooth. Mince the tomato finely and drain in a sieve. Add to the sauce.

4. Add a ladleful of hot soup to the sauce, mix well, then pour the sauce back into the rest of the soup and combine. Serve right away.

6 SERVINGS

CALF'S LIVER WITH SAGE

6 slices calf's liver, cut 1/4 inch thick

1 large sprig of fresh common sage

Juice of 1 lemon

Olive oil

1/2 cup flour

Salt and ground pepper to taste

2 beaten eggs

2 cups bread crumbs (homemade are best)

1/2 cup butter

3 tablespoons oil

Lemon slices

Sage butter:

8 tablespoons softened butter

3 tablespoons finely minced herbs (a combination of common sage, parsley, and chives — or just sage and parsley — works well)

1 tablespoon lemon juice

Continued →

1. Place calf's liver slices in an enamel or ceramic dish and bury the sage among them. Sprinkle the liver with the fresh lemon juice and olive oil. Marinate for 2 to 3 hours, covered, in the refrigerator.

2. Dry the liver with paper towels. Dip into the flour, seasoned with salt and pepper to taste, then into the beaten eggs (use a small amount of milk if raw eggs make you nervous), and finally into the bread crumbs until well coated. Place the slices on a platter and refrigerate for at least 30 minutes, but no more than 1 hour.

3. Meanwhile, make the sage butter by whipping the butter and herbs in a food processor; dribble lemon juice into the container and process until smooth. Taste to see if it needs more sage. Chill until serving.

4. Melt the 1/2 cup butter together with the oil in a large skillet. Add the calf's liver slices and sauté them over medium heat for 2 or 3 minutes. Turn and sauté on the other side until brown. You want them a little pink in the center; test with a small knife.

5. Remove to a platter. Place a little sage butter on each piece and decorate with lemon slices.

3 SERVINGS

TIPS FOR USING SAGE IN THE KITCHEN

- Add some fresh sage to your grilled cheese sandwiches on rye or other dark-grained bread.

- Make your own sage wine by steeping a cup of fresh common sage leaves in a bottle of a white or rose wine.

- Try adding some sage to a pizza topped with tomatoes, onions, and cheese.

- Make a pesto sauce with equal parts common sage, parsley, and marjoram, blended with pine nuts and Parmesan.

- Add chopped common sage to a corn-muffin mix.

- Add chopped common sage to the crumbs used for breading chicken, pork, or other meats before cooking.

Growing & Using Chives

Juliette Rogers

Illustrations by Mary Rich, Brigita Fuhrmann, Judy Eliason, Elayne Sears, and Laura Tedeschi

Deciding to Grow Chives

Chives are among the easiest and most rewarding herbs for the home gardener to grow. They are hardy and thrive in a variety of climates. In wild habitats, they manage to survive in sandy pockets of soil accumulated among rocks and on windblown mountainsides. Given their druthers, garden-variety chives prefer fertile, well-drained soil with a pH between 6 and 7. They are fond of sun but will get by with partial shade. When it comes right down to it, chives will forgive

imperfect conditions and still reward you with a long season of delicious harvests.

PLANTING CHECKLIST

Before you head out to the nursery or garden center to purchase your young chive plants, ask yourself these questions:

- Where will I grow my chives?

- Do I have a suitable piece of garden space?

- Do I want to be able to move the plants inside or outdoors seasonally?

- How many chive plants do I want, and how big do I want them to be?

- How much work am I willing to invest at the outset?

- What kind of chives do I want to grow?

STARTING POINTERS

Anybody can grow chives, but some methods of growing these tasty herbs are more challenging than others. The easiest way to grow them is to buy healthy plants from a nursery or garden center. When you're shopping for plants, look for those that are upright and brightly colored. Dull, drooping leaves are not a sign of health. Look at the bottom of the pot. Are lots of roots growing out of the drainage holes? This means that the plant has been confined to a small pot for too long, and its roots have outgrown it. Avoid these plants if you can. Ask nursery workers if the plants have been hardened off, which means they have been exposed to outdoor conditions enough to be ready for planting in your garden. Once you've made your decision and purchased some chives, they'll be ready to transplant to your garden.

> #### GARDEN NEIGHBORS
> All varieties of chives can be happily companion-planted with roses, carrots, tomatoes, and grapes.

   Starting chives from seeds is a bit more challenging than growing purchased plants. Though your total monetary investment will be modest, you will still need soil, planting trays or pots, covers, and seeds. Chives grown from seed require patience because it will take them a couple of years to grow into nice, lush plants.

Sowing from Seeds: Step-by-Step Guidelines

To start chives from seeds, freshness counts. Stick with seeds from this year's crop from a reliable supplier and discard that packet of 1987 seeds you just found in your basement.

   You can start seeds anytime, but most people sow them in spring. When it comes to planters, you have several options. Some gardeners enjoy the simplicity of peat pots, which are little pots made of compressed peat moss that can be planted directly into the garden when the plant is ready to move out into the big, bright world. Others invest in multiflats—plastic planting trays consisting of a large, rectangular base trough for proper drainage and irrigation and a top nesting tray with lots of potlike indentations, each of which gets one or two seeds. Seedlings grown in multiflats are easily popped out of these reusable trays, along with the little "cup" of soil in which they were planted—their root structures hold the soil in place while you plant them. Multiflats have the advantage of being very tidy and self-contained. Peat pots and small plastic pots need to be set into trays and can be more awkward to handle.

Any shallow container can be used to start chives from seed. Choose whatever is most convenient for you—and try to recycle old containers whenever possible!

If you already have a few empty 2- to 3-inch (5–7.5 cm) plant pots, press them into service for starting your seeds. If you have saved the six-pack plastic flats that most purchased seedlings come in, use them—they work like a charm.

Seeds need special soil to sprout and grow. Most garden suppliers carry seed-starter mixes, so you needn't mix your own. These potting mixes are formulated to be high in organic matter, such as peat moss and other moisture-holding ingredients; this keeps seeds moist and their environment hospitable to growth. Seed-starter mixes have a finer texture than ordinary potting or garden soil. They are not very rich nutritionally because a sprouting seed does not use as many nutrients as a growing and flowering plant does.

STEP-BY-STEP SOWING TECHNIQUES

1. Fill your plant pots or planting trays by sprinkling soil over them until they are overfull.

2. Scrape excess soil off the top, leaving the soil level with the tops of the pots, and lightly tap the pots to make the soil settle. The soil should settle somewhere between 1/4 and 1/2 inch (6–13 mm), depending on the depth of your pots. Use a piece of scrap wood to even out the surface.

3. Water gently with a watering can.

Step 4

4. Sprinkle chive seeds onto the prepared soil, with a density of about four seeds to each inch (2.5 cm) of surface. The seeds need light to germinate, so don't cover them with soil.

5. Many seed-starter kits come with clear plastic covers that transform the setup into a miniature greenhouse. If you are using a multiflat with a "greenhouse" top, place it over the tray and put it in a warm spot to germinate. If you don't have such a top, you can purchase one separately or rig up a similar system with household and salvaged objects. Commercial bakery boxes for cakes and cookies often come in clear plastic, and small plant pots can be put inside them to keep moisture and warmth. Small flats and plant pots can also be placed in a plastic bag; close lightly and cut small vent holes.

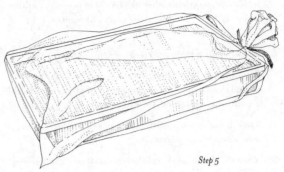

Step 5

6. Put your starter pots in a warm place away from direct light and wait for the seeds to germinate, keeping the soil moist but not soaking wet.

7. When you begin to see small shoots of green peeking up through the soil (be patient, as this may take anywhere from 2 weeks to several months), open up the "greenhouse" to allow air to circulate.

8. Keep the soil moist and grow the chives until they are about 1 or 2 inches (3–5 cm) tall. It is now time to transplant them to your garden or to a growing container.

Introducing Chives to the Great Outdoors

If you will be growing your chives outside, you have to prepare the fledgling seedlings for the vagaries of the outside world. This process is called hardening off, and it entails getting the plants gradually used to direct sun, wind, and fluctuations in temperature.

Choose a mild day to start hardening off. Place your seedlings in a shady outdoor location that is protected from the wind. If you have trouble finding such a spot, you can place your potted seedlings inside a cardboard box with its top taped open so that it will block gusts of wind but still allow some light to reach the plants directly.

Bring the plants in every night. After 4 or 5 days, move the seedlings to a more exposed position where some breezes and sunshine can reach them. Continue bringing them in at night until all chance of a frost has passed. Then the seedlings will be ready to transplant to the spot you've picked out for them.

STEP-BY-STEP TRANSPLANTING TIPS

Plants are best transplanted early in the morning, when the sun is gentler and the soil is still moist with dew.

1. Prepare the chives' new home in the garden by watering it well the night before transplanting. Also, loosen up the soil immediately before you move the seedlings to the garden.

Continued ➡

2. Water the seedlings to help their roots and soil stay together; this prevents trauma to the roots.

3. Dig a hole a little wider and deeper than the dimensions of the rootballs of the plants you have started.

4. If you are using peat pots, simply plant the entire pot. Otherwise, very gently tip the seedlings from their starter pots, avoiding any pressure on the chive sprouts. With multiflats, you might find it helpful to press on the bottom of each "pot" to pop out the roots and soil. If you have rigid pots, gently tip each one upside down over your other hand, held in a cupped position, so you catch the dirt around the edges without flattening the plants.

5. Set the plants into the prepared hole.

6. Carefully use the soil left from the hole to fill in the spaces around the transplanted seedlings, and gently firm up the soil by patting it in place with your fingers.

7. Water thoroughly but gently. Leave at least 6 inches (15 cm) between each clump of seedlings.

8. When the chives bloom, cut the blossom stems from the plant at the base. This will ensure continued new growth throughout the season.

From here on your chives should largely take care of themselves; just give them a little extra water during dry spells until they are well established. Sprinkling compost around the base of the clump will keep the soil rich, but chives are hardy enough to thrive in most soils without such special treatment.

FUTURE MAINTENANCE

As your chives mature, they will outgrow their pots, so it's essential to break up the clumps every 3 to 4 years.

Divide the mother plant by gently pulling it apart into smaller clumps. Each clump should be composed of at least 10 plantlets.

1. In the spring, after the chives have begun to show healthy growth, dig up the whole clump. Be careful to dig deep enough to get all the roots.

2. Pull apart the clump with your fingers, or cut it apart with a sharp knife. Make one clump the size you wish for the old location and set the remainder aside for planting elsewhere. Each clump should have at least 10 plantlets to ensure that it will be strong enough to survive on its own.

3. Refresh the soil by mixing a handful or two of compost or rotted manure into the soil before replacing the clump and patting soil back around the roots.

4. Put the extra plants elsewhere in your garden if you want more chives, preparing the beds as you did for the replaced clump above. You can plant some chives in a pot to keep inside for a year-round crop. You can also pot them and give them to friends, or just add them to your compost pile and let them feed the surviving plants in the months to come.

Harvesting Time

Chives can be harvested from the moment they begin to grow in spring through the early frosts of autumn. Chives delight gardeners by being among the first shoots of green to appear in the herb garden. Still, do let the plant grow to at least 6 inches (15 cm) in height before you begin tentatively pruning for your kitchen. This will ensure that growth will continue throughout the season.

While you could mow down an entire chive plant for its greens, careful harvesting will keep your chive plants healthy and good looking. Always cut each leaf or flower stalk off at the lowest point you can reach. Whatever is left of a stalk will turn brown and hard after you cut it, and leaves will become brown at the cut ends. Neither of these features makes an attractive addition to your garden. Cut off stalks and leaves in a scattered distribution, never taking more than a few leaves from one part of the plant, so you don't get "bald spots" in your chive plants.

Avoid cutting the blooming stalks with your leaves for dinner. Once a bud begins to open, its stalk begins to change into a sturdy stem to support the weight of a flower. Such a stem will be tough, fibrous, and lacking in flavor.

To harvest chive blossoms themselves, cut them off at the base of their stems. If you just pop these flowers off, the stems will quickly turn into unattractive sticks that will get in the way whenever you try to cut chives later in the season.

When harvesting, use a sharp knife to trim stalks and leaves close to the base of the plant.

Storing and Preserving Techniques

Since chives are primarily used fresh, the best way to enjoy them year-round is to keep a pot on your windowsill. Of course, chives can also be dried or frozen for later use.

SHORT-TERM FRESH STORAGE

A freshly cut bunch of chives, especially if cut to include blossoms, makes a simple, rustic floral arrangement that secretly doubles as a condiment. Chives kept in a glass or vase of fresh water will stay fresh and flavorful for over a week.

For longer storage, wrap the base of the bunch of chives in a paper towel and wet thoroughly. Place the bundle in a plastic bag and lightly twist shut the top. You don't want to close the bag completely, because some air circulation helps the chives stay fresh longer. Store the chives in the crisper drawer of your refrigerator, where they should keep for about 3 weeks. When the cut ends look dry, frayed, brown, or darker green, or are beginning to curl and split, the chives are getting old and dried out and should be discarded

DRYING CHIVES

Dried chives tend to be shadows of their former, glorious selves. You may need to increase the amount you use in a dish if the recipe calls for fresh chives. On the other hand, the subtlety of dried chives can be pleasantly mellow in contrast to the sharpness of the fresh kind.

Drying chives is easy. Just follow these steps:

1. Rinse the chives.

2. Lay the chives out on a paper towel spread over a wire cake rack and set them someplace safe to dry. Look for a well-ventilated spot that's out of direct sunlight. Avoid areas that are dusty, smoky, or exposed to kitchen odors.

3. After a few days, do a dryness test. Completely dried chives are brittle to the touch.

4. Crumble the chives and store in airtight containers.

FREEZING CHIVES

Freezing is the best way to preserve the flavor of chives. However, frozen chives suffer in texture, turning into limp, semitranslucent stalks that are not as tender as they were when they were fresh.

Still, frozen chives can be used in many cooked dishes that call for fresh chives. Dishes that incorporate chives into a marinade or sauce work well with frozen chives. To disguise the soft texture, cut the frozen chives into smaller pieces. For some recipes, of course, it's better to wait until you have the fresh herb.

To freeze chives, rinse freshly cut herbs and lay them on a towel to dry completely. Do not try to dry them by patting with the towel, or they could end up bruised.

When the chives are dry, cut them to fit into a freezer-quality bag; one that has a zip closure will be the most convenient for repeated use. Line the chives up in clumps, tying each clump together with another chive, and lay the bundles side by side in the freezer bag. Seal, pressing out any excess air gently so as not to bruise the hollow stalks. Keep in the freezer. Whenever you need some, just snip off the ends of a whole clump at once, using scissors.

Home Cooking with Chives

What chives can do for food! Their fresh, sharp bite adds zest to many dishes, especially with a potato, cheese, or egg base. Chives are standard additions to omelets and to baked potatoes with sour cream. The following recipes offer you some creative ways to add chives to other main dishes, side dishes, appetizers, soufflés, soups, dressings, spreads, and muffins. Bon appétit!

> ### FRESH OR DRIED?
> Remember, if you're using dried chives instead of fresh, increase the amount of chives—try using twice as much as the recipe calls for.

PASTA FRITTATA OF HAM AND CHIVE

6 tablespoons (90 ml) extra-virgin olive oil, divided

1/4 cup (60 ml) chives, minced

1/2 cup (120 ml) cooked ham, chopped or shredded

A pinch of freshly ground black pepper

1/4 cup (60 ml) grated Fontina cheese

1/2 pound (230 g) capellini pasta, cooked and drained

4 large eggs, beaten

1. In a skillet over medium heat, warm 2 tablespoons (30 ml) of the olive oil and sauté the chives and ham for 2 minutes. Add pepper.

2. In a large bowl, combine the ham mixture with the cheese, cooked pasta, and eggs.

3. In a 12-inch (30 cm) skillet (preferably nonstick), heat 3 tablespoons (45 ml) of the olive oil over a medium-high flame until hot (starting with hot oil helps prevent sticking). Pour in the pasta mixture, using the back of a spatula to flatten its top surface to fill in the pan, and reduce the heat to medium. Periodically reposition the pan over the flame so that the heat gets equal time under every portion of the frittata, cooking and browning it evenly. After 8 to 10 minutes, the top of the frittata will begin to show signs that the eggs have set, and it is time to turn the frittata over.

4. Set a large plate top down over the top of the skillet. The plate should be larger than the skillet. Holding the skillet handle in your left hand, place your right hand on the bottom of the plate and press them firmly together. Quickly flip the pan and plate over, allowing the frittata to tip onto the plate intact.

5. Replace the pan on the stove and set the plate of frittata aside. Put the remaining 1 tablespoon (15 ml) of olive oil into the skillet and allow it to get hot. Hold the plate of frittata over the skillet and gradually slide it in, with the uncooked side now facing downward.

6. Cook over medium heat, rotating periodically to aid in even cooking, until the frittata is set and its bottom is golden brown, about 8 to 10 minutes.

7. Turn out the frittata onto a serving plate the same way you turned it over. Let it cool and set for at least 5 minutes before cutting it into wedges and serving. Because this frittata is best served at room temperature, you can make it a couple of hours in advance and let it cool before serving.

SERVES 4 FOR DINNER OR 8 FOR LUNCHEON OR BRUNCH

Continued ➜

CHINESE PORK, SHRIMP, AND CHIVE DUMPLINGS

2 teaspoons (10 ml) vegetable oil

1 cup (240 ml) garlic chives, washed, dried, and minced

1 tablespoon (15 ml) finely minced fresh ginger

1/4 cup (60 ml) water chestnuts, rinsed, drained, and diced

1/4 pound (114 g) shrimp, cooked, peeled, and minced (canned is acceptable)

1/2 pound (230 g) lean ground pork

1 teaspoon (5 ml) roasted sesame oil

1 teaspoon (5 ml) soy sauce

1 teaspoon (5 ml) sugar

2 teaspoons (10 ml) cornstarch

A pinch of freshly ground black pepper

20–30 round dumpling wrappers (found in the vegetable section of most grocery stores; if round ones are not available, cut square wonton wrappers into 3-inch, or 7.5 cm, circles with kitchen scissors)

For the Sauce:

1 tablespoon (15 ml) soy sauce

1 tablespoon (15 ml) Shao-Hsing wine, mirin, or sherry

1 teaspoon (5 ml) roasted sesame oil

1 teaspoon (5 ml) finely chopped garlic chives

1. In a skillet over high heat, swirl the vegetable oil to cover the whole pan. When it is hot, add the chives and stir until they are brilliantly green, about 30 seconds.

2. Remove the pan from the heat and place the chives in a mixing bowl. Add the ginger, water chestnuts, shrimp, ground pork, sesame oil, soy sauce, sugar, cornstarch, and pepper. Mix thoroughly with a wooden spoon or your bare hands, pressing the ingredients into a cohesive mass.

3. Cover the bowl and let it rest in the refrigerator for at least 2 hours.

4. When you're ready to assemble the dumplings, prepare a small dish of water and a plate or baking sheet for the finished dumplings.

5. Place one dumpling wrapper on the palm of your left hand. Scoop up about 1 tablespoon (15 ml) of the filling mixture and place it in the center of the dough.

6. Dip a fingertip on your right hand into the water and use it to dampen the outer edge of the dumpling wrapper. Fold the wrapper in half over the filling and pinch along the edges to seal. Set aside and continue making dumplings until the filling is used up.

7. Keep the dumplings covered to prevent them from drying out. At this point, they may be refrigerated or frozen for later use.

8. Make the dipping sauce by stirring together all the ingredients. Place in an attractive bowl.

9. When you're ready to cook the dumplings, bring a pot of salted water to a boil. Drop the dumplings into the water carefully and boil for 4 to 5 minutes, stirring to keep them from sticking together.

10. Drain and serve immediately with dipping sauce.

MAKES 20–25 DUMPLINGS; SERVES 4 AS AN APPETIZER OR 2 AS A MAIN COURSE

CHIVED OVEN FRIES WITH A TANGY DAIRY DOLLOP

1/4 cup (60 ml) plain nonfat yogurt

2 tablespoons (30 ml) sour cream

4 tablespoons (60 ml) chives, finely chopped, divided

1 large garlic clove, minced

1 teaspoon (5 ml) salt

5 tablespoons (75 ml) olive oil

Salt and freshly ground black pepper

5 medium red potatoes

1. Preheat the oven to 400°F (205°C). Whip together the yogurt, sour cream, and 1 tablespoon (15 ml) of the chives. Set aside in the refrigerator to allow the flavors to blend.

2. In a blender, process the garlic, remaining chives, salt, and olive oil until they form a chunky paste. Scrub the potatoes clean and cut them into 1/8-inch-thick (3 mm) slices. With a pastry brush (or your fingertips), coat each potato slice with the chive mixture and set it on a baking sheet, leaving a small space between slices.

3. When each sheet is filled, add salt and pepper to taste, then bake for 20 to 30 minutes, until tender and golden.

4. Serve the fries hot with the yogurt sauce as a dip. Sprinkle a pinch of chives on the yogurt as a garnish.

SERVES 4 AS A SIDE DISH

CHIVED GREEN BEANS

1 pound (454 g) fresh green beans, washed, stems snapped off

2 tablespoons (30 ml) butter

1/4 cup (60 ml) chives, chopped

1 teaspoon (5 ml) white wine vinegar

Salt and freshly ground black pepper

1. Steam or boil the green beans until just tender, then drain.

2. In a saucepan, melt the butter over medium-low heat and add the chives. Stir for 1 minute, then add the green beans and continue stirring for another 2 minutes.

3. Add the vinegar and salt and pepper to taste, then remove from the heat and serve immediately.

SERVES 4 AS A SIDE DISH

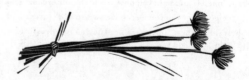

GARLIC-CHIVE POTATO SALAD

4 red boiling potatoes, scrubbed clean, with skins on

4–5 tablespoons (60–75 ml) red wine vinegar

4 celery stalks

1 cucumber

2–3 tablespoons (30–45 ml) garlic chives, to taste

2–4 tablespoons (30–60 ml) mayonnaise

1 teaspoon (5 ml) prepared mustard

Salt and freshly ground black pepper

1. In a large pot of boiling water, boil the potatoes until they can be pierced easily with the tip of a knife, about 20 minutes. Drain and let them cool until they can be handled.

2. Cut the potatoes, skin and all, into rough 3/4-inch (19 mm) cubes and place them in a large bowl. Stir in the red wine vinegar and let sit, stirring occasionally, while you prepare the other ingredients.

3. Scrub the celery and cut it into small chunks. Peel the cucumber, seed it, and cut it into small chunks. Rinse the garlic chives, dry them, and chop finely, reserving a few attractive tips for garnish.

4. When the potatoes are cool, stir in the vegetables, chives, mayonnaise, and mustard. Season to taste with salt and pepper, and adjust the mayonnaise-to-vinegar ratio to suit you.

5. The salad tastes best if it is left to sit in the fridge for a couple of hours before serving to allow the flavors to mingle. Stir well before serving and arrange the reserved chive tips on top.

SERVES 4 AS A SIDE DISH

GARLIC, CHIVE, AND GINGER CHICKEN

2 tablespoons (30 ml) vegetable oil, divided

4 skinned boneless chicken breasts

1/4 cup (60 ml) garlic chives, minced

2 garlic cloves, minced

1 tablespoon (15 ml) fresh ginger, minced

3/4 cup (180 ml) chicken broth

1/4 cup (60 ml) rice wine vinegar

2 tablespoons (30 ml) hoisin sauce

1 teaspoon (5 ml) brown sugar

12 garlic chive leaves, cut into 2-inch (5 cm) lengths

1. In a large skillet over medium-high heat, swirl 1 tablespoon (15 ml) of the vegetable oil to coat the pan. When the oil is hot, place the four chicken breasts in the skillet.

2. Sear the chicken breasts (to seal in their juices) until they are golden brown on both sides, about 5 minutes total. Remove to a plate and set aside.

3. Return the skillet to medium heat and add the remaining tablespoon (15 ml) of vegetable oil. When heated, add the garlic chives, garlic, and ginger and sauté until the garlic is soft (about 1 minute).

4. Add the broth, vinegar, hoisin sauce, and brown sugar and bring to a simmer, stirring, until the mixture begins to thicken (2 to 4 minutes).

5. Return the chicken to the pan with the other ingredients and cook over low heat until the breasts are cooked throughout.

6. Just before the chicken is done, add the lengths of chive. Stir to coat them in sauce and bring out their color. Serve immediately.

SERVES 4 AS A MAIN COURSE

CHEDDAR CHIVE SOUFFLÉ

3 cups (710 ml) milk

1 cup (240 ml) chives, chopped

3/4 cup (180 ml) cornmeal

3/4 cup (180 ml) grated Cheddar cheese

3 egg yolks, slightly beaten

1/2 teaspoon (3 ml) salt, divided

A pinch of freshly ground black pepper

A pinch of cayenne pepper

7 egg whites

1. Heat the oven to 400°F (205°C).

2. Prepare two 6-cup-capacity (1.5 l) soufflé pans by generously buttering them to the top rim and then dusting them with cornmeal, tapping out the excess.

3. Bring the milk and chives to a simmer over medium heat, and whisk in the cornmeal gradually. Keep stirring until the mixture has thickened, about 3 minutes.

4. Remove from the heat and let cool, covered, for 15 minutes.

5. Stir in the cheese, the egg yolks, 1/4 teaspoon (1 ml) of the salt, and pepper. Beat until completely incorporated.

6. In a large mixing bowl, beat the egg whites and remaining 1/4 teaspoon (1 ml) of salt until soft peaks form.

7. Spoon one-quarter of the egg whites into the cornmeal-chive mixture, then whisk to incorporate and lighten the texture.

8. Transfer the chive mixture into the bowl with the remaining egg whites and fold them together.

9. Gently spoon the batter into the two prepared soufflé pans and smooth over the tops.

10. Place the soufflés in the oven, reduce the heat to 375°F (190°C), and bake for 30 to 35 minutes, until golden brown and nicely puffed. Serve immediately. You can expect this soufflé to deflate a little as it cools, due to its rich cheese and cornmeal content, so be sure to have your appreciative audience assembled as you take it from the oven to the table.

MAKES 1 SOUFFLÉ, ENOUGH FOR 4 SERVINGS

Continued →

GOAT CHEESE TARTLETS

3 cups (710 ml) plus 1 tablespoon flour, divided

1/2 teaspoon (3 ml) salt, divided

1 cup (240 ml) chilled butter

3–8 tablespoons (45–120 ml) ice water

10 ounces (280 g) soft fresh goat cheese

1/2 cup (120 ml) cultured buttermilk

1 egg

1/4 cup (60 ml) chives, chopped coarsely

Tips of chive stalks, for decorating tops of tartlets

1. Preheat the oven to 400°F (205°C). Butter 12 cups in a muffin tin and set aside.

2. In a bowl, combine 3 cups (710 ml) of the flour and 1/4 teaspoon (1 ml) of the salt. With a fork or pastry blender, work in the butter until it is in pea-sized or smaller pieces. Blend in the ice water gradually, until the dough begins to clump together in the center but remains crumbly at the edges of the bowl. The amount of water necessary will depend on the day's humidity.

3. Quickly work the dough together with your hands to form a rough ball. Place this on a flour-dusted work surface and roll out to a thickness of about 1/8 inch (3 mm).

4. Cut the dough into 3-inch (7.5 mm) circles and press each into one of the prepared muffin tin cups to form pastry shells about 1/2 inch (13 mm) deep. Prick the bottom of each shell with a fork.

5. Bake the shells for 8 to 10 minutes, until just golden. Remove from the oven, reduce the heat to 375°F (190°C), and allow the shells to cool while you prepare the filling.

6. In a mixing bowl, use an electric mixer to blend the goat cheese, buttermilk, and egg until they are light and fluffy. Sift in the remaining tablespoon of flour, add the chives and remaining 1/4 teaspoon (1 ml) of salt, and blend.

7. Spoon the mixture into the prebaked shells, smoothing over the top surface. Bake for about 20 minutes, or until puffed and golden on top.

8. Remove the pan from the oven, let set for 5 minutes, then remove the tartlets from the pan to finish cooling on a wire rack.

9. Before serving, arrange chive tips on the top of each tartlet.

MAKES 12 TARTLETS

LANDSCAPING AND SPECIALTY GARDENS

Landscaping with Bulbs

Ann Reilly

The Magic of Bulbs

When you plant bulbs, you are planting a self-contained package of foliage and flowers that will reward you with color year after year. Triggered into motion by time or temperature, bulbs are one of the most reliable of plants, welcoming spring when most needed or filling the summer garden with unusual beauty.

WHAT IS A BULB?

True bulbs, such as daffodils, lilies, bulbous iris, hyacinths, glory of the snow and others, are actually complete plants within a tiny package. Slice into a bulb at planting time, and you will see the future roots, stems, leaves and flowers. Fleshy scales surrounding this future growth contain all the necessary food for the bulb to grow. After the bulb has bloomed, food for the next season is manufactured in the leaves and transferred to the underground portion to start the chain again the following year. On the outside of a bulb you will find a thin, brown covering similar to that you find on an onion.

As bulbs grow, tiny **bulblets** are formed around the base. These bulblets can be separated from the main bulb to form new plants. A few bulbs, such as lilies, form bulbils in the leaf axils of the parent plant.

Corms, which include crocus, freesia and gladiolus, are modified stems filled with food storage tissue. They are usually short and squat and covered with a mesh-like material. Look closely, and you will see growth eyes at the top. After a corm blooms, the original corm disappears and a new one forms for next year's growth. Some corms also produce cormels which, like bulblets, are baby plants that can be separated from the parent and grown into new plants.

Rhizomes such as iris are thick storage stems that grow along the soil surface. Growth buds form on a rhizome for next year's leaves and flowers; the original rhizome will not reflower and in time will need to be dug out.

Tubers, including Grecian windflower, caladiums and tuberous begonias, are underground food-storing stems. Unlike rhizomes, they do not creep along the ground. Tuberous roots are actually roots, not stems, with thick, fleshy food-storing parts that resemble tubers. Chief among these are dahlias.

All of these plants are generally referred to as "bulbs" because of their unique food-storing capabilities and their growth habits. All are planted while dormant and then grow, bloom, and store food before going dormant again. Because of their many similarities, they are usually grouped together.

SPRING VS. SUMMER

You will hear and see the terms "spring bulbs" and "summer bulbs" whenever the subject is discussed. Spring bulbs are winter hardy: they are planted in fall, grow and bloom in spring, and then lie dormant for a year. They do not need to be dug out of the ground except when they need to be divided. Summer bulbs are not winter hardy: they are planted in spring, grow and bloom in summer, and are then dug from the ground and stored in a frost-free area over the winter until they are replanted the following spring.

Planning the Bulb Planting

The first decision to make in planning a bulb planting is whether you want a **formal or informal look** for the garden. The style of your home and the rest of the garden may determine this for you. The formal garden, as the name implies, is a more symmetrical garden with regular borders; it should be planted with formal bulbs such as tulips and hyacinths and should use blocks of one or two colors. Informal beds are more natural in look, with bulbs planted in natural-looking drifts and in a rainbow of colors.

Selection of **flower color** sets the theme in the garden. Bright reds, yellows, and oranges are warm, happy and exciting colors while blue, pink, white, and lavender are more cooling and soothing to the eye and create a more tranquil effect.

You can chose from several **color harmonies.** Buy a color wheel from an art store to help you with this. **Monochromatic** color harmony is achieved when you plant bulbs of the same color, such as pink tulips and hyacinths. **Analagous color harmony** is the use of three colors in a row on the color wheel, such as pale yellow hyacinths, golden daffodils and orange tulips. **Complementary color harmony** is the use of opposites on the color wheel, such as red-orange tulips with purple-blue grape hyacinths. When selecting bulbs for planting, remember to harmonize with and complement existing trees and shrubs, the house, and other garden features as well.

When choosing bulbs for the garden design, select a number of types so that you will have color from late winter until early summer. By ensuring the **succession of bloom**, you ensure continuous color.

Almost without exception, bulbs look better when planted in **clumps of at least three**. The smaller the bulb, the more flowers you need in the clump. For example, plant four clumps with three tulips in each clump across a 9-foot section of the foundation planting, rather than planting the tulips single file, 9 inches apart in an empty-looking line.

Bulbs can also be **naturalized** into an informal look, particularly appropriate in woodland settings. Bulbs can be planted to look natural and then left to multiply on their own to increase the colony. If you want to achieve this effect, select a spot for your naturalistic planting that will not have to be disturbed until after the flowers and foliage have faded away.

After bulbs have bloomed and the foliage has died down, you will be left with empty spaces. If you interplanted bulbs with **ground cover**, you have no further plans to make. In flower beds, **add annuals** as soon as they can be planted in spring. No harm is done to bulb plantings to overplant them with annuals.

Perennials also make excellent companions to bulbs, starting to come into bloom about the time the bulbs fade. If possible, divide and replant both the bulbs and the perennials in the spring when you can see the location of both, avoiding accidental injury to bulbs and roots.

Summer bulbs can be integrated into the landscape, filling in spaces that need color or adding a unique look to the flower bed or border. Since summer bulbs are dug up and stored each winter, you can **plant them in a different spot each year**, achieving a different design scheme as well.

Plant bulbs of the same type and color in clusters. To achieve a natural look, scatter the bulbs on the bed and then plant them where they lie.

A **garden plan** will help you to achieve your desired effect. Sketch out your garden, indicating the position of trees, shrubs and permanent features. Select bulbs for each location based on light, existing color, desired color and a continuity of bloom times. Graph paper is an excellent way to sketch out the planting, as it makes it easy to measure the size of the beds and the number of plants that you will need.

Geometric patterns are very effective in bulb plantings. These can be circles, arcs, swales or any pattern that you find pleasing. Again, sketch this out on graph paper in advance of planting, and use the plan to mark the location of the various components of the pattern prior to planting.

Planting Spring-Flowering Bulbs

Until you plant your bulbs, be sure to store them in a dark, dry, and cool but not freezing area so they will not grow, rot, or shrivel up. A good place to store them is in a covered box inside the garage; do not keep them in the house as the heat will cause them to start growing.

You can plant spring flowering bulbs any time in fall until the soil freezes; if you can't plant them all at once, start with the smaller, earlier flowering bulbs. Begin with crocus, squills, glory-of-the-snow, winter aconite and other tiny bulbs; and with tulips and daffodils.

Bulbs in general prefer full sun to light shade. When you are planting, you may note that the bulbs seem to be in heavy shade if you are planting under a large tree. Since most bulbs bloom before trees leaf out, this shade is not a problem. However, if many hours of shade are cast from the side of the house, that will be a problem and the planting site should be moved.

SOIL PREPARATION

Good soil preparation is critical to a successful bulb garden. Because bulb roots reach deep, you'll need to spade and prepare the bed to a depth of 12 inches.

The soil for all bulbs must have good drainage and aeration to prevent the bulbs and roots from rotting and to allow for pore spaces

Continued →

into which roots can grow. Before you plant, add organic matter equal to 25% of the soil volume. This organic matter may be peat moss, compost, leaf mold or something similar.

PLANTING

When it's time to plant, assemble your bulbs and tools and hopefully pick a day when the weather is pleasant. You can prepare holes by one of two methods: you can either dig individual holes for each bulb, or you can dig out an entire area, put the bulbs in place and restore the soil. The latter is the better idea if you are planting a large number of bulbs.

When planting bulbs, you can use a narrow trowel or a special bulb planting tool. Some of these tools come with long handles so you do not have to bend over or kneel on the round. When deciding upon planting depth, consult the charts provided or plant a bulb to a depth three times its width.

Remember that bulbs look better when planted in a clump rather than individually lined up or scattered. The number in the clump depends on the size of the bulb. The larger the bulb, the less you need in the clump. For large bulbs such as tulips and daffodils, you can use only three in a clump.

Formal or informal, bulb plantings look best when individual clumps do not contain more than one color and sometimes not more than one variety. When you plan out your design, figure on enough bulbs to fill out your area based on the planting distances for the bulbs.

If you want your bulb plantings to look natural, arrange them in an informal design. Toss bulbs randomly onto the planting bed, and then plant them where they fall. You may have to adjust them slightly to maintain correct spacing, but the effect will not be as contrived as if you tried to arrange them.

Although bulbs contain their first season's food supply, fertilizing fosters future growth. To encourage root growth, add phosphorus-rich bonemeal to the bottom of each planting hole and place the bulb on top of it. Then return the soil to the hole and tamp down gently.

AFTER PLANTING

If squirrels, chipmunks or other small animals are a problem in your area and tend to make breakfast of your bulbs, place the bulbs in a wire basket or cage and plant them inside this protection. Another method of keeping animals from digging up bulbs is to spread chicken wire on to the bed after it's planted. Secure the wire at the corners, and cover it with mulch.

After planting, water the beds well and mulch them with oak leaves, bark chips or other organic mulch. One watering should be sufficient until growth starts the following spring. Label the bed so you know what's where, including the variety names. In spring, remove the mulch as soon as you see growth start, especially from low-growing varieties. Leaving mulch on too long in spring will cause foliage to be yellow and may smother the flowers of low-growing varieties.

Caring for Spring-Flowering Bulbs

Spring-flowering bulbs are about the easiest of garden plants to care for. Care requirements are minimal once planted, although a few chores in spring will keep bulbs at their blooming best.

FERTILIZING

Even though you properly prepared your bulb bed at planting time, you will need to add extra fertilizer each year to keep the bulbs healthy and flowering at their peak. When bulb foliage begins to emerge in spring, sprinkle fertilizer on the ground and water in. For maximum results, feed again as the foliage starts to yellow. Use an all purpose fertilizer such as 5-10-5 or a specially prepared bulb food.

WATERING

Once bulbs start to poke their way through the ground in spring, they will need a lot of moisture, so water deeply if spring rain does not fall. Proper flowering and growth depend on sufficient water reaching deep into the root zone.

SPRING-FLOWERING BULBS
Heights, depth of planting, and blooming times

Flower	Height	Blooming Time	Depth	Spacing
Snowdrop	4–6"	Early spring	4"	2"
Crocus	3–5"	Early spring	3–4"	3"
Anemone blanda (Wildflower)	5"	Early spring	2"	4"–6"
Grape hyacinth (*Muscari*)	6–10"	Early spring	3"	4"
Early tulips	10–13"	Early spring	6"	4"–6"
Hyacinth	12"	Early spring	6"	6"
Daffodil	12"	Midspring	6"	6"–12"
Darwin hybrid tulips	28"	Midspring	6"	4"–6"
Crown imperial (*Fritillaria imperialis*)	30–48"	Midspring	5"	18"
Late tulips	36"	Late spring	6"	4"–6"
Dutch iris	24"	Late spring	4"	3"–4"
Allium giganteum	48"	Late spring	10"	4"–12"

AFTER-BLOOM CARE

When tulips, daffodils, hyacinths and other large bulbs have finished blooming, cut off the flowers (called "deadheading") to prevent seed formation and to direct energy to the bulb. Smaller bulbs can be left to go to seed, which will scatter and increase the colony.

The future of the bulb garden depends on providing strength to the bulb as and after it blooms. As we have seen, three important aspects of this are water, fertilizer and deadheading. The fourth is maturing of foliage. Never remove leaves until they have completely browned and pull away from the plant easily.

Where neatness counts in a flower or shrub bed, braid the foliage of larger bulbs or twirl it into a circle until the foliage ripens. If the look is a natural one, the leaves can be left as is to mature. When bulbs are planted in a lawn, do not mow the grass until the foliage as browned.

One consideration with bulb plantings is the empty spaces they leave behind. If bulbs were planted into a lawn, shrub bed or under ground covers, there is no concern. A perennial border will start to fill in about the time the bulbs are finished, and annuals can be added on top of bulbs after danger of frost has passed. Be careful when planting annuals not to break or damage the bulbs in any way. Bulbs are particularly useful in rose beds as the rose foliage starts to fill out after the bulbs have passed their peak of bloom.

It's an especially good idea to mulch bulbs as mulch can help to keep the smaller bulbs from heaving out of the ground during the winter. Use an organic mulch such as leaf mold, compost, bean hulls, wood chips, or pine needles to enrich the soil as the mulch breaks down.

Glory of the snow (Chionodoxa) and other small bulbs can stay forever where you plant them.

DIVIDING AND REPLANTING

Many small bulbs, such as *Puschkinia, Chionodoxa* and squill, can be forgotten once planted, while daffodils and crocus will need to be dug and divided every five or six years when the clumps get too large, and bloom size and number decline. The best time for this is in spring right after the foliage starts to yellow. It's easier to locate bulbs in spring when

you can still see the leaves. Also, you're apt to cut or damage bulbs when you dig in fall as it's uncertain where they are. When you replant bulbs in the spring, you'll know where gaps are in the garden and you won't plant them on top of each other.

When moving bulbs, dig them carefully so as to not disturb the roots and replant them immediately just as you would plant new bulbs in the fall. Leave the foliage in place after planting and let it mature as though the bulb had not been moved.

Tulips and hyacinths do not multiply in the climate found in most parts of this country, and so diminish in size and need to be replaced every several years. Daffodils and crocus, on the other hand, multiply quickly and can be divided often. Grape hyacinths and the "minor" bulbs will also propagate from seeds they drop and will fill in a planting bed or add early spring color to the lawn within several years.

New bulbs will format the sides of the parent bulb and can be carefully pulled off and replanted to propagate the variety. Don't expect too much the first year, but in time they'll be as good as the original.

Summer-Flowering Bulbs in the Landscape

Summer-flowering bulbs (which actually can be bulbs, tubers, rhizomes, roots, or corms) are less hardy than their springtime cousins. Because they are sensitive to freezing temperatures, such tender bulbs must be planted in the spring and dug up and stored over winter each fall.

Planting Summer Bulbs

Soil with excellent drainage is required for summer-flowering bulbs. Before planting each spring, be sure the soil is rich in organic matter and well prepared as outlined here. Work the soil several inches deeper than the planting depth of the bulb.

While bulbs can be planted directly into the ground after all danger of frost has passed in spring, it is better to give some a head start indoors about four to six weeks before planting time outside. The ones most in need of this are tuberous begonias, caladiums and calla. Start them in a flat with a growing medium of 50–50 sphagnum peat moss and perlite. Set in a warm spot with bright light but not direct sun, and keep moist. Plant outdoors after frost danger is past.

Large bulbs should be planted individually. Smaller bulbs look better planted in clumps for a massed effect.

WATERING

All summer bulbs like to be watered deeply and often. If possible, apply water to the soil, not to foliage or blooms, to prolong flowering and keep disease to a minimum. A mulch of organic material about 2 to 3 inches thick will help conserve moisture while keeping roots cool as temperatures climb. All summer bulbs also benefit from heavy feeding with a balanced fertilizer.

WINTER CARE

All summer bulbs need to be lifted from the ground and stored over winter as they cannot withstand freezing temperatures. Tuberous begonias are best dug up before the first fall frost. Others should remain in the ground until the foliage is blackened by frost. Be careful when digging not to cut or damage the roots, corms, tubers or bulbs.

Continued ➜

After digging up bulbs, wash off as much soil as possible with a gentle spray of water, and dry them in a sunny spot for several days. Store bulbs in a dark, dry area at 40 to 50°F. A good method of storage is in dry sphagnum peat moss in a plastic bag.

Check the bulbs often to make sure they are in good condition. If they have started to grow, they need a cooler spot. If they have started to rot, allow the packing material to dry out somewhat.

DIVIDING

If your summer bulbs need dividing, do it in spring just prior to planting. Cut roots and tubers with a sharp knife, making sure that each division contains at least one growing shoot or eye. True bulbs and corms produce offsets called bulblets or cormels, which can be pulled from the parent and planted separately. They may not bloom during their first year of growth, but in time they will mature to full size.

OTHER CARE TIPS

Some summer bulbs, primarily dahlias, benefit from disbudding. As flower buds develop, pinch out the side buds and allow only the center bud to develop. It will become much larger than if it had been left in a spray of flowers. To produce more compact, stockier plants with more flowering stems, pinch out the growing tip during the first four to six weeks of growth, encouraging side shoots.

Some taller growing summer bulbs, such as gladiolus and tall dahlias, will probably need to be staked. Stakes should be set into the ground at planting time so bulbs will not be injured later on. Stems can be secured to a stake with a twistie; be careful not to injure the stem. Large plants or clumps of smaller plants can be staked with a hoop or cage.

CONTAINER BASICS

Summer bulbs are a natural for containers. While tuberous begonias, dahlias and dwarf canna come to mind first, many others are suitable. Look for compact types in proportion to the size of the container.

Be sure the container has drainage holes in the bottom to keep bulbs from rotting. Use a 50–50 soilless medium of sphagnum peat moss and perlite. Keep the medium evenly moist, mist the foliage when it's very hot, and fertilize every week or two with a soluble plant food to produce an array of colorful blooms all summer long.

STARTING FROM SCRATCH

Some more serious gardeners like to grow their own plants from seed. True, this is more time consuming, and some summer bulbs will not flower the first year. Dahlias are the most successful summer bulbs you can try using this method. Start seeds indoors six weeks before planting outdoors, keeping the medium slightly moist and the seed flat in bright light but not full sun. Dahlias are easy to grow, so easy that you do not have to save the tubers over winter if you don't want to. Know, however, that flowers will not be true to type or color.

Forcing Bulbs Indoors

Spring comes early when you force bulbs into bloom indoors. While winter winds howl outside, tulips, hyacinths, daffodils and crocus will bring bright colors, lovely scents, and the cheer of fresh flowers into your home. Paperwhite narcissus and amaryllis are two other excellent choices for indoor forcing. Any of these bulbs can be potted in fall for holiday decorations or in winter for spring cheer.

Depending on sunlight and temperature, it takes twelve to fourteen weeks to force tulips, hyacinths, daffodils and crocus, and four to eight weeks to force paperwhites and amaryllis. Weekly planting will ensure continual color all winter.

HOW TO PLANT

Bulbs can be used alone or in a group for a massed effect. One hyacinth can be grown in a carafe. A 6-inch container will accommodate six tulips, three daffodils or hyacinths; or fifteen crocus, grape hyacinths, or small iris. A 10- to 12-inch pot will hold sixteen paperwhite narcissus bulbs.

SUMMER-FLOWERING BULBS
Heights, depth of planting, and planting time

Flower	Height	Planting Time	Depth	Spacing
Acidanthera	20"	early Spring	2"	5"
Anemones de Caen, St. Brigid	18"	South-Sept.–Jan.; North-Early Spring	2"	3"
Dahlia				
large varieties	48"	—	4"	24"
dwarf varieties	12"	after last frost	4"	6"
Galtonia	40"	April – May	5"	10"
Gladiolus				
large flowering	60"	—	3–4"	6"
small flowering	30"	April–mid June	3–4"	6"
Lily	3–7'	Fall or early Spring	8"	8"
Montbretia	24"	April–end of May	4"	4"
Ranunculus	12"	South-Sept.–Jan.	2"	8"
Tigridia	16"	early Spring	3"	6"

Select a container that is at least twice as deep as the bulbs. Fill the pot 3/4 full with a lightweight potting soil. Place bulbs a pinkie's width apart on top of the soil, then gently press them into the soil so that the growing tip or nose of the bulbs is even with the top of the pot. When planting tulips, set the flat edge of the bulbs at the outside of the container. Add more soil around the bulbs to fill the pot to within 1/4 inch of the rim. Water thoroughly, then keep soil evenly moist. Label each pot, and record planting and bloom dates for reference next year.

Forced hyacinths, narcissi, tulips, amaryllis, and crocuses enhance a windowsill garden.

BEFORE-BLOOM CARE

After you plant and water the bulbs, keep the container in a location where it is between 35° and 45°F for twelve to fourteen weeks, to trick the bulbs into thinking they have spent the winter outdoors. You can use a refrigerator, unheated garage or porch, cool basement, cold frame, or outdoor trench. If you use a trench, dig it 6 inches deeper than the largest pot and line the bottom with gravel for drainage. Place pots in the trench, cover with soil, and apply a 3- to 4-inch layer of mulch to prevent the soil from freezing. Water all pots only to keep the media in the pots from drying out.

To avoid the twelve- to fourteen-week cooling period, you can buy prechilled bulbs and start them growing right away. Treat them as you would the precooled bulbs planted in media.

Bring the pots inside when shoots are two to three inches tall. For the first ten days, keep the pots in indirect sun at a temperature of 55 to 60°F. After that, you can move them to a sunny spot, but keep them away from heat and drafts. To provide adequate humidity, set the pots on pebbles in trays of water. Within 3 to 4 weeks, the flowers will appear, transforming your winter-weary home into springtime. Prolong blooming by keeping the pots as cool as possible. In a greenhouse, keep them out of direct sun.

AFTER-BLOOM CARE

After the flowers fade, move pots to a cool, sunny spot so leaves can naturally ripen while bulbs gain strength for new growth. Most bulbs forced indoors cannot be forced again, but can be planted outdoors and will bloom the following year. Paperwhite narcissus and amaryllis are two exceptions to this rule. Discard paperwhite bulbs after they bloom, for they will not bloom satisfactorily again; amaryllis can be repotted and rebloomed the following year after a dormant period.

Blooms will last longer if you keep the pots in a cool place.

Landscaping with Annuals

Ann Reilly

Photographs by Ann Reilly

Instant beauty, and spectacular and diverse color: these are the advantages and charms of annual flowers. By definition, an annual is a plant that grows, flowers, sets seed, and dies in the same season. The term "annual" is also applied to tender perennials that survive the winter only in the mildest of climates but are grown during the summer in other areas. The real meaning of the term "annual" is a myriad of color, size, beauty, and form that will burst forth in the landscape from spring frost to fall frost. Every year, there's the anticipation of a new look and new colors with flowers that are readily available at minimum cost.

BEDS OR BORDERS?

The impact that flowers make is a measure of professionalism in the home landscape. Wherever space permits, annual flower beds and/or borders should be included in the overall design. Flower beds are those plantings that are accessible from all sides. An example is an island planting in the middle of the lawn. Borders, on the other hand, are at the edge of an area, be it the lawn, walkway, driveway, foundation, shrub planting, or fence.

Because borders can usually be worked from only one side, do not plan them any deeper than 5 feet at the most, or maintenance will be difficult. Up to that point, they can be as wide as space and looks permit. Beds should be planned in relation to the surrounding area; don't try to situate too large a bed in a small grassed area, or it will be out of proportion.

Annual cutting garden.

Continued ➡

You can locate beds and borders anywhere on your grounds, uniting plantings of evergreens and flowering trees and shrubs with ribbons of living color.

Besides adding aesthetic value, beds and borders can be used to either highlight or camouflage areas or even to direct foot traffic. If you want to draw attention to your front door, frame it with color. If you want to conceal your trash cans, let an annual vine climb on a trellis in front of them. If you don't want the children cutting across the front lawn, plant a border of annuals to make them walk around the lawn to the path.

Vinca

COLORING YOUR ANNUAL WORLD

Color is probably the most striking aspect of flower bed design. It reflects the personality and mood of your home. Warm tones of yellow, gold, orange, and red attract attention to those sections of the garden where they are used. Blue and violet, on the other hand, create a quieter, more tranquil mood. Warm colors make a planting appear smaller than it actually is, while cool colors make it appear larger.

Keep color schemes simple. Use more than one or two colors only in a bed of the same plant, such as zinnias, impatiens, dahlias, or celosia.

DESIGNING YOUR ANNUAL WORLD

Design is the next step in creating your colorful world. Decide which plant sizes will best conform to the surroundings. Small beds or edgings along low hedges or beneath foundation plantings demand a low-growing choice, such as ageratum, alyssum, or begonias. In larger areas, you can vary the height to make the effect more interesting, especially if the ground is flat. In a freestanding bed, place taller plants in the center, stepping down to an intermediate-sized plant and then to a ground-hugging annual in front. For a border against a fence or wall, use the tallest in the back and work down to the front.

For a mixed bed or border, choose three sizes of plants. This can be done by combining three varieties of the same plant, such as zinnias or marigolds, in different heights; or by combining three different plants, such as tall spider flowers and medium-sized dahlias trimmed with a carpet of low-growing petunias.

Plants also grow in many different shapes, a mixture of which is most attractive in a mixed bed. Imagine a combination of spiked snapdragons intermingled with mounded begonias and edged with

Geraniums

low-growing lobelia. Annuals also grow upright and bushy (African marigolds) or in an open, informal manner (cosmos). Again, try to work in groups of three.

When you shop for bedding plants or seeds you will notice that many annuals come in a "series." For example, there are 'Super Elfin Pink,' 'Super Elfin Red,' and 'Super Elfin Blush' impatiens; 'Pink Pearls,' 'Azure Pearl,' and 'White Pearl' petunias; and 'Inca Yellow,' 'Inca Gold,' and 'Inca Orange' marigolds. If you are planning a massed bed of the same plant in mixed colors, you will achieve greater success if you use plants from the same series. They will be more uniform in height, plant shape, and bloom size.

Growing the Annual Garden

GETTING DOWN TO BASICS—SOIL

No matter how well you plan your garden or how high the quality of your plants, you will not succeed, without a good foundation: a proper soil. Before planting, you should prepare the soil, especially if a flower bed has never before been in the location where planting will be done. After laying out the area, remove all grass, weeds, stones, and other debris.

Incorporate organic matter such as peat moss, leaf mold, or compost at a rate of about 25% of soil volume into the areas where the roots will be growing, which is approximately the top 8 inches. Organic matter will improve moisture retention and drainage. Wetting agents can also help achieve the same results. Fertilizer should also be mixed in; choose a kind whose ratio of nitrogen-phosphorus-potassium (N-P-K) is 1:1:1 or 1:2:1, and apply according to label directions. Normal rate of application on new beds is 1 to 2 pounds of 5–10–5, 10–10–10, or similar ratio per 100 square feet. On established beds, a soil test is recommended; normally, 1 pound per 100 square feet would be sufficient. Spade, rototill, or otherwise mix the soil well until it is uniform. Then level it off.

Soil for most annuals should be slightly acid to neutral, with a pH of 5.5 to 7.0. Have your soil's pH tested at your extension service, or test it yourself with a soil-test kit.

Beds should not be worked in early spring when the soil is still wet, or the texture will be ruined. Beds can be worked the previous fall, or in spring just before planting.

PLANTING

If you purchase bedding plants instead of growing your own annuals from seeds, look for deep green, healthy plants that are neither too compact nor too spindly. It is better if they are not yet in bloom. Most annuals will come into full bloom faster in the garden if they are not in bloom when planted.

Most bedding plants are grown in individual "cell packs," although they may be in flats or individual pots. If you can't plant them right away, keep them in a lightly shaded spot and be sure to water them as needed. Just before planting, the bedding plants should be well watered, as should the soil in the bed or border.

Petunias

Do not try to jump the gun at planting time! Tender annuals cannot be planted until after all danger of frost has passed and the soil is warm. Half-hardy annuals can be safely planted if nights are still cool as long as there will be no more frost. Hardy and very hardy plants can be planted in early spring as soon as the soil can be worked.

When planting time has come, carefully lift plants from cell packs or pots, keeping the root ball intact in order to avoid damage. The best way to do this is to either gently squeeze or push up the bottom of the container if it is pliable enough, or turn it upside down to have the plant fall into your hand. If the plant does not slide out easily, tap the bottom of the container with a trowel. If the root ball is moist, as it should be, it should slip out easily without being disturbed.

Occasionally, you will find plants in a flat without individual cells. If you do, just before planting separate the plants gently by hand or with a knife so that the roots do not dry out. Other times, plants may be growing in individual peat pots. In this case, either peel most of the pot away, or be sure the top of the pot is below soil level after planting.

If roots are extremely compacted, loosen them gently before planting. Dig a hole slightly larger than the root ball, set the plant in place at the same level at which it was growing, and carefully firm the soil around the roots. Water well soon after planting, and again frequently until plants are established and new growth has started. Then an application of soluble fertilizer high in phosphorus will encourage root growth.

To reduce transplanting shock, plant on a cloudy or overcast late afternoon. Petunias are the most notable exception to this rule, tolerating planting even on hot and sunny days.

To reduce maintenance needs, use one of the commercially available pre-emergent herbicides labelled for ornamental use. Since these generally work best if they are not disturbed after application, apply them to the soil right after planting and water them in as required. Another method of weed prevention is the use of black plastic. Be sure to punch numerous holes into the plastic with a garden rake to ensure adequate water penetration. A thin layer of decorative mulch will hide the plastic.

Keeping the Garden Colorful

The first steps to a beautiful flower garden, as we have seen, are good soil preparation and proper planting. After that, keeping color at its peak is up to you and Mother Nature. If maintenance is a consideration, choose less demanding annuals.

FERTILIZING

Most annuals do not require high levels of fertilizer, but will do much better if adequate nutrients are available. Notable exceptions are nasturtium, spider flower, portulaca, amaranthus, cosmos, gazania, or salpiglossis, all of which like to be grown in poor, infertile soils. With these, the fertilizer incorporated before planting is adequate. With other annuals, you can fertilize once or twice more during the growing season with 5–10–5 or a similar ratio at the rate of 1 to 2 pounds per 100 square feet. As an alternative, you may use a soluble fertilizer such as 20–20–20, following label directions and applying every four to six weeks. Over-fertilizing will cause a build-up of soluble salts in the soil, especially if it is heavy soil, and result in damage to the annuals. Over-fertilizing can also result in heavy foliage growth and few flowers.

WATERING

Heavy but infrequent watering encourages deep root growth. Annuals should be watered only as often as the lawn. When annuals need less water than the surrounding lawn and shrubbery, or where soil drainage is poor, raised beds are a "must" for uniform and successful growth.

Keep foliage dry during watering. Using soaker hoses is a good way to achieve this. However, if overhead sprinklers must be used, as early in the day as possible you should water those annuals that are disease-prone (zinnias, calendula, grandiflora petunias, and stock in particular) so that the foliage will dry out before nightfall, lessening the chance of disease. When you use annuals for cut flowers, not watering them overhead will prevent water damage to the blooms. Where dry soil and dry skies prevail and irrigation is not possible, choose a drought-resistant annual such as portulaca, celosia, cosmos, sunflower, amaranthus, candytuft, dusty miller, gazania, spider flower, sweet alyssum, or vinca.

MULCHING

After your annuals are planted, adding a 2- to 3-inch layer of mulch will not only add a note of attractiveness, it will also reduce weeds and conserve soil moisture, resulting in better growth. The best mulches are organic, and include bark chips, pine needles, shredded leaves, peat moss, or hulls of some kind. The following year, the mulch can be incorporated into the soil before planting, thereby enriching it. Additional mulch can be added each spring, resulting in better soil structure and therefore better growth as years pass.

WEEDING

In addition to supplying the basic requirements for good growth, you will want to weed your plants in order to keep beds and borders as appealing as possible. Weeds may appear even though you used mulch and pre-emergent herbicide. Be sure to remove weeds as soon as possible, so that they do not compete with the flowers for water and nutrients. Remove weeds carefully, especially when the annuals are young, so you do not disturb the annuals' roots.

Continued →

Zinnia

RESEEDING

Some annuals, notably impatiens, portulaca, salvia, and nicotiana, will reseed from one year to the next. As many annuals are hybrids, the seedlings may not be identical to the parent and will often be less vigorous. It is best to remove these seedlings and replant all flower beds and borders each year for maximum effect. In most areas, the seedlings will never grow large enough to be showy.

MANICURING

Some annuals, chiefly begonias, impatiens, coleus, alyssum, ageratum, lobelia, vinca, and salvia, require little additional care. Their flowers fall cleanly from the plant after fading and do not need to be removed by hand. Others, such as marigolds, geraniums, zinnias, calendula, or dahlias, will need to have faded flowers removed. This is known as deadheading and keeps the plants attractive and in full bloom, while preventing them from going to seed or becoming diseased. Deadheading can be performed with pruning shears or sometimes with the fingers.

To be kept compact and freely flowering, a few annuals, primarily petunias, snapdragons, and pansies, may need to be pinched back after planting or after the first flush of bloom. As new hybrids are created, this is becoming less of a maintenance requirements. Sweet alyssum, candytuft, phlox, and lobelia may tend to sprawl and encroach on walks, the lawn, or other flowers. They can be headed back with hedge clippers. This shearing will also encourage heavier blooming.

In the fall, after frost has blackened their tops, annual plants should be removed so that the beds will not be unsightly through the winter.

INSECT AND DISEASE CONTROL

Proper care will help protect annuals from insects and disease. Those annuals mentioned as being prone to diseases should be planted in areas where the air circulation is good, and if possible the foliage should be kept dry. When this cannot be done or when rain is frequent, fungicide treatment may be necessary.

The most common problem insects that might appear are aphids, white fly, or spider mites; these again are easily controlled with a number of pesticides. Mites and white fly are less of a problem when moisture levels are high and plants are frequently watered. When temperatures are high, insect populations will increase and more frequent pesticide treatments will be necessary.

Where slugs and snails are common, you will find that they can feast on young annuals, especially marigolds, petunias, and salvia. Place slug bait near new plantings in late afternoon, and replenish it as necessary. Many of the baits lose their potency after irrigation or rain.

Plant Selection

Once you've decided to beautify your home with annuals, you must decide which plants to use. There are two considerations: matching the right plant with your growing conditions, and selecting plants for their visual appeal.

On the following pages are lists of plants to be used under a variety of climatic conditions: sun, shade, wet, dry, hot, cool. After you've studied these carefully, consider how much time you can devote to the garden. If your time is limited, choose a low-maintenance plant.

Then decide how much space to allocate to flower beds, estimating your ability to maintain the total space available.

The rest is personal preference. Do you have a color scheme you want to follow? Massed beds or mixed borders? Again, that depends on your layout, your style of home, and personal preferences.

Before you do any planting, lay out on graph paper the plan of your garden beds and flowers. This will allow you to decide, in advance, the shape and size of the borders and beds. It will also help you determine how many plants you will need to grow or buy.

ANNUAL CHOICES FOR SPECIAL PLACES

Most annuals are happiest when bathed in sunlight, rooted in average soil, and receiving moderate temperatures. The notable exceptions are:

Plants for Heavy Shade.

Begonia, browallia, coleus, fuchsia, impatiens, monkey flower, wishbone flower.

Plants for Part Shade.

Ageratum, aster, balsam, black-eyed Susan vine, dianthus, dusty miller, forget-me-not, lobelia, nicotiana, ornamental pepper, pansy, salvia, sweet alyssum, vinca.

Plants for Driest Conditions.

African daisy, amaranthus, celosia, dusty miller, gomphrena, kochia, petunia, portulaca, spider flower, statice, strawflower.

Plants for Moist Areas.

Aster, balsam, tuberous begonia, black-eyed Susan vine, Browallia, calendula, flowering cabbage and kale, forget-me-not, fuchsia, gerbera, impatiens, lobelia, monkey flower, nicotiana, ornamental pepper, pansy, phlox, salpiglossis, stock, wishbone flower.

Plants for Hottest Spots.

Amaranthus, anchusa, balsam, celosia, coleus, creeping zinnia, Dahlberg daisy, dusty miller, gaillardia, gazania, gloriosa daisy, gomphrena, kochia, triploid marigold, nicotiana, ornamental pepper, petunia, portulaca, salvia, spider flower, statice, strawflower, verbena, vinca, zinnia.

Plants for Cool Climates.

African daisy, tuberous begonia, browallia, calendula, clarkia, dianthus, flowering cabbage and kale, forget-me-not, lobelia, monkey flower, pansy, phlox, salpiglossis, snapdragon, stock, sweet peas, wishbone flower.

Plants for Alkaline Soil.

Aster, dianthus, salpiglossis, scabiosa, strawflower, sweet pea.

Plants for Fragrance.

Dianthus, scabiosa, snapdragon, spider flower, four o'clock, stock, sweet alyssum.

Plants for Hanging Baskets.

Begonia, black-eyed Susan vine, browallia, coleus, creeping zinnia, fuchsia, impatiens, ivy geranium, lobelia, petunia, portulaca, sweet alyssum, verbena, vinca.

Plants for Cut Flowers.

Ageratum, aster, calendula, cornflower, cosmos, dahlia, gerbera, marigold, salvia, snapdragon, spider flower, stock, zinnia.

Hardy Annuals.

African daisy, calendula, clarkia, cornflower, flowering kale and cabbage, forget-me-not, hibiscus, lavatera, pansy, phlox, snapdragon, stock, sweet alyssum, sweet pea.

ANNUAL SELECTION GUIDE

	Planting Distance	Maintenance	Plant Height	* Light	** Moisture	*** Temperature	**** Hardiness
African daisy	8–10"	medium	10–12"	S	d	c	H
Ageratum	5–7"	low	4–8"	S, PSh	a–m	m	HH
Amaranthus	15–18"	medium	18–36"	S	d	m–h	HH
Anchusa	8–10"	medium	9–18"	S	d–a	m–h	HH
Aster	6–18"	high	6–30"	S, PS	h	mm	HH
Balsam	10–15"	low	12–36"	S, PS	h	mh	T
Begonia, tuberous	8–10"	low	8–10"	PSh, Sh	m	c–m	T
Begonia, wax	7–9"	low	6–8"S,	PSh, Sh	a	m	HH
Black-eyed Susan vine	12–15"	medium	3–6"S,	PSh	m	m	HH
Browallia	8–10"	low	10–15"	PSh, Sh	m	c	HH
Calendula	8–10"	high	3–4"	S, LSh	m	c–m	H
Candytuft	7–9"	low	8–10"	S	d	any	HH
Celosia	6–8"	low	6–15"	S	d	m–h	HH
Clarkia	8–10"	high	18–24"	S, LSh	d–a	c	H
Coleus	8–10"	low	10–24"	PSh, Sh	a–m	m–h	T
Cornflower	6–12"	medium	12–36"	S	d–a	m	VH
Cosmos	9–18"	medium	18–30"	S	d–a	m	HH
Creeping zinnia	5–7"	medium	5–16"	S	d–a	m–h	HH
Dahlberg daisy	4–6"	low	4–8"	S	d–a	m–h	HH
Dahlia	8–10"	high	8–15"	S, LSh	a–m	m	T
Dianthus	7–9"	low	6–10"	S, PSh	a	c–m	HH
Dusty miller	6–8"	low	8–10"	S, PSh	d–a	m–h	HH
Flowering cabbage, kale	15–18"	low	15–18"	S	m	c	VH
Forget-me-not	8–12"	low	6–12"	PSh	m	c	H
Four o'clock	12–18"	low	18–36"	S	d–a	any	T
Fuchsia	8–10"	high	12–24"	PSh, Sh	m	m	T
Gaillardia	8–15"	medium	10–18"	S, LSh	d–a	m–h	HH

Continued ➜

	Planting Distance	Maintenance	Plant Height	* Light	** Moisture	*** Temperature	**** Hardiness
Gazania	8–10"	high	6–10"	S	d–a	m–h	HH
Geranium	10–12"	high	10–15"	S	a–m	m	T
Gerbera	12–15"	medium	12–18"	S	m	m	HH
Gloriosa daisy	12–24"	low	18–36"	S, LSh	a	m–h	HH
Gomphrena	10–15"	medium	9–30"	S	d	m–h	HH
Hibiscus	24–30"	medium	48–60"	S, LSh	m	m	H
Impatiens	8–10"	low	6–18"	PSh, Sh	m	m	T
Ivy geranium	10–12"	medium	24–36"	S	a	m	T
Kochia	18–24"	low	24–36"	S	d	m–h	HH
Lantana	8–10"	medium	10–12"	S	a	m	T
Lavatera	12–15"	medium	18–30"	S	d–a	m	H
Lobelia	8–10"	low	3–5"	S, PSh	m	c–m	HH
Marigold, African	12–15"	high	18–30"	S	a	m	HH
Marigold, French	3–6"	high	5–10"	S	a	m	HH
Mexican sunflower	24–30"	medium	48–60"	S	d	m–h	T
Monkey flower	5–7"	low	6–8"	PSh, Sh	m	c	HH
Nasturtium	8–12"	low	12–24"	S, LSh	d	c–m	T
New Guinea impatiens	10–12"	low	10–12"	S, LSh	m	m	T
Nicotiana	8–10"	low	12–15"	S, PSh	m	m–h	HH
Ornamental pepper	5–7"	low	4–8"	S, PSh	m	m–h	HH
Pansy	6–8"	medium	4–8"	S, PSh	m	c	VH
Petunia	10–12"	medium	6–12"	S	d	m–h	HH
Phlox	7–9"	low	6–10"	S	m	c–m	H
Portulaca	6–8"	low	4–6"	S	d	h	T
Salpiglossis	10–12"	medium	18–24"	S	m	c	HH
Salvia	6–8"	low	12–24"	S, PSh	a–m	m–h	HH
Scabiosa	8–12"	high	12–24"	S	m	m	HH
Snapdragon	6–8"	medium	6–15"	S	a	c–m	VH
Spider flower	12–15"	low	30–48"	S	d	m–h	HH
Statice	12–24"	medium	12–36"	S	d	m–h	HH
Stock	10–12"	high	12–24"	S	m	c	H
Strawflower	7–9"	medium	15–24"	S	d	m–h	HH
Sunflower (dwarf)	12–24"	high	15–48"	S	d	h	T
Sweet alyssum	10–12"	low	3–5"	S, PSh	a–m	m	H
Sweet pea	6–15"	medium	24–60"	S	m	c–m	H
Verbena	5–7"	medium	6–8"	S	d–a	h	T
Wishbone flower	6–8"	low	8–12"	PSh, Sh	m	c	HH
Vinca	6–8"	low	4–12"	S, PSh	any	m–h	HH
Zinnia	4–24"	high	4–36"	S	d–a	m–h	T

*Light:

S = Full sun
LSh = Light shade
PSh - Part shade
Sh - Full shade

**Moisture:

d = dry
a = average
m = moist

***Temperature:

c = cool (below 70°F)
m = moderate
h = hot (above 85°F)

****Hardiness:

VH = very hardy, will withstand heavy frost
H = hardy, will withstand light frost
HH = half hardy, will withstand cool weather, but not frost
T = tender, will do poorly in cool weather, will not withstand frost

Creating a Wildflower Meadow

Henry W. Art

Illustrations by Hyla Skudder

In addition to providing low-maintenance landscaping, wildflowers are extremely versatile. If portions of your yard are too dry or too wet for the usual lawn grasses, certain wildflowers mixed with native grasses may be a beautiful solution to the problem. Many species (such as black-eyed Susan, butterfly weed, and purple coneflower) will attract butterflies to your garden. Scarlet sage and standing cypress, with their bright red flowers, are pollinated by hummingbirds. These species and others (such as gayfeather, blanketflower, and wild bergamot) make excellent cut flowers as well.

Selecting Wildflowers

The wildflowers I suggest you consider have been selected because they are native to North America, reasonably easy to grow, and are well behaved once established. Although some of these wildflowers are native only to a specific region, all of them can be grown over a wide range of environmental conditions in other regions as well. There are many other species that could easily be added to your backyard and you might want to consult *A Garden of Wildflowers* or *The Wildflower Gardener's Guide*.

When I use the term "wildflower" I am referring to species of plants that can grow on their own with little or no attention from the gardener. While some species such as ox-eye daisy and chicory may be attractive, they also may become aggressive and take over your backyard. The following is a short list of alien (non-native) wildflower species that should be avoided for that reason.

ALIEN WILDFLOWER SPECIES

African daisy	Four-o'clock
Baby's breath	Foxglove
Bachelor's button	Ox-eye daisy
Bouncing Bet	Purple loosestrife
Candytuft	Queen Anne's lace
Chicory	St. John's-wort
Corn poppy	Silene
Cornflower	Sweet alyssum
Dame's rocket	White yarrow

For best results, the wildflowers you choose should be compatible with the environmental conditions typical to your region. The list of wildflowers is keyed to the regional map below and can be used as a general guide for the selection of wildflowers.

WILDFLOWER & GRASS REGION MAP

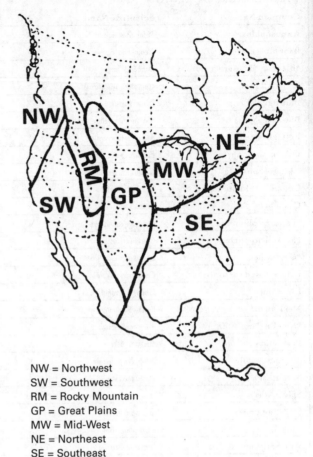

NW = Northwest
SW = Southwest
RM = Rocky Mountain
GP = Great Plains
MW = Mid-West
NE = Northeast
SE = Southeast

Some wildflowers are "hardy" and tolerate freezing temperatures, while others are "tender" and are killed by frosts. Take your local climate into consideration when selecting wildflowers, remembering that sunny southern slopes are usually warmer, and shady northern slopes may be substantially cooler, than the average climate of a region. For example, if you live in a northern region you may be able to grow more southerly wildflowers on south-facing, protected slopes.

You will probably want to plant several different species of wildflowers, drawn from a rich palette of complementary colors and giving a seasonal succession of bloom. To help you make your choices, the tables below arrange the wildflowers by color and by season of flowering.

Continued ➡

WILDFLOWERS BY REGION

Common Name	Scientific Name	NE	MW	SE	GP	RM	SW	NW
Annual phlox	*Phlox drummondii*	X	X	X	X	X	X	X
Baby blue-eyes	*Nemophila menziesii*	X	X	X	X	X	X	
*Black-eyed Susan	*Rudbeckia hirta*	X	X	X	X	X	X	X
Blanketflower	*Gaillardia aristata*	X	X	X	X	X	X	X
Blue flax	*Linum lewisii*	X	X	X	X	X	X	X
Blue-eyed grass	*Sisyrinchium bellum*						X	X
Butterfly weed	*Asclepias tuberosa*	X	X	X	X	X	X	X
California poppy	*Eschscholzia californica*	X	X	X	X	X	X	X
Chinese houses	*Collinsia heterophylla*		X	X		X	X	X
Colorado columbine	*Aquilegia caerulea*					X	X	X
Cosmos	*Cosmos bipinnatus*	X	X	X	X	X	X	X
*Eastern columbine	*Aguilegia canadensis*	X	X	X	X	X		X
Farewell-to-spring	*Clarkia amoena*			X		X	X	X
*Gayfeather	*Liatris pycnostachya*	X	X	X	X	X	X	
Lance-leaved coreopsis	*Coreopsis lanceolata*	X	X	X	X	X	X	
Linanthus	*Linanthus grandiflorus*					X	X	X
Mexican hat	*Ratibida columnifera*		X	X	X	X	X	
*New England aster	*Aster novae-angliae*	X	X	X	X	X		X
Pasqueflower	*Anemone patens*	X	X		X	X		X
*Purple coneflower	*Echinacea purpurea*	X	X	X	X	X	X	X
Scarlet sage	*Salvia coccinea*			X	X		X	X
Spiderwort	*Tradescantia virginiana*	X	X	X		X		X
Standing cypress	*Ipomopsis rubra*	X	X	X	X		X	X
Tidy tips	*Layia platglossa*	X	X	X	X	X	X	X
Wild bergamot	*Monarda fistulosa*	X	X	X	X	X		
Wind poppy	*Stylomecon heterophylla*						X	X
		NE	MW	SE	GP	RM	SW	NW

*requires cold treatment for germination of seeds

How to Obtain Wildflowers

Wildflowers should never be dug from the wild except as part of a rescue operation to save plants that would otherwise be destroyed. Wildflowers are usually propagated either by making cuttings and divisions or by planting seeds. There are a growing number of reputable wildflower propagators who grow their own stock rather than digging plants from the wild. Many of these suppliers will take phone and mail order requests for wildflowers. However, live plants are quite expensive, perhaps prohibitively so if you intend to plant a large area.

By far the least expensive means of growing wildflowers is from seed. The quickest way to obtain wildflower seeds is to purchase them from a reputable supplier. Seeds are generally available year-round and can easily be sent through the mail. If you are planning to plant large areas, you should inquire about wholesale prices for wildflower and native grass seeds.

Use caution before using prepared wildflower seed mixtures. Although some suppliers will carefully formulate mixes especially for your region using high-quality native species, others simply add the cheapest, most readily available seeds regardless of their desirability. If you are going to spend your money on wildflower seeds, you might as well purchase species that will survive well in your region and not pay for roadside weedy wildflowers that you wouldn't want in your backyard. So find out what is in the mixture of wildflower seed before you buy the can or packet.

COLD TREATMENTS

A few of the wildflowers presented here have seeds requiring exposure to cold temperatures in order to germinate. These species are marked with an asterisk (*) on the wildflower list. Typically these are wildflowers from regions with cold winters and have evolved this protection to prevent their seeds from germinating in the autumn only to have the

COLOR

Species	White	Pink	Red	Orange	Yellow	Blue	Purple	Lavender
Linanthus	X							
Cosmos	X	X	X					
Colorado columbine	X					X		
Pasqueflower	X					X	X	
Farewell-to-spring		X	X					
Eastern columbine		X	X	X				
Annual phlox		X	X				X	
Scarlet sage			X					
Standing cypress			X					
Wind poppy			X	X				
Blanketflower			X	X	X			
Mexican hat			X		X			
Purple coneflower			X					X
Black-eyed Susan				X	X			
Butterfly weed				X				
California poppy				X				
Lance-leaved coreopsis					X			
Tidy tips					X			
Blue flax						X		
Baby blue-eyes						X		
Blue-eyed grass						X	X	
Spiderwort						X	X	X
Chinese houses						X	X	X
New England aster							X	
Wild bergamot								X
Gayfeather								X

FLOWERING PROGRESSION

Species	E Sp	M Sp	L Sp	E S	S	L S	E F	F
Pasqueflower	X							
Baby blue-eyes	X	X						
Blue-eyed grass	X	X						
Wind poppy		X						
Chinese houses		X	X	X				
Tidy tips		X	X	X				
Eastern columbine		X	X	X	X			
Linanthus		X	X	X	X			
Spiderwort		X	X	X	X			
Farewell-to-spring			X	X				
Annual phlox		X	X	X	X	X		
Lance-leaved coreopsis			X	X	X			
Colorado columbine			X	X	X			
Butterfly weed			X	X				
Wild bergamot			X	X				
Standing cypress				X				
Blue flax				X				
California poppy	X	X	X	X	X	X	X	X
Cosmos				X	X	X	X	X
Mexican hat			X	X	X	X	X	
Purple coneflower				X	X	X	X	
Black-eyed Susan			X	X	X	X		
Scarlet sage			X	X	X	X	X	X
Gayfeather					X	X	X	X
Blanketflower					X	X	X	X
New England aster						X	X	X

Key:

E Sp—Early Spring **S**—Summer

M Sp—Mid-Spring **L S**—Late Summer

L Sp—Late Spring **E F**—Early Fall

E S—Early Summer **F**—Fall

tender seedlings killed by frost. However, most of these wildflowers can be grown successfully even in regions with mild winters if the seeds are first given an artificial cold treatment. Once established, these wildflowers will produce flowers and seeds, but the new seeds will not germinate unless they also receive cold treatments.

If you live in a region with cold winters, it is best to plant the seeds of these wildflowers outdoors in the autumn. If you live in a region with mild winters and want to give these species a try, or if you want to plant the seeds in the spring rather than in the autumn, give them an artificial cold treatment before planting peat moss, place them in a zip-closure bag (labeled in waterproof ink with the name of the species), and put the in the refrigerator for 2–3 months. This treatment will enable the seeds to germinate quickly in the spring. If some of the seeds

sprout during the cold treatment, just plant them in the spring, being careful not to disturb their fragile root systems.

Selecting Grasses

Natural meadows and grasslands are a combination of wildflowers and grasses. The grasses provide support and the ideal amount of competition for the wildflowers to grow straight and tall. Without the grasses some of these wildflowers might become scraggly or "leggy." In northern regions the dead remains of the grasses provide additional insulation, protecting the over-wintering roots of the wildflowers.

Not all grasses, however, are the same; different species grow in different ways. Some grasses form "sod," which is ideal for lawns, tennis

Continued ➔

courts, and putting greens, where a continuous, tight cover is required, but is not much of an environment for growing wildflowers. Other grasses form distinct clumps or "bunches" when they grow, allowing space for wildflowers to coexist. When establishing your wildflower meadow, the grasses you interplant with the wildflowers should be bunch grasses. Avoid planting ryegrasses or bluegrasses, which would form sod turfs and crowd out the wildflowers.

Some grass species grow better in some regions than in others. To help you select grasses suited to your region, the table of suggested species is keyed to the map. Native wildflower seeds should be combined with a mixture of native grasses suited to your region.

Grasses should comprise about 60–90% of the seed mixture. The wildflower and grass seed mixture should be sown at a rate of 5–20 pounds of live seeds per acre, depending on the species composition. If species with small seeds (such as switch-grass and California poppy) make up the bulk of the mixture, the seeding rate should be lower than when the mixture is composed mainly of species with large, heavy seeds (such as northern dropseed and wild bergamot). If you purchase wildflower and grass seed in bulk, the supplier can make specific seeding-rate recommendations, but typically 6–7 pounds of wildflower seeds are mixed with enough grass seeds to sow an acre.

When to Plant

In general, wildflower seeds germinate in response to ample moisture and warm temperatures, although some seeds require cold treatment before they will respond. Ideally you should plan to plant the wildflower and grass seeds to take advantage of the natural precipitation and temperature patterns of your region. Obviously you would not want to plant a meadow in midsummer, when, in most parts of North America, heat and droughty conditions might make it difficult for seeds to germinate and seedlings to become established. Pay attention to the regional and local climate and plan your planting accordingly. Here are a few suggestions for the various wildflower growing regions:

The Northeast (NE) has ample rainfall throughout the year, with cold winters and mild summers. The best time to plant is in the autumn (October to early November) and the next-best time is in mid-spring (late April to mid-May). The best time to plant most western wildflowers in the Northeast, however, is in the spring.

The Southeast (SE) region also has precipitation that is ample and evenly distributed throughout the year. Summers are hot and humid, and winters are generally mild, though frosts may occur anywhere except on the south coasts of Florida and Texas. The autumn (October and November) is the best time to plant, and in the spring after frost danger has passed is the second choice.

Midwest (MW) has cold winters and hot summers. There is increasing tendency for periodic summer droughts toward the west, where there is generally less precipitation than in the east. The optimum planting time is in the early spring as soon as the ground can be worked (mid-March to late April). Mid-autumn (October and November) is the next-best time to plant.

The Great Plains (GP) stretch from Canada to Texas and have a range in winter temperatures from very frigid to cold. Summer temperatures are generally hot. There tends to be less precipitation here than in the Midwest or Southeast since the Great Plains lie in the rain shadow of the Rocky Mountains. Soil moisture is more plentiful in the spring than in other seasons, so it is best to plant in the late fall,

BUNCH GRASS SUGGESTIONS

Common Name	Scientific Name	NE	MW	SE	GP	RM	SW	NW
Big bluestem	Andropogon gerardii	X	X	X		X		
Blue grama	Bouteloua gracilis		X	X	X	X	X	
Broomsedge	Andropogon virginicus	X	X	X	X			
Buffalo grass	Buchloe dactyloides		X	X	X	X	X	
California oat grass	Danthonia californica					X	X	X
Tufted hair grass	Deschampsia caespitosa	X	X	X	X	X	X	X
Indian grass	Sorghastrum nutans	X	X	X	X		X	
Indian ricegrass	Oryzopsis hymenoides				X	X	X	X
June grass	Koeleria cristata		X	X	X	X	X	X
Little bluestem	Andropogon scoparius	X	X	X	X	X		
Needlegrass	Stipa spartea	X	X	X	X	X	X	X
Northern dropseed	Sporobolus heterolepsis	X	X	X	X	X		
Poverty three-awn	Aristida divaricata				X	X	X	
Sheep fescue	Festuca ovina	X	X	X	X	X	X	X
Side oats grama	Bouteloua curtipendula	X	X	X	X	X	X	
Silver bluestem	Bothriochloa saccharoides			X	X		X	
Switch-grass	Panicum virgatum	X	X	X	X		X	
Western wheatgrass	Agropyron smithii	X	X	X	X	X	X	X

746

before the ground freezes, to allow the wildflowers and grasses to take full advantage of the natural moisture.

The Rocky Mountains (RM) region typically has cold winters and warm summers with low humidity. Most of the precipitation accumulates in the form of snow during the winter and is released in the spring when most of the wildflowers bloom. The best planting in this region is during the autumn.

The Southwest (SW) is an area of scanty rainfall. In southern coastal California, most of this rain comes during the winter. Summer thunderstorms occur more frequently inland. The summer and early autumn temperatures are frequently in the 90–100°F. range. Winter temperatures range from cold in the north to balmy in the southern portions of California and Arizona. The best time to plant is in the late autumn just before the winter rains start.

The Northwest (NW) has cool winters and mild summers with considerable amounts of rainfall throughout the year, especially during the winter. Whether to plant in the spring or fall depends upon the species of wildflowers and grasses being planted. Spring-flowering wildflowers should generally be planted in the early fall, and autumn-flowering wildflowers should be planted in the spring.

Preparing Bare Ground

The easiest time to create a wildflower meadow is when the land is bare and you do not have to deal with established, competing grasses, weeds, herbaceous plants, or woody seedlings. If you are planting a large area of bare ground it may be easiest to hire a landscaper to disk and then rake the soil surface with tractor-drawn equipment. Smaller areas can be raked by hand. Most of these wildflower and grass species benefit from additions of rotted manure, compost, or other appropriate seed-free organic matter along with ground limestone at the time the soil is being prepared.

If time permits, have the ground raked again about three weeks later. The second raking will help kill any weeds that sprouted from seeds brought to the surface by the initial soil preparation. Then plant the wildflower and grass seed mixture. If you cannot plant your meadow until the following planting season, sow a cover crop of buckwheat, oats, or annual rye on the area in the fall, and plow it under as a green manure before sowing the wildflower and grass seeds.

HOW TO PLANT SEEDS

It is best to sow the wildflower and grass seeds on a windless day, broadcasting them by hand or using a whirlwind seeder. Try to apply the seeds as uniformly as possible over the ground surface. If large areas are to be planted it may be worthwhile hiring a landscaping contractor to use a seed drill to plant them. Hopefully your planting has been timed to take advantage of natural rainfall, but if the rains should fail, keep the soil moist, but not wet, until the seeds have germinated and seedlings start to become established. A light covering of seed-free straw will help conserve moisture and reduce erosion until the meadow is established. Do not use baled field hay, which is likely to contain the seeds of exotic grasses, species you want to prevent from invading your meadow.

Transforming an Existing Field

Instead of bare ground, you are more likely to be confronted with an existing lawn or field that you want to convert to a wildflower meadow.

Resist any impulses to use herbicides or fumigants to kill the existing vegetation. Herbicides are more likely to create problems for the wildflower enthusiast than solve them. They cause damage to the environment, and are not likely to save you any time in establishing a wildflower meadow.

The least effective way to try to create a wildflower meadow is to simply scatter seeds into an existing lawn or meadow. Most of the seeds won't make it through the existing grass but will be consumed by insects or small mammals. Few of the seeds will germinate and become established. The best way to turn an existing field into a wildflower meadow is to start on a small scale and not tackle the entire back 40 at once.

Two strategies can be deployed in your battle against existing sod: spot seeding and transplanting live plants that you have raised. In either approach you need to carefully prepare the site before planting. It is best to start a year in advance, or at least start in the previous spring for fall planting or in the late summer for spring planting.

As soon as the soil can be worked at the beginning of the growing season, dig up patches of the field, turning them over with a sharp spade or rototiller. The patches should be 3–8 feet in diameter and dug in a random pattern, to create a more natural effect than would result from placing them in straight rows. Remove as many of the existing grass roots as possible, and water the soil to encourage the germination of weed seeds that have been stirred up in the process. Then cover the patch with heavy-gauge black plastic sheet mulch, pieces of discarded carpet, or even thick sections of newspaper. If you do not care for the sight of such coverings, you can spread a layer of bark mulch or soil on top of them. If the covering is thick enough, it will eventually shade out and kill off any remaining grass and the newly germinated weed seedlings. Enough rain will soak through or get under the coverings to keep the ground below moist.

Leave the coverings on the patches throughout the growing season, then remove them at planting time. (If black plastic mulch or carpet sections have been used, it may be possible to use them again to create the next year's patches). Rake the ground surface, and plant the grass and wildflower seeds, gently raking them below the soil surface. Alternatively, the seeds can be mixed with an equal volume of soil and the mixture broadcast in the bare patches.

Instead of planting wildflower seeds in the patches you may wish to transplant live plants. These may be raised in your own nursery beds or in plastic trays with small conical depressions, producing "plugs" of wildflowers. Grass seed can also be planted in small pots to make plugs. If you plant seeds in containers, use a mixture of sand and peat moss as a starter soil. Whether you sow the seeds in beds, flats, or trays, do it at the beginning of the growing season. By the time the patches are prepared, the plants will be ready for transplanting.

Plant the plugs in the patch, spacing the grass clumps 12–15 inches apart, and placing the wildflowers in between them. Alternatively, wildflower plants can be transplanted into the patches, and the grass seed sown around them. In either method, the meadow will benefit from an initial watering and a light mulch of seed-free straw.

If your meadow already has bunch grasses, and you do not care to introduce new grass species, live wildflowers can be planted directly into the field. Clear a small patch about a foot in diameter with a cultivator and pick out the grass roots. Set the wildflowers so the bases of their shoots are at ground level. Press them down firmly so the roots are in good contact with the soil beneath, and water well.

Continued →

Repeat the steps each year until you are satisfied with your wildflower and native grass meadow. It may be a slow process, but even in nature a beautiful wildflower meadow, resplendent with a great diversity of desirable plants, is rarely produced in a single year.

Wildflower Meadow Maintenance

Once the wildflower meadow is established it is relatively easy to maintain. Mow the meadow once a year with a rotary mower, after the growing season is over and the seeds have set; otherwise the natural process of succession may eventually turn your field into a forest. Woody plants will be clipped off and eventually eliminated by mowing, but grasses and wildflowers will be relatively unaffected.

Meadows, grasslands, and prairies can also be maintained by periodic burning, which kills invading shrub and tree seedlings. Do not burn a meadow until after the second season, but then you can burn it every several years. Meadows are best burned in the dormant season on windless days, when the grass is dry but the soil is still wet and the humidity is sufficiently high to minimize any fire danger to surrounding areas. If the meadow grass is too thin to support the fire, dry straw can be scattered about and ignited. Be careful to observe local, state, and federal regulations concerning outdoor burning, in addition to the usual safety practices. Check with your local fire department about obtaining an outdoor burning permit.

In some suburbs there are ordinances dictating aesthetic standards for landscaping. If you live in such a community you might want to check with city hall before turning your front yard into a prairie. If there are prohibitions, you can always try to change the law to encourage landscaping with native plants. Native plants are rarely the "weeds" that these ordinances are trying to prohibit, and it is unlikely that your black-eyed Susans or wild bergamots are going to march through your neighbor's Kentucky bluegrass.

Species of Wildflowers

Annual Phlox *Phlox drummondii*

The common annual phlox listed in many seed catalogs is native to east Texas, where masses of them add brilliant pink, red and purple hues to the spring landscape. Annual phlox is a "winter annual" which blooms in the early spring. Its seeds are dormant until the autumn Texas rains stimulate germination.

COLOR: Pink, red, and purple
FLOWERING: Summer
FRUITING: Summer
HEIGHT: 6–20 inches
GROWTH CYCLE: Annual

Baby Blue-Eyes *Nemophila menziesii*

There are several variations on the blue and white theme in this wildflower. The flowers are usually blue at the tip, and white with flecks or radiating streaks of blue at the base. Other forms are all blue, or sky blue with dark blue dots at the base of their petals. Baby blue-eyes flowers open and close in response to air temperature, the petals folding inward at night or in the cold.

COLOR: Blue and white
FLOWERING: Late winter to early spring

FRUITING: Spring to early summer
HEIGHT: 10–20 inches
GROWTH CYCLE: Annual

Black-Eyed Susan *Rudbeckia hirta*

Black-eyed Susan is a hardy perennial which can be grown as an annual in most locations. The 2-to 3-inch flower heads, with dark brown centers and yellow or yellow and orange outer petals, are borne on a relatively long stalk, making the black-eyed Susan an attractive cut flower.

COLOR: Yellow and orange
FLOWERING: Summer
FRUITING: Summer to early fall
HEIGHT: 1–3 feet
GROWTH CYCLE: Annual, biennial, or perennial

Blanketflower *Gaillardia aristata*

This wildflower blankets parts of the Great Plains with yellow and red daisy-like flowers all summer long. Blanketflower has long been cultivated as a cut flower and was introduced into Europe as a garden plant in the early 1800s.

COLOR: Yellow and red
FLOWERING: Summer to frost
FRUITING: Late summer to fall
HEIGHT: 2–4 feet
GROWTH CYCLE: Hardy perennial

Blue Flax *Linum lewisii*

This widely distributed wildflower of the western two-thirds of North America is a relative of the European species from which linen is made. Individual flowers usually last only a day, withering in the hot sun, but new flowers in the cluster bloom each day.

COLOR: Blue
FLOWERING: Summer
FRUITING: Mid-summer to fall
HEIGHT: 1–4 feet
GROWTH CYCLE: Hardy perennial

Blue-Eyed Grass *Sisyrinchium bellum*

This wildflower is a member of the iris family, though its flowers don't look much like those of most garden irises. Blue-eyed grass has small, saucer-shaped, purple-blue to lilac flowers. The petals, which open with the sun and close at night and when cloudy, have blunt tips with a projecting point.

COLOR: Purple-blue to lilac
FLOWERING: Early to mid-spring
FRUITING: Late spring
HEIGHT: 6–12 inches
GROWTH CYCLE: Tender perennial

Baby Blue-Eyes

Blue-Eyed Grass

California Poppy

Black-Eyed Susan

Annual Phlox

Blanketflower

Blue Flax

Butterfly Weed

Butterfly Weed *Asclepias tuberosa*

The orange, flat-topped clusters of butterfly weed flowers are one of the most striking summer sights in North American prairies. The fused petals of the flower form a crown with 5 projecting horns, which surround masses of sticky pollen. The pollen attaches to the feet of butterflies that visit to drink sweet nectar from the fragrant flowers.

COLOR: Orange
FLOWERING: Late spring to summer
FRUITING: Early to mid-fall
HEIGHT: 1–2 1/2 feet
GROWTH CYCLE: Hardy perennial

California Poppy *Eschscholtzia californica*

California poppy flowers have a shiny luster to their golden-orange petals, which open in the sunshine and close at night and on cloudy days. Flowers produced early in the spring tend to be larger than those produced later in the season.

COLOR: Golden-orange
FLOWERING: Spring to fall
FRUITING: Late spring to fall
HEIGHT: 1–2 feet
GROWTH CYCLE: Tender perennial, self-seeding and growing as an annual in northern regions

Chinese Houses *Collinsia heterophylla*

The common name Chinese houses refers to the whorled pagoda effect of the tiers of blue and white flowers, which encircle the top of this plant's stem. Chinese houses grows nicely in partial shade.

COLOR: Blue and white
FLOWERING: Mid-spring to early summer
FRUITING: Summer
HEIGHT: 1–2 feet
GROWTH CYCLE: Annual

Continued ➡

Colorado Columbine *Aquilegia caerulea*

The most common variety of Colorado columbine has sky blue and white flowers, while other varieties are all white or all light blue. They are pollinated primarily by hawkmoths and bumblebees, although some bumblebees take a shortcut and consume the nectar without pollinating the flower, by chewing off the knob at the tip of the spur.

COLOR: Blue and white
FLOWERING: Late spring to mid-summer
FRUITING: Summer
HEIGHT: 1–2 1/2 feet
GROWTH CYCLE: Hardy perennial

Cosmos *Cosmos bipinnatus*

This native of Mexico has found its way farther north and into many seed catalogs. Its flower heads are borne atop long stems, a feature which makes cosmos an excellent cut flower.

COLOR: Red, pink or white
FLOWERING: Late spring to early fall
FRUITING: Summer to fall
HEIGHT: 3–5 feet
GROWTH CYCLE: Annual, but self-seeds even in northern areas

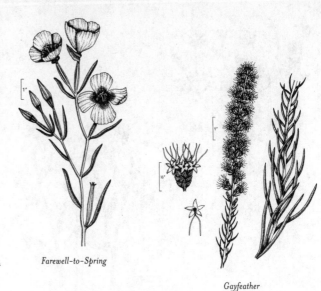

Farewell-to-Spring

Gayfeather

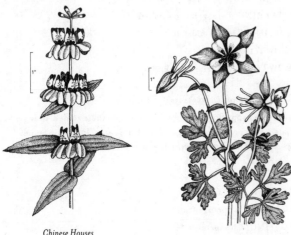

Chinese Houses

Colorado Columbine

Cosmos

Eastern Columbine

Eastern Columbine *Aquilegia canadensis*

The showy, nodding flowers are borne on leafy stems at the top of the plant. The flowers, which may be up to 2 inches across, have 5 spurred, scarlet petals which cover the yellow centers. Bumble-bees pollinate the flowers as they hang upside down to extract the sweet nectar from the spurs.

COLOR: Scarlet and yellow
FLOWERING: Mid-spring to early summer
FRUITING: Summer
HEIGHT: 1–2 feet
GROWTH CYCLE: Hardy perennial

Farewell-to-Spring *Clarkia amoena*

This native of California and Oregon, named in honor of Captain William Clark, was introduced into Europe as a garden flower not long after the Lewis and Clark Expedition. Each of the fan-shaped petals has a darker red botch toward its base.

COLOR: Red
FLOWERING: Late spring to early summer
FRUITING: Summer
HEIGHT: 1–3 feet
GROWTH CYCLE: Annual

Gayfeather *Liatris pycnostachya*

The graceful lavender spikes of gayfeather sway in the summer winds of the prairies of the U.S. heartland. The opening of the flower heads starts at the top and progresses toward the bottom.

COLOR: Lavender
FLOWERING: Mid-summer to mid-fall
FRUITING: Fall
HEIGHT: 1–5 feet
GROWTH CYCLE: Hardy perennial

Lance-Leaved Coreopsis *Coreopsis lanceolata*

The 2-inch daisy-like, yellow flowers are borne on long, smooth, slender stems, making this species an excellent cut flower. The resemblance of the seed to a tick has given this plant one of its common names, tickseed.

COLOR: Yellow
FLOWERING: Late spring to summer
FRUITING: Mid- to late summer
HEIGHT: 8–24 inches
GROWTH CYCLE: Hardy perennial

Linanthus *Linanthus grandiflorus*

Linanthus is a strikingly beautiful spring wildflower of the Coastal Ranges in California. The inch-long, trumpet-shaped, silky flowers are white, and tinged with pink or lavender. They appear in dense clusters at the tops of the stems.

COLOR: White with pink or lavender
FLOWERING: Mid-spring to mid-summer
FRUITING: Summer
HEIGHT: 4–20 inches
GROWTH CYCLE: Annual

Pasqueflower

Purple Coneflower

Lance-Leaved Coreopsis

Linanthus

Mexican Hat *Ratibida columnifera*

The flowers of this member of the aster family have brown centers protuding 1/2–2 1/2 inches above the drooping outer petals, giving them the appearance of sombreros. As the dark purple tubular flowers start to bloom from the base of the disc, the hats even appear to have hatbands.

COLOR: Yellow or yellow and red
FLOWERING: Late spring to early fall
FRUITING: Late summer to fall
HEIGHT: 1–3 feet
GROWTH CYCLE: Hardy perennial

New England Aster *Aster novae-angliae*

This species is the stock from which many of the horticultural varieties of hardy asters have been bred. Its dense leaves are covered with bristly hairs. The flowers produce 1/8-inch-long fuzzy seeds.

COLOR: Violet-purple with yellow
FLOWERING: Early to mid-fall
FRUITING: Fall
HEIGHT: 1–3 feet
GROWTH CYCLE: Hardy perennial

Pasqueflower *Anemone paten*

The solitary, 2-to 3-inch flowers have 5–7 pointed, petal-like parts which range in color from lavender to pale blue to white. The long plumes of seed-like fruits give rise to one of pasqueflower's other common names, prairie smoke.

COLOR: Lavender to blue to white
FLOWERING: Early spring
FRUITING: Mid- to late spring
HEIGHT: 6–9 inches
GROWTH CYCLE: Hardy perennial

Mexican Hat

New England Aster

Continued ➜

Purple Coneflower *Echinacea purpurea*

Though frequently listed in flower seed catalogs around the world, purple coneflower is native to midwestern prairies and dry open woods of the southeastern U.S. It is an excellent cut flower, having long-lasting single flower heads on long stems.

COLOR: Dull purple to crimson
FLOWERING: Late spring to early fall
FRUITING: Fall
HEIGHT: 2–4 feet
GROWTH CYCLE: Hardy perennial

Scarlet Sage *Salvia coccinea*

This native of the Southeast should not be confused with *Salvia splendens*, the commonly cultivated scarlet sage which is a native of Brazil. The North American native has all of the color of its South American relative, but lacks its harshness.

COLOR: Scarlet and purple
FLOWERING: Late spring to frost
FRUITING: Summer to fall
HEIGHT: 1–2 1/2 feet
GROWTH CYCLE: Tender perennial that can be grown as an annual in northern gardens

Spiderwort *Tradescantia virginiana*

Spiderwort is an old garden favorite which sometmes escapes back into its native habitat, the woods and meadows of the eastern United States. This species can be somewhat invasive, so keep an eye on it and take proper control measures if it starts to crowd out other wildflowers.

COLOR: Light blue to lavender to rose
FLOWERING: Mid-spring to mid-summer
FRUITING: Summer
HEIGHT: 6–18 inches
GROWTH CYCLE: Hardy perennial

Standing Cypress *Ipomopsis rubra*

This native of the Southeast and Mexico was once a favorite in northern gardens. It is attractive to both humans and hummingbirds, the latter being the main pollinator of the species. Individual flowers open for 2–5 days, but the overall flowering season is quite long, with a progression of bloom downward from the top of the stem.

COLOR: Scarlet
FLOWERING: Summer
FRUITING: Late summer to early fall
HEIGHT: 3–5 feet
GROWTH CYCLE: Biennial

Scarlet Sage

Spiderwort

Standing Cypress

Tidy Tips

Wild Bergamot

Wind Poppy

Tidy Tips *Layia platyglossa*

The three-toothed petals of this member of the aster family have white tips and deep yellow bases. While most of the flowers have both colors, some individuals have flowers that are all white or all yellow.

COLOR: White and yellow
FLOWERING: Spring to early summer
FRUITING: Summer
HEIGHT: 6–12 inches
GROWTH CYCLE: Annual

Wild Bergamot *Monarda fistulosa*

Wild bergamot is a member of the mint family and has the square stems characteristic of that family. Its common name refers to the similarity between the aromas in the pungent foliage of this plant and the fruit of the bergamot orange tree of Europe.

COLOR: Lilac to pink
FLOWERING: Early to mid-summer
FRUITING: Summer to early fall
HEIGHT: 2–4 feet
GROWTH CYCLE: Hardy perennial

Wind Poppy *Stylomecon heterophylla*

The wind poppy is native to western California, where its bright blossoms sway in the spring breezes. The 1 to 2-inch-wide flowers have four broad, silky, vermilion petals with dark purple spots at their bases. Its petals are delicate and fall off easily; therefore it does not make a particularly good cut flower.

COLOR: Red
FLOWERING: Spring
FRUITING: Summer
HEIGHT: 1–2 feet
GROWTH CYCLE: Annual

Suppliers

Applewood Seed Company
5380 Vivian Street 14590
Arvada, CO 80002

J.L. Hudson, Seedsman
P.O. Box 1058
Redwood City, CA 94064

W. Atlee Burpee Company
300 Park Avenue
Warminster, PA 18974

Lafayette Home Nursery
R.R. Box 1A
Lafayette, IL 61449

Clyde Robin Seed
P.O. Box 2366
Castro Valley, CA 94546

Native Seeds, Inc.
Triadelphia Mill Road
Dayton, MD 21036

Harris Moran Seed Company
3670 Buffalo Road
Rochester, NY 14624

Natural Gardens
113 Jasper Lane
Oak Ridge, TN 37830

Prairie Seed Source
P.O. Box 83
North Lake, WI 53064

Wild Seed
P.O. Box 27751
Tempe, AZ 85282

Siskiyou Rare Plant Nursery
2825 Cummings Road
Medford, OR 97501

Woodlanders, Inc.
1128 Colleton Avenue
Aiken, SC 29801

Grow a Hummingbird Garden

Dale Evva Gelfand

Illustrations by Mallory Lake and Alison Kolesar

About Hummingbirds

If asked to name the most ethereal and captivating creature to be found on our planet, most of us would be hard-pressed to top the hummingbird. Their minute size (some species weigh only a fraction of an ounce), their beauty (iridescent plumage courtesy of special structures in their feathers), their incredible aerobatic ability (hummingbirds can fly in any direction, including backward), their extraordinary appetites (hummingbirds eat half of their weight in sugar every day), even their aggression (hummingbirds are fierce protectors of their territory and nests) add up to a singularly fascinating family. A little planning of the design of and the plants in your garden is all it takes to make your yard the kind of environment that will readily attract these flying jewels.

A perfect hummingbird habitat is also a relatively simple one: food sources, water for bathing (liquid intake is generally provided by nectar), lookout perches, shade and shelter, and nesting sites and materials. You should be able to provide these requirements in even the smallest of gardens.

FOOD

Hummingbirds are extremely active creatures with an astonishing metabolic rate that requires high caloric intake of both nectar and insects—which means hundreds of food forays during their waking hours, primarily to flowers. Obviously those flowers that produce lots of nectar and also attract tiny insects are more beneficial, and therefore more appealing, to hummingbirds.

This attraction forms part of one of Nature's many interdependent relationships: Hummingbirds, while stopping for a meal, act as inadvertent pollinators for the plants they rely upon. Depending on their particular shape, the deep-tubed blossoms that are most suitable to a hummingbird's long tongue deliver pollen from the anthers—the male organs—onto hummingbirds' heads or bills or chins, and when the nectar-sipping visitors go on to probe neighboring blossoms of the same variety, that pollen is delivered to the stigmas—the female organs—for fertilization. In fact, hummingbirds are some of the most essential bird pollinators for flora in North America.

Equally as important as the nectar that the flowers provide are the tiny insects living within them. Insects are an indispensable source of protein in the hummingbird diet and, like the hummingbirds that prey upon them, insects are attracted to the nectar. When hummingbirds aren't catching them on the wing (or, in the case of small spiders, snaring them in their own webs), they find them inside flowers. Happily

Continued ➔

for gardeners and other outdoors lovers, these insects include many garden pests such as aphids and gnats.

WATER

Like all birds, hummingbirds need to bathe, and they are resourceful in employing water sources that match their tiny size—such as beads of water left on leaves after a rain or the fine spray from a waterfall. Hummingbirds prefer moving water, and are fond of flying through the spray of lawn sprinklers. If you want to set up a sprinkler for a hummingbird bath, use a nozzle that gives off a continuous fine spray. In a pinch, hummingbirds will also use birdbaths, provided they're shallow enough for hummingbirds to stand in. Adding various-size rocks to a birdbath creates different depths for different-size bird species. Hummingbirds prefer not to come to ground for their water, so if you can help them avoid this, they may well use your accommodations.

PERCHES

Having a place from where they can survey their territory is essential to hummingbirds. (For creatures so tiny to be so protective of their domain may seem peculiar, but considering how important ample food sources are to hummingbirds' survival, the ability to oversee their territory and quickly defend it from intruders is crucial.) Hummingbirds prefer a perch that directly overlooks the flowers on which they feed. The male partner of one ruby-throated hummingbird couple that takes up residence in my garden every summer prefers the slender bottom branch of an enormous hemlock tree that anchors the shady end of my garden. From there it's but a short flight to all of the flowers and to the nearer of the two hummingbird feeders, as well. It's likely that his mate also perches on the hemlock, but I haven't seen her there, as females generally prefer to remain sheltered within the interior of a tree, shrub, or vine.

SHADE AND SHELTER

Although we think of hummingbirds as being constantly on the wing, in fact they spend about equal amounts of time locating food and resting between meals. Males will rest anywhere from exposed branches to clotheslines to TV antennae, but females and immature birds seek the shade and protection of foliage. Dense foliage for shelter from the elements—evergreens are excellent windbreaks—and for roosting at night is also important to these tiny birds. The ideal balance for a hummingbird habitat is about one-half full sun and one-quarter each shade and partial shade.

NESTING SITES

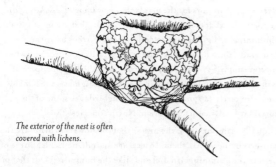

The exterior of the nest is often covered with lichens.

It's doubtful that you'll ever see a hummingbird nest—or if you do see one, you may not realize what it is. These tiny, usually lichen-covered structures are only 1 to 1 1/2 inches (21/2–4cm) in diameter, and are so effectively

camouflaged that you would assume they're but a knot on a branch. Hummingbirds nest in both deciduous and evergreen trees, anywhere from 4 to 50 feet (1.2–15m) up but most frequently in the 10- to 20-foot-high (3–6m) range, often bordering or over a stream. Although there are no guarantees in tempting a hummingbird pair to set up housekeeping in your yard, by planting both food sources and those trees and shrubs that provide nesting materials, you'll make it more appealing for them to do so. Primary among the latter is downy plant material, which makes up the bulk of hummingbird nests. An excellent—and favored—source of downy fibers are the filaments of willow seeds; additionally, willow flowers provide both nectar and the insects attracted to it. Consider planting shrub willow in your garden if your yard has a favorable site for this moisture-loving tree. Other trees that provide nesting material for hummingbirds include cottonwoods, aspens, and sycamores.

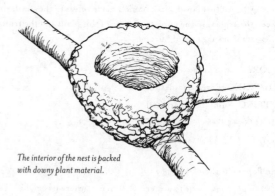

The interior of the nest is packed with downy plant material.

A Hummingbird Gallery

Hummingbirds are strictly a New World phenomenon, of Central American origin. North America is home to eight common species of hummingbirds and several more rare species. Hummingbirds follow a migratory pattern and are seen in the United States mainly during the summer months, although several species are known to take up permanent residence in coastal California, coastal Oregon, southern Arizona, and southern Florida. In some areas of the country, the ranges of certain species may overlap, although if you live anywhere east of the Mississippi, identification is usually easy: The ruby-throated hummingbird is the only regular visitor to that area.

A QUICK GEOGRAPHICAL STUDY

Eastern and Midwestern Hummingbirds

Ruby-throated

Southeastern and Gulf Coast Hummingbirds

Common	Uncommon
Black-chinned	Allen's
Buff-bellied	Anna's
Ruby-throated	Bahama woodstar
Blue-throated	
Broad-billed	
Broad-tailed	
Calliope	
Magnificent	
Rufous	

Rocky Mountain Region Hummingbirds

Common	Uncommon
Black-chinned	Magnificent
Broad-tailed	
Calliope	
Rufous	

Southwestern Hummingbirds

Common	Uncommon
Allen's	Berylline
Anna's	Cinnamon
Black-chinned	Lucifer
Blue-throated	Plain-capped starthroat
Broad-billed	Violet-crowned
Broad-tailed	White-eared
Calliope	
Costa's	
Magnificent	

West Coast Hummingbirds

Common	Uncommon
Allen's	Ruby-throated
Anna's	
Black-chinned	
Broad-tailed	
Calliope	
Costa's	
Rufous	

Designing a Hummingbird Garden

Yes, it's true, many hummingbirds have a preference for red flowers, and for a very good reason: They have learned through experience that red flowers frequently have more nectar than others. Ruby-throated hummingbirds in particular have the strongest attraction to red, while this characteristic is less pronounced in many of the western species. However, hummingbirds also feed at pink, orange, purple, yellow, and even white blossoms. In short, there are innumerable tubular-shaped flowers, both cultivated and wild, that can justly be called hummingbird flowers.

With so many flowers to choose from, narrowing down your selection will take some work. Obviously, not all flowers that hummingbirds are attracted to will be hardy to your area, but if you're among those lucky enough to live in a zone suitable to a wide and varied range of plant life, your selections will be limited only by personal preference and space considerations.

CHOOSING PLANTS

When choosing plants for your hummingbird garden, select varieties with overlapping periods of bloom. You can select combinations of annuals, perennials, flowering shrubs and vines, and even some vegetables and herbs. Plant species that are native to your region,

especially wildflowers. These will be much better nectar producers than nonnative plants and cultivars.

To ensure an adequate supply of nectar at all times, plant a variety of flower-producing plants in sizable numbers each. Nectar production in some plants can slow or stop altogether when it's too hot, too cold, too wet, or too dry. Having an assortment of plants blooming in your garden at any one time should minimize this problem.

Most gardens have a combination of perennials (herbaceous plants that live at least three years, although most will happily bloom for far longer than that) and annuals (which, as the name implies, bloom for one season only, although many will self-seed for the following year). However, although perennials will reappear year after year, they bloom for only three or four weeks in any one season, whereas many annuals will produce flowers all summer long. Bear in mind, however, that a zone 8 perennial, such as the nasturtium, will be available at a zone 4 garden shop as an annual simply because the plant can't survive that region's cold winters. And some plants, such as begonias, that are designated annuals in colder climes can be dug up in autumn, potted, enjoyed through the winter as houseplants, and then put back in the garden the following spring, after the last frost.

LAYING OUT YOUR GARDEN

Once you have a good idea of the hummingbird-attracting plants that will be appropriate for your region, zone, and soil conditions, you're ready to begin breaking ground for your garden. Remember that hummingbirds prefer areas with trees and/or shrubs that will provide perching locations, sheltering foliage, and protected roosting sites. The ideal hummingbird habitat has about one-half full sun and one-quarter each full shade and partial shade.

Group the plants in your garden so that their blossoms are easily accessible to hummingbirds, with ample room for hovering and flight maneuverability. Flowers are visually more interesting when they're tiered, with the tallest ones in back and the shorter ones in front, and a tiered design will also provide better hummingbird access to all of the blossoms in your garden.

Don't overlook your decks and porches—or even apartment balconies—as potential hummingbird garden sites. Being fearless creatures, hummingbirds will visit container plants and hanging baskets just as often as they do more traditionally embedded flora. In fact, a hanging basket of fuchsia set outside after wintering indoors may well be the only nectar source around during the early warm days of spring, when many hummingbirds return from a winter sojourn in Central America.

Hanging pots, window boxes, and containers of flowers will lure hummingbirds to your deck, porch, or balcony.

Continued →

Flowers for Hummingbirds

When planting, consider some of the following flowers for your hummingbird garden, depending on your planting zone and sun and soil conditions. The zone listings specify the zones in which each plant may be grown as a perennial—most plants can be grown as annuals in any zone. The specified heights include flower stalks as well as foliage, which may often be very short by itself. This is followed by the period in which the plant is in flower. For more comprehensive information on any of the plants referenced here, consult a gardening manual.

Beard-tongue (*Penstemon barbatus*)

Zones: 3–9

Height: 8"-36" (20–90cm)

Blooming season: Late spring to midsummer

The individual blossoms of this easy grower are reminiscent of foxglove, although its loose clusters of flower heads are more like annual phlox. Plant in moist, well-drained soil and full sun or light shade.

Bee balm (*Monarda* spp.)

Zones: 4–9

Height: 2'-4' (60–120cm)

Blooming season: Summer

Beard-tongue

Hummingbirds, bees, and butterflies alike all love the shaggy blossoms of bee balm. Most often seen in red, bee balm also blooms in purple, pink, and even white. Deadhead the spent blossoms regularly to keep these easy growers blooming, and plant in moist soil in full sun or very light shade.

Begonia (*Begonia* spp.)

Zones: 6–10

Height: 6"-24" (15–60cm)

Blooming season: Summer through autumn

Bee balm

Plant begonias in shades of red, pink, or white in your garden or in containers. Give them rich, moist soil in sun where it's cooler and partial shade in hotter climes.

Blazing star (*Liatris* spp.)

Zones: 3–10

Height: 2'-6' (.6–1.8m)

Blooming season: Summer to early autumn

These rocket-shaped, pink-purple beauties (also known as gayfeather and snakeroot) will perk up any garden. Although preferring a sandy, rich soil, *Liatris* will tolerate even poor, dry soil, as long as their planting medium is very well drained. They prefer full sun to light shade.

Bleeding heart (*Dicentra spectabilis*)

Zones: 3–9

Height: 2'-3' (60–90cm)

Blooming season: Mid- to late spring

This traditionally favorite plant with fernlike foliage and sprays of heart-shaped pink and white blooms at the tips of long, slender stems will impart elegance and charm to your garden. Plant in partial sun or partial shade—more shade is required in hotter areas—in rich, moist, well-drained soil.

Bugleweed (*Ajuga* spp.)

Zones: 3–10

Height: 4"-10" (10–25cm)

Blooming season: Mid-spring to midsummer

Carpet bugleweed (*Ajuga reptans*), a fast-spreading ground cover that's wonderful under trees or other places too shady for grass to grow, sprouts a forest of purple-blue flowers on a carpet of green and bronze-purple leaves. In rock gardens and mixed shade plantings, try Geneva bugleweed (*Ajuga genevensis*) and upright bugleweed (*Ajuga pyramidalis*), which are less invasive. This plant thrives in either sun or shade and just about any soil, even dry, poor soil, provided it drains well (note that in dry soil, bugleweed needs to be shaded).

California fuchsia (*Zauschneria californica*)

Zones: 9–10

Height: 12"-24" (30–60cm)

Blooming season: Late summer to October

Spikes of vivid red, tubular flowers are a good reason that this plant also goes by the name hummingbird flower. Plant in a warm, sunny spot in light, well-drained soil.

Cardinal flower (*Lobelia cardinalis*)

Zones: 2–9

Height: 3' (90cm)

Blooming season: Summer

California fuchsia

The dazzling red spikes of the cardinal flower are a surefire magnet for hummingbirds. Lobelias do best if given afternoon shade, moist soil (they thrive near running water), and good drainage for regular waterings.

Century plant (*Agave americana*)

Zones: 6–10

Height: Varies; can grow as high as 40 feet (12m)

Blooming season: Summer

These bold succulents with fleshy, sword-shaped leaves and giant flower spikes are highly prized desert hummingbird plants. Plant them in well-drained sandy soil in full sun.

Columbine (*Aquilegia* spp.)

Zones: 3–9

Height: 6"–48" (15–120cm)

Blooming season: Mid-spring to early summer

Columbine

These beautiful spurred flowers are hummingbird favorites. The red-and-yellow-flowered wild columbine native to the East, *Aquilegia canadensis*, will freely reseed itself—be careful it doesn't become a pest. In the West, plant crimson columbine, *Aquilegia formosa*, native to California, Oregon, and Nevada. All columbines like moist soils with light to moderate shade. Columbines do well in rock gardens.

Coralbells (*Heuchera* spp.)

Zones: 3–9

Height: 12"–36" (30–90cm)

Blooming season: Late spring to early autumn

Delicate sprays of small tubular, red, white, or pink flowers rise on tall, wiry stems out of compact clumps of scalloped foliage. Keep this plant neat by removing the flowering stems once they've bloomed. Grow in light, well-drained soil in full sun in northern zones and partial shade in warmer climes.

Creeping phlox (*Phlox stolonifera*)

Zones: 3–9

Height: 6"–8" (15–20cm)

Blooming season: Early to late spring

These spreading perennials form beautiful beds of star-shaped flowers in varying shades from white to purple to blue, although the bright, hot pink ones will attract hummingbirds most readily. Phlox prefer a rich, well-drained, moist soil and will grow in either full sun or partial shade.

Delphinium (*Delphinium* spp.)

Zones: 3–9

Height: 18"–84" (.5–2m)

Blooming season: Late spring through autumn, depending on species

These statuesque spires of blossoms—some single flowered, some double—are beautiful in any garden. Also known as larkspur, delphiniums bloom in blue, purple, pink, yellow, and white. Plants over 18 inches (46cm) tall will need to be staked to keep them upright. Although short-lived, fading out after only two or three years, delphiniums can be propagated by cuttings from new spring growth. Grow these beauties in rich, moist, well-drained soil.

Fire pink (*Silene virginica*)

Zones: 4–9

Height: 10"–24" (25–60cm)

Blooming season: Late spring to early summer

Fire Pink

These masses of dark pink and crimson blooms will stay ablaze for quite some time. Plant in well-drained, humus-rich soil in full sun or light shade (more shade in hotter climates).

Four-o'clock (*Mirabilis jalapa*)

Zones: 8–10

Height: 24"–48" (60–120cm)

Blooming season: Midsummer to late autumn

Coming from the tropics, these lovely blooms, in shades from rosy purple or red to white and yellow, are perennials only in the warmest climates. Elsewhere cultivate as container plants in well-drained soil.

Foxglove (*Digitalis* spp.)

Zones: 3–9

Height: 24"–60" (60–152cm)

Blooming season: Late spring to late summer, depending on species

The tall spires of these plants look majestic in any setting—and depending on the species and your conditions (they prefer cool, moist climates), they'll grow just about anywhere, from full sun to full shade (the hotter the summer, the more shade necessary). Foxgloves come in creamy yellow, pink, salmon, and orange. All have freckled interiors. Give these beauties moist, rich soil, and they'll happily self-seed.

Fuchsia (*Fuchsia* spp.)

Zone: 10

Height: 1'–6' (30–180cm)

Blooming season: Late spring to autumn

With its pendulous blossoms, this plant is much esteemed for hanging baskets and comes in shades of bright red, fiery pink, purple, white, and various combinations of them all. It does best in full or half shade—I hang my fuchsia basket from a sturdy lower pine branch several feet away from a feeder—in a rich, moist soil.

Geranium (*Geranium* spp.)

Zones: 3–10

Height: 4"–36" (10–90cm)

Blooming season: Spring through late summer, depending on species

We usually associate the name "geranium" with the familiar velvet-leafed houseplant with bright red flowers, but those belong to the *Pelargonium* genus. Geraniums are hardy, carefree plants with lovely lacy leaves and red, pink, or purple blooms, depending on the species and

Continued ➤

cultivar. They'll grow in average, well-drained soil, but when planted in rich soil, they'll spread rapidly. Plant in full sun in colder climates and in partial shade in warmer southern climates.

Hollyhock (*Althea* spp.)

Zones: 5–9

Height: 2'-6' (60–180cm)

Blooming season: Summer to early autumn

This wonderful, old-fashioned, upright plant is available in just about every color. Use the older, taller species as back border plantings, along a fence, or against a cottage wall; the newer, shorter species can go anywhere. Although favoring rich, well-drained, moist soil, they'll tolerate dry soil, too—but not excessive heat and humidity.

Hollyhock

Impatiens (*Impatiens* spp.)

Zones: Can be grown in any zone as an annual

Height: 12"-24" (30–60cm)

Blooming season: Late spring through first frost

Impatiens are grown as annuals in most of the country since they are unable to survive frost. With their vibrantly colored, long-lasting blossoms, they are ideal hummingbird flowers. Mass them under trees or in containers under your porch overhang, since most species prefer full shade. They also like a rich, moist soil.

Lily (*Lilium* spp.)

Zones: 3–9

Height: 2'-6' (60–180cm)

Blooming season: Late spring through autumn, depending on species

Lilies have large and exquisite, usually multiple, trumpet-shaped flowers on long, strong stems—eye-catching either singly or when massed together in any garden. Lilies require moist, well-drained, usually slightly acidic soil in full sun or light shade.

Lupine (*Lupinus* spp.)

Zones: 4–8

Height: 18"-60" (46–152cm)

Blooming season: Spring to midsummer

Lupines give any garden a boost, even when there are only a few. When massed, the effect of the pink, purple, blue, and red flower spikes is spectacular. Many species thrive in areas with relatively cool summers, although others will tolerate hotter climes. Give them a rich and moist but well-drained soil in either full sun or light shade.

Mammillaria (*Mammillaria setispina*)

Zones: 9–10

Height: Various; ball-like

Blooming season: Late spring to summer

This member of the cactus family produces dark red flowers beyond its spines, which makes it a fine place for desert hummingbirds to sup. If you don't live in the Southwest, the mammillaria makes an excellent houseplant that can summer outdoors in half shade. As with most cacti, plant in a light and porous yet stable soil with excellent drainage (a mixture of sandy and clay soils works well).

Monkey flower (*Mimulus* spp.)

Zones: 3–9

Height: 8"-36" (20–90cm)

Blooming season: Spring to autumn, depending on species

Monkey flower

Depending on the species suitable for your location, these trumpet-shaped, lipped flowers come in all sizes and will want either full sun or partial shade. Check a reference guide for more detailed information. Coming in hues of red, orange, pink, and yellow, these plants grow best in moist, rich soil.

Montbretia (*Crocosmia* spp.)

Zones: 5–8

Height: 12"-48" (30–120cm)

Blooming season: Summer

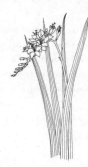

Montbretia

Spectacular branches of funnel-shaped flowers in red, orange, or yellow emerge from fans of stiff, swordlike foliage. Like the iris the foliage resembles, these plants grow from corms and spread to form clumps. Grow in sun to partial shade in average, well-drained soil.

Nasturtium (*Tropaeolum majus*)

Zones: Can be grown in any zone as an annual

Height: 12"-48" (30–120cm)

Blooming season: Summer to late autumn

These annuals have bold and beautiful yellow, orange, and red spurred blossoms that are a wonderful contrast to their rounded green leaves. Nasturtiums prefer summers that are mild and dry with cool nights. They do well even in poor soil so long as it's well drained and slightly acidic. Plant in full sun to partial shade.

Obedient plant (*Physostegia* spp.)

Zones: 2–9

Height: 12"-48" (30–120cm)

Blooming season: Midsummer to autumn

The pink, purple, or white blooms on these vigorous, easy-care plants—also known as false dragonhead—grow in long, regimented rows. *Physostegia* enjoy any good garden soil in either full sun or partial shade.

Petunia (*Petunia* spp.)

Zones: Can be grown in any zone as an annual

Height: 12"-18" (30–46cm)

Blooming season: Late spring to frost

Petunias are one of the most widely grown annuals due to their tireless (and seemingly endless) blooming period. The cheery trumpet-shaped flowers are borne on long stems that work well in hanging baskets. To make them bushier, pinch back young plants. When planted in the garden, put them in moist, well-drained soil in full sun or very light shade.

Red-hot-poker (*Kniphofia uvaria*)

Zones: 5–9

Height: 2'-4' (60–120cm)

Blooming season: Midsummer

Also known as torch lily, *Kniphofia* (knee-FOE-fia) has blossoms of fiery red, yellow, and orange on thickly clustered spikes that are dramatic in any setting. Plant in rich, moist, and well-drained soil. Give full sun in moderate climes, partial shade where summers are very hot.

Scarlet sage (*Salvia splendens*)

Zones: Can be grown in any zone as an annual

Height: 1'-3' (30–90cm)

Blooming season: Summer to autumn, depending on species

Scarlet sage is a tender perennial most often grown as an annual. Its usually bright red spikes are wonderful for creating splashes of color in your garden. Give it well-drained soil and full sun or partial shade.

Spider flower (*Cleome hassleriana*)

Zones: Can be grown in any zone as an annual

Height: 3'-4' (.9–1.2m)

Blooming season: Summer through late autumn

Although annuals, these odd-looking plants will self-seed with wanton regularity, so be careful where you plant them. Give these long bloomers average soil and lots of sun. If your summers are very hot, give them half shade.

Sweet William (*Dianthus barbatus*)

Zones: Can be grown in any zone as an annual, or sometimes a biennial

Height: 6"-24" (15–60cm)

Blooming season: Late spring to summer

Choose the crimson variety of this plant with its cushiony, tightly packed blooms. Sweet William self-sows readily and prefers rich, well-drained slightly alkaline soil in the sunny or lightly shaded part of your garden.

Verbena (*Verbena* spp.)

Zones: 3–10

Height: 4"-24" (10–60cm)

Blooming season: Late spring to frost

These showy plants with tightly packed flower heads are rather short-lived and are best grown as annuals. Choose from pink, white, purple, and red blossoms. Plant in full sun in any well-drained soil.

Yucca (*Yucca* spp.)

Zones: 3–10

Height: 3'-30' (.9–9m)

Blooming season: Early summer to autumn, depending on species

An impressive spike of white, bell-shaped flowers stands like a sentinel over the yucca's straplike evergreen leaves. This very tough, drought-resistant plant likes full sun and average or sandy well-drained soil. Some species need protection in winter in colder climates.

Vines, Shrubs, and Trees

Some of the most favored blossoms of hummingbirds are those of vines, shrubs, and trees, which also provide shelter for resting, roosting, and nesting. If you can, make room in your garden for one or more of these beauties.

VINES

Many of these vines, having densely packed foliage, are ideal homes for hummingbirds.

Morning-glory (*Ipomoea* spp.)

Zones: 5–10

Blooming season: Midsummer through autumn

These twining vines with their blue, lavender, pink, or white flowers will wrap themselves around just about anything—and will also grow in just about anything, including poor, dry soil. Grow in full sun.

Morning-glory

Scarlet runner bean (*Phaseolus coccineus*)

Zone: 10

Blooming season: Midsummer to frost

Annuals everywhere but tropical climates, scarlet runner beans make everyone happy—hummingbirds for the nectar in the clusters of flowers, humans for the beans. Grow in full sun against a trellis to appreciate fully the brilliant red flowers.

Continued ➤

Trumpet creeper (*Campsis radicans*)

Zones: 4–9

Blooming season: Midsummer through fall

This vigorous, twining perennial vine with its bold, trumpet-shaped (hence the name) scarlet flowers prefers full sun and a rich, moist, well-drained soil. It will need strong supports in your garden.

Trumpet honeysuckle (*Lonicera sempervirens*)

Zones: 3–9

Blooming season: Early to late summer

Rich orange, scarlet, or yellow clumps of blossoms punctuate this semi-to evergreen vine (depending on your climate); in areas subject to much frost it needs protection. Grow in cool, semishady areas, in porous, well-drained, fertile soil.

SHRUBS

Azalea (*Rhododendron* spp.)

Zones: 5–8

Blooming season: Early spring

In colder climes, grow this decorative species of the classic rhododendron as a houseplant and put it outdoors after the last frost. Give it a rich, moist soil—an azalea needs lots of water—and shade.

Butterfly bush (*Buddleia davidii*)

Zones: 5–9

Blooming season: Midsummer to autumn

Also known as summer lilac, butterfly bush—which obviously also attracts butterflies—has profuse white, pink, red, or purple blossoms in long clusters. Grow this and other *Buddleias* in any soil in full sun.

Cape honeysuckle (*Tecomaria capensis*)

Zones: 9–10

Blooming season: Year-round

Those in more tropical climes can enjoy the scarlet blossoms of this evergreen all year long. This beautiful shrub, which will reach 8 feet, should be grown in fertile soil in full sun.

Flowering quince (*Chaenomeles* spp.)

Zones: 4–9, depending on species

Blooming season: Spring

The showy flowers on these deciduous shrubs, not the fruit, are the main attraction for both hummingbirds and humans—although if the yield is bountiful, you can make preserves from the fruit. Plant in fertile soil in a sunny spot.

Hibiscus (*Hibiscus* spp.)

Zones: 5–10, depending on species

Blooming season: Mid- to late summer

Hibiscus are often thought of as strictly tropical shrubs, but they also include some hardier species such as rose-of-Sharon (*Hibiscus syriacus*). Grow in a sheltered, sunny spot in any well-drained soil and enjoy masses of pink, purple, orange, yellow, or scarlet blossoms, depending on the species.

Honeysuckle (*Lonicera* spp.)

Zones: 4–9

Blooming season: Late spring to early summer

Hibiscus

These bushy shrubs have tubular blossoms in creamy white, pale yellow, pink, and even hot pink, depending on the species. Honeysuckles generally prefer well-drained soil and full sun to partial shade.

Lantana (*Lantana camara*)

Zones: 8–10

Blooming season: Year-round

This 6-foot-tall evergreen shrub produces compact clusters of orange-yellow, orange, red, or red-and-white flowers. Grow in any well-drained soil in full sun.

Mealberry (*Arctostaphylos uva-ursi*)

Zones: 2–10

Blooming season: Mid- to late spring

The drooping clusters of blossoms on this dwarf evergreen shrub give way to brilliant red berries. This species prefers soil that is sandy or acidic, but will grow in almost any type of soil. Prefers full sun but will tolerate some shade.

Rosemary (*Rosmarinus officinalis*)

Zones: 6–10

Blooming season: Early spring

The stems of the fragrant herb we get at our greengrocers are actually branches of an evergreen shrub that grows to 7 feet tall—yet another plant that satisfies the needs of both humans and hummingbirds. The latter appreciate the lovely lilac-blue flowers. Rosemary grows best in light, well-drained soil in a warm, sunny spot.

Weigela (*Weigela florida*)

Zones: 4–9

Blooming season: Spring

This hardy shrub is generally easy to cultivate. It has tubular or funnel-shaped flowers in all shades of pink from deep carmine to almost white. Weigela thrives in any moist, well-drained soil in full sun.

TREES

Trees don't usually come to mind when we're thinking of flowers for hummingbirds, but many species have spectacular blossoms.

Chinaberry (*Melia azedarach*)

Zones: 7–10

Height: 30'-40' (9–12m)

Blooming season: Late spring

This member of the mahogany family produces lovely sprays of lilac-colored flowers. A good shade tree, it grows best in full sun. Chinaberry is often considered a weed species, as its wood breaks easily during heavy storms.

Cockspur/Cry-baby tree (*Erythrina crista-galli*)

Zone: 10

Height: 15' (5m)

Blooming season: Late summer

This small to average-size tree produces clusters of dark red, waxy flowers. It prefers moist but well-drained soil. Plant in full sun.

Eucalyptus (*Eucalyptus* spp.)

Zones: 9–10

Height: 30'-100' (9–30m)

Blooming season: Winter to summer

Eucalyptus provide both nectar and shelter for hummingbirds. These Australian imports have flowers that range from white to showy red and for the most part prefer full sun in moist soil.

Flowering crabapple (*Malus* spp.)

Zones: 2–6

Height: 15'-25' (5–8m)

Blooming season: Mid- to late spring

This is another species that benefits both hummingbirds (nectar) and humans (fruit for preserves—if the blue jays don't eat them first). Flowers range in color from white to pink to bright red. Grow in any well-drained, fertile soil in full sun.

Poinciana (*Caesalpinia* spp.)

Zone: 10

Height: 15'-20' (5–6m)

Blooming season: Summer

This fast-growing small tree (or shrub) is a member of the pea family. Beautiful clusters of white or yellow pealike flowers with prominent red stamens are framed by delicate fronds. Grow in full sun in well-drained, dryish soil.

Red horse chestnut (*Aesculus x carnea*)

Zones: 3–7

Height: 30'-40' (9–12m)

Blooming season: Late spring to early summer

As its name implies, the large clusters of blooms on this spectacular tree have rose red panicles that can reach 6 to 8 inches in length in the spring. Grow in moist, well-drained soil in full sun to light shade.

Siberian peashrub (*Caragana arborescens*)

Zones: 2–7

Height: 15'-20' (5–6m)

Blooming season: Spring

Lovely yellow flowers dress up this tree's feathery leaves. It does well in all soil types and prefers full sun.

Silk tree (*Albizia julibrissin*)

Zones: 6–9

Height: 20'-35' (6–11m)

Blooming season: Late spring to late summer

This small tree, also called mimosa tree, produces beautiful bristly clusters of flowers—looking like so many bottle brushes—that are white at the base and bright pink at the tips. Grow this member of the sun-loving pea family in full sun; it does well in all soil types.

Tulip poplar (*Liriodendron tulipifera*)

Zones: 4–9

Height: Can grow to 200 feet (60m)

Blooming season: Spring to early summer

This tall, stately tree, also known as tulip tree, produces—no surprise—tuliplike greenish yellow flowers lined with orange. Grow in rich, moist soil in full sun.

Grow a Butterfly Garden

Wendy Potter-Springer

Illustrations by Alison Kolesar and Elayne Sears

Why a Butterfly Garden?

Few sights are more delightful than that of a butterfly dancing on the breeze. But sadly enough, butterflies have become all too rare in our rapidly expanding world. The sheer beauty of butterflies has, in the past, prompted the collection and sale of these insects. Twenty years ago this could have been blamed for their disappearance, but it is unusual in this day and age for a collector to capture and kill a butterfly. Most modern-day collectors capture their beautiful specimens on film.

So where have the butterflies gone?

The disappearance of butterflies must largely be blamed on ourselves. Condominiums and shopping malls have taken over the fields and grassy meadows that served as the breeding grounds for many of our butterflies, and the misuse of backyard pesticides has left them with no alternative environment in which to live and multiply.

Continued ➡

By growing a few chosen plants in your yard, you will be making a major contribution toward the preservation of these fragile insects, supplying them with a haven in which to live and breed.

How a Butterfly Garden Works

Monarch butterfly with asters.

There are two kinds of butterfly flowers: food plants for caterpillars, and nectar plants for adults. Although butterflies need a shady spot to find respite from the sun during those days we consider scorchers, for the most part they spend their time in the sunshine. This is due to a butterfly's need to raise its body temperature in order to fly. Butterflies perch on flowers and shrubs to bask in the sun and absorb the solar benefits until their bodies reach a temperature of 86 to 104°F.

So it should come as no surprise that most butterfly flowers are those of the sun-loving variety. Many of the plants listed in this bulletin are sun lovers, providing butterflies with just the right spot to get going each day.

The colors in a butterfly garden also play a major role in their attraction. Scientists now know that butterflies have the ability to identify colors. Purple, pink, yellow, and white are the colors most often preferred by butterflies, so when planning your garden you'll want to keep these colors in mind.

Attracting Specific Butterflies

You may have noticed the absence of specific butterflies that were once common in your neighborhood. This could very well be due to the use of pesticides.

Pesticides have no place in your butterfly garden. Their sole purpose is to destroy insects, and while many who use them are not thinking about killing off their butterflies, this is the inevitable outcome. You can also work to minimize the use of aerial pesticides (used for "mosquito control") and herbicides (used for "roadside weed control") by your local government agencies.

If you would like to help reestablish a rare or endangered species that was once common to your neighborhood, you'll need to do some research. Check in with your local natural history, conservation, or ecological associations for more information about butterfly species native to your area and their population status. You may even be able to assist in programs led by local experts attempting to reintroduce lost species of butterflies to your area.

Another way to help native butterfly species maintain or boost their population is to grow the known food or host plant of those species.

If you grow host plants, be sure to leave them intact when the growing season is over. Do not use them for cut flowers or cut them back in the fall—you may destroy hibernating adult butterflies, their pupae, or their eggs.

Here, you will find a list of some known host plants. For more information, consult with your local chapter of the National Audubon Society.

List of Host Plants for Caterpillars

The plants on which a butterfly will lay eggs are called host plants. When the eggs hatch caterpillars, the host plant provides the food and shelter that the caterpillars need to survive. Some caterpillars will feed on only one specific plant species, while others can feed on many different plants within the same family. For example, the caterpillars of Black Swallowtail butterflies are found on many different members of the Carrot (*Umbelliferae*) family, such as carrot, dill, fennel, and Queen Anne's lace. It's important to check with local resources, such as the National Audubon Society, a natural history museum, or any local nature, conservation, or ecological association, for information about caterpillar plant preferences in your area. You can also identify butterflies already present in your garden and consult a butterfly reference book to see what its caterpillars will eat.

Although butterflies may lay hundreds of eggs, very few caterpillars survive—most fall prey to predators and parasites. This is the natural way of balancing the environment. On average, only two to three of every hundred caterpillars live long enough to go through metamorphosis and emerge as butterflies.

Below is a list of some common butterfly species and the plants that are most attractive to them as host plants for their caterpillars. Several of these plants are considered wildflowers and may already be growing in your yard or neighborhood. The butterflies are listed first by their common name, then by their genus. Again, before planting a host plant to attract a specific butterfly, be sure to check with local experts or a butterfly reference guide to make sure that butterfly is common to your area.

SWALLOWTAILS

Giant Swallowtail (*Papilio cresphontes*). Preferred host plants are prickly ash (*Zanthoxylum* spp.), hop tree (*Ptelea trifoliata*), rue (*Ruta graveolens*), and varieties of citrus trees.

Pipevine Swallowtail (*Battus philenor*). Preferred host plants are varieties of birthwort, also known as Dutchman's Pipe (*Aristolchia* spp.).

Black Swallowtail (*Papilio polyxenes*). Preferred host plants belong to the Carrot (*Umbelliferae*) family, including dill, parsley, fennel, and Queen Anne's lace (*Daucus carota*).

Zebra Swallowtail (*Eurytides marcellus*). Preferred host plant is pawpaw (*Asimina triloba*).

Eastern Tiger Swallowtail (*Papilio glaucus*). Preferred host plants are black cherry (*Prunus serotina*), tulip tree (*Liriodendron tulipifera*), sweet bay (*Magnolia virginiana*), aspen (*Populus tremuloides*), and cottonwood (*Populus deltoides*).

Western Tiger Swallowtail (*Papilio rutulus*). Preferred host plants are aspen (*Populus tremuloides*), willow (*Salix* spp.), alder (*Alnus* spp.), ash (*Fraxinus* spp.), and lilac (*Syringa* spp.).

SULPHURS

Cloudless Sulphur (*Phoebis sennae*). Preferred host plants are varieties of senna (*Cassia* spp.).

Orange Sulphur (*Colias eurytheme*). Preferred host plants are species of the Pea (*Leguminosae*) family, including alfalfa (*Medicago sativa*), vetch (*Vicia* spp.), and sweet white clover (*Melilotus alba*).

Clouded Sulphur (*Colias philodice*). Preferred host plants are clover (*Trifolium* spp.), alfalfa (*Medicago sativa*), sweet white clover (*Melilotus alba*), trefoil (*Lotus corniculatus*), and vetch (*Vicia* spp.).

BLUES

Spring Azure (*Celastrina ladon*). Preferred host plants are shrubs with clusters of flowers, including dogwood (*Cornus* spp.), ceanothus (*Ceanothus* spp., especially New Jersey tea, *Ceanothus americanus*), blueberry and cranberry (*Vaccinium* spp.), and viburnum (*Viburnum* spp.).

Ceraunus Blue (*Hemiargus ceraunus*). Preferred host plants belong to the Pea (*Leguminosae*) family, including alfalfa (*Medicago sativa*), vetch (*Vicia* spp.), and sweet white clover (*Melilotus alba*).

Eastern Tailed Blue (*Everes comyntas*). Preferred host plants are vetch (*Vicia* spp.), clover (*Trifolium* spp.), alfalfa (*Medicago sativa*), and other members of the Pea (*Leguminosae*) family.

HAIRSTREAKS

Mallow Scrub Hairstreak (*Strymon columella*). Preferred host plants are members of the Mallow (*Malvaceae*) family, including mallow (*Malva* spp.) and hibiscus (*Hibiscus* spp.).

Gray Hairstreak (*Strymon melinus*). Preferred host plants are many, but especially clover (*Trifolium* spp.), vetch (*Vicia* spp.), tick-trefoil (*Desmodium* spp.), mallow (*Malva* spp.), hollyhocks (*Alcea* spp.), and hibiscus (*Hibiscus* spp.).

MILKWEED BUTTERFLIES

Monarch (*Danaus plexippus*). Preferred host plants are varieties of milkweed, also known as butterfly flower (*Asclepias* spp.).

Queen (*Danaus gilippus*). Preferred host plants are varieties of milkweed, also known as butterfly flower (*Asclepias* spp.).

BRUSHFOOT BUTTERFLIES

Hackberry (*Asterocampa celtis*). Preferred host plants are varieties of hackberry (*Celtis* spp.).

Question Mark (*Polygonia interrogationis*). Preferred host plants are elms (*Ulmus* spp.), hackberry (*Celtis* spp.), hops (*Humulus* spp.), nettle (*Urtica* spp.), and false nettle (*Boehmeria cylindrica*).

Milbert's Tortoiseshell (*Nymphalis milberti*). Preferred host plants are varieties of nettle (*Urtica* spp.).

Comma (*Polygonia comma*). Preferred host plants are varieties of nettle (*Urtica* spp.), false nettle (*Boehmeria cylindrica*), hops (*Humulus* spp.), hackberry (*Celtis* spp.), and elm (*Ulmus* spp.).

Mourning Cloak (*Nymphalis antiopa*). Preferred host plants are willow (*Salix* spp.), hackberry (*Celtis* spp.), cottonwood (*Populus deltoides*), birch (*Betula* spp.), elm (*Ulmus* spp.), and quaking aspen (*Populus tremuloides*).

Red Admiral (*Vanessa atalanta*). Preferred host plants are nettle (*Urtica* spp.), false nettle (*Boehmeria cylindrica*), wood nettles (*Laportea canadensis*), and hops (*Humulus* spp.).

American Painted Lady (*Vanessa virginiensis*). Preferred host plants are pearly everlasting (*Anaphalis margaritacea*), hollyhocks (*Alcea* spp.), and everlastings (*Gnaphalium* spp.).

Buckeye (*Junonia coenia*). Preferred host plants are plantain (*Plantago* spp.), snapdragon (*Antirrhinum* spp.), false foxglove (*Aurelaria* spp.), monkey flower (*Mimulus* spp.), and figwort (*Scrophylaria* spp.).

Gulf Fritillary (*Agraulis vanillae*). Preferred host plants are varieties of passion flower (*Passiflora* spp.).

Bordered Patch (*Chlosyne lacinia*). Preferred host plants are members of the Composite (*Compositae*) family, especially sunflowers (*Helianthus* spp.).

Pearl Crescent (*Phyciodes tharos*). Preferred host plants are smooth-leaved asters (*Aster* spp.).

Great Spangled Fritillary (*Speyeria cybele*). Preferred host plants are violets (*Viola* spp.).

Meadow Fritillary (*Boloria bellona*). Preferred host plants are violets (*Viola* spp.).

Regal Fritillary (*Speyeria idalia*). Preferred host plants are violets (*Viola* spp.).

White Admiral (*Limenitis arthemis*). Preferred host plants are birch (*Betula* spp.) and aspen (*Populus tremuloides*).

Viceroy (*Limenitis archippus*). Preferred host plants are willow (*Salix* spp.), aspen (*Populus tremuloides*), cottonwood (*Populus deltoides*), and apple, plum, and cherry trees.

Lorquin's Admiral (*Limenitis lorquini*). Preferred host plants are willow (*Salix* spp.), aspen (*Populus tremuliodes*), cottonwood (*Populus deltoides*), and chokecherry (*Aronia* spp.).

California Sister (*Adelpha brewdowii*). Preferred host plants are varieties of oak tree (*Quercus* spp.).

Continued →

SKIPPERS

Silver-spotted Skipper (*Epargyreus clarus*). Preferred host plants are black locust (*Robinia pseudoacacia*), indigo bush (*Amorpha fruticosa*), and wisteria (*Wisteria* spp.).

Wild Indigo Duskywing (*Erynnis baptisiae*). Preferred host plants are wild indigo (*Baptisia tinctoria*) and false indigo (*Baptisia australis*).

Fiery Skipper (*Hylephila phyleus*). Preferred host plants are weedy grasses, including crabgrass (*Digitaria ischaemum*), bermuda grass (*Cynodon dactylon*), bentgrass (*Agrostis tenuis*), and sugar cane (*Saccharum officinarum*).

Long-Tailed Skipper (*Urbanus proteus*). Preferred host plants are beans (*Phaseolus* spp.) and other climbing legumes.

After you have identified the host or food plant of a particular butterfly, you may want to witness the various stages of a butterfly firsthand. Once you have discovered the eggs, this is a fairly easy thing to do.

When you have found your butterfly eggs, take the whole leaf and a few extra, and place them in a plastic bag until you get them safely home.

To protect your eggs from being devoured by predators and to keep your food plant alive, you are going to need a container. A coffee can with both the top and bottom removed makes a good container.

Cover the bottom of the can with a piece of cardboard into which you've made pin holes (jiggle the pin around to slightly enlarge the holes) for the stem of the food plant to fit through. Cut the cardboard long enough to extend beyond the coffee can.

Place the can over a dish of water so that the cardboard rests on top of the dish, but the stems of the leaves reach the water. This keeps the food plant alive longer and should keep your eggs dry.

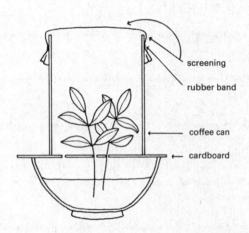

screening

rubber band

coffee can

cardboard

Cover the can with screening and secure it with a rubber band. Keep this container in a cool spot but one that receives some sun; not direct sun or the container will become too hot.

Once your caterpillars emerge, you may want to move them to a larger container. An old aquarium or glass cookie jar is fine, just make sure that air can circulate. Caterpillars require very little air, but you don't want to encourage mold.

Supply your caterpillars with plenty of leaves from their food plant and lots of dry twigs or branches on which to climb and pupate (the stage between larvae and adult butterfly). Remove any caterpillar droppings from the container daily.

Remove the top of your container as soon as your butterflies emerge. They will need some time to dry their wings and raise their body temperatures, but soon they will be airborne.

Choosing Butterfly Flowers for Your Garden

Some of the plant descriptions have been excerpted in part from *From Seed to Bloom*, by Eileen Powell (Storey Publishing, 1995).

An excellent way to gather ideas for laying out a butterfly garden is to first visit local botanical gardens, nature centers, or garden nurseries. Watch carefully to see which plants are attracting the most butterflies, and ask the gardeners at these places which plants they would suggest, based on their experience and expertise, for a butterfly garden.

Butterflies usually prefer plants in full sun. Because color plays such a vital role in attracting butterflies, it is to your advantage to plant groups or masses of a plant in one particular color, rather than single plants of different colors. A group of purple coneflower and a mass of white phlox will have a better chance of attracting butterflies than single flowers in each color. This will also give your garden a more uniform and attractive look to your human visitors. If you want your garden to be populated by butterflies throughout the summer, it is also important to plan your garden so that it has plants that are flowering throughout the growing season—chart the blooming seasons of the plants you decide to include in your butterfly garden and make sure that you'll have at least two or three plants flowering at any given time. Mix together host plants and nectar flowers to increase the number of butterflies visiting your garden.

Aster (*Aster* spp.)
ZONES: 2–9, varying by species
HEIGHT: 6 inches to 6 feet
BLOOMING SEASON: Spring through late autumn
There are hundreds of varieties of asters. They produce daisylike blooms, most commonly in shades of lavender and purple, but also in white, deep blue, pink, red, and rose. Encourage larger blooms by pruning young shoots in the spring, leaving 6 to 8 shoots per plant to develop. Taller species may need to be staked. Plant in full sun in average soil.

Baja Fairy Duster (*Calliandra californica*)
ZONE: 10
HEIGHT: To 4 feet
BLOOMING SEASON: Midsummer
Native to southern California, this tender perennial is most often grown as an annual in the greater United States. It is a showy, spreading shrub with purple blossoms. Plant in rich, moist, but well-draining soil.

Bee balm (*Monarda* spp.)

ZONES: 4–9

HEIGHT: 2 to 4 feet

BLOOMING SEASON: Summer

Hummingbirds, bees, and butterflies alike love the shaggy blossoms of bee balm. Most often seen in red, bee balm also blooms in purple, pink, and even white. Deadhead the spent blossoms regularly to keep these easy growers blooming. Plant in moist soil in full sun, and mulch well.

Black-eyed Susan (*Rudbeckia hirta*)

ZONES: 3–9

HEIGHT: 2 to 3 feet

BLOOMING SEASON: Summer

These North American natives will tolerate almost any soil that is well-drained. They have abundant yellow or orange daisylike flowers with prominent brown eyes, and are inclined to become invasive, so pick off the flower-heads after blooming to prevent self-seeding. Plant in full sun, or in partial shade where summers are very hot.

Coneflower (*Echinacea* spp.)

ZONES: 3–9

HEIGHT: 2 to 4 feet

BLOOMING SEASON: Early summer to autumn

These easy-to-grow perennials bear white, red, pink, or light purple, daisylike flowers with large pincushion eyes. Although they prefer average, well-drained soil, they will tolerate poor, dry soil. Plant in full sun or light shade.

Cosmos (*Cosmos bipinnatus*)

ZONES: 7–10

HEIGHT: 1 to 4 feet

BLOOMING SEASON: Late spring through early autumn

Cosmos will flower more abundantly in poor soil than rich. Their stems and flower foliage are topped with daisylike blooms in pink, red, orange, yellow, and white. Plant in full sun.

Dogbane (*Apocynum androsaemifolium*)

ZONES: 3–9

HEIGHT: 1 to 4 feet

BLOOMING SEASON: Midsummer

Dogbane is an herbaceous perennial native to most of the eastern United States. Its pink or white blooms will appear for only a short period in midsummer. Plant in full sun.

Eupatorium (*Eupatorium* spp.)

ZONE: 3–8

HEIGHT: 2 to 10 feet

BLOOMING SEASON: Midsummer to early autumn

Eupatoriums, native to North America, are all very popular with butterflies. They include white-flowered boneset (*Eupatorium perfoliatum*), pink- and purple-flowered Joe-pye weed (*Eupatorium purpureum*), and lavender-colored mistflower (*Eupatorium coelestinum*). Joe-pye weed may be cut back to encourage branching and more compact plants. Plant in full sun; preferred soil conditions differ between varieties.

Fleabane (*Erigeron* spp.)

ZONES: 2–9, depending on species

HEIGHT: 4 to 36 inches

BLOOMING SEASON: Summer to early autumn, depending on species

These easy-to-grow annuals and perennials resemble the aster in appearance, with neat foliage and fine-petalled, daisylike flowers of pink, purple, white, yellow, or orange with yellow eyes. Plant in full sun or light shade in average, well-drained soil.

French Marigold (*Tagetes patula*)

ZONES: Can be grown in any zone as an annual

HEIGHT: 6 to 18 inches

BLOOMING SEASON: Summer through frost

Marigolds prefer moist, well-drained soil enriched with organic matter, but will withstand quite dry soil. Plant in full sun, with afternoon shade where summers are very hot. Deadhead to prolong the blooming season. Single-flowered varieties tend to be the best nectar plants.

Gayfeather (*Liatris* spp.)

ZONES: 3–10

HEIGHT: 2 to 6 feet

BLOOMING SEASON: Summer to early autumn

Also known as blazing star, these rocket-shaped, pink-purple beauties will perk up any garden. Although preferring a sandy, rich soil, *Liatris* will tolerate even poor, dry soil, as long as their planting medium is well-drained. Plant in full sun to light shade.

Small Globe Thistle (*Echinops ritro*)

ZONES: 3–9

HEIGHT: 1 to 3 feet

BLOOMING SEASON: Summer to autumn

The small globe thistle is an unusual perennial with globelike blue flowers borne atop fleshy white wands. Will tolerate almost any soil that is well-drained, but species grown in very rich soil will require staking. Plant in full sun. Russian globe thistle (*Echinops exaltatus*), which can grow to 5 feet in height, is another good choice for a butterfly garden.

Goldenrod (*Solidago* spp.)

ZONES: 3–9

HEIGHT: 6 inches to 8 feet

BLOOMING SEASON: Summer to early autumn

Most goldenrods range in height from 2 to 4 feet, with spikes of tiny yellow flowers. They are inclined to spread rapidly—deadhead after flowering to prevent unwanted self-seeding and cut back completely in autumn. Plant in full sun or partial shade in moist, well-drained soil. Very rich soil will produce lush foliage but few flowers.

Continued →

Heliotrope (*Heliotropium arborescens*)

ZONES: 9–10

HEIGHT: 1 to 4 feet

BLOOMING SEASON: Early spring through early autumn

These violet to deep purple blooms have a sweet vanilla scent. Deadhead regularly to prolong blooming. Plant in full sun in rich, well-drained soil.

Honesty (*Lunaria annua*)

ZONES: 6–9

HEIGHT: 1 to 3 feet

BLOOMING SEASON: Summer

Also known as moonwort and moneyplant, honesty is an upright, bushy plant with purple or white blossoms followed by showy, silvery papery seed pods that are popular in dried flower arrangements. Honesty will grow in nearly any soil, and is happiest in partial shade.

Impatiens (*Impatiens* spp.)

ZONES: Can be grown in any zone as an annual

HEIGHT: 12 to 24 inches

BLOOMING SEASON: Late spring through first frost

Impatiens are grown as annuals in most of the United States since they are unable to survive frost. With their vibrantly colored, long-lasting flowers, they are ideal for both butterfly and hummingbird gardens. Plant in rich, moist soil. Most species prefer shade, but all will tolerate more sun where summers are cool.

Mexican Sunflower (*Tithonia rotundifolia*)

ZONES: Can be grown as an annual in any zone

HEIGHT: 2 to 6 feet

BLOOMING SEASON: Midsummer to frost

The brilliant orange flowers of this annual beauty are eye-catching, and butterflies love them. Deadhead to promote longevity of blooming period. Plant in full sun in average or sandy soil. Is quite tolerant of drought—water only during prolonged dry spells.

Milkweed (*Asclepias* spp.)

ZONES: 3–10

HEIGHT: 1 to 6 feet

BLOOMING SEASON: Summer

North America hosts many different species of milkweeds, which serve as host plants for monarch butterflies and nectar plants for a variety of other butterfly species. These sturdy plants prefer average, sandy soil; most species will tolerate dry soil but not heavy clay or chalk conditions. Plant in full sun to light shade. Bright orange butterfly weed (*Asclepias tuberosa*) is one of the best butterfly nectar plants.

Mountain mints (*Pycnanthemum* spp.)

ZONES: 4–8

HEIGHT: To 3 feet

BLOOMING SEASON: Summer to frost

These members of the mint family have small, pink-flecked white flowers that attract many different species of butterflies. They are long-flowering and the leaves smell wonderful. They are native to this country but are not easily available from nurseries. *Pycnanthemum* will tolerate almost any soil. Plant in full sun.

Pentas (*Pentas lanceolata*)

ZONES: Can be grown as an annual in any zone

HEIGHT: To 4 feet

BLOOMING SEASON: Early spring to frost

These tropical blooms, one of the best butterfly-attracting plants, are grown as annuals in most of the United States. Also known as starflower, this flower has striking blooms of pink, red, lilac, or white. Plant in full sun to partial shade. Water frequently.

Phlox (*Phlox* spp.)

ZONES: 3–9, depending on species; some species are annual

HEIGHT: 5 inches to 4 feet

BLOOMING SEASON: Spring to early autumn, depending on variety.

Phlox are well-known for their show-stopping floral display with blooms of red, pink, purple, white, or blue. Plant in full sun or partial shade in rich, moist, well-drained soil. Deadhead frequently to extend the blooming period.

Pincushion Flower (*Scabiosa* spp.)

Zones: 3–9

Height: 6 to 24 inches

Blooming season: Summer to early autumn

These beauties feature delicate, flowering of purple, pink, light blue, or white borne singly on long stems. Plant in full sun in humus-rich, well-drained soil, and deadhead regularly.

Rabbitbrush (*Chrysothamnus nauseosus*)

ZONES: 8–10

HEIGHT: 2 to 4 feet

BLOOMING SEASON: Late summer through autumn

This shrubby perennial is native to the western United States. Prune well for better flower production, and water sparingly. Plant in full sun in almost any well-drained soil.

Red Bird of Paradise (*Caesalpinia pulcherrima*)

ZONES: 10–11

HEIGHT: To 10 feet

BLOOMING SEASON: Summer

This tropical woody shrub can spread to a width of up to 10 feet. Its feathery foliage is accompanied by red, orange, and sometimes yellow blooms. Plant in rich, sandy soil.

Red valerian (*Centranthus ruber*)

ZONES: 4–9

HEIGHT: To 3 feet

BLOOMING SEASON: Spring to midsummer

This hardy perennial has tiny but fragrant deep red blooms. Prefers full sun and well-drained soil. Water plants sparingly. Cut back after flowering to encourage a second bloom

Scarlet sage (*Salvia coccinea*)

ZONES: 8–10

HEIGHT: 2 to 3 feet

BLOOMING SEASON: Summer to autumn

Scarlet sage is a tender perennial, most often grown as an annual, with profuse bright red (or sometimes white) spikes of blooms. Hummingbirds are attracted to the tubular flowers. Plant in full sun in well-drained soil.

Sunflower (*Helianthus* spp.)

ZONES: 3–10

HEIGHT: 3 to 10 feet

BLOOMING SEASON: Midsummer to mid-autumn

This large genus includes the familiar annual sunflower, as well as a wide variety of perennial sunflowers. They have large, showy, daisylike flowers of yellow, orange, and cream with very large, very flat eyes. Tolerant of both wet and dry soils, but stronger plants will be produced in deep, rich, well-drained soil. Taller species may need to be staked.

Sweet William (*Dianthus barbatus*)

ZONES: Can be grown in any zone as an annual, or sometimes a biennial

HEIGHT: 6 to 24 inches

BLOOMING SEASON: Late spring to summer

Choose the crimson variety of this plant with its cushiony, tightly packed blooms. Sweet William self-sows readily and prefers rich, well-drained slightly alkaline soil in the sunny or lightly shaded part of your garden. The taller varieties are wonderfully fragrant and much-loved by butterflies.

Tickseed (*Coreopsis* spp.)

ZONES: 3–10

HEIGHT: 8 to 30 inches

BLOOMING SEASON: Summer through early autumn

These versatile plants are grown for the reliable abundance of yellow or orange daisylike blooms they produce. Deadhead regularly to prolong the blooming season. *Coreopsis* prefer a rich, well-drained soil but will tolerate almost any soil condition. Plant in full sun.

Verbena (*Verbena* spp.)

ZONES: 3–10

HEIGHT: 4 to 24 inches

BLOOMING SEASON: Late spring to frost

These showy plants with tightly packed flower heads are rather short-lived and are best grown as annuals. Choose from pink, white, purple, or red blossoms. Plant in full sun in well-drained soil.

Zinnia (*Zinnia* spp.)

ZONES: Can be grown in any zone as an annual

HEIGHT: 8 to 36 inches

BLOOMING SEASON: Summer to frost

Zinnias have intensely colored, extravagant double blooms held singly on tall stems. Colors range from light pinks and whites to deep reds and oranges. Plant in full sun in well-drained soil enriched with manure.

Butterfly garden, summer.

If you are going to plant butterfly flowers in an existing garden, you'll simply be adding to the flowers you already have. But if you are planning a brand-new garden, you'll need to choose a spot that gets sun for much of the day. A butterfly garden that receives full sun for 5 to 6 hours a day should do well.

The size of your butterfly garden is really a matter of how much time you want to put into it. Although many butterfly flowers require little care, they still need some attention from time to time, so remember, a garden that is 10 feet square is going to require more work than one that is 4 feet square.

Butterfly Trees and Shrubs

There are many trees and shrubs that attract butterflies. Here is a list of just a few flowering bushes that you may wish to incorporate into your landscaping.

Abelia (*Abelia* spp.)

ZONES: 5–9

BLOOMING SEASON: Late summer through frost

This late-flowering shrub produces small, hanging, bell-shaped flowers in pink and white. Will tolerate almost all soil conditions, but growth may be inhibited by dry soil. Early in the spring, prune some of the older shoots to encourage new flowers. Plant in full sun.

Azalea (*Rhododendron* spp.)

ZONES: 4–6, with many exceptions

BLOOMING SEASON: Spring to late summer

Azaleas are a group of flowering shrubs within the genus *Rhododendron* that are particularly favored by butterflies. Blooms come in a variety of colors, including white, pink, apricot, red, yellow, and purple. Plant in full sun to light shade in well-drained soil.

Continued →

Butterfly bush (*Buddleia davidii*)

ZONES: 5–9

BLOOMING SEASON: Midsummer to frost

Also known as summer lilac, butterfly bush is probably the most renowned butterfly-attracting plant. There are many different cultivars available with white, pink, lavender, magenta, purple or yellow blossoms. Deadhead as needed to ensure profuse blooming. Heights of the shrubs vary—some will grow to nine feet—but remember to cut them back hard in the spring. Plant in well-drained soil in full sun.

Buttonbush (*Cephalanthus occidentalis*)

ZONES: 5–10

BLOOMING SEASON: Summer to early autumn

The creamy white flowers of buttonbush are abundant and extremely fragrant. Prefers moist, sandy soil, but will tolerate most soil conditions if given adequate water. Prune vigorously every two to three years to encourage profuse blooming.

Honeysuckle (*Lonicera* spp.)

ZONES: Vary by species

BLOOMING SEASON: Varies by species

Lonicera includes a wide range of species whose tubular, fragrant flowers reflect the full spectrum of color. Plant in full sun or light shade.

Lantana (*Lantana camara*)

ZONES: 8–10

BLOOMING SEASON: Year-round in warm areas; spring to frost in colder areas

This shrub produces compact clusters of orange-yellow, orange, red, or red-and-white flowers. Grow in any well-drained soil in full sun. Water deeply during the summer. Can be invasive in warmer climates.

Trailing Lantana (*Lantana montevidensis*)

ZONES: 8–10

BLOOMING SEASON: Mid-summer to frost

This woody shrub is often used as a groundcover. It has long, trailing branches that can extend as much as three to six feet and clusters of small, pink-purple flowers. Plant in full sun. Prefers infrequent, deep waterings.

Lilac (*Syringa vulgaris*)

ZONES: 3–7

BLOOMING SEASON: Early spring

This early bloomer, seen in purple, white, pink, and lavender, serves as a nectar source in the spring when little else is available. Deadhead as necessary. Plant in full sun in well-drained soil.

Spicebush (*Lindera benzoin*)

ZONES: 4–9

BLOOMING SEASON: Early spring

Also known as wild allspice, snapweed, and feverbush. Has vibrant yellow flowers that appear stunning against its nearly black bark. Plant in full sun in moist, well-drained soil.

Sweet pepperbush (*Clethra alnifolia*)

ZONES: 3–9

BLOOMING SEASON: Mid- to late summer

This easy-to-grow, late-flowering shrub bears delightfully fragrant white blooms that are favorites among bees and butterflies. Plant in full sun in moist, acidic soil that has been supplemented with organic matter. Prune in the spring.

Viburnum (*Viburnum* spp.)

ZONES: Vary by species

BLOOMING SEASON: Varies by species

Beautiful viburnums, with clusters of pink or white flowers, are available in many different varieties. Many have wonderful berries that are enjoyed by the birds in the fall. Viburnums will tolerate almost any soil condition. Plant in full sun.

Garden Pests

We know that pesticides are forbidden in a butterfly garden, but what can we do when pests invade?

First of all, invasions themselves can often be avoided. Many common garden pests can be stopped if their presence is detected early on. A daily inspection of your butterfly garden is helpful.

Keeping the perimeter of the garden free of weeds is often a good idea, as many pests such as aphids first hide among the weeds. But don't forget that weeds are often the plants that butterflies are most attracted to.

If you do detect the onset of aphids in your butterfly garden, a fine spray of the garden hose should get rid of them. The same goes for many beetles.

Beetles are large enough to be picked off by hand, however; aphids are more difficult to see.

Health and Well-Being

BEAUTY AND BATH

Essential Oils in the Bath

excerpted from *The Essential Oils Book*
by Colleen K. Dodt

Buying Pure Essential Oils

When I refer to essential oils I mean the pure plant distillates and extracts that are excellent allies in yesterday's, today's, and tomorrow's world of home health care. They are naturally derived, and should be respected as powerful substances to be used with caution and education. Pure essential oils are extracted directly from different parts of plants, depending on the oil concerned. Some are extracted from flowers, others from leaves, stems, the rind of fruit, berries, resin, or roots using a variety of extraction methods.

The resulting oil is a highly concentrated, volatile substance that is made up of many different elements, including alcohols, esters, hydrocarbons, aldehydes, ketones, phenols, terpene alcohols, and acids. Chemists have tried to re-create essential oils in the laboratory, but, to date, they have not been 100 percent successful.

As a buyer, you must beware of imitations! Better yet, be educated! Synthetic aromatic chemicals have become the norm for so long that many folks are used to them, and are unaware of the choices they have from nature's bounty.

FIND REPUTABLE SUPPLIERS

Knowing the supplier you are buying oils from is the first step. You can shop from the suppliers listed on page 774 with confidence that they are doing their best to supply only the finest, high-quality pure essential oils. Questions as to the origin and purity of an oil are usually met with enthusiasm by someone who is proud of their suppliers.

Always look for pure essential oils packaged in full, dark glass bottles, preferably with built-in droppers. These allow you to dispense the oil one drop at a time. Some oils are more viscous than others and may take a while to drop out. Some companies have adjusted the size of the dropper or bottle-neck accordingly. You can also use a separate glass eyedropper, but do not store it in the bottle because the oil will eventually break down the rubber bulb at the top, which will then contaminate the oil.

Read the label carefully. Look for the term "pure essential oil" and for cautions such as "Keep out of reach of children," and "For external use only." Seeing these warnings on a bottle is a sign of a responsible company that understands the effects of its product.

BUY IN SMALL QUANTITIES

Whenever possible, buy small bottles. Air in unfilled bottles can accelerate the deterioration of pure essential oils. Keep the bottles cool, dark, and well filled. I will often transfer small quantities of oils to a smaller bottle if I do not need them for a while.

Continued ➜

Precautions and Cautions

Working with pure essential oils can be rewarding in many ways. However, it can also be dangerous if certain precautions and cautions aren't observed. Remember that everyone is different and will react to individual essential oils in varying manners. The following simple precautions can make your experiences much more pleasant.

KEEP AWAY FROM EYES

Never use essential oils too near the eyes. Keep your hands away from the face, genitals, and mucous membranes when they have been in contact with oils. Always wash your hands before and after working with oils. I wear eye protection when pouring essential oils, and recommend it for you as well. If you do get some oil in the eye, wipe it with a cotton bud that has been moistened with sweet almond oil. Water will just disperse and spread the oil.

KEEP OUT OF THE REACH OF CHILDREN

Pure essential oils can be toxic if ingested in large amounts, and harmful to the skin and eyes if improperly spilled or undiluted. Children have no place playing with oils unless properly supervised and cautioned.

The use of essential oils on babies is debatable. Some sources say yes, some no. I would not use them on an infant without proper supervision and direction, such as reading *Aromatherapy for Pregnancy and Childbirth* by Margaret Fawcett, attending classes or workshops on the subject, or visiting a qualified aromatherapist or doctor with experience in this area. I have seen success with using oils on children as young as two years old, and successfully employed them with my own daughter, Christina, over the years.

Children's reactions to pure essential oils vary greatly. Just like adults, children take time to adjust to new things, including new scents. Let their noses be their guides. Ask them which scents they like and why. The olfactory anchors you create today can span a lifetime.

ESSENTIAL OIL SAFETY TIPS

- Dispense by the drop, carefully, and count. Record your recipe accurately.

- Dilute, dilute, dilute. Very seldom is an oil used "neat" or undiluted.

- Be careful where you set your essential oil bottles and wipe them clean first. Essential oils can mar surfaces, especially plastic ones. Always make sure bottle caps are twisted on securely.

- Practice aromatic etiquette. Many scents may be perceived as offensive to others. Use essential oils and perfumes in moderation in public, and check with family members to make sure your precious vapors aren't causing anyone else distress because of allergies, asthma, or just personal preference.

- Label everything—for your own convenience and others' safety. Clearly label and put up away from children any potentially harmful substances. Labeling is a great chance to be creative, too.

PRACTICE CAUTION DURING PREGNANCY

There are conflicting opinions on the uses of essential oils during pregnancy. I have heard that absolutely no essential oils should be used in pregnancy, but I also have books detailing just how much you can use. I would advise extreme caution, especially in the first trimester. Many oils can stimulate the uterus, which may be great as birth approaches, but not at two months into the pregnancy.

I have attended births where pure essential oils were used along with jasmine with absolutely marvelous results. If you are interested in this use, I advise working with a doctor, midwife, or aromatherapist who specializes in this area. I have heard reports of a reduction in stretch marks when a combination of pure essential oils and high-quality carrier oils were used faithfully on the skin after the first trimester.

FOR EXTERNAL USE ONLY

Pure essential oils are meant for external use only. There are those who practice internal use, but they are doctors or professionals trained in the practice of Medicinal Aromatherapy, primarily in Europe. Using pure essential oils internally would require a great amount of training and testing before it became acceptable in America. I do not suggest that anyone use them internally for any reason.

AVOID SUN EXPOSURE

Some essential oils, including bergamot and other citrus oils, such as lemon and orange, may increase the skin's sensitivity to the sun. The citrus oils can also increase the skin pigmentation in some people. If not properly blended and applied evenly, darkening and skin irritation could result. You can purchase bergamot with the bergaptene (the component of the oil that can lead to increased pigmentation of the skin) removed. Lemongrass, a fast-growing grass often used in culinary arts, may also increase sensitivity to the sun and have an irritant effect when used directly upon the skin, due to some of the key chemical constituents it contains.

REMEMBER THE OILS ARE CONCENTRATED

Pure essential oils and absolutes are very concentrated. Many pounds of herbs, flowers, resins, or fruits are used to produce small amounts of oils. Only small amounts of oil are needed to gain results. "Less is best" is what I tell my work-study students and clients. Many people think that if two drops of an oil will help them feel better, then five or six drops will lead to greater relaxation or stimulation—not so! Using too much essential oil can sometimes have a boomerang effect and aggravate, rather than soothe, symptoms. Essential oils can be expensive, and using less is smart in a financial sense as well.

BEWARE OF MEDICINAL CLAIMS

I always advise caution regarding healing and medicinal claims made by some when referring to the powers of pure essential oils. Always consult qualified help when deciding whether to use oils for something other than simple home use. Be sure to consult your doctor before changing any medications or healing practices.

Adding Essential Oils to the Bath

Essential oils should be added to a bath just before you enter the tub. If added to the water while the tub is filling, much of the oils' precious essences goes up in steam and very little is left to be absorbed by the skin. Then you get the benefit of inhaling the scents, but you miss out on the benefits to the skin.

Once you have added the oils, be sure to mix them into the water well. It is very important to avoid direct skin contact with undiluted essential oils that may irritate or cause skin sensitivity. You can also dilute the essential oils in a carrier oil before adding them them to the bath or, as some people prefer, in 1/4 cup (59 ml) milk or cream.

Remember that less is best. Adding more essential oils will not necessarily help you feel better than a small amount of oils will. These are very concentrated and should be used sparingly and well diluted. As you become familiar with the oils, their intensity, and your own personal reaction to each of them, then you may feel comfortable experimenting with a larger number of drops of selected oils. But, generally, err on the side of too little rather than too much. Pure essential oils are much more concentrated than the herbs in the leaf or flower state and deserve your respect.

Bath Recipes

Following are several recipes for combining essential oils in a bath. While specifically designed for baths, these blends may also be used with a base oil (such as sweet almond, jojoba, or grapeseed oil) to create wonderfully aromatic and healthful personal care products. Add oils directly to a tub full of warm water and mix well.

WAKE UP BATH

3 drops rosemary

3 drops lemon

2 drops eucalyptus

For a massage oil, add blend to 1 ounce base oil.

PMS BATH

It's no fun being out of sorts, bloated, and cranky. I've found that personalized herbal formulas and the use of pure essential oils can significantly reduce painful and distressing PMS symptoms.

PMS Bath I	PMS Bath II
3 drops clary sage	*2 drops clary sage*
3 drops lavender	*3 drops lavender*
2 drops rose absolute or otto	*2 drops chamomile (Roman)*
	2 drops rose geranium

For bloating: Add oils to 1/2 ounce base oil and 2 drops juniper and massage into the abdomen.

COLD CARE BATH

This pungent blend opens the nose and soothes aching muscles. It is effective when a cold is coming on. Before using, apply it to a small patch of skin on the inside of the arm to test for skin sensitivity.

5 drops eucalyptus

2 drops peppermint

2 drops lavender

As an inhalant, add blend to a simmer pot in a sick room. Be sure to watch the water level.

For a massage oil, add blend to 1/2 ounce base oil and massage into the chest.

CHEST COLD CARE BATH

I have found this blend useful when I feel that congested, tight feeling in my chest that often accompanies a cold or flu.

3 drops frankincense

3 drops hyssop

6 drops eucalyptus

The blend can also be used as an inhalant in a bathroom sink or large bowl of warm water, with a towel placed around the head to help direct the vapors up the nose. The scent is warm and spicy and feels good as you inhale.

As a massage oil, add blend to 1 ounce base oil and massage into chest, arms, neck, and abdomen. The vapors are released by body heat. It's nice to take a warm bath with the essential oils before a massage with the base-oil blend.

If this blend smells too medicinal to you, add a drop or two of a favorite oil such as ylang-ylang, rose geranium, or jasmine absolute to sweeten it to your taste. I have found that the addition of 1 to 2 drops chamomile (Roman) or clary sage helps me relax and stay in bed—and resist that urge to get up and work when I obviously need rest!

RELAXING BATH

5 drops lavender

2 drops ylang-ylang

2 drops rose absolute or otto

For a massage oil, add to 1/2 ounce base oil and 2 drops Roman chamomile (optional) and massage over the body before rest. This blend smells wonderful.

ANTIDEPRESSANT BATH

3 drops bergamot

3 drops rosewood

3 drops lavender

2 drops rose otto

For a massage oil, add essential oils to 1/2 ounce base oil and massage over the entire body, especially the heart area. For a full body massage, double the amounts in the recipe.

GRIEF BATH

3 drops sweet marjoram

3 drops lavender

3 drops rose absolute

1 drop cypress

For a massage oil, add essential oils to 1/2 ounce base oil and massage into the heart area.

Continued →

Aromatic Bath Salts

Sea salt detoxifies the body and conditions the water and skin. Adding pure essential oils to sea salt makes wonderful bath salts. This method is especially useful when using very expensive oils such as jasmine and rose absolute since it only takes a few drops added to 2 cups (500ml) of sea salt to make an elegant blend. While 1 or 2 drops of these oils alone does not seem like much for enhancing a bath, when mixed thoroughly into sea salt these drops are extended and make for a very pleasant bath. (Sea salt is great for scrubbing the oily film off your tub as well!)

Base oils such as sweet almond, apricot kernel, or grapeseed oil can also be added to the sea salt/essential oil blend to make a salt glow.

There are endless combinations of essential oils for bath salts. These are a few favorites that work well. The recipes can easily be doubled to make more.

BATH SALTS COMBINATION #1

These essential oils are known to help cleanse toxins from the body, and the scent is clean and fresh.

3 drops lavender

3 drops grapefruit

2 drops juniper

2 cups (500ml) sea salt

For relieving cellulite: Make sure the oils are well mixed with the salt to avoid skin irritation. Then take a "skinny bath" in these salts, which have been found to help relieve cellulite. Follow up the bath with an application of the oils blended in 1/2 ounce base oil to particular areas where cellulite is a problem.

BATH SALTS COMBINATION #2

An earthy, grounding blend that men tend to especially like.

3 drops sandalwood

3 drops patchouli

3 drops lavender

2 cups (500ml) sea salt

BATH SALTS COMBINATION #3

A balancing, refreshing blend. If desired, add 1 or 2 drops of a citrus oil such as lemon, sweet orange, or tangerine to brighten this blend.

3 drops rosewood

3 drops bergamot

2 drops frankincense

2 cups (500ml) sea salt

BATH SALTS COMBINATION #4

This is a great blend to bathe in when a cold is coming on.

3 drops eucalyptus

2 drops peppermint

2 drops benzoin absolute resin

2 drops cypress

2 cups (500ml) sea salt

Children's Baths

Children are always destined for a warm bath. They are also very much in tune to the sense of smell, so combinations of pure essential oils are an effective and fun way of enticing them into the tub.

These recipes are great evening bath blends that help an active child unwind. A follow-up massage can be a great opportunity to spend quality time with a child and a wonderful way to show you care and are there to listen. A parent's caring touch is an oasis in an often challenging world.

> **Caution:** Always exercise caution when using essential oils with children. Stick to mild oils and remember: less is best. Make sure the oils are well diluted in the water and that the water is the proper temperature. Improper dilution can result in skin irritation, especially with the citrus oils, so resist the urge to use just a little more.
>
> Children must always be supervised when using pure essential oils, and never allowed to make their own bath without guidance.

CHRISTINA'S CREAMSICLE BATH

This blend smells yummy and makes it a bit easier to get a dusty 5-year-old to come in from play.

2 drops sweet orange

2 drops vanilla oleoresin

LEMON DROP BATH

This blend is especially good at getting a grubby child squeaky clean. Lemon is so cleansing and refreshing.

2 drops grapefruit

2 drops lemon

SLEEP-EASY BATH

This soothing, relaxing blend that helps to ease away a day's stresses and strains also seems to help ease some of the emotional lumps and bumps of childhood.

2 drops ylang-ylang

3 drops lavender

Aromatic Foot Baths

Sometimes there is not a tub or the time available for a full body bath. This is when an aromatic foot bath is greatly appreciated. We do not often realize just how important our feet are. We stuff them into ill-fitting shoes, stand on them for long hours, and never give them much notice until they are blistered or in pain.

DISH BASIN METHOD

The basic equipment you need for a foot bath is a vessel that is large and deep enough to allow your feet to fit comfortably and holds enough water to cover the feet up to the ankles. I prefer a plastic dish basin or enamel wash basin because it is deep enough to keep the water from sloshing over the sides when carried, or overflowing when the feet are submerged. I have not used essential oils in the automatic foot baths that vibrate and massage the feet. My concern would be for the internal plastic parts, if any, that might deteriorate as a result of contact with the oils.

A dish basin is also easy to clean and portable—you can sit in front of the TV, or read and relax on the couch, while soaking tired feet. It is good to keep a kettle of water heating on the stove so you can keep warming up the foot bath as needed. Remember to set a towel next to your soaking area so you have it ready to wrap up those relaxed toes when you are finished.

Begin the bath by washing your feet before putting them into the basin to soak. Essential oils should be added to the basin just prior to immersing your feet. A total of 8 to 10 drops of essential oil is enough, and the combinations are endless. I prefer varying combinations using peppermint, rosemary, lemon, patchouli, rose geranium, bergamot, lavender, eucalyptus, tea tree, and clary sage. As with a tub bath, you must make sure the oils are well dispersed in the water before entering the water.

SPECIAL TREATMENT FOR SORE OR SWOLLEN FEET

A cold-water foot bath is a great treatment for swollen feet or a foot or ankle injury. Keep some ice cubes nearby, too, for extra soothing.

I use homeopathic arnica gel or ointment to treat any sore, overworked muscles or sprains. This works wonders for bruises, swelling, and stiffness caused by physical trauma. Arnica montana is an herb that is respected for its healing properties. Although the herb itself is not taken internally, homeopathic preparations in the form of homeopathic pellets and/or tincture, available in most major health food stores, have been found safe and effective. The ointment and gel are used externally on unbroken skin. Arnica gel has helped ease the sore feet of this world traveler and I would never leave home without it. Arnica massage oil is also very useful for massaging sore feet or an overworked back. Arnica ointment should be put on last, following an essential oil massage blend.

TUB METHOD

Another way to take a foot bath is to just sit on the side of the tub on a thick towel and dangle your feet. Wash your feet with soap first, drain the tub, then add enough warm water to cover your feet up to the ankles. Add the essential oils after the tub is full, and sit and enjoy inhaling their aromatic vapors while your feet soak in their beneficial effects. More warm water can be easily added as the water cools. This is also a foot bath you can share with a loved one or friend. Children usually enjoy foot baths, as well, and several of them can sit on the edge of the tub at once to clean up grubby little toes. Liquid soap dissolves any oily residue left in the basin or tub.

I use the tub method when I have been outside gardening and my feet are covered with earth. Also, after a long day on my feet it is easier and quicker than hauling out the dish basin.

When traveling, blend your foot bath oils ahead of time and carry them with you. In a hotel, the tub method works best.

FOOT BATH RECIPES

Individual needs and the condition of the feet being bathed should guide you in choosing the most appropriate essential oils. Foot baths are especially helpful in treating tired, aching feet, cases of ingrown nails, foot fungus problems such as athlete's foot or ringworm, injuries, and sprains.

These foot bath blends should be added to 2 gallons (8 liters) of warm water and mixed well. One cup (250ml) of Epsom or sea salts can be a nice addition to these foot baths. The essential oils can also be mixed with base oils and added to the warm water in this form.

> **Caution:** Pure essential oils mixed in an oily base before being added to a bath may make the tub surface slippery. Watch your step when entering and leaving the tub!

TIRED TOOTSIES BLEND

This blend comes in handy when I have been on my feet all day and still have things to do at home before I can totally relax. The lavender soothes the feet and the rosemary and lemon refresh, revive, and stimulate circulation.

3 drops lavender
3 drops rosemary
4 drops lemon

BURNING FOOT BATH/BLISTER BUSTER

This is a favorite for worn, weary feet that have been moving all day. The peppermint cools, and the lavender and chamomile soothe both feet and spirit.

3 drops peppermint
4 drops lavender
3 drops chamomile (Roman)

MY ACHING FEET BATH

This combination is for those occasions when you know you should have brought along more comfortable shoes. This blend is refreshing and soothing. A follow-up application of arnica gel will put you right back on your feet!

3 drops lavender
3 drops eucalyptus
4 drops rosemary

ATHLETE'S FOOT BATH

This combination of pure essential oils works wonders for people plagued with chronic athlete's foot problems. Tea tree is antifungal, as is lavender. The sandalwood conditions, softens, and soothes sore, cracked feet and toes. Its antiseptic and soothing properties help keep

Continued ➔

feet safe from secondary problems that can arise from the open, cracked skin. Patchouli could be substituted for sandalwood as a skin regenerator. Patchouli also has fungicidal properties.

4 drops tea tree

4 drops lavender

2 drops sandalwood

Sources and Resources

The companies listed below offer pure, high-quality essential oils and aromatherapy-related products including diffusers, blends, skin care products, and bath salts.

The American Society of
Natural Perfuming
Francois Michel
Natural Perfumer
P.O. Box 95
Wallingford, PA 19086
(610) 876–9432

Aromaland
RR 20 Box 29 AL
Sante Fe, NM 87501
1–800–933–5267

Boericke & Tafel, Inc.
2381 Circadian Way
Santa Rosa, CA 95407
663–9128

Amirita Quality of Life Products
Christoph Streiche
P.O. Box 2178
Fairfield, IA 52556
(515) 472–8672

Aroma Vera
Marcel Lavabre
5901 Rodeo Drive
Los Angeles, CA 90016–4312
1–800–669–9514

Aromatherapy Quarterly
P.O. Box 421
Iverness, CA 94937–0421
(415) 663–9519

The Essential Oil Company
Dorene Peterson
P.O. Box 206
Lake Oswego, OR 97034
1–800–729–5912

Frontier Co-Op Herbs
3021 78th St.
P.O. Box 299
Norway, IA 52318
1–800–669–3275

Lavender Lane
5321 Elkhorn Blvd.
Sacramento, CA 95842
(916) 334–4400
Carries hard-to-find herbalware: bottles,
droppers, essential oils, and labels

Herbal Endeavours Ltd.
Colleen K. Dodt
3618 S. Emmons Ave.
Rochester Hills, MI 48307–5621
(810) 852–0796
Catalog: $2.00
Colleen is available for lectures and book
signings.

National Association for Holistic
Aromatherapy
P.O. Box 17622
Boulder, CO 80308

Oshadi/R. J. F. Inc.
Gary Bernhardt
32422 Alipaz Suite C
San Juan, CA 92675
(714) 240–1104

For additional English sources write to:

The International Society of Professional Aromatherapists

The Annexe, Hinckley and District Hospital

Mount Rd., Hinkley, Leicestershire, LE10 1AG, England

25 Aromatherapy Blends for De-Stressing

Victoria Edwards

Illustrations by Alison Kolesar and Laura Tedeschi

Using Aromatherapy

My first profound experience with aromatherapy occurred while treating a terrible sunburn—my own. I was in pain and had already tried various sunburn remedies, but nothing helped. When a blend of herbs and oils quickly brought soothing relief, it got my attention. I began to inquire into the properties of various oils and to explore their many possible applications.

Then at the age of 34 I contracted an infectious liver disease. It was a very frightening experience. I was severely ill, and my health remained fragile for many months after I had recovered from the most acute stage of the illness. It was during my recovery that I learned to trust in the profound healing power of essential oils. My liver had become so compromised during my illness that my body rejected food and medicines. I'm convinced that the essential oils I used during that time restored my liver to its full function.

There are so many different ways to use aromatherapy in your own life. Essential oils can be applied directly to the skin as part of a massage, reflexology, or meridian treatment. They can be dispersed in a bath, inhaled, or diffused into the atmosphere of a room. Specific oils affect specific systems throughout the body. You can target these various systems if you know how to select an essential oil for its properties, and how to select an effective and efficient means of delivery in each case.

EFFECTIVE APPLICATION TECHNIQUES FOR PARTICULAR BODY SYSTEMS	
Essential Oil Application	**Internal Organs and Systems Affected**
Inhalation with diffusers	Respiratory, pulmonary
Internal uses; douches and boluses; suppositories	Digestive, eliminative, oral
Bath or spa therapy; massage and frictions; "aroma glows"	Works energetically on organ meridians
Algae, seaweed, and thalassotherapy; herbal aromatic body wraps; poultices	Endocrine system
Inhalation with diffusers	Neurochemical responses
Subtle work; essences, crystals, color lights; homeopathy	Emotional responses

Airborne Scent

One of the miracles of aromatherapy is its absolute simplicity. Just a whiff of the right oil can adjust your attitude, clarify your thinking, steady your resolve, even ease your pain. I'm rarely without a small vial containing some blend to help me through the day. Lavender is often in my pocket for brief inhalations whenever stress is beating me down. A whiff of lemon invariably clears my head and refreshes my thought processes. Inhalations are a practical way to incorporate aromatherapy into your day.

JET LAG INHALATION

5 drops geranium essential oil
5 drops bay laurel essential oil
5 drops lavender essential oil

Combine the oils in a small glass vial with a tight stopper.

To use: Carry a vial in your pocket or purse while traveling. Sniff periodically throughout the day to forestall the exhaustion and brain fog of jet lag.

STRESS-BUSTER #1

Stress wreaks havoc on the immune system. This blend will help give it a healthy boost.

5 drops niaouli essential oil
5 drops ravensara essential oil

Combine the oils in a small glass vial with a tight stopper.

To use: Carry a vial in your pocket or purse and sniff periodically.

STRESS-BUSTER #2

This is a very calming blend.

5 drops lavender essential oil
2 drops Roman chamomile essential oil
34 drops ylang-ylang essential oil

Combine the oils in a small glass vial with a tight stopper.

To use: Carry a vial in your pocket or purse to sniff periodically throughout the day.

MEDIA OVERLOAD

5 drops clove essential oil
3 drops nutmeg essential oil
10 drops sandalwood essential oil

Combine the oils in a small glass vial with a tight stopper.

To use: Carry a vial in your pocket or purse. If you're working at a computer terminal for extended periods, sniff periodically throughout the day.

THE AROMATIC DIFFUSER

There are many ways of scenting an environment. Incense has been used to deliver scent for thousands of years. More recently candle burners, simmering potpourri pots, and lightbulb rings have all become popular methods of dispersing scent atmospherically. Although these methods are aesthetically pleasing, they are not the best choices for aromatherapy. Commercial incense and potpourris are often rounded out with synthetic scents; their purity is unreliable. Additionally, incense smoke may transmit harsh, and even carcinogenic, chemicals along with its pleasing aroma. Candle burners and lightbulb rings can overheat delicate essential oils, changing their chemical makeup.

Diffusers act quite differently. Without altering or heating oils, they disperse them into the environment via an air-jet pump connected to a glass bell. A nebulizer within the glass bell diffuses a fine mist of negatively charged, scented ions into the atmosphere, much the same way that nature spreads fragrance.

The aromatic diffuser first appeared in Paris in 1960, when Dr. Bidault demonstrated the germicidal action of aromatic essences on tuberculosis, whooping cough, and influenza. His clinical observations indicated that disinfection of the air surrounding a patient had a therapeutic preventive effect. At the University of Paris School of Pharmacy, students tested his theories by collecting samples of air from an urban factory, the forest of Fontainebleau on the outskirts of the city, and a Parisian flat. By diffusing various essential oils into sealed chambers containing the air samples, they were able to validate the effectiveness of the essential oils against airborne bacteria and molds.

DIFFUSER BLENDS FOR DE-STRESSING

- For colds and flu: Oregano, lavender, eucalyptus, thyme, clove, cinnamon, peppermint

- To calm: Lavender, marjoram, geranium, chamomile

- For nervous tension: Lemon, orange, neroli

- For meditation: Clary sage, fir, cedar

- For depression: Bergamot, geranium, clary sage

The modern aromatic diffuser is a natural alternative to aerosol deodorizers and chemical air fresheners. A diffuser is a safe and convenient method of dispersing essential oils throughout a home, school, or workplace.

By using a diffuser, it is possible to dispense a therapeutic aromatherapy treatment to a number of people simultaneously. It is an excellent way of purifying the environment as well as administering the uplifting, rejuvenating, or relaxing effects of selected oils or blends to a group.

In the home environment, the therapeutic effects of diffused oils on the respiratory system are especially helpful during the cold and flu season, because the diffuser destroys airborne bacteria. When outside air is polluted, a diffuser can help create a safe, peaceful, and uplifting atmosphere indoors.

Continued →

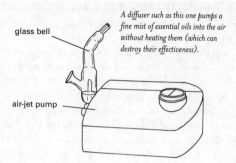

glass bell

air-jet pump

A diffuser such as this one pumps a fine mist of essential oils into the air without heating them (which can destroy their effectiveness).

ASTHMA WITH NERVOUSNESS AND ALLERGIES BLEND

5 ml (1 teaspoon) mandarin essential oil

5 ml (1 teaspoon) tarragon essential oil

5 ml (1 teaspoon) rosemary 'verbenon' essential oil

Combine the oils in a small, dark glass vial with a tight stopper and shake to mix.

To use: Use this blend in a diffuser during flare-ups of asthma. The blend can also be carried in a small glass vial in the pocket to be sniffed frequently throughout the day.

DETOXIFICATION BLEND

10 ml (2 teaspoons) lemon essential oil

5 ml (1 teaspoon) rose geranium essential oil

5 ml (1 teaspoon) everlasting essential oil

Combine the oils in a small dark glass vial and shake to mix.

To use: Use this blend in a diffuser when detoxifying or working on breaking a smoking, alcohol, or drug habit. This blend can also be carried in a small glass vial in the pocket to be sniffed frequently throughout the day.

RELAXATION BLEND

5 drops petitgrain essential oil

10 drops mandarin essential oil

20 drops lavender (Lavandula angustifolia) essential oil

Combine the oils in a small dark vial and shake to mix.

To use: Use in a diffuser to encourage relaxation.

MEDITATION BLEND #1

4 drops myrrh essential oil

5 drops sandalwood essential oil

10 drops frankincense essential oil

2 drops clove essential oil

2 drops cistus essential oil

2 drops rose essential oil

Combine the oils in a small, dark glass bottle and shake well.

To use: Add to a diffuser and use to support meditation.

MEDITATION BLEND #2

10 drops clary sage essential oil

4 drops vetiver essential oil

2 drops cistus essential oil

20 drops cedarwood essential oil

5 drops fir essential oil

Combine the oils in a dark glass vial and shake well.

To use: Diffuse to support and enhance meditation.

AROMATHERAPY BATHS

You can create your own spa experience with just a few oils and a tub of hot water. An aromatherapy bath is the ultimate luxury. Experiment with 3 to 5 drops of several different, complementary oils, adjusting the total amount to suit your individual taste. You can add the oils directly to the bath or, for added luxury, disperse them in a cup of milk first. Here are some combinations of essential oils that you might try for the bath.

OTHER BATH ADDITIVES

Essential oils combine well with all other bath additives. Try adding any of the following to your aromatherapy bath:

- Epsom salts, sea salts, and algae to mineralize the water and increase buoyancy

- Oatmeal or honey to soothe and nourish the skin

- Bicarbonate of soda to "soften" the water

- Fresh or dried herbs and flower petals for their aesthetic and therapeutic qualities

---

SOOTHE YOUR WORRIES AWAY

Lavender essential oil

Chamomile essential oil

Geranium essential oil

FLORAL ESCAPE

Rose essential oil

Bois de rose essential oil

Ylang-ylang essential oil

PAMPERED & SCENTED

Bois de rose essential oil

Frankincense essential oil

Clary sage essential oil

Geranium essential oil

LUXURIOUS SOAK

Roman chamomile essential oil

Angelica essential oil

Neroli essential oil

Clary sage essential oil

DEEP FOREST POOL
Pine essential oil

Rosemary essential oil

Eucalyptus essential oil

ESCAPE TO THE WOODS
Sandalwood essential oil

Neroli essential oil

Cedarwood essential oil

VITALITY
Ravensara essential oil

Thyme essential oil

MQV essential oil

VERY CALM NIGHT SOAK
Marjoram essential oil

Cypress essential oil

Lavender essential oil

A FEW WORDS ON WATER
Drinking and bathing in high-quality water are the most natural way to hydrate your body and preserve and promote your good health. Most tap water from public water supplies is loaded with chlorine, and often laced with other chemicals as well. Some of these chemicals are intentionally added to protect our health—fluoride, for example, is a highly controversial additive intended to harden children's teeth and prevent tooth decay—but other chemicals slip through in minute particles as traces of environmental pollution. If your skin is dry or irritated after bathing, and particularly if you notice a white residue on your skin, you might want to invest in a water filtration system.

Aromatherapy Massage from Head to Toe

Edited by Blair Dils and Nancy Ringer
Illustrations by Laura Tedeschi,
Alison Kolesar, and Kathy Bray

The physician must be experienced in many things, but most assuredly in rubbing.

—Hippocrates

Using Essential Oils

An essential oil is the life force or the "soul" of the plant. Each precious, aromatic, highly volatile, concentrated drop of an essential oil contains hundreds of powerful chemical constituents that act on our bodies either physiologically or psychologically. The therapeutic and mood-enhancing qualities of essential oils are undeniable—and extensive studies have borne this out.

Essential oils are natural ingredients for massage oils. When we inhale the gaseous vapor they release into the air and apply them to the body externally, essential oil molecules are absorbed into the bloodstream. This is an essential oil's single most important property: The molecules are small enough to penetrate the skin, reaching the dermis layer and interacting with sensory nerves, blood vessels, lymph vessels, hair follicles, and the sebaceous and sweat glands. Essential oils have a proven ability to promote elimination of waste matter and dead cells while increasing regeneration of cells.

Many massage oil recipes call for an essential oil of your choice. Choose fragrances that you find pleasing and calming. A scent may have different effects on different people, depending on past associations and life experiences, but lavender and chamomile are the fragrances most often chosen for relaxation. Bergamot, frankincense, neroli, patchouli, rose, sandalwood, and ylang-ylang are also relaxing. Patchouli, sandalwood, and frankincense are earthy; the others are more flowery. To find the essential oils that will best suit you, visit a store that carries them and use tester bottles to sample various scents.

Massage Basics

There are a variety of massage practices, but they may not all be styles that you enjoy. Some people appreciate a gentle massage; others prefer a deeper, more vigorous massage. And most of us give someone the type of massage we like to receive. Don't hesitate to tell your masseuse what you like, and to remind her as often as you need to. It's important that you receive the kind of massage you will enjoy most.

There are many different techniques and styles of massage. For more information, look for a mini-course on massage at your local adult education center. It's worth exploring all the options.

GETTING READY
Preparation is essential in creating a quality massage experience. Select a place of solitude where you won't be interrupted. For a full-body, a massage table adjusted for your height is ideal, but cushioning a long table or even using a bed or sofa can also be effective. Set up the table so that you can get around all sides, if possible. Make up the table or bed with both a bottom and a top sheet.

Another important factor is warmth. Warmth helps the muscles relax and is essential to a good massage. When lying in the prone position, the body tends to lose heat. Oil on the skin results in it becoming easily chilled. Make sure the room is warm when you start; bring in a space heater if necessary. Also use blankets as needed. Select music that is soothing and pleasing to your "client," whether that be yourself, your partner, or a friend.

BASIC MASSAGE STROKES FOR REVITALIZATION
There are many different types of massage and therapeutic touch, and plenty of good books on the subject. Here is a simple explanation of a few beginning strokes you can do at home that are quite beneficial.

Effleurage
This is a gliding stroke over the surface of the skin, usually done with oil or a massage cream. Massage normally starts with light effleurage to gently connect with the person, soothing her nervous system. Gradually, deeper strokes with more pressure may be applied to increase the circulation of blood and lymph.

Continued ➜

Petrissage

This kneading movement lifts, presses, and rolls muscle tissue away from the bone to increase circulation of blood and lymph and to detoxify the muscles.

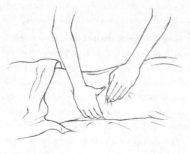

Petrissage is a kneading movement that lifts muscle tissue away from the bone.

Compression

Compression is direct pressure to the body and affects muscular, nervous, and energy systems. This technique is done with the thumbs, the whole hand, and even the elbows.

Rocking

Rocking is a smooth, rhythmic motion that soothes the nervous system. Gently shaking the limbs or rocking parts of the torso encourages the receiver to let go of tension.

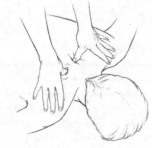

Rocking is a rhythmic shaking of a limb or a part of the torso.

Compression is direct pressure applied with the thumbs, hands, or elbows.

Massage Oils and Lotions

Once you have chosen a massage technique, you need to decide what kind of massage oil will be best for you. Plain vegetable oil is the simplest choice. The next step up is aromatherapy oils, which are easy to make and offer the healing elements of both the herbs and their aroma. A third option is an herbal infused oil. These are a bit more work, but they offer the healing elements of the herbs you choose to infuse. You can also create a product with both aromatherapy oil and herbal infused oil if you want to get really fancy: Simply infuse the oil with herbs, then scent with a complementary essential oil.

CARE AND STORAGE OF OILS

Once you've made your massage oils, remember that oils are delicate. Light and heat destabilize them; protect your oils from both. Destabilized oils become rancid. Rancid oils are linked to cancer, so it is important to heed safeguards in making, using, and storing products with oils. Dark amber and cobalt blue bottles afford the most protection from light.

Unfortunately, even the oils purchased at health food stores are rarely packaged in dark containers, with the exception of olive oil, which is the least light-sensitive. If you can, purchase oils in bulk from a supplier who has them in a dark container. If you've purchased oil in a clear glass container, either transfer it to a darker bottle or tape brown paper around the glass.

People who live in hot climates may need to refrigerate oil products for most of the year. Those in cooler climates may be able to get away with storing them in a cool, dark basement. Make small quantities, and refrigerate products that you have heated to make if you are not using them daily.

AROMATHERAPY SCENTED OILS

When making aromatherapy massage oils, choose the essential oils that call to you. For the simplest formula, combine one scent with one main oil, an antioxidant oil, and a few drops of vitamin E oil.

WHY USE NATURAL OILS?

Synthetic oils, petroleum products, and mineral oils create a barrier on the skin. This may seem helpful, but they do not allow the skin to breathe. Vegetable oils are closer to natural human oils and are better for people. Unfortunately, most commercial cosmetics contain mineral or synthetic oils. And if you go for a massage, a budget-conscious masseuse may also be using these products. Ask for a natural vegetable oil. And certainly do not skimp at home, either.

RED ROSE OIL

Rose essential oil has antidepressant, sedative, and aphrodisiac properties and is known as a restorative.

2/3 cup grapeseed oil

1 teaspoon alkanet root

1/3 cup wheat germ oil

10 drops vitamin E oil

6 drops rose essential oil

To make:

1. Pour the grapeseed oil and the alkanet root into the top of a double boiler.

2. Gently heat the water bath of the double boiler on the lowest heat.

3. Once the desired degree of redness is achieved in the oil, remove from heat and strain out the alkanet.

4. Add the wheat germ oil, vitamin E, and essential oil to the red oil.

5. Pour all ingredients into a dark bottle that has a spout.

6. Shake well.

To use:

1. Shake well before each use.

2. Pour the oil into your hands to warm before putting it on the body.

3. Massage into body using a circular motion.

YIELD: 8 OUNCES

SIMPLE LAVENDER OIL

Lavender is often recommended for its relaxing, soothing properties.

2/3 cup grapeseed oil

1/3 cup wheat germ oil

10 drops vitamin E oil

6 drops lavender essential oil

To make:

1. Pour all ingredients into a dark bottle that has a spout.

2. Shake well.

To use:

1. Shake well before each use.

2. Pour the oil into your hands to warm before putting it on the body.

3. Massage into body using a circular motion.

YIELD: 8 OUNCES

HERBAL OIL

This is a terrific conditioning oil for all hair and scalp types. It can also be used as a body massage oil.

1 tablespoon dried chamomile flowers

1 tablespoon dried rosemary

1 tablespoon dried horsetail

1 cup almond or sesame oil

To make:

1. Combine the ingredients in an airtight container. Let stand for several days (or even weeks, if time allows), stirring or gently shaking the mixture frequently.

2. Strain off the oil and discard the spent herbs. Store in dark glass bottles in a cool, dark place. Will keep for 3 to 4 weeks.

To use:

Use as an oil treatment for your hair, a scalp massage (as described on next page), or a massage oil for your body.

YIELD: APPROXIMATELY 1 CUP

CREAMY LOTION

Use the essential oil of your choice to scent this wonderful massage lotion.

2 tablespoons fresh chamomile

2 tablespoons fresh rose buds

2 tablespoons fresh comfrey

2 tablespoons fresh lavender

2 tablespoons fresh calendula

2 fresh sage leaves

1 sprig fresh rosemary

2 tablespoons dried witch hazel bark

2 tablespoons fresh lemon balm

1 sterilized, 12-ounce widemouthed jar

1 1/4 cups apricot kernel, almond, or grapeseed oil

1/4 cup cocoa butter

2/3 cup coconut oil

5 drops essential oil (optional)

To make:

1. Harvest fresh herbs in mid-morning, if possible.

2. Place the herbs on paper towels and allow to wilt overnight.

3. Fill the jar with the wilted herbs.

4. Completely cover the herbs with apricot, almond, or grapeseed oil.

5. Each day for the next week, poke the herbs down into the oil to release any captured gases. For the three following weeks, do this once a week.

6. After 4 weeks, strain the herbs from the oil.

7. Add the cocoa butter and coconut oil to the infused oil. Warm until all ingredients melt together. Scent with the essential oil of your choice.

To use:

1. Pour oil into the palm of your hands to warm.

2. Gently massage into the skin.

YIELD: APPROXIMATELY 12 OUNCES

Step-by-Step Full-Body Massage

The technique described here is a simple technique. You may want to learn other massage techniques through your local adult education center. Ideally, you should take the course with your massage partner.

Continued →

- Space heater (if necessary)
- Relaxing music
- Massage lotion, oil, or cream
- Bowl
- Pillow
- Top and bottom sheets
- Blanket or two

1. Make sure the room is comfortably warm; use a space heater if necessary. Put on a tape of relaxing music.

2. Wash your hands thoroughly before the massage and trim your fingernails if necessary.

3. Pour 4 ounces of oil into the bowl to start for easy access.

4. Oil your hands and rub them together to warm the oil.

5. Start with your "client" lying faceup with his or her head on a pillow and the body covered by a sheet (and blanket, if needed). Apply the oil to the throat using gentle side-to-side strokes.

6. Gently swipe across the chin, above the lips, and then across the forehead.

7. Using the fingertips, gently massage in upward strokes, starting at the jaw outside the mouth, coming up along the side of the nose, then across the bridge of the nose.

8. Make several spiraling, circular motions spanning the entire forehead, ending up above and outside the eyes.

9. Press the cheekbones using slight pressure from the outside to the inside.

10. Use a spiral, circular stroke on the cheeks.

11. Press along the sides of the neck, working outward to the shoulders.

Step 12

12. Massage the crown of the head using the fingertips. Press gently, working down and around to the back of the skull.

Step 13

13. Uncover one arm, leaving the rest of the body draped. Gently holding the wrist, shake the arm from side to side. With both hands around the arm, gently squeeze. Work back and forth starting at the shoulder and working down to the hand.

14. Do the same on the other arm and then each leg.

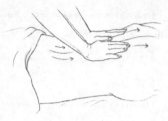

Step 15

15. Have the "client" turn over, and work on the back. Starting at the base of the spine, gently push on the spine, working up to the top of the shoulders. Rub the shoulders and top of the back all over.

Scalp Massage and Oil Treatments

Used for their stimulating, strengthening, and moisturizing properties, pre-shampoo scalp treatments loosen and slough off the dead surface cells on the scalp and provide nourishing emollient and antioxidant benefits. Oil treatments render the scalp more flexible, normalize both oily and dry itchy scalp conditions, and increase blood circulation to all the hair "roots." The protein and essential fatty acids found within these treatments will serve to fortify and smooth the hair while imparting a healthy shine. If you tend to use a lot of styling products, pre-shampoo oil treatments may have a softening effect on any film or buildup on your hair and scalp. These treatments are also especially beneficial for treating dandruff and dermatitis.

In contrast to most conditioners, which are applied after shampooing, hair and scalp oil treatments are generally administered before your bath or shower, when your hair is dry, and then shampooed from the hair. They can also be applied in the evening, left in overnight, and shampooed out the next morning, giving the oil a chance to provide optimal benefits. You will find that when you use an oil massage on a regular basis (which you should not do if you have oily hair and scalp or fine hair), your hair will not need an after-shampoo conditioner but, rather, an after-shampoo hair rinse.

This soothing and simple treatment requires about 45 minutes of your time—most of it spent relaxing!

1. Pour 2 tablespoons of vegetable oil, fruit oil, nut oil, Herbal Oil, or Ayurvedic Scalp Massage Oil into a plastic bottle with a flip-up spout top or into a cup. If desired, add 15 to 30 drops of an essential oil of your choice and mix thoroughly.

2. Although you can certainly use it unheated, you may want to warm the oil by setting the container in hot water for a couple of minutes before using. Warming the oil will enhance your hair's ability to absorb it to a degree (although the true absorption of the oil is really related to its molecular makeup, coupled with the degree of porosity of your hair).

3. Put some oil on your fingertips and work between your hands. Beginning at the top front hairline area, massage the oil with small circular strokes onto your scalp, working back toward the crown. Put more oil on your fingertips as needed.

Step 3

4. Repeat this procedure from the temple area back to the lower crown and through the nape area. Be gentle yet thorough, massaging your entire scalp for at least 3 minutes. Remember to massage with the pads of your fingertips in small circular movements along the scalp, not on top of the hair.

5. Next, put some oil into your palms and work it between your hands. Massage this oil into the hair from your scalp out to the ends with a gentle stroking or massaging motion.

Step 5

6. Cover your hair with a plastic cap and close off with a clip. (Use and recycle a plastic bag from your whole food market, or try a reusable shower cap.) You can wrap a hot, damp towel around the plastic cap if you want to maximize the effect in the shortest amount of time (20 to 30 minutes), or if time permits, take a bath, meditate, or simply luxuriate around the house while your own body heat enhances the absorption of the treatment. If you want to leave the oil on overnight, pin up your oiled hair and sleep with a towel over your pillow.

7. Shampoo, condition with a detangling formula (especially useful for long hair) or herbal rinse if required, and then style.

8. If any of this recipe is left over, use it on your body, especially on your elbows and feet. If you opt to save the oil for another day, keep it refrigerated and use within 3 weeks.

AYURVEDIC SCALP MASSAGE OIL

Use the herb *bhringaraj*, called "ruler of the hair" in Ayurveda, to create a highly effective medicated oil that is famous in India for removing grayness and reversing hair loss. Or you can select your favorite herb(s) and use in combination with bhringaraj to create your own individualized scalp oil.

1/4 cup dried herbs of choice

1 cup water

2 cups sesame oil

3–5 drops essential oils of choice (optional)

To make:

1. Combine the herbs and water in a stainless-steel or glass pan. Bring to a boil, reduce the heat, and then simmer, uncovered, until approximately half of the liquid has evaporated. Strain off the herbs.

2. Add the decoction to the sesame oil in a stainless-steel pan, bring to a boil, then immediately turn down the flame as low as possible and let this mixture simmer very slowly for at least an hour. The oil will be ready when all of the liquid from the decoction has evaporated and a drop of water added to the oil makes a crackling sound.

3. Add a few drops of essential oils. Store this oil in an airtight glass bottle in a cool, dark location.

To use:

Use for scalp and hair massages.

YIELD: APPROXIMATELY 2 CUPS

FLOWER ESSENCE SCALP MASSAGE

Flower essences can work wonders to calm the nerves and soothe anyone who is stressed out. The essences are subtle healing substances extracted from flowers. Edward Bach developed a procedure for extracting the essences in the early 1900s. Rescue Remedy, the most popular, is actually a combination of five flower essences and is available in most health food stores. Incorporating flower essences into a scalp treatment benefits both the hair and the emotional and mental state of the recipient. This treatment, which is offered at finer spas, is remarkably easy to make and enjoy at home.

Flower Essence Number 1

1/4 cup apricot kernel oil

3 drops red clover flower essence

3 drops lavender flower essence

Flower Essence Number 2

3 drops Rescue Remedy flower essence (or other flower essence combination of your choice)

3 drops lavender essential oil

1 plastic bag that will fit over your hair

To make:

1. First add the apricot kernel oil, then the flower essences and essential oils, to a lotion jar.

2. Shake well to disperse all ingredients.

3. Let sit for 24 hours in a cool, dark place; shake again before use.

To use:

1. Rinse hair with warm water.

2. Warm 1 tablespoon of the oil in the palms of your hands.

3. Using your fingertips (not nails), in a circular motion gently massage the oil into the scalp.

4. Repeat until the entire scalp has been massaged.

5. Rub the shafts and ends of your hair with the remaining oil.

6. Place a plastic bag over your hair, secure with a hair clip or clothespin, and allow the oil to remain for at least 15 minutes.

7. Rinse well, then shampoo as you normally would.

YIELD: 1 TREATMENT

Continued ➔

Hand Massage

Often neglected when people think of massage, hands demand some "touching" attention. For a hand massage, rub on a moisturizing cream. You can also mix 1 tablespoon of gently warmed avocado oil with 3 to 5 drops of your favorite pure essential oil and allow your hands to savor the experience.

1. Palm rub. Rub your palms together briskly to create some warmth, then rub the back of each hand.

2. Back of hands press. Clasp the fingers of both hands together with the palms facing. Squeeze the fingertips against the back of your hands. Hold for 5 to 10 seconds. Relax. Breathe deeply. Repeat.

3. Web pinch. The space between each of your fingers is the web. Pinch between the thumb and the index finger, hold for a moment, then rub. Repeat this process between each of the fingers on both hands. Eastern therapies hold that applying pressure on the finger's web sites (not the Internet!) helps to dispel headaches and move toxins from the body.

Step 3

4. Finger circles. Use your opposite hand to gently stretch and make little circles with each finger and thumb. Reverse direction of finger rotation. Repeat on the other hand.

5. Wrist compress. Support the wrist of one hand with the palm, fingers, and thumb of the other and squeeze lightly for about 5 seconds. Next, create the motion of a washing machine by gently rotating back and forth the wrist being held in the grasp of the supporting hand, while gently moving the holding hand in the opposite direction. Give the other wrist the same gentle treatment.

Step 5

6. Forearm press. Knead the outer muscle of the forearm below the elbow. Push the tips of your four fingers sensitively into the skin, using the thumb as an anchor, and work slowly up and down the arm, about three times, as if you were kneading bread dough. Repeat on the other arm.

7. Elbow rub. Take this opportunity to moisturize the elbow and forearm with your favorite cream or lotion by massaging with the fingertips of the opposite hand in circular movements from the elbow down to the wrist, then over the hand and fingers.

8. Arm and finger stretch. Interlace the fingers of both hands with the palms facing and then slowly turn the palms outward. Stretch your arms in front of you and give the fingers and arms an easy, relaxed stretch. Release and shake out your hands as if you were trying to dry your nails.

Foot Massage: Relief for Tired Feet

If your nerves are frayed, your energy level is running on empty, and your feet are simply worn out, then by all means partake of an aromatherapy foot massage. It will soothe your spirits, reduce your stress, put the spring back into your step, and soften your feet. What's good for the body is good for the "sole"!

FOOTSIE ROLLER MASSAGE

Wooden footsie rollers have been around for many years. They come in all shapes and sizes, from single to double or triple rollers. Some are handheld and some sit on the floor. Ones with raised ridges going from one end to the other are particularly successful. If you don't have a footsie roller, a wooden rolling pin can be used in a pinch. Simply place the footsie roller or rolling pin on the floor and, while bearing down comfortably, roll the entire length of your foot over the tool, back and forth, concentrating on your arches. Do this for 5 to 10 minutes per foot. This exercise relieves fatigue and cramping, especially in your arches.

Foot roller massages can relieve fatigue and cramping, especially in your arches.

TECHNIQUES OF FOOT MASSAGE

A foot massage can be performed at any time you wish or as a part of a home pedicure procedure. The following illustrations depict some standard foot massage techniques that a nail technician might perform on her client during a pedicure. If you do not have a willing partner to give you a massage, never fear. These techniques are just as easily done (with a minor bit of alteration) by yourself on your own feet.

If a partner is involved, have the one receiving the foot massage recline against a big pillow on the sofa or bed to fully relax the entire body. Foot massage feels really great if the whole body is at ease.

If you're going solo, find a comfortable chair, preferably one with padded arms and a foot rest, such as a recliner. Sit back, prop one foot in your lap and let the other rest extended in front of you, and massage those feet until they smile or you fall asleep!

Note: If using massage oil or lotion, a towel or two will come in handy to protect furniture and clothing.

Rub oiled or creamed hands together vigorously to warm them before beginning foot massage. Complete all six steps on one foot before moving on to the other.

1. Stroking. Stimulates circulation and warms the foot. Holding your partner's foot in your hands, on the top of the foot begin a long, slow, firm stroking motion with your thumbs, starting at the tips of the toes and sliding back away from you, all the way to the ankle; then retrace your steps back to the toes with a lighter stroke. Repeat this step three to five times.

Now stroke the bottom of the foot with your thumbs, starting at the base of the toes and moving from the ball of the foot, over the arch, to the heel, and then back again. Use long, firm strokes, slightly pressing the sole with your thumbs as you stroke. Repeat this step three to five times.

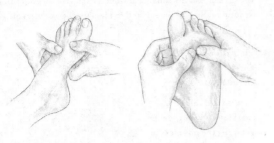

Step 1

2. Ankle rotation. Loosens joints and relaxes feet. Cup one hand under the heel, behind the ankle, to brace the foot and leg. Grasp the ball of the foot with the other hand and turn the foot slowly at the ankle three to five times in each direction. With repeated foot massages, any stiffness will begin to recede. This is a particularly good exercise for people suffering from arthritis.

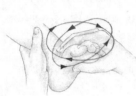

Step 2

3. Toe pulls and squeezes. Toes, like fingers, are quite sensitive to the touch. This massage step is unbelievably calming. Grasp the foot beneath the arch. With the other hand, beginning with the big toe, hold the toe with your thumb on top and index finger beneath. Starting at the base of the toe, slowly and firmly pull the toe, sliding your fingers to the top and back to the base. Now repeat, but gently squeeze and roll the toe between your thumb and index finger, working your way to the tip and back to the base. Repeat these two movements on the remaining toes.

Step 3

4. Toe slides. Grasp foot behind the ankle, cupping under heel. Insert the index finger of the other hand between each pair of toes and slide back and forth three to five times.

Step 4

5. Arch press. Releases tension in the inner and outer longitudinal arches. Hold foot as you did in step 4. Using the heel of your other hand, push hard as you slide along the arch from the ball of the foot toward the heel and back again. Repeat five times. This part of the foot can stand a little extra exertion on your part; just don't apply too much pressure.

6. Stroking. Repeat step 1. This is a good way to begin and end a foot massage.

Step 5

FOOT MASSAGE ELIXIR RECIPES

Foot massage can be performed with or without oils and creams. It's easier to grip your own or your partner's foot if it's dry, but you can use a small amount of oil or cream fragranced with essential oils. Don't overdo it, though, or the foot you're working on will be too slippery and difficult to hold.

The following recipes are very easy to make and have a relatively long shelf life in case you decide to double or triple a formula and store it for later use. The ingredients are especially good for dry, neglected feet and will leave your paws exceptionally soft and pampered.

RELAXING FOOT MASSAGE OIL

After washing and exercising your feet, use this fabulous aromatherapy herbal oil to further enhance your relaxed mood and soften any rough skin.

2 teaspoons soybean, jojoba, extra-virgin olive, or almond oil

2–6 drops (depending on strength desired) lavender, German chamomile, orange, or clary sage essential oil

To make: Mix all ingredients thoroughly in a small bowl.

To use: Massage into feet using a firm, strong hand. Apply pressure as needed to alleviate fatigue and tension in your feet. Put on socks afterward. You may be ready to climb into bed at this point.

YIELD: 1 TREATMENT

WHEN NOT TO RECEIVE A FOOT MASSAGE

Since foot massage increases the circulation, it may do more harm than good if you suffer from high blood pressure, a heart condition, or have had a stroke. Most nail technician training courses recommend that people with these conditions consult their physician prior to receiving a foot massage.

Continued ➜

POST-WORKOUT FOOT MASSAGE OIL

This formula will help feet feel cool and refreshed and aid in deodorizing.

2 teaspoons castor, soybean, jojoba, or extra-virgin olive oil

1 drop peppermint essential oil

1 drop eucalyptus essential oil

1 drop rosemary essential oil

To make: Combine all ingredients in a small bowl. Stir thoroughly.

To use:

1. Use about 1 teaspoon per foot and massage into feet completely.

2. Put on socks after massage to absorb excess oil and soften feet.

YIELD: 1 TREATMENT

AGONY OF THE FEET RELAXING MASSAGE OIL

2 teaspoons castor, jojoba, soybean, or extra-virgin olive oil

3 drops lavender essential oil

1 drop German chamomile essential oil

1 drop geranium essential oil

To make: Combine all ingredients in a small bowl. Stir thoroughly.

To use:

1. Use approximately 1 teaspoon per foot and massage in completely. Inhale the aroma on your hands before you massage, and continue to breathe deeply, as these particular oils are extremely calming.

2. Put on socks after massage to absorb excess oil and soften feet.

YIELD: 1 TREATMENT

FOOT REFRESHER AND DE-STRESSOR

This combined exercise and foot soak is designed to relax tired, aching feet, relieve toe cramps, and strengthen weak foot muscles that support the plantar fascia, which runs the length of the bottom of your foot from the heel to the ball. This one is also good if you suffer from hammertoes and pain in the ball of your foot.

Foot tub

40–60 medium to large marbles

2 tablespoons yarrow or sage

2 tablespoons wintergreen

5–10 drops lavender, camphor, peppermint, rosemary, or eucalyptus essential oil

1/4 cup sea salt, baking soda, or Epsom salts

Large towel

To make:

1. Place the foot tub with the marbles in it in front of a comfortable chair.

2. Boil enough water to fill the foot tub to above ankle level.

3. Remove the water from the heat and add the yarrow or sage and the wintergreen tied tightly in cheesecloth. Cover and steep for 15 minutes. Remove the herbs. (You can add the spent herbs to your compost.)

4. Fill the foot tub with the hot tea, and add the essential oil and the sea salt, baking soda, or Epsom salts. Swish the ingredients around to dissolve the salt and to blend in the essential oil.

To use:

1. Place your feet in the tub and roll them around on the marbles.

2. Pick up and release marbles with your toes by grasping the marbles tightly, squeezing your toes, then releasing. Do this for 10 to 15 minutes.

Step 2

3. Dry your feet roughly with a towel.

4. Slather with a thick moisturizer and put on socks.

YIELD: 1 TREATMENT

NATURAL HOME REMEDIES

10 Essential Herbs for Lifelong Health

Barbara Heller, M.S.W.

Illustrations by Laura Tedeschi

Ten Essential Herbs

In today's marketplace, there are many "popular" herbs renowned for their medicinal qualities. The ten herbs discussed here are among those that are particularly well known. Because they are also easy to use, widely available, and recommended for treating an amazingly wide range of ailments, they are well suited for presenting a basic overview and introduction to the ways in which herbs can help create health, happiness, and harmony in your life.

---

10 HERBS AT A GLANCE

Although each herb can be used in many different ways, here is a quick summary of their primary uses.

Herb	Primary Use
Calendula	Applied externally in the form of salves and ointments for treating skin irritations
Chamomile	Taken as a tea that calms and relaxes; also good for stomachaches
Echinacea	Taken in tincture or capsule form to boost the immune system and help fight off colds and flu
Garlic	Eaten or applied raw as an antibacterial and anti-viral and for cardiovascular benefits; eaten cooked, retains only cardiovascular benefits

Herb	Primary Use
Ginger	Eaten raw or in capsule form to combat motion sickness, nausea, indigestion, and inflammation
Lavender	The herb and essential oil are used in baths and compresses to treat insomnia, headaches, and burns
Lemon balm	Taken as a tea that acts to calm, soothe, and uplift
Peppermint	Taken as a tea that soothes stomachaches and headaches and eases symptoms of colds and flu
St.-John's-wort	Taken as a tea or in tincture or capsule form to treat mild to moderate depression or anxiety
Valerian	Taken in tincture or capsule form to relieve anxiety and nervous tension

Calendula (Calendula officinalis)

Calendula is a versatile plant that has been used for its medicinal, culinary, and cosmetic qualities and as a dye. Used in salves and ointments, calendula is a potent skin healer. Its primary culinary use is as an edible flower garnish. The brightly colored and mildly flavored calendula flower petals, fresh or dried, can be added to salads, soups, and muffins. Dried and ground, calendula can be substituted for the more expensive saffron.

CALENDULA IN THE GARDEN

Also known as pot marigold, calendula is an easy-to-grow, long-blooming annual. A sun-loving plant, it is said that one can predict the weather by its blossoms: If they do not open in the early morning, it is a forecast for rain. The plant usually grows 6 to 18 inches (15–45 cm) tall and blooms from June through October. Some of the newer varieties have stronger stems, growing to 30 inches (75 cm), and make lovely cut flowers. The centers of the flowers differ, some are light and others dark, which creates a beautiful contrast in the garden.

HEALTH BENEFITS

With antibacterial, antifungal, antiviral, and immune-stimulating properties, calendula is perfectly designed for soothing and healing the skin. It is primarily used in external preparations for myriad skin conditions. Calendula soothes cuts, bruises, diaper rash, eczema, hemorrhoids, burns, and other mild or chronic conditions. Germany's Commission E recommends calendula to speed wound healing and treat skin inflammations.

Some herbalists also recommend calendula in mouthwashes to treat sores and gingivitis. Calendula tea or tincture can be used for heartburn relief and as a part of ulcer treatment because of its ability to lower stomach acid levels.

HOW TO USE CALENDULA

A soothing calendula skin salve, store-bought or homemade, makes a great addition to a medicine kit. Diluted calendula tincture may be used externally for topical skin care or internally for acid stomach. A cooled brewed tea of calendula can be used as a wash for minor skin complaints.

Dried and ground calendula makes a good base for a body powder when mixed with cornstarch. Many baby soaps and lotions contain calendula because of its mild, soothing properties.

SOOTHING CALENDULA SKIN SALVE

Use this salve to soothe and heal mild burns, bruises, cuts, and rashes.

1 cup (237 ml) calendula infused oil (see recipe below)

2 ounces (56 g) beeswax, grated

4–10 drops lavender essential oil

1 200 IU vitamin E capsule

1. Combine the infused oil with the beeswax in the top of a double boiler. Heat gently until the beeswax has melted, stirring frequently. Remove from heat and allow to cool until you can touch it.

2. Add the lavender essential oil and the contents of the vitamin E capsule. Pour the mixture into small containers. The salve will solidify as it cools.

Note: The ratio of oil to beeswax is flexible and varies according to personal preference. To test the salve's consistency, put a spoonful of the beeswax mixture on a spoon and place in the freezer for 1 minute. If you want a firmer salve, add additional grated beeswax. For a softer salve, add more oil.

CALENDULA INFUSED OIL

You can use the infused oil by itself for topical healing of minor skin irritations.

2 parts extra-virgin olive oil

1 part dried calendula blossoms

1. Combine the olive oil and calendula blossoms in the top of a double boiler. Simmer gently for approximately 1 hour.

2. Strain the cooled mixture through a double layer of cheesecloth. Store in a cool, dark location, where it will keep for 3 to 6 months.

SAFETY AND CAUTIONS FOR CALENDULA

James Duke, botanist and author, points out that people who have hay fever may have an allergic reaction to this herb, especially if taken internally; he advises that a person stop taking it at the first sign of any itching or other discomfort. The *PDR for Herbal Medicines* states that there are no known health hazards or side effects when calendula is used in normal doses.

Chamomile (Matricaria recutita)

Chamomile's pretty white flowers with yellow centers make a lovely, mild, relaxing tea. (In the children's book, Peter Rabbit's mother served him a cup of chamomile after his escape from Mr. McGregor's garden.) Chamomile is good in baths for sleepless adults or fussy babies.

Continued →

Many herbalists also recommend this gentle herb as a colic remedy.

CHAMOMILE IN THE GARDEN

German chamomile, a tall annual, has small, daisylike flowers with a wisp of apple scent. The flowers can be picked and dried to make tea. Both German chamomile and Roman chamomile (Chamaemelum nobile), a somewhat similar-looking perennial, are widely cultivated for commercial purposes.

HEALTH BENEFITS

Chamomile has a relaxing effect on the nervous and digestive systems. In addition to being a sleep aid, chamomile has traditionally been used to treat stomachaches, ulcers, menstrual cramps, and arthritis. Chamomile tea is served to soothe heartburn, indigestion, and acid reflux.

Externally, chamomile has been used to heal wounds because of its anti-inflammatory properties. Compresses and baths made with infused flowers soothe irritated and inflamed skin. Several German studies have shown that applying a topical cream significantly reduced dermatitis. It is included on the list of herbs that the FDA deems "generally regarded as safe."

HOW TO USE CHAMOMILE

Serve chamomile as a soothing, sweetly scented tea. Although I often recommend infusing medicinal teas for a longer period of time, if you desire a mild, pleasant-tasting tea, don't steep chamomile for more than 10 minutes. It becomes bitter the longer it is steeped. You can brew it alone or in combination with other calming herbs, such as lemon balm. It is a major ingredient in many commercial tea blends, such as Celestial Seasonings Sleepytime tea. Extracts are also available.

Chamomile can also be used externally in baths or ointments, and its scent makes it a wonderful addition to potpourri, wreaths, and other aromatic herbal crafts.

CALMING CHAMOMILE BATH BAGS

A warm bath with these fragrant sachets provides a gentle way to wind down from a stressful day. This recipe will make enough for eight baths.

2 cups (473 ml) dried chamomile flowers

1 cup (237 ml) dried lavender flowers

1/2 cup (118 ml) dried hops flowers

1/2 cup (118 ml) dried passionflower

Combine all ingredients. Place 1/2 cup (118 ml) of the mixture in the middle of a piece of permeable fabric and tie it closed. When running the bath, loop the tie over the faucet so that the water runs through the bag as the tub fills.

SAFETY AND CAUTIONS FOR CHAMOMILE

As with all herbs, individual reactions may differ. Some people have an allergic reaction to chamomile, especially those who have hay fever and ragweed allergies, although the PDR for Herbal Medicines says that chamomile has a very weak potential for sensitization.

Echinacea (Echinacea angustifolia, E. pallida, or E. purpurea)

Also known as purple coneflower, echinacea makes a lovely addition to the garden. There are at least three echinacea species that have been used for their different medicinal properties. Although it is native to America, echinacea's medicinal effectiveness as a powerful immunity booster has been extensively studied in Germany.

ECHINACEA IN THE GARDEN

Purple coneflower is a tall, regal plant that adds wonderful end-of-the-season color to the perennial garden. It resembles a black-eyed Susan, but with purple rays.

The root of an established plant, three to four years old, is the primary part used medicinally. The plant may be dug in the autumn and the root divided and then dried before use. (Because of concerns about the overharvesting of echinacea, however, harvest only those plants you grow in your own garden.) Depending on the species of echinacea, however, commercial products may incorporate the whole dried plant.

PRESERVING THE MEDICINE

Many naturalists are concerned that echinacea is being overharvested, possibly threatening its survival. If you purchase echinacea, be sure that it has been cultivated (preferably using organic methods), not wildcrafted.

HEALTH BENEFITS

Echinacea is an immune-system enhancer with antibacterial and antiviral properties. It boosts the white blood cells that fight infection, helps stave off colds and flu, and lessens the duration and severity of symptoms once they occur.

Recent European studies conclude that echinacea is most effective when taken at the first sign of symptoms. Supplemental vitamin C at this time may also help lessen the severity of the sickness.

Taken internally, this plant medicine can also help to treat middle ear, urinary tract, vaginal yeast, and other recurring infections. Applied as a topical liquid, echinacea acts as a topical anesthetic, raising the area's pain threshold, and promotes healing of all kinds of skin wounds, burns, sores, and eczema. Echinacea's effectiveness as a treatment for rheumatoid arthritis and cancer is also being studied.

Some people take echinacea as a daily supplement in an attempt to prevent illness. Most authorities discourage its daily use, which can create a tolerance of the herb and negate its positive effects.

HOW TO USE ECHINACEA

Echinacea can be prepared in many forms: internally as a capsule, tablet, juice, tincture, or tea and externally in liquid form (juice, diluted tincture, or cooled tea) as a base for a poultice or skin wash. For medicinal purposes, most herbal practitioners recommend the tincture form; the tea is generally not strong enough. The usual dose is 1 dropperful of the tincture up to four times a day. Capsules of the freeze-dried extract are also a good choice for a potent dose. Follow the directions on the individual product label.

It is common for the tincture to create a tingling sensation on the tongue when ingested. This reaction is harmless—and some say it's a sure sign of the echinacea's potency.

ECHINACEA-ROOT TEA

Start drinking this tea at the first sign of a cold or flu. You'll know it's potent when your tongue feels a bit tingly after downing a mug.

1 teaspoon (5 ml) dried echinacea root, or 1 tablespoon (15 ml) fresh
1 cup (237 ml) water
Honey (optional)

Combine the echinacea and water in a saucepan. Bring to a boil, cover, and let simmer for 20 to 30 minutes. Remove from heat and strain. Sweeten with honey, if desired, and drink.

SAFETY AND CAUTIONS FOR ECHINACEA

Echinacea use may cause mild digestive side effects; no major side effects have been reported at recommended doses. Those allergic to flowers in the Daisy family may experience an allergic reaction and, if so, should discontinue use.

Echinacea may worsen the symptoms of autoimmune illnesses, including lupus, multiple sclerosis, and rheumatoid arthritis. People with AIDS are also cautioned against using this herb.

Garlic (Allium sativum)

Garlic, also called the stinking rose, is a culinary and medicinal wonder. A member of the onion family, this pungent bulb has been revered for eons as a natural remedy. As a popular food, garlic has inspired festivals, monocrop farms, and a multitude of cookbooks and gardening books.

GARLIC IN THE GARDEN

Garlic is a compound bulb made up of 4 to 15 cloves encased in a papery sheath. Plant garlic in the fall for the next summer's harvest or in the spring for fall harvest. In spring and summer, cut the flowers from the plant to encourage additional bulb growth. To prolong their shelf life, cure the bulbs by letting them sit in sun for 3 to 5 days, which will toughen their outer papery sheaths for winter storage.

HEALTH BENEFITS

Garlic's many therapeutic qualities include decreasing cardiovascular risk by lowering overall cholesterol levels, thinning the blood, reducing high blood pressure, and increasing circulation. Studies have shown that eating just one garlic clove a day reduced cholesterol in test subjects by 9 percent, which is equivalent to an 18 percent decrease in heart attack risk.

Garlic is purported to have antibacterial, antibiotic, antifungal, and antiviral properties. So even if you don't abide by the old folk custom of wearing garlic around the neck, eating garlic will enhance the immune system, lessen the risk of getting sick, decrease cold and flu symptoms, and help to fight infection.

Garlic may also be an important addition to a cancer-preventing lifestyle. Studies show that among people who eat a garlic-rich diet, there are 30 percent fewer cases of colon cancer and 50 percent fewer stomach cancers than in those who eat little of this powerful herb. Garlic has also proved helpful in preliminary studies with AIDS patients.

HOW TO USE GARLIC

The most potent way to take garlic is to eat it raw. Some practitioners recommend eating one raw clove, finely chopped, three times a day, but this amount may cause reactions in the stomachs of those eating it as well as in the noses of those around them! In terms of its antibiotic properties, it is estimated that an average-size garlic clove is equivalent to one-fifth of an average dose of penicillin.

Cooking garlic lessens its antibacterial and antiviral action—the heat deactivates allinase, one of garlic's healing enzymes. But one study showed that if peeled cloves are left to sit for 10 minutes before cooking, their healing compounds are not lost. Since there have been no definitive conclusions, more research is being done on the comparative value of cooked and raw garlic.

Even if cooking lessens garlic's healing qualities, it does not eliminate them. Cooked garlic still retains many of its active compounds. There are many tasty dishes that can help you incorporate garlic into your diet. In addition to various soups, entrées, and garlic bread, try salad dressings and vinegar spiked with garlic.

Garlic powder supplements are also available and are about as active as cooked garlic.

BAKED GARLIC

Baking a whole head of garlic softens its texture and taste. Individual cloves spread onto bread or baked potatoes are delicious, may help stave off a cold, and are a tasty way to include garlic's cancer-fighting and cholesterol-lowering qualities into your diet.

1 full head of garlic
Olive oil

1. Trim the top of the bulb slightly and cut the bottom so that it sits flat (do not peel off the papery sheath). Place on a baking dish and drizzle with the olive oil. Cover with aluminum foil. Bake at 350°F (175°C) for 1 hour, or until soft.

Continued ➤

2. After the garlic has cooled, remove the foil. The roasted cloves will pop out easily when squeezed.

Ginger (Zingiber officinalis)

What plant has been used to treat digestive difficulties for more than 25 centuries? What plant's root is used today for its powerful antinausea effects and as a treatment for rheumatoid arthritis? A container full of its ground essence probably sits on your spice shelf. The answer is ginger, the powerful attributes of which have been affirmed by historical, anecdotal, and scientific evidence.

GINGER IN THE GARDEN

Ginger is a tropical perennial. In the United States, this showy plant grows outdoors in Hawaii, Florida, and other states with hot steamy weather. Gingerroot, the rhizome or underground stem, is the plant part used medicinally. Limited quantities can be grown indoors from a cutting of a piece of store-bought ginger, although the older, toughened ginger most often available has a low propagation rate. The leaves grown from such a cutting are milder than the root, but may be used to enhance the flavor of cooked foods.

HEALTH BENEFITS

Ginger's primary use is as a remedy for motion sickness, nausea, and indigestion. Due to its anti-inflammatory qualities, it is also used to treat rheumatoid arthritis. A popular European remedy, ginger has been approved by Germany's Commission E. It is also listed as "generally regarded as safe" by the U.S. Food and Drug Administration.

Sailors and other travelers, take note: In multiple studies, ginger prevented motion sickness better and had fewer side effects than the leading over-the-counter motion sickness medication. Ginger's effectiveness has been proved in tests on Swedish seafaring naval cadets and on folks subjected to a tilting rotating chair and other simulated test situations intended to induce nausea. Ginger has also been hailed as an aid for postoperative nausea and to lessen the side effects of chemotherapy.

Ginger has a distinct advantage over conventional over-the-counter (OTC) antinausea medications. The OTCs act on the central nervous system and have a wide range of possible side effects, most notably fatigue. Ginger appears to avoid these adverse effects because it works on the digestive system instead of the central nervous system.

James Duke, former USDA botanist and author of *The Green Pharmacy*, lists more than 40 conditions that ginger is purported to help treat, including colds and flu, and cites it as a preventive against heart attack and stroke. Externally, ginger can be used in a massage oil to relieve lower back pain or in a wash to treat athlete's foot and other fungal infections.

HOW TO USE GINGER

Pungent ginger can be enjoyed many ways. Fresh ginger is often available in the produce section of food markets; jars of dried powdered ginger are sold in the preserved herb and spice section. Ginger beverages are also popular. Ginger ale (the old-fashioned kind made without refined sugar, which negates ginger's actions) can soothe a stomachache. You can also make a tasty ginger tea. Try candied ginger, ginger cookies, and various spiced soups and dinner entrées as a way to increase your ginger intake.

Capsules of ground ginger are especially convenient during travel as a remedy for motion sickness. Take two 500 mg capsules (which contain about 1 gram of dried ginger) about a half hour before boarding. Take another dose if you become nauseated. Effects should last about 4 hours. A 1-inch (2.5-cm) square piece of candied ginger or two cups of brewed tea can be substituted for a 500 mg capsule. Varro Tyler, a leading expert on herbs and plant-derived medicine, recommends a maximum daily dose of 4 grams.

GINGER TEA

This pungent remedy will help ease the symptoms of nausea or indigestion.

1 cup (237 ml) water

1 teaspoon (5 ml) grated or powdered ginger

1. Bring the water to a boil. Remove from heat, add the ginger, and cover. Let steep for at least 10 minutes.

2. Strain and enjoy!

Variations:

- Grate up to 1 tablespoon (15 ml) fresh ginger into a cup of brewed black or green tea.

- For a homemade ginger ale, mix a cup of strongly brewed ginger tea with carbonated water and lemon.

Lavender (Lavandula officinalis)

The beauty of its deep color and its highly evocative scent have made lavender a favorite for many centuries. Wonderfully versatile, it has been used as an ornamental plant, in cosmetics and perfumes, and for its medicinal and culinary qualities.

LAVENDER IN THE GARDEN

Lavender is a beautiful and relatively easy-to-grow garden perennial. Its scented silvery foliage is complemented by long flower spikes of various purple hues. Check out local garden suppliers for the variety best suited for your climate and gardening zone. Lovely fields of lavender are cultivated in French provinces and the British countryside. Commercially, an acre of lavender yields 12 to 20 pounds of the essential oil. To dry your own garden lavender, pick the stalks just before the flowers open, tie in small bundles, and air-dry upside down.

HEALTH BENEFITS

Lavender has a long-standing reputation for its medicinal attributes. It is used externally to help combat insomnia, nervousness, and headaches and to soothe wounds, burns, and skin irritations. It is purported to have antispasmodic, analgesic, antidepressant, and antiseptic qualities. It has been shown to reduce the size of breast cancer tumors in mice; current studies are investigating its possible cancer-fighting components.

HOW TO USE LAVENDER

Use luscious lavender in the bath, as a soothing compress for the head and neck, or in a sleep pillow. A mild tea, for external or internal purposes, can be brewed from lavender flowers and leaves. Lavender essential oil, in dilution, is convenient to use in bath salts, in massage oils, and for application to insect bites and other skin irritations.

LAVENDER HEADACHE COMPRESS

This compress is wonderful for the relief of tension headaches.

1/2 cup (118 ml) dried lavender flowers (and leaves, if available)

2 cups (473 ml) boiling water

1. Put the lavender in a teapot or similar container. Pour water over the plant matter and steep, tightly covered, for 20 minutes.
2. Strain the tea into a bowl. Soak a clean cloth in the tea and gently wring it out. Drape this warm aromatic compress on the forehead and eyes or on the back of the neck.

SAFETY AND CAUTIONS FOR LAVENDER

There are no health hazards reported with the normal use of lavender, although isolated cases of contact dermatitis have been reported in sensitive people using products containing the essential oil.

Lemon Balm (Melissa officinalis)

The luscious citrus taste and aroma of lemon balm are relaxing and good for stomachaches. Lemon balm is also called melissa, which comes from the Greek word for honeybee, a fitting name because the plant's fragrance has always attracted swarms. Use this versatile herb as a great-tasting and relaxing tea. It also makes a lovely culinary garnish for salads.

LEMON BALM IN THE GARDEN

Lemon balm is a low-growing tender perennial with deeply veined light green leaves and pink and white flowers. It grows up to 3 feet (90 cm) tall but may also spread low in the garden. Lemon balm can be grown from seed; it self-seeds so easily that some gardeners curse it as a weed. But even if it is a little wild, many think the wonderful scent makes up for the inconvenience.

HEALTH BENEFITS

Lemon balm makes a great herbal remedy for insomnia. In studies using a combination extract of valerian and lemon balm, the effects were shown to be as powerful as pharmaceutical sleep medications. In addition to its mild tranquilizing effect, it has antibacterial and antiviral properties and relieves anxiety, menstrual cramps, and mild digestive problems.

HARVESTING HINTS

Lemon balm must be gathered before the plant flowers, because after blooming the plant's essential-oil content drops dramatically. In addition, dried lemon balm has an extremely short shelf life—2 to 3 months at best.

HOW TO USE LEMON BALM

Tea made from fresh or dried lemon balm is refreshing anytime. A tincture or extract is good for a stronger medicinal dose. The glycerin tincture maintains a wonderfully potent lemon flavor: a sure pick-me-up for the winter doldrums. Lemon balm's calming qualities are put to good use in bath bags and sleep pillows.

LOVELY LEMON-LAVENDER SLEEP PILLOW

To help ease away anxiety and sleeplessness, try a sleep pillow.

2 parts dried lemon balm leaves

1 part dried lavender flowers

1 part hops strobiles

Combine the herbs. Put the mixture in a small drawstring bag or sew into a flat pillow and place between your pillow and pillowcase.

SAFETY AND CAUTIONS FOR LEMON BALM

The *PDR for Herbal Medicines* reports that "no health hazards or side effects are known in conjunction with the proper administration of designated therapeutic dosages." However, Michael Castleman, author of *Healing Herbs*, cautions that because lemon balm can interfere with a thyroid-stimulating hormone, those who have a thyroid problem should consult a medical practitioner before using it.

Continued →

Peppermint (Mentha x piperita)

Peppermint and its mint cousins are some of the most popular garden herbs. As a commercial additive, mint can make your mouth zing when used as flavoring for after-dinner mints, other candies, over-the-counter cough remedies, and dental products. The mints can be used for a variety of medicinal, culinary, cosmetic, and craft purposes.

PEPPERMINT IN THE GARDEN

Mints are enthusiastic perennials with square stems. Growing about 2 feet tall, peppermint has sharply toothed, lance-shaped leaves and spreads by surface runners. Its flowers are small, pink to lavender, with four lobes. Mints can be invasive; to contain your peppermint, plant it in a pot in the ground.

Gardeners who are also cooks are in for a treat. The delicious medley of mint choices includes apple, chocolate, and pineapple.

HEALTH BENEFITS

Peppermint's potent healing is derived from its aromatic oil, menthol. Menthol is antispasmodic, relaxing the muscles of the digestive tract. It's a wonderful digestive aid, mild enough to soothe children's stomachaches and excellent for adult indigestion and stomach upset. Studies show that menthol may also prevent stomach ulcers and stimulate bile secretion. Germany's Commission E has officially approved peppermint as an effective treatment for irritable bowel syndrome (IBS).

The decongestant action of peppermint also makes it a helpful adjunct in the treatment of many so-called winter ailments—the stuffiness and fever of colds and coughs as well as pneumonia. Peppermint chest rubs can ease the respiratory symptoms of colds.

SAFETY AND CAUTIONS FOR PEPPERMINT

There are no reports of problems caused by peppermint (the plant) in normal doses. Never ingest pure peppermint essential oil, which can be lethal. In rare cases, allergic reactions have been reported with external use of peppermint essential oil. Those with a tendency to have heartburn and gastroesophageal reflux should not ingest any form of peppermint; it irritates the condition. People with gallstones may experience digestive problems if they use peppermint products.

If you get peppermint oil in an eye or in an open wound, wash it out carefully with whole milk—the fat in the milk will bind with the oil. Do not use products with peppermint essential oil on the faces of young children because in rare cases, asthmalike symptoms and respiratory failure have been reported.

HOW TO USE PEPPERMINT

The most common and delicious way to enjoy peppermint is as a tea. A strong peppermint infusion makes a delicious morning pick-me-up, especially for those weaning themselves from coffee. Tinctures and

capsules (enteric-coated ones are recommended for treating IBS) are also available. Diluted peppermint essential oil can be used in many external applications, including the treatment of tension headaches. Peppermint can also be added to the bath or used for compresses and steams.

Peppermint also seems to repel mice; put sprigs of dried peppermint near known rodent entrance holes to discourage mouse occupation. Try cotton balls sprinkled with peppermint essential oil as a deterrent to mice in the pantry.

BREATHE-EASY PEPPERMINT STEAM

Easy to prepare, a steam can help clear up the congestion of a cold.

2–4 cups (476–943 ml) boiling water

1/2 cup (118 ml) dried peppermint or 4–6 drops of peppermint essential oil

Place the dried peppermint in a metal or glass bowl and pour the boiling water over the herb, or add the essential oil to the water in the bowl. Tent a towel over your head and the bowl. Being careful not to burn yourself, breathe in the warm scent for a few minutes.

St.-John's-Wort (Hypericum perforatum)

St.-John's-wort is a sunny plant that may brighten up dark dispositions. As a wild or cultivated plant, the vivid yellow flowers and green foliage produce a lovely dark red oil.

ST.-JOHN'S-WORT IN THE GARDEN

St.-John's-wort stands 1 to 3 feet (30–91 cm) tall and bears bright yellow flowers. The leaves of this hardy perennial are perforated with many small holes, which can be seen when a leaf is held up to a light. When pinched, the leaves, flowers, and unopened buds all produce a red oil.

HEALTH BENEFITS

St.-John's-wort is used internally for depression and anxiety and externally in the treatment of wounds, bruises, and first-degree burns.

St.-John's-wort's recently coined nickname, the Prozac of Plants, attests to its use as a highly effective and safe treatment for mild to moderate depression. It has been used extensively in Europe, and its popularity soared in the United States during the late 1990s. Studies show that St.-John's-wort is as effective as many prescription antidepressants, with a much lower rate of side effects. Many sufferers of Seasonal Affective Disorder, a type of depression caused by low levels of light, seem to react well to a boost of St.-John's-wort, especially when it is combined with lemon balm.

Researchers are also now investigating St.-John's-wort's antiviral potential, including its use as a very promising treatment against HIV infection, Epstein-Barr virus, influenza, herpes, and viral hepatitis infection.

HOW TO USE ST.-JOHN'S-WORT

St.-John's-wort is often recommended for the treatment of mild to moderate depression. Currently products are standardized to a certain percentage of one of two components: hypericin or hyperforin. The recommended dosage is 900 mg daily, taken in three separate doses of 300 mg each. The positive effects of St.-John's-wort are not immediately evident; it may take 2 to 6 weeks of use before results are noticed.

Standardized St.-John's-wort capsules and tablets are showing up on the shelves of supermarkets and pharmacies as well as in natural-food stores. Tinctures are also often available. In addition, St.-John's-wort infused oil or salve is used to treat external skin conditions. Homeopathic formulations of St.-John's-wort, labeled with the plant's Latin name, *Hypericum perforatum*, are used for the treatment of nerve pain.

ST.-JOHN'S-WORT OIL

This infused oil is wonderful for topical treatment of bruises and sprains.

2–3 ounces (56–84 g) dried or fresh-wilted St.-John's-wort leaves

1 pint (473 ml) olive oil

1. Put the St.-John's-wort in a jar and add the oil, making sure there are 2 to 3 inches (5–7.5 cm) of oil on top of the herb.

2. Place the jar in a warm, dry spot (such as a sunny windowsill) for 2 weeks. Gently shake the jar every 2 or 3 days.

3. Strain and press the oil from the St.-John's-wort. Let the oil sit until any residual water separates out; then pour off the oil and store it in an airtight container in a cool, dark location, where it will keep for 3 to 6 months.

SAFETY AND CAUTIONS FOR ST.-JOHN'S-WORT

When ingested, St.-John's-wort may cause photosensitivity. This side effect was initially observed in animals grazing on large quantities of the wild plant. Since that finding, researchers have questioned whether this effect is replicated in humans and, if so, if it would affect all people or only fair-skinned users. The *PDR for Herbal Medicines* states that photosensitivity in humans is unlikely with the administration of therapeutic dosages. In any case, those taking photosensitizing medications, such as tetracycline, should be careful of sun exposure if supplementing with St.-John's-wort.

A second important caution is for those wanting to treat depression. Depression is not just feeling down or blue; it is a medical condition with possible serious consequences. A depressed person should confer with a professional to get a correct diagnosis, including an evaluation of the severity of symptoms. Do not take St.-John's-wort while taking any other antidepressant, and if you are taking prescription antidepressants, do not abruptly stop their use to switch to St.-John's-wort.

Valerian (Valeriana officinalis)

Cats love valerian, maybe for the same reason that most people are repulsed by it—valerian stinks! There are palatable ways to ingest this powerful herbal sedative. Valerian is the premier herb for restless nights and is also a wonderful muscle relaxant, alleviating back pain and menstrual cramps.

VALERIAN IN THE GARDEN

A perennial plant, valerian grows wild in North America and is grown commercially in Europe. It is adored by many gardeners for its good

looks and shunned by others because of its fetid smell. Those who like the aroma describe it as a spicy scent reminiscent of the deep woods. The plant grows up to 5 feet (1.5 m) and has long fernlike leaves. The white to pink and lavender flowers are small and grow in branched clusters at the top of the plant. The root of valerian, which has a particularly definitive strong odor, is the part of the plant used medicinally.

HEALTH BENEFITS

Valerian is the herb of choice for insomnia and stress. It also works well for reducing menstrual cramps, headaches associated with the menstrual cycle, other muscle cramps, and intestinal upsets. The FDA places it on its list of herbs "generally regarded as safe."

German studies have substantiated its benefits as a relaxant without dreaded sedative side effects. Those who take it at night have been rewarded with deep sleep and wake refreshed in the morning. Valerian eliminates the morning-after grogginess associated with chemical tranquilizers. Herbalists recommend valerian as a nonaddictive and non-habit-forming remedy.

Animal studies have indicated that valerian may be helpful in lowering high blood pressure and as an anticonvulsant.

HOW TO USE VALERIAN

The root of the valerian plant is used medicinally. Various preparations are available. The recommended dose of valerian, as with other herbs, depends on the form and brand taken. Many herbalists recommend a dropperful of the tincture in some water at bedtime to benefit from its relaxing qualities. Dr. Andrew Weil, the well-known physician and author, believes that valerian can be especially helpful to those weaning themselves off synthetic sleep aids.

Valerian's primary drawback is its strong, unpleasant odor, often compared to the smell of dirty socks. To overcome this real aesthetic disadvantage, I recommend taking valerian in its more palatable forms, either as a capsule or as a tincture, and not as a tea. Although the strong taste is still evident in the tincture, this form may be chosen for its strength. Combining it with tastier herbs like chamomile, catnip, peppermint, and lemon balm is a good alternative. As a secondary ingredient blended with other, sweeter-scented herbs, valerian can also be used effectively in soothing herbal baths.

VALERIAN TEA

Excerpted from Rosemary Gladstar's *Herbs for Reducing Stress and Anxiety*, by Rosemary Gladstar (Storey Books, 1999).

A hearty, relaxing blend, this tea is one of the better-tasting valerian blends.

1/2 part dried licorice root

Water

1 part dried valerian root

2 parts dried lemon balm

Continued ➜

1. Combine the licorice and water in a large pot. Use approximately 1 cup (237 ml) per teaspoon (5 ml) of herb. Bring to a boil, cover, and simmer for 15 minutes. Remove from heat.

2. Add the valerian and lemon balm. Cover and let steep for 45 minutes.

3. Strain; drink as much and as often as needed.

SAFETY AND CAUTIONS FOR VALERIAN

In larger-than-recommended dosages, valerian can cause morning grogginess, nausea, headache, and blurred vision. In a small percentage of users, valerian causes the opposite effect of what is desired—it is stimulating rather than relaxing. These symptoms immediately disappear when the herb is discontinued. Some herbalists assert that long-term valerian use may exacerbate depression.

Natural & Herbal Family Remedies

Cynthia Black

Illustrations by Alison Kolesar

Introduction

When you're working with herbs and other natural ingredients, it's important to pay close attention to the recipe instructions. More is not always better—5 teaspoons of an herb in a hot-oil infusion will not necessarily work better than 2 teaspoons, and may in fact be harmful to your skin. Remember, the proportions called for in each recipe have been tested over time for best efficacy, so prepare the recipes as directed. In addition, use the recipes as directed—a remedy that is effective when applied externally may be toxic if taken internally.

EQUIPMENT

These recipes require only common utensils that can usually be found in your kitchen. Here's a list of the basic equipment you'll need:

- Stainless-steel, enamel, or glass pot or saucepan
- Wooden spoon
- Double boiler
- Cheesecloth, colander, and/or press
- Nonmetal containers with lids
- Bottles of various sizes with caps

Recipes for Health and Healing

SKIN AFFLICTIONS

Acne or broken skin: To soothe and smooth acne or broken skin, make a cold-oil infusion of plantain leaves and calendula petals and apply directly to your face with a moistened cotton ball.

Warts: To remove warts, rub them with fresh garlic or the white latex (sap) of dandelion stems.

Eczema: Make a cream using chickweed and violas. Apply directly to the rash.

Insect bites I: Rub a minute amount of basil juice (which may be found at or ordered from a local natural foods store or herb shop) onto insect bites to help relieve itching.

Insect bites II: Make an ointment from 1 cup of fresh basil, 1/2 cup of fresh oregano, and 1 cup of fresh rosemary or fresh savory with 2 cups of petroleum jelly. Spread over the bites. (Lesser quantities can be made by halving or quartering the recipe.)

Varicose veins and hemorrhoids: This astringent (for external use only) made from a decoction of witch hazel bark and leaves will shrink swollen tissue and ease varicose veins and hemorrhoids. Cut a branch of witch hazel into 2-inch pieces until you have 1/2 cup. Boil the pieces in 2 cups of water for 1 hour. Strain and add the resulting liquid to 1 1/2 cups of water and 1 1/2 cups of alcohol. Apply directly to your skin with a moistened cotton cloth, or fill a spray bottle and spritz it on. Store in the refrigerator for an extra cooling effect. You can also sprinkle some of this decoction in your bathwater.

Ringworm: This is an old remedy from my grandmother. Fill a small glass with vinegar, and then drop in 2 copper pennies. When the pennies are corroded and green, take them out and apply the vinegar to the ringworm.

ACHES AND PAINS

Sore muscles I: Make a cold-oil infusion of sage and basil and massage into sore muscles.

Sore muscles II: A hot-oil infusion of comfrey and thyme will soothe aching muscles. Use 5 large comfrey leaves and 6 sprigs of thyme in 4 cups of oil. Heat in the top part of the double boiler for 3 hours.

Tense temples: Make a hot-oil infusion of 2 tablespoons of lavender and 1/2 cup of rose petals per 1 1/2 cups of oil. Massage gently into tense temples.

Cuts and scrapes: For fast healing, mix a cream using calendula petals and apply directly to the affected area. Calendula cream is great to have in a first-aid kit.

Raw or aching gums: Make a hot infusion using 1 cup of water and 1 teaspoon each of rosemary, sage, and mint. Allow the herbs to steep for 30 minutes before straining. Use as a mouthwash to ease sore gums.

Toothaches: My husband had a very sore tooth one evening, and as we live in a rural area, all the stores were closed. I remembered that my grandmother would rub clove oil on our gums when we had a toothache. Unfortunately, I did not have any clove oil for my husband, but I did have some cloves. He placed a clove on top of the molar that was bothering him, and although it did not totally eliminate the pain, the clove was warming and helped stop the intense throbbing. Although I do not recommend using cloves or clove oil in place of care from a dentist, it sure helped us until we could get to one.

Sore and inflamed feet: Use a small plastic tub or large pot to steep a couple of tablespoons of oregano in warm water. Soak your feet in the infused mixture.

Your Immune System

Echinacea flower and rooté

TINCTURE OF ECHINACEA

Echinacea is a powerful herb that helps stimulate the immune system. Use it only when you feel an illness coming on.

3 good-size pieces of root of echinacea (purple coneflower)

1 cup vodka

1/2 cup boiled water, cooled

Combine the root of echinacea and the vodka in a nonmetal container and cover. Allow to steep for 3 weeks. Strain liquid and mix with water. Store in a dark glass bottle in a cool place.

To use: Place 3 drops of this tincture on your tongue several times a day until you are feeling better.

Sore Throats and Colds

HOMEMADE PASTILLES

Pastilles (pronounced *pas-tee*) are throat soothers and can easily be made at home.

1 1/2 cups water

1 teaspoon dried horehound leaves

1/8 teaspoon dried thyme

A pinch of dried mallow flower (if mallow is not available, you can use hollyhock or musk mallow)

2 teaspoons dried mint leaves

2 1/4 cups sugar

1/2 teaspoon cream of tartar

In a saucepan, bring the water to a boil and then remove from heat. Mix in the horehound, thyme, mallow flower, and mint and allow to steep for 1 hour. Strain into a separate pot. Add the sugar and cream of tartar to the strained liquid and stir over medium heat until the sugar is dissolved. Then cook without stirring until the mixture reaches the hard-crack stage (300°F). Pour into a greased pan. When it has cooled a bit, score into pieces. When completely hardened, break into smaller pieces.

For a lemon flavor, mix 1 teaspoon of dried horehound, a pinch of mallow, 2 tablespoons of fresh lemon balm, 1/2 teaspoon of lemon thyme, 2 teaspoons of dried mint, and a few drops of lemon oil. Proceed as directed above.

SYRUP TO SOOTHE THE THROAT

1 1/2 cups water

1 tablespoon hyssop (the flowering tips of the plant are best)

1/2 teaspoon angelica

1/2 teaspoon mallow

1 cup rose hips

1/2 cup honey

In the top of a double boiler, combine the water, hyssop, angelica, mallow, and rose hips. Heat over boiling water for about 20 minutes, or until the hips are soft. Press through a colander and add honey to the strained liquid. Store in a covered container in the refrigerator.

GARGLES TO SOOTHE THE THROAT

Use this gargle when your throat is feeling scratchy.

1/2 teaspoon grated garlic or grated horseradish

3/4 cup warm water

2 tablespoons honey

Mix the ingredients and gargle. Do not swallow!

For a simpler recipe, my grandmother added 1/2 teaspoon of salt to a glass of warm water and used this as a gargle.

TURNIP AND HONEY SYRUP TO SOOTHE THE THROAT

Another old recipe for a scratchy throat is this old turnip-and-honey remedy.

1 medium-size rutabaga (also called a winter turnip)

Honey

Wash and peel the rutabaga. Slice it straight across the bottom to make it level so that it can sit up without falling over. Then cut the turnip into four equal wedges.

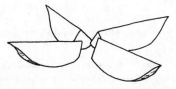

Slice the turnip across the bottom and then cut it into four equal wedges.

Continued ➔

Re-form the turnip and set it in a bowl to catch the juice.

Spread the cut sides of each wedge with a liberal amount of honey and then put them back together again, re-forming your turnip. Set in a bowl to catch the juice. Cover the bowl and allow to sit for 24 hours, or until you see that you have collected a good amount of liquid in the bowl. Store the liquid in your refrigerator, and drink to soothe a scratchy throat.

OLD-FASHIONED MUSTARD PLASTER FOR CHEST COUGHS

Here is an old remedy for chest coughs. Before penicillin and other antibiotics became widely available, pneumonia was a serious threat during the bitter winter months. My mother remembers using this mustard plaster during her yearly bouts with pneumonia.

1/4 cup dry mustard

1/4 cup flour

3 tablespoons molasses

Softened lard or thick cream

Mix the dry mustard with the flour and then stir in the molasses. Add enough softened lard or thick cream to make a workable ointment. Cover the sick person's throat and upper chest with a piece of flannel that has been dipped in warm water and wrung out. Apply the mustard plaster to the throat and chest on top of the flannel cloth. Leave on for 15 minutes, or until the skin starts to redden.

Caution: This plaster can really heat up the skin, so monitor it carefully. Do not use if irritation develops.

CHEST RUBS FOR CHEST COLDS

These are two good chest rubs we use with good success.

Basil and Anise Chest Rub

1/2 cup basil

1/4 cup anise or hyssop

2 cups oil

Mint and Thyme Chest Rub

1/4 cup mint

1/4 cup thyme

2 cups oil

Make a hot infusion using the herbs and oil. Massage into the chest area.

Warning: Do not use Basil and Anise Chest Rub during pregnancy. Potent applications of basil can have a stimulating effect on the uterus.

GARLIC

When you feel a cold coming on, chew up a clove of garlic twice a day. Garlic has many medicinal properties and is an antiseptic. We consider it a wonder plant. However, fresh garlic eaten alone can irritate the stomach if consumed in large quantities. To get around this, chop up a clove of garlic and sprinkle it on a nice green salad.

Healing Herbal Teas

In Europe, herbal teas are popularly called tisanes. This term comes from the Latin ptisana, which refers to a watery barley tea that was fed to the unwell. Today "tisane" can mean any healing or pleasurable tea of herbs. Tisanes are made as hot infusions. Boil your water and then remove from heat. Don't boil the tea once the herbs have been added! Pour the hot water over the herbs and cover. Let steep for 5 to 15 minutes, depending on how strong you want your tea to be. Strain and enjoy.

These are some recipes for teas that we have used for years. We try to use fresh ingredients. However, you can always substitute dried herbs for fresh—use 1 part of dried herbs in place of 2 parts of fresh herbs called for in the recipe.

FEMALE TEA

This tea serves as a wonderful relaxant during menstruation.

1 teaspoon fresh lemon basil

1 teaspoon fresh raspberry leaves

1 1/2 cups water

HEADACHE TEA

This is a good remedy for a tension headache.

2 teaspoons fresh catnip

1 1/2 cups water

RELAXING TEA

Chamomile is a well-known relaxant—drink this tea after a stressful day or as you're preparing for bed.

2 teaspoons fresh chamomile

1 1/2 cups water

GASTROINTESTINAL RELIEF TEA

Fennel and anise will both work to relieve flatulence.

1 teaspoon fennel

1 teaspoon anise

1 1/2 cups water

DIGESTIVE TEA

This tea will help ease digestion problems.

1 teaspoon fresh mint

1 teaspoon fresh bee balm

1 1/2 cups water

CURE-ALL TEA

This is my all-time favorite tea. I've used it for just about every health problem.

1 tablespoon fresh lemon balm

1 tablespoon fresh mint

2 teaspoons chamomile

2 teaspoons chopped rose hips

2 1/2 cups water

Recipes for Healthful and Healing Foods

Eating healthful and healing foods is an important part of caring for yourself. These traditional family recipes range from healing soups to eat when you are ill to healthful vegetable flours that you can use as a substitute in recipes that call for processed, bleached white flour. Adapt the recipes to suit your own palate, and enjoy!

HEALING SOUPS

HERBAL BROTH

This herbal concoction is a wonderful source of nutrition during all types of illnesses. The warm steam of a hot soup soothes sore throats and lungs, and the clear liquid is easy to digest.

4 cups water

1 tablespoon fresh basil leaves

1 tablespoon fresh chervil leaves

1 tablespoon fresh parsley sprigs

1 tablespoon fresh spinach leaves

1 tablespoon fresh tarragon leaves

1 tablespoon fresh watercress leaves

In a medium-size saucepan, bring the water to a boil. Add the herbs, cover, and simmer for 10 minutes. Remove from heat and strain. Serve hot.

VITAMIN SOUP

Our favorite vitamin-rich soup is great during the winter months. If you put your crockpot on low, you can simmer this soup almost all day. Try different combinations of herbs until you find your favorite tastes.

1 cup dried beans, any variety

1/3 cup dried peas

2 cups carrots, diced

2 cups potatoes, peeled and diced

2 cups parsnips, diced

1 cup rutabaga (turnip), diced

1 medium-size onion, chopped

2 teaspoons dried summer savory

1/2 teaspoon dried thyme

1/2 cup fresh or frozen parsley, chopped

2 cups cooked chicken (optional)

1 cup zucchini or pumpkin, grated (optional)

Soak the dried beans and peas in cold water for 8 hours (or overnight).

Fill the crockpot one-third full with water. Add the carrots, potatoes, parsnips, rutabaga, onion, beans, and peas. (If you decide to include them, add the cooked chicken and pumpkin or zucchini as well.) Let simmer for 3 hours, or until the vegetables are almost tender.

Add the summer savory, thyme, and parsley. Let simmer for another 1 to 2 minutes, or until vegetables are completely tender. Serve hot.

WHOLESOME BROTH

4 cups water

1 tablespoon sorrel, chopped

1 tablespoon lettuce, chopped

1 tablespoon chervil leaves, chopped

1/2 cup carrots, cut into matchsticks

1/4 cup celery, cut into matchsticks

1 tablespoon green onion tops, chopped finely

In a medium-size saucepan, bring the water to a boil. Add the sorrel, lettuce, and chervil leaves and cook until tender (about 4 minutes). Remove from heat, cover, and let stand for 15 minutes. Strain the mixture through a cheesecloth-lined colander. Return to heat, add the carrots and celery, and simmer until the vegetables are tender. Top with green onion, cook for 1 more minute, and then remove from heat. Serve hot.

VEGETABLE BOUILLON

This soup is delicious on its own, and also makes a great base for other dishes.

3 cloves garlic

4 medium-size onions

4 stalks celery

6 carrots

6 spinach leaves

4 tomatoes

2 tablespoons parsley

1 teaspoon thyme

2 teaspoons summer savory

Continued ➧

Fill a large pot with water. Add all the ingredients and simmer until the vegetables are tender. Strain. (Our hens are more than happy to eat the resulting vegetable pulp.) If you wish, you can add some noodles or rice to the broth for a thick and delicious homemade soup. You can freeze the leftover vegetable bouillon.

VINEGAR TONICS

CIDER TONIC

Cider tonic is a popular, healthful drink. It can ease indigestion and morning sickness, mitigate pain from arthritis and sinusitis, and reduce high blood alkalinity (which is often associated with chronic fatigue syndrome).

1 large glass water

1 teaspoon cider vinegar

1 teaspoon honey

Mix ingredients well and drink. You can substitute sparkling water or tonic for the water.

RASPBERRY SUMMER TONIC

This is an old family recipe that went down well after a hard day working on the farm.

1/2 cup sugar or honey

5 cups cider vinegar

3 cups fresh raspberries

Heat the sugar or honey in the vinegar until it is well dissolved. Remove from heat, let cool, and place in a large crock or glass jar. Add the fresh raspberries and cover. Make sure that the berries are totally covered. Allow to stand for 1 week, stirring or shaking gently each day. Then strain and bottle.

To use: Add 2 spoonfuls to 1 cup of water. Mix well and drink. More sugar or honey can be added if desired. You can substitute sparkling water or tonic for the water.

HEALING WITH YOGURT

Yogurt has been used for centuries by physicians to help alleviate intestinal inflammations. You can also use yogurt as a substitute for cream cheese, cutting down on the fat and calories in your recipes.

YOGURT CHEESE

2 cups plain, no-fat (or low-fat) yogurt

Chives or other herbs of choice

Secure a cheesecloth across the top of a bowl. I lay a wooden spoon across the top of the bowl and then tie the corners of the cheesecloth around the middle of the spoon, so that the cloth hangs over the bowl like a pocket. Spoon the yogurt onto the cheesecloth and allow to drain overnight. The next day you should have yogurt cheese, the same consistency as cream cheese. Add herbs to taste (roughly 2 1/2 tablespoons for me), mix well, and store in the refrigerator.

Recipes for Mothers and Infants

Natural and herbal recipes make wonderful soothing and gentle remedies for mothers and babies. With infants, remember to test small amounts of any recipe before moving on to full-size doses or applications.

SITZ BATH

Comfrey has been traditionally used in sitz baths for perineal tears or soreness after childbirth.

2 cups comfrey leaves

4 cups water

Make a hot infusion of the comfrey leaves and water, allowing the herbs to steep for 1 hour. Strain.

Fill the tub with about 3 inches of water that is a bit warmer than usual, but not hot. Add 3 cups of the comfrey infusion. Sit in this bath, exposing the inflamed parts to the water as best you can. This will also soothe hemorrhoids.

DIAPER RASH OINTMENT

First check with your health care provider to diagnose any rash the baby may have. For a regular mild diaper rash, you can try this ointment. After application, let the baby go without a diaper for a while to let the air help heal the rash. When I first made this ointment, I tested it on the inside of my elbow for a week. When no irritation developed, I then tried a minute amount on my baby's bottom. Please do not use large amounts of any homemade ointment on your baby's skin until you are sure that it will not cause irritation.

2 cups unscented petroleum jelly

1 tablespoon chamomile flowers

1 tablespoon calendula flowers

1/2 cup plantain leaves

1 tablespoon lemon balm

2 teaspoons comfrey

Heat the herbs in the petroleum jelly in the top part of a double boiler for 3 hours. Then strain the mixture through a cotton cloth and store in jars. Apply sparingly to the irritated area.

RELAXING TEA FOR MOTHERS AND BABIES

Breast-feeding mothers can prepare this infusion, which always seems to settle nursing babies. I'm not really sure if this infusion calmed me and thus calmed the baby or if it calmed the baby via the breast milk!

2 teaspoons chamomile flowers

1 teaspoon fennel seeds

1 teaspoon catnip

2 cups heated water

Infuse the herbal ingredients in the heated water. Drink the infusion as a tea with some honey.

Growing Herbs for Cold & Flu Relief

Dorie Byers

Illustrations by Charles Joslin, Beverly Duncan,
Alison Kolesar, Randy Mosher, and Louise Riotte

What Are Cold and Flu Herbs?

Each of the herbs discussed here is specially suited for soothing and relieving the coughs, sore throats, and congestion that come with colds and flus. Growing these herbs in your garden will help you become familiar with each one, as well as provide you with a beautiful, varied, wonderfully scented garden, plus natural remedies right at your fingertips. You'll find some recipes using these herbs here; recipes for cold and flu relief in other herbals will also call for many of these plants. So please, expand your medicine chest to include herbal teas, tinctures, infusions, and even stir-fry dishes that will chase away the symptoms that have you hiding under a blanket!

COLD AND FLU HERBS

Catnip	Peppermint
Cayenne	Rosemary
Echinacea	Thyme
Garlic	Yarrow
Ginger	

Catnip (Nepeta cataria)

A member of the Mint family, this Mediterranean native was once thought to symbolize love, beauty, and happiness. In pre-Elizabethan England, people drank catnip tea in the afternoons. In fact, many gardens in colonial America included catnip.

MEDICINAL USES

Commonly thought of as a treat for cats and frequently found stuffed in cat toys, this useful herb can also promote rest, improve digestion, calm and soothe stomach upsets, and relieve the symptoms of colds, flu, and fevers. It even contains antiseptic properties with which minor skin lesions can be treated. The volatile oils contained in catnip can absorb intestinal gas, so it is an age-old remedy for childhood colic. Taken before meals, it can be used to stimulate the appetite. The fresh leaves contain vitamins A, B, and C.

Catnip (Nepeta cataria)

Catnip's ability to help you relax and sleep has been compared to valerian's. It is calming without being disruptive of the next day's activities.

CAUTIONS

Catnip has many and varied uses with just one caution: You should not use catnip if you are pregnant.

CATNIP TEA

A cup of this tea in the evening hours will help you relax and prepare for sleep. Use the same infusion to alleviate cold and flu symptoms and to help settle a stomach upset from indigestion and/or gas.

Water

1–2 teaspoons (5–10 ml) of dried catnip per cup of water

Bring the water to a boil. Place the herbs in a nonreactive container and pour the boiling water over them. Cover the container to keep the volatile oils from evaporating and let the infusion steep for 15 to 20 minutes, then strain and drink.

DECONGESTANT INHALANT

This versatile mixture is for external use only. Simmer it in a pan or place it in a reusable muslin bag for the same soothing effect.

Equal parts dried catnip and dried rosemary

Eucalyptus essential oil

A muslin tea bag

Mix the herbs together. For each cup of dried mixture, add 4 or 5 drops of eucalyptus essential oil. Place the mixture in a muslin tea bag.

To relieve congestion, occasionally squeeze and bring this bag close to your nose to inhale. You also can place the bag on a warm register or in a sunny window to distribute the aroma into the air. Alternatively, put 1/4 to 1/2 cup (59–118 ml) of the mixture in 1 quart (946 ml) of simmering water in a noncorrosive pan and let the aroma drift through your house.

When you're traveling, place the muslin bag on the dashboard of your car. The heat from the sun and the defroster will help disperse the aroma.

Cayenne Pepper (Capsicum spp.)

Grown in India, Africa, and the New World, cayenne was brought to Europe by Christopher Columbus. It was used in food preparation, and was specifically used in Africa to induce skin-cooling sweats, no doubt quite welcome in the tropical climate. The plant symbolized fidelity to some. Columbus would have been disappointed to learn that in the 17th century, European herbalists believed cayenne emitted dangerous vapors. It's not hard to see where this opinion came from, though: If someone unfamiliar with the herb takes a close whiff, it will result in reddened, watery eyes and a sharp intake of breath.

Cayenne pepper
(Capsicum annuum)

MEDICINAL USES

Despite such misgivings, cayenne's uses are many. It enhances circulation, helping hot conditions cool off and cold conditions warm up. When used topically it is a counterirritant, bringing blood to the surface of the skin and causing reddening. As such, it is used to help relieve the pain of arthritic joints. Cayenne promotes digestion, increases appetite, promotes sweating, and is stimulating and energizing. Nutritionally it contains vitamins A, C, and E and is also a natural antioxidant.

Continued →

Cayenne's active ingredient is capsaicin. The hotter the pepper, the more capsaicin it contains. A low concentration of capsaicin in topical creams for muscle and joint aches and pains has been available commercially the last few years. Consistent topical use four or five times a day for at least 4 weeks seems to block pain pathways to affected areas. Additional research is being done on using cayenne to treat cluster headaches.

Aside from the topical application, eating cayenne is the best way to reap its benefits. Regularly including cayenne in your diet is said to enhance your circulation and improve digestion. It will also clear up sinus congestion.

A SURE-FIRE WARM-UP

For colds and chills, place 1/4 to 1/2 teaspoon (1.3–2.5 ml) dried cayenne in 1 pint (473 ml) tomato juice and warm the mixture, stirring until the cayenne is distributed. Sip 1/2 to 1 cup (118–237 ml) at a time for a heat-producing, sinus-clearing, vitamin-packed drink. Store the remainder in the refrigerator for later use and rewarm before drinking.

CAUTIONS

Always use caution when handling cayenne. Wear gloves when preparing it, keep it away from your eyes, and do not apply cayenne to damaged skin.

HANDLING THE HEAT

To decrease the heat of cayenne in your mouth, eat some rice or bread or drink milk; water only spreads the oil around. To remove cayenne residue from your skin, use a rinse of vinegar or milk.

Cayenne is not recommended for people with active ulcers. In addition, ingesting large amounts of this herb can be harmful to the digestive tract and, possibly, the kidneys. The negative effects of cayenne on the digestive system can be counteracted, however, by eating a high protein, low-fat diet. Some people have heartburn when eating cayenne—to avoid that situation, start by adding just a pinch at a time and increase the amount to suit your palate and your stomach.

Echinacea
(Echinacea purpurea, E. angustifolia, and E. pallida)

Commonly known as the purple coneflower, the name "echinacea" seems to be on everyone's lips these days, and it is widely touted in print as well. Best known for their ability to boost the immune system, echinacea pills fill the shelves of health-food stores as well as drugstores. The plant is well known not only by people familiar with herbs but also by those who aren't usually in the "herbal know."

MEDICINAL USES

Commission E, a special committee of the German Federal Department of Health, reviews the effects of herbs and their safety and publishes the results. It has approved echinacea for combating recurring infections and as a local application for treatment of hard-to-heal wounds. This latter use has been justified by studies that show an accelerated healing rate of bacterial skin infections when echinacea is applied.

The plant's other properties include antiseptic, antimicrobial, lymphatic, and tonic. Usually echinacea's root is the part used, although the aerial part of the plant has been used successfully in some preparations. By and large echinacea is best known for its ability to stimulate and/or

The flowering top and root of echinacea (Echinacea purpurea)

support the body's immune system against bacterial and viral attacks. At the first sign of cold or flu, start taking echinacea—the tinctured form is the most reliable. Take doses of echinacea during waking hours for 2 days, then stop. It is meant to be taken only as an immune-system booster—not on a regular basis. Echinacea will not cure a cold or flu if you take it after the illness has taken hold.

CAUTIONS FOR ECHINACEA

Echinacea should be used with caution by pregnant women. In addition, do not use echinacea if you suffer from any of the following conditions:

- an allergy to sunflowers
- a severe systemic immune disorder such as multiple sclerosis or tuberculosis
- a collagen disease such as lupus or scleroderma

ECHINACEA TINCTURE

Echinacea's active ingredients aren't all water soluble; a tincture is the best way to obtain its benefits.

3/4 cup (177 ml) pure grain alcohol or 80 to 100 proof (40 to 50% alcohol) vodka or brandy or glycerin

3/4 cup (177 ml) distilled water

1 1/2 ounces (42 g) echinacea root, chopped

To make:

1. Combine the alcohol with the distilled water in a jar with a tight-fitting lid.

2. Add the echinacea root. Run a knife or chopstick around the edges of the jar to release any trapped air bubbles.

3. Replace the lid and set the jar in a cool, dark place for 2 weeks. Shake the mixture every day.

Step 2

4. Strain the mixture to remove the herb. This must be done quickly or the alcohol will evaporate. I usually pour the mixture into a strainer lined with an unbleached paper coffee filter and place it in the refrigerator as it strains, to slow the evaporation of the alcohol. After straining, squeeze the filter to remove as much of the liquid as possible.

5. Store the tincture in a tightly sealed glass container in a cool, dark location, where it will keep for up to 5 years. Be sure to label the bottle first!

To use:

At the first sign of cold or flu's onset, herbal experts recommend 30 drops of tincture every 3 hours for the first 2 days only. Once you have developed a full-blown case of a cold or flu, echinacea probably will not cure it.

If you are unable to take the alcohol in the tincture, add the tincture to a small glass of warm water and stir gently. The warm water will cause the alcohol to evaporate.

Garlic (Allium sativum)

Garlic (Allium sativum)

Because this plant has been around for millennia, it is difficult to know where to start when discussing garlic. It's one of the oldest-known cultivated herbs. The Egyptians believed that it prevented illness and increased strength and endurance. It is even rumored that the workers who built the pyramids ate garlic to sustain them in their labors.

Greek athletes ate garlic before participating in races, and Greek soldiers ate garlic before battle. When the Romans conquered Gaul, they brought garlic with them. Nowadays garlic, also known as the stinking rose, is believed to help alleviate many ailments. It's also said to symbolize protection and healing. Perhaps that is why, in folklore, it is believed that wearing a garland of garlic will protect you from vampires.

MEDICINAL USES

Garlic's properties include antiseptic, antiviral, diaphoretic, cholagogue, hypotensive, and antispasmodic. It has sulfur-containing compounds, enzymes, B vitamins, minerals, and flavonoids. In its raw form garlic can act on bacteria, viruses, and alimentary parasites. For this reason it can be used as a preventive in many infectious conditions. The volatile oils that give garlic its scent are excreted by the lungs and through the skin.

The best news on garlic seems to be its effect on the cardiovascular system. Studies have suggested that, with regular use, garlic helps reduce blood cholesterol levels and blood pressure. This has helped to make garlic a best-seller in the vitamin and supplement world today. To lower cholesterol, you must eat the equivalent of two cloves a day.

Other positive studies imply that garlic may help AIDS patients by increasing killer-cell activity and possibly inhibiting malignant-cell formation. The downside to all of this news is that garlic can cause heartburn in susceptible people. Additionally, its odor is offensive to some individuals. (If you're concerned about odor, there are deodorized garlic preparations available.)

The best way to take garlic is by eating it. There are many wonderful recipes that include this flavorful bulb—keep in mind that it is most effective when eaten raw. Cutting or crushing the cloves before eating them allows garlic to be more effective, because its active ingredients are released readily into your system. If you are concerned about your breath, chew some fresh parsley after eating garlic.

CAUTIONS FOR GARLIC

Garlic can thin the blood, so avoid using it if you are already taking blood thinners or before surgery. The use of garlic other than in culinary amounts during pregnancy and nursing is not recommended. In addition, excessive topical use of this herb can cause irritation.

GARLICKY HERBAL BROTH

This flavorful, warming broth is packed full of vitamins.

6 minced garlic cloves

1 tablespoon (15 ml) olive oil

2 cups (473 ml) water or vegetable broth

1 teaspoon (5 ml) finely chopped fresh cayenne pepper, or 1/2 teaspoon (2.5 ml) dried powdered cayenne

1 teaspoon (5 ml) finely chopped fresh rosemary, or 1/2 teaspoon (2.5 ml) dried

1/2 teaspoon (2.5 ml) fresh thyme, or 1/4 teaspoon (1.3 ml) dried

A pinch of salt, if the vegetable broth is unsalted

1. In a large saucepan, combine the garlic and olive oil and sauté over high heat briefly, until the garlic starts to change color.

2. Add the broth or water, turn down the heat to medium-low, and simmer for 20 minutes.

3. Add all of the herbs and salt to taste. Simmer for 5 more minutes, then serve. Sip slowly.

Ginger (Zingiber officinale)

Ginger (Zingiber officinale)

In the United States, ginger is commonly thought of as a baking spice. For the last few years, though, the fresh root has also been available in Asian dishes, giving them a warm to hot, distinctively spicy flavor. I have come to enjoy this tropical rhizome so much that I keep it on hand to use and have even started growing it.

Ginger was prominent in Chinese herbal practices circa 3000 B.C., and in India ginger has been widely used in Ayurvedic medicine. The herb was brought to Europe via the trade routes from the Far East, and Spanish conquistadors brought the herb to the New World via Jamaica.

MEDICINAL USES

Nowadays, fresh ginger is becoming more popular in our country. It is rich in volatile oils whose properties include stimulant, antispasmodic, anti-inflammatory, carminative, rubefacient, and diaphoretic. The spicy rhizome also contains powerful antioxidant properties. Ginger's actions on the digestive tract are notable. It works indirectly to increase the availability of dietary nutrients for digestion and metabolism. It promotes the gastric secretions that aid in digestion of food. Ginger is also a gastrointestinal tract stimulant. While it will aid in relieving nausea and indigestion from various causes, it can also reduce the nausea associated with motion sickness; some studies have found ginger to be superior to pharmacological substances in this.

Continued ➤

Ginger is also stimulating to the peripheral circulation, making it a good topically applied treatment for minor muscle aches and pains. It relaxes peripheral blood vessels, bringing blood to the skin's surface and causing a counterirritant. Taken as a tea, ginger can help to alleviate cold and flu discomfort, including sinus congestion. For feverish conditions, it can promote perspiration.

CAUTIONS FOR GINGER

Although culinary use during pregnancy is all right, larger quantities of ginger during pregnancy are not recommended. Avoid excessive intake if you suffer from peptic ulcers. Ginger may raise blood pressure, so avoid it if this is a problem for you. Ginger may increase the activities of blood-thinning drugs.

DUAL-PURPOSE GINGER STIR-FRY

Have some of this recipe to both please your palate and help give you relief from congestion. This can be served as a side dish or over rice for a vegetarian main course. And though this recipe can help kick a cold out the door, you don't have to be congested to enjoy it!

Nonstick cooking spray or 1 teaspoon (5 ml) vegetable oil

6 cups (1.4 l) cabbage cut into 4-inch (10 cm) slices

1 tablespoon (15 ml) fresh ginger, grated

1/4 cup (59 ml) water

A pinch of cayenne

A pinch of salt

1. Spray a saucepan with nonstick cooking spray, or coat the surface with about 1 teaspoon (5 ml) of vegetable oil. Place the pan on your stovetop over high heat; add the cabbage and ginger and sauté in the oil for a couple of minutes, stirring frequently.

2. Pour the water over the cabbage. Stir and cook the cabbage until it is crisp-tender, 10 to 15 minutes.

3. Turn the stovetop heat down to medium-low. Add the cayenne and salt; stir the seasonings into the cabbage. Serve immediately.

Peppermint (Mentha x piperita)

Peppermint appeared as a sterile crossbreed in the late 1600s in England, so any history of the plant starts there. However, the mint cousins, such as spearmint and watermint, from which it derived have been around through the ages. The Egyptian Pharisees paid tithes to the pharaoh with mint; in the early medical record known as Egyptian Ebers Papyrus of 1550 B.C., it was recommended that mint tea be used to alleviate indigestion. In Greece soldiers rubbed their weapons with mint before battle for good luck. The Romans chewed mint after meals, and, as with other herbs that they used, took it with them when they moved, thus spreading mint to other parts of the world.

Peppermint
(Mentha x piperita)

In early Christian times the herb was such a valuable medicine that the Church accepted it as a payment of tithes. Medieval Europeans used it as a strewing herb and rubbed it on their teeth for fresh breath. They also used the herb to relieve toothaches. Colonists in North America grew mint in their gardens, and there it has grown ever since.

Medicinal Uses

Peppermint's useful properties include carminative, antispasmodic, aromatic, diaphoretic, antiseptic, analgesic, and nervine. Peppermint's volatile oil contains menthol, an ingredient that is familiar to us in many products. It is known to relax visceral muscles. Peppermint contains calcium, vitamins A and C, and riboflavin. The aroma encourages alertness and wakefulness.

You can use peppermint infusions, or teas, to relieve a variety of digestive-tract ailments; they stimulate bile production, thereby enhancing digestive activity. They will also help relieve gas and accompanying abdominal pain. The volatile oil acts as a mild anesthetic to the stomach wall, helping decrease nausea and vomiting. Externally, peppermint stimulates cold-perceiving nerves below the surface of the skin. It can relieve itching and be useful for easing achy muscles.

CAUTIONS FOR PEPPERMINT

Although peppermint is a wonderful medicinal herb and is safe for use by almost everyone, there are a couple of cautions:

- Those suffering from anemia should be careful, because large amounts of peppermint tea can inhibit the absorption of iron in severely anemic people and can also be toxic.

- Don't give peppermint tea to babies and small children—the volatile oils can cause them to have a choking sensation.

PEPPERMINT TEA

1 cup (237 ml) boiling water

1 tablespoon (15 ml) fresh chopped peppermint or 1 teaspoon (5 ml) dried

Pour the boiling water over the peppermint. Cover and let steep for 10 to 20 minutes.

PEPPERMINT INHALATION

When suffering from congestion due to a cold and/or a sinus condition, peppermint can be helpful simmered in water as an inhalation.

1 quart (946 ml) water

1/2 cup dried (118 ml) or 1 cup (237 ml) fresh peppermint

Combine the water and peppermint in an enamel or stainless-steel saucepan. Bring to a boil, reduce heat, and allow to simmer, uncovered, on the stovetop; this will release the peppermint aroma into the air. You will enjoy greater benefits if you are in the same room as the mixture.

An alternative way to prepare the inhalation is in a small simmering potpourri pot, which is more portable and can be placed in any room you choose. Do not allow the mixture to boil dry; add more water if needed.

Rosemary (Rosmarinus spp.)

Greek students wore rosemary in garlands on their heads when they were taking exams; they felt that it improved their memory. Medieval households used rosemary-scented water for hand washing. It was believed that rosemary refused to grow in gardens of evil people, an idea that is disconcerting to me, given that there have been some years when I can't keep a single plant alive! In the Middle Ages people carried sprigs of rosemary in their pockets to ward off evil spirits and placed sprigs under their pillows to prevent nightmares.

Rosemary
(Rosmarinus officinalis)

Rosemary has been burned in sick chambers to purify the air, and branches were strewn in law courts to protect those present from jail fever, also known as typhus. Likewise, during the Middle Ages it was believed that the reason rosemary flowers are blue is that the Virgin Mary laid her blue cloak across a rosemary bush when it was in bloom, coloring the flowers. The herb was woven into bridal wreaths as a symbol of fidelity and constancy. Rosemary's natural antioxidant properties, which slow food spoilage, made it appropriate for food preservation in the days before refrigeration.

MEDICINAL USES

Rosemary contains antioxidant, antiviral, carminative, antibacterial, anti-inflammatory, and circulatory stimulant properties. Recent research has shown that rosemary enhances the cells' intake of oxygen, which aids in cerebral function. Rosemary contains calcium, magnesium, phosphorus, sodium, potassium, and vitamins A and C.

STIMULATING ROSEMARY BATH

For a stimulating soak that will relieve a tired, achy body, add a rosemary infusion to your bath or footbath!

1 cup (237 ml) dried rosemary

2 quarts (1.9 l) boiling water

Pour the boiling water over the rosemary. Cover and let steep for 10 minutes, then strain. For a footbath, add the infusion to a basin of warm water. For a full bath, add the infusion to a warm tub.

ROSEMARY-GINGER TEA

Here is something warm and aromatic for you to sip while you lounge around in your bunny slippers, recuperating from the tiring effects of a cold or the flu.

1 cup (237 ml) boiling water

1 tablespoon (15 ml) fresh ginger, grated

1 teaspoon (5 ml) dried rosemary, or 2 teaspoons (10 ml) fresh

Honey (optional)

Pour the boiling water over the ginger and rosemary. Cover the mixture and let steep for 10 to 20 minutes. Strain, add honey to taste, and sip slowly.

CAUTIONS FOR ROSEMARY

Due to its stimulating properties, rosemary should be used as an internal infusion for a maximum of 2 cups a day for no longer than a week at a time. In addition, people with high blood pressure should avoid rosemary in other than culinary uses.

Thyme (Thymus vulgaris)

The ancient Greek physician Hippocrates and his contemporaries prized thyme highly for its medicinal qualities. In Greece a supreme compliment was to say that someone "smelled of thyme." It was burned as incense in ancient Greek temples. In ancient Rome thyme was burned as a deodorizer, and Roman soldiers bathed in it for vigor. The Egyptians used it medicinally, too. The Crusaders brought the seeds home with them, and thyme became a common addition to their families' gardens and households. Early Europeans used the herb for strewing and to make an infusion that combated excessive body lice.

Thyme (Thymus vulgaris)

Thyme's essential oil is strongly antiseptic, and during World War I it was used for that reason. Throughout various periods in history thyme has been used for such diverse complaints as colic, melancholia, sore throat, insomnia, nightmares, hangovers, and alcohol addiction. Thyme symbolizes health, healing, sleep, psychic powers, love, purification, and courage.

MEDICINAL USES

Thyme's properties are carminative, antimicrobial, antispasmodic, expectorant, stimulant, relaxant, and astringent. Research done in Japan shows that thyme works as an antioxidant as well. It contains vitamins A and D, niacin, phosphorus, potassium, calcium, iron, magnesium, and zinc.

Thyme's best medicinal use, in my opinion, is as an adjunct in treating sore throats, colds, and congestion. An infusion, or tea, made from the herb will help soothe a sore throat and act as an expectorant, due to an active constituent found in thyme called thymol. German studies have found thyme to be effective for the treatment of symptoms of bronchitis, coughs, and colds.

Thyme's antimicrobial property makes it a good choice for use in skin care. A cool infusion, or tea, of the leaves and flowers can be used as a facial lotion for blemished skin.

THYME TEA

1 cup (237 ml) boiling water

1 teaspoon (5 ml) dried thyme, or 2 teaspoons (10 ml) fresh

Honey

Pour the boiling water over the thyme. Cover and steep the infusion for 10 to 20 minutes, then strain. Adding honey increases the infusion's effectiveness.

Continued ➔

THYME-INFUSED HONEY

This is a most pleasant way to ingest thyme when you're suffering from a cold and congestion.

1 cup (237 ml) honey

1/2 cup (118 ml) fresh thyme, or 1/4 cup (59 ml) dried

1. Combine the two ingredients in a saucepan and heat gently over low heat for 15 to 20 minutes, making sure the honey does not boil or scorch. Remove from the heat and allow the honey to cool.

2. Strain out the herbs, then bottle the honey and label it.

To use: To relieve colds, coughs, and sore throats, take 1 teaspoon (5 ml) of honey three times a day. You can also add a teaspoon to a cup of regular hot tea and sip slowly.

CAUTIONS

Do not give thyme preparations to children under the age of 3. In addition, avoid all but culinary uses of thyme if you:

- have thyroid problems

- have high blood pressure

- are pregnant

Yarrow (Achillea millefolium)

Yarrow is said to be named for the ancient hero Achilles, who was supposed to have used the herb to treat his wounded soldiers. Yarrow was indeed a popular wound treatment for the ancient Greeks, and continued to be popular into the mid-19th century, when it was used by field doctors in the American Civil War. Native Americans used yarrow to halt bleeding and promote wound healing. It's not known whether European settlers introduced yarrow to the New World or if it is native to North America. Nevertheless, it is quite a useful plant.

Yarrow
(Achillea millefolium)

MEDICINAL USES

Yarrow's properties are diaphoretic, hypotensive, astringent, antiseptic, hemostatic, and anti-inflammatory, and it was traditionally used to treat wounds. To treat a minor cut or scrape that is bleeding, take a clean leaf or two of yarrow, crush it, and apply to the wound. The hemostatic and antiseptic properties should help to stop the bleeding and promote healing. Its diaphoretic property gives yarrow infusions the reputation of being helpful in feverish conditions.

BREATHE-FREE HERBAL INHALER

The aromas from this herbal infusion will aid in clearing your stuffy nose.

2 quarts (1.9 l) water

1/4 cup (59 ml) fresh yarrow, or 2 tablespoons (30 ml) dried

1/4 cup fresh (59 ml) peppermint, or 2 tablespoons (30 ml) dried

1 tablespoon (15 ml) fresh rosemary, or 2 teaspoons (10 ml) dried

1 tablespoon (15 ml) fresh thyme, or 2 teaspoons (10 ml) dried

Place the water in a saucepan on the stove. Add all of the herbs. Simmer, uncovered, over low heat for 30 to 45 minutes. This allows the herbal essences to drift through the house.

Caution: Do not allow the contents to boil dry.

YARROW INFUSION

1 cup (237 ml) boiling water

1 teaspoon (5 ml) dried yarrow, or 2 teaspoons (10 ml) fresh

Pour the boiling water over the yarrow. Cover and let steep for 10 to 20 minutes. Sip slowly. Drink no more than 3 cups (711 ml) of the infusion a day.

CAUTIONS

As with all herbs, moderation is in order. Consider the following precautions:

- Taking too much yarrow over a prolonged period can cause headaches and vertigo.

- Prolonged use of yarrow can interfere with the absorption of iron and other minerals.

- When combined with other herbs, yarrow can intensify their medicinal actions—consult a qualified herbal practitioner before you decide to take it regularly.

- Prolonged use of yarrow can make the skin light-sensitive.

- Yarrow is a member of the Daisy family, so do not use it if you have related allergies.

- Yarrow should not be ingested if you are pregnant.

An Herbalist's Guide to Growing & Using Echinacea

Kathleen Brown
Illustrations by Alison Kolesar, Laura Tedeschi, Nancy Hull, and Randy Mosher

Echinacea's Medicinal Uses

Echinacea is currently one of the trendiest plants in the herbal kingdom. It is one of the five top-selling herbal medicines in North America and accounts for nearly 10 percent of the total sales of herbal supplements.

The good news is that people trying herbs for the first time are likely to have a good experience with echinacea. Taken at the first sign of cold or flu symptoms, especially with nasal congestion present, echinacea's infection-fighting, immune-boosting power is strong and effective medicine. The bad news is that because of echinacea's popularity, people begin using it for everything, regarding it as a cure-all. It is very effective for many things, but not for everything.

Of all botanical immune-system stimulants, echinacea is the most studied and has the best safety record. After hundreds of years of use, no toxicity or severe side effects have been noted. Allergic reactions have been rare and mild, occurring mostly in people with allergies to plants in the Daisy family, like chamomile and ragweed. Although the plant is native to North America, most of the research on echinacea has been done in Germany. Since 1950, more than 400 studies have been conducted, including one study of 200 schoolchildren that showed that those who took echinacea had fewer colds and had fewer days of fever when they did get sick.

Echinacea is not only potent medicine, but it also has a beautiful flower prized in many a flower garden.

Echinacea is potent not only when taken internally but also when incorporated into creams, lotions, and gels in defense against all sorts of external conditions, such as acne, athlete's foot, bites and stings, minor cuts and scrapes, and wrinkles. For treating problems related to a bacterial, fungal, or viral infection, and as a blood purifier in cases of blood poisoning or poisonous spider and snakebites, echinacea is the herb of choice. It also makes an effective cleanser for glands and the lymphatic system, relieves acute inflammatory conditions, and speeds regeneration of new tissue for faster healing of wounds.

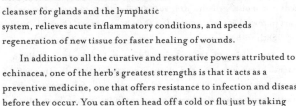

In addition to all the curative and restorative powers attributed to echinacea, one of the herb's greatest strengths is that it acts as a preventive medicine, one that offers resistance to infection and disease before they occur. You can often head off a cold or flu just by taking echinacea—as tea, as a tincture, or in capsules, by itself or in combination with other herbs. So during the winter season when colds and flu are most likely to strike, be sure to have plenty of echinacea on hand.

HOW IT WORKS

Echinacea possesses strong antibiotic, antiseptic, and digestive properties. It stimulates infection-fighting white blood cells, enabling them to dispose of toxins and damaged cells. Some studies suggest that echinacea prevents the formation of hyaluronidase, an enzyme that destroys the natural barrier between healthy tissue and unwanted organisms, such as cold germs. It's thought to act like interferon, the body's own antibacterial compound. Echinacea also stimulates production of alpha-1 and alpha-2 gamma globulins, which ward off viral infections, and the effect may be boosted if you hold the tincture in your mouth before swallowing (it is believed to stimulate the lymph nodes located there). It may have some preventive effect on cancer, as tumor growth is said to be inhibited by the creation of cellular immunity. In addition, echinacea stimulates the growth of healthy new tissue, which is important for wound healing. Its anti-inflammatory action reduces soreness, swelling, and redness.

Echinacea's biochemical constituents include flavonoids, cichoric acid, essential oil, polysaccharides, and echinacoside, a triglycoside of caffeic acid that reacts with the body's cells to facilitate wound healing. It also contains humulene, caryophylene, sesquiterpenes, polyacetylenes, isobutylalkamines, betaine, and inulin. Researchers don't know exactly which constituents, or combination of constituents, are responsible for echinacea's great immune-system-boosting power. To illustrate echinacea's strength, consider that 6 milligrams of one of its components, glycoside, has the same effectiveness as 1 unit of penicillin, making it effective against both staph and strep infections.

NUTRIENTS AND FLAVOR

Echinacea is very high in aluminum, cobalt, silicon, and zinc and contains significant amounts of chromium, iron, manganese, niacin, riboflavin, selenium, and vitamin C. It also contains beta carotene, vitamin E, iodine, copper, sulfur, and potassium.

> ### HERBAL INSIGHT
> Try eating an *E. purpurea* leaf daily as an immune tonic. It's purported to have an "interesting" flavor—one that you might grow to like!

Echinacea tastes mildly sweet at first, then bitter. Really potent echinacea causes a "buzz," or tingling sensation, in your mouth, which is caused by a high concentration of isobutylamides; if it's missing the buzz, either it isn't fresh or it's *E. pallida*, which doesn't have the same concentration.

ATTRIBUTED USES

You will see from this lengthy and varied list that echinacea may, after all, be close to being a "cure-all" herb. The herb has been used to treat:

- Allergies
- Bites and stings
- Blood and food poisoning
- Burns
- Candidiasis
- Colds and flu
- Digestive problems
- Earaches
- Enlargement and weakness of prostate gland
- Gangrene
- General infections
- Glandular infections
- Herpes
- Poison oak and poison ivy
- Psoriasis, boils, and eczema
- Staph infections
- Strep throat and tonsil infections
- Syphilis and gonorrhea
- Mouth and gum infections and toothaches
- Respiratory infections and bronchitis
- Urinary tract infections
- Wounds, especially when infected

CAUTIONS AND CONCERNS

Don't use echinacea if you have any autoimmune disorder, such as tuberculosis, multiple sclerosis, HIV, lupus, or any collagen disease. People who are allergic to other members of the Daisy family, such as ragweed or chamomile, may also be allergic to echinacea.

Continued ➤

Growing Echinacea

Echinacea purpurea, the species most often grown in the garden, has a 1- to 2-inch-high (2.5–5 cm) cone and yellow pollen. Unlike the other species, which have a taproot, *E. purpurea* has a fibrous root system. Native to many states in the eastern United States, *E. purpurea* needs plenty of moisture in the heat of summer.

E. pallida has smaller, narrower leaves, white pollen, and pale purple flowers. Native to the plains, it is found over a broad section of eastern North America. The plants will grow in poorer soils that are not overly moist; it flowers in early June to July and grows quickly and vigorously.

GROWING AT A GLANCE

PLANT CYCLE:

Perennial (Zones 3–9)

SOIL REQUIREMENTS:

Echinacea angustifolia and *E. pallida*, poorer and not overly moist soil; *E. purpurea*, richer soil with regular watering

LIGHT REQUIREMENTS:

Full sun

WATER REQUIREMENTS:

Low to moderate

SPACING REQUIREMENTS:

Set plants 12 inches (30 cm) apart

E. angustifolia has shorter petals, toothless leaves, and less drooping rays. It will grow in less fertile soil and needs minimal water, but it does require excellent drainage. It prefers hot summers and very cold winters and grows primarily in the central to northern plains region.

Both *E. purpurea* and *E. pallida* can grow 2 to 4 feet (60–120 cm) high and up to 3 feet (90 cm) wide, while *E. angustifolia* typically grows only 12 to 18 inches (30–46 cm) high and about 9 inches (23 cm) wide.

With the right soil conditions, all members of this genus are hardy in Zones 3 to 9. The herb prefers full sun but will tolerate light shade, and it grows in almost any kind of soil—rocky, slightly alkaline or acidic soil is acceptable, but raised beds amended with compost, kelp, and rock phosphate provide optimal growing conditions. Be careful not to overwater: Echinacea's native habitat is dry prairies, open woods, and roadsides, and the plant is drought tolerant.

A relatively slow-growing plant, echinacea's flowering period ranges from June through October; it's often the last plant in the garden to go dormant. The flower starts as short, stiff, greenish rays upturned around a dark cone. As the rays elongate and curve downward, they turn colors, ranging from pink and red to purple, and the cone turns a coppery brown. In late summer, the center grows to form a large cone with tiny, yellow flowers in between the larger spikes; the cones remain after the petals drop. Leaves range from 3 to 6 inches (8–15 cm) long and are usually coarsely toothed. This is an excellent plant to situate in the rear of a bed or along a fence or wall—small clusters create a stunning effect.

Cultivated varieties of echinacea include 'Bright Star', which grows 2 to 2 1/2 feet (60–75 cm) high and has rosy red flowers and a maroon center; 'Alba', which has white flowers; 'White Lustre,' which features ivory petals and a bright orange cone; 'Sombrero', which has crimson-purple rays; 'The King', with bright crimson rays; and 'White Swan', a compact variety. A rare English strain, New Colewall, has 6- to 7-inch (15–18 cm) heads with a greenish bronze center.

THE FIVE TOP GROWING TIPS

- If your soil is poor, mix in composted manure before planting, adding lime if necessary to obtain a pH between 5.5 and 7.5.

- Echinacea doesn't compete well with weeds; try to eliminate all weeds before planting, and weed often while it's growing.

- Once the plants are growing, provide moderate water for *E. purpurea* and light water for the other species.

- Echinacea prefers dry feet—if you're in a wet area, grow echinacea in raised beds.

- During cold, dry winters, cover the plants with hay or evergreens to prevent root damage.

The easiest way to get your echinacea off to a good start is to buy plants at a nursery. However, echinacea can also be started from seed or propagated by root cuttings or divisions.

PROPAGATING BY SEED

Echinacea purpurea seeds can be sown directly in the garden in early spring, when light frosts are still possible but the soil is workable. Press the seeds into moist, well-draining soil, spacing them 12 inches (30 cm) apart in rows that are 2 to 2 1/2 feet (60–75 cm) apart. Cover the seeds very lightly with soil.

E. angustifolia and *E. pallida* seeds need exposure to moist and cold in order to break dormancy and sprout. You can sow them in sandy soil in a protected area, such as an open cold frame, in the fall or artificially stratify them in the refrigerator and plant in the spring. To stratify seeds in the spring, 2 months before planting time for *E. pallida* and 3 to 4 months for *E. angustifolia*, plant the seeds in a multiflat or pot filled with a damp mixture of potting soil and sphagnum peat moss, cover with a plastic bag, and let sit in the refrigerator. You can also simply refrigerate the seeds in a resealable plastic bag filled with damp sand or slightly damp sphagnum peat moss. Then plant the seeds in early spring as described above.

Echinacea cultivated from seed will probably not flower in its first year.

PROPAGATING BY DIVISION

Echinacea is easy to grow from divisions. Divisions should be made in spring or late summer in colder regions and in fall or spring in warmer regions.

1. Start by loosening the soil around the perimeter of a mature plant's root system. Then spade under the plant and lift it up. Shake the soil from the roots.

2. Pull the root clump apart, or cut it apart with a sharp knife. Each division should have its own root and stem.

3. Plant each clump in newly fertilized soil and water well. Watch for new growth, a sign that the plants are established.

Harvesting Time

Although echinacea still grows in the wild in many areas, its natural habitat is being developed, destroyed, or overgrazed, and it is being overharvested at an alarming rate. Echinacea is an "at risk" plant on the United Plant Savers primary list, and two species, *E. laevigata* and *E. tennesseensis*, are listed as endangered by the U.S. government. Therefore, please do not harvest echinacea from wild populations—instead, grow your own!

ROOTS

Harvest echinacea roots in the fall, after the plant has gone to seed and preferably after several hard frosts. Plants propagated by division can be harvested as soon as 2 years after planting; those sown from seed need to grow for 3 to 4 years before they'll provide a sizable root crop.

1. Use a sharp knife to make a clean cut from the root, being sure to leave enough rootstock that the plant can continue to grow.

2. Once you've harvested the roots, cut any pieces larger than 1 inch (2.5 cm) in diameter into smaller pieces to avoid mold growth during the drying process. Thoroughly wash the roots, then gently pat them dry.

3. Hang or lay the roots on screens in a well-ventilated area away from direct sunlight. Depending on their size, they should dry in a week to several weeks.

4. When completely dry, store the roots in tightly covered glass jars in a cool, dark place. Be sure to label and date your harvest so you can monitor its freshness. The roots should keep for about a year.

FLOWERING TOPS

For the best quality, wait until echinacea plants are 2 or 3 years old before harvesting the aboveground portions of the plant. The best time to harvest is when the flowers start to open.

1. Using a sharp knife, cut the plants at the point where the first healthy leaves are growing.

2. Lay the tops on a screen or hang them in bundles out of direct light, making sure they aren't piled or tied too thickly.

3. When completely dry—when the leaves crumble to the touch—store the tops in airtight glass containers in a cool, dry place. Be sure to label and date your harvest so you can monitor its freshness—the dried herbs should keep for about a year.

HARVESTING SEEDS

If you haven't harvested the tops, you may harvest the seed in year two or three. The most common method for collecting seeds is to hang the ripe flower heads upside down, enclosed in paper bags. This allows them to release their seeds into the bags when they are ready. This is a simple task, provided that you harvest the spent flower heads at the right time.

1. Watch the flower heads and seeds closely. The seeds are carried in the cone that forms the center of the flower head. Five or 6 weeks after the flowers fade, the cones turn gray, signaling that the seeds are mature.

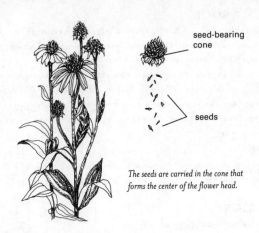

The seeds are carried in the cone that forms the center of the flower head.

seed-bearing cone

seeds

2. Hang the stems in bundles upside down and secure paper bags, with a few small air holes punched through them, around each of the flower heads. The seeds should release themselves into the bags.

3. When the seed heads are dry and the seeds have fallen, separate out the individual seeds and remove any plant debris or chaff—a kitchen strainer may be helpful. Then spread out the seeds on a layer of newspaper for 8 to 12 days.

4. When they seem thoroughly dry, pour the seeds into a glass container. Label, date, and store in the refrigerator, where they'll remain viable for up to a year.

STORAGE TIPS

Here are some simple but very important considerations for storing dried herbs:

- Store the herbs immediately after drying to best preserve the volatile oils, color, texture, and flavor.

- Store in glass containers. Dark glass is especially good because it prevents light from lessening the vitality of the herbs. If using clear glass, store in a dark place, if possible, but at least away from direct light.

- Use airtight containers to keep out dust.

- Label every container carefully, noting the date so you can monitor freshness.

- Be sure that roots are completely dry before putting them into a container; otherwise, they will turn moldy.

- Check the containers regularly to make sure there is no condensation. If there is any moisture, remove the roots and check them for signs of mold or any deterioration. If they seem all right, allow them to dry out further and then restore them to a dry, clean, airtight container.

Purchasing Echinacea and Echinacea Remedies

If you don't want to grow your own echinacea, or if you can't grow it in the quantities you'll need to make herbal medicines, you can buy the herb in several different forms. Here's a look at what's available.

Continued ➔

WHOLE ROOT

It's always best to buy echinacea root in large pieces rather than powdered. Once powdered, the root loses its potency much more quickly. When buying the root, be sure that it has been cultivated—organically!—and not wildcrafted. Always buy the freshest quality available from a reputable source. Echinacea, like all herbs, loses potency when exposed to air, warmth, or moisture, so store the root in airtight, dark containers in a cool, dry place, where it will keep for 1 to 2 years.

When you're ready to use the roots for tea, break them into smaller pieces and decoct. If making capsules, grind the roots in a coffee grinder (one that's used only for grinding herbs, not for coffee).

TINCTURES

Your body absorbs the potent healing properties of herbs most quickly when they're in tincture form. A tincture is like a very strong, concentrated tea. Tinctures are highly portable, convenient, and cost effective. They retain their potency for 4 to 5 years if stored properly in dark bottles. To check your echinacea tincture for potency, put a few drops on your tongue. If your tongue tingles, the tincture is probably acceptable. Tinctures may be more palatable than tea, but some people object to using them because they are usually alcohol based. If you make your own, however, you can use glycerin or apple cider vinegar instead of alcohol.

CAPSULES OR TABLETS

Echinacea capsules and tablets are cost effective and convenient but usually less effective than tinctures or homemade teas. Look for those packaged in glass rather than plastic. If capsules and tablets are available only in plastic packaging, look for opaque rather than clear plastic, because it will prevent exposure to light. Always look at the manufacturer's date, not the expiration date, and buy the most recently packaged product. Avoid products with a manufacturer's date more than a year old. If there's no date on the package, don't buy it, since you have no way of knowing when it was processed or packaged. The shelf life of capsules and tablets is 1 to 2 years.

A Word about Dosages

The key to using echinacea effectively is small, frequent doses, and if treatment is begun at the onset of a cold, flu, or infection, relief will usually arrive within a few days. Echinacea seems to work best in a 10-day regimen. After 10 days, your immune system may become accustomed to large doses of echinacea, and its blood-purifying action lessens. Take large doses for acute conditions only when needed, or try a 10-day-on, 5-day-off cycle. The maintenance or "prevention" dose may be taken for up to 9 months to form a shield of protection.

- **Tinctures:** For acute illness, take 1 to 2 dropperfuls of tincture every 2 hours for 10 days. For prevention of colds and flu (maintenance), take 10 to 15 drops daily.

- **Capsules or tablets:** For acute conditions, take 3 to 4 capsules every 2 hours. For chronic conditions, take 2 capsules two times per day.

- **Tea:** For acute conditions, take 1/2 cup (120 ml) every 2 hours. For chronic conditions, take 1/2 cup (120 ml) three times per day.

- **External use:** Dust skin conditions like boils or eczema directly with the powdered root, or apply tincture to a cotton pad and fix it in place with a bandage. For a wash, mix 1 part echinacea tincture with 3 parts water, apply to affected area, and cover with a gauze bandage; reapply every 2 hours.

TINCTURE FOR CHILDREN

Because children are more sensitive to herbs than adults are, you'll want to talk to your doctor before using echinacea at home. As a general rule, here's what herbalists recommend for children of different ages. Consider the following to be maximum amounts, which can be given two or three times per day.

Age	Maximum Dose
Under 6	10 drops
7 to 10	20 drops
11 to 13	30 drops
14 to 16	1 dropperful

Echinacea Teas

There are two methods for preparing herbal tea: infusion and decoction. An infusion is best for brewing a plant's leaves, flowers, berries, or seeds. These ingredients easily release their essential oils and valuable nutrients when steeped in hot water—and easily lose them when simmered. A decoction is made from roots, barks, and the more woody parts of the plant. Simmering is necessary for these materials to release their valuable properties.

COLD COMFORT TEA

Use fresh herbs, if possible, or good-quality dried herbs to make this tea. It's excellent for speeding recovery from a really bad cold. The yarrow can cause heat flushing, which is good for breaking a fever.

1 part echinacea root

1 part peppermint leaf

1 part catnip leaf

1 part yarrow leaf

1 part lemon balm leaf

Honey and lemon (optional)

Decoct the echinacea root using the directions in Appendix G. Remove from heat and add the remaining herbs. Stir well, cover the pot, and allow to steep another 10 to 20 minutes. Strain; add honey and lemon, if desired. Drink 1 cup (235 ml) every 2 hours.

directions in Appendix G. Remove from heat and add the dandelion leaf and aniseed. Stir well, cover the pot, and allow to steep another 10 to 20 minutes. Strain; add honey and lemon, if desired.

VAGINITIS VANISH

Both antiseptic and antibiotic, this blend helps with vaginal infections and irritation. This is quite bitter as a tea, so mix it with a little fruit juice to sweeten the taste.

1 part echinacea root

1 part Oregon grape root

1 part osha root

1 part crushed garlic

1 part peppermint leaf

1 part usnea lichen

Fruit juice

For tea, decoct the roots using the directions in Appendix G. Remove from heat and add the garlic, peppermint, and usnea. Stir well, cover the pot, and allow to steep another 10 to 20 minutes. Strain; sweeten with fruit juice to taste.

To make a tincture from this formula, follow directions in Appendix G.

VIRUS FIGHTER

The herbs in this formula all have active antiviral properties and are effective against herpes, shingles, flu, warts, and other viral infections. Ginger is very warming and increases circulation. Take this internally or apply externally.

1 part echinacea root

1 part gingerroot

1 part osha root

1 part boneset leaf

1 part chaparral leaf

1 part St.-John's-wort leaf and flower

1 part usnea lichen

Honey and lemon (optional)

Remove from heat and add the remaining herbs. Stir well, cover the pot, and allow to steep another 10 to 20 minutes. Strain; add honey and lemon, if desired.

LUXURY LAX

This cleansing formula soothes the lower intestine and promotes elimination. In addition to adding a sweet, licorice-like taste, anise is good for easing symptoms of indigestion, nausea, and flatulence.

1 part echinacea root

1 part barberry root

1 part dandelion root and leaf

1 part licorice root

1 part marsh mallow root

1 part buckthorn bark

1 part aniseed

For tea, decoct the echinacea root, barberry root, dandelion root, licorice root, marsh mallow root, and buckthorn bark using the

SORE-THROAT SPRAY

When you've got a sore throat, you want some RELIEF! Sucking on a lozenge is good, but it's gone all too quickly. To ease sore-throat pain, spray some of this formula directly in your throat from an atomizer bottle, use it as a gargle, or drink it as tea.

1 part echinacea root

1 part Oregon grape root

1 part licorice root

1 part osha root

1 part myrrh gum

1 part usnea lichen

1/4 part cayenne powder

Remove from heat and add the myrrh, usnea, and cayenne. Stir well, cover the pot, and allow to steep another 10 to 20 minutes. Let

Continued ➡

cool, then strain out the herbs, using cheesecloth to squeeze out all the liquid.

SUPER IMMUNITY

Garlic fights off colds, coughs, and the flu with its strong antiviral and antibacterial action.

2 parts echinacea root, leaves, and flowers

2 parts licorice root

1 part usnea lichen

1/2 part garlic

Follow the directions for making a tincture described in Appendix G. See "A Word about Dosages" on this page 806 for correct use.

BURN RELIEF

A mixture of these tinctures will help relieve the pain and soreness of sunburn and other mild burns.

1 teaspoon (5 ml) calendula tincture

1 teaspoon (5 ml) St.-John's-wort tincture

1 teaspoon (5 ml) Oregon grape root tincture

1/4 cup (60 ml) very cold water

Combine the tinctures in the cold water. Soak a clean cloth in the mixture and apply to the affected area several times a day.

CANKER ANGST

This rinse will help ease the pain of those awful canker sores.

1–2 dropperfuls echinacea tincture

1 glass water

Add the tincture to the water, then swish it around in your mouth and spit. Repeat two or three times per day.

ANTIFUNGAL SALVE

Consider this your solution for any fungal problems.

2 parts chapparal leaf *1 part echinacea root*

2 parts black walnut hulls *1 part Oregon grape root*

1 part myrrh gum *1–2 drops tea tree essential oil*

Combine all ingredients. Follow the directions for making a salve in Appendix G.

MAKING A POULTICE OR PLASTER

To make a poultice, simply moisten herbs with hot water, witch hazel, herbal tea, liniment, or tincture. (In the wild, you can chew the herbs into a pulp.) Apply directly to the affected area.

INSECT BITE POULTICE

Be sure to bring along some green clay and echinacea tincture when you go camping—this recipe is a quick fix for the mosquitoes, flies, bees, and wasps that are sure to find you!

Green or bentonite clay

1 teaspoon (5 ml) echinacea tincture

1 teaspoon (5 ml) water

Mix enough clay with the liquids to make a paste. Dab onto the bite, then cover with gauze or a bandage. Change twice a day.

HAPPY THROAT SYRUP

This soothing syrup in a base of honey or glycerin is excellent for sore throats and laryngitis. You'll be singing in the shower in no time.

1 part echinacea root

1 part coltsfoot leaf

1 part slippery elm bark

Combine all the ingredients. Follow the directions given above for making a syrup. Take 1 teaspoon (5 ml) four to six times per day.

GINGER COLD SYRUP

Ginger is one of the most versatile herbal stimulants. It relieves symptoms of colds, the flu, and coughs, especially when taken at the onset, so it combines very well with echinacea. In addition, ginger increases circulation, warms the body, and boosts energy. Because ginger also relieves nausea, this syrup would be good to take with you when traveling, both for boosting immunity and for easing travel sickness.

1 part gingerroot, grated or chopped

1 part echinacea root

Combine all the ingredients. Follow the directions for making a syrup. Take 1 teaspoon (5 ml) four to six times per day.

Variations: Add wild cherry bark and licorice root for coughs, valerian for insomnia, or elecampane for respiratory infection.

An Herbalist's Guide to Growing & Using Goldenseal

Kathleen Brown

Illustrations by Laura Tedeschi

An Herb in Danger

Goldenseal (*Hydrastis canadensis*) has been used for centuries to treat digestive complaints, allergies, eye irritation, and dozens of other common conditions. Along with echinacea, ginseng, and ginkgo, it's among the most versatile and potent of the medicinal herbs. Rosemary Gladstar, a well-known herbalist and founder of United Plant Savers, says goldenseal is "quite possibly one of the most useful and valuable plants of North America."

And demand for goldenseal has never been higher—so much so that the survival of this impressive plant is in serious jeopardy. Goldenseal is being harvested at a rate that exceeds its ability to grow back. It's becoming increasingly rare and expensive. As demand and prices rise, it's often produced in adulterated forms, either by mixing the powder with other herbs or by grinding up the entire plant and selling it as "root." In either case, the lower potency means people have to take more, and this in turn has led to even heavier harvesting. Unless alternatives are found, the demise of this precious herb may be close at hand.

Growing Goldenseal

Goldenseal is a member of the *Hydrastis* genus in the Ranunculaceae, or Buttercup, family. It can be found growing in the wild in rich, shady woods and damp meadows. Its range extends from southern Canada down through Minnesota to Arkansas, across to Georgia, and back up to Quebec. It's a woodland perennial that does well in Zone 4 and possibly warmer parts of Zone 3.

Goldenseal grows to about 12 inches (30.4 cm) in height, with a spread of 6 to 12 inches (15.2–30.4 cm). The rootstock is yellow, from 1/2 to 3/4 inch (1.3–1.9 cm) thick, about 2 inches (5.1 cm) long, and covered with skinny fibrous rootlets. From the long, knotty root, or rhizome, sprouts a single, hairy stem. The stem has two to five light green, deeply toothed hairy leaves near the top. In late spring, a small, single flower emerges. The flower is short-lived, lasting only a week or

so. The flower is replaced by a soft red berry resembling a raspberry, containing 10 to 30 black seeds.

GROWING AT A GLANCE

PLANT CYCLE:

Perennial (Zones 3–9)

LIGHT REQUIREMENTS:

Shade to partial shade

WATER REQUIREMENTS:

Moderate

SOIL REQUIREMENTS:

Adaptable, but prefers rich soil filled with composting leaves of hardwood trees

SPACING:

Plant 8 to 10 inches (20–25 cm) apart

SOIL REQUIREMENTS

Goldenseal grows naturally in rich, humus-filled soil that has excellent drainage. You'll want to re-create its natural habitat as best you can. Drainage seems to be a critical factor; without good drainage, you could lose the whole crop.

When creating the soil, be sure to add lots of organic matter, such as leaf mold, compost, peat moss, sand, bonemeal, and cottonseed meal. You'll want to create a bed of amended soil extending down as much as 10 inches (25 cm). Use granular fertilizers, especially those containing potassium and phosphorus.

THE BEST LOCATIONS

A good location to plant goldenseal rootlets is under young trees or in beds shaded on top and on the sides with arbors of lattice or lath strips. Goldenseal seems to grow best on shady north slopes, where there is lots of humidity.

PROPAGATION BY SEED

Goldenseal is very difficult to propagate from seed. It requires a huge investment of time and effort, with a spread of five years from seed to harvest. However, while germination is difficult, it can be done.

1. **Harvest the berries.** If you're going to attempt it, it's critical that you harvest the seed-bearing berry as soon as it's ripe, then clean to eliminate the juice and separate the seeds.

2. **Stratify the seeds.** Place the fresh, cleaned seeds in moist sand in small pots or multiflats. Store in a cool, humid location over the summer. In early fall, plant the seeds for overwintering: Either set them in their containers in a cold frame, or sow the seeds in flats filled with rich soil, set outside, and cover with loose burlap.

3. **Plant the seeds.** In the spring, sow the seeds 1/2 to 1 inch (1.3–2.5 cm) deep in rich soil. If the seeds were already sown and overwintered in flats, simply place the flats in a shady area outdoors. Germination can take up to 6 months.

Continued ➔

4. **Transplant the rootlings.** In the fall, plant the tiny roots outdoors in their permanent, woodland locations.

PROPAGATION BY DIVISION

The easiest way to propagate goldenseal is by root divisions. Buds form on the fibrous roots that grow from the main root. These small pieces can be cut from the mother plant and planted separately. One mature plant can produce three to five divisions. While some divisions will not produce any leaf growth the first year, they generally will the second year.

1. **Divide the mother plant.** Divide the roots in either spring or fall. (Before dividing in the fall, however, wait until the mother plant dies back after a frost.) Uproot the mother plant carefully, removing all dirt clumps. Cut some of the shoots, making sure each root stalk has a bud on it, then replant the mother plant. Rootlets can be overwintered in damp sawdust or planted immediately.

2. **Plant the rootlets.** Plant the divisions about 1/2 inch (1.3 cm) deep at 6-inch (15.2) intervals in rows about 6 to 12 inches (15.2–30.4 cm) apart. You'll want to plant the divisions in a moist, shady location. Goldenseal requires 70 to 75 percent shade (possibly less in northern climates), either natural or artificial.

SEASONAL TASKS

In spring or early summer, dress with a complete organic fertilizer, such as kelp, or add compost, then mulch with aged sawdust to hold in moisture. Cut back the aboveground growth in late autumn and mulch with leaves, hay, or chopped legume vines. This will help protect the plants through the colder months, although goldenseal is very hardy and will tolerate temperatures as low as –20°F (–29°C).

Harvesting Time

For the most part, the medicinal potency of goldenseal resides in the rhizomes. These are harvested in the fall or early spring, either by hand or using a root digger. Since it's critically important to protect wild stands of goldenseal, you should refrain from collecting from the natural habitat, a practice called wildcrafting. Harvest only cultivated plants. You'll get 2 pounds (908 g) of root from approximately 32 plants.

1. **Dig up the roots.** To harvest goldenseal you must, unfortunately, dig up the entire plant (which is a contributing factor to goldenseal's increasing scarcity). Dig up the roots in the fall just after the tops die back.

2. **Wash and dry the roots.** Once you've harvested the roots, wash them carefully and set them out in a dry, shady place with plenty of ventilation. Turn them daily for the first few days for even drying. About 70 percent of the root is water, so depending on its size, it will take two to three weeks for each root to dry thoroughly.

3. **Store the roots.** Once dried, place the roots in an airtight glass container and store in a cool, dry location, where they'll keep for several years.

STORAGE TIPS

After investing so much time in cultivating goldenseal, you'll want to be sure the roots stay fresh and retain their potency. Here are a few things you should consider.

- The roots must be completely dry before putting them into a container. Otherwise they'll mold.

- To preserve the volatile oils, color, texture, and flavor, store the roots immediately after drying.

- Label every container, noting the date so you can monitor freshness.

- Check the containers regularly to make sure there is no condensation. If there is any moisture, remove the roots and check them for signs of mold or any deterioration. If they seem all right, allow them to dry out further and then restore them to a dry, clean, airtight container.

WHEN'S THE RIGHT TIME TO HARVEST?

When you've grown goldenseal from seed, you'll want to wait at least five years to harvest the roots. Those grown from divisions or rootlets may be harvested sooner, usually after the third or fourth year (most experts believe the medicinal potency is greatest after the fourth year).

Purchasing Goldenseal

If you happen to live in an area where goldenseal won't grow, or if you don't have the space or the time to garden, the only way to obtain goldenseal is to buy it. There are three simple tests you can perform to make sure that the goldenseal you're buying is of the highest quality:

- **Color.** Whether you're buying it fresh or dried, look for a vivid yellow color. Products with a greenish tinge may contain the relatively inactive leaf powder.

- **Taste.** Goldenseal should have a distinctively bitter taste.

- **Organic cultivation.** In all cases, check the labels. You want to buy goldenseal that has been cultivated, not wildcrafted, and that has been grown using only organic materials.

Goldenseal is widely available in health food stores, and it comes in a variety of forms. Here's what to look for.

WHOLE ROOT

It's always best to buy the whole root or large pieces of root rather than the powdered form. Once goldenseal is powdered, it loses its potency quickly. The roots, however, will retain their medicinal properties for years as long as they've been properly dried. Just be sure you're buying cultivated goldenseal and not wildcrafted herb.

The roots store well, but they'll still lose potency when they're exposed to air, warmth, or moisture, so be sure to put them in airtight bottles and keep them in a dark, cool, dry place.

CAPSULES AND TABLETS

Capsules and tablets are probably the least effective way to take goldenseal, for two good reasons:

- Manufacturers often use the dregs, or poorest-quality powder, when putting goldenseal in capsule or tablet form.

- Capsules and tablets have to dissolve before being assimilated into the body. (And when you're ill, the body's ability to absorb the healing compounds may be further impaired.)

Still, capsules and tablets are convenient and cost-effective, as long as the herb used was of good quality. It's best to buy capsules and tablets that are packaged in glass rather than plastic. If they are packed in plastic, they'll be freshest when the plastic is opaque. As with some foods, herb packages often include an expiration date, as well as the date of manufacture. You always want to buy products that were packaged most recently. Properly packaged goldenseal has a shelf life of up to two years.

Some people combine the convenience of capsules with the natural potency of fresh herbs by making their own! Most health food stores (and some mail-order sources) sell encapsulating trays, along with capsules in various sizes. It's easy to fill the capsules with powdered herbs, although the process is a bit time-consuming.

TINCTURES

The fastest way to get the benefits of goldenseal is to take it in tincture form. Tinctures, which are concentrated liquids, are absorbed very quickly into the bloodstream. They're a good choice because goldenseal roots are extremely bitter—few people can bring themselves to drink the tea, but a dose of tincture is so small that the bitterness is tolerable. In addition, tinctures are convenient, easy to carry, and relatively inexpensive. And they'll retain their potency for four or five years as long as they're stored in a cool, dark location. Plus, you can make your own tinctures, which is less expensive than buying them ready-made.

One drawback of commercial tinctures is that often they aren't standardized. In other words, they may not contain reliable amounts of the medicinal compounds. Also, some herbalists believe that the alcohol used in tinctures makes the medicine less effective because the larger molecules in the herb aren't alcohol-soluble. However, high-quality tinctures do appear to give adequate medicinal benefits. The shelf life of tinctures is four to five years.

Medicinal Uses for Goldenseal

The herbalist Jethro Kloss has called goldenseal "one of the most wonderful remedies in the entire herb kingdom." The range of conditions that can be treated with goldenseal is truly impressive. Like echinacea, goldenseal is often used as a natural antibiotic. It's recommended for colds because herbalists say it helps strengthen mucous membranes and removes excess mucus from the body. As a bitter herb, it enhances digestion. It is also thought to stimulate the organs, especially the liver, kidneys, lungs, and colon.

THE ANTIBIOTIC DEBATE

Despite its popular use as an antibiotic, you have to be careful when using goldenseal to treat infections. Some experts believe that goldenseal, as with any other antibiotic, will destroy beneficial bacteria in the intestines along with the harmful germs causing the infection. They usually recommend using goldenseal for no more than one month, followed by taking probiotics—capsules that contain cultures of healthful bacteria.

However, many herbalists feel this isn't really an issue. Because goldenseal has milder effects than prescription antibiotics, it's unlikely to disrupt the intestines' normal bacterial balance. After all, some of the active ingredients are found in other plants. It's likely, herbalists say, that the beneficial bacteria in the body have evolved to coexist with these compounds.

Another explanation is that goldenseal is not an internal antibiotic. Instead, it increases the flow of mucus, which is naturally antibiotic, in the gut. This could explain why some studies have shown that while high doses of goldenseal can prevent diarrhea, they do not affect populations of malevolent *E. coli*.

MANY USES, FEW FACTS

Because so little research has been done on goldenseal, no one can say for sure how wide-ranging its benefits really are. In some cases, its reputation probably owes more to folklore than to actual improvements in health. In other instances, science may eventually show that "old-time" healers knew what they were doing. Either way, it's interesting to see just how widely goldenseal has been used. Some of the claims include:

- Alleviates eczema
- Relieves liver disorders such as cirrhosis and hepatitis
- Is a remedy for vaginitis and itching
- Acts as a natural antibiotic for urinary tract infections
- Works as an antiseptic mouthwash for gum and mouth problems, such as pyorrhea
- Relieves nasal congestion
- Eases a multitude of skin problems, including sores and ringworm
- Provides antibacterial action in the intestines
- Acts as a general tonic for the female reproductive tract and relieves male discharges
- Stimulates digestion and reduces intestinal inflammation and food sensitivities
- Eases middle ear infections
- Stimulates bile production and secretion

HERBAL CAUTIONS

With herbs no less than drugs, there are many potential side effects. Because so little research has been done on goldenseal, it's difficult to know which side effects are truly cause for concern and which may have been exaggerated. Adding to the confusion is the fact that everyone reacts differently to herbal treatments. People who are sensitive to one or more compounds in a given herb may have a serious reaction, while others can take it without any problems.

Some of these cautions are purely common sense. For example, ingesting very large amounts of goldenseal could be dangerous. Women who are pregnant and people with medical problems such as high blood pressure or hypoglycemia shouldn't take goldenseal (or any other herbal treatment) without first consulting with their primary healthcare practitioner.

Reported side effects from goldenseal include ulcerations of mucous tissue, respiratory failure, convulsions, nausea, and vomiting.

Continued →

These and other side effects sound scary, but it's important to keep things in perspective. Goldenseal and other medicinal herbs have been used for hundreds, even thousands of years. The only reason they've been used so long is that many people have found them to be effective as well as safe.

Still, it's always wise to be cautious. It's a good idea to talk to an experienced herbalist or a physician before treating any condition herbally.

USING IT SAFELY

Unlike drugs, which are identical from one batch to the next, herbs vary widely. Growing conditions, the times harvested, and the parts of the plants that are used all affect the potency. Over the centuries, however, herbalists have developed a pretty good sense of how much goldenseal to use. Here's what they advise.

For Teas

Decoctions of goldenseal root or infusions of the leaf or powder are most often used as a base for other remedies. However, if taking internally, the dose is 1 to 2 teaspoons (5–10 ml) three to six times a day.

For Capsules

Take one or two "00" capsules up to four times a day. During the acute phase of an illness, you can take up to 25 capsules daily for as long as 10 days.

For Tinctures

If you're using tinctured goldenseal for a sinus problem, you can take 10 to 25 drops up to five times a day. For other conditions, follow these guidelines:

- *When the tincture is made from fresh leaf*, take 15 to 30 drops up to four times a day.
- *When the tincture is made from dried leaf*, take 30 to 75 drops up to four times a day.
- *When the tincture is made from dried root*, take 20 to 50 drops up to four times a day.

Tinctures for Children

Because children are more sensitive to herbs than adults are, you'll want to talk to your doctor before using goldenseal at home. As a general rule, here's what herbalists recommend for children of different ages. Consider the following to be maximum amounts, to be given no more than three times a day.

AGE	DOSE (IN DROPS)
Up to 3 months	2
3 to 6 months	3
6 to 9 months	4

AGE	DOSE (IN DROPS)
9 to 12 months	5
12 to 18 months	7
18 to 24 months	8
2 to 3 years	10
3 to 4 years	12
4 to 6 years	15
6 to 9 years	24
9 to 12 years	30
13 to 16 years	1 dropperful

Goldenseal Recipes for Health and Healing

So far we've discussed how to grow and harvest goldenseal, and how the different forms are made and used. Let's focus now on some recipes for using this powerful healing herb. We'll start with formulas for internal use, including some basic teas and tinctures. Then we'll discuss formulas for making salves and poultices.

Note: Unless otherwise indicated, the ingredients are given in "parts." A part can be 1 teaspoon (5 ml) or 1 cup (237 ml), depending on the quantity you wish to make.

HERBAL ALTERNATIVES TO GOLDENSEAL

All of the recipes here call for goldenseal, but if you can't grow your own, can't purchase organically cultivated supplies, or wish not to use it, you can also use the herbal substitutes listed.

THE BASIC INFUSION

The simplest recipe of all is the basic tea, or infusion. It can be taken internally or used as the base for making washes, douches, and compresses.

1 pint (473 ml) water

1 teaspoon (5 ml) goldenseal root powder

Bring the water to a boil, then remove from the heat and add the herb. Let stand until cold.

If using internally, take 1 cup (237 ml) of tea three times a day.

RESPIRATORY RELIEF TINCTURE

This is recommended for treating acute respiratory infections. Take 1/4 teaspoon (0.6 ml) every hour. For treating other types of infections, omit the pleurisy and horseradish roots.

2 parts pleurisy root

1 part goldenseal root

1 part echinacea root

1 part myrrh

1/2 part osha root

1/4 part horseradish root

1/4 part cayenne

See the tincture-making technique in Appendix G.

COLITE-FUL

This is a tincture formula designed to ease symptoms of colitis.

3 parts wild yam

2 parts bayberry

1 part goldenseal root

1 part agrimony

1 part comfrey root

Caution: Comfrey should not be used for more than 4 to 6 weeks at a time and should be avoided by nursing mothers.

DETOXIFY

This is an especially good formula for supporting and strengthening the body during the detox process. Both burdock and dandelion purify the blood and neutralize toxins. In addition, dandelion has diuretic properties, due to its high levels of potassium. Buckthorn bark has a laxative action. Be sure to use dried buckthorn bark rather than fresh, which could cause cramping.

1 part goldenseal root

1 part echinacea root

1 part burdock root

1 part dandelion root or leaf

1 part aniseed

1/2 part buckthorn bark (dried)

1 part yarrow leaf

To make a tea, decoct the roots, aniseed, and buckthorn bark following the instructions in Appendix G. Remove from the heat, add the remaining herbs, and stir well. Cover the pot and steep 10 to 20 minutes.

BOIL POWER

This tea, taken internally, is excellent for treating boils and purifying the blood. Or you can apply it directly to a boil, followed by a sprinkle of goldenseal root powder.

2 parts yellow dock root

2 parts burdock root

1 part Oregon grape root

1/4 part echinacea root

1/4 part goldenseal root

To make a tea, follow the directions for making a decoction in Appendix G.

VAGINITIS VANISH

This blend has both antiseptic and antibiotic properties. It's recommended for treating vaginal infections and irritation. It's quite bitter when used as a tea, so you may want to mix it with a little juice or take it as a tincture. You can also use the tea as an effective douche.

1 part goldenseal root

1 part echinacea root

1 part osha root

1 part garlic bulb, crushed

1 part peppermint leaf

1 part usnea lichen

To make the tea, decoct the goldenseal, echinacea, and osha, following the directions for making a decoction in Appendix G. Remove from the heat, add the garlic, peppermint, and usnea, and stir well. Then cover the pot and steep 10 to 20 minutes.

FOOT POWDERS

Here are two good antifungal powders to keep handy for those irritating outbreaks of athlete's foot. If you're going to put on socks after applying the powders to your feet, be sure that they're dark colored—goldenseal has a propensity to stain clothing.

Recipe #1

1 teaspoon (5 ml) goldenseal root powder

1 tablespoon (15 ml) chaparral powder

1 tablespoon (15 ml) black walnut hulls powder

1 teaspoon tea tree oil

1/4 cup (59 ml) white cosmetic-grade clay or arrowroot powder

Mix all ingredients and store in a shaker bottle. Apply the mixture to your feet once or twice a day, shaking the bottle before each use.

Recipe #2

2 parts clay

1 part black walnut hulls powder

1/4 part goldenseal root powder

1/4 part myrrh powder

1/4 part sandalwood powder

Mix all ingredients and store in a shaker bottle. Apply the mixture to your feet once or twice a day, shaking the bottle before each use.

EYEWASHES

Goldenseal infusions have traditionally been used as eyewashes. Many experts feel it's best to be safe and use only commercial eye-care preparations. However, if you do decide to make your own eyewash, be sure to strain every bit of plant matter from the liquid before using it.

Continued →

Recipe #1

1 teaspoon (5 ml) goldenseal root powder

1 tablespoon (15 ml) comfrey root powder

1 cup (237 ml) boiling water

Make an infusion following the instructions in Appendix G. Strain and cool to room temperature. Wash your eyes with the solution several times a day, using either an eyecup or a dropper. Keep any leftover infusion in the refrigerator, where it will remain potent for two to three weeks.

Recipe #2

1 pint (473 ml) water

1 teaspoon (5 ml) goldenseal root powder

1 teaspoon (5 ml) boric acid

Bring the water to a boil, then add the goldenseal and boric acid. Stir, cover, let cool, and strain. Add 1 teaspoon (5 ml) of this mixture to 1/2 cup (118 ml) water. Wash your eyes with the solution several times a day, using either an eyecup or a dropper. Keep any leftover infusion in the refrigerator, where it will remain potent for two to three weeks.

EYEWASHES WITHOUT GOLDENSEAL

For an effective eyewash treatment that doesn't use the endangered goldenseal, follow the instructions for Recipe #1 but using equal parts Oregon grape root, usnea, and rose hips instead of goldenseal and comfrey.

THE TERRIBLE TOOTH

Anyone who's had a toothache knows how painful it can be, especially when you have to wait a week to see your dentist! Keep these ingredients "at the ready" for emergency toothache relief.

1 part goldenseal root powder

1 part myrrh powder

1 part turmeric powder

1 drop clove oil

Blend the herbs and make into a paste, using a little water. Add the essential oil, then make a poultice using the directions in Appendix G and apply to the affected area.

GUM BALL

This solution is easy to make and is useful for any kind of soreness in the mouth or gums.

1/2 teaspoon (2.5 ml) or 1 capsule goldenseal root powder

1/4 teaspoon (1.3 ml) salt

1 cup (237 ml) warm water

Mix, then use two or three times a day as a disinfectant. The goldenseal won't dissolve completely, so swish it around in your mouth for about a minute, then spit it out.

TAMPON SOAK

For women who suffer from vaginal itching or yeast infections, this formula can make a big difference.

1 cup (237 ml) water

1/2 teaspoon (2.5 ml) goldenseal root powder

1 teaspoon (5 ml) calendula flowers

5 drops tea tree essential oil

Combine the water, goldenseal, and calendula in a saucepan. Bring to a boil, then remove from the heat, cover, and let steep for 30 minutes. Strain, then add the essential oil. Soak a tampon in the liquid, then insert. Remove after 30 to 60 minutes. Repeat as necessary.

Note: When soaking the tampon, leave it in its protective cylinder. Otherwise, it will expand too much to use comfortably.

BLADDER-BUSTER CAPSULES

For women who have frequent bladder infections, these capsules can be very helpful.

1 part goldenseal root powder

1 part myrrh powder

1 part gingerroot powder

1 part marshmallow root powder

Mix the ingredients and put the powder into "00" capsules. Take two capsules every 3 hours during the acute phase.

YEAST RELIEF

Here's a formula for relieving yeast infections.

1 tablespoon (15 ml) goldenseal root powder

2 tablespoons (30 ml) black walnut hull powder

2 tablespoons (30 ml) myrrh powder

1 cup (237 ml) fine white clay

1/2 cup (118 ml) cornstarch

1–2 drops tea tree essential oil

Blend the ingredients with a wire whisk. Put the mix in a jar with a shaker top. Apply externally around the vaginal area. This will help keep the area dry, which will discourage the growth of yeast, fungi, and bacteria. The mixture will last indefinitely as long as it's kept dry.

FAST FIRST AID

You may want to keep goldenseal capsules in your first-aid kit or carry them with you when you go hiking. If you get a small cut, open a capsule and sprinkle the powder directly on the cut. It will help speed healing and prevent infection.

ANTIFUNGAL SALVE

For any fungal infection on the skin, this formula can help.

2 parts chaparral bark

2 part black walnut hulls

1 part goldenseal root

1 part myrrh

1 part echinacea root

1–2 drops tea tree essential oil

PIMPLE SOLUTION

This antibacterial blend helps get rid of pimples fast, and the clay will help draw out infection.

1/2 teaspoon (2.5 ml) goldenseal root powder

1/2 teaspoon (2.5 ml) green or bentonite clay

12 drops tea tree essential oil

12 drops grapefruit seed extract

Mix the ingredients to make a paste. If it's too runny, add more clay; if it's too thick, add 1 or 2 drops more of either liquid. Apply to blemishes at night, then rinse off with warm water in the morning.

GREAT GRAINS

This an excellent mixture for use as a daily cleanser and scrub.

1 cup (237 ml) oatmeal

1/4 cup (59 ml) ground almonds

2 tablespoons (30 ml) lavender flowers

2 tablespoons (30 ml) chamomile flowers

1/4 cup (59 ml) clay

1 teaspoon (5 ml) goldenseal root powder

1 teaspoon (5 ml) slippery elm powder

Grind the oatmeal, almonds, and flowers until the mixture is a fine consistency. Add the clay and powders, then store in a jar with a tight-fitting lid. To use, mix a small amount of the blend with either water or yogurt to make a paste. Scrub your face gently with the mixture, then rinse with warm water.

ADDITIONAL HERBS, GREATER POWER

Goldenseal is often used in combination with other herbs, depending on the condition being treated. For example:

- Goldenseal combined with powdered chaste tree berry (*Vitex agnus-castus*) may help relieve hot flashes and sweats associated with menopause.

- Goldenseal combined with eyebright (*Euphrasia officinalis*) is thought to be good for lowering fever.

- One part goldenseal mixed with 1/4 part myrrh (*Commiphora* spp.) is reputed to ease stomach ulcers and tonsillitis.

- Combined with skullcap (*Scutellaria* spp.) and hops (*Humulus lupulus*), goldenseal acts as a tonic for the spinal nerves.

- Goldenseal combined with skullcap and cayenne (*Capsicum* spp.) is said to strengthen the heart.

- Goldenseal combined with echinacea (*Echinacea angustifolia* and *E. purpurea*) makes an excellent antihistamine.

- For stomach conditions, goldenseal combines well with meadowsweet (*Filipendula ulmaria*) and chamomile (*Matricaria recutita*).

- For ear pain, combine goldenseal with mullein (*Verbascum thapsus*).

- A combination of goldenseal infusion and witch hazel (*Hamamelis virginiana*) makes a good external wash for irritation and itching.

- For infections, try mixing goldenseal with echinacea, cayenne, and myrrh. Or combine goldenseal and garlic (*Allium sativum*).

Herbal Alternatives to Goldenseal

Because wild goldenseal is in serious decline, herbalists have been looking for ways to get the benefits of the herb without threatening the species. Some laboratory studies have shown that the aerial parts of the plant, while less potent than the root, may be used interchangeably. This practice is encouraged to protect wild plant populations.

Most experts believe that goldenseal should be used only when other herbs won't work. As it turns out, there are many herbs that provide the same or similar benefits, and they can be substituted for goldenseal in many healing recipes.

HERBAL ACTION	ALTERNATIVE TO GOLDENSEAL
Respiratory antiseptic	Chaparral (*Larrea* spp.), echinacea (*E. angustifolia* and *E. purpurea*), elecampane (*Inula helenium*), pleurisy (*Asclepius tuberosa*)
Decongestant	Cayenne (*Capsicum annuum*), eucalyptus (*Eucalyptus* spp.), ginger (*Zingiber officinalis*), lobelia (*Lobelia inflata*), yerba mansa (*Anemopsis californica*)
Blood purification	Burdock (*Arctium lappa*), dandelion and liver cleansing (*Taraxacum officinalis*), echinacea (*Echinacea angustifolia* and *E. purpurea*), stinging nettle (*Urtica dioica*), plantain (*Plantago* spp.), red clover (*Trifolium pratense*), sassafras (*Sassafras albidum*), yellow dock (*Rumex crispus*)
Digestive bitter	Yellow gentian root (*Gentiana lutea*), horehound (*Marrubium vulgare*), wormwood (*Artemisia absinthium*)
Topical infections	Barberry (*Berberis* spp.), coptis (*Coptis* spp.), Oregon grape root (*Mahonia* spp.), usnea lichen (*Usnea* spp.)

An Herbalist's Guide to Growing & Using St.-John's-Wort

Kathleen Brown
Illustrations by Laura Tedeschi, Elayne Sears,
and Alison Kolesar

An Herb for All Uses

St.-John's-wort has a history of versatility. It has been, at different times, tossed with salads, used to flavor liqueurs and brandy, and added to bread to improve its texture. Because of the wonderful violet-red color it yields as a dye, weavers use it extensively, although it's reported to dye only silk and wool, not cotton. In craft projects, fresh or dried sprigs enhance the beauty of wreaths and floral arrangements. But despite its many uses over the course of history, most people today recognize St.-John's-wort as a treatment for depression.

Does St.-John's-Wort Cure Depression?

Renowned herbalist Rosemary Gladstar says that St.-John's-wort was "quite possibly the number-one herb for depression and anxiety, the happy herb of the '90s." In one study of 3,000 men and women, 80 percent who used St.-John's-wort felt improved or free of depression; this means that the herb is as effective as other commercial antidepressants but without the side effects. In addition, St.-John's-wort is thought to stop the multiplication of retroviruses, and this may prove helpful in treating AIDS. Because of its antibiotic properties, St.-John's-wort is also being investigated for use as a food preservative.

St.-John's-wort is not the ultimate solution, however. No pill is going to "cure" depression. An antidepressant herb such as St.-John's-wort should be used in conjunction with lifestyle changes, and possibly psychiatric counseling, for more permanent results.

A CHEMICAL BREAKDOWN

It's known that St.-John's-wort helps normalize cortisol secretions. When we're under stress, our cortisol levels rise and lessen our immune response, which leads to depression. However, no one knows exactly how St.-John's-wort really works. Traditionally it was thought that hypericin, one of the herb's chemical constituents, was the primary source of St.-John's-wort's medicinal value, as it seems to protect the brain's "feel-good" chemicals, such as serotonin, and to stimulate secretions of dopamine, the pleasure hormone. Currently, researchers tout hyperforin, another chemical constituent, as the primary active ingredient and more powerful than hypericin.

However, other biochemical constituents may be involved in the herb's therapeutic action. Unlike pharmaceuticals, which typically contain a single synthetic compound, St.-John's-wort contains a number of active compounds, so the herb may have a variety of effects on the nervous and immune systems.

IT'S MORE THAN AN ANTIDEPRESSANT!

As long ago as 1988, studies with AIDS patients revealed St.-John's-wort's clinical potential as a medicinal herb. In recent studies, AIDS patients who were given a tincture of St.-John's-wort reported reduced fever and lymph node swelling, improved appetite, more energy, and better mood.

Despite the media circus about its value as an antidepressant, St.-John's-wort also possesses sedative, astringent, antiviral, antibiotic, anti-inflammatory, antiseptic, analgesic, and diuretic properties. Externally, it's effective when rubbed on painful joints or muscle inflammation, especially when paired with yarrow. It's also helpful in healing wounds, bruises, varicose veins, sprains, and other injuries, including sciatica. Even herpes sores are eased by dabbing a little infusion on the affected areas.

A combination of St.-John's-wort tincture or tea working from the inside and St.-John's-wort oil working from the outside effectively relieves pain. For burns, the herb promotes faster healing and less scarring, especially when lavender essential oil is added. One German study found that St.-John's-wort tincture and salve healed first-degree burns in 48 hours.

Several researchers have cited St.-John's-wort as an effective treatment for bed-wetting, especially when the urinary problems are of a nervous nature. Rubbing the base of the spine with the infused oil or taking 5 to 10 drops of an infusion before going to sleep was recommended.

Some tout St.-John's-wort as a tonic for the liver and gallbladder, while others say the herb affects the nervous system. It does seem to have a gentle, calming effect and to relieve anxiety, tension, and irritability that have persisted long enough to lead to fatigue or depression. In addition, St.-John's-wort is reputed to work well in easing irritability and anxiety during menopausal changes.

Growing St.-John's-Wort

> **GROWING AT A GLANCE**
>
> PLANT CYCLE:
>
> Perennial (Zones 3–8)
>
> SOIL REQUIREMENTS:
>
> Well-draining soil; St.-John's-wort prefers disturbed areas
>
> LIGHT REQUIREMENTS:
>
> Full sun, partial shade
>
> WATER REQUIREMENTS:
>
> Low to moderate
>
> SPACING REQUIREMENTS:
>
> Set plants 8 to 10 inches (20–25 cm) apart

St.-John's-wort prefers to grow in full sun, so first you'll need to pick out a sunny spot. (It will tolerate partial shade but won't flower as profusely.) In the wild St.-John's-wort commonly grows in wastelands, so just about any soil is acceptable—average to poor, acid to alkaline, even limestone. But for best results, amend the soil with plenty of compost to obtain a pH of 6 to 7 before planting.

St.-John's-wort likes well-drained soils but will tolerate some moisture. It is a drought-tolerant plant but does best when watered regularly, because the oil content of the plant increases with moisture. Water your plants once a week for the first year, then every 2 to 3 weeks once they are established.

In nature, St.-John's-wort reproduces from seeds or spreads from underground rhizomes at the base of the stem, so it can be propagated from seeds, from root divisions made in spring or fall, or from spring cuttings. During the first year, the plants grow slowly, and it's best to keep them well weeded so that they have a chance to become established without competition. Mulching in autumn and spring will help cut down on the weeds and protect the soil. In addition, give the plants a good dressing of all-purpose garden or rose fertilizer in early spring. After the plants have established themselves, cut them back slightly every second year to encourage healthy new growth.

STARTING FROM SEEDS

St.-John's-wort is very easily grown from seeds. You can plant seeds in spring or fall; spring-planted seeds need to be stratified for 6 to 8 weeks before planting. Fall-planted seeds will be stratified naturally by the cold and thaw of winter.

To stratify seeds in the spring, simply plant the seeds in a multiflat or pot filled with a damp mixture of potting soil and sphagnum peat moss, cover with a plastic bag, and let sit in the refrigerator. You can also simply refrigerate the seeds in a resealable plastic bag filled with damp sand.

To stratify seeds, plant them in a damp mixture of potting soil and sphagnum peat moss, cover with plastic, and set in the refrigerator for 6 to 8 weeks.

Seeds need some light in order to germinate, so when sowing just barely cover the seeds with a good potting mix. Do not plant deeply, or the seeds will not germinate. Germination usually takes 3 to 4 weeks. At 6 weeks, thin the seedlings as necessary.

Seedlings started indoors will be ready to transplant into the garden at 12 weeks.

If you've started the seeds indoors, the seedlings will be ready to plant at 12 weeks. Transplant them into the garden or field in late spring or early summer, spacing the plants 8 to 10 inches (20–25 cm) apart, with 24 to 30 inches (60–75 cm) between rows.

GROWING FROM CUTTINGS

To grow St.-John's-wort from cuttings, cut nonflowering stems in spring or early summer, when the plants are putting forth their most vigorous growth and you have plenty of new tips to choose from.

1. Select healthy stems and cut each stem just below a set of leaves, about 3 to 5 inches (7.5–12.5 cm) from the top.

2. Remove the lowest leaves and insert the cuttings firmly into moist sand. Cover the cuttings with a glass jar or plastic bags to maintain humidity while they're getting established. Keep the pots indoors or in the shade, away from direct sun.

3. After 4 to 6 weeks, check for roots by gently tugging on the cuttings. If you feel resistance, new roots have formed and the cuttings are ready to transplant.

GROWING FROM DIVISIONS

St.-John's-wort is best propagated by removing leafy, rooted runners in autumn or early spring, when the air temperature is cool and soil moisture is highest. Dividing your plants every few years will not only give you more St.-John's-wort but will also help to keep your plants vigorous and healthy.

1. Start by loosening the soil around the perimeter of the plant's root system. Then spade under the plant and lift it up. Set the clump on the ground.

2. Divide the clump into smaller clumps. Each division should have its own root and stem. Once the shoots are separated, cut back any ragged tops and shorten the stems.

3. Plant each clump in a hole filled with well-rotted compost at approximately the same depth at which the plant was growing before. Water with a diluted solution of organic fertilizer to minimize transplant shock.

Harvesting Time

Contrary to what you might think, cutting leaves and flowers from St.-John's-wort actually benefits the plant, helping it become even more vigorous and abundant. By pinching off dying leaves, you're making room for new, healthy growth. Your plants will thank you for taking such good care of them.

You can think of this pinching off as giving the plant a haircut—but a trim, not a full buzz cut! When gathering, use scissors to get a clean cut rather than picking with your fingers, which could damage branches or pull up the roots. Afterward, you'll be amazed at how quickly the plants will produce new growth.

St.-John's-wort typically doesn't flower until the second year, and this is thought to be its most productive year. Harvest the upper 6 to 12 inches (15–30 cm) of the flowering top when the flowers are just opening. The best time of day to harvest is in the morning, when the plant's oil content is highest.

Although dried leaves and flowers will keep for two years when stored in a sealed container in a cool, dark location, it is best to use St.-John's-wort fresh, because its hypericin dissipates somewhat in the drying process. Other means of preserving the fresh herb include infusing it in oil or incorporating it into other products. Be aware that St.-John's-wort bruises easily and starts to decompose quickly, so whether you're drying it, infusing it, or making products with it, keep the harvested herb cool and process it quickly.

DRYING

To ensure maximum flavor, it's important to process St.-John's-wort as quickly as possible after picking. As you're gathering, be sure to keep the herbs out of strong light to prevent their color and flavor from

Continued →

fading. Once you've gathered them, shake the plants gently to remove dust and insects.

Drying in the oven. To dry herbs quickly, spread them on a mesh rack and place in a slow oven set between 100 and 125°F (38–52°C). Don't set the temperature any higher or the volatile oils in the plants will be destroyed. Leave the oven door open and stand nearby because the leaves will be dried in a few moments.

Air-drying. When air-drying herbs, make sure they are not left in places that could be attacked by insects or rodents. In cold climates, mildew is another factor to consider. The drying area should be dry, well ventilated, and out of direct light. In damp or cold climates, some artificial heat may be necessary to supplement the natural drying process.

You can hang the plants in small bunches to dry—if the bunches are too large, the leaves could turn black or moldy. You can hang air-drying herbs inside paper bags to keep the dust off; just be sure to punch many holes into the bags to let air in and moisture out. St.-John's-wort will also dry very well when spread on screens or trays.

The plant matter is about 75 percent water, so it will dry in 3 to 7 days, depending, of course, on climate. Leaves gathered when the moon is waning tend to dry most rapidly because they retain less sap in their leaves and stems.

STORAGE TIPS

Don't let all your hard work go to waste by improperly storing your dried herbs. Here are some simple but very important considerations:

- Choose the proper container. Glass is best, and dark glass is especially good, since it prevents light from damaging the vitality of the herbs. If you use clear glass, store the container in a dark place, if possible.

- Use airtight containers to keep out dust.

- Be sure the roots are completely dry before putting them into a container; otherwise, they will mold.

- Store herbs immediately after drying to best preserve the volatile oils, color, texture, and flavor.

- Label every container carefully, noting the date so you can monitor freshness.

- Check the containers regularly to make sure there is no condensation. If there is any moisture, remove the roots and check them for signs of mold or deterioration. If they seem all right, allow them to dry further and then restore them to a dry, clean, airtight container.

Purchasing St.-John's-Wort

If you prefer not to grow your own St.-John's-wort, here are some tips for buying various products. It's best to seek products that are clearly labeled MADE FROM ORGANIC MATERIAL.

LEAVES AND FLOWERS

A lot of the St.-John's-wort leaves and flowers that are available in the marketplace are of poor quality, with more stems and twigs than anything of value, so look for the dried yellow flowers. It's always best to buy whole plant matter rather than powdered; once powdered, the herb loses its potency very quickly. Always buy the freshest herb available

from a reputable source. St.-John's-wort, like all herbs, loses potency when exposed to air, warmth, or moisture, so make sure it is stored in airtight, dark bottles in a cool, dry place.

CAPSULES OR TABLETS

Capsules and tablets are probably the least effective form of St.-John's-wort, since they have to pass through your entire digestive system before being assimilated. In addition, powdered herbs are often of the poorest quality, and you have no way of knowing when the plant material was processed.

Still, buying St.-John's-wort in capsules or tablets is convenient and even cost-effective if you can verify the quality. One good way to do that is to make the capsules yourself! At most natural food stores and through some mail-order sources, you can buy both an encapsulating tray and capsules in several sizes, called 0, 00, and 000. Filling the capsules with crushed, dried herb is very simple, though a bit time-consuming.

If you're buying capsules or tablets commercially, look for those that are packaged in glass rather than plastic. If only plastic is available, opaque rather than clear is better because it will prevent exposure to light. Always look at the date of manufacture—*not* the expiration date—and buy the most recently packaged product. Don't buy products with a manufacturer's date that's more than a year old. If the package isn't dated, don't buy it, since you have no way of knowing when it was processed or packaged. The shelf life of capsules and tablets is one to two years.

TINCTURES

A tincture, which is similar to a strong, concentrated tea, is the form of herbal product that is most quickly absorbed by the body. In addition, tinctures are highly portable, convenient, and cost effective; they retain potency for four to five years if stored in a cool, dark location. Another benefit is that you can make your own tinctures for even greater savings; see the instructions in Appendix G.

Tinctures may be more palatable than tea, though some people object to them because they are usually alcohol based. But if you make your own, you can use glycerin or apple cider vinegar instead of alcohol.

DOSAGES

St.-John's-wort is not recommended for continuous internal use lasting more than 6 to 8 months. In cases of chronic and acute depression, St.-John's-wort therapy may be necessary for a longer period of time, but medical supervision is recommended in these cases. In addition, when taking St.-John's-wort on a regular basis, it's a good idea to monitor your own vital signs, energy level, mood, and sleep patterns. If you're taking this herb for extended periods of time, have routine blood studies done, as well.

Most researchers studying the effectiveness of St.-John's-wort for depression have used a dosage of 300 milligrams of herbal extract, three times a day, though some studies show that lower doses can be effective for mild depression.

For homemade preparations, here are the dosages recommended by most herbalists and naturopaths:

- For tinctures, take 1/2 teaspoon (3 ml, or about 20 drops) with water two to three times per day. Remember that St.-John's-wort is not a fast-acting herb; it requires from three to six weeks to take effect.

- For tea, make an infusion following the directions in Appendix G. You'll need to drink 1 or 2 cups (235–475 ml) daily for at least four weeks before you'll see any results.

Use these dosages as general guidelines for all of the tea and tincture recipes in this bulletin unless instructed otherwise.

DON'T MIX MEDICATIONS
Many herbalists discourage the use of St.-John's-wort with other antidepressants, particularly Prozac. No studies have been published on the efficacy of using St.-John's-wort with other antidepressants, but any use of this herb in combination with another medication should be closely monitored by your primary medical practitioner.

A WORD OF CAUTION
While many benefits are associated with St.-John's-wort, there are also some concerns about taking this herb over too long a period of time. Medical supervision is suggested for any long-term use (beyond 8 months). Taking large doses or using St.-John's-wort for extended periods could cause the following:

- Inflammation of mucous membranes and toxic reactions
- Photosensitivity (a sensitivity to sunlight)
- Nausea, insomnia, weakness, and edginess

There has not been enough study to conclusively prove the safety of St.-John's-wort for pregnant women, nursing mothers, and their children. Therefore, I recommend that pregnant and nursing women avoid using St.-John's-wort until more research has been conducted.

Making Your Own Herbal Remedies
Now that you are familiar with St.-John's-wort, you're probably ready to jump right in and start making some of your own medicine. In the following pages you'll find everything you need to know, from basic infusions and decoctions for tea to making your own tinctures, capsules, sprays, oils, salves, lotions, and potions.

LEAVES OR FLOWERS?
Most of the recipes in this bulletin call for St.-John's-wort flowers because much of the available dried plant material is of poor quality—mostly twigs and stems. If you're using dried materials, look for the yellow flowers. However, if you can verify the quality (for example, by using material from your own garden), use the leaves as well as the flowers.

MOOD SWING TEA
This tea is good hot or iced. It is particularly useful for easing the effects of wild mood swings. Teens will find it especially helpful when hormones and moods are running amok.

1 part St.-John's-wort flowers
1 part oatstraw
1 part skullcap leaves
1 part passionflower leaves
1/2 part spearmint leaves
1/10 part lavender flowers (organic)

Make an infusion as directed in Appendix G. Sweeten lightly with honey, if desired. Drink 2 to 4 cups (470–950 ml) daily.

SPIRIT LIFTER
When stress, worry, and anxiety are taking over your life, this tea soothes the most frazzled of nerves and has an excellent tonic effect.

1 part St.-John's-wort flowers
1 part chamomile flowers
1 part hawthorn flowers, leaves, and berries
1 part lemon balm leaves
1 part oatstraw
1 part skullcap leaves
1/8 part lavender flowers
1–2 dropperfuls ginseng tincture

Use all the herbs to make an infusion, following the directions in Appendix G. Add the ginseng tincture to the last few sips of tea. Drink up to 3 cups (700 ml) per day.

PMS PLEASER
Start drinking this tea about a week before menstruation begins. It calms, soothes, tones, and nourishes the nervous system and helps ease the most common symptoms of PMS, such as moodiness and irritability.

1 part St.-John's-wort flowers
1 part lemon balm leaves
1 part lemon verbena leaves
1 part nettle leaves
1 part oatstraw
1 part passionflower leaves

Make an infusion following the directions in Appendix G. Drink up to 2 cups per day as needed.

WITHDRAWAL WHEREWITHAL
For those of you in the throes of cigarette withdrawal, this tea will ease your cravings for tobacco. Oatstraw is both nourishing and soothing

Continued →

and works well, when combined with St.-John's-wort, to support the entire body during this process.

2 parts oatstraw
1 part St.-John's-wort flowers

Make an infusion following the directions in Appendix G. Drink up to 3 cups per day as needed.

GOOD NIGHT

For all the days when you're overworked, overstressed, and overly tired and can't get to sleep despite the fact that you're exhausted, this tea is a gentle way to relax the nerves and ensure a good night's rest.

1 part St.-John's-wort flowers
1 part catnip leaves
1 part lemon balm leaves
1 part linden blossoms
1 part oatstraw
1 part passionflower leaves

Make an infusion following the directions in Appendix G. Drink 1 cup (235 ml) and you'll be off in dreamland by the last sip!

SORE MUSCLE AND BRUISE SPRAY

This is a versatile recipe. You can use the herbs to make an infusion and store it in an atomizer bottle for use as a spray, or you can infuse the herbs in oil to make a salve. The arnica and calendula serve to enhance the healing power of St.-John's-wort, for they both are useful in soothing skin irritations of all types.

1 part St.-John's-wort flowers
1 part arnica flowers
1 part calendula flowers

To make a spray, infuse the herbs using the technique on page 1030. Allow to cool, then strain out the herbs. Spoon the spent herbs into the center of a piece of cheesecloth; fold the cloth over the herbs and squeeze tightly to extract every last drop of the precious liquid. Pour the infused liquid into an atomizer bottle and store in the

refrigerator, where it will keep for up to 10 days. Spritz onto sore muscles and bruises as necessary.

To make a salve using these ingredients, see page 1029.

SPRAIN PAIN RELIEF

This is a nice massage oil for soothing strains, sprains, and pains of all kinds. See page 791 for instructions for making an infused oil.

1/2 cup (120 ml) arnica infused oil
1/2 cup (120 ml) St.-John's-wort infused oil
1/2 cup (120 ml) valerian root infused oil
3–5 drops tea tree essential oil
3–5 drops wintergreen essential oil
Contents of a vitamin E capsule

Combine the infused oils of arnica, St.-John's-wort, and valerian root. Add a few drops of tea tree and wintergreen essential oils and vitamin E oil. Stir well. Store in the refrigerator, where the oil will keep for up to 6 months. Apply as needed.

OIL OF O YEA!

This oil provides quick, soothing relief for the pain of varicose veins and hemorrhoids.

1 ounce (30 ml) St.-John's-wort infused oil (see page 791)
8 drops chamomile essential oil
8 drops palma rosa essential oil
8 drops cypress essential oil

Combine the St.-John's-wort oil with the chamomile, palma rosa, and cypress essential oils. Store in the refrigerator, where the oil will keep for up to 6 months. Apply as needed.

MONTHLY OIL CHANGE

To ease the severe cramping and bloating that accompany menstruation, try this wonderfully soothing oil massage.

1 ounce (30 ml) St.-John's-wort infused oil (see page 791)
8 drops lavender essential oil
8 drops marjoram essential oil
8 drops chamomile essential oil

Combine all the ingredients. Store in the refrigerator, where the oil will keep for 6 months. Rub this soothing oil on the lower abdomen and lower back.

VAPOR DECONGESTANT SALVE

A close herbal relative to Vick's VapoRub, this blend may be used as a rub, placed in the vaporizer, or smeared on a tissue and inhaled as a decongestant.

1 part St.-John's-wort flowers

1 part camphor leaves

1 part cloves, whole or powdered

1 part lavender flowers

1 part mint leaves

1 part peppermint leaves

1 part wintergreen leaves

BABY BOTTOM BOON

In addition to providing relief for baby's diaper rash, this salve helps heal cuts, scrapes, rashes, and wounds of all sorts.

1 part St.-John's-wort flowers

1 part comfrey leaves

1 part comfrey root

1 part calendula flowers

An Herbalist's Guide to Growing & Using Violets

Kathleen Brown
Illustrations by Laura Tedeschi, Brigita Fuhrmann, Louise Riotte, and Alison Kolesar

Introduction

Few flowers inspire as much rhapsodic praise as violets. Beloved for both their beauty and their sweet and gentle fragrance in the garden, they've also been used for centuries in cooking and as an ingredient in an eclectic range of products—from soaps and perfumes to medicinal home remedies. It's no wonder that AnneBelle Rice of Long Beach, California, treasurer of the International Violet Society, describes herself as being "passionate" about violets.

In today's commercial products, the natural fragrance of violet has been largely replaced with synthetic scents. Among home gardeners and crafters, however, violets have never lost their popularity. The flowers are often used as garden ornamentals. As the herbalist Maurice Messegue poetically put it, violets "show up like amethysts in the hedgerows." In addition, for centuries people have used the fresh flowers to make delicately fragrant potpourris. And because the dried flowers retain their beautiful colors (if not their fragrance), they've traditionally been used for making decorative bookmarks.

The violet is also popular among creative cooks, who use the edible flowers—often in a crystallized form—on cakes, puddings, ice cream, and candy. The flowers, fresh or candied, are also used as a colorful and peppery-tasting garnish for salads and main meals.

WHICH VIOLETS HAVE MEDICINAL PROPERTIES?

Viola odorata (sweet violet) and *V. tricolor* (Johnny-jump-up) are the two species most commonly used in herbal medicine. For the most part, it doesn't matter whether you use *V. odorata* or *V. tricolor* for healing—they're nearly interchangeable. There are some exceptions, however:

- *V. odorata* is considered a better expectorant than *V. tricolor*.
- *V. odorata* is recommended for chronic bronchial conditions.
- *V. odorata* is said to have more pronounced effects against tumors in the lungs, throat, breast, stomach, and intestines.

Growing Violets

The violet genus (*Viola*) is one of the more than 20 genera of the family Violaceae. There are more than 500 species of violets, and many more varieties. Most species of violets are native to the Northern Hemisphere, and nearly 20 percent are indigenous to the United States.

Violets are easy to recognize by their little flowery "faces" and leaves, which unroll from the base as they mature. The lobes stand more or less erect while remaining inwardly curled. The lowest of the petals has a spur, which contains the sweet perfume and nectar.

One of the most popular violets, renowned both for its aromatic beauty and its potent healing properties, is the sweet violet (*Viola odorata*). This rhizomatous perennial has small, heart-shaped, green leaves. It grows to a height of 4 to 6 inches (10–15 cm) and has a spread of 6 to 12 inches (15–30 cm). The sweet violet blossom has three petals on its upper side and two below. The 1/2-inch (13 mm) or larger flowers range

---

GROWING AT A GLANCE

PLANT CYCLE:

Annual or perennial, depending on species

SOIL REQUIREMENTS:

Will tolerate most conditions but thrive in deep, rich, moist soil

LIGHT REQUIREMENTS:

Shade or semishade

WATER REQUIREMENTS:

Most species prefer moist soil

SPACING REQUIREMENTS:

6 to 12 inches (15–30 cm)

Continued ➔

in color from white and pink to pale lavender, rose, and blue-purple. Sweet violets produce a rosette of foliage from which downy runners emerge and grow along the ground. They create a springtime carpet of lovely, sweet-smelling flowers, whether in the garden or growing wild. A clump of sweet violets can live between 8 and 14 years.

In the wild, clumps of violets grow in rich soil in shady, moist locations.

CARE AND MAINTENANCE OF MEDICINAL VIOLETS

In general, *V. odorata* (sweet violet) and *V. tricolor* (Johnny-jump-up) need very little care. They're hardy from Zones 4 through 8 and do best in shady or semishady spots. They will tolerate some sun as long as the temperatures are mild. They tolerate almost any soil but thrive in deep, moist, humus-rich soil with a pH of 5.5 to 7.0.

When you're planting sweet violets and Johnny-jump-ups, dig in plenty of organic matter, such as leaf mold and compost. These are deep-rooted plants, but the soil should be kept moist, especially in dry weather. If you have light or gravelly soil, add extra compost. Once or twice a summer, fertilize the plants with a liquid organic fertilizer, such as a seaweed or fish emulsion.

Violets spread prolifically by runners. Be sure to give them room to spread, or be prepared to divide them frequently. Under ideal growing conditions, violets may become invasive—although it's hard to imagine having too much of their fragrance and flowers!

When transplanting violets from the wild, try to duplicate their natural growing conditions as closely as possible. For example, if the plants were growing in a shady, moist area, try to locate them in a similar spot in your garden. It's generally a good idea to plant violets with other plants that enjoy similar growing conditions. These include angelica, comfrey, foxglove, horsetail, lady's-mantle, penny-royal, sorrel, sweet flag, sweet woodruff, and valerian.

PROPAGATION BY SEEDS

Violet seeds germinate more uniformly and vigorously if they've first been stratified, or subjected to a cold treatment. You can sow them in sandy soil in a protected area, such as an open cold frame, in fall or artificially stratify them in the refrigerator and plant in spring. To stratify in the fall, plant the seeds in a tray containing soil-based compost. Water, then cover the tray with a sheet of glass or plastic. Put the tray in a corner of the garden and cover with mulch or set it inside a cold frame. In the spring, transplant them to the spot you've picked out.

To stratify in the spring, 6 to 8 weeks prior to planting, set the seeds in a multiflat or pot filled with a damp mixture of potting soil and sphagnum peat moss, cover with a plastic bag, and let sit in the refrigerator. You can also simply refrigerate the seeds in a resealable plastic bag filled with damp sand or slightly damp sphagnum peat moss.

To stratify seeds in the spring, sow them in a multiflat, cover with plastic, and set in the refrigerator for several weeks.

In warmer regions, sow seeds outdoors in early spring, covering them with just enough soil to eliminate light. In colder areas, start the seeds indoors in trays or multiflats 10 to 12 weeks before transplanting outdoors. Place them in a dark closet or cover the trays with an opaque material, such as aluminum foil, until germination takes place. Then remove the cover. Harden off the seedlings and then transplant outside, up to a month before the last frost or in late autumn, for fresh color until frost. Seeds take 1 to 3 weeks to germinate. Space or thin the plants so that they are growing 6 to 12 inches (15–30 cm) apart.

When grown from seeds, violets may not flower until their second year.

VIOLETS THROUGH THE SEASONS

Here's an annual calendar of the basic maintenance that your medicinal violets will require:

· In spring. Sow seeds and put rooted runners into pots or replant them in the garden. You should also divide established plants. Cut back plants after their first bloom to encourage a second flowering.

· In summer. Deadhead the flowers to prolong the season. Renew mulch to keep plants cool.

· In autumn. Sow seeds for spring flowers.

· In winter. Put on a light, even mulch of well-rotted manure or compost.

By giving your violets just a little attention every season, you'll enjoy them for many years to come.

After they've been hardened off, seedlings started indoors can be transplanted to the garden.

PROPAGATION BY RUNNERS

Many species of violets, including sweet violets and Johnny-jump-ups, produce runners—long creeping stems that root at various places along their length. Propagating violets from runners is very easy and can be done in either autumn or spring. In northern climates where winter comes early, however, it's best to propagate violets by runners in spring.

When you're taking runners in fall, gently remove them from the parent plant. Plant them in cell trays with a bark-and-peat soil. Their root systems will develop over the next few weeks.

When propagating violets from runners in spring, plant them directly into the ground, making sure that the base of each crown (the point from where the leaves rise and the roots form) is flush with the soil. It's a good idea to plant three crowns together for a better show and as insurance against loss.

PROPAGATION BY DIVISIONS

Violets bloom better when they're divided every year. The best time to divide is early spring, when the violets are just beginning their fresh burst of growth. A division that's made in spring will usually become full sized in one season.

1. Start by loosening the soil around the perimeter of the plant's root system. Then spade under the plant and lift it up. Set the clump on the ground.

2. Divide the plant into smaller clumps. Each division should have its own root, stem, and leaves.

3. Plant each clump in a hole or pot filled with well-rotted compost at approximately the same depth at which the plant was growing before. Water with a diluted solution of organic fertilizer to minimize transplant shock, and continue to water well until the plants are established.

You can also divide violets in summer, but this requires more careful handling. Provide a slow, deep watering before dividing the plants. Divide them early in the day or in the evening so the sun won't stress them. Keep as much soil around the roots as possible, and plant the divisions immediately. If you can't plant right away, wrap them in damp newspaper and place in plastic bags for moisture retention.

Harvesting Time

As always, it's better to harvest plants from your own garden than from the wild. However, if you decide to "wildcraft" violet leaves, it's important to practice ethical wildcrafting. Harvest only a few leaves from each plant, and be sure to clip plants above the ground so as not to disturb the roots.

When harvesting violets for cooking, gather blossoms and young, tender, bright green leaves. Wash them thoroughly to remove dirt, then snip the leaves into 1/4-inch (6 mm) shreds with kitchen shears.

FLOWERS

When they are fully open, pick sweet violet flowers early in the day. Keep the stems in water until you're ready to use them. A tiny container of cut flowers will fill a room with fragrance. Don't think that you're harming the plants by harvesting their flowers: The more you pick, the more the plant produces.

Dry the flowers in the same manner in which you dry leaves. However, if you're going to be drying the flowers, keep them away from light as much as possible because exposure to light will cause them to give up their scents along with their colors.

ROOTS

The roots contain most of the active ingredients that make violets such a popular herbal remedy. These compounds will be most active when you dig up violets in autumn.

1. Dig up the plants. Using a sharp knife, snip the roots from the stems. (Save the leaves and flowers for drying because they contain many of the same healing properties as the roots.)

2. Once you've harvested the roots, cut any pieces larger than 1 inch (2.5 cm) in diameter into smaller pieces to avoid mold growth during the drying process. Thoroughly wash the roots, then pat dry.

3. Hang or lay the roots on screens in a well-ventilated area away from direct sunlight. Depending on their size, the roots should dry in a week to several weeks.

4. When completely dry, store the roots in tightly covered glass jars in a cool, dark place. Be sure to label and date your harvest so you can monitor its freshness. The roots should keep for about a year.

LEAVES

Leaves from violet plants contain many of the same healing properties as the roots, although in lesser amounts. They should be harvested in summer.

1. With a sharp knife, clip the leaves from the stems of the plants.

2. Lay the leaves on screens and let them dry for about seven days, turning them regularly so they don't mat and mold.

3. Once they are dry, place the leaves in an airtight glass container and store in a cool, dry location, where they'll keep for up to a year.

STORAGE TIPS

Dried violet leaves, roots, and flowers will store well, but you must take a few precautions in order to preserve their potency:

- Roots must be completely dry before they're stored; otherwise, mold will form.

- Store dried roots, leaves, and flowers in airtight glass containers. Dark glass is especially good because it prevents light from fading the herbs and reducing their medicinal potency. If you do use clear glass, be sure to put the jars in a dark place, or at least out of direct light.

- Store roots, leaves, and flowers immediately after drying. This will help preserve their volatile oils, color, texture, and flavor.

- Label the containers carefully, noting the date they were stored. This will allow you to monitor freshness.

- Check the containers regularly to make sure there is no condensation. If there is any moisture, remove the roots and check them for signs of mold or any deterioration. If they seem all right, allow them to dry out further and then restore them to a dry, clean, airtight container.

Continued →

Are Violets Really Medicine?

Violets have a long history of healing. In ancient times, Hippocrates classified the violet as a "moist" plant, best used for treating liver disorders as well as bad tempers. As seventeenth-century herbalist Nicholas Culpeper put it, "All the violets are cold and moist while they are fresh and green, and are used to cool any heat or distemperature of the body." Culpeper himself recommended using violet remedies for treating a variety of eye and skin disorders, as well as for constipation and congestion. As far back as the 16th century, the English used syrups made from violets as mild laxatives for children. Adults took violet remedies for epilepsy, pleurisy, and jaundice.

Many of the traditional medicinal powers of violets have undoubtedly been exaggerated, and a long history of folklore use isn't the same as scientific evidence. However, scientists today have found that violets—the flowers as well as the roots and leaves—do contain a variety of healing compounds.

Research has shown, for example, that *Viola odorata* contains, among other things, phenolic glycosides, saponins, flavonoids, alkaloids, tannins, and mucilage. These compounds act in a variety of ways to promote healing. For example:

- The flavonoids act as diuretics, which could be helpful for people with elevated blood pressure.

- The alkaloids may affect blood pressure because they have vasodilating effects—that is, they cause the blood vessels to relax, allowing blood to flow more easily.

- The saponins and mucilage act as soothing expectorants, which can help relieve harsh, irritating coughs and other bronchial problems.

- Violets contain salicylic acid, a painkilling and anti-inflammatory compound that's similar to the active ingredient in aspirin. This might be helpful for people who are trying to reduce the discomfort of arthritis or other joint problems.

- According to herbalist and plant expert James A. Duke, Ph.D., violet flowers contain significant amounts of rutin, a compound that seems to significantly strengthen the capillaries. For people with inflammation, this means less "leakage" from the blood vessels and less swelling and pain.

- Finally, violets are rich in the antioxidant compounds beta carotene and ascorbic acid (vitamin C). A 1/2-cup (140 ml) serving of violet leaves provides as much vitamin C as four average-sized oranges and more than the USDA Recommended Daily Value for vitamin A (beta carotene is converted to vitamin A in the body).

In Germany, an expert panel called Commission E, which judges the safety and effectiveness of herbal medicines, has approved violet tea as a remedy for some skin problems. And herbalists around the world have found that violets are, in fact, helpful for treating a wide variety of health problems.

A FRAGRANT MEDICINE CHEST

Despite the dearth of scientific evidence for their medicinal effects, violets are very widely used as healing herbs. It's interesting to see just how many conditions they've been used for—not only in the past, but today. According to herbalists, violets may:

- Detoxify the body
- Eliminate lymphatic congestion
- Relieve eczema and other chronic skin problems
- Regulate immunity
- Reduce inflammation
- Ease constipation
- Relieve itching
- Work as a mouthwash
- Strengthen blood vessels
- Improve the functioning of the urinary system
- Relieve incontinence
- Ease the discomfort of menopause
- Relieve colds and flu
- Reduce fatigue and stress
- Lower blood pressure
- Promote healing of wounds

CAUTIONS AND CONCERNS

It's important to remember that violets are commonly used both as a laxative and to induce vomiting. Therefore, whatever the condition being treated, you need to be aware that violets may have some uncomfortable side effects.

Professional singers may have a unique issue to contend with: The essential oils in fresh violets and in violet-based perfumes, in some cases, cause the vocal cords to swell. You may not want to give a violet bouquet to your favorite singer before a performance!

> **CAUTION**
> Keep in mind that African violets are not related to *Viola* spp., and they are not edible. Do not substitute African violets for violets in any recipe!

The main danger isn't so much from the violets themselves as it is from accidentally picking the wrong plant when harvesting. Unless you're an experienced wildcrafter, it's best to harvest violets only when the plants are in flower. Otherwise, the heart-shaped leaves may be confused with those of other plants—which may be toxic.

Violet Recipes

Now it's time to take a look at some of the ways to prepare this wonderfully versatile herb. In the following pages, you'll find recipes for violet teas and tinctures, violet garnishes for salads, violet vinegar, and even violet mousse. Plus, there's even a recipe for crystallizing violet—a natural way to get extra vitamin C!

VIOLET TEA

Most teas have a dull, brackish appearance, but not this one. Unlike most flowers, violets readily give up their colors when they're steeped in hot water, making violet tea very beautiful to look at. Herbalists recommend violet tea for sore throats because it acts as a mild sedative and has a slight anesthetizing effect and because mucilage from the flowers coats the throat and relieves irritation. Violet tea can also be used as a gargle, a mouthwash for sore gums, and a wash for rashes.

1 handful violet leaves

1 cup water

Follow the instructions for making an infusion in Appendix G. Drink 1/2 cup (120 ml) every 2 to 3 hours.

MENOPAUSE FORMULA

This herbal blend will help support and balance the body's hormones. It's good for hot flashes and other types of menopausal discomfort and also seems to boost energy.

1 part dandelion root

1 part dong quai root

1 part fenugreek seeds

1 part wild yam root

1 part alfalfa leaves

1 part chickweed leaves

1 part horsetail

1 part motherwort leaves

1 part nettle leaves

1 part red clover blossoms

1 part red raspberry leaves

1 part violet leaves

Decoct the dandelion, dong quai, fenugreek, and wild yam, following the instructions given in Appendix G. Then add the remaining herbs and steep, covered, for 15 to 20 minutes. You can also use this remedy in tincture form; see the instructions in Appendix G.

SPRING FLING TEA

This is a light, refreshing tea. Many people use it as a palate-cleansing follow-up to the heartier "spring cleansing" teas. To maximize the fresh, lively taste, it's best to use fresh herbs rather than dried.

2 parts violet leaves and flowers

2 parts sweet cicely leaves

1 part nettle leaves

1 part raspberry leaves

1 part mint leaves

Mix 10 to 12 tablespoons (150–180 ml) of fresh herb, or 5 to 6 tablespoons (75–90 ml) of dried, in 2 to 3 cups (470–700 ml) of cold water and let sit for several hours. Drink warm or cool.

Variation: When you're in a hurry, mix the herb in the water, cover, and slowly heat until almost boiling. Then remove from heat and let steep, covered, for 5 to 10 minutes before drinking.

> **QUICK TIP**
> Tinctures contain such concentrated essences of the plant that they often taste very bitter. To make them more palatable, mix the dose with a small amount of hot water, tea, or juice, then drink.

DECREASE CYSTS

This formula, best used as a tincture, improves lymphatic drainage, which can help prevent cysts from forming in breast tissue. It also helps support and balance the body's glands.

2 parts calendula flowers

2 parts violet leaves

2 parts vitex berries

1 part cleavers leaves

1 part dong quai root

1 part astragalus root

Take 25 to 50 drops of tincture three times a day for 2 to 3 weeks.

> **VIOLET EYEWASH**
> If you'd like to use violet for soothing sore eyes, make a violet infusion following the instructions in Appendix G. Let the liquid cool to room temperature, then use it to flush and bathe the eyes. Refrigerate any leftovers and use within a week.
>
> Some herbalists, incidentally, believe that eating violet petals and leaves will improve vision.

BLADDER RELIEF

Nearly every woman will eventually have to deal with a painful bladder infection or cystitis attack. This recipe will provide quick relief.

1 part juniper berries, crushed

1 part bearberry (uva ursi) leaves

1 part violet leaves

1 part goldenrod leaves

Make an infusion following the instructions in Appendix G. Drink 1 cup (235 ml) six times a day during the acute phase of cystitis.

MIGRAINE TEA

Many healers believe that a plant's appearance and habits reflect its healing abilities. Sweet violet hides from the sun and loves shade—just as many people do when a migraine is coming on! Plus, this tea has the advantage of working very quickly.

Rosemary is an essential ingredient in this recipe because it dilates the blood vessels, promoting blood flow.

6 parts rosemary leaves

4 parts violet leaves

4 parts peppermint leaves

4 parts lemon balm leaves

3 parts feverfew leaves

1/2 part violet flowers

Make an infusion following the instructions in Appendix G. Drink 1 cup (237 ml) a day, or as needed to relieve migraines.

VIOLET VINEGAR

Herbal vinegars are all the rage these days, and violet vinegar is especially flavorful. Use it as a base for salad dressing, drizzle a few

Continued ➨

drops over fruit, or splash it on your face as an after-cleansing aromatic toner.

3 ounces (84 g) violet flowers

1 quart (950 ml) high-quality white wine vinegar

Combine the flowers and the vinegar. Cover and let sit for several weeks in a warm place, shaking daily. Strain the herb using cheesecloth, then bottle. Store in a cool, dark location, where the vinegar will keep for up to 2 years.

CRYSTALLIZED VIOLETS

This is a great way to get more vitamin C, and it's fun, too!

10–20 violet flowers

Powdered egg-white mix

Fine castor sugar

1. Gently wash the violet flowers, then lay on paper towels to dry.

2. Prepare the egg white according to the package directions so that you have an amount equal to about 1 egg white, beaten.

3. Using a fine brush, coat each flower with the egg white. Dust with fine castor sugar. Snip the stems and set aside in a warm place (but not in direct sunlight) until dry, usually about 24 hours.

4. Store the violets in a sealed jar between layers of paper. Keep the jar in a cool, dark location.

VIOLET MOUSSE

This delicate dessert is perfect after a big meal. It refreshes the palate while providing a little extra shot of vitamins and minerals.

1 teaspoon (5 ml) gelatin or agar

1/4 cup (60 ml) water

Powdered egg white mix

2 cups (470 ml) milk

2 tablespoons (30 ml) sugar

1 cup (235 ml) whipping cream

1/2 teaspoon (3 ml) violet tincture

Violet flowers

1. In a saucepan, combine the gelatin and water. Bring to a boil and cook for 2 minutes. Remove from the heat.

2. Prepare the egg white according to the package directions, making enough to equal about three egg whites, stiffly beaten.

3. When the gelatin mixture has cooled slightly, stir in the milk. Fold in the stiffly beaten egg whites and sugar, stirring until thick. Mix in the cream and violet tincture.

4. Pour into a mold and refrigerate until set. Garnish with violet flowers.

VIOLET HONEY

Violet honey was very popular in Victorian England as a spread and a flavoring for sauces. The violets give honey color, fragrance, flavor, and body. Violet honey can be used to sweeten tea and punches or as a sugar substitute in jellies, salad dressings, and frostings. It's delicious when blended with yogurt.

1 cup (235 ml) honey, room temperature

1/2 cup (120 ml) violet leaves and flowers, bruised

1. Put the honey in the top of a double boiler. Stir in the violets, cover, and cook for 10 minutes over low heat. (High heat damages honey, so don't let it boil.)

2. Remove from the heat, pour into sterilized jars, and seal. Let sit for 7 days at room temperature so the flavors will blend. Then rewarm over low heat, strain the herbs, and rebottle. Store in a cool, dark location, where the honey will keep for at least 2 years.

CHILDREN'S COUGH SYRUP

This formula is good for sore throats as well as coughs, and children love the taste.

2 cups (470 ml) water

2 tablespoons (30 ml) fresh violet leaves and flowers, or 1 tablespoon (15 ml) dried

2–4 tablespoons (30–60 ml) honey

1. Bring the water to a boil. Stir in the violets, cover, and simmer for 20 to 30 minutes.

2. Stir in the honey, remove from the heat, and let cool. Take 1 to 2 tablespoons (15–30 ml) every morning and evening as needed. The syrup will keep for 2 to 4 weeks in the refrigerator.

VIOLET JAM

Because this wonderful jam doesn't require cooking, you'll get its great taste along with the maximum amount of nutrients.

1 cup (235 ml) violet flowers, tightly packed

1 1/2 cups (360 ml) water, divided

Juice of 1 lemon

2 1/2 cups (590 ml) sugar

12-ounce (56 g) package powdered pectin

1. Add the flowers, 3/4 cup (180 ml) of the water, and the lemon juice to an electric blender. Blend into a smooth paste. Slowly add the sugar and blend until dissolved.

2. Stir the pectin into the remaining 1 cup (180 ml) of water and bring to boil. Boil hard for 1 minute. Pour the cooked pectin into the blender. Blend for about 1 minute, then spoon into jars and seal tightly.

This jam keeps for about 3 weeks in the refrigerator. For longer storage, put it in the freezer.

VIOLET WATER

For a long time, violet water was a popular gift, especially for birthdays and saints' days. It's a tradition worth reviving. The aromatic water can be used as a fragrant refresher, like a splash.

2 1/2 cups (590 ml) white wine vinegar

1 1/4 cups (300 ml) distilled water

4 cups (950 ml) violet flowers

1. Combine the vinegar and water in a saucepan and bring to a boil. Pour over the flowers. Stir, cover, and let sit in a warm place for 3 weeks, stirring daily.

2. Strain through a nonmetal strainer, pressing the flowers to release more fragrance. Pour into bottles and store in a cool, dark location, where it will keep for up to 1 year.

VIOLET MOUTHWASH

This formula is recommended for tooth, gum, and mouth problems. The addition of sage is said to help whiten the teeth.

1 part chamomile flowers

1 part comfrey leaves

1 part lemon balm leaves

1 part rosemary leaves

1 part sage leaves

1 part sorrel leaves

1 part thyme leaves

1 part violet flowers and leaves

Make an infusion of the ingredients following the instructions in Appendix G. Let cool, then use as a mouthwash as needed. Store the leftovers in the refrigerator, where they will keep for 1 to 2 weeks.

VIOLET-SAGE CREAM

This cream helps relieve cold sores and soothes and protects chapped lips.

2 tablespoons (30 ml) finely chopped fresh sage

2 tablespoons (30 ml) finely chopped sweet violet leaves

8 tablespoons (120 ml) almond oil, divided

4 tablespoons (60 ml) melted beeswax

1. Mix the sage and sweet violet leaves with 4 tablespoons (60 ml) of the almond oil in a small jar. Seal and leave in a warm place for about 1 month, shaking each day.

2. Combine the remaining 4 tablespoons (60 ml) of almond oil with the melted beeswax in the top of a double boiler. Blend.

3. Strain the infused liquid and combine with the melted fats. Mix until cool and thick. Store in an airtight jar in a dark, cool place, where it will keep for 1 to 2 years. Apply twice a day, or as needed.

RECIPES AND ELIXIRS

15 Herbs for Tea

Marian E. Sebastiano

Illustrations by Charles H. Joslin

What Is Tea?

If you sit down with a rabid tea-aholic, you will quickly learn that the only real tea is the traditional black or green tea made from leaves of the plant *Camellia sinensis*. All herbal teas are more properly called tisanes or infusions. But as the popularity of herbal teas skyrockets, the word *tea* has come to mean any drink made by steeping plant parts in water.

There are three main types of teas. Traditional tea is made from *Camellia sinensis* and comes in many varieties, depending on the region in which the tea was grown, as well as three classifications, depending on the level of fermentation. Herbal tea contains no traditional tea but is made from one or a blend of more than one other plant—like chamomile. Flavored teas fall between these two categories. They are usually part black tea and part other plants or flavorings. Earl Grey is black tea flavored with the oil of bergamot.

Planting a Tea Garden

It is not necessary to grow your own plants for herbal teas. The "Sources" section (page 834) lists outlets where you can purchase dried herbs in bulk. By growing your own, however, you can guarantee that only the freshest herbs go into your teas. You also gain the satisfaction of working with these fragrant and easy-to-grow plants. And quality control is in your hands. You know your teas are pesticide-free, picked at peak flavor, and packaged fresh. Purists package only what they grow, but you will probably find that some purchased ingredients—cinnamon, orange peel, and some exotic herbs—will expand your tea repertoire. So plant a few herbs, and experiment, experiment, experiment.

GOOD SOIL

A tea garden can be part of an existing bed or set apart. If you have limited garden space, or none, you can still have a lovely tea garden by using a large barrel or container. The key to good tea herbs, however, is good soil. And the keys to good soil are pH, texture (drainage), and nutrients. So start with a soil pH test, which will tell you how acidic your soil is. The local Cooperative Extension Service can perform one for you, or you can buy a simple test kit from a garden center. Take samples from wherever you want to plant tea herbs. Herbs generally prefer a pH in the range of 6.5 to 7.0—neutral to slightly acidic. If your soil is too acidic, a light dusting of ground limestone in early spring before planting time, or in fall when you're putting the beds to rest, will correct it. If your soil is too alkaline, organic matter such as peat moss will usually fix it.

Soil texture and nutrients are also important. Take a handful of your moist (but not wet) soil and squeeze it as if to make a snowball. If the snowball forms and then crumbles away when you press a thumb into it, you have good soil. If it fails to form a ball but pours through your fingers, you probably have sandy soil. And if it forms a heavy, solid clump that refuses to crumble, you probably have soil with too much clay. One of the easiest fixes for less-than-perfect soil is compost.

Continued →

Simply till good organic compost into your garden bed, or mix it into your container. Compost will allow soil that is too sandy to hold water, and soil that contains too much clay to drain better. And compost is rich in nutrients to help your herbs do well. If you do not have access to your own compost, you can buy bags of good organic compost at most garden centers.

SITING THE TEA BED

Choose a location that drains well, because only mints will tolerate wet feet. Unlike most perennials, herbs like dry conditions. So look for a dry site and soil that drains well. If you are using a container, make sure it has good drainage. If your only option for a tea bed is a damp area, consider building a simple raised bed there; this will improve drainage substantially.

Most herbs need lots of sun. Plant where they will get at least 4 to 6 hours of sun daily. Mints will tolerate some shade, so if your bed is partially shaded, plan to put the mints in the shaded areas. If you have a sunny windowsill, you can grow some of these herbs indoors, or bring them indoors over winter.

Designing your tea bed is simple. Once you've picked a site, and tilled and amended the soil, think about how you want the bed to look. Here are some simple guidelines:

- Place taller plants in the back of the garden and shorter herbs in the front. If your tea bed is circular and visible from all sides, plant the tallest herbs in the center and work outward toward the shortest.

- Give the plants room for growth. Allow 12 to 18 inches between annuals and 18 to 24 inches between perennials.

- Make sure all mints are "contained." They can be planted in bottomless buckets buried in the soil with a 2-inch rim protruding above the ground. I use chimney tiles for this purpose, although these are taller and require a 4-inch rim above the soil line. Or you can simply grow your mints in containers. Mints are extremely invasive, and if you don't take precautions, they will take over your garden.

- Label your herbs, or you may forget what is coming up! You don't want to weed out plants that self-sow, and you won't if you know where to expect them. Ideas for labels include pieces of slate that can be written on with a white paint pen; wooden spoons stained or painted and then coated with polyurethane spray; and odd teacups from garage sales—write the plant names on the insides with a permanent marker pen and place one near each plant. Even Popsicle sticks make good plant markers. Just write on them with a permanent marker. Whatever you use, make sure rain and weather will not fade or wash away the letters.

MAINTENANCE

Many herbs are native to the Mediterranean region, and therefore thrive in less-than-ideal conditions. In general, herbs prefer dry, slightly sandy soil and need little maintenance.

After planting, I treat my herbs to occasional feedings of soluble fertilizer. A blend of fish emulsion and liquid seaweed provides micronutrients as well as major nutrients. It's also much better for beneficial soil organisms than the traditional commercial 20–20–20 fertilizers. (The numbers refer to the concentration of three main nutrients, nitrogen, potassium, and phosphorus.) If you decide to use the traditional fertilizer, follow the dilution directions on the container for vegetables, and then dilute by half. If fertilizer is too strong, it dilutes the concentration of essential oils in herbs, and thus weakens the taste and smell.

After that, I find my garden pretty carefree. Herbs usually do not need as much watering as flowering annuals would, and I have found that the insect problems are minimal. A "mint beetle" appears in my area in early summer, but the phenomenon is short lived, and the bugs can be hand picked or ignored until they disappear. Organic gardeners learn that a few nibbles won't impair flavor or fragrance.

A few weeks into spring, after the ground is sufficiently warmed up, I mulch my herb beds. The main purposes of mulch are to prevent weed growth and to retain moisture in the soil. My favorite mulch is cocoa shell hulls, a by-product of the manufacture of chocolate. These have a nice color and texture, don't blow away, and smell wonderful! Also, cocoa shell mulch will not rob the soil of nitrogen when it breaks down, as some bark mulches do, and like all organic mulches, it adds organic matter upon decomposition. Other readily available mulches include shredded bark, decomposed leaves, and compost.

The Herbs in My Tea Garden

Anise hyssop (*Agastache foeniculum*)

A perennial favorite in the tea garden, hardy in Zones 5 through 9, this plant was second in popularity only to lavender in Victorian days. It has toothed leaves on square stems, and flowers in summer and fall. It is very fragrant; hummingbirds just love the purple spikes of flowers. You will want to plant this at the back of the tea garden, because it can grow to 4 feet tall. The leaves and flowers are used in teas for their delicate blend of mint and sweet anise flavors. Sometimes this plant is called the licorice plant or root beer plant. Members of the Chippewa and Cheyenne tribes drank anise hyssop tea for respiratory problems and chest pains.

The flowers also dry well and are popular in dried floral designs. New seedlings appear in spring and are happily accepted here! New cultivars give gardeners a choice of flower colors as well.

Basil (*Ocimum basilicum*)

Basil is an annual that will not tolerate any frost. Grow as an annual in Zones 3–9, and as a perennial in Zone 10. It should be set out only after all danger of frost has passed. The plants grow 12 to 18 inches tall, so they can be placed near the front of the garden. Pinch off the flowers to encourage more leaves, and pinch growing tips to make the plant bushier. Basil comes in a variety of colors and flavors, so plant several for variety. Sweet basil leaves have a spicy clove flavor said to promote digestion, which makes basil a good after-dinner tea. The flowers are flavorful; add these to your teas, too. Some of the scented basils include cinnamon (*O. basilicum* 'Cinnamon'), anise (*O. basilicum* 'Anise'), and lemon (*O. basilicum* 'Citriodorum'). These varieties each combine

Basil

basil flavor with a hint of the spice they are named for. These plants also make delicious herbal jellies.

Calendula (*Calendula officinalis*)

Calendula is often called pot marigold. It grows up to 2 feet tall and produces flowers resembling marigolds in yellow, orange, cream, and gold. The flowers are valued not just for tea making but also to add color and flavor to soups, stews, and breads. The petals have even been used in place of saffron to color and flavor rice. The tea made from the petals is not strongly flavored if you pull them from the flower heads and dry them. If you use the entire flower head, though, the tea will be more bitter tasting and may need to be sweetened with honey. I use the petals to add their orange and yellow colors to my tea blends, especially the lemony blends. Try adding a handful to your orange cookie or scone recipe, too.

Calendula

An added benefit of this plant in the tea garden is its hardiness. Because it can survive light frosts and early snows, it adds color through fall and even into winter, until the temperature dips into the 20°F range. It often self-sows, making it very popular in herb gardens. For beauty in the garden and tea blends, add calendula to your tea herb collection.

Catnip and catmint (*Nepeta* spp.)

Catnip, or *N. cataria*, is a member of the Mint family. It is best grown in Zones 4 through 9, where it can grow up to 3 feet tall and is definitely a back-row plant. It is a hardy perennial that self-sows; you will be weeding the seedlings out next year. Cats in your neighborhood will find you. One year I had to put a tomato cage over my plant because every morning it was crushed down to the ground! Catnip has a stimulating effect on cats that nibble it; they'll roll in it and bat it around. The effect on people is said to be the opposite—calming. The flavor is minty. I use it in iced tea. The

Catnip

leaves are best harvested before the plant flowers in late summer; after that it becomes rangy and sparse.

Another *Nepeta*, catmint (*N. mussini* and *N. x faassenii*), makes a wonderful border for the herb bed. It is closely related to catnip and perennial in the same zones. Depending on the cultivar selected, catmint can have a short, creeping growth habit (some, like 'Six Hills Giant', are very tall, so read plant and seed information carefully). It doesn't attract cats like catnip. In spring the plant is covered with blue blossoms. The flavor of the leaves is also minty.

Chamomile (*Matricaria recutita*)

There are two common kinds of chamomile: Roman (*Chamaemelum nobile*), which is a perennial ground cover in Zones 3 through 8, and German (*Matricaria recutita*), an annual that is more upright. German chamomile has delicate, fernlike leaves and white flowers that resemble daisies. Both plants have similar-looking apple-scented flowers. Tea is brewed from the flowers, so the annual variety is most often used for teas because its flowers are more abundant and pungent. The plant comes

into bloom in early June, and grows about 18 inches tall. Harvest and dry the flowers in June for tea in the winter. You will need to buy chamomile only once, because it self-sows so readily you will be weeding the seedlings out of cracks in the walkway next spring! It is very easy to grow from seeds, which can be scattered on the ground in spring.

Chamomile

I have found that chamomile tea becomes bitter if it is brewed too long. Traditionally used for a bedtime tea, it is supposed to promote sleep and help an upset stomach. The herbal jelly made from chamomile flowers tastes remarkably like honey.

Lavender (*Lavandula angustifolia*)

There are countless lavender varieties, but I prefer to grow the English lavender 'Munstead'. It is very hardy (to -20°F), has a deep-colored flower, and reaches a compact height of only 18 or 20 inches. Most lavenders are hardy in Zones 5 through 8, and they produce lavender-blue flowers in midsummer. Their aromatic foliage is silver-green and needle shaped. When growing lavender, take care to provide well-drained soil. Lavender loss over winter is usually because of water around the roots. Trim back to the new growth each spring to keep the plant from becoming woody. The oil concentration is highest in the flower bud. You can make tea from the buds or flower heads. The taste is cooling and aromatic. I like it combined with other herbs, as well: It makes an exotic-flavored tea. Historically, lavender tea has been used to cure insomnia and nervousness.

Lavender

Lemon balm (*Melissa officinalis*)

This lemon-scented herb is also in the Mint family, and hardy in Zones 5 through 8. Because of its spreading habit, I have relegated this plant to the back of the house or next to the garage, where the lawn mower keeps it in check! Don't make the mistake of putting it into a bed of mixed plants, because it will take over. It is one of the few herbs that grow well in partial shade; it may sunburn in full sun unless it is given compost-rich soil to grow in. This herb is best used fresh in herbal teas—it doesn't hold its flavor well when dried. It is also better before it goes into flower. This herb is excellent by the handful in sun tea. (See page 833.)

Lemon balm

Nicholas Culpeper, a prominent British herbalist of the 17th century, noted that lemon balm "causeth the mind and heart to become merry, and driveth away all troublesome cares." Later, a study on laboratory mice indicated the herb seemed to have a sedative effect on the nervous system. Other studies showed the oil of

Continued →

lemon balm seemed to inhibit viruses and bacteria. If nothing else, its lemony flavor may lift your spirits!

'Lemon Gem' and 'Orange Gem' marigolds (*Tagetes tenuifolia*)

These annual flowers are some of the many types of Tagetes. They grow easily from seed and often will self-sow for next year. They reach a height of about 1 foot—perfect for a border plant. The lacy foliage is covered with masses of dainty yellow ('Lemon Gem') or orange ('Orange Gem') blossoms that are edible. Both the flowers and foliage have a pungent citrus flavor and aroma. Besides using them for teas, you can sprinkle them on salads and fruit desserts.

Another fine marigold for herbal tea is called Mexican mint marigold or sweet marigold (*Tagetes lucida*). This plant grows to 2 feet tall, and its leaves are used for a soothing tea that has a sweet anise or tarragon type of flavor.

Lemon verbena (*Aloysia triphylla*)

Although a tender perennial (hardy in Zones 9 and 10) that has to be wintered indoors in northern climates, this plant is worth the trouble. Its lance-shaped leaves have the strongest lemon scent of any herb, and, unlike lemon balm, it dries well. Lemon verbena can get tall and twiggy after two or three growing seasons; remove growing tips regularly to keep it smaller and spreading. For herbal teas it can be combined with mints or fresh lemon balm. It is also good in sun tea. When you bring this herb indoors to winter over, cut back stems and cut back on the water. Usually by late winter all its leaves will have dropped off, and you will be quite sure it is dead. Do not throw the plant away—nine times out of ten, new leaves will grow from the dead-looking branches when it is time to once again put the plant outside!

Lemon verbena

Mints (*Mentha* spp.)

By far the most popular and easy-to-grow tea herbs, mints come in a variety of flavors, from citrus to peppermint. Many people do not realize how many mint varieties there are. They do best in Zones 5 through 9. And remember the warning I gave you earlier about containing mint plants—they can be invasive. In the center of my tea garden is a row of sunken chimney tiles, each with a different type of mint planted inside.

You should obtain mint plants from a rooted plug or cutting or as seedlings from a reliable source, because mints cross-breed easily. Make sure you label your mints, as they look somewhat alike. Handfuls of these fresh mints are absolutely essential in iced tea or sun tea (see page 833). Use less dried.

Often taken after dinner, mint tea is said to promote digestion. The menthol in peppermint has been found to relieve indigestion, flatulence, and nausea. It may also help relieve menstrual cramps.

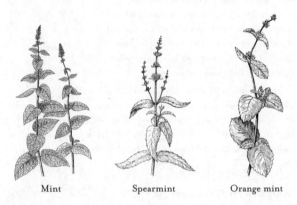

Mint   Spearmint   Orange mint

Monarda (*Monarda didyma*)

Also called bee balm, bergamot, and Oswego tea, monarda is a perennial in the Mint family. The most common cultivar, *M. didyma* 'Cambridge Scarlet', has bright red flowers and is a hardy perennial in Zones 4 through 9. This plant is best suited for the back of the herb bed—it grows into quite a large clump, about 3 feet tall. The Native Americans from the region of Oswego, New York, taught the colonists to make tea from this native plant as a substitute for highly taxed tea from England. To make tea from monarda, you can use the flowers or leaves. It has a pungent, minty flavor that requires a longer brewing time (about 15 minutes), and may need honey. Historical uses for monarda tea have included relieving stomach problems such as nausea, and soothing coughs and sore throats.

Monardae

Monarda is one of the few tea herbs susceptible to problems. Powdery mildew, a powdery white fungus that grows on leaves, can infect your monarda. To prevent this, thin your patch by removing stems to allow good air circulation. If you do get powdery mildew, another tea herb can be called in to help fight the problem: Oddly enough, chamomile tea, sprayed on the leaves of infected plants, can combat this disease! And if your conditions favor powdery mildew no matter what you do, consider planting a mildew-resistant cultivar like 'Marshall's Delight'.

MINT VARIETIES

Apple mint (*M. suaveolens*)

Chocolate mint (*M. x piperita* 'Chocolate')

Curly mint (*M. aquatica* var. *crispa*)

Ginger mint (*M. spicata* 'Ginger')

Grapefruit mint (*M. suaveolens x piperita*)

Orange mint (*M. x piperita* var. *citrata*)

Peppermint (*M. x piperita*)

Pineapple mint (*M. suaveolens* 'Variegata')

Spearmint (*M. spicata*)

Pineapple sage (*Salvia elegans*)

A tender perennial, pineapple sage has a wonderful pineapple scent. It is the last plant to bloom in the herb garden, and has scarlet red flowers. Many years I have to cover it to protect it from frost while waiting to see the blooms; then I bring it into the greenhouse to overwinter. To save space in your greenhouse, or if you only have a windowsill and no greenhouse, take cuttings, which grow readily in pots. The leaves of this tea herb are best used fresh. They can also garnish a cold beverage or fruit salad. The plant can get quite tall—it is a back-row plant.

Rosemary (*Rosmarinus officinalis*)

This is a tender perennial shrub hardy in Zones 8 through 10. Elsewhere it must winter indoors. It has very fragrant, needlelike leaves and clusters of small pink, white, or blue flowers. The tea made from rosemary is piney and aromatic. It has been used for clearing a stuffy head, treating migraine headaches, and relaxing tension. It is quite pungent and may need honey—or you can combine it with other herbs.

Rosemary

The key to overwintering rosemary is to keep it moist. This is not an easy task in the dry heat of the modern household. Try placing the pot of rosemary on a tray of wet pebbles to promote a moist environment around the plant. A cool sunporch that maintains a 50°F temperature is ideal for overwintering. Such cool temperatures will also promote blooming, which is unlikely at average household temperatures.

Sage (*Salvia officinalis*)

The word *salvia* is from the Latin *salvere*, which means "to be well." There are over 900 different species of sages, many of which can be used in tea. Garden sage has beautiful silver-green leaves on plants that can reach a height of about 2 to 3 feet. It is hardy in Zones 4 through 8. To add color to your sage bed, try growing purple sage (*S. officinalis*, 'Purpurascens'), which has purple-gray foliage. Or try 'Tricolor' (gray-green leaves variegated pink and ivory) or 'Icterina', which has yellow variegated leaves and grows 24 to 32 inches. To keep sage plants from getting "woody" after three or four growing seasons, cut back old growth in spring, and divide plants every 2 to 3 years to

Sage

rejuvenate. In winter, sage is an excellent tea. It has been used to soothe colds and sore throats. This is a good tea to keep in the pot on the stove and dilute with hot water to keep you warm throughout a cold winter day. In summer it is best enjoyed iced with lemon and sugar. Sage is traditionally associated with immortality, wisdom, and a long life.

Scented geraniums (*Pelargonium* spp.)

These plants are native to South Africa, and therefore perennial in Zone 10; they're tender in temperate climates. They are grown for their scented leaves; the flowers are neither large nor showy. There are many species, with a bevy of scents from rose to fruit and spices like nutmeg. The leaf shapes and growth habits also vary with the cultivar. In short but hot summers they can grow to be quite large; in winter, take cuttings and bring them indoors. You can dig up the entire plant and bring it in, but sometimes it is difficult for the plant to survive this, because its strained roots have such a large top growth to sustain. Take cuttings for insurance.

Geranium

MORE SCENTED GERANIUMS

Apple (*P. odoratissimum*)

Nutmeg (*P. x fragrens*)

Coconut (*P. grossularioides*)

Apricot (*P. scabrum*)

Strawberry (*P. x scarboroviae*)

Lemon rose (*P. graveolens* 'Rober's Lemon Rose')

Peppermint (*P. tomentosum*)

The citrus scents lemon and lime—*P. crispum* and *P. x nervosum*—make light flavored teas, but can be added to lemon verbena or mint teas. Rose geranium (*P. graveolens*), with its rose-scented leaves, makes a very interesting and enjoyable tea. The flavor is best if you use fresh leaves, but dried are acceptable. The selection of these interesting plants seems to keep growing.

Harvesting Tea Herbs

When you are ready to harvest, choose a dry day and pick after the dew has dried. The essential oil concentration is said to be highest in the morning. Remember, essential oils give the plant its fragrance, flavor, and any health benefits that may be attributed to the herb. Because the oil content is higher in a plant before flowering, many herb gardeners recommend picking before the plant flowers. But I've harvested at all stages of growth. The best way is to experiment with different times. You might prefer the more delicate flavor of small, new leaves, especially for the more pungent herbs.

The easiest way to clean herbs for harvesting is to rinse them off with a garden hose. Make sure your hose is set to a light spray or mist; you don't want dirt splashing up onto the plants. Soak them well and let them dry in the sun before you harvest. If you choose instead, to rinse them after cutting, use a salad spinner to remove the excess water.

Drying

After harvest, you will want to dry your tea herbs quickly but with gentle, even heat to preserve their delicate flavors. If you're using a food dehydrator, place 4- to 6-inch sprigs in a single layer on each tray. You can dry all the trays in several hours. When they are "chip dry," the leaves can be stripped off and stored in airtight tins or jars. Check the containers for moisture (condensation) within 24 hours and redry if any moisture is visible.

Another way to dry the herbs is in a slow (100° to 125°F) oven for several hours. Keeping the door slightly ajar will allow moisture to

Continued ➨

escape the oven. You have to check the progress often to determine when the leaves are dry; different herbs dry at different rates. To preserve flavor, it might be better to dry one type of herb at a time. You don't want your lemon verbena smelling of basil! If your oven doesn't have a setting this low, heat it to 150°F, turn it off, and then put the herbs in.

A microwave lined with paper towels also works. Just set the timer for a minute or less at a time and keep a vigilant watch to prevent scorching or burning. Leave the microwave door open for a minute or two between each use to keep moisture levels inside down.

A simple drying rack

COMMERCIAL HARVESTING

If you choose to collect the tea herbs and dry them systematically for packaging, rather than picking a few leaves whenever you want to try a new blend, plan to take about a third of the plant each month of the growing season. You can take the entire annual plant at the end of the season. For perennials, the last harvest of the season should be lighter. This will give the plant a chance to recover before winter. Before your first harvest, make sure you have adequate drying space, and enough containers for all the herbs you will end up with.

Although the herbs can be bunched with rubber bands and hang-dried, take care to hang them in a dry place—never in a garage or basement, where they will mold or absorb adverse odors. I prefer to process herbs for dried floral designs by hang-drying, and to process those for teas and culinary uses quickly to get them in an airtight container and not have them hanging around getting dusty. If hanging is your only alternative, place the herb bunches in paper bags that have been slit for ventilation. This will keep them dust-free, although it will slow drying time. Make sure you label each bunch you hang. I once had a friend make a spaghetti sauce with catnip—which, when dried, looks like oregano! Start checking for dryness after 2 weeks. Once the herbs are dry, simply strip off the leaves and place in airtight, clearly labeled containers.

Containers

Once your herbs are dry, you want to preserve their quality. The secret is to keep the dried tea herbs away from moisture, sunlight, and extreme heat to preserve the flavors. Many sources sell glass jars with lids that seal tightly. Baby-food jars are a good size for preserving small quantities of herbs. For bigger bunches, try canning jars or even mayonnaise jars—just make sure they are well washed and completely dry before use. Zipper-locking plastic bags, which come in a multitude of sizes, are another good choice. Just fill and label and store away from light. I store small zippered bags in an old cookie tin. If you have tins that once held loose tea, wash them well, dry, and use them. Make sure to label. When you begin making tea blends, store fine powders (like cinnamon) and ingredients with natural oils (like orange peels) in plastic bags or glass jars. Tins can corrode, and powders can also get lost in their seams.

Another idea for preserving and storing your harvest is to freeze some or all of it. Freezing herb sprigs in zipper-locking bags is an excellent way to preserve delicate flavors lost in drying. Some herbs, such as basil, will blacken in the freezer, but this does not affect their flavor. Make sure you label the bag. Herbs that freeze well include tarragon, parsley, basil, marjoram, thyme, rosemary, dill, lemon balm, lemon verbena, and mints. To use the herbs, take out a few sprigs and mince them with a sharp knife.

An alternate freezing method, which is very popular for iced teas, is to place petals, leaves, or sprigs of herbs in an ice cube tray. Cover with water and freeze. Once frozen, remove from the tray, label, and store in plastic bags. Use the cubes to add interest and flavor to iced teas and punches.

Brewing a Cup of Herbal Tea

Once you've grown, picked, and preserved your tea herbs, you'll want to test them in a cup of tea. The first thing you should know is that herb teas brew differently from traditional teas: They tend to take longer, and usually have little color. With dried herbs and herb blends, use 1 teaspoon per person, and then 1 extra "for the pot." In season, fresh herbs are preferable. Add a sprig per person—about a tablespoon of fresh leaves.

BREWING BY INFUSION

Infusion works best with fresh or dried herb leaves, petals, and flowers. Start by bringing cold water just to the boiling point in a pan or teapot, preferably an enameled one. Because herb teas are more delicately flavored, any metallic taste picked up from a metal pot may be more noticeable.

Use a ceramic or glass teapot for the infusion, for the same reason. Warm the teapot by rinsing with hot water. The tea can be put directly into the pot and then strained before drinking, or you can use one of the many infusers sold to hold the loose tea, such as metal balls, mesh balls, bamboo strainers, and muslin bags. You can also buy empty paper tea bags; see supplier list on page 834. Adding loose tea to the pot and then straining allows for the most water contact with the leaves, and therefore the most flavor.

Consider bruising fresh herbs by tearing and crushing them before adding them to the teapot. This will help release the oils from the plant that give the tea its taste.

Pour boiling water over the tea. Allow to steep for at least 5 minutes before tasting. You may want to go longer; 15 minutes is not unreasonable. Seasoned herb tea drinkers often simply allow the infusion to steep on the back of the stove all day. When you're ready, fill a cup halfway with the infusion, and top it off with boiling water.

You will acquire a taste for the pure and simple flavors of herb tea, but newcomers may have to add honey. If a brew seems bitter, try using a tad more herb with less brewing time. Sometimes the bitter flavors come out over time, so cutting back on the steeping time may be preferable for mellow flavors.

BREWING BY DECOCTION

You will see that some teas are brewed from leaves; others use flowers, roots, seeds, peel (oranges), or hips (the fruits of the rose). When seeds, bark, or whole spices are called for, they can be crushed before steeping, or passed through a spice grinder. This will release the oils for maximum flavor. You should use about a tablespoon of seeds for every 2 cups of water.

Because seed, bark, and peel oils are harder to release than those from leaves and flowers, bring water to a boil on the stove. Add the crushed or whole seeds and other ingredients and simmer gently. Taste the tea after 5 minutes. Continue steeping and tasting until the tea is to your liking.

Tea Blends

Below are some ideas for combinations and blend recipes—but I will admit that one fall, as time was running short for harvest, I picked all my tea herbs, dried them, combined them in a tin I labeled HERB GARDEN TEA, and the result was delicious! I only wish it could be duplicated.

JULY EVENING TEA

This tea is made to be shared with a friend on the front porch during a lovely summer night. Steep 1 large fresh monarda flower with about a dozen fresh lavender flower heads in 2 cups of water for 10 minutes. Pour over ice cubes and enjoy! Compatible additions include lemon balm leaves, lemon verbena leaves, and chamomile flowers.

LAVENDER MINT TEA

Mix 1 part lavender flowers and 2 parts mint leaves. Additions for more interesting blends include rosemary, lemon balm or lemon verbena, and rose geranium.

SUN TEA

Make sun tea by placing 6 tea bags in a glass gallon jug filled with water. Add handfuls of any of the lemon herbs and mints. Steep in the sun all day; at suppertime remove the herbs and tea bags, add 1/3 cup sugar and the juice of a lemon, and pour over ice.

ANISE TEA

Make a jar of anise-flavored tea by using dried anise hyssop leaves and a few spoonfuls of fennel seed. Lemon verbena or anise basil leaves can be added to the blend. Boil the seeds in the water, then remove from heat and pour over the leaves to steep.

ROSE GERANIUM TEA

Mix dried rose-scented geranium leaves with a few whole cloves and crushed cinnamon sticks. Add dried lemon peel, or add fresh lemon after brewing. Adding a tea bag when brewing this herbal tea gives it body.

NIGHTTIME TEA

Some herbs are known for calming and soothing properties. Try making this tea with 1 part catmint, 1 part chamomile, and 1/2 part catnip.

ORANGE MINT TEA

Use a citrus-flavored mint, such as orange bergamot, or any mint herb. Add grated dried lemon and orange rind, cloves, cinnamon, and calendula petals or 'Lemon Gem' marigold leaves.

LEMON BLEND TEA

Mix equal parts of fresh lemon balm leaves and fresh or dried lemon verbena leaves. Add grated and dried lemon peel (about 1 tablespoon per cup of lemon herbs). Steep about 1 cup of the mixture per teapot of water for about 20 minutes. Optional lemon herbs may be added, such as lemon-scented geranium leaves and lemon thyme. Then add some calendula petals for color.

SWEET ORANGE TEA

Mix 1 part each of orange mint, peppermint, and cinnamon basil, plus 1/2 part dried orange peel. Add a little minced vanilla bean to the mixture.

APPLE-SAGE TEA

Mix 3 cups of apple mint leaves, 1 cup of sage leaves, and 5 crushed cinnamon sticks. Additional spices may be added, such as cloves, allspice, and cardamom. You can also add cinnamon basil or a lemon herb if you wish.

BODY-FRESHENING TEA

This tea is believed to keep you fresh and help eliminate body odor. It comes from the book *The Herbal Home Spa* by Greta Breedlove.

Steep either 1 tablespoon fresh or 1 teaspoon dried thyme or peppermint in boiling water for 20 minutes. Drink three times a day.

OTHER TWO-INGREDIENT BLENDS

Agrimony with licorice

Alfalfa seed with mint

Alfalfa leaf with lemon verbena

Alfalfa leaf with red clover blossomswith

Angelica root with juniper berries

Chamomile with hibiscus flowers

Dill seed with chamomile flowers

Licorice root with any other herb

Marigold petals with mint

Mullein with sage

Mullein with chamomile

Strawberry leaves sweet woodruff

Yarrow with pep permint

—From *The Herbal Tea Garden* by Marietta Marshall Marcin

Continued ➡

Some Things to Be Careful About

Herbal teas are generally considered safe because they are not concentrated. Sensitive people can be allergic, however. For example, people who are allergic to asters, chrysanthemums, ragweed, or yarrow can react to chamomile.

Some plants that were once considered edible are now considered toxic, including comfrey, wormwood, pennyroyal, tansy, and sassafras. These plants should not be ingested.

CONVERTING RECIPE MEASUREMENTS TO METRIC

Use the following formulas for converting U.S. measurements to metric. Since the conversions are not exact, it's important to convert the measurements for all of the ingredients to maintain the same proportions as the original recipe.

When the Measurement Given Is	Multiply It by	To Convert to
teaspoons	4.93	milliliters
tablespoons	14.79	milliliters
fluid ounces	29.57	milliliters
cups (liquid)	236.59	milliliters
cups (liquid)	.236	liters
cups (dry)	275.3	milliliters
cups (dry)	.275	liters
pints (liquid)	473.18	milliliters
pints (liquid)	.473	liters
pints (dry)	550.61	milliliters
pints (dry)	.551	liters
quarts (liquid)	946.36	milliliters
quarts (liquid)	.946	liters
quarts (dry)	1101.22	milliliters
quarts (dry)	1.101	liters
gallons	3.785	liters
ounces	28.35	grams
pounds	454	grams
inches	2.54	centimeters
degrees Fahrenheit	5/9 (temp. -32)	degrees Celsius (Centigrade)

While standard metric measurements for dry ingredients are given as units of mass, U.S. measurements are given as units of volume. Therefore, the conversions listed above for dry ingredients are given in the metric equivalent of volume.

The information here is not intended as advice regarding potential medicinal, therapeutic, or other effects of plants and is for informational and study purposes only. Historical uses mentioned for the herbs are not to be considered substitutes for professional medical advice. It is strongly advised that you educate yourself on plant usage and keep current as new information continues to emerge, which may contradict old studies and beliefs.

Sources of Plants and Supplies

PLANTS AND SEEDS

Companion Plants, Inc.
7247 North Coolville Ridge Road
Athens, OH 45701
E-mail: complants@frognet.net
Offers 600 varieties of herb plants and seeds; catalog $3.

Richters
357 Highway 47
Goodwood, Ontario, Canada L0C 1A0
(905) 640–6677
E-mail: conrad@richters.com
Free catalog listing over 700 herb plants and seeds.

Sandy Mush Herb Nursery
316 Surrett Cove Road
Leicester, NC 28748

TEA SUPPLIES

Frontier Cooperative Herbs
3021 78th Street
P.O. Box 299
Norway, IA 52318
www.frontierherb.com
Free catalog of bulk dried herbs, spices, and tea products.

San Francisco Herb Company
250 14th Street
San Francisco, CA 94103
(800) 227–4530

Herbal Teas for Lifelong Health

Kathleen Brown
Recipe development by Jeanine Pollak
Illustrations by Randy Mosher, Beverly Duncan, Laura Tedeschi, and Elayne Sears

Brewing Herbal Teas

There are essentially two ways to prepare the perfect cup of herbal tea: an infusion, in which the herbs are steeped, and a decoction, in which the herbs are simmered for a period of time. Both techniques are covered in detail below, along with information on the tools and utensils you'll need, whether to use fresh or dried herbs, the ratios to use, what kind of water is best, and so forth. Let's start.

INFUSE OR DECOCT?

An infusion is the better technique for brewing teas when leaves, flowers, or crushed berries or seeds are used. These ingredients easily release their essential oils and valuable nutrients while steeping in hot water. The basic rule of thumb is to pour boiling water over the herbs, cover the pot, and allow to steep anywhere from 10 to 30 minutes. The longer a tea steeps, the stronger it will taste, but herbalists agree that, for some formulas, a longer steeping time allows nutrients to be extracted more fully.

Decoctions, on the other hand, are the method of choice when brewing teas from roots, barks, and more woody parts of herbs. In this case, the plant material must be simmered in boiling water—at least 20 minutes and as long as 60 minutes, depending on the size of the pieces—to release its valuable properties.

BREWING WITH BERRIES AND SEEDS

It's best to crush berries and seeds and infuse them with the leaves and flowers rather than decoct them with the roots, which destroys the more volatile properties released during crushing.

You're probably wondering, what if you're using a combination of ingredients, both leaves and roots, for example? The basic technique is actually to both infuse and decoct—simmer the roots 20 minutes in a covered container, remove the pot from the heat, add the leaves, stir well, cover, and steep 10 to 20 minutes.

BREWING IN LARGE QUANTITIES

You can always brew enough tea at a time to last you a whole day, or even 2 or 3 days. Leftover teas should always be refrigerated, though—you can warm them up again over a stove top or in a microwave oven.

This next tip is so important it's worth highlighting: *Use organic herbs whenever possible.* Your tea is going to be only as good as the herbs you put in it. If you're gathering fresh herbs in the wild, be absolutely certain they have not been sprayed or exposed to pesticides or pollution, such as those growing alongside a road. If you're using roses and some of the other flowering plants and trees, be especially careful they haven't been sprayed.

RULES OF THUMB

For an infusion: Pour boiling water over the herbs. Stir well, cover the pot, and steep 10 to 30 minutes.

For a decoction: Add the herbs to boiling water and stir well. Cover the pot and simmer on low heat from 20 to as long as 60 minutes, if, for example, you're using large, whole roots such as ginseng.

TOOLS OF THE TRADE

Besides a little knowledge, you'll also need some tools and utensils. There are many types of strainers and other tools for brewing tea, some fancy, others very simple. A fine-mesh metal strainer is the tool of choice for many herbalists who believe the herbs need to float happily and unencumbered while brewing, without being confined by the ubiquitous tea ball or spoon. Some like bamboo strainers, others collect brewing gadgets (okay, I confess), but whether your tea tool is aesthetic or practical, simple or ostentatious, it's up to you. Tea balls and spoons are convenient to use at work or when traveling, though some hard-core herbalists have been known to carry a porta-pot—a portable teapot, that is!

Another way of taking your tea with you—whether to work or when traveling—is to make your own tea bags. You can purchase empty tea bags from many health food stores or herb shops, or you can buy or make small cloth bags with drawstrings into which you put your tea blends. Cheesecloth cut into small squares and fastened with string, thread, or, in a pinch, a rubber band works well. Place 1 teaspoon (5 ml) of tea blend into the bag or fabric, and you'll have tea to go!

Tea balls and bamboo strainers are among the most useful, and thus most popular, utensils for making herbal teas.

CHOOSING THE RIGHT CONTAINER

Glass, stainless steel, enamel, and most types of pottery (check to make sure the glaze is lead-free!) are the best types of containers in which to make tea. Glass makes a particularly wonderful brewing container because you additionally experience the visual aspect of watching the tea brewing.

You don't need a fancy teapot, however, or any teapot, for that matter. The simple quart canning jar is not only the most utilitarian for brewing tea, it may be the best for preserving the aromatic oils and other volatile properties of the plants as well. It's simple: Just put the herbs in a jar, pour boiling water over them, stir well, cover, and steep. As far as how long to let it sit, use the suggestions for standard infusions and decoctions discussed earlier until you become familiar with the tastes and times involved in brewing your favorites.

Glass canning jars make some of the best containers for infusing.

FRESH OR DRIED HERBS?

Dried herbs will never equal fresh in providing the nutritive value, vitality, flavor, color, and texture, so using fresh herbs in your tea is always preferable.

If you are lucky enough to have your own garden, you can harvest and dry the bounty yourself, thus ensuring organic quality and freshness. Or you might try purchasing locally grown herbs from reputable growers. If these are not options, attempt to obtain the best-quality dried herbs available, organic if possible, again from a reputable source. There are several mail-order sources included in the Resources section for your reference.

Dried herbs do have the advantage of longer storage time, and it's acceptable to use both fresh and dried together.

Continued ➜

MEASURING SYSTEMS

As you become more familiar with the art of making tea, the "handful" method most herbalists enjoy as their system of measurement will seem more understandable. Before long, you too will be throwing a handful of this or that into the pot and won't even need the proportions that are given in our recipes. For now, though, the ratios provided will help you get more, shall we say, rewarding results. To be as consistent as possible and avoid confusion, the ingredients are shown as "parts" rather than precise measurements such as teaspoons, cups, or whatever. This is also for your convenience, so you can make any quantity you desire. For instance, if 1 part valerian, 1 part hops, and 1 part chamomile are listed, it just means that the combination will contain one third of each herb. If your total amount is 3 tablespoons (15 ml) of herb, then you'll use 1 tablespoon (5 ml) of each herb.

In the fresh-versus-dried question, the ratio is usually 1 teaspoon (5 ml) dried or 2 teaspoons (10 ml) fresh (roughly double) per 1 cup (237 ml) of water, or 1 ounce (28 g) of herb to 1 quart (946 ml) of water. We'll use these standards, although a recipe can vary with strength, density, taste, and color of the herbs in the mix. This is really a guideline, so adjust accordingly and feel free to experiment.

WATER PURITY

Since the basis of all teas is water, start with the purest water you can. If you are lucky to have good tap water, use it. If not, consider distilled or bottled water.

If not expressly noted in a recipe's instructions, use 1 quart (946 ml) of water to start with, making the herbal ingredients (parts) equal approximately 1 ounce (28 g) of plant material.

AS GOOD AS IT GETS

Above all else, when selecting ingredients for your herbal teas, be sure to use only organic herbs and plant parts with:

- No chemical sprays
- No pesticides
- No exposure to pollution (as may occur alongside a road)

FINDING THE RIGHT TASTE

Tart	Minty	Sweet	Rooty
Hibiscus	Catnip	Anise	Burdock
Rose hips	Peppermint	Licorice	Dandelion
	Spearmint	Rehmannia	Dong quai
Spicy	Violet	Stevia	Ginseng
Allspice	Wintergreen	Vanilla	Oregon grape
Cardamom			Yellow dock
Cinnamon	**Licorice**	**Citrus**	
Coriander	Anise	Lemon balm	**Grassy**
Fenugreek	Fennel	Lemongrass	Alfalfa
Ginger	Licorice	Lemon peel	Horsetail
Vitex	Star anise	Lemon verbena	Oatstraw
Yerba santa		Orange peel	

Obtaining the Herbs

Almost all the herbs in our recipes can be grown in your garden for the absolutely freshest ingredients, or they can be fairly easily obtained at your local natural foods store, more frequently fresh, but consistently in dried form. Many of them can also be wildcrafted, that is, found growing in the wild and gathered ethically. As many herbalists caution, though, if wildcrafting: Be absolutely certain what plants you're collecting. Some herbs look identical, but their properties can vary greatly from beneficial to toxic, and even deadly poisonous. In addition, due to overharvesting and the destruction of natural habitat, some plants are rapidly becoming endangered. Consult a good wildcrafting guide or herbalist before heading out into the wilds. Whatever source you choose, try to find organic if possible, and certainly the best quality available. Your teas will be only as good as the quality of the herbs you're using.

HARVESTING HERBS

Grab your favorite basket or trug and go out into the garden on a dry, sunny morning. The best time of day is after the dew has evaporated but before the sun is hot enough to dry all the volatile oils and properties from the plants. This is just a rule of thumb, however, and varies from plant to plant. Gathering from mid-morning to early afternoon is fine for something like mints, for instance, where a little sun and warmth bring the volatile oils to the peak of perfection. Don't pick the herbs when they're wet if you're planning to dry them, as they may become moldy; if you're going to use them fresh, you can pick them even in the rain!

Contrary to what you might think, cutting the leaves and flowers from the herb actually is beneficial to the plant and helps it to grow even more vigorous and abundant. Besides, it improves the morale of plants when yellow and dying leaves are picked off, making room for new, healthy leaves. Your plants will thank you for taking such good care of them!

Think of it as giving the plant a haircut, but a trim, not a full buzz cut! Use scissors when gathering the herbs, to get a clean break, rather than picking with your fingers, which could pull up the roots. And gather the tips rather than full stems to get the most tender parts. If harvesting from small plants, leave at least two sets of leaves at the base of each stem so the plant has something with which to continue growing. You'll be amazed how quickly the plants produce new growth. Be especially careful not to pick herbs that have been exposed to weed killers or chemicals of any kind, car exhaust, or excessive dust.

For aromatic, leafy herbs such as mint, the best time to harvest is just before the plant flowers, as this is when the greatest abundance of natural oils is concentrated in the leaves. This is especially important when the herbs are to be dried and stored, as the oils provide the best flavor, therapeutic value, and color.

USING FRESH HERBS

Okay, you have the herbs in your basket and have tidied up your plants. Now what? If you want to make tea from fresh herbs, first wash them thoroughly in clean cold water, then shake or pat them dry with a towel. Herbs that grow close to the ground, like parsley and thyme, need to be washed carefully because they are the most likely to have soil on their leaves. Remove stems and any dead and imperfect leaves, chop or bruise the herbs, and pop the green goodies into a teapot with some boiling water. It's that simple! But if you want to dry and store them, read on.

FREEZING HERBS

Freezing works very well for some herbs—dill, lemon balm, lemon verbena, mint, rosemary, and thyme, to name a few. Wash the herbs well and pat them dry with towels. You can freeze them whole or chopped. Plastic bags work well, as they take up little space when stacked flat. Or add a little water and freeze the herbs into ice cube trays. When frozen, pop the cubes from the trays into plastic bags, and take a few out when needed. Another good technique for freeze storing is to put about 1 part chopped herb in 2 parts butter and freeze. The butter preserves the color and flavor and is great for cooking, too.

Drying the Herbs

An important thing to remember when drying herbs is to process them as quickly as possible after picking to ensure maximum flavor. Once gathered, shake gently to remove dust and insects. It's important to keep the herbs out of strong light and sun to prevent the color and flavor from fading. Be sure to keep the herbs separate and well identified, because as they dry, many look the same.

TO DRY HERBS QUICKLY

Spread the herbs on a mesh rack and place the rack in a slow oven set from 100° to 125°F. (Using more heat will cause the volatile oils in the plants to be destroyed.) Leave the oven door open, and stand nearby because some leaves dry quickly.

> **LUNAR TIP**
> Leaves gathered when the moon is waning tend to dry most rapidly because they retain less sap in their leaves and stems.

TO AIR-DRY HERBS

Make sure the herbs are not left in places that could be attacked by insects or rodents. Vermin are especially common in hot, humid climates. In cold climates, mildew is a factor to consider.

The drying area should be dry, well ventilated, and out of direct light. In damp or cold climates, some artificial heat may be necessary to supplement the natural drying process. If you're hanging the herbs in bunches, don't make your bunches too large, or the leaves could turn black or moldy. You can hang air-drying herbs inside paper bags to keep the dust off, but just be sure to punch many holes into the bags to let the air in and keep moisture out.

Hang-dry bunches of herbs inside paper bags to keep the dust off them.

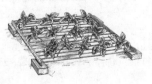

Many herbs can be dried on trays or racks. When working with thick-leaved plants, be sure to spread them out so that air can circulate freely around each herb.

Some herbs dry very well when spread on trays, but don't spread them too thickly. Parsley leaves, for instance, are so thick they can be spread only one layer deep. Thyme, however, holds so little moisture that you can just leave a big pile to dry in a basket.

When you are drying small-leaved herbs such as thyme, pick branches instead of leaves and hang them in bundles. Once they're dry, it's easy to strip the leaves from the stems by running your fingers gently backward down either side. The larger-leaved herbs like mint and sage are better picked separately from the branches before drying.

In a warm, dry spot, most herbs will air-dry in anywhere from 4 to 7 days, depending on climate. Heavy-leaved herbs may take several weeks, however. To check if your herbs are totally dry, crumble a bit between your fingers. If they're crispy and break cleanly, they're dry. If they bend and are still flexible, they need more time to dry. Leaves, properly stored, may last one to two years but are usually best used within one year. If you're drying your own

When completely dry, herbs should crumble and break cleanly in your hands.

herbs, at least you know the date they were dried. When buying dried herbs commercially, you really don't know when they were processed.

WORKING WITH FLOWERS

Harvest flowers when they are fragrant and most lovely. If they're past their prime, they won't be as aromatic and flavorful. Shake gently to remove any dust or insects. Long-stemmed flowers such as lavender dry best hung upside down in bunches. Rose petals and other flowers with more delicate blossoms are best dried on screens and in baskets. Remember, don't dry in direct sun. A dry, shady place with good air circulation is best. Flowers are best when used within one year.

WORKING WITH SEEDS

Gather seeds when they're barely ripe, as soon as they begin to look brownish, because just a day or so later they will be blowing all over, and it'll be too late: Instead of preserving your harvest, you'll have planted next year's army of new plants! Pick seeds early in the morning, snipping off the entire seed head. Drop them into a paper bag or cut the whole plant and place it, upside down, in a bag. Puncture the bag and hang it in a warm, airy, shady place. Once dried, all the seeds fall to the bottom of the bag. Seeds can remain viable for years, because they have a natural wrapping to hold in their oils.

WORKING WITH ROOTS

A plant from which roots are to be gathered usually needs to reach a certain maturity before its valuable properties are developed, several years in some cases. Autumn is usually the best

> **LUNAR TIP**
> Try to gather roots when the moon is waxing; the roots will be the most tender then.

time to harvest roots, once you've determined that the plant is sufficiently aged. Dig or gently pull up the plant, shake off any excess dirt, then cut off part of the root, leaving enough to support the plant's continued growth. Then replace. Wash the roots in cool water, trimming off side roots, which don't have much flavor. Split the roots in

Continued ➜

half lengthwise and chop so they'll dry more quickly. To preserve flavor, keep them in coarsely chopped pieces until you're ready to use. At that time, powder them in a coffee grinder to release the flavor. Properly stored in dark glass jars in a dark, cool place, roots can last two to three years.

Storing Dried Herbs

Here are some simple, but very important, considerations in storing dried herbs.

- The type of container is vital, with glass or metal being the best. Dark glass is especially good, as it prevents light from fading the herbs' vitality. If using clear glass, store in a dark place, if possible, out of direct light.

- Herbs must be completely dry or they will mold.

- Store immediately after drying to best preserve volatile oils, color, texture, and flavor.

- Use airtight containers to keep out dust and vermin.

- Package each herb separately and label every container carefully.

- Monitor containers regularly to make sure there is no condensation.

- Store in a cool, dry, dark place for best results.

Recycled glass jars are ideal for storing herbs. If the containers are of clear glass, store them in a dark place, out of direct light.

THE DAILY REGIMEN

If making teas for daily tonic purposes, to bolster and nourish the body, drink two to three cups per day. If you're sick, drink four to six cups per day, or drink as much as you can. Get a good thermos, and take your tea with you. For children ages 3 and up, usually 1/4 to 1/2 cup (59–119 ml) is given. For elderly people, or if the tea is very strong and bitter, 1/2 cup (119 ml) is recommended. These are general guidelines, however, so note the specific instructions given with each recipe.

Tea Blend Recipes

These teas are as nourishing as they are tasty and simple to prepare, making it easy to incorporate this pleasant and healthful habit into your daily routine.

NOURISHING DAILY BLEND

This recipe tastes great with cinnamon added, but if you are drinking it daily, add the cinnamon only occasionally, as it's too strong and drying to use every day.

1 part burdock root

1 part chamomile flowers

1 part nettle leaves

1 part oatstraw

1 part red clover blossoms

1/10 part cinnamon chips (optional)

1. Add the burdock root to boiling water, reduce heat, and simmer for 15 to 20 minutes in a covered pot.

2. Turn off the heat and add the rest of the herbs.

3. Stir well, cover, and steep 15 to 20 minutes.

VIOLET-ROSE VITALITY BOOSTER

A superior, vitamin-rich booster for daily health enhancement, this blend is absolutely delightful.

1 part oatstraw

1 part rose hips (organic)

1 part violet leaves and flowers

1/4 part orange slices (organic)

1/8 part rose petals (organic)

1. Combine all the herbs in a pot and pour boiling water over them.

2. Stir well, cover, and steep 15 to 20 minutes.

NOURISHING ENDOCRINE ELIXIR

Wonderful for balancing and strengthening the female being, this formula supports the hormonal and glandular systems. It's yummy and nourishing and can be made as a tea or tinctured in brandy. As a tea, drink one to two cups daily. As an elixir, take 1 to 2 dropperfuls two to four times per day.

1 part dandelion root

1 part dong quai root

1 part cooked rehmannia root

1 part sarsaparilla root

1 part Siberian ginseng root

Blackstrap molasses (if making the elixir; available in most health food stores)

Brandy (if making the elixir)

To make a tea:

1. Add all the herbs to boiling water, reduce heat, and simmer for 15 to 20 minutes in a covered pot.

2. Turn off the heat and steep, covered, 15 to 20 minutes.

To make an elixir:

1. Add all herbs to boiling water, reduce heat, and simmer for 40 minutes in a covered pot. Then turn off the heat and steep 20 minutes.

2. Strain, squeezing all the excess liquid from the herbs.

3. Measure the volume of the infused liquid, then add half to three quarters as much molasses and 1/4 part brandy.

DANDELION POWER

If you think you've never used dandelion as medicine, guess again. It's a prime ingredient in over half of all herb blends on the market, including formulas for weight loss, PMS, detoxification, and rejuvenation, along with liver, digestive, kidney, and skin ailments! Dandelion is such a wondrous source of minerals, vitamins, fiber, micronutrients, lecithin, and biologically active substances that there is probably no existing condition that would not benefit from regularly consuming dandelions.

—excerpted from *The Herbal Home Remedy Book*, by Joyce A. Wardwell (Storey Books, 1998)

HERBAL IRON TONIC

Use this great tonic for blood-building during pre- and postnatal times and also during PMS and menopause. Make it once or twice a year, then imbibe several times a week as a blood-enriching, iron and mineral boost. It will keep for several months if refrigerated.

1 part nettle leaves

1 part oatstraw

1 part red raspberry leaves

1 part rose hips (organic)

1 part dried cherries

1 part dried apricots, raisins, or currants

1/2 part yellow dock root

Blackstrap molasses (available in most health food stores)

Brandy

Raspberry vinegar (available in most health food stores)

1. Add all the herbs and fruits to boiling water (1 quart per 1 ounce of herbs), reduce heat, and simmer for 2 hours, covered.

2. Remove from the heat and allow to steep 2 hours, covered, stirring occasionally.

3. Strain out all the solids, squeezing all liquid through cheesecloth.

4. Measure the volume of tea, then add half to three quarters as much molasses, 1/4 part brandy (to preserve), and a couple of dashes of raspberry vinegar.

5. Keep refrigerated, taking 1 to 2 tablespoons (15–30 ml) as needed.

Note: If you can't find raspberry vinegar in a store, you can make your own using 1 cup (237 ml) crushed, fresh or frozen raspberries infused overnight in 2 cups (474 ml) white wine vinegar. Strain, and voilà!

GINSENG SWING

Here's a great tonic for overall energy, stamina, and mental clarity. The hawthorn nourishes the heart, the dandelion tones the liver and digestive system, and the ginseng, sarsaparilla, and licorice nourish the adrenals and male glandular system. Drink half a cup twice per day.

2 parts Siberian ginseng root

1 part dandelion root

1 part hawthorn berries

1 part sarsaparilla root

1/8 part cinnamon chips

1/10 part licorice root

1/10 part orange peel (organic)

1. Add all the herbs to boiling water, reduce heat, and simmer in a covered pot for 20 minutes.

2. Remove from the heat and steep, covered, 30 minutes.

HEART-REVIVAL TEA

This heart-nourishing formula has the classic tonic actions of hawthorn, combined with the strengthening properties of rose hips and ginkgo. Siberian ginseng safely helps the body adapt to stress and strengthens adrenal and glandular body functions. Nettle is one of the best blood and adrenal nourishers, rich in chlorophyll, beta-carotene, vitamin C, and iron. This gentle, yet effective, strengthening tea for overall heart health can also be used by anyone who is recovering from a heart attack.

2 parts hawthorn berries

2 parts Siberian ginseng root

3 parts hawthorn leaves and flowers

2 parts ginkgo leaves

1 part linden blossoms

1 part nettle leaves

1 part rose hips (organic)

1. Add the hawthorn berries and ginseng root to boiling water, reduce heat, and simmer for 20 minutes in a covered pot.

2. Remove from the heat and add the remaining herbs.

3. Steep, covered, 15 to 20 minutes.

HEART'S EASE TEA

An excellent tea for relaxing and nourishing the heart and cardiovascular system, this formula is particularly valuable in easing angina. Hawthorn and ginkgo provide cardio-tonic flavonoids, and motherwort brings cardio-active glycosides to the blend. In addition, motherwort, linden, oatstraw, and crampbark have relaxing and antispasmodic properties that work wonderfully with hawthorn and ginkgo to aid a "stressed-out" heart. Violet is added for its nourishing vitamin and mineral content and for its beautiful heart-shaped leaves. Appropriately enough, violets have, since ancient times, been affectionately known as heartsease. Drink two to three cups per day.

Continued ➡

3 parts hawthorn leaves and flowers

2 parts hawthorn berries

2 parts ginkgo leaves

2 parts motherwort leaves

2 parts oatstraw

2 parts violet leaves and flowers

1 part crampbark

1 part linden blossoms

1. Combine all the herbs in a pot and cover with boiling water.

2. Stir well, cover, and steep 15 to 20 minutes.

FIVE-ROOT REVIVAL

Traditionally, these roots were brewed into old-fashioned root beer and imbibed as a healthful liver- and blood-cleansing beverage. Drink one to two cups per day for mild to moderate skin problems.

1 part burdock root

1 part dandelion root

1 part sarsaparilla root

1 part yellow dock root

1/4 part sassafras root bark

1. Combine the herbs in boiling water, reduce heat, and simmer for 15 to 20 minutes in a covered pot.

2. Remove from the heat and steep, covered, for 30 minutes.

STRONG BONES TEA

Here's a blend that gently provides minerals for the entire body. All these herbs are nutritious and tend to be good sources of absorbable calcium, magnesium, iron, and other important trace minerals. Drink two to four cups per day as a gentle bone-building tonic.

2 parts oatstraw

1 part alfalfa leaves

1 part horsetail

1 part red clover blossoms

1 part rose hips (organic)

1 part violet leaves and flowers

2 parts nettle

1. Combine the herbs in a pot and cover with boiling water.

2. Stir well, cover, and steep 15 to 20 minutes.

IF ONLY I HAD A BRAIN TEA

When you have to study, write, or think brilliant thoughts, this tea is great for mental clarity. Drink two or three cups per day.

2 parts Siberian ginseng root

1 part ginkgo leaves

1 part gotu kola leaves

1 part peppermint

1. Add the ginseng root to boiling water, reduce heat, and simmer in a covered pot for 20 minutes.

2. Turn off the heat, add the remaining herbs, and steep 20 minutes.

HEART & SOUL TONIC

Rich in beta-carotene and bioflavonoids, this yummy raspberry-based cordial is a true tonic that's fun to take. It increases circulation to and from the heart and brain and increases the integrity of tissues and capillaries, making it excellent for people who bruise easily and heal slowly. It's useful as a pre- and postsurgery tonic and helpful in healing any structural injury to bones, ligaments, tendons, and muscles. Take 1/2 teaspoon (2.5 ml) once or twice a day, three to five times a week, or daily for the two-week periods before and after surgery.

If you'd prefer the wonderful tonic qualities as a tea, steep the ingredients (except the raspberries) in 1 quart boiled water 15 to 20 minutes in a covered pot. Drink one or two cups per day.

2 parts ginkgo leaves

2 parts hawthorn flowers and leaves

2 parts hawthorn berries

1 part orange slices (organic)

1 part raspberries (fresh or frozen)

1 part rose hips (organic)

Brandy

2 tablespoons honey (per pint of strained liquid)

1. Grind all the herbs and place in a widemouthed jar, then cover with three times as much brandy. Let stand one month.

2. Strain, squeezing all liquid from the herbs. Sweeten with honey.

Mail-Order Resources for Herbs

American Botanical Pharmacy
P.O. Box 9699
Marina del Rey, CA 90292
Info: (310) 453–1987
Orders: (800) 437–2362

Avena Botanicals
219 Mill Street
Rockport, ME 04856
(207) 594–0694

Dry Creek Herb Farm
13935 Dry Creek Road
Auburn, CA 95602
(530) 878–2441

Jean's Greens Herbal Tea Works
119 Sulphur Springs Road
Norway, NY 13416
(315) 845–6500
Fax: (315) 845–6501
Web site: www.jeansgreens.com

Motherlove Herbal Company
P.O. Box 101
LaPorte, Co 80535
(970) 493–2892
Fax: (970) 224–4844
Web site: www.motherlove.com

Mountain Rose Herbs
20818 High Street
North San Juan, CA 95960
(800) 879–3337
Fax: (530) 292–9138
Web site: www.botanical.com/mtrose/

Sage Woman Herbs™
406-B South 8th Street
Colorado Springs, CO 80904
(888) 350–3911
Fax: (719) 473–8873
Web site: www.sagewomanherbs.com

San Francisco Herb & Natural Foods Co.
P.O. Box 40604
San Francisco, CA 94140
(510) 547–6345

Green Tea: Antioxidants in a Cup

Diana Rosen
Illustrations by Alison Kolesar, Mary Rich, and Kathy Bray

Is Green Tea Really Good for You?

Happily, I can say that not only is tea enjoyable, it's good for you. For centuries, China has praised the health benefits of its native plant.

Scientists around the world have researched and examined the leaf exhaustively, and they feel now that they know some of the reasons this simple beverage does so much. Tea provides benefits for bones and teeth. Its vital chemical compounds have been found to fight cancer, help stabilize diabetes, and do much to prevent cardiovascular disease. Tea can even make your skin healthier and prettier.

And the most beneficial, most healthful tea is the barely processed leaf from the *Camellia sinensis* bush—green tea.

The Medical Stamp of Approval

For thousands of years, healers and monks have noted the many benefits of tea, particularly green tea—its ability to offer refreshment, increase alertness, and stave off disease. Yet it is reassuring to know that pharmacologists, chemists, physicians, nutritionists, and others in the field of health science are recognizing the health-giving properties of tea when used consistently all through life.

Studies of tea's value to maintaining good health have been reported in medical journals throughout the world. Most notable have been studies conducted by the *Journal of the Japanese Society of Food Science and Technology*, Tufts University, Harvard University, the National Cancer Institute, and U.S. teaching hospitals such as Johns Hopkins and Reed College. All of these studies concur on one point: Green tea is an inexpensive, healthful drink with possible long-range benefits, especially if taken daily throughout one's life.

The studies suggest that green tea may help lower the risk of cancer, inhibit aging, reduce the risk of cardiovascular disease, help lower blood-sugar levels, fight viral infections, and even prevent cavities, bad breath, and gum disease. While drinking green tea will certainly cause no harm, the best reason to drink it is that it does have time-tested benefits such as antioxidation of fats and possible anticancer properties.

Buying Green Tea

Appearance and color are not always clues to quality. Sometimes a tea can be nicely rolled but its taste is mediocre. Also, high-grade greens are sometimes more gray than green in their dried form. Your tea merchant should really know his or her inventory and be able to answer questions about how old the tea is, how it was stored prior to delivery, and how it is stored in the shop. Teas can last for months, but the finest tea will lose its flavor profile in days if not properly stored.

TESTING FOR FRESHNESS

Green tea is a beverage that is most readily enjoyed visually because of the delicate color of its infused liquor. It is important that the tea be fresh, and the best way to test its freshness is to close your fist tightly around a small amount, breathe in with your nose, then release your fingers.

Smell the aroma that has been released from the tea. Is it sweet? Grassy? Pleasant? If there's no odor or a very faint aroma, the tea is most likely not fresh enough; discard it. Although this method will tell you much, nothing will reveal the true essence of the tea like cupping it—steeping it with the correct amounts of tea leaves and water heated to the right temperature for the proper amount of time.

Whenever possible, ask for a taste sample before buying teas. While one can often tell much from the dried leaf and the smell of the brewed leaf, the ultimate test is in the mouth. Although there are many variations in color, your tea merchant should be able to tell you what to expect. If the brew of a green tea is dark gold or orange-amber, that tea

Continued ➜

may be of a low quality. Most high-quality greens should brew up pale green to yellow-green. Brewed leaves should have a clean "chestnut" flavor, plus a pleasant vegetative flavor, and the better ones will have even more complexity.

Can't quite make the transition from tea bags to loose leaf? To make sure your box of tea bags is fresh, remove one bag and take out the tea. Pour hot water over just the paper tea bag. If the ensuing infusion tastes just like water, hooray. If it tastes more like tea, uh-oh—the paper has absorbed the flavor and the tea is simply too old.

How to Store Tea

The enemies of tea are light, moisture, and odors from other foods, so a tightly constructed opaque container is important, and the size of the container should match the amount of tea. If too little tea is put into a large container, the tea will continue to oxidize. Glass and ceramic are inert and very good for teas; tins often leak because they've been soldered. Tea can be stored at room temperature, but if you live in a very humid or very hot environment, store your packages of tea in a cool, dry, dark cupboard for extra protection.

TO REFRIGERATE OR NOT?

Some green-tea sellers recommend refrigeration, but unless the packaging is airtight, storing tea in the refrigerator makes it vulnerable to odors and moisture. If you have the advantage of a very stable storage unit, and it can be used only for tea, you might consider that. Temperatures should be kept between 30 and 40°F (1–4°C), and you can store the tea for up to six months.

In general, forget about freezing unless you are confident that your high-quality greens have been packaged very carefully. Otherwise, the water condensation that occurs when the tea is defrosted can greatly damage it. Besides, the best protection for preserving tea is to buy it fresh, in season, and in small quantities—two to four ounces (56–112 g) at most. Since an ounce of tea should generate 15 to 30 cups, that should hold you for a little while!

Brewing a Perfect Cup of Green Tea

The first consideration in brewing green tea is to think of it as a delicate food, to be handled tenderly and with respect. One can compare green tea to fresh leaf vegetables. Just as a chef handles produce gently, with grace, so should you handle tea. For example, if spinach is tossed into boiling water, the result is that much of the chlorophyll and the taste go into the cooking water, leaving you with shriveled, overcooked leaves. However, if the leaves are gently laid into a steamer, and water is allowed to waft up, what results is a vegetable with more flavor and color.

SELECTING THE WATER

Ideally, springwater that runs freely near where your tea grows is the best water to use. Since that's nearly impossible for those of us who live outside the green-tea centers of Asia, bottled springwater is our best choice.

It is critical that the bottled water be springwater, taken directly from its source. Much bottled water is filtered city water and, while better than water directly from the tap, it is not the best for making tea. Some fine bottled waters are so pure and so free of minerals that they make a very flat tea. Canadian, Italian, and Polish springwaters are some of the best available, but many fine American bottlers use water from pure springs.

Never use distilled water; it will always make your tea flat because minerals have been removed that are essential to bringing out the flavor of tea. Distilled water is for your irons, not tea.

The third choice would be to use a good filter system on your tap or a commercial filtering pitcher. Both are adequate.

> ### ASK YOUR TEA MERCHANT
> If you patronize a local tea merchant rather than an on-line or catalog source, ask his or her advice about which bottled waters are best in your area. (You may be one of those lucky people who live in a city where the tap water is superb.) When you pay a premium for fine tea, it makes good sense to infuse it in the best water you can find.

Just as you must use your palate to guide you to teas that taste best to you, you must taste waters and decide which ones bring out the best flavor in your teas without making them flat-tasting, chemical-tasting, or off-tasting in any way.

MEASURING THE WATER AND THE TEA

Before brewing tea, always fill a measuring cup with water (8 fluid ounces; 240 ml) and pour it into your teacup or teapot to determine exactly how much water it holds. The styles and shapes of cups and pots vary tremendously. One pot may look small and actually hold 12 ounces (360 ml); another may look generous and yet actually hold only 6 ounces (180 ml).

Now that you know how much water your vessel holds, you can gauge the amount of tea to use. The ratio of tea to water is based on weight, because a teaspoon of smaller leaves weighs more than a teaspoon of larger leaves. Given equal amounts of water, a teaspoon of large leaves results in an insipid drink, while a teaspoon of small, dense leaves will give you a satisfyingly strong cup of tea.

It is always a good idea to purchase a well-calibrated scale or a well-built small food scale. A teaspoon is simply not as accurate a measuring tool as a scale. It is important to repeat that the lighter the leaves, the more you will use; the smaller, denser leaves require smaller quantities. This is probably the most critical point to learn in brewing tea: Always measure your tea. If you drink the same type all the time, the amount will become second nature to you, but until then, learning how to use a fine scale that indicates both grams and ounces will make the measuring simple.

A second critical point is to always weigh the tea to match the amount of water you will be using. Vessels vary greatly in the amount of liquid they can hold. Once you become accustomed to your teapot or teacup, and how each of your favorite green teas should taste to you, this, too, will become much simpler.

Three grams (.105 oz) of tea to five ounces (140 g) of water is best for brewing tea in a small teapot. Four grams (.140 oz) of tea to eight ounces (224 g) of water is best for every other method. The smaller *guywans*, or covered bowls, take two grams

When working with a new tea, use a reliable scale to measure the amount of tea you're using. Keep notes, and keep experimenting until you find just the right amount of tea for your pot or cup.

(.070 oz.) of tea to four ounces (112 g) of water. Good-quality tea leaves sink to the bottom after they have infused, so one can drink directly from the *guywan* or pour the liquor into smaller cups.

Tea drinkers quickly learn to be flexible. Tea is not an exact beverage; the exceptions are the rules. Trust your palate. Whenever you are not sure about amounts, use your tea merchant's guidelines. You can always adjust to your own tastes from then on.

The secret to learning how to brew tea is not unlike the answer to the age-old question "How do you get to Carnegie Hall?"

"Practice, practice, practice!"

WHAT'S A *GUYWAN*?

Guywans are Chinese cups made of nearly transparent pale green or white porcelain. These cups are ideal for drinking tea because they do not keep the tea so hot that it is uncomfortable to drink, the saucer protects the hands, and the cover becomes a clever paddle to push the leaves gently back and forth to help them infuse fully.

A guywan is a traditional Chinese teacup.

STEEPING THE TEA

Pu-erh, an intentionally aged black tea from China, is the only tea that requires roiling boiling water. Most blacks and oolongs do best with nearly boiling water, about 195 to 200°F (91–93°C), though the lower temperatures are best for oolongs and the higher temperatures are best for blacks.

For greens, much lower temperatures are necessary to get the best flavor and the most infusions. The suggested temperature range is 160 to 170°F (71–76°C), though some jasmines benefit from slightly higher temperatures (175–185°F; 79–85°C). Brewing green tea with cooler water and a shorter time results in a better flavor. Covering the pot is also critical to helping the tea leaves unfurl, and it will consistently provide multiple infusions.

DETERMINING BREWING TIME

Generally, 30 seconds to 1 minute of steeping is best for greens, but there are exceptions. Some Ceylonese, Vietnamese, Nepalese, and Indian greens—particularly Nilgiri and Darjeeling greens—can stand longer brewing times, and some Chinese Long Jing (Dragon-well) teas do quite well at 6 or 7 minutes of brewing. Always ask your tea merchant for recommendations on time and temperature.

USING A THERMOMETER

Quickly gauging the temperature of water becomes a matter of being sensitive to your teakettle and the sounds it makes. Until you reach that feeling of familiarity, get yourself a simple candy thermometer; they're about five dollars in most hardware stores, chef's shops, and major supermarkets.

To determine water temperature, simply dip the metal gauge into the water, wait a few seconds for the temperature dial to move, and read the temperature. If

Use a candy thermometer to test the water temperature.

it has reached its peak, remove the kettle from the heat source. If not, continue to heat until it's right. If you do this two or three times, you will be able to gauge the time and temperature easily.

You will soon become so familiar with your kettle that you will hear the bubbles as they grow from tiny to large to roiling. As with everything worthwhile, it just takes a little practice.

BREAKING THE "CRUST"

Having said all the above, I must confess that these are my personal procedures for the truest, sweetest, clearest infusions for green tea. Some tea merchants, far more experienced than I, continue to suggest that the water nearly reach the boiling point, if only to liberate or free up the oxygen content, or "break the oxidized crust." The water is then allowed to cool to the suggested lower temperature, and then the steeping begins.

I suggest you try both methods:

· Heat to near boiling, then cool to 170 to 185°F (76–85°C) and infuse; *or*

· Heat only to 170 to 185°F (76–85°C) and infuse immediately.

As Confucius said, "Let your palate be your guide."

Specialty Green Teas

There are many kinds of green tea. You can always buy a box of generic green tea bags at the grocery store, but walk into your local coffee shop or teahouse and you'll see an entire row of containers filled with dark and aromatic tea leaves, each with its own label. What are the differences? Well, the taste, fragrance, and color of green tea vary depending on where it was grown and how it was processed. For example, most green teas are cultivated in China, Japan, India, Taiwan, and Sri Lanka. Not only teas grown in different countries, but even teas grown in different regions within the same country have different tastes and aromas.

Following are descriptions of some of the most common types of green tea available for sale in North America.

HOW TEA LEAVES ARE PROCESSED

When harvested, only the top two leaves and the leaf bud are plucked from the tea plant. These leaves are tender, have fullness of flavor, and can be twisted or rolled into a variety of shapes. This precision handpicking requires dexterity and concentration, and it must be done while enduring heat, altitude, and long hours. Tea plucking is, for the most part, women's work—and hard work, at that.

After the tea leaves are plucked, they must be dried. The heat destroys natural enzymes in all tea leaves. These complex proteins are present in plant cells and serve as a catalyst for chemical reactions from heat and cold. Heat prevents oxidation of polyphenols—the antioxidants that help protect against disease—yet preserves the flavonols that give tea its unique crisp taste. There are three common methods for heating and drying the leaves: (1) They are laid on racks to wither, (2) they are pan-fired, or (3) they are steamed and then dried.

The leaves are then rolled or pressed, by hand or with machinery, into the different shapes that you see piled together in glass tea canisters in shops. Rolling the tea leaves is done not just to create a decorative look but also to ensure a regulated release of natural substances and flavor when the leaves are steeped in the cup.

Continued ➜

ASSAM

India's most plentiful tea district, Assam contains about 200 tea gardens that produce as much as one third of all the tea of India. The area is located along the border of China, Burma, and Bangladesh, about 127 miles east of the area of Darjeeling. In the 19th century, Scottish Maj. Robert Bruce "discovered" *Thea assamica* on the high plateau along the banks of the Brahmaputra River. Thus began the modern history of growing tea in India. The Assam tea bush has larger, wider leaves but is only slightly different from the Chinese tea bush, *Camellia sinensis*. Assam teas are grown for "strength" in aroma and body, and only a tiny part is processed as green teas. Not surprisingly, these greens have a hearty taste and are favored by those new to the taste of green tea.

Bherjan Estate. An organic-green-tea estate, Bherjan produces a crop with small, dark leaves that infuse to a pleasant, light-tasting green tea. This is an excellent everyday, all-day tea.

Khongea. The green version of this tea is clean-tasting and yields several crisp infusions of delicate green liquor.

BANCHA

Low tea on the totem pole, this tea is ordinary, dark, and rough. Mixed with stems, stalks, and low-grade teas, it is the everyday drink of Japan. Bancha has a slightly astringent taste and produces a yellowish liquor. Green bancha is bitter when cool. To brew bancha, use 3 rounded tablespoons (45 ml) of bancha leaves for a pot of 3 cups (720 ml) of boiling water. Steep 2 or 3 minutes and pour into warmed cups. Do not allow the leaves to continue to steep; pour off all the tea at once. For a single cup, use about 1 level teaspoon (5 ml) in 6 ounces (180 ml) of hot water (180°F; 82°C) and steep about 2 minutes. Bancha may be reinfused, and it is frequently served with sake.

BAOZHOUNG (POUCHONG)

These are the tea leaves used most often as a base for jasmine because of the large, flavorful leaves and slightly longer oxidation, which holds the scent of the night-blooming jasmine so well.

CHUNMEE (PRECIOUS EYEBROWS)

Also spelled Chun Mei or Zhen Mei, the name is given to these springtime greens because the leaves are twisted into small, curved shapes—not unlike the eyebrows of a beautiful doll. A high-grown tea from the Yunnan province of China, it produces a remarkable aftertaste from its light amber infusion that is reminiscent of plums. Multiple infusions are quite common from this subtle yet provocative tea.

DARJEELING

Some 83 gardens grow tea in Darjeeling, the district on the southern hills of the Himalayan Mountains along the border of Nepal, Sikkim, and Bhutan. Darjeelings, often referred to as the champagne of teas, are among the most sought after for their tender, highly aromatic leaves from the first flush of spring and for the more flowery teas of the autumnal picking. Here, as elsewhere in India, green-tea processing is very limited, but the teas are exquisite—delicate yet with that distinctive Darjeeling astringency that is so admired.

Caveat emptor: As with all Darjeelings, try to buy single-estate green teas only. It is a truism in the tea business that more Darjeeling is sold than could ever be manufactured; each year, 11 million kilos are grown, but more than 50 million kilos are reported sold! People blend it with other things (which is fine) but call it Darjeeling (which is not fine). A blend can produce a good cup of tea, but it should be called a blend and not passed off as one type of tea.

Ambootia Tea Estate. This estate grows several grades of green that produce a light, lovely cup. Its teas are frequently found in many commercial brands of organic greens.

Arya Green. An aromatic, gentle green from Darjeeling, this tea is equivalent in looks and style to a sencha but much more flavorful.

Makaibari Tea Estate. This tea estate produces a biodynamically grown, world-class tea with elegant, long, full leaves that infuse several times. A multiple award winner, the tea offers the essence of Darjeeling and the lightness of a green. Add to that the care and integrity of an organic leaf, and you have an enormously satisfying cup.

Risheehat Estate. A Darjeeling green produced from a limited crop, this is sought after for its fruity aroma and mild, delicate, sweet taste. It yields a lovely fragrance and clear green-yellow liquor.

Seeyok (Swek Chiyakaman). Located on the Indo-Nepal border facing Rongbong Valley, Seeyok produces a green with the classic organic Darjeeling character.

Semabeong (Abode of the Bear). This tea garden, located at perhaps the highest altitude in Darjeeling, was only recently revived and produces an interesting organic green tea.

DRAGONWELL (LONG JING OR LUNG CHING)

From Hangzhou in Zhejiang province comes the favorite green tea of mainland China. Its fresh, sweet taste has inspired poetry from Lu Yu's time to today. Its leaves are flat, long, and vibrant green and will yield several infusions of delicate, flowery aroma and flavor from its yellow-green liquor.

Up to eight spring grades of Dragonwell are possible. Each grade is different—sometimes slightly, sometimes radically—but each has that distinctive Dragonwell taste.

GENMAICHA

This tea is a mixture of bancha or medium-quality green tea, popcorn, and toasted, hulled rice kernels. This is a nutty, simple drink that tastes quite wonderful with traditional Japanese foods. Genmaicha is not a fine tea in any sense of the word but, rather, an inexpensive, everyday tea drink that is fun, flavorful, and satisfying. Brew one teaspoon in six ounces of 180°F (82°C) water for about 1 1/2 minutes.

Genmaicha tea is filled with popped corn and toasted, hulled rice kernels.

GREEN PEARLS (SILK BALLS)

Rolled "pearls" unfurl into three or four leaves that include a delicately pale tea-leaf bud. These pearls, also called balls or pellets, yield a lovely aromatic brew of a golden liquor with three to seven infusions. These are delightful to prepare for people new to green teas. The "dance of the leaf" is spectacular, and the ensuing drink always satisfying. Some smaller pearls are infused with jasmine flowers, but the plain ones, typically the size of a 6-millimeter pearl, are definitely fragrant without the additional scent of a flower.

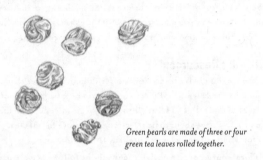

Green pearls are made of three or four green tea leaves rolled together.

GUNPOWDER

This is a tea shaped to look like small pellets that imitate the gunpowder pellets used for ammunition during the 17th century. It was one of the first teas to be exported from China to Europe and, as a result, remains one of the best known there. The original idea for rolling the leaves into tight balls, or pellets, was to help preserve their freshness for the long trip from China to Europe. The pellets are still lightly rolled combinations of buds and young green leaves. They unfurl as they infuse, offering a visual demonstration of the "agony of the leaves," the process so dramatically named in which the curled or rolled dried leaves are infused with water and open up "agonizingly."

Originally hand rolled, most gunpowders are rolled by machine today. To test the freshness of gunpowder, pinch or squeeze a pellet in your hand. It should resist pressure if it's fresh; it will crumble if it's stale. However, as always, the truest test of freshness and goodness is to cup the tea, drink it properly brewed, and let your palate be the final arbiter.

Gunpowder is frequently used in a tea blend for Moroccan mint, which incorporates a sweet digestive—the native Moroccan spearmint—with the clean, crisp taste of gunpowder green tea.

Gunpowders are most commonly from Zhejiang province, and many come from other provinces, such as Qinghai, Anhui, Hunan, and Fujian, in a variety of grades. They brew up a dark liquor.

Gunpowder (Xiao Qiu). This type of gunpowder brews dark green with a pungent but pleasant flavor and long-lasting aftertaste. It lends itself well to additional flavors such as lemon and mint.

Gunpowder Pinhead Temple of Heaven. This is similar to Gunpowder Temple of Heaven, but usually smaller. Considered a premier gunpowder type, it lends itself to multiple infusions.

Gunpowder Temple of Heaven. A premier gunpowder from Zhejiang province, it provides an aromatic cup with a sweet, grassy taste, much more delicate than the other grades.

As you might infer from its name, gunpowder green tea is rolled into tiny pellets.

GYOKURO (GEM OF DEW DROP, JEWEL DEW, OR PRECIOUS DEW)

Gyokuro has been referred to as "history, philosophy, and art in a single cup." It is the best green tea of Japan. This is a premier, noble green tea made from single buds that are picked once a year. The leaves are small and extremely fragrant and tender. Gyokuro should be made with about five heaping teaspoons of long, thin leaves with about 1/2 cup of water at 120°F (49°C). Steeped for about 1 1/2 minutes, the tea is poured off completely. The leaves can then be reinfused with slightly hotter water.

HOUJICHA

This tea is a bancha that is lightly roasted, which gives it a nutty flavor. Not at all a connoisseur tea, this is a fun everyday tea drink that goes well with Japanese foods, particularly sukiyaki, or any food strongly flavored with soy sauce. Its liquor is a tawny brownish color that has a smoky taste. Although best when served hot, it also can be served cool but not cold. It is excellent at nighttime, as it is very light and low in caffeine.

JASMINE

The jasmine flower, thought to have arrived in China from Persia, has been used to scent green teas for nearly 10 centuries, at least since the Song dynasty (A.D. 960–1279). Jasmine is unique among flowers blended with tea because it opens up only at night. As a result, scenting tea with jasmine is also done at night, by covering a bamboo tray or screen of fresh green tea leaves with a blanket of buds or flowers.

This is done in several layers, and in the morning the flowers are removed. This process is repeated, often as many as 11 times, before the delicate fragrance becomes a part of the tea itself. The quality of both the green tea and the jasmine differentiates each of the following styles of jasmine teas. Those from Fujian province are considered to be the best. The following is a partial list.

Jasmine Chun Feng (Spring Peak Jasmine). With a wonderful aroma, this green tea is a Chinese classic of uniform-sized leaves with large numbers of silver tips. The uniformity reflects careful sorting and grading. A minimum of three infusions is common.

Jasmine Hummingbird's Nest. Considered a showplace tea, this is an exquisite jasmine that is pressed and rolled to form a little "nest" and carefully protected with delicate paper folded in tight pleats. The paper is unwrapped, and the nest is placed in a tumbler or wineglass and infused gently with water, about 150°F (65.6°C). It will then blossom into leaves and proffer its exquisite jasmine scent. This is a great way to enchant guests.

Continued →

Jasmine Monkey King. A classic green tea with the divine jasmine scent that is marvelous for afternoon tea, this is an excellent marriage of good Chinese green tea and a lovely fragrance.

Jasmine Pearl. This tea is scented with the buds of the jasmine flower to create an intense and very fragrant tea. The leaves and the buds are rolled into small balls, or pearls, that unfurl as they are steeped, showing off their beautiful, graceful leaves. It will yield six or seven infusions. (A similar grade is sometimes referred to as Dragon Phoenix.)

Jasmine Yin Hao Silver Tip. Also called Fragrant Petal, this provides multiple infusions that do not fade in flavor. Its lingering aftertaste is superb. Often made with the very flavorful pouchong teas and allowed to oxidize slightly longer than most green teas, this jasmine is infinitely more aromatic than others in this category. Although pouchong tea is technically an oolong, a good grade is closer in taste to the great greens. A fine pouchong brews a pale green that is light, delicate, and without the "fired" taste typical of most oolongs.

Jasmine flowers lend a delicate fragrance to green tea leaves.

MATCHA UJI (FROTH OF LIQUID JADE)

This is the famous powdered green tea made from pulverizing the highest-quality gyokuro tea into a fine powder the consistency of talc. Matcha is used primarily in chanoyu. It is made by pouring hot water (about 185°F; 85°C) onto the powdered tea in a warmed small bowl, rather than a teapot. A dampened bamboo whisk is used to stir up the matcha and water into a frothy drink that is at once sweet and astringent. Use about 1/2 teaspoon of tea to 1/4 cup of water for thin tea, or two level teaspoons to 1/2 cup of water for thick tea.

SENCHA (INFUSED TEA)

Hunter green, needlelike leaves mark the sencha, which brews up to a delicate green liquor that is both grassy sweet and cleanly astringent. The grades are numerous, and even the mediocre sencha can be a delight; but if you can afford the better ones, be prepared for a treat. Many Pan-Asian countries are now processing greens to imitate Japanese sencha and to meet the growing demand worldwide. China and Vietnam both make senchas, though most are exported to Japan.

Sencha is referred to as a "guest tea" because it is of higher quality than, say, bancha or houjicha. Usually, it is prepared with great ceremony in a special small teapot with its spout at "9 o'clock" and its handle at "6 o'clock" instead of opposite each other. Called *kyusu*, the pots are used with small handleless cups made of porcelain. Sencha is excellent with sushi.

To brew, warm a small *kyusu* with hot water and empty it. Place 2 rounded teaspoons (10 ml) of sencha leaves in the pot and add about 1 cup (240 ml) of hot water (175°F; 80°C). Steep for just 1 minute and pour a little tea into each warmed cup. Repeat until the cups are filled. In this way, each guest receives the same quality and amount of tea. Completely pour off the liquor. Sencha is particularly rich in vitamin C and may be infused several times.

Sencha Rose. This is a traditional sencha scented or flavored with the essence of roses—quite a mélange of aromatic and taste sensations.

Sencha Sakuro. Drinking this tea is like capturing springtime in Japan. It is a sencha green tea scented with the country's famous cherry blossoms. Some commercial brands use maraschino cherries.

Mail-Order Resources

Check to see if there is a teahouse or coffee shop in your area that offers fine-quality green tea. Quality tea merchants are passionate about the teas they buy and sell, and all are (or should be) mini-encyclopedias of intimate knowledge about their selections. They love to "talk tea," so ask them for details about suggested brewing times and serving ideas.

If local sources are unavailable, consult the following mail-order and Internet sources for loose-leaf green teas and accessories. Although there are many more places to buy teas and accessories, this list includes companies that are known for selling high-quality loose-leaf green teas.

Manufacturers of green teas sold in tea bags and widely distributed in supermarkets and natural foods stores are not included in this list, because they are so readily available.

> ### "NATURAL" FLAVORINGS
> Green teas need not be organic to be healthful, but it's self-defeating to buy green teas that contain propylene glycol (PPG) to enhance flavors, particularly fruit flavors. Packaged teas may sometimes list PPG as simply "natural flavoring." Always ask what that natural flavoring is.

Choice Organic Teas, Granum, Inc.
2901 NE Blakely Street
Seattle, WA 98105
(206) 525–0051
Fax: (206) 523–9750
Web site: www.granum-inc.com
High-quality boxed organic line with nice greens.
Also available at most upscale and natural foods stores.

East India Tea and Coffee Co.
1933 Davis Street, Suite 308
San Leandro, CA 94577
(510) 638–1300
Fax: (510) 638–0760
Garden-estate green teas in nicely designed packages.

Guy's Tea
Empire Tea Services
5155 Hartford Avenue

Columbus, IN 47203

(812) 375–1937

Fax: (812) 376–7382

www.guystea.com

Excellent selection of Ceylonese teas from Sri Lanka.

Harney & Sons

11 East Main Street, Village Green

P.O. Box 638

Salisbury, CT 06068

(800) TEA TIME

Fax: (203) 435–5044

www.harney.com

John Harney and sons Michael and Paul have long played a major role in educating North America's tea consumers. Harney teas are found in fine hotels and gift shops everywhere. Their superb selection of greens continues to grow and includes fine teas from China, Japan, and other major suppliers throughout the world. Ask about Thera-greens I.P.P., a nutritional tea supplement reputed to help reduce the risk of cancer.

Himalayan Highland Tea Company

1702 South Highway 121

Suite 607–189

Lewisville, TX 75067

(800) 580–8585

Fax: (972) 221–6770

"Tea Grown on the Roof of the World." Importers of a variety of teas from Nepal.

Holy Mountain Trading Co.

P.O. Box 457

Fairfax, CA 94978

(888) 832–8008

Fax: (415) 751–6149

www.holymtn.com

Exceptionally fine green teas and a terrific Web site.

La Société du Thé

2708 Lyndale Avenue South

Minneapolis, MN 55405–3319

(888) 871–5148

Fax: (612) 874–0239

www.teashoppe.com

Mail-order company with exceptional green teas from around the world.

Leaves Pure Teas

1392 Lowrie Avenue

South San Francisco, CA 94080

(650) 583–1157

Fax: (650) 583–1163

Web site: www.leaves.com

An extensive list of fine green teas. This is a company that is committed to providing high-quality teas at affordable prices.

The Republic of Tea

8 Digital Drive, Suite 100

Novato, CA 94949

(800) 298–4TEA

Fax: (800) 257–1731

Web site: www.republicoftea.com

Offers green teas, including some organic, in loose leaf or tea bags.

Serendipitea™

P.O. Box 81

Ridgefield, CT 06877

(888) TEA LIFE

Fax: (203) 894–9649

www.serendipitea.com

Young, energetic company dedicated to educating your palate. Ecologically sensitive packaging for fine green teas.

Simpson & Vail Inc.

3 Quarry Road

Brookfield, CT 06804

(800) 282-TEAS

Fax: (203) 775–0462

www.svtea.com

Mail-order catalog lists a respectable selection of fine greens from around the world.

Stash Teas

P.O. Box 910

Portland, OR 97207

(800) 547–1514

Fax: (503) 684–1514

www.stashtea.com

Carries an impressive selection of green teas for every taste and every budget. Complex and fascinating Web site.

Upton Tea Imports

231 South Street

Hopkinton, MA 01748

(800) 234-TEAS

www.upton.com

Tom Eck established this exemplary mail-order company in 1989, and his extensive catalog currently lists about 120 teas from around the world, including stellar greens.

Water and Leaves

690 Broadway

Redwood City, CA 92063

(800) 699–4753

Fax: (650) 559–1754

www.wayoftea.com

Well-chosen green teas in beautiful packaging.

THE HISTORY OF TOFU

Tofu was first made in China about 2,000 years ago. It was then introduced into Japan during the eighth century, and the Japanese began using it extensively. First called *okabe*, *kabe*, or *shirakabe*, tofu finally received its current name sometime between the 14th and 16th centuries. Tofu became a common ingredient in Asian cuisine during the Edo period (1603–1867), but its popularity really began to soar in 1965, when packaged tofu first became available in Japan. Today, of course, packaged tofu is available everywhere.

Sensational Soy: Recipes for a Healthy Diet

Miriam Jacobs
Illustrations by Mary Rich and Laura Tedeschi

What Is Tofu?

Tofu is curdled soybean milk. Sounds horrible, doesn't it? But if you think of soybeans as milk, then tofu is cheese. Cow's milk or goat's milk is, of course, separated into curds and whey during cheese production, and soy milk is so separated to produce tofu.

Tofu comes in two different textures: regular and silken. Regular tofu is usually called simply "tofu." It has a fibrous, spongelike texture. Silken tofu has a creamier, custardlike texture. Silken and regular tofu are packaged in three different forms:

- Soft
- Firm
- Extra firm

These forms translate into dense, denser, and densest. The denser the tofu, the greater its caloric content. But not to worry. A 2 1/2-ounce serving has only 120 calories, or about the same as an equivalent piece of turkey, while packing a much greater nutritional wallop: 13 grams of protein, 8 milligrams of iron, and 120 milligrams of calcium.

Tofu has a very mild flavor—in fact, many people consider it to be flavorless. Why eat something that has no flavor? First, for its nutritional value. Tofu is a complete protein, meaning that it contains all eight amino acids essential to human health. It is loaded with nutrients and offers a healthful alternative to meat. Second, it adds texture and substance while soaking up the flavors of the foods it's cooked with. Need to beef up your vegetarian chili? Toss in some chopped firm tofu. Wish your vegetable spread was a little creamier? Mix it up with some silken tofu. Want more hamburgers per pound of ground beef? Add in some mashed tofu.

As the popularity of tofu increases, so does the availability and variety of tofu products. And they're not always the plain, bland tofu-in-a-box that we're accustomed to. You can now find flavorful tofus—smoked, grilled, marinated, or seasoned—in natural foods stores and most grocery stores.

HOW IS TOFU MADE?

To make tofu, raw, high-grade soybeans are first soaked, then drained and pulverized. Boiling water is poured over them until they form a consistency similar to mashed potatoes. This mash is then ladled into more boiling water, which allows the undigestible enzyme in soy protein to be broken down, making the result fit for human consumption. Next, the soy milk is filtered from the pulp and a coagulant is added—the Japanese traditionally use sea salt, which contains the coagulant magnesium chloride. Finally, the curds are scooped off the whey and put into a cheesecloth-lined container. After several hours, a custardlike cake of tofu is born.

WHAT ABOUT OTHER SOY PRODUCTS?

The soybean is a true chameleon—it becomes whatever you want it to be, serving as the bland yet nutritionally substantial base for its companion ingredients. Tofu is the most common soy product, but there are many others to experiment with.

Miso is a salty paste made from fermented soybeans. It is primarily used as a seasoning and in soup stocks. It is also very good for you, containing calcium and vitamin B12, which is otherwise sorely lacking in a vegetarian diet, as well as lactobacillus, the lactic-acid-forming bacteria that help the body digest dairy products. (Because miso contains these live bacterial organisms, it is important not to boil it but rather add it at the end of the cooking process.)

Soy milk is the rich, creamy liquid pressed from soybeans. It is lactose-free. Some brands, like dairy milk, are fortified with vitamins. It is available in regular and low-fat varieties.

Soy sauce is a familiar condiment for most of us. It is a salty, dark brown liquid made from fermented soybeans. There are three types: tamari, which is a by-product of miso production; shoyu, which is combined with wheat; and teriyaki sauce, which is thicker and is often mixed with sugar, vinegar, and spices.

Tempeh is made from fermented soybeans and grains, such as rice and barley. It is fibrous and firm and has a mushroomlike flavor. Because of its chewy texture, many people use tempeh as a meat substitute. It is high in B vitamins, calcium, and iron.

Textured soy protein is used to make soy-based meat alternatives. Whether you're a vegetarian looking for alternatives to meat products or simply a health-conscious consumer looking for ways to cut down on fat and cholesterol and increase your soy intake, you should acquaint yourself with the many excellent soy-based meat alternatives. Choose from burgers, hot dogs, sausages, bacon, luncheon meats—whatever meat product you're looking for, you're sure to find a tasty soy alternative to satisfy your craving. Be sure to check the label, though, to be certain that it contains good amounts of soy protein and that it's not loaded with fat.

Is Soy Really Good for You?

Vegetarians and other fans of good health have long known that soy protein is preferable to animal protein. Lately the rest of society has been jumping on the soy bandwagon, recognizing that these so-called leaf eaters apparently know what they are talking about.

Aside from being abundant, economical protein sources, soy products have been cited for their many health benefits, and it has been shown that they can actually safeguard or improve your health. Even the U.S. Food and Drug Administration (FDA) has recognized—and approved statements about—the health benefits of soy protein, based on dozens of controlled clinical studies.

Researchers are regularly adding to the list of known soy health benefits. Currently, the following points have been established:

- Soy seems to reduce the risk of cardiovascular disease. According to the FDA, eating 25 to 50 grams of soy protein per day can lower cholesterol levels by 10 to 24 percent. This is significant because a 1 percent decrease in total cholesterol can be equivalent to a 2 percent decrease in the risk of heart disease.

- Soy may slow the progression of arteriosclerosis and decrease the risk of stroke. This, too, is significant because strokes cause hundreds of thousands of deaths per year.

- Soy protects the kidneys from disease.

- Soy reduces menopausal symptoms such as hot flashes without the side effects often generated by hormone replacement therapy (HRT).

- Soy may help decrease the symptoms of osteoporosis by increasing bone density and preventing bone calcium loss.

- Soy may reduce the risk of breast, colon, and prostate cancer.

SOY FOR COMPLETE PROTEIN

Protein is an important source of essential amino acids that must come from food. Nonessential amino acids are produced in the body. Unlike many other beans, soybeans offer complete protein, meaning that they contain all eight of the essential amino acids. All this and no cholesterol—is it any wonder the soybean is often called the "miracle" bean?

MEETING THE FDA'S RECOMMENDED DAILY PORTION

In late 1999, the FDA approved statements claiming a relationship between consumption of soy protein and reduced risk of heart disease. Based on evidence from more than 50 studies, the FDA concluded that 25 grams of soy protein a day, as part of a diet low in saturated fat and cholesterol, may reduce the risk of heart disease.

> **DID YOU KNOW?**
> The FDA has allowed heart-healthy labeling for a specific food product only twice before: first for oat bran, then for psyllium.

So if you want to reap the heart-smart benefits of soy, you have to eat enough of it. But that's easy. For example:

- 4 ounces of firm tofu contains 13 grams of soy protein
- 4 ounces of soft or silken tofu contains 9 grams of soy protein
- 8 ounces of soy milk contains 10 grams of soy protein
- 1/2 cup of cooked soybeans contains 16 grams of soy protein
- 1/2 cup of tempeh contains 19 grams of soy protein

With numbers like these, it's easy to accrue 25 grams daily.

My Favorite Soy Recipes

A cookbook writer's family lives by what the author dishes up. If it were up to my son, for example, you would be reading recipes for chocolate desserts or croissants—probably anything but soy-based foods. I'm telling you this so you know that soy did not begin with a great reputation in my household. My family, like many, was a bit suspicious of anything made with tofu. You may feel the same.

Rest assured that all the recipes here have been taste tested by regular people—occasionally even people with a reluctance to try something new—and if a recipe didn't pass the taste test, it didn't make the cut.

I've included plenty of vegan recipes to show you how soy products can pinch-hit for both meat and milk proteins. In fact, the first recipe you might want to try to become familiar with soy products is the soy milk fruit smoothie (see page 853), which is vegan.

Cooking an interesting meal using soy protein requires only a willingness to experiment. Use my recipes as a jumping-off point for further soy cuisine exploration, and enjoy!

MISO SOUP

Miso soup is the Asian equivalent of chicken soup. It is mild, it will soothe an upset tummy, and it just feels healing. A simple cup of hot water with a tablespoon of miso dissolved in it is one of my favorite ways to stop the midafternoon munchies. This recipe is a bit more involved, but the extra ingredients are well worth the effort.

3 cups water

1 carrot, sliced thin

1 scallion, finely chopped

10 string beans, cut on the diagonal into thin slices

1 thin slice fresh ginger

3 tablespoons miso

1/2 cup cubed firm tofu

1. In a saucepan, bring the water to a boil. Add the carrot, scallion, string beans, and ginger and simmer for 10 minutes, or until the vegetables are soft.

2. Place the miso in a small bowl. Add a little of the water from the saucepan. Stir the miso with a spoon until it is dissolved in the hot broth.

Continued ➜

3. Add the tofu to the broth and simmer for 2 minutes. Remove the pot from the heat. Add the miso and stir to mix. Remove the slice of ginger and serve the soup immediately.

Note: If you want to reheat it, don't bring the soup to a boil again.

MAKES 2 TO 4 SERVINGS

HOT AND SOUR SOUP

Adapted from *Herbal Soups*, by Ruth Bass (Storey Books, 1996)

The blending of textures and flavors in this soup, with the added bite of cilantro, is extraordinary.

Pork Marinade

1 teaspoon soy sauce

1 teaspoon white wine

3 teaspoons cornstarch

2 teaspoons sesame oil

Soup Ingredients

1/4 pound boneless pork

1 tablespoon Chinese tree ears (a type of mushroom generally available at Asian markets; also called wood ears)

16 tiger lily buds

5 medium-size shiitake mushrooms

2 tablespoons tofu

2 tablespoons cornstarch

3 tablespoons cold water

1 egg

1 teaspoon sesame oil

1 1/2 tablespoons soy sauce

2 tablespoons red wine vinegar

Freshly ground black pepper

1 teaspoon hot chili oil

4 cups chicken broth

2 teaspoons fresh cilantro, minced

1. Cut the pork into 1/4-inch slices. Stack the slices and shred them. Place the pork in a bowl and marinate with the soy sauce, white wine, cornstarch, and oil. Refrigerate.

2. Soak the tree ears and tiger lily buds in separate bowls of warm water until they are expanded and soft.

3. Rinse the tree ears and tiger lily buds. Remove the tough stems of the tree ears and the knobby ends of the lily buds. Shred both in the same manner as the pork.

4. Thinly slice the shiitake mushrooms and cut them into 1-inch lengths.

5. Cut the tofu into 2-inch pieces, 1/4 inch thick.

6. Dissolve the cornstarch in a small bowl with the cold water. Beat the egg with the sesame oil in a separate bowl.

7. Combine the soy sauce, red wine vinegar, black pepper to taste, and hot chili oil and place the mixture in a serving bowl.

8. In a large soup pot, bring the chicken broth to a boil. Add the shiitake mushrooms and tiger lily buds. Reduce the heat and simmer about 5 minutes. Add the pork, bring to a boil, then add the tree ears and tofu. Reduce the heat again and simmer 5 minutes.

9. Stir the cornstarch mixture and add it to the soup slowly, stirring constantly. Pour the beaten egg in wide circles over the surface of the soup, breaking up the resulting ribbons with a spoon.

10. Pour the hot soup into the serving bowl containing the soy sauce mixture and sprinkle the cilantro over the top.

MAKES 6 TO 8 SERVINGS

RED AND GREEN PASTA SALAD

This recipe is open to endless variation. The ground rules are simple: Cook pasta, add extras, toss with dressing, place on lettuce-lined plate, and serve. The green in this particular version of the recipe is parsley, but you could also use basil, rosemary, or mint, adjusting the quantity to taste. The red component could be red pepper, tomato, or pimento, or . . . do you catch the drift? A fresh herb and some nuts are essential to make this dish stand out in the crowd, but otherwise you are limited only by what is fresh in the marketplace.

When I am truly in the swing of things, I make this salad right after we eat pasta for dinner, using the leftover pasta and whatever is fresh in the refrigerator. It is as easy to make this as it is to put the leftovers away! The next afternoon I have lunch ready and waiting.

3 cups rotelli or other small-size pasta	*1/4 cup chopped parsley*
3 ounces smoked tofu, cut into 1/2-inch dice	*1 tablespoon vegetable oil*
3/4 cup diced red pepper	*1 tablespoon vinegar*
3/4 cup corn kernels	*1 tablespoon mustard*
1/3 cup roughly chopped almonds	*Salt and freshly ground black pepper*
1/4 cup chopped niçoise olives	*Lettuce to line plates*

1. Cook the pasta according to package directions, then strain it.

2. Place the cooked pasta in a large bowl. Add the tofu, red pepper, corn, almonds, olives, and parsley and mix gently.

3. In a small bowl, mix the oil, vinegar, and mustard. Pour over the pasta salad and toss thoroughly. Add salt and pepper to taste. Place the salad in the refrigerator to chill.

4. Serve on lettuce-lined plates.

MAKES 4 SERVINGS

POTATO SALAD

This old standby can be given a fresh twist with some interesting ingredients. The smoked tempeh gives the salad depth without the additional cholesterol that bacon might.

4 medium red potatoes

1 apple, chopped

1 tablespoon onion, minced

3 strips smoked tempeh, chopped

1 tablespoon salad olives, chopped

1/4 cup mayonnaise

2 tablespoons cilantro, minced

1. Dice the potatoes and place them in a steaming basket. Bring a pot of water to a boil, set the basket over the pot, and steam the potatoes for 20 minutes, or until they are soft when pierced with a fork.

2. Meanwhile, place the apple, onion, tempeh, and olives in a mixing bowl. Add the mayonnaise and mix well.

3. When the potatoes are done, add them to the mixing bowl. Toss the mixture carefully but thoroughly to combine. If you have the time, let the salad sit in the refrigerator for an hour to let the flavors mingle.

4. When you are ready to serve, place the salad in a serving bowl and sprinkle the cilantro over the top.

MAKES 4 SERVINGS

SILKEN SALAD DRESSING

This dressing started out as an attempt to make a mayonnaise, but it ended up too thin. However, as so often happens in the development of a cookbook, I think this is one of the best recipes I made!

10 ounces silken tofu

2 tablespoons lemon juice

1 tablespoon Dijon mustard

1/4 teaspoon salt

1/8 teaspoon freshly ground black pepper

2 tablespoons olive oil

1. Place the tofu, lemon juice, mustard, salt, and pepper into the bowl of a blender. Process until well mixed and creamy, scraping down the sides several times.

2. With the blender running, pour in the oil, 1/2 teaspoon at a time. Make sure each bit of oil is incorporated before you add the next bit.

3. Store the dressing, covered, in the refrigerator, where it will keep for about 5 days.

   Green Dressing variation: Add 1/4 cup parsley and 5 leaves of fresh basil at the end and blend well.

MAKES 1 1/4 CUPS

TEMPEH CHILI

This chili works well over rice, but I like it even better wrapped up in a soft tortilla with some avocado and lettuce.

1 cup flour

Salt and freshly ground black pepper

8 ounces tempeh

2 tablespoons vegetable oil

1 medium onion, chopped

2 cloves garlic, minced

30 ounces crushed canned tomatoes

2 teaspoons chili powder

1/4 teaspoon salt

Cayenne

1. Season the flour with salt and pepper to taste.

2. Dice the tempeh into 1/2-inch cubes. Dredge the cubes in the seasoned flour.

3. In a skillet, warm the oil over medium-high heat. Add the floured tempeh and sauté until the cubes begin to turn a golden brown. Add the onions and continue sautéing until all the cubes are golden and the onions are translucent.

4. Add the garlic to the skillet and sauté for 20 seconds. Add the tomatoes, chili powder, and salt and mix well. Reduce the heat to low, cover the pan, and let the chili simmer for 15 minutes.

5. Add cayenne to taste. Serve warm over rice or cooled in soft flour tortillas.

MAKES 4 SERVINGS

PASTA WITH ASPARAGUS, SUN-DRIED TOMATOES, AND SOY SAUSAGE

This is an easy, fresh springtime dish. Invite a few friends over and dig in!

14 pieces sun-dried tomatoes

1 cup water

30 asparagus stalks

8 ounces sausage-flavored soy meat substitute

3 cups pasta shells

2 tablespoons grated Parmesan cheese

Freshly ground black pepper

1. Soak the sun-dried tomatoes in 1 cup of water for 15 minutes, or until the tomatoes are soft and pliable. Pour the tomatoes and the water into a food processor or blender and process until smooth.

2. Snap off the woody, hard ends of the asparagus and cut the spears into 1-inch pieces. Place in a steamer basket and steam until bright green. Set aside.

3. Heat a nonstick skillet for 20 seconds and add the meat substitute. Cook, stirring constantly with the end of a wooden spoon to break up the contents.

4. Cook the pasta according to the package directions. Time it so that the pasta, asparagus, and meat substitute are done at the same time.

5. Drain the pasta. Mix the hot pasta, asparagus, and meat substitute together with the tomato sauce in a warm serving bowl. Sprinkle the cheese over the top and grind pepper to taste over all.

Continued →

TEMPEH IN PEANUT SAUCE

A spicy peanut sauce gives tempeh all the oomph it needs to become a favorite. Adjust the cayenne as needed: Children will love this sauce if you consider their sensitive taste buds.

1 cup all-natural peanut butter (no sugar or salt added)

1/2 cup boiling water

1/4 cup apple cider vinegar

1/4 cup tamari soy sauce

2 scallions, minced

1 tablespoon honey

Cayenne

2 blocks (8 ounces) tempeh

2 tablespoons extra-virgin olive oil

1. Place the peanut butter in the bowl of a food processor. Add the boiling water and process until smooth. Add the vinegar, soy sauce, scallions, honey, and cayenne to taste and process until smooth, scraping down the sides occasionally.

2. Cut the tempeh into 1/2-inch cubes. In a wok or nonstick skillet, warm the oil over medium-high heat. Add the cubed tempeh and sauté until brown and crisp.

3. Divide the tempeh among four plates. Drizzle a bit of peanut sauce on each plate, and serve the rest of the sauce on the side.

STIR-FRY BROCCOLI

This is a basic recipe that is amenable to all sorts of variations. You can add other vegetables, such as thinly sliced carrots or water chestnuts, or bits of leftover cooked chicken, beef, or pork. A handful of chopped peanuts or cashews is also a great idea. Serve this dish over plain cooked noodles or rice. The only secret to the dish is that you must have all the ingredients prepped and assembled before you start cooking.

3 tablespoons soy sauce

1 tablespoon sherry

1 teaspoon sesame oil

1 teaspoon sugar

1 pound firm tofu, cut into 1-inch cubes

1 tablespoon oil

2 scallions, chopped

1 1-inch slice ginger

2 cloves garlic, minced

1 cup small broccoli florets

1 cup chicken or vegetable broth

1 tablespoon cornstarch

1. In a shallow bowl mix the soy sauce, sherry, sesame oil, and sugar. Add the tofu and mix so that the marinade covers the tofu. Set aside to marinate for 20 minutes to several hours.

2. In a wok or nonstick skillet, warm the oil over high heat. Add the scallions and ginger and sauté until the scallions start to darken. Add the garlic and stir to mix. Add the broccoli florets and 1/2 cup of broth. Mix, cover the pan, and reduce the heat. Let the broccoli steam in the simmering broth for about 5 minutes.

3. Add the cornstarch to the remaining 1/2 cup of broth. Stir until the cornstarch is dissolved.

4. Add the tofu and the marinade to the pan and stir to mix. Raise the heat to high and let the broth come to a full boil. Push the vegetable mix to one side and add the cornstarch broth to the boiling broth. Stir constantly until the mixture loses its milky consistency and thickens, forming a uniform consistency.

5. Serve hot over cooked rice or noodles.

MISO SOBA NOODLES

The first time I ate soba noodles, it was clear to me that this must be comfort food for the Japanese. Nourishing and filling, it's a great vegetarian counterpart to chicken soup.

1 pound soba noodles

2 cups water

2 carrots, sliced

2 scallions, minced

3 cups chopped fresh spinach

1 1/2 cups diagonally sliced snow peas

3 tablespoons sweet miso

1. Cook the soba noodles in a large pot of water for 6 or 7 minutes, or until cooked al dente. Rinse immediately under cold water and set aside.

2. Bring the water to a boil. Add the carrots and simmer for 10 minutes, or until they soften. Add the scallions, spinach, and snow peas. Cook for 3 minutes more.

3. Add the soba noodles and heat through. Remove from the heat and stir in the miso. Serve hot in deep bowls.

MAKES 4 SERVINGS

DESSERTS

When was the last time that you had a melt-in-your-mouth, delightfully sweet, soft and creamy dessert that was also low fat? Welcome to the pleasures of soy-based desserts!

CHOCOLATE PUDDING

Instant, low fat, creamy, filling, healing—what else could you possibly want from a pudding? If you prefer, you can make this recipe with honey, but the consistency will be somewhat thinner.

10 ounces silken tofu
1/4 cup light brown sugar
1/8 cup cocoa powder
1 teaspoon vanilla extract

Place all the ingredients in the bowl of a food processor and process until the mixture is very creamy and smooth. Cover with plastic wrap and refrigerate for 1 hour, or until it's as firm as you desire.

Chocolate Mint Pudding variation: Substitute 1/2 teaspoon of mint extract for the vanilla.

MAKES 2 SERVINGS, IF YOU CAN SHARE

FROZEN SMOOTHIE

This makes an excellent dessert, but it can serve equally well as a breakfast drink. You can vary the proportions depending on the fruit you have. To make the smoothie sweeter, add more orange juice concentrate.

1 cup soy milk
1 banana, frozen, cut into 1-inch chunks
3/4 cup frozen strawberries, blueberries, or mixed berries
2 tablespoons orange juice concentrate (undiluted)

Place all the ingredients into the bowl of a blender and process until smooth. Pour into a large glass and serve immediately.

MAKES 1 SERVING

VANILLA BANANA CREAM

This smooth, sweet cream is perfect on top of cakes, pies, cobblers, and just about anything else you might think of topping with a dollop of whipped cream.

1 cup silken tofu
1 banana
1 teaspoon vanilla extract
1/4 cup honey
1 tablespoon lemon juice, freshly squeezed

Place all the ingredients in the bowl of a food processor and process until smooth and creamy. Pour the cream into a bowl, cover with plastic wrap, and chill for 1 hour.

MAKES 1 1/2 CUPS

APRICOT PIE

This delicately flavored pie is "easy as pie" to make! You can experiment with other fruits—just be sure that the mixture isn't too wet.

1 piecrust in the pan (if it's a frozen crust, prebake according to the package directions, then cool for 10 minutes)
26 ounces canned apricots in heavy syrup
19 ounces silken tofu
2 tablespoons white sugar
1/4 teaspoon orange extract

1. Preheat the oven to 350°F (180°C).

2. Drain the apricots.

3. Drain the tofu on some paper towels.

4. Place the apricots, tofu, sugar, and orange extract in the bowl of a blender and process until very smooth.

5. Pour the apricot filling into the crust and smooth the top. Bake for 50 minutes, or until a knife inserted in the center comes out clean. Cool completely before serving.

MAKES 8 SERVINGS

Continued →

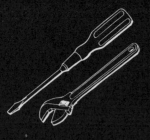

Home

INSIDE THE HOUSE

Simple Home Repairs

Repair a Leaking Faucet

Your Problem:

- Leaking faucets waste water.
- Dripping faucet may cause a spot in the sink.
- Constant dripping is annoying.

What You Need:

- A box of assorted-size washers, unless you know the size.
- A screwdriver.
- An adjustable wrench.

How-To:

1. First turn off the water at the shut-off valve nearest to the faucet you are going to repair. Then turn on the faucet until the water stops flowing. (*fig.* 1)

(fig. 1)

2. Loosen packing nut with wrench. (*fig.* 2) (Most nuts loosen by turning counterclockwise.) Use the handle to pull out the valve unit. (*fig.* 3)

3. Remove the screw holding the old washer at the bottom of the valve unit. (*fig.* 4)

4. Put in new washer and replace screw. (*fig.* 5)

5. Put valve unit back in faucet. Turn handle to the proper position.

6. Tighten the packing nut. (*fig.* 6)

7. Turn on the water at the shut-off valve.

(fig. 2)

(fig. 3)

(fig. 4)

(fig. 5)

(fig. 6)

Faucets may look different, but they are all built about the same. Mixing faucets, which are used on sinks, laundry tubs, and bathtubs are actually two separate units with the same spout. You'll need to repair each unit separately. *(fig. 7)*

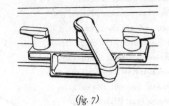

(fig. 7)

Is water leaking around the packing nut? Try tightening the nut. If there is a washer under it, replace the washer. If there's no washer, you may need to wrap the spindle with "packing wicking." *(fig. 8)* Then replace packing nut and handle, and turn water back on at the shut-off valve.

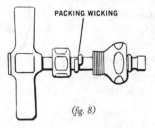

PACKING WICKING

(fig. 8)

Your Reward:

- Lower water costs.
- Spots in sink prevented.
- You save money by doing the job yourself.

Electric Plugs — Repair or Replace

Your Problem:

- Lamps or appliances do not work right.
- A damaged plug is dangerous.
- It's hard to hire help for small repairs.

What You Need:

- New plug—if your old one cannot be used. (Buy one with a UL label.)
- Screwdriver
- Knife

How-To:

1. Cut the cord off at the damaged part. *(fig. 1)*
2. Slip the plug back on the cord. *(fig. 2)*
3. Clip and separate the cord. *(fig. 3)*

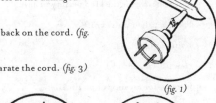

(fig. 1)

(fig. 2)

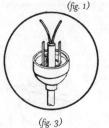

(fig. 3)

4. Tie Underwriters' knot. *(fig. 4)*
5. Remove a half-inch of the insulation from the end of the wires. **Do not cut any of the small wires.** *(fig. 5)*
6. Twist small wires together, clockwise. *(fig. 6)*
7. Pull knot down firmly in the plug. *(fig. 7)*
8. Pull one wire around each terminal to the screw. *(fig. 8)*

(fig. 4)

(fig. 5)

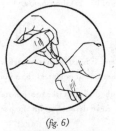

(fig. 6)

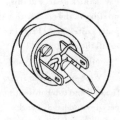

(fig. 7)

(fig. 8)

9. Wrap the wire around the screw, clockwise. *(fig. 9)*
10. Tighten the screw. Insulation should come to the screw but not under it. *(fig. 10)*

(fig. 9)

11. Place insulation cover back over the plug.

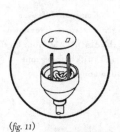

(fig. 10)

(fig. 11)

- The appliance or lamp is back in working condition.

- You have eliminated a possible cause of a fire or shock.

- You have saved money by doing the repair yourself.

Fill the Crack Around Bathtub or Shower

Your Problem:

There's a crack between the bathtub and wall. It should be filled to keep water out. Water can damage the walls and house frame. The crack catches dirt and looks bad.

What You Need:

There are two types of waterproof filler. Choose one:

1. Waterproof grout

2. Plastic sealer

Grout comes in powder form. It must be mixed with water. You can mix it in small amounts at a time. Grout costs less than plastic sealers.

Plastic sealer comes in a tube. It looks like toothpaste. It is easier to use than grout, but costs more. Read directions on the package before you begin your project.

How-To:

Prepare the surface:

1. Remove the old crack filler from the crack. (fig. 1)

2. Wash the surface to remove the soap, grease, and dirt.

3. Dry the surface well before you make repairs.

(fig. 1)

Using Grout:

Put a small amount of grout in a bowl. (fig. 2) Slowly add water and mix until you have a thick paste. Put this mixture in the crack with a putty knife. (fig. 3) Press in to fill the crack. (fig. 4) Smooth the surface. (fig. 5)

Wipe excess grout from the wall and tub before it gets dry and hard. Let the grout dry well before anyone uses the tub.

Empty any left over grout mixture. (**Not down the drain!**) Wash your bowl and knife before grout dries on them.

(fig. 2)

(fig. 3)

Using plastic sealer:

You can squeeze plastic sealer from the tube in a ribbon along the crack. Use a putty knife or spatula to press it down and fill the crack. Smooth the surface. **Work fast!** Plastic sealer dries in a very few minutes. Keep the cap on the tube when you're not using it. (fig. 6)

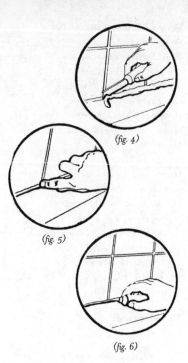

(fig. 4)

(fig. 5)

Your Reward:

- A better looking bathroom.

- No water damage to the house.

- You save money by doing the job yourself.

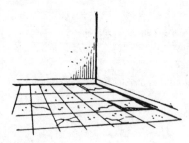

(fig. 6)

Setting Tile

Your Problem:

- Tiles have come loose from walls or floor.

- Tiles are damaged, need replacing.

- It's hard to get help to do small repairs.

What You Need:

- Something to mix in.

- Tile adhesive for the kind of tile you have.

- Paint brush or putty knife.

- Knife or saw.

- New tile (if needed.)

- Grout—for ceramic or plastic tile.

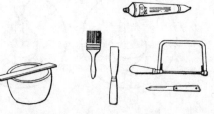

How-To:

Flexible Tile:

1. Remove loose or damaged tile. A warm iron will help soften the adhesive. (*fig.* 1)

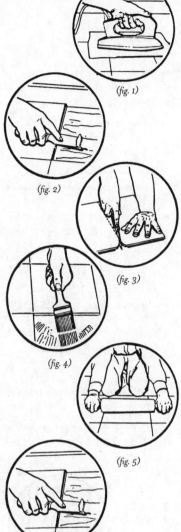

(*fig.* 1)

(*fig.* 2)

2. Scrape off the old adhesive from the floor or wall. Also from the tile if you're going to use it again. (*fig.* 2)

3. Fit tiles carefully. Some tile can be cut with a knife or shears, others with a saw. Tile is less apt to break if it is warm. (*fig.* 3)

(*fig.* 3)

4. Spread adhesive on the floor or wall with a paint brush or putty knife. (*fig.* 4)

(*fig.* 4)

5. Wait until adhesive begins to set before placing the tile. Press tile on firmly. (A rolling pin works well.) (*fig.* 5)

(*fig.* 5)

Ceramic or Plastic Tile:

1. Scrape off the old adhesive from the floor or wall. Also from old tile if you use it again. (*fig.* 6)

(*fig.* 6)

2. If you are using new tile and need to fit it, mark it carefully to size. Cut it with a saw. You can make straight cuts on the tile by scoring it first. Then it will snap off if you press it on the edge of a hard surface. (*fig.* 7)

(*fig.* 7)

3. Spread adhesive on the wall or floor and on the back of the tile. Press tile firmly into place. (*fig.* 8)

4. Joints on ceramic tile should be filled with grout after the tile has firmly set. Mix grout (powder) with water to form a stiff paste. Press the mixture into the joints with your fingers. Smooth the surface. (*fig.* 9)

(*fig.* 8)

5. Carefully remove excess grout from the tile surface before it dries. (*fig.* 10)

6. Empty excess grout mixture. (**Not down the drain!**) Clean up surfaces and tools. (*fig.* 11)

7. Let grout dry overnight before it gets wet again.

(*fig.* 9)

(*fig.* 11)

(*fig.* 10)

Your Reward:

· A better looking place to live.

· Larger and more costly repairs prevented later.

· You save money by doing the job yourself.

Repairing Screens

Your Problem:

· Insects come in through holes in screens.

· Small holes tend to become larger.

· New screens cost money.

· Help is hard to get.

What You Need:

· Screening or ready-cut screen patches.

· Shears

· A ruler or small block of wood with a straight edge.

· Fine wire, or nylon thread.

Continued →

HOW-TO:

1. Trim the hole in the screen to make smooth edges. *(fig. 1)*

2. Cut a rectangular patch an inch larger than the hole.

3. Remove the three outside wires on all four sides of the patch. *(fig. 2)*

4. Bend the ends of the wires. An easy way is to bend them over a block or edge of a ruler. *(fig. 3)*

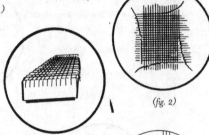

(fig. 1)

(fig. 2)

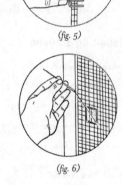

(fig. 3)

5. Put the patch over the hole from the outside. Hold it tight against the screen so that the small, bent wire ends go through the screen. *(fig. 4)*

6. From inside, bend down the ends of the wires toward the center of the hole. You may need someone outside to press against the patch while you do this. *(fig. 5)*

(fig. 4)

(fig. 5)

Mending—You can mend small holes by stitching back and forth with a fine wire or a nylon thread. Use a matching color. *(fig. 6)*

Your Reward:

· Insects kept out.

· The house looks better.

· You save money by doing the job yourself.

(fig. 6)

Replace a Broken Window

Your Problem:

· A window is broken.

· Heat is lost around windowpanes where putty is missing or dried out.

What You Need:

· Window glass—correct size

· Putty or glazing compound

· Putty knife

· Hammer

· Pliers

· Glazier points

How-To:

1. Work from the outside of the frame. *(fig. 1)*

2. Remove the broken glass with pliers to avoid cutting your fingers. *(fig. 2)*

3. Remove old putty and glazier points. Pliers will be helpful to do this. *(fig. 3)*

(fig. 1)

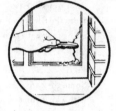

(fig. 2)

(fig. 3)

4. Place a thin ribbon of putty in the frame. *(fig. 4)*

5. Place a glass firmly against the putty. *(fig. 5)*

(fig. 4)

(fig. 5)

6. Insert glazier points. Tap in carefully to prevent breaking the glass. Points should be placed near the corners first, and then every 4 to 6 inches along the glass. *(fig. 6)*

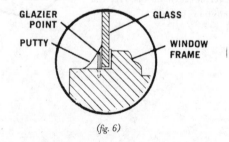

GLAZIER POINT   GLASS

PUTTY   WINDOW FRAME

(fig. 6)

7. Fill the groove with putty or glazing compound. Press it firmly against the glass with putty knife or fingers. Smooth the surface with the putty knife. The putty should form a smooth seal around the window. (fig. 7)

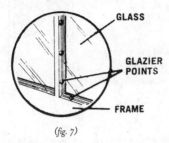

GLASS

GLAZIER POINTS

FRAME

(fig. 7)

Your Reward:

· Rain, cold, dust, and insects are kept out.

· The house looks better.

· You save money by doing the job yourself.

Patch Holes in Wallboard or Plaster

Your Problem:

· There's a hole or crack in the wall.

What You Need:

· Choose one of the two types of patching compounds:

Spackling compound is convenient for small jobs but is more expensive. It can be bought as a powder or ready-mixed.

Patching plaster can be bought in larger packages and costs less. Both spackling powder and patching powder need to be mixed with water.

· Putty knife

· Knife

· Sandpaper—medium grit

· Old cloth or a paint brush

How-To:

1. Remove any loose plaster. With a knife, scrape out plaster from the back edges of the crack until the back of the crack is wider than the front surface. (fig. 1)

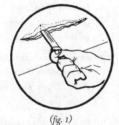

(fig. 1)

2. Thoroughly dampen the surface of the crack with a wet cloth or paint brush. (fig. 2)

3. Prepare patching compound according to directions on package. Mix only a small amount the first time. (fig. 3)

(fig. 2)

4. You can fill small holes with the patching mixture. Be sure to press the mixture until it completely fills the hole. Smooth the surface with the putty knife. (fig. 4) After the patch has dried, you can sand it. Wrap the sandpaper around a small piece of wood. This makes the surface even. (fig. 5)

5. Larger holes or cracks should be filled step-by-step. First, partly fill the hole. Let the patch dry. This gives a base for the final fill. Add a second batch of compound. Let dry. Sand until smooth. (fig. 6)

6. You may need to fill in behind large holes with wadded newspaper. Start patching by working in from all sides. Let dry. Apply another layer around the new edge. Repeat until the hole is filled. After the patch has dried, sand until smooth. (fig. 7)

(fig. 3)

(fig. 4)

(fig. 5)

(fig. 6)

(fig. 7)

(fig. 8)

If the walls have a textured surface, you'll want to make the patch match it while the plaster is still wet. You might need a sponge or comb to do the texturing. (fig. 8)

Fix Problem Doors

Your Problem:

· Doors squeak.

· Door knob rattles.

· Doors stick or drag.

· Door may not close because it strikes the frame.

· Lock may not catch.

What You Need:

· Oil

· Graphite

Continued ➡

- Screwdriver
- Hammer
- Sandpaper
- Pliers

How-To:

For noise:

1. You can usually stop a door squeak by putting a few drops of oil at the top of each hinge. Move the door back and forth to work the oil into the hinge. If the squeaking does not stop, raise the pin and add more oil. *(fig. 1)*

(fig. 1)

2. Noisy or squeaking locks should be lubricated with graphite. You can buy this at a hardware store. *(fig. 2)*

3. To stop the rattle in the knob, loosen the set-screw on the knob. *(fig. 3)* Remove the knob. Put a small piece of putty or modeling clay on the knob. *(fig. 4)* Put the knob back on. Push it on as far as possible. Tighten the screw.

(fig. 2)

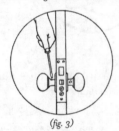

(fig. 3)   *(fig. 4)*

For Sticking or Dragging Doors:

1. Tighten screws in the hinges. If screws are not holding, replace them, one at a time, with a longer screw. Or insert a matchstick in the hole and put the old screw back in. *(fig. 5)*

2. Look for a shiny spot on the door where it sticks. Open and close the door slowly to find the spot. Sand down the shiny spot. Do not sand too much, or the door will not fit as tight as it should. *(fig. 6)*

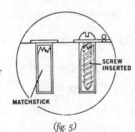

MATCHSTICK   SCREW INSERTED

(fig. 5)

(fig. 6)

3. If the door or frame is badly out of shape, you may have to remove the door and plane down the part that drags. *(fig. 7)*

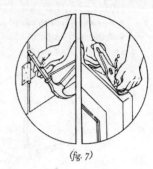

(fig. 7)

Note:

Sand edges of the door before painting to prevent a paint buildup. This can cause the door to stick.

Locks:

If the lock is tight or won't turn, you may need to lubricate it with graphite.

Repairing Drawers

Your Problem:

- Drawers stick.
- Handles or knobs are loose or broken.

What You Need:

- Screwdriver
- Sandpaper
- Candle wax or paraffin

How-To:

For Handles and Knobs:

1. Tighten handles or knobs with screwdriver from the inside of the drawer. (fig. 1)

2. You can buy knobs, or use small spools to replace lost knobs.

SCREW   KNOB

(fig. 1)

For Sticking Drawers:

1. Remove the drawer. Look for shiny places on top or bottom edges or on the sides. *(fig. 2)*

2. Sand down these shiny areas. Try drawer to see if it moves more easily. Repeat sanding if it still sticks. *(fig. 3)*

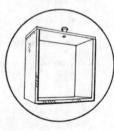

(fig. 2)

3. Rub the drawer and the frame, where they touch, with candle wax, paraffin, or soap. This makes drawers glide easier. This is important if drawers are usually filled with heavy items. *(fig. 4)*

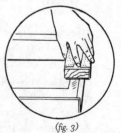

(fig. 3)

4. If glides are badly worn, the drawer may not close all the way. The drawer front strikes the frame. The drawer needs to be lifted. Remove it and insert two or three large smooth-head thumbtacks along the front of each glide. (*fig. 5*)

5. Do drawers stick only in damp weather? When weather is dry, and drawers are not sticking, coat the unfinished wood with a penetrating sealer or with wax.

CANDLE WAX

(*fig. 4*)

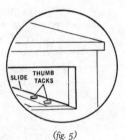

SLIDE   THUMB TACKS

(*fig. 5*)

Using Basic Tools

HAMMER:

A medium weight (12–13 ounce) claw hammer is good for general purposes.

- Hold a hammer near the end of the handle for more hitting power. To start a nail, hold it in place and tap it gently a few times until it is firmly set. Hit it straight in. (*fig. 1*)

(*fig. 1*)

- To avoid hammer marks on wood, use a nail set (*fig. 2*) or another nail to drive a nail the last one-eighth inch into the wood.

(*fig. 2*)

- To remove a nail use claw end of hammer. Place a small block of wood under the head of the hammer to avoid marking the wood. (*fig. 3*)

(*fig. 3*)

SCREWDRIVER:

You need two types of screwdrivers for household repairs: **Straight blade** (*fig. 4*) and **Phillips** (*fig. 5*). Both come in various sizes. The blade of the screwdriver should fit the slot in the screw. (*fig. 6*)

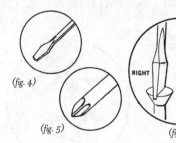

(*fig. 4*)

(*fig. 5*)

RIGHT   WRONG

(*fig. 6*)

- When using the screwdriver, push against the head of the screw as you turn it. (*fig. 7*)

(*fig. 7*)

(*fig. 8*)

- It's easier to put a screw into wood if you make a hole first with a nail or drill. (*fig. 8*) Rub wax or soap on the screw threads to make it go in easier.

PLIERS:

A **slip joint pliers** can be used for many jobs around the house. (*fig. 9*)

- Use pliers to hold a nut while you turn a bolt with a screwdriver. (*fig. 10*)

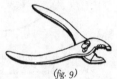

(*fig. 9*)

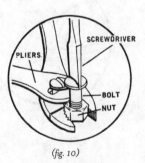

PLIERS   SCREWDRIVER

BOLT   NUT

(*fig. 10*)

(*fig. 11*)

- Use it to remove nails or brads. Pull the nail out at the same angle it was driven. Use small blocks under the pliers if you need leverage. (*fig. 11*)

- Use it to bend or cut wire or to straighten a bent nail. (*fig. 12*)

- Use it to turn nuts. Wrap tape or cloth around the nut to avoid scratching it. (*fig. 13*)

(*fig. 12*)

(*fig. 13*)

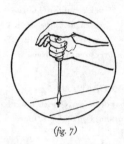

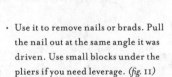

Continued →

An adjustable wrench is adjustable to fit different sizes of nuts. *(fig. 14)*

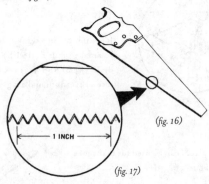

(fig. 14)

- If a nut is hard to loosen, apply a few drops of penetrating oil or kerosene. *(fig. 15)* Let it soak a couple of hours or overnight. If the wrench has a tendency to slip off, try turning it over.

(fig. 15)

HANDSAW:

A handsaw *(fig. 16)* with about 10 teeth to the inch is good for most household work. *(fig. 17)*

(fig. 16)

1 INCH

(fig. 17)

- Mark where you want to cut. Pull the saw back and forth several times to start a groove. Let the weight of the saw do the cutting at first. If you are sawing a board, it will be easier if you support it and hold it firmly near where you're cutting. *(fig. 18)*

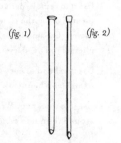

60°

(fig. 18)

Nails, Screws, and Bolts

Nails, screws, and bolts each have special uses. Keep them on hand for household repairs.

Nails come in two shapes.

- **Box nails** have large heads. Use them for rough work when appearance doesn't matter. *(fig. 1)*

(fig. 1)   *(fig. 2)*

- **Finishing nails** have only very small heads. You can drive them where looks are important, as in putting up panelling or building shelves. *(fig. 2)*

Screws are best where holding strength is important. *(fig. 3)* Use them to install towel bars or curtain rods, to repair drawers, or to mount hinges. Where screws work loose, you can refill the holes with matchsticks or wood putty and replace them. Use molly screws or toggle bolts on a plastered wall where strength is needed to hold heavy pictures, mirrors, towel bars, etc.

- **Molly** screws have two parts. *(fig. 4)* To install, first make a small hole in the plaster and drive the casing in even with the wall surface. Tighten screw to spread casing in the back. Remove screw and put it through the item you are hanging, into casing, and tighten.

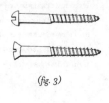

(fig. 3)

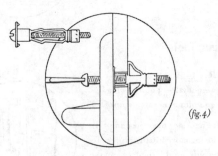

(fig. 4)

- **Toggle bolts.** *(fig. 5)* Drill a hole in the plaster large enough for the folded toggle to go through. Remove toggle. Put bolt through towel bar or whatever you are hanging. Replace toggle. Push toggle through the wall and tighten with a screwdriver.

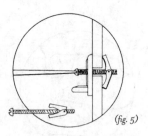

(fig. 5)

- **Plastic anchor screws** *(fig. 6)* should be used where you want to attach something to a concrete wall. To install, first make a small hole in the wall and drive casing in even with the wall surface. Put screw through item and into the casing, and tighten.

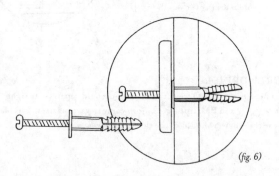

(fig. 6)

Restoring Hardwood Floors

Mary Twitchell
Illustrated by Alison Kolesar

Removing Old Floor Coverings

First, remove all furniture from the room. Because the refinishing may take from three days to a couple of weeks, store the furniture out of the way.

Removing old floor coverings and refinishing floors create a lot of dirt and sawdust. Take precautions to protect your furnishings as well as the rest of the house. Dirt and sawdust particles are extremely fine and have an amazing ability to travel.

If you cannot remove the curtains, slip them onto coat hangers hung from the curtain rods and enclose them in plastic bags. Remove heat registers. Shut doors to adjoining rooms; open all windows; and tape plastic over hallways, heat register openings, and built-in shelving.

WALL-TO-WALL CARPET

Wall-to-wall carpeting is stretched between tackless strips nailed along the perimeter of the room. The strip, made of plywood, is full of pins which stretch the carpet and hold it tight to the baseboard.

Once you have loosened a corner of the carpet, pull up the carpet along one wall. Then with a helper, walk along parallel walls to release the carpet on three sides. Continue until all carpet is free of the tackless strip.

Because carpeting is heavy and awkward to carry, fold it over in the center of the room and, with a matte knife, cut it in half through the backing fabric. This will allow you to roll up and remove the carpet in two (or more) sections.

Next, remove the felt, sponge rubber, or foam padding. If it is stapled to the floor, remove all the staples. (Any staples left protruding from the floor will rip the sandpaper off the floor sander.) Remove the staples with pliers or slip the flat side of a slotted screwdriver under the staple head and gently lift the staple free.

The tackless strip will be nailed to the floor. Carefully work a prybar under one end of the strip where it has been nailed into the floor. Once the nail loosens, work your way along the strip, gradually prying it up until it can be removed.

Remove the metal threshold strips used to secure the carpeting in doorways in the same manner.

Vacuum the floor thoroughly.

LINOLEUM OR TILE

If you bend old linoleum over on itself, it will usually snap, making it easy to remove in pieces. Scrape any old adhesive off the floor with a putty knife. Very small bits of stubborn adhesive may be sanded off when the floor is sanded.

Linoleum installed before 1985 that has a white backing could contain asbestos. Dampen the remaining adhesive with water and scrape. Put the linoleum and the adhesive scrapings in plastic bags and seal. Always wear a face mask and protective eyewear when scraping or sanding.

Flooring adhesives are flammable. Using a propane torch or heat gun to loosen linoleum or its adhesive is dangerous. Chemical adhesive solvents are available but not recommended. If you choose to try them, test in an inconspicuous area first.

Vacuum the floor thoroughly.

Evaluating the Floor

With the wood exposed, assess the condition of the floor and the amount of work involved. Some floors may require more work than you are willing to undertake. For badly damaged floors, you may want the advice of a professional.

Large cracks between boards can be filled, but when the floor is refinished, the filler may show. In addition, large patches of filler may come loose with time. Deep and multiple grooves, deep burns, or large stains may be impossible to sand away.

If there is extensive patching, if walls have been relocated, if there is evidence of rot, or if replacement boards were added to fill in the holes left when woodstove stacks were removed, refinishing your floors may not be worth the effort. It is important to know that you will have a floor worth showcasing for your time and money.

It may be more practical to paint your floors if they are in poor condition or badly discolored. Porch and deck enamels come in all colors. Apply two or three coats to a floor free of dirt, grease, and wax.

Some tongue-and-groove floors may have been sanded before, in which case there may be too little wood left above the grooves. If there is less than 1/8 inch between the top surface of the floor and the groove, further sanding will so weaken the wood that it will splinter along the edges.

Refinishing floors is a dirty, noisy, unpleasant, back-breaking task. You may want to get an estimate from a professional. He/she will quote you a figure based on the number of square feet to be refinished.

Preparing the Surface

To prepare the floor for refinishing, remove the shoe molding around the perimeter of the room. Run the blade of a matte knife between the shoe molding and the baseboard. This will separate the paint and make the shoe molding easier to dislodge. If you intend to reuse the molding, pry it off carefully with two prybars or a prybar and a slotted screwdriver. Slowly loosen the molding by working along the edge, applying pressure at each nail location. Once the molding is removed, countersink any exposed nails.

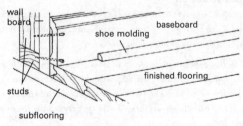

Cross-section shows flooring with baseboard and shoe molding. Baseboard is nailed into studs behind wallboard.

Continued ➜

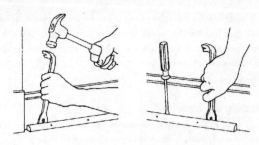

Use a prybar to remove shoe molding. A screwdriver holds the loosened piece away from the baseboard.

On the unpainted surface, number each piece of molding so that it can be renailed in the same location. With a pair of vise grips, remove the finishing nails still attached to the shoe molding. Grasp the nail shank where the nail entered the floor or baseboard with the vise grips and slowly bend the nail to a 45-degree angle. This will pull the nail head through the wood and prevent the molding from splintering. (Splintering invariably occurs when the nails are hammered out rather than pulled through the wood.) The nail holes can later be filled with wood putty.

If there is no shoe molding, remove the baseboard. Pry it off carefully, number the boards, and remove the nails.

Next go over the entire floor with a broad spackling knife. Remove grit and debris, and staples or tacks which protrude above the flooring. With a nail set, sink any nail heads to 1/8 inch below the floor surface, and fill the holes with wood putty. Nail heads, staples, and tacks will rip the sandpaper when you sand the floor. Working your way around the floor will give you ample opportunity to assess any problems.

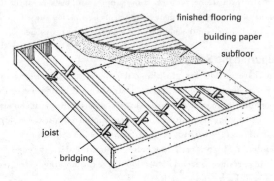

finished flooring
building paper
subfloor
joist
bridging

Floor Construction

To understand why certain problems occur in floors, it is necessary to understand something about floor construction. Residential floor construction consists of four elements:

- The floor framing is made up of **joists**. These are usually 2x6s, 2x8s, or 2x10s and are laid edgewise at 16-inch intervals. They are supported by the house foundation at one end and at the other end by a carrying beam located midway between the foundation walls.

- To keep the joists evenly spaced and to increase the rigidity of the frame, **bridging** of 1x2s is nailed in the form of an X between adjacent joists. The bridging also prevents the joists from twisting over time.

- On top of the joists is the **subflooring**. Today subfloor is usually 5/8-inch or 3/4-inch plywood laid so that the joints are staggered. In older homes, 1x6 or 1x8 tongue and groove boards were laid at a 45-degree angle to the joists.

- The **finished floor** is laid on top of the subflooring over building paper. Hardwood floors, usually of oak or maple, are laid perpendicular to the joists.

TYPES OF WOOD FLOORING

- **Strip flooring**, by far the most common, comes in random lengths and is available in widths of 1 1/2 inches to 2 1/4 inches and thicknesses of 3/8 inch, 1/2 inch, or 25/32 inch. The lumber has been milled so that there is a tongue along one edge and a groove along the other; the boards are laid in a random pattern of end joints and the strips interlock as they are laid tongue to groove. The interlocking prevents the floor from moving or squeaking. The strips, 2 feet to 16 feet in length, are nailed every 10 to 12 inches through the tongue at a 50-degree angle; the nail heads are countersunk and in the finished floor are invisible because they are covered by the groove of the next board.

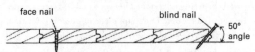

face nail

blind nail

50° angle

Interlocking pattern of tongue-and-groove flooring.

- **Plank flooring** also is tongue and groove; the lumber comes in random widths of 3 to 9 inches. Originally the planks were pegged into the subfloor; today the pieces are bored, the screws countersunk, and the holes plugged to simulate the wooden pegs.

- **Block flooring**, which looks like parquet, is made up of short strips of hardwood that have been glued together in a rectangle or square. It is sold in tongue-and-grooved squares of 6x6 inches, 9x9 inches, or 11 1/4 x 11 1/4 inches. Usually the strips are of oak, and are fastened together, then the blocks are glued with the grains at right angles to the surrounding ones.

- **Softwood flooring** (usually southern pine, Douglas fir, redwood, or western hemlock) is less costly to install and less wear resistant than hardwood flooring. Softwoods are easily marred and will show scratches whenever furniture is carelessly moved. They are best used in bedrooms or closets where the traffic is light. Softwood floors can be sanded, but because the wood is less dense than hardwood, they soon become too thin to resand.

Problems and Solutions

Before refinishing floors, certain problems should be corrected.

LOOSE BOARDS

Nails may work loose when floor boards shrink or the edges cup. Resecure these boards by predrilling holes with a bit slightly smaller than the diameter of the annular-ring flooring nails. Nail through the warped area into the subflooring below. This forces the high points back into position. Drive the nails in pairs.

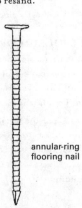

annular-ring flooring nail

Angle the nails and drive them in opposite directions for the best grip. Sink the nail heads with a nail set and fill the holes with wood putty matched to the wood of the floor. Space the nails at least 1/2 inch in from the edges of the floor board so that you don't crack the wood.

CRACKS

Small cracks between boards or between butt ends may occur if the wood was insufficiently cured before it was installed. These cracks can be filled with wood filler. Buy filler to match the color of your floor after it has been sanded or stripped. Or you can make your own wood filler by mixing the sawdust produced by sanding your floor with glue. Be sure to clean the cracks with a wire brush before applying the filler. Rub with a fine steel wool when dry.

Deep scratches and gouges can be filled in the same manner although the wood putty may loosen in larger cracks. If the cracks are substantial, it may be necessary to fill them with thin strips of wood cut to fit. Place a strip of wood on top of the crack and hammer it gently into place. Face nail and sand the strip.

SPOTS AND BURNS

Spots of wax, grease, or oil can be removed with turpentine. Surface burns will disappear when the floor is sanded. To get rid of deep burns, the scorched boards will have to be removed. See Replacing Damaged Flooring (page 867).

STAINS

Some stains will be removed when the floor is sanded. If the stains persist even after sanding the floor with three grades of sandpaper (coarse, medium, and fine grit), try removing them with undiluted household bleach, a commercial bleach, or a half-cup of oxalic acid crystals mixed in one quart of water. Be sure to wear gloves and goggles. Apply a small amount of the solution to the center of the stain and let dry. Wait a few minutes after the first application. If necessary, apply more of the solution until the stained area blends in with the rest of the floor. You don't want to lighten the spot too much. When you get the right tone, wash the bleached area with warm water and let dry.

SQUEAKS

Many old floors squeak and/or sag. Changes in humidity cause various members to shrink or swell at different rates and, although you may think squeaks and sags are proof of the house's vintage, charm, or value, it usually means that something structural is amiss. Potential causes may be that the dimension lumber was undersized; the joists were spaced too far apart; the wood wasn't sufficiently seasoned; the house settled unevenly; the flooring was laid with insufficient nails; or the house is just suffering from old age. In some instances, major reconstruction may be necessary. In other cases, creaks, squeaks, and sags may be relatively easy to eliminate.

Squeaks mean that there is slack in the floor structure. As a result, there is an audible sound whenever adjacent members (flooring, subflooring, joist, beam) rub against one another. This occurs each time the floor is loaded, and then the load removed.

The squeak may result from a loose board rubbing against a nail or another floorboard; from the finish flooring which has warped and pulled loose from the subflooring; from the subflooring which has warped or pulled loose from the joists; from the joists which have warped, shrunk, or pulled loose from a beam; or from nails which have pulled loose somewhere within the floor structure. To determine the cure, you have to determine which structural members are involved.

Squeaks between Joists and Subfloor. To locate the squeak, have someone walk on the floor while you listen from the basement below. If the squeak is above a joist (they usually are), the subfloor will move when weighted; once the load is removed, the subfloor will spring back into place. This occurs because too few nails were used to anchor the subfloor to the joists or because the joists have shrunk or twisted as the wood seasoned.

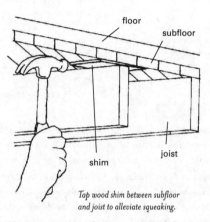

Tap wood shim between subfloor and joist to alleviate squeaking.

To prevent the subfloor from moving, fill the gap between subfloor and joist with a wooden shim shingle of the proper width. Dip the tapered shim in wood glue. Tap the shingle until it is snug; the glue will hold it in place. Do not force the shingle or you risk loosening the subfloor further which will separate the floor boards above.

Another way to eliminate friction between a joist and the subfloor is to screw a 2x2-inch cleat flush with the top of the joist and directly under the squeak. (Use cleats on both sides of a joist if there are a number of loose floor boards.) Screw through the cleat into the subfloor to pull it down tight with the joist. You may need to have someone stand on the floor above to force down the subfloor.

Be sure the screws aren't so long as to penetrate the top surface of your hardwood flooring.

If there is a finished ceiling below the squeak, you will have no access to the joists, in which case you will have to face nail through the finished floor and subfloor into the joist below.

Joists are usually laid on 16-inch centers, and can be located by using a small block of wood and a hammer. Tap the block as you move it along the finished flooring. When the tapping sounds dull, there is probably a joist below.

Predrill the holes in the finished floor. Angle them toward each other for greater holding power; then countersink the nail heads and fill with wood putty. Mound the wood putty slightly; then sand when dry.

If the nails don't hold, use wood screws. Predrill a hole at the center of the squeak. As you drill, pay attention to the resistance you experience. If the bit passes through the floor and subfloor after which there is no resistance, your squeak is between joists; however if the bit hits resistance after the subfloor, your squeak is over a joist. In this case, use longer screws to pull the flooring and subfloor tight to the joist.

Since the screws should be countersunk, you will have to drill two holes. The pilot hole is drilled first. The diameter of the drill bit should

Continued ➡

be slightly smaller than that of the screw shank. For the countersink holes, use a bit the diameter of the screw head.

A screw digger, which performs both processes simultaneously (countersinks and counterbores), makes this process even quicker.

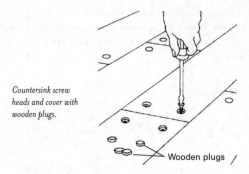

Countersink screw heads and cover with wooden plugs.

Fill the screw holes with wood putty or wooden plugs. Plug cutters can be used with the drill to obtain discs of the same wood as the floor. Place glue in the hole and on the plug, then tap the plug into place.

Weakened or twisted joists can be strengthened by adding bridging. In older homes bridging was made of 1x3s nailed crisscross in a diagonal position between adjacent joists. Today solid bridging, or blocking, of 2x6s or 2x8s, is used and end nailed between the joists every 8 feet. Cut the blocking to fit between the joists. Toenail into the subfloor before end-nailing into the joists. The bridging will hold the joists in a vertical position and increase the floor's rigidity.

Where the subflooring moves up and down between joists, push the solid bridging up against the subfloor and end nail it to the joists.

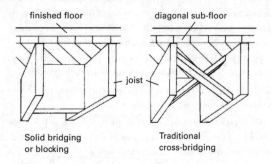

Solid bridging or blocking

Traditional cross-bridging

Sometimes bridging is present but isn't snug; pull out the loose nails and drive in longer ones.

Squeaks between Subfloor and Finished Floor. Whenever there is a gap between the subfloor and the finished floor, buckling has usually occurred and will cause the floor to squeak. Floorboards which have lifted may be very visible; some are harder to see.

The buckling may occur because the flooring material wasn't adequately cured before it was installed. Ideally, flooring should be stored for three days in the room where it will be laid. This gives the boards sufficient time to adjust to the house humidity. In new construction, flooring should be delivered after the doors and windows have been installed, and all masonry, drywall, and plastering have been completed. The flooring should then cure for three weeks in post-construction moisture conditions. This usually means closing up the

house and turning on the heat to decrease the excessive humidity caused by masonry and drywall work.

Seasonal expansion and contraction across the grain is normal for wood. To allow for this, 3/4-inch gaps are left around the perimeter of the room between the floor and the wall. Floors laid without this gap tend to buckle.

If sufficient space has not been left, remove 3/4 inch from the first and last floor boards. Shoe molding is added to hide this gap.

Boards will also buckle if they have been exposed to excessive water (from watering plants or a leaky roof or absorbing water from a moist basement below).

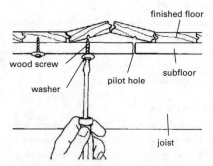

Flatten buckled flooring by pulling down with screws from beneath the subfloor.

If the floor is accessible from the cellar, buckled flooring can be flattened by drilling pilot holes through the subfloor and part way into the finished floor. The screw should not penetrate further than 1/4 inch from the top surface of the finished floor. Therefore it is important to choose the right screw length. This is determined by combining the thickness of the two flooring elements. If, for example, the subflooring is 5/8-inch plywood and the hardwood flooring is 3/4 inch, screws of 1 inch to 1 1/8 inches in length are appropriate. Choose a drill bit slightly larger than the screw shank for drilling through the subfloor, and a drill bit slightly smaller than the screw shank for drilling into the finished floor. To prevent the screw head from penetrating the subfloor, slip a washer over the screw.

Before drilling into the finished flooring, mark the depth of the hole on the drill bit with electric or masking tape. If you use washers, adjust the length for the added width of the washer. Then screw into both of the offending boards.

SAGS

Sagging usually occurs in older homes and is most common on the first floor; if sagging occurs on the second floor, an entire ceiling or floor may have to be torn out to get at the joists. Sags result in sloped floors, sticking doors and windows, cracks in the ceiling and/or walls, roof leaks, and leaky plumbing. If the first floor bows, it will affect all the floors above.

Sagging may be caused by lumber which warped as it dried, undersized joists, or joists spaced too far apart. If this is the case, the floor will flex whenever weight is applied. The bowing will cause abutting floorboards to squeak as their top edges rub together, which in turn will work the flooring nails loose. The sagging will increase over time, especially if excessively heavy objects (such as pianos or refrigerators) are placed on an already weakened part of the floor.

The sagging may, however, indicate more severe structural problems beyond the floor itself. The center structural support posts may have settled, the foundation may be crumbling under the ends of the joists or under a carrying beam, or the foundation walls may be settling unevenly.

If the sagging occurs on the first floor and the joists are accessible from below, the situation can sometimes be remedied with reinforcements.

To determine the extent of the sag, move furniture from the sagging portion of the room. If there is a rug, roll it back. Stretch a string taut across the floor at right angles to the joists. Tack each end of the string to the floor at opposite sides of the room. Mark the spot in the floor where the sag is the greatest.

Stretch the string at a 90-degree angle between the other two walls and check for the low spot. Corrective measures should be taken where these low spots intersect.

Have a helper rap on the center of the sag while you try to locate the offending member(s) in the cellar. Once located, try to determine the extent to which the joist has been weakened; you may have to strengthen only a portion of the joist, or the entire load-bearing member may need to be replaced.

Bridging. Loose diagonal bridging allows the joists to move. Check for loose nails and renail. If necessary, add further bridging. Cut to the proper joist spacing and end nail through adjoining joists into blocking.

If there is no bridging, prefabricated steel bridging is available. It requires no nails. Near the top of one joist, hammer in the pronged end. Near the bottom of the adjacent joist, hammer in the L-shaped clawed end. Alternate the crisscross bridging pattern and continue from joist to joist as needed.

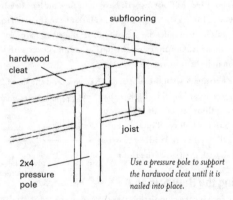

Use a pressure pole to support the hardwood cleat until it is nailed into place.

Hardwood Cleats. If only a small portion of a joist has been weakened by twisting, warping, checking, or cracking, cut a piece of hardwood longer than the defective section of the joist and force it tightly against the subfloor. To apply pressure, cut a 2x4 slightly longer than the distance from the floor to the undersurface of the piece of hardwood. Wedge it in until the hardwood is tight against the subfloor. Then nail or screw the cleat into the adjoining joist, and remove the pressure-pole.

Crossbeams. If sagging occurs only when weight is applied from above or if the permanent dip in the floor is slight, it may be possible to eliminate squeaking by adding a new carrying beam beneath the midspan of the sag.

A crossbeam will add rigidity to the floor by reducing the distance spanned by the joists. In order to install a crossbeam, however, the floor must be lifted either by an adjustable jack post or by a house jack. Since any jacking can cause considerable structural damage, you should seek outside assessment and advice before attempting it on your own.

Frequently a bow in the floor is the result of many years of stress, in which case attempting to level the floor may not be advisable. Extreme and constant pressure from below may dislodge the joists, causing damage to framing members, walls, ceilings, and floors above.

New Joist. Sometimes squeaks are the result of a weakened joist. The joist may have warped, cracked, rotted, or be infested with termites, leaving the floor above it unsupported.

To strengthen the joist, a new one has to be added. Again, the floor will have to be lifted, risking further structural damage, and you should consult a professional.

Permanent Sagging. In the worst-case scenario, the sagging is permanent because the floor can't support its own weight, or the joists were undersized, or they were spaced too far apart. Attempting to remove the sagging under these conditions may crack the walls and plaster throughout the house. In these instances, the floor framing may be reinforced by adding new joists adjacent to the existing ones. This will not level the floor, but will prevent further sagging.

One way to do this is to scribe new joists to make exact copies of the existing ones. Apply construction adhesive to the top of the new joists where they come in contact with the floor above, and wood glue along the faces that will touch the existing joists. Rest both ends of the new joists on top of the sill. Tap into place, and bolt or nail the two together with 16d nails.

Second Floor. Sagging may occur on a second floor if, for example, an attic was converted into additional living space. Since the attic wasn't originally designed to carry this additional load, it begins to bow with age.

If a second floor sags, the first floor sags as well. You must level the first floor before trying to level the second floor. To reach the joists of the second floor, however, you will have to remove the ceiling on the first floor. Obviously, this involves a major renovation and you may wish to consult a professional for evaluation and advice.

Replacing Damaged Flooring

There is no easy way to remove damaged flooring because of the interlocking of tongue and groove. However, it is worth the effort if the hardwood floor is in good condition except for a small section which has warped, cupped, or splintered and needs to be replaced.

Mark off the area to be removed with a rafter square. The lines should be perpendicular to the edge of the flooring. Cut where the wood is again sound and try to stagger the butt ends of the boards by at least 6 inches.

With a drill and 1/2-inch bit, bore a series of overlapping holes at either end of the area to be removed; the holes should follow the

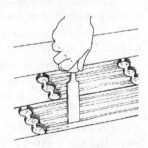

Use a chisel to remove damaged floorboards.

Continued →

lines which you have drawn across the grain of each floorboard. Drill only through the finished flooring, not the subfloor.

Begin in the center of the damaged area. With an electric circular saw set to the depth of the flooring, saw down the center of the board. Or use a 1-inch chisel to split the board down the middle along the grain. Pry the piece loose. Work toward the tongue, then toward the groove, dislodging pieces until the first section of flooring has been removed.

Continue until all the damaged boards have been pried loose. With a hammer and chisel, square up the jagged ends left by the bored holes. Use a sharp chisel to get as clean an edge as possible.

You may want to bevel the ends around the damaged area at a 45-degree angle. If so, then also bevel the ends of the replacement boards so that they will fit snugly.

A simpler method is to mark off a square or rectangular area with the rafter square (illus. 1, below). Ensure that the edges are drawn along wood which is sound. Make a pocket cut with the circular saw using an old blade because you may encounter nails (illus. 2). Slip a pry bar between the boards (illus. 3). Work it back and forth until one of the boards lifts; the others will pry out easily. Remove any remaining nails in the subfloor.

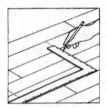

1. Mark damaged area with a rafter square.

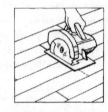

2. Make a pocket cut with a circular saw.

3. Loosen boards with a pry bar.

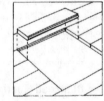

4. Cut replacement boards to fit.

Although this method is much easier, the patch will be more visible because the butt ends of the boards are no longer staggered.

If you don't know what kind of hardwood your floor is, take a sample to the lumberyard where they will match it.

Check that all nail heads are countersunk and that the boards of the original floor lie flat against the subfloor. If any of the boards are loose, blind nail them whenever possible; otherwise face nail them to the subfloor.

To lay the new boards, start from the existing course which has its tongue exposed. Check that the board is firmly nailed to the subfloor. If not, use annular ring-shank flooring nails to blind nail at a 50-degree angle through the tongue and into the subfloor. Countersink the nails

so that the nail heads won't prevent the grooved edge of the next board from fitting over the tongue.

Cut the first piece of new flooring to length. It should fit snugly. Then remove and lay a bead of construction adhesive on the subfloor where the flooring will go. Insert the replacement piece. Fit a scrap piece of flooring tongue-in-groove with the replacement piece. Tap this with a hammer until the replacement board fits tightly against the original flooring. Blind nail through the tongue into the subfloor. Continue by fitting the groove of each new piece into the tongue of the adjacent board.

If the repairs are done in winter, there may be gaps between the existing boards; heat from the furnace will have dried the boards, causing them to shrink across the grain. In this case, use shims (such as metal washers) to maintain the same spacing as the original floor.

The configuration of your patch may mean that a replacement board(s) will need to be inserted in pieces because of the interlocking of tongue with groove.

Some boards, including the last one, will have to be inserted from above. Cut the board to length. Then turn it over and chisel off the lower half of the groove. Or with a circular saw, remove the bottom lip of the groove. Fit the tongue of this board into the groove of the adjacent floorboard and using a wood block, gently tap it until the replacement board slips into place.

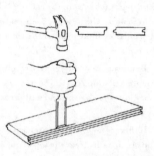

Turn last replacement board over, chisel off lower half of groove.

This last piece of flooring will have to be face nailed. Predrill the holes every 12 inches with a bit slightly smaller than the flooring nails. There should be two holes at each end of the board and along the edges for longer boards. Countersink the nail heads and cover with a wood putty to match the flooring.

Take extra care with these boards when you sand the floor. Replacement boards will be higher than the existing floor, especially if the floor has been sanded before. Replacement patches will need extra sanding to bring them flush with the rest of the floor.

last replacement board

existing floor

lower half of groove removed

Exposing the Raw Surface

Once the repairs are completed, it is time to prepare for sanding or stripping your floor of its old finish and applying a new one.

SANDING

To refinish your floors, you will need an upright drum sander for the open spaces and an edger (or disc sander) for cutting in along the baseboards. These are available at tool rental centers, which will also supply you with ample sandpaper (coarse, medium, and fine grit). There is usually no charge for the unused sandpaper that you return.

Before leaving the rental store, be sure the sanders are in working order. You don't want to be lifting the drum sander any more than is absolutely necessary. Also ask the clerk to show you how to mount sandpaper on both machines. It is quite easy, but machines do differ.

Other tools you may need include a hammer, chisel, paint scraper, and a hand-held finish sander.

The Drum Sander. Drum sanders are very heavy, very noisy, and create a mini dust bowl even though they are fitted with dust bags. You will want ear protectors and a respirator.

Before connecting the drum sander to a power source, tilt back the sander and drum cover in order to mount the coarse sandpaper.

Begin in one corner of the room. Position the sander to go in the direction of the grain. Before turning it on, rock the sander back, then turn it on and let the motor rev up. Slowly bring the drum into contact

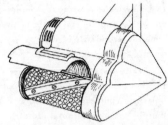

Install sandpaper over drum according to instructions.

with the floor. The sander will pull you forward; hold it in check so that you move at a slow, steady pace throughout the process.

ear protectors

face mask

cable over shoulder

controls

dust bag

Wear face mask and ear protectors when using sander.

As you reach the other side of the room, tilt the sander back from the floor. Move the electric cord so that when you walk backwards, you won't trip on it. Then as you retrace your steps, lower the drum and pass over what you have already sanded. At the beginning and end of each pass, be sure to rock the sander back. Remember, if you lower the sander too quickly or raise it too slowly, the sandpaper will gouge the floor.

Also keep the drum sander in constant motion; otherwise the sandpaper will dig troughs that will be very visible once the floor is sealed.

As you move to an unsanded area, overlap the previous pass by two or three inches. Make as many passes as necessary to expose the bare

wood. If you are making no progress with the coarse sandpaper because the floor is badly cupped, try making diagonal passes.

Continue until the entire floor is done. You won't get closer to the baseboards than 6 inches. This border must be done with the edger.

When you want to stop sanding, turn off the machine but keep the drum tilted away from the floor until the belt stops turning.

For parquet floors, use only a fine grade of sandpaper; the coarser grades are too abrasive.

Since the grain of parquet floors runs in two directions, it is difficult to avoid cross-grain scratching. With the drum sander, make one pass at 45 degrees, then a second at right angles to the first. Use a medium-fine sandpaper for the diagonal passes, then a very fine grade for along the room's length.

The Edger. Since sanders are rented by the day, it makes sense to have a helper follow you with the disc sander (or edger). Edgers are used to sand edges, corners, doorways, closets, around radiators, and other places which you cannot reach with the drum sander.

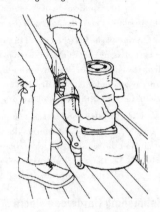

An edger gets close to corners and around radiators.

To fit the disc sander with sandpaper, turn the machine upside down. With the wrench supplied, loosen the lock nut. Remove the bolt and washer. Center the new sanding disc on the sander, insert the bolt and washer on the disc and tighten.

Grasp the edger firmly with two hands before turning it on. Move the edger in a semi-circular pattern. The edger will be sanding across the grain, and the circular action of the sandpaper will tend to leave ring marks on the floor. Therefore don't press down on the machine or let the machine linger; the swirl marks will show once the floor is sealed.

Continue the process with both the edger and the drum sander using a medium, and then a fine grit sandpaper.

Empty the dust bags as necessary. The dust is very combustible and should be disposed of carefully.

Hard-to-get-to areas will have to be done by hand. A paint scraper should remove most of the old finish; sometimes it is necessary to use the back side of the chisel blade for especially stubborn areas. Chisel away from yourself, and scrape towards yourself. When using the scraper, apply pressure to the blade with your free hand and scrape with the grain. Wear protective eyewear.

Collars around radiators and plumbing fixtures can be removed for easier access.

Sand all hard-to-get-to areas with a hand-held sandpaper block or with an electric hand sander.

Vacuum the floor thoroughly with the brush attachment. Then wipe it down with a tack cloth (a rag moistened with turpentine) to pick up all the dust.

The floor is now ready to be stained, varnished, shellacked, or urethaned.

Continued →

STRIPPING

You have no option except to strip floors which are too thin to be resanded. Regular household ammonia and steel wool work best although the fumes are intense and may irritate your eyes and sinuses. Be sure to open all the windows; you may even want to use an electric fan set to vent out.

Wear gloves when using the ammonia. Pour a cupful directly on the floor and let it stand for a few minutes. Then rub the ammonia with the grain. Once the old finish begins to dissolve, wipe off the residue with rags.

After you have finished, let the floor dry for a few days.

If the first application of ammonia doesn't completely dissolve the old finish, you may have to repeat the process.

Stains can be bleached out of the wood with laundry bleach. In a bucket mix one part of bleach to ten parts of water. Apply with a mop. Soak the entire floor. Wait five minutes, then neutralize with white vinegar or ammonia. Mop dry. If there is fuzz from the wood fibers, scrub the floor with steel wool. Let dry, then vacuum.

There are also wood bleaches on the market that come in two-part solutions. Apply the first solution liberally, or scrub it in with steel wool. Wait the required length of time before applying the second solution. Let them work overnight before neutralizing with bleach. Wait 24 hours before sanding the surfaces to remove the wood grain fuzz.

Refinishing Hardwood Floors

If the floor has been stripped, wait until it is thoroughly dry before applying a finish; if the floor has been freshly sanded, apply the finish as soon as possible. An untreated surface will begin to absorb moisture immediately and is always in danger of being scratched or marred by heel prints.

You can apply either a surface finish or a penetrating finish. Penetrating finishes are absorbed by the pores of the wood until they seal the wood fibers. They produce a velvety sheen without a shiny plastic look.

Penetrating finishes are wear resistant, easy to apply, and easy to repair. The finish resists stains and does not chip or crack.

A surface finish (varnishes, shellacs, and polyurethanes) creates a durable surface film on top of the wood which protects the floor from moisture.

Choose the finish depending on the use of the room. Floors which carry heavy traffic or are exposed to frequent spills (kitchens, for example) should be sealed with a surface film. Of the floor finishes, polyurethane provides the hardest and most durable protective film.

PENETRATING FINISHES

Stain. Light stains emphasize the beauty of the wood's grain—oil stains give the most natural finish although most stains dry darker than the original wood color. Experiment on a sample of your flooring; you can control the color by the length of time you let the stain penetrate the wood. If the stain is too dark, moisten a cloth with the thinner recommended by the manufacturer; wipe the floor area to wash away some of the pigment.

Stain should be applied only over itself or on raw wood. Apply liberally with a brush, cloth, or roller; remove excess with a clean cloth and let dry before applying the second coat.

Make sure the stain you choose is compatible with the protective finish you plan to apply. After eight hours, the polyurethane, shellac, varnish, or lacquer can be applied.

Sealer. A penetrating sealer is applied with a rag or brush (squeegee or lamb's wool applicator). Wear rubber gloves. Use a rag to spread the sealer along the grain with long sweeping strokes. Begin along the wall farthest from the door so that after the sealer is applied you can leave the room without walking over the wet floor.

Apply generously over a strip two to three feet wide. Allow the sealer to penetrate the wood (10 to 15 minutes). A helper should then follow you with a couple of rags to mop up the excess. Simultaneously you can apply the second strip of sealer. Always keep your knees on untreated wood.

Let the sealer dry for eight hours. Once dry, wood putty which matches the tone of the sealed floor can be applied to cracks and small holes with a putty knife. To ensure a color match, make your own wood putty by mixing a paste of sawdust from the final sanding with enough sealer to create a thick paste. Remove excess putty, let dry, and hand sand with fine sandpaper.

To smooth the sealed wood, buff with a floor polisher (available from a tool rental center) fitted with a steel wool pad. The steel wool will eliminate any puddles in the sealer coat. Hand scour the edges, under radiators, doorways, and other hard-to-reach areas with steel wool pads.

Vacuum the room carefully and go over it with a tack cloth.

SURFACE FINISHES

Polyurethane. Polyurethane actually seals the floor with plastic; it provides a rugged, durable, clear, mar-resistant, water-resistant surface. Polyurethane should not be used on softwood floors; softwoods are so porous that they absorb many coats of sealer before the finish is presentable.

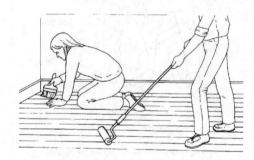

Polyurethane comes in dull, satin, or high-gloss finishes. High gloss is generally used in offices where there is constant daily traffic. It is quite shiny, but has the greatest resistance to wear.

Before the urethane is applied, the room must be free of sawdust particles. For example, don't sweep the floor just before applying the urethane; the sawdust particles will settle back down and show up in the finished floor.

Ensure that there is plenty of cross ventilation during application and drying times. Apply at temperatures between 60° and 90°F. You may have to turn on the house heat to hasten the drying process.

Stir, don't shake, the urethane. To apply, use a natural bristle brush for the corners, edges, and hard-to-reach areas; use a long-handled roller for the main part of the floor. Work along the grain, applying the finish slowly and carefully. Be sure the floor area is well lit—it is very easy to miss spots in the floor or to leave bubbles in the urethane.

Avoid the vapors and close the can after use. If you experience watery eyes, headaches, or dizziness, increase the fresh air, and wear a respirator. Avoid contact of the urethane with your skin.

Wait eight hours or until the finish has dried. To test for dryness, press your thumb down on the surface; if it leaves a thumbprint, the first primer/sealer coat isn't ready. Once dried, buff the floor with steel wool, or sand lightly. Vacuum and clean with a lint-free tack cloth. Apply a second finish coat of urethane, and let dry.

If the room is a heavily trafficked area, apply a third coat. Let dry. Then replace the shoe molding, pipe collars for plumbing and radiators, floor registers, and furniture.

Clean the brushes and rollers in paint thinner.

There is now available a water-based acrylic urethane wood finish. Unlike most urethanes, it is "environmentally friendly" and non-toxic. This waterborne urethane finish is applied in the same fashion. Although it looks milky when applied, it will dry to a clear luster.

Water-based urethane can be cleaned from brushes and rollers with soap and water.

Varnish. Varnishes produce a deep luster and are glossier than other finishes. Although once widely used on floors, varnishes don't penetrate the wood very deeply. They are less expensive than urethane, but darken with age and show scratches easily. Consequently they have been surpassed in popularity by polyurethane.

Before applying a varnish, vacuum the floor thoroughly; particles left from sanding will appear as bumps in the floor finish. During application, close any forced air furnace ducts. Apply two or three coats with a brush, allowing each coat to dry for 24 hours.

If bubbles appear as the varnish is spread, apply more varnish and continue to brush until the bubbles are worked out.

Shellac. Shellac will not darken the color of wood. However, it provides only light protection and should not be used where moisture or stains may be a problem. Shellac is economical and durable although it has a shelf life of only four to six months.

Apply two or three coats; let dry for two hours between coats, and sand lightly before applying the next coat.

Wash brushes in household ammonia and warm water.

Wax. Wax can be applied over varnish or shellac once the finish is thoroughly dry; it can also be used alone if you want the floors to look as natural as possible. Do not use wax on polyurethaned floors; it will preclude refurbishing the floor with an additional coat of polyurethane when the finish begins to wear.

Apply a thin coat of wax with a soft cloth. Let dry before applying a second coat. Polish by hand with a soft cloth or with an electric polisher.

Care and Maintenance

DAY-TO-DAY

A few precautions will keep your floors looking like new. Frequent sweeping or vacuuming will remove dust, crumbs, and grit that can get ground into the finish with every step.

Tiny stones in the grooves of athletic shoes and other non-leather-soled shoes can scratch and gouge both the finish and the floor beneath. Get into the habit of checking your shoes for pebbles before walking on hardwood floors, or, better yet, have a special place to leave shoes at the door. Stockinged feet are natural buffers!

Beware your high-heeled friends! If a person weighing 120 pounds and wearing a size seven flat-soled shoe walks across your floor, those 120 pounds are distributed over 30 square inches of floor per step—about four pounds per square inch. If that same person is wearing high heels, the entire 120 pounds are concentrated on a single one-inch-square piece of floor! In other words, every step leaves an indent in your newly refinished floor! Provide comfortable slippers at the door.

Wipe up spills immediately, wash with cool water, and dry with a soft cloth. Do not allow water spots to air dry.

WEEKLY CLEANING

There are industrial cleaners available from commercial cleaning services and flooring contractors, a variety of detergents available in grocery and hardware stores, and a number of home-brewed floor cleaners touted by friends and neighbors. What's the best for your floor?

Start with a good vacuuming, then a bucket of cool water and a mop. Most everyday dirt will come up with a simple damp mop followed by a drying cloth (old cloth diapers work best). Hot water should be avoided as it will make the top layer of finish just tacky enough to set the dirt.

If a stronger solution is needed, use a very small amount of a mild detergent, such as Ivory Liquid dish soap or Murphy's Oil Soap, in cool water. Always dry hardwood floors with a soft cloth after mopping.

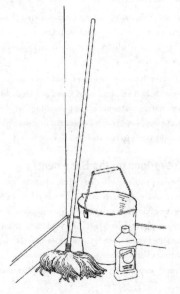

Continued ➜

For very dirty floors, gradually strengthen the cleaning solution, avoiding cleaners with ammonia. The rough side of a kitchen or bath sponge, used gently, will help remove tough scuff marks and set-in dirt. If you are uncertain about the effect a cleaner will have on the finish on your floor, test it in an inconspicuous place first.

WEAR AND TEAR

Worn spots or stains can be touched up by rubbing them with steel wool. Feather the edges and apply the same finish to the affected area.

If they have never been waxed, polyurethaned floors can be refurbished by running a polisher with steel wool over the floor and then adding another coat of finish.

Keeping Basements Dry

Larry Diamond

With the costs of single-family homes climbing out of sight these days, many homeowners have reason to take a long, second look at the house they already have. A full basement is often the largest room in an entire house and offers the potential for serving several purposes—as additional living, working, and storage space. And converting a basement to living space is unquestionably cheaper than buying a new home, with the additional long-run benefit of increasing the value of the house.

If dampness or even occasional flooding is preventing you from enjoying your basement, this booklet will help you identify the source and cause of the wetness and will describe specific remedial action you can take.

First you need to spend some time "down cellah," as they say in northern New England. In most older homes, the basement was designed only to be the place where the foundation of the house was located. It was never meant to be part of the living space. It was where pipes and wires came into the house and where conduits carried out waste water and sewage. It was where food and other things not subject to rust or mildew could be stored.

When the water table rose during a rapid spring thaw or after a heavy rain, it rose right into the basement. In anticipation of possible flooding, storage space in old basements was on shelves or platforms above the highest water mark.

Today, furnaces, hot-water heaters, and other major appliances are placed in basements and an occasional flood can be disastrously expensive. Fortunately, waterproofing technology has improved with the times so that homeowners can be assured of getting high-quality products to remedy their particular problem.

What Are Your Plans for the Basement?

The degree of waterproofing will depend on what the space will be used for. If you plan to use it regularly as a den, recreation room, or bedroom, then a high degree of dryness will be necessary to make the room comfortable. If you plan to use it just for a workshop or utility room space, then you will be able to tolerate a little more dampness, though it is wise to keep a light coating of oil on bare metal tools to prevent rust from forming. The method of waterproofing will be different depending on the usage.

In a workshop or utility room where function is more important than decoration, an unsightly floor drain into a sump at the low point in the basement will control any flooding. But if the room is to be completely finished off and used as regular living space, then you will want to be sure that the foundation walls are repaired and completely waterproofed, and that any drains or pumps be located outside of the living space. This is a more costly solution, but it is also more thorough as well as esthetic.

Few homes today have dirt floor basements. When asked how to convert a dirt floor with stone wall foundation into regular living space, a University Extension Service agent replied, "Build an addition." He explained that it would probably be cheaper in the long run because the cost of pouring a cement floor and installing extensive drainage systems would be enormous. He suggests converting the attic or adding on as better ideas.

It basically comes down to this: If your basement has a severe flooding problem, complete waterproofing will be very expensive and time consuming. If you are willing to put up with minor water problems in return for using the space more for utility purposes than living space, your cost savings will be substantial.

Where Does the Water Come From?

Life exists on this planet because of an interchange between the earth and the sun, an interchange lubricated with water. The ground we walk on is designed to be an enormous spongy repository of water that can deliver nutrients to the roots of plants that become food on the table. When we enter the moist, life-sustaining skin of the earth by digging or excavating for the foundation of a house, we must keep in mind that we are intruders. Unless we take substantial action, the water and the soil will try to reclaim the space we have taken.

It will be helpful to take a moment to understand the nature of the beast—water—and how it behaves underground. Gravity is our main ally. It takes the rain water or snow melt and tends to draw it straight down through the soil. Water will not move very far in a lateral or sideways direction unless something gets in its way such as a layer of heavy clay beneath the surface—high ledge, large stones, or other subsurface debris, either natural or manmade (such as building scraps filled in by the contractor). The direction the water moves underground is referred to as drainage. All things being equal, if the drainage area is of porous soil and free of obstructions, then a dry basement should be relatively simple to maintain. Few are that fortunate, however.

Even in areas with the best drainage, there is still a considerable amount of water near the surface. Water clings to soil particles like a sponge. This normal level of moisture is the culprit for dampness problems. Because the soil is right up against the foundation walls, any cracks or weak spots will let the dampness into your cellar.

The foundation walls must not only hold back tons of soil but also the water contained in that soil. That water can exert a tremendous amount of pressure against the foundation. Soil itself is not a problem because its particles are so relatively large. The liquid water, however, can find its way through the tiniest opening. Pressure the water exerts on floors and walls is called hydrostatic pressure. Water seeks its own level, the accurate folk wisdom goes, and your foundation is in the way. The ground water surrounding your foundation behaves the same as water in a container such as a tin can. As long as there are no holes in the can, no water will get out. But if you think the water only wants to come out the bottom, take a nail and poke a hole in the side of the can. The water spurts out until the level in the can is below the hole.

Standing water exerts pressure against every surface with which it is in contact, and the deeper the water, the greater the pressure. That is why your ears pop at the bottom of the deep end of the swimming pool, not the shallow end. It is the nature of basements that the weakest point, the wall-floor joint, is also at the deepest level and exposed to the greatest hydrostatic pressures.

So before we start spending lots of money on repairs, we now know what is going on down there. Like prisoners digging an escape tunnel with a spoon, hydrostatic pressures are slowly working away on the foundations of our homes. We are as oblivious as the prison guards until after one spring downpour we discover the basement is flooded.

How Does the Water Get Inside?

Water gets into your basement by means of any one or a combination of these ways: leakage, seepage, and condensation. Seepage is sometimes referred to as capillary action, which is not entirely accurate. Capillary action will be discussed under seepage because that is the behavior it most closely resembles.

LEAKAGE

Leakage refers to the condition where water freely enters and flows into the basement. Leaks tend to occur at any point where there is a break in the wall or floor surface. For example, leaks frequently occur at the point where pipes pass through the wall, at corner and floor joints, around basement window frames, at support post footings, or through a crack in the surface caused by settling or poor construction.

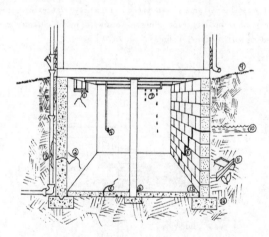

Figure 1. Composite picture of causes of basement leaks

1 — Crack at window frame
2 — Crack in poured wall
3 — Cracked or broken downspout
4 — Pipe entrance through wall
5 — Crack in floor slab
6 — Crack at floor post footing
7 — Condensation on cold pipes
8 — Crack in block wall
9 — Grade pitched toward house
10 — High water table
11 — Rotted backfill
12 — Lack of foundation drain
13 — Unsealed floor slab/wall joint

Leaks occur when a large amount of water builds up against the walls or floor of your basement and cannot adequately drain away. Seeking its own level, the water forces its way through a weak point and pools up on your floor.

PATCHING CRACKS

Materials needed: hydraulic cement, pointed trowel, hammer, masonry chisel, wire brush, water

If you are certain that water is leaking in at only one or two obvious places and the rest of the foundation is reasonably well waterproofed, it may be very possible to cure the leak with hydraulic cement. This cement can be used even as the leak occurs because it must be applied to a wet surface. The cement works by expanding as it sets, thereby filling and sealing the crack. To prepare the surface for the cement, use a hammer and masonry chisel to enlarge the crack so that it forms a kind of dovetail shape, narrower at the surface and wider at the rear. (See Figure 2.) The purpose of the dovetail shape is that the cement will have the firm support of the masonry to hold it in place.

Use a wire brush to remove any chips and loose pieces of masonry. Following the directions on the cement package, mix only as much as you need immediately because it sets very quickly. The area to be patched should be soaked thoroughly with water before applying the cement. This prevents rapid hydration and improper setting. Then fill the crack and hold until it stiffens.

Hydraulic cement can also be used along the joint of the floor and wall. Make sure the surface is free of all dirt and dust. Chip away any loose mortar and make a dovetail-shaped opening along the joint (Figure 2). A vacuum cleaner does a good job of removing dust particles. After wetting the area, mix only as much cement as you need. Use a pointed trowel to force the cement into the opening, and smooth the surface.

Check the basement after the next several rains. If the leak has been repaired, turn to the section on interior wall treatments to complete dampproofing the walls. If wetness persists, read on.

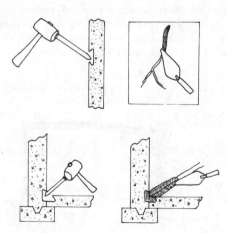

Figure 2. Patching cracks with hydraulic cement

Above — Wall crack

Below — Joint crack

Severe Water Problems: When Does It Leak?

Major basement flooding cannot be stopped by patching with cement, but determining the real problem is not easy. The first question to be answered is: When does it leak?

If the answer is:	Your major problem is:
1. After nearly every rainfall	Poor drainage around the foundation
2. Only at the height of spring thaw and after heavy rains	High water table
3. After every rainfall (a little) and especially at height of spring thaw and after heavy rainstorm	Combination of poor drainage and high water table
4. After using washing machine, dishwasher, shower, or tub and no other time.	Break in sewage pipe or clogged leach field

Solutions to poor drainage problems will be discussed next. For high water-table problems, go right to the sections on excavation and exterior wall treatment. For breaks or leaks in pipes or a backed up, clogged leach field or septic tank, you will need the services of a plumber to fix the leak, or a contractor to repair the septic system.

Poor Drainage: What Causes It?

For problems caused by poor drainage around the foundation of the house, there are some steps that should be taken before attempting any repairs.

Step outside and inspect your house. Do you have roofline gutters? If so, where do the downspouts drain the water? They should carry the water either to a storm sewer (where permitted), or a dry well. If there is neither of these, there should be splash guards at the bottom of the downspouts that will carry the water at least 8 to 10 feet from the house. Check the gutters and clean them of leaves, nests, and other debris. During a rainstorm, go outside and check for breaks or leaks. Repair any damage to the gutters caused by ice and snow. Many basement flooding problems caused by poor drainage have been corrected by the proper installation and repair of roof gutters and properly positioning the downspouts (Figure 3). Should the basement still leak after making the repairs, it should at least be less than before. (Not much consolation, but a good gutter is a worthwhile investment in any case.)

Next check the grade of land away from the house. There should be a gradual sloping away so that the surface water will tend to run off before being absorbed into the soil. You can check the grade using a straight 2" x 4" x 8' board and a four foot level. Lay the board perpendicular to the foundation and place the level on the board. The bubble should be off center toward the house. If the bubble is dead center or off center away from the house, you probably have some regrading to do.

Before calling a contractor for several loads of fill, it is a good idea to examine your soil. You can do this yourself or get the assistance of the local agricultural agent or a representative from the U.S. Department of Agriculture Soil Conservation Service (SCS) who deals with homeowner problems. In many areas of the country, SCS has detailed soil maps and can be of great assistance in helping you decide what action to take to improve the drainage around the house.

Dig out a hole down to the base of the footing. This will serve two purposes. One, it will show what you have for soil and its relative moisture-holding capacity, and two, it will show what your house has as waterproofing on the exterior wall.

Even if the walls appear well protected, poor workmanship frequently is the cause of basement leaks. Improper mixing of cement with too much sand and other time- and cost-saving "shortcuts" may have kept down the purchase price of the house at the expense of major repairs sooner and more frequently than expected.

If the soil in the test hole is loose, crumbly and easy to shovel, then you have a medium to light loamy or sandy soil. These soils will provide good drainage under most conditions. With adequate waterproofing on the wall, simple surface regrading should solve your problem (Figure 4).

If the soil is extremely hard-packed with a heavy clay texture, then it is likely that it is partly responsible for your water problem, and simply regrading will be of little value.

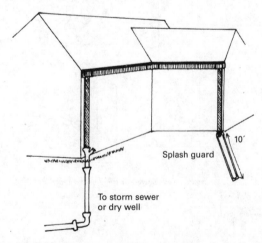

Figure 3. Proper position for downspouts

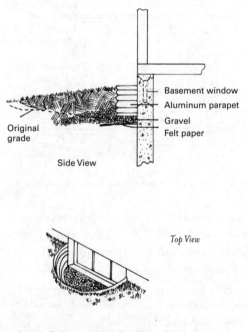

Figure 4. Surface regrading and installation of window parapet

Moisture-holding Capacity of Various Soil Types

Sandy (light)—1.25" of water per foot of soil

Loam (medium)—2.25" of water per foot of soil

Clay (heavy)—3.67" of water per foot of soil

This chart makes clear that the heavier soils have a significantly higher carrying capacity, which means much more ground water is kept near the surface in the vicinity of the foundation. More water also means that greater pressure is exerted against the walls and floor. In heavy soils, the only satisfactory solution is to excavate the perimeter of the foundation and install drain tile and waterproof the wall.

If there is no waterproofing on the wall (there should be a coating of tar or other water-repellent material) then regardless of the soil type, excavation and waterproofing will be necessary.

Excavation is a job for a person handy with a shovel, or for someone with a couple of strong-backed friends. Otherwise, consult several contractors for estimates before deciding which one to hire. Contractors generally give estimates in terms of dollars per linear foot. To get the total cost, measure the perimeter of the house and multiply that number by the cost per foot.

(Homeowners are warned to beware of advertisements for services claiming to be able to waterproof the exterior walls of the foundation without excavation. Several companies report success using a clay injection or a pressure pumping system that forces a waterproofing material down evenly spaced holes drilled around the foundation. They state that the material spreads out underground and fills in the space between the holes. There are currently, however, numerous law suits filed around the country by homeowners for recovery of payment in cases where the treatment failed to stop the leaks.)

EXCAVATION

Materials needed: pick, shovel, cart

Whether you are installing drain tile, waterproofing the wall, or both, excavation should go down to the base of the wall footings (Figure 5) and be out far enough from the wall to allow a comfortable working space. Be careful when digging around pipes and underground wires. Working in a narrow trench is not pleasurable and there is the temptation to work quickly. Have patience. This is a dirty, messy, and expensive job. Do it right the first time. Wall treatments will be discussed first, then installation of drain tile.

EXTERIOR WALL TREATMENT

Materials needed: asphalt base foundation sealer, elastic roof sealer, hydraulic cement, trowel, stiff bristle brush, waterproofing membrane

Optional: chalk line, reinforced polyethylene sheet, muriatic acid or etching product

All exterior wall treatments, regardless of other local conditions, are based on at least one application of an asphaltic base, a tar-like sealer designed for exterior foundation walls. For most homes, a properly applied coat of foundation sealer should prevent any water from entering the basement.

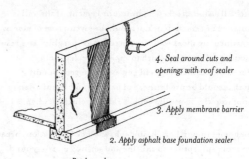

4. *Seal around cuts and openings with roof sealer*

3. *Apply membrane barrier*

2. *Apply asphalt base foundation sealer*

1. *Patch cracks*

Figure 5. Exterior wall treatment

If your home is in a low spot or in a chronically high water-table area, the enormous pressures exerted by the water against the walls will require more than a coat of sealer to prevent leakage. For these conditions, the only solution is to install a membrane, a continuous layer of material impervious to water, against the exterior wall. In the past, the installation of a membrane was referred to as the "sandwich method" because a layer of heavy 30-lb. felt paper was sandwiched between two coatings of tar. This method is still perfectly good, its disadvantages being that it is time-consuming to install, and that felt paper comes in relatively narrow rolls requiring overlapping to form a good seal.

Today, new membrane systems and materials such as those from Miradri, Sona Born, and W. R. Grace, offer almost foolproof water protection. Applied to the exterior of the foundation, these impenetrable membranes can withstand changes in temperature, continuous exposure to water, and are relatively easy to apply. These membranes range in price from $1.05 to $1.25 per square foot.

Equally effective and easier to install is a fiberglass reinforced polyethylene sheeting that comes in rolls up to 8 feet wide. Do not use a standard unreinforced polyethylene sheet. It tears too easily, negating its purpose. A single roll of this sheeting will cover the entire wall of most homes without any horizontal overlapping. It is available at well-stocked masonry supply outlets under a variety of brand names.

If a contractor is doing the job, ask if he is going to install a membrane barrier. If he says no, find out why. It doesn't take that much time to install and for the extra material cost, it may be well worth it, especially if you have any doubts about the condition of the walls and the local water-table height.

REMEMBER: If your house is in a high water-table area, water may still come up through the floor, and for obvious reasons it is impossible to place a membrane barrier on the exterior side of the floor. In an extreme case it might be possible to tear up the floor, put down a membrane and pour a new floor, but that seems an excessive solution. Good perimeter drain tile should keep the water table below the level of the floor slab.

After excavating a comfortable work space, clean the wall with a stiff brush and a garden hose. If there is a lot of sediment or crystallized deposits on the wall, wash it thoroughly with a weak muriatic solution or use a commercially prepared etching product (UGL Drylock Etch, for example). Always wear eye and hand protection when working with these products.

Continued ➜

Patch all visible cracks with hydraulic cement. If the wall is bare concrete or cement block, it should be given a coat of mortar. This treatment on block walls is referred to as "parging" and results in a smooth surface upon which to apply the sealer. Being introduced on the market is a fiber glass reinforced bonding cement that could be used instead of parging and forms a dampness barrier of its own. The wall should be absolutely clean when using it, however.

Few homes in northern latitudes have block foundations because they are more susceptible to shifting and settling due to ground movement caused by deep penetration of frost. Block foundation homes in northern climates must install a membrane barrier to insure dryness.

Once the wall is thoroughly cleaned and prepared, elastic roof sealer should be applied around any pipes, wires, or conduits that pass through the wall. Elastic roof sealer is different from roof cement in that the roof sealer can be applied to a wet surface and remains more pliable. Use roof sealer to coat the wall-footing joint, to fill any depression or holes in the surface, and to seal any other joints or corners that look like potential weak spots.

Now apply the foundation sealer. Measure the square feet covered after using the first can. The amount of coverage should correspond with the manufacturer's recommendation. If more space has been covered, then it is being spread too thin. Roof sealer and foundation sealer are available at any building-supply store, and can be purchased in one- or five-gallon cans.

To apply the reinforced polyethylene sheet, start in a few feet from a corner and strike a vertical mark with a chalk line. Press the edge of the sheet up to the line and secure it with a coating of roof sealer. The top can be temporarily tacked to the bottom of the house frame and the bottom held down with a shovel full of gravel. Roll it out tightly around the house as if you were wrapping a Christmas present. Any cuts to fit the sheet around pipes or wires should be completely sealed with roof sealer. When you get back around to the starting point, overlap at least 12 inches and completely seal the joint with the roof sealer. The same procedure is followed on any vertical joint if a second roll is necessary. After the trench is backfilled, the excess at the top can be cut off down to the level of the grade.

FOUNDATION DRAINS
Materials needed: drain pipe (PVC, flexible, or ceramic), felt paper (for ceramic pipe), pea gravel or crushed stone

Perimeter foundation drains should be installed after the walls have been treated. Drain pipe or drain tile comes in three types: PVC (polyvinyl chloride), flexible molded, and ceramic. The type you choose will depend on the price and on how much you wish to support the petrochemical industry. In any case, the pipe comes in standard 4-inch diameter size. PVC is perforated and comes in 10-foot lengths, the molded flexible pipe comes in rolls of up to 250 feet, and ceramic pipe comes in 4-foot lengths.

Lay the pipe on a 3-inch bed of pea gravel or crushed stone. If ceramic pipe is used, place the sections 1/4 inch apart and wrap the joint with an 8-inch strip of felt paper. This keeps soil and silt from clogging the joint while allowing the water to get under the paper and into the drain.

Install PVC pipe with the perforations facing down, to minimize silting. Flexible pipe needs no special treatment.

Because the purpose of installing perimeter drains is to carry the excess ground water away from the building site, you need to be concerned with where the runoff will go. If permissible in your locality, you can run the water off into a storm sewer. If you live in the country and the house is on a slope, you can simply run the pipe from the low end of the foundation to the surface some point below the house. If your lot is level and local building codes prohibit connections to storm sewers or if no sewer is nearby, then there are at least two alternatives to consider.

One is the construction of a dry well or modified leach field. These are subsurface water-collection points that allow for normal absorption into the soil at a distance from the house. The second alternative is to connect the perimeter drain to a sump and then pump the water to the surface (see the section on interior drainage and installation of sump pumps).

For dry wells there is no rule of thumb concerning the proper size. A "dry" well simply holds the water until the soil can absorb it naturally. If your soil is heavy, the well will drain more slowly and you will need a larger well. The opposite is true for sandy soils; the same size house will need a smaller well. Before installing a dry well, it is recommended that a soil engineer or representative from the SCS be consulted. A percolation test should be performed to determine the rate of absorption, and you will need an estimate of the maximum expected water flow from your drainage system. The dry well can then be constructed based on the maximum rate of flow and the soil absorption rate. A well that is too small could back up your system resulting in a flooded basement—which is what you are trying to prevent!

BACKFILLING
Materials needed: pea gravel or crushed stone, sand, gravel, felt paper, top soil, cart, shovel, rake

After the drain pipes have been laid and connected to an outlet, double-check the system using a four-foot level to make sure the water will flow toward the outlet.

The material used for backfilling should encourage rapid drainage to the pipes. DO NOT shovel dirt back into the trench. Backfill with these materials (Figure 6):

6" of pea gravel or crushed stone on top of the pipe

12" of sand

gravel filled to within 24" of the surface

a layer of felt paper

24" of topsoil graded at the surface away from the house

After the first several rains, inspect the area for any slight settling and have enough extra topsoil to fill in any small holes or depressions. Minor settling is expected as the gravel and sand work their way into permanent position.

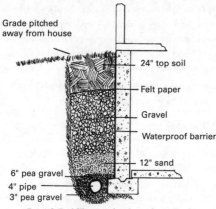

Grade pitched
away from house

24" top soil

Felt paper

Gravel

Waterproof barrier

12" sand

6" pea gravel
4" pipe
3" pea gravel

Figure 6. Backfilling over foundation drain pipe

PVC
(perforated)

Flexible molded
(with slits)

Ceramic

Figure 7. Types of foundation drain pipe

SURFACE GRADING

Materials needed: topsoil, cart, shovel, rake

Optional: gravel, aluminum window parapet

When regrading around foundations, make sure there is a slight sloping away from the house at least 8 feet from the wall. Keep a straight 2" x 4" x 8' board and a level handy to maintain an even slope. If raising the grade is necessary to maintain the proper slope, be sure to consider the area around the basement windows. An attractive and functional way to protect the windows is with an aluminum parapet. They can be purchased pre-shaped, or you can just bend a piece of corrugated roofing. Put in a good layer of gravel around the window to drain any water that gets into the well. Then have the topsoil graded to within an inch of the top of the aluminum (Figure 4).

Seepage

Wetness that results from no obvious visible source is probably caused by seepage. To make sure, perform this test: Take a 12-inch piece of aluminum foil and tape it securely to the basement wall in a spot where you have noticed dampness in the past. Be sure the tape seals all four edges. Wait a few days, then inspect the foil. If the top is dry but the surface against the wall is wet, you have a seepage problem. If the top is wet and the surface against the wall is dry, your problem is excessive moisture in the air causing condensation. If the cold water pipes are wet, you will know right away that condensation is causing some of the problem. There may be wetness on both sides of the foil, telling you that the problem is a combination of seepage and condensation. Either problem is minor compared to leakage and can generally be dealt with successfully without resorting to excavation. It is a good idea, though, to check the grade and inspect the gutters and downspouts first.

Interior Drainage and Installation of Sump Pumps

Materials needed: pick, shovel, cement, sump pump, hardware cloth

First, patch any cracks and fill in any spaces at the wall-floor joint as explained earlier in the section on patching cracks.

In a basement used for utility space only, a mild seepage problem can be dealt with most easily by installing an interior drainage system. Determine the low point around the edge of the floor. With a pick, dig out a hole three feet deep by 24 inches in diameter (Figure 8). Line the sides and bottom with heavy chicken wire or hardware cloth and finish with a 1-inch coat of cement. Make sure the bottom is troweled flat.

At the high point in the floor, begin to chip out a groove along the edge of the wall and run it along the walls to the sump. Finish the groove with fresh cement and smooth it out with the bottom edge of a bottle. Keep a level handy to make sure the pitch is toward the sump.

Install the sump pump and adjust the floats to automatically turn on the pump when the water reaches a height 12 inches below floor level. The hose can be run out through a window to the surface and drained at least 10 feet from the house.

An exterior drainage system can be connected to an interior sump pump by running a piece of drain tile under the footing to the sump. This is particularly useful if the house is on a level spot and there is no storm sewer or dry well to handle the runoff. Connect the drain tile to the upper part of the sump and adjust the float to turn the pump on when the water reaches a height just below the tile.

high point

Top View

hose to carry
water outside

Side View

Figure 8. Interior drain and sump pump showing connection to foundation drain

INTERIOR WALL TREATMENT

Materials needed: wire brush, muriatic acid or etching product, portable work lamp, waterproofing paint or silicone spray, stiff short bristle brush, face mask

To use the basement for living space, you will want a more esthetic solution than gutters and sump pumps. First you must pay close attention to the walls. They must be thoroughly cleaned. This cannot be emphasized enough. Remove any loose or broken pieces of mortar. Use a wire brush to remove dirt, dust, and other crusted material. Inspect the surface carefully, especially in the lower portion of the wall. Soluble salts in the ground water can crystallize on the interior surface as the seepage evaporates into the basement. These light-colored salt deposits must be removed before any wall treatment can be applied.

A weak muriatic acid solution (one part acid to four parts water) or a commercially prepared etching product must be used to remove the salt

Continued ➡

deposits. CAUTION: Eye and hand protection must be worn. Avoid splattering, because the acid will damage clothing.

Surface preparation can be a painstaking process. Keep in mind that the water will find the one weak spot in the wall if you give it a chance. The main reason for cleaning is that the waterproofing treatments work by soaking into the wall surface. If the wall is clogged with dirt or other deposits, the waterproofing will be unable to penetrate and will be ineffective in stopping the moisture. It will stay on the surface rather than soak into it.

After cleaning, use a portable work lamp and inspect the walls closely. Hairline cracks should be enlarged and patched with hydraulic cement. The area around pipes, wire, and conduits that pass through the walls should be patched with cement if necessary. Also inspect around window frames, floor-post footings, and doorways. Cement any places that even look weak.

Now the waterproofing can be applied. There are three types of products on the market: silicone sprays, powdered cement-base paints, and premixed cement-base paints. All operate on the principle of soaking into the wall to form a stronger barrier than a plain surface coating.

The silicones have been on the market only recently and their effectiveness has not been widely reported as yet. Purchase a brand recommended for interior use. Do not use a cement-base paint on a wall that has been treated with silicone. While the spray is easier to apply, the paints have the added feature of providing color to the basement walls. Your choice of products will depend on how the space will be used.

The paints have a much thicker consistency than latex or oil-base paints and must be applied with a stiff, short bristle brush. Standard bristle brushes do not work well with cement-base paints.

CAUTION: Proper ventilation must be maintained when using any of these products. Inhalation of the solvent vapors can be extremely dangerous. Use of a face mask is highly recommended.

Paints can be purchased in powdered or premixed form and are available in a variety of colors and some can be painted over. The premixed paints can be tinted as well. In tests conducted by a well-known independent research laboratory, it was determined that the premixed paints produce a better moisture barrier than the powdered paints. After applying the first gallon, measure the area covered. It should be within the manufacturer's recommended coverage of square feet per gallon. If it is more, than you are applying it too thin.

Paint a first coat on the lower portion of the wall where seepage is most serious. Be sure to work the paint into the wall with the stiff bristle brush. Let it dry for 24 hours before applying a second coat to the entire wall. After this dries, inspect the wall carefully with a portable work lamp and touch up any open pores and pin holes. It must be emphasized that applying cement-base paint is tiresome, arm-weary work and not recommended for the weak of hand or heart. It should present no problem, however, for the average do-it-yourselfer.

Small drops of water may appear on the surface after a few days. Repeat the aluminum foil test to determine whether the cause is condensation. If mild seepage persists, another coat of paint may be applied. Premixed paint works best when applied to a warm (more than 50°F), dry surface. Plan your work accordingly. Powdered paints must be applied to a wet surface. After preparing the wall, soak it with water before painting.

Wetness caused by capillary action can be prevented using the same procedures as for seepage problems. Capillary action is sometimes referred to as "wick action" and describes that behavior of a liquid which soaks upward into a porous material, like water into a sponge or kerosene up the wick of a lamp.

Use paints on the walls and a concrete floor sealer to prevent water from entering the basement by capillary action.

CONDENSATION

This condition occurs generally in the warmer months of the year. Open basement windows allow warm, moist outside air to come in contact with cold foundation surfaces, cold water pipes, and cold metal appliances. Like a glass of iced tea in summer, beads of water form on the cold surfaces. This rarely occurs in winter because the windows are closed and the furnace (if it is in the basement) keeps the room relatively warm in comparison to outside air temperatures.

The solution to condensation problems is to prevent the moist air from coming in contact with the cold surfaces. This can be done by:

1. Keeping the basement heated in summer, thereby eliminating the temperature difference

2. Insulating pipes, thus preventing direct contact with the air

3. Maintaining excellent ventilation or keeping the air moving with a portable fan. This prevents prolonged contact and helps evaporate moisture before it can accumulate

4. Operating a dehumidifier to remove moisture from the air.

It is a good idea to close basement windows on rainy, muggy days and keep them open on clear dry days. Clear away ferns and heavy ground vegetation that tend to trap moist air in front of basement windows. Adequate cross ventilation is essential to preventing wet and dry rot from occurring on wooden floor joists.

What to Do When the Power Fails

Revised and Updated
Mary Twitchell
Illustrations by Keith Holister

Before the Power Fails

The best way to prevent a power outage from becoming a catastrophe is to plan ahead. Assess the potential disaster, natural or man-made, that you might face, and plan to eliminate or minimize its impact on your household. Start by considering your needs. Physical survival comes first. Can you provide your family with adequate food, water, and heat until power is restored? Can you guarantee the family's safety? Are there infants or elderly people in your home whose health would be threatened by loss of heat or cooling? What about animals and family pets?

After physical safety is ensured, think about your home and furnishings. Will your pipes freeze in a prolonged outage? Do you have an alternate source of power? Do you need one? Do you know what to do to prevent ruined appliances due to power surges and spoiled foods from lack of refrigeration?

Educating yourself and your family is the first step toward surviving a power failure. Start with the infrastructure of your house.

KNOW YOUR PLUMBING

If you do not know how your plumbing works, you will be unable to drain your pipes to prevent a freeze-up. Before the next power failure, locate the main-supply shutoff. Usually it is a large blue handle located near the water meter in your basement, but it could be near the hot-water tank, under the kitchen sink (in a house with no basement), hidden behind some paneling, outside the house near an outdoor spigot, or in a curb box. If you cannot locate the main shut-off valve, ask your plumber to locate it for you, then label the handle with a tag and make sure all family members know its location and function. If a wrench is needed to close the valve, be sure you can find it quickly in an emergency. You may want to practice draining the system if your heat comes from circulating hot water. Details for draining a hot-water system are given on page 883. Don't wait until an emergency to discover you have a basement full of valves and no idea what they connect. If you find there is no easy way to drain your system, talk to a plumber about other solutions, including installing additional shutoffs.

ELECTRICAL PREPAREDNESS

Locate your main electrical box and make sure everything is clearly labeled. Know which appliances should be unplugged during an outage to prevent damage. Keep a list. Choose a lamp as your "tell-tale" and label the switch, if possible, so you will know which position is on and which is off—when a power outage occurs during peak hours, you may not remember which lights and appliances were on. During an outage, leave on this lamp at all times. It will tell you when power is restored.

GATHER FOOD AND SUPPLIES

Store supplies that are essential for survival: food, water, and fuel (in winter). When gauging quantities, figure that an outage may last two to four days. You can stay in your home during longer outages (two to four weeks) if you have an alternative heat source, adequate water, and a well-stocked pantry.

BRIGHT IDEA

Power failures due to snowstorms, sleet, hurricanes, and other natural disasters are often preceded by a warning. In such cases, heat stews, soups, beans, spaghetti, and other one-pot meals and pour them into insulated thermos bottles, where they will keep warm for up to 12 hours.

EMERGENCY SUPPLIES

Battery-operated radio and extra batteries

Bottled water

Camp stove

Candles

Can opener

Cooking and eating utensils

Emergency blankets and/or sleeping bags

Fire extinguisher

First-aid kit

Flashlight and extra batteries

Household essentials (detergent, towels, etc.)

Jackknife

Kerosene or gas lantern

Masking or duct tape

Matches

Medications

Nonperishable foods

Personal care items (soap, toothbrush, toothpaste, shampoo, etc.)

Pet food

Sanitary supplies

Spare fuel

Warm clothing

Water purification tablets

COOKING ALTERNATIVES

If the power fails, you may be without your usual cooking facilities. Electric ranges will be inoperative during a power outage; even home gas stoves ignite electrically. Know in advance what your alternative cooking source will be.

Fireplaces can be adapted for cookout-style cooking. Take a grate from a barbecue pit or gas grill (or even an oven shelf), support it with bricks in the hearth, and prepare one-pot meals using an old pot or kettle. Pots used in a fireplace will be easier to clean if their outer surface is rubbed first with soap. Woodstoves are also great for cooking during an outage. Any one-pot meal can be cooked on a woodstove, and, depending on the size of the top cooking surface of your woodstove, entire meals can be prepared easily.

Two- and three-burner Coleman stoves that burn white gas and stoves that use disposable propane cylinders are available for a modest investment. If your family camps, you may already have one. These stoves are good in an emergency, but before buying one, check that you have pots that will fit the stove; the cooking area for a two-burner stove may be a small 13 inches by 20 inches. Long-distance hikers use even smaller stoves that consist of a fuel container attached to a simple burner. These are inexpensive and easy to store, but limit you to one pot at a time. **All of these stoves should be used in a well-ventilated space because they consume oxygen.** The safest place to use them is outdoors, and they should never be used in a tight, enclosed room. Remember, you will need an ample supply of fuel on hand.

Sterno stoves or canned-heat burners can be used safely indoors. Pry off the cover and touch the contents with a lighted match. Extinguish the flame by sliding the cover on top of the flame. Once the can has cooled, the cover can be secured.

Charcoal grills and hibachi stoves must be

EMERGENCY FOOD IDEA LIST

MAIN DISHES IN A CAN

Baked beans

Beef stew

Chicken and noodles

Chili

Corned beef hash

Pork and beans

Sardines

Soups that do not require additional water

Spaghetti/macaroni dinners

Tuna or salmon

FRUIT

Canned fruit

Dried fruit

Fresh fruit

SNACKS

Cereals

Cookies

Crackers

Dried fruits and nuts

Swedish hardtack

CANNED VEGETABLES

All kinds

BEVERAGES

Bottled water

Canned and bottled fruit juices

Canned and bottled vegetable juices

Canned milk

Coffee and tea

Non-refrigerated milk

Powdered milk

Soda and seltzer

Continued →

used outside the house. The fuel gives off carbon monoxide, which can be fatal in a closed room. Because this gas is colorless and odorless, you may not be aware that you are inhaling it. Therefore, use charcoal for outdoor cooking only—never for heating. Three or four briquettes in a small (8" x 8") hibachi or charcoal grill will generate enough heat to cook a simple meal. And charcoal briquettes store well.

Don't forget your outdoor gas grill. Even if the weather is freezing, your gas grill can be used for cooking outside in an outage. It can even heat water for bathing. If you have warning of an outage, make sure you have enough fuel to cook several meals.

DRINKING WATER SAFETY AND STORAGE

Water is your body's most critical need. You can probably live two to four weeks without food, but you can only live a few days without water. At the very minimum, each person needs 2 quarts of water per day. If possible, store a gallon per person per day, and to be safe, store a two-week supply. Half of the supply will be for drinking and food preparation, the other half for dishwashing, teeth cleaning, and handwashing. Remember to count juice from stored canned goods as part of your water supply.

If you receive pump-driven water from your own well, water will be an immediate necessity in the event of a power failure. Drilled wells depend on a submersible pump, and if the power fails, you will have no water. Dug (or shallow) wells depend on a pump, too, but in an outage, you may be able to remove the well cover and dip water from a shallow well using a bucket and rope. If you do this, make sure to sterilize the water and, after the power is restored, sterilize the well. And make sure you replace and secure the well cover after every use.

Also check with your town fire or water district. In prolonged outages, the town may offer emergency water supplies to residents.

City water is usually pumped to storage towers, then gravity-fed to homes. In addition, water departments may have backup generators for their pumps. In either case, you may have water for quite some time. But check with your municipal water authority so you know what to expect in a power failure.

If you wait until the disaster, you may discover that your water service has been interrupted or contaminated (as in an earthquake or flood) no matter what your supply. So to be safe, store a supply of drinking water. Plastic is a better container than glass because it is lightweight and shatterproof, but do not use plastic containers previously used for foodstuffs, chemicals, or commercial drinks for long-term water storage. Containers will need tight-fitting lids to prevent evaporation. Store your water supply in a dark place; sunlight has an adverse effect on plastics. Properly stored water should have a shelf life of a few years. To be safe, rotate your water supply every month for purity and taste.

For longer-term storage, water should be sterilized or disinfected. To sterilize, fill glass canning jars with water, leaving 1" of headroom at the top. Place a sterilized lid on each jar and process in a boiling water bath—20 minutes for quarts.

To disinfect, treat each gallon of water (stored in plastic or glass containers) with 16 drops (or 1/4 teaspoon) of liquid chlorine bleach, which will kill or inhibit the growth of microorganisms. Sterilized or disinfected water should be safe for many years.

Water from sinks, showers, water lines, toilet tanks, and hot-water tanks is potable (fit to drink). However, water used from hot-water tanks for emergency drinking water should be free of sediment and rust. Drain the tank every month until the water is clear to ensure 40—60 gallons of potable water.

TWO WAYS TO PURITY WATER

- Boil the water for 5 minutes. For every 1,000 feet above sea level, boil 1 additional minute.

- Add 1 halazone tablet to each quart of water. Let it stand for a half hour. If the water is murky, double the number of tablets and the amount of time you let it stand. Halazone tablets are available at camping stores and pharmacies.

Keep in mind that in a power outage, electric hot-water tanks will no longer be under pressure. Before water can be drawn, the system will need to be vented. Usually this can be accomplished by opening a faucet in the hot-water line. Then drain off just what you need from the tank each time. If you have not maintained a sediment-free tank, filter the water before drinking or cooking with it.

Use water drained from a heating system or from waterbeds only for toilet flushing and hand washing—never for drinking. Swimming pool water is not potable, but water from refrigerator ice cube trays is.

BRIGHT IDEA

In the warning time before an outage, **store as much water as possible.** Fill your washing machine, sinks, bathtub, and any clean containers. Buckets, dishpans, empty soda bottles, barrels, large cookpots, plastic storage bins, and even sturdy plastic bags can be used to hold water for a few days.

If the outage is weather related, you may have access to unlimited water supplies (snow in the North and rain in the South). Use this water for sanitation, or purify for drinking.

LET THERE BE LIGHTS

Light will be an immediate need, so always keep a flashlight handy. It is a good idea to have more than one flashlight, perhaps even one for every member of the family, kept in each bedroom (the power always seems to go off at night), and a large four-battery flashlight for the kitchen or living room. Have spare batteries and bulbs (in the middle of a prolonged outage, they will vanish quickly from store shelves), and check them every three months to be sure they are still good.

Rechargeable, long-life flashlights are available, as are rechargeable batteries. Rechargeable batteries have a shorter life than conventional batteries, something to be aware of in a prolonged outage. Rechargeable flashlights plug into household current to keep the batteries at full charge; whenever there is a power failure, it serves as a flashlight.

Although candles may be romantic, they are also dangerous. Candles can be tipped over or allowed to burn so low that they become a fire hazard. In addition, too many candles are required to provide just minimal lighting. Never leave candles unattended. Consider buying candle lanterns, popular with campers. They consist of a long-burning candle inside a metal-and-glass lantern and often come with hooks and handles for hanging and carrying. They are much less dangerous than are bare candles, and provide a steadier light, as the flame is protected by the glass chimney.

Kerosene lamps yield better light than either flashlights or candles, although they are potentially hazardous. Kerosene is highly flammable; it should be kept in a special can and stored outside, if possible, until needed. For maximum light, the wicks should be trimmed and the chimneys cleaned. On a quart of fuel, a kerosene lamp will burn 10 to 12 hours.

Aladdin-brand kerosene lanterns have incandescent mantles that increase the light output from the wick, but the flame must be adjusted carefully to avoid charring. These lanterns are relatively expensive, but produce the equivalent amount of light of a 75-watt bulb. When not in use, they should be taken apart and the fuel emptied into bottles for storage, because kerosene evaporates quickly when exposed to air.

Single-mantle and double-mantle propane lanterns are another option. A disposable propane gas cylinder attaches to the burner. The single-mantle lantern provides light equivalent to a 100-watt bulb and burns for 10 to 14 hours, while the double-mantle lantern provides light equivalent to a 200-watt bulb with a burning time of 5 to 7 hours. Use these in a properly ventilated room.

KEEPING WARM

Heat will be one of your major concerns if you live in the North and the outage occurs, as they often do, in winter. The first thing to do is to dress warmly.

Clothing. Clothing insulates the body, but it does not necessarily follow that the more you wear, the warmer you will be. Generally, each sweater increases the body temperature by 3.7 degrees, but it is the warm air between the layers of clothing that insulates the body. Waffle weaves, fishnet, quilted, bonded, and pile fabrics and sweaters create air spaces and should be worn close to your skin. Very tight layers leave fewer air spaces, so make sure you have comfortably large outer layers. Outdoor sports companies sell a vast array of cold-weather clothing, from silk underwear to fleece jackets and hats. In an emergency, even newspapers can be used as an insulating layer.

Long johns add leg warmth. If you don't have long johns, try tights, pajama bottoms, or leggings. Lined slippers, slipper socks, down-filled and fiber-filled booties, even plastic bags help insulate your feet. Mittens are warmer than gloves—or you can use socks. Because your body loses a great deal of heat from your head, you should wear a hat, especially when sleeping.

Bed is the warmest place in the house. Several lightweight blankets are better than one very heavy blanket. Beds can be further warmed with hot water bottles or bricks warmed by a wood or coal fire, then wrapped in towels. And of course there is body warmth. Children and elderly people get cold more quickly and should sleep with others during a cold-weather outage. If the outage is a prolonged one, plan on having the family sleep together in one or two beds relocated to the warmest room. You will all lose less body heat this way.

Other Heat Sources. If your home depends on electricity for heat, you may want to think about auxiliary heating systems. Fireplaces will slow any temperature drop and at close range provide some comfort, but they may pull more warm air from the house than they provide. To increase efficiency, a fireplace can be fitted with heat-circulating metal inserts or with hollow tube grates.

Portable space heaters that use oil or gas are also available. Propane catalytic heaters are another option. They have a wick that draws fuel from a tank. The heater is relatively cool and is safe, clean, and efficient. These space heaters are especially beneficial when placed near vulnerable water pipes.

Use any space heaters with care. Every year, hundreds of house fires are caused by space heaters placed too close to flammable materials, being tipped over, or being used improperly. Before buying one, check that it is UL-approved, has a thermostat to prevent overheating, and has a grille to protect the combustion chamber. And never store flammable fuels in the vicinity of a space heater.

Wood-burning, coal-burning, or combination wood- and coal stoves may be the best backup systems, but they involve a substantial investment. If you do not intend the appliance for permanent use, buy a stove that is practical for emergency use only. Follow the manufacturer's installation and venting instructions. And make sure your chimney is kept clean. If you have a wood- or coal stove you use rarely, remember to keep a good supply of fuel on hand; in an outage, suppliers may run low or may be unable to reach your home with a fresh supply.

CONTACT WITH THE OUTSIDE WORLD

A battery-operated radio will keep you informed about the severity of the blackout, as local radio stations are usually a primary source for disaster instructions. But if you have a medical or other emergency, you need to think about how to contact help, because phone lines may not be functional.

A battery-operated or car-based CB radio may be helpful, as police routinely monitor certain citizens bands. Unless you have a cellular phone, this may be the only way to contact emergency services for people in rural areas trapped by storm damage.

Consider the purchase of a cellular phone. A battery-powered cell phone will still work in a power outage and you can use it to contact authorities. But keep in mind that you will have to pay monthly fees to keep a cell phone active.

TRANSPORTATION

During an outage, you may have to travel for medical help or for supplies. During a prolonged outage you may need a way to leave your home for an emergency shelter. If you have warning of a storm, fill the car with gasoline and park it where you will have the best access to traveled roads. Protect the car from blowing snow, and make sure it is parked clear of trees, branches, phone poles, and other things that could damage it or block access to it. Store blankets, a shovel, flashlight, jumper cables, flares, and a bag of sand in the car, and be sure the snow tires are on. Take food and water in case you become stranded on the road. If you are stranded in a car in a storm, stay in the car and run the engine occasionally for warmth, leaving a window open a crack and making sure the tailpipe is clear of obstructions.

Continued ➜

If you live in a flood-prone area, plan to evacuate before the water rises high enough to strand you in the house. Remember that flooded rivers are swift and dangerous, and often full of fast-moving downed trees and other hazardous debris. If you are trapped, contact emergency authorities. The best plan is to park a car on high ground with a good route to safety, and to evacuate before the water rises too high.

If you have to travel on foot, dress warmly. Skis or snowshoes are useful in winter, a bicycle in summer. No matter what the season, in an outage due to weather or natural disaster, be prepared to encounter obstacles. If you must leave your home, take water, a first-aid kit, an emergency blanket, and food. And watch for fallen power lines. You may have to detour to avoid them.

Steps to Take during a Blackout

PROTECT YOUR HEATING SYSTEM

There are things you need to do to ensure that your heating system is not damaged during an outage or when the power goes back on.

Step 1. Check your heating system to see if it is still working.

Gas Systems. The main gas burner must be operating if you are going to have heat in the house. If the burner has a manual control, this will be easy. Look for a button or switch on the gas line feeding the burner that allows for manual operation. If there is no such control, there is no way of getting gas to the main burner.

Whatever you do, do not try to light the burner with a match. A great deal of gas is fed into the main burner, and it may flare when ignited. To use the control, press or turn it until the main burner lights. The initial flame is provided by the pilot.

If there is an interruption in the gas supply, the gas company should be immediately on hand to turn off the gas to your house. However, you may be able to do this yourself. Just shut off the main gas-control valve to your home. The valve will be located near the meter and may be inside or outside your house. If you suspect a problem and cannot shut off the gas, get in touch with the fire department and gas company and leave the house immediately. Gas is poisonous to breathe and extremely explosive. If you do manage to shut off the gas to your house, open all windows and doors to ensure that any residual gas escapes. Don't light any matches, or even turn on or off electric lights in the presence of free gas. Tiny sparks in the light switch resulting from the action of the switch could set off an explosion.

Hot-water Systems. Open the flow valve on the water feed line and shut off the pump motor. This allows heated water to be gravity-fed through the system. There will not be as much heat as when the pump is operating, but there will be some.

Hot-air Systems. A hot-air system can provide heat (by gravity) even though the furnace will have to operate without the blower. Remove the filter(s) and shut off the blower motor. Some warm air will rise through the registers, which is better than nothing.

Coal Furnaces. Stoker-fed coal furnaces can be fed with a shovel. If the fire has to be restarted, fill the furnace with paper and kindling just as you would to start a fire. Then hand-feed the coal. Regulate the fire by opening or closing the manual air damper.

There may be a buildup of pressure and temperature inside any furnace operated manually. If there is a throttle on the gas line that permits you to raise and lower the flame, as with a kitchen range, lower the flame for 10 minutes every half hour or so to allow the furnace to cool. If there is no throttle, shut it off with the manual control for 10 minutes every half hour. Once electricity is restored, make sure the manual controls are turned off, then return the system to normal automatic operation.

Step 2. Conserve your heat.

If you still have an operable furnace, conserve heat in case fuel deliveries are delayed. If your heating system is not operable, and you are planning to heat with a small stove, a space heater, or a fireplace (none of them is too efficient), conservation of heat is even more critical.

Choose a living space in which you can wait out the power failure. An inside room loses heat the most slowly. Outside rooms with lots of windows lose heat more quickly. Isolate your chosen room as completely as possible from the rest of the unheated house, but do not cut it off from the basement. The earth usually stays around 50°F, which means the basement should provide some warmth. If the furnace is still warm or giving off heat, move into the basement while preparing another area of the house.

Close all doors to your chosen living room; stuff newspapers or sheets between the door and the frame. Roll up a throw rug, towels, newspapers, or blankets and push them against doors to prevent drafts. Plan openings and closings of doors (especially of exterior doors) to prevent excessive heat loss. Hang blankets, bedding, drapes, or shower curtains over the windows and secure them to the window jambs with masking tape to prevent as much movement of cold air as possible.

If your power failure extends over a long period, leave south-facing windows exposed on sunny days so that they will let in the much needed warmth. But cover the windows at night, or you may lose as much heat as was gained during the day. In a hot climate, do the reverse. Open windows at night to cool your living area, but close them and cover windows during the heat of the day to help keep the living area as cool as possible.

You will be more comfortable in a tightly closed room with no heat source whatsoever than in a room that is properly ventilated for a space heater—at least until the house temperature drops below 50°F. Likewise, until the house temperature drops below 50°F, you will lose more heat through the chimney with a roaring fire in the fireplace than you will gain. If, however, you have an air-tight, wood-burning or coal-burning stove that is properly installed and requires no ventilation, you can fire it up at any time.

Step 3. Start your alternative heat source, if necessary.

No matter how careful you are with your heat, if the power failure extends over a long enough period, your interior house temperature will drop below 50°F in winter. This is the time to start up your alternative heat source.

Fireplaces can burn firewood, wood chips, scrap lumber, corn cobs, magazines, and twigs. Ideally, burn dry wood that has seasoned one to two years, but if there is an emergency, such patience may be impossible. Both ash and sumac burn well even when wet and green.

Fireplace fires can be dangerous; never leave a fire untended. If the heat is essential, take turns watching the fire, or make a cover of sheet metal to block off the fireplace at night. Glass doors are ideal fireplace covers, but in an emergency, you may have to improvise. Spark screens are helpful but in no way foolproof, nor do they prevent a downdraft in the chimney from pushing noxious gases out into the room. Move all flammable materials like rugs, furniture, and curtains out of range of flying sparks. Do not burn trash or briquettes indoors; both give off highly toxic gases.

Space heaters can also be dangerous. Asphyxiation is possible from insufficient oxygen and an excess of poisonous gas. Be sure to provide cross ventilation. For safety, open a window on each side of the heater and have a person awake at all times. If you begin to feel drowsy, there is inadequate ventilation. To prevent plumbing and heating systems from freezing, set up the space heater in the basement near water pipes and in the area of the boiler (if you have a hot-water system).

WATER CONCERNS

During an outage, there are three main concerns with respect to water. You need to have enough to meet all your drinking and eating requirements. You need to prevent your pipes from freezing because they may cause a great deal of damage when they thaw. And you need additional water for sanitation purposes.

Once you have stockpiled sufficient water to meet your drinking requirements, the safety of your water pipes is your next concern. Frozen pipes can be costly and messy. If the power goes out for an extended period and the outside temperatures are below freezing, the pipes, regardless of how well they are insulated, may freeze. **Take the following steps to prevent frozen pipes.**

- Set the faucets on the first floor at the rate of a fast drip. Water enters a house at above freezing temperatures; if kept moving, the water will not have a chance to freeze.

- Open the hot water faucets every three or four hours and let the hot water run for 5 minutes. You can do this only if you have a gas or solar hot-water heater. Opening the faucets periodically will

warm the hot-water pipes and prevent them from freezing. The cold-water faucets, however, should be kept open and allowed to drip continuously.

- Oil or propane space heaters should be kept operating in the basement near the boiler or in the area of the pipes. Be sure to leave a window opened an inch to adequately vent the heater.

- For plumbing systems in danger of freezing, the pipes may have to be drained. When water freezes, it expands; this expansion will crack the pipes. When the water thaws, the pipes will begin leaking; and if the main supply valve has not been closed, water will gush out of the crack(s), flood your basement, cause thousands of dollars of damage, and create a terrible mess.

DRAINING YOUR HOT-WATER HEATING SYSTEM

Hot-water heating systems circulate hot water, heated in a boiler, through pipes and radiator units. These will have to be drained. For a time after a power failure, the water will still circulate without being pumped, but cold weather and a prolonged outage may endanger these pipes, too.

To drain, attach a hose to the drain valve that is in the lowest part of the system, generally at the base of the boiler. Open and drain water from all radiator bleeder valves. The expansion tank for the hot-water system must also be drained.

There will still be water in some of the pipes. Look for a vertical shut-off valve to drain the water stored in the pipes between the water meter and the hot-water tank. Open this valve to drain the lowest part of the system. There is still a short section of pipe between the water meter and the vertical shutoff. With a hacksaw, saw this section of pipe in half. Bend the two parts of pipe to drain both sections. Once the power has been restored, solder these pipes together before the water is turned on.

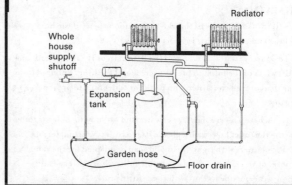

Radiator

Whole house supply shutoff

Expansion tank

Garden hose

Floor drain

Continued ➜

DRAINING YOUR PIPES

Before draining your system, turn off the hot-water-tank heat source. Then close the water supply to the heater and close the main shut-off valve—usually a blue handle located near your water meter in the basement. Turn the handle clockwise to shut off water to the house.

Turn on all water faucets, including tub and shower faucets, and flush all toilets. Next, drain water from the lowest faucet, usually at the boiler or at a basement laundry washer. Save all this water if water is in short supply.

Dip water out of the toilet bowls and tanks with a sponge. Then add 8 ounces of antifreeze, kerosene, or alcohol to the toilet bowls to keep any remaining water from freezing. Run the dishwasher and washing machine a few minutes to pump out water already in the units. Also drain ice makers and humidifiers. Showers, sinks, and tubs have drainage traps; add kerosene or antifreeze (2 to 3 ounces) to prevent the trap water from freezing.

To drain the water heater, be sure the gas or electricity that heats the tank is turned off and that the valve between the water supply and the heater is closed. Reduce the amount of water to be taken out by opening the house hot-water faucets to remove water in the pipes. Also open the hot-water faucet in the lowest part of the system.

Let the remaining water in the tank cool. Then attach a hose to the drain cock near the bottom of the tank and run the hose to a floor drain to the outside. If you use a plastic garden hose, the hot water will weaken the plastic and may ruin the hose. Use a rubber hose instead. If necessary, the water can be removed by bucketfuls.

If you have a hot-water heating system, see the box at left for instructions on draining that system.

You may not have to drain the entire system. Begin by draining all endangered pipes, including hot-water pipes to unheated spaces. Then protect all exposed pipes. This way you may avoid draining the entire system if the outage is neither severe nor prolonged.

If you have to abandon your house because of an outage, turn off the water and drain the pipes if there is any danger of freezing.

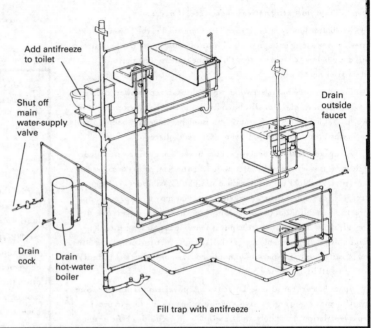

Add antifreeze to toilet

Shut off main water-supply valve

Drain outside faucet

Drain cock

Drain hot-water boiler

Fill trap with antifreeze

SANITATION

You will think longingly of the old-style outdoor privy if the outage lasts very long and your water is in short supply.

To conserve water, disconnect the lift chain or the trip lever from the lift wires of the toilet to prevent accidental flushing. Put used toilet paper in a covered container, and flush the toilet only to prevent clogging.

If you have a severe shortage of water and no snow to melt for toilet use, line the toilet bowl with a plastic bag to collect waste materials. Metal containers with tight-fitting lids can be adapted for the same purpose, or you can purchase a portable toilet. Store garbage and human waste outside in cans with tight-fitting lids.

APPLIANCES

Immediately disconnect all appliances that run continually on electricity, such as freezers, refrigerators, electric pumps of water systems, and furnace blowers on forced-air systems. Also disconnect air conditioners and ovens, which have high starting-wattage requirements. This is done to safeguard the appliances. When power is turned on after an outage, it is often initiated at half the usual voltage. The motors of appliances will work faster, trying to draw the missing voltage. If the half voltage continues for an extended period, the result can be a burned-up appliance motor. Also, power spikes and surges are common during lightning storms and when power is being restored. Vulnerable electronics like TVs, VCRs, and computers can suffer significant damage if not unplugged.

To keep informed of the status of electric power, leave a light turned on in a conspicuous area of the house. When the power comes on at half voltage, the lamp's bulb will glow dimly. Wait a half hour after the lightbulb glows normally before reconnecting your appliances.

Protect the food in your refrigerator and freezer from spoiling.

· Keep the doors closed as much as possible.

· Insulate the freezer with blankets.

For longer outages:

· Move the food to a friend's refrigerator or freezer, or

· Place a 25- to 50-pound block of dry ice on a piece of cardboard in the freezer, or

· If outside temperatures remain consistently below 0°F for freezer foods, or below 40° for refrigerator foods, place the food outdoors, but out of the sun.

A full, well-insulated freezer will keep food frozen for two days if left unopened; a half-full freezer will keep food frozen for a day. Larger freezers will preserve food longer than will smaller units. Cover the freezer with blankets to keep in the cold.

Dry ice will hold the freezer at 0°F for 36 hours. **If you decide to use dry ice, remember to handle it very carefully.** Wear thick gloves; dry ice is solid carbon dioxide gas that melts at minus 109°F. It will damage bare skin instantly.

SAFETY TIPS

· Unplug all major appliances to prevent them from being damaged when the power is restored. Unplug all lights except one so that you will know when the power returns.

· Have emergency telephone numbers listed and kept in an accessible location, preferably next to the telephone.

· Make preparations and review plans with everyone living in your house. If infants or elderly people will be involved, make plans to take them to relatives or neighbors if they will be better cared for there. If you are friendly with neighbors, or have relatives living nearby, find out if they have such things as a portable generator or woodstove. Make emergency plans together.

> ### EMERGENCY EVACUATION CHECKLIST
>
> · Turn off power at the circuit-breaker box.
>
> · Drain water pipes and heater.
>
> · Pour antifreeze into all water traps.
>
> · Store canned and bottled foods on inside walls to prevent freezing.
>
> · Take pets, plants, and valuables with you.
>
> · If possible, check your house daily.

· Check into community emergency food and fuel supplies, emergency shelters, and evacuation plans.

· Be sure your supplies of fuel and medication are out of the reach of children. Do not store them where they can contaminate food and water.

· Provide adequate venting for any alternative heating equipment. Asphyxiation is possible if there are excess poisonous gases and insufficient oxygen. Open windows to provide cross ventilation.

· Repair windows broken in the storm with heavyweight clear plastic and some tape, staples, or tacks.

When Power Is Restored

When power is restored, restart your heating system, thaw any frozen pipes, restore your appliances to working condition, and evaluate your food for spoilage. Keep in mind that power companies have priorities for power restoration. They work with local authorities to restore power first to critical areas and services (hospitals, municipal water facilities, and police and fire stations). Then their priority is to restore power to the greatest number of customers first. So if you live in an outlying area or on a street of few houses, you may have to wait several days or even weeks for power to come back at your house.

TO THAW FROZEN PIPES

Usually pipes do not freeze their entire length; they freeze at points where they are exposed to the cold, especially near sills, exterior walls, and uninsulated spaces. To locate the freeze-up, turn on the water faucets. Follow the frozen pipe back to a juncture. Then test water taps off this second pipe to determine whether the pipe has frozen farther downstream.

Once you have located the culprit section of pipe, you probably can pinpoint the location of the freeze-up by deciding where the pipe is the coldest. Open the affected faucets to allow for the expansion of the frozen water.

Try to thaw pipes with hot water poured on rags wrapped around the pipe (left), or try a propane torch with safety shielding behind it.

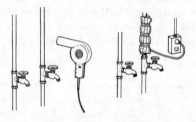

You can also try to thaw frozen pipes with a hair dryer (left), or with an electric heating pad if you have an outlet nearby.

TURNING THE HEAT BACK ON

Gas. The gas company has emergency crews to restore power as well as to reignite pilot lights. However, there are usually instructions for relighting the pilot on the front of most units. Follow the manufacturer's instructions.

Hot-water System. To refill a hot-water heating system, open the water-supply inlet to the boiler. Keep the venting valve open on the entire system, until you hear water filling the pipes and water drains from open hot-water faucets. Close the venting valves and then restart the water heater. Late in the day, vent all valves to release the trapped air.

Electric. Turn your thermostat way down; then, at half-hour intervals, raise the thermostat by two degrees. This helps to evenly spread the electric load of your community.

FOOD

When the power is restored, refreeze partially thawed foods only if they contain ice crystals. The ice crystals show that the food has remained at 40°F or below. Food with no ice crystals left in it is said to be defrosted and generally should not be refrozen. Fruit can be refrozen but with a

Continued →

decrease in quality, and bread can be refrozen. Label it and use it first. Bacteria that cause spoilage are not destroyed by freezing; they are kept inactive only as long as the food remains at 0°F. Should the food thaw, the bacteria will start to grow, and food poisoning is possible. Therefore, examine all food for spoilage before refreezing.

Sharpening Hand Tools

Max Alth

The Cutting Edge

No edge remains sharp with use. The edge dulls as the metal wears. The sharper the edge, the more quickly it wears, and the more often it requires sharpening to maintain an ultrafine edge.

Corrosion is another enemy of a sharp edge. Visible rust prevents a knife from sliding smoothly through the substance being cut. There is also invisible corrosion, which can be caused by fruit juices attacking the metal blade. This is why when you cut something acidic, even with a stainless steel knife, it is good practice to wipe the knife dry immediately afterwards.

Just how thick must an edge be to be considered dull? This is a matter of application. A sharp knife would be quite dull when used as a razor. Technically, when an edge exceeds 1/200 (0.02) of an inch, it is pretty dull; but in general a knife is too dull when it will not cut for you.

METALS

Ordinary steel is a mixture of iron and carbon. The more carbon, the harder the steel. The harder the carbon steel, the sharper the edge it can be given and will hold. Unfortunately, the harder carbon steel is made, the more brittle it becomes. Therefore, it is impractical to make an edged tool from the hardest carbon steel possible. For example, an ax made out of brittle steel would be very sharp, but you would lose a chunk of it the first time you hit a frozen knot or a stone. In addition, you would have a difficult time trying to hand-sharpen it in the field. Axes are, therefore, made from comparatively mild steel.

The solution to the problem of brittleness is toughness. This is the ability of a hard metal to give a little so that it does not break. Toughness is produced by tempering and adding exotic metals such as chromium, vanadium, molybdenum, tungsten, and nickel. Unfortunately, with the exception of nickel, all the exotic metals are expensive.

Stainless steel is made by the addition of chromium and nickel. The stainless steels that hold the best edge depend almost entirely on chromium for their resistance to corrosion. The less expensive steels, which resist corrosion much better, contain the less expensive, softer nickel. The alloy found best for cutlery is the so-called "400" series of stainless alloys. The best in this series is "440-C" which has a 17-percent to 19-percent chromium content.

Commercial cutlery used by professional butchers and chefs are straight-carbon blades made from an alloy of steel that is primarily carbon and iron. The mix contains 50 to 80 parts of carbon to 1,000 parts of iron. Less carbon makes for a steel that is easily dulled. More carbon makes for a steel that is easily nicked and difficult to sharpen. Add sufficient carbon and you get steel that is almost as hard as a diamond and just as brittle. In any case, without the addition of chromium and/or nickel, these straight-carbon blades corrode, stain, and rust. They must be kept dry or oiled.

BEVELS

The angle or bevel that forms the cutting edge of a tool is called its edge bevel. The edge bevel that you find on a tool (unless it has been altered by age or error) is that bevel best suited to the steel that makes up the tool and the way the tool is used. If you alter the edge bevel to make it longer and narrower, you weaken the edge. It will dull more quickly and chip more easily. If you shorten the bevel and broaden the angle, the cutting ability of the tool will be reduced. The angle formed by the edge bevels of common cutting tools ranges from 10 to 50 degrees. The sharper the angle, the better the tool cuts or slices, but the weaker the edge because there is less metal behind it. Here are some common edge bevel angles.

Razors	10 degrees
Pocket knives	15 degrees
Cutlery	25 to 35 degrees
Chopping edges	35 to 45 degrees
Mauls and wedges	50 degrees

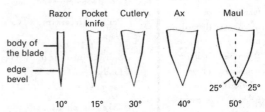

Typical edge bevel angels of various cutting tools. All are double bevels.

Basic Techniques

The process of sharpening any tool consists of restoring the original cutting edge(s) by removing a little metal. This is accomplished in two steps, which sometimes can be subdivided into a number of separate steps. The first step is called beveling, which some call grinding. The second step is called honing, or polishing, finishing, or stropping. With experience and the correct tools, both steps need not take more than five minutes for simple cutting edges, like knives and plane blades. Multiple blades, like saws, may require thirty minutes to an hour or more, depending on the number of teeth to be sharpened.

BEVELING

Beveling reestablishes the original edge bevel angle of the tool. Just how much metal has to be removed depends on the nature of the tool and the amount of metal that has worn or broken away.

Assume that you are working on the edge of an old door, and you are planing away with vim and pleasure. Suddenly your plane strikes an old, unseen nail. A chip, perhaps 1/8 inch deep, breaks from the blade of the plane. You can, if you wish, continue planing, but the plane will leave a ridge with every pass. To enable the plane to cut smoothly and true again, you will have to remove sufficient metal from the edge of the blade to restore the full and original bevel.

Assume another situation. You are in the field and have neither the time nor the tool with which to sharpen your ax properly. Instead you just touch it up a little with a file. In a short while, there is no semblance of the original bevel; the edge is rounded. To return this edge to its original bevel a lot of metal has to be removed.

In both cases, and in similar instances where an edge has been terribly dulled or damaged, grinding is the only practical way to restore the bevel.

Grinding is accomplished with a coarse stone. You can place the tool in a vise or on your workbench and move the stone over the edge of the tool, making certain to hold the stone at the correct angle to the cutting edge at all times. Or you can place the stone on the bench and run the edge of the tool across the stone. In either case, it is a lot of work if there is a lot of metal to be removed.

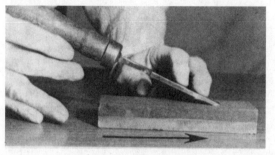

Basic position of tool and sharpening stone. In this example, a chisel is sharpened on a combination bench stone, coarse side up. Two hands are used to make certain the angle of the chisel blade against the stone remains the same. The arrow shows the direction in which the tool is moved. On the return stroke, little or no pressure is applied to the tool.

The easier way to grind is to use a power grinder. There are several kinds. There is the old-fashioned whetstone, the modern bench grinder, and the grindstone mounted on an electric drill.

To use an old-fashioned whetstone, turn the grindstone with your hand or your foot and keep the edge of the tool pressed firmly against the edge of the revolving stone. Wear gloves and safety glasses when using a bench grinder, and take care not to apply too much pressure. Otherwise, you might overheat the edge of the tool, which will soften it. The tricky part here is getting the tool to pass over the grindstone evenly and at the same angle and pressure over the entire length of the blade. This is very hard to do freehand. If you can rig up some apparatus to rest the blade on at the proper angle, it makes the job much easier.

The drill-mounted grindstone is the least desirable arrangement because it is difficult to hold the edge of the wheel correctly against the edge of the tool. However, it is a lot easier than hand-grinding. The tool must be placed firmly in a vise. Again, you need to wear gloves and safety glasses. Apply little pressure and stop frequently to examine the edge of the tool.

When the grindstone is thicker than the width of the edge of the tool, and that edge is straight, maintaining the proper tool-to-wheel angle is no problem; just hold the tool steady. When the edge of the tool is wider than the thickness of the grindstone, hold the tool-to-wheel angle steady, and move the tool from side to side so that the stone touches all of the edge evenly. Avoid a swinging motion or your corners will become rounded. When the edge of the tool is curved, swing the tool in an arc, always holding the tool-to-stone angle steady.

HONING

When the original bevel has been restored with a fine-graded stone, the marks left by the fine-grit stone are removed by an even harder stone

with a still finer grit. If you examine the bevel at this point, you will see that it is beginning to shine. The next step is honing, or stropping. Very simply, you polish the beveled edge with the rough side of the strop and then the smooth side. Five or ten strokes are all that are needed. For the ultimate in sharpness, the blade is then drawn across the palm of your hand a half dozen times. If you are not sharpening soft stainless steel, the edge should be sharp enough to cut a hair without bending it, or cut a sliver from your fingernail without pulling.

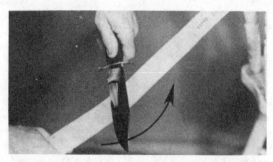

Stropping a knife on the back of a man's belt. The blade is drawn in a direction away from its edge; in the wrong direction, you would shave the belt.

Tools for Sharpening

Sharpening is the process of removing metal. For rapid metal removal, use a stone, natural or man-made, that consists of comparatively coarse abrasive particles or grains. The coarse abrasives leave a rough edge; so after using a "coarse" stone, follow with a second stone having very fine abrasive particles or grit. Instead of a stone, you might use a file to remove metal. Finally, use leathers for the final honing.

STONES

Stones and abrasives are graded by grit and hardness. They come in various shapes.

Grit. *Grit* refers to the size of the particles or grains that comprise the stone or abrasive. It is measured by the size of the smallest hole through which a particle of grit can pass. Grit ranges from 8 to 600, meaning the number of holes per linear inch. The lower the grit number, the rougher the surface the stone produces; the finer the grit, the smoother the surface it produces; and the more slowly it cuts.

Here are some general guidelines you can follow to choose stones. If the stones you have do not carry grit numbers, you can safely follow the manufacturers' suggestions.

Fast metal removal	24 to 35 grit
Moderately rapid metal removal	36 to 55 grit
Coarse beveling	55 to 65 grit
Fine beveling	65 to 120 grit
Honing	120 to 200 plus grit

In a combination stone for sharpening axes and the like, a 35/75 stone would be about right. For sharpening chisels and planes, a 50/100 stone would be about right. For sharpening knives and similar sharp edges, you might select a 65/120 stone.

Grade. Hardness, called *grade* in commercial stones, refers to the strength of the bond between grains. The harder the stone, the longer it will last, the longer it will remain flat under use, and the finer the edge

Continued →

it will produce compared to a softer stone of identical grit size. Unfortunately, the harder the stone, the higher its cost, and the more likely it will shatter if dropped on a concrete floor.

Usually the harder synthetic stones like aluminum oxide (which is sold under the tradenames India and Alundum) or silicon carbide (sold by the name Crystolon) are used for beveling. Natural stones, such as queer creek, soft Arkansas, or hard Arkansas, are used for honing.

Shapes. Wheel-shaped abrasives are known as *grindstones. Handstones* may be any size and shape and may even have a handle. *Bench stones* are rectangular with parallel surfaces and are designed to be placed on a workbench. *Slipstones* have flat surfaces plus curved edges. Long, thin sharpening stones, which may have round, square, or triangular cross sections, are called sticks.

Care. There are two schools of thought on caring for stones. One holds with oil, the other with water. The oil people soak their new stones overnight in 10-weight or 20-weight automotive oil (never vegetable or cooking oil). They add a few drops of oil to the stone every time they use it. When the stone becomes glazed, they clean it with alcohol, gasoline, or kerosene. The water people use their stones dry. When the pores of the stone clog up, they clean them with warm soap and water and a scrub brush. I hold with the water people.

A piece of sandpaper wrapped around a block of wood serves as a makeshift replacement for a bench stone.

FILES
Files are sometimes used instead of stones. You can remove more metal, stroke for stroke, with a file than with an equally coarse stone. Also, long, thin files are much stronger than long, thin stones and less likely to break in your hand. In the case of sharpening saws, files are the only practical tools to use. Stones are sometimes used to hone saw teeth, but never to bevel them.

LEATHERS
Leather is used for the final honing. If you can secure a barber's leather strop, fine. If not, you can make do with an unpainted leather belt. Or, you can purchase a length of strap leather from a hardware store. A piece two or more inches wide is best. A little neat's-foot oil on the leather every now and then will help preserve it and keep it soft.

OTHER SHARPENING TOOLS
There are times when you do not have a sharpening stone at hand, and there are tools that are more easily and quickly sharpened with other devices. You can use sandpaper and field stones for grinding and steels for honing.

Sandpaper. Sandpaper is graded by grit size as are abrasive stones. However, for reasons unknown, sandpaper grit is coarser than abrasive grit. For example, for the same job that would require a 100-grit stone, you would use 200-grit paper (and still, you would not get the same smoothing effect).

To use sandpaper, either place the paper flat on your bench and bring the tool to the paper; or fasten the paper in a standard holder and bring the holder to the tool, just as you would use a handstone.

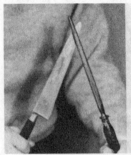 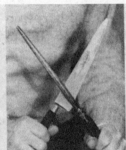

Honing with a steel. The tip of the edge of the knife is pressed against the steel (left). Then the knife and the steel are crossed, causing the steel to slide across the length of the edge of the knife (right). Repeat the operation a few times and you are ready to resume carving the roast.

Power sanders. For an occasional rough-beveling job, you can use a sanding disk mounted on a drill motor. The larger drills are preferable, as the motors have a slower speed. You can also use motor-driven belt sanders for sharpening. In all cases, wear protective glasses, as the belt tends to throw grains of sand and bits of metal. *Use a minimum of pressure*; it is easy to bear down too hard. If you force its edge into the paper, the tool may jerk out of your hands violently and fling the paper in your face. Several light passes do the best job.

Field stones. Any brick or stone that has one reasonably flat surface can be used for sharpening. A field stone or brick is used exactly as you would a sharpening stone.

Honing with steel. A steel is used to hone the edge of a carving knife after every three or four slices. It is a long, thin, round bar of steel. The steel is made of a harder alloy than the knife, and the surface has been roughened by tiny slits. In effect, the steel is a fine-toothed file. But a file is used in a drawing motion and is pulled away from the work, the steel is pushed against the knife edge.

Sharpening Techniques for Individual Tools
Now that we have covered the basic terminology and equipment used with sharpening, it is time to reemphasize that proper tool sharpening is an art that takes time to master.

Approach each task carefully. If it seems that you will have difficulty holding the tool steady against the stone, rig up a guide to hold the tool at the proper angle. Maintaining the proper tool-to-stone angle is the whole secret of proper sharpening.

PLANE IRONS
Plane irons or blades are easy to sharpen because they have a single, straight bevel. The iron itself is flat. Only the cutting edge is beveled.

You will need a two-grit stone with a fine-grit side of 100 or more and a very steady hand or a guide for holding the blade. You can purchase a guide in a hardware shop, or make one yourself. In either case, the guide can be used for a number of tools.

A plane iron has been clamped in a homemade jig, the blade positioned in the jig so that the edge bevel is just right. Now the blade and jig can be pushed along the length of the stone several times, until the blade is sharpened.

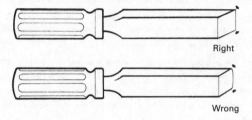

Right

Wrong

The end of the bevel must make a right angle with the side of the blade.

1. Remove and examine the blade. Remove whatever rust is present with steel wool. View the bevel in good light. The width of the bevel should be equal across the full width of the blade. The end of the bevel must make a right angle with the side of the blade. Note if there are any visible nicks more than 1/64 of an inch deep. If the bevel width is uneven, if the end of the steel is not square with the side, or if there are deep nicks, considerable metal must be removed. This is best done by grinding.

2. Use a wheel in the 55-grit to 65-grit range, 1-inch thick, and preferably thicker. (It is easier to grind an even and accurate bevel when the face of the wheel is as wide or wider than the tool to be ground.) Do not attempt to position the iron by hand alone; use a guide, making certain the guide is parallel to the face of the stone. Some craftsmen also tighten a pair of machinist's parallel clamps across the blade. Pressing the clamp edge against the guide keeps the blade at right angles to the face of the wheel.

   If possible, restore the bevel to its original angle. If not, grind the edge back to 30 degrees. The angle is not critical, you can estimate it. Generally the angle is correct when the bevel is roughly twice the thickness of the plane iron blade.

   Use little pressure and stop as soon as you have corrected the bevel—removed the nicks, evened the width of the bevel, and made it straight across. Remember, the bevel must be one flat surface.

3. The next step is coarse-beveling. Place the coarser side of the bench stone up. Fasten the blade in the guide. Check the angle by making certain the bevel lies flat on the stone before you tighten the guide. Position the end of the blade at the end of the

stone and push it forward along the length of the stone. (Dragging the blade produces a wire edge, a fine curl on the edge, which has to be removed.) Use little pressure and full strokes. Five or ten strokes should be sufficient. Examine the bevel. It should be a single, shiny surface.

4. Turn the stone over and with the tool still in the guide, give the blade five or so light strokes. If you wish, you can repeat this with a still finer-grit stone; but for most work, this is not necessary.

WOOD CHISELS

Old-time wood chisels have little or no bevel in their blade sections. But the blade is twice as thick as a plane iron. This makes for a very wide edge bevel, which may look like it is considerably less than 30 degrees, but rarely is. Modern wood chisels have shorter bodies with a more pronounced bevel to their blades. Still, you want the same 30-degree edge bevel on these tools. If someone, in error, has cut a second, shorter bevel on their edge, either you must grind or coarse-bevel the edge back to where it belongs. Wood chisels are then sharpened exactly the same as plane irons.

STRAIGHT-EDGED KNIVES

If the original edge bevel of the knife is clear enough to be followed, it is best to stick with the manufacturer's original angle. If the angle has been worn off or distorted by inaccurate sharpening, pick an angle from 25 to 35 degrees. For cutting soft things like bread, you want an acute angle. If you expect your knife to run into bone, you had best try for an angle of 35 degrees.

1. Hold the knife to the light. Ascertain whether there is a single-edge or a double-edge bevel. A single bevel means that you work from one side only. A double bevel means that you work both sides equally and that you split the angle. In other words, with a double bevel, if you are aiming for an edge bevel of 30 degrees, hold the knife at 15 degrees to the surface of the stone when you do each side.

Since the edge of the knife is longer than the width of the stone, to sharpen the knife you must hold the blade at the correct edge bevel angle, and as you move the knife forward along the stone, you must slide it sideways across the stone, so that the stone is brought to bear on the entire cutting edge of the knife.

2. Start at the near end of the coarse side of the bench stone. Hold the entire knife at the proper angle to the stone, its tip on the near end of the stone, the edge of the knife at a right angle to the stone. Move the knife toward the far end of the stone. As you do so, slide the knife diagonally across the stone. In this way you pass the entire edge of the knife across the stone. Keep the blade of the knife at right angles to the stone, and hold the flat of the knife at the same fixed angle to the stone. Repeat this action five or six times. If the knife has a double bevel, turn the knife over and rough-bevel the other side also.

Continued ➔

3. Hold the knife edge up to the light. The bevel or bevels should be one smooth, narrow band without visible nicks or scratches. If not, rough-bevel some more. (This is where practice will tell.) When the bevels are smooth, turn the stone over and hone the knife exactly as you rough-beveled it.

4. For a still finer edge, strop the edge. Pull the knife edge toward you, across the rough side of the leather, four or five times on each bevel. Then turn the leather and pull the edge across the smooth side of the leather four or five times.

5. As an alternative to stropping, you can touch up the edge with a steel. Hold the steel by its handle and the knife by its handle. Spread your hands apart. Touch the tip of the steel to the tip of the knife. Now, push the steel and knife together so that the steel slides across the knife edge, and the knife and steel cross near their handles. Do both bevel edges, if there are two. A few light passes of the steel are all that is needed.

CURVED-EDGED KNIVES

Sharpening curved edges is more difficult than sharpening straight edges. You have to turn the knife as you slide it across the stone. There is no simple jig that you can make for this movement, which means you need lots of good hand control and plenty of practice to produce a fine cutting edge.

1. Place the tip of the knife on the near end of the stone. Hold the body of the blade at its edge bevel angle to the stone. Tilt the body of the blade so that the edge bevel at the tip of the blade lies flat against the stone.

2. Push the knife away from you across the stone. As you do so, swing the handle of the knife around, away from you, so that the main body of the blade forms a right angle with the body of the stone. At the same time, slide the knife sideways across the stone. What you are doing is making a sweeping, curving motion, a motion that keeps the edge bevel of the blade flat on the stone and at the same time moves the bevel across the stone.

3. When you have coarse-beveled both edge bevels, repeat the process with the fine side of the bench stone.

4. If you wish, go on to a finer stone still; then strop the blade with a leather.

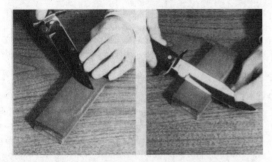

Sharpening a curved-edged knife. The tip of the blade is held against one end of the stone. The blade body is held at an angle to the stone. The blade is lifted until the edge bevel at the tip of the blade lies flat against the stone (left). As you push the knife forward against the stone, swing the knife across the stone. Shown here (right) is the finishing position. To continue sharpening, lift the blade and reposition it as shown on the left.

HUNTING KNIVES

Hunting knives differ from curved-edged, cutlery knives only in the thickness of their blades and their edge bevels. Since hunting knives are used primarily for dressing game, there is a good chance they will strike bone. Therefore, their edge bevels are designed to be on the order of 30 to 35 degrees. Usually, their cutting edges are double-beveled.

Sharpen hunting knives just as you would a curved-edge knife. Pay special attention to the tip; it is important that it be sharp for making the entering cut.

BRUSH KNIVES

Brush knives are used when and where there is no need for the heavier bush ax—and sickles, scythes, or grass hooks will not do. Brush knives include machetes, which have fairly straight cutting edges, and bolo knives, which have curved, scimitar-shaped cutting edges.

Although most of these knives come sharpened to an edge bevel of 24 degrees to 30 degrees, this bush hacker believes a 30-degree to 35-degree cutting edge to be preferable. The more acute cutting edge becomes dull much too quickly.

When sharpening a machete, treat it just as you would any straight cutting edge. You can ignore the curved end of the blade because that portion of the blade is rarely used for cutting. However, after repeated sharpenings, you must rough-bevel the end of the blade to keep the cutting edge straight.

Bolo knives are sharpened the same way as curved-edged knives. The only difference is that the edge bevel should be 30 to 35 degrees, as suggested for the machete. From an economy of labor point of view, you do not have to sharpen the blade all the way out to its tip. Like the machete, the end of the bolo knife does not do much cutting.

STRAIGHT-EDGED HATCHETS AND AXES

The edge bevels of hatchets and axes are treated exactly like straight-edge knife bevels. The only difference lies in the quantity of metal removed.

1. Examine the cutting edge. If it has been chipped or incorrectly sharpened, you will have to reshape the edge bevel. You can do this with a bench stone or a grindstone. In the latter case, take care not to apply so much pressure the metal is overheated and softened.

2. If you have used a grindstone, rework the bevels on the rough side of a bench stone. Bear in mind the angle you want. Spend sufficient time to make the edge bevel one single smooth band. If you have been rough-beveling with a bench stone, just make certain you reach the same condition before you go on to honing.

3. Next the bevels are honed. Just how much honing and the grit of the stone to use depends on how sharp you want your hatchet or ax.

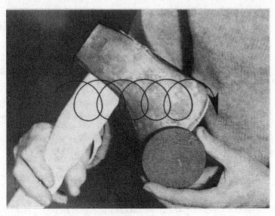

Using a round handstone to sharpen an ax.
The stone is rubbed in a circular motion against the edge of the ax.

CURVED-EDGED HATCHETS AND AXES

1. Examine the cutting edge. Rough-bevel it down to where it should be. But now, instead of simply moving the ax or hatchet straight across the stone or wheel, you have to swing the handle of the tool so that the head passes against the stone in an arc that conforms to the curve of the cutting edge. This requires a steady hand, a good eye, and lots of practice.

2. Rough-bevel the edge as required; then hone the edge bevels to whatever degree of sharpness you wish.

Field sharpening hatchets and axes. The round handstone with its two grits is probably the easiest tool to use for field sharpening hatchets, axes, and the like. Since it is round, it is easily carried.

To use the round handstone, simply press it against the edge bevel and work the stone in a circle, taking care to work it evenly against the entire surface of the edge bevel. Hone with the finer-grit side of the stone.

You will get much faster cutting action sharpening with a file—if you use both hands to develop the necessary pressure. You cannot do this with a file stone because you might crack it if you press down on its ends while its center is over the ax edge. To use a file, grip the tool head between your knees at a comfortable angle. Hold the file by its two ends, maintaining the correct edge bevel angle, and pull the file against the cutting edge.

SCYTHES

Stand the scythe on the end of its handle, with the blade in a horizontal position. Place the stone against the blade so that the stone touches both the backbone of the blade and the cutting edge. Then, with one graceful sweep, draw the stone across the full length of the blade. The thickness of the backbone is such that you will secure the correct edge bevel. Generally, scythes have two bevels of 10 degrees each, making for a 20-degree cutting edge.

SICKLES

Generally, a sickle has a single bevel. Some sickles are made with a backbone, which you can use as a beveling guide, as suggested for sharpening scythes. Others have no backbone; in such cases you must gauge the bevel by eye. The sharpening stone is pushed along the blade, just as with a scythe.

SCISSORS

Scissors cut as the edges of the two blades come together and pass closely across each other. If you examine the cutting edges you will see that they have been ground to a bevel of about 80 degrees. It is these edges that do the cutting. When these edges become rounded with wear, the scissors fail to cut properly. It is a simple matter to resharpen these edges. Never sharpen the insides of the blades, the surfaces that meet. This would remove metal so that the surfaces would no longer touch, and the scissors would no longer cut. Only sharpen the existing beveled edges.

1. Open the scissors and place one blade in a vise, cutting edge up.

2. Place a medium-grit stone atop the cutting edge. Pull or push the stone directly across the blade, taking care to hold the stone parallel to the cutting edge. Repeat this operation over the entire blade length.

3. Do the same to the other blade edge.

4. Hone to remove any wire edges that may form.

COMPOUND TIN SNIPS

If you examine the blades of compound tin snips, you will see that the edge bevel is a continuous curve that wraps around the blade terminating at the flat side of the blade. To sharpen these tools you need to take the blades apart. Then follow the curve with a fine-grit stone, pushing the stone along the edge bevel from the curve towards the flat of the blade.

SNAP-CUT SHEARS

Snap-cut shears cut by the action of a steel knife striking against a brass anvil. If you examine the blade you will see a very narrow, double-edge bevel of about 30 degrees. To sharpen, touch these edges up with a fine-grit stone. Be careful to bevel each side of the blade equally. If the bevel is skewed, it will not strike the anvil properly, and the cutting action will be greatly reduced.

AUGER BITS

An auger bit has a screw that acts to pull the bit against the wood. As the bit is turned, two spurs projecting forward cut a circle in the wood. Two flat cutting edges remove the wood from within the circle cut by the spurs. Sharpening is not difficult but it must be done carefully if the bit is to cut smoothly and evenly.

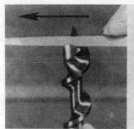

Sharpening an auger bit. First the inside edges of one spur are sharpened (left). Then the edges of the other spur are sharpened. Make sure you do not rub the file against the screw head. Then the cutting edges are sharpened (right). Note carefully the relation of the file to the cutting edge. Only the inside of the cutting edge should be sharpened.

Continued →

1. Examine the spurs. With a fine file, an auger-bit stone, or any small abrasive stick, touch up the edge bevels on the two spurs. Work from the inside only. Take care not to bevel one spur more than the other, or to reduce the height of one spur in relation to the other. This done, carefully remove any wire edges that may have formed. Never sharpen these spurs from the outside.

2. Position the bit point down. Use the same stone or file to edge-bevel the two cutting edges. Apply the stone or file to the upper side of these cutting edges only. Think of them as two tiny planes going round and round in a circle. Remove whatever wire edges may have formed.

3. Go over all the cutting edges with a fine stone to hone them.

CURVED-BLADED PRUNING SHEARS

Curved-bladed pruning shears, lopping shears, and tree trimmers have one curved, beveled blade that works against a flat-surfaced hook or bar. Although the edge of this bar or hook is not sharpened, its edge has to be at right angles to the beveled blade.

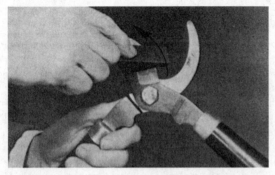

Sharpening a pair of curved-bladed pruning shears. A small stone is swung along the curved edge of the blade. The edge bevel is very narrow and has an angle of about 50 degrees; do not alter it.

1. Open the shears as far as they will go. Place the shears in a vise or prop against a bar or fence.

2. To bevel, swing a coarse stone along the curved edge of the blade. Note that the edge bevel is very narrow and angled at about 50 degrees.

3. Run a bar stone along the inside curve of the hook so as to make its edges perfectly square and clean.

HANDSAWS

1. The first step is leveling the height of the teeth. Place the saw, teeth up, in a saw vise, or improvise one from an ordinary vise and two strips of wood. Run a flat file down the length of the saw, holding the file flat with its length on top of the teeth. If all the teeth are the same height, the file will leave a shiny mark on all of them. If some are shorter, file the high teeth down. But do not file the teeth down to the height of a broken tooth; you'll end up with no teeth at all. Now, some of the teeth will have flat tops. The next step will restore the triangular shape to the teeth.

2. Select a triangular file twice as thick as the depth of each gullet (space between teeth). With the saw still in the vise, note that the leading edge of the teeth on ripsaws is perfectly vertical; the

leading edge of teeth on crosscut saws is usually angled at about 14 degrees. With the file held horizontally, follow the angle of the end, unworn teeth. Work with steady, forward-cutting strokes and apply pressure as you move the file forward only. Don't worry about the constant 60 degrees between teeth. The triangular file takes care of that. On crosscut saws, file every other tooth at the proper angle, then file the remaining teeth in the opposite direction. Stop filing when you have brought the top of each tooth to a point.

3. Next, the teeth have to be set. This consists of bending the top half of each tooth to the side for a distance equal to approximately the thickness of the saw blade. Crosscut saws should be set to each side about 1/4 the thickness of the blade; ripsaws are set 1/3 the thickness of the blade. Bend direction alternates from tooth to tooth. Setting causes the saw's teeth to cut a slot (kerf) twice as wide as the blade itself. A saw with unset teeth (they straighten with use) binds. Do not try to set a saw with hairline cracks near the teeth; they will crack under pressure.

Using a pair of pliers to set the teeth of a handsaw. The bend direction alternates with each tooth. Be careful not to bend the teeth too far, or they will break off.

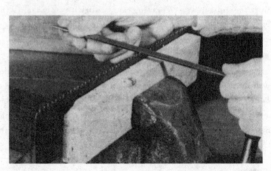

Sharpening a ripsaw. File straight across the saw blade. Apply light strokes to each tooth to achieve uniform results.

The best way to set saw teeth is to use one of the tooth-setting jigs available in most hardware shops. The second best method is to bend the teeth with the corner of a pair of pliers. Use the angle of the pliers as a guide to the angle at which you set each tooth. The second best method is far inferior to the first method, but it is a heck of a lot better than nothing. Do not overbend. Saw teeth break easily.

4. The last step is sharpening. To sharpen a ripsaw, file straight across the saw blade. To sharpen a crosscut saw, you have to hold the file horizontal and at an angle that will permit the file to sharpen (or bevel) the leading edge of one tooth and the trailing edge of another. The file is held at an angle of 45 to 60 degrees,

depending on how the teeth were originally beveled. Do not file too much, as doing so will shorten the tooth you are beveling. Use light strokes and apply the same number of strokes to each tooth for strokes and apply the same number of strokes to each tooth for uniform results. There are guides made for this job, but it is not too difficult to do without a guide if you work carefully. Start with a new file and be prepared to discard it after sharpening just one average-size handsaw.

Chair Caning and Seat Weaving

Cathy Baker

Cane Seating

The type of cane used for chair seating is made from the outside bark of the rattan, a climbing palm of the jungles of Borneo, Sumatra, and Malaysia. When the rattan reaches the desired length and diameter, it is cut and gathered for export. The outside bark is stripped from the vine and machine-cut into various widths and thicknesses. The best cane has a brightness or luster and is smooth and shiny on one side. It should be strong but pliable, and unbroken where the eyes, the joints where the leaves were attached, were shaved smooth.

Chair cane is normally purchased in hanks. These are bunches of about 1,000 feet. Each hank will cover a woven area of about four square feet. Smaller amounts may be purchased, but the length of these will vary depending on the individual supplier.

In addition to regular cane, a strip of binder cane is needed. This strip should be about two sizes wider than regular cane, and one and one-half times the length of the perimeter of the chair seat.

Size of Chair Caning	Approx. Size of Drilled Holes	Approx. Distance Apart Center to Center
Carriage	1/8" or less	5/16" to 3/8"
Superfine	1/8"	3/8"
Fine fine	3/16"	7/16" to 1/2"
Fine	3/16" to 1/4"	1/2" to 9/16"
Narrow medium	1/4"	9/16" to 5/8"
Medium	1/4"	5/8" to 3/4"
Common	5/16"	3/4" to 7/8"

HAND CANING—A SIX-WAY PATTERN

Hand caning a chair is not difficult but care and patience are required. The work is done in stages. These must be started and completed in order, as each stage locks the previous one in place.

This six-way pattern is a traditional method used in the restoration of old as well as modern chairs. It may be worked in one or two sizes of cane, excluding the binder. If you chose to use two sizes, work the first four stages in one size and the last two stages in a slightly larger cane. This will give the seat a little extra strength.

The size of cane to be used is determined by the diameter and spacing of the holes in the individual chair. The previous chart may be used as a guide.

Tools

A small hammer or mallet

A utility knife

Scissors or side cutters

Awl or ice pick

A clearing tool. Or use a small screwdriver, about two inches long, with the blade cut off, or with a two-inch, small-headed nail

Round-nosed pliers (optional)

Pegs. Golf tees may be used as temporary pegs, but you will need permanent ones as well. These may be whittled down from softwood, cut from a dowel, or purchased ready-made

A bar of paraffin (optional). If you wax the underside of the cane during weaving, it will slide along easier

A drill and drill bit (optional). Only if you need to remove the old pegs

A towel or rag to wrap the damp cane in while in use

Procedure

Stage 1

1. Clear the old cane from the seat. Cut around the inside of the seat frame to remove the center of the seat. Cut away the cane over the holes.

2. Knock the pegs out of the holes with a clearing tool and hammer. If the pegs have been glued or varnished in, drill them out.

3. Repair the chair if necessary.

4. Prepare the cane. Put a few lengths of cane into tepid water for about ten minutes, then wrap them in a slightly damp cloth. This will keep them from drying out while you are using them. Take out one piece at a time to use, and leave the rest wrapped.

5. Find the center holes in the front and back rails of the chair. Mark them with temporary pegs. If there is an even number of holes in these rails, mark the two center holes. The marked holes should be aligned from front to rear.

6. Remove the peg in the back rail. Pull a long piece of cane down through the hole. If you have marked two holes, thread the cane down through the left hole. When you have reached one-half of the cane's length, peg it in place with a temporary peg. Half of the cane is now on top of the back rail and half of it is underneath the rail. See Figure 1.

Starting Stage 1

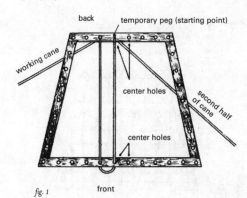

fig. 1

Continued →

7. Use the cane that is on top of the rail first. Bring the strand forward to the front rail; remove the peg in the corresponding marked hole, and thread the cane down through it. Make sure that the cane is straight and firm, but not too tight, and that the shiny, smooth side is up. If it is twisted, you will not be able to correct it later. Refer to Figure 1.

8. Peg the cane in place with a temporary peg. Peg each hole after you have run the cane through it so that it is held firmly in place while you go on to the next hole. The pegs can be moved along as you work. The only pegs that should be left in place are the ones holding the ends of the cane in place which are left under the seat.

9. Thread the cane up through the next hole to the left on the front rail, and bring it back to the corresponding hole in the back rail. Continue in this manner until all of the holes in the back rail, except the corner holes, have cane in them. Refer to Figure 1.

10. If you have extra holes in the front rail, complete them as shown in Figure 2. If at any time you run out of cane, peg a new piece in the corresponding hole in the opposite rail to the one you have just finished with a temporary peg. This may be removed and replaced when you run later pieces of cane through the hole. Always leave about a three-inch end below the seat.

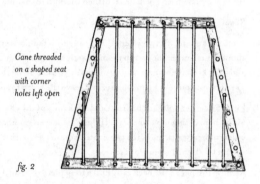

Cane threaded on a shaped seat with corner holes left open

fig. 2

Stage 2

11. Stage 2 is worked from side to side. The steps are exactly the same as in Stage 1. The cane is run on top of the first stage canes. Again leave the corner holes open. See Figure 3.

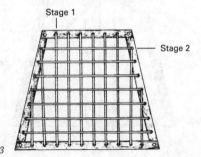

Layout: Stage 2

fig. 3

Stage 3

12. Stage 3 repeats Stage 1. It is worked on top of Stage 2. As you work, try to move the cane from Stage 1 slightly to the left so that the cane in this stage will lie just next to it on the right and not on top of it. This places the cane in the proper position for Stage 4. See Figure 4.

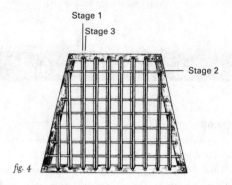

fig. 4

Stage 4

13. This stage is woven from side to side working from the front to the back. Start at the right side, as you face the front of the chair. Peg a piece of cane into the first hole from the corner in the front. It will help if you wax the back of the cane for this stage and the next two for ease in weaving.

14. Weave the cane over the first and under the second cane of each pair of vertical canes. Make sure that it is placed to the front of the horizontal canes of Stage 2. Do not pull the cane through more than four vertical pairs at a time or you may break them. See Figure 5.

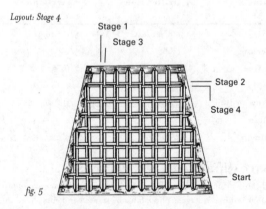

Layout: Stage 4

fig. 5

15. When you reach the left side rail, bring the cane down through the corresponding hole, peg it, and then bring it up through the adjacent hole. You can clear the holes a bit with your awl.

16. Weave the cane back to the right, under the first and over the second cane of each pair of vertical canes. Continue in this manner until you have filled all of the holes in the side rails, except the corner holes. Refer to Figure 5. Remember to place the canes to the front of the horizontal canes of Stage 2.

Stage 5

17. This is the first diagonal stage. It may be woven with the same size cane as you used in the first four stages or with a slightly larger cane. For example, if I started with fine fine cane, I would now use fine cane for these last two stages.

    While you are weaving, run the cane through your fingers to straighten it. Do not let it twist during this stage.

    As you face the chair, start this stage by pegging a piece of cane into the right front corner hole. Leave a three-inch end below the seat. See Figure 6.

18. Weave the cane under stages one and three, the vertical strands, and over stages two and four, the horizontal strands. Weave toward the back left corner. Unless your chair is perfectly square, the cane will probably not come out at the back left corner hole. It should be threaded down whichever hole it reaches after forming a true diagonal. The hole will be on the left side rail or the back rail. See Figure 6.

Layout: Stage 5

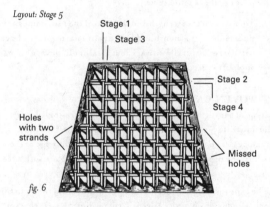

fig. 6

19. Up until this stage all of the other holes have two strands of cane in them. On this stage and stage 6, you must work out your diagonals so that you get two strands of cane in each corner hole. It is important not to miss any holes in the front or back rails. If you have to make adjustments, they should be done on the side rails. On the standard type of dining room chair, there are usually two holes that are missed on one side and two holes with two strands of cane in them on the other side. See Figure 6. If you are working a chair with rounded corners you may have to put more than one pair of canes into the corner holes, see Figure 7.

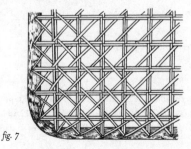

fig. 7

Placement of cane strands on a chair with rounded corners

20. Finish the first half of the chair. The final strands of cane will go across the corners if you have worked the pattern correctly. Start in the center again and work the other half of the seat. Refer to Figure 6.

Stage 6

21. Stage 6 is the reverse of Stage 5. Peg a piece of cane into the front left corner and work toward the back right corner. Weave the cane over stages 1 and 3, the vertical canes, and under stages 2, 4 and 5. The two horizontal stages and one diagonal stage. The adjustments on the sides will be reversed. Where you skipped holes in Stage 5, you will now put in double strands of cane and where you had double strands you will now skip the holes. See Figure 8.

Detail: Stage 6

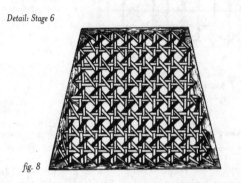

fig. 8

Finishing

There are two methods of completing a hand-caned seat. The first method is to peg every hole. Many old chairs are done this way. You will need tight-fitting pegs that are a little shorter than the depth of the rails. Put the peg in the hole and hammer it lightly. With the aid of your clearing tool, set the top of the peg just below the surface of the rail. Never hammer directly on the seat. You may damage it. When every hole has been pegged, cut the ends of the cane underneath the seat and even with the seat.

The second method of finishing a seat is to put on a binder of wider cane to cover the holes.

1. With this method you must peg every other hole, leaving open the corner holes and the two holes next to them. Always count the holes from the corners in case you have an even amount of holes. This will allow you to put two pegs together or two holes in the center of the rail. Mark the holes to be pegged with temporary pegs. See Figure 9.

2. All of the ends of the cane left underneath the seat must now go into one of the marked holes. To do this thread the ends up or down the non-peg holes and into the adjacent or pegged hole. If you have cane that is threaded up a peg hole, be careful that it does not form a loop underneath the rail when you put in your permanent peg.

Continued ➜

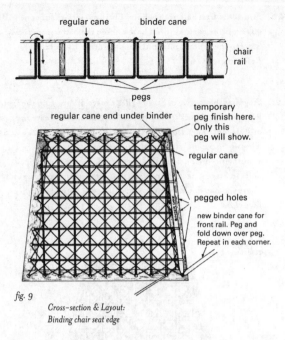

regular cane | binder cane

chair rail

pegs

regular cane end under binder

temporary peg finish here. Only this peg will show.

regular cane

pegged holes

new binder cane for front rail. Peg and fold down over peg. Repeat in each corner.

fig. 9

Cross-section & Layout:
Binding chair seat edge

3. When all of the marked holes are permanently pegged, cut off the ends of the cane closely on the top and bottom of the rail.

4. Prepare four lengths of binder cane and a long length of the cane you used to weave the seat. Each length of binder cane should be a little longer than the length of the rails.

5. Thread about four inches of the regular cane down through the hole next to the corner hole at the back of the right rail, and then up through the corner hole. You should now have the short end of the cane coming out of the corner hole and the long end coming out of the adjacent hole.

6. Lay the short end down over the holes in the right side rail.

7. Thin the end of one of the lengths of binder cane.

8. Push the thinned end of the binder cane down into the corner hole so that it will lie over the short end of the regular cane. Peg it in place with a temporary peg. Refer to Figure 9.

9. With the long end of regular cane, go over the binder cane and down through the same hole. This will hold the binder firmly in place.

10. Pass the long end of regular cane along underneath the rail to the next open hole. Go up this hole, over the binder and down through the same hole. You may need to clear the holes a bit with your awl. Be careful not to split any of the cane that is already in the holes. Refer to the cross-section view of the chair rail in Figure 9.

11. Continue this threading until you reach the corner. The regular cane should be in the last hole before the corner hole. Take the regular cane across the corner underneath the seat and come up in the first after the corner hole on the front rail. See the right front corner of the chair seat in Figure 9.

12. Trim and thin the end of the binder cane and put it into the corner hole.

13. Take a new piece of binder cane, thin the end and put it into the same corner hole at right angles to the first piece. Peg the ends in place with a permanent peg. See the right front corner of the chair in Figure 9.

14. Lay the new piece of binder down over the holes in the front rail. It should cover the corner peg that you just put in. Continue binding across the front rail and complete the corner as you did before. Work the left hand and back rail in the same manner.

15. When you have completed the back rail and have reached the starting point, remove the temporary peg. Thread the end of the regular cane up the corner hole and back under the last binder cane so that it is covered.

16. Trim and thin the end of the binder cane and push it into the corner hole. Peg it in place with a permanent peg. This is the only peg that should show.

17. To maintain the strength and tautness of the seat, dampen the underside once a month and let it dry in a warm place. The cane will darken naturally with age, but a stain, oil, or varnish may be applied to speed up the process.

PRE-WOVEN CANE WEBBING

This type of caning material is usually used in the restoration of modern furniture where there are no holes through which the cane can be drawn. There is a small groove around the edge of the seat into which the pre-woven cane is driven and held in place with a reed spline.

The cane webbing can be purchased in widths from twelve to thirty-six inches and in any length desired. To determine the size that you need for your chair, measure from the outside edges of the spline at the widest part, front to back, and side to side. Add one inch to these measurements for driving into the groove. For example, if you have a seat that is 12" x 12", you would purchase a piece 13" x 13".

To purchase the proper size spline, measure the length of the spline needed and width of the groove.

Tools

Hammer

Wood chisel slightly smaller than the width of the groove

Wooden wedge

Utility knife

Scissors or side cutters

Fine grit sand paper

White glue—Elmer's or any water-soluble glue

Procedure

1. Cut away the old cane. Remove the old spline by tapping lightly around its outside and inside edge with a chisel and hammer. Pry it out gently with the chisel. Be careful not to damage the

seat. Sand away any remaining debris. This will ensure that the new cane and spline will adhere to the surface. See Figure 13.

Preparing chair seat

fig. 13

2. Cut the pre-woven cane one-half inch larger than the outer edges of the groove.

3. Soak the pre-woven cane in tepid water for about ten minutes. Remove it from the water and let it drip for two minutes before you use it. Soak the spline in tepid water for about twenty minutes.

4. Place the pre-woven cane on the seat frame. Line up the horizontal canes with the straight edge of the front rail. If you have a rounded rail, line up the horizontal canes with the seat joints. See Figure 14.

Attaching pre-woven cane

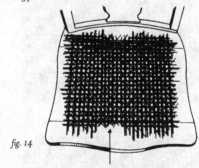

fig. 14

↑ tap the cane into the groove

5. Attach the cane to the seat. Start by tapping an area of cane about four inches long into the center of the back groove with your blunt wooden wedge and a hammer. Move to the front of the chair and straighten and pull the cane taut. Tap a four-inch area into the groove. Move to the back rail and tap a few more inches in place. Do the same to the front. Continue with this alternate method until the front and back rail are completed. Use the same method to attach the side rails. See Figure 14.

6. Cut the spline to fit the seat. The ends should be about 1/4" longer than needed. They will be cut exact later.

7. Apply a thin, even bead of glue into the groove on top of the cane.

8. Insert the spline into the groove and tap it down tightly with a wooden wedge and hammer. The corners may be mitered if you wish.

9. Trim away the excess cane carefully.

10. Let the glue set for twenty-four hours before you use the chair. If the seat is not tight after twenty-four hours, wet the underside of the cane and place it near heat or in the sun until it dries. This should tighten it.

11. To maintain the seat, dampen the underside once a month and let it dry in a warm palce. The seat may be stained, oiled, or varnished.

SEA GRASS AND CORD SEATING

Sea grass and cord seating must be used on a chair with raised corners.

Sea grass is a Chinese product made from twisted grass which resembles rope. It is sold by the coil in various thicknesses and colors.

Cord may also be purchased in coils varying in thicknesses and colors.

Any cord may be used as long as it is strong and does not stretch.

Tools

Hammer

Three- or four-ounce tacks

Scissors or utility knife

A dowel 1/2" in diameter for a tension rod. The dowel should be longer than the width of the seat

Ruler

Pencil

Upholsterer's needle

Procedure

1. Prepare the seat frame. Remove old material, tacks, and dirt. Repair any defects in the chair.

2. Coil a few lengths of sea grass or cord so that it will be easy to work with.

3. Put the tension stick across the center of the seat. See Step A in Figure 20.

4. Start the warp, the cords that run from front to back. Knot one end of the cord and tack it to the inside of the left rail. Bring the coiled end under the front rail. See Step A in Figure 20.

5. Wrap the cord around the front rail once and bring the coiled end over the tension stick to the back rail. See Step A in Figure 20.

6. Make one wrap around the back rail and thread the end up between the left rail and the first warp cord. See Step B in Figure 20.

7. Bring the end over the warp cord and back down and under the back rail. This movement should form a loop over the warp cord. Now bring the end over the back rail and thread it through the loop. See Step C in Figure 20.

Continued ➜

8. Bring the end over the tension stick to the front rail. Go over the front rail. Be sure to keep the warp cords even and taut. There should be about the same amount of tension on each cord. Refer to Steps C and D in Figure 20.

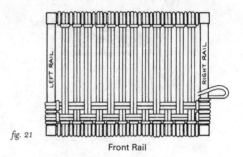

fig. 20 *Starting the warp — steps A–D*

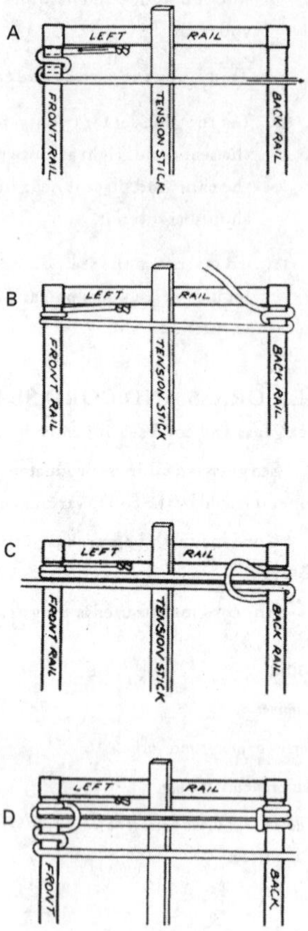

9. Thread the end up between the left rail and the first warp cord and make a loop over both warp cords. See Step D in Figure 20.

10. Bring the end down under the front rail and make another wrap around it. Repeat the process. This should give you two cords through each loop and a short wrap between each pair of warp cords. If you have to add new cord lengths, make sure that the knots are on the inside of the rails so that they will not show. Refer to Step D in Figure 20.

11. When you have finished the warp, use the upholsterer's needle to thread the end of the cord under some of the warps on the inside of the rail and tack it in place. Remove the tension stick. You are now ready to start weaving, inserting the cord from side to side. The process of attaching the strands to each side rail is the same as you just used for the warp.

12. Pick a pattern. See A, B, and C in Figure 22. Patterns B and C are variations of the basic pattern A. Start the weave on the front of the right rail and read the pattern from right to left. Each square represents one pair of warp or weave strands. The black sections designate that you weave over the warp strands and the white squares designate that you weave under the warp strands.

13. Thread one end of new coil under some of the wraps on the front rail. When this is done, tie a knot in the same end and tack it in place.

14. Bring the coiled end under the right rail and wrap the cord around the rail once. Refer to A in Figure 20 and to Figure 21.

15. Make one wrap around the left rail and bring the end up and over the woven strand and back down and around the left rail and through the loop.

16. Weave the end back cover and under the same strands. When you reach the right side, go over the rail and bring the end up and

over the two strands to form a loop. Make another wrap around the rail and weave through to the left rail. Follow the weaving pattern closely.

17. When you have finished the pattern, thread the end of the cord through some of the wraps and tack it in place.

fig. 21

Front Rail

fig. 22 *Patterns for seagrass and cord seats*

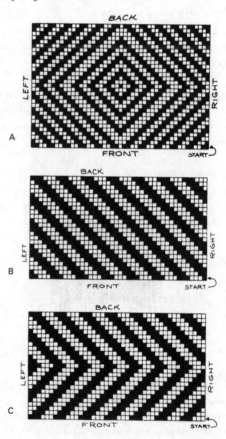

SPLINT SEATING

Splint seating is usually used on chairs with raised corners of early American design. During colonial times, splint was hand cut out of various hardwoods such as hickory, oak, or ash.

Today several types of prepared splint are readily available, flat reed splint, oval reed splint, ash splint and a synthetic, flat fibre splint.

Flat reed splint is cut by machines from the larger sizes of the rattan core. It is flat on both sides. The top is smoother than the bottom. The individual strands are usually more than eight feet long, and are available in various widths. Flat reed splint is sold in hanks or one-pound bundles. One bundle is enough to weave an average chair seat, fourteen inches wide and twelve inches deep.

Flat oval reed is also cut from the rattan plant and is flat on the bottom and oval on the top. It is also available in different widths and is sold in hanks or one-pound bundles. One bundle will cover an average seat.

Ash splint is hand-cut from select second-growth timber. The individual lengths of splint are from six to eight feet long. The number of different widths available will depend upon the individual supplier. Ash splint is sold in hanks, one-pound bundles or coils. It takes a one-pound bundle or three coils to cover an average chair seat. Ash splint is best to use if you are restoring an antique chair.

Flat fibre splint is made from a tough grade of paper fibre and should only be used on indoor chairs. It is sold in one-pound bundles. One bundle will cover an average seat.

Tools

Hammer

Three- or four-ounce tacks

Ordinary stapler

A spring clamp

A ruler

Very fine sandpaper, if you are using one of the natural splints

A can of stain or equal parts linseed oil and turpentine for finishing a natural splint, or thin shellac for fibre splint

Procedure

The Herringbone Pattern

1. Clear the chair of all of the old splint, tacks, and staples. Repair any defects in the chair frame.

2. Prepare the splint. Soak four to six strands at a time in tepid water for about one-half hour. As the strands are taken from the water, replace them with others so that you will always have a ready supply of damp, pliable splint. Remove a length of prepared splint to work with. Determine which is the right and wrong side of the strand. To do this, bend the splint. The right side will remain smooth, while the wrong side will splinter. Eliminate this step if you are using flat fibre splint.

3. Tack one end of the length of splint to the inside edge of the back rail. Allow about four inches to overlap the rail. See Figure 23.

4. Bring the free end under and over the left rail. Figure 23.

5. Bring the end across to and over and under the right rail, and then back under and over the left rail. See Figure 24.

6. Continue wrapping both side rails, moving back and forth until you reach the end of the strand. The warp strands should be straight and firm but not too tight, as they will shrink as they dry. Refer to Figure 25. To add new splint, clamp the last wrap in place, overlap the two ends underneath the seat and staple the two ends together with four or five staples. The warp strands are always put on first, no matter which way they run on the chair.

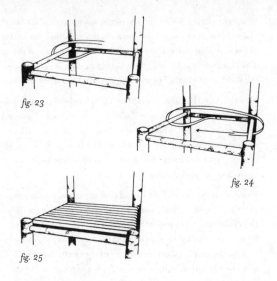

fig. 23

fig. 24

fig. 25

7. Continue wrapping and attaching new splint until both side rails are covered. Tack the end to the inside of the front rail. Leave about a four-inch overlap on the rail. Dampen the seat to keep it pliable.

8. Start the weave. If the front rail is longer than the back rail, you will need to square the design with filler strands. Measure the front and back rails. When you have found the difference, divide it in half and mark each half off from each corner post on the front rail. See Figure 26.

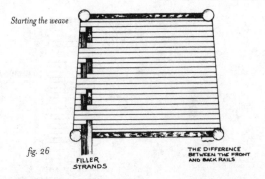

Starting the weave

fig. 26

FILLER STRANDS

THE DIFFERENCE BETWEEN THE FRONT AND BACK RAILS

9. Select a new strand of splint about three times as long as the width of the chair and begin weaving on the front left corner. Weave over the first warp strand and under three; over three; and under three until you reach the corner. Pull the end through until you have about an equal amount of splint hanging out on each end of the weave. The length of this will depend on the individual chair. The end in the back corner will hang under the chair. Let the ends hang until all of the filler strands are in place. An average chair usually requires two filler strands to square the design to start with and two or three to end with. This will vary depending upon your chair. See Figure 26.

10. Begin the second filler next to the first filler strand on the front rail. Weave over two and under three, over three, under three until you reach the back corner. Equalize the hanging ends as you did in Step 9. Figure 26.

Continued →

11. When the chair is filled and the pattern is squared off, turn the chair sideways and weave the two hanging ends into the bottom of the seat. The pattern should be the same as the top of the seat. The two ends should lie directly on top of each other and overlap the width of the seat. The overlapping will hold them in place.

12. Now that the fillers are in place on the left side of the seat, you can start a continuous weave. Start the third length of weave next to the second filler. This strand will start at the front rail and be woven on the bottom of the seat first. The line of the weave will go over three and under three until you reach the back rail. Stop there. Do not pull the end through.

13. Weave the other end of the strand over three and under three on the top of the seat until you reach the back rail. Go over the back rail and continue to weave the pattern as shown in Figure 27. When you come to the end of the splint strip, cut it to end right behind the front rail on the bottom of the chair. Figure 28. To add a new length of splint, weave it from the front rail to the back rail directly on top of the previous piece. This overlapping will keep both ends firmly in place. Follow Figure 27 for the rest of the pattern.

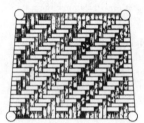

fig. 27

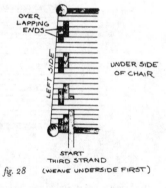

fig. 28 (WEAVE UNDERSIDE FIRST)

14. If you are working a square or rectangular chair, start the continuous weave right away. Begin at the left front corner. Weave the strip in on the bottom first over one and under three, over three, and under three until you reach the back rail. Stop there. Now weave the other end over one and under three, over three and under three on the top of the seat. When you reach the back rail, go over it and weave over two and under three, over three and under three on the bottom of the chair. Do the same on the top. Now look at Figure 26. Find the third strand in from the left front corner and follow the pattern from there. It should go over three and under three evenly across the chair seat shown.

15. When the back rail is filled, weave the final end in on the bottom of the seat. If you need fillers, weave them in the same manner as you did on the left side. Refer to steps 9 and 10 and to Figure 26.

16. If you have used natural splint, cut and sand away the hairy residue on the seat surface. Allow it to dry for twenty-four hours and stain or oil it.

17. If you have used fibre splint, apply two to three coats of thin shellac.

Building Simple Furniture

Cathy Baker

Look over the wood furniture projects in this bulletin. See something you need? A small table for the hallway, perhaps, or the Adirondack chair or picnic set for enjoyable outdoor living.

Here's a surprise for you.

You don't need a basement full of power tools to build them. Just the simple hand tools listed below.

And you don't have to be a master carpenter, either. Just follow the step-by-step instructions, and the illustrations. It's simple.

You'll enjoy the furniture you build, and get even deeper satisfaction from having built it yourself.

Tools

Hammer	Router Plane
Crosscut saw, back saw	Chisel
Coping saw	Screw Driver
Pencil	Two C-clamps
Measuring tape	Brace or hand drill
Try-square	Drill bits, numbered 1/8, 9/64, 7/32, 3/8,
Smooth or block plane	1/4, 23/64, 5/16, 1/2, 5/8 and 1 inch

(Materials for these projects may be purchased at hardware stores, lumberyards and building supply stores.)

Whenever there is a common stock name of the measure of an article it will be given in parentheses after the listing of the actual measurement of that article. For example, a piece of wood with the thickness of one and one-half inches and the width of three and one-half inches, commonly called a two-by-four. If you ask for an article by its common stock name, you will save time and avoid confusion.

Wall Shelf

Need a place for those little, breakable items you've collected, or those spice jars? Here it is, and it's a snap to build.

Bill of Materials

Pieces	Use	Dimensions: thickness	width	length
2	sides	5/8"	7"	27 1/2"
1	top	1/2"	7"	10"
1	upper shelf	1/2"	5"	10"
1	middle shelf	1/2"	6"	10"
1	lower shelf	1/2"	7"	10"

4–penny finish nails

cardboard for patterns

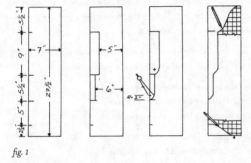

fig. 1

Procedure

1. Cut, plane and square the boards to the sizes given in the bill of materials.

2. Make a full-sized cardboard pattern of the shelf side. Lay it out on the boards as shown in *fig. 1*.

3. Saw the sides to shape with a coping saw. Start with the upper curve, then saw the two middle curves and finish with the lower end.

4. Sand all rough surfaces.

5. On both surfaces of the sides draw two light lines where each shelf is to be fastened. Refer to the side view of *fig. 2*.

6. Start the nails through the outside of the shelf side until the points just come through on the inside. See *fig. 3*.

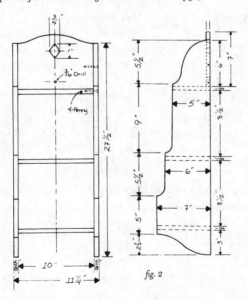

fig. 2

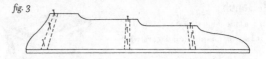

fig. 3

7. Press the first shelf against the nail points. *fig. 4*.

8. Brace the opposite end of the shelf against a flat area and drive the nails in. *fig. 5*. Continue in this manner with the other shelves.

fig. 4

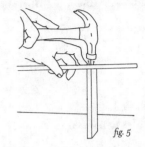

fig. 5

9. When all of the shelves have been nailed to one side, turn the nailed side down so that it is resting on a flat area and nail the second side on. Be sure to keep it square. *fig. 6*.

10. Make a pattern for the top piece as shown in *fig. 7*. Lay it out and saw to shape.

11. Drill a hole in the diamond, insert the coping blade and saw the diamond to shape. Sand. Refer to *fig. 2*.

12. Nail the top to the sides and top shelf.

13. Do a final sanding and paint, stain or varnish your shelf.

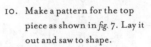

fig. 6

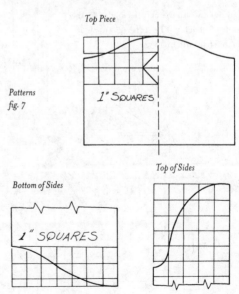

Top Piece

Patterns
fig. 7

1" SQUARES

Top of Sides

Bottom of Sides

1" SQUARES

Small Bench

Or call it a side table if that's what you need. It's sturdy, handy and decorative.

Bill of Materials

Pieces	Use	Dimensions:		
		thickness	width	length
2	seat	1 1/2"	5 1/2"	18" (2x6)
2	rails	1 1/2"	1 1/2"	9 1/4" (2x2)
4	legs	1 1/2"	2 3/4"	21" (2x3)
1	dowel	5/8" round x 17 1/4" long		

8-penny finishing nails

8 2" #8 flat-head screws

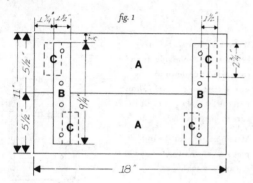

fig. 1

Procedure

1. Cut all stock to the sizes given in the bill of materials.

2. Nail the rails (B), to the underside of the seat pieces (A) as shown in *fig. 1*.

3. Lay out and cut the parallel angles on the ends of each leg. The finished length of each leg should be 18 1/2". *fig. 2*.

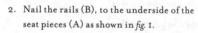

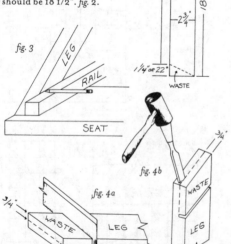

fig. 2

fig. 3

fig. 4a

fig. 4b

4. Place the seat on a flat area bottom side up. The rails will be exposed.

5. Lay out the rabbet joints at the tops of the legs. Hold each leg in place in turn. Placement may be determined by the dotted lines, marked C, in *fig. 1*. Draw a line along the leg where the top of the leg meets the side. See *fig. 3*.

6. Cut the rabbet joint. Cut into the leg 3/4 of an inch along the drawn line. Chisel out the waste. *fig. 4*.

7. After making trial assemblies of the legs, drill starter holes for the screws and attach the legs to the rails. *fig. 5*.

8. Drill 5/8" holes through the center of the cross formed by the legs. Be sure they are in the same position on both sides.

9. Pound the dowel through the holes. *fig. 6*.

10. Sand the bench.

11. This project may be stained or painted.

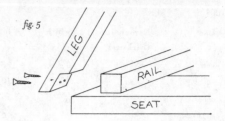

fig. 5

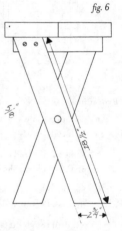

fig. 6

Pump Lamp

Children will love this lamp in their bedrooms, showing how the operation of the pump handle produces a flood of light.

Bill of Materials

Pieces	Use	Dimensions:		
		thickness	width	length
1	base	3/4"	4 3/4"	9 1/4"
1	pump	3 1/2"	3 1/2"	8 1/4" (4x4)
1	top of pump	3/4"	4"	4"
1	pump handle	3/8"	1J"	7"
2	sides of trough	1/4"	1 1/2"	4"
1	large end of trough	1/4"	1 5/8"	1 1/2"
1	small end of trough	1/4"	1 1/4"	1 1/2"
1	dowel (spout)	1/2" round x 2" long		

brass-shell pull chain socket, threaded for 1/8" pipe

continuous-threaded pipe 1/8" x 1" long

brads — 3/4" #20, 1 1/2 #15

2" finish nails   lamp shade

wall plug   white glue

lamp cord   plastic wood

Procedure

1. Cut and plane all stock to the sizes given in the bill of materials.

2. Bevel the edges on the base.

3. Lay out and plane the camfers on the corners of the pump. See *fig.* 1.

4. Lay out the hole for the pump handle in one of the sides. Bore 3/8" holes about 3/4 of an inch deep and as close together as possible. Clean out with a chisel. Chisel the 30° angle at the bottom of the hole. *fig.* 1.

5. Bore a hole for the spout. Glue the spout into place. *fig.* 1.

6. Bevel the edges on the pump top. See *fig.* 4.

7. Make full-size patterns for the pump handle and trough sides and transfer them to the wood pieces. See *fig.* 3.

8. Saw and sand the pieces to shape. Use a coping saw.

9. Fasten the handle in place. Drill as far as the hole from one side. Fit the handle in the hole so it will swing low enough to switch off the light. Bore hole in handle. See *figs.* 1 & 2.

10. Drive the 2" finish nail into the side and through the handle to the opposite side. *fig.* 2.

11. Place the pump in its proper position on the base and mark around it with a pencil. *fig.* 2.

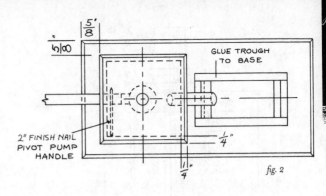

fig. 2

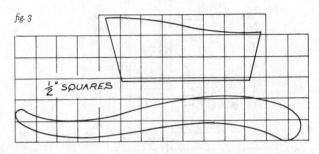

fig. 3

12. Remove the pump from the base. Drill nail holes through the base 3/8" in from the drawn lines.

13. Nail the base to the pump.

14. Fasten the pump top to the pump in the same manner as was done with the base. *fig.* 2.

15. Drill a 23/64" hole through the center of the top down through to the bottom of the base. See *figs.* 1 & 2.

16. From the bottom of the base, widen the hole through the base to one inch as seen in *fig.* 1.

17. Drill a 3/8" hole from the center of the back of the base through to the 1" hole. *fig.* 1.

18. Assemble the trough. Be sure to keep the top of the ends even with the top of the sides.

19. Plane or chisel and sand the bottom of the ends level with the sides. *fig.* 1.

20. Glue the trough to the base.

21. Screw the threaded pipe into the top.

22. Thread the wire through the base.

23. Take the socket apart and fasten the wires. Screw the base of the socket to the pipe before reassembling the socket to avoid twisting the wires.

24. Attach the plug to the other end of the wire.

25. Locate the point on the handle where the chain will just clear the top. Refer to *fig.* 1.

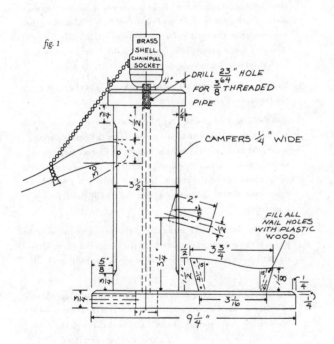

fig. 1

Continued ➔

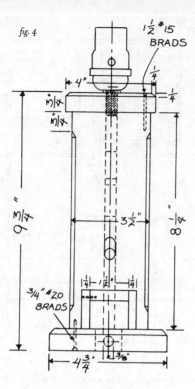

fig. 4

$1\frac{1}{2}$ #15 BRADS

4"

3/4"

3/4"

9 3/4"

8"

1/4"

1/4"

1/4"

3 1/2"

1/4"

1/4"

1/2"

1/4"

3/4" #20 BRADS

4 3/4"

3/8"

26. Drill the hole through the handle.

27. Remove the bell from the chain and thread the chain through the hole. Refasten the bell.

28. Fill all nail holes with plastic wood.

29. Sand.

30. This project may be stained, varnished or painted.

Storage Box

This box is large enough to hold a lot of tools, winter hats and boots, etc. Note that strength of this box is increased by use of rabbet joints on sides and bottom.

Bill of Materials

Pieces	Use	Dimensions: thickness	width	length
1	top	3/4"	12"	16"
2	front & back	3/4"	12"	16"
2	sides	3/4"	11 1/4"	12"
1	bottom	3/4"	11 1/4"	15 1/4"

1 16" long box hinge & screws

1 hasp

15 1/2" #10 brass plumber's chain

2 #2 round-head wood screws

3' length of 5/16" nylon rope

4-penny finish nails or 1 1/2" #15 brads

1 1/2" #6 flat-head wood screws

white glue

wood putty

Procedure

1. Cut, plane and square all boards to the sizes given in the bill of materials.

2. Lay out and cut the rabbet joints on the sides of the front and back pieces. This may be done with a backsaw and chisel or with a router plane. If you do it with the router plane, clamp the two pieces side by side on the top of your workbench. Cut along the rabbet line on the inside of the side pieces with a knife, using a straight edge to keep the knife line straight. Cut the rabbets on both sides simultaneously with a router plane. *figs. 1 & 2.*

3. Lay out and cut the rabbet joints on the inside of the bottom of the front, back and side pieces. *fig. 1.*

4. Assemble the side pieces. Start the nails through one side of the rabbet joint until the ends just protrude on the inside. Apply some glue to the joint. Press the end of the shorter side piece against these protruding points, then, resting the opposite end of the short side on the bench, drive the nails home. Attach the other short side in the same manner and finally the opposite long side.

5. Attach the bottom piece to the sides. Apply the glue to the rabbet joints at the bottom of the sides. Put the bottom in place. Drill starter holes and screw the bottom in place. See bottom view in *fig. 1.*

6. Drill 5/16" holes in the sides for the rope handles. Cut the rope in half, tie a knot on one end of the piece and thread it from the inside of the box through one hole and back through the other. Finish off the handle by tying a knot on the second end of the rope.

7. Chisel out a 1/16" deep groove 3/4" wide and 16" long on the top edge of the back of the box for the box hinge. Do the same on the underside of the back edge of the top piece. See side and top views in *fig. 1.* See also the finished view.

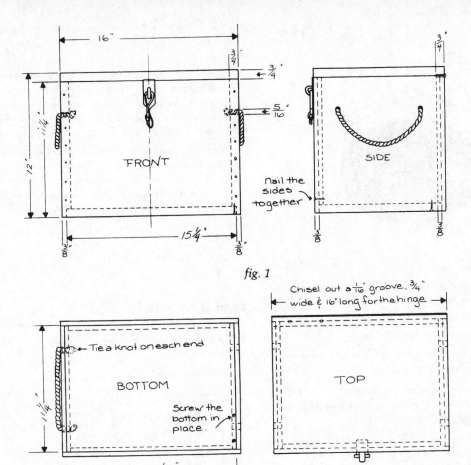

fig. 1

8. Attach the box hinge to the top piece.

9. Attach the hasp to the center front under-side of the top piece. See the front and top view on *fig. I*.

10. Attach the top to the back of the box.

11. Fit the chain to the box and top so that the lid falls back slightly. See the finished view.

12. Fit the catch to the hasp.

13. Fill all nail holes with wood putty.

14. Sand. Paint, stain or varnish as suits your intended use.

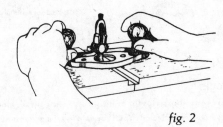

fig. 2

Braiding Rugs

Nancy Bubel

The craft of rug braiding, like so many other good things, is rooted in necessity. Americans of an earlier day found that they could use what they had—in this case, "rags" of worn clothing—to create the rugs they needed for warmth in the drafty floors of their inefficiently heated homes.

Braided rugs have never really gone out of "style" (whatever that is!), but today there are more reasons than ever for using this time-honored craft to produce the rugs we need for our homes.

The most important ingredient of a braided rug—outside of the care and craftsmanship that go into it—is the recycled fabric from which it's made. You'll want to use wool that has not been worn threadbare, of course, or your finished product won't be worth your time or (if you sell it) the buyer's money. Woolen fabric—or a blend of wool and acrylic or other man-made fiber—is the best choice. Synthetics lack that springy, alive quality and cotton—while attractive—is stiff to work with and quick to wear out.

Continued ➜

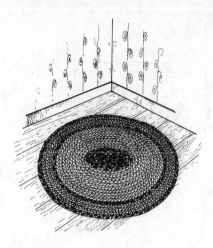

Fabrics to Avoid

Plenty of woolen garments are discarded for reasons that have nothing to do with the amount of wear left in them, however. You can usually afford to be discriminating in your choice of fabric.

For example, you will want to avoid:

1. Open, coarsely woven fabric that is likely to ravel and show wear on the individual threads.

2. Threadbare fabrics (but if only elbows or knees are worn on an otherwise sound piece of clothing, you can cut out the weak spots and use the rest).

3. Garments with many seams: a many-gored skirt or highly styled jacket with many darts and short sections of fabric sewn together. This is a matter of individual preference, though; if the garment is free, the fabric is good, and you have plenty of time, you may not mind doing the extensive piecing that will be necessary to join many short lengths of wool together.

4. Hard-finish wool fabric from men's suits—although unsuitable for some purposes, it is useful for others. Such fabric wears well if the entire rug is made from the same thin, flat, nap-free wool. The range of colors available in men's suiting runs heavily to gray, brown, black and blue, so the resulting rug would have more texture than color interest. The one thing you should not do is to combine a flat, hard-finish wool fabric with softer napped fabrics in making a rug. The braid will be crooked and wear will be uneven.

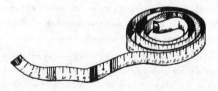

The Best Garments

Many kinds of discarded clothing can be valuable braided rug ingredients...old wool bathrobes (especially good because they yield nice long strips), out-of-style coats, torn slacks, moth-eaten blankets, a skirt that shrank or a wool dress that no longer fits. If you ask around a

bit, especially at fall and spring cleaning times, you'll probably find that friends and relatives have usable discards that will give you a good start for your rug.

After you've raided all available attics, you may want to build up your collection of rug wool further by shopping at rummage sales and thrift shops—always good sources for used clothing at reasonable and often extremely low prices. (Hint: try on some of your best finds. Perhaps you'll want to wear them for a while before cutting them up!)

Many rug makers routinely wash clothing purchased at such sales. The easiest way to do this is to run a load of the wool garments through your washing machine. Hot water and rapid agitation usually cause some shrinkage, but that only serves to tighten the weave of the fabric and detracts in no way from its usability in the rug.

Supplies You Need

The other supplies you'll need, in addition to the wool fabric, are basic hand sewing supplies found in most households or easily purchased if not readily at hand:

1. *Sharp sewing scissors.*

2. *Thread:*

   a. *Heavy duty for piecing strips.*

   b. *Button and carpet thread for lacing braids together. Note: do not use nylon thread to lace together wool braids. The nylon may cut through the wool in time, as the rug wears.*

3. *Bodkin–a flat, blunt "poker" used to lace the braids together.*

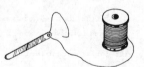

4. *Knife or seam ripper.*

5. *Tape measure or yardstick.*

How to Begin

First, prepare your wool strips for braiding by cutting up the clothes and yard goods you've collected. You'll be able to salvage most of the wool if you'll rip the seams open.

Next, cut or tear the wool into strips. Some heavy fabrics don't tear readily and must be cut. To tear light and medium weight wool, cut three-inch notches all along the short edge and then tear off the strips one by one. Children often enjoy doing this job. If the fabric has an accumulation of dust and lint in the seams, you might want to do your tearing outdoors.

WIDTH VARIES

The width of the strips varies with the weight of the fabric. Cut the heavier woolens into strips two inches wide. (Never less, or the raw edges will not stay rolled in.) Use a three-inch width for lighter weight fabrics that require more self-padding as they're folded together. Don't cut strips any wider than three inches; any fabric that needs that much self-padding is not heavy enough for your rug.

These strips of fabric must be sewn together to make a continuous length which will form one-third of the braid. You can sew together all of the strips of one kind of fabric before starting the rug if you wish, but you will find that you have a lot of untangling to do as you braid. It is simpler to sew together only a few strips at a time. Keep the strips together by rolling them into a wheel, fastening the last loose strip with a pin. Then, when you come to a break in the continuity of the strip as you use up the wheel of wool, you can join the cut ends with hand stitches.

As you accumulate wheels of the prepared strips, it's a good idea to sort the colors, at least into rough categories.

SEW ON BIAS

Strips are always sewn together on the bias . . . that is, at an angle. If you were to sew them straight across the ends, you would have a bulky, hard-to-manage lump to braid around. The diagonal seam distributes the bulk and keeps the braid pliable.

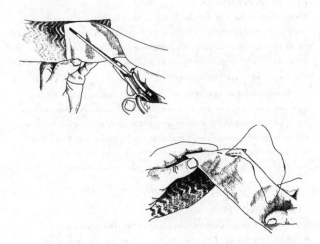

It is not difficult to find the true bias of the fabric you're working with. The bias runs diagonally at a 45° angle across the straight-of-the-goods. To make a true bias cut, overlap the two strips to be joined—right sides up—for as many inches as they are wide (two-inch overlap for two-inch-wide strips, for example) and cut diagonally across the double layer of fabric from one corner to the other. Then, with the right sides facing, line up the newly cut edges at right angles and sew them firmly together, using either a tight machine stitch or a back-hand stitch by hand. Use double thread, preferably heavy-duty, for hand stitching. It isn't necessary to match the thread color to the wool exactly, but avoid, for example, black thread to piece a very light colored strip.

TIME TO BRAID

And now to braid! There is no single, absolutely correct way to begin a braided rug. Any method that produces an attractive, sturdy result is acceptable. The procedure that follows has been used for many years with excellent results. Start here, at any rate, and work out your own variations as you gain experience.

Start the braid by folding each of three strips—good side out—in fourths. To do this, fold each side in to the center and then crease the resulting double strip of fabric along its imaginary center line, bringing both outer folded sides together, and forming a four-layer strip or tube of fabric. The strips will not hold this folded position for any great length, of course, but when you have them formed correctly from the beginning, they are headed in the right direction when they come to your hand and you will find that you can smooth and control the folds easily as you braid.

STARTING THE BRAID

There are several acceptable ways to start the braid. The old country way, which I learned first, is to place the three four-ply strips on top of each other and sew them together across the cut ends.

Another, more polished method covers all the raw edges.

Suppose you are beginning your rug with three colors. Sew a strip of color A to a strip of color B in a bias seam as described (call this strip AB).

Continued →

Fold color C into a four-ply tube-strip with raw edges inside.

Fold raw edges of strip AB in to meet at center of strip.

Insert raw edge of folded strip C at seam joining colors A and B and sew firmly in place.

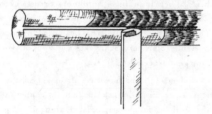

Fold top half of strip AB down to cover raw edges of strip C. You now have a "T" with color C sandwiched between layers 1 and 2, and 3 and 4, of strip AB.

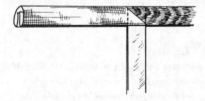

FLAT EDGES

No matter which way you choose to start the braid, the process of braiding is the same. Start braiding just as you would braid hair or yarn, except that you must take extra care to fold the strips around to make flat rather than twisted edges. Braiding is simple, but in case you don't know how, study the illustration, and you'll quickly learn. If you are learning, it is easier to work with three different colors.

Put 3 over 2 toward the left.

Put 1 over 3 toward the right.

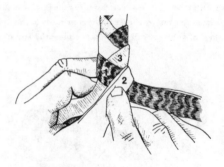

Put 2 over 1 toward the left.

Put 3 over 2 toward the right.

Put 1 over 3 toward the left.

Put 2 over 1 toward the right.

Put 3 over 2 toward the left, etc.

It is good to try this a few times, even if you have braided other materials before, to practice getting a tight, plump and even braid.

TENSION NEEDED

When starting the rug, for the first few feet, the braid will seem to be everywhere and nowhere. You need to put some tension on it in order to get an even braid. Pin, tie or clamp it—or close a window or drawer on the end of the braid—so that you can pull on it gently as you work. This will help to keep it straight and even.

Braid about two or three yards before beginning to lace the rug together. For a hit-or-miss rug in which color planning is not critical, you could let your braid accumulate a bit longer, but not too long, or it will be tangled and unruly when you try to form the rug. In a highly structured rug with a very exact color plan, you will want to braid and lace alternatively at short, regular intervals so that you can tell when it is time to change colors.

WHAT LENGTH?

How do you determine the proper length for your starting braid? Simple mathematics. The projected length of the rug minus its projected width equals the length of the starting braid. For a 7' x 9' rug, then, you would plan on an initial center braid two feet in length. Allow a few extra inches, say about three inches for every two feet of the starting braid, to make up for the slight shrinkage effect caused by lacing the braids together. Thus, for a 7' x 9' rug, you would measure out an actual 2'3" for your center braid.

DOUBLE THE BRAID BACK

Mark the end of the starting length of braid with a safety pin, and double the braid back on itself at this point, so that you have two rows of braids side by side. Force both sections of the braid to lie flat as you form this rounded corner. When lacing a rug together, always lay your work on a hard, flat surface.

Thread your bodkin (a blunt needle) with a double strand of heavy button-and-carpet thread about a yard long. Using a longer thread won't save any time and it is almost sure to tangle. Knot the end of the thread and, starting at the pin-marked corner, poke the bodkin between the braid folds. Take several stitches to secure the thread and then begin to lace by inserting the bodkin through every other braid fold, alternating from left to right. Pull firmly with your right hand as you hold the braids flat with your left.

At no time should the bodkin pierce the fabric. It always leads the thread *between* the folds of fabric. This is what makes the rug reversible.

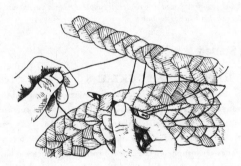

When you have laced your first length of braid down to the turning point, you will begin to see where craftsmanship comes into play. If you sew too tightly around corners, your rug will not lie flat; too loosely, and the rounds will gap unattractively. Rounding the corners on a braided rug requires judgment and common sense; there are no hard-and-fast rules, just guidelines. Loops on the sewn-on braid should match loops on the rug. As you hold that first braid around the corners, you can see what needs to happen.

TO KEEP IT FLAT

For the first six to ten rounds—*at the corners only*—the stitches on the body of the rug must be closer together than those on the braid you're attaching. So after lacing through a loop on the outer braid, and then through the next loop on the body of the rug, you then skip a loop on the outer braid and lace the following loop to the very next loop on the body of the rug. (Skip a loop on the new braid; don't skip on the rug body.)

In this way, you "hold back" the attaching braid so that it stays flat. Too many of these double stitches, though, will cause the rug to ripple rather than buckle. Later, as the project grows and the turns are less sharp, you won't need to hold back the outside braid as often in order to match the loops, as you had to during the first few rounds. The process

soon becomes second nature. That old folk saying seems to be true here: "Well begun is half done."

For a round rug, of course, there's no need to compute the length of a starting braid. Just snail the braid around and around as you hold it flat and continually correct for the increasing by making the "skip" stitches every few inches in the beginning, and only each foot or so as the rug enlarges.

START OVER

If it ever appears that your rug is buckling or rippling, you lose nothing but time by unlacing the piece and starting again from shortly before the point where it begins to look misshapen. Even the thread can be used again. Ripping out completed work may be painful but the results are worth it.

Dimples or folds in the braids are the result of using uneven tension in braiding or combining fabrics of varied weight, or of folding the strips unevenly.

Whenever you join on a new lacing thread, tie it to the old one on a firm knot, leaving 3/4" ends which can be tucked back between the loops.

COMPLETING THE RUG

Complete the rug by tapering the last 6"–8" of the braid. To do this, trim each strip so that it tapers to about half its original width at the cut end. Braid these narrow ends, carefully rolling in the edges, and lace the tapered butt firmly to the rug, retracing the last few lacing stitches for extra firmness. Leave a 2"-3" length of the lacing thread and weave it back between the braids, using a crochet hook, to form a secure, invisible ending.

SQUARE RUGS

In addition to the traditional round and oval forms, rugs may be braided in squares and in long straight mats for stair or hallway carpeting. To make square or rectangular rugs, compute the length of the center strip as you would for an oval rug. In place of the gradual increases made at the shoulders of the rounded rugs, the squared-off rugs are laced straight down each side, with an extra fold made in the braid at the point where it turns the corner, forming an L-joint that gives the rug its squared-off shape. Skip the loop at the point of the corner when lacing the rug together.

A runner or stair carpet may be made by lacing together parallel braids. In planning the length of such a rug, allow at least one inch per foot of shrinkage in the laced rug, and be sure to figure in any additional length needed to go around the lip of each stair tread.

Continued ➜

Barbara Farkas Casey

Illustrations by Alison Kolesar

I hope you're as excited as I am about the decorating possibilities presented by making your own curtains, and that you're eager to get started.

Tools and Materials

pad and pencil

dressmaker's chalk

tape measures (preferably 1 cloth, and 1 metal tape measure or yardstick)

straight pins

sewing machine (curtains can be sewn by hand; however, there's significantly more time involved)

iron

ironing board

sharp scissors (dressmaker shears are ideal)

large flat cutting surface (a clean hardwood or linoleum floor works well)

fabric and matching thread (quantity you'll need will be determined in the following pages)

heavyweight interfacing or drapery buckram (stiffening) for tab curtains only! (See page 912 for amounts.)

DEFINITIONS

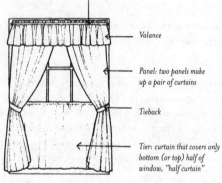

Casing: part of curtain through which rod is threaded

Valance

Panel: two panels make up a pair of curtains

Tieback

Tier: curtain that covers only bottom (or top) half of window, "half curtain"

Cross-grain of fabric

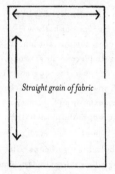

Straight grain of fabric

Heading: lining that finishes off upper edge of wrong side of tab curtain (finished length is usually four inches)

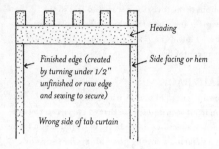

Heading

Finished edge (created by turning under 1/2" unfinished or raw edge and sewing to secure)

Side facing or hem

Wrong side of tab curtain

Seam allowance: the extra edge of fabric allowed for sewing two pieces of fabric together (usually 5/8")

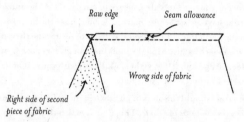

Raw edge

Seam allowance

Wrong side of fabric

Right side of second piece of fabric

Drapery buckram or stiffening: used to add body to the upper edge of tab curtains (usually 3–4" wide), can be purchased by the yard

Getting Started

TRADITIONAL VS. TAB CURTAINS

I have over ten different styles of curtains in my own home, and they are all variations of two basic designs—the traditional straight curtain and the tab curtain. I'll simply refer to them as traditional and tab from here on. As you can see in the diagrams below, their only difference is in the way they are hung from the curtain rod. The traditional has a sewn casing through which the rod is threaded; in the case of the tab, the rod is threaded through the fabric tabs affixed to the upper edge of the curtain.

In the following pages, you'll find clear, simple directions that will walk you through making these two types of curtains. You'll also be introduced to variations of these designs that are sure to inspire other ideas of your own.

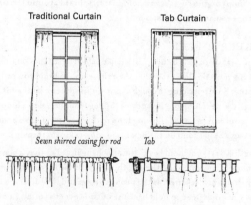

Traditional Curtain

Tab Curtain

Sewn shirred casing for rod

Tab

Simple Variations of Traditional and Tab Curtains

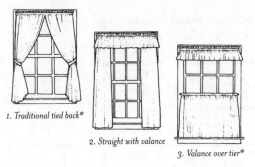

1. Traditional tied back*

2. Straight with valance

3. Valance over tier*

4. Tier over tier

5. Traditional tied back with tier*

7. Extra long straight curtain tied back tight and puffed out

Solutions for extra-wide windows

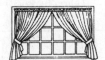

6a. One pair of curtains with valance running full width of windows

6b. Two pairs of curtains tied back to back

* Also appropriate for tab style

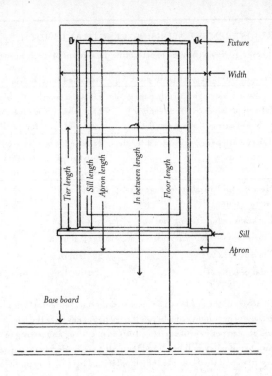

Fixture

Width

Tier length
Sill length
Apron length
In between length
Floor length

Sill

Apron

Base board

TYPES OF CURTAIN RODS

A standard extension rod or the brass café rod can be used for hanging a valance or a traditional straight curtain or tier. The café rod can also be used for tab curtains; in most cases, however, when hanging tab curtains, I prefer the look of a wooden rod. The only exception I can think of is when you're using tab curtains in a "valance over tier" design. The bulkier wooden rod would look awkward in this case. Finally, a tension rod can be used to hang traditional curtains on windows with a fairly deep sill, so that the curtain actually hangs inside the window casings.

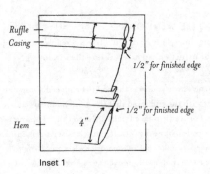

Ruffle
Casing

1/2" for finished edge

1/2" for finished edge

Hem   4"

Inset 1

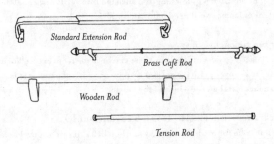

Standard Extension Rod

Brass Café Rod

Wooden Rod

Tension Rod

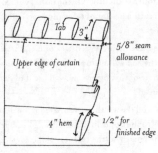

Tab   3"

5/8" seam allowance

Upper edge of curtain

4" hem   1/2" for finished edge

Inset 2

Continued →

ADJUSTMENTS TO FINISHED LENGTH AND WIDTH

These figures will be used to determine the amount of fabric needed. They will also be the guidelines for cutting out the curtains.

Style of Curtain or curtain piece	Adjusted length	Adjusted width
Traditional straight curtain panel (also applicable to tiered version), cut 2 (or 4 if using tier over tier design)	Finished length +9"* (extra 9" accommodates 4" bottom hem, plus 1/2" for finished edge, 1" casing for rod plus 1/2", and 1 1/2" for ruffle above casing - see Inset 1)	Finished width +4" (extra 4" accommodates 1 1/2" facing plus 1/2" for finished edge on each side of panel)
Tab curtain panel—cut 2 (or 4 for tier over tier style)	Finished length +2 1/8" (4 1/2" for bottom plus 1/2" finished edge, less 3" tab, plus 5/8" for seam allowance on upper edge of curtain—see Inset 2)	Finished width +4"
Heading for lining upper edge of tab curtain (cut 2)	6 1/4" length	Finished width +3"
Buckram or interfacing (cut 2)	3–4" length	Finished width
Fabric tabs (for tab curtains)**	7 1/4" length	4 1/4" wide
Tiebacks (cut 2)	22" length	7 1/4" width
Valance (cut 1)	Desired length (usually 10–12") +9"*	1 1/2–3 times the finished width of the window.

*The size of the ruffle can be increased if preferred. Simply double the amount you want it to increase by, and add it to the 9". **NOTE: To estimate the number of tabs you'll need per panel, take the finished width and divide by 4. Double this number to determine number of tabs you'll need per pair of curtains. Instead of cutting and sewing individual tabs, it may be easier to take the 7 1/4" length, multiply by the total number of tabs you'll need, and then cut 4 1/4" wide fabric strips (however many you need to total this length of fabric needed for tabs). We'll sew first, and then cut into individual tabs. This will be explained further. These measurements allow for a finished tab that is 1 1/2" wide and 3" long. A wider tab may be preferable on longer curtains; a shorter tab for tier style. In either case, you'll need to adjust the cutting measurements accordingly.

MEASURING THE WINDOWS

After determining the style curtain you'd like to create and the type of rod you'll likely be using, we can now measure the windows. (*See illustration of window.*)

First determine where you want the rod to be placed. Long tab curtains look best with the rod set so that the 3-inch tabs are above the window opening. For traditional curtains, the rod should hang 1–2 inches above the window opening. Or, if you've chosen a tension rod, this should be placed 2 inches below the upper window casing to accommodate the 1 1/2-inch ruffle above the casing. If you want a larger ruffle, you need to adjust the placement of the rod accordingly.

Next you need to decide where you want the bottom of the curtain to fall—well below the windowsill, pulling the extra fabric up to create a "puffed" look? (See illustration 7) Or, so the bottom of the curtain just barely touches the sill? Or the sash? Almost any length is acceptable, and is really a matter of taste and practicality. Avoid covering vents or radiators.

Measure (using a yardstick or metal tape measure) from the top of where the rod will be to the finished length you've decided upon. Make note of this figure, as we'll use it to determine how much fabric you'll need.

To find the width, measure from the outer edge of the casing of the window to the opposite outer edge. This measurement can be less precise than the length, as the fullness of the curtains will be forgiving here.

ADJUSTING MEASUREMENTS

We now need to adjust these two measurements to allow for hems, facings, and fullness of curtains. (See chart for adjustments.)

DETERMINING YARDS OF FABRIC TO BUY

Now we're ready to determine the amount of fabric you'll need per window. (NOTE: At least on your first attempt at making custom curtains, I would suggest staying away from wider than average windows—windows with a width that exceeds the average 45–54-inch wide fabric.) If you do want to make a curtain for an extra wide window, you might consider a solution as shown in illustrations 6a or 6b.

We can proceed with simple rules:

For traditional and tab curtain panels

Assuming the adjusted window width is less than the fabric width, double the adjusted window length, translate into feet, and divide by three to get the number of yards of fabric you'll need per window. (NOTE: If you're making curtains for very small windows, you may be able to get two panels from one width of fabric; the adjusted window width needs to be less than or equal to half of the fabric width in this case. The adjusted window length translated into yards will equal the amount of fabric you'll need per window.)

For two tie backs

You'll need 1/4 yard of fabric or these can be made from excess fabric (only for all-over prints or solids) if adjusted width of panel is at least 7 1/4 inches less than the width of the fabric.

Buckram or interfacing (for tab curtains only)

Use buckram for medium to heavyweight fabrics. It can be purchased at most fabric centers by the yard. It's usually between 3–4 inches wide. You'll need to buy an amount equal to two times the width of the window. Heavy interfacing can be used instead of buckram, and for lighter fabrics is actually preferable. You'll need to buy about 1/4 yard per pair of curtains.

Tabs

For allover prints or solid fabrics, you'll need an additional 5–6-inch length of fabric for approximately six tabs or about 1/2 yard of fabric for eighteen tabs. For one-directional fabric patterns (e.g., stripes) you'll need 1/4 yard of fabric for approximately ten tabs, assuming a finished tab width of 1 1/2 inches.

Valances

For fullness, it's desirable for a valance to be one and a half to three times the adjusted width of the window. To achieve this, it may be necessary to piece the valance from two to three widths of fabric. Plan on an additional 3/4 yard if only one width of fabric is needed, 1 1/2 yards if two widths are needed, 2 1/4 yards if three widths are needed, and so on.

Headings (two for each pair of tab curtains)

You'll need 1/4 yard of fabric if finished width plus 3 inches is less than or equal to half the fabric width. If not, you'll need 3/8 yard of fabric.

SOME TIPS ON BUYING FABRIC

At least on your first attempt at custom curtains, I'd recommend using a relatively inexpensive fabric. Remnants, costing on the average between one dollar and four dollars per yard, are ideal. That is, if you can get your hands on enough yards for your curtains. Muslins and cotton/polyester blends are another cost-effective alternative. Also, for best results, the fabric should be of medium weight with medium body. If the fabric is too stiff or bulky, the curtain won't hang nicely. If the fabric is too limp or flimsy, the curtain will be droopy.

I'd recommend staying away from plaids and one-directional patterns. Allover prints or solids are much easier to work with, and they're much more forgiving of imperfections such as a seam that is not as straight as it could be or a hemline that's a bit off. Loosely woven or very sheer fabrics should also be avoided. The raw edges of the woven fabric will unravel easily and are difficult to work with—cutting and sewing very sheer fabric is tricky business.

Most fabrics are prewashed or sized these days. As a general rule, I'd recommend **against** washing the fabric before making your curtains. The fabric will lose a lot of its body, and your curtains won't look as crisp and new as possible. Muslin or unsized 100 percent cotton, on the other hand, should be washed beforehand, as they will shrink significantly. If necessary, they can be starched to bring back their body.

Finally, if you have the luxury, I'd advise you to bring home swatches of fabric you're considering and live with them for a couple of days before making a final decision. Get the reactions of others in your household; they have to live with the curtains, too.

CUTTING OUT THE CURTAINS

It's likely you've decided to make curtains for a room with more than one window. Even though this may be the case, I'd still recommend cutting the pieces, sewing, and hanging only one pair of curtains before proceeding with the pairs for the other windows. Maybe you inadvertently made a mistake measuring the windows, or you

misjudged the fabric or style for the curtains. You'll save yourself a lot of time and frustration by catching the error after constructing only one pair of curtains. Measurements can be adjusted for the remaining curtains, or if the fabric is not as appropriate as you thought it would be, it can be saved and used for another project.

Let's get started. For this phase of making your curtains, you'll need scissors, straight pins, dressmaker's chalk, a cloth tape measure, pad and pencil, a clean, flat cutting surface, and your fabric. If your fabric is wrinkled (possibly you decided to prewash it or it's a remnant that has been sitting folded in a pile for some time), you should iron it.

Since we're not using any patterns per se, we'll be cutting the different pieces for the curtains one item at a time. We'll begin with the panels. You'll need two (four for tier over tier style) per window, and the cutting procedure will be the same for both traditional and tab styles. (See illustrations.)

Step 1: Make certain the unfinished edge of the fabric is straight. If not, cut to adjust.

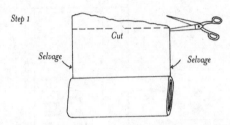

Step 2: a. If you can get two panels from one width of fabric, fold lengthwise matching selvage edges of the fabric. **b.** If not, fold the fabric horizontally to accommodate the adjusted length of the panel. Cut through the top fold.

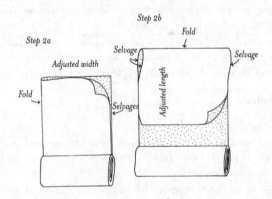

Step 3: Measuring from the unfinished top edge, mark off the adjusted length of the curtain with chalk. From here on, when measuring and marking lengths and widths of pieces, repeat the process at various locations across the fabric. The multiple chalk marks will serve as a cutting guide to ensure that you achieve a straight edge.

Continued →

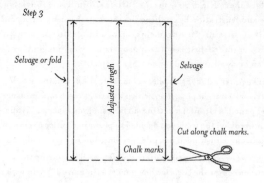

Step 3

Selvage or fold | Adjusted length | Selvage

Chalk marks | Cut along chalk marks.

Step 4: With pieces you've just cut, mark off adjusted width of curtain, measuring from selvage edges to opposite selvage edges or fold if you've been able to get two panels from one width of fabric. Cut.

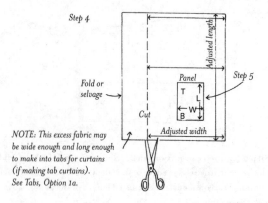

Step 4

Fold or selvage → | Adjusted length | Step 5

Panel — T L W B

Cut | Adjusted width

NOTE: This excess fabric may be wide enough and long enough to make into tabs for curtains (if making tab curtains). See Tabs, Option 1a.

Step 5: Label pieces, noting "length," "width," and if you're using a one-directional print, "top" and "bottom."

If you've opted for a straight, traditional curtain (no tiebacks or valance), believe it or not, you're ready to begin assembling your curtains. Directions begin on page 916. Otherwise, read on.

Variations

TIEBACKS

Tiebacks are a simple addition to a straight curtain (tab or traditional), yet really do provide a different look. What I would describe as a "softer" look. (See illustrations.)

To cut, match selvage edges of fabric. Measure 7 1/4 inches from the unfinished top edge of the fabric, mark, and cut. With the piece you've just cut, measure 22 inches from selvage edges to opposite fabric fold, mark, and cut. Label pieces. As you get more and more experienced at making curtains, you'll find you may be able to get tiebacks out of excess fabric left after cutting other larger curtain pieces like the panels. This is especially true if you're using an allover print or solid fabric. Keep in mind other savings and shortcuts like this as you're making your curtains.

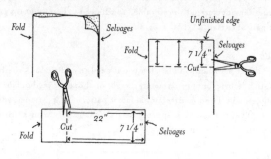

Fold | Selvages | Unfinished edge | Fold | 7 1/4" | Selvages | Cut

Fold | Cut | 22" | 7 1/4" | Selvages

VALANCE

Step 1: With fabric opened to full width, measure 22 inches for a 12-inch-long finished valance. Adjust accordingly if you want a shorter or longer valance, or ruffle at the top of your valance. Mark and cut.

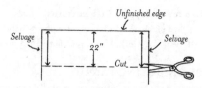

Unfinished edge

Selvage | 22" | Selvage

Cut

Step 2: The valance piece you've just cut will be sufficient if the width of the fabric is at least one and a half times the width of the window. If not, cut however many widths of fabric you'll need to piece together (following procedure in Step 1) to get a valance that is one and a half to three times the width of the window, depending on how full you would like your valance to be.

TABS

You have two alternatives for cutting the tabs. Proceed with Option 1 if your fabric has a definite one-directional pattern (e.g., a stripe) or if your fabric is extra wide or your windows are extra small so that you'll have long 4 1/4-inch strips (or multiples thereof) left over after cutting the panels.

Otherwise, I think it's easier to follow the procedure as outlined in Option 2 where we'll ignore the usual rule of cutting the pieces on the straight grain of the fabric. (See illustration.)

Option 1

We determined the total length of fabric you'll need to make the tabs for each pair of curtains. **a.** If there is enough fabric remaining after cutting the panels for the curtains (see Step 4) to use for tabs, measure 4 1/4 inches from long unfinished edge to opposite long unfinished edge, mark, and cut. Repeat process as many times as necessary to achieve total length needed to make tabs. Label pieces. We'll sew first, before cutting into individual tabs. **b.** Otherwise, with fabric opened to full width (single weight of fabric), measuring from either selvage edge mark off 4 1/4-inch intervals across the width of the fabric. Count the number of 4 1/4-inch sections (tabs) you get from one width of fabric. Divide into the total number of tabs you need (rounding up to the nearest whole number—two and two-thirds rounds to three) to determine total number of 7 1/4-inch tab fabric strips you'll need.

Option Ia.

Refer to NOTE in Step 4 of Panels.

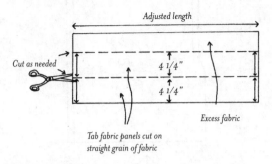

Mark off 7 1/4-inch sections along selvage edge of fabric. Only cut along last 7 1/4-inch interval marks. With same piece, cut into 4 1/4-inch wide tab fabric strips. Label the pieces. To save a bit of time, we'll cut into individual tabs after sewing.

Option Ib.

In this illustration, there are 6 4 1/4" intervals. Can get 6 tabs from 1 width of fabric. If you need 16 tabs (16÷6 = 2 2/3 which rounds to 3), you'll need to measure 3 fabric strips that are 7 1/4" long.

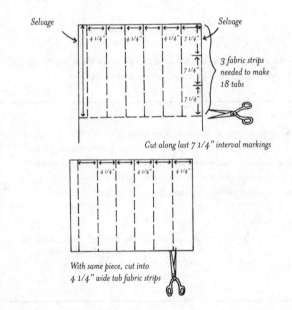

Option 2

We determined the total number of tabs per pair of curtains, and the length of fabric we'll need to make these tabs. To determine how many widths of fabric (tab fabric panels) we'll need to cut to equal this length, divide this length by the fabric width, rounding to the nearest whole number.

Match selvage edges of fabric. Measure 4 1/4 inches from unfinished edge, mark, and cut. This tab fabric panel you've just cut can be used as a pattern to cut remaining tab fabric panels that you need.

Option 2

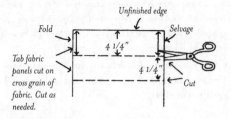

HEADING FOR TAB CURTAINS

For tab curtains, we'll need to cut two heading pieces (four for tier over tier style) to line the top portion of the two curtain panels.

Option 1

If you can get two headings from one width of fabric (i.e., the finished width plus 3 inches is less than or equal to half of the fabric width) match up the selvage edges of the fabric.

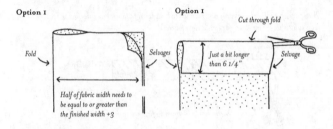

Cut 2, one for each panel

Option 2

If not, double the fabric just enough to accommodate 6 1/4-inch length. Cut through top fold.

Step 1: Measure 6 1/4 inches from the unfinished top edge of the fabric, mark, and cut.

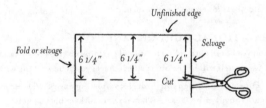

Step 2: With the same pieces, measuring from selvage edges to opposite selvage edges or fold, mark off finished width plus 3 inches and cut. Label pieces.

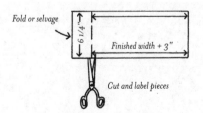

Cut and label pieces

Continued →

Buckram or Interfacing (for tab curtains only)

Use buckram for medium to heavyweight fabrics. It can be purchased at most fabric centers, and usually is between 3–4-inches wide. Heavy interfacing can be used instead of buckram, and for lighter weight fabrics is actually preferable.

Step 1: If you decide to use interfacing, you'll need to mark off 4 inches from long unfinished edge and cut. Repeat for second interfacing strip if needed.

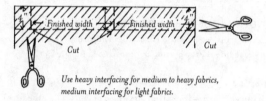

Use heavy interfacing for medium to heavy fabrics, medium interfacing for light fabrics.

Step 2: For both buckram and interfacing, measure two lengths equal to the finished width, mark, and cut. Label pieces.

Buckram (for tab curtains only and medium to heavyweight fabric) or Interfacing (can be used as a substitute for buckram for lightweight fabrics)

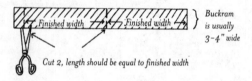

Sewing Curtains

We're now ready to move on to the next phase of making your curtains. You'll need scissors, tape measure, thread which matches your fabric, an iron, an ironing board, and a sewing machine.

Set up your sewing machine. Adjust the tension so that you're getting a taut, straight stitch on your curtain fabric. Stitch length should be set to ten stitches per inch.

TRADITIONAL CURTAIN PANELS

If you've chosen a straight, traditional curtain (no tiebacks or valance), the two panels will be the only pattern pieces you'll be working with.

For clarity, I'll step you through completing one panel from start to finish. You may find it easiest, however, to work on both panels simultaneously. For example, if you're ironing one hem, why not go ahead and iron the hem of the other panel?

SIDE FACINGS

Step 1: With wrong side of fabric facing you, iron under 1/2 inch on side edges of panel.

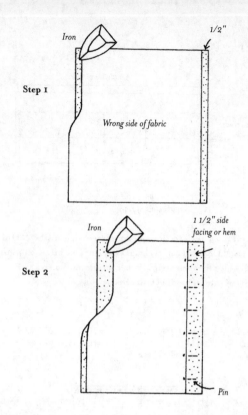

Step 2: Turn under an additional 1 1/2 inches on the same side edges to form side facings or hems. Iron and secure with straight pins.

Inset 1

When stitching all seams, make certain to secure beginning and end, either by using the reverse feature on your machine (if it has one) or by manually manipulating the fabric so that you stitch the same portion of the seam three times (once forward, then backwards, and then forward again).

Machine stitch forward about 1/2". Reverse. Stitch over the same 1/2" seam in opposite direction. Machine stitch forward again. Repeat this same process at end of seam.

Step 3: With wrong side of panel facing you, stitch through all thicknesses of fabric as close to inside edge of side facing as possible (no more than 1/4 inch from edge). Repeat opposite side.

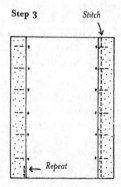

TOP HEM AND CASING

Step 1: Clip 3/8 inch off top corners of panel. With allover prints or solids, there will be no difference between top and bottom.

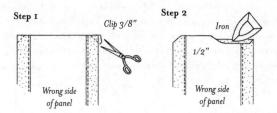

Step 2: With wrong side of panel facing you, iron under 1/2 inch on upper edge of panel.

Step 3: Turn under an additional 2 1/2 inches or more if you've allowed for a deeper ruffle at the top of your curtain. Iron and secure with straight pins.

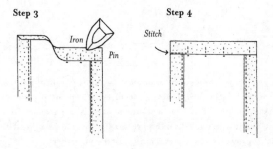

Step 4: Sew as close to inside upper hem edge as possible. Remember to secure beginning and end of seam.

Step 5: Measure 1 inch from this seam, marking in several locations across top of panel to use as sewing guide. Stitch along chalk marks. It's critical to firmly secure beginning and end of this seam, as it will form the casing for the rod, and will be subject to more stress than most seams. You may even want to stitch entire seam a second time.

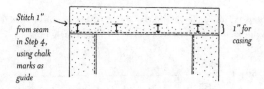

BOTTOM HEM

At this point, you may want to make certain you're happy with the finished length of the curtain. Simply pin up the 4 1/4-inch hem on the bottom of the panel, actually thread the rod through the casing, and hang to see if the length is to your liking. Shortening is no problem; simply mark off new finished length with chalk or straight pins, cut excess fabric if you think the new hem will be too deep and proceed with the directions that follow.

Lengthening up to 1 1/2 inches, mark new finished length with chalk or straight pins, and follow directions below, keeping in mind the need to adjust the depth of the hem. Lengthening more than 1 1/2 inches will be a problem because you won't have enough fabric to form a hem. You may want to consider other solutions—maybe add a ruffle at the bottom of the curtain.

Step 1: With the wrong side of the panel facing you, iron under 1/2 inch along bottom edge.

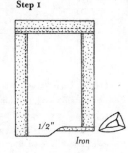

Step 2: Turn under an additional 4 inches or whatever amount is needed to achieve the finished length, iron, and pin to secure.

Step 3: Stitch through all thicknesses of fabric as close to edge as possible, securing beginning and end of seam.

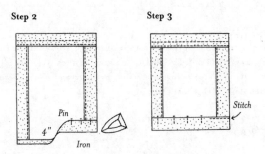

If all has gone well, you should have one completed panel or two, if you've decided to work on both simultaneously. Otherwise repeat process for other panel. Before hanging panels, clip any stray threads, get rid of any chalk marks with a damp washcloth, and iron—maybe even use spray starch for an extra crisp look. Hang the curtains, adjusting placement on rod so they fall nicely.

NOTE: If you decided not to add tiebacks or a valance to your curtains, you'll have completed assembling one pair of curtains for your room.

TIEBACKS

Step 1: With the right side of the piece facing you, fold in half, matching long 22-inch edge to opposite 22-inch edge. Wrong side of fabric will now be facing you. Pin edges together.

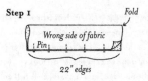

Step 2: Stitch 5/8 inch from unfinished 22-inch edges.

Step 3: On one side only, stitch 5/8 inch from short unfinished edge. Cut 1/4 inch from both seams and corners.

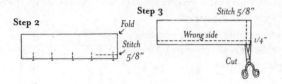

Step 4: Turn tieback to right side by threading pencil (eraser end first) or suitable long, thin, blunt object through tieback. Start by placing eraser end of pencil at sewn short edge of tieback. Carefully work fabric over pencil until piece is completely turned to right side. Remove pencil. If needed, pull out sewn corners with a straight pin to square off tieback.

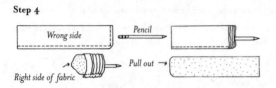

Step 5: Iron under 5/8 inch on unfinished edge. Iron entire tieback. Slipstitch open end closed by hand, or machine topstitch as close to edge as possible. If you're especially good at sewing straight seams, you may want to topstitch along all edges of tieback.

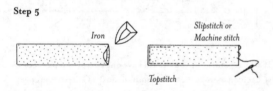

VALANCE

Much like the addition of tiebacks, a valance will lend a different look to a straight curtain. A valance can also be used effectively alone. In my own kitchen, I have one very large window which looks out onto our backyard. To take advantage of light and the view, I've simply used a fairly deep valance that runs along the top of the window. It's a perfect window solution, and extremely inexpensive!

If your valance is going to be composed of more than one width of fabric, you'll have to decide upon one of two ways to piece the valance together.

Technique 1

In this case, you'll simply treat each width of fabric as a valance. For example, if you determined that you needed three widths of fabric for the valance, you'll be making three valances. After completing all three, you'll thread them continuously onto the rod to get the full look you want. In most cases, if the fabric is of medium weight and the valance is full enough, the breaks won't be noticeable. The real benefit of this method is flexibility. If you

choose, sometime down the road, you can use these same valances on smaller windows.

Technique 2

With this method, the number of fabric widths you need for the valance will be sewn (or "pieced") together first. After piecing, we'll finish completing and treating the valance as one long unit. The bonuses of this approach are: no matter how full your valance is, there won't be any "breaks," and you'll save some time proceeding this way; you won't have as many side facings to iron and sew.

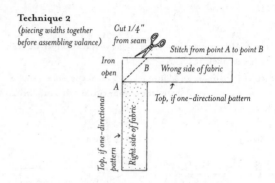

To piece widths together, overlap two sections at right angles (right side of fabric facing in). If using a one-directional print, pay attention to top and bottom. Stitch from point A to point B, clip 1/4 inch from seam, and iron open. Repeat this process as many times as needed, attaching next section to pieces you've just sewn together.

ASSEMBLING VALANCE(S)

Side facings

Step 1: With wrong side of fabric facing you, iron under 1/2 inch on side edges of valance(s).

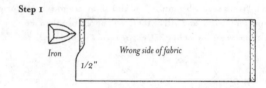

Step 2: Turn under an additional 1 1/2 inches on same side edges to form side facings or hems. Iron and secure with straight pins.

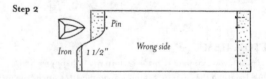

Step 3: With wrong side of valance facing you, stitch through all thicknesses of fabric as close to inside edge of side facing as possible. Repeat for other side facing, other facings, or other valance pieces if applicable.

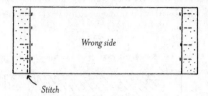

Top hem and casing

Step 1: Clip 3/8 inch off top corners of valance. With allover prints or solids, there will be no difference between top and bottom before sewing.

Step 2: Iron under 1/2 inch on upper edge of valance.

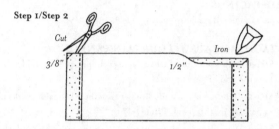

Step 3: Turn under an additional 2 1/2 inches or more if you've allowed for a deeper ruffle at the top of your valance when you cut out the pattern. Iron and secure with straight pins.

Step 4: Sew as close to inside upper hem edge as possible. Remember to secure beginning and end of seam.

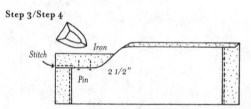

Step 5: Measure 1 inch from this seam, marking in several locations across the top of the valance to use as a sewing guide. Stitch along chalk marks, securing beginning and end of seam.

Step 5
Stitch 1" from seam you just completed to form casing for rod

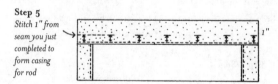

Bottom hem

Step 1: With wrong side of valance facing you, iron under 1/2 inch along bottom edge.

Step 2: Turn under an additional 4 inches, iron, and pin to secure.

Step 3: Stitch through all thicknesses of fabric, securing beginning and end of seam.

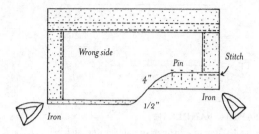

Before hanging valance(s) clip any stray threads, get rid of any chalk marks with a damp washcloth, and iron. Thread the valance(s) onto the rod, adjusting the shirring so the valance will fall nicely. Voila! You should have a beautiful new valance that you've made yourself!

Believe it or not, we've covered all the fundamentals you'll need to know to create the seven different styles of curtains for your own home. You can now create traditional straight curtains, tiebacks, valances, and even tier curtains which are simply half-curtains. Though the length of the panels is different for tier curtains, the method for assembling is exactly the same as for traditional curtains. You will, however, need to cut four panels per window.

The only procedure we still need to cover is assembling tab curtains. After these steps, you should be quite experienced at designing your own curtains with a distinctive country look. As I mentioned earlier, most curtains are simply a variation of these two types of curtains. Let's begin.

ASSEMBLING TAB CURTAINS
Heading

Step 1: With wrong side of heading facing you, iron under 1/2 inch on each side.

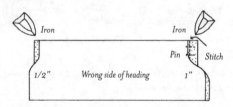

Step 2: Iron under an additional 1 inch on each side, pin to secure, and stitch as close to inside edge of side facing. Repeat for other side facing.

Step 3: Iron under 1/2 inch on bottom edge of heading. If using an allover print or solid fabric, there will be no difference between top and bottom.

Step 4: Turn under an additional 1 inch, iron, pin to secure, and stitch, securing beginning and end of seam. Set heading piece aside.

Continued →

Step 3/Step 4

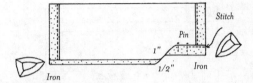

TAB FABRIC PANELS

For clarity, I'll step you through assembling one tab fabric panel at a time. You'll have to repeat the process as many times as needed to end with the total tabs you'll need per pair of curtains.

Step 1: With right side of fabric facing you, match up long unfinished edge of tab fabric panel to opposite long unfinished edge. Wrong side of fabric will now be on outside. Pin edges together.

Step 1/Step 2

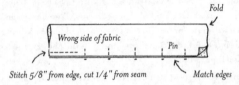

Step 2: Stitch 5/8 inch from long unfinished edges, securing beginning and end of seam. Trim seam to 1/4 inch.

Step 3: Attach large safety pin to one side of unsewn (open) end of tab fabric panel. Thread the safety pin through the casing that's been formed, carefully working fabric over the pin to turn tab fabric panel to right side out.

Step 3

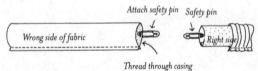

Step 4: Iron tab fabric panel flat. Cut into 7 1/4-inch-long pieces to make individual tabs. Set aside.

Step 4

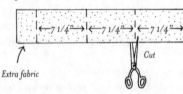

Follow above procedure for all tab fabric panels that have been cut out.

ATTACHING BUCKRAM OR INTERFACING TO PANEL

With wrong side of the fabric facing you, measure 2 inches from upper left-hand corner of curtain panel. Mark. From this point, start pinning drapery buckram (or interfacing) across the wrong side of the top of the panel. You should finish with 2 inches excess on right portion of panel as well. Baste 1/2 inch from top unfinished edge, using longest machine stitch available on your machine (six stitches per inch in most cases).

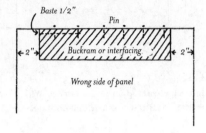

SIDE FACINGS

See pages 417–418 for constructing side facings.

ATTACHING TABS TO CURTAIN PANELS

Step 1: With right side of fabric facing you, pin one tab (folded in half) to each end of top of panel.

Step 2: Determine the midpoint between these two tabs, mark and center next tab on this mark. Pin to secure.

Step 3: Determine the midpoint between the upper right-hand tab and the middle tab, mark and center next tab on this mark. Pin in place. Determine the midpoint between the upper left-hand tab and the middle tab, mark and center next tab on this mark. Pin.

Step 1/Step 2   **Step 3**

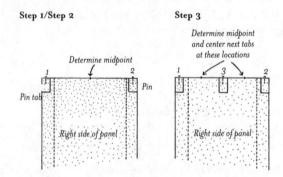

Step 4: Repeat this process until tabs are evenly spaced 3–5 inches apart across top of panel.

Step 5: Machine baste (using long stitch length) 1/2 inch along upper edge of panel through all thicknesses to secure tabs.

Step 4/Step 5

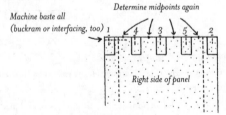

ATTACHING HEADING

Step 1: With right side of fabric facing you (tabs will also be facing you), match upper edge of panel to top edge of heading (right sides of fabric together). Pin to secure.

Step 1

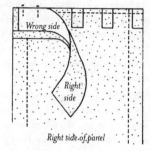

Pin heading to right side of panel (right side of heading facing in)

Wrong side

Right side

Right side of panel

Step 2: Stitch 5/8 inch from top edge through all layers of fabric, securing beginning and end of seam. You'll be working with a number of layers of fabric (the panel, the buckram or interfacing, the heading, and the tabs), so don't be surprised if stitching this seam is a bit awkward or cumbersome.

Step 3: Cut 1/4 inch from seam. Once again, cut through various layers of fabric.

Step 2/Step 3

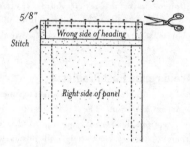

Cut 1/4" from seam

5/8"

Stitch

Wrong side of heading

Right side of panel

Step 4: Turn heading to right side of panel. Iron open.

Step 4

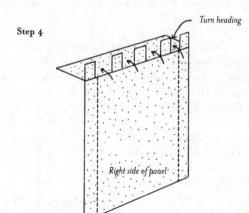

Turn heading

Right side of panel

Step 5: Machine topstitch as close to upper edge (just below tabs) as possible. (Stitching this seam, once again, may be a bit awkward.) With right side of panel facing you, match up left edge of panel to left edge of heading. Pin to secure, and machine topstitch as close to edge as possible. Repeat on right side.

Step 5

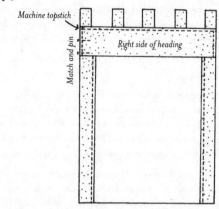

Machine topstitch

Match and pin

Right side of heading

BOTTOM HEM

See page 919 for bottom hem construction.

You've now completed one pair of tab curtains. Tiebacks and valances can be added to your tab curtains. Simply follow the directions as outlined in the section on traditional curtains. If you're satisfied with your efforts, cut and assemble remaining pairs of curtains.

FENCES, ORCHARDS, OUTBUILDINGS AND MORE

The Best Fences

James FitzGerald

Illustrations by Brigita Fuhrmann

How to Plan Ahead

Four basic indoor planning steps and an equal number of outdoor planning steps are needed to keep you away from mistakes or miscalculations in building a fence.

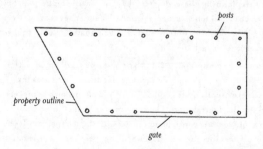

posts

property outline

gate

Continued →

1. Draw a map of your property on 1/4-inch graph paper (1/4 inch equals one foot).

2. Using a ruler, sketch in the contemplated fence line. Try to keep the scale accurate.

3. From your anticipated traffic pattern, locate the gate area first. Mark out the gate posts, then the corner posts, and finally each line post. If you find that the distance between gate post and the corner post is not evenly divisible by eight feet or six feet or whatever your section length will be, you have two choices.

a. Shorten each section a bit so that all sections have identical lengths.

b. Plan for a shorter section next to each corner post. This second option is usually preferred because it wastes less time and materials. It would be very time-consuming if every eight-foot board, for instance, had to be trimmed by 7 1/4 inches. Also, these short sections make excellent braces for the corner posts.

4. Write down the various lengths. For the first time in your life you may be confronted with working in rods. Pasture land boundaries are frequently measured in rods, and rolls of barbed wire always come in rods. Don't panic. A rod is simply 16 1/2 feet.

From the above data you can calculate the answers to these basic questions.

a. How many corner posts, bracing posts, and line posts will you need?

b. How many boards, pickets, rails, or bales of wire will you need?

c. How many gates and gate posts will you need?

Once satisfied with your graph paper version, go outside and re-create your ideas on the ground in the next four steps.

1. Place a stake at the site of each gate post. By starting your fence at each side of the main gate and proceeding with standard size sections toward the corners, you can maintain perfect symmetry around the gate area where fence asymmetry or other defects would be most noticeable.

2. Place stakes at the corners.

3. Pull mason's twine tightly between the gate posts and the corner posts after clearing any brush or obstacles that may be in the way.

4. Lay a board or rail or any unit of horizontal "stringer" material along the twine to locate each successive line post location. Mark each spot with a stake.

In this planning phase, don't be shy about asking for help. People who own beautiful fences are very proud of them. They are usually delighted to give you all of the details and help that you want. So if you see a terrific fence, ask about it.

Most of the giant catalog stores have at least a small fence section mixed in with garden supply or hardware sections. The prices for materials are usually quite good, especially for items such as pickets, should you like their design. The amount of information you can obtain about fencing construction varies with the salesperson. If you want to talk fencing, the local hardware store personnel are usually unbeatable. They know the local soils and weather conditions, and have a lot of experience with do-it-yourself problems in your area.

If you need professional help with the planning or construction, look in the yellow pages under landscape design, contractors, or fencing materials. Even if you only want help with your plans, ask about estimated costs for their time and services.

How to Construct a Legal Fence

First, make sure you are putting the fence on your own property. It is embarrassing to construct a fence on someone else's land, and it can also result in a loss of ownership. Consult your own survey maps or verify your boundary lines at the recording clerk's office. Find out if there are any restrictions such as height limits, set-back rules, or construction codes.

If you plan to run the fence exactly on the boundary line between your property and your neighbors', talk with them about it. Even if you fear the possible response, try it. You may get more cooperation than you expect. There are many possible responses. Here are some suggestions for handling the two extreme positions.

1. Your neighbor may be willing to share construction and maintenance costs, thereby effectively flipping Robert Frost's statement into good neighbors make good fences. If you and your neighbor agree on certain aspects of fence construction, write down what you agree upon so that the details don't get distorted as time goes on.

2. If you are not fortunate enough to have a concurring neighbor, make sure your fence is located a foot or so inside your property boundaries so there is no ownership dispute.

In addition to laws that may restrict your fence variables, some laws may require you to build fences. Frequently, it is mandatory to construct a barrier to attractive nuisances such as swimming pools and excavation sites.

How to Avoid Fence Post Problems

Most fences share a need for posts every few feet to support the wood or wire in the horizontal sections. The classic Virginia zigzag rail fence is one of those exceptions; it does not require posts when constructed with angles less than 135 degrees. Nevertheless, the post is the most common denominator to all fences. It will become the backbone of your system, and it demands careful selection. A good fence post should demonstrate three basic characteristics: stability, survivability, and straightness.

STABILITY

Generally, one-third of the fence post should be well anchored underground. If you want a four-foot post above ground, start with a six-foot post. Before you dig the hole, it pays to check out a couple of things. Avoid ledges and rocks, buried cables and water pipes, leach fields and septic systems.

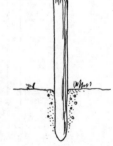

A post often can be set without even digging a hole. Thrust a long iron bar downward several times in the same spot. It should go a little deeper each time. After it penetrates the ground a foot or two, grasp the top of the bar with both hands and rotate it as if you were stirring a witch's cauldron. Next place your nicely sharpened fence post into the earthen tunnel you just created and pound it in. You finish with posts that are held tightly by compressed soil, and avoid having to fill in a large hole.

POUNDING THE POSTS

Be careful when you are pounding the post into the ground. If you are using a sixteen-pound sledgehammer or a maul, make sure the head is not loose and the handle is not cracked just below the head. Position yourself so that the head of your sledge hits the post at approximately the level of your waist. Unless you are eight feet tall, you should stand on something stable such as the back of a pickup truck to start each post. Face the post directly, spreading your feet apart (so if you miss the post the sledge will be headed between your feet and not at one of them), get balanced, and look exactly at the spot you want the maul to hit the post. Don't blink. If you blink just at the moment of impact or a fraction of a second before, you risk splitting the post, cracking the sledge handle on the top of the post, or smashing some toes. Watch carefully as you are striking the post, don't blink, and wear protective glasses.

PLANTING THE POSTS

If you can't punch a hole with an iron bar, you can plant your posts. Making the hole may be tedious but it is simple. Use an iron bar to loosen the dirt and rocks, and a shovel to empty the hole. The advantage of this method is that you do not need sharp posts and you can construct a post enclosure that is well drained and allows the post to be solidly wedged with rocks and dirt. Frost is less likely to heave this post.

USING CONCRETE

For an extremely solid post, a wide ring of concrete at the base may be built. Place the concrete in an open collar around, but not under, the post so that the moisture can drain down along the post as the post shrinks or decays with age. Avoid sticking the post in concrete as if you were sticking a candle in frosting. This creates a moisture chamber around the post and tends to hasten its deterioration.

Mix the concrete a little bit on the dry side. Use two parts of cement, three parts sand, and five parts gravel with just enough water to make the mixture fluid but still somewhat firm.

If you use concrete, make the top of the hole two or three feet wide, mix the concrete, put the pole in position, and pour the concrete around it. To increase the bond between a post and the concrete, nail small flanges or cross pieces to the bottom of the post before putting it in position. Smooth the surface of the concrete so that the highest point is next to the post. This allows the water to drain away. It is also a good idea to let the concrete cure for a day or two before you use the post.

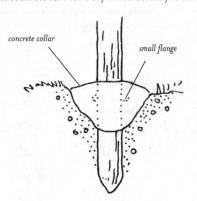
concrete collar

small flange

SURVIVABILITY

It would be great to find a post that would resist rot or rust forever, but there aren't any. Post rot usually occurs at the ground level because that is where the combination of food supply, oxygen, and moisture is ideal for the growth of fungi. Woods decay at different rates, depending on the type of soil they stand in and on the amount of natural fungus-retarding chemicals present. The core of every cylindrical tree trunk (heartwood) contains more of these chemicals than the remaining wood (sapwood).

This table describes the hierarchy of preferable fence post heartwood.

DURABILITY OF UNTREATED HEARTWOOD

Resistance	Tree Type	Life Expectancy
Extreme Decay Resistance	Western Juniper Osage Orange	20–30 years
Good Decay Resistance	Sassafras White Oak Red Cedar Cherry	10 years
Poor Decay Resistance	Birch Beech Ash Elm Hemlock Hickory Maple Red Oak Poplar Willow	2 years

The lifetime of fence posts can be lengthened. Peeling them is one method. Some oldtimers believe that posts set in the ground upside down rot sooner.

"Weak" wood such as maple can be converted into a "strong" wood by a variety of techniques. A simple method that offers limited protection consists of placing the lower half of the fence post in a fire long enough to produce a layer of char.

In the past, builders of fences have soaked the posts in either pentachlorophenol or creosote. Now the U.S. Environmental Protection Agency has placed restrictions on the use of these, limiting it to persons who have passed a course on the safe handling of hazardous materials, and restricting sale of these to these certified applicators.

As a result, we must recommend that you use copper naphthenate, which long has been recommended for use around gardens, since it will not kill plants, as the other two will. Follow the directions on the container. As with all wood preservatives, the wood is best protected if it is dipped into the liquid, rather than being painted, if the work is done in the shade, and if the wood is clean and, particularly, unpainted.

Continued →

STRAIGHTNESS

Make sure that the posts are standing straight and in a straight line. This is important cosmetically as well as practically, particularly when using wire fencing, because any post that is out of line is subject to enormous stress. If it bends over, the wire along the entire fence will be loosened.

To get each post standing straight, use a carpenter's level.

To get the posts in a line, run two pieces of twine between two corner posts. Tie one at the bottom of both posts, the other near the top. Place each post so that it just touches each string, keeping all posts on the same side of the strings.

BRACING

If you think that one post will encounter more horizontal stress than the others, brace it. All corner posts and gate posts should be braced, with corner posts braced in two directions. Here's how to do it.

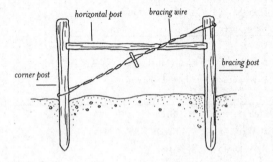

horizontal post   bracing wire

bracing post

corner post

1. The anchoring post should be larger than the other posts and should be set deeper, if possible. Try to bury about 3 1/2 feet of an eight-foot post.

2. Set another large post four to six feet down the line.

3. Place a strong horizontal post between the two posts about a third of the way down from the top of the posts. This horizontal post should be set in a dado joint, or at least blocked for stability.

4. Circle eleven-gauge wire twice around these posts, running it from the top of the bracing post to the base of the corner post. Twist the ends of the wire together and staple it to the post.

5. Insert a strip of wood at the midpoint of the bracing wire and twist it like a tourniquet to tighten the wire.

6. Anchor it with wire against the horizontal bar.

The physics of this bracing system is simple. Any force tending to pull the top of the corner post down the fence line is indirectly shared with the solid base of the same post. Through triangulation with a rigid horizontal bar and tight wire, two simple posts have been changed into a system of counterlevers. Remember, if you run the wire in the opposite direction (from the top of the corner post to the base of the bracing post), it will be useless.

How to Choose the Right Type of Fence

There are almost as many kinds of fencing materials as there are varieties of ice cream. The selection depends principally on which materials are the most readily available, least expensive, and will do the job properly. A five-strand barbed wire fence may be great for containing cattle but it just won't do around a school yard. The table gives you an idea of the popular options.

VIRGINIA RAIL FENCE

This type of fence can still be seen as an aging monument to classic fencing beauty reminding us of an age when materials were in abundance and inexpensive. Very few new zigzag fences are built because they consume an enormous amount of expensive material and also because their rambling design wastes acreage. Nevertheless, it is a distinctive fence and may be exactly the statement you want to make.

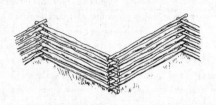

FENCE VARIETIES

Requirements	Favorite Options
Decoration	Virginia Zigzag Picket
Post and Rail	(two-rail variety) Boards
Deflection of	
Wind, Noise	Solid Boards
People	Chain Link
Domestic Animal	
Management:	
Cows	Wire: Barbed, Electric, or Woven
Horses	Boards
Sheep, hogs, goats	Woven Wire or Electric

SPLIT-RAIL FENCE

A much more economical approach to the use of material came with the development of techniques for splitting timber into rails. Two- or three-rail fences are handsome and serve as very sturdy enclosures. Unfortunately, the posts need extra work. Holes must be chiseled or drilled through the fence posts at heights corresponding to the desired rail levels. To avoid the tough job of making holes in fence posts, an alternative method is to use two posts at each position instead of one. A horizontal connection between the two posts is made with a pin or a dowel to hold up the rails.

This type of fence will be more expensive than woven wire, barbed wire, or electric unless you can make your own rails.

THE BOARD FENCE

With the increasing availability of machined boards and nails, the board fence has become more popular. Painted or unpainted, a board fence is the aristocrat of the fencing world. It can be seen surrounding horse pastures or dressing up estates like an elegant frame on a masterpiece. Horses will need a six-foot high fence with fewer horizontal boards. A decorative fence need not be as high.

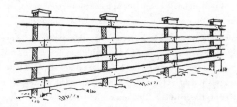

The cost of board fencing will be more than for split rail or electric fencing but probably less than woven wire fencing.

BARBED WIRE FENCE

The invention of barbed wire was one of the major events of the 19th century. Joseph Glidden gets a lot of the credit for the invention, but the first patent was given to Michael Kelly in 1868. Glidden popularized barbed wire by perfecting an easy way to manufacture it. By 1900 there were at least 1,000 different designs with many clever wire weaves and points. Old barbed wire "cuts" (eighteen-inch lengths) are extremely valuable collector's items today. Despite that history of a large variety of types of barbed wire, today there are fewer than six standard styles. A 16 1/2 -gauge two-point wire is the favorite for cattle owners, who use three to five strands of it. It is effective, economical, and durable. A barbed wire fence costs less than split rails, boards, or woven wire but probably more than electric fencing.

WOVEN WIRE FENCE

Woven wire makes a very gentle yet formidable fence. It is simply a net of wire with no sharp features. It can be used for all kinds of livestock and is particularly good for sheep because it has no barbs to catch the wool. It has a tight grid pattern close to the ground that makes it ideal for containing small animals such as hogs. Its height of four feet makes it quite adequate for cows and horses. Because woven wire has no electric shock or barbs to discourage animals, it may be subject to more stress than other types of fence. To discourage larger animals from leaning over the fence and bending it, string a strand of barbed wire along the top of the post above the woven wire.

As with barbed wire, there are variables to consider. In addition to choosing the gauge and the protective coating, you must choose the type of grid pattern you want. You need to understand how to decipher the code number. The last two numbers tell you the height of the fence in inches, and first two numbers tell you the total number of horizontal wires in the pattern. For example:

Style 1155. The fence is fifty-five inches tall and there are eleven wires.

Style 726. Stands twenty-six inches with seven wires.

ELECTRIC FENCES

For many years barbed wire had no competition as the most economical and popular type of livestock fencing. Like barbed wire, electric fencing was another United States invention that found its way around the world. After being patented here, it was exported to New Zealand in 1937. Today, ironically, New Zealand and Australia are two of the major suppliers of electric fencing materials to the United States.

To be truly effective, livestock should learn to respect the electric wire. Feed should be placed around and under a live wire so that the animal will contact it once or twice and learn to avoid it in the future.

PICKET FENCES

The all-American white picket fence carries all the neatness and formality of white gloves. Construction of a handsome picket fence requires patience, precision, and an attention to detail such as constantly measuring little distances and checking alignments with a bubble level. The designs of pre-cut pickets available in most lumber yards are quite limited. With a little extra effort and imagination, you can customize a picket top and have it cut out by a lumber yard. You could also do it yourself with a C clamp and a saber saw.

The cost of constructing a picket fence is roughly comparable to that of a split-rail fence. The picket fence is mainly a decorative item. Its low height and openness make it a friendly and attractive boundary statement that deflects wandering pets and people but not motivated intruders. The picket fence also seems to have a unique capacity for unlimited absorption of all of the creativity that you can give it.

How to Select the Right Tools

Some of the tools used in constructing fences are simple and yet ingenious. You should be familiar with the ones listed below so that you can make your fencing job as easy as possible.

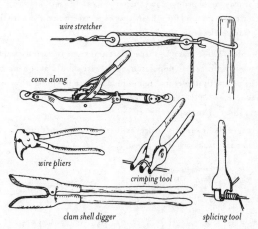

wire stretcher
come along
wire pliers
crimping tool
clam shell digger
splicing tool

The metal post driver. A metal post is very hard to hit with a sledgehammer because the top is so small. The metal post driver is a heavy pipe welded on the sides so that you can pick it up and drop it a few times on the fence post. If you have trouble finding one to buy, you can have one welded for you locally.

Fence pliers/staple puller. This tool can do a million things. It can grasp wire, cut it, or twist it. It can dig out staples or hammer them in. It can even be used as a lever to stretch wire.

Continued ➜

Wire stretcher/splicer. This is a device that has a greater leverage than pliers for the job of stretching a strand of wire. One end connects to the wire and the other attaches to a tree or dummy post for wire stretching or attaches to another wire for splicing.

Come along. When stretching the multiple strands of wire in a woven wire fence, a comealong can be very useful. One or two of these can be attached to the dummy post or tree and then connected to the wire which has been clamped between two bolted boards. Two come alongs make it much easier to distribute the tension between the top and the bottom of the fence, especially with bigger sizes of woven wire.

Wire splicer. This simple tool allows you to wind wire around itself easily. Some have holes with varying diameters to accommodate varying gauges of wire.

Nails. The most frequently used nails in fencing operations are called "common" nails and "box" nails. The common nails are sturdier. Both can be obtained with a galvanized coating which prevents rusting.

Carpenter's level. This metal device is at least one foot long. It has two bubble tubes set at 90 degrees from each other.

Plumb bob. This is a metal weight suspended on a string and is used to insure proper vertical alignment.

Wire Tighteners.

- **Crimping tool.** These funny-looking pliers deform wire in an attempt to tighten it. By making a straight wire wavy, they can take the sag out of the fences. The crimps, however, may not last very long and soon you may be back where you started. This device may be quite useful on older wire that can't take much bending or twisting.

- **Wire reels (Reel-tight).** The sagging wire can be wound around a pair of metal fingers until the desired tightness is reached. These sturdy metal prongs come in many sizes and are a very fast, effective method for eliminating sags, except in older wire that may break easily.

Staples. These sharp U-shaped fasteners come in various lengths and gauges. Contrary to popular practice, wire should not be mashed into the post with staples, but rather held close to the posts allowing for some movement of the wire. For very hard wood posts, such as locust, use very short, thin staples.

Hinges. Four kinds of hinges are used for light, medium, heavy, and very heavy tasks involving gates.

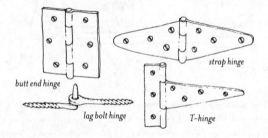

butt end hinge

lag bolt hinge

strap hinge

T-hinge

- **Butt end hinges** are used primarily for light jobs. The leaves of this hinge attach to interfacing surfaces between the gate and the gate post.

- **The strap hinge** is designed for stronger work and attaches to the front surface of both the gate and the gate post.

- **The T-hinge** is a hybrid of the first two.

- **The lag-bolt strap hinge system** is the most useful for very heavy tasks.

Latches and bolts. There are many different ways to close gates. The most common ones are thumb latches and dead bolts.

Hand auger. This device allows one or two people to drill a beautifully cylindrical hole every time. The principle of this tool is the same as the corkscrew.

Power auger. This machine replaces people power with horsepower. Renting one of these hole-diggers for a day can save an enormous amount of time and backache, although the motorized nature of this tool does move you out of the frontiersman class temporarily.

Clam shell digger. This device is basically two narrow shovels hinged together. With the long handles held together, the clam digger is jammed into the soil. Sharp blades help a great deal here. Then the handles are pushed apart, trapping dirt between the blades. With a little twisting action, the unit is pulled out of the ground with its plug of dirt. The maneuver is repeated several times until you have created a nice, narrow, cylindrical hole about two feet deep. At this point, you can deepen the hole with your long iron bar, thrusting and stirring. The beauty of this technique is that it leaves the surrounding soil undisturbed, ready to be compressed by the driven post.

How to Use the Best Construction Technique

Good construction technique starts with stable, long-lasting fence posts. The steps involved vary with the type of fence you choose to build.

THE VIRGINIA RAIL FENCE

1. Lay out the fence with stakes and twine.

2. Set each bottom rail on solid flat rocks or concrete to keep it off the ground so it will not decay as quickly.

3. Lay adjacent rails at a 130-degree angle with an overlap of approximately one foot.

4. Continue stacking the rails one row at a time.

5. If the fence is not circular, the rails in the first and last sections can be set on the ground in a fan pattern, set in a mortised end post, or held between a pair of end posts supported on dowels.

THE SPLIT RAIL FENCE

Splitting the Timber. The first technique to master with this type of fence is splitting rails. It is usually possible to divide a fifteen-inch timber into four pieces quite easily. If you can then divide each of these poles in half again to get a total of eight poles, that's great. If you push to get sixteen poles you may end up with stockade fencing instead of split rails.

1. Some people advocate notching the butt end of the timber with a chainsaw along each of the diagonals that you intend to split. This step is not essential, but helpful.

2. Drive a steel wedge into the notch until splitting starts.

3. Drive additional wedges into the log until it splits. Continue splitting pieces to get four or eight rails.

4. Repeat the process with the remaining timbers.

Mortising the Posts. Making slots through the posts to accept the rails is called mortising. It should be done before setting the posts in the ground. A two-rail fence, with two mortises per pole, is most common.

1. Mark the area of the wood to be removed. Measure down from the tops of the poles.

2. Use a two-inch drill to remove most of the wood, then complete the job with a mallet and chisel.

3. Taper the ends of the rails so they will fit together in the mortise. They can be overlapped either vertically or horizontally.

Setting out the Fence.

1. Plan on setting posts about two feet closer together than the length of the rails—six feet apart if you are using eight-foot rails.

2. Set one post firmly in place. Put the second post in the hold at the proper depth, so rails will be parallel to the ground. Put the two rails in position in both posts, get a tight fit of the rails, then tamp the second post into position. Repeat this process, each time putting rails in the second post before tamping it into position.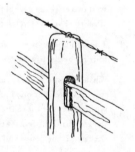

3. Heavy animals will rub against rails, loosen them, and eventually knock them down. To halt this, run a strand of barbed wire across the top rail.

THE BOARD FENCE

1. Plan on setting posts a distance apart that equals half the length of the boards—six feet apart for twelve-foot boards, for example. In that way, each board is supported by three posts.

2. Arrange the boards so that each line post will support the center of some boards and the junctions of others.

3. Mark each post at the points where the top of each board will cross it.

4. As with the split-rail fence, place the first post firmly in position, then put the second in the hole at the proper depth, but don't tamp it into position until you've measured its exact position with the boards that will be nailed to it.

5. Place the boards on the same side of the posts as the livestock. This way the fence will be supported by the posts as well as the nails.

6. Nail the boards in place, being careful not to split the wood by nailing too close to the edge of the board. Also, stagger the pattern of nails so that they are not all in the same vertical line, to avoid splitting the posts.

7. Nail a small batten vertically over the board junctions at each line post for additional support and trim.

8. The top of each board should be beveled to shed water. A small block of wood can be used to cap each post, or an additional board can be run along the top of the beveled post. This creates an excellent "roof" for the posts.

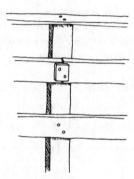

THE BARBED WIRE FENCE

The principal job is to stretch the wire from the first to the last post in a straight line and then staple the wire on the posts in the middle. The posts in the middle don't contribute to the tightness of the wire; they keep it at the right height and provide stability in any situation that puts stress on the fence.

1. Set posts eight feet apart and brace the end posts. In some situations where stress on the fence will be slight, posts can be placed as much as sixteen feet apart.

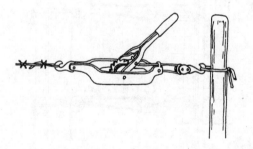

2. Wind barbed wire around the first post and then wind it around itself, using the wire splicer.

3. Unroll the wire around the inside (your property side) of the line posts. This is easier if two people hold the ends of a crowbar which has been inserted through the hole of a bale of barbed wire, then walk down the fence line, letting the wire unreel.

Continued ➡

4. Go beyond the last post to a dummy post or a tree which is in line with the line posts.

5. Attach the wire stretcher to the dummy post, then attach it to the barbed wire.

6. Stretch the wire cautiously by working the stretcher. Don't use a motor vehicle to stretch barbed wire.

7. The wire has two strands. Cut one of them about two feet past the last post and remove any barbs.

8. Wind that strand around the post and then around itself. This allows the single wire strand on the stretcher to hold the tension of the whole line of the barbed wire while you are securing the other strand to the post.

9. Cut the remaining strand and repeat the wiring process.

10. Staple the wire to the line post. Avoid setting the staple legs in a straight vertical line because the post may split. Don't try to make the staple squish the wire into the post because this weakens the wire and ruins its protective coating.

THE WOVEN WIRE FENCE

1. Set up a braced end post and line posts set eight feet apart.

2. Unroll the fence along the inside of the posts.

3. Make sure that the narrow grid portion is on the bottom of the fence posts.

4. Wrap each horizontal wire around the post and then around itself.

5. Do the top horizontal wire first, then the bottom horizontal wire, then the middle ones. You may have to cut a few vertical lines in order to get enough wire to work with. When the fence is fastened securely to the initial post, unroll the entire length of the fence.

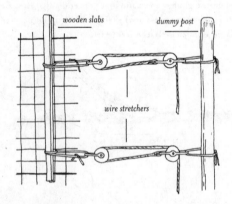

wooden slabs   *dummy post*

wire stretchers

6. Go beyond the braced end post to a dummy post or a tree and set up your wire stretchers. One way to do this is to bolt wooden slabs together through the fence and pull on the slabs with one or two or more wire stretchers or a come-along. Using the wooden slabs distributes the tension more evenly along the fencing and helps to avoid breaking the wire.

7. Stretch the fence carefully. Most woven fencing has built-in kinks along the horizontal wires. These help to maintain tightness. When you stretch the wire out, don't pull the wire so hard that you straighten out these kinks. Stop at the point where they just start to flatten a little. A few loosely placed staples holding the top wire to the line posts will hold the fence in the right position as you stretch. When the fencing is in place, start connecting it to the end anchor post, the one nearest the stretchers. Free enough of the central horizontal wire so that you can wrap it around the post and then around itself. Next, repeat the procedure with the horizontal wire halfway between the central wire and the top wire. The next wire to attach is the one that is halfway between the central wire and the bottom wire. Then do the remaining horizontal wires, saving the top one for last.

8. Go to each of the line posts and staple in the horizontal wires.

THE PICKET FENCE

1. Plan the distance and materials on paper as discussed previously.

2. Place stakes in the ground at post sites six feet apart and then dig the holes.

3. Set the posts two feet deep on gravel and surround with concrete.

4. Check all alignments.

5. Wait two or three days before continuing the fence in order to allow the concrete to cure.

6. The wooden posts most commonly used measure four inches by four inches by five feet and have been treated with preservatives.

7. While you wait, cut the rails and the stringers and the pickets. A typical picket is one inch by three inches by three feet. The typical stringer is two inches by four inches. There are several ways to build the framework to hold the pickets. An easy method that avoids the dados and mortise joints calls for butt ending stringers along the tops of the posts with a mitered joint at each corner. The lower stringer should be supported by blocks and toenails.

8. Attach the pickets to the framework using a spacer bar that is a little narrower than the pickets. If the pickets are three inches wide, the spacer should be approximately two inches wide. Hang the cleated spacer bar  from the top stringer to determine the exact place for each picket to be nailed. Use galvanized nails. When nailing the picket, it is helpful to also run a temporary board between the posts at the level of the bottom of the picket. This board keeps the bottom of the pickets on a level and will thus keep the tops aligned. Check the alignment frequently with the bubble level.

THE ELECTRIC FENCE

1. Establish sturdy corner posts that are braced.

2. Set a fence post every 150 feet if the terrain is level. If the land is uneven or if you can identify any area that must withstand unusual animal stress, use posts more frequently.

3. Unroll the wire from a flat reel set in the ground to work like a lazy susan. If you plan to have more than one strand of electrified fence, work with one strand at a time to avoid getting tangled up. The thinner the wire you choose, the tougher it is for your animals to see it. Make it noticeable by tying bright plastic ribbons on it, especially if it is sixteen gauge or thinner and you're only using one strand.

4. Attach the wire to the corner post with an end insulator.

5. Attach the wire to all the other insulators on the posts or on offset brackets, making sure the wire is allowed to slide freely at all points. If you are using one strand, set it thirty-six inches above ground. If you're using two strands, set one at seventeen inches and one at thirty-six inches.

6. Attach springs to the wire, if desired. Then by winding wire tighteners, the tension from the springs can be brought to about 200 pounds.

7. Use spring-loaded plastic handles at each gate area.

8. Plant the grounding rods properly. Then attach the controller to both the grounding rods and the fence wire.

How to Construct Workable Gates

Regardless of the style of fence you construct, you will need at least one gate. Figure on four feet for entering lawn equipment; up to sixteen feet for farm equipment. There are three areas that must be given careful attention in gate building to avoid big mistakes.

- Foremost, the support post must be sturdy.

- The post itself should be bigger, taller, and set deeper than the remaining line posts. It is not uncommon to use a 6 x 6 or 8 x 8 preservative-treated post set at least three feet deep in a collar of concrete and braced well to an adjacent post.

- The gate must be hung properly. Sagging gates are ugly and irritating to use. If the gate is supported by blocks and guy wires while it is being hung, you won't have to fight the gate while attaching it to the rest of the fence. Flimsy hinges, improper bracing, and poor alignment can all be avoided easily.

- The gate must be structurally sound. A gate must be as light as possible and yet strong. This is the reason aluminum gates are so popular with farmers.

- A satisfactory wooden gate can be constructed with less cost by using good quality, dry, strong, pressure-treated wood, using correct bracing techniques, using the appropriate hardware, and by following the simple construction steps listed below.

Basic Gate Construction

1. Make sure you have very strong gate posts as mentioned previously for wide (twelve to sixteen feet) hanging gates. You may want to use a very tall gate post so that you can add support to the gate by running a cable from the top of the post to the latch side of the gate and tightening it with a turnbuckle.

2. Measure the opening for the gate. Measure it from top to bottom on both sides and measure the distance between the gate posts at the top and at the bottom to make sure that the gate is constructed as a true rectangle.

3. Working on a flat surface, construct a frame for the gate that is one inch shorter than the horizontal measurement made in the previous step so that the gate can swing without interruption. Using pressure-treated two-by-fours, make dado joints or rabbet joints for the corners. Also block these joints and use large wood screws.

4. Brace this basic frame with a strong diagonal strut. The alignment of this supporting structure is very important. The low end of this bracing bar must be placed on the hinged side of the gate, allowing the high end to be attached to the left side. For additional support, a cable and turnbuckle can also be used. To be effective, this system must be set on the opposite diagonal from the wooden brace.

   Following the placement of these bracing systems, the corners of the gate should be blocked with rectangular or triangular pieces of wood.

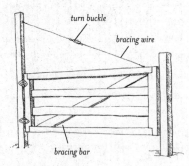

turn buckle

bracing wire

bracing bar

5. Nail the pickets or boards or other fencing trim in the proper pattern to match the remaining fence.

6. Set the gate on blocks in the same position you want it to be when you finish. Wire it into place temporarily with guy wires if necessary.

7. Attach the hinges by using large wood screws to attach the gate-side hinged leaf first. You should choose the largest wood screws that will go through the holes of the hinges but not through to the back side of the wood. Gates are usually too heavy for butt hinges, so strap hinges are usually used. For large gates, you will get much more long-lasting support from a lag and strap hinge system.

8. Attach the gate post hinge leaf with similar screws.

9. Undo the guy wires and remove the blocks. If necessary, trim the end of the gate so that it can swing freely for attaching the latch.

10. Set the latch or bolt system of your choice.

11. Place a stop-board on the post behind the latch.

Continued ➜

How to Build Safely

Fencing materials and tools can be very dangerous. Barbs are sharp, electricity can kill, one strand of wire under tension can snap back with enough force to cripple you. Here is a list of some basic fencing dos and don'ts to remember.

DON'TS

- Don't carry staples in your mouth.
- Don't steady a post with your hands while someone else hits the top of it with a sledgehammer.
- Don't wear loose clothing around power augers and barbed wire.
- Don't let your feet or legs stay in the arc of the swing when you are pounding posts into the ground—just in case you miss.
- Don't shortcut a good controller in your electric fencing.
- Don't work with fencing materials in a lightning storm.
- Don't stretch wire with a tractor. If it breaks you are in big trouble.
- Don't try to clear the weeds and brush beneath a wire fence by burning it. The fire may weaken the posts and ruin the protective zinc coating on the wire.

DOS

- Wear some eye protection, especially when hammering staples into very hard wood, hitting a metal post with a metal maul, or breaking up rock in a post hole.
- Anticipate the whipping action of wire, especially when stretching a new line of wire or when unstapling an old line.
- Stay on the side of the post away from the wire.
- Avoid getting chemicals from treated fence posts onto your skin or into your eyes.
- Place a grounding rod somewhere along non-electric fencing unless you are using metal fence posts.
- Always wear gloves.

Building Stone Walls

Charles McRaven

Illustrations by Carl Kirkpatrick, Carolyn Bucha, Doug Merriles, and Brigita Fuhrmann

Why Build Stone Walls?

Why stone? Well, a better question might be, why not? For building or landscaping, you simply can't do better. Stone is weatherproof, ratproof, insectproof, and long lived. Stone is quietly elegant and looks expensive; whether you use it in rustic or formal designs, it signifies good taste.

Getting to Know Stone

The stone you choose to work with should match the environment in which you are placing it. Your stone should match native stone; if you can't find any native stone to work with, look for some that matches it as closely as possible.

SANDSTONE AND QUARTZITE

Sandstones and quartzites are the most versatile building stones. They range from coarse, soft, crumbly rocks to dense, fine-grained creek quartzites so hard that they ring when struck.

Sandstone is a good stone to learn on because it cuts well, occurs in layers, and is porous enough to age quickly after shaping. It comes in as many colors as sand itself—grays, browns, whites, roses, and blues (the most common, though, are grays and browns)—and is composed of fine sand particles fused together under great pressure. Many sandstones have a definite grain along them that can be split easily. Therefore, sandstone is best laid flat, the way it was formed. Set on edge, it may weather in such a way that the layers separate. The sandstone you may have access to could be soft or hard, weak or strong. In mortared work, the stone should be at least as hard as the mortar.

Sandstone usually splits into even thicknesses in nature, so the critical top and bottom surfaces are already formed. If any shaping is necessary, it may be nothing more than a bit of nudging on the face of each stone to give an acceptable appearance. When making your selection, of course, try to find stones that are already well shaped, thereby keeping any necessary shaping to a minimum. Any sandstone can be worked to the shape you desire, but there's a logical limit. If you spend all your available time shaping, then efficiency plummets.

LIMESTONE

Limestone has always been a favorite stone for builders. Dense but not hard, it can be worked to almost any shape. Before concrete blocks were invented (around 1900), limestone was the accepted standard for commercial stonework.

Newly cut limestone has a slick surface that is unattractive; weathered, top-of-the-ground limestone, on the other hand, is often rough, fissured, pockmarked, and interesting.

GRANITE

Granites are generally rough-textured stones that are not naturally layered. When weathered, their exterior provides a welcoming environment for lichens and mosses. Strong and hard granites vary in color. Along the East Coast, the familiar light gray granite is plentiful. Formed principally of feldspar and quartz, it's a favored landscaping stone. There are also dark blue, dark gray, greenish, and even pink granites.

If you use granite, try to find stones naturally endowed with the desired shapes, as they can be hard to shape. Granite can often be recycled from foundations, chimneys, and basements of abandoned buildings.

STONES TO AVOID

Shale, slate, and other soft, layered stones are not very good as building stones. Other odd stones, such as the hard and flashy quartz, are hard to work with and rarely look natural.

> **WORKING WITH MIXED LOTS**
>
> If you have a limited supply of stones, try mixing types to give added texture to a wall and keep it from visually fading into the landscape.

THE BEST STONE FOR MORTARLESS WALLS

In drystone work—that is, stonework without mortar—both sandstone and limestone are ideal because of their evenly layered strata. The more bricklike the stones are in shape, the easier it is to lay drystone. And with the inevitable sprouting of plants from the crevices, these walls age well.

Finding a Source for Good Stone

Before you can work with stone, you have to get the stuff. And where you get it depends a lot on where you happen to be. However, whether you plan on buying stone from a stone lot or want to head out into the back woods of your property to collect loose rock, there are four points to remember that will simplify your task:

- Because one criterion for good stone is that it be as native to the environment as possible, start your search close to home.

- Especially when you're prospecting, look for usable shapes, such as a flat top and bottom, with the appearance you're looking for on what will be the stone's face. When you find some, there'll usually be more of the same nearby, because stone tends to fracture naturally along the same lines in a given area.

- If a stone looks doubtful for laying, pass it up. Bring home only the very best—you'll still have a lot of rejects. Every stone will fit somewhere, but not necessarily where and when you want it. It's not worth the added weight to haul a rock you won't use.

- If you're looking for a particular type of stone, seek the help of your state geology or mineral resource headquarters. Field geologists map stone underlayment and can tell you where certain stones occur.

RULES OF ETIQUETTE FOR PRIVATE LANDS

Excerpted from *Natural Stonescapes*, by Richard L. Dubé and Frederick C. Campbell (Storey Books, 1999)

There are many sources of stones on private lands. However, there are also some important standards of etiquette that you must be aware of before venturing out into the countryside on a stone-collecting mission:

1. Don't trespass. Ask the landowners for permission to explore the property.

2. Communicate with the landowners. Share with them what you are doing. The more they know, the more apt they are to let you onto their property.

3. Leave the site in better shape than you found it. For example, repair your ruts.

4. Never take more than you need.

5. Do not mark stone with spray paint; use a chalk or removeable marker, such as ribbon.

6. Be careful not to remove stones that could initiate or exacerbate an erosion problem.

7. Pay a fair price for the stones. This will vary by region and stone availability. You can find out what's a fair price by checking in with a local stone center, pit, or stone broker (a person who buys stone for redistribution to masons, stone centers, and landscape contractors).

When dismantling an old stone wall, to the greatest extent possible watch out for, and try to avoid disturbing, its inhabitants.

BUYING STONE FROM COMMERCIAL VENDORS

Stone yards are an obvious place to begin. Most mine local stone for riprap (irregular stone used for fill) and crush it for roadway gravel. But they usually also import fieldstone and quarried stone for veneer, paths, patios, and solid stonework. Newly quarried stone is fresh and sterile and will look that way for many years. Fieldstone, which is found on top of the ground, will be weathered, often with lichens, and have a patina of age.

PROSPECTING FOR STONE IN THE WILDS

Fields and byways, woods and country roadsides provide plenty of rocks lying on top of the ground. That's where the quarries get their fieldstone. Go prospecting, but remember that the stone you find already belongs to someone; check with the landowners and get permission to remove it. You will need a pickup—even a flatbed truck if you will be transporting large stones—and one or two helpers, depending on the size of the stones.

It's cheaper to find your own stone than to buy it at the quarry. It's more work, too, but it gives you an excuse to get out into the country. So lay a sheet of plywood in the bed of your pickup truck to protect it, and have fun prospecting.

Please note: You absolutely must have permission from the local forest service or park management before removing stones from public land.

Tools and Techniques for Handling Stone

Even in this high-tech age, most stoneworkers still pick up, load, stack, select, shape, and place stone by hand. In a single day, a mason may handle 10 tons (9,000 kg) of stone, one stone at a time, and many of the same stones several times.

Incorrect lifting

Correct lifting

Continued →

MOVING AND LIFTING

With a substance as unforgiving as stone, it is hard to overemphasize the importance of lifting properly. Learn to *squat and lift with your legs*. If you can't do it that way, don't do it at all. When in doubt, use heavy equipment to move and place stones.

For those stones you decide you can lift, the procedure is simple. Grab the stone in what would be a normal position, and then drop your rear another 2 feet (60 cm). When lifting, hug the stone close. It's a lot easier on your back and arms.

The wheelbarrow will be your handiest tool for moving small- to medium-size stones. You can lay it on its side, slide a stone in, and stand the wheelbarrow up by yourself to move it. (You may, however, need help laying the stone when you get it where you want it.) On rocky or steep ground, load the wheelbarrow back near the handles. You'll lift more, but the wheel will go over obstacles better. With the weight on the wheel, it's harder to push; even a pebble can stop you.

To load a large stone, lay the wheelbarrow on its side, slide the stone in, and pull the wheelbarrow upright.

You can also use simple plank "slides" to push heavy stones from the ground up to truck beds or the top of a wall. Just make sure the bottom of the plank is well anchored, set the top of the plank on the desired destination at a relatively low angle, and push the stone up the plank, flipping it end over end. For large stones with a nice flat base, you can even place rollers between the stone and the plank, which will allow you to simply slide the stone up the plank.

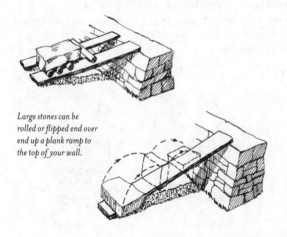

Large stones can be rolled or flipped end over end up a plank ramp to the top of your wall.

MOVING THE BIG ONES

For really big stones (those requiring more than two people to handle), you may want to use machinery. This includes everything from a single pry bar, block and tackle, or come-along (a hand-operated ratchet hoist) to an electric winch, a hydraulically activated boom mounted on a truck, a hydraulic jack, or a tractor with bucket. It depends on where you are and how much room you have to maneuver. Unlike big commercial construction sites with flat, uncluttered access, most stone-gathering and stone-laying sites are among trees, on sloping ground, or against walls, where there is little room.

Lifting and loading devices for large stones are many and ingenious. You will seldom have heavy equipment out in the woods where you find stone, but you can rig a tripod, even if there are no trees handy. Make it tall, of doubled 2-by-4s about 12 feet (3.7 m) long. Wrap chain around the apex and hold it in place with some 20-penny spikes. Hook a come-along into this chain and wrap another chain around the stone. Set the legs of the tripod far enough apart to allow your pickup truck to back between. Lift the stone, back under it with the truck, and let the stone down. The process isn't fast, but a large stone will cover more area than several smaller ones and will look better, too.

One of the simplest loading devices is a small swiveling crane that mounts in a corner of a pickup bed. It is raised by a simple hydraulic jack and will lift more weight than you should subject the average pickup to. You can block under the rear bumper and load large stones with this little crane, but watch the limits of mounting bolts and braces.

You don't have to use big stones at all, but the stonemason's adage that a small one takes just as long to lay as a big one is largely true. And big stones look good. Generally, your work will be just fine with maximum two-person rocks, which can easily be 2-foot (60 cm) expanses and maybe 6 inches (15 cm) thick.

As you work with various stones, you'll come up with your own ingenious devices for getting them into place. In general, you can move small quantities of stone by hand in the time it takes to set up machinery. If you're in reasonable physical shape and don't overdo it, you can get by with a wheelbarrow and pickup truck. If you do a lot of work, consider the advantages of more equipment. Stonemasons are a lot like anglers and mechanics, though—they collect all sorts of tools they rarely use. Unless you plan to do a great deal of stonework, don't bother investing in expensive machinery.

Staying Safe

Safety equipment is essential. Use a hard hat, goggles, gloves, steel-toed boots, and a dust mask around stone. Sand, chips, and dust are always around. And no matter how careful you are, use goggles; a stone chip will eventually fly straight at your face.

Gloves help keep your hands from getting scratched, but not your fingers from getting smashed. (Your toes will be more fortunate if you encase them in steel-toed boots.) Your hands do get rough without gloves, and in winter tend to crack, chap, and bleed no matter how much lotion you use.

Safety goggles and sturdy work gloves are essential for stonework.

Cutting and Shaping Stone

Good fieldstone masons will only true up—that is, make level or plumb—the shapes they find, not try to create new ones. A long, triangle-faced stone might get its corners chipped to match others in a wall. Or a curved edge could get straightened for a better fit in a ledge pattern. A thick stone might need to be split for veneer work—and if you're lucky, you'll get two stones. Minimal shaping is always recommended, because newly cut stone faces glare from an aged wall. It takes years for these fresh cuts to blend in, so try to avoid them where they will show.

USING A HAMMER AND CHISEL

To cut a corner off a stone, lay the stone on something soft to absorb the shock. Sand in a box is good, or use a table padded with old rugs. Try to get the work area elevated to about counter height (36 inches; 90 cm). Bending down to work at ground level is hard.

To mark the cut you want, make a series of light hits with a striking hammer on a stone chisel, then go over this line again, this time striking harder. After about the third pass, turn the stone over and mark that side, too. Repeat the procedure, using more force with each repetition. If you're working near the edge of the stone, lean the chisel out a bit to direct it into the mass of the stone. (If you hold it perpendicular, the stone will tend to chip off instead of breaking all the way through.)

Remember that a light tap will tend to chip the stone out toward the edge; a heavier hit will crack it deeper, usually closer to where you want it. Sometimes the stone will break toward the edge anyway, leaving a ridge on the edge face. Slope the chisel sharply, just enough for it to bite into the surface, striking into the mass near the ridge. Take off small chips from both sides this way until you have dressed the surfaces sufficiently. Ideally, the stone will break all the way through from marked line to line, but don't count on it the first few thousand times.

A large stone-breaking maul, which has an edge to it, will create small stones from big ones. Use a 12-pounder (5.4 kg) for this if there's no way to utilize big stones as they are. Hit the line lightly, as with the chisel, then go back over it harder. You'll have to smooth your breaks afterward with the hammer and chisel, because the maul gives you approximates only. Splitting sedimentary stones, such as sandstone and limestone, is quick with a maul if your aim is good. It's a lot like splitting wood, but it doesn't go quite as quickly.

THE ELUSIVE "PERFECT FIT"

Masons have always been fascinated by cutting mortises and steps in stones for the perfect fit. It's rarely worth the time it takes, and too often a stone breaks after hours of shaping. Try to use the spaces between stones creatively rather than going for a tight fit every time. Often, you can proceed much more efficiently if you lay a stone that leaves a space you can fill with a shim or chip.

The dry-stack look requires closer fitting and therefore more shaping. Dry-stack is mortared stone, but none of the mortared joints shows, so it looks like tightly laid dry-stone work. Sometimes it will allow more chips and shims, sometimes not. If large stones are required for a job, there are just two solutions: Search more or shape more.

For a tight fit at the edges, you may have to take down a hump. To do this, stand the stone on edge and dress the offending surface with a chisel or a stone point, which is just what it sounds like: a chisel that comes to a point. It is used to chip off bits of stone. Slow; but it works.

The most important thing to remember about shaping stones: Don't attempt it unless you must. If you have a lot of extra stone, you may be able to find the right fit, even if you must use two or more to fill the gap. You'll find cutting frustrating enough to want to avoid it, even with easily shaped sandstone. If you're using harder stones, like granites, just find the right ones.

Building a Drystone Wall

A freestanding drystone wall is the simplest and most attractive structure you can build of stone. There's no footing, no mortar, no cracking with freezing. If you use stones gathered from the top of the ground, they'll have lichens and an aged appearance. So a new drystone wall will look as if it's centuries old.

Building a basic drystone wall means simply placing stones on top of other stones, with some intelligent constraints. (If it falls down, for instance, it isn't a wall.) A freestanding drystone wall should have stones on each face that slope inward against each other. Each stone, if possible, should push against its neighbor in a controlled situation that doesn't let either move. Thus, the stone in drystone walls stays in place without mortar because gravity and friction hold it in place—if it has been laid properly.

MATERIALS AND TOOLS

To build a freestanding wall, 3 feet (90 cm) high and 2 feet (60 cm) thick, you'll need the following:

Materials

1 ton (0.9 t) of relatively flat (tops and bottoms) stones, 6–24 inches (15–60 cm) wide and 2–6 inches (5–15 cm) thick, for every 3 feet (90 cm) of wall length

Tools

Stone chisel	*Tape*
Striking hammer	*4-foot (1.2 m) level*
Mason's hammer	*Pry bar (straight or crowbar)*

STONE BY WEIGHT AND VOLUME

One ton (0.9 t) of stone makes about 3 running feet (90 cm) of stone wall, 3 feet (90 cm) high and 2 feet (60 cm) thick. You can buy a ton of stone at a stone and gravel yard or some home and garden centers. If you gather stone in the field, a ton of stone is about 17.5 cubic feet (3.5 by 5 by 1 feet, or 1.1 by 1.5 by 0.3 m) or a full-size pickup truck loaded about 6 inches (15 cm) deep.

STEP 1: DIG A TRENCH FOR THE BASE

The stability of a drystone wall is based on gravity; the stones lean into each other, thereby holding each other in place. How do you get the stones in your wall to slope inward? Dig the topsoil at the base of the wall into a shallow trench that's 24 inches (60 cm) wide and 4 to 6 inches (10 to 15 cm) deep, but with a slight V-slope; it should thus be about 2 inches (5 cm) deeper in the center. Keep the ditch level lengthwise; if the ground slopes, step the trench to keep it level.

Continued →

STEP 2: LAY THE FIRST COURSE OF STONES

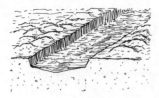

The trench should form a slight V-shape.

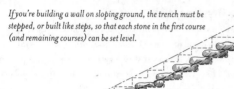

If you're building a wall on sloping ground, the trench must be stepped, or built like steps, so that each stone in the first course (and remaining courses) can be set level.

Walls are built in courses, or layers. To lay the first one, place stones along the bottom of the trench in pairs, with each sloping toward the center. Use stones that have a relatively even outside edge and that reach approximately to the center of the trench. If a stone extends 2 to 3 inches (5–8 cm) past the center, adjust the soil for it, and use a narrower one opposite it. If both stones are short, fill the center space with broken stones.

Place uneven surfaces down on this first course, digging out as necessary. Leave as smooth a top surface as possible, matching stone heights.

Leave as smooth a surface as possible on the first course.

STEP 3: LAY THE REMAINING COURSES

Begin the next course with similar stones, taking care to cover the cracks between the first-layer stones. If you have spanned the 24-inch (60 cm) trench with one 15-inch (38 cm) stone on, say, the right side and a 9-inch (23 cm) one on the left, reverse this now. If the stones were 12 inches (30 cm) long (along the length of the wall), use shorter or larger ones on this second layer to avoid vertical running joints. Try to use stones of uniform thickness (height) in each course. Where this is impossible, use two thin ones alongside a thick one for an even height.

Span cracks in the first course with solid stone in the second course to avoid vertical running joints.

Place a 24-inch (60 cm) stone as a tie-stone (see the box below) across the width of the wall every 4 feet (1.2 m) along a course and in every third course in any given location in the wall. Because this will be seen on both wall faces, it should have relatively straight ends. Use the hammer and chisel, if necessary, to shape these faces.

When you use a tie-stone, it probably won't have a convenient dip in the middle, so you'll have to reestablish the V-slope with the next course. Tapered stones are the obvious answer, but you can also wedge up the outside edges with chips, or shims. These shims must not themselves be tapered, however, or they will gradually work their way out of the wall with the flexing and movement inherent to drystone work. Use thin rectangular chips from your shapings or break thin stones for shims. Properly laid, wedged-in shims and stones won't shift, even if they are used as steps, where they get jostled a lot.

wedge

Wedges help reestablish the sloping angle that holds the stones in place.

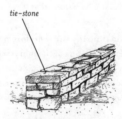
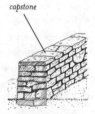

FIVE SECRETS FOR SUCCESS WITH A DRYSTONE WALL

1. **Establish an even plane.** The surface of a stone wall is never even, but if you establish a plane that you go back to often, the stones in the wall can jut out or be recessed without appearing sloppy. If you've been careful to align the outer edges of the stones in the wall, the tie-stone ends can vary in appearance and overhang without seeming out of place.

2. **Use step patterns on sloping ground.** When building a drystone wall that runs downhill, keep the stones level by removing the topsoil at the base of the wall in a stepped pattern (see preceeding page) and repeating this pattern with the capstones. Stones that slope or are laid at an angle will move over time, and even though it may take them a while to do this, you don't want your wall to fall down. Build it right the first time.

When working with a stepped base, the top of the wall must be stepped as well.

3. **Lay stones with their best edges out.** Lay the slightly sloped stones with their best edges out. If that leaves gaps in the center of the wall, fill these with rubble—that is, any scrap stone not usable otherwise. More than likely, your supply of neat stones with nice edges will be limited or nonexistent, so you'll have to shape at least one end for a face (see preceeding page).

4. **Work with thin stones.** It's simpler to build a drystone wall with thin stones; they're easier to handle and can be shaped more easily than thick ones.

5. **Avoid vertical running joints.** Always lay stones side by side with the top edge parallel to the ground, and make sure to cover the crack between them with a stone on the next course. If you don't, you'll have a running joint, or vertical crack, which will weaken the wall too much. A joint that is two courses deep is permissible but not desirable.

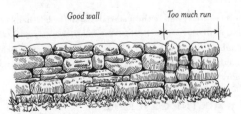

Good wall Too much run

Vertical running joints will compromise the strength and durability of your wall and should be avoided at all costs.

STEP 4: CAP THE TOP

Begin and end the wall vertically (A), or step it down to the ground (B). If the ground rises, keep the wall top level until it fades into the grade (C). Use as many tie-stones as possible for the top layer. These are called capstones, and they are easily dislodged unless they're large and heavy. The best stones should be saved for capstones, because piecing this top layer will make it unstable.

A

B

C

Building a Mortared Wall

A mortared wall seals out water and roots, does not flex appreciably with temperature changes, and is much stronger than a drystone wall. Properly laid on a footing and with joints raked 1/2 to 1 inch (13–25 mm) deep to let the stones stand out, a mortared wall is very attractive. It's more than a dry wall with cement in it, however. Because it cannot flex, mortared stonework must be set on a footing, or base, that extends below the frost line. The footing can be as high as the surface of the ground or as low as 6 inches (15 cm) below it. A footing, which is wider than the wall, distributes the wall's weight over a larger area, reducing its downward pressure. Building codes vary, but usually anything that calls for a foundation such as a footing requires a building permit.

A 3-foot-high (90 cm) mortared stone wall can be narrower than a comparable drystone wall; a width of 12 inches (30 cm) provides adequate stability for a straight wall. The footing should be twice the width of the wall thickness.

STORING CEMENT INGREDIENTS

Because of the time it takes to mix and pour, and the resulting small batches of concrete that you work with, you won't be able to mix and pour all of the cement required by a wall at once, so be sure to store Portland up off the ground, wrapped in plastic or under a roof. Don't secure the plastic to the ground or ground moisture will condense under it and get the cement wet. And don't store Portland for more than a month. There's often enough moisture in the air to start the chemical process of setting up, which you don't want until after you mix and pour.

Continued ➡

STEP 1: PREPARE A TRENCH FOR THE CONCRETE FOOTING

To lay a footing, you'll first need to dig a ditch 24 inches (60 cm) wide to below the frost line in your area. Building inspectors require that you set rebar grade stakes in the ditch to determine the thickness of the footing. Drive these in every 4 feet (1.2 m) or so, and level their top ends at the height to which you will fill the ditch with concrete. Use a 4-foot level, line level, water level, or transit for this. The inspector will want to see these set, along with step bulkheads and smooth, solid ditch bottoms and sharp ditch corners, before he or she will approve the pour.

STEP 2: CALCULATE HOW DEEP THE FOOTING SHOULD BE

The depth or thickness of the footing concrete is largely up to you, beyond the 6-inch (15 cm) minimum for a hypothetical 3-foot-high (90 cm) wall. It is commonplace to lay concrete blocks below ground level on the footing instead of wasting good stones where they will not be seen. In our situation, it's actually cheaper to buy ready-mixed concrete and fill the ditch to ground level. Additional labor and materials to bring the wall up to the surface are too expensive.

LAYING GRAVEL FOOTINGS

Another type of footing that is much cheaper, but not as long lived or as strong, is a gravel footing. With this, you dig a ditch well below frost line but only as wide as your wall thickness. Then you dump in gravel or crushed stone to a minimum of 6 inches (15 cm) deep—but you must keep the top below frost line. Then level off and start laying stone.

The theory here is that water won't get into the wall and freeze, because the mortar seals it out. It doesn't freeze below the wall and cause it to buckle because it drains to below the frost line. And because the water soaks through the gravel and runs off quickly, the wall stays stable.

There are, however, two drawbacks to this kind of footing. It does nothing to distribute the weight of the wall, which can settle and crack. And eventually the gravel gets dirt washed into it, the water stops percolating through it, and the wall essentially sits on dirt. In addition, tree roots do a lot more damage when they can get under a wall this easily. But a gravel footing can serve you well for a long time, and given the expense of the concrete footing, a gravel-based wall may be the way to go.

If you're in a place a concrete truck can't access and you're mixing concrete for the footing by hand or in a mixer, however, the equation can change, especially if your wall is going to be a long one, in which case it may take too much concrete to fill the ditch that way. If you have lots of good stone, you can afford to hide some of the less-than-gorgeous pieces belowground. Keep in mind, though, that really misshapen stones hidden down there won't hold up the wall properly unless they're embedded in concrete.

QUICK TIP

If the wall runs up- or downhill, step it to keep it level. Step heights can vary, but because concrete blocks are commonly set on footings, most are 8 inches (20 cm) deep. Put steps in place using "bulkhead" boards set in grooves cut into the sides of the ditch and then braced with short pieces of reinforcing rod.

When working with a concrete footing on sloping ground, use boards to demarcate the steps in the trench.

The quantities given in the materials list in the left-hand column assume you will dig to 18 inches (45 cm) and fill to the grade. Of course, you can substitute 12-inch (30 cm) concrete blocks or stone below grade, on the footing. However, as noted above, it is quicker and not too much more expensive to fill the trench to grade.

STEP 3: MIX THE CONCRETE

You can buy ready-mixed concrete at most building supply and garden shops, but it tends to be slightly more expensive than mixing your own.

Cost versus convenience—it's your choice. If you're mixing your own, the basic mix is:

> 1 **part Portland cement**
>
> 2 **parts sand**
>
> Water
>
> 3 **parts gravel,** 1 **inch (2.5 cm) or less in size (what quarries call six-to-eights)**

Calculate how much footing you'll need before you start. At 2 feet (60 cm) wide and a minimum of 6 inches (15 cm) deep, you'll be mixing and pouring at least 1 cubic foot (28 cudm) per running foot of ditch. For a 50-foot (15 m) wall, that's a minimum of 50 cubic feet (1.4 cu m) of concrete (more, if it has steps in it), for which you'll need about 2 cubic yards (1.5 cu m) of gravel, allowing for spills and settling. That amounts to several loads in your pickup truck, so you might want to have the quarry deliver it. Its crushed rock generally makes stronger concrete than rounded creek gravel, too, although you can dig the latter yourself. Add to that two-thirds as much sand and about 13 cubic-foot sacks of Portland.

The concrete mixture should be firm enough to hold stiff peaks.

Mix concrete footings in small quantities so that the concrete won't dry out faster than you can use it; if you have a wheelbarrow, you'll be mixing 1 cubic foot (28 cu dm) at a time; if you have a small- to medium-size mixer, you'll be mixing 2 to 3 cubic feet (56–84 cu dm) at a time. Start with 4 shovels of sand, then add 2 shovels of Portland cement. Dry-mix, then add water until the mix is wet and loose. How much water you need varies a lot; the key factor is how dry or wet the sand is when you start. Add roughly 6 shovels of gravel last, working it into the wet mix a little at a time.

The finished concrete should be dry enough to hold shaped peaks when you shovel it into place, but wet enough to level out when it is shaken with a hoe. If water puddles up on the mixture, it is too wet. Excess water will leave air pockets when the concrete dries, which will weaken it.

STEP 4: POURING AND REINFORCING THE CONCRETE

You'll need reinforcing rods, or rebar, typically 1/2 inch (13 mm) thick, in the footing to strengthen it. Steel makes cement strong. Otherwise, soft spots in the ditch bottom, or places where it goes from bedrock to dirt, can settle and crack your stone wall. Set the rebar in the concrete halfway up the footing thickness. Don't prop the rod up on bricks or rocks, because that leaves a hairline crack for water to seep into, which will rust the steel. Instead, pour 4 inches (10 cm) of

QUICK TIP

Always try to pour the concrete all at once. If a section has as much as an hour to set up before you join it with another, you get a "cold" joint, which is another place for water to seep in and thus weaken the concrete.

concrete, then place two rods 1 foot (30 cm) apart in the center of your 3-foot (90 cm) ditch. Overlap the rebar ends 6 inches (15 cm). Then pour the rest of the footing.

Establishing a rough level is close enough if you're laying stone on top of the footing, but it must be smoother for concrete blocks. You can dump wheelbarrow loads in, then smooth them with a hoe. As you even out the surface, feel around for the tops of the rebar grade stakes that mark off a level surface.

Let the cement dry for 2 days.

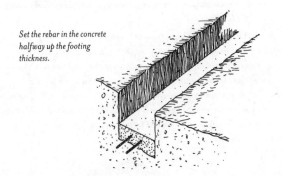

Set the rebar in the concrete halfway up the footing thickness.

STEP 5: PLAN THE LAYOUT

After 2 days, remove bulkhead boards, if any. Whether you've built to ground level with concrete, concrete blocks, or stone, you're ready now to lay stone that will show. Your work will be judged by this, so it needs to be right. For strength, a basically horizontal or ledge pattern is best. Too many same-size stones look monotonous, so vary the sizes often. Just remember to return as much as is practical to the horizontal arrangement.

Dry-fit 3 to 4 feet (0.9–1.2 m) of wall length, keeping the outside faces even and top surfaces level. Be sure each stone will stay in place dry. Shape with hammer and chisel where necessary. Leave a 1/2-inch (13 mm) space between each stone. You may use two stones for the 12-inch (30 cm) wall thickness.

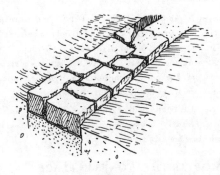

Dry-fit the stones before you mortar them in place.

STEP 6: MIX THE MORTAR

A heavy contractor's wheelbarrow is ideal for mixing mortar. You can move it to the sandpile, to where your Portland cement and lime are stored, and to the part of the site you're working on. The basic mix for stonework mortar is:

Continued ➡

9 parts sand

2 parts Portland cement

1 part lime

Water

Start with the sand and add the Portland cement and lime, so that the wheelbarrow is no more than half full. A medium-size shovel used for the measuring produces a good batch of mortar.

Mix dry first, using the shovel, a hoe, or both. Then move the dry mix away from one end of the wheelbarrow pan and pour in about 1/2 gallon (1.9 l) of water.

With the hoe, begin "chopping off" thin slices of the dry mix into the water. Work each bit until it is wet throughout, then chop some more. When this water is used up, open a hole beyond the mixed mortar for more water and repeat the process. Be sure you don't leave dry pockets of mix down in the corners as you go. When you get to the end of the wheelbarrow using this process, you should be finished. Take care not to add too much water at a time or the mix can get overly wet. It should stand in peaks.

Mix mortar by "chopping off" slices of dry mixture and working each slice with water.

If the sand is wet from rain, you'll need very little water for the mix. As you get near the end of the batch, use only a small amount of water at a time. It's easy to go from too dry to too wet with just a cupful of water.

The consistency should be as wet as possible without running or dripping. If the mix is too wet, add sand, Portland cement, and lime in proportionate amounts and mix until the batch stiffens up. Or you can leave it for 20 minutes or so; excess water will float to the surface, where you can pour it off. The mortar at the bottom will thicken enough for use, and you can scrape aside the soft stuff to get to it.

As you use the mortar, it will dry out more. This will help amend too-wet mortar and will mean you have to add water to an ideal mix. Use all mortar within 2 hours of mixing.

STEP 7: MORTAR THE STONES IN PLACE

Follow the principles of drystone work: Minimize mortar but seal out water and make the wall rigid. If you elect to try for a dry-stack, mortarless look, you have a big job ahead of you. Aim for joints between 1/2 and 1 inch (13–25 mm), recessed deeply (1 inch or so) so that they're not noticeable. A substantial mortar joint will bond well, keep out water better, and take up the irregularities in the stones more easily.

Lay a base of 3/4 inch (2 cm) of mortar on the concrete footing, removing and replacing the prefitted stones as you go. Rock each stone

just a bit to work out air pockets. If mortar gets pushed out to the face, trim it off and rake out the joint with the pointing tool. Don't let mortar get onto the stone faces at all; the stains are hard to get off. Fill between the stones, using the pointing tool to push mortar off the trowel into the cracks. Recess visible joints at least 1/2 inch (13 mm). You may extend the first course as far as you like before beginning the second one. Keep the mortar wet for at least 2 days.

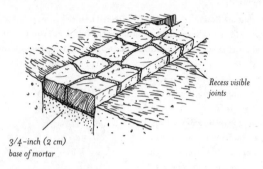

Recess visible joints

3/4-inch (2 cm) base of mortar

Recess visible joints of mortar at least 1/2 inch (13 mm).

Repeat the dry-stacking and subsequent mortaring of stones for the entire wall, mixing new mortar as necessary. Step hill walls and lay stones flat instead of up on edge unless they are very thick. Lay several feet horizontally, working with the full width of the wall so that you create the outside faces together. Then go back and work on the second course.

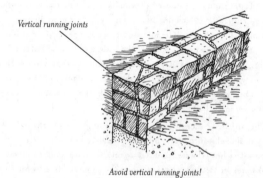

Vertical running joints

Avoid vertical running joints!

For the second and succeeding courses, avoid exterior and interior vertical running joints, just as in drystone work. Here, too, tie-stones are necessary. For this narrow wall, there will probably be no need to fill the center with small pieces. Fill small gaps with mortar, for strength. Work out all air spaces by packing with the pointing tool.

STEP 8: RAKE THE JOINTS

Within 4 hours of applying mortar, use the pointing tool to rake the mortar out of the joints onto a trowel for reuse. The raked-out joints should have a uniform depth of at least 1 inch (2.5 cm); no matter how deeply you want the mortar joints struck, or recessed, this depth should be consistent. It's probably impossible to use just the right quantity of mortar every time, so count on raking some out every day. At this point the mortar will probably still be wet enough that it will smear, so don't expect to do a complete job now.

STEP 9: CLEAN THE JOINTS AND FACES

Within 4 hours of applying mortar, use a pointing tool to rake out the joints to a consistent depth.

After the mortar is dry enough not to smear, use a wire brush to clean up and make the mortar neat. Raking will leave grooves, pits, and uneven places, but the wire brush will smooth them. Wet the mortar thoroughly afterward, using any method you like, when you're sure that the mortar is dry enough not to run down the faces of the stones.

Use the wire brush for additional cleanup. Keep the mortar wet with a spray, or slosh water on, for at least 2 days. Normally four or five wettings a day will suffice.

A wire brush and water will eventually remove mortar stains from stone.

STEP 10: CAP THE WALL

It isn't necessary for all the capstones to be large and heavy, because they are mortared in place, but make sure mortared joints are tight, so that water won't get into the wall and freeze. If it does, stones will break off the wall.

A mortared hill wall need not be stepped on top. The individual courses should be level, and if odd-shaped accent stones are used, return to a level again. If the top is to be sloped instead of stepped, you must use sloped stones—those thicker on one edge—and lay them flat on the stones below them.

In contrast to a drystone wall, a mortared wall built on a stepped trench on sloping ground does not need to be stepped on top.

7 SECRETS FOR SUCCESS WITH MORTAR

1. **Lock the ends.** If your wall has a freestanding vertical end—if it doesn't end against a building or fade into the ground—alternate short and long stones so that the end is even but each course is locked together. It's like using half bricks to end every other course. Cover the crack between two stones with the stone above.

2. **Keep the wall straight.** Most masons use stretched string to keep the wall straight.

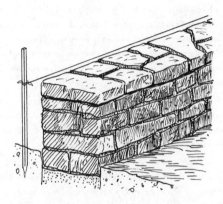

You can use a guide string to keep your wall straight. Just tie the string to tall stakes driven in the ground, and elevate the string as necessary.

3. **Test before mortaring.** Dry-fit a few stones to see how they look before you actually mortar them. Don't do too many, though, for the mortar will change the dimensions. Then set this half dozen or so, rake the excess mortar from the joints, and stand back and admire your handiwork.

4. **Fill wide joints with stone chips.** Fill any wide mortar joints with appropriately shaped chips. There will be a lot of bits from your shaping, but few of them will be shaped to the places they will fill. So lay an almost-good stone, and count on a shim to take up the slack.

5. **Avoid vertical running joints.** After laying stones side by side on one course, be sure to cover the crack between them with a stone on the next course. If you don't, you'll have a running joint, or vertical crack, which will weaken the wall too much. A joint that is two courses deep is permissible but not desirable.

6. **Prepare for the next day's work.** When you stop for the day, leave stone in steps, rather than leaving a vertical end, so it's easier to tie onto the next time.

7. **Keep the mortar wet.** Moisture is important to curing mortar, which is a chemical process that goes on for several days. If the mortar dries out too soon, the process stops and the stuff has little strength. So wet it thoroughly about four times during the day after you lay mortared stone. In very hot weather, drape plastic sheeting over it to hold in the moisture. After 2 days, it doesn't matter much; the process naturally slows down.

Continued ➔

Jay Heinrichs
Illustrations by Charles Joslin

As the demand for renewable resources such as trees escalates, and as rules for taking wood out of government land get stricter, the forest industry predicts that it is going to turn more to the small-woodlot owner for forest products. That will mean higher prices for wood, and more intensive lobbying for woodlot tax relief.

If you own less than ten acres of forest, you may not find it practical to manage your woods for timber production. But you can produce healthier, faster-growing trees and supply more wood for your stove. In addition, a few exceptionally valuable old hardwood trees might be worth a logger's trouble to remove them individually—and could bring you a tidy sum.

Most woodlots are overcrowded, with competition among the trees so intense that the wood grows about half as fast as it could. Without careful management, opportunities for recreation are diminished, and the forest does not support the wildlife that it could.

There are people who say you should walk softly on the land and take care not to disturb the natural balance of the forest. These same people will tell you to cut only what you need from your forests and let nature take care of itself. Well, if humans had never walked the earth, this system of forest management would work just fine. But in most wooded tracts in the United States, the natural balance has been seriously upset, and a great deal of work is necessary to set it right.

There is a real temptation to avoid the long wait for trees to grow valuable. But using your woodlot just for burning or selling firewood for a fast buck can be like burning your dining room furniture to cook dinner. It pays to plan ahead.

How Much Forest Do You Need?

Even with a relatively small woodlot, you can produce enough wood to heat your home forever. Exactly how small it can be depends on the energy efficiency and size of your home, and the efficiency of your stove. In the old days, when wood was there for the taking, inefficient stoves and fireplaces burned wood in large, drafty houses at the rate of ten to fifteen cords per year. But the average modern house in a northern climate can now be heated year-round with only three to eight cords.

GROWTH PER ACRE

The growth rate per acre in most forests is between one-quarter and three-quarters of a cord per year, depending in part on the climate, soil, kinds of trees, and the degree of management. In much of the East, for example, the volume of wood in the forests doubles every ten to twenty years. If it is harvested under intensive-management techniques, a good crop of trees can be obtained on the same woodlot every twelve to fifteen years. Most foresters say that a vast majority of woodlots in this country could double the amount of wood they produce—if cared for properly. Some of the management techniques include thinning, selective cutting, planting

faster-growing species of trees, and harvesting trees before they become "overmature" and slow their growth rate. Many trees send out shoots from stumps, which develop into fast-growing trees whose root systems are already established. Usually, these sprouted trees do not grow straight and tall for timber production, but they make perfectly good firewood.

In short, a carefully managed woodlot need be only five acres or more to give you year-round fuel for heating and cooking. If your woodlot is larger, you might have enough wood left over to sell some firewood. If it is larger than ten acres, you should get professional or governmental help and consider managing it for timber. But before you do anything to your woods, you should go see what you have.

Woodland Inventory

Part of a good forest inventory involves making sure the trees you cut are yours. So, if you have not done so already, get your neighbors to walk along the borders of your lot with you. In many woodlots, boundary corners are marked with metal rods or small piles of rocks. Mark the boundaries themselves by painting boundary trees; but if you do, use quick-drying enamel or a caulking compound. Aerosol paint can lead to decay in trees. Use aerosol spray only to mark trees that are about to be cut. Be especially careful to mark the points where the boundary lines change direction.

The Soil Conservation Service in the U.S. Department of Agriculture can supply you with a map or aerial photos that can give you a general idea of the shape of your woodland, and should tell something about the kinds of trees on it. Soil maps can tell you how good the land is for growing trees. The agricultural extension agent for your county should be listed in the phone book; he or she can tell you how to get maps and photos.

KNOW YOUR TREES

Now for the inventory itself. The most important expertise you need to carry into the woods with you is the ability to distinguish between different species of trees. A good tree guide is indispensable. You cannot beat the *Audubon Society Field Guide to North American Trees* by Elbert L. Little. It comes in both eastern and western region editions.

The best wood for burning is *hardwood*, found in most broadleaf (decidous) trees. Most of these trees lose their leaves in the winter. *Softwood*, found in needleleaf (evergreen) and some decidous trees, can also be burned, although the burning qualities of softwood are inferior to those of hardwood. But in some parts of the country, you have no choice—you may not *have* any hardwood.

Although you will do most of your firewood cutting in the late fall and early winter, it is a good idea to take inventory in the spring or summer. That is when the leaves and fruit are on most of the trees, making them easy to identify. You can distinguish a tree by the color, texture, and the smell of its bark; by the characteristics of its leaves, fruit, and twigs; and by the shape and size of the whole tree.

In the spring and summer, you can identify trees by their seeds and leaves.
Here is a sampling of some good timber trees.

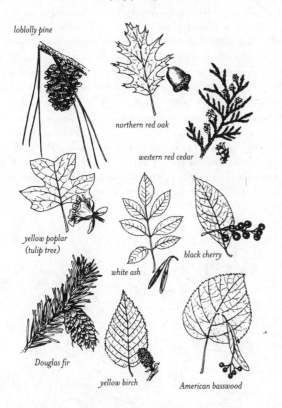

loblolly pine

northern red oak

western red cedar

yellow poplar
(tulip tree)

white ash

black cherry

Douglas fir

yellow birch

American basswood

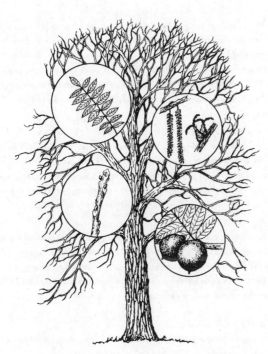

*Here a black walnut is identified. Notice the scaly bark, the compound leaves,
the alternate buds on the twig, the characteristic fruit and flowers.*

Managing for Firewood

The key to managing for firewood is knowing what to cut and when. A *selective cut*, in which you carefully choose the trees you want to take out, is the opposite of a *clearcut*, in which all the trees are harvested indiscriminately. Clearcuts result in *even-age management*, because when the stand is reforested, all the trees that grow back are the same age. A selective cut allows you to ensure a variety of ages in your forest. Although even-age management is good in many situations, in most cases your woodlot is better off with a mixture of ages. A mixed-age forest is less susceptible to diseases and pests, and it is more interesting to look at.

SELECTIVE CUTTING

Plan to remove the poorly growing wolf trees, and the trees that are growing skinny and crooked. In addition, you may have to remove some of the best-growing trees—the "dominant crown trees." These are the ones whose branches reach over the branches of others, and which have the most opportunity for growth. These dominant crown trees should be carefully spaced for maximum growth.

Cutting Formula. To determine whether two of these dominant crown trees are too close to each other, take their average diameter in inches (add them and divide by two) and then add six (a constant figure). The resulting figure is the proper distance in feet between the dominant trees. For example, the distance between a twelve-inch dominant tree and a twenty-two-inch dominant tree should be twenty-three feet (12 + 22 divided by 2, plus 6, equals 23). But use your judgment; some trees with particularly large crowns need more space. Others need less. Hardwoods generally need more room in the forest than softwoods. If you are managing your woodlot for firewood and you find two straight, tall trees right next to each other, cut down the larger one. But if you are managing your land for saw timber, cut the smaller one, leaving the crop tree for future harvesting.

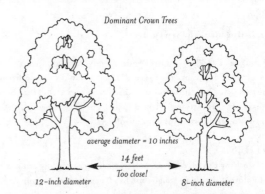

Dominant Crown Trees

average diameter = 10 inches

14 feet
Too close!

12-inch diameter

8-inch diameter

*To determine whether two dominant crown trees are spaced too closely, take their
average trunk diameter in inches and add 6. This gives you the proper spacing in feet.
If you are managing for firewood, remove the larger tree. If you are managing
for timber, you cull the smaller one.*

When you determine which dominant tree to cut, do not take out everything between those trees; some smaller trees should be left. Plan to cut about the same number of small trees as large trees, leaving enough space for light and nutrients.

This does not mean necessarily that you should immediately go in and cut all that wood. If you cut too many trees at once, you will expose the forest soil to drying or invasion by shrubs, and you may let the wind in, which also dries the soil. Some competition among trees is good for *self-pruning*, in which a tree drops branches that have been shaded out. This produces a straight, tall tree that is relatively free of knots.

CLEARCUTTING

If a portion of your woods has been badly abused and is growing a tangle of small, crooked trees, you might consider a clearcut. Despite all the bad things you have heard about logging abuses, a small clearcut can be sound forestry. It gives you a chance to plant the kind of trees you want to grow. Scientists have developed special fuel wood trees that grow very rapidly. The new hybrid poplars, for example, can grow to a foot in diameter in five to eight years. If used to stock a woodlot in the Northeast, they can almost double its energy production. Some states offer hybrid tree seedlings at nominal cost for firewood production. To learn more about clearcutting and reforestation, consult your county extension agent or state forester.

TOOLS FOR THE WOODLOT OWNER

Now that you have decided what to cut and what not to cut, you have to prepare yourself for taking the trees down and processing them for burning. There are three basic steps to this operation: felling, bucking (cutting trees into four-foot or smaller logs), and splitting. You will need a number of fairly specialized tools; but you do not need all those that I list. Before you invest in hundreds or thousands of dollars worth of equipment, decide how much wood you will be cutting each year. It might be cheaper and easier to rent the more expensive equipment. Here are the tools you might want.

- **chain saw**
- **crosscut saw**
- **felling wedges (plastic, aluminum, or magnesium)**
- **axes**
- **bow saw**
- **peavey**
- **splitting maul and steel wedges**

If you are cutting a lot of firewood, you might want to invest in a mechanical wood splitter. There are all kinds of fancy wood splitters, but the best is the hydraulic splitter, which rams logs at 15,000 pounds per square inch. It costs over $1,500 to buy, but you can probably rent one to split several cords over a couple of days.

CLOTHES

Proper clothing can increase your safety when you are using a chain saw. All your clothes should fit snugly, and by all means, tuck in your scarf before turning on your saw! You should also have goggles or glasses and a hardhat. Wearing a hardhat is always a good idea in the woods, especially during a period of high winds or drought.

The noise a chain saw makes is well above established safety levels. Buy shooters' earplugs or the muffs worn by airport-runway workers. You should wear heavy shoes for all work in the woods. Get loggers' knee pads—half of all chain saw accidents involve the knees.

Felling a Tree

The healthy respect you should have for your chain saw should extend to the tree the saw is cutting. Safety is one reason you should cut in the late

fall: with the leaves off, you can easily determine which way a tree is leaning, and plan your attack accordingly.

Before you actually start to cut, take a pair of lopping shears or a handsaw and clear away brush around the tree. Plan the landing zone—you should fell your tree in the general direction of its crown lean and the angle of its trunk. But you can "aim" the tree so that it does not get hung up in another tree or smash young saplings. Finally, plan your escape route and walk along it. When it comes time to clear out, you do not want any surprises tripping you up.

Notch cut. Your first cut is the notch cut, made on the side of the tree toward which it will fall. First, make a cut parallel to the ground more than a quarter and less than a third of the way into the trunk. Then cut down into this first cut to make a forty-five-degree notch. Be careful when cutting into a wolf tree with several trunks; the trunks have a tendency to separate just when you finish the notch.

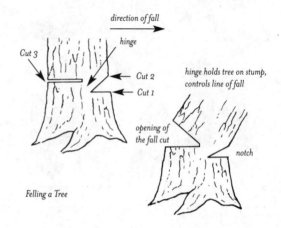

Felling a Tree

Fall cut. Now comes the back, or fall, cut, which should be parallel to the bottom of the notch cut and about three inches above it. The point is to create a hinge that controls the fall of the tree and keeps it from flipping up or rolling during descent. You can control the angle of fall slightly by making one side of the hinge fatter than the other; this is called "holding a corner." The tree will fall in the direction of the deepest cut.

Take it easy during the beginning of your fall cut, but keep your saw running at full speed. When you reach the middle of the cut, apply a little more pressure and cut as fast as the saw can comfortably go. This makes the tree go down faster and prevents hangups. There are several ways to release a hung-up tree. We recommend enlisting the help of an experienced friend. Such booby traps are best left to the experts.

If your saw gets bound while you are felling, stop the saw and tap a wedge or two (or three) into the back cut, behind the saw. The tree will tend to fall in the direction in which you point the wedge, so aim carefully. Use an ax or hammer and continue to tap the wedge in occasionally as you resume cutting.

FELLING WOLF TREES

Wolf trees are tricky, even after you have made the notch cut. How you attack them depends on their shape, size, and the direction of their trunks. If a wolf tree is forked close to the ground, cut one trunk at a time and allow it to fall in the direction of its own lean. Cut a couple of feet above the fork to avoid the separation of another trunk. If the fork is too high for you to get your saw above it, you will have to cut below the fork. Remember that each trunk may act as a separate tree; but be aware that the other trunks may be affected by what you do to one. You may not be able to make a good back cut. Your back cut may actually have to be a side cut, supported by strategically placed wedges to help control the angle of fall. If the trunks are not too big, you can actually help push each one over. Try to remove the smallest trunks first, then work on the bigger ones.

Bucking and Splitting

Once the tree is down, the limbs should be removed (limbing) and the log cut into smaller pieces (bucking). First make sure the tree has settled properly on the ground. Then lop off trunk limbs, keeping the crown intact at first. When cutting large limbs, make your first cut from the bottom, then finish off from the top.

Buck the wood into lengths about four inches shorter than the length of your firebox. If you plan to sell the firewood, cut it into four-foot lengths. Cut all limbs three inches or more in diameter. Cut from the butt of the tree toward the crown, which acts as an anchor. The easiest way to buck is to cut downward until the saw threatens to bind. Then roll the log over with a peavy and finish the job. On large trees, saw about a fourth of the way through on the top of the log, then finish the cut from underneath. Keep the log off the ground, if you possibly can, to protect your chain saw.

Do not bother to cut branches less than three inches thick. Spread the leftover branches on the forest floor to decompose. Do not pile branches around the base of a tree—it's a fire hazard. But small piles of brush create good wildlife habitats.

SPLITTING

Although most moisture leaves logs through the ends, wood dries faster when it is split. Logs larger than eight inches in diameter should be split in quarters or smaller pieces.

Some woods split easier than others. Oak, ash, and beech should not cause you too much trouble. Hickory, elm, and ironwood are especially tough. Most wood splits easier when green; so split your wood shortly after cutting.

To split, use a splitting maul, and aim toward the center of the unended log. Split with the grain, taking advantage of cracks that exist naturally in the wood.

DRYING

If you can possibly manage it, dry your wood in the woods, close to where it was cut. Dry wood is much lighter than green wood, and so it is easier to transport. Wood should be dried to 20 percent moisture before it is suitable for burning. This takes six months to a year. Dry wood feels dry to the touch when the bark is peeled off, and its ends contain deep cracks. Check your wood carefully before you burn it; wood that is still green causes creosote to build up in your chimney, which can cause disastrous chimney fires.

Wood dries faster with a "solar drier," which is simply a sheet of heavy-duty clear plastic secured over your pile. Leave the end that faces

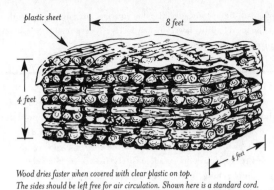

Wood dries faster when covered with clear plastic on top. The sides should be left free for air circulation. Shown here is a standard cord.

the prevailing wind open for plenty of air circulation. Set logs lengthwise along the bottom of the pile for a base. Logs dry most effectively when stacked log-cabin style, with each level set at right angles to the one below it. If you do not cover your wood, stack it with the bark facing up. If you do cover it, the split sides should face up.

Selling Firewood

If you have more than enough wood and woodlot to grow your own fuel wood, you might consider selling some. The rocketing prices for firewood may give you a chance to cull much of your unwanted wood at once, getting your forest into shape very quickly.

DON'T SELL TIMBER FOR FIREWOOD

Call your county extension agent for free advice—and possible financial aid—for "timber-stand improvement." The advice could come in handy, because the first thing you should check when examining the wood market is whether you are cheating yourself by selling high-value wood for firewood. No matter how good the prices are for fuel, they will never beat the prices for lumber. And you might be surprised to learn what kind of wood is bought for other uses.

Call local pulp mills and sawmills to ask about the species bought, and prices paid, for delivered wood. The cooperative extension service offices in most states have reporting services that give prices for fuel wood, pulpwood, saw timber, peeler and veneer logs, chips, poles, crossties, fuel residues, and dimension lumber. Call your county extension agent or state forestry representative for information on this service.

MARKETS FOR FIREWOOD

You can sell your firewood through local retailers and brokers. Again, make sure you know the value of your wood first. If possible, get yourself listed in your state's directory of fuel wood suppliers. Not all states have one, but an increasing number do. The simplest way to sell is to advertise the availability of "cut-your-own" stumpage, and let people come and remove it themselves. Mark the trees you want to come out. You should be able to build up a steady clientele over several seasons. But of course you cannot expect a lot of money per cord; one-fifth the price of delivered, bucked wood would be excellent money if you can get it. Ask the visitors to clean up after themselves. If you are unable or unwilling to cut wood for your own use, you can let friends cut cord-wood "shares," and take as payment for yourself something like a third

Continued →

of each load. Before you advertise that you have cut-your-own wood, check the local liability laws; you may be legally responsible if someone is injured on your property.

WHAT IS A CORD?

A cord of wood is a stack 8 feet long, 4 feet deep, and 4 feet high. Its volume is therefore 128 cubic feet. But because the stack is not solid wood, about 20 percent of that volume is air. Different kinds of wood weigh differently, of course, but the average cord weighs about 1 1/2 tons. It contains about thirty-five 10-inch-diameter logs 16 inches long, or about ten trees measuring 8 inches in diameter at about the height of your breast. (If you count the branches, though, a medium-size tree can produce half a cord.) An average cord produces the same heat energy as 166 gallons of No. 2 oil, or 3/4 ton of hard coal, or about 5,000 kilowatt-hours of electricity.

More and more states are requiring firewood sellers to specify the volumes of their loads. An increasing number of jurisdictions forbid sales of "loads" or "racks" of wood, because the meaning of these terms is indefinite. Another unit is the "thrown" cord, which is wood thrown into a 144-cubic-foot truck body. Maine accepts this as a standard measure, but New Hampshire still uses the 128-cubic-foot cord of tightly stacked wood as a standard. Call your state forestry representative to see what regulations apply to you. Many departments establish fuel wood grades, specify permissible species and sizes, and state forms, condition of wood, sizes to be split, and so on. The state forester can also give you a good idea of fair firewood prices.

Some states allow firewood dealers to sell by the *face cord*, which is a stack of wood four feet high, eight feet long, and just about any depth four feet and under. A face cord is a useful measurement for selling wood that has been cut to a specified length to fit a firebox, but it is often used to cheat unwary buyers. When you sell a face cord, let your buyer know how much smaller it is than a standard cord.

Stack your firewood reasonably tight, but expect to be paid for a high-volume cord. The actual volume of wood in a standard cord varies between 60 and 100 cubic feet, depending on the kind of wood, the lengths and thicknesses of the logs, and how they are stacked. The cord with the least wood volume is the one in which the wood has been stacked one log on top of the other. The most wood volume is obtained when the logs are staggered, with small pieces squeezed between the gaps, and then the logs are short. If you sell your firewood by the truckload, make sure you know the volume of what you are selling. A cord of log lengths should sell for less than a cut-up cord.

One final piece of advice about delivering wood: use a good truck, and do not overload it. A cord of hardwood can weigh well over two tons. If you plan to sell wood regularly, do not use a car to deliver it! No load of firewood is worth the sacrifice of an axle. Drive slowly, and be careful when stopping—your brakes just won't seem as efficient when your truck is groaning under a full load.

Man Does Not Live on Fuel Alone

There are many uses of a forest that may be much more valuable than producing firewood. The most important of these is lumber. Call local sawmills and find out what kinds of wood are sold for lumber in your area, and what the prices are. Thanks to a rising housing demand, timber prices are rising twice as fast as the prices of other crops in this country.

But suppose your woodlot is a small one—ten acres, say. Is it worth a logger's while to take out such small amounts of timber? Is it worth your while to go through the trouble of selling the timber? All that depends on what you have on that small lot. A single huge, flawless black walnut tree can sell for several thousand dollars (one such tree reportedly brought $30,000 on the stump).

Before you consider selling any of your trees, get help from the government. A county or state forester will give you advice on whether you have timber to sell, and how to get more help to sell it. A word to the wise: seek advice. If you do not have experience in selling wood products, you risk ruining your woods and depleting your bank account.

One way to find out whether or not you have timber to sell is to conduct your own informal "cruise," or inventory, and see what you have. By conducting your own cruise, you can estimate the number of trees that should be removed to increase the vigor of the trees that remain. Then you can get a forester to help you find out the prices you can get for the trees you remove, and whether the trees are good for firewood or for other uses. If you are interested only in producing firewood, do not discount the possibility that you will want to sell timber in the distant future.

EXAMINE A SAMPLE PLOT

The best way to estimate how many trees can be removed to increase the health of the woods is to examine a sample plot. First, mark the trees that you do not want to cut, for reasons of economic value, beauty, contribution to wildlife, or ability to restock the stand. Put a spot of paint at the base or tie a ribbon around each trunk. Then pick out a typical part of your woodland—if there is any typical part—a tenth of an acre in size. A tenth of an acre has a thirty-seven-foot radius, and you can measure a circular sample plot with a piece of rope that long. Within the sample plot you have measured out, pick out the ten best trees to save, counting the ones you have already marked. If the stand is composed of good softwoods, mark about twenty trees. The trees you mark should be the straightest, healthiest-looking trees. The leaves should be relatively clear of defects that might show disease. Where branches have naturally fallen off, the wounds should have healed cleanly.

Now count the number of trees that you want to cut down—the ones that you have not marked. That will determine how much firewood you have to use or sell. If you think that the "junk" wood might be good for something else, ask the government forester. Multiply the amount of "junk" by ten, and you will have the approximate number of firewood trees per acre. Take a look at the trees you have marked to save. If you can, get the forester to look at them. Do they show promise for timber? Did you have to look hard just to come up with ten good trees in your sample plot? Then you may need to get advice on a different form of management. Small, single-acre clearcuts replanted with fast-growing trees might be a solution, or the forester might tell you how to manage for pulpwood production. Beware of choosing favored trees that are too close to each other; follow the formula mentioned on page 941, for thinning dominant crown trees.

The above inventory should be used only to help you decide what to do with your woodlands. If it appears you have a large number of big, slow-growing, healthy trees, you may already have a woodland sufficient for immediate timber sale. If so, get your county extension agent to recommend some good consulting foresters to help you with the sale.

The majority of small woodlots in this country, however, are in serious need of restoration. Most of them have suffered under a practice called *high-grading*, in which the best trees were taken out, leaving genetically inferior ones to reseed the stand naturally. In many cases, the best practice is to do the reverse; take the worst trees out and leave the best to spread their superior genes around. Before the boom in woodburning stoves, it just didn't pay to remove the "worthless" trees. But now those trees are worth something, and a stand can be improved profitably. You get firewood now, and more timber in the years to come. Still, a firewood sale does not always pay off enough for you to hire a professional consultant to help. In this case, you can do a cruise yourself, deciding what to cut and when.

Managing for Timber

If your initial inventory has indicated that your woodland has saw timber, you will want to mark all the trees you plan to save for timber.

CRUISING FOR TIMBER

Start ten to twenty feet from your property line or the edge of the woods. Mark a *crop tree*, a straight, tall tree that you want to save for lumber some day. Like the trees you marked in the sample plot, a crop tree should be free of signs of internal disease: swollen stem, seams or breaks in the bark, open wounds, or poorly healed branch stubs. After marking your first tree, pace off twenty feet parallel to the property line or the edge of the stand. Mark the closest crop tree, or one that might become a crop tree. If there are no trees within five to seven feet around you, take another couple of steps and try again.

Keep this up until you reach the end of the stand or the edge of the plot you want to work with. Turn at a right angle and pace off another twenty feet. Pick a crop tree, mark it, then turn again and go back, parallel to the first line. Continue this process, marking all the crop trees in your lot.

SELLING TIMBER

A paid consulting forester will help you draw up a prospectus that tells the amount of timber you wish to sell. This private forester will also draw up a timber-sale contract and send it to at least six possible buyers. The buyer with the highest bid, or the most attractive logging plan, can then do the logging for you. This is called selling timber "on the stump." A good forester can mark the trees to go out (a government forester will occasionally do this for free), and can make sure that the logging techniques are environmentally sound.

Make your desires clear to the forester; if you want a beautiful old tree to stand, say so before the contracts get sent out. If you do not want an old stone wall to be torn down to make way for logging equipment, mention it before it is too late. In fact, most of these decisions should be made even before you hire a consultant. That way the government people can tell you whether a paid consultant is worth the money in the first place. Your timber sale should make at least enough money to pay costs for help and cover taxes on your profit. But if you are serious about producing timber on your land, local timber companies might give you free consulting work in exchange for first bids on the timber.

You can, if you want, sell wood directly to the sawmill. Some mills will come out and pick up logs that you stack by the roadside. You will get higher prices for cut wood, of course; but you need some expertise and some equipment. Some woodland owners have been known to rig their own log "deckers," which stack trees that have been stripped of their limbs. A few cannibalized truck parts and an old winch do the job. A good four-wheel-drive vehicle skids the logs to the site, with the aid of a logging chain and winch. Don't age the wood as you would firewood. Sawmills and kilns are expensive, so you will probably want to sell your logs green.

Trees that are not good enough for lumber can be used to make pulp, which goes into making paper, corrugated boxes, particle board, and many chemicals. Trees four to ten inches in diameter often make the best firewood; but some straight, tall trees of the right species can make fence posts and poles. Locust and ash make good heating wood, for example, but they are highly valued as fence posts that can stand without rotting for decades. Huge hardwood trees are sometimes cut individually for veneer and bring great prices. These logs are often shipped to Germany or Japan, where they are sliced into strips hundredths of an inch thick. Pines, particularly in the South, can be tapped for naval stores, and they make better pulp than firewood. But again, before you seriously consider selling any of your trees, get the advice of a good forester.

Recreational Uses for Land

You can make money from your woods without touching a single tree: by charging users for recreation. Many landowners are justifiably leery of visitors. Visitors have an annoying tendency to litter, leave gates open, tear down fences, shoot up signs, and rut trails with off-road vehicles. Worst of all, they sometimes get themselves hurt and hold the landowners liable—whether or not they were aware of the visitors' presence in their woods. But as the saying goes, when you've got a lemon, make lemonade. By selling user permits to responsible groups of people, you can establish direct contact with the people using your land.

CHARGING FOR RECREATIONAL USE

There are several ways to charge for recreational use. The most common—and profitable—is hunting and fishing fees. You do not own the wildlife on your land—the state does. But you do own access to that wildlife, and you can charge for it. Write your state fish and wildlife agency for local regulations.

With a small investment you can build a year-round campsite and charge for its use. A small cabin, piped-in water, outdoor toilet, and facilities for garbage disposal are a lot of trouble, but they may bring you more income than any amount of woodcutting you could do.

According to the Heritage Conservation and Recreation Service of the U.S. Department of the Interior, the fastest-growing sport in the nation is cross-country skiing. In parts of the Northeast, city folk are scrambling after uncrowded trails, which are harder and harder to find. If you have a trail or two with a total winding length of a few miles or more, you can lease trail rights. If your trail leads into your neighbor's property, you might consider banding together to rent the trails. Each landowner could be responsible for the trails on his or her own property.

Again, check your insurance coverage and local liability laws before you enter any agreements.

Continued →

Managing for Wildlife

A great many woodland owners have just one other purpose for their woodlots beyond firewood. They use their forests for attracting wildlife. No matter how small your woodland is, you can manage it to attract and sustain a much larger number of animals than it presently does. Your state fish and wildlife agency can recommend ways to build nesting boxes and plant vegetation that attract wildlife. Some states sell game birds at a nominal cost for release on woodland. (A dozen quail make a great gift for the woodland owner who thinks he has everything!)

Your tree harvest can be worked around wildlife amenities. When you see an old, dead tree, think twice about cutting it up. The wood may be too rotten for burning, anyway; but the tree may be a wildlife heaven for the animals on your property. Woodpeckers and other birds feed on the insects the tree harbors. Raccoons, squirrels, owls, snakes, and other animals can use it for their dens. The U.S. Forest Service spends a great deal of money making sure that a minimum number of dead trees, called *snags*, remain standing after timber harvests over much of the national forest land.

The best kind of forest for wildlife has trees of all ages. It also has patches of seedlings or sprouts, called *openings*, interspersed with taller shade trees and cover. You can produce openings with small clearcuts. If you want to supplement the natural food with food of your own, make sure you *always* leave food. Many a deer has starved after the friendly couple that left oats in the winter did not spend the season in the country one year.

Help!

Conservationist Dorothy Behlen, in a column she used to write for *American Forests* magazine, described a program that the Tennessee Valley Authority designed in cooperation with the U.S. Forest Service. It is a computer program called WRAP, for Woodland Resource Analysis Program. For a small fee, the computer analyzes information collected by a forester who makes an on-site inspection; it then matches this information with the goals of the landowner, be they maintaining wildlife, scenery, fishing, hunting, timber, Christmas trees, or some combination of uses. The computer printout gives an inventory of the land, a list of the management practices needed to achieve the landowner's goals, and a year-by-year plan for each acre of land.

Unfortunately, WRAP is available only in Alabama and Kentucky. But it may someday be available for nationwide use. In the meantime, you can get some free help to devise a program of your own and come up with an inventory, list of management practices, and step-by-step plan. Public foresters do not have a whole lot of time to spend with each landowner, and it may take a while to get one to come out; but the free advice can help steer you to a decision on whether to hire a consulting forester.

FREE HELP

For managing the land, a lot of free government advice is out there for the taking. The following agencies offer forestry help.

State Foresters. Many states have a forester in every county. The department or division of forestry is often contained within the department of natural resources or environmental resources, or the department of agriculture.

State Woodland-Owners' Associations. Your state forester can help steer you toward landowners who have banded together to share advice, buy equipment in bulk, and lobby local and state governments. Such organizations are springing up all over the country, particularly in the Northeast and parts of the South. Some of them are affiliated with the state forestry association, whose address the state forester can also provide.

U.S. Forest Service. This federal agency works with states in the Rural Forestry Assistance Program. It gives good advice through the land-grant university extension foresters. It also doles out financial assistance to woodlot owners through the Forestry Incentives Program and the Agricultural Conservation Program. The Forestry Incentives Program allows the federal government to share up to 75 percent of the cost of planting trees and improving a small owner's forest stand. For the nearest forest service office, look in the phone book under U.S. Department of Agriculture.

U.S. Soil Conservation Service. The Soil Conservation Service can give you advice on soil conditions of your land. Like the Forest Service, it is a branch of the U.S. Department of Agriculture.

Professional Consultants. Timber companies often provide professional help to landowners, with just one string attached: the company gets the right of first refusal on the sale of the timber.

Consulting information is also available from the American Tree Farm System, a nationwide community of nearly 70,000 landowners. Effective management includes producing continuous crops of trees to supply the demand for wood products, while simultaneously maintaining the forest to be aesthetically pleasing and beneficial to wildlife. To qualify for membership, you must have ten or more acres of woodland, and have your land inspected by one of the 10,000 foresters who donate time to the system. Lands are reinspected at least every five years to ensure they are being managed properly. It costs nothing to join, and accepted landowners receive the quarterly *Tree Farmer* magazine, which keeps the woodland owner up-to-date with recent forestry techniques and legislation that could affect them. Write to the American Forest Council, 1250 Connecticut Avenue NW, Suite 320, Washington, DC 20036, for more information.

If you decide to hire a consulting forester to come out and give some management advice, be prepared to pay twenty-five to forty dollars or more per hour (fees vary greatly). For a nationwide list of consultants, write for the *Directory of Consulting Foresters* from the Society of American Foresters, 5400 Grosvenor Lane, Washington, DC 20014.

Taxes

If you have not done so already, look into your tax situation. Many a conscientious woodland owner has been forced into environmentally unsound practices—or even into sale of the land—because of poor tax planning. They say that nothing is as inevitable as death and taxes, but modern medicine can prolong life well beyond ancient expectations. It is not the same for taxes; no amount of political wizardry has yet managed to make a landowner feel chipper come April.

If you market firewood or any other product of your land, you will have to pay federal tax, and probably state tax as well, on the income. But profits on sales of your timber can be classified as "capital gains," and you can avoid paying more than half the tax on it. If the woodcutting was done to improve the woodlot, however, added value of the forest could increase your property tax—except in areas where innovative laws have alleviated this problem. And do not forget estate taxes, which could force your heirs to butcher the woods or sell some of the land to get the government off their backs.

In many cases, you can write off, or delay paying, taxes on some of your woodlot expenses, such as tools and reforestation. A few months before President Jimmy Carter left the White House, he signed a bill that includes a reforestation incentive. This law gives a 10 percent tax credit for reforestation expenses—site preparation, labor and tools, and depreciation of equipment used in planting or seeding. For example, if you spend $2,000 to replant cut-over woodland on your property, you will be allowed to subtract $200 from the taxes you would normally pay that year. In addition, a seven-year amortization on the first $10,000 of capitalized reforestation expenditures each year allows further tax relief. What all this means is that you can deduct a certain amount when you state your adjusted gross income each year for seven years on your tax form.

Most important to a woodland owner, particularly an elderly one, is estate planning. Without good planning for the future, all your woodland work could go down the drain. But, by giving parts of your land to heirs in parcels every year, you could end up saving them thousands of dollars in taxes later.

To help you with all these problems, find a lawyer familiar with timber taxation. Write your state forester or your state bar association for referrals. Some timber-tax lawyers even specialize down to estate taxes. Figure out what kind of advice you want in advance. To help you understand some of the tax jargon, write to the American Forestry Association, 1516 P Street NW, Washington, DC 20005, for information on timber taxes.

The final solution to paying property tax is to avoid it by getting the government to buy or trade tax relief in exchange for rights to your property. If your woodlot is important to a city's watershed, or to an area's aesthetic value, or if it has special qualities like wildlife or rare plants, you might be able to get the state or local government to agree to a conservation easement. In return for your promise not to develop the land, the government relieves you of the tax burden. In many cases, landowners are still allowed to cut their timber and to exercise other good management practices. Write to the Nature Conservancy, 1815 North Lynn Street, Arlington, VA 22209, for more information on easements.

Build a Pole Woodshed

Mary Twitchell

Getting the full heat value from a piece of wood is very simple. The wood must be allowed to dry, and preferably for two years. (Seasoning times vary with the climate; in the desert wood dries much more quickly, in colder wetter areas drying may take two years or more.)

Over this two-year period, the green wood dries at various rates. Much of the moisture evaporates very quickly. In the first three months the seasoning is half complete and the fuel value is 90 percent of what it will be when thoroughly dried (evaporation also depends on temperature and humidity). In the next six to nine months, the wood is reasonably dry; in two years it will be as dry as it will get.

If you have invested time, energy, and money in a wood stove installation, it's foolish to forgo a further savings by burning green wood. It requires no work to let wood season, and in the process you are increasing its heat value; the wood will be lighter, ignite better, and produce less smoke and fewer sparks.

The following pages outline various ways to speed the seasoning process—from no-cost methods of stacking the wood properly to building a low-cost, pole-built storage shed.

PREPARING WOOD FOR STORAGE

After a tree is felled, it should be bucked to length, then split. Splitting is easiest when the wood is green and preferably frozen. Wood can be left round if under six inches in diameter. If the logs are of greater diameter, they should be split to prevent decay and accelerate the drying process. Since wood dries more rapidly along the grain, it is necessary to break the water barrier—the bark—to let this process occur. Splitting also increases the surface area which speeds up drying.

It is essential to split birch and alder or they will rot. Don't be shy about splitting wood; you can always use kindling. In addition, splitting reduces the sizes to be burned, and wood stoves/furnaces burn cleaner and more efficiently if fed splits of no more than six inches in diameter.

OPEN-AIR STACKING

Indoor or basement storage may seem the most logical way to dry wood, but you will probably have to contend with dirt and insects. There will be fewer problems if the wood is stored outdoors with a week's supply stacked in the basement or on an enclosed porch for easy access.

Wood piled outdoors against an exterior wall of the house is conveniently located, and you won't have to negotiate cellar stairs with armloads of wood. It also keeps the dirt and insects outside, but the exterior house walls will cut down on air circulation to the pile, water may drain off the house onto it, and it may dry very slowly, if at all.

Continued →

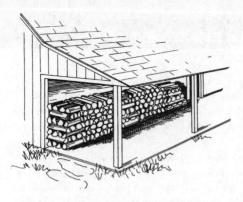

Wood stacked on a porch for seasoning.

If you have a concrete patio, wood can be piled there. Otherwise, locate the pile within a reasonable distance of the house. If the pile is located too far away, getting to it will be difficult in winter; if located too close, insects may be a problem, fire a hazard, and good air circulation more difficult to achieve.

Avoid damp places or depressions where water will collect after a rainfall or during the spring runoff. Loose soils dry the fastest; clayey soils the slowest. The wood should have maximum exposure to the sun and wind. The best location is on a hilltop or knoll where there are more air currents.

Consider the prevailing winds. The longer dimension of the pile should be exposed to the summer winds.

Lay down two stringers (poles of three to four inches in diameter) running the length of the pile. Anything can be improvised for support (stones, 2 x 4s, metal pipes) as long as it raises the pile about four inches off the ground to prevent decay and rot. Place the stringers a foot or so apart, and leave plenty of space between the piles.

The stringers can be of any length, but if you're curious about the number of cords of wood that you've cut, they should be eight feet long. At either end, drive in stakes to prevent the pile from collapsing. Cut them so that when driven in they are four feet high. Stack the splits so that they straddle the stringers.

Stacking wood on stringers speeds curing.

It is a real annoyance to have a pile tip over in the middle of winter. As a precaution, pile the last two splits in every row crosswise and tilt them slightly towards the pile to give it more stability.

The splits will air-dry more quickly if, after the first layer, the entire next layer is laid criss-cross, and the direction of the splits alternated with each tier until the pile starts to wobble. Leave the splits stacked criss-cross for three months, then restack them in the normal, parallel fashion.

Wood without bark will dry faster, but stripping it is impractical. Strip elm of bark to prevent the further spread of Dutch elm disease. This bark should be burned or the beetle will continue its nefarious activities once the weather warms.

If wood is totally exposed to the elements to air-dry, the moisture content of the wood may vary considerably with the season and the humidity. In some areas wood will dry rapidly in May and June; reabsorb water in July and August; dry out again in September; reabsorb in October.

The pile will be somewhat protected if the top layer of splits is turned bark-side-up. The bark will help shed rain. Even better is to cover the top of the pile with clear plastic sheeting, a tarp, pieces of tin, or any non-porous covering which will protect the wood from the worst of the weather.

SOLAR DRYER

A more permanent solution and one which will hasten drying is to build a solar dryer.

Four poles, two of which are one foot taller than the pile and two which are three feet taller, should be driven in six to twelve inches beyond each of the four corners with the shorter poles on the windward side. Then cover the pile with 4-mil clear polyethylene. The plastic should be stapled to the poles to form a shed-like structure, with a vent at the top of the high side. Don't let the plastic touch the pile and don't let it go all the way to the ground on any of the sides because air must be able to pass from the bottom of the pile through the splits and out the top vent. If there is no way for the air to escape, the water vapor which is released from the wood will condense on the surface of the plastic, and later be reabsorbed by the wood.

In sunny weather, the temperatures within the dryer will rise much higher than the outside temperatures. This heat will eliminate beetle and insect problems, while producing air-dried wood in three months.

The disadvantage of a solar dryer is that the intensity of the summer sun will deteriorate the plastic. Consequently this method is best for spring, fall, and winter protection. During the summer, the pile may have to be re-roofed.

ATTACHED WOODSHED

Some homes can be adapted for an attached wood storage facility, or it can be designed into houses under construction. Attached sheds with a pass-through door allow easy access from the house, and you won't have to don winter clothes to bring in the wood. Every week the shed may have to be reloaded or the wood rearranged. Be sure the door fits tightly.

For convenience, have a woodshed close to the house, and a door through which wood can be loaded into an inside wood box.

Wood Storage Shed

Open-air drying reduces the moisture in wood 14–25 percent; a woodshed will reduce it another 10–15 percent; indoor drying will add another 5–15 percent. For best results wood should be dried one year outdoors, then one year in a woodshed, with a week's supply dried indoors just before it is used. This means that to solve the problems of storing and seasoning wood, the serious woodburner should think about building a permanent, free-standing woodshed. The shed keeps insects and dirt to a minimum, while allowing the wood to dry under ideal conditions.

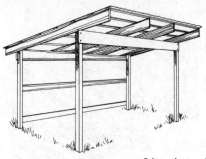

Pole wood storage shed.

LOCATION

The best location for your woodpile is also perfect for your storage shed. Since the wood will probably spend a year drying in the open air and then be moved into the shed, the piles should be located close to one another. The wood for burning will come from the shed, so it should be situated closer to the house. A short trip from shed to house will be appreciated all winter.

In choosing the location of the shed, consider water runoff and the soil composition. Loose soil dries fastest and makes a solid base for the foundation posts. The shed should be oriented with maximum exposure to the sun and wind. In cold regions the long dimension should run north/south to get the most heat from the morning and afternoon sun. If possible, the longer and most exposed side should be open to the summer winds, with the least exposure to blustery winter winds which will fill the shed with rain and snow. (Consider the location of buildings, trees, hills, or other barriers which might offer protection.) Usually the shed should face south or southwest. If the north side is unprotected, trees might be planted, or the north side of the shed enclosed.

Siting the shed will depend on the prevailing winds and the many variables of a location.

PRELIMINARIES

Pole construction is one of the cheapest, easiest, and most appropriate ways to build a storage shed. The only excavation required is digging holes for the poles. No foundation or slab is necessary; since wood piles have to be raised anyway for ventilation, it would needlessly add to the expense. Pole buildings are suspended between load-bearing members which are embedded in the ground. Therefore load-bearing walls can be omitted without structural weakness. This cuts down on the amount of lumber that would be used if the shed were built using conventional construction techniques.

Pole buildings can be erected rapidly because the construction is simple. Very little carpentry skill is required. Two people will be needed to set and plumb the posts; the rest of the work can be done by any unskilled worker. These buildings are easy to construct; simple to maintain—and cheap.

The initial cost of a pole building is low, and can be even lower if you scrounge some of the materials. You may be able to buy used utility poles from the telephone company. Metal roofing may be salvaged from a barn or house which is being re-roofed.

POSTS

The corner posts can be poles of at least six inches in diameter at their tips or 4 x 4s spaced at eight-foot intervals and sunk to below the frost line. Since these posts serve as the structural framework, it is essential that they be protected from decay. Wood deteriorates because of insects, dampness, bacteria, and fungi. To retard this process, wood can be sprayed with a fungicide and then pressure-impregnated with a preservative. You may prefer to creosote the wood yourself. However the creosote will not penetrate as far into the wood as pressure treatment and the wood will rot eventually. Cedar and hemlock are more naturally rot-resistant than other woods but still lack the longevity of those which have been pressure-impregnated. The pressure-treated poles of the telephone company will last forty to fifty years.

SIZE

The size of your shed will depend on your wood heating needs and the methods you intend to use for drying your wood supply. Since wood is cheaper to buy green, you should be buying your wood a year in advance of when you will be burning it. This means that, ideally, you will need storage space for at least one year's supply (if you plan to air-dry the wood for one year before moving it into the shed). If you don't want to move the wood, the shed should be large enough to store a two years' supply.

A homestead heated solely with wood will require seven to ten cords per year. Smaller homes which are tight and well-insulated may burn only two to three cords a year.

WOOD MEASUREMENTS

Wood is measured by divisions of a *standard cord*, which is a neatly stacked pile eight feet long by four feet wide by four feet high covering 128 cubic feet. Only 60–110 cubic feet of the 128 may be solid wood because wood cannot be stacked without air space. (Usually a cord runs between eighty to ninety cubic feet with more solid wood content in round wood than split.) Few people have four-foot fireplaces and many lack the equipment to reduce four-foot lengths to stove dimension. Therefore wood sold in face cords, or lengths corresponding to either fireplace dimension (twenty inches) or stove dimension (twelve to sixteen inches), is more common. A *face cord* is a pile neatly stacked eight feet long by four feet high by whatever dimension you specify. A *rick* usually refers to sixteen-inch lengths.

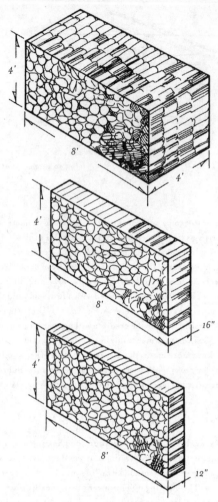

Full cord is 8 x 4 x 4. Face cords or runs measure eight feet long, four feet high, and the width of one row of wood stacked, such as twelve or sixteen inches.

A *run* is also a face cord, and varies in size depending on wood length. For example, wood cut to twenty-four-inch lengths means there are two runs in a cord; cut to sixteen-inch lengths, three runs to the cord; cut to twelve-inch lengths, four runs to the cord. To complicate matters further, there is a *unit* which is 1/24 of a standard cord, or a pile two feet by sixteen inches by two feet—the amount of wood which will fit into a station wagon or car trunk.

These measurements are important particularly if you are buying wood and want to be sure you have received what you paid for. They also will help you gauge how much firewood you will need for the heating season.

How Much Wood?

Can you figure out how much wood you will need to heat your home if you haven't used a wood stove before?

The University of Wisconsin Extension Service in its publication, *Wood for Home Heating*, suggests this method. "The easiest way to figure how much fuel wood you will need for a heating season is to convert your present fuel consumption to wood equivalents.

"Below are figures to help convert your present fuel to wood equivalents. A standard cord of wood is a stack 4' x 4' x 8'; it includes 80 cubic feet of solid wood. The heavier (better) hardwoods weigh, per standard cord, between 3,000 to 4,000 pounds when air-dry, so you can use an average of 3,500 pounds per cord for your estimate.

"1 gallon of #2 fuel oil = 22.2 pounds of wood

"1 therm (100 cubic feet) of natural gas = 14 pounds of wood

"1 gallon of propane gas = 14.6 pounds of wood

"1 kilowatt-hour of electricity = 0.59 pounds of wood

"1 pound of coal = 1.56 pounds of wood.

"Using #2 fuel oil as an example, if you burn 1,000 gallons of fuel oil, then 1,000 x 22.2 = 22,200 pounds of wood. Dividing 22,200 by 3,500 means you would need 6 1/3 standard cords of wood."

Gauge your firewood needs for the coming winter by using your last year's heating fuel requirement. Convert this number into cords and double it if you plan to store a two years' supply of wood in the storage shed.

But doubling the storage space will mean you're building quite a large woodshed. If your requirements were ten cords a year, for example, you would need a woodshed that measured 8 x 8 x 40 for a total of 2560 cubic feet. A two-year supply for three cords per year would call for a woodshed 8 x 8 x 12.

There's another approach, to cut the size of the woodshed required. Plan to store the wood supply for the following winter in the woodshed, and the supply cut for the next year after that under plastic for a year. The only disadvantage of this is that you will have to move the wood from the plastic covering to the woodshed.

The 8 x 8 x 8 structure is very practical, holding four cords. If your demand for a woodshed is less than this, hold to this minimum size rather than not making full use of the pole design.

BIG ENOUGH

When deciding on the size of your woodshed, build large enough so that your wood supply can be stored easily. For example, if reaching high with wood is impossible for you, plan your woodshed so your supply can be contained if your pile is not more than six feet high.

Building instructions here are for the 8 x 8 x 8-foot module. For more space, the shed easily can be made to an 8 x 8 x 16-foot or 8 x 8 x 24-foot size. For more space, increase the length, while keeping the eight-foot height and width. If the shed is made any higher, stacking the wood becomes a problem; if the shed is wider, air will not circulate through it as well.

MATERIALS

Lumber

Amt.	Dimension	Use
2	4'x4'x12' (Pressure-treated)	corner posts (front)
2	4'x4'x10' (Pressure-treated)	corner posts (back)

(Poles can be substituted for the posts; they should be of the same heights, and approximately six inches thick at the tips. Be sure they have been pressure-treated. See Pole Depth for possible need for longer poles.)

4	2"x6"x12'	rafters
2	2"x8"x8'	girders
7	2"x4"x8'	purlins
1	2"x4"x12'	batter boards (can be scrap lumber)
4	1"x6"x10'	batter boards (can be scrap lumber)

Scrap lumber (1"x2" or furring strips)

Hardware

1 1/2 lbs. 10d nails	1/2 lb. 16d nails

Tools

Tape measure	Handsaw
Mason's cord	Line level
2 8-foot ladders	Post hole digger
Plumb bob	Crowbar (may not be necessary)
Chalkline	Hand shovel
Hammer	Combination square
4' or 2' carpenter's level	

The Construction Process

SITE PREPARATION

Drive in stakes eight feet apart with a nail in the top of each to roughly mark the corners of the shed. Consider the terrain enclosed by this area. An excessive slope may necessitate some grading; a natural depression which will fill with rain or snow runoff may need to be leveled. Avoid these conditions, if possible.

Once the approximate corners have been established, check whether the area is square by measuring the diagonals—the lines between opposite stakes. Adjust the stakes until the diagonals are of the same length.

Outside the stakes at each of the four corners, erect *batter boards*. Drive three 2 x 4 stakes into the ground, spaced four to five feet apart, and to these nail 1" x 6" x 5' boards so they form a right angle. These boards should be about ten to eighteen inches above the ground.

SQUARE IT

Level strings should be stretched taut between the boards; where they intersect should mark the outside corners of the building. Drop a

plumb bob from the intersection of the two strings to the nail head to establish the precise corners. The strings will probably need adjustment.

Another way to check for squareness is to use the 3–4-5 principle (Pythagorean theorem). Measure from one corner three feet along one edge and mark this point with a stake. From this same corner, measure along the other leg of the right angle four feet and mark it. The distance between these two points should be five feet. Again, adjustments may be made to insure you have squared up the shed corners. Any multiple of these numbers can be used; if you are building a larger shed, 6–8-10 may be more accurate since it means you are checking the angle of a corner over a longer distance.

Cut a notch a saw kerf in width at precisely the place where the string is located on each of the batter boards. This allows you to remove the strings while the holes are being dug yet to replace them whenever you want to check the alignment of the holes.

Check the strings for level. Rest a four-foot carpenter's level on the string, or use a line level. The saw kerf may need to be adjusted so that all strings will read level.

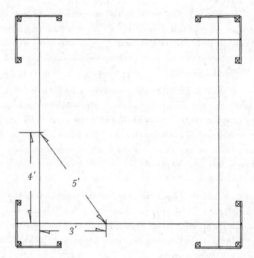

Batter boards and strings are used for locating the four corners of the shed. To check for squareness, measure from one corner three feet along one edge. Measure four feet along the other leg of the right angle. The distance between these two points should be five feet, if the corner is a true right angle.

POLE SPACING

It is most convenient to space the poles so that dimension lumber can be used. The strings mark the *outer* perimeter of the shed. The center of the post holes should be marked before digging, and these points will depend on whether you will be using round poles or 4 x 4s. This "center" point should be adjusted further to allow for the girders. Move the corner posts towards the center of the shed an extra 1 1/2 inches (see illustration). This allows the girders a 1 1/2-inch overhang beyond each corner post on which the end rafters will rest.

Sketch your layout plan on a piece of paper to insure that you have calculated the dimensions correctly.

Continued ➜

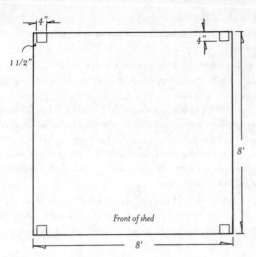

Pole spacing. Moving poles in from corner as shown permits placement of girders with slight overhang, where rafters will rest.

POLE DEPTH

As a rule 4" x 4" posts should be sunk 4'4" in poor soil; 3'6" in average soil; and 2'8" in good soil. If your soil is loose or sandy, the posts will be more secure set in concrete. Generally, posts sunk three feet should be secure enough if the soil is relatively stable, and earth or gravel is tamped around the base.

Remove the strings. With a post hole digger, dig the holes. A shovel will disturb the earth too much. For posts which will be tamped with earth or gravel, make the hole twice the post's diameter. Angle the digger so that the hole widens towards its bottom if the post will be set in concrete. Add another six inches to the depth of the hole for gravel. This will provide drainage and prevent the butt of the pole from sitting in a puddle of water.

Gasoline-powered augers can be rented and should be used by those with bad backs or by those with more holes to dig than they can handle. Periodically the bit will have to be raised and cleaned of dirt. If you hit a rock, stop the motor and remove the auger. A crowbar or pick will have to be used to pry the rock loose.

SETTING AND ALIGNING THE POSTS

Setting and aligning the posts is the most important step in constructing a shed because the weight of the structure is borne by these posts. You will need a helper or two.

Draw a couple shovelfuls of gravel in the hole. On top of this, place a flat rock on which the pole will rest. Begin with the two 10-footers of the rear of the shed. They will be lighter to handle. With two or three people, lift the pole hand over hand into an upright position. Try to disturb as little soil as possible. A 1" x 4" placed under the butt of the pole may help in allowing you to lift against the board rather than against the edge of the hole.

Once the pole is in place, drive two stakes on adjacent sides of it, on the north and east sides, for example. To these nail a 1" x 2" which will be long enough to span a diagonal from the stake to the post.

Before bracing a pole, check carefully so that it is turned with the squarest side of the pole facing the eave. This will make it easier when nailing in the rafter.

Rest a 2- or 4-foot carpenter's level against the post and plumb the side adjacent to the 1 x 2 bracing. When this side is plumb have your helper nail the 1 x 2 to the post. Plumb the side adjacent to the second brace; nail the 1 x 2.

After both 10-footers are braced, replace the perimeter string. Measure from the string to the top of the posts. This distance should be the same on both poles.

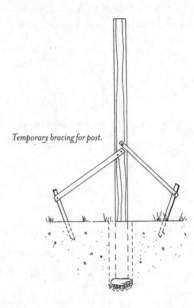

Temporary bracing for post.

You can adjust for uneven ground by changing the depth of the hole; add or remove gravel to make minor adjustments in height. Larger adjustments can be made by digging a deeper hole. Poles can even be cut later to the right height with a chain saw but this involves dangerous cutting from a ladder.

Erect the twelve-foot posts, align, plumb, and brace them. Check them for height. Then if the structure is larger than an 8' x 8' x 8' shed, erect the intermediate posts. Plumb these posts by stretching two strings between the end posts—one six to twelve inches from the ground, the second near the top of the posts. Intermediate posts should align with these strings. Have a helper sight along the strings to insure the posts are plumb.

SECURING THE POSTS

One person should be constantly checking the posts for plumb, while a second person secures the posts in place. Shovel a layer of dirt into the hole and tamp it down with a hoe or the head of a crowbar. Add a second layer and continue the process. Near the top of the hole, use the heel of your boot to pack the earth as tightly as possible. At the top of the hole, shape a conical earth mound around the hole. Tamp this down and add more dirt if necessary so that there will be a cone left around each post. You want to insure there will still be a mound to divert runoff water from entering the hole.

If you intend to set the posts in concrete, use a concrete mix of one part cement, three parts sand, five parts gravel. Put the hole in place, then fill the hole, leaving a slight mound at the top which should be leveled towards the edges to lead runoff water away from the pole.

The post should be checked for plumb and adjusted, if necessary, while the concrete is drying. Wait twenty-four hours before removing the braces.

FRAME CONSTRUCTION

Two girders of 2" x 8" x 8' are nailed to the front and back of the shed to support the rafters. If you've calculated correctly, the girders should overhang 1 1/2 inches on each end. This gives the rafters something to sit on.

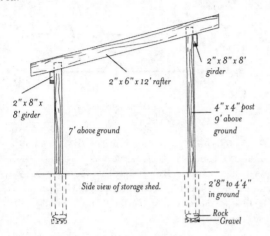

Side view of storage shed.

You will need two 8-foot ladders and a helper for nailing the girders in place. Nail them so that the top edge of the 2" x 6" x 12' rafters will clear the posts. Otherwise the posts will interfere with the roof.

If the poles are at slightly different heights, you can adjust now. Hold one end of the girder about five inches down on the taller post. Drive in a 16d nail part way. With a helper holding the other end of the girder, move your ladder to the center of the girder and with a two- or four-foot level, adjust the girder until it reads level. If this leaves enough space on the posts to nail the end rafters, the girder can be nailed in place permanently. Use five 16d nails for each post. To lessen the chances of splitting, stagger the nails so that they aren't entering the same grain in the wood.

For sheds larger than 8' x 8', the girders should have 1 1/2-inch overhang at each end, but be butted where they meet at intermediate posts. You may have to square the ends of the girders to make a better butt joint.

RAFTERS

There will be four 2" x 6" x 12' rafters for an 8' x 8' shed. For each additional eight-foot section, three more rafters will be needed.

See the illustration on spacing the rafters. Note that the spacing between the two on the left is 30 1/2 inches, while the space between the second and third and third and fourth is 32 inches.

Facing the front of the shed, begin at the left end of the front girder, and measure in 30 1/2 inches, mark and square off this point with a combination square. Put an X to the right of the line. Continue this pattern down the girder, measuring for the next two in thirty-two-inch increments.

Do exactly the same on the rear girder, remembering to work from left to right and to make the X to the right of the line. Put one of the end

rafters in place, leaving a 1 1/2-foot overhang on the lower eave. This rafter should rest on the 2" x 8" girders. Nail the end rafters into the posts or toe-nail them into the girders with three 10d nails.

The intermediate rafters should be nailed in place. Toe-nail them with two or three 10d nails, at least one on each side.

SHED ROOF

Conventional roofs are sheathed with plywood or tongue-and-groove boards, over which felt paper is stapled, then roll roofing or asphalt shingles are laid. Metal roofing can be put down on top of decking and felt paper. However, there are metal roofs which are even easier and cheaper to install. Purlins are nailed at right angles to the rafters twenty-four inches on center and to these the metal roofing is nailed. This saves time and materials.

Metal roofs are lightweight, fire resistant, and under normal conditions will last longer than a conventional roof. Installation is simple, and for a shed or garage where heat retention is of no concern, metal roofs are more than adequate.

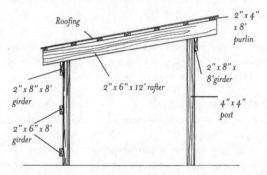

Roofing details of shed.

PURLINS

In order to have something to support the metal roofing, 2" x 4" purlins are added on top of and perpendicular to the roof rafters. Place these on twenty-four-inch centers. Beginning from the lower eave, measure twenty-four inches. Use a combination square to mark the location, draw an X. From this line measure 24 inches, draw a line, then the X. Do likewise on the opposite side of the shed, being sure the Xs fall to the same side of the line. (Before placing the purlins, check the roof manufacturer's instructions. Spacing varies from sixteen inches to twenty-two inches with different metal roofs.)

You will find it easier to nail the purlins with a helper. With one eight-foot ladder at either end of the shed, line up the first purlin with the rafter tails. Nail it in place with two 10d nails at each rafter. Stagger the nails so that they don't enter the same grain of the wood.

Place the next purlin in place. To be sure you have made your Xs to the same side of the line, check the distance between the rafters. (It should be 20 1/2 inches.) Continue with all seven purlins.

Continued ➡

Types of Metal Roofing

Flat and ridged metal roofs are laid with locked or soldered joints. These roofs come in rolls and need to be laid on top of decking—purlins won't provide sufficient support because of the flexibility of the metal.

Ribbed, corrugated and V-crimp sheets of galvanized steel or aluminum roofing are commonly used on farm buildings and are recommended. The corrugations add rigidity to the metal. Further rigidity is possible by buying a lower gauged metal; No. 28 gauge should be ample. These sheets are available in lengths of six to thirty-two feet; they come in widths up to four feet. Therefore large areas can be covered quickly.

Buy ribbed or corrugated panels in twelve-foot lengths for this shed. One sheet usually covers twenty-four inches after the side lap allowance. You will need four twelve-foot sheets. If you buy sheets in four-foot widths, you will need only two panels.

There are various lapping techniques for metal roofing: V-crimp, prime rib, double rib, grand rib, and corrugated, and the sheets can be made of either galvanized steel or aluminum.

ACCESSORIES

Most manufacturers sell the accessories made to fit their products, such as proper nails, trim, filler strips and sealants. Follow their instructions and use the same style and type of roofing throughout. Do not mix metals.

Should any of the panels need to be trimmed, cut the metal with tin snips. A circular or jig saw can be used with a metal cutting blade. If the sheet is to be cut lengthwise, score it with a utility knife and bend the sheet back on the scoring line.

CORRUGATED ROOFING

Some corrugated, galvanized-steel sheets are 26 inches wide with 1 1/2-inch corrugations. Others are 27 1/2 inches wide with 2 1/2-inch corrugations, but when the sheets are lapped the usable widths will be 24 inches. The larger the corrugation, the stronger the panel. Even though sheets of 1 1/2-inch corrugations will have more ridges, the sheet will not be as strong as the 2 1/2-inch pattern.

The aluminum sheets come with corrugations of 1 1/4 and 2 1/2 inches.

Apply the sheets vertically, working towards the direction of the prevailing winds. Then wind, rain, and snow will blow over, not under, the laps.

Align the first sheet with care or the whole roof will be out of square. The galvanized-steel sheets should be fastened at the laps with galvanized-steel ring- or screw-shank nails and lead or neoprene washers. The galvanized steel protects against rust; the washers will seal the nail holes and protect against leakage.

HOW TO NAIL

For aluminum roofing, use aluminum nails with neoprene washers under the heads.

The nails should be driven through the high part of a corrugation. Be sure they are long enough to fasten the roofing tightly to the purlins. The nails should penetrate the 2 x 4s by at least one inch; to determine the nail length, add one inch to the thickness of the corrugation (a 1 3/4- or 2-inch nail should be sufficient).

At both eaves nail every other corrugation. Nail every third corrugation on the intermediate purlins.

Do not under-drive the nails; they may work themselves loose. Do not over-drive the nails; this will compress or damage the washers and either dimple or flatten the corrugation.

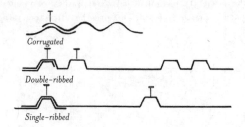

How to nail various types of roofing

To keep from driving a nail that misses a purlin, align and secure the sheet both top and bottom. Mark off two-foot centers on the panel with a chalkline. Have a helper hold one end of the line over the purlin. Stretch the cord over the 2 x 4 and snap a line which will locate the center of the purlin. Do this for all the intermediate purlins.

Should you inadvertently miss a purlin, pull out the nail and fill the hole with a sheet metal screw or rubber sealant recommended by the manufacturer. The same thing should be done if you discover an enlarged nail hole.

RIBBED ROOFING

V-crimp sheets of metal roofing with two to three crimps should be laid with a side lap of one crimp. Sheets with five crimps should be laid with a side lap of two crimps. The five-crimp sheets provide a more watertight seal than sheets with only one overlap.

Ribbed roofing can be single or double ribbed. Nail the manufacturer's gable trim along the rake with roofing nails at twelve-inch intervals. The molded-rubber filler strip should be tacked to the eave. The nails which will pass through the metal roofing will secure this strip.

Start at the edge furthest from the prevailing winds to prevent rain or snow from leaking into the structure between the sheets. The panel should be squared and nailed at both eaves and at the intermediate purlins. Do not nail down the last rib since it will be secured when the next panel is nailed. Overlap the second panel by one rib for both double-rib and single-rib sheets and complete the nailing pattern according to the manufacturer's instructions.

Continue across the roof with screw-type or ring-shank nails with protected heads or neoprene washers.

PRESERVING A METAL ROOF

Galvanized steel, which is steel with a coat of zinc, won't rust until the zinc wears off. The durability of the metal depends on this coating. The heavier the zinc, the longer the life. The gauge of the steel has nothing to do with the thickness of the zinc. To indicate a thicker coating of zinc, the metal is marked with the 2-oz. "Seal of Quality" which specifies a heavier coating of zinc on galvanized-steel sheets. Look for this "Seal of Quality" if you live in an area of extremely rigorous weather conditions or highly corrosive industrial or seashore atmosphere.

The galvanized steel should weather for at least one year before being painted; in fact the steel should give years of service before it will need painting. Although the steel can be painted immediately, weathering is desirable (but not necessary) to achieve good adhesion when the correct paint is used.

Buy zinc-rich paint and purchase only the top grade of paint—at least for the first coat. Zinc-dust paints adhere the best. Do not use aluminum paints. They will bleed because the two metals are incompatible. Two coats are better than one, but the second coat can be ordinary house or trim paint.

Don't wait too long before you paint; the best time is when the first rust begins to show. Before painting, clean the roof thoroughly. Remove loose dirt and rust spots with a stiff broom or wire brush. Remove oil or grease with a solvent and wash the entire surface with a brush and water. Check the nails. Some may have to be re-nailed.

Paint the roof in warm, dry weather (at least 40°F). Apply the zinc-base paint with a brush, high-pressure sprayer, or long nap roller.

Aluminum doesn't need to be painted, and if the steel is coated with aluminum or aluminum-zinc, the steel can be left unpainted.

REPAIRS

Repairs to metal roofs are simple. Sometimes the sheets pull away at the side laps. Remove the nails and reset them to make a tighter fit. If the nails will not hold, use sheet metal screws to pull the sheets together. Drill a small hole through the two sheets at the peak of the corrugation and screw in a size 12 or 14 sheet metal screw. Drive in a new nail one inch away. Enlarged nail holes should be filled this way with extra nails added along the sides.

Leaks can be stopped with a coat of roofing cement or a drop of solder. Larger holes should be covered with a new piece of the same metal. (A fiberglass patch should be used for aluminum which cannot be soldered, and for any roof that has been coated with tar or roofing cement.) Cut a patch at least two inches larger than the hole. Snip off the corners and turn back the edges 1/2 inch. Sand the turned edge to a shine. Coat it and the corresponding roof surface with flux. Lay the patch in place; weigh it down with bricks or stones. Use an electric soldering iron and heat the edge of the patch until the solid-core solder flows freely into the joint. Work around all four sides. Wipe away the residue.

STORM DAMAGE

If a bad storm has partially ruined the roof, remove the damaged sheets and replace them, keeping the same overlap pattern. Be careful not to damage the usable sheets when removing nails.

Remember that aluminum and galvanized steel aren't compatible. Do not make repairs with aluminum panels on a roof of galvanized steel or vice versa. The two metals have a corrosive effect on each other.

If leakage occurs along an entire side lap, the two sheets should be caulked. Butyl rubber or a caulking compound recommended by the manufacturer may be used. Loosen the side lap nails with a screwdriver. Pry up the top sheet and force the sealant between the sheets in a continuous bead. Reset the nails and caulk the nail holes carefully. If any are enlarged, fill them with sealant or sheet metal screws, and renail one inch away.

Stacking the Wood

Wood will season much more quickly if it is stacked, with some accommodation for ventilation. If space is no problem, wood stacked criss-cross (for six months, then in a parallel fashion) will dry more rapidly. If storage is a problem or you don't relish the prospect of restacking the pile, then it can be stacked in parallel fashion in the storage shed. Remember that if stacked in long rows it will take much longer to dry and the lower layers may rot before they season.

When stacking the wood, some provision must be made to keep it off the ground. Stringer can be laid down approximately a foot apart and the wood stacked on these, or wood pallets can be used if they are available locally.

Criss-cross the end logs as you build up on the pile and tilt these logs slightly towards the center of the pile. You may even want to pile a set of splits criss-cross in the center of the pile for greater stability. End braces shouldn't be necessary but can be used if you have difficulty stacking wood, or if the pile collapses at either end.

The piles should go the long way of the shed, and with space between the rows for ventilation.

Since dry wood has more heat value than green, keep close track of which wood you've stacked where. Use the first-cut wood first, particularly since wood can be stored too long. Decay will markedly reduce the wood's heat value. Unsplit wood with its bark still on will become moist and punky inside because the bark has prevented water loss. Birch will rot quickly; hickory, beech and hard maple are susceptible to rot and fungi; cedar, oak, black locust and black walnut are most durable.

You may wish to separate hardwoods and softwoods. The softwoods ignite more easily and burn more rapidly than the hardwoods. Therefore they are ideal for kindling.

In one portion of the shed build a bin for kindling, twigs, birch bark, shavings, pine cones, corn cobs, dried citrus peels, lath, scraps from lumberyards, or whatever else you may collect during the year for tinder. It can also be a receptacle for wood chips found around the chopping block.

HOW TO CHECK FOR GREEN WOOD

Even with a storage shed, you may run out of wood, and have to use wood cut this year. Since some woods may be greener than others, it will be useful to know how to identify green wood—just split a piece. The core will look wet and shiny; dry wood looks dull and the saw marks are much less pronounced.

Green wood is almost twice as heavy as seasoned wood and will make a dull thud when two sticks are hit together. Green wood is hard to handle, hard to light and burns slowly. Much of its heat value is lost in heating, then evaporating, the excess moisture.

As wood dries, the moisture evaporates naturally and the wood begins to shrink. (Wood even when air dry is still 20–25 percent moisture.) Since wood dries unevenly, cracking and checking of the wood occurs. Dried wood can be recognized by the weathered ends and by the cracks which will radiate like spokes out from the heartwood.

Continued ➜

Green wood can be used to dampen an excessively hot fire or used at night to help hold a fire overnight. It tends to smoke more than dry wood and therefore increases creosote deposits and soot. If you must use green wood, use it during the day when the fire is the hottest.

To be more scientific about the process, you can weigh a split just after it has been cut; then weigh it again in nine months and figure the weight loss. Oven-drying will also give you an indication of moisture loss. Weigh the wood, then leave it in the oven at a low setting. After a few hours, you should know how much by weight the wood has lost.

SEASONED WOOD

In order to avoid burning green wood, it is important to establish a wood storage routine which hastens the drying of your wood fuel supply. A pole-built shed is a simple, practical method of insuring you get the full heat potential from the wood. In addition, you will be increasing the burning efficiency of your stove while decreasing the possibility of chimney fires.

APPROXIMATE WEIGHTS AND HEAT VALUES FOR DIFFERENT WOODS

	Weight/cord		Available heat (Million BTU)	
	Green	Air dry	Green	Air dry
Ash	3840	3440	16.5	20.0
Aspen	3440	2160	10.3	12.5
Beech, American	4320	3760	17.3	21.8
Birch, yellow	4560	3680	17.3	21.3
Elm, American	4320	2900	14.3	17.2
Hickory, shagbark	5040	4240	20.7	24.6
Maple, red	4000	3200	15.0	18.6
Maple, sugar	4480	3680	18.4	21.3
Oak, red	5120	3680	17.9	21.3
Oak, white	5040	3920	19.2	22.7
Pine, eastern white	2880	2080	12.1	13.3

Making Maple Syrup

Noel Perrin

The basic process of making maple syrup is extremely simple. All you do is boil maple sap down to about 1/35th of its original volume.

If you intend to sell any of what you make, there are some further steps, such as getting the syrup to precisely the right density. And filtering it through a good felt strainer. And grading it. And hot-packing it at a temperature of at least 180°F. Many people do all these things with syrup for home use, as well. But they don't have to.

The equipment for making syrup can be as simple as two or three spouts, some large tin cans, and a kettle. Or it can be as complicated as a full-scale sugarhouse with evaporator, finishing rig, holding tank, and

so on through twenty or thirty other pieces of equipment. At that point you have an investment of $10,000 or $20,000.

The Sugar Maple

The first equipment for making maple syrup is to be able to recognize a sugar maple. Most people who started life in cities cannot. (Many years ago this writer paid a neighbor's teenage son $3 to walk through his newly bought woods with him, pointing out the sugar maples while he frantically marked them with red paint.)

There are two other maples to distinguish a sugar maple from: one that you'll find in yards, and one that you'll find in the woods. In yards, the other common variety is an import from Europe called the Norway maple. At first glance a Norway and a sugar look very much alike. Both have the classic maple leaf, such as can be seen on the Canadian flag. Both are large, handsome trees. But the leaf of the Norway looks as if it had been put sideways through a clothes wringer; it's about twice as wide as a sugar maple leaf, and much larger altogether. And the bark, if you look closely, has a fine, almost diamond-shaped pattern. Sugar maples lack this.

In the woods, the other common variety is the red maple—also called soft maple and swamp maple. In the fall, it's absurdly easy to tell one from a sugar maple—it is among the first of all trees to turn color, and it turns bright scarlet. A sugar maple will turn pink-yellow-orange several weeks later. In the summer it's still pretty easy to tell them apart, because red maples have small saw-toothed leaves, while the edges of a sugar-maple leaf move in smooth curves.

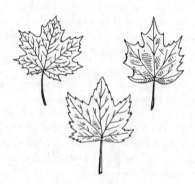

From left, Norway, red, and sugar maple leaves.

IDENTIFY EARLY

In the winter and spring, however, it can sometimes be hard to tell—unless you have very good eyes, and can see the large red buds of the red maple, way up there in the top of the tree. Moral: If you're going to tap maples in a woodlot, identify them the fall before you plan to start. It won't be any disaster if you don't; red maples can also be tapped, and they make a perfectly edible syrup. But you have to boil down just about twice as much sap to get the same amount of syrup—and you end up with an inferior product. Most people avoid the reds.

All right, now you know how to spot a sugar maple, at least when it has its leaves. You have some in your yard or your woods, or you have permission to use a neighbor's trees. You furthermore know that early spring is when you make maple syrup. (It's possible to make some in the fall, as the sap goes down to the roots for the winter, and it's possible to make a little on any warm, sunny winter day. But early spring is the only time you can make a serious quantity.) Finally, you know that your part of the country has to have sunny days and freezing nights in early spring, or your maples won't yield any sap to mention. English visitors in the 18th century didn't know this, and wasted a lot of time digging up sugar maples and taking them back to England. But the climate was wrong—as it also is in, for example, all of Virginia except a few hill counties. No syrup got made. Where is the climate right? In virtually all of New England, in New York State right down to the outer suburbs of New York City, in western Pennsylvania, in a broad sweep of the Middle West, especially Ohio, Indiana, Michigan, and Wisconsin.

System One

Suppose you have just one sugar maple in your front yard, or suppose you have a whole hillside covered with them, but want to experiment before you commit yourself to buying equipment. Here is a system, for one to five taps.

First buy one to five spouts. New ones will cost you 75¢ to $1.00 each at almost any hardware store in sugaring country, or by mail from the manufacturers. There are four or five varieties of spouters, each favored by a group of farmers. I favor spouts that come with pre-cast hooks, like the Warner and Soule. But any of the metal spouts on the market will work just fine.

Now see if you have a 7/16" bit for a hand drill. If you don't, you may have to buy one. Those specially designed for sugaring start at around $8. But for this one year you could probably get away with a 3/8" or a 1/2" bit, especially if you use Grimm spouts.

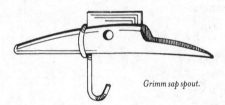

Grimm sap spout.

CONTAINERS

The next step is to get some containers. If you were operating on a larger scale, you would get proper sap buckets, or else use tubing. As it is, plastic gallon jugs, such as cider and milk come in, will do nicely. For that matter, even coffee cans will do, though you have to empty them pretty often.

Decide how you're going to boil the sap down. The simplest way is to put it in an ordinary cookpot on the kitchen stove. There are myths, dating back a century, of all the wallpaper in a kitchen coming loose and sliding to the floor, when a pot of sap was kept boiling day after day. But if the myth were ever true, it isn't now. Exhaust fans have outdated it.

USE WOOD STOVE

A more serious objection is that at the price of electricity and gas it is simply too expensive to make syrup on a kitchen range. It's better to do it instead on the top of a wood heating stove, and just use the range as a finishing rig. Some people—especially those whose families hate mess in the house—do their boiling in the yard, on an outdoor fireplace. But use an indoor woodstove if you possibly can.

The next step is up to nature. You've got your spouts, and a drill, and containers; you know where you will boil. Now you wait for the right day to tap. The right day is a sunny one, with the temperature at least 40°F, after a freezing night. If there's no wind, that's better still.

Depending on where you live, such days will begin to occur anywhere from late February to late March. If you tap too early, your spouts will dry up before the season is over. The tree can usually close off the flow of sap in four to six weeks. This becomes a problem if you tapped on a freak early warm day, which is then followed by a couple of weeks of cold weather, and no sap runs. On the other hand, if you tap too late, you miss the early runs. A good rule of thumb is to tap about a month before the last snow usually goes. If your snow is usually all gone by April 10, you'd tap about March 10.

THE DAY ARRIVES

Let's say the right day has now come. You have two sugar maples in your yard, and you are going to tap them. The old rule is that you don't tap a maple until it's ten inches in diameter—and then you can add one tap for each additional six or eight inches of diameter, up to a maximum of four. But this year, though your maples are both fairly big, you are just going to put one tap in each.

Get your drill, the spouts, and a hammer. Drill a hole about two and a half inches deep in each tree, about two feet above the ground. (The lower the tap, the better the sap run.) If you want to be professional, drill your hole very slightly upwards, to take advantage of gravity flow. But a horizontal tap will work almost as well.

Slant slightly upwards when drilling hole.

Now drive the spout in with the hammer—and if it's a hookless spout like a Grimm, remember to put a hook on, facing outwards, before you do. Tap it in with several light strokes. If you drive it in too hard, you will split the bark, and a good deal of sap will leak out through the split and be lost. And if you drive it in too lightly, it may pull out under the weight of a full container. Neither of these will hurt the tree, but why waste sap? Besides, the dark stain running down the bark amounts to a public confession that you tapped badly.

If you're using tin cans, just make a hole near the rim, and hang one on the hook. If you're using gallon plastic jugs, you make two holes, both in the handle. The small lower hole goes on the hook. The larger upper one is where the sap runs into the jug from the end of the spout. The holes have to be in the handle, because that's the only strong part of the jug.

If you picked the right day, and if you got the jugs up by ten o'clock or so, they should both be full by suppertime. In fact, if it was a really

Continued ➡

good day, you may have to empty them twice. About then you'll wish you had a gathering pail—and for an operation this size a cheap plastic bucket will work nicely.

Plastic jug makes a fine sap bucket. And it's cheap.

START BOILING

As soon as you've gathered, you can start boiling. A pot that will hold at least two gallons is obviously preferable. Just leave it on the woodstove all night. At this stage, no special precautions are necessary.

In the morning, if you're lucky, the volume will be down about half, and by afternoon it will be down to about a quarter. At this point, you will need to decide whether to keep adding fresh sap or to finish off each batch separately. Since two gallons of sap usually make less than a cup of maple syrup, it's a good idea to add fresh sap at least once. That way you can make a pint at a time.

Either way, once the sap has boiled down to about a tenth of its original volume, you should shift it to the kitchen range, and start watching it. By now it has a faint color, and is quite sweet. It has begun to develop a layer of thick white foam on top, which you skim off with a strainer and throw away. It is also very likely to boil up abruptly, if you get the heat too high. One drop of cream will send it right back down, and enable you to keep boiling fast.

A professional sugarer would determine when he or she had syrup either with a hydrometer or a sugaring thermometer. If you have a candy thermometer, you can use that. It should read seven degrees above the boiling point of water—219°F. if you live near sea level. But if you don't, dip an ordinary spatula in the boiling sap, and hold it vertically over the pot. If you've got syrup, a thin "apron" of maple will appear at the bottom of the spatula. It looks a little like a bubble-gum bubble, only much prettier. If the sap is still too thin, it will simply drip back into the pot.

FILTERING

All right, it aproned. You have syrup. Since this is for home use, you can immediately can it in a pint glass jar with a tight lid. The next day, however, there will be quite a lot of unattractive sediment at the bottom of the jar. The old-timers just poured off the clear syrup from above it. But you may prefer to filter before you can, and avoid the inevitable waste. To do a perfect job, you need a special felted-wool filter. None is made in the tiny size you would need. But you can do a pretty good job with a paper coffee filter, or even with a funnel lined with paper toweling.

You keep repeating these steps until the season ends or you get tired, whichever comes first. Sugaring in the house is so slow a process that fairly often people do get tired while the sap is still running. In that case, they simply pull out their spouts and stop.

END OF SEASON

But suppose you don't get tired? How will you know when to stop? One of two ways. The more likely way is that your cans or jugs will begin to fill more and more slowly, until one afternoon you go out to gather and you find that they contain either nothing or else a small quantity of pale yellow sap. Occasionally it's even bright yellow. That means the tree is ready to bud, and the sap is worthless for making syrup. Throw it out, and call the season over.

The other way is that you're still getting plenty of sap, but when you boil it you get a dark syrup—not just amber but actually brown. It has an overpowering and not altogether pleasant flavor. Such syrup is commonly called Grade C. Big producers often make large quantities of it, and sell the best of it to health food stores as a kind of maple molasses, and the rest to tobacco companies and other bulk buyers. But it is not worth anyone's while to make it in the house. Pull your spouts and quit.

If you did keep going until the end of the season, you should have about two quarts of syrup—a quart per tap is a fair average production.

Where to Get Sugaring Supplies

There are several principal manufacturers of sugaring equipment:

The Leader Evaporator Company
25 Stowell Street
St. Albans, VT 05478
(802) 524–4966

G. H. Grimm Company
#2 Pine Street
Rutland, VT 05701
(802) 775–5411

Mann Lake Supply
501 First Street
Hackensack, MN 56452
(218) 675–6688

Each company also has a string of distributors and agents who sell their supplies. Some are independent farmers; some are store owners. Write to any of these companies for a list of their distributors and agents or for supplementary information and catalogues.

In addition, many other hardware and general stores in sugaring country stock a variable selection of equipment. Prices will usually be slightly higher.

Easy Composters You Can Build

Nick Noyes

Illustrations by Alison Kolesar

Introduction

Composting, which in its most basic form is simply the process of decomposition, began long before we humans ever took it upon ourselves to make it an organized activity. Given enough time and the proper conditions, organic matter breaks down. Composting, as we use the term in the modern sense, is a system for enhancing, and thus accelerating, the natural process of decomposition. Since composting is going to take place with or without us, we can make the process as simple or as complex as we choose and be assured of success every time.

Why Make Compost in a Bin?

Although they are not strictly required for composting to occur, compost bins are useful for a number of reasons. First, bins are tidy. Piles out in the open are harder to control, especially to keep piled up and properly aerated and watered, than ones that are contained. Frequent turning accelerates composting, and a pile in a bin is easier to turn without making a mess. Bins help hold in heat as the compost "works," increasing the likelihood that weed seeds and pathogens will be destroyed, an especially important factor if you will use the compost on your garden.

Another good reason for a bin is animals. Animal problems are second only to odor problems as the factors that gave early composting efforts a bad name. Both problems are easily avoided. With minimum effort, a properly designed and managed compost heap will not create any problems with animals. Period.

Common sense dictates that compost piles in urban residential neighborhoods without fences should be protected from animals, especially pets, rats, and mice. Because of the danger of encouraging rodents, some states require rodent-proof compost bins in urban areas. A rodent-proof bin really is a necessity if you plan to compost food waste in urban areas, and you may find that it is a good idea wherever you are. Pets, especially dogs, will sometimes "prospect" around untended piles. Some gardeners use an enclosed composter for food wastes and have a separate open bin system to handle yard wastes. Food waste may also be composted by burying it in the garden, at least 8" deep.

If you should encounter a problem with animals, you may be using the wrong materials in your pile (i.e., fat, oils, grease, meat, bones, or dairy products), or not turning it often enough (thereby creating an "attractive" odor), or the bin might not be sufficiently restricting to pests.

COMPOSTING SYSTEMS AT A GLANCE

Type	Advantages	Disadvantages
Slow outdoor pile	Easy to start and add to. Low maintenance.	Can take a year or more to decompose. Nutrients are lost to leaching. Can be odorous and attract animals and flies.
Hot outdoor pile	Fast decomposition. Weed seeds and pathogens are killed. More nutrient-rich because less leaching of nutrients. Less likely to attract animals and flies.	Requires lots of effort to turn and aerate and manage the process. Works best when you have lots of material to add right away, as opposed to a little bit at a time.
Bins and boxes	Neat appearance. Hold heat more easily than a pile. Deter animals. Lid keeps rain off compost. If turned, decomposition can be quite rapid.	Costs you time to build the bins or money to buy them.
Tumblers	Self-contained and not messy. Can produce quick compost. Relatively easy to aerate by turning the tumbler. Odor not usually a problem. No nutrient leaching into ground.	Tumblers are costly. Volume is relatively small. Works best if material is added all at once.
Pit composting	Quick and easy. No maintenance. No investment in materials.	Only takes care of small amounts of organic matter.
Sheet composting	Can handle large amounts of organic matter. No containers required. Good way to improve soil in large areas.	Requires effort to till material into the soil, Takes several months to decompose.
Plastic bag or garbage can	Easy to do year-round. Can be done in a small space. Requires no back labor.	Is mostly anaerobic, so smell can be a problem. Can attract fruit flies. Need to pay attention to carbon/ nitrogen ratio to avoid a slimy mess.
Worm composter	Easy. No odor. Can be done indoors. Can be added to continuously. So nutrient-rich it can be used as a fertilizer. Good way to compost food waste.	Requires some care when adding materials and removing castings. Need to protect worms from temperature extremes. May attract fruit flies.

Continued ➜

WIRE MESH COMPOST BINS

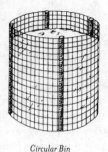

Circular Bin

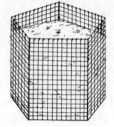

Five-Panel Bin

Materials

Circular Bin (3 1/2-foot diameter)

12 1/2 feet of 36" wide 1" poultry wire, or 1/2" hardware cloth, or

18-gauge plastic-coated wire mesh

4 metal or plastic clips, or copper wire ties

three or four 4-foot wooden or metal posts to support poultry wire bins

Five-Panel Bin

15 feet of 24" wide 12- to 16-gauge plastic-coated wire mesh

20 metal or plastic clips, or plastic-coated copper wire ties

Tools

heavy-duty wire or tin snips

pliers

hammer or metal file

work gloves

CONSTRUCTION DETAILS

Circular Bin:

Roll out and cut 12 1/2 feet of poultry wire, hardware cloth, or plastic-coated wire mesh. If using poultry wire, roll back 3 to 4 inches at each end of cut piece to provide a strong, clean edge that will be easy to latch and won't poke or snag. Set wire circle in place for compost pile and secure ends with clips or wire ties. Space wood or metal posts around perimeter inside wire circle. Pound posts firmly into the ground while tensing them against wire to provide support.

If using hardware cloth, trim ends, flush with a cross wire to eliminate loose edges that may poke or scratch hands. Apply file to each wire along cut edge to ensure safer handling when opening and closing bins. Bend hardware cloth into circle and attach ends with clips or ties. Set bin in place for composting. Bins made with hardware cloth should be strong enough to stand alone without posts. Plastic-coated wire mesh bins are made in the same manner, except that bending this heavier material into an even circular shape will require extra effort. Also, filing the wire ends may cause the plastic coating to tear. Striking the end of each wire with a hammer a few times will knock down any jagged edges.

Five-Panel Bin:

Cut five 3-foot-long sections of 24" wide wire mesh. Make cuts at the top of the next row of squares to leave 1" long wires sticking out along one cut edge of each panel. This edge will be the top of the bin. Use a pair of pliers to bend over and tightly clamp each wire on this edge. This provides protection against scraping arms when adding yard wastes to the bin. Attach panels using clips or wire ties.

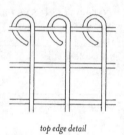

top edge detail

Bin designs for "Wire Mesh Compost Bins" and "Wood and Wire Stationary 3-Bin System" were developed by Seattle Tilth Association for Seattle's Master Composter Program. Reprinted with permission from Seattle Tilth and the Seattle Engineering Department.

Plans for Compost Bins and Boxes

The following plans offer compost containers that fit a variety of composting styles and composter locations. While some offer exact specifications for dimensions and materials, the plans can also be used simply as guidelines. The desire to recycle materials on hand seems to be an integral personality trait of those who compost. My neighbor cuts 15-foot lengths from an old reinforced rubber conveyor belt, wires together the ends, and makes great, sturdy bins. Others use plastic or wood snow fencing arranged in a circle. Experiment, adapt, innovate!

The plans of the Seattle Tilth Association are included (with thanks for their use) because they are well thought out and understandably popular. However, some people, especially those with

physical handicaps, may find the bins are too tall for them to easily reach in and turn materials, or that it is too cumbersome when aeration is done by lifting and moving the bin. While the taller bin is optimum for making a hot pile, compost may be made just as well in a lower, wider bin.

Many prefer to use pressure-treated wood for outdoor projects (and the "wood and wire stationary 3-bins system" specifies its use). You may wonder if this wood is safe for use around materials, such as compost, that will come in contact with plants that you might eat. The jury is still out, although some experts insist that the toxic compounds in pressure-treated wood do not leach out and affect plants. I choose not to use pressure-treated materials anywhere near my compost bins or my vegetable gardens. If you want to build with pressure-treated wood, check with the manufacturer for the latest safety information regarding your intended use.

Although these are mostly simple projects, don't neglect safety when making them. Unwrap wire carefully: prepackaged hardware cloth (which, by the way, is not cloth at all, but a stiff wire mesh) is often "spring loaded." When making composters that use hardware cloth or poultry wire, make sure there are no wire ends sticking out on your completed project. Cover all exposed wire edges with wood trim where practical. Finally, always wear the ear and eye protection appropriate for building your project.

A QUICK AND EASY COMPOSTING SYSTEM FOR WIRE MESH COMPOST BINS

1. Set up a wire collector. Choose a well-drained spot, preferably a shady one that's not too far from the house or garden. Don't forget that it's nice to be near a water source, too. If you want, you can loosen the soil up a little where the collector sits. This will help drainage.

2. Make the first layer. Loosely place leaves, hay, straw, or other good compost materials in the bottom of the collector in a layer about 2 inches thick.

3. Add protein material. Sprinkle a large handful of alfalfa meal or other protein-rich meal over the first layer. Dust the entire surface.

4. Do it again. Repeat steps 2 and 3 by adding the same amounts of organic matter and meal as before.

5. Sprinkle with water. Moisten the pile thoroughly. Compost piles that don't "work" well are usually too dry or too wet. The material should be moist but not soaked. In warm, dry weather you may have to water the pile every three or four days to keep it in good working condition.

6. Keep the center loose—never compact the center of the pile. The composting process depends on the ability of the air, water, and activator to contact all the material as completely as possible. Good circulation is a must. A good compost pile is a balance of thirds: one-third air, one-third material, and one-third moisture.

7. Fill the collector. Whenever material becomes available, repeat steps 2 through 6, until the collector is full. Keep everything loose and never tightly packed down.

8. Turn the pile in a week. If the pile is made correctly, the temperature should reach 140° to 150°F. within two or three days. After a week or so of heating and decomposing, it's time to turn the pile.

Lift off the wire collector, set it up beside the pile, and then fork all the material back into it. Put the outside, drier material in the center of the new pile. If the material seems too dry, moisten it. The heating process will start up again. It should be ready to use—but still coarse—in 15 days.

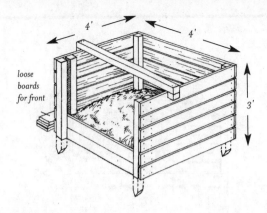

loose boards for front

NEW ZEALAND COMPOST BOX

The New Zealand Box was designed by Sir Albert Howard, a far-sighted British horticulturist who developed composting systems during the World War II era. A very precise man, Howard's methods and composting processes were quite specific, as were his instructions for making this bin.

This box requires two ten-foot lengths of 2" x 2" wood and twelve eight-foot lengths of 1" x 6" wood. Cut the 2x2s into six 39" pieces, and cut the 1x6 wood into twenty-four 48" pieces. Assemble the pieces as illustrated, taking care to leave a half-inch space between each of the side boards to allow for aeration. Use galvanized screws (preferably) or nails to join the pieces. The uprights should be pushed into the ground approximately 3" (loosen the soil if necessary). The front boards (which will likely need to be trimmed a bit for an exact fit) slide in and out to make filling and emptying the box easier.

Two of these boxes side by side would make an ideal system. Adding a crossbar across the top is strongly recommended to increase the stability of the sides.

The box may be primed and painted with latex paint for greater durability, or built with treated wood if you don't object to using it in contact with your composted materials. Some have suggested making the uprights longer to create a taller box. This might be a good idea if you often have a lot of bulky materials to compost.

Sir Albert Howard's compost-making system is called the Indore method, named after Indore, India, where he conducted research. This method will make great compost, but frankly most of us aren't that organized. But if you have built the box, perhaps you're a composting purist, and will want to follow Sir Albert Howard's instructions for using it, too.

The Indore method calls for building a series of layers with a three-to-one ratio of green matter to manure:

- first: six inches of green matter (weeds, leaves, etc.)
- second: two inches of manure, garbage, or other high-nitrogen source
- third: a sprinkling of soil (plus ground limestone and ground phosphate rock)

Repeat layers until the pile is four or five feet high. Moisten each layer as you build the pile so it is about as wet as a squeezed-out sponge. Poke holes in it with a rod to aid aeration. Turn the pile in six weeks and use it after three months.

Continued →

Wood and Wire Stationary 3-Bin System

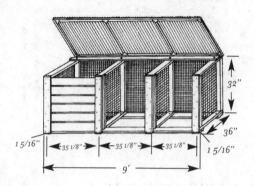

32"

36"

1 5/16" ←— 35 1/8" —→←— 35 1/8" —→←— 35 1/8" —→ 1 5/16"

9'

Materials

two 18-foot treated 2x4s

four 12-foot, or eight 6-foot treated 2x4s

one 9-foot and two 6-foot 2x2s

one 16-foot cedar 2x6

nine 6-foot cedar 1x6s

22 feet of 36" wide 1/2" hardware cloth

twelve 1/2" carriage bolts 4" long

12 washers and 12 nuts for bolts

3 lbs. of 16d galvanized nails

1/2 lb. 8d galvanized casement nails

250 poultry wire staples or power stapler w/1" staples

one 12-foot and one 8-foot sheet 4 oz. clear corrugated fiberglass

three 8-foot lengths of wiggle molding

40 gasketed aluminum nails for corrugated fiberglass roofing

two 3" zinc-plated hinges for lid

8 flat 4" corner braces with screws

4 flat 3" T-braces with screws

Tools

hand saw or circular power saw

drill with 1/2" and 1/8" bits

screwdriver

hammer

tin snips

tape measure

pencil

3/4" socket or open-ended wrench

carpenter's square

(option — power stapler with 1" long galvanized staples)

safety glasses and ear protection

CONSTRUCTION DETAILS

Build Dividers: Cut two 31 1/2" and two 36" pieces from each 12-foot 2x4. Butt end nail the four pieces into a 35" x 36" square. Repeat for other three sections. Cut four 37" long sections of hardware cloth, bend back edges 1". Stretch hardware cloth across each frame, check for squareness of the frame and staple screen tightly into place every 4" around edge.

Butt end nail detail

Set Up Dividers: Set up dividers parallel to one another 3 feet apart. Measure and mark centers for the two inside dividers. Cut four 9-foot pieces out of the two 18-foot 2x4 boards. Place two 9-foot base boards on top of dividers and measure the positions for the two inside dividers. Mark a center line for each divider on the 9-foot 2x4. With each divider, line up the center lines and make the base board flush against the outer edge of the divider. Drill a 1/2" hole through each junction centered 1" in from the inside edge. Secure base boards with carriage bolts, but do not tighten yet. Turn the unit right side up and repeat the process for the top 9-foot board. Using the carpenter's square or measuring between opposing corners, make sure the bin is square, and tighten all bolts securely. Fasten a 9-foot-long piece of hardware cloth securely to the back side of the bin with staples every 4" around the frame.

Front Slats and Runners: Cut four 36" long 2x6s for front slat runners. Rip-cut two of these boards to 4 3/4" wide and nail them securely to the front of the outside dividers and baseboard, making them flush on top and outside edges. Save remainder of rip-cut boards for use on back runners. Center the remaining full-width boards on the front of the inside dividers flush with the top edge and nail securely. To create back runners, cut the remaining 2x6 into a 34" long piece and then rip-cut into four equal pieces, 1 1/4" x 2". Nail back runner parallel to front runners on side of divider leaving a 1" gap for slats. Cut all the 1x6 cedar boards into slats 31 1/4" long.

Fiberglass Lid: Use the last 9-foot 2x4 for the back of the lid. Cut four 32 1/2 inch 2x2s and one 9-foot 2x2. Lay out into position on ground and check for squareness. Screw in corner braces and T-braces on bottom side of the frame. Center lid frame, brace side down on bin structure and attach with hinges. Cut wiggle board to fit the front and back 9-foot sections of the lid frame. Predrill wiggle board with 1/8" drill bit and nail with 8d casement nails. Cut fiberglass to fit flush with front and back edges. Overlay pieces at least one channel wide. Predrill fiberglass and wiggle board for each nail hole. Nail on top of every third hump with gasketed nails.

CEMENT BLOCK BINS

Stacked Block Composter

Stacked cement block bins are my hands-down favorite quick-to-build composting bins. They cost more than some other styles, but they last virtually forever. In addition to being durable, they are easy-to-use, and because they are not mortared

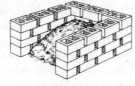

Cement Block Bin

together, may be arranged in myriad and quickly changed bin designs to accommodate a variety of personal composting styles.

Be sure to select a level site for a stacked cement block composter. It is especially important that the blocks that form the base of the bin be on firm, level ground because the blocks are not mortared together. Stagger the seams in each row to interlock the blocks, rather than making a simple series of stacks of blocks that could easily topple. For bins that use blocks placed with holes vertically, iron pipe or wooden stakes may be placed through at intervals and driven into the ground for added stability, if desired.

To build the bin, first calculate the approximate size bin you want. Approximately fifty blocks will make a decent-sized bin, although the exact number you need will depend upon how you lay the blocks. Next, either lay the blocks with the holes sideways to promote air circulation, or, if laying the blocks with the holes vertically, leave spaces between each block. Half blocks can be purchased for the front edges of the walls, to fill the gaps due to staggering the alternating rows. With a cement block bin it is easy to create a two or even three bin system: simply lengthen the back wall and add an additional side wall or two.

The only real drawback of open cement block bins is that they offer no protection against visits from animals, so they are not practical for urban areas. To discourage small pets from visiting the bin a four-sided bin may be constructed, although this makes adding materials and turning the compost more difficult. This bin would need a lid, which can be a simple wood frame constructed of two by fours, with chicken wire or hardware cloth stapled to it. The lid would simply lift off for access.

Mortared Composter

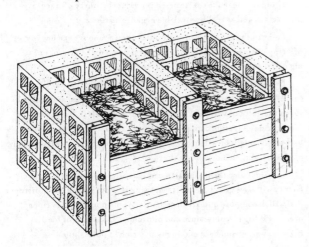

An alternative to the stacked open bin is a two-bin closed container using concrete blocks held in place with mortar. Because it is mortared, this bin may be somewhat taller than a stacked block bin and the wall seams do not have to be staggered. The bin pictured features a removable front made of wood.

To make the front of the bin, bolt 1" x 8" boards through a spacer board to the cement blocks. Make sure that the space between the 1x8s and the blocks is slightly greater than the thickness of the boards that will slide in to face the front, so that they may be inserted and removed easily. One way to accomplish this is to make spacers by ripping 2 1/2-inch-wide pieces from some of the 1-inch wood. Then just shim the spacers out from the blocks with a couple of washers when you install the bolts.

BARREL COMPOSTERS

If you have limited space or just need a small, quickly made bin, you can compost in a garbage can or a steel drum. This is a great system if you are concerned about rodents and if you don't generate large quantities of compostable materials that require a bigger bin. Either galvanized metal or heavy duty polyethylene cans will work. I prefer the polyethylene ones with a locking lid for this purpose. Lids that don't lock will have to be

secured—using a rubber tie-down strap run from one can handle over the top to the other handle. This is a very quick and secure system. Punch or drill 1/4 inch holes in the bottom, sides, and lid for drainage and aeration. Set the can up on bricks or concrete blocks so that it will drain properly. As you fill this composter, cover each layer of waste materials with a layer of soil. This system holds water well, but may need additional water at times. To prevent odors, stir the material once in a while, as barrel compost bins receive less natural aeration than other types of bins.

It usually takes at least a couple of months to get usable compost from a barrel composter. Fully composted material will settle toward the bottom and the uncomposted top material will have to be removed to reach and use the finished stuff.

It helps to have two barrels set up. When one barrel is full, begin filling the second barrel. The first barrel should be fully composted and ready to use when the second barrel is full.

Selecting the Compost Pile Location

The basic rules for situating a compost pile are to set it up in a location protected on three sides, with the opening, if the bin loads from the side, facing south. And when the various options are considered, putting the pile directly on the ground in a level area seems to work best, as opposed to going to the work of elevating the pile and/or putting in a concrete or plastic sheeting base. But don't hesitate to experiment—perhaps you have an ideal natural location or a great new technique that doesn't fit these suggestions.

Virtually any location, from full sun to total shade, will work for composting. In northern New England a partially shady location has

Continued ➜

functioned best for me. In cooler climates a sunny location will enhance composting for those who want a quick-working pile. A bin in full sun in warm climates, however, will tend to dry out quickly and require more frequent watering to keep things working.

Consider where items to be composted will be loaded from. If most of the waste will come from the kitchen, select an area convenient to that sort of disposal. I have always located my compost piles at least 25 or 30 feet from the house, which, as much as I enjoy composting, is close enough to suit me. Remember, though, if you live in an area with snowy winters you'll have to clear a path to it. Also keep in mind that the less frequently you turn the pile, the more odor your bin will give off. Unfortunately, the more lazy a composter you are, the further from the house (and heavily used areas of the yard) the bin should be.

Locating your compost bin close to a source of water is another factor to consider. I rarely add water to my piles (laziness again), but in some climates this is a frequent necessity, especially for piles that you want to compost very quickly.

The proximity of your pile to your garden may also be important. A close bin saves hauling, and you'll probably find more uses for compost if the pile is handy to the garden.

Finally, consider the size of the pile that you want. I find that piles that are a moderate size, say 3 to 5 feet square and 3 to 4 feet tall, are the most manageable. Smaller piles don't heat up much, so they don't decompose as quickly. On the other hand, large piles are difficult to manage because they require frequent turning to aerate all of the material. Also, very large piles require very large bins. For me, making two or three medium piles keeps things going much better than one big one.

Ingredients for Compost: What to Use, What to Avoid

To get a compost pile working well, it's essential to have several layers of an activator throughout the pile. An activator is a source of both nitrogen and protein—ingredients that help all the various microorganisms and bacteria break down compost material.

Alfalfa meal is one of the cheapest, quickest-acting activators. If you can't find it at your garden or feed store, look in the supermarket for Litter Green, a cat litter product that's 100 percent alfalfa meal.

Every time you add new material to the compost pile, dust it thoroughly with alfalfa meal and moisten the pile a little. Alfalfa meal is an excellent source of nitrogen and protein. Made from alfalfa hay, it is usually 14 to 16 percent protein. Other good activators include barnyard manure, natural products such as bone meal, cottonseed meal, blood meal, and good, rich garden soil. Any time you add to your compost pile, dust it with a little activator.

RECIPE FOR COMPOST

To get organic material to compost properly, mix materials so that the mixture is about 30 parts of carbon to 1 part of nitrogen. There is nothing precise about this, but be aware that a mixture with too much carbon, such as a pile of leaves, will not heat up, while a mixture with too much nitrogen will manufacture ammonia—and the nitrogen will be wasted.

In the following list, the figure given is the amount of carbon per 1 part of nitrogen:

Straw	150–500
Ground corn cobs	50–100
Sawdust	150–500
Pine needles	60–110
Oak leaves	50
Young weeds	30
Grass clippings	25
Manure with bedding	25
Vegetable trimmings	25
Animal droppings	15
Leguminous plants	15

FINDING ADDITIONAL MATERIALS FOR GREAT COMPOST

While compostable materials from around the house and yard are more than enough for most backyard compost makers, many gardeners find the need to go further afield to secure even larger quantities of usable materials, such as some of the more exotic ones listed below.

The next most immediate source is your neighborhood. People are often glad to give away raked leaves for the favor of not having to haul them to the local landfill. The same is often true of lawn clippings. Fireplace and woodstove ashes are high in phosphorus and potassium.

If you live near the sea, seaweed is a valuable source of trace minerals as well as readily available organic matter.

Folks in the country can sometimes obtain manure at a low cost by offering to clean out a neighbor's horse stable, chicken coop, or pig pen.

Even the local barber shop can be a source of fertility for the garden. Human hair contains about 12 percent nitrogen and will help speed the decomposition of other organic materials in the garden. If you provide a separate container and make regular collections, the barber just might be willing to save his refuse and give you a free supply of clean, light, rich organic matter.

Consider also the manufacturing activities in your area. A shoe factory will have quantities of leather scraps, a potent source of nitrogen that will decompose quickly in compost. Apple pomace from cider pressing is high in potassium and phosphorus, basic plant foods. Brewer's waste from beer making is also rich in potassium.

Feathers from poultry processing contain about 15 percent nitrogen; while eggshells contain roughly 1 percent. Scraps and lint from wool and cotton cloth manufacture also contain fertilizing elements.

Cannery wastes are another good source of organic matter. Pea and bean pods, potato skins, corn cobs, peanut shells, and the like will all boost soil fertility.

SUGGESTED MATERIALS FOR COMPOST

"You can work at compost as if you're cooking a wonderful French ragout," says a gardener who savors her product. "Try to make it as interesting and diverse as possible."

With a little imagination and the initiative to scavenge a bit, the time spent in building your soil will bring lush crops that grow with less of your midsummer energy.

Here's a handy basic list of items that you can use on your compost pile:

- apple pomace (by-product of cider making)
- bird-cage cleanings
- brewery wastes
- buckwheat hulls
- cannery wastes
- castor bean pomace
- chaff
- cheese whey
- cocoa bean hulls
- corn cobs and husks
- cottonseed hulls and gain trash
- dust from vacuum cleaner
- evergreen needles
- feathers
- felt waste
- garden residues (spent plants and vines, beet and carrot tops, corn stalks, etc.)
- gelatin processing waste
- grape pomace (by-product of winemaking)
- grass clippings
- hair
- hay
- kitchen wastes (vegetable and fruit rinds, parings, eggshells, coffee grounds and filters, tea leaves. etc.)
- leather waste and dust
- leaves
- manures (horse, cow, goat, pig, rabbit, poultry)
- milk, sour
- mill wastes of lignin, wool, silk, and felt
- nut shells
- oat hulls
- olive residues
- peanut hulls
- pine needles
- pond weeds
- rice hulls
- salt hay
- sawdust and shredded bark
- seaweed, kelp, eelgrass
- straw
- sugar cane
- tanbark
- tobacco stems and dust
- wood chips and rotted wood

GRASS CLIPPINGS:
IDEAL FOR IMPROVING GARDEN SOIL

These days many folks are content to let their grass clippings remain on the lawn to decompose back into the ground. However there are times when clippings must be removed, and grass clippings can be a great soil amendment if handled properly. Don't leave fresh clippings in a pile, or they will quickly turn to a smelly, brown mess. And, don't pile them too high if you're using them as mulch, or the same thing will happen.

Here are several ways to use grass clippings:

- Add them to the compost pile. They'll give you the nitrogen you need to make the pile "cook." Mix them well with other materials, such as weeds, leaves, or hay.

- Spread them around the garden area, then till them in. They're an excellent green manure.

- Spread them in thin layers when green, or let them dry before spreading them in the garden, and they'll provide one of the best mulches you can find.

The waste from the local supermarket can be a fortune in free organic materials. To please the eye of the shopping public, produce managers trim away unsightly parts of vegetables and discard all but the best produce. The culls are generally free for the asking. It is best to provide your own container and collect the refuse regularly. What can't be sold can be recycled through the soil into vegetables far better than you could find in any market.

Saw mills can also supply you with organic materials for free or at a minimal cost. Keep in mind that tree wastes are largely deficient in nitrogen and some fertilizing elements will have to be added to hasten decay of wood materials. In order to keep saw blades sharp longer, most mills use debarking machines to peel off the outer layers of the logs and the dirt and stones stuck in the bark. This bark will be coarse and should probably be composted first, using a liberal dose of nitrogen. Screen the finished product well to remove inorganic debris.

Sawdust will cost a few cents per cubic foot as it has other uses, such as for animal bedding. Unless your garden soil is already in a high state of fertility, avoid incorporating sawdust into the soil, as nitrogen necessary for good plant growth will become tied up in the decay of the sawdust. When the sawdust is used as a mulch material, this fixation is less likely to occur. Sawdust is an easy mulch to apply to give uniform coverage around plants and makes for an attractive garden. If the plants begin to slow in their growth and exhibit a yellowing of the foliage, a nitrogen deficit probably exists and can be corrected with a side dressing of high-nitrogen fertilizer.

Continued ➔

LEAF MOLD

In a hurry-up world, the making of leaf mold is largely forgotten. Because leaves have little nitrogen, they decompose slowly and do not heat up as they would if high-nitrogen material were added to them.

The two-year process of decomposition can be hastened by running the leaves through a shredder before piling them. Fence in the pile with wire netting to keep the leaves from spreading back across your lawn. Stamp the pile down. Expect to see it half its original size when the leaves have turned to leaf mold and are ready for use.

After a year, turn the pile, cutting and mixing it as much as possible. In this stage it can be used as a mulch, and will be welcomed by the earthworms in your garden.

STUFF TO KEEP OUT OF THE COMPOST PILE

Not all organic materials are suitable for composting. Animal bones and other animal waste are inappropriate, as are grease and oils because they take a long time to break down and may attract animal pests. Sewage sludge may contain heavy metals that you don't want in your garden.

Chicken manure is so strong that we are warned about the danger of it burning crops, while sawdust has such a high carbon content that we are told to add it sparingly to compost piles and never to put it on the garden without first giving plants a "booster" feeding of nitrogen. But sawdust and chicken manure together are an ideal combination—the acidity of the sawdust offsets the alkalinity of the chicken manure. But remember, sawdust from pressure-treated wood is a no-no.

Any woody material takes a long time to break down and is best avoided unless you can chip or shred it. Don't add anything whole to the pile that cannot be easily broken with the edge of a shovel. Also avoid eucalyptus, which contains an oil that inhibits plant growth, and magnolia leaves, because they don't break down easily. Avoid Bermuda grass, nut grass, morning glory, buttercup, English ivy, and other plants that may be noxious weeds or tough-to-stop spreaders.

Diseased garden plants should not be added to the compost pile. They should be burned, even if you think that your compost pile is hot enough to kill any pathogens. Why take a chance?

Wood ashes are fine, but coal ashes contain iron and sulfur in amounts that may harm plants. Leftover charcoal briquettes are to be avoided, as they refuse to break down.

Some experts now say that it is OK to compost newspaper (but never colored paper). I have never composted newspaper, and I don't see the point since so many communities now offer newspaper recycling. And, maybe because I am a former newspaper journalist, I just don't like the look of a compost pile with newspapers in it. (I realize that this is a ridiculous line of reasoning, but even compost heaps must have some standards.) Some inks used in printing contain toxins, and though many newspapers have gone to soy and other biodegradable inks, I still don't think composting newspapers is worth it. But if you really want to compost your daily paper, give the newspaper's pressroom a call and ask if the ink that they use is safe for composting.

Finally, don't throw cat or dog litter or feces on your compost pile—they can harbor pathogens.

Using Compost

Your compost is ready to use when it resembles black, fluffy soil and has a sweet, "earthy" smell. Compost is best used within a few months of being ready—the longer it is kept the more nutrients will decompose and leach away. As the compost continues to break down, it's soil texture-improving qualities diminish as well.

While compost is not a substitute for fertilizer, it is most often used for enriching soil. Large-scale addition of compost to a garden is best done in the fall. It may be simply spread on the ground, or better, tilled in. Finished compost may also be worked in the same way several weeks before planting in the spring. Many gardeners insist that nothing can take the place of a shovelful of compost mixed in planting holes for tomatoes, peppers, eggplant, and members of the cabbage family. Melons, cucumbers, and squash need compost's richness to send out strong, healthy vines.

Compost is also used to side-dress hungry crops. Screen the compost with a sieve, then mix it into the seedbed, or use it to cover fine seeds during planting. The screened mixture can also be used to top-dress lawns in the spring or fall, or mixed 1 part compost to 2 parts potting soil for a rich potting mix. And don't forget to brew up and use plenty of compost tea. Your plants will love you for it.

Building & Using Cold Frames

Charles Siegchrist

Imagine your Thanksgiving table graced with a beautiful salad of crisp baby lettuce, tangy onions, crunchy radishes, and your very own tomatoes.

While this may sound like the northern gardener's fondest fantasy, you can make it come true through the use of a simple, inexpensive cold frame.

A cold frame is nothing more than a box of boards set on the ground outdoors and topped with a second-hand storm window, but its simplicity belies its usefulness.

Involving a day's work with readily available materials and simple hand tools, construction of a cold frame is quick and economical. The cost of a cold frame—no more than $30—will be repaid many times over in pleasure, pride, and plain good eating.

SELECTING A SITE

In order to trap the maximum amounts of heat and light, a cold frame should face south. Should this prove impractical for your location, a southeasterly exposure is next preferred. A site close to a south-facing wall will get extra heat and protection.

The ground on which the frame is to be set should be well drained, free of large stones, and reasonably level. Placing the cold frame within your regular vegetable patch will save the bother of drawing in soil to fill the bottom. Such a location will also save many steps at transplanting time.

Choose the spot in the garden carefully so that the cold frame does not become a hindrance to routine cultivation. A location near perennial plants such as asparagus and rhubarb may serve well. Soil near such crops is usually rich and friable, and further, the location is out of the way of yearly garden chores such as rototilling.

FOUNDATION

How ambitious are you?

A foundation for this cold frame is not essential for most uses. But an insulated foundation will retain heat in the cold frame, and permit you to use the frame even longer in both spring and fall.

If you decide to build one, plan on going down two feet or more with it, use concrete blocks, add two-inch Styrofoam insulation on the outside, and attach it to the blocks with plastic roofing cement. For most of us, this foundation isn't needed. In cold climates, or for the gardener needing maximum heat for the plants he's raising, the extra heat stored in the cold frame will be appreciated.

MATERIALS

Cold frames may be built as grand or as humble as the owner desires. Plans given here are for a durable, low-budget model.

This is a portable structure which can be easily collapsed for storage in an area of about three feet by six feet by one foot.

The work should be a weekend project for anyone who has access to a basic collection of hand tools and the skill to use them.

The primary component of the cold frame is wood. In selecting the type of wood to be used, utmost consideration should be given to decay resistance. Being out in the weather most of the year and in direct contact with the soil, the wooden parts should be of species such as cedar, cypress, or redwood. These materials are listed in ascending order of cost.

If lumber of those types should prove unavailable or too expensive, consider using hemlock. It is an inexpensive, tough wood and should give good service despite its drawbacks.

Its shortcomings include knots as hard as steel, a tendency to crack and twist if improperly cured, and relative unattractiveness compared to such a lovely wood as redwood. Hemlock is rugged enough to see service as bridge planks on our Vermont back roads.

List of Materials

Whatever type of wood you select, you will need the following dimensions and quantities:

Amt/Dimension

1" 1 x 1" x 10' (cut into four pieces of 7"; four pieces of 10"; three pieces of 11")

12" x 2" x 8'

11" x 8" x 12' (cut into one piece of 69"; two pieces of 35I")

11" x 4" x 3' (cut to 35I")

11" x 6" x 12' (cut into two pieces of 69")

Your hardware needs for the project are as follows:

1/4 lb. 6d common nails

36 1 1/4" slotted wood screws

1 1/8" x 1/2" x 12' weatherstripping

1 set 4" T hinges. These usually are sold with screws included. If not, buy a dozen 1" slot head wood screws as well.

TOOLS NEEDED

Tools necessary for the job include a measuring tape, square, hammer, hatchet, saw, screwdriver, and pencil. A bar of soap will be handy for easing the driving of screws. If you plan to use an old storm window, you will need a putty knife and glazier points. If you build your own window, get a chisel.

You will also need to get a transparent lid for the cold frame. Directions are given below for the construction of a lid 36 x 72 inches. A more durable and economically comparable substitute is a used storm window of those dimensions. Look for one at a cost of about $5 at a garage sale, junk store, or the like. If you have a choice of storm windows, choose the one with the fewest panes of glass. It will cast fewer shadows on the growing plants.

Finally, secure a quart of good quality wood preservative and an inexpensive small paint brush. Do not use creosote, as its fumes are toxic to plants. Ask your dealer for a stain or sealer suitable for the project. Cuprinol is a good choice.

PREPARATIONS

Assuming you have chosen to use an old storm window, scrape away all cracked and loose paint, and the putty if it is cracked and dry. Saturate the cleaned areas with wood preservative and allow ample drying time.

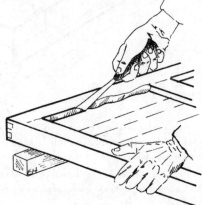

Continued →

Check the recessed joint where wood meets glass. When the window is tilted in position atop the cold frame, these areas will tend to collect rainwater. Thus they deserve special attention now.

Look where the putty was for small, triangular pieces of metal which hold the glass in position. Each pane of glass should have at least two of these glazier points along each of its four sides. If more are needed insert them into the wooden part of the window with firm pressure from the tip of a screwdriver.

Once the glass is secured, ready some glazing compound. Knead a small wad of compound until it is soft and pliable. Using a putty knife work small dabs of the compound into the recess where glass meets wood until a uniform depth has been applied around the perimeter of the glass.

Starting at a corner of the pane, hold the putty knife at such an angle as to form a triangle of glazing compound that is flush to the top of the surface of the wood and extends about 1/4 inch out onto the glass. Steadily and evenly, draw the knife down the joint until a corner is reached. Reposition the knife and continue to the next corner, repeating until all the putty is new.

Next paint the window with a good grade of exterior enamel trim paint to provide a long-lasting and attractive finish.

BUILDING THE WINDOW

If you can't find a satisfactory storm window, and decide to build your own, follow these instructions.

Amt	Dimension
1	2" x 2" x 10' (cut into three pieces of 36")
1	2" x 2" x 12' (cut into two pieces of 72")

On the three pieces 36 inches in length, mark and square off a line 1 1/2 inches in from each end.

Lay one of the pieces flat with the squared line facing up. On the two edges draw lines from the 1 1/2 inch mark down 3/4 inch and continue this line along half the thickness of the piece.

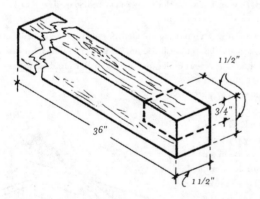

With the saw make several crosscuts from the squared line toward the end of the stick, sawing down only to the halfway mark. Remove the sawed section from the end to the square mark with a sharp wood chisel.

Repeat this procedure at the ends of the other 36-inch pieces, which at conclusion should appear as follows:

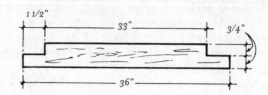

The ends of the 2" x 2" x 72" pieces are marked, sawed and chiseled identically. On one of these long window pieces, measure and make marks from one end at 35 1/4 inches and at 36 3/4 inches. Square these marks and mark the edges to a 3/4-inch depth as was done to all the end joints; saw halfway through the stick and chisel out the joints as before. The 72-inch pieces should appear as below when you are done:

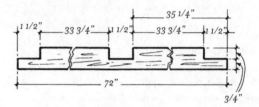

Lay the two 72-inch side rails parallel 33 inches apart and lay the three 36-inch pieces into place across them. The joints should fit flush, square, and snug. Check for fit, chisel to level any high spots in the joint faces, and coat all these pieces with wood preservative.

ASSEMBLY

Once all the components are dry, assembly can begin.

The window frame will be held together with a half-dozen wood screws 1 1/4 inches in length. If you are using softwood for the frame, you may wish to pre-drill the holes to prevent the wood from splitting. Use a drill bit which is one size smaller than the diameter of the screw shank. Place a screw through each part of the lap joints at corners and centers. The completed product is illustrated here.

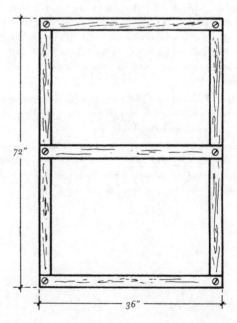

To cover this window frame will require a piece of plastic film measuring 39 by 75 inches; one 12-foot and one 9-foot strip of wood approximately 1/4 x 1 inch; and 36 brads 3/4 inch long. Cut the 12-foot strip into two lengths of 7 inches. From the 9-footer cut two strips of 36 inches and one of 34 inches.

Lay the sheet of plastic atop the window frame so the sheet and frame are flush at one corner and along two edges. From the flush corner lay a 36-inch strip of wood atop the plastic and flush along the narrow end of the window. Tack it in place.

Start brads in the other 36-inch wooden strip and lay it atop the piece of plastic at the opposite end of the window. Using the excess edge of the plastic as a handle, draw the sheet tightly across the surface of the window. Position the wooden strip flush to the edge of the window and drive the brads.

The two long wooden strips will go along the long sides of the frame. First nail one and then draw the plastic tightly before nailing the second. The 34-inch strip of wood secures the plastic to the middle rail of the window frame. Trim off excess plastic with a knife.

BUILDING THE FRAME

You are now ready to build the frame.

First, saw the 2" x 2" piece into four lengths, two at 18 inches and two at 20 inches. On each of these measure up 8 inches from an end. With the hatchet hew down this 8-inch section to a point. These are the posts that will anchor the cold frame in the ground.

Take the board 1" x 4" x 35 3/4" and lay a straightedge from the lower right corner to the upper left corner. Mark that line and saw along it to form two identical triangles. Try to hold the saw perpendicular to the surface of the board.

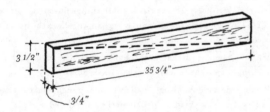

Next, saw the 1" x 1" piece into cleats. Four of these will be 7 inches long, four 10 inches, and three 11 inches.

Coat all the lumber with preservative. The sawed ends and edges will be especially absorbent.

The two triangular pieces that were cut from the 1" x 4" x 35 3/4" board will form the tops of the east and west walls of the cold frame. The bases of these end walls are the pieces 1" x 8" x 35 3/4", which should now be laid edge to edge with the triangular boards. When placed together the end wall components should appear as below:

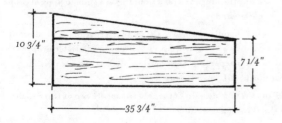

THE END WALLS PARTIALLY ASSEMBLED

It is now time to apply the 1" x 1" cleats which will serve both to hold the end wall boards together and to fix in place the north and south walls of the cold frame.

Start at the wide end of one of the end walls. Lay a 10-piece of the 1" x 1" stock flush with the ends of the boards and centered vertically. Mark locations for two screw holes, taking care to avoid knots, splits, or other defects.

Remove the cleat and drive a nail in at the marks, then extract it to leave pilot holes for 1 1/4-inch screws. If you have a drill, use a bit one size smaller than the screws for the pilot holes. Push the screws into a bar of soap to coat the ends. Lay the cleat back on the wide end of the board and screw it into place.

After the first cleat is fixed, lay a second piece of 1" x 1" x 10" alongside it and draw a pencil line along the edge of the second cleat toward the center of the end wall. Move the second cleat over and flush to this pencil line, leaving a gap of slightly more than 3/4 inch between the two cleats. Mark the second cleat for screw holes, make pilot holes, reposition the cleat and screw it down.

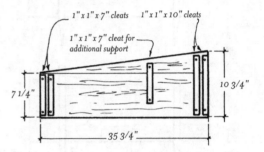

Using 7-inch cleats at the narrow end of the boards, repeat this procedure by putting one cleat flush to the edge, marking a 3/4-inch gap and applying the second cleat of 7 inches to the inside of the mark.

The other pairs of cleats are applied in similar fashion to the opposite end wall. From the remaining 1"x 1" stock, you may want to cut two additional 7-inch strips to be screwed 12–14 inches in from the wide end. These cleats will further strengthen the connection between the two boards.

Once the cleats are all in place, the end walls should appear as below:

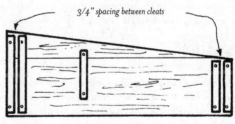

Inside of end walls

Now turn over the end walls end for end so that the cleated sides are down. From each end measure in 8 inches. At the narrow end, lay one of the posts of 2" x 2" x 18" stock so that it lies between the lines but is flush against the 8-inch mark. The top of this post should protrude

Continued ➔

about an inch above the edge of the triangular upper board. The sharpened end of the post should extend beyond the base of the 1" x 8" about 8 inches. Nail this in place with 6d nails. Be sure that at least one nail fastens the post to the base board and another to the triangular piece.

Use a 2" x 2" x 20" at the wide end of the end walls. Lay it to the inside of the 8" mark. Again, the square end of the stick should be about 1" above the triangular piece and the sharp end about eight inches below the base. Nail it.

Duplicate this pattern on the other end wall. The completed end walls should appear as on the next page.

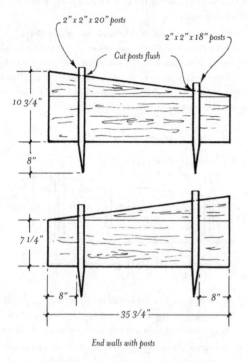

End walls with posts

THE END WALLS WITH POSTS INSTALLED

Using a handsaw, cut off the tops of the posts flush with the tops of the end walls. These components are now completed. Now lay the two boards 1" x 6" x 69" edge to edge lengthwise. Measure in from each end two inches. Lay in position two of the 1" x 1" x 11" cleats. Mark them for screw holes, make pilots, and install them, using four screws in each cleat. The remaining cleat should be centered and screwed into place.

CONSTRUCTION

The cold frame is now ready to go up.

Move the wooden components to your selected site, taking along pencil, hammer, screwdriver, nails, measuring tape, hatchet, hinges and screws, weatherstripping, and a scrap of sturdy lumber.

Position one of the side walls so that its high point is to the north and the cleats are toward the area you wish to enclose.

Lay the scrap of heavy lumber atop one of the posts and start driving it in with the hatchet. When the post is halfway home, drive the other post until it too is about halfway down. Tip the top of the wall so that it

leans slightly toward the area to be enclosed, and finish driving the posts.

Slip the end of the 1" x 8" x 69" board into the groove between the cleats at the narrow end. At the wide end, slip the cleated 1" x 6" 69" boards into the gap between the cleats.

Make a mark in the soil along the ends of these boards. Remove the boards. The cleated side of the second end wall should line up with these marks. Align the second end wall so that these marks fit into the gaps between the cleats.

Drive each post halfway, tilt the end wall inward slightly, and complete the driving of the posts.

The slight cants of the end walls should make for secure placement of the north and south walls of the cold frame. Slip the ends of the 1" x 8" x 69" board into the grooves between the cleats at the narrow ends of the end walls. Tap it into place until its top aligns with the end walls.

The cleated pair of 1" x 6" x 69" boards will fit similarly into the grooves at the high ends of the end walls, completing the framework. Tap it until it aligns with the end wall.

If the north and south walls are not snug within their channels, drive nails through the end walls and into the ends of the long walls. Leave the nail heads exposed about 1/4" for ease of disassembly in the future.

WINDOW INSTALLATION

Position the window on top of the walls so that the ends of the window extend about 1/2" beyond the edges of the end walls and the north edge of the window is flush to the outside top of the north wall.

With the window so located, mark in eight inches from each end of the northern edge of the window. Position a hinge to the inside of one of these marks with the rectangular leg of the hinge flush to the upper edge of the window, and the triangular leg hanging down the north wall of the cold frame.

With the hinge so placed, mark the six screw holes. Position the second hinge as was the first and mark those six holes.

Remove the window. Using a nail as a center punch, make shallow pilot holes at the centers of the pencil marks along the edge of the window. Attach the rectangular legs of the hinges to the window using 1" screws.

Replace the sash on top of the cold frame walls and line up the triangular straps over the pencil marks. Make six more shallow pilot holes and drive in the remaining screws.

Trace a pencil line along the outside of the east, south, and west walls of the cold frame onto the underside of the window. Prop open the window and apply to the inside of this pencil mark the piece of self-sticking weatherstripping.

No weatherstripping should be applied to the underside of the window along the hinged edge. It would act as a shim to prevent proper closure of the window.

A simple handle attached to the southern edge of the window will prove useful, as will a notched stick to use as an adjustable prop for the window. An inexpensive thermometer located as high as possible on the inside north wall is handy as well.

Bank the outside walls of the cold frame with two or three inches of dirt and the structure is done.

USING THE COLD FRAME

The completed cold frame is essentially a simple solar collector. The small, protected environment within its walls will trap tremendous amounts of heat, even on cloudy days. On clear winter days, with an outside temperature of 0°F, temperatures may soar in the afternoon as high as 100°F within the cold frame.

While different types of plants vary in their temperature preferences nearly all of them fare poorly in excessive heat. At about 99°F most plants lose water through their leaves more rapidly than they are able to take water up through their root systems.

When this excessive transpiration takes place, the plants sensibly take a siesta until cooler weather occurs. This is visible as wilt, a condition which saves the plant but produces no progress for the gardener.

The thermometer inside the cold frame should read near 75°F for the optimum growth of most plants.

The most convenient gadget for making sure the plants in the cold frame don't become overheated is a thermostatically controlled window prop. These non-electric units will adjust the opening of the window to allow sufficient ventilation to raise or lower the temperature toward the optimum. Check with greenhouse operators or supply firms to find where these can be located.

A notched stick and a bit of experience with the cold frame will serve adequately, however.

When the outside temperature is cool and the sun is shining, prop open the window slightly at first and check the temperature inside the cold frame in about 10 minutes. Adjust the window as necessary.

During hot weather and full sun, even with the window of the cold frame opened completely, it may be impossible to keep the inside temperature low enough without the use of artificial shade. This can be easily provided by placing a piece of window screen or cheesecloth over the top of the cold frame walls. These materials will allow ventilation but still greatly filter the sunlight.

BEWARE THE COLD

The other side of the coin is obviously a climate too cool for good plant growth.

Many of the plants suitable to growth within a cold frame are hardy to a touch of frost. Lettuce, spinach, onions, and radishes can be planted safely within a cold frame as soon as the ground can be worked.

The protected interior of the cold frame allows the sowing of such seeds as early as mid-March in northern climates, but these plants will not withstand a hard freeze of below 26°F.

Extra protection from bitter weather can be provided economically. Fill plastic grain sacks with leaves, straw, or other coarse, dry material and bank the bags around the outside walls of the cold frame. These can stay in place until the advent of warmer weather.

HEAT LOSS THROUGH GLASS

While the banking materials will help prevent infiltration of cold air, the bigger culprit will be heat loss through the window atop the cold frame. Glass is a notoriously poor insulator.

Check first that the weatherstripping on the underside of the window is snug. A simple test is to open the window and lay a sheet of paper on top of the wall of the cold frame. Close the window and try removing the paper. If it comes out only with an effort, all is well. If it slips out easily, the seal needs improvement.

To cut heat loss through the glass, a heavy blanket or canvas laid over the window will suffice. Good timing of the application of this covering can be added insurance against cold temperatures.

For example, assume that it is a sunny day in late March. Tiny lettuce and spinach seedlings are just popping up in the cold frame. The window is propped open and the inside temperature reads 70°F.

The afternoon weather forecast predicts overnight lows of about 15°F. About 3 P.M. close the cold frame window and allow the inside temperature to inch up toward 90°F. Then apply the blanket over the window.

The seedlings may miss an hour or so of light, but you have trapped as much heat as practical and the seedlings should survive the chilly night in good condition.

The same technique can be used in the late fall and early winter to protect small stands of salad greens.

HOTBEDS

If you resort to artificial means of heat inside the cold frame, it is a cold frame no longer but rather a hotbed. These are generally more expensive and elaborate than cold frames.

The least expensive way to conserve heat in these is to stack up old bricks on the inside of the north wall. While this will cut about three

Continued ➜

square feet of growing space out of the interior, the bricks will act as solar collectors, rising to the temperature that prevails inside the cold frame during the day.

Due to their mass, the bricks will dissipate their accumulated heat, but slowly, affording substantial protection overnight to the young plants. The heat-absorbency of the bricks can be heightened by painting them flat back.

HEAT FROM DECOMPOSITION

An alternative is to take up the cold frame and shovel a pit two feet deep and six inches wider and longer than the outside dimensions of the cold frame.

Into the pit shovel fresh manure to a depth of four inches. Pack this down, add four more inches, and tread down and proceed in this manner until the pit is filled within eight inches of the surface of the surrounding ground.

Top off the pit to level with good soil and reassemble the cold frame.

As the manure rots, it will give off heat for a period of from six to eight weeks. For the first week, leave the cover of the cold frame—now a hotbed—open so that fumes given off by the manure can escape.

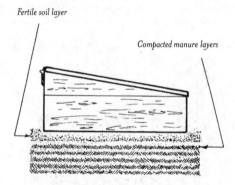

Fertile soil layer

Compacted manure layers

After a week tie a thermometer to a long stick and plunge the instrument into the heart of the manure pile. Leave it for five minutes or so. If the temperature is 90°F or below, you may safely set seeds into the soil.

Of all the means of providing artificial heat for a hotbed, this is the least desirable. It involves excavating a cubic yard of earth and securing a like amount of fresh manure. The rate of decomposition of and thus the heat given off by the manure pile is also subject to a number of variables, including:

- The amount of bedding or plant material in the manure. The higher the proportion of pure manure, the hotter the pile will become.

- The type of manure used. Generally speaking, the smaller the animal, the richer its manure. Poultry dung will make much more heat than that from a cow.

- The diet of the animal from which the manure is secured. A pig on a diet of straight grain will give a richer manure than one eating table scraps, garbage, and hay.

The combination of these unknowns and the amount of labor involved make manure heating the least attractive method of warming a hotbed.

ELECTRICITY

For steady temperatures and reliable heat, electricity is unsurpassed for use in the hotbed.

An extension cord feeding a light bulb inside the cold frame is the simplest procedure. It serves to warm the air inside and will ward off frost adequately.

The light bulb trick is not ideal for the plants, however, as they prefer warmth from below to maintain soil temperature.

The better solution, and the more expensive, is to install a soil heating cable, available from most garden supply stores at a cost of from $40 to $60. During the course of a growing season such a cable may consume about 50 kilowatt hours of electricity.

With reasonable preparation of the ground, the cable should last indefinitely. The thermostatic control makes its use safe, economical, and very convenient.

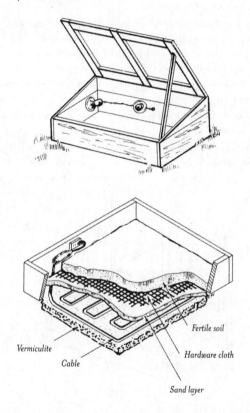

Fertile soil

Hardware cloth

Vermiculite

Cable

Sand layer

Further advantages of the cable over manure are control and cleanliness. The electricity can be turned on whenever the gardener desires, rather than waiting for the temperature of the manure heap to become appropriate. When outside temperatures get hot the electricity can be shut off, while the manure heap might still be hot.

The case for electricity can also be argued on the grounds of economy, unless one has ready access to a supply of free manure and the means to haul it.

To install the cable, first excavate the interior of the cold frame to a depth of 12 inches. At the bottom lay a pad of vermiculite 2 inches thick. This will insulate the interior of the frame from cold coming from below and will also provide adequate drainage so no water will stand around the cable.

On the inside of the cold frame wall install an electrical outlet. Plug in the soil cable and drape it evenly over the layer of vermiculite. Cover the cable with a 2-inch layer of sand and top this with a sheet of 1/2-inch mesh hardware cloth. This tough mesh will prevent the cable from being inadvertently cut by a trowel.

Cover the hardware cloth with a layer of fertile soil 8 inches deep. This soil should contain one-sixth part sand for good drainage and one-sixth part shredded peat moss for good water retention.

SOIL FOR THE COLD FRAME
The soil within the cold frame should be the finest that you have. It is the very foundation of success for growing plants.

The least expensive source of soil is from the garden. It should be prepared for use by the addition of organic matter, fertilizer, and possibly limestone.

First, dig up enough soil to fill the cold frame to a depth of about 3 inches. Add one-sixth the volume in clean sharp sand and a like amount of organic matter in the form of leaf mold, shredded peat moss, rotted straw or the like. Add another sixth of well-rotted manure or compost. Blend these ingredients thoroughly.

Across the top of an empty garbage can lay a piece of 1/2 inch mesh hardware cloth and sift the soil through it.

This should provide a well-drained, moisture-absorbent medium for growing your cold frame plants.

While soil contains many organisms beneficial to plant life, it can also harbor pathogens which can cause a complete crop failure. Any soil disease that is present in the cold frame will wreak havoc rapidly due to the close quarters.

If you're a conscientious gardener you will want to remove these harmful organisms.

The accepted technique is to raise the soil temperature to 180°F, and maintain that temperature for 30 minutes. This will render harmless most weed seeds, insects and eggs, as well as pathogens.

The common way to do this for small amounts of soil is to heat it in an oven. That's also expensive and the smelliest way, and almost impossible with the amount of soil required for the cold frame.

Another alternative is to purchase sterilized potting soil, about five cubic feet. Again—expensive.

For these larger amounts of soil, it is worthwhile to set up a steam pasteurizer. A large sheet of perforated metal is set on top of a pan of water of equal size. Up to ten inches of soil can be placed on the perforated sheet. This is covered with foil, heavy plastic, wet burlap bags, or any material that will retain heat and moisture. The water must be kept boiling for several hours, until the top of the soil reaches 180°F. Then the heat is turned off and the soil left for thirty minutes before removing the cover.

Think about how you will use your cold frame before going to the work of pasteurizing the soil. It is particularly important when starting seeds and cuttings.

SOIL TESTS
A couple of tablespoons of the soil should be set aside for testing. This can be done at home with a relatively inexpensive kit available through most garden supply houses, or by the local cooperative extension service, usually for a nominal charge.

Soil tests determine the level of nutrients and the acidity of the soil sample.

Acidity is evaluated in terms of pH level. Soils testing pH 7 are neutral, neither acid nor alkaline. Alkaline soils are rated from 7 to 14 while acid soils are rated from 7 to 0. Most bacteria and plants function best in a slightly acid soil at a pH level of between 5.5 and 6.5.

Soils with a pH level lower than 5.5 can be corrected by adding ground limestone, calcium carbonate. Soils above pH 7 can be reduced in alkalinity by adding acid organic matter such as pine needles or oak leaves, or by sprinkling a diluted solution of household vinegar on the soil.

If your soil sample is sent to the extension service, be sure to indicate where the soil will be used so that their recommendations can be scaled down. Advice to add two tons of lime to the acre will hardly be useful to your purposes.

The soil test will also indicate any deficiencies of the three major plant foods. These are nitrogen, phosphorus, and potassium. They are always listed in that order when describing the contents of a fertilizer. A 5–10-20 formulation of fertilizer contains 5 percent nitrogen, 10 percent phosphorus, and 20 percent potassium, for example.

All three are important to rapid, balanced plant growth.

Nitrogen is responsible for rapid growth, especially of leaves of plants. Phosphorus encourages root growth, the early development of seeds, fruits, and flowers, and the transmission of other nutrients within the plant. Potassium is used in large amounts by plants, affecting the sturdiness of branch and stem growth as well as the color and health of fruits and flowers.

The scope of your project should cause some consideration as to whether you choose to use organic or chemical fertilizers. On a field scale an error of 200 pounds of chemical fertilizer to the acre might not be of any great impact, but an error of one ounce of chemical within the confines of the cold frame could spell disaster.

The chemical fertilizers are quick-fix, quick-feed amendments to the soil, and if applied too heavily to tiny plants they can easily cause burning of roots.

Organic fertilizers feed the plants more slowly, but also in a sustained manner. If the organic nutrients are applied sparingly, the chances for plant damage are minimal. Any shortcomings of the plant's food supply can be quickly remedied with chemicals if need be.

Organic sources of nitrogen include cottonseed meal, dried blood, and manures. Bonemeal or ground rock phosphate will supply phosphorus organically, and wood ashes are a good source of potassium.

Apply these according to the test indications and watch for any signs of deficiency as the plants are growing. A nitrogen shortage will show as stunted plants with yellowish leaves. Reddish margins about the leaves indicates a lack of phosphorus, while a potassium shortfall will appear as soft, lush growth and rubbery stems and branches.

Once the soil has been sifted, pasteurized, limed, and fertilized it can be placed within the cold frame and gardening can begin.

Continued →

Cold Storage for Fruits & Vegetables

Illustrations by Cathy Baker

Do you want to save what could be wasted garden surpluses? Want to lower food costs, and gain deep personal satisfaction?

Try storing food the natural way, in storage rooms and root cellars, in pits and trenches, or even in the garden.

Here's a way to keep large quantities of food that is cheaper, less work, and far more energy-efficient than canning or freezing. And for many fruits and vegetables, it's the best way to keep them as close as possible to their just-picked or just-dug peak of quality.

It's not difficult, either, if you follow a few simple rules.

One of those rules is that crops are particular about where you store them. They want just the right humidity and temperature. You probably have ideal conditions for some of them in your home right now, and, with little effort, can provide satisfactory conditions for the others.

Another rule to remember is that the maximum storage time for vegetables and fruits varies enormously. Ripe tomatoes and peppers can be held for only a few weeks, winter squash will last through the winter, dried peas and beans can be stored for several years. None should be stored and forgotten. They must be checked often, once a week is not too frequent, to make certain conditions are as ideal as possible, and to remove any produce showing decay.

A third general rule is that you should plan your gardening so that your storage crops reach maturity—no more and no less—just when you wish to store them, which in most cases is before the truly hard frosts that signal the approach of winter. Most of the crops require only drying in the sun for several days before being stored. They should not be washed before being stored, although dried dirt can be brushed off them, and they should be handled carefully at all times, so bruises do not invite speedy decay.

Storage Tips

Here are some tips on storage, aimed at enabling you to store more food for longer periods with less loss.

1. Select the best of the crop for storage. Vegetables should be mature, but not too old, and not damaged by disease or handling. One bad apple will spoil the whole barrel, and the rule applies to most vegetables as well.

2. Don't handle crops for storage when they are wet.

3. Proper ventilation is important. Air should circulate around the stored produce as much as possible.

4. Get your crops in before a hard freeze. Some may not be damaged by heavy frosts; many of them will be.

5. Turnips, rutabagas and cabbages give off strong odors. This is a good reason for storing them in an outdoor pit or mound.

6. Sort potatoes carefully for storage. Use as quickly as possible those that are not mature or whose skins have been broken while being dug up.

7. Most vegetables need to be cured before being stored. Check directions for individual vegetables. Proper curing will do much to increase the maximum storage time.

8. Root crops must retain their moisture to keep their freshness. Store them in boxes of damp sand or sawdust, and keep the storage material damp. Or try perforated polyethylene bags.

9. Most crops store best if kept in the dark. Light is not needed for any of them.

Building Your Storage Room

For most vegetables that need damp, cool storage conditions, a cold storage room or root cellar is the most satisfactory answer.

The homeowner has control over it, control over its temperature and humidity, and control enough to exclude hungry mice that may want to share the feast. The produce is available when he wants it. Carrots can be stored just fine in the garden or in a pit, but retrieving them in the midst of a snowstorm can be trying.

The homeowner must aim for certain conditions in his root cellar:

1. Light should be excluded, but light for use when working in the cellar should be provided.

2. The room should have access to fresh air. That's why we recommend building it to include a cellar window. This air is needed for maintaining low temperatures and to provide the ventilation most crops require.

3. The room should be insulated off from the rest of the house. This is essential if low temperatures are to be maintained. And it's far better for your comfort and heating bills if the cold air of the cellar can't find its way up through the ceiling and into your house.

4. It should provide ample space. The sample storage room we picture is 10' x 10', more than ample for a family of four.

5. Bins, boxes, shelves, and slatted duckwalks should be used to keep all produce off the concrete floor.

6. Humidity must be high. Water can be sprinkled on the floor. Some persons use damp sawdust, which is fine if you don't mind cleaning up that trail of sawdust you will leave through the house each time you leave the cellar. Try a layer of gravel or crushed stone instead. You'll find extra water will be needed most in the fall, when the storage room may be at its warmest and the most air is being circulated.

7. The entire room, including all bins and storage areas, must be built with an eye toward easy cleaning. A good scrubbing of the entire room and all containers with a detergent and disinfectant is a must after each storage season. Thus painting the room with a moisture-proof paint will aid in this effort to keep the room clean and free of vegetable-spoiling disease and fungi. A concrete floor is recommended.

8. The storage room should be in the coolest part of the cellar, not close to the furnace, have a window, and, to minimize the construction costs, be in a corner. The north side is usually coolest.

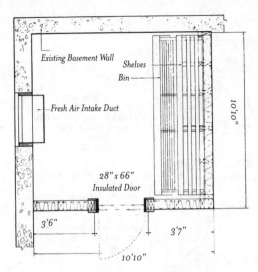

Existing Basement Wall

Shelves

Bin

Fresh Air Intake Duct

10'10"

28" x 66"
Insulated Door

3'6"

3'7"

10'10"

Top view of plan for storage room in corner of basement.

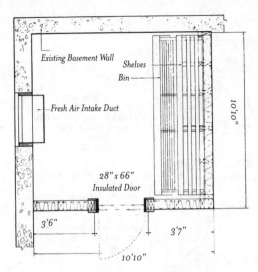

The design we use as an illustration is from the Agriculture Canada Publication 1478, *Home Storage Room for Fruits and Vegetables.*

The first step in construction is to mark off the two walls to be built, then build forms and pour concrete for a 4" x 4" concrete footing. The purpose of this is to raise the wooden wall and its insulation above the level of any water used within the room to maintain high humidity and thus protect them from rotting. Some may skip this step, planning to use care so that the water does not come in contact with the walls.

Use 2" x 4" studs to frame the walls, spacing them properly for the insulation that will be fitted between them. Batts of insulation are cut to fit between studs set on 16-inch or 24-inch centers. If batt type insulation with a vapor barrier is used, that vapor barrier should be on the warm side of the wall. If there is no vapor barrier, use 4 mil polyethylene on the warm side of the insulation. Plywood hardboard or lumber can be used for sheathing on both sides of the insulation.

Use 2" x 2" material for framing an insulated door. Weatherstrip it if necessary to get a tight fit.

Any hot water pipes that pass through the room should be insulated. Circular insulation for just this purpose is available at building supply stores. Hot air ducts, too, should be insulated.

The ceiling should be insulated, too, with the vapor barrier above the insulation and thus on the warm side. There should be no break between walls and ceiling in either the vapor barrier or the insulation. The outer concrete walls should not be insulated.

The ventilation system can be of varying degrees of sophistication and effectiveness. Most simple is a window that is opened when fresh or colder air is needed. This lets in unwanted light as well as air, and does not ensure a good circulation of air.

Far better is a system of vents so that air is exhausted from the top of the room, and flows in at near-floor level. Adding an electric fan to the exhaust will increase its efficiency. This system should include dampers so that air circulation can be halted when it is not wanted.

More expensive but more effective is the system shown in the cross-section view of the sample room. This system is automatic, with a fan

and louvers set in the upper half of the basement window. These are controlled by a differential thermostat, which measures outside and inside temperatures, and kicks the system into operation when inside temperatures are too high, and outside air is cooler. The system forces the warm air out of the room, and thus air is drawn back into the room through the intake system, with its outlet extending nearly to floor level. Both inlet and outlet have screening at the window openings to keep out bugs and rodents.

The builder should look ahead to decide what and how he will be storing before he designs and builds shelves and bins. A cardinal rule: Keep all produce, including those stored in boxes, at least four inches off the floor.

There are several advantages to using crates and boxes placed on shelves rather than building bins for crop storage. One, the boxes are cheaper. Two, they're easier to move out and clean in the spring. Three, and probably most important, boxes can be loaded in the garden, then carried into the cellar for storage. This eliminates one transfer of food from one container to another, and thus eliminates one possibility of damaging the produce and thus reducing its storage life. Boxes can be stored one on top of another. Usually it's wise to put small slats of wood between them, to permit better ventilation.

Two instruments are valuable in the storage room. One is the thermometer, to make certain temperatures are as close to freezing as possible, but not below that level. And the second is a sling psychrometer, which measures humidity. It can be purchased from scientific instrument companies.

If too-cool temperatures are a problem in your storage room you may wish to install a low-temperature warning system, which consists of a thermostat in the storage area, connected to a buzzer outside and set so that the buzzer sounds if the temperatures reach dangerously low levels. This equipment and the differential thermostat we mentioned earlier are available at electrical supply houses.

In some storage rooms, where temperature fluctuations are a problem, it may be necessary to insulate the window, at least for part of the winter.

If you construct a storage room, you'll find it is valuable for many uses. It can be used for most fruits, or for vegetables (although you may get in trouble with unwanted flavor transfers if you mix the two). You'll find its weather is ideal for root crops and for potatoes. It's also an ideal spot for short-term storage of other crops. Here's the place for those end-of-season surpluses you've rescued from the frosts. Eggplant can be saved in here for a few weeks, and so can grapes, cauliflower, kohlrabi, cantaloupes, and watermelons. As with the other crops you've stored here, you'll want to keep a close eye on these short-timers, since they should be eaten as quickly as possible, and they will not last long, no matter how ideal the conditions.

Keep Out Canned Goods

If you preserve food in glass jars, perhaps you're planning on shelves in your storage room just for those. That way you keep all of your stored food together. We advise against it. Sure, the temperature is just right—cool—for those canned goods. And they should be in the dark, too, just the same as your stored vegetables. But remember that high humidity. It's fine for vegetables, but it will rust the metal on those cans, and eventually may cause leaks, leading to spoilage.

Continued ➜

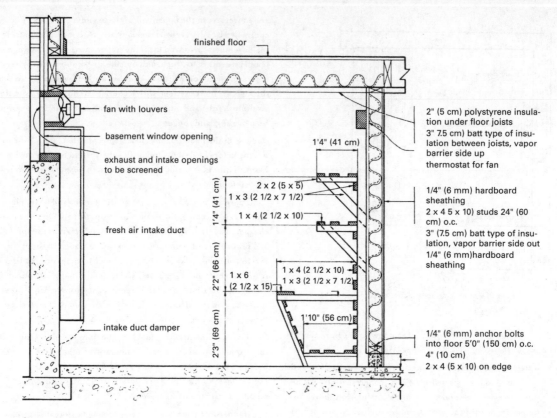

fan with louvers

basement window opening

exhaust and intake openings to be screened

fresh air intake duct

intake duct damper

finished floor

2" (5 cm) polystyrene insulation under floor joists
3" 7.5 cm) batt type of insulation between joists, vapor barrier side up
thermostat for fan

1/4" (6 mm) hardboard sheathing
2 x 4 5 x 10) studs 24" (60 cm) o.c.
3" (7.5 cm) batt type of insulation, vapor barrier side out
1/4" (6 mm)hardboard sheathing

1/4" (6 mm) anchor bolts into floor 5'0" (150 cm) o.c.
4" (10 cm)
2 x 4 (5 x 10) on edge

1'4" (41 cm)

2 x 2 (5 x 5)
1 x 3 (2 1/2 x 7 1/2)

1 x 4 (2 1/2 x 10)

1 x 6
(2 1/2 x 15)

1 x 4 (2 1/2 x 10)
1 x 3 (2 1/2 x 7 1/2)

1'10" (56 cm)

1'4" (41 cm)
2'2" (66 cm)
2'3" (69 cm)

Cross–section view of a storage room.

Instead, while you're building those walls for the storage room, add shelves on the outside for all of those cans and jars of food. Do this, of course, only if yours is a dry cellar.

Pits and Trenches

The storage room is crammed full, and you still have more carrots and beets and cabbages to harvest. Or you don't have time or money or ambition enough to build a root cellar. Or you just want to try different storage methods.

Trenches and pits may be for you.

Be alert for possible troubles, though, since pits and trenches seem to operate on the theory that if something could happen, it will. The spot you choose may look like the Sahara in September, but turn into a dowser's dream of plenty in November. Mice and other tiny animals will find their way in vast numbers into your trench or pit, given so much as a nose-width invitation. And the weather can offer combinations that produce a layer of frozen moisture that's hard as a banker's heart, and will bar you from those carrots or cabbages as effectively as that banker's vault doors.

You've been warned. Now let's try building some of these.

First, you're trying to create conditions in these that are very similar to those in a root cellar. Cool temperatures, but not below freezing. High humidity, but not cold running water. Ventilation. And protection from insects, rats, mice, squirrels, the neighbor's dog, woodchucks, and other creatures with four legs and curiosity or an appetite for vegetables or fruits. Remember all of these, as you try the following suggestions, or your own variations on them.

FIRST, THE PITS

They can be used for the root crops (beets, carrots, celeriac, parsnips, the large winter radishes, rutabagas, salsify, and turnips), as well as potatoes, Brussels sprouts, cabbages, kohlrabi, and apples and quinces.

Consider your area temperatures before deciding to try pits. They aren't practical if winter temperatures in your area don't average 30°F or less. If you live in areas of hard winter weather such as New Hampshire, the Dakotas, and the other states in that belt, they can't be used for winter-long storage, since the freezing cold will get to those crops, no matter how high the straw, hay or soil is piled.

Pits are best if they're small. In this way, food enough for a short time can be packed away in one, and all removed at the same time. Try a week's supply in a pit, and remove all of the food at one time. Repacking a pit can be difficult when the ground is frozen, there's a foot of snow on the ground, and the hay or straw has been scattered.

Try digging a hole one foot deep and three feet square in an area of good drainage. Line it with two to four inches of straw, salt hay, hay, or leaves. Make a pyramid of the week's supply of vegetables—carrots, beets, parsnips, and others. This pile can be as much as two or three feet high. Don't throw the vegetables in. That may damage them. Place them in position. Now cover them with a deep layer of straw or hay or leaves. A six-inch layer is adequate—a foot-thick layer is better. Add a layer of soil, and the deeper it is the longer those vegetables can be left in cold weather without freezing. If mice are a problem, cover pile with hardware cloth before you add those layers of straw and soil.

What have we forgotten? Ventilation. Simply letting the straw or hay stick up through the layer of soil will provide enough ventilation for the vegetables. Another method used is to cut both ends off a tin can, and set that in place on the vegetable pyramid, sticking up through those layers above the pyramid. A screen of some sort over the top of the can will prevent it from becoming Mouse Alley.

The final step is to dig a ditch around the pile, and provide a runoff from your ditch so any rain that accumulates can flow away. If you were a Girl Scout or a Boy Scout, you remember how you did this when raising a tent. Same method, and for the same purpose, to keep dry what the ditch surrounds.

Cabbages can be stored in a similar fashion, but with differences that let you get the cabbages when you need them. Cover a storage area with straw or hay, marking out a space that will be wide enough for four cabbages abreast and not touching, and long enough for as many cabbages as you plan to store. Pull up the cabbages, roots and all, and put them head-down on the blanket of straw or hay. Support them by packing hay or leaves around them, so that this insulating material is as much as a foot deep over the roots. Shovel soil over this pile until the soil is at least six inches deep. Dig a runoff ditch around the pile. A few cabbages at a time can be taken from this pile without ruining the layers of insulation protecting the others.

There are many variations on these pits. These include the use of boxes, barrels, and even garbage cans in the pit. There are advantages to using these containers. They tend to protect the produce from mice and water.

There are several rules you should follow if you try the pit method.

One is to use the stored produce as quickly as possible. Just cutting down the storage time reduces the chances of loss of fruits and vegetables due to hungry rodents, abnormally cold weather, rain, or other calamities not yet imagined.

Another is to store in a cool, damp place any produce removed from the pit and not used immediately. The root cellar of course is fine for this, too.

If your produce freezes, don't throw it away. Try letting it thaw gradually, then using it. Carrots and most of the root crops will not be harmed, and cabbages may survive.

Finally, don't be afraid to experiment with this method. You're looking for a system that will fit your vegetable or fruit supply in your weather conditions, and some trying and learning are necessary.

TRENCHES

Trenches are used for leafy vegetables, including cabbages, celery, and Chinese cabbage. This method works very well, although here in northern Vermont, we can't recommend it for all-winter storage. But for a few months—fine.

Dig a trench one foot wide by two feet deep by whatever length you find you need for these crops. If your soil is loose, you may want to prop up the sides of this trench with boards, to prevent cave-ins. Dig up your plants, roots and all. Transplant them into the trench, packed closely together, with soil covering the roots, and the plants deep enough so that their tops are below ground level. Water them as you replant them, keeping water off the tops. Leave them for several hours at least to settle. Place boards over the top of them, followed by hay, straw, or leaves up to a foot in depth, then cover the entire pile with a piece of plastic.

Visualize what's down there: Your plants have their roots in the soil, so, while they're not growing and prospering, they are getting moisture from the soil. They're protected from the cold, but they do have air. And, when eating time comes, one end of the trench can be opened, a few plants can be removed, and the trench can be closed again.

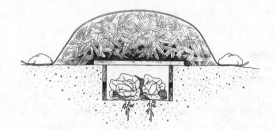

GARDEN STORAGE

Here's the method the lazy man prefers.

It works well with certain crops, simply leaving them in the ground until they are needed. For some, the protection of a blanket of hay or straw or leaves is advised. For others, even this is not needed.

Let's run down through a list of the vegetables that can be stored in this way.

But, before we do that, one suggestion. Plan on this storage when you are planting your garden. Some of these crops should be planted in mid-summer so they mature in the late fall. Try to keep all of the "storage" crops in one area of your garden. It makes for easier work in the fall, when you should be cleaning out your garden, rototilling it, and planting a cover or green manure crop. If all of those storage crops are in one area, cleaning will be much easier. And so will harvesting, in the dead of winter when finding the vegetables can be a task.

Kale is a hardy vegetable and can be harvested and used like spinach well past Christmas in even the coldest parts of the country. Just let it grow.

Jerusalem artichokes are poor "keepers," but keep well if left undisturbed in the ground. Dig them up when you want them. If the digging promises to be hard in colder areas, put down a layer of hay or leaves, and the digging will be easier. You'll miss a few of the 'chokes as you harvest them, and those will provide you your next season's crop.

Cabbage can be left in the garden until well after the first frosts. Halloween or severe freezes may finish the cabbages. Brussels sprouts will produce long after the first frosts, too.

For winter harvesting of the root crops, spread a heavy layer of leaves, hay, or straw over them. This prevents the possibility of alternate freezing and thawing, which can injure them, and makes it easy to retrieve them when they're wanted.

Continued →

Mark both ends of each row with stakes. It will simplify finding the crops after a snowstorm.

Notice the flavor of these crops as you harvest and eat them. We think some improve with the cold. These include carrots, parsnips, salsify, and turnips. See whether you agree.

Storage Crops

APPLES

Store apart from vegetables, since apples may pick up some flavors, as from potatoes and onions, and may make carrots bitter. Keep temperatures as close as possible to 32°F. Lawrence Southwick, a veteran grower, recommends cooling picked apples as quickly as possible. Root cellar conditions are ideal for apples. Don't try to store windfalls or bruised fruit. They will only spoil the others. Apples that mature in late fall store best. (See Table 3 on page 982 for keeping quality of varieties.) Apples are stored best in crates that can be stacked on top of each other. Those who store apples in deep bins find the weight of the pile will damage those on the bottom, causing them to decay.

BEETS

Harvest after first light frosts, let dry in sun, then cut off tops, leaving at least two inches of tops so beets won't bleed. Discard any that are immature, damaged, or show signs of decay. Store as described for carrots. Beets do not store as well as carrots, so plan to use them as quickly as possible.

CABBAGES

For keeping, grow winter cabbages. Cabbages should be mature, and feel heavy for their size. Their odor can permeate a home, so if you place them in your root cellar, cut off the root and outer leaves, then wrap them in several layers of newspaper. Other ways to store: outside in a pit or trench, or hung up by the root in shed or garage, or simply left in the garden, to harvest before severe frosts.

CARROTS

Most varieties store well, the thicker varieties keep best. Can be heavily mulched in the garden, and dug up all winter. Or dig up, let dry in the sun, then store in boxes in root cellar. One method is to put a heavy layer of sand in the box, then layer carrots (they can touch, but don't jam too many together), more sand, and another layer of carrots, repeating until box is filled. Sand must be kept damp to keep carrots in good, unshriveled condition. They'll also keep well in outside pits.

CELERIAC

This lesser-known cousin of celery is nutritious, tasty, and a good keeper. Start a late crop to harvest in the late fall, then store as described for carrots.

CELERY

Giant Pascal is a good keeper. Use trench method described for outside storage. Or take up plants with roots, pack them in a box with roots in soil, and store in root cellar. Keep sand or soil moist, but keep water off the tops. In areas having temperate winters, leave plants in the ground, mulch heavily with leaves or hay, and harvest as needed.

GARLIC

Harvest and keep like onions. Garlic can add beauty to your home if braided and hung on the wall.

JERUSALEM ARTICHOKES

Dug up, they're poor keepers, no matter what method you try. But they store just fine if left in the ground. Dig them up when they're needed—and dig up no more than will be used in a week. If frozen ground may halt your digging, try a heavy mulch over the area, after you have cut back the lengthy stalks. Remember, too, that chokes are fine for eating when dug early in the spring.

LEEKS

Mulch heavily, and dig up as needed.

ONIONS

The stronger the taste, the better they keep. Late-maturing onions will keep best. Also those with thin necks. Good keepers include Ebenezer, Southport, and Yellow Globe. Harvest when most of the vegetation has fallen over. Let them cure for several weeks in a warm, dry, and well-ventilated area. Can be in the sun. Skins will rustle when they're ready to be stored. Use, don't store, those with wide necks or green stalks. Place in open-weave bags or open slatted crates, in cool, dry room. Attics are often ideal.

PARSNIPS

Can be stored like carrots in root cellar or, better still, a pit. Far easier to leave them in the ground, mulch heavily, and dig them up when they're needed. Cold weather improves their taste, so they're best when dug in the early spring.

POPCORN

Harvest when the stalks and leaves are dry. Let ears cure for about three weeks in a warm, dry area, then shell by twisting off kernels with hands. If kernels cling, let the ears cure longer. Store kernels in closed jars in room temperature. For decorations—as well as eating, pull back the husks, braid them, and hang them in your home. Remove as needed for popping,

POTATOES

Harvest after most of the tops have died down, and potatoes are mature. Harvesting can be delayed as much as six weeks without harming the crop. Let potatoes dry on the ground for several hours after digging, then store them in the dark, to avoid having them turn green. Don't store them near apples. Pick out all immature potatoes, any that were damaged while digging, and any that show signs of rot.

Potatoes can be put in boxes. They need ventilation. Ideal temperatures are between 40° and 50°F. If stored at cooler than 40°, potatoes tend to become sweet, but can be returned to original flavor by leaving them in room temperature for a week or two before eating them.

A method of outdoor storage is the potato mound. Around the area to be used, dig a shallow drainage ditch. Also dig an X of trenches crossing the bottom of the mound area. Cover the trenches with wire screening to keep out rodents, but allow air to enter and ventilate the mound. Construct a circular vent of screening that will extend vertically from the trenches to the top of the mound like a chimney.

The floor of the mound should be layered with one foot of clean hay. Pile the potatoes into the area around the vertical vent and over the cross-ventilation trenches. Cover the potatoes with about six inches of hay for insulation. A final insulating layer of soil about 6"-12" thick should be placed over the hay. The circular vertical vent should extend about six inches above the surface of the mound, and must be covered with a lid to keep out water. An inverted tin can works well. When the temperature falls below freezing, the cross-ventilation trenches should be blocked with soil. For a rough rule-of-thumb, pile the potatoes so that the height of the mound is about one-half its diameter.

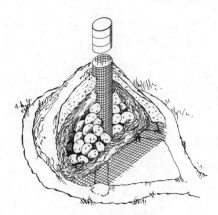

PUMPKINS

Harvest and store as described under squash.

RUTABAGA

Harvest before heavy frost. Must be kept moist to avoid shriveling. Follow directions for carrots.

SALSIFY

Can be stored like carrots, in root cellar or in outdoor pit. It's far easier to leave them in the ground, mulch heavily enough to keep ground from freezing, and dig up as wanted.

SQUASH

Good keepers are Hubbard, Butternut, Acorn. Leave on plant until fully matured, but pick before heavy frost, leaving a stem on the squash. Leave in sunny field for several weeks, or cure in a dry warm place for two weeks. They're ready to store when a fingernail won't penetrate the skin. Don't cure the Acorns. They may lose moisture, turn orange, or become stringy. Store squash on shelves, preferably not piled up, in warm (50°-60°F), dry area.

SWEET POTATOES

Harvest before frost. Cure potatoes in high humidity and 80°-85°F temperatures for two weeks to toughen skins. Then store in warm (55°-60°F), relatively dry area. Light won't affect sweet potatoes as it will their Irish brethren.

TOMATOES

Green tomatoes are well worth harvesting. Those in the light green stage will ripen, providing good eating long after the vines have been killed by frosts. Harvest before those frosts. Try one of several methods to save them. One is to pull up the entire plant, roots and all, and hang it upside down in a place where frost will not reach it. Or pick the light green tomatoes, wrap them in newspapers individually, then keep them in temperatures of 55°–60°F, where they will ripen during the next six weeks.

TABLE 1.

Storage life expectancies, recommended storage temperatures, and relative humidities of fresh fruits *

Fruit	Temperature °F	(°C)	Relative humidity %	Approximate length of storage period
Apples	30	(-1.1)	85–90	as per variety
Apricots	32	(0.0)	85–90	1–2 weeks
Blackberries	same as raspberries			
Cherries				
sweet	32	(0.0)	85–90	2–3 weeks
sour	32	(0.0)	85–90	few days
Cranberries	36–40	(2.2–4.4)	80–85	2 months
Grapes, American	32	(0.0)	85–90	1 month
Peaches	32	(0.0)	85–90	2 weeks
Pears				
Bartlett	30	(-1.1)	85–90	2–3 months
fall and winter	30	(-1.1)	85–90	3–5 months
Plums				
Early, Japanese type	40	(4.4)	85–90	few days
Other types	32	(0.0)	85–90	4–6 weeks
Raspberries	32	(0.0)	85–90	few days
Strawberries	32	(0.0)	85–90	5–10 days

* Based on information from Canada Department of Agriculture Publications 1532, *Storage of fruits and vegetables*, by S. W. Porritt.

TABLE 2.

Storage life expectancies, recommended storage temperatures, and relative humidities of fresh vegetables *

Vegetable	Temperature °F	(°C)	Relative humidity %	Approximate length of storage period	Suggested methods for extended preservation
Asparagus	32	(0.0)	95	3 weeks	freeze or can
Beans					
green or snap	45–50	(7–10)	85–90	8–10 days	freeze or can
lima					
shelled	32	(0.0)	85–90	2 weeks	freeze or can
unshelled	32	(0.0)	85–90	2 weeks	
Beets					
bunched	32	(0.0)	90–95	10–14 days	
topped	32	(0.0)	90–95	1–3 months	
Broccoli					
Italian or sprouting	32	(0.0)	90–95	1 week	freeze
Brussels sprouts	32	(0.0)	90–95	3–4 weeks	freeze
Cabbage					
early	32	(0.0)	90–95	3–4 weeks	
late	32	(0.0)	90–95	3–4 months	
Carrots					
bunched	32–34	(0.0–1.1)	95	2 weeks	
topped	32–34	(0.0–1.1)	95	4–5 months	

TABLE 2.

Storage life expectancies, recommended storage temperatures, and relative humidities of fresh vegetables *

Vegetable	Temperature °F	(°C)	Relative humidity %	Approximate length of storage period	Suggested methods for extended preservation
Cauliflower	32	(0.0)	90–95	2 weeks	freeze
Celery	32	(0.0)	95+	3 months	
Corn, sweet	32	(0.0)	90–95	8 days	freeze or can
Cucumbers	45–50	(7.2–10)	95	10–14 days	
Eggplants	45–50	(7.2–10)	85–90	10 days	
Endive or escarole	32	(0.0)	90–95	2–3 weeks	
Garlic, dry	32	(-1.1–0.0)	70–75	6–8 months	
Horseradish	30–32	(-1.1–0.0)	90–95	10–12 months can	
Kohlrabi	32	(0.0)	90–95	2–4 weeks	freeze
Leeks, green	32	(0.0)	90–95	1–3 months	
Lettuce	32	(0.0)	95 (head lettuce)	2-weeks	
Melons					
Cantaloupe or muskmelon	32–45	(0.0–7.2)	85–90	2 weeks	
honeydew	45–50	(7.2–10)	85–90	2–3 weeks	
watermelon	36–40	(2.2–4.4)	85–90	2–3 weeks	
Mushrooms, cultivated	32	(0.0)	85–90	5 days	freeze
Onion sets	32	(0.0)	70–75	5–7 months	
Onions, dry	32	(0.0)	50–70	5–9 months	
Parsnips	32	(0.0)	95	2–4 months	
Peas, green	32	(0.0)	95	1–2 weeks	freeze or can
Peppers, sweet	45–50	(7.2–10)	85–90	8–10 days	freeze
Potatoes					
early-crop	50	(10)	85–90	1–3 weeks	
late-crop	39	(3.9)	85–90	4–9 months	
Pumpkins	45–50	(7.2–10)	70–75	2–3 months	
Radish					
spring, bunched	32	(0.0)	90–95	2 weeks	
winter	32	(0.0)	90–95	2–4 months	
Rhubarb	32	(0.0)	90–95	2–3 weeks	freeze
Rutabaga or turnip	32	(0.0)	90–95	6 months	
Salsify	32	(0.0)	90–95	2–4 months	
Spinach	32	(0.0)	90–95	10–14 days	freeze or can
Squash					
summer	45–50	(7.2–10)	70–75	2 weeks	
winter	45–50	(7.2–10)	70–75	6 months	
Tomatoes					
ripe	50	(10)	85–90	3–5 days	
mature green	55–60	(12.8–15.6)	85–90	2–6 weeks	

* Based on information from Canada Department of Agriculture Publications 1532, *Storage of fruits and vegetables*, by S. W. Porritt.

Continued ➡

TABLE 3.
Normal and maximum storage periods for some common apple varieties *

| | Storage Period | |
| | Normal | Maximum |
Variety	months	months
Wealthy	0–1	3
Grimes Golden	2–3	4
Jonathan	2–3	4
McIntosh	2–4	4–5
Cortland	3–4	5
Spartan	4	5
Rhode Island Greening	3–4	6
Delicious	3–4	6
Stayman	4–5	5
York Imperial	4–5	5–6
Northern Spy	4–5	6
Rome Beauty	4–5	6–7
Newton	5–6	8
Winesap	5–7	8

* Based on information from Canada Department of Agriculture Publications 1532, *Storage of fruits and vegetables*, by S.W. Porritt.

Build Your Own Underground Root Cellar

Phyllis Hobson
Illustrations by Ed Epstein

Having a root cellar in your backyard is like having your own private supermarket of fresh fruits and vegetables. Any time you need potatoes for dinner or an apple for a snack, just open the door and walk inside. Anything you need is right there on the shelves.

A good root cellar should provide cool, above-freezing temperatures and good circulation of moderately humid air. The dirt floor takes advantage of the naturally cool, even temperature of the earth. It also cuts costs and provides needed humidity.

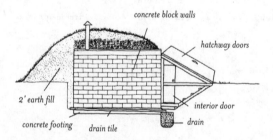

Here is a cutaway view of the completed root cellar.

The concrete block walls are durable and sturdy, with a middle core of air, which acts as an insulator. In extreme climates, the cores can be filled with loose insulation to keep temperatures more even. Concrete block walls are simple to work with. And you can lay a few blocks whenever you have a little time, then resume where you left off the next time.

The walls are topped by a wood frame roof made of 2 X lumber, which can be handled by 1 person. The roof is protected by sheathing, roll roofing, and plastic film, then covered with 2 feet of soil.

Entrance to the cellar is through an air lock created by a 4-foot-wide hatchway at the top of the stairway and another door at the bottom of the stairs. The doors and the entrance wall are insulated to protect the cellar interior.

The cellar is vented for good air circulation, and a drainage system protects the interior from water seepage.

So here it is. This is one root cellar you can afford. This is one you can do all by yourself. And you can build it in your spare time.

But first, let's decide where to put this 8-foot by 12-foot cellar.

The Right Location

The ideal location for a root cellar is on a hillside or slope facing away from prevailing winds. Even without a slope, choose the highest ground you have for the best drainage possible. Avoid any low-lying areas, or your cellar may fill up with water in the spring.

If possible, pick a spot convenient to both the kitchen and garden. Remember, from harvest season until early summer—during the worst weather of the year—you will probably be visiting it almost every day.

Stay away from large trees, if you can. Tree roots sometimes reach out an incredible distance, and they not only hamper digging, they can invade your cellar walls eventually.

Consider the type of soil. If it is rocky or hardpan clay, hand digging will be difficult, so you will need excavation equipment. If it is too sandy, the dirt walls will collapse as you dig, and you will have to dig the hole larger to allow for sloping walls. If you encounter either condition, it is probably best to look for another location.

TOOLS

Many of the tools you will need are already in your garage or workshop. Some specialized tools, such as a heavy-duty wheelbarrow, can be rented. Here's what you will need and what you will need them for.

- *Pointed-ended, long-handled shovel* to dig the excavation and the footing trench and to move wet concrete and gravel.

- *Square-ended trench shovel* for squaring up the sides and bottom of the footing trench.

- *Garden hoe* to spread wet concrete in the footing trench and mix concrete and mortar.

- *Metal tape measure* at least 20 feet long.

- *Sturdy wheelbarrow*.

- *Masonry trowel* to apply mortar between blocks. The end of the wooden handle is useful to tap the blocks in place.

- *Mortarboard* to hold mortar as it is applied.

- *Jointer tool* to compact mortar in the joints.

- *Level*, 36 to 48 inches long, to check plumb and level of the wall as it is built.

- *Plumb bob* to lay out the footing trench.

- *Wooden float* to level off the top of the concrete footing.

- *Straight 1 x 6 board*, measuring 8 feet, marked every 8 inches to check the level of each course of blocks and the accuracy of the horizontal mortar joints. Sometimes called a storyboard.

- *Pair of mason's line stretchers* to hold a line taut between corner blocks as a guide for each course.

- *Masonry chisel* to cut blocks.

- *Hammer* to pound chisel, stakes, and nails.

- *Crosscut saw* to cut lumber to fit.

- *Saber or keyhole saw* to cut the vent hole in the roof.

- *Carpenter's plane* to trim roof rafters.

- *Screwdriver* to attach hinges and door handles.

- *Wrench* to tighten nuts on top plate.

- *Caulking gun* to caulk around footing and air vent.

- *Applicator* (brush, roller, trowel, or 6-inch putty knife) to apply waterproofing to wall exterior.

MATERIALS

Here are the materials you will need to build a low-cost, 8-foot by 12-foot by 8-foot concrete block root cellar. The list is divided into construction steps, so you can buy the materials as you go along, and budget the costs over time. You may find, however, that you can save on delivery costs by buying all of 1 type of material at the same time.

For Step 2

16 stakes to mark off footing: 2" x 2" x 3'?

8 boards: 1" x 3" x 4'6"

mason's line or stout string: 150'

For Step 4

30 stakes: 1" x 2" x 12"

ready-mix concrete: 1 cubic yd. (or 6 bags of cement, 12 cubic ft. of sand, and 24 cubic ft. of 1" gravel)

For Step 5

24 hollow core concrete blocks: 8" x 8" x 16"

4 hollow core corner blocks: 8" x 8" x 16"

1 strip of 3/8" plywood: 2" x 8"

masonry cement: 14 bags (for Step 8 as well)

mortar sand: 11 cubic yd. (for Step 8 as well)

For Step 6

perforated plastic drain tile: 40'

90° elbows for drain tile: 2

1" to 1 1/2" gravel or stone: 2 cubic yd.

For Step 7

2 boards: 2" x 8" x 69"

2 boards: 2" x 8" x 32"

scrap lumber for bracing and props

For Step 8

262 hollow core concrete blocks: 8" x 8" x 16"

56 hollow core corner blocks: 8" x 8" x 16"

6 lintel blocks: 8" x 8" x 8"

reinforcing bars

2 boards: 1" x 2" x 69"

concrete mix: 1 cubic yd. (for Step 10 as well)

For Step 9

loose insulation: 50 cubic ft.

1/4" mesh hardware cloth: 20 sq. ft.

14 anchor bolts: 5/8" x 10"

For Step 10

Stairway wall: use pressure-treated lumber

2 boards: 2" x 4" x 96"

2 boards: 2" x 4" x 30 1/2"

2 boards: 2" x 4" x 39"

2 boards: 2" x 4" x 98 3/4"

2 boards: 2" x 4" x 70 1/2"

2 boards: 2" x 4" x 86 3/4"

4 sheets 1/2" exterior plywood: 4' x 8'

wood preservative (copper naphthenate): 2 gal.

Stairway: use pressure-treated lumber

2 boards: 2" x 12" x 74"

10 boards: 2" x 4" x 12"

5 boards: 2" x 12" x 36"

4 pieces scrap 2 x 4s: about 2' long

Interior door

2 sheets 1/2" plywood: 4' x 8'

2 x 4 boards: 20? (can be pieced together)

insulation (foam, batt, or loose)

Hatchway doors

2 sheets 1/2" exterior plywood: 4' x 8'

2 x 4 boards: 40' (can be pieced together)

insulation (foam, batt, or loose)

1 board: 1" x 6" x 8'

For Step 11

2 boards for the top plate: 2" x 8" x 12'

2 boards for the top plate: 2" x 8" x 6'9"

2 boards for headers: 2" x 10" x 11'9"

2 boards for end rafters: 2" x 12" x 8?

11 boards for rafters: 2" x 12" x 7'9"

Continued →

3 sheets of 3/4" or 1" exterior plywood: 4? x 8?

I roll tar paper roofing: 4' x 80'

roofing nails

For Step 12

3/4" plywood: 7 1/2" x 7 1/2"

2 boards: 1" x 2" x 7 1/2"

3/4" leaf hinge

hook and eye

self-stick weatherstrip foam: 30"

plastic screen: 8" x 8"

4" solid plastic sewer pipe: 4'

plastic flange with inner diameter of 4"

I galvanized hood to fit sewer pipe

For Step 13

roofing tar: 4 gal.

12 bales straw

6-mil plastic sheeting: 100-foot roll

waterproof plastic tape: 1 roll

foundation coating

cement plaster

caulking compound

For Step 14

Interior door

2 boards: 2" x 4" x 6'

2 boards: 2" x 4" x 3'

6" T-hinges: 3

I board: 1" x 2" x 69"

2 pieces of scrap lumber: 2" x 4" x 8"

door handle: 1

hook and eye

Hatchway doors

3 boards: 2" x 6" x 102 1/4"

2 boards: 2" x 6" x 39"

4 boards: 2" x 4" x 96"

6" T-hinges: 6

door handles: 2

All lumber should be treated with a wood preservative, such as copper naphthenate sold under various brand names. Wood should be soaked in the liquid, if possible, or generously painted with the solution, according to the manufacturer's directions. Be prepared to store all materials under cover to keep them as dry as possible before and during construction.

Concrete blocks and lumber should be stacked on planks off the ground and covered with tarps or plastic sheeting. Keep bags of cement well protected in a dry place, especially after the bag has been opened. Even the sand and gravel should be kept as dry as possible. Wet sand will add a great deal of water to the concrete mix and possibly weaken it.

While you are waiting for the materials to be delivered, you can get out your tape measure and shovel. You are ready to start digging.

Building the Cellar

STEP 1 EXCAVATING

For your 12-foot by 8-foot root cellar, dig a hole 16 feet long by 12 feet wide by 4 feet deep with an entrance ramp 4 feet wide and sloping 6 feet, 2 inches from the ground level to the bottom of the hole. The floor should be as level as possible.

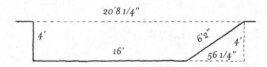

Step 1. Here is a cutaway view of the excavation. The excavation is 12 feet wide.

STEP 2 MARKING OFF

Beginning 32 inches from the entrance end, pound 4 stakes in the ground to mark off an area 6 feet, 8 inches wide by 10 feet, 8 inches long, keeping the stakes equidistant from the dirt walls.

Check to make sure the corners are square by measuring diagonally from corner stake to corner stake. The distance should be equal. Adjust, if necessary.

Stretch a cord along the ground around the outside of the 4 stakes and tie the ends together. This line marks the inside dimensions of the block walls.

To mark off a footing trench, pound 4 more stakes in a rectangle 1 1/2 feet outside the marked area. Again, measure diagonally to be sure the corners are square.

This next step will help you mark off right angles for your corners. Pound 2 more stakes at right angles to each of the new stakes, at least 4 feet away. Nail 2 batter boards (1 x 3s) near the top of the stakes to tie the stakes together. Check that the corners are square by measuring from the corner stake 3 feet down 1 leg and 4 feet down the other. The distance between these 2 points (the hypotenuse of the triangle) should be 5 feet. Adjust the stakes and batter boards if necessary.

Using nails in the top of the boards to keep the cord in place, stretch a line between the batter boards exactly 4 inches inside the original line (which measures 6 feet, 8 inches by 10 feet, 8 inches).

Pull up the original 4 stakes and cord. The new line above the ground marks the inside edge of the footing trench. Now stretch another line 16 inches outside the new line. Nail to the top of the batter boards as you did the first line.

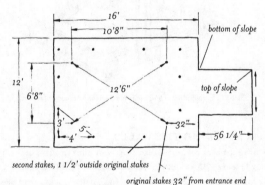

Step 2. Marking the foundation.

1. *Pound 4 stakes to mark off an area 6 feet, 8 inches by 10 feet, 8 inches. The corners are square if the distances from corner to corner are equal.*
2. *Pound a second set of 4 stakes 1 1/2 feet outside the original stakes.*
3. *To square the corners made by these new stakes, measure 3 feet in 1 direction and 4 feet in the other direction, so that the distance between them makes a 5-foot line, as shown in the lower left corner.*

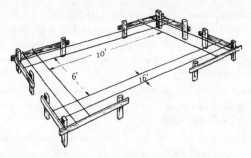

Step 2. Once the stakes are in place, batter boards are nailed to the top of the stakes, and lines are stretched between the boards to mark the footing trench. The inside line is exactly 4 inches inside the original line. The outside line is 16 inches beyond that.

STEP 3 DIGGING THE FOOTING

Dig a trench 16 inches wide and 9 inches deep all the way around the hole between the 2 lines. Keep the corners square and the bottom level.

When the trench is dug, check from each corner, eyeing the length of the string lines to make sure the trench is straight. Make any adjustments necessary before pulling up the batter board construction.

STEP 4 POURING THE FOOTING

To insure a level footing for the block walls, pound the 1 x 2 stakes in the ground down the center of the trench every 2 or 3 feet. The tops of the stakes should extend 8 inches from the bottom of the trench and should be perfectly level. Use a mason's level and a straight 2 x 4 board cut 8 feet long to check the level.

When the stakes are all in place, dampen the trench with a garden hose or a few buckets of water; then fill the trench with wet concrete. Level it just to the tops of the stakes, using a wooden float. There is no need to pull up the stakes.

A 1:2:4 concrete mix (1 part cement, 2 parts sand, 4 parts gravel) is recommended for footings. If you mix your own, a clean, dry water bucket makes a good measure. Mix the dry ingredients thoroughly in a wheelbarrow, then add just enough clean water to make a stiff mixture. Too much water will make a weak concrete, so be careful not to use more than 5 or 6 gallons of water for each bag of cement.

It's easier, but more expensive, to buy ready-mixed concrete. You can have large amounts delivered in a mixer-truck, but most dealers have small trailers to haul behind your car for the small amount you will need.

When the wet concrete is leveled, lay scrap pieces of 2 x 4s or other wood in the center of the footing. Remove the wood as soon as the concrete sets up. This will create a groove for the mortar to lock the bottom row of blocks to the footing.

Give the wet concrete at least 3 days to cure before you start laying the blocks. Spray the surface with water once a day to keep it damp. In cold or very hot weather, keep it covered with straw, canvas, or old blankets.

STEP 5 LAYING THE FIRST COURSE

To make sure the blocks are going to fit the footing, make a trial run by setting the first course (1 row of blocks all the way around) in place without mortar.

Place the blocks 4 inches in from the inside edge of the concrete footing, and slip a 2-inch by 8-inch strip of 3/8-inch plywood between

Continued →

each 2 blocks to allow for the mortar. Lay 9 blocks lengthwise down the 2 side walls. Then place 5 blocks between them on the 2 end walls. Blocks should always be placed with the large core side down. Adjust, if necessary, to make the blocks fit, then mark the placement on the footing with chalk. Remove the blocks.

Starting at I corner, spread a layer of mortar along the chalk line from the corner down both walls. The mortar should be I inch thick by 8 inches wide by the length of 2 blocks.

Set a corner block on the mortar and tap it into place with the trowel handle until the block is level and plumb, and the mortar is 3/8 inch thick. Scrape off excess mortar under the block on both sides.

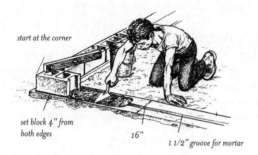

start at the corner

set block 4" from both edges   16"   1 1/2" groove for mortar

Step 5. Spread the mortar 1 inch thick. Tap the block in place and scrape off excess mortar.

Spread mortar 1/2 inch thick on the end of a stretcher block, and set it in place end to end with the first block in the bed of mortar. Again tap the block into place and scrape off all excess mortar. This mortar can be used again.

Repeat with another block placed at right angles to the first along the other wall.

Continue laying blocks all the way around the footing, spreading mortar on the footing and on the end of each block and checking to be sure each block is level before setting the next. Use corner blocks on each corner. Spread mortar on both ends of the last block in the course and carefully ease it in. It may take a couple of tries.

As the mortar between the blocks and between the blocks and the footing begins to stiffen, it will pull away slightly from the blocks. To correct this and make the walls more waterproof, run a mason's jointer or a metal or wooden rod along the joints to force the mortar in the cracks. This operation is called tooling, and it will leave a concave impression between blocks.

Tool all joints and wipe off any excess mortar.

STEP 6 LAYING THE DRAIN TILES

With the first course of blocks in place, pour 2 inches of gravel around the outside perimeter. Then, lay a line of 4-inch perforated plastic drain tile on top. Be sure the holes on the tile face down on the gravel. Slope the tile 2 inches from back to front. Join sections of tile according to manufacturer's directions, using 90-degree elbows at the corners. Make sure the tiles are not clogged with dirt.

At each front end of the drain tiles, dig a hole about 3 feet in diameter (or as large as possible) and 3 feet deep. Fill both holes with gravel, and lay tile to the center of each. Cover the tiles with 12 inches of crushed stone or gravel.

If your land is wet, and if the ground slopes away from the root cellar, it is a good idea to run the drain tile all the way to the outside to allow the water to drain on the ground.

STEP 7 MARKING THE DOORWAY

Mark off a 32-inch rough opening in the center of the entrance wall. The doorway should be opposite the entrance ramp and should be positioned as evenly with the blocks as possible to avoid the time-consuming job of cutting blocks to fit. The door is set on top of I course of blocks to discourage mice, chipmunks, and water from entering the cellar.

To make the door frame, nail together the 2 x 8 lumber as shown, with a I x 2 centered on and nailed into the side jambs. The I x 2s will be mortared into the grooves of the concrete blocks. Brace the door frame temporarily with scrap lumber. The sill should be flush with the outside edge of the concrete blocks.

Step 6. The drain tiles are laid when the first course of blocks are in place. Slope the tile 2 inches from back to front. The tiles drain into a 3-foot drain filled with gravel.

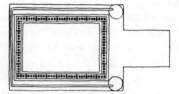

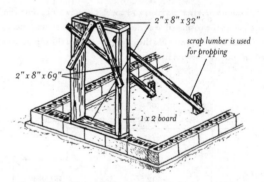

2" x 8" x 32"

scrap lumber is used for propping

2" x 8" x 69"

1 x 2 board

Step 7. The door frame is propped in place on the first course of blocks.

STEP 8 BUILDING THE WALLS

Beginning at a back corner, spread mortar on the top edges of the first course of blocks 2 blocks long in each direction. Build the corner 3 blocks high. Repeat on all 4 corners, using corner blocks where needed.

Hook a mason's line around the ends of the corner blocks and stretch a taut line from corner to corner. Using this line as a guide, fill in the second course of blocks along I wall, then move the line to the next wall. Continue building up the walls, first on the corners, then filling in the course, all the way around. As you finish each course, move the mason's line up to the next corner block. Tool all joints as they begin to stiffen. Build the entrance wall around the door frame, using blocks cut to fit. Continue until the walls are 11 blocks high all the way around.

Over the doorway, insert the lintel. To make the lintel, lay 6 lintel blocks end to end so a channel is formed. Place reinforcing bars in the channel and fill with concrete. Let dry. Turn the lintel over and gently set in place. Adjust until the mortar joint is the same thickness as the other horizontal joints.

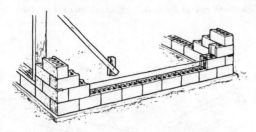

Step 8. Stretch a taut line from corner block to corner block to align each course of blocks.

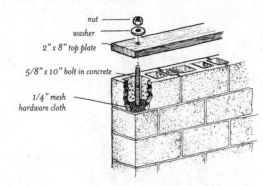

nut
washer
2" x 8" top plate
5/8" x 10" bolt in concrete
1/4" mesh hardware cloth

Step 9. This cutaway view of the top course shows the placement of the hardware cloth, anchor bolt, and top plate.

Step 8. Build the entrance wall around the door frame. To cut a block to fit around the frame, use a hammer and chisel to mark a cutting line all the way around the block. Place the chisel on this line and rap sharply with the hammer. It may take a few tries to cut through. Trim off any rough edges.

STEP 9 INSULATING AND TOPPING THE WALLS

Before laying the top course of blocks, insulate the entrance wall by filling the cores of the blocks with sawdust or commercial insulation pellets. In a northern climate, you may want to insulate all walls.

Cut 1/4-inch mesh hardware cloth into 6-inch-wide strips, and lay the strips over the tops of the eleventh course of blocks on all 4 walls. The strips should be cut in pieces as long as possible.

Now proceed with the final course of blocks, spreading the mortar on the hardware cloth as necessary.

When the final course is in place, mix a batch of 1:2:4 concrete, and fill the cores of the top course of blocks, smoothing off the top. As you fill the cores, imbed a 5/8-inch by 10-inch anchor bolt in the concrete every other block. The nut end should protrude from the concrete about 2 inches.

Allow the mortar and concrete fill to cure at least 3 to 5 days. If the weather is very cold or very hot, keep it covered, but do not wet down.

Meanwhile, you can work on the stairway and doors.

STEP 10 BUILDING THE STAIRWAY AND DOORS

Stairway Wall. Using pressure-treated lumber, build a framework for a stairway wall and hatchway door support as illustrated. Cover the outside of the framework with 1/2-inch exterior grade plywood that has been painted with wood preservative.

Stairway. Dig 4 holes 6 inches in diameter and 3 feet deep at the top and bottom of the stairway slope.

To make the stringers, cut 2 pieces of 2 x 12s to measure 74 inches. Trim the ends to fit the slope of the entrance ramp.

Securely nail 10 12-inch pieces of 2 x 4s to form braces on both stringers for treads. The first braces should be nailed so that the top edges of the braces are 8 inches above the bottom edges of the stringers. The other braces should be nailed 9 1/2 inches apart, measuring from the top of one brace to the top of the next brace.

Make 5 treads from 2 x 12s to measure 36 inches, and nail them in place on the top edge of the braces.

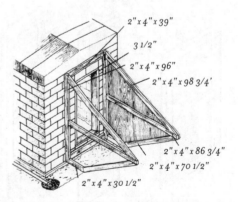

2" x 4" x 39"
3 1/2"
2" x 4" x 96"
2" x 4" x 98 3/4'
2" x 4" x 86 3/4"
2" x 4" x 70 1/2"
2" x 4" x 30 1/2"

Step 10. To make the stairway wall and hatchway door support, construct a frame of 2 x 4s around door opening, as shown. Attach the frame to the block wall, using concrete nails. At right angles to the pieces that frame the door, build a 2 x 4 frame for the stairway wall. The bottom 2" x 4" x 70 1/2" board should match the ground slope. Nail securely in place and repeat on other side of the doorway.

Set the stairway in place on the slope. Nail 2-foot-long pieces of 2 x 4s to the inside of the stringer so they extend into the holes you dug. Place a few rocks in the bottom of each hole. Then fill the holes with wet concrete mixture to hold the stairway in place.

Continued ➡

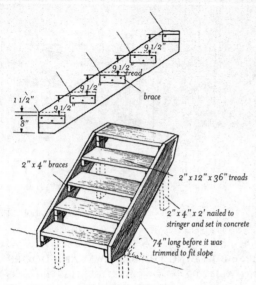

Step 10. The stairway is set in place on the entrance slope.

Taper both ends of the 13 rafter boards with a saw or plane. Set aside.

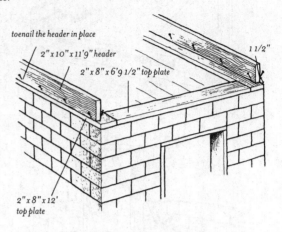

Step 11. Set the header on edge and toenail to the top plate 1 1/2" from each end.

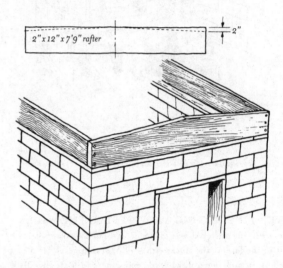

Step 11. Attach the end rafters first. Then attach the middle rafters. The rafters can be sawed or planed to achieve the 2" slope.

Interior Door. Nail 2 x 4 pieces along the outside edge and across the middle of 1 of the 28 7/8-inch by 68 7/8-inch plywood pieces. Fill the 2 recesses with insulation and top with the other plywood sheet. Nail in place.

2 Hatchway Doors. Cut the 1/2-inch plywood to make 4 pieces measuring 21 1/2 inches by 96 inches. Frame 2 of the pieces with 2 x 4s as you did the interior door. Nail in place. Fill the center cores with insulation and nail the other 2 pieces of plywood on top.

Nail a 1 x 6 board the length of the right-hand door on the edge with the board extending 2 inches over the edge. This board will overlap the opening and shut out drafts when the doors are closed.

The headers should be set on edge on the 12-foot top plate you bolted to the top of the block walls and toenailed in place 1 1/2 inches from each end.

Set the 2 full-length 2-inch by 12-inch by 8-foot rafters on edge at each end of the headers. Nail to the top plate and to the ends of the headers, creating an open box on the block walls.

One at a time, set the 11 rafters in place across the top of the building between the 2 headers every 12 inches the length of the building. Toenail the rafters to the top plate, and nail through the headers into the ends of the rafters on each end.

When all the rafters are nailed in place, cover the top with 3/4-inch or 1-inch exterior grade plywood, and nail in place. Fill any holes around the edge of the roof with batt insulation, stapled in place. Then cover the entire roof with layers of roll roofing. Begin the layers at each side, overlapping each layer 2 inches and extending it at least 1 foot over on all sides. Nail in place, using blind nailing cement.

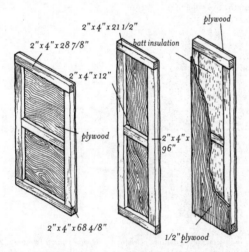

Step 10. The partially completed interior door (left) and hatchway doors (right) are constructed with 2 x 4 frames with plywood backing.

STEP 11 ROOFING THE CELLAR
Attach 2 x 8 boards to the top of the block walls by drilling holes in the boards for the bolts you embedded in the concrete. The 2 x 8s may be pieced together, if necessary. Fasten the top plate securely with nuts.

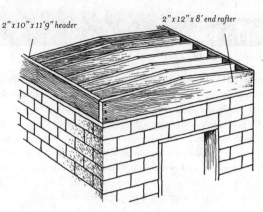

2" x 10" x 11'9" header

2" x 12" x 8' end rafter

Step 11. Nail the rafters in place between the 2 x 10 headers.

STEP 12 INSTALLING THE AIR VENT

Between the second and third rafters from the rear wall, drill a small hole in the roof. Using a saber saw or a keyhole saw, and starting from the hole you made, cut a 6-inch hole in the roof, centered between the rafters.

Cut an 8-inch square of screen. Staple this to the underside of the hole to keep out insects.

Cut 2 pieces of 1 x 2s to measure 7 1/2 inches long. Nail these to the rafters on both sides of the hole you just cut. Cut a piece of 3/4-inch plywood to measure 7 1/2 inches square. Attach the plywood piece to one side of the 1 x 2s with a 3/4-inch leaf hinge. Close the plywood hatch door against the other piece of 1 x 2 with a simple hook and eye. Weatherstrip around the edges of the plywood.

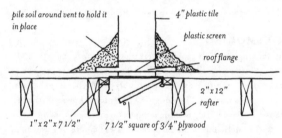

pile soil around vent to hold it in place

4" plastic tile

plastic screen

roof flange

2" x 12" rafter

1" x 2" x 7 1/2"

7 1/2" square of 3/4" plywood

Step 12. Side view of roof vent assembly.

On top of the roof, screw the plastic flange to the plywood, centering it over the hole. Knock out the center, if necessary, by tapping it with a hammer. Then slip a 4-foot length of plastic sewer pipe into the flange. Caulk around the bottom of the vent and install the galvanized hood on top.

STEP 13 WATERPROOFING THE EXTERIOR

Cover the roof with roofing tar. Pile soil around vent pipe to hold it in place. Over the rest of the roof, place 1 1/2 feet to 2 feet of baled straw "slices." Top this with 2 to 5 layers of 6-mil plastic sheeting. Fold the plastic over the edges on all sides well below the top plate. The soil covering will hold it down securely.

Cover the exterior of the block walls with a 1/2-inch coating of cement plaster (1 part cement, 3 parts sand). Then coat with foundation coating.

Caulk well along the bottom edge between the first layer of blocks and the footing with commercial caulking.

STEP 14 INSTALLING THE DOORS

Interior Door. Remove the props and braces from the door frame installed in Step 7. Insulate around the frame by stuffing pieces of batt insulation into any gaps between the concrete blocks and frame.

Nail 2 x 4 lumber to the edge of the door frame all the way around on the outside of the wall. Shim, if necessary, to form a snug fit.

Attach the interior door to the 2 x 4 frame with screws, using 3 6-inch T-hinges. Install a latch or hook and eye on the outside to hold the door closed. Nail a 1 x 2 stop to the side jamb located on the inside of the root cellar along the edge of the door.

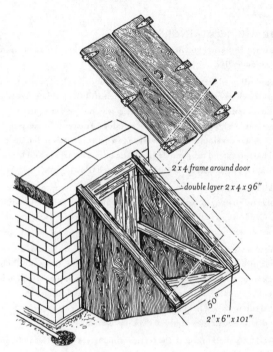

2 x 4 frame around door

double layer 2 x 4 x 96"

50"

2" x 6" x 101"

Step 14. Face the stairway wall frame built in Step 10 with 2 x 6s and 2 x 4s. Then attach hatchway doors to the frame.

Attach an easy-to-grasp handle (metal or homemade) at a convenient height.

Hatchway Doors. Face the top of the stairway wall frame with 4 2 x 6s laid flat and flush with the inside edge of the 2 x 4 supports to make a frame 50 inches wide. Attach 2 sets of double 2 x 4s (3 inches thick) to the outside edge of the 2 x 6 frame. The doors will fit between these and be hinged to them.

Lay the 2 doors on the frame and attach with 6-inch T-hinges on each door. Attach large handles at a convenient height for opening.

STEP 15 COVERING THE CELLAR

Using the soil you removed in Step 1, first fill in around the 3 sides of the block walls, tamping it down well as you go by walking on it. Pile the dirt up to the roof, then cover the roof, being careful not to disturb the air vent or the roofing.

Continued ➤

Cover the roof with 2 feet of soil, gradually tapering it out to the sides so there is at least 1 1/2 feet covering all 3 sides. Pile the soil carefully around the hatchway door frames, packing it well.

You may need to bring in additional soil, but earth is the cheapest insulator for your cellar, so don't stint on this step. When the cellar is well covered, seed with a good ground cover to make the area more attractive and hold the soil in place in heavy rains.

Get the Most from Your Root Cellar

With a few thermometers and a humidity gauge, you can learn to take advantage of the natural temperature and humidity differences that will exist in your cellar. Usually, the coolest, most humid area is near the door on the floor. The warmest, driest area is at the ceiling toward the back.

STORAGE CONTAINERS

Almost any container you have on hand or can buy cheaply can be used in your root cellar.

You will need crates or baskets for those foods, such as potatoes and apples, which need containers through which air can circulate freely. For those foods, such as onions and garlic, which need warm, dry storage, mesh bags—the kind onions, potatoes, and fruits sometimes come in—are excellent. Other produce can be stored in wooden or metal barrels, metal tubs and pails, plastic or metal garbage and trash containers, or sections of 18-inch and 24-inch tile.

All floor containers should be raised off the dirt floor to prevent rotting and rusting of containers and mold and insect infestation of the food. Crude wood pallets, sometimes available for free at building or garden centers or appliance stores, are ideal for this purpose.

You can buy heavy-duty metal shelving or make your own of 2 x 12 lumber with 2 x 4 shelf braces. For maximum strength, there should be a vertical support every 4 feet, and these supports should be attached to the roof supports. A piece of scrap aluminum or plastic under the vertical supports will help retard rotting. The boards also may be treated with 2 coats of commercial wood preservative.

Nail 2 x 4 shelf braces to the vertical supports. Cut shelves to fit and set in place, but do not nail down so that shelves may be removed for cleaning and airing.

Root Cellar Maintenance

A well-constructed root cellar does not require much maintenance, but you will need to check it at least once a day the first winter to make sure the temperature stays above freezing.

In very cold weather, you will need to close the air vent, and you may want to supply a small amount of heat with a kerosene lantern or a couple of 100-watt light bulbs. Be careful, though; a kerosene or electric heater gives off too much heat.

Once a year the cellar should be cleaned and aired thoroughly to avoid plant disease and insect infestation. Choose a dry day in early summer just before harvest, when the shelves and bins are almost empty. During the annual clean-up, open the doors as far as possible for 2 or 3 days, take out all the containers and shelves and scrub them well with soapy water, then let them air in the sun a day or 2. Sweep or rake the floor and whitewash the walls.

Remove and discard any sand, sawdust, or leaves in which root vegetables were stored. Replace with new material in the fall.

Build a Smokehouse

Illustrations by Ed Epstein

Some of the most mouth-watering, epicurean delights in gourmet stores are smoked hams, breasts of turkey, pheasants, eels, salmon, whitefish, and trout. These delicacies are also very, very expensive, and most of us buy them in miniscule amounts for special occasions. But if you have your own smokehouse, you can enjoy these luxuries and dozens of superbly flavored foods from smoked homemade sausages, venison, beef, and lamb, to wild game birds, clams, oysters, shrimp, squid, and freshwater fish. If you fish or hunt or farm livestock, your costs will be a fraction of what you might pay at the delicatessen counter.

In recent years dozens of commercial smokers have appeared on the market, most of them expensive, hard to clean, and none of them more efficient than a homemade smoker. You can make a simple smoke box or barrel that works very well, or you can build a strong, tight smokehouse that will endure for decades. In southern hog-raising country, smokehouses a century old are still doing service.

What Is Smoking?

Smoking is an ancient food preservation technique that probably goes back to the first delighted efforts of human beings to cook meat and fish over fire. Smoking lowers the moisture content of food and seals the exterior with a hard, golden-brown film; the complex chemical reactions between the smoke, the meat protein, and the internal moisture inhibit the growth of undesirable microorganisms. The temperature of the heated air that accompanies the smoke, the construction and venting of the smoker, the length of time the meat is exposed to the heat and smoke, as well as the slightly different flavors given off by various woods, all contribute to the unique tastes, textures, and keeping qualities of each smoked food product.

HOT SMOKING

Hot smoking is a fairly rapid process that both cooks the meat and flavors it with smoke at the same time. The reason steaks and fish cooked over an open campfire taste so memorably good is because they are crudely "hot smoked." The slower the hot smoking process, the more intense the flavor. Hot smoking temperatures range from 85°F to 250°F. The delicious foods prepared this way should be eaten right away or kept under refrigeration less than a week.

COLD SMOKING

Cold smoking is a long, slow process that can last weeks with temperatures never exceeding 85°F. Often just a trickle of smoke flows over the meat, very gradually permeating the tissue to give a mellow and delicate flavor. Cold smoked products keep for months.

CURING AND SMOKING

There are several ways to cure meat before smoking it, but the traditional methods are dry curing and brine curing.

Dry Curing. This is a salt dehydration process, now little used, that involves rubbing the meat with a mixture of salt, sugar, and often a small amount of sodium nitrate. Then the meat is stored at cool temperatures, allowing three days for each pound of meat. The salt gradually draws the moisture from the meat tissues. Large hams and bulky cuts often take longer than a month to cure. When the curing is finished, the meat is soaked a few days to draw off excess salt, air dried, then cold smoked. Food preserved this way is salty but almost indestructible.

Brine Curing. This involves soaking the meat in a pickling solution of salt, sugar, spices, and often a tiny amount of sodium nitrite at a rate of two to four days per pound. A six-pound pork shoulder takes about twenty-four days to brine cure; a big fifteen-pound ham must stay in the brine for two months. Often brine is injected along the bone of a big ham with a hypodermic needle. After the meat is cured, it may be soaked in fresh water a few days, dried, and then smoked.

Smoking cured meats improves their flavor immeasurably; the famous cured smoked hams of Virginia are a testament to this slow, careful process which makes hams, bacon, and sausages of premium quality.

Very often cured cold smoked meats, especially hams and bacon, are finished off at the end of the smoking period with a brief burst of hot smoking until the internal temperatures reach 140°F. Cured meats also can be hot smoked from the beginning at graduated temperatures for briefer periods than cold smoking demands, though gourmets and connoisseurs agree the results are not as fine.

An oven thermometer is a must for smokehouse equipment.

How Smokers and Smokehouses Work

The most efficient smoking is not done over a campfire, but in the confines of a closed shelter with a smoke source at one end and a vent at the other.

THE PARTS OF A SMOKEHOUSE

Vents. The smoker or smokehouse must have a top vent, or vents, not only to keep the smoke-laden air moving over the meat, thus drawing out moisture and evenly distributing the smoke, but also to prevent too dense an accumulation of smoke—and even soot and creosote—on the meat. A bottom vent near the smoke source helps control air, smoke, and heat flow over the meat.

Baffles. Baffles are useful in a smaller smoker; they force the smoke to take a slower, longer journey through the smoker, rather than a swift straight run from smoke inlet to vent. Baffles encourage an even dispersion of smoke through the enclosure, and wring the last drop of flavor from every wisp of smoke. Baffles also permit some measure of temperature control.

Racks and Hooks. Inside the smoker there should be adjustable pegs and hooks from which to hang the slabs of bacon, fish, sausages, hams, and the hens and turkeys in their net bags. Movable benches and racks are the place to lay the more tender fish fillets, or such fragile or small food as frogs' legs, woodcock, oysters, shrimp, and nuts.

Smoke. The smoke can come from a variety of green hardwoods, hardwood chips, or sawdust. Maple, hickory, apple, birch, ash, oak, and dry willow all give excellent flavor. The traditional smoke for hams is from green hickory wood and hickory sawdust. Corncobs can be used, but the smoke flavor is inferior to good hardwood.

Never, never use softwoods, such as spruce, pine, cedar or fir in a smokehouse—a black, sooty deposit, bits of flying ash, and a strong and unpleasant flavor of evergreen essence will ruin the meat. Experts advise not even using softwood kindling to get your smoke fire going, nor crumpled paper, nor any kind of starter or kerosene, for all of these impart their distinctive aromas to the meat and may contribute an unsightly residue of flying ash.

If you get hardwood sawdust from a furniture factory or woodworking mill, be very sure it is not from plywoods. In the smoke of such sawdust are evil-smelling, poisonous gases from the glue used to bind the plys together.

Rat-proofing. Covers and stoppers to fit the smoke and vent holes should be rodent-proof and left in place when the smoker is unused.

How to Make Smokers and Smokehouses

Here are three different smokers and smokehouses you can build—from a smoke pit to a permanent concrete smokehouse.

The simple smokers should serve the needs of the family that raises only one pig or has an occasional lucky day fishing, or keeps a few chickens.

For the homestead or farm family with a good-sized poultry yard and livestock, or for the hunting-fishing family that regularly brings home venison, waterfowl, game birds, rabbit and hare, pike, salmon, and trout, a sturdy, permanent smokehouse that can hold up to twenty-four hams at a time is a good investment. In a rural community a neighborhood smoking project can preserve the meats of several families at once.

Making a permanent, well-constructed smokehouse is not a building project for someone who has never picked up a hammer before; some carpentry or masonry experience is very helpful. On the other hand, the project is both small enough and detailed enough to be an excellent learning experience preparatory to building your own house or barn. The key to success is to proceed slowly and carefully.

A slightly modified USDA plan for a concrete smokehouse is shown here. It is widely recommended because of its fire-resistant qualities, relatively low cost, and simple construction.

Project 1: The Hot Smoke Pit

This extremely simple hole in the ground turns out delicious hot-smoked chickens, roasts, and fish. It is ideal for a Fourth of July picnic. (Be sure to surround the hole with a circle of temporary fencing to prevent anyone from accidentally stepping into it.)

The grill used in a hot smoke pit should not be galvanized or chromed. Half an old picnic grill or the grill from a hibachi is ideal.

Materials	Tools
flat rocks	*shovel*
vent rock	
nongalvanized sheet metal for lid	
nongalvanized grill	

1. Dig a fire pit about 2' deep and wide enough to accommodate the grill.

2. Line the hole with flat rocks so that the grill is supported about 12" to 15" above the level of the coals.

Continued ➔

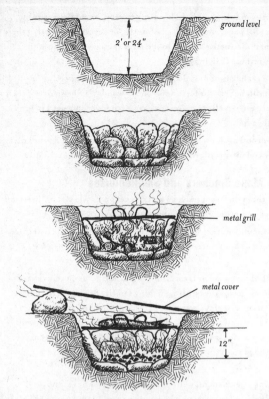

Figure 1. A hot smoke pit, dug 2' below ground level, lined with stone, and covered with a metal lid makes an ideal temporary smoker.

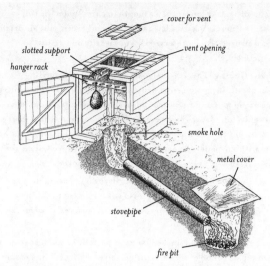

Figure 2. A box smoker can cold smoke twice as much as a barrel smoker.

USING THE HOT SMOKE PIT

Half an hour before starting the hot-smoke process, build a good hardwood fire in the fire pit, and let it form a bed of red hot coals. Then cover the coals with several handfuls of dampened hickory or other chips or small green hardwood twigs from apple, pear, maple, oak, or birch. Set the grill in place, and arrange the food to be smoked on the grill. Chickens will cook more rapidly if they are halved or quartered, but you lose much of the juices.

Put on the cover, adjust the vent rock under it to allow some smoke to escape. The narrower the vent opening, the more intense the smoke flavor, and the more slowly the meat will cook. The wider the opening, the more subtle the smoke flavor, the more rapid combustion (and heat) of the wood, and the higher the cooking temperatures. It will take the meat slightly longer to cook than in the kitchen oven—an additional 15–20 minutes for every hour.

You can put the food to be smoked on the grill with no preparation; sweet corn in the husk is very fine when hot smoked. Or you can marinate meat 4–6 hours in your favorite marinade. Here is a marinade recipe to try. It is especially good with chicken.

MARINADE

1/2 cup cider vinegar	1 clove garlic, crushed
1/2 cup hard cider or wine	ground pepper to taste
1 tablespoon salt	

Combine all the ingredients. Pour the marinade over the meat, fish, or poultry; cover and refrigerate. Turn the meat occasionally so that the marinade is distributed evenly. Marinate for 4–6 hours.

Project 2: The Box Smoker

If you want a small smoker with a little more control, you can build a versatile smoke box in a few hours. Make it larger than a barrel for the increased capacity. A 4' x 3' box smoker is a convenient size that can take 6–8 hams at once, but you can vary the dimensions to suit your needs.

This box smoker is made from materials readily available from any lumberyard. To cut costs, you can use rough-cut boards or lumber from wooden shipping pallets.

Materials

Amount	Size	Tools
10 boards	1" x 6" x 8'	shovel
5 boards	1" x 6" x 12'	saw
1 board	1" x 6" x 10'	hammer
4 boards	2" x 3" x 8'	level
1 board	2" x 3" x 10'	wood chisel
1 board	1" x 4" x 5'	tape measure
1 board	1" x 3" x 10'	T-square
1 board	1" x 3" x 12'	screwdriver
1/4 lb.	10d common nails	brace and 1/2" bit
3/4 lb.	6d common nails	electric drill and bits
1/5 lb.	8d common nails	
40	1 1/4" wood screws	
1	1/2" x 2' hardwood dowel	
1	10–12' of 6" stovepipe	
1 pair	2 1/2" butt hinges and screws	
1	hook and eye latch for the door	
1	3' x 3' metal cover for the fire pit	

1. To build the back of the smoke box, cut nine 1 x 6s to 46 1/2". Cut two 2 x 3s to 49 1/2". Lay the two 2 x 3s on a flat surface parallel to each other and 41 1/2" apart. Between these, align the first 1 x 6 on top, flush with the sides and ends of the 2 x 3s.

   Nail the 1 x 6 into place with two 6d nails. Position the second 1 x 6 edge to edge with the first 1 x 6. Align the ends with the outside edges of the 2 x 3s and nail into place. Continue until the nine boards have been nailed into the 2 x 3 corner supports. Set aside.

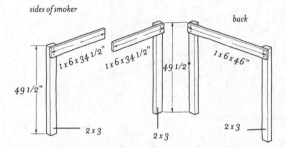

Figure 3. Assembly for back and sides of the box smoker (steps 1 and 2).

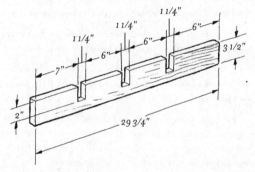

Figure 4. Hanger rack support (step 4).

2. For each of the two sides, you will need nine 1 x 6 x 34 1/2" pieces and one 2 x 3 x 49 1/2" length. Lay the 2 x 3 on a flat surface. Perpendicular to it, align the first 1 x 6 with the end and outside edge of the 2 x 3. Nail together with two 6d nails.

   Continue until the nine 1 x 6s have been nailed into place. (You may want to raise the other ends of the 1 x 6s with a scrap piece of 2 x 3 to make nailing easier.)

   Complete the second side.

3. There will be runners along the top edge of each side to which the lid will later be nailed. Cut two 29 3/4" lengths from the 2 x 3 stock. Lay one of the sides flat on a work surface with the corner support facing down. Slip one length of 2 x 3 under the side so that it butts against and is perpendicular to the corner support. It also should be flush with the outside edge of the end board. Nail into place.

   Follow the same procedure for the second side.

   Cut one 2 x 3 to 41 1/2". This runner will be nailed between the two back corner supports in the same manner.

4. Cut two hanger rack support boards to 29 3/4" from the 1 x 4 stock. Lay one of the pieces on a flat work surface. Measure in 7" from one edge and mark for a slot 1 1/4" wide and 2" deep. From the edge of the slot, measure in 6" and mark for a second slot. The third slot will also be separated by 6". This will leave 7" at the end of the board.

   Saw along both sides of the slots to the 2" depth. With a chisel and hammer, chisel out the waste wood.

5. Screw the slotted supports on the inside of the side walls. The supports should sit on a line 12" from the top edge (the edge with the runner), and be screwed into place with 1 1/4" wood screws. Predrill the screw holes so that the wood doesn't split.

6. Turn the back on edge so that it rests on one of the corner supports. Set one of the sides at right angles so that the sawn ends are flush with the outside of the back. Approximately 1 1/8" in from the edge, nail each side board into the back corner support with two 6d nails per board.

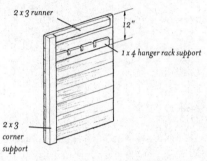

Figure 6. Attaching the hanger racks to the side walls (step 5).

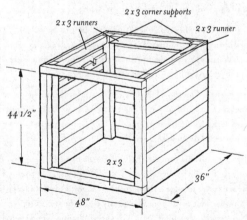

Figure 6. Box assembly (steps 7, 8, and 9).

7. Rotate the box so that the side rests on your work surface. Set the second side in place with its sawn ends flush with the outside of the back. Be sure the runners for the lid are opposite each other. Nail through the side boards into the back corner support.

   You should now have a three-sided box with 2 x 3 supports in each corner. Set the box aside.

Continued ➡

8. For the door frame, cut two 2 x 3s to 48" and two to 44 1/2". Rest one of the 48" lengths on edge. Into it, toenail the shorter uprights, one at either end, using 8d nails.

    Lay the second 48" length on edge. Tip up the U-shaped 2 x 3s so that the shorter uprights can be toenailed into the bottom cross rail.

9. Rest the three-sided box on its back. Set the door frame on top so that the top and bottom cross rails align with the outside edges of the sides. Measure in 1 1/8" along the uprights and nail the frame to the corner supports with 10d nails.

10. The box smoker will have a cover and a movable vent cover. For the cover, cut four pieces of 1 x 6 to 48". Cut six pieces to 12", and rip two of these to 3" wide. Also cut two 1 x 3 x 36" lengths for the cleats.

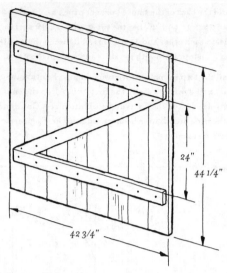

Figure 8. Door assembly (step 13).

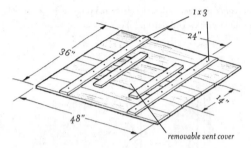

Figure 7. Box smoker lid (step 10).

    On a flat surface, lay out the pieces so that the ends of three 12" lengths are 24" from the other three 12" lengths. (In each set of three there should be one of the 3" x 12" boards.) To the top and bottom of these, place two 48" lengths. There will be a 24" x 14" hole in the center for the vent.

    To either side of the vent opening, place a 1 x 3 cleat. They should run perpendicular to the cover boards. Nail through the cleats into the lid boards with 4d nails. On the underside of the lid, bend over the nails with your hammer.

11. Place the lid on top of the box. Along the sides and back, measure in 1 1/8" and nail the lid to the box corner supports and runners with 6d nails. Along the front, measure in 3/4" and nail the lid down with 6d nails.

12. For the movable vent cover, cut three 1 x 6s to 24" lengths. Rip one to 3" wide. Also cut two 1 x 3s to 17" pieces. Lay the 1 x 6 boards edge to edge. Align the sawn edges. Perpendicular to the movable vent cover boards, equally space the two 1 x 3 pieces. Nail together with 6d nails. On the underside, bend the nails over with your hammer.

13. Cut eight 1 x 6 boards to 44 1/4" lengths for the door. Rip one of the eight to 4 1/4" wide. Then cut two 1 x 3 boards to 42" long.

    Lay the 1 x 6s edge to edge on a flat surface. Place the two 1 x 3 battens for the Z-brace perpendicular to the 1 x 6s, and 24" apart from inside edge to inside edge. Be sure they are centered on the door. Screw them into the 1 x 6s with 1 1/4" wood screws. Each board should be screwed top and bottom into the battens.

    Measure for the 1 x 3 diagonal brace between the battens (approximately 48") and screw it into the vertical door boards.

14. Hang the door using the hinges, spaced about 5" from the top and bottom of the door. Screw into place and lift the door into the opening.

    Put a piece of scrap lumber or a match book under the door to center it in the door frame. Mark the hinge placement on the smoker side edge. Remove the door and chisel out a slight depression to receive the hinge plate. Replace the door and fasten the hinges to the frame. Check that the door swings freely.

15. Close the door. At a convenient height, screw an eye to the door frame and a hook to the door. This allows you to latch the door tightly.

16. Cut two hanger racks to 46 1/4" from 1 x 3 stock. They should fit between the slotted supports. Drill 1/2" holes 6" apart and at a slight upward angle for the dowels. Cut 3" dowel lengths and pound them gently but firmly into place.

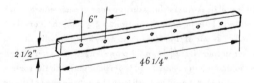

Figure 9. Hanger rack assembly (step 16).

Set the hanger racks into the slotted supports. Now the box smoker is ready to be positioned.

17. Locate the box smoker uphill from the fire pit. Dig a smoke hole, fire pit, and trench. Place the smokepipe in the trench (or use drain tile or a board-covered trench) and cover with earth. Mound the earth around the base of the box smoker.

Project 3: Concrete Block Smokehouse with a Concrete Floor

Permanent smokehouses can be made of stone, logs, concrete, or wooden framing members, and should be large enough to meet the needs of an average family (usually a 6' x 8' x 8' structure). For these buildings, a concrete floor is necessary to protect the house from rodents, with concrete footings set below the frost line to insure a sturdy, durable structure. The fire pit, located outside the building, is vented through the floor into the smokehouse.

Experienced builders will have no trouble erecting a permanent smokehouse; less experienced builders may want to consult manuals on masonry and wood-framing techniques.

THE SITE

The site for a smokehouse should be at least 50' away from other buildings as a fire hazard precaution, especially if you will be building a frame structure. The firebox should be located at least 4' (preferably more) from the smokehouse. The drawings here are for only 4' of tile for the smoke channel; buy additional tile if your firebox is farther away. The firebox smoke hole should be lower than the smokehouse floor smoke hole to facilitate upward smoke movement; the optimum pitch is 30 degrees. Placing the smokehouse on a knoll is also helpful.

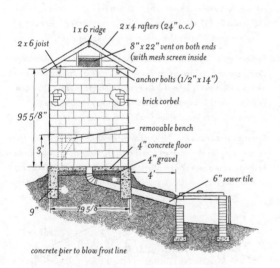

Figure 10. Concrete block smokehouse.

The foundation of both the smokehouse and the firebox should extend below the frost line for your area. (This may mean relocating your smokehouse if your soil is full of boulders.) In cold regions with a deep frost line, you will need more sand, gravel, and cement than specified in the list of building materials.

Only a concrete block smokehouse is described in detail; however, the design and foundation for any permanent smokehouse are quite

similar (the exception: the foundation walls for the frame building are only 6" wide; for the concrete block building, they are 9" because of the additional weight of the walls). The rest of a log or frame building is erected according to standard building techniques.

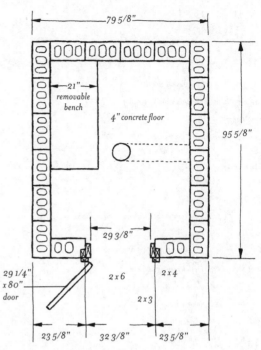

Figure 11. Concrete block smokehouse floor plan.

Materials

Masonry

Concrete: 1:3:5 of cement, sand, and gravel

Mortar: 1:3 plus 10% hydrated lime (in total: 14 bags of cement, 1 1/2 cubic yards of sand, 2 cubic yards of gravel, and 65 pounds of hydrated lime)

Amount	Size
145	8" x 8" x 16" smooth face concrete blocks
12	8" x 4" x 16" smooth face concrete blocks for the corbel section
2	8" x 4" x 8" smooth face concrete blocks
14	8" x 8" x 8" smooth face half concrete blocks
52	8" x 8" x 16" corner concrete blocks
8	8" x 8" x 8" lintel blocks
10	8" x 8" x 16" jamb concrete blocks
10	8" x 8" x 8" half jamb concrete blocks
100	common bricks

Lumber

Amount	Size
12 boards	2" x 4" 8'
7 boards	2" x 4" x 10'
6 boards	2" x 4" x 6'
1 board	1" x 3" x 8'
4 boards	1" x 4" x 10'

Continued →

1 board	1" x 6" x 6'
6 boards	1" x 6" x 7'
1 board	1" x 6" x 8'
1 board	1" x 6" x 10'
3 boards	2" x 3" x 8'
6 boards	2" x 6" x 7'
2 boards	2" x 6" x 8'
1 board	2" x 6" x 10'
3 pieces	1" x 3' hardwood dowels

120 square feet plywood or board sheathing for roof

1 roll roofing paper

shingles or roofing to cover 100 square feet

Miscellaneous

Amount	Size
8	4" lag bolts
10	1/2" x 14" anchor bolt with nuts and washers
1 pair	8" T-hinges
2 pairs	2" x 2" tension hinges
4 linear feet	#30 mesh screening 10" wide
1/2 lb.	6d common nails
1 lb.	8d common nails
1/2 lb.	10d common nails
2 lbs.	16d common nails
1/4 lb.	16d casing nails
20	2" wood screws

hanging hooks (optional)

stucco, stone, or brick facing (optional)

8' rebar

1 latch and strike plate

at least 4' of 6" sewer tile and elbow

Firebox

7 bags cement, 1/2 cubic yard sand, 1/3 cubic yard gravel

450 common bricks

90 firebricks

4 pieces 1/4" steel rods 44" long

4 pieces 1/4" steel rods 36" long

2 pieces 1 1/4" pipe 36" long

24" x 32" metal sliding door

24" x 48" light gauge metal strip

36" x 44" piece 1/4" hardware cloth

LOCATING THE SMOKEHOUSE

1. Decide on the exact location of the 79 5/8" x 95 5/8" smokehouse; then dig the foundation trenches to below the frost line. In firm soil, foundation forms aren't needed for the concrete walls.

2. Locate and mark off for the 44" x 52" firebox. Dig trenches for the fire pit to below the frost line.

Also dig a trench for the 6" tile, remembering to pitch it up towards the smokehouse. Join and place sections of tile in the trench. Attach the elbow so that the pipe will reach through the concrete floor and into the smokehouse.

Cover the floor surface of smokehouse with 4" of 1/2" gravel or broken stone.

3. Pour concrete footings for smokehouse and firebox; let harden. Then level the gravel layer on the smokehouse floor, plug the tile opening with a metal or wooden ring stopper, and pour a 4" concrete slab.

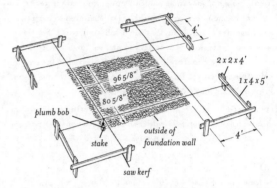

Figure 12. Mark off the four outside corners of the foundation wall. Then erect batter boards. Run masons cord between the batter boards and adjust until the line accurately outlines the foundation. Check that the lines are level and the corners are square. Building lines are removed during excavation but can be replaced whenever necessary (step 1).

FIREBOX COVER

4. The firebox cover is made of concrete. Build a 36" x 44" form from 1 x 6s. Nail the form together and lay on level ground. Along the inside, draw a line 1" down from the top edge. Add a 1/2" sand bed in the bottom of the form to make it easier to remove the slab after the concrete has hardened.

5. From the 24" x 48" metal sheet, cut a semicircle 48" in outside diameter and 36" in inside diameter. You can improvise a compass with a nail, a 30" piece of string, and a Magic Marker. Rivet the ends of the strip together so that it forms a circle with a 24" diameter and tapered sides. Stake this in the center of the form.

6. On the top of the sand, lay the hardware cloth (you will have to cut an opening for the tapered metal circle). Twist short sections of wire at the joints to lock the reinforcing rods in place, and fit the grid around the metal circle. Let grid rest on top of the hardware cloth.

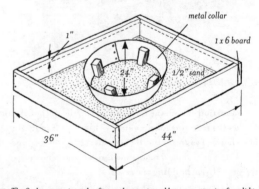

Figure 13. The firebox cover is made of poured concrete and leaves an opening for a lid to control combustion rates.

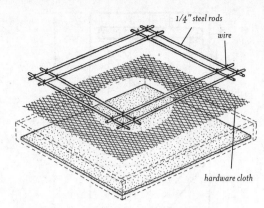

Figure 14. The firebox cover is reinforced with 1/4" steel rods (step 6).

Dampen the sand and pour in concrete until it reaches the line along the inside of the form; do not pour any concrete into the center circle. Allow to harden; then remove the form and metal circle.

7. Use the metal circle to separately cast a 4" concrete lid. Place a sturdy metal handle in the center before the concrete hardens. Once cured, the tapered concrete plug should fit neatly into the center of the concrete lid.

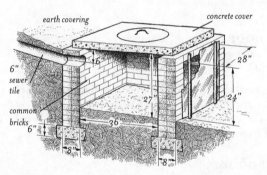

Figure 15. Smokehouse fire pit (step 8).

THE FIRE PIT

8. Lay up the walls from the footings to the fire pit with common bricks. Thereafter use firebricks for the inner row. A 24" x 28" door opening must be left for access to the fire pit. On top of the firebox, center the 36" x 44" concrete cover and cement into place.

SMOKEHOUSE WALLS

9. Lay up eight courses of concrete blocks on top of the smokehouse foundation walls. Remember to alternate between jamb and half jamb blocks around the doorway; the 2" x 4" indentation on these blocks is for the door framing which will be added later.

10. Begin the ninth row from the doorway and work to either corner. Down the sides set 8" x 4" x 16" blocks on edge and flush with the outside edge of the wall. Mortar the brick corbelling into place on the remaining interior lip. The corbelling makes a strong continuous ledge for the removable 2 x 4 hangers to rest on.

11. Frame the doorway. Some jamb blocks come with predrilled holes to accept lag bolts. If so, use lag bolts to fasten the 2 x 4s to the block walls on either side of the doorway. If you have blocks without predrilled holes, drill them yourself using a mortar bit. Then attach with lag bolts.

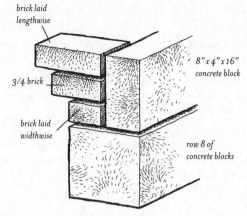

Figure 16. Corbel detail (step 10)

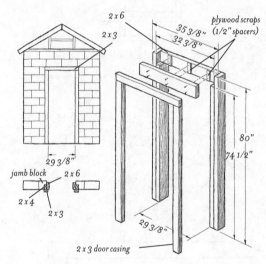

Figure 17. Door framing (step 11). The 2 x 3 door casing is attached in step 18.

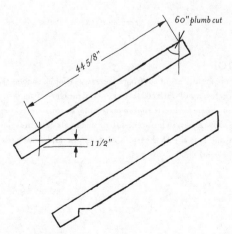

Figure 18. Rafters cuts (step 13).

Continue laying up the eleventh and twelfth tiers of concrete blocks, setting a lintel of eight lintel blocks and two sections of rebar, each 48" long, over the doorway.

12. After the top tier of blocks has been laid, set the anchor bolts in place. Bolt the 2 x 6 top plate to the concrete walls.

13. To frame the roof, use 2 x 4 x 5' rafters with a 60° plumb cut and spaced on 24" centers. Nail these into the 1 x 6 x 10' ridge.

14. On both gable ends of the smokehouse, there will be an 8" x 22" vent. Frame these using scrap 2 x 4 stock.

15. Cut three 2 x 6 joists to span the distance between the two side walls; they will sit on the top plate. Nail joists into the second, third, and fourth sets of rafters.

16. Blocking is necessary before the fly rafters for the overhang can be nailed into place. Cut twelve 2 x 4s to 10 1/2". Nail these to the existing end rafters at 1' intervals from the ridge. Then nail fly rafters into ridge and into blocking.

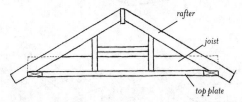

Figure 19. The joists are nailed to the rafters. Joist tops will have to be trimmed to match the angle of the roof pitch.

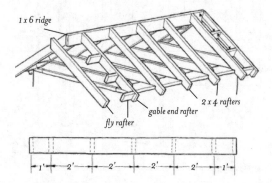

Figure 20. Nail the fly rafters into the ridge and into the blocking attached to the end rafters (step 16).

THE ROOF

17. There are different roofing materials available, such as asphalt shingles, hand-split cedar shakes, and metal roofing. You may want the smokehouse roof to match that of your house, or you may have access to leftover roofing materials. The most common method is to sheath the roof with plywood, and cover with felt paper and asphalt shingles.

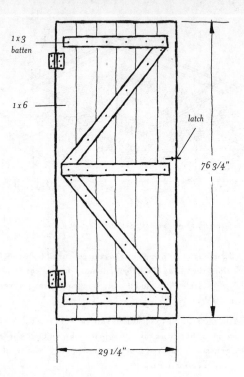

Figure 21. Board and batten door (step 19).

THE DOOR

18. Align the 2 x 3 casing pieces flush with the outside edge of the door framing and nail into place.

19. Build a 29 1/4" x 76 3/4" board and batten door out of 1 x 6 and 1 x 3 stock. Mount the hinges 8" from the top and bottom of the door, and lift door into place. Predrill and screw hinges to frame. Then mount the latch and strike plate.

VENT DOORS

20. Trim the vent door opening with 2 x 3s. Cut two pieces of plywood to 8" x 22" and hinge to top trim piece using the tension hinges. Around the inside of the vent opening, staple the wire screening to keep out insects. Close in gable ends with plywood.

HANGER RACKS

21. To span the distance between the brick corbelling on the interior side walls, cut six or as many 2 x 4 x 71" hanger racks as you will need. The hangers can be pegged with 1" doweling as in the Box Smoker rack hangers.

For greater capacity in your smokehouse, suspend a tier of lower level hangers on an additional support instead of building the removable bench.

BENCH

22. If desired, construct a bench along one wall. Most useful may be a slotted bench of hardwood strips to hold small or delicate foods that cannot hang.

FINISHING TOUCHES

23. Heap earth over the tile. Drive two sections of 1 1/4" pipe into the ground in front of the firebox opening. Slide the metal door into place, and the smokehouse is ready for use.

24. When using the smokehouse, always open the firebox door with a long-handled poker.

The gable vents are opened from the inside with a long pole; the tension hinges will hold them open at the desired angle.

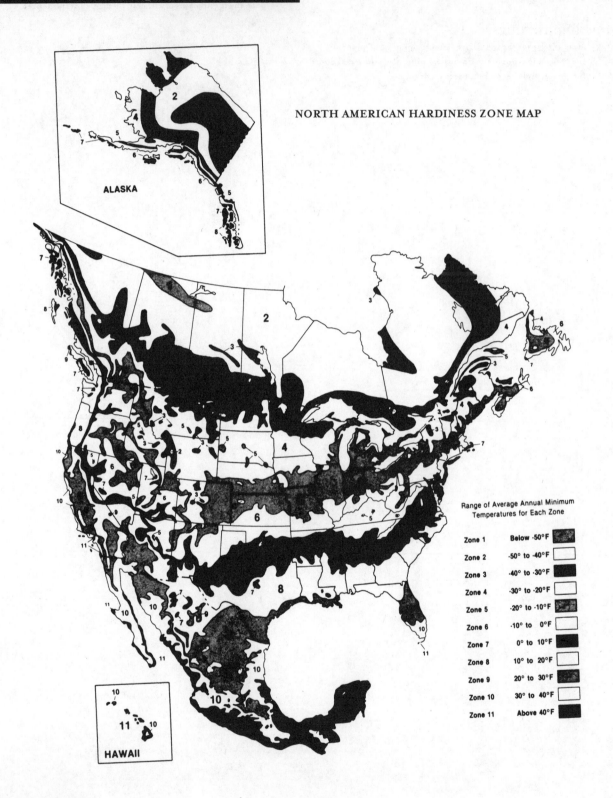

NORTH AMERICAN HARDINESS ZONE MAP

ALASKA

HAWAII

Range of Average Annual Minimum
Temperatures for Each Zone

Zone 1	Below -50°F
Zone 2	-50° to -40°F
Zone 3	-40° to -30°F
Zone 4	-30° to -20°F
Zone 5	-20° to -10°F
Zone 6	-10° to 0°F
Zone 7	0° to 10°F
Zone 8	10° to 20°F
Zone 9	20° to 30°F
Zone 10	30° to 40°F
Zone 11	Above 40°F

Appendix B: Gardening Answers

Seed companies are well aware of the itchiness that gardeners develop as snow drifts deepen, and they time delivery of their catalogs to coincide with the onset of cabin fever. A common reaction to the glossy pictures and glowing praises of each new variety is to overreact and order more seeds than the entire neighborhood could use. To avoid this, plan your garden carefully.

Decide on the size garden you want. The information contained in this bulletin can be applied to any size area.

Next, determine what vegetables your family enjoys. If just one person enjoys rutabagas, does it make sense to plant an entire row of them?

Also, consider the local climate. Eggplant may be a great delicacy, but are chances for success with this vegetable good in an area with a short growing season?

Table I indicates how much seed or how many plants of most popular vegetables are needed to plant a 50-foot row and to produce a season's supply of each vegetable for one person. Distances between rows are also suggested.

Draw up a plan for your garden on a piece of graph paper. Locate the tallest plants near the northern edge of the garden so that they will not shade shorter neighbors.

The row spacing in Table I is the minimum. If your garden soil is rich, the plants will probably be crowded and it would be advisable to increase the distance between rows by about 30 percent.

When making out your garden plan, also consider what type of cultivating equipment you will use. If you plant to use a hoe, rows may be spaced irregularly. If you intend to use a rototiller, plan your rows so the machine will fit between them and won't disturb the plants once they have begun to grow.

Soil Types

Soils are classified by the size of their particles. Generally, they range from coarse to fine or from light to heavy. Here are some soil types:

Type	Characteristics
Sandy	Easily tilled
Sandy loam	Well drained
Loam	Warms quickly
	Poor nutrient retention
Silty loam	Hard to work
Clay loam	Slow drainage, great moisture retention
Clay	Warms slowly
	Excellent nutrient retention

The coarser the soil, the earlier it warms in the spring and the earlier it can be worked. Coarse particles of sand retain less moisture than fine particles of clay. Coarse soils require less spring sunshine to reach a temperature suitable for seed germination.

Delay working the soil until it is dry enough so that a compressed ball of soil will break apart when dropped from the height of your hip.

Soil that is worked when too moist forms compact clods and makes root growth difficult.

Soil Analysis

The ideal garden soil is rich in organic matter, well drained, slightly acidic, and replenished with plant nutrients. How good is your soil? The amount of nutrients and the level of acidity can be determined by soil tests.

These tests are performed by the Extension Service at little or no charge. Or, you can do your own test, using a kit purchased through the mail, or at better garden and hardware stores.

If you use the Extension Service, contact the nearest office and request specific instructions. In general, these are the guidelines many Extension Service offices recommend:

· Use a trowel to recover small amounts of soil at a depth of about six inches.

· Take several samples from across the garden. Mix these in a bucket to get an accurate indication of average soil conditions.

· Avoid soil where peas, beans, or other nitrogen-fixing crops have been grown in previous years.

· Dry two or three handfuls of the soil from the bucket at room temperature. Drying with a stove can lead to a false indication of the need for lime. Send a small plastic bag of dry soil to the nearest Extension Service office.

I. GARDEN PLANNING CHART

Vegetable	Seeds or Plants for a 50' Row	Distance Between Rows in Inches	Feet of Row Per Person	Spacing Between Plants in Inches
Beans, dry	4 oz.	18	20–30'	6–8
Beans, shelled	4 oz.	18	30'	8–10
Beans, snap	4 oz.	18	30'	2–4
Beets	1/2 oz.	12	10–15'	2–4
Broccoli	25 plants	24	5 plants	12–24
Brussels sprouts	25 plants	24	5 plants	12–24
Cabbage	25 plants	24	10 plants	12–18
Cauliflower	25 plants	24	5 plants	14–24
Carrots	1/8 oz.	12	10'	1–3
Corn	1 oz.	24	25'	9–15
Cucumbers	1/4 oz.	48	10–15'	12
Eggplant	25 plants	24	5 plants	18–36
Endive	1/8 oz.	18	10'	8–12
Kale	1/8 oz.	18	12'	18–24
Kohlrabi	1/8 oz.	18	10'	3–6
Lettuce, head	1/8 oz.	15	5–10'	10–15
Lettuce, leaf	1/8 oz.	12	5–10'	10–12
Muskmelons	12 plants	48	3 plants	12
Onion sets	1 lb.	12	10–20'	2–4

Continued →

Vegetable	Seeds or Plants for a 50' Row	Distance Between Rows in Inches	Feet of Row Per Person	Spacing Between Plants in Inches
Parsnips	1/4 oz.	18	5–10'	3–6
Peas	8 oz.	24	50–100'	1–3
Peppers	33 plants	18	5 plants	12–24
Potatoes	33 plants	30	50'	9–12
Pumpkins	1/4 oz.	60	1 hill	36–60
Radishes	1/2 oz.	12	5'	1–2
Salsify	1/2 oz.	18	5'	2–4
Spinach	1/2 oz.	15	20'	2–6
Squash, summer	1/4 oz.	60	1 hill	24–48
Squash, winter	1/2 oz.	60	3–5 hills	24–40
Swiss chard	1/4 oz.	18	5'	3–6
Tomatoes	12–15 plants	30	5 plants	12–24
Turnips	1/4 oz.	15	10'	2–6
Watermelon	30 plants	72	2–3 hills	72–96
Zucchini	1/4 oz.	60	1 hill	24–48

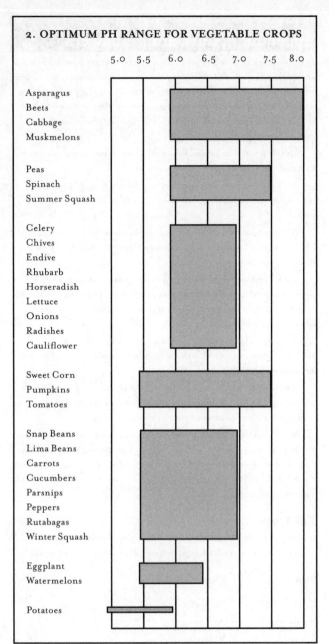

2. OPTIMUM PH RANGE FOR VEGETABLE CROPS

Another tip: Do your soil test in the fall. Extension Service offices are often swamped with requests in the spring, causing delays of up to a month. By having the soil test results on hand early, you will be able to purchase the necessary fertilizers during the winter. And, you'll be gardening in the first good spring weather, rather than fighting crowds at the local garden supply store.

The acidity or alkalinity of the soil (the pH level) is an important factor. Most plants have a specific pH range within which they thrive and outside of which they perform poorly, if at all. A pH level of 7 represents neutrality, when the soil is neither acid nor alkaline. Levels higher than 7 indicate alkalinity, while numbers below 7 indicate an acid state.

Table 2 indicates the optimum pH range for various popular vegetables.

Adjusting Soil pH

Excessive soil acidity is usually corrected by adding lime, in one of three forms: ground limestone (the most commonly used form), burned lime (not recommended), and hydrated lime. The latter two are derived from the first.

Ground limestone is calcium carbonate (CaC_3). When burned, the carbon dioxide is driven off, resulting in burned lime (CaO). The volume of the ground limestone is reduced by 44 percent, but its neutralizing value is unimpaired. Hydrated lime is made by adding water to burned limestone.

You may adjust the pH of your soil, if necessary, by applying lime or other materials as suggested in Table 3. Spread the material as evenly as possible and work it into the top three or four inches of soil uniformly. (If you should need to substitute one form of lime for another: 100 pounds of ground limestone equals 74 pounds of hydrated lime.)

3. TO RAISE SOIL ONE UNIT OF PH

	Hydrated Lime	Dolomite	Ground Limestone
Light Soil 100 sq. ft.	1 1/2 pounds	2 pounds	2 1/2 pounds
Heavy Soil 100 sq. ft.	3 1/2 pounds	5 1/2 pounds	6 pounds

TO LOWER SOIL ONE UNIT OF PH

	Sulphur	Aluminum Sulphate	Iron Sulphate
Light Soil 100 sq. ft.	1/2 pound	2 1/2 pounds	3 pounds
Heavy Soil	2 pounds	6 1/2 pounds	7 1/2 pounds

Note: The amount of lime you use doesn't have to be as precisely measured as this chart suggests.

Fertilizers

Most fertilizers contain varying amounts of the three essential plant foods: nitrogen, phosphorus, and potassium. On the label of commercial fertilizer bags, the elements are listed in the order given above. A bag of fertilizer listed as 10–15-20, for example, would contain 10 percent nitrogen, 15 percent phosphorus, and 20 percent potassium.

Fertilizers are also available in organic forms, that is, derived from animal, vegetable, or mineral sources. Commercially prepared organic fertilizers tend to be more expensive than chemicals and slower acting, but they provide a more sustained feeding of the plants and generally improve the soil condition.

Fertilizing elements have different effects upon plants. Table 4 indicates what aspect of plant growth is governed by each of the major elements and gives sources for each, and signs of deficiency and excess.

4. PRIMARY PLANT FOOD ELEMENTS

Element Symbol	Function in Plant	Deficiency	Symptoms of Excess	Sources Symptoms
Nitrogen N	Gives dark green color to plant. Increases growth of leaf and stem. Influences crispness quality of leaf crops. Stimulates rapid early growth.	Light green to yellow leaves. Stunted growth.	Dark green. Excessive growth. Retarded maturity. Loss of buds or fruit.	Urea Ammonia Nitrates
Phosphorus P	Stimulates early formation and growth of roots. Gives plants a rapid and vigorous start. Is important in formation of seed. Gives hardiness to fall-seeded grasses and grains.	Red or purple leaves. Cell division retardation.	Possible tie up of other essential elements.	Super-phosphate Rock phosphate
Potassium K	Increases vigor of plants and resistance to disease. Stimulates production of strong, stiff stalks. Promotes production of sugar, starches, oils. Increases plumpness of grains and seed. Improves quality of crop yield.	Reduced vigor. Susceptibility to diseases. Thin skin and small fruit.	Coarse, poor colored fruit. Reduced absorption of Magnesium and Calcium.	Muriate or Sulphate of Potash

Continued →

Manures

The most common organic fertilizers are manures. Table 5 shows the approximate nutrient contents of different types of manures and natural fertilizers. The age of the manure, its state of decomposition, and the diet of the animal from which it comes affect its nutrient content. Figures indicate percentage by weight.

5. APPROXIMATE COMPOSITION OF NATURAL FERTILIZER MATERIALS

Material	Nitrogen (N)	Phosphorus (P)	Potassium (K)
Manures			
Bat guano	10.0	4.5	2.0
Cow manure, dried	1.3	0.9	0.8
Cow manure, fresh	0.5	0.2	0.5
Hen manure, dried, with litter	2.8	2.8	1.5
Hen manure, fresh	1.1	0.9	0.5
Horse manure, fresh	0.6	0.3	0.5
Pig manure, fresh	0.6	0.5	0.4
Sheep manure, dried	1.4	1.0	3.0
Sheep manure, fresh	0.9	0.5	0.8
Vegetative and Animal Concentrates			
Bonemeal, steamed	2.0	22.0	—
Castor pomace	6.0	1.9	0.5
Cocoa shell meal	2.5	1.5	2.5
Cottonseed meal	6.0	3.0	1.0
Dried blood meal	13.0	1.5	0.8
Fish meal	10.0	6.0	—
Fish scraps	5.0	3.0	—
Garbage tankage	1.5	2.0	0.7
Hoof & horn meal	12.0	2.0	—
Sewerage sludge	2.0	1.4	0.8
Sewerage sludge, activated	6.0	3.0	0.1
Soybean meal	7.0	1.2	1.5
Wood ashes	—	1.8	5.0

6. SECONDARY PLANT FOOD ELEMENTS

Element	Symptoms of Deficiency	Symptoms of Excess	Sources
Magnesium	Loss of yield. Chlorosis of old leaves.	Reduced absorption of Calcium and K.	Magnesium Sulphate (Epsom Salts); Dolomite is 1/3 Magnesium.
Manganese	Mottled chlorosis of the leaves. Stunted growth.	Small dead areas in the leaves with yellow borders around them.	Manganese Sulphate (Tecmangam)
Copper	Multiple budding. Gum pockets.	Prevents the up-take of iron. Causes stunting of roots.	Copper Sulphate; Neutral Copper
Zinc	Small, thin, yellow leaves. Low yields.	None known.	Zinc Sulphate
Iron	Yellowing of leaves, the veins remaining green.	None known.	Iron Sulphate (Copperas); Chelated Iron
Sulphur	Looks like Nitrogen deficiency.	Sulphur burn from too low pH.	Sulphur Superphosphate
Calcium	Stops growing point of plants.	Reduces the intake of K and Magnesium.	Lime; Basic Slag; Gypsum
Molybdenum	Symptoms in plants vary greatly.	Poisonous to livestock.	Sodium Molybdate
Boron	Small leaves. Heart rot and corkiness. Multiple buds.	Leaves turn yellowish red.	Borax

Conversions

Manufacturers of fertilizers and other garden or farm materials sometimes suggest that these materials be applied by the ton to an acre of crops. For small gardeners, these figures are often meaningless. Here are some guidelines to follow, when reducing large application rates:

- For each ton recommended per acre, apply 4 3/4 pounds per 100 square feet.
- For each 500 pounds recommended per acre, apply 1 1/4 pounds per 100 square feet.

Table 7 provides some additional helpful conversions.

7. CONVERTING FERTILIZER APPLICATION FROM POUNDS PER ACRE TO POUNDS PER SQUARE FEET

Area in Sq. Ft.	Fertilizer to apply, where amount to be applied per acre is:		
	100 lbs.	400 lbs.	800 lbs.
100	0.25	1	2
500	1.25	5	10
1,000	2.50	10	20
1,500	3.75	15	30
2,000	5.00	20	40

POUNDS PER ACRE TO POUNDS PER ROW

Distance Between Rows in Feet	Row Length in Feet	Fertilizer to apply, where amount to be applied per acre is:		
		100 lbs.	400 lbs.	800 lbs.
2	50	0.25	1.0	2.0
2	100	0.50	2.0	4.0
2 1/2	50	0.30	1.2	2.4
2 1/2	100	0.60	2.4	4.8
3	50	0.35	1.4	2.8
3	100	0.70	2.8	5.6

Planting Dates in Relation to Frost

Table 8 indicates the sensitivity of certain vegetables to frost and suggests their planting times in relation to frost.

8. PLANTING DATES IN RELATION TO FROST

HARDY Plant as soon as ground can be prepared.	SEMI-HARDY Plant 1–2 weeks before average date of last frost.	TENDER Plant 1 week after date of last frost.	VERY TENDER Plant 2 weeks after average date of last frost.
Asparagus	Cauliflower	New Zealand spinach	Cucumber
Beet	Potato	Snap Bean	Eggplant
Broccoli		Sweet Corn	Lima Bean
Cabbage		Tomato	Muskmelon
Chard			Pepper
Carrot			Pumpkin
Kale			Squash
Lettuce			Watermelon
Onion			
Parsnip			
Pea			
Radish			
Spinach			
Turnip			

Continued →

9. SOIL TEMPERATURE CONDITIONS FOR VEGETABLE SEED GERMINATION[1]

Crop	Minimum, °F	Optimum Range, °F	Optimum, °F	Maximum, °F	Crop	Minimum, °F	Optimum Range, °F	Optimum, °F	Maximum, °F
Asparagus	50	60–85	75	95	Onion	35	50–95	75	95
Bean	60	60–85	85	95	Parsley	40	50–85	75	90
Bean, lima	60	60–85	85	85	Parsnip	35	50–70	65	85
Beet	40	50–85	85	95	Pea	40	40–75	75	85
Cabbage	40	45–95	85	100	Pepper	60	65–95	85	95
Carrot	40	45–85	80	95	Pumpkin	60	70–90	95	100
Cauliflower	40	45–85	80	100	Radish	40	45–90	85	95
Celery	40	60–70	702	85[2]	Spinach	35	45–75	70	85
Chard, Swiss	40	50–85	85	95	Squash	60	70–95	95	100
Corn	50	60–95	95	105	Tomato	50	60–85	85	95
Cucumber	60	60–95	95	105	Turnip	40	60–105	85	105
Eggplant	60	75–90	85	95	Watermelon	60	70–95	95	105
Lettuce	35	40–80	75	85					
Muskmelon	60	75–95	90	100					
Okra	60	70–95	95	105					

[1] Compiled by J.F. Harrington, Dept. of Vegetable Crops, Univ. of Calif. at Davis.

[2] Daily fluctuation to 60° or lower at night is essential.

Transplants

Plants started in the home or greenhouse offer a gardener a chance to harvest early, have a succession of ready crops, and harvest vegetables that could not usually be grown in his climate. Normally, transplants are started several weeks prior to outdoor planting. Table 10 indicates the number of weeks needed to grow plants before setting them in the ground outside.

10. VEGETABLES SUITABLE FOR TRANSPLANTING AND METHODS OF SOWING SEED

Easy to transplant. Can be sown in flats in rows and transplanted bare root.	Must be started in individual containers and transplanted without disturbing roots.
Broccoli (5–7)	Cantaloupe (3–4)
Brussels sprouts (5–7)	(all muskmelons) (3–4)
Cabbage (5–7)	Cucumbers (3–4)
Cauliflower (5–7)	Squash (3–4)
Celeriac (7–12)	(summer & winter)
Celery (7–12)	Watermelon (5–7)
Chinese Cabbage (5–7)	†
Collards (5–7)	
*Eggplant (6–8)	
Lettuce (5–7)	
Onion (8–10)	
Parsley (8–10)	
*Peppers (6–8)	
Sweet Potato (3–4)	
(start from tuber and not seed)	
*Tomato (6–8)	

* Sometimes sown in flats and then transplanted into individual containers before transplanting to garden.

† Many vegetables like corn, beans, and beets can be started early in pots and flats, but seldom are because the large number of pots needed is impractical.

( ) Number in parentheses is approximate time (weeks) from sowing seed to transplanting to garden.

Response to Transplanting

Transplanting checks growth. The severity of the checking depends on the vegetable planted, the number of times the vegetable is moved, causing roots and root hairs to break, and the plant size. The larger the plant, the greater is the check in growth.

Other factors include the length of time the plant has a reduced water supply due to root damage; the conditions that affect transpiration from the leaves until root replacement occurs; the damage to the root system and rate at which new roots are formed; and the rate of growth. Slow-growing plants suffer less than rapidly growing ones. See Table 11 for a classification of selected vegetables according to their response to transplanting.

11. VEGETABLE RESPONSE TO TRANSPLANTING		
Easily Survive Transplanting	Require Care in the Operation	Not Successfully Transplanted by Usual Methods
Beet	Carrot	Bean
Broccoli	Celery	Corn
Brussels sprouts	Eggplant	Cucumber
Cabbage	Onion	Lima bean
Cauliflower	Pepper	Muskmelon
Chard	Salsify	Pea
Lettuce		Turnip
Tomato		Watermelon

* The crops in the last group will usually suffer a very serious check if the roots are disturbed. The cucurbit members of this group can be seeded in a row and then placed in containers before the first true leaves have appeared.

Leftover Seeds

In case you have seeds left over, Table 12 shows which ones will germinate after a given amount of time. In general, vegetable seeds should be stored in a cool, dry, dark location.

Cultivation and Care

- Cultivate early. One hour of weeding in late May is worth a full day in August. The best time to kill weeds is when they sprout.

- Don't weed right after a rainstorm. Weeds on moist ground will re-root rapidly. Wait until the soil is workable and dry.

- Thin ruthlessly. If your beets, carrots, or lettuce are to grow well, they must have room. Leave enough space between plants so they can mature easily.

- Be careful around the plants. One careless swipe of the hoe can destroy a lot of work and future vegetables.

- Stay out of a wet garden. Rust disease of beans and other diseases are easily spread when a picker goes through a row of wet plants.

12. AVERAGE SEED STORAGE TIMES		
Dependable 1 Year	2 or 3 Years	4 or 5 Years
Onion	Asparagus	Beets
Sweet corn	Peas	Cabbage
Parsley	Beans	Cauliflower
Parsnips	Carrots	Cucumber
	Peppers	Eggplant
		Lettuce
		Muskmelon
		Pumpkin
		Spinach
		Squash
		Turnip
		Tomato
		Watermelon

- Water the ground, not the plants. Wet foliage can cause fungus diseases. Apply water to the base of the plant at sundown, so the heat of the day will not deplete its moisture. The garden should receive an inch of water per week.

- Keep weeds under control by tillage or mulching. Weeds take moisture, light, and nutrients away from vegetable plants. Be systematic about weeding; set aside some time each day so the weeds don't get ahead of you.

Mulching

You may want to lay mulch between the rows and around the plants to keep the ground cool in hot weather, conserve moisture, prevent the possibility of erosion, and help control weeds.

Table 13 lists common mulching materials and mentions benefits and disadvantages of each.

13. MULCHING MATERIALS

Material	Pros	Cons
Straw/Hay	Cheap; generally available; adds organic matter	Can contain weed seed, insects and/or disease
Leaves	Readily available; generally free; rich in nutrients	Can mat down or be too acidic for some plants
Grass clippings	Easy to get and apply; good source of nitrogen	Can burn plants; may contain weed seeds
Pine needles	Attractive; easy to apply	Large quantities hard to collect; may be too acid
Wood shavings	Weed and disease free; easy to apply; available	Can be acid; tends to tie up nitrogen in soil
Manure	Great source of fertility and organic matter	Should be well-rotted; expensive to buy; usually contains weeds
Newspaper	Easy to get and apply; earthworms thrive in it	Decomposes very fast; must be weighted down
Plastic	Total weed control if opaque is used; warms soil for early start; heavy plastic can be used more than one season	Expensive, unattractive; adds nothing to soil; must be weighted down and cleaned up in the fall

Composition of Organic Mulchers

Table 14 gives the approximate percentage composition of selected organic mulches.

14. APPROXIMATE COMPOSITION OF BULKY ORGANIC MULCHES

Material	Nitrogen (N)	Phosphorus (P)	Potassium (K)
Alfalfa hay	2.5	0.5	2.0
Bean straw	1.2	0.3	1.2
Grain straw	0.6	0.2	1.0
Olive pomaces	1.2	0.8	0.5
Peanut hulls	1.5	—	0.5
Peat	2.3	0.4	0.8
Sawdust	0.2	—	0.2
Seaweed (kelp)	0.6	—	1.3
Timothy hay	1.0	0.2	1.5
Winery pomaces	1.5	1.5	0.8

Insects

Your garden is an artificial environment with row on row of delicacies that insects love. Table 15 lists common vegetables and the pests which regularly afflict them. Check with your local extension agent for availability and legality of these insecticides.

15. VEGETABLE INSECTS

	Insect	Crop	Dust Formula	Spray Formula	Remarks
	Aphid*	Cabbage Cucumbers Melons Peas Potatoes Tomatoes	5 percent malathion	2 tsp. 50–57 percent emulsifiable malathion *or* I tsp. 64 percent emulsifiable dibrom in I gal. water	Apple on foliage when aphids appear. Repeat weekly as needed.
	Blister beetle	Potatoes Corn Tomatoes Beans	5 percent sevin	2 tb. wettable sevin in I gal. water	
	Cabbage worms	Broccoli Cabbage Cauliflower Greens	4 percent dibrom	I tsp. 64 percent emulsifiable dibrom in I gal. Water *or* *Bacillus thuringensis* biological insecticide	Thorough treatment is necessary. Repeat weekly as needed. Begin treatment when worms are small.
	Corn earworm (2/3 nat. size)	Sweet corn Tomatoes	5 percent sevin	Inject I/2 medicine dropperful of mineral oil into silk channel as silks start to dry *or* 2 tb. wettable sevin in I gal. water	Dust or spray silks with sevin every other day for IO days. Dust or spray tomatoes with sevin 3 to 4 times at IO-day intervals; begin when first fruits are small.
	European corn borer	Sweet corn	5 percent sevin *or* 5 percent sevin granules	2 tb. wettable sevin in I gal. Water *or* 2 tb. 25 percent diazinon in I gal. water	Apple insecticide four times at 5-day intervals beginning with egg hatching near mid-June. Avoid early spring plantings. On late corn dust as for corn earworm.
	Striped cucumber beetle	Cucumbers Melons Squash	5 percent sevin	2 tb. wettable sevin in I gal. Water	Treat as soon as beetles appear. Repeat when necessary.
	Cutworm	Most garden Crops		2 tb. 25 percent diazinon in I gal. water	At transplanting, wrap stems of seedling cabbage, pepper, and tomato plants with newspaper or foil to prevent damage by cutworms.
	Flea beetle	Most garden Crops	5 percent sevin	2 tb. wettable sevin in I gal. water	Apply as soon as injury is first noticed. Thorough application is necessary.
	Grasshopper	Most garden Crops	5 percent sevin	2 tb. wettable sevin in I gal. water	Treat infested areas while grasshoppers are still small.

Continued →

	Insect	Crop	Dust Formula	Spray Formula	Remarks
	Hornworm (1/2 nat. size)	Tomatoes	5 percent sevin	2 tb. wettable sevin in 1 gal. water	Ordinarily hand-picking is more practical in the home garden.
	Leafhopper	Beans Carrots Potatoes Cucumbers Muskmelons	Use sevin dust or 5 percent methoxy-chlor dust	2 tb. wettable sevin in 1 gal. water	Spray or dust once a week for 3 to 4 weeks, beginning when plants are small. Apply to underside of foliage.
	Mexican bean beetle	Beans	5 percent sevin	2 tb. wettable sevin in 1 gal. water	Apply insecticide to underside of foliage. Also effective against leafhoppers on beans.
	Potato beetle	Potatoes Eggplant Tomatoes	5 percent sevin	2 tb. wettable sevin in 1 gal. water	Apply when beetles or grubs first appear and repeat as necessary.
	Squash bug	Squash	5 percent sevin	2 tb. wettable sevin in 1 gal. water	Adults and brown egg masses can be hand picked. Trap adults under shingles beneath plants. Kill young bugs soon after they hatch.
	Squash vine borer	Squash	5 percent sevin	2 tb. wettable sevin in 1 gal. water	Dust or spray once a week for 3 to 4 weeks beginning in late June when first eggs hatch. Treat crowns of plants and runners thoroughly.

* Where two drawings are shown, the smaller one is the natural size.

The plants listed in Table 16 help prevent the presence of various destructive insects.

16. INSECT DETERRENT PLANTS

Asters	Most insects
Basil	Repels flies and mosquitoes
Borage	Deters tomato worm—improves growth and flavor of tomatoes
Calendula	Most insects
Catnip	Deters flea beetle
Celery	White cabbage butterfly
Chrysanthemum	Deters most insects
Dead Nettle	Deters potato bug—improves growth and flavor of potatoes
Eggplant	Deters Colorado potato beetle
Flax	Deters potato bug
Garlic	Deters Japanese beetle, other insects and blight
Geranium	Most insects
Horseradish	Plant at corners of potato patch to deter potato bug
Henbit	General insect repellent
Hyssop	Deters cabbage moth

Marigold	The workhorse of the pest deterrents. Plant throughout garden to discourage Mexican bean beetles, nematodes, and other insects
Mint	Deters white cabbage moth and ants
Mole Plant	Deters moles and mice if planted here and there
Nasturtium	Deters aphids, squash bugs, striped pumpkin beetles
Onion family	Deters most pests
Petunia	Protects beans
Pot Marigold	Deters asparagus beetles, tomato worms and general garden pests
Peppermint	Planted among cabbages, it repels the white cabbage butterfly
Radish	Especially deters cucumber beetle
Rosemary	Deters cabbage moth, bean beetle, and carrot fly

Rue	Deters Japanese beetle
Sage	Deters cabbage moth, carrot fly
Salsify	Repels carrot fly
Southernwood	Deters cabbage moth
Summer Savory	Deters bean beetles
Tansy	Deters flying insects, Japanese beetles, striped cucumber beetles, squash bugs, ants
Tomato	Asparagus beetle
Thyme	Deters cabbage worm
Wormwood	Carrot fly, white cabbage butterfly, blackflea beetle

Beneficial Insects

Lest the entire insect kingdom be given a black eye, it should be pointed out that several bugs are on your side. Two of these, the lady bug and the praying mantis, can be purchased through some of the larger garden supply houses.

Garden Problem Guide

Symptoms of common garden problems and their possible cures are given in Table 18.

17. BENEFICIAL INSECTS

Insect	Benefit
Braconid Wasps	Females lay eggs in body of tomato hornworm which the larvae then consume as their first meals.
Lace Wing Fly	Thrives on aphids. Pale green, fly-like bug.
Calosoma Beetle	Hard-shelled, 2-inch long, loves to eat caterpillars.
Hover Fly	Larvae of this four-winged fly feed on aphids and scale insects.
Ichneumon Fly	Lays eggs in caterpillars and their pupae, which the young flies then consume.
Lady Bug	Eats its weight in aphids daily.
Praying Mantis	Up to three inches long; feasts on pests, including mosquitoes.
Spiders	Many arachnids subsist on garden pests.
Wheel bug	Gray, 1 1/2-inch long, preys on soft-shelled pests; in profile it looks as if a cogged wheel were attached to its back.

18. GARDEN PROBLEM GUIDE

Symptoms	Possible Cause	Possible Cures
Dying young plants	Fertilizer burn	Mix fertilizer thoroughly with soil.
	Disease (damping-off)	Treat seed; don't over-water.
Stunted plants pale to yellow	Low soil fertility	Soil test for fertilizer recommendations.
	Low soil pH (too acid)	Soil test for lime recommendations.
	Poor soil drainage	Drain and add organic matter.
	Shallow or compacted soil	Plow deeper.
	Insects or diseases	Identify and use control measures.
	Nematodes	Soil test for treatment recommendations.
Stunted plants purplish color	Low temperature	Plant at recommended time.
	Lack of phosphorus	Add phosphorus fertilizer.
Holes in leaves	Insects	Identify and use control measures.
	Hail	Be thankful it was not worse.

Continued ➤

Symptoms	Possible Cause	Possible Cures
Spots, molds, darkened areas on leaves and stems	Disease	Identify, spray or dust, use resistant varieties.
	Chemical burn	Use recommended chemical at recommended rate.
	Fertilizer burn	Keep fertilizer off plants.
Wilting plants	Dry soil	Irrigate if possible.
	Excess water in soil	Drain.
	Nematodes	Soil test for treatment recommendations.
	Disease	Use resistant varieties if possible.
Weak, spindly plants	Too much shade	Remove shade or move plants to sunny spot.
	Plants too thick	Seed at recommended rate.
	Too much nitrogen	Avoid excess fertilization.
Failure to set fruit	High temperature	Follow recommended planting time.
	Low temperature	Follow recommended planting time.
	Too much nitrogen	Avoid excess fertilization.
	Insects	Identify and use control measures.
Tomato leaf curl	Heavy pruning in hot weather	Don't.
	Disease	Identify and use control measures.
Dry brown to black rot on blossom end of tomato	Low soil calcium	Add liming material.
	Extremely dry soil	Irrigate.
Misshapen tomatoes (catfacing)	Cool weather during blooming	Plant at recommended time.
Abnormal leaves and growth	2, 4-D weed killer	Don't use sprayer that has previously applied 2, 4-D.
		Don't allow spray to drift to garden.
	Virus disease	Remove infected plants to prevent spreading. Control insects that transmit.

Tomato Varieties

19. SELECTED TOMATO VARIETIES

This is only a sampling of tomato varieties. See your local extension agent for the best varieties for your area.

Variety	Days to Maturity	Comments	Variety	Days to Maturity	Comments
Beefeater	60	Meaty; short season areas	Hastings Brimmer	83	Pink, often seedless
Better Boy	72	All-purpose northern variety; needs staking	Heinz 1439	75	Fleshy, good processing fruit from the ketchup kings
Bonny Best	74	Acid flavor	Marglobe	73	Sweet, all-purpose
Burpeeana	58	Good yields, mild flavor	Ottawa	78	Does well in clay soil
Campbell 1327	69	A good canner from the soup company	Pixie	52	A good early tomato
			Rocket	50	A hardy Canadian variety
Coldset	68	Seed will sprout at 50°F	Roma	76	Tops for paste
Crimson Giant	90	Canning and slicing, good size	Snowball	70	A novelty type with white skin and low acid content
Dwarf Champion	73	Can be grown in tubs			
Globemaster	65	Resists cracking	Sub-Arctic	56–64	Several varieties, very early, good in cold climates
Golden Boy	80	Low-acid, yellow fruit			

Variety	Days to Maturity	Comments
Sweet 100	60	A cherry type that grows fruit in grapelike clusters
Tropic	80	Firm, resistant to disease and hot growing conditions
Ultra Boy	72	Large, juicy type for the northern gardener
Veeset	66	Good canner
Wisconsin Chief	80	Mature fruit can be left on vine 2 weeks

Harvesting

Table 20 gives average harvesting times which you can adjust according to your local conditions and preference.

20. APPROXIMATE DAYS FROM PLANTING TO MATURITY

Crop	Early Variety	Common Type	Late Variety
Bean, broad	. . .	120	. . .
Bean, bush	46	. . .	65
Bean, pole	56	. . .	72
Bean, lima, bush	65	. . .	78
Bean, lima, pole	80	. . .	95
Beet	50	. . .	80
Broccoli, sprouting[1]	70	. . .	150
Broccoli raab	. . .	60	. . .
Brussels sprouts[2]	90	. . .	100
Cabbage[2]	62	. . .	110
Carrot	60	. . .	85
Cauliflower, snowball type[2]	55	. . .	65
Cauliflower, winter type[2]	120	. . .	180
Celeriac	. . .	110	. . .
Celery, green[2]	98	. . .	130
Chard, Swiss	50	. . .	60
Chervil	. . .	60	. . .
Chicory	65	. . .	150
Chinese cabbage	70	. . .	80
Chives	. . .	90	. . .
Collard	. . .	75	. . .
Corn	70	. . .	100
Cucumber	60	. . .	70
Eggplant	70	. . .	85
Endive	80	. . .	100

Crop	Early Variety	Common Type	Late Variety
Florence fennel	. . .	110	. . .
Kale	60	. . .	90
Kohlrabi	55	. . .	65
Leek	. . .	150	. . .
Lettuce, cos	. . .	70	. . .
Lettuce, head	60	. . .	85
Lettuce, leaf	40	. . .	50
Melon, casaba	. . .	120	. . .
Melon, honey ball	. . .	105	. . .
Melon, honey dew	. . .	115	. . .
Melon, Persian	. . .	115	. . .
Muskmelon	83	. . .	90
Mustard	40	. . .	60
New Zealand spinach	. . .	70	. . .
Okra	50	. . .	60
Onion	85	. . .	120
Parsley	70	. . .	85
Parsnip	100	. . .	130
Pea	58	. . .	77
Pepper, hot[2]	70	. . .	95
Pepper, sweet[2]	60	. . .	80
Potato	90	. . .	120
Pumpkin	110	. . .	120
Radish	22	. . .	40
Radish, winter type	50	. . .	60
Rutabaga	. . .	90	. . .
Salsify	. . .	150	. . .
Sorrel	. . .	69	. . .
Southern pea (Cowpea)	62	. . .	80
Spinach	40	. . .	50
Squash, bush	50	. . .	68
Squash, vining	80	. . .	120
Sweet potato[3]	120	. . .	150
Tomato[2]	65	. . .	100
Turnip	40	. . .	75
Watercress	. . .	180	. . .
Watermelon	75	. . .	95

[1] For a direct-seeded crop. Transplanting may delay maturity by a few weeks, depending on environmental conditions.

[2] For a transplanted crop additional time needed from seed sowing to transplanting.

[3] Under good growing conditions enough roots may have reached number 1 size by 120 days after field seeding to justify harvesting for an early high-priced market.

Continued ➜

Selecting Seeds

Seeds are available from a number of sources, and since the federal government has laws regarding purity and germination, any dealer working interstate must meet high minimum standards.

Seed catalogs are fun to browse through, and once you order from one company you will probably receive catalogs from others, as many sell their mailing lists among themselves.

The seed suppliers listed in this book are not intended as an endorsement or advertisement for these companies. Rather, it is a list of those with interesting catalogs, good reputations, and, by and large, good merchandise.

Businesses relocate frequently. We try, but it is not always possible to keep our lists up-to-date. See your local extension agent for additional sources.

Appendix C: How to Take a Soil Sample

The quality of your test results depends on the quality of your sample. Remember that a very small amount of soil is going to have to represent your whole garden area. Professional soil labs may provide specific instructions or a kit for collecting samples; if so, follow their directions carefully. If you're using a home kit or the lab doesn't provide its own instructions, follow the steps here.

You'll need a separate sample for each part of the yard; sample lawn in one test, the vegetable garden in another, and flower beds in a separate test. If any part of your garden seems significantly different (looks or feels different, collects more water, or plants grow differently there), take a separate sample from there to find out what's causing the difference.

1. Take small amounts of soil from as many as six or eight different spots. First remove any plants, leaves, thatch, or other litter from the soil surface.

2. Dig a hole 6 inches deep in garden beds; if you're testing lawn areas, 4 inches is deep enough. Carve a thin slice of soil from the side of the hole and put it in a clean bucket or similar container.

3. If the soil you've selected is at all wet, spread it on a cloth or piece of clean plastic to dry. Then put all of your various samples in a single clean container and mix them together as thoroughly as you can. Save only about half a pint of this mixture.

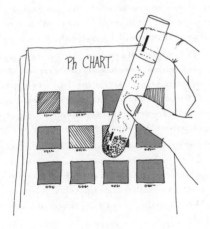

4. If you're using a home kit, follow instructions for the amount of soil (from your blended sample) and amount of indicator chemical to use for each test. Mix as directed, allow to settle for the specified amount of time, and compare the test tube to the colored chart supplied in the kit.

5. If you're sending your sample off to a lab, place your collected sample in a clean zipper-lock bag and label it, including the date and which part of the garden you sampled. Add a note explaining the history and intended use of the site (new bed, vegetable garden, lawn, etc.): The lab's fertilizer recommendations, based on your test results, will differ for lawns and vegetables and flowers.

It's a good practice to sample your soil once a year for the first two or three years. After that, you shouldn't need to sample more than every four years, unless your garden isn't growing well.

FERTILIZER BY THE NUMBERS

If the big numbers on a package of commercial fertilizer say "10–6–4," this means that the fertilizer contains 10 percent nitrogen (N), 6 percent phosphate (P) (a common form of phosphorus), and 4 percent potash (K) (a common form of potassium). Different fertilizers contain different NPK amounts. Fertilizers such as 10–6–4 that contain all three of the heavy-hitter major nutrients are called "complete" fertilizers. Superphosphate (0–20–0) is called "incomplete" because it only contains phosphate and no significant percentage of either nitrogen or potash.

"Complete" is an odd term for these fertilizers because they don't contain all the essential nutrients. Manufacturers rarely tell you much about the sulfur, magnesium, or calcium content; you have to check the fine print. Synthetic fertilizers contain few if any micronutrients; you need to use them in conjunction with sources of organic matter such as compost to keep plants supplied with micronutrients.

Most organic fertilizers contain a good supply of micronutrients. In addition, one of the biggest advantages of organic fertilizers is that they don't release all their nitrogen at once but keep supplying small amounts over a much longer time. Standard, concentrated synthetic fertilizers supply nitrogen in its most mobile form; while this means it's available quickly, it also means it can wash away quickly.

Appendix D: Pruning Trees, Shrubs, & Vines

What, When, & How

What is pruning? It is cutting away unwanted parts of a plant for a better shape or more fruitful growth.

What is involved in pruning? To do the job well, you need to know when (in what season) to prune, what to cut away, and how to do the cutting. For most jobs, all you will need are a few simple hand tools, although power tools are sometimes handy.

Is pruning really necessary? Nature does its own pruning. The woods are full of dead limbs and branches pruned by nature's ruthless wind, snow, and ice storms. Weak branches die and drop off neglected trees; rubbing branches kill one another. Thick undergrowth frequently kills trees by its dense shade. But, nature's pruning is a slow, haphazard process; you can get better results with pruning shears.

There are four basic reasons for pruning. Careful pruning enables you to control the shape and growth of your plant, to increase its productivity through more blooms and larger fruits, and to maintain the health of the plant.

When should you prune? When to prune depends on many things. First, it depends on the plant. Trees are usually pruned while they are dormant. If pruned in the spring—or even late winter—certain trees will bleed too much sap; others, if pruned in the summer or early fall, may develop new soft growth that will not withstand the winter. For these same reasons, grapevines are also pruned while dormant. Hedges, on the other hand, are trimmed several times a growing season to stimulate denser growth.

There are no absolute rules to follow. Many growers prefer to prune "heavy bleeders"—maples and birches—late in the summer. In areas where the winter is not severe, fall pruning may not lead to growth that can be winter-killed as it would in northern areas.

The growth habit of the plant is an important consideration. With flowering shrubs, you need to know whether blooms are produced on year-old growth or on new growth. Early spring pruning stimulates growth for shrubs that will bloom on the new shoots; but pruning after flowering is best for shrubs like forsythia that bloom on year-old wood.

Any time is a good time to prune away dead growth or broken or diseased limbs. Feel free to snip away water sprouts or remove suckers as they appear. Undesired growth drains energy from the plant.

The Basics

The mistake that many home growers make is usually either too little or too much pruning. The extent to which a plant needs to be pruned depends on the habits of the species and also on how old the plant is. A young tree, vine, or shrub will need more formative pruning to get it off to a good shape. Many ornamental trees and vines can be left pretty much alone once they have matured.

Check the table in the back of this appendix for the special pruning requirements of many commonly grown plants. Always keep in mind to what purpose you are training your plant—as a privacy hedge or fruit-bearing tree, for example—and let your common sense guide you.

TOOLS

There is a large assortment of pruning equipment on the market, and only trial and error will enable you to find the tools you like to work with best. But a few hand tools will get you started.

Whether or not you want to invest in power tools is another decision. For most jobs, hand tools—shears, clippers, saws, and knives—will do. Pole pruners can extend your reach far enough for most jobs.

Pruning Equipment. *Pruning shears,* hand clippers, or hand pruners, as they are variously called, will be your most used and useful tools. Many gardeners make it a practice to carry a pair with them always. That way they are ready to snip off any unwanted water sprouts, suckers, or faded blooms.

The ideal pruning shear is lightweight, cuts easily, and makes clean cuts which heal over quickly. Some gardeners have several pairs; one kept especially sharp for fine pruning of roses and shrubs, and others for rough work like cutting roots and separating clumps of perennials.

Pruning shears come in a variety of styles. Some operate with a thin, sharp blade that cuts against an anvil. There is also a scissors-type pruner. Personal preference will determine which one is best for you.

Long-handled lopping shears will give you additional leverage and reach for taller, bigger branches. Some lopping shears are gear-driven for additional leverage. A *tree pruner,* for cutting those very high branches, up to an inch in diameter, is extremely useful on tall shrubs, and high-growing vines. These are simply clippers mounted on top of poles. The cutting action is activated by a rope and spring.

For large tree limbs, a *pruning saw* is necessary—an ordinary hand saw won't do; it tends to gum up. Pruning saws also come in a variety of styles. There are both straight-bladed and curved saws for general purpose work, and fine-tooth saws for finer work. A lightweight *bow saw* is also handy. A *pole saw* is similar to a pole pruner—it is a saw mounted on a long pole.

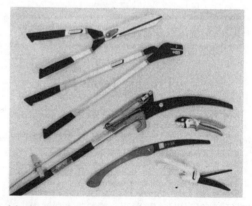

A few simple hand tools are all you need for most jobs. From top to bottom: *hedge trimmers, lopping shears, pole pruner, hand pruner, pruning saw, and grass trimmer.*

A sharp *knife* is another essential. It will enable you to trim wounds left when tree branches are removed.

Don't be tempted to use a heavy-duty pruner where a saw is appropriate. It may squeeze the branch rather than cut it, and the wound will be much greater. A good rule of thumb is a branch beyond one inch in diameter should be cut with a saw.

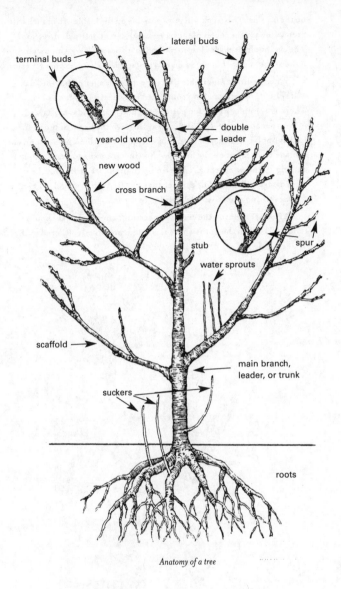

terminal buds

lateral buds

year-old wood

new wood

cross branch

double leader

stub

water sprouts

spur

scaffold

main branch, leader, or trunk

suckers

roots

Anatomy of a tree

Pruning Terms

Axil: The angle formed by branch and leaf and the part of the plant from which it arises.

Bearing tree: A fruit tree that has reached the age of producing blossoms and fruits.

Branch: A shoot that has grown for more than one season.

Bud: An unexpanded flower or vegetative shoot. Buds may develop into flowers or into leaves and shoots. They may be terminal, as at the top of a shoot, or lateral, as in the axil of a leaf.

Candle: New terminal growth on a pine from which needles will emerge.

Cane: A long, healthy branch, usually referring to the growth on brambles or vines.

Central leader: A style of pruning that leaves one single, strong trunk from which side branches are allowed to grow.

Columnar: Referring to a tree that naturally grows in a tall, narrow shape.

Crotch: The angle between two branches or shoots near the point of their union.

Deshoot: Removal of young shoots from a tree during growing season to aid in training it to a desirable shape.

Disbud: Selective removal of flower buds so that the remaining buds become bigger and produce showier blooms.

Dormant: Resting, or not growing.

Espalier: A tree or shrub trained to grow flat against a trellis or wall.

Fruiting wood: Shoots or branches carrying flower buds and having the potential for bearing fruit.

Hanger: A drooping branch on a tree that does not normally have branches which grow downward. These should be removed.

Head: The extension of the tree trunk above the first branches.

Heading back: Cutting away a portion of the terminal growth of a branch or shoot, usually to control the size of the tree or shrub.

Latent bud: A bud that does not open within the season it is formed. These may develop into new growth if existing branches are broken or pruned.

Lateral: A shoot or branch arising from a side (lateral) bud of another shoot or branch.

Lateral bud: A bud on the side rather than tip of a stem.

Leader: A developing trunk that is stronger and taller than any laterals.

Modified leader: A system of pruning, usually a fruit tree, where the central stem is kept part way up the tree, and then is allowed to branch more freely.

Open vase: A system of pruning, usually fruit trees, when the main trunk is kept short and the center of the tree is kept open, with the limbs growing around the open center.

Pinch: Heading a growing shoot by removing the top with your fingernails.

Shearing Equipment. Because shearing involves cutting soft growth, instead of wood, different tools are used. A *long-handled hedge shear*, electric- or hand-powered, is the main tool.

Make sure the model you choose is the right one for the job you have to do. Are the handles long enough to enable you to reach the top of your shrub? Are the blades heavy enough to cut coarse-twigged shrubs, or will they just chew them up? Electric tools are handy for big jobs, and some electric hedge clippers are available without cords.

Maintenance. Keep your tools in good condition. Most blades can be kept sharp with a grindstone or whetstone. Saws should be sharpened professionally. Clippers and pruners need an occasional drop of motor oil to keep them operating smoothly. Protect the metal surfaces from rust by keeping them dry and occasionally oiled. Clean off sap and pitch with a little kerosene.

Continued →

Pyramidal: Referring to a tree with a broad base tapering to a pointed top.

Scaffold: A branch arising from the trunk.

Scion: The cutting of one plant that is grafted to the rootstock of another.

Shoot: Vegetative growth produced from a bud, generally during the current growth season.

Spur: Short, thick growth producing flowers on apple, pear, and cherry trees.

Standard: A plant not normally grown as a tree that has been trained to a single trunk with a round head. Roses are often grown to a standard.

Stone fruit: Represented by peach, plum, apricot, and cherry.

Sucker: A vigorous shoot arising from the rootstock or from the lower portion of the trunk. These should be removed immediately.

Terminal bud: The bud at the end of the trunk or branch that extends the growth of the plant.

Topiary: To shape a tree or shrub into an unnatural form for ornamental purposes.

Water sprout: A vigorous shoot arising from a latent bud on the trunk or on older branches. These may be caused by overpruning and should be promptly removed.

How to Cut

The cardinal rule of pruning is *cut cleanly and leave no stubs*. A dead stub will rot, die, and is vulnerable to infections that can spread to the rest of the tree. Either cut close to the main branch or immediately above a bud.

Only the stub on the far left has been cut properly. From left to right: *the first cut is done correctly; the second cut leaves too much surface; the third cut leaves too long a stub; and the fourth cut was made too close to the bud.*

Make your pruning cut just above the bud that grows in the direction you want the new growth to take.

When cutting above a bud, which will stimulate new growth, make the cut just above a bud that grows in the direction the new growth is desired. A bud

on the outside of a branch will grow out; one on the inside of a branch will grow in toward the center of the tree—usually an undesirable direction. The cut should be made close to the bud so it does not leave a long stub, and it should be angled, but not so sharply that it leaves a long, exposed surface.

When sawing off a sizable limb, the main danger is that the limb will split off before you have completed your neat and clean saw cut. There is a simple three-step cutting method that avoids this hazard. Make a cut about one-third of the way through the branch, ten to fifteen inches out from the main trunk. Saw from the bottom up. A second cut is made farther out on the branch, this time from the top down and cutting all the way through. The limb will often break off, but the jagged edge will extend no farther than the first cut you made. Then cut the remaining stub flush and parallel to the main trunk.

After performing the cutting operation, any loose bark should be trimmed back to the point where it is sound and firmly adhered to the

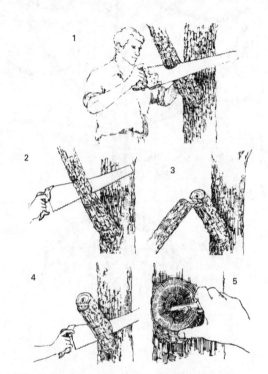

Step 1. Make a cut about one-third of the way through the branch, ten to fifteen inches out from the trunk. Step 2. Saw completely through the branch a few inches farther out on the branch. Step 3. The bark will tear only as far as the first cut. Step 4. Saw the remaining stub close to the trunk. Step 5. Trim the edges of the wound with a sharp knife.

wood. For the quickest healing results, the wound should be trimmed clean with no ragged edges. Use your knife to smooth over the wound and surrounding bark.

Every cut of more than 1 1/2 inches in diameter should have a protective coating of wound dressing. The primary reason for coating a large wound is to keep out moisture and to accelerate the healing process. Healing is quicker if the wound is trimmed in an oval shape. It sometimes takes years before a wound is covered with bark, so a seasonal repainting is advisable. Although any paint will seal out the insects and the effects of weather, a commercial tree-paint preparation contains antiseptic as an additional protection against disease.

Practical Pruning Tips

- Cut off a diseased, dead, or broken branch from any tree or plant at any time.

- Prune the weaker of two rubbing or interfering branches that are developing bark wounds—the quicker the better.

- Always prune flush to the parent branch or trunk. If only the end of a branch is dead, cut just beyond and close to a bud. Note: Be sure the branch is dead—not dormant—by slicing the bark and looking for green wood.

- In pruning, don't leave stubs or ragged cuts. Always use sharp, clean-cutting pruning tools.

- All bark wounds over 1 1/2 inches in diameter should have a protective coating of dark paint.

- Prune a hedge so that the plants grow wider at the base than at the top.

- Pruning top terminal branches produces a low spreading tree. By pruning lateral or side branches the tree will grow upwards—less bushy.

- Burn what you cut to avoid spreading disease and attracting rot organisms.

- Keep pruning shears sharp and well-oiled, and use the right tool for the job.

- In the garden it's always good practice to carry hand clippers.

- Keep trees out of foundation plantings. Never let trees and shrubs block windows of the house.

- Keep your feet on the ground. Don't use stepladders, chairs, or other make-shifts to prune the upper branches—use long-handled pruners or tree pruners and pole saws.

- Don't climb trees—it's too hazardous—that's the job for a professional arborist who has proper equipment and knows how to use it.

CONDENSED PRUNING GUIDE

	When	How
FRUITS		
Apple	Winter or early spring	Train tree for low head. Prune moderately. Keep tree open with main branches well spaced around tree. Avoid sharp V-shaped crotches.
Blackberry	After bearing and summer	Remove at ground canes that bore last crop. In summer cut back new shoots 3 1/2 feet high.
Cherry	Winter or early spring	Prune moderately, cut back slightly the most vigorous shoots.
Currant	Early spring	Remove old unfruitful growth. Encourage new shoots.
Gooseberry	Early spring	Same as currant. Cut back new shoots at 12 inches high and side shoots to two buds.
Grape	Late winter or early spring, before sap starts	Requires heavy pruning of old wood to encourage new bearing wood. Remove all old branches back to main vine. Cut back the previous year's new growth to four buds.
Peach	Early spring	Prune vigorously—remove one-half of the previous year's growth, keep tree headed low, and well thinned-out.
Plum	Early spring	Remove dead and diseased branches, keep tree shaped up by cutting back rank growth. Prune moderately.
Quince	Early spring	Cut back young trees to form low, open head. Little pruning of older trees required except to remove dead and weak growth.
Raspberry	After bearing and in summer	Remove at the ground in fall canes which bore last crop. In summer head back new canes 20 inches to 22 inches high.
SHRUBS		
Barberry	Early spring	Little pruning required except to remove a few old branches occasionally to encourage new growth. Head back as necessary to keep plant in shape.
Butterfly Bush	Early spring	Cut out all dead wood. Remove some old branches and head in as necessary to keep plant properly shaped.

Continued ➔

	When	How
Clematis	Spring	Cut out weak growth but save as much old wood as possible.
Crab	Early spring	Prune moderately. Cut out dead and broken branches and suckers.
Deutzias	After flowering	Remove a few older branches and all dead wood. Do not let growth get too dense.
Dogwood, Flowering	After flowering	Remove dead wood only.
Dogwood, Other	Spring	Varieties grown for colored twigs should have the old growth removed to encourage bright-colored new shoots.
Elderberry	After fruiting	Prune severely. Remove one-half of season's growth.
Forsythia	After flowering	Remove a few older branches at the ground each year and head back new growth as necessary.
Honeysuckle, Bush	After fruiting	Cut out some old branches. Keep bush open.
Hydrangea	Early spring	Hills of Snow variety: cut back to ground. Others: remove dead and weak growth, cut old flowering stems back to two buds.
Laurel, Mountain	After flowering	Prune very little. Remove a few old branches at the ground from weak, leggy plants to induce growth from the roots.
Lilac	After flowering	Remove diseased and scaly growth, cut off old flower heads, and cut out surplus sucker growth.
Mock-Orange	After flowering	Cut out dead wood and a few old branches to thin out plant.
Rhododendron	After flowering	Treat same as Laurel, Mountain.
Roses, Climbing	After flowering	Cut out about one-half of old growth at the ground and retain the vigorous new shoots from the root for next year's flowers. Head back as necessary.
Roses: Tea, Hybrid, Perpetual	Spring after frosts	Cut away all dead and weak growth and shorten all remaining branches or canes to four buds for weak growers and five buds for vigorous varieties.
Rose of Sharon	When buds start	Cut out all winter killed growth back to live wood.
Snowberry	Early spring	Thin out some old branches and cut back last season's growth of that part remaining to three buds.
Trumpet Vine	Early spring	Prune side branches severely to the main stem.
Viburnum	Early spring	Prune lightly. Remove all dead, weak, and a few of the old branches.
Virginia Creeper	Spring	Clip young plants freely. Older plants require little pruning except to remove dead growth and some thinning.
Weigela	After flowering	Prune lightly, remove all dead, weak growth and head in as necessary. Cut out a few old branches at the ground to induce new growth.
Wisteria	Spring	Cut back the new growth to the spurs at the axils of the leaves. This can be repeated in midsummer.

Appendix E: Pest-Proofing Your Garden

by Ruth Harley

Illustrations by Barbara Carter

Introduction

Your approach to getting rid of the unwanted animals in your garden will be determined by your own philosophy, influenced by the appetites of those intruders. If you are concerned about the environment and dislike using poisonous substances or killing animals, your attitude will differ from the person who is intent on having the perfect garden and getting rid of the rascals, no matter what method is employed.

Suggestions for protecting plants presented here cover a wide range. Undoubtedly you will find some of the methods more useful than others. The tricks that deter one gardener's predators may not faze the animals that are ruining your crop.

The methods you choose may be determined by the amount of time and money you wish to invest. If you are sharing a community garden for a season, your approach will not be the same as the gardener who plans to cultivate the same plot indefinitely.

A FENCE STOPS SOME

A fenced garden fares better than one open to traffic. A fence keeps out the neighbor's dog, your own children, a few rabbits and cats. But a simple picket or wire fence does not stop everything: groundhogs (or do you call them woodchucks?) and moles dig under, raccoons and squirrels climb over, deer hurdle it, slugs ignore it, and birds perch on it while digesting your delicacies. Fences can be expensive and the barrier designed to keep out absolutely all invaders is not only exorbitant in price but also impractical.

It's a good idea to garden for a while in an area to find out just who your enemies are. Identify the animals and birds that are determined to share your garden with you and watch to see which vegetables are most attractive to them. Then you can take steps to repel the culprits and concentrate on protecting specific crops. Unfortunate indeed is the gardener who is attempting to raise vegetables in an area inhabited by all the creatures discussed in the following paragraphs!

Rabbits

Only about 7 percent of all rabbits live to be a year old, but you may feel that the entire surviving population is in your neighborhood. Rabbits mate early and often, and produce several litters each year, ranging in number from four to seven. They do not hibernate and are usually active during the day. They are particularly destructive to young fruit trees, garden vegetables, and tulip leaves.

To protect fruit trees from rabbits, build a cylindrical fence of chicken wire or hardware cloth around the trunk, or purchase the perforated plastic strips offered through seed catalogues or garden stores. They can be wound around the tree to a height of twenty-four inches and make it difficult for the rabbits to make a meal on the bark. These protections for fruit trees will discourage mice, too.

Perforated plastic wrapped around tree trunks will help stop rabbits (left). Or use chicken wire or hardware cloth (right).

RABBITS FRIGHTEN EASILY

Fortunately, rabbits are timid creatures and are easily frightened. A toy snake or even an old piece of garden hose left in the garden will fool them, at least temporarily. A dog tied near the garden will keep rabbits away. The family cat, if a good hunter, may eliminate them altogether.

Dried blood meal, available in farm and garden centers, is a good deterrent and is also beneficial to the soil. It can be sprinkled near the plants. Rains wash it away, so it must be replaced. Some dislike using it, saying it attracts dogs.

Powdered rock phosphate can also be tried. Sprinkle it on the leaves of young plants.

Chemical repellents on the market to keep animals away from ornamental plants should not be used on vegetables. Read the label to find out what the ingredients are, and follow the directions carefully. It is possible to soak a clothesline in a repellent and suspend it from stakes a few inches from the ground, or stretch such a line along your fence.

Other repellents, recommended by some gardeners, may or may not work on your rabbits, but you may wish to try them. Moth balls or moth crystals should be used with caution, especially where children may be playing. Additional substances to scatter around tulips and young plants are powdered aloe, tobacco dust, cayenne or black pepper, wood ashes, and cow manure.

TRY FISH SPRAY

In her book *Companion Planting*, published by Garden Way, Louise Riotte points out that rabbits dislike the odor of fish. She gives directions for making a spray that will repel rabbits and insect pests at the same time:

Take three to four ounces of chopped garlic bulbs and soak in two tablespoons of mineral oil for one day. Add a pint of water in which one teaspoon of fish emulsion has been dissolved. Stir well. Strain the liquid and store in a glass or china container, as it reacts with metals. Dilute this, starting with one part to twenty parts of water, and use as a spray.

Rabbits dislike onions, so it is a good idea to interplant onions with cabbage, lettuce, peas, and beans. Another plant that rabbits seem to stay away from is Dusty Miller (*Cinerara diamond*), an attractive ornamental that—even if it fails to discourage the rabbits—will improve the looks of your garden. As with any companion planting, get it into the ground early so that it will be thriving before your lettuce comes up.

Continued →

One approach that brings cheers from some gardeners and jeers from others is to bury empty soda bottles along the border with their tops about four inches above the ground. The theory is that the wind blowing across the openings makes a sound that either frightens the rabbits or hurts their ears so they will stay away. Another "glassware" remedy is to fill bottles or jars with water and place them around the garden. This time the theory is that the rabbits and other small animals will be frightened by the reflections of lights or of themselves.

A BURIED FENCE

The best method to keep out rabbits is to enclose the garden with a poultry fence. Get 48-inch fencing and bury the lower ten inches. While few rabbits will burrow under a fence, by burying it you will keep out the rabbits as well as the burrowing animals. If building a fence involves more time and expense than you wish to invest, try making a portable cage (see illustration) that can be placed over a few plants and used at the stage when the plants are most attractive to birds and beasts.

Before you condemn all rabbits as troublemakers, there is something to be said on their behalf. Sal Gilbertie, an author of gardening books, recommends keeping a couple of pet rabbits (of the same sex) in a cage so that you can use the rabbit manure. The rabbits eat relatively little while producing a surprising quantity of beneficial fertilizer with a high nitrogen, phosphorus, and potash content. Rabbit manure pellets can be used directly on a garden. If you're familiar with commercial fertilizers like 10–10-10, think of rabbit manure as 2.4–1.4–0.6.

A portable garden cage used at the right time can save your young corn or strawberries.

Groundhogs or Woodchucks

It is not difficult to study the habits of a groundhog. If there is one living on your property (and it may sometimes seem as if you are living on *its* property), you will notice that it comes out for breakfast shortly after the sun is up. It samples any dewy thing that pleases it and blandly stares down any intruders. Other than dogs, the groundhog—and a woodchuck is the same animal—has no natural enemies.

During the middle of the day, it stays in its burrow, digesting the tremendous amount of greenery it has chewed up. Late in the afternoon, it emerges and once again gobbles up the salad stuff, then waddles off to retire for the night.

Groundhogs are diurnal. Unlike the nocturnal marauders, the skunks and raccoons, groundhogs are active during the day. They hibernate, are herbivorous, and eat astronomical amounts of food.

Almost every gardener has a home remedy for discouraging groundhogs. None of them is 100 percent sure. Some of them are as hard to believe as the legend about Groundhog's Day. The trick that deters one groundhog may not bother yours.

A DOG MAY HELP

It helps to tie the family dog near the garden. In at least one instance, however, the groundhog seemed able to judge the exact length of the dog's chain and calmly ate the vegetables anyway.

Some gardeners advocate planting a double row of soybeans around the perimeter of the vegetable bed. Soybeans are favorites of both groundhogs and rabbits and, theoretically, they will feast heavily on the soybeans and leave the other plants alone. The difficulty is that the soybeans may attract animals that would otherwise have bypassed your garden entirely.

Another scheme is to place bottles or jars of water throughout the garden. Seeing reflections is supposed to frighten the animals.

Scattering the same ill-smelling substances that deter rabbits is also recommended—red pepper, black pepper, powdered aloe, and dried blood. Sprinkle it on the ground, not on the foliage.

If there is tall grass around the garden, try spraying it lightly with a mixture of half diesel fuel and half kerosene. (A heavy application will kill the grass.) Animals dislike having the oily, smelly substance on their fur and will stay away.

A good fence is the best protection against groundhogs. The bottom should be buried at least ten inches below the surface or, even better, the underground portion should be bent outward at a 90° angle. The groundhog may never discover that he should back up before he starts to dig.

A good woodchuck fence, sunk ten inches below the surface and bent outward to foil furry tunnelers.

A CAGE TRAP

Tenderhearted gardeners can solve the groundhog problem—at least for themselves—by trapping the animals in a cage-type trap and transporting them to another area. Havahart traps are made of steel mesh and open on both ends. The traps come in many sizes and strengths to take care of animals from the size of a mouse to that of a coyote or large dog. The captives are not injured. Neighborhood pets, if captured, can be released easily (and their owners encouraged to keep them at home).

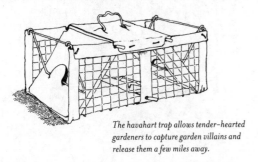

The havahart trap allows tender-hearted gardeners to capture garden villains and release them a few miles away.

If you have no aversion to killing groundhogs, you may wish to buy gas capsules to put into the groundhog's tunnel. The difficulty here is in locating the tunnel and all of its openings. The gas capsules are available in garden and hardware stores. Read the directions carefully before you attempt to use the capsules.

Moles

At least one good thing can be said for moles: They eat slugs, white grubs, Japanese beetles, and other soil insects. After that, moles are bad news for the gardener. They eat the earthworms that are the gardener's friend. Although they do not eat plants or seedlings, in digging their tunnels they may uproot them or disturb the roots so that they dry out and die.

How do you know if the damage is being done by a mole? By a network of ridges throughout the lawn and garden. Their nests are inside a circular mound of earth (gopher mounds are crescent-shaped). Moles dig the subways that are commonly used by mice and voles. It is these animals that leave behind the bits of debris from bulbs, grass roots, or other vegetable matter found in mole tunnels.

Any season is mole season: They are active throughout the year. They spend almost their entire lives underground and their bodies are highly specialized. They have short legs with powerful broad front feet and sharp claws, and no visible eyes or ears. A hairless nose is sensitive to touch and serves as a guide. Their fur is dark, soft, and velvety.

MOLES DISLIKE CASTOR BEANS

Castor plants are repulsive to moles. Try dropping castor beans in the mole holes or plant a border of castor plants around the garden. They are attractive ornamentals. Since the seeds and leaves of this plant are poisonous, take care about using them in areas where children may be playing. Instead, try making an emulsion of two parts castor oil and one part liquid detergent in the blender. Add an equal amount of water, then put two tablespoons of the solution in a sprinkling can of water and pour it over the area where the moles are at work.

DEAD FISH

Another suggestion is to place a dead fish in the mole tunnel. If the tunnel is near your home or where you are working, you may prefer to co-exist with the mole rather than endure the smell.

A few other tricks that may encourage the moles to move on: Stuff raspberry bushes or other thorned branches into mole tunnel openings; sprinkle red pepper around tunnel entrances; keep a cat.

Moles have an acute sense of hearing. A soft drink bottle buried so that the top is just above ground acts as a whistle when the wind blows over it. Moles, like rabbits, are supposed to dislike this noise intensely. Small toy windmills placed outside the tunnel entrance may have the same effect, because the mole dislikes the vibration transmitted into the ground.

Mouse traps (right) or specially designed mole traps (left) may help when fences are useless.

Mouse traps can be used to catch moles, but care should be taken to handle the traps with gloves to keep from leaving a scent. Place the trap at right angles to the hole and cover it with a basket or bucket. Mole traps, especially designed for the purpose, are available at hardware stores. Instructions for the traps advise flattening down the ridges that the mole has made, then waiting to see which ridges are reopened. The trap is placed above one of the tunnels that is in use. The pan of the trap is placed in a flattened portion. When the mole opens the tunnel, he springs the trap and is impaled on its metal rods.

Deer

White-tailed deer are the most numerous kind in the United States today. There are about 30 varieties of deer and they are found in all types of habitat, from suburban areas to dense wilderness. They commonly are found near the edges of forest areas where they can feed on berries and young trees—as well as on garden produce.

Before our country was fully settled, the deer's natural enemies held their numbers within the limits of their food supply. Today there are believed to be well over five million deer—many more than 200 years ago. Their natural predators—wolves and cougars—have almost disappeared. Hunting seasons and highway mishaps decimate their ranks, but in many regions there is still an overpopulation. When the animals are in danger of starving, they become bolder in their search for food and move in closer to inhabited buildings.

White-tailed deer browse, like most members of the deer family. They eat buds, twigs, and bark of shrubs and trees. They also like the tender vegetables growing in the garden. Because they are curious and adaptable, they are willing to sample new food and live under new conditions. In other words, they may be able to get along very nicely on the new, high-priced hybrids you choose to plant. Records of deer damage to crops go back to the earliest days of farming in this country.

Deer are able to leap an eight-foot fence, so simply fencing your garden is not sufficient. A four-foot width of chicken wire spread flat on the ground around the garden may be a better barrier against deer than the same chicken wire fastened to upright posts. Deer dislike walking on the wire. If you do not lay the wire completely around the garden, place it at the points where the deer usually enter and leave. Stake it down. Black plastic also discourages deer crossings, but to a lesser degree.

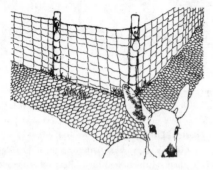

The high-jumping deer may be turned away by a width of chicken wire laid flat on the ground around the garden.

Deer have a highly developed sense of smell. One of the best repellents is dried blood meal put into small cloth bags—similar to tobacco pouches—and hung along the fence at intervals. Hanging the ill-smelling blood on the fence or on the lower branches of trees you wish to protect seems to be more effective than spreading it on the ground. As stated before, however, this may attract dogs.

The Cooperative Extension Service of Orange County, New York, recommends hanging bags of human hair in trees to discourage browsing by deer. The hair can be collected from barber shops or beauty parlors and stuffed into old nylon stockings or plastic mesh produce bags, such as onion bags. A bag about the size of a softball should be hung in the tree to be protected. If the problem is severe, try hanging a bag in every tree.

A number of deer repellents are on the market for use in spraying shrubbery and ornamental plants. Read the directions carefully and note the ingredients before deciding to use these near your vegetables.

A dog tethered near your garden will frighten off the boldest deer.

Raccoons

Although gardeners like to believe that they are clever enough to outwit all the other animals, the raccoon gives them a hard time. Raccoons are particularly fond of fresh, juicy corn, but they also enjoy fish, birds, eggs, fruit, and other vegetables as well. In short, they are omniverous.

Raccoons not only pay nocturnal visits to the garden, they raid your garbage can as well. They are extremely intelligent. A crafty raccoon can open a trash container without knocking it over and delicately help

himself. If you are mystified as to the identity of the garbage thief that comes in the night, study the clues. A dog will knock over the can, tear open all your neat brown paper bags, and strew the debris over a wide area. An opossum takes what it wants and drags it along the ground while it eats, leaving a trail. A raccoon chooses its menu, washes it carefully, then stays to eat.

A teaspoon of ammonia in each trash can and a little sprinkled around the garbage can area will help to discourage dogs, raccoons, opossums, and skunks. Ammonia is also a good disinfectant.

The best thing for keeping the greatest number of animals out of your garden is a good fence. Raccoons are not deterred by a two-foot—or even a four-foot—fence. They can climb over easily. Some gardeners keep coons out of the corn by surrounding the rows of corn with a high fence and topping it with a roof of fencing. The "coon cage" must be equipped with a screen door with a good latch. The difficulty in building the cage and the discomfort of cultivating in a cage may discourage you from trying it.

ELECTRIC FENCE

An alternative to the coon cage is a length of electrified wire or two stretched above a conventional fence. If your garden is on a farm or in a sparsely populated area, the electric fence can be the ultimate solution to the entire animal pest problem. However, electric fences in residential areas are a touchy subject.

Many cities and towns have ordinances prohibiting the use of electric fence controllers—particularly homemade units. Prior to using electric fencing, consult your local officials about ordinances.

There are companies that manufacture components for electric fences designed for use with large domestic animals in rural settings. They do not recommend electric fencing in urban areas for small animals. However, the gardeners who are using just such fences are enthusiastic about them. They believe a combination of chicken wire or snow fence and electric fencing is the best solution to all animal pest problems. The electric charge is not sufficient to harm a child or pet, but is dangerous to the person with heart trouble who has a pacemaker.

The cost of erecting an electric fence must be balanced against the value of your crop. Certainly its use is not justified to protect a row of lettuce and a few radishes. To build an electric fence using new components—a UL fence controller, wire, posts, insulators, battery, etc.—costs a bare minimum of $50.

For raccoons, a combination of buried chicken wire and electric strands works best.

A LIVING FENCE

The oldest method is to plant pumpkins, cucumbers, watermelon, or squash close together around the edge of the rows of corn. Raccoons like to be able to stand up and look around and the large leaves and tangle of vines make that difficult. If you decide to plant one of these living fences, don't leave any gaps or the coons will find them and slip through.

- Plant a Kentucky Wonder bean or a cucumber seed when you plant each hill of corn. The vines will climb the stalks and deter the raccoons.

- Use a three- or four-foot fence of chicken wire leaving a loose overhang of wire about two feet high at the top. The shaky wire keeps the heavy raccoon from climbing over.

- Sprinkle red or black pepper on the corn silks. It will not affect the taste of the corn.

- If the crop is not too large, slide a nylon stocking over each ear.

- Light the corn patch at night. If it is too far from a source of electricity, use a lantern.

- Run barefoot around the patch each night.

- Place a transistor radio in a plastic bag and turn it on to an all-night station. (If the raccoons are not frightened, they will at least have dinner music.)

- Encourage the youngsters in the family to sleep out in the garden in their sleeping bags when the corn is nearly ripe.

- Press cloves of garlic into the ground around the vegetables.

- If there is grass around the garden, spray it lightly with a mixture of kerosene oil and diesel oil. Raccoons are tidy creatures and dislike having the oily substance on their coats.

- Place dog droppings between the plants. If you have access to the manure of a larger beast, try it.

One final word of advice: Never put off picking until tomorrow the corn that is ready today. Invariably the coon will beat you to it.

Birds

Symbiosis is a word that refers to the living together of two species in a manner that is advantageous to both. The word might apply very well to the humans and the birds who have an interest in the same garden. Both wish to obtain food with the least amount of work. Humans tend to the garden; birds tend to many of the harmful insects.

A little bird-watching throughout the season will help you to determine what methods to use to protect your crops from the birds. Different things attract and repel various species. Your purpose is not to get rid of all birds—you will need some of them. The same birds that torment you by pulling up the corn seedlings or eating your ripe strawberries are also very useful at gobbling up bugs and slugs. The trick is to devise a plan whereby both you and the birds benefit.

More than one expert will tell you that wild berries are more attractive to birds than cultivated ones and if you allow wild plants to grow up near your garden, the birds will leave your strawberries alone. You may or may not believe this. Your experience may have been that the birds are attracted to the wild fruit and linger on to sample the cultivated berries as well.

SCARECROWS INEFFECTIVE

Scarecrows give a certain picturesqueness to the garden, but after the first day, they fool no one—especially the crows. It is better to use your skills constructing other devices.

First, be neat when you are planting. Do not drop seeds on the surface and leave them uncovered. The crow might have missed seeing you at work, but it will be sure to spy a random kernel of corn here and there and then discover the whole row.

At the risk of inviting slugs, you might try covering your newly planted corn with mulch. By the time the sprouts are poking through their blanket of hay or straw they will be so large that the crows won't be interested. After the plants are well started, pull the mulch aside.

Another solution is to make the seeds unpalatable to the crow. A commercial repellent is on the market or you may soak the seeds briefly in turpentine (one teaspoonful per pound). The crows will not sample more than one. Some repellants retard seed germination.

One determined gardener plants garlic prior to planting corn. After the crows have pulled up the garlic sprouts several times, they lose interest. She then plants the corn and it develops undisturbed. Another method is to plant corn in a shallow trench, and cover the trench with fine mesh poultry wire.

Newly sprouted lettuce leaves seem to be particularly attractive to sparrows and finches. Place a few extra stakes around the garden, then tie thread or string to the stakes, criss-crossing it over the rows. Once the seedlings have a good start, the network can be removed.

Garden net is readily available in several sizes at garden stores. Throw it over berry bushes, dwarf peach and cherry trees, or across strawberry patches. Equally effective and easy to handle is ordinary nylon net available in fabric and variety stores.

The portable cage, described and pictured earlier, is useful to place over strawberry plants as the berries start to ripen.

Cover bunches of grapes with sections of nylon stockings.

Stretch a string over the row of ripening strawberries and suspend strips of aluminum foil or small aluminum pie plates to dangle in the breeze.

A child's whirling toy windmill may help.

The practice of exploding firecrackers in the garden—an old-time remedy—is not greeted enthusiastically in some neighborhoods. If you are trying this method as a last resort, better check your local ordinances.

Opossums

Statistics indicate that other animals cause far more trouble in the garden than does the common opossum, but if the common opossum is troubling you, statistics are not important.

This strange-looking animal has a body length of twelve to twenty inches with a naked tail ten to eighteen inches long. Its hair is extremely soft and shaggy, and its face and ears are hairless. The tiny Marsupial babies are no longer than kidney beans when born. They are carried within the mother's pouch for four to eight weeks, then they are "self-supporting."

The opossum has a reputation for playing dead when cornered—and it usually does. However, never trust an opossum. They have been known to attack and their sharp, curved teeth can inflict painful wounds.

Opossums will eat almost anything—roots, fruit, insects, garbage, birds, and reptiles—and sometimes each other. They are tree dwellers and excellent climbers. Like raccoons, they are nocturnal and wash their food.

To keep the opossums out of your garbage can, fasten the lid on tight and sprinkle ammonia around the area. You can catch opossums easily in a box-type trap using almost anything for bait. Turn them loose a mile or so away from your property or ask the humane society to dispose of them for you.

Squirrels and Chipmunks

Some of the tricks that keep the rabbits, woodchucks, and birds out of your garden will also repel squirrels. Fences are not particularly useful as the squirrels are great climbers and acrobats. Squirrels dislike having anything greasy or sticky on their fur coats, so the mixture of diesel fuel and kerosene sprayed on high grass around the garden will also discourage them.

Squirrel repellent is available, but read the directions carefully and proceed cautiously. Many of the products that are safe around ornamentals and on the bark of fruit trees should not be used in the vicinity of your vegetables. Dried blood or blood meal spread around the garden is a good deterrent but it never should be put directly on the plants.

Squirrels, like raccoons, have a real hankering for juicy sweet corn. If your crop is not too large, protect individual ears with bags, old nylon stockings, or aluminum foil. Sprinkling pepper on the silk will not affect the flavor of the corn.

One gardener plants sunflowers in with the corn as the squirrels in his area seem to prefer the sunflower seeds to the corn. However, if the sunflowers are the desired crop, you have a different problem. About the best thing you can do to protect the seeds is to cover the sunflower heads with old stockings or nylon net.

Live traps can be used to capture the squirrels so that you can carry them to the woods and release them.

Chipmunks usually do little damage in the garden, but they may attack bulbs. Plant your bulbs in wire baskets for protection, or livetrap chipmunks and carry them off to a more appreciative neighborhood. A cat will also deter chipmunks from your garden.

Mice

Knowing that many of the "field mice" that are eating your seeds and bulbs are actually voles doesn't make them any easier to catch. Voles live on the ground, usually in a grassy area. They travel along inch-wide pathways and are active night and day, winter and summer. They can swim and dive. In addition to their athletic prowess, voles manage to eat twice their own weight every twenty-four hours and reproduce at an astounding rate. Meadow voles are usually brown above and lighter beneath. Six inches long, they are slightly larger than a house mouse.

A cat is the best deterrent to field mice in the garden. Voles can be caught in the same traps as house mice or by using one of the live box-type traps designed for catching rats and other small animals. Other "better mouse traps" are on the market and can be purchased from mail order houses.

Mice can be particularly destructive to the bark of young fruit trees. The same plastic wraparound covers used to prevent rabbit damage can be used, or trunks can be surrounded with wire mesh or foil. To prevent damage to flower bulbs, plant mothballs at the same time that the bulbs are planted. In beds where mice and voles are particularly destructive, gardeners sometimes plant their bulbs inside mesh cages. Mice do not like daffodils, hyacinths, scilla, or grape hyacinths. In the vegetable garden, companion plantings of onions and mint will help to keep the mice away. Since heavy mulching provides cover for mice, delay mulching until late in the season.

Skunks

For all their bad reputation, skunks are not major criminals in the vegetable garden. They are helpful in that they eat rats, mice, and insects. They also like fruit, berries, and corn but are not so brazen as the raccoons in going after the corn. There are many tales of skunks eating the leftovers of the corn crop after the raccoons have brought down the ears and eaten what they wanted. They may dig up your lawn in search of grubs.

Skunks sleep by day and feed at night. They are about the size of large house cats, averaging twenty-two to thirty-two inches long, have a plumelike tail, and are easily identified by the white stripes forming a V on their back.

If having a family of skunks near your home makes you uneasy, the best method is to help them move to another neighborhood. A trapped skunk does not use its scent gland and spray unless it is alarmed. Once the skunk has entered the cage of the box trap, it can be safely covered with a cloth and transported. Good bait for the trap is canned cat food or sardines.

The level at which skunks show alarm, and so pungently demonstrate their discomfort, varies with the individual. Thus extreme caution is urged when handling skunks in live traps. In case of failures, we recommend repeated washing with tomato juice, and shampooing the hair with this same juice.

Slugs

You may not object to sharing your vegetables with a cotton-tailed rabbit or a cagey raccoon, but it is hard to love a slug. If a poll were to be taken, slugs would emerge as the #1 enemy of gardeners. All garden crops are attractive to slugs. They eat plant leaves, stems, and roots.

Don't mistake slugs for grubs, the pupa stage of the insect class. Slugs, unfortunately, will not turn into something else. A grub looks a little like a miniature armadillo. A slug is a greasy, gray flat worm with two pairs of tenticles. Its eyes are on the outer end of the longer pair. Slugs are snails that lack shells, and there are about thirty varieties of them. They are hatched from eggs and may reach a length of four inches, if they find enough to eat. They crawl, leaving a wake of slime which tells you where they've been—if you can't tell by the appearance of the plants they have ravaged!

SLUGS WORK AT NIGHT

Knowing something about slugs helps a little in getting rid of them. They cannot survive in areas of high temperature and low humidity. They seek cool, damp places and usually work at night. In the daytime they seek protective covering.

This last characteristic can be particularly frustrating for the gardener. The mulch that keeps the soil moist also provides protection for the slugs. If slugs have become a major problem in your garden, cultivate between the rows, clean up the old debris or mulch, and pile it a distance from the garden or in your compost pile. The slugs will help the composting process.

Slugs seek cover in the daytime, making them a little easier to catch and kill. Lay a few boards or shingles between the rows. The slugs will collect under them and can easily be killed. In fact, a sprinkle of salt causes them to shrivel up and die.

Empty grapefruit rinds or cabbage leaves left in the garden attract slugs. After they have collected under the damp object, they can be easily killed. (If there are children for hire in your neighborhood, pay them a penny apiece for every slug they eradicate—or set your own pay scale. While you're negotiating, you might also establish rates for cabbage worms and other insects.)

Today's gardening literature abounds with homey tips on how to get rid of slugs. The most popular notion is that a container of beer will attract the slugs: They will overimbibe, fall in, and drown. Containers of various shapes and sizes are recommended depending on the authority. One "expert" says that shallow saucers or widemouth jar tops should be used. Another says that beer evaporates too rapidly in open containers. He plants throwaway bottles in the rows with just the tops sticking out, and puts about two inches of beer in the bottom. Beetles as well as slugs fall in. The bottles are replaced a couple of times during the season.

Other authorities claim it is not the beer that attracts the slugs but the yeast that the beer contains. A little "working" sourdough from the kitchen or one teaspoon of dry yeast mixed with three ounces of water may be substituted for the beer with equally good results. But does the beer or yeast attract slugs that would not have come in the first place? Scientists at the Ohio Research and Development Center, Wooster, think it does.

Appendix F: Converting Recipe Measurements to Metric

Use the following chart for converting U.S. measurements to metric. Since these conversions are not exact, it's important to convert the measurements for all of the ingredients to maintain the same proportions as the original recipe.

To convert to	From	Multiply by
milliliters	teaspoons	4.93
milliliters	tablespoons	14.97
milliliters	fluid ounces	29.57
milliliters	cups	236.59
liters	cups	0.236
grams	ounces	28.35

Appendix G: Tinctures, Elixirs, Syrups, Creams, Decoctions, Salves, Ointments, Poultices, and Infused Oils

Making Tinctures, Elixirs, and Syrups

Many tinctures, elixirs, and syrups can be made from the same blend of herbs used to make an herbal tea. As herbalist Gail Ulrich of Blazing Star Herbal School says, the stronger and less-pleasant-tasting herbs may best be prepared as tinctures or capsules. There are some excellent books on making medicinal preparations, so we won't go into a lot of detail here, but will just include a brief introduction to get you started if you want to make tinctures and the like.

MAKING TINCTURES

This is tincture making at its most *simple*, which, interestingly, is the term traditionally applied to single-ingredient tinctures, or simples. In a way, a tincture is a tea, only stronger. In a tea, the herb's properties, or values, are extracted in water, with heat. In a tincture, the values are extracted into a different medium, over time.

It's incredibly easy to make a tincture. You may find it even easier than making tea. Tincturing has some other important advantages. It's more potent and sometimes more palatable than tea. A bottled tincture is infinitely portable, assimilated immediately, can be preserved almost indefinitely, and is attractively cost-effective.

Chop or grind the herbs to release their volatile oils.

Continued ➔

Step 1. If using fresh herbs, coarsely chop or mince. If using dried herbs, powder them first in a coffee grinder or mortar and pestle. Either way, you are trying to release the essential oils and volatile goodies.

Run a knife around the edges of the jar to release air bubbles.

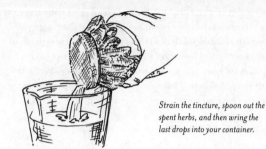

Strain the tincture, spoon out the spent herbs, and then wring the last drops into your container.

TINCTURING WITH ALCOHOL

If tincturing with alcohol, use 80 to 100 proof (40 to 50 percent alcohol), like vodka. Forty percent alcohol is usually sufficient to effectively extract an herb's constituents. When tincturing very resinous herbs such as black sage and yerba santa, or herbs from which it's harder to extract their properties, however, you'll need a higher percentage of alcohol, probably 70 to 90 percent. Brandy has a slightly sweeter taste that many herbalists prefer for throat and lung blends, digestive bitters, and some tonic formulas, and, though it is only 80 proof (40 percent alcohol), it is sufficient for most tinctures.

Caution: Never use isopropyl alcohol (also called rubbing alcohol) for internal use.

Step 2. Place the processed herbs in a widemouthed jar in which the herbs make up about a quarter of the volume. For example if the herbs represent 1/2 cup (119 ml), the container should hold 2 cups (474 ml) total. Cover the herbs with twice as much liquid if using fresh herbs and three times as much liquid if using dried herbs. Use the liquid of your choice: apple cider vinegar, glycerin, and alcohol such as brandy or vodka are the most common. Blend well, then run a dull knife around the edges of the jar to release any lingering air bubbles.

Step 3. Close the jar tightly. If you're tincturing in vinegar, you may want to cover the top of the jar with plastic wrap to prevent the corrosive action of vinegar from rusting the lid shut. Label and date the jar.

Step 4. Store the jar in a cool, dark place and let sit for 2 to 4 weeks. Shake the jar daily, making sure that the plant material remains covered by alcohol.

Step 5. Strain the liquid through a piece of cheesecloth into a glass or stainless-steel bowl. Then spoon the spent herbs out onto the cheesecloth. Gather the cheesecloth around them and wring out any additional tincture.

Step 6. Using a funnel, pour the tincture into a glass bottle, preferably of dark glass. (Don't forget to label your bottles, or you won't know what you have when you're done!) Store at room temperature. If you prefer, bottle into smaller dark glass bottles with eyedropper tops for more convenient use.

Bottle the tincture in a dark glass container.

TINCTURE DOSAGES

Obviously, when you have a wide range of human health, weight, and constitutions to factor into an equally varied range of herb properties and strengths, the proper dosage for a tincture will vary just as much. Generally, though, 1 to 2 dropperfuls of tincture one to five times per day is appropriate. You may add the tincture to a little water or tea. Be aware, however, that a dropperful of bitter tincture can make an entire cup of tea bitter. We suggest pouring off 2 tablespoons (30 ml) of tea and adding the tincture to that. Let the tea sit for 5 minutes, and most of the alcohol will evaporate. Now you're drinking 2 tablespoons (30 ml) with a strong taste, not an entire cup. You'll thank us for this tip! This technique also works well for those not wanting to ingest alcohol.

MAKING ELIXIRS

An elixir is a delicious, fruity, and festive concoction, typically a tonic formula to nourish and support a particular body system such as heart, brain, or immune. The basic method is to choose your herbs, cover with three times as much brandy, add any of the yummy and nourishing flavor-enhancing ingredients from the list in the box, and tincture as you would normally, for 2 to 4 weeks. When done, strain and add 1/10 part maple syrup or honey. Take 1 teaspoon (5 ml) to 1 tablespoon (15 ml) once or twice per day.

MAKING SYRUPS

Here's an interesting technique for making syrups, what could be described as the "Super Bowl of herbal teas." These are thick, soothing, highly flavorful, and potent beverages, usually made with fruit and sipped as needed for tonic benefits.

First, prepare a tea, simmering for 1 to 2 hours in a covered pot. Remove from heat and allow to steep another 1 to 2 hours, stirring occasionally. Strain out all the solids, squeezing all the liquid through cheesecloth. Measure the volume of tea, then add half to three quarters as much molasses plus 1/4 part brandy (as a preservative). Other recipes will vary slightly, but this is the basic method.

MAKING CREAMS

Herbal creams are easy to make. At your drugstore, buy a cream base that is hypoallergenic. Put this in the top of a double boiler and heat over boiling water, with the selected herbs, for 2 hours. (Unless otherwise directed, use about 1 ounce of dried herbs or 2 1/2 ounces of fresh herbs per 10 ounces of cream base.) Remove from heat, strain through a cheesecloth, and pack into jars. Seal tightly and keep in a cool, dark place.

MAKING A BASIC DECOCTION OR INFUSION

There are two ways to prepare herbal tea. You can make an infusion, in which the herb is steeped, or you can make a decoction, in which the plant matter is simmered over time.

Infusions. To extract medicinal properties from leaves, flowers, berries, or seeds, you'll want to infuse them. These ingredients easily release their essential oils when they're steeped in hot water—and they easily lose their value when they're simmered. To infuse a cup of tea, pour 1 cup (237 ml) boiling water over 1 to 2 teaspoons (5–10 ml) dried herbs or 2 to 4 teaspoons (10–20 ml) fresh herbs. Cover, let steep 10 to 15 minutes, strain well, and drink.

Decoctions. Decoctions are made by simmering root, bark, and other woody parts of the plant, then drinking the cooled liquid. The simmering is necessary to extract the valuable properties. To decoct a cup of tea, add 2 teaspoons (10 ml) dried root to 1 cup (237 ml) water. Cover, bring to a boil, then simmer 15 to 20 minutes. Strain the herbs (they make a nice addition to your compost pile!) and enjoy.

Combinations. When you're making a tea with both roots and leaves, you'll both infuse and decoct: Simmer the roots 20 minutes, remove the pot from the heat, add the leaves and stir, then cover and steep 10 to 20 minutes.

MAKING A SALVE

Salves are used for a variety of skin problems, as well as to provide protection against the elements. At room temperature, they'll last for several months; in the refrigerator, they'll keep for up to a year.

Step 1: Cover the herbs with oil. Gather 2 to 3 ounces (56–84 g) of dried or freshly wilted herb and 1 pint (473 ml) of olive oil. Then use one of two methods for infusing the herbs in the oil:

- **Stovetop method.** Combine the herbs and oil in the top part of a double boiler. Heat over boiling water for at least 40 minutes, then remove from heat.

- **The sun method.** Put the herb in a jar and cover with oil, making sure there are 2 to 3 inches (5–8 cm) of oil over the top of the herb. Run a knife around the edge of the jar to release any trapped air bubbles. Set the jar in a warm, dry place, such as a sunny windowsill or on top of a water heater, for 2 to 6 weeks.

Step 2: Strain the oil. Press the mixture through cheesecloth to separate the oil from the spent plant matter.

Step 3: Add beeswax. To give the salve the proper consistency, combine the infused oil with 1/4 cup (59 ml) grated beeswax for each cup of oil in the top of a double boiler. Heat until the beeswax is completely melted and the ingredients are thoroughly combined.

Step 4: Test the consistency. You can test the consistency by taking a spoonful of the mixture and putting it in the refrigerator for a minute or two. If it becomes too hard, add more oil. If it doesn't harden, add a bit more beeswax.

Heat the beeswax in a double boiler, stirring constantly so that it doesn't burn.

Continued ➜

Step 5: Bottle. When the consistency of the salve seems right to you, divide the mixture among several glass containers. Allow to cool, then seal them tightly. Store in the refrigerator, where the salve will keep for up to two years.

MAKING AN OINTMENT

Unlike a salve, ointments aren't absorbed into the skin. Rather, they form a layer over it, protecting it from moisture. Like salves, they'll keep for several months at room temperature, and up to a year in the refrigerator.

Step 1: Melt the base. In the top of a double boiler, melt about 20 ounces (560 g) of either petroleum jelly or paraffin wax for every 2 ounces (56 g) of herb.

Step 2: Add the herb. Stir in the herb and heat about 2 hours.

Step 3: Strain and bottle. Now strain the mix into glass jars. Allow to cool before sealing tight.

MAKING POULTICES AND PLASTERS

Poultices and plasters are applied directly to the skin to relieve inflammation, blood poisoning, venomous bites, and the like. They help cleanse the area and draw out infection, toxins, and foreign bodies. They also relieve pain and muscle spasms.

Poultices. A poultice is a warm, moist mass of powdered or crushed fresh herb. To make a poultice, moisten the herb with hot water, witch hazel, herbal tea, or herbal tincture and apply to the skin. If necessary, reapply after it cools. (In a pinch, you can also make a poultice by chewing the herbs and applying them directly to the skin.)

Plasters. A plaster is just like a poultice except that the herb is placed between two thin pieces of cloth instead of applied directly to the area.

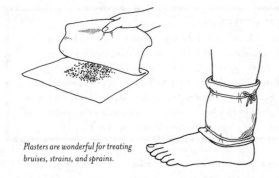

Plasters are wonderful for treating bruises, strains, and sprains.

MAKING INFUSED OILS

The Sun Method

Begin with top-quality extra-virgin olive oil.

Step 1. Fill a clean, dry, widemouthed glass jar to the top, loosely packed, with fresh flowers. Cover with the oil and stir with a nonmetal utensil—such as a wooden spoon or chopstick—to release any trapped air bubbles. Top off with more oil, seal, and set in a warm, dry spot, such as a sunny windowsill or the top of a water heater, for 2 to 6 weeks.

Step 2. Press the oil through cheesecloth to filter out the spent plant matter. Then let the oil stand so any water will separate. Pour off the water and store the oil in a sealed container in the refrigerator, where it will keep for up to 6 months.

The Stovetop Method

Step 1. For a yield of 2 cups (475 ml), use 2 cups (550 ml) of dried herbs to 4 cups (950 ml) of oil. Place the herbs in a double boiler, then cover with the oil. Heat, uncovered, over boiling water for about 3 hours. Don't let the oil bubble or smoke—long, slow cooking produces the best result.

Step 2. Strain the oil by lining a wire strainer with muslin or a coffee filter. Place the herbs in the strainer, then press to remove as much liquid as possible.

Step 3. Bottle the liquid and store in the refrigerator, where it will keep for up to 6 months.

Appendix H:
Buying Country Land

By Peggy Tonseth

Illustrations by Elayne Sears

So, you want to move to the country? Give up dirty air, noise, and congestion? You want to live the good life, you say. Grow your own food. Be self-sufficient. Good. Do it.

But before you do, know what you are getting into. Learn which of your dreams you can fulfill easily, which will require time and money. And then, go for it.

First, let's start with you and what you want to do with your country property.

The kind of land you look for will be determined by what you intend to make of it. Your requirements will be very different if you are planning to live in town and vacation on your land than if you plan to homestead. Do you want a vacation home with good fishing? Then buy land near bodies of water. Are you a hunter? Then you will want to be near good woodland. If you want to homestead, you will need tillable land, a woodlot, and, probably, pasture land.

Some people buy land with several uses in mind. For example, they may want to vacation on it now and retire to farm it later.

Here are a few things for you to think about, before you start looking for land. How important are neighbors to you? While it is romantic to visualize yourself independently facing the elements, away from everyone, private, quiet, and alone, these things can have their harsh sides in times of emergency, especially for older people and those who live alone. Also consider the distance to a general store and to a decent hospital. Each is vital in its own way.

If you have children or are anticipating them, consider schools and facilities for child care. Don't look just at the quality, but also check out things like distance to travel, costs, and opportunities for outside activities for the children.

Transportation is an item to think about for everyone living in the country. Rarely will you find any form of public transportation. People who commute to work or transport marketable items must think about the effect gasoline shortages and increased prices will have. For the family depending on the farm income to live, the gasoline issue will be among the very serious ones.

SERVICES

Some rural areas do not have the services that most of us take for granted: water and sewage disposal, for instance, and trash collection. Ask at the town or county clerk's office about road maintenance to make sure that the property you are looking at is on a maintained road.

There are places that have no electricity or telephone lines. Can you afford to extend these lines? In most places, the telephone company and the power company work together to install their lines. You will want to ask both companies what the current procedure and prices are.

Finally, be sure to look at the property in different seasons. Land features which are apparent at one time of year may be hidden or very different at another time. For example, in the spring, there may be plenty of water to use for farming and building a pond; but by August, it may have dried up, no available water at all.

How to Find Pieces of Land

Begin your search by visiting the area you have chosen to move to, subscribing to local newspapers, and getting in touch with several real estate people.

The real estate advertisements in the local papers will give you introductory information, what price ranges to consider, and where land is available. In addition, you can find legal notices of properties to be sold for delinquent taxes, mortgage foreclosures, and estate settlements (more about these later). The real asset in having the local paper is in learning about the area in which you plan to make a large investment.

REAL ESTATE AGENTS

If you have decided to use a real estate agent, begin by contacting several of them. Tell them what you are looking for and see how they react to you. If you do end up purchasing land through an agent, you will want to know that person well enough to understand his or her idiosyncrasies.

After trying a few agents, you can decide how you will interact with the real estate people. Some buyers choose the agent they like most and stick loyally to him or her. There are some advantages to this. One broker told me that if a customer is looking exclusively with her, she works harder, knowing that she will have a sale, that it is only a question of her finding the right property. She begins to build up a relationship with the customer, challenging herself to find the right property. She throws herself into the project as though it were her own.

The other side of the coin is that some agents will become complacent knowing that you are their client only. These brokers will work harder for you if there is the element of competition with others who have property listings in the same area.

Keep in mind that you need pay nothing to be shown property. Real estate dealers have many services for you the buyer, but their money comes from the seller. They may make you feel that they have your interests at heart, and because you are the prospect with the money, perhaps they do; legally they represent the sellers. This may seem like a minor point, but it is worth remembering.

PRIVATE SALES

As you look at properties with the real estate agents, you should follow up on private sales advertisements as well. Find them in both local

Continued ➔

newspapers and magazines that specialize in country living, newspapers of nearby cities, and real estate advertisements.

When you see what you like, make an appointment; visit the property; walk the boundaries with the owners; talk to them about their experiences with the property. Any information you can get now will help you later.

If you become interested in the property, visit the neighbors and talk to local residents who might know something about the land. If you are very certain that you want to buy the property, retain the services of a good, *local* lawyer. He will know the people you are dealing with, and he can get the legal work done more easily.

It is especially important in private sales that you protect yourself from well-meaning, uninformed sellers. For example, the owner may be happy with his "100 acres more or less" and may have spent his whole life making a living on that amount of land. In fact, the "100 acres more or less" may turn out to be 60 or 120 acres. The only way to know for sure is to have a survey done. Then you will not be in the position of having purchased two-thirds of what you expected.

Old-timers will tell you that most "more or less" deeds actually have many more acres than stated. I know a couple who had a plot of land which was described as "178 acres more or less." It turned out to be 265.5 acres when surveyed. However, fewer stories are told about the purchaser of "60 acres more or less" who ended up with 39.1 surveyed acres. These stories are not as much fun to tell.

Reputable real estate dealers should be able to recommend qualified surveyors.

FERRETING OUT LAND FOR SALE

There is another way to find private sales. Properties may not actually be on the market. A farmer may be decreasing his production and may welcome the idea of extra income from a land sale. Perhaps there is property for sale that just is not being advertised for some reason. Ferreting out this kind of property can be an adventure and a challenge.

SURVEYING

Surveying costs are relative to the difficulty of the job. A local (Vermont) survey company charges $50 per hour for a two-person crew and $75 per hour for a three-person crew for field work. Office work is $50 per hour. An average small survey (one to three acres) for this company is about $600–$1000. This includes paying the people to do the field work, pinning every corner, setting out metes and bounds from which deeds can be drawn, a plan (map) which is recorded in the registry of deeds, and all environmental tests.

Start by becoming familiar with local people. Patronize the general store and the local eatery. Talk to people and tell them what you want. Usually people are happy to be helpful and will tell you about land they know is for sale or about to become for sale. These contacts will get you started talking to others. In addition, you will become acquainted with the local history and customs. It's a long process, one of building relationships and trust.

Perhaps the most effective way to get to know a community and become comfortable there is to rent a home in the area while you are looking to buy. People may consider you more as a new neighbor this way than as an out-of-towner.

Many books suggest that you go out and find pieces of property that appeal to you. Then approach the owners to ask if they are willing to sell.

I asked several landowners near me how they felt about that suggestion. I thought they might feel that it was an invasion of their privacy. Consistently they said that it was appropriate or not, according to the approach that people used.

For example, one woman said that when prospective buyers inquire in a straightforward manner, she respects their quest and tries to think of other landowners who they may call. She recalled one man, however, who telephoned and insisted that she show him a parcel of her land. He implied that since she owned "so much land" she must be willing to sell him some. When she told him none was for sale, he continued pressuring her. She felt his behavior was uncalled for and did not suggest other people for him to call.

AUCTIONS

Another source of property for sale is the land auction. Usually these sales occur when the owner has defaulted on a mortgage, has not paid property taxes for a long time, or when the property is part of an estate settlement.

You will find land auctions advertised in local papers. They are similar to any other kind of auction; the parcels are sold to the highest bidder.

Some auctions are conducted with sealed bids. This means you submit a sealed offer to the bank estate executor, or person in charge of the sale. At an appointed time, the offers are opened, and whoever made the highest bid is awarded the sale.

There is a risk in mortgage default and delinquent tax sales. In most places, a waiting period is provided after the sale, during which the previous owner can reclaim his property. It is the buyer's responsibility to protect himself from this complication. Contact the auctioneer or local authorities to know the exact situation before getting involved. Procedures may vary from auctioneer to auctioneer and from town to town.

Sources of Information on Land

Accurate information is probably the best safeguard against buying the wrong property.

Where can you find accurate information? Books, magazine articles, and bulletins are good first sources. They will get you asking the kinds of questions you need to have answered. Be wary of publication dates, however; accurate information ten or twenty years ago could be very misleading today.

Next, you might want to go to the local real estate people. They can give you general ideas about how to get started looking for property. If you already have found a piece of land, the real estate person can answer specific questions about it, such as whether any studies, soil tests, water investigations, or surveys have been done and who did the testing.

MAPS

Several different types of maps can be consulted for a variety of information.

The local planning board should have maps that detail planned growth within the town. The zoning commission will have a map of the town showing zones and the restrictions within the zones. Check with the town clerk for these maps.

The United States Geological Survey has prepared "quadrangle" maps for the entire United States. Also called "topos" (topographic maps), they indicate elevation with contour lines. These maps include towns, roads, railroads, bodies of water, rivers, and other geographic features. It is useful to compare these maps to aerial photographs.

An aerial photograph can help you see other geographical features that you would not notice from the ground—especially, the extent of erosion, vegetation, and timber. Most of the land mass of the United States has been photographed systematically. The town or county clerk, or the soil conservation agent, can tell you how to find aerial photos for the land you are looking at.

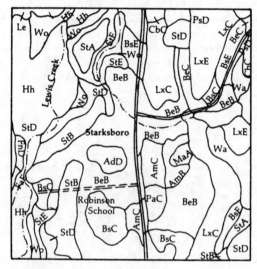

Scale 4 inches = mile

AdD	Adams 12 to 30% slopes
AmB	Amenia stony, 0 to 8% slopes
AmC	Amenia stony, 8 to 15% slopes
BeB	Berkshire and Marlow, 3 to 12% slopes
BeC	Berkshire and Marlow, 12 to 25% slopes
BsC	Berkshire and Marlow extremely stony, 3 to 20% slopes
BsE	Berkshire and Marlow extremely stony, 20 to 50% slopes
CbC	Cabot extremely stony, 0 to 15% slopes
FaC	Farmington extremely rocky, 5 to 20% slopes
Hh	Hadley, frequently flooded
Le	Limerick
LxC	Lyman-Berkshire very rocky, 5 to 20% slopes
LxE	Lyman-Berkshire very rocky, 20 to 50% slopes
MaA	Massena stony, 0 to 3% slopes
PsD	Peru extremely stony, 20 to 50% slopes
StA	Stetson, 0 to 5% slopes
StB	Stetson, 5 to 12% slopes
StD	Stetson, 12 to 30% slopes
StE	Stetson, 30 to 50% slopes
Wa	Walpole
Wo	Winooski

Soil survey maps will provide you with invaluable information. Soil survey maps locate the extent of different kinds of soils, as shown in this drawing. Each soil type mapped is described in terms of its color, texture, depth, drainage capacity, and so on. A soil survey map can tell you whether the land is suitable for farming, forestry, and building (including the possibility for adequate septic tank filter fields).

GOVERNMENT AGENCIES

Cooperative Extension Service. Each county has a cooperative extension agent for agriculture, home economics, youth, community resources and development, energy, and farm family rehabilitation. Each of these agents has a differing area of expertise. The agriculture agent, in particular, is able to discuss land fertility, different crops, markets, and agricultural opportunities, and can provide in-depth information about all aspects of farming in that particular locale. Some agents may walk over the land with you, pointing out strong and weak points. Some may even give you personal advice about purchasing and people to contact.

Soil Conservation Service. There is a soil conservation service agent in almost every county in this country. One agent told me that he was willing to go out on the prospective land and walk around with the purchaser to discuss the water and erosion problems. He can tell whether a farm pond is feasible, whether the soil is deep or shallow, and what the remedies might be for each type of erosion problem.

Supposing the real estate broker tells you that there is a pond site on the property. You go there to look, and sure enough there is a marshy, swampy area. If you consult the soil conservation agent, however, you may find that there is no possible way to build a pond at that site, either because of the conditions now, or because of the conditions which would result after the pond is built.

Perhaps the house was recently built on a clayey soil which shrinks and swells. It could mean that the foundation and walls will crack, forcing continual expensive maintenance work. The soil conservation agent can alert you to that kind of hazard.

The Soil Conservation Service provides maps and information on all of the following for specific areas within their county:

· Detailed soil identifications (and explanations of soil types)

· Seasonal high water table

· Flood plains

· Degree of slopes

· Depth to bedrock

· Potential for farming

· Potential for forestry

· Potential for septic systems

Character of the Land

Your introduction to the land will be a walk with the owners or real estate people. Presumably, they will be talking to you about the larger features: the view, the hills, the buildings. These things are important

Continued ➜

for the first impression. As you walk over the land looking for views and nice building sites, check the soil and water, make some notes about the character of the land. I always draw a profile of the land as it appears to me. Then I compare it with the real estate broker's ideas and the written description in the office.

First, I look at the degree and direction toward which the land slopes. Gently rolling hills will be easier to build on, more tillable, and more open to sunlight than steep banks.

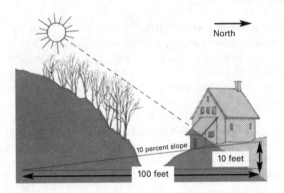

Both degree and direction of slope are important considerations. This south-facing slope has the potential for providing the home with solar energy. In general, the site will be warmer and drier than a north-facing slope. The house was built on a steep slope (the grade here is 10 percent, meaning that every 100 feet, the elevation increases by 10 feet). This slope will make road building and maintenance difficult and the land would be somewhat steep for farming.

The easiest soils to cultivate are level, or sloping slightly. For most agricultural purposes, land should not slope more than 12 to 15 percent. This is the same for house building. Although roads can be built on steeper grades, towns will not accept maintenance of such roads. For pastures and woodlands, there need be no concern for slope. The old story that cows will develop two shorter legs on their uphill side if they graze on steep mountainsides has yet to be proven to my satisfaction!

The best slope for most crops is to the south. The soil gets more sun longer in the day on a southern slope. The sun provides warmth earlier in the spring and helps dry out wet soil. Seeds germinate earlier in the southern exposure, too.

Other things I note in my land profile are: How much rocky, ledgey land is there? What is the altitude and will that make a difference in the use? How much is wooded and how much is open land? If the cultivated fields are to be restored, how much work will have to be done?

How much is swampy, wet land? Two other important aspects of the land have to do with water: flood plains and seasonally high water tables. A flood plain is the flat land near a river which may be covered with water when the river floods. Flooding may happen only once in a hundred years, but there is always that danger. As a potential landowner, you should at least be aware of the possibility, and be wary of buying land that is wholly on a flood plain.

The water table refers to the level in the soil below which it is saturated with water. If you dig a hole below the water table, it will fill up with water. The water table goes up and down according to the season and the amount of precipitation. Some land has a large seasonable variation in the levels of water. Thus, if you buy land with a seasonably

high water table, you may experience floodlike conditions in the spring: cellars full of water, plant roots drowned. Late summer may bring droughtlike conditions or no water at all.

Once you have your land character profile made and you have compared it to others, you will be able to see how well the land will fit in with your plans.

Looking at the Soil

The foundation of any land is the soil. It is the basis for everything you will do with your land: plant crops, raise animals, build buildings, transport water, or use your land recreationally.

Especially important if you are planning to farmstead is knowing what soils there are and what can be done to make the land support your needs.

Important aspects of soil information are the fertility (what nutrients it has), the composition, and the depth.

Some of the following things you can check on your first visits to the land. Others take more time. If everything looks green and healthy, the first indications are good. Then you need to look more closely. Since it is important to return in different seasons, you should have plenty of opportunity to check out the kinds of vegetation the soil supports.

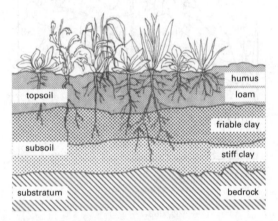

The depth of soil is determined by the total thickness of the topsoil and subsoil. These are the areas that plant roots can be expected to extend through. Deep soils extend at least thirty-six inches; moderately deep soils extend down twenty to thirty-six inches; shallow soils are ten to twenty inches deep; and very shallow soils are less than ten inches deep.

SOIL TESTS

An ideal soil would be moderately fine textured, deep (3 to 5 feet of topsoil), teeming with bacteria and fungi, adequately moist, well-aerated, well-drained, have a neutral pH, be easy to cultivate (have good tilth), and be level (not sloping).

Texture. The best soil texture is a mixture of sand and silt, stirred up with rotting organic material. A handful should be friable (easily crumbled), and should have a mixture of granule sizes.

Depth. Dig a hole and see how much loose, friable soil there is before you hit the tightly packed subsoil. When you hit bedrock or ledge, measure depth of soil to bedrock.

Organic decomposition. Dig out a shovelful of topsoil. Are there rotting leaves or roots and stems? Look for earthworms and evidence of bacteria and fungi. Take a handful. Is it blackish and crumbly and even a bit smelly? If so, then there is organic action.

Adequately moist. The soil should make a ball but not be sticky and wet feeling.

Well aerated. When you took your shovelful out, did the particles break up easily? Did you see lots of tiny air spaces? If it is stuck together so that you could not break off a handful easily, it is probably too dry and not well aerated.

Well drained. Poorly drained soil has standing water or evidence of water having "sat around" on top of the soil. For a crude check: pour buckets of water on the soil and see how quickly it soaks in. Well-drained soil will absorb the water easily.

Testing pH. Make a ball of earth, cut it in half, and sandwich a piece of litmus paper (easily purchased in hardware stores or drugstores) between the two halves. The color, reds for acidity, blues for alkalinity, can be matched up to a chart to determine pH values from 4.5 (very acidic) to 7.5 (alkaline).

Tilth. This is the looseness, or mellowness, of the soil—the result of good cultivation. If a handful of soil is friable, if it crumbles easily in your hand, if it is rich-looking, it has good tilth.

What is soil? Soil is basically mineralized rock particles. It was formed over thousands of years from the bedrock deposited by the glaciers. Vegetation grew, died, and became part of the soil. Microbes,

worms, and insects broke down the vegetation into usable nutrients for more plant growth. Most natural soils that have not been cultivated will have three basic layers: the bedrock (substratum), soil particles on top of bedrock (subsoil), and the soil particles mixed with organic matter above that (topsoil).

DEPTH OF THE SOIL

Most of the growing for vegetables, grains, trees, weeds, and flowers takes place in the topsoil. It is the element that should concern you most.

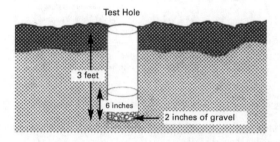

A percolation test will determine how quickly water will drain, a factor in locating a septic system. Dig at least six test holes, each three feet deep and twelve inches in diameter. Add two inches of gravel; then fill with twelve inches of water. Maintain that water level for four hours. Then let the water drain to six inches above the gravel. Next, measure the drop in water level every thirty minutes. Multiply by two to determine the percolating rate per hour. Determine the average rate from the test holes. A drainage rate slower than 2 1/2 inches per hour is insufficient for sanitation.

Topsoil can be lost in two ways. Nutrients can be taken out by continual planting and harvesting. If the nutrients are not replaced, then the soil gets used up. It becomes a sterile medium and will not grow healthy crops. The other way topsoil is lost is through wind and water erosion. In some places, all the topsoil has been blown away leaving subsoil bare to the elements. If there is no topsoil, the nutrients for growth may be locked in the subsoil.

Soil (topsoil and subsoil) that is less than three to six inches down to bedrock will grow virtually nothing and cannot be cultivated by usual means. Frequently, in New England, there is practically no topsoil. Where there is no subsoil, either, cultivation is nearly impossible. Where there is deep subsoil, remedial action can be taken in the form of adding manure, compost, and fertilizers, and a great deal of work.

For forestry pursuits, depth of soil to bedrock must be more than sixteen inches to sustain tree growth. Shallower soil may support shrubs, Christmas trees, or berry bushes, but not timber trees.

A final comment about soil depth is that septic tank effluent requires certain depths of soil. There are no rules of thumb, but the denser the soil and the smaller the particles, the greater the depth needed to absorb the effluents. Clayey soil is very dense. The converse is that gravel soil will absorb more effluent more quickly and can be shallower than fine silt to do the same job.

SOIL DRAINAGE

Soil must be well drained and well aerated for organic action to take place. This means that it will crumble easily in your hand and that water soaks into it rapidly. If the soil is wet and tightly compacted, it will retard growth and be unsuitable for septic systems. A percolation test will tell you whether the soil drains well.

INDICATORS OF POOR SOILS

scrub or bear oak

Jersey or scrub pine

ox-eye daisy

common mullein

wild carrot

Continued →

SOIL ACIDITY

All soils are "sour" (acidic) or "sweet" (alkaline). A neutral soil has a pH of 7. Usually, soils are naturally acidic (low pH) because the by-product of organic decay is hydrogen (acid). Usually, cultivated plants prefer a more neutral soil than is found naturally. Farmers often compensate by spreading crushed limestone to make the soil "sweeter." You can test for soil acidity easily with a home soil sample test kit.

Add a tablespoon of soil and a few drops of ammonia to a glass two-thirds filled with rainwater. Stir. Check the water in two hours. Clear water indicates sweet, or alkaline, soil; dark indicates a sour, or acidic, sample.

Checklist for Evaluating the Soil

As a potential homesteader, you should make yourself aware of as much as possible about the soil.

_____What is the condition of the topsoil? Is it fertile?

_____Is it shallow or deep?

_____How deep is the total soil to bedrock?

_____Is there good aeration, drainage, moisture, and organic material?

_____Is the soil acidic or alkaline?

_____What is the potential of the land for farming or for forestry?

Water

To support life, there must be water. The land you look at may have access to town water. Generally, though, rural land is too far from the town source, and, thus, you must provide your own.

EXISTING WATER SYSTEMS

If the property has a developed water system in place, get as much information as you can about it. Ask the owners, or real estate agent, then consult the farm agents, well-drillers, and neighbors to verify what you learn.

Checklist for Existing Water Systems

Source of water

_____Spring

_____Dug well

_____Drilled or driven well

Pump System

_____None, gravity feed (Source is high enough above the house to create plenty of pressure.)

_____Pump at site

_____Submersible

_____Above ground

_____Pump in house

Check the condition and age of pump, pipes, holding tanks, and well houses.

Quality of Water

_____Needs filtering

_____Is easily contaminated

_____Is hard or soft

Quantity of Water

_____1/2 gallon or less per minute (720 gallons or less a day)

_____1/2 gallon to 2 gallons per minute (720 to 2,880 gallons a day)

_____2 gallons to 5 gallons per minute (2,880 to 7,200 gallons a day)

Variability of water supply

_____Constant throughout the year

_____Plenty in spring, little in late summer

LOOKING FOR WATER SOURCES

When buying undeveloped land, do not expect any water system on the property. But the owner may have identified springs and other sources of ground water.

If there is no knowledge of water on a piece of land, take the initiative and walk over it looking at the wet spots. Do they "spring" out of the ground? If there appear to be springs, dig carefully around the wet area and look for the source. You may have found a true spring, or it may be a small stream that has gone underground for a little way.

Theoretically, springs are clear, cool water coming from deep underground. The water is purified by filtering through many layers of soil. This type of source is considered ground water. Although frequently pure, springs can be contaminated by surface water (rain, snow melt, brooks, lakes). If you decide to rely on springs on the land, you should have them tested for purity. Contact the local health officials.

Another way to find water is to dig a well. A hand-dug well usually is done where there is known water—a small marshy spot in the midst of a dry woodsy area, or a stream beginning on a hillside.

If the owner will permit it, dig a deep hole and observe what the water does over time. Try to drain the hole by bailing out the water and then timing how long it takes to fill up. The longer you can watch—days, weeks, months—the better.

A major difficulty with springs and dug wells is their unreliability. They may dry up during the summer, and they are easily polluted. Many people who have springs or wells will live with the drying up summer after summer. Eventually they may turn to the well-driller and seek a more reliable source of water.

Record to the second the time it takes a one-gallon or two-gallon bucket to fill. Then convert that figure to gallons per minute.

1036

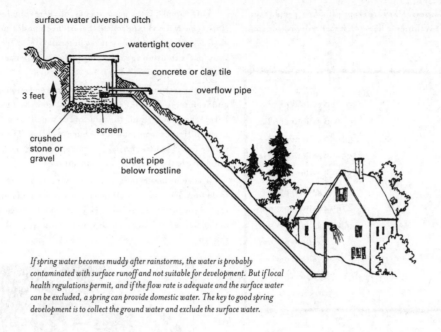

If spring water becomes muddy after rainstorms, the water is probably
contaminated with surface runoff and not suitable for development. But if local
health regulations permit, and if the flow rate is adequate and the surface water
can be excluded, a spring can provide domestic water. The key to good spring
development is to collect the ground water and exclude the surface water.

VARIOUS TYPES OF WELL CONSTRUCTION

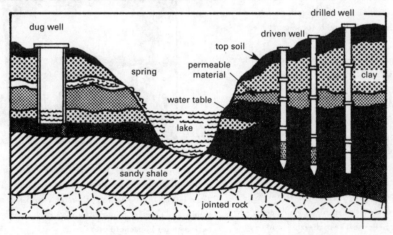

DRILLING FOR WATER

If you find a piece of land on which there is no obvious water, no
springs, and you have no luck finding places to dig for water, you will
want to consult a well-driller for advice.

Our county extension agent has a list of "Landowner Services"
which names a variety of services, the types of equipment the services
use, and the distances they will travel. The list is free. It includes well-
drillers, fence-builders, field mowers, haulers, and many more. Check
to see if this information is available in the area you are considering.

Drilling for water is a chancy business. Some drilling companies
will tell you where they think they should drill for water. Others refuse
to take that responsibility; they ask you to decide where they should
drill.

A local driller told me that in Vermont and New Hampshire the
average cost for a drilled well is $2,500 to $3,500 (1988 prices). This
includes drilling the well, installing the casing down to bedrock, the
cost of the pump, and its installation. The **average** depth of wells in that
area is 220 to 230 feet. He cautioned that this is only an average.

There is no scientific way to determine where water is, nor how far
down one would have to drill. For example, several wells on one side of a
hill might be about 130 feet deep, and wells on the other side could be
400 to 500 feet deep. The deeper you go, the more it will cost you.

Should you trust a dowser to locate water on your land? That's a
completely individual decision. Dowsers, or "water witches," hold
forked sticks or metal rods on pendulums in such a way that they point
downward when underground sources of water are located. Many people

Continued ➔

swear by the accuracy of dowsers. Many are skeptical. Some people are willing to try many different things in hopes that each will provide some usable information.

Water is a necessity. Beware of the person who treats this subject with nonchalance. If water is unknown, get as much information as you possibly can prior to purchasing. Take samples of the soil, do tests, do anything you can to determine whether the gamble for water is reasonable.

A soil conservation service agent I talked to commented that "there is no way anybody can guarantee water... It's one of the chances a purchaser has to take. He can get the best information available if he looks for it, but it's still a chance."

The main thing is to try to be as certain as possible that there is good water, that it is reliable throughout the year, and that the system functions well with a minimum of maintenance.

Value of Land

The value of land depends largely on the needs of the person evaluating it.

The most basic way to look at value is to determine your needs. Any land that satisfies your particular needs will be high-value land to you.

Another way to look at it is to find the monetary value of land per acre at today's market value. Look at similar parcels that have sold within the recent past and are reasonably close to the piece you are trying to evaluate. Calculate their value by applying one of the many formulas to those sales. These formulas can be found in books or gotten from the local assessors. The simplest formula, but perhaps a slightly misleading one, is to divide the purchase price equally by the number of acres. You will come up with a dollar-value per acre which you can use for rough estimation.

Be sure to research land sales to make certain that the asking price on the parcel you are considering is not out of line with other real estate in the area. Records of sales in town or county clerks' offices are one source of information. Checking around among real estate people is another.

A third way to view the idea of value is to determine what cash crops can be raised on the land, find a dollar value of projected income from these crops, and calculate from there.

For example, if the property has four acres of fair-quality land that slopes gently toward the south, that has been under cultivation, that is slightly acidic, you may view it as a potential strawberry farm. Contact your local extension agent for cultivation costs per acre for equipment, plants, cash expense, and possible cash return.

Other cash crops to consider are cordwood, timber, maple syrup, and fruit trees. See your extension agent for assistance. A few cautions here. When considering the value of cordwood, be aware that one wood is very different from another in burning value. The best burning value will be found in hickory, oak, hard maples, and beech. The poorest woods are balsam, aspen, and white pine.

To decide how many acres you must have, first decide what you want to do for work, what you will need for income, and how much available capital you have to invest in stock and equipment. Keep in mind that the dollar figures will vary according to area, time, weather, and health of the crop.

When considering the value of apple trees, be aware that trees left to grow wild will be extremely difficult to prune back into production. Trees left on their own more than ten years often are not commercially viable, and trees let go more than twenty years may never be brought back even for household use.

When considering maple syrup production, be aware that access to the trees during the end of the winter and beginning of spring is a serious matter. If you are making a gallon of syrup for your own kitchen, you may not mind clomping through snow and slush to collect sap two or three times a day. If you are producing quantities, this becomes a huge burden.

To you, the purchaser, the value of land must be at least equal to the price and that price must be within your capacity to pay.

RESALE

You haven't even bought your country property, yet, and I'm talking about resale. That's a bit premature, isn't it? No, not really.

You must be aware that once you have purchased your land, your plans may not work out. Regardless of the reasons, it will help you at that time to have some idea of how easy or difficult it will be to resell your property. Certainly you do not want to have an albatross if the country living experiment does not work out.

A ballpark resale figure can be arrived at by averaging the rate of inflation over some years back, adding that to the purchase price, and adding in what you estimate it will cost you to improve or renovate the property. Thus, if you buy a farm for $50,000 and the average rate of inflation is 12 percent, and if you figure you will have to invest $20,000 in the farm over a two-year period, at the end of that time you will have to sell your farm for a minimum of $82,720 just to get your money back.

$50,000	purchase price
6.0012	percent inflation first year
6.27012	percent inflation second year
	($50,000 + $6,000)
20,000	improvements over 2 years
$82,720	Total

Another ballpark figure can be obtained by hiring a real estate assessor. He or she is a person who makes a living determining the monetary value of real estate.

Access to the Land

In most cases, you will find that there is direct access to the land you are considering. There will be frontage on a public road, or there will be a deeded right-of-way across private land. There is the possibility, however, that there will be no legal access to the property.

Let's speculate for a moment. Supposing a piece of land, a hilltop farm, say, is completely surrounded by privately owned land. The town road passes by about a quarter of a mile down the hill. There is a driveway from the town road to the farmhouse. It crosses one of the privately owned fields.

When you are shown this farmstead, the real estate person or the owner may tell you what he believes to be true, that the driveway is a legal right-of-way. On the other hand, he may know that it is not, and may tell you not to worry because it has always been this way. The people who own the field, he may say, are happy to have you cross it to get to the house. This may be true at the time. The land may change hands, however, or the people may change their minds, and then you might be stuck.

If there is no legal right-of-way drawn up, be sure to get one. If you don't, you may be setting yourself up for a great deal of trouble, the most extreme being that you would not be permitted access to your own property.

Usually the major access problem that you will have to consider is the physical aspect, not the legal one. Is the town road passable in all seasons? Will you have to build a long driveway to your house site? Will that involve going across water, or bridging a stream? Will you have to install culverts, bring in a lot of gravel and fill?

Answers to these questions will help you decide the value of that property. High-priced acreage that includes a driveway may be more economical than lower-priced land that requires complicated road building.

Public rights-of-way and road maintenance are the responsibility of the individual town or county depending on the state where you are looking. If the road near a piece of property is impassable or unmaintained during any part of the year, find out immediately whose responsibility it is to have it reconditioned.

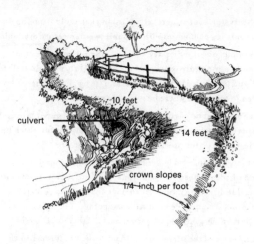

Building a driveway can be an expensive proposition. The driveway should be at least ten feet wide at the straight parts; fourteen feet wide at curves. To enable a graveled surface to shed water, you must provide a crown that slopes 1/4 to 1/2 inch per foot. Without trees to break the wind, snow fencing may be necessary. A gravel drive will need more care and maintenance than a concrete drive; every few years, additional gravel should be added to the rutted surface.

In 1968, the town of Norwich, Vermont, totally rebuilt one and a half miles of old dirt road from our house to our nearest neighbor. Eleven gravel trucks drew gravel constantly for five days; graders, bulldozers, and men worked for weeks to make it a year-round passable road. It cost the town $8,000. All this for one couple who had bought a run-down farm on a town right-of-way. It was not a personal favor, however; it was town policy in those days.

Today, Norwich town policy is quite different. Landowners who want impassable town right-of-ways rebuilt are responsible for doing it themselves. After the road is constructed according to town standards, the town will take over the maintenance.

Do not rely on hearsay. Go to the officials involved and learn what the current policy is in the area where you are looking.

All Those Other Things

Although having a title search seems obvious, many people get into trouble because they do not have an accurate search done. The person who sells the property ought to have a clear title to it. If there are covenants, restrictions, and liens on the property, these must show up in the title search. It is very important to have all these things written down carefully.

I know a woman who recently sold her house to a young couple. She had bought the house two years ago with what she thought was a clear title. The search had been done by a reputable lawyer. When she was ready to sell the house, however the young couple's lawyer found a $1,000 lien on the appliances left over from the owner previous to my friend. In this case, the lien was discharged immediately, taken care of without litigation or lengthy complications. That lien could have fouled the sale and tied up the property indefinitely.

RIGHTS

Rights can get very complicated. All rights sold to the owner of the property or sold away from the property ought to be in the public records. A careful search should, but does not always, turn them up.

Continued ➔

One still hears stories of mineral rights having been sold from the property to mining companies with no public written record available.

For example, one summer day, a few years ago, I noticed a man walking across our pasture in front of the house. He headed directly for our brook and proceeded to take samples and tie brightly colored plastic on branches of trees near where he took the samples.

When asked what he was doing, he replied that the copper mine not far from there had sold its mineral rights to the company for which he worked. He was surveying possible future mining sites.

In fact, my husband and I were unaware that any mineral rights to our property had ever been sold to anyone. I went to see our town clerk, who was an elderly man, a native. He told me that "everyone up there sold their mineral rights when the mine was going." There was no record to be seen, he said; he just knew that the rights had been sold.

Nothing came of the survey so we did nothing. But it remains that there was no mention of that sale of rights in our deed nor in the deeds belonging to several of our neighbors.

Water rights are commonly sold to and away from pieces of land. If you have no water on your land and your neighbor has a good spring that he is not using, he might sell you the right to use the water. Once that is legally transacted, the right to that spring remains with the property to which it was sold.

Other types of rights that may be sold or given away are hunting and fishing rights. If they have been sold, usually to the state, the owner has no authority over how his land will be used for hunting and fishing, and he cannot sell you that authority.

Recently people have been deeding the development rights to their property to the state or to environmental groups. The reasoning for this is that without the development rights a property is less valuable; thus the taxes are lower. When the property is sold, the development rights remain with the state or the environmental group. Consequently, the purchaser cannot develop the property.

COMMUNITY REGULATIONS

Zoning regulations of any community may be a limiting factor for the prospective buyer. Check into the type of zoning in force in the community where you plan to buy. It may turn out that you would not be permitted to do what you have in mind for a particular piece of land.

This information usually can be found at the town or county clerk's office. Sometimes the zoning regulations are statewide. If you are doing business with someone who says that there is no zoning, that may be true. Or there may be regulations he or she does not know about.

Check the town plan, if there is one, to see what the "town founders" envision for growth. It may be a shock to buy a nice piece of rural land through which a road is planned in the next ten years or next to which a shopping center is projected. For example, interstate highways were built through valuable and productive farmland under the authority of eminent domain in many areas of this country.

Other regulations to check out are the environmental restrictions that the town, county, or state may have placed on certain tracts of land. If your land is designated as a wildlife preserve, you may not be allowed to plant fields of corn.

Perhaps the most critical aspect of an old house is the soundness of its foundation. Check the foundation for general deterioration that would allow moisture or water to enter the basement. Then check for uneven settling of the foundation walls. In this drawing, uneven settling of the foundation has distorted the eave line, caused the roof ridge to sag, and the doors and windows to loosen and bind.

Environmental agencies can be identified by the real estate people, the town or county clerk, or the extension agent.

TAXES

To determine your annual costs, you will need to calculate expenses like mortgage payments, insurance, living expenses, renovation costs, loans, and transportation expenses. Don't forget hidden property taxes, too.

Ask your real estate person or the town/county clerk to explain the property tax system to you. There are many systems, and they vary from state to state and town to town.

There is a fair market value, which is based on what a property is selling for currently. There is current use evaluation, in which you are assessed according to the use you make of the land. Any reduction in taxes under this system is made by the taxing authority when the use changes or when the property is sold. Some towns base their taxes on full valuation, some on half valuation.

Find out what the tax rate, the assessment, and the actual taxes have been over the past several years. Look into more properties than you are actually interested in to get an idea of the trend. By this you will see how fast the rate rises and how often properties are reevaluated.

Some people I know were unpleasantly surprised when their tax bill was three times what they were told it had been for the previous owners. They had not bothered to check the system and did not understand that the property had not been reassessed for the past twenty years. Their purchase of the property jogged the assessors into doing a more up-to-date assessment. Thus without warning, my friends owed their town far more than they had anticipated.

Index

Continued ➜

1043

Continued ➜

Continued →

Continued →

1061
Notes